"I remember, when I was a student writing exegesis essays, making frequent use of the 1993 *Dictionary of Paul and His Letters*. The study of Paul has changed enormously in the three decades since that volume was published. But McKnight, Cohick, and Gupta, with their excellent team of contributors, have now brought the whole discussion up to date for a new generation of students, clergy, and laypersons."
Matthew V. Novenson, University of Edinburgh

"Rather than an update, the second edition of *The Dictionary of Paul and His Letters* is a completely new work that draws on the expertise of a diverse group of male and female scholars writing from a variety of hermeneutical perspectives. Academic but accessible essays summarize theological (e.g., law, grace, justification) and cultural (e.g., adoption, sexuality, women) topics from a Pauline perspective. So many interesting entries! An outstanding resource."
Sandra L. Glahn, Dallas Theological Seminary

"The publication of this new edition of the *Dictionary of Paul and His Letters* brings to students, pastors, and scholars fresh, up-to-date orientation to Paul, Paul's letters and theology, and numerous key issues in the contemporary study of Paul. A signal achievement and wonderful gift to all readers of Paul! I will be keeping this volume handy as well as recommending it widely."
Joel B. Green, senior professor of New Testament interpretation at Fuller Theological Seminary

"A staple of syllabi and a first stop for research, the original *Dictionary of Paul and His Letters* became a fixture in the landscape of Pauline studies. Much has changed in the past three decades, and this completely new dictionary, with contributions from no less than 141 scholars, provides an authoritative overview of the present state of Pauline scholarship. From Abraham and Adam to worship and wrath, and from classic theological topics to matters of pressing contemporary concern, the broad coverage of this remarkable project will be welcomed by novice student and seasoned scholar alike."
David Lincicum, University of Notre Dame

"For thirty years, the *Dictionary of Paul and His Letters* has provided readers with informed and scholarly introductions to key areas in the study of Paul from a broadly evangelical perspective. This new and thoroughly revised edition will bring today's readers up to date with this vibrant, important, and diverse field of study; it will again prove to be an invaluable resource."
David G. Horrell, University of Exeter

GENERAL EDITOR: SCOT McKNIGHT

ASSOCIATE EDITORS: LYNN H. COHICK *and* NIJAY K. GUPTA

DICTIONARY OF PAUL AND HIS LETTERS

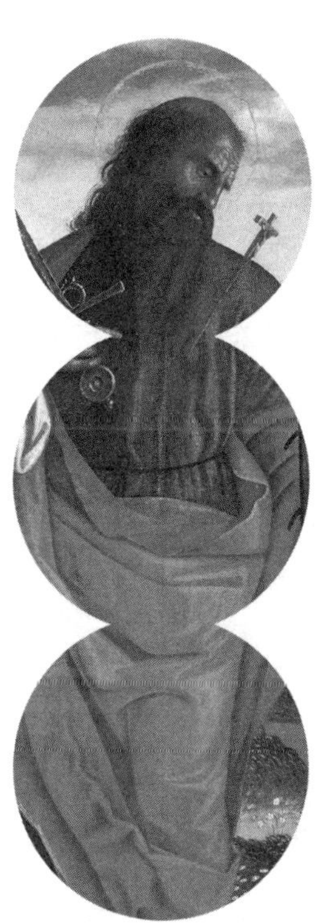

SECOND EDITION

A Compendium of Contemporary Biblical Scholarship

Academic
An imprint of InterVarsity Press
Downers Grove, Illinois

InterVarsity Press
P.O. Box 1400 | Downers Grove, IL 60515-1426
ivpress.com | email@ivpress.com

InterVarsity Press® is the publishing division of InterVarsity Christian Fellowship/USA®. For more information, visit intervarsity.org.

All Scripture quotations, unless otherwise indicated, are the author's own translation.

The publisher cannot verify the accuracy or functionality of website URLs used in this book beyond the date of publication.

Cover design and image composite: Cindy Kiple

ISBN 978-0-8308-1785-6 (print) | ISBN 978-0-8308-4936-9 (digital)

Printed in the United States of America ♾

Library of Congress Cataloging-in-Publication Data
A catalog record for this book is available from the Library of Congress.

30 29 28 27 26 25 24 23 | 13 12 11 10 9 8 7 6 5 4 3 2 1

InterVarsity Press

Project Staff

Project Editors
Anna Moseley Gissing
Rebecca F. Carhart

Managing Editor
Elissa Schauer

Copyeditor
Claire VanderVelde Brubaker

Rights and Contracts Coordinator
Subaas Gurung

Editorial Services Team
Alberto I. Bonilla-Giovanetti
Ashley Davila
Zachary Gordon
Kaitlin Murphy
Lisa Renninger
Sheila Urban

Consulting Editor
Daniel G. Reid

Proofreader
Adam Stevenson

InterVarsity Press

President and Publisher
Terumi Echols

Divisional Vice President of Editorial
Cindy Bunch

Associate Publisher, IVP Academic
Jon Boyd

Production Manager
Ben McCoy

Print Coordinator
Ethan Lunow

Associate Director, Rights and Contracts
Ellen Hsu

Academic Publicity and Marketing
Karin DeHaven
Alexandra Horn

Contents

Preface

In the space of only three years, we closely observed the soliciting of scholarly essays for two books exploring various perspectives on the apostle Paul's theology and mission. One book explored four views (Reformation, New Perspective, Apocalyptic, Participationist) and the other explored five entirely different views (Roman Catholic, Traditional Protestant, New Perspective, Paul Within Judaism, and Gift). Even then, both books were quick to acknowledge that there were still so many other voices on Paul that could have been included.

The first edition of this dictionary, published in 1993, spilled considerable energies in the spaces occupied by the Old and New Perspectives. However, so much has changed in the last thirty years that a new edition updating the discussions on all the topics was needed. In addition, many new topics have risen to the surface, and we have done our best to present as wide a view of these studies as can be mustered in one hefty volume.

The DPL2, as we editors call it, is not a mere touch-up of the original DPL but truly a completely new dictionary. Fifteen articles were revised or reused from the first edition, but the rest were written specifically for this edition (though some draw from their DPL1 predecessors). Some of the authors of the original volume have passed into the hands of our Lord, while new authors have entered the lecture hall with new ideas and fresh expressions of old and new topics. Any study of Paul has to discuss justification and the church, for example, but in the hands of our authors fresh light has been shed on these topics. New topics—such as ecology, patronage, and various historical and cultural interpretations—also deserve a place at the table, and readers of the DPL2 will discover their distinct insights for reading the letters of the apostle.

IVP Academic's design is for these volumes to be useful to pastors and professors, so our aim is to be comprehensive, accessible, and suggestive. We have also worked to make the essays accessible enough for beginning students as well as the educated layperson who wants to dig deeper into the apostle's writing. The bibliographies will serve a new generation of readers for a long time. Each author was given the freedom to work out their ideas as deemed most appropriate, which will mean the reader keen on comparison may well find tensions at times between articles—such is the cacophony of voices in the conversation about the apostle Paul today.

In the last decade more than one academic has approached editors at IVP to inquire if a new edition was in the making. We are honored to be those contacted by the publisher to determine entries and solicit authors. To harvest these exceptional entries appearing in this volume was a privilege for us. We express our gratitude to Jon Boyd, Anna Moseley Gissing,

Rebecca Carhart, and the rest of the IVP staff for their ability to turn a massive bundle of digital manuscripts into a final product fit for publication. They did so with customary grace, technological adaptations, and collegiality as they worked with several professors whose skills in at least one of those areas just mentioned was lacking.

You hold in your hands the work of 141 scholars and editors who have devoted their time to forming a tool accessible for the next generation of Paul's students. One of our contributors informed us that he spent 140 hours writing his entry, demonstrating how much our writers have done out of love.

We also wish to celebrate here the contributions of the first edition's editors, Gerald F. Hawthorne, Ralph P. Martin, and Daniel G. Reid, and we honor the Pauline scholars whose scholarship changed the landscape but who have passed since the first DPL was published.

Finally, to quote Paul in Philippians: "This is my prayer: that your love may abound more and more in knowledge and depth of insight, so that you may be able to discern what is best and may be pure and blameless for the day of Christ, filled with the fruit of righteousness that comes through Jesus Christ—to the glory and praise of God" (Phil 1:9-11 NIV).

Scot McKnight
Lynn H. Cohick
Nijay K. Gupta

How to Use This Dictionary

Abbreviations
Comprehensive tables of abbreviations for general matters and for scholarly, biblical, and ancient literature may be found on pages xiii-xxii.

Authorship of Articles
The authors of articles are indicated by their first initials and last name at the end of each article. A full list of contributors may be found on pages xxv-xxx, in alphabetical order of last name. The contribution of each author is listed following their identification.

Bibliographies
A bibliography at the end of each article contains works cited in the article and other significant related works. Bibliographical entries are listed in alphabetical order by the author's name, and where an author has more than one work cited, they are listed chronologically by publication date. Bibliographies for most Pauline letters include a special listing of commentaries on that letter.

Cross-References
This dictionary has been extensively cross-referenced in order to aid readers in making the most of material appearing throughout the volume. Three types of cross-referencing are used.

1. One-line entries appearing in alphabetical order throughout the dictionary direct readers to articles where a topic is discussed:

Abba. *See* ADOPTION; GOD; SON OF GOD.

2. An asterisk before a word in the body of an article indicates that an article by that title (or a closely worded title) appears in the dictionary. For example, "*Christology" directs the reader to an article titled "Christology." Asterisks typically are found only at the first occurrence of a word in an article.

3. Cross-references have been appended to the end of articles, immediately preceding the bibliography, to direct readers to articles significantly related to the subject.

See also JUSTIFICATION; RIGHTEOUSNESS.

Indexes
A Scripture index is provided to assist readers in gaining quick access to the numerous Scripture texts referred to throughout the dictionary.

Since most of the dictionary articles cover broad topics in some depth, the subject index is intended to assist readers in finding relevant information on narrower topics that might, for instance, appear in a standard Bible dictionary. For example, while there is no article titled "Expiation," the subject index might direct the reader to pages where the topic is discussed in the articles "Atonement" and "Romans, Letter to the."

A full list of articles appears in the table of contents. Those who wish to identify the articles written by specific contributors should consult the list of contributors at the front of the book.

Transliteration
Hebrew and Greek words have been transliterated according to a system set out on page xxiii.

Abbreviations

General Abbreviations

//	parallel text(s)	Lat.	Latin
Aram.	Aramaic	lit.	literally
cf.	confer, compare	mg.	margin
esp.	especially	MS(S)	manuscript(s)
ET	English translation	par(s).	parallel passage(s)
flor.	*floruit*	pl.	plural
frg(s).	fragment(s)	repr.	reprint
Gk.	Greek	sg.	singular
Heb.	Hebrew	s.v.	*sub verbo*, under the word

Ancient Texts, Text Types, and Versions

LXX	Septuagint	OT	Old Testament
MT	Masoretic Text	Theod.	Theodotion
NT	New Testament		

Modern Editions

NA[28]	*Novum Testamentum Graece*, Nestle-Aland, 28th ed.	UBS[5]	*The Greek New Testament*, United Bible Societies, 5th ed.
SBLGNT	The Greek New Testament: SBL Edition		

Translations of the Bible

ASV	American Standard Version	NET	New English Translation
CEB	Common English Bible	NETS	*A New English Translation of the Septuagint*
CEV	Contemporary English Version	NIV	New International Version
CSB	Christian Standard Bible	NJB	New Jerusalem Bible
ESV	English Standard Version	NLT	New Living Translation
GNT	Good News Translation	NRSV	New Revised Standard Version
HCSB	Holman Christian Standard Bible	REB	Revised English Bible
KJV	King James Version	RSV	Revised Standard Version
LEB	Lexham English Bible	TLV	Tree of Life Version
NABRE	New American Bible, Revised Edition	WEB	World English Bible
NASB	New American Standard Bible		

Books of the Bible

Old Testament	1-2 Kings	Is	Mic	Lk	1-2 Tim
Gen	1-2 Chron	Jer	Nahum	Jn	Titus
Ex	Ezra	Lam	Hab	Acts	Philem
Lev	Neh	Ezek	Zeph	Rom	Heb
Num	Esther	Dan	Hag	1-2 Cor	Jas
Deut	Job	Hos	Zech	Gal	1-2 Pet
Josh	Ps (Pss)	Joel	Mal	Eph	1-2-3 Jn
Judg	Prov	Amos	*New Testament*	Phil	Jude
Ruth	Eccles	Obad	Mt	Col	Rev
1-2 Sam	Song	Jon	Mk	1-2 Thess	

Apocrypha and Septuagint

Add Esth	Additions to Esther
Bar	Baruch
Jdt	Judith
1-2 Esd	1-2 Esdras
1-4 Kgdms	1-4 Kingdoms
1-4 Macc	1-4 Maccabees
Sir	Sirach
Tob	Tobit
Wis	Wisdom of Solomon

Old Testament Pseudepigrapha

Apoc. Ab.	Apocalypse of Abraham
Apoc. Dan.	Apocalypse of Daniel
Apoc. Mos.	Apocalypse of Moses
Apoc. Zeph.	Apocalypse of Zephaniah
As. Mos.	Assumption of Moses
2 Bar.	2 Baruch (Syriac Apocalypse)
3 Bar.	3 Baruch (Greek Apocalypse)
1 En.	1 Enoch (Ethiopic Apocalypse)
2 En.	2 Enoch (Slavonic Apocalypse)
4 Ezra	4 Ezra
Jos. Asen.	Joseph and Aseneth
Jub.	Jubilees
L.A.B.	Liber antiquitatum biblicarum (Pseudo-Philo)
LAE	Life of Adam and Eve
Let. Aris.	Letter of Aristeas
Ps.-Phoc.	Pseudo-Phocylides
Pss. Sol.	Psalms of Solomon
Sib. Or.	Sibylline Oracles
Testaments of the Twelve Patriarchs	
T. Ash.	Testament of Asher
T. Benj.	Testament of Benjamin
T. Dan	Testament of Dan
T. Jos.	Testament of Joseph
T. Jud.	Testament of Judah
T. Levi	Testament of Levi
T. Naph.	Testament of Naphtali
T. Reu.	Testament of Reuben
T. Sim.	Testament of Simeon
T. Ab.	Testament of Abraham
T. Job	Testament of Job
T. Mos.	Testament of Moses
T. Sol.	Testament of Solomon

Dead Sea Scrolls

CD	Damascus Document
1QH[a]	1QHodayot[a]
1QpHab	1QPesher to Habakkuk
1QS	1QRule of the Community
1Q28a (1QSa)	1QRule of the Congregation
1Q28b (1QSb)	1QRule of Benedictions
1Q33 (1QM)	1QWar Scroll
1Q34 + 1Q34bis (1QLitPr)	1QFestival Prayers
1Q35 (1QH[b])	1QHodayot[b]
2Q23 (2QapocrProph)	2QApocryphon Prophecy
4Q161 (4QpIsa[a])	4QIsaiah Pesher[a]
4Q164 (4QpIsa[d])	4QIsaiah Pesher[d]
4Q174 (4QFlor)	4QFlorilegium
4Q177	4QCatena[a] (Midrash Eschatology[b])
4Q185	Sapiential Work
4Q215a	4QTime of Righteousness
4Q246	4QApocryphon of Daniel
4Q252 (4QcommGen A)	4QCommentary on Genesis A
4Q258 (4QS[d])	4QRule of the Community[d]
4Q259 (4QS[e]) + 4Q319 (4QOtot)	4QRule of the Community[e] + 4QOtot
4Q369 (4QPEnosh?)	4QPrayer of Enosh (?)
4Q372 (4QapocrJoseph[b])	4QApocryphon of Joseph[b]
4Q379 (4QapocrJoshua[b])	4QApocryphon of Joshua[b]
4Q382	4Qpapyrus paraphrase of Kings et al.
4Q394 (4QMMT[a])	4QHalakhic Letter[a]
4Q395 (4QMMT[b])	4QHalakhic Letter[b]
4Q396 (4QMMT[c])	4QHalakhic Letter[c]
4Q397 (4QMMT[d])	4QHalakhic Letter[d]
4Q398 (4QMMT[e])	4QHalakhic Letter[e]
4Q399 (4QMMT[f])	4QHalakhic Letter[f]
4Q416	4QInstruction[b]
4Q417	4QInstruction[c]
4Q427 (4QH[a])	4QHodayot[a]
4Q458	4QNarrative A
4Q460	4QNarrative Work and Prayer
4Q471b	4QSelf-Glorification Hymn[b]
4Q491	4QMilḥamah[a]
4Q504 (4QDibHam[a])	4QDibre Hameʾorot[a] or Words of the Luminaries[a]
4Q509 + 4Q505 (4QPrpapFêtes[c])	4Q Festival Prayers[c]
4Q521	4QMessianic Apocalypse
4Q525 (4QBéat)	4QBeatitudes
11Q13 (11QMelch)	11QMelchizedek
11Q19 (11QT[a])	11QTemple[a]

Naḥal Ḥever/Seiyal

8ḤevXII gr	Naḥal Ḥever Minor Prophets Greek

Tractates in the Mishnah, Tosefta, and Talmud

m.	Mishnah
t.	Tosefta
b.	Babylonian Talmud
y.	Jerusalem Talmud
Abod. Zar.	Abodah Zarah
Abot	Abot
ʿArak.	ʿArakin
Ber.	Berakot
Giṭ.	Giṭṭin
Kel.	Kelim
Ketub.	Ketubbot
Mak.	Makkot
Meg.	Megillah
Pesah.	Pesahim
Qidd.	Qiddushin
Rosh Hash.	Rosh Hashanah
Shabb.	Shabbat
Sanh.	Sanhedrin
Sotah	Sotah
Sukkah	Sukkah
Ta'an.	Ta'anit
Yebam.	Yebamot
Yoma	Yoma (= Kippurim)

Other Rabbinic Works

Avot R. Nat.	Avot of Rabbi Nathan
Pesiq. Rab.	Pesiqta Rabbati
Pirqe R. El.	Pirqe Rabbi Eliezer

Apostolic Fathers

1-2 Clem.	*1-2 Clement*
Barn.	*Epistle of Barnabas*
Did.	Didache
Herm.	Shepherd of Hermas
Ign. *Eph.*	Ignatius, *To the Ephesians*
Ign. *Phld.*	Ignatius, *To the Philadelphians*
Ign. *Pol.*	Ignatius, *To Polycarp*
Ign. *Rom.*	Ignatius, *To the Romans*
Ign. *Smyrn.*	Ignatius, *To the Smyrnaeans*
Pol. *Phil.*	Polycarp, *To the Philippians*

Inscriptions and Papyri

CIIP	*Corpus Inscriptionum Iudaeae/Palaestinae*, 6 vols. (Berlin: de Gruyter, 2010–)
CIJ	*Corpus Inscriptionum Iudaicarum*, ed. J. B. Frey, 2 vols. (Rome, 1936–1952)
CIL	*Corpus Inscriptionum Latinarum*, 17 vols. (Berlin: Berlin-Brandenburg Academy of Sciences and Humanities, 1871–)
IBM	*Ancient Greek Inscriptions in the British Museum*, 4 vols. (Oxford, 1874–1916)
IEph	*Die Inschriften von Ephesos*, 10 vols. (Bonn, 1979–1984)
IG	*Inscriptiones Graecae*, Editio Minor (Berlin: de Gruyter, 1924–)
IGRR	*Inscriptiones Graecae ad res Romanas pertinentes*, ed. R. Cagnat, 3 vols. (Paris, 1906–1927; repr., Chicago, 1975)
IKorinthKent	*Corinth*, 8.3, *The Inscriptions, 1926–1950*, ed. J. H. Kent (Princeton, 1966)
IKorinthWest	*Corinth*, 8.2, *Latin Inscriptions, 1896–1926*, ed. A. B. West (Cambridge, 1931)
ILS	*Inscriptiones Latinae Selectae*, ed. H. Dessau, 3 vols. (Berlin, 1892–1916)
IOlympia	*Die Inschriften von Olympia*, ed. W. Dittenberger and K. Purgold (Berlin, 1986)
MAMA	*Monumenta Asiae Minoris Antiqua*, 10 vols. (Manchester and London, 1928–1993)
NewDocs	*New Documents Illustrating Early Christianity*, ed. G. H. R. Horsley et al. (North Ryde, NSW: Macquarie University, 1981–)
OGI	*Orientis graeci inscriptiones selectae*, ed. W. Dittenberger, 2 vols. (Leipzig, 1903–1905)
P.Dura	Dura-Europos Papyri
P.Mich.	Papyrology Collection of the University of Michigan Library
P.Oxy.	Oxyrhynchus Papyri
P.Ryl.	Papyri in the John Rylands Library
P.Tebt.	Tebtunis Papyri
P.Zen.	Papyri from the Zenon Archive
SEG	Supplementum epigraphicum graecum
SIG	*Sylloge inscriptionum graecarum*, ed. W. Dittenberger, 4 vols, 3rd ed. (Leipzig, 1915–1924)
Tab. Vindol.	Vindolanda Writing Tablets

Greek and Latin Works

Aelian (Claudius)
Var. hist. *Varia historia (Various History)*
Appian
Bell. civ. *Bella civilia (Civil Wars)*
Apuleius
Metam. *Metamorphoses (The Golden Ass)*
Aristotle
Ath. pol. *Athenaion politeia (Constitution of Athens)*
Eth. nic. *Ethica nichomachea (Nichomachean Ethics)*
Poet. *Poetica (Poetics)*
Pol. *Politica (Politics)*
Probl. *Problemata (Problems)*
Rhet. *Rhetorica (Rhetoric)*
Virt vit. *De virtutibus et vitiis (Virtues and Vices)*
Arrian
Epict. diss. *Epicteti dissertationes*
Augustine
Bapt. *De baptismo contra Donatistas (Baptism)*
C. Jul. op. imp. *Contra secundam Juliani responsionem imperfectum*
Opus (Against Julian: Opus Imperfectum)
Civ. *De civitate Dei (City of God)*
Conf. *Confessionum libri XIII (Confessions)*
Doctr. chr. *De doctrina christiana (On Christian Instruction)*
Faust. *Contra Faustum Manichaeum (Against Faustus the Manichaean)*
Fid. op. *De fide et operibus (Faith and Works)*
Fort. *Contra Fortunatum (Against Fortunatus)*
Gen. Man. *De Genesi contra Manichaeos (On Genesis against the Manichaeans)*
Gest. Pelag. *De gestis Pelagii (Proceedings of Pelagius)*
Grat. Chr. *De gratia Christi, et de peccato originali (The Grace of Christ and Original Sin)*
Nat. grat. *De natura et gratia (Nature and Grace)*
Peccat. mer. *De peccatorum meritis et remissione et de baptismo parvulorum (On Merits and Remission of Sin, and Infant Baptism)*
Perf. *De perfectione justitiae hominis) Perfection in Human Righteousness)*
Praed. *De praedestinatione sanctorum (The Predestination of the Saints)*
Quaest. Hept. *Quaestiones in Heptateuchum (Questions on the Heptateuch)*
Serm. *Sermones (Sermons)*
Serm. Dom. *De sermone Domini in monte (Sermon on the Mount)*
Spir. et litt. *De spiritu et littera (The Spirit and the Letter)*
Tract. Ev. Jo. *In Evangelium Johannis tractatus (Treatise on the Gospel of John)*
Trin. *De Trinitate (The Trinity)*
Util. cred. *De utilitate credendi (The Usefulness of Believing)*
Cassius Dio
Hist. *Historia romana (Roman History)*
Cicero
Acad. *Academicae quaestiones*
Arch. *Pro Archia*
Att. *Epistulae ad Atticum (Letters to Atticus)*
Brut. *Brutus* or *De claris oratoribus*
Dom. *De domo sua (On His House)*
Fam. *Epistulae ad familiares (Letters to Friends)*
Fin. *De finibus (On the Ends of Good and Evil)*
Flac. *Pro Flacco (In Defense of Flaccus)*
Inv. *De inventione rhetorica*
Leg. *De legibus (Laws)*
Nat. d. *De natura deorum (On the Nature of the Gods)*
Off. *De officiis*
Opt. gen. *De optimo genere oratorum*
Orat. *De oratore (On the Orator)*
Quint. fratr. *Epistulae ad Quintum fratrem*
Rep. *De republica*
Tusc. *Tusculanae Disputationes*
Verr. *In Verrem (Against Caius Verres)*
Clement of Alexandria
Ecl. *Eclogae propheticae (Extracts from the Prophets)*
Paed. *Paedagogus (Christ the Educator)*
Strom. *Stromata (Miscellanies)*
Demosthenes
Timocr. *In Timocratem (Against Timocrates)*
Dio Chrysostom
1 Regn. *De regno i (Or. 1) (Kingship 1)*
1 Tars. *Tarsica prior (Or. 33) First Tarsic Discourse*
2 Tars. *Tarsica altera (Or. 34) (Second Tarsic Discourse)*
3 Regn. *De regno iii (Or. 3) (Kingship 3)*
4 Regn. *De regno iv (Or. 4) Kingship 4*
Alex. *Ad Alexandrinos (Or. 32) To the People of Alexandria*
Avar. *De avaritia (Or. 17) (Covetousness)*
Compot. *De compotatione (Or. 27) (Symposia)*
Dei cogn. *De dei cognitione (Or. 12) (Man's First Conception of God)*
Invid. *De invidia (Or. 77/78)*
Ven. *Venator (Or. 7) (The Hunter)*
Virt. *De virtute (Or. 8) (Virtue)*
Diodorus Siculus
Bib. hist. *Bibliotheca historica (Library of History)*
Diogenes Laertius
Vit. *Vitae philosophorum (Lives of Eminent Philosophers)*
Epictetus
Diatr. *Diatribai (Dissertationes)*
Epiphanius
Pan. *Panarion (Adversus haereses) (Refutation of All Heresies)*

Euripides
Hipp. *Hippolytus*
Iph. aul. *Iphigenia aulidensis (Iphigenia at Aulis)*
Eusebius
Hist. eccl. *Historia ecclesiastica (Ecclesiastical History)*
Praep. ev. *Praeparatio evangelica (Preparation for the Gospel)*
Herodotus
Hist. *Historiae (Histories)*
Hesiod
Op. *Opera et dies (Works and Days)*
Theog.. *Theogonia (Theogony)*
Hippolytus
Comm. Dan. *Commentarii in Danielem (Commentary on Daniel)*
Haer. *Refutatio omnium haeresium (Refutation of All Heresies)*
Trad. ap. *Traditio apostolica (The Apostolic Tradition)*
Homer
Il. *Iliad*
Od. *Odyssea (Odyssey)*
Horace
Ars. *Ars poetica*
Carm. *Carmina (Odes)*
Ep. *Epistulae (Letters)*
Sat. *Satirae (Satires)*
Irenaeus
Epid. *Epideixis tou apostolikou kērygmatos (Demonstration of the Apostolic Preaching)*
Haer. *Adversus haereses (Against Heresies)*
Jerome
Comm. Eph. *Commentariorum in Epistulam ad Ephesios libri III*
Jov. *Adversus Jovinianum libri II*
Vir. ill. *De viris illustribus (On Illustrious Men)*
John Chrysostom
Hom. 2 Cor. *Homiliae in epistulam ii ad Corinthos (Homilies on 2 Corinthians)*
Hom. 2 Thess. *Homiliae in epistulam ii ad Thessalonicenses (Homilies on 2 Thessalonians)*
Hom. Eph. *Homiliae in epistulam ad Ephesios (Homilies on Ephesians)*
Hom. Phil. *Homiliae in epistulam ad Philippenses (Homilies on Philippians*
Hom. Rom. *Homiliae in epistulam ad Romanos (Homilies on Romans)*
Nom. hebr. *De nominibus hebraicis (Liber nominum)*
Virginit. *De virginitate*
Josephus
Ag. Ap. *Against Apion (Contra Apionem)*
Ant. *Jewish Antiquities (Antiquitates judaicae)*
J.W. *Jewish War (Bellum judaicum)*
Life *The Life (Vita) Fragmenta (Fragments)*
Justin
1 Apol. *Apologia i (First Apology)*
2 Apol. *Apologia ii (Second Apology)*
Dial. *Dialogus cum Tryphone (Dialogue with Trypho)*
Juvenal
Sat. *Satirae (Satires)*
Livy
Hist. *The History of Rome (Ab urbe condita libri)*
Lucian
Alex. *Alexander (Pseudomantis) (Alexander the False Prophet)*
Fug. *Fugitivi (The Runaways)*
Hermot. *Hermotimus (De sectis) (Hermotimus, or Sects)*
Nigr. *Nigrinus*
Salt. *De saltatione (The Dance)*
Tox. *Toxaris (On Friendship)*
Syr d. *De syria dea (The Goddess of Syria)*
Marcus Aurelius
Comm. *Commentariorum quos ipse sibi scripsit (Meditations)*
Martial
Epig. *Epigrammata (Epigrams)*
Origen
Cels. *Contra Celsum (Against Celsus)*
Comm. Rom. *Commentarii in Romanos (Commentary on Romans)*
Princ. *De principiis (First Principles)*
Orosius
Adv. Pag. *Historiarum Adversum Paganos Libri vii (Seven Books of History Against the Pagans)*
Ovid
Con. Liv. *Consolatio ad Liviam (Consolation to Livia)*
Metam. *Metamorphoses*
Pausanias
Descr. *Graeciae descriptio (Description of Greece)*
Philo
Abr. *De Abrahamo (On the Life of Abraham)*
Aet. *De aeternitate mundi (On the Eternity of the World)*
Agr. *De agricultura (On Agriculture)*
Cher. *De cherubim (On the Cherubim)*
Conf. *De confusione linguarum (On the Confusion of Tongues)*
Congr. *De congressu eruditionis gratia (On the Preliminary Studies)*
Contempl. *De vita contemplativa (On the Contemplative Life)*
Decal. *De decalogo (On the Decalogue)*
Det. *Quad deterius potiori insidari soleat (That the Worse Attacks the Better)*
Deus *Quad Deus sit immutabilis (That God Is Unchangeable)*
Ebr. *De ebrietate (On Drunkenness)*
Flacc. *In Flaccum (Against Flaccus)*
Fug. *De fuga et inventione (On Flight and Finding)*
Gig. *De gigantibus (On Giants)*
Her. *Quis rerum divinarum heres sit (Who Is the Heir?)*

Hypoth. *Hypothetica (Hypothetica)*
Ios. *De Iosepho (On the Life of Joseph)*
Leg. *Legum allegoriae (Allegorical Interpretation)*
Legat. *Legatio ad Gaium (On the Embassy to Gaius)*
Migr. *De migration e Abrahami (On the Migration of Abraham)*
Mos. *De vita Mosis (On the Life of Moses)*
Mut. *De mutatione nominum (On the Change of Names)*
Opif. *De opificio mundi (On the Creation of the World)*
Post. *De posteritate Caini (On the Posterity of Cain)*
Praem. *De praemiis et poenis (On Rewards and Punishments)*
Prob. *Quad omnis probus liber sit (That Every Good Person Is Free)*
QE *Quaestiones et solutiones in Exodum (Questions and Answers on Exodus)*
QG *Quaestiones et solutiones in Genesin (Questions and Answers on Genesis)*
Sacr. De sacrificiis Abelis et Caini (On the Sacrifices of Cain and Abel)
Sobr. *De sobrietate (On Sobriety)*
Somn. *De somniis (On Dreams)*
Spec. *De specialibus legibus (On the Special Laws)*
Virt. *De virtutibus (On the Virtues)*

Philostratus
Vit. Apoll. *Vita Apollonii (Life of Apollonius)*
Vit. soph. *Vitae sophistarum (Lives of the Sophists)*

Plato
Def. *Definitiones (Definitions)*
Euthyd. *Euthydemus*
Leg. *Leges (Laws)*
Menex. *Menexenus*
Parm. *Parmenides*
Phaedr. *Phaedrus*
Prot. *Protagoras*
Resp. *Respublica (Republic)*
Symp. *Symposium*
Tim. *Timaeus*

Pliny the Elder
Nat. *Naturalis historia (Natural History)*

Pliny the Younger
Ep. *Epistulae (Letters)*
Ep. Tra. *Epistulae ad Trajanum*

Plutarch
Adv. Col. *Adversus Colotem (Against Colotes)*
Alex. *Alexander*
Alex. fort. *De Alexandri magni fortuna aut virtute*
Amat. *Amatorius (Dialogue on Love)*
Ant. *Antonius*
Cat. Min. *Cato Minor (Cato the Younger)*
E Delph. *De E apud Delphos*
Frat. amor. *De fraterno amore*
Galb. *Galba (Life of Galba)*
Is. Os. *De Iside et Osiride (Of Isis and Osiris)*
Mor. *Moralia (Morals)*
Pel. *Pelopidas*
Pomp. *Pompeius (Life of Pompey)*
Quaest. conv. *Quaestionum convivialum libri IX (Table Talk)*
Sept. sav. conv. *Septem sapientium convivium*
Tu san. *De tuenda sanitate praecepta (Advice About Keeping Well)*

Q. Cicero
Comm. pet. *Commentariolum Petitionis*

Quintilian
Inst. *Institutio oratoria (Institutes of Oratory)*

Rhet. Her. Rhetorica ad Herennium

Seneca
Ben. *De beneficiis (On Benefits)*
Clem. *De clementia*
Const. sap. *De constantia sapientis (On the Constancy of the Wise Man)*
Contr. *Controversiae*
Dial. *Dialogi*
Ep. *Epistulae morales (Moral Epistles)*
Helv. *Ad Helviam*
Herc. Ot. *Hercules Otaeus*
Lucil. *Ad Lucilium*
Nat. *Naturales quaestiones*
Prov. *De Providentia (On Providence)*
Tranq. *De tranquillitate animi (On the Tranquility of the Mind)*

Strabo
Geogr. *Geographica (Geography)*

Suetonius
Aug. *Divus Augustus (Augustus)*
Claud. *Divus Claudius (Claudius)*
Gramm. *De grammaticis (On Grammarians)*
Jul. *Divus Julius*
Tib. *Tiberius*
Vesp. *Vespasianus (Vespasian)*
Vit. *Vitellius*

Tacitus
Agr. *Agricola*
Ann. *Annales (Annals)*
Hist. *Historiae (Histories)*

Tertullian
Adv. Jud. *Adversus Judaeos (Against the Jews)*
An. *De anima (The Soul)*
Apol. *Apologeticus (Apology)*
Bapt. *De baptismo (Baptism)*
Idol. *De idolatria*
Marc. *Adversus Marcionem (Against Marcion)*
Mon. *Monogamia (Monogamy)*
Praescr. *De praescriptione haereticorum (Prescription against Heretics)*
Pud. *De pudicitia (Modesty*
Res. *De resurrectione carnis (The Resurrection of the Flesh)*
Scorp. *Scorpiace (Antidote for the Scorpion's Sting)*
Spect. *De spectaculis (The Shows)*

Valerius Maximus
Fact. dict. *Factorum et dictorum memorabilium libri IX (Memorable Doings and Sayings)*

Virgil
Aen. *Aeneid*

Xenophon

Anab.	*Anabasis*
Cyr.	*Cyropaedia*
Hell.	*Hellenica*
Mem.	*Memorabilia*

Periodicals, Reference Works, and Serials

AB	Anchor Bible
ABD	*Anchor Bible Dictionary*, ed. D. N. Freedman, 6 vols. (New York: Doubleday, 1992)
ABQ	*American Baptist Quarterly*
AcBib	Academia Biblica
AGJU	Arbeiten zur Geschichte des antiken Judentums und des Urchristentums
AIL	Ancient Israel and Its Literature
AJEC	Ancient Judaism and Early Christianity
AJP	*American Journal of Philology*
AJPS	*Asian Journal of Pentecostal Studies*
AnBib	Analecta Biblica
ANEM	Ancient Near East Monograph Series
ANRW	*Aufstieg und Niedergant der römischen Welt: Geschichte und Kultur Rom sim Spiegel der neuren Forschung*, ed. H. Temporini and W. Haase (Berlin: de Gruyter, 1972–)
ANTC	Abingdon New Testament Commentaries
ANTF	Arbeiten zur neutestamentlichen Textforschung
ANWAW	Abhandlungen der Nordrhein-Westfälischen Akademie der Wissenschaften
ARel	*Archiv für Religionsgeschichte*
ARGU	Arbeiten zur Religion und Geschichte des Urchristentums
AThR	*Anglican Theological Review*
AUSS	*Andrews University Seminary Studies*
AYB	Anchor Yale Bible
AYBRL	Anchor Yale Bible Reference Library
BAFCS	The Book of Acts in Its First-Century Setting
BAR	*Biblical Archaeology Review*
BBR	*Bulletin for Biblical Research*
BDAG	F. W. Danker, W. Bauer, W. F. Arndt, and F. W. Gingrich, *Greek-English Lexicon of the New Testament and Other Early Christian Literature*, 3rd ed. (Chicago: University of Chicago Press, 2000)
BECNT	Baker Exegetical Commentary on the New Testament
BETL	Bibliotheca Ephemeridum Theologicarum Lovaniensium
BFCT	Beiträge zur Förderung christlicher Theologie
BHT	Beiträge zur historischen Theologie
Bib	*Biblica*
BibInt	Biblical Interpretation Series
BibInt	*Biblical Interpretation*
BJRL	*Bulletin of the John Rylands Library*
BMCRE	*Coins of the Roman Empire in the British Museum*, 6 vols. (London: British Museum Press, 1923–1962)
BNTC	Black's New Testament Commentaries
BPC	Biblical Performance Criticism
BR	*Biblical Research*
BSac	*Bibliotheca Sacra*
BSL	Biblical Studies Library
BT	*Bible Translator*
BTB	*Biblical Theology Bulletin*
BTF	*Bangalore Theological Forum*
BTS	Biblical Tools and Studies
BZ	*Biblische Zeitschrift*
BZNW	Beihefte zur Zeitschrift für die neutestamentliche Wissenschaft
CBET	Contributions to Biblical Exegesis and Theology
CBQ	*Catholic Biblical Quarterly*
CCCM	Corpus Christianorum: Continuatio Mediaevalis
CCT	Contours of Christian Theology
CIM	Christianity in the Making
ClQ	*Classical Quarterly*
COMS	Civitatum Orbis Mediterranei Studia
ConBNT	Coniectanea Biblica: New Testament Series
COQG	Christian Origins and the Question of God
CSEL	Corpus Scriptorum Ecclesiasticorum Latinorum
CTQ	*Concordia Theological Quarterly*
CurBR	*Currents in Biblical Research*
CurTM	*Currents in Theology and Mission*
DBWE	Dietrich Bonhoeffer Works in English
DJG[2]	*Dictionary of Jesus and the Gospels*, 2nd ed., ed. J. B. Green, J. K. Brown, and N. Perrin (Downers Grove, IL: IVP Academic, 2013)
DNTB	*Dictionary of New Testament Background*, ed. C. A. Evans and S. E. Porter (Downers Grove, IL: IVP Academic, 2000)
DOTHB	*Dictionary of the Old Testament: Historical Books*, ed. B. T. Arnold and H. G. M. Williamson (Downers Grove, IL: IVP Academic, 2005)
DOTP	*Dictionary of the Old Testament: Prophets*, ed. M. J. Boda and J. G. McConville (Downers Grove, IL: IVP Academic, 2012)
DOTWPW	*Dictionary of the Old Testament: Wisdom, Poetry and Writings*, ed. T. Longman III and P. Enns (Downers Grove, IL: IVP Academic, 2008)

DPL — *Dictionary of Paul and His Letters*, ed. G. F. Hawthorne, R. P. Martin, and D. G. Reid (Downers Grove, IL: IVP Academic, 1993)
DSD — *Dead Sea Discoveries*
EC — *Early Christianity*
ECL — Early Christianity and Its Literature
EDNT — *Exegetical Dictionary of the New Testament*, ed. H. Balz and G. Schneider, ET, 3 vols. (Grand Rapids, MI: Eerdmans, 1990–1993)
EEC — Evangelical Exegetical Commentary
EJL — Early Judaism and Its Literature
EKKNT — Evangelisch-katholischer Kommentar zum Neuen Testament
ES — Emerging Scholars
ETL — *Ephemerides Theologicae Lovanienses*
EvQ — *Evangelical Quarterly*
EvT — *Evangelische Theologie*
ExpTim — *Expository Times*
FC — Fathers of the Church
FRLANT — Forschungen zur Religion und Literatur des Alten und Neuen Testaments
FzB — Forschung zur Bibel
GE — F. Montari. *The Brill Dictionary of Ancient Greek* (Leiden: Brill, 2015)
GELS — T. Muraoka, *A Greek-English Lexicon of the Septuagint* (Leuven: Peeters, 2009)
GTJ — *Grace Theological Journal*
HALOT — L. Koehler, W. Baumgartner, and J. J. Stamm, *The Hebrew and Aramaic Lexicon of the Old Testament*, trans. and ed. under the supervision of M. E. J. Richardson, 4 vols. (Leiden: Brill, 1994–1999)
HBT — *Horizons in Biblical Theology*
HeyJ — *Heythrop Journal*
HSM — Harvard Semitic Monographs
HThKNT — Herders Theologischer Kommentar zum Neuen Testament
HTR — *Harvard Theological Review*
HUCA — *Hebrew Union College Annual*
HUT — Hermeneutische Untersuchungen zur Theologie
IBC — Interpretation: A Bible Commentary for Teaching and Preaching
ICC — International Critical Commentary
IDB — *The Interpreter's Dictionary of the Bible*, ed. G. A. Buttrick, 4 vols. (New York: Abingdon, 1962)
Int — *Interpretation*
IRM — *International Review of Mission*
IVPNTC — IVP New Testament Commentaries
JA — Judaisms of Antiquity
JAOS — *Journal of the American Oriental Society*
JBL — *Journal of Biblical Literature*
JCBRF — *Journal of the Christian Brethren Research Fellowship*
JCTCRSS — Jewish and Christian Texts in Contexts and Related Studies Series
JECS — *Journal of Early Christian Studies*
JETS — *Journal of the Evangelical Theological Society*
JFSR — *Journal of Feminist Studies in Religion*
JGRChJ — *Journal of Greco-Roman Christianity and Judaism*
JJS — *Journal of Jewish Studies*
JPTSup — Journal of Pentecostal Theology Supplement Series
JQR — *Jewish Quarterly Review*
JRA — *Journal of Roman Archeology*
JRASup — Journal of Roman Archeology Supplement Series
JRE — *Journal of Religious Ethics*
JRH — *Journal of Religious History*
JRS — *Journal of Roman Studies*
JSHJ — *Journal for the Study of the Historical Jesus*
JSJ — *Journal for the Study of Judaism*
JSJSup — Supplements to the Journal for the Study of Judaism
JSNT — *Journal for the Study of the New Testament*
JSNTSup — Journal for the Study of the New Testament: Supplement Series
JSOTSup — Journal for the Study of the Old Testament: Supplement Series
JSP — *Journal for the Study of the Pseudepigrapha*
JSPSup — JSPSup Journal for the Study of the Pseudepigrapha Supplement Series
JSPHL — *Journal for the Study of Paul and His Letters*
JSS — *Journal of Semitic Studies*
JSSR — *Journal for the Scientific Study of Religion*
JTC — *Journal for Theology and the Church*
JTI — *Journal for Theological Interpretation*
JTS — *Journal of Theological Studies*
L&N — J. P. Louw and E. A. Nida, eds., *Greek-English Lexicon of the New Testament: Based on Semantic Domains*, 2nd ed. (New York: United Bible Societies, 1989)
LCL — Loeb Classical Library
LNTS — Library of New Testament Studies
LSJ — Liddell, H. G., R. Scott, and H. S. Jones, *A Greek-English Lexicon*, 9th ed. with rev. supplement (Oxford: Clarendon, 1996)
LW — *Luther's Works* [American edition], 82 vols. planned (St. Louis: Concordia; Philadelphia: Fortress, 1955–1986, 2009–)
NCBC — New Cambridge Bible Commentary
Neot — *Neotestamentica*
NIB — *The New Interpreter's Bible*, ed. L. E. Keck, 12 vols. (Nashville: Abingdon, 1994–2004)
NIBC — New International Biblical Commentary
NICNT — New International Commentary on the New Testament
NIDNTT — *New International Dictionary of New Testament Theology*, ed. C. Brown, 4 vols. (Grand Rapids, MI: Zondervan, 1975–1978)

NIGTC New International Greek Testament Commentary
NIVAC New International Version Application Commentary
NKZ *Neue kirchliche Zeitschrift*
NovT *Novum Testamentum*
NovTSup Supplements to Novum Testamentum
NPNF[1] *The Nicene and Post-Nicene Fathers*, Series 1, ed. P. Schaff (1886–1889, 14 vols.; repr., Peabody, MA: Hendrickson, 1994)
NSBT New Studies in Biblical Theology
NTC New Testament in Context
NTL New Testament Library
NTM New Testament Monographs
NTR New Testament Readings
NTR *New Theology Review*
NTS *New Testament Studies*
NTTSD New Testament Tools, Studies and Documents
NTT New Testament Theology
OBT Overtures to Biblical Theology
OCD *Oxford Classical Dictionary*, ed. S. Hornblower and A. Spawforth, 3rd ed. (Oxford: Oxford University Press, 1996)
OECS Oxford Early Christian Studies
OTP *Old Testament Pseudepigrapha*, ed. J. H. Charlesworth, 2 vols. (New York: Doubleday, 1983–1985)
PBM Paternoster Biblical Monographs
PG Patrologia Graeca [= *Patrologia Cursus Completus*: Series Graeca], ed. J.-P. Migne, 162 vols. (Paris, 1857–1886)
PGM *Papyri Graecae Magicae: Die griechischen Zauberpapyri*, ed. K. Preisendanz, 2nd ed. (Stuttgart: Teubner, 1973–1974)
PL Patrologia Latina [= *Patrologia Cursus Completus*: Series Latina], ed. J.-P. Migne, 217 vols. (Paris, 1844–1864)
PNTC Pillar New Testament Commentary
PPSD Pauline and Patristic Scholars in Debate
PriscPap *Priscilla Papers*
PRSt *Perspectives in Religious Studies*
PSN Paul's Social Network
PzB *Protokolle zur Bibel*
RB *Revue biblique*
RBS Resources for Biblical Study
ResQ *Restoration Quarterly*
RevQ *Revue de Qumran*
RGRW Religions in the Graeco-Roman World
RRA Rhetoric of Religious Antiquity
RRBS Recent Resources in Biblical Studies
RSECW Routledge Studies in the Early Christian World
R&T *Religion and Theology*
RTR *Reformed Theological Review*
SBL Studies in Biblical Literature
SBLDS Society of Biblical Literature Dissertation Series
SBLMS Society of Biblical Literature Monograph Series
SBLSBS Society of Biblical Literature Sources for Biblical Study
SBT Studies in Biblical Theology
SCJ *Stone Campbell Journal*
SE *Studia Evangelica*
SemeiaSt Semeia Studies
SERAPHMIE Studies in Education and Religion in Ancient and Pre-Modern History in the Mediterranean and Its Environs
SGBC Story of God Bible Commentary
SHBC Smyth & Helwys Bible Commentary
SJT *Scottish Journal of Theology*
SNTSMS Society for New Testament Studies Monograph Series
SNTW Studies of the New Testament and Its World
SP Sacra Pagina
ST *Studia Theologica*
STDJ Studies on the Texts of the Desert of Judah
StBibLit Studies in Biblical Literature
Str-B H. L. Strack and P. Billerbeck, *Kommentar zum Neuen Testament aus Talmud und Midrasch*, 6 vols. (Munich, 1922–1961)
StPatr *Studia Patristica*
SwJT *Southwestern Journal of Theology*
SymS Symposium Series
TANZ Texte und Arbeiten zum neutestamentlichen Zeitalter
T@C Texts@Contexts
TDNT *Theological Dictionary of the New Testament*, ed. G. Kittel and G. Friedrich, trans. G. W. Bromiley, 10 vols. (Grand Rapids, MI: Eerdmans, 1964–1976)
TDOT *Theological Dictionary of the Old Testament*, ed. G. J. Botterweck and H. Ringgren, trans. J. T. Willis et al., 8 vols. (Grand Rapids, MI: Eerdmans, 1974–2006)
TECC Theological Explorations for the Church Catholic
TENTS Texts and Editions for New Testament Study
TGST Tesi Gregoriana, Serie Teologia
THAT *Theologisches Handwörterbuch zum Alten Testament*, ed. E. Jenni, with C. Westermann, 2 vols. (Munich: Chr. Kaiser Verlag; Zürich: Theologischer Verlag, 1971–1976)
THNTC Two Horizons New Testament Commentary
ThSt Theologische Studiën
TLNT *Theological Lexicon of the New Testament*, C. Spicq, trans. and ed. J. D. Ernest, 3 vols. (Peabody, MA: Hendrickson, 1994)
TLZ *Theologische Literaturzeitung*
TNTC Tyndale New Testament Commentaries
TrinJ *Trinity Journal*
TS *Theological Studies*

TSAJ	Texte und Studien zum antiken Judentum
TU	*Texte und Untersuchungen zur Geschichte der altchristlichen Literatur*
TynBul	*Tyndale Bulletin*
TZ	*Theologische Zeitschrift*
USQR	*Union Seminary Quarterly Review*
VC	*Vigiliae Christianae*
VCSup	Supplements to *Vigiliae Christianae*
VT	*Vetus Testamentum*
WA	*D. Martin Luthers Werke: Kritische Gesamtausgabe*, 66 vols. (Weimar: Hermann Böhlaus Nachfolger, 1883–1987)
WA DB	*D. Martin Luthers Werke: Kritische Gesamtausgabe: Deutsche Bibel*, 12 vols. (Weimar: Hermann Böhlaus Nachfolger, 1906–1961)
WBC	Word Biblical Commentary
WC	Wisdom Commentary
WGRW	Writings from the Greco-Roman World
WGRWSup	Writings from the Greco-Roman World Supplement Series
WMANT	Wissenschaftliche Monographien zum Alten und Neuen Testament
WUNT	Wissenschaftliche Untersuchungen zum Neuen Testament
WEC	Wycliffe Exegetical Commentary
WTJ	*Westminster Theological Journal*
WW	*Word and World*
ZBK	Zürcher Bibelkommentare
ZCINT	Zondervan Critical Introductions to the New Testament
ZECNT	Zondervan Exegetical Commentary on the New Testament
ZNW	*Zeitschrift für die neutestamentliche Wissenschaft und die Kunde der älteren Kirche*
ZSNT	Zacchaeus Studies—New Testament
ZTK	*Zeitschrift für Theologie und Kirche*

Transliterations

HEBREW

Consonants						*Short Vowels*			*Long Vowels*		
			ל	=	l						
א	=	ʾ	מ	=	m	◌ַ	=	a	◌ָה	=	â
ב	=	b	נ	=	n	◌ֶ	=	e	◌ֶי	=	ê
ג	=	g	ס	=	s	◌ִ	=	i	◌ִי	=	î
ד	=	d	ע	=	ʿ	◌ָ	=	o	וֹ	=	ô
ה	=	h	פ	=	p	◌ֻ	=	u	וּ	=	û
ו	=	w	צ	=	ṣ				◌ָ	=	ā
ז	=	z	ק	=	q	*Very Short Vowels*			◌ֵ	=	ē
ח	=	ḥ	ר	=	r	◌ֲ	=	ă	◌ֹ	=	ō
ט	=	ṭ	שׂ	=	ś	◌ֱ	=	ĕ			
י	=	y	שׁ	=	š	◌ְ	=	ĕ (if vocal)			
כ	=	k	ת	=	t	◌ֳ	=	ŏ			

GREEK

Α	=	A	θ	=	th	Π	=	P	ψ	=	ps
α	=	a	Ι	=	I	π	=	p	Ω	=	Ō
Β	=	B	ι	=	i	Ρ	=	R	ω	=	ō
β	=	b	Κ	=	K	ρ	=	r	Ῥ	=	Rh
Γ	=	G	κ	=	k	Σ	=	S	ῥ	=	rh
γ	=	g	Λ	=	L	σ/ς	=	s	ʽ	=	h
Δ	=	D	λ	=	l	Τ	=	T	γξ	=	nx
δ	=	d	Μ	=	M	τ	=	t	γγ	=	ng
Ε	=	E	μ	=	m	Υ	=	Y	αυ	=	au
ε	=	e	Ν	=	N	υ	=	y	ευ	=	eu
Ζ	=	Z	ν	=	n	Φ	=	Ph	ου	=	ou
ζ	=	z	Ξ	=	X	φ	=	ph	υι	=	yi
Η	=	Ē	ξ	=	x	Χ	=	Ch			
η	=	ē	Ο	=	O	χ	=	ch			
Θ	=	Th	ο	=	o	Ψ	=	Ps			

Contributors

Adewuya, J. Ayodeji, PhD. Professor of Greek and New Testament, Pentecostal Theological Seminary, Cleveland, Tennessee: **Gifts of the Spirit; Sacrifice, Offering**.

Anderson, Garwood P., PhD. Dean and Professor of New Testament, Nashotah House Theological Seminary, Nashotah, Wisconsin: **Freedom/Liberty; Law**.

Arnold, Clinton E., PhD. Research Professor of New Testament, Talbot School of Theology, Biola University, La Mirada, California: **Magic**.

Barber, Michael Patrick, PhD. Professor of Scripture and Theology, Augustine Institute Graduate School, Greenwood Village, Colorado: **Interpretation: Augustine**.

Barclay, John M. G., PhD. Lightfoot Professor of Divinity, Durham University, Durham, United Kingdom: **Grace; Jesus and Paul**.

Barnett, Paul W., PhD, ThD. Lecturer Emeritus, Moore College, Sydney, Australia: **Tentmaking**.

Bates, Matthew W., PhD. Professor of Theology, Quincy University, Quincy, Illinois: **Gospel**.

Baum, Armin D., ThD. Professor of New Testament, Freie Theologische Hochschule Giessen, Giessen, Germany: **Pseudepigraphy/Forgery**.

Beers, Holly, PhD. Associate Professor of Religious Studies, Westmont College, Santa Barbara, California: **Demons and Exorcism**.

Bertschmann, Dorothea H., PhD. Tutorial Fellow of Biblical Studies, College of the Resurrection, Mirfield, and Visiting Fellow at the Department of Theology and Religion, Durham, United Kingdom: **Wrath, Destruction**.

Bevere, Allan R., PhD. Professional Fellow in Theology, Ashland Theological Seminary, Ashland, Ohio: **Colossians, Letter to the**.

Bird, Michael F., PhD. Academic Dean, Ridley College, Melbourne, Australia: **Christology; Righteousness; Supersessionism**.

Blackwell, Ben C., PhD. Professor of Early Christianity, Houston Theological Seminary, Houston, Texas: **Interpretation: Patristic**.

Blomberg, Craig L., PhD. Distinguished Professor Emeritus of New Testament, Denver Seminary, Littleton, Colorado: **Jesus, Sayings of**.

Bormann, Lukas, PhD. Professor of New Testament, University of Marburg, Marburg, Germany: **Interpretation: Modern Europe**.

Briones, David E., PhD. Professor of New Testament, Westminster Theological Seminary, Glenside, Pennsylvania: **Financial Support; Friendship**.

Brookins, Timothy A., PhD. Associate Professor of Classics, Houston Baptist University, Houston, Texas: **Corinthians, First Letter to the; Hellenism, Roman**.

Brown, Jeannine K., PhD. David Price Professor of Biblical and Theological Foundations, Bethel Seminary, Saint Paul, Minnesota: **Hermeneutics/Interpreting Paul; Philippians, Letter to the**.

Burge, David K., PhD. Senior Pastor, Drummoyne Presbyterian Church, Sydney, Australia: **Jerusalem, City of**.

Burke, Trevor J., PhD. Tutor in New Testament, Cambridge Theological Federation, and Visiting Lecturer, London School of Theology, London, United Kingdom: **Kinship Language in Paul**.

Byron, John, PhD. Dean of the Seminary and Professor of New Testament, Ashland Theological Seminary, Ashland, Ohio: **Man of Lawlessness and Restraining Power; Philemon, Letter to**.

Canty, Aaron, PhD. Professor of Religious Studies and Theology, Saint Xavier University, Chicago, Illinois: **Interpretation: Medieval**.

Capes, David B., PhD. Director, Lanier Theological Library, Houston, Texas: **Lord**.

Chester, Stephen J., PhD. Lord and Lady Coggan Professor of New Testament, Wycliffe College, Toronto, Ontario, Canada: **Conversion and Call of Paul; Interpretation: Luther**.

Ciampa, Roy E., PhD. S. Louis and Ann W. Armstrong Chair of Religion and Chair of the Department of Biblical and Religious Studies, Samford University, Birmingham, Alabama: **Abraham; Old Testament in Paul**.

Clarke, Andrew D., PhD. Honorary Professor of New Testament, University of Aberdeen, Aberdeen, Scotland: **Leadership; Servant, Service**.

Cohick, Lynn H., PhD. Provost and Dean of Academic Affairs, Professor of New Testament, Northern Seminary, Lisle, Illinois: **Ephesians, Letter to the; Households and Household Codes; Paul and Judaism**.

Colijn, Brenda B., PhD. Professor Emerita of Biblical Interpretation and Theology, Ashland Theological Seminary, Columbus, Ohio: **Atonement**.

Croasmun, Matthew D., PhD. Associate Research Scholar, Yale Divinity School, New Haven, Connecticut: **Sin, Guilt**.

Crook, Zeba, PhD. Professor, Carleton University, Ottawa, Ontario, Canada: **Social-Scientific Approaches to Paul**.

Danylak, Barry N., PhD. Executive Director, SEE Global, Calgary, Alberta, Canada: **Singleness and Celibacy**.

Darko, Daniel K., PhD. Wilson-Ockenga Professor of Biblical Studies, Gordon College, Wenham, Massachusetts: **Hope**.

Das, A. Andrew, PhD. Niebuhr Distinguished Chair and Professor of Religious Studies, Elmhurst University, Elmhurst, Illinois: **Narrative**.

Davies, Jamie P., PhD. Tutor of New Testament, Trinity College, Bristol, United Kingdom: **Apocalyptic Paul**.

deSilva, David A., PhD. Trustees' Distinguished Professor of New Testament and Greek, Ashland Theological Seminary, Ashland, Ohio: **Honor/Shame**.

Dickson, John P., PhD. Jean Kvamme Distinguished Professor of Biblical Evangelism and Distinguished Fellow in Public Christianity, Wheaton College, Wheaton, Illinois: **Gentiles; Witness**.

Diehl, Judith A., PhD. Retired, Denver Seminary, Denver, Colorado: **Anthropology, Pauline; Purity and Impurity**.

Dodson, Joseph R., PhD. Craig L. Blomberg Chair of New Testament, Denver Seminary, Denver, Colorado: **Philosophy**.

Downs, David J., PhD. Clarendon-Laing Associate Professor in New Testament Studies and Laing Fellow in Theology and Religion, Keble College, University of Oxford, Oxford, United Kingdom: **Almsgiving and Rewards; Collection for the Saints**.

Dunne, John Anthony, PhD. Associate Professor of New Testament and Director of the Doctor of Ministry Program, Bethel Seminary, St. Paul, Minnesota: **Food Laws and Customs, Jewish and Roman**.

Easter, Matthew C., PhD. Director of Christian Studies and Associate Professor of Bible, Missouri Baptist University, St. Louis, Missouri: **Faith of Christ**.

Edwards, Dennis R., PhD. Seminary Dean and Vice President of Church Relations, North Park Theological Seminary, Chicago, Illinois: **Interpretation: African American; Preaching from Paul Today; Slave, Slavery**.

Evans, Craig A., PhD. John Bisagno Distinguished Professor of Christian Origins, Houston Baptist University, Houston, Texas: **Prophet, Paul as; Qumran and Paul**.

Fiensy, David A., PhD. Professor Emeritus of Biblical Studies, Kentucky Christian University, Grayson, Kentucky: **Urban Setting of Paul's Churches**.

Flemming, Dean, PhD. Professor Emeritus of New Testament, MidAmerica Nazarene University, Olathe, Kansas: **Mission**.

Fox, Nickolas A., PhD. Adjunct Professor, Crown College, St. Bonifacius, Minnesota: **Hermeneutics/Interpreting Paul**.

Frederick, John, PhD. Pastor of Discipleship, The Falls Church Anglican, Falls Church, Virginia: **Colossians, Letter to the**.

Gill, Justin K., MA. Director of the Seth Wilson Library and Professor of Critical Backgrounds, Ozark Christian College, Joplin, Missouri: **Sexuality, Sexual Ethics**.

Gombis, Timothy, PhD. Affiliate Professor of New Testament, Fuller Theological Seminary, Pasadena, California: **Cosmology; Flesh; Justification**.

Gooder, Paula, DPhil. Chancellor, St. Paul's Cathedral, London, United Kingdom: **Body; Church Structure; Coworkers, Paul and His**.

Goodrich, John K., PhD. Professor of Bible, Moody Bible Institute, Chicago, Illinois: **Apocalypticism**.

Gordley, Matthew E., PhD. Dean of the College of Arts and Sciences, Carlow University, Pittsburgh,

Pennsylvania: **Firstborn; Hymns, Hymn Fragments, Confessions.**

Gorman, Michael J., PhD. Raymond E. Brown Chair in Biblical Studies and Theology, St. Mary's Seminary and University, Baltimore, Maryland: **Church; Cruciformity; In Christ.**

Gosbell, Louise A., PhD. Principal, Mary Andrews College, Sydney, Australia: **Disability and Paul.**

Gray, Patrick, PhD. Professor of Religious Studies, Rhodes College, Memphis, Tennessee: **Apocryphal Pauline Literature.**

Gundry, Judith M., ThD. Research Scholar and Associate Professor (Adjunct) of New Testament, Yale Divinity School, Yale University, New Haven, Connecticut: **Foreknowledge, Divine.**

Gupta, Nijay K., PhD. Professor of New Testament, Northern Seminary, Lisle, Illinois: **Ethics; Faith; Interpretation of Paul; Thessalonians, Letters to the.**

Gurry, Peter J., PhD. Associate Professor of New Testament and Codirector of the Text & Canon Institute, Phoenix Seminary, Scottsdale, Arizona: **Textual Criticism.**

Guthrie, George H., PhD. Professor of New Testament, Regent College, Vancouver, British Columbia, Canada: **Baptism.**

Hanlon, Daniel J., DMin. Rector, Christ the Foundation Anglican Church, Kailua, Hawaii: **Wisdom.**

Hardin, Justin K., PhD. Vice President for Academic Affairs and Professor of Biblical Studies, Ouachita Baptist University, Arkadelphia, Arkansas: **Discipline, Church; Judaizers; Judgment.**

Harris, Dana M., PhD. Professor of New Testament, Department Chair, Trinity Evangelical Divinity School, Deerfield, Illinois: **Cross.**

Heim, Erin M., PhD. Tutor in Biblical Studies, Wycliffe Hall, University of Oxford, Oxford, United Kingdom: **Adoption.**

Heiser, Michael S., PhD. Executive Director and Professor, Awakening School of Theology, Jacksonville, Florida: **Principalities and Powers.**

Hill, Wesley A., PhD. Associate Professor of New Testament, Western Theological Seminary, Holland, Michigan: **God.**

Hoklotubbe, T. Christopher, ThD. Director of Graduate Studies and Professor of Biblical Studies, NAIITS: An Indigenous Learning Community: **Savior.**

Hood, Jason B., PhD. Senior Pastor, North Shore Fellowship, Chattanooga, Tennessee: **Imitation of Paul / of Christ.**

Hubbard, Moyer V., DPhil. Professor of New Testament, Talbot School of Theology, Biola University, La Mirada, California: ***Cursus Honorum*; Religions, Greco-Roman.**

Humphrey, Edith M., PhD. William F. Orr Professor Emerita of New Testament, Pittsburgh Theology Seminary, Pittsburgh, Pennsylvania: **Tradition; Visions, Ecstatic Experience.**

Instone-Brewer, David, PhD. Honorary Research Fellow, Tyndale House, Cambridge, United Kingdom: **Marriage and Divorce, Adultery and Incest.**

Jacob, Haley, PhD. Associate Professor of Theology, Whitworth University, Spokane, Washington: **Glory, Glorification.**

Jipp, Joshua W., PhD. Associate Professor of New Testament, Trinity Evangelical Divinity School, Deerfield, Illinois: **Christ, Messiah; Hospitality; Kingdom of God/Christ.**

Jobes, Karen H., PhD. Gerald F. Hawthorne Professor Emerita of New Testament Greek and Exegesis, Wheaton College, Wheaton, Illinois: **Peter.**

Johnson, Andy, PhD. Willard H. Taylor Chair in Biblical Theology, Nazarene Theological Seminary, Kansas City, Missouri: **Holiness, Sanctification.**

Johnson, Dru, PhD. Associate Professor of Biblical and Theological Studies, The King's College, New York, New York: **Knowledge and Mind.**

Keener, Craig S., PhD. F. M. and Ada Thompson Professor of Biblical Studies, Asbury Theological Seminary, Wilmore, Kentucky: **Tongues.**

Kidson, Lyn M., PhD. Honorary Research Fellow, Macquarie University, Sydney, Australia: **Pastoral Epistles.**

Kugler, Chris, PhD. Research Associate, Keble College, University of Oxford, Oxford, United Kingdom: **Adam and Christ; Creation and New Creation.**

Lamerson, Samuel, PhD. Distinguished Professor of Biblical Studies, Knox Theological Seminary, Ft. Lauderdale, Florida: **Forgiveness.**

Lang, T. J., PhD. Senior Lecturer in New Testament, University of St. Andrews, St. Andrews, Scotland: **Mystery.**

Lee-Barnewall, Michelle, PhD. Senior Affiliate Professor of New Testament, Talbot School of Theology, Biola University, La Mirada, California: **Man and Woman**.

Leese, J. J. Johnson, PhD. Independent Teacher and Scholar, Seattle, Washington: **Ecological Paul**.

Licona, Michael R., PhD. Associate Professor of Theology, Houston Baptist University, Houston, Texas: **Resurrection**.

Lim, David S., PhD. President, Asian School of Development and Cross-cultural Studies, MetroManila, Philippines: **Fullness**.

Lyons, Thomas M., PhD. Director of Library Services and Education Technology, Northern Seminary, Lisle, Illinois: **Holy Spirit**.

McCaulley, Esau, PhD. Associate Professor of New Testament, Wheaton College, Wheaton, Illinois: **Galatians, Letter to the**.

McKnight, Scot, PhD. Julius R. Mantey Chair of New Testament, Northern Seminary, Lisle, Illinois: **James and Paul; Romans, Letter to the**.

McNutt, Jennifer Powell, PhD, FRHistS. Franklin S. Dryness Associate Professor of Biblical and Theological Studies, Wheaton College, Wheaton, Illinois: **Interpretation: Calvin**.

Miller, Becky Castle, PhD Student. Wheaton College Graduate School, Wheaton College, Illinois: **Ascension**.

Miller, James C., PhD. Professor of Inductive Biblical Study and New Testament, Asbury Theological Seminary, Orlando, Florida: **Ethnicity in Paul's World**.

Mitchel, Patrick, PhD. Director of Learning, Senior Lecturer in Theology, Irish Bible Institute, Dublin, Ireland: **Eschatology; Love**.

Moses, Jay L., DMin. Adjunct Professor of Religion, Elmhurst University, Elmhurst, Illinois: **Interpretation: Jewish**.

Myers, Jason A., PhD. Associate Professor of Biblical Studies, Greensboro College, Greensboro, North Carolina: **Fellowship, Communion, Sharing; Lord's Supper; Rhetorical Criticism**.

Nordling, Cherith Fee, PhD. Sessional Lecturer in Theology, Regent College, Vancouver, British Columbia, Canada: **Ascension**.

Odor, Judith A., PhD. Adjunct Professor, Asbury University, Wilmore, Kentucky: **Birth Pangs, Maternal Imagery; Women Named in Paul**.

Oropeza, B. J., PhD. Professor of Biblical and Religious Studies, Azusa Pacific University and Seminary, Azusa, California: **Covenant**.

Paul, Ian B., PhD. Adjunct Professor, Fuller Theological Seminary, Pasadena, California: **Universalism**.

Peeler, Amy L., PhD. Associate Professor of New Testament, Wheaton College, Wheaton, Illinois: **Son of God**.

Peppiatt, Lucy, PhD. Principal, Westminster Theological Centre, Cheltenham, United Kingdom: **Women**.

Perrin, Nicholas, PhD. President, Trinity International University, Deerfield, Illinois: **Salvation; Temple**.

Peterson, Ryan S., PhD. Associate Professor of Theology, Talbot School of Theology, Biola University, La Mirada, California: **Image of God**.

Pifer, Jeanette Hagen, PhD. Affiliate Professor of New Testament, Biola University, La Mirada, California: **Fruit of the Spirit**.

Pinter, Dean, PhD. Rector, St. Aidan Anglican Church, Moose Jaw, Saskatchewan, Canada: **Light and Darkness; Mercy; Name; Stumbling Block**.

Porter, Stanley E., PhD. President, Dean, Professor of New Testament, and Roy A. Hope Chair in Christian Worldview, McMaster Divinity College, Hamilton, Ontario, Canada: **Fear, Reverence; Travel in the Roman World**.

Rapske, Brian M., PhD. Professor Emeritus of New Testament, Northwest Baptist Seminary, Langley, British Columbia, Canada: **Legal System, Roman; Prison, Prisoner**.

Reasoner, Mark, PhD. Professor of Theology, Marian University, Indianapolis, Indiana: **Citizenship; Political Systems; Roman Christianity; Strong and Weak**.

Reeder, Caryn A., PhD. Professor of New Testament, Westmont College, Santa Barbara, California: **Violence**.

Reeves, Rodney, PhD. Senior Pastor, First Baptist Church, Jonesboro, Arkansas: **Ministry; Spirituality**.

Reid, Daniel G., PhD. Retired Editorial Director, IVP Academic, InterVarsity Press, Westmont, Illinois: **Satan, Devil; Triumph**.

Rhee, Helen, PhD. Professor of Church History, Westmont College, Santa Barbara, California: **Wealth and Poverty**.

Richards, E. Randolph, PhD. Research Professor of New Testament, Palm Beach Atlantic University, West Palm Beach, Florida: **Canon of Paul's Letters; Letters, Letter Forms; Patronage**.

Riesner, Rainer, Dr. theol. habil. Professor Emeritus of New Testament, University of Dortmund, Dortmund, Germany: **Chronology of Paul; Syrian Antioch**.

Roberts, Mark D., PhD. Senior Strategist, Max De Pree Center for Leadership, Fuller Theological Seminary, Pasadena, California: **Call, Calling; Pastor, Paul as**.

Rosner, Brian S., PhD. Principal, Ridley College, Melbourne, Australia: **Identity**.

Schnabel, Eckhard J., PhD. Mary F. Rockefeller Distinguished Professor of New Testament, Gordon-Conwell Theological Seminary, Hamilton, Massachusetts: **Jerusalem, Council of**.

Schreiner, Thomas R., PhD. James Buchanan History Professor of New Testament Interpretation, The Southern Baptist Theological Seminary, Louisville, Kentucky: **Circumcision**.

Shiell, William D., PhD. President and Professor of Pastoral Theology and Preaching, Northern Seminary, Lisle, Illinois: **Performance; Preaching, First-Century**.

Simmons, William A., PhD. Professor of New Testament Studies and Greek, Retired: **Prophecy, Prophesying**.

Sosa Siliezar, Carlos Raúl, PhD. Associate Professor of New Testament, Wheaton College, Wheaton, Illinois: **Interpretation: Reading Paul *Latinamente***.

Sprinkle, Preston M., PhD. President of the Center for Faith, Sexuality & Gender, Boise, Idaho: **Homosexuality**.

Staples, Jason A., PhD. Assistant Teaching Professor, North Carolina State University, Raleigh, North Carolina: **Body of Christ; Empire**.

Still, Todd D., PhD. Charles J. and Eleanor McLerran DeLancey Dean and William M. Hinson Professor of Christian Scriptures, Baylor University, George W. Truett Theological Seminary, Waco, Texas: **Truth**.

Stokes, Ryan E., PhD. Director of Graduate Theological Studies and Associate Professor of Biblical Studies, Carson-Newman University, Jefferson City, Tennessee: **Cursed, Accursed, Anathema**.

Strait, Drew J., PhD. Assistant Professor of New Testament and Christian Origins, Anabaptist Mennonite Biblical Seminary, Elkhart, Indiana: **Idolatry; Peace, Reconciliation**.

Sumney, Jerry L., PhD. Professor of Biblical Studies, Lexington Theological Seminary, Lexington, Kentucky: **Opponents of Paul**.

Thomas, Matthew J., DPhil. Assistant Professor of Biblical Studies and Theology Department Chair, Dominican School of Philosophy and Theology, Berkeley, California: **Israel; Works of the Law**.

Thornhill, Anthony Chadwick, PhD. Professor of Biblical and Theological Studies, Liberty University Rawlings School of Divinity, Lynchburg, Virginia: **Apostasy; Election and Predestination**.

Trebilco, Paul R., PhD. Professor of New Testament Studies, Theology Programme, University of Otaga, Dunedin, New Zealand: **Ephesus; Travel and Itinerary Plans**.

Tupamahu, Ekaputra, PhD. Assistant Professor of New Testament, Portland Seminary, Portland, Oregon: **Interpretation: Asian and Asian American; Interpretation: Postcolonial**.

Twelftree, Graham H., PhD. Professor of New Testament and Early Christianity, London School of Theology, London, United Kingdom: **Healing, Illness; Signs, Wonders, Miracles**.

Vaughan, Joy, PhD. Assistant Professor, Asbury University, Wilmore, Kentucky: **Tongues**.

Walton, Steve, PhD. Professor of New Testament, Trinity College, Bristol, United Kingdom: **Paul in Acts**.

Weima, Jeffery A. D., PhD. Deppe Family Chair of New Testament, Calvin Theological Seminary, Grand Rapids, Michigan: **Prayer**.

Westfall, Cynthia Long, PhD. Associate Professor of New Testament, McMaster Divinity College, Hamilton, Ontario, Canada: **Apostle; Head**.

Whisenand Krall, Amy, ThD. Assistant Professor and Assistant Program Director of Biblical and Theological Studies, Fresno Pacific University, Fresno, California: **Worship**.

White, B. G., PhD. Assistant Professor of Biblical Studies, The King's College, New York, New York: **Corinthians, Second Letter to the; Knowledge and Mind**.

Wilson, Todd, PhD. President, Center for Pastor Theologians, Chicago, Illinois: **Law of Christ**.

Winter, Bruce W., PhD. Former Principal, Queensland Theological College, and Warden, Tyndale House, Cambridge, United Kingdom: **Corinth**.

Wood, Shane J., PhD. Dean of Graduate Studies and Professor of New Testament, Ozark Christian College, Joplin, Missouri: **Afterlife; Death; Joy, Rejoicing; Politics and Power**.

Wu, Siu Fung, PhD. Independent Scholar, Australia: **Suffering**.

Yinger, Kent L., PhD. Professor of New Testament, Retired, Portland Seminary, Portland, Oregon: **Complete, Mature (Perfect); Gnosis, Gnosticism; Interpretation: New Perspective; Teaching, Teachers.**

ABBA. *See* ADOPTION; GOD; SON OF GOD.

ABRAHAM

In Paul's letters Abraham is explicitly named in Romans 4:1-3, 9, 12-13, 16; 9:7; 11:1; 2 Corinthians 11:22; and Galatians 3:6-9, 14, 16, 18, 29; 4:22 (he is always called Abraham in the NT, and never his original name, Abram). Of course, Abraham is discussed in surrounding texts as well, despite not being mentioned by name (e.g., Rom 4:10-11, 17-23; Gal 3:17; 4:23-31 [obliquely]). Abraham plays an important role in Paul's argument in his letters to the Galatians and to the Romans, especially for the purposes of supporting Paul's arguments about *justification, the nature of God's blessing of the nations/*Gentiles, and the identifying marks of God's *covenant people in *Christ.

1. Abraham in the Old Testament
2. Abraham in Second Temple Judaism
3. Abraham in Galatians
4. Abraham in Romans
5. Abraham in 2 Corinthians
6. Circumcision as Abrahamic Material
7. Common Themes in Paul's Discussions of Abraham

1. Abraham in the Old Testament.

Abraham's story is told in Genesis 11:26–25:10. He is called to leave his family and homeland to travel to Canaan with the promise that he will be blessed and become a great and powerful nation (Gen 12:1-3) that will be the source of great blessing. *God promises that Abram will have innumerable descendants, and when Abram believes that promise God credits that *faith to him as *righteousness (Gen 15:6). God then establishes a covenant with Abram that includes the gift of the land "from the river of Egypt to . . . the river Euphrates" (Gen 15:18 NRSV). A significant part of the narrative revolves around the fact that Abraham and his wife, Sarai, are unable to have children. He takes his wife's slave-girl, Hagar, and has a son by her, Ishmael (Gen 16). God changes Abram's name to Abraham because he will be the father of many peoples, and Sarai's name to Sarah, and he establishes *circumcision as the sign (and requirement) of his covenant, which includes a reiteration of the earlier promises (Gen 17).

God's plan is to provide a son through Sarah, despite the fact that both Abram and Sarai are elderly. Abraham's behavior seemingly undermines the promise when, more than once, he allows his wife to be taken into the harem of another man, until God intervenes (Gen 12:10-20; 20:1-18). God eventually provides a son, Isaac, through Sarah (Gen 21). At one point God asks Abraham to offer up Isaac (who is referred to as his "only son") as a *sacrifice, and Abraham is ready to complete that sacrifice when God intervenes and accepts a ram in Isaac's place (Gen 22). Abraham lives a long life, dying at the age of 175. The promises given to Abraham are reiterated to Isaac on the grounds that "Abraham obeyed my voice and kept my charge, my commandments, my statutes, and my laws" (Gen 26:5 NRSV).

In the rest of the OT Abraham's name is most frequently invoked when identifying God as "the God of Abraham [Isaac, and Jacob]" or when referring to the promises God gave to Abraham (on which Israel's hope depended) or to his role as the father of the nation (see Gen 28:13; 31:42, 53; Ex 3:6, 15, 16; 4:5; 1 Kings 18:36; 1 Chron 29:18; 2 Chron 30:6; Ps 47:9; Is 41:8; Jer 33:26).

2. Abraham in Second Temple Judaism.

Abraham is referred to in innumerable Second Temple Jewish texts. One of the major themes is that Abraham is the father of the Jewish people, with whom God established his covenant with *Israel, and the belief that God will continue to show Israel *mercy and *forgiveness for the sake of Abraham and the covenant (e.g., T. Levi 15.4; T. Asher 7.6-7;

Pss. Sol. 9.8-11; As. Mos. 3.8-10; 4.2-5; 4 Ezra 3.13-15; Josephus, *Ant.* 1.233-234; 11.169). Abraham is often presented as the archetypal proselyte, who rejected *idolatry and turned to the God of Israel instead (see Jub. 12.1-14; Apoc. Ab. 1–8).

Another key theme has to do with Abraham's unique righteousness and faithfulness to God (e.g., Josephus, *Ant.* 1.225). The opening lines of the Testament of Abraham say, "All the years of his life he lived in quietness, gentleness, and righteousness, and the righteous man was very hospitable" (T. Ab. 1.1; *OTP* 1:882). At 4.7 Michael the archangel tells God about Abraham, "I have not seen upon earth a man like him—merciful, hospitable, righteous, truthful, God-fearing, refraining from every evil deed" (*OTP* 1:884). Throughout the book he is referred to as "righteous Abraham." Many texts present Abraham as one who obeyed the *law of Moses even before it was given, including the Levitical laws and festivals (Sir 44:19-22; Jub. 15.1-2; 16:20, 26; 17:17-18; 23:10; CD III, 2-41; XVI, 6; 1 Macc 2:50-52; T. Levi 9.1-14; T. Benj. 10.2-5; T. Ab. 17; 2 Bar 57.1-3). According to Jubilees 23.10, "Abraham was perfect in all of his actions with the Lord and was pleasing through righteousness all of the days of his life" (*OTP*).

Philo's treatment of this theme (*Abr.* 1.5; 46.275-276) reflects a (seemingly Platonic) distinction between the law of Moses and a natural law that Abraham obeyed that anticipated that given to Moses (see 2 Bar. 57.1-3; also see Bekken's explorations of various differences and parallels between Philo's treatment of Abraham and Paul's arguments, including the redemption of Gentiles as proselytes who remain Gentiles, the distinction between Abraham's faithfulness and obedience to the law of Moses, and the reception of the Spirit as a result of believing in God). Philo's presentation presents Abraham as the ideal representation of the best of Greek *philosophy. Along the way, Philo repeatedly returns to Genesis 15:6 and the theme of Abraham's faith in God (Philo, *Leg.* 3.228; *Deus* 4; *Migr.* 44, *Her.* 90-95, 101; *Mut.* 177, 181-182, 186, 218; *Abr.* 262-274; *Virt.* 216-218; *Praem.* 27-30, 49-51). Philo argues on the basis of Genesis 17:17 that Abraham had a fleeting doubt about God's promise (because he was a mortal man and not God), but by speaking of what Abraham thought in his mind, "Moses has represented the doubt not as long-lived, or prolonged to reach the mouth and tongue, but staying where it was with the swiftly moving mind. . . . So then in the case of the virtuous man the swerving was short, instantaneous and infinitesimal, not belonging to sense but only to mind, and so to speak timeless" (Philo, *Mut.* 177-182 [LCL]).

Abraham's faithfulness in the midst of testing and trials is a common motif, especially (but not exclusively) with respect to the offering of Isaac (Sir 44:19; Jub. 17.17-18; 19.8; 1 Macc 2:50-52; Jdt 8:25-27). Anachronism is not infrequently present, with Abraham's faithfulness given as the grounds for the granting of the covenant or his being reckoned righteousness (e.g., in 1 Macc 2:50-52 Mattathias declares that Abraham was "found faithful when tested, and it was reckoned to him as righteousness" [NRSV], and Sir 44:19-22 suggests God's promises [in Gen 12] were given because Abraham had kept God's law).

Josephus presents Abraham as the consummate philosopher and polymath (*Ant.* 1:154-156, 165-168) who (in what seems to be Josephus's interpretation of Gen 15:6) "began to have more lofty conceptions of virtue than the rest of mankind, and determined to reform and change the ideas universally current concerning God. He was thus the first boldly to declare that God, the creator of the universe, is one" (LCL, 155). In the context of his offering of Isaac, Josephus says that Abraham submitted himself to God as a response to his *grace (225, 229).

3. Abraham in Galatians.

A key question regarding both Galatians and Romans is why Paul spends so much time on Abraham to make his arguments. Is it because his opponents are using Abraham in their arguments, and he must counter them? Does Paul need to provide a foundation based on Abraham because in a Jewish debate about soteriology any proposal that "does not work for Abraham . . . simply cannot be correct" (Gathercole, 156)? Is it because Abraham, as the father of Israel, provides the paradigm of faith that prefigures that of the Messiah (Hays 2005, xii-xiii)? Or is Paul expounding on the Abrahamic promises and covenant to show that the revelation of God's righteousness entails the fulfillment of these ancient promises (Wright 2013, 208)? Although the exact combination of motivations may differ between Galatians and Romans, it seems likely that a combination of the factors above is involved. Paul has not simply found Abraham to be a convenient but random biblical prooftext for his understanding of justification by faith.

In his letter to the Galatians, Paul's interest in Abraham is focused on the question of the identification of Abraham's true descendants (an issue that seems to have been a live one within Second Temple Judaism) and the blessings that he received and that are also received by his "children." Abraham is mentioned for the first time in Galatians 3:6, where Paul quotes Genesis 15:6 to indicate that believers' experience of miracles and the presence of God's Spirit (Gal 3:1-5) is predicated on their faith (or *pistis*), just as in Abraham's case his experience of being reckoned righteous by God took place when he believed God's promise about having innumerable descendants (Gal 3:6). In fact, faith that emulates Abraham's faith is what marks people as Abraham's descendants (Gal 3:7). That argument underwrites the assertion, involving a personification of Scripture, that Abraham had had the *gospel preached to him beforehand in the form of the promise that all the Gentiles (or nations) would be blessed in him, because Scripture had foreseen that God would one day justify Gentiles (reckon them righteous) on the basis of faith (Gal 3:8). So, Paul argues, those who believe (*in Christ) are, inasmuch as they experience justification through their faith, experiencing the blessing that Abraham experienced (Gal 3:9, reinforcing again the idea that such people are Abraham's true children).

Although Abraham is not mentioned in Galatians 3:10-13, that Paul mentions him again in Galatians 3:14 as he brings that passage to a conclusion suggests he has never been far from mind. Rather, all that was said about Christ being the key to being redeemed from a *curse was to show how Christ made it possible for Gentiles who have faith like Abraham did to experience "the blessing of Abraham," which would include justification and the promised Spirit (Gal 3:14 NRSV). Regarding the relationship between Abraham and reception of the Spirit in Galatians 3:1-5, 14, see the suggestion of Jarle Bekken (151-58, 198-202) that there is a parallel in Philo, *De virtutibus* 212-219, in that when Abraham believed God he received the divine Spirit, and the same would happen to other proselytes (see also Hays's suggestion that Is 44:1-3 provides the key background [Hays 2002, 182-83]).

Paul continues in Galatians 3:15-18 to explain how it is that the promises to Abraham are realized in Christ, addressing the question of the relationship between the promises given to Abraham and the establishment of the law of Moses. Paul's argument trades on the fact that the Greek word used for "covenant" (*diathēkē*) was the word for a testament or will, and Paul argues that such a legal document, once ratified, cannot be annulled or revised. Since God made his promises to Abraham in the form of a *diathēkē*, the law, which was not given until later, cannot be construed in a way that would make it an annulment or revision of the promise given earlier. Scholars debate whether Paul's use of *diathēkē* suggests he has a will or a covenant in mind. Bradley Trick argues for the former, positing that Paul has testamentary *adoption in mind and that Paul understands the Abrahamic *diathēkē* as God's testamentary adoption of the patriarch and of Christ as Abraham's unique seed who also shares in that inheritance. It seems Paul may be exploiting the polyvalence of the term *diathēkē* and blending together concepts related to covenants and testamentary adoptions. He is specifically concerned with the terms according to which the promised blessings are realized, wanting to establish that it cannot be on the basis of keeping the law since it was not introduced until "four hundred thirty years later" (Gal 3:17 NRSV). Interestingly, in this passage, Paul refers to the promises given to Abraham as a *diathēkē* but does not use the same term when referring to the law (although Gal 4:24-26 suggests he understood the latter to simply be another, later, *diathēkē*). The semantic domain of fatherhood and descendants is still essential, as Paul's argument turns on his understanding of laws of inheritance.

Significant attention has been given to Paul's argument in Galatians 3:16 based on the singular grammatical form (and referent, in his argument) of the word translated "offspring" or "seed" (*sperma*). Paul's argument across Galatians is to the effect that all those who have faith in Christ are Abraham's children or offspring, as Galatians 3:29 makes perfectly clear (see also Gal 3:7; 4:28-31). But here he exploits the fact that the word *sperma*, as a collective noun (a noun that denotes a group of individuals), is grammatically singular to interpret it (for the purposes of the argument in the near context, at least) as a reference to Jesus Christ. Here Christ is highlighted as the messianic descendant of Abraham in whom (as Paul understands it) all people of faith find their status as children of Abraham to be established. Paul thus draws a straight line from Abraham to Christ, and from the promises given to Abraham (and their anteriority to the giving of the law) to their fulfillment in Christ and those who have faith in Christ.

Paul had previously argued that those who have faith are children of Abraham based on their sharing of the family resemblance inasmuch as they also have faith (Gal 3:6-7), and has just argued that Jesus Christ is the exclusive referent of the term *sperma* in the promises to Abraham (Gal 3:16). In

Galatians 3:27-29 Paul argues from believers' union with Christ through *baptism (with faith implied) that they are all Abraham's *sperma* (seed/descendants) and heirs entitled to the promises given to Abraham.

Paul comes back to Abraham again in Galatians 4:21-31 (or Gal 5:1). Here Paul interprets the Genesis narratives about the births of Abraham's sons, Ishmael (Gen 16) and Isaac (Gen 18; 21), allegorically. The focus is more on the mothers (Hagar and Sarah) and sons than on Abraham himself, but the argument is ultimately about distinguishing the true children of Abraham. Scholars debate whether Paul means to say the Genesis texts themselves are an allegory, or whether he simply means he finds an allegorical interpretation appropriate for the purposes of distinguishing two types of Abrahamic descent, one that is by natural descent and one that is by spiritual descent. This is again about who counts as a child of Abraham, with the right to inherit (Gal 4:30) the blessing from their ancestor ("father") Abraham. Paul's reference to "two covenants" in Galatians 4:24 concerns not the covenant with Moses and the new covenant (the two that come most naturally to the Christian mind) but instead God's covenants with Abraham and with Moses (see Hays 1989, 114-15). Here Paul perhaps takes the people referred to in the text he quotes from Isaiah (Is 54:1) as references to Sarah (the "childless one" who bears no children and who endures "no birth pangs"; "the desolate woman"; Gal 4:27 NRSV) and Hagar ("the one who is married"; Gal 4:27 NRSV). Or he simply sees Sarah and Hagar fitting a pattern in which God eventually blesses barren women with more children than those who did not struggle to give birth (it would be odd to think a reference to "the one who is married" would refer to Hagar rather than Sarah, if Isaiah actually had these two women in mind).

In Galatians 4:28-31 Paul makes it clear that his interest in the two sons of the two women is based on the desire to identify different communities with each of the sons. The (predominantly Gentile) believers in Galatia are identified with Isaac as a "true" (or covenantal) son of Abraham (through Sarah). Those of Jewish/Judean descent and insisting on circumcision as a mark of God's covenant people are identified with Ishmael (and his mother, Hagar). Paul highlights the two different ways in which Abraham's sons were born (with Isaac understood to be the result of a miraculous intervention by God and Ishmael understood to have been conceived in the normal, natural, or "fleshly" way). His argument is that those of Jewish/Judean descent (and all who are circumcised) are children of Abraham by mundane or worldly means while the Galatian (Gentile) believers are children of Abraham by a more supernatural or spiritual means, thus having a stronger claim to the line of Isaac. It seems quite likely that Paul is turning the tables on an argument by which his opponents in Galatia argued that the Gentile believers were not yet proper sons of Abraham because they were not circumcised—so, if they had any relationship with Abraham, it was more along the lines of Ishmael, who had a connection but did not count as a son of Abraham for the purposes of God's covenant promises about Abraham's innumerable descendants.

Having reviewed the passages in Galatians where Paul explicitly mentions Abraham, it is now suitable to consider a few places where he or his story are or may be in mind even if he is not mentioned by name. It has been suggested (see especially Ehorn) that Paul's hypothetical reference to "an angel from heaven" (Gal 1:8 NRSV) preaching a contrary gospel may have Abraham's own well-known experience of receiving divine messages from angels in mind, especially given Paul's extensive engagement with Abraham traditions in the rest of the letter.

Even though Paul does not mention Abraham and quote Genesis 15:6 explicitly until Galatians 3:6, his discussion of being "justified by faith in Christ" in Galatians 2:15-16 may well already have him (and Hab 2:4) in mind. This is suggested by his extended argument in Galatians 3 to the effect that believers' experience of justification by faith results from following the footsteps of Abraham, who also was reckoned righteous based on his faith in God's promise. It is also consistent with Paul's argument that the promise that Abraham believed was about his offspring/seed (*sperma*), which Paul identifies as referring specifically to Christ in Galatians 3:16. Paul may well have understood that for Abraham to believe God about his *sperma* is equivalent to saying Abraham believed God about Christ and was reckoned righteous for that faith.

4. Abraham in Romans.

Paul introduces Abraham in Romans 4:1, and he remains at the center of the argument throughout Romans 4. He is brought up again in Romans 9:6-9 and in Romans 11:1.

The meaning of Paul's introduction to Abraham in Romans 4:1 has been debated. It is usually translated as in the NRSV ("What then are we to say was gained by Abraham, our ancestor according to the *flesh?") or the NET ("What then shall we say that Abraham, our ancestor according to the flesh, has discovered regarding this matter?"). Richard Hays and N. T. Wright, among others, have proposed it should rather be translated as "What shall we say? Have we found [on the basis of Scripture] that Abraham is our forefather according to the flesh?" (Hays 1985) or "What shall we say, then? Have we found Abraham to be our ancestor in a human, fleshly sense?" (Wright 2013). They point out that much of Paul's argument undermines the idea that "fleshly" descent from Abraham is the descent that matters, and certainly in Romans 4:11b-25 the spiritual or theological nature of Abrahamic descent is central to Paul's argument. However, in the near context (Rom 3:21-31; 4:2-11a) the argument seems to be more focused on whether righteousness is conferred on people on the basis of faith (*pistis*) or of the works of the law (esp. Rom 3:28; 4:2-8; see R. N. Longenecker, 486-91).

4.1. Abraham, "Works," and Faith. Paul argues in Romans 4:2-5 that Abraham was not justified (or reckoned righteous) by God on the basis of works but on the basis of his faith in God. "Works" or "*works of the law" are usually understood to refer to adhering to those things required by the covenant and law of Moses, and in this case Paul may have in mind the common Second Temple *tradition that Abraham kept the law of Moses (or a more universal set of divine laws) despite the fact that it was not yet established by God. The tradition that Abraham had kept all of God's laws (and that obedience was the foundation for God's blessing being extended through him) finds clear and early precedent in Genesis 26:4-5, where God tells Isaac, "I will make your offspring as numerous as the stars of heaven, and will give to your offspring all these lands; and all the nations of the earth shall gain blessing for themselves through your offspring, because Abraham obeyed my voice and kept my charge, my commandments, my statutes, and my laws" (NRSV).

Paul argues that Abraham's experience of justification had nothing to do with his performance of God's law or commandments but was a matter of trusting God as one "who justifies the ungodly" (Rom 4:5 NRSV). It may be that Paul here echoes the Jewish tradition about Abraham as the first and archetypal proselyte: that he had been an idolater (from a family of idolaters) and had come to faith in God. Thus Paul would hold that Abraham's status was as one of "the ungodly" up to the time he believed God's promise to him and was reckoned righteous as a result. Abraham's experience of being reckoned righteous by faith (Gen 15:6) is identified by Paul as the blessing to which David refers in Psalm 32 when he talks about the blessedness of not having *sin reckoned but having iniquities forgiven instead (Rom 4:6-8). However, the totality of Paul's treatment of Abraham leaves some ambiguity concerning whether Paul understands Abraham to have been included among "the ungodly."

4.2. Abraham's Chronology as an Interpretive Key for Paul. As in Paul's argument in Galatians 3, a key part of Paul's argument in Romans 4 turns on his understanding of the chronological sequence of the Abraham narrative in Genesis. In Galatians 3 Paul emphasizes that the law was established 430 years after the promises were given to Abraham. In Romans 4 it is crucial to Paul's argument and understanding of Genesis that Abraham was not yet circumcised (which is recounted in Gen 17) when the promises were given in Genesis 12 and when Abraham was reckoned righteous based on his faith in Genesis 15. Abraham had not yet had the opportunity to hear or respond to God's requirement of circumcision. Having been declared or reckoned righteous *before* the introduction of circumcision (Rom 4:9-11), this reckoning could not have been based on "works."

4.3. The Nature of Abrahamic Descent. Having established that Abraham was justified while uncircumcised (Rom 4:1-11a), Paul again (as in Galatians) moves to establish faith as the key to Abrahamic descent and inheritance, making him the father or ancestor "of all who believe without being circumcised" (Rom 4:11b NRSV) and also "of the circumcised who are not only circumcised but who also follow the example of the faith that our ancestor Abraham had before he was circumcised" (Rom 4:12). The argument that faith is the key to Abraham descent is reiterated again in Romans 4:16-17, where Paul asserts that the promise (which "depends on faith") is "guaranteed to all [Abraham's] descendants, not only to the adherents of the law but also to those who share the faith of Abraham (for he is the father of all of us, as it is written [citing Gen 17:5], 'I have made you the father of many nations')" (Rom 4:17 NRSV). Paul reiterates the promise of Genesis 17:[4-]5 in Romans 4:18 ("he believed that he would become 'the father of many nations,'" NRSV) and connects that to the original promise of Genesis 15:5: "according to what was said, 'So numerous shall your descendants be'" (NRSV). In Romans 4:23-24 Paul does not explicitly mention the idea of Abrahamic fatherhood or descent, but the previous argument leads the reader to understand that the words from Genesis 15:6, "it was reckoned to him" (Rom 4:23 NRSV), will apply not only to Abraham but also to Christian believers because Paul has already established that it is faith like Abraham's that establishes the family tie as far as the covenant is concerned.

Paul briefly returns to the nature of Abrahamic descent in Romans 9:6-9, where he rehearses an argument reminiscent of the one in Galatians 4:21-31 about the difference between "children of the flesh" and "children of the promise," with only the latter "counted as descendants" (Rom 9:8 NRSV). This supports Paul's statement that "not all Israelites truly belong to Israel, and not all of Abraham's children are his true descendants" (Rom 9:6 NRSV), since in Genesis 21:12 God says, "It is through Isaac that descendants shall be named for you" (NRSV). The children of the promise are those who have a supernatural conception, rather than a natural or fleshly one.

The question of Abrahamic descent is mentioned one last time in Romans 11:1, where Paul identifies himself as "an Israelite, a descendant of Abraham, a member of the tribe of Benjamin" (NRSV) as part of his argument that God has not rejected the people of Israel. In this case, Paul has natural or physical descent in mind; the question being addressed is that of God's faithfulness to the Jewish people in light of the rejection of the gospel by the majority of that community.

4.4. Abraham as a Paragon of Faith. In his extended portrayal of Abraham's faith in Romans 4:18-21, Paul presents Abraham as a perfect paragon of unstinting faith:

> He did not weaken in faith when he considered his own body, which was already as good as dead (for he was about a hundred years old), or when he considered the barrenness of Sarah's womb. No distrust made him waver concerning the promise of God, but he grew strong in his faith as he gave glory to God, being fully convinced that God was able to do what he had promised. (Rom 4:19-21 NRSV)

It was this remarkable faith in God's power to deliver what he promised that "was reckoned to him as righteousness" (Rom 4:22 NRSV). Of course, the rest of the Abraham narrative suggests this portrayal of unblemished faith does not reflect the whole story of his life. In Genesis 12:10-20 and in Genesis 20 Abram has Sarai identify herself as his sister, for his own protection. In Genesis 16, in what does seem to be a failure of faith as he "considered the barrenness of Sarah's womb" (Rom 4:19 NRSV), Abraham agrees to take Hagar as a second wife in order to have children through her rather than Sarai. It remains unclear whether Paul followed the line of Jewish interpretation that tended to overlook Abraham's weaknesses to present him as a consistent paragon of faith throughout his life, whether Romans 4:18-21 is concerned merely with Abraham's immediate response in Genesis 15:6 to the promise given in Genesis 15:4-5, or whether Paul has a more radical definition of "doubt" in mind (Schliesser's discussion of this issue is helpful).

Before his encounter with Christ, Paul would probably have seen adherence to the law of Moses and faith in God as perfectly complementary concepts. But he now perceives a strong distinction or even opposition between adherence to the law and adherence to faith in Christ (Rom 4:13-14), with the latter (unlike the former) being accessible to both Jews and Gentiles (that is, not requiring Gentiles to become Jewish proselytes). Abraham and his portrayal in Genesis is a key to this distinction.

4.5. Abraham as Heir of "the World." In Romans 4:13, Paul refers to "the promise that [Abraham] would inherit the world" and says that it "did not come to Abraham or to his descendants through the law but through the righteousness of faith" (NRSV). There are at least two interesting features of this verse. One is the suggestion that Abraham was promised that he would inherit "the world." The other is that this promise is said to have come to Abraham "through the righteousness of faith."

First, regarding the promise coming "through the righteousness of faith," one notes that God promises Abraham the land of Canaan in Genesis 12:7 and reiterates this promise in Genesis 13:14-15, 17, all of which is before Abraham is reckoned righteous by faith in Genesis 15:6. But the promise continues to be reiterated (and possibly reinterpreted) in Genesis 15:7, 18-20; 17:8; 26:3; 28:13-14. Inasmuch as the promise is given (Gen 12–13) before the establishment of the covenant of circumcision (Gen 17) or the giving of the law of Moses (Exodus), Paul's primary point may be that the promise was independent of and prior to any obedience to those covenants and thus has more to do with "the righteousness of faith" than the law, however the latter was conceived. Certainly, the contrast between faith and law (as two possible warrants for God's blessing) governs Romans 4:13-16.

Second, regarding the idea that Abraham was promised that he would inherit "the world," it seems that already in the OT some had come to understand that God's intention was not merely to give his people the land of Canaan but the whole world as the object of God's redemptive concern (see, e.g., Is 55:3-5). Perhaps the promise regarding Abraham's inheritance came to be understood in light of Psalm 2:7-8, where God promises to give the Davidic king "the nations" as his heritage/inheritance and "the ends of the earth" as his possession (see Ps 72:8, 11; Mic 5:1-4; Zech 9:9-10). Some Second Temple texts also suggest Israel's inheritance will be of a global nature (e.g., Sir 44:21; Jub 22.14; 32.19; 2 Bar. 14.13; 51.3). Other references in the NT suggest that the hope regarding the inheritance God had in mind for his people had been transformed, including Matthew 5:5 ("inherit the earth," NRSV); Matthew 19:29; Mark 10:17; Luke 10:25; 18:18 ("inherit eternal life," NRSV); and Matthew 25:34 ("inherit the *kingdom," NRSV). Paul himself talks about inheriting "the kingdom of God" (1 Cor 6:9-10; 15:50; Gal 5:21 NRSV; see also Eph 5:5), and elsewhere in the Pauline letters there are other indications that the anticipated inheritance has to do with something other than land (1 Cor 15:50b; Gal 3:18; 4:30; Eph 1:11, 14, 18; Col 1:12; 3:24).

4.6. Echoes of Abraham in Romans 8:32. Although Abraham is not explicitly mentioned, many find an allusion to his sacrifice of Isaac in Romans 8:32 ("He who did not withhold his own Son, but gave him up for all of us, will he not with him also give us everything else?"; NRSV) with that sacrificial offering serving as the prism through which Paul presents God's own offering of Christ (see Segal and many Romans commentaries, including those of Cranfield; Moo; R. N. Longenecker; Wilckens).

5. Abraham in 2 Corinthians.

Paul's only explicit reference to Abraham outside Galatians and Romans is found in 2 Corinthians 11:22, where Paul is responding to those he calls superapostles (*hyperlian apostolōn*) in 2 Corinthians 11:5; 12:11. Speaking of them and their supposed credentials, he asks, "Are they descendants of Abraham?" and answers, "So am I" (2 Cor 11:22 NRSV). Once again, Abrahamic descent is the issue, but in this case, Paul has natural or physical descent in mind, as traditional Jewish heritage is the credential being claimed in this case.

6. Circumcision as Abrahamic Material.

Given the clear and ancient direct association between Abraham and the covenant requiring circumcision (Gen 17), Abraham's story may be lurking just under the surface whenever Paul refers to circumcision as a requirement of God's covenant (e.g., Gal 2:3; 5:2-3; 6:6, 12-15; 1 Cor 7:19; Phil 3:3, 5; Col 2:11; 3:11; Rom 2:25-3:1; 3:30; 15:8 [not to mention the numerous references to circumcision in Rom 4, where Abraham is explicitly key to Paul's argument]).

7. Common Themes in Paul's Discussions of Abraham.

Most of Paul's discussions of Abraham revolve around the motif of his role as father of Israel and the implication of that fatherhood for the promises God made to him. The heirs of those promises and thus the correct identification of the children of Abraham are recurring themes. Abraham's descendants are to be identified not on the basis of genetic descent or a combination of genetic descent and family resemblance based on a similar obedience to God's law, but on the basis of family resemblance based on a similar faith in God and in God's promised seed of Abraham (in this case, Jesus Christ). In the Abraham narrative not all who descend from Abraham are counted as his children (e.g., Isaac and Jacob but not Ishmael and Esau), and for Paul that means that physical descent may not be a valid factor at all, but rather faith like Abraham's is the determinative factor. This faith is a marker of a spiritual or supernatural conception (analogous to that of Isaac) as opposed to a merely natural one (as in the case of Ishmael). In this the motif of father Abraham's role as the archetypal proselyte remains, but it is conceived in a way that does not entail, for Gentiles, full assimilation into the Jewish identity, but rather a way of being children of Abraham while remaining Gentiles. Some key Jewish themes regarding Abraham are abandoned (e.g., Abraham as one who was the ideal keeper of God's law and whose personal righteousness was the foundation for God's *election), others are maintained (e.g., Abraham's trust in God and the centrality of the promises to Abraham in God's redemptive plans), and some are radically transformed (e.g., the criteria for the identification of Abraham's children and the inclusion of Gentiles along with Jews in the Abrahamic family).

See also CIRCUMCISION; CORINTHIANS, SECOND LETTER TO THE; COVENANT; FAITH; GALATIANS, LETTER TO THE; GENTILES; ISRAEL; JUDAIZERS; JUSTIFICATION; LAW; OLD TESTAMENT IN PAUL; RIGHTEOUSNESS; ROMANS, LETTER TO THE; WORKS OF THE LAW.

BIBLIOGRAPHY. **W. B. Barcley,** "The Law and the Promise: God's Covenant with Abraham in Pauline Perspective," in *Perspectives on Our Father Abraham: Essays in Honor of Marvin R. Wilson*, ed. S. Hunt (Grand Rapids, MI: Eerdmans, 2010), 138-52; **P. J. Bekken,** *Paul's Negotiation of Abraham in*

Galatians 3 in the Jewish Context: The Galatian Converts Lineal Descendants of Abraham and Heirs of the Promise, BZNW 248 (Boston: de Gruyter, 2021); **L. L. Belleville,** "'Under Law': Structural Analysis and the Pauline Concept of Law in Galatians 3:21–4:11," *JSNT* 26 (1986): 53-78; **A. Borrell,** "Abraham and His Offspring in the Pauline Writings," in *History and Identity: How Israel's Later Authors Viewed Its Earlier History*, ed. N. Calduch-Benages and J. Liesen, Deuterocanonical and Cognate Literature: Yearbook (Berlin: de Gruyter, 2006), 359-68; **J. E. Bowley,** "Abraham," in *The Eerdmans Dictionary of Early Judaism*, ed. J. J. Collins and D. C. Harlow (Grand Rapids, MI: Eerdmans, 2010), 294-95; **B. Byrne,** *Son of God—"Seed of Abraham": A Study of the Idea of the Sonship of God of All Christians in Paul Against the Jewish Background* (Rome: Biblical Institute, 1979); **R. E. Ciampa,** "Abraham and Empire in Galatians," in *Perspectives on Our Father Abraham: Essays in Honor of Marvin R. Wilson*, ed. S. Hunt (Grand Rapids, MI: Eerdmans, 2010), 153-68; **M. Cranford,** "Abraham in Romans 4: The Father of All Who Believe," *NTS* 41 (1995): 71-88; **S. M. Ehorn,** "Galatians 1:8 and Paul's Reading of Abraham's Story," *JTS* 64, no. 2 (October 2013): 439-44; **C. A. Evans,** "Abraham," in the *Encyclopedia of the Dead Sea Scrolls*, ed. L. H. Schiffman and J. C. VanderKam (New York: Oxford University Press, 2000), 1:2-4; **G. D. Fee,** "Who Are Abraham's True Children? The Role of Abraham in Pauline Argumentation," in *Perspectives on Our Father Abraham: Essays in Honor of Marvin R. Wilson*, ed. S. Hunt (Grand Rapids, MI: Eerdmans, 2010), 126-37; **S. J. Gathercole,** "Justified by Faith, Justified by His Blood: The Evidence of Rom 3.21-4.25," in *Justification and Variegated Nomism*, vol. 2, *The Paradoxes of Paul*, ed. D. A. Carson, P. T. O'Brien, and M. A. Seifrid, WUNT (Tübingen: Mohr, 2004), 147-84; **G. W. Hansen,** *Abraham in Galatians: Epistolary and Rhetorical Contexts* (Sheffield: JSOT Press, 1989); **R. B. Hays,** "'Have We Found Abraham to Be Our Forefather According to the Flesh?' A Reconsideration of Rom 4.1," *NovT* 27, no. 1 (1985): 76-98; idem, *Echoes of Scripture in the Letters of Paul* (New Haven, CT: Yale University Press, 1989); idem, *The Faith of Jesus Christ: The Narrative Substructure of Galatians 3:1–4:11* (Grand Rapids, MI: Eerdmans, 2002); idem, *The Conversion of the Imagination: Paul as Interpreter of Israel's Scripture* (Grand Rapids, MI: Eerdmans, 2005); **N. L. C. Koyzis,** *Paul, Monotheism and the People of God: The Significance of Abraham Traditions for Early Judaism and Christianity* (London: T&T Clark International, 2004); **J. L. Kugel,** *Traditions of the Bible: A Guide to the Bible as It Was at the Start of the Common Era* (Cambridge, MA: Harvard University Press, 1998); **C.-C. Lee,** *The Blessing of Abraham, the Spirit, and Justification in Galatians: Their Relationship and Significance for Understanding Paul's Theology* (Eugene, OR: Pickwick, 2013); **A. T. Lincoln,** "Abraham Goes to Rome: Paul's Treatment of Abraham in Romans 4," in *Worship, Theology and Ministry in the Early Church*, ed. M. J. Wilkins and T. Paige, JSNTSup 87 (Sheffield: JSOT Press, 1992), 163-79; **B. W. Longenecker,** *The Triumph of Abraham's God: The Transformation of Identity in Galatians* (Nashville: Abingdon, 1998); **R. N. Longenecker,** *The Epistle to the Romans: A Commentary on the Greek Text*, ed. I. H. Marshall and D. A. Hagner, NIGTC (Grand Rapids, MI: Eerdmans, 2016); **D. J. Moo,** *The Epistle to the Romans*, NICNT (Grand Rapids, MI: Eerdmans, 1996); **P. Perkins,** *Abraham's Divided Children: Galatians and the Politics of Faith* (Harrisburg, PA: Trinity Press International, 2001); **B. Schliesser,** "'Abraham Did Not "Doubt" in Unbelief' (Rom. 4:20): Faith, Doubt, and Dispute in Paul's Letter to the Romans," *JTS* 63 (2012): 492-522; **A. F. Segal,** "'He Who Did Not Spare His Only Son . . . ': Jesus, Paul, and the Akedah," In *From Jesus to Paul: Studies in Honour of Francis Wright Beare*, ed. P. Richardson and J. C. Hurd (Waterloo, ON: Wilfrid Laurier University Press, 2006), 169-84; **J. Siker,** *Disinheriting the Jews: Abraham in Early Christian Controversy* (Louisville, KY: Westminster, 1991); **T. H. Tobin,** "What Shall We Say That Abraham Found? The Controversy Behind Romans 4," *HTR* 88, no. 4 (1995): 437-52; **B. Trick,** *Abrahamic Descent, Testamentary Adoption, and the Law in Galatians: Differentiating Abraham's Sons, Seed, and Children of Promise*, NovTSup 169 (Leiden: Brill, 2016); **U. Wilckens,** *Der Brief an die Römer*, 3 vols., EKKNT 6 (Zurich: Neukirchener, 1978–1982); **M. Wilcox,** "The Promise of the 'Seed' in the New Testament and the Targumim," *JSNT* 5 (1979): 2-20; **N. T. Wright,** "The Seed and the Mediator: Galatians 3.15-20," in *The Climax of the Covenant* (Minneapolis: Fortress, 1991), 157-74; idem, "Paul and the Patriarch: The Role of Abraham in Romans 4," *JSNT* 35 (2013): 207-41.

R. E. Ciampa

ACTS. *See* Chronology of Paul; Paul in Acts; Travel and Itinerary Plans.

ADAM AND CHRIST

For Paul, the juxtaposition "Adam and *Christ" signals some of the deepest and most profound, if also some of the least appreciated, elements of his theological vision. This juxtaposition concerns not only his doctrine of *sin and his soteriology but also his *Christology and his theological *anthropology. Paul's "Adam and Christ" discourse, and not least the way in which it presupposes and sometimes explicitly evokes the notion of the *imago Dei* from Genesis 1:26-28, reflects Paul's macro-theological vision.

1. Adam in the Old Testament
2. Adam in Second Temple Judaism
3. Adam in Paul

1. Adam in the Old Testament.
The Hebrew word of which the English word *Adam* is a transliteration appears first in Genesis 1:26-27, where the text states,

> Then God said, "Let us make humankind [Heb. *ʾādām*; Gk. *anthrōpos*] in our image, according to our likeness; and let them have dominion over the fish of the sea, and over the birds of the air, and over the cattle, and over all the wild animals of the earth, and over every creeping thing that creeps upon the earth."
>
> So God created humankind [Heb. *ʾādām*; Gk. *anthrōpos*] in his image,
> in the image of God he created them;
> male and female he created them. (NRSV)

That these early instances of Hebrew *ʾādām* refer to humanity in general and not to the primogeniture in particular is indicated both by the third-person plurals ("let *them*") and by the reference to creating *ʾādām* "male and female." The singular figure "Adam" is not in view until Genesis 2:7, where one first encounters Hebrew *ʾādām* in conjunction with first-person pronouns. Adam is not referenced again in the OT after Genesis 5:5: "Thus all the days that Adam lived were nine hundred thirty years; and he died" (NRSV).

2. Adam in Second Temple Judaism.
There was, however, considerable reflection on and speculation about Adam in later Second Temple sources. The most obvious examples are the Apocalypse of Moses and the related Latin Life of Adam and Eve, but there are similar themes in Jubilees 1–4; 4 Ezra 3–4; 6–7; 2 Baruch 4; 17–18; 23; 48; 54–56; and Philo (see especially Levison; Kugler, 61-88). These texts and traditions concern an array of issues: (1) theological anthropology: Adam's/humanity's relationship to *God (often as a creature made in his *image and likeness; e.g., LAE 12–16); (2) Adam's/humanity's vocation as stewards of God's *creation (e.g., throughout Apocalypse of Moses and Life of Adam and Eve); (3) the nature and consequences of the fall (e.g., Apocalypse of Moses; Life of Adam and Eve; 4 Ezra 3–4; 6–7; 2 Bar. 4; 17–18; 23; 48; 54–56); and (4) the relationship between the original creation and the *temple, the Torah, and the requirements of the latter for proximity to the former (e.g., Jub. 1–4). Moreover, there is also a relationship between Adam in the original creation and the high priest in the temple (e.g., Jub. 1–4; Sir 49:16–50:21; see Fletcher-Louis, 69-113). In some texts and traditions, the high priest was and is in the microcosm of the temple what Adam was created to be in the macro-temple of creation.

3. Adam in Paul.
Paul presents Christ in some kind of explicit typological (see the use of Greek *typos* in Rom 5:14) relationship to Adam in Romans 5:12-21 and 1 Corinthians 15:20-49. The connection is implicit in passages where Paul refers to the image of God (Rom 8:29; 1 Cor 11:2-16; 15:35-49; 2 Cor 3:18; 4:4; Col 1:15-20; 3:9-10). Moreover, a theology of Adam/humanity and of the consequences of the fall is presupposed in Pauline passages about *baptism (esp. Rom 6:1-11; Col 3:9-10; Eph 4:22-24). Likewise, Paul even, however subtly and implicitly, presents *Israel apart from the Messiah as no better than the rest of Adamic humanity (esp. Rom 7:11).

3.1. Christ and Adam: The Typological Relationship. In Romans 5:12-21, Christ and Adam stand in typological relationship. Adam is presented as the prototype of sinful humanity, the one through whose disobedience Sin and *death came into the world and so spread to all people. Christ, on the other hand, is presented as the prototype of the new humanity, the one through whose obedience "many will be made righteous" (Rom 5:19). Similarly, in 1 Corinthians 15:20-49, Paul depicts Adam as the one through whom death came into the world, and Christ as the one through whom comes the *resurrection of the dead. In other words, Christ more than reverses the effects of Adam's disobedience.

Whence, however, comes this explicit typology into Paul's thought? That some Jews reflected deeply on Genesis 1–3 is clear from (e.g.) the Apocalypse of Moses; the Life of Adam and Eve; Jubilees 1–4; 4 Ezra 3–4; 6–7; 2 Baruch 4; 17–18; 23; 48; 54–56; and Philo. But, in the Pauline typology, the emphasis lies on the way in which the resurrection that comes through Christ overcomes the death that had come through Adam. In other words, a major impetus for Paul's thinking in the area of his Adam-and-Christ typology is the meaning of the resurrection of Christ. Because, for Paul, Jesus was raised as the firstfruits of the general resurrection (Rom 8:23; 1 Cor 15:20, 23), and because, therefore, Jesus was raised ahead of the eschaton and *all by himself*, it was perhaps natural for Paul to contrast Jesus directly with the singular primal man through whom Sin and death came into the world.

There is, however, even more to this typology. Paul is also interested in the way in which Jesus and his people assume the sovereignty that God had originally intended for Adam but which the latter forfeited to the forces of Sin and death (Rom 5:14). This sovereignty will fully and finally be reclaimed in the resurrection by those in the Messiah (Rom 5:17; 8:18-23). This is also, moreover, at the heart of the argument of 1 Corinthians 15:20-58. In and through the death-defeating victory of the Messiah's resurrection, and in and through believers' participation in such, they will reign with the Messiah and so inherit God's eschatological rule (i.e., God's "*kingdom"; 1 Cor 15:50).

3.2. Adam and Image Christology. Furthermore, there is in 1 Corinthians 15:35-49 and particularly in 1 Corinthians 15:42-49 something also evident in Paul's other image-of-God passages: namely, a little-noticed but crucial teleological dimension to his thought. Adamic humanity, as a creation of the good creator God, was good, but it was created to grow into the *fullness of the incarnate, crucified, resurrected, and glorified image of the second, heavenly man.

Paul's other image-of-God passages likewise reflect this teleology. For Paul, the preexistent Jesus himself was and is the cosmogonical (i.e., the creating) and protological image of God according to which Adam was made and toward the eschatological fullness of which he was destined (Rom 8:29; 1 Cor 15:45-49; 2 Cor 3:18; 4:4; Col 1:15-20; 3:9-10). This image Christology is present not only in Colossians (which, for many, is deutero-Pauline) (see Col 1:15-20; 3:9-10), but it is also presupposed in the terse, famous statement of Paul's macro-theological vision in Romans 8:29: "For those whom he foreknew he also predestined to be conformed to the image of his Son, in order that he might be the firstborn within a large family" (NRSV).

Is Paul's image Christology, however, an Adam Christology or something else? J. D. G. Dunn influentially argued that one could detect here resonances of both Adam and *wisdom traditions (Dunn, 98-128, 163-212). But Dunn's reductionistic construal of wisdom Christology has tempted some "early high christologists" to reject a wisdom Christology in Paul altogether (so, e.g., Fee, 595-619, with discussion in Kugler, 24-26). Strictly speaking, it is correct to see Paul's image Christology as a wisdom Christology rather than an Adam Christology (Kugler). On the one hand, for Paul, indeed, there is a tight typological connection between Adam and Jesus, insofar as the former brought death into the world and the latter brought the resurrection of the dead. On the other hand, however, for Paul, Jesus is not to be conceived simply on a parallel with Adam but as the cosmogonical and protological image of God according to which Adam himself was made and toward the eschatological fullness of which he was destined (esp. Rom 8:29; Col 1:15-20; 3:9-10). Nor is this any small point.

Paul, like John (Jn 1:1-18) and the author of Hebrews (Heb 1:1-6), ascribes to Jesus some kind of preexistence and a role in the creation of the *kosmos*. For this purpose, he made christological use of the Jewish wisdom *tradition and of Middle Platonic intermediary doctrine (Cox; Kugler, 89-110). The Jewish wisdom tradition had already said that God's divine Wisdom—in Proverbs 8; and Sirach 1; 24, probably only as a literary personification—was present with God before the creation of the *kosmos*, existing as a mediator between God and humans and the rest of creation, imbuing the latter with divine Wisdom and enjoining humans to a life of wisdom. But it is later strands of this tradition, particularly Wisdom 7 and Philo, that provide the strongest parallel to Paul's image Christology. These Jewish traditions adopt elements of Middle Platonic intermediary doctrine, within which a distinct, divine ontological status is assigned to intermediary *sophia* ("Wisdom") and/or *logos* as God's cosmogonical and archetypal image (Cox; Kugler, 95-104).

Paul further uses this image-of-God concept to make a number of other exegetical and theological moves. First, this concept allows him, à la the Jewish wisdom tradition (Wis 7:26; Philo), to present the preexistent Jesus in Wisdom's place and so as the means by which the one God created the *kosmos* (especially Col 1:15-20). Furthermore, because of the resonances of the image-of-God concept in the Greek philosophical and cosmological tradition, and because of the way in which elements of the latter had already been taken up into traditions such as Wisdom 7 and Philo, Paul was able to present the preexistent Jesus not only as the cosmogonical and protological image of God but also as the teleological image of God toward the eschatological fullness of which humanity was destined. Finally, because of the use of the concept of the image of God in Genesis 1:26-28, Paul was able to ground his macro-christological and macro-theological vision in the foundational creation narrative of his sacred Scriptures (Kugler, 95-104).

*3.3. **The Old and New Humanity.*** Moreover, in Paul, Adam and Jesus respectively originate and represent the old and new humanities. This comes to particularly potent expression in Paul's theology of baptism. The old, Adamic humanity has been crucified and buried through baptism, while the new humanity has been proleptically raised in Christ and by the Spirit (Rom 6:1-11; Eph 4:20-24).

*3.4. **Adamic Israel.*** Paul also makes the point, especially in the difficult section of Romans 7:7-25, that Israel too is corrupted by an Adamic humanity. In Romans 7:7-25, Paul offers a speech-in-character where he assumes the role of a typical, Torah-faithful Israelite apart from the Messiah. There he contends that—not unlike what he had argued in Romans 2–3—though Israel had been called by God and given the Torah, because she was "fleshly" like the rest of Adamic humanity, Sin was able to seize an opportunity through Torah and so "deceive [Israel] and . . . kill [her]" (Rom 7:11). The language of "deceiving" and "killing" reflects an allusion to Genesis 3:13 and thereby makes the point that, despite and even through Torah, Sin and death had come upon Israel just as much as it had come upon the rest of Adamic humanity.

In many ways, the Adam and Christ juxtaposition refers to and represents the macro-vision within which Paul did much of his theologizing, living, church planting, pastoring, and teaching. He and his churches are "in Christ," but the "in Adam" nature rumbles along during the overlap of the ages and the overlap of the two kinds of humanity. But for Paul, all is not discontinuity here. After all, the preexistent Son created Adam in view of the day when the latter might grow in to his own incarnate, crucified, resurrected, and glorified fullness.

See also CHRISTOLOGY; COLOSSIANS, LETTER TO THE; CORINTHIANS, FIRST LETTER TO THE; CORINTHIANS, SECOND LETTER TO THE; CREATION AND NEW CREATION; DEATH; IMAGE OF GOD; RESURRECTION; ROMANS, LETTER TO THE; SALVATION; SIN, GUILT.

BIBLIOGRAPHY. **C. K. Barrett,** *From First Adam to Last* (London: A&C Black, 1962); **K. Barth,** *Christ and Adam: Man and Humanity in Romans 5* (Edinburgh: Oliver & Boyd, 1956); **R. Bultmann,** "Adam and Christ According to Romans 5," in *Current Issues in New Testament Interpretation: Essays in Honor of O. A. Piper*, ed. W. Klassen and G. F. Snyder (London: SCM Press, 1962), 143-65; **R. Cox,** *By the Same Word: Creation and Salvation in Hellenistic Judaism and Early Christianity*, BZNW 145 (Berlin: de Gruyter, 2007); **C. E. B. Cranfield,** *The Epistle to the Romans*, 2 vols. (Edinburgh: T&T Clark, 1975); **W. D. Davies,** *Paul and Rabbinic Judaism*, 4th ed. (Philadelphia: Fortress, 1980); **J. D. G. Dunn,** *Christology in the Making: A New Testament Inquiry into the Origins of the Doctrine of the Incarnation*, 2nd ed. (Grand Rapids, MI: Eerdmans, 1996); **G. D. Fee,** *Pauline Christology: An Exegetical-Theological Study* (Grand Rapids, MI: Baker Academic, 2007); **C. Fletcher-Louis,** "The Temple Cosmology of P and Theological Anthropology in the Wisdom of Jesus ben Sira," in *Of Scribes and Sages: Early Jewish Interpretation and Transmission of Scripture*, ed. C. A. Evans, Library of Second Temple Studies 50, Studies in Scripture in Judaism and Early Christianity 9 (Sheffield: Sheffield Academic Press, 2004), 69-113; **M. D. Hooker,** *From Adam to Christ: Essays on Paul* (Cambridge: Cambridge University Press, 1990); **L. J. Kreitzer,** "Christ as Second Adam in Paul," *Communio Viatorum* 32 (1989): 55-101; **C. Kugler,** *Paul and the Image of God* (Lanham, MD: Lexington Books/Fortress Academic, 2020); **J. Levison,** *Portraits of Adam in Early Judaism: From Sirach to 2 Baruch* (New York: Bloomsbury, 2015); **R. Scroggs,** *The Last Adam* (Oxford: Basil Blackwell, 1966); **M. Thrall,** "Christ Crucified or Second Adam? A Christological Debate Between Paul and the Corinthians," in *Christ and Spirit in the New Testament: Studies in Honour of C. F. D. Moule*, ed. B. Lindars and S. Smalley (Cambridge: Cambridge University Press, 1973), 143-56; **N. T. Wright,** *The Climax of the Covenant: Christ and the Law in Pauline Theology* (Minneapolis: Fortress, 1989).

C. Kugler

ADOPTION

The term *adoption* (*huiothesia*) does not appear frequently in Paul's letters (Gal 4:5; Rom 8:15, 23; 9:4; Eph 1:5), but it is a term of significant importance for understanding those passages where it appears. In each instance, Paul's use of the term builds on the logic of the Roman practice of adoption while also incorporating themes and echoes from the OT. It bears mentioning at the outset that *huiothesia* is a gendered term, meaning "adoption to sonship" and not "adoption as children." Paul uses the term *sonship* to forge a clear link to inheritance, and therefore this article will speak of "sons" rather than "children" to reflect the logic of Roman adoption. However, it is equally important to note that Paul is not privileging men nor excluding women by his use of a gendered term. In Paul's letters both men and women are equal inheritors of the promise and together are coheirs with Christ (Rom 8:17).

1. Adoption in Greek and Roman Practice
2. The Old Testament and Pauline Adoption
3. Adoption in the Pauline Texts

1. Adoption in Greek and Roman Practice. Since ancient adoption practices differ substantially from contemporary Western notions of adoption, it is necessary to first examine the practice itself. In scholarly treatments on Pauline adoption that emerged in the 1970s and 1980s, there was some disagreement on whether the term *huiothesia* (adoption to sonship) was best understood as *adoption* specifically, or with the more general term *sonship*. However, this question has been largely settled by J. M. Scott, whose 1992 monograph conclusively demonstrated that *huiothesia* always connotes adoptive sonship in particular and never is used to describe more general sonship. Yet, it is also important to point out that *adoption* describes an event that results in a permanent change in status—that is, adoption results in the *sonship* of the adopted son. Through adoption, a son of one father becomes the legal son of another father and is legally estranged from the family of his birth. All of his debts are canceled, and he is the heir apparent in his adoptive family.

There are some small distinctions between Greek and Roman practices of adoption, but it is likely that the term *adoption* in Paul's letters is trading primarily on the Roman concept, since Greek adoption practices were in decline by the time of Paul's writing (Heim). In any case, the two systems share much in common. In both earlier Greek practices and then Roman practices, the purpose of adoption was to secure the lineage and legacy of a father and a household, rather than to protect a vulnerable child. In both Greek and Roman adoptions, a father, through adoption, would name an adult male to be his son and heir in order to pass on his family name, inheritance, and estate.

There are three types of Roman adoption—testamentary adoption, *adrogatio*, and *adoptio*—all of which illuminate the inner logic of the Roman *familia* and so are relevant to discussion of the Pauline adoption texts. In Roman adoption the *paterfamilias* (the head of a Roman *household; usually the oldest male) chose an adult male (usually a younger son of a relative, or at least of a family of similar social status) to name as his son through an act of *huiothesia*. As son and heir, the adopted son of a Roman *paterfamilias*, upon the death of the father, inherited the father's power as the head of the household (*patria potestas*), and his estate. The son (as the new *paterfamilias*) was also tasked with the maintenance of the *gens* (family name and religion) of his adoptive family. In most instances, adoptions were testamentary; the adopted son and heir was named in the last will and testament of the deceased *paterfamilias*. Testamentary adoptions also feature most prominently in extant legal sources, likely because they were the most contested since the adoptive son was not named while a father was still living.

The two forms of adoption that involved a living father naming a new son and heir (*adoptio* and *adrogatio*) were likely less common but still highly recognizable cultural practices. *Adrogatio*, which was the rarest form of adoption, was the practice by which one *paterfamilias* adopted another *paterfamilias* along with his whole household. This was a serious matter, since it extinguished the *gens* of the adopted *paterfamilias*, and so *adrogatio* only took place after an investigation of the Roman pontiffs, and the adoption needed to be validated by the Roman *curia* (and so took place only in Rome). In contrast to the public affair of *adrogatio*, *adoptio* was a private transaction between the *paterfamilias* of an adoptive family and the *paterfamilias* of an *in potestate* (a son still under the authority of his *paterfamilias*) son's natural family, which was carried out before a local magistrate. As in the practice of Roman emancipation of sons to release them from the *potestas* and the right to their inheritance (*emancipatio*), a *paterfamilias* who wished to give his son in adoption sold his son three times, which nullified his *potestas* over the son. Upon the third instance, the adoptive *paterfamilias* claimed *potestas* over the adoptive son, thereby securing the son's place as the son and heir of his new *paterfamilias*. In the legal practice of Roman adoption, an adopted son's status in the family matched a natural firstborn son's status in every way, and thus adoption was a legitimate and legal way of establishing kinship ties apart from (and sometimes as a remedy for) biological lineage.

The three practices of Roman adoption illuminate several important cultural assumptions that likewise are present in Paul's own use of the term. Significantly, the practices of adoption uphold the logic and structure of the patriarchal society of the Roman *Empire. In order to adopt, one had to possess *patria potestas* (the power of the father), and thus one had to be male. The purpose of Roman adoption was to pass on one's *patria potestas*, and since women could not possess *patria potestas*, women were also not typically adopted (there are rare exceptions, but the term used in those instances is typically *thygatrothesia*, "adopted as daughter," and never *huiothesia*). The wife of the adoptive *paterfamilias* did not become a mother to the adopted son; however, the children of the *paterfamilias* did become the adopted son's sisters and brothers. Thus adoption was, in every respect and in keeping with Roman social norms, centered on the *paterfamilias*. Nowhere was this more evident than in imperial adoptions. The emperor, who was the Pater Patriae ("Father of the Fatherland"), adopted his successor beginning with the adoption of Octavian by Julius Caesar, and continuing throughout the time the NT authors were writing. These imperial adoptions were marked through public celebrations and broadcast on coinage and through monuments.

2. The Old Testament and Pauline Adoption. In some respects, Paul's use of *huiothesia* is unprecedented. The word group of Greek adoption terms does not appear anywhere in the LXX, and indeed Israelite religion and Second Temple Judaism do not contain evidence of a practice of adoption that is analogous to the adoptions practiced by the Greeks and Romans. However, in Romans 9:4 Paul lists *huiothesia* among the historic privileges of the Israelites, and thus it is equally clear that he sees *Israel's sonship of *God as *adoptive sonship* in particular.

Scott has argued that although the Greek word group is absent from the LXX, some OT texts (esp. 2 Sam 7:14) contain a Hebrew adoption formula. According to Scott, this formula, which in 2 Samuel 7:14 reads, "I will be a father to him, and he will be a son to me," signifies God's adoption of the Davidide as the representative Israelite. Scott also argues that Paul has this text and its reception in mind in all of his uses of *huiothesia*.

However, it is also possible that Paul does not have a particular text in mind when he speaks of Israel's adoption in Romans 9:4, but instead is evoking Israel's identity as God's son (e.g., Exod 4:22; Deut 8:5; 14:1; Is 1:2; Mal 3:16-17) in order to highlight the nature of sonship (which Paul, uniquely, sees as *adoptive sonship*). If this is the case, then Paul both evokes and reinterprets the sonship texts of the OT in his use of *huiothesia* in Romans 9:4.

3. Adoption in the Pauline Texts. Although the various cultural and textual influences from Greek, Roman, and Jewish sources must be taken into account when interpreting each of the Pauline occurrences of *huiothesia*, in each instance Paul has taken a term from his surrounding cultural context and put it to use within his own theological matrix, which is conditioned not only by his surrounding culture, but also, more importantly, by his encounter with the risen *Christ and his commission to preach the *gospel to the *Gentiles. It is most fruitful to examine each instance of *huiothesia* individually since each occurrence contains subtly different emphases.

3.1. Adoption in Galatians. In Galatians, which Paul wrote in order to combat the "agitators" who were attempting to compel the Galatian Gentiles to observe the Jewish *law, the adoption metaphor forms an integral component of Paul's larger argument for Gentile inclusion in the people of God on the basis of the Spirit rather than by their observance of Jewish law (Gal 3:1–5:1). The word *adoption* itself appears in the context of an extended analogy about an underage heir in a household (Gal 4:1-7). Paul offers this analogy in order to explain further how the Galatians, through Christ, have also become descendants of *Abraham (Gal 3:29). Appealing to the Galatians' shared experience of receiving the Spirit (Gal 3:1), Paul explains that the presence of the Spirit testifies to their adoption into Christ, and thus also into the lineage of Abraham.

The analogy Paul uses in Galatians 4:1-7 has several oddities that further reveal his theological reasoning. First, the heir introduced at the beginning of the analogy is presumably the natural heir of the household (Gal 4:1), but Paul insists that he is no different from a *slave when he is underage. While it is true that the *paterfamilias* over a Roman household had authority over his children, it is a striking statement indeed to claim that the freeborn children of a Roman father were no different from slaves. Likewise, in Paul's analogy the sons do not come of age but instead are delivered from slavery at the time appointed by the Father and through the coming of his *Son. The Galatians' sonship is therefore solely the prerogative of the Father, and the son in God's household in Galatians 4:1-2 turns out *not* to be a natural-born heir (Gal 4:5). Furthermore, the Son's coming effects the redemption of those under the law and secures their adoption to sonship, and Paul insists that the household of God therefore has many heirs rather than a solitary son who is the heir apparent. Finally, the Spirit testifies to their adoption, crying out, "Abba, Father," from the hearts of believers. Thus adoption in Galatians 4:1-7 is a trinitarian action that resulted in a new status and familial bonds for the Galatian believers.

3.2. Adoption in Romans. Paul uses the term *huiothesia* three times in his letter to the Romans, in relatively short succession in Romans 8–9. In Romans 8:15-23, Paul uses the term *huiothesia* twice, and these two instances have puzzled interpreters since they are seemingly at odds with each other. Indeed, some ancient manuscripts elide the second occurrence of *huiothesia*, presumably because of a perceived contradiction with Romans 8:15. However, the weight of the manuscript tradition favors viewing both occurrences of the term as original to Paul's letter.

The two occurrences of *huiothesia* in Romans are embedded in Paul's contrast between life according to the Spirit and life according to the *Flesh (*sarx*), which, in this context is Paul's word for anti-God powers. Life in the Spirit endows the believer with the mind of the Spirit (Rom 8:5), which leads to *peace and *righteousness. In contrast, those who live according to the Flesh have the mind of the Flesh, which is destined for *death, and those of the Flesh are unable to submit to God's law. In Romans 8, the Spirit and Flesh are best viewed eschatologically; they are the two possible modes of existence that have been brought about by the death and *resurrection of Christ. Those in the Flesh belong to the old order of *creation, which is destined for death and is passing away because it has been co-opted by the anti-God powers (*Sin), and those in the Spirit are participants in God's new creation. In Romans 8, *huiothesia* is primarily functioning as a term of eschatological transfer between the realm of the Flesh and the realm of the Spirit, and it likewise captures the change in believers' allegiance inherent in that transfer. In Romans 8:15 the believers' participation in the Spirit is marked by the Spirit's own testimony that they are sons of God and thus co-heirs with Christ. However, their participation in the age to come highlights their current displacement within the present age. Thus in Romans 8:23 Paul can likewise insist that those who have the Spirit groan inwardly as in the pains of childbirth as they eagerly await their adoption, which will be consummated upon the redemption of their bodies.

The occurrence of *huiothesia* in Romans 9:4 shares the least in common with Paul's use of the term elsewhere, though like the other occurrences it does still draw on the notion of sonship by decree. In Romans 9:4, Paul lists *huiothesia* in the privileges of the Israelites, which also include the giving of the law, the covenants, *temple *worship, and the promises (Rom 9:4). Some interpreters have posited that Paul is evoking Exodus 4:22 (Israel is my firstborn son), and others have seen Paul identifying Israel's adoption with the giving of the law at Sinai. However, Paul has likely chosen the term in order to emphasize the nature of Israel's sonship (sonship by divine decree/election), which nicely foreshadows his defense of God's faithfulness to Israel in Romans 9–11.

3.3. Adoption in Ephesians. In Ephesians, *huiothesia* occurs in the letter's opening benediction, as part of a series of rich and superlative blessings that are lavished on believers. In Ephesians, Paul speaks of believers being predestined in Christ for adoption (Eph 1:5), which marks adoption out as the *telos* of human existence. As in Galatians, adoption in Ephesians is a trinitarian act. The *Father* (Eph 1:3) has predestined believers for adoption *in Christ* (Eph 1:5), and they are marked by the **Holy Spirit* as a sign and seal of their inheritance (Eph 1:13-14). Paul is also clear that this trinitarian action is grounded in the *love of God, and that it takes place before the foundation of the world (Eph 1:4). Such a statement makes clear that God's plan was always to welcome his people through divine adoption (rather than through biology); God's adoption of his people, both Jew and Gentile, was not a savvy political calculation (as in Roman adoption) but an expression of his lavish love and the good pleasure of his will.

Although the occurrences of *huiothesia* in Paul's letters do not speak in unison, and therefore each must be taken on its own terms, they do speak in harmony with one another. All draw on the logic of Roman adoption, which entails kinship by the decree of the Father. In every case of *huiothesia* in the Pauline letters, it is the Father who acts to graciously bring many children into his family though the mission Son. These believers are joined together through the Spirit as children of God and as brothers and sisters of one another. Having received the Spirit, they groan with one another and with all of creation as they wait for their final redemption, which is the very thing God had planned for them from the foundation of the world.

See also EPHESIANS, LETTER TO THE; FLESH; GALATIANS, LETTER TO THE; HOLY SPIRIT; KINSHIP LANGUAGE IN PAUL; MAN AND WOMAN; OLD TESTAMENT IN PAUL; ROMANS, LETTER TO THE; SON OF GOD.

BIBLIOGRAPHY. **T. Burke,** *Adopted into God's Family*, NSBT (Downers Grove, IL: IVP Academic, 2006); **B. Byrne,** *"Sons of God"—"Seed of Abraham": A Study of the Idea of the Sonship of God of All Christians in Paul Against the Jewish Background* (Rome:

Pontificio Istituto Biblico, 1979); **K. Corley,** "Women's Inheritance Rights in Antiquity and Paul's Metaphor of Adoption," in *A Feminist Companion to Paul*, ed. Amy-Jill Levine (Cleveland: Pilgrim, 2004), 98-121; **E. M. Heim,** *Adoption in Galatians and Romans* (Leiden: Brill, 2017); **C. Johnson Hodge,** *If Sons, Then Heirs: A Study of Kinship and Ethnicity in the Letters of Paul* (New York: Oxford University Press, 2007); **R. B. Lewis,** *Paul's "Spirit of Adoption" in Its Roman Imperial Context* (London: Bloomsbury, 2016); **F. Lyall,** "Roman Law in the Writings of Paul: Adoption," *JBL* 88 (1969): 458-66; **M. Peppard,** *The Son of God in the Roman World* (New York: Oxford University Press, 2011); **J. M. Scott,** *Adoption as Sons of God: An Exegetical Investigation into the Background of ΥΙΟΘΕΣΙΑ in the Pauline Corpus* (Tübingen: Mohr, 1992); **J. C. Walters,** "Paul, Adoption, and Inheritance," in *Paul in the Greco-Roman World: A Handbook*, ed. J. Paul Sampley (Harrisburg, PA: Trinity Press International, 2003), 42-76.

E. M. Heim

AFFLICTIONS. *See* Suffering.

AFTERLIFE

Christ's life, *death, *resurrection, and *ascension brought a portion of the eschaton into the present as a revelation that heaven and earth, then and now, are no longer separate. The veil between heaven and earth, between eternity and the present, has been removed. Paul calls attention to this heavenly inbreaking and instructs Christians to live Spirit-centered lives as God's new *creation.

1. Removing the Veil
2. Reorienting Space and Time in Christ
3. Living on Earth as Present in Heaven
4. Conclusion

1. Removing the Veil.

Prior to *Christ, heaven was considered the abode of God and earth the abode of humanity, each space separated by a veil that, on occasion, *God uniquely penetrated to accomplish his purposes. This veil between heaven and earth was assumed to be quite thick. As Psalm 115:16 declares, "The highest heavens belong to God, but the earth he has given to humanity" (NIV, slightly modified). Even God's presence in the *Jerusalem *temple was considered an aberration (1 Kings 8:27), and death provided little resolution, whether envisioned as Sheol (Job 7:9; Ps 88:3-6) or the later paradise (2 En. 8.5-6; 2 Bar. 50.1–51:16; cf. Lk 16:19-31). Humanity and, to some extent, God were confined to their designated locations behind the veil.

Yet, according to Paul, Christ removes the veil (2 Cor 3:12-18). Christ's incarnation, death, resurrection, and ascension disrupt the separation between heaven and earth, God and humanity. Christ pierces the veil by making visible what was invisible (Col 1:15), by escorting the future into the present (2 Tim 1:10), by reorienting space and time under his sovereignty (Eph 1:20-21; Rom 14:8-9). This is all so that, by Christ's *light, believers can have "the eyes of [their] heart[s] enlightened" to his "incomparably great power" (Eph 1:18 NIV) on earth and in heaven, both now and in the age to come.

2. Reorienting Space and Time in Christ.

Removing the veil offers a new perspective on humanity's access to God. In fact, Paul compels Christians to gaze heavenward to correct their earthly perception: "We do not fix our attention on what is seen, but the things unseen. For what is seen is temporary, but what is unseen is eternal" (2 Cor 4:18). Paul wants believers to see that, through Christ, heaven is invading earth and vice versa.

Because of Christ, space and time do not function as before, now offering avenues of intimacy heretofore unknown. So, in 2 Timothy 4:16-17a, Paul is deserted by *human* presence at his defense, yet he claims, "But the Lord stood beside me and strengthened me"—a heavenly presence similar to Christ's intercession in heaven on behalf of Christians on earth (Rom 8:34; cf. 1 Cor 10:20-22). Thus, heaven invades earth even as the events of earth echo in heaven's halls.

Even death no longer separates humanity from God's presence (1 Cor 15:12-19), in contrast to the common portrayal in Jewish literature (see section 1 above). To some extent, the dead in Christ hold a more privileged position than the living (1 Thess 4:13-16; 5:10). Paul argues, however, that Christians alive on earth are still uniquely connected to heaven in Christ: "Even when we were dead in *sin, [God] made us alive together with Christ . . . and raised us up together and sat us together in the heavenlies in Christ Jesus, so that in the coming ages, he might demonstrate the incomparable richness of his *grace in kindness toward us in Christ Jesus" (Eph 2:5-7). Christ's life, death, resurrection, and ascension reorient space and time, and humanity's interaction with them, for Christians on earth are present in heaven in ways that defy understanding.

Indeed, Paul himself appears perplexed narrating the report of "a man in Christ" who, some "fourteen years ago," was "caught up to the third heaven" (2 Cor 12:2 NIV; cf. 2 En. 8.1; Apoc. Mos. 37.5; T. Levi 2.6-10; 3.1-9). Recounting this heavenly journey, Paul exclaims twice in two verses, "whether in the *body or outside the body I do not know, only God knows" (2 Cor 12:2-3). But what Paul *does* know is that, in Christ, the abode of God is a present reality for Christians, alive or dead (2 Tim 2:11). God is present with believers, and they with him, now and in the age to come, for through Christ Christians can "take hold of eternal life" today (1 Tim 6:12).

3. Living on Earth as Present in Heaven.
This is not to say that living on earth is no different from living in heaven. Paul is quite clear that "to depart and to be with Christ . . . is better by far" (Phil 1:23 NIV). In Christ, the perishing of the physical body results in life eternal (1 Cor 15:22-23), the defeat of all enemies (1 Cor 15:24-26, 54-55), and a bodily resurrection—the perishable clothed with the imperishable, the ignoble resurrected in glory, the forlorn transformed to power, the mortal replaced with immortality (1 Cor 15:42-43, 53). Or as Paul celebrates this metamorphosis, "Just as we bore the image of the dust, we will also bear the image of the heavenly" (1 Cor 15:49).

However, because of Christ, embracing death in the present (Gal 2:20) allows Christians to live as new creations on earth today (2 Cor 5:17). Christ's death led to a resurrection (1 Cor 15:3-4), releasing him to traverse earth unfettered by space and time (1 Cor 15:5-8) even in bodily form (1 Cor 15:42-44). As citizens of heaven on earth (Phil 3:20), the same is true for believers: "If then you were raised together with Christ, seek the things from above, where Christ is sitting at the right hand of God. Set your minds on things from above, not on things from the earth, for you died and your life has been hidden with Christ in God" (Col 3:1-3). The resurrection of Christ, then, does not just give Christians unique access to heaven in the future, but frees them to "reap eternal life" in the present (Gal 6:8 NIV), to harvest *fruit of the Spirit (Gal 5:16-26) as God's new creations living on earth (Gal 6:15). To be sure, there is also a future resurrection and new creation at the eschaton (1 Cor 15:12-23, 29-34; cf. 2 Tim 2:17-18). Yet, because Christ reoriented space and time, the *Holy Spirit, living in Christians, does not have to wait until the consummation to start transforming them into new creations (2 Cor 5:17; cf. 2 Cor 1:21-22; Eph 1:13-14), even if what is *now* is only "in part" and will be made whole when "completeness" comes (1 Cor 13:9-12; 2 Cor 5:1-5; 1 Tim 4:8-10).

4. Conclusion.
In the incarnation, heaven came to earth, eternity came to humanity, and Christ removed the veil between *glory and mortality. His death, resurrection, and ascension did not diminish this evolution but enhanced it. Now the *church as the *body of Christ (Eph 1:23), entrusted with "every spiritual blessing in the heavenly places" (Eph 1:3 NRSV), can, like Christ, traverse earth as an entry point to heaven. Christians can live in the present in light of the future as answers to the Lord's prayer: "Let your *kingdom come. Let your will be done, on earth as it is in heaven" (Mt 6:10).

See also CORINTHIANS, SECOND LETTER TO THE; CREATION AND NEW CREATION; DEATH; EPHESIANS, LETTER TO THE; ESCHATOLOGY; HOLY SPIRIT; RESURRECTION.

BIBLIOGRAPHY. **W. Baird,** "Visions, Revelation, and Ministry: Reflections on 2 Cor 12:1-5 and Gal 1:11-17," *JBL* 104, no. 4 (1985): 651-62; **P. R. Gooder,** "Eden and Beyond: Images of Paradise in Biblical and Extra-biblical Literature," *New Blackfriars* 83, no. 971 (2002): 3-15; idem, *Only the Third Heaven: 2 Corinthians 12.1-10 and Heavenly Ascent*, LNTS 313 (New York: T&T Clark, 2006); **M. J. Gorman,** *Cruciformity: Paul's Narrative Spirituality of the Cross* (Grand Rapids, MI: Eerdmans, 2001); **J. B. Hood,** "The Temple and the Thorn: 2 Corinthians 12 and Paul's Heavenly Ecclesiology," *BBR* 21, no. 3 (2011): 357-70; **A T. Lincoln,** *Paradise Now and Not Yet: Studies in the Role of the Heavenly Dimension in Paul's Thought with Special Reference to His Eschatology*, SNTSMS 43 (Cambridge: Cambridge University Press, 1981); **J. A. Loubser,** "Paul and the Politics of Apocalyptic Mysticism: An Exploration of 2 Cor 11:30–12:10," *Neot* 34, no. 1 (2000): 191-206; **C. R. A. Morray-Jones,** "Paradise Revisited (2 Cor 12:1-12): The Jewish Mystical Background of Paul's Apostolate, Part 1: The Jewish Sources," *HTR* 86, no. 2 (1993): 177-217; idem, "Paradise Revisited (2 Cor 12:1-12): The Jewish Mystical Background of Paul's Apostolate, Part 2: Paul's Heavenly Ascent and Its Significance," *HTR* 86, no. 3 (1993): 265-92.

S. J. Wood

AGE TO COME. *See* AFTERLIFE; APOCALYPTICISM; COSMOLOGY; ESCHATOLOGY.

ALLEGORY. *See* OLD TESTAMENT IN PAUL.

ALMSGIVING AND REWARDS

Provision of material support for the needy was a key practice of the Pauline *mission (Rom 12:13, 16;

15:25-32; 1 Cor 11:17-34; 16:1-4; 2 Cor 8:1–9:15; Gal 6:9-10; Eph 4:28; Phil 4:10-20; 1 Thess 5:14; 1 Tim 5:3-16; 6:17-19; Titus 3:14). As in other strands of early Christianity, the Pauline letters depict almsgiving as a deed that will be recognized and rewarded by *God, both in the present life and in the eschatological future.

1. Almsgiving and Reward in the Old Testament, Other Jewish Writings, and Early Christian Tradition.
In order to comprehend the relationship between almsgiving and reward in the Pauline epistles, at least two frameworks for gift giving need to be emphasized. The first is the widespread assumption and cultural practice in the ancient Mediterranean that gifts ought to be reciprocated. Although this conception of gift exchange may stand in tension with modern, Western notions of the free gift, an extensive body of literature has explored the connection between giving and reciprocity in the Greco-Roman world (see Barclay, 11-65; Downs, 1-26). A second key framework, perhaps not identical to the first but not unrelated to it, is the Jewish and Christian concept of eschatological *judgment on the basis of one's deeds, a notion clearly reflected in Paul's letters (e.g., Rom 2:5-11, 15-16; 14:10; 1 Cor 3:5-17; 4:1-5; 5:13; 11:31-32; 2 Cor 5:10; 11:15; 2 Tim 4:1, 8) but also represented in the literature of Second Temple Judaism (e.g., Jub 5:11, 15; 1 En. 38.1-2; 41.1; 95.5; 100.7. L.A.B. 64.7; 2 Bar 54.21; Pss. Sol. 9.1-5; 1QS 3-4; 4Q215a; T. Ab. 13.11-13) and other early Christian texts (Acts 10:42; 17:30-31; 24:25; Heb 6:2; 10:30; 13:4; 2 Pet 3:7; Rev 11:18; 20:11-15), including particularly the canonical Gospels (e.g., Mt 7:21-23; 10:15; 11:22-24; 12:36, 41-42; 13:37-43, 47-50; 16:27; 18:35; 19:28-30; 25:31-46; Jn 5:28-29).

A link between almsgiving and reward is established in numerous OT passages and in other Jewish writings. In the OT, almsgiving is a merciful deed that results in reward for those who share resources with the needy. Often recompense for almsgiving is described as divine blessing (e.g., Deut 14:22-29; 15:9-11; 24:13; 26:13-15; Prov 19:17; 22:9), and charity can result in material abundance (Prov 3:9-10; 11:25; cf. Prov 8:18-21) or *honor for God (Prov 14:31). Conversely, abuse and neglect of the poor may evoke divine *wrath, cursing, judgment, or financial ruin (Ex 22:21-24; Deut 27:19; Is 10:1-4; Jer 2:34-35; 5:27-29; Prov 21:13; 22:16; 28:27; Ezek 16:49-50; 22:22-23; Amos 2:6-8; 4:1-3; 8:4-14; Zech 7:8-14; Mal 3:5). In the LXX, at least two texts frame care for the poor as an act that can atone for *sin (LXX Dan 4:24; LXX Prov 15:27). This connection between almsgiving and atonement for sin is continued in Jewish apocryphal writings (e.g., Tob 12:8-9; Sir 3:30-31). At the same time, almsgiving is also depicted as a reciprocal exchange in which those who are generous to the needy will receive assistance in return, if donors later find themselves in distress (Tob 4:6-11; Sir 29:11-13).

In the canonical Gospels almsgiving is perhaps linked with atonement for sin in Luke 11:41 (cf. 1 Pet 4:8). But the stronger emphasis in Jesus' teaching is that care for the poor leads to heavenly or eschatological reward (Mk 9:41; Mt 6:2-4, 19-21; 10:40-42; 25:31-46; Lk 12:32-34; 16:1-9), although Mark 10:29-31 (cf. Lk 18:29-30) indicates that those who abandon possessions and family will receive reward both "now in this life—houses and brothers and sisters and mothers and children, and fields, with persecutions—and in the age to come eternal life."

2. Almsgiving and Reward in the Pauline Epistles.
In the Pauline epistles, there is no indication that sins can be cleansed, covered, removed, or redeemed by charity. Yet Paul does advance the notion that care for the poor will be recognized and rewarded by God, both in the present life and in the eschatological future.

In the context of his acknowledgment of the Philippians' partnership and material support in Philippians 4:10-20, for example, Paul indicates that their sharing with him "in the matter of giving and receiving" results in "the profit that increases to your account" (Phil 4:15, 17). This exchange of material gifts for spiritual reward is similar to Paul's assertion that the Macedonians and Achaians had received "spiritual blessings" from Christ-followers in *Jerusalem following the *Gentiles' financial support of the *collection for the saints (Rom 15:27). Similarly, when Paul remembers how the Galatians welcomed him in the midst of a physical affliction (Gal 4:12-15), he implies that his readers received divine blessing for their care for the *apostle (Gal 4:15).

In the context of his attempt to encourage the Corinthians to support the Jerusalem collection in 2 Corinthians 8–9, Paul twice highlights the theme of recompense for giving. In the first instance, the recompense is not from God but from the recipients of the offering, as Paul reminds the Corinthians that their generosity will establish a relationship of reciprocal exchange that might prompt the needy among the church in Jerusalem to support the Corinthians at some point in the future (2 Cor 8:14; see Schellenberg). At the same time, in 2 Corinthians 9:6-12, Paul states, "The one who sows sparingly will also reap sparingly, and the one who sows blessedly will also reap blessedly" (2 Cor 9:6). Returning to this image of sowing, Paul then cites LXX Psalm 111:9: "As it is written, 'He scatters abroad; he gives to the poor; his *righteousness endures forever.'" Given Paul's appeal for charity among the Corinthians, it is likely that he has transformed the subject of the psalm so that it refers to the one who generously supports the needy: righteousness is the blessed reward for the one who sows blessedly.

Finally, the most direct connection between heavenly reward and almsgiving in the Pauline corpus is found in 1 Timothy 6:17-19, which indicates that those who do good are rich in good works, generous, and willing to share "store up for themselves a good foundation for the future, so that they may take hold of the life that is truly life" (1 Tim 6:19).

The practice of providing material assistance to the needy was regularly advocated by Paul. While Paul offers numerous reasons that his assemblies should care for the poor—including, among others, to avoid God's judgment (1 Cor 11:27-34), to establish solidarity among geographically disparate communities (Rom 15:25-31), and to imitate the self-giving love of Jesus Christ (2 Cor 8:9)—one key motivation is that charity will result in divine reward.

See also ATONEMENT; COLLECTION FOR THE SAINTS; FINANCIAL SUPPORT; JUDGMENT; MISSION; WEALTH AND POVERTY.

BIBLIOGRAPHY. **J. M. G. Barclay,** *Paul and the Gift* (Grand Rapids, MI: Eerdmans, 2015); **D. Downs,** *Alms: Charity, Reward, and Atonement in Early Christianity* (Waco, TX: Baylor University Press, 2016); **N. Eubank,** "Justice Endures Forever: Paul's Grammar of Generosity," *JSPHL* 5 (2015): 169-87; **R. S. Schellenberg,** "Subsistence, Swapping, and Paul's Rhetoric of Generosity," *JBL* 137 (2018): 215-34; **K. L. Yinger,** *Paul, Judaism, and Judgment According to Deeds*, SNTSMS 105 (Cambridge: Cambridge University Press, 1999).

D. J. Downs

AMEN. *See* PRAYER.

ANATHEMA. *See* CURSE, ACCURSED, ANATHEMA.

ANGELS. *See* APOCALYPTICISM; MAGIC; PRINCIPALITIES AND POWERS.

ANTHROPOLOGY, PAULINE

For Paul there is no anthropology without theology. Humanity is to be understood in its relationship to the Creator *God and the incarnation of the *Son of God, through whom men and women enter a new reality. It is helpful to see Paul's anthropology in light of how humanity was viewed in his own day and in relationship to dualistic conceptions of humanity, both ancient and modern.

1. Greek Philosophy
2. Old Testament Background
3. Dualism
4. Paul's Inner and Outer Person
5. Condition of Humanity
6. Death and the Resurrected Body
7. Conclusion

1. Greek Philosophy.

Hundreds of years before Paul, philosophers such as Plato, Socrates, and Aristotle molded Greek and, later, Roman thought, influencing social *ethics, politics, religion, and anthropology. Paul encountered numerous Hellenistic philosophies that were distinct from Judaism as he traveled in his *ministry. Acts 17:18-33 records Paul's speech in Athens before a group of Epicurean and Stoic philosophers, who viewed life and humanity very differently. The Epicureans thought that the supreme good for humans was happiness, and their goal was a contented life. By the time of Paul, Epicurean ideas had fallen into a more "carnal" understanding of life (Croy). The pantheistic Stoics emphasized ethics and believed that happiness was achieved through virtue and excellence; they were also known for their attempts to tolerate *suffering through "calmness" (Thom). Paul answered their philosophies with the *gospel of Jesus *Christ and the immanent God who created the world.

Plato determined that the "soul" part of a person was a composite of three parts: reason is in the head (the mind), spirit is the upper one-third of the body's torso, and appetite is the lower one-third of the torso. *Death and the *afterlife were topics of much discussion among the ancient philosophers, and it was Plato who suggested that, as the essential part of the human being, the soul continues to live after physical death (Brown, "Soul").

Thus the Greeks perceived an obvious dualism in the world and in the human being. For the Greeks, the world was perpetually in a conflict of good versus evil, and some adhered to the notion that the physical was bad and the spiritual innately good. Virtuous inner qualities such as compassion and generosity were always in conflict with the physical desires of gluttony and greed. In this dualistic conception, matter and spirit were two realms in opposition, and restoration meant the release of the human soul from the heavy burden of the physical *body. This idea of separation and release is completely different from Paul's view of God's redemption and restoration plans for humanity. Paul did not adhere to the idea that all matter is evil and only the spiritual is good. His understanding was shaped by the Hebrew creation story, in which human bodies are indeed "very good" because God created them (Gen 1:31; Ps 139:13-16; Col 1:15).

2. Old Testament Background.
In contrast to the Greeks, the ancient Israelites viewed the person as a whole being. Steeped in Jewish culture, Paul believed that the person was one whole entity, designed and given life by God. The Hebrew word *nepeš* in Deuteronomy 6:5 is a difficult word to translate into English, but it commonly refers to "life" (Job 12:10; Dan 5:23); it can also be translated as simply "person," "someone," or "living being" (Gen 2:7). The meanings of the various terms used to describe a human being in the OT often overlap in sense and referent. Therefore, it is wise not to place too much distinction between these terms as they relate to the complex human being created by God.

2.1. Shema. As a Jew Paul was deeply informed by the Hebrew *Shema*: "Hear, O Israel: The Lord our God, the Lord is one. Love the Lord your God with all your heart and with all your soul and with all your strength" (Deut 6:4-5 NIV; see also Deut 4:29). The *Shema* underscores that, first, human beings are not divine; second, every person has heart, soul, and strength. The three terms do not necessarily imply that the human being has three parts. For the Hebrews, the *Shema* was much more about God and much less about the human being. It was a description of the whole, undivided person loving one, undivided God. The Israelites believed that the "heart" (*lēbāb*) was the center of human will, conscience, courage, mind, and understanding. The idea of the heart is common in the OT, where it is often connected with *love for God (Deut 10:12; 13:3; 30:6), and especially common in the Psalms (see Ps 119). This means that loving God must be a total commitment and active obedience to him. The *Shema*, then, is a Hebrew confession of *faith that promises that the love that humans have for God is to be total and complete, engaging one's whole being (Miller).

2.2. Person as God's Creation and Imago Dei. In line with the OT tradition, Paul promoted the idea that human beings, both male and female, were created by God as his ultimate creation. Humanity was created in God's "*image and likeness" (Gen 1:26-27; Col 1:15). A caring God "crowned" humanity with "*glory and honor" (Ps 8:3-6 NIV). People were appointed to "rule" (or "have dominion") with respect and integrity over all creation, disclosing the nature and plans of God (Gen 1:28; Ps 8:6-8). Because humans are created in God's image, they can reflect the very characteristics of their Creator, such as "*righteousness and *holiness" (Eph 4:24) and "*knowledge" (Col 3:10). Paul calls on believers to be "conformed to the image of his Son" (Rom 8:29 NIV), and as the bearers of the image of God, human beings are to replicate the love and righteousness of Creator God over all the earth (Rom 1:17-20).

However, the divine image in humans was marred by human *sin. Genesis 3 records the refusal and denial of God by human beings as their divine Creator and sole deity. Humanity failed to rule over *creation, to image God correctly, and to demonstrate his glory. Instead, people began to worship objects *within* creation, such as animals, reptiles, the sun, the moon, and rain. Paul writes, "Although they claimed to be wise, they became fools and exchanged the glory of the immortal God for images made to look like a mortal human being and birds and animals and reptiles" (Rom 1:22-23 NIV). Thus, by dishonoring their Creator and breaking their portion of God's covenantal agreements, the ancient peoples tarnished their reflection of God's image with their sinful desires, ingratitude, and rebellion. Paul retells this story in Romans 1:21-25. In losing its glory, humanity damaged its relationship with God and severely injured their relationships with one another. Paul recalls the long history of natural human depravity (Rom 1:28-31), including degrading the human body (Rom 1:24). He considers such behavior "foolishness" (Rom 1:22). Clearly, Paul viewed the original image of humanity as having been stained by sin and lawlessness (Rom 4:15; 5:12-13).

Losing the glory of God does not mean that humans are the same as animals and other creatures. Lawson Stone notes that Genesis 2:7 helps to define the differences between God's creatures: "Then the Lord God formed a man from the dust of the ground and breathed into his nostrils the breath of life, and the man became a living being" (NIV). The verb *form* is used to describe God's creation of both animals and people (Gen 1:21, 25; 2:19). Both humans and animals are given the "breath of life" (*nepeš hayyâ*, Gen 1:30 NIV; Job 33:4). This implies a physical connection between humans and animals, but *only* human beings are made in the image of God (Gen 1:27). The physicality of human beings is vital to their existence, but they possess something spiritual that connects them to God (who is Spirit; 2 Cor 3:18). Therefore, as Paul would say, *worship, devotion, and love are reserved for the "immortal God" and should not be given to any other created being (Stone).

3. Dualism.

For these purposes, dualism may be defined as binary principles that exist together, often in opposition to each other. N. T. Wright enumerates various distinctive types of dualism in first-century Judaism. Some early Jews divided the world into two realms: the good and the evil. They would have been conscious of a deep connection between the god dimension (the realm of the divine) and the human, earthly realm. This is demonstrated in the Qumran scroll War of the Sons of Light Against the Sons of Darkness (1QM; Wright 1992, 252). These Jews had a sense of cosmic dualism, which is the contrast of *light and darkness, day and night, hot and cold, even human beings and the divine.

Cosmological duality was the common position of Plato, who determined that the physical, material world is a copy or shadow of the "real" world, which is only perceived by the minds of informed, enlightened people. This view filtered down into the age of the Greco-Roman *empire (in various versions). What was perceived in the physical world was subordinate and inferior to what was encountered by the human mind and/or spirit. In a similar sense, anthropological duality regards the human being as a combination of physical body and soul, with the soul being superior to the body (Wright 1992, 253).

Ethical or moral dualism is the realm of human behavior, or the idea of right versus wrong, moral versus wicked. This is reflected in the beliefs of Zoroastrianism and some forms of *Gnosticism. In fact, most religions presume some kind of distinction between right and wrong in human behavior. In addition, early Judaism believed that humans had two inclinations, a good one and a bad one. So, people have to make choices between the two antagonistic inclinations. This idea may be applied to the "two spirits" or the "two ways" doctrines found in the Qumran scrolls (Wright 1992, 253-54). Most Jews also held to an eschatological dualism, which was the idea of two ages: the present age, which is evil, and the age to come, which is good (Wright 1992, 253).

3.1. Descartes's Dualism. In the seventeenth century, French philosopher and scientist René Descartes developed a philosophy of mind/body dualism. In his *Meditations* (1641) and *The Passions of the Soul* (1649), Descartes envisions a dualism of the human mind and matter (or the body), which are separate but "closely joined." The human being is a union of mind and body, but priority is given to the mind. The mind (or soul) is defined as thinking, while the body is explained as matter or "unthinking." The human being is a rational being; thus, Descartes famously deduced, "I think, therefore I am" (*cogito ergo sum*). Descartes argues that the mind can exist without a body, but the body cannot exist without a mind.

This dualistic understanding of the human being led to a number of unresolved questions. Descartes's dualism was challenged by people involved in the scientific fields and by those who viewed the soul as divine. Nevertheless, the mind/matter dualism of Descartes affected modern research, and his influence is felt in the study of physics, metaphysics, epistemology, and even theology. Consequently, for centuries, an anthropological dualism has prevailed in the West, with the human creature seen as a divided person with a body and a soul (Green, Palmer and Corcoran).

3.2. Undivided Unity. Paul, however, would declare that the person is an undivided entity; the intangible cannot exist without the tangible. Genesis 2:7 describes the human being, Adam, as a physical being created by God "from the dust of the ground"; God then put the "breath of life" into the "living being" (NIV). There is no mention of an abstract, disembodied, separate portion of the person created by God that is strictly spiritual (Green, "Resurrection"; 2008; Green, Palmer, and Corcoran).

Paul clearly enunciates his concept of two aspects of one complete person in his discussion of the *flesh and the spirit (or "mind"): "Those who live according to the flesh have their minds set on what the flesh desires; but those who live in accordance with the Spirit have their minds set what the Spirit desires" (Rom 8:5 NIV). In addition, he lists the "acts of the flesh" in contrast to the *"fruit of the Spirit," insisting that his readers should "walk by the Spirit" (Gal 5:16-26). To the Corinthians he writes, "Therefore, since we have these promises, dear friends, let us purify ourselves from everything that contaminates body and spirit, perfecting holiness out of reverence for God" (2 Cor 7:1 NIV).

4. Paul's Inner and Outer Person.

*4.1. **Outer Person.*** Yet, why did Paul conceive of an inner and an outer person? He uses these contrasting terms as metaphors for two different facets of a person; one is temporary and one is permanent. The inner and outer aspects of the whole person are distinguishable, but both are necessary to complete a living person. The outer body is the temporal "fleshly," "physical," or "natural" body (*sarkikos*, 1 Cor 15:39, 44, 50; Eph 6:12). The outer body (*sōma*) is the material aspect of a person, which is "wasting away" (2 Cor 4:16). He compares the outer body to an "earthly tent" (flimsy and temporary) in which "we groan and are burdened" (2 Cor 5:1, 4 NIV). A person has a body and is a body that houses the immaterial, inner spirit. The outer body is the human creatureliness, showing all human frailties, desires, and weaknesses, and is the basic condition of all living creatures (1 Cor 15:38-39). In addition to "wasting away," Paul says that the outer body is "subject to death" (Rom 7:24 NIV) and must be "controlled" (1 Thess 4:4).

*4.2. **Inner Person.*** Paul also speaks of the inner being, the interiority of the person, and its various aspects—mind, heart, spirit, soul, and will. As N. T. Wright puts it, for Paul the human "spirit" (*pneuma*) is "the human seen in terms of an interiority which is open to the presence and power of the creator (not least by his spirit)" (Wright, *Paul and the Faithfulness of God*, 492). The work of God's Spirit eludes containment in any particular term—whether guiding, calling, challenging, testifying, or empowering. This work is "different on the one hand from his presence in Jesus but different on the other hand from his presence everywhere else" (Wright, *Paul and the Faithfulness of God*, 1369). The Spirit is the deposit, or the beginning, of the spiritual transformation of the inner being into a "new creature" (2 Cor 1:22; 5:5). The outer change in a person is the visual expression of the inner Spirit of Christ in the person's life. "The Spirit himself testifies with our spirit that we are God's children" (Rom 8:16 NIV; see 1 Cor 2:10-11). Paul instructs believers to yield to the direction and guidance of the *Holy Spirit, who is working within them (Rom 8:6-8).

Because of the work of Christ and with the filling of the Holy Spirit, a new reality exists for the person who follows Christ. Paul teaches the Ephesians that their "former way of life" (in the flesh) was changed by the "*truth that is in Jesus" (Eph 4:21-22 NIV). Therefore, they are to "put off your old self [the outer person], which is being corrupted by its deceitful desires; to be made new in the attitude of your minds [the inner person]; and put on your [whole] new self, created to be like God [as one entity] in true righteousness and holiness" (Eph 4:22-24 NIV).

The Spirit is the power at work in those "in Christ." The Spirit "testifies" with the human spirit (Rom 8:16); he "helps us in our weakness" and "intercedes for us" (Rom 8:26 NIV). It is the Spirit who changes, renews, and enlivens the spirit of the person "as we wait eagerly for our *adoption to sonship, the redemption of our [physical] bodies" (Rom 8:23 NIV). Paul can liken the human body to a clay jar that holds the treasure of the true gospel of Christ (2 Cor 4:7). It may be frail and fragile, but the physical person holds great value because the Spirit of Christ is in the spirit of the person (2 Cor 5:6-10). "If the Spirit of him who raised Jesus from the dead is living in you, he who raised Christ from the dead will also give life to your mortal bodies because of his Spirit who lives in you" (Rom 8:11 NIV). By God's plan, then, the outer, frail, vulnerable aspect of the human being is temporary and will be replaced someday with a new body. The inner, spiritual, immortal facet is permanent and yet transformed by God's Spirit.

*4.3. **Soul.*** The Greek word *psychē* is generally translated as "soul"; it is an unusual word in Paul's letters. While it occurs over 900 times in the Greek LXX, it can be found only 101 times in the NT. In fact, it is found only 13 times in the Pauline letters. When it does appear in the NT, it is usually used to denote simply life itself, or the center of human life. In some NT passages, *psychē* can imply the whole natural being, or it can mean the inner life of a person, not unlike the ego or personality. *Psychē* is used as "human being" in Romans 2:9 and as "everyone" in Romans 13:1. It is used as "a living being" in 1 Corinthians 15:45 and "my life" in 2 Corinthians 1:23. As one example, Barnabas and Paul are said to be men who risked their "lives" *(psychē)* "for the *name of our Lord Jesus Christ" (Acts 15:26 NIV; Brown, "Soul," 682-83). The nonphysical soul/spirit is the foundation for human *spirituality. It is how humans can enjoy a relationship with God, and it is a bridge between this earthly life and the next life (Green, *What About the Soul?*).

Even so, in his closing prayer to the Thessalonians, Paul writes, "May your *whole* spirit [*pneuma*], soul [*psychē*] and body [*sōma*] be kept blameless at the coming of our Lord Jesus Christ" (1 Thess 5:23 NIV). This is not a declaration of a trichotomous understanding of the human being. It is a literary way of expressing a contrast between the soul/spirit and the body (Brown, "Soul," 684). In this letter, Paul is asking God to redeem and sanctify his readers "through and through," inside and out, to make them completely clean and totally "blameless at the coming of our Lord Jesus Christ" (1 Thess 5:23 NIV).

5. Condition of Humanity.

5.1. The Power of Sin. The behavior of humans is not their essence or fundamental nature, although their actions may result from their essence. As God's created beings, humans should love, obey, and be devoted to their Creator. However, falling short of their duties and obligations, humanity is subject to God's *judgment. The human condition has been blemished by rebellion against God, as seen in the laments of Job and in Psalms (e.g., Ps 55:4-5, 11). Paul summarizes the human condition:

> For since the creation of the world God's invisible qualities—his eternal power and divine nature—have been clearly seen, being understood from what has been made, so that people are without excuse. For although they knew God, they neither glorified him as God nor gave thanks to him, but their thinking became futile and their foolish hearts were darkened. (Rom 1:20-21 NIV)

Paul experienced the true condition of humanity for himself, and it is possible to view Romans 7:14-24 as reflecting his own experience. He fully recognized his own "sinful nature" as a nonbeliever, when he was "sold as a *slave to sin" (Rom 7:14 NIV): "What a wretched man I am!" (Rom 7:24 NIV). Even when he tried to be good, he could not. In Romans 7, Paul presents the war raging within the person: the spiritual and the unspiritual, the good and the evil, the mind and the body, the good *law and the sinful proclivities; all of the human being is subject to the power of sin and to opposing forces. The "old self" can be another expression of a pre-Christian lifestyle, with "deceitful desires," practices, and incorrect thinking (Rom 6:6; 12:2; Eph 4:22; Col 3:9).

Yet, it is for this reason that Jesus was sent to redeem the failing human condition. Paul's conclusion is, "Thanks be to God, who delivers me through Jesus Christ our Lord!" (Rom 7:25 NIV). Jesus was sent "in the likeness of sinful flesh to be a sin offering" to redeem humanity (Rom 8:3 NIV). Slavery is a Pauline image used to demonstrate the human condition. In the realm of the flesh, humanity is enslaved and condemned by the power of sin, but believers are free from this realm to live in the power of the Holy Spirit (Rom 6:4-6, 16-23). In view of the *cross, there are two mindsets among humanity: those who are living according to the flesh and those who are being governed by the Spirit (Rom 8:5-6, 8). Thus, the new self is "being renewed in knowledge in the image of its Creator" (Col 3:10 NIV). The condition of humanity, though still dire in the world, was radically changed by the work of Christ and by the indwelling Holy Spirit (Rom 6:11-14).

5.2. The New Reality. The gift of a new reality is a promise; it may not be completely visible today. Paul insists that "we fix our eyes not on what is seen, but on what is unseen, since what is seen is temporary, but what is unseen is eternal" (2 Cor 4:18 NIV). Patrick Miller argues, "What therefore is to be said about the human cannot be confined to general statements about humanity apart from God. In Christ, we see who we really are." In terms of *eschatology, ultimately who we are is yet to come. The new reality for humans is eternal life with Jesus, body and spirit, finally living with no tears but with *joy and *peace. Christians cannot see it now, but they do see Jesus, and he is the example (Miller, 63-73).

This new reality of redemption and restoration of humanity is initiated by God and accomplished by Christ (2 Cor 5:17). In spite of sin and disobedience, God did not leave people in a tumultuous condition (Rom 4:5; 5:6). He sent his Son to be a human being on earth and to redeem the human condition (Gal 4:4; Rom 5:8; 8:3). The true essence of humanity is defined in the salvific act of Christ. Although people are sinful in thought, word, and deed, they are created by God and are redeemable. The salvific work of Jesus Christ creates a new reality for humanity in which people are justified not by their own essence but by Christ's (2 Cor 5:18-21; Gal 3:11-13; Schnelle).

6. Death and the Resurrection Body.

6.1. Physical Death. For Paul, human life is to exist in and for Christ. In his life, he placed "no confidence" in his own physical abilities and achievements (the flesh, Phil 3:3-4). But "I have been crucified with Christ, and I no longer live, but Christ lives in me. The life I now live, I live by faith in the Son of God, who loved me and gave himself for me" (Gal 2:20 NIV). In contrast, physical death is the penalty for the sinful human condition, rejection of God, and disobedience (Rom 5:12-14). Whatever interrupts or interferes with human life is not part of God's original plan and desire for his people, including disease, destruction, and even death. Perhaps Paul was facing his own physical death when he wrote his later *letters to his churches; he desires to depart this life and "be with Christ," but he knows he has to continue his ministry "in the body" (Phil 1:23-24 NIV).

Thus, Paul clearly teaches his readers that they are redeemed from complete annihilation at physical death. There is some kind of direct presence and *fellowship with Christ after the separation of the temporary human body from the eternal human spirit at death. Constantine Campbell suggests that Paul implies that there is an intermediate state for the person, prior to bodily *resurrection, and that Paul expects to be "consciously with Christ" at that time (Campbell, 445). Then the physical body will finally be resurrected into a new, permanent body (Rom 8:23). "By his power God raised the Lord from the dead, and he will raise us also" (1 Cor 6:14 NIV). Putting Philippians 1:21-24 together with 2 Corinthians 5:1-10, Paul's emphasis is on the fact that this life is inferior to the life that is to come. That is, at death, "the body and the spirit/soul are temporarily separated, while the latter enjoys the presence of Christ and the former awaits its redemption" (Campbell, 448).

6.2. "Perishable and Imperishable." In 1 Corinthians 15 Paul defends the resurrection of Jesus and the resurrection of the human beings who belong to Christ by faith. The Corinthians were asking the same kinds of questions people ask today: "How are the dead raised? With what kind of body will they come?" (1 Cor 15:35 NIV). There are only hints about resurrection in the OT. Redemption was understood to be a divine promise of the restoration of the entire nation of *Israel, not of the individual person (Is 43:14; 44:6, 22; 63:8-9). *Hellenism had various beliefs about the afterlife, and there was no consensus about death and resurrection in Second Temple Judaism. So, what Paul had to say about the death and the resurrection of Christians was unprecedented and revolutionary.

Using images from nature, Paul likens human resurrection bodies to plant life (1 Cor 15:36-39). Like a seed, the earthly body will die and decay and then will be transformed into another, perfect body, like a living plant from the seed, that will serve God's purposes forever (see Jn 12:23-24). He then compares the new body to fleshly creatures (animals and birds, 1 Cor 15:39) in that they will all be different. Finally, he compares the spiritual body to various celestial bodies (sun, moon, and stars, 1 Cor 15:40-41) with their differing splendor. In biological terms, human death is the conclusion of life in the earthly body. As a consequence of sin, creatures really die, and the human being does not morph into another spiritual being such as an angel. Human bodies are always in the process of formation, as cells live and die; in the same manner, the physical body must be changed and renovated to live eternally with God (1 Cor 15:48-51). The future resurrection of the human body is guaranteed by the indwelling Holy Spirit, who "gives life" even in the present (Rom 8:10-11).

Thus, at the bodily resurrection, a new and different body is given to believers so that their new personhood is without sin but alive in Christ and with Christ (Rom 6:6-11). There is continuity, but there is also change; at the eventual return of Christ, "we will all be changed" (1 Cor 15:51 NIV). New bodies are not a reward for good behavior; they are a gift of God's *grace and love so that believers can be with him for eternity. In addition, Paul uses the metaphor of sleep to picture an interim time between physical death and human resurrection (1 Cor 15:18, 20; see Mt 9:24; Lk 8:52; Jn 11:11-14). Paul encourages his readers by using the image of "those who sleep in death," so the grief, *fear, and finality of death are removed by the assurance of the resurrection of believers, who are "in him" and "will be with the *Lord forever" (1 Thess 4:13-14, 17 NIV).

In the meantime, the human spirit is "being transformed into his image with ever-increasing glory, which comes from the Lord, who is the Spirit" (2 Cor 3:18 NIV). The transformation of the human spirit, then, begins on earth, when the Holy Spirit fills the believer (Rom 8:1-2, 6-11). God will complete this spiritual transformation in the end times: "Now the one who has fashioned us for this very purpose is God, who has given us the Spirit as a deposit, guaranteeing what is to come" (2 Cor 5:5 NIV). Redemption is the fulfillment of God's purposes for all of creation in Christ, through whom all things were made (Col 1:16), and the whole world is changed into a totally new creation (Rom 8:19-23). That is, the resurrection of human beings is not a rescue *from* the fallen world but a transformation *with* it. Everything in the corrupt cosmos must be restored and renewed by God to be in his presence. The transformation of the entire human being, body and soul/spirit, will accompany the transformation of the entire world (Green, "Resurrection").

Paul writes, "Death has been swallowed up in victory" (1 Cor 15:54 NIV). We know this victory is sure because of the death and resurrection of Jesus (Rom 6:5). Jesus was the firstfruits of all believers, who die and will be resurrected (1 Cor 15:20, 23). After his resurrection, his disciples saw him, finally recognized him, ate with him, and touched him. His body was the same but not the same. Paul tells the Corinthians that if they do not believe in the resurrection and transformation of the human being, they are denying the resurrection of Jesus Christ (1 Cor 15:12-17).

7. Conclusion.
Paul's anthropology is a theological anthropology. The human creature is a unique, individual entity, created and sustained by God. In the current state of humanity, it is difficult to even imagine human creatures existing eternally, but such is the plan of God, confirmed by Paul in his letters. Paul recognized the nature of human beings in the present world. In this life, the human creature is bound by the constraints of the physical, material, and corrupt cosmos. Yet at the return of Christ to earth, Christ-followers will receive new, transformed bodies for life with God. The Creator God, who made humans as body and soul/spirit, will redeem and restore his creation completely so that redeemed humanity can live and serve and enjoy being in the presence of a holy, righteous God forever.

See also Body; Cosmology; Creation and New Creation; Death; Flesh; Identity; Image of God; Philosophy.

BIBLIOGRAPHY. **M. F. Bird,** *Introducing Paul; The Man, His Mission and His Message* (Downers Grove, IL: InterVarsity Press, 2008); **C. L. Blomberg,** *A New Testament Theology* (Waco, TX: Baylor University Press, 2018); **C. Brown,** "Holy Spirit," in *NIDNTT* 3:689-709; idem, "Soul," in *NIDNTT* 3:676-89; **W. Brown, N. Murphy, and M. Newton,** eds., *Whatever Happened to the Soul? Scientific and Theological Portraits of Human Nature* (Minneapolis: Fortress, 1998); **C. R. Campbell,** *Paul and the Hope of Glory: An Exegetical and Theological Study* (Grand Rapids, MI: Zondervan, 2020); **J. W. Cooper,** *Body, Soul, and Life Everlasting: Biblical Anthropology and the Monism-Dualism Debate* (Grand Rapids, MI: Eerdmans, 1989); **N. C. Croy,** "Epicureanism," in *DNTB*, 324-27; **S. G. Eastman,** *Paul and the Person: Reframing Paul's Anthropology* (Grand Rapids, MI: Eerdmans, 2017); **D. F. Ford,** "The What, How, and Who of Humanity Before God: Theological Anthropology and the Bible in the Twenty-First Century," *Modern Theology* 27, no. 1 (2011); **B. Gladd and D. Gurtner,** eds., *From Creation to New Creation: Biblical Theology and Exegesis* (Peabody, MA: Hendrickson, 2013); **T. G. Gombis,** "Participation in the New-Creation People of God in Christ by the Spirit," in *The Apostle Paul and the Christian Life*, ed. S. McKnight and J. B. Modica (Grand Rapids, MI: Baker Academic, 2016), 103-24; **J. B. Green,** "Resurrection of the Body: New Testament Voices Concerning Personal Continuity and the Afterlife," in *What About the Soul?*, ed. J. B. Green (Nashville: Abingdon, 2004), 85-100; idem, ed., *What About the Soul? Neuroscience and Christian Anthropology* (Nashville: Abingdon, 2004); idem, *Body, Soul, and Human Life: The Nature of Humanity in the Bible* (Grand Rapids, MI: Baker Academic, 2008); **J. B. Green, S. Palmer, and K. Corcoran,** *In Search of the Soul: Four Views on the Mind-Body Problem* (Downers Grove, IL: InterVarsity Press, 2005); **D. Groothuis,** "New Age Spiritualities," in *Dictionary of Contemporary Religion in the Western World*, ed. C. Partridge and D. Groothuis (Downers Grove, IL: InterVarsity Press, 2002); **R. H. Gundry,** *Sōma in Biblical Theology: With Emphasis on Pauline Anthropolgy*, SNTSMS (New York: Cambridge University Press, 1976); **A. A. Hoekema,** *Created in God's Image* (Grand Rapids, MI: Eerdmans, 1986); **P. K. Jewett,** *Who We Are: Our Dignity as Humans* (Grand Rapids, MI: Eerdmans, 1996); **R. Jewett,** *Paul's Anthropological Terms: A Study of Their Use in Conflict Settings* (Leiden: Brill, 1971); **D. B. Laytham,** "Looking at What Cannot Be Seen: Reading 2 Corinthians Through the Lens of Ascension," *JTI* 15, no. 2 (2021): 305-17; **M. D. Litwa,** "2 Corinthians 3:18 and Its Implications for 'Theosis,'" *JTI* 2, no. 1 (2008): 117-33; **J. Maston,** "Christ or Adam: The Ground for Understanding Humanity," *JTI* 11, no. 2 (2017): 277-93; **P. D. Miller,** "What Is a Human Being? The Anthropology of Scripture," in *What About the Soul?*, ed. J. B. Green (Nashville: Abingdon, 2004), 63-73; **D. Moo,** *A Theology of Paul and His Letters: The Gift of the New Realm in Christ* (Grand Rapids, MI: Zondervan, 2021); **U. Schnelle,** *The Human Condition: Anthropology in the Teachings of Jesus, Paul, and John* (Minneapolis: Fortress, 1996); **L. G. Stone,** "The Soul: Possession, Part, or Person? The Genesis of Human Nature in Genesis 2:7," in *What About the Soul?*, ed. J. B. Green (Nashville: Abingdon, 2004), 47-62; **J. C. Thom,** "Stoicism," in *DNTB*, 1139-42; **N. T. Wright,** *The New Testament and the People of God* (London: SPCK, 1992); idem, *Surprised by Hope: Rethinking Heaven, the Resurrection, and the Mission of the Church* (New York: HarperCollins, 2008); idem, *Paul and the Faithfulness of God* (Minneapolis: Fortress, 2013); idem, *Pauline Perspectives; Essays on Paul, 1978–2013* (Minneapolis: Fortress, 2013).

J. A. Diehl

APOCALYPTIC PAUL

The word *apocalyptic* derives from Greek *apokalypsis*, "unveiling." In the field of biblical studies, it has a narrower focus on the visions recorded in revelatory literature, and in particular the book of Revelation, whose "title," *apokalypsis Iōannou*, provided the label for the genre apocalypse. The recognition of this origin and focus has been useful but has not completely cleared the "cloudiness of current definitions" of the word (Koch). Certainly, defining apocalyptic is a challenge, and one on which much depends.

One locus of confusion is the relationship between an "apocalyptic Paul" and the wider corpus of Jewish and Christian apocalyptic literature. It is sometimes suggested that the two fields of inquiry are using the word *apocalyptic* in entirely different ways. However, while it is not always immediately evident, the apocalyptic perspective on Paul has shared this commitment to examining the apostle's thought in relation to the theology and/or worldview expressed in the Second Temple Jewish and Christian apocalypses. The majority of the scholars discussed below acknowledge this relationship, variously understood, in their discussions of Paul's apocalyptic thought.

That is not to say, of course, that the challenge of definition is illusory. Every significant apocalyptic *topos* is debated among Pauline scholars. Examinations of apocalyptic literature have highlighted *eschatology, *cosmology, soteriology, and epistemology as key themes. The first of these, eschatology, has been a particular focus in discussions of apocalyptic, while the last, epistemology, has received significantly less attention. Likewise, approaches to Paul as an apocalyptic theologian have largely focused on one or more of these four themes. The importance of Paul's christological reworking of this theological framework must not, however, be underestimated, and it is here that crucial questions and differences often emerge in the debate over the apocalyptic Paul.

1. History
2. Contemporary Scholarship
3. Criticisms and Prospects

1. History.

1.1. Albert Schweitzer. The recent history of apocalyptic in Pauline scholarship begins in a less than promising position. It was certainly a concern in the late nineteenth-century German *Religionsgeschichtliche Schule* ("history-of-religions school"), as demonstrated by the work of Johannes Weiss and Wilhelm Bousset, for whom the imminent eschatology expressed in the Jewish apocalypses was a profound influence on NT thought. However, it was generally considered a feature of late Judaism to be treated with suspicion, certainly in relation to the message of Jesus but also for Paul. Far from the center of Pauline theology, post-Enlightenment liberal theology saw apocalyptic as something from which the *apostle needed to be saved.

It was thus against the grain of scholarship when Albert Schweitzer highlighted positively the importance of a Jewish apocalyptic worldview in NT thought. In his discussions of *Jesus and Paul, Schweitzer argued that early Christianity must be understood against this Jewish apocalyptic background. Though he rarely uses the term *apocalyptic* to describe his approach (preferring *spätjüdischen Eschatologie*, "late Jewish eschatology," or *Mystik*, "mysticism"), he repeatedly anchors this idea in Jewish apocalyptic thought. In his discussions of Paul, particularly in *The Mysticism of Paul the Apostle*, Schweitzer consistently draws on the Jewish apocalypses and the apocalyptic worldview (*Weltanschauung*) as source and context.

Schweitzer's discussion of Pauline mysticism has three defining characteristics. First, there is the theme of "thoroughgoing eschatology," the keystone of which is a commitment to the imminent end of the world and a dualistic contrast of two ages. Second, this eschatology is coupled with a belief in angelic or demonic powers, signaling the cosmic dimension of *salvation, understood not as individual transaction but as a "cosmologically conceived" view of redemption as "world-event." Third, these two characteristics of Paul's mysticism, eschatology and cosmology, are bound up in Schweitzer's central theme: the doctrine of "being-in-Christ," or Christ-mysticism. For Schweitzer's Paul, the "prime enigma" of Pauline theology is that the believer, through union with *Christ, participates now in the age to come and the cosmic redemption it brings (Schweitzer, 3). The Christian life in the present age is characterized by a cosmic struggle with angelic powers until the (imminent) eschatological consummation. This is the "Christ-mysticism" that constitutes the architectonic framework of Schweitzer's Pauline theology, the "main crater" within whose rim the doctrine of *righteousness by *faith is formed as a "subsidiary crater" (*Nebenkrater*; Schweitzer, 225).

1.2. Rudolf Bultmann. Schweitzer may have placed apocalyptic back on the radar of NT scholarship, but it nevertheless remained "unfashionable" (Käsemann 1969, 108), and his ideas were somewhat sidelined from Pauline exegesis and major reference works produced in the period between the two world wars. However, a generation after Schweitzer, a debate began that turned the tide and brought apocalyptic to the center in Pauline theology, and it remains crucial to understanding the ongoing conversation about the apocalyptic Paul.

Rudolf Bultmann, whose ideas on the question were already taking shape in the 1920s, agreed with Schweitzer that the apocalyptic mythological worldview was central to Paul's thought. The question was what to do with it. For Bultmann, the answer lay in his (in)famous program of *demythologization*, the classic formulation of which came in his 1941 essay "Neues Testament und Mythologie: Das Problem der Entmythologisierung der neutestamentlichen Verkündigung" (ET: "The New Testament and Mythology: The Problem of Demythologizing the New Testament Proclamation"). Bultmann argues that the prescientific cosmology and eschatology of the Pauline apocalyptic "mythical world picture" (*mythische Weltbild)* are not credible for the contemporary world. Adopting such an understanding of the cosmos would be both impossible and pointless for the contemporary Christian—it must instead be reinterpreted. Bultmann saw potential for such reinterpretation in an anthropological (which for him meant *existential*) approach to the interpretation of myth. When stripped of its mythological garments, apocalyptic became a way of understanding present authentic human existence. Apocalyptic cosmology, eschatology, *anthropology, and soteriology are all passed through this interpretative process. Language of cosmic powers is interpreted as way of understanding people's present captivity to their own fallenness, and future eschatology is transposed into a present eschatology located in the moment of individual responsibility and existential decision. Apocalyptic thus remained a central concern for Bultmann, but in what Koch calls a "completely negative respect" (Koch, 66).

1.3. Ernst Käsemann. Bultmann's strongest challenge came from one of his own students. In a bombastic series of essays, Ernst Käsemann agreed with his teacher about the centrality of apocalyptic for understanding Paul but insisted that Bultmann's demythologizing program, fueled by an individualistic and existential anthropology (influenced by Martin Heidegger), anachronistically prevented the apostle from speaking on his own terms. Where Bultmann felt the demythologizing imperative, Käsemann affirmed the opposite, insisting on the positive significance of apocalyptic in Paul. This was a concern for Bultmann and his allies, many of whom continued to view "primitive" Jewish apocalyptic mythology with suspicion.

Käsemann famously declared that "apocalyptic was the mother of all Christian theology" (Käsemann 1969, 102), though his explorations took particular shape in his disagreements with Bultmann's work on Paul. The battle lines between them can be most clearly seen on the question of anthropology and cosmology. Where Bultmann had transposed cosmology into anthropology, Käsemann went the opposite direction, placing anthropology within an apocalyptic cosmological frame. In his 1957 essay "Neutestamentliche Fragen von Heute" (the title essay of the 1969 collection, ET: *New Testament Questions of Today*), Käsemann argues that Bultmann's individualism had denied Paul's apocalyptic vision of humanity its cosmic breadth. For Käsemann's Paul, the world is not neutral ground but a battlefield in the war between cosmic powers. Humankind is therefore defined, as it were, from outside, caught up in the contested cosmos—not as individuals faced with the moment of decision but combatants. Anthropology, for Käsemann, is thus cosmology "*in concreto*" (Käsemann 1971, 27). The apocalyptic center of Paul's thought is not the crisis of decision but the question "To whom does the sovereignty of the world belong?" (Käsemann 1969, 135). This, he argues, is what it means to understand Paul's anthropology apocalyptically. Yet this was not simply a return to Schweitzer. In this cosmological-apocalyptic frame, Käsemann places a doctrinal emphasis not on mysticism but on the centrality in Pauline doctrine of the *dikaiosynē theou* (righteousness of *God), understood not as the salvation of the individual but as the militant saving power of God in recapturing the embattled cosmos for himself.

Käsemann's theological concern was not limited to a refutation of Bultmannian demythologization, however. He was also challenging Krister Stendahl (who was himself responding to Bultmann in other ways) and Oscar Cullmann with respect to their approach to the question of salvation history. Käsemann insisted that Paul remained an apocalyptic thinker who believed in future eschatology and who looked for an imminent *parousia*. Here it may be tempting to think that Käsemann's apocalyptic Paul meant a straightforward rejection of salvation history, but this would be a misreading. Käsemann was clear in his affirmation of salvation history as an indisputable horizon for Pauline theology, but he nevertheless remained vigorously resistant to any construals of this as an "immanent evolutionary process" (Käsemann 1971, 63). Here Käsemann does not mask the importance of his own experience as one of the "burnt children" of Nazism, which was for him a "secularised and political form" of nineteenth-century liberal progressive-evolutionary theology (Käsemann 1971, 64). Salvation history's importance as the horizon of Pauline thought is only defensible if such smooth continuities are rejected, and history is instead construed as an apocalyptic battlefield between the power of *death and life, *sin and salvation, and therefore as the locus of the promise and *triumph of God.

1.4. J. Christiaan Beker. The apocalyptic motif of God's cosmic triumph has left an indelible mark on apocalyptic treatments of Paul ever since, and an example of this is found in J. Christiaan Beker. In 1980, Beker published his most expansive treatment of Pauline theology, *Paul the Apostle: The Triumph of God in Life and Thought.* In its opening chapters, Beker outlines the architectonic theme of his Pauline theology: "contingency" and "coherence" in Paul's letters. In seeking to describe the coherent center of Paul's *gospel, he follows Käsemann in protesting against introspective distortions, offering as a correction an exposition of the Christ-event as "the reversal of the ages" and the righteousness of God as "God's liberating act for his creation" (Beker 1980, 7).

This center, Beker stresses, must not be understood as a dominant theme or symbol in Paul's thought, suggesting that this was the methodological error at the heart of Käsemann's fusion of righteousness by faith with apocalyptic. Rather, the center should be construed as a "symbolic structure," the linguistic expression of Paul's encounter with the risen Christ. The language Paul deploys to express his thought is that of Jewish apocalyptic, christologically intensified and modified. Thus understood, Christian apocalyptic constitutes the "heart of Paul's gospel" (Beker 1980, 17). Beker sees here a way through the Bultmann-Käsemann impasse. Although Bultmann had recognized (rightly, in Beker's view) the arbitrariness of the liberal distinction between "husk" and "core," he still considered Paul's apocalyptic thought as an existential projection of the human plight, and thus an obsolete myth to be reinterpreted, rather than the reality of God's triumph and the heart of Paul's gospel. He therefore still "surrenders the integrity of Paul's thought, although in a more sophisticated way" (Beker 1980, 141). Käsemann, on the other hand, fused apocalyptic with the theme of the righteousness of God and identified this theme as the Pauline center. Both were mistaken, Beker thinks, in failing to identify that apocalyptic is not a *theme* but the *texture* of Paul's gospel. Thus, a "consistent apocalyptic interpretation of Paul's thought" (Beker 1980, 143) is, for Beker, the only way to reframe the quest for the *Mitte* (logical center) of Pauline doctrine and demonstrate coherence in his epistles.

That is not to say, of course, that the matter of contingency had been forgotten. For Beker, the letters of Paul demonstrate considerable variety in the deployment of the apocalyptic texture of his thought according to the contextual situation. The "indicative" of God's triumph in Christ is linked in various ways to the "imperative" of his epistolary arguments to diverse audiences. In 1 Corinthians, the apocalyptic texture is clearly imposed on the (Hellenistic) situation. In Galatians, it is suppressed in response to a different (Judaizing) challenge.

In investigating the apocalyptic texture of Paul's thought, Beker relies heavily on interpretations of the Jewish apocalypses by Philipp Vielhauer and Klaus Koch (whom he prefers). Apocalyptic, for Beker, "revolves around three basic ideas: (1) historical dualism; (2) universal cosmic expectation; and (3) the imminent end of the world" (Beker 1980, 136). Paul's gospel modifies these essential apocalyptic ideas in the light of the Christ-event. For instance, the stark historical dualism of the "two ages" of the Jewish apocalyptic worldview is, for Beker, both tempered and intensified in Pauline apocalyptic. The "old age" is not straightforwardly an age of sin and death but contains the "hidden presence of God's promises" (Beker 1980, 151). It is crucial, therefore, that an apocalyptic interpretation of Paul marries the liberative core of his gospel—the triumph of God—to a salvation-historical scheme, properly understood as God's faithfulness to his promises and the climax of his plan of redemption. Nevertheless, Beker does not allow this tempering of historical dualism to lead to an evolutionary understanding of redemption history, since the Christ-event also represents the "incursion" of the age to come into the present, intensifying an eschatological crisis of conflict between the powers of death and life.

1.5. J. Louis Martyn. Two years after publication, Beker's *Paul the Apostle* was reviewed by a scholar sharing a debt to Käsemann, J. Louis Martyn. Martyn considers Beker's work "the strongest and the most compelling" attempt at a comprehensive treatment of Paul's thought and agrees that the best hope for coherence was to be found in a "consistent apocalyptic interpretation" (Martyn 1982, 194, 196). He takes issue, however, with what he sees as an unwelcome relegation of apocalyptic eschatological dualism in favor of historical linearity in Beker's marriage of apocalyptic and salvation history. Martyn's opinion is that this marriage was "rather more arranged by Beker than discovered in Paul" (Martyn 1982, 196).

Martyn's own apocalyptic approach to Paul developed over the next three decades but is best encapsulated in two influential volumes: the collection of essays published as *Theological Issues in the Letters of Paul* and his Anchor Bible commentary on Galatians. Beker would have considered this an unlikely hunting ground for an apocalyptic Paul, having judged Galatians an example of Pauline contingency that suppressed the apocalyptic theme of his gospel. Käsemann, likewise, makes almost no reference to the letter in his various essays on Pauline apocalyptic. Martyn, however, makes Galatians the keystone, a move made possible by his demonstration that Pauline apocalyptic, properly construed, is not suppressed there. For Martyn, Beker and Käsemann's reliance on a view of apocalyptic focused on imminent expectation and future triumph has the effect of blinkering their vision when it came to Galatians. Crucial to the shedding of these blinkers is allowing Galatians to inform a fresh reconsideration of the apocalyptic heart of Paul's gospel. After all, as Martyn earlier said to Beker, in this letter Paul repeatedly states "with unmistakable emphasis that the truth of the gospel is a matter of apocalypse (Gal 1.12, 16; 2.2, 5, 14)" (Martyn 1982, 196; in the preface to the second edition of *Paul the Apostle*, Beker accepts Martyn's critique regarding the value of Galatians).

Pauline apocalyptic, for Martyn, should be oriented not around an imminent *parousia* but the theme of *invasion*, a theme that shapes Paul's apocalyptic epistemology, eschatology, cosmology, and soteriology. The revelation of Jesus Christ constitutes, first, an "epistemological crisis" at the turn of the ages. This apocalyptic epistemology, Martyn argues, is inadequately captured by language of "unveiling mysteries" but should be seen in more radical irruptive terms, a "disjunctive apocalypse" constituted by the dawn of the new *creation. For Martyn, the apocalypse of Jesus Christ results in "a radically new perception of time" best understood in a punctiliar, rather than linear, mode (Martyn, *Galatians*, 104). The eschatological question "What time is it?" receives its answer as Christ comes "onto the scene" of history at a time selected by God: it is therefore the end of the "present evil age" (Gal 1:4) and "the dawn of the new creation" (Martyn, *Theological Issues*, 122).

In this way, Martyn rejects linear redemptive-historical schemes in favor of a polemically punctiliar and singular invasion, and argues that this polemic is crucial to Paul's logic in Galatians. With this apocalyptic temporal-spatial invasion of enemy-held territory, and the warfare it begins, comes a new cosmos, one in which the antinomies that characterized the present evil age (Jew/Greek; *slave/free; male/female) are dissolved and in which new antinomies (*flesh/Spirit; faith in Christ/*law) emerge. The *cross of Christ is an invasion that launches a war against the enslaving powers of the present evil age, resulting in an apocalyptic anthropology and soteriology oriented "not towards personal guilt and forgiveness but toward corporate enslavement and liberation" (Martyn, *Galatians*, 101).

2. Contemporary Scholarship.

2.1. Martinus de Boer. Martyn's influence on today's discussion of the apocalyptic Paul is hard to overestimate. A number of former students and colleagues have taken up his framework and extended his lines of inquiry. Among them is Martyn's former doctoral student Martinus de Boer, whose 1983 dissertation (published as *The Defeat of Death*) traces its genealogy from Schweitzer, Käsemann, Bultmann, and Beker to Martyn. De Boer then develops his own lines of Pauline inquiry with reference to the Jewish apocalypses since, for de Boer, the scholarly construct "apocalyptic eschatology" signaled the presence of "conceptual affinities" between Paul and Jewish apocalypticism.

One feature of de Boer's work, which Martyn hails as "extraordinarily perceptive" and "essential to the reading of Galatians" (Martyn, *Galatians*, 97n51), is his analysis of "two tracks of Jewish apocalyptic eschatology" (de Boer 1989, 180). In subsequent publications, including his own Galatians commentary, de Boer argues that Jewish apocalyptic literature has two forms of eschatology, dubbed "forensic apocalyptic eschatology" and "cosmological apocalyptic eschatology." While both apocalyptic "tracks" espouse a revelatory epistemology and an eschatology of the two ages, there are considerable cosmological/soteriological differences between them. "Forensic apocalyptic eschatology" is characterized by a view of sin as human transgression against God's law, resulting in death in the present age and a final *judgment in the age to come, with reward for the righteous and punishment for the wicked. In contrast, "cosmological apocalyptic eschatology" attributes sin and death to a primordial angelic rebellion, resulting in cosmic warfare between God and his enemies, and expecting an imminent divine invasion and final battle ending in God's triumph and the deliverance of his world. The two ages are thereby primarily understood as two radically opposed "spheres of power."

While careful to insist that this two-track model is heuristic, de Boer considers it crucial for investigating Paul's christologically determined apocalyptic eschatology. Observing significant similarity between the forensic/cosmological tracks of apocalyptic thought and the Bultmann/Käsemann debate, de Boer sides with the latter, arguing that Paul's apocalyptic logic is of the cosmological type, christologically modified. The presence of forensic elements in Paul's letters (say, in Rom 1–4) is explained as a rhetorical tactic against his opponents. Such motifs, de Boer argues, are decidedly overtaken or circumscribed by Paul's cosmological apocalyptic eschatology. Pauline apocalyptic thus signals a profound disjunction between the ages, with no human possibility of moving from one to the other. Paul's gospel, for de Boer, is that God has destroyed the power of sin and death in the cosmological-apocalyptic triumph of the cross of Christ, rectifying the cosmos and bringing it into the sphere of life.

2.2. Beverly Gaventa. The martial-cosmological tenor of Paul's apocalyptic theology is also emphasized in the work of Beverly Gaventa, whose apocalyptic reading of Paul has three emphases that display the influence of Martyn, Beker, and Käsemann. First, Gaventa highlights Paul's cosmic soteriology, a commitment to the divine salvific invasion of the contested territory that is the present world in the death and *resurrection of Jesus Christ. Second, this is an invasion with epistemological consequences, retrospectively revealing the extent of the world's captivity to the powers of Sin and Death, which seek to enslave and separate it from its rightful sovereign. Third, over against merely forensic accounts of salvation (whether individual or corporate), salvation is conceived in fundamentally liberative terms as God having delivered the world from these enslaving powers. The community of Christ is those who have been rescued by God's invasion of the present evil age and who therefore join with creation in groaning for the birth of the age to come.

One of Gaventa's signature contributions to the discussion is her examination of the maternal metaphors in Paul, collected in her book *Our Mother Saint Paul.* At first glance this might appear an unlikely locus for an exposition of such a dramatic, irruptive, and martial vision of Paul's gospel. But, far from being an exposition of cozy motherly imagery, Gaventa's work with this theme in Paul provides the context for her exposition of his apocalyptic theology. Apocalyptic eschatological expectation is frequently connected to the anguish of childbirth, not only in the imagery used by Paul (and other apocalyptic writings) but also, Gaventa argues, in the apocalyptic logic of his thought. The labor pains of Paul's own eschatological expectation (Gal 4:19) are connected to those of the whole world (Rom 8:22) in the framework of apocalyptic theology, as both Paul and creation eagerly await the apocalypse of Jesus Christ.

2.3. Alexandra Brown. The weight of discussion in the apocalyptic Paul conversation is placed (as so often in Pauline studies) on Galatians and Romans and on questions of eschatology, cosmology, and soteriology. In her 1995 book *The Cross and Human Transformation*, however, Alexandra Brown gives sustained attention to 1 Corinthians and to Paul's apocalyptic epistemology and anthropology.

Following Martyn's exposition of Pauline "epistemology at the turn of the ages," Brown develops the claim that Paul's apocalyptic battleground is the "realm of human perception" (Brown, xvii). The revelatory word of the cross has invaded the epistemological landscape, transforming the Corinthian perception of the world and thus their way of being in it. The proclamation of the gospel is thus an "apocalyptic speech act" that not only communicates but transforms its hearers' minds and worlds (Brown, 20).

Here Brown notes Paul's connection to the theological perspective of the Jewish apocalypses, while also drawing attention to his radical christological extension and transformation of it. However, in assessing the epistemological question of revelation and *wisdom, central to 1 Corinthians, Brown is careful not to rely on a sharp dichotomous distinction between those two streams of Jewish theology. In addition to the apocalyptic literature, she argues, Paul is also indebted to the Hellenistic Jewish wisdom tradition. The joining of these two streams, and the transformation of both in the light of the decisive apocalyptic event of the cross, is what generates Paul's epistemology. As with Martyn's antinomies, this is precisely not to say that all dualities are dissolved. For Brown, there are two profoundly antithetical ways of knowing: the human wisdom of the present age versus the revealed wisdom and power of God. In the light of the revelation of Jesus Christ, wisdom must therefore now be qualified as "apocalyptic wisdom." The apocalypse of the cross effects a new way of knowing and being.

2.4. Douglas Campbell. Douglas Campbell has been tentative in adopting the word *apocalyptic*, but his theological concerns nevertheless express similar commitments to the genealogy described above. In his 2005 book *The Quest for Paul's Gospel*, he eschews the label "apocalyptic" for his vision of Pauline theology, suggesting instead the acronym PPME (pneumatologically participatory martyrological eschatology). However, his subsequent treatment of the doctrine of justification in Paul (*The Deliverance of God*) embraces the term. Campbell's approach affirms the implicit link to the Jewish apocalypses, though he ultimately questions the value of this background for Pauline theology, judging it a species of arguing from the general to the particular and less than helpful in settling important Pauline debates. The value of the label is primarily to be found, for Campbell, in identifying his theological alignment with Martyn.

Among Martyn's conclusions regarding apocalyptic in Paul, Campbell places greatest emphasis on Paul's christologically reworked and "emphatically retrospective" apocalyptic epistemology (Campbell 2009, 110). For Campbell, this epistemology, which owes a great deal to the (early) work of Karl Barth, is "the *sine qua non* of valid Pauline interpretation" (Campbell 2016). This methodological starting point is starkly contrasted with what he considers its opposite, the "deadly methodological heresy" of foundationalism (Campbell 2016, 78).

Along with this retrospective epistemology, Campbell's Paul bears witness to the new reality thus disclosed: a fundamentally unconditional and noncontractual paradigm of soteriology, which generates Campbell's apocalyptic rereading of *justification. An apocalyptic soteriology construed in invasive, liberative, and unconditional terms is fundamentally incompatible, in Campbell's view, with traditional views of salvation bound up with an irretrievably forensic, individualistic, and contractual paradigm. The latter he dubs "justification theory" and subjects it to a full-scale critique. The presence of forensic motifs in Romans 1–4 is explained as speech-in-character, or ironic speech, rather than Paul's own views. To understand Paul in "a consistently apocalyptic fashion" means, for Campbell, to endorse the liberative and retrospective model over against the forensic, foundationalist approach of justification theory (Campbell 2009, 192).

2.5. Susan Eastman. A final scholar who owes a great deal to Martyn is Susan Eastman, who has recently placed the old (and somewhat neglected) question of Pauline anthropology in an apocalyptic light. Like Bultmann, Eastman insists that Pauline anthropological language must be comprehensible in today's terms, and so she addresses the question in dialogue with contemporary scientific understandings of personhood. Unlike Bultmann, however, Eastman does not view apocalyptic as a myth to be translated into existentialist and individualist terms. Rather, her forays into philosophical anthropology and contemporary neuroscience lead her in the opposite direction, to an understanding of the self that is irreducibly relational. Eastman does not anachronistically impose this modern framework onto Paul, nor does she demythologize Paul into contemporary psychology, but rather explores how Paul's apocalyptic anthropology can be brought into fruitful conversation with such insights.

The results of Eastman's interdisciplinary investigation resonate strongly with Käsemann's apocalyptic and cosmological reframing of Pauline anthropology. Human persons, in Eastman's view, are not autonomous individuals but are "relationally constituted agents who are both embodied and embedded in their world" (Eastman 2017, 2). The person, for Paul, is thus conceived in relation to a relational matrix of "cosmic and corporate powers," which is to say within an apocalyptic cosmology (Eastman 2017, 20). Under the enslaving power of sin and death, human agency is diminished. When brought into the liberating dominion of the power of *grace, however, human beings find a new divinely gifted agency. The liberative action of God in Christ thus reconstitutes the person, hitherto constituted by the cosmic powers of sin and the flesh. This newly constituted personhood is anchored in the new creation, not the present world, and as such there exists an eschatological tension in Paul's experience of selfhood. This apocalyptic reframing of anthropology, Eastman argues, is what one finds expressed in the Pauline "I" of Romans 7; Philippians 2; and Galatians 2.

3. Criticisms and Prospects.

One of the more common challenges to the apocalyptic Paul movement is that its version of apocalyptic bears little resemblance to what scholars of Jewish and Christian apocalyptic literature describe, and that their consideration of apocalyptic themes in Paul offers little to no engagement with those texts, thus cutting its historical roots. The above summary has shown, however, that, consideration of contemporary apocalyptic literature has, to varying degrees, usually been in view when it comes to describing Paul's apocalyptic thought. Of course, since there is considerable theological diversity among that corpus, there remains the question of discerning which apocalyptic themes are affirmed by Paul and which are not. Moreover, in examining Paul's deployment of these themes, a more fundamental and enduring challenge lies in evaluating how they are transformed in the light of the revelation of Jesus Christ. Here some of the more insightful and constructive criticisms are located.

3.1. Apocalyptic Eschatology: Continuity and Discontinuity. Given the importance of Käsemann's fight against an evolutionary *Heilsgeschichte* (salvation history), it is hardly surprising that the question of apocalyptic and salvation history remains the most contested issue in the debate. It is certainly the focus of the trenchant critiques of Martyn and his followers offered by one of the movement's most vocal critics, N. T. Wright. For Wright, salvation history is integral to Paul's own thought in Galatians and not, as Martyn argued, a category used by his *opponents. In Wright's view, the rejection of salvation history found in Martyn's "invasion" language, and in the subsequent development of this theme in contemporary scholarship, represents a form of *supersessionism.

Part of the problem is that the issue is often presented in dichotomous terms, offering a stark choice between an irruptive (apocalyptic) discontinuity versus a progressive (salvation-historical) continuity. But it need not be so. Martyn's apocalyptic Paul certainly contrasts the punctiliar and the linear, but in addressing the problem of continuity and discontinuity he argues that Paul's apocalyptic thought contains a distinction between "theological continuity" and "anthropological discontinuity" (Martyn 1991, 176). While finding this helpful, Susan Eastman critiques Martyn for being insufficiently nuanced and for failing to account for the gospel's intersection with human history. In Eastman's view, the divine creation of human history and the concomitant intersection of divine and human action problematize Martyn's sharp distinction.

One Pauline scholar who has offered a solution to this problem is John Barclay, who argues that Galatians "combines apocalyptic motifs with a salvation historical outlook" (Barclay 2005, 104). Barclay suggests divine *promise* as a helpful category for combining apocalyptic and salvation history. The "radical caesura" of the Christ event is related to the continuous narrative trajectory of the divine plan articulated in the promise of God, first given to *Abraham. For Barclay, any continuity in Paul's theology lies in the history of God's promise and not at the level of human history, in which the Christ-event remains radically discontinuous. While this approach to the problem is similar to Martyn's, Barclay views the latter's emphasis on the punctiliar nature of the Christ-event as true only in respect to its relationship to human history, not to the continuity of the divine promise. On the other hand, Barclay challenges construals of salvation history that straightforwardly locate continuity on the human level.

In a similar vein, Grant Macaskill has argued that the doctrine of *providence* provides a framework for Paul's apocalyptic thought within which both apocalyptic discontinuity and salvation-historical continuity might coherently be located. Macaskill's framing of the debate in this theological account of history resists both the overly punctiliar tendencies of one side and the potentially naturalistic view of history characteristic of the other.

3.2. Apocalyptic Epistemology: Revelation and Wisdom. Closely connected to this eschatological dichotomy is an epistemological one, present in different ways in the work of Martyn and Campbell. Martyn's apocalyptic epistemological contrast is between wisdom and revelation, whereas for Campbell it is between prospective and retrospective. These antitheses, too, have not gone unchallenged.

In respect to the first, there have been some insightful developments. Macaskill, along with many who have studied the epistemology of the Jewish apocalyptic literature, argues that wisdom and apocalyptic are not incompatible epistemological streams but are in fact often found together in that corpus. This is also noted by Brown, who acknowledges that wisdom and apocalyptic are sometimes found together in the Jewish apocalypses. Moreover, she argues that these two epistemological streams are joined in the epistemology of 1 Corinthians. Crucially, for Brown, this is not to say that human wisdom remains unaffected by divine apocalypse, and as such she examines Paul's christological reworking of wisdom. The apocalyptic event of the life, death, and resurrection of Jesus Christ, she argues, effects perceptual transformation such that human wisdom, while still epistemologically valid, nevertheless cannot remain unchanged. Therefore, the category of "apocalyptic wisdom" (Brown) or "revealed wisdom" (Macaskill) offers potential for integrating the two modes of knowing.

In respect to the second dichotomy, the centrality of retrospective epistemology in Pauline apocalyptic seems to have met with growing agreement, though the old challenge of the ordering of the Pauline plight and solution is unlikely to disappear any time soon (namely, which comes first in the logic of Paul's thought: Does he move from the "plight" of sin to the "solution" of the Christ-event, or vice-versa?). Richard Hays, while joining other Pauline scholars in critiquing the "apocalyptic Paul" movement for espousing a false dichotomy between apocalyptic and salvation history, insists that a retrospective epistemology provides the key to solving this problem. Hays argues that Paul deploys an apocalyptic epistemology that works retrospectively, thereby rereading and not repudiating the story of *Israel. Continuity is found as one "reads backwards."

The work of Wright regularly serves as the foil (explicitly or otherwise) to this retrospective epistemology. Though both Wright and Hays are famously committed to this narrative hermeneutic in their approaches to Paul, their epistemological starting points are significantly different. Wright's first major book on Paul is titled *The Climax of the Covenant*, indicating the importance that his Pauline theology has placed on the prospective narrative trajectory of God's *covenant with Israel, reaching its climax in Christ. In the light of that climax, Paul "reworks" or "reimagines" the foundational categories of Jewish thought, but the forward-moving *narrative remains paramount. Yet this is not, Wright insists, an endorsement of the epistemological foundationalism Campbell decries. Wright agrees with Martyn that the apocalypse of Jesus Christ reveals the nature of the problem to which the gospel is the solution, though he argues that this should not be understood in a manner radically discontinuous with Second Temple Jewish descriptions of the problem prior to Christ. Paul's plight is not simply retained from his prior convictions, but neither is it created *ex nihilo* in response to an unanticipated solution: it is, in Wright's words, a "plight revised" (Wright 2013, 752-64).

Without rejecting his commitment to the covenantal narrative trajectory of Paul's theology, Wright's more recent discussions of Pauline epistemology adopt a decidedly retrospective approach. In Wright's Gifford Lectures (published with the Bultmannian title *History and Eschatology: Jesus and the Promise of Natural Theology*), he argues that Christian theology has a renewed mode of knowing that is consequent to the resurrection. The resurrection is the epistemological starting point, bringing its own ontology and epistemology. For Wright, this new ontology, this new world, happens within the old, thus making sense of and retrospectively validating it; as such (and only as such) we may speak of "natural theology." The same is true, Wright argues, of salvation history, a narrative of promise that is validated and radically modified by the resurrection. This, it should be clear, is an account of history that is emphatically retrospective; in Wright's words, it "start[s] with Easter and looks back" (Wright 2019, 191). There is no doubt still debate to be had, particularly in respect of *how* revelation transforms wisdom, but the conversation over Paul's apocalyptic epistemology seems to have more common ground than is sometimes thought.

3.3. Apocalyptic Soteriology: Captivity and Complicity. One can trace a third and final dichotomy in recent work on Paul's apocalyptic soteriology, though its origins (as with so much) can be tracked back to Bultmann. In his 1941 essay "New Testament and Mythology," Bultmann describes a contradiction in the NT between cosmic and existential definitions of sin and human agency, resolvable only by dissolving the former into the latter. Käsemann, of course, rejected Bultmann's demythologization and pressed in the other direction. More recently, this debate surfaced in de Boer's heuristic two-tracks analysis, contrasting cosmological and forensic themes in apocalyptic eschatology, subsequently developed into strict antithesis in some approaches to Pauline soteriology. One example of this is Campbell, who dramatically contrasts the forensic soteriology of justification theory with his reading of Paul's cosmological-apocalyptic gospel. But again, it need not be the case that the two soteriological paradigms are so dichotomous, and this was not, after all, de Boer's intended conclusion. Examination of the apocalyptic texts has shown that the two soteriological paradigms regularly overlap and intersect. Can the same can be said of Paul? For most scholars (Campbell being a notable exception), the answer is yes.

But how might cosmological and forensic apocalyptic soteriologies be coherently integrated? In later assessments of the issue, Martyn articulates a more nuanced view than the stark dualism implied by his earlier account, arguing for the interrelationship of guilt and deliverance. While still seeing slavery/deliverance as "primary" and guilt/*forgiveness as "secondary," he sees these two soteriological patterns not as a strict dichotomy but bound up together in tension. Interpretative help, he suggests, can be found in the category of *complicity* (to summarize the argument of Martyn's afterword in Gaventa 2013). This is a potentially helpful category, allowing the affirmation of both the reality of human responsibility and the enslaving cosmic power of Sin. A significant contribution along these lines is Susan Eastman's work on anthropology and human agency, discussed above. Taking her cue from Käsemann,

Eastman offers an analysis of Paul's view of the person, particularly as developed in the overlapping narratives of Romans 1–8, as *both* culpable sinner *and* slave to the cosmic power of Sin. Her participatory account of Paul's anthropology thus contributes to an analysis of his apocalyptic soteriology that integrates both forensic forgiveness and cosmological deliverance.

Systematic theologian Philip Ziegler has recently developed this line of inquiry. For Ziegler the notion of complicity is instructive for Pauline soteriology in an "apocalyptic key." He argues that Martyn's emphasis on a cosmological apocalyptic soteriology captures well the approach of the early Barth. However, Barth's more mature work integrates this with a more clearly forensic account of salvation, and thus Martyn's account, Ziegler argues, is weakened by its overemphasis on the earlier, more sharply dichotomous explication of Pauline soteriology. Ziegler's own proposal, developed in dialogue with Käsemann, is that Paul's apocalyptic theology integrates human captivity to and complicity with sin, to which the gospel offers both liberation and forgiveness as "two aspects of the one rectifying moment of God's sovereign grace" (Ziegler, 61).

Finally, a third recent investigation of Pauline hamartiology that offers a framework for the integration of the two soteriological categories is that of Matthew Croasmun. In his recent monograph *The Emergence of Sin*, Croasmun presses beyond "Bultmannian reduction" and "Käsemannian dualism" not through resolving in favor of one or the other, nor through offering a middle way, but through an account of Paul's apparent "personification" of s/Sin in Romans that integrates both the cosmological and forensic themes of his apocalyptic soteriology, "because both extremes recognize important features of the Pauline text" (Croasmun, 13). Sin, for Croasmun, is *at once* a matter of human individual culpability, a feature of human social structures, and a cosmic tyrant. What prevents this threefold assertion from being merely an exercise in affirming paradox is Croasmun's use of "emergence theory," an interdisciplinary discourse that allows various ontologies to be deployed at different levels of analysis simultaneously. Applied to Paul's doctrine of sin, this approach speaks of s/Sin as at once a cosmic and forensic phenomenon, thereby offering a resolution to the Bultmann-Käsemann debate without taking either side.

See also Apocalypticism; Cosmology; Creation and New Creation; Eschatology; Gospel; Paul and Judaism; Salvation; Sin, Guilt.

BIBLIOGRAPHY. **J. M. G. Barclay,** *Obeying the Truth: Paul's Ethics in Galatians* (Vancouver: Regent College Publishing, 2005); *Paul and the Gift* (Grand Rapids, MI: Eerdmans, 2017); **J. C. Beker,** *Paul the Apostle: The Triumph of God in Life and Thought* (Philadelphia: Fortress, 1980); idem, *Paul's Apocalyptic Gospel: The Coming Triumph of God* (Philadelphia: Fortress, 1982); **B. Blackwell, J. Goodrich, and J. Maston,** eds., *Paul and the Apocalyptic Imagination* (Minneapolis: Fortress, 2016); **M. de Boer,** *The Defeat of Death: Apocalyptic Eschatology in 1 Corinthians 15 and Romans 5*, JSNTSup 22 (Sheffield: Sheffield Academic Press, 1988); idem, "Paul and Jewish Apocalyptic Eschatology," in *Apocalyptic and the New Testament: Essays in Honor of J. Louis Martyn*, ed. J. Marcus and M. L. Soards (Sheffield: Sheffield Academic Press, 1989): 169-90; idem, "Paul and Apocalyptic Eschatology," in *The Encyclopaedia of Apocalypticism*, ed. J. J. Collins and B. McGinn (London: Continuum, 1998), 345-83; **A. R. Brown,** *The Cross and Human Transformation: Paul's Apocalyptic Word in 1 Corinthians* (Minneapolis: Fortress, 2008); **R. Bultmann,** *Theology of the New Testament*, vol. 1 (London: SCM Press, 1952); idem, *The New Testament and Mythology and Other Basic Writings* (Minneapolis: Fortress, 1984); **D. C. Campbell,** *The Quest for Paul's Gospel: A Suggested Strategy* (London: Continuum, 2005); idem, *The Deliverance of God: An Apocalyptic Rereading of Justification in Paul* (Grand Rapids, MI: Eerdmans, 2009); idem, "Apocalyptic Epistemology," in *Paul and the Apocalyptic Imagination*, ed. B. Blackwell, J. Goodrich, and J. Maston (Minneapolis: Fortress, 2016), 65-86; **M. Croasmun,** *The Emergence of Sin: The Cosmic Tyrant in Romans* (Oxford: Oxford University Press, 2017); **J. P. Davies,** *Paul Among the Apocalypses: An Evaluation of the "Apocalyptic Paul" in the Context of Jewish and Christian Apocalyptic Literature* (London: T&T Clark, 2016); idem, *The Apocalyptic Paul: Retrospect and Prospect* (Eugene, OR: Cascade, 2022); **J. B. Davis and D. K. Harink,** eds., *Apocalyptic and the Future of Theology: With and Beyond J Louis Martyn* (Eugene, OR: Cascade, 2012); **S. Eastman,** *Recovering Paul's Mother Tongue: Language and Theology in Galatians* (Grand Rapids, MI: Eerdmans, 2007); idem, *Paul and the Person: Reframing Paul's Anthropology* (Grand Rapids, MI: Eerdmans, 2017); **B. R. Gaventa,** "The Singularity of the Gospel: A Reading of Galatians," in *Pauline Theology*, ed. J. M. Bassler (Minneapolis: Fortress, 1991) 1:147-59; idem, *Our Mother Saint Paul* (Louisville, KY: Westminster John Knox, 2007); idem, ed., *Apocalyptic*

Paul: Cosmos and Anthropos in Romans 5–8 (Waco, TX: Baylor University Press, 2013); **R. B. Hays,** "Apocalyptic *Poiēsis* in Galatians: Paternity, Passion, and Participation," in *Galatians and Christian Theology*, ed. M. W. Elliot et al. (Grand Rapids, MI: Baker, 2014), 200-219; **E. Käsemann,** *New Testament Questions of Today* (London: SCM Press, 1969); idem, *Pauline Perspectives* (London: SCM Press, 1971); **L. Keck,** "Paul and Apocalyptic Theology," *Int* 38 (1984): 229-41; **K. Koch,** *The Rediscovery of Apocalyptic* (London: SCM Press, 1972); **G. Macaskill,** "History, Providence, and the Apocalyptic Paul," *SJT* 70, no. 4 (2017): 409-26; **J. Marcus and M. L. Soards,** eds., *Apocalyptic and the New Testament: Essays in Honor of J. Louis Martyn* (Sheffield: Sheffield Academic Press, 1989); **J. L. Martyn,** review of *Paul the Apostle: The Triumph of God in Life and Thought*, by J. Christiaan Beker, *WW* 2, no. 2 (1982): 194-98; idem, "Events in Galatia: Modified Covenantal Nomism Versus God's Invasion of the Cosmos in the Singular Gospel: A Response to J. D. G. Dunn and B. R. Gaventa," in *Pauline Theology*, ed. J. M. Bassler (Minneapolis: Fortress, 1991), 1:160-79; idem, *Galatians: A New Translation and Commentary* (New Haven, CT: Yale University Press, 1997); idem, *Theological Issues in the Letters of Paul* (Edinburgh: T&T Clark, 1997); idem, "The Apocalyptic Gospel in Galatians," *Int* 54, no. 3 (2000): 246-66; **R. B. Matlock,** *Unveiling the Apocalyptic Paul: Paul's Interpreters and the Rhetoric of Criticism*, JSNTSup 127 (Sheffield: Sheffield Academic Press, 1996); **B. McCormack,** "Can We Still Speak of 'Justification by Faith'? An In-House Debate with Apocalyptic Readings of Paul," in *Galatians and Christian Theology*, ed. M. W. Elliot et al. (Grand Rapids, MI: Baker, 2014), 159-84; **A. Schweitzer,** *The Mysticism of Paul the Apostle* (London: A&C Black, 1931); **R. E. Sturm,** "Defining the Word 'Apocalyptic': A Problem in Biblical Criticism," in *Apocalyptic and the New Testament: Essays in Honor of J. Louis Martyn*, ed. J. Marcus and M. L. Soards (Sheffield: Sheffield Academic Press, 1989), 17-48; **N. T. Wright,** "Paul in Current Anglophone Scholarship," *ExpTim* 123, no. 8 (2012): 1-15; idem, *Paul and the Faithfulness of God* (London: SPCK, 2013); idem, *Paul and His Recent Interpreters* (London: SPCK, 2015); idem, *History and Eschatology: Jesus and the Promise of Natural Theology* (Waco, TX: Baylor University Press, 2019); **P. G. Ziegler,** *Militant Grace: The Apocalyptic Turn and the Future of Christian Theology* (Grand Rapids, MI: Baker, 2018).

J. P. Davies

APOCALYPTICISM

Apocalypticism is a religious worldview that emerged in ancient Judaism and significantly affected early Christianity, Paul's theology included. Commonly understood to comprise motifs germane to the literary genre "apocalypse," apocalypticism is an ideology consisting of three core beliefs: "the world is mysterious and revelation must be transmitted from a supernatural source, through the mediation of angels; there is a hidden world of angels and demons that is directly relevant to human destiny; and this destiny is finally determined by a definitive eschatological judgment" (Collins 2016, 9). In other words, apocalypticism centers on what has been called *apocalyptic epistemology*, *apocalyptic *cosmology*, and *apocalyptic *eschatology*. While some dispute whether apocalypticism was a distinct theological movement, and whether Paul's adoption of these theological emphases makes him anything other than generically Jewish, the apocalyptic configuration of Paul's theology has been copiously examined in modern scholarship. The results of such inquiry, however, have reached conclusions that emphasize different, even competing, dimensions of the apostle's thought.

1. Jewish Apocalypticism
2. Paul and Apocalypticism

1. Jewish Apocalypticism.

The term *apocalypticism* and its cognates originate from the Greek word *apokalypsis* ("revelation"), which is the description given by John of Patmos to his own literary-visionary work (Rev 1:1). Borrowing from John, biblical scholars have long applied transliterations of *apokalypsis* to designate the worldview, literary genre, and theological perspective represented by Revelation and shared by other early Jewish and Christian texts, particularly the book of Daniel. Employing terms that indicate approximation to a single literary-theological work, however, hardly provides clarity. Thus, scholars have used the terms *apocalypticism*, *apocalypse*, and *apocalyptic* inconsistently, such that the precise content and boundaries of these concepts have remained contested for nearly as long as their existence has been recognized. The following survey will illustrate some of these debates and highlight significant developments in scholarship on Jewish apocalypticism.

1.1. Surveying Scholarship on Jewish Apocalypticism. The modern study of apocalyptic literature has its beginnings with Friedrich Lücke, who sought to illuminate the book of Revelation by examining the "still extant apocryphal apocalypses"—namely, 1

Enoch, 4 Ezra, the Sibylline Oracles, the Testament of the Twelve Patriarchs, the Ascension of Isaiah, and the Shepherd of Hermas (Lücke, 52). Related texts have since been rediscovered and classified alongside the collection recognized by Lücke—including 2 Enoch, 2 and 3 Baruch, Jubilees, the Apocalypse of Abraham, the Testament of Abraham, and various works from the Dead Sea Scrolls.

As the collection of Jewish apocalypses (ca. 200 BC–AD 200) expanded and became available, particularly through the English-language editions of R. H. Charles, opinions about the defining features of apocalypticism and apocalypses also evolved. Thus, by the middle of the twentieth century H. H. Rowley explained that apocalypses divide history into a predetermined number of ages, with a particular emphasis on "the great final act of history," when *God will overturn a time of domination by evil spiritual forces and of unprecedented *suffering for the righteous, urgently and definitively ushering in God's promised *kingdom (Rowley, 154). Alternatively, D. S. Russell simply highlighted four characteristics that distinguish apocalyptic writings from *prophecy, namely, that they are "esoteric in character, literary in form, symbolic in language, and pseudonymous in authorship" (Russell, 106).

As these and other perspectives accumulated, an important and impassioned plea for clarity came in 1970 from Klaus Koch, who lamented that while scholarship was experiencing an "apocalyptic renaissance" (Koch 1972, 13), biblical scholars and theologians (particularly in his native Germany) were nonetheless "baffled before apocalyptic" (a more literal translation of the title of Koch's book). This confusion, Koch insisted, applied not only to definitions but to apocalypticism's origins, its relation to Jesus, and its reuniting not only the two Testaments but historical-critical and theological studies. Concerning semantics, Koch defined an *apocalypse* as a "literary type" with six formal literary features: discourse cycles, spiritual turmoils, parenetic discourses, pseudonymity, mythical images rich in symbolism, and composite character. This Koch differentiated from *apocalyptic*, which he claimed was an "historical movement" characterized by eight ideas largely associated with eschatology, including eschatological urgency and cosmic catastrophe, the impact of angelic and demonic beings, and the agency of God's throne.

Koch also provided a significant early critique of his teacher Gerhard von Rad on the origins of apocalypticism. Discussion about Jewish apocalyptic writings and their attendant ideologies has often centered on their historic and genealogical development, including their relationship to Hebrew prophetic and wisdom traditions, to ancient Near Eastern and Hellenistic mythologies, and their *Sitz im Leben*. Although scholars have recognized the influence of a variety of contexts on apocalyptic thought, theories about Jewish apocalypticism being the child of Hebrew prophecy have been advanced since the beginning of the project. For von Rad, however, a derivative relationship "is completely out of the question," because their respective views of history conflict—the prophets respect salvation history, the apocalypses disregard it (von Rad, 2:303). In place of prophecy, von Rad maintained that apocalypticism originated from the wisdom tradition, though this theory forced him to downplay the prominence of eschatology in apocalyptic literature: "if we pay attention only to apocalyptic predictions about the *eschaton* we narrow the whole field of reference for these writings" (von Rad, 2:307). Koch objected: "Eschatology is not simply added on [to apocalyptic], as one additional theme among many others . . . ; it is the absolutely dominating centre, round which all other material . . . is grouped" (Koch 1972, 46).

An even firmer defense of prophecy's influence on apocalypticism arrived shortly thereafter by Paul Hanson. Deepening an interpretive trajectory that long preceded even Rowley, Russell, and Koch, Hanson demonstrated that several significant apocalyptic features—for example, future divine intervention, hope for new *creation, and deployment of mythological language—derive early from the Hebrew prophetic tradition (e.g., Is 24–27; 55–66; Zech 9–14). According to Hanson, "the rise of apocalyptic eschatology is neither sudden nor anomalous, but follows the pattern of an unbroken development from pre-exilic and exilic prophecy" (Hanson 1975, 7-8).

A second of Hanson's enduring contributions concerns definitions. In a pair of influential dictionary entries, Hanson distinguished between *apocalypticism*, *apocalypse*, and *apocalyptic eschatology* in a way that stabilized scholarly discourse for the subsequent generation. Hanson describes an apocalypse as "(1) a *revelation* . . . given by God, (2) through a *mediator* . . . , (3) to a *seer* concerning (4) *future events*" (Hanson, "Apocalypse, Genre," 27 [emphasis original]). He then defined *apocalyptic eschatology* as "a religious perspective, a way of viewing divine plans in relation to mundane realities" (Hanson, Apocalypticism," 29). Finally, *apocalypticism* is "the symbolic universe in which an apocalyptic movement codifies its identity and interpretation of reality" (Hanson, Apocalypticism," 30).

Additional semantic clarity arrived in 1979 when a Society of Biblical Literature group tasked with defining *apocalypse* published their initial results. The team, led by John Collins, famously issued the following: "Apocalypse is a genre of revelatory literature with a narrative framework, in which a revelation is mediated by an otherworldly being to a human recipient, disclosing a transcendent reality which is both temporal, insofar as it envisages eschatological salvation, and spatial insofar as it involves another, supernatural world" (Collins 1979, 9). Five years later, Collins published the first edition of *The Apocalyptic Imagination*, a classic introduction to the relevant ancient texts, now in its third edition (Collins 2016). According to Collins, among the Jewish apocalypses there exist two main subtypes: *historical apocalypses*, which review sacred history (e.g., Daniel, 4 Ezra, Animal Apocalypse, Apocalypse of Weeks), and *otherworldly journeys*, which tour the cosmos (e.g., Book of the Watchers, the Similitudes, 2 Enoch, T. Levi 2–5). Regardless of a work's subtype, what is important is that these accounts describe a "transcendent reality." In other words, the seer is granted either a behind-the-scenes peek of *this* world or a glimpse into an altogether different realm. In either case, what is being reported is entirely invisible or at least not as things appear to the naked eye (see Rowland).

Many advances have followed the seminal work of Hanson and Collins, not only in articles and monographs but in conference proceedings, encyclopedias, and commentaries (see Hellholm; DiTommaso; Collins, *Encyclopedia of Apocalypticism*; 2014). Nuanced discussions on semantics have continued to surface, as have original insights on the function of apocalyptic discourse. Missing, for instance, from the Society of Biblical Literature group's definition is any suggestion about purpose or function. Thus, a later publication modified the group's original description, adding that an apocalypse "was intended to interpret present, earthly circumstances in light of the supernatural world and of the future, and to influence both the understanding and the behavior of the audience by means of divine authority" (Yarbro Collins, 7).

No consensus has yet to emerge on precisely how apocalyptic writings sought to aid their readers. Some have suggested they provide hope for the marginalized, others that they supply ideological ammunition for resistance to imperialism (Horsley; Portier-Young 2011). Indeed, forced assimilation profoundly affected Second Temple Jewish communities. Although some acquiesced, others opposed Greek and Roman tyranny. But anti-imperialism cannot, and need not, explain every apocalypse. Apocalyptic writings, Anathea Portier-Young concedes, could "embody discursive resistance as well as aim to motivate and sustain a program of resistance to domination and hegemony. But this was not a necessary function of the genre apocalypse. Resistance literature proves to be an apt category for some apocalyptic literature, but by no means all" (Porter-Young 2014, 146; cf. Collins 1979, 4).

The modern apocalyptic project has only continued to gain traction as new scholarship has built on the foundational work that appeared in the final quarter of the twentieth century. Yet scholars are now in a moment when basic vocabulary has been established. Hanson's conceptual distinctions continue to be widely respected—*apocalypticism* is a worldview, *apocalypse* a literary genre, and *apocalyptic (eschatology)* a religious perspective. Likewise, Collins's definitions of *apocalypse* and *apocalypticism* have become standard: "Apocalypse is a genre of revelatory literature with a narrative framework, in which a revelation is mediated by an otherworldly being to a human recipient, disclosing a transcendent reality which is both temporal, insofar as it envisages eschatological salvation, and spatial insofar as it involves another, supernatural world" (Collins 1979, 9). *Apocalypticism* is the worldview projected in apocalypses, the "essential ingredients of [which] were a reliance on supernatural revelation, over and above received tradition and human reasoning; a sense that human affairs are determined to a great degree by supernatural agents; and the belief that human life is subject to divine judgment, culminating in reward or punishment after death" (Collins, "From Prophecy to Apocalypticism," 157). With these distinctions and definitions in place, it is now appropriate to further unpack apocalypticism by probing deeper into its three essential ingredients: *epistemology*, *cosmology*, and *eschatology*.

1.2. Jewish Apocalyptic Epistemology. It is appropriate to begin with the epistemological dimension of apocalyptic literature, for none of the apocalyptic realities to be discussed are knowable apart from divine revelation. Due to the transcendent nature of various cosmic secrets, God must dispatch angelic messengers and grant *visions and dreams (2 Bar. 36.1; 52.8–53.1) to human agents to mediate heavenly mysteries about the structures of the universe, the actors governing its movements, and the events that have and must take place within it. Otherworldly beings, such as Uriel in 4 Ezra and Ramiel in 2 Baruch, disclose and interpret discrete visions of forthcoming earthly events. Other mediators, such as the cast of seven angels in 1 Enoch 17–20, guide the seer through a tour of the cosmos and explain its significance for the eschatological future. In each case, divine mysteries are communicated to the human recipient, whose report does not simply review abstracted information but conveys a narrative in which he *sees* a vision and *hears* a message obtained through a multisensory revelatory experience.

Despite their emphasis on revelation, apocalyptic writings do not flatly reject human reason or *wisdom. The presence of wisdom literature among, for example, the Dead Sea Scrolls demonstrates how a community can author original wisdom texts from an apocalyptic worldview (Goff 2007). Criticism of wisdom occasionally surfaces in apocalyptic literature (1 En. 42.1-3), though the compatibility of revelation with wisdom is apparent elsewhere in the apocalyptic corpus (1 En. 37–71, 2 Enoch, 4qInstruction), where the religious community lives in accordance with what Grant Macaskill calls "revealed wisdom" (see also Goff 2014). The same is true of the compatibility between revelation and reason. For example, the Book of the Watchers begins with an indictment of rebellious humanity in which all people are instructed to engage in natural theology so they might infer from the created order God's work in fashioning and finetuning the cosmos as well as the natural world's obedience to God's sovereign programming (1 En. 2.1–5.3).

1.3. Jewish Apocalyptic Cosmology. An apocalyptic worldview ordinarily divides the universe into two major parts—the heavens and the earth. Earth is the location of normal human activity, whereas the heavens are the unseen realm where God and angelic beings rule and reside. The heavens are often multitiered, having three, five, seven, or even ten distinct levels, each with its own occupants and operations (T. Levi 2–3; 2 En. 3–22). Among the cosmic agents who abide in the heavens are angelic armies, rebellious angels, and other magnificent creatures with anthropomorphic and zoomorphic features (2 En. 7:1-3; 12:1-2; 17:1; 18:1; 21:1).

Despite the duality of the universe, neither the heavenly nor terrestrial realms are impenetrable. The entire premise of the apocalypse is that the boundaries separating the various cosmic arenas are porous, such that human and nonhuman beings alike can pass from one to the other. For example, some of the earliest apocalypses report the arrival of Watchers onto primordial earth, where they interbreed with women and introduce humanity to technological advances with harmful effects (1 En. 6–8; Jub. 4.15). In response, God commissions archangels to descend from heaven to bring judgment on these rebellious spirits and their mixed-race kin (1 En. 9–11; 15), causing their malevolent spirits to populate the earth and provoke evil for posterity (Stuckenbruck). Conversely, human seers are granted revelatory access to the heavens and the farthest reaches of the cosmos. Thus, in various apocalyptic accounts, the biblical patriarch Enoch is portrayed as the human counterpart to the Watchers who journeys through the heavens (1 En. 12–16, 17–36, 37–71, 72–82). Mirroring the divide between good and evil in the heavens, apocalyptic communities portray the human population likewise as divided into two groups, the righteous and the wicked. This anthropological dualism is most famously expressed in the Dead Sea Scrolls, where various texts divide humanity into the sons of *light and the sons of darkness, the former possessing the spirit of *truth and the latter possessing the spirit of darkness (1QS III, 13–IV, 26; cf. 1QM).

1.4. Jewish Apocalyptic Eschatology. If cosmic dualism represents the vertical (spatial) axis, temporal dualism represents the linear (time) axis. Apocalypticism emphasizes the existence of two major temporal ages—the present and the future. As 4 Ezra announces, "the Most High has made not one world but two" (7.53), namely, "this world" and "the world to come" (4 Ezra 8.1; cf. 1 En. 71.15). Apocalyptic literature might also survey human history by dividing the past, present, and future into numerous (sometimes four, seven, or twelve) distinct historical phases in order to demonstrate God's providence over all human affairs (1 En. 93.1-10; 91.11-17). Despite such periodization of *covenant history, the past and present are clearly distinguishable from the eschatological future. In the age to come, God will bring history to completion by defeating evil, issuing eternal *judgment on all creatures (retribution for the wicked and *resurrection for the righteous), and ushering in a state of *peace where the righteous will prosper eternally. According to 4 Ezra, "This present world is not the end; the full glory does not abide in it. . . . But the day of judgment will be the end of this age and the beginning of the immortal age to come, in which corruption has passaged away, sinful indulgence has come to an end, unbelief has been cut off, and righteousness has increased and truth has appeared" (7.112-114 NRSV).

Eschatological scenarios, however, are presented variously by individual apocalypses, sometimes differently even in the same apocalypse. Some scenarios include a regal deliverer (Pss. Sol. 17–18), a messianic kingdom, resurrection, rewards, and retribution (Collins 2010; Elledge). In the Apocalypse of Weeks (in which all of human history is divided into ten periods), the seventh week (following Israel's dispersion) will be marked by the proliferation of evil and the election of the righteous, who during the eighth week will defeat the wicked, rebuild the *Jerusalem *temple, and restore the kingdom of *Israel; this will be followed by universal *righteousness and *law observance in week nine, and then the final judgment of the Watchers and the installation of the new heavens in week ten, leading afterwards to innumerable weeks of righteous and sinless existence (1 En. 93.1-10; 91.11-17). Even the simplicity of Ezra's presentation above is complicated earlier in its own narrative, where the end comprises an entire series of eschatological events—the end will commence with the arrival of the Messiah and his people for four hundred years, after which all humanity will die and remain dead for seven silent days; this will then be followed by the resurrection of the dead and the final judgment, the righteous being rewarded with rest and paradise, the unrighteous receiving torment and fire (4 Ezra 7.26-44).

Appealing to the past is also a method for providing *hope in the present. Sometimes Israel's history is retold with an emphasis on how God has already defeated evil in the past (e.g., the flood, the exodus) as a way of encouraging and even modeling the defeat of evil in the present and future (1 En. 10.16-22; 15.3–16.4; 91.5-10; 106.13–107.1; Jub. 5.1–10.11). According to Loren Stuckenbruck, "some writers of apocalyptic texts demonstrated a concern with divine activity as a constant," and not only as an instrument of forthcoming eschatological deliverance (Stuckenbruck, 252).

2. Paul and Apocalypticism.

Just as disagreement has characterized the study of Jewish apocalypticism, so it is with Paul's worldview. Few deny that Paul's theology is in some sense apocalyptic, but no consensus has yet to emerge about what this means (see Blackwell, Goodrich, and Maston). What follows is a brief sketch of the development of apocalyptic in Pauline scholarship before showing how the apostle's theology contains the three essential ingredients of apocalypticism outlined by Collins.

2.1. Surveying Scholarship on the Apocalyptic Paul. Reading Paul's letters alongside Jewish apocalyptic writings found its most enduring early endorsement from Albert Schweitzer, who lamented how "scholarship of the period after Baur . . . takes scarcely any notice of what remains of the Late-Jewish non-Hellenistic literature," by which Schweitzer meant especially "the parallels in Enoch, the Apocalypse of Baruch, the Apocalypse of Ezra, and here and there in the Testaments of the Twelve Patriarchs" (Schweitzer 1951, 51). For Schweitzer, it is Paul's notion of "being-in-Christ" and especially Paul's eschatology—namely, "the Parousia, the resurrection, the judgment, and the Kingdom of the Last Times" (Schweitzer 1951, 52)—that resonate within "late Judaism" and thereby demonstrate the apostle's apocalyptic framework. Indeed, "Since Paul lives in the conceptions of the dramatic world-view characteristic of the late Jewish Eschatology, he is by consequence bound to the logic of that view" (Schweitzer 1998, 11).

Karl Barth was also an early proponent of the apocalyptic reading of Paul's letters. While Barth showed little interest in contextualizing Paul within Judaism, he nevertheless saw in Paul's writings the same dualisms observed in the Jewish apocalypses. According to Barth, God's radical transcendence necessitated an equally radical revelatory act to redeem humanity:

> In [Jesus'] name two worlds meet and go apart, two planes intersect, the one known and the other unknown. The known plane is God's creation, fallen out of its union with Him, and therefore the world of the "flesh" needing redemption. . . . This known plane is intersected by another plane that is unknown—the world of the Father, of the Primal Creation, and of the final Redemption. The relation between us and God, between this world and His world, presses for recognition, but the line of intersection is not self-evident. The point on the line of intersection at which the relation becomes observable and observed is Jesus. (Barth, 29)

For Barth, the knowledge and realities of *salvation—which are unrealizable prior to the Christ-event—"breaks forth, like a flash of lightning" in Christ (Barth, 331), signifying the epistemological and cosmic separation between God and humanity.

The next phase of apocalyptic Pauline interpretation was ushered in by Ernst Käsemann, whose contributions appeared mainly in critical response to his teacher, Rudolf Bultmann. The latter regarded apocalypticism as prescientific and thus of limited value to the modern church. Paul's letters therefore require "demythologizing"—being stripped of their "ancient world-view which is obsolete" (Bultmann, 36). Bultmann's project of demythologization effectively reduced Paul's theology to the *justification of the individual, and thus *anthropology. Käsemann, conversely, famously declared that "apocalyptic was the mother of all Christian theology" (Käsemann, 102), and that humanity could not be separated from the larger fabric of the cosmos: "in Paul the depth of redemption as it affects the individual corresponds to its cosmic breadth" (Käsemann, 14). Paul's apocalyptic *gospel centers on the lordship of *Christ and the righteousness of God, which Käsemann deemed basically synonymous, such that the proclamation of God's righteousness laid claim on the human: "God's power reaches out for the world, and the world's salvation lies in its being recaptured for the sovereignty of God" (Käsemann, 182).

In Anglophone scholarship, Käsemann's reading was mediated through and modified by J. Christiaan Beker and J. Louis Martyn. With Käsemann, Beker believed that "Paul's thought is anchored in the apocalyptic world view," and "the coherent center of Paul's gospel is constituted by the apocalyptic interpretation of the Christ-event," by which he meant Jesus' resurrection (Beker, 135). For Beker, apocalyptic had three main components: "(1) historical dualism; (2) universal cosmic expectation; and (3) the imminent end of the world" (Beker, 136). Martyn, on the other hand, famously shifted the focus of apocalyptic from the second advent of Christ to the first—particularly the *cross—as the apocalyptic linchpin of Paul's theology, at which time God invaded the world to liberate it from evil powers. According to Martyn, "There, in the thoroughly real event of Christ's crucifixion, God's war of liberation was commenced and decisively settled, making the cross the foundation of Paul's apocalyptic theology" (Martyn, *Galatians*, 101).

The twentieth-century work on Paul by Schweitzer, Barth, Käsemann, Beker, and Martyn has proven influential on countless twenty-first-century interpreters, including Beverly Gaventa (2007), Douglas Campbell (2009), John Barclay, Susan Eastman, and Martinus de Boer. Yet this "apocalyptic Paul"—as he has come to be known (see Gaventa 2013)—also has had critics (see Matlock; Wright; Davies). These scholars often grant Paul's proximity to apocalypticism yet protest the manner and inconsistency with which scholars apply the label to Paul, as well as the infrequency with which the Jewish apocalypses are brought into scholarly discussions. Some critics are content to refer to Paul as "apocalyptic," though when doing so they typically emphasize different aspects of his theology (see Blackwell, Goodrich, and Maston). This raises some important questions: Is Paul really an apocalyptic theologian? If so, how? What follows seeks to show that Paul's letters do exhibit the three essential ingredients of apocalypticism introduced by Collins, thus demonstrating that Paul does indeed deserve the adjective *apocalyptic*.

2.2. Paul's Apocalyptic Epistemology. Although Paul wrote no apocalypses, he purportedly received "visions and revelations of the Lord" (2 Cor 12:1 NRSV). These refer at least to the episode reported thereafter to the Corinthians. Paul, readers are told, was caught up to the "third heaven" (2 Cor 12:2), an experience so bewildering he can neither confirm that he was inside the *body nor repeat what he heard (2 Cor 12:3-4). Paul was also the recipient of a revelation of the risen Jesus that resulted in his *conversion and apostolic commission (Gal 1:12, 15-16). While he might have received other revelations during his *ministry (1 Cor 11:23), he certainly received and routinely relayed divine *mysteries (Rom 11:25; 16:25; 1 Cor 15:51; Eph 1:9; 3:3, 6; Col 1:26; 2:2; 4:3). Indeed, so central to Paul's apostolic identity was proclamation of previously hidden *knowledge that he refers to himself as one of the "stewards of God's mysteries" (1 Cor 4:1 NRSV).

Beyond his ecstatic experiences, Paul's writing attends closely to the topic of epistemology. For Paul, being *in Christ is not only a soteriological concept; it is also a reality that elicits what Martyn calls an "epistemological crisis" (Martyn, *Theological Issues*). In Christ, the Christian's way of knowing is recalibrated to the value system of the cross (1 Cor 1–2). From this new vantage point, Christians perceive the world as those who now participate in the new creation (2 Cor 5:16-17). This reality is related to the cognitive transformation Paul refers to elsewhere as having the mind of Christ (1 Cor 2:16; Phil 2:5-8), renewing the mind (Rom 12:2), and setting one's mind on things above (Col 3:1 [see A. R. Brown; Campbell 2016]). But just as the apocalypses rely on revelation without discarding reason and wisdom, so Paul affirms that reason and wisdom remain instrumental in Christian cognition (Rom 1:18-32; 1 Cor 1:17–2:16). As Ian Scott explains, "The message of the cross is thus not anti-rational. It is, rather, calculated to subvert the essentially idolatrous tendencies which pervert all fallen human thought, by forcing the believer to abandon his or her usual standards of evaluation" (Scott, 29).

2.3. *Paul's Apocalyptic Cosmology.* Similar to Jewish apocalyptic writings, Paul maintained the distinction between heaven and earth (1 Cor 15:40, 47; 2 Cor 5:1-2; Eph 1:10; 3:15; Phil 2:10; 3:19-20; Col 1:16, 20; 3:1-2). Apart from explicit heaven language, Paul refers to the heavenly realm as "above" (Col 3:1-2), as "the Jerusalem above" (Gal 4:26), and as the locus of the reign of God and of Christ at God's right hand (Rom 8:34; Eph 1:20; Col 3:1). The schematics of heaven remain ambiguous. Paul only once explicitly mentions its multitiered structure, speaking of the "third heaven," which he identifies with "paradise" (see 2 En. 8). This is probably the highest heavenly tier, where God himself resides (2 Cor 12:1-4). Elsewhere Paul refers to the plurality of "the heavens" (2 Cor 5:1; Eph 4:10) and its synonym "the heavenlies" (Eph 1:3, 20; 2:6; 3:10; 6:12 [Brannon]), yet without specifying their number or discrete functions.

Nevertheless, the undifferentiated heavens are clearly the abode of good and evil beings alike. Heaven is the locus of angels (Gal 1:8; 2 Thess 1:7), of God (Rom 1:18), and of the exalted Christ (Phil 3:20; Eph 6:9; Col 4:1; 1 Thess 1:10; 4:16; 2 Thess 1:7 [Orr]). The "rulers and authorities" also reside in the heavenlies (Eph 6:12), though probably at a lower tier, outside the immediate presence of God and beneath Christ's exalted station (Eph 1:21). These rulers are likely rebellious spirits since they are contrasted with angels (Rom 8:38); it is not clear they are the diminutive gods of the *Gentiles (Wasserman, 122-28). *Satan, the chief demonic being, whose influence warrants the moniker "the god of this age" (2 Cor 4:4 [D. R. Brown]), leads these powers as they misdirect the sons of disobedience (Eph 2:2; 6:12), whereas the children of light are directed by the *Holy Spirit (Eph 5:8, 18).

In apocalyptic accounts of Paul's theology, these personal powers are not alone in their opposition to God. The powers of *Sin, *Death, and the *Flesh should likewise be identified as antigod powers that hold the world captive following the transgression of *Adam (Rom 5:12), and not merely as rhetorically advantageous personifications (see Gupta and Goodrich). The power of Sin resides within the human body such that all people remain "under Sin" (Rom 3:9; 7:14; Gal 3:22) and are linked to the enslaved creation (Rom 8:18-25). Yet these impersonal powers, along with evil spiritual beings, have been preliminarily disarmed through the Christ-event (Col 2:15) and will be finally defeated at the return of the second Adam (1 Cor 15:24-27).

2.4. *Paul's Apocalyptic Eschatology.* Jewish apocalyptic literature stressed the distinction between the present age, in which existed significant opposition to God's people and purposes, and the future age, characterized by God's intervention into human history and the installation of his long-awaited covenant promises. Paul maintains this temporal duality by differentiating between "the present evil age" (Gal 1:4 NRSV; cf. Rom 12:2; 1 Cor 2:6-8; 2 Cor 4:4; Eph 2:2) and "the one to come" (Eph 1:21 NIV; cf. Eph 2:7), also referred to as the "new creation" (Gal 6:15; 2 Cor 5:17) and "God's kingdom" (1 Cor 6:9-10; 15:24, 50; Gal 5:21; 2 Tim 4:1, 18). He also contrasts "present" things with things "to come" (Rom 8:38; 1 Cor 3:22) and the ages of Adam and of Christ (Rom 5:12-21; 1 Cor 15:21-22). The blessed future will be fully installed when Jesus descends suddenly from heaven and escorts in resurrected bodies those who belong to him (1 Thess 4:13-18; 1 Cor 15:22-23). This will be followed by "the end," when Jesus will deliver the kingdom to the father after defeating all evil powers, including "the *man of lawlessness" and Death (2 Thess 2:3-12; 1 Cor 15:24-28). Included in this scenario is Jesus' judgment of humanity, which will include redemption and rewards for his righteous people (Rom 2:7, 10; 1 Thess 1:10; 5:9) and retribution for the unrighteous (Rom 2:8-9 [see C. R. Campbell]). Paul can refer to this series of eschatological events as "the day" (Rom 2:6; 13:12; 1 Cor 3:13; 2 Tim 4:8), "the day of wrath" (Rom 2:5), "the day of redemption" (Eph 4:30), and other variations.

The separation of the present age from the future age has been complicated by the death and resurrection of Jesus, which inaugurated the eschaton so that Paul considers the *church as those "on whom the end of the ages has come" (1 Cor 10:11 ESV) and those who already participate in Christ's kingdom (Col 1:13) and the new creation (2 Cor 5:17 [Jackson]). The present moment consists of an overlapping of the ages, in which the present evil age remains in place, yet the blessings of the eschaton have been introduced (Eph 1:3). Thus, believers have already received "the promised Holy Spirit" as a seal of God's still-future deliverance (Eph 1:13 NRSV; see Eph 4:30; 2 Cor 1:22). Moreover, Paul can announce that those who are in Christ are already saved (Rom 8:24; 10:9; Eph 2:5, 8; 2 Tim 1:9; 3:5), justified (Rom 5:1, 9; 8:30; 10:9; 1 Cor 6:11), raised/alive (Rom 6:11, 13; Eph 2:5-6; Col 2:12; 3:1), seated at Christ's right hand (Eph 2:6), and so on, even if those salvific blessings retain a still-future realization at Christ's return, when the present age suddenly terminates and the fullness of the eschaton climactically arrives.

Jewish apocalypticism remains an area of focused research by ancient historians, the results of which have immediate implications for the study of early Christianity, Paul's letters in particular. This brief analysis of epistemology, cosmology, and eschatology in Jewish apocalyptic literature and in Paul's letters suggests that the apostle's theological architecture was akin to the conceptual structure of the apocalypses. It is appropriate, therefore, to conclude that Paul operated within the worldview of Jewish apocalypticism.

See also Adam and Christ; Apocalyptic Paul; Conversion and Call of Paul; Corinthians, Second Letter to the; Cosmology; Creation and New Creation; Eschatology; Principalities and Powers; Romans, Letter to the; Sin, Guilt; Thessalonians, Letters to the; Visions, Ecstatic Experiences.

BIBLIOGRAPHY. **J. M. G. Barclay,** *Paul and the Gift* (Grand Rapids, MI: Eerdmans, 2015); **K. Barth,** *The Epistle to the Romans*, trans. E. C. Hoskyns (Oxford: Oxford University Press, 1933); **J. C. Beker,** *Paul the Apostle: The Triumph of God in Life and Thought* (Philadelphia: Fortress, 1980); **B. C. Blackwell, J. K. Goodrich, and J. Maston,** eds., *Paul and the Apocalyptic Imagination* (Minneapolis: Fortress, 2016); **M. C. de Boer,** *Paul, Theologian of God's Apocalypse: Essays on Paul and Apocalyptic* (Eugene, OR: Cascade, 2020); **M. J. Brannon,** *The Heavenlies in Ephesians: A Lexical, Exegetical, and Conceptual Analysis*, LNTS 447 (London: T&T Clark, 2011); **A. R. Brown,** *The Cross and Human Transformation: Paul's Apocalyptic Word in 1 Corinthians* (Minneapolis: Fortress, 1995); **D. R. Brown,** *The God of This Age: Satan in the Churches and Letters of the Apostle Paul*, WUNT 2/409 (Tübingen: Mohr Siebeck, 2015); **R. Bultmann,** *Jesus Christ and Mythology* (New York: Scribner, 1958); **C. R. Campbell,** *Paul and the Hope of Glory: An Exegetical and Theological Study* (Grand Rapids, MI: Zondervan Academic, 2020); **D. A. Campbell,** *The Deliverance of God: An Apocalyptic Rereading of Justification in Paul* (Grand Rapids, MI: Eerdmans, 2009); idem, "Apocalyptic Epistemology: The Sine Qua Non of Valid Pauline Interpretation," in *Paul and the Apocalyptic Imagination*, ed. B. C. Blackwell, J. K. Goodrich, and J. Maston (Minneapolis: Fortress, 2016), 65-85; **R. H. Charles,** ed., *The Apocrypha and Pseudepigrapha of the Old Testament*, 2 vols. (Oxford: Clarendon, 1913); **J. J. Collins,** "Introduction: Towards the Morphology of a Genre," *Semeia* 14 (1979): 1-20; idem, ed., *The Encyclopedia of Apocalypticism, vol. 1, The Origins of Apocalypticism in Judaism and Christianity* (New York: Continuum, 1998); idem, "From Prophecy to Apocalypticism: The Expectation of the End," in *The Encyclopedia of Apocalypticism, vol. 1, The Origins of Apocalypticism in Judaism and Christianity*, ed. J. J. Collins (New York: Continuum, 1998), 129-61; idem, *The Scepter and the Star: Messianism in Light of the Dead Sea Scrolls*, 2nd ed. (Grand Rapids, MI: Eerdmans, 2010); idem, ed., *The Oxford Handbook of Apocalyptic Literature* (Oxford: Oxford University Press, 2014); idem, *The Apocalyptic Imagination: An Introduction to Jewish Apocalyptic Literature*, 3rd ed. (Grand Rapids, MI: Eerdmans, 2016); **J. P. Davies,** *Paul Among the Apocalypses? An Evaluation of the "Apocalyptic Paul" in the Context of Jewish and Christian Apocalyptic Literature*, LNTS 562 (London: Bloomsbury, 2016); **L. DiTommaso,** "Apocalypses and Apocalypticism in Antiquity (Part I)," *CurBR* 5, no. 2 (2007): 235-86; idem, "Apocalypses and Apocalypticism in Antiquity (Part II)," *CurBR* 5, no. 3 (2007): 367-432; **S. G. Eastman,** *Paul and the Person: Reframing Paul's Anthropology* (Grand Rapids, MI: Eerdmans, 2017); **C. D. Elledge,** *Resurrection of the Dead in Early Judaism, 200 BCE–CE 200* (Oxford: Oxford University Press, 2017); **B. R. Gaventa,** *Our Mother Saint Paul* (Louisville, KY: Westminster John Knox, 2007); idem, ed., *Apocalyptic Paul: Cosmos and Anthropos in Romans 5–8* (Waco, TX: Baylor University Press, 2013); **M. J. Goff,** *Discerning Wisdom: The Saptiential Literature of the Dead Sea Scrolls* (Leiden: Brill, 2007); idem, "Wisdom and Apocalypticism," in *The Oxford Handbook of Apocalyptic Literature*, ed. J. J. Collins (Oxford: Oxford University Press, 2014), 52-68; **N. K. Gupta and J. K. Goodrich,** eds., *Sin and Its Remedy in Paul* (Eugene, OR: Cascade, 2020); **P. Hanson,** *The Dawn of Apocalyptic: The Historical and Sociological Roots of Jewish Apocalyptic Eschatology* (Philadelphia: Fortress, 1975); idem, "Apocalypse, Genre," in *Interpreter's Dictionary of the Bible*, supplementary vol. (Nashville: Abingdon, 1976), 27-28; idem, "Apocalypticism," in *Interpreter's Dictionary of the Bible*, supplementary vol. (Nashville: Abingdon, 1976), 28-34; **D. Hellholm,** ed., *Apocalypticism in the Mediterranean World and the Near East: Proceedings of the International Colloquium on Apocalypticism, Uppsala, August 12–17, 1979* (Tübingen: Mohr Siebeck, 1983); **R. A. Horsley,** *Revolt of the Scribes: Resistance and Apocalyptic Origins* (Minneapolis: Fortress, 2010); **T. R. Jackson,** *New Creation in Paul's Letters: A Study of the Historical and Social Setting of a Pauline Concept*, WUNT 2/272 (Tübingen: Mohr Siebeck, 2010);

E. Käsemann, *New Testament Questions of Today*, trans. W. J. Montague (Philadelphia: Fortress, 1969); **K. Koch,** *Ratlos vor der Apokalyptik: Eine Streitschrift über ein vernachlässigtes Gebiet der Bibelwissenschaft und die schändliche Auswirkungen auf Theologie und Philosophie* (Gütersloher: Gütersloher Verlagshaus, 1970); idem, *The Rediscovery of Apocalyptic: A Polemical Work on a Neglected Area of Biblical Studies and Its Damaging Effects on Theology and Philosophy*, trans. M. Kohl, SBT 2/22 (London: SCM Press, 1972); **F. Lücke,** *Versuch einer vollständigen Einleitung in die Offenbarung Johannis und in die gesammte apokalyptische Litteratur* (Bonn: Eduard Weber, 1832); **G. Macaskill,** *Revealed Wisdom and Inaugurated Eschatology in Ancient Judaism and Early Christianity*, JSJSup 115 (Leiden: Brill, 2007); **J. L. Martyn,** *Galatians: A New Translation with Introduction and Commentary*, AYB 33A (New York: Doubleday, 1997); idem, *Theological Issues in the Letters of Paul* (Nashville: Abingdon, 1997); **R. B. Matlock,** *Unveiling the Apocalyptic Paul: Paul's Interpreters and the Rhetoric of Criticism*, JSNTSup 127 (Sheffield: Sheffield Academic Press, 1996); **P. C. Orr,** *Exalted Above the Heavens: The Risen and Ascended Christ*, NSBT 47 (Downers Grove, IL: IVP Academic, 2018); **A. E. Portier-Young,** *Apocalyptic Against Empire: Theologies of Resistance in Early Judaism* (Grand Rapids, MI: Eerdmans, 2011); idem, "Jewish Apocalyptic Literature as Resistance Literature," in *The Oxford Handbook of Apocalyptic Literature*, ed. J. J. Collins (Oxford: Oxford University Press, 2014), 145-62; **G. von Rad,** *Old Testament Theology*, trans. D. M. G. Stalker, 2 vols. (Edinburgh: Oliver & Boyd, 1965); **C. Rowland,** *The Open Heaven: A Study of Apocalyptic in Judaism and Early Christianity* (New York: Crossroad, 1982); **H. H. Rowley,** *The Relevance of Apocalyptic: A Study of Jewish and Christian Apocalypses from Daniel to the Revelation*, 2nd ed. (London: Lutterworth, 1947); **D. S. Russell,** *The Method and Message of Jewish Apocalyptic: 200 BC–AD 100* (Philadelphia: Westminster, 1964); **A. Schweitzer,** *Paul and His Interpreters: A Critical History* (New York: MacMillan, 1951); idem, *The Mysticism of Paul the Apostle*, trans. W. Montgomery (Baltimore: Johns Hopkins University Press, 1998); **I. W. Scott,** *Paul's Way of Knowing: Story, Experience, and the Spirit* (Grand Rapids, MI: Baker Academic, 2009); **L. T. Stuckenbruck,** *The Myth of Rebellious Angels: Studies in Second Temple Judaism and New Testament Texts*, WUNT 335 (Tübingen: Mohr Siebeck, 2014); **E. Wasserman,** *Apocalypse as Holy War: Divine Politics and Polemics in the Letters of Paul* (New Haven, CT: Yale University Press, 2018); **N. T. Wright,** *Paul and His Recent Interpreters: Some Contemporary Debates* (Minneapolis: Fortress, 2015); **A. Yarbro Collins,** "Introduction: Early Christian Apocalypticism," *Semeia* 36 (1986): 1-11.

J. K. Goodrich

APOCRYPHAL PAULINE LITERATURE

As early as the second century, there appeared an assortment of noncanonical works about the *apostle Paul or written in his name. They typically take some element from the Acts of the Apostles or the canonical letters as a point of departure and expand the narrative of Paul's *ministry or adapt his teachings to new situations. These works are usually labeled "New Testament Apocrypha."

1. Letters
2. Acts
3. Apocalypses
4. Other Works

1. Letters.

Given the influence of Paul's correspondence, it is surprising that pseudonymous *letters composed in his name are so few, even if one includes the deutero-Pauline or "disputed" letters found in the NT. The Muratorian Canon (late second century) mentions letters to the Alexandrians and to the Laodiceans, "both forged in Paul's name to [further] the heresy of Marcion, and many others." Only a brief letter to Laodicea is extant, and it is not Marcionite in theological orientation. Marcion, furthermore, appears to have identified the canonical letter to the Ephesians as the Laodicean letter. Some modern scholars believe canonical Ephesians originated as a circular letter intended for several churches in the region. The surviving Letter to the Laodiceans was composed in the late second or third century, its author taking a cue from Colossians 4:16, where Paul urges the Colossians and Laodiceans to exchange letters he has sent to each community. It is a pastiche written in Latin, drawing on Pauline language, especially from Philippians, and consisting of exhortations to *prayer, perseverance, and good works. It was rejected in the East but can be found in many Western biblical manuscripts until the Reformation, including the English translation of John Wycliffe.

Misunderstandings about the *resurrection in 1 Corinthians 15 provided an occasion in the second century for a letter purporting to be from Corinthian presbyters along with a reply from Paul. This exchange, known as 3 Corinthians, is embedded in the Acts of Paul (see below) but also circulated as a separate document. Whether it is integral to that narrative or has been interpolated—for example, to bring it into closer conformity with orthodox doctrine—is uncertain. The text describes how Simon and Cleobius have upset the Corinthians' *faith with their Gnostic teachings. In his response, Paul strongly affirms the inspired status of the prophets, the resurrection of the *body, the incarnation, and the divine *creation of the world. For centuries 3 Corinthians was included in many Armenian Bibles (Hovhanessian).

A fourteen-letter correspondence between Paul and Seneca, the Stoic philosopher and adviser to Nero, is first mentioned by Jerome (*Vir. ill.* 12). These letters (eight by Seneca, six by Paul) were written in the fourth century, though shifts in style suggest multiple hands at work in writing them (Kappler). In the correspondence, Seneca, who has apparently read 1–2 Corinthians and Galatians, mixes gentle criticism of Paul's Latin style with praise for his moral *teaching. Paul's easy manner among the Greco-Roman elite, whose respect he enjoys in these friendly letters, may have sought to neutralize the cultural stigma attached to Christianity for much of antiquity. The letters were widely considered authentic, if not canonical, until the Renaissance.

2. Acts.

The longest and best-known example of apocryphal Pauline literature is the Acts of Paul. At thirty-six hundred lines (according to the *Stichometry* of Nicephorus), it was roughly a third longer than the canonical Acts of the Apostles, though much of the original Greek has been lost. Portions of the text are also extant in Latin, Coptic, Syriac, Ethiopic, and Armenian. A date of composition in the mid- to late second century is likely based on patristic references (Tertullian, *Bapt.* 17.5; Hippolytus, *Comm. Dan.* 3.29; Origen, *Princ.* 1.2.3). Three sections of the Acts circulated independently as the Acts of Paul and Thecla, 3 Corinthians (see above), and the Martyrdom of Paul. Many of the stories are probably drawn from popular oral traditions, separate from the canonical Acts. Scholars are divided on whether the Acts of Paul should be understood as a sequel, a supplement, or a corrective to the Acts narrative, or else entirely independent of the canonical account of Paul's ministry. By the conventions of ancient physiognomy, the famous description of Paul as short, bald, bow-legged, "of noble mien, with eyebrows meeting, rather hook-nosed, and full of grace" (Acts of Paul 3 [trans. Elliott]) is generally positive, though its correspondence with historical realities, if any, is uncertain (Omerzu).

Paul's missionary *travel provides the literary structure, which in many respects resembles that of ancient novels, with its exotic locales and dangerous adventures, interspersed here with speeches delivered by the protagonist. The plot follows Paul from Damascus to *Jerusalem and then on to several other cities: *Syrian Antioch, Iconium, Pisidian Antioch, Myra, Sidon, Tyre, *Ephesus, Philippi, *Corinth, and finally Rome. Unlike ancient novels, however, the Acts of Paul deemphasizes romantic elements in favor of an asceticism that drives the plot at key moments. Paul's success in converting *Gentiles to the Christian faith, especially the wives and daughters of Greek and Roman elites who embrace his message of sexual abstinence, generates opposition from various government officials along the way. This message—expressed, for example, in the form of beatitudes pronouncing blessings on "those who have kept the flesh chaste" and "those who have wives as not having them" (Acts of Paul 5-6 [trans. Elliott])—may be traced to Paul's comments on celibacy in 1 Corinthians 7:1-9.

Thecla, a virgin from a prominent family in Iconium, becomes engrossed in Paul's discourses on chastity, upsetting her fiancé and family. She visits Paul in jail and learns at his feet. For her devotion to him and his subversive teachings, she is condemned to be burned naked at the stake but is miraculously preserved from harm by a timely storm. During subsequent travels with Paul, she is again condemned after rebuffing the advances of another man—this time to be eaten by wild animals. Following a series of miraculous rescues, Thecla baptizes herself by jumping into a pool with ravenous seals. Upon hearing her testimony, Paul authorizes her to teach the word of *God (Acts of Paul 41), shortly after which the narrative shifts to his own itinerant *preaching and miracle working. Among the memorable episodes is one involving a conversation with a lion sent to devour him in the stadium. In this Christianized version of Androclus and the Lion, perhaps inspired by the apostle's remarks (1 Cor 15:32; 2 Tim 4:17), the beast refuses when it recognizes Paul as the man who previously baptized him.

In the martyrdom account, Nero becomes agitated when his cupbearer, who has been healed by Paul, says he will fight for *Christ, the "king of the ages." When other guards proclaim their solidarity, Nero issues an edict that all "soldiers of Christ" be executed. Paul's apocalyptic warnings when he is questioned seal his fate and cause Nero to persecute the Roman Christians. The method of execution—beheading—is reflected in early iconography, in which Paul is typically pictured with a sword.

Much discussion of the Acts of Paul focuses on its value as evidence for the status of *women in second-century Christianity (Dunn). According to Tertullian (*Bapt.* 17.5), its author was an Asian presbyter wanting to honor the apostle, and it was invoked—wrongly, in Tertullian's view—as a precedent for the teaching and baptizing office of women in the *church. Paul's letters indicate the presence of women among his *coworkers (Rom 16:1; 1 Cor 1:11). It has been suggested that stories about Thecla were told and perhaps written by virgins, widows, and other women who had embraced celibacy and rejected *marriage (Davies). The challenge to the patriarchal social ethic of Greco-Roman society of any such movement is readily apparent, as one may infer, for example, from the importance attached to marriage and childbearing in 1 Timothy 2:11-15. Pauline teaching thus accommodated both conservative and radical interpretations in the second century, and could be appropriated by proponents of antinomianism as well as asceticism. The relationship of Thecla traditions to the Pastoral Epistles remains a matter of debate. Whereas some scholars view the Acts of Paul as a response to what its author perceives as a regressive social agenda, others believe the Pastoral Epistles are attempting to combat a nascent form of the egalitarianism implicit in the story of Thecla. From an early date, Thecla was venerated in the East and the West, most enthusiastically in Seleucia in the fourth to sixth centuries. Her feast day was removed from the Roman Catholic liturgical calendar in 1969 over questions of historicity.

Paul appears as a major or minor character in a number of later Acts, such as the Acts of Titus (sixth century) and book 2 of the Apostolic History of Pseudo-Abdias (seventh century). The Acts of Barnabas (fifth century) invents a background for the conflict concerning Mark between Paul and Barnabas mentioned in Acts 15:36-39. In the Acts of Andrew and Paul (fourth century?), Paul visits the underworld by diving into the ocean, leaving behind his cloak, which restores sight to a blind woman when it accidentally touches her eyes. A sixth-century Latin manuscript of the Acts of Peter (Actus Vercellenses) depicts Paul in a Roman *prison, where he converts the warden and his wife and hears a heavenly voice announcing that he will be put to death by Nero, before embarking on a *mission to Spain mentioned in Romans 15 (one of his converts there is the protagonist of the fourth-century Acts of Xanthippe, Polyxena, and Rebecca).

The Acts of Peter and Paul (seventh century) expands on Paul's travel between Malta and Rome briefly described in Acts 28:10-15, including an unfortunate case of mistaken identity when one of his bald converts is seized and beheaded. A latter section of the work draws on the sixth-century Passion of Peter and Paul of Pseudo-Marcellus, also known as the Martyrdom of Peter and Paul. A longer version of this Martyrdom has Paul joining Peter in his contest with Simon Magus in Rome, thus angering Nero, who orders their execution. The narrative places Paul's grave on the Via Ostia, where now stands the Basilica of Saint Paul Outside the Walls. The Syriac History of Paul (fifth century?) reports legends about the *healing powers of a tree that sprang up from his shed blood, mingled with that of *Peter on the same spot.

3. Apocalypses.

Paul's brief description of a mystical ascent through the heavens in 2 Corinthians 12:2-4 prompted the composition of at least two apocalypses in the second and third centuries (see Tertullian, *Praescr.* 24.5-6; Hippolytus, *Haer.* 5.8; Epiphanius, *Pan.* 38.2.5, mentions an Ascension of Paul, "full of filthy lewdness" [trans. Williams], that is not extant). A Gnostic Apocalypse of Paul survives in two hundred lines of Coptic discovered at Nag Hammadi (V 2). Paul is taken up to the third heaven by the *Holy Spirit in the form of a child, witnesses *judgment scenes in the fourth and fifth heavens, and encounters an old man, who unsuccessfully attempts to stop his further ascent in the seventh. As Jewish apocalypses locate Yahweh here, the old man represents the Jewish God, regarded by Gnostics as the inferior Demiurge (Irenaeus, *Haer.* 2.30.7). Paul likewise surpasses the twelve apostles, whom he meets in the eighth heaven on his way to joining "fellow spirits" in the tenth.

Much lengthier and more influential is another Apocalypse of Paul with a complicated textual history. Originally written in Greek, probably in the third century, it was translated into Latin, Syriac, Coptic, Armenian, Ethiopic, Slavonic, and Arabic, and appeared in both shorter and longer redactions as well as with alternate introductions and conclusions. The earliest surviving form of the apocalypse is a sixth-century Latin version, the Visio Pauli, which opens with an account of its purported discovery (together with Paul's shoes!) in 388 under the foundation of a house in Tarsus and its subsequent delivery to the Emperor Theodosius. This introduction was added to an earlier version that drew on the still earlier Apocalypse of Peter. Its literary conceit—the work purports to disclose revelations that, according to 2 Corinthians 12:4, must not be disclosed—raised the hackles of Augustine (*Tract. Ev. Jo.* 98.8) but otherwise caused no doctrinal consternation among patristic authorities troubled by the Gnostic Apocalypse's heterodox content.

This apocalypse recounts the apostle's *vision of heaven and hell in the form of a tour led by an angelic guide. Geographic features of the *afterlife combine elements drawn from the Bible (paradise as a land flowing with milk and honey) and Greek myth (the Acherusian lake to be crossed). Paul hears the testimony of all creation concerning the sinfulness of humanity and God's desire for their repentance, witnesses scenes of judgment of the righteous and the wicked, and arrives at paradise and the walls of the heavenly Jerusalem, where God is praised in song for eternity. Most memorable are the vivid descriptions of the damned in the service of moral admonition. Punishments are meted out according to the *sin, such as those guilty of infant exposure being torn apart by beasts. That Paul is frequently moved to tears also suggests a desire to address questions of theodicy about the justice of hell.

Although it is condemned in the Gelasian Decree, the Visio Pauli had the largest influence of the Christian apocalypses, not least through its translation into several European vernaculars (Bremmer and Czachesz). Popular beliefs about the afterlife can be traced back to its narrative and imagery, such as the notion that the damned receive a respite from their torments on Sundays. A later Ethiopic Apocalypse of the Virgin also circulated, in which Mary receives the same visions of heaven and hell in place of Paul. Dante's debt to the work is evident not only in the scheme of punishments but also in the reference in *Inferno* 2.28 to the visit of the "chosen vessel" (see Acts 9:15).

4. Other Works.

A short Prayer of the Apostle Paul is copied onto the front flyleaf of Codex I of the Nag Hammadi Library. It echoes Paul and the Psalms as well as the language of Hermetic and magical texts, and bears the stamp of third-century Gnostic teaching. Pseudo-Cyprian, in *De Rebaptismo* 17 (third century?), mentions an otherwise unattested Preaching of Paul and corrects the historical and theological errors it contains, such as its teaching that Jesus had sins of his own to confess and that Peter and Paul met for the first time in Rome. The Epistula Apostolorum is a second-century revealed dialogue in which the risen Jesus foretells the *conversion and ministry of Paul, whom the apostles are to catechize, written perhaps to reclaim Paul for orthodoxy. Although he is not named, many scholars believe that Paul is the figure attacked as the "enemy" opposing Peter and James in the Pseudo-Clementine literature (Recognitions; Homilies; Epistula Petri).

See also Apocalypticism; Canon of Paul's Letters; Gnosis, Gnosticism; Paul in Acts; Pseudepigraphy/Forgery; Women.

BIBLIOGRAPHY. **F. Bovon et al.,** eds., *Les Acts Apocryphes des Apôtres* (Geneva: Labor et Fides, 1981); **J. N. Bremmer,** ed., *The Apocryphal Acts of Paul and Thecla* (Kampen: Kok Pharos, 1996); **J. N. Bremmer and I. Czachesz,** eds., *The Visio Pauli and the Gnostic Apocalypse of Paul* (Leuven: Peeters, 2007); **S. L. Davies,** *The Revolt of the Widows: The Social World of the Apocryphal Acts* (Carbondale: Southern Illinois University Press, 1980); **P. W. Dunn,** "Women's Liberation, the *Acts of Paul,* and Other Apocryphal Acts of the Apostles: A Review of Some Recent Interpreters," *Apocrypha* 4 (1993): 245-61; **D. L. Eastman,** *Paul the Martyr: The Cult of the Apostle in the Latin West,* WGRWSup 4 (Atlanta: Society of Biblical Literature, 2011); idem, *The Ancient Martyrdom Accounts of Peter and Paul,* WGRW 39 (Atlanta: SBL Press, 2015); **J. K. Elliott,** ed., *The Apocryphal New Testament* (Oxford: Clarendon, 1993); **M. Himmelfarb,** *Tours of Hell: An Apocalyptic Form in Jewish and Christian Literature* (Philadelphia: University of Pennsylvania Press, 1983); **V. Hovhanessian,** *Third Corinthians: Reclaiming Paul for Christian Orthodoxy,* StBibLit 18 (New York: Peter Lang, 2000); **R. Kappler,** "Correspondance de Paul et Sénèque," in *Écrits apocryphes chrétiens,* ed. F. Bovon and P. Geoltrain (Paris: Gallimard, 1997), 1579-94; **D. R. MacDonald,** *The Legend and the Apostle: The Battle for Paul in Story and Canon* (Philadelphia: Westminster John Knox, 1983); **H. Omerzu,** "The Portrayal of Paul's Outer Appearance in the *Acts of Paul and Thecla*: Re-considering the Correspondence Between Body and Personality in Ancient Literature," *R&T* 15 (2008): 252-79; **R. I. Pervo,** *The Making of Paul: Constructions of the Apostle in Early Christianity* (Minneapolis: Fortress, 2010); **W. Schneemelcher and R. McL. Wilson,** eds., *New Testament Apocrypha,* 2nd ed., 2 vols. (Louisville, KY: Westminster John Knox, 1991); **G. E. Snyder,** *Acts of Paul: The Formation of a Pauline Corpus,* WUNT 2/352 (Tübingen: Mohr Siebeck, 2013); **P. Tite,** *The Apocryphal Epistle to the Laodiceans: An*

Epistolary and Rhetorical Analysis, TENTS 7 (Leiden: Brill, 2012); **F. Williams,** *The* Panarion *of Epiphanius of Salamis: Book I* (Leiden: Brill, 1987).

P. Gray

APOLLOS. *See* COWORKERS, PAUL AND HIS; EPHESUS.

APOSTASY

Among the many controversial topics in Pauline theology is the question of apostasy in Paul's letters. Can genuine believers, those who once were initiated and were genuine followers of *Christ, abandon or renounce their belief and thus reject God's gift of *salvation? Various theological traditions posit different answers to this question, and to some extent one can find support for either the reality of apostasy or the eventual "perseverance of the saints" (i.e., the idea that true believers cannot "fall away") in Paul's letters.

1. Paul and Judaism
2. Terminology
3. Paul as Apostate
4. Warnings Against Apostasy in Paul's Letters
5. Examples of Apostasy in Paul's Letters
6. Perseverance and "Eternal Security"

1. Paul and Judaism.

The reality of apostasy is observed within the Judaism of Paul's day. Various Jewish texts evidence markers of inclusion and exclusion and speak with some frequency of those who were once in the community of *faith who have been removed from it or abandoned it on their own volition. The standards for this abandoning of a faith community vary within the Jewish literature, as different sects and strands of Judaism held different beliefs and practices in varying priority. First Maccabees 1:15 describes those who allied with the *Gentiles and adopted their customs as having "abandoned the holy covenant." In the *Qumran literature, 1QS II, 11-18 describes the possibility of those who have entered into the *covenant and yet succumb to iniquity as being sentenced to everlasting destruction and being cut off from the "sons of light." The Animal Apocalypse of 1 Enoch frequently refers to apostates as those who have become blind or dim (e.g., 1 En. 90.6-7). Likewise, the Book of Luminaries condemns sinners and apostates to *judgment (1 En. 81.7-9).

Though different writings and communities held different standards for how apostasy was judged, often it was connected to improper *circumcision; improper Sabbath observance; ritual impurity, especially concerning dietary matters; sexual immorality; association with Gentiles; failing to observe the correct calendrical and festival cycles; accommodating *idolatry; failing to maintain personal piety; and rejection or embrace of the *temple, depending on the disposition of the group with regard to the *Jerusalem *leadership. It is not unreasonable, in fact, to consider that the Jewish leadership in Paul's own day considered him an apostate, or someone on the verge of such, for his supposed rejection of the *law of Moses and Jewish customs (see Acts 21:17-26). His frequent recounting of his conflict with Jewish leaders (e.g., 1 Cor 11:22-32) represents an ironic reversal given his own former status as a persecutor of those followers of Jesus whom he at one time viewed as apostates themselves (see Gal 1:13-14).

2. Terminology.

There are several terms in the NT frequently used to reference apostasy. *Apostasia* and *apostasi* similarly reference defying, denying, or rebelling against a community or authority structure. While these terms often convey a religious meaning, they can refer to rebellion against a king or superior as well. In Paul's letters, *apostasia* is used only in 2 Thessalonians 2:3, to refer to the "rebellion" of the *"man of lawlessness." Paul himself is referred to as one spreading apostasy in Acts 21:21 by instructing the Jews to forsake (*apostasian*) the law of Moses. Other terms factor in more frequently to Paul's discussions of apostasy. In Galatians 5:4, Paul speaks of those who have "been estranged" (*katargeō*) from Christ and "fallen away" (*ekpiptō*) from *grace because of their pursuit of *righteousness in the law. Likewise, in Romans 11:11, Paul describes the rejection of Jesus as Messiah by many of his Jewish contemporaries as a "fall" (*piptō*) and notes that *God deals severely with those who have fallen (Rom 11:22), though he also suggests their fall could be reversed if they repented (see also 1 Cor 10:8-12).

3. Paul as Apostate.

Recent scholarship, with a heightened interest in the relationship between Paul and Judaism, has given some attention to the question of Paul's own *identity in relation to apostasy (see Segal). The major divide centers on whether Paul saw himself as an apostate of a former religion, which he now encouraged other Jews to leave as well, or whether Paul saw his following of Jesus as a continuation of his former religious identity now transformed. As John Barclay has recognized, the question of apostasy in Paul must be seen both from the angle of his own self-descriptive statements (e.g., Gal 1:11-24; Phil 3:1-11) and from what his Jewish contemporaries thought of him (e.g., 2 Cor 11:24, 26; 1 Thess 2:15). Barclay concludes, "Paul was frequently viewed by his fellow Jews with the deepest distrust" (Barclay, 116). As Sigurd Grindheim demonstrates, Paul, however, turns these apostastic tables on his Jewish opponents in Galatians 3:1-14 and pronounces the covenantal *curse on them for their disloyalty to God through their disloyalty to Jesus. It is thus possible to answer the question of whether Paul was an apostate with both a yes and no, depending on which *tradition one is viewing him from within. Paul may have seen his own *ministry as existing in continuity with Jewish belief while being viewed by Jewish leaders as an apostate.

4. Warnings Against Apostasy in Paul's Letters. Though the main terms linked with the word group for "apostasy" in the NT occur sparingly in Paul's letters, warnings against such are prevalent. In the face of their dilemma with the *Judaizers, Paul writes to the Galatians that he fears they are turning back to their former enslavement to the spiritual forces of darkness and thinks his efforts for them might be wasted (Gal 4:8-11). Paul warns them also that those who exhibit immoral, selfish, and indulgent behaviors will not inherit the *kingdom of God (Gal 5:21; see also 1 Cor 6:9-11), and those who "sow to the *flesh" will reap destruction (Gal 6:8). In his first letter to the Thessalonians, Paul warns that succumbing to sexual immorality constitutes a rejection of God and the Spirit (1 Thess 4:8). Though not as clear, in Romans 14:21, Paul, in his discourse about "the weak and the *strong" as it relates to certain practices of *purity and *holiness, warns the Roman believers not to cause a weaker brother or sister to fall (*proskoptō*). Though the context does not make it clear that Paul has apostasy in mind, since the term is often used to describe those who are separated from God for various causes of stumbling (e.g., Rom 9:32; 1 Pet 2:8), such an inference is possible here as well.

The Pastoral Epistles, though debated as to Pauline authenticity, are replete with references to apostasy and rejecting sound *teaching and practice. First Timothy 4:1 predicts a future abandoning of the faith (presumably by former believers) and following deceiving spirits, which will occur because of false teachers. In the context of commands to support widows, in 1 Timothy 5:8 it is declared that those who do not provide for those of their own *household have "denied the faith" and "are worse than an unbeliever." Paul's letters thus warn about rejection of the faith arising through immoral practices, acceptance of false teaching, or denying the *truth of the *gospel.

5. Examples of Apostasy in Paul's Letters. Paul also refers to instances of apostasy in his letters where those within the community have rebelled against and rejected the authority of Jesus' teachings or the community's standards. In his letter to the Galatians, Paul seems to suggest some of the Galatian believers have already been cut off from Christ. He remarks that their pursuit of circumcision will result in Christ being useless to them and states that some have already been estranged from Christ and fallen away from grace (Gal 5:1-4).

Perhaps one of the clearest instances of apostasy in Paul's letters occurs in 1 Corinthians 5:1-13. Here Paul details the case of a man who "has the wife of his father" (probably his stepmother rather than birth mother). Paul refers to this *sin as taking place "among you," which would seem to put the offender within the community of believers in *Corinth. Paul states the community should have removed the man from their midst, and instructs them to do so now and to hand the man over to *Satan for the "destruction of his flesh [*sarx*]," that his Spirit "might be saved on the day of the *Lord." Paul concludes the instructions with a command to "remove the wicked person from among yourselves" (1 Cor 5:13), quoting from a similar command that occurs throughout Deuteronomy (Deut 13:5; 17:7; 19:19; 21:21; 22:21, 24; 24:7), always in the context of an Israelite who has violated the covenant and is now being cut off from the covenant community. In Deuteronomy, this often occurs with the implication of capital punishment. The nature of the punishment in 1 Corinthians 5:5 ("destruction of his flesh") is debated, and Paul appears to hold out *hope for the repentance and restoration of the individual, though such a hope is not portrayed as definitive but rather possible.

Another clear instance of apostasy in Paul's letters occurs in Romans 11. Here Paul describes his Jewish compatriots who have rejected Jesus as Messiah as having stumbled, fallen away, and been "cut off" from the tree of God's people. Paul declares that this fall is not "beyond recovery" (Rom 11:11; i.e., repentance and restoration is possible), but being "broken off" (Rom 11:17) is a reasonable indication that he views them as formerly being counted among God's people and now having been removed from them. Paul warns his Gentile readers as well that such a fate is not out of the realm of possibility for them either. If they hold their faith with arrogance and lack kindness, they too could be "cut off" (Rom 11:17-24). In both cases in this text, Paul speaks of those formerly counted among God's people who have been or could be cut off for their lack of loving loyalty to God and his purposes.

Finally, the Pastoral Epistles contain several texts that indicate that apostasy had occurred by certain members of the believing community. First Timothy 1:18-20 contains the identification of possible apostates (Hymenaeus and Alexander) who have "rejected" the faith, have "suffered shipwreck," and have been handed over to Satan, though it is not clear whether there is intention or hope for restoration as in 1 Corinthians 5. Likewise, in 1 Timothy 6:10, it is affirmed that, because of the love of money, some have already "wandered from the faith." In these passages, Paul identifies those once part of the believing community who have now been cut off, have been removed, or have otherwise abandoned the faith through a rejection of Jesus or through lack of repentance for their immoral practices.

6. Perseverance and "Eternal Security."
Part of the challenge of reconciling the warnings against and examples of apostasy in Paul's letters is his strong statements that seem to indicate the security of believers against any threat to their standing with God. The sequence of Romans 8–11 illustrates this tension well. In Romans 8:28-39, Paul assures the Roman church of the unfailing *love of God for them, from which nothing in the created order is able to separate them. However, in Romans 11:11-24, Paul warns these same recipients against the potential for them to be cut off from the tree of God's people should they live in sinful arrogance against God.

This tension is demonstrated in various ways throughout Paul's other letters, though it is clearly more pronounced in some than in others. In 1 Corinthians, a letter that contains both examples of apostates within the community and warnings against apostasy, Paul can also write reassuringly that God will keep the Corinthians "firm to the end, so that you will be blameless on the day of our Lord Jesus Christ" (1 Cor 1:4-9), and that "God is faithful, who will not let you be tempted beyond what you can bear" (1 Cor 10:13). In 2 Thessalonians, Paul can declare in the very same passage that the Thessalonian believers are chosen, sanctified, called, and awaiting future glory (2 Thess 2:13-14), while also commanding them to stand firm and praying that God would strengthen them to stand firm in the truth (2 Thess 2:15-17). Likewise, in 2 Timothy, there is a "trustworthy saying" that affirms: "If we died with him, we will also live with him; if we endure, we will also reign with him. If we deny him, he will also deny us; if we are faithless, he remains faithful, for he cannot deny himself." The tension in perspectives here is readily apparent as affirmations of future assurance ("we will live with him," "we will reign with him") are combined with both conditions ("if we endure") and warnings of judgment ("he will deny us").

As a result of these tensions, interpreters have affirmed opposite conclusions concerning Paul's theology of apostasy and perseverance. While some emphasize the perseverance of the elect (i.e., those who have been chosen will persevere, and those who do not persevere were never chosen), others emphasize that abandonment of the faith, either through rejection of Jesus or through unrepentant sin, is a genuine possibility for believers (see Pinson). While theological motives often drive these interpretive results, contextual factors—including Paul's background and Jewish context, the context and purpose of his letters, the identity of his various audiences, and the interconnections of his various theological themes—remain necessary factors in attempting to bring a resolution to the tension found on matters of salvation, perseverance, and apostasy in the writings of Paul.

See also Conversion and Call of Paul; Corinthians, First Letter to the; Election and Predestination; Pastoral Epistles; Paul and Judaism; Romans, Letter to the; Salvation.

BIBLIOGRAPHY. **J. M. G. Barclay,** "Paul Among Diaspora Jews: Anomaly or Apostate?," *JSNT* 60 (1995): 89-120; **J. D. G. Dunn,** "Paul: Apostate or Apostle of Israel?," *ZNW* 89 (1998): 256-71; **S. Grindheim,** "Apostate Turned Prophet: Paul's Prophetic Self-Understanding and Prophetic Hermeneutic with Special Reference to Galatians 3.10-12," *NTS* 53 (2007): 545-65; **R. H. Gundry,** "Grace, Words, and Staying Saved in Paul," *Bib* 66 (1985): 1-38; **J. M. Gundry Volf,** *Paul and Perseverance: Staying In and Falling Away*, WUNT 2/37 (Tübingen: Mohr, 1990); **G. Harris,** "The Beginnings of Church Discipline: 1 Corinthians 5," *NTS* 37 (1991): 1-21; **I. H. Marshall,** *Kept by the Power of God: A Study of Perseverance and Falling Away* (Minneapolis: Bethany, 1975); **B. J. Oropeza,** *Apostasy in the New Testament Communities*, vol. 2, *Jews, Gentiles, and the Opponents of Paul* (Eugene, OR: Cascade, 2012); **J. M. Pinson,** *Four Views on Eternal Security* (Grand Rapids, MI: Zondervan, 2002); **T. R. Schreiner and A. B. Caneday,** *The Race Set*

Before Us: A Biblical Theology of Perseverance and Assurance (Downers Grove, IL: InterVarsity Press, 2011); **A. Segal,** *Paul the Convert: The Apostolate and Apostasy of Saul the Pharisee* (New Haven, CT: Yale University Press, 1990); **A. C. Thornhill,** *The Chosen People: Election, Paul, and Second Temple Judaism* (Downers Grove, IL: IVP Academic, 2015); **B. W. Witherington III,** *The Problem with Evangelical Theology* (Waco, TX: Baylor University Press, 2005); **A. Yarbro Collins,** "The Function of Excommunication in Paul," *HTR* 73 (1980): 251-63.

A. C. Thornhill

APOSTLE

Scholarly understanding of the early Christian role or position of apostle is overwhelmingly dependent on the Pauline epistles and Luke-Acts, which is associated with the Pauline *mission. Out of eighty occurrences, *apostolos* occurs thirty-four times in the Pauline epistles, and thirty-four times in Luke-Acts. The Pauline epistles not only reflect Paul's understanding of his role as an apostle of *Christ, but they also offer insight into the qualifications for apostles in the early *church.

1. Critical Issues
2. *Apostle* in the Gospels and Acts
3. Paul's Description of and Criteria for an Apostle of Christ
4. Paul's Description of Other Apostles
5. Paul's Description of His Apostleship
6. Conclusion

1. Critical Issues.

There are a number of critical issues that frame the scholarly discussion of Paul's use of the word *apostle*.

1.1. Greek Origins of Apostolos. *Apostolos* emerged as a technical term in early Christianity distinct from its general use in Greek. The use of the word *apostolos* was relatively rare in Greek literature before the NT was written. Referents, whether people or things, were generally associated with naval operations (Rengstorf, 407-8). *Apostolē* is a related word that means "dispatching" or "sending on a journey," but in the NT it means "apostleship" (Acts 1:25; Rom 1:5; 1 Cor 9:2; Gal 2:8). Both *apostolos* and *apostolē* are likely derived from the much more common cognate verb *apostellō,* which is "to send off or send away."

1.2. Origin of* Apostle *as a Technical Term in Early Christianity. There are three views on the origin of *apostolos* as a technical term in early Christianity: a Christian origin; a derivation or influence from *šālîaḥ* of late rabbinic Judaism, a legal institution in which a surrogate messenger was used (Rengstorf); and a Gnostic background (Schmithals). The known occurrences of *šālîaḥ* and the Gnostic redeemer myths postdate Paul's writings, but whereas the *šālîaḥ* origin has received scholarly support, the Gnostic origin has not been widely received. Neither can convincingly account for the technical term *apostle* in the NT better than a direct derivation from the Greek word *apostolos* and the cognate verb *apostellō.* The specific scenario that accounts for the term's emergence would be Jesus' desire to give the disciples a special name when he appointed them in order to send them away on missions (Mk 3:14; Lk 6:13).

1.3. Gospels and the Oral Tradition. According to the majority of scholars, the Gospels postdate the Pauline epistles, so that Paul could not have used them as sources. However, as Richard Bauckham convincingly argues, the Gospels are based on the accounts of eyewitnesses, which is explicitly claimed in Luke 1:2. Furthermore, Paul makes a similar appeal in one of his most important passages on apostles (1 Cor 15:1-11). He cites the oral *tradition he has received and passed on (1 Cor 15:3), and he makes a point of saying that hundreds of eyewitnesses were still living at the time he was writing, circa AD 55 (1 Cor 15:6). Therefore, it is plausible that the authors of the Gospels and Paul were drawing from the oral tradition(s) originating in Jerusalem, which allows for exploring plausible linkages.

1.4. Relationship Between Luke-Acts and the Pauline Epistles. A trend in Pauline studies, due to the influence of F. C. Baur, is to challenge Luke's knowledge of Paul due to alleged discrepancies between the Paul of Acts and the Paul of the Pauline epistles. Ernst Haenchen claims that the author of Acts missed Paul's major claim to apostleship, which he gives as one of five reasons that the author could not have been one of Paul's companions (Haenchen, 114). However, Paul and Barnabas are called apostles (Acts 14:4, 14), and in the immediate context, Acts 14:3 states that the Lord "testified to the word of his grace by granting *signs and wonders to be done through them" (NRSV), which Paul designates as the signs of a true apostle (2 Cor 12:12). Luke repeats the narrative of Paul's commission on the Damascus road three times (Acts 9:1-19; 22:3-16; 26:9-18), which parallels what Seyoon Kim argues is the centrality of the Damascus road experience in Paul's vocabulary and thought. Stanley Porter rightly observes a high degree of similarity in usage of *apostolos* in Acts and the Pauline Epistles that allows for differences but not contradictions (Porter, 197).

1.5. Authorship of the Pauline Epistles. When dealing with themes in the Pauline corpus, various challenges to Pauline authorship can be a consideration for how one would compile the data and what weight one may give to disputed letters. However, most of the key passages that give information on the meaning and function of an apostle and that reflect challenges to Paul's apostleship are located in undisputed epistles (Romans, 1–2 Corinthians, Galatians, 1 Thessalonians).

1.6. Junia's Apostleship. The apostleship of Junia in Romans 16:7 has become prominent in the discussion of Paul's use of the term *apostle* since Eldon J. Epp published a survey of text-critical scholarship on Romans 16:7 in 2005. Epp demonstrated that between 1927 and 1998, the GNT critical editions replaced the well-attested feminine name *Junia* with a poorly attested masculine variant (Junias) because of their biased belief that a woman could not be an apostle. Since the publication of Epp's monograph, the consensus of scholarship is that Junia was a woman and that she was an apostle. Yii-Jan Lin offers an excellent survey and analysis of several new counterarguments that have emerged and further supports Junia's status as a prominent apostle with the context of Paul's rhetoric.

2. *Apostle* in the Gospels and Acts.

The Synoptic Gospels present a fairly unified picture of Jesus' appointment of the Twelve, their designation as apostles, their commission to preach, the power and authority to heal and do exorcisms, and their representation of Jesus. When Jesus appoints the twelve disciples, Mark and Luke make the point that he chose to call them apostles (Mk 3:14; Lk 6:13). He appoints them to be with him as companions (Mk 3:14), but he also appoints them in order to send them out on missionary journeys to preach the *gospel (Mt 10:7; Mk 6:12; Lk 9:2), and he gives them the authority and power to heal the sick, raise the dead, cure lepers, and drive out *demons (Mt 10:1, 8; Mk 6:7, 12; Lk 9:1). In Matthew's instructions to the Twelve before they are sent out (Mt 10:5-42), he makes it clear that the apostles represent Jesus: "Whoever welcomes you welcomes me, and whoever welcomes me welcomes the one who sent me" (Mt 10:40 NRSV).

The term *apostle* receives further development in Luke-Acts. After sending out the Twelve in Luke 9:1-6, Jesus appoints and sends out "seventy others" (or "seventy-two others" in some manuscripts) in Luke 10:1-20. Luke uses repetition of the same criteria to identify the "seventy others" as apostles; they have been known as apostles in the Eastern Christian tradition. Therefore, in Luke, the term *apostle* has a broader definition than the Twelve. An apostle is recognized by the criteria and activity modeled by the Twelve and the Seventy.

As is often noted, Luke most often uses the term *apostle* as a reference to the Twelve in Acts 1–11 (see also Acts 15; 16:4). He emphasizes the apostles' authority, power, and prophetic *knowledge, as well as their many signs and wonders (e.g., Acts 4:30; 5:12), but the Twelve also practice administrative oversight that becomes extended over all the churches (e.g., Acts 4:30–5:11; 6:1-7; 15:1-35; 21:17-26). Luke also portrays Paul as meeting apostolic criteria. In addition to describing Saul/Paul's commission by Jesus on the Damascus road three times (Acts 9:1-19; 22:3-16; 26:9-18), Luke portrays Barnabas and Saul/Paul as appointed and sent by the *Holy Spirit (Acts 13:2, 4), with a ministry of preaching the gospel that was characterized by signs and wonders (e.g., Acts 14:3). It is in this context that Luke explicitly designates Barnabas and Saul/Paul as apostles (Acts 14:4, 14), but it is clear in Acts 15 that Luke does not confound the apostleship of Barnabas and Paul with that of the Twelve in *Jerusalem and their oversight of all the churches.

3. Paul's Description of and Criteria for an Apostle of Christ.

In his letters, Paul appeals to readers' shared knowledge about apostles and their qualifications in order to make various arguments, or to support his own apostleship and/or gospel.

3.1. Foundation of the Church. Paul saw apostles as essential to the existence of the church, based on not only his metaphorical description of the God's people as a building in Ephesians 2:20, but his ordering of spiritual *gifts in which "apostle" is placed first (1 Cor 12:28; cf. Eph 4:11). The specific ways in which the apostles provide a foundation are expressed in the other criteria.

3.2. Eyewitnesses of the Resurrected Jesus. In his defense of his apostleship to the Corinthians, Paul links being an apostle with having seen the *Lord (1 Cor 9:1). Later in the letter in defense of the *resurrection from the dead, he provides a brief survey of the eyewitnesses of Jesus' resurrection (1 Cor 15:3-8). The eyewitnesses include Cephas/Peter, then the Twelve, five hundred people, James the brother of Jesus, and then "all the apostles." Then Paul states that Jesus' last postresurrection appearance was to him. The eyewitnesses of the resurrected Jesus had an important apostolic status and role in the early church, Paul is making a claim to membership in that group, and membership to that group is closed. A claim to belong to the Twelve, the Seventy, or the eyewitnesses of the resurrected Jesus would be a claim to apostolic status, but Jesus' postresurrection appearance to Paul does not appear to be the endpoint of apostolic appointment, as Paul Barnett argues (Barnett, 48). Rather, it is a claim to a prominent subcategory of apostleship in the same way that the Twelve are a prominent subcategory of apostleship. A third subcategory, which Paul also claims to belong to in Galatians 2:7-9, includes a variety of others whose apostleship is based on the pragmatic evidence that they have the spiritual gift of apostleship (see section 4 below).

3.3. Called/Appointed/Sent. In the salutations of the Pauline epistles, the direct role of God the Father and Jesus Christ in his appointment are prominent, as it is in the description of his calling (Gal 1:15-16). However, in 1 Corinthians 12:28, the spiritual gift of apostle is distributed by the Holy Spirit (1 Cor 12:4, 7, 11), though God the Father is the one who places apostles in the church (1 Cor 12:28). Similarly, in Acts 13:2-4, the Holy Spirit tells the church to set apart Saul/Paul and Barnabas, and the Holy Spirit sends them through the church.

3.4. Signs, Wonders, and Mighty Works. Paul asserts that the indicators of a true apostle are signs, wonders, and mighty works (2 Cor 2:12; cf. Rom 15:18-19), which is consistent with the Gospels' descriptions of apostles being appointed by Jesus to heal and perform exorcisms, and the subsequent performance of *healings and miracles by the apostles in the Acts account. These criteria appear to be overlooked in most studies, but they appear to have been central in the early church in the effective preaching and spreading of the gospel.

3.5. Faithful Spread and Transmission of the Gospel. Paul expresses an apostolic responsibility and commitment to preach and transmit the gospel (Rom 1:1-3; 1 Cor 1:17; Gal 1:11-16; 1 Thess 2:4; 2 Tim 1:11). That responsibility includes not only founding churches but also transmitting and maintaining the traditions about Jesus to churches and individuals (1 Cor 11:21-26; 1 Cor 15:3-6; cf. 2 Tim 1:13; 2:2). Paul depicts "the other apostles" as conducting mission trips (1 Cor 9:5), so that being "sent" as an apostle retains the core meaning of travel to spread the gospel.

3.6. A Spiritual Gift. As said above, apostle is listed by Paul as one of the spiritual gifts that are being distributed to each one as the Spirit determines for the edification of the church (1 Cor 12:11, 28; Eph 4:11). This would indicate that it is available with the other spiritual gifts and the calling is determined by pragmatic evidence, which best accounts for the people called apostles who do not belong to the subcategories of the Twelve or the eyewitnesses of the resurrected Christ.

3.7. Status. Paul places apostles first in the ranking of the spiritual gifts, as they are essential to the spread, transmission, and defense of the gospel. Paul supports the status and rights of apostles in the churches, though he personally waives those rights. He tells the Thessalonians that apostles of Christ are entitled to make demands (1 Thess 2:6-7). He claims that apostles have basic rights to material support from the people to whom they minister (1 Cor 9:1-18). On the other hand, he accepts the public humiliation of apostles as the normal state of affairs, comparing it to being the final captives in a triumphal procession who are condemned to die in the arena (1 Cor 4:9).

4. Paul's Description of Other Apostles. Paul acknowledges the title of apostle for a variety of others, particularly the apostles before Paul (Gal 1:17), who were numerous. In 1 Corinthians 15:5-7, he is appealing to the apostolic witness of hundreds for the resurrection of Jesus Christ.

In Galatians, Paul describes Peter as having a unique or foundational *call (Gal 2:7-8) and he acknowledges the apostles of Jerusalem as leaders and pillars (Gal 2:2, 6, 9), particularly Peter, John, and James. By seeking their affirmation, he acknowledges their administrative oversight of the churches (Gal 2:6-10). However, he disparages their celebrity among the churches (Gal 2:6), relativizes the importance of their affirmation (Gal 2:6), and deems their admonition to remember the poor as unnecessary (Gal 2:10). He tells of how he confronted Peter for hypocrisy (Gal 2:11-14) and suggests that James was complicit in undermining his mission to the *Gentiles (Gal 2:12). None of this contradicts his theology of apostleship or undermines what he considers to be the proper status of the apostles since he believes and practices the public confession of error.

Paul refers to a number of people as apostles who are associated with him, including Barnabas (1 Cor 9:6; cf. Acts 14:4), Silas and Timothy (1 Thess 2:6; cf. 1 Thess 1:1), two "brothers" (2 Cor 8:23), Epaphroditus (Phil 2:25), and Andronicus and Junia (Rom 16:7). None of them, except possibly Andronicus and Junia, who were in

Christ before Paul, would be eyewitnesses of the resurrected Christ.

Paul's use of the technical term *apostle* encompasses distinct subcategories. Paul acknowledges the apostleship of the Twelve, and their unique role in Jerusalem and all the churches, and according to Luke, Matthias would be the last member of that group (Acts 1:15-26). In addition to the Twelve, Paul also acknowledges other eyewitnesses of the resurrected Jesus as apostles with an important function in transmitting the gospel, and he counts himself as the last member of that group. A third group would be those who, after the ascension of Jesus, are identified as having the spiritual gift of apostle in the same way that prophets and teachers are identified—their appointment or call is based on pragmatic evidence of their ministry that conforms to the criteria (see Gal 2:7-9).

5. Paul's Description of His Own Apostleship. As said above, Paul's general description of apostles is extracted from arguments that he is making either to support his own apostleship or to support another argument that he is making.

5.1. Foundation of the Gentile Churches. Paul assigns himself a more specific role as the apostle who is foundational in the establishment of Gentile churches in a way that is parallel to Peter's role (Gal 2:7-8). Paul's strategy is to break new ground in his ministry so that he does not "build on someone else's foundation" (Rom 15:20).

5.2. Eyewitness of the Resurrected Jesus. In 1 Corinthians 15:8, Paul states that the Damascus road experience was Christ's last postresurrection appearance, but that is not the same as making the claim that he was the last apostle. Since Christ appeared to Paul after Jesus' ascension, he is like "one untimely born" (1 Cor 15:8 NRSV). Among other things, he associates Jesus' postresurrection appearance to him with his apostleship (1 Cor 9:1) and to stress the divine origin of his call and his gospel (Gal 2:15-16).

5.3. Called, Appointed, and Sent. The salutations of most of the Pauline epistles emphasize the theme that Paul is divinely and directly appointed to be an apostle by the will in of God, which draws on his commission on the Damascus road. In Galatians 1:1 Paul stresses the specifics: he has a divine commission and was sent from Jesus Christ and God the Father, as opposed to having a human commission or being sent from human authorities. He elaborates on this in Galatians 1:11-24, indicating that he received his gospel directly from God, which was how he understood the Gentiles to be saved by *faith.

5.4. Signs, Wonders and Mighty Works. Paul claims that the proof that he is a true apostle is his performance of signs, wonders, and mighty works (2 Cor 12:12). He similarly tells the Roman church that his mission to the Gentiles was accomplished through what he said (his gospel) and by the power of signs and wonders that show the power of God (Rom 15:18-19). The importance of Paul's performance of signs and miracles is consistent with the prominent pattern of performance of miracles, healing, and exorcisms by the Twelve and the Seventy in the Gospels and Acts.

5.5. Faithful Spread and Transmission of the Gospel to the Gentiles. Paul emphasizes his priority and commitment to preach the gospel to the Gentiles and the specific content that he was *preaching to the Gentiles throughout the Pauline epistles (Gal 1:11–2:3; 1 Tim 2:7; 2 Tim 1:11). *Travel was a central aspect to Paul's function as an apostle (Marquis, 3). He describes his commitment to being a pioneering apostle, with the ambition and strategy of proclaiming the gospel where it has not been heard before (Rom 15:19b-24).

5.6. The Spiritual Gift. In Galatians 2:8, Paul indicates that the Jerusalem apostles acknowledged him as an apostle based on pragmatic evidence rather than on his claim to be an eyewitness to the resurrected Jesus. They saw that God was at work in Paul as an apostle to the Gentiles in the same way that he was at work in Peter as an apostle to the Jews. Similarly, Paul says to the Corinthians: "If I am not an apostle to others, at least I am to you: for you are my seal of my apostleship in the Lord" (1 Cor 9:2 NRSV). Even if Paul had not encountered the risen Christ and had not been called to be an apostle to the Gentiles, his work with the Corinthians was pragmatic evidence that he was their apostle and that God had placed him in the church at its foundation.

5.7. Status. In regards to Paul's personal status, on the one hand he claims the same apostolic status as Peter (Gal 2:7). On the other hand, in 1 Corinthians 15:9, he states that he is the least of the apostles, not because he was the last to see the postresurrected Christ but because he persecuted the church of God (see 1 Tim 1:13-16). Paul's understanding of God's *grace compels him to recognize and publicly confess the error of his ways as an expression of gratitude (Joubert, 74). Furthermore, he waives the status, privileges, and rights of being an apostle at the same time that he defends them (1 Thess 2:7; 1 Cor 9:12; 2 Cor 11:7-9, 12:12). He considers his weaknesses and *suffering as opportunities to display God's power (2 Cor 11:16–12:10) and to participate in Christ's sufferings (Phil 3:10). However, his apostolic status was challenged in *Corinth and Galatia. He was attacked in Corinth in part for his weaknesses (Schreiner, 84-85), in part for waiving his rights, and in part because his *leadership was challenged by "superapostles" who more closely represented the Greco-Roman concepts of status and *honor (2 Cor 10–11).

In Galatians, the authority and integrity of the gospel he preached was undermined by "*Judaizers" from Jerusalem. If one accepts 2 Timothy's representation of Paul, at the end of his life, Paul's message faced harmful opposition (2 Tim 2:17-18; 4:14-15), and he was deserted by most of his support, partly because they were "ashamed of" his "chains" (2 Tim 1:15-16; see 2 Tim 4:9-12), so that he stresses his appointment as an apostle (2 Tim 1:11-12) and the transmission of the gospel (2 Tim 1:13-14; 2:2; 4:1-2). As N. H. Taylor argues, these conflicts and challenges were complex and diverse, but they provided the occasions in which Paul most clearly defined and defended his *identity as an apostle and to defend Christlike leadership.

6. Conclusion.

Paul appeals to characteristics of apostles in the early church who were before him (1 Cor 15:5-7). Paul makes reference to three subcategories of apostles: the Twelve, the eyewitnesses of the resurrected Christ, and others who demonstrate pragmatic evidence that they have the spiritual gift of apostleship. Apostles are divinely appointed to spread and transmit the gospel and the oral traditions and to plant churches. They represent Christ wherever they go. Their ministry is characterized by mission trips, preaching, and demonstrations of the power of God. Paul claims that he qualifies as an apostle because he is an eyewitness of the resurrected Christ and was commissioned by him at that time to be an apostle to the Gentiles. However, he also claims he is an apostle because of the evidence of signs, wonders, and mighty works, and the establishment of churches through his preaching.

See also Church; Conversion and Call of Paul; Corinthians, First Letter to the; Galatians, Letter to the; Gifts of the Spirit; Gospel; Mission; Paul in Acts; Signs, Wonders, Miracles; Travel in the Roman World; Women; Witness.

BIBLIOGRAPHY. **P. W. Barnett,** "Apostle," *DPL*, 45-51; **C. K. Barrett,** *The Signs of an Apostle* (Philadelphia: Fortress, 1972); **R. Bauckham,** *Jesus and the Eyewitnesses: The Gospels as Eyewitness Testimony,* 2nd ed. (Grand Rapids, Eerdmans, 2017); **A. Ehrhardt,** *The Apostolic Ministry,* SJT Occasional Papers 7 (Edinburgh: Oliver & Boyd, 1958); **E. J. Epp,** *Junia: The First Woman Apostle* (Minneapolis: Fortress, 2005). **E. Haenchen,** *The Acts of the Apostles: A Commentary,* trans. B. Noble et al. (Philadelphia: Westminster, 1971); **S. Joubert,** "'Seeing the Error of My Ways': Revisiting Paul's Paradigmatic Self-Critical Remarks in 1 Corinthians 15:8-10," *Acta Theologica* 33, no. 2 (2013): 74-89; **S. Kim,** *The Origins of Paul's Gospel* (Grand Rapids, MI: Eerdmans, 1981); **Y. J. Lin,** "Junia: An Apostle Before Paul," *JBL* 139, no. 1 (2020): 191-209; **T. L. Marquis,** *Transient Apostle: Paul, Travel and the Rhetoric of Empire* (New Haven, CT: Yale University Press, 2013); **J. Munck,** "Paul, the Apostles and the Twelve," *ST* 3 (1949): 36-68; **S. E. Porter,** *Paul in Acts,* Library of Pauline Studies (Peabody, MA: Hendrickson, 2001); **R. Rengstorf,** "ἀπόστολος," *TDNT* 1:407-47; **W. Schmithals,** *The Office of Apostle in the Early Church* (Nashville: Abingdon, 1969); **R. Schnackenberg,** "Apostles Before and During Paul's Time," in *Apostolic History and the Gospel: Biblical and Historical Essays Presented to F. F. Bruce*, ed. W. W. Gasque and R. P. Martin (Exeter, UK: Paternoster, 1970), 297-303; **T. R. Schreiner,** *Paul, Apostle of God's Glory in Christ: A Pauline Theology,* 2nd ed. (Downers Grove, IL: IVP Academic, 2020); **N. H. Taylor,** "Conflict as Context for Defining Identity: A Study of Apostleship in the Galatian and Corinthian Letters," *TS* 59, no. 3 (2003): 915-45.

C. L. Westfall

APOSTOLIC FATHERS. *See* Interpretation: Patristic.

APOSTOLIC PAROUSIA. *See* Travel and Itinerary Plans.

AQEDAH. *See* Abraham; James and Paul; Romans, Letter to the.

ARMOR OF GOD. *See* Ephesians, Letter to the; Triumph.

ARTEMIS. *See* Ephesus; Religions, Greco-Roman.

ASCENSION

The ascension, exaltation, and enthronement of the crucified and risen *Lord Jesus is the apogee of

Paul's *Christology. The church's destiny and that of all *creation are ultimately fulfilled in Christ's incarnate life at the Father's right hand, where he embodies and mediates the present and future *hope of the world in the power of the Spirit. Paul proclaims Jesus' *death and *resurrection as God's good news from the perspective of Jesus' current reign as ascended king, priest, and Lord. Having met the ascended Jesus of Nazareth on the Damascus road, Paul comes to understand that Jesus' glorified life (and thus his continuing incarnation) is the essential climax and eschatological hope of God's human children, who are being conformed into Christ's gloriously renewed human image as children of resurrection.

1. Paul and the Ascended Lord Jesus Christ
2. Aspects of Jesus' Ascension
3. Implications for the Church

1. Paul and the Ascended Lord Jesus Christ.

1.1. Met, Called by, and Conformed to Jesus Ascended. Jesus of Nazareth, ascended and enthroned as God's human-divine King, revealed himself to Saul of Tarsus on the Damascus road as the crucified, resurrected Lord of heaven and earth, now united to his persecuted disciples by the Spirit. In this life-transforming encounter described by Luke (Acts 9:1-31; 22:2-21; 26:4-20) and Paul (1 Cor 9:1; 15:8), Jesus' true *identity is displayed, giving his death and resurrection divine significance, and thus reordering Paul's messianic expectations and eschatological understanding of God's new *covenant, along with all this implies for God's people as children of the resurrection (Gorman 2016). In this Lord and *Christ their glorious, embodied inheritance has been sealed by the *Holy Spirit, who is outpoured from Jesus' place of exaltation with the Father (Lk 20:36; Acts 2:32-36; Eph 1:13-14).

Though it is unlikely that Paul interacted with Jesus before his death, he certainly knew of him and the claims about him (Maile). Saul/Paul perceived him to be a human messianic pretender from Nazareth cursed by *God (Gal 3:13; see Deut 21:23) yet worshiped by some as risen and ascended Lord and Christ (in fulfillment of Ps 110:1 and therefore sharing YHWH's divine identity and authority). Hence Saul's vicious persecution of believers after the death of Stephen. To Saul, Stephen's testimony before the Sanhedrin, subsequent *vision of Christ, and dying prayer offered to Jesus as Lord at the Father's right hand were the height of blasphemy (Acts 7). Yet on the Damascus road this same Jesus, risen, ascended, and exalted, met Saul in blinding *glory, thereby reshaping Paul's entire experience and understanding.

It was by Jesus' own authority that Paul was subsequently healed of his blindness, baptized with water and the Spirit, commissioned for Gentile *ministry, and uniquely instructed as an *apostle of the Lord Jesus Christ in the power and *wisdom of the Spirit (Gal 1:1, 11-22). Distinct from yet united with the apostles who had been with Jesus since his *baptism, Paul became an eyewitness to the risen Lord Jesus (Acts 9:1-6; 26:14; 1 Cor 15:8). With them, Paul worships and proclaims the risen Christ Jesus to be both Mary's Son, descended from Abraham and David, and God's *Son, descended from on high, now "ascended higher than all the heavens, in order to fill the whole universe" as still incarnate Lord (Eph 4:10 NIV; see Rom 1:3-4; 1 Cor 1:17-18; 11:23-27; Col 3:16; Gal 3:16; 4:4; 1 Tim 3:16).

Paul understands his whole life and ministry—and that of the *church—as united to the ongoing life and ministry of the ascended Lord Jesus. He not only preaches Jesus as Lord but demonstrates that his *kingdom "is not a matter of talk but of power" (1 Cor 4:20 NIV). Paul's eschatological hope is to be like the risen and ascended Christ, through participation in the *fellowship of Jesus' earthly *suffering and glory and ultimately through resurrection (2 Cor 12:9; Phil 3; Gorman 2019). Thus, Paul also calls the church to embody this hope of renewed human glory—"the redemption of our bodies" (Rom 8:23 NIV)—presently embodied by Jesus in full and final glory. Therefore, by the power of the Spirit, God's people are now to put on the "new self, which is being renewed in knowledge in the image of its Creator" (Col 3:10 NIV) and thus find themselves increasingly "conformed to the *image of his Son" (Rom 8:29 NIV), who is the "*firstborn over all creation," "firstborn from among the dead" (Col 1:15, 18 NIV), and "firstborn among many [eternally human] brothers and sisters" (Rom 8:29 NIV; Jacob).

1.2. The Exalted Lord of Psalm 110:1: Paul's Christology and That of the Early Church. Though Jesus' ascension and enthronement are not explicitly mentioned in every book of the NT, they nevertheless undergird and orient every Gospel and letter written to a suffering church. The church's eschatological hope and present authority come from this real, living person, crucified, raised to new life through the glory of the Father, and exalted as Lord to reign in anticipation of his final parousia and of creation's renewal. Hence when Paul speaks of the risen Lord Jesus and of the church's life "hidden with

Christ in God" (Col 3:3 NIV), he has in view all the ascension implies (Fee).

In alignment with the Christology of all other NT authors, Paul proclaims what he has received from the Lord Jesus Christ, using traditional Christ *hymns and creeds regarding Christ's death, resurrection, and exaltation "according to the Scriptures" (1 Cor 15:3-8 NIV; Phil 2:6-11; Col 1:15-20; 1 Tim 3:16). Foundational to these christological affirmations as prophetic fulfilment is Psalm 110:1. Referred to more than twenty times in the NT, either by allusion or by direct quotation, Psalm 110:1 is the basis for the church's understanding of Jesus' unprecedented yet unequivocal ascension as Davidic, messianic Lord. Jesus uses this Scripture regarding his messianic claim (Mt 22:41-45; Waltke). Shortly after Jesus' ascension Peter cites it again in his Pentecost speech to contextualize Jesus' giving of the Spirit from his place of enthronement:

> But God raised him from the dead. . . . Exalted to the right hand of God, he has received from the Father the promised Holy Spirit and has poured out what you now see and hear. For David did not ascend to heaven, and yet he said,
>
> "The Lord said to my Lord:
> 'Sit at my right hand
> until I make your enemies
> a footstool for your feet.'"
>
> Therefore let all Israel be assured of this: God has made this Jesus, whom you crucified, both Lord and Messiah. (Acts 2:24, 33-36 NIV)

Peter's epistle also speaks of Jesus enthroned in exaltation and authority (1 Pet 3:22). The author of Hebrews preaches of glorified, holy human life made possible through the Lord Jesus. John's apocalyptic vision centers on the authority and *worship of the enthroned Lamb at God's right hand, who will return in glory (Rev 5:1-13; 22:8, 20), and James and Jude affirm the same (Jas 5:7-9; Jude 14, 21).

Like these other authors, Paul too recognizes that Jesus' triumphant demonstration of his kingship on earth reached its zenith in his heavenly ascension. Paul's *gospel also has Psalm 110:1 in view: "[Christ] appeared in the *flesh, was vindicated by the Spirit . . . was believed on in the world, was taken up in glory" (1 Tim 3:16 NIV). His letters proclaim that God's Son was taken up to rule "until he has put all his enemies under his feet" (1 Cor 15:25 NIV), both in the present age and "in the [age] to come" (Eph 1:21 NIV; see 1 Cor 15:24-28; Acts 13:30-33; 17:31; 2 Cor 4:5).

2. Aspects of Jesus' Ascension.

2.1. The Identity and Authority of the Ascended Lord. "Who are you, Lord?" Paul answers his own question on the Damascus road based on his encounter with Christ Jesus and in concert with the early church: Not only is he God's messianic king and the faithful recapitulation of Israel as God's Son, but he also shares God's divine identity and prerogatives as "Lord," or *kyrios* (the word in the LXX most often rendering God's *name). Jesus received this title at his ascension, having been given "the name that is above every name" (Phil 2:9 NIV; see Is 45:23) and thus royal lordship over the living and the dead and over all powers and authorities in the created order (Col 1:15-20; Eph 1:20-23). Paul speaks of Jesus' lordship in both human and divine terms: "regarding [God's] Son, who as to his earthly life was a descendant of David, and who through the Spirit of holiness was declared with power to be the Son of God by his resurrection from the dead: Jesus Christ our Lord" (Rom 1:3-4 NIV). "Being in very nature God" and "taking the very nature of a *servant" (Phil 2:6-7 NIV), the divine-human Jesus fulfills Israel's messianic hopes and exercises divine authority over the whole cosmos (Gal 3:16; 2 Cor 5:19). Moreover, the Father extends to cosmic proportions the salvific rule of his beloved Son, through whom "God was reconciling the world to himself" (2 Cor 5:19 NIV; see Rom 8:29; Col 1:13; Ex 4:22-23, Deut 32:6).

That the Father has exalted the ascended Lord Jesus to his right hand as creator and Lord over all things is nowhere more straightforward than in 1 Corinthians, where Paul echoes the Shema (Deut 6:4 NIV: "Hear, O Israel, the Lord our God, the Lord is one") to profess the one God and Lord of the church: "for us there is but one God, the Father, from whom all things came and for whom we live, and there is but one Lord, Jesus Christ, through whom all things came and through whom we live" (1 Cor 8:6 NIV). Although the ascended Christ shares the divine identity and prerogatives belonging to him as God's eternal Son, he "did not consider equality with God something to be used to his own advantage" (Phil 2:6 NIV) but became a human servant even unto death, thus manifesting the true character of God on the earth. Jesus descended in self-emptying obedience unto death, and thus he was raised as Lord to the "highest place" by the Father, bearing "the name that is above every name" (Phil 2:9 NIV; see Is 45; 52–53; Fee; Bauckham 2008).

Paul describes the power that "the glorious Father" exerted "when he raised Christ from the dead and seated him at his right hand in the heavenly realms, far above all rule and authority, power and dominion, and every name that is invoked, not only in the present age but also in the one to come" (Eph 1:17, 20-22 NIV). Aligning Jesus' destiny with the church as his metaphorical *body, Paul continues, "God raised us up with Christ and seated us with him in the heavenly realms" in eschatological hope and participation (Eph 2:6 NIV). Having already been raised with Christ, God's people do not follow the world but rather set their "hearts on things above, where Christ is, seated at the right hand of God" (Col 3:1 NIV; see Col 1:15-16; Phil 2:6; 1 Tim 1:15; 2). From that place of cosmic authority, the ascended Jesus manifests and mediates the hope of *salvation (Rom 8:23). Thus, Jesus' location at the Father's right hand not only refers to his supreme cosmic authority but also speaks to his divine-human life in and with God as well as the cosmological reordering of all things in heaven and earth from and to him. (Hence, rather than asking "Where is Jesus?" from our sense of dimensionality, one can ask in what ways one is held—in every relational and eschatologically sense—*by him* who is the true center of all that is; see Farrow; Orr).

2.2. "Man with God Is on the Throne": The Ascension of God's Glorified Image Bearer. Jesus ascended reveals human destiny in all its splendor. In the glorified Son, raised to newness of life "through the glory of the Father" (Rom 6:4 NIV), the triune God has taken humanity into God's being forever (Canlis). Thus, Christopher Wordsworth's hymn resounds with the fulfillment of Psalm 110:1, "Man with God is on the throne."

Having seen God's risen, image-bearing Son in the flesh, Paul sees a foretaste of the glory of God's human image-bearing children as Christ's co-heirs. Paul described Jesus as the new *Adam, the incarnate restoration of God's true image in creation. In Adam's fall, God's human children gave away their original inheritance—their divine image-bearing glory and stewardship over creation—thus enslaving all things to death and decay. However, as the ascended second Adam, Jesus restores humanity's eternal inheritance and vocation (Rom 8:14-21). Jesus ascended reveals not only the reign of God's Son but also that of restored humanity, rightly reordering their rule with him in submitted obedience as God's vice regents over creation: "you have made them a little lower than the angels and crowned them with glory and honor. You made them rulers over the works of your hands; you put everything under their feet" (Ps 8:5-6 NIV; McCartney).

Echoing both Psalm 8:6 and Psalm 110:1, Paul speaks of God having already put all things under Jesus' feet, with his enemies as his "footstool," even while human beings and all of creation still await the day when death is permanently destroyed and the immortal glory of the children of God is revealed. Because their life is already "hidden with Christ in God" (Col 3:3 NIV), what has happened to the ascended Jesus will happen to them; they will "bear the image of the heavenly man" (1 Cor 15:49 NIV; see 1 Cor 15:24-27; Eph 1:22; Rom 8:19; Jacob; Fee; Gorman).

Joined to the death and ascended life of this second Adam, Jesus' disciples are being transformed to his glorious image by the Spirit: "When Christ, who is your life, appears, then you also will appear with him in glory" (Col 3:4 NIV), for "if the Spirit of him who raised Jesus from the dead is living in you, he who raised Christ from the dead will also give life to your mortal bodies because of his Spirit who lives in you" (Rom 8:11 NIV; see Phil 3:21; 2 Cor 3:18; Rom 5:17, 21; 6:3-5; 8:20-23, 33).

2.3. Priestly Mediator and Returning King. Psalm 110 both brings forward the kingly lordship of the Son and foreshadows his priestly function in the order of Melchizedek, the "king of Salem" and "priest of God Most High" (Gen 14:18-19 NIV; see Ps 110:4). Though Paul's priestly language is less explicit than that of Hebrews, his description of Jesus as both sin offering and faithful intercessor alludes to the priestly aspect of Jesus' ascension (Dawson): "For there is one God and one mediator between God and humankind, the man Christ Jesus, who gave himself as a ransom for all people" (1 Tim 2:5-6 NIV). Having become like his people in every way yet without *sin, faithful unto death, and raised in human-divine glory, Jesus alone is humanity's mediating intercessor: "Christ Jesus who died—more than that, who was raised to life—is at the right hand of God and is also interceding for us" (Rom 8:34 NIV). Thus, his ascension necessarily involves his human absence in terms of identity and function as well as location (all of which are presently mediated to us by the Spirit; Orr).

Though everything already belongs to him "at the Father's right hand," Jesus must nonetheless "reign until he has put all his enemies under his feet," including death (1 Cor 15:25 NIV). At that time, he will hand over the kingdom to his Father so that "God may be all in all" and bring all things to their end as a new beginning (1 Cor 15:28 NIV, echoing Ps 8:6; 110:1; 2 Cor 5:17). Jesus, who "has ascended into heaven" (Heb 4:14 NIV), will come again to earth as he departed, and God will raise his children in glory with Jesus and renew all things in justice (Acts 1:11; Phil 1:6; 3:20; 1 Thess 3:13; 4:16; 5:2; 2 Thess 1:5-10).

3. Implications of Ascension for the Church. Paul knows the biblical story of "God with us" as one of descent and ascent: sending his Son to unite human life to God's own life, renewing humanity through his human obedience unto death, and raising humanity to divine exaltation, in vicarious ascension with Christ, with the promise of descending once more to gather God's children up with him in ascended glory. Thus in Jesus' ascension God has (1) reconciled the world to himself, (2) restored the immortal human glory of his image-bearing children, (3) empowered those eschatologically "seated . . . in the heavenly realms in Christ Jesus" (Eph 2:6 NIV) with the life of his Spirit, and (4) guaranteed the consummation of heaven and earth in union with God.

See also CHRISTOLOGY; CONVERSION AND CALL OF PAUL; GOD; RESURRECTION.

BIBLIOGRAPHY. **R. Bauckham,** "The Sonship of the Historical Jesus in Christology," *SJT* 31 (1978): 245-60; idem, *Jesus and the God of Israel* (Grand Rapids, MI: Eerdmans, 2008); **P. Beasley-Murray,** "Colossians 1:15-20: An Early Christian Hymn Celebrating the Lordship of Christ," in *Pauline Studies*, ed. D. A. Hagner and M. J. Harris (Grand Rapids, MI: Eerdmans, 1980), 169-83; **F. F. Bruce,** *Paul and Jesus* (Grand Rapids, MI: Baker, 1974), 77-87; **J. Canlis,** *Calvin's Ladder: A Spiritual Theology of Ascent and Ascension* (Grand Rapids, MI: Eerdmans, 2010); **G. S. Dawson,** *Jesus Ascended* (Edinburgh: T&T Clark, 2004); **J. D. G. Dunn,** "I Corinthians 15:45—Last Adam, Life-Giving Spirit," in *Christ and Spirit in the New Testament*, ed. B. Lindars and S. S. Smalley (Cambridge: Cambridge University Press, 1973), 127-42; idem, *Christology in the Making* (Philadelphia: Westminster, 1980); **D. Farrow,** *Ascension and Ecclesia: On the Significance of the Ascension for Ecclesiology and Christian Cosmology* (Grand Rapids, MI: Eerdmans, 1999); **G. D. Fee,** *Pauline Christology* (Grand Rapids, MI: Baker Academic, 2013); **M. J. Gorman,** *Apostle of the Crucified Lord* (Grand Rapids, MI: Eerdmans, 2016); idem, *Participating in Christ* (Grand Rapids, MI: Baker Academic, 2019); **W. H. Harris,** "The Ascent and Descent of Christ in Ephesians 4:9-10," *BSac* 151 (1994): 198-214; **M. Hengel,** *The Son of God* (Philadelphia: Fortress, 1976); idem, "'Sit at My Right Hand!' The Enthronement of Christ at the Right Hand of God and Psalm 110:1," in *Studies in Early Christology* (Edinburgh: T&T Clark, 1995), 119-225; **H. G. Jacob,** *Conformed to the Image of His Son: Reconsidering Paul's Theology of Glory in Romans* (Downers Grove, IL: IVP Academic, 2018); **J. F. Maile,** "Exaltation and Enthronement," *DPL*, 275-78; **D. G. McCartney,** "*Ecce Homo*: The Coming of the Kingdom as the Restoration of Human Vicegerency," *WTJ* 56 (1994): 1-21; **P. C. Orr,** *Exalted Above the Heavens: The Risen and Ascended Christ* (Downers Grove, IL: InterVarsity Press, 2019); **A. Schlatter,** "The Easter Account," in *The History of the Christ* (Grand Rapids, MI: Baker, 1997), 375-89; **B. K. Waltke,** "'He Ascended and Sitteth . . . ' Reflections on the Sixth Article of the Apostles' Creed," *Crux* 10 (June 1994): 4-8; **J. Ziesler,** *Pauline Christianity*, rev. ed. (Oxford: Oxford University Press, 1990).

C. F. Nordling and B. C. Miller

ASCETICISM. *See* GNOSIS, GNOSTICISM; INTERPRETATION: PATRISTIC; MARRIAGE AND DIVORCE, ADULTERY AND INCEST; SEXUALITY, SEXUAL ETHICS; SINGLENESS AND CELIBACY.

ASTROLOGY. *See* MAGIC; RELIGIONS, GRECO-ROMAN.

ATHENS, PAUL AT. *See* PAUL IN ACTS; PHILOSOPHY.

ATONEMENT

Atonement refers to what *God has done in Jesus *Christ for human *salvation, with special attention to the problem of human *sin. The Greek words most often translated as "atonement" belong to the *hilasmos* word group. The only instance of this word group in Paul's letters occurs in Romans 3:25, which is variously translated as propitiation (KJV), expiation (RSV), *sacrifice of atonement (NIV, NRSV), place of atonement (NRSV mg.), atonement cover on the ark of the *covenant (NIV mg.), place of sacrifice where *mercy is found (CEB), and mercy seat (LEB).

The English word *atonement* comes from an old expression *at onement*, meaning reconciliation. Two parties who were at odds have been brought together. In Christian theology, it has become a technical term referring to the restoration of relationship between God and human beings brought about by Christ.

1. Overview
2. New Covenant
3. Redemption
4. Sacrifice
5. Justification and Righteousness
6. Other Relational Metaphors
7. Metaphors of Transformation
8. Special Issues
9. Conclusion

1. Overview.

The Pauline letters offer no systematic doctrine of atonement. Instead, like the other NT writers, Paul uses a variety of conceptual metaphors drawn from the OT and the Greco-Roman context to describe the work of Christ. Paul's letters generally do not rehearse his basic teaching on the work of Christ, which he would have communicated verbally to his converts (1 Cor 15:1-11).

Paul often draws on the work of Christ in the service of other aims. For example, in 1 Corinthians 15:1-11, he refers to traditional teaching about Christ's *death and *resurrection in order to counter the Corinthians' skepticism about the resurrection of believers. In Philippians 2:1-11, he urges the believers in Philippi to imitate the humble obedience shown by Christ in his incarnation and death, likely drawing on a preexisting *hymn into which he inserts the *cross. Ephesians and Colossians exhort believers to forgive one another as Christ has forgiven them (Eph 4:32; Col 3:13).

While the cross is predominant, and forgiveness of sins is its central effect, Paul does not restrict Christ's work to the cross or to forgiveness. Just as the human predicament is multifaceted, the work of Christ is multifaceted. In the Pauline letters, the whole career of Christ has salvific significance—his incarnation, life, ministry, death, resurrection, present reign, and future *judgment.

- In his incarnation, Christ became poor so that his followers might become rich (2 Cor 8:9; cf. Phil 2:1-11). He was born an Israelite so that he could redeem those under the *law (Gal 4:4-5).
- In his life of obedience, even unto death, he overturned the disobedience of *Adam to become the source of *righteousness and life for those who trust him (Rom 5:19; cf. Paul's references to the faithfulness of Jesus in Rom 3:22; Gal 2:16; 3:22 and the discussion in Gal 5:2).
- In his ministry, he inaugurated the *kingdom or reign of God, into which his followers could be transferred to escape from the dominion of evil (Col 1:13-14). God's kingdom is both a present reality (Rom 14:17; 1 Cor 4:20) and a future inheritance (1 Cor 6:9-10; 15:50).
- In his death, he dealt with sin and ratified the new covenant prophesied by Jeremiah and Ezekiel (Rom 4:25; 8:3; 1 Cor 11:25; 2 Cor 3:6; see Jer 31:31-34; Ezek 36:25-27).
- In his resurrection, he defeated death and the powers of evil, opening the way to eternal life (1 Cor 15:22; Col 1:15; 2 Tim 1:10).
- In his reign as *Lord, having become a "life-giving spirit" (1 Cor 15:45), he mediates the sending of the promised *Holy Spirit (Titus 3:6), the Spirit of Christ, to indwell and transform his followers (Rom 8:9-11).
- Even now he advances the Father's reign on earth (1 Cor 15:25), interceding for believers at the Father's right hand (Rom 8:34).
- Because Jesus is the exalted Lord, he can save those who call on his *name (Rom 10:12-13). He is the source and model of Christian maturity (Eph 4:11-16).
- At his return, he will bring the kingdom to completion (1 Cor 15:24-28) and save believers from divine *wrath at the final judgment (Rom 5:8-10).

Since discussions of atonement usually restrict themselves to what Christ has accomplished to restore the relationship between God and human beings, the rest of this article will focus on Christ's finished work. Because the time of fulfillment had dawned—evidenced by the resurrection of Jesus and the gift of the Holy Spirit—the NT writers reframed the death of Christ on a cross. Rather than the definitive proof that Jesus was not the Messiah (see Luke 24:19-21), the cross was the centerpiece of God's redemptive action.

However, the death and resurrection of Christ should not be divorced from the pouring out of the Spirit, for which it was the necessary preparation. While Paul associates forgiveness of sins with Christ's death, he associates new life with Christ's resurrection and the sending of the Spirit. The Holy Spirit is an essential part of God's solution to the problem of human sin.

2. New Covenant.

The new covenant serves as a foundational concept for Paul's thinking about atonement. Paul may draw on the Servant Songs of Isaiah for the connection between Christ and the new covenant: Isaiah predicts that the Servant (*pais*, LXX) will be a covenant to the people and a light to the nations (Is 42:1, 6). Paul declares that Jesus became a *servant (*diakonon*) to the Jews in order to fulfill God's promises to them and to show God's mercy to the *Gentiles (Rom 15:8-9).

Paul uses three different metaphors to credit Jesus with bringing about the new covenant through both his life and his death. First, playing on the meaning of *diathēkē* as both covenant and testament, Paul argues that Christ is the heir of the Abrahamic covenant and thus the inheritor of the Abrahamic blessing, which Paul interprets as *forgiveness of sins (Rom 4:6-12) and the Holy Spirit (Gal 3:13-18), drawing from the new-covenant promises in Jeremiah 31:31-34 and Ezekiel 36:25-27. Believers in Christ become co-heirs with him and thus share in his blessings (Rom 8:14-17; cf. Gal 4:7).

Interpreting the new covenant as the fulfillment of the Abrahamic covenant enables Paul to resolve the problem of the Mosaic law, which excludes Gentiles from God's covenant with *Israel. The Abrahamic covenant is earlier and thus takes precedence over the Mosaic covenant. When it is fulfilled in the new covenant, the law is no longer needed, because God writes his law on his people's hearts (Gal 3:17-26; Rom 8:2-4; Jer 31:33).

Second, Paul depicts Jesus' death as the sacrifice that ratifies the new covenant. In Paul's version of the Last Supper, which he says he learned directly from the Lord, Jesus declares, "This cup is the new covenant in my blood" (1 Cor 11:23, 25; cf. Exod 24:8). Paul's version agrees with Luke 22:20 and is slightly more explicit than the statements in Mark 14:24 and Matthew 26:28: "this is my blood of the covenant."

Paul himself is a minister of this new covenant. Comparing the new covenant with the old, he describes it as a covenant of Spirit rather than letter, which brings life rather than death. The old covenant, while glorious, was a ministry of condemnation and death, while the new covenant, even more glorious, is a ministry of *justification and life (2 Cor 3:6-11). With the coming of the new, lasting covenant, the old has been set aside (2 Cor 3:7).

Third, in his crucifixion, Jesus dies the death of someone cut off from the covenant, cursed by God (Gal 3:13; cf. Deut 21:23; Dunn, 227). Just as Israel suffered under pagan oppression when it turned away from God, Jesus suffers under Israel's Roman oppressors. But Paul overturns the shame of the cross by declaring that Jesus suffered "for us" so that Gentiles could receive the Abrahamic blessing—the promise of the Spirit—through *faith in him (Gal 3:14). Jesus endures the consequences of human faithlessness, brings the old covenant to an end, and inaugurates the new, which is open to both Jews and Gentiles (Eph 2:11-18). For further discussion, see 8.2 below.

3. Redemption.

The new covenant is based on the new and greater redemption accomplished by Jesus. The comparison of the cross and resurrection to the exodus is implicit in Jesus' reinterpretation of the Passover meal in terms of his coming death (1 Cor 11:23-26; cf. Exod 24:6-8). Ransom refers to the liberation of someone in captivity, usually by the payment of a price, while redemption derives from the practice of freeing *slaves or prisoners of war, again through payment.

3.1. Ransom and Redemption. First Timothy 2:5-6 identifies Christ as the only mediator between God and human beings, declaring that he gave himself as a ransom for everyone. This statement may reflect the ransom saying in the Jesus *tradition (Mk 10:45), although it uses *antilytron* instead of *lytron* to express ransom, emphasizing the sense of exchange. By implication, human beings were held in captivity but were liberated by Jesus' offering of himself on their behalf or (more likely) in their place. The ransom is Jesus himself, and the captor is not identified; however, 2 Timothy 2:25-26 states that nonbelievers are held captive by the devil.

Redemption (*apolytrōsis*) can refer to the eschatological "day of redemption" (Eph 4:30) when believers' *bodies will be set free from decay in the general resurrection and believers will receive their inheritance (Rom 8:23; 1 Cor 15:50-57; Eph 1:14). Believers' present experience of the Holy Spirit is the pledge of, or down payment on, that future inheritance (Eph 1:14).

However, redemption is also a metaphor for Christ's completed work, which involves the justification of believers (Rom 3:24) and the forgiveness of their sins (Col 1:14). This redemption is accomplished by Christ's death (Eph 1:7) and is embodied in Christ himself (Col 1:28). Gentiles are redeemed from their slavery to idols, while Jews are redeemed from their slavery under the law (Gal 4:8-9; 5:1-5, using *exagorazō*). Jesus' faithful obedience unto death broke the cycle of law-sin-death for Jews and opened covenant membership to Gentiles. Believers are no longer slaves, because they have been bought (*agorazō*) with the price of Jesus' death (1 Cor 6:20; 7:23). The Holy Spirit, who indwells them, is the stamp of Christ's ownership (Eph 1:13). Because they now belong to Christ, they must not become slaves to immorality or to other people.

3.2. Jesus' Victory. In order to redeem believers, Jesus had to achieve victory over the powers that held them in slavery. All powers on earth and in heaven were originally created through Christ and for him (Col 1:16). However, these powers became enmeshed with earthly systems that kept people in bondage (Col 2:18-23). Through the cross, Christ triumphed over all these powers. God disarmed them by forgiving human sin, which had made human beings subject to them (Col 2:13-15). Sin itself, according to Paul, is an enslaving power from which believers have been freed (Rom 6:1-11).

Because of Christ's faithfulness unto death, the Father raised him from the dead and exalted him above all spiritual or material powers (Phil 2:5-11; Eph 1:20-21). Believers acknowledge Christ's victory in their confession that "Jesus is Lord" (Rom 10:9-10). As exalted Lord, Christ can save those who belong to him. Moreover, Christ's exaltation was the necessary condition for the sending of the Spirit, who is the ultimate answer to the human sin problem. The Spirit can do what the law could not—namely, transform sinners so that they might fulfill the intent of the law by following the Spirit (Rom 8:3-4).

While Christ's victory is complete in principle, it will not be final until the day of resurrection, when Christ destroys death, the last enemy. Then he will have triumphed over all rulers, authorities, and powers (1 Cor 15:24-26). As he works toward that goal, Paul describes his own ministry as a triumphal procession of the victorious Christ (2 Cor 2:14-16). The final triumphal procession will take place in the general resurrection, when believers rise to meet Christ at his return (1 Thess 4:15-17).

3.3. Freedom. The result of Christ's redemption is *freedom. Believers have been set free from their slavery to sin in general, and from their slavery to the law of sin and death in particular (Rom 6:18, 22; 8:2). The mark and agent of this freedom is the Holy Spirit (2 Cor 3:17). Besides freedom from sin, believers have freedom of conscience in regard to nonessentials, although Paul urges them to use their freedom to serve others rather than themselves (1 Cor 10:23-33; Gal 5:13).

Freedom in Christ affects one's social status as well. Because enslaved and free believers share the same Spirit, they are members of one body, the *body of Christ (1 Cor 12:12-13). Their new relationship as brothers and sisters in Christ supersedes the divisions created by their social status (Gal 3:28; Col 3:11; see Philemon for a case study). Their new identity in Christ thus contains the seeds of social transformation.

4. Sacrifice.

Sacrifice metaphors in Pauline literature usually express Jesus' self-giving on behalf of sinners. For example, Ephesians 5:2 states that Christ, because of his *love for us, handed himself over on our behalf as an offering and sacrifice to God that was a "fragrant aroma" (see Gal 2:20). The Ephesians are to imitate God's character (Eph 5:1), which is demonstrated supremely in the loving self-giving of Christ. Paul also uses sacrifice language to express his own self-giving for the sake of the *gospel (Phil 2:17).

In 1 Corinthians, Paul uses the metaphor of the Passover lamb to make an ethical point: he exhorts the Corinthians to remove all leaven of sin from their lives because Christ, their Passover lamb, has been sacrificed (1 Cor 5:6-8). By implication, believers are to reflect the *purity of Christ, the unblemished lamb.

The most significant doctrinal passage in which sacrifice language is used is Romans 3:21-26. Paul states that God puts forth Jesus as a *hilastērion* in his blood (Rom 3:25). Despite translations that render *hilastērion* as an expiatory or propitiatory sacrifice, such meanings are unlikely (Jersak and Hardin, 256-57; Morris 1965, 144-213; Snyder Belousek, 244-64; Wright 2016, 327-39). The word *hilastērion* occurs elsewhere in the NT only in Hebrews 9:5, where it refers to the mercy seat, the lid of the ark of the covenant. In the LXX, with rare exceptions (in Amos and Ezekiel, where it refers to architectural features), *hilastērion* refers to the mercy seat as well.

In the context of Paul's argument, Jesus is the new mercy seat, the mercy seat of the new covenant, where the presence of God can be found and both Jews and Gentiles can receive forgiveness of sins. As Paul explains, there is now no distinction between Jews and Gentiles in regard to salvation (Rom 3:21-24). Unlike the mercy seat of the old covenant, which benefited Israel alone, Jesus is available to all who have faith in him. Unlike the former mercy seat, which was consecrated with the blood of animals, Jesus has consecrated himself with his own blood (Rom 3:25). In other words, through his death Christ has become the mediator of salvation for all people.

According to Paul, God has made Christ the new mercy seat in order to show his righteousness "through the passing over of previous sins in the forbearance of God" (Rom 3:25-26). If the righteousness of God in Romans 3:21 refers to God's justice in punishing sins, as some interpretations would suggest, Paul is saying that the cross is God's self-justification, vindicating him as just *in spite of his failure* to punish previous sins (see, for example, the NIV, which uses the phrase "left . . . unpunished" instead of the "passing over" in the text). However, if the righteousness of God refers to God's covenant faithfulness, Paul is saying that in the cross God demonstrates his covenant faithfulness *precisely by his forbearance* in forgiving previous sins (as he had promised he would in the new-covenant prophecies). The latter is the more natural reading of the Greek (Travis, 191-93). The language of passing over or passing by also recalls Paul's comparison of Jesus to the Passover lamb.

Some would see sacrifice language in 2 Corinthians 5:21, where God makes Jesus *hamartian* for our sakes. Most translations render this word as *sin*, but some propose *sin offering* (NIV mg., HCSB mg.). While *hamartia* seems to mean sin offering in some LXX passages (e.g., Exod 29:14; Lev 4:3), that meaning is unlikely here. See the discussion in 8.2.

Other passages similarly underscore Jesus' self-giving. For example, Jesus tells his disciples at the Last Supper, "This is my body, which is for you" (1 Cor 11:24). Similarly, the language of giving (*didōmi*) or handing over (*paradidōmi*) often appears in connection with the cross. Jesus "gave himself for our sins so that he might deliver us from the present evil age" (Gal 1:4); He "gave himself for us so that he might redeem us from all lawlessness and purify for himself a special people, zealous for good works" (Titus 2:14). Jesus handed himself over for us (Eph 5:2) or for the *church (Eph 5:25) because of his love (Gal 2:20).

5. Justification and Righteousness.

Christ accomplished the justification of believers and established a new way of righteousness. Paul ascribes justification to both Jesus' death (Rom 5:9) and his resurrection (Rom 4:25). It seems likely that, like other aspects of salvation, justification is accomplished by Christ and applied to human beings by the Spirit.

5.1. Justification as Covenantal. Justification is often understood as purely forensic and paradoxical—that is, as the legal declaration, on the basis of Christ's payment for sin, that believers are not guilty of sin, even though they actually are sinners and remain so. However, a strong case can be made for a nonparadoxical relational or covenantal understanding of justification (Colijn, 196-217).

When Paul discusses the righteousness of God in Romans 3:3-7, he places the righteousness of God, the faithfulness of God, and the *truth or integrity of God in parallel, implying that these concepts are similar in meaning. These parallels suggest that Paul understood the righteousness of God as something like God's covenant faithfulness, his fidelity to his promises and obligations.

If this is correct, it would make sense that the righteousness God expects from human beings is a similar covenant faithfulness. The appropriate human response to God's offer of salvation in Christ would be an initial trust followed by ongoing fidelity. Justification would then be best understood as God's initiation of covenant relationship or God's declaration that someone is in such a relationship—in other words, reconciliation or vindication (Colijn, 209-17; Wolterstorff, 243-82; Wright 2013, 925-1032). Paul's parallel between justification and reconciliation in Romans 5:9-10 supports a relational understanding of justification.

When God justifies the ungodly, he reckons their faith as righteousness (Rom 4:5). In the usual Protestant understanding, God considers people righteous (legally faultless), even though they are not. In a relational understanding, however, God is reconciling them, bringing them into covenant relationship with himself. God considers their faith to be righteousness because it is their first trusting step in their reconciled relationship with him. God himself is said to be justified in Romans 3:4, one instance in which "vindicated" is surely the meaning. At the final judgment, God will be vindicated as having been faithful to both Jews and Gentiles.

The atonement resolves the central question of Paul's *ministry, which is how both Jews and Gentiles can be the people of God despite the Mosaic law that divides them. Formerly, a faithful covenant relationship with God was marked by the works of the Mosaic law (Gal 3:12). However, Paul declares that Christ is the end of the law—in the related senses of goal, fulfillment, and termination—in order to make righteousness available to all those who believe (Rom 10:4). Because of Christ's work, righteousness now comes by faith in Christ rather than by the works of the law (Gal 2:16; Rom 3:28). Paul associates this development especially with Christ's death (Gal 2:21). Thus covenant relationship is now open to both Jews and Gentiles.

5.2. Pistis Christou. The expression *pistis Christou* has been much debated in contemporary Pauline scholarship (Hays; Bird and Sprinkle; Wright 2013, 836-51). Protestant Bibles often translate this phrase as "faith in Christ," even though it literally says "*faith of Christ" or "faithfulness of Christ," perhaps because this translation accords with the Protestant emphasis on justification by faith. However, if the expression means "the faithfulness of Christ" rather than human faith in Christ, the connection between atonement and justification becomes even clearer. The expression occurs in several statements in which the faith of believers is also mentioned. For example, Paul declares that the righteousness of God has been revealed "through *pisteōs Iēsou Christou* for all those who believe" (Rom 3:22; cf. Rom 1:17). He says similarly that Scripture has confined all things under sin, so that the promise "from *pisteōs Iēsou Christou* could be given to those who believe" (Gal 3:22).

Protestants have traditionally understood these verses to say that God's righteousness is revealed through faith in Christ for those who believe. However, interpreting *pistis Christou* as the faithfulness of Christ turns a mere redundancy into a significant statement about the atonement: God's righteousness (covenant faithfulness) has been revealed through the faithfulness of Messiah Jesus for all those who trust in him (or are faithful to him).

Believers have come to trust Christ so that they could be justified "through *pisteōs Iēsou Christou*" rather than by the works of the law, which cannot justify anyone (Gal 2:16). The faithfulness of Christ, exemplified supremely by the cross, has power for salvation (1 Cor 1:17-24). Justification is an act of God's grace, which is received by faith rather than by doing the works of the law (Eph 2:8-9). Understanding *pistis Christou* as the faithfulness of Christ emphasizes that Christ's atonement, rather than human faith, is the foundation of justification. Human faith is trust in Christ and what Christ has done.

6. Other Relational Metaphors.

6.1. Reconciliation. Christ reconciles people to God and to one another. God reconciles the world to himself through Christ's death and calls the reconciled to become reconcilers themselves (2 Cor 5:18-20). Colossians makes an even more expansive claim: God reconciles all things in heaven and earth to himself through the cross (Col 1:20). This cosmic reconciliation is applied to human beings at conversion (see Rom 5:10-11).

Paul speaks of both interpersonal and ethnic reconciliation. By reconciling both Jews and Gentiles to God, Jesus reconciles them to one another. The two groups have become one through the literal body of Christ, given for them, and fellow members of the spiritual body of Christ through the Holy Spirit given to them. The law, which had divided them, has been abolished because Christ himself is their *peace (Eph 2:11-18; cf. Col 1:19-22; 1 Cor 11:24). In order to reconcile the Gentiles to himself, God has temporarily rejected Israel, with the ultimate aim of saving both groups (Rom 11:11-15, 25-27).

As the God of peace (1 Thess 5:23; Phil 4:9), God is always the subject, never the object, of reconciliation. That is, God reconciles human beings to himself through Christ; Paul never suggests that God must be reconciled to human beings. This point is relevant to the issue of God's wrath (see 8.3 below).

For Paul, believers are not only reconciled to God; they are adopted as God's children (Gal 4:4-7; Eph 1:4-6). The Holy Spirit is both the means of and the *witness to this *adoption (Rom 8:14-16). Adoption is a present reality, but the experience is not yet complete. The final adoption takes place when believers' bodies are redeemed in the general resurrection (Rom 8:23).

6.2. Solidarity Through the Spirit. The most intimate relational metaphor for the work of Christ could be called solidarity through the Spirit. Paul most often uses participation language in reference to the reception of salvation, but the work of Christ makes this way of salvation possible. Through his death, his resurrection, and the sending of the Spirit, Jesus creates a new reality in which believers can participate through their union with him.

Paul expresses the old and new realities by comparing Christ with Adam (Rom 5:12-21; 1 Cor 15:20-22, 45-49). Through his obedience, Christ has achieved something greater than Adam did through his disobedience. While Adam brought about condemnation and death for all those in solidarity with him, Christ has brought about justification and life for all those in solidarity with him. While death comes to all those "in Adam," those "in Christ" will experience resurrection life. Jesus identified fully with the human condition to the point of death. As the raised and exalted Lord, he enables believers to participate in his life through the Holy Spirit, who indwells them (1 Cor 6:17; cf. 1 Cor 15:45; Gal 2:19-20).

In fact, Paul declares that believers participate in Christ's death, resurrection, and exaltation. Because Christ has died for all, all have died (2 Cor 5:14). Christ has abolished death through his resurrection and opened the way to eternal life (2 Tim 1:10). Believers have died and risen with Christ (Rom 6:3-11; cf. Col 2:12), so that they are now seated with Christ in heaven (Eph 2:4-6). All the blessings of salvation are granted to believers "in Christ" (see Eph 1). Believers are members of Christ and of one another (1 Cor 12:12-13; Rom 12:5). The church's relationship with Christ is as intimate as marital sexual union (Eph 5:31-32). Believers' participation in Christ extends to Paul's description of the Eucharist as a sharing in the body and blood of Christ (1 Cor 10:16). Union with Christ creates a new *identity for believers (Rom 6:6; Eph 4:22-24).

7. Metaphors of Transformation.

7.1. New Creation. The new reality brought about by Christ is so transformative that Paul calls it a new *creation. As with other metaphors of atonement, Christ's work makes the new creation possible, and the Holy Spirit makes it actual in people's lives. For individuals, the new creation is expressed as regeneration and sanctification. As Paul says, although believers' bodies are still subject to decay, their inward selves are being renewed by the Spirit. They can be confident that the Spirit will eventually redeem their physical bodies as well in the resurrection (2 Cor 4:16; Rom 8:10-11). Even the creation itself will participate in the final redemption (Rom 8:19-21). Until that time, anyone who is "*in Christ" is evidence that God's new-creation project is underway (2 Cor 5:17). Believers should put off the corrupted "old self" and put on the "new self" that resembles God as humans were supposed to when they were created in God's *image (Eph 4:22-24). For those "in Christ," there is no longer a division between Jews and Gentiles; only the new creation matters (Gal 6:15).

7.2. Sanctification. Sanctification is a transformational metaphor drawn from the context of *worship. In the OT, priests were set apart, or consecrated, for their service in the *temple (Exod 29:1-37). Even the furnishings of the temple had to be consecrated for divine service (Exod 30:22-29).

Sanctification has two senses in Pauline literature. One aspect of sanctification has the same sense as in the OT: believers are set apart by Christ to belong to God and serve him. Their consecration allows them to appear in the presence of God without fear. The other aspect of sanctification is a process of growth in Christlikeness brought about by the Holy Spirit with human cooperation.

Paul captures both senses when he addresses the Corinthian believers as "the church . . . having been sanctified in [or by] Christ, called [to be] saints" (1 Cor 1:2). Because of the work of Christ, the Corinthians have a new identity as consecrated people, and they have been called to a vocation of *holiness. Paul commonly calls believers "saints" in the sense that they have already been consecrated (see Rom 1:7; 2 Cor 13:12; Phil 4:22). Paul describes his own ministry as the "priestly service" of presenting the Gentiles before God as an acceptable offering, sanctified by the Spirit (Rom 15:16). He describes the church—even the fractious Corinthians—as God's holy temple, in which the Spirit dwells (1 Cor 3:16-17).

Believers' initial consecration is accomplished by Christ and applied to individuals at conversion. Paul tells the Corinthians that they have a new identity because they were "washed . . . sanctified . . . [and] justified in the name of the Lord Jesus Christ and in the Spirit of our God" (1 Cor 6:11). The association of sanctification with justification and *baptism suggests that Paul is speaking of a consecration that occurs with initial salvation. Ephesians declares similarly that Christ gave himself for the church in order to sanctify it, "cleansing [it] by the washing of water in the word" (Eph 5:25-26). Believers' sanctification depends on their union with Christ: they have life "in him" because he became for them "righteousness and sanctification and redemption" (1 Cor 1:30; see the discussion of solidarity with Christ in 6.2 above).

8. Special Issues.

8.1. Forgiveness. Forgiveness of sins is one of the central effects of the atonement. Paul declares that God sent his Son to deal with sin (literally, "concerning sin"; Rom 8:3). First Timothy 1:15 quotes a saying that is "worthy of all acceptance"—namely, that "Christ Jesus came into the world to save sinners." Ephesians and Colossians specifically define redemption in Christ as the forgiveness of sins (Eph 1:7; Col 1:14). In fact, forgiveness is an aspect of redemption, in that it frees recipients from their sin.

The forgiveness of sins is a new-covenant blessing. Paul foregrounds this connection in his version of Jesus' words at the Last Supper. Whereas in the Gospels, Jesus says that his blood is poured out for the forgiveness of sins (Mt 26:28), Paul quotes Jesus as saying that the cup is "the new covenant in my blood" (1 Cor 11:25; cf. Rom 11:27; Jer 31:31-34). Paul also associates forgiveness of sins with the blessing of Abraham (Rom 4:7).

Paul usually associates forgiveness with the cross: for example, the tradition that he passed on to his converts taught that Christ "died for our sins according to the Scriptures" (1 Cor 15:3). However, Christ's death should not be divorced from his resurrection. Paul tells the Corinthians that if Christ has not been raised, their sins have not been forgiven (1 Cor 15:17). This does not necessarily mean that the resurrection brought about their forgiveness; Paul may be suggesting that the resurrection legitimates Jesus' claims to forgive sins or that it demonstrates that the new-covenant promise of forgiveness of sins has been realized in Christ.

Even justification is associated with both Christ's death (Gal 2:21) and his resurrection (Rom 4:25). Connecting forgiveness with Christ's resurrection emphasizes the new life that believers have as a result of Christ's work. Both Ephesians and Colossians declare that believers were dead because of their sins but have been made alive with Christ (Eph 2:1-7; Col 2:13-14).

Paul never describes the mechanics of the cross—that is, how Christ's death brought about forgiveness of sins. He comes closest to an explanation in two passages: 2 Corinthians 5:14-21 and Colossians 2:13-14. In the former passage, Paul declares that God reconciled the world to himself in Christ, "not reckoning their trespasses to them" (2 Cor 5:19). Forgiveness is a requirement before reconciliation can take place, since the offense that caused the broken relationship must be dealt with. God chooses not to count people's sins against them so that they can be reconciled to him (2 Cor 5:19). For a discussion of 2 Corinthians 5:21, see 8.2 below.

The Colossians passage is similar but more detailed: "And you, being dead in trespasses and the uncircumcision of your *flesh, [God] made you alive together with [Christ], having forgiven you all [your] trespasses. Having wiped away the record of debts in the ordinances which was against us, he has taken it out of the way, having nailed it to the cross" (Col 2:13-14). This passage is talking specifically about Gentiles, who were uncircumcised and therefore outside the covenant, but the use of "us" and the similar statement in 1 Corinthians 5 about "the world" suggests that this declaration would apply to all believers.

The cross is the event of divine pardon. Because of Christ, God chooses to set aside the condemnation of the ordinances in order to forgive people's sins. God writes off the debt of human sin, bearing the consequences of that sin without requiring compensation from the offenders (Jersak and Hardin, 280-85; Moule, 19-26; Wolterstorff, 165-77). Divine forgiveness brings with it the obligation to forgive others (Eph 4:32; Col 3:13). The indwelling Spirit enables believers to fulfill this obligation.

8.2. Punishment. Because of the influence of Roman law in Western culture, the Western Christian tradition has often conceived of sin and atonement in metaphors of crime and punishment. The Eastern tradition, by contrast, has gravitated to more transformative metaphors, such as sickness and *healing or deification. The penal-substitution theory of atonement, widespread in Western contexts, asserts that Jesus suffers the punishment for our sins in our place. This theory has achieved near-dogmatic status in some evangelical contexts.

The difficulty with deriving this theory from Pauline literature, however, is that Paul never suggests that Jesus is punished on the cross. He does talk about punishment and divine vengeance (*ekdikēsis*) in connection with the final judgment (2 Thess 1:5-10; cf. Rom 12:19). He also describes discipline as necessary for growth, whether administered by oneself (1 Cor 9:25-27) or by God (1 Cor 11:30-32). Similarly, he uses the word *punishment* (*epitimia*) in connection with church *discipline (2 Cor 2:6). Those who reject God for idols and turn to sexual immorality are already "receiving in themselves the recompense for their error" (Rom 1:27). However, Paul never uses punishment language for what Jesus suffers on the cross.

The idea that Jesus is punished on the cross is usually based on the assumption that the OT sacrifices are examples of vicarious punishment in which the animal substitutes for the one who offers it (Beilby and Eddy, 82-86). However, it seems more likely that the sacrifices have to do with ritual purity rather than punishment (Jersak and Hardin, 265-67; Milgrom; Snyder Belousek, 171-91; Wright 2016, 329-31). For example, the blood of the sacrifices was sprinkled on the sanctuary as well as on the worshipers, indicating that the sanctuary had become polluted by the sin of the people and had to be reconsecrated along with the people (see, e.g., Lev 16:14-16).

However, even if the sacrifices were examples of vicarious punishment, the particular sacrifice metaphor that Paul uses for Jesus is the Passover lamb, which is unrelated to punishment (Exod 12:1-13). The Passover lamb is sacrificed so that its blood on the doorpost will shield Israelite households from God's judgment that is coming on the Egyptians because of Pharaoh's refusal to free God's people. The metaphor aptly reflects the reality that Jesus' death will spare his followers from God's (final) judgment (Rom 5:9-10).

Nevertheless, while Jesus is not punished on the cross, something else is condemned. In Romans 6–8, Paul deals with the question of why the law is inadequate to deal with human sin. He declares that there is nothing wrong with the law itself; it is holy and just and good (Rom 6:12). However, there is something in the nature of fallen human beings that foils the intent of the law and even uses it as an inspiration for further sin (Rom 7:7-12). Paul identifies this agent variously as the "body of sin" (Rom 6:6), "passions of sin" (or sinful passions; Rom 7:5), "my flesh" (Rom 7:18), the "body of death" (Rom 7:25), and the "law of sin that is in my members" (Rom 7:23).

He is referring not to the body itself, but to something in the body or its "members" that works against righteousness. He personifies this "flesh," ascribing agency and power to it and blaming it for human beings' captivity to sin (Rom 6:6). In a speech in character, he declares that if "I" desire to obey the law but sin instead, the guilty party is not "I" but that personified indwelling sin (Rom 7:17, 20). This "sin in the flesh" is judged and condemned on the cross (Rom 8:3). It has been destroyed through being crucified with Christ (Rom 6:6), who is himself "in the likeness of the flesh of sin" (Rom 8:3). The law, which was "weakened through the flesh," as Paul describes in Romans 7:14-25, could not enable sinners to become righteous. The work of Christ and the indwelling Spirit, however, can (Rom 8:3-4).

Some scholars also see punishment in Paul's claim that Christ became a curse for us (Gal 3:10-14; Beilby and Eddy, 89-93; Demarest, 171, 174). In Galatians 3, Paul is explaining that the blessings of *Abraham come to those who have faith. By contrast, anyone who relies on the law is under a curse (Gal 3:10), because failure to maintain everything in the law brings down the curses specified in the covenant. In Deuteronomy 27:26, the people explicitly invoke this curse as they vow to uphold the law. It would make no sense for Gentiles to place themselves under this curse when they can share the blessings of Abraham through faith in Christ.

Christ redeemed people from that curse by suffering another: "Cursed is everyone who is hanged on a tree" (Gal 3:13, quoting Deut 21:23). While this curse is described in the law, it occurs in a section describing the execution of criminals rather than one about covenant breaking (Deut 21:22-23). Jesus died the death of a criminal, apparently cursed by God but actually suffering this curse "for us" (Gal 3:13). Paul may be thinking of Isaiah's Servant, who appears to be struck down by God but is actually suffering because of the sins of others (Is 53:4-5). Christ "becomes" or embodies the curse of crucifixion in order to establish the way of righteousness through faith in him. The way of righteousness through faith opens covenant membership to Gentiles (Gal 3:14) and frees Israel from the threat of judgment (Wright 2016, 82-83).

The theory of penal substitution posits that Jesus can be justly punished for human sin because an exchange takes place in which human sin is imputed to Christ and Christ's righteousness is imputed to believers. This exchange is said to be described in 2 Corinthians 5:21 (Beilby and Eddy, 90; Demarest, 337). However, that verse is the summary of Paul's argument that God's reconciliation of believers has positioned believers to take on a ministry of reconciliation themselves (2 Cor 5:18-21). Second Corinthians 5:21 does not say that believers receive Christ's righteousness or that they are credited with it; it says that believers *become the righteousness of God* in Christ. If God's righteousness is understood in a relational or covenantal sense, as God's covenant faithfulness, then 2 Corinthians 5:21 is not an exchange but a mission statement. Just as Jesus embodied sin, as he died the death of one apparently cursed by God, believers can embody the saving faithfulness of God as they carry out the ministry of reconciliation that God has entrusted to them (Wright 2013, 881-85). Just as Jesus became righteousness for us, in that he mediates God's saving faithfulness to us, we become God's righteousness for others, in that we are the instruments through which the gospel reaches them.

8.3. Divine Wrath. Christian tradition has given a prominent place to divine wrath in the work of Christ. In the penal-substitution theory of atonement, the cross is said to satisfy God's wrath as well as God's justice. This idea may originally have been a solution to the medieval fear of God's wrath exacerbated by events such as the Black Death. For example, Calvin begins his discussion of atonement in the *Institutes* by declaring that all people who examine themselves will realize that God is angry at them (2.16.1). His discussion refers to an uneasy conscience several times (2.16.5, 6, 12, 18). This emphasis on wrath has been carried on in translations that render the word *hilastērion* in Romans 3:25 as *propitiation* (for example, KJV, NASB, and ESV), suggesting that the cross had to turn away God's wrath before God could forgive sins (Beilby and Eddy, 87-88; Demarest, 178-80; Morris 1965, 144-213).

However, just like the language of punishment, the language of wrath appears in Paul's discussions of the final judgment rather than the cross (see Rom 5:9). Paul observes that God must exercise wrath in order to judge the world (Rom 3:5-6). People who commit sinful acts in the present and refuse to repent are accumulating wrath toward that day (Rom 2:4-10).

As noted above, *hilastērion* in Romans 3:25 likely refers not to a sacrifice but to the mercy seat. However, even if *hilastērion* did mean an atoning sacrifice (NRSV, NIV), it would be a sacrifice *made by God*, not *offered to God*. It is God himself who sets Jesus forth as a *hilastērion*; thus it is not a propitiation. God does not need to be propitiated, since his love is the wellspring of the atonement (Rom 5:6-8). While some scholars would argue that God in Christ propitiates his own wrath (Morris 1965, 210-11), that idea creates the strange picture of a God who must use human intermediaries to work out his own internal conflicts (see the discussion of love, justice, and forgiveness in Wolterstorff).

For Paul, the cross is not an event in which the Father pours out his anger on the *Son. However, Paul describes God's wrath in the present as God giving people over to experience the consequences of their sinful choices (Rom 1:24, 26, 28). God also hands Jesus over for all of us (Rom 8:32) for our sins (Rom 4:25). The linguistic parallel suggests that God's role in the cross was to release Jesus into the hands of the sinful people who tortured and killed him.

Thus Jesus can be said to experience God's wrath in this carefully qualified sense—namely, that he experiences the desolation that results from God handing people over to experience the consequences of sin (Snyder Belousek, 209-19; Travis, 194-200). The idea of wrath as abandonment or exclusion is consistent with discussions of church discipline in 1 Corinthians 5:5, 13 and the final judgment in 2 Thessalonians 1:9. It is also consistent with an *honor/shame culture like those of the NT context.

8.4. Atonement and Violence. Considerable recent scholarship has reflected on the *violence of the cross, asking to whom the violence should be attributed (Boersma; Girard, 141-262; Jersak and Hardin; Sanders). According to the Gospel accounts, some Jewish leaders incited mob action regarding Jesus and turned him over to the Roman authorities, who tortured and executed him. However, speaking theologically, did God demand the *suffering and death of his innocent Son as the price of forgiving human sin? This question is particularly acute for the penal-substitution theory, which identifies God the Father as the one whose holy character requires punishment and whose anger at sin must be satisfied.

Paul does not address this question directly, but his statements about the cross suggest that God is not the agent of Jesus' suffering and death. For example, he tells the Corinthians, who are so enamored of *wisdom, that he speaks God's wisdom, which differs from the wisdom of this age and its rulers: "None of the rulers of this age has known [it]; for if they knew [it], they would not have crucified the Lord of *glory" (1 Cor 2:6-8). The actions of the authorities who crucified Jesus did not reflect God's wisdom, which "God predestined before the ages for our glory."

Similarly, Paul asserts that the Jewish leadership in Judea had opposed God's plans rather than carrying them out: they "killed both the Lord Jesus and the prophets," and "they do not please God and are hostile to everyone" (1 Thess 2:14-16). He describes them as the objects of God's wrath. He associates God's agency with the resurrection rather than with the crucifixion: Jesus was "crucified because of weakness but lives because of God's power" (2 Cor 13:4). (Paul describes sin as weakness in Rom 5:6.)

The cross is certainly part of God's redemptive plan. For example, Paul includes the cross in his assertion that "God chose the weak things of the world to shame the strong things" (1 Cor 1:27; cf. 1 Cor 1:18). God presumably arranged for Jesus to die "at the right time" (Rom 5:6). Jesus' *mission is part of God's plan to save both Jews and Gentiles (Rom 10:8-13), and God has predestined believers to be conformed to Christ (Rom 8:29). Furthermore, God gave Jesus over into the hands of those who killed him, so he clearly permitted the violence to take place. However, Paul does not seem to say that God demanded it. He leaves the responsibility for Jesus' torture and death squarely on the shoulders of human beings.

8.5. Representation and Substitution. Jesus represents Israel specifically and human beings more generally. This is not a mere legal representation but a spiritual solidarity. In that solidarity, he suffers vicariously on behalf of sinful human beings. In their turn, believers experience such solidarity with Christ that Paul can speak of sharing in Christ's sufferings (Phil 3:10; cf. Col 1:24).

Jesus not only represents but also substitutes for human beings. This is implied by the use of the word *antilytron* to express ransom (1 Tim 2:5-6) and Jesus' experiencing the curse of crucifixion to redeem others from the curse of the law (Gal 3:10-14). Substitution also takes place in the forgiveness of sins. God in Christ substitutes for human beings in the same way that anyone who forgives substitutes for the one who offended: the one who forgives chooses to absorb the cost of the offense rather than requiring it from the offender, allowing the offender to go free and creating the possibility of reconciliation (see Col 1:19-20; 2:13-14; Moule; Wolterstorff).

9. Conclusion.

Pauline literature does not provide a systematic doctrine of atonement but offers instead a rich, overlapping set of conceptual metaphors that emphasize relationship, participation, and transformation. Jesus demonstrates his Father's covenant faithfulness through his own faithfulness as Messiah, opening salvation to anyone who trusts and follows him. While central to the atonement, the cross should not be separated from Jesus' resurrection and the sending of the Spirit, both of which are essential to the accomplishment of salvation. Thus the atonement is fully trinitarian, motivated throughout by God's love. Atonement is also organically related to mission: believers' solidarity with Christ moves them into the world to carry on his ministry until his return (2 Cor 5:14-15; Gal 2:19-20).

See also Adam and Christ; Adoption; Christology; Covenant; Creation and New Creation; Cross; Curse, Accursed, Anathema; Death; Faith; Faith of Christ; Flesh; Forgiveness; Freedom/Liberty; Gospel; Holiness, Sanctification; Holy Spirit; In Christ; Justification; Peace, Reconciliation; Resurrection; Righteousness; Sacrifice, Offering; Salvation; Sin, Guilt; Triumph; Violence; Works of the Law; Wrath, Destruction.

BIBLIOGRAPHY. **J. Beilby and P. R. Eddy,** eds., *The Nature of the Atonement: Four Views* (Downers Grove, IL: IVP Academic, 2006); **M. F. Bird and P. M. Sprinkle,** eds., *The Faith of Jesus Christ: Exegetical, Biblical and Theological Studies* (Peabody, MA: Hendrickson, 2010); **H. Boersma,** *Violence, Hospitality, and the Cross: Reappropriating the Atonement Tradition* (Grand Rapids, MI: Baker, 2004); **G. A. Boyd,** *The Crucifixion of the Warrior God: Interpreting the Old Testament's Violent Portraits of God in Light of the Cross*, 2 vols. (Minneapolis: Fortress, 2017); **D. Brondos,** *Paul on the Cross* (Minneapolis: Fortress, 2006); **G. Cole,** *God the Peacemaker: How Atonement Brings Shalom* (Downers Grove, IL: IVP Academic, 2009); **B. B. Colijn,** *Images of Salvation in the New Testament* (Downers Grove, IL: IVP Academic, 2010); **O. Crisp,** *Approaching the Atonement: The Reconciling Work of Christ* (Downers Grove, IL: IVP Academic, 2020); **B. Demarest,** *The Cross and Salvation* (Wheaton, IL: Crossway, 1997); **D. A. deSilva,** *Honor, Patronage, Kinship & Purity: Unlocking New Testament Culture* (Downers Grove, IL: IVP Academic, 2000); **J. Driver,** *Understanding the Atonement for the Mission of the Church* (Scottdale, PA: Herald, 1986); **J. D. G. Dunn,** *The Theology of Paul the Apostle* (Grand Rapids, MI: Eerdmans, 1998); **C. A. Eberhart,** *The Sacrifice of Jesus: Understanding the Atonement Biblically*, Facets (Minneapolis: Fortress, 2011); **R. Girard,** *Things Hidden Since the Foundation of the World* (Stanford, CA: Stanford University Press, 1987); **M. Gorman,** *The Death of the Messiah and the Birth of the New Covenant: A (Not So) New Model of the Atonement* (Eugene, OR: Cascade, 2014); **J. B. Green and M. D. Baker,** *Recovering the Scandal of the Cross: Atonement in New Testament and Contemporary Contexts* (Downers Grove, IL: IVP Academic, 2000); **C. Gunton,** *The Actuality of Atonement: A Study of Metaphor, Rationality, and the Christian Tradition* (New York: T&T Clark, 2003); **W. R. Hastings,** *Total Atonement: Trinitarian Participation in the Reconciliation of Humanity and Creation* (Minneapolis: Fortress, 2019); **R. B. Hays,** *The Faith of Jesus Christ: The Narrative Substructure of Galatians 3:1–4:11*, 2nd ed. (Grand Rapids, MI: Eerdmans, 2002); **S. M. Heim,** *Saved from Sacrifice: A Theology of the Cross* (Grand Rapids, MI: Eerdmans, 2006); **M. Hengel,** *Crucifixion in the Ancient World and the Folly of the Message of the Cross* (Philadelphia: Fortress, 1977); idem, *The Atonement: The Origins of the Doctrine in the New Testament* (Philadelphia: Fortress, 1981); **C. E. Hill and F. A. J. L. James,** eds., *The Glory of the Atonement: Biblical, Historical and Practical Perspectives: Essays in Honor of Roger R. Nicole* (Downers Grove, IL: IVP Academic, 2004); **B. Jersak and M. Hardin,** eds., *Stricken by God: Nonviolent Identification and the Victory of Christ* (Grand Rapids, MI: Eerdmans, 2007); **P. J. Leithart,** *Delivered from the Elements of the World: Atonement, Justification, Mission* (Downers Grove, IL: IVP Academic, 2016); **R. Letham,** *The Work of Christ*, CCT (Downers Grove, IL: IVP Academic, 1993); **D. Macleod,** *Christ Crucified: Understanding the Atonement* (Downers Grove, IL: IVP Academic, 2014); **I. H. Marshall,** *The Work of Christ* (Palm Springs, CA: Ronald N. Haynes, 1981); **R. P. Martin,** *Reconciliation: A Study of Paul's Theology* (Grand Rapids, MI: Zondervan, 1989); **S. McKnight,** *A Community Called Atonement* (Nashville: Abingdon, 2007); **J. Milgrom**, *Leviticus: A Book of Ritual and Ethics*, CC (Minneapolis: Fortress, 2004); **L. Morris,** *The Apostolic Preaching of the Cross*, 3rd ed. (Grand Rapids, MI: Eerdmans, 1965); idem, *The Atonement: Its Meaning and Significance* (Downers Grove, IL: IVP Academic, 1984); **C. F. D. Moule,** *Forgiveness and Reconciliation and Other New Testament Themes* (London: SPCK, 1998); **J. I. Packer and M. Dever,** *In My Place Condemned He Stood: Celebrating the Glory of the Atonement* (Wheaton, IL: Crossway, 2008); **B. Pitre, M. P. Barber, and J. A. Kincaid,** *Paul, a New Covenant Jew: Rethinking Pauline Theology* (Grand Rapids: Eerdmans, 2019); **E. P. Sanders,** *Paul and Palestinian Judaism* (Minneapolis: Fortress, 2017); **J. Sanders,** ed., *Atonement and Violence: A Theological Conversation* (Nashville: Abingdon, 2006); **D. W. Snyder Belousek,** *Atonement, Justice, and Peace: The Message of the Cross and the Mission of the Church* (Grand Rapids, MI: Eerdmans, 2011); **A. Spence,** *The Promise of Peace: A Unified Theory of Atonement* (New York: T&T Clark, 2007); **J. Stott,** *The Cross of Christ* (Downers Grove, IL: InterVarsity Press, 1986); **F. Thielman,** *The New Creation and the Storyline of Scripture* (Wheaton, IL: Crossway, 2021); **D. Tidball, D. Hilborn, and**

J. Thacker, eds., *The Atonement Debate: Papers from the London Symposium on the Theology of Atonement* (Grand Rapids, MI: Zondervan, 2008); **S. H. Travis,** *Christ and the Judgment of God* (Peabody, MA: Hendrickson, 2009); **J. R. Treat,** *The Crucified King: Atonement and the Kingdom in Biblical and Systematic Theology* (Grand Rapids, MI: Zondervan, 2014); **N. Wolterstorff,** *Justice in Love* (Grand Rapids, MI: Eerdmans, 2011); **N. T. Wright,** *Paul and the Faithfulness of God*, 2 vols. (Minneapolis: Fortress, 2013); idem, *The Day the Revolution Began: Reconsidering the Meaning of Jesus' Crucifixion* (New York: HarperCollins, 2016).

B. B. Colijn

AUTHORITY. *See* Church Structure; Discipline, Church; Freedom/Liberty; Head; Leadership; Politics and Power.

AUTOBIOGRAPHY, PAULINE.
See Conversion and Call of Paul; Galatians, Letter to the.

B

BAPTISM

Among the writings of the earliest Christians, Paul's letters have by far the greatest volume of teaching on baptism and, correspondingly, had a great deal of influence on the ways that baptism came to be understood in the history of the *church (Taylor 2016, xvii-xviii). Rather than providing a systematic treatment of the significance and practice of the rite, the *apostle touches on baptism in the course of dealing with a variety of pastoral and theological matters (Byars, 61). Clearly, he assumes that all of those who confess Jesus as their *Lord would have been baptized and would have been instructed in baptism's significance (Rom 6:3; Gal 3:27). In the apostle's *teaching, baptism stands as related to his understanding of conversion and thus in a place of vital importance for his *mission. Although Paul did not place a priority on personally baptizing those who responded to his *gospel (1 Cor 1:14-17), it is clear that he considered baptism directly associated with the life-transforming experience of the gospel of Jesus *Christ. In speaking of baptism, the apostle drew from his broader Jewish and Christian contexts but also crafted new paths of theological reflection on its power and import for believers.

1. Paul and the Language of Baptism
2. The Background of Paul's Understanding and Practice of Baptism
3. Baptism in Paul's Epistolary Reflections and Exhortations

1. Paul and the Language of Baptism.

Three terms are used with reference to baptism in Paul: the verb *baptizō* and its two cognates, *baptisma* and *baptismos*. The apostle never uses the term *baptistēs*, "baptizer" or "baptist," a word occurring in the NT only in the Gospels as they speak of the ministry of John the Baptist (Mt 3:1; 11:11-12; 14:2, 8; 16:14; 17:13; Mk 6:25; 8:28; Lk 7:20, 33; 9:19).

In the broader culture, the verb *baptizō* meant "to plunge, dip, or wash" (BDAG, 164-65). Used straightforwardly with reference to physical water, the term normally connoted various forms of immersion (Ferguson 2009, 48-49). For example, the word was used of a person immersing or bathing in water for cleansing (2 Kgs 5:14; Jdt 12:7 LXX), including cultic washing (Sir 34:25 LXX), or of a ship plunging beneath the waves of the sea (Josephus, *Ant.* 9.212), or of a person being dunked under the water until drowned (Josephus, *Ant.* 15.55; *J.W.* 1.437; 3.423). The verb also was used of a sword being "plunged" into a person's *body (*J.W.* 2.476). These various uses had metaphorical counterparts. For example, the word could be employed of a person being "flooded," or overwhelmed, with *fear (Is 21:4 LXX), or submerged in passions (Philo, *Leg.* 3.18), or "drowned" in drunkenness (Josephus, *Ant.* 10.169; Philo, *Prob.* 1.97; *Contempl.* 1.46).

The verb occurs seventy-seven times across sixty-four verses in the NT, and thirteen of these occurrences are found in Paul's writings, twice in Romans, once in Galatians, and ten times in 1 Corinthians. Paul uses the word of the Christian rite, but also of spiritual realities associated with the rite, such as being baptized into Christ or by the Spirit (Rom 6:3; 1 Cor 12:13; Gal 3:27). There is no sharp distinction between the rite of baptism and the spiritual dynamic, the two being closely associated.

Of the two cognate nouns, *baptisma* and *baptismos*, the first is the primary one used of the water ceremony, baptism, in the ministries of John (Mt 3:7; 21:25; Mk 1:4; 11:30; Lk 3:3; 7:29; 20:4; Acts 1:22; 10:37; 13:24; 18:25; 19:3-4) and the early Christian movement (Acts 19:4; Rom 6:4; Eph 4:5; 1 Pet 3:21). The term is also employed figuratively in Mark 10:38-39 and Luke 12:50 of Jesus' persecution and *death, thus being plunged into an intense personal experience. It may be that OT word pictures of river and flood, used as images of one being overwhelmed by calamities (e.g., Ps 42:7; 69:2, 15; Is 43:2), lie behind this use of *baptism* as traumatic experience (Dunn, 11-12). The word *baptismos*, on the other hand, connotes primarily various kinds of ceremonial washings in the practice of Judaism (Mk 7:4; Heb 6:2; 9:10), though in Colossians 2:12 the term is used of the Christian rite (however, see the textual variant there).

2. The Background of Paul's Understanding and Practice of Baptism.

Various suggestions have been made as to the primary influences on Paul's theology and practice of baptism. It is clear that water rites of cleansing were practiced widely in the Greco-Roman world, whether in civic cults, in sanctuaries focused on *healing and reception of communication from the gods, in forms of magic, or in the mystery *religions (Ferguson 2009, 25-37). Yet, attempts to draw direct correlations between Paul's concept of baptism and these expressions in the broader culture have been unproductive. For instance, the suggestion that Paul's form of baptism was taken from the initiation rites of the mystery religions has been shown to lack evidence (so Wedderburn, 70-71). Others suggest that bathing practices in a context of *patronage, with a person being washed while nude and then anointed with oil, may have had some influence on the Christian rite, constituting a ritual practice that shaped social *identity (Tucker, 174; Ferguson 2009, 37).

Be that as it may, a general consensus seems to point rather to Judaism as a nearer backdrop for the practice of baptism. In the past some scholars suggested that the nearest correlation lay in the Jewish practice of proselyte baptism (e.g., Jeremias, 29-40). Yet the silence of Second Temple Jewish texts on the practice is thunderous. No evidence exists that would suggest that proselyte baptism was present in Judaism prior to the ministry of John the Baptist (McKnight, 85; Smith, 32).

A more certain course understands Christian baptism to have arisen from rituals of cleansing in broader Judaism, which signified renewal or maintenance of relationship with *God and association with God's people (McGowan, 135). In the OT law, the foundations had been laid with instructions on various kinds of lustrations (e.g., Lev 11:24; 14:5, 50-53; 15:5-13; 16:14-15; Num 19:17-20), and the extensive archaeological evidence for *mikveh* bathing in the Second Temple period bears witness to its cultural and religious development and importance, as well as immersion being a standard practice (Sanders 2016, 221, 364-75, 696-97, 735-36). This dynamic of ritual ablutions combined with the words of the prophets, who told of a future cleansing of God's people by the pouring out of the Spirit (Ezek 36:25-26; Ferguson 2009, 61-64), formed a backdrop for groups such as the sectarians at Qumran, who understood their community as a fulfillment of such prophetic announcements. They also practiced ritual cleansing as normative for their followers (1QS III, 7-9; IV, 21; 1QH XVI, 12; Dunn, 9-10). Yet, the washings at Qumran were self-administered and practiced in an ongoing manner, distinct from the pattern of baptism in the ministries of John, Jesus, and the early Christian movement. John's ministry, oriented as it was to the wilderness, used the Jordan River as a *mikveh*, "since there was plenty of water there" (Jn 3:23), facilitating the baptism of large groups of people. The location was significant historically, the Jordan having formed the boundary of transition for the wilderness generation into the Promised Land (Josh 1:2; 3:1-17). The river also may have symbolized the eschatological renewal of Israel, associated with "a way in the wilderness" for God's people (Is 41:18; 43:19-20).

It seems clear that Paul received baptism as a normative practice that had existed prior to his own confession of Jesus, which took place just three to four years after Jesus' death and *resurrection (Acts 9:18; Carlson, 255). This suggests that the rite had been part of the Christian movement from the very beginning (Beasley-Murray 1993, 60), indeed originating in the ministry of Jesus (see Jn 3:25-26; 4:1-3), which arose in the wake of John the Baptist's movement (Mt 3:7; 21:25; Mk 1:4; 11:30; Lk 3:3; 7:29; 20:4; Acts 1:22; 10:37; 13:24; 18:25; 19:3-4). While there was continuity from the baptism of John to that of the first Christians—baptism was still an act involving repentance and *forgiveness of *sins (Acts 2:38; 22:16)—the latter added "in the *name of Jesus" and understood baptism as related to the gift of the *Holy Spirit (Acts 2:38; 8:14; 19:5-6; Paroschi, 94-95). Thus, the Christian practice, and consequently Paul's appropriation of the rite, should be conceived of as Jewish in its orientation, arising primarily from the ministries of John, Jesus, and the first Christians.

3. Baptism in Paul's Epistolary Reflections and Exhortations.

As noted above, there are some sixteen references to baptism in the writings traditionally attributed to Paul. These offer a rich, though partial, window into the apostle's understanding of the significance and practice of the rite. As to practice, those baptized almost certainly, upon their entrance to the faith, were baptized in the name of Jesus (1 Cor 6:11; Acts 2:38), were probably baptized by a leader of the church (1 Cor 1:13-17), and may have experienced the rite as part of a broader *household (e.g., 1 Cor 1:16; Acts 11:14; 16:15, 34). As to mode: the lexical meaning of the verb in this period, the practice of full immersion in the use of Jewish purification baths, descriptions in the NT of going into or coming up from a place of abundant water (e.g., Mt 3:16; Mk 1:5, 9; Jn 3:23; Acts 8:38-39), and the imagery of baptism as burial (Rom 6:4; Col 2:12) all point to immersion as the most likely mode of baptism in the early church (see Ferguson 2009, 95-96, 857-60).

The motifs on which Paul touches, offered as he refers to baptism in the course of addressing a variety of topics, form a network of interrelated theological convictions surrounding baptism. These convictions are set in an eschatological background of thought, grounded in the life-transforming work of God's Spirit, associated with Jesus Christ, especially his death, and foundational for unity in the church.

3.1. Eschatological Frame. In considering Paul's thoughts on baptism, one must first put them in their broader, eschatological framework, the worldview that understands God as breaking into the world and shaping the ages of the world to accomplish his purposes of *salvation for his people (Tsui, 416). Romans 6:3 reads, "Or don't you know that all of us who were baptized into Christ Jesus were baptized into his death?" (Rom 6:3 NIV). Here Paul speaks of baptism as deeply related to the Christ-event, and that event is evoked as part of a larger *narrative structure involving the entrance of sin into the world, through Adam, as a dominating power (Rom 5:12). God's provision of *grace through Christ, with the gift of *righteousness (Rom 5:17), has led to a transformation of people by the Spirit and given them the ability to live a new life free from the dominion of sin and death as well as to live the requirements of God (Rom 6:4, 22; 8:4). This inaugurated, new form of life ultimately will be consummated in resurrection life at the end of the age (Rom 6:5). Thus, baptism marks much more than entrance to a new association with an organization. Rather, it pictures a transformative initiation into a new reality, a new eschatological community (Crowley, 291), in which old barriers have been broken down and all those involved have been made heirs to the promises of *Abraham (Gal 3:26-29). In terms of this broader framework, baptism thus as "a divinely-wrought event" entails the negation of a life under the dominating power of sin and death, an inauguration of new patterns of life by the Spirit, and the anticipation of resurrection life at the end of the age (Carlson, 255). In short, baptism is part of a large sacred story being written on the world.

3.2. The Foundational Work of the Spirit. In that sacred story, the bestowal of God's Spirit on his people in an age of renewal is foretold by the prophets and spoken of in images connoting cleansing with, or the pouring out of, water. Ezekiel writes, "I will sprinkle clean water on you, and you will be clean; . . . I will put my Spirit in you" (Ezek 36:25, 27 NIV), and "I will no longer hide my face from them, for I will pour out my Spirit on the people of *Israel, declares the Sovereign LORD" (Ezek 39:29 NIV). This pouring out of the Spirit is also spoken of in Isaiah (Is 32:15; 44:3), Zechariah (Zech 12:10), and, of course, Joel (Joel 2:28-32), a text taken up by *Peter on the day of Pentecost (Acts 2:16-21). In Acts 2 the author associates the pouring out of the Spirit with the hearers' repentance, forgiveness of sins, and baptism "in the name of Jesus Christ" (Acts 2:37-39; 11:15-17; 15:8-9). The baptism in the Holy Spirit had been anticipated in the preaching of John the Baptist as an essential descriptor of what Jesus would accomplish in his ministry (Mt 3:11; Mk 1:8; Lk 3:16) and heralded as well by Jesus' own anointing with the Spirit (Jn 1:33).

The eschatological outpouring of the Spirit for cleansing, forgiveness, transformation, and reconstitution of God's people was foundational to an early Christian understanding of entrance into new life *in Christ (Titus 3:5; see also 1 Pet 3:21) and thus directly associated with water baptism. Yet, the NT never makes a direct correlation between baptism in the Spirit and the rite of baptism in water, with the second, at least at times, following from the first (e.g., Acts 9:17-19; 10:44-48). The most one can say is that, in the NT generally and in what Paul seems to assume particularly, water baptism and the ministry of the Spirit are deeply associated at the beginning of the Christian experience (Fee, 604).

Thus for Paul the reception of the Holy Spirit by *faith (Gal 3:26-27) constitutes the *sine qua non* of entrance to Christian life as a part of Christ's church (Rom 8:9-11; 2 Cor 3:17-19; Fee, 603), and this reception is described as "immersion" in the Spirit. With Spirit baptism God's presence resides in the Christ-follower, empowering the Christ-follower for life and ministry in the church (Taylor 2016, 48; Vassiliadis, 19-20). In 1 Corinthians 12:13, in a passage speaking of unity within the church, the apostle writes, "For in one Spirit we were all baptized into one body" (NET). Although many translations read the preposition *en* as communicating agency ("by";

cf. 1 Cor 12:9), the use of the phrase "baptize in . . ." elsewhere in the NT points to a locative use, people being "immersed" in water presented in parallel to immersion "in the Spirit" (so Fee, 606; Mt 3:11; Mk 1:8; Lk 3:16; Jn 1:26, 31, 33; Acts 1:5; 11:16). The implication in context concerns Christian unity, the people of God unified by their common experience of the Spirit in the *body of Christ.

3.3. An Association with the Lord Jesus Christ. Most essentially, by the indwelling, cleansing, and transformation effected by the Spirit, believers live in relationship of participation in Christ Jesus, baptized in his name, incorporated into one body with other Christ-followers, "clothed" in Christ, and identified with him in his death and resurrection.

3.3.1. Baptized in the Name of Jesus. To do something "in the name of" someone forms a common idiom in the NT, the preposition varying between the use of *en* and *eis* or *epi*. Jesus as son of David came "in the name of the Lord" (Ps 118:25-26; Mt 21:9; 23:39; Mk 11:9; Lk 13:35; Jn 12:13; *en onomati kyriou*). John's Gospel explains that those who do not believe in Jesus are condemned because they have not believed "in the name [*eis to onoma*] of the one and only *Son of God" (Jn 3:18 CSB). In the so-called Great Commission, Jesus commands his followers to baptize disciples "in the name of the Father and the Son and the Holy Spirit" (Mt 28:18-20 NET; *eis to onoma tou patros kai tou huiou kai tou hagiou pneumatos*).

It is not surprising, therefore, that in both Acts and Paul, people are baptized "in the name of Jesus Christ" (e.g., Acts 2:38 [*epi tō onomati Iēsou Christou*]; 8:16 [*eis to onoma tou kyriou Iēsou*]; 10:48 [*en tō onomati Iēsou Christou*]; 1 Cor 1:13-14). At 1 Corinthians 1:13-17 Paul addresses factionalism in the church at Corinth, writing, "Is Christ divided? Was Paul crucified for you? Were you baptized in the name of Paul [*eis to onoma Paulou*]? I thank God that I did not baptize any of you except Crispus and Gaius, so no one can say that you were baptized in my name" (1 Cor 1:13-15 NIV). The assumption, of course, is that the Corinthians rather were baptized "in the name of Jesus Christ."

Both the Greek and Hebrew backgrounds of the idiom have been probed. From the broader Greek context and taken from the world of banking and commerce, some have understood the phrase to connote "to the account of" a person, as in a deed of transfer (e.g., Heitmüller, 105; Dunn, 123), that is handed over to the possession of another person. Others have suggested that a Hebrew idiom forms a more appropriate backdrop, generally meaning "with respect to" as affirming the establishment of a relationship of some kind (Str-B, 1054-55; Beasley-Murray 1993, 61).

However, in seeking to understand the significance of the idiom, one must consider that in the NT a great number of other actions are done "in the name of Jesus" or "of Jesus Christ" or "of the Lord": healing (Acts 3:6; *en tō onomati Iēsou Christou*), speaking or teaching (Acts 4:18; 5:40; *epi tō onomati;* Acts 9:27-28, *en tō onomati tou Iēsou* or *tou kyriou*), exorcising a *demon (Acts 16:18, *en onomati Iēsou Christou*), gathering the church (1 Cor 6:11, *en tō onomati tou kyriou Iēsou Christou*), giving thanks to God (Eph 5:20, *en onomati tou kyriou hēmōn Iēsou Christou*), any talk or task (Col 3:17, *en onomati kyriou Iēsou*), an authoritative command (2 Thess 3:6, *en onomati tou kyriou [hēmōn] Iēsou Christou*), *prayer and anointing for healing (Jas 5:14, *en tō onomati tou kyriou*), and believing (Jn 1:12; 2:23; 3:18; 1 Jn 3:23; 5:13, *tō onomati tou huiou autou Iēsou Christou/eis to onoma tou huiou tou theou*). Notice that most, though not all, of these use the formula in a context in which authority is being wielded.

The variation of prepositions, both in the texts having to do with baptism and other uses, may offer shades of nuance, though given the fluidity of prepositions in the Koine of this period, this should not be overinterpreted. It may be that "in [*en*] the name" refers to an act done on behalf of or in the authority of Jesus, "on [*epi*] the name" perhaps constituting a calling on Jesus' name, and "into [*eis*] the name" a Semitic expression for an act, especially of *worship, directed to Jesus (Ferguson 2009, 182). Yet, all connote some form of special relationship with Jesus. Notice that in Acts, the baptismal formula varies in use, taking up each of these three prepositions in the baptismal formula, seemingly interchangeably (Acts 2:38, *epi*; Acts 8:16, *eis*; Acts 10:48, *en*).

Therefore, one can conclude that for Paul baptism "in the name of Jesus" would have communicated the evoking of a relationship to Jesus Christ, the name often expressing an authoritative basis for the act being carried out on his behalf or as his person(s). When in 1 Corinthians 1 Paul asks the Corinthians, "Were you baptized in the name of Paul [*eis to onoma Paulou*]?" he challenges the posture of choosing one of their church leaders as the primary person around whom they gather, displacing Jesus from his rightful place as Lord at the heart and *head of the church. That foundational relationship then formed the basis for church unity, all the members of the church understanding themselves to live in a common relationship with Jesus Christ as Lord.

3.3.2. *Baptized into Christ.* In addition to the use of the Greek preposition *eis* in the baptismal formula, there are a number of places where Paul writes that believers are baptized "into" something or someone. It could be that this is a shortened form of the baptismal formula, "in [*eis*] the name of Christ" (so Beasley-Murray 1993, 61), but something more seems to be going on in Paul's theological reflections, for baptism "into" Christ has several parallels that should be noted. At Romans 6:3 Paul writes, "Or don't you know that all of us who were baptized into Christ Jesus were baptized into his death?" (NIV). Again, one must not make a false dichotomy between the physical reception of baptism and the spiritual realities with which that rite is associated. The two, spiritual and the physical, are neither identical nor separate in Paul's thought but coexistent. That the Roman believers already know what he is about to say suggests that he appeals to foundational Christian principles that they would have been exposed to upon entrance to the church through the waters of baptism.

Specifically, Paul speaks of the believer's incorporation "into Christ," that is, being transferred to a place of relational union "*in Christ" or "with Christ" (Moo, 360; cf. the parallel with the wilderness wanderers being "baptized into Moses," 1 Cor 10:2). Believers also, therefore, participate in events of the Christ's narrative, including his death. Michael Gorman notes, "Participation is not merely one aspect of Pauline theology and spirituality, or a supplement to something more fundamental; rather, it is at the very heart of Paul's thinking and living" (xviii). Accordingly, in his writings the apostle uses the phrase "in Christ" (*en Christō*) or one of its variations seventy-six times (e.g., Rom 3:24; 6:11, 23; 8:1-2, 39; 15:17; 1 Cor 1:2, 4; 16:24; Gal 2:4; 3:14; Philem 1:23). The phrase has been understood variously but should probably be interpreted primarily as a dative of association, "in relation to Christ." In a thorough treatment of the "in Christ" theme, Constantine Campbell summarizes his insights on this Pauline motif as involving not only incorporation and participation, but also union and identification (420). Thus, in their baptism by the Spirit, which is reflected in the baptism in water, believers are incorporated into Christ, participate in the events of Christ's narrative, identify with Christ and his kingdom, and have union with Christ. This multifaceted reality of being in Christ has several implications for Paul—key baptismal realities that serve as foundational for life in the church and the world.

First, it means that the believer shares in the death of Christ and lives as dead to sin (Rom 6:11; 2 Cor 5:14-15; Gal 2:19-20). Again, at Romans 6:3 Paul asserts that all of those incorporated into Christ through baptism "were baptized into his death," and he continues in the next verse, "We were therefore buried with him through baptism [*baptismatos*] into death in order that, just as Christ was raised from the dead through the *glory of the Father, we too may live a new life" (Rom 6:4 NIV). Being baptized "into Christ Jesus" (*eis Christon Iēsoun*) corresponds to being baptized "into death" (*eis ton thanaton*), specifically, into *his* (*autou*) death, and baptism by immersion in water serves as a fitting picture of burial and resurrection to new life.

Similarly, in Colossians 2:12 one reads of believers as "having been buried with him in baptism, in which you were also raised with him through your faith in the working of God, who raised him from the dead" (Col 2:12 NIV). Thus, Paul's soteriological move, connecting the believers' "death to sin" and new life in Christ, with the death and resurrection of Christ, points to a powerful, cosmic, spiritual reality (Tsui, 403). By the transformational work of the Spirit and incorporation into a living relationship with the Lord Christ, believers have the spiritual resources to live as God's holy people in the world, demonstrating that sin's dominion over humanity with its deadly implications has been broken in the death of Christ (Paroschi, 99). Sin no longer rules the lives of believers, nor does it control their conduct (Carlson, 258-59), and the only way to this resurrection life is through death (Crowley, 297).

A second, positive implication of being baptized into Christ is that believers have been "clothed with Christ" (see Col 3:9-11): "So in Christ Jesus you are all children of God through faith, for all of you who were baptized into Christ have clothed yourselves with Christ. There is neither Jew nor *Gentile, neither *slave nor free, nor is there male and female, for you are all one in Christ Jesus. If you belong to Christ, then you are Abraham's seed, and heirs according to the promise" (Gal 3:26-29 NIV). Whereas death connotes the turning away from a life under the dominion of sin, being in Christ also means being dressed for new life, and this act of being clothed evokes imagery of sonship, being identified with Christ the son as Abraham's descendants and heirs of the promise (Gal 3:29). Thus, the image of being clothed with Christ speaks of transformation to a new status as sons and daughters in one family, a theological reality with ethical and relational implications (Tsui, 407-8).

The third implication follows from the second. Believers are baptized by the Spirit "into one body" (*eis hen sōma*; 1 Cor 12:13), spirit baptism and its physical counterpart forming the basis for unity in the church. This is why in life under God, "There is one body . . . one Lord, one faith, one baptism" (Eph 4:4-5 NIV). Again, at Galatians 3:28 the apostle notes, "for you are all one in Christ Jesus" (NIV). So, baptism creates one new, human family out of fragmented humanity, torn by sin along religio-ethnic, social, and gender boundaries (Carlson, 259). This new *creation manifests the glory of God by walking and working together for the *kingdom under their one Lord, believers' common baptism projecting a picture of the dominion of Christ over sin, confessing Christ's lordship over the world, and anticipating the new creation of the world to come.

See also Church; Creation and New Creation; Eschatology; Holy Spirit; In Christ; Lord; Magic; Name; Purity and Impurity; Religions, Greco-Roman.

BIBLIOGRAPHY. **G. R. Beasley-Murray,** *Baptism in the New Testament* (Grand Rapids, MI: Eerdmans, 1973); idem, "Baptism," in *DPL*, 60-66; **M. Bockmuehl,** "The Baptism of Jesus as 'Super-Sacrament' of Redemption," *Theology* 115 (2012): 83-91; **R. P. Byars,** *The Sacraments in Biblical Perspective*, Interpretation (Louisville, KY: Westminster John Knox, 2011); **C. R. Campbell,** *Paul and Union with Christ: An Exegetical and Theological Study* (Grand Rapids, MI: Zondervan, 2012); **R. P. Carlson,** "The Role of Baptism in Paul's Thought," *Int* 47 (1993): 255-66; **J. Crowley,** "Baptism as Eschatological Event," *Worship* 62 (1988): 290-98; **J. D. G. Dunn**, *Baptism in the Holy Spirit: A Re-examination of the New Testament Teaching on the Gift of the Spirit in Relation to Pentecostalism Today*, SBT 2/15 (London: SCM Press, 1970); **G. Fee**, *The First Epistle to the Corinthians*, NICNT (Grand Rapids, MI: Eerdmans, 1987); **E. Ferguson,** "Baptism," in *DJG*², 66-69; idem, *Baptism in the Early Church: History, Theology, and Liturgy in the First Five Centuries* (Grand Rapids, MI: Eerdmans, 2009); **M. J. Gorman,** *Participating in Christ: Explorations in Paul's Theology and Spirituality* (Grand Rapids, MI: Baker Academic, 2019); **W. Heitmüller,** *Im Namen Jesu, eine Sprach-U religionsgeschichtliche Untersuchung zum Neuen Testament, speziell zur altchristliche Taufe,* FRLANT 1/2 (Göttingen: Vandenhoeck & Ruprecht, 1903); **J. Jeremias,** *Infant Baptism in the First Four Centuries* (Philadelphia: Westminster, 1962); **A. B. McGowan,** *Ancient Christian Worship: Early Church Practices in Social, Historical, and Theological Perspective* (Grand Rapids, MI: Baker Academic, 2016); **S. McKnight,** *A Light Among the Gentiles: Jewish Missionary Activity in the Second Temple Period* (Minneapolis: Fortress, 1990); **D. J. Moo,** *The Epistle to the Romans*, NICNT (Grand Rapids, MI: Eerdmans, 1996); **W. Paroschi,** "Acts 19:1-7 Reconsidered in Light of Paul's Theology of Baptism," *AUSS* 47 (2009): 73-100; **S. E. Porter and A. R. Cross,** *Dimensions of Baptism: Biblical and Theological Studies*, LNTS 234 (New York: Sheffield Academic Press, 2002); **M. C. Salter,** "Does Baptism Replace Circumcision? An Examination of the Relationship Between Circumcision and Baptism in Colossians 2:11-12," *Themelios* 35 (2010): 15-29; **E. P. Sanders,** *Judaism: Practice and Belief, 63 BCE–66 CE* (Minneapolis: Fortress, 2016); **D. C. Smith,** "Jewish Proselyte Baptism and the Baptism of John," *ResQ* 25 (1982): 13-32; **N. Taylor,** "Baptism for the Dead (1 Cor 15:29)?," *Neot* 36 (2002): 111-20; idem, *Paul on Baptism: Theology, Mission and Ministry in Context* (London: SCM Press, 2016); **T. K.-Y. Tsui,** "'Baptized into His Death' (Rom 6,3) and 'Clothed with Christ' (Gal 3:27): The Soteriological Meaning of Baptism in Light of Pauline Apocalyptic," *ETL* 88 (2012): 395-417; **J. B. Tucker,** "Baths, Baptism, and Patronage: The Continuing Role of Roman Social Identity in Corinth," in *Reading Paul in Context: Explorations in Identity Formation*, ed. K. Ehrensperger and J. B. Tucker (London: Bloomsbury, 2010), 173-88; **P. Vassiliadis,** "The Biblical (New Testament) Foundation of Baptism: Baptismal Theology as a Prerequisite of Eucharistic Theology," *Greek Orthodox Theological Review* 60 (2015): 11-44; **A. J. M. Wedderburn,** "The Soteriology of the Mysteries and Pauline Baptismal Theology," *NovT* 29 (1987): 53-72.

G. H. Guthrie

BARNABAS. *See* Coworkers, Paul and His.

BIRTH PANGS, MATERNAL IMAGERY

Paul's appeal to the figure of a pregnant woman in the throes of her labor pains in 1 Thessalonians 5 marks a sharp contrast to the more familiar gentle, nurturing image of a nursing mother earlier in the letter (1 Thess 2:7-8). Yet Paul clearly finds the image a compelling eschatological metaphor: not only does he use it here to highlight the unexpected and sudden nature of Christ's return and *judgment (1 Thess 5:3), but he also employs it to describe the painful and often uncertain process of becoming a new *creation, adopted and redeemed by *Christ (Gal 4:19; Rom 8:22). From the perspective of patriarchal first-century Mediterranean culture, Paul's appeal as a man to the vulnerability and pain of woman's labor likely seemed at least noteworthy, if not just odd. Like Jesus' parables, such a metaphor was meant to force a mental pause, a shift in perspective in order to bring new insight. Of those who have ventured into the metaphor, Beverly Gaventa's *Our Mother Saint Paul* has contributed significantly to the understanding of Paul's use of the labor metaphor, as have Conrad Gempf and Susan Eastman in their analyses of these metaphors and Paul's use of maternal language in general.

1. Contexts of *Hōdines*
2. Galatians 4:19, 27
3. 1 Thessalonians 5:3
4. Romans 8:22
5. Conclusion

1. Contexts of *Hōdines*.

Galatians 4:19; 1 Thessalonians 5:3; and Romans 8:22 all use the *hōdines/hōdinō* family to describe Paul's felt experience. However, since this word family is not common throughout NT texts, it is essential to examine the larger contexts of the words in order to accurately identify how Paul may have intended them and how his first audiences would most likely have understood them. Most frequently, one finds *hōdines* to be quite straightforward in that the vast majority of uses refer to the painful labor and delivery of an infant. The term encapsulates the pain, uncertainty, and dogged endurance of labor. But Paul's metaphorical use requires one to look beyond the literal and straightforward into the figurative and idiomatic. These may be significantly more helpful in identifying the literary milieu Paul draws from—a milieu that may also have helped shape his message to the churches.

Metaphorical uses of *hōdines* and the related verb *hōdinō* in Greco-Roman literature are most commonly found in the context of war, where the verb is used intransitively to focus on the pain of wounds sustained, comparing that pain to the life-threatening anguish of labor (e.g., Homer, *Il.* 5.115-120; *Od.* 9.415). Much later, in the third century CE, Plotinus uses *hōdis* to describe the anguish of nature in the "birthing" of the lower hypostases and the loss of unity entailed by that separation (*Enneads* 1.5.7.13). Again one finds the focus of *hōdines* and *hōdinō* to be painful *suffering, often combined with emotional anguish. This emphasis is heightened to a sense of corporate solidarity in suffering with *synōdinei* (Rom 8:22; see Aristotle, *Eudemian Ethics* 7.6).

In the Greek OT, one finds that *hōdines* also describes corporate distress in the face of war (Jer 6:24; 50(27):43; cf. Jer 4:31), with some emphasis on physical exhaustion due to anxiety and physical stress (Nahum 2:11). The term is also employed in the context of Israel's birth as a nation (Hab 3:10). Yet the majority of figurative uses of *hōdines* occur in the context of the day of the *Lord, where the pain and suffering of war and disaster are cast within the framework of the *hope of *salvation (Jer 30:5-6; 48:41; 49:22; Is 66:7-9; Jer 30:7-8; Mic 4:9). Here one sees with Gempf the tension of hope versus frustration and despair, yet these are clearly eschatological contexts as well that bring the metaphor's focus toward the pain of the process of bringing about new life.

This focus on present pain with the hope of eschatological restoration emerges even more clearly in Second Temple literature. The Teacher of the *Qumran community identifies himself as experiencing the pain of labor in his efforts to bring the community into the eschatological age (1QH[a] III, 7-10; V, 30-32). In addition, 2 Esdras parallels the eschatological focus of Mark 13:8 on enduring through the final day of the Lord, while 4 Esdras 4:42 emphasizes the pain of new birth into the *resurrection. In the same way, Jesus' use of *hōdines* and *hōdinō* also looks forward into the last days: the present pain indicates that the time has come for the final judgment, but also for the final salvation and renewal of creation (Mk 13:8; Mt 19:28; see also Rev 12:2).

2. Galatians 4:19, 27.

Paul's use of the imagery of labor pains in Galatians 4:19, 27 has relatively little in common with classical usage: though Homer's heroes were likewise men, Paul clearly links the sense of suffering not with war but with the painful process of labor, thus placing himself firmly within the feminine space. While classical authors used the verb *hōdinō* intransitively to focus on the anguish and uncertainty of suffering in war, Paul uses the verb *hōdinō* transitively to further focus the attention not just on the suffering of labor but also on its purpose: the product of the pain is a new life. Like a mother, Paul anticipates the birth with *joy; there is no sorrow like that of Plotinus at the parting of parent and offspring. Instead, Paul situates himself within the Jewish literary tradition, enduring the birthing pain in order to rejoice over the new life of God's people (Is 66:7-9).

Yet there is more than an emotional appeal to the Galatians or a foretaste of new creation at work in Paul's metaphor, though he does frequently address his audience emotionally and frame the believer in these terms (e.g., Gal 6:15; 2 Cor 5:17). Readings that stop at Paul's more common language of the new creation born in Christ through identification with his suffering and *death fall short of grasping Paul's odd metaphor in Galatians 4:19. Instead of resolving the figure in the expected way (with the birth of new life), he intentionally truncates the metaphor: it is not a new creation Paul labors to bring forth but rather Christ formed *in* the Galatians. The sudden change to the passive *mophōthē* signals that Paul is no longer the acting, laboring subject; rather, *God becomes the unstated subject, the one who actually births ("forms") Christ in the Galatians (compare Is 66:9). Paul intentionally shifts the metaphor to make a theological point: it is not by anyone's doing but God's alone that Christ is formed in and *righteousness is credited to the believer (Gal 3).

In addition, Paul speaks to the Galatians as a corporate *body, not as individuals, thus highlighting his claim that being "*in Christ" (as Christ is in Paul; see Gal 2:20) changes the reality of the individual, making meaningless any previous distinctions or separations with the body (Gal 3:28). Gaventa's description is apropos: "Paul's labor is that of an individual who knows that the world has been invaded by a new reality: a crucified Lord who confronts and overturns the world" (194). In this emotional metaphor, Paul links the Galatians' situation with his claim that the *gospel given him by Jesus is apocalyptic in nature, revealing God's ultimate plan to restore all of creation, and within which the believers in Galatia have the privilege of experiencing the radically new life Christ brings to all believers as the firstfruits of that cosmological labor.

Susan Eastman's analysis of Paul's "mother tongue"—his use of passionate and relationally focused language—in his letter to the Galatians helpfully identifies how Paul's rhetoric unites himself and the Galatians in their *faith and in a uniquely "in Christ" corporate life. However, her argument that Paul's discussion of pain here in Galatians 4:19 reflects his earlier comments in Galatians 4:13 draws Paul's metaphor of labor pains down to a merely personal level, eradicating the bold theological claim Paul is making in Galatians 4:19. That claim links his relational plea with the apocalyptic nature of the gospel with its cosmological implications. Paul's truncated metaphor in fact intentionally functions as a hinge linking the theological arguments of Galatians 2–4 and their implications—new life and a redefined *freedom—in Galatians 5–6 (see Gaventa).

3. 1 Thessalonians 5:3.

Here Paul reverts to the more familiar OT motif of labor pains as a metaphor for the sudden and unpredictable pain and anguish of disaster. Unlike his appeal in Galatians 4:19, Paul employs the intransitive verb common to classical literature, with the focus of the image squarely on the pain and uncertainty of labor. There is no new life in view here, particularly for those facing the judgment at the sudden and unexpected parousia of Christ. Instead Paul echoes Jesus' words in Luke 21:34 and Mark 13, and both Paul and Jesus draw on imagery describing the day of the Lord in the OT and Second Temple literature (Ps 48:6; Is 26:17; 66:8; Jer 30:6-7; Mic 4:9-10; 2 Esd 16:37-39; 4 Ezra 16.35-39; 1 En. 62.1-6). The metaphor highlights not only the unexpectedness of that day but also the urgency of Paul's warnings to the Thessalonians: because no one knows when the day will come, all must heed Paul's words now or risk being surprised by the parousia when they are not ready for it (see also Mt 24:15-31 for thematic echoes).

4. Romans 8:22.

At first glance Romans 8:20-23 does not appear to share in the imagery of labor pains, and so many commentators glance over the groaning without fully grasping the metaphor Paul employs here. However, the context of groaning and the anticipation of new life and the firstfruits of the Spirit justify a closer look at Paul's language. In Romans 8:22 one finds the verb *synōdinei*, with its echoes of corporate birthing pain. The *syn-* prefix to the familiar *hōdin-* root (found in Gal 4:19; 1 Thess 5:3) focuses attention on the groaning in unison of a corporate body in distress (see, e.g., Aristotle, *Eudemian Ethics* 7.6). OT uses of the verb include Genesis 3:16 and Jeremiah 4:31, while occurrences of the verb in Greco-Roman literature include Heraclitus's description of the cyclical return of spring as the earth's yearly groaning, giving birth to what has been forming within her through the winter (*Quaestiones Homericae* 39).

Yet those who read Romans 8 in terms of spring's rebirth miss Paul's claim that life in Christ is a completely new creation (2 Cor 5:17). Rather, as with Galatians 4:19, the OT context is a far better fit with Pauline theology, and Paul seems to draw on the OT motifs quite deliberately. Both the eschatological context of Jeremiah 4:31 and the *curse of Genesis 3:16 are profoundly meaningful backdrops for Paul's claim that in Christ, the curse is defeated and the promised day of the Lord has come. But instead of disastrous judgment, those who are in Christ experience a foretaste of the prophesied eschatological reality of Christ's presence as adopted children awaiting the full realization of their redemption.

Thus one sees that where Gempf reads *synōdinei* here to focus only on the "helplessness and frustration" of labor, Paul on the contrary clearly links the joy of new birth to the pain of labor. While all of creation (including those in Christ) groans, all also look eagerly ahead to the final result. In fact, both Qumranic and later rabbinical literature reflect this theology of travail before the age of the Messiah, though it is difficult to determine whether the rabbinical strands of tradition in particular were current with Paul or later (1QH III, 3-18; 1 En. 62.4; later, b. Sanh. 98b; b. Shabb. 118a; Str-B 1:950). Instead, it may be that Paul is relying more heavily on an OT motif of birth in which the onset of labor is a metaphor for waiting for events that are beyond one's control (Ps 48:6; Is 13:8; 26:17-18; Jer 13:21; Mic 4:9). So Paul tempers the current distress by the hope of the "freedom of the *glory of the children of God" (Rom 8:21 NRSV), and the hope of all creation is entirely contingent on God's intervention, on his choice of when to step into history and bring this labor to a successful and joyful resolution.

But as with his truncated metaphor in Galatians 4:19, Paul refuses to resolve this metaphor in the expected way. The joy at the resolution of labor is typically the birth of a son or daughter, but here the eagerly awaited outcome is *adoption, not birth. Gaventa notes that while this shift of the second half of the metaphor echoes that of Galatians 4:19, here is essentially a double shift in that the awaited adoption is in fact the redemption of the body (Rom 8:23). This redemption should be read quite literally, as *apolytrōsin* suggests: as a release from captivity or *slavery to the forces of *sin and death that Paul has so clearly described in the previous chapters (particularly bearing the echoes Paul's narrative of humanity's descent into sin and death in Rom 1). The singular *sōmatos* (body) that will be redeemed foreshadows Paul's vision (Rom 9–11) of a unified body composed of both Jews and *Gentiles, apocalyptically revealed in the final day of the Lord (i.e., the parousia of 1 Thessalonians).

5. Conclusion.
Surface-level readings of Paul's metaphors of labor and delivery typically focus on Paul's use of emotional appeals or a Pauline theology of the new man. Many readings simply miss the fundamental shift Paul introduces in the metaphors he employs in Galatians 4:19 and Romans 8:22. However, a deeper reading demonstrates that these shifts in fact reflect the heart of Paul's message within those *letters and reveal a Paul wholly convinced of the cosmic implications of his apocalyptic gospel, as (with the exception of Thessalonians) labor pains lead to an adoption that heralds the already-accomplished and soon-to-be-consummated invasion of God's life and freedom that overturns and transforms the broken world.

This is the Paul who urges churches to expand their concept of the gospel, to grasp that God's revelation in the person of Jesus invades and eclipses all of the norms and standards of this world, releasing all of creation from its enslavement to sin and death. It is a revelation that rewrites the rules of behavior and relationship, redefines freedom, and reorients all of creation around what Paul describes in Romans as "the *love of God in Christ Jesus our Lord" (Rom 8:39 NRSV).

See also ESCHATOLOGY; MAN AND WOMAN; ROMANS, LETTER TO THE; SUFFERING; WOMEN.

BIBLIOGRAPHY. **S. G. Eastman,** *Recovering Paul's Mother Tongue: Language and Theology in Galatians* (Grand Rapids, MI: Eerdmans, 2007); **B. R. Gaventa,** *Our Mother Saint Paul* (Louisville, KY: Westminster John Knox, 2007); **C. Gempf,** "The Imagery of Birth Pangs in the New Testament," *TynBul* 45, no. 1 (1994): 119-35.

J. A. Odor

BOASTING. *See* CORINTHIANS, FIRST LETTER TO THE; OPPONENTS OF PAUL; ROMANS, LETTER TO THE; SUFFERING.

BODY

The term *sōma* (body) occurs ninety-one times in the Pauline corpus as a whole, with a particular focus of usage in Romans, 1 and 2 Corinthians, Ephesians, and Colossians.

The term has a wide range of meanings. It is used to refer to the physical body (e.g., in 1 Cor 5:3 Paul talks about being absent in the body, or in Gal 6:17 bearing the marks of Christ in his body), but it is also used to mean more than just physical bodies, to refer to the entirety of a person, what we might term the body, mind, spirit, and soul. Woven into the heart of Paul's use of the term *sōma* is his belief in the *resurrection of the body, which takes the form of an embodied existence after *death and hence links to *eschatology and his understanding of redemption. In addition to all this, Paul does not just use the term to refer to the bodies of individuals but speaks of a corporate dimension, the *body of Christ, to refer to Christian corporate identity and relationship in *Christ.

1. *Sōma* (Body), *Sarx* (Flesh), *Psychē* (Soul), and the Self
2. The Resurrection of the Body
3. Participation in the Body of Christ
4. Concluding Observations

1. *Sōma* (Body), *Sarx* (Flesh), *Psychē* (Soul), and the Self.

While it is important to be careful to avoid simplistic distinctions between Jewish and Hellenistic thought—that is, to assume that Jewish thought was not influenced by the Hellenistic world that surrounded it—in some areas such as Paul's teaching about the body it is possible to trace a greater reliance on Hebrew concepts than on Hellenistic ones. Many scholars agree that Paul's *anthropology does seem to be more influenced by Jewish thinking than by the Hellenistic world. In particular, this affects his understanding of the human self, which throughout the Pauline corpus is a unified whole including the body. As E. Best observes, a person "cannot be divided into an 'I' and a non 'I,' a soul and a body" (Best, 217). The predominance of this thinking has caused scholars such as R. Jewett to argue that the more Hellenistic terminology found in Paul's writings is made up of borrowed phrases from his *opponents in order to argue against them (Jewett 1971).

1.1.* Sōma *(Body) and* Sarx *(Flesh). One of the confusions that arises over Paul's use of the term *sōma* is its assumed conflation with the term *sarx* (flesh). Although the terms are used alongside each other in Paul's writings, by and large *sarx* has a more negative connotation than *sōma*. When Paul wants to contrast life in the Spirit with something else, most of the time he uses *sarx* rather than *sōma*.

The most common translation of *sarx* is "*flesh," but this may not be the most helpful rendering of the word (see the discussion in Jewett 1971, 49-166). In the Pauline writings the term *sarx* rarely refers literally to the soft substance of muscle and fat that sits between the skin and the bone. The term is used more often with a derogatory meaning to denote the limitations of the human condition (Gal 4:13), to refer to moral weakness (Rom 3:20), and most importantly of all to refer to mortality and destruction (Rom 8:6). J. D. G. Dunn views *sarx* as referring to the whole "continuum of human mortality" (Dunn, 66). It is worth noting, however, that *sarx* is not universally evil. In Paul's mind the problem arose when *sarx* was given a power it should not possess (as in Rom 8:6 NRSV, "set[ting] the mind on the flesh"). If flesh is mortal and will come to an end, setting the mind on it can only lead to destruction.

In contrast to *sarx*, *sōma* commonly has a much more positive association in the Pauline corpus. In 1 Corinthians, Paul states that the Corinthians' bodies are members of Christ (1 Cor 6:15) and that the bread that is broken is a participation in Christ's body (1 Cor 10:16). He also uses the body of Christ as a primary metaphor for talking about Christian community (1 Cor 12:12-27; Rom 12:4-5) and commands Christians to respond to the mercy of God by presenting their bodies to him (Rom 12:1-2). Indeed, the only time that body is used negatively is when it appears with a negative qualifier: the body of *sin (Rom 6:6), the body of death (Rom 7:24), or the mortal body (Rom 8:11). These uses are so unusual in the Pauline corpus that Jewett argues that they are phrases taken over from Paul's Gnostic opponents (Jewett 1971, 254-304).

The contrast between the use of the two terms is so great in Paul's writings that it suggests he was attempting to make a distinction between *sarx* and *sōma* where one had not existed previously in either Greek or Hebrew. Although there are a few instances where it appears as though Paul uses *sōma* and *sarx* interchangeably (most notably 1 Cor 15:39, where Paul breaks off from an extensive discussion of *sōma* to use *sarx* before reverting to *sōma* once more), most of the time he maintains a clear distinction between the two. This is made all the more noticeable by the fact that there is no separate word for "body" in Hebrew. The closest word was *bāśār*, which is much nearer to *sarx* in meaning than "body."

In identifying *sarx* as a more negative concept, marked almost entirely by the mortality of the age that is coming to an end, and *sōma* as a more positive term, associated with this age of sin and death but also with the resurrection body in the age to come, Paul was making a careful distinction that had not been made previously. This allowed him to introduce a positive strand to the use of *sōma*. As Dunn notes, "We could say that Paul's distinction between *sōma* and *sarx* made possible a positive affirmation of human createdness and *creation and of the interdependence of humanity within its created environment. Sadly, however, this potential in

Paul's theology was soon lost as the distinction itself was lost to sight" (Dunn, 73).

1.2.* Sōma *(Body) and* Psychē *(Soul). This distinction between *sōma* and *sarx* is in some ways connected to Paul's use of the term *psychē* (soul). Unlike Plato, who in the *Phaedo* in particular describes the all-knowing soul as existing before it was entombed within the body and as continuing to exist after the body's death, Paul viewed the *psychē* as integral to the body. While he does contrast *sarx* (flesh) and *pneuma* (spirit), he never contrasts *sōma* with *psychē*. Indeed, there is a broad consensus among NT scholars that the thirteen times that *psychē* appears in Paul's writings (Rom 2:9; 11:3; 13:1; 16:4; 1 Cor 15:45; 2 Cor 1:23; 12:15; Eph 6:6; Phil 1:27; 2:30; Col 3:23; 1 Thess 2:8; 5:23), its usage is much closer to the Hebrew term *nepeš*, which might be better translated as "life force," than to Plato's notion of the soul.

J. Green observed the drop in uses of the word *soul* in modern English translations and tied it to this rough consensus about Paul's usage of the term *psychē*, noting that in the NT the KJV translation (1611) contains the word *soul* 39 times, whereas it appears only 34 times in the ASV (1901), 27 times in the RSV (1952), 22 times in the NRSV (1989), 20 times in the NIV (2001), 15 times in the NABRE (2011), and only three times in the CEB (Green 2013). This list omits two significant exceptions to this: the ESV, first published in 2001, has 43 uses of the word *soul* in the NT, and *The Message*, first published in 1994, has 32. Nevertheless, the waning confidence in the word *soul* as a good translation of Paul's use of *psychē* is ably demonstrated in many of the modern English translations.

The key problem is that the English term *soul* conjures up a view of the self that can be removed easily from a body while still continuing to exist. Thus the word itself evokes a concept that Paul would never have intended. Paul's use of *psychē* most often implies the whole self, a self that would have included, not excluded, the body. For example, in Romans 13:1 Paul declares that every person (*psychē*) should be subject to the governing authorities; or in Romans 16:4 he mentions Prisca and Aquila, who risked their necks for "my life" (*psychē*, NRSV). Similarly, Colossians 3:23 commands slaves to "put yourselves [*ek psychēs*]" into every task (NRSV). In each of these examples, Paul uses the word to refer to the whole of oneself, including one's body. In this his use is very close to a Hebrew understanding of the self. OT scholars have long made the point that the "Hebrew idea of the personality is an animated body, and not an incarnated soul" (H. Wheeler Robinson, 362) and that therefore human beings do not *have* a body; they *are* a body (J. A. T. Robinson, 14). Just as it would be impossible to remove the *nepeš* from a living being, since it is located in the blood (Gen 9:4; Lev 17:11) so too for Paul it would be impossible to remove the *psychē* from the *sōma*.

This has led Green to view Pauline anthropology as monist, having a single *identity, so that "at death, the person *really dies*; from the perspective of our humanity and sans divine intervention, there is no part of us, no aspect of our personhood that survives death" (Green 2008, 179). Others argue for two identifiable, if not easily separable, parts to the human identity—such as J. Cooper, who argues for holistic dualism or dualistic holism. There is just one verse (1 Thess 5:23) in the Pauline corpus that suggests that Paul's anthropology is trichotomous (spirit, soul, and body) apparently supported by Hebrews 4:12. Although this is a popular view in non-academic circles (see, e.g., Nee), few academics hold a trichotomous view of Pauline anthropology. The key argument against 1 Thessalonians 5:23 maintaining a trichotomous view of identity is that the verse emphasizes wholeness in two words, *holotelēs* and *holoklēros*, which stress the wholeness and unity of the human person. Paul's prayer is that they might be held together in perfect balance—a holy wholeness—not separated in any way.

1.3. Dualism and Duality. The separation of body and soul often draws on a dualistic view of the world, which splits the world into two categories, good and bad, and which sometimes also establishes an opposition between two powers or gods, such as that between *God and a powerful devil. Paul's love of contrasts can suggest that he too was fueled by dualism and hence that he, along with other dualists, viewed the body as bad to the soul's good. N. T. Wright has argued, however, that it is wrong to view Paul as a dualist, that his contrasts are better understood as dualities rather than as full-blown dualism (Wright, *Paul and the Faithfulness of God*, 1043-1268). It is clear that Paul was thoroughly monotheistic and that the whole of creation has been reconciled to God (2 Cor 5:19) and awaits the final consummation of redemption alongside the human race (Rom 8:19-23). Where Paul *does* draw a contrast is between this age and the age to come. The previous age, symbolized by *Adam, was marked by sin and the need for *law along with, crucially, mortality, as this age would come to an end; the age to come, symbolized by Christ, is imbued with the Spirit and will never end. In terms of the body, while flesh belongs to this age and will end, the body belongs both to this age and to the age to come. Bodies are a gift of God to be cherished and nurtured, not an encumbrance to be endured.

1.4. The Body as the Self. If human beings *are* a body rather than just having a body, this explains why Paul can use the word *sōma* as a circumlocution for himself. In 1 Corinthians 9:27 he says, "I punish my body [*sōma*]" (NRSV), and in Philippians 1:20 he says, "Christ will be exalted . . . in my body [*sōma*]" (NRSV), both of which use *sōma* as an indirect way of saying "myself" or "me."

In a similar way he uses *body* elsewhere to refer to the whole person. Two particularly clear examples of this are Romans 8:23 and Romans 12:1. Romans 8:23 refers to waiting for the "redemption of our bodies" (NRSV). There is no suggestion here that Paul means just the physical self, nor is there any implication that what is being awaited is redemption from our bodies. Romans 8 describes the waiting for redemption of the whole created order alongside humanity. The redemption, when at last it comes, will involve transformation—the transformation of the whole self, not just the physical body. Similarly, in Romans 12:1, when Paul instructs the Roman Christians to present their bodies as a living *sacrifice, as Dunn observes, there is no suggestion that they should place their limbs on an actual altar (Dunn, 58). Presenting their bodies as a living sacrifice involved the whole self in an act of dedication. The word *sōma* does of course include the physical body but is not reduced to it. Unlike in the modern world, for Paul the term *sōma* refers to human identity as a whole, including but not limited to the physical body.

2. The Resurrection of the Body.

One of the pillars of Paul's more positive theology of the body is his extensive discussion of resurrection in 1 Corinthians 15. It is clear from this passage that, although the Corinthians had no problem in believing that Jesus rose from the dead (1 Cor 15:12), they were uncertain that they themselves would rise from the dead. It is far less clear, however, what the exact nature of their belief about resurrection or life after death was.

Much of twentieth-century NT scholarship in this area focused on the question of what form the so-called Corinthian heresy took. There is little agreement on the answer. A. Thiselton categorizes the many different theories into four main strands: that the Corinthians denied any kind of existence after death, that they maintained that the resurrection had already happened in some spiritual way, that they could not conceive of a resurrection of the *body*, or that Paul was speaking to more than one group in Corinth, and hence was addressing more than one problem (for an extensive discussion of the options see Thiselton, 1276-81). While it is impossible to identify with any certainty the precise nature of the Corinthian views on resurrection, D. Martin argues persuasively that the problem can probably be traced to some form of Greek philosophical view that split the soul from the body at death and struggled to comprehend the possibility of a body being immortal (Martin, 116).

2.1. The Continuity and Discontinuity of the Resurrected Body. The second half of 1 Corinthians 15 explores the nature of the resurrected body. Paul introduces this issue in 1 Corinthians 15:35 with the question: "But someone will ask, 'How are the dead raised? With what kind of body do they come?'" to which he responds "Fool!" (NRSV). The Greek is not quite as dismissive as the usual English translation suggests and instead suggests a senseless question (in other words, one that could be answered independently with the application of common sense). Wright suggests that the original question as cited in 1 Corinthians 15:35 was asked by a skeptic who was deliberately not applying common sense to the query (Wright 2003, 342).

The analogy that Paul uses to illustrate his point about the nature of the resurrected body is an agricultural one. In using this analogy, he makes clear that his view of resurrection differs from some of his Jewish contemporaries. Rabbi Shammai, for example, argued that the dead would be raised to the same body as they had had prior to death (Cavallin, 172). The agricultural analogy that Paul used in 1 Corinthians 15:35-55 emphasizes the transformation that will take place from the seed sown to the plant grown. While this theme is present from 1 Corinthians 15:35 onward, Paul states it explicitly in 1 Corinthians 15:51 ("Listen, I will tell you a mystery! We will not all die, but we will all be changed"; NRSV).

The analogy Paul uses also introduces the concept of continuity and discontinuity. There is a continuity in that the plant grown emerges from a seed sown; there is a discontinuity in that the plant grown looks significantly different from the seed sown. This theme of continuity and discontinuity between the pre- and postresurrection body is something that can also be observed in accounts of Jesus' resurrection body in the Gospels. There Jesus' resurrection body is continuous with his previous body in that it still bears the scars of his crucifixion (Lk 24:38-40; Jn 20:27) and discontinuous in that he is apparently not immediately recognizable (see Lk 24:16; Jn 20:14). In addition, he can eat but can also pass through locked doors. Wright terms Jesus' body "trans-physical" to draw attention to the idea that, while it is transformed, it is still an actual body (Wright 2003, 477).

2.2. A Body Fit for Its Context. The nature of the transformation of the body is to ensure that the resurrection body fits its context in the new heaven and the new earth. The next stage of Paul's argument (1 Cor 15:39-41) establishes that God gives the body what is needed for its context: birds need one type of body, whereas fish need another type. Into this discussion Paul introduces a potentially confusing term: "heavenly bodies" as opposed to "earthly bodies" (1 Cor 15:40 NRSV). Some see this as a reference to nonphysical bodies as opposed the physical bodies we have now. Martin argues that this is the case, maintaining that a heavenly body is the nonphysical body needed for existence in the heavenly realms after death (Martin, 117-20, 123-36).

Others disagree, noting that this would be the only reference in this chapter to going to heaven when we die. Further, if it is such a reference, it is somewhat oblique. Another option is to note that the following verse, 1 Corinthians 15:41, moves on to talk about the moon and stars, which exist in the heavens. "Heavenly bodies," therefore, probably refers to the bodies of those who already dwell in heaven, that is, angels. Indeed, J. Héring notes that there is a strong connection between the bodies of angels and of stars because some angels appear as stars (Héring, 174).

The key feature of Paul's argument, therefore, is that just as God gives the body that is needed now to, for example, birds, fish, and angels, so after the resurrection God will give the body that will be needed for the new heaven and the new earth. It does not answer the question of 1 Corinthians 15:35, "With what kind of body do they come?" (NRSV), but it does provide some hints.

2.3. A Spiritual Body. These hints are expanded in 1 Corinthians 15:42-46. There Paul provides four contrasts between bodies now and then. Each of these contrasts is introduced by the formula "it is sown a . . . it is raised a . . ." (NRSV). The first of the contrasts is notoriously complex to translate. It is often translated as *perishable* and *imperishable*, but Thiselton argues that this is an inadequate rendering of the words. He argues that *perishable* and *imperishable* are static words, whereas *phthora*, which lies behind both of these words in Greek (*phthora* versus *aphtharsia*) implies a process or a dynamic. He maintains that whereas our current bodies move toward decay and death, resurrection bodies will move in the opposite direction, toward greater life and energy (Thiselton, 1271-72).

The fourth contrast is the one that has garnered the most discussion. It is commonly translated as "It is sown a physical body, it is raised a spiritual body" (NRSV). This obviously suggests that the resurrection body is not, after all, an actual body but one made of an entirely different substance—spirit or, as some argue, "heavenly light" (see Thiselton, 1276-81, for a discussion of the full range of the different views). Other scholars, and notably Wright, argue that the common translation does not give an adequate rendering of *sōma psychikos* and *sōma pneumatikos*, not least because the use of "physical" to translate *psychikos* implies that a *pneumatikos* body will not be physical (Wright 2003, 341).

When used elsewhere by Paul, *psychikos* is used in contrast to *pneumatikos*, where *pneumatikos* means "that which pertains to the spirit" and *psychikos* "that which does not pertain to the spirit" (see in particular 1 Cor 2:13-14). In the epistles of James and Jude this contrast between the two terms is even more exaggerated: in James 3:15-16 *psychikos* is associated with the terms "earthly" (*epigeios*) and "demonic" (*daimoniōdēs*); in Jude 1:19 *psychikos* people are said not to have the Spirit and to have caused divisions. In 1 Corinthians the term *psychikos* does not have quite the negative connotations that it does in James and Jude; nevertheless, it is contrasted with *pneumatikos*. The impact of the contrast can be seen most clearly in 1 Corinthians 15:45, via a quotation from Genesis 2:7: "Thus it is written, 'The first man, Adam, became a living being' [*psychēn zōsan*]; the last Adam became a life-giving spirit [*pneuma zōiopoioun*]" (NRSV). In other words, *psychikos* bodies are like those of Adam, animated by the *psychē* but mortal; *pneumatikos* bodies will be like those of the risen Christ, animated by the *pneuma* and immortal. Both *psychikos* and *pneumatikos* bodies are real bodies, making up a self that includes but is not limited to the physical body; one is needed for life in the old creation, and the other is needed for resurrection life.

3. Participation in the Body of Christ.
Jewett observes that, in Paul, bodies do not just make up the whole self; they are also the means by which a person relates to the world around them (Jewett 1971, 301-4). So, for example, when Paul

encourages the Romans to present their bodies as a living sacrifice to God, one of the themes he goes on to talk about is relationships with other Christians (Rom 12:4-19; 15:1-3). Although present in numerous places in Paul's writings, the place where the connection between the individual body and relationship becomes particularly clear is in 1 Corinthians, where Paul moves seamlessly between talking about individual bodies and their actions and talking about the body as a whole.

3.1. From the Individual to the Community and Back Again. Paul's anthropology leads him to draw a deep connection between the body of an individual and the body of the community, which in 1 Corinthians 12 (and also Rom 12:4-7) he describes as the body of Christ. In 1 Corinthians 6:12-20 Paul counters what appears to be an argument put forward by the Corinthians themselves that what they do with their bodies has little significance because ultimately their bodies will come to an end (see the discussion in Murphy-O'Connor). Paul's argument, begun in 1 Corinthians 6 and continuing until at least 1 Corinthians 12, if not 1 Corinthians 15, is that an individual's body, and what someone does with it, has a profound impact on the body of the community as a whole. Whom someone has sex with, what they eat, and how they conduct themselves in the midst of conflict all affect the well-being of the corporate body, the body of Christ, the community of Christians. In the middle chapters of 1 Corinthians Paul moves so swiftly from talking about individual bodies and their identity as temples of the *Holy Spirit to talking about Christ's body in the Last Supper and about the community of the body of Christ that it is often difficult to ascertain where one ends and the other begins. It is important to remember that Paul's anthropology focuses as much on the identity and well-being of the corporate body as on the identity and well-being of the individual body.

3.2 Putting to Death the Deeds of the Body. The importance of the corporate body in Paul's thinking is often obscured in English by the fact that modern English language struggles to differentiate between the plural and the singular. Romans 8:13 is an important example of this: "If by the Spirit you put to death the deeds of the body, you will live" (NRSV). At first glance, this verse appears to advocate the mortification of the body, an attitude that suggests a less positive relationship with the body than has been explored thus far in Paul's writings. This changes when one recognizes that the *you* in the verse is plural, not singular, and therefore refers to the corporate body, not the individual body. As Jewett points out, the "death that Paul has in mind is collective; the fleshly mode of behaviors shaped by traditional obligations of honour, by a chronic suppression of the truth, and by lethal competition is like a plague that destroys a house or tenement church and everyone in it" (Jewett 2006, 494). In order for the body of Christ to thrive, behaviors that mar the body must be extinguished.

4. Concluding Observations.
Paul's use of the word *sōma* draws on a Hebraic understanding of the self but at the same time develops a new distinction between *body* and *flesh*. This distinction makes it possible for Paul to condemn what will come to an end while at the same time holding open a positive attitude toward embodiment. For Paul the word *body* refers to much more than simply physical identity and is often used to describe the whole self, including but not limited to the physical body. It is this self that Paul envisages will be transformed into a resurrection body at the end of time, a resurrection body that will be animated by the Spirit and not just the *psychē*, as our current bodies are.

The connection between bodies and identity is what makes it possible for Paul to talk about corporate bodies as well as individual bodies. He argues that participation in the body of Christ means that the actions of individuals in their bodies affect the relationship and identity of the whole body, the body of Christ.

See also ADAM AND CHRIST; AFTERLIFE; ANTHROPOLOGY, PAULINE; BODY OF CHRIST; CORINTHIANS, FIRST LETTER TO THE; CREATION AND NEW CREATION; DEATH; ESCHATOLOGY; FLESH; IN CHRIST; RESURRECTION; ROMANS, LETTER TO THE.

BIBLIOGRAPHY. **A. J. Avery-Peck and J. Neusner,** *Judaism in Late Antiquity: Death, Life-After-Death, Resurrection and the World-to-Come,* JA 4 (Leiden: Brill, 2000); **R. Bauckham,** "Life, Death and the Afterlife in Second Temple Judaism," in *Life in the Face of Death: The Resurrection Message of the New Testament,* ed. R. N. Longenecker (Grand Rapids, MI: Eerdmans, 1998), 80-95; **E. Best,** *One Body in Christ* (London: SPCK, 1955); **H. C. C. Cavallin,** *Life After Death: Paul's Argument for the Resurrection of the Dead in I Cor. 15* (Lund: Gleerup, 1974); **J. W. Cooper,** *Body, Soul, and Life Everlasting: Biblical Anthropology and the Monism-Dualism Debate.* (Grand Rapids, MI: Eerdmans, 2000); **J. D. G. Dunn,** *The Theology of Paul the Apostle* (Edinburgh: T&T Clark, 1998); **P. Gooder,** *Heaven* (London: SPCK, 2011); idem, *Body* (London: SPCK, 2016); **J. B. Green,** *Body, Soul, and Human Life: The Nature of Humanity* *in the Bible* (Grand Rapids, MI: Baker Academic, 2008); idem, *On Doing Without a Soul: A New Testament Perspective*, 2013, Biola University, www.youtube.com/watch?v=SDqm9rCq2Mo; **R. H. Gundry,** *Sōma in Biblical Theology: With Emphasis on Pauline Anthropology* (Cambridge: Cambridge University Press, 1976); **M. J. Harris,** *Raised Immortal: Resurrection and Immortality in the New Testament* (Grand Rapids, MI: Eerdmans, 1985); **D. W. Hayter,** "How Are the Dead Raised? The Bodily Nature of Resurrection in Second Temple Jewish Texts," in *The Body in Biblical, Christian and Jewish Texts*, ed. J. E. Taylor (London: Bloomsbury, 2014), 123-43; **J. Héring,** *The First Epistle of Saint Paul to the Corinthians* (London: Epworth, 1973); **R. Jewett,** *Paul's Anthropological Terms: A Study of Their Use in Conflict Settings* (Leiden: Brill, 1971); idem, *Romans: A Commentary*, Hermeneia (Minneapolis: Fortress, 2006); **D. Martin,** *The Corinthian Body* (New Haven, CT: Yale University Press, 1999); **J. Murphy-O'Connor,** "Corinthian Slogans in 1 Cor. 6:12-20," *CBQ* 40 (1978): 391-96; **W. Nee,** *Spiritual Man* (New York: Christian Fellowship, 1969); **J. A. T. Robinson,** *The Body: A Study in Pauline Theology* (London: SCM Press, 1952); **K. O. Sandnes,** *Belly and Body in the Pauline Epistles*, SNTSMS (Cambridge: Cambridge University Press, 2009); **A. F. Segal,** *Life After Death: A History of the Afterlife in Western Religion* (New York: Doubleday, 2004); **A. C. Thiselton,** *The First Epistle to the Corinthians*, NIGTC (Grand Rapids, MI: Eerdmans, 2001); **H. Wheeler Robinson,** *The People and the Book* (Oxford: Clarendon, 1952); **N. T. Wright,** *The Resurrection of the Son of God* (London: SPCK, 2003); idem, "Mind, Spirit, Soul and Body: All for One and One for All; Reflections on Paul's Anthropology in His Complex Contexts," in *Pauline Perspectives: Essays on Paul* (London: SPCK, 2013), 453-73; idem, *Paul and the Faithfulness of God*, 2 vols. (London: SPCK, 2013).

P. Gooder

BODY OF CHRIST

The phrase "body of *Christ" refers to three things in the Pauline corpus: (1) the physical *body of Jesus, (2) the bread of the *Lord's Supper/Eucharist, and (3) the *church, composed of those having been incorporated in Christ by receiving the spirit of Christ. The exact phrase itself appears only four times (Rom 7:4; 1 Cor 10:16; 12:27; Eph 4:12), but related expressions occur another seventeen times: "my body" (1 Cor 11:24), "body of the Lord" (1 Cor 11:27), "his glorious body" (Phil 3:21), "his body of *flesh" (Col 1:22), "his body" (Eph 1:23; 5:30; Col 1:24); "the body" (1 Cor 11:29; Eph 5:23; Col 1:18; 2:19); "one body" (Rom 12:5; 1 Cor 1:17; 12:13; Eph 2:16; 4:4; 3:15). In Romans and 1 Corinthians, Paul appeals to body imagery only in the context of ethical instruction (paraenesis) and appeals for unity (see Gundry; Jewett; Wedderburn). But in Colossians and Ephesians, the body concept is also used to emphasize the headship and authority of Christ over the growing organism of the church (Col 1:15-20; Eph 1:22-23; 4:15; 5:23), which is, by union with Christ, both a heavenly and earthly entity.

Many proposals have been made about possible sources from which Paul may have derived the "body of Christ" idea, but the metaphorical or analogical use of *body* to denote a group of people was sufficiently common in Greco-Roman antiquity that it is unlikely to have been drawn from a single source. For example, the state was regularly compared to a body in political speeches arguing for unity within a given civic body or group of persons (Martin, 38-47; Mitchell, 157-64). Such orations regularly compared the group to a body of members with different roles needing to cooperate for the common good of the body as a whole—exactly the argument Paul employs with the Corinthians (1 Cor 12:12-27). Plato similarly compares the state to a body in the *Republic* and the cosmos to an ensouled body in the *Timaeus* (see also *Philebus* 29D-E). This image became especially popular in Stoic *philosophy, where it provided a foundation for basic ethical obligations and decisions (Lee, 46-102; Moule, 84-85). An especially close contemporary parallel to the Pauline usage of the concept may be observed in Seneca's address of Nero as "the soul of the republic [which] is your body" (*Clem.* 1.5.1), depicting the Roman *Empire as a unified body that actualizes the purposes and intentions of its ruler (see *Ep.* 95.52).

Paul takes this image a step further than its usual metaphorical or analogical sense. For the *apostle, the "body of Christ" is not just a metaphor for individuals unified by belief in Jesus but an ontological and relational reality in which persons, receiving the "spirit of Christ" (Rom 8:9), thereby become incorporated into Christ himself. Believers actually become the "body of Christ" by being "baptized into one body by one spirit" (1 Cor 12:13). Thus Paul's most common way of referring to believers is as those *"in Christ," and he declares that "if anyone is in Christ, this person is a new *creation" (2 Cor 5:17). The body concept is therefore closely connected with Paul's conception of spirit (*pneuma*). In the same way the breath within a person animates, inspires, and unifies that person's body, those who have received Christ's spirit are animated and unified as Christ's body, functioning as the active agents through whom *God works in the world (1 Cor 2:10-16; 3:9; see Mt 10:40-42 and pars.). Here the image of the church as body of Christ naturally connects with the church as God's *temple (1 Cor 3:16-17; 6:16, 19; Eph 2:21), as each image represents the church as the locus of God's presence in the world.

While *baptism marks one's initial incorporation into Christ's body, to participate in the Eucharist is to participate in or commune (*koinōnia*) with the body, represented in the one loaf broken and distributed among the many members (1 Cor 10:16-17). By consuming the same loaf, each individual comes to be composed of the same substance (1 Cor 10:17)—Moule's objection that "*eating* the body is not *being* the body" (87) overlooks that a body is composed of what that body consumes, so that *eating* the body is to *become* the body. Participation in the Lord's Table thus reconstitutes the various individuals as the one people of God, obliging them to live according to the unity of one body, in which there is "neither Jew nor Greek, neither *slave nor free, nor male and female" (Gal 3:28).

As such, the regular practice of Communion carries significant ethical implications, suggesting that one's place within the body is not a static or irrevocable status permanently conferred through baptism but rather a relational status that depends on maintaining the unity of the spirit manifested through *love of neighbor. Those having received the spirit remain in the body of Christ by walking according to the spirit (Rom 8:4-13; see Gal 5:16), while those who "eat the bread or drink the cup in an unworthy manner will be guilty of the body and blood of the *Lord" (1 Cor 11:27). Similarly, those who quench or grieve the spirit (1 Thess 5:19; Eph 4:30) may thereby be cut off from the body (Rom 11:22; see 2 Cor 13:5), having lost connection with the *head (Col 2:19), and participation in the Eucharist while behaving in an unloving manner is to "eat and drink *judgment" against oneself (1 Cor 11:29) and to contaminate or fracture the unified wholeness of the body of Christ (see 1 Cor 1:10-17; 5:6-7, 13; 11:18-19).

See also Body; Church; Head; In Christ; Lord's Supper.

BIBLIOGRAPHY. **E. Best,** *One Body in Christ: A Study in the Relationship of the Church to Christ in the Epistles of the Apostle Paul* (London: SPCK, 1955); **B. Brock,** "Theologizing Inclusion: 1 Corinthians 12 and the Politics of the Body of Christ," *Journal of Religion, Disability & Health* 15, no. 4 (2011): 351-76; **K. Butting,** "Pauline Variations on Genesis 2.24: Speaking of the Body of Christ in the Context of the Discussion of Lifestyles," *JSNT* 23, no. 79 (2001): 79-90; **J. D. G. Dunn,** "'The Body of Christ' in Paul," in *Worship, Theology, and Ministry in the Early Church: Essays in Honor of Ralph P. Martin*, JSNTSup (London: Bloomsbury, 1992), 146-62; **E. E. Ellis,** *Pauline Theology: Ministry and Society* (Grand Rapids, MI: Eerdmans, 1989); **R. Y. K. Fung,** "Ministry, Community, and Spiritual Gifts," *EvQ* 56, no. 1 (1984): 3-20; idem, "Body of Christ," in *DPL*, 76-82; **A. K. Grieb,** "People of God, Body of Christ, Koinonia of Spirit: The Role of Ethical Ecclesiology in Paul's 'Trinitarian' Language," *AThR* 87, no. 2 (2005): 225-52; **R. H. Gundry,** *Sōma in Biblical Theology: with Emphasis on Pauline Anthropology*, SNTSMS 29 (Cambridge: Cambridge University Press, 1976); **J. R. Hollingshead,** *The Household of Caesar and the Body of Christ: A Political Interpretation of the Letters from Paul* (Lanham, MD: University Press of America, 1998); **A. R. Hunt,** *The Inspired Body: Paul, the Corinthians, and Divine Inspiration* (Macon, GA: Mercer University Press, 1996); **J. Jeremias,** *The Eucharistic Words of Jesus*, trans. A. Ehrhardt (Oxford: Blackwell, 1955); **R. Jewett,** *Paul's Anthropological Terms: A Study of Their Use in Conflict Settings*, AGJU 10 (Leiden: Brill, 1971); **E. Käsemann,** *Leib und Leib Christi: eine Untersuchung zur paulinischen Begrifflichkeit von Ernst Käsemann*, BHT (Tübingen: Mohr, 1933); idem, "The Theological Problem Presented by the Motif of the Body of Christ," *Perspectives on Paul* (1971): 102-21; **A. J. Kelly,** "'The Body of Christ: Amen!': The Expanding Incarnation," *TS* 71, no. 4 (2010): 792-816; **S. Kim,** *The Origin of Paul's Gospel* (Tübingen: Mohr, 1981); **M. V. Lee,** *Paul, the Stoics, and the Body of Christ*, SNTSMS 137 (Cambridge: Cambridge University Press, 2006); **S. Liubinskas,** "The Body of Christ in Mission: Paul's Ecclesiology and the Role of the Church in Mission," *Missiology: An International Review* 41, no. 4 (2013): 402-15; **D. B. Martin,** *The Corinthian Body* (New Haven, CT: Yale University Press, 1995); **I. Melniciuc-Puică,** "'The Two Will Become One Flesh': Argumentative Function of Genesis 2:24 in 1 Corinthians 6:16b," *Analele Ştiinţifice ale Universităţii »Alexandru Ioan Cuza« din Iaşi. Teologie Ortodoxă* 21, no. 1 (2016): 7-16; **M. M. Mitchell,** *Paul and the Rhetoric of Reconciliation* (Louisville, KY: Westminster John Knox, 1992); **R. Moses,** "Discerning the Body of Christ: Paul, Poverty, and the Powers," *JSNT* 40, no. 4 (2018): 473-93; **C. F. D. Moule,** *The Origin of Christology* (Cambridge:

Cambridge University Press, 1977); **P. T. O'Brien,** "The Church as a Heavenly and Eschatological Entity," in *The Church in the Bible and the World: An International Study*, ed. D. A. Carson (Grand Rapids, MI: Baker, 1987), 88-119; **G. M. M. Pelser,** "Once More the Body of Christ in Paul," *Neot* 32 (1998): 525-45; **A. C. Perriman,** "'His Body, Which Is the Church. . . ': Coming to Terms with Metaphor," *EvQ* 62, no. 2 (1990): 123-42; idem, "The Head of a Woman: The Meaning of ΚΕΦΑΛΗ in 1 Cor. 11:3," *JTS* 45, no. 2 (1994): 602-22; **J. A. T. Robinson,** *The Body: A Study in Pauline Theology*, SBT 5 (London: SCM, 1952); **B. Wannenwetsch,** "Owning Our Bodies? The Politics of Self-Possession and the Body of Christ (Hobbes, Locke, and Paul)," *Studies in Christian Ethics* 26, no. 1 (2013): 50-65; **A. J. M. Wedderburn,** "The Body of Christ and Related Concepts in I Corinthians," *SJT* 24, no. 1 (1971): 74-96.

J. A. Staples

BONDAGE. *See* SERVANT, SERVICE; SLAVE, SLAVERY; TRIUMPH; WORKS OF THE LAW.

C

CALL, CALLING

The language of calling appears in the letters of Paul to describe what *God has done in the lives of all believers. Though Paul can speak of God calling him in a distinct way to be an *apostle, he affirms that God has called all Christians to be saints and to participate in the *fellowship of Christ. The summons of God is an expression of his sovereignty and *grace. He takes the initiative by calling people into relationship with himself through *Christ and into a life of faithful service as they walk worthy of their calling.

1. The God Who Calls
2. God Calls All Saints
3. God Calls Through the Good News
4. Calling Reframes Ordinary Life
5. Walking Worthy of the Calling
6. Calling and God's Future

1. The God Who Calls.

In Pauline theology, calling is not so much something believers have as it is something God does in their lives (1 Cor 1:9). Calling is so essential to God's activity that Paul can refer to God simply as "the one who called you" (Gal 1:6 NRSV; see 1 Thess 5:24).

God calls people on the basis of God's own sovereign choice and purpose (Rom 8:28-30). One's calling does not depend on one's own works or worthiness (though one is to walk worthy of our calling; see section 5 below). Rather, God calls people "according to [God's] own purpose and grace" (2 Tim 1:9 NRSV; also Gal 1:6).

Seeing the Christian life in terms of calling underscores the authority and initiative of God. Those who know God through Christ are not initiators in this relationship but responders to the initiating, calling God. Christians are to believe and live in response to the God who calls them "into his own *kingdom and *glory" (1 Thess 2:12 NRSV; Messenger and Preece).

2. God Calls All Saints.

Paul introduces himself as one who is "called to be an apostle of Christ Jesus by the will of God" (1 Cor 1:1 NRSV; see Rom 1:1). He understands his apostolic calling as similar to the calling of prophets in the OT (compare Gal 1:15 and Jer 1:5; Fee, 6-11).

Yet Paul does not reserve the language of calling for himself and others who have a distinctive role to play in the *church. Rather, all who accept God's grace through Christ are "called to belong to Jesus Christ" (Rom 1:6 NRSV). First and foremost, the call of God is to a relationship with God through Christ. This is emphasized in believers' calling to be saints, that is, to be people set apart by God for relationship with God and participation in his work in the world (1 Cor 1:2; Fee, 11-14).

Though Christians are called personally by God, their calling is not individualistic. Rather, they are "called to be saints, along with all of those who call upon the name of the Lord Jesus Christ in every region" (1 Cor 1:2). Just as God once called *Israel to be his special people, so Christians share together in a corporate calling embodied in a common life. (God's call to Israel remains intact even as *Gentile believers in Jesus are now numbered among "the called." See 1 Cor 1:24; Rom 11:29; Volf, 17-47).

3. God Calls Through the Good News.

The call of God to *faith in Jesus Christ comes "through the good news" (2 Thess 2:14). This phrase points to the preaching of the *gospel, which summons the hearer to accept God's grace through faith. Though the words being preached have a human source, they are a means by which God calls someone to Christ. The word *calling*, therefore, can identify what others might refer to as the time or experience of conversion (see 1 Cor 7:17-24).

4. Calling Reframes Ordinary Life.
Though God sometimes calls people—Paul is a good example—to make major changes in their lives (Gen 12:1-3), one's calling to God through Christ does not require that one alter the external particulars of one's life. In fact, Paul makes sure the Corinthians understand that they are free, if not even obligated, "to remain in the calling in which they were called" (1 Cor 7:20). The CEB rightly captures the sense of Paul's language here: "Each person should stay in the situation they were in when they were called." Though some commentators refer to this situation itself as a calling, Paul's point is that one's calling by God can be lived out faithfully in whatever situation one finds oneself. If one is married, for example, one should remain married (1 Cor 7:12-17).

Yet, being called by God does not mean one experiences life as one did before one's calling. Instead, one's calling reframes one's lives. If, for example, one was a *slave when God called, then one can remain a slave and find ways to live out one's calling in one's particular situation. But, because of one's divine calling, one can see oneself as a freed person of the Lord, even as actual freed persons see themselves as slaves of Christ (1 Cor 7:21-22; Tucker, 39-94; Volf, 150-72; Fee, 18-21).

5. Walk Worthy of the Calling.
In Ephesians 4:1 Paul urges the recipients of his letter "to walk worthy of the calling with which [they] were called" (similarly, 1 Thess 2:12). God's calling is a summons to a new way of living, one in which believers walk in the "good works" God has planned for them (Eph 2:10).

At times, Paul specifies the behavioral implications of calling. Christians are called to *freedom, not for the sake of pleasing their selfish desires, but in order to serve others in *love (Gal 5:13). They are called to shalom-shaped relationships with brothers and sisters in Christ (Col 3:15). They are called not to impurity but to holy living (1 Thess 4:7). Walking worthy of one's calling means treating others with humility, gentleness, and patience as one seeks to preserve the unity of one's Christian community (Eph 4:1-3).

6. Calling and God's Future.
When talking about calling, Paul usually refers to something that God has done in the past. But the call of God also has a future dimension. Paul tells the Thessalonians that God is calling them "into his own kingdom and glory" (1 Thess 2:12 NRSV). In Ephesians Paul prays that the letter recipients "may know what is the *hope to which [God] has called you" (Eph 1:18 NRSV; see Eph 4:4).

God invites Christians into his glorious future. Yet this future has present implications. Paul urges Timothy to "take hold of the eternal life, to which you were called" (1 Tim 6:12 NRSV). The *fullness of eternal life lies in the future, but Timothy is to grab hold that life in the present.

See also APOSTLE; CONVERSION AND CALL OF PAUL; HOLINESS, SANCTIFICATION; SERVANT, SERVICE.

BIBLIOGRAPHY. **G. D. Fee,** *Offer Yourselves to God: Vocation, Work, and Ministry in Paul's Epistles* (Eugene, OR: Wipf & Stock, 2019); **W. Messenger and G. Preece,** *Calling: A Biblical Perspective* (Cambridge, MA: Theology of Work Project, 2013); **D. J. Schuurman,** *Vocation: Discerning Our Callings in Life* (Grand Rapids, MI: Eerdmans, 2004); **J. B. Tucker,** *Remain in Your Calling: Paul and the Continuation of Social Identities in 1 Corinthians* (Eugene, OR: Wipf & Stock, 2011); **M. Volf,** *Work in the Spirit: Toward a Theology of Work* (Eugene, OR: Wipf & Stock, 2001).

M. D. Roberts

CANON OF PAUL'S LETTERS

By the end of the fourth century (AD 397), the *church recognized a list of fourteen letters of Paul, the traditional thirteen plus Hebrews. Evidence for a collection (canon) can be discussed under three categories: early lists, evidence from early writers (quotations and allusions indicating the writer was aware of multiple letters of Paul), and manuscript evidence (demonstrations of collected letters). Each type of evidence has strengths and weaknesses; nonetheless, the evidence makes a compelling case for a collection at least by the third century. Scholars are left to conjecture the process between Paul dispatching his letters and those collections.

1. Early Lists
2. Evidence from Early Writers
3. The Manuscript Evidence
4. Theories About Collecting the Letters

1. Early Lists.
From the second Christian century, there are one—possibly two—sources providing lists of Paul's letters. First, Marcion (writing ca. 130–140) is said by his opponents to hold to a Pauline canon of ten letters: Galatians, 1–2 Corinthians, Romans, 1–2 Thessalonians, Laodiceans (seemingly Ephesians), Colossians, Philippians, and Philemon. U. Schmid argues Marcion inherited a ten-letter collection,

but E. Scherbenske counters that Marcion instead "corrected" the texts to fit his hermeneutic (94-112). Given Marcion's demonstrated willingness to edit Scripture, one cannot be confident what his list means. Are these all the letters he knew or only those he approved? The second document, the Muratorian Fragment, is a canon list, possibly from the second century. This list of twenty-two NT books in a Latin manuscript from the seventh century is thought to be a translation from a Greek original. The value of the list depends on when the (hypothetical) Greek exemplar was composed. Traditionally, scholars dated the composition circa 170, because, among other reasons, it seems to refer to Pius I (140–155) as "recent," thus suggesting a collection of Paul's letters in Rome by the mid-second century, listing the thirteen Pauline letters but not Hebrews. A. C. Sundberg Jr. argued for a fourth-century composition in the eastern empire. B. Metzger says Ferguson "sufficiently refuted (not to say demolished)" Sundberg's arguments (193). G. Hahneman considered Metzger's rebuttal to be "brief and dismissive" (3), arguing, for example, that the Fragment contains a Latinized form of a nickname for the Montanists (211-12), a point Ferguson (1993) vigorously disputes (see Hill). More recently, C. Rothschild suggests the Fragment is a fourth- or even ninth-century Roman fake, but C. Guignard aggressively disagrees.

2. Evidence from Early Writers.
The author of 2 Peter refers to "all letters" of Paul (2 Pet 3:16). This passage is largely dismissed as second-century pseudepigrapha. The main reason often seems to be that since there could not have been a collection of Paul's letters in Rome in the early 60s, then this letter must be from the second century, when such collections did exist. On the other hand, if the letter is Petrine, then it becomes the earliest known reference to some collection of Paul's letters (Richards 1998, 160-62). "All letters" does not speak to the size or contents of the collection. Clement, an early bishop of Rome (ca. 96), is the only other first-century witness to Paul's letters. R. P. Martin thinks that Clement "at best knows only four Pauline letters" (2:277). R. M. Grant sees in Clement references to Romans, 1 Corinthians, Galatians, Ephesians, and Philippians (81-83), and D. Hagner (135) sees most of Paul's letters. Absence of evidence, though, is not evidence of absence. Clement may well have known more letters than he referenced. One is left with Clement's suggestion of the existence of a collection, but not a suggestion as to its contents.

Other witnesses to a collection before circa 200 include Ignatius, who refers or alludes to all but 2 Thessalonians, 1–2 Timothy, Titus, and Philemon, while Polycarp alludes to all but Colossians, 1 Thessalonians, Titus, and Philemon. Tatian accepts Titus but rejects 1–2 Timothy (so Jerome, PL 26.556). Neither Irenaeus nor Clement of Alexandria mention Philemon, but it is not clear whether they rejected it. Tertullian and Origen, both in North Africa, seem to agree with subsequent church fathers on a collection with thirteen letters and Hebrews. Origen is perhaps more noteworthy since "Origen's typical practice is to acknowledge doubts regarding authorship where they are present" (Thomas, 603). Thus, even though Papias, Barnabas, and Justin show no evidence of familiarity with Paul's writings (Grant, 62-107), it is still possible to maintain that the second century demonstrates a more dispersed familiarity with Paul's letters. In summary, early references show awareness of multiple letters but cannot speak to the size of the Pauline canon.

3. The Manuscript Evidence.
Aside from the five small fragments of P30 (recently dated 175–225), the earliest extant copy of any of Paul's letters is the papyrus codex P46, often dated about 200. Although damaged, the codex has (in sequence) Romans, Hebrews, 1–2 Corinthians, Ephesians, Galatians, Colossians, and 1 Thessalonians (through 1 Thess 5:28). The unusual location of Hebrews and the reversal of Ephesians and Galatians can be seen clearly. F. Kenyon, the original examiner of the manuscript, estimated there was sufficient space for only 2 Thessalonians and 1 Timothy, leaving Kenyon (vii) to assert P46 did not originally contain the Pastorals but rather left the final four leaves blank. Kenyon's conclusions are often cited; for example, Marshall merely comments, "As is well-known, P46 lacks the *Pastoral Epistles" (10). Kenyon's conclusions have since been challenged. Ancient scribes typically calculated the lines (stichometry) needed for a book and then the required number of pages. If the scribe had not planned to include the Pastorals, then from his stichometry, he was able to calculate that he had plenty of blank pages. Yet, about midway the scribe of P46 began increasingly to compress his writing. There is debate over how much the scribe was compressing and whether it would have been sufficient for the Pastorals. D. Wallace, executive director of the Center for the Study of New Testament Manuscripts, has argued in blogs and seminars that the compression suggests the scribe realized partway that there would

not be room for the pastorals, but E. Ebojo counters the compression does not necessarily imply that the scribe was trying to include the Pastorals (204-35). At the least, it seems unwise to cite P46 as evidence of a Pauline collection without the Pastorals. As to the other letters, D. Trobisch makes a compelling argument that P46 arranged the "letters of Paul" strictly by length and so explains the placement of Hebrews after Romans and the inversion of Galatians and Ephesians (16-17).

The five major uncial manuscripts present a consistent sequence of Paul's letters (with two minor variations). Codex Sinaiticus (א 01, fourth century), Codex Alexandrinus (A 02, fifth century), and Codex Ephraemi Rescriptus (C 04, fifth century) are all thought to be independent of one another; yet all present the same sequencing: Romans, 1–2 Corinthians, Galatians, Ephesians, Philippians, Colossians, 1–2 Thessalonians, Hebrews, 1–2 Timothy, Titus, and Philemon. Codex Claromontanus (D^p 06, sixth century) nearly follows the traditional sequence of Pauline letters, with Hebrews at the end of the Corpus Paulinum, but Colossians and Philippians are reversed in sequence, perhaps influenced by the Latin tradition, which is not as consistent in the placement of Colossians. Trobisch suggests Hebrews was added "later" (13), but this is too much conjecture (Richards 2021). Last, in Codex Vaticanus (B 03, fourth century), Hebrews follows 2 Thessalonians (as in the other manuscripts of the fourth and fifth centuries), but the original manuscript breaks off at Hebrews 9:14. The remaining text is a minuscule, from when the original codex was repaired in the fifteenth century. Vaticanus shows at least two peculiarities. First, when repaired, the Pastorals and Philemon were not included. Omitting the Pastorals is, in the minds of many Vaticanus scholars (e.g., Grenz), accidental and not indicative of the fourth-century text. Second, the fourth-century section numbers in Vaticanus imply Hebrews was placed between Galatians and Ephesians in an earlier exemplar.

Two conclusions seem justified from the manuscript evidence. First, all nonfragmentary manuscripts of Paul's letters show a complete collection (thirteen letters) at least as early as the mid-300s. Second, the sequence of the thirteen letters is nearly fixed even in our earliest manuscripts, with only two variations: Ephesians-Galatians in P46 and Colossians-Philippians in Claromontanus (Trobisch, 22). The other evidence provides first- and second-century knowledge of multiple letters of Paul, and thus a potential collection, but does not indicate the size of the canon. Marcion appears to not have known (or to have excluded) the Pastorals. The impact of the Muratorian Fragment depends entirely on the dating. If the earlier date is accurate, then it provides evidence of a thirteen-letter collection at least in Rome before the end of the second century. The question becomes, When and how did letters dispatched to at least nine locations come to be a collection?

4. Theories About Collecting the Letters. Paul encourages the church in Colossae (Col 4:16) to acquire a copy of his letter to Laodicea. Polycarp had copies of Ignatius's letters and sent copies to Philippi (Pol. *Phil.* 13.2). P. N. Harrison suggested that when a church treasured its own letter(s) of Paul, it began to collect copies of other letters (Harrison, 236), and so regional collections of Paul's letters arose, perhaps in the late first or early second century, leading to fuller collections (P46?) and eventually to the complete collections represented in the majuscules of the fourth and fifth century. S. E. Porter labels this the "gradual collection or Zahn-Harnack theory" (99-103). Despite the attractive logic, manuscripts provide no evidence for partial collections. This approach fell out of vogue, and scholars began to build on an older theory by Goodspeed, who suggested that after the publication of Acts, someone decided to collect from the various churches copies of the dispatched letters of Paul (1927). E. J. Goodspeed then suggested this disciple wrote Ephesians as the preface to the collected letters (1933). J. Knox, a student of Goodspeed, identified the disciple as Onesimus. The Goodspeed-Knox theory, also called the "lapsed interest theory," has not prevailed, although the underlying approach remained attractive. As H. Y. Gamble notes, subsequent theories retained the idea of "an occasion, an agent and a motive" (39). C. F. D. Moule and others have suggested clever theories that all share that an individual (or an individual school) took the initiative to collect the dispatched letters of Paul (see Porter, 99-103).

Since 1991, Richards noted *collection* often suggests an active process, that someone collected the letters. Such a view is often built on two presuppositions. First, it assumes the published set arose from making copies of the dispatched letters. Second, it assumes no collection existed until someone desired to publish the letters. As a corollary, Paul's letters would need to be esteemed (by someone) before a collection could exist. Richards distinguishes collection from publication, suggesting the original collection was Paul's personal set.

Ancient letter writers commonly retained copies of their *letters. Gamble notes, "In antiquity, collected editions of letters were nearly always produced by their author or at their author's behest, often from copies belonging to the author" (101; see also Tyrrell and Purser, 59). Suetonius knew three sets of Caesar's letters, and the *Epistulae ad senatum* seem to have been published by Caesar himself: "Some letters of his to the senate are also preserved, and he seems to have been the first to reduce such documents to pages and the form of a note-book" (Suetonius, *Jul.* 56.6 LCL). There is evidence of letter writers retaining personal copies among the Roman aristocratic elite. Cicero mentions dashing off a letter but keeping a copy in his notebook (*Fam.* 9.26.1). A letter he had sent to Caesar had become so wet as to be unreadable, so he sent another copy (*Quint. fratr.* 2.12.4). The practice has earlier roots. According to Plutarch, Alexander the Great in a fit of rage burned his secretary's tent. He regretted losing the documents and required his officials to send back copies to replace the lost ones (Plutarch, *Eumenes* 2.2-3). The uncovered archive of Petaus (ca. AD 185), a village scribe in Greco-Roman Egypt, had sixty-four copies and drafts of letters he had dispatched; see other examples of making (P.Mich. 855), retaining (Tab. Vindol. 2.299), sending (P.Zen. 43), or using a copy (P.Tebt. 32) of a letter. Across the empire, those who troubled to write significant letters retained their own copies. Likely Paul followed custom and retained copies.

Sometimes, ancients mentioned copies of letters were made into *membranae* (Latin), that is, parchment notebooks. Imprisoned in Rome, Paul requests (2 Tim 4:13) his books and *membranas* (Greek), using what appears to be a Hellenized form of the Latin (see Roberts and Skeat, 30). Perhaps the first collection of Paul's letters was his personal set in Rome, suggesting why the earliest references are from Rome (Richards 1998). Whether as early as the first century or later in the second, the evidence suggests Paul's letters from the onset were distributed as a collection of thirteen letters.

See also Letters, Letter Forms; Textual Criticism.

BIBLIOGRAPHY. **E. Ebojo,** "A Scribe and His Manuscript: An Investigation into the Scribal Habits of Papyrus 46" (unpublished thesis, University of Birmingham, 2014); **E. Ferguson,** "Canon Muratori: Date and Provenance," *StPatr* 17, no. 2 (1982): 677-83; idem, "Review of Hahneman, Geoffrey Mark, *The Muratorian Fragment and the Development of the Canon*," *JTS* 44 (1993): 691-97; **H. Gamble,** *The New Testament Canon: Its Making and Meaning* (Philadelphia: Fortress, 1986); **E. Goodspeed,** *New Solutions to New Testament Problems* (Chicago: University of Chicago Press, 1927); idem, *The Story of the New Testament* (Chicago: University of Chicago Press, 1933); **R. M. Grant,** *Heresy and Criticism: The Search for Authenticity in Early Christian Literature* (Louisville: Westminster John Knox, 1993); idem, *The Formation of the New Testament* (New York: Harper & Row, 1965); **J. Grenz,** "The Scribes and Correctors of Codex Vaticanus," PhD diss., University of Cambridge, 2020; **C. Guignard,** "The Muratorian Fragment as a Late Antique Fake? An Answer to C. K. Rothschild," *Théologie et souffrance* 93 (2019): 73-90; **D. A. Hagner,** *The Use of the Old and New Testaments in Clement of Rome*, SNTSMS 34 (Leiden: Brill, 1973); **G. M. Hahneman,** *The Muratorian Fragment and the Development of the Canon* (Oxford: Clarendon, 1992); **P. Harrison,** *Polycarp's Two Epistles to the Philippians* (Cambridge: Cambridge University Press, 1936); **C. E. Hill,** "The Debate over the Muratorian Fragment and the Development of the Canon," *WTJ* 57 (1995): 437-52; **F. G. Kenyon,** *The Chester Beatty Biblical Papyri Descriptions and Texts of the Twelve Manuscripts on Papyrus of the Greek Bible: Fasciculus III; Pauline Epistles and Revelation* (London: Emery Walker, 1934); **I. H. Marshall,** *The Pastoral Epistles*, ICC (Edinburgh: T&T Clark, 2004); **R. P. Martin,** *New Testament Foundations*, rev. ed., 2 vols. (Eugene, OR: Wipf & Stock, 2000); **L. M. McDonald,** *The Biblical Canon: Its Origin, Transmission, and Authority* (Peabody, MA: Hendrickson, 2007); **B. M. Metzger,** *Canon of the New Testament* (Oxford: Clarendon, 1987); **C. Moule,** *The Birth of the New Testament*, 3rd ed. (London: A&C Black, 1962); **A. G. Patzia,** *The Making of the New Testament: Origin, Collection, Text and Canon*, 2nd ed. (Downers Grove, IL: InterVarsity Press, 2011); **S. E. Porter,** "When and How Was the Pauline Canon Compiled? An Assessment of Theories," in *The Pauline Canon*, ed. S. E. Porter (Leiden: Brill, 2004), 95-127; **E. R. Richards,** "The Codex and the Early Collection of Paul's Letters," *BBR* 8 (1998): 151-66; idem, "The Pauline Canon," in *Canon Formation: Tracing the Role of Sub-collections in the Biblical Canon*, ed. W. E. Glenny and D. R. Lockett (London: Bloomsbury T&T Clark, 2021); **C. H. Roberts and T. C. Skeat,** *The Birth of the Codex* (London: Oxford University Press, 1983); **C. K. Rothschild,** "The Muratorian Fragment as Roman Fake," *NovT* 60 (2018): 55-82; **E. Scherbenske,** *Canonizing Paul: Ancient Editorial Practice and the Corpus Paulinum*

(Oxford: Oxford University Press, 2013); **U. Schmid,** *Marcion und sein Apostolos: Rekonstruktion und historische Einordnung der marcionitischen Paulusbriefausgabe*, ANTF 25 (Berlin: de Gruyter, 1995); **A. C. Sundberg Jr.,** "Canon Muratori: A Fourth Century List," *HTR* 66 (1973): 1-41; **M. J. Thomas,** "Origen on Paul's Authorship of Hebrews," *NTS* 65 (2019): 598-609; **D. Trobisch,** *Paul's Letter Collection: Tracing the Origins* (Minneapolis: Fortress, 1994); **R. Tyrrell and L. Purser,** *The Correspondence of M. Tullius Cicero*, 7 vols. (London: Longmans, Green, 1901–1933).

E. R. Richards

CAPTIVE. *See* Prison, Prisoner; Triumph.

CELIBACY. *See* Marriage and Divorce, Adultery and Incest; Sexuality, Sexual Ethics; Singleness and Celibacy.

CENTER OF PAUL'S THEOLOGY. *See* Hermeneutics/Interpreting Paul; Interpretation: Modern European; Justification.

CHARISMATA. *See* Gifts of the Spirit; Prophecy, Prophesying; Tongues.

CHILDREN OF GOD. *See* Adoption; Kinship Language in Paul; Son of God.

CHRIST, MESSIAH

There are close to 270 references to *Christos* in the canonical letters of Paul. English versions of the Bible usually translate the term as either "Christ" (emphasis on the name) or "Messiah" (emphasis on the title). Paul can refer to Jesus as simply "Christ" or "Jesus Christ" or "Christ Jesus." Both the frequency of occurrences and the flexibility of usage have perplexed interpreters, who have wondered whether *Christos* retains its titular sense of "Messiah" or is simply now a proper *name. Recent scholarship has largely confirmed the titular sense and has demonstrated that Paul's *Christology is in large part, though not exclusively, indebted to his interpretation of messianic texts and oracles in the Scriptures of *Israel. This article will engage in a selective but representative examination of scholarship and set forth an argument primarily (though not exclusively) with respect to Paul's letter to the Romans that demonstrates how Jesus' messiahship is critical to significant Pauline theological arguments and themes.

1. Messiah as Name or Title in Paul's Letters?
2. Paul's Messianic Christology

1. Messiah as Name or Title in Paul's Letters?

1.1. Meaning and Context of Term. The biblical origins of the word *Christos* are found in Israel's Scriptures, where it is associated with the act of anointing or smearing with oil. In ancient Near Eastern culture, anointing a person or an object with oil was understood as marking out said person or object for a sacred task or use. Within the OT, this anointing with oil is usually associated with the consecration of kings (1 Sam 2:10; 24:7, 11; Ps 2:2) and priests (e.g., Lev 4:5, 16; 6:15; see Novenson 2017). The OT often speaks of the Messiah as "the Anointed *of the *Lord*," thereby indicating that the anointed king is subordinated to and works in congruence with Yahweh (e.g., 1 Sam 16:6; 24:7, 11; 26:9, 11, 16, 23; Lam 4:20). The Anointed of the Lord, not unlike kings and rulers in the ancient Near Eastern and Greco-Roman cultures, is the elected agent of the gods or Yahweh (portions of what follows are adapted from Jipp 2015; 2020).

First and Second Samuel narrate the beginnings of Israel's monarchy, and here Saul and then David are presented as those consecrated and thereby established as Yahweh's anointed (see 1 Sam 16:1-13; 2 Sam 2:1-7; 5:1-5; Abernethy and Goswell, 49-66). So too Solomon is anointed as king over Israel, and this is understood as designating him as Yahweh's earthly agent (1 Kings 1:28-40; see also 2 Kings 9:1-13; 11:4-20; Johnson, 14-15). The Davidic king was gifted with a covenantal relationship with *God such that he was referred to as God's *Son, and this further marked him out as one invested with God's authority to rule (2 Sam 7:12-14; Ps 2:6-9; 89:26-28). Further marking out the Davidic king as sacred and ruling on God's behalf is the gift of God's Spirit to the king (1 Sam 16:13; Pss. Sol. 17.22, 27; 18.5-7). Messianic *prophecies sometimes forecasted a coming messianic ruler, whose reign would be marked by the powerful workings of God's Spirit (e.g., Is 11:1-5). The Anointed of the Lord was expected to shepherd God's people with justice and *righteousness, protect them from their enemies, and establish God's people in *peace and prosperity (e.g., Ps 72:1-16; 132:15; Is 11:1-10; Ezek 34; see Abernethy and Goswell, 174-76).

1.2. Christos as Name or Insignificant Title? Despite the abundant references to Jesus of Nazareth as *Messiah*, many interpreters have not seen Paul's favorite title for Jesus as holding much interest or significance. Thus, Jesus' Davidic ancestry and messianic kingship has rarely been emphasized as a defining feature of Paul's Christology. There are a variety of reasons for this. The frequency with which

Messiah occurs in Paul's letters has led some to see *Christos* as a proper name for Paul, and one that had lost the connotations of "the Lord's Anointed" (Dahl; Bultmann; Zetterholm). When Paul speaks of "Christ," it is true that his statements are entirely understandable if simply referring to a proper name (Hengel). Some have assumed that the Jewish designation *Messiah* would have been of no interest or even unintelligible to non-Jewish readers of Paul's letters. Nowhere do we find Paul explicitly saying "Jesus is the Messiah," as we do in other NT writings (e.g., Jn 20:30-31; Acts 17:2-3).

One culprit here is W. Bousset's *Kyrios Christos,* which set forth a highly influential argument for the development of early Christology. Bousset argued for a division between Palestinian and Hellenistic Christianity. The latter's preferred title for Jesus was *Lord,* and the community had little interest in Jesus' Davidic ancestry (see Bousset; Heitmüller). Instead, so the argument goes, Jesus' Davidic-messianic descent was only intelligible and interesting to Jewish Christians for whom a "nationalist" Messiah was of importance (e.g., Mt 9:27; Lk 1:27, 31-35; Rev 5:5; see Hahn, 240-46). More recently, it is often held that Paul assumes Jesus is the Davidic Messiah, but the notion plays only a small role in the development of Paul's Christology or theological argumentation (see Chester).

1.3. The Importance of Jesus' Messianic Identity for Paul's Christology in Select Recent Scholarship. But recently there have been numerous adjustments and even whole-scale attacks on those arguments that dispense with Jesus' messianic identity for Paul's Christology. N. T. Wright has been one of the most vocal examples of those pointing to places in Paul's letters where his argument depends on Jesus' messianic identity. Wright, among others, has emphasized the *inclusio* in Romans that begins by defining the *gospel with respect to Jesus the Davidic Messiah (Rom 1:1-4) and concludes with Jesus' messiahship (Rom 15:7-12; Wright, 818-21; Whitsett; Jipp 2009, 258-59). Many have shown that Paul's interpretation of Jesus' *resurrection and enthronement takes place against the framework of God's promises to David to raise up a son and seat him on God's throne to rule over his people (2 Sam 7:12-14; Ps 2:7; 89:26-27; see Novakovic; Juel). A. Collins argues that Paul's initial proclamation of the gospel to his churches clearly included the claim that Jesus was the Messiah of Israel (Collins and Collins, 122). R. Hays has made the influential observation that Paul's depiction of Christ praying the psalms in Romans 15:1-12 only works on the assumption that Jesus is the descendent of the Davidic Messiah of the Psalter (Hays). Paul thus appropriates the Psalms as foreshadowing the life and work of the Messiah (Rom 11:9 [Ps 68:23-24]; Rom 15:3 [Ps 68:10]; Rom 15:9 [Ps 18:49]; Rom 15:11 [Ps 117:1]; 2 Cor 4:13-14 [Ps 115:1]). D. Campbell has written an important essay showing that Romans 8 operates with an underlying narrative of "ascent through resurrection to glorification and heavenly enthronement," and that Paul has been deeply influenced here by Israelite royal ideology, particularly Psalm 89 (Campbell, 116). Others have also noted that Romans 8 is infused with messianic exegesis. H. G. Jacob, for example, shows this to be the case with Paul's claims about the messianic Son of God in Romans 8:29, 34 (Jacob, 177-233). W. Horbury's *Jewish Messianism and the Cult of Christ* shows how the worship of Christ, particularly the granting of acclamations, *hymns, and honorifics, has its origins in Jewish messianism and Greco-Roman depictions of kingship (Horbury). A similar argument comes from L. Hurtado, who also sees Paul's Christology as a distinctive reflection of Jewish messianism and notes that the exalted Jesus is portrayed as worthy, along with God, of receiving worship (Hurtado 2016). Somewhat surprisingly, confirmation of the importance of Jesus' messiahship for Paul has come from many Continental philosophers, who have argued for a vision of Paul's messianism as setting forth a politics of sovereignty that takes its starting point from a crucified Messiah (see Taubes; Agamben).

1.4. Christos as Honorific or Name? A critical source for Paul's Christology is Jewish messianic and Greco-Roman traditions of the good king (Jipp 2015; also J. Smith). One of the most important voices here is that of M. Novenson, who has conclusively demonstrated that Paul's uses of *Christos* do everything one would expect of an honorific in antiquity (Novenson 2012). Along the lines of Seleucus *the Victor*, Judah *Maccabee*, or Alexander *the Great,* so Jesus' honorific is *Christ.* Honorific designations can identify an individual apart from their proper name or can be used in combination with the person's name. Honorifics are found in abundance among kings and rulers, and often signify the individual's identity as a military hero, great benefactor, or wise ruler (Novenson 2012, 64-97). Novenson notes that Paul's usage of "Jesus Christ," "Christ Jesus," and "Christ" conforms to conventions of ancient honorifics (138). Thus, there are no good reasons to claim "Christ" is a name that has lost its meaning of Messiah. Novenson has shown that Paul's Christ language is Messiah language because it "could be used meaningfully . . . because it was deployed in the context of a linguistic community whose members shared a stock of common linguistic resources" (47). Thus, Paul is one example among other Second Temple Jews who used the honorific *Christos* in tandem with scriptural Messiah language to speak about a Jewish Messiah. Furthermore, if A. Collins is right that Paul's initial proclamation of the gospel to his churches included the claim that Jesus was the Messiah (in other words, the churches were already convinced Jesus was the Messiah), then we should not expect Paul's messianic Christology to conform to what we find in the Synoptic Gospels, John's Gospel, or Acts (Novenson 2012, 103).

2. Paul's Messianic Christology.

Paul uses the honorific *Christos* to speak of Jesus of Nazareth as God's anointed messianic ruler as it pertains to Paul's understanding of the specific narrative of Christ—centering primarily on his death, resurrection and enthronement, and the renewed world as his cosmic inheritance. Paul consistently interprets this particular narrative of Jesus the Messiah through the use of messianic honorifics (e.g., "Christ," "Son of God," "Lord"), the application of messianic Scriptures and Jewish traditions, and activating royal motifs and scenarios.

2.1. The Death of the Messiah. The death of the Messiah was a traditional component of the early Christian *kerygma* (also 1 Cor 11:23-26; 15:3-5; Gal 3:1; see Dodd). Paul repeatedly uses the title *Christos* when he speaks of Jesus' death and resurrection (e.g., Rom 5:5-6, 8; 14:9, 15; 1 Cor 5:7; 8:11; 15:20; Gal 2:21; 3:13). L. Hurtado states what others have also noted, namely, that this "seems to reflect an emphasis on Jesus' death and resurrection in particular as *messianic* acts or events—an emphasis that likely originated in circles of Aramaic-speaking and Greek-speaking Jews and was then echoed and developed by Paul" (Hurtado 2016, 111; see also 2003, 100-101). Paul puts together *Messiah* and *crucifixion* in ways that are surprising and serve to make the point that the Jewish Messiah's identity is inextricably connected to his death on the *cross. So 1 Corinthians 1:23: "We proclaim a crucified Messiah—a *stumbling block for the Jews and foolishness for the *Gentiles." Again, in 1 Corinthians 2:2 Paul reminds the Corinthians that his *kerygma* was simply "Jesus the Messiah and this one crucified." As noted earlier, Hays, among others, has shown how Paul used the Psalter as a means of interpreting the *suffering, death, and resurrection of Jesus the singular Davidic Messiah (see 1.3 above). In this, Paul is in company with many other early Christian readings of the Psalter (e.g., Mk 15:16-32; Lk 24:24-27, 44-49; Acts 2:22-36; Heb 1:5-13). Paul uses the depiction of the suffering, righteous king from the Davidic psalms to make sense of God's resurrection of Messiah Jesus from the dead (e.g., Ps 44:22 in Rom 8:36; Ps 68:10 in Rom 15:3; Ps 68:23 in Rom 11:9-10; Ps 115:1 in 2 Cor 4:13; Ps 2:1-3 in Eph 1:20–2:3).

To give just one extended example: In Romans 15:1-12, Paul depicts Christ as the messianic king who speaks two Davidic psalms. To validate his claim that the church in Rome should look out for the interest of their neighbors, Paul writes: "for even the Christ [*ho Christos*] did not please himself, but as it has been written, 'the insults of those insulting you have fallen upon me'" (Rom 15:3). Jesus is here speaking the language of David's royal psalm in Psalm 69:9 (68:10 LXX). So also in Romans 15:9, the speaker of the Davidic Psalm 18—"I will confess you among the Gentiles, and I will praise your name" (Ps 18:50 [17:50 LXX])—is "the Christ" of the preceding verses (Rom 15:7-8). The reader should not be surprised to see Paul identify "the Christ" with the anointed Messiah of the Psalter, given that Romans begins with identifying Christ Jesus as God's "son . . . who was born from the seed of David according to the *flesh" (Rom 1:3). The epistle concludes by marking him out, with the language of Isaiah 11:10, as "the root of Jesse and the one who has been raised up to rule over the Gentiles" (Rom 15:12). Paul describes here a ruler who is "the Christ" (Rom 15:3, 7-8), a speaker of the psalms of David (Rom 15:3, 9), and one who is the son of Jesse (Rom 15:12). He is the one who rules over the nations (Rom 15:7-12). As such there are excellent reasons for viewing Paul as characterizing Christ as Israel's singular messianic king in Romans 13:8–15:13 (Horbury, 142-43). Throughout this section of Romans, Paul draws together the depiction of the suffering, righteous king of the Psalter with Jesus' other-regard leading to his crucifixion in order to advance the claim that "we who are *strong ought to bear the weakness of the weak and to not please ourselves [*mē heautois areskein*]. Let each of us please our neighbor [*hekastos ēmōn tō plēsion aresketō*] for the good of building up the neighbor" (Rom 15:1-2). The Messiah's primary activity is seen in Romans 15:3: "even the Christ did not please himself" (*kai gar ho Christos heautō ēresen*).

2.2. The Resurrection and Exaltation of the Messiah. Paul interprets God's resurrection of Jesus from the dead as the act whereby God vindicated Jesus of Nazareth as his anointed Messiah, positioned him to a place of powerful rule over his people and the cosmos, and enacted his defeat and dethroning of *Satan and his powers (e.g., Rom 1:4; 1 Cor 15:43-45; Eph 1:20–2:6). As the resurrected and enthroned Messiah, his establishment to a place of cosmic rule is the event that demonstrates him to be both Lord and Messiah (e.g., Phil 2:9-11). Paul's frequent application of Psalm 110:1 implies that the risen Jesus is currently sitting in a position of power in heaven as he reigns "until all enemies are put under his feet" (e.g., Rom 8:34; 1 Cor 15:25-28; Eph 1:20-23; Col 2:14-15). He is, therefore, the judge of heaven and earth and all people (2 Cor 5:9-10).

In 2 Timothy 2, Paul (or a later Pauline follower) reminds Timothy of the gospel and its saving implications: "Remember Messiah Jesus, raised from the dead, from the seed of David, according to my gospel" (2 Tim 2:8). Paul's understanding of the Davidic Messiah's suffering, death, and resurrection provides the ground for his claims that those who share in the suffering of the Messiah can also have the expectation that they will reign together with the resurrected Messiah (Marossy, 90-99). "The saying is trustworthy: For if we die together with him, we will also live with him; if we endure, we will also reign together with him" (2 Tim 2:11-12).

Paul sets out the messianic significance of Christ's resurrection most clearly in Romans 1:4. There Paul declares that God's Son is "installed" (*tou opisthentos*) as "Son of God in power." The depiction of Jesus as "appointed" as "the Son of God" evokes Israel's royal enthronement language, particularly Psalm 2:7: "I will tell of the decree of the Lord: He said to me, 'You are my son; today I have begotten you'" (Whitsett, 676). God's resurrection of his son from the dead is the means by which he installs his "Son-of-God-in-power" in a position of rule. Jesus' installation as God's Son places him in a position of heavenly rule now marked by divine power. Paul frequently speaks of power as an attribute of God that is on display particularly in God's act of raising Jesus from the dead (1 Cor 6:14; 15:24, 43; 2 Cor 13:4; Eph 1:19-20; Phil 3:10, 21). The Son of God's resurrection and installation to a place of powerful rule is related to "the Spirit of *holiness" now marking his new resurrection existence. This is similar to Paul's claim in 1 Corinthians 15:44-45, where he argues that Christ's resurrection marks him out as a "life-giving Spirit." Just as God elected his anointed king and consecrated him with oil and the Spirit, so the Son of God is enthroned through God's resurrecting him from the dead by the life-giving Spirit (Kirk, 42-43). Paul also describes "Messiah Jesus" here as "our Lord" (Rom 1:4). Paul's claim that the Davidic Messiah is "Lord" and associated with God is likely influenced by Psalm 109:1 LXX—"The Lord said to my lord [*Eipen ho kyrios tō kyriō mou*], 'Sit at my right hand until I make your enemies a footstool under your feet'" (Eskola, 247-48). In Romans 8:33-34, Paul uses the language of Psalm 109 LXX to speak of the enthroned Son as seated at God's right hand and interceding for his people (Rom 8:33-34). Paul's understanding of the Messiah's resurrection and enthronement to lordship is indicated by the association he makes elsewhere between Jesus' resurrection, his divine lordship, and his judicial powers (Rom 2:16; 8:33-34; 10:5-13; 14:8-12; Bates, 94).

2.3. The Messiah's Inheritance. Israel's Scriptures contain promises that the messianic king will rule with peace and justice over the Gentile nations. Some of the poetic seams in the Pentateuch anticipate a coming ruler from the tribe of Judah, "the expectation of the nations" (Gen 49:8-12), and one "who will rule over many nations, whose *kingdom will be exalted above God, and his kingdom will be increased" (Num 24:7). Balaam further prophesies that the non-Jewish nations will be the king's "inheritance" (Num 24:17-18; also Num 23:21). It is well known that the Psalter also contains numerous royal hymns that speak of a Davidic king's righteous reign over the earth. Here too the Gentile nations will come and worship Yahweh's designated ruler (e.g., Ps 72:1-18; 89:1-28). God even promises his enthroned king, the Son of God, the nations as his inheritance (Ps 2:6-8). Isaiah also looks forward to a time when the Davidic king will rule the nations with justice (Is 11:1-15).

Romans contains a messianic *inclusio* (Rom 1:3-4; 15:7-12), as noted above, but it is also clear that these verses indicate how Paul viewed his own apostolic task as "bringing gentiles to the worship of the true god" through "his proclamation of Jesus as the scion of David's house" (Fredriksen, 136-37). The echo of Psalm 2:7-8 in Romans 1:3-4, where God promises his Anointed that he will give him the nations as his inheritance, shows that Paul conceptualizes his apostolic task as procuring the inheritance of the Messiah as he secures "the obedience of faith among all the nations" (Rom 1:5). This phrase alludes to Genesis 49:8-12, an oracle that looks forward to a ruler from the tribe of Judah who will receive "the obedience of the nations" (Gen 49:10 MT; cf. Num 24:17-19; Is 11:10). The LXX reading has the phrase "he is the expectation of the nations [*prosdokia ethnōn*]" (see Garlington). Thus, Paul situates his ministry within the larger messianic framework to procure "the obedience of *faith among the nations" (Rom 1:5). This is confirmed when we look at the catena of scriptural quotations in Romans 15:9-12, texts that celebrated the risen Lord's entrance into his messianic inheritance as he rules over the nations (note that all of the quotations in Rom 15:9-12 share the language of *ta ethnē*).

Paul also speaks of the Messiah's eschatological inheritance in Romans 8, where the Messiah and his people reign in the renewed cosmos. The restoration of the entire world will correspond to humanity's eschatological adoptive sonship (Rom 8:19-23). Paul had earlier marked out *Abraham *and his seed* (*ē tō spermati autou*) as receiving the promise of the entire world as an inheritance (*to klēronomon auton einai kosmou*, Rom 4:13). Paul has interpreted the patriarchal promises to Abraham and his seed in Genesis as the expectation that they will inherit and rule the entire world (see Jacob, 213-14). But this inheritance to Abraham and his seed only takes place through God's "giving life to the dead" (Rom 4:17), and it is precisely God's resurrection of Jesus and royal enthronement to a place of cosmic rule that enables Abraham's seed, the Messiah, to inherit the cosmos. Thus, Paul's interpretation of the Abrahamic promises in Genesis is connected to his eschatological expectation for a renewed world over which the Messiah reigns in Romans 8:18-39. Here Paul expects the renewed *creation to be marked by the undoing of the creation curses (Gen 3:17-19). This renewed cosmos will instead be marked by *glory (Rom 8:18, 21), *freedom (Rom 8:21), incorruption (Rom 8:21), the Spirit (Rom 8:23), and glory-filled human *bodies (Rom 8:18, 23).

Again, Paul understands Israel's Scriptures as anticipating a time of peace and fertility when the Messiah enters into his eschatological rule over the cosmos (e.g., Ps 71 LXX; Is 11). Paul's quotation of Isaiah 11:10 ("the root of Jesse will come, and one will rise to rule the nations, the nations will hope in him," Rom 15:12) connects the Messiah's rule with the oracle's expectation for a Spirit-empowered ruler who brings peace to all of creation (Wright, 820). The scriptural promises that David and his seed will be the recipients of the promises to Abraham for worldwide dominion and blessing of the nations (e.g., Gen 15:18; Ps 71:21-22 LXX; Jer 33:14-26) provide the framework for Paul's claims that the Messiah is the one marked out as the heir of God's promise for sovereignty over all of creation and the nations (see also the promise to the seed in Gen 12:15; 17:8; 24:7; Juel; Whitsett, 87, 671-72). Thus, when Paul speaks of the Messiah's inheritance (Ps 2:7-8; Rom 4:13; 8:17), he anticipates the eschatological renewal of the entire cosmos as his dominion (Rom 8:18-25).

See also CHRISTOLOGY; KINGDOM OF GOD/CHRIST; RESURRECTION; ROMANS, LETTER TO THE.

BIBLIOGRAPHY. **A. T. Abernethy and G. Goswell,** *God's Messiah in the Old Testament: Expectations of a Coming King* (Grand Rapids, MI: Baker, 2020); **G. Agamben,** *The Time That Remains: A Commentary on the Letter to the Romans*, trans. P. Dailey (Stanford, CA: Stanford University Press, 2005); **M. W. Bates,** *The Hermeneutics of the Apostolic Proclamation: The Center of Paul's Method of Scriptural Interpretation* (Waco, TX: Baylor University Press, 2012); **W. Bousset,** *Kyrios Christos: A History of the Belief in Christ from the Beginnings of Christianity to Irenaeus*, trans. J. E. Steely (Nashville: Abingdon, 1970); **R. Bultmann,** *Theology of the New Testament*, 2 vols. (New York: Scribner's, 1951); **D. A. Campbell,** "The Story of Jesus in Romans and Galatians," in *Narrative Dynamics in Paul: A Critical Assessment*, ed. B. W. Longenecker (Louisville: Westminster John Knox, 2002), 97-124; **A. Chester,** "Christ of Paul," in *Redemption and Resistance: The Messianic Hopes of Jews and Christians in Antiquity*, ed. M. Bockmuehl and J. C. Paget (London: T&T Clark, 2008), 109-12; **A. J. Collins and J. J. Collins,** *King Messiah as Son of God* (Grand Rapids, MI: Eerdmans, 2008); **N. A. Dahl,** "The Messiahship of Jesus in Paul," in *Jesus the Christ: The Historical Origins of Christological Doctrine*, ed. D. H. Juel (Minneapolis: Fortress, 1991), 15-25; **C. H. Dodd,** *The Apostolic Preaching and Its Developments* (New York: Harper & Row, 1964); **T. Eskola,** *Messiah and the Throne: Jewish Merkabah Mysticism and Early Christian Exaltation Discourse* (Tübingen: Mohr Siebeck, 2001); **P. Fredriksen,** *Paul: The Pagans' Apostle* (New Haven, CT: Yale University Press, 2017); **R. H. Fuller,** *The Foundations of New Testament Christology* (New York: Charles Scribner's Sons, 1965); **D. Garlington,** "Israel's Triumphant King: Romans 1:5 and the Scriptures of Israel," in *Jesus and Paul: Global Perspectives in Honor of James D. G. Dunn for His Seventieth Birthday,* ed. B. J. Oropeza, C. K. Robertson, and D. C. Mohrmann, LNTS 414 (London: T&T Clark, 2010), 173-83; **F. Hahn,** *The Titles of Jesus in Christology: Their History in Early Christianity* (New York: World, 1969); **R. B. Hays,** "Christ Prays the Psalms: Paul's Use of an Early Christian Convention," in *The Future of Christology: Essays in Honor of Leander E. Keck*, ed. A. J. Malherbe and W. A. Meeks (Minneapolis: Fortress, 1993), 122-36;

W. Heitmüller, "Zum Problem Paulus und Jesus," *ZNW* 13 (1912): 320-37; **M. Hengel,** "'Christos' in Paul," in *Between Jesus and Paul: Studies in the Earliest History of Christianity* (Philadelphia: Fortress, 1983), 65-77; **W. Horbury,** *Jewish Messianism and the Cult of Christ* (London: SCM Press, 1998); **L. W. Hurtado,** *Lord Jesus Christ: Devotion to Jesus in Earliest Christianity* (Grand Rapids, MI: Eerdmans, 2003); idem, "Paul's Messianic Christology," in *Paul the Jew: Rereading the Apostle as a Figure of Second Temple Judaism*, ed. G. Boccaccini and C. A. Segovia (Minneapolis: Fortress, 2016), 107-31; **H. G. Jacob,** *Conformed to the Image of His Son: Reconsidering Paul's Theology of Glory in Romans* (Downers Grove, IL: InterVarsity Press, 2018); **J. W. Jipp,** "Ancient, Modern, and Future Interpretations of Romans 1:3-4: Reception History and Biblical Interpretation," *JTI* 3 (2009): 241-59; idem, *Christ Is King: Paul's Royal Ideology* (Minneapolis: Fortress, 2015); idem, *The Messianic Theology of the New Testament* (Grand Rapids, MI: Eerdmans, 2020); **A. R. Johnson,** *Sacral Kingship in Ancient Israel* (Cardiff, UK: University of Wales Press, 1967); **D. Juel,** *Messianic Exegesis: Christological Interpretation of the Old Testament in Early Christianity* (Philadelphia: Fortress, 1988); **J. R. D. Kirk,** *Unlocking Romans* (Grand Rapids, MI: Eerdmans, 2008); **M. D. Marossy,** "The Rule of the Resurrected Messiah: Kingship Discourse in 2 Timothy 2:8-13," *CBQ* 82 (2020): 84-100; **L. Novakovic,** *Raised from the Dead According to Scripture: The Role of Israel's Scripture in the Early Christian Interpretations of Jesus' Resurrection*, JCTCRSS (London: T&T Clark, 2012); **M. V. Novenson,** *Christ Among the Messiahs: Christ Language in Paul and Messiah Language in Ancient Judaism* (Oxford: Oxford University Press, 2012); idem, "Oil and Power in Ancient Israel," in *The Grammar of Messianism: An Ancient Jewish Political Idiom and Its Users* (Oxford: Oxford University Press, 2017), 34-64; **J. C. H. Smith,** *Christ the Ideal King: Cultural Context, Rhetorical Strategy, and the Power of Divine Monarchy in Ephesians*, WUNT 2/313 (Tübingen: Mohr Siebeck, 2011); **J. Taubes,** *The Political Theology of Paul*, trans. D. Hollander (Stanford, CA: Stanford University Press, 2004); **C. G. Whitsett,** "Son of God, Seed of David: Paul's Messianic Exegesis in Romans 2[*sic*]:3-4," *JBL* 119 (2000): 661-81; **N. T. Wright,** *Paul and the Faithfulness of God* (Minneapolis: Fortress, 2013); **M. Zetterholm,** "Paul and the Missing Messiah," in *The Messiah in Early Judaism and Christianity*, ed. M. Zetterholm (Minneapolis: Fortress, 2007), 33-55.

J. W. Jipp

CHRIST HYMN. *See* CHRISTOLOGY; HYMNS, HYMN FRAGMENTS, CONFESSIONS; JESUS AND PAUL; PHILIPPIANS, LETTER TO THE.

CHRISTOLOGY

The scholarly quest for the *centrum Paulinium* has erroneously focused on soteriological categories (e.g., *justification, reconciliation, participation), whereas the real center of Paul's thought should be sourced in Paul's Christology (Fitzmyer, 37-38). Put broadly, Paul's theological project consists of Jewish monotheism as redrawn around Jesus and the Spirit (N. T. Wright 2013); put specifically, in the middle of that project is the profession that *God is one and Jesus is *Lord (Nicholson, 5). The continuity across Paul's letters is not in any particular doctrine but the presence and power of God in *Christ Jesus. It was his experience of Christ that animated Paul's Christ devotion and his *mission to the *Gentiles (Hurtado 2017, 525). The *apostle was devoted to Jesus as the *Son of God, who loved him and gave himself for him (Gal 2:19-20); he was driven by the *love of Christ, who died and was raised to rescue Gentiles (2 Cor 5:14-15); he remained captivated by the surpassing value of knowing Christ (Phil 3:8); and he could not erase from his memory his encounter with God's *glory in the face of the risen Christ (2 Cor 4:6). This devotion does have specific content. Jesus is for Paul an Israelite prophet, the Messiah, God's Son, the definitive divine agent of redemption, exalted Lord, and part of God's very own *identity. However, there are several complexities in Paul's portrayal of Jesus that give impetus to scholars to dispute the background, origins, content, development, and significance of Paul's Christology (see Smith).

1. The Origins of Paul's Christology
2. The Preexistence of Jesus
3. The Earthly Jesus
4. The *Diakonia* of Jesus
5. Worship of Jesus
6. Titles for Jesus
7. The Father and Jesus
8. The Spirit and Jesus
9. Paul's Divine Christology

1. The Origins of Paul's Christology.

The emergence of Paul's Christology is shaped by Jewish and Hellenistic categories for divine agents, configured by Paul's *conversion experience and influenced by Paul's reception of early Christian traditions.

1.1. Judaism. The Jews of the Second Temple period held by and large to both monolatry (worship of one god) and monotheism (belief in one god even if there were lesser supernatural beings). This is demonstrated by the identification of Israel's God as the Creator, reverence for the divine *name, and exclusive *worship of this God (Deut 6:4; Is 44:6, 8; 45:14, 21; 46:9; Jer 10:10; 2 Macc 1:24-25; Let. Aris. 132; Philo, *Decal.* 65; Add Esth 13:12-14; Acts 10:25-26; Rev 19:10; 22:9; Tacitus, *Hist.* 5.5.4). Even so, in the Hebrew Bible and in Second Temple Jewish literature, several intermediary beings are presented as God's agents and act on God's behalf (see Philo, *Conf.* 170, 171, 175). In some cases, these figures are a personification of God (Wisdom, Word); in other instances they are a human agent with a divine commission (Israel's king), a patriarch exalted to a heavenly position (Enoch), sometimes an angelic figure (angel of the Lord, Michael, Yahoel), or else a heavenly being sent to earth (Son of Man). Some of these figures are even called "god"; they receive types of veneration from human subjects, and they participate in divine acts of revelation and redemption.

All of this raises questions as to whether Jewish monotheism was strict or flexible, whether divinity was ontological, functional, or honorific, and whether humans could be promoted to divine status and receive divine honors. For example, Philo asserts an uncompromising monotheism by declaring that there is "but one God, the most high, and to honor him alone; and do not permit polytheistic doctrine to even touch the ears of any person who is accustomed to seek after the truth, with a clean and pure of heart" (*Decal.* 65, trans. C. D. Yonge), and he rejects ideas of both incarnation and deification since "sooner could God change into a man than a man into God" (*Legat.* 118 [LCL]). At the same time, Philo refers to Moses as "God and King of the whole nation" and calls the Logos a "second God," which would seem injurious to a strict monotheism (Philo, *Sacr.* 9-10 [LCL]; *Mos.* 1.156-58; *Conf.* 146-47; *QG* 2.62). Paul's thought is immersed in and structured by Israel's sacred traditions, with their conceptions of God and God's relationship to the world, by a suite of royal, priestly, and prophetic types, and multiple intermediary beings. Yet we are left to work out the precise nature of Paul's monotheism and messianism, the aptness of comparisons between Paul's Christ and various intermediary figures, and how this all relates to the specifically Jewish sense in which someone can be considered divine.

1.2. Hellenism. Paul was raised and educated in Jewish environs, in a Jewish family in Tarsus, in the province Cilicia, bordering Syria, Cappadocia, and Galatia. However, Paul's Judaism was not siloed; it was embedded within the religious atmosphere of the Greco-Roman world. The Jewish Scriptures were the most formative text for his religious devotion, but Hellenistic philosophy, rhetoric, and culture surrounded Paul as well. The eastern Mediterranean was teeming with gods. There were gods for all stages of life, all activities of life, all vocations of life, all situations and emotions, and all regions. There were holidays, festivals, plays, literature, and dances associated with the gods. Cities were littered with temples, altars were placed at crossroads and street corners, and shrines and statues were visible in domiciles, while businesses including bathhouses, brothels, and bakeries were decorated with images of gods (see Hopkins, 14). Paul undoubtedly knew the stories of Zeus visiting earth and copulating with women, the healing powers attributed to Asclepius, tales of the apotheosis of Herakles, the postmortem deification of Julius Caesar and Augustus; Paul used coins that called Tiberius the "Son of the divine Augustus" and perhaps received invitations from the leatherworkers' guild to "dine at the table of Lord *Serapis* in the Serapeum" (P.Oxy. 3.523). Paul lived in Greco-Roman cities filled with "many 'lords'" (1 Cor 8:5 NIV); deities evoked in myths, *magic, and mystery cults; temples bustling with the sounds and smells of prayers and sacrifices; festivals with readings of the poetry of Homer and Virgil; markets swirling with folk beliefs about *curses and cures; speeches in the forum complaining about the neglect of traditional cults and the introduction of Eastern cults—all the time cognizant that a fusion of Rome's military power and pantheon of gods comprised the "rulers of this age" who "crucified the Lord of glory" (1 Cor 2:8 NIV).

Although Paul retained standard Jewish aversion to idols and pagan practices (1 Thess 1:9; 4:5; Rom 1:18-32; 1 Cor 5:1; 6:9-11; 10:1-22; 12:2; 2 Cor 6:16-18; Gal 5:20), the question remains, To what extent did Paul imitate, parody, or counter pagan notions of deity in his own titles and stories attributed to Jesus? How does Paul's monotheism and Christology compare to the anthropomorphic polytheism of antiquity, where gods visited earth as human and humans ascended to become gods? An older generation of scholarship believed that Paul was partly responsible for transforming the Judean Jesus movement into a Hellenistic Christ cult by indigenizing Christianity into the world of Hellenistic religion, a position that has been thoroughly refuted (Hengel 1976; Hurtado 2003, 5-26; 2017, 11-37). Even so, comparisons between Mediterranean deities and divinized humans with Pauline Christology and its devotional practices continue to stimulate discussions about any analogical and genealogical relationships between them (Zeller; Yarbro Collins 1999; Ehrman; Litwa).

1.3. Paul's Conversion Experience. Paul's conversion experience was an arresting encounter with the Lord Jesus and entailed an immediate transformation of his prior beliefs about Jesus (Gal 1:11-23; 1 Cor 15:8-10; Acts 9; 22; 26). Paul's Christophany meant (1) Jesus was alive, resurrected, which was world shattering because *resurrection was meant to happen at the *end* of history to *all* *Israel (Dan 12:2; 2 Macc 7:14; Jn 11:24), and yet God had raised one man in the middle of history. This required an instant christological and chronological recalibration to Paul's entire symbolic universe (N. T. Wright 1997, 49-51). For a start, it meant that the future age had invaded the present (Eph 1:21) and Jesus was the "*firstborn" and "firstfruits" of the general resurrection (Rom 8:29; Col 1:18; 1 Cor 15:23). (2) It would have been nakedly evident that Jesus was not a pseudo-Messiah; much to the contrary, he was the risen Messiah, who had been crucified and cursed for Israel's redemption (Gal 3:13; 4:4-5), and revealed to Paul as God's Son (Gal 1:16). (3) The visually resplendent nature of Paul's Christophany led him to identify Jesus with God's glory and *image (2 Cor 4:4, 6; Col 1:15). (4) Jesus' apparent authority meant he had been exalted by God to a position of *honor and power at the Father's right hand (Rom 8:34; Col 3:1; Eph 1:20), implying Jesus' coregency as the Son of God (Ps 110:1; Rom 1:4) and exercising authority as the eschatological *Adam (Ps 8:4-6; 1 Cor 15:25-27; Eph 1:22). (5) God revealed to Paul that his task was to proclaim Jesus as Israel's Messiah to the nations (Gal 1:16), which was a call through *grace and to testify to grace (Rom 1:5; 15:15; Gal 1:15-17; Acts 20:24), and to bring God's *salvation to the nations (Rom 15:8-13, 15-17; Gal 3:14; Eph 3:1-12; Col 1:27; 1 Thess 5:9; 1 Tim 2:7).

1.4. Early Christian Tradition. Paul received traditions about Jesus from churches in Damascus, *Jerusalem, and Antioch (Rom 6:17; 1 Cor 11:2, 23; 15:3; 2 Thess 2:15). While we cannot always be certain which texts were inherited by Paul, augmented by Paul, or creations of Paul, generally scholars identify passages such as Romans 1:3-4; 4:25; 10:9; Philippians 2:6-11; 1 Corinthians 8:6; 15:20-28; 16:22; Colossians 1:15-20; and 1 Timothy 3:16 as Paul's rehearsal or reworking of traditional christological materials (see Sumney). These are texts that refer to Jesus' preexistence, messianic status, exalted lordship, and eschatological agency, and imply veneration of his person. It is amazing, declares M. Hengel (1983, 31; 1995, 383-84), that prior to Paul's letters, fewer than twenty years since the crucifixion of the Galilean Jew, that Jesus was elevated by his followers to a dignity that matched Jewish monotheistic worship and exceeded ordinary pagan deification categories, given that preexistence, the mediation of *creation, and the revelation of the identity of the one God were attributed to the man Jesus of Nazareth.

2. The Preexistence of Jesus.

Several texts suggest that Paul regarded Jesus as a preexistent person who was sent by God to earth and became human. However, we must first consider the many senses of preexistence. Does Paul envisage Jesus as preexistent in the sense of having a name and role foreordained by God (Ps 109:3 LXX; 1 En. 48.2-3; T. Mos. 1.14; 4 Ezra 7.28; 12.32; 13.25-26)? Is Jesus retrospectively identified with God's *wisdom as the divine agent through whom God creates and whom God sends to humanity in the form of Torah (Prov 8:22-31; Wis 7:22-26; 9:9-10, 17; Sir 1:4; 24:1-23; Bar 3:9–4:1; cf. 1 Cor 1:24, 30)? Is Jesus preexistent with Israel in a typological sense, with persons from biblical history such as Adam, Abel, Isaac, Joseph, Moses, or David somehow prefiguring Christ (Melito, *Pascha* 59-69)? Is Jesus preexistent as a fully divine person within a tripersonal Godhead, or preexistent like a supreme angel (the essence of the fourth-century debates about Jesus as divine)?

2.1. Philippians 2:5-11. The Christ *hymn (or poem) presents Jesus as "existing" (*hyparchōn*) in the "form of God" (*morphē theou*), which is the outward display of divine splendor and is further defined as being "equal with God" (*isa theō*), which is tantamount to sharing in divine honors (Philo, *Conf.* 170). Yet rather than choosing to exploit this state for his own self-aggrandizement, Jesus voluntarily emptied himself—not by laying aside any divine attribute but by taking on human existence, and so entered the experience of slavery, humiliation, and *death. The shift from "form of God" to "form of a *slave" implies a transition from a heavenly position to human form. The text thus implies a V-shaped narrative, with Jesus' divine preexistence (Phil 2:6), humanity and humiliation (Phil 2:7-8), and subsequent exaltation (Phil 2:9-11).

2.2. Galatians 4:4 and Romans 8:3. Paul twice declares that God "sent" his "Son." These descriptions cannot be generalized, as if God sent the Son the same way that he sent *Abraham, Moses, or David. That is because Paul specifies that the Son's mission entails being "born from woman" and taking "the likeness of sinful *flesh," which would be redundant for a mere human figure but underscores the Son's origins with God and his full participation in humanity (see Gathercole, 29; Hill, 90).

2.3. 1 Corinthians 15:47. Paul, in the midst of a discussion about the nature of the resurrection *body, contrasts Adam, as a man created "from the dust of the earth," with Jesus, who came "from heaven."

2.4. 1 Corinthians 8:6 and Colossians 1:16. Jesus' preexistence is required by Paul's reference to Jesus as the one "through/in whom all things were created" (1 Cor 8:6; Col 1:16), who is even "before all things" (Col 1:17). Noticeably, there is a distinction of roles, as creation is *from* the Father (1 Cor 8:6; Rom 11:36) yet *through* Christ (Gathercole, 27). There is a genuine parallel with wisdom traditions, but Jesus is otherwise depicted as God's mediatorial agent in creation (see Jn 1:3, 10).

2.5. 2 Corinthians 8:9. When discussing the Jerusalem *collection, Paul sets forth Jesus as an example of generosity: "For you know the generous act of our Lord Jesus Christ, that though he was rich, yet for your sakes he became poor, so that by his poverty you might become rich" (NRSV). Paul does not specify what the states of riches and poverty precisely correspond to in Christ's existence. Most likely, Paul is reminding the Corinthians that the Lord Jesus Christ, though he was rich in the glory of his preexistent heavenly life, became impoverished in comparison by becoming human, and through that poverty Christ has made them rich.

2.6. Romans 10:6-8. Paul's gloss on Deuteronomy 30:12-14 in Romans 10:6-8 implies that the events of Jesus' incarnation and resurrection need not be repeated. One need not go to heaven to "bring Christ down," nor enter into the abyss "to bring Christ up from the dead," because the benefits of Christ's coming and return are already accessible through the "word of *faith." The same Deuteronomic language is used for Wisdom, who is likewise heralded as accessible (Bar 3:29-30) and present (Bar 3:37–4:1).

2.7. 1 Corinthians 10:4 and Romans 15:3, 9-11. Paul warns the Corinthians by way of reference to Israel's example in its wilderness wanderings and stresses the continuity between the ancient Israelites and the Corinthians themselves. The Israelites were baptized into Moses in the Red Sea, and they ate the spiritual food and drank the water from the spiritual rock (Ex 16:13-16; 17:6), and Paul adds that "the rock was Christ" (1 Cor 10:4 NRSV). Whereas Jewish tradition allegorically identified the water-giving rock with divine Wisdom (Wis 11:4; Philo, *Leg.* 2.86), Paul sees the provision of the rock as a typological prefiguration of Christ based on a Christotelic rereading of Scripture (Enns, 149-51). In addition, Paul engages in an instance of prosopological exegesis, where someone is regarded as the person speaking in a text, when he portrays Christ speaking in the first person in a series of OT citations, including Psalm 69:9 (Rom 15:3); Psalm 18:49 (Rom 15:9); Deuteronomy 32:43 (Rom 15:10); and Psalm 117:1 (Rom 15:11; see Bates, 240-55). Paul thus uses typological and prosopological techniques to locate Jesus in Israel's sacred history.

Affirmation of Jesus' preexistence is detected in *tradition materials in circulation prior to the late 40s, when Paul began writing. The preexistence of Jesus perhaps emerged based on Jesus' own consciousness of his unique divine sonship (Mk 12:6, 35-37; 13:32; Lk 10:22//Mt 11:27) and the early church's messianic exegesis of Psalm 2:6 and Psalm 110:1 (Lee, 314-15). Or else—and these are not mutually exclusive—preexistence was postulated based on a rereading of Scripture in light of the early church's experience of Jesus as risen and robed in divine glory, and in light of their beliefs that Jesus was mediator of God's salvation and harbinger of the new age. If the one true God had worked so dramatically through Jesus to redeem and re-create the world, then there was every reason to believe that Jesus' mediating role reached back to the very origins of creation (McDonough 2009, 235-36).

Accordingly, if Jesus was the "firstborn from among the dead" (Col 1:18 NIV), then one might infer that he also was the "firstborn of all creation" (Col 1:15 NRSV). If Jesus had ascended to the heavens (1 Thess 1:10; 2 Thess 1:7; Phil 2:9-11; 3:20), then he must have originally been sent from heaven (Gal 4:4; Rom 8:3; 1 Cor 15:47). If Jesus was the chief agent of the new creation (2 Cor 5:17;), then he must have been the chief agent who had brought the first creation into being (Col 1:16; 1 Cor 8:6). The early church's religious experience of Jesus' presence, power, and lordship, combined with its christologically centered rereading of Scripture, led it to the conclusion that whoever Jesus is—Son of God and Lord—he must have always been in some form or another (Hengel 1976, 66-76; Hurtado 2003, 124-26; Bird 2017, 30-32).

3. The Earthly Jesus.

The extent of Paul's knowledge of Jesus' earthly life and *ministry is a matter of debate (see Holzbrecher). An older generation of scholarship took Paul's remark that he did not want to know Christ "according to the flesh" (2 Cor 5:16 ESV) to mean that, apart from the crucifixion, Paul disparaged knowledge of the historical Jesus and wanted to know Christ only according to the realm of faith. But that is to misconstrue Paul's words, as Paul is only rejecting a *knowledge of Christ according to worldly measures. It is possible that Paul encountered Jesus during his itinerant movements in Galilee and Judea (see Porter), although we have no solid evidence that he did so. It is more likely that Paul learned about Jesus and the Jesus tradition from the Christ-followers he persecuted (1 Cor 15:9; Gal 1:13, 23; Phil 3:6), then later from the churches of Damascus, Antioch, and Jerusalem—specifically from prominent leaders such as Barnabas and John Mark, from members of Jesus' family such as James, and from the first disciples, including Peter and John (Gal 1:17-23; 2:7-9). Ultimately it would be astounding if someone who proclaimed the "one man, Jesus Christ" (Rom 5:15, 17 NRSV; cf. 1 Tim 2:5), who baptized in Jesus' name (1 Cor 1:13, 15; 6:11), who considered himself co-crucified with Christ (Gal 2:19), who longed to be with him (Phil 1:23), would be uninterested in Jesus' life, teaching, and earliest followers (Dunn 1998, 185). Paul could not call people to imitate the example of Jesus if nothing about Jesus was known in the early churches (1 Thess 1:6; 1 Cor 11:1; Phil 2:5-11).

The historical anchor is Jesus' crucifixion, because Paul considered Jesus' death as the climax of his life, the means of *atonement, and the presupposition for his risen life and exalted status. Paul strenuously insisted on a unity between the earthly Jesus and the exalted Lord Jesus Christ (Hurtado 2015, 121-22; Dunn 2006, 369), as demonstrated in his identification of the crucified Jesus with the Lord of glory (2 Cor 2:6; 13:4) and in the eucharistic communal meal that celebrated the memory of Jesus' death as much as it looked forward to his return as the eschatological judge (1 Cor 11:23-26). This unity is confirmed by Paul's condemnation of anyone who "preaches a Jesus other than the Jesus we preached" (2 Cor 11:4 NIV). Paul was of the firm conviction that Jesus lived, died, and lived again. As such, the life of the earthly Jesus was fundamental for his thought (Murphy-O'Connor, 91).

The sketch of Jesus' life that we get from Paul is that

- Jesus was human (Rom 8:3; Phil 2:7), born to a woman under the Torah, that is, as a Jew (Gal 4:4);
- Jesus was of Israelite ancestry (Rom 9:5), descended from a Davidic family (Rom 1:3);
- Jesus had brothers, including James (1 Cor 9:5; Gal 1:19);
- Jesus served (Phil 2:7) Israel (Rom 15:8);
- Jesus was a prophet (1 Thess 2:15);
- Jesus gave instructions about divorce (1 Cor 7:9-11) and taught that those who proclaim the *gospel should get their living from the gospel (1 Cor 9:14);
- on the night he was betrayed, Jesus hosted a meal that instituted the new *covenant (1 Cor 11:23-25);
- Jesus was obedient to his messianic task (Phil 2:7; Rom 5:18-19), to the point of being crucified and dying on the *cross (Phil 2:8; 1 Cor 1:23; 2:2; 15:3);
- Jesus was buried (1 Cor 15:4) and was raised three days later (1 Cor 15:4, 20; 1 Thess 4:14; 2 Cor 5:15); and
- afterwards Jesus was seen by Peter, James, the disciples, many others, and also by Paul (1 Cor 15:5-8).

Paul appears to have echoed some of Jesus' teachings, such as the "Abba" prayer (Rom 8:15-17; Gal 4:6-7) and love command (Rom 13:8, 10; Gal 5:14), but does not discuss them at length in his letters, either because such knowledge might have simply been assumed as part of the tradition that his readers already knew (1 Thess 4:2; 2 Thess 3:6; Rom 6:17; 1 Cor 11:2, 23-25; Col 2:6) or else because the matters he dealt with could rarely be addressed by way of reference to the Jesus tradition (e.g. circumcision, eating *food sacrificed to idols, the Jerusalem collection).

4. The *Diakonia* of Jesus.

Jesus' person cannot be separated from Jesus' work any more than Yahweh's person can be known apart from Yahweh's deliverance of Israel in the exodus, his covenant relationship with Israel, the giving of the Torah, *temple worship, and the prophetic word ringing from him (see Fee, 8). Jesus' person is known through the redemptive story underlying Paul's letters. Paul's gospel declares what God has accomplished in Jesus' mission (Rom 15:8), primarily in Jesus' death and resurrection, reflecting a tradition Paul received (Rom 4:25; 1 Thess 4:14; 1 Cor 15:3-5; 2 Cor 5:5) and himself amplifies (Rom 3:21-26; 5:6-11; 8:1-4; Gal 2:19-20; 3:13-14).

Jesus' death is "for" believers in the sense of atoning for their sins and yielding a variety of salvific dividends, including redemption, reconciliation, *forgiveness, cleansing, justification, rescue from evil powers, life, victory, and deliverance from *wrath (1 Thess 5:10; Gal 2:19; 3:13; Rom 5:6-11; 8:3; 14:15; 1 Cor 5:7; 6:11, 20; 8:11; 15:3; 2 Cor 5:21; Col 1:14-15; 3:13; Eph 1:7; 4:32). The resurrection is also prominent as the instrument of justification (Rom 4:25), forgiveness (1 Cor 15:17), and the prototype of the believer's own resurrection (Rom 8:11; Phil 3:21). It is by the agency of the Spirit and by the instrument of faith that believers have union with Christ in his death, resurrection, and exaltation, and so participate in the redemption that he brings, the risen life that he possesses, and the reign that he will usher in (Rom 6:1-14, Gal 2:19-20; Col 2:12; 3:1; Eph 2:6; 2 Tim 2:11-12). In the future, Jesus will return to rescue believers (1 Thess 1:10; 4:15-17; 2 Thess 1:7), and to inaugurate the general resurrection (Phil 3:20-21; 1 Cor 15:22, 51-56) and the final *judgment (Rom 2:16; 1 Cor 15:24-28; 2 Cor 5:10; 2 Tim 4:1). For Paul, Christ Jesus is God's definitive agent in the redemptive saga of rescuing Israel, redeeming the Gentiles, and renewing creation.

5. Worship of Jesus.

In the Pauline assemblies, Jesus was venerated as God's eschatological agent, the exalted Lord, and the source of life and redemption, and a person's relationship to God was mediated through Jesus. To this end, psalms and hymns celebrating his exaltation by God, acclaiming him as Lord, and offering thanks for God's work of salvation through him were part of the churches' devotional life from the very beginning, including the Pauline churches (Hengel 1983, 78-96). Various hymns make Jesus the object of praise (Phil 2:6-11; Col 1:15-20; Eph 5:19; 1 Tim 3:16), so "the one who functions as God naturally receives divine worship, not of course as a competitor or supplanter of God in the community's worship, but as God's plenipotentiary whose praise redounds to God's glory" (Bauckham, *ABD* 3:815). In Pauline doxologies glory is given to God through Jesus (Rom 16:27; 2 Cor 1:20; Phil 1:11) and directly to Jesus (2 Tim 4:18). Whereas God is "blessed" or "praised" (*eulogētos*) by Paul (Rom 1:25; 2 Cor 1:3; 11:31; Eph 1:3), he confers the same blessedness/praise on Jesus alone (Rom 9:5). There are prayers offered to Jesus (1 Cor 16:22; 2 Cor 12:8-9; 1 Thess 3:11-13; 2 Thess 2:16-17; 3:5, 16) and mention of "calling on the name of our Lord Jesus Christ" (1 Cor 1:2; cf. Rom 10:12-14; 2 Tim 2:22).

*Baptisms are performed in the name of Jesus (1 Cor 1:15; 6:11), which also means to "put on Christ" (Gal 3:27 ESV). Paul makes a triadic benediction (2 Cor 13:14) and Jesus-only benedictions (Rom 16:20; 1 Cor 16:23; 1 Thess 5:28; 2 Thess 3:18). The "*Lord's supper" (1 Cor 11:20) is a memorial meal, which Paul compares to the rituals in pagan temples, but it is no mere tribute to a dead hero, because "Jesus is perceived as the living and powerful *Kyrios* who owns the meal and presides at it, and with whom believers have *fellowship as with a god" (Hurtado 2003, 146). These forms of devotion are all the more startling within the Jewish tradition, where God's uniqueness was principally expressed by the restriction of worship to God alone. Yet Jesus was worshiped alongside God the Father, not as a rival object of worship; rather, Jesus was worshiped *within* the worship of the one God (Bauckham, *ABD* 3:812-19; Hurtado 2003, 134-53; 2015, 103-30).

6. Titles for Jesus.

It is inadequate to rely on titles to expound Paul's Christology when narratival, functional, and intertextual aspects illuminate the identity and person of Jesus in Paul's letters. However, the titles remain significant because they do partly explicate the roles and relationships Paul attributes to Jesus. The primary titles for analysis are Messiah, Lord, Son of God, and last Adam.

6.1. Messiah. Paul uses *Christos* 270 times, a Greek word meaning "anointed," "consecrated," "smeared," or "plastered" (GE), but which is used to translate the Hebrew *māšîaḥ* and Aramaic *məšîḥā* for an anointed figure such as a prophet, priest, king, or the eschatological Davidic deliverer known as the Messiah (BDAG). However, whether *Christos* in Paul's letters is a proper name, a messianic title, or an honorific designation is a matter of dispute (see Bird 2009, 15-22; Novenson; Hurtado 2017, 539-58). A glance at 1 Thessalonians, arguably Paul's earliest letter, reveals that *Christos* is part of an honorific designation for the "Lord Jesus Christ" (1 Thess 1:1, 3; 5:9, 23, 28), that it nominates Jesus as Paul's apostolic patron in referring to "Christ's apostles" (1 Thess 2:7), that there is an incorporative sense of being "*in Christ" (1 Thess 2:14; 4:16; 5:18), and that it designates Jesus as the object of Paul's gospel in the "gospel of Christ" (1 Thess 3:2).

Even if *Christos* functions as a proper name for Jesus in Paul's letters, there are clear indications that the royal-messianic connotations were maintained: (1) Paul valorizes ethnic Israel as the hereditary progenitor of the Messiah and so connects Jesus to the messianic role (Rom 9:5). (2) Paul was aware that *Christos* means "anointed one," given the wordplay he makes where God established believers in the *Christos* and "anointed" (*chrisas*) them. (3) Paul connects *Christos* to Jesus' Davidic heritage (Rom 1:4) and to Isaianic expectations of a Davidic deliver (Rom 15:12 = Is 11:10). (4) The references to Jesus Christ as future judge (Rom 2:16; 2 Cor 5:10) and as the royal arbiter of God's *kingdom present Jesus in a role akin to other Jewish representations of the Messiah (1 Cor 15:24-28). (5) Paul was aware that to proclaim the *Christos* as crucified was a *stumbling block to Jews because it implied the failure, humiliation, and subjugation of Israel's divinely appointed deliverer (1 Cor 1:23; 2:2). Consequently, Paul's Christology should be situated in ancient Jewish messianic discourse, and there is no reason to think that his Gentile congregations could not pick up on that.

6.2. Lord. Another common title for Jesus, used 189 times in the Pauline corpus, is that of "Lord" (*kyrios*). It can be used in a nonreligious sense for "master" or "boss" (e.g., Eph 6:5, 9). Otherwise it is notable that the *kyrios* title was used in oriental cults for deities such as Isis, Adonis, and Serapis; in Hellenistic ruler cults in Egypt, Thrace, and Syria; and in imperial cults and public proclamations about the Roman emperor; and the sacred name Yahweh in the Hebrew Scriptures was translated as *kyrios* in the Greek Scriptures. Jesus is addressed as *kyrios* in the sense of "master" by disciples and supplicants (e.g., Mt 8:21; 9:28; 17:4; Jn 11:3, 21), but he also describes himself as *kyrios* in an elevated sense (Mk 12:35-37; Lk 6:46; Mt 10:24-25; Jn 13:13; 15:15, 20). The Aramaic-speaking church identifies Jesus as the eschatological *mareh* for "Lord" (1 Cor 16:22; Did. 10.6; cf. Jas 2:1; 5:7-8); the designation was common among the Jerusalem church (Acts 2:21, 34, 36, 39; 7:59) and was prevalent too in Greek-speaking circles for Jesus (Phil 2:11; Heb 13:20; 1 Pet 3:15; Rev 11:8). Paul regards the lordship of Jesus as central to his proclamation (2 Cor 4:5) and the substance of the tradition that his congregations received (Col 2:6). Confession of Jesus as Lord was the very definition of being a Christ-follower (Rom 10:9-10) and the decisive test of spiritual *truth (1 Cor 12:3).

The conviction that Jesus was the risen Lord (Rom 4:24; 1 Cor 6:14; 2 Cor 5:15; Rom 10:9; 14:9) led Paul to follow tradition and apply Yahweh passages from Israel's Scriptures to Jesus as Lord, including Deuteronomy 6:4 (1 Cor 8:6); Psalm 110:1 (Rom 8:34; 1 Cor 15:25; Col 3:1; Eph 1:20); Isaiah 40:13 (1 Cor 2:15); Isaiah 45:23 (Phil 2:9-11); Jeremiah 9:24 (2 Cor 10:17-18); and Joel 2:32 (Rom 10:13). This is evidence that Paul felt "obliged to read Scripture in profound, new ways, programmatically situating the Lord Jesus in Scripture texts reserved for YHWH" (Capes, 183).

On the whole, there are three specific contexts in Paul's letters where Jesus is referred to as *kyrios* (Hurtado 2003, 117): (1) in hortatory statements where Jesus is Lord/Master, whose teaching and example are authoritative for believers; (2) in eschatological expectations as one who returns as God the Father's agent; and (3) in passages designating the unequaled status given to Jesus by God within settings that are indicative of Christian worship practices. Notably, Paul does not equate the Lord Jesus with the totality of Israel's "Lord God" (*kyrios ho theos* in the LXX). Paul retains the distinction between God the Father and the Lord Jesus (e.g., 1 Cor 1:3; Gal 1:3, Rom 1:7; 1 Cor 8:6). Moreover, Jesus is exalted to lordship by God the Father (Phil 2:9; Eph 1:20-22), he delivers his eschatological reign up to God the Father (1 Cor 15:24), and he is the conduit for glory to be given to God the Father (2 Cor 1:20; Phil 1:11; 2:11; Col 3:17; Rom 16:27). Nonetheless, Paul regarded Jesus as uniquely Lord in salvation, the vice regent of God's kingdom, and possessing an unprecedented position within the orbit of divine sovereignty. To call Jesus *kyrios* was to profess his superlative authority over all things, to accent his special divine status relationally distinct from but organic to God the Father, and to highlight the subservience of his subjects before him and the worthiness of their worship of him.

6.3. Son of God. Jesus' sonship, referred to sparsely by Paul, pertains to his intimate relationship with God, his unique standing under God, and God's direct work through his messianic office (Hurtado 2003, 104). The divine sonship of Jesus is basic to Paul's gospel, as he refers to the "gospel of/concerning his Son" (Rom 1:3, 9; 2 Cor 1:19). The roots for this lie, first, in the Jewish tradition with David and his descendants formally appointed by God as a "son" chosen to rule over Israel, so representing a royal ideology, which, when combined with restoration eschatology, becomes messianism (2 Sam 7:12-16; Ps 2:7; 89:3-4, 19-37).

Second, influence emerges from the Jesus tradition, which emphasized Jesus' divine sonship (e.g., Mk 1:11; 9:7; 15:39). Importantly, Jesus' sonship for Paul is preexistent, as God sends his Son to fulfill a redemptive mission (Gal 4:4-5; Rom 8:3). Jesus is a divine son by virtue of his Davidic heritage (Rom 1:3), and yet this divine sonship came into a new eschatological function after the resurrection (Rom 1:4). Paul explains the Son's reconciling death (Rom 5:10) by allusion to the Aqedah tradition, so that just as Abraham did not spare his son Isaac from sacrifice (Gen 22:12-16), so too God did not spare his only Son but gave him up (Rom 8:32). This is mirrored in Paul's moving remark that the Son of God "loved me and gave himself for me" (Gal 2:20 NRSV). For Paul, to be saved means to experience a new exodus and be transferred to the "kingdom of the Son of his [God's] love" (Col 1:12-13), identical to "the kingdom of Christ and God" (Eph 5:5). Jesus' sonship is also eschatological in that Jesus is the Son who will return from heaven to save believers from wrath (1 Thess 1:9), to subjugate all anti-God opposition, and to then subject everything to the Father's dominion (1 Cor 15:24-28; Phil 3:21).

Furthermore, Jesus' divine sonship is something to be shared with believers; since believers are adopted as the Son's siblings and thereafter address God as "Abba, Father" (Rom 8:15; Gal 4:6), they are the Son's co-heirs (Rom 8:17; Gal 4:7) and are destined to be conformed to the Son's image, with the Son as the firstborn of a new-creation family (Rom 8:29). Jesus' sonship is filial, preexistent, Davidic, redemptive, eschatological, and participatory.

6.4. Last Adam. Paul depicts Jesus as the eschatological counterpart of the primeval Adam (Dunn 1998, 200). Just as the first Adam through his disobedience was the conduit by which *sin, death, and condemnation entered the world, so too is Jesus the new Adam, and through his obedience there is *righteousness, grace, life, justification, and resurrection now available (Rom 5:12-18; 1 Cor 15:20-21). Paul also engages in a christological reading of Psalm 8:6, where Jesus will fulfill the divinely given role for humanity to reign on behalf of God the Father over creation (1 Cor 15:24-28; Phil 3:21; Eph 1:22). In addition, whereas the first Adam became a "living soul" that was subject to corruption and mortality, the last Adam became a "life-giving spirit" in the sense that the risen Jesus has a heavenly body fit for the new creation, one that is imperishable, glorious, and immortal (1 Cor 15:45).

7. The Father and Jesus.

Paul stands in the Jewish monotheistic tradition (Rom 3:30; Gal 3:20; 1 Cor 8:4; Eph 4:6; 1 Tim 2:5). He acclaims God as the "father of us all" (Rom 4:16; Eph 4:6), and Jesus is "his Son" in a special sense (Rom 5:10; 8:3, 29, 32; 1 Cor 1:9; Gal 1:16; 4:4, 6; Col 1:13; 1 Thess 1:10). Paul construes Jesus as the agent of God the Father, especially in the salutations of letters, where Paul extends wishes of grace and *peace to his readers from God our Father and the Lord Jesus Christ (Rom 1:7; 1 Cor 1:3; 2 Cor 1:2; Gal 1:3; Eph 1:2; Phil 1:2; 1 Thess 1:1; 2 Thess 1:2; 1 Tim 1:2; 2 Tim 1:2; Titus 1:4; Philem 3). Elsewhere God is blessed as the Father of the Lord Jesus (2 Cor 11:31), or the Father is thanked in the name of Jesus (Col 3:17; Eph 5:20). It appears that God the Father is God toward believers only through the Lord Jesus, and Jesus is Savior to believers only on behalf of God the Father.

Paul's "gospel of God" centers on what God achieved in the work of the Son, while the Son's mission and person is indiscernible apart from God's relationship to him. Clearly, then, when Paul and his *coworkers and congregants spoke about God, they had to speak about Jesus; and when they spoke about Jesus they had to include God as well. Viewed this way, Paul's "Theology" implied a "Christology" and "Christology" affected "Theology" (de Jonge, 130; Schnelle, 392-93, 475). Consequently: "Jesus's first followers found themselves not only (as it were) permitted to use God-language for Jesus, but compelled to use Jesus-language for the One God," for the relation of Jesus to the Father is such that "one cannot now speak of this God without thinking of Jesus, or of Jesus without thinking of the one God, the creator, Israel's God" (N. T. Wright 2013, 655, 666).

Many detect here not a flexible monotheism with God the Father and a divinized human subject, nor ditheism split between a senior Father and lesser son, but what amounts to a binitarian monotheism (Hurtado 2003, 151-53) or a christological monotheism (Bauckham 2008). If there is no separation between God's being and action in Jewish discourse, so that Yahweh's action in the exodus constitutes Yahweh as the redeeming and covenanting God, then similarly, God the Father's sending, raising, and exalting of the Son is what defines the nature of the Father's god-ness. Jesus the Son is intrinsic to the Father's own identity as God, and that is a statement both about who God is and about who Jesus is (Watson, 105-6, 111-12). In effect, then, Jesus is defined in relation to God the Father, and the Father is defined in relation to the Son, in which case the Father-Son relationship is mutually constitutive for each other's identity as a divine person (see Richardson, 307; Watson, 111-19; Yeago, 375-77; Hill, 78; Bates 2015).

8. The Spirit and Jesus.

Paul does not have the Lukan and Johannine conception of Jesus as the giver of the Spirit. It is God who gives the *Holy Spirit (1 Thess 4:8; Gal 3:5; 4:6; 2 Cor 1:21-22; 5:5; Rom 5:5; Eph 1:17; 2 Tim 1:7). The Spirit is how God acted on Jesus in his resurrection (Rom 1:4; 8:11), and the conferral of the Spirit comes through Jesus, specifically through his death (Gal 3:14; Rom 5:5; 2 Cor 11:4; Titus 3:5-6). Intriguingly, though, Paul does refer to the "Spirit of Christ," which is parallel to the "Spirit of God" and is the proof that one belongs to God (Rom 8:9 NRSV; cf. Phil 1:19). The context of Romans 8:9-11 makes clear that the indwelling of the Spirit is the mode by which Christ inhabits believers and renders someone a child of God. Moreover, in Israel's sacred literature the experience of the Spirit was the experience of God as Spirit. Therefore, when the Holy Spirit conveys and communicates the presence of the risen Jesus, we are right to associate this with an experience as God as mediated by the Spirit. If Spirit-language is God-language, then the use of such language to depict Christ's presence and activity assumes that Christ is in some sense divine (Fatehi).

Interesting too are the several ways that Paul coordinates Jesus and the Spirit. Paul can make the "Lord Jesus Christ" and the "love of the Spirit" the basis for his exhortations to *prayer (Rom 15:30 NRSV). Imitation of the Lord is accompanied by *joy inspired by the Holy Spirit (1 Thess 1:6). A believer is washed, sanctified, and justified "in the name of the Lord Jesus Christ and in the Spirit of our God," indicative of a dual christological and pneumatological action in salvation (1 Cor 6:11 NRSV). There is a triadic account of salvation, which Paul proclaims as the "*mystery of God" revealed in "Jesus Christ, and him crucified" with "a demonstration of the Spirit and of power" (1 Cor 2:1-4; cf. Eph 3:2-6 NRSV), and a triadic benediction from "grace of the Lord Jesus Christ, the love of God, and the communion of the Holy Spirit" (2 Cor 13:13 NRSV). God's wisdom is provided by the Spirit's illumination, which in turns furnishes someone with the "mind of Christ" (1 Cor 2:16 NRSV). Paul can describe the Spirit as the "Lord" leading the church into the *freedom of a renewed knowledge in Christ (2 Cor 3:17-18), and elsewhere make the Spirit the agent of Jesus (Phil 1:19). Worship of God happens by the Spirit, with accompanying boasting in Christ Jesus (Phil 3:3) and confessing Jesus as Lord (1 Cor 12:3). Paul's strong binitarian focus on God the Father operating in/through/from Jesus Christ should not obscure the Spirit's role in a triadic economy of salvation, where the Spirit unites the believer to Christ, conveys Christ's presence to them, empowers service to Christ, illuminates believers with the mind of Christ, and ensures the inclusion of Christ in divine worship.

9. Paul's Divine Christology.

To what extent does Paul's Christology embody, anticipate, or align with the statements of the Nicene Creed (AD 381) that Jesus is the "only-begotten Son of God," "begotten, not made," "true God from true God," and "of one substance with Father" (see Rowe; Hill; Rosner)? Nicene trinitarianism was not built on a collection of prooftexts as much as it was a hermeneutical framework necessary to make sense of how Scripture affirmed God's oneness and Jesus' participation in God the Father's being. Put simply, Nicene Christology represents a synthetic convergence of Pauline and Johannine motifs as constructed through the process of patristic exegetical discussion and as articulated as part of the search for a scripturally sound and philosophically coherent conceptualization of God's god-ness and the relationships between the three divine persons.

Paul cannot be regarded as Nicaean in any exact sense; some passages sound prima facie subordinationist (1 Cor 3:23; 11:3; 15:24-28) or give succor to Arian interpretation (Col 1:15), and the divine nature of the Spirit is relatively underdeveloped (2 Cor 3:17-18). In addition, Paul's christological grammar is far more agential and relational and only implicitly ontological. However, Paul's christological affirmations provided the basic material for subsequent debate about the specificity of Jesus' divine nature and his shared nature with the Father and Spirit. Paul contributed pressures to think in directions that would eventually crystallize into fourth-century Nicene trinitarianism (Rowe). Several things suggest this:

First, Paul does make explicit identifications of Jesus as God. While the grammar of Romans 9:5 is disputed, it is rightfully rendered "the Messiah, who is God over all, forever praised" (NIV; see B. J. Wright; N. T. Wright 2013, 707-9; Carraway). Similarly, in Titus 2:13, there is reference to the "blessed *hope and the manifestation of the glory of our great God and Savior, Jesus Christ," which also predicates divinity of Jesus (see Stettler, 328). But then again, Moses (Philo, *Mos.* 1.158) and Melchizedek (11Q13 2.10) are called "god" in Jewish tradition, and so are Roman emperors such as Augustus in inscriptions and papyri (P.Oxy. 1143.4). So, in what sense is Jesus a divine being (Gieschen, 31-33; Yarbro Collins 2007, 57-61; Ehrman, 43-45)? Does it mean transcendent, heavenly, supernatural, angelic, humanly deified, semidivine, or a mode of being that is the same as or similar to God the Father? And if Jesus is as fully divine as the Father, what does it mean for monotheism, or does it imply modalism? Several scholarly proposals are worth exploring in this space.

L. Hurtado (2003; 2015; 2017; 2018) argues that the species of monotheism reflected generally in Second Temple literature and specifically in the NT was a strict monotheism. Furthermore, whereas ancient Judaism knew of divine chief agents who acted on behalf of God, the chief-agent category was adopted by the early church for Jesus, except that the experience of Jesus as the risen Lord caused a mutation in this category so that Jesus began to receive devotional and cultic attention in ways ordinarily reserved for the worship of Israel's one God. What emerged was a form of binitarian devotion in Jewish Christians circles loyal to Israel's ancestral traditions, which then migrated to Pauline communities.

G. Fee undertakes a rigorous exegetical approach, focusing on Christ's person rather than work, stressing Christ's preexistence and accenting how Christ shares in divine roles and prerogatives in Paul's thought. C. Tilling focuses on how Second Temple Judaism enunciated a unique relationship between God and Israel. Tilling notices that Jesus' relationship to the church in Paul's letters parallels how Yahweh relates to Israel in the Jewish Scriptures. Paul portrays a Christ-relation with believers in 1 Corinthians 8–10 using terms and categories drawn from the Jewish Scriptures that describe the relationship between Yahweh and Israel over against *idolatry.

R. Bauckham argues that Israel's God was unique by virtue of the divine name Yahweh, the distinction between Creator and creation, the covenant relationship with Israel, and the exclusive worship offered to him; this is what constitutes God's unique identity (Bauckham, *ABD* 3:812-19; Bauckham 2008). This identity is not *what* God is, but *who* God is, a matter of character, story, and relationships. Added to that, Bauckham argues that early Christian exegesis of the OT, especially passages such as Psalm 110:1, led early Christians to include Jesus precisely and unambiguously within the unique divine identity. Jesus is consistently portrayed as exalted above all powers and *principalities and does not emerge from the intermediary order (Col 1:16; Eph 1:21-22). Jesus is not, then, an intermediary figure correlated with God by virtue of performing a few divine functions. Such figures are never said to share in God's rule, participate in God's creative work, or receive God's worship, whereas Jesus does. Jesus shares in what makes God unique from creation.

N. T. Wright (2013, 644-709) regards Jewish monotheism to be creational and cultic. Beyond that, Wright finds that the overarching framework for Paul's Christology is the prophetic hope for the long-awaited return of Yahweh to Zion, which happens in the person of Jesus. It is in Jesus that God returns as king to visit his people and redeem them. Paul's christological tapestry combines the threads of exodus, redemption, tabernacle, Yahweh's return, wisdom, and kingship. This amounts to an eschatological monotheism: God comes in and as Jesus himself to put things to right. Thus, to see God's glory in the face of Jesus is to attribute to Jesus the return of God's glorious presence, which had been withdrawn since the exile (2 Cor 4:4-6; Ezek 43:4-5; 1 En. 22.14; 25.3, 7), and to acclaim Jesus as the exalted Lord in the language of Isaiah is to proclaim that God has returned to be enthroned as Israel's true king and as king of the world in Jesus (Phil 2:9-11; Is 45:23).

Second, Paul's use of OT Yahweh passages to describe Jesus is evidence for a strong identification of Jesus with God's sovereignty and self (see Capes). This is especially apparent in 1 Corinthians 8:6 and Philippians 2:9-11, where Jesus is incorporated within the monotheistic language of Deuteronomy 6:5 and Isaiah 45:23. The inescapable effect of this christologizing of monotheism is that Jesus is directly and uniquely associated with God (Hurtado 2003, 112), and it illustrates a conceptual overlap between God the Father and Christ Jesus (Kreitzer, 116). This is, says N. T. Wright, "A small step for the language; a giant leap for the theology. Jesus is not a 'second God': that would abrogate monotheism entirely. He is not a semi-divine intermediate figure. He is the one in whom the identity of Israel's God is revealed" (N. T. Wright 2013, 666). The combination of Christology and monotheism is "explosive," as it means that

> At the centre of his Jewish-style monotheism is a human being who lived, died and rose in very recent memory. Jesus is not a new God added to the pantheon. He is the human being in whom YHWH, Israel's one and only God, has acted within cosmic history, human history, and Israel's history to do for Israel, humanity and the world what they could not do for themselves. (N. T. Wright 2013, 684-83)

Importantly, the exaltation of Jesus does not add to God's identity; it reveals God's identity precisely in the exaltation of Jesus. For the Father's unique way of being Israel's God and Lord does not sparingly spill over onto Jesus, nor does Jesus somehow encroach on it in an invasive fashion; rather, Jesus is said here to belong to that which makes God unique in that he shares in the divine name *kyrios* (Rowe, 303; Hill, 95-96).

Third, Paul's articulation of Jesus' sonship anticipates the Nicene definition of "begotten, not made." Jesus is never adopted to divine sonship, nor elevated to divine honors in Paul's discourse (Bates 2014, 76-79; Bird 2017). Rather, Jesus' sonship is preexistent (Gal 4:4; Rom 8:3), and if God is the Father of the Son, and if God's Fatherhood is eternal, then by inference the Son's sonship likewise exists in eternity. Understood this way, "There is only one God, but the one God is never without his only begotten Son" (Yeago, 377). This is the biblical root of the Son's eternal begottenness, in that he eternally relates to the Father as the Son. The title "firstborn of all creation" (Col 1:15 NRSV) does not mean that Jesus was the first created being within creation. The title is not one of procreative order but of privileged position and preeminent status. Israel is designated God's "firstborn son" compared to other nations (Ex 4:22; Jer 31:9; 4 Ezra 6.58; Pss. Sol. 18.4), and Israel's king is likewise referred to as the "firstborn" compared to other kings (Ps 89:27). The designation "firstborn of all creation" operates as an "eschatological inheritance and as the title for Israel," and denotes Jesus' "rulership and supremacy over every creature" (Kim, 188-89). Jesus is the firstborn as the eschatological embodiment of Israel, the messianic ruler of God's kingdom, and the mediator of creation. Jesus, then, possesses an unsurpassed preeminence over God's creation, God's people, and God's kingdom. What is affirmed is both Jesus' kinship with creation and his kingship over creation. Jesus relates to creation in terms of his priority and primacy, sustaining its unity and enjoying its purpose (Col 1:16-17). H. Langkammer (*EDNT* 3:190-91) regards "firstborn" here not as a "matter of purely temporal priority of the pre-existence of Christ, but rather of a superiority of essence [compared to creation]." In effect, Jesus enters creation but is not from creation; he has a unique relationship to humanity within creation and represents God as the mediator of creation.

Fourth, Paul's Christology can be said to tacitly support Jesus' divine nature in an ontological sense. When the pro-Nicaeans called Jesus "true God from true God," they meant divine in a strong sense, not semidivine or mostly divine but divine in the same way as the Father (Ayres 2004, 2-5). Paul would likely have agreed with this sentiment even if he himself never expressed it that way. Paul did nothing to suggest that recognition of Jesus' divinity was merely the honorific and reflexive action of supplicants offering divine titles to a savior figure in the same way that a city might confer divine titles on an emperor who lifted a siege against them ("Emperor Caesar [Augustus], son of god, god Sebastos has by his benefactions to all men outdone even the Olympian gods" [IOlympia 53]). Paul did not think of Jesus as a "hero" or "immortal" (Herodotus, *Hist.* 2.44), or a kind of in-between demigod (Plutarch, *Is. Os.* 360-61), but closer to the categories of "eternal and unbegotten" (Plutarch, *Pel.* 16.5 [LCL]), and divine by "nature" not "decree" (Antisthenes, frg. 29 [LCL]). Paul did not consider Greco-Roman deities/*demons to have a "nature" or "being" comparable to God (1 Cor 8:4; 10:20; Gal 4:8).

In contrast, Paul does align Jesus with the authority, attributes, and actions of Israel's God, so that he functions as God's agent in creation, redemption, and consummation. Yet Paul exceeds a functional mode for Jesus' divinity. He does that, first, by locating Jesus within the Creator side of the Creator/creature distinction (1 Cor 8:6; Col 1:16). This was very important because the pagan gods had not made the world—yes, some stories involved them, but they were the mightiest part within the world and did not stand outside it (O'Donnell, 67). Then, second, Paul makes what are effectively ontological claims by stating that Jesus is in "very nature God" and has "equality with God" (Phil 2:6 NIV), which is the outward display of God's being and glory and expresses the inner reality of God's nature (Martin and Nash, 117). Paul declares too that in Jesus "all the fullness of the Deity dwells in bodily form" (Col 2:9) about which can be inferred: "The man Jesus Christ, now exalted, is not one of a hierarchy of intermediary beings, angelic or (in some sense) 'divine.' He is, uniquely, 'God's presence and his very self' . . . Christ is not a second, different Deity: he is the embodiment and full expression of the one God of Abraham, Isaac and Jacob" (N. T. Wright 1986, 108). The Nicaean description of Jesus as *homoousios* ("same substance") with the Father is a theological explication of Pauline judgments about Jesus sharing the form, equality, glory, and divinity of the Father in language that ruled out a radical disparity between their natures (Yeago, 379-80; Bauckham 2008, 59).

Thus, on the one hand, Paul arguably implies a divine ontology for Jesus, but on the other hand, his worship of Jesus also created a divine ontology for

Jesus. The continuous worship of Jesus in Pauline congregations created a symbolic reality where Jesus was honored not *as to* a god (see Pliny, *Ep.* 10.96.7), but *as* God the Son of creation, redemption, and consummation (see *2 Clem.* 1.1). The continuous worship of Jesus created its own type of ontology, as the liturgical acclamation reified Jesus' divine status into a divine nature shared between Jesus and the Father. One can surmise that Jesus' functional divinity gave rise to the worship of Jesus and so generated an ontic Christology already within the Pauline communities (Bauckham, *ABD* 3:815).

In conclusion, there are torrid debates over how Israel's God was unique compared to other deities and deified beings in antiquity, whether Jesus was included as God within monotheistic formulas or alongside God in those formulas, what constituted worship and whether Jewish worship ever incorporated angelic and human figures, whether Jesus was worshiped as God or beside God, how to move from functional to ontological divinity for Jesus, and how to explain Jesus as fully divine if he remains economically subordinated to the Father (see, e.g., McGrath; Dunn 2011). Even so, the overall impression one gets is that Paul's christological discourse operates in a theater that retains God's oneness and unique identity, God's relationship to both creation and to Israel, and God's role as Savior; and yet simultaneously seeks and somewhat struggles after language to redefine that identity, relationship, and role by way of reference to the Lord Jesus Christ. In Pauline idiom, God is "for us" in the Son (Rom 8:31) only as the messianic Son is "God over all, forever praised" (Rom 9:5 NIV). Similarly, the climax of new creation is where God is "all in all," filling everything in every way, pervading the universe with divine sovereignty and love, which proves to be coordinate with Christ filling and fulling everything so as to be "all in all" (Eph 1:23 NRSV; see Eph 4:10). In the end, God's communion with the universe will be christological, so that eschatological monotheism will be christological monotheism.

Paul's basic tenets are that Israel's God is one, the blessed Lord of creation, the faithful Lord of the covenant, and the Father of Jesus; while Jesus the Son is associated with God's unique divine name and glory, cosmic lordship, divine functions in creation and salvation, aversions to idolatry, worthiness of divine worship, and a mutually constitutive Father-Son relationship. Thus, the Father and Son (and Spirit) are distinct while integrated together in a complex web of authority, agency, binitarian devotion, belonging, fatherhood, filiality, functions, coordinations, relations, reciprocations, shared being, redemptive story, and redounding glory. The most reasonable explanation for Paul's christological discourse is that *God* is a rightful predicate for Jesus, and the remaining task is to establish what adjectives or imagery have the greatest utility to explain that predication in a sense compatible with Paul's discourse in its religious context and generative of the church's discussion about Jesus' unitive relationship to the Father.

See also Adam and Christ; Christ, Messiah; Conversion and Call of Paul; Creation and New Creation; Firstborn; God; Hellenism, Roman; Holy Spirit; Hymns, Hymn Fragments, Confessions; In Christ; Jesus and Paul; Lord; Name; Old Testament in Paul; Paul and Judaism; Religions, Greco-Roman; Resurrection; Salvation; Servant, Service; Son of God; Tradition; Wisdom; Worship.

BIBLIOGRAPHY. **L. Ayres,** *Nicaea and Its Legacy: An Approach to Fourth-Century Trinitarian Theology* (Oxford: Oxford University Press, 2004); **M. Bates,** *The Hermeneutics of the Apostolic Proclamation: The Center of Paul's Method of Scriptural Interpretation* (Waco, TX: Baylor University Press, 2012); idem, *The Birth of the Trinity: Jesus, God, and Spirit in New Testament and Early Christian Interpretations of the Old Testament* (Oxford: Oxford University Press, 2015); **R. Bauckham,** "The Worship of Jesus," *ABD* 3:812-19; idem, *Jesus and the God of Israel* (Carlisle, UK: Paternoster, 2008); **M. F. Bird,** *Jesus Is the Christ: The Messianic Testimony of the Gospels* (Downers Grove, IL: InterVarsity, 2009); idem, *Jesus the Eternal Son: Answering Adoptionist Christology* (Grand Rapids, MI: Eerdmans, 2017); **D. C. Capes,** *The Divine Christ: Paul, the Lord Jesus, and the Scriptures of Israel* (Grand Rapids, MI: Baker, 2018); **G. Carraway,** *Christ Is God over All: Romans 9:5 in the Context of Romans 9–11* (London: Bloomsbury T&T Clark, 2013); **J. D. G. Dunn,** *The Theology of Paul the Apostle* (Edinburgh: T&T Clark, 1998); idem, *Unity and Diversity in the New Testament: An Inquiry into the Character of Earliest Christianity*, 3rd ed. (London: SCM Press, 2006); idem, *Did the First Christians Worship Jesus? The New Testament Evidence* (London: SPCK, 2011); **B. D. Ehrman,** *How Jesus Became God: The Exaltation of a Jewish Preacher from Galilee* (New York: HarperOne, 2014); **P. Enns,** *Inspiration and Incarnation: Evangelicals and the Problem of the Old Testament* (Grand Rapids, MI: Baker, 2005); **M. Fatehi,** *The Spirit's Relation to the Risen Lord in Paul: An Examination of Its Christological Implications*

(Tübingen: Mohr Siebeck, 2000); **G. D. Fee,** *Pauline Christology: An Exegetical-Theological Study* (Peabody, MA: Hendrickson, 2007); idem, *Jesus the Lord According to Paul: A Concise Introduction* (Grand Rapids, MI: Baker, 2018); **J. Fitzmyer,** *Paul and His Theology: A Brief Sketch* (Englewood Cliffs, NJ: Prentice Hall, 1989); **S. J. Gathercole,** *The Pre-existent Son: Recovering the Christologies of Matthew, Mark, and Luke* (Grand Rapids, MI: Eerdmans, 2006); **C. Gieschen,** *Angelomorphic Christology: Antecedents and Early Evidence* (Leiden: Brill, 1998); **M. Hengel,** *The Son of God: The Origin of Christology and the History of Jewish Hellenistic Religion* (London: SCM Press, 1976); idem, *Between Jesus and Paul* (London: SCM Press, 1983); idem, *Studies in Early Christology* (London: T&T Clark, 1995); **W. Hill,** *Paul and the Trinity: Persons, Relations, and the Pauline Letters* (Grand Rapids, MI: Eerdmans, 2015); **F. Holzbrecher,** *Paulus und der historische Jesus: Darstellung und Analyse der bisherigen Forschungsgeschichte* (Tübingen: A. Francke, 2007); **K. Hopkins,** *A World Full of Gods: Pagans, Jews and Christians in the Roman Empire* (London: Phoenix, 2000); **L. W. Hurtado,** *The Lord Jesus Christ: Devotion to Jesus in Earliest Christianity* (Grand Rapids, MI: Eerdmans, 2003); idem, *One God, One Lord: Early Christian Devotion and Ancient Jewish Monotheism*, 3rd ed. (Philadelphia: Fortress, 2015); idem, *Ancient Jewish Monotheism and Early Christian Jesus-Devotion: The Context and Character of Christological Faith* (Waco, TX: Baylor University Press, 2017); idem, *Honoring the Son: Jesus in Earliest Christian Devotional Practice* (Bellingham, WA: Lexham, 2018); **M. de Jonge,** *God's Final Envoy: Early Christology and Jesus' Own View of His Mission* (Grand Rapids, MI: Eerdmans, 1998); **K. S. Kim,** *The Firstborn Son in Ancient Judaism and Early Christianity* (Leiden: Brill, 2019); **L. J. Kreitzer,** *Jesus and God in Paul's Eschatology* (Sheffield: JSOT Press, 1987); **A. H. I. Lee,** *From Messiah to Preexistent Son* (Eugene, OR: Wipf & Stock, 2005); **M. D. Litwa,** *Iesus Deus: The Early Depiction of Jesus as a Mediterranean God* (Minneapolis: Fortress, 2014); **M. Martin and B. Nash,** "Philippians 2:6-11 as Subversive *Hymnos*: A Study in the Light of Ancient Rhetorical Theory," *JTS* 60 (2015): 90-138; **S. M. McDonough,** *Christ as Creator: Origins of a New Testament Doctrine* (Oxford: Oxford University Press, 2009); **J. F. McGrath,** *The Only True God: Early Christian Monotheism in Its Jewish Context* (Chicago: University of Illinois Press, 2009); **J. Murphy-O'Connor,** *Paul: A Critical Life* (Oxford: Oxford University Press, 1997); **S. Nicholson,** *Dynamic Oneness: The Significance and Flexibility of Paul's One-God Language* (Eugene, OR: Pickwick, 2010); **M. Novenson,** *Christ Among the Messiahs: Christ Language in Paul and Messiah Language in Ancient Judaism* (Oxford: Oxford University Press, 2012); **J. J. O'Donnell,** *Pagans: The End of Traditional Religion and the Rise of Christianity* (New York: Ecco, 2016); **S. E. Porter,** *When Paul Met Jesus: How an Idea Got Lost in History* (Cambridge: Cambridge University Press, 2016); **N. Richardson,** *Paul's Language About God* (Sheffield: Sheffield Academic Press, 1994); **B. S. Rosner,** "Paul and the Trinity," in *The Essential Trinity: New Testament Foundations and Practical Relevance*, ed. B. D. Crowe and C. R. Trueman (Nottingham, UK: Inter-Varsity Press, 2016), 107-21; **C. K. Rowe,** "Biblical Pressure and Trinitarian Hermeneutics," *Pro Ecclesia* 11 (2002): 295-312; **U. Schnelle,** *Apostle Paul: His Life and Theology* (Grand Rapids, MI: Baker, 2005); **B. D. Smith,** "What Christ Does, God Does: Surveying Recent Scholarship on Christological Monotheism," *CurBR* 17 (2019): 184-208; **H. Stettler,** *Die Christologie der Pastoralbriefe* (Tübingen: Mohr Siebeck, 1998); **J. L. Sumney,** *Steward of God's Mysteries: Paul and Early Church Tradition* (Grand Rapids, MI: Eerdmans, 2017); **C. Tilling,** *Paul's Divine Christology* (Grand Rapids, MI: Eerdmans, 2012); **F. Watson,** "The Triune Divine Identity: Reflections on Pauline God-Language, in Disagreement with J. D. G. Dunn," *JSNT* 80 (2000): 99-124; **B. J. Wright,** "Jesus as THEOS: A Textual Examination," in *Revisiting the Corruption of the New Testament: Manuscript, Patristic, and Apocryphal Evidence*, ed. D. B. Wallace (Grand Rapids, MI: Kregel, 2011), 232-33; **N. T. Wright,** *Colossians and Philemon* (Downers Grove, IL: InterVarsity Press, 1986); idem, *What Saint Paul Really Said* (London: Lion, 1997); idem, *Paul and the Faithfulness of God*, 2 vols. (London: SPCK, 2013); **A. Yarbro Collins,** "The Worship of Jesus and the Imperial Cult," in *The Jewish Roots of Christological Monotheism*, ed. C. D. Newman, J. R. Davila, and G. S. Lewis (Leiden: Brill, 1999), 234-57; idem, "'How on Earth Did Jesus Become a God?': A Reply," in *Israel's God and Rebecca's Children: Christology and Community in Early Judaism and Christianity*, ed. D. Capes et al. (Waco, TX: Baylor University Press, 2007), 55-66; **D. S. Yeago,** "The New Testament and the Nicene Dogma: A Contribution to the Recovery of Theological Exegesis," *Sewanee Theological Review* 45 (2002): 371-84; **D. Zeller,** "New Testament Christology in its Hellenistic Reception," *NTS* 46 (2001): 312-33.

M. F. Bird

CHRONOLOGY OF PAUL

Chronology is the backbone of history. For writing a history of early Christianity in the first century AD, the Pauline chronology is indispensable. If Luke–Acts was written by a part-time companion of Paul, then such a chronology is made possible by the combination of data from this work and the undisputed letters of the *apostle.

1. Evaluation of the Sources
2. Methodological Considerations
3. Individual Historical Data
4. Chronological Hints and Sequences of Events in the Pauline Epistles
5. A Synthesis of Events in the Pauline Epistles and Acts
6. The Beginning and End of Paul's Life
7. Chronological Synthesis

1. Evaluation of the Sources.

In NT studies there is no consensus about the chronology of Paul's life and his letters, due to different evaluations of the sources and opposite methodologies. In this article the integrity of the seven undisputed Pauline letters (Galatians, 1 Thessalonians, 1 Corinthians, Philippians, Philemon, 2 Corinthians, Romans) is assumed: it is not possible to rearrange hypothetical fragments into a certain chronological sequence. The six disputed letters are of limited value for establishing a chronology. The "lawless one" from 2 Thessalonians 2:3 cannot be identified with a certain Roman emperor, and Ephesians is too general an epistle to draw chronological conclusions. Compared to the letter to Philemon, the personal notes and geographical hints point to an origin of Colossians in Paul's lifetime (see 5.3 below). Scholars such as F. F. Bruce (1977, 443) and I. H. Marshall (57-92) assume that the Pastoral Epistles (1–2 Timothy, Titus) are expanded from shorter genuine Pauline letters and contain valuable historical information.

In line with the early church tradition, the Acts of the Apostles is attributed to Luke (Hengel and Schwemer, 6-11; Schnabel 2012, 21-28). As a part-time coworker of Paul (Philem 24), Luke was present at crucial stages of the apostle's career, as the "we" sections of Acts testify (Acts 16:10-16; 20:5-15; 21:1-18; 27:1–28:16). Luke could also gain firsthand information about other periods of Paul's life, either from Paul himself or from other coworkers. Therefore, Acts should not be classified as a secondary source (Keener, 166-257). In some cases the NT data can be supplemented by secular sources or traditions of the post-NT church.

2. Methodological Considerations.

Attempts to emancipate Pauline chronology from the historical framework of Acts differ rather widely (Knox, 68; Lüdemann, 262-63; Campbell, 412-14). This approach involves many subjective decisions and produces only uncertain results. To the contrary, chronological reconstructions that hold to Acts as a reliable source show remarkable agreement for the time from Paul's conversion until his arrival at Rome (Dunn, 512; Porter; Riesner 2011, 22-23; Schnabel 2012, 43-45). The following reconstruction proceeds in five steps:

1. By combining NT data and extracanonical sources, we ascertain as much individual chronological data as possible.
2. We gain some chronological hints, as well as the sequences of some events, from the Pauline epistles.
3. We attempt a combination of the sequences of events both in the Pauline epistles and in the book of Acts.
4. I offer an addendum with suggestions about the beginning and the end of Paul's life.
5. We integrate all the available data in a chronological synthesis.

3. Individual Historical Data.

3.1. The Crucifixion of Jesus. Jesus was condemned by Pontius Pilate, the prefect of Judea from 26 to 36 CE (Josephus, *Ant.* 18.89-95.122-126). Jesus was crucified on a Friday (Mt 27:62; Mk 15:42; Lk 23:54; Jn 19:31) and the following Sabbath was the first day of Passover (Jn 18:28; 19:14). Paul knew that Jesus was executed at the time of the slaughtering of the Passover lambs (1 Cor 5:7). Hence, according to the Jewish calendar, Jesus was crucified on Nisan 14. He could be called "first fruits [*aparchē*]" (1 Cor 15:20), because he rose on the "third day" (1 Cor 15:4), which was Nisan 16, when the firstfruits of corn were offered in the *temple (see Lev 23:10-11). Between the years 26 and 36, Nisan 14 fell on a Friday only two times, namely, April 7, 30, or April 3, 33. The year 30 is to be preferred on several grounds: John the Baptist began his preaching "in the fifteenth year of the reign [*hēgemonia*] of Emperor Tiberius" (Lk 3:1 NRSV). Counted from the coregency with Augustus in 12/13, the career of the Baptist started in 26/27. Jesus appeared in public forty-six years after the (re)construction of the Jerusalem temple by Herod the Great (Jn 2:20). This leads to 27/28 (see *Ant.* 15.380), followed by an activity of two or three years (Jn 2:13; 6:4; 12:1), so Jesus' *death can be dated between 29 and 31. Clement of

Alexandria knew April 7 as the crucifixion day (*Strom.* 1.21.146), and Tertullian placed the death of Jesus in "the year of the Gemini" (*Adv. Jud.* 8). Since this calculation probably originated in Egypt, where the year began in August, 30 and not 29 is meant. The crucifixion of Jesus in 30 is a fixed date after (*terminus post quem*) which the *conversion of Paul must have happened.

3.2. Paul's Conversion. A tradition dating the stoning of Stephen (Acts 7:54–8:1) seven years after the *resurrection is rather late and can be explained by speculations about epochs providentially fixed by symbolic numbers of years. The earliest tradition about the time of Paul's *call goes back to the second century at least, and since it is attested in very different sources it seems reliable. The Jewish-Christian Ascension of Isaiah (9.16), the Gnostic Apocryphon of James (Nag Hammadi Codex 1.2.19-24), and the apocryphal Acts of Paul (*TU* n.s. 7/2, 130) place the conversion either one and a half years after the resurrection or "in the second year after the *ascension." From the year 30 this would lead to 31/32.

3.3. Flight from Damascus. Paul had to leave "when the ethnarch of King Aretas guarded the city of the Damascenes" (2 Cor 11:32). Since the Nabataean king Aretas IV is the only person mentioned both in the undisputed Pauline letters and in secular sources, some scholars thought they had found an absolute date for anchoring a chronology (Campbell, 182-89). But neither the literary sources nor the numismatic evidence proves that Damascus was handed over to Aretas by the emperor Caligula between 37 and 39, or that it was violently occupied by the Nabataeans around the same time (Hengel and Schwemer, 129-31). The term *ethnarchēs* is also used for the overseer of the Jewish quarter in Alexandria (Josephus, *Ant.* 14.117; Strabo, *Geogr.* 17.798), and indeed a Nabataean colony existed in Damascus (Donfried, 1020-21). The mention of Aretas only means that the flight of Paul must have occurred before the death of the king in 40 (*terminus ante quem*).

3.4. Persecution by Agrippa and Famines Under Claudius. Agrippa I, called "Herod" in Acts since as a grandson of Herod the Great he belonged to his dynasty, ruled from 41 to 44 (Josephus, *Ant.* 19.343). *James, son of Zebedee, was "killed with the sword" (Acts 12:1-2 NRSV) around the beginning of his reign. Agrippa's order should demonstrate his unrestricted authority to inflict the death penalty as the new Jewish king (*ius gladii*) and also win the support of the majority population by persecuting a dissident religious minority. Around the same time (39/40) the antipathy against the new messianic movement increased as Jews took part in riots directed against the community, a mixed group of Jews and *Gentiles (Acts 11:19-26), in the Syrian metropolis Antioch (*Chronicle of John Malalas* 244-245). The reign of Emperor Claudius (41–54) was marked by a series of severe aridities (*assidue sterilitates*; Suetonius, *Claud.* 18.2). The Jewish Christians of Judea also experienced a famine (Acts 11:28), which was particularly catastrophic in 44/46 (Josephus, *Ant.* 20.51-53.101). Around the time of Agrippa's death in early 44 (see Acts 12:19-23), Barnabas and Paul brought a collection from Antioch to *Jerusalem (Acts 11:29-30; 12:25). A visit in 44 of Queen Helena of Adiabene, a convert to Judaism (*Ant.* 20.51-53), served the same purpose to bring help in the time of famine (Riesner 1998, 132-33).

3.5. Sergius Paullus. According to the time frame of Acts, Barnabas and Paul met the proconsul Sergius Paul[l]us (Acts 13:6-12) on a first missionary journey after the death of Agrippa in 44 on Cyprus. An inscription from Soloi on this island mentioning a proconsul Paulus, dated around 124 AD (IGRR III 930), is too late. Another inscription from Cypriote Kytheria, variously dated under Tiberius, Caligula, or Claudius, mentions a Quintus Sergius (IGRR III 935). But the completion of the fragment into "Paulus, the proconsul" must be regarded as pure conjecture. An inscription from Rome names a certain L. Sergius Paullus, who was apparently curator of the Tiber in 41/42 (CIL VI 31545). Following the usual Roman **cursus honorum*, this office would fit to a later proconsulship of a senatorial province such as Cyprus and into the chronological framework of Acts as well. The family of the Sergii owned much land in southern Galatia (MAMA VII 319.321.330/31.485); hence a recommendation by the proconsul would have supported the *mission in this region.

3.6. Expulsion of Jews from Rome. As the earliest source, Acts 18:2 testifies to an expulsion of Jews from Rome by Claudius, and in about AD 130, Suetonius did the same (*Claud.* 25.4). Matters are complicated because Cassius Dio mentions an edict against Jewish assemblies in the capital (*Hist.* 60.6.6). It is not at all clear whether Dio dates this ban to the accession of Claudius (41/42) or whether he offers a summary of measures from his entire reign beforehand. Ancient historians prefer the solution that an original ban was later aggravated by an expulsion, which Orosius (fourth/fifth century) dates to 49 ("the ninth year of Claudius"; *Adv. Pag.* 7.6.15-16). Orosius cannot have inferred the date from Acts; indeed, he says he knows it from another source, perhaps from second-century Jewish Christian historian Hegesippos (Riesner 1998, 180-87). From Suetonius's report, one may deduce that the expulsion was caused by riots about the new messianic belief ("*impulsore Chresto*") preached in Roman synagogues. The years around 48/49 were generally troublesome for early Christianity because of Zealot uprisings in Judea (Josephus, *J.W.* 2.232-246) and a Jewish persecution in Antioch (*Chronicle of John Malalas* 247).

3.7. ***Gallio, Proconsul of Achaia.*** In 1905, E. Bourguet published an inscription from Delphi, to where a few more fragments were later assigned (SIG 801). This rescript of Claudius dates the beginning of the proconsularship of L. Iunius Gallio in the senatorial province of Achaia to July 1, 51. Paul stood before his law court in *Corinth (Acts 18:12-17), and so 51/52 is an absolute date for the life of the apostle. It seems that Gallio did not serve the full year of office but had left the province capital earlier out of fear for his health (see Seneca, *Ep.* 104.1), possibly before the end of the Mediterranean naval season in October 51. Before the interrogation Paul met "Aquila . . . who had recently [*prosphatōs*] come from Italy . . . , because Claudius had ordered all Jews to leave Rome" (Acts 18:1-2 NRSV). Hence, Paul's arrival to Corinth must be dated between 49 and 51. The interrogation happened more likely at the beginning of Gallio's term in 51, when the synagogue leaders had not yet known his anti-Jewish feelings (see Acts 18:12-17).

3.8. ***Paul in Ephesus.*** When Paul stayed in the capital of Asia Minor he became the target of riots (Acts 19:23-40). Normally, Luke refers to proconsuls by their name, but in connection with these disturbances, he uses an undefined plural expression for the leading local authorities (*anthypatoi*, Acts 18:8). Perhaps it can be linked with the confusion in *Ephesus after the death of Claudius in October 13, 54 (Bruce 1990, 421). Immediately, at the latest in December 54 or January 55, his wife Agrippina gave orders to kill Silanus, the proconsul of Asia Minor (Tacitus, *Ann.* 1.3.1; Cassius Dio, *Hist.* 61.6.4-5). While the office was vacant the city was led by three deputies.

3.9. ***The Last Journey to Jerusalem.*** A "we" narrative describes a journey from Philippi to Jerusalem, where Paul planned to celebrate Pentecost (Acts 20:6–21:15). As an eyewitness of this trip, Luke gives quite concrete chronological details. Apparently the apostle left Philippi immediately "after the days of Unleavened Bread" (Acts 20:6 NRSV). According to Lukan usage (Lk 24:1), the "first day of the week," when Paul stayed at Troas (Acts 20:7 NRSV), must refer to a Sunday. Since Luke counts the day from sunrise to sunrise (Acts 4:3-5; 10:3-23), the Christian meeting did not take place on Saturday but on Sunday evening and the subsequent departure on Monday morning. Paul stayed for seven days (counted inclusively) in Troas (Acts 20:6), and so he must have arrived on the Tuesday of the previous week. If one subtracts the five days of travel from Philippi (Acts 20:6), one arrives at a Friday for the departure, so that the Passover began and ended on a Thursday. Astronomical calculations make it probable that between 52 and 60, Nisan 14 as the beginning of the Passover fell on a Thursday only once, on April 7, 57 (Jewett, 47-50).

3.10. ***Paul in Jerusalem.*** When Paul visited the temple, a riot based on false accusations broke out, and he was rescued only by Roman soldiers (Acts 21:27-36). The interrogating tribune thought that Paul might be a certain "Egyptian who recently stirred up a revolt and led the four thousand assassins out into the wilderness" (Acts 21:38 NRSV). The rebel leader had escaped (Josephus, *Ant.* 171-172), and there was fear that he might ignite another uprising. The revolt occurred after the death of Claudius in October 54 (*J.W.* 2.261-263; *Ant.* 20.167-172) and after a series of actions by the new emperor, Nero (*Ant.* 20.158-164). The earliest possible dating of the revolt is 55, and it might have been influenced by apocalyptic expectations linked to the Sabbath year 55/56.

3.11. ***From Felix to Festus.*** Paul was *prisoner in Jerusalem and Caesarea under the procurators Felix and Festus. Felix was protected by his brother (Josephus, *Ant.* 20.182) even after Pallas was suspended as head of the Imperial finance administration in 55 (Tacitus, *Ann.* 13.14), because he was rehabilitated in the next year (*Ann.* 13.23) and remained very influential until his assassination under Nero in 62 (Cassius Dio, *Hist.* 62.14.3). Hence the change of procuratorship from Felix to Festus (Acts 24:27) could have happened after 55 and may be dated by numismatical evidence (Riesner 1998, 223). The last coins, certainly issued under Felix, are from the first year of Nero's rule (54/55). Coins from 56/57 are still missing, but in the fifth year of the emperor (58/59), an extraordinary large number of coins were struck in Judea, which points to the arrival of a new procurator. The conflicting dates of the change in Eusebius (*Hist. eccl.* 2.22;

Chron.) may be explained by his misunderstanding of a source attesting to the year 59.

3.12. Synthesis of Individual Data.

Table 1.

Year	Event
30	Crucifixion of Jesus
31/32	Paul's call, near Damascus
before 40	Flight from Damascus Under Aretas IV
after 41/42	Meets proconsul Sergius Paulus on Cyprus
around 44	With Barnabas in Jerusalem
49	Expulsion of Jews from Rome; afterwards Paul meets the exiled Aquila in Corinth
51	Paul in Corinth under Gallio
54/55	Paul in Ephesus
57	From Philippi to Jerusalem
59	Festus procurator of Judea; Paul prisoner in Caesarea

The sequence of all the individual data is in agreement with the narrative framework of Acts.

4. Chronological Hints and Sequences of Events in the Pauline Epistles.

4.1. The Autobiographical Retrospective in Galatians 1–2. After his call, Paul went to "Arabia" and returned to Damascus (Gal 1:17). "After three years" he went to Jerusalem (Gal 1:18) and then stayed in Syria and Cilicia (Gal 1:21). "After fourteen years" he ascended again to Jerusalem (Gal 2:1). Some questions cannot be answered on the basis of the letter, only by integrating the notes in an overarching chronological framework (see 5.4 below): (1) Are the "three years" and "fourteen years" to be counted consecutively or onward from the call? (2) Did the conflict with *Peter in Antioch (Gal 2:11-14) take place after the second journey to Jerusalem, or was it placed out of chronological sequence for a rhetorical purpose? (3) When were the Galatian communities founded?

4.2. A Series of Events Based on First Thessalonians. Before founding the community in Thessalonica, capital of the province Macedonia, Paul visited the Roman colony Philippi (1 Thess 2:2; cf. Phil 4:15-16). After his departure from Thessalonica he went to Athens in Achaia (1 Thess 3:1).

4.3. Events Linked to a Collection. The sequence of three letters is established, because the *collection was announced in 1 Corinthians (1 Cor 16:1-4), completed at the time of 2 Corinthians (2 Cor 8:1–9:15) and close to its delivery to Jerusalem when Romans was written (Rom 15:25-27). Whether the collection mentioned in Galatians 2:10 is the same must be discussed in connection with the dating of Galatians (see 5.4 below). First Corinthians was written in Ephesus (1 Cor 16:9). Second Corinthians looks back on an "affliction in Asia [Ephesus]" (2 Cor 1:8-10) and on a stay at Troas (2 Cor 2:12). Evidently, the letter was written in Macedonia (2 Cor 2:13). A future trip to Judea is announced (2 Cor 1:16; cf. 1 Cor 16:3-4), which will be preceded by a visit to Corinth (2 Cor 9:4). Afterward, missionary work in unreached regions is planned (2 Cor 10:16). The letter to the Romans, written in Corinth (see 5.1 below), looks forward to a mission in Spain after Paul would have visited Jerusalem and Rome (Rom 15:22-29).

4.4. The Interrelation of the Three Sequences. It is impossible to deduce from the letters alone how much time elapsed between Paul's sojourn in Ephesus and his certainly earlier visit to Corinth. In addition, it cannot be decided whether his visits to Macedonia and Achaia, attested by the second sequence, if related with the first sequence, should be placed before or after the apostolic meeting of Galatians 2:1-10. An answer might only be conjectural, if the evidence of Acts is excluded (Knox, 40-52).

5. A Synthesis of Events in the Pauline Epistles and Acts.

5.1. From Macedonia to Jerusalem and Rome (Acts 20–28). For this sequence, it is possible to combine a significant number of data from Acts and external sources. The sending of Paul to trial in Rome (Acts 24:27) happened after the change of procuratorship of Judea in 59 (see 3.11 above). Indeed, in this year, the Day of Atonement as the critical date for a sea voyage (Acts 27:9) fell very late (Jewett, 50-52). This strengthens the credibility of the detailed chronological indications within the "we" report about the trip from Philippi to Jerusalem pointing to 57 (see 3.9). If Paul was in Jerusalem for Pentecost in 57, he could have been mistaken for the Egyptian rebel (Acts 21:38) whose uprising was possibly connected to the Passover in 56 (see 3.10 above). According to this reconstruction, two years elapsed between Paul's arrival at Jerusalem in 57 and his sending to Rome in 59, corresponding to a "two-year imprisonment" at Caesarea (Acts 24:27). Therefore, one might also trust "the two whole years" for a subsequent captivity in Rome (Acts 28:30), bringing the narrative of Acts to an end in 62.

Acts 20:1-3 agrees with 2 Corinthians 2:13 in stating that the voyage to Jerusalem was preceded by a visit to

Macedonia and Achaia. "Erastus, the city treasurer" who is greeted in Romans 16:23 (NRSV) can be identified with a high Roman officeholder from Corinth (IKorinthKent 99-100). Luke knew that Paul planned to travel to Rome via Jerusalem (Acts 19:21) and also refers to the Jerusalem collection briefly (Acts 24:17). Paul made his travel plans for the first time known in Ephesus (Acts 19:21-22), matching the first undisputed mentions of the collection (1 Cor 16:1-4; 2 Cor 8-9). A date of Romans in early 57 could explain why Paul had to deal with the question of paying taxes (Acts 13:1-7). The order of a severe tax by Nero incited strong opposition in 58 (Tacitus, *Ann.* 13.50-51).

5.2. From the Apostolic Council in Jerusalem to Ephesus (Acts 15–18). Possibly Paul already tried to realize his long-cherished plan to visit Rome (Rom 1:13; 15:22-23) on the second missionary journey. He could have followed the Via Egnatia from Thessalonica to Dyrrhachium in Illyria and from there sail on to Brundisium in Italy. But in early 50 at the latest Paul learned about the expulsion of Jews from Rome in 49 (see 3.6 above), and he went to Achaia (Acts 17:15). Paul stood before Gallio at the beginning of his office in summer 51 (see 3.7 above), and he left Corinth soon after (Acts 18:18). Paul's one-and-a-half-year stay at Corinth (Acts 18:11) points to a beginning of his mission in the city in 50. Here is a remarkable chronological fit of three independent sources: the Gallio inscription, Acts, and Orosius. The departure from Corinth in the second half of 51 and his travels to Syria and Judea via Ephesus (Acts 18:18-22) must have happened before the end of the naval season in October. Since the Taurus Mountains were impassable in winter, a journey from Jerusalem and Antioch to Ephesus, through the Phrygian part of the province Galatia (Acts 18:22-23; 19:1), would only be possible in early 52 (Riesner 1998, 313).

Starting from Paul's well-dated first stay in Corinth, one can establish data of the preceding second missionary journey. The churches in Philippi and Thessalonica (Acts 16:11–17:9) were founded in 49/50. The majority of scholars date 1 Thessalonians to the beginning of Paul's stay in Corinth in 50, since he had to leave Thessalonica very soon (see 1 Thess 2:17-18). The sharp polemic in 1 Thessalonians 2:14-16 may relate to reports about Jewish persecutions in Syria and Judea in 48/49 (see 3.6 above) and to the disappointment about a failed mission in Rome because of Claudius's expulsion edict in 49 (see above). The journey from Jerusalem via Antioch across the Taurus Mountains to visit the churches in the southern part of the province of Galatia, and then along through the western part of Asia Minor to the Aegean Sea (Acts 15:30–16:8), could not have taken place entirely in 49. Therefore, the apostolic council of Acts 15 must be dated to 48. Luke's sequence of the foundation of the churches in Philippi, Thessalonica, Athens, and Corinth is confirmed by Paul (1 Thess 2:2; 3:1; Phil 4:15-16; 2 Cor 11:7-9).

5.3. From Ephesus to Achaia (Acts 18–20). Here the sequence of events can be placed chronologically with the help of the previous and the subsequent series (see 5.2 and 5.1 above). From Paul's arrival in the first half of 52, a stay of slightly less than three years in Ephesus (Acts 20:31) leads to a departure at the end of 54 or early 55, when local riots were dangerous for the apostle (see 3.8 above). Since 2 Corinthians 1:8-10 looks back to a relatively recent life threat in Ephesus (see 4.3 above), the letter should be dated to 55/56. The abolition of Claudius's expulsion edict after his death in 54 explains why, by the time of 2 Corinthians 10:16 already, Paul could plan a trip to Spain via Rome (see Rom 15:20-24). His travels after the stay in Ephesus probably required two winters rather than one (Riesner 1998, 300-301). Perhaps Paul undertook a mission in the eastern part of Macedonia and as far as Illyricum (see Rom 15:19) in this period (Schnabel 2004, 1250-57). Acts and Paul agree in stating an activity at Troas, preceded and followed by stays in Macedonia (2 Cor 2:12-13; Acts 20:1-6).

First Corinthians, being written in Ephesus (1 Cor 16:8-9), should probably be placed toward the end of Paul's stay in 54 (before Passover?; 1 Cor 5:8). Despite increasing opposition (1 Cor 15:32; 16:5-9), he delayed a trip to Corinth to complete his present missionary work. To conjecture an intermediate visit to Corinth is not necessary because the phrase "This is the third time I am coming to you" (2 Cor 13:1 NRSV) can mean the third attempt of a visit after two failed ones (see 2 Cor 1:15-16). Early church tradition identified the "tearful letter" (see 2 Cor 2:3-4; 7:8-9) with 1 Corinthians (Ambrosiaster). When writing Philippians, Paul expected his release from prison and planned a visit to Philippi (Phil 1:18-27; 2:24). This almost excludes a composition during a Roman imprisonment (see 6.2 below) and points to an Ephesian arrest in 54/55 (Riesner 1998, 212-16). Evidently, Philemon belonged to the community of Colossae (see Col 4:9, 17 with Philem 2, 10-11). Paul met Philemon's slave Onesimus during an imprisonment (Philem 10) that could neither have been in distant Caesarea nor Rome but in nearby Ephesus. According to the ancient Marcionite Prologue, Colossians was written during an Ephesian imprisonment, and this would apply to Philemon, too.

5.4. From the Conversion to the Apostolic Council in Jerusalem (Acts 9–15). A majority of scholars identify the meeting in Galatians 2:1-10 with the apostolic council in Acts 15. But a growing number of exegetes identify the collection visit of Barnabas and Paul (Acts 11:28-30; 12:15) with Galatians 2:1-10 (Porter; Schnabel 2012, 44). This reconstruction offers a sequence of events that corresponds to Acts without any problems and is also historically plausible. When Galatians was written, no fundamental decision about the inclusion of Gentiles had been made, so Paul could only refer to a precedent: at his second visit to Jerusalem, Titus was not compelled to be circumcised (Gal 2:3). After the growth of mixed communities in Syria and the foundation of largely Gentile Christian churches in southern Galatia, the growing threat by Zealot persecutions in 48 (see 3.6 above) explains Peter's and Barnabas's concern for the Judean Jewish Christians (Gal 2:13-14) and made a clear decision necessary (Acts 15:13-21).

Since a mission to the region of Galatia in the middle of Anatolia is attested neither by Acts (Acts 16:6; 18:23 [Schnabel 2012, 668, 782-83]) nor by Galatians, this letter was addressed to the communities in the Phrygian and Lycaonian parts of the *provincia Galatica* with their influential Jewish communities. Galatians had been written very soon (Gal 1:6) after the founding at the first missionary journey (Acts 13–14) and in immediate reaction to the Antioch incident (Gal 2:11-14). If dated before and not after the apostolic council of 48, it is understandable that, in around 54, Paul could report effortlessly to Peter, Barnabas, and the Lord's brothers (1 Cor 9:1-6). Galatians 2:10 can be understood as a retrospect to the collection of 44/45 (Schnabel 2004, 988-91). If twelve to thirteen years (Gal 2:1) are subtracted, there is a clear match with Paul's call in 31/32 (see 3.2 above). This speaks against a consecutive counting of the "fourteen years" from the first visit to Jerusalem on. This visit (also mentioned in Acts 9:26-29), two to three years after the call (Gal 1:18), would have taken place in 33/34, followed by a stay in Syria-Cilicia (Gal 1:21), then in Tarsus/Cilicia (Acts 9:30).

Luke knew nothing of a Pauline Gentile mission in Nabataea (Acts 9:23-25), which some scholars conjectured from Galatians 1:17. According to Acts 22:17-21, Paul received a corresponding call through a *vision in the temple during his postconversion visit in 33/34, making Jerusalem the starting point of his Gentile mission (see Rom 15:19). This vision cannot be identified with the ecstatic experience "fourteen years" before writing 2 Corinthians (2 Cor 12:2-9), because it was communicated in understandable words. Isaiah 6 stands behind both Luke's description of the vision and Paul's explanation of the *mystērion* of God's salvific plan for the Gentiles revealed to him (Rom 11:25). In Isaiah 66:18-21, the apostle found the way of his mission prophetically announced (Rom 15:16-28) in terms of ancient geography: Jerusalem, Tarsus, Cilicia, Lydia in Asia Minor, Mysia, Bithynia, Macedonia/Greece, and the western end of the world. This corresponds closely with the route of his mission in Acts (Riesner 1998, 245-53; Dunn, 541-44).

6. The Beginning and End of Paul's Life.

6.1. The Birth of Paul. Paul earned Roman citizenship from his father (Acts 22:28). According to Jerome, his parents had been enslaved during a Jewish rebellion (*Vir. ill.* 3.5). Indeed, their native city Giscala in Upper Galilee was a Zealot stronghold (Josephus, *J.W.* 2.585; 4.84). Such a scenario would explain how an anti-Roman Pharisee (Phil 3:5-6; Gal 1:14) could obtain citizenship, since his father got it automatically when he was freed by his master (*manumissio*). Following the death of Herod the Great in 4 BC (*J.W.* 2.11-13) and after the installation of a direct Roman rule over Judea in AD 6 (*J.W.* 2.117-118), revolts broke out. Thus, one may date the birth of Paul in Tarsus (Acts 22:3) around the turn of the era, which would correspond to notes stating that at the stoning of Stephen in 31/32 (Acts 7:58) Paul was a *neanias* (one under forty) and around 54/55 an older man (*presbytēs*; Philem 9).

6.2. After the End of Acts. According to Luke the legal situation of Paul was rather favorable (Acts 25:24-27), which rules out an execution already at the end of his Roman imprisonment in 62. The unanimous church tradition testifies to his martyrdom in connection with the Neronian persecution after the fire of Rome in July 64 (Eusebius, *Hist. eccl.* 3.25.4-8). According to ancient local tradition, Paul was exiled and reached "the farthest limits of the West" (*1 Clem.* 5.5-7, trans. Lightfoot and Harmer). Apparently, the first Roman trial had ended neither with the death penalty nor with a release but with an exile to Spain (see Muratorian Canon 38-39). From Philippians 2:24 and the Pastoral Epistles (1 Tim 1:3; Titus 1:5; etc.), some infer a last journey to the East. Such a reconstruction presupposes that Paul had abandoned his crucial Spanish plan, and Acts 20:38 almost eliminates the possibility that, after his visit to Milet in 57, he would see Asia Minor again. Additionally, Philippians had more likely been written around 54/55 in Ephesus and not in Rome (see 5.3 above). Second Timothy seems to presuppose a second Roman imprisonment leading to death (2 Tim 1:16-17; 4:6-18; Schnabel 2004, 1270-71).

7. Chronological Synthesis.

Table 2.

Contemporary History	Paul and Early Christian Events
26–36: Pilate prefect of Judea	30: Crucifixion of Jesus
	31/32: Paul's call
	33/34: Paul in Jerusalem
	ca. 34–42: Paul in Syria and Cilicia
37: Death of Tiberius 37–41: Gaius Caligula	39/40: Jewish persecution in Antioch
41: Agrippa I king of Judea	41/42: Martyrdom of James, son of Zebedee
	ca. 42–44: Paul in Antioch
44: Death of Agrippa I	44/45: Paul with Barnabas in Jerusalem (collection)
After 41/42: Sergius Paullus, Cypriote proconsul	Between 45 and 47: Paul with Barnabas in Cyprus and southern Galatia
48/49: Zealot uprisings in Judea; Jewish persecution in Antioch	ca. 48: Antiochean conflict (*Galatians written*) 48: Apostolic council in Jerusalem
49: Expulsion of Jews from Rome by Claudius	49/50: Paul in Macedonia (Philippi, Thessalonica)
	50: Paul in Corinth (*1 Thessalonians written;* soon after *2 Thessalonians written?*)
51: Gallio proconsul of Achaia	51: Paul's trial before Gallio; journey to Jerusalem
	52–55: Paul in Ephesus (54: *1 Corinthians written*)
54: Death of Claudius 54/55: Murder of Silanus, proconsul of Asia Minor	54/55: Paul imprisoned in Ephesus (*Philippians, Philemon, Colossians written; Ephesians written?*)
	55: Paul in Troas
55/56: Sabbath year in Judea	55/56: Paul in Macedonia (*2 Corinthians written*)
56: Uprising of "the Egyptian" in Judea	56/57: Paul in Corinth (57: *Romans written*)
	57: Paul's arrest in Jerusalem
Until 59: Felix procurator of Judea	57–59: Paul imprisoned in Caesarea
59: Festus procurator of Judea	59: Paul sent to Rome
	60–62: Paul imprisoned in Rome
	62/63: Paul in Spain (exile?)
64: Fire of Rome, persecution by Nero	Around 64: Paul's martyrdom in Rome (short letter behind *2 Timothy*)

Table is lightly adapted from Riesner 2011.

See also COLLECTION FOR THE SAINTS; CONVERSION AND CALL OF PAUL; CORINTHIANS, FIRST LETTER TO THE; CORINTHIANS, SECOND LETTER TO THE; COWORKERS, PAUL AND HIS; *CURSUS HONORUM*; EPHESUS; GALATIANS, LETTER TO THE; JERUSALEM, CITY OF; JERUSALEM, COUNCIL OF; PASTORAL EPISTLES; PAUL IN ACTS; PHILIPPIANS, LETTER TO THE; PRISON, PRISONER; ROMAN CHRISTIANITY; THESSALONIANS, LETTERS TO THE; TRAVEL AND ITINERARY PLANS; TRAVEL IN THE ROMAN WORLD.

BIBLIOGRAPHY. **F. F. Bruce,** *Paul: Apostle of the Free Spirit* (Exeter, UK: Paternoster, 1977); idem, *The Acts of the Apostles* (Grand Rapids, MI: Eerdmans, 1990); **D. A. Campbell,** *Framing Paul: An Epistolary Biography* (Grand Rapids, MI: Eerdmans, 2014); **K. P. Donfried,** "Chronology: New Testament," *ABD* 1:1011-22; **J. D. G. Dunn,** *Christianity in the Making*, vol. 2, *Beginning from Jerusalem* (Grand Rapids, MI: Eerdmans, 2009); **K. Haacker,** "Paul's Life," in *The Cambridge Companion to Paul*, ed.

J. D. G. Dunn (Cambridge: Cambridge University Press, 2003) 19-33; **M. Hengel and A. M. Schwemer,** *Paul Between Damascus and Antioch: The Unknown Years* (London: SCM Press, 1997); **R. Jewett,** *A Chronology of Paul's Life* (Philadelphia: Fortress, 1979); **C. S. Keener,** *Acts*, vol. 1, *Introduction and 1:1–2:47* (Grand Rapids, MI: Baker Academic, 2012); **J. Knox,** *Chapters in a Life of Paul*, ed. D. R. A. Hare (Macon, GA: Mercer University Press, 1987); **J. B. Lightfoot and J. R. Harmer,** trans., *The Apostolic Fathers*, 2nd ed., ed. and rev. M. W. Holmes (Grand Rapids, MI: Baker 1992); **G. Lüdemann,** *Paul, Apostle to the Gentiles: Studies in Chronology* (Philadelphia: Fortress, 1984); **I. H. Marshall,** *The Pastoral Epistles*, ICC (New York: T&T Clark, 1999); **S. E. Porter,** "Chronology. New Testament," *DNTB* 201-8; **R. Riesner,** *Paul's Early Period: Chronology, Mission Strategy, Theology* (Grand Rapids, MI: Eerdmans, 1998); idem, "Pauline Chronology," in *The Blackwell Companion to Paul*, ed. S. Westerholm (Oxford: Wiley-Blackwell, 2011), 9-29; **E. J. Schnabel,** *Early Christian Mission*, vol. 2, *Paul and Early Christianity* (Downers Grove, IL: IVP Academic, 2004); idem, *Acts*, ZECNT 5 (Grand Rapids, MI: Zondervan, 2012).

R. Riesner

CHURCH

The *ekklēsia*, the church, is not a footnote to Pauline theology; it is at the very heart of that theology. According to both the letters and Acts, when Paul encountered the resurrected, crucified *Messiah Jesus, he received a commission to take the *gospel to the nations. His *mission would be to establish, by God's power and *grace, an *empire-wide network of communities *worshiping the one true *God, embodying the saving narrative of the living Lord Jesus in the power of the *Holy Spirit, and bearing public *witness to the gospel.

1. *Ekklēsia* in Context
2. Additional Sociological Dimensions
3. Practices of the *Ekklēsia*
4. Images of the *Ekklēsia*
5. Marks of the *Ekklēsia*
6. Conclusion

1. *Ekklēsia* in Context.

***1.1.* Ekklēsia.** Paul considered each community an *ekklēsia*, or "assembly" (see further at 1.2 below). *Ekklēsia* is most often translated "church," which indicates its foundational status in and continuity with the Christian church(es) throughout history. Since the Pauline *ekklēsia* was neither a building nor an occasional meeting but an ongoing group focused on regular meetings and relationships, "congregation" or "community" is also an appropriate gloss. The word *ekklēsia* appears in the Pauline letters sixty-two times: five in Romans, all in Romans 16; twenty-two in 1 Corinthians, including nine in 1 Corinthians 14; nine in 2 Corinthians, including five in 2 Corinthians 8; three in Galatians, all in Galatians 1; nine in Ephesians, including six in Ephesians 5; two in Philippians; four in Colossians; two each in 1 Thessalonians and 2 Thessalonians; three in 1 Timothy; and one in Philemon. Only 2 Timothy and Titus lack the word.

For Paul, "while the church is local, churches are united into the nascent universal church" (Thompson, 21). In the singular, *ekklēsia* can refer to an individual assembly in one house (e.g., Rom 16:5; Phil 3:6; Col 4:15-16; Philem 1:2), the community of believers in one city (Rom 16:1; 1 Thess 1:1; 2 Thess 1:1; Col 4:16), or the entirety of Christ-followers (1 Cor 12:28; Phil 3:6). The phrase "the whole church" (Rom 16:23; 1 Cor 14:23) probably refers to an assembly of smaller assemblies. "The assembly [*ekklēsia*] of God" seems normally to mean the church as a single, empire-wide entity (1 Cor 10:32; 11:22?; 15:9; Gal 1:13) that is also manifested in particular locations (1 Cor 1:2; 11:22?; 2 Cor 1:2). In 1 Timothy 3:5, 15, both a local and a wider sense may be at play.

In the plural, *ekklēsia* (sometimes qualified with an additional phrase) can refer to a regional group of assemblies (Rom 16:16, "all the [local] churches of Christ"; 1 Cor 16:1, 19; 2 Cor 8:1; Gal 1:2, 22; cf. 1 Thess 2:14), a major portion of the entire network (Rom 16:4, "of the *Gentiles"), or the entire network (e.g., 1 Cor 7:17; 11:16; 14:33-34; 2 Cor 8:18-19, 23-24; 11:28; 2 Thess 1:4, "churches of God").

It is often said that in Colossians and Ephesians the *ekklēsia* is not (or not primarily) a local assembly but a single, universal, cosmic, heavenly entity (Eph 1:22; 3:10, 21; 5:23-32; Col 1:18, 24). This is an important aspect of the church in these letters but not the complete picture. Colossians 4:15-16 knows of the house church, and Ephesians 4–5 speaks of functions and activities that are clearly at the grassroots level. Likely a circular *letter, Ephesians is naturally attentive to the church's universality.

1.2. Context. In Paul's world, the word *ekklēsia* could refer to various meetings and groups, including the civic assembly of a city, or citizens council. Because piety was part of both daily life and politics, such assemblies generally included *prayers and *sacrifices to deities. Their primary functions, however, were furthering group solidarity and making decisions for the group's (or the general) common good. For Paul, the *ekklēsia* in Christ was somewhat similar to a civic assembly but more inclusive, like the congregation (Heb. *qāhāl*) of *Israel/YHWH (though obviously much smaller). The LXX frequently translates *qāhāl* as *ekklēsia*, either by itself (e.g., Deut 9:10) or in combination with "of Israel" or "of YHWH": *kyriou* ("of the *Lord"; e.g., Deut 23:2-4, 9). Nehemiah 13:1 alone has "assembly of God" (see Beale). Some Jewish assemblies used the term *ekklēsia* (Korner, 81-149). In Paul the OT/Jewish usage continues, including eleven occurrences of *hē ekklēsia theou* (or a variant thereof): "the assembly [or "assemblies"] of God."

While Paul may see the *ekklēsia* as somewhat similar to the civic assembly, as the "honorable assembly of God" (Park), he likely envisions the church even more as an *alternative* to the civic *ekklēsia*. In Philippians, for example, Paul uses political language (*politeuesthe* in Phil 1:27 and *politeuma* in Phil 3:20, related to *polis*), probably to indicate the nature of the church as a different sort of political body, a colony of heaven rather than of Rome. But whether the *ekklēsia* was in some sense counterimperial (e.g., Elliott, Harrison, and Maier in Winn) or not (e.g., Korner) cannot be decided on terminology alone. As with words such as *christos*, the significance of *ekklēsia* lies in the content with which it is filled.

As for its concrete social form, the Pauline *ekklēsia* was similar to a small association. Associations came in several types, including occupational guilds, cultic associations, neighborhood associations, *ethnic/immigrant clubs, and family *collegia* (Kloppenborg; Ascough), though many associations were hybrids. Pauline assemblies shared characteristics of some of these kinds of associations, including the main Jewish association (the synagogue). They also had practices and goals in common with certain *philosophical schools, such as moral formation. It is also likely that an *ekklēsia* sometimes consisted largely or partially of a particular *household (*oikos*; see Gehring). There were differences among the various churches, even though there were common aspects, images, and practices (discussed below).

Despite similarities to various social bodies, the Pauline *ekklēsia* should be recognized as unique, an entity sui generis. Especially distinctive, sociologically, was its inclusive composition with respect to gender, socioeconomic status, and ethnicity. Theologically, the *ekklēsia* was to be a foretaste, a "microcosmos" (Wright, 1492), of the new *creation inaugurated in Jesus' coming, death, and *resurrection and soon to be consummated at his parousia. It was intended to be an alter-assembly, even an alterculture: a different way of coming together and of being human in the world. Specifically, the *ekklēsia* was to be an alternative to the first-century Roman world of power, inequality, mistreatment of the weak, polytheism, and *sexual immorality and exploitation (see 5.1-6 below).

2. Additional Sociological Dimensions.

Describing the Pauline congregations is challenging because direct evidence is relatively minimal. Interpreters consider the letters in light of material evidence (archaeological discoveries, inscriptions, iconography, and coinage) as well as literary sources.

2.1. Meeting Places and Size. The Pauline *ekklēsiai* are often called "house churches," though hard evidence is scarce. Interestingly, all four references to the church meeting in a residence connect those communities to *women (Rom 16:5; 1 Cor 16:19; Col 4:15; Philem 2). Homes in which assemblies gathered were likely of various sizes: small units in tenement apartment buildings (*insulae*), modest homes of the middling class, and villas of the elite. The norm was likely the small, modest home.

Like other associations, Christ-assemblies probably also met in *tabernae*, small workshops that included living quarters, as well as restaurants, taverns, warehouses, and rented spaces (Adams; Kloppenborg). They may also have met outdoors, in public spaces or at the properties of those with means. Smaller spaces would have been adequate for many *ekklēsiai*, but at least in *Corinth and probably Rome (and possibly elsewhere), larger accommodations would have been needed when the "whole" *ekklēsia*—multiple smaller groups—gathered. We have no statistics, but a range for the size of the assembly from about a dozen to no more than sixty to one hundred for "the whole church" seems likely.

2.2. Group Composition. Assemblies founded and/or addressed by Paul consisted largely of Gentiles—converted pagans and "God-fearers." But Paul understood the church to be multicultural (Rom 9:24; 1 Cor 1:24; 12:13; Gal 3:28; Col 3:11; Eph 2:11-22), and there were Jews in many, if not all, assemblies (e.g., 1 Cor 7:18). Yet the church is something novel, for Paul can divide humanity into three components: Jews, Greeks (Gentiles), and the *ekklēsia* of God (1 Cor 10:32). In the Jewish Messiah and universal Lord Jesus, ethnic identity is preserved yet ultimately transcended, as "one new humanity" (*anthrōpos*; Eph 2:15) has been created.

There has been much debate about the socioeconomic status of the Pauline churches and about a relevant key text: "not many of you were wise . . . powerful . . . of noble birth" (1 Cor 1:26 NRSV). Although the precise meaning of this text is difficult to ascertain, it suggests to most interpreters that the Corinthian community was largely drawn from the lower end of the socioeconomic scale, with a few exceptions. Given the conditions in the empire and the evidence of the letters, several significant studies (e.g., Longenecker) conclude that many in Corinth and elsewhere would have hovered around or below subsistence-level existence, with some enjoying modest surpluses and very few, if any, having significant *wealth and/or social status. Yet there was diversity among the congregations; the Macedonian communities, for example, had fewer material resources than the Corinthians (2 Cor 8:1-6).

3. Practices of the *Ekklēsia*.

3.1 Assembly/Worship. The Pauline *ekklēsia* was a group devoted to the Jewish god and his *Son, the Messiah and Lord Jesus. Unlike other associations, this *ekklēsia* was cultically exclusive; participants could not acknowledge other gods or lords (1 Cor 8:5-6), including emperors. It practiced a form of "christological monotheism" that included what some have termed "binitarian" worship (Hurtado, 79-153). But participants also experienced the presence and power of a third, related person/party: the Spirit of the Father and the Son. (For "of the Son," see Rom 8:9; Gal 4:6; Phil 1:19.)

When the *ekklēsia* assembled—probably at least weekly, on the "first day of every week" (1 Cor 16:2)—it was an event of *koinōnia* (communion, participation, solidarity) with the divine triad of Father, Son, and Spirit and with one another (e.g., 2 Cor 1:21-22; 13:13; Phil 2:1). This meant sharing *food and engaging in related cultic and community-building activities. First Corinthians and other letters attest to numerous practices, including two major rituals (see 3.2 below): (1) a *koinōnia* meal, called the *Lord's Supper, culminating in a symbolic sharing of one cup and one loaf (1 Cor 11:17-34); and (2) *baptism, an (occasional) entrance ritual for new converts (e.g., 1 Cor 1:14-16; 12:13; Eph 4:5).

Additionally, there was (3) prayer: individuals speaking *to* God on behalf of the assembly and for others (1 Cor 11:2-16; 1 Thess 5:17-18; Eph 6:18; Phil 1:9), including praise, thanksgiving, and congregational "Amens" (Eph 5:20; 1 Cor 14:16; 2 Cor 1:20); (4) *prophecy/revelation: individuals speaking *for* God to the assembly (1 Cor 11:2-16; 14; 1 Thess 5:19-21), subject to communal testing and discernment (1 Cor 14:29-33; 1 Thess 5:21); (5) additional *charismata/pneumatika* (grace-gifts/spiritual *gifts), including glossolalia, *tongues interpretation, and *healing (1 Cor 12; 14); (6) recitation of acclamations, such as "Jesus is Lord"(1 Cor 12:3; Phil 2:11) and "Our Lord, come!"/*maranatha* (1 Cor 16:22), as well as creed-like texts (1 Cor 8:6; 15:3-8) and other liturgical material (e.g., 1 Cor 11:23-25); and (7) singing of psalms and *hymns (1 Cor 14:15, 26; Eph 5:19; Col 3:16).

Further, there was (8) mutual care, including the sharing of participants' joys, sufferings, and practical needs (Rom 12:9-13; 1 Cor 12:22-26; Phil 2:1-4; 1 Thess 5:11-15); (9) reading and interpretation of Scripture (e.g., Rom 15:4; 1 Tim 4:13); (10) reading and interpretation of apostolic correspondence (1 Thess 5:27), including letters originally sent to other assemblies (Col 4:16); (11) *teaching, including moral admonition, both from leaders and among participants (1 Cor 4:17; 14:6, 26; 1 Thess 5:14; Eph 4:14-16; Col 3:16; 1 Tim 4:13); (12) *discipline (1 Cor 5:1-13); (13) *collection of funds for internal needs (Rom 12:13; Gal 6:2?), apostolic mission work (Rom 15:24, 28-29; Phil 4:10-19), and support of other churches (Rom 15:25-28; 1 Cor 16:1-4; 2 Cor 8-9; cf. Gal 2:10); (14) welcoming visitors and guests (Rom 12:13; 1 Cor 14:16; Philem 22); and (15) exchanging holy kisses (Rom 16:16; 1 Cor 16:20; 2 Cor 13:12; 1 Thess 5:26).

Active participation by all assembled, including women, was the norm, with possibly some (local?) restrictions on women (1 Cor 14:33b-36, if authentic; 1 Tim 2:11-15, which may reflect a post-Paul practice). The range and nature of these activities suggest regular, perhaps more than weekly, community interaction.

3.2. Baptism and the Lord's Supper. Baptism functioned as the means of entrance into the assembly and of initial participation in it. This was simultaneously and inseparably entrance into and initial participation in Christ. The Greek preposition *eis* ("into") expresses both dimensions: converts are "baptized *into* Christ" and are thus "one in Christ Jesus" (Gal 3:27-28) because they have been "baptized *into* one *body" (1 Cor 12:13 NRSV). Through this complete immersion into Christ, the convert begins a new life of resurrection-infused, *cruciform existence as God's *servant because immersion into Christ is immersion into his death and resurrection

(Rom 6; cf. Col 2:12). Done in the *name of the Lord Jesus Christ (1 Cor 1:13, 15; 6:11), baptism conveyed the Lord's character ("name") to the baptized. Both individuals and entire households could be baptized (1 Cor 1:14-16; 16:15).

Although the Lord's Supper is mentioned only in the letter addressing its abuse (1 Cor 10:15-22; 11:17-34), Paul undoubtedly handed the practice on to all churches. It was one of the primary means of ongoing *koinōnia* in the assembly, meaning simultaneously and inseparably *koinōnia* among the participants and with the risen Lord Jesus. The Lord's Supper was based on the Passover meal but also had elements of the ancient banquet and its *symposium*, or time of after-dinner discussion, entertainment, or drinking (Smith)—an occasion for *koinōnia*, but also possibly for inappropriate behavior.

As a regular practice of ongoing participation in Christ and his body, the Lord's Supper complemented the one-time initiating event of baptism. As an act of devotion to and *koinōnia* with Christ, who was both the Supper's host and its central guest, this participation with him was exclusive (1 Cor 10:20-22; cf. 2 Cor 6:13-18). As an act of *koinōnia* with others, it was intended to express gospel values, including concern for the poor and weak. When it failed to do so, it was no longer the Lord's Supper (1 Cor 11:20) until repentance and change occurred. This especially involved "discerning the body" (1 Cor 11:29), likely a double entendre referring to both the one loaf and the assembly as Christ's body. Practiced appropriately, the Lord's Supper was an event of grace, memory (like the Passover meal), solidarity, *covenant renewal, and proclamation, as well as a foretaste of the messianic banquet.

Significantly, these two rituals gave expression to the universality of the church as one body of the Messiah (1 Cor 10:17; 12:13).

3.3. Life Together and in the World. Paul's pastoral mission was to form communities that lived worthily of the gospel, as a sort of living exegesis of that good news. This means an internal life of mutual care, and an external life of care for outsiders and public witness to the gospel. This dynamic of the community's centripetal and centrifugal existence requires consistency between these two dimensions of its life (Phil 1:27–2:16). One way the community's internal life finds expression is in phrases containing the reciprocal pronoun "one another," while phrases such as "and all" express its obligations to outsiders.

With various reciprocal-pronoun constructions, Paul calls those in the *ekklēsia* to embody the gospel of God's grace by doing good to one another (1 Thess 5:15). Such phrases stress mutual *love, affection, care, servanthood, and burden bearing (Rom 12:10; 13:8; 1 Cor 12:25; Gal 5:13; 6:2; 1 Thess 3:12; 4:9; 2 Thess 1:3). Paul also urges mutuality in encouragement and edification (1 Thess 4:18; 5:11), *honor (Rom 12:10), pursuit of harmony (Rom 12:16; 15:5; 2 Cor 13:11), welcome (Rom 15:7; 1 Cor 11:33), forbearance and *forgiveness (Eph 4:2, 25; Col 3:13), submission (Eph 5:21), and instruction (Rom 15:14; Col 3:16). In slightly different language, he also calls for suffering and rejoicing together (1 Cor 12:26), and for occasional mutual correction (Gal 6:1). Such mutual concern does not, however, eliminate individual responsibility to bear one's own load (Gal 6:5; 2 Thess 3:7-12). Paul also exhorts the communities to refrain from mutual envy and fighting (Gal 5:15, 26), lying (Col 3:9), judgmentalism about nonessential matters (Rom 14:13), and lawsuits (1 Cor 6:7).

Some have argued that Paul does not expect the church to be "evangelistic" or "missional." Much depends on how one defines such terms, but there are several significant indicators that Paul expects those in the *ekklēsia*, corporately and individually, to proclaim the gospel in word and deed (Phil 2:14-16), both publicly and privately—and thereby to participate in the divine saving mission (Gorman 2015).

First, several of the ecclesial practices expressed in "one another" exhortations (and similar texts) extend these practices into the world. Certain references to "all" (versus "one another" or "the holy ones/saints") reveal that Paul expects the church to do good to nonbelievers (Gal 6:10), with specific exhortations to practice love, *peace, patience, nonretaliation, kindness, and humility (Rom 12:14, 17-18; 1 Thess 3:12; 5:14-15). This even includes *financial generosity (2 Cor 9:13; lit. "all," not NRSV, "all others"). These exhortations are grounded in God's grace and love toward all (e.g., 2 Cor 9:15; 1 Tim 2:4-6). The most radical of Paul's exhortations—to love and bless enemies and persecutors—are grounded in God's own love for enemies (Rom 5:10) and exemplified by Paul and his *coworkers. Paul does not provide many details about these various missional practices; apparently, each *ekklēsia* must discern the particulars in context.

Second, the church's public life is to be distinguished from that of nonbelieving pagans (e.g., 1 Thess 4:5, 13). However, believers' abandonment of idolatrous and immoral practices deemed normal by their culture leads naturally to questions, criticism, and opposition from family members, business associates, and others. Believers could not avoid explaining their behavior, a form of witness in deed and word (Col 4:6). The evidence of suffering among many of the assemblies attests to this dynamic of public witness and negative response.

Third, Paul expects participants in his communities to share in his mission, and not just financially (Ware). He says that the persecuted Thessalonian and Philippian communities are sharing in the same sort of struggle and suffering as he experiences (Phil 1:29-30; 1 Thess 2:13-16). He calls the church to maintain, as he did (1 Cor 9:19-23), a "salvific intentionality" (Barram) in its interactions with outsiders (e.g., 1 Cor 7:10-16; 10:31–11:1; cf. 1 Cor 14:20-25) as well as insiders (1 Cor 8:1-10).

Fourth, Paul envisions the *ekklēsiai* as participants in an *apocalyptic battle against the forces of *Sin and the *devil. They are "weapons" (not merely "instruments") of God's *righteousness, or justice (Rom 6:13), embodying that justice (2 Cor 5:21) as they participate in the divine warrior's mission, but only with the "armor of God," the weapons of the Spirit: (Eph 6:10-18; cf. 1 Thess 5:8). This is how the church proclaims "the gospel of peace" (Eph 6:15), even as it meets opposition to its life and message. Despite whatever persecution it may experience, the Pauline community is not permitted to turn in on itself and abandon the outside world.

4. Images of the *Ekklēsia*.

Paul's theological understanding of the church's life is highly relational, expressed in several interconnected images of *koinōnia* with the God of Paul's proto-trinitarian experience and theology (1 Cor 12:4-6; 2 Cor 13:13; see Grieb), and with one another.

4.1. Assembly of God/Community of the New Covenant. Paul believes that the Christ-assemblies as a whole constitute the *ekklēsia tou theou*; each local assembly is an instantiation of that one global entity. As noted above, the *ekklēsia* is a continuation of the congregation of Israel (*qāhāl YHWH*). It is the people of the (new) covenant of shalom promised by the prophets (Ezek 11:17-20; 36:23-28; 37:21-28; Jer 31:31-34) and inaugurated by God in the sending, death, and resurrection of the Messiah and the gift of the Spirit (Gal 4:4-6).

Although the phrase "new covenant" appears only twice in Paul's letters (1 Cor 11:25; 2 Cor 3:6), the reality permeates his writings. The community of the new covenant is gifted with the promised indwelling Spirit so that the participants may live in a way that pleases God/the Lord Jesus (1 Thess 4:1; Phil 4:18; Col 1:10; Eph 5:10) and fulfill the "just requirement of the *law" (Rom 8:4 NRSV). Such a life entails embodying the two basic demands of God's covenant with Israel: love for, or faithfulness to, God and love of neighbor (Rom 13:8-10; Gal 5:14), demands that have been reworked in light of the story of the crucified Messiah as "the obedience of *faith" (Rom 1:5; 16:26 NRSV) and "the *law of the Messiah" (1 Cor 9:21; Gal 6:2).

Being part of God's new-covenant people is thus dependent on being related to the Messiah Jesus and having his Spirit. Of particular importance is the argument of Galatians that there is one promised "seed"/offspring (*sperma*) of *Abraham, namely the Messiah (Gal 3:13-29). To belong to Christ is to be (part of) that singular seed: a recipient of the Abrahamic promise and blessing, which Paul interprets as the Spirit (Gal 3:14). Gentiles who acknowledge Jesus as Lord have been "grafted in" (Rom 11:17, 19 NRSV) to the people of God as equal members (Rom 9:24-30; 15:7-13). Paul designates this mixed community as "the Israel of God" (Gal 6:16 NRSV). Although there is debate about this text, the immediate context and the letter's overall argument strongly suggest it means the community where "neither *circumcision nor uncircumcision is anything; but a new creation is everything" (Gal 6:15 NRSV; cf. Gal 5:6; Rom 3:27-31; Eph 2:11-13). For Paul, the circumcision that effects entrance into the people of God is of the heart (Rom 2:25-29; cf. Col 2:11-12; Deut 30:1-6, 8). The inauguration of the new *covenant* means also the start of the prophetically promised new *creation* (see 2 Cor 5:17; Is 65:17-25).

That the Christ-assemblies constitute God's *ekklēsia* does not, however, mean Paul loses respect and concern for ethnic Israel, because God's faithfulness guarantees Israel's *salvation (Rom 9–11). As the prophets also promised, Paul envisions the nations "coming" to Israel's God by the work of the Spirit through himself and others, creating a multiethnic *eschatological people of God. This is the "new humanity" (Eph 2:15 NRSV); the Spirit is remaking diverse people in the image of the Messiah Jesus, the *image of God (2 Cor 3:17–4:4; Col 1:15; 3:10). The means of entering this new-covenant people of God is the same for all: confession of Jesus as Lord in faith and baptism, by which a person is moved "into" Christ (Rom 6; 10).

4.2. Being in Christ/the Body of Christ. *4.2.1. Being in Christ.* For Paul, the geographic and socioeconomic location of an *ekklēsia* is secondary to its fundamental identity. The saints who happen to be in Philippi or Corinth or wherever are above all **in Christ* (e.g., 1 Cor 1:2; Phil 1:1), where they find the ongoing, transformative activity of God (1 Cor 12:6, 11; 2 Cor 5:21; Phil 1:6; 2:13; 1 Thess 3:12-13). This is a place of radical resocializing—ongoing conversion. Paul uses the image of getting dressed to portray the nature of the church's identity: "putting on Christ" (Gal 3:27) is both a one-time event and an ongoing responsibility (Rom 13:14; Eph 4:24; cf. Col 3:9-14). The essential mark of the community in Christ is therefore Christlikeness.

"In Christ" (or "in the Messiah"; also "in the Lord" and "in him") therefore expresses the essential identity of both the individual believer and the community as a whole, and thus also of the bond, the *koinōnia*, that exists among those who share this identity (1 Cor 1:9; 10:16; 2 Cor 13:13; Phil 2:1; Philem 6). This *koinōnia*—the lifeblood of the *ekklēsia*—involves both communion between the *ekklēsia* and the one, true triadic God (Father, Son, and Spirit) and communion among the human participants. It does not, however, exist with nonbelievers (2 Cor 6:14). *Koinōnia* is more than a sentiment; with Christ, it entails suffering (Phil 3:10); with others, it involves common commitment and mission, including financial sharing with those in *ministry (e.g., Phil 1:5; 4:15) and those in financial need (Rom 15:26-27; 2 Cor 8:4; 9:13), as well as sharing in others' suffering and comfort (2 Cor 1:7).

4.2.2. The Body of Christ. A particularly close relationship exists between Paul's "in Christ" language and the image of Christ's body. In using this image, Paul adopts and transforms a common ancient metaphor of human community. Body-of-Christ imagery appears briefly several times in the Pauline correspondence (Rom 12:4-5; 1 Cor 6:15; 10:17; 11:29; Col 1:18, 22, 24; Eph 5:23) and at length in 1 Corinthians 12 and Ephesians 4:1-16.

In 1 Corinthians 12 Paul uses the language of Christ's body in connection with spiritual gifts (*charismata*/*pneumatika*) to convey a paradoxical combination of interdependent equality and cruciform hierarchy in the *ekklēsia* so that it can function as a living exegesis of the gospel.

The equality of divinely given gifts means that no member of the body should feel either superior and self-sufficient or inferior and unneeded. This equality of giftedness is preceded by an even more fundamental equality: common confession of Jesus' lordship (1 Cor 12:2-3). Moreover, Paul attributes the community's giftedness to the divine triad of Father, Son, and Spirit (1 Cor 12:4-6), with special emphasis on the Spirit's work within the body (1 Cor 12:7-11). This divine activity empowers the body to function properly and interdependently as a unity in diversity, like the human body (1 Cor 12:14-21, 26). Although the focus of 1 Corinthians 12 is diversity of gifts, this diversity also includes socioeconomic and ethnic differences (1 Cor 12:13-14; cf. Gal 3:28; Col 3:11).

Notions of unity in diversity and solidarity through interdependence are common in antiquity, but Paul's understanding of the body as encompassing a cruciform hierarchy is unique. It has two aspects: elevating weak members and prioritizing gifts that edify others rather than self. Honoring the weak (1 Cor 12:22-25) is a necessary corollary of the gospel, for God works through the weakness of Christ's *cross and Paul's ministry for the benefit of the weak (1 Cor 1:18–2:5). Considering gifts that edify others (1 Cor 12:7), such as teaching and prophecy, as the "greater gifts" (1 Cor 12:31 NRSV)—rather than gifts such as glossolalia that supposedly indicate higher social or spiritual status—derives similarly from the gospel. Christlike love means putting others before self (1 Cor 13:5), expressed in part by preferring the others-edifying use of prophecy to the self-edifying use of tongues (1 Cor 14).

The image of the body of Christ is more than a metaphor, for the church is how and where Christ is present in the world. Not only are believers in Christ, but he is present in the individual members of his body (Gal 2:20) and among them as a whole (Rom 8:9-10)—a relationship of mutual indwelling. This present Christ continues to enact his faithfulness and love in and through the body, while simultaneously offering *hope to its members: "the Messiah among you, the hope of your future *glory" (Col 1:27).

As noted above, there is for Paul ultimately but one *ekklēsia*, one body of the Messiah, to which all the baptized belong and in which all participate at the Lord's Supper (1 Cor 10:17; 12:13), even if gifts are deployed primarily locally. This singular, universal understanding of the body is emphasized in Colossians and especially Ephesians. In these letters, Jesus the Lord is identified as the *head of the church (Col 1:18, 24; Eph 1:22; 4:15; 5:23; contrast 1 Cor 12:21). Participants in the body, therefore, belong to one another (Rom 12:5; Eph 4:25), both locally and globally.

In Ephesians 4, the emphasis is on a sevenfold theological and experiential basis of unity (Eph 4:4-6) that provides the framework within which gifts, given by the ascended Lord (Eph 4:7-10), are to be lovingly exercised for the unifying and maturing of Christ's one body (Eph 4:11-16). Thus the one body is connected to one Spirit, one hope, one Lord, one faith, one baptism, and one God and Father. The purpose of the gifts ("*apostles . . . prophets . . . evangelists . . . pastors and teachers") is to "equip the saints for the work of ministry" (*diakonia*; Eph 4:11-12 NRSV) in the edification of the body; leaders enable the ministry of all. As with 1 Corinthians 12, edification is the primary goal, and every member of the body must work properly to ensure that the community's common life is marked by love (Eph 4:15-16). Because the *ekklēsia*'s proper working and maturity include faithful public witness, the body-of-Christ image implies mission in the world.

4.3. Temple and* Koinōnia *of the Holy Spirit. In 1 Corinthians 3, Paul speaks of the church as God's field and building, the latter particularly as the *temple of the Holy Spirit (1 Cor 3:16-17; cf. 2 Cor 6:16; Eph 2:21-22). Although the field and building images have many ecclesial implications (Schnabel), the temple image is particularly significant. It indicates that the *ekklēsia* is the location of the personal presence and power of God—Father, Son, and Spirit. Paul also identifies the individual believer as the temple of the Holy Spirit (1 Cor 6:19). As with Christ, the Spirit's presence in and among believers is one of mutual indwelling (Rom 8:1-16).

Paul's letters indicate that the participants in each *ekklēsia* had palpable experiences of the Holy Spirit. These experiences started with conversion (Gal 3:1-5), baptism (1 Cor 6:11; 12:13), and confession of Jesus as Lord (1 Cor 12:3). They continued to include sensing God's love (Rom 5:5); being empowered to fulfill covenant obligations (Rom 8:1-4); knowing peace, *joy, and hope (Rom 5:5; 14:17; 15:13); and much more. Moreover, the *Holy* Spirit makes the holy ones holy.

As the temple of the Spirit, the *ekklēsia* experiences a common life that Paul calls *koinōnia* of the Spirit (2 Cor 13:13; Phil 2:1). The Spirit creates a Christlike, cruciform community (Phil 2:1-4)—one that is holy and pure, living in covenant with God (2 Cor 6:14-18). The Spirit's activity in his temple may be summarized in terms of *fruit (Gal 5:22-23) and gifts (noted in 4.2.2 above): the work of moral transformation/sanctification and the work of edification and ministry. The two are inseparable, for there can be no common good or ministry if the gifts are not exercised in love, or if the "works of the *flesh" destroy the body through factious and unholy activity devoid of the Spirit (Gal 5:19-21).

Colossians and Ephesians use the language of God's "filling" the individual believer and the *ekklēsia*, which also implies the temple image (see Ex 40:34-35; 1 Kings 8:5-11; 2 Chron 5:8-13; Is 6:1-4; Ezek 10:1-4). In a way analogous to Christ's being the *fullness of God in bodily form (Col 1:19; 2:9), the church has now "come to fullness in him [Christ]" (Col 2:10 NRSV). And yet this fullness can increase: the community can perpetually be "filled with all the fullness of God" (Eph 3:19 NRSV). This requires ecclesial intentionality, so the church is even counseled to be filled with the Spirit (Eph 5:18).

4.4. Family. The *ekklēsia* as a place of *koinōnia* is a place of belonging, intimacy, and loyalty: a family, or "society of siblings" (Bartchy; cf. Aasgaard). This is expressed especially in Paul's pervasive language of "brothers" (*adelphoi*), meaning "brothers and sisters"—as many recent translations recognize. (The word *adelphos* appears 133 times in the Pauline letters; the noun "sister," *adelphē*, only six.) Some versions, however, do not render *adelphoi* as inclusive of women, while others that do so occasionally translate *adelphos/adelphoi* as "believer(s)," "beloved," "members of the church," or even "Christian." Both kinds of interpretation detract from the content and significance of Paul's family image.

Family relationships are possible and necessary in the *ekklēsia* because each participant is an *adopted child of God (Rom 8:14-23; Gal 4:4-7; Eph 1:5), with God as Father and Christ, his Son, as the elder brother (implied in Rom 8:17, though Paul does not stress that fraternal role). This is the family of God. Both Ephesians 2:19 and 1 Timothy 3:15 refer to the church as God's household (*oikeios/oikos*). At the same time, there may be pseudo-siblings in the assembly—those whose lives or teachings deny the gospel (2 Cor 11:26; Gal 2:4; cf. 2 Cor 11:13).

This sort of family imagery and language, which was also used by certain other groups, is sometimes called "fictive *kinship." For Paul, however, these relationships are very real and consequential. In many ways, the community is expected to behave according to certain ancient family values: for example, a sibling must not sue a sibling (1 Cor 6:1-11). But family values are also transformed and radicalized: the believing *slave becomes his believing master's brother, no longer his property (Philem 15-16); the male head of household must treat the entire household with respect and love, not as property (Eph 5:21–6:9; Col 3:17–4:4).

While considering all believers his siblings, Paul also sees himself as the father of the communities he has founded, and even as their mother (1 Cor 4:14-21; Gal 4:19-20; 1 Thess 2:5-12; cf. Philem 10). The church needs maternal care as well as fatherly instruction and discipline.

5. Marks of the *Ekklēsia*.

Despite certain similarities between Pauline communities and other Greco-Roman groups, there are critical, fundamental differences. As an alter-culture determined by the narrative of Jesus' death and resurrection, the *ekklēsia* is a place of transformative participation in Christ—of resurrection-infused cruciformity, or "Christoformity" (McKnight). The result is—or should be—certain distinguishing features, or marks. These marks derive from the images just discussed and are expressed concretely in the various practices, both internal and external, enumerated earlier.

5.1. Faith/Faithfulness, Hope, and Love. A frequent triad in Paul's letters, from the earliest to the latest, is faith/faithfulness (*pistis*), hope (*elpis*), and love (*agapē*). In some cases these three appear in terse or annotated list form (1 Thess 1:3; 5:8; 1 Cor 13:13; Col 1:4-5), with endurance (*hypomonē*) occasionally joining or replacing hope (1 Thess 1:3; 2 Thess 1:3-4; Titus 2:2). Sometimes the three appear in close proximity to one another (Rom 5:1-5; Gal 5:5-6).

5.1.1. Faith/faithfulness. Perhaps the most obvious mark of a Pauline assembly is faith, specifically faith in Christ and in the gospel of God (Rom 1:16-17). Forms of the "faith/believe" (*pistis/pisteuō*) word family occur more than two hundred times in the Pauline correspondence. The church is a family, or household, of faith (Gal 6:10), continuing the Abrahamic tradition of faith (Rom 4; Gal 3:6-8). As the proper response to the gospel, faith entails confessing Jesus as Lord (Rom 10:8-14) and also, for Gentiles, turning from idolatry to the true, living God (1 Thess 1:9-10). Faith is therefore the mode of *justification, of restoration to right relations with God and entrance into the community of the new covenant (Gal 2:15-21; Rom 3:21-26). But *pistis* is not merely the means of entering the *ekklēsia*; it is a permanent characteristic. Although Paul prefers terms such as "brothers" and "saints/holy ones," he occasionally characterizes participants in the *ekklēsia* as "believers" (*pisteuontes*; 1 Cor 14:22; 1 Thess 1:7; 2:10, 13; perhaps also, e.g., Rom 1:16; 3:22; 4:11; 10:4; 1 Cor 1:21; Eph 1:19).

The faith/believe word family has a variety of senses (Gupta). In addition to assent (1 Cor 15:2) and trust (1 Cor 2:5), it can also signify faithfulness (Gal 5:22; 1 Thess 3:5-7) and can therefore be inclusive of obedience to God (Rom 1:5; 16:26). The phrase "believing allegiance" is thus frequently an appropriate gloss.

5.1.2. Hope. The people of God, according to Paul, has always been a hopeful people, beginning with Abraham (Rom 4:18). In the *ekklēsia*, the basis of this hope is God's resurrection of Jesus (1 Cor 15); hope is God- and Christ-centered (Eph 1:12; 1 Tim 1:1; 4:10). Essential to the community's life, hope is a gift to be received and celebrated together (Rom 12:12; 15:13; Eph 4:4). As the future tense of faith, hope is oriented to the eschatological glorification of God's people and the salvation of all creation, especially in the face of persecution and other forms of suffering (Rom 8:18-39; 2 Cor 1:7-10; Gal 5:5; Eph 1:17-19; Col 1:5, 23, 27; Titus 1:2; 2:13; 3:7). This hope also gives meaning to present existence (1 Cor 15:58; Eph 1:12; 2:11-13), with practical consequences in daily life together. It also means reassurance about community participants who have died and is thus one of the marks that distinguishes the church from "Gentiles," who lack such hope (1 Thess 4:13-18). Hope is a form of public witness.

5.1.3. Love. Love is the first dimension of the fruit of the Spirit (Gal 5:22) and the greatest of the faith-hope-love triad (1 Cor 13:13). Participants in the *ekklēsia* are God's beloved (e.g., Rom 1:7; Eph 5:1; 1 Thess 1:4), recipients of God's love demonstrated in Christ's death and made tangible by the Spirit's presence (Rom 5:5, 8; 8:35, 39; 2 Cor 5:14; Gal 2:20). Genuine, self-giving, others-regarding love must therefore be the modus operandi of all activity in the church (e.g., Rom 12:9-10 [*philadelphia*]; 13:8-10; 1 Cor 8:1; 13; 16:14; Gal 5:6, 13-14; Col 3:12, 14; Eph 3:17; 4:32–5:2; 1 Thess 3:12; 4:9 [*philadelphia*]; 1 Tim 4:12). According to the household codes of Colossians and Ephesians, the love expected of everyone in the *ekklēsia* is expressed within the believing household as mutual submission (Eph 5:21) and respect, significantly undermining the power and rights of the male Roman head of household. The community's love must also extend beyond the local congregation (2 Cor 8:8, 24; 1 Thess 4:10) and to nonbelievers—even enemies (e.g., Rom 12:14-21). Although love in Paul is primarily about loving people, the *ekklēsia* is also where God is loved (Rom 8:28; 1 Cor 2:9).

5.2. "One, Holy, Catholic, and Apostolic." The Nicene-Constantinopolitan Creed of AD 381 famously characterizes the church with these four adjectives. Although such descriptors may seem anachronistic when applied to Pauline assemblies, they are actually quite appropriate. The beginning of 1 Corinthians, for example, provides a mini-ecclesiology indicating these marks are appropriate (Gorman 2015). The "church of God" in Corinth consists of those "sanctified in Christ Jesus, *called to be saints": set apart and called to be *holy* (1 Cor 1:2 NRSV). Paul identifies them as part of a universal, or *catholic*, community: "together with all those who in every place call on the name of our Lord Jesus Christ, both their Lord and ours" (1 Cor 1:2 NRSV). This catholic identity implies that they are *one*, but Paul urges them to embody their unity: "that all of you be in agreement . . . no divisions among you . . . united in the same mind and the same purpose" (1 Cor 1:10 NRSV). The Corinthians must also heed Paul's counsel, spoken in the name of the Lord (1 Cor 1:10), because they are an *apostolic* assembly guided by their God-appointed founder (1 Cor 1:1). These four complementary marks can be found throughout 1 Corinthians and the Pauline corpus.

5.2.1. Unity and Holiness. For Paul, unity in Christ is not a human invention but a divinely constituted reality to be expressed and maintained (1 Cor 1:10; 12:12-13; Gal 3:28; Eph 4:3). The gospel unites people of different genders, socioeconomic stations, and ethnicities (on equality, see 5.3 below). Paul calls for unity as a basic ecclesial practice (Phil 2:2), with special emphasis where there is division (1 Cor 1:10-13; Phil 4:2), and he has strong warnings for those who would threaten this oneness (1 Cor 3:17). Unity in Christ is embodied in various ways, but particularly in the intimate *koinōnia* of meals (Gal 2:11-14), especially as they culminate in the Lord's Supper, which focuses on "one bread" (1 Cor 10:17) and should therefore unite rather than divide the community (1 Cor 11:17-34).

Just as the *ekklēsia* must *be* one because it *is* one, so also it must *be* holy because it *is* holy—an alterculture, set apart for God's purposes (see Brower and Johnson). Like Israel (e.g., Lev 11:45), it is called to share in God's *holiness; this is the work of the Holy Spirit (1 Thess 4:1-8). "Saints," or "holy ones" (*hagioi*), is a basic designation for all individuals and communities in Christ. Although Paul sometimes addresses letters simply to a church or churches, more often his letters designate the recipients as holy ones/saints (Rom 1:7; Eph 1:1; Phil 1:1; Col 1:2, with *adelphoi*) or as the church consisting of holy ones/saints (1 Cor 1:2; 2 Cor 1:1). In other parts of the letters, too, believers are frequently referred to as holy ones/saints (e.g., Rom 8:27; 12:13; 1 Cor 6:1-2; 2 Cor 13:12; Eph 5:3; 1 Tim 5:10).

As a holy alter-culture, the *ekklēsia* must recognize its difference from outsiders and acknowledge boundaries (1 Cor 1:18; 5:12-13; 1 Thess 4:12-13; 5:5). Converts undergo a transformation from "then" to "now" (Rom 6; 1 Cor 6:11; Eph 2:1-10; Col 1:21; 3:5-11) that is also, in essence, from "there" (outside Christ) to "here" (inside Christ). Of particular concern is abstention from idolatry and sexual immorality, two basic vices thought by many Jews and early Christians to be characteristic of pagans (Rom 1:18-32). Paul urges the saints to flee (*pheugete*) from such pagan practices (1 Cor 6:18; 10:14).

Paul also expects those who share in God's holiness to participate in God's righteousness/justice (*dikaiosynē*); the justified community is, or should be, the community that practices justice because it is being transformed into the justice of God (2 Cor 5:21). The *dikai-* word family is especially prominent, for example, in 1 Corinthians 6:1-11 (1 Cor 6:1, 7, 8, 9, 11), indicating the alter-cultural character of the church as the realm of cruciform justice. Unfortunately, many English translations miss the linguistic and theological connections between justification and justice both here and elsewhere.

5.2.2. Catholicity and Apostolicity. As already noted, Paul understands the church to be both global and local, and in both aspects it is and must be inclusive: male/female, slave/free, Gentile/Jew, elite/nonelite, "*strong"/"weak" (e.g., Rom 14:1–15:13; 1 Cor 8:1-11; Gal 3:28). Locally, this means, for instance, that those of some means must take care of "those who have nothing" at the Lord's Supper (1 Cor 11:22 NRSV). Globally, it means, for example, that the largely Gentile churches need to financially support the Jewish believers in *Jerusalem (Rom 15:25-29; 1 Cor 16:1-4; 2 Cor 8–9).

As apostle for the nations, recipient of a revelation of Jesus and emissary of God (e.g., Gal 1:10-17), Paul believed deeply that the communities he founded and/or addressed needed to heed his teaching and *imitate his Christlike example (1 Cor 11:1; Phil 3:17; cf. 1 Thess 1:6). Yet he also believed there were apostolic norms that were not merely Pauline but universal. The decision of the pillars/apostles in Jerusalem regarding Gentiles was universally binding (Gal 2:1-14). The tradition about Jesus' Last Supper (1 Cor 11:23-25), the early creedal statement (1 Cor 15:3-7), and other traditions (1 Cor 11:2) were received and handed on as globally authoritative teachings, also most likely from the Jerusalem leadership. Even certain customs (1 Cor 7:17; 11:16; 14:33b-36, if authentic) seem to be universal in application. The church cannot be one or holy or apostolic if its practices are inconsistent with its catholic traditions.

5.3. Equality and Respect for Leaders. One of the most important descriptions of the Pauline *ekklēsia* is this: "There is no longer Jew or Greek, there is no longer slave or free, there is no longer male and female; for all of you are one in the

Messiah Jesus" (Gal 3:28; cf. 1 Cor 12:13; Col 3:11). As social-identity interpreters have stressed, this sentence does not eliminate these distinctions but validates and unites each and all of the binaries. This dynamic is at play in the composition of the assemblies individually and as a network.

Regarding "Jew or Greek," Paul expects the fractured community at Galatia to end disputes about table fellowship and circumcision. The indwelling and unifying Spirit, present among both circumcised and uncircumcised believers, means they cannot remain separated at table (Gal 2:1-14) and cannot value circumcision as the distinguishing mark of the "Israel of God" (Gal 5:6; 6:15-16; cf. 1 Cor 7:19). Similarly, Paul expects the two factions (possibly representing several assemblies) in Rome—one largely, though not exclusively, Jewish and one largely, though not exclusively, Gentile—to cease their mutual judgmentalism about nonessential, cultural matters (what the Stoics called *adiaphora*). They are to embody the reality into which they have been called: a unified community of mutual love and respect, *hospitality and worship (Rom 14:1–15:13). Ephesians sums up this Pauline theme, and a main section of that letter (Eph 2:11-22), in the phrase "one new humanity" (Eph 2:15 NRSV).

As for "slave or free," one way Paul asserts believers' equality in Christ is by positing their common slavery to and *freedom in Christ: "whoever was called in the Lord as a slave is a freed person belonging to the Lord, just as whoever was free when called is a slave of Christ" (1 Cor 7:22 NRSV; cf. Eph 6:9; Col 4:1). This equality plays out concretely at the *ekklēsia* in Philemon's house: Philemon and his slave Onesimus are both now in Christ, brothers in the Lord (Philem 10-16).

The equal status of "male and female" in the church is summarized in the phrase "sons and daughters," indicating the members of God's holy people (2 Cor 6:18). This equality comes across especially in 1 Corinthians, despite questions about how to handle 1 Corinthians 14:33b-36. Women and *men belong to each other in marriage (1 Cor 7:1-4) and have an equal role in the fate of a mixed *marriage (1 Cor 7:10-16). Women and men, or husbands and wives, are interdependent in the Lord (1 Cor 11:11-12). Furthermore, women and men both pray and prophesy in the assembly (1 Cor 11:4-5). Also important are the designations "coworker" and "apostle" Paul gives equally to men and women (e.g., Rom 16:7, 9, 12, 21; 2 Cor 8:23; Gal 1:17, 19; Philem 24).

Such designations demonstrate that, while there is equality within the assemblies, there is also a need for *leadership and a corollary need for respect for leaders—not merely for Paul. Leadership is among the church's gifts (Rom 12:8; 1 Cor 12:8). Because even 1 Thessalonians, probably the earliest letter, refers to leaders who care for the *ekklēsia* and therefore merit respect (1 Thess 5:12-13), it is likely that each *ekklēsia* had several such leaders. Philippians mentions "overseers and servants" or "guides and caregivers" (Phil 1:1; *episkopoi, diakonoi*; cf. Phil 2:25-30). Other congregations likely had similar leaders, as did most associations. Like Paul and other ministers (e.g., 1 Cor 3–4; 2 Cor 3–4), such leaders are to exercise their leadership as cruciform servants of God and the people (Clarke).

There are some leaders who have transecclesial roles, whether named colleagues such as Timothy and Titus or groups of unnamed ministers such as apostles and evangelists (1 Cor 12:28; Eph 4:11; cf. Eph 2:20). In addition to men such as Timothy and Titus, among the church's named leaders are women, including the apostle Junia (Rom 16:7); Phoebe, a *diakonos* and benefactor/*patron (Rom 16:1-2); Prisca, coworker with Paul and cohost of house churches (Rom 16:3; 1 Cor 16:19; 2 Tim 4:19); Mary, Tryphaena, and Tryphosa (Rom 16:6, 12); and probably Euodia and Syntyche (Phil 4:2). Despite Paul's own general practice of self-support, it is at least sometimes expected that certain leaders (teachers) be remunerated (e.g., Gal 6:6; 1 Tim 5:17).

Only the *Pastoral Epistles furnish detailed obligations of specific leaders: 1 Timothy names three distinct roles: overseer(s) (*episkopos/episkopoi*, 1 Tim 3:1-7); deacons/servants/ministers (*diakonoi*, 1 Tim 3:8-13); and elders/presbyters (*presbyteroi*, 1 Tim 5:17-19). (The "real widows" of 1 Tim 5:3-16 may also have some *diakonos*-like role in the church.) Titus mentions two: elders/presbyters (*presbyteroi*, 1 Tim 1:5-6) and overseer/bishop (*episkopos*, 1 Tim 1:7-9; the context suggests a plurality). These positions are similar to leadership roles in the Jewish synagogue and other ancient associations. Their primary role in the *ekklēsia* is not to establish order or control but to ensure faithfulness to the gospel (Thompson).

All three positions require moral virtue and piety, and being married only once. The overseer in both 1 Timothy and Titus must practice hospitality and be a good, knowledgeable teacher; 1 Timothy adds the requirement of having a good reputation among outsiders and proven household managerial skills, while Titus forbids greed. These suggest formational, administrative, and external responsibilities. The *diakonoi* in 1 Timothy must hold to the faith but are not required to teach, though they too may not be greedy and need household management experience, suggesting administrative and financial tasks. Significantly, 1 Timothy 3:11 likely refers to female deacons (such as Phoebe), rather than deacons' wives. Elders in 1 Timothy are said to "rule," with some being teachers and preachers, while no specific tasks are clearly named in Titus.

*5.4. **Grace, Mercy, and Peace.*** The greeting found at the start of each Pauline letter is not a mere formality or casual "hello." Rather, it indicates a pair or trio of gifts God constantly bestows on the assembly—grace and peace (usually) or grace, *mercy, and peace (1 Tim 1:2; 2 Tim 1:2). Wishes for grace and/or peace are also found toward the end of every letter (Rom 15:13, 33; 16:20; 1 Cor 16:23; 2 Cor 13:13; Gal 6:18; Eph 6:23-24; Phil 4:23; Col 4:18; 1 Thess 5:23, 28; 2 Thess 3:16, 18; 1 Tim 6:21; 2 Tim 4:22; Titus 3:15; Philem 25). Paul's greetings and parting wishes remind believers that such blessings should form them into a community of grace, mercy, and peace.

The members of the *ekklēsia* are both recipients and channels of these divine blessings. They "stand" in the abundant grace and mercy they have received (Rom 5:2, 15-21; cf. 1 Cor 1:4; Eph 1:6; 2:4-9; Phil 1:7; Titus 3:4-7) and the additional gifts that come from grace, which they share with others (e.g., Rom 12:6; 1 Cor 12: *charismata*; Eph 4:7). They are also called to imitate Paul and other churches in extending grace, or generosity, beyond themselves (2 Cor 4:15; 8:1-6). Even believers' speech should be grace-filled, edifying others (Eph 4:7, 29).

Similarly, those in Christ "have" peace with God (Rom 5:1), the God of peace (1 Thess 5:23). In Christ, the Lord of peace (2 Thess 3:16), God has made peace between Jews and Gentiles (Eph 2:11-22), has brought peace to "all things" (Col 1:20 NRSV) and continues to grant peace (Phil 4:7-9). Thus the church should practice peace; it is part of the Spirit's fruit (Gal 5:22). This practice of peace is to occur both inside and outside the assembly (Rom 12:18; 14:17, 19; 1 Cor 7:15; 2 Cor 13:11; Eph 4:3; 6:15; 1 Thess 5:13); it is to "rule" in the participants' hearts (Col 3:15).

The *ekklēsia* "in Christ," then, is a place of forgiveness, reconciliation, and peacemaking (Rom 12:18; 14:17-19; 2 Cor 2:5-11) because God was in Christ effecting forgiveness, reconciliation, and peace (Rom 5:1-11; Eph 1:7-8; Col 1:13-14). Ephesians 4:31-32 makes that link between theology and ecclesial practice especially clear.

*5.5. **Honor and Humility.*** For anyone in the ancient world, but especially those near the bottom of the social ladder, being made children of God was a high honor—and that honor is precisely what all those baptized into Christ receive (Oakes). This honor is not, however, grounds for any sort of pride; rather, humility is the standard in the *ekklēsia* (Phil 2:3; Eph 4:2; Col 3:12). Believers are to seek honor for others rather than themselves (Rom 12:10), reversing the normal Roman pursuit of glory. The only sort of legitimate boasting is directed at the Lord, specifically the *crucified* Lord (1 Cor 1:31), who humbled himself and was crucified in weakness (2 Cor 13:4; Phil 2:6-8). Moreover, as noted earlier, because this honor springs from the paradoxical divine power-in-weakness of the cross that effected the justification of the weak (Rom 5:6; 1 Cor 1:18-31), the *ekklēsia* must above all welcome, assist, and even honor the weak and lowly—the socially, spiritually, economically, and physically marginalized (Rom 12:16; 15:1-6; 1 Cor 8:1-11; 12:21-26; Gal 2:10; 1 Thess 5:14; see Works).

*5.6. **Suffering and Joy.*** Finally, Paul claims that both suffering and joy are normal features of life in Christ. The community is to receive joy as a gift and experience it together (Rom 12:12, 15; 14:17; 15:13; Phil 2:29). Joy is part of the fruit of the Spirit, who works within the community (Gal 5:22). As a community experience, joy can be shared within and across communities, and it can bolster the spirits of other people (2 Cor 2:1-4; 7:5-16; Phil 2:23-30; 1 Thess 3:9), for experiencing joy sometimes necessitates assistance from others (2 Cor 1:24; Phil 1:25).

At the same time, the church, like Paul, should expect hostility. "All who want to live a godly life in Christ Jesus will be persecuted" (2 Tim 3:12 NRSV; cf. Rom 8:17) summarizes the Pauline perspective. Suffering in various forms—social, economic, and even physical—is the natural consequence of faithful witness to the gospel (e.g., 1 Thess 3:3-4). It is even something to receive as a grace (Phil 1:29), for it is participation in Christ's sufferings (Phil 3:10), the ultimate form of cruciformity.

Joy in Christ is possible—indeed necessary—even during times of trouble (Phil 2:17-18; 1 Thess 1:6-7; Col 1:11-12). Surprisingly, in affliction joy can lead to loving, missional acts, providing for the physical and spiritual needs of others (2 Cor 8:1-6). But joy requires attention and cultivation, so it is appropriate for the *ekklēsia* to be encouraged to rejoice together at all times (Rom 12:15; 1 Cor 12:26; Phil 3:1; 4:4; 1 Thess 5:16), even during periods of trial or grief (Rom 12:12, 15; cf. 2 Cor 6:10). Exhortations to joy are therefore combined with calls for prayer, patience, and trust (Rom 12:12; Phil 4:4-7; 1 Thess 5:16-17).

6. Conclusion.

The *ekklēsia* is the community "in Christ" that Paul depicts as the people, family, and household of God; the multigifted, multiethnic body of Christ; and the temple and communion of the Holy Spirit. Both local and universal, it is the people of the new covenant and new creation effected by Jesus' coming, death, and resurrection that exists in *koinōnia* with this triadic God and with one another. The participants' alter-cultural life together in Christ and in mission to the world is a sign of God's intention for humanity. The *ekklēsia* is a *new* humanity, in contrast to "normal" human existence and in anticipation of the arrival of the new creation in its fullness. It therefore challenges its host culture, including the empire, not by means of a political agenda but simply through the content of its gospel and character of its life. The church's life of allegiance to Jesus the Lord is distinguished by resurrection-suffused cruciformity and the fruit of the Spirit, manifested in a variety of distinctive marks, from faithfulness and love to unity and holiness to suffering and joy.

See also Body of Christ; Church Structure; Discipline, Church; Ephesians, Letter to the; Fellowship, Communion, Sharing; Gentiles; Gifts of the Spirit; Head; Hospitality; Households and Household Codes; Israel; Leadership; Pastor, Paul as; Temple; Urban Setting of Paul's Churches; Worship.

BIBLIOGRAPHY. **R. Aasgaard,** *"My Beloved Brothers and Sisters!" Christian Siblingship in Paul*, JSNTSup 265 (London: T&T Clark, 2004); **E. Adams,** *The Earliest Christian Meeting Places: Almost Exclusively Houses?*, rev. ed., LNTS 450 (London: Bloomsbury T&T Clark, 2015); **R. S. Ascough,** "What Are They Now Saying About Christ Groups and Associations?," *CurBR* 13 (2015): 207-44; **R. J. Banks,** *Paul's Idea of Community: Spirit and Culture in Early House Churches*, 3rd ed. (Grand Rapids, MI: Baker Academic, 2020); **M. D. Barram,** *Mission and Moral Reflection in Paul* (New York: Peter Lang, 2006); idem, "Pauline Mission as Salvific Intentionality: Fostering a Missional Consciousness in I Corinthians 9:19-23 and 10:31–11:1," in *Paul as Missionary: Identity, Activity, Theology, and Practice*, ed. T. J. Burke and B. S. Rosner (London: T&T Clark, 2011), 234-46; **S. S. Bartchy,** "Undermining Ancient Patriarchy: The Apostle Paul's Vision of a Society of Siblings," *BTB* 29 (1999): 68-78; **G. K. Beale,** "The Background of ἐκκλησία Revisited," *JSNT* 38 (2015): 151-68; **K. E. Brower and A. Johnson,** eds., *Holiness and Ecclesiology in the New Testament* (Grand Rapids, MI: Eerdmans, 2007); **A. D. Clarke,** *A Pauline Theology of Church Leadership*, LNTS 362 (London: T&T Clark, 2008); **R. W. Gehring,** *House Church and Mission: The Importance of Household Structures in Early Christianity* (Peabody, MA: Hendrickson, 2004); **M. J. Gorman,** *Becoming the Gospel: Paul, Participation, and Mission* (Grand Rapids, MI: Eerdmans, 2015); idem, "First Corinthians and the Marks of God's *Ekklēsia*: One, Holy, Catholic, and Apostolic," in *One God, One People, One Future: Essays In Honor of N. T. Wright*, ed. J. Dunne and E. Lewellen (Minneapolis: Fortress, 2018), 167-90; **A. K. Grieb,** "People of God, Body of Christ, Koinonia of Spirit: The Role of Ethical Ecclesiology in Paul's 'Trinitarian' Language," *AThR* 87 (2005): 225-52; **N. Gupta,** *Paul and the Language of Faith* (Grand Rapids: Eerdmans, 2020); **P. Harland,** *Associations, Synagogues, and Congregations: Claiming a Place in Ancient Mediterranean Society* (Minneapolis: Fortress, 2003); **J. Harrison and J. D. Dvorak,** *The New Testament Church: The Challenge of Developing Ecclesiologies* (Eugene, OR: Pickwick, 2012); **L. W. Hurtado,** *Lord Jesus Christ: Devotion to Jesus in Earliest Christianity* (Grand Rapids, MI: Eerdmans, 2003); **J. S. Kloppenborg,** *Christ's Associations: Connecting and Belonging in the Ancient City* (New Haven, CT: Yale University Press, 2019); **R. J. Korner,** *The Origin and Meaning of Ekklēsia in the Early Jesus Movement*, AJEC 98 (Leiden: Brill, 2017); **B. W. Longenecker,** *Remember the Poor: Paul, Poverty, and the Greco-Roman World* (Grand Rapids, MI: Eerdmans, 2010); **D. Maben,** "Pauline Ecclesiology: A Paradigm of Unity, Reciprocity and Universality: The Image of Body in the Corinthian *ekklēsia*," *BTF* 42 (2010): 59-73; **W. A. Meeks,** *The First Urban Christians: The Social World of the Apostle Paul*, 2nd ed. (New Haven, CT: Yale University Press, 2003); **S. McKnight,** *Pastor Paul: Nurturing a Culture of Christoformity in the Church* (Grand Rapids, MI: Brazos, 2019); **P. Oakes,** *Reading Romans in Pompeii* (Minneapolis: Fortress, 2009); **C. Osiek, M. Y. MacDonald, and J. H. Tulloch,** *A Woman's Place: House Churches in Earliest Christianity* (Minneapolis: Augsburg Fortress, 2006); **Y-H. Park,** *Paul's Ekklēsia as a Civic Assembly: Understanding the People of God in Their Politico-Social World*, WUNT 2/393 (Tübingen: Mohr Siebeck, 2015); **J. Peterson,** "'In the Churches of Macedonia': Implicit Ecclesiology in Paul's Letters to the Thessalonians and Philippians," in Harrison and Dvorak, *New Testament Church*, 148-63; **E. J. Schnabel,** "The Community of the Followers of Jesus in 1 Corinthians," in Harrison and Dvorak, *New Testament Church*, 103-29;

D. E. Smith, *From Symposium to Eucharist: The Banquet in the Early Christian World* (Minneapolis: Fortress, 2003); **J. W. Thompson,** *The Church According to Paul: Rediscovering the Community Conformed to Christ* (Grand Rapids, MI: Baker Academic, 2014); **J. Ware,** *Paul and the Mission of the Church: Philippians in Ancient Jewish Context* (Grand Rapids, MI: Baker Academic, 2011); **A. Winn,** ed., *An Introduction to Empire in the New Testament* (Atlanta: SBL Press, 2016); **C. S. Works,** *The Least of These: Paul and the Marginalized* (Grand Rapids, MI: Eerdmans, 2020); **N. T. Wright,** *Paul and the Faithfulness of God* (Minneapolis: Fortress, 2013).

M. J. Gorman

CHURCH STRUCTURE

One question that has fueled passionate debate among NT scholars for many decades is that of church structure and whether it is possible to discern patterns of church structure in the earliest Pauline communities. The question is not an abstract one, since evidence discerned often affects current practice. James Burtchaell has observed that, inevitably, commentators on the area discern a structure of the *church that coheres with their own current views and practice:

> Some, because they acknowledge apostolic succession and ordained office as essential to authentic Christianity, have claimed to see enough hints and harbingers of office in the New Testament to verify a radical continuity between the two periods (and indeed between the polity then and the polity in their present church). Scholars of a contrary loyalty and interpretation have seen a radical discontinuity and have taken the earlier "unofficered" church as the inspired norm. (Burtchaell, 274)

This debate continues on and is unlikely to be resolved easily. It finds its roots in the early nineteenth-century consensus among Protestant scholars who saw all early Christian communities as autonomous and democratic (i.e., with no structure at all) and in the responses to this consensus particularly of Edwin Hatch, Adolph von Harnack, and Rudolph Sohm (see discussions in Burtchaell, 1-179). Many, though not all modern commentators, now accept some form of early church structure both between churches and in the roles and structures of *ministry, though some still maintain that there was no discernable structure at all until developments in the post-NT era.

The question of church structure in Pauline churches focuses attention on three key areas:

1. Connections and Relationships Between the Different Pauline Churches
2. Models That Lie Behind the Different Communities
3. Roles and Structures of Ministry Within the Pauline Communities
4. Conclusion

1. Connections and Relationships Between the Different Pauline Churches.

While there is insufficient evidence to enable one to identify how different Christian communities related to each other in the NT period, it is possible to discern Paul's own view about their connections.

1.1.* Ekklēsia *as Local and Universal. *Ekklēsia,* the Greek word commonly translated "church," means a gathering of people, but very quickly in the Pauline writings it came to be used to refer to a reality that existed whether the people were actually gathered or not. It is also interesting to note that Paul uses the same word *ekklēsia* both for a local church meeting in a house (Rom 16:5) and to refer to the universal church (Gal 1:13). Indeed, Paul draws these two concepts together in 1 Corinthians 1:2, where he speaks to the church of *God that is in *Corinth alongside "those who in every place call on the name of our *Lord Jesus *Christ" (NRSV), demonstrating that he had in mind both a local gathering and a more abstract universal church made up of a large number of local gatherings. The ability to move seamlessly between these two concepts indicates that Paul did not just use the word *ekklēsia* functionally to describe a local autonomous gathering; he also had in his mind "church" as an abstract concept.

1.2. The Collection. Paul's language regularly balances an awareness of local needs and concerns with a consciousness of the universal church. He encouraged individual Christians to see themselves as belonging to the wider *body "the church" and not just their local gathering (Eph 2:19). He had both a theological and a practical understanding of universal church, seeing Christ as the *head of the body, the church (Col 1:18), and therefore expected each member of local congregations to care for the whole. This was particularly evident in the *collection for the saints. Despite the breakdown of the Jerusalem agreement that took place following the Antioch incident (Gal 2:11-14), Paul continued to encourage the churches he visited to collect money for the Jerusalem church (2 Cor 8:1-15) and in doing so to serve others "in material things" (Rom 15:27 NRSV; see discussion in Georgi 1992).

The connection between the different local communities was also maintained by Paul and his companions traveling constantly from community to community. This was certainly the means by which the collection was received, but it also seems to have been the means by which Paul attempted to enforce *discipline on the communities. Indeed, the tensions between Paul and the Corinthians emerged both through the letters he wrote (e.g., 2 Cor 2:4) and by the visits he did or did not manage to make (2 Cor 2:1). During the visits he did make, he seems to have passed on news of other congregations and by doing so created a sense of greater interconnectedness between the churches.

2. Models That Lie Behind the Different Communities.

Another factor that affects views on church structure is the model that is imagined as lying behind and informing the church communities. Wayne Meeks, in his seminal 1983 book, *The First Urban Christians*, identifies four key models: the *household, the voluntary association, the synagogue, and the philosophical or rhetorical school, although he argues that it was the household/extended family unit that was not only the primary unit in Roman society but also the primary unit within Christian communities: "Our sources give us good reason to think that [the household] was the basic unit in the establishment of Christianity in the city, as it was, indeed, the basic unit of the city itself" (Meeks, 29). The importance of recognizing these different models as informing early Christian communities is that different models suggest different levels of implicit structure. The more structured the model, the more structured the Christian community.

This is evidenced in James Burtchaell's work, which examines the influence of synagogue *worship on the earliest Christian communities. His argument, drawing on the work of Eric Meyers and James Strange, is that, as it is not easy to locate evidence of physical archaeological identifiers of Christianity until the fourth to fifth century AD, it is probable that Christian communities grew up in or alongside Jewish synagogues. This would mean that the structures of synagogue worship would have imprinted onto Christian communities from an early stage.

The reality is that there was probably a wide diversity of models and structures used by the earliest Christians, some based on extended families and households, others on synagogues, and others still on other social groupings. The model that lay behind the particular community would certainly have influenced the level of formality of structure found within that community, but there was probably a wide variety of experience within the different first-century communities, from the largely charismatic and nonstructured communities identified by some scholars to the more formal, institutional settings proposed by others.

3. Roles and Structures of Ministry Within the Pauline Communities.

3.1. Itinerant and Resident Leaders. One of von Harnack's most influential theories is that there were two basic forms of early Christian *leadership: (1) itinerant apostles, who were later replaced in local communities by (2) episcopal leadership (von Harnack, 398-461). Gerd Theissen expands on this theory by identifying two parallel strands of itinerant leaders: those who can be traced back to the Gospels and Jesus' missional commands and who accepted support along the way (Mk 6:7-13; Mt 10:5-15; Lk 9:1-6; 10:1-12), and those represented by Paul and Barnabas, who were still itinerant but were community organizers and who supported themselves as they traveled (Theissen, 28). As David Horrell observes, however, one must not allow these two forms of itinerant leadership to distract one from the recognition that a key dynamic in the first century was the shift from itinerant leadership to resident leadership.

Itinerant leadership is linked with apostleship, since **apostle* means at its basic level "agent" or "one who is sent." In the Gospels themselves the term *apostle* is associated with the Twelve (Mt 10:2; Mk 3:14; 6:30; Lk 6:13; 9:10; 11:49; 17:5; 22:14; 24:10), and in Acts 1:2 Matthias is said to be added to the eleven apostles. In the Pauline writings, however, the term appears to be differently defined, since it is used of Paul himself and of the so-called superapostles (2 Cor 11:5), and is even listed as a gift (1 Cor 12:28-30; Eph 4:11). There is no hint in the Pauline corpus that the term was restricted to the Twelve in any way, nor that it was used as a title. It does, however, appear to have some level of authority associated with it, since in 2 Corinthians the dispute between Paul and the Corinthians seems to be focused around the issue of Paul's apostleship and authority, and in 1 Corinthians 1:10-12 different people within the congregation of Corinth claim allegiance to *Peter, Paul, or Apollos, all of whom were itinerant.

As time went on, however, there appears to have been increasing problems with verifying who was and was not an authentic itinerant leader. For example, 2 John 9 cautions against welcoming anyone who "does not abide in the *teaching of Christ, but goes beyond it" (NRSV). The Didache, an early Christian document that might be dated as early as the late first century AD, is even more explicit about the problems of itinerant leaders:

> 1 Let everyone who "comes in the Name of the Lord" be received; but when you have tested him you shall know him, for you shall have understanding of true and false. 2 If he who comes is a traveller, help him as much as you can, but he shall not remain with you more than two days, or, if need be, three. 3 And if he wishes to settle among you and has a craft, let him work for his bread. 4 But if he has no craft provide for him according to your understanding, so that no man shall live among you in idleness because he is a Christian. 5 But if he will not do so, he is making traffic of Christ; beware of such. (Did. 12 [LCL])

In contrast, while itinerant leaders appear to be associated with the title "apostle," even if that title changed its meaning from just the Twelve to others who acted as envoy or agent, resident leaders do not always appear to have been given a formal title. First Thessalonians 5:12, in referring to Christian leaders, says, "respect those who labor among you, and have charge of you in the Lord and admonish you" (NRSV), but with no apparent title associated with them. R. Alastair Campbell argues extensively that leaders of local communities were heads of households under the authority of the patron-style leadership to which Greek households were accustomed (Campbell, 126). There is certainly evidence that heads of households were leaders in this period, but Horrell argues that leaders were not restricted to this category, citing Fortunatus and Achaicus (Rom 16:17) as evidence that those who were members of a household were also acknowledged as leaders (Horrell 1997, 327). This would certainly accord with Edward Adams's work demonstrating that the earliest Christians did not just meet in houses (Adams 2013).

The distinction between itinerant and resident leadership has been helpful in identifying patterns of leadership in the earliest communities and the shift of authority that took place from itinerant to resident leadership as time went on. However, we should not push the theory too far. While Paul traveled extensively, there is little evidence that, for example, James or John, who are acknowledged by Paul as "pillars" (Gal 2:9), traveled anything like as much. They were, nevertheless, influential leaders in the earliest church.

3.2. Episkopoi, presbyteroi, *and* diakonoi. One of the biggest contentions among NT scholars is whether there is any connection at all between the terms *episkopoi* (bishops or overseers), *presbyteroi* (elders), and *diakonoi* (deacons) and formal roles within the churches, and, of course, between them and modern church practice. The debate is so contentious that it is impossible in an article as short as this to provide any helpful adjudication on the subject. However, a few observations may be helpful.

The first point to note is that elders (*presbyteroi*) are not generally mentioned alongside *episkopoi* and *diakonoi* in the NT. For example, Philippians 1:1 mentions *episkopoi* and *diakonoi* but not *presbyteroi*; even 1 Timothy, which contains all three terms, does not refer to them together. First Timothy 3 discusses what *episkopoi* and *diakonoi* should do, but the expectation of considering *presbyteroi* worthy of double honor does not come until 1 Timothy 5:17. This separation of the terms leads some to see this as evidence that there were two separate systems running parallel in this period, *episkopoi* and *diakonoi* on the one hand and *presbyteroi* on the other; others argue that *episkopoi* and *diakonoi* are terms more connected with worship and *presbyteroi* with practical arrangements; others still argue that Acts 20:28 indicates that *presbyteroi* and *episkopoi* are used interchangeably, since in Acts 20:17 Paul addresses elders but later calls them overseers. It is also worth noting that Dieter Georgi argues that the *episkopos* and *diakonos* in Philippians 1:1 are synonymous and not two distinct functions or roles (Georgi 1986, 20).

The key dispute is whether these three terms refer to functions (overseers, elders, and servants) or to roles—bishops/overseers, presbyters, and deacons. The problem is that the NT is not consistent in its usage. The noun *diakonos* is used regularly in Paul's writing to describe the role of being a *servant of Christ (Rom 1:1; Gal 1:10); it is also used of Phoebe, whom Paul describes as a *diakonos* of the church at Cenchreae in a way that implies she occupied a role that the Roman Christians would recognize.

4. Conclusion.

The lack of agreement among scholars about church structure and the roles or functions of ministry might in fact point to something important: that the lack of clarity among modern scholars on this subject reflects the lack of clarity in the earliest Pauline communities. Some communities might have had more structure than others; some might have had more clearly defined roles than others. The difficulty that scholars find in discerning what happened in all the churches might have as much to do with the fact that no one thing happened in them all as it does with divergences between modern practices and beliefs.

See also Apostle; Body of Christ; Church; Collection for the Saints; Households and Household Codes; Ministry; Pastoral Epistles; Philosophy; Travel and Itinerary Plans.

BIBLIOGRAPHY. **E. Adams,** "First-Century Models for Paul's Churches: Selected Scholarly Developments Since Meeks," in *After the First Urban Christians: The Social-Scientific Study of Pauline Christianity Twenty-Five Years Later*, ed. T. D. Still and D. G. Horrell (Edinburgh: T&T Clark, 2009), 60-78; idem, *The Earliest Christian Meeting Places: Almost Exclusively Houses?* (London: T&T Clark, 2013); idem, "The Shape of the Pauline Churches," in *The Oxford Handbook of Ecclesiology, ed. P. Avis* (Oxford: Oxford University Press, 2018); **R. Banks,** *Paul's Idea of Community: The Early House Churches in Their Historical Setting* (Grand Rapids, MI: Eerdmans, 1980); **J. T. Burtchaell,** *From Synagogue to Church: Public Services and Offices in the Earliest Christian Communities* (Cambridge: Cambridge University Press, 1992); **R. A. Campbell,** *The Elders: Seniority Within Earliest Christianity, SNTW* (Edinburgh: T&T Clark, 1994); **D. Georgi,** *The Opponents of Paul in Second Corinthians: A Study of Religious Propaganda in Late Antiquity* (Philadelphia: Fortress, 1986); idem, *Remembering the Poor: The History of Paul's Collection for Jerusalem* (Nashville: Abingdon, 1992); **R. Haight,** *Christian Community in History*, vol. 1 (London: Continuum, 2004); **A. von Harnack,** *The Expansion of Christianity in the First Three Centuries*, 2 vols. (London: Williams & Norgate, 1904); **E. Hatch,** *The Organization of the Early Christian Churches* (London: Longmans, 1888); **D. Horrell,** "Leadership Patterns and the Development of Ideology in Early Christianity," *Sociology of Religion* 58 (1997): 323-41; **W. A. Meeks,** *The First Urban Christians: The Social World of the Apostle Paul*, 2nd ed. (New Haven, CT: Yale University Press, 2003); **E. M. Meyers and J. F. Strange,** *Archaeology, the Rabbis, and Early Christianity* (Nashville: Abingdon, 1981); **H. Ridderbos,** *Paul: An Outline of His Theology* (Grand Rapids, MI: Eerdmans, 1982); **R. Sohm,** *Kirchenrecht*, vol. 1 (Munchen: Duncker & Humblot, 1892); **A. C. Stewart,** *The Original Bishops: Office and Order in the First Christian Communities* (Grand Rapids, MI: Baker Academic, 2014); **T. D. Still,** "Organizational Structures and Relational Struggles Among the Saints: The Establishment and Exercise of Authority Within Pauline Assemblies," in *After the First Urban Christians: The Social-Scientific Study of Pauline Christianity Twenty-Five Years Later*, ed. T. D. Still and D. G. Horrell (Edinburgh: T&T Clark, 2009), 79-98; **G. Theissen,** *The Social Setting of Pauline Chrisitianity: Essays on Corinth* (Edinburgh: T&T Clark, 1982).

P. Gooder

CIRCUMCISION

Paul's insistence that circumcision not be imposed on *Gentile male converts led to one of the most serious and fundamental controversies in the early *church. The controversy over Paul's stance on circumcision is reflected in Acts 15, the letters to the Galatians and to the Romans, Philippians 3, and perhaps Colossians 2.

1. The View of Paul's Opponents on Circumcision
2. Paul's Response to His Opponents
3. The Circumcision of Timothy and Titus

1. The View of Paul's Opponents on Circumcision.

Those who opposed Paul on the circumcision question have traditionally been called *Judaizers, although that moniker is disputed by some since the debate is among Jews and since Gentiles are considering the practice. Judaizers were Jews who confessed Jesus as Messiah, believing also that the Mosaic *law and particularly the rite of circumcision should be required of Gentiles for conversion. The views of the Judaizers are explicitly cited in Acts 15:1, 5 and can be inferred from Galatians, Philippians 3, and Romans 2:25-29; 4:1-12.

1.1. The Scriptures. Some Jewish teachers found support in the OT for their understanding of circumcision, for Genesis 17:9-14 says that circumcision was the *covenant sign for the people of *God and that refusal to take on the covenant sign would result in being cut off from the people of God. Moreover, Genesis 17:13 specifies that this covenant is an "everlasting" one. Therefore, the Jewish teachers probably concluded from Genesis 17 (see also Ex 4:24-26; Lev 12:3; Josh 5:2-9) that circumcision was an indispensable sign of the covenant, and thus they taught that "unless you are circumcised according to the custom of Moses, you cannot be saved" (Acts 15:1).

1.2. Other Jewish Literature. Evidence from extrabiblical literature also shows that the majority of Jews considered circumcision necessary for conversion (see Esther 8:17 LXX; Jdt 14:10; Josephus, *Ant.* 13.9.1 §§257-258; 13.11.3 §§318-319; 20.2.4 §§38-41; *J.W.* 2.17.10 §454; Philo, *Migr.* 89-93). John Nolland (contra McEleney) argues persuasively that in the intertestamental period circumcision was typically required for one to become a proselyte to Judaism. Moreover, during the reign of Antiochus Epiphanes Jews had practiced circumcision at the risk of losing their lives (1 Macc 1:60-61; cf. 2 Macc 6–7). Thus any diminution of the rite would naturally inflame both the cultural and religious passions of Jews.

2. Paul's Response to His Opponents.
This brief examination of the OT and the intertestamental period demonstrates that circumcision was considered to be crucial for membership in the people of God. The question that arises is, How could Paul defend the idea that Gentiles could be part of the people of God without being circumcised? Paul marshaled at least four arguments for his position.

2.1. Argument from the Spirit. The presence of the Spirit in the lives of the Galatian believers, apart from their being circumcised, proved that circumcision was unnecessary for membership in the people of God (Gal 3:1-5). No one could be a part of the new community who has not received the Spirit (Rom 8:9), and since God had seen fit to give the Galatians the Spirit apart from circumcision, it followed that circumcision was not essential for membership among the people of God (see Acts 10:44-48; 15:8-9).

2.2. Argument from the Scriptures. In order to convince Jewish believers of the tenability of his theology, Paul had to defend his view from the OT. Paul pinned his case on *Abraham, arguing from Genesis 15:6 that Abraham was justified by *faith, not by his performance of the law (Gal 3:6-9; Rom 4:1-8). Indeed, circumcision could not have been decisive for Abraham's entrance into the people of God because Abraham was already righteous in God's sight before he was circumcised (Rom 4:9-12). In this latter passage, Paul claims that circumcision was a "seal" (*sphragis*) of Abraham's *righteousness by faith gained before he was circumcised, indicating that righteousness does not depend on circumcision. Circumcision as a seal ratifies and confirms one's faith. Abraham was circumcised so that he could be the father of Jewish believers in the covenant God, and his righteousness by faith prior to circumcision made him the father of Gentile believers in *Christ (Rom 4:11-12). Paul writes autobiographically in Philippians 3:2-9. The adversaries boasted of circumcision but Paul has the same credential, contending that righteousness does not stem from the law but through faith in Christ.

2.3. Argument from Salvation History. Paul's view of circumcision raises the question of the place of the law in *salvation history. Granted that Abraham was righteous before he was circumcised, objectors might still point out that the OT commands circumcision. In Galatians 3:15–4:7 Paul provides his perspective on salvation history (see also 2 Cor 3:4-18).

The Mosaic covenant, as a means by which the people of God were identified, was never intended to be in force forever. It was a temporary covenant designed for an interim period until the promise that was made to Abraham reached its fulfillment. Now that the Christ has come, the promise made to Abraham has been fulfilled, and thus the covenant with Moses is no longer in force. Paul considered circumcision to be part of the covenant with Moses, and so he concluded that since the Mosaic covenant was no longer operative, circumcision was unnecessary. Moreover, the arrival of the new covenant (Jer 31:31-34; Ezek 36:26-27), which is really a fulfillment of the covenant made with Abraham, involved the outpouring of the *Holy Spirit, who enables believers to fulfill what circumcision in the OT pointed to—inclusion in the people of God. For now the true circumcision, the circumcision of the heart, has become a reality (Rom 2:28-29; Phil 3:3).

In Paul's thinking circumcision and the law are intertwined in yet another way. Those who think they can be righteous before God by receiving circumcision (Gal 5:2-6; Phil 3:2-11)—that is, by doing the works of the law—are on the wrong path. No one can be justified by the *works of the law (Gal 3:1-5, 10-14), for no one can perform perfectly the works required by the law.

2.4. Argument from the Cross. Peder Borgen also points out that for Paul the *cross had replaced circumcision as the way of entrance into the people of God, as a covenant requirement. In Galatians Paul wages a consistent polemic against circumcision and the law because they diminish the cross (Gal 1:4; 2:21; 3:1, 13; 5:11; 6:12, 14). And the context of Colossians 2:11-14 suggests that Jesus' *death is portrayed as his circumcision in Colossians 2:11, indicating that the new circumcision for believers is accomplished in the cross.

3. The Circumcision of Timothy and Titus.
The explanation offered above explains why Paul refused to circumcise the Gentile Titus (Gal 2:3-5). The requirement of circumcision for salvation was a compromise of the *gospel of *grace and a denial of the arrival of the age of fulfillment. Paul's decision to circumcise Timothy (Acts 16:3) consequently seems inconsistent, and many scholars claim that

the incident is not historically credible. The traditional resolution of this problem postulates that Paul did agree to circumcise Timothy since Timothy's mother was Jewish. This would, according to Jewish law, make Timothy a Jew. According to this interpretation, Paul circumcised Timothy for cultural reasons so that he could bring his Jewish brother with him into synagogues when he preached the gospel.

Shaye Cohen (1986), however, raises three objections to this common resolution. (1) The most natural reading of Acts 16:3 is that Timothy was circumcised because he was a Gentile, not because he was a Jew, for Luke does not inform the reader that Timothy's mother was Jewish in this verse but simply says that "they all knew that his father was Greek." (2) Most interpreters from the second to the eighteenth century believed that Timothy was a Gentile. (3) There is no firm pre-mishnaic evidence that in Jewish circles a son born to a Jewish mother and a Gentile father was considered a Jew.

Christopher Bryan shows that Cohen's conclusion is not as convincing as it appears on first examination. Acts 16:1 introduces Timothy by saying that "he was the son of a Jewish woman who was a believer." Since Luke particularly notes that Timothy was the son of a Jewish woman and a Greek father, he has hinted to the reader before he describes Timothy's circumcision in Acts 16:3 that the latter's national status is ambiguous. Moreover, it is difficult to see how the circumcision of Timothy as a Gentile fits the Lukan story line. In Acts 15 Paul has just won a victory over those who would require circumcision of Gentile converts, and in Acts 16:4 he delivers the results of this decree to the churches. It contradicts the Lukan context if in Acts 16:3 he portrays Paul as circumcising the Gentile Timothy contrary to the decree.

Nevertheless, Cohen is right in asserting that there is no evidence contemporary with the NT that sons of a Jewish mother and a Gentile father were legally considered Jewish. Such a fact is not damaging to the theory that Paul circumcised Timothy because the latter was considered to be Jewish. The rabbinic law on the status of children born to a Jewish mother and a Gentile father was probably established by early in the second century of the Common Era, and thus it is likely that in the previous century there was ongoing discussion and uncertainty about the status of such cases. Paul agreed to circumcise Timothy because there was some doubt regarding his nationality. He wanted to show that he did not forbid circumcision if there was any connection with the Jewish people. Thus by circumcising Timothy Luke shows that Paul did not forbid Jews from practicing the law (Acts 21:21-26; cf. 1 Cor 9:19-23). Paul had no animosity toward circumcision as a cultural practice; neither circumcision nor uncircumcision was anything significant in itself (Gal 5:6; 6:15; 1 Cor 7:19). But when circumcision was required for salvation, then Paul resisted it adamantly.

See also Abraham; Gentiles; Judaizers; Law; Paul and Judaism; Salvation; Works of the Law.

BIBLIOGRAPHY. **J. M. G. Barclay,** *Obeying the Truth: A Study of Paul's Ethic in Galatians* (Edinburgh: T&T Clark, 1988); **P. Borgen,** "Observations on the Theme 'Paul and Philo': Paul's Preaching of Circumcision in Galatia (Gal 5:11) and Debates on Circumcision in Philo," in *The Pauline Literature and Theology*, ed. S. Pederson (Göttingen: Vandenhoeck & Ruprecht, 1980), 85-102; idem, "Paul Preaches Circumcision and Pleases Men," in *Paul and Paulinism: Essays in Honour of C. K. Barrett*, ed. M. D. Hooker and S. G. Wilson (London: SPCK, 1982), 37-46; **C. Bryan,** "A Further Look at Acts 16:1-3," *JBL* 107 (1988): 292-94; **S. J. D. Cohen,** "Was Timothy Jewish (Acts 16:1-3)? Patristic Exegesis, Rabbinic Law, and Matrilineal Descent," *JBL* 105 (1986): 251-68; idem, "Contesting Conversion: Genealogy, Circumcision, and Identity in Ancient Judaism and Christianity," *CBQ* 75 (2013): 379-81; **G. F. Dowden,** "Circumcision of Christ," *Church Quarterly Review* 162 (1961): 400-407; **J. R. Edwards,** "Galatians 5:12: Circumcision, the Mother Goddess, and the Scandal of the Cross," *NovT* 53 (2011): 319-37; **R. G. Fellows,** "Paul, Timothy, Jerusalem, and the Confusion in Galatia," *Bib* 99 (2018): 544-66; **J. Garroway,** "The Pharisee Heresy: Circumcision for Gentiles in the Acts of the Apostles," *NTS* 60 (2014): 20-36; **M. E. Glasswell,** "New Wine in Old Wine Skins: VIII, Circumcision," *ExpTim* 85 (1974): 328-32; **J. K. Hardin,** "'If I Still Proclaim Circumcision' (Galatians 5:11a): Paul, the Law, and Gentile Circumcision," *JSPHL* 3 (2013): 145-63; **N. J. McEleney,** "Conversion, Circumcision, and the Law," *NTS* 20 (1974): 319-41; **R. Meyer,** "Περιτέμνω, κτλ.," *TDNT* 6:72-84; **J. Nolland,** "Uncircumcised Proselytes?," *JSJ* 12 (1981): 173-94; **P.-B. Smit,** "In Search of Real Circumcision: Ritual Failure and Circumcision in Paul," *JSNT* 40 (2017): 73-100; **M. Thiessen,** "Paul's Argument Against Gentile Circumcision in Romans 2:17-29," *NovT* 56 (2014): 373-91; **W. O. Walker,** "The Timothy-Titus Problem Reconsidered," *ExpTim* 92 (1981): 231-35.

T. R. Schreiner

CITIZENSHIP

Political citizenship, whether of a city or of the Roman Empire, was a matter of considerable advantage for *travel in the first-century Mediterranean world. Paul's understanding of the issues bound up in citizenship allowed him to use a fitting metaphor for participation in the *kingdom of *God.

1. Political Citizenship
2. Heavenly Citizenship

1. Political Citizenship.

Acts presents Paul as a citizen both of the city of Tarsus and of the Roman Principate.

1.1. Municipal Citizenship. Cities across the first-century Mediterranean world extended citizenship to their residents and honored friends, both to guard their residents' political rights and to advance the city's presence in its region. According to Acts 21:39, which records Paul's words to the Roman tribune in *Jerusalem, Paul was a citizen of Tarsus. Mark Antony had declared Tarsus a free city and granted it immunity from Roman taxation around 41 BC, so Paul's citizenship in Tarsus could be viewed as citizenship in a client city of Rome.

1.2. Roman Citizenship. Roman citizenship brought economic, political, and social advantages to its holders. It usually involved tax immunity, the right to vote for certain officeholders, and the right to marry another citizen. Roman citizenship was granted so readily in the republic that it surprised the Greek world. Specifically, the Greeks found it remarkable that *slaves of Romans received citizenship on full manumission and that cities or other social bodies could be granted citizenship. In the provinces of the early *empire while Paul lived, Roman citizenship would protect its holders from the *imperium* (supreme rule) vested in a proconsul or prefect and offer tax immunities, as in the republic. Claudius, who reigned from 41 to 54, returned to the policies of Caesar and Augustus in awarding Roman citizenship in order to extend Rome's dominance in the world.

Roman citizenship was more thickly textured than is usually pictured. During the republic cities could be granted *optimo iure* citizenship with the right to vote, or *sine suffragio* citizenship without such a right. In addition to full Roman citizenship, there were also other provisions of citizenship that offered some reciprocities with Roman citizenship. For example, during the republic, the Latin right that certain communities possessed allowed members to marry Roman citizens and to trade with the Romans. Magistrates of communities who held the Latin right were also routinely granted Roman citizenship. Those slaves not manumitted according to the proper protocol did not become Roman citizens, but under the *lex Iunia* of either Augustus or Tiberius, these freed slaves' legal category became Latin. At death, their property reverted to their former master. The child of two Roman citizens was a Roman citizen. If a man with Roman citizenship fathered a child with a noncitizen woman who possessed the legal right to marry a Roman, their child would still be a Roman citizen.

Acts explicitly presents Paul as claiming Roman citizenship in Acts 16:37-39; 22:25-29. If one accepts the accounts of Paul's trials and passage to Rome in Acts, then indirect evidence for Paul's citizenship may come from the scene in which he appeals to Caesar. But there is evidence that controversial noncitizens were arrested and sent as prisoners to Rome from this time period (Josephus, *Ant.* 20.6.2-3; 20.8.5; 20.10.1), as may also have been the case later with Ignatius, bishop of Antioch. In terms of the narrative strategy of Acts, it is worth noting with Wolfgang Stegemann that Paul's citizenship is never mentioned in the descriptions of his appeal to Caesar and passage to Rome.

Those who question the historicity of Paul's Roman citizenship do so on the grounds of anomalies in the narratives of Acts. First, there is the unexplained timing of Paul's declaration of his citizenship in Philippi. The resulting portraits of a vindicated or honored Roman, Paul, and discredited Roman officials seem to be part of the author's preferred way of ending the citizenship scenes (Acts 16:35-40; 22:25-29). With regard to the portrait in Acts of Paul's arrest in Jerusalem, Hans Conzelmann considers it impossible that a Roman centurion would leave a citizen of Rome bound and in *prison overnight, and then turn him over to be interrogated by the Jews (Acts 22:27–23:19). Klaus Wengst contrasts the view of Roman citizenship one could infer from Paul's letters with the view of Roman citizenship that one sees in Acts. In the letters, it seems that Paul puts no pride in his citizenship. In the book of Acts, Paul seems to take some pride in this citizenship and wants it recognized, in the first case even when such recognition is not necessary for escaping persecution (Acts 16:37-39; 22:28). Arguments from silence for doubting Paul's Roman citizenship may refer to 1 Corinthians 9:21-22 and Philippians 3:4-6, where Paul makes no mention of Roman citizenship when presenting his personal accommodations when evangelizing and his human advantages. In the end, one's position on whether Paul was a citizen rests on one's understanding of what sort of history Acts presents.

In addition to the explicit testimony to Paul's Roman citizenship in Acts 16:37-39; 22:25-29, other arguments for this citizenship include Paul's use of the names of Roman provinces (Rom 15:26; 1 Cor 16:1, 5; 2 Cor 8:1; 9:2-4; Gal 1:2), his *mission strategy of *church planting in Roman colonies (Philippi, *Corinth) or a city loyal to Rome (Thessalonica), and the way that he tells his audience in Romans to pay taxes, while not mentioning that he pays them. (If he were not a citizen, he would have to pay taxes to Rome.) If Paul indeed was both a citizen of Tarsus and a citizen of Rome, then such dual citizenship may have provided an analogy for his point in Philippians, that all believers—with varying citizenships on earth—have a heavenly citizenship.

2. Heavenly Citizenship.

Paul, who does not compartmentalize a believer's political and spiritual identities and was executed by the Romans, envisioned a believer's relationships in ways informed by the provisions of Roman citizenship while transferring the citizen's loyalties to *Christ. For example, Paul can treat the *freedom from slavery to *sin that *baptism brings as an entrance into a completely new existence, as slaves fully manumitted by their Roman owners became Roman citizens (Rom 6:17-23). Paul viewed churches as holding a corporate citizenship in the kingdom of God, much as whole cities could be granted Roman citizenship (1 Cor 1:2; Phil 3:20-21). A parent's identity "*in Christ" also rendered the spouse and children as somehow within God's sanctifying influence (1 Cor 7:14), as a Roman father could ensure citizenship for his progeny.

There is no evidence in Paul's letters that he could conceive of a Christ-follower who showed equal loyalties to the kingdom of God and to a given nation or political entity on earth. The citizenship in heaven that Paul taught eclipsed all political relationships on earth, since the Christ Paul followed ruled over every power on earth (Phil 2:9-11; 3:18-21; Col 1:15-20). Paul's own mission to bring the nations to the obedience of *faith, rendering them an acceptable offering to God, can be viewed as a Christ-inspired, counterimperial agenda (Rom 1:5; 15:15-21; 1 Cor 1:1-2). The alternative citizenship that Paul taught, influenced by the practical implications of Roman citizenship in the first century, can best be encapsulated with Paul's own terminology as "heavenly citizenship" (Phil 3:20).

While explicit language relation to heavenly citizenship is rare in Paul, the metaphor of heavenly citizenship influences both Paul's *ethics and his *eschatology. Paul uses this citizenship to inform his ethical injunctions and orient his readers toward their participation in the eschatological kingdom of God.

2.1. Ethical Injunctions. Paul presents his church members' heavenly citizenship with full cognizance of their participation in civil society (1 Cor 5:9-10; Rom 13:1-7). In this sense it is possible that Paul has in mind the legal status of a dual citizen (Phil 1:27; 3:20–4:1). Since Christians are citizens of both earth and heaven, Paul describes his *ministry as that of an ambassador who helps believers live on the basis of their heavenly citizenship (2 Cor 5:18-21; Eph 6:19-20). As citizens of heaven, Christians are responsible to think consistently with their citizenship (Col 3:1-4) and live holy lives (Rom 13:12-14; 15:15-16). Paul's idea of his own citizenship freed him to be all things to all people (1 Cor 9:19-23). First Peter 2:11 in context develops Paul's idea of heavenly citizenship by describing believers on earth as sojourners, temporarily exiled from heaven. Philippians 3:20 (in the light of Phil 1:27) provides the most explicit terminology for heavenly citizenship in Paul. This citizenship grounds Paul's commands to avoid thinking in an earthbound way (Phil 2:3-4; 3:19) and instead to follow his example (Phil 3:17) as befits believers who rejoice in God's goodness, praying and thinking in God-centered ways (Phil 4:1-9). The description of Christians' heavenly citizenship in Philippians 3:20 also is linked to the expectation of the parousia and the physical transformation it will bring to believers (Phil 3:20 21).

2.2. Eschatological Descriptions. The conviction that believers possess a citizenship in God's kingdom is a powerful force in Paul's theology. Thus one sees in 1 Thessalonians 4:13–5:24 how an understanding of the rights and destiny of the citizen leads to holy living now. In Romans 8:12-30, the prospect of participation as a citizen in the new *creation is inextricably linked both to one's status as a child of God and the concomitant behavior that such future citizenship and *adoption necessarily imply for the present. Paul's eschatological understanding of heavenly citizenship includes the conviction that the Christian is not ultimately subject to *death and ought therefore to live for values that will outlast life on earth (1 Cor 15:53-58). For those who worship the one granted the *name above every name, the one through whom and for whom all things were created, Paul emphatically values heavenly citizenship over any political citizenship here on earth (Phil 2:9-11; Col 1:15-20).

See also Eschatology; Ethics; Kingdom of God/Christ; Paul in Acts; Politics and Power; Prison, Prisoner; Travel in the Roman World; Urban Setting of Paul's Churches.

BIBLIOGRAPHY. **H. Conzelmann,** *Acts of the Apostles*, trans. J. Limburg, A. T. Kraabel, and D. H. Juel, Hermeneia (Philadelphia: Fortress, 1987); **M. H. Crawford,** "Citizenship, Roman," *OCD*, 334-35; **A. H. M. Jones and S. Mitchell,** "Tarsus," *OCD*, 1476; **A. D. E. Lewis,** "Ius Latii," *OCD*, 790-91; **B. Nicholas,** "Latini Iuniani," *OCD*, 821; **A. N. Sherwin-White,** *The Roman Citizenship* (repr., Oxford: Clarendon, 1996); **W. Stegemann,** "War der Apostel Paulus ein römischer Bürger?," *ZNW* 78 (1987): 200-229; **H. Strathmann,** "πόλις, κτλ.," *TDNT* 6:529-35; **K. Wengst,** *Pax Romana and the Peace of Jesus Christ*, trans. J. Bowden (Philadelphia: Fortress, 1987); **G. M. Zerbe,** *Citizenship: Paul on Peace and Politics* (Winnipeg: CMU Press, 2012).

M. Reasoner

CIVIL AUTHORITY. *See* Empire; Legal System, Roman; Political Systems; Politics and Power.

CLEAN. *See* Food Laws and Customs, Jewish and Roman; Purity and Impurity.

COLLECTION FOR THE SAINTS

A significant element of Paul's missionary activity in Achaia, Macedonia, and Galatia was his effort to organize a collection of funds among the congregations of those regions for Christ-followers in *Jerusalem. This project is often called "the collection for the saints," a term Paul uses in 1 Corinthians 16:1 (NRSV). Paul himself also labels the fundraising project a "partnership-forming contribution" (*koinōnia*, Rom 15:26; 2 Cor 9:13), a "service" (*diakoneō/diakonia*, Rom 15:25, 31; 2 Cor 8:4, 19-20; 9:1, 12-13), a "gift/benefaction" (*charis*, 1 Cor 16:3; 2 Cor 8:4, 6-7, 19; cf. 2 Cor 1:15), a "blessing" (*eulogia*, 2 Cor 9:5), a "lavish gift" (*adrotēs*, 2 Cor 8:20), and a "*ministry of service" (*hē diakonia tēs leitourgias*, 2 Cor 9:12). The energy and time that Paul expended in order to deliver this collection to Christ-followers in Jerusalem—in spite of some resistance among the churches of his *mission and the possibility of the gift's rejection by its intended recipients (Rom 15:31)—testify to the importance of the effort for Paul's mission among the *Gentiles.

1. History of the Collection
2. Frameworks for the Collection

1. History of the Collection.

It is difficult to piece together a narrative of Paul's efforts to bring material relief to the Christ-following community in Jerusalem. It is often suggested that the origin of the Pauline collection for the saints lies in the request of the leaders of the Jerusalem church—James, Peter, and John among them (Gal 2:9)—that Paul and his associates "remember the poor" (Gal 2:10 NRSV), an appeal made at the meeting that Paul recounts in Galatians 2:1-10. According to this view, Paul's efforts to organize funds among the largely Gentile churches of his mission reflect the fulfillment of a compact reached between him and the leaders of the Jerusalem church on the occasion of the conference recounted in Galatians 2:1-10 (so Nickle; Joubert).

Others have tied the request that Paul, Barnabas, and Titus "remember the poor" in Galatians 2:10 to the delivery of material assistance from Antioch to Jerusalem narrated in Acts 11:27-30 (Downs). That is, as a representative of the church in Antioch, Paul had been involved in the dispatch of a relief fund to Jerusalem at a time of famine (Acts 11:28), and perhaps Paul reports that he was eager to fulfill the request to "remember the poor" because the visit recounted in Galatians 2 refers to the same episode described in Acts 11. On the other hand, B. W. Longenecker has put forward a strong argument that the request from the leaders of the Jerusalem church that Paul and his associates "remember the poor" should not be interpreted in a local sense at all. Instead, Longenecker, with support from the early history of interpretation of Galatians 2:10, sees the entreaty to "remember the poor" as a call that "demarcates caring for the poor without geographical restriction of specificity" (Longenecker, 182), this is a reflection of the fact that the agreement at the Jerusalem conference commissioned Paul to bring the gospel to the Gentiles. Since Gentiles, in contrast to Jews shaped by the teachings of Torah, did not, for the most part, value or embody practices of care for the needy, it was important for the leaders of the Jerusalem church, according to Longenecker, to insist that Paul, in the context of his mission to Gentiles, not neglect the responsibility to "remember the poor," a request that Paul indicates he was eager to accept and that coheres with the stress on caring for the poor and weak found elsewhere in the Pauline letters (e.g., Rom 12:13, 16; 1 Cor 11:17-34; Gal 6:9-10; Eph 4:28; 1 Thess 5:14; 1 Tim 5:3-16; Titus 3:14).

Whatever the origins of Paul's attempt to organize an offering for Christ-followers in Jerusalem, the project appears to have consumed his attention over the course of several years and is mentioned explicitly in 1 Corinthians 16; 2 Corinthians 8–9; and Romans 15. Paul's first explicit comments about the collection indicate that the Galatians were already informed about the project and procedures for gathering funds (1 Cor 16:1-4). Paul offers the Corinthians guidance on how to do the same, namely, that on Sundays "each of you is to put aside and save whatever extra you earn, so that collections need not be taken when I come" (1 Cor 16:2 NRSV). At this point, Paul apparently intends to dispatch the gift to Jerusalem via Corinthian delegates, although he holds out the possibility that he might accompany the offering himself (1 Cor 16:3-4).

By the time of Paul's extended comments about the collection in 2 Corinthians 8–9, much had happened to imperil the fundraising effort in Corinth (and perhaps elsewhere). Paul's reference to a conflict between him and the Corinthians over his change in *travel plans (2 Cor 1:15–2:4) may imply Corinthian displeasure at the apostle's fundraising practices (2 Cor 1:15; cf. 2 Cor 11:7-15; 12:13-18) and perhaps even charges of financial impropriety against Paul (see 2 Cor 2:5-11; so Downs, 43-47). The material about the collection for the saints in 2 Corinthians 8–9 was written from Macedonia after Paul had received news of the Corinthians' reconciliation to him (2 Cor 7:2-16); it is a cautious attempt to encourage the Corinthians to resume gathering funds for the Jerusalem church. Here Paul mentions "the *grace of God that has been granted to the churches of Macedonia; for during a severe ordeal of affliction, their abundant *joy and their extreme poverty have overflowed in a wealth of generosity on their part" (2 Cor 8:1-2 NRSV). Thus, the generous willingness of the Macedonians to support the Jerusalem collection is offered as a model for the Corinthians to imitate. Interestingly, nowhere in 2 Corinthians does Paul mention participation in the collection by the Galatians, in spite of the fact that the churches of Galatia had earlier served as something of an example for the Corinthians (1 Cor 16:1-4). Whether this might imply that the Galatians had abandoned participation in the collection is impossible to determine.

That the Corinthians did ultimately join with Macedonian Christ-followers and contribute to the collection for the saints is suggested by Paul's final comments about the project in Romans 15:14-33. Paul writes to the Romans that from his present location in *Corinth he intends to travel to Jerusalem and then to Rome, "for Macedonia and Achaia were pleased to make a certain partnership-forming contribution [*koinōnian tina*] for the poor among the saints in Jerusalem" (Rom 15:26). Although in Romans 15 Paul stresses only his own plans to deliver the funds (e.g., "So, when *I* have completed this, and have delivered to them what has been collected," Rom 15:28 NRSV; "that *my* ministry to Jerusalem may be acceptable to the saints," Rom 15:31 NRSV), elsewhere the apostle implies that representatives from Achaia (1 Cor 16:3-4) and Macedonia (2 Cor 8:18-22; 9:3-5) may travel or are traveling to Jerusalem with the collection.

As the origins of the collection for the saints are unclear, so is its outcome. It is impossible to say anything certain about the delivery of the collection for the saints because there is no explicit reference to any fundraising effort in the account of Paul's activities in the Acts of the Apostles. Nowhere does the author of Acts mention or allude to Paul's labors to organize a relief fund among the churches of his mission, and Acts is silent about the conveyance of any collection in its account of Paul's final journey to Jerusalem. In a speech at Caesarea before Felix, the Roman governor of Judea, the *apostle does indicate after his arrest that he came to Jerusalem "to bring alms to my nation and to offer *sacrifices" (Acts 24:17 NRSV). While many interpreters find in Acts 24:17 a reference to the collection (Joubert, 211), such an identification is not supported by reading the narrative of Acts on its own terms, for Acts nowhere intimates that Paul organized a monetary fund for the Jerusalem church prior to his final journey to Jerusalem. Without the information about the collection for the saints that can be gathered from Paul's letters, the apostle's reference to *almsgiving in Acts 24:17 might simply highlight Paul's depiction of himself as a pious, faithful Jew in his speech before the Roman governor (Downs, 60-70).

As he is preparing to bring the collection to Jerusalem, Paul does ask the Romans to join him "in earnest *prayer to God on my behalf, that I may be rescued from the unbelievers in Judea, and that my ministry to Jerusalem may be acceptable to the saints" (Rom 15:30-31 NRSV). To take Paul's prayer seriously is to reckon with the possibility that his "ministry" (*diakonia*), that is, the collection for the saints, might not have been acceptable to Christ-followers in Jerusalem. Did the author of the Acts of the Apostles fail to mention the Jerusalem collection because he was aware of its rejection? Unfortunately, the available sources do not allow confident answers to the question of why the narrative of Acts is silent regarding the collection for the saints.

2. Frameworks for the Collection.

Scholars have typically identified several potential, and not necessarily mutually exclusive, reasons behind and frameworks for Paul's effort to collect funds for the Jerusalem church.

2.1. Material Relief. Among the purposes of the collection for the saints, the alleviation of material distress among recipients in Jerusalem is presented by Paul as a key motivation. In a socioeconomic context in which subsistence existence was the norm for the vast majority of inhabitants of the Mediterranean region, a materialist interpretation of the Jerusalem collection emphasizes the present and potential deprivation faced by both the recipients of and, to judge from Paul's statements, contributors to the relief fund (see Friesen; Longenecker). Paul calls the beneficiaries of the collection "the poor among the saints at Jerusalem" (Rom 15:26 NRSV), a designation that almost certainly refers to material deprivation, and he speaks of the gift as relieving the material need of those who receive it so that there might be equity (*isotētos*) between givers and recipients (2 Cor 8:13-15). At the same time, Paul acknowledges that the Macedonians have contributed to the collection in spite of their own poverty (2 Cor 8:1-5), and he implies that the Corinthians, though they possessed comparative material abundance at the time the apostle wrote 2 Corinthians, might in the future require financial assistance from the saints in Jerusalem (2 Cor 8:13-15). The collection for the saints represents a communal survival strategy among Christ-followers for whom poverty and deprivation were ever-present realities (Harland and Last, 135-49).

2.2. Communal Solidarity. While the collection for the saints ostensibly aimed to meet very real material needs, Paul also depicts the gift as an ecumenical offering to symbolize the unity of the largely Gentile churches of his mission with Jewish Christ-followers in Jerusalem. In Romans 15:26-27 Paul frames the collection as an exchange of material blessings from those whom Paul calls "the Gentiles" for spiritual blessings shared by "the poor among the saints at Jerusalem" (NRSV). Paul not only indicates that the Gentiles were pleased to contribute to Christ-followers in Jerusalem but that the Gentiles were "obligated" (*opheilousin*, Rom 15:27) to bless those in whose spiritual blessings the Gentiles have come to share, a point explored in S. Joubert's study on the collection and reciprocal exchange (see Barclay). The frequency with which Paul employs the noun *koinōnia* and its cognates (Rom 15:26; 2 Cor 8:4, 23; 9:3, 13; cf. Gal 2:9) in discussions of the offering emphasizes both the social relationships formed by the gift and the material sign of those relationships, thus the ungainly translation "partnership-forming contribution." For this reason, the possible rejection of the offering by Jewish Christ-followers in Jerusalem would, from Paul's perspective, be an affront to the legitimacy of his mission among the Gentiles and potentially imperil the unity of Jews and Gentiles in the one *body of Christ (see Rom 12:4-5; 1 Cor 12:27).

At the same time, it should be stressed that the collection also established or increased solidarity among the various Gentile churches of Paul's mission that participated in the project, especially as representatives of churches from Macedonia (and possibly Asia) traveled to Corinth to assist with the organization of the fund and to ensure that contributions were handled properly. While there are numerous examples of collective assistance among voluntary associations (including Jewish synagogues) in Greco-Roman antiquity, the translocal nature of the Pauline collection for Jerusalem is notable (so Downs; cf. Kloppenborg).

2.3. Eschatological Pilgrimage. Drawing on a number of OT texts that envision an eschatological pilgrimage of either Diaspora Jews or Gentiles to Jerusalem (Is 2:1-4; 60:5-14; 66:18-20; Jer 3:17; Mic 7:12-17; Hag 2:7; Zech 8:21-23; 14:16), scholars have argued that the Pauline collection was a symbolic act of eschatological provocation (e.g., Nickle). According to this view, Paul intended his group of gift-bearing Gentiles to provoke non-Christ-believing Jews to jealousy (see Rom 11:14), causing Jews to believe that Jesus was Israel's Messiah because prophetic texts regarding Gentiles bringing offerings to Zion had been fulfilled. That Paul does not cite any eschatological pilgrimage texts in his discussions of the Jerusalem collection, and that Paul's contribution was intended for "the poor among the saints" rather than the *temple in Jerusalem, raise challenges for this view of the collection, although it still has articulate proponents (e.g., Auler).

2.4. The Collection as Anticolonial Act and Challenge to Roman Patronage. Other aspects of the Jerusalem collection might be emphasized, including the sociopolitical dimensions of the offering. S. Wan, for example, has framed the collection as an "anticolonial act" through which Paul "constructed an all-embracing sociopolitical order that stood in contradistinction to and in criticism of colonial powers" (Wan, 192), and similarly J. M. Ogereau has suggested that the collection aimed to establish "a new order of socio-economic equality and solidarity among the emergent Christ-believing communities, at both a local and global level, and across socio-cultural and ethnic divides" (Ogereau, 360). Finally, D. J. Downs has interpreted Paul's rhetorical strategies vis-à-vis the collection for the saints in light of gift-giving practices in the ancient world, including Paul's implicit challenge to the cultural assumption that donors should receive public honor for their beneficence: "Paul metaphorically frames his readers' responsive participation in the collection as an act of cultic *worship, and in so doing he underscores the point that benefaction within the community of believers results in praise to *God, the one from whom all benefactions ultimately come" (Downs, 121).

Recent research on gift-giving in Greco-Roman antiquity has emphasized the importance of reciprocity and the key role that gifts play in establishing and strengthening social ties (so Barclay). The collection for the saints in Jerusalem was clearly an important endeavor for the apostle Paul, a gift from the Gentile churches of his mission that he was ostensibly willing to risk his own life to deliver. This particular effort to "remember the poor" stands as a signal example of Paul's commitment to exhort Christ-followers to care for the needy.

See also Almsgiving and Rewards; Corinthians, Second Letter to the; Fellowship, Communion, Sharing; Gentiles; Jerusalem, Council of; Ministry; Mission; Paul in Acts; Romans, Letter to the; Sacrifice, Offering; Servant, Service; Travel and Itinerary Plans; Wealth and Poverty.

BIBLIOGRAPHY. **S. Auler,** "More Than a Gift: Revisiting Paul's Collection for Jerusalem and the Pilgrimage of Gentiles," *JSPHL* 6 (2016): 143-60; **J. M. G. Barclay,** *Paul and the Gift* (Grand Rapids, MI: Eerdmans, 2015); **D. J. Downs,** *The Offering of the Gentiles: Paul's Collection for Jerusalem in Its Chronological, Cultural, and Cultic Contexts* (Grand Rapids, MI: Eerdmans, 2016); **S. J. Friesen,** "Paul and Economics: The Jerusalem Collection as an Alternative to Patronage," in *Paul Unbound: Other Perspectives on the Apostle*, ed. M. D. Given (Peabody, MA: Hendrickson, 2010), 27-54; **P. A. Harland and R. Last,** *Group Survival in the Ancient Mediterranean: Rethinking Material Conditions in the Landscape of Jews and Christians* (London: T&T Clark, 2020); **S. Joubert,** *Paul as Benefactor: Reciprocity, Strategy and Theological Reflection in Paul's Collection*, WUNT 2/124 (Tübingen: Mohr Siebeck, 2000); **J. S. Kloppenborg,** "Fiscal Aspects of Paul's Collection for Jerusalem," *EC* 8 (2017): 153-98; **B. W. Longenecker,** *Remember the Poor: Paul, Poverty, and the Greco-Roman World* (Grand Rapids, MI: Eerdmans, 2010); **K. F. Nickle,** *The Collection: A Study in Paul's Strategy*, SBT 48 (Naperville, IL: Allenson, 1966); **J. M. Ogereau,** "The Jerusalem Collection as Κοινωνία: Paul's Global Politics of Socio-economic Equality and Solidarity," *NTS* 58 (2012): 360-78; **S. Wan,** "Collection for the Saints as Anticolonial Act: Implications of Paul's Ethnic Reconstruction," in *Paul and Politics: Ekklesia, Israel, Imperium, Interpretation*, ed. R. A. Horsley (Harrisburg, PA: Trinity Press International, 2000), 191-215.

D. J. Downs

COLLECTION OF PAUL'S LETTERS.
See Canon of Paul's Letters.

COLOSSIANS, LETTER TO THE

Paul's letter to the Colossians, one of his shorter *letters by comparison, was written to the *church in the city of Colossae, situated in the Lycus Valley in the Roman province of Asia. The church was founded through the work of Epaphras, a fellow laborer with Paul. Colossians offers a high *Christology, a universal ecclesiology, and an *eschatology more realized than futuristic. The epistle is often connected in similarity to Ephesians and connected in time and geography to Philemon. Paul and Timothy write to the church to respond to a problem in the congregation that has been variously identified by modern scholarship. A recent survey has concluded that over forty theoretical proposals about the precise nature of the Colossian problem were extant in contemporary scholarship through 1977 alone, "a number that certainly has increased and continues to increase" (Copenhaver, 1-33). The proposals can be split into perspectives that propose that the primary influence on the problematic philosophy was *Gnosticism, pagan religion, Hellenistic *philosophy, or Judaism. Writers find the solution to the threat before the church in a Christology that has made possible reconciliation embodied in the church, the *body of which Christ is the *head.

1. Contextual Matters
2. Theology
3. The Letter Proper
4. Major Themes
5. Conclusion

1. Contextual Matters.

1.1. Authorship. The writers identify themselves as "Paul, an *apostle of Jesus *Christ by the will of *God, and Timothy our brother" (Col 1:1 NRSV). It has been disputed whether Paul is the author or whether it was written by someone else after the apostle's *death. Writing in the name of a respected *teacher or leader (pseudonymity) was not unheard of in the ancient world. In some quarters it was not necessarily an unacceptable practice, but neither was it universally welcomed. It was not until the modern era that the Pauline authorship of Colossians was questioned.

The current state of Colossians scholarship evidences a significant degree of variation even among those interpreters who argue for genuine Pauline authorship. A consensus view does not exist at this time. Among those who argue for the Pauline authorship, interpreters postulate Paul's precise role in the production of the epistle to have operated in a number of different ways. Scholars arguing in favor of Pauline authorship can, for example, propose that the epistle was either written by Paul or "authorized" by Paul (Thompson, 4), that the epistle was written or dictated by Paul with "eventual revisions, made by one or several aides" (Barth and Blanke, 125), or that the epistle was written by Paul simply because the evidence against Pauline authorship cannot convincingly and sufficiently establish that Colossians was written by someone else (see Gupta 2013, 8-10; Beale, 1-8). All of these qualify as arguments in favor of Pauline authorship, but each uniquely describes the parameters and possibilities pertaining to how the epistle was authored in relation to Paul.

Those who argue against genuine Pauline authorship typically do so on the basis of statistical analyses of lexical differences between Colossians and the undisputed Pauline epistles (Schweizer 1982, 18-19), the absence of key Pauline concepts such as *justification and *righteousness, or a perceived theological incongruence with the undisputed epistles on issues such as eschatology, ecclesiology, Christology, and baptismal theology (Canavan, 25). Witherington (118-19) observes a correlation between those scholars (such as Lohse, Lincoln, and MacDonald) who argue for a primarily Hellenistic, syncretistic, or proto-Gnostic provenance for the Colossians problem and the corresponding tendency to attribute authorship to someone other than Paul. Among those who argue for non-Pauline authorship of the epistle, theories abound and include many hypothetical proposals, such as the view that Timothy (Schweizer 1982, 25-26) or a disciple of Paul such as Epaphras (Canavan, 27-29) could be the author.

The real difference between Colossians and the undisputed Pauline letters is one of style, but a pseudonymous author is not the only explanation. Colossians 1:1 identifies Paul *and Timothy* as coauthors of the letter. This could suggest that Timothy was the one who actually penned the letter, with Paul giving it his final approval (see, e.g., Thompson, 4). In Colossians 4:18 Paul puts his own hand to his personal greeting, suggesting that the rest of the letter was not penned by him. In other letters, Paul made use of amanuenses (editors given leeway to compose). What is not known is how much freedom he gave these various writers to shape the letters that bore his name. This is true not only of Colossians but of Romans and Galatians as well. Perhaps it is better to speak less of Pauline authorship and instead highlight Paul's authority behind the whole Pauline corpus.

1.2. Date and Imprisonment. If Colossians carries the authority of the still-living Paul, then it must have been written before a devastating earthquake destroyed Colossae in AD 60–61. Paul wrote the letter from *prison (Col 4:3), but it is not clear which prison. The majority view is that Paul was under house arrest in Rome, as indicated in Acts 28:16-31, but that position has recently been challenged in favor of *Ephesus. A third view positing a Caesarean imprisonment represents a clear minority position (Barth and Blanke, 127-29).

Moo indicates a "slight preference" for a Roman imprisonment, indicating that it best explains the circumstances in Philemon and best accords with the movements of Paul known through other NT writings (46). F. F. Bruce (in O'Brien, l-li) is likewise firmly convinced of a Roman provenance, arguing that a large imperial city is the most likely location that the runaway *slave Onesimus would remain successfully hidden. Some commentators hold to a mediating position of Rome or Ephesus (but not Caesarea), noting that "it is hard to be confident about whether Paul wrote from Ephesus or Rome" (Beale, 8).

Hypotheses positing an Ephesian imprisonment are well represented and on the rise in some of the most recent commentaries on Colossians. Bird leans slightly toward an Ephesian imprisonment as being "marginally less problematic" than a Roman imprisonment (9-15), based on the closeness of Ephesus to Colossae, which lends to a more likely scenario for all of the comings and goings articulated in the epistle (see Schweizer 1982, 25-26; Beale, 8); on the hardships that Paul endured in Asia Minor (see, e.g., 1 Cor 15:32; 2 Cor 1:8, albeit without explicit mention of an imprisonment); and finally on the fact that Timothy (who is with Paul in Col 1:1) is not said to accompany Paul to Rome in Acts 28 but is situated with Paul in Ephesus according to 1 Corinthians 16:8-10. Additionally, Romans 15:14-33 indicates that Paul was intending to go to Spain after his time in Rome and not to return to Asia Minor.

Despite an Ephesian imprisonment not being made explicit in the extant NT literature, it is reasonable to give consideration to the fact that Paul was imprisoned on more than a few occasions in other places that are not mentioned in Acts or the Pauline corpus (see 2 Cor 6:5; 11:23). Given the proximity of Ephesus to Colossae and the other churches in the cities of Asia Minor, and considering Paul's traveling companions and their locations chronologically and that Rome was twelve hundred miles from Colossae (see Barth and Blanke, 127), which made traveling long, difficult, and expensive, Ephesus is likely the best option for the place of composition, but even that conclusion must be drawn cautiously.

1.3. The City of Colossae. When Paul and Timothy wrote to the Colossians, the glory days of the city had long faded into memory. Pliny the Elder (AD 23–79) refers to Colossae as an insignificant and dwindling city (*Nat.* 2.3-7). Colossae's closest neighbor, Laodicea, and Hierapolis were larger. The area was known for its production of wool. "Colossian wool," as it was called, was dark red. The Lycus Valley, in which Colossae was situated, produced figs and olives.

The city's location in Asia Minor (modern-day Turkey) made it susceptible to earthquakes. A large earthquake in AD 60–61 destroyed Laodicea and Colossae. The evidence suggests that the city lay uninhabited until the second century AD.

Prior to the earthquake, Colossae was less a city and more of a large town with a cosmopolitan feel. Located on a major coastal trade route, Colossae benefited from the exchange of both commerce and culture, which can be observed in the artifacts retrieved in recent excavations (Canavan, 21). The population consisted of native-born Phrygians from west-central Turkey and Greek immigrants who settled there several generations before. In the second century BC Antiochus III brought around two thousand Jewish families from Mesopotamia and Babylon to settle in the region (Josephus, *Ant.* 12). Jewish influence was felt in the area along with a mixture of pagan religious practices. This religious context makes it difficult to diagnose the problem Paul and Timothy address in their letter.

1.4. The Colossian Church. The letter to the Colossians suggests that the church was founded by Epaphras (Col 1:16-17). While it is possible that Paul traveled through Colossae on one of his missionary journeys, there is no reason to believe that he stayed there for any significant length of time. He never visited the church in person (Col 2:1). The size of the Christian population of Colossae is unknown, but it is not unreasonable to think that it consisted of several house churches. From Philemon 2 it is clear that a church did gather at Philemon's home in Colossae. Depending on the nature of the Colossian philosophy that Paul and Timothy address, it could have been the case that the Christian congregations were large enough in that small town to get noticed by those outside the church.

While it cannot be ruled out that a minority of Jews made up the Colossian church, by and large the congregations consisted of *Gentiles. Paul's language in the letter clearly indicates this (see Col 1:12, 21, 27; 2:13; 3:5).

1.5. The Reason for the Letter. Perhaps even more controversial than the question of authorship is the reason for the letter's composition. Just what is the Colossian philosophy (Col 2:8)?

The residents of Colossae were exposed to an amalgam of pagan religious practices as well as Jewish religious influence. The characteristics of the philosophy are revealed in the so-called polemical core of Colossians 2:8-23. Markus Barth and Helmut Blanke identify some forty-four views present in scholarship at that time (38). The various possibilities presented on the philosophy's nature can be classified into two general groupings. The first is that the Colossian philosophy contained a mixture of religious practices or a religious syncretism. Various amalgams have been suggested to describe the philosophy.

John Barclay provides a concise explanation of the most dominant theories in the history of interpretation (Barclay, 40-48). These theories include everything from Jewish Gnosticism (J. B. Lightfoot and later Günther Bornkamm) to the syncretistic Christian adoption of a pagan mystery cult (Martin Dibelius). Others posit the influence of various Hellenistic philosophies on the Colossian believers, such as neo-Pythagoreanism with its focus on the physical elements (*stoicheia*) of the world (Schweizer), a syncretistic morphing of Middle Platonism and Jewish religion (DeMaris), and a Colossian philosophy that is developed to deal with the problem of Cynic criticism of Christian doctrine and practice in the church (Martin). Last, Clinton Arnold argues on the basis of his survey of literature and artifacts from the Lycus Valley that what one finds in Colossians is a mix of Jewish and folk religious practices designed to ward off evil powers and curb the effect of *magic through amulets, religious practices, and the invocation of angels (Barclay, 40-48).

Those who promote the syncretistic thesis disagree on what are the most significant elements of the philosophy or whether even certain components are present. Nevertheless, if this first option is correct, then there appears to have been some pressure coming from a group within the church, or from the outside, to incorporate these syncretistic elements into the Christian practice of the Colossian believers.

The second option, which has gained more traction with recent studies such as those by Marianne Meye Thompson, Charles Talbert, and Ben Witherington III (see Gupta 2010, 12), is that the character of the Colossian philosophy was essentially Jewish in nature and that its proponents were Jews either from within the church or from the synagogue in town who were promoting their Judaism to the church, arguing that the Colossian Christians had distorted the ancestral faith by not embracing certain Jewish practices in their life and *worship (see too Wright 2008, 97-98, though he does note that "no scholarly consensus whatever" exists). Such practices were badges of Jewish *identity and marked off Jews as God's people in the first century—*circumcision, *food laws, and Sabbath and holy day observances.

For James Dunn, "the number of distinctly and definitively Jewish features" makes it very unlikely that the core of the philosophy was non-Jewish in nature (Dunn 2014, 34). The focus on circumcision (Col 2:11), food and drink restrictions, festivals, new moons, and most particularly Sabbath (Col 2:16) indicates a clear Jewish center to the philosophy, not a peripheral Jewish syncretism (Dunn 2014, 156-59, 173-77). Paul wrote to warn the Christians of the dangers of incorporating these identity markers, arguing that their identity is to be found in Jesus Christ alone. Thus, they must hold "fast to the head [Christ], from whom the whole body" (the church) is "nourished and held together by its ligaments and sinews" (Col 2:19 NRSV). Others, such as Fred Francis, have argued for an exclusively Jewish philosophy at play in Colossians, but one characterized by a mystical Jewish focus on heavenly ascent to worship among the angels mediated through a severe regimen of fasting (Barclay, 44-45).

The tone of the letter is quite calm, suggesting the Colossians had not embraced the practices of the synagogue but may have been entertaining the possibility. This contrasts with Galatians, where Paul offers an angry response to the churches that appear to have taken up these practices.

2. Theology.

Paul is first and foremost a missional theologian. His theology is worked out in the context of the church and its purpose for existence. Thus, his theology resists systemization, but that does not mean that a construction of his theology is impossible. A brief statement of the following three doctrines mentioned in Colossians forms an understanding of Paul's theology and its practical implications.

2.1. Christology. Colossians affirms what has been traditionally called a high Christology. Jesus is "the image of the invisible God, the *firstborn of all *creation," and the dwelling place for the "*fullness of God" (Col 1:15, 19 NRSV). Scot McKnight summarizes the teaching of Paul's Christology in Colossians 1:15-20 by noting that Jesus is presented as preeminent above the rest of creation because "temporally he is before all things, hierarchically he is above all things, and ontologically he sustains all things" (McKnight, 194). Yet, while the majority of literature on Christology in Colossians focuses on the Christ *hymn of Colossians 1:15-20, theological arguments of christological import are woven throughout the entire epistle, and most of them demonstrate how Jesus is the fulfillment of Judaism.

Jesus is presented as the fulfillment of and dwelling place for Jewish *wisdom, which had formerly been equated with the Torah (Col 2:3; cf. Col 1:9, 28), and he is presented as the substance of which the boundary-marking *works of the *law were merely a shadow (Col 2:16-17). As God's beloved *Son, Jesus completes the missional and vocational task of Israel's sonship (Ex 4:22), and as "Israel-in-Person" (Wright 2013, 521, 842, 930) he expands the inheritance of sonship through *Israel to the entire cosmos, bringing about a new redemptive exodus through his death and *resurrection (Col 1:12-14). He is the culmination, completion, and perfection of the old *covenant system of blood *sacrifices, "making *peace through the blood of his *cross" (Col 1:20 NRSV) and thereby establishing the reconciliation and *holiness of those who are found in him (Col 1:22). Finally, he is Christ the victor over *sin and death, triumphing over the *principalities and powers through his death and resurrection (Col 2:11-15). A high Christology is certainly concentrated within the Christ hymn, but the same Christ in whom "all things hold together" binds the coherence of the entire epistle together through his persistent and pervasive presence as the one in whom the church, the creation, and the cosmos is "all in all" (Col 1:15-20; 3:11).

2.2. Ecclesiology. It is often claimed that Ephesians is focused on ecclesiology (the doctrine of the church) while Colossians is unique in its realized eschatological perspective. In terms of lexical statistics, it is true that Ephesians uses the word *ekklēsia* roughly twice as much as Colossians (nine times as compared to four). However, apart from that rather inconsequential lexical metric, Colossians holds as high a view of the church as it does Christology. The Christology of Colossians functions not only to exalt Christ but to exalt his body, the church. In particular, the theme of participation in Christ as the means and goal of Christian perfection is inseparably connected to participation in the church. The prepositional phrase *en Christō* ("*in Christ") occurs three times in Colossians and usually indicates union with Christ through inclusion in Christ by belonging to his body, the church (see, e.g., Col 1:2, "to the saints and faithful brothers and sisters in Christ at Colossae" [NRSV]; cf. Col 1:27-28). This is participation "in Christ" (*en Christō*) is also described as union "with Christ" (*syn Christō*)—union with Christ in his death (Col 2:20) and resurrection ("made . . . alive together with him"; Col 2:13 NRSV).

For Paul in Colossians, ecclesiology is not merely a peripheral topic to be tagged on to the end of an otherwise more soteriologically significant systematic theology. Rather, ecclesiology is itself soteriological in Colossians. Ecclesiology in Colossians is not so much about polity as it is about participation. This participation in Christ, Paul says, is fundamental to how believers are presented perfect "in Christ," that is, by his person and through his body.

Even the so-called ethical sections of Colossians do not actually ever shift away from theology. Just as ecclesiology is soteriological in Colossians, so too *ethics is theological, and theology is ethical. This can be observed in that the renewal in *knowledge according to the image of the Creator that takes place in Colossians 3:10 is a result not so much of personal behavioral choices but of the corporate clothing of believers in a new domain and power of existence. In Colossians 3:9-10, the verbs "put off" and "put on" are second-person plural, while that which is taken off is, in both instances, third-person singular. The result of this is profoundly important for understanding the role of the church in Paul's ecclesial ethic. The life of Christian transformation takes place when one is removed from the corporate inclusion in the sinful way of life characterized by the first *Adam and one is individually inducted into the corporate clothing of the new Adam, namely, Jesus Christ. "Here" (Gk. *hopou*), Paul says, "is no longer Greek and Jew, circumcised and uncircumcised, barbarian, Scythian, slave and free; but Christ is all and in all!" (Col 3:11). Thus, the true focus of the "ethics" of Colossians 3 is not individual virtue formation but ecclesial cruciformation, spiritual formation in the way of the cross as Christ's body, through Christ's life, by the power of Christ's self-giving *love embodied, enacted, and received. This love binds the church together, leading them to perfection through participation in Christ together (see Col 3:14; Frederick 2019, 187, 193-97; Barth and Blanke, 424; Montague, 82, 108, 153).

2.3. Eschatology. The eschatology of Colossians is partially realized, with an emphasis on living in Christ as the new age has already dawned (see Still). While Colossians often does speak in terms of the accomplished result of *salvation with reference to the believer (i.e., "you have been raised with Christ" [Col 3:1 NRSV]; "you have died" [Col 3:3 NRSV]), salvation is also presented as very much in the process of being applied (e.g., "When Christ who is your life is revealed, then you also will be revealed with him in *glory" [Col 3:4 NRSV]; "Put to death" [Col 3:5 NRSV]; "Clothe yourselves" [Col 3:12 NRSV]). Therefore, while there are some unique aspects to the way that salvation is portrayed in a realized sense in Colossians, it is in no way out of sync or incommensurate with what one finds elsewhere in the undisputed Pauline epistles.

A consensus on the precise nature and articulation of eschatological realities in Colossians is, of course, an object of disagreement among Colossians scholars, and it is common to find a link between scholars who argue against Pauline authorship and a perceived significant incongruence between the Christology and ecclesiology of Colossians along with the way these aspects of theology are approached in the undisputed epistles (Canavan, 25). Thus, the verdicts on the authorship and the degree to which the eschatological perspective of Colossians appears to be novel typically go hand in hand. Like the OT fulfillment that one finds in the Christology of Colossians, the eschatology of the epistle is likewise situated within the framework of the fulfillment of the covenant promises of God in Christ. For example, in addition to all the ways that Jesus fulfills the old covenant (all of which could also rightly be labeled eschatological as well as typological), the "peace" achieved by Christ's blood is eschatological and messianic. As Barth and Blanke show, the messianic peace prophesied in 2 Samuel 7:14; Isaiah 9:5; and Micah 5:1-4 comes to the people of God in its fullness and eschatological inbreaking through Jesus Christ (Barth and Blanke, 216-17).

3. The Letter Proper.

3.1. *Outline.*

I. Opening greeting (Col 1:1-2)
II. Thanksgiving for faithful saints (Col 1:3-14)
III. The Christ hymn (Col 1:15-23)
IV. The call and the testimony (Col 1:24–2:7)
V. Living life in Christ's fullness (Col 2:8-23)
VI. Living the heavenly life on earth (Col 3:1-17)
VII. Living in the Christian household (Col 3:18–4:1)
VIII. Final instructions, greetings, and benediction (Col 4:2-18)

3.2. Opening Greeting (Col 1:1-2). In referring to himself as "an apostle of Jesus Christ by the will of God" (Col 3:1 NRSV), Paul is bolstering his credentials, which in some other contexts were considered suspect (Gal 1:11–2:10).

Paul characteristically refers to the recipients of his letters as "saints," "holy ones" (Gk. *hagios*; Latin *sanctus*), whom God has set apart for a specific purpose. In this designation, Paul reminds the Colossians that they too are called by God.

Finally, Paul and Timothy conclude their greeting with a wish of "*grace and peace from God our Father" (Col 1:2 NRSV), a typical Pauline greeting in which Paul affirms the Colossians are members of the covenant at God's initiative as well as his desire for their well-being in all aspects of life.

3.3. Thanksgiving for Faithful Saints (Col 1:3-14). The authors always thank God the Father of the Lord Jesus Christ when they pray for the Colossians. There is a Christ-centered quality to Paul's thankfulness. The Colossians' faith in Christ and the fruit it has produced have come to them because other faithful saints brought these to them. Fruit produces more fruit.

Paul and Timothy move from their thankfulness to a reminder of their continual *prayers for the Colossians. Their prayers are persistent. Moreover, their prayers for the Colossians are specific: "asking that you may be filled with the knowledge of God's will in all spiritual wisdom and understanding, so that you may lead lives worthy of the *Lord, fully pleasing to him, as you bear fruit in every good work and as you grow in the knowledge of God" (Col 1:9-10 NRSV), which is to be known through "spiritual wisdom and understanding."

Such wisdom, knowledge, and understanding are divine gifts given to aid the Colossians in their life together as the church. Recent scholarship on intertextuality in Colossians has identified the influence of Isaiah 11:1-9 on Colossians 1:9-10. Isaiah 11 is widely known to have been read messianically in Second Temple and rabbinic Judaism. A connection has now been shown to exist between the messianic function of the themes of wisdom, knowledge, and the Spirit in Isaiah 11:1-9 and Colossians 1:9-10 (Beetham, 72).

In Colossians 1:12-14 the authors connect the church as God's chosen people in continuity with God's chosen Israel. One can hear echoes of the OT in these verses—echoes that hark back to the exodus from Egypt and Israel's entrance into the Promised Land of Canaan—delivering and sharing in the inheritance. The Gentile Christians now share in the inheritance of deliverance and salvation given to Israel by God's grace.

3.4. The Christ Hymn (Col 1:15-23). It is generally agreed that Colossians 1:15-20 is a hymn or poem written in the early decades of Christianity and likely used in worship. Scot McKnight, however, notes that some recent scholarship on Colossians 1:15-23 leans away from interpreting the section as an inherited hymn and favors the view that it is more of "an on-the-spot poetic creation by the apostle Paul." While still referring to the section as a "hymn," he argues against interpretations that speculate about a pre-Pauline provenance for the hymn, adding that one must maintain the possibility that Paul himself composed the hymn "perhaps on the basis of preexisting confessional lines that he perhaps also had a hand in himself" (McKnight, 136-37). Whether written by others or Paul himself, it is employed in the letter to persuade the Colossians of Christ's centrality in all things, including worship. Here there is a high Christology emphasizing Jesus' divinity. Jesus is both in the *image of the invisible God and the one who reconciles all things. The term and concept of "image" can refer to the making "visible and concrete" of the invisible God through the incarnation (Thiselton, 33-35) or to Christ's likeness to God in his eternal preexistence, which he bore even before he was incarnated (Beale, 80-85), or to both.

As Jesus embodies the image of the invisible God, so the church embodies the image of Jesus. "He is the head of the body, the church" (Col 1:18 NRSV). The cosmic significance of Jesus reveals the universal importance of the church. As Jesus is the incarnation of God, so the church is to embody Christ for the world. The emphasis is missional. The *mission is nothing less than the reconciliation of all things. It is Christ who accomplishes the work of reconciliation by the "blood of his cross" (Col 1:20), but the church is the vehicle by which reconciliation is made known to the world.

This work of reconciliation includes earthly aspects and institutions, albeit those that operate under the control of spiritual powers. Interest in the intersection between Paul's theological concepts in Colossians and Roman imperial themes is evident in the studies of A. Deissmann, P. Wendland, A. Harnack, and H. Leitzmann dating back to the beginning of the twentieth century (see Maier, 323-24). While it is debatable whether Colossians was primarily written as an anti-imperial epistle (among other things), the contrasting lordship of Jesus in a culture that proclaimed the lordship of Caesar would certainly have had (and continues to have) religious and political implications that were pertinent to the way the cruciform *kingdom of God operated in contrast to the crucifying kingdom of Caesar. Likewise, Harry Maier shows how the terminology and concepts of Colossians 1:15-23 echo imperial terms and ideas that were applied to the emperor Nero, depicting him as the head of the body and an incarnate deity (Maier, 329-40). The point, Maier argues, is not merely that the words resonate in an imperial context but also that Paul uses them to "reverse" imperial claims in order to reorient and repopulate them with the *gospel of Jesus Christ (329). Others do not necessarily reject these views but caution interpreters to avoid "mistaking context for content" (Bird, 91).

In seeking to interpret Colossians in its original, cultural and historical context, it is appropriate, beneficial, and indeed necessary to consider the way the themes of Colossians would have been perceived in a first-century imperial setting. As Maier argues in the prolegomena to his influential 2005 article, paying exegetical "attention to imperial themes and imagery cannot give a complete account of Colossians, nor does it supplant other exegetical treatments" (Maier, 326-27). It is more common, however, in contemporary Colossians scholarship to see imperial themes ignored rather than incorporated. Yet, it is certainly valid to consider the contrast of the Pauline gospel of fruitfulness, which results in "the practice of justice and sacrificial faithfulness," with the Roman use of the term *euangelion* ("gospel") to refer to military might and success (Walsh and Keesmaat, 74-75). It is also crucial, however, to balance exegetical contrasts with Roman imperial culture in ways that reflect the entirety of the biblical position. While it is true, for example, that the kingdom of God will result in "fruitfulness and safety for the whole creation" (Walsh and Keesmaat, 73), it will also result in *judgment. It is therefore possible either that Colossians in this regard could be best conceived of as a "thinly veiled protest against the power and propaganda of the Roman state" (Bird, 91) or that Colossians bears a more pervasive "imperial imprint" that suggests Paul is intentionally drawing on imperial themes in order to reverse them through "a dramatic reorientation of prevailing ideals" (Maier, 329, 336). The evidence seems to lean in the direction of the latter view.

3.5. The Call and the Testimony (Col 1:24–2:7). Paul spends much more time on his testimony than his call in this passage, but his labors for the gospel of Jesus Christ and all he endured would not have been possible without his *calling. In Colossians 1:25 Paul writes, "I became its servant according to God's commission that was given to me for you, to make the word of God fully known" (NRSV).

Paul does not know the Christians at Colossae personally, so his reflections on his calling and his work serve as an introduction to them. Paul designates himself as a *servant, a humble *diakonos*, a table servant. This is not a title for a dignitary or someone of high rank. Here Paul is reflecting the attitude of Jesus, who also referred to himself as one who came to serve (Mk 10:34). The character of God's call on the apostle Paul and on every believer is one of service to Jesus Christ and to others.

Paul wants the Colossians to know that his striving or struggling is also for the sake of believers he has never met personally. His calling is one of service to the church, and such service has led to *suffering for Paul. Nevertheless, he accepts and embraces such difficulties because they are for the sake of the church and its mission, including his service to the Colossians. Paul claims such calling to the church there, even though the apostle did not establish that particular community of *faith. Paul does not specify how the Colossians benefit from his mission, but he could possibly have in mind his almost singular focus on bringing the gospel to the Gentiles, which has opened the door for others to engage in such mission.

Paul interprets his sufferings as providing valid testimony to his calling as an apostle. He wants the Colossians and the church at Laodicea (Col 2:1) to be aware of his trials, so that they too will be encouraged in the midst of their trials and that as a community of faith they will "be encouraged and united in love" (Col 2:2 NRSV). Difficult times often remind people of what is most important in life. But how would Paul's struggles on behalf of the Colossians serve as an encouragement? Evidencing his own commitment to Christlike servanthood, Paul's prose here exudes a cruciform pattern. Paul's struggle on behalf of the Colossians is intended to encourage them to exhibit the same kind of love toward one another, thus leading to their being "united in love" (Col 2:2 NRSV). Strikingly, this suffering-for-the-other love, Paul asserts, not only leads to ecclesial unity; but this ecclesial unity has as its goal something even more profound and transformational, namely, the ability "to reach all the riches of full assurance of understanding and the knowledge of God's *mystery, which is Christ" (Col 2:2-3 ESV). In order to know Christ fully, one must love like Christ in community, and the essence of the love that leads to unity can be observed in Paul's own others-centered activity on behalf of the Colossians.

The mystery now revealed in Christ is that from the beginning God intended to offer salvation to the Gentiles as equally as to Jews. The covenant and promises made to Israel were for the ultimate purpose of offering the new covenant and God's promises to the world. The plan of salvation comes through Israel, but it is not offered solely to Israel.

The mystery now revealed in Jesus Christ fulfills the vision and *hope of *Abraham and Sarah that their descendants would number the stars in the night sky and the grains of sand on the seashore (Gen 15:1-6; 22:17). It is only in Christ that these treasures of wisdom and knowledge are found.

3.6. Living Life in Christ's Fullness (Col 2:8-23). In Colossians 2:8-23 Paul gets to the heart of his argument. The Gentile Christians in the Colossian church are being told that their faith in Christ is insufficient and that to be the true people of God they have to take on themselves the observance of Torah. The Jewish practices Paul highlights are beliefs and practices that by the first century AD had become identity markers for the Jewish people, specifically circumcision, the observing of certain food laws, and Sabbath observance. The synagogue in Colossae was criticizing the church for claiming to share in Israel's inheritance in Jesus Christ without taking up the outward practices that marked God's people off from everyone else.

3.6.1. Circumcision. In Paul's day, circumcision had become one of the most important visible marks of the people of God, the nation of Israel. It was fundamental to Jewish identity. Circumcision was a mark of the Jew and the covenant people. It bore witness to one's nationality and one's status as a member of the covenant. As a Jew, Paul had believed in the solidarity of the ethnic people of God. Colossians in no way rejects the solidarity of the people of God. What is rejected is solidarity defined in ethnically bounded terms. The people of God are a people, but they are no longer marked by a rite tied inextricably to one ethnic group. Paul suggests that those who have received this "circumcision without hands" need no other circumcision. The Jewish rite of circumcision is unnecessary and unimportant for faith in Christ and the membership of the people of God.

3.6.2. Sabbath and Special Days. By the time of Jesus and Paul, Sabbath and special days and feasts had become marks of distinction associated with Israel, the people of God, and a critical sign of a Jew's faithfulness as a member of Israel. In Jubilees the seasons and festivals are ordained as "feasts for a memorial forever" (Jub. 6.23-29; see also Jub. 6.17-22, 35; 16.28-29; 49). The evidence indicates that the Sabbath was an observance unique to the people of Israel, and by the first century AD it was a distinctively Jewish practice.

3.6.3. Food Laws. Food laws prescribed in the law of Moses were also a clear mark of Jewish identity in the first-century world. Leviticus and Deuteronomy contain admonitions concerning foods that are unclean in and of themselves as well as foods offered to idols (Lev 3:17; 7:26-27; 11; 17:10-14; Deut 12:16, 23-24; 14; 15:23). Diaspora Jews were particularly concerned over whether both food and drink had previously been offered to the pagan gods. In Colossians 2:21, where the authors are possibly quoting the Colossian philosophers, "Do not handle, Do not taste, Do not touch" (NRSV), an OT flavor can be detected (T. Mos. 7.9-10; Mak. 3.7). It is clear that such dietary concerns were an important feature of Jewish life in the Jewish world of Paul.

All of these practices, as "a shadow of what is to come" (Col 2:17 NRSV), are reminiscent of Hebrews 10:1—"Since the law has only a shadow of the good things to come and not the true form of these realities, it can never, by the same sacrifices that are continually offered year after year, make perfect those who approach" (NRSV). These badges of Jewish ethnic identity, which marked out Israel as God's people, were a shadow—a foreshadowing—of what was to come. Nowhere in his letters does Paul ever suggest that Christianity has made Judaism irrelevant; rather, Christianity is the fulfillment of

Judaism, which represented the shadow of what God now intends in Jesus Christ.

3.7. Living the Heavenly Life on Earth (Col 3:1-17). That the Colossians participate in Christ is crucial to Paul's ethical admonitions to come. All the various themes of Paul's ethics in Colossians are inevitably connected to Christ. Indeed, it is well established in recent scholarship that the virtues that believers are to "put on" are terms that are used elsewhere throughout Scripture to describe the characteristics of God and Christ (see, e.g., Witherington, 179; Frederick 2019, 1-2, 133-62, 221-24; Thompson, 74, 80; Schweizer 1982, 211; MacDonald 2008, 140; Lindemann, 60; Barth and Blanke, 418; Cannon, 65).

The Christians in Colossae are encouraged to look heavenward, not to escape this world but rather to put this world in heavenly context. To "seek the things above" is, therefore, to bring the resurrection realities of heaven to earth by recontexualizing earthly life around the power and presence of Christ and his resurrection life.

Paul and Timothy tell the believers in Colossae to put to death the vices within them and put on the clothing of the resurrected life. Right from the beginning of Colossians, Paul wants to remind the Colossians that their whole Christian existence is bound up with Jesus Christ. To participate in the new life in Christ is to be directed onward toward the "things above." Indeed, in Colossians 3:3-4 Paul asserts that "your" [pl.] life [sg.] is Christ." Using a structure of grammatical apposition, Paul equates the communal ecclesial participation in Christ with participation in his resurrection life, which leads to a transformed personal and communal character in accordance with Christ. Therefore, what is "hidden in Christ in God" is not one's own individual, existential life but rather the mutually nourishing divine life of Christ himself, which enlivens one through faith. Thus, central to Paul's counterpoint to the erroneous Colossian philosophy is not merely an argument against the necessity of Jewish religious customs; it is a substantive theological focus on the centrality of *theosis* (or union with Christ, participation in Christ) as fundamental to the experience of Christ's fullness and Christian transformation (see Frederick 2019; Blackwell). Since all that Paul will say in the remainder of Colossians 3:1-17 is linked to the life of Christ, George Montague is correct to note that, far from simply presenting a Christianized version of Greco-Roman ethics, "growth in these virtues is, properly speaking, growth in the divine life" (212). Thompson notes that in Colossians, believers participate in Christ through his death and resurrection and thereby receive "the life that is his" (12, 176).

In addition to a focus on the soteriological effect of Christ's life on believers' sanctification, the emphasis in Colossians on the wisdom and understanding of God is the key that unlocks wisdom itself.

The Colossian Christians have been tempted to look for God's wisdom elsewhere. Paul and Timothy are clear that the Colossians have access to divine wisdom through Jesus Christ. It is true that there is still a hiddenness to their lives in Christ, yet to be revealed (Col 3:4). This is part of that mystery of which Paul speaks in Colossians 2:3. Yet the revelation of Jesus Christ in the lives of the Colossians is a process already begun as well. The "mystery" revealed is that the Gentile believers are reconciled to Christ and are being formed after Christ's image to be holy and blameless. The only requirement given to the Colossians to continue on this journey is that they continue securely established in the faith, without shifting from the hope promised (Col 1:23).

The resurrection of Jesus makes the believer strong, able to endure all things patiently (Col 1:11). The Colossians through faith have been transferred into the kingdom of his beloved Son (Col 1:13), in whom they find *forgiveness that is only possible because of his death (Col 1:20) and resurrection (Col 2:13). The cross of Christ and his resurrection are kept close together at all times throughout the letter, especially in Colossians 2:11-15, when mention is made of the Colossians' burial with Christ in *baptism and their resurrection with him through faith.

The foundation of the moral instruction in Colossians is the community's participation in the cross and resurrection of Christ. Paul and Timothy continually remind their readers of this throughout the letter. Colossians 2:20 reads, "If with Christ you died to the elemental spirits of the universe, why do you live as if you still belonged to the world?" (NRSV). The Colossians are admonished "to put to death" all that is "earthly" (Col 3:5 NRSV) as they have stripped off "the old self with its practices" (Col 3:9 NRSV).

The "old self" is more literally rendered "the old man." A significant degree of variation exists at this point with regard to the precise referent of the terminology. Some believe it refers to believers' own former, individual, sinful lives (Wilson, 251; Schweizer 1982, 197; MacDonald 2000, 137), while others emphasize that it is more properly understood as believers' former individual and corporate participation in the sinful way of life represented by the old man, Adam (Moo, 268, "our Adamic identification with its servitude to sin"; Barth and Blanke, 412). The most comprehensive interpretation explicitly incorporates both the individual and corporate aspects of the "old man" (Harris, 119, 151; Moule, 119; Dunn 2014, 221).

It is interesting to note that as the first ethical reference to the resurrection of Christ comes in Colossians 3:1—"So if you have been raised with Christ" (NRSV)—Paul next describes how that resurrection life is to look in the church, God's Easter people. Paul uses the language of clothing. The Christians at Colossae must put on the new self with its practices, listed in Colossians 3:12-17. Here too the language of "new self" is literally "the man who is being renewed in knowledge according to the image of his creator." While some interpret the new man to be Christ himself (Moo, 274) or the new individual person (Lindemann, 58), it is more precise (and more theologically coherent) to see the "new man" as a reference to the new humanity or the corporate participation of the community and individuals in Christ (Wilson, 264; Moule, 119; Hanson, 119; Frederick, 2019, 207-19). While the corporate view of the new humanity in Christ accords best with the parallel to the old humanity in Adam, it is worth noting that included within the corporate reality is the experience of converted individuals who make up the community. Christopher Beetham's view of the new man as "the resurrected existence of the new age that is acquired by incorporation or union with the risen Christ" helpfully incorporates both aspects within the larger, overarching framework from which Paul is working in Colossians 3, namely, union with and participation in Christ (Beetham, 241).

The admonitions of Paul to strip off the old way of life with its vices and evil practices are not optional for those who are in Christ. In the work of Christ God has brought into existence the church, a new and redeemed community unified by the power of the *Holy Spirit and diverse in the gifts offered in the fulfillment of that mission. A new humanity leads to a new way of life. Colossians 3:11 marks a transitional verse from the vices to the virtues. The vices already mentioned are a reminder of what hinders unity; the virtues are the habits that bring unity. But this unity in Christ is not just about diverse people getting along and tolerating each other. This unity is radically new and unlike anything seen before. Paul describes that renewal in Christ in Colossians 3:11: "Here there is no longer Greek or Jew, circumcised and uncircumcised, barbarian, Scythian, slave and free; but Christ is all and in all!" (NRSV).

This new humanity that is birthed from Christ's work is indeed a unity. Paul and Timothy do not have in mind some kind of natural equality, whatever that might mean, but rather they envisage people from diverse backgrounds and cultural stations gathered together by one common Lord. Their allegiance to that Lord means something for the way these Christians live in relationship to each other, even though they continue to live in the roles determined by the world. Salvation defined in nationalistic, ethnic, cultural, or economic terms will do nothing but divide the church.

As love binds together all the good dispositions of character, so it binds the community in "perfect harmony." In fact, many scholars argue that a more precise translation of the Greek here indicates that love is a "perfecting bond" or that love itself is the bond that leads the community together toward maturity and perfection by binding the people (rather than the virtues) together in unity (Schweizer 1982, 208; Lohse, 149; Lohmeyer, 228; Garland, 211; Barth and Blanke, 424; Sumney, 219; MacDonald 2000, 141). This love stands not as an abstract, sentimental notion. It is the love the Colossians have experienced by virtue of their participation in Christ, and the love that was exemplified in the life and death of Christ. It is the kind of love that can only be practiced in the church that has died to the old order and has been resurrected to participate in the new. Love is the bond of unity secured by Christ in the power of the Holy Spirit, in which a new humanity is brought together made up of Jew and Gentile, slave and free.

It is God's will that his people live in peace and harmony. This is not the kind of peace that can be found simply through dialogue and mutual understanding. It is in Christ that such peace is possible and finds concrete expression. The distinctions and behaviors that stand in the way of this peace have been abolished and can no longer be tolerated. It is Christ's love embodied in his life, death, and resurrection, along with his teaching, that gives expression to the kind of peace that is to reign in the midst of the congregation. The believers in Colossae, though they are Gentiles, participate in this unity, which is God's new creation. Therefore, everything they do should be done not according to the law of Moses but in the *name of Christ Jesus (see 1 Cor 5:4; 6:11; Phil 2:10). As wisdom found a home in Israel, so the word of Christ should be at home in the church. The garments of Christian virtue worn well lead to a church that is faithful and loving and at peace.

3.8. Living in the Christian Household (Col 3:18–4:1). The major concern of NT household codes is the good management of the *household. These households were no doubt diverse in reference to the level of Christian commitment among the family members. Some households might have been entirely Christian, while others might have had only one or two followers of Jesus in the family. Nevertheless, Paul has some instructions for how Christians are to behave toward others in the household in which they live.

The concern for good household management in the early church not only reflects an interest in living in the "already" brought near in Christ, but also it reveals that the early Christians were well aware of the fact that the "not yet" of Christ's return had still to arrive. (This is quite different from a failure to arrive.) Thus, the household code in Colossians could indicate, to some extent, a compromise with the form of the current age. For example, the hierarchical ordering of the family and the institution of slavery are not customs that were created by Paul but rather realities assumed in the cultural milieu into which Paul was writing (Thompson, 92). Yet, accommodation does not adequately describe the character of Colossians 3:18–4:1. While the household code expresses concern over good household management, an interest shared in common with Jews and Romans, the orientation by which the Colossian Christians order their households is the same as in every aspect of their lives—the foundation of the household is Jesus Christ, the Lord. All relationships in the household must be pleasing to him. The new world in Jesus Christ invited and challenged the first-century Christians to reorder their lives according to that new creation, while having to exist in the old order that was now passing away and would one day cease to exist.

The household codes, read within the context of the epistle's broader focus on the peace that comes through Christ's cruciform love rather than Rome's crucifying force, unsettle "the traditional rule and exploitation of Greco-Roman *paterfamilias* over their subordinates" and therefore run "counter" to the dominant cultural usage of the codes (see Maier, 347). The inclusion of the common household code form in Colossians does not, therefore, imply a simple capitulation to the dominant culture but a missional engagement of the culture through the transformation of one of its most recognized literary *topoi*. (See more on the Colossian household codes in 4.3 below.)

3.9. Final Instructions, Greetings, and Benedictions (Col 4:2-18). Paul and Timothy offer some final instructions to the Colossians, some of it by way of a reminder that was written earlier. The Colossians are to devote themselves to prayer. As Paul remembers the Colossians in prayer continually, he thanks God for the Colossians (Col 1:3) and prays for their faithfulness (Col 1:9). The Colossians are to pray as well. They too are to offer thanksgiving, a theme already referred to (also Col 1:12; 2:7; 3:17), and they are to pray for Paul and his missionary work, specifically that an opportunity will present itself to "declare the mystery of Christ" (Col 4:3 NRSV). Paul's reference to the door opening to the possibility of *preaching could very well be a not-so-veiled reference to his imprisonment, which has hindered his evangelistic work. Thus Paul is asking the Colossians to pray for his release. The irony is that it was precisely Paul's preaching that put him in prison in the first place. As one not to be detoured from his calling, he is asking that he will be freed so he can resume the work that led to his arrest. Paul's main concern does not seem to be his *freedom in and of itself but that his freedom is necessary to continue his work. Paul is singularly focused on the calling he received while traveling the Damascus road many years before (Acts 9:1-19).

Finally, Paul turns his greetings outward to other Christians. He greets the sisters and brothers in Laodicea, which appears to be strange since this letter is addressed to the Colossians. But in Colossians 4:17, Paul instructs the Colossians to take this letter to Laodicea to have it read to the church there after it is read to the Colossians. The greetings make sense in that context. The perplexing question, however, is why Paul would not greet the Laodiceans in the letter written to them.

Paul ends with the typical benediction wishing God's grace to the Colossians. God is the giver and sustainer of grace. Jesus' followers are to demonstrate that divine grace in their lives. In so doing, they offer the presence of God to others. Paul's chains do not raise questions about God's grace in Paul's life; rather, they are a reminder to Paul of the grace of God that called him to preach the gospel. It is God's grace that has liberated Paul whether he is in prison or free to travel. As Paul says to King Agrippa, "I pray that you . . . might become such as I am, except for these chains" (Acts 26:29 NRSV).

4. Major Themes.

4.1. The Christ Hymn. The Christ hymn should be understood in the context of mainstream Judaism, that is, it reflects a Jewish worldview. This Jewish character of the hymn makes it intelligible in the context of the letter to the Colossians. Several important terms present in this passage help in understanding what Paul believes about Christ and the cosmic extent of his redemptive work.

4.1.1. Wisdom. Wisdom played a very important role in the theology of Jesus' day. In the OT, wisdom was the means by which God created the world (see e.g., Prov 8; Wis 7; Thompson, 30). In texts such as Ben Sira 6:23; 19:20, wisdom is derived from obedience to the Torah and considered to be the fulfillment of the Torah. Scholars such as Eckhard Schnabel, E. Zenger, W. D. Davies, and M. Hengel argue that the Torah not only facilitated wise behavior but was itself identified with wisdom in Ben Sira and in the writings of Second Temple Judaism (see Schnabel, 12, 69). In Colossians, the wisdom formally attributed to the Torah is relocated in its fullest exposition in the person of Jesus Christ (Col 2:3). This theme is also present elsewhere in 1 Corinthians 1:24, 30, an undisputed Pauline letter that likewise asserts that Christ is the wisdom of God.

4.1.2. Firstborn. This term refers to Jesus as the *Savior of the world as one who has priority over all creation. *Firstborn* here in Colossians and throughout Scripture (see, e.g., Gen 25:29-34) refers to "rank and status in the family," which was linked to the reception of the inheritance (Gupta 2013, 55). The term can also be used as a metaphorical designation that indicates preeminence. It is applied in this way to Israel (Ex 4:22), David (Ps 89:27), and Wisdom (Prov 8:22) (McKnight, 149). The purpose of the world and the universe is found in Jesus Christ. Christ has supremacy over all of creation because he is the firstborn "from the dead" (Col 1:18). He is the first installment of the future resurrection of his people. Reading Colossians 1:15 in light of Colossians 1:18, one finds Paul presenting Christ's supremacy over creation (Beale, 93) and Christ's priority and perfect preeminence as the firstborn of the new creation (Seitz, 97). In this way Colossians presents "a tension between the two senses in which Christ is 'all in all'" (Barclay, 82).

4.1.3. Thrones, Dominions, Rulers, and Powers. As firstborn, Christ is supreme over all of creation, including natural and supernatural powers. In Greco-Roman and Jewish literature, the words translated "thrones," "dominions," "rulers," and "powers" could refer to either earthly authorities or spiritual beings, depending on the context (Wink 1984, 10-11). So, Paul probably has both spiritual and earthly authorities in mind here. Perhaps, however, overly specific attempts to delineate and identify the powers are unnecessary since the Bible elsewhere teaches that the earthly nations are indeed under the direction of spiritual forces (Lk 4:5-7). It is unlikely that the forces here represent benevolent powers, since the need for their reconciliation that Paul refers to here would make little sense if so (Moo, 64). Rather, with Wink (1984, 5-6; cf. 1986, 50) it is wise to conceive of the thrones, rulers, dominions, and powers as spiritual beings that work through tangible hosts, such as human beings, cultures, and institutions. Such a view refuses to separate the "earthly" from the "spiritual," a position that, while perhaps a meaningful distinction to contemporary thinkers, would have been quite foreign to the ancient cultural and social plausibility structures of first-century people (see Maier, 330).

In whatever precise way one might conceive of the nature of the thrones, dominions, rulers, and powers, the tension between the concepts of reconciliation (Col 1:20) and what appears to be the defeat of the powers (Col 2:15) should not be simplistically resolved. Reconciliation may come through either destruction or redemptive reintegration. As Barclay notes, "The important point is that the most powerful forces of disintegration and hostility in the universe have been dealt with decisively through the crucifixion and resurrection of Christ" (Barclay, 85).

4.1.4. Fullness. In Colossians 1:19 Paul and Timothy write, "For in him [Christ] all the fullness of God was pleased to dwell" (NRSV). In the OT the fullness of God's presence means that God is imminent and closely involved in the world (Ps 72:19; Jer 23:24; Ezek 43:5; 44:4), and creation itself reflects the fullness of God's glory (Ps 24:1). Paul picks up this theme again in Colossians 2:9, where readers learn that in Christ "the whole fullness of deity dwells bodily" (NRSV) and that believers have been filled by (or in) him. While full-blown Gnosticism is too late to have been fully operative in Colossae at this time, it is likely that an early set of ideas, perhaps associated with Greco-Roman mystery religions, later to be parsed out more fully into Gnostic systems of thought such as Valentinianism, were operative in Colossae in germinal form. If that were the case, then Paul's use of the concept of fullness in relation to the divine identity of Jesus Christ could be seen as a theological, literary, and conceptual subversion of erroneous Greco-Roman religious ideas resituated and recalibrated around the fullness of God in Christ (see, e.g., Foster, 195-96).

*4.2. **Vices and Virtues.*** Since Paul has highlighted the cross of Christ and its importance, it is not a surprise that he refers to the Colossians' old selves as something to be killed, something that must be put to death (Col 3:5). This former earthly way of life in solidarity with humanity under sinful Adam, which the letter has previously referred to as "estranged and hostile in mind, doing evil deeds" (Col 1:21 NRSV), is contrary to the resurrected life the Colossians now enjoy. One cannot pretend to live in light of Jesus' death and resurrection while living as Christ's reconciling, redemptive work never happened. Paul goes into specific detail as to the character of that earthly life by listing a series of vices, behaviors that are unacceptable for God's people in Christ.

4.2.1. Fornication. The Greek word translated "fornication" is *porneia*, from which comes the English word *pornography*. *Porneia* can refer specifically to prostitution and generally to all sorts of extramarital sexual behavior (see, e.g., Sir 41:8, 17; Wis 14:9, 12; Acts 15:20, 29; 21:25). It can also function metaphorically to refer to unfaithfulness to God (Philo, *Spec.* 1.282; see Philo's use of the related form *porneuō* in *Fug.* 153; *Spec.* 1.281; cf. Prov 2:18).

4.2.2. Impurity. Akatharsia, which is often translated "impurity," elaborates on the first word, *porneia. Akatharsia* can refer to religious and moral impurity (e.g., Plato, *Spec.* 4.716e). The LXX translates the Hebrew word for impurity, linking it to ritual *purity (Gen 7:2; Lev 4:12). Since moral purity is important in Israel's worship of God, it inevitably is connected to ritual purity (practices of worship). However, recent research using a cognitive-linguistic approach has shown that—even within its original OT context, and certainly before the period of early Christianity and the composition of the NT—many OT cultic texts (such as Lev 1–16) also functioned symbolically to express ethical convictions (see, e.g., Trevaskis, 1-10). Paul uses the word here to present sinful behavior within the metaphorical ethical paradigm of cultic impurity, signifying thereby the problem that sin introduces with regard to proximity to God and the believer's state of purity before God.

4.2.3. Passion. In Stoic philosophy persons who let themselves be controlled by their emotions can be described by the word *passion*, which in Greek is *pathos*. Here in Colossians it refers to those desires that lead to sexual excesses. In Greco-Roman philosophy, *pathos* could function in a number of different ways. In the writings of Aristotle (e.g., *Eth. nic.* 1095a; 1101a; 1104b; 1128b; 1132a; 1134a) passion is neither a virtue nor a vice, and its ethical value is determined to be either good or bad based on how an individual reacts to it in relation to the ethical mean that Aristotle envisions as the virtuous sweet spot between ethical excess and deficiency. The Stoics, however, viewed passion itself as fundamentally disordered behavior, a mental illness, and something to be eradicated at all costs. This can be seen, for example, in Dio Chrysostom's view that the virtuous person should be "wholly unaffected" (2 *Tars.* 33) and by Musonius Rufus's instruction that virtue is formed by developing an apathetic disposition not only to emotional disturbances but also to physical pain caused by exposure to extreme weather, thirst, hunger, and scarcity of food (Musonius Rufus, *Lecture* 6.4 [*Stobaeus* 3.29.78]). While Paul is closer to the Stoics in this regard, viewing passion itself as a vice, he does so without adopting the Stoic aversion to empathy and feeling.

4.2.4. Evil Desire. While the word *epithymia* is not always employed in negative fashion (Jesus uses the term in Lk 22:15 to refer to his desire to eat the Passover with the disciples), its use in this context makes it clear that Paul is using the term negatively. Not all desires are evil, but Paul specifically has evil desires in mind in Colossians.

4.2.5. Greed (Which Is Idolatry). The last two vices listed in Colossians 3:5 are connected: *pleonexia* (greed) and *eidōlolatria* (idolatry). In Jewish thinking greed reveals a central focus on oneself and is a form of self-worship—*idolatry. It is a worship of creation and not the Creator.

4.2.6. Anger, Wrath, Malice. After a brief reminder to the Colossians that the way of these vices was formerly familiar to them but no longer, Paul and Timothy return to their list of vices in Colossians 3:8-9. The Greek word *thymos* refers to a resentful and grudging hatred that views other individuals as less than human and not worthy of being treated as imagers of God. This is especially true when used with the next vice listed, *wrath. Such anger and wrath are signs of malice or wickedness, which speaks directly to the character of those who exhibit such vices.

In Colossians 3:8-9 Paul and Timothy also list the practices the Colossians are to rid from their lives, slander and abusive language—demeaning another's reputation and uttering obscenities toward them. These practices are exhibited by those who have embodied the vices mentioned. Such practices tear at the fabric of unity the church is supposed to embody instead and display in its communal life. Being raised with Christ means a new community with unity at its heart.

Next Paul turns his attention to the way of life that displays the unity of the body. Paul has spent some time listing the dispositions that are not in keeping with those who participate in the resurrected life of Christ and that divide the church. Now he turns his attention to the virtues, the dispositions that reflect the new life in Christ and the new humanity embodied in the church, the body of Christ.

4.2.7. Compassion. The Greek *splanchna oiktirmou* can be translated "heartfelt *mercy." *Splanchna* refers mainly to the entrails of sacrificial animals (hence the KJV translation "bowels of mercies"), and later the term was used to refer to the sacrificial meal itself, where the viscera were eaten (Aristophanes, *The Birds* 984). Paul charges the Colossians to clothe themselves with the gut-wrenching compassion of Christ, a compassion that is not merely intellectual but visceral. Comparing this with the Roman Stoic Epictetus, a near contemporary of Paul, shows the uniqueness of Christian ethics over against pagan approaches to morality. As A. A. Long has shown, while Epictetus would not have been opposed to showing sympathy, he, like all of the Stoics and most Greco-Roman philosophers, would perhaps have allowed "'sharing in another's groans' provided that one does not 'groan within oneself'" (*Enchiridion* 16 in Long, 253; cf. Epictetus, *Diss.* 3.24).

4.2.8. Kindness. The NRSV translates the word *chrēstotēta* as "kindness," but perhaps "goodness" or "generosity" is better. The word is also used to refer to someone who is honest and decent (Sophocles, *Oedipus Tyrannus* 609-610; Aristotle, *Poet.* 15, 1454a, 16-18). In the LXX, this word denotes the sense of excellence in reference to things genuine (Jer 24:2-3, 5) and costly (Ezek 27:22; 28:13). It appears in the Psalms many times as both a noun and an adjective, and often functions there as an attribute of God (see, e.g., [Ps 25:7 (LXX 24:7); Ps 52:9 (51:11); Ps 69:16 (68:17); Ps 104:28 (103:28); Ps 145:7 (144:7)]). Psalm 112:4-10 demonstrates the sort of kindness that is intended by *chrēstotēta*. There the person who is "righteous," "compassionate," and "kind" (using the adjectival form *chrēstos*) is described as one who has "distributed freely . . . to the poor." Thus kindness, for the OT and for Paul, is not the equivalent of mere dispositional warmth or modern niceness, but rather shows itself through sacrificial acts of other-centered benevolence and equity. Just as God's kindness is more than a descriptive term of the Almighty's mood, so too Christian kindness, modeled after the character of God and Christ, becomes incarnate through deeds when "heartfelt mercy" (*splanchna oiktirmou*) comes to fruition in heartfelt action (*chrēstotēta*).

4.2.9. Humility. It is interesting that Paul lists humility (*tapeinophrosynēn*) as a Christian virtue. The Greeks did not consider humility a virtue at all. Humility was a sign of weakness and was considered a vice (Homer, *Od.* 17.322-323; Plato, *Leg.* 5.728e; 6.744c; 7.791d; Euripides, *Andromache* 164-165; Xenophon, *Cyr.* 5.1.5; Dio Chrysostom, *On Tyranny*).

The NT background of *tapeinophrosynēn* is to be found not in a Roman context but in a Jewish one. In Judaism, humility was not shameful but something necessary in one's relationship to God. The word *humility* and its related terms are used approximately 270 times in the LXX. It is used negatively in the sense of "oppress" or "afflict" (e.g., Gen 34:2; Deut 21:14; 2 Sam 13:12-14; Ezek 22:10-11), but for the most part this word group refers to what God has done to bring down the proud and haughty and lift up the poor and lowly (e.g., 1 Sam 1:11; 2:8; 7:13; 2 Sam 22:5, 28; Ps 10:17-18; 22:5, 28; 25:18; Amos 2:6-7; Zeph 2:3; 3:12).

4.2.10. Meekness. The Greek word *prautēs*, which the NRSV translates as "meekness," denotes that which is gentle and pleasant (Plato, *Leg.* 10.888a; Xenophon, *Symposium* 1.10). *Prautēs* reveals high ideals and social virtue. Most significantly for NT ethics and for the ongoing theme of conformity to Christ in Colossians, *prautēs* is used to describe the moral character of Jesus (2 Cor 10:1; see the related form *praus* in Mt 11:29; 21:5).

4.2.11. Patience. In the LXX *makrothymia* often marks an attribute of God, who restrains himself when it comes to the judgment of his people (Ex 34:6; Num 14:18; Ps 86:15; 103:8; Joel 2:13; Nah 1:3). Since God is patient with his people, they too must be patient with others (Prov 14:29; 16:32; 25:15).

These virtues the Colossians are to clothe themselves with find their meaning in the reorientation of their lives "in Christ," "in the Lord." The Christian community lives by reflecting in its life the gospel it proclaims.

4.3. The Household. Household management was very important in the ancient world. It was believed by the Romans that the family unit was the center and the foundation of the *empire. If the family were to break down, so would the empire.

Dunn makes five observations regarding household codes: First, household management was a common concern of Christians in the third and fourth generations, and this concern centered on the relationships between husbands and wives, fathers and their children, and masters and their slaves. Second, there was no standard pattern being passed along, meaning there was no written form, a catechesis (introductory religious instruction), for example, from which the household codes were drawn. Third, the threefold pattern (husband/wife, father/child, master/slave) reflects the typical family structure of the time. Fourth, the household code undoubtedly reflects the patriarchal character of the first century AD. This cannot be denied, in spite of such passages as Colossians 3:19 and especially Ephesians 5:25-33. Such passages were meant to temper a husband's treatment of his wife. Egalitarian concerns were simply not in mind. The concern in the household was not equality but unity. Fifth, slaves were quite prominent in first-century households and were regarded as part of the household (Dunn 1996, 43, 47-48).

Roman, Jewish, and Christian documents clearly reveal the general interest in household management. Seneca is a fine example of the interest in this three-paired relationship one finds in Colossians (*Ep.* 94.1). But it was not only the Greeks and the Romans who shared such concerns; Jews did as well (Ps.-Phoc. 175-227; Philo, *Hypoth.* 7.14; *Decal.* 165-167; *Spec.* 2.224-241; Josephus, *Ag. Ap.* 2.199-208). So did Christians (Did. 4.9-11; *1 Clem.* 21.6-9; *Barn.* 19.5-7; Pol. *Phil.* 4.2-3; Ign. *Pol.* 4.1–5.2). All these documents reflect varied interest in the relationships of husband/wife, child/father, and slave/master.

NT scholars have debated for decades whether the background of the NT household codes is primarily Roman, Jewish, or uniquely Christian. In one sense these three contexts all serve as the background for the household codes because the good ordering of the household was of common concern in the first-century world. On the other hand, there are really no precise parallels to the household codes. It would be going too far to say that the NT household codes are uniquely Christian, but it is correct to say that the household codes are decisively Christian in their concern that all believers in whatever station they may have in life act in a way that honors the Lord Jesus Christ, whom they serve. To this point James Hering cites several unique aspects of the Christian approach to households that are reflected in the household code in Colossians but that have no parallels in the comparative literature of the time, most notably the function of *agapē* love in the Christian codes and the "socially-leveling" lordship of Christ (Hering, 87).

Early in the twentieth century, NT scholars were generally of the opinion that the concerns expressed in the Colossian household code had very little if nothing to do with the interests of the rest of the letter. This meant that the household code was independent from the rest of the letter. Paul and Timothy put it in there as an aside. The consensus of scholarship was that the first generation of Christians were expecting Jesus to return in their lifetime. As that generation aged and as second-generation Christians were coming into their prime, the church had to contend with how to live in the world with the delay of the Christ's second coming. Faced with continued life in the world, the early Christians had to consider how they would live in their everyday relationships and affairs. The household code was the result of that consideration.

It does appear to be the case that there were at least some Christians in the first generation who expected the imminent return of Jesus during their lives, as seems to be the case in 2 Peter 3:3-4, but the situation in the early church was more complex than simply assuming the majority of the first Christians expected Christ to return soon. Indeed, it seems by the context of Colossians that the purpose of the household code was not how Christians should live now that the end had been delayed, but rather how believers should live as citizens of the new age that had already dawned. Throughout Colossians the Christians are reminded that they are in Christ and now in the Lord—for example, they are to live as citizens of the kingdom of God's beloved Son (Col 1:12)—and this includes three reminders in the household code. The household code in Colossians clarifies further in the letter how believers are to live in the dawn of the new age, not how one is to live because of the failure of the new age to arrive.

Yet it must also be said that the concern for good household management in the early church not only reflects an interest in living in the "already" brought near in Christ but also reveals that the early Christians were well aware that the "not-yet" of Christ's return had still to arrive. Thus, the household code in Colossians does betray to some extent a compromise with the form of the current age. But accommodation does not adequately describe the character of Colossians 3:18–4:1. While the household code expresses the concern over good household management, an interest shared in common with Jews and Romans, the perspective by which the Colossian Christians order their households is the same as in every aspect of their lives—the foundation of the household is Jesus Christ, the Lord. All relationships in the household must be pleasing to him. While the slavery and "subordinated relationships" present in the culture of the time are not abolished, Hering shows how the theme of submission to Christ in the Colossian code has fundamentally reordered the nature of the "stratified relationships within the church" so that they operate in ways that have introduced "remarkable changes in a previously inequitable relationship." The key to rightly interpreting the codes, then, is reading them within the christological context of the entire letter, on which the codes remain theologically dependent. Apart from this context, and "when removed from the interpretative paradigm found in the person of Christ," the codes cannot be rightly interpreted in distinction from the broader ubiquitous use of *Haustafeln* in the larger cultural and historical context (Hering, 104-5).

5. Conclusion.

In Colossians, Paul and Timothy bring Christology, ecclesiology, and eschatology together. Jesus the image of the invisible God is reflected in the church, the body of Christ, as God's imagers in this world living the new life that has dawned in the present age. A high Christology in which Christ is temporally, ontologically, and sovereignly preeminent in all things is the foundation of a global and missional ecclesiology that remains in force until the end of the age.

See also CHRISTOLOGY; CHRONOLOGY OF PAUL; CHURCH; ESCHATOLOGY; ETHICS; HOUSEHOLDS AND HOUSEHOLD CODES; HYMNS, HYMN FRAGMENTS, CONFESSIONS; WISDOM.

BIBLIOGRAPHY. ***Commentaries:*** **J. M. Barclay,** *Colossians and Philemon*, T&T Clark Study Guides (New York: T&T Clark, 2004); **M. Barth and H. Blanke,** *Colossians*, trans. A. B. Beck, AB (New Haven, CT: Yale University Press, 1994); **G. K. Beale,** *Colossians and Philemon*, BECNT (Grand Rapids, MI: Baker Academic, 2019); **M. F. Bird,** *Colossians and Philemon*, New Covenant Commentary Series (Eugene, OR: Cascade, 2009); **F. F. Bruce,** *The Epistles to the Colossians, to Philemon, and to the Ephesians*, NICNT (Grand Rapids, MI: Eerdmans, 1984); **J. D. G. Dunn,** *The Epistles to the Colossians and to Philemon*, NIGTC (Grand Rapids, MI: Eerdmans, 2014); **P. Foster,** *Colossians*, BNTC (New York: Bloomsbury T&T Clark, 2016); **D. E. Garland,** *Colossians/Philemon* (Grand Rapids, MI: Zondervan, 1998); **N. K. Gupta,** *Colossians*, SHBC (Macon, GA: Smyth & Helwys, 2013); **M. J. Harris,** *Colossians and Philemon*, EGGNT (Grand Rapids, MI: Eerdmans, 1991); **E. Lohmeyer,** *Die Briefe an die Philipper, an die Kolosser und an Philemon* (Göttingen: Vandenhoeck & Ruprecht, 1964); **E. Lohse,** *Colossians and Philemon*, Hermeneia (Philadelphia: Fortress, 1971); **M. Y. MacDonald,** *Colossians and Ephesians*, SP (Collegeville, MN: Liturgical Press, 2000); **S. McKnight,** *The Letter to the Colossians*, NICNT (Grand Rapids, MI: Eerdmans, 2018); **D. J. Moo,** *The Letters to the Colossians and to Philemon*, PNTC (Grand Rapids, MI: Eerdmans, 2008); **C. F. D. Moule,** *The Epistles of Paul the Apostle to the Colossians and to Philemon* (Cambridge: Cambridge University Press, 1958); **P. T. O'Brien,** *Colossians-Philemon*, WBC (Nashville, TN: Thomas Nelson, 1982); **D. W. Pao,** *Colossians and Philemon*, ZECNT (Grand Rapids, MI: Zondervan Academic, 2012); **E. Schweizer,** *The Letter to the Colossians: A Commentary*, trans. A. Chester (London: SPCK, 1982); **C. R. Seitz,** *Colossians*, Brazos Theological Commentary on the Bible (Grand Rapids, MI: Brazos, 2014); **J. L. Sumney,** *Colossians: A Commentary*, NTL (Louisville, KY: Westminster John Knox, 2008); **C. H. Talbert,** *Ephesians and Colossians*, Paideia (Grand Rapids, MI: Baker Academic, 2007); **A. C. Thiselton,** *Colossians: A Short Exegetical and Pastoral Commentary* (Eugene, OR: Cascade, 2020); **M. M. Thompson,** *Colossians and Philemon*, THNTC (Grand Rapids, MI: Eerdmans, 2005); **R. M. Wilson,** *Colossians and Philemon*, ICC (New York: T&T Clark, 2005); **B. Witherington III,** *The Letters to Philemon, the Colossians, and the Ephesians: A Socio-Rhetorical Commentary on the Captivity Epistles* (Grand Rapids, MI: Eerdmans, 2007); **N. T. Wright,** *Colossians and Philemon*, TNTC (Downers Grove, IL: IVP Academic, 2008).

Studies: **C. E. Arnold,** *The Colossians Syncretism: The Interface Between Christianity and Folk Belief at Colossae* (Grand Rapids, MI: Baker, 1996); **H. H. Attridge,** "On Becoming an Angel: Rival Baptismal Theologies at Colossae," in *Religious Propaganda and Missionary Competition in the New Testament World: Essays Honoring Dieter Georgi*, ed. L. Bormann, K. Del Tredici, and A. Standhartinger (Leiden: Brill, 1994); **D. L. Balch,** "Household Codes," in *Greco-Roman Literature and the New Testament: Selected Forms and Genres*, ed. D. E. Aune (Atlanta: Scholars Press, 1988); idem, "Neopythagorean Moralists and the New Testament Household Codes," *ANRW* 26.1, (1992): 380-411; **C. A. Beetham,** *Echoes of Scripture in the Letter of Paul to the Colossians* (Leiden: Brill,

2008); **A. R. Bevere,** *Sharing in the Inheritance: Identity and the Moral Life in Colossians*, JSNTSup (London: Sheffield Academic, 2003); **B. Blackwell,** "You Are Filled in Him: Theosis and Colossians 2-3," *JTI* 8, no. 1 (2014): 103-23; **R. Canavan,** *Clothing the Body of Christ at Colossae*, WUNT 2/334 (Tübingen: Mohr Siebeck, 2012); **G. E Cannon,** *The Use of Traditional Materials in Colossians: Their Significance for the Problems of Authenticity and Purpose* (Macon, GA: Mercer University Press, 1983); **W. Carr,** *Angels and Principalities: The Background, Meaning, and Development of the Pauline Phrase hai archai kai hai exousiai* (Cambridge: Cambridge University Press, 1981); **A. Copenhaver,** *Reconstructing the Historical Background of Paul's Rhetoric in the Letter to the Colossians*, LNTS 585 (New York: Bloomsbury, 2018); **R. E. DeMaris,** *The Colossian Controversy: Wisdom in Dispute at Colossae*, JSNTSup 96 (Sheffield: JSOT Press, 1994); **J. D. G. Dunn,** "The Colossian Philosophy: A Confident Jewish Apologia," *Bib* 76 (1995): 153-81; idem, "The Household Rules in the New Testament," in *The Family in Theological Perspective*, ed. S. Barton (Edinburgh: T&T Clark, 1996), 43-48; **F. Francis,** "Humility and Angel Worship in Col 2:18," in *Conflict at Colossae: A Problem in the Interpretation of Early Christianity Illustrated by Selected Modern Studies*, ed. F. O. Francis and W. A. Meeks (Atlanta, GA: Society of Biblical Literature, 1975), 163-95; **J. Frederick,** *Worship in the Way of the Cross: Leading Worship for the Sake of Others* (Downers Grove, IL: InterVarsity Press, 2017); idem, *The Ethics of the Enactment and Reception of Cruciform Love: A Comparative Lexical, Conceptual, Exegetical, and Theological Study of Colossians 3:1-17*, WUNT (Tübingen: Mohr Siebeck, 2019); **N. K. Gupta,** "New Commentaries on Colossians: Survey of Approaches, Analysis of Trends, and the State of Research," *Themelios* 35, no. 1 (2010): 7-14; **S. Hanson,** *The Unity of the Church in the New Testament: Colossians and Ephesians* (Uppsala: Almqvist & Wiksells, 1946); **J. P. Hering,** *The Colossian and Ephesian Haustafeln in Theological Context: An Analysis of Their Origins, Relationship, and Message*, American University Studies (New York: Lang, 2007); **M. D. Hooker,** "Were There False Teachers in Colossae?," in *Christ and Spirit in the New Testament: Studies in Honour of Charles Francis Digby Moule*, ed. B. Linders and S. Smalley (Cambridge: Cambridge University Press, 1973); **A. T. Lincoln,** "The Household Code and Wisdom Mode of Colossians," *JSNT* 74 (1999): 93-112; idem, *Paradise Now and Not Yet: Studies in the Role of the Heavenly Dimension in Paul's Thought, with Special Reference to His Eschatology*, SNTSMS 43 (Cambridge: Cambridge University Press, 2004); **A. Lindemann,** *Der Kolosserbrief* (Zürich: Theologischer Verlag, 1983); **A. A. Long,** *Epictetus: A Stoic and Socratic Guide to Life* (Oxford: Clarendon, 2002); **M. Y. MacDonald,** *The Pauline Churches: A Socio-historical Study of Institutionalization in the Pauline and Deutero-Pauline Writings*, SNTSMS 60 (Cambridge: Cambridge University Press, 1988); **H. O. Maier,** "A Sly Civility: Colossians and Empire," *JSNT* 27, no. 3 (2005): 323-49; **T. W. Martin,** *By Philosophy and Empty Deceit: Colossians as Response to a Cynic Critique* (Sheffield: Sheffield Academic, 1996); **G. Montague, TSM,** *Growth in Christ: A Study in Saint Paul's Theology of Progress* (Fribourg: St. Paul's, 1961); **E. J. Schnabel,** *Law and Wisdom from Ben Sira to Paul: A Tradition Historical Enquiry into the Relation of Law, Wisdom, and Ethics* (Tübingen: J. C. B. Mohr, 1985); **E. Schweizer,** "Slaves of the Elements and Worshipers of Angels: Gal 4:3, 9 and Col 2:8, 18, 20," *JBL* 107 (1988): 455-68; **C. Spicq, OP,** *Agape in the New Testament*, vol. 2, *Agape in the Epistles of St. Paul, the Acts of the Apostles and the Epistles of St. James, St. Peter, and St. Jude*, trans. Sister M. A. McNamara, OP, and Sister M. H. Richter, OP (London: Herder, 1965); **T. D. Still,** "Eschatology in Colossians: How Realized Is It?," *NTS* 50, no. 1 (2004): 125-38; **L. M. Trevaskis,** *Holiness, Ethics, and Ritual in Leviticus*, Hebrew Bible Monographs 29 (Sheffield: Sheffield Phoenix, 2011); **B. Walsh and S. Keesmaat,** *Colossians Remixed: Subverting the Empire* (Downers Grove, IL: InterVarsity Press, 2004); **W. Wink,** *Naming the Powers: The Language of Power in the New Testament* (Philadelphia: Fortress, 1984); idem, *Unmasking the Powers: The Invisible Forces That Determine Human Existence* (Philadelphia: Fortress, 1986), **B. Witherington III and G. F. Wessels,** "Do Everything in the Name of the Lord: Ethics and Ethos in Colossians," in *Identity, Ethics, and Ethos in the New Testament*, ed. J. G. vander Watt, BZNW 141 (Berlin: de Gruyter, 2006); **N. T. Wright,** *The Climax of the Covenant* (Philadelphia: Fortress, 1993); idem, *Paul and the Faithfulness of God* (Minneapolis: Fortress, 2013).

A. R. Bevere and J. Frederick

COMMUNION. *See* Collection for the Saints; Fellowship, Communion, Sharing; Lord's Supper.

COMMUNITY. *See* Church; Church Structure; Fellowship, Communion, Sharing; Kinship Language in Paul.

COMPLETE, MATURE (PERFECT)

Paul assumes believers can reflect the divine design for human beings, that they can be *teleios.*

> Let those of us then who are mature [*teleioi*] be of the same mind. (Phil 3:15 NRSV; KJV has *perfect*)

> Among the mature [*teleiois*] we do speak wisdom. (1 Cor 2:6 NRSV; KJV has *perfect*)

Although he can use this language for things other than persons (such as *knowledge and revelation [1 Cor 13:10; 14:20], the will of *God [Rom 12:2], and mutual *love [Col 3:14]), this article will focus on Paul's use of this language for believers.

1. Linguistic Background
2. Paul's Sources
3. Already or Not Yet Complete?
4. Paul, the Law, and Perfection
5. Eschatological Perfection?

1. Linguistic Background.

In most such texts a form of the Greek adjective *teleios* or verb *teleioō* is used. Both speak of something or someone who has reached their *telos,* their goal or purpose. They fulfill their design and are thus complete, finished, whole, or mature. Since the Greek term does not imply sinless or flawless character, most translations now generally avoid rendering this with *perfect.*

The same is true in the Hebrew OT, where *tāmîm* and *šālēm* are most commonly used. Both refer to those who are whole and complete in accord with God's *covenant design. They live wholeheartedly for the *Lord and for others, though again without any suggestion of sinlessness. For this reason, even flawed characters such as Noah and Job can be presented in the Bible as whole or complete (Gen 6:9; Job 1:1).

2. Paul's Sources.

Some have suggested that Paul drew inspiration for his perfection ideas from Greek *philosophy, mystery religions, or Gnosticism, since these also employed similar linguistic and conceptual elements. For instance, a *teleios* in some mystery religions was one initiated into these rites.

Most, however, see Paul's Jewish environment as his main wellspring (Du Plessis; Walters). Both the language (*tāmîm, šālēm*) and the idea of human wholeness are found regularly throughout the OT and contribute to its view of human persons. Alongside *righteousness, *holiness, and so on, such completeness describes the divine aim for humanity. Thus, *Abraham was called to "walk before me, and be *tāmîm*" (Gen 17:1 NRSV). This same Jewish tradition recurs in the Dead Sea Scrolls, which call members "men of perfect [*tāmîm*] holiness" (CD B XX, 2). It is carried on by Jesus in his call to "be perfect" (Mt 5:48).

3. Already or Not Yet Complete?

As in the two verses cited above in the introduction, Paul can speak of himself and of other believers as *already* complete or mature. That is, they are adhering to *Christ and his way faithfully and wholeheartedly. They are leading lives "worthy of the *gospel" (Phil 1:27 NRSV; see also 1 Thess 2:12; Col 1:10; Eph 4:1) and can be equally described now as saints or holy ones (*hagioi*; e.g., Phil 1:1).

In other texts, however, such human *teleios* constitutes a *future* expectation. "It is [Christ] whom we proclaim, warning everyone and teaching everyone in all *wisdom, so that we may present everyone mature [*teleion*] in Christ" (Col 1:28 NRSV; see also Eph 4:13). Paul and his *coworkers pray for the believing communities toward this end, "so that you may stand mature [*teleioi*] and fully assured in everything that God wills" (Col 4:12 NRSV). Interpreters remain divided as to whether such a future presentation as complete is envisioned in this life before the watching world or before God at a final *judgment. In either case it remains a future expectation, not yet realized.

Such a conundrum (already complete—not yet complete) calls for resolution. Traditionally, the notion of *teleios* as perfection (perfect, sinless righteousness) has been assumed. Thus, the already-obtained perfection must be a relative, forensic, or positional perfection, since believers are clearly not behaviorally flawless in this life. On this reading, only the future *teleios* is true moral perfection, which occurs at the eschatological transformation.

However, once *teleios* is understood as covenantal wholeness or completeness rather than perfection, the tension is resolved. Paul can refer to imperfect but faithful Christ-followers as already *teleioi,* while simultaneously calling them to continue in that walk of faithful discipleship to the eschatological end (1 Thess 3:8). Their wholeness is not a static thing but a relationship that must be cultivated and maintained.

One verse might seem to counter the idea that Paul saw the completion (*teleios*) of believers in this life as realistic and expected. "Not that I have already obtained this or have already reached the goal [*teteleiōmai*; NIV has 'have already been made perfect']; but I press on to make it my own, because Christ Jesus has made me his own" (Phil 3:12 NRSV). The context, however, suggests that the goal in this verse is not moral transformation but participation in the *resurrection of the dead (Phil 3:11).

4. Paul, the Law, and Perfection.

Did Paul think the OT law demanded perfect obedience? At least since Martin Luther, many would answer yes. For them this explains why "as many as are of the *works of the *law are under a *curse" (Gal 3:10 NKJV), because no one can keep the law's demands flawlessly, perfectly. However, this does not seem to be the perspective of the OT itself. Those considered righteous, upright, and "perfect" were not flawlessly obedient but wholeheartedly faithful to God and his ways. Paul represents this same point of view when he states of himself, "as to righteousness under the law, blameless [*amemptos*]" (Phil 3:6 NRSV).

5. Eschatological Perfection?

Paul did expect a radical transformation of some sort at the eschaton. "Listen, I will tell you a *mystery! We will not all die, but we will all be changed, in a moment, in the twinkling of an eye, at the last trumpet" (1 Cor 15:51-52 NRSV). However, he is speaking here not of moral transformation or sinlessness but of the change in human bodies ("this mortal *body must put on immortality," 1 Cor 15:53 NRSV). See the similar thought in Philippians 3:21 ("transform the body of our humiliation," NRSV).

As second *Adam, Christ is the image and measure for Paul of what it means to be a whole and complete human *creation. Thus, for the Pauline *church, authentic *ministry aims to bring all believers "to maturity [lit. to the complete human being, *eis andra teleion*], to the measure of the *full stature of Christ" (Eph 4:13 NRSV).

See also COVENANT; ESCHATOLOGY; FAITH; GLORY, GLORIFICATION; GNOSIS, GNOSTICISM; PHILOSOPHY; RIGHTEOUSNESS; WORKS OF THE LAW.

BIBLIOGRAPHY. **P. J. Du Plessis,** *Teleios: The Idea of Perfection in the New Testament* (Kampen: Kok, 1959); **H. K. LaRondelle,** *Perfection and Perfectionism: A Dogmatic-Ethical Study of Biblical Perfection and Phenomenal Perfectionism*, 2nd ed. (Berrien Springs, MI: Andrews University Press, 1975); **F. Mussner,** "Perfection: Later Judaism, the New Testament," in *Encyclopedia of Biblical Theology: The Complete Sacramentum Verbi*, ed. J. B. Bauer (New York: Crossroad, 1970), 663-67; **J. R. Walters,** *Perfection in New Testament Theology: Ethics and Eschatology in Relational Dynamic*, Mellen Biblical Press Series 25 (Lewiston, ME: Mellen Biblical, 1995); **K. L. Yinger,** *God and Human Wholeness: Perfection in Biblical and Theological Tradition* (Eugene, OR: Cascade, 2019).

K. L. Yinger

CONSCIENCE. *See* ANTHROPOLOGY, PAULINE; APOSTASY; ETHICS; FOOD LAWS AND CUSTOMS, JEWISH AND ROMAN; LAW; LAW OF CHRIST; STRONG AND WEAK.

CONTENTMENT. *See* PHILOSOPHY; WEALTH AND POVERTY.

CONVERSION AND CALL OF PAUL

"If you were to ask the average person, 'What is conversion?' chances are that he or she would reply: 'It's what happened to St Paul on the Damascus road'" (Peace, 17). In popular imagination Paul is the archetypal convert. Paul's Damascus road experience and his letters also profoundly shape modern conversion studies, with Pauline images cropping up frequently in scholars' analyses and definitions of conversion (see Yates). Nothing seems more obvious than that Paul was a convert. Yet significant voices within recent NT scholarship argue that Paul was not converted but instead called to the specific role of *apostle to the *Gentiles. Paul is not only the archetypal convert but also a disputed one. The reasons for this are embedded in the treatment of Paul's conversion in historical-critical scholarship and its relationship to dominant perspectives in conversion studies.

1. History of Reception, Part 1: Christian Convert or Jewish Apostle?
2. History of Reception, Part 2: Jewish Convert or Unconverted Jew?
3. Paul and the History of Conversion
4. Pauline Texts and Paul's Conversion
5. Acts and Paul's Conversion
6. Paul's Reshaping of Conversion
7. Paul's Conversion and Paul's Theology
8. Paul and Later Definitions of Conversion

1. History of Interpretation, Part 1: Christian Convert or Jewish Apostle?

In early twentieth-century scholarship Paul was often pictured as psychologically prepared for his Damascus road experience by an internal struggle with his inability to obey the *law. This struggle was resolved by his encounter with *Christ, as a result of which Paul's attempts to be justified through the law were replaced by *justification through *faith in Christ. Paul left behind his Pharisaic Judaism for nascent Christianity and held his new faith "not as a type of Judaism, but as an independent religion distinct from that of the Jews" (Burton, 44). Such characterizations of Paul's experience fitted with the description of conversion advocated by William James in his influential study *The Varieties of Religious Experience* (1902). Here an unhappy divided self "becomes unified and consciously right superior and happy, in consequence of its firmer hold upon religious realities" (James, 189).

The applicability of this to Paul is sharply challenged by Krister Stendahl in *Paul Among Jews and Gentiles* (1976). Key texts in which Paul describes his experience (Gal 1:11-24; Phil 3:3-17) show that, rather than struggling with guilt, Paul had a clear conscience. The false assumption that Paul struggled with guilt was prompted by the introspective experiences of influential later Christian figures such as Augustine and above all Martin Luther. Far from leaving behind his Judaism, Paul experienced a *call like that of the prophets of the Hebrew Bible. He was to be an apostle to the Gentiles, bringing them the good news of Israel's Messiah. It was through fulfilling this role that Paul began to emphasize justification by faith as the means by which Gentiles could now be included in the people of God. Paul did not change religions and should be understood as a Jewish apostle and not as a Christian convert.

2. History of Interpretation, Part 2: Jewish Convert or Unconverted Jew?

Stendahl's argument was successful in important respects. That Paul had a robust conscience was widely accepted, as was the need to emphasize Paul's continued commitment to central aspects of Judaism. Early Christianity was not in the mid-first century a separate religion but still itself a Jewish movement with a majority of Jewish members. Yet the argument that Paul was called but not converted was not widely accepted. It faced three key challenges:

1. Stendahl made unsupported sweeping generalizations connecting the assumption of a guilty conscience on Paul's part with what he regarded as erroneous perspectives on justification in the Western theological tradition (see Martin Luther).

2. Stendahl sharply contrasted the category of conversion and Paul's use of the vocabulary of calling. Yet Paul uses the vocabulary of calling to refer back to the point at which his readers became Christ-followers: "Were you a *slave when called?" (1 Cor 7:21 NRSV). Far from carrying a meaning that contrasts with conversion, the vocabulary of calling is a way in which Paul describes conversion: "Paul uses it to mark the point when God applies salvation" (Hussey, 85). This application of *salvation is not restricted to Gentiles, for Paul twice, in strongly soteriological contexts, specifically refers to Jewish as well as Gentile Christ-followers as called by *God (Rom 9:24; 1 Cor 1:24). Only Paul is called to be apostle to the Gentiles, but all who believe, both Jewish and Gentile, are called to follow Christ. The vocabulary of calling fits Paul's apostolic role so appropriately because his role is to proclaim the *gospel, through which God calls Gentiles. His apostolic calling cannot be used to deny that Paul was a convert (Chester, 153-59).

3. The adequacy of Stendahl's definition of conversion was questioned. Alan Segal, himself Jewish, argues in *Paul the Convert* (1990) that "in modern usage and social science the word *conversion* can denote moving from one sect or denomination to another within the same religion, if the change is radical" (Segal, 6). Paul's shift of communities from Pharisaic Judaism to participation in predominantly Gentile communities of Christ-followers makes him a convert. Paul retains his commitment to Judaism but expresses it, precisely as apostle to the Gentiles, in a highly novel way. Paul was not a convert to Christianity, but he was a Jewish convert whose Judaism was transformed through his Damascus road experience.

At the close of the twentieth century it therefore appeared that a consensus was developing that Paul was both called and converted. However, in the first decades of the twenty-first century this has been challenged by a movement to interpret Paul's texts under the banner "Paul within Judaism" (Nanos and Zetterholm). On this view, Paul's letters address Gentile Christ-followers and their relationship to the law. Nothing he says is intended to apply generally to Jews and Judaism or to call into question the continued importance for Jewish Christ-followers of observing the law. Both traditional Protestant perspectives, which regard Paul as critiquing Jewish works-righteousness, and the "new perspective on Paul," which regards Paul as critiquing Jewish ethnic exclusivity, go astray in considering Paul to have a critique of Judaism. Paul's slogan that justification is not by *works of the law is formulated as a statement about the justification of Gentiles.

In turn, if Paul has no critique of Judaism, then the application of the concept of conversion to his own experience becomes strained. What did he convert from if he did not regard his new life as a

Christ-follower as any more or less Jewish than his previous one? The Christian tradition of treating Paul as a convert lacks any basis in his letters and is nothing more than a covert way of implying that Christianity is true religion and Judaism false (Eisenbaum, 132). From this perspective, it is essential to maintain Stendahl's position that Paul was not a convert against Segal's position that he was a Jewish convert whose Judaism was transformed. Only if Paul abandoned Judaism would it be accurate to term him a convert. He was an unconverted Jew. The contrast between this position and the earlier view that Paul converted to nascent Christianity is stark, but the understanding of what constitutes conversion is remarkably unchanged.

3. Paul and the History of Conversion.
It is doubtful that any contemporary Pauline scholar regards Paul as having left behind Judaism for nascent Christianity. Paul remained deeply committed to the God of *Israel and to the Scriptures of Israel. He was also completely convinced that the God of Israel would never abandon the Jewish people. Despite the failure of the majority to accept Jesus as Messiah, the gifts and the calling of God given to their ancestors are irrevocable (Rom 11:29). A hardening has come upon Israel only until the full number of the Gentiles has come in (Rom 11:25), and God's ultimate purpose is *mercy (Rom 11:31-32). Yet does it follow that Paul was therefore not a convert? Some of the ways in which Paul remained most deeply Jewish are ways in which Christianity, shaped by Paul's texts, was itself to remain most recognizably Jewish (Westerholm, 14-16). Further, while Paul has no doubts about his own continuing Jewishness, he regards those who have not become Christ-followers as having gone astray. They have stumbled (1 Cor 1:23; Rom 9:32-33), have sought to establish their own *righteousness (Rom 10:3), and are like broken-off branches (Rom 11:20). Paul can even say that not all Israelites currently belong to Israel (Rom 9:6) and that he is anguished concerning their situation (Rom 9:3). For Paul, acceptance of Jesus as Messiah is now a defining issue for Judaism.

The rigid tying of the issue of whether Paul was a convert to the continuation of his Jewish *identity is therefore unhelpful. For Paul his Jewish identity continued but was reshaped by the conviction that Jesus was Messiah. Yet simply to conclude from this that Paul was a convert is itself unsatisfactory. Conversion is not a static, timeless concept into which an individual in any historical context either fits or does not. Conversion has a history, and Paul's own experience and his apostolic career form a particularly crucial episode in that history. One's focus in studying the relevant texts should be on how Paul's experience and his writings shape conversion. Only then will it be possible to ask important related questions such as how Paul's experience influenced his theology, whether he treats Jews and Gentiles coming to faith in Christ in the same way, whether his theology establishes his own experience as a normative paradigm of conversion for subsequent Christianity, and whether modern definitions of conversion can be helpful in studying Paul.

An essential first step is to understand the history of conversion prior to Paul. The English verb "to convert" derives from the Latin *convertere,* meaning "to turn around." It could therefore be used to translate the Greek verbs *epistrephō*, "I turn back to" or "I turn toward," and *metanoeō*, "I change my mind" or "I repent." The LXX uses these Greek terms to render the Hebrew terms *šûb* (return, repent) and *nāḥam* (regret something). In such texts, conversion means that a people who have been unfaithful in their relationship with God now return to God, demonstrating the change through renewed ethical conduct and covenantal fidelity (e.g., 2 Kgs 17:13; Jer 15:19). This prophetic concept of conversion reappears in the *preaching of John the Baptist, who calls for repentance (Mt 3:2, 8). The Gospels, however, add a ritual element of conversion in *baptism that, while not a central part of Jesus' own *ministry, reappeared as an essential practice of the first churches. Already conversion itself is changing and developing. The approach of God's *kingdom in Jesus also provides a new eschatological context in which the call to conversion is no longer primarily to a nation as a whole. The ministries of John and of Jesus were to "to the lost sheep of the house of Israel" (Mt 10:6 NRSV), but Israel will turn out to include both wheat and chaff (Mt 3:12). Individuals, *households, and towns must decide where they stand, and some will repent, while others will not (Mt 10:35-36). The history of conversion therefore begins not between Judaism and other religious traditions but within Judaism. The question of whether Paul could both be a convert and remain Jewish makes little sense. The issue that faced him and other Christ-followers was instead whether and on what basis conversion could be extended to Gentiles.

As they grappled with this issue, they were not entirely without antecedents within Judaism. The God of Israel's lordship over the nations is proclaimed by the prophets. God's *judgment of evil and God's willingness to forgive the repentant are understood by Jeremiah to structure God's dealings with other nations and not simply Israel alone (Jer 18:7-10). Through the ministry of Jonah, the people of Nineveh "turn from their evil ways" (Jon 3:8 NRSV). There were also Jewish apocalyptic traditions, expressed in both biblical and intertestamental texts (e.g., Is 2:1-4; Tob 14:5-6), that speak of the nations abandoning their idols and turning to the God of Israel in the last days. Once the *death and *resurrection of Jesus and the pouring out of the Spirit were identified as the inauguration of the last days (Acts 2:17), the issue of the Gentiles and conversion was likely to arise. It was in this context that Paul stepped onto the Damascus road and into the history of conversion.

4. Pauline Texts and Paul's Conversion.

Paul gives a direct account of his Damascus road experience only at Galatians 1:11-24, with much briefer references at 1 Corinthians 9:1; 15:8-10. Philippians 3:2-11 provides instead a description of the change wrought by Paul's experience, contrasting the sources of his identity before and afterward. In the letters of which authorship is disputed, 1 Timothy 1:12-17 is similarly concerned with a contrast between Paul's identity before and after his experience. One further text, Romans 7:7-25, was often interpreted in nineteenth- and early twentieth-century scholarship as evidence of Paul's preconversion struggle with his inability to obey the law. This contradicts the clear indications in Galatians 1 and Philippians 3 that Paul's conscience was robust, and the notion of a preconversion struggle seems to satisfy all too neatly the need to provide a psychological explanation for events that precritical interpreters ascribed to divine intervention. Romans 7 continues to generate a multiplicity of readings, but a majority today either regard it as describing a struggle with *sin Paul experienced as a Christ-follower or as describing his preconversion self from a later perspective—that is, Paul now recognizes that his former life was under the power of sin, but this was not how he would have described it at the time (Chester, 183-95). Either way, it does not refer directly to Paul's conversion.

4.1. 1 Corinthians 9:1; 15:8-10. Despite their brevity, these texts offer vital information. Without them we would not know that Paul understood his experience in such strongly visual terms. Paul's rhetorical question at 1 Corinthians 9:1, "Have I not seen Jesus our *Lord?" (NRSV) confirms that he understands his experience as a *vision of Christ. At 1 Corinthians 15:8-10 he describes it at the climax of a list of Jesus' resurrection appearances. Despite its separation from Jesus' initial resurrection appearances by several years (the appearance is "as to one untimely born," 1 Cor 15:8 NRSV), Paul places his experience in the same category as Jesus' other appearances. This positions Paul in a complex manner in relation to other apostles. He is the least of them, and the most undeserving, because he persecuted the *church (1 Cor 15:9), but he is also what God has made him, and he and his apostolic ministry are a unique token of the invincibility of divine *grace (1 Cor 15:10).

4.2. Galatians 1:11-24. In relation to the content of his experience, Paul here too emphasizes that he encountered Jesus ("apocalypse of Jesus Christ," Gal 1:12). He also says very strongly that this was how he received the gospel that he preaches among the Gentiles and, in doing so, makes his own experience part of the argument of the letter. For the Galatians to accept *circumcision and take on observance of the law would be to abandon the gospel that Paul preaches (Gal 1:6-9), and this gospel was given to him in direct encounter with the risen Jesus. Paul frames his conversion experience as the source of the content of his gospel, a gospel through which the Galatians will be justified by faith (Gal 2:16).

Paul further emphasizes the divine origin of his gospel by presenting a biography of reversal, contrasting his past as a persecutor of the church (Gal 1:13) with his present proclamation of the gospel (Schütz, 133-34). This biography is an expression of divine sovereignty, for God had set Paul apart before his birth (Gal 1:15) for the particular purpose of proclaiming Christ among the Gentiles (Gal 1:16). Even Paul's persecuting activity, directed against the church of God (Gal 1:13), is ultimately contained within God's providential purpose. It is the remarkable nature of Paul's reversal from persecutor to apostle that results in *glory being given to God (Gal 1:23-24). This emphasis on overarching divine sovereignty is strengthened even further by Paul's use of vocabulary drawn from Isaiah 49:1-6 and Jeremiah 1:5 to describe how God intervened in his life. Both texts not only speak of divine appointment (the calling of the figure of the Servant in Isaiah, the setting apart of the prophet in Jeremiah) but do so in ways that include references to the Gentiles in the explanations of God's purposes provided (Is 49:6; Jer 1:5; also Jer 1:10). God's actions in and through Paul stand in continuity with God's prior speaking in the Scriptures of Israel.

All this helps to account for striking features of Paul's description of his "former way of life in

Judaism" (Gal 1:13-14 NET). When converts present biographies of reversal, they frequently denigrate their former lives. Their past becomes a straightforwardly negative foil to the present and is presented in terms that the converts themselves would previously have rejected. They engage in biographical reconstruction, emphasizing the positive nature of the changes brought by conversion. Yet aside from his persecuting activity, there is little for Paul to regret. He had advanced in Judaism beyond many of his contemporaries because of his zeal for "the traditions of my ancestors" (Gal 1:14 NRSV), a phrase that likely references commitment to specifically Pharisaic reliance on oral traditions in interpreting and obeying the law (Ortlund, 141-45). Paul no longer defines his way of life in this way, but neither will he denigrate his past. He portrays his former life not as a demonstration of Judaism's inadequacy, or as an inadequate form of Judaism, but rather as the best of Judaism.

*4.3. **Philippians 3:2-11.*** Paul here presents another biography of reversal. He contrasts the sources of his identity before his conversion, which he terms reasons for "confidence in the *flesh" (Phil 3:4 NRSV), with Christ as the primary source of his new identity (Phil 3:7-11). When describing his previous life Paul specifically states that he was a Pharisee (Phil 3:5), and he confirms the impression given at Galatians 1:13-14 by linking his persecuting activity to his zeal (Phil 3:6). He persecuted the church as a misguided expression of devotion to God. It is the same devotion that led Paul to persecute that also allows him to say that he was "blameless" (Phil 3:6 NRSV) in relation to righteousness under the law (Ortlund, 158). As in Galatians 1, Paul emphasizes the positive nature of his previous life and does so for a rhetorical purpose. This purpose emerges when he goes on to depict these positive sources of his previous identity as "loss" and "rubbish" (Phil 3:7-8 NRSV) compared to knowing Christ. Prior to his conversion Paul would not have described his Jewish identity as "loss" or "rubbish" even in comparative terms. Yet Paul's refusal to offer an outright negative characterization of his previous life remains significant. It is the "surpassing value of knowing Christ" (Phil 3:8 NRSV) that Paul wishes to emphasize. This superlative value cannot be demonstrated by a comparison with something worthless but only with that which apart from knowing Christ would itself represent the best possible human identity. Paul goes on to express the gain that Christ represents by expressing the *hope of being found in him eschatologically, no longer relying on his own righteousness but on the righteousness from God that comes through Christ (Phil 3:9). He therefore links his conversion experience to justification, just as in Galatians 1 he connects it with fidelity to the gospel, through which the Galatians will be justified by faith.

*4.4. **1 Timothy 1:12-17.*** These verses present yet another biography of reversal but with some significant differences from Galatians 1 and Philippians 3. Here Paul is categorized as having been the greatest of sinners because of his persecuting activity (1 Tim 1:12-15), whereas in the other texts such labeling is avoided. There it is the retrospectively anomalous juxtaposition of Paul's persecuting activity with the unimpeachable rectitude of every other aspect of his identity that serves his rhetorical purpose. Here it is also not only Christ whom Paul encounters but Christ who appoints Paul (1 Tim 1:12) and is patient with him (1 Tim 1:16), in contrast to the calling activity of God in Galatians 1. Yet if one looks beyond these rhetorical differences to what the text tells readers about Paul's life then, whether 1 Timothy was written by Paul or someone else, the content is familiar. The sense expressed of the gravity of Paul's persecuting activity coheres with 1 Corinthians 15:9-10, and the explanation that Paul acted "ignorantly in unbelief" (1 Tim 1:13 NRSV)—that is, he persecuted believing that he was doing right—coheres with Galatians 1 and Philippians 3. As in Galatians 1:23-24, Paul's transformation from persecutor to apostle results in glory being given to God (1 Tim 1:16-17).

5. Acts and Paul's Conversion.

The conversion of Paul is recounted three times in Acts, once as a major event in the narrative of the book (Acts 9:1-19) and twice in subsequent speeches of Paul defending his ministry before potentially hostile audiences (Acts 22:1-21; 26:2-23). These texts naturally provide fuller narrative details than the references in the Pauline letters. From Acts one learns that Paul was journeying to Damascus in order to engage in persecuting activity (Acts 9:1-2; 22:5; 26:12), that he was accompanied by others (Acts 9:7; 22:9; 26:13), that there was a bright *light from heaven that caused Paul to fall to the ground (Acts 9:3-4; 22:6; 26:13), that Jesus spoke to him (Acts 9:4; 22:7-10; 26:14-18), and that he was temporarily struck blind (Acts 9:8; 22:11). Also from Acts one learns of the role of Ananias (Acts 9:10-17; 22:12-13) and that Paul was immediately baptized (Acts 9:18; 22:16).

There are some significant differences between the three accounts. Acts 9:7 says that Paul's companions heard the voice of Jesus but saw no one, whereas Acts 22:9 says that they did not hear the voice. Acts 26:2-23 is a condensed account in which the part played by Ananias is left out and Paul's commission to preach to the Gentiles comes directly from Jesus (Acts 26:16-18). At Acts 22:15 Ananias says that Paul will be Christ's *witness "to all people" (NET), but the explicit command to go to the Gentiles is reserved for a subsequent vision experienced while Paul was praying in the *Jerusalem *temple (Acts 22:17-21). In Acts 9 God's will for Paul to go to the Gentiles is revealed to Ananias (Acts 9:15), but its communication to Paul is unrecorded.

There are also some differences in emphasis from the information given in Pauline texts. Acts does not explicitly link Paul's encounter with Christ to his status as an apostle or use the vocabulary of calling. Paul emphasizes seeing Jesus, whereas Acts places a very strong emphasis on the auditory elements of his experience, although it is acknowledged that Paul has seen the Righteous One (Acts 22:14). In Acts Paul hears the voice of Jesus, with a double address "Saul, Saul," reminiscent of the experiences of Moses (Ex 3:4) and Samuel (1 Sam 3:4, 10). The identification of Jesus with the churches is stressed (Acts 9:4; 22:8; 26:14): to persecute them is to persecute him (Keener, 1635). However, despite all these differences in detail, at a more general level the picture provided by Acts reinforces that given in the Pauline texts. In all three accounts in Acts it is clear that the purpose of Paul's conversion is for him to take the gospel to the Gentiles (Acts 9:15; 22:21; 26:17-18), in all three accounts Paul's experience is an encounter with Jesus (Acts 9:5; 22:8; 26:15), and in all three accounts Paul's prior persecuting activity is emphasized (Acts 9:1-2; 22:3-5; 26:9-11). For all that the motif of Paul's blindness is unique to Acts, its symbolism fits Paul's own reflections. His temporary literal blindness ironically reflects his previous spiritual blindness, and he will now go to the Gentiles, whose blind eyes must be opened to God's *truth (Acts 26:18) just as Paul's have been. Acts therefore gives no hint that Paul was anything other than sincere in his persecuting activity, which Acts 22:3 mentions alongside his zeal (Keener, 3222-25).

6. Paul's Reshaping of Conversion.

The major common themes that emerge from the accounts of Paul's conversion in the NT are that he persecuted the church convinced that he was doing God's will, that his experience was an encounter with Christ, and that God's purpose was for him to take the gospel to the Gentiles. This combination had decisive consequences in the history of conversion. For when Paul constructs biographies of reversal for his Gentile converts, he characterizes their previous lives using a vice list detailing multiple transgressions (1 Cor 6:9-11). Many of these transgressions may not have appeared to them as transgressions at the time (e.g., for Gentiles the sin of *idolatry was simply the proper practice of piety), but Paul expects that looking back they will now recognize the sin-infested nature of their lives. The contrast with his own list of reasons for confidence in the flesh is striking. In terms of the ethical change involved, conversion appears very different for Paul and for his Gentile converts. Yet it was Paul the ideal Jew and not these Gentile sinners who rejected Jesus as Messiah and persecuted the church. He did so not as a lapse from his devotion as a Pharisaic Jew but as an expression of his zeal. Despite all the myriad ways in which now he wishes the ethics of his Gentile converts to become more Jewish, Paul perceives his position before God prior to his conversion as fundamentally similar to theirs. Both he and they were the perpetrators and victims of unrecognized sin. Other Jewish Christ-followers could embrace Gentile conversion, but not all could join Paul in recognizing that "both Jews and Greeks are under the power of sin" (Rom 3:9 NRSV). Those Jewish followers of Christ who insisted against Paul that it was necessary for Gentile believers to be circumcised were not rejecting Gentile conversion but construing it in terms of traditional conversion within Judaism, where it would involve turning back to fidelity to the law. Whether or not Paul thought that he and his fellow Jewish followers of Christ were obligated to continue to practice the law, he is clear that, because of the law's weakness in the face of sin, of which his former life provided a paramount example, fidelity to the law could no longer define conversion. It must now be understood with an exclusively christological focus (Gal 2:21).

Alongside this recasting of conversion as constituted primarily in relationship to the Messiah rather than the law, Paul's conviction that his *mission to the Gentiles was divinely directed also shaped the subsequent history of conversion. For the gospel going to first Jew and then Greek without distinction is part of God's reclamation of all of God's *creation (Rom 8:21). Under the pressure of this unlimited scope of Christ's lordship (Phil 2:9-11), Paul speaks about conversion using a cluster of images that describe it not as the changing or transforming of an existing person but as the creation of a new person. He speaks plainly of a new creation (2 Cor 5:17; Gal 6:15). Paul also compares God's act of converting Gentiles through his own ministry to the calling into being of things that do not exist (Rom 4:17; 1 Cor 1:26). The corollary of this creation of a new person is the death of the old one. To walk in newness of life can result only from sharing in Christ's death (Rom 6:3, 6), something ritually enacted in baptism (1 Cor 12:13). Paul can say quite literally that, since he has been crucified with Christ, he no longer lives but rather Christ lives in him (Gal 2:19-20). The metaphor of turning is not left behind, and Paul speaks to the Thessalonians of "how you turned to God from idols" (1 Thess 1:9 NRSV), but it has been decisively supplemented. Paul significantly expands the concept of conversion.

7. Paul's Conversion and Paul's Theology. If this portrayal of Paul as one of the principal architects of conversion within the later Christian tradition is correct, then it is likely that his own conversion and reflection on it was significant to his theology (Kim). The alternative view that Paul developed his central theological commitments only in response to later practical issues in Gentile mission (Räisänen) does not take seriously enough Paul's rooting of his gospel in his Damascus road experience (Gal 1:11-12). Yet it does not necessarily follow that the theology expressed in Paul's letters emerged fully formed in the immediate aftermath of Paul's experience. Converts' accounts of their experience and the present purposes these accounts serve exist in a complex relationship with each other (Chester, 18-25). It could be that Paul reacted to later issues in Gentile mission differently from others precisely because he could relate them to his own experience and came to identify that experience as similar in fundamental ways to Gentile conversion. Paul's claim to have received his gospel through his conversion does not, for example, necessarily imply that he immediately formulated a theology of justification identical to that expressed in Galatians. If Paul's claim is accurate, however, it does follow that, whenever it reached a mature form, he regarded the content of this theology as an essential expression of the gospel he received through his conversion. Rejection of it constitutes rejection of his gospel (Gal 1:6-9; 5:2-4).

8. Paul and Later Definitions of Conversion. Christians have unsurprisingly always used Paul's texts as a basis for their own understanding and praxis of conversion. He has been enormously influential in defining expectations about what Christian converts must believe and how they should behave. In some Protestant traditions there has been an additional emphasis on the dramatic nature of Paul's experience and its marking of a specific point in time from which his commitment to Christ began. In recent decades some evangelical scholars have questioned whether this aspect of Paul's conversion should be regarded as an expectation for others, urging more attention to other NT material consistent with a gradual transformation (Peace; McKnight).

These calls for greater flexibility in expectations concerning conversion have often also appealed to approaches to studying conversion in the social sciences. The more an account of conversion in the NT coheres with contemporary conversion studies, the more compelling its argument (McKnight, 176). However, the relationship between contemporary definitions of conversion and study of Paul is rarely as simple as this makes it appear. A. D. Nock's classic study of conversion in the ancient world has often been accused of bias in arguing that conversion is found only in Judaism and Christianity among the traditions of the ancient world (Nock, 1-16). The dominant response has been to attempt to construct more neutral, inclusive definitions of conversion applicable to any tradition (Rambo, 5-19). Yet given Paul's crucial role in generating dominant images and metaphors of conversion, these ostensibly secular tools of analysis may contain unacknowledged Pauline elements. Metaphors of transformation are prominent in both Paul's letters and *social-scientific approaches to studying conversion (Segal, 28-29), but does such a fit objectively demonstrate that Paul was a convert or simply highlight his significance in the history of conversion?

Rather than providing static definitions of conversion, contemporary conversion studies are better used as a heuristic resource, allowing NT scholars to formulate appropriate research questions. The emphasis placed in this article on Paul's reshaping of conversion is partly stimulated by that of many late twentieth-century sociological studies, themselves reacting against James's psychological approach, on the active convert (Richardson). Here it is recognized that converts make use of means of personal transformation offered by particular communities and engage in the reconstruction of their own identity. Paul does so in a way that affects not only himself but also the resources available to subsequent converts. Similarly, the emphasis within conversion studies in the early twenty-first century on conversion careers, and the recognition that conversion is not an event that is automatically sustained (Gooren), could help the formulation of worthwhile research questions about how Paul maintains his conversion and that of others. It is time for study of the conversion and call of Paul to move beyond a narrow focus on the question of whether Paul was a convert.

See also CHRONOLOGY OF PAUL; CORINTHIANS, FIRST LETTER TO THE; GALATIANS, LETTER TO THE; PASTORAL EPISTLES; PAUL AND JUDAISM; PAUL IN ACTS; PHILIPPIANS, LETTER TO THE.

BIBLIOGRAPHY. **G. Boccaccini and C. A. Segovia,** eds., *Paul the Jew: Rereading Paul the Apostle as a Figure of Second Temple Judaism* (Minneapolis: Fortress, 2016); **E. D. W. Burton,** *The Epistle to the Galatians,* ICC (Edinburgh: T&T Clark, 1921); **S. J. Chester,** *Conversion at Corinth: Perspectives on Conversion in Paul's Theology and the Corinthian Church* (New York: T&T Clark, 2003); **Z. Crook,** *Reconceptualising Conversion: Patronage, Loyalty, and Conversion in the Religions of the Ancient Mediterranean* (Berlin: de Gruyter, 2004); **A. Despotis and H. Löhr,** eds., *Religious and Philosophical Conversion in the Ancient Mediterranean Traditions* (Leiden: Brill, 2022); **T. Donaldson,** *Paul and the Gentiles: Remapping the Apostle's Convictional World* (Minneapolis: Fortress, 1997); **P. Eisenbaum,** *Paul Was Not a Christian* (San Francisco: HarperOne, 2007); **P. Fredriksen,** *Paul the Pagan's Apostle* (New Haven, CT: Yale University Press, 2017); **B. R. Gaventa,** *From Darkness to Light: Aspects of Paul's Conversion in the New Testament* (Minneapolis: Fortress, 1986); **H. Gooren,** *Religious Conversion and Disaffiliation: Tracing Patterns of Change in Faith Practice* (New York: Palgrave MacMillan, 2010); **J. B. Green,** *Conversion in Luke-Acts: Divine Action, Human Cognition, and the People of God* (Grand Rapids, MI: Baker, 2015); **I. Hussey,** *The Soteriological Use of Call by Paul and Luke* (Eugene, OR: Wipf & Stock, 2018); **W. James,** *The Varieties of Religious Experience* (New York: Longmans, Green, 1902); **C. S. Keener,** *Acts: An Exegetical Commentary,* 4 vols. (Grand Rapids, MI: Baker, 2012–2015); **S. Kim,** *The Origin of Paul's Gospel,* 2nd ed. (Tübingen: Mohr Siebeck, 1984); **D. W. Kling,** *A History of Christian Conversion* (Oxford: Oxford University Press, 2020); **R. N. Longenecker,** ed., *The Road from Damascus: The Impact of Paul's Conversion on His Life, Thought, and Ministry* (Grand Rapids, MI: Eerdmans, 1997); **S. McKnight,** *Turning to Jesus: The Sociology of Conversion in the Gospels* (Louisville: Westminster John Knox, 2002); **D. S. Morlan,** *Conversion in Luke and Paul: An Exegetical and Theological Exploration* (New York: Bloomsbury T&T Clark, 2013); **M. Nanos and M. Zetterholm,** eds., *Paul Within Judaism: Restoring the First-Century Context to the Apostle* (Minneapolis: Fortress, 2015); **A. D. Nock,** *Conversion: The Old and New in Religion from Alexander the Great to Augustine* (Oxford: Oxford University Press, 1933); **D. C. Ortlund,** *Zeal Without Knowledge: The Concept of Zeal in Romans 10, Galatians 1, and Philippians 3* (New York: T&T Clark, 2012); **R. Peace,** *Conversion in the New Testament: Paul and the Twelve* (Grand Rapids, MI: Eerdmans, 1999); **H. Räisänen,** "Paul's Conversion and the Development of His View of the Law," *NTS* 33 (1987): 404-19; **L. R. Rambo,** *Understanding Religious Conversion* (New Haven, CT: Yale University Press, 1993); **L. R. Rambo and C. E. Farhadian,** eds., *The Oxford Handbook of Religious Conversion* (Oxford: Oxford University Press, 2014); **J. T. Richardson,** "The Active vs. Passive Convert: Paradigm Conflict in Conversion/Recruitment Research," *JSSR* 24 (1985): 163-79; **A. Segal,** *Paul the Convert: The Apostolate and Apostasy of Saul the Pharisee* (New Haven, CT: Yale University Press, 1990); **J. H. Schütz,** *Paul and the Anatomy of Apostolic Authority* (Cambridge: Cambridge University Press, 1975); **K. Stendahl,** *Paul Among Jews and Gentiles* (Philadelphia: Fortress, 1976); **S. Westerholm,** *Law and Ethics in Early Judaism and the New Testament* (Tübingen: Mohr Siebeck, 2017); **T. Yates,** "Christian Conversion 1900–2000: William James to Lewis Rambo," in *Previous Convictions: Conversion in the Present Day,* ed. M. Percy (London: SPCK, 2000), 124-37.

S. J. Chester

CONVERTS. *See* GENTILES; PASTOR, PAUL AS; PAUL AND JUDAISM.

CORINTH

Paul founded a church in the city of Corinth (1 Cor 4:15) and wrote two of his longest epistles, 1 and 2 Corinthians, to its members.

1. Sources
2. History
3. City Layout
4. Economy
5. Government
6. Demographics
7. Religion

1. Sources.

The most detailed description of Roman Corinth and its surrounding area, book 2 of *Description of*

Greece, was written in the second century by Pausanias (ca. AD 110–180). His work is an important primary source for reconstructing certain aspects of city life in Corinth. His overall focus on Greece was primarily on its sanctuaries, statues, tombs, and the legends connected with them, but his comprehensive work also describes towns, villages, roads, and the natural geography, principally in the vast peninsula that comprised southern Greece.

The American School of Archaeology has been exploring Corinth for over a century, and its endeavors have been a major source for understanding the ancient city. Its resources on Corinth (published by Harvard University Press) are invaluable for comprehending life in this prestigious Roman colony.

It is notable that Corinth minted its own currency. A large number of different coins were struck in Corinth from the reign of Julius Caesar through to that of Nero (*Roman Provincial Coinage*, nos. 1116-1209). Many have the head of the reigning Roman emperor on one side, some with his spouse alongside, and others with symbolic figures aiming to remind their users of different aspects of life in Corinth.

The imperial images, including those engraved on coins, were propaganda tools reminding Corinthians of their obligation of loyalty to the Roman Empire and its reigning emperor, whom they worshiped as a god on the official imperial high and holy days throughout the year. Extant evidence such as coins can help throw light on those aspects of the Corinthian lifestyle that later constituted a challenge for the first generation of Christians residing in Corinth.

2. History.
Prior to 146 BC, Corinth was the head of the Achaian League of cities in southern Greece. It was destroyed by Rome that year because it led other cities in the region in a revolt against Roman rule. Rome's policy with such rebellions was to both kill the inhabitants of the city and demolish all of the city itself. Corinth was rebuilt from "the ashes" almost a century later, in 44 BC. Strabo (ca. 64 BC–ca. AD 24) records, "Now after Corinth had remained deserted for a long time, it was restored again, because of its favourable position, by the Deified Caesar, who authorised its colonisation with people from Rome who belonged for the most part to the freedmen class" (*Geogr.* 8.6.23 [LCL]).

Ancient Corinth was destroyed after an earthquake in 1858. The modern town of Corinth, known as New Corinth, lies approximately seven kilometers to the northeast of the ancient city.

3. City Layout.
Roman Corinth's residential houses were erected along some eighty-three parallel streets within the city's wall. These were laid out symmetrically according to the Roman centuriation pattern for town planning. Its temples and commercial, civic, and legal buildings in the civic center, however, did not have the same level of organization, as they were erected on the foundations of previous buildings from the Greek era. Despite the lack of symmetry, the stone buildings were well constructed, reflecting the grandeur of Roman architecture.

The forum was the official center of the city. It was a large public square where the commercial, political, legal, religious, and social activities of the city took place. Pausanias records that the marketplace in Corinth was where most but not all of the sanctuaries were (*Descr.* 2.6).

Commerce, courts, and cults as well as shrines and temples located in the forum functioned alongside one another. Commercial transactions could be legally undertaken only there because it was the official place where all goods were bought and sold by and to its citizens. A tax was levied on all commercial transactions, and the revenue went into the city treasury.

4. Economy.

4.1. Corinth as a Strategic Trading Location. Once rebuilt, Corinth quickly regained its reputation of being the thriving commercial center that it was in the Greek era. Strabo writes, "Corinth is called 'wealthy' because of its commerce, since it is situated on the Isthmus and is master of two harbours, of which one leads straight to Asia and the other to Italy; and it makes easy the exchange of merchandise from both countries that are so far distant from each other" (*Geogr.* 8.6.20-23). Cargo on ships from the Roman East was downloaded and transported on wheeled vehicles across to the port on the other side on the track, named the Diolkos, a term derived from a Greek verb meaning "to haul across." It was then loaded on a ship bound for the Italian port Puteoli (where the apostle Paul arrived, having been sent to Rome for his trial before the emperor; see Acts 28:13). Ships could avoid storms rather than sailing around the major portion of southern Greece, known as the Peloponnese. Corinth, at its northern tip, grew to become a significant commercial center in the province as well as its capital.

Roman poet Horace (65–8 BC) speaks of "twin sea'd Corinth" (*bimarisve Corinthi moenia*), given its geographic location between the Gulf of Corinth and the Saronic Gulf (*Carm.* 1.7.2).

4.2. Women as Benefactors. Among the inscriptions located in Corinth is one to Junia Theodora, the official patron of a league of cities in the province of Lycia on the other side of the Aegean Sea. The longest set of inscriptions to any woman in the public domain in the first century is dedicated to her. It was found in 1954 in Corinth, where she later lived, and consists of two official letters to the Corinthians as well as three decrees from the provincial assembly of Lycia, including an official letter to "the Council and the people of Corinth."

This inscription is a reminder that there were official roles for wealthy *women in the public square as well as benefactors of individuals. Hence, "Greetings from the Federal Assembly of the Lycians and the Lycian magistrates to the magistrates, the council and the people of Corinth. By an honorific decree made in favour of Junia Theodora, living among you . . ."

It is significant that Paul in his personal greetings to a large number of Christians known to him in Rome includes women and commences with, "I commend to you our sister, Phoebe, a *servant of the *church in Cenchreae . . . for she has been a patron of many and of myself as well" (Rom 16:1-2). In the church located close by Corinth in its harbor city of the Aegean Sea, she played a significant role.

4.3. Food Supply Issues. There is evidence of a serious food crisis in Corinth after Paul left. A number of inscriptions to Tiberius Claudius Dinippus, a leading citizen of Corinth, record the prestigious roles he held. He was "President of the Neronea Caesarean and of the Isthmian and Caesarean Games," which were held near Corinth, but he was also "three times curator of the grain supply" (*curator annonae*). This is a clear signal that the city had experienced serious food crises, and in response he had subsidized the grain supply at his own expense (IKorinthKent, nos. 158-63).

In AD 40–41 Seneca the Younger records, "We were threatened with the worst evil that can befall men even during a siege—the lack of provisions . . . very nearly at the cost of the city's destruction and famine and the general revolution that follows famine" (*On the Shortness of Life*, LCL). If this is the "distress" to which Paul refers (1 Cor 7:26), it may be this was what caused Christians to have to bring their own meal to the *Lord's Supper. Some did not have the food to bring, and others left intoxicated (1 Cor 11:22).

5. Government.

5.1. The Legal System. The governors of the province were appointed by Rome and resided for their term of office in Corinth. They were also responsible to Rome for the running of the province and undertook the annual assize to the cities for the hearing of criminal cases.

Lucius Junius Gallio Annaeanus and his brother, Seneca the Younger, had been sent by their father, Seneca the Elder, to Rome for the equivalent of tertiary education that included the study of Roman law. Gallio was appointed proconsul of Achaia in AD 51. When Jews in Corinth proposed a legal case against Paul at the *bema* (stage or platform) in the city center Gallio immediately dismissed it, declaring that Paul had not committed a "felony" or "a political misdemeanor" under Roman law, as the charge against Paul was a breach of "your own law" (Acts 18:12-16), hence the case could not proceed to court.

Gallio was already a Roman senator when he came as governor to Corinth. He later became the personal tutor of Nero.

5.2. Civil Court. The task of the civil court was to try claims concerning legal possession, breach of contract, damages, fraud, and personal injury. Civil courts had also been long been a legitimate means of pursuing personal grievances on minor issues. What Paul calls "trivial cases" were not settled impartially by the jury, but their decision was based primarily on which person in the case possessed the highest social status in Corinth (1 Cor 6:2). The alternative procedure was for both parties to agree to have a private arbitrator so that there could be an amicable resolution.

5.3. Public Offices. Roman citizens in Corinth could nominate themselves for election to public offices for the administration of the city. These were regarded as prestigious positions for their holders. The policy was for a candidate to make an election promise called *pollicitatio* that would benefit the city, and if they were successful in being elected they legally had to fulfill it.

For example, there is an inscription recording, "Erastus laid this pavement at his own expense in exchange for his *aedileship* i.e., 'the city treasurer'" (IKorinthKent, no. 232). The lettering would have stood out, as it was in bronze. The pavement was outside the entrance to the theater and alongside the road to the nearby city of Sikyon. It measured 19 by 19 meters and consisted of slabs of Acrocorinth limestone. He was in effect the city business manager, being responsible for the upkeep and welfare of city property such as streets, public buildings and especially the market place as well as the public revenue from there (IKorinthKent, no. 27).

The Erastus on this inscription is believed to be the same "Erastus the city treasurer" who later sent "his greeting" to Roman Christians from Corinth (Rom 16:23).

6. Demographics.

Paul was in Corinth just over a century since its reconstruction. There were still a large number of Greeks living in Corinth as well as Romans, whose names bear witness—Erastus, Aquila, and Gaius, for example. There was also a significant Jewish population, enough to require a synagogue, whose ruler, Crispus, a convert to the Christian faith, was baptized by Paul (Acts 18:8).

A legal process existed whereby residents who were not citizens by birth could obtain Roman *citizenship. They entered into a legal contractual agreement as a bonded servant in the *household of a Roman citizen. After serving for seven years, they were eligible for manumission and thereby gained citizenship as freedmen, with their children also to become Roman citizens after a certain age (1 Cor 7:21).

7. Religion.

7.1. Temples and Shrines. Archaeological evidence bears witness to eight temples and shrines to different gods in the forum as well as to other gods who were worshiped outside the forum. Pausanias records, "On the market-place, where most of the sanctuaries are, stands Artemis, the names of the shrines and temples that had been built in the forum where the Corinthians could worship their many gods" (*Descr.* 2.6-3.1). Citizens went to specific temples because the particular god(s) there had something to offer that they wanted or needed.

For example, in the case of illness one would go to the Asclepion *temple located below the theater. Archaeologists have uncovered rooms next to that temple, which are assumed either to have contained beds for those who had to stay while they were treated—something comparable to a hospital—or have been a place where doctors were located. The latter had access to many different drugs and sophisticated surgical instruments.

The temple of Demeter and Kore was on the road leading up to the Acrocorinth. People would go to this particular temple to call on these gods to curse a person or persons who had offended them. They would write a *curse on the person on a piece of lead and invoke these or other relevant gods verbally to curse the offender while stabbing the metal with a nail. The gods themselves were never cursed.

7.2. Federal Imperial Cult Festivals. After Paul's departure, a major change occurred in Corinth. In AD 54-55 federal imperial cult celebrations were introduced. These festivities lasted for a whole week.

Gaius Julius Spartiaticus was responsible for organizing these. An inscription records that he was already a leading person in the life of the city, having held a number of public roles. He had been "magistrate of the fifth year twice" and also "the president of Isthmian and Caesarean Sebastian Games," after which he was made a "high priest for life of the Augustan house," that is, the imperial one. The inscription adds, "He was the first of the Achaeans to hold this office on account of his excellence and unsparing and most lavish generosity both to the divine family [*domus divina*] and to our colony" (IKorinthWest, no. 68).

It was his official duty to invite representatives from all cities in the province of Achaia to attend these annual celebrations. They came to Corinth to venerate the reigning emperor along with Corinthians whose right it was to attend by reason of their social status. As guests, such people had the right to attend the festive dinner each evening as part of the whole week's celebration. The precinct surrounding the large imperial temple was an appropriate location for these official imperial cult feasts. Those participating were expected to express their loyalty by drinking a toast to the divinity of the emperor during the feast (the word Greek *daimon* and the Latin *genius* were used to indicate divinity). A coin was issued declaring Nero to be *Gen. Col*, "the *genius* of the colony" (*Roman Provincial Coinage*, no. 1189). Paul refers to the cup of *demons and the table of demons in 1 Corinthians 10:20-22.

See also CORINTHIANS, FIRST LETTER TO THE; CORINTHIANS, SECOND LETTER TO THE; POLITICAL SYSTEMS; RELIGIONS, GRECO-ROMAN; URBAN SETTING OF PAUL'S CHURCHES.

BIBLIOGRAPHY. **A. Burnett, M. Amandry, and P. P. Repolle,** *Roman Provincial Coinage: From the Death of Caesar to the Death of Vitellius*, 2 vols. (London: British Museum Press, 2006); **A. D. Clarke,** "Another Corinthian Erastus Inscription," in *Secular and Christian Leadership* (Leiden: Brill, 1993), chap. 4; **D. E. Epstein,** *Personal Enmity in Roman Politics 218-43 B.C.* (London: Routledge, 1989); **D. Fishwick,** "*Genius* and *Numen*," in *The Imperial Cult in the Latin West*, vol. 2, *Studies in the Ruler Cult of the Western Provinces of the Roman Empire*, part 2.1 (Leiden: Brill,

2005), 373-87; **P. Garnsey,** *Social Status and Legal Privilege in the Roman Empire* (Oxford: Clarendon, 1970); **K. Hopkins,** *Conquerors and Slaves: Sociological Studies in Roman History* (Cambridge: Cambridge University Press, 1978); **R. A. Kearsley,** "Women in Public Life in the Roman East: Iunia Theodora, Claudia Metrodora and Phoebe, Benefactress of Paul," *TynBul* 50, no. 2 (1999): 189-211; **J. Murphy-O'Connor,** *St. Paul's Corinth: Texts and Archaeology* (Collegeville, MN: Liturgical Press, 2002); **Pausanias,** "Corinth: Book II," in *Description of Greece* (Cambridge, MA: W. Hermann and Harvard University Press, 1959); **D. G. Romano,** "Post-146 B. C. Land in Use in Corinth, and Planning of the Roman Colony of 44 B.C.," in *The Corinthia in the Roman Period,* ed. T. E. Gregory, JRASup 8 (Ann Arbor, MI: Journal of Roman Archaeology, 1994), 9-30; **R. S. Stroud,** *The Sanctuary of Demeter and Kore: The Inscriptions of Corinth* (Princeton, NJ: American School of Classical Studies at Athens, 2013); **C. K. Williams II,** "Roman Corinth as a Commercial Center," in *The Corinthia in the Roman Period,* ed. T. E. Gregory, JRASup 8 (Ann Arbor, MI: Journal of Roman Archaeology, 1994), 31-46; **B. W. Winter,** *After Paul Left Corinth: The Influence of Secular Ethics and Social Change* (Grand Rapids, MI: Eerdmans, 2001); idem, *Divine Honours for the Caesars: The First Christians' Responses* (Grand Rapids, MI: Eerdmans, 2015).

B. W. Winter

CORINTHIANS, FIRST LETTER TO THE

Among the extant letters of Paul, 1 Corinthians has been among the most influential from the beginning. Surviving references occur already among Christian writings of the late first century (1 Clem. 37.5; 47.1-3; 49.5) and early second century (Ign. *Eph.* 16.1; 18.1; Ign. *Rom.* 5.1). Today 1 Corinthians stands among the core group of letters whose Pauline authorship modern scholarship has virtually never doubted. Second only to Romans in length, 1 Corinthians includes unique material concerning several important Pauline theological motifs (his theology of the *cross, 1 Cor 1:18–3:23; the nature of spiritual *gifts, 1 Cor 12:1–14:40; an extended discussion of the general *resurrection, 1 Cor 15:12-58); the earliest extant testimony of the *Lord's Supper *tradition (1 Cor 11:23-26) and of the postresurrection appearances of Jesus (1 Cor 15:1-11); and some of the most memorable passages in the Pauline corpus (1 Cor 13:1-13). The letter is a pure illustration of the occasional nature of Paul's letters. Paul had founded the Corinthian *church himself (1 Cor 4:15) and according to Acts spent eighteen months among the Corinthians before his departure (Acts 18:11). In his absence things fell quickly into disorder. His response, 1 Corinthians, is a letter about their problems.

1. Introductory Issues.

1.1. The Authorship of 1 Corinthians. Like several other letters in the Pauline corpus (2 Cor 1:1; Phil 1:1; Col 1:1; Philem 1; cf. Gal 1:2), 1 Corinthians names a co-sender in the address line: "Sosthenes the brother" (1 Cor 1:1). Sosthenes is probably to be identified as the same man whom Acts describes as the "leader of the synagogue" in *Corinth. He apparently accompanied Paul when Paul left Corinth and was now present with him in *Ephesus (1 Cor 16:8). The extent to which co-senders of Paul's letters played a role also as coauthors is debated, a question whose relevance increases in the case of 1 Corinthians due to the presence of two passages in which the perspective shifts from the first-person singular into the first-person plural (1 Cor 1:18-31; 2:6-16).

1.2. The Founding of the Corinthian Church. According to Acts, Paul first came to Corinth during what is generally known as his second missionary journey (Acts 15:36–18:22). Having come directly from Athens (Acts 17:16-34), Paul arrived in Corinth and met up straightaway with two Jewish Christians named Priscilla and Aquila, with whom he took up residence, since they shared his trade as "tentmakers" (Acts 18:1-3). Acts depicts Paul's ministry in Corinth as highly successful. Following the conversion of Crispus, the leader of the synagogue and apparently a man of note, "many of the Corinthians" believed and were baptized (Acts 18:8). Being assured in a *vision that no one would lay a hand on him there, since the *Lord "has many people in this city" (Acts 18:10), Paul remained in Corinth for eighteen months, teaching God's word among the people (Acts 18:11). "The Jews," however, rose up against him and, dragging him before the governor, made a complaint that Paul was "persuading people to *worship *God in ways that are contrary to the *law" (Acts 18:13). The governor, however, dismissed the case as one concerning the Jewish law rather than civic affairs. Sosthenes, nevertheless, fell victim to the *violence of the crowds, thanks to his relationship with Paul. Wary of his safety, Paul bade Corinth farewell (Acts 18:12-18).

In his absence, others came to minister in Corinth. According to Acts, an eloquent Alexandrian man named Apollos so impressed the Christian leaders in Ephesus that they sent him on to Corinth, letters of recommendation in hand (Acts 18:24-28). Apollos's *ministry in Corinth is corroborated by 1 Corinthians. By the time Paul wrote the letter, Apollos had not only been to Corinth but had attracted a group of believers around himself (1 Cor 1:12; 3:5–4:6) though he had now departed (1 Cor 16:12). Whether Peter himself visited Corinth after Paul's departure is impossible to determine, though it seems that he too had become known to the Corinthians and attracted partisans of his own (1 Cor 1:12; cf. 1 Cor 3:22; 9:5). Apart from these ministers, the local Christians had recognized leaders of their own. The "household of Stephanas" had been among Paul's first converts in Corinth (1 Cor 1:16; 16:15). Paul's emphatic endorsement of Stephanas and his *household at the close of the letter (1 Cor 16:15-16) may suggest that, after being established in his role during Paul's time in Corinth, respect for his *leadership had more recently weakened.

1.3. The Church's Members. The church was diverse in every way. Both Acts and Paul's letters reveal that the church contained both Jews (Acts 18:2, 8, 17; 1 Cor 7:18) and *Gentiles (Acts 18:7-8; 1 Cor 7:18). Undoubtedly, the greater part consisted of Gentiles, for even apart from Acts' attestation that Paul turned in Corinth from the Jews to the Gentiles (Acts 18:6), Jewish names make up a minority of the named individuals in the church (see below). Many of the church's problems can only be explained reasonably in connection with Gentiles (meat sacrificed to idols, 1 Cor 8:1-11:1; or former *idolatry, 1 Cor 8:7; 12:2) or were more likely to arise in a Gentile cultural context (an infatuation with Greek "wisdom," 1 Cor 1:18–4:21; sexual immorality, 1 Cor 5:1-13; 6:12-20; appeal to pagan courts, 1 Cor 6:1-11; denial of a bodily resurrection, 1 Cor 15:12-58).

Culturally, Corinth was both Greek and Roman. Though geographically situated in Achaia (Greece), the city had been refounded in 146 BC as a Roman colony. Its political institutions were Roman and its social structures driven by Roman ideology. Six known members of the Corinthian church had Roman names (Crispus, Gaius, Fortunatus, Tertius, Quartus, and Titius Justus), and at least three of them may have been Roman citizens (Crispus, Gaius, Titius Justus). The city's Roman qualities, however, blended with its Greek cultural heritage to make it a truly Greco-Roman city. Greek remained the language of a majority of the population, and traditional Greek religious cults continued to flourish. Several members of the Corinthian church bore Greek names (Erastus, Stephanas, and possibly several individuals cited in Rom 16).

Socioeconomic stratification seems to have been greater among the Corinthian Christians than in other Pauline communities. Markers of above-average economic means (e.g., the ability to *travel, the possession of *slaves, the ability to provide financial support, Roman *citizenship, the holding of public office) are evident in connection with most of the Corinthians whom either Paul or Acts names explicitly, including Chloe (1 Cor 1:11), Phoebe (Rom 16:1-2), Crispus (Acts 18:8; 1 Cor 1:14), Stephanas (1 Cor 1:16; 16:15-16), Prisc(ill)a and Aquila (Acts 18:2-3; 1 Cor 16:19), Titius Justus (Acts 18:7), Gaius (1 Cor 1:14; Rom 16:23), and Erastus (Rom 16:23). While much controversy has surrounded the figure of Erastus, the balance of evidence leans in favor of the theory that he held the office of *aedile* in Corinth (Weiss, 139-41), one of the highest offices in the city's administration and a sure marker that he possessed means beyond a majority of people. Stratification between the church's higher- and lower-status members offers a sound explanation for some of the problems encountered in the letter (e.g., segregation according to social group at meetings for the Lord's Supper, 1 Cor 11:17-34; those who considered themselves "wise" may have been among the more educated, 1 Cor 1:18–3:23; see 1 Cor 6:5).

Estimates of the church's size vary between about forty and two hundred persons. The lower limit is set by a count of those whom Paul and Acts name explicitly, together with those in their households. Acts may suggest a much larger number in its depiction of great missionary success, and Paul's extended stay, in Corinth. Apollos's (and Peter's?) continuation of Paul's ministry after his departure would have augmented growth further. The church apparently met in cell groups in multiple houses and more rarely came together as a "whole church" (Rom 16:23; 1 Cor 14:23). While only a large house could accommodate more than forty or fifty people, a variety of rented public spaces could accommodate many more. The adscriptions in both 1 and 2 Corinthians suggest that the *faith had spread widely throughout the region, the first letter being addressed to "the church at Corinth . . . with all those *in every place*" (1 Cor 1:2) and the second to "the church at Corinth, with all the saints *in all of Achaia*" (2 Cor 1:1).

The believers in Corinth remained well integrated with secular society. To have dinner at the house of a nonbeliever was apparently a likely scenario (1 Cor 10:27-29). The presence of "outsiders"

(1 Cor 14:16, 23-24) and "unbelievers" (1 Cor 14:23-24) at the church's meetings for worship was to be expected. Some believers had nonbelieving spouses (1 Cor 7:12-16). The Corinthians' apparently peaceful coexistence with their nonbelieving neighbors probably explains why, in contrast to other letters, Paul's letters to the Corinthian church contain no hint of persecution against the church. No, the problems in the Corinthian church were internal.

1.4. Date and Provenance. External evidence supplies at least two important anchors for dating 1 Corinthians. According to Acts, upon arriving in Corinth Paul immediately encountered two Jews, named Priscilla and Aquila, who had been displaced to Corinth in Claudius's expulsion of Jews from Rome (Acts 18:1-2). Based on the evidence of Suetonius (*Claud.* 25.4), this event can be dated with some assurance to the year AD 49. Acts also indicates that the end of Paul's first visit coincided with Gallio's administration as governor of Achaia (Acts 18:12-18). Since governors served a term of exactly twelve months, and since epigraphical evidence puts Gallio in office in the year AD 52 (IG 7:1676; SIG 2:801), Paul's eighteen-month stay in Corinth must have taken place somewhere within the limits of AD 50 and 52.

Leaving Corinth after his meeting with Gallio, Paul returned to his home church in Antioch (Acts 18:22), before setting out again through Galatia and Phrygia (Acts 18:23), and then settling for two and a half years in Ephesus (Acts 19:1-41). It was from Ephesus that Paul wrote 1 Corinthians (1 Cor 16:8), after receiving news about the church from several sources: Chloe's people (1 Cor 1:11), a letter sent from the Corinthians (1 Cor 7:1), and a report from three Corinthians who delivered that letter (1 Cor 16:17).

Establishing a date for the composition of 1 Corinthians has to take several factors into account. First, sufficient time was needed for Paul to have returned to Antioch, to have ministered in Galatia and Phrygia, and then to have come to Ephesus. Second, sufficient time was needed for the conflict in Corinth to arise and for reports of it to have reached him through Chloe's people and the Corinthians' letter to him. Third, Paul had resided in Ephesus for months if not more than two years by the time he wrote, for not only had his ministry there already been fruitful (1 Cor 16:8-9) but he was now preparing to travel the Corinthians' way within only a few months (1 Cor 16:5-7). Finally, one must take into account that this was not Paul's first letter to the church but his second (his first, referenced in 1 Cor 5:9, has not survived); since 1 Corinthians reflects Paul's awareness of the Corinthians' response to the earlier letter, sufficient time is needed for him to have sent the letter and to have received their reply. If that letter too was written from Ephesus, 1 Corinthians would have been written well into his time in Ephesus. These factors establish a range most likely between AD 53 and 55 for the composition of 1 Corinthians, some two to four years after his departure. Chronologies that prioritize the data in Paul's letters over the data of Acts allow for an alternate dating, perhaps as early as the early 40s (Donfried, 72-75), though the earlier dating has found little acceptance among scholars.

The time of year during which the letter was composed can be determined roughly based on Paul's comments about his immediate *travel plans. He wishes to remain in Ephesus until Pentecost (1 Cor 16:8). Since Pentecost took place in spring, and the possibility of travel was limited during the winter months, the present letter was written and delivered most likely in the fall.

1.5. Audience and the Corinthian Slogans. The letter's prescript identifies the audience as the whole "church of God at Corinth" (1 Cor 1:2). Throughout the letter Paul addresses his audience almost exclusively in the second-person plural, without any explicit restriction of the audience. The letter, however, addresses a variety of problems, and it is evident that not everyone was equally in focus in every case. While Paul opposes factionalism in general and not any faction in particular (1 Cor 1:10-17), interpreters have agreed almost universally that one faction was probably more generative of the problems than others. In some cases, a single individual is identified as a culprit. At several points, Paul refers to an offender or offenders as "someone" (*tis*), "such a person" (*toioutos*), "some people" (*tines*). "Some" are "puffed up" (1 Cor 4:18), "someone" has had his father's wife (1 Cor 5:1), "some" have denied the resurrection of the dead (1 Cor 15:12). Paul frequently refers to "any such person" (1 Cor 1:15; 3:4, 12-17, 18). Some (or someone), but not all, of the church's members were suing each other (1 Cor 6:1-11). Those who considered themselves "wise," "spiritual," and "knowledgeable" surely made up a more exclusive group, for they appear to be denigrating others as "immature," "unspiritual," and "weak" (1 Cor 1:18-31; 2:6–3:3; 3:18-23; 8:1-11). Finally, Paul's endorsement of the leadership of Stephanas and his household (1 Cor 16:15-16) likely suggests that they at least were not a primary target of the criticism. Whether or not the antagonists in Corinth represented a well-defined group, it seems likely that a group of self-proclaimed "wise" and "knowledgeable" people, perhaps gathering around a single influential individual, were behind many of the problems.

First Corinthians is unique in that it contains what appear to be citations of claims made by the audience, or rather, by some of them. While these slogans, as they are often called, are not marked as quotations in the original Greek, the context and various other clues in the text bring these to light at many points throughout 1 Corinthians 6–15. Paul cites these slogans in 1 Corinthians 6:12a, c, 13a-b, 18b; 7:1; 8:1b, 4, 5a, 6; 8:8a-b; and at 1 Corinthians 15:12, he cites the Corinthians ("some") in the form of an indirect report. These slogans are vital for understanding the nature of the problems that occasioned the letter.

2. The History of Scholarship.

2.1. Explaining the Corinthian Factions. The "divisions" referenced in 1 Corinthians 1:10-12 (Paul describes the Corinthians as dividing their loyalties between Paul, Apollos, Cephas, and *Christ) have been a dominant focus of Corinthians scholarship since the early nineteenth century. The dynamics of the rivalries have been variously explained.

(1) Although Paul references four individuals who are respectively favored by the Corinthians, scholarship has commonly conjectured that the rivalry was primarily only two-sided. (a) Building on the work of J. E. C. Schmidt (1801), F. C. Baur proposed that the church had separated into four parties, but that the parties of Paul and Apollos had formed an alliance, and likewise the parties of Cephas and Christ. According to Baur, these alliances formed over a conflict between Paul's (Gentile) law-free *gospel and Peter's (Jewish) law-focused gospel. (b) The two-sided view of the conflict remained popular through the early and mid-twentieth century. During this period, several important studies took the view that the conflict existed primarily between the Paul group and a Christ group, and that the latter consisted of spiritual enthusiasts (Lütgert) or Gnostics (Schmithals). (c) Since the final third of the twentieth century, it has been most common to view the Paul and Apollos groups not (as Baur proposed) as allies but as the primary participants in the conflict, and the conflict as one stemming from the Corinthians' varied assessments of these ministers' rhetorical abilities (Litfin). In this configuration, the Cephas and Christ parties are usually understood to be inventions of Paul, contrived for rhetorical purposes.

(2) A three-party view remains common, with the slogan "I am of Christ" being understood not as the slogan of a Christ party but as Paul's personal response to the slogans of the Paul, Apollos, and Cephas parties (Prothro). (3) Some have taken 1 Corinthians 1:12 as a straightforward description of four real parties (Barrett). (4) Over the last several decades, it has become increasingly common to understand the parties as simplifications of a more complex situation, in which parties were not so sharply defined and may not have existed as such at all (Dahl). Those who take the no-party view ground their perspective above all in the fact that Paul makes no mention of a Cephas or a Christ party after 1 Corinthians 1:12; that Paul nowhere defines the parties in terms of specific, clashing theological viewpoints; and that Paul does not single out any particular group for correction but rather confronts the entire church.

The common thread in all of these positions has been the view that 1 Corinthians 1–4 is essentially apologetic (defensive) and that Paul aims to restore his authority and control over the community against one or more factions or against a drifting church.

Paul's mention of *baptism immediately following reference to the rivalries (1 Cor 1:13-16) has led many to believe that baptism played a role in determining the church's allegiances, and that the Corinthians had vowed allegiance to the particular minister who had baptized them, perhaps believing that baptism united them with the minister in some mystical way (Chester, 295). Others have contested this view, pointing out that Paul appeals to the Corinthians' baptism only as a reminder of their unity: they ought not to be divided since they were all baptized, as one, into Christ (Mitchell, 201).

Because Paul's discussion of the divisions (1 Cor 1:10-17) belongs within a larger unit (1 Cor 1:10–4:21) focused on his denunciation of the "wisdom of the world" (1 Cor 1:20; 3:19) and his presentation of the—fundamentally different—"wisdom of God" (1 Cor 1:21, 30), scholarship has taken the virtually unanimous view that the matter of *wisdom was the predominant problem contributing to the divisions. Thus, most reconstructions of the letter's occasion are built on efforts to understand the Corinthians' brand of "wisdom." The theories are numerous and for the most part can be identified as trends representative of particular periods of scholarship (see below).

2.2. The Integrity and Coherence of the Letter. The relationship between 1 Corinthians 1–4 and the remaining twelve chapters of the letter is not easy to understand. The tight coherence of the first four chapters as a discrete unit has led some to conjecture that these chapters constituted what was originally a separate letter, compiled with other material to form 1 Corinthians (J. Weiss). In recent decades, however, scholarship has almost unanimously affirmed 1 Corinthians' original integrity (Mitchell). The unity of the letter is then explained in any of three ways: (1) 1 Corinthians 1–4 establishes a theological preface, in light of which Paul treats the problems that follow; (2) the Corinthians' wisdom as referenced in 1 Corinthians 1–4 generated, in part or in whole, the problems treated in the chapters that follow; or (3) the letter consists in a collection of topics that do not all relate to one another in a coherent way.

2.3. Theological, Religious, and Philosophical Influences. A perennial goal in the modern history of interpretation has been to explain the "content" of the Corinthians' wisdom (1 Cor 1:10–4:21). In this regard, several points have been thought to have special relevance: that the Corinthians portrayed themselves not only as "wise" (1 Cor 1:18–2:16; 3:18-23) but also as "perfect" (1 Cor 2:6-16), "spiritual" (1 Cor 2:6-16; 12:1–14:40), and "knowledgeable" (1 Cor 8:1-11); that they possessed great enthusiasm for manifestations of the Spirit (1 Cor 2:6-16; 12:1–14:40); and that they apparently tended toward an anthropological dualism (e.g., 1 Cor 15:12-58) and indifference toward matters of the *body (1 Cor 6:12-20; 8:1–11:1).

The Corinthians' perspective has in turn been thought to explain the rise of many of the church's problems as addressed in the chapters that follow: their justification of illicit sexual conduct (1 Cor 5:1-11; 6:12-20) and indiscriminate eating (1 Cor 6:13-14; 8:1–11:1), their infatuation with spiritual gifts (1 Cor 12:1–14:40), and their rejection of a bodily resurrection (1 Cor 15:12-58), among other things.

During the late twentieth century, several scholars advocated the view that the Corinthians' wisdom was not a product of direct external influences but rather consisted in an overrealized *eschatology, stemming from the Corinthians' own distortion of Paul's teaching (Käsemann, 125-26; Thiselton 1978). It has been more common, however, to attribute the Corinthians' wisdom to external influences. Through the early and mid-twentieth century, scholars commonly explained their wisdom as a syncretistic blend of Greek religious and philosophical elements (Conzelmann, 14-16). Others posited more specific influences. The view that the Corinthians' wisdom was "Gnostic" in nature persisted until the final third of the twentieth century (Schmithals), when the existence of first-century Gnosticism was finally disproven (Yamauchi).

Following the demise of the Gnostic thesis, and still up to the present, many have sought to demonstrate that the Corinthians' wisdom betrays distinct influences from Hellenistic Judaism in the vein of Philo of Alexandria (Horsley), or else from one or another of the Hellenistic philosophies, including Epicureanism (Tomlin), Cynicism (Downing), or Stoicism (Brookins 2014). Critical in assessing these options is the relevance of Paul's description of wisdom as a "Greek" pursuit (1 Cor 1:22), along with the technical ties that "wisdom" language had developed in the first-century world in reference to *philosophy (*sophia*, *sapientia*) and the philosopher (*sophos*, *sapiens*), especially in connection with Stoicism.

That a common intellectual culture underlay the many disparate religious and philosophical systems of the time may explain why all of these theses offer potential, if only partial, explanations for the Corinthians' wisdom. Genealogical relationships between systems were not always direct, and elements could be combined from various places to form new patterns of thought. This point does not of necessity prove the view that the Corinthians' wisdom reflected only a generic *Hellenism, for the possibility of more diffuse and indirect influence in some cases does not exclude the possibility of more direct borrowing in others, nor does it dissolve all entities into the same thing. Thus, two points continue to be subject to debate: first, whether specific influences on the Corinthians can be determined, and second, the extent to which the Corinthians introduced their own innovations.

2.4. Social Factors. From the 1970s onward, scholars have given less attention to religious and philosophical influences in the church and more to its social dynamics. (1) Gerd Theissen has shown that socioeconomic disparity (see 1.3 above) offers a possible explanation for both the church's disagreements over the eating of idol-meat (1 Cor 8:1–11:1) and their segregation at the Lord's Supper (1 Cor 11:17-34). (2) Studies have pointed to various aspects of "secular" culture that could have contributed to the church's problems. For instance, the Corinthians' lawsuits may have been motivated by inheritance disputes (1 Cor 6:1-11), as were common in the first-century world (Peppard). It has been proposed that the church's factions (1 Cor 1:10–4:21) were rooted in an application of secular criteria in assessing leaders (Clarke): the church evaluated Paul and other ministers according to the criteria of eloquence, education, power, *wealth, and in general social status as measured by the standards of the world. By attaching themselves to leaders who were the most educated or most powerful, or of the highest social status, the Corinthians sought in turn to enhance their own prestige. Other studies have interpreted the Corinthians' relationship with church ministers through various social institutions, including the patron-client system, *honor and shame orientation, the conventions of *friendship, or self-support practices.

(3) A renewed interest in ancient rhetoric among biblical scholars in the 1980s spurred a new theory that the Corinthians' wisdom was not so much a matter of "content" as of "form" (Litfin; Winter 2002). Specifically, the Corinthians were obsessed with eloquence (or wisdom) and were for that reason drawn to Apollos, whom Acts describes as "learned" (*logios*, Acts 18:24). While the theory harks back to aspects of earlier studies, it separates wisdom from Greek philosophy and religion in a way unseen in those studies. (4) Other studies take a more "political" view of the situation. According to Larry Welborn (1997), in 1 Corinthians 1–4, Paul faced a power struggle. The Corinthians declared allegiance to rival ministers, whom they supported in the fashion of clients and citizens who were partisans of their chosen political candidates. According to this perspective, the language of 1 Corinthians 1–4 constructs a conception of the church as a new commonwealth, with its own Christ-centered political theology as its constitution. (5) Straddling the line between theological and social explanations are studies that view the church's controversies as rooted in the ideologies of elite culture, with its philosophical assumptions and social values (Martin).

2.5. Text- and Audience-Centered Approaches. Over the last thirty years, a number of studies have focused on the meaning of the text as conceived independently of its background. According to one influential study (Mitchell), 1 Corinthians takes the form of a "deliberative speech" aimed at persuading the Corinthian church to reunify, and the content of the letter resembles contemporary political rhetoric used to address discord in the city. Others have sought to locate Paul's rhetoric in relation to contemporary institutions such as that of education, but with a view to audience reception, or how the Corinthians would have heard his words, and not a view to the letter's background (White). Still other studies have focused on Paul's self-portrayal (Welborn 2005).

The rationale for many such studies is the supposition that Paul's description of the situation does not in every way correspond with the real situation and that his representation of the audience may not always be fair. In this regard, some studies, including several coming from a feminist perspective (Wire), have approached the letter through a stronger hermeneutic of suspicion, presupposing a misrepresentation of the audience and seeking to redeem the audience by reading against the grain of Paul's rhetoric.

2.6. Conclusions. More integration is needed both methodologically and exegetically to provide coherence to the vast array of interpretive insights proposed across the history of modern interpretation, especially since the rise of studies oriented more toward the Corinthians' social world. Studies in the social trajectory have veered to varying degrees away from an interest in the Corinthians' "wisdom," and while studies in this vein most often presuppose some version of the theory that the Corinthians' wisdom was related to rhetoric or eloquence, it is not always clear how the various social lines of interest integrate to explain the tight connection between the divisions and wisdom in the letter. Proposals for social explanations are often presented as supplementing explanations focused on the religious or philosophical aspects of the Corinthians' wisdom, though at many points the social explanations really constitute irreconcilable alternatives, and some decision must be made as to which explanation should be preferred.

Relatedly, more careful nuance is needed in describing the relationship between theological and social approaches. Theological and social factors neither exclude one another nor simply supplement one another, but are themselves embedded in one another. Finally, recent studies have been more helpful in providing a deep description of the Corinthians' cultural backgrounds than in close analysis of the text. Consequently, the hypothetical reconstruction has sometimes taken precedence over the detailed exegetical work needed to test these theories.

3. The Contents of 1 Corinthians.

Apart from sporadic challenges throughout much of the twentieth century, it is now the virtually unanimous position of scholarship that 1 Corinthians represents a single, unified letter. The letter, however, does not address a single, specific problem but rather a variety of problems, which are sometimes but not always closely related.

Scholars have offered various explanations of the letter's structure. Some find the logic of organization in Paul's use of his sources: having learned about the church's divisions from "Chloe's people" (1 Cor 1:11) he addresses their divisions in 1 Corinthians 1:10–4:21; and having received a letter from the Corinthians about various issues (1 Cor 7:1), he responds point-by-point throughout much of 1 Corinthians 7:1–16:12, so that the order of issues in his letter is dictated by the order of topics in theirs. Others have attempted to outline the letter according to the traditional parts of an ancient speech, with varying results. Others offer outlines based on the theology of the letter. No theory of the letter's organization has found universal acceptance.

While the logic of the letter's organization is more difficult to explain, the main units of the letter are readily identifiable: 1 Corinthians 1:1-9; 1:10–4:21; 5:1–6:20; 7:1-40; 8:1–11:1; 11:2–14:40; 15:1-58; 16:1-24.

3.1. 1 Corinthians 1:1-9. Hints of Paul's reasons for writing appear already in the letter's prescript (1 Cor 1:1-9). His description of the church as "sanctified" and called to be "saints" (1 Cor 1:2) anticipates the moral problems with which most of the letter is occupied, particularly those involving sexual immorality (1 Cor 5:1-11; 6:12-20). In thanking God for all that he has "given" the Corinthians in Christ Jesus, and thanking him that they have been "enriched in him" in word and knowledge and that they "do not lack any spiritual gift" (1 Cor 1:4-7), Paul alludes to the Corinthians' pretensions of *spirituality and their emphasis on charismatic gifts (1 Cor 2:6-16; 12:1–14:40). His addressing of the letter not only to the whole church in Corinth but to "all those in every place who call upon the *name of the Lord" (1 Cor 1:3), and his reminder of the Corinthians' corporate "*fellowship" with Jesus Christ (1 Cor 1:9), emphasizes the oneness of the many churches that exist throughout the region, and anticipates and indirectly challenges that the Corinthians are divided among themselves.

3.2. 1 Corinthians 1:10–4:21. The first unit of the letter's body puts front and center the problem of the church's "factions" (1 Cor 1:11). Some of the Corinthians say, "I am of Paul," but others "I am of Apollos," or "I am of Cephas," or "I am of Christ" (1 Cor 1:12).

The unity of 1 Corinthians 1:10–4:21 suggests that the various recurring themes that appear here relate in some way to the divisions as well as to one another. While wisdom features as the most prominent theme, the themes of status and boasting are also prominent. Read as a whole, a coherent picture of the problem in Corinth arises. There were some in Corinth who claimed to be wise and, in their wisdom, better than others in the community. The wise made up but one of the factions, perhaps claiming that they received their wisdom from their teacher, Paul (distorted as their interpretation was). Those who did not belong to the group of the wise fell into groups of their own and attached themselves by name with alternative teachers.

After introducing the problem of divisions in 1 Corinthians 1:10-12, Paul immediately raises the matter of baptism (1 Cor 1:13-17a). The church's divisions, he suggests, run contrary to the church's *salvation experience. His logic begins from the premise that the church is one, since all were baptized into fellowship with Christ. If, however, the church is one, claiming allegiance to Paul is valid only if the church's oneness in fact arose from baptism into Paul. Of course the church was not baptized into Paul, so their divisions are absurd.

In 1 Corinthians 1:17b, Paul transitions into a discussion of the main theme of the unit, and the main cause of the church's divisions, that is, wisdom. Here Paul poses a contrast that he will elaborate in several subsections across 1 Corinthians 1:17b–3:23. The contrast puts on one side what he calls the "wisdom of the world" (1 Cor 1:20; 3:19; cf. 1 Cor 1:21) or "human wisdom" (1 Cor 2:5, 13), and on the other side, the "wisdom of God" (1 Cor 1:21, 24; 2:7). Paul has in mind the "content" of wisdom, understood in terms of value systems and the logic that underlies them. The wisdom of the world elevates the value of status, especially status as measured by ordinary social criteria, such as fame, esteem, importance, and achievement. Through this lens the gospel appears as "foolishness" (1 Cor 1:18, 21, 23; 2:14; 3:19), for it claims that God approved a man executed in the most shameful way possible (1 Cor 1:23-24) and that God elected those who were foolish, weak, and without any value by the standards of the world. Christ embodied God's wisdom not only in his death for the unworthy but also by demonstrating a pattern of life characterized not by the pursuit of his own honor, but by his renunciation of honor for the benefit of others. The logic of the cross thus reverses the value system of the world: what the world values, God does not, and what the world does not value, God does.

In 1 Corinthians 2:1-5, Paul reminds the Corinthians that he too lives after the cruciform pattern—or the way of Jesus and the cross—and puts himself forward as an example. When he came to the Corinthians he did not promote himself or advertise his credentials. Preaching the gospel message of lowliness, he conducted himself with lowliness. This was the gospel in which they had put their faith.

As Paul continues, he emphasizes that, because this message is counterintuitive with respect to the world's wisdom or way of thinking, one comes to see it as valid only through a transformation of the mind (1 Cor 2:6-16). Responsible for this transformation is the Spirit. The "spiritual" person (1 Cor 2:15), then, is not the one who advertises and seeks credit for their high level of spiritual achievement, but the person who becomes "less" so that others may become "more." Ironically, the "spiritual" people in Corinth are therefore not spiritual, but "carnal" and "immature" (1 Cor 3:1).

Paul returns in 1 Corinthians 3:4 to the church's divided loyalties. They claim to belong some to Paul, some to Apollos. This reflects a misunderstanding about their leaders. Specifically, they have misunderstood the *roles* of Paul and Apollos. Pointing to themselves again as human examples of God's wisdom, Paul observes that he and Apollos are only "*servants" (1 Cor 3:5), living embodiments of *cruciformity. Moreover, they serve God not competitively, but in cooperation with each other, that is, as a unity (1 Cor 3:6-9).

This is God's wisdom. Using a metaphor of building, Paul now issues a warning to anyone who would distort God's wisdom by "building upon" the work already done by God's "*co-workers" Paul and Apollos (1 Cor 3:9). This subsequent building, as 1 Corinthians 3:18-23 indicates, is the introduction of wisdom contrary to the wisdom of God, the human wisdom that elevates the value of status and boasts in self. Having denounced this wisdom, in 1 Corinthians 3:21 Paul solemnly enjoins the Corinthians not to boast in their humanity. This injunction echoes Jeremiah 9:23 but also parallels a wider OT theme that humanity should not boast in themselves but in God. Thus Paul concludes that all that the Corinthians have, including the service of God's ministers to them, they have received from God, for they belong to God.

In the final chapter of the unit (1 Cor 4:1-21) Paul again appeals to his own example, as well as that of Apollos. Paul and Apollos are Christ's "assistants and stewards" (1 Cor 4:1). The Corinthians, like them, should have no concern for status in the eyes of humanity. The final judge of status will be God (1 Cor 4:1-5). With that, Paul reveals that the purpose of all his discussion about himself and Apollos (1 Cor 3:5–4:5) has been to offer the Corinthians an example (1 Cor 4:6). The Corinthians boast that they are better than others (1 Cor 4:8-10); Paul and the apostles live after the cruciform pattern of Christ, being weak, powerless, hungry, and reviled, and having all the qualities that the world finds contemptible.

In 1 Corinthians 4:14-21, Paul brings the first unit of the letter to a close. Reminding the Corinthians that he is their spiritual "father" (1 Cor 4:15), he makes an appeal, for the first time explicitly, for the Corinthians to imitate his example (1 Cor 4:16), that is, his example as an embodiment of the wise message of the cross and of lowliness. Some follow a different pattern and are "puffed up" (1 Cor 4:18-19) in themselves. He will discover such people when he visits.

3.3. 1 Corinthians 5:1–6:20. With a distinct change in topic in 1 Corinthians 5:1, the letter moves to a new unit, consisting of three main sections (1 Cor 5:1-13; 6:1-11; 6:12-20). Tying these sections together are the themes of sexual immorality (1 Cor 5:1; 6:9, 18), boundaries between insiders and outsiders (1 Cor 5:2, 9-13; 6:1-6), and *judgment within the community (5:2-5, 12-13; 6:1-5).

The first (1 Cor 5:1-13) and third (1 Cor 6:12-20) sections share a focus on sexual immorality. In 1 Corinthians 5:1-13 Paul rebukes the community for allowing a man to continue a sexual relationship with his stepmother (his "father's wife," 1 Cor 5:1). This a community matter, for the impurity of the man contaminates the church as a whole. Thus Paul advises a pronouncement of church *discipline, expelling the man from the community both to restore *purity to the community and to restore the man to repentance.

Paul returns to the issue of sexual immorality in 1 Corinthians 6:12-20, though the situation is now different. The statement repeated in 1 Corinthians 6:12a and c, "All things are permitted for me," is a slogan of the Corinthians. The Corinthians had used the slogan to justify loose sexual behavior consisting in the free use of prostitutes. In 1 Corinthians 6:13a-b Paul cites another Corinthians slogan, this one claiming *freedom in matters of diet. In 1 Corinthians 6:18b a third slogan appears, claiming that "every *sin that a person commits is committed apart from the body." The second and third slogans clarify that the Corinthians' grounding for the first was theological and anthropological. They believed, perhaps by virtue of their new "spiritual" nature (1 Cor 2:15), that the body and what one did with it, whether in *food or in *sex, was no longer morally relevant. One committed sins only with the mind or intellect.

Between these two sections sits a discrete section concerned with the matter of lawsuits (1 Cor 6:1-11).

Someone in the community had issued a suit against another with appeal to the secular courts. This action reflected a failure in the community—who on the last day will participate in judging both the world (1 Cor 6:2) and angels (1 Cor 6:3)—to serve even as judges between right and wrong among those who belong within the community of the faithful. The problem, then, is twofold: first, the committing of injustices against one another and retaliating for them; second, the failure of the community to arbitrate on behalf of its members and their abdication of responsibility to nonbelievers.

3.4. 1 Corinthians 7:1-40. After countering the position that believers possess wide sexual freedom (1 Cor 6:12-20), Paul now addresses the opposite position: that "it is good for a man not to touch a woman" (1 Cor 7:1). The topic, and the wording, comes from a letter sent to Paul by the Corinthians themselves ("now, concerning the letter that you wrote"). Since the slogans in 1 Corinthians 6:12a, c, and 1 Corinthians 7:1b reflect opposing positions on sexual matters, the second may derive from a separate group and represent a reaction to the position of the first. They now inquire of Paul regarding the disagreement.

This citation opens up an extended discussion about the value of *marriage (1 Cor 7:1-40). The unit divides into three main sections.

The first (1 Cor 7:1-16) discusses the issue of marriage in relation to groups of varying marital statuses. Paul's response to the slogan in 1 Corinthians 7:1 reveals that he agrees, with some qualification. Paul emphasizes that celibacy, his personal preference, is in general a more ideal lifestyle for believers (for reasons that will be spelled out more clearly in 1 Cor 7:25-35). His position, however, is not articulated in terms of absolutes. While it is better not to marry, marriage can help restrain sexual misconduct by providing a context for more controlled satisfaction; while it is better not to marry, believing couples should not divorce; and while Jesus himself forbade divorce, divorce is permissible in cases of believers living in disharmony with a nonbelieving spouse.

The second section (1 Cor 7:17-24) shifts into a brief excursus on social roles parallel to those of the married/unmarried: circumcised/uncircumcised (1 Cor 7:18-19) and slave/free (1 Cor 7:21-22). These two pairs illustrate the central principle that drives Paul's advice on marriage. The point is not "remain as you are" (though that is sometimes a fitting course of action), but only that roles within the social domain of the world are of lesser importance than one's status as a believer, and if inordinately prioritized can distract from this more paramount status. The two analogies to marriage status, then, do not exactly run parallel to each other. While the circumcised/uncircumcised should make no effort to change their status, on balance, it is preferable to be free than to be a slave, and "if you are *able* to be free," Paul says, "rather take the opportunity to do so."

Returning to the issue of marriage, the final section of the unit (1 Cor 7:25-40) explores several further marital issues before offering a final recapitulative summary of Paul's personal conviction about the impracticality of marriage. Here it becomes further evident that Paul's advice regarding social roles is driven not so much by the ideal of maintaining the social status quo as by the practical advantages or disadvantages of one's respective status. While Paul continues to acknowledge that there are situations in which marriage is permissible (1 Cor 7:28, 36-37), he maintains a strong conviction that for most people it will introduce unnecessary troubles (1 Cor 7:26, 28, 35) and distract from a single-minded commitment to Christ (1 Cor 7:32-33).

The final verses of the chapter encapsulate the kind of balance, but also strong leaning toward celibacy, that characterizes Paul's whole discussion: marriage is good, but celibacy is better (1 Cor 7:38, 40).

3.5. 1 Corinthians 8:1–11:1. A transitional formula in 1 Corinthians 8:1 indicates a shift to a new topic: "Now concerning idol-meat" (1 Cor 8:1a). As in 1 Corinthians 7:1b, discussion opens with the citation of a Corinthian slogan: "We know that we all have *knowledge" (1 Cor 8:1; cf. 1 Cor 7:1b). This knowledge—received presumably through faith in Christ—consists in knowing that one has "freedom" (1 Cor 8:9). On the basis of this knowledge, some within the community have claimed that they have "freedom" to eat idol-meat; those with convictions against eating idol-meat the knowledgeable Corinthians disparage as "weak."

Paul's response in 1 Corinthians 8:1–11:1 consists of three main parts. The first part (1 Cor 8:1-13) issues a direct response to the slogan cited in 1 Corinthians 8:1. This section alternates between Paul's own words and several additional Corinthian slogans (1 Cor 8:4, 5a, 6, 8a-b). Paul's response shows that, as in his discussion of marriage, he appears to agree with the sloganeers in part. Believers do have "knowledge"; idols are in fact "nothing," since there is only one God (1 Cor 8:4, 6); food in itself has no bearing on one's status before God (1 Cor 8:8a-b). Yet, knowledge without love puffs the knower up in arrogance (1 Cor 8:1-3) and puts a principle before people (1 Cor 8:7-12). Some of the Corinthians eat idol-meat on grounds that they "know" that they have the freedom to do so, but in doing so they cause those whose conscience tells them it is wrong to conform to the same behavior, thus doing what they feel to be sin. Paul asserts that it is worse to be knowledgeable and use the freedom that derives from that knowledge to destroy the faith of others than, lacking this knowledge, to be "weak." Paul himself would rather conform to the choices of the "weak," so as not to offend, or worse, destroy them (1 Cor 8:13).

The unit then carries into a brief interruption presenting positive (1 Cor 9:1-23) and negative (1 Cor 10:1-13; or cautionary, 1 Cor 9:24-27) examples that illustrate Paul's views about idol-meat. Paul first presents himself as an example. He has freedom to eat and drink (certain things), the right to bring a wife along on his missions, and a right to receive support for his ministry (1 Cor 9:1-17). Dwelling on his right to support, he explains that he has waived that right because, should he have exploited it, some might see his preaching of the gospel as a mercenary endeavor, thus calling his motives into question and hurting the success of his ministry. This section is no digression but an example of the principle that Paul says ought to drive one's use of freedom with regard to idol-meat. Just because one can does not mean that one should. The practical consequences are more important than the principle. One must do what is best for others.

The next two examples are cautionary. Believers must remain wary of the possibility of falling. Paul knows that he himself must remain faithful, for he may still be disqualified (1 Cor 9:24-27). The example of *Israel (1 Cor 10:1-13) brings the illustration back closer to the central topic, that of idol-meat. Despite the spiritual blessings Israel had received, many committed idolatry and fell in destruction.

Continuing in the vein of idolatry, 1 Corinthians 10:14–11:1 completes the circle back to the topic of idol-meat. Those who eat idol-meat endanger not only other believers, but even themselves. While an idol in itself is lifeless, and indeed "nothing" (1 Cor 8:4), it is possible to become so comfortable with idol-meat that one finds oneself banqueting at a feast dedicated to foreign divinities and in fact to "*demons" (1 Cor 10:14-22). The final words of the unit reiterate the idea of the opening section: one must act not according to one's right but according to what is beneficial to others (1 Cor 10:23-31).

3.6. 1 Corinthians 11:2–14:40. Holding together the next main unit is a thematic focus on the church's official gatherings for worship. Treated here are three separate issues: gender and head-covering practices (1 Cor 11:2-16), practice of the Lord's Supper (1 Cor 11:17-34), and the exercise of spiritual gifts (1 Cor 12:1-31; 14:1-40), with a brief interlude comparing spiritual gifts and *love (1 Cor 13:1-13).

The particulars of the church's problem in 1 Corinthians 11:2-16 are obscure. Paul's primary point is that, in contexts of worship (involving praying and prophesying), male and female should be differentiated by what covers the head. Less certain is the nature of the head covering. The covering is either some kind of synthetic covering, like a veil, or the hair of the head itself (the language is vague in the original Greek). From Paul's discussion, one may infer that the church, apparently the *women, were not observing the distinction. Paul supports his directive for distinction with five separate arguments: an argument from the order of *creation (1 Cor 11:3), an argument from cultural conceptions of honor and shame (1 Cor 11:4-6), a second argument from the order of creation (1 Cor 11:7-10), an argument from nature (1 Cor 11:13-14), and an argument from the practice of the churches (1 Cor 11:16). While Paul's arguments indicate that he objected to their practices on theological principle ("nature teaches that it is shameful for a man to wear his hair long, and for a woman to wear her hair short," 1 Cor 11:14-15; the arguments from natural order in 1 Cor 11:3, 7-10), he must also have been concerned about the practical consequences. If 1 Corinthians 12–14 is any indication, the issue of head covering had generated disorder and disunity in the church's gatherings.

With a statement of disapproval in 1 Corinthians 11:17 ("I do not commend you"), Paul transitions to the church's next problem in their gatherings. When they gather for the Lord's Supper—in which they share a full meal—they are divided. Some, perhaps arriving early, consumed all that was available before others had an opportunity to take their portion (1 Cor 11:17-22). Paul addresses the problem by rehearsing the Lord's Supper tradition as it was handed down by those who shared the Last Supper with Jesus (1 Cor 11:23-26). He finds in the tradition a warning (1 Cor 11:27-34). Employing the term *body* in multiple senses, he observes that those who take the bread (body of Jesus) without first examining themselves and without properly "discerning the body" (the church) eat and drink to their own judgment. That is, they are aware neither that *they are a part of* the body of Christ / the church nor that the body/bread that they eat represents *the corporate entity of the church*. They do not, then, understand that the elements represent a unified entity, the body/church/Christ. Echoing 1 Corinthians 11:21, Paul's concluding words in 1 Corinthians 11:33 show that the divisions are quite physical. When gathering to eat the Lord's Supper, they should "wait for each other." The irony is that divisions manifest themselves in a ritual that centers on unity.

Paul gives lengthy treatment to the next, and final, issue that demanded attention in the church's gatherings for worship (1 Cor 12:1–14:40). Recalling 1 Corinthians 2:6-16, this unit depicts the Corinthians as enthusiasts for the "Spirit" (see 1 Cor 12:1; 14:12), obsessed especially with the spiritual gift of "*tongues" (which appears in all three lists of spiritual gifts: 1 Cor 12:8-10, 28-30; 13:1-3). Paul's discussion in 1 Corinthians 12:1-31 suggests that their perspective was misguided on at least two counts: they failed to recognize that all believers possess spiritual gifts, each as the Spirit has given (1 Cor 12:4-11, 28-30); and they failed to recognize that each member, equipped with their own gift, plays a part in contributing to the well-being of the whole "body of Christ" (1 Cor 12:12-27). As Paul picks up again in 1 Corinthians 14:1-40, further problems with the Corinthians' orientation toward the gifts become evident. They had ordered the gifts into a de facto hierarchy, with tongues at the top, a hierarchy that replicated the kind of two-tier classification of believers seen in 1 Corinthians 1:18–4:21 ("spiritual" vs. "unspiritual," "mature" vs. "immature") and 1 Corinthians 8:1-13 (the knowledgeable and the "weak").

In a digression placed between 1 Corinthians 12:31 and 1 Corinthians 14:1, Paul offers an alternative hierarchy. Better than any of the gifts is love, first, because love gives the gifts their value (1 Cor 13:1-3), and second, because love is permanent and the gifts only temporary (1 Cor 13:8-13). If one wanted to compare gifts, moreover, one would find that *prophecy is "greater" than tongues, since the former builds up the whole church body, whereas the latter builds up only oneself (1 Cor 14:1-19). In the unit's final point of emphasis (1 Cor 14:20-36), Paul urges that all manifestations of the Spirit should be carried out in an orderly way, not in a confused din of noises, both to ensure that one's messages for the church are intelligible and able to edify, and to present a good impression to outsiders and attract them to the faith. The conclusion to the unit summarizes two of the overarching principles of the discussion: all gifts serve a purpose (1 Cor 14:39) and all things must be done in an orderly fashion (1 Cor 14:40).

3.7. 1 Corinthians 15:1-58. Paul saves for last the critical issue of the general resurrection. As he reports in 1 Corinthians 15:12, "some" of the Corinthians were saying that "there is no resurrection of the dead." With this they denied not the resurrection of Christ but the general resurrection, an eschatological event in which God's people—from a Pharisaical perspective the Jewish people (Acts 23:6-8), and from Paul's perspective Christ's people—would participate.

Comprising 1 Corinthians 15:1-58, this final unit divides into three parts. First (1 Cor 15:1-11), Paul reviews the tradition that he had handed over to the Corinthians on his visit, and that he in turn had received from others, regarding the resurrection of Jesus. The tradition takes the form of a creed, whose content depicts the resurrection as an empirical event that happened in history and that can be confirmed by a host of witnesses to whom Jesus appeared, including Paul himself.

By reaffirming the early Christian consensus about the resurrection, shared by missionaries and their converts alike, Paul establishes a common reference point that he will leverage next in a case against the Corinthians' denial of the general resurrection (1 Cor 15:12-34). In the first place, the Corinthian deniers are inconsistent: if Christ has been raised from the dead, as they agree he has been, then they ought also to agree that believers will be raised, since the two events are integrally connected (1 Cor 15:12-28). Moreover, if Christ has not been raised from the dead, then that renders pointless both the Corinthians' practice of baptism "on behalf of the dead" and Paul's risking of life and limb in proclaiming the gospel (1 Cor 15:29-34).

Paul last challenges the theological and philosophical grounds on which the Corinthians have staked their position (1 Cor 15:35-58). Their objection, as the question in 1 Corinthians 15:35 makes evident, is grounded in their thinking about the nature of the human body. Perhaps a part of a person will survive into a blessed afterlife in the presence of God, but this is impossible for the body, subject as it is to corruption and decay. Paul answers their objection not by disputing their claim about the body but by posing a distinction between the present body and the one to come. Just as there are many kinds of bodies in the created order, so also are there different types of human bodies. Yes, the present body is corruptible, shameful, and weak, but the resurrection body will be incorruptible, glorious, and strong. The first kind of body is like that of the first man, *Adam; the latter will be like that of the "last Adam," Christ (1 Cor 15:45). Likewise, just as Christians have borne the *image of the man "from earth," so also will Christians, at the resurrection, put on the image of the man "from heaven," Christ (1 Cor 15:49). All those in Christ will be changed, and *death, mortality, and corruption will give way to life, immortality, and incorruption.

3.8. 1 Corinthians 16:1-24. With Paul having addressed the Corinthians' denial of the general resurrection, the body of the letter comes to a close. The letter concludes with instructions about a "*collection for the saints" (1 Cor 16:1-4), a preview of Paul's and his associates' travel plans (1 Cor 16:5-12), some final exhortations (1 Cor 16:13-18), closing greetings (1 Cor 16:19-21), and a postscript consisting of a curse (1 Cor 16:22) and a benediction (1 Cor 16:23-24).

Paul's brief discussion of the collection "for the saints," or believers in *Jerusalem, suggests that the Corinthians were already familiar with the initiative. While several churches participated in the collection, only here does Paul give instructions for the process of collecting funds and for delivery of the gift.

In the meantime, Paul is making tentative travel plans. He is in Ephesus at present, where he intends to stay until Pentecost (see 1.4 above). From there he will go immediately to Macedonia, and after passing through there, intends to return to the Corinthians. These plans, however, did not unfold as he now tells them, for according to 2 Corinthians 1:16 he actually visited the Corinthians directly from Ephesus before moving on to Macedonia, thus traveling to the Corinthians directly by sea and following a course in the opposite direction to the one originally planned. In any case, he now indicates that he will wait in Ephesus for Timothy and "the brothers" before departing; before that, the Corinthians should expect a visit from Timothy (1 Cor 4:17; 16:10-11).

Before closing, Paul makes mention again of two figures introduced back in 1 Corinthians 1:10-17. Both references may be motivated by concerns over loyalties. Some indeed say, "I am Paul," and others, "I am of Apollos" (1 Cor 1:12). It is not clear, however, whether Paul's curt remark that Apollos was not willing to return to them at present was calculated either to hurt their feelings about Apollos or to communicate that he and Apollos entirely agreed that their loyalties were unhealthy. In the case of Stephanas, Paul affirmed earlier that he had baptized him (1 Cor 1:16), and he here enjoins the Corinthians to "be subject" to him and his household (1 Cor 16:15-16); Paul's endorsement may suggest that some had slighted him in favor of other leaders.

With some closing greetings (1 Cor 16:19-21), and a postscript consisting of a curse (1 Cor 16:22) and a benediction (1 Cor 16:23-24), the letter comes to an end.

4. The Theology of 1 Corinthians.

To speak of the theology of 1 Corinthians is to acknowledge that Paul does not articulate a theology in the abstract but in response to a situation. Thus, while the theology of the letter draws from a symbolic matrix that in its essence transcends the occasion, its theology is nonetheless situationally embodied and contingently articulated. A deep grasp of the letter's theology, then, requires some speculation into the church's circumstances, and indeed, into the church's own theology and the behavior that embodied it.

Approached in this way, the letter's main theological motifs could be articulated in terms of several theological antitheses.

4.1. Division and Unity. The problem of division in the church occupies first place in the main body of the letter. While it may be overgeneralizing to say that the entire letter is about disunity (if being "*in Christ" is an essentially corporate experience, all problems among believers everywhere could be generalized as problems of disunity), disunity sits at the heart of many of the issues addressed. The church's allegiances varied between different Christian ministers (1 Cor 1:10-17); they wronged one another and took legal retaliation (1 Cor 6:1-11); they failed to understand their interdependence and thus the importance of each and every person in the community (1 Cor 12:1-31); and their disorder and dysfunction in gatherings for worship, in a way, demonstrated a profound lack of concord (1 Cor 14:20-36). In response, Paul makes, in the letter's opening verses, a direct appeal for unity (1 Cor 1:10); he pronounces that it is better to endure injustice than to retaliate (1 Cor 6:7); he emphasizes that the members of the church are a body, and that all its parts serve one another for the good of the whole (1 Cor 12:12), and that the "greater" gifts are the ones through which the body is edified (1 Cor 14:5).

4.2. Status and the Cross. The divisions are a problem in a final sense, but they are partly a symptom of an underlying theological, or ideological, problem. One of the main causes of the church's divisions is the wisdom of the world (1 Cor 1:20; 3:19). Some in the church, professing to be "wise" (1 Cor 1:18–3:23), fancied themselves superior to others, being more "mature," more "spiritual" (1 Cor 2:6-16). They were "*strong," "wellborn" "rich," "kings" (1 Cor 1:26; 4:8). They had "knowledge" that "an idol is nothing" (1 Cor 8:4), while those still short of this knowledge were "weak" (1 Cor 8:7, 9-10). Those with the greater gifts were more spiritual than others (1 Cor 12–14). In short, they bought into the value system of the world, where honor and self-promotion were intuitively more to be desired than humiliation and self-disinterest. Sitting apart from others in honor, they also sat apart from them in fellowship.

Against that worldly wisdom Paul sets the "wisdom of God" (1 Cor 1:21, 24; 2:7), which is the message of the cross. Against human intuition, true wisdom consists in humility and *sacrifice in the interest of others, a wisdom embodied most of all in the symbol of Christ crucified (1 Cor 1:23; 2:2), and imitated by Paul and the apostles (1 Cor 2:1-5; 4:8-13). This is the wisdom that directs one to place the well-being of others above one's own "rights" (1 Cor 8–10) and the wisdom that views the chief purpose of spiritual gifts as the edification of the body rather than the elevation of the individual (1 Cor 12–14). In an ironic way, it is those who follow the wisdom of humiliation whom God finally exalts. Paul's discussion of the resurrection of believers at the climax of the letter, then, is not literarily detached from the first fourteen chapters. In a way, it presents the assurance that those who humble themselves will be exalted, after the pattern of Jesus.

4.3. Life in the Body and Life in the Spirit. The "wise" in Corinth saw their transcendent status largely as a matter of spiritual achievement, or rather as a matter of their transcendence of the body through their status in the Spirit. Having received the Spirit through Christ, they had relegated the body to too low a level, of little importance. The body had become morally irrelevant—irrelevant in matters of sex (1 Cor 5:1-13; 6:12-20) and diet (1 Cor 6:13; 8:1–11:1)—and one sinned only with the mind (1 Cor 6:18). The body was irrelevant because it would be destroyed (1 Cor 6:13), and in fact, would have no place in the *afterlife (1 Cor 5:12). Paul reasserts the importance of the body. The body is not for immorality but for the Lord (1 Cor 6:13); God will resurrect believers' bodies as he resurrected Christ's (1 Cor 6:14); God has bought believers with a price, so believers must glorify God with their bodies (1 Cor 6:19-20). Others in the church push in the opposite direction, wanting to deny the body its pleasures (1 Cor 7:1). For Paul, this too entails too low a view of the body. As embodied people, sexual urges are strong, and for many people an outlet is a necessary good (1 Cor 7:2-5, 36-37). Clinching the case for the body is the fact of resurrection itself—since God raised Jesus from the dead, he will also raise believers (1 Cor 15:1-58).

See also BODY; CORINTH; CORINTHIANS, SECOND LETTER TO THE; CRUCIFORMITY; GIFTS OF THE SPIRIT; LORD'S SUPPER; RESURRECTION; RHETORICAL CRITICISM; STRONG AND WEAK; WISDOM.

BIBLIOGRAPHY. ***Commentaries:*** **R. E. Ciampa and B. S. Rosner,** *The First Letter to the Corinthians*, PNTC (Grand Rapids, MI: Eerdmans, 2010); **R. Collins,** *1 Corinthians*, SP 7 (Collegeville, MN: Liturgical Press, 1999); **H. Conzelmann,** *1 Corinthians*, Hermeneia (Philadelphia: Fortress, 1975); **G. Fee,** *The First Epistle to the Corinthians*, NICNT (Grand Rapids, MI: Eerdmans, 1987; rev. ed., 2014); **J. Fitzmyer,** *First Corinthians*, AB 32 (New Haven, CT: Yale University Press, 2008); **D. E. Garland,** *1 Corinthians*, BECNT (Grand Rapids, MI: Baker Academic, 2003); **R. B. Hays,** *1 Corinthians*, Interpretation (Louisville, KY: John Knox, 1997); **R. Horsley,** *1 Corinthians*, ANTC (Nashville: Abingdon, 1998); **P. Perkins,** *First Corinthians*, Paideia (Grand Rapids, MI: Baker Academic, 2012); **W. Schrage,** *Der erste Brief an die Korinther*, 4 vols, EKKNT 7 (Zürich: Benziger, 1991-2001); **A. C. Thiselton,** *The First Epistle to the Corinthians*, NIGTC (Grand Rapids, MI: Eerdmans, 2000); **B. Witherington III,** *Conflict and Community at Corinth: A Socio-Rhetorical Commentary on 1 and 2 Corinthians* (Grand Rapids, MI: Eerdmans, 1995).

Studies: **E. Adams and D. Horrell,** eds., *Christianity at Corinth: The Quest for the Pauline Church* (Louisville, KY: Westminster John Knox, 2004); **C. K. Barrett,** "Christianity at Corinth," *BJRL* 46 (1964): 269-97; **F. C. Baur,** "Die Christusparti in der korinthischen Gemeinde, der Gegensatz des paulinischen und petrinischen Christentums in der altesten Kirche, der Apostel Petrus in Rom," *Tübinger Zeitschrift für Theologie* 4 (1831): 61-206; **B. Bitner,** *Paul's Political Strategy in 1 Corinthians 1–4: Constitution and Covenant* (Cambridge: Cambridge University Press, 2015); **T. A. Brookins,** *Corinthian Wisdom, Stoic Philosophy, and the Ancient Economy*, SNTSMS 159 (Cambridge: Cambridge University Press, 2014); idem, *Reading 1 Corinthians*, Reading the New Testament (Macon, GA: Smyth & Helwys, 2020); **S. J. Chester,** *Conversion at Corinth: Perspectives on Conversion in Paul's Theology and the Corinthian Church*, Studies of the New Testament and Its World (London: T&T Clark, 2003); **J. Chow,** *Patronage and Power*, JSNTSup 75 (Sheffield: JSOT Press, 1992); **A. Clarke,** *Secular and Christian Leadership in Corinth: A Socio-historical and Exegetical Study of 1 Corinthians 1–6* (New York: Brill, 1993); **N. Dahl,** "Paul and the Church at Corinth According to 1 Corinthians 1:10–4:21," in *Studies in Paul: Theology for the Early Christian Mission* (Minneapolis: Augsburg, 1977), 40-61; **K. P. Donfried,** *Paul,*

Thessalonica, and Early Christianity (Grand Rapids, MI: Eerdmans, 2002); **F. G. Downing,** *Cynics, Paul, and the Pauline Churches* (New York: Routledge, 1998); **M. Finney,** *Honour and Conflict in the Ancient World: 1 Corinthians in Its Greco-Roman Social-Setting* (London: Continuum, 2012); **E. Käsemann,** "On the Subject of Primitive Christian Apocalyptic," in *New Testament Questions of Today* (Philadelphia: Fortress, 1969), 108-37; **D. Litfin,** *St. Paul's Theology of Proclamation: 1 Corinthians 1–4 and Greco-Roman Rhetoric* (Cambridge: Cambridge University Press, 1994); **W. Lütgert,** *Freiheitspredigt und Schwarmgeister in Korinth* (Göttingen: C. Bertelsman, 1908); **P. Marshall,** *Enmity in Corinth: Social Conventions in Paul's Relations with the Corinthians*, WUNT 2/23 (Tübingen: Mohr Siebeck, 1987); **D. B. Martin,** *Corinthian Body* (New Haven, CT: Yale University Press, 1995); **M. M. Mitchell,** *Paul and the Rhetoric of Reconciliation* (Louisville, KY: Westminster John Knox, 1993); **M. Peppard,** "Brother Against Brother: *Controversiae* About Inheritance Disputes and 1 Corinthians 6:1-11," in *The First Urban Churches 2: Roman Corinth*, ed. J. R. Harrison and L. L. Wellborn (Atlanta: SBL Press, 2016), 133-52; **J. B. Prothro,** "Who Is 'of Christ'? A Grammatical and Theological Reconstruction of 1 Cor 1.12," *NTS* 60 (2014): 250-65; **J. E. C. Schmidt,** *Bibliothek für Kritik und Exegese des Neuen Testaments und älteste Christengeschichte* (Hadamar, 1801); **W. Schmithals,** *Die Gnosis in Korinth: Eine Untersuchung zu den Korintherbriefen* (Göttingen: Vandenhoeck & Ruprecht, 1969); **G. Theissen,** *The Social Setting of Pauline Christianity* (Philadelphia: Fortress, 1982); **A. C. Thiselton,** "Realized Eschatology at Corinth," *NTS* 24 (1978): 510-26; **G. Tomlin,** "Christians and Epicureans in 1 Corinthians," *JSNT* 68 (1997): 51-72; **A. Weiss,** *Soziale Elite und Christentum: Studien zu ordo-Angehörigen unter den frühen Christen* (Boston: de Gruyter, 2015); **J. Weiss,** *Der erste Korintherbrief* (Göttingen: Vandenhoeck & Ruprecht, 1910); **L. L. Welborn,** *Politics and Rhetoric in the Corinthian Epistles* (Macon, GA: Mercer University Press, 1997); idem, *Paul, The Fool of Christ: 1 Cor 1–4 in the Comic-Philosophic Tradition* (London: T&T Clark, 2005); **D. L. White,** *Teacher of the Nations: Ancient Educational Traditions and Paul's Argument in 1 Corinthians 1–4*, BZNW 227 (Boston: de Gruyter, 2017); **B. W. Winter,** *After Paul Left Corinth: The Influence of Secular Ethics and Social Change* (Grand Rapids, MI: Eerdmans, 2001); idem, *Philo and Paul Among the Sophists: A Hellenistic Jewish and a Christian Response*, 2nd ed. (Grand Rapids, MI: Eerdmans, 2002); **A. C. Wire,** *The Corinthian Women Prophets: A Reconstruction Through Paul's Rhetoric* (Philadelphia: Fortress, 1990); **E. M. Yamauchi,** *Pre-Christian Gnosticism: A Survey of Proposed Evidences* (Grand Rapids, MI: Eerdmans, 1973).

T. A. Brookins

CORINTHIANS, SECOND LETTER TO THE

The document known as 2 Corinthians is arguably one of the most difficult and least understood in the Pauline corpus. Although its authorship by Paul has never been seriously questioned, interpreters still debate its literary integrity, how it was written, and the *identity of Paul's *opponents in *Corinth. Beyond these preliminary questions lies the enigmatic heart of the argument: Paul's proclamation of the strength-in-weakness paradox (e.g., 2 Cor 1:8-11; 4:7; 6:3-10). The best example of this paradox, which can be defined in a literary sense as two opposed realities that occur simultaneously (see, e.g., G. Hotze), is found in the well-known climax of the material. As Paul prays for the removal of his "thorn in the flesh" (2 Cor 12:7), he receives a revelation from the risen Jesus: "My *grace is sufficient for you, for my power is perfected in weakness" (2 Cor 12:9). Paul responds that he will "boast all the more gladly in weaknesses" since "when I am weak, then I am strong" (2 Cor 12:10). The convoluted nature of this passage helps one to see why Alfred Plummer thought that moving from 1 Corinthians to 2 Corinthians is like going "from the somewhat intricate paths of a carefully laid-out park to the obscurity of a pathless forest . . . thick with roots which trip one up" (xiii). Nonetheless, the poet George Herbert believed that 2 Corinthians was Paul's most pastoral epistle, and Michael Gorman (2016) calls it the sleeping giant of Pauline theology. It is beloved by Christians for Paul's vulnerable self-presentation and his unwavering affirmation that divine power is present in human weakness. The key task for interpreters is appreciating the complexity of 2 Corinthians and the different interpretive options without losing sight of Paul's distinctive presentation of his *gospel, which varies considerably from his other letters.

1. Historical and Literary Questions.

1.1. Authorship. Second Corinthians is attributed to Paul in its salutation and demonstrates every historical, literary, and theological evidence of Pauline authorship. Although the document is not clearly attested until Marcion's canon (AD 140), it is a member of the Pauline corpus from then onward, and its authorship is undisputed today. Some interpreters believe that the vocabulary and subject matter of 2 Corinthians 6:14-7:1 indicate that Paul adopted this passage from a previous writing, or from a non-Pauline source (often associated with the Essene movement or Qumran documents), or from a Jewish-Christian *tradition. But even if one accepts that this passage originated elsewhere, the entire discourse is fully integrated into the argument of 2 Corinthians.

1.2. Occasion and Literary Integrity. Paul's founding of the community at Corinth, recorded in Acts 18, took place in AD 49–51 as part of Paul's second missionary journey. When Paul left Corinth after eighteen months, it seems the community was flourishing. At some point later Paul wrote a *letter to the Corinthians, a document that is no longer extant, to deal with issues being faced by the new believers. But the Corinthians had difficulty understanding Paul's instructions and misapplied them to their context (1 Cor 5:9-13). The community then sent a letter to Paul by the hands of the messengers listed in 1 Corinthians 16:15-17 to receive clarification. In response to this Paul wrote canonical 1 Corinthians. In the meantime, he sent Timothy to visit the Corinthians on his behalf (1 Cor 16:10-11; Acts 19:22). Timothy found the tension between Paul and the community to have escalated, due most probably to the arrival of opponents from outside of Corinth.

In response, Paul set out for Corinth for what became a "painful visit," during which his authority and gospel were called into question by the community. Paul was offended during the visit (2 Cor 2:1, 5-8; 7:8-13; 11:4), causing him to leave with the determination not to make another "painful visit" (2 Cor 2:1-2). Instead, he sent Titus with a "tearful letter" as an attempt to win back the Corinthians (2 Cor 2:3-9; 7:8-12). Titus was also supposed to organize the *collection (2 Cor 8:6), which indicates that Paul still had hope for the community and did not consider them beyond repentance. While this "tearful letter" is probably lost, some scholars have tried to identify it with 1 Corinthians or 2 Corinthians 10–13 (e.g., J. H. Kennedy, F. Watson, L. L. Welborn), although neither option has attained anything close to a consensus.

As Paul waited for Titus to return with his report on the impact of the new letter, his mind could not rest due to his anxiety over the Corinthian situation (2 Cor 2:12-13). So Paul left Troas to find Titus, and when he did, Titus gave Paul the good news that his "tearful letter" had indeed won back many of the Corinthians (2 Cor 7:6-13). Moreover, because the community had responded positively, Paul could now plan to visit them again (2 Cor 2:3; 9:5; 12:20–13:1). In anticipation of this third visit, Paul wrote 2 Corinthians. However, the continuing existence of pain in the community (see section 2 below) requires Paul to comfort the members while at the same time defending his apostleship. This balancing act is complicated by the ideologies of the opponents that seem to animate the Corinthians' objections. Paul's basic circumstantial goal in writing, therefore, is to prepare for his next visit to the Corinthians, in which he will have to judge those who persist in their rejection of him. Paul did return to Corinth (Acts 20:2), where less than a year later he wrote his letter to the Romans.

Given the reconstruction above, interpreters have cause to scrutinize the thematic tensions in 2 Corinthians, not least two sets of evidence that raise questions about the material's literary integrity: (1) the seemingly abrupt transitions and change of subject matter and (2) the sudden and sometimes contradictory shifting of Paul's tone. Specifically, interpreters have been puzzled by the apparent breaks in thought between 2 Corinthians 2:13 and 2 Corinthians 2:14; between 2 Corinthians 7:4 and 2 Corinthians 7:5; between 2 Corinthians 6:13 and 2 Corinthians 6:14; and between 2 Corinthians 7:1 and 2 Corinthians 7:2; by the seemingly separate treatments of the collection in 2 Corinthians 8 and 2 Corinthians 9; and by the distinct unit of 2 Corinthians 10:1–13:14.

If each of these transitions denotes a separate document, 2 Corinthians becomes a composite of the following six major fragments, which were then unified into a single letter: 2 Corinthians 1:1–2:13 and 2 Corinthians 7:5-16; 2 Corinthians 2:14–6:13; 2 Corinthians 6:14–7:1; 8; 9; 10–13. These proposed documents are commonly slotted into the history of Paul's interactions with the Corinthians. Typically, 2 Corinthians 10–13 is viewed as the "tearful letter"; 2:14–6:13 is a part of a lost letter of defense; 1:1–2:13 and 7:5-16 are viewed as Paul's letter of reconciliation after Titus's report; and 6:14–7:1 is taken to be yet another lost Pauline or non-Pauline writing, part of the "tearful letter" or even the "previous letter" of 1 Corinthians 5:9 (e.g., G. Bornkamm, H. D. Betz, D. Georgi, M. M. Mitchell).

Alternatively, a growing minority of scholars maintain the unity of the entire letter (e.g., C. D. Land, F. J. Long, I. Vegge). Those who hold this position explain the integrity of the transitions within the letter at each point (e.g., an intentional rhetorical move, a sleepless night, a break between writing sessions). They may also explain the changes in subject matter and tone as the result of the mixed nature of the Corinthian community (some were pained by Paul's previous letter more than others, some are more faithful to the opponents than others, etc.). In short, the question of literary integrity typically hinges on whether one thinks the changes in subject and tone are evidence of Paul's disjointed composition, of the mixed nature of the Corinthian community, or of some combination of both. Since a consensus has yet to emerge, this article assumes the unity of 2 Corinthians for the sake of simplicity.

*1.3. **Paul's Opponents.*** Paul writes to the Corinthian community as a whole (2 Cor 1:1) and only addresses the opponents in the third person; however, they are a distinct group within the community, and he pejoratively calls them super-apostles (2 Cor 11:5). The consensus is that these influencers are distinct from the Corinthians and presumably originate from outside Corinth, yet they are also clearly within the community, and many of their beliefs have been taken up by the Corinthians. The key passages for identifying Paul's opposition in Corinth have often been 2 Corinthians 3:1-18; 11:4, 22-23. The opponents are also widely believed to be the animating force behind the accusation that Paul's "appearance is weak and his speech contemptible" (2 Cor 10:10). From these texts some conclude that Paul's opponents were Jews who were familiar with the Hellenistic world and espoused Sophist values and rhetorical techniques, but beyond this bare sketch—if it is even correct—the identity and theology of the opponents is a matter of conjecture. Taking a position on this issue could nevertheless be considered important if one is to achieve a historically plausible reading of 2 Corinthians.

In modern times, interpreters have offered at least three basic theories about the identity of the opponents in 2 Corinthians. These hypotheses are constructed primarily by reading Paul's arguments as a direct contrast to the positions of his opponents (i.e., the "mirror reading" technique). The proposals are as follows: (1) Gnostics, (2) "legalistic" *Judaizers on a par with those Paul supposedly fought elsewhere, and (3) Jews with a mixture of Gnostic and/or pneumatic ideologies of various persuasions. The most forceful positions of the mid- to late twentieth century were drawn by the following interpreters, and their hypotheses remain the most influential today: Rudolf Bultmann and Walter Schmithals (the Gnostic hypothesis), C. K. Barrett (the Judaizer hypothesis), and Dieter Georgi (Hellenistic Jewish pneumatics of Palestinian origin with a "divine man" theology centered on Moses).

Given the amount of reconstruction necessary to identify the opponents, Jerry Sumney's proposal of a "minimalist approach" for identifying them is to be welcomed. Sumney's proposal includes (1) an emphasis on the priority of exegesis in a "text-focused method," (2) an insistence on a sound evaluation of proper sources, (3) a "stringently" limited application of the mirror reading technique, and (4) a rejection of the attempt to approach the text with a previously determined reconstruction. However, these guidelines have not led to any breakthroughs or new leading theories. The Gnostic hypothesis has died due to a lack of evidence for a robust *Gnosticism in the pre-Christian or NT era, and Georgi's proposal has been met with serious criticism concerning his reconstruction of early Jewish missionaries and of their understanding of Moses. Finally, Barrett's thesis is hopelessly dated in its views of Judaism. All of this leaves one to wonder whether the opponents represent such a vague and broad category that they have become a blank canvas for interpreters to sketch the opposite of their imagined Paul.

2. Paul's Relationship with Corinth.

As with all of Paul's letters, the relationship between Paul and the community is fairly determinative for interpretation. With Corinth, it is an especially dynamic relationship of growing conflict that develops over multiple visits and letters. How one narrativizes the conflict is complicated by the prevalence of partition theories that slice the material in different ways and often into a sequence that does not follow the canonical progression (e.g., many interpreters believe 2 Cor 1:1–2:13 and 2 Cor 7:5-16 comprise a final, conciliatory letter). This raises questions about how exactly one might describe the community's relationship with Paul in the various stages of the conflict. Even if one favors a unity theory, the relationship between *apostle and community is still complex. At one time, Paul is somewhat pleased with the Corinthians (e.g., 2 Cor 7:11-13), and at another he seems completely perturbed by them (e.g., 2 Cor 11:1-4).

One of the variables within the Paul-Corinth relationship that has gained attention recently, not least for its constructive theological implications, is the shared identification with *Christ between apostle and community. When Paul asks whether "Christ is in you" (2 Cor 13:5), his word choice suggests that he expects the community to answer in the affirmative. Although the Corinthians have become interested in "another Jesus" (2 Cor 11:4), it is indeed Jesus with whom they have interest. Paul thus envisions the community sharing both "sufferings" and "comfort" with him despite their rebellion (2 Cor 1:7). One could wager that Paul's entire strategy in 2 Corinthians—that is, to accept the Corinthian charge of weakness and to demonstrate how he finds power within it—would collapse if the Corinthians were uninterested in how one suffers in Christ. Paul assumes that his experience is generally applicable to the community—it is "Christian existence written large" (Seifrid, xxiv). As such, one must carefully consider the distance between Paul and the Corinthians since, lurking subtly below the surface, there are the ties that bind and they are not yet severed.

Some interpreters have started to read 2 Corinthians with the community's participation in Christ in the foreground. Dustin Ellington doubts that Paul's use of the singular pronoun can be taken as a singular reference—it is a participatory "I" (e.g., 2 Cor 10:1; 12:10). This means that whenever Paul speaks of his experience in suffering, he is implicitly advising the Corinthians. Thomas Stegman similarly argues that Paul's autobiographical discourses have a didactic function. Paul is not merely defending himself; rather, his life offers the Corinthians a model of true *faith. In other words, the line of inquiry being developed here begins to implicitly or explicitly question the dominant reading over the last century or more, which has been that 2 Corinthians is a defense of Paul's *ministry against proud, rebellious Corinthians. To be fair, no serious interpreter doubts that Paul defends himself (e.g., 2 Cor 11:1-15; 3:1-6). But the overlooked variables in the Paul-Corinth relationship suggest the need for a reevaluation of how one understands the purpose of 2 Corinthians and what it achieves for the community.

One of the problems with these emerging readings, however, is that they do not demonstrate in historical terms how the field has misunderstood the Corinthian conflict. Why would the Corinthians care to learn about suffering and weakness *if they are not suffering*? A potential solution is found in the work of Larry Welborn, who proposes that the chief background of 2 Corinthians is the community's pain created by Paul's previous visit and letter (2 Cor 2:1-7; 7:5-16; see Welborn, "Paul and Pain"). The language used for this pain indicates a very negative psychological experience. This suggests that rather than merely defending himself, Paul must console a community that can no longer be construed as completely rebellious or as some being faithful and others being rebellious. All have been affected by serious pain (2 Cor 2:2, 5). These claims have been developed by B. G. White (2021) to show that there are multiple types of pain envisioned in 2 Corinthians 2:1-7. These include bitterness and despair, thus differentiating the Corinthians' pains from the fleeting "godly grief" (2 Cor 7:5-16) and confirming that these pains would have been alive and ongoing as Paul penned each part of 2 Corinthians. The community then occupies an altogether ironic position: they accuse Paul of weakness yet feel ongoing pains concerning his most recent letter. An implication of this reading is that the Corinthians are not merely "the strong" but are experiencing a form of weakness too, meaning that Paul's strength-in-weakness paradox becomes relevant to them in ways that have been previously unexplored.

Even if one disagrees about the importance of the Corinthians' pains, there are still reasons to think that the relationship between apostle and community possesses overlooked complexities. Paul explicitly states in the programmatic thanksgiving that his task is not merely to confront but to console (2 Cor 1:3-7), thus suggesting that the Corinthians know deprivation in some sense and may in their desperation look not merely to the opponents but also to their antagonistic apostle for insight, relief, and transformation.

3. Content and Argument.

3.1. The Salutation (2 Cor 1:1-2). The salutation in 2 Corinthians 1:1-2 follows the same pattern as 1 Corinthians 1:1-3, though both the identification of the sender and of the recipients are now abbreviated, probably due to the advanced state of correspondence between Paul and Corinth. Paul's apostolic identity is expressed, with Timothy noted as the cosender. Although there has been considerable discussion concerning whether the plural pronouns in 2 Corinthians 1–7 refer to a wider circle of *coworkers (e.g., 2 Cor 1:19; 8:16-23), the themes and style of the material suggest that Paul remains the main author. The recipients are the believers in Corinth.

3.2. The Opening Thanksgiving (2 Cor 1:3-7). Unlike the situation he faced in 1 Corinthians, Paul now finds his legitimacy as an apostle being severely called into question. This situation creates the need to defend himself and may explain why he begins 2 Corinthians not by thanking *God for his work of grace among the Corinthians but by praising God for his work of comfort and deliverance in his own life (2 Cor 1:3-7). However, this section is subtly directed at the Corinthians, who "share in our sufferings" and thus "in our comfort" (2 Cor 1:7). In the absence of explicit explanation, Paul is presumably referring to their shared experience of pains concerning his previous visit (2 Cor 2:1-7). This rhetorical decision to refer to shared *suffering—one could argue that Paul and the Corinthians have very different types of pain at this moment—creates a sense of solidarity between the two opposed groups. The thanksgiving thus establishes the pastoral focus of what is to follow: Paul will use his autobiographical discourses to address the Corinthians' own experience of pain and suffering, which allows him to simultaneously defend himself and present Jesus anew to the community.

3.3. Paul's Affliction in Asia and the Corinthian Response (2 Cor 1:8-11). In this section Paul formulates the first instance of the strength-in-weakness paradox, which occurs as he experiences a surprising rescue. The precise event is unknown to us, but the implications are more important. Paul says that he had to experience the "sentence of *death" to trust more deeply in the God who raises the dead (2 Cor 1:9). The apostle characteristically concludes this episode by appealing to the Corinthians. Such appeals have been explained by past interpreters as fixtures of Paul's defense—the apostle experienced God's power, and the community should acknowledge this. But a more compelling explanation, given the shared suffering noted above, would be that the Corinthians may be more willing to give thanks (2 Cor 1:11) as they learn that weakness and strength are not merely separate entities—that there is some way in which Christ's resurrection power comes to them amidst their pains (2 Cor 1:8). In other words, an experience of strength in weakness results in a broader transformation: of one's attitude (2 Cor 1:9), emotions (2 Cor 1:10), and behavior (e.g., 2 Cor 11). All of this is predicated on the christological shape of the narrative, an apparent participation in the life and death of Jesus (2 Cor 1:9).

3.4. Paul's Defense of His Plans and Recognition of Corinthian Pains (2 Cor 1:12–2:11). Paul then moves to the theological rationale for the unexpected change in his *travel plans (2 Cor 1:15-16). Paul's purpose is to demonstrate that his behavior has been an expression of sincerity that only God can discern (2 Cor 1:12). Conversely, Paul's actions have not been the result of "fleshly *wisdom" (2 Cor 1:12) and the vacillations of one who makes his plans "according to the *flesh." Paul's point in 2 Corinthians 1:15–2:4 is that his earlier decision not to visit Corinth on his way to *Jerusalem from Macedonia (1 Cor 16:5-9) but to come directly to Corinth first (2 Cor 1:15), as well as his later decision not to return to Corinth a second time (2 Cor 1:23), was the action of one who is "sealed by the Spirit" and is therefore acting in a Christlike manner. Paul changed his travel plans in order to give the Corinthians the chance for repentance (2 Cor 7:8-13), deciding not to come back to Corinth after his "painful visit" but writing the "sorrowful letter" instead (2 Cor 2:1-5).

In 2 Corinthians 2:1-7 Paul fixes his attention on the Corinthians and their pain, a reality that is likely ongoing given the types of pain in view and the persistent nature of human emotions (see section 2 above). He explains that he did not intend pain but *joy (2 Cor 2:3), and he offers instructions to the loyal Corinthians on how to forgive the "offender"—presumably the ringleader of the accusations against Paul during his painful visit. They must welcome this one back, lest he be "overwhelmed by excessive pain" (2 Cor 2:7). Moreover, just as Paul's actions toward the Corinthians demonstrate his genuine apostolic standing, their willingness to extend mercy to this person takes on the character of a test of their faith (2 Cor 2:9).

3.5. The Nature of Paul's Ministry (2 Cor 2:12–3:18). Rather than calling the legitimacy of his apostleship into question, Paul's suffering leads him once again to praise God in 2 Corinthians 2:14. At the heart of his explanation of his ministry is the twofold argument in 2 Corinthians 2:14–3:6 for his sufficiency and boldness as an apostle. On the one hand, Paul is sufficient for the apostolic *calling (2 Cor 2:16) precisely because his life of suffering, as the means of revealing the *knowledge of God, brings about the same effect in the world that Paul attributed to the word of the *cross in 1 Corinthians 1:18-25. Moreover, unlike his opponents, Paul has willingly taken up this suffering by preaching the gospel free of charge as evidence of his sincerity and call (2 Cor 2:17). Paul can point to the Corinthians themselves as additional evidence for his sufficiency, since their own conversion and life in the Spirit, brought about through Paul, testify to the genuine nature of Paul's ministry among them (2 Cor 3:2-3). Paul's ministry of suffering and the Spirit thus combine to support his assertion that his sufficiency is from God and that God has made him a minister of the "new *covenant" of the Spirit in fulfillment of Ezekiel 36 and Jeremiah 31 (2 Cor 3:4-6).

In 2 Corinthians 3:7-18, one of the most complex passages in the Pauline corpus, Paul proceeds to compare his role as an apostle of the "new covenant" established by Christ to that of Moses' role as mediator of the "old covenant" established at Sinai. But if Paul has been called like Moses, how then is his ministry different from that of Moses? Paul answers this question by contrasting the events of Exodus 32–34 and their significance for understanding the nature and purpose of the old covenant to the new covenant in Christ.

Paul's main point is that from the very beginning the *law functioned to "kill" Israel by condemning it for its sinfulness. This was not because the law itself was somehow deficient but because the vast majority of *Israel was left in a hardened condition so that it was unable to keep the covenant (Ex 32:1-10; 33:3, 5; 34:9). As a result, Israel could not endure the *glory of God without being destroyed (Ex 33:3, 5). Moses had to veil himself, therefore, not because the glory was fading but so that the effects of God's glory might be brought to an end (2 Cor 3:7, 11-12, in view of Ex 34:29-35). This would make it possible for God's presence to continue in Israel's midst in spite of Israel's hardheartedness.

Crucially, believers may now encounter in the Spirit the same glory of God that Moses encountered "with unveiled faces" (2 Cor 3:16-17). Rather than being judged and destroyed by the presence of God, they are transformed by it into the very *image of God himself (2 Cor 3:18). Whereas Moses had to veil himself (2 Cor 3:12-13), as an apostle of the new covenant Paul can be bold in his declaration of the gospel because he is confident that he has been called to a ministry of the Spirit (2 Cor 3:8). Inasmuch as Paul's ministry thus mediates the glory of God to those whose hearts have been changed and thus need not fear their destruction, his ministry "outshines" that of the old covenant (2 Cor 3:10-11), and those in Christ are transformed from one degree of glory to another (2 Cor 3:18).

3.6. The Paradox Revisited (2 Cor 4:1-18). In 2 Corinthians 4:1-6 Paul draws the necessary conclusion from his preceding argument. On the one hand Paul's apostleship demonstrates, through his preaching and his way of life, the "light of the gospel of the glory of Christ, who is the image of God" (2 Cor 4:4). This was the purpose of Paul's own call, pictured in 2 Corinthians 4:6 in terms of a new *creation in which God "shone in our hearts to give the light of the knowledge of the glory of God in the face of Christ." On the other hand, this can only mean that those who reject Paul and his message do so because their own minds have been hardened by *Satan, the "god of this age" (2 Cor 4:3-4).

In 2 Corinthians 4:7-18, Paul returns to his suffering, developing once again the strength-in-weakness paradox. He memorably states, "We have this treasure in jars of clay to show that this surpassing power is from God and not from us" (2 Cor 4:7). Here the metaphor appears to refer to Paul's possession of the good news in his frail body. The metaphor is intricately crafted, with the treasure only perceptible within the jar and the jar only fully understood when one sees the treasure inside. Neither is removed or separated from the other. This, then, is one of the most developed paradoxes of 2 Corinthians, where one sees Paul's argument most clearly: he should not be rejected for his weaknesses because divine power simultaneously comes to him. While Paul's weaknesses are not removed, they are always qualified by *resurrection power and only understood in that light.

Continuing the pattern of moving from himself to the Corinthians, Paul enters into a catalogue of sufferings that subtly invokes the Corinthian community with a reference to "despair" and to being "crushed"—both words/images that are semantically and conceptually related to "pain" in antiquity (cf. 2 Cor 2:1-7). He then explicitly addresses the community, indicating that he selflessly serves them in order that that they may have life (2 Cor 4:12). In this sense, there is an outward movement of the paradox in which Paul passes along the resurrection life given to him because—unlike the Corinthians—he is not stuck in his weaknesses nor held back from entering a death for those who could be deemed lesser than him. Here Paul becomes an exemplar to the Corinthians.

3.7. Eschatological Implications (2 Cor 5:1-21). Paul's confidence in his future vindication, when he will be "at home with the *Lord" (2 Cor 5:8), is based on the guarantee of his present possession of the *Holy Spirit (2 Cor 5:5). His envisioned life will no longer be in tension; rather, he will shed this "earthly tent" and be fully glorified (2 Cor 5:1). In other words, the strength-in-weakness paradox appears to resolve in eschatological life. For the interim time, Paul has a ministry of reconciliation that, rather than being strictly concerned with himself—though it is concerned with interpersonal reconciliation—is more accurately understood as a ministry from Christ to the Corinthians (2 Cor 5:20). Here Paul's role as a conduit between the community and Christ is made clear and gives further clues as to how Paul understands his purpose in writing—not as a defense but as a proclamation of Christ to the Corinthians.

3.8. The Paradox and Reconciliation (2 Cor 6:1-13). Paul's focus on reconciliation continues through the catalogue of suffering in 2 Corinthians 6:3-13, which supports his legitimacy as an apostle and demonstrates for the Corinthians how they can be transformed, even reconciled, with Paul and thus with Christ.

First, Paul delivers a set of paradoxes, demonstrating that every aspect of his life is touched by this tethering of weakness and power. Notably, some of these paradoxes implicate the Corinthians, not least "as pained, yet always rejoicing" (2 Cor 6:10). The different paradoxes touch on Paul's attitude, emotions, and behavior, once again demonstrating their broader importance for the apostle's life.

Paul then moves into a discourse about the Corinthians, this time making it clearer than ever that what stands in the way of reconciliation is their pains. He says, "Open wide your hearts to us" (2 Cor 6:13). The use of *hearts* is an implicit reference to the community's pains—elsewhere Paul says pain is a matter of the heart (Rom 9:2). His reference to their "restrained . . . affections" (2 Cor 6:13) also suggests that Corinthian pains are in view here. In antiquity, pain was often depicted as shrinking one's inner being. But why does Paul address the Corinthians' pains so delicately? It is worth remembering that he was more explicit in 2 Corinthians 2:1-7; here, however, he probably treads lightly because he does not want to dwell on an experience for the Corinthians that could be causing shame (see Welborn, *End to Enmity*). Paul's solution, even to a problem as knotty as reconciliation, is to once again appeal to an experience of strength in weakness. If only the community could comprehend and experience the paradoxical power of Jesus Christ, they would be able to embrace, without *fear, the so-called weakness required to make amends with an apostle as "weak" as Paul.

3.9. Pain Revisited (2 Cor 7:1-16). In 2 Corinthians 7:2-16 Paul resumes his account of the recent events in Corinth, focusing on the good news he received when he finally met Titus. Although Paul initially regretted having sent them such a severe reprimand, Paul is relieved that his letter of rebuke (2 Cor 7:5-8) brought about among the majority of Corinthian believers the kind of godly sorrow that leads to repentance rather than "worldly grief," which merely brings death (2 Cor 7:9-13). Paul's reflection on his apostleship in 2 Corinthians 2:14–7:16 consequently ends with a great expression of joy, comfort, and confidence in the Corinthians as a whole, since their positive response to Paul's previous warnings and to Titus's *mission is a sure sign of the genuine nature of their faith and of the bond between Paul and his *church (2 Cor 7:2-5, 11-16).

Paul's envisioned distinction between pains—the godly pain and the worldly pain (2 Cor 7:10-11)—also confirms that interpreters are on the right track when they understand Paul to be addressing the community's pains with the strength-in-weakness paradox. Paul is continually thinking about how the Corinthians' pains can be redeemed without being removed, through an experience of Christ's resurrection power. It seems that, in punishing the offender, they have already had such an experience. They have exhibited not those characteristics that come from naked power or naked weakness but a clothing of the two with one another. The community does not exhibit acts indicative of one entity alone (e.g., the overt power of rebellion or the extreme weakness of complacency). Rather, their pains are being redeemed by Christ's resurrection power into useful longing, intention, and an interest in justice (2 Cor 7:11) (see section 4 for more on the meaning of the metaphor here).

3.10. The Collection (2 Cor 8–9). In 2 Corinthians 8:1–9:15 the subject matter changes completely. Paul now takes up the theological foundation and practical administration of the collection for the believers in Jerusalem that he had initiated in Corinth but that due to the problems in the church had not been completed as anticipated (2 Cor 8:6-7, 10-11; 9:2). The necessity for the collection is based not only on the needs of the church in Jerusalem and the ability of the Corinthians to give (2 Cor 8:14-15) but also on the implications of Christ's own self-giving for those under his lordship (2 Cor 8:8-9). Giving to the needs of others therefore becomes a test of the genuineness of one's faith (2 Cor 8:8, 24; 9:13), with Titus providing an example of just such a genuine faith and the *love it produces (2 Cor 8:16-17). Two unnamed but well-known and respected brothers will be sent by Paul with Titus to ensure the completion and credibility of the collection to the glory of God (2 Cor 8:18-23; 9:1-5).

In 2 Corinthians 9:6-15 Paul then concludes his discussion of the collection by returning to its theological foundation. The collection is necessary because it expresses the church's trust in God to meet their needs to such a degree that they are willing and able to give cheerfully to others (2 Cor 9:6-9). God is faithful, and he will respond to such acts of faith by working to supply the needs of those who give and then by rewarding those who use their resources for the benefit of others (2 Cor 9:8, 10-12). In going forward with the collection the Corinthians will therefore glorify God by affirming with their actions the gospel of Christ (2 Cor 9:13) and causing others to join them in glorifying God (2 Cor 9:12). The collection will also create a unity of prayer and appreciation between the Corinthians and the church in Jerusalem (2 Cor 9:14), which leads Paul in response to close this section by praising God for his own "inexpressible gift" (2 Cor 9:15).

3.11. Paul's Final Proclamation and Defense (2 Cor 10:1–13:10). In the last major section of 2 Corinthians, 10:1–13:10, the tone, style, and subject matter change dramatically. Paul is largely on the offensive here, though the consolatory dimensions persist and have been overlooked. Perhaps the most important literary cue is Paul's highlighting of the accusations against him (2 Cor 10:10). Here one must take seriously both that Paul is being called weak and that the Corinthians think his letters are weighty and strong (probably because they have been pained by one). From Paul's perspective, the community is trying to ride the coattails of these superapostles (2 Cor 11:5) who do not really care about them and are actually "slapping them in the face" (2 Cor 11:20). Nonetheless, the wounded Corinthians put up with this arrangement if it means that they can possess the power of "another Jesus" (2 Cor 10:4). Given the Corinthians' disdain of weakness, this is presumably an artificial Jesus of pure resurrection power, what Martin Luther ironically called a "theology of glory."

Since God has already commended Paul through his apostolic work, the need to boast in one's own behavior or accomplishments is "foolish" (2 Cor 11:1, 16-21; 12:11). Yet in 2 Corinthians 11:1–12:10 Paul feels forced to do just that in order to counter the claims of his opponents and to win back those who have fallen under their sway. At the heart of the issue is the opponents' claim that they, not Paul, represent eminent apostles. Paul endeavors to show that he is a genuine apostle, on a par with the leaders of the mother church (2 Cor 11:5; 12:11), while his opponents, claiming some connection with the Jerusalem leaders, are in fact "false apostles" and "deceitful workers" who disguise themselves as "servants of *righteousness" (2 Cor 11:12-15).

In this final section Paul therefore "boasts" first in his decision to preach the gospel free of charge in Corinth (2 Cor 11:7-12) and then in his other sufferings (2 Cor 11:23-33) as the true marks of his legitimacy as an apostle, only to boast finally in his own spiritual experiences. In this last case, however, Paul is exceedingly hesitant, knowing that this is the epitome of foolishness and the very thing concerning which God has given him a "thorn in the flesh" to keep him from doing (2 Cor 12:6-10). Here Paul reaches the high point of 2 Corinthians, a climactic proclamation that declares the strength-in-weakness paradox in vivid terms: rather than removing Paul's thorn, the risen Jesus says to Paul, "My grace is sufficient for you, for my power is perfected in weakness" (2 Cor 12:9). Crucially, Paul turns to the Corinthians in 2 Corinthians 12:15, stating poignantly, "If I love you more, am I to be loved less?"

Much like in 2 Corinthians 6:10-13, Paul reasons that his experience of the paradox allows him to love even when he is weak or the beloved is weak, whereas the Corinthians, without a thorough grounding in his gospel, fail to love. Love is the natural product of the paradox, and it is likewise described elsewhere as consisting of strength and weakness (1 Cor 13:4-7). Paul concludes by noting what the Corinthians are lacking in order to possess his paradigmatic, paradoxical experiences: faith in *the crucified and risen* Jesus (2 Cor 13:5). This suggests that there is indeed a Pauline gospel in 2 Corinthians: a grace given in weakness for the transformation of lives that become more fully devoted to a crucified and resurrected Jesus.

3.12. Final Greetings (2 Cor 13:11-14). In 2 Corinthians 13:11-14 Paul ends his letter by calling his church to mend its ways, heal its rivalries, and live in unity and *peace with one another. This closing appeal is based on the promise that in doing so "the God of love and peace" will be with them.

4. Gaining an Interpretive Foothold: Two Events.

Given all of the debates and interpretive possibilities for the reader of 2 Corinthians, one naturally searches for a constructive way to frame the material that is plausible, is applicable to most approaches, and yields useful theological and practical insights. As mentioned above, no matter how one understands the composition of 2 Corinthians or the question of its literary integrity, Paul's strength-in-weakness paradox is found across the letter and seeps into nearly every possible division of it. Paul's paradoxical formulation stems from two distinct motifs—or for Paul, more accurately, events—the death and resurrection of Jesus (e.g., 2 Cor 13:3-4). How one interprets these events, particularly their relationship to one another, lies at the heart of how one reads 2 Corinthians.

This may seem like a strange thing to say given that these are historical events that were said to occur sequentially, only days apart. But Paul's largely nonsequential process of reasoning about the paradox stems from a revelation delivered by the risen Jesus, which offers creative license to distill the events into a paradox (2 Cor 12:9; see S. J. Kraftchick). Paul is clearly at pains throughout 2 Corinthians to articulate the intricacies of the relationship between strength and weakness given that he returns to it time and again, using both metaphor (e.g., a treasure in jars of clay) and distinctive vocabulary (e.g., "perfected," 2 Cor 12:9). Conversely, the Corinthians, and especially the opponents, have embraced "another Jesus," who—if their accusations against Paul are any indication (2 Cor 10:10)—is a Jesus of resurrection power removed from any weakness whatsoever. What divides Paul and the Corinthians is arguably their view of Jesus' human life, the nature of the death that he died, and how much, if at all, the resurrection has silenced the cry of dereliction.

In interrogating the relations between strength and weakness (or crucifixion and resurrection), interpreters have tended to favor one side or the other. A recent emphasis of scholarship on 2 Corinthians, particularly with the rise of ideological criticisms, has been that Paul uses his apostolic power for his own gain and that his confession of weakness is accordingly insincere and manipulative (e.g., E. Castelli). While it is true that Paul forcefully applies his authority, and one must always think critically about Paul and his actions, such proposals do not provide a sufficient explanation for the external accusations about Paul's weakness (2 Cor 10:10). The apostle's poor health and appearance are among the most commonly cited characteristics of the historical Paul, which suggests that Paul cannot be plainly read from the perspective of Nietzsche's "will to power." One could say that approaches to 2 Corinthians that focus on power relations tend to do so at the expense of subtly articulating both sides of the paradox. Such approaches could be adjusted by deconstructing the apostle with his own cipher: the strength-in-weakness paradox. As Karl Plank rightly notes, Paul often risks the integrity of his own paradoxical constructs by leaning too far into power at certain times or into weakness at other times. For instance, Paul's "tearful" letter produced pain in Corinth (2 Cor 2:4-5), and it seems to have left an impression in the community that the apostle's letters are "strong" (2 Cor 10:9-10). This may demonstrate Paul's culpability in distorting the paradox and vindicate, in a different way, those who criticize Paul's use of authority. On the other hand, Paul's potential failure is a reminder that even our best guides to this paradox may struggle to embody strength in weakness in their ethics, and such a paradox will ultimately give trouble to any interpreter who tries to articulate what Paul could only begin to grasp by revelation.

Other interpreters—especially those in confessional contexts—tend to focus on weakness. This is resonant with the Christian tradition, which prizes humility and charity above all else. What is not sufficiently understood, however, is that there is a difference between humiliation and humility. For instance, with his *cruciformity motif (now rearticulated as "resurrectional cruciformity"), Michael Gorman (2021) tends to emphasize the cross to the detriment of the resurrection, even going so far as to say that the goal of Paul's strength-in-weakness paradox is human powerlessness and that human life climaxes in suffering. While Gorman is a far more cautious interpreter than most, this repeated isolation of weakness from resurrection power resolves the paradoxical congruence and risks the charge of theological masochism. A probable example of the latter occurs in the work of John Caputo, who both is inspired by Paul and openly eschews his finely tuned articulations in favor of a "God of frailty" whose power is dissolved in weakness (see the response by J. Heavin).

Beyond those interpreters who approach Paul with clear ideological or theological goals, there are a host of exegetes who try to articulate the strength-in-weakness paradox but may distort or even resolve it by their efforts. Some of the most utilized terms to describe the relationship between strength and weakness include an "emphasis" (e.g., G. Guthrie, 253), a "mingling" (e.g., E. B. Keller, 13), and a "positive evaluation" of weakness (e.g., R. Pickett, 135). In each case, the description fails to robustly describe the dyadic (i.e., both/and) nature of a paradox, and thus turns Paul's complex construct into a singular proposition. A better approach is offered by Andrew Boakye, who suggests that "resurrectiformity" and "cruciformity" together are the "headline" of Pauline theology generally and 2 Corinthians in particular. Even this approach, though, does not capture the sense in which these opposite ends of the paradox are mutually qualified rather than merely coexisting. Boakye's articulation thus appears more like a dialectic than a genuine paradox.

Finally, on a more theological note, the majority of interpreters have tended to envision a competitive relationship between strength and weakness (e.g., T. Savage, M. Gorman, M. Thrall). In other words, they suggest that human agency must step back in order for divine agency to operate properly. This leads to a reading of the paradox in which Paul, or those in Christ generally, bring weakness into the paradoxical equation while God alone is the arbiter of power. Such readings fail to acknowledge that the infamous "thorn in the flesh" is divinely "given" (2 Cor 12:7), and even God himself possesses "weakness" (1 Cor 1:25). All of this suggests that God is, so to speak, on *both sides* of the paradox. Without acknowledging this, one is left to think of the paradox as a contrast between two items in the same ontological class. But God and humanity are not at all in the same class! To put it another way, the paradox is more than a literary construct. It is a divine gift given to Paul and to those in Christ. This allows the paradox to be truly alien to Paul's experience and to thus be a paradox in a theological sense. Furthermore, conceptualizing the paradox in this way allows one to make sense of how the paradox works in Paul's life. His agency and power do not shrink. These are simply redefined in light of a new understanding and experience of the relationship between strength and weakness. Paul clearly says that the resurrection power belongs to God (2 Cor 12:9), but then it becomes his: "when *I* am weak, then *I* am strong" (2 Cor 12:10). It is this complementary growth of divine and human agency that becomes so essential for interpreting 2 Corinthians as a whole and understanding how Paul can repeatedly move from experiences of the paradox to moral and ethical admonitions (e.g., 2 Cor 1:11; 6:12-13; 12:15).

However one determines to interpret the paradox at the heart of the material, one must offer an accurate and robust articulation. As Plank rightly says, a paradox "erupts to wreak havoc" on unsuspecting interpreters (132). The following principles of Pauline paradox should be followed carefully (see White 2022):

- Pauline paradox involves at least two opposed realities or experiences.
- The paradox's meaning is not found in one opposite alone, nor in two that coexist, but in an equal distribution of two opposed-yet-congruent entities.
- The opposites occur simultaneously and mutually qualify one another ad infinitum.
- Both opposed entities must originate from a transcendent realm (to prevent the paradox from being reduced to contrasting viewpoints in the same ontological class).

While one might question the tedium of paradoxical grammar and its utility for exegesis, such fine distinctions are necessary to preserve the integrity of Paul's argument. For instance, if the paradox is improperly articulated or otherwise misunderstood, it could lead an interpreter to think that Paul emphasizes his weaknesses in 2 Corinthians. While Paul may do this rhetorically at times, it is hardly a sound description of his theology or pastoral strategy. For the pained Corinthians, an emphasis on weakness would sound a lot like masochism and raise serious questions about Paul's credibility as an apostle with "anxiety for all the churches" (2 Cor 11:28). It hardly seems like a sound pastoral strategy to tell a pained community that what they need in their life is more weakness! To the contrary, the Corinthian tendency to isolate weakness and strength—to place Paul in the "weakness" camp and themselves in the "strength" camp—is combatted by the paradoxical congruence that Paul envisions between these opposites. If the Corinthians' pains can be redeemed by resurrection power and thus converted into useful experiences of humility, there may be hope that they can eventually commit the ultimate act of strength in weakness: love. For the Corinthians to reconcile with Paul, they need to return his love (2 Cor 12:15), an act which includes, from Paul's perspective, elements of strength and weakness (1 Cor 13:4-7). In this sense, the paradoxical form of Paul's argumentation is crucial for the apostle's moral and ethical agenda in Corinth, and it allows him to envision a useful role for human weakness without saying it is inherently redemptive (it is redemptive only insomuch as it is being simultaneously redeemed by Christ's resurrection power).

5. Three Interpretive Approaches.

In an attempt to thread together the various interpretive issues described so far, there are three identifiable paradigms by which interpreters approach the material. The dominant approach today and arguably the most attested in the past may be called the apologetic reading. This reading takes all or most of the material to be a defense of Paul's apostolic authority. An emphasis is placed on the rhetorical back-and-forth between Paul and the opponents, and most of Paul's autobiographical discourses are read through the lens of an *apologia*. The Corinthians are proud, rebellious, and in need of a verbal drubbing that reasserts Paul's authority. In this case, the identity of the opponents is considered important for understanding the nature of the Corinthian conflict, and the focus on this conflict often causes the interpreter to favor a partition theory where one can project the partitions onto the various stages of the drama. While one may commonly discuss the nature of Paul's ministry or worldview within this paradigm, the pastoral components of Paul's argument are usually reduced to confrontation and rebuke (e.g., T. Savage).

In the late twentieth century several interpreters subtly departed from the primary view and now offer—depending on how one views it—either a modified version of the apologetic reading or an entirely new option altogether. This position may be called the didactic view, which emphasizes Paul's self-exposition and his attempt to teach the Corinthians the true nature of life in Christ through his own example. The opponents thus take a lesser place, and interpreters are more likely to favor a unity theory of composition since the autobiographical discourses are distributed evenly across the material. In fact, this paradigm is helped by a shift in how scholars view Paul's autobiographical discourses generally: they are not merely tools of apologies but have something constructive to say for the recipients (see G. Lyons). Another point of emphasis is the connection between Paul's experience in Christ and that of his hearers. For some, Paul presents a vision of ethical training—Paul wants the Corinthians to learn how to love, or how to persevere, by following his example—while for others he is defending his ministry but with some space reserved for admonition or consolation. Leading interpreters here include T. D. Stegman, D. Ellington, L. Bowens, and M. J. Gorman.

More recently another permutation has emerged that builds on the increasing focus on the Corinthian community. Using the insights of Welborn (2001, "Paul and Pain"), a fresh background is developed for 2 Corinthians—the Corinthians' pains—and this approach then traces how this issue is addressed by the various distinctions of Paul's strength-in-weakness paradox throughout the material (see esp. White 2021). The apostle thus presents himself as a living paradigm for experiencing divine power in weakness and the subsequent transformation of his attitude, emotions, and behavior that occurs as a result of this participation in Christ's dying and rising. This view—what one might call the kerygmatic view—arguably leans more than the others into Paul's concluding statement that "all this time you have been thinking that we are defending ourselves to you. . . . Actually . . . we have spoken for your building up" (2 Cor 12:19). Paul's purpose is largely and ultimately pastoral, and it is specifically concerned with the proclamation of Jesus' grace in the midst of weakness, both for Paul and for the Corinthians *in their weakness*. This represents a fresh embodiment of the Pauline kerygma, or gospel, which is highly paradoxical and deeply focused on the incongruous and effective gift of a Jesus whose crucifixion cannot be understood without his resurrection and vice versa.

6. Theology.

A striking and often overlooked feature of 2 Corinthians is its view of the divine. On the one hand, 2 Corinthians emphasizes the difference between God and humanity—for example, "not that we are competent in ourselves to claim anything for ourselves but our competence comes from God" (2 Cor 3:5)—making God appear powerful but removed and transcendent. On the other hand, one would be poorly mistaken to approach the divine in 2 Corinthians solely from the top down. In ways that are clearer than many of his other letters, Paul tends to define God in terms of Christ rather than Christ in terms of God. The "weakness of God" (1 Cor 1:25) is on full display in 2 Corinthians, where Christ's participation in humanity is essential for bridging the gap between the divine and the human. Both divine transcendence and divine immanence are necessary for Paul's argument. Without the former, there could be no paradox, no higher solution for how to deal with weakness that moves beyond the stultifying effects of pain; without the latter, there would be no way for the paradox to descend to humanity and fill those in Christ with resurrection power.

One of the practical implications of Paul's focus on the incarnate Lord is captured well by Adolf Schlatter: the cross destroys our idols. Paul shows that the cross relativizes the artificial and competitive drama of human life. Highly coveted certificates of proficiency are no more (e.g., 2 Cor 3:1-2), the skills that purportedly separate the elite from the plebians are useless (e.g., 2 Cor 10:12-13), and all supposed signs of strength have been set aside. If one wants to be like God, one must embrace the narrative of death and resurrection that the Spirit creates for those united to Christ.

Finally, an interpretive matter that has yet to be fully appreciated and explored in Anglophone scholarship—but is commonly acknowledged in German scholarship—concerns the function of the strength-in-weakness paradox. The first and most common view has been labeled by Gerald O'Collins as the revelatory view, which suggests that weakness *reveals* divine power more clearly. This perspective tends to echo the Stoics and their conviction that power resides within (in one's reason, attitude, etc.) and is not captured by physical appearance. The divine power operative in Paul's life, then, becomes more conspicuous *because of* his weak appearance. Weakness possesses a hermeneutical function, and thus the paradox is largely concerned with the production of true knowledge and a heavenly perspective that allows one to perceive the power that functions in weakness (e.g., J. T. Fitzgerald, T. Savage, G. Hotze).

The other view, which O'Collins has dubbed the ontological perspective, emphasizes the *arrival* of divine power. It is in human weakness, typically understood as humility or repentance, that divine power comes to humanity (e.g., J. Lambrecht, H. Windisch). This view is typically accompanied by a sense of sequence rather than a simultaneous experience of weakness and power, and among some interpreters it has even come to mean that weakness is a prerequisite to power (see the critique by Heckel that this view is often "Pelagian"). O'Collins notes that the perspectives are not mutually exclusive and both are arguably too narrow. He proposes that the two should be combined, and this broader perspective has slowly begun to gain more adherents. With greater attention to the question of pain in the Corinthian community, perhaps future interpreters will think more broadly about how the paradox transforms the Corinthians. An initial reading along these lines is provided by B. G. White (2021), who offers a "transformative" view of the paradox, which shows how Paul's construct responds to Corinthian pains and converts their weaknesses into useful attitudes, emotions, and behaviors.

7. Modern Reception.

In many ways, 2 Corinthians has been left behind as other purportedly apologetic letters—perhaps Galatians and Philippians chief among them—are liberated from an abstract hermeneutic and subjected to greater analysis of what they do for the community that receives them. Even if the interpreter wishes to continue spotlighting an *apologia* in 2 Corinthians, the evidence of modern reception may speak the best word of caution since the material has rarely been understood in this way. For instance, while Martin Luther loved Romans and Galatians, he cites 2 Corinthians 12:9 more often than almost anything else in the NT, and it was his favorite verse for *Seelsorge* (soul care). One can also detect the influence of Paul's strength-in-weakness paradox in the spiritual writings of Henri Nouwen, particularly *The Wounded Healer*. More recently, Sarah Williams has appropriated Paul's strength-in-weakness motif to reflect on the vulnerability of childbirth and the life of the unborn and the sick, while Tim Gombis has used it to take aim at strength-based models of *leadership and ministry in the church.

In the philosophical world, however, 2 Corinthians has not always fared so well. Some philosophers have appreciated its interest in a "weak God" (e.g., Caputo), but far more have shuddered at its disinterest in power, competence, and mastery. One of the most influential figures in this regard is Friedrich Nietzsche, who believed that Paul, and specifically his argument in 2 Corinthians, created a religion of "weaklings." Other intellectuals have questioned the place of humility in the Western canon of thought, and these voices also tend to greet the apostle Paul's writings with a high degree of skepticism.

Finally, Lisa Bowens points to an overlooked history of reception for Paul generally, and his strength-in-weakness material specifically, which offers a helpful concluding perspective. As noted above, most readers tend to find meaning in one side of the paradox—for example, it was the acceptance of weakness that so bothered Nietzsche. However, like Paul's life itself, the paradox is best understood and appreciated by those who know deep deprivation and suffering. Bowens points to Zilpha Elaw, a black woman in nineteenth-century America who repeatedly faced racism and sexism in her efforts to preach the gospel. She looked to Paul for courage and inspiration to keep going, and he gave her a key in which to register her struggle: she was living a life of strength in weakness.

See also Collection for the Saints; Corinth; Corinthians, First Letter to the; Eschatology; God; In Christ; Letters, Letter Forms; Ministry; Opponents of Paul; Suffering; Travel and Itinerary Plans.

BIBLIOGRAPHY. ***Commentaries:*** **P. Barnett,** *The Second Epistle to the Corinthians*, NICNT (Grand Rapids, MI: Eerdmans, 1997); **C. K. Barrett,** *The Second Epistle to the Corinthians*, Harper's New Testament Commentaries (New York: Harper & Row, 1973); **R. Bultmann,** *The Second Letter to the Corinthians* (Minneapolis: Augsburg, 1985); **V. P. Furnish,** *II Corinthians*, AB 32 (Garden City, NY: Doubleday, 1984); **G. H. Guthrie,** *2 Corinthians*, BECNT (Grand Rapids, MI: Baker Academic, 2015); **P. E. Hughes,** *Paul's Second Epistle to the Corinthians*, NICNT (Grand Rapids, MI: Eerdmans, 1962); **R. P. Martin,** *2 Corinthians*, 2nd ed., WBC 40 (Waco, TX: Word, 2014); **A. Plummer,** *Second*

Epistle of St. Paul to the Corinthians, ICC (Edinburgh: T&T Clark, 1925); **T. Schmeller,** *Der zweite Brief an die Korinther*, EKKNT 2/8 (Zürich: Patmos-Verlag, 2010–2013); **M. Seifrid,** *The Second Letter to the Corinthians*, PNTC (Nottingham, UK: Apollos, 2014); **M. Thrall,** *2 Corinthians*, ICC (Edinburgh: T&T Clark, 1994); **H. Windisch,** *Der zweite Korintherbrief*, 9th ed. (Göttingen: Vandenhoeck & Ruprecht, 1970).

Studies: **L. Belleville,** *Reflections of Glory: Paul's Polemical Use of the Moses-Doxa Tradition in 2 Corinthians 3:12-18* (Sheffield: Sheffield Academic, 1991); **H. D. Betz,** "Corinthians, The Second Epistle to the," in *ABD*; **A. Boakye,** "Inhabiting the 'Resurrectiform' God: Death and Life as Theological Headline in Paul," *ExpT* 128, no. 2 (2016): 53-62; **G. Bornkamm,** "History of the Origin of the So-Called Second Letter to the Corinthians," *NTS* 8, no. 3 (1962): 258-64; **L. M. Bowens,** *An Apostle in Battle: Paul and Spiritual Warfare in 2 Corinthians 12.1-10*, WUNT 2 (Tübingen: Mohr Siebeck, 2017); idem, *African American Readings of Paul: Reception, Resistance, and Transformation* (Grand Rapids, MI: Eerdmans, 2020); **J. D. Caputo,** *The Weakness of God: A Theology of the Event* (Bloomington: Indiana University Press, 2006); **D. A. Carson,** *Showing the Spirit: A Theological Exposition of 1 Corinthians 12–14* (Grand Rapids, MI: Baker, 1987); **E. Castelli,** *Imitating Paul: A Discourse of Power* (Louisville, KY: Westminster John Knox, 1991); **J.-F. Collange,** *Enigmes de la deuxième épître de Paul aux Corinthiens*, SNTSMS 18 (Cambridge: University Press, 1972); **D. Ellington,** "Not Applicable to Believers? The Aims and Basis of Paul's 'I' in 2 Corinthians 10–13," *JBL* 131, no. 2 (2012): 325-40; **J. T. Fitzgerald,** *Cracks in an Earthen Vessel: An Examination of the Catalogues of Hardships in the Corinthian Correspondence*, SBLDS (Atlanta: SBL Press, 1988); **D. Georgi,** *The Opponents of Paul in Second Corinthians* (Philadelphia: Fortress, 1986); **T. G. Gombis,** *Power in Weakness: Paul's Transformed Vision for Ministry* (Grand Rapids, MI: Eerdmans, 2021); **P. Gooder,** *Only the Third Heaven? 2 Corinthians 12.1-10 and Heavenly Ascent*, LNTS 313 (London: Bloomsbury, 2006); **M. J. Gorman,** *Apostle of the Crucified Lord: A Theological Introduction to Paul and His Letters*, 2nd ed. (Grand Rapids, MI: Eerdmans, 2016); idem, *Cruciformity: Paul's Narrative Spirituality of the Cross*, 2nd ed. (Grand Rapids, MI: Eerdmans, 2021); **S. J. Hafemann,** "'Self-Commendation' and Apostolic Legitimacy in 2 Corinthians: A Pauline Dialectic?," *NTS* 36 (1990): 66-88; idem, *Suffering and Ministry in the Spirit: Paul's Defense of His Ministry in II Corinthians 2:14–3:3* (Grand Rapids, MI: Eerdmans, 1990); idem, "Corinthians, Letters to the," in *DPL*; **A. E. Harvey,** *Renewal Through Suffering: A Study of 2 Corinthians*, SNTW (Edinburgh: T&T Clark, 1996); **J. Heavin,** "Power Made Perfect in Weakness: Theologia Crucis in 1 Corinthians 13:3-4," *JTI* 13, no. 2 (2019): 251-79; **U. Heckel,** *Kraft in Schwachheit: Untersuchungen zu 2. Kor 10–13*, WUNT 56 (Tübingen: Mohr Siebeck, 1993); **G. Hotze,** *Paradoxien bei Paulus: Untersuchungen zu einer elementaren Denkform in seiner Theologie*, Neutestamentliche Abhandlungen 33 (Münster: Aschendorff, 1997); **M. M. S. Ibita, D. Kurek-Chomycz, T. A. Vollmer, and R. Bieringer,** *Theologizing in the Corinthian Conflict: Studies in Exegesis and Theology of 2 Corinthians*, BTS 16 (Leuven: Peeters, 2013); **E. Käsemann,** "Die Legitimität des Apostels. Eine Untersuchung zu II Korinther 10–13," *ZNW* 41 (1942): 33-71; **E. B. Keller,** *Some Paradoxes of Paul* (New York: Philosophical Library, 1974); **J. H. Kennedy,** *The Second and Third Epistles of Saint Paul to the Corinthians* (London: Methuen, 1900); **S. J. Kraftchick,** "Death in Us, Life in You," in *Pauline Theology*, ed. David Hay, vol. 2 (Minneapolis: Fortress, 1993); **J. Lambrecht,** "Paulus Vermag Alles Door de Kracht van God. Zwakheid En Sterkte," *Nederlands Theologisch Tijdschrift* 55, no. 4 (2001): 273-85; **C. D. Land,** *The Integrity of 2 Corinthians and Paul's Aggravating Absence*, NTM 36 (Sheffield: Sheffield Phoenix, 2015); **F. J. Long,** *2 Corinthians: A Handbook on the Greek Text* (Waco, TX: Baylor University Press, 2015); **G. Lyons,** *Pauline Autobiography: Toward a New Understanding*, SBLDS (Atlanta: SBL Press, 1985); **P. Marshall,** *Enmity in Corinth: Social Conventions in Paul's Relations with the Corinthians*, WUNT 2/23 (Tübingen: Mohr, 1987); **M. M. Mitchell,** *Paul, the Corinthians, and the Birth of Christian Hermeneutics* (Cambridge: Cambridge University Press, 2010); **J. Murphy-O'Connor,** *St. Paul's Corinth: Texts and Archaeology*, Good News Studies 6 (Wilmington, DE: Glazier, 1983); idem, *The Theology of the Second Letter to the Corinthians*, NTT (Cambridge: University Press, 1991); **G. G. O'Collins,** "Power Made Perfect in Weakness: 2 Cor. 12:9-10," *CBQ* 33, no. 4 (October 1971): 528-37; **R. Pickett,** *The Cross in Corinth: Social Significance of the Death of Jesus*, LNTS 143 (Sheffield: Sheffield Academic, 1997); **K. A. Plank,** "Confronting the Unredeemed World: A Paradoxical Paul and His Modern Critics," *AThR* 67, no. 2 (April 1985): 127-36; **T. Savage,** *Power Through Weakness: Paul's Understanding of the Christian Ministry in 2 Corinthians*, SNTSMS 86 (Cambridge: Cambridge University Press, 1996); **R. S. Schellenberg,**

Rethinking Paul's Rhetorical Education: Comparative Rhetoric and 2 Corinthians 10–13, ECL 10 (Atlanta: Society of Biblical Literature, 2013); **A. Schlatter,** *Gesunde Lehre* (Velbert: Freizeiten-Verlag, 1929); **T. Stegman,** *The Character of Jesus: The Linchpin to Paul's Argument in 2 Corinthians*, AnBib 158 (Roma: Pontificio Istituto Biblico, 2005); **J. L. Sumney,** *Identifying Paul's Opponents: The Question of Method in 2 Corinthians*, JSNTSup 40 (Sheffield: Sheffield Academic, 1990); **G. Theissen,** *The Social Setting of Pauline Christianity: Essays on Corinth* (Philadelphia: Fortress, 1982); **I. Vegge,** *2 Corinthians—a Letter About Reconciliation: A Psychagogical, Epistolographical, and Rhetorical Analysis*, WUNT 239 (Tübingen: Mohr Siebeck, 2008); **F. Watson,** "2 Cor. X-XIII and Paul's Painful Letter to the Corinthians," *JTS* 35, no. 2 (1984): 324-46; **L. L. Welborn,** "The Identification of 2 Corinthians 10–13 with the 'Letter of Tears,'" *NovT* 37, no. 2 (1995): 138-53; idem, "Paul's Appeal to the Emotions in 2 Corinthians 1.1–2.13; 7.5-16," *JSNT* 82 (June 2001): 31-60; idem, *An End to Enmity: Paul and the "Wrongdoer" of Second Corinthians*, BZNW 185 (Berlin: de Gruyter, 2011); idem, "Paul and Pain: Paul's Emotional Therapy in 2 Corinthians 1.1–2.13; 7.5-16 in the Context of Ancient Psychagogic Literature," *NTS* 57, no. 4 (2011): 547-70; **B. G. White,** *Pain and Paradox in 2 Corinthians: The Transformative Function of Strength in Weakness*, WUNT 2/555 (Tübingen: Mohr Siebeck, 2021); idem, "Interpreting Pauline Paradox: A Response to Gorman's Cruciformity Concept," *HBT* 44, no. 2 (2022): 172-94; **S. C. Williams,** *Perfectly Human: Nine Months with Cerian* (Walden, NY: Plough, 2018); **H. Windisch,** *Der Zweite Korintherbrief*, KEK 1/9 (Göttingen: Vandenhoeck & Ruprecht, 1924); **F. Young and D. F. Ford,** *Meaning and Truth in 2 Corinthians* (Grand Rapids, MI: Eerdmans, 1987).

B. G. White

COSMIC POWERS. *See* Apocalyptic Paul; Apocalypticism; Cosmology; Principalities and Powers; Satan, Devil.

COSMOLOGY

Paul's conception of the cosmos, or universe, including its origin and how it functions, draws from a Jewish cosmology rooted in the OT. What distinguishes Paul's understanding are features of the cosmic drama that flow from his contention that the *God of *Israel has acted in *Christ to restore all aspects of God's *creation. Because his letters largely address specific situations, he nowhere lays out a systematic presentation of his cosmology. His conception of the cosmos is dualistic in that it encompasses the present and the future (temporal dualism); divine activity in the heavens and human activity on earth, along with their interrelation (spatial dualism); and both good and evil (ethical dualism).

1. Cosmology in the Old Testament
2. Terminology in Paul
3. Spatial and Temporal Aspects
4. Correlation of Heaven and Earth
5. The Corruption of the Cosmos
6. The Enslavement of the Cosmos to Hostile Cosmic Powers
7. The Church as Prolepsis of a Renewed Cosmos

1. Cosmology in the Old Testament.

The OT portrayal of creation shapes Paul's vision of the world. A brief outline of this view serves as an entrance into Paul's cosmology. Some OT texts envision a two-tiered structure of the cosmos—"heaven and earth" (e.g., Gen 1:1; Ex 20:11), an expression meant to encompass all created things. Other passages point to a third level, the underworld, or Sheol, the abode of the dead (e.g., Deut 32:22; Ps 88:3-5).

God alone is the creator of all things, and the creation is the arena of God's glory. The cosmos is God's *temple or dwelling place. Temples in the ancient world pointed to the existence and sovereignty of a transcendent deity supposed to inhabit the temple, whose presence is indicated by an image. Because the God of Israel is the one true Creator God of all that is, the entire cosmos is his temple (Walton). The Genesis narrative portrays God's creative work from two perspectives. Genesis 1–2 portrays God as transcendent King speaking the creation into existence (Gen 1:1–2:3), and he is also immanent within creation, fashioning it with his hands (Gen 2:4-25). In his transcendence, God is judge and lord over creation, and in his immanence, he is near to creation and in genuine relationship with it.

God's *glory fills the heavens (Ps 19:1-6). On the earth, however, God's glory is seen in humanity as they are the *image of God, commissioned by God to rule creation on his behalf, bringing order to the world and fostering creation's flourishing (Gen 1:26-27). In this way, humanity is functioning as "the glory of God." Psalm 8 closely associates humanity as the image of God with God's crowning them "with glory and honor" (Ps 8:5). As the glory of God, humanity was made to be "rulers over the works of your hands" (Ps 8:6 NIV). The psalm proceeds in verses 6-8 to list the aspects of creation over which God commissioned them to rule in Genesis 1–2.

Included in Scripture's cosmological vision are divine beings that are God's creation, whom he appointed to rule over aspects of the cosmos and to determine the corporate life of tribes and nations (Deut 32:8 LXX). While Israel was God's special possession, God appointed "gods of the nations," or "the sons of God," over each nation to orient their national customs and patterns of life (see Job 1:6; Dan 10:13-14, 20-21). These cosmic beings were also intended to ensure justice among the nations (Ps 82), but because they have rebelled against the one true God and have not done this, they will ultimately face God's *judgment (Ps 82:6-7). These figures played a significant role in the Jewish apocalyptic cosmology in the time leading up to the first century, a conception of the cosmos reflected in Paul's vision (e.g., 1 Enoch; Jubilees; 1QSa II, 8-9; 1QM VII, 5-6).

2. Terminology in Paul.

Paul can use *kosmos* ("world") to speak of the created world, including heaven and earth and all the entities that fill them, much like the OT expression "heaven and earth." The term itself is not inherently cosmological but refers to the order or arrangement of things, most often the order among social groups. Paul uses it in some instances to refer merely to the inhabited world of humans or to the structure and functioning of human society (1 Cor 7:31, 33; Gal 6:14; Col 1:6). His use can occasionally have negative connotations, depending on the context in which it appears. For example, in 1 Corinthians, a letter in which Paul seeks to reinforce group cohesion over against the corrupt Corinthian culture, Paul routinely uses *kosmos* to refer to mindsets and practices that oppose the way of the *cross (e.g., 1 Cor 1:20-21; 2:12; 11:32). He also uses *ktisis* ("creation") to refer to the created world, though *kosmos* appears far more regularly.

Oikoumenē ("inhabited world") is used as more or less a synonym of *kosmos*, in the sense of the inhabited world and its various organizing systems. Paul uses *gē* ("earth") rarely and mainly in OT quotations. The expression *ta panta* ("all things") makes reference to everything created that fills the heavens and the earth (Eph 3:9; Col 1:15-17).

Paul uses *aiōn* ("age") as somewhat of a synonym of the morally negative way he uses *kosmos* to describe the corrupt ways of life and perverted ideologies that characterize human cultures and seem to be in the air. He refers to "this age" in 1 Corinthians 1:20 in this negative sense, along with "the present evil age" (Gal 1:4). *Aiōn*, of course, has a temporal meaning to it and may refer to the present or the future (Eph 1:21; 2:7).

3. Spatial and Temporal Aspects.

For the most part, Paul envisions the cosmos as a two-tiered structure, involving heaven and earth. He employs the expression "all things" (*ta panta*) to capture everything that exists in the heavens and on the earth (Rom 11:36; 1 Cor 8:6; Eph 1:10; 3:9; Col 1:16-17). In a few other places, he describes a three-tiered structure, including "under the earth" (*katachthoniōn*, Phil 2:10) or "the lower parts of the earth" (*ta katōtera merē tēs gēs*, Eph 4:9). In Ephesians 2:2, he refers to "the air" (*aēr*), a space above the earth that, in this age, is the realm of corrupt mindsets and ideologies.

Temporally, Paul associates the origins of the cosmos with God's original creative act in the distant past (Rom 1:20; 1 Cor 11:9). The character of the present for the cosmos, however, involves a transformation from Paul's inherited Jewish cosmology drawing on the OT. The prophets had looked ahead to Israel's future restoration, indicating a clear division between the present age and the future age separated by the dramatic coming of God and the renovation of the cosmos at the day of the *Lord (Is 24; Joel 3). The Jewish apocalyptic worldview, by the time of the first century, had made a clear distinction between "two ages"—the present age and the glorious one to come (4 Ezra 7.47-50; see also 1 En. 91.16; Jub. 1.29).

Unique to the NT apostolic *witness, reflected in Paul, was the vision of the new creation age being inaugurated in the *death and *resurrection of Christ. While the "present evil age" is still up and running (Gal 1:4; Eph 6:12), the new creation age has already begun (2 Cor 5:17; Gal 6:15). Paul notes that the *church is the gathering of people "on whom the culmination of the ages has come" (1 Cor 10:11 NIV). In Christ, God has "rescued us from the domain of darkness and transferred us into the *kingdom of his beloved son" (Col 1:13 NASB; cf. Gal 1:4). The current condition of the cosmos, then, is one that involves the crossover of the ages. This dualistic conception of two ages involves competing dynamics that Paul envisions as warring against each other (Gal 5:17). The new creation age exists in Christ and by the agency of the *Holy Spirit, empowering the church and shaping it into the corporate image of Christ (2 Cor 3:17-18). Paul calls the church to resist being conformed to the pattern of "this age" (Rom 12:2), discerning and standing firm against the strategies of the cosmic forces that oversee this age and seek to form them into community patterns of injustice and selfishness (Eph 6:10-18).

For Paul, the prophetic day of the Lord has been transformed into the day of Christ, that future event when Jesus Christ will return to bring to an end the present evil age and fully realize the new creation (1 Cor 1:8; Phil 1:6, 10; 2:16; see also Eph 1:21). At that time, the cosmos will be fully renewed (Rom 8:18-25) and "all things" will be subject to Christ, with God's enemies—the entities that corrupt the cosmos—fully defeated (1 Cor 15:20-28).

4. Correlation of Heaven and Earth.
Cultures across the ancient world envisioned a direct correlation of things in the heavens with things on earth, so that an event that occurred on earth had a heavenly correspondent (Longenecker). For example, if one nation defeated another in battle, ancients assumed that the god of the first nation had proved more powerful than the deity of the other. The biblical creation account reflects this interrelationship, as God's rule in the heavens was meant to be depicted on earth through humanity overseeing the spread of God's rule, bringing about creation's flourishing. A central concern among Jews in the first century was having a calendar that accurately matched heavenly realities, one of the main areas of disagreement between the community at *Qumran and the Jerusalem temple leadership.

This reality is reflected in Paul's cosmological vision in several places. In Romans 3:29-31, Paul raises the question of whether God is the "God of Jews only." The question is valid because of the issue facing the Roman churches. If they were to embody their *salvation in Christ by insisting that *Gentiles become Jews, this would signal that in the heavens the one true God was only a tribal deity, ruling only over Jews. Paul answers with the Shema, Israel's declaration that the God of Israel is the only true God, who is the great King over all the earth (Deut 6:4). Because of this, the earthly *worship of the one true God must be embodied by Jews and non-Jews joining together in Christ, welcoming one another, and enjoying the *fellowship of a common meal (Rom 15:7; cf. Gal 2:11-21).

The correspondence between heaven and earth also lies behind why Paul must explain that he is incarcerated in Ephesians 3:1-13 and urge his audiences not to be discouraged by this (Eph 3:13). The assumption across ancient cosmologies would be that if Paul were in a Roman *prison, then the God whom Paul serves as representative was defeated by the gods of Rome. Paul writes, however, that in light of the fact that God's *triumph was brought about by the death of Christ, his *apostles carry out their privileged *ministries through social locations of shame, such as imprisonment. He does the same in Philippians 1:12-26, portraying his incarceration not as a loss for the gospel but as the expected way of life for those who follow and represent the self-giving Christ (Phil 2:6-11).

5. The Corruption of the Cosmos.
The narrative of the corruption and renewal of the cosmos forms the substructure of Paul's letter to the Romans. Since "the creation of the world" (*ktiseōs kosmou*), the character of God has been clearly displayed for humanity to know and worship him, making them without excuse and liable to God's judgment (Rom 1:20). But they have refused to glorify God and give him thanks (Rom 1:21), behaviors that point to God's original intention for humanity to be "the image of God" within God's cosmic temple. Further, they "exchanged" or "changed" the "glory of the immortal God for images made to look like a mortal human being and birds and animals and reptiles" (Rom 1:23 NIV). Paul invokes OT imagery to speak of the denigration of humanity in its rebellion. That is, rather than embodying God's glory by ruling creation on God's behalf, humanity worshiped something within creation. This is a debasement of the human and resulted in the dishonoring of human bodies—the marring of the image of God and the pollution of the temple space that is the cosmos. The specific character of human *sin is that humanity has refused to play its role as image of God in God's cosmic temple.

In Romans 1:25, Paul restates that humanity "exchanged" or "changed" the *truth of God by the lie. The lie that humanity bought is that they are the image of some created thing rather than the image of the uncreated and transcendent God. Humanity corrupted the truth of God by no longer embodying God's faithfulness to his creation by managing it on his behalf. This is both a distortion of human identity and the pollution of the cosmos that is God's temple space through the behaviors Paul elaborates in Romans 1:21-32.

Following the narrative direction of Genesis 1–4, Paul notes that this rebellion has led to enslavement to the cosmic power of Sin. In Romans 3:9, Paul summarizes that both Jews and Gentiles are under the power of Sin. Paul portrays Sin throughout the rest of Romans as active to enslave humanity and disrupt the unity of the Roman churches. In

Romans 5:12-20, Sin "entered the world," and Death, Sin's cosmic companion in destruction, entered along with it. Paul depicts these figures as having wills and as active agents, and Pauline interpreters capitalize these terms to emphasize this reality. Death "reigned" (Rom 5:14, 17), and "sin reigned in death" (Rom 5:21 NIV). In Romans 7:8-11, Sin seizes an opportunity (2×) and springs to life.

Paul describes the active agency of Sin just as does the narrative of Genesis 4:1-7, in which God speaks to Cain, noting that "sin is crouching at your door; it desires to have you, but you must rule over it" (Gen 4:7 NIV). In some mysterious way, human rebellion against God's intentions has polluted the temple space of God's creation such that there are now unintended cosmic actors within God's world, with which humanity must now contend.

These cosmic actors embody the cosmic corruption of God's temple, polluting its space so that God is not glorified by humanity. Because of this cosmic pollution the creation (*ktisis*) is groaning under the weight of the *curse and frustration (Rom 8:19-21). It was subjected to futility because humanity is not currently acting as the image of God and fostering the flourishing of the creation. Its groaning is eschatologically oriented as it awaits the final transformation of the children of God (Rom 8:21). At that point, God will restore humanity to being the image and glory of God carrying out its collective task faithfully. Paul's personification of creation as groaning draws on OT texts that give aspects of it some kind of independent agency (see Lev 26:34; 2 Chron 36:21; Is 24:23; 55:12).

6. The Enslavement of the Cosmos to Hostile Cosmic Powers.

Jewish tradition drew on the OT conception of the gods of the nations to explain that the nations were disobedient and idolatrous because these cosmic ruler figures had led them astray (1 En. 69.28; Jub. 10.1-14; 1QS III, 17-26). Paul's cosmological vision reflects this apocalyptic scenario. Paul identifies these cosmic figures with various titles. They are "the rulers of this age" (1 Cor 2:6, 8 NIV); "gods" and "lords" (1 Cor 8:5 NIV); "the authorities," "the cosmic rulers of this darkness," and "the spiritual forces of evil in the heavenly realms ["heavenlies" or "heavenly places" in some translations]" (Eph 6:12 NIV); "thrones or powers or rulers or authorities" (Col 1:16 NIV); "powers and authorities" (Col 2:15 NIV); "the elements [*stoicheia*] of the world" (Col 2:8; Gal 4:3, 9).

The final term (*stoicheia*) in the previous list has been the subject of debate among Pauline scholars, who seek the appropriate background against which the term may be understood. Greek and, later, Roman writers (e.g., Aristotle, Epictetus) used *stoicheia* to speak of the physical stuff of creation—earth, air, fire, and water. Scholars cite this background to claim that Paul's expression *stoicheia tou kosmou* ("elements of the world") in Galatians 4:3 and Colossians 2:8 refers to this transient creation. Others view Paul as referring to some rudimentary teachings, rendering the expression "elementary principles of the world." It appears, however, that Paul uses *stoicheia* to refer to the same cosmic figures as the "rulers," "powers," and "authorities." His use of *stoicheia tou kosmou* in Colossians 2:8 associates them with "powers and authorities" (Col 2:15). In Galatians 4:8-9, he equates the *stoicheia* with "beings who by nature are not gods." He writes something similar in 1 Corinthians 8:5, referring to "so-called gods" in a passage where he claims that the heavens are populated with "many gods and many lords." The expression is best understood, then, against the Jewish tradition of cosmic ruler figures that lead humanity astray.

These figures are responsible for holding humanity enslaved by sowing within creation corrupt ideologies and mindsets, and providing an array of sinful patterns and practices so that humanity does not experience life within God's world as God intended. Paul envisions humanity as responsible for acts of sin, but these cosmic forces pervert human experience at a macro level, fostering systems of oppression, exploitation, and animosity between nations and groups, along with making attractive sinful ways of life characterized by selfishness, fleshly indulgence, and greed.

In 1 Corinthians 2:6-8, Paul notes that he embodied the way of the cross that is the *wisdom of God while he was among the Corinthians. He contrasts this with "the wisdom of this age or of the rulers of this age" (1 Cor 2:6 NIV). The wisdom of this age and of its rulers has to do with the corrupt cultural patterns that the Corinthians were replicating in their community—prestige seeking, power questing, exploitation of the poor by the rich, and fleshly indulgence. Just as the gods of the nations had fostered cultural patterns of injustice, for which God would judge them (Ps 82:1-8), the rulers of this age tempt humanity toward a variety of sinful ways of life that destroy human community.

Paul states that the rulers of this age do not understand the wisdom of God (1 Cor 2:8), by which he means that their character and the ways of life oriented by them run contrary to the cruciform community modes of life that make up God's way of working. Paul charges the Corinthians to learn and discern the wisdom of God so that they will embody it through renewed community dynamics. In the wisdom of God, God triumphs by the death of Christ, and this is something that the hostile cosmic rulers do not grasp. If they had understood it, "they would not have crucified the Lord of glory" (1 Cor 2:8 NIV). Here Paul puts the responsibility for the death of Christ at their feet, indicating that their corrupt ideologies of power seeking had overtaken the Jewish and Roman authorities who put Jesus Christ to death.

In 1 Corinthians 8:4-6, Paul reflects the OT and Jewish *tradition that the gods of the nations lie behind systems of *idolatry. He acknowledges that idols are "nothing at all in the world" (1 Cor 8:4 NIV), reflecting the OT theme that idols are mere human creations that are lifeless, cannot create anything, and are powerless to save (Ps 135:15-18; Is 45:20; Jer 10:11). Idols are merely fabrications spun by the rebellious gods of the nations that create apparently idolatrous realities in order to hold enslaved the nations over which they were originally appointed. Paul acknowledges that various "gods" and "lords" really do exist (1 Cor 8:5), but the church resists their influence by fleeing idolatry (1 Cor 10:14) and maintaining faithfulness to the one true God revealed in Christ. He states, "For us there is but one God, the Father, from whom all things came and for whom we live; and there is but one Lord, Jesus Christ, through whom all things came and through whom we live" (1 Cor 8:6 NIV). This is a restatement of Deuteronomy 6:4, emphasizing that the God of Israel is the only true God, who created the heavens and earth, while the idols of the nations represent nonexistent entities.

This is the scenario Paul portrays in Galatians 4:1-11. Before their conversion to Christ, the Galatians were "in *slavery under the elemental spiritual forces of the world" (Gal 4:3 NIV). He further notes that they "are not gods" but rather "weak and miserable forces" (Gal 4:8-9 NIV).

Overseeing the complex of hostile cosmic forces is *Satan, whom Paul calls "the god of this age," who blinds the minds of nonbelievers to the truth of the gospel (2 Cor 4:4 NIV). In Ephesians 2:1-2, Paul refers to Satan as "the ruler of the kingdom of the air," who also oversees "the spirit who is now at work in those who are disobedient" (Eph 2:2 NIV). For Paul, "the air" is the realm of ideologies and cultural mindsets. Rather than working on individuals in such a way as to control their minds or wills, Satan, along with the rulers of this age, orients human ways of thinking and acting so that they do not experience their humanity as God originally intended.

7. The Church as Prolepsis of a Renewed Cosmos.

God has begun the project of purifying the cosmos by liberating it from the enslaving grip of the hostile cosmic powers. In the death and resurrection of Christ, God has defeated the powers of Sin and Death, along with Satan and the powers and authorities. This is the thrust of Paul's use of the language of Psalm 110 in two strategic texts. The psalm celebrates God's installation of his appointed king, whom God commissions to subdue his enemies with God's help. In 1 Corinthians 15:25-28, Paul uses the psalm to speak of Christ's present reign and his current activity of subjecting his enemies: "For he must reign until he has put all his enemies under his feet" (1 Cor 15:25 NIV). The psalm also lies behind Paul's statement in Ephesians 1:20-22 of Christ's having been seated at the right hand of God in the heavenly places, "far above all rule and authority, power and dominion, and every name that is invoked, not only in the present age but also in the one to come" (Eph 1:21 NIV). While a triumph is not explicitly stated, the reality that God has "placed all things under his feet" (Eph 1:22 NIV) indicates that a victory has been won over the hostile cosmic powers that had enslaved creation and polluted the cosmos.

Christ rules as cosmic lord, and his presence fills not only the church but "everything in every way" (Eph 1:23 NIV). The reign of Christ, with his presence filling the cosmos, is the initial recovery of the original intention of God to rule over his creation and for his presence to fill his cosmic temple. This "already" aspect of salvation is the proleptic (i.e., an anticipated future reality experienced in the present) recovery of what will become a universal restoration of the entire creation. When Christ has completely subjected and defeated his cosmic enemies—the last one being Death—then Christ will hand the fully subjected creation over to God so that God's rule over creation will be fully and finally seen, with humans ruling creation on God's behalf and for God's glory (Rom 5:17; 8:18-21).

According to Paul, this proleptic scenario is seen in the church. In Ephesians 2:11-18, Paul narrates how God has united humanity in Christ from formerly divided ethnicities and nations. This united people have become a new building that is "a holy temple in the Lord" (Eph 2:21 NIV) and "a dwelling place of God by the Spirit" (Eph 2:22). The unified humanity within the church is a microcosm of what all humanity will become when God makes all things new at the day of Christ.

Paul's depiction here builds on the function of the temple in the OT, which was a microcosm of creation as God originally intended. While God's presence and glory were to pervade the cosmos, human rebellion had prevented this. The design of the physical temple, in which God's presence was encountered, was patterned after the creation and pointed ahead to the time when the cosmos would be renewed to its condition of flourishing (see 1 Kings 8:12-13; Ps 132).

Paul makes much of the church as temple in 1 Corinthians. This notion appears early in the letter but shapes many of the warnings Paul delivers about the church's disunity throughout. In 1 Corinthians 3:16-17, he asks, "Don't you know that you yourselves are God's temple and that God's Spirit dwells in your midst? If anyone destroys God's temple, God will destroy that person; for God's temple is sacred, and you together are that temple" (NIV). The corporate *body is the dwelling place of God, and this must be depicted by the community's remaining unified in mutual service and *love. Anyone who is an agent of division is subject to God's judgment, since they have become polluters of temple space. In 1 Corinthians 11:17-34, Paul warns the Corinthians about their corrupt practice of the *Lord's Supper, from which the rich are excluding the poor. He notes that this has made them the objects of God's judgment and is why some in the community have become sick and died (1 Cor 11:29-31).

In a remarkable passage, Paul stresses that the church has cosmic significance as God's temple, since it is the site of God's triumph that is visible to the powers and authorities. As Paul the prisoner preaches the gospel and God forms the church made up of humanity from every *ethnicity and social class into a unified people, "the manifold wisdom of God should be made known to the rulers and authorities in the heavenly realms" (Eph 3:10 NIV). The hostile cosmic powers had corrupted the cosmos to ensure that humanity would divide along tribal and ethnic lines, fostering conflict and hostility. But when the church is created and lives as unified communities, the powers' efforts are frustrated, and they come to know the wisdom of God—the wisdom of the cross and its power to renew humanity.

See also Apocalyptic Paul; Apocalypticism; Church; Corinthians, First Letter to the; Creation and New Creation; Idolatry; Principalities and Powers; Romans, Letter to the; Sin, Guilt; Temple.

BIBLIOGRAPHY. E. **Adams,** *Constructing the World: A Study in Paul's Cosmological Language*, SNTW (Edinburgh: T&T Clark, 2000); **J. C. Beker,** *Paul the Apostle: The Triumph of God in Life and Thought* (Philadelphia: Fortress, 1980); **G. B. Caird,** *Principalities and Powers* (Oxford: Clarendon, 1956); **O. Cullmann,** *Christ and Time: The Primitive Christian Conception of Time and History* (London: SCM Press, 1962); **J. D. G. Dunn,** *The Theology of Paul the Apostle* (Grand Rapids, MI: Eerdmans, 1998); **B. R. Gaventa,** *Our Mother Saint Paul* (Louisville, KY: Westminster John Knox, 2007); idem, *Apocalyptic Paul: Cosmos and Anthropos in Romans 5–8* (Waco, TX: Baylor University Press, 2013); **T. G. Gombis,** *The Drama of Ephesians: Participating in the Triumph of God* (Downers Grove, IL: IVP Academic, 2010); **B. W. Longenecker,** *The Triumph of Abraham's God: The Transformation of Identity in Galatians* (Nashville: Abingdon, 1998); **S. F. Noll,** *Angels of Light, Powers of Darkness: Thinking Biblically About Angels, Satan, and Principalities* (Downers Grove, IL: InterVarsity Press, 1998); **J. T. Pennington and S. M. McDonough,** eds., *Cosmology and New Testament Theology* (London: T&T Clark, 2008); **B. N. Peterson,** "Cosmology," *DOTP*, 90-99; **J. H. Walton,** *Genesis 1 as Ancient Cosmology* (Winona Lake, IN: Eisenbrauns, 2011); **W. Wink,** *Naming the Powers: The Language of Power in the New Testament* (Philadelphia: Fortress, 1984).

T. Gombis

COVENANT

A covenant (Gk. *diathēkē*/Heb. *bərît*) is understood generally as a solemn pledge or treaty between parties that assures promises and obligations between them are kept (Hugenberger, 168-215; Williamson 2007, 139). In biblical texts, apart from agreements made between humans, covenants involve divine-human relationships inclusive of both privileges and responsibilities, and positive or negative consequences that depend on human behavior (Bergsma and Hahn; Hahn). In Paul's letters *diathēkē* is interpreted differently depending on context, and limiting one's study to the Greek term may be too restrictive (Porter; Wells, 8-9). The word *covenant* also refers to a particular theological or hermeneutic position in Pauline studies. Likewise, Jewish Scripture is important for both exegetical and theological interpretations of Paul's covenant language.

1. Covenant Related to Jewish Scripture
2. Covenant in Paul's Letters
3. Covenantal Theology and Paul

1. Covenant Related to Jewish Scripture.

In Jewish Scripture, the establishment of covenants between humans is frequently attested (e.g., Gen 21:27; Josh 9:11; 2 Sam 3:12-13), but particularly relevant in Paul's letters are divine-human agreements. Although a covenant with Adam and *creation is sometimes proposed (Dumbrell), the first explicit mention of a covenant is God's agreement with Noah. After the deluge, and in response to Noah's obedience to divine instructions as well as his sacrificial offering, *God promises never to flood the earth again as God reestablishes stability in the created order, repeats the Adamic command for humans to multiply, and sets a rainbow in the sky as the sign of this universal covenant for "all *flesh" (Gen 6:18; 8:20–9:17).

God's next covenant is with *Abraham. In Genesis 12:1-3 Abraham departs from his father's land in response to God's command for him to go to the land that will be shown to him. God promises to make the patriarch into a great nation and that other families of the earth will be blessed through him. Abraham's obedience opens the door for a covenant to be made. Certain scholars suggest God establishes two distinct covenants with the patriarch in Genesis 15; 17 (e.g., Williamson 2007, 17-43). The covenant in Genesis 15 is considered a royal grant in which unilateral obligation is made by one party for the other party's past loyalty. God more specifically promises here that Abraham's descendants will be as numerous as the stars, a promise that Abraham believes and for which he is thus reckoned righteous. After Abraham prepares a ritualistic *sacrifice, God establishes his covenant with Abraham, promising that his offspring will inherit the land of Canaan. The covenant in Genesis 17, however, is said to be bilateral, involving obligations from both parties. Abraham is to walk blamelessly before God and establish *circumcision as a sign of the covenant for his descendants to observe. God promises that Abraham's chosen offspring will come through Sarah and that the fruitfulness of his descendants will include other nations.

Other scholars suggest a single Abrahamic covenant mentioned in regard to Abraham, Isaac, and Jacob (Ex 2:24; Lev 26:42; 2 Kings 13:23; Acts 3:25; Niehaus; Postell; Gentry and Wellum, 254-56). In this light Genesis 12:1-3 is precovenantal for Genesis 15, which in turn is either renewed or supplemented in Genesis 17 and then supplemented again in Genesis 22 with the Akedah. This view interprets Abraham's covenant as both conditional and unconditional—it requires the patriarch and his descendants' obedience, and yet God establishes and accomplishes his purpose through it. Whether one or two covenants is the best interpretation, it is noteworthy that Abraham's rites progress from animals (Gen 15) to circumcision (Gen 17) to his son Isaac (Gen 22). His benefits likewise progress from land to a dynasty to a worldwide blessing including other nations (Hahn, 134). The last point is most relevant for Paul, *apostle to the *Gentiles.

The Mosaic covenant is established on the basis of Israel's exodus from Egypt, divine deliverance, and the establishment of the Decalogue with other regulations (Ex 12; 15; 20–23). The covenant is considered bilateral, requiring human obedience and law observance (Ex 19:5-6; 20:1-17). It is ratified by sacrificial offerings and reading the Book of the Covenant (= Ex 20:22–23:33), as well as Moses sprinkling blood on the people and dining in God's presence (Ex 24:1-11; cf. Ex 19:5). This covenant is later reconfirmed at Moab upon Israel's entrance into Canaan (Deut 29:1), with observances and violation of commands explicated in Deuteronomy 26:16–32:47. *Israel will receive blessings for keeping God's laws and *curses for disobeying it, which include expulsion from the land (Deut 28:63; 30:17-18). The Deuteronomic covenant, as well as Exodus 19–24 to a lesser extent, resembles a suzerain-vassal treaty with preamble, historical introduction related to vassal loyalty, treaty stipulations, witnesses, provision and readings, blessings and curses, impositions, and a ceremony of ratification (Mendenhall and Herion, 1180-83; Weinfeld, 266). Although Israel's breaking of the covenant and exile seem expected (Deut 32), the people's repentance and restoration is also anticipated in terms of a circumcised heart (Deut 30:1-6; cf. Deut 10:16), a prelude to the new covenant that Paul adopts.

The Davidic covenant is thought to be another example of a royal grant (Hahn, 176-213), this one characterized by the promise of royal offspring, building of the Lord's house, and God's steadfast *love never departing from David's posterity (2 Sam 7:8-16; 2 Chron 13:5; Ps 89; 132). Certain scholars, however, suggest the covenant resembles a suzerain-vassal treaty and find both conditional and unconditional elements to it (Waltke; Kinzel; Freedman and Miano, 13-19). Regardless, permanency behind Davidic posterity paves the way for messianic fulfillment, with a Davidic figure or language repeatedly appearing in *prophecy (Is 9:5-7; 11:1-2, 10; 16:5; 55:3; Jer 23:5-6; 33:15-26; Hos 3:5; Amos 9:11), a point of which Paul is well aware (Rom 1:3-4; 15:12).

In prophetic writings a futuristic covenant is marked out for the restored people of God, which is new (Jer 31:31-34), brings peace (Is 54:9-10; Ezek 34:25; 37:26), and is everlasting (Is 55:3; 61:8; Jer 32:40; 50:5; Ezek 16:60; 37:26; cf. Is 42:6; 59:20-21). In Isaiah 42:1-9 the Servant of the Lord may be considered as the embodiment of this anticipated covenant, "the agent through whom God's covenant blessing will be extended to all people" (Rata, 103). The voice of Paul is perhaps interpreting Isaiah's words as fulfilled in *Christ and by Gentiles coming to the *Lord (Acts 13:47; 26:23; McConville, 749-50). In Jeremiah 31:31-34 the "new covenant" with the house of Israel and Judah will not be like Moses' covenant, which they failed to keep. This covenant will be characterized by God writing his law (or "laws," LXX) in their hearts. Thus a kinship relation is established, with God being the people's God and they being God's people, and all of them knowing the Lord, who forgives their sins and unrighteousness. It is disputed whether this covenant's dissimilarity with the Mosaic covenant means that the new one is simply a renewed Torah or an entirely different covenant, due to Israel breaking the first. Another possibility is that there is essentially one divine-human covenant in Scripture, though several from a human point of view (Christiansen, 61-62). In any case, it appears that there are both similarities and dissimilarities between the two covenants.

Ancient people who followed Christ seem to have equated Jeremiah's covenant, which is both new and everlasting (Jer 31:31; 32:40), with the everlasting covenant of other prophetic discourses such as in Ezekiel (Heb 13:20; cf. Heb 8:8-10; 10:16, 29; 12:24; 2 Cor 3:3–4:6; Oropeza 2018). In Ezekiel 36:23–37:28 (also Ezek 11:14-21; 18:30-31) the everlasting covenant of *peace (Ezek 37:26), among other things, will lead to restoration of Israel's land, people knowing their Lord, permanency, a sense of belonging, kinship with God, and purification, involving a new heart given to the people. Moral incentives will be successfully accomplished with this new heart. In addition, Ezekiel emphasizes God's Spirit renewing humans and dwelling in and among them (Ezek 36:26-27; 37:14). "David" will dwell with them, and the nations will come to know the Lord (Ezek 37:24-25, 28). This covenant is thus inclusive of a new deliverance, new Zion, and new Davidic king (Lundbom, 1088). Gentiles will also participate in it.

2. Covenant in Paul's Letters.

In 1 Corinthians Paul passes on to the Corinthians the earliest *tradition recalling Jesus' words about the new covenant (1 Cor 11:23-26). The *Lord's Supper was celebrated in a number of congregations (Acts 2:42, 46; 20:7; 1 Cor 10:3-4, 16-17, 21; Jude 12; Jn 6:48-58; Did. 9-10), and it is evident that Jesus' disciples remembered and repeated his words orally to the congregations when celebrating the meal. These words were eventually written down in the Synoptic Gospels (Mk 14:22-25; Mt 26:26-29; Lk 22:14-20). That Paul claims to receive this tradition "from the Lord" probably does not mean he received it through divine revelation but rather through the Lord's disciples, who were present at the Last Supper and heard Jesus himself speak. Perhaps Paul learned the tradition from *Peter (Cephas), whom he visited for a few weeks after becoming a Christ-follower (Gal 1:18). It seems that, after practicing this celebration in Antioch, Paul eventually passed on the tradition to the congregations he founded, *Corinth included. When he wrote 1 Corinthians, the Lord's Supper and Jesus' words pertaining to it had already been part of the Corinthians' normal *worship for many months.

Paul's recitation of Jesus' words in 1 Corinthians 11:25 follows Luke 22:20 best: "this cup is the new covenant in my blood." (The omission of Lk 22:19b-20 in Western manuscripts is to be rejected as the original witness: see Metzger, *Textual Commentary,* 148-49.) Unlike Luke's version, the synoptic parallels lack the word *new* before *covenant* in some important manuscript witnesses: "my blood of the [new] covenant" (Mk 14:24; Mt 26:28). If the longer text variant is not the original in Mark and Matthew, this still does not deter the strong possibility that even in these Gospels Jesus' words and actions associate his blood with inaugurating a new covenant (Perrin, 494; also compare Mt 26:27 with Jer 31:34). Links between the concepts of covenant, blood, a sacrifice, and dining together are reminiscent of the establishment of Moses' covenant (Ex 24:5-11), while at the same time there is allusion to Jeremiah's words and the Servant of the Lord's sacrifice (Jer 31:31-34; Is 53:5, 11-12). Such a conceptual blend seems to be the assumed background behind Paul's tradition, a variant of which is brought out more forcefully in Hebrews 8:8-10; 9:14-22; 10:29; 12:24; 13:20 (Gräbe, 125-41). The sacrifice behind this new covenant that Jesus establishes turns out to be his crucifixion, and his broken body and shed blood are represented by the unleavened bread and wine he shares with his disciples during his final meal. Paul and Luke include human obligation related to the meal: "Do this in remembrance of me" (1 Cor 11:24-25// Lk 22:19).

The importance of grounding Paul's new covenant language in the words of Jesus is at least threefold. First, this makes the language pre-Pauline, uttered by Jesus on the night he was arrested. Paul's use of the term "new covenant," then, is carried not merely by the weight of his own authority but by Jesus' authority. Second, since Jesus' words are attached to a sacred dining ritual to be practiced by his followers afterward, both Pauline and non-Pauline congregations almost surely would have been familiar with the idea of Christ establishing a new covenant at his final supper, *before* Paul wrote his extant letters. Third, if Paul uses the word *covenant* in an ad hoc manner elsewhere in his letters, this does not infringe on the importance of the more particularized term "new covenant" (*kainē diathēkē*) for Paul and his letter recipients.

One can surmise that, after the apostle first learned about Jesus' new covenant, he read and reflected further on the covenants in prophetic Scripture, which he interpreted as being fulfilled through the Christ-event. By the time he discussed the new covenant in 2 Corinthians 3:3-18, he was doubtless familiar with the term and could hardly have been using it merely as a way to offset his opponents' use of it. It is a struggle to find compelling indications that the Corinthian situation centered on conformity to Mosaic *law or that Paul's *opponents taught that the Spirit of the new covenant would enable the Corinthians to keep the law perfectly (contrast Murphy-O'Connor, 295-323; Blanton 2007; 2010). In 1 Corinthians 15:56 Paul mentions without further explanation his radical connection of the law with *sin; the probable reason he could state this simply in passing is that he knew the Corinthians already agreed with his interpretation. Their libertine ways and vice doing are clear in both letters to the Corinthians and strongly suggest their problem was not with a desire to keep the law and Jewish ways. Rather, they had accepted Paul's opponents through letters of recommendation and, incited by these interlopers, had criticized the validity of Paul's *ministry, his competency in *preaching, and his outward persona, which in their estimation lacked visible signs of divine approbation, *unlike* Moses (Oropeza 2016, 232-38, 570-78, 601-6).

In defense of his team's ministry Paul advances the self-designation "ministers of the new covenant" (2 Cor 3:6), which points back not only to Jesus' eucharistic words but also to the prophetic discourses that informed those words. Paul had long since discovered his own role in the prophetic writings as a servant-messenger of God called to reach the Gentiles with the good news about Jesus Messiah, inclusive of the awaited new covenant. The influence of prophetic Scripture on Paul's *calling is clear enough (Gal 1:15-16; 2 Cor 6:2; Rom 10:15; 15:20-21; see Is 49:1-8; 52:7, 15; Jer 1:5). Particularly in 2 Corinthians the apostle could identify with Jeremiah as a fellow Benjamite called by God from the womb, commissioned to the nations, struggling with speaking inadequacies, challenging deceptive opponents, suffering imprisonment with a "sentence of death" for his proclamations, using the imagery of tearing down and rebuilding in his messages, emphasizing that the only legitimate boast is in the Lord, and, of course, speaking of the new covenant (see references in Oropeza 2018, 407-9). Likewise, Paul's "seal" of the Spirit "in the hearts" of the believers, and the "earthenware jar" that houses the treasure of new covenant knowledge, reflect Jeremiah's object lesson of purchasing his uncle's inheritance with a document sealed in an earthenware jar, anticipating restoration from exile and the implementation of the new covenant (Jer 32[39]; see 2 Cor 1:21-22; 3:3-6; 4:7).

Paul's covenant, however, emphasizes God's Spirit (2 Cor 3:3, 6, 8, 17-18), which neither Jesus nor Jeremiah's version mentions. It is likely that either he or someone before him linked Jeremiah 31–32 with Ezekiel 36–37 via midrash technique (for example, *gezerah shawah*), as maintained by Carol Stockhausen (56-59). Hook terms such as "new," "in the heart," and "everlasting covenant" linked the two prophetic texts together so that the apostle interpreted the content of the new covenant to include God writing laws on the human heart (Jeremiah), the Spirit dwelling in those hearts (Ezekiel), and the covenant extending to Gentile nations (Ezekiel).

Paul argues that the new covenant shows itself to be more glorious than the old covenant of Moses in at least three ways (2 Cor 3:3-11). First, the new covenant is characterized by the Spirit, who gives salvific life, but the old covenant of Moses is characterized by a written code that brings *death, killing those who disobey it (see Ex 32:26-28; 33:3-6). Second, the ministry of the Spirit brings *righteousness and greater *glory, whereas the ministry of the old covenant brought condemnation, and although it came with glory, this needed to be veiled (Ex 34:27-35). Third, there is permanence to the Spirit and glory, but the glory of the old covenant is now being set aside or "rendered inoperative" (Hafemann 1996, 301-10). The new covenant ministry of the Spirit in which Paul operates, then, exceeds the old covenant ministry of Moses in benefit, intensity, and duration.

The apostle continues that the *telos* (goal + end/outcome) behind the veil that hides Moses's glory is the glory of a life transformed by the Spirit into the likeness (image) of Christ, which brings eternal glory (2 Cor 3:12–4:6). Whenever a person hearing the Torah read "turns" to the Lord (here identifying God's Spirit, who transforms the hearts of those who confess Jesus as Lord), they, too, can experience freedom from the obduracy that prevented them from comprehending Paul's *gospel. The new covenant in the Corinthian correspondence is bound up with Paul's gospel and a change of eras from old to new brought on by the Christ event. The apostle's interpretation of the prophetic covenant in 2 Corinthians 3 seems to place an accent on discontinuity rather than continuity between old and new covenants, though certain scholars would contest this (e.g., Campbell; Christiansen, 324). Even so, it must be admitted that, given the repetitive use of ministerial terminology in the text (2 Cor 3:3, 6-9; 4:1), the comparison focuses more on two ministries rather than two covenants (Hafemann 2020; 2021).

Another witness to the new covenant is argued by T. J. Deidun (19-35, 58-61), but it is at best implicit. Paul warns the Thessalonians that as a holy people they must not reject his exhortation or else they will reject "God, who gives his *Holy Spirit to you" (1 Thess 4:8). The phrase may allude to Ezekiel 36:27 or Ezekiel 37:14, which encourage moral living in a covenantal context (see Ezek 36:15; 37:23, 27).

There are more explicit uses of *covenant* in Galatians 3:15-17; 4:21-32. In the former text Paul argues that the divine promise of Abraham's seed, interpreted as Christ, cannot be nullified by the law of Moses that came 430 years after the promise. The promise is associated with a covenant that, according to typical human pacts, cannot be altered or nullified. This quotidian use of *diathēkē* in Galatians 3:15 points to a final testament or will; at the same time, the promise recalls the Abrahamic covenant (Gen 15). The quotidian aspect probably exhibits the inviolability of a will *after* a testator's death (Keener, 260-65; contrast Hahn, 238-76), though inviolability also reflects the promise of Abraham's covenant. Perhaps both aspects are valid to some extent (Christiansen, 234-39), which suggests a play on the terms *will* and *covenant*, similar to Hebrews 9:15-22. It is quite possible that Paul's use of Abraham in Galatians reflects the language of his opponents in that letter; the apostle attempts to divorce the connection the agitators made between Abraham and Moses by virtue of the patriarch's circumcision (Martyn 1997, 345-47). Allusion to Abraham's covenant here takes a backseat to the more central aspect of "promise" (Dunn 2003, 290-95; Das 2016, 74-76, 79).

This covenant surfaces again in Galatians 4:24 allegorically with Hagar and Ishmael, who are associated with such images as Sinai, *Jerusalem, the flesh, and enslavement. Sarah and Isaac are associated with Jerusalem from "above," the Spirit, *freedom, and promise. The two women represent two covenants, which in turn may represent two Gentile missions, one related to the law observances of Paul's opponents (Hagar) over against Paul's gospel *mission (Sarah), according to William Campbell. If so, Paul implies a bifurcated Abrahamic covenant. More likely, however, the Mosaic covenant, whose reception at Sinai and center of worship in Jerusalem is alluded to here, is represented by Hagar, whereas Abraham's covenant of promise is represented by Sarah. Others draw a connection between the new covenant and the Abrahamic promise here (Hahn 2009, 243; Keener, 417). Although nothing is explicitly mentioned about the new covenant in this letter, God's Spirit as prophetically realized and perhaps assumed from Ezekiel 36–37, among other texts, may be implied in such passages as Galatians 3:1-5, 14.

In Romans, circumcision of the heart intimates Gentile conversion and the Spirit's power (Rom 2:28-29). Newness plus Spirit, in contrast to oldness plus written code of the law (Rom 7:6), parallels the new covenant language of 2 Corinthians 3 (Dunn 1998, 422). In Romans 9:4-5 the plural "covenants" of Israel probably refer at least to Abrahamic and Mosaic covenants, if not Davidic and new covenants also. There is another plural use in the disputed letter of Ephesians (Eph 2:12); in that instance it is attached to the notion of promise, thus reflecting Abrahamic, Davidic, and/or new covenants. In Romans 11:26-27, when speaking of the deliverer from Zion, Paul is thought to quote Isaiah 27:9 fused with Isaiah 59:20-21: "for this is the covenant with them from me when I remove their sins." Isaiah 27:9, however, has "his sin," whereas the new covenant of Jeremiah is closer in wording by using "their sins" and "this is the covenant" (Jer 31[38]:33-34; Dunn 2003, 304; Lundbom, 1092). This may suggest that Jeremiah's passage was fused with the Isaianic texts in this quote. But even if Jeremiah were excluded from the mix, the covenant still fits comfortably under the rubric of the new covenant.

The covenant of Isaiah 59:20-21 is explained in terms of God's Spirit being with God's people forever (Is 59:21). Paul seems to believe that, at some point in the future, a large portion of Israel who currently reject the Messiah, the deliverer from Zion, will be saved and will receive the Spirit as they embrace the prophetic covenant. Given that the apostle mentioned earlier in the letter that the "law of the Spirit of life" sets free from sin and condemnation those who are in Christ (Rom 8:1-2), this reading appears to be confirmed. Apart from Gentile nations such as the Romans coming to the know the Lord (Ezek 37:28), allusions to Ezekiel 36–37 in Romans 8:1-13 include God's Spirit dwelling in believers (Ezek 36:26-27; 37:14//Rom 8:9-11), the "Spirit of life" empowering the dead to come back to life (Ezek 37:5-6, 10, 14//Rom 8:2, 6, 11), the covenant characterized in terms of a permanent divine relationship with "peace" (Ezek 37:26//Rom 8:6), and the people enabled to "walk" in God's "righteous requirements" (Ezek 36:27//Rom 8:4).

Although Paul recognizes other covenants, the most prominent for the messianic era is the new covenant as taught by Jesus, traced back to Jeremiah, and connected with the covenants of other prophetic writings, especially that of Ezekiel 36–37, through which the life-giving Spirit dwells in the hearts of the faithful.

3. Covenantal Theology and Paul.

There is currently a lively discussion about the concept of covenant as a hermeneutic by which one may interpret Paul's theology. E. P. Sanders helped spark the current trend through his studies on Second Temple Judaism, especially in *Paul and Palestinian Judaism*. Rather than accept the prevailing NT scholarly view of the time that considered Judaism as a works-righteousness religion, Sanders demonstrates that the Judaism of Paul's day was a grace-based religion. Sanders popularized the term "covenantal nomism" to describe ancient Judaism's relationship with God:

> The "pattern" or "structure" of covenantal nomism is this: (1) God has chosen Israel and (2) given the law. The law implies (3) God's promise to maintain the election and (4) the requirement to obey. (5) God rewards obedience and punishes transgression. (6) The law provides for means of atonement, and atonement results in (7) maintenance or re-establishment of the covenantal relationship. (8) All those who are maintained in the covenant by obedience, atonement, and God's mercy belong to the group which will be saved. An important interpretation of the first and last points is that election and ultimately salvation are considered to be by God's mercy rather than human achievement. (Sanders, 422; see also 75)

If such *grace is the case, then why does Paul come against the *works of Mosaic law? Sanders's explanation is that Paul worked from solution to plight to conclude that *faith in the Lord Jesus constitutes the only path to *salvation. The law, then, could not be another path, and as such, the problem with Judaism for Paul is that it is not the Christian faith (Sanders, 552).

Certain scholars contest Sanders's view by claiming that ancient Judaism was more variegated on grace than Sanders proposes (e.g., Carson, O'Brien, and Seifrid). They claim also that Paul contests the works of Mosaic law not simply because Judaism is not Christianity but, inter alia, because none could keep the law perfectly, or the law centers on legalism, or non-Jews do not need to observe Torah customs, or a change of eras took place through the Christ event that made Mosaic law invalid for Gentiles.

N. T. Wright concurs with Sanders's assessment of Second Temple Judaism and holds to covenant keeping in a more comprehensive way regarding Paul's soteriology: "Dealing with sin, saving humans from it, giving them grace, forgiveness, justification, glorification—all this was the purpose of the single covenant from the beginning, now fulfilled in Jesus Christ" (Wright 2009, 95; emphasis original). For Wright, God's righteousness is understood as covenant faithfulness, and *justification involves covenant membership as part of God's family, inclusive of all nations (Wright 1993, 203; 2009, 116, 121, 133-34; 2013, 960-61). Other scholars likewise have affirmed the importance of covenant in Paul, such as Michael Gorman, who understands justification as the "establishment or restoration of right covenant relations" (Gorman, 52); Sarah Whittle, who considers covenant making and renewal from Deuteronomy as an important cornerstone for Paul's inclusion of Gentiles and their call to *holiness (Whittle 2015); and Mary Nwachukwu, who connects justification in Romans with a creation covenant finding its theological voice in the Abrahamic and Mosaic covenants (Nwachukwu 2002).

Some other scholars, however, think that the notion of covenant, or connections between covenant and righteousness, has been overstated. They question covenant as the grand narrative in Paul, pointing out, for example, how this does not reflect the apostle's handling of *diathēkē* in Galatians, where his use appears to be ad hoc and tied in with a final will and allegory (Tatum; Das 2001; 2016; Dunn 2003).

Mark Seifrid points out how rare the occurrences are in Scripture that hold together righteousness and covenant. He asserts that covenant keeping may be righteous behavior, but not all righteous behavior is covenant keeping (Seifrid, 424-25, though for corrections, see Bird, 35-39). Reading Paul through the *apocalyptic turn of ages in Christ, others make a more definitive break between OT covenantalism and the apostle (Martyn 1991; 1997).

Deidun takes a different tack, centering Paul's salvific theology on the eschatological realization of the new covenant, which is focused on the experience of the Spirit. The Spirit of God is the agent through which humans are enabled to conduct themselves in love and are justified (Deidun, 34-35, 45-47, 227-29). Pitre, Barber, and Kincaid hold that Paul is best viewed as a new covenant Jew, self-identifying as a minister of the new covenant based on Jeremiah (2 Cor 3:6). This means that Paul's thoughts were largely shaped by the Jewish Scriptures in light of the revelation of Christ, which helped him come to a new way of reading these Scriptures (Pitre, Barber, and Kincaid 11-12, 38-63).

Richard Hays derives an interpretative approach to reading Scripture from Paul that he calls "new covenant hermeneutics" (Hays, 122-53, 183-92; contrast Sloan). For Hays, Paul's turn from a Pharisee to Jesus resulted in his interpreting Scripture with a new set of eyes, and at the heart of this rests his contrast between the Spirit/new covenant and "script"/old covenant in 2 Corinthians 3:6. Paul affirms that his ministry does not center on written words of the old covenant, which lacks power "to effect the obedience that it demands," but on empowerment of the eschatological community by the Spirit, which transforms it into the *image of Christ. With the old covenant, "Israel's knowledge of God was dependent on and limited by the mediated (and therefore veiled) written word of Torah; under the new covenant, direct experience of God is immediately given through the Spirit" (Hays, 131, 143). In this hermeneutic, "there is no true reading without moral transformation, and there is no moral transformation without true reading" (Hays, 152). Among other things, one learns through Paul's new covenant reading that Scripture is significantly a narrative about *election and covenant promises, community centered, in the service of proclamation of the gospel of Christ; and readers are to participate in the drama of eschatological redemption (Hays, 183-86, 191).

Two traditional but opposing views of covenant theology may be seen through Michael Horton's classic Reformed reading, which regards good works as an aspect of covenant theology that is evidence of forensic justification (Horton). Differently, the Eastern Orthodox approach to Pauline soteriology centers on the new covenant, and

> Justification—being or becoming righteous—by faith in God is part of being brought into a covenant relationship with Him. Salvation comes through faith in Christ, who fulfills the law. . . . Rather than justification as a legal acquittal before God, Orthodox believers see justification by faith as a covenant relationship with Him, centered in union with Christ (Rom 6:1-6). (Sparks, 1529)

Finally, Francis Watson presents criteria for determining whether covenant theology is present on the basis of (1) differentiation between Israel and the nations regarding election, (2) certain events that are scripturally attested to be foundational for a covenant relationship, (3) relational continuity grounded in divine faithfulness, and (4) the salvation-historical continuum "as the comprehensive context of theological reflection" (Watson, 102-3). He also specifies what rules out covenant theology, including individual instead of corporate focus; disinterest in Abraham, Sinai, and the exodus; stress on discontinuities generated by sinfulness, which results in divine redefining of covenant and scope; and a view of "covenantal salvation-history as one among a number of possible themes for theological reflection" (Watson, 103). Kyle Wells, however, questions whether Watson's criteria is too arbitrary and stringent; if it were applied to Qumran's *Yaḥad*, this sect would not possess a covenant theology due to its view of sin and covenantal scope, and neither would 4 Ezra, 2 Baruch, or N. T. Wright's Paul (Wells, 6-7). Watson's criteria nonetheless lays important groundwork on which to build or make one's point of departure from in future studies.

Issues surrounding a covenantal reading of Paul are far from settled. The challenge moving forward will be to fine-tune a hermeneutic of covenant that does not impose denominational and theological presuppositions onto Paul's own language from his letters.

See also ABRAHAM; CONVERSION AND CALL OF PAUL; INTERPRETATION: NEW PERSPECTIVE; JESUS AND PAUL; OLD TESTAMENT IN PAUL; PAUL AND JUDAISM.

BIBLIOGRAPHY. **R. J. Bautch,** "Covenant," in *T&T Clark Encyclopedia of Second Temple Judaism*, ed. D. M. Gurtner and L. T. Stuckenbruck (London: T&T Clark, 2020), 2:171-74; **J. S. Bergsma and**

S. W. Hahn, "Covenant," in *The Oxford Encyclopedia of the Bible and Theology*, ed. S. E. Balentine (Oxford: Oxford University Press, 2015), 1:151-66; **M. F. Bird,** *The Saving Righteousness of God: Studies on Paul, Justification, and the New Perspective* (Eugene, OR: Wipf & Stock, 2007); **T. R. Blanton,** *Constructing a New Covenant: Discursive Strategies in the Damascus Document and Second Corinthians*, WUNT 2/233 (Tubingen: Mohr Siebeck, 2007); idem, "Spirit and Covenant Renewal: A Theologoumenon of Paul's Opponents in 2 Corinthians," *JBL* 129 (2010): 129-51; **P. Buis,** "La nouvelle alliance," *VT* 18 (1968): 1-15; **W. S. Campbell,** *The Nations in the Divine Economy: Paul's Covenantal Hermeneutics and Participation in Christ* (Lanham, MD: Lexington/Fortress Academic, 2018); **D. A. Carson, P. T. O'Brien, and M. A. Seifrid,** eds., *Justification and Variegated Nomism*, 2 vols. (Grand Rapids, MI: Baker Academic, 2001–2004); **J. E. Christiansen,** *The Covenant in Judaism and Paul: A Study of Ritual Boundaries as Identity Markers*, AGJU 27 (Leiden: Brill, 1995); **A. A. Das,** *Paul, the Law, and the Covenant* (Peabody, MA: Hendrickson, 2001); idem, *Paul and the Stories of Israel: Grand Thematic Narratives in Galatians (*Minneapolis: Fortress, 2016); **T. J. Deidun,** *New Covenant Morality in Paul*, AnBib 89 (Rome: Pontifical Biblical Institute, 1980); **W. J. Dumbrell,** *Covenant and Creation: A Theology of the Old Testament Covenants*, rev. ed. (Milton Keynes, UK: Paternoster, 2013); **J. D. G. Dunn,** *The Theology of Paul the Apostle* (Grand Rapids, MI: Eerdmans, 1998); idem, "Did Paul Have a Covenant Theology? Reflections on Romans 9.4 and 11.27," in *The Concept of the Covenant in the Second Temple Period*, ed. S. E. Porter and J. C. R. de Roo, JSJSup 71 (Leiden: Brill, 2003), 287-307; **W. A. Elwell and B. J. Beitzel,** "Covenant," in *Baker Encyclopedia of the Bible*, ed. W. A. Elwell (Grand Rapids, MI: Baker, 1988), 1:530-36; **D. N. Freedman and D. Miano,** "People of the New Covenant," in *The Concept of the Covenant in the Second Temple Period*, ed. S. E. Porter and J. C. R. DeRoo, JSJSup 71 (Leiden: Brill, 2003), 7-26; **P. J. Gentry and S. J. Wellum**, *God's Kingdom Through God's Covenants: A Concise Biblical Theology* (Wheaton, IL: Crossway, 2015); **M. J. Gorman,** *Inhabiting the Cruciform God: Kenosis, Justification, and Theosis in Paul's Narrative Soteriology* (Grand Rapids, MI: Eerdmans, 2009); **L. Grabbe,** "Covenant in Philo and Josephus," in *The Concept of the Covenant in the Second Temple Period*, ed. S. E. Porter and J. C. R. de Roo, JSJSup 71 (Leiden: Brill, 2003), 251-66; **P. Gräbe,** *New Covenant, New Community: The Significance of Biblical and Patristic Covenant Theology for Contemporary Understanding* (Waynesboro, GA: Paternoster, 2006); **S. J. Hafemann,** *Paul, Moses, and the History of Israel: The Letter/Spirit Contrast and the Argument from Scripture in 2 Corinthians 3* (Peabody, MA: Hendrickson, 1996); idem, *Paul: Servant of the New Covenant: Pauline Perspectives in Eschatological Perspective*, WUNT 435 (Tübingen: Mohr Siebeck, 2020); idem, "Like and Unlike Moses: Paul's Comparative Eschatology in 2 Corinthians 3," in *Paul and Moses*, ed. F. Wilk, SERAPHMIE 11 (Tübingen: Mohr Siebeck, 2021); **S. W. Hahn,** *Kinship by Covenant: A Canonical Approach to the Fulfillment of God's Saving Promises*, AYBRL (New Haven, CT: Yale University Press, 2009); **R. B. Hays,** *Echoes of Scripture in the Letters of Paul* (New Haven, CT: Yale University Press, 1989); **A. L. A. Hogeterp,** "The Eschatological Setting of the New Covenant in 2 Cor 3:14-18," in *Theologizing in the Corinthian Conflict: Studies in the Exegesis and Theology of 2 Corinthians*, ed. R. Bieringer, M. M. S. Ibita, D. A. Kurek-Chomycz, and T. A. Vollmer, BTS 16 (Leuven: Peeters, 2013), 131-44; **M. Horton,** *God of Promise: Introducing Covenant Theology (*Grand Rapids, MI: Baker, 2006); **G. P. Hugenberger,** *Marriage as a Covenant: Biblical Law and Ethics as Developed from Malachi*, BSL (Grand Rapids, MI: Baker, 1998); **C. S. Keener,** *Galatians: A Commentary* (Grand Rapids, MI: Baker Academic, 2019); **B. J. Kinzel,** "The Davidic Covenant," in *A Handbook on Jewish Roots of the Christian Faith*, ed. C. S. Evans and D. Mishkin (Peabody, MA: Hendrickson, 2019), 22-28; **J. R. Lundbom,** "New Covenant," *ABD* 4:1088-94; **J. L. Martyn,** "Events in Galatia: Modified Covenantal Nomism Versus God's Invasion of the Cosmos in the Singular Gospel; A Response to J. D. G. Dunn and B. R. Gaventa," in *Pauline Theology: 1 Thessalonians, Philippians, Galatians, Philemon*, ed. J. M. Bassler and D. Hay (Minneapolis: Fortress, 1991), 1:161-79; idem, *Galatians*, AYB 33A (New Haven, CT: Yale University Press, 1997); **G. J. McConville,** "בְּרִית," in *New International Dictionary of Old Testament Theology and Exegesis*, ed. W. A. VanGemeren (Grand Rapids, MI: Zondervan, 1997), 1:747-55; **G. E. Mendenhall and G. A. Herion**, "Covenant," *ABD* 1:1179-1202; **B. M. Metzger,** *A Textual Commentary on the Greek New Testament*, 2nd ed., 4th rev. (Peabody, MA: Hendrickson, 1994); **J. Murphy-O'Connor,** *Paul: A Critical Life (*Oxford: Oxford University Press, 1996); **J. J. Niehaus,** "God's Covenant with Abraham," *JETS* 56 (2013): 249-71; **M. S. Nwachukwu,** *Creation-Covenant Scheme and Justification by*

Faith: A Canonical Study of the God-Human Drama in the Pentateuch and the Letter to the Romans, TGST 89 (Rome: Pontificia Università Gregoriana, 2002); **B. J. Oropeza,** *Exploring Second Corinthians: Life and Death, Hardship and Rivalry,* RRA 3 (Atlanta: SBL Press, 2016); idem, "New Covenant Knowledge in an Earthenware Jar: Intertextual Reconfigurations of Jeremiah in 2 Corinthians 1:21-22, 3:2-11, and 4:7," *BBR* 28 (2018): 405-24; **N. Perrin,** "Last Supper," in *DJG*[2], 492-501; **B. Pitre, M. P. Barber, and J. Kincaid,** *Paul, a New Covenant Jew* (Grand Rapids, MI: Eerdmans, 2019); **S. E. Porter,** "The Concept of Covenant in Paul," in *The Concept of the Covenant in the Second Temple Period*, ed. S. E. Porter and J. C. R. de Roo, JSJSup 71 (Leiden: Brill, 2003), 269-85; **S. D. Postell,** "The Abrahamic Call," in *A Handbook on Jewish Roots of the Christian Faith*, ed. C. S. Evans and D. Mishkin (Peabody, MA: Hendrickson, 2019), 13-16; **T. Rata,** "Covenant," in *DOTP*, 99-105; **S. Ruzer,** *Mapping the New Testament: Early Christian Writings as a Witness for Jewish Biblical Exegesis* (Leiden: Brill, 2007); **E. P. Sanders,** *Paul and Palestinian Judaism*, 40th anniversary ed. (Minneapolis: Fortress, 2017); **M. A. Seifrid,** "Righteousness Language in the Hebrew Scriptures and Early Judaism," in *Justification and Variegated Nomism: The Complexities of Second Temple Judaism*, ed. D. A. Carson, P. T. O'Brien, and M. A. Seifrid (Grand Rapids, MI: Baker, 2001), 1:415-42; **R. B. Sloan,** "2 Corinthians 2:14–4:6 and 'New Covenant Hermeneutics'—a Response to Richard Hays," *BBR* 5 (1995): 129-54; **J. N. Sparks,** *The Orthodox Study Bible: Notes* (Nashville: Thomas Nelson, 2008); **C. K. Stockhausen,** *Moses' Veil and the Glory of the New Covenant: The Exegetical Substructure of II Cor 3,1–4,6*, AnBib 116 (Rome: Pontifical Biblical Institute, 1989); **G. Tatum,** "Law and Covenant in *Paul and the Faithfulness of God,*" in *God and the Faithfulness of Paul*, ed. C. Heilig, J. T. Hewitt, and M. F. Bird (Minneapolis: Fortress, 2017), 311-27; **P. R. Thorsell,** "The Spirit in the Present Age: Preliminary Fulfillment of the Predicted New Covenant According to Paul," *JETS* 41 (1998): 397-413; **B. K. Waltke,** "The Phenomena of Conditional with Unconditional Covenants," in *Israel's Apostasy and Restoration: Essays in Honor of Roland K. Harrison*, ed. A. Gileadi (Grand Rapids, MI: Baker, 1988), 123-40; **F. Watson,** "Is Paul a Covenant Theologian?," in *The Unrelenting God: God's Action in Scripture; Essays in Honor of Beverly Roberts Gaventa*, ed. D. J. Downs and M. L. Skinner (Grand Rapids, MI: Eerdmans, 2013), 102-18; **M. Weinfeld,** "בְּרִית," *TDOT* 2:253-79; **K. B. Wells,** "Was Paul a Covenant Theologian? Methodological Problems and Prospects" (paper presented at the 2016 Colloquium for winners of the Manfred Lautenschläger Award for Theological Promise, 2016), 1-14; **S. Whittle,** *Covenant Renewal and the Consecration of the Gentiles in Romans*, SNTSMS 161 (Cambridge: Cambridge University Press, 2015); **P. R. Williamson,** *Abraham, Israel and the Nations: The Patriarchal Promise and Its Covenantal Development in Genesis*, JSOTSup 315 (Sheffield: Sheffield Academic Press, 2000); idem, "Covenant," in *Dictionary of the Old Testament: Pentateuch*, ed. T. D. Alexander and D. W. Baker (Downers Grove, IL: InterVarsity Press, 2003), 139-55; idem, *Sealed with an Oath: Covenant in God's Unfolding Purpose*, NSBT 33 (Downers Grove, IL: InterVarsity Press, 2007); **N. T. Wright,** *The Climax of the Covenant: Christ and the Law in Pauline Theology* (Minneapolis: Fortress, 1993); idem, *Justification: God's Plan and Paul's Vision* (London: SPCK, 2009); idem, *Paul and the Faithfulness of God*, COQG (Minneapolis: Fortress, 2013).

B. J. Oropeza

COVENANTAL NOMISM. *See* INTERPRETATION: NEW PERSPECTIVE; LAW; WORKS OF THE LAW.

COWORKERS, PAUL AND HIS

Paul is popularly perceived as a largely independent character, traveling the world with few close colleagues, an impression that can be accentuated by Paul's insistence that he was called by *God and set apart for the *gospel (1 Cor 1:1; 2 Cor 1:1; Gal 1:1). This superficial impression is soon undermined by a close reading of the Pauline writings and Acts. Depending on how broad a definition one works with, there are between eighty and one hundred people who could fall within the general category of Paul's coworkers. Not only that, but it is clear from Paul's writings that he found the support and companionship of his coworkers to be vital to his ability to proclaim the gospel, which 2 Corinthians 2:12-13 makes particularly clear. Here Paul reports arriving in Troas (Troy) to "proclaim the good news of *Christ" and that "a door was opened for me in the *Lord" (NRSV), but he was unable to rest because he could not find Titus his brother, so he continued onwards to Macedonia. This small anecdote reveals much about Paul's *ministry and relationships. Paul worked closely and collaboratively with his colleagues and found that their absence hampered his ministry.

It is also worth noting that, although the majority of Paul's coworkers were men, *women are mentioned regularly as coworkers (Priscilla/Prisca,

Rom 16:3-5; Euodia and Syntyche, Phil 4:2-3), as fellow soldiers (Prisca/Priscilla, Philem 2), as an apostle (Junia, Rom 16:7), as toilers alongside Paul (Mary, Rom 16:6; Tryphaena and Tryphosa, Rom 16:12), and as a deacon (Phoebe, Rom 16:1). There was no separate category called "female coworkers," and Paul made no distinction between his female coworkers and his male ones. As a result, there will be no separate section dedicated to Paul's female coworkers. However, given the common tendency to imagine women out of biblical narratives, it is worth noting their presence explicitly at the start.

1. Terminology
2. The Roles of Those Who Worked with Paul
3. Conclusion

1. Terminology.

1.2. Compound Nouns and Verbs. Another feature that highlights Paul's leaning toward collaboration is his use of words compounded with the prefix *syn-*. By far the most common of these compounds is *synergos*, "coworker" (used of Achaius, 1 Cor 16:15-18; Apollos, 1 Cor 3:9; Aristarchus, Philem 24; Col 4:10-11; Clement, Phil 4:3; Demas, Philem 24; Epaphroditus, Phil 2:25; Euodia and Syntyche, Phil 4:3; Fortunatus, 1 Cor 16:15-18; Justus, Col 4:10-11; Luke, Philem 24; Mark, Philem 24; Col 4:11; Philemon, Philem 1; Prisca and Aquila, Rom 16:3; Stephanas, 1 Cor 16:15-18; Timothy, Rom 16:21; 1 Thess 3:2; Titus, 2 Cor 8:23; and Urbanus, Rom 16:5). Paul uses the term quite freely even, in 2 Corinthians 1:24, maintaining that "we" are *synergoi* with "you" (i.e., all the Corinthians Christians). Such usage makes it clear that this is not a technical term for people who were particularly close colleagues with Paul and reminds us that Paul does not imagine that he is engaged in his ministry alone.

As well as *synergoi*, Paul also regularly uses the compounds *syndoulos* (co- or fellow slave) in relation to Epaphras (Col 1:7) and Tychicus (Col 4:7); *systratiōtēs* (co- or fellow soldier) of Archippus (Philem 2) and of Epaphroditus (Phil 2:25); and *synaichmalōtos* (co- or fellow prisoner) of Andronicus and Junia (Rom 16:7), Aristarchus (Col 4:10), and Epaphras (Philem 23). Paul also uses the compound verb *synathleō* (to strive together for something) to describe what Euodia and Syntyche do alongside Paul (Phil 4:2). All of these compound words indicate that Paul saw his ministry and the *suffering that came from it not as done alone but with others.

Another important word used by Paul of the people who work with him is the verb *kopiaō*, which means "to work hard so as to become weary." This verb is often used of a farmer laboring in the fields. The implication of the term is that those laboring are doing the same task as Paul and are therefore coworkers with him in the task of the gospel. In 1 Timothy 5:17 Paul explicitly uses *kopiaō* to refer to the elders (*presbyteroi*) who labor "in word and *teaching" (*en logō kai didaskalia*). Paul used the verb to describe Achaius (1 Cor 16:16), Fortunatus (1 Cor 16:16), Mary (Rom 16:6), Persis (Rom 16:12), Stephanas (1 Cor 16:16), Timothy (2 Tim 2:6), and Tryphaena and Tryphosa (Rom 16:12).

1.2. Other Terms for Coworkers. Paul also uses other words to describe his coworkers, though none of these are used exclusively of coworkers.

- *Adelphoi* (brothers and sisters). E. E. Ellis argues persuasively that where *adelphoi* is used with the article, it often means Christian workers, as opposed to the general usage without the article, where it refers to Christians more generally (1993, 13-17). Examples of this in Paul's writings include 1 Corinthians 16:19-20; Ephesians 6:23-24; Philippians 4:21-22; Colossians 4:15. It may also be used in this sense in Galatians 1:1-2, when Paul greets the Galatians: "Paul an *apostle . . . and all the members of God's family who are with me" (NRSV). Paul uses the feminine noun *adelphē* with the article in Philemon 1 of Apphia. This occurs between a description of Philemon as friend and coworker and Archippus as fellow soldier, and it points to *adelphē* being used here in the same way as the masculine noun is used elsewhere. The problem with the term *brother* or *sister* (or *brothers* and *sisters*) is that it can be hard to discern which use of the term Paul is employing at any one time.
- *Diakonos* (*servant or deacon). As with the term *adelphoi*, *diakonos* is used by Paul in the very general sense to mean a commissioned agent or servant (see discussion in Collins), but at other times it is used to describe those who are engaged in the task of proclaiming the gospel, as Paul was (see, e.g., 1 Cor 3:5; 2 Cor 6:4; Col 1:7). The term also appears to be used in a more technical sense to describe a role within the earliest Christian communities (Phil 1:1; Rom 16:1-2), though precisely what that role entailed remains unclear.
- *Apostoloi* (apostles). Although the Gospels and Acts appear to associate apostles solely with the Twelve and Matthias, who was elected to replace Judas Iscariot (Mt 10:2; Mk 3:14; 6:30; Lk 6:13; 9:10; 11:49; 17:5; 22:14; 24:10), Paul

uses the term more widely to include himself (Rom 1:1; 11:13; 1 Cor 1:1; 9:1-2), Barnabas (1 Cor 9:5), Silas (1 Thess 2:6), and Andronicus and Junia (Rom 16:7). Epaphroditus is also called an apostle by Paul (Phil 2:25 NRSV mg.), although there he uses the phrase "your apostle," implying that Epaphroditus might have been more an envoy of the Philippian church than of Christ.

2. The Roles of Those Who Worked with Paul. The question of what Paul's coworkers did now arises. Some coworkers are simply engaged in the same task as Paul: preaching, teaching, and proclaiming the gospel; others appear to have more focused tasks as missionaries, go-betweens, coauthors, and local leaders.

2.1. Itinerant Missionaries. All through his ministry Paul had associates with whom he traveled as he sought to proclaim the gospel to the ends of the earth.

The first mentioned companions are Barnabas and Titus (Gal 2:1). Barnabas was a Cypriot Jew who is first mentioned in Acts 4:36 as selling a field that belonged to him and giving the money to the apostles. He is later said to have introduced Paul to the apostles in *Jerusalem (Acts 9:27), though the text does not state how Barnabas knew Paul. They proclaimed the gospel together in Antioch and Anatolia. They both returned to Jerusalem for what is often known as the *Jerusalem Council, though whether Acts 15:1-21 and Galatians 2:1-10 record the same event is heavily disputed. After their return to Antioch, Barnabas was caught up in Paul's dispute with *Peter about whether it was right to eat with *Gentiles, with Barnabas taking Peter's side in the dispute (Gal 2:13). Barnabas and Paul subsequently parted ways following a dispute about whether John Mark should accompany them (Acts 15:36-40). Barnabas and John Mark returned to Cyprus to continue proclaiming the gospel there.

Titus appears to have been one of Paul's most long-standing coworkers, even though he is not mentioned in the book of Acts. Galatians records that he accompanied Paul and Barnabas to Jerusalem (Gal 2:1) but that despite being "a Greek" (Gal 2:3 NRSV), the Jerusalem church did not insist that he was circumcised. The epistle to Titus indicates that, following his role as envoy from Paul to the Corinthian church, he traveled with Paul again and that Paul left him behind in Crete so that he could put in order "what remained to be done" (Titus 1:5 NRSV). Second Corinthians suggests that Titus was a particularly important coworker for Paul since Paul found himself unable to proclaim the gospel in Troas after not meeting up with Titus (2 Cor 2:12-13).

Paul's other two key companions during his travels were Timothy and Silas. Timothy was from Lystra in Asia Minor. His mother was Jewish and his father a Gentile, which meant that he had not been circumcised as a child. When Paul returned to Lystra a second time with Silas, he took Timothy with him, after circumcising him "because of the Jews . . . in those places" (Acts 16:3 NRSV). Like Titus, Timothy was sent as Paul's envoy to various churches and was also with Paul in *Corinth when he wrote the epistle to the Romans (Rom 16:21). Timothy was trusted by Paul to the extent that he tells the Philippians, "I have no one like him who will be genuinely concerned for your welfare" (Phil 2:20 NRSV). He was the recipient of two epistles from Paul, which focus on the importance of establishing good church order, although many scholars dispute the letters' authorship.

Silvanus, called Silas in Acts, which is the Aramaic spelling of his name, was sent by the Jerusalem church with Paul and Barnabas (and Judas called Barsabbas; Acts 15:22) to Antioch. Following Paul's split with Barnabas, he took Silvanus with him. They were imprisoned briefly together in Philippi (Acts 16:25-37) and then went onward to Thessalonica with Timothy. Constant harassment by those who opposed them caused Paul to leave Silvanus and Timothy in Berea while he went on to Athens. They later reunited in Corinth.

Beyond these four regular companions, Acts and Paul's writings also mention Aristarchus (Acts 19:29; 20:4; 27:2; Col 4:10; Philem 24); Artemas (Titus 3:12); Crescens (2 Tim 4:10); Epaphras (Col 1:7); Demas, whom Paul recounts disapprovingly as leaving him to go to Thessalonica (Col 4:14; 2 Tim 4:10); Luke (Col 4:14; 1 Tim 4:11; Philem 24); Gaius (Acts 19:29; 20:4); Mark, who appears to have rejoined Paul following the disagreement with Barnabas (Acts 15:37; Col 4:10; 2 Tim 4:11; Philem 24); Secundus (Acts 20:4); Tychicus (Acts 20:4; Eph 6:21; Col 4:7; 2 Tim 4:12; Titus 3:12); and Trophimus.

Others also suggest that Paul's "relatives" (a word that might simply mean fellow Jews rather than family members) traveled with him from time to time (see Alexander). These "relatives" include Andronicus and Junia (Rom 16:7), Lucius, Jason, and Sosipater (Rom 16:21; he is assumed by most to be the same person as Sopater, who is reported by Acts 20:4 to have accompanied Paul). It is also worth noting that, though only temporarily, Prisca and Aquila traveled with Paul from Corinth to *Ephesus.

Such a catalog builds up a picture of a core of coworkers: Barnabas (until he went on to Crete) and Titus, Silvanus, and Timothy, who were with Paul over a longer period of time and who were supplemented from time to time by others. These were probably joined by a good number of people who are not named in either Acts or the epistles.

One person who does not fit easily into any of these categories is Apollos. Paul insists that he and Apollos are God's coworkers (1 Cor 3:9), but it is clear from 1 Corinthians 1:12 that varying allegiances to Apollos and Peter were causing tension within the community. First Corinthians 16:22 also indicates that Paul asked Apollos to visit the Corinthians but he declined. All of this combined with Acts 18:24-28, which records the need for Priscilla and Aquila to explain "the Way of God to him more accurately" (Acts 18:26 NRSV), indicates a more distant relationship between Paul and this particular coworker.

2.2. Envoys. As already observed, Paul's traveling companions also acted as envoys or intermediaries between Paul and his churches. The two key envoys were Timothy and Titus, both of whom were sent to Corinth in an attempt to shore up the crumbling relationship between Paul and this important community. Timothy was sent before 1 Corinthians was written (1 Cor 4:17) and, Paul hoped, again after the epistle had been received (1 Cor 16:12). Paul also urged Apollos to visit too, but he was unable to do so (1 Cor 16:12). Following these visits, Titus also visited the Corinthian community once or twice (2 Cor 7:6-15; 8:6). It is also clear from 2 Corinthians 2:13 that Titus was due to visit Troas on Paul's behalf but did not do so at the same time as Paul. Tychicus also seemed to act in a similar capacity toward the Ephesian community (Eph 6:21; 2 Tim 4:12) and possibly also to Crete (Titus 3:12), although Artemas is also cited as someone who might be sent to Crete.

The language Paul uses of these envoys implies that, as was common in the ancient world, the envoys were to be regarded and treated as though they were Paul himself. As L. Alexander notes, this coheres with a rabbinic dictum that "action by an agent is equivalent to action by a principal" (Alexander 2011; b. Qidd. 41b). This also fits with Paul's use of the verb *synistēmi* to describe Phoebe in Romans 16:1. This was a verb commonly used in letters of recommendation that designated the bearer a trustworthy representative of the author (White, 216).

The role of envoy also included being letter bearers. Tychicus brought the letter to the Ephesians (Eph 6:21-22) and to the Colossians (Col 4:7), and it is also highly likely, though not stated explicitly, that the deacon Phoebe brought the epistle of the Romans from Corinth to Rome. The expectation would not just have been that the letter bearers deliver the letter but that they would then be available to explain the letters to their recipients.

In addition to those who went from Paul to the various churches, there are also those who came from the churches to Paul: Stephanas, Fortunatus, and Achaius are described at the end of 1 Corinthians (1 Cor 16:17) as visiting Paul from Corinth; Epaphroditus was sent from Philippi to Paul and subsequently returned with this letter (Phil 2:25-30; 4:18); and according to 1 Timothy 1:16, Onesiphorus often visited Paul in *prison.

2.3. Coauthors. Paul's companions were not just bearers of his letters; they were also coauthors of the letters with him. Indeed, it was far more common for Paul to write his epistles with someone than on his own. The only exceptions are the epistles to the Romans, Galatians, Ephesians, and the Pastoral Epistles. It is interesting to observe that of the three general epistles (Romans, Galatians, and Ephesians) that do not record a coauthor, two of them (Romans and Galatians) give clear evidence of scribal assistance. The scribe is mentioned by name in Romans (Rom 16:22) and by implication in Galatians when Paul picks up the pen for the first time and writes with big letters (Gal 6:11).

The role of a scribe or secretary is often used to explain the striking difference in style between various of Paul's epistles, and in particular to explain why the style of 1–2 Timothy, Titus, and sometimes also Ephesians is so different from the rest (Richards; Ellis 2002). There is a difference of opinion among scholars about whether the coauthors of the epistles that are named in the greeting of a good number of the epistles were more valued and trusted scribes or were genuine coauthors alongside Paul. Timothy was the most common coauthor with Paul, assisting in writing 1 Corinthians, Philippians, Colossians, and 1–2 Thessalonians. Silvanus also assisted in the writing of 1–2 Thessalonians. Sosthenes is listed as coauthor of 1 Corinthians with Paul.

Little is known of Sosthenes outside his coauthorship of 1 Corinthians. Some assume that he was the Sosthenes cited in Acts as the chief ruler of the synagogue in Corinth (Acts 18:12-17), who was beaten by the mob in front of Gallio. On one level it would make sense for Paul to write a difficult letter to the Corinthians alongside a former leader of their synagogue. It is unclear whether, if this is the same person, why Sosthenes was now with Paul and no longer in Corinth.

2.4. Local Leaders. As noted above, Paul used the word *synergoi* to describe Christians who ministered in local churches as well as those who traveled with him on his journeys. This implies that Paul's vision of his ministry was universal as well as particular. In other words, people did not have to be physically working alongside him for him to view them as coworkers; simply being engaged in the same task was sufficient.

Paul uses *synergoi* in Philippians 4:2-3 of Euodia, Syntyche, and Clement, who were ministering in the *church in Philippi. He also uses it of Stephanas and his household (1 Cor 16:16) in Corinth and of Philemon in Philemon 1, alongside "sister" for Apphia and "fellow soldier" for Archippus, although he had not met them at this point. It is possible that this also explains Paul's regular use of the term in Romans 16 (of Mary, Rom 16:6; of Urbanus, Rom 16:7; and of Persis, Tryphaena, and Tryphosa, Rom 16:12), in that he was content to describe people as coworkers if they were engaged in the task of proclaiming the gospel even if they had never met.

Paul also described Epaphras "as a beloved co *slave" in Colossians 1:7. We learn from Colossians 4:12 that Epaphras was one of them (i.e., the Colossians) who both worked among the Colossians and accompanied Paul, so much so that he is called a coprisoner in Philemon 23.

3. Conclusion.

The evidence from both Acts and Paul's epistles indicates that Paul practiced collaborative ministry. He traveled with companions, both a core group and some who spent only a short time with him, and was so dependent on them that on at least one occasion he found himself unable to proclaim the gospel in a place without a companion he expected to find there (2 Cor 2:12). Paul's companions also acted as envoys for him, carrying messages and letters to a wide range of different churches, and as coauthors for many of the epistles that are extant in the NT. Key to understanding Paul's attitude to his coworkers is the importance of those who worked in local contexts far away from Paul himself. For Paul, the work of proclaiming the gospel was shared between himself and anyone else who joined in, whether he knew them or not. Ultimately Paul's coworkers were not his but the gospel's, coworkers together in proclaiming the good news of Jesus Christ, *Son of God.

See also APOSTLE; CHURCH; CHURCH STRUCTURE; FINANCIAL SUPPORT; KINSHIP LANGUAGE IN PAUL; LETTERS, LETTER FORMS; MAN AND WOMAN; MINISTRY; MISSION; OPPONENTS OF PAUL; PASTORAL EPISTLES; PAUL IN ACTS; SERVANT, SERVICE; TRAVEL AND ITINERARY PLANS; WOMEN NAMED IN PAUL.

BIBLIOGRAPHY. **L. Alexander,** "Paul's Coworkers," Religion Past and Present, 2011, dx.doi.org/10.1163/1877-5888_rpp_COM_124314; **F. F. Bruce,** *The Pauline Circle* (Exeter, UK: Paternoster, 1985); **J. C. C. Campbell,** *Phoebe: Patron and Emissary*, PSN (Collegeville, MN: Liturgical Press, 2015); **A. Clarke,** *Serve the Community of the Church: Christians as Leaders and Ministers* (Grand Rapids, MI: Eerdmans, 2000); idem, *A Pauline Theology of Church Leadership*, LNTS (London: T&T Clark 2013); **J. N. Collins,** *Diakonia: The Sources and Their Interpretation* (New York: Oxford University Press, 1990); **H. Conzelmann,** "Paulus und die Weisheit," *NTS* 12 (1965–1966): 231-44; **E. E. Ellis,** *Prophecy and Hermeneutic in Early Christianity* (Grand Rapids, MI: Baker, 1978), idem, *The Making of the New Testament Documents* (Leiden: Brill, 2002); **E. J. Epp,** *Junia: The First Woman Apostle* (Minneapolis: Fortress, 2005); **V. P. Furnish,** "'Fellow Workers in God's Service' [1 Cor 3:9]," *JBL* 80 (1961): 364-70; **R. Gehring,** *House Church and Mission* (Peabody, MA: Hendrickson, 2004); **D. Georgi,** *The Opponents of Paul in Second Corinthians* (Philadelphia: Fortress, 1986); **F. M. Gillman,** *Women Who Knew Paul*, ZSNT (Collegeville, MN: Liturgical Press, 1992); **D. J. Harrington,** "Paul and Collaborative Ministry," *NTR* 3 (1990): 62-71; **M. N. Keller,** *Priscilla and Aquila: Paul's Co-workers in Christ Jesus*, PSN (Collegeville, MN: Liturgical Press, 2010); **E. Lohse,** "Die Mitarbeiter des Paulus im Kolosserbrief," in *Verborum Veritas*, ed. O. Böcher and K. Haacker (Wüppertal: Brockhaus, 1970); **W. Meeks,** *The First Urban Christians* (New Haven, CT: Yale University Press, 1983); **W. H. Ollrog,** *Paulus und seine Mitarbeiter* (Neukirchen: Neukirchener, 1979); **E. B. Redlich,** *S. Paul and His Companions* (London: Macmillan, 1913); **E. R. Richards,** *The Secretary in the Letters of Paul* (Tübingen: Mohr, 1991); **E. Schüssler Fiorenza,** "Missionaries, Apostles, Coworkers," *WW* 6 (1986): 420-33; **E. G. Selwyn,** *The First Epistle of St. Peter* (London: Macmillan, 1946); **K. Stenstrup,** *Titus: Honoring the Gospel of God* (Collegeville, MN: Liturgical Press, 2010); **P. Trebilco,** "Women as Coworkers and Leaders in Paul's Letters," *JCBRF* 122

(1990): 27-36; **J. L. White,** *Light from Ancient Letters* (Philadelphia: Fortress, 1986).

P. Gooder

CREATION AND NEW CREATION

Paul's usage of the Greek word for "creation," whether in the expression translated "creature/creation" (Gk. *ktisis*) or "new creature/creation" (Gk. *kainē ktisis*), is not especially plentiful (in the so-called undisputed letters: Rom 1:20, 25; 8:19-22, 39; 2 Cor 5:17; Gal 6:15; in the so-called disputed letters: Col 1:15, 23), though his theology of creation and new creation is much more christologically developed than is usually appreciated. The Greek noun for "creator" (Gk. *ktistēs*) never occurs in his corpus (occurring in the NT only at 1 Pet 4:19), though the verbal form (Gk. *ktizō*) occurs in the undisputed (Rom 1:25; 1 Cor 11:9) and disputed letters (Eph 2:10, 15; 3:9; 4:24; Col 1:16 [2×]; 3:10; 1 Tim 4:3). The closely related concept of a "new humanity" (Gk. *kainos anthrōpos*) features both in the undisputed (implicit in Rom 6:6 and probably present in 2 Cor 5:17; Gal 6:15) and disputed letters (Eph 2:15; 4:23-24; Col 3:9-10). Paul's *hope for a new humanity/new creation, however, was not unique in his Second Temple Jewish context but was also expressed in a few OT texts and in several Second Temple sources.

1. Creation and New Creation in the Old Testament and Second Temple Judaism
2. The Corruption of Humans and the Whole Creation
3. The Scope of the New Creation
4. Paul's Teleology
5. Inaugurated Eschatology: The Firstfruits of New Creation
6. Continuity and Discontinuity
7. The Character of the New Creation
8. Galatians 6:15 and 2 Corinthians 5:17

1. Creation and New Creation in the Old Testament and Second Temple Judaism.

Most OT scholars agree that a robust doctrine of Israel's one *God as the sole creator of a good creation emerges for the first time in exilic or early postexilic sources (esp. Is 44:24; 45:18; 48:12-13). Moreover, some Jewish texts attest to a tradition in which the uniquely wise God of *Israel was the creator of a beautiful creation charged with his own unique (and divine) *wisdom, a wisdom that humans were enjoined to appreciate and to embody (Prov 1:22-33; 8:1-21; Sir 24:1-22; Wis 1:1-15; 7:7–9:18; Bar 3:9–4:4). Indeed, some Jewish texts go as far as to say that YHWH created the world by the very personified Wisdom with which he would later imbue it (Prov 8:22-31; Sir 24; Wis 7:22-30; 9:1-2; Philo). Some of these same texts go one crucial step further: this unique, divine wisdom is to be found in Torah and Torah fidelity (Sir 24:23-34; Bar 4:1-4). This is the context of Paul's so-called wisdom *Christology: that is, of his christological (and pneumatological) appropriation of the language and conceptualities of the Jewish wisdom *tradition (Rom 8:3, 14-17; 10:5-10; 1 Cor 1:30; 2 Cor 3:17-18; 4:4; Gal 4:4-6; Col 1:15-20; 3:9-10). The preexistent Jesus is the one "through whom" the creator God fashioned the *kosmos* (1 Cor 8:6; Col 1:15-16); he is the meeting place of God and Israel's *covenant faithfulness; and he is the means of redemption and new creation.

2. The Corruption of Humans and the Whole Creation.

However, though the God of Israel fashioned a "very good" creation (Gen 1:31), sundry Jewish texts and traditions say that it was corrupted as a result of the corrupt stewardship of human beings enslaved to *sin and *idolatry (Gen 3; Life of Adam and Eve; 4 Ezra 7.116-131). Paul, too, attests to this view. Ever since *Adam and Eve's sin, the *kosmos* has not been as it was intended to be (Rom 1:18-32; 3:23; 5:12-21; 8:18-22; 1 Cor 15:20-58). Human beings (Rom 1:18-32; 3:23), and even Israel itself (Rom 2:1-29; 3:19-20; 7:7-25), have been corrupted and enslaved to Sin. Consequently, the creation over which these now-corrupt human beings were set is itself subjected to corruption and futility (Rom 8:19-21). For Paul as for some of the Jewish apocalyptic thought on which he drew, the solution could only be the fresh reconstitution of human beings (for Paul, in Christ and by the Spirit, through whose stewardship the creation might be "set free from its bondage to decay" [Rom 8:21 NRSV within Rom 8:1-30 as a whole]; cf. Deut 30; Ezek 36; Is 52–55).

3. The Scope of the New Creation.

But, with his reference to "new creation" in, for example, 2 Corinthians 5:17 and Galatians 5:17, does Paul refer only to humanity or to the created order as a whole? Or is this perhaps a false antithesis? In this connection, scholars have sometimes pointed to potentially illuminating *comparanda* in the Jewish tradition. For example, in Joseph and Aseneth, when an angel visits the recently Judaized Aseneth, the angel states: "From this moment on you will be renewed and refashioned [*anakainisthēsē kai anaplasthēsē*]" (Jos. Asen. 15.4). In other words, from the perspective of this tradition, for a Gentile to become a part of the people of God is tantamount to becoming a new creation.

On the other hand, there are also texts such as Isaiah 65:17-25 (see also 1 En. 51.4-5; 2 Bar. 73–74) that envisage the recreation of the whole *kosmos*. Because, however, Paul regards the Messiah and those in the Messiah as the firstfruits of the general *resurrection and thus of the new creation (Rom 8:23; 1 Cor 15:20, 23), this is probably, at least for him, a false antithesis. Precisely as new creatures those in the Messiah are firstfruits of God's new creation.

4. Paul's Teleology.

There is, moreover, a crucial feature of Paul's christologically focused doctrine of creation that has rarely been noticed. Paul works with a particular teleology. For him, creation (Gen 1–2) was not a fixed, static, and final state, but a glorious beginning headed toward an even more glorious *telos*. He states this teleology tersely in a few key places (Rom 8:29; 2 Cor 3:18; Col 3:9-10). The logic of this teleology depends on his appropriation not simply of the Jewish wisdom tradition but also of Middle Platonic intermediary doctrine. The most famous statement comes in Romans 8:29: "For those whom he foreknew he also predestined to be conformed to the image of his Son, in order that he might be the firstborn within a large family" (NRSV). This is a dense encapsulation of Paul's macro-theological vision. God's whole purpose, he is saying, had been to create human beings according to the paradigmatic image of the preexistent Jesus and yet teleologically toward their growing into the *fullness of the incarnate, crucified, resurrected, and glorified Jesus. This is also the point of texts such as 2 Corinthians 3:18 and Colossians 3:9-10.

5. Inaugurated Eschatology: The Firstfruits of New Creation.

For Paul, the resurrection of Jesus—and, indeed, the outpouring of the eschatological Spirit—marked the beginning of the general resurrection and thus the new creation (Rom 1:4; 1 Cor 15:20 within 1 Cor 15 as a whole). This inaugurated *eschatology can be seen not least in Paul's agricultural metaphor of the eschatological harvest (Rom 8:23; 1 Cor 15:20, 23). The resurrected Messiah and those crucified, buried, and raised in the Messiah and by the Spirit *via* *baptism are the "firstfruits" of God's new creation. Moreover, as firstfruits of God's new creation, and in this sense as *images of God set over God's now-but-not-yet new world (Rom 8:18-30; Col 3:9-10), those in the Messiah are called to take up their vocation of stewarding God's now-but-not-yet new world in the power of the Spirit. That is why the Corinthian Christians should handle matters of justice "in house," as it were (1 Cor 6:1-11). They will, after all, be among the stewards of God's new world and, as those crucified, buried, and raised with the Messiah *now* through baptism and by the power of the Spirit, they should go ahead and begin to exercise some of this authority in the present. This is also the context of Paul's reference to being "seated [i.e., enthroned]" with the Messiah *in the present* (Eph 2:6). Those in the Messiah, by the power of the Spirit, anticipate their future reign on the Messiah's behalf and over God's new creation.

6. Continuity and Discontinuity.

But what does Paul mean by the *new* in "new creature/creation"? Does he imagine a *creatio ex nihilo* ("creation from nothing") or a *creatio ex vetere* ("creation out of the old [creation]")? For Paul, again and again, Jesus himself, and particularly his crucifixion and resurrection as the firstfruits of God's new creation, serves as the model of both the continuity and the discontinuity between the present creation and the future, new creation. The problem with the first creation was that it was corrupted by Sin. It was not, however, entirely beyond redemption. It retained, in other words, some original goodness. One can see this in the way in which Paul uses the resurrection of Jesus' crucified *body as the model (Rom 6:1-11; Gal 6:14-15). Neither is Jesus' body left in the tomb—which might signal the rejection and end of the original creation and a fresh *creatio ex nihilo*—nor is his resurrection body simply the resuscitation of his crucified body—which might imply that the corruption of the old creation was not so serious. Rather, it was precisely Jesus' crucified body that was raised *but also glorified*. The latter reveals, again, a teleology. The problem with human beings and the whole creation, at least for Paul, is not simply that they have been corrupted—a corruption that must, of course, be dealt with—but that they have never attained a particular *telos*. Humans were created to grow into the fullness of the incarnate, crucified, resurrected, and glorified Jesus (Rom 8:29; Phil 3:20-21); more than anything else, Sin derails this teleology.

7. The Character of the New Creation.

The new creation is, moreover, characterized through and through by the character of God revealed in Jesus and sustained by the Spirit. Those whose *flesh, through baptism, has been crucified, buried, and raised with the Messiah in the power of the Spirit exhibit the *fruits of the Spirit that will characterize God's new world: "*love, *joy, *peace, patience, kindness, generosity, faithfulness, gentleness, and self-control" (Gal 5:22-23 NRSV). New creatures within the new creation will *not* be characterized by "sexual immorality, impurity, passion, evil desire, and greed . . . anger, *wrath, malice, slander, and obscene speech" (Col 3:5, 8 NASB) but, instead, by "compassion, kindness, humility, gentleness, and patience . . . [and] love" (Col 3:12, 14 NASB). All those in the Messiah and suffused with God's Spirit will be raised with new (i.e., *creatio ex vetere*), resurrected and glorified bodies in order to steward God's new world (Rom 8:23 within Rom 8:18-25 as a whole; Phil 3:20-21).

8. Galatians 6:15 and 2 Corinthians 5:17.

The two best-known instances of "new creation" language in Paul's letters occur at Galatians 6:15 and 2 Corinthians 5:17. In Galatians 6:15, Paul writes, "For neither circumcision nor uncircumcision is anything; but a new creation is everything!" (NRSV). Within the context of the argument, Paul's point is that, insofar as the goal of creation, covenant, and Torah was the procuration and maintenance of sacred space so that YHWH could be with his people, and insofar as, in Paul's view, the latter had been achieved in Christ and by the Spirit *irrespective* of Torah fidelity in general or circumcision in particular, what matters is not circumcision but the fact that in Christ and by the Spirit Jews and Gentiles alike—as well as, in some sense, the whole *kosmos*—have been indiscriminately reconstituted as a new creation. God can now, by the Spirit, dwell with his people, which was the main goal of covenant and Torah (and circumcision) in the first place.

In 2 Corinthians 5:17, as a part of Paul's extended defense of his apostleship, he insists that Christ and the Spirit have inaugurated the new creation. As a result, reality itself and the Christian perception of such have necessarily changed. In the same way that Christ's death and resurrection marked the so-called overlap of the ages, the old and the new, so those living and ministering at the overlap of the ages in Christ and by the Spirit will be marked by the cruciform character of the Christ event. Far from invalidating Paul's apostleship, this cruciform character actually evidences its legitimacy and indicates that Paul is a new creature working amid new creatures in God's inaugurated new creation.

See also ADAM AND CHRIST; COSMOLOGY; ESCHATOLOGY; HOLY SPIRIT; RESURRECTION.

BIBLIOGRAPHY. **G. Baumbach,** "Die Schöpfung in der Theologie des Paulus," *Kairos* 21 (1979): 196-205; **N. A. Dahl,** "Christ, Creation, and the Church," in *The Background of the New Testament and Its Eschatology*, ed. W. D. Davies and D. Daube (Cambridge: Cambridge University Press, 1956) 422-43; **J. D. M. Derrett,** "New Creation: Qumran, Paul, the Church, and Jesus," *RevQ* 13 (1988): 597-608; **M. V. Hubbard,** *New Creation in Paul's Letters and Thought*, SNTSMS 119 (Cambridge: Cambridge University Press, 2002); **R. Jackson,** *New Creation in Paul's Letters: A Study of the Historical and Social Setting of a Pauline Concept*, WUNT 2/272 (Tübingen: Mohr Siebeck, 2010); **G. W. H. Lampe,** "The New Testament Doctrine of *Ktisis*," *SJT* 17 (1964): 449-62; **D. J. Moo,** "Creation and New Creation," *BBR* 20, no. 1 (2010): 39-60; **M. Parsons,** "The New Creation," *ExpTim* 99 (1987): 3-4; **L. M. Russell,** "Partnership in New Creation," *ABQ* 3 (1984): 161-71; **P. Stuhlmacher,** "Erwägungen zum ontologischen Charakter der *kainē ktisis* bei Paulus," *EvT* 27 (1967): 1-35; **L. H. Taylor,** *The New Creation: A Study of the Pauline Doctrines of Creation, Innocence, Sin, and Redemption* (New York: Pageant, 1958).

C. Kugler

CREATOR. *See* CHRISTOLOGY; CREATION AND NEW CREATION; ECOLOGICAL PAUL; GOD.

CREED. *See* HYMNS, HYMN FRAGMENTS, CONFESSIONS.

CROSS

A wooden cross was used in a gruesome form of Roman execution and/or impalement of a dead *body. The expression "the cross" is inextricably linked with Jesus' crucifixion. The crucifixion must be understood together with Jesus' *resurrection, which demonstrated God's acceptance and vindication of Jesus' sacrificial *death.

1. The New Testament Vocabulary of Crucifixion.

The primary Greek word used to indicate a cross is *stauros* ("upright stake," "cross"; 27×); cognate verbs are *stauroō* ("I crucify"; 46×) and *systauroō* ("I am crucified with"; 5×). The compound form *anastauroō* occurs only in Hebrews 6:6. One also finds *kremannymi* ("I hang [upon a tree]"; 3×; cf. Lk 23:39) and *prospēgnymi* ("I crucify"; Acts 2:23). The noun *xylon* ("tree," "wood") can also refer to Jesus' cross (Acts 13:29; 1 Pet 2:24), perhaps as an allusion to Deuteronomy 21:22-23. In the Pauline epistles, *stauros* occurs in 1 Corinthians 1:17, 18; Galatians 5:11; 6:12, 14; Ephesians 2:16; Philippians 2:8; 3:18; Colossians 1:20; 2:14; *stauroō* occurs in 1 Corinthians 1:13, 23; 2:2, 8; 2 Corinthians 13:4; Galatians 3:1; 5:24; 6:14; and *systauroomai* occurs in Romans 6:6; Galatians 2:19.

2. Historical Context.

Crucifixion, one of the cruelest forms of execution in the ancient world, was utilized by Assyrians, Persians, and Romans, among others. It was designed to maximize pain and prolong death, sometimes for days. Crucifixions could use a pole, tree, or cross (consisting of a horizontal beam, or *patibulum*, and a vertical beam). Because of the variety of methods employed for this type of torture and execution, the term *suspension* is sometimes used instead of *crucifixion*. The crucified individual was usually hung by the forearms, which necessitated pushing oneself up to breathe, in the process painfully rubbing one's back against the cross. Individuals eventually died from asphyxiation, blood loss, shock, or a combination of these. Roman crucifixion was designed to maximize shame and humiliation since the individual was usually stripped naked and flogged, and may have been forced to carry the cross beam to the place of crucifixion, usually on a public road outside the city, where the crucified individual was ridiculed and harassed by passersby.

The primary function of crucifixion was as a horrific, public deterrent against wrongdoing or rebellion (see Hengel). Shame was compounded by the fact that crucified individuals were often left unburied. In general, Roman citizens were not subject to crucifixion; instead, this "barbaric" practice was reserved for horrendous criminals, *slaves, and noncitizens. The actual procedures and instruments employed in ancient crucifixions are debated mainly because historical accounts do not provide much detail and there were various forms of crucifixion (see esp. Samuelsson). Even the Gospel accounts of Jesus' crucifixion are notably concise. The horror of and abhorrence to crucifixion must be understood to grasp the significance of the cross in the NT, especially in the Pauline epistles. The association of anything positive with crucifixion or the use of a cross as an identifying symbol is unique to Christianity.

3. Gospel Accounts of the Crucifixion.

All four Gospels record Jesus' crucifixion under Pontius Pilate and his subsequent resurrection. These accounts are preceded by Jesus' predictions of his death (Mt 16:21; 20:18-19; 26:1; Mk 8:31; 9:30-31; 10:32-34; Lk 9:22; 18:31-33; Jn 3:14; cf. Lk 24:6-7). Additionally, each Gospel records Jesus' crucifixion and resurrection extensively, including his trial (Mt 27:11-26), the people's demand for his crucifixion (Mt 27:22-23; Mk 15:13-14; cf. Lk 23:23-25; Jn 18:39-40), his being mocked by the soldiers (Mt 27:27-31; Mk 15:16-20; Lk 23:36-38; Jn 19:2-3); the forced walk to Golgotha (Mt 27:31-32; Mk 15:20-21; Lk 23:26; Jn 19:17), his crucifixion (Mt 27:35; Mk 15:23-26; Lk 23:33; Jn 19:18), the presence of others who were crucified along with Jesus (Mt 27:38; Mk 15:27; Lk 23:32-33; Jn 19:18), his being mocked by passersby (Mt 27:39-42; Mk 15:29-32; Lk 23:35-36), his death (Mt 27:45-50; Mk 15:34-37; Lk 23:46; Jn 19:28-30), and his resurrection (Mt 28:1-10; Mk 16:1-8; Lk 24:1-12; Jn 20:1-10) (see esp. Green, part 2). Somewhat surprisingly, prior to his actual crucifixion, Jesus exhorted his followers to take up their own crosses (Mt 16:24; cf. Mt 10:38; Mk 8:34-35; Lk 9:23).

Although it is often assumed that Jesus was hung on a cross with a crossbeam and vertical pole, the Gospel accounts lack sufficient detail to conclude this definitively (see Samuelsson, 245-51). The date of Jesus' crucifixion is generally thought to be April 7, AD 30, or April 3, AD 33. Several nonbiblical sources also attest to Jesus' crucifixion (Josephus, *Ant.* 18.3.3; Tacitus, *Ann.* 15.44).

4. The Centrality of the Cross in Pauline Theology.

Both the historicity of the cross and its ongoing significance are crucial to Pauline theology. The cross is at the center of Paul's preaching: "we preach Christ crucified" (1 Cor 1:23). Considering the intense shame associated with crucifixion, this claim is remarkable and indeed defies human logic. This was especially true for the *church in *Corinth, with its focus on supernatural power and manifestations of the Spirit that distorted its understanding of the *gospel. Hence Paul's resolve to know nothing apart from "Jesus Christ and him crucified" (1 Cor 2:2) among the Corinthians.

The cross is the revelation of God's *wisdom and power (1 Cor 1:18–2:16). Yet precisely because the cross involved the painful suffering and gruesome death of God's anointed, Jesus, it appeared as a scandal or *stumbling block to Jews (what sign of God's power was a dead Messiah?) and as foolishness to *Gentiles (what *philosophy would follow a crucified criminal?). Yet the cross (together with the resurrection) reveals God's glorious plan of redemption, which could not be ascertained by human wisdom (1 Cor 1:25). In the cross, the reality of human *sin, the supreme *love of *God, and the willing *sacrifice of the Son are revealed. Indeed, God's wisdom manifest through the weak, lowly, and despised things of the world (allusions to the cross) confounds, challenges, and redefines all human wisdom and power. Thus to share in Christ's resurrection power is to share in the weakness of his crucifixion (2 Cor 13:4).

Perhaps the most comprehensive outcome associated with the cross is that of reconciliation. Colossians 1:20 proclaims that God is reconciling all things back to himself "by making *peace through [Christ's] blood, shed on the cross" (NIV). Peace recalls the original state of right relationships as seen in the Garden of Eden—humans rightly related to God, each other, and the rest of creation. Human rebellion ruptured that peace on every dimension. Thus, reconciliation has both a vertical dimension (between God and sinners; see Col 2:13-14) and a horizontal dimension (between sinners; see Eph 2:14-16; 2 Cor 5:11–6:2). The context of Colossians 1:20 reveals that the cross must also be understood in terms of the *kingdom of God. Colossians 1:12-14 describes the work of God through *Christ to rescue his people from the "dominion of darkness" and deliver them to the kingdom of his beloved Son. This reconciling work involves redemption (recalling the exodus event) and the *forgiveness of sins. Moreover, the reconciliation of *all things* has cosmic implications, suggesting both reconciliation of God and redeemed humanity and the pacification of evil powers (see Phil 2:6-11).

The connection between the cross and the kingdom of God reveals the eschatological nature of the cross, which simultaneously signals the *judgment and eventual end of the present age/world and the inauguration of the age/world to come. As Jeremy Treat notes, "The kingdom is *telic* (the goal toward which everything moves) and the cross is *central* (the climax and turning-point of the story), and they intersect as the end-time kingdom breaks into history through the cross" (38, italics original). Moreover, the cross effects the ultimate fulfillment of God's promises. Galatians 3:13-14 indicates that because Christ took the *curse of the (Mosaic) *law on himself on the tree (citing Deut 21:23), the blessings promised to *Abraham might come to Gentiles through Christ.

The eschatological effect of the cross is most clearly seen in God's ultimate victory over the powers of evil. Following the revelation that the cross is central to God's work of reconciliation (Col 1:20), Paul describes Christ's disarming of the spiritual "powers and authorities" of evil in terms of triumphing over them on the cross (Col 2:15). The allusion to a Roman general's triumphal parade in Colossians 2:15 further reveals God's wisdom revealed in the cross: Jesus, crucified by Roman power, is now the one who triumphs over all "powers" by means of the cross. Had the "rulers of this age" understood this divine wisdom, they would not have crucified "the *Lord of *glory" (1 Cor 2:8).

The cross as the means by which the spiritual powers and *principalities of evil are defeated has implications for human power structures as well. Jesus' death on the cross was a political event carried out by the former enemies Pontius Pilate and Herod to serve political ends (see Elliot). Paul's repeated use of cross language to refer to Jesus' death (e.g., Phil 2:8) suggests that he intended to keep the shame and brutality of the cross in the mind of his audience. Paul's comment that the "rulers of this age" had crucified "the Lord of glory" (1 Cor 2:8) may suggest that he grasped the political nature of Jesus' crucifixion, if those rulers include both human and supernatural agents. Demetrius K. Williams argues, "Paul's understanding of the cross as a manifestation of God's power challenges the very ideology of Rome's power. Crucifixion was a primary means of maintaining the *pax Romana*," and yet Paul's "gospel of the cross was set over against the gospel of the Roman imperial system" (799, 812). Whereas the Romans used crucifixion to exert and maintain their power and control, Paul proclaims the cross as the place where God, through Christ, has defeated all powers.

Inextricably linked to the cosmic, eschatological implications of the cross is the clear connection between Jesus' death on the cross and *justification, as seen in the repeated expression "Christ died for us" or "Christ died for our sins" (Rom 5:8; 1 Cor 15:3; cf. Rom 14:15; Gal 1:4; 2:20), where the historical fact is inseparable from its ongoing significance. Romans 3:21-26 presents the death of Jesus as a "sacrifice of atonement" or "propitiation" (*hilastērion*, Rom 3:25), whereby his shed blood effects redemption (Rom 3:24) and justifies those who receive this sacrifice by *faith (Rom 3:25). Traditionally, this aspect of Jesus' death has been described as penal substitutionary atonement, where Christ willingly died on behalf of, or as a substitute for, guilty transgressors and thereby satisfied the righteous *wrath of God. In this way, the cross also reveals God's justice. So closely connected is the cross with justification and the work of Christ that those who seek to live by the *works of the law (or compel others to do so) are actually seeking to avoid the "offense of the cross" (Gal 5:11; 6:12-14).

The cross is also integral to the Pauline understanding of participation in Christ. A key text in this regard is Romans 6:1-14, in which believers' *baptism is understood as sharing in Christ's death and being raised to new life. The old self has been crucified with Christ (Rom 6:6; cf. Gal 2:19-20; 5:22-24) and yet this death is ongoing as believers are exhorted to "put to death" or crucify their sin and any sinful use of their mortal bodies. Thus participation in Christ's death on the cross is not a one-time event but a defining characteristic of the life of the believer (2 Cor 4:7-15), as demonstrated in Paul's own life (Phil 3:7-12). Participating in Christ's death is a separation from the wisdom, power, and status of the world. Such participation necessarily involves *suffering.

Closely related to participation in Christ's crucifixion is the ongoing conformity of believers to the humility and self-sacrifice demonstrated by Christ. For Paul, the supreme example of these virtues is found in Jesus' obedience to death, even death on a cross (Phil 2:5-11)—this cruciform attitude is to be adopted by the entire community of believers.

Although the benefits of the cross, such as justification, participation, and sanctification, are often understood along individual lines, the cross is the basis of the new, diverse humanity that God is creating. In this humanity, power is demonstrated through the Spirit (1 Cor 2:4); status, wisdom, and boasting are in Christ (1 Cor 1:26-31; Gal 6:14); former ethnic and socioeconomic divisions have been removed (1 Cor 1:10-17; Eph 2:11-22); and reconciliation is experienced.

5. Significance and Summary.

The significance of the cross, in Pauline theology, the rest of the NT, and indeed in theology as a whole can be inferred from the use of the definite article—*the* cross or *the* crucifixion—which underscores the uniqueness of this historical event (Rutledge, 3-4). For Paul, the cross is the fullest revelation of God's nature and will; it is the place where the eschatological reconciliation of all things and the defeat of hostile powers and authorities takes place; it is where the eschatological kingdom of God is inaugurated; it is where sinful humanity is justified and declared righteous; it is where believers participate in the life of Christ and are conformed to his image; and it is where the new humanity is formed, shaped, and called to preach the message of the cross.

See also DEATH; ESCHATOLOGY; IN CHRIST; PEACE, RECONCILIATION; PRINCIPALITIES AND POWERS; STUMBLING BLOCK; TRIUMPH.

BIBLIOGRAPHY. **A. R. Brown,** *The Cross and Human Transformation: Paul's Apocalyptic Word in 1 Corinthians* (Minneapolis: Fortress, 1995); **D. W. Chapman,** *Ancient Jewish and Christian Perceptions of Crucifixion* (Grand Rapids, MI: Baker Academic, 2010); **C. B. Cousar,** *A Theology of the Cross: The Death of Jesus in the Pauline Letters* (Minneapolis: Fortress, 1990); **N. Elliot,** "The Anti-imperial Message of the Cross," in *Paul and Empire: Religion and Power in Roman Society*, ed. R. A. Horsley (Harrisburg, PA: Trinity Press International, 1997), 167-83; **S. J. Gathercole,** "The Cross and Substitutionary Atonement," *Scottish Bulletin of Evangelical Theology* 21 (2003): 152-65; **M. J. Gorman,** *Cruciformity: Paul's Narrative Spirituality of the Cross*, 2nd ed. (Grand Rapids, MI: Eerdmans, 2021); **J. B. Green,** *The Death of Jesus: Tradition and Interpretation in the Passion Narrative*, WUNT 2/33 (Tübingen: Mohr, 1988); **M. Hengel,** *Crucifixion in the Ancient World and the Folly of the Message of the Cross*, trans. J. Bowden (Philadelphia: Fortress, 1977); **F. Rutledge,** *The Crucifixion: Understanding the Death of Jesus Christ* (Grand Rapids, MI: Eerdmans, 2015); **G. Samuelsson,** *Crucifixion in Antiquity: An Inquiry into the Background and Significance of the New Testament Terminology of Crucifixion*, WUNT 2/310 (Tübingen: Mohr Siebeck, 2011); **J. R. W. Stott,** *The Cross of Christ* (Downers Grove, IL: InterVarsity Press, 1986); **D. Tidball,** *The Message of the Cross: Wisdom Unsearchable, Love Indestructible*, The Bible Speaks Today (Downers Grove, IL: InterVarsity Press, 2001); **J. R. Treat,** *The Crucified King: Atonement and Kingdom in Biblical and Systematic Theology* (Grand Rapids, MI: Zondervan, 2014); **D. K. Williams,** "Paul's Anti-imperial 'Discourse of the Cross': The Cross and Power in 1 Corinthians 1–4," *SBL Seminar Papers* 39 (2000): 796-823.

D. M. Harris

CRUCIFIXION. *See* CHRIST, MESSIAH; CROSS; DEATH.

CRUCIFORMITY

The noun *cruciformity* comes from the adjective *cruciform* ("cross-shaped"), a term originally used primarily to describe cross-shaped churches. In the second half of the twentieth century, as biblical scholars and theologians increasingly focused on Jesus as the norm of Christian discipleship and on discipleship as a corporate, ecclesial practice, the words *cruciform* and then *cruciformity* came to be applied to the Christian *gospel and life.

Cruciformity is at the heart of Paul's spirituality. For him, the *cross is the shape as well as the source of *salvation—the essence of Christlikeness. Paul's focus on *Christ crucified (1 Cor 2:2) does not, however, deny the *resurrection, but "the cross is the signature of the risen one" (Käsemann). Paradoxically, therefore, cruciformity is suffused with resurrection life—and life in the resurrected *Lord is cruciform.

1. Central Aspects
2. Additional Aspects
3. The Paradoxes of Cruciformity

1. Central Aspects.

Cruciformity is multivalent. Especially significant is Paul's triad of essential ecclesial "marks": *faith (or faithfulness), *hope, and *love (Rom 5:1-5; 1 Cor 13:13; Gal 5:5-6; Col 1:4-5; 1 Thess 1:3; 5:8; see *hypomonē*, "endurance," for hope in 2 Thess 1:3-4; Titus 2:2). Each mark possesses a pattern and can therefore be said to have a narrative character.

The Greek word *pistis*, often translated "faith," has several senses in Paul's letters. One of the most significant is "faithfulness" or "believing allegiance," as in the rhetorical bookends of Romans: "the obedience of faith" (Rom 1:5; 16:26 NRSV). Jesus' obedience to the point of death on the cross (Phil 2:8) is the ground for believers' obedience (Phil 2:12—a reference to obeying *God, not Paul). In several places Paul likely connects believers' *pistis* with that of Jesus in his self-giving death: "the faithfulness of Christ" (*pistis Christou* and similar phrases: Rom 3:22, 26; Gal 2:16, 20; 3:22; Phil 3:9). *Pistis*, then, has a cruciform shape; it entails a Christlike narrative pattern of choosing costly faithfulness to God, especially in the face of opposition and persecution (e.g., 1 Thess 1:3-8; 3:2-10).

Hope functions for Paul as the future tense of faith and is therefore similarly cruciform. As *Abraham demonstrated in anticipation of Jesus' death and resurrection, hope is the conviction that God will bring life out of death (Rom 4:13-25). The narrative pattern of Christ's humiliation and death, followed by resurrection and exaltation, becomes the pattern of believers' hope. Their existence as God's children resembles that of the elder *Son Jesus, with whom they will co-suffer before being co-glorified with him (Rom 8:17-18; cf. Phil 3:10-11). This present co-suffering is shared with the entire *creation, which also experiences the pattern of affliction prior to *eschatological redemption (Rom 8:19-25).

Love is the most thoroughly developed aspect of cruciformity in Paul; Christ's death is the paradigmatic refusal of self-serving behavior and embrace of self-giving love (Gal 2:20; Eph 5:2). This is expressed most fully in Philippians 2:6-8, in which the Christ-poem has a narrative pattern that is echoed throughout the letters: "although *x* not *y* but *z*," meaning "although [possessing status] not [selfishly exploiting status] but [humbly relinquishing status in acts of self-giving]." (The *z* refers to both Christ's incarnation and his crucifixion.) The context shows that this is a story of love, and that such love must define the *ekklēsia* as the community that lives in Christ, animated by the Spirit (Phil 2:1-4). Paul adapts this pattern of cruciform love to characterize Christ (2 Cor 8:9; Gal 1:4; 2:20) as well as himself and other leaders (1 Cor 9; 1 Thess 2:5-9; Phil 2:19-30; cf. 2 Cor 6:10; 11:7-11), and to urge all in Christ to practice cruciform love (e.g., 1 Cor 8:1–11:1; Phil 2:1-4). Paul's frequent use of the *christological pattern found in Philippians 2:6-11 suggests it is a "master story"—a narrative of self-humbling and love for others in obedience to God the Father as the prequel to vindication and exaltation.

Cruciform love, then, means both not looking out for one's own interests and seeking the edification of others (e.g., Rom 15:1-6; 1 Cor 8:1; 10:23-33; 13:5; 14:1-6, 12). Such love also reconfigures power. Because divine power is embodied in the cross (1 Cor 1:18-31), which is the gift of divine love (Rom 5:8), human power entails benefiting others, rather than dominating or exploiting them.

Another critical aspect of cruciformity is suffering, though cruciformity does not exclusively, or even primarily, mean suffering. Paul and many of the Pauline communities suffered in various ways, and the apostle saw both his and their suffering as similar to Christ's (e.g., 1 Thess 1:6; 2:14-16). Suffering for Christ and the gospel creates a bond between believers and the apostle (e.g., Phil 1:27-30; cf. 2 Tim 1:8). Such suffering is also, more importantly, a participation in, and even a continuation of, Christ's sufferings (2 Cor 1:5; 4:10-12; Phil 3:10;

Col 1:24). Indeed, suffering is to be expected as a normal part of life in Christ (1 Thess 3:3; 2 Tim 3:12); it is an expression of cruciform faithfulness, hope, and love.

2. Additional Aspects.
Because God's generous *grace came to fullest expression in the incarnation and death of the Son, believers are *called to practice cruciform generosity toward those in need (2 Cor 8–9). This is more than charity, since God's gracious act is also the ultimate act of divine *righteousness and justice (*dikaiosynē*; 2 Cor 9:9-10). Thus Paul speaks of God's cruciform justice and of believers' participation in it (2 Cor 5:21; cf. Rom 6:13). The vocabulary of justice also permeates 1 Corinthians 6:1-11. Believers must not sue their Christian siblings; rather, they should even accept injustice because, Paul implies, Christ the sacrificial paschal Lamb did precisely that (1 Cor 5:7).

Similarly, since Christ's death is God's act of reconciliation and peacemaking (Rom 5:1-11; 2 Cor 5:18-20; Eph 2:11-22; Col 1:20-22), Christ-followers are called to participate in that death by practicing *peace with one another, outsiders, and even enemies (Rom 12:14-21; 1 Thess 5:11-15; Col 3:15). Paul's exhortations in this regard echo Jesus' teaching (see also 1 Cor 4:12-13). His spirituality of cruciformity is also consonant with the calls to discipleship Jesus attaches to his passion predictions (e.g., Mk 8:31-37; 9:30-37; 10:32-45): faithfulness even to the point of suffering, *serving others rather than self, and identifying with the weak.

The cruciform imperative is intensified for ministers of the gospel. Manual labor, physical and emotional suffering, missional adaptability, and nondominating power are examples of the normal ministerial life because they are analogous to the story of Christ (1 Cor 9; 11:1; 2 Cor 11:1–12:10; 1 Thess 2:7-12; 2 Thess 3:7-9).

3. The Paradoxes of Cruciformity.
Cruciformity has an inherent, profound paradox: just as Christ's death brought life, so also cruciformity is life giving for both its practitioners and its beneficiaries. Cruciformity means "always carrying in the *body the death of Jesus, so that the life of Jesus may also be made visible in our bodies" and "life [is at work] in [or among] you" (2 Cor 4:10, 12 NRSV; cf. 2 Cor 4:7-9). Although bodily resurrection is still future, the present life of cruciformity is *resurrectional*—filled with the power, *joy, and life of Christ's resurrection.

Cruciformity also involves another paradox of sorts. Because Christ crucified is, for Paul, not only a Christophany but also a theophany—the revelation of God's attributes and character—to be conformed to Christ, the *image of God (Rom 8:29; 2 Cor 3:18–4:4; Col 1:15; 3:10), is ultimately to be conformed to God (see, e.g., Eph 4:31–5:2). *Cruciformity* is actually *theoformity*. The process of conformity to Christ/God has been called Christification or Christosis, and deification or theosis. This transformation is not achievable by mere human effort; it requires the work of the *Holy Spirit within the community and the individual believer. The result is a holy, living (though imperfect) exegesis of the gospel and of the divine life.

See also CROSS; ETHICS; FAITH; GRACE; HOLINESS, SANCTIFICATION; HOPE; IDENTITY; IN CHRIST; JOY, REJOICING; LOVE; MINISTRY; PEACE, RECONCILIATION; SUFFERING.

BIBLIOGRAPHY. **B. C. Blackwell,** *Christosis: Pauline Soteriology in Light of Deification in Irenaeus and Cyril of Alexandria*, rev. ed. (Grand Rapids, MI: Eerdmans, 2016); **D. Bonhoeffer,** *Discipleship*, trans. Barbara Green and Reinhard Krauss, DBWE 4 (Minneapolis: Augsburg Fortress, 2001), 199-288; **W. T. Davey,** *Suffering as Participation with Christ in the Pauline Corpus* (Lanham, MD: Lexington Books/Fortress Academic, 2019); **C. A. Gieschen,** "Christian Identity in a Pagan Thessalonica: The Imitation of Paul's Cruciform Life," *CTQ* 72 (2008): 3-18; **M. J. Gorman,** *Cruciformity: Paul's Narrative Spirituality of the Cross* (Grand Rapids, MI: Eerdmans, 2001); idem, *Inhabiting the Cruciform God: Kenosis, Justification, and Theosis in Paul's Narrative Soteriology* (Grand Rapids, MI: Eerdmans, 2009); idem, "Cruciform or Resurrectiform? Paul's Paradoxical Practice of Participation," *Ex Auditu* 33 (2017), 60-83; **L. R. Hogan,** *I Live, No Longer I: Paul's Spirituality of Suffering, Transformation, and Joy* (Eugene, OR: Wipf & Stock, 2017); **L. A. Jervis,** *At the Heart of the Gospel: Suffering in the Earliest Christian Message* (Grand Rapids, MI: Eerdmans, 2007); **E. Käsemann,** "The Saving Significance of the Death of Jesus," in *Perspectives on Paul*, trans. Margaret Kohl (Philadelphia: Fortress, 1971); **H. H. D. Williams,** "Living as Christ Crucified: The Cross as a Foundation for Christian Ethics in 1 Corinthians," *EvQ* 75 (2003): 117-31; **S. F. Wu,** "Participating in God's Purpose by Following the Cruciform Pattern of Christ: The Use of Psalm 69:9b in Romans 15:3," *JSPHL* 5 (2015): 1-19; idem, *Suffering in Paul: Perspectives and Implications* (Eugene, OR: Pickwick, 2018).

M. J. Gorman

CURSE, ACCURSED, ANATHEMA

Notions of "curse" and "cursing" appear in the books of Romans, 1 Corinthians, and Galatians. In addition, two texts in the Pauline corpus likely refer to Paul's own use of a curse to discipline believers who are guilty of particularly egregious sins.

1. Curses and Cursing in Paul's Ethics
2. The Curse of the Law
3. *Anathema*
4. Handing Sinners Over to Satan

1. Curses and Cursing in Paul's Ethics.

Paul expresses his disapproval of cursing, along with other forms of malevolent behavior. In Romans 3, Paul draws on a number of OT texts in order to characterize humankind as universally guilty of *sin. Quoting Psalm 10:7, he avers that "their mouths are full of cursing [*aras*] and bitterness" (Rom 3:14 NRSV). Later in the same letter, Paul encourages the *church in Rome, "Bless those who persecute you; bless and do not curse [*katarasthe*] them" (Rom 12:14 NRSV). While it is understandable and perhaps justifiable that one would curse one's persecutors, Paul says that members of the Christian community should do the very opposite of this (see Mt 5:44).

2. The Curse of the Law.

In his letter to the Galatians, Paul addresses a theological challenge posed by the *law of Moses, namely, that the law entails a curse (*katara*) for all who fail to live up to its standards (Gal 3:10). According to Paul, Jesus has redeemed believers from the curse of the law by becoming a curse for them (Gal 3:13). To make his case, Paul cites the declaration of Deuteronomy 27:21 that everyone who does not take care to obey the laws of Deuteronomy is cursed (*epikataratos*). He then quotes Deuteronomy 21:23, which explains that a person who hangs on a tree is considered cursed (*epikataratos*). For Paul, Jesus' crucifixion entailed Jesus becoming a curse for the sake of those who needed redemption from the curse of the law.

3. *Anathema.*

In four passages, Paul uses the term *anathema* to refer to one who is cursed or accursed. The Greek word *anathema* in its most general sense indicates something that has been devoted to *God. The devoted item could be regarded positively, such as an offering presented at the *temple (Lk 21:5; Jdt 16:19). More frequently in the NT, however, it is regarded negatively, something that has been devoted to destruction or cursed. Paul employs the word exclusively in its negative sense. Paul counsels the church in *Corinth about how they can distinguish the Spirit of God from a misleading prophetic spirit (1 Cor 12:3). He instructs the Corinthians to reject any spirit who inspires the utterance "Let Jesus be *anathema*!" In contrast, the spirit who says, "Jesus is *Lord!" is the *Holy Spirit and is to be heeded. In other passages, Paul suggests that certain sinful individuals are to be regarded as *anathema*. In 1 Corinthians 16:22, Paul pronounces anyone who does not love the Lord *anathema*. Similarly, Paul tells the Galatians that they should regard as *anathema* anyone, even an angel from heaven, who proclaims a *gospel that is contrary to his (Gal 1:8-9). Paul also expresses the great lengths to which he would go (hypothetically) to see his fellow Jews come to *faith. He tells the church in Rome that he could wish that he himself were *anathema*, that is, "cut off from *Christ," for the sake of his own people.

4. Handing Sinners Over to Satan.

A couple of NT texts appear to suggest that Paul himself engaged in a sort of cursing for the purpose of disciplining sinners within the Christian community. Both of these passages mention the "handing over" of one or more persons "to *Satan" (1 Cor 5:1-5; 1 Tim 1:20). In 1 Corinthians 5, Paul instructs the church in Corinth not to tolerate egregious sexual immorality within their community. They had failed to correct a man in their church who was involved in an incestuous relationship with his father's wife. Paul tells the Corinthians that when they gather together they should "hand this man over to Satan for the destruction of the *flesh, so that his spirit may be saved in the day of the Lord" (1 Cor 5:5 NRSV). Unfortunately, Paul offers no further information about precisely what he expects the church to do or about the result that he anticipates, and interpreters have proposed various creative explanations of the apostle's enigmatic statement.

The most persuasive explanation of this passage is that Paul expects the church to call a sort of curse on the immoral person with the result that Satan would physically afflict (perhaps even kill) the sinner (e.g., Smith). Other explanations of the passage have also been offered, such as that Paul intends merely for the church to excommunicate the sinful person (e.g., Brown) or that the man was to experience a purely psychological trauma, rather than a physical one, as a result of the church's rejection (Murphy-O'Connor). That Satan would be invoked, however, to chastise a sinner physically for the purpose of restoring the errant individual to a proper standing before God fits Paul's Jewish theological context quite well (Stokes, 205-10). Presumably, 1 Timothy 1:20 has in mind a practice similar to the one presumed by 1 Corinthians 5. According to this verse, Paul has handed the wayward Hymenaeus and Alexander "over to Satan, so that they may learn not to blaspheme" (1 Tim 1:20 NRSV).

While Paul instructs the Roman believers not vengefully to curse their persecutors (Rom 12:14), the apostle's theology and ecclesiology apparently accommodate other kinds of curses. These are directed at those within the church who propagate a doctrine or live a lifestyle that Paul perceives to pose a serious threat to the spiritual well-being of a Christian community (Gal 1:8, 9; 1 Cor 5:5).

See also CORINTHIANS, FIRST LETTER TO THE; DISCIPLINE, CHURCH; ETHICS; GALATIANS, LETTER TO THE; LAW; ROMANS, LETTER TO THE; SIN, GUILT.

BIBLIOGRAPHY. **J. Behm,** "ἀνατίθημι, προσανατίθημι, ἀνάθεμα, κατάθεμα, ἀναθεματίζω, καταθεματίζω," *TDNT* 1:353-56; **D. R. Brown,** *The God of This Age: Satan in the Churches and Letters of the Apostle Paul,* WUNT 2/409 (Tübingen: Mohr Siebeck, 2015); **J. D. G. Dunn,** "Works of the Law and the Curse of the Law (Galatians 3.10-14)," *NTS* 31 (1985): 523-42; **J. Murphy-O'Connor,** *1 Corinthians,* NTM 10 (Wilmington, DE: Glazier, 1979); **D. R. Smith,** *"Hand This Man Over to Satan": Curse, Exclusion, and Salvation in 1 Corinthians 5,* LNTS 386 (New York: T&T Clark, 2008); **R. E. Stokes,** *The Satan: How God's Executioner Became the Enemy* (Grand Rapids, MI: Eerdmans, 2019).

R. E. Stokes

CURSUS HONORUM

The *cursus honorum* (Latin: "succession of honors") refers to the established sequence of public offices for aspiring aristocrats in their ascent of the sociopolitical pyramid in the Roman world. Minimum age requirements applied to each rung in the ladder, and Roman law also established a fixed minimum interval before advancing to the next post. The system was designed to ensure that civic administrators were equipped with the requisite skill sets and life experiences for upper-level governmental leadership. A well-regulated structure for advancement also curtailed the extent to which a politician's rise through the ranks could result from coercion or mere popular sentiment. While originally a product of the political organization of Rome, the system was replicated throughout the provinces as a means of legitimizing the political hierarchy and reinforcing the status and *dignitas* of provincial magistrates. Paul's letters and the record of his travels contained in Acts include references to Roman and provincial elites who were making their way through this established sequence of offices (Sergius Paulus, Acts 13:7-12; Gallio, Acts 18:12-16; Erastus, Rom 16:23), and his assemblies were established in cities governed by this political organization and the social ethos it represents.

1. Historical Development and Major Offices
2. The Quest for Honor in the Roman World
3. Paul and the *Cursus Honorum*

1. Historical Development and Major Offices. The *cursus honorum* was first formalized in 180 BC through the Lex Villia Annalis, which established the basic progression of political advancement that continued through the imperial period. Sulla introduced important reforms (80–79 BC), including age requirements, and the system continued to develop under successive emperors. While the major offices and general sequence remained stable, deviations, variations, and exceptions were not uncommon, especially as a result of imperial favor. By the NT era, the typical *cursus* of a Roman senator contained the following major posts held in chronological succession:

- *Vigintiviri*: A college of twenty men divided into several boards controlling the minting of coins, maintaining the streets in Rome, and overseeing various judicial matters
- *Military Tribune*: A military officer ranking just below the legate, the chief officer of a Roman legion
- *Quaestor*: A civic administrator with various responsibilities, including supervision of the treasuries in Rome and assisting governors in the provinces
- *Aedile*: A magistrate charged with maintaining temples and public buildings, and overseeing the grain supply, the marketplaces, and the public games
- *Praetor*: A judicial official presiding over the courts in Rome
- *Consul*: The highest political office on the *cursus honorum*. During the republic, two consuls presided over the senate and were assigned two legions for military campaigns. Under the principate, their authority was significantly curtailed.

The typical political career frequently included other military, civic, and religious posts as well. Priesthoods were particularly important and were regularly included in honorific inscriptions and funerary monuments, where Roman and provincial dignitaries heralded their achievements: "Lucius Calpurnius Fabatus: member of the board of six, military tribune, prefect, priest of the deified Augustus" (inscription from Philippi, abbreviated; Levick, 17).

2. The Quest for Honor in the Roman World. The very name, *cursus honorum,* betrays the fundamental role that *honor played in the *politics of Rome and demands that one situate this topic within the broader quest for honor so crucial in the Greco-Roman world. From Aristotle, who argued that "honor is the greatest of external goods" (*Eth. nic.* 1123b 10 [LCL]), to Cicero, who famously observed, "Nature has made us . . . enthusiastic seekers after honor, and once we have caught, as it were, some glimpse of its radiance, there is nothing we are not prepared to bear and go through in order to secure it" (Cicero, *Tusc.* 2.24.58 [LCL]), honor was the lens through which Greeks and Romans viewed the world. This resulted in a social structure characterized by fierce competition, jealous protection of accrued dignity, and hypersensitivity to any perceived loss of public esteem. The agonistic nature of public life engendered not only a concern to acquire honor but a concern for honor visibly expressed and publicly acknowledged. As J. E. Lendon summarizes, "Honor [in the Greco-Roman world] is a public thing; it is not a consequence of opinion merely, but of opinion publicly expressed" (Lendon, 54). Hence, Roman cities were chock-full of honorific monuments, with the publicly inscribed *cursus honorum* of the local elite prominent among them.

However, the quest for honor was not exclusive to the relatively small cadre belonging to the political aristocracy. Members of trade guilds, voluntary societies, military personal, and religious cults also vied for honors among their peers and similarly inscribed records of their achievements in stone: "Lucias Papius Venerus, of the tribe of Aemelia: assistant to the superintendent of the games, keeper of the flame of the Isthmian sanctuary, co-superintendent of the games, victor at the Nemean games, priest of Mars Augustus" (inscription from Corinth, abbreviated; Kent, 211). Both the lower orders and the patrician establishment were captivated by honor's "radiance" (Cicero), and each, through Paul's preaching, was confronted by the ignominious spectacle of a Messiah crucified on a Roman *cross.

3. Paul and the *Cursus Honorum*. The relevance of the *cursus honorum* and the value system it represents is evident at numerous places in Paul's letters, particularly in his dealings with the assemblies in *Corinth and Philippi, both Roman colonies with a strongly Roman ethos.

3.1. Corinth. The honorific inscriptions excavated from Roman Corinth reveal the importance of athleticism as one of the defining characteristics of this city. Corinth hosted the Isthmian games, a Pan-Hellenic athletic competition second in prestige only to the games in Olympia. Reflecting the importance of this international sporting event, the *cursus honorum* in Corinth reserved as the crowning achievement of a decurion's political career the office of *agonothete,* the superintendent of the games. Paul's letters also bear *witness to this social ethos. His extended athletic metaphor in 1 Corinthians 9:25-27 and his daring theological argumentation in 2 Corinthians, championing weakness over strength (esp. 2 Cor 12:9-10; cf. 2 Cor 10:10), seem to pointedly target this context.

The situation of Erastus represents a particularly difficult conundrum. Paul refers to him as the "city treasurer" (*oikonomos*) of Corinth (Rom 16:23), and there is a first-century inscription from Corinth that names a certain Erastus as an aedile of the city (Kent, 232). If one assumes, with most scholars, these refer to the same person, there was a Christian who was making his way through the public offices of Corinth's *cursus honorum* whose duties almost certainly involved participation in the pagan religious establishment. The responsibilities of the aedile normally involved managing local markets and temples. In Laconia, southeast of Corinth, the aedile was charged with setting up the cult statues of the emperors and supervising the sacrifices at the imperial shrine (Levick, 131-33). By the second century, Tertullian argued that city officials were so inextricably involved in *idolatry that it would be impossible for a Christian to hold public office (*Idol.* 17). How Erastus negotiated his Christian faith with his political career remains a mystery.

3.2. Philippi. Numerous honorific inscriptions have also been excavated from Roman Philippi, and their structure and content bear remarkable affinities with Philippians 3:5-6: "Circumcised on the eighth day, of the people of *Israel, of the tribe of Benjamin, a Hebrew of Hebrews . . . a Pharisee . . . a persecutor of the *church, as to *righteousness, blameless." Compare this example from the forum in Philippi: "Lucius Valerius Priscus . . . from the tribe Voltinia, decurion, irenarch, duumvir, sponsor of the games, devotee of the gods Isis and Serapis" (Pilhofer, 252, abbreviated). Joseph Hellerman has argued persuasively that Paul's repudiation of his own Jewish *cursus honorum* was intended to reconstruct honor among the Philippians. Similarly, Hellerman demonstrates that the Christ *hymn of Philippians 2:6-11 constitutes a kind of *cursus pudorum* ("succession of ignominies") in Philippians 2:6-8, followed by God's restoration of honor in Philippians 2:9-11. This striking inversion of the standard *cursus honorum* was intended to redefine honor in his honor-obsessed Roman context.

For Paul and other NT writers, honor is primarily a gift, not a pursuit. It is approval given by God and others on the basis of honorable behavior (Rom 2:10; 13:7), not a pursuit for status acquired at the expense of others. Hence, Paul commends honoring others above oneself (Rom 12:10; Phil 2:3) and embraces what others would consider dishonorable and shameful (1 Cor 4:10-13; 2 Cor 6:4-8; 12:10), if such disrepute was earned in the service of Christ. To be sure, Paul was not unconcerned about his reputation (Rom 3:8; 2 Cor 12:11; 1 Thess 2:1-12), but his determination to follow the self-abasing example of Christ (Phil 2:6-8) and his rejection of status based on mere human approval (1 Cor 1:26-29; 2 Cor 5:12; Gal 2:6) constituted a decidedly un-Roman way of thinking and living.

See also Christ, Messiah; Citizenship; Corinth; Food Laws and Customs, Jewish and Roman; Honor/Shame; Idolatry; Legal System, Roman; Politics and Power; Temple.

BIBLIOGRAPHY. **C. Barton,** *Roman Honor: The Fire in the Bones* (Berkeley: University of California Press, 2001); **H. Beck,** *Karriere und Hierarchie: die römische Aristokratie und die Anfänge des cursus honorum in der mittleren Republik* (Berlin: Akademie, 2005); **A. B. Gallia,** *Remembering the Roman Republic: Culture, Politics, and History Under the Principate* (Cambridge: Cambridge University Press, 2012); **J. H. Hellerman,** *Reconstructing Honor in Roman Philippi: Carmen Christi as Cursus Pudorum*, SNTSMS 132 (Cambridge: Cambridge University Press, 2005); idem, *Embracing Shared Ministry: Power and Status in the Early Church and Why It Matters Today* (Grand Rapids, MI: Kregel, 2013); **J. H. Kent,** *Corinth: Results of Excavations*, vol. 8.3, *The Inscriptions: 1926–1950* (Cambridge, MA: Harvard University Press, 1966); **M. L. Laird,** *Civic Monuments and the Augustales in Roman Italy* (Cambridge: Cambridge University Press, 2015); **J. E. Lendon,** *Empire of Honour: The Art of Government in the Roman World* (Oxford: Oxford University Press, 1997); **B. Levick,** *The Government of the Roman Empire: A Sourcebook*, 2nd ed. (New York: Routledge, 2000); **G. W. Peterman,** *Paul's Gift from Philippi: Conventions of Gift Exchange and Christian Giving*, SNTSMS 92 (Cambridge: Cambridge University Press, 1997); **P. Pilhofer,** *Philippi*, vol. 2, *Katalog der Inschriften von Philippi*, WUNT 119 (Tübingen: Mohr Siebeck, 2000); **R. J. A. Talbert,** *The Senate of Imperial Rome* (Princeton, NJ: Princeton University Press, 1984).

M. V. Hubbard

D

DAMASCUS ROAD EXPERIENCE.
See Conversion and Call of Paul.

DARKNESS. *See* Light and Darkness.

DAY OF THE LORD. *See* Eschatology.

DEAD SEA SCROLLS. *See* Qumran and Paul.

DEATH

In Paul, death is not merely the cessation of physical bodies. It unfolds with various dimensions that explain humanity's problem with *sin, Christ's pathway to *salvation, and patterns of living through the Spirit.

1. The Principle of Union
2. One Flesh with Death
3. Christ Unites with Death
4. Death as Life in Christ

1. The Principle of Union.

Death's multiple facets in Paul disentangle by examining union—when two become one. The principle of union appears before the fall, embedded in a hinge verse transitioning the narrative from *creation to Genesis 3: "For this reason, a man leaves his father and his mother and is united to his wife, and they become one *flesh" (Gen 2:24). On two separate occasions, Paul quotes this verse, highlighting the significance of union for sinners and saints alike.

In Ephesians 5:31, Paul cites Genesis 2:24 to conclude a discussion on the relationship between husbands and wives (Eph 5:21-30). However, in Ephesians 5:32, Paul signals a deeper application: "This [Gen 2:24] is a profound *mystery—for I am speaking about *Christ and the *church." Paul is not being crass; he is invoking the profound principle of union.

In 1 Corinthians 6:16, Paul appeals, once again, to union but in quite a different context. Amid an extended discussion on sexual immorality (1 Cor 5:1-5; 6:9-20), Paul asserts, "But the *body is not meant for sexual immorality, but for the *Lord, and the Lord for the body" (1 Cor 6:13). The two belong together, united with each other and not another. Paul emphatically continues: "So then shall I take the members of Christ and unite them with a prostitute? Never! Do you not know that the one united with the prostitute is one with her body? For, as it says, 'the two will become one flesh.' But the one united to the Lord is one with him in spirit" (1 Cor 6:15-17). For Paul, Genesis 2:24 articulates a principle of union present in acts of obedience and disobedience, salvation and sin, life and death: where two become one (Parsons, 32-33).

2. One Flesh with Death.

The principle of union in Paul is wide reaching (Campbell, 406-20). It governs *worship (1 Cor 10:21), the *Lord's Supper (1 Cor 11:23-26), the Christian community (1 Cor 12:12-26), and even one's understanding of humanity's relationship to death birthed at the fall. Paul explains, "Through one man sin came into the world, and death through sin, and in this way death spread to all humanity, because all sinned" (Rom 5:12; see also Rom 6:20-23). In Genesis 3, *Adam and Eve did not just break a rule; they employed the principle of union. Ingesting the forbidden fruit united humanity with death, two becoming one flesh (Wood, 23-50). And the results have been disastrous.

Union with death governs how humanity processes and engages reality. Death infuses the minds, desires, and actions of humans with predictable patterns of sin that isolate them from themselves, others, and *God (Rom 8:5-8; cf. Col 2:20-23). Death distorts what is holy (Rom 7:9-12) and employs sin to enslave humanity still further (Rom 6:16), separating people from the God in whose *image they were created in "in the beginning" (Gen 1:26-27). Humanity united with death bears "fruit for death"

(Rom 7:5) and acts of "sexual immorality, impurity, lust, evil desire, and greed" (Col 3:5), not to mention "fury, *wrath, malice, blaspheme, and obscene speech" (Col 3:8). Because humanity is united with death, acts that divide and destroy are more natural than acts that heal and harmonize, producing greater despair and deeper dependency on death itself. With each sin, humanity laments, "Who will rescue me from this body of death?" (Rom 7:24).

3. Christ Unites with Death.

In response, God could not merely obliterate death, for since the two became one, destroying death would also destroy humanity. Yet, God could not just stand by, for as Paul reminds his audience, "If we are faithless, he remains faithful, for he cannot disown himself" (2 Tim 2:13). So, the "image of the invisible God" (Col 1:15), refusing to repeat Adam's mistake and seize "equality with God" (Phil 2:6), became flesh, "humbled himself," and became "obedient to death—even death on a *cross" (Phil 2:8). God in the flesh united with death.

However, unlike Adam, Christ's union with death was out of obedience, not disobedience; out of faithfulness, not rebellion; out of *love, not sin. And death was unable to sustain such a union, for death was united with the God "who gives life to the dead and calls into being things that are not" (Rom 4:17). Through the incarnate Christ's crucifixion, then, the immortality of God filled the container of death, causing death to split wide open, spewing forth Christ as the "*firstborn from the dead" (Col 1:18).

Death was overcome with life, producing a *resurrection and a new iteration of death itself (2 Tim 1:9; cf. 1 Tim 2:8; 1 Cor 15:3-4). Christ's union with death, though, did not obliterate humanity's union but transformed it. Christ's death repurposed death and altered its ability and definition. In Christ, death now leads to life (1 Cor 15:22-23). Death no longer separates humanity from God but leads to union with God, both in this life and in the one to come (Rom 6:5-11; Phil 1:20-22; 2 Tim 2:11-12).

4. Death as Life in Christ.

Thus, Christians are called to die in order to unite with God, to merge their narratives with the narrative of Christ's death, resurrection, and *ascension (Phil 3:10-11; Gorman, 11-13). As Paul boasts, "I have been crucified with Christ. I no longer live, but Christ lives in me" (Gal 2:20; see also Rom 12:1). Death in Christ leads to a resurrection, a new life guided by the Spirit of God and dislodged from *slavery to sin (Rom 6:5-7, 16; Col 3:1-3).

If, therefore, Christians are dead to sin and alive to Christ, then their actions must follow (Col 2:20). Their mental processes (Phil 2:1-5) and desires (Titus 2:11-14) should transform into predictable patterns of *fruit from the Spirit (Rom 7:4-6; Gal 5:22-25). When they "put to death" (Col 3:5) their old way of living, they resurrect to a new way of life (Gal 2:20; Eph 5:8-14): a life that recaptures the "image of God" (Col 3:9-10), a life lived with Christ's death carried around in their bodies (2 Cor 4:10-12), producing life in them and in the world around them; a life that, whether alive or dead (Rom 14:8), boldly proclaims with Paul and the prophets: "Where, O death, is your victory? Where, O death, is your sting?" (1 Cor 15:55). Now, in Christ, death no longer separates humanity from God but fosters union with God today and in the age to come.

See also ADAM AND CHRIST; ATONEMENT; ESCHATOLOGY; FORGIVENESS; GLORY, GLORIFICATION; HOLY SPIRIT; IN CHRIST; SALVATION; SIN, GUILT.

BIBLIOGRAPHY. **F. Ábel,** "'Death as the Last Enemy': Interpretation of Death in the Context of Paul's Theology," *Communio viatorum* 58 (2016): 19-54; **C. C. Black,** "Pauline Perspectives on Death in Romans 5–8," *JBL* 103 (1984): 413-33; **C. R. Campbell,** *Paul and Union with Christ: An Exegetical and Theological Study* (Grand Rapids, MI: Zondervan, 2012); **M. C. de Boer,** *The Defeat of Death: Apocalyptic Eschatology in 1 Corinthians 15 and Romans 5*, JSNTSup 22 (Sheffield: JSOT Press, 1988); **M. J. Gorman,** *Participating in Christ: Explorations in Paul's Theology and Spirituality* (Grand Rapids, MI: Baker Academic, 2019); **J. A. Keiser,** "Disarming Death: Theomachy and Resurrection in 1 Corinthians 15," in *Coming Back to Life: The Permeability of Past and Present, Mortality and Immortality, Death and Life in the Ancient Mediterranean*, 2nd ed., ed. F. S. Tappenden and C. Daniel-Hughes (Montreal: McGill University Library, 2017), 375-406; **M. Parsons,** "'In Christ' in Paul," *Vox Evangelica* 18 (1988): 25-44; **F. S. Tappenden,** "Coming Back to Life in and Through Death: Early Christian Creativity in Paul, Ignatius, and Valentinus," in *Coming Back to Life: The Permeability of Past and Present, Mortality and Immortality, Death and Life in the Ancient Mediterranean*, 2nd ed., ed. F. S. Tappenden and C. Daniel-Hughes (Montreal: McGill University Library, 2017), 181-214; **S. J. Wood,** *Between Two Trees: Our Transformation from Death to Life* (Abilene, TX: Leafwood, 2019), 23-96; **N. T. Wright,** *Paul and the Faithfulness of God*, vol. 2 (Minneapolis: Fortress, 2013).

S. J. Wood

DEATH OF CHRIST. *See* ATONEMENT; CHRIST, MESSIAH; CROSS.

DEITIES. *See* IDOLATRY; RELIGIONS, GRECO-ROMAN.

DEMONS AND EXORCISM

Much modern scholarship has assumed a post-Enlightenment worldview that questions or disallows the existence of demons (and exorcism), often leading to the "demythologization" of NT texts. Some scholars have even argued that Paul himself disbelieved in the ontological reality of evil spirits or demons, though that same Paul writes about the *Holy Spirit. More recently, aided by global realities and interdisciplinary frameworks that emphasize how common beliefs in spirits are across a broad spectrum of cultures, many are reassessing the worldview(s) of the NT.

1. Relevant Terminology and Background
2. Acts
3. Paul's Letters

1. Relevant Terminology and Background.

The cognate Greek words for "demon" include the masculine noun *daimōn* and substantivized neuter adjective *daimonion*. In Greek literature from the time of Homer, these terms describe a variety of entities either good or evil (or both), including divine or semidivine entities such as gods, goddesses, (lesser or other) divine powers, beings with a status between humans and gods, divinities, spirits, fate, and even the souls of dead humans.

In Acts and the Pauline epistles the term *daimonion* is always negative when used from the perspective of the authors (*daimōn* is not used), though it appears only six times (Acts 17:18, with the neutral sense of "divinities," but on the lips of Paul's interlocutors; 1 Cor 10:20-21, 4×; 1 Tim 4:1). Many scholars have suggested that one of the reasons for the negative Jewish and Christian use of *daimonion* stems from the experience of the exile, as Babylon's spiritual dualism (systematized in Zoroastrianism) stressed opposing spiritual powers rather than powers that could be both good and evil. Jewish interest in the demonic became more (literarily) prominent during the Second Temple period, for while both Philo and Josephus use *daimonion* in the older Greek manner, most texts employ the language negatively. Especially relevant is the LXX, which translates with *daimonion* a variety of Hebrew words that refer to other gods.

Demons could be associated with a variety of afflictions, including bodily or mental harm, influence toward *idolatry, war, sex, and even famine. In response people employed amulets, prayers, incantations and other rituals, and exorcists. While in the OT the closest analogy to exorcism concerns Saul (1 Sam 16:14-23), later Jewish writers such as Josephus expand on the 1 Samuel 16 narrative (*Ant.* 6.166-168) and also describe Solomon as possessing exorcistic *knowledge and power (*Ant.* 8.45-47).

Paul nowhere discusses exorcism explicitly, though his "*signs and wonders" language may include it (e.g., 2 Cor 12:12; Rom 15:19; cf. Jesus' ministry). The relationship between the vocabulary of *daimonion* and that of *archōn/archē* (ruler; e.g., 1 Cor 2:6, 8), *exousia* (authority; e.g., 1 Cor 15:24), *dynamis* (power; e.g., Rom 8:38), *thronos* (throne; e.g., Col 1:16), *kyriotēs* (dominion, e.g., Eph 1:21), *stoicheion* (elements or elemental spirits; e.g., Gal 4:3, 8-9), and even *hamartia* (sin, e.g., Rom 6:6) is also an ongoing area of debate, as Paul does not systematize his language.

2. Acts.

In Acts 5:16, after summarizing "signs and wonders" (see Acts 2:22) that include *healings, Luke states that all those tormented by "unclean spirits" (*pneumatōn akathartōn*; see, e.g., Luke 4:33 for unclean spirits paralleled with demons) were "healed" (*etherapeuonto*). Acts 8:7 shows that Philip's "signs" in Samaria also follow this pattern of exorcisms of *pneumatōn akathartōn* and healings, though here the spirits cry out loudly as they depart (see, e.g., Lk 4:33-35).

Paul and his companions are in Philippi in Acts 16 and encounter a slave girl with a python spirit (*pneuma pythōna*), through which she predicts the future (Acts 16:16). The python spirit was associated with the Delphic oracular priestess of the god Apollo, who had conquered the python serpent in Greek mythology, and thus was probably viewed positively in the Greco-Roman world. Paul, however, successfully orders the spirit to leave her in the name of Jesus *Christ (Acts 16:18; cf. Lk 8:26-29).

This exorcism implies a negative view of the spirit for Paul and the author of Acts (who also employs *manteuomai*, "divination" or "fortune-telling," used only here in the NT and in the LXX for illegitimate religious practices), though the stated reason for the exorcism has confused many: Paul is annoyed (or deeply troubled? *diaponeomai*) because for "many days" the slave girl cried out that Paul and his companions were "*slaves of the Most High *God, who proclaim a way of *salvation to all of you!" (Acts 16:17). Both "Most High God," which described numerous gods in the Greco-Roman world (including the Delphic Apollo), and the indefinite "way of salvation" have encouraged the view that the girl's proclamation is unclear at best and dangerous at worst, at least from the perspective of Paul and the author of Acts (Klutz, 207-64). Scholars have also expressed concern for the slave girl's exploitation and the silence on her future, though Luke elsewhere highlights *women (and their liberation; Lk 8:1-3; Klutz, 247-51, 260-62).

During Paul's stay in Ephesus in Acts 19 evil spirits (*pneumata ponēra;* see Lk 7:21; 8:2) come out of people even through clothing that had touched Paul (Acts 19:11-12; objects were known as possible transmitters of power; cf. Acts 5:12-16). Afterward a failed exorcism attempted by seven Jewish *exorkistōn* (exorcists; the only NT occurrence of the term) illustrates both the power of Jesus' *name and Paul's reputation. Names were famous sources of power and were included in incantation lists, often with the verb *adjure* or *command* (though not by Jesus or his followers). Here, as elsewhere in Acts, the healing ministry of a Spirit-anointed agent demonstrates continuity with the *kingdom *ministry of Jesus and thus affects the worldview and actions of the audience.

3. Paul's Letters.

In Paul's discussion of idol food in 1 Corinthians 8–10, he first affirms that an idol is nothing (or does not exist, *ouden*; 1 Cor 8:4), but then in 1 Corinthians 10:20 specifies that pagan sacrifices benefit *daimonia*, not God (quoting Deut 32:17 LXX; cf. Is 65:11 LXX). He warns against partnership with *daimonia*, which provokes God's jealousy (1 Cor 10:21-22; see 1 Cor 10:1-13 for Israel's wilderness judgment). The idea that an idol can be nothing while idolatrous sacrifices are offered to *daimonia* (who, apparently, are something) has raised questions.

Some scholars minimize any real danger from the demons (who are simply "not God") and instead stress God's jealousy (Walton and Walton, 150-53). Others see Paul denying the ontological reality of other gods while admitting that their worshipers subjectively understand the gods to be real, a construct that has consequences (Thiselton, 773-76). More recently many argue that idols are distinct in the OT from the deities who inhabit them. An idol is thus "nothing," but the *daimonia* behind the idol are real (Williams, 145-48).

First Timothy connects apostasy with deceitful spirits (*pneumasin planois*) and teachings of demons (*didaskaliais daimoniōn*, 1 Tim 4:1). The grouping of spirits and demons likely indicates that the genitive *daimoniōn* is subjective, rendering "teachings taught by demons." Because of the clear problem of false *teaching in this community (e.g., 1 Tim 1:3-7; 4:2-3, 7), demonic teaching seems mediated by human teachers who are lying hypocrites with either disabled or perversely productive consciences (1 Tim 4:2-3).

See also Flesh; Healing, Illness; Holy Spirit; Idolatry; Magic; Name; Principalities and Powers; Religions, Greco-Roman; Satan, Devil; Signs, Wonders, Miracles.

BIBLIOGRAPHY. **M. S. Heiser,** *The Unseen Realm: Recovering the Supernatural Worldview of the Bible* (Bellingham, WA: Lexham, 2015); **T. Klutz,** *The Exorcism Stories in Luke-Acts: A Sociostylistic Reading* (Cambridge: Cambridge University Press, 2004); **A. Lange, H. Lichtenberger, and D. Römheld,** eds., *Die Damonen: Die Damonologie der israelitischjudischen und fruhchristlichen Literatur im Kontext ihrer Umwelt* (Tübingen: Mohr Siebeck, 2003); **D. B. Martin,** "When Did Angels Become Demons?," *JBL* 129, no. 4 (2010): 657-77; **R. E. Moses,** "Love Overflowing in Complete Knowledge at Corinth: Paul's Message Concerning Idol Food," *Int* 72, no. 1 (2018): 17-28; **E. Sorensen,** *Possession and Exorcism in the New Testament and Early Christianity*, WUNT 2/157 (Tübingen: Mohr Siebeck, 2002); **A. C. Thiselton,** *The First Epistle to the Corinthians*, NIGTC (Grand Rapids, MI: Eerdmans, 2000); **K. van der Toorn, B. Becking, and P. W. van der Horst,** eds., *Dictionary of Deities and Demons in the Bible* (Leiden: Brill, 1995); **G. H. Twelftree,** *In the Name of Jesus: Exorcism Among Early Christians* (Grand Rapids, MI: Baker Academic, 2007); idem, *Paul and the Miraculous* (Grand Rapids, MI: Baker Academic, 2013); **J. H. Walton and J. H. Walton,** *Demons and Spirits in Biblical Theology: Reading the Biblical Text in Its Cultural and Literary Context* (Eugene, OR: Cascade, 2019); **G. Williams,** *The Spirit World in the Letters of Paul the Apostle: A Critical Examination of the Role of Spiritual Beings in the Authentic Pauline Epistles*, FRLANT 231 (Gottingen: Vandenhoeck & Ruprecht, 2009).

H. Beers

DESTRUCTION. *See* Eschatology; Wrath, Destruction.

DEVIL. *See* Satan, Devil.

DIASPORA. *See* Hellenism, Roman; Israel; Mission.

DIATRIBE. *See* Performance; Philosophy; Rhetorical Criticism.

DISABILITY AND PAUL

While disability-related language is not as prevalent in the Pauline corpus as in the Gospel accounts, close examination of Paul's letters reveals the author's usage of disability-related language. He does so most often in relation to his own health and bodily experiences but also in a more generalized way.

1. Understanding Disability
2. Paul's Use of Disability Language
3. Paul's Disability

1. Understanding Disability.

While the English word *disability* has a relatively short history, the experience of disability itself is perennial, with texts and artwork from many ancient cultures depicting a broad range of disabling conditions. Disabilities such as vision and mobility impairments are depicted in many ancient sources, including Sumerian, Mesopotamian, and Egyptian, as well as in Jewish (e.g., Mephibosheth in 2 Sam 9) and Greco-Roman (e.g., Philip II of Macedon in Plut., *Alex. fort.* 331c) literature, inscriptions, and artwork (see Gosbell for more examples).

The World Health Organization describes disability as the result of a health condition or impairment acting in combination with various personal, social, and environmental factors. It is not simply that an individual lives with a particular health condition or impairment, but it is also the resultant impact this condition has on an individual's ability to function within society, including any experience of marginalization or stigmatization associated with the health condition or impairment. While people in all cultures and societies experience illness and impairments, the extent to which these affect a person's societal participation varies significantly between societies and across different historical periods. An individual's experience will also vary depending on the nature of their particular condition or conditions; their gender, socioeconomic status, and age; and their particular culture's expectations of individuals.

This means that, while some conditions considered a disability in the modern world would also have been considered such in ancient cultures, one cannot assume that all cultures and societies would have identical lists of conditions deemed disabling. For example, while muscular *bodies are revered by many in the modern world, heavily muscled bodies in Greco-Roman antiquity were indicative of manual labor and lower social status and were, in this respect, considered a kind of physical impairment. Likewise, infertility is not typically considered a disability by modern definitions; however, the expectation of *women to bear children in many ancient cultures meant that infertility is likely to have been considered a particularly disabling condition within those cultures. Conversely, the experience of vision loss in the ancient world would have been more disabling for people in the ancient world than in the present. For many, mild vision loss can be corrected through glasses, contact lenses, or corrective surgery. While recognizing a loss of vision, people who wear glasses in the modern world are not generally considered disabled. However, without these corrective means, even what is considered mild vision loss in the present would have been disabling for individuals in the ancient world. While modern readers may have a clear picture of the conditions that constitute disabilities in their own society and culture, readers cannot assume that their categories of disability are identical to those depicted in ancient texts. Any attempt to address disability within ancient sources, including the texts of the NT, must therefore consider these references within their own social and cultural context.

No ancient language—including the Greek of the NT—had an overarching word equivalent to the English word *disability*, especially not one that encompassed both a health condition or an impairment and its social implications. The closest equivalents in Koine Greek are *adynatos* ("unable") and *astheneia* ("weakness"). While *adynatos* is used in Greek literature to refer to physical disabilities in ancient sources (e.g., Acts 14:8), in its Pauline usage it refers more generally to powerlessness and lack of strength (e.g., Rom 8:3; 15:1). The word *astheneia* has a wide semantic range and can refer to physical weakness connected to illness or disability but can also be used in a more figurative way to refer to moral weakness, weakness of character, or weakness of *faith. While the Gospel writers employ *astheneia* almost exclusively in a physical sense (e.g., Lk 9:2; 10:9; 13:11-12), in the Pauline corpus, *astheneia* is used to refer to physical weakness or illness (Phil 2:27; 1 Tim 5:23) as well as moral and spiritual weakness (Rom 14:1; 1 Cor 8:9). However, it is not always easy to clearly demarcate one kind of usage of *astheneia* from another, which Dale Martin argues is indicative of the ancient belief in a connection between "health and status" (168).

2. Paul's Use of Disability Language.
As with other NT writers, and like OT writers before them, Paul does use disability-related language in a metaphorical sense. In his rebuke of some in the *church at Rome, Paul questions those who are "convinced that you are a guide for the blind [*typhlos*], a light for those who are in the dark" (Rom 2:19 NIV). In Romans 11, in a discussion of the members of *Israel who were hardened against a positive response to *God, Paul quotes from various passages in the OT where disability-related language is used metaphorically, in particular with the image of blinded or darkened eyes referring to those who do not respond accurately to God (Rom 11:7-10; cf. Is 29:10; Ps 69:22-23). In this sense, vision is used metaphorically to refer to knowledge. Seeing God means to know and respond to him, while having blind or darkened eyes refers to a failure to know and respond to him.

2.1. Weakness (*astheneia*). As noted, Paul uses the language of weakness (*astheneia*) in both a literal and a figurative sense throughout his letters, with the greatest concentration in Romans and 1–2 Corinthians. It is apparent that some of this usage is in relation to physical weakness, including illness (Phil 2:27; 1 Tim 5:23). However, Paul uses *astheneia* overwhelmingly in a figurative sense to refer to those who are weak in character or in faith or those who are spiritually weak (Rom 14:1; 1 Cor 8:9). Paul also speaks of weakness in a broad sense as a shared experience of humanity. Humans in their creatureliness are weak in comparison to the power and strength of the limitlessness of God (e.g., Rom 6:19). Paul also draws a contrast between the present human body, "sown in weakness," with that of the resurrected body, which will be "raised in power" (1 Cor 15:43-44 NIV).

In 2 Corinthians, Paul cites the accusations of the Corinthians that Paul has a weak (*asthenēs*) bodily presence that is inconsistent with the weighty content of his letters (2 Cor 10:10). More than simply drawing attention to an apparent disconnect between his writing and physical presence, it is likely that in a "physiognomically-conscious" culture (Harstock, 58), the Corinthians' claims form a kind of slur against Paul's character with a view to undermining his apostolic authority. Physiognomics was a pseudoscience popular in the first century Greco-Roman world. It posited an alignment between a person's physical appearance and gestures with their character. Physiognomic language was regularly employed in rhetorical arguments as a means of discrediting and belittling one's opponent. It appears that the Corinthians' accusation of Paul's weakness in body is an example of physiognomic ideals thus aimed at casting aspersions on Paul's character.

Rather than attempting to refute these claims, Paul does something unique in embracing the language of weakness to describe himself. Paul openly acknowledges that he came to the Corinthians in weakness (*astheneia*, 1 Cor 2:3), but this is not shameful because it served to ensure that the Corinthians' "faith might not rest on human *wisdom, but on God's power" (1 Cor 2:5 NIV). Paul did not consider his weakness as something that destabilized his apostolic authority, but rather his weakness served as the means through which God's power could be displayed. Paul makes this belief expressly clear in 2 Corinthians 12:9-10, when he states that God's power is made perfect in weakness (*astheneia*) and that he will "boast all the more gladly about my weaknesses [*astheneia*], so that Christ's power may rest on me" (NIV; see also 2 Cor 11:30). Such claims from Paul would have been surprising to his contemporaries, who likely would have eschewed any association with weakness in any form.

2.2. Mental Illness ("Madness") and Mental Incapacity ("Foolishness"). Although the language of mental illness and mental incapacity is not always immediately evident in English translations of the NT, Paul's letters do include examples of language associated with mental illness ("madness") or mental incapacity ("foolishness"). Similar to Paul's use of the language of weakness, Paul's use of this language of madness and foolishness is also complex and multifaceted. At times, Paul appears to shun accusations or appearances of madness (1 Cor 14:23), while at other times he appears to recognize the *gospel itself as demonstrating a form of madness. In 1 Corinthians 1, Paul declares that the message of the gospel itself is a message of foolishness (*mōria*) to those who are perishing (1 Cor 1:18; cf. 1 Cor 1:23). Even within the context of the so-called fool's speech of 1 Corinthians 11–12, Paul on one hand asserts that he is not a fool (1 Cor 11:16), but on the other hand eventually concedes that in the process of giving this particular speech he has indeed become a fool (1 Cor 12:11). The fool's speech includes Paul boasting in, among other things, his sufferings and weaknesses (2 Cor 11–12). On other occasions also, Paul embraces the experience of madness/foolishness in tandem with his experience of weakness. In 1 Corinthians 1:27 Paul asserts that "God chose what is foolish in the world to shame the wise; God chose what is weak in the world to shame the *strong" (ESV; cf. 1 Cor 4:10).

As with the accusations against Paul of his weakness, Paul also appears to respond to accusations from his Corinthian detractors that he was mad or foolish. Just as he does with the claims of his weakness, Paul also resists defying claims of his madness or foolishness but instead accepts the label for himself. Paul is at ease doing so because he recognizes that the gospel message itself has the appearance of foolishness to a perishing world. In doing so, Paul asserts that the "gospel in itself has changed the rules, and Christ's death and resurrection reinterpret what madness, as well as weakness means (1 Cor. 1:18-2:5)" (Solevåg, 109).

3. Paul's Disability.

As well as using the language of weakness and madness in a broad sense, Paul in his letters refers to his own disabling health conditions. In Galatians 4:13-14, Paul writes, "It was because of an illness [*astheneian tēs sarkos*] that I first preached the gospel to you, and even though my illness was a trial to you, you did not treat me with contempt or scorn" (NIV). In combination with Paul's reference to writing with "large letters" later in the letter (Gal 6:11) and the statement that the Galatians would have been willing to tear out their own eyes to give to him (Gal 4:15), some scholars propose that Paul's bodily ailment was related to his eyes, possibly a long-term effect of the blinding he experienced on the Damascus road (Brock, 85). Other scholars suggest Paul's condition may have been epilepsy. This view comes from a literal reading of "scorn" (*ekptyō*) in Galatians 4:13 as meaning "to spit out" rather than its metaphorical meaning of rejection. Some ancient references to epilepsy recall observers spitting at the illness as a means of warding off its contagion or bad luck (Pliny, *Nat.* 28.7). Proponents of this view argue that it is not merely that the Galatians could have scorned or rejected Paul but that it would not have been surprising if the Galatians had responded with a literal reaction of spitting at him, as one might have done in response to a person with epilepsy in the ancient world (Pakhoungte, 145; Yarbro Collins, 175). It is possible that Paul's reference to his visit to the Corinthians, where he came to them in "in weakness and *fear and much trembling" (1 Cor 2:3 NABRE), could also refer to a literal trembling associated with an epileptic seizure or another form of disability.

In 2 Corinthians 12:7, Paul states, "There was given me a thorn in my *flesh, a messenger of *Satan, to torment me." It is unclear whether this "thorn in the flesh" is a reference to the health conditions Paul has alluded to elsewhere in his letters or a different experience altogether. The precise nature of Paul's thorn has been a topic of intense debate from the time of the early church and continues to remain so among modern scholars. Some argue that the thorn Paul refers to is simply the "insults, hardships, persecutions, and calamities" he mentions in 2 Corinthians 12:10 (NRSV), in particular persecutions that were leveled at Paul by some of his Corinthian detractors (McCant, 572). Others, however, interpret the thorn as a further reference to the same "weakness in the flesh" that Paul refers to in Galatians 4:13-14, indicating a kind of illness or disability.

In contrast, R. P. Martin argues that it would have been impossible for Paul to have lived with a significant long-term illness or disability given the intensity of his itinerant ministry (415). However, given the evidence from the ancient world of people with disability serving in an array of political, military, and social roles, such a position is untenable (see Gosbell, 68-71). While an impairment would have added additional challenges to Paul's *ministry—to which he attests—a physical impairment would not have been completely incompatible with Paul's tasks and *mission. One should not be hasty in dismissing the possibility that Paul experienced at least a portion of his life with a significant disability that at times caused him physical pain as well as some mental and emotional anguish.

While investigations into the nature of the possible disability are fruitful for drawing attention to the scope of Paul's allusions to his condition, the precise nature of his disability is purely conjecture. It is simply not possible to diagnose an illness or disability from a few scant references in Paul's letters. Ultimately, it is not the nature of the condition itself, however, that is significant, but Paul's conviction that his impairments were no impediment to God being at work in and through him. Thus Susan Garrett states, "Whatever the identity of the thorn, the cross/resurrection paradigm governs Paul's reading of the divine response, for Christ's resurrection had shown 'power made perfect in weakness' (2 Cor 12:9) to be God's characteristic design for Christian life" (Garrett, 83). Irrespective of his precise condition, Paul accepted his human weaknesses and limitations, which did not disable God's ability to be at work. Far from deterring him in his ministry or impeding his abilities to fulfill God's purposes, Paul recognized his weaknesses as the means through which God demonstrated his power and limitlessness. For Paul, power was God's and thus "a human, in his or her fragile 'clay jar,' is only powerful or 'able' to the extent that the divine works through him or her" (Albl, 147).

See also BODY; HEALING, ILLNESS; STRONG AND WEAK; SUFFERING.

BIBLIOGRAPHY. **M. Albl,** "'For Whenever I Am Weak, Then I Am Strong': Disability in Paul's Epistles," in *This Abled Body: Rethinking Disabilities in Biblical Studies*, ed. H. Avalos, S. J. Melcher, and J. Schipper (Atlanta: Society of Biblical Literature, 2007), 145-58; **D. A. Black,** *Paul, Apostle of Weakness: Astheneia and Its Cognates in the Pauline Literature*, rev. ed. (Eugene, OR: Pickwick, 2012); **B. Brock,** *Disability: Living into the Diversity of Christ's Body* (Grand Rapids, MI: Baker Academic, 2021); **M. L. Edwards,** "Women and Physical Disability in Ancient Greece," *Ancient World* 29 (1998): 3-9; **S. R. Garrett,** "Paul's Thorn and Cultural Models of Affliction," in *The Social World of the First Christians: Essays in Honor of Wayne A. Meeks*, ed. L. M. White and O. L. Yarbrough (Minneapolis: Fortress, 1995), 82-99; **L. A. Gosbell,** *"The Poor, the Crippled, the Blind, and the Lame": Physical and Sensory Disability in the Gospels of the New Testament*, WUNT 2/469 (Tübingen: Mohr Siebeck, 2018); **C. Harstock,** *Sight and Blindness in Luke–Acts: The Use of Physical Features in Characterization* (Leiden: Brill, 2008); **D. Martin,** *The Corinthian Body* (New Haven, CT: Yale University Press, 1995); **R. P. Martin,** *2 Corinthians*, WBC (Waco, TX: Word Books, 1986); **J. W. McCant,** "Paul's Thorn of Rejected Apostleship," *NTS* 34 (1998): 550-72; **R. L. Pakhoungte,** *Paul's Suffering and Weakness in 2 Corinthians: Reading from a Disability Perspective* (Carlisle, UK: Langham Monographs, 2022); **A. R. Solevåg,** *Negotiating the Disabled Body: Representations of Disability in Early Christian Texts* (Atlanta: SBL Press, 2018); **A. Yarbro Collins,** "Paul's Disability: The Thorn in His Flesh," in *Disability Studies and Biblical Literature*, ed. C. R. Moss and J. Schipper (New York: Palgrave Macmillan, 2011), 165-83.

L. A. Gosbell

DISCIPLINE, CHURCH

In an entry about discipline, readers might hope that the ecclesiological formation of Paul's congregations included a community code akin to what one finds in the Dead Sea community's scrupulous Community Rule (1QS, originally dubbed the Manual of Discipline). There is no reason either from his extant letters or the evidence of Acts, however, to draw any such conclusions. To be sure, Paul did give some specific instructions that applied to all his congregations (of which he felt compelled to remind the Corinthian congregation—1 Cor 3:17; 7:17-24; 14:29-36). Paul also faithfully handed down the *gospel traditions of the *faith (1 Cor 11:2, 23-26; 15:3-8).

But one should be cautious in seeking to reconstruct a detailed community rule among the Pauline churches. This is for at least two reasons. First, Paul believed that both Jew and *Gentile had been endowed with the promised Spirit (Gal 3:13-14) and were therefore taught by *God (1 Thess 2:9; see Witmer). Because his congregations lived in the Spirit-filled age of Messiah Jesus, believers had every resource needed to live out their calling as God's holy people (1 Cor 1:2). Second, the evidence of Paul's letters suggests that discipleship is an ongoing process (e.g. his already/not yet eschatological framework), which sometimes requires Spirit-filled pastoral guidance or correction in specific instances of confusion or controversy. The very fact that Paul needed to address a wide variety of pastoral situations in his letters seems to preclude the possibility of an elaborate community rule, beyond the general guidelines that the *Jerusalem council had already set out in Acts 15:19-29 (cf. 1 Cor 8:1–11:1). Paul's famous virtue lists, for example, contrast generally the Spirit-guided and the flesh-guided life (Gal 5:13-26; see also Rom 8:1-39), without providing detailed merits and demerits based on standards of performance.

But the question remains: What constituted discipline in the Pauline congregations? The answer to this question, in part, depends on what sort of communities Paul established (see Ascough). Paul consistently calls his congregations *ekklēsia*, a term used both in the Greek world of assemblies/associations and in the LXX to refer to the assembly of God's people. Scholars who believe Paul's communities resembled the former (Kloppenborg; van Kooten), might reasonably find parallels in those organizations (see Kwon). Those, on the other hand, who believe Paul's use of *ekklēsia* is owing to his Jewish understanding of God's people (e.g., Ps 88:6 LXX; Trebilco), will look for Jewish antecedents in tracing Paul's practice of discipline among his congregations. Yet a third way forward is to answer the question regarding the social makeup of his congregations (see esp. Longenecker). E. A. Judge has vigorously argued that Paul's communities were scholastic communities. Expanding on Judge's work, Claire Smith concludes that the pervasive teaching language in his letters suggests his congregations were "learning communities" that ultimately came together under the *teaching of God and his

Word (for a reconstruction of Paul's teaching, see Edsall). Whatever the precise taxonomy of Paul's congregations, then, one may begin with the observation that Paul's pastoral guidance (discipline) consistently brings his understanding of the Scriptures to bear on the unique situations of his congregations, as seen in the extensive quotations, allusions, and narrative substructures that undergird his writings (see Bockmuehl).

It is far beyond the scope of this essay, however, to trace fully the scriptural roots of community discipline in Paul's correspondence. Instead, this discussion will seek to (1) survey briefly the expressions of "learning" and "discipleship" in his letters and then (2) discuss three examples of his *corrective* discipline in his letters.

1. Expressions of "Learning" and "Discipleship"
2. Corrective Instructions: 1 Corinthians, 2 Thessalonians, and Philippians
3. Conclusion

1. Expressions of "Learning" and "Discipleship."

The Greek word normally used for "learning" as a pupil or rearing up as a child is *paideuō* and its cognates. Paul uses this constellation of terms on eight occasions, while he employs the similar verb for "learning/discipleship" (*manthanō*) at a slightly higher rate of fifteen. The words themselves carry slight distinctions between them according to their contexts, falling broadly into three groups: preventative, corrective, and hardship training.

1.1. Preventative Expressions. First, Paul uses these terms in preventative-instructional occasions. In Romans, for example, Paul provides a warning in his letter closing to watch out for those who would contradict either in words or deeds "the teaching you learned" (*manthanō*, Rom 16:17). The letter to the Ephesians similarly contrasts their pattern of life as Gentiles with their new pattern of learning (*manthanō*) as followers of Jesus (Eph 4:20). This learning also takes shape as they watch Paul's life (Phil 4:9) and hear from others (e.g., Epaphras; Col 1:7). In his instructions to *households, Paul tells the Ephesians that children should be brought up in the training (*paideia*) and instruction of the *Lord (Eph 6:4). In his *Pastoral Epistles, he similarly encourages his protégé Timothy to remain in what he has learned (*manthanō*) since childhood in the Scriptures, which are useful for teaching, reproof, correction, and training (*paideia*) in *righteousness (2 Tim 3:14-16). Finally, Paul further explains to his coworker Titus that God's *grace "teaches [*paideuō*] us that, by renouncing ungodliness and worldly lusts, we might live self-controlled, righteous, and godly lives in the present age" (Titus 2:12-14). In all these uses, Paul emphasizes the role of God's Word and the example of God's *servants in making disciples who walk in the ways of Jesus.

1.2. Corrective Expressions. At the same time, Paul uses these terms to correct dysfunction and to troubleshoot congregational crises. One can see this most clearly in his first extant letter to the Corinthian congregation. In response to their divisions over leaders, Paul hopes the congregation will learn (*manthanō*) not to go beyond the Scriptures in turning Paul and Apollos into rival messengers (1 Cor 4:6) when they are actually servants, coworkers, and fellow stewards of God's household (1 Cor 3:1-9; 4:1-5). In response to their socioeconomic divisions at the Lord's table, Paul warns that the Corinthians are weak and sick (and some are dying), and further explains that they are being disciplined (*paideuō*) as God's community (1 Cor 11:32). In response to the chaos of their public *worship, which valued *tongues over *prophecy, Paul contends that there should be order so that everyone may learn (*manthanō*; 1 Cor 14:31, 35).

1.3. Hardship-Training Expressions. Finally and somewhat surprisingly, Paul makes use of these terms when discussing the hardships and persecutions that the apostles undergo as part of their calling as emissaries. He assures the concerned Philippians that his apostolic training has taught him (*manthanō*) to be content in all circumstances—both in hunger and in abundance (see 2 Cor 11:16–12:10). He also explains to the Corinthians that his many persecutions have disciplined him, but not unto *death (2 Cor 6:9; cf. Ps 118:18 LXX). God's discipline, in fact, is in keeping with his steadfast love, as the fruit of righteousness grows from the ashes of persecution and hardship (see Heb 12:5-11).

In all these unique expressions, the thread that holds these examples together is Paul's aim to guide the believers in the ways of Jesus according to God's Word.

2. Corrective Instructions: 1 Corinthians, 2 Thessalonians, and Philippians.

In this section, it is now necessary to turn to three test cases in Paul's letters to determine the extent to which Paul's corrective discipline is similarly based on messianic and/or scriptural reasoning.

2.1. The Sinful Man (1 Corinthians 5). The most obvious place to begin is with Paul's extensive instructions to the Corinthians. One might reasonably argue, in fact, that the majority of Paul's energies in 1–2 Corinthians are corrective. From their divisions over leaders to their denial in the bodily *resurrection of believers, the Corinthians took many of their (mis)cues from the culture of *Corinth (Winter 2001). Given the limits of the present discussion, however, one must focus on Paul's most sustained pastoral guidance regarding the sinful man.

In 1 Corinthians 5, Paul is shocked to learn that the Corinthians have endured—even while boasting—the outrageous *sin of a man who sleeps with this father's wife. In his response, Paul never actually addresses the man directly. Instead, he frames his response to the congregation by turning to the commands God gave to the exodus generation. First, the congregation must weep in corporate repentance, as God called the people to do in times of corporate sin (1 Cor 5:1-5; cf. Lev 26:40-45; Ezra 9–10). Second, the Corinthians must prepare to celebrate Passover—Messiah Jesus is, after all, the Passover lamb—by removing the leaven of sin from their midst (1 Cor 5:6-8; cf. Ex 12:14-16). Finally, the congregation must act decisively by removing the wicked person from among them (1 Cor 5:9-13; cf. Deut 22:21-24). In other words, Paul is scripting the congregation directly into the biblical narrative of God's people (see 1 Cor 10:1-13; Rosner) so they might take up their calling as God's holy people in Corinth (1 Cor 1:2).

To be sure, Paul is also concerned for the man's *salvation. Without undertaking a detailed exegesis of the complex sentence of 1 Corinthians 5:3-5, three clarifications must now be made. First, Paul's point in these verses seems to be that he has *already* passed *judgment on the sinful man precisely because the Corinthians have failed to take decisive action. Put another way, Paul is not actually asking the Corinthians to judge the man but to recognize that Paul's Spirit-filled judgment carries the power of the Lord Jesus even in his absence as they assemble together in the Lord's *name. Second, Paul's decision to hand the man over to *Satan "for the destruction of his *flesh" seems to suggest his desire that the man would come to his senses and scramble out of the sewage of Satan's sphere (see 1 Tim 1:20). Third, whatever precisely Paul means by handing the man over to Satan, Paul does not want judgment to be the final word. His ultimate hope is that the man's spirit might be saved (see the extensive discussion in Thiselton, 395-400). (Paul's instructions to the Corinthians may well have worked, especially if the repentant man in 2 Cor 2:1-11 is to be identified with the sinful man of 1 Cor 5.)

2.2. The Disruptive Congregants (2 Thessalonians 3:6-15). In 2 Thessalonians, Paul instructs his congregation on the ongoing issue of unruly (*ataktōs*) individuals within the congregation who apparently are unwilling to work for a living (2 Thess 3:6-15; see 1 Thess 5:14). The possible background of this scenario is not entirely settled among scholars, but the most likely view is that Paul is confronting clients who have become disruptive busybodies as they do the bidding of their patrons (see Winter 1989; cf. Russell). In response to this situation, Paul warns the Thessalonian believers to avoid those unruly individuals who are not walking according to the traditions given to them (2 Thess 3:6). After giving a threefold rationale (2 Thess 3:7-11), he then provides three further instructions. First, he instructs the unruly believers to earn their own living (2 Thess 3:12). Second, he encourages the congregation not to grow weary in doing good (i.e., in providing for the needs of others). Third, he warns the congregation of associating with anyone who ignores his teaching on this matter (2 Thess 3:14-15). Paul's corrective instructions here are bound up with the traditions of apostolic teaching, but without specific mention of the Scriptures.

2.3. Philippians. In his warm letter to the Philippians, Paul nevertheless tactfully tackles an acute issue of disunity. After disclosing the gospel's progress even in the midst of opposition (Phil 1:12-26), Paul encourages the Philippians to live as citizens worthy of the gospel even in the midst of opposition (Phil 1:27-30). In what seems at first blush to be general parenesis, Paul then invites the Philippians to live in harmony (literally, "to think the same thing") and to practice humility as they look after the interests of others (Phil 2:1-4). As they follow the example of Messiah Jesus (2:5-11), Paul also invites them to observe the example of Timothy (Phil 2:19-24) and Epaphroditus (Phil 2:25-30) and to follow his own example (Phil 3:1-21). In his call for response, Paul puts a fine point on these seemingly generic instructions when he urges two women in the congregation, Euodia and Syntyche, to live in harmony (Phil 4:2; see Phil 2:2) and asks another individual (it is unclear whether *syzygos* is a description of "a true companion" or his actual name) to help them in this process of reconciliation. Given his high praise of these women as fellow evangelists, along with Clement, it is unlikely that he intends to shame them into obedience. But the unbroken thread of unity and humility in the letter unquestionably leads to this final exhortation on unity. Paul's corrective instructions thus hinge on the example of Jesus himself and others who have followed in his ways.

3. Conclusion.

If the above discussion is on the right track, one can briefly reflect on the implications of Paul's practice of discipline in his congregations. First, any discussion of community discipline must begin with Paul's conviction that followers of Jesus were God's redeemed, holy, and Spirit-endowed people. Second, Paul believed that training in godliness was only possible as Jesus-believing communities lived out the scriptural story by following the ways of Jesus through the leading of the Spirit. Finally, the real-life examples in 1 Corinthians, 2 Thessalonians, and Philippians seem to be consistent with his instructions to the Galatian congregations, namely, that those caught in sin should be restored in a spirit of gentleness and watchfulness (Gal 6:1; see further Obenhaus). Rather than pointing to a fixed process for excommunication, Paul instead points to the story of God's deliverance of his people, who (as he reminds the Corinthians) have been "washed, made holy, and declared righteous in the name of the Lord Jesus the Messiah and by the Spirit of our God" (1 Cor 6:11).

See also CORINTHIANS, FIRST LETTER TO THE; ETHICS; HOLY SPIRIT; PASTOR, PAUL AS; PHILIPPIANS, LETTER TO THE; QUMRAN AND PAUL; THESSALONIANS, LETTERS TO THE; URBAN SETTING OF PAUL'S CHURCHES.

BIBLIOGRAPHY. **R. S. Ascough,** "What Are They Now Saying About Christ Groups and Associations?," *CurBR* 13 (2015): 207-44; **M. Bockmuehl,** *Jewish Law in Gentile Churches: Halakhah and the Beginning of Christian Public Ethics* (Grand Rapids, MI: Baker Academic, 2003); **B. A. Edsall,** *Paul's Witness to Formative Early Christian Instruction*, WUNT 2/365 (Tübingen: Mohr Siebeck, 2014); **E. A. Judge,** "Early Christians as a Scholastic Community," *JRH* 1 (1960): 4-15; idem, "Early Christians as a Scholastic Community: Part II," *JRH* 1 (1961): 125-37; **J. S. Kloppenborg,** "Pauline Communities and Graeco-Roman Associations," in *Receptions of Paul in Early Christiainty: The Person of Paul and His Writings Through the Eyes of His Early Interpreters*, ed. J. Schröter, S. Butticaz, and A. Dettwiler, BZNW 324 (Berlin: de Gruyter, 2018), 215-47; **G. H. van Kooten,** "Ἐκκλησία Τοῦ Θεοῦ: The 'Church of God' and the Civic Assemblies (Ἐκκλησίαι) of the Greek Cities in the Roman Empire; A Response to Paul Trebilco and Richard A. Horsley," *NTS* 58 (2012): 522-48; **O.-Y. Kwon,** "Discovering the Characteristics of Collegia—Collegia Sodalicia and Collegia Tenuiorum in 1 Corinthians 8, 10 and 15," *HBT* 32 (2010): 166-82; **B. W. Longenecker,** *Remember the Poor: Paul, Poverty, and the Greco-Roman World* (Grand Rapids, MI: Eerdmans, 2010); **S. R. Obenhaus,** "Sanctified Entirely: The Theological Focus of Paul's Instructions for Church Discipline," *ResQ* 43 (2001): 1-12; **B. S. Rosner,** *Paul, Scripture and Ethics: A Study of 1 Corinthians 5–7*, AGJU 22 (Leiden: Brill, 1994); **R. Russell,** "The Idle in 2 Thess 3.6-12: An Eschatological or a Social Problem?," *NTS* 34 (1988): 105-19; **C. S. Smith,** *Pauline Communities as "Scholastic Communities": A Study of the Vocabulary of "Teaching" in 1 Corinthians, 1 and 2 Timothy and Titus*, WUNT 2/335 (Tübingen: Mohr Siebeck, 2012); **A. C. Thiselton,** *The First Epistle to the Corinthians*, NIGTC (Grand Rapids, MI: Eerdmans, 2000); **P. Trebilco,** "Why Did the Early Christians Call Themselves ἡ Ἐκκλησία?," *NTS* 57 (2011): 440-60; **B. W. Winter,** "'If a Man Does Not Wish to Work . . .': A Cultural and Historical Setting for 2 Thessalonians 3:6-16," *TynBul* 40 (1989): 303-15; idem, *After Paul Left Corinth: The Influence of Secular Ethics and Social Change* (Grand Rapids, MI: Eerdmans, 2001); **S. E. Witmer,** "Θεοδίδακτοι in 1 Thessalonians 4.9: A Pauline Neologism," *NTS* 52 (2006): 239-50.

J. K. Hardin

DIVINE FOREKNOWLEDGE.
See FOREKNOWLEDGE, DIVINE.

DIVINE SONSHIP. *See* ADOPTION; SON OF GOD.

DIVORCE. *See* MARRIAGE AND DIVORCE, ADULTERY AND INCEST.

DOMINIONS. *See* PRINCIPALITIES AND POWERS.

DOXOLOGY. *See* PRAYER.

DYING AND RISING WITH CHRIST.
See BAPTISM; CRUCIFORMITY; DEATH; IN CHRIST; RESURRECTION.

E

EARLY CHURCH TRADITION.
See INTERPRETATION: PATRISTIC.

ECOLOGICAL PAUL

Contemporary scientific, political, and public concerns for the environment have influenced how Jewish and Christian scholars approach Scripture. New questions have redeployed the ancient biblical tradition to produce ecologically sensitive readings of the Bible. In turn there has been a burgeoning subdiscipline of ecological theology (ecotheology). In part due to modern interpreters' emphasis on *justification by *grace through *faith, Pauline scholarship has tended to focus on anthropocentric themes (i.e., human *salvation, Christian community, etc.) with little focused attention given to aspects of *creation besides humans. Due to these scholarly trajectories, the majority of ecotheological scholarship on the Pauline corpus has primarily been focused on Romans 8:18-25 and Colossians 1:15-20. This article will discuss these two passages within a broader range of Pauline theological categories: new creation, *Christology, redemption as reconciliation of all things, protology, and *eschatology. The article concludes with implications for the *church today.

While *ecotheology* is a modern term representing a conscientious effort on the part of biblical scholars and theologians to read Scripture with an ecosensitive interpretive lens, readings of Scripture that identify and celebrate creation did not originate in the modern era. Paul Santmire and others have identified writings of authors such as Irenaeus, Thomas Aquinas, Hildegard of Bingen, and St. Francis of Assisi that to varying degrees read Scripture, and indeed the Pauline letters, in ways that affirm creation and the cosmic scope of God's redeeming work in *Christ. However, the field of ecological theology goes further to address at least three issues by (1) reconsidering interpretations based on anthropocentric bias, (2) uncovering biblical texts for ecological *wisdom, and (3) highlighting the cosmic scope of God's redemptive act.

1. Ecology and New Creation.

It is suitable to begin with the expansive categories of new creation. In the Bible, the phrase "new creation" (*kainē ktisis*) is unique to Pauline writings, yet scholars regularly identify the OT concept of "new heavens and new earth" (Is 65–66) as analogous, and the phrase also appears in Second Temple Jewish literature. In two theologically important passages, Paul uses "new creation" as a descriptor of the new *reality* inaugurated by *God in Christ. These texts help to indicate the degree to which Paul may view redemption as extending beyond individual humans. Most scholars concur that in these passages Paul references individuals and a community of believers: in Galatians with the title "the *Israel of God" (e.g., Is 66:22-23; Gal 6:16) and in 2 Corinthians through the phrase "not counting their trespasses against them" (2 Cor 5:19). This parallels Paul's reference elsewhere to the "new humanity" as the church (e.g., Gal 3:26; Eph 2:14-16; 4:23-24; Col 3:9-11). Yet, 2 Corinthians further outlines the inauguration of the new creation within a temporal two-age apocalyptic concept that includes the cosmic realm (e.g., *mēketi*, "no longer," 2 Cor 5:15; *apo tou nyn*, "from now on," 2 Cor 5:16; and *nyn ouketi*, "no longer," 2 Cor 5:16; cf. Gal 3:26-28), what J. Louis Martyn refers to as a "turning point of earth-shaking proportions" (Martyn, 270). Paul further expands his thought by stating, "Therefore, if anyone is in Christ, there is a new creation. Everything old has passed away; see, everything has become new" (2 Cor 5:17). Paul clarifies that God's reconciling work in Christ creates a new community with a distinct purpose. They are given "the *ministry of reconciliation" (2 Cor 5:18) and called "ambassadors for Christ" (2 Cor 5:19), and through Christ the community becomes "the *righteousness of God" (2 Cor 5:21). Paul's understanding of new creation within an *apocalyptic vision goes beyond individual salvation or even the collective redemption of the people of God. Paul is speaking of an inauguration of a new creation sphere that echoes the Isaianic renewal of a new heaven and a new earth—an eschatological reality where Paul understands that the church has a specific role within the broader new creation.

This reading of new creation is further affirmed by its use in Second Temple Judaism. Jewish authors used this phrase for communities of faith (e.g., the righteous,; see 2 Bar. 51.1-16) and the cosmic realm, inclusive of the natural world (e.g., Jub. 4.26; 1 En. 51.4-5.1; 1QH XIII, 11). Within apocalyptic texts the dawning of a "new age" where "all things" will be transformed is regularly in view. In this literature analogous concepts include the Isaianic notion of the "new heavens and new earth" (Is 43:18-19; 65:17-22; 66:22; 2 Pet 3:13; Rev 21:1; see also 1 En. 91.15-16; 4 Ezra 7.31; 2 En. 70.9-10; Apoc. Zeph. 12.5-8; Sib. Or. 4.186; 3.92; 7.118-149; As. Mos. 10.1-10), a renewed creation (e.g., 4 Ezra 6.25; 2 Bar. 21.17; 40.3; 1QS IV, 25; 1QH XI, 10-14), and/or a return of creation to its original state (e.g., 2 Bar. 73-74). Of importance is that these texts often reflect the common Jewish worldview whereby the eschatological renewal of the temporal world is dependent, in part, on the faithful community (Jackson, 33-59, 174-75). In a similar way, the prophets attest to a worldview that linked the health of the land with the faithfulness of Israel (see, e.g., Jer 4:23-28; 9:10-11; Is 35:1-7; 41:17-20; 42:15-16; 43:19-20; 44:1-4; 55:13; 65:17-25; Ezek 34:25-31; 36:26-36; Hos 4:1-3; see also Is 11:6-9; 24:4-7). In light of the Second Temple usage and Paul's dependence on Isaiah, the majority of Pauline scholars today concur that in Galatians and 2 Corinthians Paul almost certainly has all three categories in view—the individual, the community, and the entire cosmos (see, e.g., Hahne).

2. The Cosmic Scope of Pauline Soteriology.

For ecological readings of Paul, establishing new creation as inclusive of all creation is important for affirming that the reconciliation of humanity is only one component of the larger cosmic dilemma to which the Christ-event responds. A reading of new creation limited to an anthropocentric bias has the potential to end up elevating the spiritual realm and diminishing created matter as temporal and severed from the ongoing life of the Spirit. Redemption solely bound to human *sin (Gen 3) tends to eclipse the broader divine economy (*oikonomia*) that unfolds the cosmic scope of the redeeming and reconciling work of God in Christ (e.g., Eph 1:9-10). In response to narrowly defined soteriological models, ecotheologians regularly cite Romans 8:18-25; 1 Corinthians 8:6; 15:20-28; Colossians 1:15-20; and Ephesians 1:9-10 as complementary texts to 2 Corinthians 5:17 and Galatians 6:15. These collectively affirm a cosmic Christology with Christ as the creator of all things (protology) and the final culmination of all things (eschatology).

2.1. Christ as the Creator and Reconciler of All Things. More than any other NT author, Paul incorporates OT creation themes and motifs into his theological framework, yet he reappropriates them in light of the new creation inaugurated through Christ. In contrast to the first *Adam, Christ as the "last Adam" (1 Cor 15:45) is the full expression of the "*image of God" (2 Cor 4:3-4; Col 1:15), who as "life-giving Spirit" transforms those in Christ into the "image of Christ" (Rom 8:28-30; 1 Cor 15:49; 2 Cor 3:18; Col 3:9-10). Paul further identifies Christ as the creator in the original creation (1 Cor 8:6; Col 1:15) and the one who in the *telos* will "hand over the *kingdom to God the Father . . . so that God may be all in all" (1 Cor 15:20-28; see also 2 Cor 5:19; Phil 3:21). Colossians 1:15-20 provides a concise statement that aligns Christ with the creative and redemptive purposes of God in relationship to all things (*ta panta*): "for in him all things in heaven and on earth were created . . . and through him God was pleased to reconcile to himself all things, whether on earth or in heaven" (NRSV).

A similar example is located within Paul's lengthy response to the Corinthians' question about whether they are to eat meat that has been offered to pagan gods (1 Cor 8–10). Paul grounds his response theologically by citing a modified form of the *Shema* that establishes Christ as the mediator in the original creation: "Yet for us there is one God, the Father, from whom are all things and for whom we exist, and one *Lord, Jesus Christ, through whom are all things and through whom we exist" (1 Cor 8:6 NRSV; cf. Rom 11:36). Toward the end of his three-chapter discussion, Paul affirms the Corinthians' *freedom to purchase meat in the public market because "the earth is the Lord's and everything in it" (1 Cor 10:26, citing Ps 24:1 [23:1 LXX]). In 1 Corinthians and Colossians, Paul provides a cosmological framework connecting Christ with "all things."

It is of note that the term *ta panta* was regularly used within Greek cosmologies of Paul's time to designate the collective totality of creation, a universal vision that Paul certainly maintains here (Sterling). Paul, however, goes further than other cosmologies of his time by subsuming believers into the cosmological framework, incorporating a distinct *ecclesial* component into the text. That reframing, in the Corinthian context, is partnered with an affirmation of the lordship of Christ over creation (1 Cor 10:26). Thus it becomes the theological grounding for directing the Corinthians toward restraint and/or freedom in relationship to *food. The determining factor for Paul is the proper *orientation* of believers toward the elements of creation and the resulting outcome of consumption (1 Cor 10:1-21). The criteria outlined by Paul are that consumption must be beneficial to all (1 Cor 8:7-13; 10:23-34), be done with an orientation of thanks and gratitude (1 Cor 10:30; see Rom 14:5-9), and ultimately bring glory to God (1 Cor 10:31). Paul concludes his lengthy discussion with a sweeping theocentric exhortation: "So, whether you eat or drink, or whatever you do, do all to the *glory of God" (1 Cor 10:31–11:1; for a detailed ecotheological reading of this text, see Leese 2014).

In eschatological texts, Paul likewise envisions a comprehensive cosmic reconciliation of all things, with 1 Corinthians 15:20-28 as a key text. Paul regularly uses the term *katargeō* within apocalyptic texts that envision the victory of Christ in the present and in the age to come (e.g., 1 Cor 1:26-28; 2:6; 15:24-26; 2 Cor 3:7). Unfortunately, *katargeō* is often translated as "destroy" or "annihilate"—so, for example, in 1 Corinthians 15:24 the NRSV translates, "Then comes the end, when he [Christ] hands over the kingdom to God the Father, after he has destroyed [*katargēsē*] every ruler and every authority and power." Numerous scholars have identified these translations as misguiding readers, skewing the nuance of the term, which is better translated as "nullify" or "render inoperative" (Leese 2018, 50-54). In these scenarios, Paul presents an eschatological future where Christ confronts the opposing structures of the cosmos by disarming their power instead of by destroying them; their effectiveness ceases, but their ontological existence remains. This notion comports with Paul's new creation framework that envisions the renewal and restoration of all things for the purpose of bringing God glory. This hopeful message is earth-affirming.

2.2. *Ecological Reconciliation.* Ecotheologians regularly identify the importance of texts that bind redemption with creation. In those texts human beings are defined more by their organic relationship *within* creation than by human distinctiveness or creation's obliteration. Romans 8:19-23 provides the clearest affirmation of creation's present and future condition and its symbiotic relationship with humanity. Many scholars consider these verses as the climax of an extended discussion of creation in the preceding chapters of Romans. Here, the created order is aligned with believers in both their *suffering and their expectation of freedom from bondage:

> For the creation waits in eager expectation for the children of God to be revealed. . . . The creation itself will be liberated from its bondage to decay and brought into the freedom and glory of the children of God. We know that the whole creation has been groaning as in the pains of childbirth right up to the present time. Not only so, but we ourselves, who have the firstfruits of the Spirit, groan inwardly as we wait eagerly for our *adoption to sonship, the redemption of our bodies.

Many scholars believe that the reference to the suffering of creation is an allusion to Genesis 3, where the disobedience of humanity results in a *curse being placed on the earth (Gen 3:17). Throughout Scripture, human beings are shown to have moral agency; through sin and disobedience, they have broken their relationship with God, with other humans, and with creation. In contrast, other-than-human parts of creation are never identified as moral agents but rather are recipients of the adverse effects of human sin and disobedience. The ecological corollary is that the flourishing of creation is dependent in part on right human behavior. This teaching reflects the ancient worldview that matters of justice, righteousness, and flourishing of the creation are linked with the moral actions of humanity. Texts such as this also affirm the first creation narrative(s), where humans, as uniquely created in the image of God (Gen 1:26-28), have responsibility to care for and serve the earth (Gen 1:26-28; 2:15). Additionally, humans share a kinship with the earth (Gen 2:7, 19), trees (Gen 2:9), and animals (Gen 2:19).

One early reader of Paul, Irenaeus of Lyon, marshaled the importance of these connections as he confronted Gnostic dualism of his day, which devalued material creation. Irenaeus incorporates each of the texts mentioned here, and he famously highlights Ephesians 1:9-10 as the organizing center of his theology, the eschatological *recapitulation* of all things in Christ: "God has made known to us the mystery of his will, according to the good pleasure that he set forth in Christ, as a plan for the fullness of time, to gather up all things in him, things in heaven and things in earth." He cites 1 Corinthians 15:39-44 as confirmation that God has assigned to every creature a functional ontology with "a nature suitable to the character of the life assigned them" (Irenaeus, *Haer.* 2.2.4; trans. D. Unger, further revised by J. Dillon; see Leese 2018). It is of note that Irenaeus championed texts from Paul to affirm the goodness of creation and the future renewal of the earth.

3. Ecotheology: Implications for the Practice of the Church.

What is the connection between ecology and Pauline theology? Certainly, when Paul wrote his letters, he could never have anticipated the environmental crisis facing the global community, nor could he have articulated responses to the ethical questions that people of faith ask in relationship to it. As *ad hoc* writings, the Pauline letters address the immediate needs of specific communities, yet they also outline a broader understanding of God's *love encompassing all of creation, with a cosmic vision of God's reconciliation of all things through Christ. An ecosensitive reading of Paul's letters suggest that Christian discipleship for Paul includes a concern for the flourishing of all creation. His theocentric exhortation, that all be done for "the glory of God," provides a guiding criterion whereby Christians can consider their relationship to creation as an expression of their faithfulness to the Creator and Redeemer of all things.

See also CHRISTOLOGY; COSMOLOGY; CREATION AND NEW CREATION; JUSTIFICATION; PEACE, RECONCILIATION.

BIBLIOGRAPHY. **J. M. G. Barclay,** "Food, Christian Identity, and Global Warming: A Pauline Call for a Christian Food Taboo," *ExpTim* 121, no. 12 (2010): 585-93; **R. Bauckham,** *Bible and Ecology: Rediscovering the Community of Creation*, Sarum Theological Lectures (Waco, TX: Baylor University Press, 2010); **S. Bouma-Prediger,** *For the Beauty of the Earth: A Christian Vision for Creation Care* (Grand Rapids, MI: Baker Academic, 2010); **L. J. Braaten,** "All Creation Groans: Romans 8:22 in Light of Biblical Sources," *HBT* 28 (2006): 131-59; **D. Brunner, J. Butler, and A. J. Swoboda,** *Introducing Evangelical Ecotheology: Foundations in Scripture, Theology, History, and Praxis* (Grand Rapids, MI: Baker Academic, 2014); **H. A. Hahne,** *The Corruption and Redemption of Creation: Nature in Romans 8:19-22 and Jewish Apocalyptic Literature*, LNTS (New York: T&T Clark, 2006); **D. Horrell,** *The Bible and Environment: Towards a Critical Ecological Biblical Theology* (Durham, UK: Acumen, 2013); **D. Horrell, C. Hunt, and C. Southgate,** *Greening Paul: Rereading the Apostle in a Time of Ecological Crisis* (Waco, TX: Baylor University Press, 2010); **T. R. Jackson,** *New Creation in Paul's Letters: A Study of the Historical and Social Setting of a Pauline Concept* (Tubingen, Germany: Mohr Siebeck, 2010); **J. J. J. Leese,** "Christ as Creator: Implications for Ecotheological Readings of Paul," *JSPHL* (2014): 111-28; idem, *Christ, Creation, and the Cosmic Goal of Redemption: A Study of Pauline Creation Theology as Read by Irenaeus and Applied to Ecotheology* (New York: T&T Clark, 2018); **J. L. Martyn,** "Epistemology at the Turn of the Ages: 2 Corinthians 5:16," in *Christian History and Interpretation: Studies Presented to John Knox*, ed. W. R. Framer et al. (Cambridge: Cambridge University Press, 1967), 269-87; **S. M. McDonough,** *Christ as Creator: Origins of a New Testament Doctrine* (Oxford: Oxford University Press, 2010); **J. Moltmann,** *God in Creation: An Ecological Doctrine of Creation*, trans. M. Kohl, Gifford Lectures 1984–1985 (London: SCM Press, 1985); **J. Moo,** "Romans 8:19-22 and Isaiah's Cosmic Covenant," *NTS* 54, no. 1 (2008): 74-89; **H. P. Santmire,** *The Travail of Nature: The Ambiguous Ecological Promise of Christian Theology* (Philadelphia: Fortress, 1985); **H. A. Snyder and J. Scandrett,** *Salvation Means Creation Healed: The Ecology of Sin and Grace* (Eugene, OR: Cascade, 2011); **G. E. Sterling,** "'Wisdom Among the Perfect': Creation Traditions in Alexandrian Judaism and Corinthian Christianity," *NovT* 47, no. 4 (1995): 354-84.

J. J. J. Leese

ECSTATIC EXPERIENCE. *See* HOLY SPIRIT; PROPHECY, PROPHESYING; TONGUES; VISIONS, ECSTATIC EXPERIENCE.

EDUCATION OF PAUL. *See* CONVERSION AND CALL OF PAUL; PAUL AND JUDAISM; PHILOSOPHY.

ELDERS. *See* CHURCH STRUCTURE; LEADERSHIP; MINISTRY.

ELECTION AND PREDESTINATION

"I will have *mercy on whom I have mercy, and I will have compassion on whom I have compassion" (Rom 9:14 NIV). Few ideas in Paul's letters elicit as much heated debate as Paul's discussions of what have come to be called his doctrines of election and predestination. The doctrine of "double predestination," typically associated with the Augustinian and

Calvinistic interpretive traditions, holds that *God chooses those whom he will save and withholds *salvation from those whom he will not. This is a particularly contentious and divisive doctrine, and one that finds its grounding largely in Paul's comments in Romans 9–11. Related to the question of the determination of the salvation of individual humans is the question of whether God predetermines all events in the course of human history. Various traditions have answered these questions in Pauline theology along a broad spectrum of answers, generally finding good grounding for their positions in Paul's own thought, which illustrates the challenge of interpreting Paul in these areas. Some interpreters (e.g., Räisänen) have concluded that Paul's discussions of *grace, *law, *faith, and salvation are so full of contradictions that they must simply be accepted and not resolved. Most interpreters, however, opt for an approach that seeks to find a resolution to these tensions in Paul's thought.

1. Terminology
2. Paul and Judaism
3. Election "in Christ"
4. Election and Salvation History
5. Election and Ethnic Identity
6. Predestination

1. Terminology.

There are several key terms in Paul's vocabulary of election and predestination. *Eklegomai*, *eklektos*, and *eklogē* all stem from the same word group and describe a choice or selection, or a person or entity worthy of such choice. In Paul's letters, the words occur in Romans 8:33; 9:11; 11:5, 7, 28; 16:13; 1 Corinthians 1:27-28; Ephesians 1:4; Colossians 3:12; 1 Thessalonians 1:4; 1 Timothy 5:21; 2 Timothy 2:10; Titus 1:1. Paul's focus in these passages is typically on God's choice of *Israel, God's choice of certain individuals (which may be simply descriptive, relating to their ethical character, "a choice or excellent person"), and the identity of those "*in Christ" as chosen. Paul's vocabulary of predestination includes the terms *proorizō* and *proginōskō*, which are found in Romans 8:29-30; 11:2; 1 Corinthians 2:7; Ephesians 1:5, 11. *Proorizō* generally means to "predetermine" or "decide ahead of time," and *proginōskō* to "know beforehand," though the terms are sometimes taken as roughly synonymous.

2. Paul and Judaism.

The election of Israel as God's favored *covenant people is a central theme of the OT, and this belief certainly carried over into Second Temple Judaism. With its belief in this covenantal relationship between God and Israel comes also an understanding of Israel's *identity defined primarily in its relation to God through Torah. Variations of emphasis in Second Temple literature have led to a variety of approaches by interpreters, with some emphasizing the unconditional nature of Israel's election (e.g., Gürkan and to some extent Sanders), others framing Israel's election as both unconditional and requiring obedience (e.g., Gathercole), and others still emphasizing the conditional (Elliott) or even meritorious (VanLandingham) nature of the receipt of the covenant.

A tension exists throughout the literature between the promissory nature of the covenant and the conditions that define one as an insider or outsider. These tensions manifest themselves in the same texts and arguably stem from the portrayal of the covenant in the OT itself. Pseudo-Philo, for example, at times calls into question whether the covenant promises have been forfeited due to Israel's *sin, while also expressing confidence that God will renew Israel once again (e.g., L.A.B. 12.4). Similarly, in the Psalms of Solomon, the author prays that God will provide salvation for Israel forever while also recognizing that only the devout will inherit his promises (Pss. Sol. 12.5-6). The texts from the period generally emphasize a collectivist understanding of election and the covenant, while also varying, sometimes drastically, in their definition of what markers or conditions defined covenant membership (see especially Elliott; Thornhill). These markers included practices such as *circumcision, Sabbath observance, abstinence from sexual immorality, avoidance of intermarriage with *Gentiles, proper calendrical and festival observances, rejection of pagan *worship practices, and so on. When Paul is read against this backdrop, his disagreements with his contemporaries become more apparent. Election for Paul is not then only a soteriological category but one that connects with historical and social dimensions of Jewish self-identity.

3. Election "in Christ."

A growing number of interpreters have begun to emphasize a collective or corporate approach to Paul's theology of election (e.g., Abasciano; Bates; Thornhill; Witherington; Wright). In texts such as Ephesians 1–2 (esp. Eph 1:4), some argue that what is on display is God's choice of those "in Christ," which does not specify the means by which union with *Christ is accomplished (i.e., "faith") but rather focuses on the elect as the collective identity of God's people. This would include the faithful of old covenant Israel and those united with Christ in the new covenant. One finds in Paul's letters a collective emphasis, for instance, in his agricultural metaphors (fruit, vines, trees, etc.), which are likewise used in Jewish texts of the period to identify the "true Israel" (e.g., Sir 47:22; L.A.B. 12.8-9; 1 En. 10.16-17; 84.5-6; 93.5-10). Paul utilizes similar imagery in 2 Thessalonians 2:13, where he mentions God's choice of the Thessalonian believers as "firstfruits," and in Romans 11, where he discusses the people of God as a tree to which Gentile branches have been engrafted. This is likewise displayed both in Paul and in Jewish literature with representative imagery, where individuals are discussed (e.g., Jacob and Esau) in relation to the groups which they represent. In Romans 9, Paul uses this common motif while introducing some surprising elements that are unique in some ways to his letters in how he defines the boundaries or markers of God's people (i.e., those "in Christ").

4. Election and Salvation History.
Paul's election framework undoubtedly derives from its OT context of God's choice of Israel as his covenant people. God chooses Israel as his "treasured possession" (Deut 7:6 NIV) and promises to *Abraham to make them a great nation, to bless them, to give them a land, and to bless the nations through them (Gen 12; 15; 17). Israel as the recipients of the covenant promises is clearly the focal point of the OT's theology of election. At times Paul interchangeably uses this language of covenant and election to speak of Israel historically and to speak of the *church as God's chosen people (e.g., see Rom 11:5; 2 Tim 2:10). Paul's most sustained discussion of election, found in Romans 8:28–11:36, focuses not on the question "How are people saved?" or "Why or how does God elect persons to salvation?" but rather "Can God still be regarded as faithful to the covenant when so many Jews have rejected Jesus as Messiah and so many Gentiles have submitted to his lordship?"

Paul includes throughout this section a summary of the salvation-historical narrative of Israel, beginning with Abraham, Isaac, and Jacob/Esau, progressing through Moses, and culminating in his quotations of the prophets (see especially Abasciano 2005; 2011; 2013). He establishes that the logic of election does not follow human intuitions, so the inclusion of Gentiles in God's people should not be seen as unjust on God's part. The church since Pentecost had grown more Gentile in nature, and Paul continued to receive opposition from his Jewish compatriots for his proclamation of Jesus as Messiah and fulfillment of the covenantal promises. This, along with the situation at Rome, apparently required a sustained response on Paul's part. Paul concludes in Romans 11:1-10 that God has not rejected Israel, and the current state of affairs is not final, since "whoever calls on the name of the *Lord" (Rom 10:13) will be saved, Israel included. In a similar vein, in 2 Timothy 2:10, Paul seems to indicate that election does not create the foregone conclusion of salvation, stating that he suffers for the sake of the elect in order that they might obtain salvation in Christ. Paul's verb here for "obtain" is subjunctive, apparently indicating contingency as it relates to the future salvation of the elect. Given the OT backdrop of Paul's theology of election, which involves God's choice of Israel as his covenant people, the necessity of Paul's discussion—in light of the historical developments of how the new covenant community has been formed around Jews and Gentiles together—is apparent.

5. Election and Ethnic Identity.
A unique but often overlooked feature of Paul's election texts is his focus in these passages on the ethnic identities of Jews and Greeks/Gentiles and how they now relate in the one people of God in Christ. Paul introduces Romans 9 with the admission that he wishes himself accursed from Christ from the sake of his Jewish compatriots. He asserts that it is not those of blood descent from Abraham, or those "from works" (presumably "of the law," as elsewhere in Romans) who are counted among God's people, but rather those who have answered the "*call" (Rom 9:12; see also Rom 9:7, 24-26). Paul clarifies shortly thereafter that he is speaking of those "not only from the Jews but also from the Gentiles" (Rom 9:24 NIV), quoting Hosea to support his claim. Paul continues by stating that he sees Jesus as the goal of the law (Rom 10:4) and identifies his wayward Jewish compatriots as having stumbled over this reality and missed their appropriate destination. His exposition in Romans 9–11 concludes in Romans 11:11-26 with the imagery of God's people as an olive tree. He informs his recipients that Gentiles have been grafted into this tree among the other branches (i.e., old covenant saints and Jewish believers), and that it is possible, if they hold their status with pride, that they too be "cut off" (Rom 11:21).

Ephesians 1–2 likewise involves a sustained discussion from the outset on the significance of Gentile inclusion into the covenant promises to Israel, climaxing in Paul's explanation in Ephesians 2:11-22 that God has reconciled Jews and Gentiles together through the *cross of Christ, putting to *death the enmity between them. Paul also speaks of God's choice more generally in 1 Corinthians 1:27-28 of the foolish, weak, and lowly things of the world to bring shame to the wise and powerful. This "foolishness" of God is on display, according to Ephesians 1:23-26, in the crucified Messiah and in the uniting of Jews and Gentiles in God's family. Paul's emphasis is similar in Colossians 3:12, where, prior to commanding his audience to love and forgive one another, he reminds them of their status as "God's chosen people," which does not discriminate or distinguish between "Gentile or Jew, circumcised or uncircumcised, barbarian, Scythian, *slave or free" (Col 3:11 NIV). With the OT backdrop in mind, Paul enters into substantial explanations of the recent historical developments in light of the Christ-event that have reshaped God's people to include Jews and Gentiles together in one *body. Though perhaps surprising to some of his contemporaries, Paul sees this development as a fulfillment of the promises of the prophets and advocates for the unity of God's ethnically diverse people now in both theory and practice.

6. Predestination.

While election and predestination often logically go hand in hand, the concept of predestination is focused specifically on God's "beforehand" activity, usually as it relates to the work of salvation. In Romans 8:29-30, Paul asserts that those God "foreknew he also predestined" (NIV), similar to his assertion in Ephesians 1:5 that he "predestined us for *adoption" (NIV). In both instances, Christ is described either as the goal or the means for this predestination. Paul affirms in Romans 11:2, speaking of Israel, that he did not reject his people "whom he foreknew." In 1 Corinthians 2:7, Paul states that the "*wisdom of God in secrecy" has now been revealed, which God "predestined before the ages for our *glory." Here, similar to the other texts, the plan of God revealed in Christ was not a new development but one planned "before the ages" for God to redeem his *creation.

Sometimes overlooked are the ethical and transformative dimensions of God's predetermined plan. Paul's focus in the passages on election and predestination is often on thankfulness, unity, and moral transformation. In Romans 8:29, Paul states that God determined for his people to be "conformed to the *image of his Son" (NIV) so that Christ might be the *firstborn of God's family. Likewise, in Ephesians 1:4, Paul tells his recipients they were chosen "in him" "to be holy and blameless" before God (NIV). Paul indicates then that the eternal plan was not just for the salvation of God's people in Christ but for their transformative union with him, in which they are conformed to his glorious image for all eternity as they dwell with him in eternal life.

See also Covenant; Faith; Foreknowledge, Divine; Gentiles; Holiness, Sanctification; In Christ; Interpretation: Jewish; Interpretation: New Perspective; Israel; Paul and Judaism; Romans, Letter to the; Stumbling Block.

BIBLIOGRAPHY. **B. J. Abasciano,** *Paul's Use of the Old Testament in Romans 9.1-9* (New York: T&T Clark, 2005); idem, *Paul's Use of the Old Testament in Romans 9.10-18* (New York: T&T Clark, 2011); idem, *Paul's Use of the Old Testament in Romans 9.19-33* (New York: T&T Clark, 2013); **M. W. Bates,** *Salvation by Allegiance Alone: Rethinking Faith, Works, and the Gospel of Jesus the King* (Grand Rapids, MI: Baker Academic, 2017); **G. C. Berkouwer,** *Divine Election* (Grand Rapids, MI: Eerdmans, 1960); **M. A. Elliott,** *The Survivors of Israel: A Reconsideration of the Theology of Pre-Christian Judaism* (Grand Rapids, MI: Eerdmans, 2000); **S. J. Gathercole,** *Where Is Boasting? Early Jewish Soteriology and Paul's Response in Romans 1–5* (Grand Rapids, MI: Eerdmans, 2002); **S. Grindheim,** *The Crux of Election: Paul's Critique of the Jewish Confidence in the Election of Israel* (Tübingen: Mohr Siebeck, 2005); **S. L. Gürkan,** *The Jews as a Chosen People: Tradition and Transformation* (New York: Routledge, 2009); **J. S. Kaminsky,** *Yet I Loved Jacob: Reclaiming the Biblical Concept of Election* (Nashville: Abingdon, 2007); **W. W. Klein,** *The New Chosen People: A Corporate View of Election* (Eugene, OR: Wipf & Stock, 2015); **H. Räisänen,** *Paul and the Law* (Minneapolis: Fortress, 1986); **E. P. Sanders,** *Paul and Palestinian Judaism* (Minneapolis: Fortress, 1970); **S. Storms,** *Chosen for Life: The Case for Divine Election* (Wheaton, IL: Crossway, 2007); **A. C. Thornhill,** *The Chosen People: Election, Paul, and Second Temple Judaism* (Downers Grove, IL: IVP Academic, 2015); **C. VanLandingham,** *Judgment and Justification in Early Judaism and the Apostle Paul* (Peabody, MA: Hendrickson, 2006); **D. R. Wallace,** *Election of the Lesser Son: Paul's Lament-Midrash in Romans 9–11* (Minneapolis: Fortress, 2014); **B. W. Witherington III,** *Biblical Theology: The Convergence of the Canon* (Cambridge: Cambridge University Press, 2019); **N. T. Wright,** *Paul and the Faithfulness of God* (Minneapolis: Fortress, 2013).

A. C. Thornhill

ELEMENTS/ELEMENTAL SPIRITS OF THE WORLD. *See* Colossians, Letter to the; Galatians, Letter to the; Law; Magic; Principalities and Powers.

EMPEROR WORSHIP. *See* Empire; Lord; Religions, Greco-Roman; Savior.

EMPERORS, ROMAN. *See* Empire; Political Systems; Politics and Power.

EMPIRE

The theme of empire appears frequently in contemporary studies of Paul and his *letters. How should we understand Paul's use of terms and motifs that carry resonance of the Roman *imperium*? Is Paul using coded language in a "hidden transcript" gauged to subvert the Roman empire? Or is he inverting the language at hand to proclaim and explicate the paradoxical *triumph and lordship of *Christ?

1. Understanding Empire
2. Empire and Early Judaism
3. Empire in Pauline Studies
4. The Roman Empire and Its Gospel
5. Empire in the Pauline Epistles
6. Concluding Questions

1. Understanding Empire.

An empire is a political order in which a central political body rules over diverse national/ethnic groups outside its original territorial borders. Inasmuch as empires involve a dominant center ruling over an extensive subordinate periphery, empires are distinct from nation-states in that they have flexible borders and can incorporate additional peoples, nations, and territories without affecting the basic structure or identity of the empire (Howe, 30). Whereas states are often ethnically and socially homogenous, empires are heterogenous, including a variety of ethnicities, cultures, and territories (Maier 2007, 23). Similarly, while states tend to be linguistically unified, empires typically have a multitiered language system including an imperial language needed for participation among the elite (e.g., Aramaic, Greek, Latin, Mandarin, English) and many local vernaculars. Empire has been the default form of political order in recorded history, and the discipline of history itself has tended to focus on empires (Howe).

The word *empire* itself derives from the Latin *imperium*, a word referring to power or authority to command (*imperare*) a military or governmental entity. Under the Roman Republic, *imperium* was granted to two consuls for yearly terms. As Rome's authority extended beyond the Republic to govern other territories—that is, as Rome became imperial—the term came to have a territorial dimension, referring to all the territories under Roman dominion, and *imperium* was delegated to the emperors and then the Roman people as a whole (Maier 2007, 36). The related word *colony* and the verbal form *colonize* similarly derive from the Latin *colonia*, originally a term for an estate that came to refer to settlements in other territories with direct ties back to Rome, such as the city of Philippi.

Many ancient empires would to modern eyes resemble a protection racket or cartel and could easily be described as little more than a series of military bases protecting the increasingly expansive imperial tax base needed to sustain the imperial military engine. Nevertheless, since it is typically easier for empires to govern through local elites rather than investing the resources required for direct rule, empires have tended to work closely with local allies from the subjected peoples, typically leveraging some locals against others and delegating imperial authority to local elites incentivized to work with rather than against the empire.

Within the history of *Israel and Judah, one may observe that Judah called for Assyrian aid against the alliance led by Israel and Syria/Aram (2 Kings 16:7-10) before themselves being subjected to Assyrian *violence after their own rebellion against the empire (2 Kings 18–19). Similarly, the Hasmoneans requested Roman aid against the Syrian imperial threat (1 Macc 8; 12; 15) and eventually got more "aid" than they bargained for once Rome decided Hasmonean rule was insufficiently stable to govern the area in accordance with Roman imperial interests. By the first century AD, Rome had annexed Judea as a province and governed it directly through a Roman appointee, but the day-to-day administration of the province was still managed by the high priest in Jerusalem and other Jewish elites beholden to their Roman masters.

By placing many peoples and nations under a single standardized rule, establishing a common imperial language, and building and protecting trade routes, empires facilitate the exchange of ideas, technologies, and norms across different peoples and cultures. In economic terms, empires reduce social and economic friction by diminishing transaction costs across the disparate groups within the empire (Coase 1937; Maier 2007, 57-59). In the process, empires become engines of amalgamation and hybridity, absorbing many smaller cultures that are affected by contact with one another. Over time, those subcultures become increasingly indistinct as the empire digests the smaller peoples and cultures, which become part of a hybridized superculture that incorporates elements from the various cultures the empire has consumed. After enough generations of imperial control, those from what once was the periphery become increasingly assimilated into the larger imperial culture—the scattered northern Israelites become Assyrians, the descendants of the conquered Iberians or Gauls become Roman citizens (even emperors!), Egyptian culture becomes irreversibly hybridized with that of Egypt's Arab conquerors, and those descended from tribes that resisted the Zulu Empire in South Africa reflect proudly on their common Zulu heritage.

This process of imperial digestion is slow, however, and relationship between colonizer and colonized is one of ambivalence—simultaneous attraction and repulsion—as both sides are irrevocably changed by the imperial encounter. The resulting imperial culture is therefore inevitably characterized by hybridity, as colonized and colonizer coproduce an imperial superculture through the "creative and contentious mixing of traditions and cultures" fostered by empire (Marshall, 164; Ashcroft, Griffiths, and Tiffin, 135-39; Bhabha). As Jews became Hellenized, for example, their mimicry and hybridity inevitably altered Greekness itself, contributing to the creation of a common Hellenistic (imperial) superculture (Seesengood, 23). Similarly, Roman imperial culture was nearly as Greek as it was Roman, thanks to the fusion between Roman culture and the previously Hellenized cultures of the eastern Mediterranean.

Empire also provides the conditions for the development of a scholarly and artistic class, with the consequence that most art, literature, and architecture has been produced and preserved under the auspices and influence of empire. Even the art and literature produced out of resistance to imperial oppression tends to incorporate or mimic the intellectual and literary forms—and often even the values—of the dominant culture, reflecting the mixture of resistance and accommodation inherent in imperial contexts (Newsom, 169; Moore, 10-11). After enough time, once the digestion of the smaller colonized cultures is more complete, an empire—or a portion of an empire that eventually breaks off—may begin to more closely resemble a state, with a more homogenous culture as the inhabitants of the empire increasingly identify themselves with the larger superculture. Inasmuch as powerful states may also become empires through expansion and colonization, empire and nation are reciprocally related, with each generating the other (Maier 2007, 29).

2. Empire and Early Judaism.

Although history is generally written by the victors, the story of ancient Israel and Judah is one of near-constant subjugation by external empires. The biblical narratives root Israelite identity in the exodus from Egypt, a story about Israel's *God powerfully delivering them from the most powerful empire of a past era and settling them as one people in a land God provided for them. Later Jewish self-understanding was further established in the narration of the dissolution and deportations of the kingdoms of Israel and Judah by the Assyrian and Babylonian empires, leading to a present reality in which the Israel established through the exodus no longer exists.

Nevertheless, the biblical prophets promised a future rebirth and reunification of Israel and Judah from the nations among which they were scattered, a miraculous work of Israel's God in an event even greater than the exodus itself (e.g., Jer 16:14-15; 23:5-8; see Staples). Once restored, the unjust empires of the nations will be dissolved, and all the nations will be subjected to this renewed Israel in a just empire ultimately governed by God himself (e.g., Dan 7; Ps 2). The kings and rulers of the nations may "conspire together against YHWH and his anointed" (Ps 2:2), but Israel's God will give the nations to his anointed one as a possession (Ps 2:8-12). Within this framework, the annual Passover festival not only commemorates the past exodus but looks forward to Israel's future deliverance from among the nations.

These hopes had by no means diminished under Roman rule in the first century AD, and there were repeated efforts throughout this era to initiate the promised restoration and exaltation of Israel—efforts that eventually led to the Roman destruction of Jerusalem and the *temple of YHWH in the Jewish War of AD 66–73. Jesus' own proclamation of the arrival of the *kingdom of God fits closely with the restoration expectations of his contemporaries; Jesus promises his disciples, for example, that they will "sit on twelve thrones judging the twelve tribes of Israel" (Mt 19:28). This is a plainly restorationist statement since several of the tribes had long been absent by Jesus' day. Jesus therefore proclaims the "good news" (*gospel) of the end of the era of unjust imperial domination and the beginning of the long-anticipated era of justice, a divine empire (kingdom of God) in which God rules the world through his chosen people. The political authorities in Judea certainly understood Jesus' claims in this manner, as evident by his crucifixion as a political revolutionary against Rome, with "king of the Jews" the charge posted on his *cross (Mk 15:26).

But the crucifixion did not end Jesus' restorationist movement, as Jesus' disciples—soon joined by Paul—continued to proclaim the "good news" that "Jesus is *Lord" (Acts 2:36; 1 Cor 12:3; Rom 10:9), declaring that the kingdom Jesus proclaimed had indeed been initiated. The Gospel of John makes this explicit, with Jesus explaining to Pilate, "My kingdom is not of this world" (Jn 18:36). The claim that Jesus is Lord carries the obvious corollary that Caesar is not—indeed, since all authority has been given to Jesus, even Caesar is subject to a higher king and lord (Rom 1:4; 13:1; see Mt 28:18). Again, the significance of these claims is evident in that early Christians were sometimes deemed sufficiently rebellious against Roman imperial authority that they—like Jesus himself—were executed for sedition, a circumstance surely not helped by their refusal to worship traditional gods or the emperor.

3. Empire in Pauline Studies.

Like the *apostle himself, nearly all major interpreters of Paul and his letters have written from within empires. Those imperial locations have affected Pauline interpretation, shaping the questions interpreters have brought to the text and how they have understood specific concepts and discourses within the letters. Augustine, for example, wrote from a weakening and increasingly Christianized Western Roman Empire, while Martin Luther's reading of the Pauline letters was deeply shaped by his position in the late Holy Roman Empire. Modern Pauline scholarship has similarly been shaped by various interpreters' relationship to (and within) empire. Historical-critical biblical scholarship itself emerged as the study of the Bible was increasingly removed from church control after the Protestant Reformation, arising in a period that also saw the rise of consolidated modern nation-states from numerous petty fiefdoms.

More recently, Pauline scholarship has been radically shaped by World War II and the various geopolitical phenomena in a postcolonial and now neocolonial/globalist era. One primary consequence of this shift has been a rediscovery of the fundamental Jewishness of the NT and Paul in particular. The "new perspective" on Paul, for example, is perhaps better understood as a new perspective on early Judaism, no longer characterized as a legalistic foil to Paul's gospel. More recently, those taking a "Paul within Judaism" approach have pushed further, arguing that the new perspective's presentation of Paul as a former Jew still reflects a fundamentally anti-Jewish perspective and inadequately represents the apostle, who himself must be understood as an early Jew proclaiming a fundamentally Jewish message (Fredriksen; Nanos and Zetterholm).

The international upheavals of the post–World War II period and the twentieth-century dismantlement of colonial empires were accompanied by the growth of postcolonial studies, an approach that critically analyzes the legacies of imperialism and colonialism, typically focusing on the exploitative nature of empire and its negative impacts on colonized peoples. By the late twentieth century, Pauline studies was beginning to incorporate insights and approaches from this burgeoning scholarly movement. This shift has ironically been most prominent within American (and to a lesser extent) British scholarship, as the events of the late twentieth and early twenty-first centuries further precipitated a turn to "empire-critical" scholarship (Lopez and Penner, 585).

This approach emphasizes a deep, albeit often implicit, conflict between Paul and the Roman Empire as a key to understanding the Pauline epistles and Paul's gospel in general. In this approach, Paul is frequently cast as a subversive anti-empire figure especially useful for critiques of modern Western (mostly American) hegemony and its abuses (e.g., Elliott). Such anti-imperial readings were of course anticipated decades and even centuries earlier in the work of liberation theologians and other theological readers of Paul from the margins, who have long emphasized Paul's opposition to the oppressive structures of this world. In any case, it can now hardly be doubted that Paul's presentation of his gospel engages with and is affected by Roman imperial rhetoric.

4. The Roman Empire and Its Gospel.

The early Roman Empire had its own "gospel according to Augustus" (Georgi, 36), in which the emperor was understood as savior of the republic, having ended the "tyranny" of his opponents in the Roman civil wars and inaugurated an age of *peace, justice, piety, and liberty for the whole world. Missives from Rome spreading "good news" about the emperor's rule and the peace he was bringing to the world were sent across the empire, and numerous inscriptions attest to the widespread influence of such views. For example, the bilingual calendar inscription erected in various places across Asia Minor declares the "gospel" (*euangelion*) of "the god" and "savior"

Augustus, through whom good favor came to all humanity (see Sherk, no. 101; Porter). This imperial gospel nevertheless was not a matter of propaganda imposed from above but was instead widely embraced within the culture as a whole (Harrill, 290).

At least as far as imperial rhetoric was concerned, Caesar ruled by *auctoritas* (power of patronage) rather than *potestas* (positional authority). In his *Res Gestae*, for example, Augustus emphasizes that "all Italy voluntarily [*sponte sua*] pledged allegiance to me and demanded me as leader. . . . The provinces of Spain, Gaul, Africa, Sicily, and Sardinia pledged the same allegiance" (25). Moreover, Augustus declared that Julius Caesar had been deified after his *death, making Augustus a "son of a god." Augustus himself was then declared a god at his own death, with later emperors—preservers of the peace, liberty, and justice Augustus had inaugurated—likewise claiming divine heritage and status and being widely honored as divine "sons of a god."

A variety of local cults focused on the emperor or his predecessor(s) emerged across the empire as regional elites and the general populace worshiped the emperor in their own ways, including offering *sacrifices to the emperor himself or to other gods on the emperor's behalf (Harrill, 304; Woolf, 23-34; Price 1984). Such cults should not, however, be understood as a single, centralized "imperial cult" (the early empire lacked the bureaucracy for such) but as local and decentralized manifestations of a common phenomenon (Harrill, 303-5; Beard, North, and Price, 357-58). Moreover, in Paul's day, these emperor cults were still relatively marginal; many of the cities Paul visited may not have engaged in emperor *worship at all, and in those cities where the emperor was worshiped, that was but one cultic practice among many others (Miller).

5. Empire in the Pauline Epistles.

In this context, Paul's claim to be an envoy (apostle) of "the gospel of God . . . concerning his son" (Rom 1:1-3) appointed to "bring about the obedience of fidelity . . . in all the nations" (Rom 1:5) stands in sharp contrast to the similar claims of the Roman imperial "gospel." Indeed, Paul explicitly preaches the "kingdom of God" (e.g., Rom 14:17; 1 Cor 4:20; 6:9-10; 15:24, 50; Gal 5:21; Eph 5:5; Col 1:13; 1 Thess 2:12) and that Jesus will "nullify all rule and authority and power" (1 Cor 15:24), lending at least some truth to the accusation of his *opponents in Acts that he and his *coworkers "act against Caesar's decrees, saying there is another king, Jesus" (Acts 17:7).

In the very first verse of Romans, Paul labels himself a "*slave of Christ Jesus" (Rom 1:1). Although easily overlooked by modern readers who have come to treat *Christ* as something akin to a surname, this term functions for Paul as an honorific title akin to *Caesar*, marking Jesus as a royal figure from the beginning of the book (Novenson; Jipp). This royal aspect is further reinforced by the reference to Jesus' Davidic descent two verses later (Rom 1:3). The very first verses of the letter therefore clearly establish that Paul's "good news" is about the divine authority of a royal son of God to whom all nations owe their obedience (Rom 1:4).

In what is widely understood as the thesis of the letter, Paul proclaims that his gospel amounts to the revelation of "the justice [*dikaiosynē*] of God" (Rom 1:17). Though the term *dikaiosynē* derives from the LXX, this thesis may be read in contradistinction to Rome's claim to the source of justice (*dikē/iustitia*) to the world (Wright 2011, 285); what Caesar claimed to do, Christ in fact does. Whereas others within the empire acted as though *grace or favor were disseminated by and through the Roman emperor, Paul proclaims that divine grace in fact comes through Christ (Rom 1:5; 3:24; 5:15-21; 6:14-15). Whereas Caesar styled himself a bringer of liberty, it is Christ who sets his people free from *sin and death (Rom 6:20; 8:2, 21). And whereas others understood liberty and *salvation as coming through incorporation under the Roman *imperium*, Paul argues that salvation comes to the nations by their being engrafted into the olive tree of which Christ is the root (Rom 11:17-24; 15:12).

These prior arguments give a double edge to the injunction to "be subject to the governing authorities, for there is no authority except from God" (Rom 13:1). On the one hand, Paul argues that those within the Roman Empire are obligated to submit to Roman authority, which God established "to bring *wrath on the one who practices evil" (Rom 13:4). Followers of Christ are therefore to "pay to all what is due to them" (Rom 13:7), closely paralleling Jesus' ruling to "give to Caesar what is Caesar's and to God what is God's" (Mk 12:17 and pars.), paying taxes, honor, and respect to those to whom such are due. On the other hand, this formulation serves as a reminder that Caesar himself stands under the authority of Christ and is therefore obligated to rule justly. If, on the other hand, the ruling authorities govern unjustly, they will "receive condemnation upon themselves" in the same fashion as any others who oppose "the ordinance of God" (Rom 13:2). Just as the rulers of past ages, the present ruling authorities must recognize that "the most high is ruler over the kingdom of humanity and bestows it on whomever he chooses" (Dan 4:32) or face judgment under the authority of Christ. The letter concludes by presenting Jesus as the divinely appointed ruler of the world, "the root of Jesse" who has risen "to rule the nations, and in him the nations will hope" (Rom 15:12).

Turning to 1 Corinthians, Paul argues that Christ's *resurrection is only the "firstfruits" of a larger resurrection, after which will be "the end, when he hands over the kingdom to our God and father, when he has nullified all rule and authority and power" (1 Cor 15:23-24). Christ is the one to whom "all things are put in subjection" (1 Cor 15:27). Rather than awaiting a future time in which Christ will displace the Romans, Paul proclaims that Christ *already* reigns and must do so "until he has put all his enemies under his feet" (1 Cor 15:25). At the resurrection, those in Christ receive the very sort of cosmic, astral glory ascribed to the allegedly divinized Caesar (1 Cor 15:40-49), having become immortal and set free from death (1 Cor 15:51-57).

In this light, when earlier in the letter Paul argues against the social and economic divisions that had emerged within the Corinthian *church, he is advocating for a new imperial structure under the true sovereign. The Corinthians are to be shamed for their inability to judge among themselves, resulting in appeals to outside authorities—they already stand under the authority of another king ruling above the Roman authorities and will eventually judge angels (1 Cor 6:1-6). In light of Christ's authority and inevitable just *judgment, better to suffer wrong or be defrauded than to fight with one another (1 Cor 6:7-8). Indeed, the kingdom of God does not reign through conquest or subjugation of others but rather through a hidden *wisdom, "which none of the rulers of this age has understood" (1 Cor 2:8), a wisdom reflected in the cross, a device of imperial domination through which Christ paradoxically triumphed over all the rulers and powers of this world (1 Cor 1:17-18).

In 2 Corinthians, Paul employs the imagery of triumphal processions after imperial conquests but inverts the characters—rather than the triumphant conquerors, Paul and his coworkers are among the conquered led in triumph (2 Cor 2:14-16; see Horsley 2007, 240). Paul's litany of sufferings further serves as an inversion of the boasting of imperial conquest—rather than glorying in his victories, Paul lists his sufferings and weakness as the evidence of his position in the kingdom of God (2 Cor 11:23-30), wherein *service and *suffering rather than domination reflect true authority. Paul's efforts to gather a *collection for those in *Jerusalem may also be understood as an attempt to create "an alternative society" (Horsley 2007, 241) characterized by mutual *patronage and benefaction—a circle of grace—under the ultimate authority of Christ (Porter).

In Galatians 1:4, Paul declares that Jesus "gave himself for our sins so that he might rescue us from this present evil age"—the very age celebrated across the Roman Empire as a new era of peace and justice. He goes on to pronounce a *curse on anyone who preaches "a gospel contrary to what we have preached to you" (Gal 1:8). Such a statement stands strongly at odds with the "gospel" proclamations announcing important events concerning Rome and its allegedly divine ruler (Nanos, 284-90).

The Christ *hymn of Philippians 2:6-11 presents Jesus as the "servant" whose great works—not of conquest but rather of submission to suffering and death—are the reason "God has highly exalted him and bestowed on him the *name which is above every name [YHWH]," so that every knee will bow and every tongue confess "Jesus Christ is Lord" (Phil 2:9-11). Such an account may easily be read alongside contemporary accounts of Caesar's divinization, presenting Jesus as not only having been exalted to the heavens but as exalted to the highest status, above all others who may pretend to divine power. The exhortation of Philippians 2:12, "work out your own salvation with *fear and trembling," can easily be read in contrast to the claims that the emperor had brought "salvation." Moreover, in Philippians 3 Paul tells the Philippians to imitate him (Phil 3:17) in giving up their present privileges in exchange for "*citizenship in heaven" (Phil 3:20), suggesting a natural contrast with Roman citizenship for those living in a Roman colony (Porter and Westfall 2011, 13; Wright 2011, 293-94).

First and Second Thessalonians each refer to Christ's coming with the term *parousia* (1 Thess 5:23; 2 Thess 2:1, 8), a term associated with the visitation of a royal or military official (a god). In 1 Thessalonians, this appears in an especially loaded context, as Paul has just warned that Jesus will return "when they are saying 'peace and security'" (1 Thess 5:3), terms so thoroughly associated with Roman rule that they appear together on coins from this era. In 2 Thessalonians, although the events that will immediately precede the parousia/"day of the Lord" are based primarily on exegesis of Daniel, knowledgeable first-century readers could hardly read of the coming of a "lawless one" who will exalt himself in the temple of God without thinking of the emperor Gaius's attempt to erect a statue of himself at the Jerusalem temple in AD 40.

Both Colossians and Ephesians present Jesus as "far above all rule and authority . . . both in this age and the age to come" (Eph 1:21; see Col 1:15-20), and Ephesians sees the unification of Jews and *Gentiles in Christ as central to the gospel—those previously excluded from the "citizenship [*politeia*] of Israel" (Eph 2:12) are "no longer strangers and foreigners but fellow citizens" (Eph 2:19) within the divine empire (Eph 5:5). The code of behavior for that divine empire also differs markedly from the violent ideology of earthly empire, emphasizing a "stripping off the old self" and ethic of service rather than conquest (Walsh and Keesmaat). Within the Pastoral Epistles, 1 Timothy 6:15 calls Jesus the "king of kings and lord of lords," explicitly identifying Jesus in imperial terms.

6. Concluding Questions.

Having briefly examined conceptual and verbal overlaps between Paul's gospel proclamation and the Roman imperial gospel, this article now concludes by engaging with some of the main disputed questions in recent scholarly discussions of Paul and empire.

6.1. Did Paul in His Letters Disguise Anti-Imperial Sentiments Through Coded Language Tied to an Anti-Imperial "Hidden Transcript"? Increasing recognition of the conceptual and verbal overlap between Paul's gospel and the Roman imperial gospel has led some to read Paul through the lenses of political scientist James C. Scott's concept of "the hidden transcript," the discourse space in which a subordinate group critiques the status quo outside the hearing of those who dominate them. According to Scott, although the hidden transcript itself is often inaccessible, a "coded version of the hidden transcript is always present in the public discourse of subordinate groups," resulting in literature that may seem politically complacent on the surface while containing coded critiques of the status quo throughout (Scott, 19).

Inasmuch as the Pauline correspondence might be understood as within a private space in which the oppressive authorities are not presumed to be listening, they may be defensibly understood as examples of a hidden transcript brought to light. But if one means that Paul's letters should be understood as part of the public discourse containing coded references to an otherwise unseen hidden transcript critiquing the empire, the evidence is against it. Even if such coded references were present, modern interpreters have little or no access to the hidden transcript by which they may decode the hidden messages within the public transcript of the letters with any sort of confidence (see Harrill, 309).

Moreover, although certainly at odds with the general zeitgeist, Paul's assertion that the deities of Rome (including the emperor and his predecessors) are not in fact gods is a standard Jewish claim and would hardly need to be hidden (Barclay, 381; Robinson 2021, 71). Rome also lacked the surveillance apparatus (or the interest) to spy on personal letters from a Jewish *teacher to his acolytes—letters hand-delivered by his associates at that (Robinson, 67-71). It is true, however, that even Jews who publicly disputed the divine claims of the emperor and did not participate in emperor worship could not safely claim allegiance to another (human) sovereign over and against the emperor (Heilig, 88-91). Paul's proclamation of Jesus as divinely appointed ruler of the world therefore represents a more serious challenge to imperial authority than the traditional Jewish insistence in the emperor's nondivinity, as attested by the fact that Jesus was executed for making such a claim.

Nevertheless, there is little evidence to suggest that Paul felt the need to conceal such a message from the Roman authorities, least of all in private correspondence with other followers of Jesus. Indeed, Paul explicitly proclaims that Jesus is the true ruler of all (Rom 10:12), that the kingdom of God supersedes all human rule and authority (Eph 1:21; Col 2:10), and that Jesus will bring all such rule to an end (1 Cor 15:24). Once Paul has openly proclaimed that Jesus is a king above Caesar, what is left to hide? If in his letters Paul has attempted to conceal his criticisms of Roman imperial rule or his proclamation of a competitor for Caesar's titles and lordship, he has done so very badly (Robinson, 66).

6.2. Was Paul's Gospel Fundamentally Anti-Imperial, with His Use of Imperial Language and Concepts Ultimately Aimed at Subverting Ancient Roman Imperialism? There is no question that the apostle leverages language familiar from his Roman imperial context to preach a message at odds with Roman claims of authority and sovereignty. Nevertheless, given his own use of imperial rhetoric, it is more precise to regard Paul exhibiting the sort of hybridity and ambivalence that is often the case with imperial subjects, being both shaped by and resistant to contemporary imperial discourse (Harrill). As such, Paul was not anti-empire so much as he proclaimed a new, superior empire—the long-awaited kingdom of God anticipated by many of his fellow Jewish predecessors and contemporaries. That is, he plainly counters Roman imperial rhetoric by asserting that those things claimed by the empire and its partisans are truly to be found in another empire, ruled by another Lord, to whom even Caesar is subject.

Paul's gospel is not, however, especially concerned with the Roman Empire itself because Rome is simply not important enough to be a main character in the drama Paul proclaims (Barclay, 386-87). Instead, the Roman Empire is merely the latest set of ruling authorities in the current fleshly order, this passing age that will be swept away at Christ's parousia. The struggle Paul proclaims is not, as Ephesians declares, "against *flesh and blood" but against the heavenly rulers and powers underlying and granting power to the paltry fleshly powers that imagine themselves gods (Eph 6:12). In that respect, whether the Roman Empire ceased to exist was irrelevant to Paul and his gospel; either way he would have continued to proclaim the "obedience of fidelity" (Rom 1:5) to Christ as king.

In the process, Paul does not *subvert* but rather *inverts* imperial concepts, assuming and borrowing the basic logic inherent to Roman (and earlier) imperial discourses but turning them upside-down (see Acts 17:6). That is, rather than preaching the *elimination* of hierarchy altogether and arguing for anarchism or antinomianism, he argues for a *reorientation* of authority, inverting typical societal power relationships based on the cross. Rather than an empire ruling through violent conquest, Christ's empire is won and established in weakness and servitude. True authority comes from below and by the submission to death on others' behalf rather than the subjection of others to death. Nevertheless, Christ will return in power to overthrow and judge not only the unjust fleshly rulers but the evil cosmic powers who have previously subjected the world to injustice. The end to which Paul looks is a new kingdom (empire) of God, incorporating every tribe, tongue, and nation, all under the universal (imperial) *law of Christ Jesus (Gal 6:2; see Rom 7:4-6; 8:2).

See also Gospel; Interpretation: Postcolonial; Lord; Political Systems; Politics and Power; Religions, Greco-Roman; Son of God.

BIBLIOGRAPHY. **B. Ashcroft, G. Griffiths, and H. Tiffin,** "Hybridity," in *Post-Colonial Studies: The Key Concepts*, 3rd ed., ed. B. Ashcroft, G. Griffiths, and H. Tiffin (London: Routledge, 2013), 135-39; **J. M. G. Barclay,** *Pauline Churches and Diaspora Jews*, WUNT 275 (Tübingen: Mohr Siebeck, 2011); **M. Beard, J. North, and S. Price,** *Religions of Rome* (Cambridge: Cambridge University Press, 1998); **H. K. Bhabha,** *The Location of Culture* (London; New York: Routledge, 1994); **M. G. Brett,** *Decolonizing God: The Bible in the Tides of Empire* (Sheffield: Sheffield Phoenix, 2008); **C. Bryan,** *Render to Caesar: Jesus, the Early Church, and the Roman Superpower* (Oxford: Oxford University Press, 2005); **W. Carter,** *The Roman Empire and the New Testament: An Essential Guide* (Nashville: Abingdon Press, 2010); **R. H. Coase,** "The Nature of the Firm," *Economica* 4, no. 16 (1937): 386-405; **J. D. Crossan and J. L. Reed,** *In Search of Paul: How Jesus' Apostle Opposed Rome's Empire with God's Kingdom* (San Francisco: HarperOne, 2004); **J. Diehl,** "Empire and Epistles: Anti-Roman Rhetoric in the New Testament Epistles," *CurBR* 10, no. 2 (2012): 217-63; **N. Elliott,** *The Arrogance of Nations: Reading Romans in the Shadow of Empire* (Minneapolis: Fortress, 2008); **P. F. Esler,** *The First Christians in Their Social Worlds: Social-Scientific Approaches to New Testament Interpretation* (London: Routledge, 2002); **P. Fredriksen,** "What Does It Mean to See Paul 'Within Judaism,'" *JBL* 141, no. 2 (2022): 359-80; **S. J. Friesen,** *Twice Neokoros: Ephesus, Asia, and the Cult of the Flavian Imperial Family*, RGRW (Leiden: Brill, 1993); **D. Georgi,** "Who Is the True Prophet?," in *Paul and Empire: Religion and Power in Roman Imperial Society* (Harrisburg, PA: Trinity Press International, 1997), 36-46; **M. D. Given,** ed., *Paul Unbound: Other Perspectives on the Apostle* (Peabody, MA: Hendrickson, 2010); **M. D. Goodman,** "Opponents of Rome: Jews and Others," in *Images of Empire*, ed. L. Alexander (Sheffield: Sheffield Academic, 1991), 222-38; **N. T. Haddad,** *Paul, Politics, and New Creation: Reconsidering Paul and Empire* (Minneapolis: Fortress Academic, 2020); **J. K. Hardin,** *Galatians and the Imperial Cult: A Critical Analysis of the First-Century Social Context of Paul's Letter*, WUNT 237 (Tübingen: Mohr Siebeck, 2008); **C. Harker,** *The Colonizers' Idols: Paul, Galatia, and Empire in New Testament Studies*, WUNT 2/460 (Tübingen: Mohr Siebeck, 2018); **J. A. Harrill,** "Paul and Empire: Studying Roman Identity After the Cultural Turn," *Early Christianity* 2 (2011): 281-311; **J. R. Harrison,** *Paul and the Imperial Authorities at Thessalonica and Rome: A Study in the Conflict of Ideology*, WUNT 273 (Tübingen: Mohr Siebeck, 2011); **C. Heilig,** *Hidden Criticism? The Methodology and Plausibility of the Search for a Counter-Imperial Subtext in Paul*, WUNT 2/392 (Tübingen: Mohr Siebeck, 2017); **R. A. Horsley,** ed., *Paul and Empire: Religion and Power in Roman Imperial Society* (Harrisburg, PA: Trinity Press International, 1997); idem, ed., *Paul and*

Politics: Ekklesia, Israel, Imperium, Interpretation: Essays in Honor of Krister Stendahl (Harrisburg, PA: Trinity Press International, 2000); idem, *Jesus and Empire: The Kingdom of God and the New World Disorder* (Minneapolis: Fortress, 2003); idem, *Hidden Transcripts and the Arts of Resistance: Applying the Work of James C. Scott to Jesus and Paul*, SemeiaSt (Leiden: Brill, 2004); idem, ed., *Paul and the Roman Imperial Order* (London: Bloomsbury, 2004); idem, "The First and Second Letters to the Corinthians," in *A Postcolonial Commentary on the New Testament Writings*, ed. F. F. Segovia and R. S. Sugirtharajah (London: A&C Black, 2007), 220-45; **R. A. Horsley and N. A. Silberman,** *The Message and the Kingdom: How Jesus and Paul Ignited a Revolution and Transformed the Ancient World* (Minneapolis: Fortress, 2002); **S. Howe,** *Empire: A Very Short Introduction* (Oxford: Oxford University Press, 2002); **J. W. Jipp,** *Christ Is King: Paul's Royal Ideology* (Minneapolis: Fortress, 2015); **E. A. Judge,** *The First Christians in the Roman World: Augustan and New Testament Essays* (Tübingen: Mohr Siebeck, 2008); **B. Kahl,** *Galatians Re-Imagined* (Minneapolis: Fortress, 2014); **S. Kim,** *Christ and Caesar: The Gospel and the Roman Empire in the Writings of Paul and Luke* (Grand Rapids, MI: Eerdmans, 2008); **H. Koester,** ed., *Ephesos, Metropolis of Asia: An Interdisciplinary Approach to Its Archaeology, Religion, and Culture* (London: Burns & Oates, 1995); **T.-S. B. Liew,** *Postcolonial Interventions: Essays in Honor of R. S. Sugirtharajah* (Sheffield: Sheffield Phoenix, 2009); **D. C. Lopez and T. C. Penner,** "Paul and Politics," in *The Oxford Handbook of Pauline Studies*, ed. M. V. Novenson and R. B. Matlock (Oxford: Oxford University Press, 2022), 579-97; **C. S. Maier,** *Among Empires: American Ascendancy and Its Predecessors* (Cambridge, MA: Harvard University Press, 2007); **H. O. Maier,** *Picturing Paul in Empire: Imperial Image, Text, and Persuasion in Colossians, Ephesians, and the Pastoral Epistles* (London: A&C Black, 2013); **J. A. Marchal,** "Paul and Postcolonial Studies," in *The Oxford Handbook of Pauline Studies*, ed. M. V. Novenson and R. B. Matlock (Oxford: Oxford University Press, 2022), 597-621; **J. W. Marshall,** "Hybridity and Reading Romans 13," *JSNT* 31, no. 2 (2008): 157-78; **S. McKnight and J. B. Modica,** eds., *Jesus Is Lord, Caesar Is Not: Evaluating Empire in New Testament Studies* (Downers Grove, IL: InterVarsity Press, 2013); **C. Miller,** "The Imperial Cult in the Pauline Cities of Asia Minor and Greece," *CBQ* 72, no. 2 (2010): 314-32; **S. D. Moore,** "Paul After Empire," in *The Colonized Apostle: Paul Through Postcolonial Eyes*, ed. C. D. Stanley (Minneapolis: Fortress, 2011), 9-23; **M. D. Nanos,** *The Irony of Galatians: Paul's Letter in First-Century Context* (Minneapolis: Augsburg Fortress, 2002); **M. D. Nanos and M. Zetterholm,** eds., *Paul Within Judaism: Restoring the First-Century Context to the Apostle* (Minneapolis: Augsburg Fortress, 2015); **C. A. Newsom,** "'Resistance Is Futile!' The Ironies of Danielic Resistance to Empire," *Int* 71, no. 2 (2017): 167-77; **M. V. Novenson,** *Christ Among the Messiahs: Christ Language in Paul and Messiah Language in Ancient Judaism* (New York: Oxford University Press, 2012); **L. G. Perdue and A. Lee,** eds., *Postcolonial Commentary on the Old Testament* (London: T&T Clark, 2012); **S. E. Porter,** "Paul Confronts Caesar with the Good News," in *Empire in the New Testament*, ed. S. E. Porter and C. L. Westfall (Eugene, OR: Wipf & Stock, 2011), 164-96; **S. E. Porter and C. L. Westfall,** eds., *Empire in the New Testament* (Eugene, OR: Wipf & Stock, 2011); **A. E. Portier-Young,** *Apocalypse Against Empire: Theologies of Resistance in Early Judaism* (Grand Rapids: Eerdmans, 2011); **S. R. R. Price,** *Rituals and Power: The Roman Imperial Cult in Asia Minor* (Cambridge: Cambridge University Press, 1984); **J. Rieger,** *Christ and Empire: From Paul to Postcolonial Times* (Minneapolis: Augsburg Fortress, 2007); **L. Robinson,** "Hidden Transcripts? The Supposedly Self-Censoring Paul and Rome as Surveillance State in Modern Pauline Scholarship," *NTS* 67, no. 1 (2021): 55-72; **E. Schüssler Fiorenza,** ed., *Searching the Scriptures: A Feminist Commentary* (New York: Crossroad, 1993); idem, *The Power of the Word: Scripture and the Rhetoric of Empire* (Minneapolis: Fortress, 2007); **J. C. Scott,** *Domination and the Arts of Resistance: Hidden Transcripts* (New Haven, CT: Yale University Press, 1990); **R. Seesengood,** *Competing Identities: The Athlete and the Gladiator in Early Christian Literature* (London: T&T Clark, 2007); **F. F. Segovia and R. S. Sugirtharajah,** eds., *A Postcolonial Commentary on the New Testament Writings* (London: A&C Black, 2007); **R. K. Sherk,** ed., *Rome and the Greek East to the Death of Augustus* (Cambridge: Cambridge University Press, 1984); **C. D. Stanley,** *The Colonized Apostle* (Minneapolis: Fortress, 2011); **J. A. Staples,** *The Idea of Israel in Second Temple Judaism: A New Theory of People, Exile, and Israelite Identity* (Cambridge: Cambridge University Press, 2021); **R. S. Sugirtharajah,** *The Bible and the Third World: Precolonial, Colonial, and Postcolonial Encounters* (Cambridge: Cambridge University Press, 2001); idem, *Postcolonial Criticism and Biblical Interpretation* (Oxford University Press on Demand, 2002); idem, *The Bible and Empire: Postcolonial Explorations* (Cambridge: Cambridge University

Press, 2005); idem, *The Postcolonial Biblical Reader* (London: Wiley & Sons, 2008); idem, *Exploring Postcolonial Biblical Criticism: History, Method, Practice* (London: Wiley & Sons, 2011); **J. Taubes,** *The Political Theology of Paul,* trans. D. Hollander, Cultural Memory in the Present (Stanford, CA: Stanford University Press, 2004); **B. J. Walsh and S. C. Keesmaat,** *Colossians Remixed: Subverting the Empire* (Downers Grove, IL: InterVarsity Press, 2015); **A. Winn,** *An Introduction to Empire in the New Testament* (Atlanta: SBL Press, 2016); **G. Woolf,** "World Religion and World Empire in the Ancient Mediterranean," in *Die Religion des Imperium Romanum: Koine und Konfrontationen*, ed. H. Cancik, J. Rüpke, F. Fabricius, and D. Püschel (Tübingen: Mohr Siebeck, 2009), 19-35; **N. T. Wright,** *Paul: In Fresh Perspective* (Minneapolis: Fortress, 2008); idem, "Paul and Empire," in *The Blackwell Companion to Paul*, ed. S. Westerholm (London: Blackwell, 2011), 285-97.

J. A. Staples

EPHESIANS, LETTER TO THE

Ephesians weaves an elegant tapestry of God's *salvation from threads describing the work of *God the Father, *Christ the *Son, and the *Holy Spirit. The epistle provides a spatial map of the cosmic world and its impact on human life. It sets out a timeline that stretches back before time, to the foundations of the world, and places the present era in light of the future reign of God's *kingdom. Ephesians assumes a world lost in *sin and redeemed in Christ, a world composed of Jew and *Gentile, *slave and free, wife and husband, who are brought together in Christ. It establishes salvation by *grace through *faith and encourages a life lived worthy of God's *calling. It points to the new people, the *body of Christ, guided by the Holy Spirit and growing in maturity. Ephesians offers exalted language of praise and beautiful, powerful *prayers that lift the heart and inspire the soul.

1. Style and Composition
2. Authorship
3. Relationship to Colossians
4. Household Codes
5. Destination
6. Life Setting and Purpose
7. Themes in the Letter

1. Style and Composition.

Ephesians's elevated style and soaring descriptions of God and his salvation plan have impressed readers through the centuries. John Chrysostom points to its depiction of God's kingdom and to Jesus' similar call to the faithful, namely, that he will welcome them into the kingdom prepared for them from the foundations of the world (Mt 25:34; *Hom. Eph.* 1). Jerome highlights the emphasis on confrontation with the *principalities and powers, and the letter's admonition to stand firm in the fight (*Comm. Eph.*, preface, book 1). He links the worship of Artemis/Diana, the prevalence of *magic in *Ephesus, and the encouragement to believers there to withstand the *idolatry that permeates their city, citing Acts 20:31-32 (Heine). In his tract *On the Papacy in Rome* (1520), Martin Luther drew on the letter's picture of the single body of believers united in true faith in his debate concerning the nature of the *church (Eph 4:5; LW 39). These comments highlight the epistle's focus on soteriology, ecclesiology, and discipleship.

Ephesians has been compared to a theological treatise or sermon (Jeal; Lincoln summarizes the arguments, xxxiv-xl). Most commentators, however, conclude that Ephesians is best understood as a *letter. Some scholars suggest Ephesians should be read through the lens of Greco-Roman speech conventions and outline the epistle with the categories of *exordium, narratio, probatio, peroratio* (Lincoln; Witherington). Others caution that we cannot assume Paul (or the author) was highly educated in the art of *rhetoric. They point to ancient sources that both distinguish between written and oral rhetoric, and present epistolary theory as a separate category (Classen; Bird). We should not forget that Paul grew up in Tarsus, a vibrant city known for its orators and philosophers, and spent time in *Jerusalem, where Jewish orators pressed their arguments about God's word. Paul's ear would be attuned to rhetorical expressions. Letters could take the form of an essay addressed to a wide audience and focused on *philosophy or propaganda (such as Epicurus's literary epistles), but Ephesians is better understood as a documentary letter. This category includes both official and personal letters sent to a specific audience with particular information (Reece).

Ephesians draws on *tradition, liturgy, and possibly early *hymns, as seen in the confession in Ephesians 4:4-6 and the hymn-like declaration in Ephesians 5:14. The charge to believers to sing psalms and hymns to each other in the Spirit suggests that the author models this posture in the epistle (Eph 5:19-20). The author also includes two prayers (Eph 1:15-23; 3:14-21). The first prayer reemphasizes believers' inheritance and God's *glory, Christ's redemption, and the Holy Spirit's activity presented earlier in Ephesians 1. The prayer leads to themes of God's power, Christ's exaltation, and the church's union with Christ. It trumpets Christ's victory over his enemies (Eph 1:21; 6:10-12). The second prayer addresses God as the Father of all families (Eph 3:14-15), emphasizing the salvation brought to both Jew and Gentile in Christ. The prayer underscores Christ's *love that surpasses understanding. The prayer's structure is built around three main sections, introduced by "that" (*hina*; Eph 3:16, 18, 19). It concludes with a doxology that points to God's power, evidenced by Christ's redemption and the creation of the church, his body.

Lengthy sentences with an even mixture of present and aorist verb tenses punctuate Ephesians 1–3, while shorter sentences with present tense verbs predominate in Ephesians 4–6 (Martín-Asensio). The first half focuses primarily on theological argument, and the latter chapters on discipleship and holy living. The author establishes injunctions for the moral life in the redemptive story traced in the earlier chapters.

In the beginning of the epistle, the author offers a eulogy or blessing in a single sentence that includes Ephesians 1:3-14, followed by a thanksgiving. The opening sentence's rich language suggests to some that Paul draws on a hymn or perhaps a *baptismal liturgy or even Greek poetry. However, A. T. Lincoln represents the majority opinion in his conclusion that the passage's "language and style are too similar to the rest of the first three chapters for it to be possible to isolate an entity which is clearly different" (Lincoln, 14).

Typically we would expect Paul to begin with a thanksgiving that highlights the themes found in the rest of the epistle. The eulogy provides the same framework as a thanksgiving, as it focuses on how God the Father, Christ the Son, and the Holy Spirit accomplish redemption, how they form and develop the church, and how they safeguard believers for their ultimate inheritance in God's kingdom. The eulogy emphasizes the believer's life as being "in Christ," with the remaining chapters developing images of *adoption and inheritance (Eph 1:5, 14; 3:6; 5:1-2, 5), of putting on the new self (Eph 4:24), and of being a member of God's *household (Eph 2:19) and Christ's body (Eph 1:23; 4:16, 25; 5:30). The focus on God's grace is also found in the *Qumran hymns (Barclay).

This lengthy sentence in Ephesians 1:3-14 reveals the central message of Ephesians. The blessing is best understood as the author's unstudied adoration of God, who in Christ creates and sustains his people. The subject, God the Father, and the finite verb, "to choose," shape the explanation of God's redemption plan (Eph 1:4). Participles underline God's purpose and intention as the one who blessed us (Eph 1:3) and "*predestined us" to adoption and an inheritance in Christ (Eph 1:5, 11) and "made known" to us his will (Eph 1:9). Four times in this sentence the author includes the prepositional phrase "in whom," referencing Christ (Eph 1:7, 11, 13 [2×]), as the picture of redemption through Christ's work on the *cross unfolds. Three times the author repeats the sentiment, "to the praise of his glory" (Eph 1:6, 12, 14); in the first reference, the section's emphasis is on God the Father's actions, while the second section highlights Christ's work, and the third section exalts the Holy Spirit's seal on believers. The epistle's underlying narrative emphasizes a *mystery now revealed—God's redemption plan that encompasses the past, present, and eternity, and includes both the reconciliation of Jew and Gentile in Christ, as well as the victory of Christ over cosmic forces.

The first half of the epistle focuses on facets of Christ's redemption. In Ephesians 1, Paul accentuates God the Father's salvation plan in Christ in several ways. First, God's plan extended back before time and will continue into eternity. Second, the plan is one of redemption and unity, for Christ's work both redeems humanity and will bring unity to the entire *cosmos (Eph 1:7, 10). Third, Christ is exalted by God the Father and now reigns over powers and principalities. The phrase "his mighty strength," found in Ephesians 1:19; 6:10, draws attention to his overarching theme that Christ is superior to all powers and principalities. Fourth, the *gospel message came to both Jews and Gentiles, who are in Christ and make up Christ's body, the church. The stage is set for Ephesians 2, which describes the entailments of believers' salvation from two major vantage points.

Ephesians 2 sketches the believers' redemption in relation to Christ's exaltation, and with regard to the Gentiles' inclusion with the people of God. The question arises whether the author addresses Gentiles and Jews in the first half of the chapter. The pronouns "we" and "you" are used in Ephesians 1, setting up a distinction, but the nature of the dissimilarity is debated. The picture in Ephesians 2 of believers' former life under the power of the ruler of this world suggests that the author has Gentiles in mind. The author distinguishes "you" from "we" who face struggles of the *flesh, likely here contrasting the idolatry of Gentiles with the failures of Jews to follow God's *law well (Eph 2:3). The author explicitly discusses "you" Gentiles in Ephesians 2:11-13, making the case that Gentiles were without God and without *hope until Christ reconciled Jew and Gentile into a single family, his church. The focus on

Gentile inclusion continues in the epistle, as the author describes the mystery of the gospel that Gentiles are heirs with *Israel (Eph 3:6) and warns against acting as Gentiles with darkened understanding and sinful activities (Eph 4:18). The importance of inheritance vis-à-vis Gentiles becomes clear as the author declares that the kingdom of Christ and of God awaits the faithful, but the idolatrous will fail to inherit (Eph 5:5).

The digression in Ephesians 3 establishes the role of the *apostle in declaring the gospel and explains his current situation as being in chains for the sake of "you Gentiles" (Eph 3:1). God is the implied subject in Ephesians 3:1-13, the one who assigned the apostle with the task of preaching the gospel of Christ. The chapter ends with a prayer to the Father of all families, which provides the transition to the second half of the epistle and its emphasis on living a life worthy of the gospel.

The second half of the epistle takes up the ramifications of redemption in Christ and concentrates on how believers should think and act in a holy and blameless manner (Eph 1:4; 4:1). The kerygmatic and didactic interweave in these chapters, encircled by a reference to the apostle's chains (Eph 4:1; 6:20). The tempo picks up with shorter sentences and a higher number of imperatives. The unity emphasized in the earlier chapters is elaborated by stressing maturity of the body of Christ (Eph 4:15) as each member puts on Christ (Eph 4:24) and acts with the other's best interest in mind (Eph 4:29; 5:21). Alongside the call for right living is the warning against behaving in immoral ways (Eph 4:17-19; 5:3-5). Discussion of house church *worship is followed by the household codes (see section 4 below), with the closing charge to put on the armor of God so as to stand fast against the evil that endangers believers (Eph 6:11). The treatment of God's armor links back to the opening chapter through the common phrase "his mighty strength" (Eph 1:19; 6:10). It also picks up the claim from Ephesians 3 that spiritual powers have seen the *wisdom of God in the creation of his church (Eph 3:10), and builds on the reality that the world is ruled by one who promotes disobedience and sin (Eph 2:2).

The author supports the gospel message by drawing on Scripture, evidenced by the few quotations and the more numerous allusions and echoes within Ephesians. The author pulls from the list of Ten Commandments in exhorting children to obey their parents (Eph 6:1-3), and from Genesis 2:24 in linking the one-flesh relationship of husband and wife with Christ and his church (Eph 5:31-32), and from Isaiah 59 when charging believers to put on the armor of God (Eph 6:14-17). Isaiah 57:19 forms the backdrop for the discussion about those who are far and those who are near, both receiving peace (Eph 2:13, 17), and the passage is understood to speak of Gentiles coming near to Christ. The quotation of Psalm 68:18 (Ps 68:19 MT; 67:19 LXX), plays a key role in the discussion of Christ's *ascent/descent theme (Eph 4:8-10). The quotation includes interesting variants that shift the focus from God receiving gifts from people to Christ giving gifts to people. A similar variant, with an emphasis on Moses, is found in the Targum (Stec, 131); however, the Targum's late date (fourth or fifth century) likely reflects a reaction to Christian tradition around this psalm. Our author probably shaped this quotation to demonstrate the fulfillment of God's victory, as suggested by Jerome (*Comm. Eph.*). The author alludes to Psalm 8:6 (Ps 8:7 MT, LXX), a favorite among NT authors (1 Cor 15:25), in a description of God the Father, who has put all things under the feet of his Son (Eph 1:22). The description continues that Christ is *head of all things, for the church. The picture of Christ as head takes some of its rhetorical power from the image that his feet are placed above all things. The accent on inheritance and adoption, as well as the mention of *circumcision and *covenant, makes clear the author's dependence on the milestones of Israel's history as found in Genesis, Exodus, Deuteronomy, the Psalms, and Isaiah.

2. Authorship.

For most of the church's history, Paul was considered the author of Ephesians. In the late eighteenth century, F. C. Baur challenged the consensus based on his broader theory that the early church was divided between Paul's camp, which represented Gentile Christianity, and *Peter with his Jewish Christian group. Baur's theory on the early church no longer holds sway, but other scholars have voiced concerns about Pauline authorship (Lincoln; Ehrman). Some scholars suggest that Ephesians is *pseudepigraphic, that is, written by a different person from the one named in the letter, perhaps one of Paul's *coworkers after the apostle's death. The argument assumes a genuine Pauline corpus that includes Romans, 1–2 Corinthians, Galatians, Philippians, 1 Thessalonians, and Philemon, with Colossians and 2 Thessalonians questioned, and Ephesians and the Pastoral Epistles often appraised as non-Pauline. M. Y. MacDonald concludes that Ephesians "constitutes the first interpretation of and guide to Pauline tradition in light of the disappearance of Paul" (MacDonald, 16). Within the argument for pseudepigraphy, the letter's authority is said to reside in its canonical status and not on whether the apostle Paul authored it (Childs; Fiorenza). The pseudepigraphic author is not attempting to deceive the audience but to promote Paul's teachings (Wilder). Ancient pseudepigraphic epistles often were produced in a school setting, circulated as a collection, and claimed a famous person such as Plato as their author. A forgery, on the other hand, is a document designed to deceive the audience and enrich the actual author in some way. Typically the arguments against Pauline authorship center on a few areas: (1) theology, (2) style and composition, (3) historical setting, and (4) relationship to Colossians.

2.1. Theology. Some argue that Ephesians does not include language or concepts normally associated with Paul's letters, such as *apocalyptic thought or "*justification by faith" over against "*works of the law." Ephesians does not mention "justification" and has the phrase "not by works" (Eph 2:9) once, with no additional clause "of the law." Other arguments include the claim that Pauline letters tend to speak about salvation as a future event, while Ephesians speaks of its attainment now (Eph 2:5, 6). The cross as central for *forgiveness of sins is highlighted in Romans, Galatians, and the Corinthian correspondence, while Ephesians speaks of the cross bringing together Jew and Gentile in Christ (Eph 2:13, 16). Moreover, in Ephesians, the cosmic Christ takes precedence over the Jesus of the cross. Ephesians underlines the universal church, while the Corinthian and Philippian letters highlight the local congregation. The household codes, with the emphasis on *marriage, seem at odds with Paul's injunction to the Corinthians to pursue *singleness (1 Cor 7:6-7, 29, 32-35).

However, evaluating Ephesians alongside Paul's undisputed letters reveals that the peculiarities in Ephesians are within the range of theological topics we find throughout Paul's corpus. Ephesians' use of the OT and the reliance on Israel's narrative of salvation, and its emphasis on the kingdom of God, the church as a body and as a *temple, and the conviction that believers live in a present age of darkness, are all found in the undisputed letters. The claim that Ephesians shows an overrealized *eschatology ("by grace you *have been saved*," Eph 2:5, 8) can be addressed by pointing to evidence of similar expressions in undisputed epistles, such as Paul's exclamation to the Corinthians that "now is the day of salvation" (2 Cor 6:2). He declares to the Romans that believers are justified and glorified (Rom 8:30). Ephesians insists that believers are "in Christ" and thus in some way are with him in his exalted state (Eph 2:5-6). One can also point to Ephesians's use of the image of a maturing body of Christ as a future-focused eschatology (Eph 4:15-16). Again, Ephesians contrasts the present evil age and the present need to put on the armor of God (Eph 2:2, 6:10-18), with the kingdom of Christ and God that is to come (Eph 5:5).

The church as the universal body of believers is discussed not only in Ephesians but also in 1 Corinthians (1 Cor 1:2; 12:7-14, 27-31), where the spiritual *gifts are distributed across local communities, as not every local group had its own apostle, prophet, or healer. The emphasis of Christ as head of the body, his church, reinforces the claims that Christ is ruler now and is exalted (1 Cor 15:24-27; Phil 2:9-11; Col 1:15-20). Finally, the topic of marriage serves very different purposes in the letters, for in Ephesians the discussion of marriage focuses on unity, a theme developed extensively throughout the epistle. By contrast, the analysis of marriage and singleness in 1 Corinthians centers on the church's questions concerning *sex, celibacy, and virginity in the life of a disciple.

2.2. Style and Composition. Ephesians includes numerous lengthy sentences and extensive use of synonyms, genitive phrases, and unique phrases such as "in the heavenlies" (*en tois epouraniois*, Eph 1:3, 20; 2:6; 3:10; 6:12). The quick pace we expect in Paul's letters, his rhetorical questions, and his intense arguments give way in Ephesians to lengthy sentences filled with numerous participial phrases and genitive clauses, creating ambiguities. Yet this observation holds primarily for Ephesians 1–3, which include two prayers, a doxology, and an opening eulogy—all of which draw on traditional vocabulary and liturgical rhythm. Moreover, we find that both wide divergence and significant commonality characterize the Pauline corpus. For example, Ephesians and Galatians contain about the same number of *hapax legomena* (Hoehner). Ephesians includes traditional material (Eph 4:14; 4:4-6) and scriptural quotations and allusions (Eph 1:22; 2:13, 17; 4:8; 5:31; 6:2) that account for some of its stylistic distinctives. The term *mystery* is used with a range of meaning across the Pauline corpus: describing Israel's hardening (Rom 11:25-26), highlighting the cross as wisdom of God (1 Cor 2:1, 7), celebrating the *resurrection body (1 Cor 15:51), and explaining discipleship as believers being in Christ (Col 1:27). Ephesians adds to this list in its emphasis on the mysterious union of Christ and the church, his body (Eph 3:3-9; 5:32).

2.3. Historical Setting. Ephesians provides little information on the circumstances that prompted the letter. We do not hear of any crises or false teachings, no questions arising from the Ephesians, no personal greetings from the author. Although Acts 19:9-10 indicates that Paul spent over two years in Ephesus, in our epistle the author speaks of the congregation "hearing" about him, rather than "knowing" him (Eph 3:2). Some suggest that the picture of unity between Jew and Gentile believers must represent a time later than Paul.

While it is true that Ephesians does not have the intensity and situational focus that 1 Corinthians or Galatians displays, the relative lack of historical details resembles Romans. Both Romans and Ephesians offer minimal personal references and extensive theological discourse. These two epistles spend much energy at the beginning of their communication illuminating theological truths and their ramifications before examining the impact on living a faithful life. In both cases there are references to local circumstances. In Romans, Paul speaks of paying taxes, eating kosher *food (or not), and following Sabbath (or not; Rom 14:1-23). In Ephesians, the author implicitly addresses the Artemis cult and the imperial cult in his declaration that Christ is above all names and has power over all authorities (Eph 1:20-22).

Both Romans and Ephesians emphasize a unity of Jew and Gentile within the church. The suggestion that Ephesians reveals a historical unity between Jew and Gentile has two weaknesses. First, the unity described is achieved at the level of redemption in Christ and thus is weighted theologically. Second, this unity created by Christ's redemption must be actualized daily. Therefore, the author stresses that the believers live worthy of their calling, doing their best to express the unity of the Spirit (Eph 4:3-4). Ephesians's focus on Jew/Gentile unity in Christ is drawn from Paul's reliance on Isaiah's *vision and his own eschatological conviction about Christ's church as one new humanity (Eph 2:15). And there is little evidence that the second and third generation of the church witnessed Jew-Gentile unity. Moreover, the appeal to keep unity and the bond of peace, to grow in maturity, and to put on Christ—these injunctions suggest the church has not reached unity in practice.

The remark that the congregation "heard" about him (Eph 3:2) could reflect that Paul has not been to the city for about seven years, and that he suspects that the congregation includes new members who have never met him. Additionally, the comment could reflect that Ephesus had several congregations, not all of them connected with Paul directly (Trebilco). Perhaps some were linked with Paul's coworker Apollos. Paul hoped all churches in Ephesus would read his letter, including those who were not directly connected to his *ministry there.

Another historical note is the author's declaration that he is a *prisoner. Some suggest this is a leitmotif included to increase verisimilitude (Lincoln), but it seems improbable that a pseudepigraphic author, determined to honor Paul, would take on the honor of incipient martyr.

2.4. Pseudepigraphy and Forgery in the Ancient World. The position that Ephesians is pseudepigraphic has been challenged. The Pauline corpus displays significant differences from ancient pseudepigraphy, including that the latter focused on persons deceased for centuries, were much shorter than Paul's undisputed letters, and made no attempt to create a relationship with readers. If not pseudepigraphic, is Ephesians best categorized as a forgery? B. Ehrman argues that Ephesians is better understood as a forgery, or "counterforgery," that is, a work that refutes forgeries. He suggests Ephesians and other forgeries were produced in a highly polemical context. While it is true that ancient Christian discussion about forgeries included polemics, these ancient authors focused primarily on the text's content when determining authorship, and not on rhetoric or stylistic variations. The attention paid to content and not rhetoric was due in part to the use of secretaries (*amanuenses*), who might copy down an author's exact words or serve as what we might call today a ghostwriter (Richards 2012). A final word on forgery and pseudepigraphy: both assume that we can determine with certainty what is genuinely Pauline. However, the method to do so can become circular, as we must first establish what is essential to Paul and then determine whether we find it (or not) in a given letter.

An adaptation to the pseudepigraphy theory is that Ephesians is a cover letter created when Paul's letters were collected. E. J. Goodspeed put forward this theory in 1926, and while the details have not held up to scrutiny, the overall thrust that Ephesians is a later document addressing Pauline churches with Paul's theology for a new generation retains persuasive power (MacDonald).

Those who consider Ephesians as a genuine Pauline letter point to the similarities of thought and voice with other undisputed epistles (Arnold; Barth; Cohick; Thielman; Wright, 61, "highly likely"). Moreover, one can point to the exceedingly unusual circumstance that Paul co-sent many of his letters as an explanation for certain differences. The question remains as to how influential the co-sender's voice was (Weima; Richards 2004). Romans, Philippians, and 2 Timothy do not include a co-sender, and these are often viewed as establishing Paul's theological center. First Corinthians, co-sent by Sosthenes, shows the greatest diversity from this center, based on A. Kenny's stylometric analysis, yet this epistle is determined to be authentic by most scholars.

A variation on this position is D. Campbell's argument that Ephesians is the letter written by the apostle Paul to the Laodiceans mentioned in Colossians 4:16.

3. Relationship to Colossians.
Ephesians shares with Colossians about one-third of the same terms, as well as similar concepts and worldview, such as an emphasis on Christ as cosmic ruler (Eph 1:20-23; Col 1:15-20). Tychicus's introduction is found verbatim in both (with the omission of *kai syndoulos* in Ephesians; Eph 6:21-22; Col 4:7-8). Colossians includes lengthy sentences and redundant clauses, as does Ephesians. Only in these two letters are believers identified both as "saints" and "faithful" (Eph 1:1; Col 1:2). In both letters we find versions of the household codes, with the three pairs (wife-husband, child-parent, slave-master) addressed in the same order (Eph 5:22–6:9; Col 3:18–4:1).

The similarities in themes and language between Ephesians and Colossians lead some to conclude that the author of Ephesians borrowed from Colossians. Borrowing might have occurred at the level of memory, or perhaps direct copying took place. However, beyond the similarities are distinctions that could point to two different authors. The differences between the two epistles warrant discussion before one can conclude that Ephesians relies on Colossians. Ephesians takes a topic found also in Colossians and develops it, which can be explained as a single author expressing views in nuanced ways. The structure of the two letters is different, for Ephesians does not use Colossians's opening picture of the exalted Christ (Col 1:15-20) and includes a lengthy discussion about Christ our Peace (Eph 2:14-18) as well as a second prayer (Eph 3:14-19). Ephesians "omits" the central argument of Colossians (Col 2:1–3:4) but expands greatly the household codes. Ephesians introduces the household codes by a transitional sentence that provides the key for interpretation: mutual submission out of reverence for Christ (Eph 5:21). In Ephesians, husbands are commanded to love their wives as Christ loves the church, while in Colossians, husbands are enjoined not to be harsh with their wives (Eph 5:25, 28; Col 3:19). In Ephesians, wives' submission to their own husbands serves as a model for Christian behavior.

Finally, how might one explain the verbatim note about Tychicus? This is an odd sentence to commit to memory, while the passage about the exalted Christ (Col 1:15-20) would seem a natural passage to remember. But if the letters were composed at about the same time, the secretary could have copied the letter carrier's description. In the end, it is not possible to demonstrate that Ephesians used Colossians (or vice versa), for there is no impartial way to determine priority (Muddiman). More likely, we have a single author who employed traditional and liturgical elements as well as distinctive emphases to various congregations.

4. Household Codes.
The household codes represent a sizable portion of Ephesians (Eph 5:21–6:9) and present challenges to the modern reader, particularly concerning the institutions of slavery and patriarchy. The social hierarchy of the ancient world clashes with today's standards of justice and the social worth of each individual. The household codes follow the ancient pattern established by Aristotle (*Pol.* 1260a; *Eth. nic.* 8.11.6-7), but in Ephesians, they are shaped to conform to the gospel. Ephesians 5:21 and Ephesians 5:22 are linked by repeating the participle *submitting.* Ancient listeners would have expected Paul to command the wife to obey her husband, but Paul emphasizes reciprocity, namely, that as the husband should treat his wife as his own body, so by implication the wife should see her husband as her own body (see also 1 Cor 7:1-4). As with the unity of Jew and Gentile in Christ's body, so too here the wife and husband retain their individuality, as they celebrate their one-flesh-ness in marriage. This union is an image of Christ's union with the church, a great mystery, Paul declares (Eph 5:32).

Careful analysis of the household codes lead to several proposals. First, the author stresses reconciliation as part of the redemptive work of Christ and repeats that believers are one body of Christ. This claim is reinforced in Ephesians 5:21, which calls each believer (wife or husband, child or parent, slave or owner) to submit to each other out of holy fear or reverence for Christ. Parenthetically, we should note that house churches would have included widows, widowers, relatives, stepparents and stepchildren, freedmen and -women, orphans, and others. This passage was read aloud to the church, so all heard the promises and commands.

Second, Ephesians underscores the believer's inheritance from God and a reward for faithful living. These truths challenge the social reality of a slave who has no progeny, no inheritance, and no freedom from the threat of violence. Ephesians declares that God will judge against owners who threaten their slaves, thus removing the power to dominate that secured owners' rights over their slaves (Eph 6:9). Ephesians not only proclaims a theological equality among masters and slaves in Christ but also insists on the social unity, not hierarchy, within the church. Slavery is about domination and by its very nature creates distinctions of social worth; the gospel message in Ephesians declares that each believer receives grace from Christ for works of *service. The emphasis on unity "is not asserting the obliteration of difference, but rather the obliteration of *dominance*" (Braxton, 94, emphasis original).

Third, Ephesians stresses the verbs "to love" and "to submit" throughout, including in the discussion of marriage. Husbands are commanded to love their wives as Christ did, in a selfless manner, as though the wife were the husband's own body (Eph 5:28, 33). The focus on the husband's love here is to draw a distinction from the wider culture that did not call for a husband's self-giving love. Likewise, believers are called to submit to each other, as a display of *honor that they also extend to the *Lord (Eph 5:21).

5. Destination.

The vast majority of ancient biblical manuscripts and commentators refer to our letter as sent by Paul to the church "in Ephesus" (Eph 1:1). However, in three early texts, the phrase "in Ephesus" is missing from the epistle's opening line. A third-century Alexandrian uncial, P^{46}, reads, "to the saints who are and to the faithful," while the superscription (similar to a cover page) identifies the epistle as "To the Ephesians." Two important, fourth-century Alexandrian codices, Sinaiticus (א) and Vaticanus (B), omit "in Ephesus" in the text but include it in the superscription. Third-century theologian Origen, who was originally from Alexandria but later lived in Caesarea Palestinae, used a biblical text that did not include "in Ephesus." Origen nevertheless held that the apostle Paul wrote Ephesians to believers in that city. Tertullian, who lived a generation or so before Origen, describes his opponent Marcion as wrongly identifying our epistle as to the Laodiceans. Tertullian points out that the church has always identified the letter as to the Ephesians. He dismisses Marcion's title change as of no importance because the apostle Paul wrote to the entire church. Tertullian's cryptic remarks fail to state explicitly that Marcion's biblical text did not include "in Ephesus," nor does Tertullian indicate that his biblical text includes the phrase (Tertullian, *Marc.* 5.17.1).

To explain the absence of "in Ephesus" in these three, early Alexandrian texts, some scholars suggest that Ephesians was not written by the apostle and was a circular or encyclical letter sent to churches in the wider metropolis area around Ephesus or to Laodicea and Hierapolis (Lincoln, 3). Alternatively, the label "Ephesians" could have been attached later, as the Pauline letters were collected into a corpus (Best). Most plausible is the theory that Paul kept copies of his letters, thus creating the first collection (Campbell).

Some argue that Paul wrote the epistle but deliberately omitted the place name. The letter reader, Tychicus, would have inserted the town's name as he read the letter to the various house churches. Paul instructs Tychicus to read Colossians to the Laodicean church, and the (nonextant) letter to the Laodiceans to the Colossians (Col 4:15-16). Again, Galatians is sent to several churches in the area (Gal 1:1; see also 1 Pet 1:1). However, this theory does not explain why "in" was omitted, nor why Paul did not simply write "to the churches in Asia Minor" or some other geographical marker.

While no theory has successfully answered all questions, the strong manuscript evidence, including Codex Alexandrinus (A), for the inclusion of "in Ephesus" makes it likely that the epistle initially included "in Ephesus." A few early Alexandrian texts dropped the phrase from the opening while retaining it in the superscription. The omitted phrase could be the result of a scribe hoping to generalize the epistle, much as did the scribe of Codex G, who edited out the phrase "in Rome" (Rom 1:7, 15; Thielman).

6. Life Setting and Purpose.

In the first century, Ephesus was second in size to Rome and had a population of about 250,000. The city was the guardian of the Temple of Artemis, one of the seven wonders of the ancient world. The temple, which was four times the size of the Athenian Parthenon, shaped the city's *politics and economics. City coins held Artemis's image, and civic leaders celebrated her festivals, thereby legitimating their authority (Hoag; Trebilco). Moreover, in 29 BC, Ephesus constructed a temple to Roma and the Divine Julius, and in the first century AD the imperial cult thrived in the city. The *pax Romana*, or Roman peace, came with much bloodshed and reinforced social hierarchy. Ephesians's emphasis on Christ as "our peace" is a startling contrast, as Christ sheds his blood, not that of his followers (Eph 2:14-16). This peace offers slaves an inheritance and brings unity across *ethnic and gender barriers.

We can sketch the recipients of Ephesians in broad strokes as primarily Gentile believers (Eph 2:2, 11) who were concerned about Paul's imprisonment (Eph 3:13), and needed guidance on faithful living in the midst of their pagan city (Eph 4:17). The Gentile culture relied on astrology and magic, and feared spiritual powers. It condoned practices that the author believed were unholy, sexually immoral, or greedy (Eph 5:6). E. Schüssler Fiorenza suggests that the recipients (Jews and former Gentiles) should be identified as "Jewish Messianists," those who follow a Jewish Messiah, Jesus of Nazareth. Her rhetorical move attempts to highlight that the exclusive categories of "Jew" and "Christian" had not yet emerged, historically speaking, and to avoid what she identifies as *supersessionism (Schüssler Fiorenza, lxvii).

We might know some of the recipients if we draw on 1 Corinthians, which was written from Ephesus. Paul reveals that some of Chloe's people informed him of divisions within the Corinthian church (1 Cor 1:11), making it likely that these people were part of the congregation. Paul indicates that two coworkers, Priscilla and Aquila, were part of the Ephesian believing community and that a group met in their home (1 Cor 16:19). The book of Acts explains that Paul traveled with Priscilla and Aquila to Ephesus from *Corinth, where they established a community of believers (Acts 18:18-21). Also from Acts, we learn of a group that followed Apollos's teaching and knew only John's baptism (Acts 18:24-25). Paul meets such a group as well in Ephesus (Acts 19:3-7); these believers are connected with the synagogue and are probably predominantly Jewish. This information, coupled with the likelihood that the Ephesian letter addresses a predominantly Gentile group, leads one to speculate that there could be several house churches in Ephesus. They might not have had much contact, and there is no evidence of the sort of tension we find in 1 Corinthians (Trebilco).

Some argue that the letter is best understood in the context of rituals and worship (MacDonald) or, more specifically, of baptism, based on its liturgical tone (Dahl). Others see the epistle as an attempt to move the church toward greater catholicity, paralleling a demise in an imminent anticipation of the parousia (Käsemann). The epistle's emphasis on unity could reflect a threat from an external source such as the wider pagan community or spiritual forces (Gombis; Arnold). Some suggest that Gentile believers were drawing back from *fellowship with Jewish believers (Martin). No specific crisis seems present. The focus on a moral lifestyle probably does not arise from a specific situation of sinful behaviors but rather represents the general practice to remind readers about what is good and fitting (Bruce). In a similar fashion, Dio Chrysostom states that it is not a person's ignorance of right and wrong but their failure to follow their reason that prompts him to constantly remind people to heed their reason and do what is proper (*Avar.* 17.2).

7. Themes in the Letter.

The theology expressed in Ephesians has two foci: God and the church. The epistle emphasizes God the Father's blessings for believers, Christ's work in bringing redemption and unity to believers, and the Holy Spirit's seal of salvation on believers. It describes Jesus Christ in relation to God, often with language of Father and, implicitly, Son. This suggests that the author did not hold a static monotheism into which Jesus Christ was inserted but understood God the Father and Christ the Son as defined in part by the relationship to each other (Hill; Richardson). This holds as well for the Holy Spirit, such that one cannot speak about God the Father without also involving Christ the Son and the Holy Spirit. Ephesians establishes this point in the opening sentence that praises the God and Father of the Lord Jesus Christ (Eph 1:3). It encourages believers who have hoped in Christ, are sealed with the Spirit, and receive an inheritance from God (Eph 1:12-14), and reinforces this as it speaks of one Spirit, one Lord, and one God and Father of all (Eph 4:4-6).

The redeemed life includes being saved by grace (Eph 2:5, 8) and being filled with God so as to live an upright life (Eph 3:19). The narrative that underpins this theology includes God's good *creation marred by the fall, redeemed by Christ's salvific work that brings a new creation into being—the body of Christ—and will achieve the unity of the cosmos. The penultimate chapter of this narrative is the life of the church now, as believers grow together in the Lord. The church, the body of Christ, brings the reconciling message of the gospel to the world. Ephesians focuses on right living now and the inheritance to be gained in the coming kingdom of Christ and of God (Eph 5:5). Christ's victory over spirits and powers of darkness offers sure hope as believers take up God's armor to help them stand fast now against evil (Eph 6:11-12).

*7.1. **God the Father.*** God is described as "our" Father, as the Father of Jesus Christ (Eph 1:2-3) and of all families in heaven and on earth (Eph 3:14-15). God brings salvation through his beloved, that is, Christ (Eph 1:6), whom he raised from the dead and seated at his right hand (Eph 1:20). Christ is the Son of God (Eph 4:13). Both Father and Son existed before the foundation of the world (Eph 1:4), and now God has revealed the mystery of redemption, that Gentiles are coheirs with Jews in Christ (Eph 3:6). Thus the author can speak of God as "our" Father, developing the theme of adoption into God's family (Eph 1:4-5). The author declares that God's grace was given him to proclaim redemption in Christ to Gentiles (Eph 3:2, 7-8). Believers are beloved "children of God" (Eph 5:1) who should imitate their father's generous character. Believers are able to do good works that God prepared for them to do (Eph 2:10). Moreover, they can know and understand God the Father better, for his power is extended to those who are in Christ (Eph 1:17-19; 3:20-21). Most importantly, God's great love for his children gave them life in Christ (Eph 2:4-5). Significantly, the author does not connect human fathers with God the Father here or in Ephesians 6:1-4. Human fathers are not called to model God in a particular way, perhaps because all believers are to walk in love (Eph 5:2).

*7.2. **Exalted Christ.*** The title "Christ" or Messiah, the anointed one of God, occurs quite often in the first three chapters in discussions of Christ's death and exaltation to God's right hand. In the second half of the epistle, the focus is on Christ as the active agent supporting his church. For example, Christ descended and ascended and gives gifts to his church (Eph 4:7-11). The title "Lord" is found extensively in Ephesians, referring to Christ. There is "one Lord," as proclaimed in the calling that believers share (Eph 4:5). While "Lord" is also used in reference to Jesus's resurrection (Rom 14:9), in Ephesians the connection to Christ's exaltation and its effects, namely, the establishing of the church, takes center stage. The author stresses "Lord" when enjoining believers to holy living. Believers are challenged to live worthy, for they are "light in the Lord" (Eph 5:8). The longer phrase, "Lord Jesus Christ," occurs in several places, and in each case the context stresses his relationship to God the Father (Eph 1:2-3, 17; 3:11 ["Christ Jesus our Lord"]; 5:20). Both God the Father and the Lord Jesus Christ give peace and grace to believers (Eph 1:2). Christ is exalted to God's right hand (Eph 1:20). It is in his *name that believers give thanks to God the Father (Eph 5:20). The emphasis is on Christ's oneness and mutuality with the Father.

*7.3. **Holy Spirit.*** The Holy Spirit is mentioned in all six chapters of Ephesians, for the Spirit is central to believers' redemption. Believers receive assurance of their inheritance, for they are marked with the seal of the Holy Spirit (Eph 1:13-14; 4:30). The Spirit is that deposit that guarantees the believer's inheritance (Eph 1:14). Alongside its role in confirming redemption, the Holy Spirit fills the church, the temple of God (Eph 2:22). The Holy Spirit provides access to the Father (Eph 2:18), strength and power (Eph 3:16), and unity (Eph 4:4). The sword of the Spirit, the word of God, offers protection as part of God's armor (Eph 6:17). The Spirit is grieved when believers speak against each other and fail to forgive (Eph 4:30-32). Believers are to be filled with the Spirit in their worship as they sing and praise with thanksgiving (Eph 5:18-20). Paul enjoins them to pray in the Spirit in all circumstances (Eph 6:18). The Holy Spirit is known alongside God the Father and Christ the Son as establishing and securing believers as they grow in Christ.

*7.4. **Salvation in Its Present Dimension, Including Struggle with the Powers.*** Believers both are seated with Christ in the heavenlies (Eph 2:6) and are together growing to maturity as members of Christ's body (Eph 4:15-16). They must put on their new self so as to live a holy life fitting to their calling (Eph 4:24). They are adopted in Christ and await an inheritance (Eph 1:5, 14). Redemption is personal, as each believer is "in Christ." Redemption is also corporate, as believers are members together of Christ's body. Salvation includes forgiveness of sins and membership into a new family. Salvation is by God's grace alone and is received by faith (Eph 2:5, 8). The redemption plan through Christ was established before the foundation of the world and was accomplished in the cross, resurrection, and ascension of Christ by God's power. Christ now has his enemies at his feet. In the fullness of time, the cosmos will be united in Christ.

Until such consummation, believers struggle against powers and against their own sinful nature. Ephesians discusses powers and principalities in four of the six chapters. The powers not only are spiritual forces but can be manifest within earthly institutions and human structures. The present time is overshadowed by the ruler of the air, who controls those who disobey God (Eph 2:2). The *devil seeks the downfall of God's children, promoting evil and chaos (Eph 6:11-12). Those who live in this space are "dead" in their sins, and the spotlight is shown particularly on pagan Gentiles' life before Christ (Eph 4:17-19). The Ephesians are to abandon their previous habits and attitudes that were antithetical to God's goodness and grace. They are commanded to put on God's armor and stand in God's power (Eph 6:11), for Christ already has his enemies under his feet (Eph 1:22). The author also notes the strong pull of the sinful nature toward disobedient thoughts and acts (Eph 2:3).

In the discussion about powers in the ancient world, the subject of magic arises. Acts indicates that in Ephesus, believers burned a large number of scrolls filled with magical spells (Acts 19:19). Magic was an attempt to harness power to achieve one's own ends or damage an opponent. Ephesians's emphasis on Christ's superiority over all powers cuts to the root of magic's power (Arnold).

*7.5. **The Church.*** God called the church into being through Christ's work on the cross, and its roots as the people of God stretches back in Israel's history (Eph 2:11-19). God adopts believers to be members of God's family and to receive an inheritance (Eph 1:13-14). In line with this future, believers are to live in *holiness (Eph 4:1). The church is Christ's body, emphasizing the union of Christ with believers (Eph 1:22-23; 5:30-32). This union is also expressed in the new people created through Christ's reconciling work on the cross (Eph 2:15). Only here and in Colossians does the author speak of Christ as head of the church (Eph 1:22; 4:15; 5:23; Col 1:18; 2:19).

Ephesians speaks of Christ as "our peace" (Eph 2:14). This peace reconciles Gentiles and Jews and creates a new community, a new family, a temple for God (Eph 2:15-22). The gospel of peace destroys hostilities between people, and the ethnic and social walls that divide (Eph 2:14-15). Christ's peace is thus an active force that pursues unity and tears down barriers. Believers are in Christ and therefore share this *mission of peace as they take up God's armor, stand fast, and pray in the Spirit (Eph 6:15-18). Gentiles are coheirs with Jews in God's promises (Eph 3:6). The unity within the church is related to the unity that will be accomplished for the cosmos, described as the mystery of God's will (Eph 1:9-10).

The "already/not yet" eschatology underpins the description of the church. The church is established as Christ's body, and as a body it is growing and maturing (Eph 4:15; 5:26-27). Additionally, this eschatology is shown in the dual realities of believers seated with Christ and alive with him in the heavenlies (Eph 2:5-6), and looking forward to an inheritance enjoyed in Christ's and God's kingdom (Eph 5:5).

The universal aspect of the church in Ephesians is emphasized in the claims of one baptism, one hope, and one body, and the unity created in the Holy Spirit (Eph 4:4-5). Believers abandon former pagan practices and beliefs and embrace a life worthy of the gospel (Eph 4:17-20). Ephesians draws on images of cosmic warfare in painting a picture of Christ's kingdom and the prince who rules this world and the disobedient (Eph 2:2; 6:11-12). Members of the church submit to each other out of reverence for Christ (Eph 5:21), a posture similar to soldiers, who take an oath to obey their commander. As a military unit strives for unity, so too believers are to make every effort to express their unity in the Spirit (Eph 4:3).

*7.6. **Status of Believers.*** Ephesians develops the claim that believers are "in Christ" in several ways. First, it emphasizes adoption, with believers sharing the status "in Christ" as sons and daughters of God (Eph 1:5). Second, Ephesians explains an entailment of the "in Christ" status, namely that believers are with Christ in his exaltation, raised and seated with him (Eph 2:5-6). Third, believers are "in Christ" as members of his body, the church. Ephesians 2:14 makes clear that Christ brings peace and oneness to his people. "This is the 'indicative of the gospel—that which God has done, that which is. The indicative carries within it an 'imperative'—that which now needs to be" (Gorman, 184). The church is made up of Jews and Gentiles, the latter of whom are now coheirs with Israel and receive the promise of redemption and life in the kingdom of God (Eph 3:6; 5:5-8). Finally, believers participate in Christ missionally as they stand fast in their faith (Eph 6:10), putting on the armor of God (Eph 6:11, 13) and being empowered by the Holy Spirit (Gorman).

*7.7. **The Ethical Obligation of Believers.*** Ephesians exhorts believers to "walk" worthy of the calling they have received (Eph 4:1). The verb "to walk" is rightly translated as "to live" in many English translations, but the nuance of the Greek is lost, and its connection to the Hebrew Scripture is less obvious. At the outset of the letter, the author explains that redemption includes not only forgiveness of sins but the adoption into a family characterized by holy and blameless lives (Eph 1:4). This expectation for proper lifestyle was common for any Greek philosophical group or Jewish sect, such as the Sadducees and Pharisees. Therefore, believers would not have assumed that the phrase "by grace you have been saved" implied that behavior was secondary in importance (Eph 2:5, 8). Ephesians highlights the behaviors and attitudes expected in believers' lives. The good works expected by believers flow from God, who has prepared them already for this

(Eph 2:10). God's own forgiveness of believers becomes the model that believers imitate (Eph 4:30–5:1). Christ's self-denying love charts the path that all believers should follow (Eph 5:2). Alongside promoting good behavior, Ephesians warns against sinful behavior, especially idolatry, sexual immorality, greed, and abusive speech (Eph 4:25-29; 5:3-5).

7.8. Unity of Jew and Gentile. The unity of Jew and Gentile as a single family of God carries powerful theological force in Ephesians. The plight of pagan Gentiles as without hope and without God is addressed (Eph 2:11-13), as is the promise of redemption through Christ, which brings them near to God (Eph 2:17-18). Christ's work inaugurated a unity that can overcome even this social animosity. The scene is constructed with language of opposites: enmity/peace, stranger/citizen, far/near; the division between Jew and Gentile was hostile. Christ's death destroyed the barrier wall between the two groups (Eph 2:14). Yet Christ's death did not only destroy hostility; it also created a new humanity through his powerful peace (Eph 2:16). The Gentile who follows Christ is no longer pagan but is also not Jewish; instead, the Gentile believer joins Jewish believers as part of God's family in Christ, part of the holy temple in the Lord (Eph 2:21-22).

The question remains, however, whether the Ephesian church experienced ethnic unity of Jew and Gentile. Some suggest that the author paints a picture of accomplished reconciliation and, given that such unity was not a feature of the first generation of believers, conclude that the apostle was not the author of the letter. Others deduce that the epistle does not give the impression of ethnic unity, as it calls for harmony repeatedly. While it seems best to conclude that ethnic unity is not an accomplished fact in Ephesus, we should also not presume that the emphasis on unity is primarily metaphorical or theological, for Ephesians asserts that expressions of unity in the church are specific evidence for Christ's redemption (Hodge). Moreover, unity relies on difference; unity is not a call for sameness. The diversity desired is one that does not insist on privilege but puts others ahead of oneself out of reverence for Christ, who is in each believer.

7.9. Apostle to the Gentiles. The unity presented in Ephesians, unfortunately, has been interpreted in *anti-Jewish ways. For example, Jews are represented as the typological "unbeliever" and are portrayed as ethnocentric, while Gentiles are understood as representing Christianity and are assumed to be without a culture and as universal in perspective. One antidote for this tendency is to take seriously Paul's identification as an apostle to the Gentiles. This avoids substituting "unbeliever" for "Jew," a position that can open the door to anti-Jewish views and actions. In Paul's own presentation as an apostle to the Gentiles (Eph 3:1, 8, 13), he underlines God's grace in calling him to present the gospel that Gentiles are coheirs with Israel in Christ (Eph 3:6). This gospel message supersedes all other claims, as Paul emphasizes Jesus as God's Messiah, who has accomplished redemption for all, has brought peace to all, and has created the church, his body.

Not only is Paul an apostle to the Gentiles, but this calling has led to his imprisonment (Eph 3:1; 4:1). Paul asks for prayer that he would be bold in his confession of the gospel while in chains (Eph 6:20). The confinement in this case was probably similar to what we would call today house arrest (Rapske). Paul endured social shame as well as the physical pain that went along with his chains (Phil 1:15-17). The shame of his chains made him an outcast, even as Gentiles might feel like outcasts because they were once far from God. The pain of his imprisonment reinforced his conviction that, as a servant of God, he suffers affliction even as Christ did (Eph 3:7-8; Col 1:23-29). The traditional location of Paul's imprisonment is Rome. Some suggest Ephesus, but this argument is based primarily on concluding that the other prison epistles (Colossians, Philippians, Philemon) were written from Ephesus.

See also Body of Christ; Canon of Paul's Letters; Christology; Church; Colossians, Letter to the; Election and Predestination; Ephesus; Ethics; Gentiles; God; Holy Spirit; Households and Household Codes; Hymns, Hymn Fragments, Confessions; In Christ; Lord; Magic; Mystery; Peace, Reconciliation; Principalities and Powers; Pseudepigraphy/Forgery; Salvation; Worship.

BIBLIOGRAPHY. ***Commentaries:*** **C. E. Arnold,** *Ephesians*, ZECNT (Grand Rapids, MI: Zondervan, 2010); **M. Barth,** *Ephesians*, 2 vols., AB (Garden City, NY: Doubleday, 1974); **F. F. Bruce,** *The Epistles to the Colossians, to Philemon, and to the Ephesians*, NICNT (Grand Rapids, MI: Eerdmans, 1984); **L. H. Cohick,** *Ephesians*, NICNT (Grand Rapids, MI: Eerdmans, 2020); **R. E. Heine,** *The Commentaries of Origen and Jerome on St. Paul's Epistle to the Ephesians*, OECS (Oxford: Oxford University Press, 2002); **H. W. Hoehner,** *Ephesians: An Exegetical Commentary* (Grand Rapids, MI: Baker Academic, 2002); **A. T. Lincoln,** *Ephesians*, WBC 42 (Dallas: Word, 1990); **M. Y.**

MacDonald, *Colossians and Ephesians*, SP 17 (Collegeville, MN: Liturgical Press, 2000); **J. Muddiman,** *The Epistle to the Ephesians*, BNTC (New York: Continuum, 2001); **E. Schüssler Fiorenza,** *Ephesians*, WC (Wilmington, DE: Glazier, 2017); **F. Thielman,** *Ephesians*, BECNT (Grand Rapids, MI: Baker Academic, 2010).

Studies: **J. M. G. Barclay,** *Paul and the Gift* (Grand Rapids, MI: Eerdmans, 2015); **F. C. Baur,** *Paul the Apostle of Jesus Christ: His Life and Works, His Epistles and Teachings*, 2 vols. in 1 (repr., Peabody, MA: Hendrickson, 2003 [*Paulus, der Apostel Jesu Christi*, 1845]); **E. Best,** "Recipients and Title of the Letter to the Ephesians: Why and When the Designation 'Ephesians'?," *ANRW* 25.4: 3247-79; **M. F. Bird,** "Reassessing a Rhetorical Approach to Paul's Letters," *ExpTim* 119 (2008): 374-79; **B. R. Braxton,** *No Longer Slaves: Galatians and African American Experience* (Collegeville, MN: Liturgical Press, 2002); **D. Campbell,** *Framing Paul: An Epistolary Biography* (Grand Rapids, MI: Eerdmans, 2014); **B. S. Childs,** *The New Testament as Canon: An Introduction* (Philadelphia: Fortress, 1985); **C. J. Classen,** *Rhetorical Criticism of the New Testament*, WUNT 128 (Tübingen: Mohr Siebeck, 2000); **N. A. Dahl,** "Adresse und Proëmium des Epheserbriefes," *TZ* 7 (1951): 241-64; **B. Ehrman,** *Forged: Writing in the Name of God—Why the Bible's Authors Are Not Who We Think They Are* (New York: HarperOne, 2011); **T. Gombis,** *The Drama of Ephesians: Participating in the Triumph of God* (Downers Grove, IL: IVP Academic, 2010); **M. J. Gorman,** *Becoming the Gospel: Paul, Participation, and Mission* (Grand Rapids, MI: Eerdmans, 2015); **W. Hill,** *Paul and the Trinity: Persons, Relations, and the Pauline Letters* (Grand Rapids, MI: Eerdmans, 2015); **G. G. Hoag,** *Wealth in Ancient Ephesus and the First Letter to Timothy: Fresh Insights from Ephesiaca by Xenophon of Ephesus* (Winona Lake, IN: Eisenbrauns, 2015); **C. J. Hodge,** *If Sons, Then Heirs: A Study of Kinship and Ethnicity in the Letters of Paul* (Oxford: Oxford University Press, 2007); **R. R. Jeal,** *Integrating Theology and Ethics in Ephesians: The Ethos of Communication* (Lewiston, NY: Mellen, 2000); **E. Käsemann,** "Paul and Early Catholicism," in *New Testament Questions of Today* (Philadelphia: Fortress, 1967), 236-51; **A. Kenny,** *A Stylometric Study of the New Testament* (Oxford: Clarendon, 1986); **R. P. Martin,** "An Epistle in Search of a Life-Setting," *ExpTim* 79 (1968): 296-302; **G. Martín-Asensio,** *Transitivity-Based Foregrounding in the Acts of the Apostles: A Functional-Grammatical Approach to the Lukan Perspective*, JSNTSup 202 (Sheffield: Sheffield Academic Press, 2000); **B. Rapske,** *The Book of Acts and Paul in Roman Custody*, BAFCS (Grand Rapids, MI: Eerdmans, 1994); **S. Reece,** *Paul's Large Letters: Paul's Autographic Subscriptions in the Light of Ancient Epistolary Conventions*, LNTS 561 (London: Bloomsbury T&T Clark, 2017); **E. R. Richards,** *Paul and First Century Letter Writing: Secretaries, Composition and Collection* (Downers Grove, IL: InterVarsity Press, 2004); idem, "Will the Real Author Please Stand Up?," In *Come Let Us Reason: New Essays in Christian Apologetics*, ed. Paul Copan and William Lane Craig (Nashville: B&H Academic, 2012), 113-36; **N. Richardson,** *Paul's Language About God*, JSNTSup 99 (Sheffield: Sheffield Academic Press, 1994); **David M. Stec,** *The Targum of Psalms: Translated with a Critical Introduction, Apparatus, and Notes* (Collegeville, MN: Liturgical Press, 2004); **P. R. Trebilco,** *The Early Christians in Ephesus from Paul to Ignatius* (Grand Rapids, MI: Eerdmans, 2007); **J. A. D. Weima,** *Paul the Ancient Letter Writer: An Introduction to Epistolary Analysis* (Grand Rapids, MI: Baker Academic, 2016); **T. L. Wilder,** *Pseudonymity, the New Testament, and Deception: An Inquiry into Intention and Reception* (Lanham, MD: University Press of America, 2004); **B. Witherington III,** *Jesus, Paul, and the End of the World: A Comparative Study in New Testament Eschatology* (Downers Grove, IL: InterVarsity Press, 1992); **N. T. Wright,** *Paul and the Faithfulness of God*, vol. 1 (Minneapolis: Fortress, 2016).

L. H. Cohick

EPHESUS

Ephesus was located on the west coast of Asia Minor (modern-day Turkey) at the mouth of the Cayster River. In Roman times, the city probably ranked as the fourth-greatest city in the empire, after Rome, Alexandria, and Antioch. Paul spent over two years and three months there, and a number of his letters have a connection with Ephesus.

1. History
2. The Importance of Ephesus in the Roman Period
3. The Jewish Community in Ephesus
4. Paul's Ministry in Ephesus According to His Letters
5. Paul's Ministry in Ephesus According to Acts
6. Conclusion

1. History.

According to an Ephesian foundation myth, Androclus, the son of Athenian king Codrus, founded the city, perhaps around 1000 BC. In the sixth century, the Lydians under Croesus controlled Ephesus. After Croesus was defeated by Cyrus I in 546, the Achaemenid Persians ruled until the coming of Alexander the Great in 334. In 281, Lysimachus moved the city to higher ground in the area between the hills known as Mount Pion and Mount Koressos, the site the city occupied in the Greco-Roman period. This was due to land subsidence where the preceding city and the Artemision lay (Strabo, *Geogr.* 14.1.21; Pausanias, *Descr.* 1.9.7; 7.3.4-5). Lysimachus fortified the new city with a wall that extended for more than five miles, and a new harbor was established. The city was laid out on the Hippodamian system, with the only deviation being the so-called Kouretes Street, which followed an older path.

In the third century BC Ephesus was in turn under the Seleucid kings and the Ptolemies of Egypt; in 188 BC it became part of the Attalid kingdom of Pergamum. Ephesus came within the sphere of Roman rule when Attalos III bequeathed his kingdom to the Romans in 133 BC. In 30/29 BC, the city became the capital of the Roman province of Asia and the seat of the provincial governor instead of Pergamum. The city participated in the general prosperity that resulted from the Pax Romana. In particular, as communications with the interior of Asia Minor improved, and as new cities were founded there, the importance of a city such as Ephesus at the head of two great roads to the interior increased. The extent of the city's land and sea trade also meant it benefited greatly from the growing prosperity of the whole of the province of Asia under the Pax Romana.

2. The Importance of Ephesus in the Roman Period.

There are a number of indications of the significance of the city of Ephesus in the Roman period. In 29 BC Augustus granted the right to dedicate sacred precincts to Dea Roma and Divus Julius to Ephesus and Nicaea because, according to Cassius Dio (*Hist.* 51.20.6), "these cities had at that time attained the chief place in Asia and in Bithynia respectively." Strabo (*Geogr.* 14.1.24) around AD 20 wrote that "the city, because of its advantageous situation, . . . grows daily, and is the largest emporium in Asia this side of the Taurus." Pliny (*Nat.* 5.120), after having spoken of Smyrna, wrote of Ephesus as "the other great luminary of Asia." The city also calls itself "the first and greatest metropolis of Asia" in inscriptions (IEph 647, 1541, 1543). Early in the second century AD it was said of Ephesus by Philostratus (*Vita Apoll.* 8.7.8) that it was a city that "grew in size beyond all other cities of Ionia and Lydia, and stretched herself out to the sea outgrowing the land on which she is built."

Another indication of the *wealth and significance of Ephesus was the particularly notable number of donations made and public buildings constructed in the first and second centuries AD. In the Greco-Roman city, monumental public buildings were all-important, and had become an index of city status and a dominant and crucial defining characteristic of cities. Excavations by J. T. Wood in 1863–1874 and then by the Austrian Archaeological Institute since 1895 have uncovered much of the city. Reconstruction of some buildings means the city comes alive for contemporary visitors.

In the time of Paul the notable buildings of the city would have included the temple of Artemis; the Magnesian Gate; the Heroon, now (incorrectly) called the grave of Saint Luke; the Upper or State Agora, with an Augustan Basilica and Chalcidicum; the temple of Dea Roma and Divus Julius; the Prytaneion; the Memmius monument; the Monument of Pollio; the Terrace Houses; the octagonal Tomb of Arsinoë; the Tetragonos Agora; the theater; the Gate of Mazaeus and Mithridates; the stadium; and the Koressian Gate. Many of these buildings were constructed or significantly renovated during or since the reign of Augustus. A temple of the Sebastoi was built in AD 89/90.

Ephesus was famous for its temple of Artemis, one of the seven wonders of the ancient world. In Paul's time, the temple was the fifth built on the site, having been built in the fourth century BC after the previous temple burnt to the ground. It was 67 by 130 meters and was the largest religious building in the Hellenistic world, about four times the size of the Parthenon in Athens. As well as being a religious center, the temple of Artemis was a banking center and a repository of official inscriptions, and it also offered asylum. The imperial cult was also very important in the city. Many other deities were worshiped in the city, including Aphrodite, Apollo, Asclepius, Athena, the Cabiri, Demeter, Dionysus, Ge, God Most High, Hecate, Hephaestus, Hercules, Hestia, Isis, the Mother goddess, Pluton, Poseidon, Serapis, Zeus, and other minor deities.

The population of the city in the Roman period is generally estimated at between 200,000 and 250,000. This would make it the fourth-largest city in the empire after Rome, Alexandria, and Antioch.

3. The Jewish Community in Ephesus.

The Jewish community in Ephesus was a significant community in the life of the city. We do not know when Jews first arrived in Ephesus, but by the time of Paul's mission in Ephesus around AD 52, the Jewish community may have lived in Ephesus for more than three hundred years. Although they experienced some hostility from the wider city in the second half of the first century BC, it seems likely that their interactions with the wider city in the first century AD were generally more positive. Further, documents preserved by Josephus (see *Ant.* 14.223-227, 228-229, 230, 234, 238-240, 262-264, 301-313, 314-317; 16.27-65; *Ag. Ap.* 2.39) show that the community maintained key facets of Jewish identity, including paying the *temple tax, continuing its link with *Jerusalem, and observing *food laws and the Sabbath. In addition, the documents show that it received Roman support and that it had a level of communal organization and had adopted a united, citywide organizational structure.

4. Paul's Ministry in Ephesus According to His Letters.

4.1. Opposition and Opportunity. Paul wrote 1 Corinthians from Ephesus (see 1 Cor 16:8) and gives us some information about his *ministry in the city. In 1 Corinthians 15:32 he writes of fighting wild animals in Ephesus, which is almost certainly a reference to non-Christian opponents. It is unlikely that Paul is referring to facing literal wild animals because he does not mention a fight with real animals in 2 Cor 11:23-29 (written after he left Ephesus), and "to fight wild animals" was used metaphorically by contemporary writers to describe the wise person's struggle against their own passions and against *opponents. In 1 Corinthians 16:8-9 he says there are "many adversaries" in Ephesus. He also writes in 2 Corinthians 1:8 of "the affliction we experienced in Asia; for we were so utterly, unbearably crushed that we despaired of life itself" (NRSV). We do not have further details about this hardship, but the experience may have been in Ephesus.

In 1 Corinthians 16:9 he also says that "for a wide door for effective work has opened to me, and there are many adversaries." (NRSV) in Ephesus, which clearly points to the significance of his work in the city. The greetings he gives in 1 Corinthians 16:19-20, both from the *church meeting in Aquila and Prisca's house and from "all the brothers and sisters" (NRSV), indicate the success of Paul's *mission to that point.

4.2 House Churches. We know from 1 Corinthians 16:19-20 that toward the end of the Pauline mission there were at least two house churches in Ephesus. A house church met in the home of one of its members and might have been a group of around twenty to thirty people. One house church could be reasonably independent of other groups, particularly since there seems to have been no overarching organizational structure for all Christians in the city. That the basic unit of the Christian community in Ephesus, as elsewhere, was the house church meant that variety and diversity could develop between different Christian groups in the city. Differences could develop between house churches with regard to matters such as beliefs and practices, socioeconomic level, leadership style, attitudes to outsiders, and mission. In addition, some house churches may have been made up predominantly of Jews and others predominantly of Gentiles, which might have meant that difference or disagreement between different ethnic groups could develop quite easily. In general, then, the house church structure facilitated diversity among Christians more easily than citywide unity.

4.3. Imprisonment. Writing after his ministry in Ephesus, Paul tells the Corinthians that he has been in *prison frequently (2 Cor 11:23), and many scholars have thought that one of these imprisonments was in Ephesus. This could mean that one or more of his prison epistles (Colossians, Philippians, Philemon) were written in Ephesus, but there is no consensus about this.

4.4. Ephesians. In Ephesians 1:1, there is uncertainty whether "in Ephesus" was part of the original Greek text, which means we cannot be sure that the letter was written to Ephesus. Many argue that it was a circular letter, sent to a number of destinations. Even if the intended recipients of the letter included Christians in Ephesus, the more general nature of the letter in comparison with other Pauline *letters means we gain little information about the recipients. At the least, though, it would suggest that relations between Jewish and *Gentile Christians in Ephesus was an ongoing issue in the Christian community at the time the letter was written (see Eph 2:11-22). As noted above, this issue may have been fostered by the house church structure adopted by the early Christians.

4.5. Timothy in Ephesus. The authorship of the Pastoral Epistles is disputed, with many scholars arguing that they were written by a Pauline disciple. Ephesus is mentioned in 1 Timothy 1:3; 2 Timothy 1:18; 4:12. If 1 and 2 Timothy are by Paul, then they point to Paul's further ministry in Ephesus after the close of Acts. After his first imprisonment in

Rome, Paul would have returned to Ephesus and left Timothy there before going on to Macedonia (1 Tim 1:3). After his subsequent arrest, he sent Tychicus to Ephesus to relieve Timothy, so that the latter could join Paul in Rome (2 Tim 4:12-13). If the Pastorals are *pseudepigraphical, then they were probably written to Ephesian Christians by a Pauline disciple in the generation after Paul and may indicate what was happening in the Pauline Ephesian community at that time.

Whether the letters are by Paul or are pseudepigraphical, they indicate that opponents, who are clearly Christians, had been active within the community and had had a considerable impact among the readers. At the time of writing, they posed a dangerous threat (see 1 Tim 1:3-7, 18-20; 4:1-7; 6:3-10, 20-21; 2 Tim 2:14–4:5; cf. Titus 1:10-16; 3:9-11). The opponents probably had a Jewish dimension to their *teaching (1 Tim 1:6-11) and also believed that the *resurrection (probably a spiritual resurrection) had already taken place (2 Tim 2:16-18).

5. Paul's Ministry in Ephesus According to Acts. Acts 18:24–20:38 records the beginning of the Christian community in Ephesus, including Paul's mission in the city, which lasted for more than two years and three months. There is much local color in this passage, which suggests that Luke has reliable sources for his account (see Trebilco 2007, 104-7).

5.1. Paul's First Visit to Ephesus. We learn from Acts 18:18-21 that Paul visited Ephesus briefly on his way to Jerusalem from *Corinth. Paul was well received in the synagogue he visited in Ephesus, and he promised to return. Priscilla and Aquila remained in Ephesus and continued work in the synagogue there (Acts 18:26).

5.2. Apollos, Priscilla, and Aquila in Ephesus. According to Acts 18:24-28, Apollos was active in the synagogue in Ephesus, and there he met Priscilla and Aquila, who "explained the Way of *God to him more accurately" (Acts 18:26 NRSV). We do not know exactly what was lacking in Apollos's *faith, but Priscilla and Aquila assisted him to come to a fuller understanding. Sometime afterward, Christians were to be found within the synagogue, for in Acts 18:27 we read: "And when he [Apollos] wished to cross over to Achaia, the brothers and sisters [in Ephesus] encouraged him and wrote to the disciples to welcome him" (NRSV modified). These "brothers and sisters" were Jewish believers in Jesus within the synagogue in Ephesus. We are not told how they came to faith, but the most likely supposition from within Luke's narrative is that they had been converted through the ministry of Priscilla and Aquila.

5.3. Paul Returns to Ephesus. Acts 19:1, 8-10 tells us that Paul returned to Ephesus and that he spoke in the Jewish synagogue for three months. This was a particularly long time for Paul to stay in the synagogue (compare Pisidian Antioch, Acts 13:13-14, 42, 44-52; and Thessalonica, Acts 17:2, 5-9) and shows that some Jews were receptive to Paul's preaching. However, other Jews did not accept what Paul said, and so he left the synagogue, taking with him a number of believers (Acts 19:9). He then "argued daily in the lecture hall of Tyrannus" (NRSV) for the next two years, with the result that many Jews and Gentiles heard the *gospel (Acts 19:9-10). This is by far the longest time Paul spent in any one city during his missionary travels according to Luke. The strategic location and importance of the city of Ephesus help us to understand why Paul spent so long in Ephesus. That, according to Luke, people from the whole province of Asia heard the gospel while Paul was in Ephesus (see Acts 19:10, 26) points to it being a center to which people traveled from all over the province. It is likely that Epaphras, a coworker of Paul, founded the church in Colossae at this time (see Col 1:7-9; 4:12-13).

5.4. Particular Incidents in the City. Luke also records some important incidents that occurred in Ephesus in conjunction with Paul's ministry. Paul encountered and converted twelve people who seem to have been disciples of John the Baptist (Acts 19:1-7). A number of miracles occurred through Paul (Acts 19:11-12), and when some Jewish exorcists sought to use Jesus' name in exorcisms, a man with an evil spirit leaped on them and overpowered them (Acts 19:13-16). Many believers who had practiced *magic responded to Paul's preaching by burning their very valuable books (Acts 19:18-20).

5.5. Departure from Ephesus. In Acts 19:23-41, Luke gives an account of the riot that led to Paul's departure from the city. Paul's preaching was having an impact on the sale of silver shrines of Artemis, with the result that Demetrius, one of the silversmiths who made these shrines, told his fellow artisans that "there is danger not only that this trade of ours may come into disrepute but also that the temple of the great goddess Artemis will be scorned, and she will be deprived of her majesty that brought all Asia and the world to worship her" (Acts 19:27 NRSV). This led to a crowd gathering in the theater and shouting, "Great is Artemis of the Ephesians!" for two hours (Acts 19:34 NRSV). As a result, Paul left the city for Macedonia.

5.6. Meeting with the Ephesian Elders. After ministry elsewhere, Paul met with the Ephesian elders in nearby Miletus. In addressing them in Acts 20:18-35, Paul gives an account of his ministry in Ephesus, encourages the elders, and warns them that after his departure "savage wolves will come in among you, not sparing the flock. Some even from your own group will come distorting the *truth in order to entice the disciples to follow them" (Acts 20:29-30 NRSV). That Luke records this as part of Paul's speech suggests that this did indeed happen in Ephesus after Paul's death.

6. Conclusion.

Ephesus was a very important city in the Roman *Empire, and it became an important center for early Christianity. From Paul's own letters and from the Acts of the Apostles we learn a good deal about Paul's ministry of two years and three months in the city. Paul clearly had a considerable impact in Ephesus, where he established a significant group of Christians, although he also encountered opposition in the city.

See also CHRONOLOGY OF PAUL; CHURCH; CORINTHIANS, FIRST LETTER TO THE; CORINTHIANS, SECOND LETTER TO THE; COWORKERS, PAUL AND HIS; EPHESIANS, LETTER TO THE; MISSION; OPPONENTS OF PAUL; PASTORAL EPISTLES; PAUL AND JUDAISM; PAUL IN ACTS; PRISON, PRISONER; PSEUDEPIGRAPHY/FORGERY; RELIGIONS, GRECO-ROMAN.

BIBLIOGRAPHY. **T. Georges,** ed., *Ephesos*, COMS 2 (Tübingen: Mohr Siebeck, 2017); **M. Günther,** *Die Frühgeschichte des Christentums in Ephesus*, ARGU 1 (Frankfurt am Main: Peter Lang, 1995); **J. R. Harrison and L. L. Welborn,** eds., *The First Urban Churches*, vol. 3, *Ephesus*, WGRW 9 (Atlanta: SBL Press, 2018); **H. Koester,** "Ephesos in Early Christian Literature," in *Ephesos: Metropolis of Asia; An Interdisciplinary Approach to Its Archaeology, Religion, and Culture*, ed. H. Koester (Valley Forge, PA: Trinity Press International, 1995), 119-40; **M. Meiser,** "The City of Ephesus in Early Christian Literature," *EC* 7 (2016): 368-77; **Philostratus,** *Life of Apollonius of Tyana*, vol. 2, *Books 5-8*, trans. C. P. Jones, LCL (Cambridge, MA: Harvard University Press, 2005); **Pliny,** *Natural History*, vol. 2, *Books 3-7*, trans. H. Rackham, LCL (Cambridge, MA: Harvard University Press, 1942); **G. M. Rogers,** *The Mysteries of Artemis of Ephesos: Cult, Polis, and Change in the Graeco-Roman World*, Synkrisis (New Haven: Yale University Press, 2012); **P. Scherrer,** *Ephesus: The New Guide* (Istanbul: Ege Yaginlari, 2000); idem, "The Historical Topography of Ephesos," in *Urbanism in Western Asia Minor: New Studies on Aphrodisias, Ephesos, Hierapolis, Pergamon, Perge and Xanthos*, ed. D. Parrish (Portsmouth, RI: Journal of Roman Archaeology, 2001), 57-93; **D. Schowalter, S. Ladstätter, S. J. Friesen, and C. Thomas,** eds., *Religion in Ephesos Reconsidered: Archaeology of Spaces, Structures, and Objects*, NovTSup 177 (Leiden: Brill, 2019); **Strabo,** *Geography*, vol. 6, *Books 13-14*, trans. H. L. Jones, LCL (Cambridge, MA: Harvard University Press, 1929); **R. Strelan,** *Paul, Artemis, and the Jews in Ephesus*, BZNW 80 (Berlin: de Gruyter, 1996); **M. Tellbe,** *Christ-Believers in Ephesus: A Textual Analysis of Early Christian Identity Formation in a Local Perspective*, WUNT 242 (Tübingen: Mohr Siebeck, 2009); **W. Thiessen,** *Christen in Ephesus: Die historische und theologische Situation in vorpaulinischer und paulinischer Zeit und zur Zeit der Apostelgeschichte und der Pastoralbriefe*, TANZ 12 (Tübingen: Francke Verlag, 1995); **P. R. Trebilco,** *Jewish Communities in Asia Minor*, SNTSMS 69 (Cambridge: Cambridge University Press, 1991); idem, *The Early Christians in Ephesus from Paul to Ignatius*, WUNT 166 (Grand Rapids Eerdmans, 2007); **M. Wilson,** *Biblical Turkey: A Guide to the Jewish and Christian Sites of Asia Minor* (Istanbul: Yayinlari, 2010); **S. Witetschek,** *Ephesische Enthüllungen 1: Frühe Christen in einer antiken Grosstadt Zugleich ein Beitrag zur Frage nach den Kontexten der Johannesapokalypse*, BTS 6 (Leuven: Peeters, 2008); **J. T. Wood,** *Discoveries at Ephesus Including the Site and Remains of the Great Temple of Diana* (Boston: Osgood, 1877).

P. R. Trebilco

EPISTLES. *See* LETTERS, LETTER FORMS.

ESCHATOLOGY

The word *eschatology* comes from the Greek *eschatos*, meaning "last," hence the theology of "last things." This framing of the subject leads, understandably, to the popular assumption that eschatology is exclusively concerned with the study of what the Bible says about the future, particularly around specific questions of personal destiny at the end of this world. However, within the NT, eschatology is more like the fabric of thought onto which themes such as soteriology, *Christology, pneumatology, ecclesiology, *anthropology, and *ethics are stitched. Another way of putting this is that eschatology involves a dynamic interplay between the *past* events of Jesus' life, *death, and *resurrection, *future* *hope, and *present* experience.

1. The Significance of Paul for Eschatology
2. Eschatological Language and Imagination
3. Messianic Eschatology: Past, Future, Present
4. The Origins of Pauline Eschatology, Narrative and Apocalyptic
5. Conclusion

1. The Significance of Paul for Eschatology. Major contemporary studies on Paul typically have extensive discussions of his eschatology, either in separate sections or within analysis of individual letters (e.g., Dunn 1998; Wright 2013; 2018; Gorman 2009; 2015; 2016; Schnelle; Sanders; Schreiner; Porter; Pitre, Barber, and Kincaid). This is not surprising for at least three reasons. First, Paul's letters are among the earliest recorded documents of early Christianity and capture seminal perspectives on eschatological theology. Second is the scope of Paul's contribution to the NT canon. The overarching importance of eschatology is evident within all of Paul's writings, whether one accepts the authenticity of the disputed letters (2 Thessalonians, Colossians, Ephesians, and the Pastoral Epistles) or not. This is true for a letter such as Galatians; even though it does not mention specific "end things" such as the day of the *Lord, much of its content revolves around an eschatological battle between the *flesh and the Spirit. Third, more than mere quantity, it is the depth, range, and sheer complex creativity of Paul's eschatological imagination that imprints itself on the reader. Much of this article attempts to identify the main strands of that creativity and how they have been discussed within contemporary Pauline studies.

2. Eschatological Language and Imagination. Evoking hope in an unseen future is by necessity an imaginative exercise. The allusive and imprecise nature of eschatological language is therefore a significant factor behind the diversity of perspectives on Pauline eschatology. At a broad level three interpretive approaches illustrate this point (but it applies to specific themes within the apostle's thought as well). The first is a literal hermeneutic in which the interpreter's imagination of the future is constrained by what is actual and possible in the present. Paul himself cautions against such an unimaginative reading (1 Cor 15:35). Literalist readings of Paul tend to be the domain of popular theology rather than NT scholarship. Second, following in Rudolf Bultmann's footsteps, is a postcritical or historicist understanding of eschatology in which Paul's eschatological language is merely symbolic imagery telling readers about the religious beliefs of the *apostle and his communities. In this approach, to read Paul as speaking of actual future realities is to seriously distort a Christian understanding of *salvation and leads to self-delusion (Borg).

Scholars within orthodox or evangelical constituencies in general attempt to forge a third way in which Paul's eschatological language is neither literal nor only symbolic. Paul's future-orientated imagery is understood as an exercise in creative imagination in which there is both continuity and radical disruptive discontinuity with the present (Bauckham and Hart). Yet this future hope is not purely fantastical; Paul's eschatological language of hope is founded on the past events of the *cross and resurrection of Jesus Christ.

3. Messianic Eschatology: Past, Future, Present. How to organize a synopsis of Pauline eschatology is no easy matter; such is the all-embracing impact of an eschatological perspective across his thought. The approach taken below is to work outward from the revolutionary impact of the *past* Christ-event, how it determines Paul's vision of the *future* and how, together, past and future shape his *teaching on living a life worthy of the Lord in the *present.*

3.1. Messianic Eschatology: Past. For Paul, the coming of Jesus the Messiah inaugurates a new eschatological age. This overlap of two interlocking ages surfaces in multiple ways, each highlighting how, for the apostle, a dramatic eschatological shift in the nature of reality has occurred. Dualism between two ages was a familiar concept within Jewish apocalyptic literature, and Paul is not unusual in this regard. He is radically discontinuous, however, in how it is the death and resurrection of God's Messiah, the risen Lord of both Jews and *Gentiles, that marks the arrival of the age to come within the present. The present age is described in strongly negative terms. In Philippians Paul exhorts believers to "shine like stars" within "a crooked and perverse generation" (Phil 2:15-16 NRSV). The age (*aiōn*; Rom 12:2; 1 Cor 1:20; 2:6-8; 3:18; 2 Cor 4:4) is sometimes described as "evil" (Gal 1:4, see Eph 5:13; 6:13) and in the process of "passing away" (1 Cor 7:31). Believers in Corinth, on whom "the ends [*telos*] of the ages have come," are exhorted to stand firm (1 Cor 10:11 NRSV). The term "age to come" is only specifically mentioned in Ephesians 1:21 but is implied in multiple places throughout Paul's undisputed and disputed letters.

The world (*kosmos*) often functions in a similar way and is a significant eschatological theme in the

Pauline corpus. The world will be judged by God (Rom 3:6, 19; 1 Cor 6:2; 11:32); sin and death reign in the world (Rom 5:12-14); the world's *wisdom cannot know God (1 Cor 1:20-21; 3:19; 2 Cor 1:12); God's Spirit is in opposition to the "spirit of the world" (1 Cor 2:12 NRSV); those who belong to the world are immoral, greedy, swindlers, idolaters (1 Cor 5:10); the world requires reconciliation by God in Christ (2 Cor 5:9); and in Paul's own experience "the world has been crucified to me, and I to the world" (Gal 6:14 NRSV). Galatians and Colossians connect the world with "elemental spirits" (*stoicheia*: Gal 4:3, 9; Col 2:8, 20; see 3.2.3.2 below). The Ephesian believers used to be dead in their sins, walking in the ways of the world, a domain inextricably linked with "the ruler of the power of the air" (Eph 2:2 NRSV). This eschatological framework provides the context for how Paul repeatedly refers his readers back to a decisive event that marked their new beginning in Christ. He does this using several distinct images, the most significant of which are outlined below.

3.1.1. The Resurrection. For Paul the resurrection of Jesus is an eschatological event, revealing the death of Christ as the victory of God and evidence that the new creation has broken into the present, giving hope for transformed life in the future (Rom 8:11, 23). The resurrection is inseparable from the *ascension of Jesus to the right hand of God, where he intercedes for the saints as reigning Lord. The fact of the resurrection therefore gives profound assurance to believers of the love of Christ, whatever trials or opposition come their way (Rom 8:34-38). Paul talks about resurrection in three distinct ways: first, the historical event of Christ's resurrection (Rom 6:9); second, the past resurrection of believers from spiritual death to new life (Col 2:12; Rom 6:4, 6, 13, 17); and third, the future bodily resurrection of all in Christ (1 Cor 15:52). The first two will be discussed here and the third in 3.2 below.

3.1.1.1. Jesus' Resurrection as Historical Event. Romans 1:3-4 probably contains elements of an early creedal affirmation of the gospel. Jesus' identity as the *Son of God (which is contrasted with his earthly lineage of Son of David) is inextricably linked to his resurrection from the dead. While not easy to interpret precisely, it seems that the resurrection shows, or declares, Jesus to be God's Son, who is also the promised Messiah and reigning Lord. Jesus' resurrection involves exaltation to the right hand of God. The unique identity of the risen Messiah means that his resurrection is central to God's redemptive work. A significant example is Romans 4:25, where Jesus "was raised for our justification" (NRSV). Similar examples of the saving power of Jesus' resurrection abound (Rom 5:10; 6:3-11; 1 Cor 15:3-4), without which faith is futile and sins remain unatoned for (1 Cor 15:14, 17).

3.1.1.2. Baptism, Death, and Resurrection to New Life. Within Paul's eschatological framework of overlapping ages, those in Christ have already experienced a *past* resurrection to new life in the present. Typically, this idea is pictured through the image of being baptized into Christ Jesus and his death, and subsequently raised to new life (Rom 6:3-4; Col 2:12). Believers have already "died to sin" (Rom 6:2). United to Christ in death, their old self has been crucified (Rom 6:5-6; see Gal 2:19; 6:14), setting them free from sin and its enslaving power (Rom 6:6-7, 17-18; 7:6). In Colossians, like Romans, those in Christ have moved from being dead in their sins to being "raised with Christ" (Col 3:1); they are now forgiven and liberated from any condemnation (Col 2:14; Rom 8:1-2). This past event is also explicit in Ephesians 2:6, though linked there to exaltation with Christ rather than *baptism into his death.

3.1.1.3. Death and Resurrection in 1 Corinthians 15. First Corinthians 15 is by far the most sustained discussion of the resurrection in the Pauline corpus. The influential argument that the underlying problem is a Greek dichotomy between *body (*sōma*) and soul (*psychē*) or spirit (*pneuma*), leading to an overrealized eschatology in which both the body and the resurrection (1 Cor 15:12) were denigrated by the Corinthians (e.g., Lampe), has increasingly been questioned (R. B. Hays). Regardless of precise cause, the apostle's response is to affirm, in Jewish terms, a somatic unity based on the gospel of a crucified and resurrected Messiah who appeared to witnesses (1 Cor 15:3-7). His resurrection is likened to the firstfruits of a crop, with the full harvest (the resurrection of all in Christ) assuredly to follow (1 Cor 15:20, 23). The past event is affirmed ("in fact Christ has been raised from the dead" [1 Cor 15:20 NRSV]) and forms a pattern for future resurrection and the final defeat of death (1 Cor 15:26, 56-57).

The death of Christ has major eschatological significance in this chapter and elsewhere in Paul. Death is not merely the cessation of physical life; it connotes spiritual separation from God and results from sin (Rom 5:17, 21; 6:16; 7:9-14; 8:10; Eph 2:1-3; Col 1:21). Death has destructive power and is not, as sometimes portrayed in some Christian circles, a friend to be welcomed but "the last enemy" to be overcome (1 Cor 15:26; see 1 Cor 15:54-57). God's defeat of this potent enemy *has already happened* in the death and resurrection of Jesus. Those who are asleep in Christ (a frequent Pauline term for believers who have died) will be raised because the crucified Christ has returned from the dead (1 Cor 15:17-19). This evokes a decisive apocalyptic confrontation between God and the powers of sin and death, played out at Calvary and the resurrection.

3.1.2. New Life in the Spirit. In Jewish thought the outpouring of the Spirit of God was to be a sign of the dawning of God's promised new age. Paul integrates this expectation within his messianic eschatology; the new creation has arrived (Rom 6:4; 1 Cor 5:7; 2 Cor 5:17; Gal 6:16; Eph 2:15; 4:24; Col 3:10), and it is the Spirit who bestows new life to both Jews and Gentiles through faith in Christ, thus fulfilling God's promise to Abraham (Gal 3:14). Repeatedly this is depicted as a decisive past event (Rom 8:1-2, 10; 2 Cor 3:6). The gift of the Spirit unites believers within the *body of Christ (1 Cor 12:13). Romans 5:1-11 is a striking example: Paul's use of the first-person plural likely indicates he is including himself in every believer's experience of transitioning from being unreconciled enemies under God's *wrath to justified and reconciled recipients of the Spirit, through whom "God's love has been poured into our hearts through the *Holy Spirit" (Rom 5:5 NRSV).

Various eschatological images for the Spirit appear in an unsystematic and often overlapping way within the Pauline corpus. In Romans 8:23 the Spirit is described as the firstfruits (*aparchē*), echoing the same language used of Jesus' resurrection. The image conveys how the already experienced gift of the Spirit is the basis for the future hope of completed *adoption and bodily redemption. Just a few verses earlier, adoption is described as already having happened through the Spirit (Rom 8:15), an idea reiterated elsewhere in Paul (Rom 9:4; Gal 4:5; Eph 1:5). Yet it clearly still has a future component consistent with Paul's overall inaugurated eschatological framework.

Elsewhere, the Spirit is an *arrabōn* (guarantee) of God (2 Cor 1:22; 5:5; Eph 1:14). The image is financial and its meaning unambiguous—believers are encouraged to look back at what God has already done in the gift of his Spirit as a basis that they belong to God. The verb *sphragizō* (to seal) in 2 Corinthians 1:22 makes this point explicit. Those with the Spirit can therefore be assured of future eschatological blessing; the full payment will definitely follow the down payment.

One of the most significant eschatological pictures of how the new age of the Spirit has already arrived with the Christ event is Paul's contrast of the Spirit versus the flesh (*sarx*), primarily in Romans 7–8 and Galatians 5–6 (see also Phil 3:3). The weight of contemporary scholarship has moved away from older interpretations that tended to assume an introspective Pauline anthropology of two inner natures continually at war within the believer to viewing the apostle as setting up a duality between two opposing ages or realms (Fee; Turner; Gombis; B. W. Longenecker; Mitchel 2013). This "inner conflict" view is incompatible with how the flesh is described in overwhelmingly negative terms, opposed to life within the *kingdom of God (Gal 5:19-21) and a way of life that leads to destruction (Gal 6:8; Rom 8:13).

3.1.3. Adam/Christ. Another Pauline dualism, set within an eschatological framework that bases future hope on what has already happened, is that of *Adam and Christ (Rom 5:12-21; 1 Cor 15:20-21, 44-45). In 1 Corinthians 15 the apostle compares and contrasts Adam and Jesus Christ as corporate human figures, the former representing death, the latter life/resurrection (1 Cor 15:20-21). In light of Jesus' resurrection, those "*in Christ" will be raised to life, but those "in Adam" remain in death. A related but different point is being made in 1 Corinthians 15:45-49, which look backwards to Adam and Christ's origins—one of dust, the other of heaven. Again the image is of corporate identity, but the application is more on the unbridgeable gulf between the preresurrection body ("the image of the man of dust") and the resurrection body to come ("the image of the man of heaven").

3.2. Messianic Eschatology: Future. Paul's understanding of the future appears to be a creative fusion of Jewish eschatology and high Christology, the former being reworked in light of the latter. How this process unfolded, and what influences were most significant, are matters of continuing academic debate, but what should not be missed is how utterly remarkable and unparalleled these developments were.

3.2.1. The Day of the Lord. Within the OT, the day of YHWH developed a dual significance as a time of Israel's deliverance, blessing, and salvation from her enemies as well as a time of fearsome *judgment—a "great and terrible day of the LORD" (e.g., Joel 2:31; Mal 4:5 NRSV) associated with words such as *destruction*, *wrath*, *darkness*, and *woe*. The theme is found in Jewish pseudepigraphal writings such as 1 Enoch, 4 Ezra, and 2 Baruch, as well as in some Qumran documents (1QM and 1QS; Kreitzer). The apostle adapts and builds on the OT prophetic theme of the day of the Lord (*yôm yəhwâ*) in light of the Christ-event, effectively reimagining it as "the day of the Lord Jesus Christ" when Jesus enacts judgment on God's behalf (1 Cor 1:8; Phil 1:10). The christological implications of this remarkable shift are significant.

Within the Pauline corpus a variety of phrases and ideas are used to refer to the eschatological day of the Lord Jesus Christ. *Yôm yəhwâ* appears three times (1 Thess 5:2; 2 Thess 2:2; 1 Cor 5:5), "day of Christ Jesus" once (Phil 1:6), "day of Christ" twice (Phil 1:10; 2:16), "day of the Lord Jesus" twice (1 Cor 1:8; 2 Cor 1:14), "the day" twice (1 Thess 5:4; 1 Cor 3:13), and "that day" three times (2 Tim 1:12, 18; 4:8). Assumed in such language is Paul's pervasive reference to Jesus as the risen Lord (*kyrios*) with the associated christological implications of such terminology (Hurtado 2015). Alongside this explicitly messianic eschatology there are references to the day of God's judgment. Romans mentions the "day of wrath" (Rom 2:5), and Ephesians includes reference to "the day of redemption" (Eph 4:30) and "that evil day" (Eph 6:13).

3.2.2. The Parousia of Jesus Christ. Related terms occur frequently in Paul to refer to the future appearance of Jesus Christ, with several drawing on OT apocalyptic imagery to talk of his descent from heaven to earth (e.g., 1 Thess 1:9-10; 4:13–5:11; Kreitzer). *Parousia* (coming) is significant (1 Cor 15:23; 1 Thess 2:19; 3:13; 4:14; 5:23; 2 Thess 2:1, 8-9). The *apokalypsis* (revelation) of Jesus is used with a similar meaning twice (1 Cor 1:7; 2 Thess 1:7). In the Pastoral Epistles quite different language appears; *epiphaneia* (appearance) is used in 1 Timothy 6:14; 2 Timothy 1:10; 4:1, 8; and Titus 2:3, while the verb *epiphainō* (to appear) occurs in Titus 2:11; 3:4. Within context, each of these terms relates primarily to the future manifestation of the Lord Jesus Christ. Other verbs with parallel meanings include *erchomai* (come) in 1 Corinthians 4:5; 11:26 and 2 Thessalonians 2:10; *apokalyptō* (reveal) in 2 Thessalonians 1:7; *phaneroō* (make manifest) twice (1 Cor 4:5; Col 3:4; and in 2 Cor 5:10 it is believers who must appear before the judgment seat of Christ); *telos* (end) four times in the Corinthian letters (1 Cor 1:8; 10:11; 15:24; 2 Cor 1:13); *ta telē tōn aiōnōn* (the ends of the ages, 1 Cor 10:11); and *to teleion* (the complete) in 1 Corinthians 13:10 (see 3.3.1.1 below).

A text that makes a unique contribution to Paul's future-oriented messianic eschatology is 1 Corinthians 16:22, which finishes with the invocation in Aramaic *maranatha* (Our Lord, come!). Its appearance in a letter to a Greek-speaking church indicates that Jesus was recognized as Lord (*mar*) very early within Palestinian Christianity and that expectation of his return was well established. Most scholars take it as a form of *prayer looking forward to the parousia of the Lord. How imminent that expectation was has long been a matter of dispute, which raises to the question of whether Paul was mistaken or significantly adapted his thinking in light of an unexpected delay to Christ's parousia.

Frey comments that an older scholarly consensus, that a supposed crisis caused by the delay of the parousia was a critical factor in the evolution of early Christian theology, has largely been abandoned (Frey 2011; see Kreitzer for a survey). The reason, he suggests, lies in how, while there may have been disappointment that the first generation of disciples died before Christ's return (Jn 21:22-23), the early Christian communities were able to cope with a delayed parousia since their *identity did not rest on an imminent consummation of the age but on broader eschatological themes such as their tangible experience of the Spirit, the fulfillment of biblical promises in Christ, and Jesus' exaltation as the risen Lord. Like other apocalyptic movements of the past such as Qumran (see 1QpHab VII, 3-14), or those in today's world, Frey argues the first Christians had various strategies available to rationalize a supposed delay: it was due to the work of evil powers (see 2 Thess 2:7); they could acknowledge that their previous expectations were in need of correction in light of God's superiority over time (see 2 Pet 3:8); or they could see the "delay" as an opportunity for mission (2 Pet 3:9; Mk 13:10; Acts 1:8). This sort of theological reimagining meant that any delay of the parousia did not in itself lead to a crisis of core convictions and thus the problem of a supposed delay has been overestimated. Whether one accepts Frey's language of "strategies" or not, his point has weight. Arriving at a similar conclusion by a different route, Wright contends that there is no hint in the NT of Paul and the first Christians wrestling with the failure of their eschatological hopes; they lived in the tension of an already inaugurated eschatology that had not yet come to fulfillment (Wright 2019).

This discussion links to two further issues: whether Paul, to put it bluntly, was mistaken and died disappointed that the parousia did not occur within his lifetime; and the question of development within the apostle's eschatology. On whether Paul was mistaken, Frey is dogmatic: "interpreters cannot deny the fact that at least Paul had expected to see the coming of Christ within his lifetime (*cf.* 1 Thess 4:15, 17; 1 Cor 15:52)" (Frey 2011, 5). Wright specifically rejects Frey's conclusions (Wright 2019). Similarly, Craig Blomberg argues that a text such as 1 Thessalonians 4:15 cannot support such a conclusion; at best it shows Paul thought he might live to see the parousia, but nothing suggests he was convinced it had to happen in his lifetime (Blomberg 2019). A typically independent position is taken by James Dunn, who, contra Wright, doubts that such "now and not yet" eschatologies can account for the "failure" of an imminent unfolding of final events (Dunn 2003). He suggests that within Jewish prophetic/apocalyptic tradition there was some recognition that partial fulfillment of hope did not invalidate that hope. Hope by definition is indeterminate and often "mistaken" because it looks forward into an unknowable future. More significantly, Jewish hope is centered not on hope itself, or on a timetable of events, but in *God*. Thus, Dunn speculates whether the indeterminate nature of Jewish hope, shaped by image and symbol, is one reason why the supposed delay of the parousia was not a major issue for the early Christians (see C. M. Hays et al. for wider discussion).

The question of development within Paul's eschatology has been long debated and revolves around whether there was a process of de-eschatologization of the Christian hope in Paul from an imminent parousia (particularly in the Thessalonian letters) to a more spiritualized and individual hope in the form of the believer's union with Christ (e.g., 2 Cor 5:1-10; 10–13; Phil 1:21-23). Theories abound, but Dunn's assessment is probably one of the most fair-minded and realistic (Dunn 1998). Proposals of significant eschatological development tend to overplay multiple factors: the significance of 1 and 2 Thessalonians, how relatively little is said about the parousia in subsequent letters, and an assumption of linear development in the apostle's thinking that overlooks the very different circumstances that stimulated his various epistles. The apostle's eschatology is fragmented and uncorrelated, yet has a consistency throughout the undisputed letters. Even in Colossians, the last of his letters, the expectation of Christ's return is "as calm and as confident as ever" (Dunn 1998, 313; see Col 3:4; cf. Dunn 2003). To this Frey adds social-dynamic factors that also call into question the notion that a supposed delay of the parousia can be explained as a linear development or can somehow be used as a scale for dating early Christian writings (Frey 2011).

3.2.3. Wrath and Judgment. Few topics within Pauline eschatology are as controversial as that of wrath and judgment. Wrath (*orgē*) is mentioned frequently within the Pauline corpus, nearly always belonging to God, with Romans being the most significant (Rom 1:18; 2:5, 8; 3:5; 4:15; 5:9; 9:22; 12:19; 13:4-5) but not isolated example (see Eph 2:3; 5:6; Col 3:6; 1 Thess 1:10; 2:16; 5:9). Wrath is often linked with phrases connected with *krinō* (judge; e.g., Rom 2:3, 16; 3:6-7; 1 Cor 11:32; 2 Thess 2:12; 2 Tim 4:1). Divine anger (*thymos*) appears alongside *orgē* once (Rom 2:8). C. H. Dodd famously attempted to depersonalize the wrath of God as a cause-and-effect process. While this is certainly a strand of Pauline thought, Dodd's thesis does not do justice to the apostle's complex perspective—or that of the Bible in general (Travis).

The apostle is characteristically Jewish in his conviction that history is moving toward the final victory of God, when "the present evil age" (Gal 1:4 NRSV) will come to a climactic close and when all men and women will be held accountable before God. In Romans this is taken as self-evident fact within which at least four fundamental truths apply: humans are morally accountable for their actions; God will "repay according to each one's deeds" (Rom 2:6 NRSV; see 2 Cor 5:10; Col 3:25; 2 Tim 4:14); God is an impartial judge (Rom 2:11) whose wrath is just (Rom 3:5-6); and believers were dead but now have been made alive in Christ and will be saved from God's wrath (e.g., Rom 5:1-12; Eph 2:1-7). Within his inaugurated eschatology, the apostle can say that God's wrath is already in the process of being revealed "now" (Rom 1:18) and will be fully revealed in the future.

Where Paul is innovative is how, within his messianic eschatology, divine judgment is inextricably connected with the day of the Lord (see 3.2.1), the parousia (see 3.2.2) and the resurrection of the dead (see 3.2.4), when Jesus will return as judge to enact the wrath of God. As with other themes, the picture is not systematic, with examples scattered throughout his letters. In 1 Thessalonians 3:13, Paul prays they may be "blameless before our God and Father" at the parousia of the Lord Jesus (NRSV). In Romans 2:16 God will judge all people's secrets "through Jesus Christ" on "the day." In 1 Corinthians 4:5 it is the Lord who "will bring to light" that which is currently hidden (NRSV). The God/Christ relationship in judgment even becomes interchangeable in Paul's double reference to the "judgment seat" (*bēma*; Rom 14:10; 2 Cor 5:10) before which everyone must stand. In Romans it is God's judgment seat; in 2 Corinthians it is Christ's. Christ's judgment is the judgment of God.

3.2.3.1. Judgment of Those in Christ. Eschatologically speaking, in some way the right of judgment will be extended to the saints who will judge the world and even angels (1 Cor 6:2-3). None of this, however, means that God's people will be exempt from judgment (2 Cor 5:10; see Rom 2:16). There is an eschatological tension here: while there is no condemnation for those "in Christ" (Rom 8:1), all believers will appear before the judgment seat of Christ to account for their lives. This is made most explicit in 1 Corinthians 3:11-15, where the quality of a believer's life built on the foundation of Jesus Christ will be revealed by purifying fires on "the day."

How this tension is understood is a topic of ongoing debate, with multiple scholars highlighting how participation in Christ leads not only to acquittal but to transformation within the community of the Spirit: for example, Michael Gorman (2009, theosis); Craig Keener (a renewed mind); Frank Matera (transformative *grace) and John Barclay (grace requires the obedience of faith); Constantine Campbell (union); Michael Thate, Kevin Vanhoozer, and Constantine Campbell (in Christ); James Thompson (2014, community conformity); Grant Macaskill (union). This list could be extended, the point being that the last judgment will reveal that those in Christ are already in right relationship with God through God's grace and empowered by God's Spirit. There are hints in Paul that believers will be rewarded according to "what has been done in the body, whether good or evil" (2 Cor 5:10 NRSV; see 1 Cor 3:10-15), but what this means is left unexplained. Levels of reward within the future new creation would seem difficult to square with divine grace and the gift of being in Christ's presence (Thiselton 2012). Blomberg is probably right in suggesting the rewards may be God's praise on judgment day (1 Cor 4:5) rather than throughout eternity, but Paul says too little for anyone to be dogmatic on this point (Blomberg 2018).

3.2.3.2. Judgment of the Powers. The stark eschatological duality between two opposing ages within Paul's thought provides the framework for interpreting what he says about judgment of those outside Christ or actively opposed to God. Behind the scenes, malign spiritual powers perpetrate chaos in the world and within humanity. The rehabilitation of eschatology within NT studies (Mitchel 2019), and the more recent "apocalyptic turn" (see 4.2 below), has brought renewed attention to this aspect of Paul's thought. *Satan is referred to relatively frequently in the Pauline corpus (Rom 16:20; 1 Cor 5:5; 7:5; 2 Cor 2:11; 11:14; 12:7; 1 Thess 2:18; 1 Tim 5:15) and as "the tempter" once (1 Thess 3:5). The "devil" (*diabolos*) appears occasionally in the disputed letters (Eph 4:27; 6:11; 1 Tim 3:6-7; 2 Tim 2:26). The destructive power as the "god of this world" to blind "the minds of the unbelievers" is acknowledged in 2 Corinthians 4:4 (NRSV). Ephesians 2:2 ascribes to him the title "ruler of the power of the air" (NRSV).

Active alongside Satan are a spectrum of heavenly powers hostile to God and his people (Rom 8:38-39; 1 Cor 2:6-9; 3:22; 15:24; Col 1:16; 2:15; Eph 1:20-21; 3:10; 6:12). The most common descriptions are "rulers and authorities" (*archai* and *exousiai*), but a remarkable variety are named in passing within Paul's contextual pastoral theology, including angels, powers (*dynameis*), death (*thanatos*), cosmic powers (*kosmokratores*)—which Bruce Longenecker (2016) calls "cosmos grabbers" seeking to wrestle creation away from God—dominions (*kyriotētes*), and spiritual forces (*pneumatika*). In Romans 8:38 the term *powers* frames a spiritual battle between God and destructive forces including angels and *demons. In Colossians 1 thrones and dominions, existing alongside rulers and power, suggest a hierarchy of heavenly forces with thrones at the top. From this evidence Dunn contends that Paul believed, not unusually, in several heavens, with the lower heavens populated by malign powers blocking access to the higher heavens (Dunn 1998). This clarifies somewhat Paul's intriguing reference to a spiritual journey to "the third heaven" or paradise (2 Cor 12:1-4).

Another significant term for malevolent heavenly powers is "elemental spirits" (*stoicheia*) of the world (Gal 4:3, 9; Col 2:8, 20), which enslave and captivate believers, perverting God's agenda for communities of love and unity into discordant relationships of injustice and self-interest (Longenecker 2016). To this catalogue of suprahuman cosmic forces can be added the destructive powers of sin, death, and the flesh.

A unique addition to this gallery of opponents is the "lawless one" in 2 Thessalonians 2:1-12. While his identity is opaque, and he never reappears in Paul's later letters, familiar themes of eschatological conflict are present: a power directly opposed to God, allied to Satan (2 Thess 2:9), and who draws people away from God.

However apparently intimidating these enemies are, for Paul there is no contest when it comes to God's judgment. His consistent pastoral message is that those in Christ should not fear the powers. In Colossians the rulers and authorities have *already* been disarmed, shamed, and vanquished by the cross (Col 2:14-15). In Romans nothing—including death, angels, demons, rulers, or powers—has the capacity to separate believers from the love of God in Christ the Lord (Rom 8:38-39). God will judge and defeat Satan and all forces allied with him (Rom 16:20). The *man of lawlessness will be annihilated by the parousia of the Lord Jesus (2 Thess 2:8). In 1 Corinthians, when the end comes, Christ will destroy every rule and authority and power (see Phil 2:9-11). All enemies will be vanquished including, in Paul's eschatology, the ultimate opponents of death (1 Cor 15:26, 54) and sin (1 Cor 15:56). Ultimately, God will be "all in all" (1 Cor 15:28).

Paul's negative analysis of the powers and the *kosmos* (see 3.1 above) leads to his conclusion that all who belong to its realm will "perish" (*apollyō*, "to destroy": Rom 2:12; 1 Cor 1:18; 2 Cor 2:15; 4:3; 2 Thess 2:10) and will be brought "to nothing" (*katargeō*, "to end": Rom 6:6; 1 Cor 1:28; 2:6; 15:24, 26; 2 Thess 2:8). Such people will not inherit the kingdom (1 Cor 6:9-10; 15:50; Gal 5:21; Eph 5:5), in contrast to those who will (Rom 14:7; Col 1:13; 4:11; 1 Thess 1:5; 2:12; 2 Tim 4:18). What this means precisely continues to be much debated, with exegetical study of Pauline texts being utilized within wider systematic and philosophical discussion concerning eternal conscious punishment, conditionalism, and *universalism (e.g., see Travis; Date, Stump, and Anderson; Kinghorn).

3.2.4. Death and Bodily Resurrection. The focus here is on Paul's somatic eschatology—what he says about the fate of the body after death. There are several contrasts at play, particularly between the life in present body compared to resurrection body to come. First, as discussed above (see 3.1.1), the model and basis of future bodily resurrection of those in Christ is his past resurrection (Rom 8:11; 1 Cor 15:22; Phil 3:10-11; Col 3:4). Second, while death of the body within the present age is inevitable, Paul views it as a transformation from one form of existence to another (2 Cor 4:14; 5:6-8). Death leads somehow to being with Christ. Paul typically uses the metaphor of "sleep" (1 Cor 7:39; 11:30; 15:6, 18, 20, 51; 1 Thess 4:13-15; 5:10), indicating its temporary nature. Scholars disagree on how far this metaphor can be pressed regarding a conscious intermediate state with Christ between death and resurrection (e.g., Wright 2008 "for" and Middleton "against") but are generally agreed that it is not theologically significant.

Third, at the parousia, all in Christ, whether awake (living) or asleep (already dead), will, by God's power, experience an eschatological transformation (1 Cor 15:51-52; see Phil 3:21; 1 Thess 4:13-18) from a "natural body" (*sōma psychikon*) to a "spiritual body" (*sōma pneumatikon*; 1 Cor 15:44). Fourth, in some mysterious way the resurrected body stands in both continuity and discontinuity with the mortal body of flesh and blood (1 Cor 15:51). Eschatological contrasts pepper 1 Corinthians 15's somatic imagery: heavenly/earthly, dishonor/*glory, weakness/power, image of the man of dust (Adam)/image of the man of heaven (Christ), perishable/imperishable, mortality/immortality, death/life. Fifth, these contrasts are alien to Greek dualism of a soul escaping its bodily prison; the picture is of a bodily resurrection in line with Jewish thinking that humans are a unified whole. Paul's overriding concern is to emphasize that the resurrection body is incorruptible, somehow fitted for the age to come, beyond the power of sin and death.

3.2.5. Creation Liberated. Paul's holistic somatic anthropology prevents his eschatology of the new creation from lapsing into a dualistic split between creation and salvation. Or, put more positively, the apostle exudes a confidence that individuals in Christ are already participants in the new creation, which began with the cross (2 Cor 5:17; Gal 6:14-15). In light of what God has done in Christ, personal eschatology is intrinsically bound up within the cosmic reconciliation of all things. This is particularly clear in Colossians 1, with personal salvation (Col 1:1-14) set within the broader sweep of cosmic reconciliation (Col 1:15-20) of *ta panta* (all things), "whether on earth or in heaven" (Col 1:20 NRSV). A similar pattern is visible in Ephesians 1:1-9. Within the apostle's undisputed writings, Romans 8 contains the same dynamic, where Romans 8:19-23, on the liberation of creation "from its bondage to decay" (Rom 8:21 NRSV), appears within Paul's pastoral and theological encouragements to Christians in Rome. Personal and cosmic eschatologies are inseparable (Rom 8:19). The most explicit is Romans 8:21-23, where parallels are drawn between Romans 8:22, where creation is groaning (*systenazō*, to groan) "in labor pains" (itself an apocalyptic image; Kreitzer), and how, in Romans 8:23, believers who have the Spirit also "groan inwardly" as they await their future bodily redemption.

3.3. Messianic Eschatology: Present. Paul's apostolic teaching to young Christian communities under his care represents a comprehensive, if unsystematic and contingent, educative program developed over the fifteen years or so of his letter-writing career to convert his readers' imaginations to think eschatologically about the future in order to live faithfully in the present (R. B. Hays). He does this through eschatological double vision—looking back at Christ's first coming while simultaneously looking forward to his parousia.

3.3.1. Life Within the Eschatological Community of the Spirit. Section 3.1.2 above discussed the gift of the Spirit as evidence that God's new eschatological age had already arrived. For Paul, the Christian life in the present is therefore a thoroughly eschatological enterprise. The apostle's overwhelming concern for believers under his care is for their moral transformation in the present (Thompson 2011; 2014), a goal only made possible through the "empowering presence" of the Holy Spirit (Fee). This calling, for Paul, is relentlessly corporate. Common Pauline words such as *hagioi* (saints) and *ekklēsia* (assembly or church, used in the LXX as a translation of the Hebrew *qāhāl*), *adelphoi* (brothers, a family image inclusive of gender, so "brothers and sisters," NRSV), along with *laos* (a people; 2 Cor 6:16; Titus 2:14) and temple (*naos*; 1 Cor 3:16; 2 Cor 6:16; Eph 2:21; see Eskola's argument below in 4.1), populate the Pauline corpus, together conveying a theology of a set-apart community, embodying the values of a distinct body politic formed by the Spirit (1 Cor 12:13) belonging to Christ the risen Lord and reflecting his character (Phil 2:1-15).

For Paul, life in the overlap of the ages poses moral choices to believers in the present if they are to live lives worthy (*axiōs*) of their new calling (Eph 4:1; Phil 1:27; Col 1:10; 1 Thess 2:12; 2 Thess 1:11). This Pauline emphasis has been summarized as "Be who you already are." One of his most common metaphors in this regard is that believers are "to walk" (*peripateō*, often masked in modern translations) according to the age to which they now belong, rather than to the old age (Rom 6:4; 13:13; 2 Cor 5:7; Eph 2:2; 4:17; 5:8, 15; Col 2:6; 3:5-7). In Romans eschatological exhortation revolves around two distinct groups of people: one living *kata sarka* (according the flesh), the other living *kata pneuma* (according to the Spirit). The overarching issue here is power. The law is not sinful (Rom 7:7); the problem is its powerlessness to overcome sin and produce life because it belongs to the old age. Only those in Christ who live by the Spirit fulfill the law and have overcome the destructive powers of death, flesh, and sin. The apostle's warnings not to return to life of the old age are clearly not hypothetical (Rom 8:12-13; Gal 5:13, 26; 6:8), indicating that those in Christ must engage actively with life in the Spirit (Turner). This is why the tone of Galatians is so confrontational. The issue at stake is a false gospel (Gal 1:6-7) that is luring Gentile believers to reject the Spirit and "go back" under the power of the flesh (Gal 3:3).

How spiritual transformation happens within the life of the believer has been a relatively neglected area of Pauline studies. Three scholars in particular have further explored this area with significant monographs: Volker Rabens on the relational and transformative work of the Spirit, Keener on Paul's approach to the transformation of the mind, and Sarah Harding on Paul's eschatological anthropology and the dynamics of human transformation. Key to the discussion is Paul's theology of destructive passions (*pathēmata*; Rom 7:5; Gal 5:24) and desires (*epithymiais*; Rom 1:24; 6:12; 7:7-8; 13:4; Gal 5:16, 24; Eph 2:3; 4:22; Col 3:5; 1 Thess 4:5; 1 Tim 6:9; 2 Tim 2:22; 3:6; 4:3; Titus 2:12; 3:3) that belong to the old age. For the apostle, the only way not to gratify such desires is to walk by the Spirit (Gal 5:16; see Gal 5:18, 25). Such walking will lead to a community characterized by the *fruit of the Spirit (Gal 5:22-23; see Rom 8:6). Keener shows how a similar eschatological dynamic is at work in Romans 12:1-2 (a renewed mind enabled to discern right choices in the present from the perspective of the age to come); 1 Corinthians 2:15-16 (the mind of Christ versus human judgments); Philippians 2:1-5 (a Christlike mind versus acting in selfish ambition); and Colossians 3:1-2 (minds set on things above rather than things on earth; see Phil 3:19-20).

3.3.1.1. Agapē *and the Charismata.* Paul uses *to teleion* in 1 Corinthians 13:10 to describe the eschatological climax of when "the *complete" arrives, in contrast to the present imperfect world. Within context, "the complete" is inextricably linked to love (*agapē*), which, unlike spiritual *gifts, is a permanent feature of the future age. Views differ on how love is greater than faith and hope (1 Cor 13:13), but a point to note is that Paul's vision of the future age is profoundly relational. Love will flourish to its fullest unimaginable extent, and all that opposes it now (1 Cor 13:4-6) will cease to exist. God's people finally will be perfected to see God "face to face" (1 Cor 13:12). Love in the present is therefore an eschatological foretaste of God's people's future destiny in the presence of their God. This is why, in the next verse, Paul exhorts the Corinthians to "pursue love" (1 Cor 14:1) and later encourages them, "Let all that you do be done in love" (1 Cor 16:14 NRSV).

3.3.1.2. Sex and the Body. Paul's teaching on sexual ethics and the body within 1 Corinthians is also eschatologically framed. In 1 Corinthians 5 the incestuous man is like leaven that contaminates the whole batch of dough and is therefore to be excluded, left to face the destructive power of Satan in the hope of his salvation on the day of the Lord (1 Cor 5:5).

Beliefs about the future similarly shape the apostle's teaching on not using the body for sexual immorality (1 Cor 6:12-20) and on *marriage and *singleness in 1 Corinthians 7:6-40. The latter is a complex passage, but however interpreted, Paul's advice is obviously shaped by his expectation of Jesus' parousia. Because of the "impending crisis" (1 Cor 7:26 NRSV), and since "the appointed time has grown short" (1 Cor 7:29 NRSV) and "the present form of this world is passing away" (1 Cor 7:31 NRSV), those unmarried, widowed, married, and betrothed (as well as *slaves) are best to keep their current status unchanged and focus on "the affairs of the Lord" rather than "affairs of the world" (1 Cor 7:34 NRSV). How Paul's eschatological perspective on sex relates to contemporary revolutions around same-sex marriage, gender, queer theology, and identity will undoubtedly be an ongoing area of development in Pauline theology. While not designed to address such issues, Cynthia Long Westfall's *Paul and Gender* (esp. chap. 5 on eschatology) provides a significant exegetical and theological foundation.

Regarding the body itself, Paul's view holds an eschatological paradox in tension: gifted life by the Spirit, it will be resurrected, yet in the present it is like a clay jar (2 Cor 4:7) or a tent (2 Cor 5:4). The body is mortal (*thnētos*, Rom 6:12; 8:11; 1 Cor 15:43, 54; 2 Cor 4:11; 5:4), yet it will be "swallowed up by life" (2 Cor 5:4). The present mortal body is temporary; its true "home" is to be "with the Lord" (not in a Gnostic sense; Paul has the resurrection body in mind here—1 Cor 15:53; Phil 3:21). The ultimate calling of the believer is to please God "whether we are at home or away" (2 Cor 5:9 NRSV). So strong is this eschatological hope that Paul can describe physical decay as a "slight and momentary affliction," compared with inner renewal that leads to a future eternal glory (2 Cor 4:17-18 NRSV).

3.3.1.3. Suffering and Persecution. Paul's theology of the body is closely linked to his eschatological view of suffering and persecution, in which present afflictions are drastically relativized in comparison with future glory (Rom 8:17-18). For Paul, suffering is an integral part of life in the present prior to the final defeat of death and sin. Suffering is not a cause of shame; it can even be delighted in since it produces endurance, character, and hope (Rom 5:3-5; see 2 Cor 2:10; Col 1:24; 2 Tim 1:12). Violent opposition by powerful enemies will not have the last word because of hope in God's deliverance and resurrection power (2 Cor 1:1-10; Phil 1:28-30; 2 Thess 1:4-10). But even more remarkably, since through baptism believers are united with Christ in his death and resurrection (Rom 6:5; see 3.1.1.2 above), there is a strong eschatological sense within Paul that believers share in the death of Christ in the present. They suffer "with him" now so that they will be glorified "with him" (Rom 8:17). This eschatological tension is exemplified in 2 Corinthians 4:10, where Paul talks of "always carrying in the body the death of Jesus, so that the life of Jesus may also be made visible in our bodies" (NRSV).

3.3.1.4. Now Is the Day of Salvation. Numerous other examples of past-future eschatological double vision pervade Paul's teaching on life in the present. In 2 Corinthians 6:2, quoting Isaiah 49:8, he encourages the community to stay faithful since "now is the day of salvation." Their reception of God's grace (2 Cor 6:1) is, in effect, in itself an eschatological event fulfilling God's promise (Wolter). The Lord's Supper proclaims Christ's death until he comes (1 Cor 11:26). The return of the risen Lord as judge over all people and powers (see 3.2.3 above) provides one motive for living to please God in the present (Travis). Considerable debate has evolved in recent decades on how explicitly anti-imperial Paul's teaching is here (McKnight and Modica). Whatever conclusions are reached, it is clear that, for Paul, no loyalty to temporary powers, whether spiritual or political, should intrude in the present, whatever the cost. Good works in the present are also understood eschatologically as a basis of future judgment or harvest (Rom 2:6-7, 10; 2 Cor 5:10; Gal 6:10; Eph 6:8). Barclay's *Paul and the Gift* makes a significant contribution in arguing that while the divine gift is unconditioned, it is not unconditional: grace leads to the obedience of faith (Rom 1:5; 15:16-18; 16:26; see 1 Tim 2:7). Finally, turning to money, financial generosity is likened to sowing for a future reaping, motivated by thanksgiving for God's inexpressible gift in Christ (2 Cor 9:5-15).

3.3.2. Paul's Mission to the Gentiles and the Future of Israel. Often overlooked is how Paul interprets his own apostolic *mission in eschatological terms. He experiences a decisive rupture with his past identity (Phil 3:4-7; 1 Cor 15:8) and theology. Every area of the apostle's Jewish faith is drastically reimagined, including personally in terms of understanding his own calling. A good case can be made that Paul's self-understanding was rooted in his own experience of the "apocalypse" (revelation) of Jesus Christ on the Damascus road (Gal 1:11-12; R. N. Longenecker). If so, it is in light of that event that Paul does retrospective theology, now perceiving what was there in the previous narrative all the time but that had, until unveiled with the coming of

Christ, been a hidden *mystery known only to God (Rom 11:25; 16:25; 1 Cor 2:7; 4:1; Eph 1:9; 3:3-4, 9; 6:19; Col 1:26-27; 2:2; 4:3; 1 Tim 3:9, 16). His God-given commission to be an apostle to the Gentiles is therefore an eschatological event, marking a decisive and shocking new stage in God's redemptive purposes, fulfilling his promise to Abraham that all nations would be blessed through him (Rom 4:11-12; Gal 3:8, 14; Eph 3:6) and marking the end of the Mosaic covenant.

This perspective gives context to the apocalyptic imagery of 1 Corinthians 4:9, which envisions the apostles being displayed at the end of a great procession into the gladiatorial arena, condemned to die as an act of theater (*theatron*) before the *kosmos*, angels, and humanity. It is as if the apostles' appearance, and imminent execution, constitutes a final act on the stage of cosmic history (Dunn 2009). In Romans 11:13-15 (more below), the apostle understands his mission to the Gentiles in terms of a bigger eschatological canvas of provoking his own people to faith, leading to "life from the dead," a reference to the resurrection at the end of age when "out of Zion will come the Deliverer" (Rom 11:26 NRSV).

It is therefore not surprising that living by, and making known, the gospel of Jesus Christ becomes Paul's overriding passion, regardless of the cost (1 Cor 2:2; 4:9-13; 9:16-18; 15; 2 Cor 4:5-9; 6:3-10; 10:15-17; 11:21-33; Gal 5:11; Phil 3:8-10). However, it is important to note that, within Paul's missionary career, the Gentile mission was never detached from mission to Jews (Bird 2016). Practical and theological tensions arising from the inclusion of both Jews and Gentiles within the one body of Christ populate the Pauline corpus, with the apostle consistently seeking to build unity across boundaries. One of the most significant questions he faced was the place of Israel within the purposes of God now that the Gentiles had been "grafted in" to the original olive tree (Rom 9–11).

It is his own people's rejection of the climax of their story (Rom 9:4-5) that causes Paul personal anguish (Rom 9:2-3), and Romans 9–11 can be understood as the apostle seeking to resolve this tension theologically. How his argument works is complex and much disputed within modern scholarship (Das 2001; 2004; 2006; Hodge; Wright, 2013; Grindheim, critiquing Wright; Still). A minority of scholars see Paul as presenting a new path for Gentiles to be included within the people of God while Jews continue to be so through Torah observance. Jewish scholar Mark Nanos offers a nuanced version of this perspective. Others affirm that "nothing could be clearer" that Romans heralds one gospel for Jew and Gentile (Gorman 2016), leading to one multicultural new-covenant community of the church in which the weak (mainly Jews) and the *strong (mainly Gentiles) need to find room to tolerate and embrace one another (Rom 15:13-27; see McKnight).

However, if Israel is now reimagined as an eschatologically inclusive rather than an ethnically exclusive people, what then was God's purpose for ethnic Israel? Has the word of God failed? Paul's answer is an emphatic "No." Israel's unbelief is neither a failure of God's word (Rom 9:6) nor an unfair rejection of his people (Rom 11:1). Nor is the inclusion of the Gentiles a divine "plan B"; Paul sees ethnic Israel's rejection of its Messiah as part of God the potter's eternal promises (Rom 9:20-24). In the eschatological overlap of the ages, Gentiles, who had been "not my people" (Rom 9:25-26; see Hos 2:23, 1:10), are now included in "my people" (Israel). Historic Israel had stumbled in pursuing righteousness through the Torah (Rom 9:30–10:21) rather than through faith in Christ (Rom 10:4-13).

But this does not mean that "Israel" is now simply constituted of those who believe in Christ, as if the church replaces Israel. Paul still sees a crucial role for his people in God's unfolding eschatological plan (Rom 11:1-6). Jews, who have come to Christ by God's grace, form a remnant (Rom 11:5). Ironically, it is through the disbelief of the majority of Jews that salvation has come to the Gentiles (Rom 11:11-12, 30), who are branches grafted in to the olive tree (Rom 11:16-21). There is only one tree—Gentiles join Israel by God's kindness and have no basis for pride (Rom 11:18, 20-22). Paul reaches the climax of his argument with the eschatological "mystery" (Rom 11:25) that, due to the *mercy of God, the natural branches (his own people) will one day be grafted in again (Rom 11:23-25) and that when "the full number of the Gentiles has come in . . . all Israel will be saved" (Rom 11:25-26 NRSV). Opinion is divided, but it seems best to interpret "Israel" here as Paul's fellow Jews, the broken-off branches (Dunn 1998; Gorman 2016). The timing of this future event is unspecified, but it is most likely the parousia of Christ. To speculate, perhaps Paul had in mind his own experience; such a mass turning to Christ may depend on an encounter with the risen Lord.

4. The Origins of Pauline Eschatology, Narrative and Apocalyptic.

Much scholarly debate about Paul revolves around how eschatological themes within his writings relate to the thought world of the OT and Jewish *apocalypticism of the NT era. First-century Jewish apocalyptic texts such as 1 Enoch, 4 Ezra, and 2 Baruch are of particular relevance in that they represent the closest known parallels to Paul in terms of genre and sociopolitical context. Linked to this, proposals exploring the process by which Paul the Jew developed his multilayered messianic eschatology tend to wrestle with questions of where and how much the apostle reworks or innovates from the expectations of first-century Jewish messianism.

4.1. Narrative Eschatology. Various scholars reconstruct the development of a multilayered *narrative within Paul's mind in which eschatology plays a key role in fulfilling God's purposes for *Israel and the world (Wright 2013; 2018; Witherington; R. B. Hays; Eskola; Jipp; Bird 2016). While in broad agreement on many areas, not least that Paul operates within an inaugurated "now and not yet" eschatological framework, others are cautious of what they regard as overly ambitious attempts to press Paul's diverse writings into an overarching narrative (e.g., Dunn 2009; Das 2016).

N. T. Wright's inaugurated eschatology is articulated at length in his *Paul and the Faithfulness of God.* Integrating a strong emphasis on realized eschatology in the line of C. H. Dodd and George Caird with historical realism, Wright sees an essential storied coherence within diverse strands of NT eschatology. For Paul, hope both had been fulfilled through Jesus and would be fulfilled in his parousia. A consistent Wrightian theme is that the emphatically "earthy" nature of that future hope has social implications for the praxis of Christian ethics in the here and now. Wright places his inaugurated eschatology in critical dialogue with what he sees as popular Christianity's Platonized eschatology, where escaping to heaven is the goal of eschatological hope. Familiar opponents in Wright's eschatology are different forms of dualism—whether an Enlightenment split between past and present, an Epicurean separation of heaven and earth, or a dehistoricized Bultmannianism (Wright 2019). Critics such as Jörg Frey argue that Wright's grand narrative interpretation of Paul effectively neutralizes Paul's apocalypticism and distances the apostle from Jesus (Frey 2016).

For Joshua Jipp, Paul has come to understand Christ as the Davidic Messiah who shares in God's divine kingship and embodies the destiny of his people in his own person. This picture is a result of Paul taking over and transforming the scripts and motifs of ancient royal ideologies to invent a new royal ideology of Christ the king, the resurrected and enthroned ruler of the world. From this royal messianism it is but a short step to Paul's depiction of Jesus Christ as the Lord and *head over all things (Eph 1:2–2:10) and the identity of the *church as a political community under his authority and sharing his rule.

Building on the work of Wright and applying it to Paul and other NT authors, Timo Eskola takes a related but distinct tack to Jipp. His reconstruction has Jesus' self-understanding as that of a messianic vocation, the Suffering Servant sacrificing himself at the cross to effect the end of exile and reform Israel's *worship by building an eschatological *temple of renewed believers. Eskola sees this sort of restoration eschatology as permeating Paul's soteriology.

A fresh, highly regarded work from a trio of Catholic scholars explores the continuities and discontinuities between Paul and Judaism by viewing him as a new-covenant Jew whose Jewish apocalypticism has been redrawn in light of the revelation of God's Messiah. His resultant eschatology is christologically shaped. The *gospel revealed to Paul proclaims *Christ, who, through the cross, has fulfilled God's *covenant promises. The cross simultaneously is a redemptive *sacrifice that establishes the new covenant and is an apocalyptic revelation of divine *love. The *Lord's Supper is eschatological in that it is a new-covenant sacrifice representing the church's participation in the new *creation (Pitre, Barber, and Kincaid).

Michael Bird uses the notion, first suggested by John Barclay, of Paul as an "anomalous Jew" who does not fit within first-century Judaism precisely because his apocalyptic interpretation of the Messiah's death and resurrection forced him into a rereading of Jewish Scripture (Bird 2016; 2019). The result was a creative synthesis whereby "the story and symbols of Judaism were redrawn around Jesus the Messiah and his followers, who constituted the renewed Israel of an inaugurated eschaton" (Bird 2019, 189).

4.2. Apocalyptic Eschatology. More recently the development of a so-called apocalyptic perspective on Paul has sharply questioned the concept of a continuously unfolding narrative. At a literary level, apocalyptic is a particular type of literature (such as the book of Revelation), replete with dramatic symbolism, revealing transcendent realities in order to help readers (often facing persecution or *suffering of some sort) to interpret their present circumstances and live accordingly. However, building on the seminal work of Ernst Käsemann (1969), developed by J. Christiaan Beker (1980) and expanded further by J. Louis Martyn (1985), proponents of apocalyptic push beyond this narrow understanding through a hermeneutic that stresses the idea of an unexpected and *disruptive* divine revelation (*apokalypsis*) that explodes all previous frameworks (see Blackwell, Goodrich, and Maston for fuller discussion). The influence of Karl Barth is tangible here. The coming of Christ is the climactic event in a cosmic war between God and the forces of *Sin, *Law, Death, and the Devil (often capitalized as personalized powers) that enslave humanity (1 Cor 15). This is a spiritual conflict on a grand stage and has a very different theological feel from so-called old perspective soteriology, where the stress tends to be on *Abraham, *faith, and the individual's failure to keep the law of Moses. Significant names within a loose coalition of scholars include Beverly Gaventa, Martinus de Boer, Susan Eastmann, Philip Ziegler, and Douglas Campbell. Few have done more to build bridges between an academic apocalyptic perspective and Christian discipleship within the life and *witness of the church than Fleming Rutledge through her well-received books on the crucifixion (2017) and Advent (2018).

Douglas Campbell is probably the most radical in his fierce criticisms of what he calls "justification theory," characterized by the old perspective on Paul. The apostle's theology of *justification is not a logical progression from the "problem" of sin to the "solution" of salvation (plight to resolution) but results from God's intervention in Jesus Christ and can only be understood retrospectively in light of that divine irruption into human history (Campbell 2009; see Tilling for debate). Less iconoclastic than Campbell, and perhaps more influential in the long term as a result, is the work of Gaventa (2007; 2013).

Critics such as Wright are concerned that, taken to extremes, the apocalyptic perspective sets up a false dichotomy that so emphasizes discontinuity that it threatens to minimize major Pauline themes such as *atonement for sin, justification (particularly D. A. Campbell), and Paul's strong sense of a divine narrative reaching its climax in Israel's Messiah (Wright 2015; 2019). Wright argues for a both/and rather than a stark either-or choice, as do Bird (2016) and J. P. Davies.

5. Conclusion.

Pauline thought cannot be understood without appreciating how eschatology permeates every level of the apostle's experience, theology, and ethics. Paul's writings to early Christian believers about how to live in the present are framed by an eschatological double vision that simultaneously looks back to the Christ-event and forward to the end of God's redemptive action in the world. For these reasons, eschatology should, and no doubt will, continue to be at the forefront of Pauline studies. Eschatological imagery is by definition imprecise, and so no doubt academic theories and interpretative proposals of the origins and content of Paul's eschatology will continue to arise and be evaluated. His overriding concern for the authenticity of his Christian communities will point academics whose study is done in the service of the church in that ethical and pastoral direction. On a broader canvas, given major cultural and technological developments in the West and beyond, anthropological issues such as gender, *sexuality, the body, and identity are likely to be at the forefront of much academic eschatology. Finally, in a world riven by economic injustice, *violence, and totalitarian use of political power—coupled with an unfolding global environmental crisis—Paul's words about suffering, judgment, and future hope will continue to resonate powerfully with Christians, particularly within the developing world. Western academics will do well to listen to, and learn from, such voices.

See also Apocalyptic Paul; Corinthians, Second Letter to the; Flesh; Glory, Glorification; Holiness, Sanctification; Holy Spirit; In Christ; Israel; Judgment; Paul and Judaism; Resurrection; Salvation; Wrath, Destruction.

BIBLIOGRAPHY. **J. M. G. Barclay,** *Paul and the Gift* (Grand Rapids, MI: Eerdmans, 2015); **R. Bauckham and T. Hart,** *Hope Against Hope: Christian Eschatology in Contemporary Context* (London: Darton, Longman, & Todd, 1999); **J. C. Beker,** *Paul the Apostle: The Triumph of God in Life and Thought* (Philadelphia: Fortress, 1980); **M. J. Bird,** *Paul: An Anomalous Jew: Paul Among Jews, Greeks and Romans* (Grand Rapids, MI: Eerdmans, 2016); idem, "Paul, a Jew Among Jews, Greeks and Romans," in *The State of New Testament Studies: A Survey of Contemporary Research*, ed. S. McKnight and N. K. Gupta (Grand Rapids, MI: Baker Academic, 2019), 182-96; **B. C. Blackwell, J. K. Goodrich, and J. Maston,** eds., *Paul and the Apocalyptic Imagination* (Minneapolis: Fortress, 2016); **C. L. Blomberg,** *A New Testament Theology* (Waco, TX: Baylor University Press, 2018); **M. J. Borg,** *Convictions: How I Learned What Matters Most* (New York: HarperOne, 2014); **C. R. Campbell,** *Paul and Union with Christ: An Exegetical and Theological Study* (Grand

Rapids, MI: Zondervan, 2012); **D. A. Campbell,** *The Deliverance of God: An Apocalyptic Rereading of Justification in Paul* (Grand Rapids, MI: Eerdmans, 2009); **A. A. Das,** *Paul, the Law, and the Covenant* (Peabody, MA: Hendrickson, 2001); idem, *Paul and the Jews* (Peabody, MA: Hendrickson, 2004); idem, *Solving the Romans Debate* (Minneapolis: Fortress, 2006); idem, *Paul and the Stories of Israel: Grand Thematic Narratives in Galatians* (Minneapolis: Fortress, 2016); **C. Date, G. Stump, and J. Anderson,** eds., *Rethinking Hell: Readings in Evangelical Conditionalism* (Eugene, OR: Cascade, 2014); **J. P. Davies,** "What to Expect When You're Expecting: Maternity, Salvation History, and the 'Apocalyptic Paul,'" *JSNT* 38 (2016): 301-15; **J. D. G. Dunn,** *The Theology of Paul the Apostle* (Grand Rapids, MI: Eerdmans, 1998); idem, *Jesus Remembered*, CIM 1 (Grand Rapids, MI: Eerdmans, 2003); idem, *Beginning in Jerusalem*, CIM 2 (Grand Rapids, MI: Eerdmans, 2009); **T. Eskola,** *A Narrative Theology of the New Testament: Exploring the Metanarrative of Exile and Restoration*, WUNT 350 (Tübingen: Mohr Siebeck, 2015); **G. D. Fee,** *God's Empowering Presence: The Holy Spirit in the Letters of Paul* (Grand Rapids, MI: Baker Academic, 1994); **J. Frey,** "New Testament Eschatology—an Introduction: Classical Issues, Disputed Themes, and Current Perspectives," in *Eschatology of the New Testament and Some Related Documents*, ed. J. G. van der Watt, WUNT 2/315 (Tübingen: Mohr Siebeck, 2011), 3-32; idem, "Demythologizing Apocalyptic? On N. T. Wright's Paul, Apocalyptic Interpretation, and the Constraints of Construction," in *God and the Faithfulness of Paul: A Critical Examination of the Pauline Theology of N. T. Wright*, ed. C. Heilig, J. T. Hewitt, and M. F. Bird, WUNT 2/413 (Tübingen: Mohr Siebeck, 2016), 489-532; **B. R. Gaventa,** *Our Mother Saint Paul* (Louisville, KY: Westminster John Knox, 2007); idem, ed., *Apocalyptic Paul: Cosmos and Anthropos in Romans 5–8* (Waco, TX: Baylor University Press, 2013); **T. G. Gombis,** "Participation in the New-Creation People of God in Christ by the Spirit," in *The Apostle Paul and the Christian Life: Ethical and Missional Implications of the New Perspective*, ed. S. McKnight and J. Modica (Grand Rapids, MI: Baker Academic, 2013), 113-24; **M. J. Gorman,** *Inhabiting the Cruciform God: Kenosis, Justification, and Theosis in Paul's Narrative Soteriology* (Grand Rapids, MI: Eerdmans, 2009); idem, *Becoming the Gospel: Paul, Participation, and Mission* (Grand Rapids, MI: Eerdmans, 2015); idem, *Apostle of the Crucified Lord: A Theological Introduction to Paul and His Letters*, 2nd ed. (Grand Rapids, MI: Eerdmans, 2016); **S. Grindheim,** "Election and the Role of Israel in God and the Faithfulness of Paul: A Critical Examination of the Pauline Theology of N. T. Wright," in *God and the Faithfulness of Paul: A Critical Examination of the Pauline Theology of N. T. Wright*, ed. C. Heilig, J. T. Hewitt, and M. F. Bird, WUNT 2/413 (Tübingen: Mohr Siebeck, 2016), 329-46; **S. Harding,** *Paul's Eschatological Anthropology: The Dynamics of Human Transformation*, ES (Minneapolis: Fortress, 2015); **C. M. Hays et al.,** *When the Son of Man Didn't Come: A Constructive Proposal on the Delay of the Parousia* (Minneapolis: Fortress, 2016); **R. B. Hays,** *The Conversion of the Imagination: Paul as Interpreter of Israel's Scripture* (Grand Rapids, MI: Eerdmans, 2005); **J. Hodge,** "'A Light to the Nations': The Role of Israel in Romans 9–11," in *Reading Paul's Letter to the Romans*, ed. J. L. Sumney (Atlanta: Society of Biblical Literature, 2012), 169-86; **L. Hurtado,** *One God, One Lord: Early Christian Devotion and Ancient Jewish Monotheism*, 3rd ed. (London: Bloomsbury T&T Clark, 2015); **J. W. Jipp,** *Christ Is King: Paul's Royal Ideology* (Minneapolis: Fortress, 2015); **E. Käsemann,** *New Testament Questions of Today*, trans. W. J. Montague (London: SCM Press, 1969); **C. S. Keener,** *The Mind of the Spirit: Paul's Approach to Transformed Thinking* (Grand Rapids, MI: Baker Academic, 2016); **K. Kinghorn,** *But What About God's Wrath? The Compelling Love Story of Divine Anger* (Downers Grove, IL: IVP Academic, 2019); **L. J. Kreitzer,** "Eschatology II: Paul," in *DPL*, 332-50; **P. Lampe,** "Paul's Concept of a Spiritual Body," in *Resurrection: Theological and Scientific Assessments*, ed. P. Peters, R. J. Russell, and M. Welker (Grand Rapids, MI: Eerdmans, 2002), 103-14; **B. W. Longenecker,** "Faith, Works, and Worship: Torah Observance in Paul's Theological Perspective," in *The Apostle Paul and the Christian Life: Ethical and Missional Implications of the New Perspective*, ed. S. McKnight and J. Modica (Grand Rapids, MI: Baker Academic, 2016), 47-70; **B. W. Longenecker and T. Still,** *Thinking Through Paul: A Survey of His Life, Letters, and Theology* (Grand Rapids, MI: Zondervan, 2014); **R. N. Longenecker,** ed., *The Road to Damascus: The Impact of Paul's Conversion on His Life, Thought, and Ministry* (Grand Rapids, MI: Eerdmans, 1997); **G. Macaskill,** *Living in Union with Christ: Paul's Gospel and Christian Moral Identity* (Grand Rapids, MI: Baker Academic, 2019); **J. L. Martyn,** "Apocalyptic Antinomies in Paul's Letter to the Galatians," *NTS* 31 (1985): 410-24; **F. J. Matera,** *God's Saving Grace: A Pauline Theology* (Grand Rapids, MI: Eerdmans,

2012); **S. McKnight**, *Reading Romans Backwards: A Gospel of Peace in the Midst of Empire* (Waco, TX: Baylor University Press, 2019); **S. McKnight and N. K. Gupta,** eds., *The State of New Testament Studies: A Survey of Recent Research* (Grand Rapids, MI: Baker Academic, 2019); **S. McKnight and J. Modica,** eds., *Jesus Is Lord, Caesar Is Not: Evaluating Empire in New Testament Studies* (Downers Grove, IL: IVP Academic, 2013); **J. R. Middleton,** *A New Heaven and a New Earth: Reclaiming Biblical Eschatology* (Grand Rapids, MI: Baker Academic, 2014); **P. Mitchel,** "The New Perspective and the Christian Life: Solus Spiritus," in *The Apostle Paul and the Christian Life: Ethical and Missional Implications of the New Perspective*, ed. S. McKnight and J. Modica (Grand Rapids, MI: Baker Academic, 2013), 71-102; idem, "New Testament Eschatologies," in *The State of New Testament Studies: A Survey of Contemporary Research*, ed. S. McKnight and N. K. Gupta (Grand Rapids, MI: Baker Academic, 2019), 224-52; **M. Nanos,** "A Jewish View," in *Four Views on the Apostle Paul*, ed. M. F. Bird (Grand Rapids, MI: Zondervan, 2012), 159-93; **B. Pitre, M. P. Barber, and J. A. Kincaid,** eds., *Paul, A New Covenant Jew: Rethinking Pauline Theology* (Grand Rapids, MI: Eerdmans, 2019); **S. E. Porter,** *The Apostle Paul: His Life, Thought, and Letters* (Grand Rapids, MI: Eerdmans, 2016); **V. Rabens,** *The Holy Spirit and Ethics in Paul: Transformation and Empowering for Religious-Ethical Life*, 2nd rev. ed. (Minneapolis: Fortress, 2014); **F. Rutledge,** *The Crucifixion: Understanding the Death of Jesus Christ* (Grand Rapids, MI: Eerdmans, 2015); idem, *Advent: The Once and Future Coming of Jesus Christ* (Grand Rapids, MI: Eerdmans, 2018); **E. P. Sanders,** *Paul: The Apostle's Life, Letters, and Thought* (Minneapolis: Fortress, 2015); **U. Schnelle,** *Paul the Apostle: His Life and Theology*, trans. M. E. Boring (Grand Rapids, MI: Baker Academic, 2012); **T. E. Schreiner,** *Paul, Apostle of God's Glory in Christ: A Pauline Theology* (Downers Grove, IL: IVP Academic, 2001); **T. D. Still,** ed., *God and Israel: Providence and Purpose in Romans 9–11* (Waco, TX: Baylor University Press, 2017); **M. J. Thate, K. J. Vanhoozer, and C. R. Campbell,** eds., *"In Christ" in Paul: Explorations in Paul's Theology of Union and Participation*, WUNT 2/384 (Tübingen: Mohr Siebeck, 2014); **A. C. Thiselton,** *The Living Paul: An Introduction to the Apostle's Life and Thought* (Downers Grove IL: IVP Academic, 2009); idem, *Life After Death: A New Approach to the Last Things* (Grand Rapids, MI: Eerdmans, 2012); **J. A. Thompson,** *Moral Formation According to Paul: The Context and Coherence of Pauline Ethics* (Grand Rapids, MI: Baker Academic, 2011); idem, *The Church According to Paul: Rediscovering the Community Conformed to Christ* (Grand Rapids, MI: Baker Academic, 2014); **C. Tilling,** *Beyond Old and New Perspectives on Paul: Reflections on the Work of Douglas Campbell* (Eugene, OR: Cascade Books, 2014); **S. H. Travis,** *Christ and the Judgement of God: The Limits of Divine Retribution in New Testament Thought* (Colorado Springs: Hendrickson, 2008); **M. M. Turner,** *The Holy Spirit and Spiritual Gifts: Then and Now* (Carlisle, UK: Paternoster, 1996); **F. Watson,** *Paul, Judaism, and Gentiles: Beyond the New Perspective*, rev. ed. (Grand Rapids, MI: Eerdmans, 2007); **C. L. Westfall,** *Paul and Gender: Reclaiming the Apostle's Vision for Men and Women in Christ* (Grand Rapids, MI: Baker Academic, 2016); **B. Witherington III,** *New Testament Theology and Ethics*, vol. 1 (Downers Grove, IL: IVP Academic, 2016); **M. Wolter,** "The Distinctiveness of Paul's Eschatology," in *Eschatology of the New Testament and Some Related Documents*, ed. J. G. van der Watt, WUNT 2/315 (Tübingen: Mohr Siebeck, 2011), 416-26; **N. T. Wright,** *Surprised by Hope* (London: SPCK, 2008); idem, *Paul and the Faithfulness of God*, 2 vols., COQG (Minneapolis: Fortress, 2013); idem, *Pauline Perspectives: Essays on Paul, 1978–2013* (London: SPCK, 2013); idem, *Paul and His Recent Interpreters* (London: SPCK, 2015); idem, *History and Eschatology: Jesus and the Promise of Natural Theology*, 2018 Gifford Lectures (Waco, TX: Baylor University Press, 2019); **P. G. Ziegler,** *Militant Grace: The Apocalyptic Turn and the Future of Christian Theology* (Grand Rapids, MI: Baker Academic, 2018).

P. Mitchel

ETERNAL LIFE. *See* Afterlife; Death; Eschatology; Resurrection.

ETHICS

Classic studies of Paul's writings and his theology rarely ever address the area of his ethics. Yet, if we define *ethics* as the study of behavior that is good and right, clearly this was important to the *apostle. In the twenty-first century, Pauline ethics has become a discipline in its own right, and for good reason. Paul's theology was not just ideas or theories, but *knowledge of *God that is meant to form and shape the person in relationship to the *gospel of Jesus Christ.

1. Did Paul Have an Ethic?
2. Ethics and Covenantal Relationship with God
3. Approaching Biblical Ethics

4. "You Are Not Your Own": Paul's *Doulos* Ethic
5. Eschatology and Ethics
6. Pneumatology and Ethics
7. Christology and Ethics
8. Paul and the Moral Philosophers
9. Paul and the Master Virtues

1. Did Paul Have an Ethic?
Everyone believes that the apostle Paul had a theology, but did he have an ethic? For as important as a question as this may seem, it is not really one that generated much discussion before the twentieth century—more specifically, before the 1960s. There are a whole host of reasons for this historical neglect of the topic of ethics in biblical studies. To begin with, there has been the broad and superficial sense that the Bible is about "religion," and religion is a spiritual matter related to *salvation. When the Bible is read only within that framework, the notion of right-doing in the world can seem marginal.

When it comes to NT studies in particular, scholars in the twentieth century had a tendency to dismiss or minimize ethics through a variety of arguments or rationales. Some, for example, portrayed Paul as writing extensively about key theological matters in the majority of his *letters, and then he would handle "practical matters" (or implications from his theology) only briefly toward the end of an epistle (see Dodd 1944, 7-8). Even then, though, some have held that Paul's concluding advice is conventional and of a general nature, rather than specific to the letters' main concerns. That gave it a sense of being optional, or an appendix, rather than something climactic or substantial in its own right (see Dibelius, 239; Gupta 2009).

Another approach has been to argue that Paul's *eschatology was such that whatever moral advice he gave was only part of an interim ethic, temporary norms before the end of the age (see Houlden). This made his advice appear limited and perhaps even lacking a theological foundation, merely short-term advice until the final and permanent age.

Some theologians have dismissed the notion that Paul had an ethic, because *ethics* can be perceived as a rigid system or rulebook of rights and wrongs, and if Paul operated in this way, he would not be led by the Spirit or acting in true *worship of the one true God. Rather, this would amount to a form of legalism or rule following (see Bultmann).

Today, though, there is more openness to a positive answer to the Paul-and-ethics question, especially if *ethics* is given a more basic definition: a system or framework that helps a person decide what is good or bad, right or wrong. With this in mind, there is no question that Paul was interested in how, why, and whether believers do what is good and right (e.g., Rom 7:18; 2 Cor 13:7; Gal 6:9). At the same time, Paul did not directly engage with Greco-Roman moral *philosophy (see Dodson and Pitts), and it is clear that the norms, behaviors, and values that he held and expected of his readers were not tied to any explicit philosophical framework but primarily related to the believer's relationship with Father, *Son, and Spirit.

2. Ethics and Covenantal Relationship with God.
The first place to begin with Paul's understanding of morals and the discernment of right and wrong is with the human's relationship with God. Paul viewed God as creator (1 Cor 8:6) and as judge (Rom 2:16), and mortal lives exist by divine will and *grace. But more specifically, as a *Jew*, Paul would have had a totalizing social conception of God's people living in a covenantal relationship with him. A simple word search of "covenant" (*diathēkē*) will demonstrate that Paul did not often use this term (but see 2 Cor 3:6; Rom 9:4). Nevertheless, the wise reader of Paul would do well not to depend on explicit citation for demonstration of the importance of *covenant as a concept (see Pitre, Barber, and Kincaid). Truth be told, it was uncommon for Jewish writers in the Second Temple period to refer directly to covenant(s), unless they were recounting *Israel's history (see Josephus, *Antiquities*; *Jubilees*). But it appears that they would more often simply take the covenant as a given and cite OT commandments and expectations accordingly. Notice, for Paul, the way he assumes the validity and authority of Jewish covenantal expectations such as "You shall not commit adultery," "You shall not murder," "You shall not steal," "You shall not covet," and, of course, "Love your neighbor as yourself" (Rom 13:9 NRSV). Ethics, for Paul the Jew, was grounded in a relationship with God that expected obedience to the divine will. Paul regularly expressed his life goal as that of seeking to please God, that is, to please God by carrying out his will faithfully (1 Thess 2:4; 4:1; Gal 1:10; Rom 8:8; 12:1-2; 14:8; Phil 4:18).

There are two key terms that help to further underscore how Paul saw ethics as obedience to the covenantal God. First, we have his language of *glorifying* (or praising) God. *Sin, or disobedience, brings dishonor to God; obedience brings *honor (Rom 3:7; 1 Cor 10:31; Phil 1:11). Another term relevant to Paul's covenantal ethics is **faith*. We sometimes think of faith (*pistis*) as something that happens in the mind or the heart, but Paul would have seen this as a more holistic term that relates to trusting in God through Jesus Christ, the kind of loyalty and allegiance that is lived out in obedience (Gal 5:6; Rom 1:5).

Another central concept related to Paul's ethics and closely related to covenant is *holiness (Wells). Israel was commanded by God to be "holy, for I the LORD your God am holy" (Lev 19:2 NRSV). The holiness of God involves his purity and his unique *glory. Those who are graced with being near him and associated with him must also be holy (Peterson). Thus, Paul communicates that it is God's will for his people to be sanctified (1 Thess 4:3). Sanctification does not mean perfection (as in sinless). Perhaps a better translation of *hagiasmos* in 1 Thessalonians 4:3 is "consecration." Those who are *consecrated* are set apart and have a special obligation of maintaining *purity, innocence, and integrity. One of Paul's primary objectives as apostle to the *Gentiles was to prepare the Gentile believers as an offering "acceptable to God, sanctified by the *Holy Spirit" (Rom 15:16 NIV). This was clearly a matter that was constantly on his mind, as he urged his churches toward holy living (1 Thess 3:13; 5:23; Phil 1:10; 2:15; see Thompson 2006).

Did Paul derive his ethics from the OT *law? On the one hand, since Paul did not reject his Jewish heritage and faith to embrace Jesus, the answer is "yes." On the other hand, Paul was more likely to quote fulfillments from the law rather than appeal to it as commands for Christians to obey (see Rosner 2013). Furthermore, rather than forming his churches according to the law of Moses, he instead talked about the "*law of Christ" (Gal 6:2 NRSV), which probably refers to the model of the *person* of *Christ (especially focused on Christ's love), not a particular set of rituals, commands, or practices. While Paul revered the OT (which includes Israel's law) as holy Scripture (2 Tim 3:16), he came to see the Jewish law in a new light because of Jesus Christ, not as a set of covenant commandments to keep in a formal way but as God's formative *wisdom for his people summed up and concentrated in Jesus Christ.

3. Approaching Biblical Ethics.

Before we investigate what made Paul's ethics distinctive, it is helpful to consider some of the methodological questions, concerns, and insights that have led to a more robust and meaningful study of biblical ethics in recent years.

3.1. Identity and Ethics. Perhaps it can now go without saying, but one of the major discussion points of the last century or so in Pauline studies has involved human *identity and how identity shapes values, ethics, and behavior. Who we *think* we are plays a major role in how we live our lives. So, for example, the Pauline language of *kinship ("my brothers and sisters") matters greatly when it comes to how people should treat one another—not as threats to one's own livelihood or honor, but as family. This has sometimes been described as "indicative and imperative"—what is *true* about us inspires certain activity (see van der Watt).

3.2. The Theology of Ethics. Along the same lines of what has been described above as identity and ethics, we can also talk about theological ethics, or the theology of ethics. That is, ethics is not just specific behaviors but a certain way of thinking about life and existence. Christians frame this in terms of theology. Particular theological affirmations, doctrines, or values naturally lead one to reinforce or follow those truths. R. Hays, for example, identifies three key focal lenses of the "moral vision of the New Testament" as: (1) new *creation (or eschatology), (2) the *cross, and (3) life in community (see Hays). There has also been much work done in the area of how stories relate to ethics (Wenham). Just as Jesus could tell (story-form) *parables* to teach *kingdom values and how people should behave, so in general we can say stories have a way of forming moral values (Burridge). Of course, Paul did not present parables or share fictional stories in his letters, but his appeal to the biblical story and the story of Jesus (from incarnation to death, *resurrection, and new life) had a deeply formative effect on how he thought believers should live (e.g., Phil 2:5-11).

3.3. Ethos and Communal Life. Especially thanks to historical study of the ancient world, as well as insight from modern social sciences, there has been a surge of interest in biblical studies in ethics as formed *in communities*. In that sense, ethics (as a discipline) is theoretical, but in reality we often see an ethos at play in people groups. Sometimes we can conceive of ethics as an individualistic matter, focusing on a single person making a moral decision in a vacuum. But people, as members of communities, are shaped by the traditions, values, norms, and social expectations of a particular culture and community. When we consider Pauline ethics, then, we must take into account the wider Roman world around these believers in the churches, and the cultures of the churches themselves (see Horrell, 83-98).

3.4. Virtue and Character Ethics. Finally, a major development in the study of biblical ethics pertains to the classical notion of virtue ethics (sometimes called character ethics; see Harrington and Keenan; Brawley). Often, ethics is treated as the performing of certain correct or just actions, or following certain rules of right and wrong. But a virtue-ethics perspective puts the focus on the cultivation of certain values and habits (i.e., virtues) that form the good and whole person (Wright 2010). In that sense, ethics is not law based or rule based per se, but directed toward maturity and one's overall contribution to society as a person formed by virtuous habits. Sometimes character is explained as a person's "durable" moral qualities. Paul talks about "character" (*dokimē*) in Romans 5:4: perseverance produces *character*.

Most Pauline scholars interested in ethics do not align with just one of the above approaches, distinctives, or perspectives, but combine several of them and attempt to study Paul's ethics or moral reasoning with several features in mind. Below we will consider further key elements of Paul's theology of ethics.

4. "You Are Not Your Own": Paul's *Doulos* Ethic. To begin with, we can identify what could be called Paul's *doulos* ethic (see Gupta 2016). The Greek word *doulos* means "*slave," and Paul (and some of the other NT writers) used slavery metaphors to talk about commitment and obedience to God. According to Paul, believers live in such a way that their goal is to serve God like a slave serving a master (Harris). Often, when we find the word *serve/serving* in Paul, he was actually using the verb *douleuō*, which refers to slave-like work (1 Thess 1:9; Rom 12:11). This did *not* mean for Paul that humans were treated by God as property to use and abuse. Rather, it involved the person's total commitment to God; just as Jesus taught, "No slave can serve two masters" (Lk 16:13 NRSV). Indeed, the way that Paul and other NT writers naturally refer to Jesus as **lord* (*kyrios*) also evokes the slave-master relationship (Rom 12:11; 2 Tim 2:24). The point of this *doulos* imagery for Paul was not to demean the believer but to recognize the supreme authority of Jesus. A Jewish view of divine supremacy would undergird not only this notion but also a sense that God redeemed his people from slavery to sin and death. Paul communicated this explicitly to the Corinthians, saying, "You were bought at a price; do not become slaves of human beings" (1 Cor 7:23 NIV).

What does all this have to do with ethics? Paul viewed all mortals as guided in life by a master. This is made most explicit in Romans 6. There is the default position of enslavement to sin and unrighteousness. This compels or entices the person to do what is wrong. But God freed believers from slavery to sin, and they now become "slaves of *righteousness" (Rom 6:18 NRSV), that is, slaves of *God* (Rom 6:22), who are set free to do what is right, redeemed to live in holiness. Later in Romans Paul refers to those who are enslaved to their own sinful appetites (Rom 16:18). As for the Galatians (primarily Gentiles), Paul reminds them that they were once enslaved to spiritual forces (Gal 4:3, 8). Freedom in Christ does not amount to libertinism, human "freedom" to do anything one likes (which leads to reenslavement to one's own appetites). Rather, true *freedom means release from the wrong master (sin, unrighteousness, death, self) and guidance and direction by a new master (God, Christ, Spirit; see Gal 5:1). Paul's *doulos* ethic, then, involves the notion that believers belong to the Lord and live to serve at his pleasure and will. This is not drudgery or misery for Paul, but restorative and healthy because God is a benevolent, wise, and humble master and lord.

Another implication of Paul's *doulos* ethic is that believers are not only to serve *God*, but also they are to serve *others*. Repeatedly throughout his letters, Paul talks about Christian freedom as an opportunity to serve: "For though I am free with respect to all, I have made myself a slave to all, so that I might win more of them" (1 Cor 9:19 NRSV; cf. 2 Cor 4:5). Again, to the Galatians Paul explains that freedom is most genuinely expressed in humble *service to others in *love (Gal 5:13). This would have been quite a radically countercultural moral philosophy in a wider Greco-Roman world that did not value humility and reinforced social and political hierarchies of status and value. But Paul drew from the model of Jesus Christ, who humbled himself and took the form of a slave (*doulos;* Phil 2:6-11). When Paul wrote the Philippian Christ *hymn (Phil 2:5-11), perhaps he had the image of the footwashing in mind, where Jesus performed a task for the benefit of his disciples that put him in the position of a common household slave. This should be kept in mind when Paul introduces himself as "slave [*doulos*] of Christ" in Romans (Rom 1:1) and Philippians (Phil 1:1).

5. Eschatology and Ethics.
When it comes to Paul's view of the believer's capacity to do what is good and right, he treats this as a new reality made possible by God's act of new creation (Furnish; Sampley 1991). The clearest expression of a before-and-after understanding of

moral capacity in Paul is found in Ephesians 4:17-25. Paul warns readers not to live like the pagans "in the futility of their minds" (Eph 4:17 NRSV). They have twisted minds and hard hearts, easily given over to greed and lust (Eph 4:18-19). On the contrary, those who have learned about Christ and embraced Christ shun their "former way of life, your old self, corrupt and deluded by its lusts" (Eph 4:22 NRSV). With Christ and Spirit comes a renewal of spirit and mind, a new self "created according to the likeness of God in true righteousness and holiness" (Eph 4:24 NRSV).

Paul did not see the dawning of new creation in Christ as the immediate moral perfecting of believers. It was a beginning, not an instantaneous event. In Romans, Paul affirms that the first coming of Christ brought a kind of dawn to the world, and thus believers were called to wake from sleep, "For salvation is nearer to us now than when we became believers" (Rom 13:11 NRSV). This dawn created not only opportunity for good in the world but also a sense of urgency. As "the day" (the day of the Lord) draws near, there is a more pressing need to dispel darkness and don the armor of *light, requiring that the people of God "live honorably as in the day, not in reveling and drunkenness, not in debauchery and licentiousness, not in quarreling and jealousy" (Rom 13:13 NRSV). They must "put on the Lord Jesus Christ" and reject the desires of the *flesh (Rom 13:14 NRSV).

6. Pneumatology and Ethics.

What role does the Holy Spirit play for Paul in the believer's discernment of what is right and good and pleasing to the Lord? The Spirit is central to the transformation of the person toward holiness and righteousness in life (Rabens). To begin with, Paul represents the Spirit as *purifying* the believer. Those who once were bound by greediness or sexual immorality were cleansed by the Spirit, washed and put right with God to live in a new way (1 Cor 6:9-11). Second, we can also say that Paul portrays believers as *led* by the Spirit. If once they were led by the flesh, and led unto death, the Spirit put to death the bondage of the flesh by the work and life of Christ, and now they can be led by the Spirit as true children of God (Rom 8:12-14). Third, the Spirit reshapes believers' ability to discern what is true and wise (1 Cor 2:14-15; see Keener). This notion is captured well in the famous statement in Romans 12:1-2: "Therefore, I urge you, brothers and sisters, in view of God's *mercy, to offer your bodies as a living *sacrifice, holy and pleasing to God—this is your true and proper worship. Do not conform to the pattern of this world, but be transformed by the renewing of your mind. Then you will be able to test and approve what God's will is—his good, pleasing and perfect will" (NIV; see Gupta 2010). Later in Romans (Rom 15:16), Paul makes a more explicit connection between becoming a pleasing sacrifice to God and the sanctifying work of the Holy Spirit. Suffice it to say here that the Spirit is a transforming influence on the mind that resists worldly reasoning and thinking. The mind and heart are renewed and reshaped to enable the believer to conform to the image of Christ, the Son of God.

Finally, we can add that the Holy Spirit, according to Paul, gives *gifts to each believer "for the common good" (1 Cor 12:7 NRSV). Believers are not merely individuals creating social transactions, but more like different parts of one *body or organism, each one providing a life-sustaining function. The Spirit empowers and equips this body of Christ to work together and create righteousness and goodness that is greater than the mere sum of the parts.

7. Christology and Ethics.

In favor of those who might argue that Paul did not have a formal ethic, it should be noted that Paul's attitude toward life and one's behavior does not center on a set of rules or virtues per se, but primarily on living life together with Christ, what is sometimes called "union with Christ." A classic union text is Galatians 2:20: "I have been crucified with Christ and I no longer live, but Christ lives in me. The life I now live in the body, I live by faith in the Son of God, who loved me and gave himself for me" (NIV). This kind of union concept is behind the frequent use of "*in Christ" language that is ubiquitous in Paul's letters (Campbell). First Corinthians 1:2 offers a helpful expansion of how Paul conceived of what it meant to be "in Christ": "those sanctified in Christ Jesus and called to be his holy people" (NIV). To the Romans, Paul explains that believers must "count yourselves dead to sin but alive to God in Christ Jesus" (Rom 6:11 NIV). Their new life is not only *because* of (the death of) Christ, but it is also lived *in* the life of Christ (Gorman 2015).

The ethical implications of Paul's *Christology—both the lordship of Christ and what it meant to live "in Christ"—are crucial, but sometimes lost on his letter recipients. For example, Paul chastises the Corinthians for sleeping with prostitutes, exclaiming, "Do you not know that your bodies are members of Christ himself? Shall I then take the members of Christ and unite them with a prostitute? Never!" (1 Cor 6:15 NIV). The believer does not act according to their own will or whim but must recognize the presence of Christ. Christ died for all, so that those who live might live "for him who died for them and was raised again" (2 Cor 5:15 NIV).

Another formulation that Paul used is "in the Lord," which seems to function the same as "in Christ" (see Rom 16:2). Sometimes Paul employs "in the Lord" language as a way to express his concern that believers behave appropriately according to their new life with Christ. For example, the Philippians are meant to welcome their emissary Epaphroditus back home "in the Lord with all *joy, and honor such people" (Phil 2:29 NRSV). If, perhaps, they would not have shown joy or given honor, this they *ought* to do "in the Lord," as a new person with Christ alive in them. Similarly, Paul urges the Philippian *women Euodia and Syntyche to be "of the same mind in the Lord" (Phil 4:2 NRSV). Again, the inclusion of "in the Lord" appears to point to a particularly *Christian* way to come together, an attitude and behavior that is possible and expected for those who live and exist and share their being with the Lord Jesus Christ.

Being "in Christ" represents, for Paul, a new kind of life, full of new ethical possibilities. It is helpful to observe how he contrasts being "in Christ" with being "in *Adam." Presumably, to be "in Adam" is to be formed by the corrupted image of Adam, tainted by sin. The destiny of all those formed in the image of sinful Adam is death, but Christ came to renew the *image of God and forge a new path for humanity to give them life (1 Cor 15:22).

Ephesians 4:22-24 portrays aptly both the eschatological and christological dimensions of Paul's moral conception with reference to the discarding or disrobing of the old self (probably a reference to the old self "in Adam"; see Rom 6:6), which is morally twisted, and the donning of a new self, which conforms to the righteousness and holiness of God in Jesus Christ.

8. Paul and the Moral Philosophers.

It has sometimes been observed that ethics and religion did not tend to go hand in hand in the ancient world, and this is true. Put another way, Paul's letters have more in common with the writings of the ancient moral philosophers than with religious myths and sacred laws of the Greco-Roman world. One of the most active conversations in Pauline scholarship in the twenty-first century so far has involved whether or to what degree Paul thought like and engaged the moralists of his day (Malherbe; Johnson; Dodson and Briones; on Roman moral philosophy, see Morgan). Several issues play into properly answering these questions. For example, it matters what kind of education Paul had in his upbringing, where it happened, and whether it included study of rhetoric and philosophy. When it comes to Paul's work as an apostle to the Gentiles, how did he conceive of trying to "speak their language," as it were? Would it have included learning philosophy and dialoguing about the gospel in those terms? What was normal or acceptable within Jewish communities in terms of adopting or adapting Greco-Roman philosophy? (We certainly see a positive inclusion of various strands of philosophical thought in the works of Jews such as Philo of Alexandria.)

On the one hand, it is easy to affirm that the apostle Paul was a man of the world in many ways. He traveled around to many Gentile-dominant regions and did not shy away from centers of civic activity and cultural engagement. He used metaphors from sports and public events (e.g., 1 Cor 9:24) in such a way that indicates he was familiar with activities of cultural importance in the Roman world. On the other hand, we do not have irrefutable evidence that Paul quoted pagan philosophers. In 1 Corinthians 15:33, Paul does write, "Bad company corrupts good character" (NIV), an aphorism that has been linked to Greek dramatist Menander (fourth–third century BCE) and Athenian tragedian Euripides (fifth century BCE). But it must be kept in mind that Paul does not cite a source by name, and it very well may be that he was repeating a popular saying.

When it comes to Paul and the moral philosophers of his day, it is reasonable to assume he had broad familiarity with the basic teachings of the major figures. Going further than that, he would have found resonant certain perspectives, values, or themes in Platonism or Stoicism, for example. Especially when it comes to the Stoics, Paul would have naturally identified with writers such as Seneca and Epictetus, who frequently extolled the virtues of bravery, resilience, and perseverance in times of adversity and difficulty (Dodson and Briones). To say that Paul could be compared to moral philosophers on some ethical issues does not mean that he borrowed directly from their literature, nor even that he consciously adapted or echoed their ideas. Most likely, he simply shared similar moral values and occasionally utilized general ideas or images that would have been known in wider society (see Rowe).

At the broadest and most basic level, Paul shared with the moral philosophers one important value: concern for doing good. The word for "good" (*kalos*) is not a term strictly associated with ethics. As with the English word *good*, so *kalos* could refer to the quality of something, like when the banquet master in Cana refers to the wine as "good" (Jn 2:10). It was common language for something that is excellent, right, or favorable. So Paul could use this versatile adjective in many different ways. However, there are times when it appears he was using *kalos* in relation to morality, specifically in reference to behavior that meets a certain standard. In Galatians, for instance, Paul writes about continuing in the work of "doing good" (Gal 6:9 NIV; cf. Rom 7:18, 21; 2 Thess 3:13). One might naturally presume that the standard involves what *God* thinks is "good," and certainly Paul put that standard above all. But there are times where it seems Paul was using a more civic or cultural measuring stick, as when he tells the Romans, "Be careful to do what is right in the eyes of everyone" (Rom 12:17 NIV; cf. 1 Thess 5:15). Here Paul is not lowering his standards. Rather, his concern is that believers should have a respectable reputation more widely, known for their honesty, integrity, and positive contribution to society (see Phil 4:5).

9. Paul and the Master Virtues.

It is widely recognized that there were certain cardinal virtues in the Roman world, especially prudence, courage, temperance, and justice (see Aristotle, *Rhet.* 1366b). Paul never cites these virtues as some kind of conventional set, but in Philippians 4:8 he mentions *aretē* (virtue) and lists several values that would have been appreciated more widely in society. It is appropriate, then, to consider selective norms, virtues, or moral values that guided Paul's ethics.

9.1. Love and Generosity. It is sensible to begin with Paul's emphasis on the virtue of love. In the Jewish tradition and for Paul's *ministry as well, love was not primarily viewed as an emotional feeling of affection or attraction, though such feelings did exist (2 Cor 7:15). Love was first and foremost a disposition of care and concern for the other. Love could and did exist between equals and those who found mutual benefit and value from each other. Surely, there was nothing wrong with this. But Paul was especially interested in love that is generous and grace filled, going beyond normal reciprocal expectations. This was especially demonstrated in the love that God showed: "God demonstrates his own love for us in this: While we were still sinners, Christ died for us" (Rom 5:8 NIV). Not only did God make the first move to show love toward humans, but his love is perfect and unyielding. Indeed, no power or problem in heaven or on earth can separate believers from the love of God in Jesus (Rom 8:38-39). This love leaves a special impression on believers and also presents an important model. It is an essential priority that they love one another, as taught by God (1 Thess 4:9). Indeed, this is Paul's special prayer and hope for the churches that he serves (Phil 1:9). Generous and self-sacrificial love expressed mutually within a community strengthens the church (1 Cor 8:1).

Famously, 1 Corinthians 13:1-13 details the value and moral supremacy of Christian love, contrasted with the hollowness of boasting or self-centered acquisition of knowledge or power (see 1 Cor 13:1-2). Love treats the other kindly and puts the other's need before self (1 Cor 13:4). It is forgiving and good (1 Cor 13:5-6). It is not fleeting or weak but strong (1 Cor 13:7-8). It is the virtue of all virtues, the greatest of all Christian traits (1 Cor 13:13). But Paul is clear that love is not an activity that happens by accident or by sheer human grit. It is at the head of the list of the *fruit of the Spirit, the highest form of Christian virtue, but something that can only happen by God's transformative work (Gal 5:22). It is no wonder, then, that Paul can so confidently refer to the "love of God" (2 Cor 13:14) and the "God of love" (2 Cor 13:11).

9.2. Integrity and Honesty. As one reads through Paul's letters, it is easy to see that he had a lot of people who either opposed him or found his work dubious. Therefore, he takes several occasions in his writings to defend himself. Often enough, he appeals to his integrity, his honest words and actions, and his transparency. A good example of this appears in 1 Thessalonians 2:1-12. Paul does not hesitate to point his readers to his own genuine and positive motives (1 Thess 2:4), his innocence and blamelessness when it comes to money (1 Thess 2:5-6), and his practice of earning wages through manual labor, which he does in the open (1 Thess 2:9). In summary, he explains, "You are *witnesses, and so is God, of how holy, righteous and blameless we were among you who believed" (1 Thess 2:10 NIV).

Similarly, in dialogue with the Corinthian *church, with whom he had an ongoing strained relationship, Paul states matter-of-factly that he and his associates behaved impeccably among them "so that no fault may be found with our ministry" (2 Cor 6:3 NRSV). Throughout many great difficulties, they maintained purity, truthfulness, and gracious resilience (2 Cor 2:6–4:10). They spoke openly and honestly with the Corinthians at all times and revealed their heart and gave their true affections (2 Cor 6:11-13). Paul holds these qualities up as virtues to imitate for his churches as well (see Phil 1:10).

9.3. Humility and Cruciformity. In order to reckon with the importance of humility as a virtue for Paul, we need look no further than the Philippian Christ hymn (Phil 2:6-11). There we see the glorious Christ who humbled and lowered himself, taking the form of a commoner, as if a king chose to become a slave. Not only did he take on flesh and suffer many hardships, but he was also betrayed and put to death—on a cross! Crucifixion in the Roman world was the most shameful form of execution for a human, let alone for the Son of God. According to Paul, though, Christ was not a hapless victim but allowed himself to be mistreated, killed, and shamed out of his obedience toward God and his love for sinful mortals. Paul saw the action and attitude of Christ as not just a means of salvation, but a model for Christian life—*cruciformity (Gorman 2001). The word *cruciformity* refers to a disposition and activity of trusting and obeying God and imitating the self-sacrificing work of Christ such that believers *conform* to the image of Christ. This requires humility, as the believer follows Paul's counsel in Philippians 2:3-4: "Do nothing out of selfish ambition or vain conceit. Rather, in humility value others above yourselves, not looking to your own interests but each of you to the interests of the others" (NIV).

9.4. Peace, Reconciliation, and Forgiveness. Due in no small part to the challenges of bringing Jews and Gentiles together as part of his apostolic ministry, Paul was often addressing his hope for unity and *peace in the community of faith. This is famously expressed in Ephesians 2:15-19, where Paul explains that Christ preached peace both to those far away (Gentiles) and those nearby (Jews) so all would have equal knowledge and relationship with God (Eph 2:17-18). The gospel is meant to transform strangers into friends and fellow citizens, members of one *household, establishing in Christ "one new humanity out the two, thus making peace" (Eph 2:15 NIV).

Paul saw the possibility and hope of unity and reconciliation as something guided and inspired by the love and mercy of God, as he wrote to the Colossians, "Bear with each other and forgive one another. . . . Forgive as the Lord forgave you" (Col 3:13 NIV). The work of Christ turned the enmity between God and mortals into *friendship (Rom 5:10-11). This became such an important theological foundation for Paul that he saw his apostleship as a "ministry of reconciliation," ambassadors of Christ calling for people to "be reconciled with God" (2 Cor 5:18-20 NIV). This has clear and deep implications for interpersonal reconciliation. Forgiving one another, reconciling with them, and restoring them to community is an activity and process inspired by Christlike love and compassion for the other (see 2 Cor 2:7-8).

9.5. Communion and Friendship. Today, friendship can seem like leisure, and spending time with friends might appear to be a perk rather than some sort of moral imperative. But in the context of ancient attitudes toward friendship and "the good" in society, Paul would have naturally believed that friendship was necessary for growing in virtue. In Paul's view, the mission of the gospel could not be properly carried out unless God's people were acting as one, not just professionally but as intimate allies, as it were. We see this clearly in Philippians, where he refers to powerful bonds of *fellowship, love, and joy. He calls on the Philippians to give and receive love and tenderness with each other, as God poured out love on them (Phil 2:1). Going further, he urges them to be "like-minded, having the same love, being one in spirit and of one mind" (Phil 2:2 NIV). That kind of warm communion and unity would have evoked images in the ancient mind of the bond between friends. The power and necessity of this friendship can be seen throughout Philippians, for example in Paul's hopes for the cooperation and unity of Euodia and Syntyche, women leaders whom he commends as *coworkers who have "contended at my side in the cause of the gospel" (Phil 4:3 NIV).

For Paul, friendship was not *just* missional, creating synergy to accomplish a task. Friendship was also fundamentally about the human need to give and receive love. We have already discussed the theme of love above, but suffice it to say here that Paul was open about his love for others in Christian friendship and fellowship and his appreciation for reciprocal affection and care. On the former, we can observe how often Paul referred to churches or individuals as "beloved" (*agapētos*), sometimes translated "friend(s)" (e.g., Rom 12:19; 16:5-12; 1 Cor 10:14; 2 Cor 12:19; Phil 2:12; Philem 1). In terms of the latter, in Galatians 4:14-15 he reminds them how they showed deep love and concern for Paul when he was in a vulnerable and weak situation. Many times he refers to being "refreshed" by the company of trusted friends (Rom 15:32; 1 Cor 16:18; Philem 20 NIV). To the Philippians and Thessalonians, Paul expresses that they are his "joy" and "crown" (1 Thess 2:19 NIV; Phil 4:1). Such superlative statements are a clear reminder that friendship was crucial for Paul in terms of the life lived well.

9.6. Justice and Equality. We do not normally associate Paul with the concept of justice, but if justice is about upholding of the (divine) law and accountability to that law, it was a matter often on his mind (Harink). One of the reasons why it is not immediately obvious when reading Paul's letters is that justice tends to be expressed in terms of divine *judgment (and *wrath). The judgment of God is an expression of divine justice for Paul. For example, in Romans Paul explains that God will "repay" each person according to their deeds (Rom 2:6). Later in the same letter Paul warns these believers not to take revenge against those who have wronged them. Rather, they must trust God to make all things right. Then Paul quotes Deuteronomy 32:35, which says (in Paul's words), "It is mine to avenge; I will repay" (Rom 12:19 NIV).

Statements that reflect a sociology of equality and what we now think of as human rights appear throughout Paul's letters. For example, he is insistent that believers carry out good, honest labor to earn their own wages. This is not necessarily a statement against welfare or charity. Rather, it is a general expectation that each able-bodied person ought to do their part for the good of the whole community (2 Thess 3:6-12). Similarly, to the Galatians Paul affirms that "each one should carry their own load" (Gal 6:5 NIV). That simply means that, all things being equal, everyone should live within their means. Of course, there are times when it is *not* possible to carry one's own load, perhaps due to unforeseen difficulties, in which case others ought to help: "Carry each other's burdens, and in this way you will fulfill the law of Christ" (Gal 6:2 NIV).

One of the clearest arguments Paul makes for equality and balance in the community relates to supporting poorer or needier churches. His message to the Corinthians is that every community goes through its ups and downs. God does not desire for *any* community to be struggling while others have great abundance, "but [the ideal is] that there might be equality" (2 Cor 8:13 NIV). The Corinthians were experiencing *wealth at that time, and their surplus could be used to raise up those who lack. As an illustration, Paul points to the divine manna miracle, where each person was given just enough by God, "as it is written, 'The one who gathered much did not have too much, and the one who gathered little did not have too little'" (2 Cor 8:15 NIV, quoting Ex 16:18). While Paul did not engage with the state *politics of his day (except in a very basic way in Rom 13), we can see he was clearly interested in social economics, fair treatment, and justice (see 1 Cor 6:5).

9.7. Discipline and Self-Control. Paul, along with many ancient people, believed that within the person were passions and desires that could be aroused and could cause them to behave impulsively in regretful and harmful ways (see Rom 1:26; cf. Jas 1:14-15). When someone comes to believe in Jesus Christ, the passions do not simply go away (e.g., 1 Cor 7:9), but such urges must be bridled. The common term for this in Paul's world was *self-control* or *self-mastery* (*enkrateia*; see Gal 5:23). Having new life in Christ means that bondage to flesh and passions is broken, so the believer can live in freedom (see Gal 5:13). Paul reminds the Thessalonians, for example, that pagans who do not know God act in passionate lust, but believers learn how to control themselves according to holiness and honor (1 Thess 4:4-5). This requires self-discipline. In 1 Corinthians Paul offers the analogy of a serious athlete who wants to run the race and win (1 Cor 9:24-26). Athletes then, as now, present helpful models of determination and self-discipline. Paul next transitions to an analogy of a boxer who masters their own body and brings their whole self under control toward a singular goal (1 Cor 9:27). The healthy, mature believer lives out freedom in Christ by making wise choices with mind and body, shaping both into the image of Christ.

See also COVENANT; CREATION AND NEW CREATION; CRUCIFORMITY; ESCHATOLOGY; FAITH; FELLOWSHIP, COMMUNION, SHARING; FORGIVENESS; FREEDOM/LIBERTY; FRIENDSHIP; HOLINESS, SANCTIFICATION; HOUSEHOLDS AND HOUSEHOLD CODES; IDENTITY; IMITATION OF PAUL / OF CHRIST; IN CHRIST; LAW; LAW OF CHRIST; LOVE; OLD TESTAMENT IN PAUL; PEACE, RECONCILIATION; PHILOSOPHY; RIGHTEOUSNESS; SERVANT, SERVICE; SEXUALITY, SEXUAL ETHICS; SLAVE, SLAVERY; STRONG AND WEAK; WEALTH AND POVERTY.

BIBLIOGRAPHY. **S. C. Barton,** "The Epistles and Christian Ethics," in *The Cambridge Companion to Christian Ethics,* ed. R. Gill (Cambridge: Cambridge University Press, 2001), 63-73; **R. Brawley,** *Character Ethics and the New Testament* (Louisville, KY: Westminster John Knox, 2007); **R. Bultmann,** *Theology of the New Testament,* trans. G. Grobel, 2 vols. (New York: Scribner's, 1951, 1955); **R. A. Burridge,** *Imitating Jesus: An Inclusive Approach to New Testament Ethics* (Grand Rapids, MI: Eerdmans, 2007); **C. R. Campbell,** *Paul and Union with Christ* (Grand Rapids, MI: Zondervan, 2012); **D. A. Campbell,** *Pauline Dogmatics: The Triumph of God's Love* (Grand Rapids, MI: Eerdmans, 2020);

M. Dibelius, *From Tradition to Gospel,* trans. B. Woolf (London: Ivor Nicholson and Watson, 1934); **C. H. Dodd,** *The Apostolic Preaching and Its Developments* (London: Harper and Brothers, 1944); idem, *Paul and Seneca in Dialogue* (Boston: Brill, 2017); **J. R. Dodson and D. E. Briones,** eds., *Paul and the Giants of Philosophy* (Downers Grove, IL: InterVarsity Press, 2019); **J. R. Dodson and A. W. Pitts,** eds., *Paul and the Greco-Roman Philosophical Tradition,* LNTS (London: Bloomsbury, 2017); **S. G. Eastman,** *Paul and the Person: Reframing Paul's Anthropology* (Grand Rapids, MI: Eerdmans, 2017); **V. P. Furnish,** *Theology and Ethics in Paul,* 2nd ed., NTL (Louisville: Westminster John Knox, 2009); **M. J. Gorman,** *Cruciformity: Paul's Narrative Spirituality of the Cross* (Grand Rapids, MI: Eerdmans, 2001); idem, *Becoming the Gospel: Paul, Participation, and Mission* (Grand Rapids, MI: Eerdmans, 2015); **N. K. Gupta,** "The Theo-Logic of Paul's Ethics in Recent Research," *CurBR* 7, no. 3 (2009): 336-61; idem, *Worship That Makes Sense to Paul,* BZNW (Berlin: de Gruyter, 2010); idem, "Did Paul Take Up the Great Commission?," in *Ethics and Ecclesia,* ed. E. A. Jones et al. (London: T&T Clark, 2016), 99-116; **D. Harink,** *Resurrecting Justice* (Downers Grove, IL: IVP Academic, 2020); **D. J. Harrington and J. F. Keegan,** *Paul and Virtue Ethics: Building Bridges Between New Testament Studies and Moral Theology* (Lanham, MD: Rowman & Littlefield, 2010); **M. Harris,** *Slave of Christ: A New Testament Metaphor for Total Devotion to Christ* (Downers Grove, IL: InterVarsity Press, 2001); **R. B. Hays,** *The Moral Vision of the New Testament* (San Francisco: HarperSanFrancisco, 1997); **M. D. Hooker,** "Interchange in Christ and Ethics," *JSNT* 25 (1985): 3-17; **D. G. Horrell,** *Solidarity and Difference: A Contemporary Reading of Paul's Ethics,* 2nd ed. (London: Bloomsbury, 2016); **L. Houlden,** *Ethics and the New Testament* (New York: Oxford University Press, 1973); **L. T. Johnson,** *Among the Gentiles* (New Haven, CT: Yale University Press, 2010); **C. S. Keener,** *The Mind of the Spirit: Paul's Approach to Transformed Thinking* (Grand Rapids, MI: Baker Academic, 2016); **B. W. Longenecker,** *Remember the Poor: Paul, Poverty, and the Greco-Roman World* (Grand Rapids, MI: Eerdmans, 2010); **G. Macaskill,** *Living in Union with Christ: Paul's Gospel and Christian Moral Identity* (Grand Rapids, MI: Baker Academic, 2019); **A. Malherbe,** *Paul and the Popular Philosophers* (Minneapolis: Fortress, 1989); **F. Matera,** *New Testament Ethics: The Legacies of Jesus and Paul* (Louisville, KY: Westminster John Knox, 1996); **S. McKnight and J. B. Modica,** eds., *The Apostle Paul and the Christian Life* (Grand Rapids, MI: Baker, 2016); **W. A. Meeks,** *The Moral World of the First Christians* (Philadelphia: Westminster, 1986); idem, "Understanding Early Christian Ethics," *JBL* 10, no. 1 (1986): 3-11; **T. Morgan,** *Popular Morality in the Early Roman Empire* (Cambridge: Cambridge University Press, 2010); **D. G. Peterson,** *Possessed by God* (Downers Grove, IL: IVP Academic, 2001); **B. Pitre, M. P. Barber, and J. A. Kincaid,** *Paul, a New Covenant Jew* (Grand Rapids, MI: Eerdmans, 2019); **V. Rabens,** *The Holy Spirit and Ethics in Paul: Transformation and Empowering for Religious-Ethical Life,* 2nd ed. (Minneapolis: Fortress, 2014); **B. S. Rosner,** *Understanding Ethics: Twentieth-Century Approaches* (Grand Rapids, MI: Eerdmans, 1995); idem, *Paul and the Law: Keeping the Commandments of God* (Downers Grove, IL: InterVarsity Press, 2013); **C. K. Rowe,** *One True Life: The Stoics and Early Christians as Rival Traditions* (New Haven, CT: Yale University Press, 2016); **J. P. Sampley,** *Walking Between the Times: Paul's Moral Reasoning* (Minneapolis: Fortress, 1991); idem, *Walking in Love: Moral Progress and Spiritual Growth with the Apostle Paul* (Minneapolis: Fortress, 2016); **W. Schrage,** *The Ethics of the New Testament* (Philadelphia: Fortress, 1988); **W. M. Swartley,** *Covenant of Peace: The Missing Peace in New Testament Theology and Ethics* (Grand Rapids, MI: Eerdmans, 2006); **J. W. Thompson,** *Pastoral Ministry According to Paul* (Grand Rapids, MI: Baker Academic, 2006); idem, *Moral Formation According to Paul* (Grand Rapids, MI: Baker Academic, 2011); **J. G. van der Watt,** ed., *Identity, Ethics, and Ethos in the New Testament,* BZNW (Berlin: de Gruyter, 2006); **J. B. Wells,** *God's Holy People* (London: Continuum, 2000); **G. Wenham,** *Story as Torah* (Grand Rapids, MI: Baker Academic, 2004); **N. T. Wright,** *After You Believe* (New York: HarperOne, 2010); **A. Verhey,** *The Great Reversal: The New Testament and Ethics* (Grand Rapids, MI: Eerdmans, 1984); **R. Zimmermann,** *The Logic of Love: Discovering Paul's "Implicit Ethics" Through 1 Corinthians* (Minneapolis: Fortress, 2018).

N. K Gupta

ETHNICITY IN PAUL'S WORLD

In recent decades, the subject of ethnicity has gained increasing attention among scholars of Paul and his letters. Three interrelated factors drive this growing interest. First, the rise of *social-scientific criticism brings questions of collective *identity and intergroup relationships to the fore. Since primary identity for ancients was rooted in *kinship systems, questions of ethnicity naturally arise from the world of the text. Second, ethnicity has taken on greater importance within the multicultural context of modern biblical interpreters. As a result, questions of ethnicity originate from within the world of the modern reader as well. Third, Paul's apostolic work centers on incorporating the non-Jewish peoples (*ethnē*) into the children of *Abraham (Rom 4:1-25; Gal 3:3-6; cf. Eph 2:11-21), a work of ethnic reconciliation. But the practical outworking of that incorporation created no small conflict among first-generation Christ-followers. Romans, Galatians, and Ephesians contain Paul's response to this crisis, a response argued in terms of "*justification by *faith." Thus, Paul's apostolic call, the three letters long regarded as our best window into Paul's theology, and an issue central to that theology—all revolve around issues of ethnicity.

In and of itself, the term *ethnos*/*ethnē* (Gentile/*Gentiles) offers little assistance for understanding God's *mission through Paul. The term was used for anything that could be referred to collectively, including people or animals. As such, it could designate a "nation" in the sense of a people united by a shared homeland, language, history, and culture. In Paul's usage, the plural *ethnē* (usually translated "Gentiles") designates all non-Jewish peoples. He often contrasts the Gentiles (or *hellēnes*, "Greeks") in paired form with Jews. Thus, his self-description as "*apostle to the Gentiles" means he has been sent to all non-Jewish peoples. In organizing the world's peoples in this manner, Paul betrays a distinctively Jewish perspective. A Jew such as Paul could describe non-Jews as *ethnē*; non-Jews did not refer to themselves in this fashion. Scholars debate whether to refer to Paul's own *ethnos* as "Jews," a term with cultural and religious overtones, or as "Judeans." The latter carries more geographic connotations, as in "a people from the eastern Mediterranean." For the sake of this article, I will use the terms interchangeably.

Neither Gentiles nor Greeks constituted ethnic groups in Paul's time (though "Greeks" could in an earlier era; see Hall 2002). But Paul's discourse sets Gentiles in a binary contrast with the Jewish people in a context that involves non-Jews becoming part of the descendants of Abraham. In other words, the context casts Paul's construction of them in an ethnic light.

1. Defining *Ethnicity*.

The widespread use of the term *ethnicity* in modern parlance assumes a shared understanding of its meaning. But the complicated nature of ethnic identity renders the concept difficult to define. As a result, varied (though often closely related) conceptions of the issue echo through the academic literature on the subject. For this reason, the rather lengthy discussion of ethnicity that follows must precede our examination of evidence from Paul and his world. This section unpacks five central themes in the recent study of ethnicity and their significance. Together they serve as the definition of ethnicity employed in this article.

First, *contemporary scholars work with constructivist understandings of ethnicity*. Traditionally, ethnic groups were defined by the shared or essential features (kinship, customs, language, and so on) characteristic of the group. These internal features were understood to develop in isolation from other such groups and remain largely unchanged through time. Within this understanding, known as the primordial approach, to study ethnicity meant to examine these unique characteristics that distinguished one group from another.

F. Barth, however, argued that ethnicity forms through ongoing interaction between groups (Barth, 9-16). This activity generates perceptions of group similarities and differences that ultimately define boundaries between them. From this perspective, ethnicity is not the static characteristics of an isolated entity. Rather, social interaction produces a shared sense of belonging that constitutes ethnic identity. The cultural practices of an ethnic group are the product of its identity, not the identity itself. In other words, social engagement *constructs* and maintains group identity. The investigative focus therefore lies in the discursive features ("ethnic discourse") of the interaction that does this formational work. Among scholars, varying forms of constructionist views now rule the discipline.

Keep in mind that from an *emic* perspective (internal to the group), ethnicity appears much more as a given, primordial phenomenon. A constructivist perspective will be more common to an external observer (an *etic* perspective). This distinction is important since ancient witnesses to collective understanding stem from both insiders and outsiders to those groups. We will return to these categories when discussing ethnicity in the Greco-Roman world.

Second, *from a constructionist perspective ethnicity is always situationally defined.* Since the contours of ethnic identity emerge out of social interaction, the expression of that identity will be shaped by the particulars of that engagement. For example, which particular *foods a group eats (or does not eat) may serve as a focal issue in its engagement with one group but not arise at all in its relations with a second. Thus the contours and boundaries of ethnic identity will be articulated with regard to food in one instance but not in another. Ethnic identity does not exist in some pure form as if in a vacuum.

By implication, no single configuration of Judean ethnic identity existed in Paul's time. Rather, one must ask, "How did these Judeans express their perception of themselves and of others, and how were they understood by others in a particular time and place?" (Miller 2008, 173). The resulting articulation of identity will take its specific form and draw its particular emphases from the social context. Yes, continuities will appear over time. But how they become understood and expressed depends on context.

Third, *ethnic boundaries are permeable.* We speak of boundaries between groups as if these serve as impenetrable barriers. Yet the borders between groups can be crossed in any number of ways, such as marriage, *adoption, or the formation of "fictive kinship" (common in the Greco-Roman world). Once again, possibilities for crossing boundaries stem from the dynamic, situational nature of ethnicity (as we will see). But from a constructivist perspective, the porous nature of boundaries serves as a common feature of groups in antiquity.

Fourth, *ethnic identity exists in a complex, integrated relationship with other kinds of collective identity.* Ethnicity is a particular form of collective identity; but it never exists independently. It will always be intermingled with other forms in multifaceted ways that often become difficult, if not impossible, to untangle.

J. Hutchinson and A. Smith (relying on earlier work by R. Schermerhorn) proposed a widely used set of identifiers of an ethnic group that illustrates this phenomenon. Note the multiple factors that go into their definition, each a possible source of identity on its own or in combination with some other dynamics. They list the following:

1. a common *proper name*, to identify and express the "essence" of its community;
2. a myth of *common ancestry*, a myth rather than a fact, a myth that includes the idea of a common origin in time and place and that give an *ethnie* [ethnic group] a sense of fictive kinship;
3. shared *historical memories*, or better, shared memories of a common past or pasts, including heroes, events, and their commemoration;
4. one or more *elements of common culture*, which need not be specified but normally include religion, customs, or language;
5. a *link* with a *homeland*, not necessarily its physical occupation by the *ethnie*, only its symbolic attachment to the ancestral land, as with diaspora peoples;
6. a *sense of solidarity* on the part of at least some sections of the *ethnie*'s population. (Hutchinson and Smith, 6-7, emphasis original, citing Schermerhorn, 12)

The point is that these dynamics can rarely be isolated from one another; they are bound up together. What factors come to the fore as key features depends on context.

Fifth, *the distinguishing feature of ethnic identity lies in a myth of common ancestry, however fictive.* As helpful as this list is, it fails to identify what separates ethnicity from other types of collective identity. Most scholars agree that the distinguishing feature of ethnicity is a sense of common ancestry. Obviously, a sense of common ancestry necessitates shared historical memories and a common ancestral homeland (Cornell, 52). This narrative element also means that group members will share elements of a common culture. But what sets ethnic groups apart from other collectivities is the sense of common ancestry in this mix.

Two methodological issues warrant attention before proceeding. One, since ethnic identity is situational and bound up with other forms of collective identity, discerning ethnicity in ancient writings can prove difficult, if not impossible. Take the early Judean writing titled Joseph and Aseneth. It offers a fictional story to explain how the patriarch Joseph married the daughter (Aseneth) of an Egyptian priest (Gen 41:45). The story is rife with boundary-defining issues such cultic devotion to god/gods, intermarriage, and conflicting cultural customs. But the key mark of ethnicity, common ancestry, barely surfaces in the tale. Or does it? After all, religious practice, intermarriage, and cultural customs are integrally part of what it can mean to be part of the children of Abraham. In the case of Joseph and Aseneth, how do we discern genuine ethnic discourse (or its absence)? Furthermore, although Joseph and Aseneth engages issues of social boundaries between Judeans and non-Judeans (in this case Egyptians), we know little of its specific origin. Proposed dates for its composition vary over centuries (typically 200 BC–AD 200), and although most locate it in Egypt, nothing about the particulars of its context can be discerned with any confidence. How then do we discern features of ethnic identity when (1) our knowledge of its particular setting remains unclear and (2) ethnic identity cannot readily be disambiguated from other dynamics of collective identity?

Two, scholars are well aware that investigating ancient documents using concepts developed in modern Western societies requires utmost caution. Such carefulness is particularly warranted in examining subjects that entail collective identity and kinship systems. R. Kennedy, C. S. Roy, and M. L. Goldman wisely preface their introduction to their valuable collection of primary sources on race and ethnicity in antiquity by quoting L. Hartley, "The past is a foreign country; they do things differently there" (xiii, citing Hartley, 17). On this point, see C. H. Cosgrove. (For extended discussions by biblical scholars related to defining ethnicity, see Esler 2003, 40-53; Hodge; Miller 2008, 171-75; Sechrest, 31-53.)

2. Ethnicity in the Greco-Roman World.
The ancient Mediterranean world was a multilingual cultural mosaic, a region where an array of peoples migrated and intermingled. It thus provided an incubator for the formation and reformation of group identity as groups both borrowed from and contrasted themselves with others (Gruen). Modern research into the ethnic dimensions of identity in the Greco-Roman world began to flourish within the closing decades of the twentieth century. Academic interest in the subject continues unabated. This section highlights central features of ethnic discourse in antiquity.

In antiquity people drew their identity through participation in the multiple types of groups that formed the fabric of daily life. These included political affiliations within a city, trade guilds or other kinds of voluntary associations, and so on. But primary identity came through a kinship system.

Kinship ties, with their links to clan and ancestors, ascribed honor to a household or individual, thereby influencing social interaction in any number of ways. For example, such ties could regulate marriage possibilities, determine eligibility for political or cultic office, or influence economic prospects. In other words, kinship located (and legitimated the location of) a person, a *household, or other larger groups within society (see Vearncombe, 26-28).

Given the pivotal social role played by ethnicity and kinship, establishing a group's ancestry was critical. Genealogies were often constructed and used for this purpose (see examples in Kennedy, Roy, and Goldman, 15-33). Three factors about ancient genealogies must be kept in mind. First, they appear in multiple forms, including simple lists of ancestors such as those found in the Hebrew Bible and in the Gospels of Matthew and Luke. But others were structured as narratives, telling the story of a people. Second, people seldom composed genealogies to provide an accurate record of blood descent. Rather, they *constructed* an ancestry for the purpose of establishing worthiness and honor. In other words, genealogies served a rhetorical purpose and were crafted accordingly. For this reason, we find genealogies from antiquity that trace ancestry back to some mythical progenitor, even a god or gods. In this sense, genealogies constructed fictive kinship for the purpose of legitimizing a group's or individual's (who is situated within a group) honor and status.

C. J. Hodge identifies underlying assumptions that enable the persuasive power of kinship and ethnic discourse in antiquity. The core concept is what she labels the "logic of patrilineal descent." This logic assumes an organic unity between progenitor and descendants. This link depends on shared blood and appears both natural and essential. More specifically, character traits and physical features pass from male progenitors to descendants via this shared blood. Thus, kinship connections with ancestors of honor from the past, human or supranatural, ascribe character and honor to the group in the present.

In addition, Hodge demonstrates how descent was regulated by means of religious ritual. She states, "Birth did not automatically grant membership into the oikos or household. A child had to be officially—that is, ritually—admitted into the family by the father" (Hodge, 27). The creation and maintenance of kinship ties by sacrifice was the norm in antiquity.

The seemingly incompatible notions of the essential nature of patrilineal descent and the malleable constructions of kinship were held together by means of what G. Baumann (95; cited by Hodge, 21) calls "double discursive competence." By this he means that these two discourses, typically held as incompatible, actually function in a complementary manner. In fact, according to Baumann they *must* function together in the construction of kinship and ethnicity.

3. Jewish Ethnicity.

In his thorough survey of Diaspora Judaism between Alexander the Great and the Bar Kokhba revolt, J. M. G. Barclay (1996) documents the bewildering variety of political, economic, and sociocultural contexts in which Jews lived. Given the highly contextual manner in which identity becomes expressed, one therefore expects a broad array of Jewish self-description during this era.

Nevertheless, Barclay observes that scattered Jewish communities "survived *as coherent and enduring entities*" throughout these centuries (Barclay 1996, 400, emphasis original). More specifically, he argues that these communities endured with a recognizable Jewish identity intact, owing to a combination of their sense of common ancestry and their shared cultural practices (400-401). In other words, across time and place ethnic identity provided a common unifying element.

Numerous examples can be cited. Josephus begins his *Life* as follows: "Now in my case, my ancestry [*genos*] is rather distinguished, having originated with priests long ago. Just as the basis of noble birth is different among various [nations] so also among us membership in the priesthood is a certain proof of an ancestry's brilliance" (Mason, 3-4). He goes on to recount his ancestors back several generations, highlighting their priestly and royal connections. Thus, as is normal in antiquity, Josephus defines himself in terms of kinship and family. On that basis he establishes his honor and character, features that legitimize his *Life*.

Although Philo remains more difficult to interpret with regard to ethnicity, he still makes claims that echo this combination of descent and ancestral customs. He speaks of Abraham as the one from whom would issue "not a family of a few sons and daughters, but a whole nation [*holon ethnos*]" (*Abr.* 98; trans. Colson). To Moses, speaking to the Hebrew people, he attributes the following, that they are "one race [*genos*; better 'people'], the same fathers, one house, the same customs, community of laws, and other things innumerable, each of which strengthens the tie of kinship" (*Mos.* 1.324; trans. Colson).

Barclay identifies five ways in which Jewish ethnicity was displayed in the Diaspora (1996, 404-13). First, Jews described themselves in ethnic terms. Across a broad swath of early Jewish literature, writers speak of the Jewish "nation" (*ethnos*, *phylon*) or people (*genos*, *laos*) in contrast to foreigners (*alloethnēs* or *allophyloi*). Second, non-Jewish authors consistently refer to Jews as an ethnic entity. For example, Roman and Greek political authorities deal with Jews on the basis of Jews' ancestral customs (*ta patria ethnē*) or ancestral laws (*toi patrioi nomoi*), conceptions that readily illustrate the link between descent and cultural practices. Third, when foreigners adopted Jewish ways, they were resocialized into a new family and its customs. As an example, he cites Philo (*Spec.* 1.52), where newcomers receive new citizenship, family, and *friendship. Fourth, Diaspora Jews were concerned to maintain endogamy. Although mixed marriages did occur, they were discouraged. Finally, we find a consistent concern in Diaspora literature that children be instructed in the customs of their forefathers.

Although such examples could be multiplied, we must avoid oversimplifications. Judeans articulated their identity in any number of circumstances. As we would expect, these expressions do not take on uniform expression. What the evidence does allow is the certainty that a wide swatch of Jews in what is now known as late Judaism understood themselves in what we now label "ethnic" terms.

4. Paul and Ethnicity.

In Romans 1:5, Paul states that the purpose of his apostolic labors consists of bringing about "the obedience of faith among all the Gentiles" (NRSV). M. Novenson has demonstrated that Paul unpacks the meaning of this phrase when he returns to this juxtaposition of faith, obedience, and the nations in Romans 15:9-12. There Paul quotes from LXX Psalm 17 (Rom 15:11) and LXX Isaiah 11:13-14 (Rom 15:12). These texts indicate this "obedience of faith" means bringing the pagan nations into submission to the coming messianic king. According to Paul (who may be quoting early Christian tradition at this point), this king has now come (Rom 1:4). As a result, Paul calls on the nations to forsake their idols in order to serve the living *God (see 1 Thess 1:9-10). Paul's divine call therefore thrusts him into the thick of what we now label ethnic issues.

Discussions of Paul and ethnicity focus on two issues. The first concerns ethnic aspects of Paul's personal identity. The second involves Paul's call as apostle to the *ethnē*. Consideration of either or both entangles one in some of the most debated issues in Pauline studies. We will first examine Paul's own sense of identity before looking at Paul's depictions of Christ-following Gentiles in relation to Paul's own people in *Christ.

4.1. Paul's Identity. Paul's letters offer conflicting evidence regarding his assessment of his own ethnic identity. In numerous passages he explicitly locates himself within *Israel in ethnic terms. For example, he wishes himself accursed for the sake *of his own people* Israel (Rom 9:3-4). Furthermore, in Romans 11:1 Paul poses a rhetorical question, "Has God rejected his people?" (NRSV). He responds that his own existence as an ethnic Israelite provides proof that God has not rejected Israel: "I myself am an Israelite, a member of the tribe of Benjamin" (Rom 11:1 NRSV).

In Philippians 3:4-6 Paul offers his fullest account of his place within his ancestral people. Paul apparently responds (indirectly) to claims made by Jewish teachers (Phil 3:2) who opposed him and/or his *gospel. He does so by listing his reasons for possible confidence in "the *flesh" using ethnic indicators. Paul states that he was "circumcised on the eighth day, a member of the people of Israel, of the tribe of Benjamin, a Hebrew born of Hebrews; as to the *law, a Pharisee; as to zeal, a persecutor of the church; as to *righteousness under the law, blameless" (Phil 3:5-6 NRSV). For further examples of Paul's identification with Israel ethnically defined, see Galatians 2:15 and 2 Corinthians 11:22.

Paul's argument in Philippians 3, however, goes on to introduce tensions regarding these claims. In Philippians 3:7 Paul says he regards these ethnic markers as "loss" because of Christ, part of his loss of "everything" for the sake of knowing Messiah Jesus (Phil 3:8 NRSV). He then says he regards what he has forsaken, including the status brought about by his markers of Israelite identity, as "rubbish" (Phil 3:8 NRSV). In other words, in Christ Paul now seems to regard these markers of Jewish ethnicity as part of his past rather than his present.

Similar evidence appears elsewhere. Paul claims those baptized with Christ (which includes himself) are no longer "under [Mosaic] law" (Rom 6:15–7:6). Furthermore, in 1 Corinthians 9:19-23 he tells the Corinthians that he can observe or not observe the law depending on the sensitivities of his audience. A "Jew" who was not "under the law" or regarded its observance as optional would have been nearly unimaginable in Paul's time.

So Paul's letters present contrasting evidence regarding his assessment of his ethnic heritage. What are we to make of this apparent tension? Insights drawn from the processes of ethnic identity formation offer a path forward.

Ethnic identity is an ongoing process, negotiated in the midst of changing circumstances and encounters with new groups. For Paul, the apocalyptic revelation of God's righteousness manifested through Jesus the crucified Messiah and *Lord constitutes a dramatic change of circumstance. God has now inaugurated the new *covenant spoken of by Jeremiah (Jer 31:33-34) and Ezekiel (Ezek 36:36-37). Covenant membership is now defined by participation in this Messiah, as evidenced by the reception of God's Spirit. What we witness in Paul's letters (as in the rest of the NT writings) is the process of these early Jesus-followers working out the implications of this new reality.

The tensions identified above emerge on the basis of conceiving of Paul's relationship with his ethnic heritage in terms of *either* continuity *or* discontinuity with his Jewishness. But this frames the issues in false terms. Paul locates himself within ethnic Israel. But the new realities produced by God's action through Jesus the Messiah transform aspects of that identity. Within Philippians 3, for example, Paul does not deny or denigrate the truth of his ethnic heritage. Rather, he now regards the status derived from that ethnic status differently because of what God has done through Jesus. Doing so is part of assessing "all things" (Phil 3:8 NRSV) in a new light in Christ. In other words, Paul understands himself standing fully within his ethnic heritage. But the meaning and implications of that ethnic heritage have been transformed in Christ. Such transformation, although dramatic in this instance, works within the normal processes of ethnic identity formation (see Miller 2011; see Pitre et al., regarding Paul as a "new covenant Jew").

4.2. Groups. Questions about Paul and the *ethnē* focus primarily on Romans 4 and Galatians 3:6–4:7. In both passages Paul interprets key texts regarding Abraham: Genesis 15 in Romans 4, and Genesis 12 and 15 in Galatians 3–4. In each passage Paul makes extensive arguments for the inclusion of the non-Jewish peoples in Christ within the descendants of Abraham. In other words, Paul describes the status of Gentiles in Christ using ethnic categories.

Hodge's depiction of the logic of patrilineal descent (see above) illuminates Paul's reasoning in Romans and Galatians (though many scholars would disagree with her understanding of the implications of this reasoning for the status of Gentiles in Christ vis-à-vis Jews). The themes identified below permeate one or both passages. In brief, Abraham is the progenitor of God's covenant people. He was reckoned in covenant relationship with God on the basis of his faith (*pistis*). Like their progenitor, Abraham's true descendants, or "seed," will be reckoned in covenant relationship with God in the same manner. In other words, covenant relationship with God is not bounded by the Mosaic law. That would restrict the children of Abraham to Jews. Rather, covenant membership encompasses all those who bear the resemblance to their forefather Abraham in Christ. Gentiles become adopted into this new familial line through the ritual of *baptism and the reception of God's Spirit. Thus, using kinship conceptions and practices common to his world, Paul constructs the one children of Abraham in new terms. Stated differently, Paul recalibrates *election so that it paradoxically creates a single but multiethnic family of Abraham's descendants (on election in Paul, see Wright, 774-1042).

In these texts we see Paul exercising double discursive competence. For Paul, links with Abraham remain essential. But Paul can exploit the malleable nature of ethnicity to construct a path to family membership for non-Jews in Christ.

Two additional texts warrant notice here: Galatians 2:11-22 and Ephesians 2:11-21. Paul's argument in Galatians 3–4 is preceded by his account of events in Antioch in Galatians 2:11-21. Although details remain in dispute, it appears Christian Judeans (including Peter and Paul) and Christian non-Judeans were eating together without regard for meal practices rooted in Judean ethnic sensibilities. But when emissaries arrived from the Jerusalem church, Peter ceased eating with non-Judean Christ-followers. As a result, Paul rebukes Peter, characterizing Peter's earlier practice as living "like a Gentile and not like a Jew" (Gal 2:14 NRSV). The implication is that, for Gentile Christ-followers to now eat with Peter, they will have to "live like Jews" (Gal 2:14 NRSV). Paul's rhetoric indicates this means they will have to practice Jewish sensibilities with regard to eating, sensibilities supposedly derived from observing the Mosaic law.

Paul provides his rationale for this rebuke in the form of a speech to Peter in Galatians 2:15-21. Both Peter and Paul are Jews "by birth and not Gentile sinners" (Gal 2:15 NRSV). Yet such distinctions bear no significance for covenant membership. God justifies Jews and non-Jews in the same manner: in Christ rather than through "*works of the law." The latter phrase is Paul's interpretation of Peter's refusal to eat with non-Jewish Christ-followers. The upshot is that although Paul distinguishes Jews and non-Jews in Christ, the significance of those distinctions becomes irrelevant with regard to social significance and honor in Christ.

In Ephesians 2:11-21, Paul develops the implications of his argument regarding Jews and non-Jews in Christ found in Ephesians 2:1-10. In those verses, Paul argued that Jews and non-Jews were both dead in their trespasses and sins, under the control of powers hostile to God. But because of God's *mercy, God raised both groups from the dead and seated them together with Christ in the heavenlies. Therefore (*dio*), Gentiles who were formerly separate from Israel and outside the covenant people of God have now joined this people through God's work in Christ (Eph 2:11-18). As a result (Eph 2:19-22), non-Jews in Christ are now fully part of the one household of God among whom God dwells. Once again, Paul speaks of Jews and non-Jews in Christ while removing distinctions between them in the same breath.

Paul's mission, divinely given and empowered, participates in God's purpose to bring all the *ethnē* into obedience to the one true God through Christ by the power of the Spirit. Paul's letters provide glimpses into the struggles he encountered in embodying this call and at least some of the reasoning he employed to carry it out. Following the contours of these arguments takes us into highly debated issues within Pauline studies. But an awareness of Paul's use of ethnic reasoning helps to illuminate Paul's arguments as he works to form one multiethnic family of Abraham's descendants. As we explore these arguments, we must bear in mind W. C. van Unnik's counsel, "It is extremely risky at all times . . . to rummage around in ancient history with modern problems in mind" (quoted in Cosgrove, 268; see van Unnik, 77).

See also ABRAHAM; CHRIST, MESSIAH; COVENANT; EPHESIANS, LETTER TO THE; FOOD LAWS AND CUSTOMS, JEWISH AND ROMAN; GALATIANS, LETTER TO THE; GENTILES; HONOR/SHAME; HOUSEHOLDS AND HOUSEHOLD CODES; IDENTITY; ISRAEL; JERUSALEM, COUNCIL OF; JUSTIFICATION; KINSHIP LANGUAGE IN PAUL; MISSION; PAUL AND JUDAISM; PETER; ROMANS, LETTER TO THE; SOCIAL-SCIENTIFIC APPROACHES TO PAUL.

BIBLIOGRAPHY. **J. M. G. Barclay,** *Jews in the Mediterranean Diaspora* (Berkeley: University of California Press, 1996); idem, "'Neither Jew nor Greek': Multiculturalism and the New Perspective on Paul," In *Ethnicity and the Bible*, ed. M. G. Brett (Leiden: Brill, 2002), 197-214; idem, "Who Was Considered an Apostate in the Jewish Diaspora?," in *Pauline Churches and Diaspora Jews*, WUNT 275 (Tübingen: Mohr Siebeck, 2011), 141-55; **F. Barth,** "Introduction," in *Ethnic Groups and Boundaries*, ed.

F. Barth (Long Grove, IL: Waveland, 1998), 9-39; **G. Baumann,** *The Multicultural Riddle: Rethinking National, Ethnic, and Religious Identities* (New York: Routledge, 1999); **F. H. Colson,** trans., *Philo VI*, LCL (Cambridge, MA: Harvard University Press, 1936); **S. Cornell,** "That's the Story of Our Life," in *We Are a People: Narrative and Multiplicity in Constructing Ethnic Identity*, ed. P. Spickard and W. Jeffrey Burroughs (Philadelphia: Temple University Press, 2000), 42-53; **C. H. Cosgrove,** "Did Paul Value Ethnicity?," *CBQ* 68, no. 2 (2006): 268-90; **P. Esler,** *Conflict and Identity in Romans: The Social Setting of Paul's Letter* (Minneapolis: Fortress, 2003); idem, "Judean Ethnic Identity in Josephus' *Against Apion*," in *A Wandering Galilean*, ed. Z. Rodgers, M. Daly-Denton, and A. F. McKinley, JSJSup 132 (Leiden: Brill, 2009), 73-91; **M. J. Gorman,** "Pauline Theology," in *The State of New Testament Studies*, ed. S. McKnight and N. K. Gupta (Grand Rapids, MI: Baker Academic, 2019), 197-223; **E. S. Gruen,** *Rethinking the Other in Antiquity* (Princeton, NJ: Princeton University Press, 2011); **J. M. Hall,** *Ethnic Identity in Greek Antiquity* (Cambridge: Cambridge University Press, 1997); idem, *Hellenicity: Between Ethnicity and Culture* (Chicago: University of Chicago Press, 2002); **L. P. Hartley,** *The Go-Between* (New York: Knopf, 1954); **C. J. Hodge,** *If Sons, Then Heirs: A Study of Kinship and Ethnicity in the Letters of Paul* (New York: Oxford University Press, 2007); **J. Hutchinson and A. Smith,** eds., *Ethnicity*, Oxford Readers (Oxford: Oxford University Press, 1996); **R. Kennedy, C. S. Roy, and M. L. Goldman,** trans. and eds., *Race and Ethnicity in the Classical World: An Anthology of Primary Sources in Translation* (Indianapolis: Hackett, 2013); **S. Malesevic,** *The Sociology of Ethnicity* (London: SAGE, 2004); **I. Malkin,** ed., *Ancient Perceptions of Greek Ethnicity* (Washington, DC: Center for Hellenic Studies, 2001); **S. Mason,** trans., *Flavius Josephus: Life of Josephus* (Leiden: Brill, 2003); **J. Miller,** "Ethnicity in the Hebrew Bible: Problems and Prospects," *CurBR* 6, no. 2 (2008): 170-213; idem, "Paul and His Ethnicity: Reframing the Categories," in *Paul as Missionary: Identity, Activity, Theology, and Practice*, ed. T. Burke and B. Rosner, LNTS 420 (London: T&T Clark, 2011), 37-50; **T. Morgan,** "Society, Identity, and Ethnicity in the Hellenic World," in *Ethnicity, Race, Religion*, ed. K. M. Hockey and D. G. Horrell (London: T&T Clark, 2018), 23-45; **M. Nanos and M. Zetterholm,** eds., *Paul Within Judaism: Restoring the First-Century Context to the Apostle* (Minneapolis: Fortress, 2015); **M. Novenson,** "The Jewish Messiahs, the Pauline Christ, and the Gentile Question," *JBL* 128, no. 2 (2009): 357-73; **B. Pitre, M. Barber, and J. Kincaid,** *Paul, a New Covenant Jew* (Grand Rapids, MI: Eerdmans, 2019); **R. Schermerhorn,** *Comparative Ethnic Relations* (New York: Random House, 1970); **L. Sechrest,** *A Former Jew: Paul and the Dialectics of Race*, LNTS 410 (London: T&T Clark, 2009); **K. Sparks,** "Ethnicity," in *DOTHB*, 268-72; **C. D. Stanley,** "'Neither Jew nor Greek': Ethnic Conflict in Graeco-Roman Society," *JSNT* 64 (1996): 101-24; **W. C. van Unnik,** "Christianity and Nationalism in the First Centuries of the Christian Church," in *Sparsa Collecta*, part 3, NovTSup 31 (Leiden: Brill, 1983), 77-94; **E. Vearncombe,** "Kinship," in *The Ancient Mediterranean Social World: A Sourcebook*, ed. Z. A. Crook (Grand Rapids, MI: Eerdmans, 2020), 26-42; **N. T. Wright,** *Paul and the Faithfulness of God*, 2 vols. (Minneapolis: Fortress, 2013).

J. C. Miller

EUCHARIST. *See* LORD'S SUPPER.

EVANGELISM. *See* APOSTLE; MINISTRY; MISSION; PREACHING, FIRST-CENTURY.

EVE. *See* ADAM AND CHRIST; MAN AND WOMAN.

EXALTATION, ENTHRONEMENT. *See* ASCENSION; LORD; TRIUMPH.

EXAMPLE OF CHRIST. *See* ETHICS; HYMNS, HYMN FRAGMENTS, CONFESSIONS; IMITATION OF PAUL / OF CHRIST.

EXEGESIS. *See* HERMENEUTICS/INTERPRETING PAUL; OLD TESTAMENT IN PAUL.

EXILE. *See* INTERPRETATION: NEW PERSPECTIVE; ISRAEL.

EXORCISM. *See* DEMONS AND EXORCISM.

EXPIATION, PROPITIATION, MERCY SEAT. *See* ATONEMENT; ROMANS, LETTER TO THE.

F

FAITH

The language of faith was central to Paul's conception of life with *God and *salvation through the *gospel of Jesus *Christ. The three main words that Paul used in relation to faith are the noun *pistis* (faith), the verb *pisteuō* (believe), and the adjective *pistos* (faithful).

Faith was so foundational to Paul's gospel that he often used this language not only to describe the essence of one's personal relationship with God (belief/faith/trust/commitment), but also as a way of describing what we might call the Christian religion itself. In various places he refers to Christians being "in the faith," the preaching of "the faith," the "faith of the gospel," and the "family of faith" (2 Cor 13:5; Gal 1:23; Phil 1:27; Gal 6:10 NRSV; cf. 1 Tim 6:12; 2 Tim 1:5; 4:7). While believers may be different in social status, *ethnicity, and sex, they share one faith in Jesus Christ (Gal 3:26; Rom 3:30; Eph 4:5: "one faith"), hence Paul's reference to a "fellowship of faith" (Philem 6). The gospel itself, for Paul, was a word or message of faith (Rom 10:8), because it was about Christ (Rom 10:17) and involved believing in Christ. In Galatians, Paul writes about the coming of faith, which relates specifically to the coming of Christ (Gal 3:23, 25; cf. 1 Tim 3:9).

A definition of faith according to Paul could be expressed in this way: *faith is human participation in a relationship with God through Christ, empowered by the Spirit, trusting in the *truth of the gospel, hoping in the confirmation of *righteousness, relying on the person of Christ in active dependence, and living in *love and obedience.* Before attempting to unpack some of the key elements of this definition, it will be helpful to look at the historical and canonical context of Paul's faith language.

1. Faith Language in the Greco-Roman World
2. Faith According to Jewish Tradition
3. Faith According to the Jesus Tradition
4. Paul and the Language of Faith

1. Faith Language in the Greco-Roman World.

It is important for the modern reader of Paul to know that *pistis* (faith) was not a term primarily associated with religion in the ancient world (Gupta). Most ancient people took for granted the existence of gods, and rarely do we find belief language used in religious texts (as an exception, see Plutarch, *Amat.* 756AB; see Lindsey). On occasion, philosophers did discuss and debate religious views, but it was extraordinarily uncommon to see someone argue that the gods did *not* exist (see discussion by Philo, *Prob.* 127-130; cf. Whitmarsh). Philosophers may have used belief language in conversations about religion, but it was not considered technical religious terminology. Put another way, Greek writers would use the same word group related to "belief" (*pistis, pisteuō*) to say, "I *believe* Zeus will help us win the war" as they would to say, "I *believe* my sister will be late for dinner."

The noun *pistis* was commonly used in the Greco-Roman world, primarily in relation to "faith," "commitment," or "allegiance" as a social virtue (for detailed analysis, see Morgan; Gupta). Nations would pledge *pistis* to one another, business partners would as well. *Pistis* was crucial to *marriages and *friendships, as both were relationships with expectations of fidelity, mutuality, and goodwill. *Pistis* represented an active concept that involved mutuality and trust in relationship, though the context and type of relationship would determine the nature of the expectations and activities.

2. Faith According to Jewish Tradition.

In Hellenistic Jewish literature around the time of Paul, Jews used *pistis* in approximately the same way as wider Greco-Roman culture. By and large *pistis* communicated "faithfulness" or "commitment" (LXX 1 Sam 26:23; LXX Prov 3:3; LXX Hos 2:20; cf. LXX Deut 32:20). We will return to Habakkuk 2:4 below, but it is worth briefly mentioning that the Hebrew text reads "the righteous live by *their* faith[fulness]" (NRSV), whereas the Septuagint reads, "the righteous will live by *my* [*God's*] faithfulness" (Hab 2:4). The works of Philo showcase the breadth of meanings that *pistis* could have in ancient usage; indeed, Philo often uses *pistis* to refer to proofs in an argument (e.g., *Opif.* 84, 109, 116; *Sacr.* 34; *Abr.* 141; *Ios.* 149).

The verb *pisteuō* (believe) is found frequently throughout the LXX, but its uses in LXX Isaiah bear special importance for the early Christians. Isaiah offers this prophetic word, "See, I will lay for the foundations of Sion a precious, choice stone, a highly valued cornerstone for its foundations, and the one who believes [*pisteuō*] in him will not be put to shame" (Is 28:16 NETS). This is cited by Paul in Romans 9:33 (see also 1 Pet 2:6). Isaiah implies that some will not trust this cornerstone, and those who do may face challenges. Similarly, in the early section of the famous Suffering Servant passage (Is 52:13–53:12), the prophet exclaims, "Who has believed our message and to whom has the arm of the *Lord been revealed?" (Is 53:1 NIV). Again, this is quoted in Romans 10:16 (cf. Jn 12:38). There is a prophetic emphasis on divine revelation that leads to *wisdom and insight that can understand some of the strange ways of God.

3. Faith According to the Jesus Tradition. The Gospels were first circulated after Paul wrote most of his canonical *letters, but it is probable that Paul's own faith language was influenced by the teachings of Jesus he received (Morgan). Since Paul himself was not a disciple of Jesus prior to the Christ event, he learned about the *ministry and teachings of Jesus through the *apostles and early Christian *tradition (Gal 1:18-19). The four Gospels presumably record some of the church's Jesus tradition and thus help us to consider one important source of inspiration for the way Paul used the language of faith.

To begin with, we need to recognize that faith was not an entirely new concept to Jews (see above). According to Matthew 23:23, Jesus accused the scribes and Pharisees of hypocrisy and charged them with neglecting three important matters in the *law: "justice, *mercy, and faith(fulness) [*pistis*]" (NIV). More programmatically for Jesus' teachings and ministry is his call for Jews to "Repent, and believe in the good news" (Mk 1:15 NRSV). The *kingdom of God is like the seed that quickly sprouted and grew up overnight with unexpected and impossible power and life—it defies logic and requires faith (Mk 4:26-27).

In the Synoptic Gospels, Jesus often refers to belief, but rarely focuses it directly on himself. In a rare moment in Matthew, Jesus refers generally to his followers as people "who believe in me" (Mt 18:6 NRSV). This need not mean here that they believed in Jesus as *God*, but primarily relates to Jesus as the special leader who was ushering in God's new kingdom. After all, Jesus also refers to the importance of believing the message of John the Baptist (Mt 21:32). The Gospel of John draws a clearer connection between belief in Jesus and the affirmation of Jesus' divinity.

The majority of occurrences of belief language in the Synoptics involve human belief and *healing through Jesus (Mt 9:22; Mk 5:34; 10:52; Lk 8:48; 17:19; 18:42). This often involves people seeking out Jesus, trusting and hoping he will show compassion. In most cases, Jesus commends their faith and credits that for their miraculous recovery ("your faith has made you well," Mt 9:22 NRSV).

Jesus also associates faith with the disciples' ability to do amazing deeds. If they had even a small amount of true faith, they could move a mountain (Mt 17:20; 21:21). With a twist of irony, Jesus sometimes refers to his disciples by the nickname *oligopistoi*—"little-faith ones" (famously translated by KJV "ye of little faith"; Mt 6:30; 8:26; 14:31; 16:8; Lk 12:28).

The Gospel of John focuses its faith language entirely on the verb "believe" (*pisteuō*; the noun *pistis* does not occur at all in John). To receive Jesus is to believe in his *name (Jn 1:12). Jesus does miracles as **signs* that foster belief, not the other way around (see Jn 2:11; 4:48). John 3:15-16 famously refers to the blessing of eternal life given to those who believe in Jesus (see also Jn 3:36; 6:29, 40). The consequences of unbelief are death and punishment for sins (Jn 8:24). In terms of Jesus' identity, belief involves knowing that Jesus and the Father are united (Jn 10:38; 14:1, 10, 11; 17:21), and that he is the Messiah, *Son of God (Jn 11:27; 20:31). Jesus pronounces a special blessing on those who believe without visible signs (Jn 20:29).

4. Paul and the Language of Faith.

4.1. Faith, Salvation, and the Gospel. Paul is an important *witness to the fact that in the middle of the first century CE, Christians called each other "believers"—and outsiders were "unbelievers" (see Trebilco 2012, 68-120; 2017, 44-86; see Rom 15:31; 1 Cor 7:13-15; 10:27; 14:22, 24; 2 Cor 4:4; 1 Thess 1:7; 2:10). That is, for Paul, to be Christian is to believe. Believe in *what?* There are a few places where Paul offers succinct summaries of the substance of believing faith. In 1 Corinthians 15:1-11, Paul recounts the basics of the gospel that were preached to the

Corinthians: they were called to believe that (1) Christ died for sins according to the Scriptures, (2) he rose from the dead in accordance with the Scriptures, and (3) he appeared to many, including the apostles (and Paul). In Romans 1:16-17, Paul underscores that believers trust in the true gospel, the power of God for salvation (see Eph 2:8-9). The salvific work was completed by God in the atoning work of Christ, but believers receive it through faith (Rom 3:25). Thus, faith "counts" as righteousness (Rom 4:5, 22; 9:30). Put another way, mortals are justified by faith, trusting in God's saving work on behalf of sinners to redeem and transform them (Rom 5:1; Gal 2:16; 3:8, 24-26; Phil 3:9).

For Paul, Christian faith is not just past oriented (looking back to the Christ event) but also closely connected to Christian *hope, anticipating what God will do in the future. By faith and hope, holding now the deposit of the Spirit, believers "eagerly wait for the hope of righteousness" (Gal 5:5 NRSV). In the present time of waiting, they walk according to faith in what God has promised for the future, namely, consummating transformation of self and world. Ultimately, knowing Christ will include *knowledge by sight (1 Cor 13:12), but in the meantime, believers walk by faith and not sight (2 Cor 5:7).

It would be a mistake to assume, though, that faith or belief unto salvation and *justification are merely matters of thinking or believing with the mind. Paul is clear that true faith and trust in Christ lead to conviction and action (2 Cor 4:13). Christ did not die so mortals could be justified in theory or status alone. He died "so that those who live might live no longer for themselves, but for him who died and was raised for them" (2 Cor 5:15 NRSV). In 1 Timothy, we read warnings about those who do not live out the faith; they renounce it and turn to false *teachings (1 Tim 4:1). Those who do not provide sustaining care for their relatives have denied their faith (1 Tim 5:8). Paul viewed faith as a whole way of thinking and living in God through Christ (Bates).

4.2. Faith and the Christ-Relation. It is typical for modern readers to associate the word *faith* with religious beliefs about the nature of religion or religious salvation. But for Paul, faith (*pistis*) assumed a personal relationship with God through the Christ-relation. On numerous occasions Paul makes reference to the personal faith of believers (e.g., Rom 1:8: "your faith is proclaimed throughout the world," NRSV; cf. 1 Thess 1:8). Here, the focus is not on a list of beliefs to hold, but more so on the believers' commitment or loyalty to the gospel, which centers on a personal relationship with Jesus Christ. This relationship was conceived of, by Paul, as a bonding or uniting with the life of Christ. In Galatians he describes this as being crucified with Christ and allowing Christ to come alive within oneself (Gal 2:19-20; cf. Eph 3:17). In Philippians, Paul explains knowing Christ as sharing in his *sufferings and conforming to Christ's death, "if somehow I may attain the *resurrection from the dead" (Phil 3:11).

Of major significance for Paul's understanding of faith is his interpretation of Habakkuk 2:4 ("The one who is righteous will live by faith"). In the OT, this is a text that presumes a covenantal relationship between *Israel and YHWH, a bond and commitment that requires trust and obedience. In Galatians, Paul is insistent that such a relationship of faith and trust in God (as Habakkuk describes it) is a commitment to a person—and Paul understands that person to be Jesus Christ (Gal 3:11). The Christ-relation fulfills that principle of connecting God and his people by faith. Paul contrasts that with associating with God primarily by law (Gal 3:12). In Romans 1:17, Paul quotes Habakkuk 2:4 again, with the same basic intent to align that scriptural truth with faith in Christ that makes the believer right before God (Rom 3:22). Paul's rare double reference to one OT text (Hab 2:4; Gal 3:11; Rom 1:17) demonstrates the importance of this notion for his theological perspective on knowing God: faith is a way of living; it is a set of beliefs, a standard, and a lifestyle focused on commitment to God through a personal relationship with Jesus Christ.

4.3. The Faithfulness of God. To say that Paul treated faith as the means by which mortals participate in life with God in Christ is not to say that justification or salvation was primarily a matter of human will or effort. While Paul speaks often and positively about human faith as participating actively in life with God, his focus is clearly on divine initiative, divine transformative power, and divine faithfulness (Wright). God's commitment to his human creatures is not dependent on their perfect faith (Rom 3:3; cf. 2 Tim 2:13). Whenever Paul wants to instill confidence in the hopes of his converts, he points to the faithful character of the one God (1 Cor 1:9; 10:13; 2 Cor 1:8). Any Christian growth in maturity, wisdom, or *holiness cannot be attributed to human achievement, but only to the empowering and enriching work of God to complete the redemptive work to which he is committed (1 Thess 5:24; cf. Phil 1:6). Paul believed the work that he accomplished in his life and ministry was not his own achievement, but was due to the *grace of God at work in him (1 Cor 15:10). He taught these churches to be active in faith and to seek to please God, but with full knowledge that it is God "who is at work in you, enabling you both to will and to work for his good pleasure" (Phil 2:13-14 NRSV).

4.4. Faith like Abraham. In Paul's letters, especially Galatians and Romans, the patriarch *Abraham is highlighted as a model of faith. Some Jews in Paul's day held up Abraham as the father of obedience to God's law(s) (*Jub.* 24.11; Sir 44:19-20; cf. Philo, *Abr.* 60). Paul instead places the focus on Abraham's *faith*: Abraham "believed God, and it was reckoned to him as righteousness" (Gal 3:6 NRSV, quoting Gen 15:6; cf. Rom 4:3). Abraham dared to trust this God and step out in faith. Though his physical *body was "as good as dead" and Sarah's womb was barren, he trusted that God would make new life where there could not be life (Rom 4:19 NRSV). That deep trust models belief for those who become "children of Abraham" in Christ (Gal 3:7 NIV). Abraham was given sure promises from God about his well-being and the greatness of his progeny (Gal 3:16).

Abraham was not acceptable to God because of his achievements (Rom 4:2). Nor was he blessed because of his *circumcision. It was his faith that was counted as righteousness before God (Rom 4:9). Therefore, he is the father of faith (Rom 4:12; cf. Rom 9:7). While Paul makes these forceful arguments about believers identifying with Abraham as the father of faith, Paul continues to recognize Abraham as the physical patriarch of Jews, including himself (Rom 11:1).

4.5. Faith and Works of the Law. On several occasions, Paul sets up a contrast between faith and *works of the law. Humans cannot be put right by works of the law, but only by faith in Jesus Christ (Gal 2:16; cf. Rom 3:28). It is important to note here that Paul does not criticize works themselves but observes that they cannot justify. Furthermore, while it can appear that Paul treated the Jewish law as problematic (Gal 3:12), nevertheless, he recognized that it had an important role in God's relationship with his people before the time of Christ (Rom 9:4), and the law points to the holy and just character of God (Rom 7:12). Faith in Christ does not undermine the purpose of the law, but its goal is upheld and fulfilled (Rom 3:31; 10:4). Paul can write about a new "law of faith" (Rom 3:27 NRSV) and *"law of Christ" (Gal 6:2 NRSV) that establishes a kind of rule of life based on believing in Christ, living in Christ, and imitating Christ (Rosner).

4.6. Faith, Obedience, and Perseverance. Above I have considered many facets of the relationship between faith and salvation in Jesus Christ. Here I examine the goal of faith according to Paul. Paul does not view faith as a static doctrine or belief to hold, like coins in a purse. Rather, it is a dynamic part of being and living in relationship to something outside oneself. Faith is a particular kind of commitment or allegiance to a person and a set of promises and expectations. Within that framework, it makes sense that Paul treats faith as something that is expected to *grow* (2 Cor 10:15; 2 Thess 1:3; cf. Titus 1:13; 2:2). Faith is meant to become firm (Col 2:5) and naturally work itself out in obedience (Rom 1:5; 16:26). There will be many occasions in life that will test believers' faith, and Paul calls them to be strong and courageous, standing strong in their faith (1 Cor 16:13; cf. Eph 6:16; 1 Tim 1:13). Paul commends the Philippians for their strong faith, able to stand firm in the face of resistance and hostility. They are so resilient that they would be willing to face death, to *sacrifice themselves out of loyalty to Christ (Phil 2:17). When it comes to the Thessalonian believers, they too persevere in faith, but Paul is so concerned that he sends Timothy to support them (1 Thess 3:5-8). Paul recognizes the reality that one can weaken in faith, even lose one's faith (1 Tim 1:19; 6:10).

4.7. Faith Weak and Strong, Faith as Gift. On occasion, Paul refers to having more or less faith. In his letter to the Romans, he mentions those who are "weak in faith," those whose faith is not fully formed. Paul also addresses the *"strong" (Rom 15:1; Paul includes himself in this category). Being "weak" in this context involves a believer feeling the need to "find assurance in added practices" (Fitzmyer 688). This does not assume the weak have a major deficiency in their understanding of Christ or the Christ event; rather, weakness in faith involves "weakness in assurance that one's faith permits one to do certain things" (Fitzmyer 689). As for the strong, Paul does not mean that they are more holy as believers, but simply that they do not believe their faith necessitates certain rituals of practice or abstinence. Furthermore, Paul criticizes both groups (weak and strong) for judging the other disrespectfully (Rom 14:3). As it relates to faith (*pistis*), Paul is insistent that one's practices should be aligned with what one believes. Faith should lead to conviction and firm commitment, and this should determine action (or abstinence). Paul states, "Those who have doubts are condemned if they eat, because they do not act from faith; for whatever does not proceed from faith is sin" (Rom 14:23 NRSV; cf. Rom 14:22).

In his first letter to the Corinthians, Paul mentions the gift of faith. In 1 Corinthians 12:7, he presents it in a list alongside many other *gifts "of the Spirit for the common good": utterance of wisdom, utterance of knowledge, *faith* (*pistis*), healing, miracle-working, prophecy, discernment of spirits, various kinds of *tongues, interpretation of tongues (1 Cor 12:8-10). The gift of faith is treated by Paul as a special gift given only to some believers, so it is not referring here to the faith expected of all Christians (Garland 581-82). Given that this gift appears alongside gifts such as healing and miracle-working, it probably involves an extra measure of trust in God that puts confidence in his power to do the impossible. In 1 Corinthians 13:2, Paul describes the kind of powerful faith that can displace a whole mountain.

4.8. Faith and the Spirit. Paul links the Spirit to the inspiration of faith in 2 Corinthians 4:13 (see Fee 323-25). The Spirit empowers and elicits faith, causing the believer to know and confess God as "Abba! Father!" (Gal 4:6). At the time same, the Spirit is given *by* faith (Gal 3:2; cf. Gal 3:14). With some measure of paradox, Paul affirms that human faith leads to the endowment of the Spirit, but after the Spirit resides in a special way inside the believer, the Spirit also enables faith to flourish and grow, transforming the mind and the whole person (see Keener). The presence itself of the Spirit gives the believer faith and hope, because the Spirit is a guarantee and promise of the consummating transformation and redemption that is yet to come (2 Cor 1:22; 5:5; Gal 5:5). Therefore, just as the Spirit is a Spirit of faith, so too Paul acknowledges the Spirit as a Spirit of hope (Rom 15:13).

4.9. Faith as a Social Virtue. In the above discussion of how *pistis* is used in Greek literature more widely, I observed that it is often employed in reference to a social virtue of fidelity, firm commitment, or allegiance. On many occasions, Paul talks about faith as something that believers *do* in respect to God as well as in respect to others. To the Galatians, Paul explains that the highest aim is to demonstrate "faith working through love" (Gal 5:6 NRSV). Similarly, when Paul refers to the metaphorical armor of the "breastplate of faith and love" (1 Thess 5:8 NRSV), he is probably imagining faith (*pistis*) and love (*agapē*) as features demonstrating a relational commitment to God. In fact, this may have formed a hendiadys, such that it should be translated as something like "fully committed love." In Paul's list of the fruit of the Spirit, *pistis* appears alongside love, *peace, *joy, goodness, kindness, patience, gentleness, and self-control (Gal 5:22-23; see also 1 Tim 6:11; 2 Tim 2:22; 3:10). The majority of these items are recognizable qualities of noble friends, good coworkers, or responsible fellow citizens. In these kinds of contexts, it is best not to take *pistis* as something like "beliefs," but rather as fidelity, loyalty, faithfulness, or firm commitment. Of course, Paul would have viewed this *pistis* as inspired and empowered by God.

4.10. Faith Remains. At the end of a long discourse on the nature of love (1 Cor 13:1-13), Paul refers to the famous triad of faith, hope, and love, singling out the third element as the greatest (1 Cor 13:13). This triad appears elsewhere in Paul as well (1 Thess 1:3; Gal 5:5-6; Rom 5:1-5) and in other early Christian writings (Heb 6:10-12; 10:22-24; 1 Pet 1:3-9; *Barn.* 1.4; 11.8; Pol. *Phil.* 3.2-3). What does Paul mean when he writes that "faith, hope, and love abide" (1 Cor 13:13 NRSV)? One view argues that faith and hope abide only until the end of this age, when "faith will become sight and hope will be fulfilled" (Witherington, 271). In that case, love is greater than these because it alone is eternal. But this interpretation of faith (*pistis*) assumes that here Paul only means that kind of faith that does not know fully (see 2 Cor 5:7). This is possible, but more likely is the view that sees the faith Paul refers to in 1 Corinthians 13:13 as "confident trust in God and appropriation of his grace," which is important in this age *and* in the age to come (Thiselton, 1072). Love is not the greatest because it lasts longer than faith and hope, but because it is the intended demonstration and outcome of true faith and true hope.

See also ABRAHAM; COVENANT; FAITH OF CHRIST; GALATIANS, LETTER TO THE; GIFTS OF THE SPIRIT; GOSPEL; HOLY SPIRIT; HOPE; JUSTIFICATION; LAW; RELIGIONS, GRECO-ROMAN; RIGHTEOUSNESS; ROMANS, LETTER TO THE; SALVATION; SIGNS, WONDERS, MIRACLES; STRONG AND WEAK; WORKS OF THE LAW.

BIBLIOGRAPHY. **M. W. Bates,** *Salvation by Allegiance Alone* (Grand Rapids, MI: Baker Academic, 2017); **R. Carlson,** "Whose Faith? Reexamining the Habakkuk 2:4 Citation with the Communicative Act of Romans 1:1-17," in *Raising Up a Faithful Exegete: Essays in Honor of Richard D. Nelson,* ed. K. L. Noll and B. Schramm (Winona Lake, IN: Eisenbrauns, 2010) 293-324; **V. P. Chiraparamban,** "The Translation of Πίστις and Its Cognates in the Pauline Epistles," *BT* 66 (2015): 176-89; **D. J. Downs and B. Lappenga,** *The Faithfulness of the Risen Christ* (Waco, TX: Baylor University Press, 2019); **J. D. G. Dunn,** "ΕΚ ΠΙΣΤΕΩΣ: A Key to the Meaning of ΠΙΣΤΙΣ ΧΡΙΣΤΟΥ," in *The Word Leaps the Gap,* ed. J. R. Wagner, C. K. Rowe, and A. K. Grieb (Grand

Rapids, MI: Eerdmans, 2008), 351-66; **G. D. Fee,** *God's Empowering Presence* (Peabody, MA: Hendrickson, 1995); **J. Fitzmyer,** *Romans* (New York: Doubleday, 1993); **J. Frey, B. Schliesser, and N. Überschaer,** eds., *Glaube: Das Verständnis des Glaubens im frühen Christentum und in seiner jüdischen und hellenistisch-römischen Umwelt,* WUNT 373 (Tübingen: Mohr Siebeck, 2017); **D. Garland,** *2 Corinthians,* BECNT (Grand Rapids, MI: Baker Academic, 2003); **N. K. Gupta,** *Paul and the Language of Faith* (Grand Rapids, MI: Eerdmans, 2019); **R. B. Hays,** "Jesus' Faith and Ours: A Rereading of Galatians 3," in *Conflict and Context: Hermeneutics in the Americas,* ed. M. L. Branson and C. R. Padilla (Grand Rapids, MI: Eerdmans, 1986), 257-68; idem, "Πίστις and Pauline Christology: What Is at Stake?," in *The Faith of Jesus Christ* (Grand Rapids, MI: Eerdmans, 2002), 272-98; **D. Heliso,** *Pistis and the Righteous One: A Study of Romans 1:17 Against the Background of Scripture and Second Temple Jewish Literature,* WUNT 2/235 (Tübingen: Mohr Siebeck, 2007); **C. S. Keener,** *The Mind of the Spirit* (Grand Rapids, MI: Baker Academic, 2016); **D. Konstan,** "Trusting in Jesus," *JSNT* 40 (2018): 247-54; **D. Lindsay,** *Josephus and Faith* (Leiden: Brill, 1993); **T. Morgan,** *Roman Faith and Christian Faith* (Oxford: Oxford University Press, 2017); **P. Oakes,** "Πίστις as a Relational Way of Life in Galatians," *JSNT* 40 (2018): 255-75; **J. H. Pifer,** *Faith as Participation: An Exegetical Study of Some Key Pauline Texts,* WUNT 2/486 (Tübingen: Mohr Siebeck, 2019); **B. Rosner,** *Paul and the Law* (Downers Grove, IL: IVP Academic, 2013); **B. Schliesser,** *Abraham's Faith in Romans 4: Paul's Concept of Faith in Light of the History of Reception of Genesis 15:6,* WUNT 2/224 (Tübingen: Mohr Siebeck, 2007); idem, *Was ist Glaube? Paulinische Perspektiven,* ThSt (Zurich: TVZ, 2011); idem, "'Christ-Faith' as an Eschatological Event (Galatians 3.23-26): A 'Third View' on Πίστις Χριστοῦ," *JSNT* 37 (2016): 277-300; **A. Thiselton,** *The First Epistle to the Corinthians,* NIGTC, (Grand Rapids, MI: Eerdmans, 2000); **P. Trebilco,** *Self-Designations and Group Identity in the New Testament* (Cambridge: Cambridge University Press, 2012); idem, *Outsider Designations and Boundary Construction in the New Testament* (Cambridge: Cambridge University Press, 2017); **T. Whitmarsh,** *Battling with the Gods: Atheism in the Ancient World* (New York: Vintage, 2016); **B. Witherington,** *Conflict and Community in Corinth: A Socio-rhetorical Commentary on 1 and 2 Corinthians* (Grand Rapids, MI: Eerdmans, 1995); **N. T. Wright,** *Paul and the Faithfulness of God,* 2 vols. (Minneapolis: Fortress, 2013); **G. Zerbe,** "Believers as Loyalists: The Anatomy of Paul's Language of *Pistis,*" in *Citizen: Paul on Peace and Politics* (Winnipeg: CMU Press, 2012), 26-47.

N. K. Gupta

FAITH OF CHRIST

*Faith is an important category for Paul. The noun *pistis* appears 142 times, the verb *pisteuō* 54 times, and the adjective *pistos* 33 times in the thirteen books attributed to Paul. *Pistis* has received much scholarly attention recently, highlighting the multivalent nature of the word (see Bates; Downing; Gupta; Morgan). *Pistis* evokes a number of concepts, such as faith, belief, trust, faithfulness, loyalty, and credibility. Assuming Pauline authorship of Ephesians, Paul pairs the head noun *pistis* with a genitive referring to Jesus eight times: Romans 3:22 (*pisteōs Iēsou Christou*); Romans 3:26 (*pisteōs Iēsou*); Galatians 2:16 (twice: *pisteōs Iēsou Christou* and *pisteōs Christou*); Galatians 2:20 (*pistei tou huiou tou theou*); Galatians 3:22 (*pisteōs Iēsou Christou*); Ephesians 3:12 (*pisteōs autou*); and Philippians 3:9 (*pisteōs Christou*). First Thessalonians 1:3 should perhaps receive more attention in this discussion as well (see Ulrichs, 71-93). These phrases are abbreviated *pistis Christou.* Scholars debate the relationship between the head noun *pistis* with the genitive that follows. The most popular options are "faith in *Christ" (objective genitive), "faith of Christ" or "faithfulness of Christ" (subjective genitive), "Christ-faith" (genitive of quality, or the so-called third view), or some mix thereof. The objective and subjective genitive readings are occasionally referred to as the "anthropological" and "christological" interpretations, respectively (as in Campbell 1994, 271-72; Easter, 33-34), but the anthropological/christological distinction has been critiqued as a false dichotomy between divine and human agency (see Barclay, 382; Gupta, 185-90; Hagen Pifer, 176; Rusam, 70; Watson, 159). The meaning of *pistis Christou* extends beyond the phrases themselves to the whole of Paul's theology, including such dense phrases as "from faith to faith" (Rom 1:17) or "the coming of faith" (Gal 3:23-26), and Scripture quotations such as Genesis 15:6 (Rom 4:3; Gal 3:6) or Habakkuk 2:4 (Rom 1:17; Gal 3:11).

1. History of the *Pistis Christou* Debate
2. Objective Genitive: "Faith in Christ"
3. Subjective Genitive: "Faith(fulness) of Christ"
4. "Third View": "Christ-Faith"
5. Intentionally Multifaceted

1. History of the *Pistis Christou* Debate. The church fathers are unclear regarding *pistis Christou*, yielding different interpretations among modern scholars. R. A. Harrisville and M. W. Elliot find objective genitives in the Fathers, whereas I. G. Wallis finds subjective genitives until the threat of Arianism dictated otherwise (Harrisville 1994; 2006; Elliot 2009; on this shift, see especially Wallis, 200-212). M. D. Hooker shows how Athanasius, Augustine, and Thomas Aquinas read the phrase objectively but in each case are "driven by their presuppositions regarding Christ's divinity and humanity" (2016, 49). Martin Luther makes the objective genitive clear in his translation ("der Glaube an Jesum Christum"), and Protestant exegesis followed this tradition (Hooker 2016, 50).

The origin of the *pistis Christou* debate is often attributed to J. Haussleiter in 1891 (as in Campbell 1994, 265; Hays 2002a, 142; Hooker 2016, 50), but B. Schliesser has catalogued proponents of the subjective genitive interpretation dating to as early as the 1820s (Schliesser 2015). The first English-language articles on the debate appear in 1955 (Hebert) and 1957 (Torrance), which argue that *pistis* in the NT is influenced by the Hebrew *ʾĕmûnâ*. While some interpreters followed G. Hebert and T. F. Torrance in connecting *pistis* to *ʾĕmûnâ* (e.g., M. Barth, 365), no recent proponents for the subjective genitive argue along these lines (especially since Barr). P. Vallotton, writing in French, argued at length for the subjective genitive reading in 1960, but few interpreters have interacted extensively with his work. The recent debate stems from R. B. Hays's 1983 dissertation, *The Faith of Jesus Christ* (republished in 2002). Since 1983, the debate has largely been an English-speaking phenomenon, with some exceptions (e.g., Rusam; Ulrichs; note also Ota 1997; 2014). Most of the debate has swirled around the objective and subjective options, but the "third view" has gained ground in the last decade. P. M. Sprinkle, who coins the name "third view" (167-74), catalogues a series of scholars dating to at least 1929 who advocate a position outside the standard subjective and objective genitive options. Schliesser also argues for the third view (2016; see also Gupta, 174, who is "sympathetic to Schliesser's proposal"). Recent studies on ancient semantics (Downing) and early Roman and Christian uses of *fides* and *pistis* (Morgan) demonstrate how a phrase such as *pistis Christou* could intentionally evoke more than one meaning. This may open new interpretive avenues previously unexplored.

2. Objective Genitive: "Faith in Christ." The objective genitive interpretation of *pistis Christou* renders the phrase "faith in Christ." This is the traditional reading, reflected in most modern English translations (e.g., ESV, NASB, NIV, NLT, NRSV). By this reading, Christ or *God's work in Christ is the object of faith: "Primarily, it is acceptance of the kerygma, that is, subjection to the way of *salvation ordained by God and opened up in Christ" (Bultmann, 217). Faith extends beyond mere assent or belief in historical fact but is itself "the act in virtue of which a man, responding to God's eschatological deed in Christ, comes out of the world and makes a radical reorientation to God" (Bultmann, 216). In sum, then, the objective genitive sees individual humans as the subjects, and Christ as the object of their faith.

One of the earlier defenses for the objective genitive involves the presence or absence of an article before *pistis*. A. Hultgren suggests that whenever Paul uses *pistis* followed by a subjective genitive, the article always appears before *pistis* (253). Of the *pistis Christou* phrases in Paul, only Ephesians 3:12 has an article before *pistis*. S. E. Porter and A. W. Pitts show how all thirty-three instances of *pistis* without an article in Paul carry an "abstract conceptual notion unconnected to a particular individual" (50). Arguments centered on the article have not convinced scholars in both the objective (Silva, 227) and subjective (Campbell 2009b, 66-67n28) camps (see also the discussion in Kugler, 246-47).

The grammatical discussion extends into the manuscript tradition. Regarding Galatians 3:26, R. B. Matlock notes the difference between the most likely reading (*dia tēs pisteōs en Christō Iēsou*) and the variant reading in P46 (*pisteōs Christou*). If the scribe made this change intentionally, it suggests for Matlock that Greek speakers of the era understood *pisteōs Christou* as "faith in Christ" (2003, 437). Similarly, Porter and Pitts note the shift in Codex Alexandrinus from the most likely reading of *dia pisteōs Iēsou Christou* to *dia pisteōs en Christō Iēsou*. They attribute this to a "conscious change on the part of the scribe" to indicate Jesus as the object of faith (Porter and Pitts, 52; see also Porter, 416-18). However, arguments hinging on supposed scribal intention are difficult to prove (see the rebuttal to Matlock in Campbell 2009a, 877-78, 1099-1101n11; see also Kugler, 247-48; cf. Porter, 403-19).

In both Romans and Galatians, the first time Paul introduces the phrase *pistis Christou*, he immediately clarifies the phrase by referring to humans believing. In Galatians 2:16, two *pistis Christou* phrases (*dia pisteōs Iēsou Christou*; *ek pisteōs Christou*) sandwich a clear reference to faith in Jesus (*eis Christon Iēsoun episteusamen*). Likewise, in Romans 3:22, Paul follows *pistis Christou* with *eis pantas tous pisteuontas*, "for all who believe." In so doing, Paul disambiguates the potentially ambiguous *pistis Christou* phrases for the hearers of his letters (Barclay, 380; Keener, 181). Beyond these verses, Paul depicts Jesus as object of faith using other language (Gal 3:26; Eph 1:15; Phil 1:29; Col 1:4; 2:5; Philem 5; cf. 1 Tim 1:14; 3:13; 2 Tim 1:13; 3:15). Nevertheless, even the staunchest advocates of the subjective genitive interpretation usually allow that Paul wishes Christians to believe in Jesus (e.g., Campbell 2020, 303, 320). That Paul wants humans to believe in Jesus does not require an objective genitive reading of every *pistis Christou* phrase.

*Abraham is an example of faith for Paul (Rom 4:3, 16; Gal 3:6). Abraham is remembered for believing in God rather than being faithful to God, which suggests that Abraham's *pistis* is a model of *faith* and not *faithfulness*. If *pistis Christou* follows this example of Abraham's *pistis*, then the phrase would be about a human's faith rather than Christ's faithfulness (Dunn 2002, 265, 270-71; Hunn 2016). This comparison introduces theological questions of its own: "If Abraham could be justified by trusting God, why should we need to believe in Christ to be justified? Why not simply put our trust in God, as Abraham did?" (Hays 2002a, 151, italics original; cf. Hays 2002b, 290). Furthermore, Galatians 3:23 speaks of a time "before faith came." If faith had not come in Abraham's time, how then can he model faith now (Campbell 2009a, 1162-63n130)?

*Works of the *law and *pistis* are often contrasted (Rom 3:28; 4:5, 13-16; 9:32; 10:4; Gal 2:16; 3:2, 5, 11-12, 23-26; Eph 2:8; Phil 3:9). Supporters of the objective genitive have argued that since works of the law are a human work, *pistis* must also be a human response. As such, *pistis Christou* would be a human's faith in Jesus in contrast to a human's efforts (Dunn 2002, 270-71; Hultgren, 258-59; Hunn 2006, 30-33). Supporters of the subjective genitive reading acknowledge this contrast between works of the law and *pistis* but argue that the distinction is between human action (works of the law) and divine action (*pistis Christou*; M. Barth, 368-69; Hooker 1989, 336, 341; Martyn, 271). However, as Barclay shows, the objective genitive does not disregard God's initiating action. The emphasis with "faith in Christ" is on Christ: "Paul has no interest in 'faith' as such, as a special cognitive mode or subjective experience, only in *faith in Christ*, which is the mark of those whose lives have been reconstituted and reordered by the death and life of Christ" (Barclay, 379, italics original; see also Hagen Pifer, 147-51).

3. Subjective Genitive: "Faith(fulness) of Christ."

The subjective genitive interpretation of *pistis Christou* renders the phrase "faith of Christ" or "faithfulness of Christ." Few modern English translations follow this reading (e.g., CEB, NET), although others include this option in a footnote (e.g., NIV, NRSV). The KJV translates the phrases as "faith of Christ," but it is unclear whether this was intentionally a subjective genitive reading or an example of the translation's overliteral tendencies (Hooker 2016, 49).

The meaning of "faith of Christ" or "faithfulness of Christ" is not self-evident (see the challenges in Dunn 2002, 259; Hagen Pifer, 28). Hebert understands the phrase as fragile humans taking refuge in Christ's faithfulness, similar to the psalmist's refuge in God's steadfastness (374). For Torrance, Jesus is the representative human, who is faithful to the faithful God on humanity's behalf (114; see also K. Barth, 97). G. M. Taylor reads *pistis Christou* in light of the Roman *fidei commissum*, such that Christ's faith is his "reliability as a trustee" who distributes the benefits of the Abrahamic promise to those who are not naturally heirs (72, 75). Similarly, G. Howard takes the faith of Christ as "the fulfilment of the promise given to Abraham that all the nations will be blessed in him" (*ABD* 2:760). For E. R. Goodenough, the faith of Christ "is simply his trusting that the *cross would not be the end, and that God would save him from death because God is *pistos*" (Goodenough and Krabel, 45). Hays reads *pistis Christou* "as a reference to the faithfulness of 'the one man Jesus Christ' whose act of obedient self-giving on the cross became the means by which 'the promise' of God was fulfilled" (2002a, 161). His treatment of *pistis Christou* is in service to his central thesis, that "a story about Jesus Christ is presupposed by Paul's argument in Galatians, and his theological reflection attempts to articulate the meaning of that story" (Hays 2002a, xxiv). Most recent subjective genitive interpreters follow Hays in understanding *pistis Christou* as Jesus' faithfulness to death on a cross. D. J. Downs and B. J. Lappenga go beyond Jesus' death to read *pistis Christou* as a reference to "the faithfulness of the risen Christ Jesus who will remain faithful to those who, in their own faith, are justified through union with Christ, risen and exalted" (Downs and Lappenga, 3; see also Vallotton, 128). Along similar lines, S. Ota understands the phrase as

"Christ's faithfulness to humanity, that is, in the sense of Christ's being steadfast, truthful, and trustworthy as God's Christ" (1997, 80). T. Morgan understands the faithfulness of Christ as being both toward God and human beings (303-4).

Advocates of the subjective genitive have suggested that when *pistis* is followed by a person in the genitive case, it never refers to faith in that person (Howard 1967, 460-61; Robinson, 78-79; Wallace, 116; Wallis, 88). However, Mark 11:22; Acts 3:16; James 2:1; Revelation 2:13; 14:12 appear to link *pistis* with an objective genitive of a person (Dunn 2002, 253; Moo, 225). Still, the extent to which these passages apply to the *pistis Christou* constructions in Paul is debatable (see Easter, 39; Kugler, 248-49).

Advocates for the subjective genitive have noted redundancies if following the objective genitive. For example, Romans 3:22 reads in the NRSV, "the *righteousness of God through faith in Jesus Christ [*pisteōs Iēsou Christou*] for all who believe." The objective genitive reading of *pisteōs Iēsou Christou* creates a redundancy ("faith in Jesus Christ . . . all who believe"). If Paul intends a subjective genitive, then the redundancy is removed (M. Barth, 368; Hays 2002a, 158; Hooker 1989, 322, 336; Morgan, 271-72). However, this repetition could be for emphasis or other reasons (Dunn 1988, 166; Matlock 2002, 307).

Paul quotes Habakkuk 2:4b in Romans 1:17 and Galatians 3:11. A number of supporters of the subjective genitive have argued for a christological reading of Habakkuk 2:4b, such that the "righteous one" is Jesus, who is faithful to death and lives in the sense of being resurrected (Campbell 1994, 281-85; 2009a, 613-16; Hanson, 40-45; Hays 2002a, 132-41; 2005, 119-42; Wallis, 110-11). Furthermore, Campbell has shown how Paul derives his *ek pisteōs* and *dia pisteōs* constructions from Habakkuk 2:4b, suggesting the clauses allude to the Scripture quotation (Campbell 1992, 100-101; 2009a, 377-78). Watson makes this same observation, crediting Campbell, but uses Habakkuk 2:4b to argue for the objective genitive (Watson, 147-63; see also Hunn 2012). Cranfield questions how likely it is that the hearers of Romans would have understood Habakkuk 2:4 christologically, given that the immediately preceding *pistis* is "all who believe" in Romans 1:16 (Cranfield, 88; see a similar challenge with respect to Hab 2:4 in Gal 3:11 in Johnson, 189-90).

Paul speaks of the arrival of a singular, external *pistis* in Galatians 3:23. The NRSV translates the verse, "Now before faith came, we were imprisoned and guarded under the law until faith would be revealed." As an external reality arriving at a singular time, *pistis* cannot be each individual's belief. Furthermore, given that *pistis* in Galatians 3:23 and "the seed" in Galatians 3:16, 19 are both "coming" and linked to "the promise," *pistis* and "the seed" point to the same thing. Paul insists that the singular seed is Christ (Gal 3:16), the law was put in place until the arrival of this seed (Gal 3:19), and humanity was enslaved under the law until *pistis* would be revealed (Gal 3:23). If this is the same expected coming and the same law under which people are held, then the seed and *pistis* would both refer to Christ. A number of supporters of the subjective genitive have made this argument (such as Campbell 2005, 196, 225-30; 2009a, 869-74; Choi, 475; Hays 2005, 139; Wallis 87-88, 113), and these insights are important to the "third view" as well.

The NRSV translates Romans 3:21-22 with an objective genitive: "But now, apart from law, the righteousness of God has been disclosed, and is attested by the law and the prophets, the righteousness of God through faith in Jesus Christ [*dia pisteōs Iēsou Christou*] for all who believe." By this translation, "faith in Jesus Christ" is the means by which "the righteousness of God" is revealed, which some interpreters find theologically problematic (e.g., Campbell 1994, 272-76; 2009a, 379, 610; 2009b, 67-70; Choi, 476; Hays 2002a, 158-60; 2002b, 283; Robinson, 80). Furthermore, as C. Kugler notes, "What sense does it make to move from definitive moments in space and time—namely, actual Jewish texts and figures from Israel's history—only to make a generalized statement about how human faith can work at any time or in any place?" (251). Instead, defenders of the subjective genitive argue, the definitive action of God through the faithfulness of Christ reveals God's righteousness.

Outside the *pistis Christou* phrases, Paul narrates the story of Jesus in such a way to evoke concepts of faithfulness, even though the phrase is not used (e.g., Rom 5; 2 Cor 4:13-14 [Campbell 2009a, 913-24]; Phil 2:5-11; 2 Thess 3:3 [Downs and Lappenga, 21-37]; see also 2 Tim 2:8-13 [Downs and Lappenga, 4-10]). Critics of the subjective genitive note that if Paul wished to speak of Jesus' faithfulness, he missed some key opportunities (such as in Rom 4, where Abraham is the model of faith; see Dunn 1988, 166).

4. "Third View": "Christ-Faith."

The "third view" reads *pistis Christou* as a singular entity ("Christ-faith") rather than separating *faith* and *Christ* into either "faith in Christ" or "faith(fulness) of Christ." Christ-faith refers to the eschatological saving Christ event and in this way is nearly synonymous with the *gospel (Sprinkle, 180; Schliesser 2016). The third view shares commonalities with both the subjective and objective genitive positions. Similar to the subjective genitive, the third view places the Christ event (rather than human faith) as that which reveals God's righteousness (*ek pisteōs* in Rom 1:16; *dia pisteōs Christou* in Rom 3:22; Sprinkle, 175). Similar to the objective genitive, Abraham's faith (not Christ's) is the example for believers (Schliesser 2016, 284).

Central to the third view is the coupling of *faith* with *gospel*. Paul makes a similar move in Galatians 1. In Galatians 1:23, the first time *pistis* appears in Galatians, Paul notes the churches in Judea heard it said that Paul is now "preaching the faith [*tēn pistin*] he once tried to destroy" (NIV). Just a few verses earlier in Galatians 1:16, Paul notes that God apocalypsed his *Son in him so that he might "preach him to the *Gentiles." Comparing these two verses, *faith* and *him* (Christ) are parallel. Paul makes a similar parallel in Romans 10:8 ("word of faith") and Romans 10:17 ("word of Christ"; Sprinkle, 177-78). Furthermore, as noted above, supporters of the objective genitive have a difficult time explaining the singular arrival of faith in Galatians 3:23-26. Faith in this passage is "apocalyptically revealed," which does not align with an individual's religious attitude or decision but rather with an external objective event (Sprinkle, 179). Hays's understanding of *pistis Christou* as referring to the story of Christ's life, death, and *resurrection is not far from this third view's emphasis on eschatological event. As such, these third-view readings of Galatians 1; 3 may equally support the subjective genitive.

Schliesser understands the Christ-faith as an orbit into which humans are incorporated: "All of these passages affirm the correspondence between faith and Christ, as both share a core meaning in terms of a *Machtbereich* into which individuals are incorporated and under whose influence a new *communitas* is created" (2016, 287). This locative reading of participation extends even to *ek pisteōs* in Romans and Galatians (from Hab 2:4), an interpretation Schliesser claims Paul derived from the Hebrew *Vorlage* (Schliesser 2016, 288-29; see critiques in Bates, 183-84; Oakes, 262-63).

5. Intentionally Multifaceted.

Momentum is gathering for reading *pistis Christou* as intentionally multifaceted (see Bates). That is, as Schliesser notes, "Some of the most recent studies on the subject agree that one should finally move beyond the somewhat naïve philological assumption of a subjective-objective-genitive dichotomy" (2016, 289). The push for multiple meanings is coming from different angles.

First, F. G. Downing has demonstrated the intended imprecision in ancient semantics. Downing's research into ancient semantics shows how "no word and no set of words 'encapsulates' let alone itself defines 'the idea.' It is always outside and beyond the words; and, *a fortiori*, there is no attempt to discriminate—let alone then to prioritise and exclude—various possible senses, connotations, of the various individual terms deployed" (Downing, 146). Ancient authors did not share modern concerns for connotative precision (see also Ulrichs, 19-23). As such, when Paul uses a phrase such as *pistis Christou* without clearly disambiguating the statement, he may expect his hearers to derive more than one meaning.

Second, advances in the lexicography of *pistis* suggests a multifaceted meaning of the word itself. Morgan's massive study on the meaning of *pistis* and *fides* in the early Roman Empire and early churches has demonstrated how *pistis* is "first and foremost, neither a body of beliefs nor a function of the heart or mind, but a relationship which creates community" (Morgan, 14; see also Bates). As a relationship of trust, *pistis* has a "Janus-faced quality," involving the qualities and practices of both partners in the relationship. Christ is faithful to God and worthy of God's trust. Christ is worthy of human trust, and humans in turn trust him. *Pistis Christou*, then, involves the multiple elements of Christ's trustworthiness or faithfulness to God and human faith in or loyalty to Christ (Morgan, 273-74; see also Bates, 198; Campbell 2020, 303; Downing, 160; Gupta, 176; Hays 2005, 297; Hooker 2016, 62; Keener, 181-82; Lee, 253-55; Oakes, 272; Taylor, 71-72).

See also Ephesians, Letter to the; Faith; Galatians, Letter to the; Gospel; In Christ; Justification; Law; Old Testament in Paul; Philippians, Letter to the; Romans, Letter to the; Salvation; Textual Criticism; Works of the Law.

BIBLIOGRAPHY. **J. Barclay,** *Paul and the Gift* (Grand Rapids, MI: Eerdmans, 2015); **J. Barr,** *The Semantics of Biblical Language* (London: Oxford University Press, 1961); **K. Barth,** *The Epistle to the Romans*, 6th ed., trans E. C. Hoskyns (Oxford: Oxford University Press, 1968); **M. Barth,** "The Faith of the Messiah," *HeyJ* 10 (1969): 363-70; **M. W. Bates,** "The External-Relational Shift in Faith (Pistis) in New Testament Research: Romans I as Gospel-Allegiance Test Case," *CurBR* 18, no. 2 (2020): 176-202; **R. Bultmann,** "πιστεύω, πίστις, κτλ.," *TDNT* 6:174-228; **D. A. Campbell,** "The Meaning of Πιστις and Νομος in Paul: A Linguistic and Structural Perspective," *JBL* 111, no. 1 (1992): 91-103; idem, "Romans 1:17—A Crux Interpretum for the Πιστις Χριστου Debate," *JBL* 113, no. 2 (1994): 265-85; idem, *The Quest for Paul's Gospel: A Suggested Strategy* (London: T&T Clark, 2005); idem, *The Deliverance of God: An Apocalyptic Rereading of Justification in Paul* (Grand Rapids, MI: Eerdmans, 2009); idem, "The Faithfulness of Jesus Christ in Romans 3:22," in *The Faith of Jesus Christ: Exegetical, Biblical, and Theological Studies*, ed. M. F. Bird and P. M. Sprinkle (Peabody, MA: Hendrickson, 2009), 57-71; idem, *Pauline Dogmatics: The Triumph of God's Love* (Grand Rapids, MI: Eerdmans, 2020); **H. Choi,** "ΠΙΣΤΙΣ in Galatians 3:5-6: Neglected Evidence for the Faithfulness of Christ," *JBL* 124 (2005): 467-90; **C. E. B. Cranfield,** *On Romans and Other New Testament Essays* (Edinburgh: T&T Clark, 1998); **F. G. Downing,** "Ambiguity, Ancient Semantics, and Faith," *NTS* 56 (2009): 139-62; **D. J. Downs and B. J. Lappenga,** *The Faithfulness of the Risen Christ: Pistis and the Exalted Lord in the Pauline Letters* (Waco, TX: Baylor University Press, 2019); **J. D. G. Dunn,** *Romans 1–8*, WBC 38A (Dallas: Word, 1988); idem, "Once More, ΠΙΣΤΙΣ ΧΡΙΣΤΟΥ," in *The Faith of Jesus Christ: The Narrative Substructure of Galatians 3:1–4:11* (Grand Rapids, MI: Eerdmans, 2002), 249-71; **M. C. Easter,** "The Pistis Christou Debate: Main Arguments and Responses in Summary," *CurBR* 9, no. 1 (2010): 33-47; **M. W. Elliot,** "Πίστις Χριστοῦ in the Church Fathers and Beyond," in *The Faith of Jesus Christ: Exegetical, Biblical, and Theological Studies*, ed. M. F. Bird and P. M. Sprinkle (Peabody, MA: Hendrickson, 2009), 277-89; **E. R. Goodenough with A. T. Kraabel,** "Paul and the Hellenization of Christianity," in *Religions in Antiquity: Essays in Memory of Erwin Ramsdell Goodenough*, ed. J. Neusner (Leiden: Brill, 1968), 23-68; **N. Gupta,** *Paul and the Language of Faith* (Grand Rapids, MI: Eerdmans, 2020); **J. Hagen Pifer,** *Faith as Participation: An Exegetical Study of Some Key Pauline Texts* (Tübingen: Mohr Siebeck, 2019); **A. T. Hanson,** *Studies in Paul's Technique and Theology* (London: SPCK, 1974); **R. A. Harrisville,** "ΠΙΣΤΙΣ ΧΡΙΣΤΟΥ: Witness of the Fathers," *NovT* 36 (1994): 233-41; idem, "Before Πιστις Χριστου: The Objective Genitive as Good Greek," *NovT* 48 (2006): 353-58; **J. Haussleiter,** "Der Glaube Jesu Christi und der christliche Glaube: Ein Beitrag zur Erklärung des Römerbriefes," *NKZ* 2 (1891): 109-45; **R. B. Hays,** *The Faith of Jesus Christ: The Narrative Substructure of Galatians 3:1–4:11* (Grand Rapids, MI: Eerdmans, 2002); idem, "ΠΙΣΤΙΣ and Pauline Christology: What Is at Stake?," in *The Faith of Jesus Christ: The Narrative Substructure of Galatians 3:1–4:11* (Grand Rapids, MI: Eerdmans, 2002), 272-97; idem, *The Conversion of the Imagination: Paul as Interpreter of Israel's Scripture* (Grand Rapids, MI: Eerdmans, 2005); **G. Hebert,** "Faithfulness and Faith," *Theology* 58 (1955): 373-79; **M. D. Hooker,** "ΠΙΣΤΙΣ ΧΡΙΣΤΟΥ," *NTS* 35 (1989): 321-42; idem, "Another Look at πίστις Χριστοῦ," *SJT* 69, no. 1 (2016): 46-62; **G. Howard,** "Notes and Observations on the 'Faith of Christ,'" *HTR* 60 (1967): 459-84; idem, "Faith of Christ," *ABD* 2:758-60; **A. Hultgren,** "The Pistis Christou Formulation in Paul," *NovT* 22 (1980): 248-63; **D. Hunn,** "ΠΙΣΤΙΣ ΧΡΙΣΤΟΥ in Galatians 2:16: Clarification from 3:1-6," *TynBul* 57, no. 1 (2006): 23-33; idem, "Pistis Christou in Galatians: The Connection to Habakkuk 2:4," *TynBul* 63, no. 1 (2012): 75-91; idem, "Galatians 3:6-9: Abraham's Fatherhood and Paul's Conclusions," *CBQ* 78 (2016): 500-514; **H. W. Johnson,** "The Paradigm of Abraham in Galatians 3:6-9," *TrinJ* 8 (1987): 179-99; **C. S. Keener,** *Galatians: A Commentary* (Grand Rapids, MI: Baker Academic, 2019); **C. Kugler,** "ΠΙΣΤΙΣ ΧΡΙΣΤΟΥ: The Current State of Play and Key Arguments," *CurBR* 14, no. 2 (2016): 244-55; **S. M. Lee,** "Christ's Πίστις vs. Caesar's Fides: Πίστις Χριστοῦ in Galatians and the Roman Imperial Cult," *ExpTim* 130, no. 6 (2019): 243-55; **J. L. Martyn,** *Galatians*, AB 33A (New York: Doubleday, 1997); **R. B. Matlock,** "'Even the Demons Believe': Paul and πιστις Χριστου," *CBQ* 64 (2002): 300-318; idem, "ΠΙΣΤΙΣ in Galatians 3.26: Neglected Evidence for 'Faith in Christ'?," *NTS* 49 (2003): 433-39; **D. Moo,** *The Epistle to the Romans*, NICNT (Grand Rapids, MI: Eerdmans, 1996); **T. Morgan,** *Roman Faith and Christian Faith: Pistis and Fides in the Early Roman Empire and Early Churches* (New York: Oxford, 2015); **P. Oakes,** "Pistis as Relational Way of Life in Galatians," *JSNT* 40, no. 3 (2018): 255-75; **S. Ota,** "The Absolute Use of ΠΙΣΤΙΣ and ΠΙΣΤΙΣ ΧΡΙΣΤΟΥ in Paul," *Annual of the Japanese Biblical Institute* 23 (1997): 64-82; idem, "ΠΙΣΤΙΣ ΧΡΙΣΤΟΥ: Christ's Faithfulness to Whom?," *Hitotsubashi Journal of Arts and Sciences* 55, no. 1 (2014): 15-26; **S. E. Porter,** "The Rhetorical Scribe: Textual Variants in Romans and Their Possible Rhetorical Purpose," in *Rhetorical Criticism and the Bible: Essays from the 1998 Florence Conference*, ed. S. E. Porter and D. Stamps, JSNTSup 195 (London: Sheffield Academic, 2002), 403-19; **S. E. Porter and A. W. Pitts,** "Πίστις with a Preposition and Genitive Modifier: Lexical, Semantic, and Syntactic Considerations in the πίστις Χριστοῦ Discussion," in *The Faith of Jesus Christ: Exegetical, Biblical, and Theological Studies*, ed. M. F. Bird and P. M. Sprinkle (Peabody, MA: Hendrickson, 2009), 33-53;

D. W. B. Robinson, "'Faith of Jesus Christ'—a New Testament Debate," *RTR* 29 (1970): 71-81; **D. Rusam,** "Was versteht Paulus unter der πίστις (Ἰησοῦ) Χριστοῦ (Röm. 3,22.26; Gal. 2,16.20; 3,22; Phil. 3,9)?," *PzB* 11, no. 1 (2002): 47-70; **B. Schliesser,** "'Exegetical Amnesia' and ΠΙΣΤΙΣ ΧΡΙΣΤΟΥ: The 'Faith of Christ' in Nineteenth-Century Pauline Scholarship," *JTS* 66, no. 1 (2015): 61-89; idem, "'Christ-Faith' as an Eschatological Event (Galatians 3.23-26): A 'Third View' on Πίστις Χριστοῦ," *JSNT* 38, no. 3 (2016): 277-300; **M. Silva,** "Faith Versus Works of Law in Galatians," in *Justification and Variegated Nomism*, vol. 2, *The Paradoxes of Paul*, ed. P. T. O'Brien, D. A. Carson, and M. A. Seifrid (Grand Rapids, MI: Baker, 2004), 217-48; **P. M. Sprinkle,** "Πίστις Χριστοῦ as an Eschatological Event," in *The Faith of Jesus Christ: Exegetical, Biblical, and Theological Studies*, ed. M. F. Bird and P. M. Sprinkle (Peabody, MA: Hendrickson, 2009), 165-84; **G. M. Taylor,** "The Function of ΠΙΣΤΙΣ ΧΡΙΣΤΟΥ in Galatians," *JBL* 85, no. 1 (1966): 58-76; **T. F. Torrance,** "One Aspect of the Biblical Conception of Faith," *ExpTim* 68 (1957): 111-14; **K. F. Ulrichs,** *Christusglaube: Studien zum Syntagma pistis Christou und zum paulinischen Verständnis von Glaube und Rechtfertigung*, WUNT 2/227 (Tübingen: Mohr Siebeck, 2007); **P. Vallotton,** *Le Christ et la Foi: Etude de théologie biblique*, Nouvelle série théologique 10 (Geneva: Labor et Fides, 1960); **D. B. Wallace,** *Greek Grammar Beyond the Basics* (Grand Rapids, MI: Zondervan, 1996); **I. G. Wallis,** *The Faith of Jesus Christ in Early Christian Traditions*, SNTSMS 84 (Cambridge: Cambridge University Press, 1995); **F. Watson,** "By Faith (of Christ): An Exegetical Dilemma and Its Scriptural Solution," in *The Faith of Jesus Christ: Exegetical, Biblical, and Theological Studies*, ed. M. F. Bird and P. M. Sprinkle (Peabody, MA: Hendrickson, 2009), 147-63.

M. C. Easter

FAITHFULNESS OF GOD. *See* Faith; Faith of Christ; God; Righteousness.

FALLING AWAY. *See* Apostasy.

FALSE APOSTLES. *See* Apostle; Judaizers; Opponents of Paul.

FAMILY. *See* Church; Church Structure; Households and Household Codes; Identity; Kinship Language in Paul.

FATHER. *See* Adoption; God; Kinship Language in Paul; Son of God.

FEAR, REVERENCE

Fear and *reverence* occupy two different semantic domains. *Fear* (L&N 25V, "Fear, Terror, Alarm") encompasses a number of Greek words that represent the normal human response of fear, terror, or alarm caused by a variety of circumstances. *Reverence* (L&N 53G, "Worship, Reverence") encompasses a number of Greek words, some of which overlap the above, that speak of respect and *worship (though this article only touches briefly on the topic of worship). The semantic connection between the two domains is that some of the words used of fear are then metaphorically extended to denote an appropriate response, usually before *God, of holy fear or reverence. There is therefore a continuum between these literal and metaphorical meanings that sometimes makes it difficult to distinguish them.

1. Fear
2. Reverence

1. Fear.

Human fear, terror, or alarm is a natural response to a variety of circumstances, and there are many circumstances within the NT, including within Paul's letters, that speak of human fear. For example, human fear is a normal part of one's emotional reactions to troubling situations. Paul tells the Corinthians that he is afraid (*phobeomai*) that they may be deceived (2 Cor 11:3). Paul says that he himself had fear (*phobos*) when he came to the Corinthians (1 Cor 2:3), and that when he traveled to Macedonia, due to outward conflicts, he had internal fear (*phobos*; 2 Cor 7:5). He says that his letter to the Corinthians had the effect of producing fear (*phobos*) in them (although this may have a more metaphorical sense of reverence; 2 Cor 7:11), even though he did not want to make them fear (*ekphobeō*) through his letters (2 Cor 10:9). He says that they also had "fear [*phobos*] and trembling" when they received Titus (2 Cor 7:15). Paul says that he is afraid (*phobeomai*) that if he comes the Corinthians may not meet his expectations, and he theirs (2 Cor 12:20). Paul has similar concerns regarding the Galatian situation, speaking of Peter fearing (*phobeomai*) those from the *circumcision (Gal 2:12) and his own fearing (*phobeomai*) lest he had worked in vain (Gal 4:11). He likewise encourages the Philippians not to be frightened (*ptyromai*) by those who oppose them (Phil 1:28), and the Thessalonians not to be frightened (*throeomai*) by unsettling teaching regarding the Lord's return (2 Thess 2:2). The reason for this ability not to fear is that God did not give believers a spirit of enslavement so that they live in fear (*phobos*) but a spirit of *adoption (Rom 8:15), nor did he give believers a spirit of fearfulness or cowardliness (*deilia*; 2 Tim 1:7).

Paul extends the scope of fear from personal human interaction to the fear of authority. The primary place for this discussion in Paul is Romans 13:1-7. This is a widely misunderstood passage, as it does not call for unqualified obedience to authorities, but it does call for appropriate respect to be paid and obedience to just and fair authorities (see Porter, 243-50). Paul tells the Romans that rulers (just rulers) are not a fear (*phobos*) to one doing good, only to one doing evil (Rom 13:3), and says that if they do not want to fear (*phobeomai*) authority they should do good (Rom 13:3), but if they want to do evil, then they should fear (*phobeomai*; Rom 13:4). Paul concludes his discussion about authority by saying that one should give appropriate regard to earthly authorities, and one expression of this regard is fear (*phobos*; Rom 13:7), as well as *honor. Paul similarly tells *slaves at *Ephesus to have "fear [*phobos*] and trembling" toward their masters (Eph 6:5). Within the *church, Paul tells Timothy that the *discipline of elders is important so that others take note and are fearful (*phobos*; 1 Tim 5:20), whether this is fear of falling into *sin or fear of God.

2. Reverence.

Reverence is a figurative or metaphorical extension of fear that is reserved for those contexts in which one is responding appropriately to being in the presence of God or Christ, or being in another suitable circumstance demanding such a response. This context is usually indicated by reference to the fear being directed toward or in respect of God or Christ. Fear of or reverence for God or Christ is found in a number of different contexts within the Pauline letters, along with some contexts that also commend reverence for other humans as appropriate.

In Romans, Paul states from the outset that the basic human problem is that human beings worship (*sebazomai*) the creature rather than the creator (Rom 1:25), when the opposite should be the case. As a result, humans, both Jew and *Gentile alike, stand condemned under sin. In Romans 3:18, Paul supports this statement with a quotation of Psalm 36:1: "there is no fear of God before their eyes" (NRSV). In other words, rather than keeping the *image of God before them, "fear, reverence, or awe for God is unknown to them" (Porter, 90). In Romans 11:20, Paul tells his Gentile Roman readers that they should not be arrogant because God has grafted them into the olive tree and cut off unbelieving Jews; rather, they should fear (*phobeomai*), here a fear of God, lest they should be cut off as well. This passage well illustrates the metaphorical connection between fear and reverence, in that fear is the emotion reflected in the appropriate response of reverence for God.

Paul speaks of fear of or reverence for God in a number of his other letters. In 2 Corinthians 5, Paul grounds his confidence regarding the state of believers after *death (2 Cor 5:6-10) in the "fear [*phobos*] of the *Lord" (2 Cor 5:11 NRSV). This serves as a transition to his defense of his Corinthian ministry of reconciliation (2 Cor 5:11-21). Believers are obligated to respond by cleansing themselves from defilement and perfecting themselves in sanctification, a passage probably influenced by cultic terminology. Sanctification is grounded "in fear [*phobos*] of God" (2 Cor 7:1), with "in" referring to the sphere or arena in which sanctification occurs.

There are several passages that exemplify the continuum of literal-metaphorical language in use of the language of fear and reverence. Such language occurs in *household code passages. The first is Colossians 3:22. Paul commands slaves to be genuinely obedient, "fearing [*phobeomai*] the Lord" (NRSV). The Lord, here Christ (see Col 3:24) rather than an earthly master, serves as the backdrop for all of the commands in the Colossian household code (see Col 3:18, 20). This may reflect language of the OT (see, e.g., Ex 1:17, 21; Lev 19:14, 32; 25:17 for similar phrasing), in which service is to be rendered to God. The next passage is Ephesians 5:21-33. There is major debate over whether Ephesians 5:21 is the conclusion to the previous section (variously defined as Eph 5:6-20 or Eph 5:15-20), whether it is the introduction to Ephesians 5:22–6:9, or whether it is a transition. In any case, the verse consists of a participle clause, "being obedient to each other in fear [*phobos*] of Christ," introducing Christ as the object of fear or reverence, and placing Christ in a similar position to God, as in 2 Corinthians 7:1. However, the household code continues with Ephesians 5:33, which says a wife is to "fear [*phobeomai*] her husband." Whereas this may reflect the emotion of human fear in light of ancient gender relations, the reciprocal nature of the Pauline household codes, in which in Ephesians 5:25 husbands are told to love their wives as Christ loved the church and gave himself for it, encourages readers to think that this instruction to the wife is for appropriate reverence and respect for her husband.

There are several passages noted above that speak of "fear and trembling" (1 Cor 2:3; 2 Cor 7:15;

Eph 6:5 NRSV) as normal human emotions, but only Philippians 2:12 speaks of Christians working out their *salvation with "fear [*phobos*] and trembling." Whereas one may recognize the sociologically based use of the phrase in Paul's dealings with others (see Michael), this does not seem to be appropriate in the Philippian context. After his christological passage of Philippians 2:6-11 regarding Christ's example, Paul tells his audience to be similarly obedient and to work out their salvation with "fear [*phobos*] and trembling" (Phil 2:12 NRSV). The sense of salvation here is soteriological, with Paul apparently endorsing the idea that believers are actively engaging in accomplishing, developing, and fulfilling their salvation with reverence toward God (Silva, 117, "godly fear").

See also Households and Household Codes; Joy, Rejoicing; Romans, Letter to the; Salvation.

BIBLIOGRAPHY. **J. H. Michael,** "'Work Out Your Own Salvation,'" *Expositor* 9, no. 2 (1924): 439-50; **S. E. Porter,** *The Letter to the Romans: A Linguistic and Literary Commentary*, NTM 37 (Sheffield: Sheffield Phoenix, 2015); **M. Silva,** *Philippians*, 2nd ed., BECNT (Grand Rapids, MI: Baker, 2005).

S. E. Porter

FELLOWSHIP, COMMUNION, SHARING

Community was at the center of Paul's life, theology, and *ministry, as fellowship is a theological necessity of the proclamation of the *gospel. The new *creation issues forth a new community and is keenly concerned with a set of distinctive practices for the flourishing of its members (Barclay, 439). Therefore it should not be surprising to see that these ideas permeate Paul's correspondences. The community of Jesus' followers, their relationship to one another, and the activities therein are represented by multiple terms and images. The most important are *koinōnia* and its various cognates, the verbs *metechō* and *merizō*, and Paul's image of the community of *God as a *body. The concept of community transcends any single term or image. Community for Paul is both spiritual and social, both economic and practical.

1. Fellowship/Sharing with the Triune God
2. Fellowship/Sharing with the People of God

1. Fellowship/Sharing with the Triune God. All life together begins with the initiation of God to humanity in sharing God's life with God's creation—his people. *Koinōnia* is not something Paul or his communities create. In 1 Corinthians, Paul says that God's people are called by him into the fellowship (*koinōnia*) of his son (1 Cor 1:9), and this forms the basis of their relationship with one another. It is the antithesis of the factions in Corinth. Paul grounds their fellowship with one another in their participation in the life of God together. All such activity comes as a result of the *grace of God (Phil 1:9), which Paul says he and believers share in (*synkoinōnous*) together. Believers also share in the blessings of the gospel (1 Cor 9:23). Sharing also involves incorporation with others on behalf of God. In Romans 11:17, Paul reminds his (mostly) *Gentile readers that they share (*synkoinōnos*) in something that was not originally theirs and did not start with them. Rather, they have been incorporated into a fellowship "long cultivated by God" in his *covenant with *Abraham (Dunn 1988, 2:673).

2. Fellowship/Sharing with the People of God. For Paul believers both share in and share with one another. They participate with Jesus (Phil 2:1) and have communion with one another (Phil 2:2-3). Paul invites Gentiles into this new fellowship marked by inclusion and generosity, a community that preceded Paul's involvement (see Acts 2:42). In Romans 12 and 1 Corinthians 10; 12, Paul uses his preferred ecclesiological metaphor of the body to refer to his communities (Dunn 1998, 548). The metaphor of the body was a frequent image of community in the Greco-Roman world, going as far back as the fourth century BC (Aristotle, *Eth. nic.* 8-9). Various writers used the body metaphor to discuss the political organization, and the metaphor was commonly employed to combat divisions within a community (Mitchell, 157-58). *Koinōnia* in this context was sharing something in common with someone else, thus forming a fellowship and associating with them. In the ancient world, this was structured along the lines of status and honor, *ethnicity, gender, and economic factors.

Paul assumes this context yet radically transforms the notion of *koinōnia* and community in the ancient world with the makeup of the social gathering (Gal 3:28). Paul's sense of communal identity and its related set of practices are not rooted in biological or sociological common ground but in the radical work of *Christ, who died for "all" and now lives in "all" by the power of the Spirit. The Spirit acts as the binding agent in the community of the new creation (Gal 4:6-7; 2 Cor 13:13). More importantly, when Paul expounds on the nature of the Christian community (Rom 12:4-8; 1 Cor 12:4-27;

Eph 4:7-16), it is a charismatic community (Dunn 1998, 548). For Paul, the community is graciously created by God and unremittingly sustained by the Spirit. In this sense one participates in the Spirit (2 Cor 13:13), revealing that the sine qua non of Christian existence and community is the indwelling and experience of the *Holy Spirit both in and amid its members. This sharing of the Spirit is a gift given by God and joins believers with God, so the expectation is that it will create new vistas and avenues for the experience of community in creative and radical ways.

Fellowship is both local and supra-local in its outlook. Attention should be paid to the word *all* in Paul's understanding of Christian community (Eastman, 210). For example, in 1 Corinthians 1:2, Paul writes that the Corinthians are "together with all those who in every place call on the *name of our *Lord Jesus Christ" (NRSV), revealing the longitudinal relationships that extend beyond the Corinthian community itself. Paul's community and sense of fellowship are linked geographically with others (in contrast to the Corinthians' limited sense). These links are not just spiritual or theological but include concrete ways of sharing in a common life, both locally and globally. Paul commends the Macedonian churches as an example to follow for radical generosity amid their extreme poverty, which abounded in sacrificial giving for another Pauline community (2 Cor 8:1-3; Rom 15:26). Paul describes this as a sharing (*koinōnia*) in the ministry to the saints (2 Cor 8:4).

*Women also played a substantial leadership role in the formation of the fellowship and sharing of Pauline communities. Women such as Phoebe (Rom 16:1), whose description ("she has been a benefactor of many and of myself," Rom 16:2 NRSV) implies that she was a person of substantial *wealth, were commissioned by Paul to lead house churches and would have been responsible for *sharing* their resources in concrete and practical ways with the Roman community(ies) (Jewett, 946-47).

Sharing in community is also a *suffering with one another (Phil 4:14; 2 Cor 1:3-7) in light of the broader sharing (*koinōnia*) in the sufferings of Christ (Phil 3:10). Scholars have noted that this sharing is particularly noteworthy as believers participate in the *cross, rehearse this sharing in the *Lord's Supper, and orient their lives toward suffering for others (Bird and Gupta, 148). Believers share in the *cruciformity that marked the life and *death of Jesus and subsequently marks those who are united with Jesus (Gorman, 349-67).

See also Body of Christ; Church; In Christ; Lord's Supper.

BIBLIOGRAPHY. **R. Banks,** *Paul's Idea of Community*, rev. ed. (Grand Rapids, MI: Baker, 1994); **J. M. G. Barclay,** *Paul and the Gift* (Grand Rapids, MI: Eerdmans, 2015); **E. Best,** *Paul and His Converts* (Edinburgh: T&T Clark, 1988); **M. F. Bird and N. K. Gupta,** *Philippians* (New York: Cambridge University Press, 2021); **J. Y. Campbell,** "κοινωνία and Its Cognates in the New Testament," in *Three New Testament Studies* (Leiden: Brill, 1965), 1-28; **J. D. G. Dunn,** *Romans*, 2 vols. (Grand Rapids, MI: Eerdmans 1988); idem, *The Theology of the Apostle Paul* (Grand Rapids, MI: Eerdmans, 1998); idem, *Beginning from Jerusalem* (Grand Rapids, MI: Eerdmans, 2009); **S. G. Eastman,** "What Did Paul Think God Was Doing in Christian Communities?," in *The New Cambridge Companion to St. Paul*, ed. B. W. Longenecker (New York: Cambridge University Press, 2020), 210-24; **M. J. Gorman,** *Cruciformity: Paul's Narrative Spirituality of the Cross* (Grand Rapids, MI: Eerdmans, 2001); **J. Hainz,** *Koinonia. "Kirche" als Gemeinschaft bei Paulus*, Biblische Untersuchungen 16 (Regensburg: Pustet, 1982); **F. Hauck,** "κοινός, κτλ., " *TDNT* 3:797-809; **R. Jewett,** *Romans* (Minneapolis: Fortress, 2006); **R. P. Martin,** *The Family and the Fellowship* (Grand Rapids, MI: Eerdmans, 1979); **J. M. McDermott,** "The Biblical Doctrine of ΚΟΙΝΩΝΙΑ," *BZ* 19 (1975): 64-77, 219-33; **M. M. Mitchell,** *Paul and the Rhetoric of Reconciliation* (Louisville, KY: Westminster John Knox, 1992); **G. Panikulam,** *Koinōnia in the New Testament: A Dynamic Expression of Christian Life*, AnBib 85 (Rome: Biblical Institute, 1979); **H. Seesemann,** *Der Begriff ΚΟΙΝΩΝΙΑ im Neuen Testament*, BZNW 14 (Giessen, 1933); **M. J. Suggs,** "Koinonia in the New Testament," *Mid-Stream* 23 (1984): 351-62.

J. A. Myers

FINAL JUDGMENT. *See* Eschatology; Judgment.

FINANCIAL SUPPORT

Although Paul provided for himself as a leatherworker (Acts 18:3; see Still, 781), he nevertheless had the apostolic right to receive financial support from the churches he planted. That he availed himself of this right with some and not all gave rise to several accusations. Was he inconsistent in his financial policy? Why did he accept from some but refuse from others? Was he even an *apostle if he refused payment?

1. Paul's (Inconsistent?) Apostolic Right to Financial Support.

Paul had every right to obtain financial support from his churches. This much is clear from 1 Corinthians 9:1-18. He asks seventeen questions, employs four vocational images, and appeals to the *law (1 Cor 9:9-10) and even the *Lord himself (1 Cor 9:14), all in order to assert his apostolic right (*exousia*) in the *gospel to live from the gospel (1 Cor 9:11, 14). But this rhetorical tour de force ends up being surprisingly anticlimactic. He forthrightly asserts his *exousia* simply to give it up (see 1 Thess 2:1-12, where he adopts the same approach).

This is where the charge of inconsistency comes in. On the one hand, he adamantly refuses financial support from the Corinthians, not only in 1 Corinthians 9 but also in 2 Corinthians 11–12. He insists that he refrained from being a financial burden and will refrain in the future (2 Cor 11:9), even during his third visit to Corinth (2 Cor 12:14). On the other hand, however, Paul happily accepts financial support from the Philippians, with whom he shares a *koinōnia* (a *fellowship in Christ and partnership in gospel advancement; Phil 4:15; cf. 2 Cor 11:9). They delivered a gift to Paul in *prison through the hands of Epaphroditus (Phil 4:10-20; 2:25-30).

How does one explain this seemingly inconsistent financial policy? In search of an answer, many have turned to ancient forms of financial support.

2. Ancient Forms of Financial Support.

R. Hock identified four means to financial support available to Paul: (1) the charging of fees (practiced by the sophists), (2) entering the household of a patron (practiced by philosophers, rhetors, and grammar teachers), (3) begging (practiced by Cynic philosophers), and (4) working a trade (practiced by rabbis and Cynic philosophers; Hock, 52-59). Recently, J. Ogereau argued that another option should be added: a financial partnership called *societas unius rei*, which Paul transformed into a *societas evangelii*. It involves the *church depositing money into a common fund, from which Paul may withdraw what is necessary for his missionary activities (Ogereau, 289, 337).

Scholars are divided on which approach Paul adopted. Some emphasize Paul's Jewish upbringing, which combined the study of Torah with working a trade (e.g., Hengel; Harvey). Others connect him to the itinerant ministry of Jesus, where the apostle would engage in "charismatic begging" (Theissen, 34-35). Still others situate Paul in the Socratic-Cynic tradition of plying a trade as a leatherworker (see Acts 18:3; Hock; Malherbe). But the most influential view was first advanced by E. A. Judge, who insisted that Paul accepted *patronage by entering the household of the rich. Many have built on Judge's rich contributions to explain Paul's seemingly inconsistent financial policy.

3. The Patronal Approach to Paul's Financial Policy.

P. Marshall, one influential proponent of this approach, argues that the Corinthians offered a gift to Paul under the guise of *friendship, but Paul saw through their so-called gift. It was, in reality, a gift with strings attached. They sought to make Paul their client and so become his patron. Not wanting these oppressive ties of obligation with their attendant power plays, he refused the "gift" of these would-be benefactors.

This view has been widespread since the early 1970s, but it suffers from four faulty assumptions about Paul that render it improbable:

(1) Paul does not evade obligation. Compare Philippians 2:30, where he speaks of the Philippians' obligatory service (*leitourgia*) of sending a gift, or the way he crafts the Jerusalem *collection as something "owed" (Rom 15:26-27). Scholars anachronistically impose modern assumptions about obligation and debt onto Paul. No ancient person would deny that those elements exist in gift giving.

(2) Money does not necessarily represent patronage. Just because the Corinthians offered Paul money does not mean they attempted to make Paul their client. Patronage depends on the context. Paying a professor through one's tuition does not render the professor a client to the student. Knowledge is a greater commodity. In the same way, immaterial gifts have a greater value than material gifts in Paul's perspective (1 Cor 9:11 ESV: "If we have sown spiritual things among you, is it too much if we reap material things from you?"; see also 1 Cor 9:14; Rom 15:27). More than that, there were other relationships of exchange in the Greco-Roman world (i.e., father-child, friend-friend, teacher-pupil, etc.). One cannot see patronage behind the exchange of every gift.

(3) Offering a gift to Paul does not turn the Corinthians into his patron. Advocates of this view assume their gift to Paul is the initial gift. In a patron-client relationship, the patron gave the first gift, so it makes sense that the Corinthians would be considered the patron and Paul the client. In this instance, though, Paul gave the initial (immaterial) gift, the gift of the gospel. He sowed "spiritual things" first (1 Cor 9:11 ESV), so their gift should be considered a return (material) gift.

Related to this, 1 Corinthians 9 is not Paul's response to the Corinthians' gift (a common assumption among patronal proponents, who read 2 Cor 11–12 into 1 Cor 9). It is actually a response to their response to Paul's initial gift of the gospel at Corinth. They wondered why he refused their countergift of money while he spiritually labored among them.

(4) The patronage model itself only accounts for two parties, Paul and the Corinthians, or a patron and a client. But, for Paul, every human relationship involves *God as the divine party, and his presence necessarily reconfigures the way humans relate to one another.

So, our initial questions remain: Why did Paul accept financial support from the Philippians but refuse from the Corinthians? Was he inconsistent? Was he even an apostle?

4. A Sociotheological Approach to Paul's Financial Policy.

When the relational dynamics among God, Paul, and the Philippians are compared to those between God, Paul, and the Corinthians, one discovers the answers to the questions above.

On the social level, Paul never accepted financial support when initially entering a city. Whether at Philippi (Phil 4:15), Thessalonica (1 Thess 2:9), or *Corinth (1 Cor 9:12, 15, 18), Paul consistently worked as a leatherworker and refused fiscal aid. This allowed him to disassociate himself from the sophists and distinguish his gospel ministry from those itinerant philosophers who sought financial gain. He proclaimed the gospel "free of charge" (1 Cor 9:18 ESV).

On the theological level, this specific policy enabled Paul to highlight the true giver of the gospel. God is the source of the gospel, not Paul (see 1 Thess 2:2, 4, 8-9, 13; 2 Cor 11:7). Paul is "entrusted with a stewardship" (1 Cor 9:17 ESV). He mediates a divine commodity. If a return had came to Paul during his initial visit, recipients would have been liable to mistake him as the source of what he provided. His role as a mediator of God's *grace was fundamental to what it meant to be an apostle of Christ.

Nevertheless, after initially preaching the gospel "free of charge" and departing the newly founded church, he began to accept financial support from them while ministering in a new city, where he refused support. This is why Paul accepted gifts from Philippi during his initial entrance at Thessalonica (Phil 4:16) and Corinth (2 Cor 11:9). He is not inconsistent, accepting money under the table while supposedly preaching "free of charge." We are simply witnessing the overlapping of two stages in Paul's gospel ministry. The Philippians progressed from stage one (Paul's initial preaching) to stage two (financially supporting Paul), but the Corinthians never progressed past stage one.

But we are still left asking, Why? Why did he accept from the Philippians but not from the Corinthians? Two primary points of comparison stand out.

(1) Whereas the Philippians acknowledged God as a divine party in their relationship with Paul (as a close examination of Philippians makes clear; see Briones, 58-130), Paul continually had to remind the Corinthians that God was the source and owner of all their possessions (see 1 Cor 1:4-9; 2:12; 3:16, 21-23; 4:7; 8:6; 11:12), and that apostles were simply mediators of divine beneficence (see 1 Cor 3:5; 4:1; 9:17). They thought otherwise.

(2) Whereas the Philippians exhibited a life transformed by divine grace, as they suffered social dislocation in Christ for the sake of the gospel (Phil 1:27-30), the Corinthians exhibited an indigenized *faith, enraptured by the status-enhancing way of the world, and so are labeled "infants in Christ" (1 Cor 3:1 ESV). Their spiritual immaturity was further exacerbated by their financial support of the superapostles (1 Cor 11:20), those who displayed all the honorable and worldly features that they looked for in Paul. As the slogans of 1 Corinthians 1:10 and their support of these superapostles demonstrate, the Corinthians wrongly looked to humans as the source of their gift instead of looking up to God, the one from whom and through whom and to whom are all things (Rom 11:36).

Consequently, Paul's sociotheological approach provides answers to key questions related to financial support. Paul refuses financial support to distinguish himself from sophists and itinerant philosophers and to highlight God as the ultimate Giver. But Paul accepts support when his churches exhibit the right perspective of God as the source of the gospel and of Paul as an apostolic mediator, and when they embody the countercultural gospel in a world gone awry.

See also Apostle; Collection for the Saints; Corinthians, Second Letter to the; Fellowship, Communion, Sharing; Mission; Patronage; Philippians, Letter to the; Wealth and Poverty.

BIBLIOGRAPHY. **D. Briones,** *Paul's Financial Policy: A Socio-theological Approach*, LNTS 494 (London: T&T Clark, 2013); **A. E. Harvey,** "'The Workman Is Worthy of His Hire': Fortunes of a Proverb in the Early Church," *NovT* 24 (1982): 209-21; **M. Hengel,** *Acts and the History of Earliest Christianity* (London: SCM Press, 1979); **R. Hock,** *The Social Context of Paul's Ministry: Tentmaking and Apostleship* (Eugene, OR: Wipf & Stock, 1980); **E. A. Judge,** *Social Distinctives of the Christians in the First Century: Pivotal Essays by E. A. Judge* (Peabody, MA: Hendrickson, 2008); **A. Malherbe,** "Gentle as a Nurse: The Cynic Background to 1 Thess. 2," *NovT* 12 (1970): 203-17; **P. Marshall,** *Enmity in Corinth: Social Conventions in Paul's Relations with the Corinthians*, WUNT 2/23 (Tübingen: Mohr Siebeck, 1987); **W. Meeks,** *The First Urban Christians: The Social World of the Apostle Paul* (New Haven, CT: Yale University Press, 1983); **J. Ogereau,** *Paul's Koinonia with the Philippians: A Socio-historical Investigation of a Pauline Economic Partnership*, WUNT 2/377 (Tübingen: Mohr Siebeck, 2014); **T. Still,** "Did Paul Loathe Manual Labor? Revisiting the Work of Ronald F. Hock on the Apostle's Tentmaking and Social Class," *JBL* 125 (2006): 781-95; **G. Theissen,** *The Social Setting of Pauline Christianity: Essays on Corinth*, trans. and ed. J. Schütz (Philadelphia: Fortress, 1982); **S. Walton,** "Paul, Patronage and Pay: What Do We Know About the Apostle's Financial Support," in *Paul as Missionary: Identity, Activity, Theology, and Practice*, ed. T. J. Burke and B. S. Rosner, LNTS 420 (London: T&T Clark, 2011), 220-33.

D. E. Briones

FIRST ADAM. *See* Adam and Christ.

FIRSTBORN

The term *firstborn* (Greek *prōtotokos*) occurs three times in the Pauline letters (Rom 8:29; Col 1:15, 18). Outside Paul's letters it occurs three times in Hebrews (Heb 1:6; 11:28; 12:23), once in Luke (Lk 2:7), and once in Revelation (Rev 1:5). Both within and outside the NT usages, the term can have a literal meaning (i.e., denoting the first child to be born to a mother) or a figurative one (i.e., denoting a special status or privilege). Paul uses the term figuratively in each case and in reference to Jesus. The context of each use must be carefully considered to determine its significance in that instance.

1. In Romans.

In Romans 8:29, the term relates to the supremacy of *Christ in the age of eschatological renewal. Paul explains that God's ultimate goal of believers' being conformed to Christ's image is that Christ might be "the firstborn among many brothers." Here family and *kinship associations are clearly in view. The larger context of Romans 8 is filled with familial language, including that those who are led by the Spirit are "sons of God" (Rom 8:14), *adoption as sons (Rom 8:15), *God as Father (Rom 8:15), children of God (Rom 8:16), and "heirs of God and fellow heirs of Christ" (Rom 8:17). There is also metaphorical birth language about the sons of God being revealed (Rom 8:19), children of God (Rom 8:21), childbirth (Rom 8:22), and waiting eagerly for adoption (Rom 8:23). In the context of these metaphors for the people of God, the term *firstborn* is the literal language neither of birth nor of temporal priority but rather has the meaning of preeminence within a familial relationship. For believers, Christ is both the model to which they will be conformed and the preeminent one in the family of God.

2. In Colossians.

In Colossians, the term appears twice as a structuring element in the majestic Colossian *hymn (Col 1:15-20). Each usage follows an introductory phrase "who is the . . ." which it helps to explain, and is then followed by a clause that provides the rationale for the titles of preeminence. Joined with other theologically rich titles such as *eikōn* (image) and *archē* (beginning), the phrases "firstborn over all *creation" (Col 1:15) and "firstborn from the dead" (Col 1:18) draw attention to the supremacy of Christ in both creation and redemption. The former may reflect earlier Jewish reflection on the *Wisdom of God, inspired by passages such as Proverbs 8 and taken up by Hellenistic Jewish writers such as Philo. The supremacy of Christ in creation is not then that he was temporally the first to be created but rather, as following phrases make clear, as the mediator of creation himself and the one through whom all things were created, Christ holds the place of primacy. In Colossians 1:18 "firstborn from the dead" is a reference to the *resurrection, ultimately making the point that "in all things he might have the supremacy" (Col 1:18), including in the work of reconciliation. As such, these two uses of *firstborn* contribute to a prose hymn that takes up Jewish traditions about wisdom and about the eschatological age of renewal to describe the person and work of Jesus in exalted ways.

See also ADOPTION; COLOSSIANS, LETTER TO THE; HYMNS, HYMN FRAGMENTS, CONFESSIONS; KINSHIP LANGUAGE IN PAUL; ROMANS, LETTER TO THE; SON OF GOD.

BIBLIOGRAPHY. **J. D. G. Dunn,** *Christology in the Making* (Philadelphia: Westminster, 1980); **K. S. Kim,** *The Firstborn Son in Ancient Judaism and Early Christianity* (Leiden: Brill, 2019); **W. Michaelis,** "πρωτότοκος," *TDNT* 6:871-82.

M. E. Gordley

FIRSTFRUITS. *See* CREATION AND NEW CREATION; HOLY SPIRIT.

FLESH

Interpreters have sought to determine the proper background for Paul's uses of *sarx* (often translated "flesh"), whether Jewish or Hellenistic. In the last few decades, a consensus has emerged that the lines between cultural contexts cannot be so easily discerned. Further, while there are some similarities between Paul's theological conception of *sarx* and the manner in which Jewish texts portray human sinfulness in relation to demonic or cosmic entities, Paul's use of *sarx* is unique, and comparisons are less than illuminating. Particular instances of Paul's use of the term must be regarded on a case-by-case basis.

One of the most significant advances in Pauline studies, beginning with Ernst Käsemann and furthered by scholars influenced by J. Louis Martyn, is an increased awareness among interpreters of Paul's apocalyptic frame of thought. For many generations, and certainly among modern interpreters until the 1970s and beyond, the focus of Paul's theology was assumed to be the individual. That is, Paul was regarded as focusing his theological reflections on the individual human's relationship to *God and to the world. Since Käsemann, many interpreters have come to envision Paul's theology through an apocalyptic lens, a framework that encompasses the entire cosmos, involving activity in the heavens and on earth. This has significant bearing on Paul's uses of *sarx*.

1. Flesh in the Old Testament and Jewish Literature.

In the LXX, *sarx* refers to generic human existence, to the skin of humans and animals, and to all humanity. It appears in contexts that refer to the realm of human relationships ("he is our brother, our own flesh," Gen 37:27 NRSV). It denotes human existence that can suffer injury and perish (Job 2:5). It is used to refer to *circumcision of Israelite male children ("circumcise the flesh of your foreskins," Gen 17:11 NRSV; cf. Lev 12:3), and to those who are non-Israelites ("uncircumcised in heart and flesh," Ezek 44:7, 9 NRSV). *Sarx* refers to all humanity (Gen 6:12; Num 16:22; Is 66:23), and it can indicate humanity in its weakness and limitation, especially in passages that mention *sarx* along with God's Spirit (e.g., Gen 6:3). In Jewish texts, *sarx* can be used to refer to the physical—as opposed to nonphysical—aspect of a person (Wis 9:15), the realm of merely human existence on earth (1QH XV, 16-17), and humanity in its sinfulness (1QS XI, 9; 1QM XII, 12).

2. The Apocalyptic Frame.

It is important to set Paul's use of *sarx* within his apocalyptic theological vision for two reasons: (1) While Paul refers to humans and corporate human life as "flesh," he also uses *sarx* with reference to one of the cosmic powers ("Flesh") that determines the course of human life on earth (Gal 5:17). Further, (2) while Paul refers to humans and corporate human life as "flesh," the character of that existence is thoroughly shaped by the larger cosmic reality that there are two cosmic realms—or fields of power—in existence simultaneously. Abstracted from this apocalyptic framework, human existence as "flesh" may be regarded as morally neutral. Yet all the appearances of the term refer to human existence in the present evil age, which is determinative for how Paul's uses of the term must be understood (de Boer).

Along with most Jews of his day, Paul's conception of reality was cosmic in scope, encompassing activity on earth and in the heavens. The mundane realities of daily life among humans were directly tied to activity in the heavens. All of reality was cosmically contested space, involving God (Father, Son, and *Holy Spirit) and a range of other cosmic actors. For Paul, apart from God's saving action in *Christ, humanity existed in disobedience and was subject to *judgment. This was not merely because of the choices of individual humans but also because all *creation, along with humanity, was enslaved to hostile cosmic powers, which held creation in their grip.

2.1. The Present Evil Age. According to Scripture, God's design was for humanity to function as the image of the Creator God within creation, reflecting his character in their conduct toward one another and in their care for creation, fostering its flourishing. That cosmic-wide conception was how activity on earth would have related to activity in the heavens: God's rule being reflected within creation through humanity, God's image bearers. Because of human rebellion, that design has gone wrong, and life on earth has been filled with chaos, destruction, and oppression. Humanity no longer depicts God's heavenly rule but the apparent triumph of evil. The prophetic Scriptures of *Israel speak of a time in the future when God will finally triumph over evil, redeem Israel, and cleanse the cosmos (the heavens and the earth) of its pollution.

Paul regarded the time before that future renewal as "the present evil age" (Gal 1:4), "this age" (Rom 12:2), "the age of this world" (Eph 2:2), or "this present darkness" (Eph 6:12). This evil age, in which "the days are evil" (Eph 5:16), is overseen by hostile cosmic powers that seduce humanity into various forms of disobedience and *idolatry. These hostile cosmic powers see to it that humanity and the nonhuman creation do not experience God's intentions for their flourishing.

2.2. Hostile Cosmic Powers. At the head of what some interpreters have called "the apocalyptic power alliance" (Beker) is *Satan, whom Paul calls "the god of this age" (2 Cor 4:4) and "ruler of the power of the air" (Eph 2:2). "The air," in Paul's conception, is the realm of ideologies, mindsets, cultural assumptions, prejudices, hopes, fears, and national and tribal commitments that are held over against others. Satan disguises himself as "an angel of light" (2 Cor 11:14), perhaps in reference to his strategy of tempting humans to achieve apparently good ends through means that foster human *suffering (e.g., exclusion of others, oppression, the marginalization of the weak and vulnerable).

Allied with Satan are the powers and authorities, to which Paul refers with various titles (Gal 4:3, 9; Eph 1:21; 3:10; 6:12; Col 2:8, 13; Rom 8:38-39; 1 Cor 2:6, 8). Jewish *tradition, based on Scripture, held that God had granted authority over the lives of nations to archangelic ruler figures (Deut 32:8-9; Jub. 15.31-32). They were to uphold justice and foster cultural patterns among the nations so that humanity experienced the flourishing God intended (Ps 82). These have rebelled against God and now orient human cultures toward idolatry and disobedience, seducing humanity to pursue lives of selfishness, sinful sensuality, destructive competition, quests for prestige and prominence, and the exploitation and oppression of others.

In league with these figures are entities Paul portrays in personified terms. They are cosmic entities that act, exercise will, and have aims and intentions. In Romans 5, Paul portrays *Sin and *Death as entering the cosmos (Rom 5:12). Death spreads to all humanity and exercises dominion (Rom 5:12, 14). In Romans 7, Sin, "seizing an opportunity" with the giving of God's holy *law, "produced in me all kinds of covetousness" (Rom 7:8 NRSV). Sin sprang to life, "deceived me and through [the commandment] killed me" (Rom 7:11 NRSV). In these texts, Sin and Death are active agents, not merely things that humans do (i.e., they sin, they die). These personified entities turn God's good gifts toward the end of human degradation, division, and destruction. Discussed below is the inclusion of Flesh as one of these cosmic figures personified by Paul (Gal 5:17).

2.3. Cosmic Significance of the Death of Christ. According to Paul's *gospel, God in Christ has broken the enslaving grip of the apocalyptic power alliance over creation. God sent Jesus Christ to take on the form of humanity subject to these hostile cosmic powers (Rom 8:3; Gal 4:4-5), and in his death, God judged the present evil age and dealt a fatal blow to the powers that oversaw its corruption. But, in contrast to the Jewish expectation that God's saving action would bring the present age to an end and initiate the fullness of the renewed creation, God's transformation of creation is taking place in two stages. At the death and *resurrection of Christ, the destruction of the present age and the defeat of its rulers has begun and will be completed at the future day of Christ (1 Cor 2:6; 15:24-26). The new creation age has begun in Christ and by the Spirit, but it will only come in its fullness on that future day. This is the "already but not yet" of NT theology. *Salvation and judgment have *already* begun, but the *fullness of God's work is *not yet* finished.

The present moment, for Paul, is one in which these two ages overlap. The *church exists at the intersection of the present evil age and the new creation age in Christ. God's people experience the pull and tug of these two cosmic realms and the powers that animate them. Paul exhorts his churches throughout his letters to orient community behaviors and attitudes so that they are living less and less within the cosmic space of the present age and increasingly within the cosmic space of the new creation (Rom 12:1-2; Eph 4:22-24; Col 3:1-11).

3. Flesh as Merely Human.

Flesh, in continuity with some OT uses, appears in contexts that indicate existence as merely human or that which belongs to the merely human realm (Barclay). At the same time, some of Paul's uses, because of his apocalyptic framework, indicate what is merely human *in contrast* to God's activity or the way of life God commands and commends.

3.1. Morally Neutral Human Existence. In certain passages, *flesh* indicates the realm of human relationships and points to normal procreative processes. In Romans 1:3, Jesus Christ "was descended from David according to the flesh" (NRSV). Even though Paul follows this by noting that Jesus was declared to be "*Son of God with power according to the spirit of *holiness" (Rom 1:4 NRSV), there does not appear to be any denigration of his human line of descent. The same applies to Paul's lament about the condition of his fellow Israelites in Romans 9:1-5, referring to them as "my own people, my kindred according to the flesh" (Rom 9:3 NRSV).

It is likely in this sense of mere human existence that Paul refers to whatever weakness or *disability was given to him by God after his heavenly journeys: "a thorn was given me in the flesh, a messenger of Satan to torment me, to keep me from being too elated" (2 Cor 12:7 NRSV). Likewise, Paul relays to the Colossians how much he labors for them and for others who have not seen him *en sarki* (NRSV, "face to face"; Col 2:1).

In Philemon 15-16, Paul suggests that Onesimus, using a divine passive, "was separated from" Philemon for a time so that he might receive back Onesimus as "a beloved brother—especially to me but how much more to you, both in the flesh and in the *Lord" (Philem 16 NRSV). "In the flesh" denotes the realm of human relationships, while "in the Lord" obviously points to the new relationship now established by the inclusion of Philemon and Onesimus "in Christ" (Philem 8, 20; see also Philem 6). Though some commentators suggest that the phrase "in the flesh" indicates that Philemon and Onesimus share a common humanity, it is also possible that they are blood brothers—either sharing the same two human parents or half-brothers (Callahan). In the Greco-Roman world, the widely shared assumption was that a nobleman (Philemon) and a *slave (Onesimus) did not share a common humanity. Slaves were regarded as less than human.

In uses such as these, there is no moral judgment made about the realm of normal human relationships. That is, it goes too far to note about such appearances of "flesh" that they indicate any sort of existence that designates humanity in its sinfulness. It must be said, however, that while Paul uses *sōma* ("*body") to refer to both present earthly existence and future "heavenly" existence (i.e., the life of the new creation), his uses of *sarx* refer only to existence in the present age (1 Cor 15:39-40).

3.2. Human Existence in Its Limitation. Other uses of *flesh* to denote existence as merely human represent humanity in its limitation—a slight move along a continuum toward a more negative judgment. In two passages, Paul states that a person is justified before God "by *faith in Christ" (or "by the faithfulness of Christ") and not from "*works of law" (Gal 2:16; Rom 3:20). In the negative statement regarding "works of law" in each passage, Paul refers to all humanity with the same expression: *ou dikaiōthēsetai pasa sarx* ("all flesh will not be justified"). While *pasa sarx* ("all flesh") simply refers to every living person, it pointedly indicates all humanity as belonging to the present evil age and facing an absolute limitation when it comes to *justification. Humanity stands entirely in need of God's action to justify in the sense of being set right with God and transformed into participants in the new creation reality in Christ.

A similar instance of *sarx* as merely human existence, but with this note of limitation, is found in Paul's description of his transformed life as a result of being "crucified with Christ" (Gal 2:19-21). This reality has transformed Paul's entire identity so that "it is no longer I who live, but it is Christ who lives in me" (Gal 2:20 NRSV). Yet, he is still alive in the world, in the realm of everyday human existence (Martyn, *Galatians*). He describes this as "the life I now live in the flesh," which he lives "by faith in the Son of God." That his life "in the flesh" now is qualified by a new mode of existence characterized by participation in Christ casts a negative light on the realm of what is merely human (de Boer).

This transformed reality whereby believers simultaneously inhabit an existence on earth and in the new creation reality by virtue of being baptized into Christ appears in Colossians 2:11-13. The Colossians formerly existed in the "uncircumcision of your flesh"—that is, outside the holy people of God—but by virtue of their *baptism, they have put "off the body of the flesh in the circumcision of Christ" (NRSV).

Similar uses of *flesh* occur in Philippians 3:3-6. Paul celebrates the identity of the true people of God as those who "boast in Christ Jesus and have no confidence in the flesh—even though I, too, have reason for confidence in the flesh" (Phil 3:3-4 NRSV). He goes on to say that he has more reason than anyone else "to be confident in the flesh." In this passage, to "boast in Christ Jesus" is to claim as one's current *identity one's existence in Christ, and to stake one's entire claim for future justification on one's participation in Christ (Phil 3:9-11). The contrast is with those who put their "confidence in the flesh," in that they claim their social credentials for their current identity and stake their claim for future justification on their merely human identity. Paul is not, then, casting an absolute negative moral judgment on flesh here, since he is referring to what is true of a person by birth and progression through life. *Flesh* is indeed limited to the merely human realm and takes on a slight negative connotation in comparison with identity determined by participation in Christ. He decries, however, the human tendency to assume that one's social status inherited or earned within the merely human realm has any value when it comes to one's standing before God.

3.3. *Morally Negative Human Existence.* In other passages, Paul's uses of *sarx* convey a morally negative judgment. Throughout 1 Corinthians 2, Paul contrasts the *wisdom and power of God with human wisdom and the wisdom of this age. The latter is determined by "the rulers of this age"—hostile cosmic powers who make available within human culture corrupt ideologies and practices. He further sets "the spirit of the world" against "the Spirit that is from God," who teaches "those who are spiritual" about "the gifts bestowed on us by God" (1 Cor 2:12-13 NRSV). "Those who are unspiritual" do not understand God's gifts "because they are spiritually discerned," while "those who are spiritual discern all things" (1 Cor 2:14-15 NRSV).

This contrast determines the appearances of *sarx* ("flesh") and *sarkinos* ("fleshly") in 1 Corinthians 3:1-4. Rather than regarding the Corinthians as "spiritual people," they are "people of the flesh" (*sarkinois*, "fleshly ones"). Their practice of splitting into factions (1 Cor 3:4) demonstrates that they are operating according to the wisdom of this age and of its rulers. The so-called wisdom at work among them is a corrupt logic drawn from the merely human realm, oriented by destructive competition and quests for social honor. Because of this, Paul addresses them "as infants in Christ"—as people who have just barely crossed over the divide between what is "spiritual" and what is "worldly" (1 Cor 3:1). The "wisdom of God" is not operative among them; the spirit animating their social practices is thoroughly worldly. Because "there is jealousy and quarreling among" them, they are "of the flesh," indicating their belonging to the wrong side of the spiritual/fleshly divide (1 Cor 3:3).

Referring to what is merely human with a negative moral judgment likely characterizes Paul's use of *sarx* in Galatians 3:1-5. Paul asks them whether, having "started with the Spirit, are you now ending with the flesh?" (Gal 3:3 NRSV). The contrast between "the Spirit" and "the flesh" here lines up with the contrast in Galatians 3:2, 5 between "works of the law" and "believing what you heard." Paul is not here criticizing Judaism or works of law as pointing to a Jewish identity in the abstract. Rather, he relegates to the realm of the flesh the recently arrived teachers and their teaching that in order to be fully and faithfully Christian, the non-Jewish Galatians must take on a Jewish identity and share in Jewish practices. Paul envisions this teaching as flesh in that it is a merely human way of thinking, running in opposition to the apostolic gospel.

4. Flesh as a Cosmic Power.
An apocalyptic scenario explains some of Paul's uses of *sarx* in Galatians. The cosmic situation of God's deliverance of his people from the present age into the new creation reality in Christ orients the framework within which the letter should be understood. In the opening, he states that the Lord Jesus Christ "gave himself for our sins to set us free from the present evil age" (Gal 1:4 NRSV). Near the close of the letter, in Galatians 6:14, he maintains that "the world has been crucified to me, and I to the world" (NRSV), indicating the cosmic situation in which he finds himself and in which he wants the Galatians to locate themselves. The death of Christ, and their inclusion in it by the Spirit, represents their removal from participation in that age, which has been judged and proleptically destroyed. He follows this by stating that the distinction between circumcision and uncircumcision no longer matters; what matters is the "new creation" (Gal 6:15). Paul and his audiences have experienced cosmic realm transfer by virtue of their participation in the death of Christ. They no longer inhabit the present evil age but live in the new creation.

Within this apocalyptic frame, Paul personifies Flesh as one of the hostile cosmic powers that corrupts the mode of life within the present age. That the appearances of *sarx* in Galatians 5:16-19 do not refer to humans or desires within humans is evident from his setting the Spirit's work in opposition to Flesh. Flesh is here described as having "desires," and both Flesh and Spirit "are opposed to each other, to prevent you from doing what you want" (Gal 5:17 NRSV). Personification is evident here in that Flesh is a subject that acts—it "desires" and "opposes." So, when Paul states in Galatians 5:16 that the Galatians must "not gratify the desires of the flesh," he is prohibiting the Galatians from being participants in Flesh's desires to subject them again to the enslaving dynamics of the present evil age. Alternatively, they must fully live into their new cosmic location by living in accordance with the Spirit, the animating power of the new creation age ("Live by the Spirit," Gal 5:16).

Paul's setting *sarx* in opposition to God's Spirit further supports regarding Flesh as a cosmic power. While Flesh is one of the cosmic powers in league with Sin and Death to enslave humanity and prevent its flourishing, the Spirit is the animating power with the cosmic realm of Christ—the new creation.

Paul counsels the Galatians that they can determine which animating power is at work among them by looking at the sorts of practices that are found among them. In Galatians 5:19-21 he lists a range of vices and destructive community patterns that reveal behaviors "of the Flesh." Where there is bitterness, outburst of anger, and malice, they can be sure that their community is functioning within the cosmic realm of the present age. But when their community life is characterized by virtuous social behaviors (Gal 5:22-26), they know they are behaving in the cosmic realm empowered by God's Spirit.

It is a consensus among scholars that in Romans 5:12–8:39 this same apocalyptic framework is evident, and the appearance of *sarx* in Romans 8:1-17 is similar to that in Galatians. In Romans 8:2, Paul sets "the Spirit of life in Christ Jesus" over against Sin and Death, with reference to the Mosaic law. Paul is referring to the Roman Christians using Torah inappropriately to foster division and the boasting of one group in their superiority over another, when he refers to "the law of sin and of death." That is, because they are using the law to divide the church, they have unwittingly turned it into a weapon in the hands of the cosmic powers of Sin and Death. Alternatively, when they read the law to foster a community dynamic of faithfulness and unity, it becomes a tool of the Spirit to build the church. The church's corporate conduct and community patterns of behavior draw on the powers operative in alternative cosmic realms.

Paul refers to *sarx* as one of these powers that had hijacked God's good gift of the Mosaic law. Because Torah was given within a cosmically enslaved situation, Flesh as a hostile cosmic power had prevented it from doing its work (Rom 8:3). But within the liberated cosmic space of Christ Jesus himself, the law's righteous work is now produced among God's people (Rom 8:4). Paul goes on to contrast *sarx* with the Holy Spirit as the animating powers of alternative cosmic realms and exhorts the Romans to have minds set on the Spirit's priorities for their community rather than on the priorities of Flesh, which are destructive competition and division. After all, the Roman believers are not cosmically located under the power of Flesh (Rom 8:9) but "in the Spirit," since the Spirit of God dwells among them.

Understanding *sarx* in this way may also explain its appearance in Colossians 2:23. The use of *stoicheiōn* in Colossians 2:20 points to an apocalyptic scenario, a reference to hostile cosmic powers that orient the life of the present evil age. These entities appear in Colossians 2:8 with reference to corrupt ideologies that are handed down through human tradition, in close connection with "rulers and authorities" over whom God has triumphed in Christ. Paul also mentions the *stoicheia* in Galatians 4:3, 9 as cosmic entities that enslave through corrupt human *teaching. In Colossians 2:20, Paul states that the Colossians have died with Christ to these enslaving powers and they no longer belong to the world. They should therefore resist submitting to rules and regulations that "are simply human commands and teachings" (Col 2:22 NRSV). While they have the appearance of wisdom, such teachings have no value "against the desire of the flesh" (Col 2:23). Most English translations envision sinful human desires here, but the apocalyptic framework of Colossians and the similarities with Galatians 5 point to *sarki* as a possible reference to Flesh as a hostile cosmic power.

Another text in which some interpreters see an appearance of Flesh is in Ephesians 2:3. Paul states in Ephesians 1:20-23 that God has accomplished a victory over the powers and authorities and that his presence now fills the church. He then describes God's victory in Ephesians 2:1-10 in terms of God's liberation of his people from enslavement to hostile cosmic powers, including Satan and "the spirit that is now at work among those who are disobedient" (Eph 2:2 NRSV). Those now liberated formerly lived "in the passions of our flesh," a clear reference to sinful desires within people (Eph 2:3). He goes on to claim, however, that they previously were "doing the desires of Flesh and of the imagination." While the first use of *sarx* is an obvious reference to sinful human desires, the apocalyptic context of cosmic enslavement points to the second appearance of *sarx* as likely referring to Flesh as a hostile cosmic power.

Paul's uses of *sarx*, then, have reference to human existence within the present age, subject in some sense to Flesh as a cosmic power and its desires, aims, and intentions. Salvation is the liberation of humanity from this form of existence into the full and final transformation of the new creation. In this way, Paul's use of *sarx* differs from his use of *sōma*, which can indicate existence as a human in both the present age and the future age of transformation.

See also ANTHROPOLOGY, PAULINE; APOCALYPTIC PAUL; APOCALYPTICISM; BODY; COSMOLOGY; DEATH; PRINCIPALITIES AND POWERS; SIN, GUILT.

BIBLIOGRAPHY. **J. M. G. Barclay,** *Obeying the Truth: A Study of Paul's Ethics in Galatians* (Edinburgh: T&T Clark, 1988); **J. C. Beker,** *Paul the Apostle: The Triumph of God in Life and Thought* (Philadelphia: Fortress, 1980); **M. C. de Boer,** *Galatians: A Commentary*, NTL (Louisville, KY: Westminster John Knox, 2011); **A. D. Callahan,** *Embassy of Onesimus: The Letter of Paul to Philemon* (Valley Forge, PA: Trinity Press International, 1997); **D. A. Campbell,** *The Deliverance of God: An Apocalyptic Rereading of Justification in Paul* (Grand Rapids, MI: Eerdmans, 2009); **J. D. G. Dunn,** *The Theology of Paul the Apostle* (Grand Rapids, MI: Eerdmans, 2006); **R. Gundry,** Sōma *in Biblical Theology: With Emphasis on Pauline Anthropology* (Cambridge: Cambridge University Press, 1976); **R. Jewett,** *Paul's Anthropological Terms: A Study of Their Use in Conflict Settings* (Leiden: Brill, 1971); idem, *Romans: A Commentary*, Hermeneia (Minneapolis: Fortress, 2007); **E. Käsemann,** *Commentary on Romans*, trans. G. W. Bromiley (Grand Rapids, MI: Eerdmans, 1980); **J. L. Martyn,** *Galatians*, AB 33A (New Haven, CT: Yale University Press, 1997); idem, *Theological Issues in the Letters of Paul* (Nashville: Abingdon, 1997).

T. Gombis

FOOD LAWS AND CUSTOMS, JEWISH AND ROMAN

Broadly speaking, Jews and Romans shared a common diet. Nevertheless, Jewish distinctives endured during the time of the Roman Empire, and some of these scruples are discernible in the writings of Paul.

1. Mediterranean Diet
2. Food Laws and Taboos
3. Meals
4. Food and Unity in Paul

1. Mediterranean Diet.

Ancient diets were affected by a variety of factors, including famine, socioeconomic means, trading and distribution routes, rural versus *urban settings, and so on. Food allocation seems to have favored men as the most productive members of the *household in the Roman world (Garnsey, 100-101), and the lower-than-average heights of female skeletons indicate the same for ancient *Israel (MacDonald, *What Did the Ancient Israelites Eat?*, 87).

The content of the ancient Mediterranean diet mostly consisted of the "Mediterranean triad" of olive oil, wine, and grain (Garnsey, 12-17; MacDonald, *What Did the Ancient Israelites Eat?*, 8, 91). Grain in particular, whether boiled into porridge or baked into bread, would have constituted the bulk of the caloric intake. Despite the extensive cultivation of grain, neither Jews nor Romans were major beer consumers (Nelson, 67, 71). The Romans typically diluted their wine with two or three parts water to one part wine (Faas, 90-91; Dunbabin, 20). The evidence that Jews diluted wine is not as clear (MacDonald, *Not Bread Alone*, 61; *What Did the Ancient Israelites Eat?*, 23), though some contend that they generally did not (McGovern, 235; see Is 1:22).

Other foods were consumed such as fruits, vegetables, legumes, and fish. Both Jews and Romans used their fingers to eat, though spoons or knives were used with soups and stews alongside breads for dipping (Kraemer, 409; Faas, 74-76; Borowski, 74). Meat often had a cultic connotation for both Romans and Jews, being ceremonially offered before consumption. Recent osteoarcheological research on skeletal remains suggests that meat was consumed more often in Roman contexts than previously thought, though access to quality meats and a wide variety of meats was not always economically viable (Tite). Cattle, sheep, goats, and chickens were farmed mostly for their secondary uses: labor, wool, eggs, and milk (Garnsey, 16-17; MacDonald, *What Did the Ancient Israelites Eat?*, 71). Due to the lack of ability to preserve milk, it was mostly processed into butter, cheese, or yogurt.

As a result of their limited diets, ancient Mediterraneans were probably nutritionally deficient in vitamins A and C and in iron (Garnsey, 43-61; MacDonald, *What Did the Ancient Israelites Eat?*, 91-92, 97-98). Roman and Jewish literature does not necessarily give this impression, however, because (1) the authors had greater access to food than the general population (Grimm, 354-55; MacDonald, *What Did the Ancient Israelites Eat?*, 9); (2) much of the literary focus is on special rather than mundane circumstances, that is, sacrificial offerings in

Jerusalem did not affect daily life for most Jews throughout the land; and (3) there may be ideological purposes at work, for example, in Roman literature, there are examples of philosophical and satirical critiques of indulgence (Gowers), and in the OT, "milk and honey" were not major foodstuffs in the everyday diet (MacDonald, *Not Bread Alone*, 55; *What Did the Ancient Israelites Eat?*, 3-9).

There was clear dietary overlap between Jews and Romans. Yet, of course, one place where distinction was to be found was in the area of regulation.

2. Food Laws and Taboos.

Food taboos were not common among the Romans (Garnsey, 83; Grimm, 354). However, they did have some scruples regarding meat. Meat per se was not taboo, but the Romans were concerned about consuming it (1) uncooked, (2) in excess, (3) without manners, and (4) without other food items (Garnsey, 124). Abstention from meat altogether was not common, though some, such as Porphyry and Pythagoras, did articulate philosophical reasons for abstaining (Garnsey, 85-91; Osborne; Grimm, 362-66).

As for Jewish food laws, the Mosaic diet chiefly encoded in Leviticus 11 and Deuteronomy 14, which later contributed to *kashrut* (i.e., the kosher diet), was concerned with the content and preparation of meat.

2.1. Content of meat. "Clean" animals were permissible to eat, and "unclean" animals were not. Land animals were permitted only if they both chewed the cud and had cloven hooves (Lev 11:3-4; Deut 14:6), which excluded the camel, the hyrax, the rabbit, and the pig, who did not do both (Lev 11:4-8; Deut 14:7-8). Abstention from consuming pork was the best-known taboo, being satirized and mocked by non-Jews (e.g., Juvenal, *Sat.* 6.158-160; 14.98-99; Macrobius, *Saturnalia* 2.4.11). Water animals had to have fins and scales (Lev 11:9-12; Deut 14:9-10). Predatory birds were excluded, but the rationale for their exclusion is not expressly provided (Lev 11:13-19; Deut 14:11-18). Some winged and hopping insects were permitted, such as locusts and grasshoppers (Lev 11:20-23; Deut 14:19-20).

Both Leviticus 11 and Deuteronomy 14 point to the special election of Israel as the grounds for distinguishing clean from unclean (Lev 11:44-47; Deut 14:2; see also the virtue argument in Let. Aris. 142-171). Scholars have proposed various ideas to find a unifying theory behind these food laws (most notably Douglas), but most contend that one is not likely to be found. Given the fixation of these food laws on meat, it seems that meat may have been prominent in the Jewish diet, since the prohibitions do not pertain to other foods, such as vegetables, for example (Grimm, 367-68). However, Jacob Milgrom makes the point that, regardless of the rationale behind the prohibitions, they were intended to limit meat consumption, because meat was to be offered to *God and consumed at an altar (Milgrom, 733-35).

2.2. Preparation of meat. Blood had to be thoroughly drained from the animal before it could be consumed, due to the belief that life was in the blood (Lev 17:11, 14). Also, eating carrion or animals that were found dead was not permitted (Lev 11:39-40; 17:15; Deut 14:21). Another prohibited preparation of meat was that a goat could not be cooked in its mother's milk (Ex 23:19; 34:26; Deut 14:21); as Milgrom explains, this law arises from "the fusion and confusion of life and death *simultaneously*" (Milgrom, 741).

In the light of exile and diaspora, concern arose of cultic influence on Gentile preparation of food, and by extension mealtime association with *Gentiles became an issue. Diet was one of the chief ways for Jews to distinguish themselves vis-à-vis Gentiles. Although Jewish scruples regarding food may have been negotiated in different ways in the diaspora with varying degrees of assimilation and accommodation, the literary evidence points to Jews maintaining their dietary practices in large measure (Barclay 1996, 435-36).

3. Meals.

The main meal of the day for Romans was the *cena*. Originally occurring at midday, it was eventually moved to the late afternoon, replacing the *vesperna* (Faas, 40). Breakfast (*ientaculum*) and lunch (*prandium*) were much lighter meals for the Romans; the same was true for the Jews, who likewise had one main meal at the end of the workday (Borowski, 74).

A well-known communal meal in the ancient world was the Greek banquet. The banquet comprised two main events: the meal (*deipnon*) and the subsequent drinking party (*symposium*). These two parts of the banquet were formally separated by a libation of wine. After the libation the *symposiarch* (either the host or an honored guest) would combine wine with water in a common vessel (*krater*) to be consumed by all guests during a time of philosophical conversation, games (esp. *kottabus*), and sexual escapades.

The Roman counterpart to the *deipnon/symposium* was the *cena/convivium*. The *sine qua non* of the banquet was the reclining posture of the guests during the meal (Smith 2012, 24; Taussig, 68-69). During such a banquet, Romans reclined on a three-couch structure, known as the *triclinium,* in which there were typically three guests per couch, approximating to a group of around nine guests (Dunbabin, 38-39). In distinction from the Greek *symposium*, the Roman *convivium* regularly welcomed women as reclining guests at the meal (Garnsey, 136; Dunbabin, 22). In Roman banquets, wine was consumed before, during, and after the meal, and, additionally, Romans mixed the wine individually rather than in a common vessel (Dunbabin, 21-22). These types of banquets were not everyday experiences, however. Mary Beard explains, based on archeological evidence from Pompeii, that formal dining was something that relatively wealthier people did on special occasions and that most homes did not have *triclinia.* More commonly people would eat their meals throughout their homes or even away from their residences (Beard, 95-97, 219, 221-22, 225-33).

Jews celebrated special days weekly (Sabbath), monthly (New Moon), and annually (e.g., Passover); each had its own respective rituals that included feasting or fasting. The evidence from Qumran is the most extensive there is for Jewish communal meals, even though it is not broadly representative of Second Temple Judaism. Josephus, writing for a Roman audience, describes the meals of the Essenes, who possibly occupied Qumran, as *quiet* and *sober* (*J.W.* 2.129-233), which William den Hollander interprets as a positive portrayal of Judeans to a Roman audience in contrast to the typical characteristics of the *symposium* (den Hollander, 21-22). At Qumran there was both literarily and archaeologically a strict concern for ritual *purity and order at meals. The Community Rule describes how inductees waited a year before participating in the "pure meal" (1QS VI, 16-17) and yet another year for the "drink of the congregation" (1QS VI, 20-23; VII, 20). Once admitted, various behaviors could lead to privation of these communal meals (1QS VI, 24–VII, 25). Prior to meals these sectarians had to bathe for ritual purity (1QS V, 13-14). If one accepts that the sectarian texts were written by the occupants of Khirbet Qumran, the presence of *mikvaot* (ritual bathing sites) at the entrance to dining centers corroborates this (Magness, 127). Furthermore, the abundance of individual dishes found at the site might suggest that the occupants did not share common dishes, presumably for purity concerns (Magness, 117). Although communal meals at Qumran are not broadly representative, they do highlight the concern within Judaism regarding one's mealtime associates.

4. Food and Unity in Paul.

When Paul addresses food it is in response to communal discord and includes a pastoral call for unity. Private food practices are not what created tension as much as the gathering of diverse people for communal meals. Paul could have called for fasting when the communities were gathered together—fasting being a common Jewish practice, including for Paul (e.g., Acts 13:2; 14:23; 27:9; and possibly 2 Cor 11:27; cf. Harris, 808-10)—and that would have ostensibly solved the problem. Given the differing food customs and the varying levels of socioeconomic access to food, eating together created tension in the Pauline communities, but it also provided an opportunity for a unique social expression. For Paul, nothing should jeopardize the common Christian *identity that believers share, and that common identity should be demonstrated through sharing meals together. In the light of this, Michael Wolter argues that, since *baptism and *faith were not observable boundary markers that distinguished insiders and outsiders, it was the communal meal where early Christian identity and ethos were chiefly experienced and discerned (Wolter, "Identität und Ethos bei Paulus"; "Primitive Christianity as a Feast"). Indeed, what Paul says about food in his letters reveals some of his deepest values and theological commitments about the nature of the people of God.

4.1. The Antioch Incident. When *Peter withdrew from eating with Gentiles in Antioch (Gal 2:11-14), which may have been a eucharistic meal, Paul gave him a strong rebuttal because of the problematic implications of this action (Gal 2:14-21). Since *"works of the *law" do not justify believers before God, dietary restrictions should not be enforced on Gentiles, nor should *circumcision be enforced in order to permit Jews and Gentiles to eat together. Rather, baptized believers of all backgrounds should be able to eat together as members of the same Abrahamic family centered in *Christ (see Gal 3:26-29).

4.2. Romans 14–15 and 1 Corinthians 8–10. In these passages, Paul offers pastorally sensitive admonitions for those without food scruples to accommodate those who have them in order to keep the so-called weak from stumbling (Rom 14:13, 15, 19-21; 15:1-2; 1 Cor 8:9-13). In each situation Paul reveals a principle of conscience that ought to guide individuals (Rom 14:14, 22-23; 1 Cor 8:7; 10:25-28). As examples of accommodation for the churches to follow, Paul emphasizes Christ's *hospitality (Rom 15:1-13) as well as his own *imitation of Christ in laying down his rights (1 Cor 9:19-23; 11:1).

These two passages, however, are not neatly symmetrical. First Corinthians 8–10 is chiefly concerned with meat offered to idols, whereas Romans 14–15 does not mention *idolatry. Thus, Robert Karris argues that Romans 14–15 is a general exhortation that despecifies the contents of 1 Corinthians 8–10 for a broader audience. Although idolatry is explicitly lacking, the fact that readers are told that the weak eat only vegetables (Rom 14:3) and keep certain days as sacred (Rom 14:5) makes the passage in Romans specific rather than general (Barclay 2016, 38). The chief difference in these texts regarding food scruples, then, appears to be *preparation* (1 Corinthians) and *content* (Romans).

Gerd Theissen famously proposed that the discord at the meals in Corinth was aggravated by a socioeconomic divide in the church, evinced especially in 1 Corinthians 1:26, where the poorer members of the church had access to meat only through cultic means. This reconstruction has been refuted by Tite on the basis of osteoarcheological research of ancient skeletal remains in Roman Corinth and the broader Roman Empire, which suggests that meat was more accessible than Theissen proposed. Instead, the problem in Corinth was how common meals should be conducted by those with varying understandings of how meat offered to idols related to their new group identities (Tite, 206-13).

In Romans there is more to say about the *content* of the food scruples. Jewish food laws did not categorically restrict the consumption of meat. The group abstaining from meat might not have been homogenous in its makeup, nor united in its motivations (Reasoner, 1-23, 136-38, 218-20). On balance, however, most scholars find it preferable to view vegetarianism here as a Jewish tactic in Gentile-dominant settings to avoid potential pollution by idols (see Barclay 2015, 508-16; Watson, 175-77). This strategy is similarly reflected in Daniel 1:8-16; Judith 12:1-4; and Additions to Esther 14:17 LXX. Additional features of Romans 14–15 help to confirm that a broad Jew-Gentile issue informs the discourse, including (1) the use of "common" (*koinos*) in Romans 14.14, (2) an implied Sabbath reference in Romans 14:15, (3) the parallel contrast of eating/faith and law/faith, and (4) that Romans 15:7-13 speaks of Jews and Gentiles being hospitable to each other (Watson, 176-77).

In these two passages one can see that Paul is content with a diversity of beliefs and practices regarding food so long as this does not threaten the unity of the congregations, symbolized in their ability to eat together. This emphasis on unity at mealtime is chiefly expressed in 1 Corinthians 11, with its focus on the central communal meal of the *Lord's Supper.

4.3. The Lord's Supper in 1 Corinthians 11. Eating together as an expression of unity is central to this passage, but various aspects of it are debated. In regards to food customs, the most notable scholarly discussion relates to the background of this communal meal and the *tradition about the Lord's Supper (1 Cor 11:23-26). Smith and Klinghardt argue that the Lord's Supper was modeled on the Greek banquet. Their main observation from 1 Corinthians 11 is that the "cup" is blessed "after the supper," which they argue maintains an essential division between the *deipnon* and the *symposium* (see Smith 2003, 188). This cup would then have been offered as a libation in keeping with this background (see the discussion on the cup being "poured out" in Lk 22:20 in Klinghardt 2012, 12).

Against the banquet typology of a sharp separation between the meal and the *symposium*, Charles Cosgrove highlights Greek, Roman, Jewish, and Christian texts where there is a lack of reference to libations and/or where wine is consumed during the meal. Furthermore, Cosgrove argues that the lack of direct concern for libations by Paul suggests that they must not have been as pervasive as Smith and Klinghardt contend. This is because libations would have created an immediate concern relative to meat offered to idols. Unless offered to household gods/idols, the meat would be offered previously and at a separate cultic space, whereas libations would have occurred directly in front of those at the meal. In fact, in the Mishnah, wine receives the bulk of the treatment on offerings to idols due to the concern that it may have been used in a libation (m. Abod. Zar. 2:3-4; 4:2, 8-11; 5:1-5, 8). The lack of these concerns in Paul is therefore highly suggestive.

If the later Mishnaic tradition that four cups of wine were consumed at the Passover meal extends back to the time of Jesus, then the cup that is blessed "after the supper" in 1 Corinthians 11 would not have been the first cup of wine consumed that evening. In the Mishnaic tradition, the four cups also received their own blessing (m. Pesah. 10:1-9). The last one was to be accompanied by a *hymn (m. Pesah. 10:7; see Mt 26:30; Mk 14:26). Some see this rabbinic tradition as a post-AD 70 invention due to the inability to perform the requisite *sacrifices and also as a means of providing an alternative to the Greek *symposium* (so, e.g., Hauptman; Kraemer, 414-15). Whether or not the tradition extends back to the time of Christ, the Gospel accounts suggest that wine was consumed during the meal (Mt 26:26-29;

Mk 14:22-25) and that there was more than one cup (Lk 22:17, 20). The words of Exodus 24:8, with its reference to the "blood of the *covenant," seem to inform and influence the wording of 1 Corinthians 11 and the Gospel accounts, which further anchors the Lord's Supper in the Passover tradition rather than the Greek banquet.

Regardless of the precise background, it is clear that the unity of the *church as it gathers to celebrate this central communal meal is the focus of the passage. Paul is critical of some of the Corinthians for eating privately rather than communally (1 Cor 11:20-21), leading to some going hungry while others get drunk (1 Cor 11:21-22). He recounts the tradition he received about the Lord's Supper (1 Cor 11:23-26) and uses it to conclude that improper celebrations of the Supper will lead to *judgment (1 Cor 11:27-32), so the celebration ought to promote unity (1 Cor 11:33-34).

See also Corinthians, First Letter to the; Ethics; Galatians, Letter to the; Hospitality; Idolatry; Law; Lord's Supper; Romans, Letter to the; Strong and Weak; Stumbling Block; Works of the Law.

BIBLIOGRAPHY. **J. M. G. Barclay,** *Jews in the Mediterranean Diaspora: From Alexander to Trajan (323 BCE–117 CE)* (Berkeley: University of California Press, 1996); idem, *Paul and The Gift* (Grand Rapids, MI: Eerdmans, 2015); idem, "Do We Undermine the Law? A Study of Romans 14.1–15.6," in *Pauline Churches and Diaspora Jews* (Grand Rapids, MI: Eerdmans, 2016), 37-59; **M. Beard,** *The Fires of Vesuvius: Pompeii Lost and Found* (Cambridge, MA: Harvard University Press, 2008); **O. Borowski,** *Daily Life in Biblical Times* (Atlanta: Society of Biblical Literature, 2003); **C. H. Cosgrove,** "Banquet Ceremonies Involving Wine in the Greco-Roman World and Early Christianity," *CBQ* 79 (2017): 299-316; **M. Douglas,** *Leviticus as Literature* (Oxford: Oxford University Press, 1999); **K. M. D. Dunbabin,** *The Roman Banquet: Images of Conviviality* (Cambridge: Cambridge University Press, 2003); **P. Faas,** *Around the Roman Table: Food and Feasting in Ancient Rome,* trans. S. Whiteside (New York: Palgrave Macmillan, 2003); **P. Garnsey,** *Food and Society in Classical Antiquity* (Cambridge: Cambridge University Press, 1999); **E. Gowers,** *The Loaded Table: Representations of Food in Roman Literature* (Oxford: Oxford University Press, 1993); **V. E. Grimm,** "On Food and the Body," in *A Companion to the Roman Empire,* ed. D. S. Potter (Oxford: Blackwell, 2006), 354-68; **M. J. Harris,** *The Second Epistle to the Corinthians,* NIGTC (Grand Rapids: Eerdmans, 2005); **J. Hauptman,** "Thinking About the Ten Theses in Relation to the Passover Seder and Women's Participation," in *Meals in Early Judaism: Social Formation at the Table,* ed. S. Marks and H. E. Taussig (New York: Palgrave Macmillan, 2014), 43-57; **W. den Hollander,** "Dining with Dignity: Josephus's Rhetorical Use of the Essene Common Meals," in *T&T Clark Handbook to Early Christian Meals in the Greco-Roman World,* ed. S. Al-Suadi and P.-B. Smit (London: T&T Clark/Bloomsbury, 2019), 19-30; **R. J. Karris,** "Romans 14:1–15:13 and the Occasion of Romans," *CBQ* 25 (1973): 155-78; **M. Klinghardt,** *Gemeinschaftsmahl und Mahlgemeinschaft: Soziologie und Liturgie fruehchristlicher Mahlfeiern* (Tübingen: Francke Verlag, 1996); idem, "A Typology of the Communal Meal," in *Meals in the Early Christian World: Social Formation, Experimentation, and Conflict at the Table,* ed. D. E. Smith and H. E. Taussig (New York: Palgrave Macmillan, 2012), 9-22; **D. Kraemer,** "Food, Eating, and Meals," in *The Oxford Handbook of Jewish Daily Life in Roman Palestine,* ed. C. Hezser (Oxford: Oxford University Press, 2010), 403-19; **N. MacDonald,** *Not Bread Alone: The Uses of Food in the Old Testament* (Oxford: Oxford University Press, 2008); idem, *What Did the Ancient Israelites Eat? Diet in Biblical Times* (Grand Rapids, MI: Eerdmans, 2008); **J. Magness,** *The Archeology of Qumran and the Dead Sea Scrolls* (Grand Rapids, MI: Eerdmans, 2002); **P. E. McGovern,** *Ancient Wine: The Search for the Origins of Viniculture* (Princeton, NJ: Princeton University Press, 2013); **J. Milgrom,** *Leviticus 1–16: A New Translation with Introduction and Commentary,* AB 3 (New York: Doubleday, 1991); **M. Nelson,** *The Barbarian's Beverage: A History of Beer in Ancient Europe* (London: Routledge, 2005); **C. Osborne,** "Ancient Vegetarianism," in *Food in Antiquity,* ed. J. Wilkins, D. Harvey, and M. Dobson (repr., Exeter: University of Exeter Press, 1995), 214-24; **M. Reasoner,** *The Strong and the Weak: Romans 14.1–15.13 in Context,* SNTSMS 103 (Cambridge: Cambridge University Press, 1999); **D. E. Smith,** *From Symposium to Eucharist: The Banquet in the Early Christian World* (Minneapolis: Fortress, 2003); idem, "The Greco-Roman Banquet as a Social Institution," in *Meals in the Early Christian World: Social Formation, Experimentation, and Conflict at the Table,* ed. D. E. Smith and H. E. Taussig (New York: Palgrave Macmillan, 2012), 23-33; **H. E. Taussig,** *In the Beginning was the Meal: Social Experimentation and Early Christian Identity* (Minneapolis: Fortress, 2009); **G. Theissen,** *The Social Setting of Pauline Christianity: Essays on Corinth,* trans. J. H. Schütz (Philadelphia: Fortress, 1982); **P. L. Tite,** "Roman Diet and Meat Consumption: Reassessing Elite Access to

Meat in 1 Corinthians 8 and 10," *JSNT* 42 (2019): 185-222; **F. Watson,** *Paul, Judaism, and the Gentiles: Beyond the New Perspective,* rev. ed. (Grand Rapids, MI: Eerdmans, 2007); **M. Wolter,** "Identität und Ethos bei Paulus," in *Theologie und Ethos im frühen Christentum,* WUNT 263 (Tübingen: Mohr Siebeck, 2009), 121-69; idem, "Primitive Christianity as a Feast," in *Feasts and Festivals*, ed. Christopher Tuckett, CBET 53 (Leuven: Peeters, 2009), 171-82.

J. A. Dunne

FOOLISHNESS. *See* Cross; Knowledge and Mind; Philosophy; Wisdom.

FOREKNOWLEDGE, DIVINE

Paul refers to God's foreknowledge twice (Rom 8:29; 11:2). In both cases, God's foreknowledge denotes not prescience but initiation of a relationship with a person(s) for the sake of bestowing favor on them. *God "foreknew" those who love God, or inclined with favor toward them before they loved God. God "foreknew" or inclined with favor toward *Israel before Israel was God's people. Paul deploys the motif of divine foreknowledge to illustrate God's sovereignty and faithfulness in relation to human beings.

1. The Semitic Use of "Know" as the Background for Paul's Use of "Foreknow"
2. God's Foreknowledge and Sovereignty
3. God's Foreknowledge, Faithfulness, and Power

1.The Semitic Use of "Know" as the Background for Paul's Use of "Foreknow."

Paul's use of the verb "foreknow [someone]" (*proginōskein*) reflects the Semitic use of "know [someone]" (Heb. *yādaʿ*; Gk. *ginōskein*) for "know with affection, predilection" (Fitzmyer, 525). For example, God "knew" with predilection Jeremiah, even before God formed him in the womb (Jer 1:5), and *Abraham (Gen 18:19), and Moses (Ex 33:17). God "knew" with predilection the people of Israel in contrast to other nations (Hos 13:4; Amos 3:2; Hos 12:1 LXX). In these and other OT texts and in the Qumran literature (Fitzmyer, 525), divine *knowledge refers to a special relationship that God initiates, as in God's *election to set favor on someone.

The verb "know" (*ginōskein*) is used in the same sense in the Pauline corpus. The one who loves God "is known with predilection [*egnōstai*] by him" (1 Cor 8:3). Those who "know [*gnontes*] God" "were known with predilection [*gnōsthentes*] by God" (Gal 4:9). The one who "was fully known with predilection [*epegnōsthēn*]" (by God) "will know fully [*epignōsomai*]" (1 Cor 13:12). "Those who are his" are the ones "the *Lord knows with predilection" (*egnō*; 2 Tim 2:19, citing Num 16:5 LXX). Although none of these texts refers explicitly to God's foreknowledge, it is assumed.

2. God's Foreknowledge and Sovereignty.

When Paul refers explicitly to God's *fore*knowledge, there is a specific reason to stress the chronological priority of God's knowing people with predilection, or initiating a relationship with them to benefit them. In Romans 9–11, this motif contributes to Paul's argument concerning God's sovereignty in dealing with Israel (see esp. Rom 9:6-33; 11:7-24). Israel is the people "whom God foreknew [*proegnō*]" (Rom 11:2), that is, prior to Israel's having done anything to put God in its debt. By the same token, Israel is the people whom "God has not rejected" (Rom 11:2), despite Israel's having disbelieved the *gospel and rejected Messiah Jesus *en masse*. God is sovereign in dealing with Israel and has willed to harden part of Israel (Rom 11:7, 18), albeit temporarily (see Rom 11:25-26). (Against the alternative translation of Rom 11:2, "God has not rejected his people whom he foreknew," implying that that some were *not* foreknown and *were* rejected, see Moo, 674).

In a similar statement about "God's knowledge" (echoing Rom 11:2), Paul praises how deep it reaches, even down to human beings, who are always in God's debt: "Oh God's deeply rich *wisdom and knowledge [or "Oh the depth of the riches of God's wisdom and knowledge"; Schreiner]. . . . Who has given beforehand [*proedōken*] to him, that he/she might be repaid?" (Rom 11:33, 35; see Gundry; Barclay, 556). God's affectionate knowing of people is both before and beyond that which human beings can muster.

3. God's Foreknowledge, Faithfulness, and Power.

In Romans 8, Paul refers explicitly to God's foreknowledge of "those who love God" as part of a larger argument concerning whether it is possible to be separated from the *love of God, and thus the hope of final *salvation, by evil powers in the world (Rom 8:31-39). Paul denies this by affirming the identicality of "those whom [God] foreknew [*proegnō*]" and "those whom [God] predestined . . . and called . . . and justified . . . and glorified" (Rom 8:29-30). The "golden chain" representing God's continuous, unbroken favor on those who love God in the midst of present *suffering stretches clear from the distant (premundane?) past when God foreknew (*proginōskein*) and predestined (*proorizein*) them for a predetermined purpose (*prothesis*) to a yet future time when God will have glorified them (described proleptically as past: "he glorified"). God's faithfulness is implied.

See also Covenant; Election and Predestination; Israel; Knowledge and Mind; Romans, Letter to the.

BIBLIOGRAPHY. **J. M. G. Barclay,** *Paul and the Gift* (Grand Rapids, MI: Eerdmans, 2015), 493-561; **J. A. Fitzmyer,** *Romans: A New Translation with Introduction and Commentary*, AB (New York: Doubleday, 1992); **J. M. Gundry,** "'Or Who Gave First to Him, So That He Shall Receive Recompense?' (Rom 11:35): Divine Benefaction and Human Boasting in Paul and Philo," in *The Letter to the Romans*, ed. Udo Schnelle, BETL 226 (Leuven: Peeters, 2009), 25-53; **J. Gundry-Volf,** *Paul and Perseverance: Staying in and Falling Away*, WUNT 2/37 (Louisville: Westminster John Knox, 1990); **D. J. Moo,** *The Epistle to the Romans*, NICNT (Grand Rapids, MI: Eerdmans, 1996); **T. R. Schreiner,** *Romans*, BECNT, 2nd ed. (Grand Rapids, MI: Baker Academic, 2018).

J. M. Gundry

FORGIVENESS

Paul not only teaches theologically about forgiveness but also shows several applications in process. Simply searching for Greek words that can be glossed as "forgiveness" is an inadequate method for studying this concept. Paul's view of forgiveness is very close to the Gospels' view, but Paul's is more fleshed out by human examples.

1. The Language of Forgiveness
2. The Need for Forgiveness
3. The Application of Forgiveness in Paul's Letters

1. The Language of Forgiveness.

If one were to examine Matthew's use of the Greek term *aphiēmi* (BDAG, 156) compared to Paul's use of the same Greek word for "forgiveness," one might mistakenly conclude that Paul was not very concerned with this concept. In fact, one might encounter claims that, on the one hand, Paul generally speaks of forgiveness rather than *justification or, on the other, that Paul rarely uses the term *forgiveness*, preferring instead the language of justification.

This shows how easily one might confuse concept with word usage. While Paul uses the Synoptic Gospels' common word for forgiveness only five times, the need for, application of, and means of forgiveness are consistent throughout his writings.

The verb *aphiēmi*, which is used mainly in the Synoptics, especially Matthew, is used by Paul twice in Romans (all statistics are from NA[28]). It appears in Romans 1:27 (with the primary meaning "give up" rather than "forgive") and in Romans 4:7 (quoting Ps 32) with the meaning "forgive." Paul also uses the verb in 1 Corinthians three times (1 Cor 7:10-16), all with the meaning of "divorce" or "let go of a spouse" rather than "forgive."

The noun form of this word, *aphesis*, is used seventeen times, mostly by Luke–Acts. In fact, while Luke's reported speech of Paul in Acts 13 has Paul using this noun (Acts 13:38), in Paul's own writing he uses the noun only twice, in Ephesians 1:7 and Colossians 1:14. Both times it carries the meaning "forgiveness" or "justification." Other than these, the student of Paul must turn to other words to find the notion of forgiveness.

Paul uses the term *charizomai* much more frequently (16×, including the disputed epistles), sometimes with the sense of "forgive." Yet one must be careful not to assume the same meaning in every usage (see Carson, 46-49). Paul does not always use the term to mean forgiveness. While *aphiēmi* carries with it the idea of wiping away a debt or letting go of a spouse, *charizomai*, in its range of meaning, carries more of the idea of graciously giving, perhaps as a favor.

A fairly rare word (4× in the NT, all in Paul or the disputed epistles) is *exagorazō*. Paul can use this term to mean "redeem," "buy back," or "deliver," and does so twice in Galatians (Gal 3:13; 4:5). In both cases he is speaking of the redemption from the *curse of the *law. In Colossians 4:5 and Ephesians 5:16 the term is not used to speak of forgiveness.

By far the most consistent term that Paul uses to speak of those who find themselves in the proper *covenant relationship with *God is *pistis*. This term, while a very common one both in the NT and in Greek literature of the Second Temple period, is used by Paul more than forty times in Romans alone. (Of course, not all of these can be connected to forgiveness through Christ.) The word often has the sense of placing one's belief in a person or thing. Forgiveness is based on the reliability of that which is trusted. Paul very frequently uses the term to speak of a people who have placed their belief/trust in *Christ as Messiah. This faith thus shows that the person or group who hold it are Christ-people, a people who have trusted that the covenant Messiah will provide them not only with forgiveness but with much, much more (e.g., *peace, generosity, kindness, and other virtues).

A second common phrase used often by Paul to speak of having a proper covenant relationship with God through Christ is *en Christō* ("in Christ"; the preposition takes the dative). Paul uses this term over 140 times (including the disputed epistles), and the vast majority of times it means that one has been forgiven/justified by becoming one with Jesus.

The technical term that the apostle uses most often to speak of being forgiven or "set right" with God is the term *dikaiaō*. The verbal form of this term (the noun is used twice in Romans 4:25; 5:16) is used twenty-five times in the uncontested epistles and once each in 1 Timothy and Titus.

This word often means "render a favorable verdict" or "be found not guilty of charges." While *sin in the Gospels is often seen as a debt to be repaid (see Mt 6:12; 18:23-35), Paul frequently sees sin as a breaking of the law, and thus the need for a positive court verdict (e.g., see Rom 3:20 [Ps 142:2], 24, 28; 4:2; 5:1, 9; 1 Cor 4:4; Gal 2:16-17 [Ps 142:2]; 3:11, 24; 5:4). Since the central metaphor for wrongdoing is different between the Gospels and Paul, one should expect the image of forgiveness to be different as well. The Gospels see sin and forgiveness in the marketplace. Paul sees these concepts in the court of law.

Another term, comparatively rare in surviving Greek documents and used only ten times in the NT (eight of those by Paul), is *apolytrōsis*. This term seems to originate in setting a *slave free by paying a ransom. In Colossians 1:14, the author uses the term to speak of being forgiven of one's sins. Later in the same letter (Col 2:14) Paul speaks of our wrongdoing having been "nailed to the cross." Once again, one sees the concept of forgiveness and not necessarily the particular term. Whether or not one holds to the Pauline authorship of Colossians, this is clearly in line with the other uses of the word (either *apolytrōsis* or *lytrōsis*) by Paul in the undisputed *letters. The Colossians 1:14 passage seems to have been a poem that points to both the need of the Messiah and the only means of forgiveness (through this Messiah, Jesus).

One place where the reader might expect to see Paul speaking specifically about the forgiveness of sin, yet does not, is in his directions for the *Lord's Supper. Matthew, in speaking of this event, quotes Jesus as saying that this cup is his blood that is "poured out for many for the forgiveness [*aphesin*] of sins" (Mt 26:28 NRSV). Paul, in giving instructions to the Corinthians about the sacrament, says much about the horrible consequences for taking the cup in an unworthy manner but nothing about the drinking of the cup leading to or showing forgiveness (1 Cor 11:23-33). This is likely because Paul is endeavoring to set right the problems around the Lord's Table rather than give a full-fledged explanation of the sacrament.

While it is clear that the *apostle Paul does not use the same vocabulary for forgiveness as the Gospels, and his metaphor for the remission of sins is usually drawn from the law court rather than the marketplace, this difference of vocabulary and metaphor is not unexpected. Rather, it goes along with Paul's understanding of his beloved *Israel. Many examples the apostle uses in his writings come not from the success of Israel but from the failure to be faithful to the covenant that Israel's God has given them. These examples are the very opposite of any kind of victory tales, yet in the end God still offers redemption/forgiveness. This concept of covenantal faithfulness, while certainly including much more than forgiveness, has the remission of sin at its core.

2. The Need for Forgiveness.
Despite the fact that Paul does not speak in the same terms as the Gospels, he is no less clear in pointing out the need for forgiveness or peace with God and one another. In fact, one could argue that in the apostle's brief letter to Philemon, Paul implies that the follower of Christ transcends the usual categories of punishment, forgiveness, and justice in order to have peace between Christ-followers. Sin and forgiveness is not the central theme of Philemon, but it is a work in which much is implied. One can hardly read Philemon without concluding that Paul is asking for a slave to be treated on the same level as a free man, which would have included forgiveness.

Paul is much more explicit in his statement of the sin of humankind and the need for forgiveness in his letter to the Romans. In Romans 1:18-22 Paul states that the "*wrath of God is revealed to everyone." While there is some contention about the genitive use of *anthrōpōn* (people, everyone) and whether it refers to all people or only to *Gentiles, it is clear that later in the letter Paul attributes sin to everyone (Rom 3:23). Elsewhere in Romans 3, Paul makes it very clear that one is not justified by any work, but only through *faith in Christ. This argument that everyone needs some method of escape from the consequences of wrongdoing or covenant breaking is carried out throughout the rest of the book.

There is no epistle of Paul that can be read correctly without the background of the hearer/reader's need for forgiveness/justification. The Corinthians have a variety of moral problems; the Thessalonians have misunderstood the day of the *Lord and because of this some refuse to work; the Galatians have been falsely led to believe that one cannot be a Christian (or obtain forgiveness) without first becoming a Jew. The reader of Paul could go on, but the point is made. The need for forgiveness in the *teaching and writing of Paul is very clear.

3. The Application of Forgiveness in Paul's Letters.

There are two very clear cases in which Paul instructs the group to whom he is writing concerning the offering of forgiveness by the *church and thus by the Lord, in 1 and 2 Corinthians. In both letters there seems to be some sort of issue of behavior that has caused a man to be worthy of being excommunicated. In 1 Corinthians 5 Paul speaks of a man who is guilty of immoral sexual behavior that is not even allowed among the Gentiles (1 Cor 5:1). This statement ("not even tolerated among pagans") may be an echo of the kind of behavior denounced among the Greeks in the play *Oedipus Rex*. In the work, a child, later called Oedipus, is saved from exposure on a mountaintop and is raised in Corinth by the childless King Polybus. This child then grows up and then makes his way back (unknowingly) to his real homeland, where he (again unknowingly) marries his mother. This is such a crime against nature that when Oedipus realizes what he has done he blinds himself. It seems likely that a good portion of the Corinthians hearing Paul's letter would have known of Sophocles's use of their city in what seems to have been one of his most famous plays.

Whether or not this is a deliberate echo on the part of Paul, and even though it is unlikely that the man in 1 Corinthians 5 married his actual mother, it is clear that this was considered by Corinthians outside the church to be an obvious wrong. That the church had not dealt with it was shocking to the apostle. He is clear in his instructions that the man should be put out of the church. The intended consequence of this action (and any such excommunicative action) is both to cleanse the church and to show the person the seriousness of their sin and drive them back to Christ and the church in desperate need of forgiveness. In this case, Paul instructs the church (enigmatically; there are at least six major interpretations) to turn this man over to *Satan so that his spirit may be saved in "the day of the Lord."

Second Corinthians 2:5-11 has more to say about forgiveness. In this case the man has already been put outside the church (this is almost certainly not the same person as in 1 Cor 5; see commentaries). It seems as if he committed some sort of action that the church and perhaps Paul himself found offensive (2 Cor 2:5). Yet Paul speaks very strongly about the need for the church to forgive the man and welcome him back into the church. He specifically says that the punishment that has been placed on him by the "majority" is enough. The word translated here "majority" (*pleionōn*) is used hundreds of times in the NT and twenty-four times in 2 Corinthians. It is often translated "many" or "most." In this case it almost certainly indicates that there was a minority who thought that the punishment placed on him was not enough.

In spite of this minority, Paul indicates that to punish the man more might cause him to despair, which was not the aim of this action. The point of the action was to drive the man back to the church and thus back to his need for forgiveness. This is perhaps the most significant example of practical forgiveness in all of Paul's letters. It shows that not to forgive not only harms the repentant person but also gives a possible advantage to the evil one.

Paul is a faithful missionary/*pastor who wants to share the covenant blessings of Israel with those outside his own race. In an effort to do so, he uses terms and metaphors that his hearers would be familiar with. There is no doubt that he longs for forgiveness both for Israel and those outside his national people. Forgiveness comes as a benefit of the covenant God has made with anyone who is a Messiah person rather than any one race.

See also Corinthians, First Letter to the; Corinthians, Second Letter to the; Discipline, Church; Faith; Fellowship, Communion, Sharing; Justification; Peace, Reconciliation; Sin, Guilt.

BIBLIOGRAPHY. **J. M. G. Barclay,** *Paul and the Gift* (Grand Rapids, MI: Eerdmans, 2015); **D. A. Carson,** *Exegetical Fallacies* (Grand Rapids, MI: Baker, 1996), 47-52; **I. H. Marshall,** *New Testament Theology: Many Witnesses, One Gospel* (Downers Grove, IL: IVP Academic, 2004); **R. P. Martin,** "Reconciliation and Forgiveness in Colossians," in *Reconciliation and Hope*, ed. R. Banks (Grand Rapids, MI: Eerdmans, 1974), 104-24; **S. McKnight,** *Reading Romans Backwards* (Waco, TX: Baylor University Press, 2019); **D. J. Moo,** *A Theology of Paul and His Letters* (Grand Rapids, MI: Zondervan, 2021); **L. Morris,** "Forgiveness," *DPL*, 311-13; **T. R. Schreiner,** "Paul and Perfect Obedience to the Law: An Evaluation of the Work of E. P. Sanders," *WTJ* 47 (1985): 245-78; idem, *Paul, Apostle of God's Glory in Christ* (Downers Grove, IL: IVP Academic, 2001);

M. Seifrid, *Christ, Our Righteousness: Paul's Theology of Justification* (Downers Grove, IL: IVP Academic, 2000); **N. T. Wright,** *Paul and the Faithfulness of God* (Grand Rapids, MI: Eerdmans, 2013); idem, *Justification: God's Plan and Paul's Vision*, 2nd ed. (Downers Grove, IL: IVP Academic, 2016).

S. Lamerson

FREEDOM/LIBERTY

While Paul's vision for Christian existence is not easily summarized, a central component must include his repeated insistence on the freedom granted those who are *in Christ. Yet because freedom is, both then and now—and also for Paul—a multifaceted notion and potentially ambiguous, both the nature of that freedom as Paul conceives it and its corollaries require close examination.

1. Terminology and Use in Paul
2. Context: Freedom(s) in Paul's World
3. Freedom in Paul's Letters: Leading Themes

1. Terminology and Use in Paul.

The Pauline notion of freedom will most frequently attach to the Greek terms of the *eleuther-* root (noun, *eleutheria*, "freedom," "liberty"; adjective, *eleutheros*, "free"; verb, *eleutheroō*, "I set free"). On this evidence alone, Paul's preoccupation with the notion stands unparalleled within early Christian discourse. For example, of the forty-one NT uses, thirty are in the Pauline corpus, albeit notably concentrated in Galatians, Romans, and the Corinthian correspondence. Paul's advocacy of freedom in a theological context is nearly unparalleled in broadly contemporary Jewish literature and is a theme largely set to the side in earliest Christian literature outside the NT.

But the conceptual field is considerably larger than that which maps to one set of cognates. The interpreter must thus keep in mind that, no less for Paul than for people today, freedom is not limited to a singular vocabulary or social context. In Paul's writings, the notion of freedom draws from a diverse lexicon reflecting a breadth of backgrounds including especially liberty from enslavement, literal and metaphorical; deliverance or rescue from an oppressing force (*sōtēria/sōzō, apolytrōsis, rhyomai*); the "authority" or "right" (*exousia*) to self-determine without compulsion (e.g., *anankē*); the "release" from obligation entailed in "*forgiveness" (*aphiēmi, aphesis*); an internal bearing that renders external compulsion unnecessary (*parrēsia*); and so on. By this standard, Paul's interest in freedom is expansive well beyond a particular vocabulary, demonstrating that he understood the Christ-event as fundamentally liberative in character, effecting a multifaceted transformation of the human condition. Thus, not only for the ubiquity of the theme but for its peculiarity to the Pauline corpus, interpreters of Paul are justified to claim the centrality of this theme within a constellation of related ideas (e.g., Longenecker; Richardson; Epp).

2. Context: Freedom(s) in Paul's World.

Ancient cultures expressed diverse notions of freedom—political, moral, religious, and psychological—and freedom was the locus of a wide-ranging political and philosophical discourse. This background being both diverse and dynamic, it resists summary and generalizations (see, e.g., Betz; Raaflaub; Schlier; Wirszbuski). Beyond a sketch of the general milieu in which Paul's discourse is located, demonstration of direct influence on the *apostle remains largely speculative. Because Paul's context evinces at least as much conceptual diversity as today's, there is always a danger of mapping misaligned modern notions on to ancient ones.

2.1. Slavery and Freedom. Paul's writings traffic in a world in which *slavery was an assumed and long-pervasive social structure. As such it provides the metaphorical root for all discourse concerning freedom, not only in Paul's writings but for all ancient reflection on the theme. Lacking its own positive content, freedom cannot be described other than as the antithesis to slavery, actual or metaphorical. For example, Israel's national freedom gained in the exodus is routinely described in the OT as a redemption from slavery (Lev 25:42; 26:13; Deut 6:21; 7:8; 13:5; 15:15; 24:18). Similarly, ancient political and philosophical reflection on freedom presumes a metaphorical donation from the slavery-freedom construct. Paul's discourse on freedom must likewise be understood against that background, and not only in such passages in which the freedom of slaves is the matter at hand (e.g., 1 Cor 7:21-23; Philemon).

2.2. Jewish Background. Jewish notions of freedom are predicated literally and conditioned metaphorically on Israel's formative exodus event, the liberation of the nation from its Egyptian oppressors. This event proved foundational to all subsequent national and ethnic self-understanding and posits freedom or liberation as fundamental to Jewish identity. This basic political conception of freedom came to the fore in the Hellenistic era, not least in the literature of the Maccabean revolt. For Paul, however, while Israel's political conditions can never have been unrelated to his "religious" concerns (Wright, 145-338), neither Israel's political status nor its fortunes in the Roman Empire factors prominently in his writings (Barclay). While Paul takes up the language of Israel's political deliverance to fund soteriological metaphors, such as redemption, deliverance, and *salvation, in his discussion of freedom itself Paul's frame of reference is typically abstract, theological, and metaphorically derived from a slavery-freedom, rather than a political, framework.

Where, however, Paul's view of the law and freedom overlaps with his fellow Jewish contemporaries, one finds the apostle's assertions novel and provocative. While, at least for his *Gentile converts, Paul posits a freedom *from* the *law (see 4.1 below), antecedent and contemporary Judaism would assert the opposite: the law itself was an instrument of human freedom. At critical points in Israel's history, rediscovery of the law (e.g., 2 Kings 23; 2 Chron 34) or returning to law observance (e.g., 2 Kings 18; 2 Chron 31; Neh 7–13) became the means of overturning national calamity or as the grateful response to restored fortunes. In the Psalter, the law is the object of devotion and delight, a privilege to obey and no burden (e.g., Ps 1:2; 19:7-11; 40:8; 119; and throughout), and in keeping it one *finds* freedom: "I shall walk at liberty, for I have sought your precepts" (Ps 119:45 NRSV). In the second century BC, Torah infidelity was understood as the cause of Israel's misfortune (e.g., 1 Macc 1:11-15), and a return to Torah devotion galvanized resolve to throw off the Seleucid oppression. True and lasting freedom was unthinkable apart from fidelity to the law.

The same conviction is widely attested in later sources. For example, Pirqe Abot invents a wordplay on Exodus 32:16 to make the claim that the law is itself the source of freedom:

> And it is written, *And the tables were the work of God, and the writing was the writing of God, graven* [*haruth*] *upon the tables.* Read not *haruth* ["graven"] but *heruth* ["freedom"], for thou findest no freeman excepting him that occupies himself in the study of the Law; and he that occupies himself in the study of the Law shall be exalted. (m. Abot 6:2, italics original)

In the same way that Roman political *philosophy would assert law as necessary to social freedom (Betz), Paul's Jewish antecedents and contemporaries would ascribe a parallel function to Torah. As Paul's near contemporary Philo would put it, "Those in whom anger or desire or any other passion, or again any insidious vice holds sway, are entirely enslaved, while all whose life is regulated by law are free" (*Prob.* 45 [LCL]).

Thus, it may be that Paul's novelty on this matter is the cause of a polemical contrary claim in *James: "the perfect law, the law of liberty" (Jas 1:25; cf. Jas 2:12 NRSV). Whether polemically motivated or not, the author of James reflects the more mainstream Jewish perspective. Paul's claim that the law could be a counterproductive constraint on human freedom is unprecedented, and the notion of "freedom from the law," which Paul regards as a fruit of his *gospel, would seem at best an oxymoron to his contemporaries.

2.3. Greco-Roman Context. Ancient Western notions of freedom—concrete and abstract—find their conceptual roots in the socioeconomic structure of slavery, on the one hand, and as the slave-free binary is translated by metaphorical extension to the political realm—the relation of persons to the state and law—on the other. Thus, by providing its metaphorical frame, the social givens of the ancient world dictated the terms on which further moral and philosophical reflection would take place. In contrast to modern, especially Western and democratic, norms, the ancient world did not experience freedom in every dimension as a default human condition or as though a birthright. One might have been born a slave or fallen into subjugation to slavery for economic or political reasons, and even if manumission was not uncommon, the resulting freedom was not necessarily absolute. Likewise, by modern standards, virtually any ancient political regime would have been authoritarian, if not tyrannical and despotic, even where more democratic virtues were espoused. And, religiously and philosophically, most ancients would have seen themselves subject to impersonal fate itself or to personal divine sovereignties, which, if perhaps subject to human influence, were beyond human control. Beyond all of this, the discourse of moral philosophers reveals a self-consciousness of a natural captivity to appetites and unruly passions such that self-control was a rare achievement. Thus, freedom in the ancient world would have been both relative and elusive, and its acquisition or maintenance in any dimension would have been cherished.

Freedom being coveted yet elusive, it is understandable that philosophical reflection should inquire of the ways a kind of freedom could be experienced that was not dependent on circumstances beyond one's control. The practical and populist philosophies of Cynicism and, especially, Stoicism made the acquisition and maintenance of this freedom a matter of first importance. While scholars have explored certain striking parallels between each of these schools and primitive Christianity, whether this demonstrates a direct influence or merely illustrates something of a shared milieu is a question that continues to intrigue scholars (e.g., Engberg-Pedersen 1995; 2000; Rowe; Eastman 2017).

Nonetheless, that there are certain elements of correspondence between Paul's notion of freedom and that of the Stoics is evident, even if, in the end, the ground and structure of the superficial similarities are found to be different. With the Stoics, Paul conceives of freedom in abstract and personal terms, with a strong noetic dimension. For the Stoics, enslavement and liberty are elected dispositions and are irrespective of social location. Freedom is attained especially through *apatheia* (an elective freedom from passion) and correlates, a dispassionate engagement with the life's stimuli that concedes sovereignty to fate as the condition of existential liberation. Paul's exhortations to exercise freedom (e.g., Gal 5:1, 13; 6:11-13) demonstrate that he also understands that freedom can and must be chosen and realized existentially. Paul also models and counsels a studied indifference to life's hardships so as not to be enslaved to circumstance (Phil 1:12-26; 4:10-14; 1 Cor 9:1-27; 2 Cor 12:10).

Although this elective and existential character to freedom is thoroughly Pauline, it is promised only to those who participate in the objective victories of *Christ, and it is premised on the extrinsic influence of the Spirit. From Paul's vantage, humans are not free enough to will their own freedom. Whereas Epictetus would ascribe a freedom of volition (*prohairesis*) divinely granted and inalienable, Paul understands humans as fundamentally enslaved to *sin and *flesh, incapable of sustained choices for good and self-control. Thus, whatever *apatheia* (a term not used by Paul) believers might muster toward nonultimate matters, it is morally conditioned on the self-renouncing, cruciform pattern of Christ, a participation in his sufferings.

Likewise, although Paul renders much of worldly existence as though *ta adiaphora* ("matters of indifference," though, again, not Pauline terminology), Pauline freedom is radically conditioned by an *eschatology that nullifies the ultimacy of narrowly mundane concerns. In the face of the possible or even presumed imminence of the eschaton, Paul regards the stations and circumstances of the mortal life as consequential but nonultimate. The radicality of this stance is most clearly articulated in 1 Corinthians, where neither *marriage, nor sex, nor slavery, nor *circumcision is regarded as an ultimate concern (1 Cor 7:29-31): "For the present form [*schēma*] of this world is passing away" (1 Cor 7:31 NRSV). But rather than a consequence of a self-disciplined psyche or a learned behavior, Paul's counsel derives from a new account of the world understood through the eschatological revelation of Christ and the advance of the gospel (e.g., Phil 1:12-26; 1 Cor 9:19-23).

3. Freedom in Paul's Letters: Leading Themes. One can note that Paul's treatment of freedom is not singular; Christian freedoms are several. Given the contextual circumstances of his letters, it is also not surprising that certain aspects of the theme are featured in certain letters, not to say absent entirely in the others. The following is a summary of those themes with particular attention to the letter in which it is most prominent.

3.1. Freedom from the Law: Galatians. Among Paul's letters, none has a more repeated and sustained reflection, albeit contextually occasioned, on the theme of freedom. This freedom is fundamentally a freedom from a law observance that was being imposed on the Gentile converts by Paul's antagonists. Galatians is a sustained argument that these converts need not—indeed, must not—"Judaize."

Already in the letter's *narratio*, Paul writes that his Judean *opponents insinuated themselves to spy on "the freedom we have" and to "enslave" them (Gal 2:4 NRSV). In the context, the primary freedom to which Paul refers is from obligation to Torah observance and such liberties as will follow consequently, such as unhindered Jew-Gentile commensality (see Gal 2:11-14).

Provocatively, Paul characterizes this enslavement in Galatians 4:1-11 as to "the elemental spirits" (Gal 4:3, 9 NRSV; *ta stoicheia*, alternatively, "the rudiments," ASV), which he describes as the status of "minors" (*nēpioi*) "under the law." While Paul's precise use of this language remains opaque, this enslavement to the apparently personified and nefarious *stoicheia* casts the law into an even more oppressive role. Yet freedom from enslavement to the *stoicheia* is enjoyed by those who once "under the law" now come of age, redeemed to their new status as fully adopted "sons" (*huioi*; Gal 4:4-5). The freedom-slavery binary also forms the basis of one Paul's most creative appropriations of the OT. In his extended allegorization of Sarah and Hagar

(Gal 4:21-31), Paul describes Sarah as the "free [woman]" (*eleuthera*) and Hagar as "slave woman" (*paidiskē*), in order to map theological claims to these social identities. The line of argument is complex and counterintuitive, the subject of many detailed treatments (see, e.g., Eastman 2007, 127-60). For the purposes of this article, the following observations are salient. (1) For his theological argument, Paul wishes to exploit the "slave" status of Hagar. She provides a ready antithesis to Sarah, whom Paul dubs "the free woman," an identification, though inferable, not found in Genesis 21:10 (see Gal 4:30). (2) It is this distinction that Paul uses to identify Sarah and her offspring as the *covenantally* free and Hagar's offspring as enslaved. (3) Polemically, Paul thus identifies nonbelieving Judaism—"Mount Sinai in Arabia," "the present *Jerusalem" (Gal 4:25 NRSV)—as the offspring of Hagar(!), descended from the child born according to the flesh, while the children of Sarah are the children of the promise, the "Jerusalem above" (Gal 4:26 NRSV). "So then, friends, we are children, not of the slave [woman] but of the free woman" (Gal 4:31 NRSV). Thus, those incorporated into *Abraham, his true children of promise through Sarah, are free, above all from the demands of Sinai.

That this freedom is not incidental to Paul's message is indicated by the summative declaration of Galatians 5:1: "For freedom Christ has set us free. Stand firm, therefore, and do not submit again to a yoke of slavery" (Gal 5:1 NRSV). Following on the Sarah-Hagar allegory, again, it must be a freedom from law observance that is primarily in view. Freedom from Torah observance must not be compromised by yielding to the pressure to be circumcised, for to receive circumcision is to be "obliged to obey the entire law" (Gal 5:3 NRSV), a choice if taken that would nullify the saving work of Christ. Thus, Paul regards this freedom not simply as a benefit of *justification apart from *works of the law but as its proper end.

Yet Paul no doubt understands that this is an objectionable and even precarious claim; this freedom from Torah observance might be mistaken for a thoroughgoing antinomianism, which would be to misunderstand the nature of the freedom altogether. "For you were called to freedom, brothers and sisters; only do not use your freedom as an opportunity for self-indulgence, but through *love become slaves to one another" (Gal 5:13 NRSV; see 1 Pet 2:16). As always in Paul, the alternative to freedom from the law is not freedom tout court but to an alternative "enslavement" (Rom 6:16, 18, 22; 1 Cor 7:22; 9:19), in this context, through love being obliged as slaves to one another. Freedom is never merely *from* but always *for*.

That those who are in Christ are emancipated from the law is arguably Paul's most basic claim with respect to freedom (Gal 3:23-25; 5:18; 1 Cor 9:20; Rom 6:14-15; 7:3-4; 8:3; Eph 2:15) and perhaps the genesis of his reflection on the theme altogether (Richardson). It follows from two premises: (1) inclusion into the covenant people is not dependent on observance of the Torah and (2) obedience to the law does not secure or inspire the transformative *righteousness wrought by the Spirit. Paul is well aware that the gift of such freedom might easily be perverted into an antinomian libertinism. But this is a profound misunderstanding if not a deliberate perversion of the freedom granted in Christ. (Rom 3:8; 6:1, 15; perhaps 2 Pet 3:16). In Galatians, Paul anticipates and rebuts such objections; in 1 Corinthians he checks a libertine spirit apparently already in play; in Romans, he shows such an outcome to be a theological impossibility. Under several complementary figures, Paul maintains that law from which believers are freed does not leave a vacuum, nor does it in any sense disoblige those set free from an obedience to *God. Rather, being "led by the Spirit" is the prior condition for not being under the law (Gal 5:18 NRSV); the command to love neighbor fulfills the law and conditions the whole of Christian behavior (Gal 5:14; Rom 13:8-9); and Christians are obliged, in any case, to obey the *law of Christ (Gal 6:2; 1 Cor 9:21). Thus, Paul's freedom from the law is a thoroughly positive emancipation toward a singular goal of free and wholehearted obedience to God.

3.2. Freedom from Freedom: 1 Corinthians. Although Galatians is understandably tagged as Paul's treatise on freedom, 1 Corinthians is likewise saturated with the theme in an especially nuanced treatment, applied to moral, communal, and missional priorities. Here Paul seeks to weave a course that at once affirms the genuine freedom wrought in Christ while rejecting a facile libertinism that might be—and apparently has been—wrongly deduced from that premise. In response, Paul affirms a freedom that, while conditioned, precisely as such is more radical than a libertine might imagine.

Paul's vision of this radical freedom is exemplified by the discourse of 1 Corinthians 7, in which Paul subverts the ultimacy of social station for Christian existence: "Let each of you lead the life that the Lord has assigned, to which God called you. This is my rule in all the churches. . . . Let each of you remain in the condition in which you were called. . . . In whatever condition you were called, brothers and sisters, there remain with God" (1 Cor 7:17, 20, 24 NRSV). Thus, illustrating by various states of marriage and *sexuality, circumcision, and slavery, Paul insists that Christian freedom is such that social station bears inconsequentially on one's capacity to live a life holy and pleasing to God. This relative indifference to matters of otherwise great significance demonstrates how thoroughgoing is the liberation wrought in Christ. That noted, Paul's high-minded indifference to the mundane is not absolute. While relativizing the significance of social circumstance, Paul maintains a pragmatism as concerns lust and sexual self-control (1 Cor 7:5, 9, 36) and seems also to endorse slaves availing themselves of manumission should it come to them (1 Cor 7:21, 23; albeit debated). Nonetheless, freedom from worldly preoccupation enables a single-hearted devotion to the *Lord and his work.

Perhaps the most elevated discussion of freedom in Paul is found in 1 Corinthians 9, a personal and rhetorically purposeful digression amid Paul's extended discussion of *food offered to idols in 1 Corinthians 8; 10. If the propriety of eating such food is the occasion and theme of this discourse, 1 Corinthians 9 shows that the larger subtext is the question of Christian freedom. Assuming with most scholars that Paul is engaging Corinthian slogans (e.g., "food is meant for the stomach and the stomach for food," 1 Cor 6:13 NRSV; "It is well for a man not to touch a woman" 1 Cor 7:1 NRSV; "all of us possess *knowledge," 1 Cor 8:1 NRSV; "no idol in the world really exists"; "there is no God but one," 1 Cor 8:4 NRSV), apparently some among them were flaunting their liberty toward harmful outcomes. As is frequently the case, Paul's response to their sloganeering is a concession to the substance of the claim while offering a profound recasting within a larger framework. "Yes, it is true that idols as such are not real beings, but this does not mean that practices acknowledging their existence are morally neutral." "Yes, it is true that you enjoy a certain kind of freedom, but your exercise of this freedom could be woefully misguided."

Thus, in 1 Corinthians 9, Paul inserts himself—his freedom and his panoply of apostolic prerogatives—as a case study in the proper exercise of freedom. Leading with the rhetorical question, "Am I not free?" (1 Cor 9:1 NRSV), Paul goes on to itemize his many apostolic honors and prerogatives (1 Cor 9:1-12a, 13-14), while insisting that he has not availed himself of such privileges, though having every right to do so (1 Cor 9:12b, 15). Rather, his various "freedoms" (*exousia*; "authority," "right") are employed or even obviated toward the singular goal of preaching the gospel as widely and persuasively as possible (1 Cor 9:16-27). Thus, while the Corinthians also have true freedom and "rights" (1 Cor 8:9) that they exploit toward libertarian ends, perhaps even smugly, Paul's freedom (1 Cor 9:1, 19; 10:29) and "rights" (1 Cor 9:4, 5, 6, 12, 18), though far exceeding theirs, he subordinates and employs to the greater good of preaching the gospel to all.

Though free of all persons, in one sense, Paul *chooses* a kind of slavery for the sake of the spread of the gospel: "For though I am free from all, I have made myself a servant [*doulos*] to all, that I might win more of them" (1 Cor 9:19 ESV). For Paul, freedom does not terminate in its exercise for the benefit of the free person, but rather in the latitude that it grants him to exercise a far-reaching flexibility to reach all. Thus, Paul can "become" a Jew and "become" law-observant for the sake of Jews and those under the law, though not under the law himself. Just as readily, he can become as one outside the law to win those outside the law; he can become weak for the sake of the weak: "I have become all things to all people, that by all means I might save some" (1 Cor 9:22 ESV). Yet, this liberality of spirit is anything but unprincipled or undisciplined. These diverse stances are united under the singular principle of availing as many as possible of the gospel, a slavery Paul freely chooses. By this standard, the Corinthians' proud exploitation of their prerogatives as a means of displaying a supposed spiritual advancement is shown for the rank immaturity that it is.

Freedom in Christ is always conditioned by love, specifically concretized in community, which is to override the freedom that might otherwise be intrinsic to the individual. This is the pervasive theme not only of 1 Corinthians 8–10 but also a broadly analogous discourse in Romans 14:1–15:6, even if these treatments originate from somewhat different controversies. Behaviors within the "rights" (*exousia*) of the individual, even if being themselves objectively just, are not necessarily commended, lest they reap deleterious effects on fellow brothers and sisters or the community as a whole. The violation to the life of the community is chiefly the disturbance of another's more scrupulous conscience, which may either scandalize their sensibilities, producing inevitable judgment and division, or, no less seriously, embolden or even pressure a brother or sister to behave contrary to their conscience. But the lived unity of the community is paramount, and the conscience of another believer "for whom Christ died" (Rom 14:15 ESV) is sacrosanct. Thus, paradoxically, the freedom that Paul espouses is not to become captive to itself, such that what one could do by rights must not determine what one ought to do in fact. Freedom is conditioned by love and in deference to a community.

*3.3. **The Freedom of the New Covenant: 2 Corinthians.*** Second Corinthians evinces only a single occurrence of "freedom" vocabulary: "Where the Spirit of the Lord is, there is freedom" (2 Cor 3:17 ESV). The absence of immediate contextual clues renders this watchword subject to a variety of interpretations, including even the unlikely conjecture that it is an interpolation. However, in the context of Paul's densely constructed argument, he contrasts the limited and fading access Moses had to the face of God (Ex 34:29-35) and the former dispensation that it illustrates, an old dispensation, to the superiority of the new *covenant. This freedom can be understood broadly as the numerous prerogatives availed by the new covenant—unrestricted access to God by the Spirit, and release from the externality of the letter in favor of a wholehearted and unconstrained obedience as the fulfillment of new covenant promise (Jer 31:31-34; see 2 Cor 3:3-4). Given that, in the near context (2 Cor 3:7-11), Paul has described the adverse experience of life under the former dispensation as "dispensation of *death" and of "condemnation," and a "fading *glory"—freedom from the condemnatory and inert character of the law is likely in mind. This is set in contrast to the "confidence" (2 Cor 3:12; *parrēsia*, "boldness," "openness") enjoyed before God, unveiled faces beholding the glory of God and transformed from one degree of glory to another.

*3.4. **Freedom, Anthropology, Allegiance, and Eschatology: Romans.*** Of the various expositions of freedom in Paul's letters, Romans offers the most theological—more particularly, anthropological—treatment. While freedom from the law is reasserted in Romans (e.g., Rom 6:14; 7:1-6; 10:4) as in Galatians, it is not the singular or even primary concern. Likewise, in a manner broadly parallel to 1 Corinthians 8–10, Romans 14:1–15:6 insists that the exercise of genuine freedom is constrained by the edification of the community as a whole, especially in consideration of its most vulnerable members.

But the stage in Romans is a larger one. Paul's concern is not only with the law or merely to check a Judaizing impulse, but also with humanity's cosmic adversaries: sin, death, the flesh, and the fallen *creation in entropy. It is impossible to lay hold of Paul's understanding of freedom apart from engaging his theological *anthropology. The human dilemma extends beyond objective guilt (esp. Rom 1:18–5:11) to the tragedy of human corruption (esp. Rom 5:12–8:39), whereby human beings find themselves unfree to exercise fealty and obedience to their Creator, wills disabled, judgment impaired, motives corrupted. This, as Paul describes it, is the consequence of slaveries to entities unworthy of human allegiance and destructive of human well-being—in short, sin (*hamartia*). Here sin (or better, Sin) is not simply such individual actions as transgress the moral will of God, nor even their aggregate, but a reified or personified power that is at work exploiting fallen human weakness and oppressing its subjects into a powerless subjugation, out of which they cannot will themselves. This futility is itself an enslavement more profound than any other, from which believers are set free by Christ's breaking of the power of the stronghold of Sin, on the one hand, and by the gift of the indwelling power of Christ by the Spirit, on the other. Yet, apart from this fundamental and thoroughgoing transformation, Paul would regard a vaunted "freedom" to do as one pleases both illusory and catastrophic.

Apart from the liberation wrought by Christ, humanity is "enslaved to sin" (Rom 6:6 NRSV; see Rom 6:16-20; 7:25). The inevitable corollary of this enslavement to Sin is its "reward," death (Rom 5:12; 6:16, 23; 7:13; 8:2, 10; see also 1 Cor 15:56). While "death" (*thanatos*) refers to the termination of physical life, it also names more broadly a *telos* of alienation from God and the tragedy of self-destruction. A willing accomplice in this enslavement leading to death is the "flesh" (*sarx*), the mortal, appetitive self in rebellion against the righteousness of God. As Paul understands it, Sin exploits the weakness of the flesh, so as to exercise dominion over the enslaved person unto ultimate reprobation. This circle is vicious, the flesh lacking the wherewithal to overcome the power of Sin and becoming subject to the wages of death.

If the solution to these human enslavements is freedom, it is a paradoxical freedom wrought by a new slavery to God and obedience to righteousness. For Paul, genuine freedom requires a transfer of allegiance rather than an unqualified autonomy. Nowhere is this articulated more directly than in Romans 6, where, by *baptism into Christ's death, the believer dies a death to Sin and is brought to new life with Christ in solidarity with his *resurrection. In doing so, the believer exchanges a former allegiance to Sin for an allegiance to Christ, becoming a "slave to righteousness." Sardonically, Paul characterizes that former enslavement as its own kind of "freedom": "you were free in regard to righteousness"

(Rom 6:20), taunting that the bitter "fruit" of that slavery was death (Rom 6:20-23). A parallel transfer of loyalty described under a different figure follows immediately in Romans 7:1-6, turning from the metaphor of slavery to that of the legal status of marriage. By incorporation into the death of Christ, obligation to the law is nullified, so that the believer—cast as the bride—is free to marry another, Christ, now willingly bearing fruit unto God.

From Paul's vantage, human beings are always and inevitably in a condition of slavery. Apart from Christ's saving intervention, they are unwitting and involuntary slaves of Sin, captive to their own fleshly passions and self-interests. There is no release from these apart from a willing yielding of one's mind and bodily members to the liberating authority of Christ that is on offer by means of the objective victory of Christ's death and resurrection. Thus, Paul's only notion of freedom involves a transfer from one sphere of slavery to another sphere of "slavery": from the law to the Spirit, from the power of sin to obedience to Christ as Lord, from self to love of others.

Freedom, thus, for Paul, is never naked autonomy but a properly located fealty; one is always subject to what one serves. Rather than unconstrained action, it is a newfound capacity for the believer to will and to do what pleases God and edifies neighbor. Such freedom is not an achievement of the believer but gifted by the victory of Christ over sin and death. But neither is freedom a condition enjoyed automatically. Those objectively liberated by Christ must "reckon [them]selves to be dead to sin, but alive to God in Christ Jesus"; they must not "let sin reign in [their] mortal bodies; they must rather "present [their] members to God as instruments of righteousness" (Rom 6:11-13, 19). Yet, this willing and self-offering is itself only a gift made accessible by the victory of Christ.

Because Paul's notion of personal freedom requires this transfer of allegiance by which believers are made "slaves of righteousness" (Rom 6:18 NRSV), it never succumbs to libertinism. Paradoxically, Paul considers this new allegiance, unlike the former state, to be a liberation. It is thus neither incidental nor a mere rhetorical flourish that Paul's chosen titular moniker for himself and fellow Christian servants is "slave" (*doulos*; Rom 1:1; 1 Cor 7:22; 2 Cor 4:5; Gal 1:10; Eph 6:6; Phil 1:1; 2 Tim 2:24; Titus 1:1) or "*servant" (*diakonos*; Rom 16:1; 1 Cor 3:5; 2 Cor 3:6; 6:4; 11:23; Eph 3:7; 6:21; Col 1:7, 23, 25; 4:7; 1 Tim 4:6). In so designating himself, he names his freedom as an exclusive and thoroughgoing submission to Christ, the "master" (*kyrios*).

In their enslaved state, humans stand under condemnation and the ultimate consequence of sin, death. Those in Christ are liberated from these ends and delivered from the fear of them (Rom 5:1, 16; 6:5; 8:1-2, 11, 34; see also 1 Cor 6:14; 2 Cor 4:14; Col 2:13; Eph 2:5-6). Instead, "the law of the Spirit of life in Christ Jesus has set you free from the law of sin and of death" (Rom 8:2 NRSV). But this destiny of unalloyed freedom is not for humans alone but for the whole creation:

> The creation was subjected to futility, not of its own will but by the will of the one who subjected it, in hope that the creation itself will be set free from its bondage to decay and will obtain the freedom of the glory of the children of God. We know that the whole creation has been groaning in labor pains until now; and not only the creation, but we ourselves, who have the first fruits of the Spirit, groan inwardly while we wait for *adoption, the redemption of our bodies. (Rom 8:20-23 NRSV)

Thus, the ultimate release of redeemed humanity from the oppression of Sin, the corruption of the flesh, and the threat of death will coincide with the emancipation of the whole creation from its "bondage to decay" at the "freedom of the glory of the children of God." Freedom is humanity's destiny, and it is bound up with the freedom of the cosmos from the oppression of the fall. Thus, all Christian freedom enjoyed on this side of the eschaton is but an earnest toward an ultimate liberty that escapes the sway of sin altogether and in every dimension.

Popular Stoic philosopher Epictetus offers a classic ancient definition of freedom in the opening words of his fourth discourse, "About Freedom": "He is free who lives as he wills, who is subject neither to compulsion, nor hindrance, nor force; whose choices are unhampered, whose desires attain their end, and whose aversions do not fall into what they would avoid" (*Diatr.* 4.1.1 [LCL]). While both Paul and the Stoic understood that a person cannot be free if under external compulsion, Paul understood that an internal compulsion—the good of the other born of love—liberates a person to act with a radical freedom on which not even freedom itself cannot lay claim. Paul's vision of freedom is not the right to live as one pleases but the unimpeded internal capacity to live so as to please God and neighbor.

See also CORINTHIANS, FIRST LETTER TO THE; CORINTHIANS, SECOND LETTER TO THE; CREATION AND NEW CREATION; FLESH; GALATIANS, LETTER TO THE; IN CHRIST; LAW; LOVE; PHILOSOPHY;

Romans, Letter to the; Sin, Guilt; Slave, Slavery; Strong and Weak.

BIBLIOGRAPHY. **J. M. G. Barclay,** "Why the Roman Empire Was Insignificant to Paul," in *Pauline Churches and Diaspora Jews* (Grand Rapids, MI: Eerdmans, 2016), 363-87; **H. D. Betz,** *Paul's Concept of Freedom in the Context of Hellenistic Discussions About the Possibilities of Human Freedom* (Berkeley, CA: Center for Hermeneutical Studies in Hellenistic and Modern Culture, 1977); **R. Bultmann,** *Theology of the New Testament,* trans. Kendrick Grobel, 2 vols. (New York: Scribner, 1951); **S. J. Chester,** "Reception and Theology: Who Is Freedom For? Martin Luther and Alain Badiou on Paul and Politics," in *Paul, Grace, and Freedom: Essays in Honour of John K. Riches,* ed. P. Middleton, A. Paddison, and K. J. Wenell (New York: T&T Clark, 2009); **S. G. Eastman,** *Recovering Paul's Mother Tongue: Language and Theology in Galatians* (Grand Rapids, MI: Eerdmans, 2007); idem, *Paul and the Person: Reframing Paul's Anthropology* (Grand Rapids, MI: Eerdmans, 2017); **T. Engberg-Pedersen,** "Stoicism in Philippians," in *Paul in His Hellenistic Context,* ed. T. Engberg-Pedersen (Minneapolis: Fortress, 1995), 256-90; idem, *Paul and the Stoics* (Louisville, KY: Westminster John Knox, 2000); **E. J. Epp,** "Paul's Diverse Imageries of the Human Situation and His Unifying Theme of Freedom," in *Unity and Diversity in New Testament Theology: Essays in Honor of George E. Ladd,* ed. G. E. Ladd and R. A. Guelich (Grand Rapids, MI: Eerdmans, 1978), 100-116; **L. E. Galloway,** *Freedom in the Gospel: Paul's Exemplum in 1 Cor 9 in Conversation with the Discourses of Epictetus and Philo* (Leuven: Peeters, 2004); **M. J. Harris,** *Slave of Christ: A New Testament Metaphor for Total Devotion to Christ,* NSBT 8 (Downers Grove, IL: InterVarsity Press, 2000); **E. Käsemann,** *Jesus Means Freedom: A Polemical Survey of the New Testament* (London: SCM Press, 1969); **L. E. Keck,** "Paul's Understanding of Freedom," in *Christ's First Theologian: The Shape of Paul's Thought* (Waco, TX: Baylor University Press, 2015); **R. N. Longenecker,** *Paul, Apostle of Liberty: The Origin and Nature of Paul's Christianity* (Grand Rapids, MI: Baker, 1976); **M. Luther,** *The Freedom of a Christian, 1520,* ed. T. J. Wengert (Minneapolis: Fortress, 2016); **D. B. Martin,** *Slavery as Salvation: The Metaphor of Slavery in Pauline Christianity* (New Haven, CT: Yale University Press, 1990); **J. Murphy-O'Connor,** *Becoming Human Together: The Pastoral Anthropology of St. Paul* (Wilmington, DE: Glazier, 1982); **K. A. Raaflaub,** *The Discovery of Freedom in Ancient Greece* (Chicago: University of Chicago, 2004); **P. Richardson,** *Paul's Ethic of Freedom* (Philadelphia: Westminster, 1979); **C. K. Rowe,** *One True Life: The Stoics and Early Christians as Rival Traditions* (New Haven, CT: Yale University Press, 2016). **H. Schlier,** "ἐλεύθερος, κτλ.," *TDNT* 2:487-502; **R. Schnackenburg,** "Christian Freedom According to Paul," in *Christian Existence in the New Testament,* ed. R. Schnackenburg and F. D. Wieck (South Bend, IN: Notre Dame University Press, 1969), 31-53; **C. Wirszubski,** *Libertas as a Political Idea at Rome During the Late Republic and Early Principate* (Cambridge: Cambridge University Press, 1960); **N. T. Wright,** *The New Testament and the People of God,* COQG 1 (Minneapolis: Fortress, 1992).

G. P. Anderson

FRIENDSHIP

Paul never uses the term "friend" (*philos*) or "friendship" (*philia*), nor does he provide an explicit definition of friendship (unlike, for instance, Aristotle in *Eth. nic.* 8.2.3-5). But that does not mean the concept of friendship is absent in Paul's writings, or that it mattered little to him. He clearly addresses relationships of affection, of which friendship is a subset. Such bonds of affection were essential not only to the health of the *church but especially to Paul's theology. In fact, friendship (or relationship) is the paradigm through which Paul theologizes—friendship with God and one another in union with Christ.

Several Greek words and images (e.g., the *body) are employed by Paul to describe this overtly theological friendship, but this article will focus on *koinōnia* ("partnership, *fellowship, participation") and its cognates, *phroneō* ("a way of thinking, feeling, and acting"), and *allēlōn* ("one another"). Although scholars generally agree that these terms depict friendship, they fundamentally disagree as to the precise type of friendship envisioned by Paul. After briefly outlining different perspectives, this article will consider the Pauline hallmarks of friendship *in Christ. They can all be found in Philippians, a letter that has drawn the most attention when considering the topic of friendship in Paul's writings. No wonder the Philippian congregation held a special place in the apostle's heart.

1. Friendship in the Ancient World
2. Scholarly Perspectives on Friendship
3. The Pauline Hallmarks of Friendship in Christ

1. Friendship in the Ancient World.

Friendship—known as *philia* among the Greeks, *amicitia* among the Romans—was a common point of interest among philosophers in the ancient world. Plato, Aristotle, Cicero, Seneca, and many others thought deeply about friendship and communicated their ideas not simply to challenge common conceptions of friendship but also to encourage people to practice it (see Konstan). Of course, these writers employ different strategies to expound on the virtue of friendship. Plato's *Lysis*, *Symposium*, and *Phaedrus*, as well as Cicero's *On Friendship*, are dialogues on friendship. Seneca reveals his perspective through *letters written to friends in his *Moral Epistles*. And Aristotle devotes two entire books to friendship in his philosophical treatise, *Nicomachean Ethics* 8-9.

Among these, Aristotle's work is considered to be "the fullest and most probing classical study of friendship" (Pangle, 2). He distinguished among friendships based on utility, pleasure, and virtue, elevating virtue friendships above the rest. Friends in this relationship reciprocate goodwill, *love, and material goods. They seek the good of the other person for their own sake, not for selfish gain. They possess one mind or soul, share all things in common, and are equals in virtue. Since Aristotle employs similar terminology found in Philippians, it is unsurprising to see so many scholars comparing Paul with this ancient philosopher (see, e.g., Fitzgerald 1996).

2. Scholarly Perspectives on Friendship.
After a well-known lecture by A. Malherbe in 1990, where he called on scholars to investigate friendship language in Paul and the Greco-Roman world, many began to mine the depths of Philippians (see Fitzgerald 1996). What resulted was placing Paul within a much larger discussion on friendship and its relational dynamics, in which Plato, Cicero, Seneca, Aristotle, and many others participated. Comparing Paul and ancient philosophers led these scholars to ask specific questions about the exact kind of relationship that Paul and the Philippians enjoyed. Was it equal or unequal? Did it contain the element of obligation or not? Could it be traced back to other kinds of relationship in the ancient Greco-Roman world? Different answers emerged from this exploration.

2.1. A Roman Consensual Societas. Recently, J. Ogereau has revived the thesis (first developed by Fleury and later expounded by Sampley) that Paul's understanding of friendship stems from a Roman consensual *societas*. This relationship was a legally binding, reciprocal partnership between two or more parties that aimed at a common goal. By arguing that *societas* is the Latin equivalent of *koinōnia*, in addition to many other arguments, these scholars insist that the relationship between Paul and the Philippians should be considered a *societas Christi* that advances the *gospel (see Sampley, 72). What results is a legally binding friendship among Christians, though entered into freely and voluntarily (see Ogereau, 341). But it is neither clear that *koinōnia* is the Greek equivalent of *societas* nor certain that Paul meant to import that meaning into his theological (rather than purely socioeconomical) use of *koinōnia*.

2.2. An Equal Friendship. Others veer away from a legally binding *societas Christi* and instead affirm an equal relationship between Paul and the Philippians. L. White crafts it in terms of a *patronage relationship, but one that is a symmetrical friendship. Paul, he contends, is their "spiritual patron," and the Philippians are his "economic patron" (see White, 214-15n59). This is an overtly Christian take on patronage as existing among equals. In the ancient world, patrons related to socially inferior clients, whom they would, at times, call friends. But, obviously, the symmetrical term *friend* only disguised the obvious asymmetry between them. What developed was an *ideal* perspective on friendship as symmetrical and the *reality* that it was actually asymmetrical. Scholars holding this view recognize the *ideal-reality* distinction but nevertheless maintain that Paul and the Philippians experienced an equal Christian friendship.

2.3. An Unequal Friendship. Many other scholars are not so idealistic. Instead, they argue that Paul affirms the *reality* of unequal friendship. B. Witherington, for example, argues that Paul's "partnership with the Philippians is not one of complete equality," since he is an authoritative *apostle who can issue commands (see Witherington, 168n19). Unlike in the previous perspective, Paul is a superior patron and the Philippians are his inferior clients, and this asymmetrical relationship is what he calls friendship.

2.4. A Nonobligatory Friendship. Over against perspectives on friendship that affirm the presence of obligation, such as Roman *societas*, M. Ebner and G. Peterman deny its exploitative presence in Paul's relationship with the Philippians. To be sure, these scholars recognize obligation to be an inherent element of friendship in the Greco-Roman world. They just think it is completely foreign to Christian friendship. Thus, Ebner contends that Paul corrects the Philippians' wrong understanding of "der Verpflichtungscharakter der Freundschaft" ("the obligatory nature of friendship") by affirming his dependence on *God in Philippians 4:13 (see Ebner, 358).

Peterman highlights the absence of the term *obligation* in Philippians and entirely excludes this exploitative element from the relational equation.

So, what kind of friendship did Paul and the Philippians enjoy? Was it analogous to a Roman consensual *societas*? Was it equal or unequal? Did it include the ties of obligation? However one answers these questions, one must be careful not to put the cart before the horse. A more fundamentally theological question must be asked before determining the relational hallmarks of their friendship: Were Paul and the Philippians in friendship with God? This seemingly simplistic question contains profound implications when determining the hallmarks of friendship in Paul.

3. The Pauline Hallmarks of Friendship in Christ.

3.1. Friendship with God and One Another. Christian friendships are *koinōnia* relationships between the triune God and believers, and these relationships are marked by vertical and horizontal dimensions. Horizontally, Paul and the Philippians have a *koinōnia* in "gospel" advancement (Phil 1:5, 7), in "*grace" (Phil 1:7), in "*suffering" (Phil 4:14), and in "giving and receiving" (Phil 4:15). They are human partners in these endeavors or experiences. But the horizontal is rooted in the vertical. Their *koinōnia* is also said to be a mutual participation in grace (Phil 1:7), in the "Spirit" (Phil 2:1), and in the "sufferings" of *Christ (Phil 3:10). More than this, God partners with them by working through them. For example, Paul and the Philippians have a *koinōnia* in the gospel, but it is God who advances (*prokopē*) that gospel through them (see the *inclusio* of Phil 1:12, 25). "From him . . . are all things" (Rom 11:36 ESV), and believers possess nothing that cannot be labeled a divine gift (1 Cor 4:7). So, God energizes (*energeō*) their labors (Phil 2:13) and works in and through them as the vertical party. They are therefore mediators of *his* gospel and *his* grace.

Koinōnia or Christian friendship is a tripartite relationship. It consists of friendship with God and one another in Christ by the Spirit.

3.2. The Christological Shape of Friendship. Having "one mind" or "one soul" is essential to ancient (as well as modern) friendship. That is why friends are considered another self. They think, feel, and act the same way toward one another, so as to become one whole person. Paul desired the Philippians to share such a mindset. The word frequently used by ancient writers is *phronēsis,* or the verbal form *phroneō*. Yet Paul employed the verb in a christologically distinct way from other ancient writers. In Philippians 2:2, Paul calls them to be "of one mind [*phronountes*]" and "of the same mind [*phronēte*]" (ESV). But, intriguingly, when he shows them where to find this mindset, he points to their union with Christ. "Have this mind [*phroneite*] among yourselves, which is yours *in Christ Jesus*" (Phil 2:5 ESV). The rest of Philippians 2:5-11 fleshes out this christological mindset, which can essentially be boiled down to lowering oneself for the sake of others. Paul is not calling them solely to intellectually ponder their union with Christ but also to demonstrate it. Christian *phronēsis* is a humble, sacrificial, self-giving posture toward others, as one thinks, feels, and acts in a way that accords with the self-giving love of Christ (see Fowl, 28). It is the natural effect of union with Christ and the indwelling of the Spirit.

We see this humble, self-giving posture in Paul's friendship with the Philippians. Paul believes it is right for him to "feel" or "think" (*phronein*) a certain way about the Philippians. They are his "beloved" (Phil 4:1), his "joy" and "crown" (Phil 4:1), and his "boast" (Phil 2:16). He loves and longs for them, holding them in his heart (Phil 1:7), yearning for all of them with "the affection [*splanchnois*] of Christ Jesus" (Phil 1:8 ESV), and desiring to build them up in the *faith (Phil 1:25 27; 2:24). In fact, Paul's love turns into action as he embodies the gospel of Christ in Philippians 2:5-11. He likens his *ministry to a sacrificial drink "offering" (*thysia*) and "service" (*leitourgia*) for their faith (Phil 2:17). He is even willing, like Christ, to suffer on their behalf inside and outside *prison walls (Phil 1:12-18), as the gospel advances through Paul's suffering for the edification of the Philippian church (Phil 1:25). Although he desires to be with Christ, he lowers himself for their sake, choosing to remain in the *flesh so they might be exalted (Phil 1:21-26). One can easily see that Christ lives in Paul (Gal 2:20).

But this christological mindset also resides in the Philippians. God revived the Philippians' "concern" (*phroneō*) for Paul (Phil 4:10), which they tangibly expressed through their gift to him in prison (Phil 4:18). Not that they stopped caring about Paul. They just lacked opportunity (Phil 4:10). But now they can send Epaphroditus to act as their personal presence with their imprisoned apostle and to assist him financially (Phil 2:25-30). Interestingly, Paul likens their material gift to a sacrificial "offering" (*thysia*, Phil 4:18) and "service" (*leitourgia*, Phil 2:30), the very same words he used to describe his ministry toward them. They reciprocated a christological mindset, lowering themselves to exalt the other. One can easily see that Christ lives in the Philippians.

Paul and the Philippians share a common christological mindset that replicates (in a nonidentical way) the life of Christ to one another (see Fowl 1998). This is what distinctly marks Christian friendship as *Christ*ian.

3.3. Reciprocity of Grace—"One Another." Reciprocity in Paul is summed up in the well-known phrase "one another" (*allelōn*). In his wider corpus, he calls on the church to "bear one another's [*allelōn*] burdens" (Gal 6:2 ESV), to bear "with one another [*allelōn*]" (Eph 4:2 ESV), to "serve one another [*allelois*]" (Gal 5:13 ESV), to "love one another [*allelous*]" (Rom 12:10 ESV), to "welcome one another [*allelous*]" (Rom 15:7 ESV), and the list goes on.

In Philippians, however, the phrase appears only once. "Do nothing from selfish ambition or conceit, but in humility [*tapeinophrosynē*] consider one another [*allēlous*] more significant than yourselves" (Phil 2:3). Five verses later, Paul uses the verbal form of *tapeinophrosynē* to describe Jesus, who "humbled [*etapeinōsen*] himself" for the sake of others (Phil 2:8 ESV). By connecting Philippians 2:3, 8 through the word *tapeinophrosyne*, Paul, in essence, exhorts the entire Philippian community (not just certain individuals) to embody the gospel to "one another." How? By imitating their Lord, who became a humble *servant, not considering himself more significant than others.

When it comes to depicting Paul's friendship with the Philippians specifically, he does not employ the term *allēlōn*. But although it is absent lexically, it is certainly present conceptually. One can see it in the identical use of the terms *thysia* and *leitourgia* when describing Paul's ministry toward them and their ministry toward Paul (Phil 2:17, 30; 4:18), and when he employs the term *phroneō* to speak of the Christ-shaped mindset and lifestyle that they reciprocate (Phil 1:7; 4:10). But their reciprocal friendship also appears in a key phrase Paul uses to define his relationship with the Philippians. They enjoy a *koinōnia* of "giving *and* receiving" (Phil 4:15 ESV). The Philippians received grace through Paul's preaching of the gospel, and they reciprocated by giving a gift to Paul in prison (Phil 4:10-20). That gift can be considered grace, since the most basic definition of *grace* (*charis*) is "gift." Paul and the Philippians therefore reciprocated grace to one another—Paul through the gospel, and the Philippians through *financial support (see the use of *charis* in 2 Cor 8–9). But let us not forget that a divine party mediates that grace through both parties. God is the source, whereas Paul and the Philippians are mediators of a divine surplus (Barclay, 438).

3.4. Mutual Obligation in Christ. The idea of obligation in friendship may go against modern sensibilities, but no one in the ancient world would have balked at the idea. Friends were expected—even more, obligated—to give *and* take. If not, friendship ceased to exist. Put in Pauline terms, friendship consists of "giving *and* receiving" (Phil 4:15 ESV). This relational description confirms their mutual obligation toward one another and makes sense of the way Paul describes Epaphroditus, the messenger of the Philippians' gift. Paul calls him a "minister [*leitourgon*] to my need" (Phil 2:25 ESV). A *leitourgia* in the ancient world was equivalent to benefaction, so a *leitourgos*, like a benefactor, would give gifts to the general public. It was considered his obligatory civic duty. Epaphroditus and the Philippians, however, had an obligatory Christian duty to Paul. They delivered a financial gift to "complete what was lacking in [their] service [*leitourgias*] to [him]" (Phil 2:30 ESV). Their *leitourgia* was lacking for a time, but the obligation remained intact. Their *koinōnia* of giving and receiving bound them to care for one another in time of need.

But their mutual obligation was not solely on the human level of friendship. They were mutually obligated to God. Notice how Paul theologically figures their gift in Philippians 4:18: "*I have received all things* and abound. I am well supplied, having received from Epaphroditus the gifts you sent, a fragrant offering, a *sacrifice acceptable and pleasing *to God.*" A gift to Paul is considered a gift to God (maintaining a sharp Creator-creature distinction, of course). But if giving to Paul is giving to God, then their obligation to give to Paul is also an obligation to give to God (see deSilva for a proper understanding of obligation to God). This makes sense. If God is the one who gives grace through Paul's gospel, then that grace naturally empowers the Philippians to fulfill their obligation and so render a Spirit-wrought return to God. Remember, "*from him* and through him and *to him* are all things" (Rom 11:36). But since God is not in need of anything, Christians give to God by giving themselves to their neighbor in love and good deeds.

3.5. Corporate Gratitude to God. God is the source of everything reciprocated on the human level of friendship. It therefore naturally follows that Christian gratitude would primarily go to God. Paul does this in his so-called thankless thanks in Philippians 4:10-20. The words "thank you, Philippians" never appear in that text or the letter, but that does not mean Paul is ungrateful. Rather, Paul's silence can be understood as a theological lesson. He wants them to acknowledge God as the divine source who primarily receives human gratitude (see Briones). So, Paul explains, God is the one who revived the Philippians' ability to give the gift (Phil 4:10). In other words, God gave through the Philippians. God also empowered Paul to experience "abundance" (*perisseuō*, Phil 4:13) in the past and is the one who gives "abundance" (*perisseuō*) in the present through the Philippians' gift (Phil 4:18). God also received the Philippians' gift as a "fragrant offering" and "a sacrifice acceptable and pleasing" (Phil 4:18 ESV). God rightly receives all the glory (Phil 4:20). In Philippians 4:10-20, Paul directs Christians' eyes upward so that the church will rightly render all *glory, honor, and gratitude to the Giver of all things—Father, *Son, and *Holy Spirit.

See also Fellowship, Communion, Sharing; Grace; Love; Patronage; Philippians, Letter to the.

BIBLIOGRAPHY. **J. M. G. Barclay,** *Paul and the Gift* (Grand Rapids, MI: Eerdmans, 2015); **D. Briones,** "Paul's Intentional 'Thankless Thanks' in Philippians 4.10-20," *JSNT* 44 (2011): 47-69; **D. deSilva,** "'We Are Debtors': Grace and Obligation in Paul and Seneca," in *Paul and Seneca in Dialogue,* ed. J. R. Dodson and D. E. Briones (Leiden: Brill, 2017), 150-78; **M. Ebner,** *Leidenslisten und Apostelbrief: Untersuchungen zu Form, Motivik und Funktion der Peristasenkataloge bei Paulus,* FzB 66 (Würzburg: Echter, 1991); **J. T. Fitzgerald,** *Friendship, Flattery, and Frankness of Speech: Studies on Friendship in the New Testament World* (Leiden: Brill, 1996); idem, "Paul and Friendship," in *Paul in the Greco-Roman World: A Handbook,* ed. P. J. Sampley (Harrisburg, PA: Trinity Press International, 2003); **J. Fleury,** "Une société de fait dans l'Eglise apostolique (Phil. 4:10 à 22)," in *Mélanges Philippe Meylan* (Lausanne: Université de Lausanne, 1963), 41-59; **S. Fowl,** "Christology and Ethics in Philippians 2:5-11," in *Where Christology Began: Essays on Philippians 2,* ed. R. P. Martin and B. J. Dodd (Louisville: Westminster John Knox, 1998), 140-53; idem, *Philippians,* THNTC (Grand Rapids, MI: Eerdmans, 2005); **L. T. Johnson,** "Making Connections: The Material Expression of Friendship in the New Testament," *Int* 58 (2004): 158-71; **D. Konstan,** *Friendship in the Classical World* (Cambridge: Cambridge University Press, 1997); **G. Lyons and W. H. Malas Jr.,** "Paul and His Friends Within the Greco-Roman Context," *WTJ* 42, no. 1 (2007): 50-69; **J. M. Ogereau,** *Paul's Koinōnia with the Philippians: A Socio-historical Investigation of a Pauline Economic Partnership,* WUNT 2/377 (Tübingen: Mohr Siebeck, 2014); **S. M. Olyan,** *Friendship in the Hebrew Bible* (New Haven, CT: Yale University Press, 2017); **L. S. Pangle,** *Aristotle and the Philosophy of Friendship* (Cambridge: Cambridge University Press, 2003); **G. W. Peterman,** *Paul's Gift from Philippi: Conventions of Gift Exchange and Christian Giving,* SNTSMS (Cambridge: Cambridge University Press, 1997); **J. P. Sampley,** *Pauline Partnership in Christ: Christian Community and Commitment in Light of Roman Law* (Philadelphia: Fortress, 1980); **L. M. White,** "Morality Between Two Worlds: A Paradigm of Friendship in Philippians," in *Greeks, Romans, and Christians: Essays in Honor of Abraham J. Malherbe,* ed. D. Balch, E. Ferguson, and W. Meeks (Minneapolis: Augsburg Fortress, 1990), 201-15; **B. Witherington,** *Friendship and Finances in Philippi,* NTC (Harrisburg, PA: Trinity Press International, 1994).

D. E. Briones

FRUIT OF THE SPIRIT

The expression "the fruit of the Spirit" is a metaphor used by Paul to describe virtues that manifest the realities of life in *Christ. In Galatians 5:22-23 Paul catalogs the components of the "fruit of the Spirit" (*ho karpos tou pneumatos*) as "*love, *joy, *peace, patience, kindness, goodness, faithfulness, gentleness, self-control" (ESV).

1. The Context of Galatians
2. Similar and Contrasting Metaphors
3. Paul's Sources
4. Spiritual Virtues
5. Conclusion

1. The Context of Galatians.

*Justification by *grace through *faith dominates Galatians 1–4. In Galatians 5–6, Paul expounds on what the Christian life looks like. Grounded in grace, the believer is empowered to walk by the Spirit (Gal 5:16). *Freedom, Paul explains, is the very reason Christ set believers free (Gal 5:1), but Christian freedom is not to be used to gratify the desires of the *flesh (Gal 5:13). Rather, Christians are called to serve one another in love (Gal 5:13), which can only be accomplished "through the Spirit, by faith" (Gal 5:5 ESV). The two verses outlining the "fruit of the Spirit" fit within this context of Paul's emphasis on faith and the work of the *Holy Spirit—it is through a faith that is dependent on the work of the Holy Spirit that these virtues flow out of the believer (Gal 5:5-6).

2. Similar and Contrasting Metaphors.

2.1. Other Fruit Metaphors. The precise phrase "fruit of the Spirit" appears only once in Paul's letters (Gal 5:22-23). However, similar imagery is widely used throughout the Pauline literature. The fruit metaphor specifically shows up in several places with a variety of meanings (e.g., good deeds—Phil 1:11, 22; Col 1:10; the fruit of the *gospel—Col 1:6; a gift—Rom 1:13; 15:28; or even a spiritual reward—Phil 4:17). Fruit is often used as a metaphor for Christian behavior and character. Typically, the focus is on the Spirit as the source of such Christian character growth, but the believer is also exhorted to work at growing in these virtues, especially love (Gal 5:6, 13; 6:9-10). Sometimes Paul contrasts good fruit that honors *God (Rom 6:22; 7:4) with bad fruit, representing evil deeds (Rom 6:21; 7:5). A life apart from Christ yields unfruitful (*akarpos*) works (Eph 5:11; Rom 6:1).

Closely related to "the fruit of the Spirit" is Paul's depiction of the "fruit of *light," which is found "in all that is good and right and true" (Eph 5:9-11 ESV). Also closely related are the metaphors of walking in the Spirit (Gal 5:16) and being led by the Spirit (Gal 5:18).

2.2. Flesh and Spirit. The dominant contrast in Galatians 5:16-24 is two lists: "the works of the flesh" (Gal 5:19-21 ESV) and "the fruit of the Spirit" (Gal 5:22-23 ESV). Neither list is exhaustive. Nor are the two lists arranged in a way that each wrong behavior symmetrically corresponds to each of the nine virtues. Galatians 5:17 explains that the things of the Spirit and the flesh are opposed to each other, but Paul's exhortation to "walk by the Spirit" (Gal 5:16 ESV) is followed by an emphatic subjunctive clause, "and you will not gratify the desires of the flesh" (ESV), indicating a promise. Not gratifying the desires of the flesh is a promised result of following the imperative of walking by the Spirit, for such a victory can only be a supernatural work (Betz, 278; Schreiner, 343). The discourse concludes asserting that believers ultimately defeat the flesh because "in Christ" believers have "crucified the flesh with its passions and desires" (Gal 5:24 ESV; see Gal 2:20).

3. Paul's Sources.

Virtue lists were common in antiquity, evident in sources such as the Dead Sea Scrolls and philosophers such as Philo, Seneca, Musonius Rufus, and Plutarch (Keener, 515). However, Paul does not use the qualities in a Greek way. For Paul, these virtues are always for the benefit of the *church and not merely for character formation, as was the case in Greek *ethics.

Paul's employment of "fruit" most likely stems from the variety of fruit metaphors in the Gospels: Matthew 3:7-10; 7:15-20; Mark 12:1-12; Luke 13:6-9; John 15:1-6. These draw from the OT imagery comparing *Israel to a vine (e.g., Ps 80:8-18), vineyard (e.g., Is 27:2-6), or an olive tree (Jer 11:6). Israel is also called out for failing to bear fruit (Is 5). Isaiah 32:15-16 and Joel 2:18-32 are often cited as background with their promise of the Spirit and the intended fruitfulness of the recipients (Barclay 1991, 121; Beale, 1-38; Dunn, 308; Hansen, 178; Silva, 810). Others find background in the *covenant blessings of Leviticus and Deuteronomy (Keesmaat, 207-8; Pate, 229-30).

4. Spiritual Virtues.

The godly qualities Paul lists here are prompted by the Spirit and demonstrate the work of the Spirit in believers in contrast to the "works of the flesh" (Gal 5:19-21). They are not the result of human effort. In fact, these virtues go beyond the natural bounds of virtue. For example, believers demonstrate love profoundly by not only loving the lovable but their enemies too (Rom 12:14; see Mt 5:44).

4.1. Love (*Agapē*). It is not surprising that love is first in the list—it is the foundational virtue (1 Cor 13). Love for God is the greatest command, and love for neighbor the second greatest (Mt 22:36-40). The active faith described in this letter is manifested through love (1 Cor 5:6), indeed loving service to others (1 Cor 5:13). Love fulfills the whole *law (Gal 5:14; Rom 13:8-10).

Love is fundamental to God's character. It is best understood as a self-giving action for the benefit of others, rather than an emotion. Christ's giving of himself on the *cross is the supreme example of such love (Gal 2:20; Eph 5:25). It is God's Spirit who pours out his love to believers (Rom 5:5). Love is associated with God's Spirit also in Romans 15:30; Colossians 1:8; 2 Corinthians 6:6; 2 Timothy 1:7.

4.2. Joy (*Chara*). Joy is a prevalent theme in Paul's letter to the Philippians (see Phil 1:4, 18, 25; 2:2, 17-18, 28-29; 3:1; 4:1, 4, 10). In Galatians, the word *joy* occurs only here (Gal 5:22). Joy is connected to God's character and is a work of the Spirit (Rom 14:17) that cannot be attributed to human effort. Believers are exhorted to "rejoice in the *Lord" in all circumstances and all times (Phil 4:4 ESV; see 1 Thess 5:16), and are able to experience joy even in the midst of *suffering and trials because they are rooted in God's love and grace, while filled with *hope that he works all things together for good (Rom 5:1-4; 8:28; 2 Cor 6:10).

*4.3. Peace (***Eirēnē***).* Paul uses peace in a few different ways. First, it can refer to the objective state in which believers find themselves following their justification (Rom 5:1). Believers have "peace with God" in contrast to the prior state of hostility humans have as a result of their *sin. Jesus himself is identified as "our peace" (Eph 2:14), reconciling humans to himself (Eph 2:16) and to each other (Eph 2:14-15). This relational peace is the second way Paul employs this word—it denotes the harmony and love that is possible between believers who have first found peace with God (Rom 14:19). Third, Paul at times refers to peace as an internal state of well-being. The peace of God guards believers' hearts and minds in *Christ Jesus (Phil 4:7).

*4.4. Patience (***Makrothymia***).* Patience is another work of the Holy Spirit that enables a believer to endure hardship. In the LXX, this word occurs as an adjective, describing God's character (Ex 34:6; Ps 103:8 [102:8 LXX]). In the NT, it is used to describe God and Christ's attitude toward sinful people (Rom 2:4; 9:22; 1 Tim 1:16; 1 Pet 3:20; 2 Pet 3:15). More commonly, it indicates the patience people should manifest toward one another, especially despite difficulties (L&N 25.169; Bruce 1982, 253; see 2 Cor 6:6; Eph 4:2; Col 1:11; 3:12; 2 Tim 3:10; 4:2; Heb 6:12; Jas 5:10). More simply, it can be defined as "long-tempered" (Dunn, 311).

*4.5. Kindness (***Chrestotēs***).* Only Paul employs this word in the NT. It is often used to express God's gracious offering of *salvation through Jesus Christ (Rom 2:4; 11:22; Eph 2:7; Titus 3:4). Believers are called to emulate this kindness toward others (Rom 3:12; 2 Cor 6:6; Col 3:12).

*4.6. Goodness (***Agathōsynē***).* This word is related to the term *agathos*, which in the LXX translates the Hebrew *tôb* (Grundmann, *TDNT* 1:13). In Jewish tradition, it served in the frequent confession of the Lord's perfect goodness: "Give thanks to the LORD, for he is good; his love endures forever" (1 Chron 16:34 NIV; cf. 2 Chron 5:13; Ps 118). Goodness serves as a kind of master moral category in the Jewish tradition. It refers to what is ethically good, especially as concerns the welfare of others (Keener, 521). In the NT, God alone is good (Mt 19:17). The natural person is unable to pursue good (Rom 7:18-25), but the grace of God transforms and equips believers for that purpose (Eph 2:8-10).

Among NT writers, only Paul uses *agathōsynē* (Rom 15:14; Eph 5:9; 2 Thess 1:11). It is "roughly synonymous" with *chrēstotēs* (Longenecker, 262).

*4.7. Faithfulness (***Pistis***).* *Pistis* may mean either "faith" or "faithfulness." The noun *pistis* occurs 132 times in Paul's letters, and 20 times in Galatians alone. It is mostly translated as "faith," but in this list of ethical qualities, it makes sense that *pistis* also should express an ethical quality. Faith is first an act of trust in the gospel, but it is continually exercised through active dependence on Christ and the Spirit. Thus, faith, in Paul's usage, usually entails faithfulness—it stimulates activity that produces good works (Pifer, 209). The word denotes reliability or trustworthiness.

*4.8. Gentleness (***Prautēs***).* This word shows up in other Pauline virtue lists (Eph 4:2; Col 3:12; Titus 3:2) and generally means "gentleness, "meekness," or "humility." Jesus is the model of such gentleness. In Matthew 11:29 he states that he is "gentle [*praus*] and humble in heart" (NASB; see Mt 21:5; 2 Cor 10:1). Believers who sin should be corrected with gentleness (Gal 6:1), and nonbelievers should also be instructed with gentleness in hope that they will repent (2 Tim 2:25).

*4.9. Self-Control (***Enkrateia***).* The word was widely used by Greek classical writers to convey a restraint of passion or base emotion. During Paul's lifetime, the concept was central to Hellenistic ethics (Longenecker, 264), but it is a rare word in the NT (Acts 24:25; 2 Pet 1:6; the verbal form is employed in 1 Cor 7:9; 9:25). Craig Keener identifies this last term as the "climax of the Spirit's fruit" because it combats most of the vices listed in Galatians 5:19-21 (Keener, 522-23).

5. Conclusion.

While debate remains as to whether the word *fruit* in the singular indicates a unitary concept (Betz, 286; Matera, 202) or whether fruit is simply a collective noun (Fee, 217), the significance of this list lies in their "cumulative effect" (Moo, 366). The specific virtues Paul has chosen here are those he deemed most appropriate for the situation in Galatia. The "fruit of the Spirit" builds up the church and reflects Christ's presence. For those in Galatia who fear that abandoning law for Spirit will lead to libertinism, Paul assures that "against such things there is no law" (Gal 5:23 ESV). It is the Spirit who produces fruit in the lives of Christians and provides what the law requires.

See also ETHICS; FLESH; GALATIANS, LETTER TO THE; GIFTS OF THE SPIRIT; HOLINESS, SANCTIFICATION; HOLY SPIRIT; JOY, REJOICING; LOVE; PEACE, RECONCILIATION; SPIRITUALITY.

BIBLIOGRAPHY. **J. M. G. Barclay,** *Obeying the Truth: Paul's Ethics in Galatians* (Minneapolis: Fortress, 1991); idem, *Paul and the Gift* (Grand Rapids, MI: Eerdmans, 2015); **W. Barclay**, *Flesh and Spirit:*

An Examination of Galatians 5:19-23 (Nashville: Abingdon, 1962); **J. Barr,** "Words for Love in Biblical Greek," in *The Glory of Christ in the New Testament: Studies in Christology in Memory of George Bradford Caird*, ed. L. D. Hurst and N. T. Wright (Oxford: Clarendon, 1987), 3-18; **G. K. Beale,** "The Spirit as the Transforming Agent of the Inaugurated Eschatological New Creation," in *A New Testament Biblical Theology: The Unfolding of the Old Testament in the New* (Grand Rapids, MI: Baker, 2011), 559-91; **K. Berding,** *Walking in the Spirit* (Wheaton, IL: Crossway, 2011). **H. D. Betz,** *Galatians,* Hermeneia (Philadelphia: Fortress, 1979); **F. F. Bruce,** *Paul: Apostle of the Heart Set Free* (Grand Rapids, MI: Eerdmans, 1977); idem, *Commentary on Galatians,* NIGTC (Grand Rapids, MI: Eerdmans, 1982); **W. D. Davies,** *Paul and Rabbinic Judaism,* rev. ed. (Philadelphia: Fortress, 1980); **J. D. G. Dunn,** *The Epistle to the Galatians,* BNTC (Peabody, MA: Hendrickson, 1993); **G. D. Fee,** *The First Epistle to the Corinthians,* NICNT (Grand Rapids, MI: Eerdmans, 1987); **V. P. Furnish,** *Theology and Ethics in Paul* (Nashville: Abingdon, 1968); **W. Grundmann,** "ἀγαθός, ἀγαθοεργέω, ἀγαθοποιέω, -ός, -ία, ἀγαθωσύνη, φιλάγαθος, ἀφιλάγαθος," *TDNT*; **G. W. Hansen,** *Galatians,* IVPNTC (Downers Grove, IL: IVP Academic, 1994); **C. S. Keener,** *Galatians: A Commentary* (Grand Rapids, MI: Baker Academic, 2019); **S. C. Keesmaat,** *Paul and His Story,* JSNTSup 181 (Sheffield: Sheffield Academic Press, 1999); **R. N. Longenecker,** *Galatians,* WBC 41 (Dallas: Word, 1991); **W. Longsworth,** "Ethics in Paul: The Shape of Christian Life," *The Annual of the Society of Christian Ethics* (1981): 29-56; **D. J. Lull,** *The Spirit in Galatia,* SBLDS 49 (Chico, CA: Scholars Press, 1980); **F. Matera,** *Galatians,* SP (Collegeville, MN: Liturgical Press, 1992); **D. J. Moo,** *Galatians,* BECNT (Grand Rapids, MI: Baker Academic, 2013); **C. M. Pate,** *The Reverse of the Curse,* WUNT 2/114 (Tübingen: Mohr Siebeck, 2000); **J. H. Pifer,** *Faith as Participation* (Tübingen: Mohr Siebeck, 2019); **T. R. Schreiner,** *Galatians,* ZECNT (Grand Rapids, MI: Zondervan, 2010); **E. Schweizer,** "Traditional Ethical Patterns in the Pauline and Post-Pauline Letters and Their Development," in *Text and Interpretation,* ed. E. Best and R. McLean Wilson (Cambridge: Cambridge University Press, 1979), 195-209; **M. Silva,** "Galatians," *in Commentary on the New Testament Use of the Old Testament,* ed. G. K. Beale and D. A. Carson (Grand Rapids, MI: Baker Academic, 2007), 785-812; **O. Wischmeyer,** *Der höchste Weg. Das 13. Kapitel des 1 Korintherbriefes* (Gütersloh: Mohn, 1981).

J. H. Pifer

FULLNESS

Paul uses fullness (*plērōma*) with different shades of meaning in both the passive sense, "that which is completed or filled" (as object), and the active sense, "that which completes or fills up" (as subject).

1. Totality of Space
2. Totality of Quantity
3. Totality of the Law
4. Fulfillment of Time
5. Fullness of Essence

1. Totality of Space.

In 1 Corinthians 10:26, 27 Paul quotes Psalm 24:1 LXX to defend his view that "all contents of the earth" belong to the *Lord, and thus all kinds of food can be eaten.

2. Totality of Quantity.

In Romans 11 Paul refers to "the full inclusion" or "full recovery" of *Israel (Rom 11:12), which will most probably take place soon after "the total number of the *Gentiles have come in" (Rom 11:25). In Romans 11:12, although the *plērōma* is morally neutral, the contrasting parallel, "trespass" (*paraptōma*), suggests moral or spiritual consummation. And in Romans 11:25, although it can mean that the Gentiles have "the whole time of the *church" all to themselves (see Lk 21:24), the parallel phrase "all Israel" (Rom 11:26) points to "until the great multitude is completed" (see Rev 7:9).

In Romans 15:29 the passive sense is used to refer to Paul's desire that the Roman believers share in "the full abundance" of Christ's blessing" through their financial *collection, not just to bring relief to the famine-stricken in *Jerusalem but also to strengthen the bond between Jews and Gentiles in the church (Rom 15:24-33).

3. Totality of the Law.

Another passive use is Paul's reference to *love as "the sum of the Law's demands" (Rom 13:10), which believers fulfill wholly because, by God's provision in *Christ through his Spirit, sin has no more power over them (see Rom 8:4, 9-10); the immediate context shows his concern for obedience to the whole Torah (Rom 13:8-10). But it is also possible that it has an active meaning: the Torah has been fulfilled and receives its perfection in love. Love for one's neighbor is the end or complete realization of the Torah (see Rom 13:8; Gal 5:14; 6:2).

4. Fulfillment of Time.

The active sense of *plērōma* is clearly used with reference to time. In Galatians 4:4 Paul refers to Christ's first advent as "the completion of time [*chronos*]." This may be one (or the first) of the times (*kairos*; see Lk 21:24; Acts 1:7) or ages (*aiōnes*; see Gal 3:20-21; 1 Cor 10:11; Eph 2:7), which will all find their consummation in God's ultimate objective of uniting all things in Christ (Eph 1:10). Christ is not only the source and sustainer but also the goal of the history of the whole cosmos. So here in Galatians 4:4 *plērōma* means the full realization of God's predestined plans revealed in the Scripture (Eph 1:10; cf. Mt 5:17; Mk 1:15).

5. Fullness of Essence.

5.1. Colossians 1:19; 2:9. Significant yet controversial is the usage in Colossians 1:19; 2:9. Here *plērōma* most likely means "the whole total of the Godhead," which was pleased to dwell in the person of Christ (Delling). Some scholars (Lightfoot, Bultmann) think that *plērōma* is used in Colossians 1:19 as a quasi-technical term borrowed from early *Gnosticism to refer to the space in which the entirety of intermediary beings exist between the Creator and his *creation. This assumes that Paul was using a term taken from the Colossian heretics who, under the influence of Gnostic thinking, taught that Christ is only one of the members of the heavenly mediatorial hierarchy. Paul was therefore arguing for the superiority and uniqueness of Christ, that he rules over these beings as the divinity who fills them all.

But apart from the lack of external evidence for early Gnosticism, there is also no internal evidence of a polemic against this alleged false teaching about Christ. So the active sense of *plērōma* seems best for this text: Christ has all the divine attributes in himself. This fits the OT and Hebraic usage, where the Hebrew equivalent connotes completeness and *God who, on the one hand, in his being or *glory fills the whole earth (e.g., Ps 72:19; Jer 23:24; Is 6:3; Ezek 43:5), and, on the other hand, is said to be "pleased to dwell" in a place of his choosing, Zion (Col 1:19, *eudokēsen . . . katoikēsai*; LXX Ps 67:17; cf. LXX Ps 131:13, 14; Is 8:18; 49:20). Moreover, Jewish *wisdom speculation spoke of Wisdom's universal presence and permeation of all things (Wis 7:24). Colossians 1:19 seems to indicate that the fullness the OT attributed to God and Judaism attributed to Wisdom now dwells in the place of God's choosing, Christ. Other aspects of Wisdom *Christology may be detected in the statements about the preexistent Christ and his role in creation in Colossians 1:15-16 (see the appropriation of wisdom concepts in the Johannine logos Christology in Jn 1:14, 16).

5.2. Ephesians 1:23. Another difficult text is Ephesians 1:23 (see Yates, who lists the interpretive options). It seems best to take *plērōma* as a christological title that is used in apposition to "him" in Ephesians 1:22: Christ himself is the one who has the full measure of the God who fills everything (see 1 Cor 15:28). This harmonizes with the use of the verb *plēroō* in Ephesians 4:10 and the usage in Colossians (Moule).

It seems probable that the passive sense of the church being dwelt in and "completed by Christ" may be meant. Though the immediate context can also suggest that "Christ is being filled by the church," "the church is being filled by Christ" makes better sense since the usage of the imagery of the church as Christ's *body focuses on the importance of Christ to the church and not vice versa (Eph 4:13). The church is the receptacle being filled up with the *grace and gifts of Christ (see Eph 4:7-11).

5.3. Ephesians 4:13; 3:19. *Plērōma* is used in the body metaphor of Ephesians 4:13 to denote the full realization of the unity of all believers in Christ: it attains "the measure of the stature of the fullness of Christ" (RSV), in which Christians are no longer easily swayed by false teachings (Eph 4:14).

The usage in Ephesians 3:19 is possibly similar: the growth in Christian experience is to reach "to the measure of [*eis*] all the fullness of God."

See also Body of Christ; Israel; Wisdom.

BIBLIOGRAPHY. **P. Benoit,** "Body, Head and Pleroma in the Epistles of the Captivity," in *Jesus and the Gospel*, vol. 2 (London: Darton, Longman & Todd, 1974), 51-92; **M. Bogdasovich,** "The Idea of Pleroma in the Epistles to the Colossians and Ephesians," *Downside Review* 83 (1965): 118-30; **R. Bultmann,** *Theology of the New Testament* (New York: Scribner's, 1951–1955), 2:149-52; **G. Delling,** "πλήρης, κτλ.," *TDNT* 6:283-311; **J. Ernst,** *Pleroma und Pleroma Christi: Geschichte und Deutung eines Begriffs der paulinischen Antilegomena*, Biblische Untersuchungen 5 (Regensburg: Pustet, 1970); **A. Feuillet,** "L'église plérôme du Christ d'après Éphés., 1, 23," *Nouvelle revue théologique* 78 (1956): 449-72, 593-610; **A. T. Lincoln,** *Ephesians*, WBC 42 (Dallas: Word, 1990), 72-78; **C. F. D. Moule,** "'Fullness' and 'Fill' in the New Testament," *SJT* 4 (1951): 79-86; **P. D. Overfield,** "Pleroma: A Study in Content and Context," *NTS* 25 (1978–1979): 384-96; **I. de la Potterie,** "Le Christ, Plérôme de l'église (Eph 1.22-23)," *Bib* 58 (1977): 500-524; **R. Schippers,** "πληρόω," *NIDNTTE* 1:733-41; **R. Yates,** "A Reexamination of Eph 1:23," *ExpTim* 83 (1971–1972): 146-51.

D. S. Lim

G

GALATIANS, LETTER TO THE

Galatians was written to a *church in the midst of controversy. At some point after Paul evangelized and departed from the churches in Galatia, a group of outsiders claiming official status as representatives of the church in *Jerusalem arrived. They claimed, it seems, that Paul had not properly catechized the Galatian church on what was required of followers of the Messiah Jesus and members of the church of *God. In their view, to be full members of the church and heirs of the promises made to *Abraham, the *Gentile men in the church needed to be circumcised and keep the law like Abraham (Gal 5:2; Gen 17:10). This teaching seems to have been sufficiently compelling to draw significant support, and as a result members of the congregation reported these developments to Paul (Gal 1:6-9). Paul wrote Galatians to remind them of the *gospel he preached and to keep them from adopting the views of his *opponents.

Paul's gospel includes that trust in the crucified (and risen) Messiah Jesus is sufficient to justify believing Jews and Gentiles and make them co-heirs to the inheritance that belongs to the promised heir of Abraham, Jesus the Messiah (Gal 3:16, 19). Galatians, then, is a letter that functions to unite men and women across *ethnicity and class under the banner of the king who died to reconcile them to God and each other. Paul believes that something essential to the gospel itself is lost if those who believe are not justified on the same basis, namely, *faith.

Galatians is more than a defense of a doctrine of *justification, though *righteousness/justification language does figure prominently in the letter. In the course of making his argument, Paul examines the nature of God's promises to Abraham, the role of the *law in God's purposes (Gal 3:19-22), the meaning of Christ's *death (Gal 1:4; 3:13-14; 4:4-7), and the ethical norms for Christians who live by the Spirit in community (Gal 5:22-25; 6:1-5). In short, Galatians is, in the heat of controversy, an articulation of a vision for Christian faith and practice that remains relevant today.

1. Authorship and Audience
2. Dating Galatians
3. Paul, His Opponents, and the Use of Scripture
4. Galatians, Rhetoric, and Structure
5. Galatians in Outline
6. The Argument of Galatians

1. Authorship and Audience.

Few things are less contested in Pauline scholarship than Paul's authorship of Galatians. Matters are not so simple when it comes to discerning who the Galatians were. Exploring this topic requires a brief journey through a history of the settlement of the Roman province of Galatia.

The province took its name from the Celts of central Europe, who were called "Gauls" or "Galatians" in Latin and Greek sources. In the middle of the third century BC, these Gauls migrated from central Europe to attack and eventually colonize the north-central portion of Asia Minor in what is now modern Turkey. By 232 BC the boundaries had become fixed, with the major cities being overseen by the three major Gaul tribes: Pessinus (Tolistobogii), Ancyra (Tectosages), and Tavium (Trocmi). In the Roman sources, these ethnic Gauls have a reputation of being ignorant and uncivilized. This ethnic bias should probably be viewed as propaganda justifying Roman conquest of the area.

North-central Asia Minor remained under the oversight of tribal councils and later three tribal kings until 42 BC, when Deiotarus murdered the other two kings and took power for himself. This area now known as Galatia became a client kingdom some twenty years before Deiotarus's rule due to Galatia's support of Pompey in a war against Mithridates V. In 25 BC Galatia became a province of the Roman *Empire.

In Paul's day the province of Galatia extended beyond the originally ethnically Galatian area in the north-central Asia Minor. (This included the area around the three cities Pessinus to the west, Ancyra to the north, and Tavium on the east.) Galatia grew to include parts of Pisidia, Lyconia, Paphlagonia, Pontus, and Phrygia. Its northern border stretched to the Black Sea and its southern border the Mediterranean. To the east it extended until one arrived at Cappadocia and on the west until one reached Asia and Bithynia.

As it relates to Paul's letter, *Galatia* could refer to any portion of this expansive province. The first of two major options is the ethnically Galatian area to the north, around the three major cities mentioned above. The second option is the southern part of the province, with its mixed population of Jews and Gentiles. If there were churches in the north, then Acts 16:6; 18:23 probably records their founding. However, if *Galatia* refers to the area in the south, Acts 13–14 describes Paul's missionary work in that region. The major difference between the two options is that in the south it is possible that the congregation consisted of Jewish and Gentile believers, while in the north the congregation would have most likely been completely Gentile (and ethnically Galatian).

Historically, northern Galatia was viewed as the location of the recipients of Paul's letter because by the middle of the first century, according to Acts 13–14, the southern portions of the area that Paul visited had been detached from the province. For most ancient commentators, then, *Galatia* referred to the ethnically Galatian area to the north. Today the arguments in favor of the north are: (1) Paul would not refer to an ethnically diverse group of people, especially the Phrygians or the Lycaonians living in the south, as Galatians (Gal 3:1); (2) Paul writes as if there were no Jews in the congregation, which would fit a northern location; (3) when Luke refers to *Galatia* he has in mind the north (Acts 16:6; 18:23).

The arguments for a southern location are several: (1) Acts 16:6 does not depict Paul's evangelizing in the north, only Paul's travels in the region. Luke usually describes Paul's church-planting efforts when Paul evangelizes an area (Acts 13–14; 16); (2) there is explicit mention of churches being formed in the south (Acts 13–14); (3) based on the *travel plans depicted in Acts 16, Paul would have to had travel around 125 miles out of the way to reach the populated northern cities; (4) Paul in his *letters usually refers to locales by their Roman provincial designations (1 Cor 16:19; 2 Cor 8:1; 1 Thess 2:14). This means that he could refer to the southern portions of the province as "Galatia" even if Luke did not; (5) only the elites in the north would have spoken Greek, making Paul's evangelism difficult; (6) it seems more likely that an ethnically mixed congregation that knew of Judaism would find the arguments of Paul's opponents compelling, and the southern location assumes just such a congregation.

On balance the best argument for the northern hypothesis is that Paul would not refer to an ethnically mixed group as Galatians, but it is difficult to think of a better collective for the people in those churches than "Galatians." Furthermore, there simply is better evidence, if Acts can be trusted, that Paul evangelized the south, and the cultural milieu (local knowledge of Judaism) makes it more likely that the problems the Galatians faced would arise there.

2. Dating Galatians.

The questions of when Paul wrote his letter to Galatians and the relationship between the events recounted in Galatians and the book of Acts must be handled together. In Galatians 1:11–2:14, Paul recounts the events from the time of his *conversion to his confrontation with *Peter in Antioch. He does this to prove, over against his detractors, that his gospel originates with God and does not rely on human approval. In the course of making his case, Paul acknowledges that when the *leadership in Jerusalem heard about his message, they gave him the right hand of *fellowship and approved of his *mission to the Gentiles (Gal 2:9).

During his rehearsing of events, Paul mentions two visits to Jerusalem. One occurred three years after his conversion (Gal 1:18). He then mentions a second visit fourteen years later. This could be fourteen years after his conversion or fourteen years after the first visit (Gal 2:1). This article will assume (1) that Jesus' death, *resurrection, and *ascension occurred between AD 29 and 30, and (2) that Paul was converted between AD 31 and 32. Therefore, the first Jerusalem visit occurred between AD 34 and 35. The second visit occurred between AD 44 and 49. There are two reasons for this range. First, it is unknown whether Paul counts entire years or portions of a year in his reckoning. Second, as noted above, it is unclear whether the fourteen years refers to the time since his conversion or since his first visit. It is known that Paul wrote his letter after these two visits. Thus, the *earliest* date for Galatians could be shortly after the second visit using the earliest date, namely, sometime around AD 46. (That time could be moved earlier by those who date Jesus' death and Paul's conversion at a different time from the assumptions outlined above.) The later date of composition could be any time after AD 49.

Dating Galatians is complicated by the fact that there is a second set of data—Luke's depictions of Paul's travels in the book of Acts. Acts records three visits that are relevant to the discussion here: (1) a visit following his conversion in Acts 9:26-29; (2) a visit for famine relief in Acts 11:27-30; 12:25; and (3) the *Jerusalem council in Acts 15.

A northern location for Galatians means that the letter had to be written after the events of Acts 15, because Paul evangelizes northern Galatia after those events. Luke records this in Acts 16:6. The Jerusalem council occurred around AD 48–49. In a northern account, one needs to allow time for a number of events to occur. Paul first evangelized the region. Following this evangelization, he departed, and his opponents arrived and preached their gospel. The news of trouble spread to Paul, and he composed the letter. AD 50–51 seems like a reasonable period of time. If one assumes that Galatians 4:13 refers to two trips to Galatia, then the letter would have been written after the second visit, during Paul's second missionary journey recounted in Acts 18:23. That pushes the date to sometime around AD 53–55.

This article takes the position that a southern destination for the letter is more likely, so that will be the focus here. Most agree that Acts 9:26-29 refers to the first visit to Jerusalem mentioned by Paul. The question is whether the second visit to Jerusalem that Paul recounts in Galatians 2:1-10 refers to the visit in Acts 15:1-29 or the famine visit in Acts 11:27-30.

The strongest arguments for equating the visit that Paul recounts in Galatians 2:1-10 with Acts 15:1-29 are that (1) both record Paul and Barnabas going up from Antioch to Jerusalem, (2) both deal with the issue of *circumcision and Gentile inclusion, (3) both state that there is an agreement that Gentiles need not be circumcised, (4) both record *James and Peter's consent, and (5) both recount the blessing of Paul's *ministry.

The problems most often raised when equating Galatians 2:1-10 with Acts 15:1-29 are that (1) Paul presents this as a private meeting between himself, Barnabas, Titus, and the pillars, while Acts 15:1-29 depicts a gathered church; (2) in Galatians, the central issue is Paul's apostolic *calling, while in Acts 15:1-29 the issue is Gentile inclusion; (3) Paul does not mention the decree of Acts 15, which would have been very useful in Galatia; and (4) one has to assume that Paul omits the visit of Acts 11:27-30; 12:25 even though he seems to be giving a very careful account of his activities.

There is strong evidence for both options. The differences in public versus a private meeting could be a matter of perspective. The same could be said about Paul's emphasis on the approval of his ministry in Galatians versus Luke's more detached depiction in Acts. Craig Keener notes that there are other places in Paul's letters where the decree in Acts would be useful. The Acts decree about sexual morality and *food sacrificed to idols, for example, would have been very useful in *Corinth. Nonetheless, the differences between the accounts do matter. In addition, one can be relatively confident that Paul would not omit a visit to Jerusalem when making the case about his independence from Jerusalem. Therefore, on balance the evidence favors Galatians 2:1-10 referring to the famine visit in Acts 11:27-30.

In this reconstruction, Paul met with the pillars privately, received the right hand of fellowship, and withstood pressure from the more conservative wing of the Jewish Christian movement. Paul then returned to Antioch with the positive news and interpreted this as a sign of unhindered Jewish and Gentile Christian fellowship. Peter visited and initially shared a meal with the mixed community of Jewish and Christian believers in Antioch. This visit unraveled under pressure from Jewish Christian conservatives who thought that Peter's actions would hinder the mission to the Jewish people. Paul and Peter's confrontation in Antioch was one more step along the way to finding a solution to the question of Gentile inclusion. Given the choice to favor the southern destination for the letter, and matching Galatians 2:1-10 with the famine visit in Acts 11:27-30, one can date Galatians shortly before the apostolic council in AD 48–49.

3. Paul, His Opponents, and the Use of Scripture.

Galatians is Paul's response to his opponents. One does not get their side of the story. This raises the interpretive question of how best to reconstruct the arguments to which Paul responds. While one cannot be certain that everything that Paul affirms they denied, some form of "mirror reading" is inevitable (Barclay 1987). For example, Paul makes much of the life of the Spirit to sustain the Galatians (5:5, 16-18, 22-26; 6:1, 8). One cannot assume his opponents denied the power of the Spirit. It means that the Spirit must have functioned in their theology in a way now lost. On the other hand, based on Paul's strong protest against mandatory circumcision for Gentiles (2:3; 5:6, 11-12; 6:12-15), it is safe to assume that his opponents contended for Gentile circumcision. All interpretation involves some conjecture, and the following is an attempt at sketching what was going on in Galatia.

The reconstruction that seems most plausible is that Paul came to Galatia and preached the gospel of Jesus as Messiah crucified (Gal 3:1). The result of this death is that Jews and Gentiles can be justified by faith and thereby become a part of God's people. On the understanding that the church in Galatia was a mixed congregation of Jews and Gentiles (see section 1 above), it is likely that they had some understanding of how the death and resurrection of Jesus functioned as an unexpected climax of God's promises to *Israel. In other words, it seems unthinkable that Paul did not mention the kingship of Jesus and the relationship between his death and the inclusion of the Gentiles by faith in his initial preaching mission.

The entry of Paul's opponents and their appeal in Galatia only makes sense if there is some Jewish base on which to build. Paul does say in Galatians that he told them about inheriting the *kingdom (Gal 5:21). Given the prominence of Abraham in the Jewish and early Christian theological schemas, it seems difficult to believe that Paul failed to mention that Abraham was justified by faith. Paul then would have left Galatia with the following ideas in place:

- Jesus as Israel's Messiah died for their sins and enabled justification by faith (Gal 3:1).
- All who believe are a part of God's kingdom (Gal 5:21).
- Abraham is an example of God's justifying by faith.
- Gentiles do not have to follow the Torah and should rely on the Spirit (Gal 3:1-5).

Paul's opponents were Jewish Christians who agreed that Jesus was Israel's long-expected Messiah whose death for sins was a strange and unexpected fulfillment of God's promises. Nonetheless, this did not mean that the law is done away with. Instead, it was time to do what the prophets foretold: invite the Gentiles to come and learn of the law of the Lord (Is 2:3). Therefore, when they heard of Paul's church planting in Galatia, they went to fill the Galatians in on what the law really commanded. It is possible that they pointed out that Abraham, the convert from paganism, was circumcised (Gen 17). Therefore, the circumcised were true children of Abraham and heirs to the inheritance promised to Abraham and his seed.

If it is true that, after an initial burst of enthusiasm, the church in Galatia struggled with living holy lives, Paul's opponents could have posited the law as the solution to their problems. Paul, in their estimation, had not given them all the tools at their disposal to fight temptation. God had given his people the law at Sinai to guide them as a people. In any case, they maintained that Paul was not entirely consistent. At other times he encouraged people to keep the law. Furthermore, his current ministry was somewhat rogue and unsanctioned by the church in Jerusalem, the loci of authority. They, on the other hand, had the approval of the pillars to engage in ministry.

This brief sketch is necessary because many treat Galatians merely as Paul's response to a series of scriptural texts posed by his opponents. It is vital to treat Galatians as round three in the argument, not round two. If Paul's letters are any indication of his ministry, then his *preaching was saturated with the OT. Therefore, Paul must have planted his own exegetical flag before his opponents arrived. Paul's opponents' use of Genesis 17 may have countered Paul's own use of Abraham in his preaching. Galatians is a reassertion of a central thesis in the midst of polemics. For example, Paul's discussion of Abraham in Galatians 3:6-9 could be seen as an expansion of his previous discussion of Abraham, countering his opponents' views. Therefore, as it relates to the use of Scripture in Galatians, it will not do to assume in every case that Paul is simply reinterpreting texts chosen by others. Galatians instead should be seen as a reassertion and expansion of Paul's apostolic preaching.

4. Galatians, Rhetoric, and Structure.

One development in Pauline interpretation has been the use of *rhetorical criticism to understand the types of arguments Paul makes in his letters. H. D. Betz is credited with stimulating an extensive discussion of the rhetorical structure of Galatians.

The Greco-Roman handbooks describe three main types of arguments. *Forensic* or *judicial* rhetoric was used to present a case in a legal context. In a forensic reconstruction of Galatians, Paul's opponents have accused Paul of a crime (preaching a truncated gospel without approval). Paul is the defendant, and the Galatian congregation is the jury. *Deliberative* rhetoric tries to persuade the audience to take a certain course of action or convince them that a planned course of action is unwise. In a deliberative reading, Paul was attempting to convince the Galatians to remain faithful to the gospel he preached and abandon the course set by his rivals.

An *epideictic* speech attempted to laud communal values, virtues, or character worth emulating. Few have found epideictic rhetoric to be the most helpful lens for reading Galatians.

Although Betz began the conversation about the rhetorical genre of Galatians by claiming that it was a judicial apologetic letter, deSilva (94-95) is correct to note that the most prominent feature of Galatians is Paul's attempts to convince the Galatians not to follow his opponents and to remain faithful to the gospel he preached. This would make Galatians deliberative rather than forensic. Proponents of a deliberative perspective also contend that it is not evident that Paul believed the Galatians had the authority to judge the ultimate truthfulness of his gospel. Paul believed that the risen Lord affirmed the validity of his gospel. Finally, the extensive advice on future behavior found in Galatians is not native to judicial rhetoric. Nonetheless, Paul does at points defend himself from the attacks of his opponents with evidence about his independence from Jerusalem and their approval of his message. It seems best to maintain that Galatians is not a pure manifestation of any particular genre but that Paul adapts these forms to suit his purposes.

The same adaptation can be seen when one compares the structure of Galatians to the instructions on structure in classical rhetorical manuals. Instructors suggest that speeches should have (1) an *exordium*, an introduction intended to create goodwill for the argument to follow; (2) a *narratio*, a section that lays out the pertinent facts and states the thesis; (3) a *probatio*, a defense of the main contention stated in the narration with supporting evidence; and (4) a *peroratio*, the summary and conclusion. It is plain that Galatians contains an introduction. Paul does include a narrative with relevant facts, and he concludes his argument at the end of the letter. Yet Paul's opening, in which he rebukes the Galatians, does not inspire goodwill. Furthermore, this structure does not account very well for Galatians 5:1–6:10, which includes an extensive discussion of life in the Spirit. Again, one sees Paul adapting these forms to suit his purposes.

This skepticism regarding a pure form does not mean that rhetorical analysis is without its merits. Rhetorical analysis helps one to understand the purposes certain sections of Galatians were intended to serve, and attending to ancient literary devices gives access to the cultural encyclopedia that Paul drew from in making his arguments. Nonetheless, Paul was an apostle who was willing to use whatever he felt was necessary to keep his congregation faithful to the gospel as he understood it. If some rhetoricians would have scoffed at his arguments, he may have been tempted to reply that God had made a fool of the *wisdom of the wise on the cross (1 Cor 2:1-8).

5. Galatians in Outline.

Recognizing that all scholarly outlines are attempts to make sense of the argument, an outline is provided here:

I. The origin and widespread ecclesial support of the gospel that the Galatians are on the verge of abandoning due to the false testimony of Paul's opponents (Gal 1:1–2:21)

A. Introduction and assertion of Paul's apostolic authority (Gal 1:1-5)

B. Paul's rebuke of the Galatians' potential abandonment of the gospel (Gal 1:6-9)

C. Paul's account of the origins of his call and gospel from the Messiah, and affirmation of his gospel in Jerusalem (Gal 1:10–2:10)

D. The rebuke of Peter in Antioch and reaffirmation of justification by faith (Gal 2:11-21)

II. A defense of Gentiles' justification by faith and their status as heirs to the inheritance apart from the law (Gal 3:1–5:11)

A. The Spirit is evidence that the Galatians are justified by faith and part of the eschatological community of the restored people of God (Gal 3:1-5)

B. The Galatians can either share in the blessing of Abraham through faith in the Messiah Jesus or come under the *works of the law and experience the covenant curses (Gal 3:6-14)

C. The Messiah Jesus is the promised heir, and the law was always intended to play a temporary role. Therefore, all who have been baptized in Christ are Abraham's offspring and co-heirs (Gal 3:15-29)

D. If we have moved from *slaves to adopted children and heirs, why turn back (Gal 4:1-11)?

E. A reminder of Paul's own ministry among the Galatians and their previous approval (Gal 4:12-20)

F. An allegory of Sarah and Hagar that affirms the readers' status as heirs and encourages them to hold fast to *freedom (Gal 4:21–5:1)

G. The perilous implications of coming under the law (Gal 5:2-12)

III. Spirit-enabled life together apart from the law (Gal 5:12–6:10)

A. Freedom is bounded by *love (Gal 5:12-15)

B. A Spirit-empowered life together is superior to living in the *flesh (Gal 5:16-26)

C. The importance of bearing one another's burdens and ecclesial accountability (Gal 6:1-10)

IV. Summary and conclusion: the marks of Christ and the Israel of God (Gal 6:11-18)

6. The Argument of Galatians.

6.1. The Origin and Widespread Ecclesial Support of the Gospel That the Galatians Are on the Verge of Abandoning Due to the False Testimony of Paul's Opponents (Gal 1:1–2:21). *6.1.1. Introduction and Assertion of Paul's Apostolic Authority (Gal 1:1-5).* Paul opens his letter by asserting that his apostolic call does not come from any human but from the Messiah Jesus and God the Father. Here Paul appears to be countering the claims of his opponents. They maintain that authority ultimately derives from ecclesial authorities in Jerusalem. Although Paul will later argue that Jerusalem approved of his mission, here he reminds the Galatians of the final loci of authority. Paul wants the Galatians to remember the God to whom they owe their allegiance. He does so recounting God's saving activity. God the Father is the one who raised Jesus from the dead, and Jesus is the one who gave himself for their sins to rescue them from the present evil age.

Paul's language of Jesus giving himself has its origins in the account of the servant in Isaiah, who gave himself for the sins of the nation (Is 52:13–53:12). In Isaiah's account this self-offering somehow ends the *covenant curses under which the nation suffered as a result of their corporate disobedience. This is seen in the depiction of Jerusalem as a formerly barren and now fruitful woman (Is 54:1-3). This offering also brings about a second exodus to a new inheritance (Is 54:3). In the Isaianic narrative, when God finally acted to restore Israel it would be nothing less than a new start to *creation (Is 65:17-25). Paul seems to be drawing on this idea when he says that Jesus' death for sins has rescued the Galatians from the present evil age. Jesus' death, for Paul, has brought about a whole new reality. In other places Paul draws on Isaianic self-giving to talk about Jesus' death for sins or as an act of love (Rom 4:25; Gal 2:20). Here Paul speaks of how Jesus' death brought the believer into a new epoch of history and says that their flirtation with law signals a desire to turn back the eschatological clock.

Even in a letter that will soon express his frustration with the Galatians, he still wishes them the *grace and *peace that comes from their relationship with God the Father and the *Lord Jesus Christ (Rom 1:7; 1 Cor 1:3; Phil 1:2). Through this opening Paul repeatedly speaks about the cooperation of God the Father and Jesus the Messiah in the work of redemption, which speaks to his understanding of their sharing in the divine *identity.

6.1.2. Paul's Rebuke of the Galatians' Potential Abandonment of the Gospel (Gal 1:6-9). Rather than transition to a time of thanksgiving, which is his custom in other letters (Rom 1:8; Phil 1:3; 1 Cor 1:4), Paul rebukes the Galatians for quickly abandoning the gospel he preached and pronounces an anathema on anyone who delivers another message. Here one comes to the central issue this letter addresses. There are two parties trying to persuade the Galatians about the nature of the Christian life (Paul and his opponents). Paul believes that one can be justified and included within the people of God on the basis of faith, while his opponents see some ongoing role of the law in the lives of the Galatians.

6.1.3. Paul's Account of the Origins of His Call and Gospel from the Messiah, and Affirmation of His Gospel in Jerusalem (Gal 1:10–2:10). Paul turns from a rebuke of the Galatians to assert that he is only attempting to please God. This seems to be a response to a criticism levied by his opponents that Paul adjusts his message for his audience. The implication seems to be that at times he has been in favor of law keeping and other times not (see the missionary strategy he outlines in 1 Cor 9:19-23). Behind this could also be an implicit criticism of his opponents, whose advocacy of law obedience may be influenced by a desire to appease the non-Christian Jewish community.

Paul then recounts briefly his conversion as a result of a revelation or apocalypse of the Messiah Jesus (Gal 1:12). This revelation of Jesus as Messiah marked a sharp break in his past. Before encountered Jesus, he persecuted the church of God as a manifestation of his zeal for the law and the traditions of his ancestors. Paul sees God's call of him as a display of grace that was destined even before he was born (Gal 1:15).

According to the *apostle, this call had a purpose: to preach to the Gentiles the good news that Jesus was the crucified and risen messianic Son (Ps 2:7; Rom 1:2-4; Gal 3:1) who was inviting all into his kingdom by faith. Paul sees this mission as a participation in the ministry given to the servant character in Isaiah 49:1-7. There the servant's ministry is not simply a work of restoring of Israel; the servant's vocation encompasses the salvation of Gentiles.

Paul has already described Jesus' death using another portion of Isaiah that depicts the servant (Gal 1:4; Is 53:12 LXX). Paul, then, sees his own ministry as a participation in the ministry of the servant Messiah, whose life and death brought salvation to Jews and Gentiles alike. He recounts this conversion and call to (1) demonstrate the origins of his gospel and (2) speak to his previous adherence to the law, which underwent a change after he recognized Jesus as Israel's Messiah.

Paul then recounts his activities after his conversion. He went to Arabia and Damascus (Gal 1:17). Three years later he went to Jerusalem for the first time, where the only significant people he met were Cephas and James the brother of the Lord. He left and went to Syria and Cilicia. The churches in Judea did not know him but rejoiced in his new ministry after his season of persecution (Gal 1:24). The purpose of this portion of the *narrative is to establish that he never depended on Jerusalem for approval for his mission.

Paul did at some point come into more extensive contact with the church in Jerusalem. Paul tells the church in Galatia that fourteen years after his first visit to Jerusalem, or fourteen years after his conversion, he returned to the city a second time. He brought along Barnabas and Titus, possibly because Barnabas and Titus as Jewish and Gentile believers working together in Antioch were an example of the gospel's power to bring together Jews and Gentiles by faith. Paul makes much of how Titus, a Greek, was not forced to be circumcised (Gal 2:3). Nonetheless, it does appear that a more traditional faction of Jewish Christians did force their way into the meeting and attempt to compel Paul's group and by extension to the church in Antioch into some form of adherence to the law. Paul successfully resisted this attempt, and his law-free gospel to the Gentiles received approval from Peter, James, and John (Gal 2:9). The one request that they made was that Paul remember the poor, and he does so eagerly.

At this point in the narrative Paul has responded to apparent attacks on his apostolic authority by (1) showing that Jerusalem was never the basis of his authority, but instead it was God's own call; and (2) stating that nonetheless his gospel was approved by those in authority in Jerusalem.

6.1.4. The Rebuke of Peter in Antioch and Reaffirmation of Justification by Faith (Gal 2:11-21). Peter's visit after the meeting in Jerusalem could have been seen as an approval of Jewish and Gentile fellowship (Gal 2:11-14). Things were again going well until a group claiming support from James came to Antioch. The best conjecture seems to be that James or others in Jerusalem may have been concerned that Peter's status as the leader of the Jewish mission was compromised by his transgressing food laws or at least some stricter contemporary Jewish norms about eating with Gentiles. One cannot know exactly what instructions, if any, this group had from James, but the effect of their presence was the withdrawal of Jewish believers from table fellowship.

Paul saw this as a denial of the gospel's power to bring Jewish and Gentile believers together on the basis of faith. Therefore, he rebuked Peter publicly. He seems to rehearse this story because it bears directly on the issue in Galatia.

Paul argues that all agree that believers are justified on the basis of faith in the Messiah Jesus and not works of the law. Since the two main issues raised thus far in Galatians involve food and circumcision (Gal 2:3, 11-14), it would be wrong to suggest that Paul's opponents have in mind some strict legalism that involves doing enough good works to earn salvation. What they seem to have in mind is adopting a Jewish way of life with a particular emphasis on food and circumcision but of course including the wider ethical demands of the Torah. Paul's counterpoint is that Jewish Christians were not accepted into the church on the basis of doing the works of the law. The law did not bring justification; faith in Jesus is sufficient (Gal 2:14).

Since Richard Hays's groundbreaking work (1983), scholars have questioned whether Paul grounds this justification in their "faith in Christ" or the "faithfulness of Christ" unto death for them. Both ideas have merit in Paul's wider theology. Christ's finished work is the basis for the Christian *hope, in Paul's estimation, and Paul lauds the importance of individuals' belief. In Galatians he seems to be speaking about the sufficiency of personal trust in Jesus for justification.

The Reformation brought the question of justification to the forefront of theology and Pauline interpretation. It remains so today. Since E. P. Sanders's proposals surrounding covenantal nomism, much has been made about whether Luther and others' depiction of a legalistic Judaism is accurate. It is true that post-Sanders, scholarship has articulated a much more nuanced view of the variety of Jewish beliefs about the relationship between obedience to the law and justification in the first century (see especially Barclay's *Paul and the Gift*). This debate cannot be adjudicated here. Nonetheless, in Galatians Paul rebukes any addition to faith or trust in the Messiah as the basis for justification. What he rebukes (good works, ceremonial laws, or something else entirely) is a matter of debate, but that he rebukes *something* is clear. Therefore, the arguments Paul uses against the works of the law in a first-century context could be applied to different additions to the sufficiency of faith in later generations. It falls to those appropriating Paul's argument to make it clear that they are extending his original point to a new situation.

Paul argues the death of the Messiah Jesus brought Jews and Gentiles together on the basis of faith. If his opponents are correct that their life to together is sinful, then Jesus' death led to *sin (Gal 2:17). Paul thinks that this is an absurd idea. Furthermore, his own ministry of bringing the Gentiles and Jews together would be sinful. Neither of these ideas is thinkable for Paul. Through his union with the Messiah, he died to the law and now lives to God. He believes that if works of law were necessary, then Christ died for no reason, because there would be another way to be justified besides faith in his death for them (Gal 2:21).

Paul ends his account of his apostolic ministry up until his time with the Galatians by having disproved opponents' accusations and by laying out in brief a theological rationale for justification by faith.

6.2. A Defense of Gentiles' Status as Heirs to the Inheritance Apart from the Law (Gal 3:1–5:11). *6.2.1. The Spirit as Evidence That the Galatians Are a Part of the Eschatological Community of the Restored People of God (Gal 3:1-5).* After having cleared up the past, Paul rebukes the Galatians in the present by calling them foolish for having fallen for the bewitching message of his opponents. His preaching of the Messiah Jesus should have shielded them from their tricks. With a series of questions, he reminds them that they did not receive the Spirit by doing works of the law but by trusting in the Messiah Jesus.

Paul's recourse to the Spirit as evidence is often called his argument from experience. There is more going on here. The gift of the Spirit was often tied to the eschatological restoration of Israel after the covenant curses outlined in Deuteronomy 27–30 were over. These curses included exile and death. In the prophets, when God redeemed Israel from those curses, he would provide them with the Spirit (Ezek 36:24-32; Is 32:14-20). The Galatians' reception of the Spirit is evidence that they are indeed a part of the eschatologically restored people of God based on faith.

6.2.2. The Galatians Can Either Share in the Blessing of Abraham Through Faith in the Messiah Jesus or Come Under the Works of the Law and Experience the Covenant Curses (Gal 3:6-14). Paul next turns to the example of Abraham. He contends that in the same way faith sufficed to justify Abraham, those who believe are children of Abraham. Many assert that Paul turns to Genesis 15:6 to counter the teaching of his rivals, who possibly used Genesis 17:1-27. In Genesis Abraham and his entire family are circumcised in obedience to the divine command. Paul's opponents' argument would be that if one wanted to be a part of the people of God, one must be circumcised like Abraham and his household.

It seems unlikely, given the prominence of Abraham in early Christianity and the central role that faith played in Paul's gospel before his opponents arrived, that the Galatians had not already heard about Abraham's faith (Mt 1:1; Lk 1:73; 3:8; Jn 8:38-39; Heb 6:13; 11:17; Jas 2:13). It is probable, then, that Paul mentioned Abraham and justification in his initial visit, and his opponents countered that he did not tell the whole story. Galatians 3:6-9 is a more extensive discussion in which Paul responds by maintaining that God justified Abraham *before* he was circumcised (Gen 15:6). This justification prior to circumcision for Paul is the same as Galatians' justification without circumcision.

Furthermore, he maintains that God's promise to bless the Gentiles in Genesis 12:3 is a foreshadowing of the gospel because the promise to bless the Gentiles in Abraham began an epic that climaxed with the death and resurrection of Jesus. This death brought about the end of the law as the means by which one identified the people of God and enabled Gentiles and Jews to be justified by faith. Paul's counterargument to his opponents, therefore, is that in the providence of God, he had always intended to justify Gentiles by faith, not by works of the law. Therefore, those who believe are blessed alongside Abraham the believer.

Galatians 3:10 presents the alternative to receiving justification through faith, which for Paul is receiving a curse. Many have been confused by the fact that Paul uses Deuteronomy 27:26 to suggest that those who are "of the works of the law" are cursed when Deuteronomy 27:26 says just the opposite. It stated that those who do not do the works of the law are under a curse. Some have explained this by suggesting that Paul believes that passages such as Deuteronomy 27:26 require perfect obedience to the law for justification, and since this is impossible, anyone who attempts to do the works of the law is cursed (see Das 2001, 145-70; Keener, 231-37). Others have suggested that Paul has in mind the implicit narrative of Deuteronomy 27–30. In this narrative God outlines either blessings for obedience or curses for disobedience. In Deuteronomy 27–30, the author predicts that Israel will fail to keep the law and will end up suffering the covenant curses until God acts to redeem them from the curses of the law.

Proponents of a narrative reading of Galatians 3:10, such as N. T. Wright and Richard Hays, point out that Galatians 3:10 is a mixed citation of Deuteronomy 27:26; 28:58. The latter passage speaks about Israel's corporate failure. In this reading, Paul would be suggesting that coming under the law would effectively put the Galatians into the situation that corporate Israel faced before the coming of the Messiah, namely, under the covenant curses outlined in Deuteronomy 27–30, which include exile and death.

Given that it is difficult to suggest that the law requires perfect obedience to avoid a curse, the narrative reading and its focus on the corporate curses seems best. Circumcision returns one to the community under the curse and nullifies the work of Christ. Paul's point in either case is that the coming under the law results in the curse because of either individual or corporate disobedience. Paul then argues that Christ's death redeemed Israel from the curse, enabling Gentiles to be blessed without having to come under the law, and opened the way for the eschatological Spirit to come on all.

6.2.3. The Messiah Jesus Is the Promised Heir, and the Law Was Always Intended to Play a Temporary Role. Therefore, All Who Have Been Baptized in Christ Are Abraham's Offspring and Co-Heirs (Gal 3:15-29). Paul continues his argument for the sufficiency of faith by taking a closer look at the terms of the Abrahamic covenant, which he asserts cannot be amended (Gal 3:15). His main point is that the inheritance was promised to Abraham and his singular offspring and not to corporate Israel (Gal 3:16). This singular heir is the Messiah. The law, which came 430 years later, cannot amend the terms of the covenant. If it were possible to amend the covenant and make Torah obedience necessary to inherit, the very nature of the covenant would change from a promise to something achieved through the law. The claim that the Abrahamic covenant cannot be annulled by the law given at Sinai raises the question of why the law was added at all (Gal 3:19). Paul responds that it came about "because of transgressions" and that it was only intended to be in place until the coming of the one to whom the promises had been made (Gal 3:19). Here Paul has in mind the promised heir described in Galatians 3:16, the Messiah Jesus.

Paul states that the problem was not the law but human brokenness (Gal 3:21). Thus, the law functioned in a supervisory role until the Messiah (in Gal 3:24 identified with faith) came. His goal in Galatians 3:16-25 is to sketch his own account of redemptive history and thereby locate the Galatians in the era on the other side of the law. The Galatians are in the messianic age, in which Jesus decides who becomes an heir to the inheritance.

The logical implication of Paul's argument is that if the inheritance ultimately belongs to the Messiah Jesus, then the union with Christ effected by faith and *baptism makes the Galatians Abraham's offspring and heirs to the inheritance. Status as an heir does not depend on ethnicity, gender, or social standing (Gal 3:28). In the Messiah's kingdom, one's status comes from him.

6.2.4. If the Galatians Have Moved from Slaves to Adopted Children and Heirs, Why Turn Back (Gal 4:1-11)? Paul continues this section by using a Greco-Roman analogy of an heir who is destined to inherit at a certain point in the future. While the heir waits, he is no better than a slave. Paul maintains that before the Messiah came, those under the law were enslaved by the elements of the world. This lasted until God sent his Son to redeem those under the law and bring about the *adoption of all those who believe as sons and daughters of God through the Spirit (Gal 4:4-7).

If the Galatians have this new status as heirs, it makes no sense to return to slavery (Gal 4:8-11).

6.2.5. A Reminder of Paul's Own Ministry Among Them and Their Previous Approval (Gal 4:12-20). Paul then reminds the Galatians of his initial visit and the dire circumstances surrounding his ministry among them (Gal 4:13-14). Although they had every reason to reject him, they did not. Surely, Paul maintains, if he was their friend then, he cannot become their enemy for telling the truth (Gal 4:16).

6.2.6. An Allegory of Sarah and Hagar That Affirms the Readers' Status as Heirs and Encourages Them to Hold Fast to Freedom (Gal 4:21–5:1). Paul drives home the point of this section with an analogy that has confused many. He reminds those born under the law of what the law says about two women: Hagar and Sarah. Ishmael, Hagar's son, was born as an act of human will (Abraham and Sarah's). Isaac was born as a result of God's faithfulness to the promise. Paul sees an analogy to two covenants (Abrahamic and Mosaic). He identifies Hagar with Mount Sinai and present Jerusalem. He suggests that this covenant gives birth to slaves. It is best to think of this as a further extension of his discussion of the covenant curses in Galatians 3:10-14. Before the Messiah came, Israel remained under the covenant curses outlined in Deuteronomy 27–30 (see also Neh 9:36). Therefore, those born under the law were born under the curses outlined for disobedience. Paul's point, then, is that apart from the Messiah, those under the works of the law remain under the curse from which he redeemed them from on the cross. Therefore, there is no need to turn to the law (which is personified as present Jerusalem) for justification because it results only in slavery.

The alternative in Paul's mind is the "Jerusalem from above," the believer's mother. It is no surprise that here he quotes Isaiah 54:1-3, a passage that describes the results of the servant's work described in Isaiah 52:13–53:12. In Isaiah 54:1-3, a previously barren Jerusalem becomes fruitful and expands to inherit the nations. Paul claims that the believers in Galatia are those born of the restored Jerusalem, who because of the death of Jesus for sins are set free from the law and the curse. Those who try to add the works of the law to faith in Christ will not inherit alongside the children of the promise (Gal 4:30-31).

6.2.7. The Perilous Implications of Coming Under the Law (Gal 5:2-12). Paul nears the end of this central section of the letter by encouraging the Galatians to hold on to the freedom they have (Gal 5:1). He then makes it clear that the law cannot function as a simple additive. If one is circumcised in an attempt to complete one's conversion, then one is putting one's trust in the law and will be required to keep it (Gal 5:3). It is a denial of God's gracious activity in one's life (Gal 5:4). The alternative is to trust in God and wait by faith through the power of the *Holy Spirit for the hope of righteousness (Gal 5:5). Paul reminds the Galatians that at bottom, God does not care whether one is circumcised. What God cares about is a faith that reveals itself through love (Gal 5:6).

Paul concludes this section by expressing a similar confusion about the Galatians' sudden turn that he has addressed earlier (Gal 1:6; 3:1; 4:20). They were running well until his opponents got in their way (Gal 5:8-9). He then reaffirms his earlier contention that he does not preach circumcision and hyperbolically wishes that those so intent on circumcision would castrate themselves (Gal 5:11-12)!

6.3. Spirit-Enabled Life Together Apart from the Law (Gal 5:12–6:10). Part of the reason Torah obedience may have been appealing was the ethical guidance it provided. Paul's opponents may have met the felt need of the Galatians in their struggle with sin. The law would, in Paul's opponents' account of the Christian faith, fill in what was lacking in his law-free gospel. Therefore, even if Paul has argued that law is not required for justification, he still needs to articulate some vision of the Christian life together. He turns to such matters in Galatians 5:13–6:10.

6.3.1. Freedom Is Bounded by Love (Gal 5:12-15). Paul begins by articulating that the freedom of the Christian is bounded by love. Paul maintains that the Messiah did not set them free for the sake of self-indulgence but so that they might be free to love one another (Gal 5:13). His claim that all should become slaves to one another is an example of the gospel's ability to upset social structures (Gal 3:28; 5:13). By using the Torah love command (Lev 19:18) to outline a picture of the Christian life, Paul shows that his problem is not with the law as God's word to the congregations under his charge. He has a problem with making the law a prerequisite to justification and fellowship (Gal 2:11-21). The alternative to Paul is not fruitful life under the law but a divisiveness that tears the community apart (Gal 5:15).

6.3.2. A Spirit-Empowered Life Together Is Superior to Living in the Flesh (Gal 5:16-24). What does Paul offer as the solution to human brokenness? The Spirit (Gal 5:16). He acknowledges that fallen humanity will not always desire properly. Nonetheless, the Spirit has the ability to give the Galatians a greater desire to obey God's prompting than their distorted impulses (Gal 5:17). If the Spirit orders Christian life and *ethics, then the Galatians are not organized around the law (Gal 5:18). This does not mean that the Galatians lack, because the works of unredeemed humanity are evident (Gal 5:19-21). By contrast, the Spirit brings about life as God intended, creating in the Galatians fruit such as love, patience, kindness, and self-control (Gal 5:22-26).

6.3.3. The Importance of Bearing One Another's Burdens and Ecclesial Accountability (Gal 6:1-10). This articulation of life together does not mean that Paul was not a realist. After articulating the *fruit of the Spirit, Paul describes how the Galatians should respond if someone is caught up in sin (Gal 6:1-5). He speaks of the gentle nature of Christian restoration and the need to be constantly vigilant lest their desire to exercise ecclesial discipline morph into a power that distorts their own well-being. Paul outlines a vision of the Christian life that involves the work of the Spirit on the lives of individuals in the context of communal accountability. This Spirit-drenched ecclesial life together replaces the law as the basis for fellowship.

6.4. Summary and Conclusion: The Marks of Christ and the Israel of God (Gal 6:11-18). Paul closes his letter by accusing his opponents of having faulty motives (Gal 6:11-13). They want to avoid persecution and boast in Gentile circumcision. Paul contrasts their desires with his own. Through his union with Christ, he has been crucified to the world (Gal 6:14). Therefore, there is no one he attempts to please. He does not care about circumcision or uncircumcision. What matters to him is the new creation brought into being through the death and resurrection of Jesus (Gal 6:15). Anyone who is similarly focused on the new creation can expect nothing but wishes of grace and peace from the apostle (Gal 6:16). He calls these people of the new creation the "Israel of God." He probably has in mind believing Jews and Gentiles together in the church as the fulfillment of the promise that Abraham would be the father of many nations. Closing the letter with a declaration that believers are the Israel of God supports his wider thesis that God had always intended to create one people united and justified by their faith in Christ.

Confident that he teaches the truth, Paul asserts that he is undisturbed. His confidence is not in circumcision, a mark in the flesh. His confidence is in the marks in his own *body, the wounds and the scars that he has received as a result of his proclamation of a gospel that unites Jews and Gentiles into one body (Gal 6:15-16).

See also ABRAHAM; CIRCUMCISION; CONVERSION AND CALL OF PAUL; FAITH; FAITH OF CHRIST; FREEDOM/LIBERTY; GENTILES; GOSPEL; JUSTIFICATION; LAW; OPPONENTS OF PAUL; PETER; RHETORICAL CRITICISM; RIGHTEOUSNESS; WORKS OF THE LAW.

BIBLIOGRAPHY. ***Commentaries:*** **J. Becker,** "Der Brief an die Galater," in *Die Briefe an die Galater, Epheser, und Kolosser: Ubersetzt und Erlkärt*, ed. J. Becker and U. Luz, Das Neue Testament Deutsch 8/1 (Göttingen: Vandenhoeck & Ruprecht, 1998), 9-106; **H. D. Betz,** *Galatians: A Commentary on Paul's Letter to the Churches in Galatia*, Hermeneia (Philadelphia: Fortress, 1979); **M. C. de Boer,** *Galatians: A Commentary*, NTL (Louisville, KY: Westminster John Knox, 2011); **F. F. Bruce,** *The Epistle to the Galatians: A Commentary on the Greek Text*, NIGTC (Grand Rapids, MI: Eerdmans, 1982); **E. D. W. Burton,** *A Critical and Exegetical Commentary on the Epistle to the Galatians*, ICC (Edinburgh: T&T Clark, 1980); **A. A. Das,** *Galatians*, Concordia Commentary (St. Louis, MO: Concordia, 2014); **D. A. deSilva,** *The Letter to the Galatians*, NICNT (Grand Rapids, MI: Eerdmans, 2018); **J. D. G. Dunn,** *The Epistle to the Galatians*, BNTC (Peabody, MA: Hendrickson, 1993); **G. D. Fee,** *Galatians*, Pentecostal Commentary Series (Blandford Forum, UK: Deo, 2011); **D. B. Garlington,** *An Exposition of Galatians: A Reading from the New Perspective*, 3rd ed. (Eugene, OR: Wipf & Stock, 2007); **C. S. Keener,** *Galatians: A Commentary* (Grand Rapids, MI: Baker Academic, 2018); **J. B. Lightfoot,** *St. Paul's Epistle to Galatians* (London: Macmillan, 1874); **R. N. Longenecker,** *Galatians*, WBC 41 (repr., Waco, TX: Word, 1990); **J. L. Martyn,** *Galatians: A New Translation with Introduction and Commentary*, AB 33A (New Haven, CT: Yale University Press, 1997); **D. J. Moo,** *Galatians*, BECNT (Grand Rapids, MI: Baker Academic, 2013); **H. Schlier,** *Der Brief an die Galater*, Kritisch-exegetischer Kommentar über das Neue Testament 13 (Göttingen: Vandenhoeck & Ruprecht, 1965); **S. K. Williams,** *Galatians*, ANTC (Nashville: Abingdon, 1997); **B. Witherington III,** *Grace in Galatia: A Commentary on St. Paul's Letter to the Galatians* (repr., London: T&T Clark, 2004); **N. T. Wright,** *Galatians*, CCF (Grand Rapids, MI: Eerdmans, 2021).

Studies: **M. Bachmann,** "Zur Argumentation von Galater 3.10-12," *NTS* 53 (2007): 527-44; **J. M. G. Barclay,** "Mirror-Reading a Polemical Letter: Galatians as a Test Case," *JSNT* 31 (1987): 73-93; idem, *Obeying the Truth: Paul's Ethics in Galatians* (Vancouver: Regent College Publishing, 1988); idem, *Jews in the Mediterranean Diaspora: From Alexander to Trajan (323 BCE–117 CE)* (Edinburgh: T&T Clark, 1996); idem, *Paul and the Gift* (Grand Rapids, MI: Eerdmans, 2015); **B. K. Blount, C. H. Felder, C. J. Martin, and E. B. Powery,** *True to Our Native Land: An African American New Testament Commentary* (Minneapolis: Fortress, 2007); **N. Bonneau,** "The Logic of Paul's Argument on the Curse of the Law in Galatians 3:10-14," *NovT* 39 (1997): 60-80; **B. R. Braxton,** *No Longer Slaves: Galatians and African American Experience* (Collegeville, MN: Liturgical Press, 2002); **A. B. Caneday,** "'Redeemed from the Curse of the Law': The Use of Deut 21:22-23 in Gal 3:13," *TrinJ* 10 (1989): 185-209; **D. A. Carson,**

"Summaries and Conclusions," in *Justification and Variegated Nomism: The Complexities of Second Temple Judaism*, ed. D. A. Carson, P. T. O'Brien, and M. A. Seifrid (Grand Rapids, MI: Baker Academic, 2001), 505-48; **H. C. C. Cavallin,** "Righteous Shall Live by Faith: A Decisive Argument for the Traditional Interpretation," *ST* 32 (1978): 33-43; **D. W. Chapman,** *Ancient Jewish and Christian Perceptions of Crucifixion*, WUNT 244 (Tübingen: Mohr Siebeck, 2008); **R. E. Ciampa,** "Deuteronomy in Galatians and Romans," in *Deuteronomy in the New Testament: The New Testament and the Scriptures of Israel*, ed. S. Moyise and M. J. J. Menken, LNTS (New York: T&T Clark, 2007), 99-117; **A. A. Das,** *Paul, the Law, and the Covenant* (Peabody, MA: Hendrickson, 2001); **T. L. Donaldson,** "The 'Curse of the Law' and the Inclusion of the Gentiles: Galatians 3:13-14," *NTS* 32 (1986): 94-112; **S. G. Eastman,** "The Evil Eye and the Curse of the Law: Galatians 3.1 Revisited," *JSNT* 83 (2001): 69-87; **H.-J. Eckstein,** *Verheissung und Gesetz: Eine exegetische Untersuchung zu Galater 2:15-47*, WUNT 86 (Tubingen: Mohr Siebeck, 1996); **S. J. Gathercole,** "Torah, Life, and Salvation: Leviticus 18:5 in Early Judaism and the New Testament," in *From Prophecy to Testament: The Function of the Old Testament in the New*, ed. C. A. Evans (Peabody, MA: Hendrickson, 2004), 126-45; **S. Grindheim,** "Apostate Turned Prophet: Paul's Prophetic Self-Understanding and Prophetic Hermeneutic with Special Reference to Galatians 3.10-12," *NTS* 53 (2007): 545-65; **R. B. Hays,** *The Faith of Jesus Christ: The Narrative Substructure of Galatians 3:1–4:11*, SBLDS 56 (Chico, CA: Scholars Press, 1983); idem, *Echoes of Scripture in the Letters of Paul* (New Haven, CT: Yale University Press, 1989); idem, "The Letter to the Galatians," *NIB* 11:181-348; **I-G. Hong,** "Does Paul Misrepresent the Jewish Law? Law and Covenant in Gal. 3:1-14," *NovT* 36 (1994): 164-82; **D. Hunn,** "Galatians 3.10-12: Assumptions and Argumentation," *JSNT* 37 (2015): 253-66; **Y-G. Kwon,** *Eschatology in Galatians: Rethinking Paul's Response to the Crisis in Galatia*, WUNT 2/183 (Tübingen: Mohr Siebeck, 2004); **C-C. Lee,** *The Blessing of Abraham, The Spirit, and Justification in Galatians: Their Relationship and Significance for Understanding Paul's Theology* (Eugene, OR: Pickwick, 2013); **D. Lincicum,** *Paul and the Early Jewish Encounter with Deuteronomy*, WUNT 2/284 (Tübingen: Mohr Siebeck, 2010); **B. W. Longenecker,** *The Triumph of Abraham's God: The Transformation of Identity in Galatians* (Nashville: Abingdon, 1998); **D. J. Lull,** *The Spirit in Galatia: Paul's Interpretation of Pneuma as Divine Power* (Chico, CA: Scholars Press, 1980); **E. McCaulley,** *Sharing in the Son's Inheritance: Davidic Messianism and Paul's Worldwide Interpretation of the Abrahamic Land Promise in Galatians*, LNTS (London: T&T Clark, 2019); **R. J. Morales,** *The Spirit and the Restoration of Israel: New Exodus and New Creation Motifs in Galatians*, WUNT 2/282 (Tübingen: Mohr Siebeck, 2010); **E. P. Sanders,** *Paul and Palestinian Judaism* (Philadelphia: Fortress, 1977); **M. Silva,** *Interpreting Galatians: Explorations in Exegetical Method*, 2nd ed. (Grand Rapids, MI: Baker Academic, 2001); **P. Sprinkle,** *Law and Life: The Interpretation of Leviticus 18:5 in Early Judaism and in Paul*, WUNT 241 (Tübingen: Mohr Siebeck, 2008); **F. Thielman,** *From Plight to Solution: A Jewish Framework to Understanding Paul's View of the Law in Galatians and Romans*, NovTSup 61 (Leiden: Brill, 1989); **J. S. Vos,** "Die hermeneutische Antinomie bei Paulus (Galater 3:11-12, Römer 10:5-10)," *NTS* 38 (1992): 254-70; **S. Westerholm,** *Perspectives Old and New on Paul: The "Lutheran" Paul and His Critics* (Grand Rapids, MI: Eerdmans, 2004); **J. Williams,** *Christ Redeemed "Us" from the Curse of the Law: A Jewish Martyrological Reading of Galatians 3:13* (London: Bloomsbury, 2019); **J. Willitts,** "Context Matters: Paul's Use of Leviticus 18:5 in Galatians 3:12," *TynBul* 54 (2003): 105-22; **T. A. Wilson,** "Wilderness Apostasy and Paul's Portrayal of the Crisis in Galatians," *NTS* 50 (2004): 550-71; **M. Wolter,** "God and the World in the Epistles of Paul," *In die Skriflig (Online)* 47 (2013): 1-7; **N. T. Wright,** *Paul and the Faithfulness of God* (Minneapolis: Fortress, 2013); idem, *Pauline Perspectives: Essays on Paul 1978–2013* (London: SPCK, 2013).

E. McCaulley

GENTILES

From the Latin *gens* (meaning "family, race"), the English term *Gentiles* translates the NT Greek *ethnē*, a plural noun referring in the biblical tradition to *non-Jews*, or to members of *nations* other than *Israel, or, on occasion, simply to *nonbelievers* or "*heathens*." The Greek etymology of *ethnē* is unknown, though it perhaps derives from the verb *ethō*, "to be accustomed," indicating a distinct group bound together by shared customs or characteristics. The extension to *ethnos* or "nation/tribe" (frequent already in Homer) is plausible enough.

Paul's frequent use of the plural *ethnē* simultaneously betrays his specifically Jewish frame of reference and his distinctive international Christian *mission. "Gentiles" are, for Paul, the *others* whom God is now graciously including among his *covenant people through *faith in Jesus, the Messiah of Israel and *Lord of all nations.

1. Usage in Paul's Letters
2. The Old Testament Background of Paul's Usage
3. Gentiles in Postbiblical Judaism
4. Paul's Gospel and the Gentiles

1. Usage in Paul's Letters.

Despite his self-designation as "*apostle to the Gentiles" (Rom 1:5; 11:13; Gal 2:8), Paul does not employ the noun *ethnē* throughout his letters with anything like the consistency of other key Pauline terms, such as *pistis* (faith), *charis* (*grace), or *euangelion* (*gospel). In the seven so-called undisputed epistles (Romans, 1 Corinthians, 2 Corinthians, Galatians, 1 Thessalonians, Philippians, Philemon), the term appears 46 times. However, 40 of those, or 87 percent, appear in just *two* epistles: 29 times in Romans, 11 times in Galatians. The remaining six occurrences are scattered across three of the remaining five epistles: 3 times in 1 Corinthians, once in 2 Corinthians, and twice in 1 Thessalonians. The word does not appear in Philippians and Philemon. The adverbial form *ethnikōs* ("living as a Gentile") appears in Galatians 2:14.

On a few occasions, *ethnē* carries the *negative* sense of foreigners to the faith, nonbelievers, or even sinners (1 Cor 5:1; 12:2; Gal 2:15; 1 Thess 4:5). Paul can even speak of his Gentile converts as *former* Gentiles: "when you were *ethnē*" (1 Cor 12:2). Particularly striking is his contrast between "Jews by birth" and "Gentile sinners" (Gal 2:15). It is possible Paul intends this to be ironic, adopting a typical Jewish criticism of Gentiles (Jub. 23.23-24; 1 Macc 2:48; see further below) as part of his criticism of Peter's duplicity in the dispute over dining with Gentiles. In the previous verse (Gal 2:14), Paul describes Peter's actions as "living as a Gentile," *ethnikōs*, the only instance of the adverb in the NT.

Paul was no doubt conscious of his special commission to be apostle to the Gentiles even in the letters where *ethnē* appears rarely (1–2 Corinthians, 1 Thessalonians) or not at all (Philippians and Philemon). After all, the recipients of these letters were largely *Gentiles*. The striking concentration of usage in Romans and Galatians, then, reflects the rhetorical situation of those epistles: Paul's mission and/or gospel seem to have been challenged in various ways in Galatia (Gal 4:15-20; 6:12-17) and Rome (Rom 3:8; Phil 1:14, assuming a Roman provenance for Philippians). Paul responds with a full-scale defense of his—and God's—intentions toward Gentiles. This fact draws attention to a key connotation or function of the word in Paul's letters: *ethnē* is principally a missiological term. It signals the eschatological inclusion of the once-excluded people of the nations. In this sense *ethnē* is a wholly positive term.

Romans 15 provides a particularly illuminating cluster of occurrences of the term: five occurrences of *ethnē* appear in citations from the OT (Rom 15:9, 10, 11, 12 [2×]), and a further five appear in Paul's own statements about his *calling to evangelize the nations (Rom 15:9, 16 [2×], 18, 27). Here the missiological or eschatological import becomes apparent: Paul sees himself as an Israelite "priest" (Rom 15:16) offering up to *God the *sacrifice of the Gentiles in fulfillment of the divine plan foretold in the Prophets.

These redeemed Gentiles neither become Israelites nor displace Israel. While the expression "all Israel" in Romans 11:26 and "the Israel of God" in Galatians 6:16 may be read in this way, numerous other texts suggest that, for Paul, Gentiles remain Gentiles, even as Christians. Gentiles are a "wild olive shoot" grafted onto the "natural olive tree" (Rom 11:17-24), and Paul directly addresses them as Gentiles: "I am talking to you *ethnē*" (Rom 11:13, and repeatedly in the "you" and "they" throughout Rom 11:25-31). Paul's outlook seems to be that through faith in *Christ, Gentiles have gained equal status—as Gentiles—with God's ancient covenant people who believe.

Little, if any, development in the usage of *ethnē* can be discerned in the so-called disputed Pauline epistles (2 Thessalonians, Colossians, Ephesians, 1–2 Timothy, Titus). The term appears nine times across four of the six letters (Ephesians, Colossians, 1–2 Timothy). In typical Pauline fashion, the inclusion of the Gentiles is said to be the principal *mystērion* of the apostle's calling (Col 1:27; 1 Tim 3:16). Indeed, the very point of his apostleship is to teach/proclaim Christ among the nations (1 Tim 2:7; 2 Tim 4:17). The eschatological or missiological import of *ethnē* observed already in Romans and Galatians is particularly evident in the central section of Ephesians. Indeed, the verbal and conceptual correspondences between Ephesians 2:11–3:11 and Romans 15:15-27 are striking: the coming together of Jew and Gentile into one family of God is the central purpose of Paul's calling. Yet, even here—as in 1 Corinthians 12:2 and Galatians 2:15—the author can still use *ethnē* negatively to refer to the outsider status of most Gentiles: "you must no longer live as the Gentiles live" (Eph 4:17 NIV).

The absence of any mention of *ethnē* in the disputed 2 Thessalonians and Titus is likely no more significant than the absence of the terminology in the undisputed Philippians and Philemon.

Finally, the term *Hellēn* ("Greek") in Paul is nearly synonymous with *ethnē*. It appears twelve times in the undisputed letters (six in Romans, four in 1 Corinthians, two in Galatians). It sometimes appears in synonymous parallel with *ethnē* (Rom 1:13-14; Gal 2:2-3), or, more frequently, it is paired/contrasted with *Ioudaios*, "Jew" (Rom 1:16; 2:9-10; 3:9; 10:12; 1 Cor 1:22, 24; 10:32; 12:13; Gal 3:28). It appears just once in the disputed epistles (Col 3:11), again contrasted with *Ioudaios*, in a passage strikingly similar to Galatians 3:28. *Hellēn* is principally an ethnic signifier (meaning "non-Jew"). It does not seem to carry the same eschatological overtones as the far more common *ethnē*. Paul's strong preference for *ethnē* may have been influenced by the distinctive eschatological portrait of the Gentiles in Isaiah (see below).

2. The Old Testament Background of Paul's Usage.

Overwhelmingly, the Hebrew plural noun *gôyîm* ("nations") refers to the foreign nations, as distinct from the nation of Israel. While the singular *gôy* certainly can refer to the nation of Israel (e.g., Gen 12:2), the more frequent Hebrew term for God's own nation is *ʿam* (the "people"). In the LXX, the typical Greek rendering of *gôyîm* is *ethnē*. Throughout much of the OT, the "nations" are seen as foreigners and nonbelievers. God's own people must live separately from them: "Do not defile yourselves in any of these ways, because this is how the nations [*gôyîm*/*ethnē*] that I am going to drive out before you became defiled" (Lev 18:24 NIV). Indeed, Israel's punishment for breaching the covenant is described in apposite terms: "I will scatter you among the nations" (*gôyîm*/*ethnē*, Lev 26:33 NIV). Similar usage is found frequently throughout the historical books of the OT.

A dramatic change in usage, and the likely background to Paul's own usage, comes in Isaiah. Already in the early chapters of the book, the *gôyîm*/*ethnē* are seen as future recipients of God's blessing, one day streaming to the mountain of God in an eschatological pilgrimage and finding justice and *peace for themselves (Is 2:2-4). Moreover, the Davidic descendant, the "stump of Jesse," will eventually bring *judgment for all people, so that the "earth will be filled with the *knowledge of God" and "the nations [*gôyîm*/*ethnē*] will rally to him" (Is 11:1-10 NIV). This theme largely disappears from the middle sections of Isaiah, with a striking possible exception in Isaiah 19:18-25. In these chapters, the *gôyîm*/*ethnē* are frequently said to be the object of divine punishment: "The Lord is angry with all the nations" (Is 34:1-2).

In what is often called Deutero-Isaiah (and Trito-Isaiah), Isaiah 40–66, there is a remarkable return to and extension of the themes of Isaiah 2; 11. While the *gôyîm*/*ethnē* may be said to be "like a drop in the bucket" before the Lord (Is 40:15-17 NIV), these foreign nations, or Gentiles, are also recipients of God's "justice," "teaching," and "*hope" (Is 42:1-4). The connections with Isaiah 2; 11 are obvious. Indeed, the *servant of the Lord (the Davidic descendant?) is set to become "a *light for the *gôyîm*/*ethnē*" (Is 42:6). The expression "light for/to the nations" is repeated in Isaiah 49:6, where the "light" restores both Israel and the Gentiles so that the Lord's "*salvation may reach to the ends of the earth," and again in Isaiah 51:4, where the "light" illuminates the Gentiles with divine instruction and justice. None of this contradicts the theme of the punishment of the nations prominent in the middle chapters of Isaiah, since it is clear in the closing chapters of the book that, while the nations/Gentiles are invited into the light that shines from Israel (Is 60:3), those nations that refuse to honor Israel and its God "will perish" and "be utterly ruined" (Is 60:12).

Most of the rest of the prophets refer to the *gôyîm*/*ethnē* as foreign, nonbelieving powers at odds with God's own people. The striking exception is Micah, where the eschatological pilgrimage of the nations, foreseen in Isaiah, is reiterated: "Many nations [*gôyîm*/*ethnē*] will come and say, 'Come, let us go up to the mountain of the LORD, to the temple of the God of Jacob. He will teach us his ways, so that we may walk in his paths'" (Mic 4:2 NIV).

Paul's understanding of God's purposes for the Gentiles was likely influenced by Isaiah's vision of the nations being drawn to Israel's light, giving up their disobedience, and finding the Lord's salvation (Donaldson 1997). This was not a mere liberal-minded universalism on the part of the apostle; not for a moment did Paul negate the dominant criticism of the nations found throughout the biblical tradition, as is clear from his own stock denunciation of Gentiles in Romans 1:18-32 and from his occasional use of *ethnē*, as noted earlier, to mean something like "nonbeliever" or "sinner" (1 Cor 5:1; 12:2; Gal 2:15; 1 Thess 4:5). Paul's perspective was that the grace shown to undeserving Israel has now been opened up to all undeserving nations, through the saving work of the Messiah, in fulfillment of the promises to *Abraham (Gen 12:1-3; 15:6) and the prophecies of Isaiah.

Paul's indebtedness to the Isaianic vision for the nations is evident in numerous passages, especially in Romans. In Romans 10:20 he cites Isaiah 65:1, describing the Gentiles as those who "did not seek" God but nonetheless "found" him. In Romans 15:12 he says that the eschatological pilgrimage of Isaiah 11:1-10, in which the "Root of Jesse," the Messiah, will "rule over the nations," finds fulfillment in that there are Gentile congregations in Rome. In both passages Paul explicitly names the biblical prophet: "Isaiah cries out" and "Isaiah says." In Romans 15:21 (NIV) the apostle identifies the Gentiles he has evangelized from *Jerusalem to Illyricum as the fortunate ones foretold in Isaiah 52:15: "Those who were not told about him will see, and those who have not heard will understand."

Further evidence of Isaiah's influence on Paul's understanding of the Gentiles may be found in the book of Acts, where the author—a devoted admirer of Paul—*twice* says that Paul described his own *ministry as a fulfillment of Isaiah's universal light: "We now turn to the Gentiles. For this is what the Lord has commanded us: 'I have made you a light for the Gentiles, that you may bring salvation to the ends of the earth'" (Acts 13:46-47 NIV, citing Is 49:6); and "I am saying [as Moses and the prophets did] . . . that the Messiah would suffer and, as the first to rise from the dead, would bring the message of light to his own people and to the Gentiles" (Acts 26:23 NIV, alluding to Is 49:6 or Is 51:4).

3. Gentiles in Postbiblical Judaism.

Paul was not alone among ancient Jews in looking forward to the fulfillment of Isaiah's "light for the Gentiles," even if it was also widely believed—by Paul, too—that Gentiles had no inherent claim on the favor of Israel's God. Two tendencies are observed, almost simultaneously, in the sources. Many have noted that Jews in the Second Temple period were frequently tolerant of, and even open toward, the Gentiles (Goodman; McKnight). On the other hand, numerous Jewish texts are highly critical of pagans: forbidding intermarriage (Tob 4:12), expecting future judgment on the nations (e.g., Sir 36:1-7; Pss. Sol. 17.3-7, 22-28), and generally critiquing Gentile religion and morals (Wis 13–15; Sib. Or. 3.350-488; Jub. 15.16; Let. Aris. 134-139). The Roman chronicler Tacitus castigates Jews for such social scruples, claiming (with obvious exaggeration) that they are "extremely loyal toward one another" but "toward every other people they feel only hate and enmity," adding that "those who are converted to their ways follow the same practice" (Tacitus, *Hist.* 5.5 [LCL]). Tacitus's criticism is perhaps truest with respect to the community at *Qumran. In the sectarian writings of the Dead Sea Scrolls, the Gentiles are viewed almost entirely negatively, as idolators and evildoers destined for judgment (e.g., 1QM VI, 6; XII, 11; 1QpHab XII, 13).

One concrete manifestation of both Jewish openness and antipathy toward Gentiles is the Jerusalem *temple inscription forbidding foreigners to enter the "holy place" beyond the more public square known as the Court of the Gentiles. That non-Jews were permitted within the general temple complex attests to a certain tolerance toward any pagan who was curious to learn more about Jewish *worship. On the other hand, the wording of the balustrade inscription (composed in Greek and Latin, according to Josephus, *J.W.* 5.194) struck an ominous tone: "No foreigner is to enter within the balustrade and forecourt around the sacred precinct. Whoever is caught will himself be responsible for his consequent death" (CIIP 1/1.2:42). Gentiles are, by nature, unholy and must not breach the pure-impure divide so central to the Jewish understanding of reality. It is possible, if speculative, that Paul (or pseudonymous Paul) deliberately refers to this temple balustrade with its hostile warning against foreigners when he writes that Jews and Gentiles enjoy *fellowship in Christ: "he himself is our peace, who has made the two groups one and has destroyed the barrier, the dividing wall of hostility" (Eph 2:14 NIV). This passage concludes by describing the universal *church, made up of Jews and Gentiles as a "holy temple in the Lord" (Eph 2:21 NIV).

The mention by Tacitus of those "converted" to Jewish ways raises the much-debated theme of Jewish mission to Gentiles prior to Paul. For this article's purposes, it need only be noted that the Jewish *ambivalence* toward Gentiles—both openness and critique—is the necessary precondition for the Bible's hope of Gentile restoration to Israel's God. The nations may be condemned sinners by nature, but they retain a destiny in the plans of the Creator. Thus, the pre-Maccabean Tobit looks forward to a day when "a bright light will shine to all the ends of the earth; many nations will come to you from far away, the inhabitants of the remotest parts of the earth to your holy name, bearing gifts in their hands for the King of heaven" (Tob 13:11 NRSV). Tobit 14:6 (NRSV) is more explicit: "Then the nations in the whole world will all be converted and worship God in truth. They will all abandon their idols, which deceitfully have led them into their error; and in righteousness they will praise the eternal God." Similar hopes of final Gentile inclusion among the people of God are expressed in 1 Enoch 10.21 and 90.6-42, as well as 2 Baruch 72-73, Testament of Levi 18, and Sibylline Oracles 3.716-720.

In less eschatological terms, Philo of Alexandria (25 BC–AD 50), a Jewish intellectual active in the time of Paul, expresses his hope that Gentiles might join in the proper worship of God when Israel begins to prosper on the world stage. In language reminiscent of Isaiah's "light to the nations," Philo expresses his hope "that each nation would abandon its peculiar ways, and, throwing overboard their ancestral customs, turn to honouring our laws alone." Those laws "shine brightly" in the world, "darkening the light of the others as the risen sun darkens the stars" (*Mos.* 2.44 [LCL]). Earlier in the same work, Philo describes Israel as a nation called to pray for the Gentiles that they might be "delivered from evil and participate in what is good" (*Mos.* 1.149 [LCL]). Elsewhere he expresses his conviction that the Jewish "life of temperance and every virtue" may "convert even those who seemed to be quite incurable" among Gentiles (*Ios.* 85-87 [LCL]).

A similar openness to Gentile conversion is found in Josephus's famous account of the conversion of the royal house of Adiabene in northern Mesopotamia (in modern Iraq). Josephus devotes an unusually large amount of space to the story (*Ant.* 20.17-96). Sometime around the year 30, a merchant named Ananias taught the women of the royal court how to worship the God of Israel. With the assistance of the women, Ananias then persuaded Prince Izates—soon to be king—likewise to worship God. In a remarkable historical parallel to the perspective of Paul, Ananias advised the Gentile king that he could "worship God even without being circumcised if indeed he had fully decided to be a devoted adherent of Judaism" (Josephus, *Ant.* 20.41 [LCL]). Nothing is known of Ananias's rationale. Was it a mere political expedience, or a theological conviction akin to that of the slightly later Paul? Whatever the case, in a further precedent to the mission of Paul, Ananias's circumcision-free Judaism (for Gentiles) was soon threatened by a Judaizer from Galilee. Josephus writes that a Galilean teacher named Eleazar, "who had a reputation for being extremely strict when it came to the ancestral laws," rebuked Izates for presuming to worship God without circumcision, declaring him to be "guilty of the greatest offense against the law" (Josephus, *Ant.* 20.43-44 [LCL]). The king promptly acquiesced and received the Jewish rite, thereby becoming a true Jewish proselyte. One wonders whether Ananias might have responded to this contradiction of his teaching in a similar fashion to the apostle Paul when he learned of attempts to Judaize his Galatian converts: "Who has bewitched you?" (Gal 3:1).

Nothing more can be known about Ananias or Eleazar, but these goings-on to the east of Paul's mission field, just a few years earlier, make plain that the apostle to the Gentiles was not an outlier in the period, and nor were his Judaizing opponents. One might even imagine the criticism of Jesus against certain Pharisees being directed against Eleazar of Galilee (a contemporary of Jesus): "Woe to you, teachers of the law and Pharisees, you hypocrites! You travel over land and sea to win a single convert, and when you have succeeded, you make them twice as much a child of hell as you are" (Mt 23:15 NIV).

4. Paul's Gospel and the Gentiles.

The inclusion of the nations in the purposes of God was central to Paul's self-conception and mission. It is naturally intimately related to his gospel. But what place did Gentiles have in the *content* of Paul's gospel?

Following the comprehensive success of the mission to the nations in the centuries after Paul, the frequent mention of "Jews and Gentiles" in the letters of Paul had less immediate relevance in the (almost wholly) Gentile church. In the Augustinian and later Lutheran tradition of Pauline interpretation, "Jews" in Paul's letters—like "Pharisees" in the Gospels—came to represent human beings who sought to win salvation through good works. "Gentiles," by contrast, were sinners in self-confessed need of divine grace. This hermeneutical shift pushed the concrete idea of "Gentiles" into the background of exegesis and theological reflection. Within this hermeneutical tradition, Gentiles were central to Paul's gospel mainly to the extent that they provided a symbol of humanity's need for *justification through faith. The living debate of Paul's day over the status of the nations in the plans of Israel's God faded into the background of much Pauline scholarship from the medieval period through to the twentieth century, as may be observed in the otherwise diverse commentaries on Romans by Martin Luther, Karl Barth, and Ernst Käsemann. A striking exception is the 1935 commentary on Romans by Adolf Schlatter.

Krister Stendahl's 1962 essay (1963 English translation) "The Apostle Paul and the Introspective Conscience of the West" sought to redress the hermeneutical problem, as he saw it, of emptying Paul's discussion about Gentiles of its concrete meaning and filling it with the metaphorical significance of the dilemma of the individual soul seeking justification by works.

> The Reformers' interpretation of Paul rests on an analogism when Pauline statements about Faith and Works, Law and Gospel, Jews and Gentiles are read in the framework of late medieval piety. The Law, the Torah, with its specific requirements of circumcision and food restrictions becomes a general principle of "legalism" in religious matters. Where Paul was concerned about the possibility for Gentiles to be included in the messianic community, his statements are now read as answers to the quest for assurance about man's salvation out of a common human predicament. (205-6)

By contrast, Stendahl insists that Jews and Gentiles were central to Paul's message, at least in Romans and Galatians, precisely because his gospel announced the inclusion of the foreign nations in the *wisdom of Israel's God. Stendahl's essay marked a hermeneutical revolution in the study of Paul.

The so-called new perspective on Paul, whose beginning is often credited to E. P. Sanders's 1977 *Paul and Palestinian Judaism*, brought Gentiles further to the fore of Pauline scholarship. A natural trajectory can be discerned from Stendahl to Sanders to James Dunn (and many other new perspective writers) that gives Gentiles a concrete place in Paul's gospel. According to the new perspective, "justification by faith apart from works" refers not to finding grace for salvation but to the affirmation that Gentiles really are among God's covenant people through faith in the Messiah rather than through practicing the nationalistic Jewish customs of *circumcision, *food laws, and Sabbath keeping. Gentiles need not become Jews in order to be seen as the people of God; their faith in Christ is a sufficient "badge" of their belonging to Israel's God *as Gentiles*. The merits of this revision of Paul's notion of justification continue to be debated. What has been accepted by a consensus of Pauline scholars today is that Gentiles were central to Paul's thinking. One can see this shift even in commentaries that are either not at all aligned with the new perspective (e.g., Stuhlmacher on Romans) or that may be described as *post*-new perspective (e.g., Jewett on Romans).

Whatever one says about the precise place of Gentiles in Paul's gospel, it remains clear that the *content* or *framework* of the Pauline gospel was the traditional one, passed onto him in creeds or summary statements (1 Cor 15:3-5; Rom 1:2-4; cf. 2 Tim 2:8). It concerns the birth, life, *death for sins, *resurrection, and appearances of Jesus the Davidic Messiah and Lord of the world. On the other hand, the *scope* or *basis* of Paul's gospel—certainly in Romans and Galatians—is that Gentiles may receive the gospel's blessings *as Gentiles,* that is, without in any sense *becoming Israelites* through circumcision and adherence to Israel's Torah. All of this was foreshadowed, according to Paul, in the fact that Abraham, the father of Israel, was declared righteous by faith prior to his circumcision (Rom 4:9-17; cf. Gen 15:6). Abraham was thus not only the father of Israel—a standard Jewish motif—but also the father of "many *ethnē*" (Rom 4:17). This is why Paul can even describe God's announcement to Abraham in Genesis 12:3 ("all nations will be blessed in you") as *proeuangelizomai* (Gal 3:8), a "pre-evangelization" or foreshadowing of the gospel's international scope (if not its particular christological content).

Reflection on the Gentiles today draws readers of Paul into the *mystery that animated his mission. God is graciously calling people from all nations to believe in Jesus the Messiah and Lord and so find their place among his covenant people.

See also APOSTLE; CONVERSION AND CALL OF PAUL; ETHNICITY IN PAUL'S WORLD; GOSPEL; INTERPRETATION: NEW PERSPECTIVE; MISSION; OLD TESTAMENT IN PAUL; ROMANS, LETTER TO THE.

BIBLIOGRAPHY. **F. Ábel,** ed., *The Message of Paul the Apostle Within Second Temple Judaism* (Lanham, MD: Lexington/Fortress Academic, 2019); **J. Becker,** *Paul Apostle to the Gentiles* (Louisville, KY: Westminster John Knox, 1993); **E. Best,** "The Revelation to Evangelize the Gentiles," *JTS* 35, no. 1 (1984): 1-30; **M. F. Bird,** "Gentiles," in *Encyclopedia of the Historical Jesus*, ed. C. A. Evans (New York: Routledge, 2008); idem, *An Anomalous Jew: Paul Among Jews, Greeks, and Romans* (Grand Rapids, MI: Eerdmans, 2016); **W. S. Campbell,** *Paul's Gospel in an Intercultural Context: Jews and Gentiles in the Letter to the Romans*, Studies in the Intercultural History of Christianity (Frankfurt am Main: Peter Lang, 1991); **J. P. Dickson,** *Mission-Commitment in Ancient Judaism and in the Pauline Communities: The Shape, Extent, and Background of Early Christian Mission*, WUNT 2/159 (Tübingen: Mohr Siebeck, 2003); idem, "Mission-Commitment in Second Temple Judaism," in *Introduction to Messianic Judaism: Its Ecclesial Context and Biblical Foundations*, ed. D. J. Rudolph and J. Willitts (Grand Rapids, MI: Zondervan, 2013), 255-63; **P. E. Dinter,** "Paul and the Prophet Isaiah," *BTB* 13, no. 2 (1983):

48-52; **T. L. Donaldson,** "Proselytes or 'Righteous Gentiles'? The Status of Gentiles in Eschatological Pilgrimage Patterns of Thought," *JSP* 7 (1990): 3-27; idem, *Paul and the Gentiles: Remapping the Apostle's Convictional World* (Minneapolis: Fortress, 1997); idem, *Judaism and the Gentiles: Jewish Patterns of Universalism (to 135 CE)* (Waco, TX: Baylor University Press, 2007); idem, "'Gentile Christianity' as a Category in the Study of Christian Origins," *HTR* 106, no. 4 (2013): 433-58; **J. D. G. Dunn,** "From Jewish Sect to Gentile Religion," in *Beginning from Jerusalem: Christianity in the Making* (Grand Rapids, MI: Eerdmans, 2009), 2:29-51; **C. A. Evans,** "From Gospel to Gospel: The Function of Isaiah in the New Testament," in *Writing and Reading the Scroll of Isaiah: Studies of an Interpretive Tradition*, ed. C. C. Broyles and C. A. Evans (Leiden: Brill, 1997), 651-91; **R. Feldmeier and U. Heckel**, eds., *Die Heiden: Juden, Christen, und das Problem des Fremden*, WUNT 70 (Tübingen: Mohr Siebeck, 1994); **R. W. Fisher,** "The Herald of Good News in Second Isaiah," in *Rhetorical Criticism: Essays in Honor of James Muilenburg*, ed. J. J. Jackson and M. Kessler (Pittsburgh: Pickwick, 1974), 117-32; **J. Flamming,** "The New Testament Use of Isaiah," *SwJT* 11 (1968): 89-103; **P. Fredriksen,** "Judaism, the Circumcision of Gentiles and Apocalyptic Hope: Another Look at Galatians 1 and 2," *JTS* 42 (1991): 532-64; **P. Fredriksen and J. Svartvik,** *Krister Among the Jews and Gentiles: Essays in Appreciation of the Life and Work of Krister Stendahl* (Mahwah, NJ: Paulist, 2018); **M. Goodman,** *Mission and Conversion: Proselytizing in the Religious History of the Roman Empire* (Oxford: Clarendon, 1994); **M. Hengel,** *Judaism and Hellenism: Studies in Their Environment in Palestine During the Early Hellenistic Period*, 2 vols. (Minneapolis: Fortress, 1974); idem, "The Origins of the Christian Mission," in *Between Jesus and Paul* (Philadelphia: Fortress, 1983), 48-64; idem, *The Pre-Christian Paul* (London: SCM Press, 1991); **M. Hengel and A. M. Schwemer,** *Paul Between Damascus and Antioch: The Unknown Years*, trans. J. Bowden (London: SCM Press, 1997); **K. R. Iverson,** "Gentiles," in *DJG*², 302-9; **J. Jeremias,** *Jesus' Promise to the Nations* (London: SCM Press, 1958); **R. Jewett,** *Romans* (Minneapolis: Fortress, 2007); **S. McKnight,** *A Light Among the Gentiles: Jewish Missionary Activity in the Second Temple Period* (Minneapolis: Fortress, 1991); **M. M. Mitchell,** "Gentile Christianity," in *The Cambridge History of Christianity, ed.* M. M. Mitchell and F. M. Young (Cambridge: Cambridge University Press, 2006), 1:103-24; **D. Novak,** *The Image of the Non-Jew in Judaism: The Idea of Noahide Law*, 2nd ed. (Liverpool: Littman Library of Jewish Civilization, 2011); **S. E. Porter and B. W. R. Pearson**, "Isaiah Through Greek Eyes: The Septuagint of Isaiah," in *Writing and Reading the Scroll of Isaiah: Studies of an Interpretive Tradition*, ed. C. C. Broyles and C. A. Evans (Leiden: Brill, 1997), 531-46; **R. Riesner,** "A Pre-Christian Jewish Mission?," in *The Mission of the Early Church to Jews and Gentiles*, ed. J. Ådna and H. Kvalbein (Tübingen: Mohr Siebeck, 2000), 211-50; **I. Rosen-Zvi and A. Ophir,** "Paul and the Invention of the Gentiles," *JQR* 105, no. 1 (2015): 1-41; **J. F. Sawyer,** "Isaiah and Christian Origins," in *The Fifth Gospel: Isaiah in the History of Christianity* (Cambridge: Cambridge University Press, 1996), 21-41; **K. L. Schmidt,** "ἔθνος, ἐθνικός," *TDNT* 2:364-72; **M. Silva,** "Ethnos," *NIDNTT* 2:89-93; **K. Stendahl,** "The Apostle Paul and the Introspective Conscience of the West," *HTR* 56, no. 3 (1963): 199-215; **P. Stuhlmacher,** *Paul's Letter to the Romans* (Louisville, KY: Westminster John Knox, 1994); **J. R. Wagner,** "The Heralds of Isaiah and the Mission of Paul: An Investigation of Paul's Use of Isaiah 51–55 in Romans," in *Jesus and the Suffering Servant: Isaiah 53 and Christian Origins*, ed. W. H. Bellinger Jr. (Harrisburg, PA: Trinity Press International, 1998), 193-222; **F. Watson,** *Paul, Judaism, and the Gentiles: A Sociological Approach*, SNTSMS 56 (Cambridge: Cambridge University Press, 1986); **S. Whittle,** "Paul's Priestly Ministry and the Offering of the Gentiles (Rom 15:16)," *Judaïsme Ancien* 4 (2016): 57-78; **F. Wilk,** *Jesus und die Völker in der Sicht der Synoptiker*, BZNW 109 (Berlin: de Gruyter, 2002); **S. G. Wilson,** *The Gentiles and the Gentile Mission in Luke–Acts*, SNTSMS 23 (Cambridge: Cambridge University Press, 1973); **O. L. Yarborough,** *Not Like the Gentiles: Marriage Rules in the Letters of Paul*, SBLDS (Atlanta: Scholars Press, 1985).

J. P. Dickson

GIFTS OF THE SPIRIT

Although the phrase "gift of the Spirit" does not appear in the Pauline corpus, Paul's connection of "gift" language with the activities of the *Holy Spirit in Romans 1:11 and 1 Corinthians 12–14 makes its use legitimate. However, various issues surround this subject. First, how does one identify the gift(s)? Second, what is the relationship between gifts and natural abilities? Third, because Paul exhibits a considerable degree of fluidity in his use of the terms *pneumatika* (things of the Spirit) and *charismata* (gifts of the Spirit), one wonders how Paul himself might have understood these words in relation to gifts. Fourth, the asystematic nature of the texts makes it difficult to isolate the activities that might legitimately be classified as the gifts of the Spirit. Finally, it is helpful to identify the nature of the various gifts that are mentioned.

1. The Gift and Gifts
2. Spiritual Gifts and Natural Abilities
3. Source and Nature of the Gifts
4. Gift Vocabulary
5. Texts
6. The *Charismata*
7. Purpose of the Gifts

1. The Gift and Gifts.
In discussing the gifts of the Spirit, a clear distinction is to be made between the Holy Spirit as a gift and the gifts that the Holy Spirit bestows on believers. That Paul implies that the Holy Spirit is a gift is beyond question. In 1 Thessalonians 4:8 Paul makes clear that the Holy Spirit within believers is the Sanctifier, and in Romans 5:5 the *apostle says that God gives his Spirit to believers that by him the "*love of *God may be poured out into our hearts." However, there is a difference between God's gift of the Spirit to believers and the gifts the Holy Spirit bestows on believers.

2. Spiritual Gifts and Natural Abilities.
There is frequently confusion between the natural gifts or talents of an individual and the gifts the Spirit bestows on believers. Although the distinction is not always easy to make, there are marked differences between them. On the one hand, natural gifts or talents are present in many, if not all, lives. They derive from factors such as one's environment, experience, education, and genetics. All people have potential talents that require necessary conditions for their development. On the other hand, the spiritual gifts refer to special spiritual endowments by the Spirit. They are "manifestations of the Holy Spirit in the lives of believers enabling them to minister in a means beyond their human capacity. Believers receive these gifts as a result of God's grace" (Rea, 242). Paul's letters show that natural talents are not spiritual manifestations. However, the presence of the *charismata* enhances capacities and natural functions. God touches all human abilities and potential with supernatural power (Lim, 59).

3. Source and Nature of the Gifts.
Paul's description of the gifts in 1 Corinthians 12 begins both with their source and nature. Paul uses three important words: *gifts* (1 Cor 12:4, Gk. *charismata*), *services* (1 Cor 12:5, Gk. *diakonia*), and *workings* (1 Cor 12:6, Gk. *energemata*). Paul's choice of words is not merely stylistic. While the gifts (*charismata*) emphasize the *truth of the spiritual manifestations as an expression of God's *grace, the administration of them or services (*diakonia*) suggest that the purpose of the gifts is not self-enjoyment or edification. Rather, the gifts are for loving *ministry within the *body of *Christ. No one can boast of one's spirituality or greatness. The operations or workings (*energēmata*) suggest that, in all these manifestations, God is powerfully at work through the Spirit.

Although discussions about the gifts often refer to them as "gifts of the Spirit," it is not the Spirit alone who distributes the gifts (Rom 12:2-8; 1 Cor 12:4-6; Eph 4:7-11). The source of the gifts is the triune God—Father, Son, and Holy Spirit. In 1 Corinthians 12:4-6, Paul makes deliberate reference to all persons of the triune God, "the same God . . . the same *Lord . . . the same Spirit." Based on the unity of the Godhead, Paul accentuates the coherence of the gifts that God distributes as a unity-in-diversity (1 Cor 12:14-26), thus leaving no room for rivalry and competition within the body of Christ.

4. Gift Vocabulary.

***4.1.* Charisma(ta).** Most discussions on the subject of the gifts of the Spirit usually associate the term "gift of the Spirit" with Paul's use of the word *charisma*. With the exception of 1 Peter 4:10, the word *charisma* occurs only in Paul's writings in the NT. It is rarely found otherwise in Greek literature. There are differing opinions on how the word is to be understood. On the one hand, it has been explained broadly in terms of a concrete expression of God's grace, that is, a variety of ways God's grace has been evidenced among his people (Käsemann). This is certainly plausible in some Pauline passages, such as Romans 5:15; 6:23; 11:29 and 1 Corinthians 1:7. However, such understanding of *charisma* fails to communicate what is distinctive about Paul's usage. On the other hand, *charisma* can be understood in its simple sense of "(gracious) gift," primarily unrelated to Paul's concept of grace but to other words that are in the semantic domain of *gift*. The verb *charizomai* means "to give freely" (Turner).

Charisma in Paul is closely linked with the Holy Spirit. Thus in 1 Corinthians 12:4 the Holy Spirit is the source of the *charismata*. However, its association with the Holy Spirit is not to be automatically assumed but to be determined by the context. An example of this is Romans 12:6, where there is no explicit connection of the Holy Spirit with *charismata*. Instead, there is the connection of *charismata* with grace. Undoubtedly, there are various aspects of the listing of the gifts in Romans 12 that resemble the list in 1 Corinthians 12 and imply the presence of the Spirit. Nevertheless, it remains unclear whether Paul intended the listing in Romans 12:6-8 to be thought of as "gifts of the Spirit" in the same way as the *charismata* in 1 Corinthians 12–14. As such, the distinction between "Spirit charismata" and other expressions of *charismata* that do not necessarily imply visibly evident Spirit activity is unnecessary (Fee, "Gifts of the Spirit"). Although Paul uses the term "spiritual gift" (in the singular) only in Romans 1:11, it is appropriate to use the term "spiritual gifts" of all the manifestations and abilities that Paul relates to the Spirit, even though the word *charisma* is not specifically used to describe them.

4.2. **Pneumatika.** This term is the plural of the adjective *pneumatikon*; literally, "the things of the Spirit" or "spiritual persons." Its occurrence twice in 1 Corinthians 12–14 (1 Cor 12:1; 14:1) in the context of Paul's discussion and its interchange with *charismata* suggest that it refers to spiritual gifts. There is considerable overlap between *charismata* and *pneumatika* in 1 Corinthians 12:1 and 1 Corinthians 14:1, thus generating a discussion on how the relationship between the two should be explained—whether they are synonymous or whether one is more comprehensive than the other. The best solution to this matter probably lies with taking seriously the root meaning of the two words. If the emphasis in the word *charisma* is on God's graciousness (including the gifts) toward his people, then the emphasis in *pneumatika* rests with the Spirit nature of the activity to which these various *charismata* bear witness. Paul would thus be referring to the same phenomena. Diverse *charismata* of the one Spirit they are indeed; here is how God is currently at work among his people in a variety of ways for the common good. The *pneumatika* are supernatural manifestations of the Holy Spirit, not natural abilities. However, Paul's evident preference of *pneumatikon* over *charismata* may be due to the occasional nature of his discussion and suggests that he was engaged in a theological critique of his audience. The latter had probably become so loaded with misleading associations. Hence Paul decided to use a different word.

4.3. **Dōrea.** This word, the term for "gift" proper, rarely occurs in Paul but does appear in Ephesians 4:7. Elsewhere in the NT *dōrea* can refer to the Spirit (see Acts 2:38; 8:20; 10:45; 11:17). Ephesians 4:7 is a transition from the trinitarian basis for unity in Ephesians 4:4-6 (one body, one Spirit, one *hope; one Lord, one *faith, one *baptism; one God) to several specific divine giftings God has given to the *church for its own health and service to the world. Since the Spirit is crucial to the church's unity (Eph 4:3-4), and since three of the ministries listed in Ephesians 4:11 also appear in the listing in 1 Corinthians 12:28, it is common to see Ephesians 4:11 as giving us yet one more list of "gifts of the Spirit," this time more specifically narrowed to ministries as such. Paul's use of *charis* here (which appears to be a close equivalent to *charismata*) and its connection with *dōrea* suggests that it is not farfetched to think that he might have considered these ministries as *charismata* in the sense that word is used in 1 Corinthians 12 or Romans 12.

5. Texts.

Due to the ad hoc nature of Paul's letters as well as the vagueness of the vocabulary Paul uses for the spiritual gifts, classifying the gifts into neat categories remains a difficult task. In order to explicate the nature of the gifts, interpreters should carefully study the discussions of the gifts in their contexts instead of superimposing an outside grid on Paul's arguments.

5.1. 1 Corinthians 12–14. Paul's discussion of the spiritual gifts in 1 Corinthians 12–14 is within the overarching discussion about *worship, which answers a question posed to Paul by the Corinthians. Paul's purpose in this section is to correct what he considers a misunderstanding of the gifts, particularly the use of *tongues, which he focuses on in 1 Corinthians 13–14. The Corinthians seemed to have placed a higher value on speaking in togues than on other gifts, seeing it as a mark of greater *spirituality (1 Cor 14:36-37). This misunderstanding resulted in both inordinate zeal for tongues and disorder in their assembly. Hence, in his effort to curb their misguided zeal Paul first argues for the necessity of diversity—if the community is truly to be "of the Spirit" (1 Cor 12:4-30; Adewuya). He then argues that no gifting counts for anything if love does not motivate (1 Cor 13:1-13), concluding that, in terms of Spirit manifestations, love demands that the Corinthians seek after intelligible utterances (1 Cor 14:1-25) and order (1 Cor 14:26-40). This is so the community can be built up (1 Cor 14:1-19, 26-33) and outsiders converted (1 Cor 14:20-25). In the process Paul has occasion to list various *charismata*, ministries and forms of *service, at seven different points in his argument (1 Cor 12:8-10, 28, 29-30; 13:1-3, 8; 14:6, 26), no two of which are alike (not even 1 Cor 12:28, 29-30); not only so, but they appear in ways that make systematizing nearly impossible.

5.1.1. 1 Corinthians 12:8-10. After speaking in general terms, Paul mentions different manifestations of the Spirit in 1 Corinthians 12:8-10. He begins by mentioning the word of *wisdom. This is the unique ability to speak forth the wisdom of God, especially in an important or difficult situation, as shown by Solomon (1 Kings 3:16-18), Jesus (Lk 20:20-26), Stephen (Acts 7), and Paul (Acts 23). This is followed by the word of *knowledge, a divine revelation of what otherwise could not have been known by mere human senses. There are biblical examples such as God's *judgment for Eli, given as a voice in the night to Samuel (1 Sam 3:13), and God's word to Peter regarding the arrival of messengers from Cornelius (Acts 10:19).

Next on the list is the gift of faith. Faith is an essential part of every Christian's life. Paul is not referring to the initial faith that is necessary for *salvation. The gift of faith is the unique ability to trust God in all circumstances, as Peter did when he walked out of the boat onto the water (Mt 14:22-33). Next is the gifts of *healing. The plural form of *gifts* may suggest that the manifestation of these gifts takes different forms at different times, depending on the particular needs. Moreover, it is to be observed that these gifts are for the benefit of the community. Next is the working of miracles, which seems to be a general term encompassing supernatural activity including healing. In most cases the Holy Spirit overrides the power of nature.

The gift of *prophecy refers both to the foretelling of the future and the forthtelling of the mind of God for a particular situation. Some Christians have defined prophecy as *preaching, but there are different words for preaching and for prophecy. Whereas preaching deals with proclamation, prophecy involves a supernatural revelation and words that are spoken under direct inspiration from God. Distinguishing between spirits or "discerning of spirits" (KJV) describes the God-given ability to determine whether a supernatural manifestation has its source in God. An example is that of Paul in Acts (Acts 16:16-18). The list continues with speaking in different kinds of tongues. This refers to a supernatural utterance in a language that was not learned by the speaker and may or may not be a language known to others. Last, Paul mentions the interpretation of tongues. This refers to an intelligible presentation of the content of what was spoken in an unknown tongue.

5.1.2. 1 Corinthians 12:27-30. Paul ends 1 Corinthians 12 with a list of some of the gifts God gives to the community. The emphasis remains the same: the need for diversity. Paul's juxtaposition of the special gifts and the various ministry functions in the church in 1 Corinthians 12 (see 1 Cor 12:8-10, 28) shows the close relationship between the two. Three observations are helpful here. First, God distributes gifts and callings according to his pleasure. In the same manner that the church does not bestow the gifts of healings, tongues, interpretation of tongues, and so on onto individuals, the church does not create apostles, prophets, *teachers, and other ministry functions.

Second, the list does not exactly match the earlier one in 1 Corinthians 12:8-10, which suggests that neither list is exhaustive. Paul discusses the ministry functions in dialogue with the existing situation at Corinth as well as in the light of the forms of *leadership that suited his own cultural context. Paul does not suggest that these offices are either the only or exact forms of leadership that are both timeless and universally normative.

Third, these verses in context press home Paul's argument in the entire chapter by way of summary. If these gifts are given generously as God wills (1 Cor 12:4-6), and if they are for the common good of the whole church (1 Cor 12:4), it is right to say that the gifts do not serve the purpose of comparison and competition among ministers for the sake of enhancing one's status. The members of Christ's body ought not to be in competition with one another to gain prestige, position, or power. Rather, they should work together for the well-being of the whole assembly. Paul does not suggest that there is any particular individual who functions in all these capacities. The gifts transcend the capacity of any individual to possess them. Significantly, these gifts are complementary. They function together within the community—the church.

In 1 Corinthians 12:28 Paul lists several gifts, starting with apostle. The list itself has several interesting features: (1) He begins with a list of persons, whom he seems to rank in the order of first, second, third. (2) With the fourth and fifth items ("miracles" and "gifts of healings") he revisits *charismata*, focusing on two from the list in 1 Corinthians 12:8-10. He starts both statements with "then," suggesting that he intended to continue the ranking. (3) He highlights the significance of the sixth and seventh items ("helpful deeds" and "acts of guidance"), which are deeds of service, in three notable ways: Paul does not mention both again in 1 Corinthians 12:29-30, nor elsewhere in the NT, and they appear to be different in kind. The list is representative of a whole range of ministries in the church, which were probably chosen for that reason. Notably, Paul does not grade the gifts or create a hierarchical structure. He simply enumerates them. Apostles are not limited to the twelve but also include Paul and others.

Paul brings his argument to a close in 1 Corinthians 12:29-30. He concludes that diversity of the gifts within the body of Christ is not to be considered strange but both acceptable and expected; it was God's plan for how the body of Christ would function. Thus, Paul's argument comes full circle (Adewuya).

5.2. Romans 12:6-8. This passage stands near the beginning of the paraenesis of this *letter. Although the gifts God gives are popularly labeled "spiritual gifts," appealing to 1 Corinthians 12–14, Paul nowhere explicitly refers to the Spirit in Romans 12. Each believer has received a gift as a gracious expression of God's blessing for the church (Rom 12:6). The concern here is the need for a sober estimate of oneself and mutuality in the community. The theme of unity in diversity runs through the section.

There are three similarities between this passage and Paul's discussion about the gifts in 1 Corinthians 12–14: (1) the analogy of the body—as one but with many parts, (2) that the members have *charismata* given to them (that this is done for the building up of the body is implied), and (3) the mention of prophecy as the first gift and teaching as the third. But after that, nothing is familiar. It is not surprising that prophecy appears at the head of Paul's list of gifts, in light of his discussion in 1 Corinthians 14. In contrast to 1 Corinthians but in keeping with the issues in the Roman church, the seven items in Romans 12 emphasize forms of service (including service itself), not miracles or verbal utterances. One item (*paraklēsis*, "exhortation," NRSV, NASB) is probably a verbal gift, but it also might be another form of serving ("encouraging," NIV). Each gift is qualified as to the manner in which the utterance/service is to be rendered ("according to the rule of faith," "with sincerity, earnestness, cheerfulness," etc.).

The most difficult item on this list is the sixth, *proistamenos*, which is quite ambiguous in Greek, meaning either "to manage/govern" or "to care for/give aid to." In 1 Thessalonians 5:12 Paul uses the word to describe those in leadership; its appearance here between "giving" and "showing *mercy" suggests that for Paul it usually carries the sense of "caring for" rather than "leading," even when leadership is in view. It is unlikely that Paul thinks of such leaders as duly elected church officials, but rather as those whose giftedness allows them to arise to the needs of a given occasion. On the whole, the list in Romans 12:6-8 expands how one is to view Paul's understanding of the plural *charismata*; but it helps very little in assessing whether Paul would also have thought of all of these as "gifts of the Spirit."

5.3. Ephesians 4:11. This list is unique in the Pauline corpus. It is clear from the previous discussions about the gifts both in 1 Corinthians and Romans that the fivefold list of gifted people whom Paul mentions here is not a complete enumeration of all the leadership roles within the church. Three ministries from 1 Corinthians 12:28 are mentioned (apostles, prophets, teachers). These are joined by evangelists and pastors; the latter probably are to be understood in close relationship with teachers. Paul emphasizes these five groups because they were foundational to the building of local churches (Eph 2:20) and played primary roles in ministering the word (Arnold, 256).

Although this list occurs again in a context of Spirit and body (Eph 4:4), these "gifts" are not referred to as *charismata*, nor are they suggested to be gifts of the Spirit. They are in fact given to the church by Christ, and they are not spoken of as gifts per se. Rather, they are people who function in these ways within the church for the singular aim of "equipping the saints," apparently so that the latter can do the "work of the ministry, for the building up of the body." The burning question in this list is whether these people are to be thought of in terms of their function or as holders of an office. In keeping with the prior lists, when ministries of these kinds are mentioned, the emphasis still seems to be on function. In any case, with this list one moves somewhat beyond Paul's own understanding of *charismata*, either as "Spirit manifestations" or as "forms of service." There is no indication that Paul ever considered an office in the church as a spiritual gift, either in terms of a *charisma* or as a special endowment of the Spirit.

6. The *Charismata*.

Despite the difficulties involved, the various items from these texts may be grouped under three major headings: Spirit manifestations within the worshiping community, deeds of service, and specific ministries. Whether or not one understands the term "gifts of the Spirit" in its narrower sense (as applying only to Spirit manifestations), the goal of all *charismata* is the building up of the community itself and individual members within the community. Furthermore, in the first two categories Paul highlights the universality of such gifting within the Spirit-filled community.

6.1. Gifts as Spirit Manifestations. Here is a certain grouping in Paul's letters with explicit and specific connection between the Spirit and *charismata*. The gifts appear chiefly to be supernatural manifestations of the Spirit within the community at worship. They can be further grouped into miracles as such and inspired utterance.

6.1.1. Miracles. Included here are three items from 1 Corinthians 12:9-10: faith, gifts of healings, and workings of miracles. The gift of faith is to be distinguished from ordinary faith, without which it is impossible to please God (Heb 11:6). The text implies a particular manifestation. The use of the plurals "gifts" and "workings" for the latter two may signify that the Spirit develops in different Christians not only the faith to pray for different kinds of sicknesses but also diverse kinds of workings for different miracle workers. These two gifts probably overlap. Such phenomena were a regular part of Paul's own ministry, as shown by 2 Corinthians 12:12 and Romans 15:18-19, and were expected within the Pauline churches, evidenced by Galatians 3:5 (Fee, "Gifts of the Spirit").

6.1.2. Inspired Utterance. Included here are the word of wisdom, the word of knowledge, prophecy, the discernments of S/spirits, tongues, and the interpretation of tongues from 1 Corinthians 12:10; teaching and revelation from 1 Corinthians 14:6; and (perhaps) exhortation from Romans 12:8—this category might also include singing from 1 Corinthians 14:15, 26 (see also Eph 5:19).

The language of "word of wisdom" and "knowledge" was prompted by the situation in Corinth. For Paul the "message of wisdom" is the preaching of the *cross (see 1 Cor 1:18–2:16; the terminology occurs nowhere else). "Knowledge," on the other hand, is closely related to "mysteries" in 1 Corinthians 13:2 and elsewhere stands close to the concept of "revelation" (1 Cor 13:8-9, 12; 14:6). Nevertheless, the placement of these gifts among the manifestations of the Spirit suggests that they include some measure of a supernatural operation of the Holy Spirit.

6.1.2.1. Glossolalia. Paul's term here refers to "different kinds of tongues." Based on the arguments in 1 Corinthians 13–14 one could draw some conclusions on how Paul understood the term. (1) It is Spirit-inspired utterance (1 Cor 12:7, 11; 14:2). It "consisted of a power of more or less ecstatic speech, in languages with which the speaker was not naturally familiar" (Gee). The speech is essentially unintelligible both to the speaker (1 Cor 14:14) and to the ungifted hearers (1 Cor 14:16), which is why it must be interpreted in the assembly. (2) The regulations for its community use in 1 Corinthians 14:27-28 make it clear that the speaker is not out of control. Rather, the speakers must speak in turn, and they must remain silent if there is no one to interpret. (3) It is speech directed primarily toward God (1 Cor 14:2, 14-15, 28). (4) As a gift for private *prayer, Paul held it in the highest regard (1 Cor 14:2, 4, 5, 15, 17-18).

The overall evidence suggests that Paul does not understand the language as earthly. Thus he thinks it unlikely that someone present might understand without interpretation. By making an analogy to earthly language in 1 Corinthians 14:10-12, he implies that tongues are not actually an earthly language (Fee, "Gifts of the Spirit").

6.1.2.2. Prophecy. The gift of prophecy is the one mentioned most often in the Pauline letters (1 Thess 5:20; 1 Cor 11:4-5; 12–14; Rom 12:6; Eph 2:20; 3:5; 4:11; 1 Tim 1:18; 4:14), implying the widest range of occurrence in the Pauline churches. Paul writes with such clear favor toward the exercise of the gift that he exhorts the believer to covet it (1 Cor 14:39) and even suggests that the whole assembly prophesy (1 Cor 14:24). Hence, although some people are called prophets, the implication of 1 Corinthians 14:24-25, 30-31 is that the gift is potentially available to all.

Paul's understanding of prophecy was shaped by the OT, in which prophets were those who spoke to God's people under the inspiration of the Spirit. In Paul's letters prophetic speech consists either of spontaneous, intelligible messages, orally delivered in the gathered assembly and intended for the edification or encouragement of the people, or of a "revelation" of some kind (Gal 2:2), which at times could expose the hearts of nonbelievers and lead them to repentance. Those who prophesied were clearly understood to be in control (see 1 Cor 14:29-33). Scriptural prophesying is more than ordinary preaching but provides a most essential balance to the didactic and logical ministry of the preacher, thus avoiding a purely and rational and intellectual line of ministry.

It is clear from 1 Thessalonians 5:21-22 and 1 Corinthians 12:10; 14:29 that prophecy must be regulated and requires discernment by the charismatic community. These texts imply that though a person may believe they are truly inspired by the Spirit, what is said may not come from the Spirit at all. The prophet may unwittingly or sometimes knowingly include their own thoughts. Therefore, the community must test all things, holding fast to the good and dispensing with every evil expression.

6.2. The Gifts in the Pauline Churches. Paul's clear and matter-of-fact discussion of the gifts in several passages, particularly in 1 Corinthians 12:7-11, is a clear indication that the gifts were manifested in the early church and that the worship of the early church was far more "charismatic" than has been true for most of the church's subsequent history. This is probably why some have concluded that the gifts have either ceased or were meant to remain in operation as long as the early Christians, particularly the Corinthians, remained immature. Moreover, it is sometimes argued that the gifts ceased once the NT was canonized. Such views miss the evidence in Paul as well as his point in 1 Corinthians 13:8-13 (see Fee 1987). Such reasoning could lead one to conclude or argue that the other Pauline churches did not celebrate the *Lord's Supper, since it is mentioned only in 1 Corinthians. That the first century has ceased does not mean that the spiritual gifts have ceased. There is considerable and clear evidence that a robust charismatic dimension of life in the Spirit was the normal experience of the Pauline churches. Paul directly addresses this dimension only twice (1 Thess 5:19-22; 1 Cor 12–14) because in these two contexts there were issues of abuse of the gifts. The case in Thessalonica is revealing, in fact, since it seems Paul is admonishing the church for downplaying the prophetic Spirit in its gatherings (Fee, "Gifts of the Spirit").

More telling is that, elsewhere in the Pauline corpus, Paul, offhandedly but firmly demonstrates that these phenomena are recent experiences. For example, in 1 Corinthians 11:2-16 Paul refers to worship as "praying and prophesying," the two significant ways of speaking to God and people in the assembly. In Galatians 3:4-5, he directs the attention of his audience to their past and current experience of the Spirit, including miracles. Also, in 1 Timothy 1:18; 4:14, Paul reminds Timothy of his experience of receiving prophetic utterances, an experience that he is to continue to relish and in light of which he is to continue to live and minister.

7. Purpose of the Gifts.

First, the gifts aid the church in carrying out the Great Commission given by Christ. Second, the gifts edify the church as a corporate body as well as its individual members. God's purpose in bestowing the gifts is that through their operation Christians might truly function as the body of Christ in the world. Paul indicates that the gifts are given to all the people of God for the benefit of all or the common good. The gifts are not to bring personal benefit, advantage, or status to the individual but advantage to the whole community. This advantage consists of building up the body of Christ into his image.

See also APOSTLE; BODY OF CHRIST; CHURCH; CHURCH STRUCTURE; CORINTHIANS, FIRST LETTER TO THE; EPHESIANS, LETTER TO THE; HEALING, ILLNESS; HOLY SPIRIT; MINISTRY; PROPHECY, PROPHESYING; ROMANS, LETTER TO THE; SIGNS, WONDERS, MIRACLES; SPIRITUALITY; TEACHING, TEACHERS; TONGUES.

BIBLIOGRAPHY. **J. A. Adewuya,** "The Spirit in 1 Corinthians," *Pneuma* 43, nos. 3-4 (2021): 485-95; **C. A. Arnold,** *Ephesians*, ZECNT (Grand Rapids, MI: Zondervan, 2010); **K. Berger,** "χάρισμα," *EDNT* 3:460-61; **A. Bittlinger,** *Gifts and Graces* (Grand Rapids, MI: Eerdmans, 1967); **T. J. Burke and K. Warrington,** *A Biblical Theology of the Holy Spirit* (Eugene, OR: Cascade, 2014); **J. D. G. Dunn,** *Jesus and the Spirit* (Philadelphia: Westminster, 1975); **G. D. Fee,** *The First Epistle to the Corinthians*, NICNT (Grand Rapids, MI: Eerdmans, 1987); idem, "Gifts of the Spirit," in *DPL*, 339-47; idem, *God's Empowering Presence: The Holy Spirit in the Letters of Paul* (Peabody, MA: Hendrickson, 1993); **R. Y. K. Fung,** "Ministry, Community, and Spiritual Gifts," *EvQ* 56 (1984): 3-14; **D. Gee,** *Concerning Spiritual Gifts* (Springfield, MO: Gospel, 1947); idem, *Spiritual Gifts in the Work of the Ministry Today* (Springfield, MO: Gospel, 1963); **M. Green,** *I Believe in the Holy Spirit*, rev. ed. (Grand Rapids, MI: Eerdmans, 2004); **E. Käsemann,** "Ministry and Community in the New Testament," in *Essays on New Testament Themes* (London: SCM Press, 1964), 63-94; **C. S. Keener,** *Gift and Giver: The Holy Spirit for Today* (Grand Rapids, MI: Baker Academics, 2001); **D. Lim,** *Spiritual Gifts: A Fresh Look* (Springfield, MO: Gospel, 1996); **J. Rea,** *The Holy Spirit in the Bible* (Lake Mary, FL: Creation House, 1990); **A. C. Thiselton,** *The Holy Spirit* (London: SPCK, 2013); **M. Turner,** *The Holy Spirit and Spiritual Gifts* (Peabody, MA: Hendrickson, 1996).

J. A. Adewuya

GLORY, GLORIFICATION

Glory and *glorify* were two of the weightiest theological terms used by Paul and other early Christians, and they remain so for Christians today. Until recently, however, scholars have paid relatively little attention to their meaning in Paul's letters. The result of this oversight is now the terms' common usage in Christian parlance without much commonality of meaning. Christians sing about, envision, and *hope for glory and their personal glorification but struggle to articulate what glory actually is. This is no wonder, considering both the lack of scholarly attention and Paul's own varied usage of the term throughout his epistles. The noun *doxa* occurs in Paul's letters in seventy-six instances, and *doxazō* in twelve instances. While primarily used in references to *God, the terms are also used vis-à-vis Jesus, believers, and objects, and they are used in contexts that speak both of the present and of the future.

1. *Glory* and *Glorification* in the Septuagint
2. *Glory* and *Glorification* in Paul's Epistles
3. Glory of God
4. Glory of Christ
5. Glory of Humanity
6. Glory of Objects

1. *Glory* and *Glorification* in the Septuagint. With the exception of Paul's application of the terms to Jesus, their usage in his letters primarily follow the same patterns as are established for the terms in the LXX. Though in nonbiblical literature *doxa* regularly meant "opinion" or "reputation," it was the chosen translation for the Hebrew term *kābôd*, which at its root means "heavy" or "weighty." *Glory* was used on rare occasion as a title for God (e.g., Ps 3:4 LXX), but more frequently it refers to his *honor, status, power, or character. This latter meaning of *glory* is consistently and evenly given to God in ascription (e.g., Josh 7:19 LXX), possessed by God (Is 24:14 LXX), manifested by God in various signs or symbols (e.g., Ex 15:7 LXX), and at times manifested in theophany (e.g., Ex 33:19 LXX). A similar story is told for the Septuagintal application of *doxa* to individual people, nations, and objects: it refers almost entirely to their honor, status, character, or wealth (e.g., Gen 45:13; Sir 45:2; Ps 8:6; Hos 9:11; 10:5).

2. *Glory* and *Glorification* in Paul's Epistles. Given Paul's dependence on the LXX, it is no wonder that his use of *glory* and *glorify* primarily follows their Septuagintal usage. Also of undoubted influence for Paul was the use of the terms in the parlance of the first-century Roman Empire, a culture built on both personal and social glory. The one main difference between the use of the terms in the LXX and in Paul's epistles is their application to the person of Jesus *Christ, the person who witnesses most directly to the glory of God in its various forms.

3. Glory of God.

3.1. Receive Praise, Adoration, Honor. Perhaps the most common and straightforward use of the term is in ascription of praise, adoration, or honor. Commonly found in doxologies (e.g., Rom 11:36; 16:27; Phil 4:20; Gal 1:5; Eph 3:21; 1 Tim 1:17) or in commands to glorify God, glory given to God is synonymous with giving God praise or adoration. An excellent example of the latter is 1 Corinthians 10:31—the life of the believer ought to bring praise, honor, or adoration to God (also Rom 4:20; 15:7; Phil 1:11; 2:11; 2 Cor 1:20; 4:15). *Glorify* is also used to indicate giving ascription or praise to God and is often overshadowed by translations of "honor" (Rom 1:21; 15:6, 9; 1 Cor 6:20; 2 Cor 9:13; Gal 1:24).

3.2. Possess Honor, Power, Magnitude. *Glory* is also used in reference to the honor, power, or majesty possessed by God rather than that which is given to God. Such glory pertains to the innate honor of God (see Rom 3:7) or the honor of God specifically associated with his sovereign rule (see 1 Thess 2:12; 1 Tim 1:11). In Ephesians 1:17, as is often the case in the LXX, *glory* is used as part of a title for God, "the Father of glory" (NRSV). Along similar lines is a phrase unique to Paul, "riches of his glory," found in Romans 9:23 and Ephesians 3:16 (NRSV; see also Phil 4:19). God's glory also serves as a synonym for the power or magnitude of God. In Romans 6:4 it is the glory of God that raised Christ from the dead (see also 2 Thess 1:9).

3.3. Presence of God. A number of Paul's references to the glory of God point to God's theophanic presence as seen in the Sinai traditions of the OT. Though potentially a reference to Jesus, the "glory of the *Lord" in 2 Corinthians 3:18 (NRSV) is likely Yahweh. Under the *ministry of the Spirit, a new *freedom is found in the presence of God, in which the believer (unlike Moses) beholds unveiled the glory of the Lord. This same visible presence of God, Paul then declares in 2 Corinthians 4:6, is revealed or, according to the NIV, "displayed" in the face of Christ. Again, Paul likely references this Sinai tradition in Romans 9:4, where the glory possessed by *Israel is actually that of the theophanic presence of God with Israel in the Sinai wilderness and then eventually in the *temple in *Jerusalem.

3.4. Difficult to Categorize. More difficult to assign meaning to are the references to the glory of God that do not naturally fall into a particular category. Such instances exist entirely in Romans and are historically and currently the foci of scholars' conversations surrounding Paul's use of *glory*. Three verses have consumed scholars' attentions: Romans 1:23; 3:23; 5:2. In Romans 1:23, Paul writes that humanity "exchanged the glory of the immortal God for images made to look like a mortal human being and birds and animals and reptiles" (NIV), and in

Romans 3:23 he writes that "all have sinned and fall short of the glory of God" (NIV). Then, in Romans 5:2 he proclaims that "we boast in the hope of the glory of God" (NIV). Three interpretive questions primarily abound: (1) Into which category of glory does each reference fall: the character, nature, or attributes of God, consisting principally in his honor, power, or magnitude, or the saving presence of God? (2) Is the glory of God to which Paul refers in each instance objective or subjective, that is, does humanity participate in or possess the glory of God to which Paul refers (e.g., see NRSV translation of Rom 5:2)? (3) If Paul does imply humanity's participation in or possession of the glory of God, does he also have *Adam and/or the *creation narrative in mind as a literary or theological background? Needless to say, the combined options are numerous, and persuasive arguments are made in favor of each one.

4. Glory of Christ.

4.1. Honor, Power, Rule. Paul's use of *glory* and *glorify* throughout his letters follows the patterns seen in the use of *doxa* and *doxazō* throughout the LXX. The key exception to this is, of course, the use of it in relationship to Jesus Christ. Yet, even here the glory ascribed to Jesus follows the same primary patterns of meaning: honor, rule, or power. In 1 Corinthians 2:8 Paul says the "rulers of this age" "crucified the Lord of glory" (NIV)—the *true* pantocrator. In 2 Corinthians 8 Paul writes that the *collection taken up for the Lord's people is ultimately for the "glory of the Lord" (2 Cor 8:19 NRSV), the honor of Christ. This same theme reappears only four verses later when Paul says the brothers, the messengers of the churches, are "the glory of Christ" (2 Cor 8:23 NRSV; see also 2 Thess 2:14). Such honor ascribed to Jesus is also found in the recurring phrase "to the praise of his glory" in Ephesians 1:12, 14 (ESV), as well as in the one doxology ascribed to Jesus, "to him be glory forever," in 2 Timothy 4:18 (NIV). Similar to Romans 6:4, where Jesus was "raised from the dead by the glory of the Father" (NRSV), in 1 Timothy 3:16 he was "taken up in glory" (NRSV).

4.2. Presence of God. Though the majority of the references to the glory of Christ regard his honor, power, or rule, 2 Corinthians 4:4 falls within Paul's commentary on the ministry of the Spirit and the presence of God revealed in the Spirit and in Christ Jesus. In 2 Corinthians 4:4 Paul writes that unbelievers are blind to the "*light of the *gospel of the glory of Christ," the one who reveals in his face the glory—the visible presence—of God (2 Cor 4:6; see also 2 Cor 3:18).

5. Glory of Humanity.

5.1. Eschatological Glory. Until recently, the glory or glorification of humanity was overshadowed by the use of the terms vis-à-vis God and Christ. The terms primarily fall into two categories: eschatological glory and present glory, with significant theological overlap between the two. The majority of the time, the glory or glorification of humanity refers to the honor, power, or rule of believers, whether present or future. Whether explicit or implied, believers' glory is a direct result of their association with Christ, that is, their participation in Christ's glory. Here Paul's anthropological notion of believers' union with Christ is fundamental to his understanding of believers' glory. This participatory connection to Christ is nowhere as clear as it is in Romans 8:17, 18, 21, where the glory the children of God will have is due to their participation in the glory of the firstborn Son as adopted children of God. Less in the limelight but no less explicit, 2 Thessalonians 2:14 speaks to this fundamental goal of *salvation for Paul: "For this purpose he called you through our proclamation of the good news, so that you may obtain the glory of our Lord Jesus Christ" (NRSV). Additionally, Paul offers Colossians 1:27: "Christ in you, the hope of glory" (NRSV).

At times Paul describes the hope of glory as an explicitly future reality. "When Christ who is your life is revealed, then you also will be revealed with him in glory" (Col 3:4 NRSV) is an excellent example. That same hope Paul describes as an "eternal weight of glory" in 2 Corinthians 4:17 (NRSV; see also 2 Tim 2:10), set to come when this temporary or momentary reality is turned into an eternal one (2 Cor 4:18). Though not as definitive, Romans 2:7, 10 likely fit this eschatological context of a future hope of glory. Additionally, while ambiguous in the text, it is highly likely that Paul intends believers' "hope of the glory of God" in Romans 5:2 (NIV) as an anticipated eschatological participation or sharing in God's glory.

5.2. Present Glory. What is perhaps most striking about Paul's references to believers' glory or glorification is that he thinks of such glory as not only a future reality but, because of his inaugurated *eschatology, combined with the reality of believers' union with Christ, also a lived reality in the present. In 2 Corinthians 3:18, perhaps the best-known passage on humanity's glory, Paul declares that the Christian is currently being transformed from one glory to another. Whatever this transformation implies, it is unequivocally a present transformation as much as it is a future hope. Additionally, while ambiguous in 1 Corinthians 2:7, Paul describes how the *wisdom of God was "decreed before the ages for our glory" (NRSV). Such glory is both future and present, and is intricately connected to the rightful rule of the crucified "Lord of glory" in 1 Corinthians 2:8. The same proleptic reality can be said for his use of glorified in Romans 8:30: "those he justified, he also glorified" (NIV)—a very present reality (see also Rom 9:23).

The most common use of present glory for believers, however, is in its connections to sociological honor—the meaning of glory commonly understood within the honor-shame society of the Roman Empire. As such, *glory* or *glorify* in such passages is often rightly translated as "honor" because it is used in conjunction with "shame" (*aischynē*; see Phil 3:19) or "dishonor" (*atimia*; see 2 Cor 6:8), or simply because the context warrants such a translation (e.g., 1 Cor. 12:26; 1 Thess 2:6, 20; Eph 3:13). In 1 Corinthians 11:7, Paul writes that man is the "glory of God" and that woman is the "glory of man" (NIV). Later, in 1 Corinthians 11:15, he reiterates that a woman's hair is her glory. Despite the many interpretive difficulties associated with these verses, the unequivocal meaning of *glory* here is sociological honor in contrast with sociological shame (see 1 Cor 11:4-6).

6. Glory of Objects.

While *glory* and *glorify* are used most often for God, Christ, and humanity, the terms are also found a significant number of times as modifiers of objects. The most significant use in this category is in 2 Corinthians 3, where Paul describes the glory of the "ministry of *death" that was also visible on the face of Moses (2 Cor 3:7 NRSV) and the surpassing glory of the "ministry of the Spirit" (2 Cor 3:8 NRSV). Paul then contrasts the glory of the "ministry of condemnation" with the surpassing glory of the "ministry of *justification" (2 Cor 3:9-10 NRSV). For the former, the glory was transitory; for the latter, the glory is permanent (2 Cor 3:11). This passage, perhaps more than any other, demonstrates the richness, diversity, and depth of meaning that comes with Paul's use of the term *glory*. A similar demonstration is found in 1 Corinthians 15:40-41, where Paul describes the varying glories of the sun, moon, and stars. While he may imply their varying levels of brightness, his use of the same term with the human *body in 1 Corinthians 15:43 in close association with honor and shame perhaps indicates a similar Roman use of the term for the heavenly bodies. The same consideration can be made for his use of *glory* in reference to the physical body of the risen Christ in Philippians 3:21. Other objects modified by glory in Paul's letters include God's *grace (Eph 1:6), believers' inheritance (Eph 1:18), God/Christ's power (Col 1:11), and the riches of the *mystery of Christ "in you" (Col 1:27). Finally, Paul glorifies his ministry in Romans 11:13 and asks that the word of the Lord be glorified in 2 Thessalonians 3:1.

See also FIRSTBORN; HONOR/SHAME; IN CHRIST; SALVATION.

BIBLIOGRAPHY. **D. L. Berry,** *Glory in Romans and the Unified Purpose of God in Redemptive History* (Eugene, OR: Wipf & Stock, 2016); **B. R. Gaventa,** "The 'Glory of God' in Paul's Letter to the Romans," in *Interpretation and the Claims of the Text: Resourcing New Testament Theology*, ed. J. A. Whitlark, B. W. Longenecker, L. Novakovic, and M. C. Parsons (Waco, TX: Baylor University Press, 2014), 29-42; **S. Grindheim,** "A Theology of Glory: Paul's Use of Δόξα Terminology in Romans," *JBL* 136, no. 2 (2017): 451-65; **H. G. Jacob,** *Conformed to the Image of His Son: Reconsidering Paul's Theology of Glory in Romans* (Downers Grove, IL: InterVarsity Press, 2018); **C. Newman,** *Paul's Glory-Christology: Tradition and Rhetoric, NovTSup* (Leiden: Brill, 1992); **T. R. Schreiner,** *Paul, Apostle of God's Glory in Christ* (Downers Grove, IL: InterVarsity Press, 2020).

H. Jacob

GLOSSOLALIA. *See* GIFTS OF THE SPIRIT; TONGUES.

GNOSIS, GNOSTICISM

Gnosticism refers to one or more religio-philosophical movements thought to be present in the early Christian centuries. The name derives from the Greek word for "*knowledge," "acquaintance," or "insight" (*gnōsis*) and was probably first used in the seventeenth century. Prior to that the NT and the church fathers spoke of "gnostics [*gnōstikoi*, knowers]," which leaves open the question of whether such Gnostics were adherents of something called Gnosticism. While it is clear that there were people called Gnostics who have left behind numerous writings, it may also be that "there was . . . no such thing as Gnosticism" (King).

1. Sources
2. Origin
3. Character
4. Significance for Paul and His Letters

1. Sources.

Prior to the mid-twentieth century, knowledge of Gnostics was limited largely to second- and third-century patristic sources such as Irenaeus and Hippolytus, who opposed them as Christian heretics. Irenaeus, for example, polemicized against Valentinus and other claimants to *gnōsis* in *Against Heresies* (ca. AD 180) and included extensive paraphrases of their works.

Until recently, only a few Gnostic works had come to light through individual manuscript finds (e.g., Books of Jeu [Bruce Codex], and the Apocryphon of John [Berlin Codex]), but the major impetus for renewed interest in Gnosticism came in 1945 with the discovery of thirteen leather-bound papyrus codices near Nag Hammadi in Upper Egypt. These contained fifty-two translations in the Coptic language and included the following:

- Allogenes the Stranger
- Gospel of Philip
- Gospel of Thomas
- Gospel of Truth (two versions)
- Hymn of the Pearl
- Plato, *Republic*
- Secret Book (Apocryphon) of John (three versions)
- Three Forms of First Thought (Trimorphic Protennoia)
- Three Steles of Seth
- Thunder: Perfect Mind

As can be seen from the inclusion of Plato's *Republic*, one cannot simply assume that each document testifies to Gnosticism. Rather, each must be examined individually. There is considerable ongoing debate regarding the Gnostic provenance of given treatises depending on how one defines Gnosticism.

2. Origin.

Determining the beginnings of Gnosticism is tied necessarily to the disputed question of the nature of the movement. As noted, some scholars hesitate to use the word *Gnosticism* for a coherent religion, in which case there would be no origin per se. Michael Williams and Karen King argue there never was such a clearly identifiable social entity, no distinct religion called Gnosticism with its own philosophy/theology, meetings, leadership structure, and so on. The elements one can identify—teachers such as Basilides and Valentinus, an emphasis on *salvation through gnosis, cosmic dualism, and so on—were trends throughout the early Christian centuries that could attach themselves to Christianity, Judaism, and other religio-philosophical viewpoints. Gnostics "were not adherents of a clearly discernible gnostic religion, characterized by a coherent set of ideas and rituals and practised in an identifiable social group, but they were people with a distinct gnostic mentality, a gnostic frame of mind, which could manifest itself in various religious contexts"; "the gnostic mood was in the air" (van den Broek, 8, 226).

Even for those presuming a coherent Gnostic religion, the origins remain disputed. Richard Reitzenstein, Rudolf Bultmann, and Kurt Rudolph (the *religionsgeschichtliche* school) postulated a pre-Christian Gnostic religion based especially on late Mandaean manuscripts. Others, due to the patristic perception that this was a Christian heresy, sought its origins in Gnostic deviations from Christian orthodoxy (Adolf von Harnack, Simone Pétrement). Still others, noting the frequent speculation regarding Genesis and *creation, posited an origin in Hellenistic Jewish circles (Birger Pearson, Henry Green).

3. Character.

Since many scholars accept the reality of Gnosticism in the early centuries, and since readers will encounter resources that speak of it, a brief description will prove helpful. The following beliefs and myths have been thought characteristic of Gnosticism. If there was no such thing, the following ideas will, nevertheless, have been influential to a greater or lesser extent in many gnostically oriented groups.

3.1. ***Dualism and Demiurge.*** The visible world is evil, "a kingdom of evil and darkness." For this reason, *God cannot be too closely connected with it. Thus, a series of emanations from God leads ultimately to a demiurge (Plato's "craftsman"), an inferior semidivine entity entangled with evil, who created the visible, evil world and material human beings. This demiurge is the OT Yahweh, the creator god. The ultimate God is unknown and inconceivable, utterly remote in the *plērōma* (*fullness).

3.2. ***Salvation.*** Sparks of the divine fell to earth, where they became trapped in some material human beings (the elect), who, however, remain ignorant of this reality. Through revelation these elect can be awakened to their true nature and destiny. In some forms of gnostic mythology this revelation comes through a Revealer/Redeemer. Through this *gnōsis* the inner divine spark is released from the entrapment in ignorant matter and bound for reunion with God. These are gnostics, knowers of the *truth of their origins. "If one has knowledge, he is from above" and "knows where he comes from and where he is going" (Gospel of Truth 22, trans. Robinson and Smith).

3.3. Christology. Where a *Christ figure appears, he is not to be identified with the material Jesus of Nazareth. Rather, as in some docetic Christologies, this immaterial Christ indwelt the human Jesus and departed at (before) the crucifixion.

3.4. Ethics. The antimaterial tendency led in most cases to asceticism, avoidance of material entanglements and pleasures. In some cases, at least according to the patristic sources, it may have led in the opposite direction, to licentiousness, since the already-redeemed elect could not be affected by anything in the material realm. *Women are sometimes portrayed as playing prominent *teaching and *leadership roles. Nevertheless, some texts hint that the female as such would need to be transformed into male for the eschaton.

3.5. Types. The patristic opponents of Gnostic trends mentioned numerous teachers and movements. These included Simon (tied to Simon the magician in Acts 8:9), Basilides, and Valentinus, as well as Sethian and Barbelo Gnostics. Although now disputed, a number of other early teachers and movements were at one time thought to express Gnosticism: Marcion, Gospel of Thomas, Mandaeans, and the Hermetic writings.

4. Significance for Paul and His Letters. Pauline interpreters who assumed a pre-Christian or some very early form of Christian Gnosticism (proto- or incipient Gnosticism) found evidence of its influence in Paul's letters. The First Letter to Timothy warns against "what is falsely called *gnōseōs*" (1 Tim 6:20). The *apostle opposes in 1 Corinthians some who considered themselves "spiritual [*pneumatikos*]" versus "natural [*psychikos*]" (1 Cor 1–4), rejected *marriage (1 Cor 7), possessed *gnōsis* (1 Cor 8), and viewed themselves as already raised to new life, not needing a physical *resurrection (1 Cor 15) (see esp. Schmithals). The motif of a descending/ascending redeemer (Phil 2) was thought to reflect a Gnostic redeemer myth. Thus, both Paul's language and the arguments of his letters were thought to reflect the influence of Gnosticism (as also in other NT documents, e.g., Gospel of John; 1 John).

Other NT interpreters, however, see little need to assume Gnosticism lurking behind such texts. For such interpreters the "dividing wall" (NRSV) of Ephesians 2:14 refers more reasonably to the curtain in the Jewish temple than to a gnostic myth, and references to people who are mature or perfect (e.g., 1 Cor 2:6) sound as much like the Dead Sea Scrolls or Philo than later Gnostic systems, to take only two examples. Not only is the assumption of Gnostic religion questionable for this early period, but Paul's statements can be explained equally well in light of Hellenistic Judaism and Greco-Roman *philosophy, which were well-versed in discussions of knowledge, *spirituality, dualism, asceticism, and so on (e.g., Richard Horsley, Robert Wilson, Bruce Winter, Edwin Yamauchi).

It should, nevertheless, be allowed that there was at least a growing wave of interest around Paul's time in *gnōsis*-related ideas even if he was not responding to Gnosticism per se. Such interest may have played some role in prompting Paul to comment on things such as knowledge, spirit versus *flesh, heavenly powers, and the necessity of *suffering. It was thus not by chance that Paul was a favorite author of second-century Gnostics (Pagels).

See also ELECTION AND PREDESTINATION; FLESH; HELLENISM, ROMAN; LIGHT AND DARKNESS; PHILOSOPHY; RELIGIONS, GRECO-ROMAN.

BIBLIOGRAPHY. **R. van den Broek,** *Gnostic Religion in Antiquity* (New York: Cambridge University Press, 2013); **H. A. Green,** *The Economic and Social Origins of Gnosticism,* SBLDS 77 (Atlanta: Scholars Press, 1985); **H. Jonas,** *The Gnostic Religion: The Message of the Alien God and the Beginnings of Christianity,* 3rd ed. (Boston: Beacon, 2001); **K. L. King,** *What Is Gnosticism?* (Cambridge, MA: Belknap, 2003); **B. Layton,** *The Gnostic Scriptures: A New Translation with Annotations and Introductions* (New York: Doubleday, 1995); **N. D. Lewis,** *Introduction to Gnosticism: Ancient Voices, Christian Worlds* (New York: Oxford University Press, 2013); **E. H. Pagels,** *The Gnostic Paul: Gnostic Exegesis of the Pauline Letters* (New York: Continuum, 1992); **S. Pétrement,** *A Separate God: The Christian Origins of Gnosticism* (San Francisco: Harper, 1990); **J. M. Robinson and R. Smith,** eds., *The Nag Hammadi Library in English* (Leiden: Brill, 1996); **K. Rudolph,** *Gnosis: The Nature and History of Gnosticism* (San Francisco: Harper & Row, 1983); **W. Schmithals,** *Gnosticism in Corinth: An Investigation of the Letters to the Corinthians* (Nashville: Abingdon, 1971); **M. A. Williams,** *Rethinking "Gnosticism": An Argument for Dismantling a Dubious Category* (Princeton, NJ: Princeton University Press, 1999).

K. L. Yinger

GNOSTIC PAUL. *See* APOCRYPHAL PAULINE LITERATURE; GNOSIS, GNOSTICISM; OPPONENTS OF PAUL.

GOD

Owing to the radically Christocentric themes of Paul's *letters, themes that have dominated most readers' attention, the character and activity of God has been neglected as a topic of study in its own right. NT scholar Nils Dahl wrote in 1975 of God as "the neglected factor in New Testament theology" (153). Although some of that neglect has been remedied in the intervening years (Flebbe; Hurtado), it remains the case that studies of Paul continue to prioritize other subjects, and this despite the fact that Paul's letters mention God 548 times.

This neglect of attention to God specifically is partly the result of the repeated claim that Paul does not say anything original about God. As one influential scholar concludes: "From [Paul] we learn nothing new or remarkable about God. God is a God of wrath and mercy, who seeks to save rather than to condemn, but rejection of whom leads to death. One could, to be sure, list further statements made by Paul about God, but it is clear that Paul did not spend his time reflecting on the nature of the deity" (Sanders, 509). On this widespread view, Paul simply carries forward his ancestral Jewish monotheism without making any major revisions to his pre-Christian understanding. Another scholar refers to Paul's understanding of God as "all too axiomatic" (Dunn, 28), suggesting that God is largely hidden in the background of Paul's discussions of other topics, and thus readers must consciously focus attention where Paul does not if God's centrality is to be grasped.

However, this perspective has been challenged on the grounds that when Paul treats topics that are supposedly other than *theo*logical, in the proper sense, such as *justification or *resurrection, he is describing divine *actions*, which thus implies an understanding of the divine *agent* who is their author, which is in turn to say that such "nontheological" Pauline topics turn out to be in the end properly theological: "The deity and identity of God are bound up with . . . particular divine actions. . . . For Paul, the question who God is can best be answered by reference to what God does" (Watson 2000, 104-5). Thus, to grasp Paul's teaching about God in full, one must consider the range of divine actions Paul attributes to God: for example, God's electing, predestining, and calling (Rom 8:30); God's presence in weakness and *suffering (2 Cor 4:7); God's justifying (Rom 3:21-26); God's revelation of *wrath and *judgment (Rom 1:18; 2:6-11); God's faithfulness (1 Cor 1:9; 1 Thess 5:24); God's raising to new life (1 Cor 6:14); and, centrally, God's *love revealed in Jesus *Christ and the Spirit of Christ (Rom 5:5, 8).

Paul does not retain his pre-Christian understanding of God unaltered; what Paul finds disclosed in the events concerning Jesus and the Spirit is a new, definitive understanding of God, albeit one that (Paul believed) maintained *faith with Israel's *knowledge of God as the one, supreme Creator and ruler of all. For Paul, "'God' in its fullest sense means the one whose identity is known by speaking together of the Father, the Son, and the Holy Spirit" (Rowe 2016, 91). This article will treat several themes as especially indicative of Paul's central concerns.

1. God as One
2. God as "Other"
3. God as Creator
4. God as Promise Maker and Keeper
5. God as Triune
6. Summary and Conclusion

1. God as One.

Paul's letters carry forward the conviction of Second Temple Judaism that God is one, meaning not simply that God is self-consistent but that God exists over against all reality as the Creator and judge of all (see section 3). As a Jew growing up in the Diaspora (see Acts 22:3), Paul would probably have recited Deuteronomy 6:4, known as the Shema, twice daily: "Hear, O Israel, the LORD our God, the LORD is one" (LXX; or, "the Lord our God is one Lord"). He alludes to this passage in 1 Corinthians 8:6, where he includes Jesus Christ in it (on the meaning of this inclusion, see section 5). In Romans 3:30, Paul makes God's oneness the basis for his claim that Jew and *Gentile alike will be declared righteous on the same basis, that is, faith (Hays, 69-70). Similarly, in the earlier letter to the Galatians, Paul argues that Moses had to mediate between *Israel and the one God, probably thinking of Israel's failure to uphold the ethical counterpart to God's oneness, which is exclusive fidelity ("love," Deut 6:5); Israel broke faith through their making of an idolatrous golden calf, an episode Paul alludes to both in Romans 1:23 and 2 Corinthians 3. In Galatians 3:20, Paul takes for granted that God is one and argues from that basis, as in Romans 3:30.

The later pastoral letter of 1 Timothy continues this emphasis: "there is one God; there is also one mediator between God and humankind" (1 Tim 2:5 NRSV). The same correlation between God's oneness and the unity of God's people can be found in Ephesians: "There is one *body and one Spirit, just as you were called to the one *hope of your calling, one *Lord, one faith, one *baptism, one God and Father of all, who is above all and through all and in all" (Eph 4:4-6 NRSV). As these pastoral texts focused on the church's communal life show, for Paul, monotheism is not a philosophical abstraction.

One can glimpse the congruence between God's oneness and the imperative of pursuing social unity in 1 Corinthians 8 (see section 5). Paul argues there, on the basis of some of the Corinthians' knowledge that there really is only one God, that those believers should take care not to cause those with weak consciences to stumble in their faith (1 Cor 8:7-13). God's oneness carried social and ethical implications for Paul's churches.

There has been much scholarly discussion about whether Paul's monotheism (and that of the Jewish traditions to which he is heir) is as strictly ontological or as philosophical as some later definitions (Fredriksen). Many have pointed out that Paul's cosmos is crammed with other deities: he affirms that "there are many gods and many lords," though he does qualify them as "so-called" (*legomenoi*, 1 Cor 8:5); and he refers to a nefarious entity as "the god of this world" (2 Cor 4:4 NRSV). Statements such as these, along with others from earlier in Israel's history (e.g., Ps 82:1), have caused some scholars to deny that Judaism at the time of Paul or Paul himself thought in terms of an ontological monotheism, whereby only one God may be said to exist (as opposed to something like henotheism or monolatry—supreme adherence to one God in devotion, without necessarily denying the existence of other deities).

Yet Paul and the Pauline *tradition do make use of ontological language and categories, as does Second Temple Jewish literature. To the Galatians Paul writes, "Formerly, when you did not know God, you were enslaved to beings that by nature [*physei*] are not gods" (Gal 4:8 NRSV). And in his first letter to the Thessalonians, perhaps the earliest extant piece of Pauline correspondence, he describes their conversion as a turning "to God from idols, to serve the living and true God" (1 Thess 1:9 NRSV modified). This appellation echoes the strong monotheistic affirmations of Deutero-Isaiah (Is 40:18-31; 41:21-29; 43:10-13; 44:6-20; 45:5-25; 46:1-11), which suggests that Paul is working within a polytheistic framework of thought in order precisely to undermine it: "This theology is driving an ontological division through the midst of the old category of 'gods' such that YHWH appears in a class of his own" (Bauckham, 71).

2. God as "Other."

In order to speak about God's oneness in Paul's letters, it seems necessary to underscore God's radical difference from the created realm (see section 3). Despite its unpopularity in much scholarly literature, the claim that Paul stands downstream of Greek notions of divine transcendence, immutability, eternity, and the like is increasingly recognized.

In the first place, the world of Paul's Judaism was already thoroughly intertwined with the surrounding Hellenistic environment. Paul's younger Jewish contemporary Josephus, for example, speaks in this way about the stricture in Israel's Scriptures against making images of God (see Ex 20:4-6):

> [Moses] represented [God] as one, uncreated and immutable to all eternity; in beauty surpassing all mortal thought, made known to us by his power, although the nature of his real being surpasses knowledge. . . . By his works and bounties he is plainly seen, indeed more manifest than aught else; but his form and magnitude surpass our powers of description. No materials, however costly, are fit to make an image of him; no art has skill to perceive and represent it. The like of him we have never seen, we do not imagine, and it is impious to conjecture. (Josephus, *Ag. Ap.* 2.167, 190-191 [trans. LCL])

Here is a thoroughly Hellenized description of Israel's God, offered as an interpretation of Israel's Scripture. The supposed gulf that separates Jewish "historicized" God-talk and the more "essentialized" Hellenistic God-talk is not present here.

Paul likewise portrays God as transcending creaturely limitations at key junctures in his letters, albeit more glancingly. In Romans he speaks of God's "eternal power and divine nature" being "invisible" and yet discernible through *creation (Rom 1:20; see below). Immediately following this, he uses "the immortal God" as a divine title (Rom 1:23). First Timothy exhibits the same portrait in doxological mode: "To the King of the ages, immortal, invisible, the only God, be honor and *glory for ever and ever. Amen" (1 Tim 1:17 NRSV). Further in the same letter, "It is he alone who has immortality and dwells in unapproachable light, whom no one has ever seen or can see; to him be honor and eternal dominion. Amen" (1 Tim 6:16 NRSV). This echoes and extends the paean to divine *wisdom and transcendence in the undisputed letter to the Romans: "O the depth of the riches and wisdom and knowledge of God! How unsearchable are his judgments and how inscrutable his ways! 'For who has known the mind of the Lord? Or who has been his counselor?' 'Or who has given a gift to him, to receive a gift in return?' For from him and through him and to him are all things. To him be the glory forever. Amen" (Rom 11:33-36 NRSV). The account of Paul's *preaching in Acts 17:24-25 might not simply be a Lukan invention but may well be true to the preaching of the historical Paul: "The God who made the world and everything in it, he who is Lord of heaven and earth, does not live in shrines made by human hands, nor is he served by human hands, as though he needed anything, since he himself gives to all mortals life and breath and all things" (NRSV).

One systematic theologian argues that the wider context of Romans 9–11, in which Paul wrestles through the unbelief of his fellow Jews in Jesus as Messiah, implies a strong understanding of divine transcendence, insofar as God is able to direct history without overwhelming the existence of human choices:

> In God's electing agency with creatures, creatures retain their properties and natures undiminished. The calling and election of Israel, the calling and incorporation of Gentiles, are fully historical, contingent events. To be in the presence of God's mighty working is to encounter history unfolding in its own character: it could have been otherwise. In just this way, God rules, redeems and enters his cosmos. (Sonderegger, 482)

In this way it is Paul's robust notion of divine sovereignty that leads to the conclusion that it must not simply be another, stronger agency jostling alongside that of humans; rather, it must be an agency of a different kind altogether, able to work compatibly with that of humans without evacuating the latter of all meaning.

This understanding of divine sovereignty and human *freedom not only is present in Romans 9–11 but reappears throughout the Pauline corpus. When Paul describes the Thessalonians' conversion a second time, he writes: "We also constantly give thanks to God for this, that when you received the word of God that you heard from us, you accepted it not as a human word but as what it really is, God's word, which is also at work in you believers" (1 Thess 2:13 NRSV). Here Paul uses a "not . . . but" idiom to express a "not only . . . but also" construal of the intertwining of divine and human action: "The nature of his human words is so constituted by God that their full reality is not adequately rendered by an account which does not simultaneously depict the divine as well as the human" (Moberly, 3; see Gal 2:20; 1 Cor 15:10). This implies that Paul operates with an understanding of divine life and action that does not displace creaturely means but works in and through them, which in turn suggests the otherness of God from creation. Putting the point the other way around, that Paul is able to discern divine action within the creaturely realities of decision, speech, and activity suggests an understanding of God in which God's immanence within creation must be of a categorically different sort from the intimacy of one creature to another.

3. God as Creator.

For Paul, God is the source of the cosmos, including the life of human beings. Although there are clear indications of this conviction in the undisputed letters (see especially Rom 4:17, where God is described as the one who "calls into existence things that do not exist" [NRSV], and 1 Cor 11:7, which alludes to Gen 1:27), this thought is most fully thematized in the disputed letters of Colossians, Ephesians, and 1 Timothy. Ephesians 3:9 refers simply to God "who created all things," as 1 Corinthians earlier said that "all things come from God" (1 Cor 11:12 NRSV). Presupposed in this is the affirmation of creation's goodness (1 Tim 4:4), though Paul considers creation to have been "subjected to futility" (Rom 8:20 NRSV) on account of human *sin (Rom 5:12-14). Most strikingly, the letter to the Colossians makes Jesus Christ the invisible God's agent of creation: "In [Christ] all things in heaven and on earth were created, things visible and invisible, whether thrones or dominions or rulers or powers—all things have been created through him and for him. He himself is before all things, and in him all things hold together" (Col 1:16-17). This is a more developed statement of a view that is present already in the undisputed 1 Corinthians (see section 5), in which Jesus Christ is ranked alongside God "the Father" as the source and mediator of creation: "For us there is one God, the Father, from whom are all things and for whom we exist, and one Lord, Jesus Christ, through whom are all things and through whom we exist" (1 Cor 8:6 NRSV).

God's identity as Creator is expanded to encompass his work of *new* creation, as indicated in 2 Corinthians 5:17; Galatians 6:15; and more allusively elsewhere (see, e.g., Rom 7:4-6; Gal 2:19-20; cf. Eph 4:22-24).

Along with an understanding of God as Creator goes Paul's understanding of God's governance and providence over history. Not only in Romans 9–11, where Paul unfolds his most sweeping understanding of God's purposes in hardening and *election, do readers find a notion of God guiding history toward a determined end. This thought also appears in contexts of comfort and exhortation, in which Paul frames God's ongoing sustenance of his creation as a reason to be confident that even difficult or terrible circumstances can be turned to the benefit of human beings (see, e.g., Rom 8:28-29; 15:30-32; 1 Cor 3:21-23; 10:6; 16:7; Phil 2:12-13; see also the *peristaseis kataloge* in 1 Cor 15:30-32; 2 Cor 4:7-15; 6:4-10; 11:21-29, which evoke God's providential care in the midst of affliction).

4. God as Promise Maker and Keeper.

One of the chief ways in which Paul identifies God, however, is by carrying forward the Jewish affirmation of Israel's election. While God is the universal Lord and source of all creation, Paul consistently identifies God in terms of God's unique relationship with a particular people, the family of *Abraham. Paul affirms that the Jews, the people of Israel, are the recipients of special divine revelation: "The Jews were entrusted with the oracles of God" (Rom 3:2 NRSV). More than that, to the Jews "belong the *adoption, the glory, the covenants, the giving of the *law, the *worship, and the promises; to them belong the patriarchs, and from them"—Paul says climactically—"according to the *flesh, comes the Messiah, who is over all, God blessed forever" (Rom 9:4-5 NRSV; it continues to be debated whether Paul intends *theos* here to be applied to Christ; for arguments in the affirmative, see Jewett, 568). God has chosen Israel to be the bearer of his word and to be the object of his unique commitment.

Paul treats the story of Israel's election in ways that many of his fellow Jewish contemporaries would recognize, though his reworking of that story would be surprising and scandalous to many of those same contemporaries (see 1 Cor 1:23). He traces a line of descent from God's promise to Abraham (Rom 4:13; Gal 3:16-18) through Isaac, the son of Abraham born to Sarah (Rom 9:7, 9), through Jacob, rather than Esau (Rom 9:10-13). He affirms that the presently nonbelieving Jews for whom he is in anguish owing to their unbelief are the recipients of the irrevocable gifts and *calling of God (Rom 11:28-29).

Despite many popular claims to the contrary, Paul does not usually speak of Israel's election and status before God with the language of "*covenant" (Watson 2013), preferring instead the language of "promise," which becomes important in the face of Israel's present unbelief insofar as the promise gestures toward a future in which God will act to reverse Israel's current condition and bring Israel to eschatological *salvation (Rom 11:25-32). About the promise of land given to Abraham (Gen 12:7), Paul appears to expand its reach, affirming that God in fact pledged "the world" would be Abraham and his descendants' inheritance (Rom 4:13).

Insofar as Paul makes use of affirmations about God's power and *mercy that he shares with Jews who do not share his faith in Jesus as Messiah, he extends and reshapes those affirmations in light of his convictions about how God has acted in Christ. So, while he borrows classic, liturgically inflected epithets for God such as "who gives life to the dead and calls into existence the things that do not exist" (Rom 4:17 NRSV), he concretizes those epithets with others that derive their uniqueness of what God has done in Christ. Now, in light of the Christ-event, God is known as the one who "justifies the ungodly" (something forbidden in Israel's Scripture; see Prov 17:15) and the one "who raised Jesus our Lord from the dead" (Rom 4:24 NRSV). In this way, Israel's faith is not overturned but reimagined, and it is Paul's confidence about the character of God disclosed in Christ that gives him confidence in Israel's final salvation, rather than the reverse: "All Israel will be saved because, being the God who rectifies the ungodly, God is also the one whose capacity to show mercy is more powerful than the capacity of human beings to be disobedient (Rom 11:30-31)" (Martyn, "Romans as One," 45).

5. God as Triune.

This christological shaping of Paul's theological formulations has led many scholars to speak of Paul's making a modification to his inherited Jewish monotheism: hence, "christological monotheism" (Wright, 99; Bauckham, x). The claim is that rather than portraying Jesus as an exalted mediator, who remains subservient in terms of his status as a creature to the one God, Paul has "included" Jesus within the unique divine identity by ascribing to him attributes and activities that are the exclusive prerogative of God in Israel's Scripture and Second Temple Jewish literature, thus reshaping his understanding of "God" at the most fundamental level. Richard Bauckham, in particular, intends this way of putting it as an alternative to patristic trinitarian language of "person" (*hypostasis*) and "being" (*ousia*), which are not found in Paul (see 5.6 below).

Other scholars have been readier to speak of Paul as a trinitarian, while honoring the linguistic and conceptual distance of Paul from the later fourth-century conciliar debates (Fee; Watson 2000; Rosner; Fowl). Rowe, who speaks of Paul as having a "trinitarian" understanding of God, emphasizes that Bauckham's way of framing matters is one-sided: it is not just that Paul identifies Jesus and the Spirit with God in an ascending fashion; Paul also attends, in his own first-century idiom, to the question of what it means to say that God—"the Father"—identifies himself, in a descending self-revelation, with Jesus and the Spirit. Not adoption or annexation but sending is how Paul understands Jesus and the Spirit's relation to God (Rowe 2000, 169-73).

5.1. Jesus Identified with God. One of the primary places to see Paul ascribing to Jesus names and acts that in Israel's Scripture and in first-century Judaism served to demarcate "God" over against all that is "not-God" is 1 Corinthians 8:6: "For us there is one God, the Father, from whom are all things and for whom we exist, and one Lord, Jesus Christ, through whom are all things and through whom we exist" (NRSV).

Several of the key terms here are taken from the LXX version of Deuteronomy 6:4, the Shema, discussed above: *one*, *God*, and *Lord*. "Lord" translates the Greek *kyrios*, which is the LXX translators' reverential substitute for the divine *name given in the Hebrew Bible as YHWH, the so-called Tetragrammaton. By the time of Paul, Jews would not pronounce the divine name, except for the high priest, once a year, on Yom Kippur, the Day of Atonement. Readers would substitute the Hebrew word *ʾadōnāy*, which is rendered in Greek as *kyrios*. Thus, "Lord" is, strictly speaking, not a title, as "God" is. "Lord" is an acknowledgment of the divine name, a placeholder that points to it without translating or transliterating it.

What makes Paul's use of the scriptural text unique is its apportioning these elements, all of which refer the same agent in their LXX context, the one God of Israel, to two different named figures—"one God," designated as "the Father," and Jesus Christ, designated as "one Lord." It is as though Paul has tweezed apart the Deuteronomy text and folded Jesus into the preexisting scriptural affirmation of God's oneness. Most strikingly, Paul assigns *kyrios*, the substitute for the divine name, to Jesus. This is not to say that Paul adds Jesus on to the monotheistic text, including him by attaching him to God's retinue in some subordinate mode. Rather, he apportions elements of the Deuteronomy precursor text to the one he calls "the Father," and he apportions other elements—also used to underscore God's *identity as one—to the one he calls "Jesus Christ." Paul is offering a Christian interpretation of what the Deuteronomy text affirms. To rightly identify the God to whom Deuteronomy 6:4 refers requires acknowledgment of both "God the Father" and "Jesus Christ"; where Deuteronomy 6:4 affirms, "The Lord our God is one," Christians are to understand "the Lord our God" as inclusive of both "God the Father" and the "Lord Jesus Christ."

As part of his interpretation of the Shema, Paul includes another monotheistic formula whose original form probably resembled Romans 11:36: "from him and through him and to him are all things" (NRSV). In its original form, the object of all the prepositions would have been the same figure: God. The acts of creation and eschatological consummation that this formula indicates are activities used in Scripture and Jewish texts to distinguish God as in a class by himself (e.g., in Is 40:26, 28; 42:5; 44:24; 45:12, 18, 22-23; Neh 9:6; Hos 13:4 LXX; 2 Macc 1:24; Sir 43:33; Sib. Or. 3.20-35; 4 Ezra 6.6). In Paul's adaptation of it, two of the prepositions—*from* and *to*—continue to take "God," now specified as "the Father," for their object, while the third of the prepositions—*through*—now takes the "one Lord Jesus Christ" for its object. In the same way that Paul apportioned the Shema's "one" to both God and Jesus, he now does the same with the prepositional phrases of a different monotheistic formula, in such a way that the one God whose oneness the formula safeguards is now interpreted as including both "the Father" and "Jesus Christ." The formula on which Paul draws would have originally served to signal God's uniqueness—that all of creation is from, through, and for him—but it now functions in Paul's handling to emphasize the uniqueness of God *and* Jesus together over against the "many gods" and "many lords" in 1 Corinthians 8:4-5. The "one Lord Jesus Christ" is not thereby absorbed into "God" in such a way that he ceases to remain distinct from "the Father." The identities of God and Jesus are not blurred, even as *God* must now be understood as inclusive of both "the Father" and "Jesus Christ," without infringing on God's oneness.

A similar pattern can be traced in several other texts throughout the Pauline corpus, and very similar analysis could be offered (see 2 Cor 4:3-6; Gal 4:1-11; Col 1:15-17).

5.2. Jesus as Preexistent with God. There are related passages in Paul in which Jesus is portrayed as, in a sense that Paul does not develop, preexistent with "God" or "the Father." This is probably implied in the affirmation that God sent his Son. Although the language of Jesus' sonship is taken chiefly from *son* being first a designation for the people of Israel (Ex 4:21-23) and then being concentrated on the anointed king or Messiah of Israel (Ps 2:7), thus not implying anything about Jesus' divine identity by itself, Paul apparently identifies Jesus as "son" in a pretemporal way too (Rom 8:3; 1 Cor 10:1-4; 2 Cor 8:9; Gal 4:4; see also 1 Tim 3:16). This thus implies that God did not become "Father" at the resurrection (as might be inferred from Rom 1:4, though the use of "son" in Rom 1:3 would tell against that inference) but has always been Father and Son.

5.3. The Spirit Identified with God. A similar movement of thought can be seen in 2 Corinthians 3, in which Paul offers a kind of midrash or figural interpretation of the pentateuchal account of Moses meeting with the Lord of Israel in a tent and veiling his face afterward when he would speak to the people (Ex 34:29-35). Paul reads Moses as a symbol of the law. Negatively, just as Moses experienced the glory of God in such a way that his face reflected that glory and thus needed to be veiled to protect the people, so the law, Paul says, is also veiled when Paul's contemporaries hear it read, insofar as they are kept from seeing the glory of God in Jesus Christ, which now eclipses the lesser glory of the law (2 Cor 3:7-18). Positively, Paul reads Moses as a figure for the person who, in Paul's present, turns in faith to Jesus and encounters the glory of God (2 Cor 3:18; 4:6). That person, like Moses, beholds the glory of God in "the Lord who is the Spirit" (2 Cor 3:18).

Interpreters have differed on the meaning of Paul's affirmation here and in the previous verse: "the Lord is the Spirit" (2 Cor 3:17). Does Paul mean to collapse the "persons" of Jesus and the Spirit ontologically, so that they are in some way one, not two, persons, as in a modalist understanding? This has sometimes been described as a primitive form of "Spirit Christology." Or does Paul mean to continue glossing the exodus story, saying that, in his reading, the Lord whom his Moses-like hearers presently turn to and encounter in the Corinthian *church is the Spirit, the one who mediates the presence of the risen Jesus to them in their assembly? This latter interpretation should be preferred, as is captured in the REB translation: "Now the Lord of whom [Exodus] speaks is the Spirit." Just as Jesus is the bearer of the reverential substitute for the divine name "Lord" in 1 Corinthians 8:6, so here the Spirit bears the same name. The Spirit is thereby identified with God: to ask after the identity of Israel's "Lord," one must say that he is the Spirit, just as he is Jesus.

5.4. God Identified with Jesus and the Spirit. Philippians 2:6-11 may have its origin in liturgical, hymnic traditions before Paul, but if so, Paul has added his distinctive touches and made the theology of the *hymn his own. The passage begins with a description of Christ Jesus being in the form of God. Rather than considering his preexistent equality with God as something to be used to his own advantage, he interpreted that equality in his human life of self-emptying. That humiliation is spelled out as Jesus' taking the form of a *slave, becoming human, and subjecting himself to the horror of *death on a *cross (see Gal 2:20). At this point in the Philippians text, the focus shifts from Jesus' action to God's. In Philippians 2:9, God acts to exalt Jesus after his death, bestowing on him "the name that is above every name." There follows an allusion to the eschatologically monotheistic passage Isaiah 45:23, which pictures the time at the consummation of history when every knee will bend and every mouth confess the sovereignty of Israel's one God. Paul borrows the very wording of the text in its LXX translation, but rather than apply it to "God" (Phil 2:9), he interprets the knee bending and mouth confessing as being directed to Jesus as "Lord" (*kyrios*). This designation "Lord" in Philippians 2:11 must be the "name above all names" mentioned in Philippians 2:9 (it is hard to see how, within the Jewish tradition, it could be anything else). In giving this name to Jesus, God not only exalts and honors Jesus but also identifies himself by and with that exaltation, marking out Jesus as now essential to the identity of the one Lord of Israel.

A similarly "from above," vertical movement can be seen Romans 8:9-11, which has often been described as one of the densest, richest trinitarian passages in the entire NT. It features three named "persons": Jesus, the one who raised Jesus, and the Spirit of the one who raised Jesus. But there is still further complexity insofar as the Spirit is described as "the Spirit of God," "the Spirit of Christ," and even "Christ in you." There is both identification between the persons and differentiation. Some kind of ordering appears to be in view, insofar as "God" seems to direct or shape the actions of Jesus and the Spirit, and yet at the same time Jesus and the Spirit act in ways that Scripture and the Jewish tradition reserve for God alone (i.e., giving life). More specifically, God, here the one known elsewhere as "the Father," acts to guarantee believers' resurrection by raising Jesus from the dead through the power of the Spirit. This saving action is "from above," with God marking out his own identity through what takes place with Jesus and their Spirit: "God's identity is here given by his having raised Jesus from the dead. . . . God has now identified himself by his act in Jesus Christ, making that act, indeed, the primal mark of his identity" (Martyn, *Galatians*, 85).

5.5. Trinitarian or Triadic Formulation. To these texts could be added the triadic benediction at the end of 2 Corinthians: "The grace of the Lord Jesus Christ, the love of God, and the communion of the *Holy Spirit be with all of you" (2 Cor 13:13 NRSV). This shows, at minimum, that Paul thought of the gracious divine action as requiring triadic coordinates, and it may also suggest that Paul was unwilling to parcel out the work of salvation to separate divine "agents," thus laying the groundwork for later trinitarian teaching about the indivisibility of God's action and the incomposite nature (or simplicity) of his existence.

Alongside this could be added a similarly triadic passage from 1 Corinthians, which differs in the personal ordering. Where 2 Corinthians 13:13 speaks first of Jesus, then of God (the Father), then of the Spirit, 1 Corinthians 12:4-6 begins with the Spirit, gives Paul's preferred title/name to Jesus, and showcases Paul's usual practice of reserving *theos* for God "the Father": "Now there are varieties of gifts, but the same Spirit; and there are varieties of *services, but the same Lord; and there are varieties of activities, but it is the same God who activates all of them in everyone" (NRSV). For Paul, when it comes to specifying God's identity, "God the Father and Christ and the Spirit all demand dramatically coordinating mention" (Jenson, 92).

5.6. A Trinitarian Doctrine of God "in" Paul? Having noted all these features of Paul's portrayal of God, it is possible to go one of two ways in relating them to the later church doctrine of the Trinity, usually seen as solidified at the Council of Nicaea in AD 325 and later modified at the Council of Constantinople in 381, now enshrined in the confession of faith most Christians today know as the Nicene Creed. One option is to emphasize the gulf between them: Paul does not speak explicitly of the Son's being "eternally begotten" nor of the Spirit "proceeding" from the Father (that language is Johannine, not Pauline), nor does he usually employ the idiom of Hellenistic *philosophy, as the creed does (though the creed stretches that idiom beyond what ancient philosophy would regard as recognizability, apart from faith). Another option is to understand the creed's language as providing grammatical rules that arise, in part, from observation on how Paul's God-talk actually goes. Paul speaks of "the Lord" of Israel's Scripture as God the Father of Jesus (Rom 10:13, quoting Joel 2:32), as Jesus Christ (1 Cor 8:6; Phil 2:11), and as the Spirit of God and Jesus (2 Cor 3:17-18). He maintains fidelity to Israel's confession of God's oneness, even as he encourages *prayer to Jesus (1 Cor 12:8-9; 1 Thess 3:11-13). In order to honor this many-sided linguistic phenomenon, the creed lays down rules that are not so much implications of Paul's way of speaking as they are what must be said about God if all of Paul's conceptual and linguistic moves are to remain in play (Rowe 2011).

6. Summary and Conclusion.

Paul speaks of God as the one God of Israel, the "living and true God," as opposed to the so-called gods and lords whose existence he may not have questioned but whose inferiority he was convinced of. As the one God, God transcends human limitations and categories and is capable of acting in history without overwhelming or displacing the action of human persons. In line with the Judaism of his upbringing, Paul treats God as the Creator of all things, the source and goal of the world's existence. At the same time that Paul upheld God's universal power and rule over all things, he reaffirmed the classic Jewish understanding of God's election of the people of Israel and his fidelity to the promises made to Abraham, albeit reinterpreting their referents in terms of what God had done in Jesus Christ. Ultimately, Paul's portrait of God is not one that can be gleaned simply by attending to every time he uses the word "God" (*theos*). His theological grammar is such that God's identity bears a triune shape, in which God, Jesus Christ, and their Spirit require to be mentioned together if the identity of Israel's one God, whom Paul did not renounce when he received a revelation of Jesus Christ (Gal 1:12), was to be explicated in full. For Paul, the answer to the question "Who is the God of Abraham?" is "God the Father of our Lord Jesus Christ," "the Lord Jesus Christ" himself, and "the Spirit."

See also Christ, Messiah; Christology; Creation and New Creation; Holy Spirit; Paul and Judaism; Son of God.

BIBLIOGRAPHY. **R. Bauckham,** *Jesus and the God of Israel: God Crucified and Other Studies on the New Testament's Christology of Divine Identity* (Grand Rapids, MI: Eerdmans, 2008); **N. A. Dahl,** "The Neglected Factor in New Testament Theology," in *Jesus the Christ: The Historical Origins of Christological Doctrine*, ed. D. H. Juel (Minneapolis: Fortress, 1991), 153-63; **J. D. G. Dunn,** *The Theology of Paul the Apostle* (Grand Rapids, MI: Eerdmans, 1998); **G. D. Fee,** "Paul and the Trinity: The Experience of Christ and the Spirit for Paul's Understanding of God," in *The Trinity: An Interdisciplinary Symposium on the Trinity*, ed. S. T. Davis, D.

Kendall, SJ, and G. O'Collins, SJ (Oxford: Oxford University Press, 1999), 49-72; **J. Flebbe,** *Solus Deus: Untersuchungen zur Rede von Gott im Brief des Paulus an die Römer*, BZNW 158 (New York: de Gruyter, 2008); **S. E. Fowl,** "Paul and the Trinity," in *The Bible and Early Trinitarian Theology*, ed. C. A. Beeley and M. E. Weedman (Washington, DC: Catholic University of America Press, 2018), 151-61; **P. Fredriksen,** "How High Can Christology Be?," in *Monotheism and Christology in Greco-Roman Antiquity*, ed. M. V. Novenson (Leiden: Brill, 2020), 293-319; **R. B. Hays,** "Abraham as Father of Jews and Gentiles," in *The Conversion of the Imagination: Paul as Interpreter of Israel's Scripture* (Grand Rapids, MI: Eerdmans, 2005), 61-84; **L. W. Hurtado,** *God in New Testament Theology*, Library of Biblical Theology (Nashville: Abingdon, 2010); **R. W. Jenson,** *Systematic Theology*, vol. 1 (Oxford: Oxford University Press, 1997); **R. Jewett,** *Romans: A Commentary*, Hermeneia (Minneapolis: Fortress, 2007); **Josephus,** *The Life; Against Apion*, trans. H. St. J. Thackeray, LCL (Cambridge, MA: Harvard University Press, 1926); **J. L. Martyn,** *Galatians: A New Translation with Introduction and Commentary*, AB 33A (New York: Doubleday, 1997); idem, "Romans as One of the Earliest Interpretations of Galatians," in *Theological Issues in the Letters of Paul* (Edinburgh: T&T Clark, 1997), 37-45; **R. W. L. Moberly,** *Prophecy and Discernment*, Cambridge Studies in Christian Doctrine 14 (Cambridge: Cambridge University Press, 2006); **B. S. Rosner,** "Paul and the Trinity," in *The Essential Trinity: New Testament Foundations and Practical Relevance*, ed. B. D. Crowe and C. R. Trueman (London: Apollos, 2016), 107-21; **C. K. Rowe,** "Romans 10:13: What Is the Name of the Lord?," *HBT* 22, no. 2 (2000): 135-73; idem, "Biblical Pressure and Trinitarian Hermeneutics," *Pro Ecclesia* 11 (2002): 295-312; idem, "The Trinity in the Letters of St. Paul and Hebrews," in *The Oxford Handbook of the Trinity*, ed. G. Emery, OP, and M. Levering (New York: Oxford University Press, 2011), 41-54; idem, *One True Life: The Stoics and Early Christians as Rival Traditions* (New Haven, CT: Yale University Press, 2016); **E. P. Sanders,** *Paul and Palestinian Judaism* (London: SCM Press, 1977); **K. Sonderegger,** "The Doctrine of Election in Romans 9–11," in *Between Gospel and Election*, ed. F. Wilk and J. R. Wagner, WUNT 257 (Tübingen: Mohr Siebeck, 2010), 479-82; **F. Watson,** "The Triune Divine Identity: Reflections on Pauline God-Language, in Disagreement with J. D. G. Dunn," *JSNT* 80 (2000): 99-124; idem, "Is Paul a Covenantal Theologian?," in *The Unrelenting God: God's Action in Scripture*, ed. D. J. Downs and M. L. Skinner (Grand Rapids, MI: Eerdmans, 2013), 102-18; **N. T. Wright,** "Poetry and Theology in Colossians 1.15-20," in *The Climax of the Covenant: Christ and the Law in Pauline Theology* (London: T&T Clark, 1991), 99-119.

W. A. Hill

GOD OF THIS AGE. *See* SATAN, DEVIL.

GODS. *See* IDOLATRY; RELIGIONS, GRECO-ROMAN.

GOODNESS. *See* FRUIT OF THE SPIRIT; GOD.

GOSPEL

The gospel is of utmost importance in the NT and Paul's letters. But it has often not received the scholarly attention it deserves. For the past five hundred years Protestant-Catholic polemics concerning how to systematize justification by faith have dominated to such a degree that "gospel" (*euangelion*) has not always been scrutinized within first-century categories.

The Protestant-Catholic systematic debate has made analysis of "gospel" challenging. On the one hand, many Protestants assert that personal justification by *faith alone is the gospel or its center. When popularized in this way, the gospel is primarily about how sinful humans can obtain heaven by trusting in Jesus' accomplished work on the *cross. On the other hand, justification by faith alone is denied by Catholicism. The official Catholic position, articulated at the Council of Trent, is that justification is imparted/infused as a seed of righteousness at baptism by the Holy Spirit, but subsequently one must maintain and grow one's own justification through good deeds (with God's assistance) to receive the final crown of justification at life's end.

Recent scholarship has made strides by analyzing "gospel" within a first-century framework—along with related terms. For Paul, it is certainly true that a person can be justified by faith. But that does not mean that an individual's justification by faith is part of the gospel. Paul's own description of the gospel has a considerably different shape and emphasis.

1. Definition and Related Words
2. Scholarly Context for Recent Developments
3. Recent Scholarship
4. Content or Event?
5. Gospel Content
6. Gospel as Event
7. The False Gospel in Galatians
8. The Purpose of the Gospel

1. Definition and Related Words.
For Paul, the gospel (*euangelion*) is the announcement that Jesus the Son was sent by *God (the Father) to become the victorious *king*. When the king was enthroned, the Spirit was sent to bring *benefits* and to facilitate the gospel's primary *purpose*: allegiant obedience to Jesus as the *Christ among all the nations. Greater clarity about the gospel and salvation can be achieved by distinguishing between the gospel proper and its purposes and benefits.

The *euangel-* word group appears 44 times in the LXX and 119 times in the NT, with 62 occurrences in the seven undisputed Pauline letters and 15 in the disputed. In the LXX, the highest density appears in 2 Samuel and Isaiah 40–66. Throughout the disputed and undisputed letters, occurrences are distributed in a fairly uniform fashion (only Titus is not represented). Closely related terms include *kerygma* ("proclamation") and *logos* ("word, message"). Despite the frequency of occurrences, there are only a handful of passages in the Pauline corpus that explicitly give an expanded description of the gospel or its purposes—Romans 1:1-5; 15:15-21; 16:24-26; 1 Corinthians 15:3-5; Galatians 3:8; 2 Timothy 2:8. These passages can be supplemented by other, briefer indications.

2. Scholarly Context for Recent Developments.
Leading Pauline scholars from the previous generation expressed reticence concerning a Hebraic or Jewish background to *euangelion*. It was a Christian novum. To illustrate this tendency to downplay the Hebraic background in favor of Christian newness, consider Rudolf Bultmann's analysis.

On the surface the Jewish background for "gospel" appears to have been important to Paul. But Bultmann was not convinced. Isaiah uses gospel language that Paul cites in a modified form: "like the feet of one bringing glad tidings [*euangelizomenou*] of a report of *peace, like one bringing glad tidings of good things [*euangelizomenos agatha*], because I will make your salvation [*tēn sōtērian sou*] heard, saying to Sion, 'Your God shall reign [*basileusei sou ho theos*]'" (Is 52:7 NETS; cf. Rom 10:15). Even though Paul cites this text, Bultmann underplays the importance of this gospel language in the Hebrew Bible/OT and the Greek OT manuscript traditions for Paul's theology.

For Bultmann, the Hebraic background did not significantly affect Paul or other early Christian understandings of gospel. What is vital is how the early church developed the gospel over time to fit its emerging needs. Bultmann claimed that the original "germ-cell" gospel proclamation (*kērygma*) merely included the *death and *resurrection of Jesus. But then, to meet their practical needs, early Christians began to build on this original death-and-resurrection gospel. First, the earliest Jewish Christians needed to show how the passion and resurrection fit into salvation history and *prophecy, so they added interpretative elements to the *kērygma*. Second, the *church had to account for the cultic *worship of Jesus, so miracles and teachings were appended. Next, the church needed Jesus' teachings, so moral elements were added to the gospel. Yet even still *gospel* was not yet used in the absolute sense of "the gospel" (full stop) in which one finds it in Paul's letters (Bultmann 1:86).

Bultmann rejected not only a Hebraic background for Paul's gospel but also a Greek context: "This usage of Paul, which in his footsteps became widely current, has no analogy either in the Old Testament and Judaism or in Gentile Hellenism, and the widespread view that 'evangel' is a sacral term of the emperor-cult cannot be maintained" (Bultmann 1:87).

Bultmann's emphasis on the gospel as a Christian novum was echoed by the leading scholars who followed him. For example, Ernst Käsemann approvingly cites Bultmann and then reiterates his sentiments, saying, "The antithesis between the worship of Christ and emperor worship does not play in the primitive Church the role presupposed for such a derivation" (Käsemann, 7). Moreover, Käsemann agrees with Bultmann that objections to deriving Paul's understanding of *euangelion* from Deutero-Isaiah "have not been fully met" (7). In arriving at this conclusion, Käsemann, citing Peter Stuhlmacher, finds the absence of the use of "the gospel" in an absolute sense outside early Christianity to be decisive. This is significant because Stuhlmacher's influential studies of the gospel (1968) were more optimistic regarding a Hebraic background and continuity between the Jerusalem-based church and Paul's letters.

In short, leading Pauline scholars of a previous generation were convinced that "the gospel" as an unqualified term could not go back to the earliest Jerusalem-based church. Rather, Jesus' death and resurrection were originally *gospel* (good news), but it was only as the Hellenistic church added diverse elements that such ideas became fixed as *the gospel*. Therefore, Paul's use of *the gospel* reflects all of these developments (Bultmann, 1:87-88; on past scholarship, see Twelftree, 5-9).

3. Recent Scholarship.

The theory of a pre-Pauline development from an early Palestinian (Jewish) to early Hellenistic (Greek) church is now widely rejected. Accordingly, scholarly understandings of *the gospel* have shifted. In terms of origin, Paul himself claims to have received the gospel directly from the Lord Jesus himself when the once-dead-but-now-living king was revealed to him (Gal 1:12). This, however, does not suggest that Paul's gospel had no pre-Pauline currency among followers of Jesus the Messiah.

There is every reason to believe that Paul's gospel predates Paul's letters, reaching back to the earliest distinctively Christian experiences of the Jerusalem-based church. Although they date after Paul's letters, the Gospels strongly indicate that the gospel was central to the historical Jesus' own message (e.g., Mk 1:14-15; Lk 4:16-21; 4:43). Jesus proclaimed that he was in the process of bringing about God's kingdom through his own emerging kingship. Moreover, Paul acknowledges that Peter was entrusted with the gospel before he was (Gal 2:7) and speaks of it as a *tradition that he himself received from others (1 Cor 15:3). Paul's gospel did not fully originate with Paul. Nor was the *euangel-* word group devoid of meaning in the broader Greco-Roman world.

Scholars today are more prepared to see the HB/OT, Second Temple Judaism, and the Greco-Roman world not as preparation for the Christian gospel as a novum but as the sociohistorical matrix that informed its novel content holistically. As N. T. Wright puts it: "In Paul's Jewish world the word [gospel] looked back to Isa 40:9 and 52:7, where a messenger was to bring to Jerusalem the good news of Babylon's defeat, the end of Israel's exile, and the personal return of YHWH to Zion. In the pagan world Paul addressed, the same Greek word referred to the birthday of a ruler or emperor" (Wright 2013, 415). That is, within Paul's world *euangelion* connected both to the OT promises of YHWH's return to Zion and also to announcements pertaining to the emperor and his benefactions.

The imperial context is apparent in the famous Priene Calendar inscription, in which Caesar Augustus is referred to as "savior" (*sōtēr*) and "god" (*theos*), and the day of his birth is called "the gospel [*euangelion*] for the world." An imperial framework is also in place for Josephus, when he describes the "good news" that Vespasian has become the new emperor: "And quicker than thought rumour spread the news of the new emperor in the east. Every city kept festival for the good news [*euangelia*] and offered sacrifices on his [Vespasian's] behalf" (*J.W.* 4.618 [LCL]; cf. *J.W.* 4.656).

N. T. Wright is not alone in advancing a royal gospel informed by the HB/OT, Second Temple Judaism, and the Greco-Roman context. Matthew Novenson has shown that *Christ* had not devolved into a mere name but retained royal implications as an honorific for Paul. A royal gospel is inescapable in Paul's letters because the phrases *Jesus Christ* and *Christ Jesus* ubiquitously assert that Jesus presently holds the messianic office. For scholars today, Paul's gospel might be more than a royal proclamation that God's HB/OT promises have been fulfilled—with implications for the wider Greco-Roman world—but it cannot be less.

Michael Gorman (2004, 98-114) captures the way in which Paul's gospel is holistically informed by its Jewish and Greco-Roman contexts. Paul's gospel is *theopolitical*: "It announces an event that has to do with God's intervention in history, something that must be both a 'theological' and a 'political' event" (108). Meanwhile Gorman shows that key terms such as *euangelion* ("good news"), *kyrios* ("*lord"), *sōtēr*/*sōtēria* ("*savior"/"salvation"), *basileia* ("kingdom"), *eirēnē* ("peace"), *pistis* ("faith"), *eleutheria* ("*freedom"), *dikaios*/*dikaiosynē* ("just"/"*righteousness"), *ekklēsia* ("church"), and *parousia* ("coming") are all double-voiced. Each draws from and resonates within its Jewish and Greco-Roman context but takes on additional meanings when used by the emerging church to speak of the paradoxes surrounding a crucified, risen king. Paul was well aware of the irony of a crucified Messiah, seeing the message of the cross as folly to the perishing world but nevertheless God's transformative power (1 Cor 1:18).

Those working within an apocalyptic framework also emphasize a royal gospel, although generally the theme is more muted. For example, J. L. Martyn speaks of a royal gospel (127-28) but focuses more on its eruptive, disruptive quality as a revelatory occurrence: "In a word, the gospel *happened* to Paul when God stepped on the scene, invading his life in Christ" (Martyn, 144; cf. 147-51). Beverly Gaventa strikes similar chords. Meanwhile, Douglas Campbell believes that neither justification by faith nor a salvation-historical approach can ultimately do justice to Paul's *euangelion* (Campbell 2005; 2009). Campbell advances an apocalyptic model for Paul's gospel that focuses on Spirit-led participation in Christ's death and resurrection. He calls it "pneumatologically participatory martyrological eschatology," or PPME.

Additionally, Michael Bird (2014), Scot McKnight (2011; 2019), and Joshua Jipp (2015) have furthered the emphasis on the gospel as a royal proclamation for Paul. M. W. Bates (2017; 2019), whose results regarding Paul's gospel are consolidated in the following subsections, has sought to integrate a royal gospel with other key categories such as grace, faith, and works. The most recent full-length monograph, Graham Twelftree's *The Gospel According to Paul*, continues these trends, while adding that the miraculous deeds of the Spirit should be regarded as gospel too.

In short, there is now heightened awareness that Paul's gospel (*euangelion*) was associated with Roman emperors—their patronage, benefactions, and governance. Paul's gospel is that something new has happened in world and cosmic history. God's king is now ruling: the Christ is Jesus. Although humans did not deserve the grace of the Christ-events that together constitute the gospel, nevertheless the benefits of ultimate salvation are available to all who accept this gift by giving loyalty to the king.

4. Content or Event?

Recent scholarship raises an important basic question: For Paul, does *euangelion* characteristically intend *a message with a specific content*, or is it rather *an activity or event*? Some words, such as *hope, contain a verbal idea even when used as a noun. If one has placed *hope* in a retirement account, for example, *hope* is a noun. But since it can be a verb in other contexts, it has an implied action and an object. Similarly, although *euangelion* ("good news," "glad tidings") is a noun, it has a verbal counterpart, *euangelizomai* ("to herald good news"). Much of the debate in contemporary Pauline scholarship about the gospel concerns how to correlate salvation-historical *content*, such as promise and *covenant, with cosmic and apocalyptic *events*, such as deliverance and new *creation (for discussion, see Gaventa).

Consider the English word *proclamation* as a relevant word capable of denoting content or activity. When a governor issues a proclamation pertaining to a new regulation, one might focus on the *content* proclaimed (the message), the *activity* (the event of the speech-act), or the purposes or results. It is the same for Paul and *euangelion*.

Careful inspection of Paul's usage makes it clear that *euangelion* is a proclamation, so it can intend both content and event. Douglas Moo calls this the static and active sense of *euangelion* (43). The gospel also has distinct purposes. In dividing this article's treatment into content, event, and purpose, the intention is not to suggest a tidy, nonoverlapping division in Paul's usage along these lines but to discern and discuss the weight of emphasis in the most important gospel passages.

5. Gospel Content.

5.1. Incarnation and Enthronement—Romans 1:1-4. That the gospel is central to Paul's letters and theology is apparent from the opening verse of the Pauline corpus: "Paul, *slave of the Messiah, Jesus. A called *apostle, having been set apart for the gospel of God" (Rom 1:1). Paul uses the phrase "gospel of God" (*euangelion Theou*), suggesting that God (the Father) is the gospel's author and source. Since Paul wants to stress the gospel's universal significance here, he avoids "my gospel" (Rom 2:16; 16:25; cf. 2 Tim 2:8). Since this is the gospel of the one true God, its purview is boundless.

While it would be wrong to exclude activity entirely, contextually *the content* is foregrounded in this passage as Paul continues to present the gospel (so also Moo).

> [the gospel] that he promised in advance through his holy prophets concerning his Son,
> > (X) who came into being [*tou genomenou*]
> > > (a) by means of the seed of David [*ek spermatos Dauid*]
> > > (b) as it pertains to the *flesh [*kata sarka*]
>
> > (Y) who was appointed Son-of-God-in-Power [*tou horisthentos huiou Theou en dynamei*]
> > > (b) as it pertains to the Spirit of *Holiness [*kata pneuma hagiōsynēs*]
> > > (a) by means of the resurrection from among the dead ones [*ex anastaseōs nekrōn*]
>
> Jesus the Christ our Lord [*Iēsou Christou tou kyriou hēmōn*]. (Rom 1:2-4)

5.1.1. Promised in Advance. Paul stresses that the gospel was "promised [by God] in advance [*proepēngeilato*] through his prophets in the holy Scriptures" (Rom 1:2). This clause presses uncomfortably against the tendency within earlier scholarship to angle toward the Christian gospel as a novum over against its Hebrew Bible/OT background. Three points should be made: (1) Paul's gospel presupposes God's orchestration of a divine economy, a providential arrangement of world affairs and their outworking; (2) God did not merely announce the gospel in advance but committed himself via promises, such as those made to *Abraham and David (e.g., Gen 12:3; 2 Sam 7:12-16); (3) the gospel is not an entirely unanticipated rupture within human history, since God promised it beforehand in Scripture. The gospel is not identical to the OT story but is the fulfillment of patterns and promises made within that story. This hints at an implication that Paul will tease out subsequently: the gospel vindicates God, proving that he has acted powerfully and justly within history.

Paul is probably using preexisting material in Romans 1:3-4, much as he does in 1 Corinthians 15:3-5. That is, the early church prior to Paul may have used this gospel content as part of a proto-creed or *hymn. If so, Paul may have modified its wording to adjust portions of its theology, or for irenic purposes, or both (see Jewett). But it is unlikely that Paul would have idiosyncratically redacted gospel material here. It is more probable that he presented the gospel that he and the Romans held in common, especially since he had never personally visited the churches at Rome and he is requesting their assistance in his efforts to preach the gospel in Spain (Bates 2015).

For Paul in Romans 1:2-4, the gospel pertains to God's Son. Yet what one learns about the Son is presented in a tightly structured X-a-b-Y-b-a pattern in the Greek text. The X and Y are participial phrases. The a-b-b-a pattern is carried out by the prepositions *ek-kata-kata-ek*. This structure in Greek shows that two events are primary, for the rest of the information describes and qualifies these two events. The two events are *coming into being* and *being appointed Son-of-God-in-Power*.

5.1.2. Coming into Being. In detailing the gospel, Paul stresses that the Son *came into being*. The ordinary word for human reproduction, *gennaō*, is eschewed in favor of *ginomai* ("to be, to become"), much as in Galatians 4:4; Philippians 2:7. But Paul qualifies the way in which the Son came into being in two ways. First he says this was *ek spermatos Dauid* ("by/from the seed of David"). This could merely be a statement of Davidic origin (i.e., "from the line of David"). But earliest reception history and parallelism with Romans 1:4 points at a more plausible solution—that Paul is describing *the means* by which this "coming into being" of the Son transpired. It was *by means of the seed of David*. That is, *by means of Mary*, who is called "the seed of David" in several second-century sources (Ign. *Eph.* 18.2), including Irenaeus, in what is the earliest explicit interpretation of this verse (*Haer.* 3.16.3; cf. Irenaeus, *Epid.* 36; see Jipp 2009). Second, Paul further qualifies "came into being" by saying that this was not a coming-into-being in every way but only with regard to the flesh (*kata sarka*), since he was already the Son (Rom 1:1). The key gospel event highlighted in Romans 1:3 is what subsequently would come to be termed *the incarnation*.

5.1.3. Appointed Son-of-God-in-Power. After speaking of the Son's enfleshment, Paul describes his appointment to a new station. Prior to the gospel the Son preexisted alongside the Father. But the gospel is about his installation as Son-of-God-in-Power. There is a progression from Son to enthroned Son. This interpretation takes the prepositional phrase *en dynamei* as modifying "*Son of God" rather than the participle *horisthentos* ("who was appointed"). It is not that the Son was appointed with power to be Son of God, but rather that the Son was appointed Son-of-God-in-Power.

This is the most likely interpretation because (1) Jesus is already described as the Son in Romans 1:1, so it would be odd for him to be described subsequently in Romans 1:4 as being appointed with power to be Son of God in conjunction with the resurrection—but the strangeness dissipates if the Son is being appointed to a new office, Son-of-God-in-Power; (2) it preserves the a-b-b-a structure; (3) it best explains the word order within the clause; (4) it is contextually reinforced by the royal emphasis throughout Romans 1:1-5; and (5) there is a movement from the Son's preexistence with God to his role as glorified ruler in similar texts in Paul's letters, such as Philippians 2:6-11 and Romans 8 (Rom 8:3 together with Rom 8:34; cf. 2 Cor 8:9). The content of the gospel in Romans 1:3-4 pertains to the preexistent Son of God coming into fleshly existence and to his appointment to a new office after his resurrection, Son-of-God-in-Power.

Perhaps what is most surprising about the gospel in Romans 1:1-4 is what is missing. There is no mention of the cross, faith, *forgiveness of *sins, or salvation. Even if the previous generation of scholarship is the standard, Paul's emphases are surprising inasmuch as it is not a Christian novum but draws on HB/OT and Hellenistic royal motifs. In Romans 1:2-4 the gospel pertains to God's advance promises about his Son: that he would take on human flesh by means of a seed of David and that he would be enthroned in a position of power after his resurrection from the dead. In Romans 1:1-4, *the gospel is about God's promise of the Son's incarnation and enthronement*.

5.2. The Raised King—2 Timothy 2:8. Second Timothy 2:8 is among the few passages that spell out the content of the gospel explicitly. But due to its brevity and disputes over its authorship, it is woefully neglected. "Remember Jesus the Christ, raised from among the dead ones, of the seed of David, according to my gospel" (2 Tim 2:8). In contradistinction to the "gospel of God" in Romans 1:1, with his "my gospel," Paul makes his personal stake in the gospel clear. Yet, as in Romans, one is immediately reminded that above all the gospel is about *the Christ, the Messiah,* the Jewish but nevertheless universal *king.* The gospel is not just about Jesus; it is about Jesus in his kingly capacity.

The resurrection of Jesus the king is fronted: "raised from among the dead ones" (2 Tim 2:8; cf. Rom 1:4). The point is not that Jesus as a singular individual happened to die and be raised up—a neat one-of-a-kind miracle. Rather, Paul emphasizes that the Messiah was in a condition of death among others who were dead too (the word *dead* is plural in the Greek) and that God raised the king up. It suggests that the king upon his death was with others who were dead until he was raised on the third day. It also hints that the resurrection of the king has implications for all his subjects. The Messiah is the firstfruits of resurrection life, but there will be a full harvest for all the king's people (1 Cor 15:35-58). As in Romans 1:3, Paul describes the Messiah as "from/by the seed of David," implying God's faithfulness to his covenant promises to David.

*5.3. **The Crucified-Risen King—1 Corinthians 15:3-5.*** Although Paul is capable of summarizing the gospel without mentioning the cross at all, in 1 Corinthians 15:3-5 Paul locates the king's death for humanity's sins alongside other key events. Paul begins by reminding the Corinthians that "the gospel that he proclaimed" (*to euangelion ho euēngelisamēn*—"the gospel that he gospeled") to them was part of an intentional process for reliably transmitting tradition. Hence they "received" it.

5.3.1. An Idiosyncratic Gospel? Was Paul's gospel unique or weird in comparison with other early Christian articulations of the gospel? The gospel one finds in Paul's letters is not Paul's alone, but rather part of the common property of the church. Consider five reasons: (1) Paul states that he himself received the gospel and passed it to the Corinthians (1 Cor 15:3). So it did not originate with Paul—even if he personally received core elements of the gospel when Jesus the Messiah revealed himself in his resurrected state to Paul (Gal 1:11-12; cf. Acts 9:3-9; 22:6-11; 26:12-18). (2) Paul asserts that this same gospel was proclaimed by the other apostles: "Whether then it was I or they, thus we preach and thus you believed" (1 Cor 15:11). (3) Other apostles, including Peter, had almost certainly visited *Corinth (1 Cor 1:12; 3:22), so if Paul was dissimulating in asserting a common gospel, the Corinthians would have known better—so there is every reason to believe Paul. (4) No portion of *the content* of Paul's actual gospel as one can reconstruct it here or elsewhere was a matter of dispute among those elsewhere called apostles in the NT. (5) Paul's gospel is in harmony with the presentation of the gospel found in the four canonical Gospels and in the remainder of the NT. For example, there is no genuine discrepancy between the gospel in Paul's letters and the gospel presented as Paul's in Acts. Acts faithfully summarizes Paul's gospel, "The Christ is Jesus" (Acts 18:5; cf. 9:22; 17:2-3). In short, there is no evidence that any portion of the content of Paul's gospel was disputed by any apostle or apostolic *witness. Paul's gospel was not idiosyncratic but a participation in the common, united apostolic testimony.

5.3.2. The Saving Gospel. Paul's gospel, properly weighed, is not a procedure for how to get saved. But it certainly is a saving message. Paul affirms that it is by this gospel that the Corinthians are "being saved"—that is, if they continue to cling to it (1 Cor 15:3). What is the content of this saving gospel? "That the Christ *died* in behalf of our sins in accordance with the Scriptures, and that he was *buried,* and that he has been *raised* on the third day in accordance with the Scriptures, and that he *appeared* to Cephas, then to the Twelve" (1 Cor 15:3-5). In presenting the gospel here, Jesus' royal office is fronted to such a degree that Jesus' name is not even mentioned, merely his honorific title, *the Christ.* The gospel is a royal proclamation. Paul mentions four distinct events that constitute the good news about this king: death, burial, resurrection, and appearances.

Two of the events, death for sins and resurrection on the third day, are given primacy inasmuch as they are said to be "according to the Scriptures." What seems to be in view with the "according to the Scriptures" is not one or two specific texts from the OT but numerous passages involving a righteous sufferer who is subsequently vindicated by God. Meanwhile the other two events, burial and appearance to others, serve a secondary role. They confirm the truthfulness of the primary events. Burial certifies the reality of the king's death for sins. Appearances to numerous witnesses certify the truthfulness of the resurrection on the third day. A brief word about the two primary events is in order.

5.3.3. The King Died for Our Sins According to the Scriptures. The cross is theologically central to the gospel, even if it is not the gospel's definitive theological center. The death of the king is described as "for our sins," or even better, "in behalf of our sins" (*hyper tōn hamartiōn*). The king stands in humanity's place as a substitute (see Rom 8:3; 2 Cor 5:21). Elsewhere Paul elaborates on this substitution, saying that the king redeemed humanity from the curses associated with the old covenant when he "became a *curse for us" as he hung on the cross (Gal 3:13).

5.3.4. The King Was Raised on the Third Day According to the Scriptures. The resurrection is as vital as the cross to the saving message of the gospel. "Jesus our Lord," as Paul puts it elsewhere, "was delivered up on account of our trespasses," but that alone did not result in full vindication for humanity (Rom 4:25). He was also "raised on account of our justification" (Rom 4:25). Human justification depends not just on Jesus' death but also on his resurrection. If believers live, it is only because he was raised to everlasting life.

5.4. The Gospel of Blessing to All Nations—Galatians 3:8. Paul gives the content of the gospel in another passage—Galatians 3:8. It is quite different, and hence it is neglected as a gospel-defining passage. Paul is explaining to the Galatians that they received the Spirit not by performing *works of the *law but rather by *pistis* ("faith," "faithfulness," or "allegiance")—and that the same is true for Abraham. "The Scripture foresaw that that God would justify the *Gentiles by allegiance [*ek pisteōs*] and announced the gospel in advance to Abraham, 'All nations will be blessed through you'" (Gal 3:8, see Gen 12:3; 18:18; 22:18).

Paul makes several intriguing claims about the gospel in Galatians 3:8. Paul personifies the Scripture here, giving it independent speaking agency as a character in the divine drama. The text of Genesis is made by Paul to herald the good news to Abraham even though historically the book of Genesis did not yet exist so as to speak to Abraham. Paul is not making a historical blunder but unveiling his high view of God's providence. Not only does God orchestrate a vast divine economy, arranging correspondences between past, present, and future historical events, but God also controls Scripture formation as part of that process—to such a degree that the text of Genesis can be ushered on stage as an advance witness to the good news about Jesus the king (cf. Rom 10:6-8, in which "the righteousness by faith" and other characters speak). Scripture announces the gospel in advance to Abraham.

What Paul identifies as the content of the gospel spoken to Abraham via the text of Genesis is arresting. It is not "justification by faith," as if Abraham learns the good news that trust alone is efficacious for obtaining a right standing in God's presence. Abraham does trust and is reckoned as righteous. But this is not what Paul identifies as the gospel. Rather, the gospel Abraham hears is "All nations will be blessed through you" (Gal 3:8).

When one teases out Paul's argument in Galatians further, one discovers that Abraham's seed, the Messiah, is in view as the vehicle of that blessing and that "the righteous will live by *pistis*" (Gal 3:11, citing Hab 2:4; cf. Rom 1:17). This pertains especially to the king's *loyalty* in redeeming his people (Gal 3:13). This redemption is purposed toward the *loyalty* of the nations to Jesus the king, as the Gentiles receive the *Holy Spirit and are integrated into the worldwide family that God is creating (Gal 3:14). Paul's description of the gospel's content, "All nations will be blessed in you" (Gal 3:8), is a reminder that the gospel pertains to Jesus the king's rule over the nations as facilitated by the Holy Spirit. Similar motifs arise in the passage discussed next, Romans 1:16-17, Paul's most famous statement about the gospel.

5.5. Summarizing the Content. In sum, what is the *content* of Paul's gospel? It is the common apostolic gospel. According to Paul's own witness, the following elements are prominent:

The gospel is that Jesus the king

1. preexisted as God the Son,
2. was sent by the Father,
3. took on human flesh in fulfillment of God's promises to David,
4. died for our sins in accordance with the Scriptures,
5. was buried,
6. was raised on the third day in accordance with the Scriptures,
7. appeared to many witnesses,
8. *is enthroned at the right hand of God as the ruling Christ*,
9. has sent the Holy Spirit to his people to effect his rule, and
10. will come again as final judge to rule. (Bates 2019, 86-87)

Jesus' present rule as the Christ is italicized because it best summarizes the gospel's content for Paul.

Since these ten events are derived from passages in which Paul explicitly gives the gospel's content, other texts that fit this pattern but are not called "gospel" by Paul can be identified as expressing important aspects of it (e.g., Rom 8:3; Gal 1:3-5; 4:4-5; 2 Cor 8:9; Phil 2:6-11). Moreover, in pondering these ten events, one should not fail to observe the gospel's trinitarian shape: the Son is sent by the Father, so they can send the Spirit. The gospel reveals the Trinity.

6. Gospel as Event.

Since Romans 1:16-17 is widely recognized as Paul's thesis statement in Romans, what Paul says in it has decisively influenced theological reconstructions of the gospel's content and center of gravity. For Protestants the influence of this passage is even more pronounced, for it was Martin Luther's meditations on Romans 1:16-17 that, by his own later reports, led to his breakthrough tower experience. On the basis of the close identification between the gospel and justification by faith in this passage, Luther considered the latter the doctrine by which the church stands or falls. Paul, however, does not say that he is giving the gospel's content in Romans 1:16-17. Paul has already done that in Romans 1:2-4.

Paul's reference to the gospel in Romans 1:16-17 is designed to bring readers back to his previous description in Romans 1:2-4. Now he needs to explain how the gospel's content—God's promises about the Son's enfleshment and enthronement—is *able to save*. Paul's focus in Romans 1:16-17 is not on the gospel's content but on the gospel as activity or event—what sort of power and effects the royal good news of the Son's incarnation and enthronement have thrust into the world. "For I am not ashamed of the gospel, for it is the power of God for salvation for everyone who performs the *pistis* action, to the Jew first and also to the Greek. For in the gospel the righteousness of God is revealed by *pistis*, for *pistis*, as it is written, 'But the righteous [one] by *pistis* will live'" (Rom 1:16-17, citing Hab 2:4).

6.1. The Revelation of God's Righteousness. Paul asserts that the gospel is able to effect salvation for Jew and Greek alike—for everyone who performs the *pistis* action. Paul does not equate the gospel and "justification by faith." Rather, he says something slightly different: the righteousness of God is revealed in or through the events that together constitute the gospel.

It would be going too far afield to enter here into a scholarly discussion of the righteousness of God (for its history, see McGrath; for a recent exegetical attempt, see Irons). But on the level of a biblical theology, it can be summarized this way: "The righteousness of God is *God's resurrection-effecting verdict that Jesus the wrath-bearing, sin-atoning, allegiant king is alone righteous—a verdict that all who are united to Jesus the representative king share*" (Bates 2017, 181). So ultimately, when one is in the Messiah, "the righteousness of God" is a standing or benefit that one can enjoy (2 Cor 5:21). The righteousness of God is unveiled in the gospel because, although it was previously attested in Scripture, it is not attainable by works of the law, but only by the *pistis* of the Messiah and by those who perform the *pistis* action in relationship to him (Rom 3:21-22; Gal 3:21-23).

6.2. Paul's Citation of Habakkuk 2:4. In Romans 1:17, Paul cites Habakkuk 2:4: "The righteous [one] by *pistis* will live." In the OT, the Hebrew word *pistis* translates *ʾĕmûnâ. ʾĔmûnâ* is best glossed "steadfastness," "trustworthiness," "faithfulness," "honesty" (*HALOT* 1:62). A covenantal framework helps make sense of the meaning. Habakkuk is querying God's justice in using Babylon as his instrument for judging his people. God replies that the righteous man will live by staying *faithful* or *loyal* to God and God's covenant during this difficult season.

Paul's use of the OT is made complex by the textual witness. One can summarize it as follows:

- The righteous man will live by *his [own] fidelity* (MT)
- The righteous [one] will live by *my [God's] pistis* (LXX)
- The righteous [one] will live *by pistis* (Paul's quotation of the OT)

In the MT, the righteous man will live because of *his own* fidelity. In considering how the LXX and Paul's citation differ from the MT, there are two things to observe. First, the LXX uses *my* instead of *his*: "But the righteous one will live by *my pistis*." The translator understood the faithfulness to belong to God rather than to the righteous man. The translator believed it was God's *own fidelity* that would uphold the righteous man throughout this time of *judgment. Second, in citing Habakkuk 2:4, Paul follows neither the MT nor the LXX precisely. Unlike the MT, Paul does not say "*his* pistis" (*the righteous man's* fidelity). And unlike the LXX, Paul does not say "*my* pistis" (*God's own* fidelity). Paul has no pronouns at all, just a solitary *pistis*. This makes it uncertain whether Paul intends to speak of divine or human *pistis*.

6.3. By the King's Loyalty, for the People's Loyalty. Paul's omission of pronouns before *pistis* in the Habakkuk citation in Romans 1:17 appears to be calculated. Christopher Stanley has convincingly demonstrated that Paul's modifications to his OT citations are often theologically motivated. Omission of the pronouns allows Paul to include both divine and human *pistis*. God shows himself to be faithful to his promises through the king's faithfulness, but this is purposed toward stimulating human allegiance to the king in response.

6.3.1. Faith's Agency and Direction. Paul prefaces the citation with an opaque expression: "in the gospel the righteousness of God is revealed *by fidelity for fidelity* [*ek pisteōs eis pistin*]" (Rom 1:17). Paul is using compressed language to express dual agency and the bidirectional movement of faith (*pistis*): "in the gospel the righteousness of God is revealed *by [the Messiah's] fidelity, for [our human] fidelity*." That is, two agents are in view: (1) the king and (2) the people loyal to the king. Twin agency is probable here for *pistis*—the king's first, and then other humans' second—because the same twin agency can be found in closely related passages such as Romans 3:22; Galatians 2:16; and Galatians 3:22. Moreover, the bidirectional movement of *pistis*—from the king toward God and from the people toward the king—is also probable on the basis of these passages.

6.3.2. Instrumental Means and Purpose. The translation "by loyalty, for loyalty" in Romans 1:17 is reinforced by contextual clues that suggest *instrumental means* and *purpose*. Since in Habakkuk 2:4, *ek pisteōs* expresses the instrumental means by which life is achieved, "by loyalty" or "by allegiance," this is also likely for Paul in Romans 1:17—especially given the royal framework for the gospel for Paul. Meanwhile, the "*for* [*eis*] the obedience of *pistis*" in Romans 1:5 suggests that purpose is in view for *eis pistin* in Romans 1:17. Confirming evidence can be found in Romans 3:22, where Paul circles back to expand on themes he introduced in Romans 1:17. Paul indicates the righteousness of God has been revealed "*through* [*dia*] the *pistis* of Jesus the Christ *for* [*eis*] all who perform the *pistis* activity" (Rom 3:22). In Romans 3:22 instrumental means, purpose, and twin agents—the Christ and other humans—are in view for the *pistis* word family, just as has been proposed for *ek pisteōs eis pistin* in Romans 1:17. In sum, although alternatives are possible (Longenecker 2016, 178-80, has a helpful discussion), *ek pisteōs eis pistin* most likely intends *instrumental means* (*ek pisteōs*) and *purpose* (*eis pistin*).

6.3.3. "The righteous by allegiance will live." For Paul, Habakkuk makes a prophetic declaration, "The *righteous* [one] by *allegiance* will *live*" (Rom 1:17; cf. Gal 3:11), which finds its answer in the Messiah's *allegiance* to God (the royal Father) in his obedient life and climactic death (see Rom 5:17-21). In view of the Messiah's allegiance, God justified Jesus as *the righteous one*. God's justifying verdict with respect to Jesus the Messiah was confirmed by his resurrection. As Son-of-God-in-Power, the raised king now *lives* forever, having defeated death once for all. When Paul refers to "the righteous [one]," he first has the Messiah in view (see Acts 3:14; 7:52; 22:14; Rom 5:17-19), but secondarily all who imitate his pattern.

The same by-*pistis*-the-righteous-will-live pattern is found in Paul's prosopological exegesis of Psalm 116:1 in 2 Corinthians 4:13 (see Bates 2012, 304-25; 2019, 79-82; Downs and Lappenga, 75-80, 110-13). Paul finds the Messiah saying to the Father, "I performed the *pistis* action, therefore I spoke." This speech was a plea to God for rescue (Ps 116:4) that culminated in deliverance to the land of the living (Ps 116:9).

In sum, Paul's expression "*The righteous* [*one*] *by allegiance* will *live*" (Rom 1:17) refers to Jesus the king's allegiance and resurrection life first. But secondarily the Christ's fidelity in his death, ongoing mediation at the right hand of God (Rom 8:34), and Spirit-sending enables allegiance and resurrection life among his followers. As for the king, so also for the king's people: trusting loyalty results in vindication unto life in the presence of God: "the righteous by allegiance will live." The purpose of the king's allegiance was *for believers' allegiance*, that humanity might enter into his allegiant pattern. The aim of Jesus' allegiance was so that people might declare allegiance to him as king, so they can share in the saving benefits that belong to the king's people (e.g., *adoption, justification, and life).

6.4. Justification, Allegiance, and Life. In Romans 1:17 Paul refers to the gospel as a royal proclamation, but the focus is on the new saving power released into the world in these events. In the events of the gospel—including the king's incarnation, death for sins, resurrection, enthronement, and Spirit-sending—the righteousness of God is revealed *ek pisteōs eis pistin* ("by loyalty for loyalty"). For the king first and secondarily his people, the verdict of righteousness is attained by *trusting allegiance* and results in resurrection *life*.

For Paul, the gospel has a specific content that demands a response—Jesus has now become the Christ. It is also an event. Furthermore, because it unleashes transformative power, the gospel has fixed results and aims. Paul's language in Galatians shows that the gospel demands a unique response and generates specific communal benefits that cannot be compromised.

7. The False Gospel in Galatians.

Paul never says that his gospel is personal "justification by faith." Nor does he ever include it as a component of the gospel. The same can be said for the rest of the NT. The closest one gets is Paul's presentation of the gospel in his speech in Pisidian Antioch (Acts 13:13-41), where he is described as mentioning justification by faith (Acts 13:39). But even there Paul is not portrayed as straightforwardly indicating that the principle is part of the gospel.

But given Paul's ardent and urgent warnings about a "different gospel" (a nongospel) that is threatening the churches of Galatia (Gal 1:6), is one not compelled to equate the gospel with justification by faith? After all, when Paul details the problematic teachings in Galatia that are causing consternation, he has in view certain works-of-the-law activities that compromise the unique role of *pistis* in justification (e.g., Gal 2:11-21; 3:10-14; 5:1-6). The equation is tempting.

A better solution is that justification is a *benefit* or *result* of the gospel that has been objectively won by the king for his people. But the personal receipt of the benefit of justification is not part of the gospel. When the gospel of Jesus' saving kingship is proclaimed (that is, the ten events or a likeminded summary), personal receipt of justification is conditioned on whether that individual has declared loyalty (by *pistis*) to the king.

7.1. Peter Violated the Gospel's Results. When Paul first broaches the topic of justification by *pistis* in Galatians, he does not say that Peter denied the gospel's *content*. Rather, Peter was not walking straight with regard to "the *truth of the gospel" in his actions (Gal 2:14; cf. Gal 2:5). Peter's actions had compromised the truth of the gospel by violating not its raw content but the truth that the gospel *results* in one and only one justified family—and that this family is defined by *pistis* (both by the king's *pistis* and by those who yield *pistis* to the king)—not by works of the law. Peter's action had created a false division and tiers within that one justified family. Paul knew these divisions and tiers were false because *pistis* uniquely avails with God (Gal 5:6).

7.2. Communal Justification First. God's justification of Jesus is part of the gospel, since Jesus' resurrection and enthronement give evidence that God has judged and vindicated him. Moreover, the King poured out his Spirit on Pentecost, justifying his followers. It is part of the gospel that the king "died for *our* sins" and then sent the Spirit to his people. The establishment of a forgiven or justified community—the church—on the basis of the king's work is gospel.

But an individual's justification by faith is not part of the gospel. Rather, an individual's justification is a benefit of the gospel, conditioned on an allegiant response. The benefit of justification is only realized when a person performs the *pistis* action (e.g., Rom 3:22; Gal 2:16). It is the *pistis* response to the gospel that moves a person into the justified community. When an individual *by faith declares allegiance to King Jesus,* the community benefit of *justification* is actualized for that individual.

7.3. Not Content but Response and Benefits. In the warnings against turning to a different gospel in Galatians 1:6-9, Paul is using metonymy (see Bates 2019, 107-8). The content of Paul's gospel is the proclamation that Jesus is the Christ-King (variously summarized; see section 5.5 above). But Paul uses metonymy to refer to other close associations.

Within metonymy, via contextual implicature, a reference to a thing (e.g., "the gospel") can intend a reference to responses, effects, or other close associations (e.g., faith and justification). For example, Paul uses metonymy in Galatians 2:7, where he speaks of "the gospel of the foreskin" and "the gospel of *circumcision." This is metonymy because Paul intends not the content of the gospel but its effect or result for the noncircumcised and circumcised. In Galatians 2:7 Paul uses the phrase "the gospel" but intends its results.

Metonymy also makes the best sense of Paul's warnings about the gospel in Galatians 1:6-9. The content of Paul's gospel was not being violated in Galatia, but rather works of the law compromised the uniqueness of *pistis* ("trusting loyalty") as the only effective response to the royal gospel. Works of the law also compromised the gospel benefit of justification, because they threatened to divide the one people of the king. The true gospel can result in one and only one justified family.

In sum, that an individual can be justified by faith is vitally important to Paul. But it is not the gospel. The content of Paul's gospel pertains to Christ-events, not personal justification by faith. For the individual, *faith* (trusting allegiance) is the only saving *response* to the gospel, and *justification* (right-standing with God) is one of its key *benefits*. Paul speaks in strong terms in Galatians about compromises to the gospel using metonymy because the exclusive means (trusting allegiance) to one of the gospel's most important benefits (justification) was under threat. This takes seriously Paul's own explicit royal descriptions of the gospel while also making sense of Paul's language in Galatians. The cogency of this solution is sharpened when one considers Paul's statements about the purpose of the gospel.

8. The Purpose of the Gospel.
The required response to the gospel and its results align with the gospel's purposes. In short, the gospel is purposed toward stimulating loyal obedience to the king in order to restore glory. Through allegiance, the benefits of Jesus' kingship are delivered to humans and creation, all of which redounds to God's ultimate honor. Allegiance to the king brings restoration.

8.1. Loyal Obedience to the King. The most overt statement of the purpose of the gospel is found near the end of Romans. Although the authenticity of this portion of the letter has been questioned, Pauline authorship has been capably defended (see Hurtado). The whole of Romans 16:25-26 is a description of the gospel, while the final line is a purpose statement about the gospel.

> ... *my gospel and the preaching about Jesus the Messiah*
> which has been made manifest
>
> according to the revelation of *mystery kept silent for eternal ages
> but which now has been made known through the prophetic writings
>
> according to the command of the eternal God
> *for the obedience of* pistis *for all the* nations. (Rom 16:25-26)

The content of Paul's gospel is given in summary form as "the preaching of Jesus the Messiah" (*to kērygma Iēsou Christou*), best understood as an objective genitive ("preaching about Jesus the Messiah"). It is further described as a long-concealed mystery that has suddenly been unveiled. Yet it was not without witness in the prophetic writings of the OT. Now that the gospel has been revealed, it can be shown to have been made known in advance through the prophetic writings (see Rom 1:2).

The matching bookend to Romans 16:26 can be found in Romans 1:5. Immediately after Paul gives the content of the gospel in Romans 1:2-4, he speaks of its purpose: "[the gospel about the Son,] Jesus the Christ our Lord, through whom we received *grace and apostleship *for the obedience of* pistis *in all the nations* in behalf of his *name" (Rom 1:4-5). The "in behalf of his name" refers back to Jesus, who is called Lord, Christ, and Son-of-God-in-Power in the immediate context. His royal titles are ubiquitous. What is the purpose of the gospel? It is the "obedience of *pistis* in all the nations" unto King Jesus.

Given Paul's stress on Jesus' sovereignty, "the obedience of *pistis*" (Rom 1:5; 16:26) is best translated as a descriptive genitive—"the obedience characterized by loyalty" or "allegiant obedience." Put more simply in contemporary English language idiom: the purpose of the gospel is to cultivate allegiance to King Jesus in every nation.

8.2. Obeying the Gospel. Allegiant obedience to the king is why elsewhere Paul speaks of not just belief or trust but obedience as a necessary response to the gospel. Paul, with reference to Jesus' lordship, can grieve, "not all have *obeyed the gospel*" (Rom 10:16) and can express confidence that all who fail to "*obey the gospel*" will experience wrath when the Lord Jesus is fully revealed in his coming (2 Thess 1:8). Elsewhere Paul summarizes the purpose of the gospel, saying that he has "fulfilled the *ministry of the gospel of the Christ" by bringing "the nations to obedience" (Rom 15:18-19).

God's final judgment, exercised through his king, is also said to be part of the gospel (Rom 2:16). This judgment for eternal life or condemnation will be according to deeds (Rom 2:6-8; cf. Rom 14:10; 1 Cor 3:12-15; 2 Cor 5:10; Eph 6:8; 1 Tim 5:24; 2 Tim 4:14; Mt 16:27; Jn 5:28-29). Thus, the gospel requires bodily obedience. One can best make sense of this by seeing salvation as solely by *pistis* (faith; loyalty) to King Jesus. *Pistis* unites one to the king and his benefits. But it is not merely mental. *Pistis* is externalized, relational, and embodied, so that with the Holy Spirit's assistance saving deeds are within allegiance's purview, allowing a person to meet the law's righteous requirements (Rom 2:27-29; 8:4, 12-14).

Similarly the necessity of obedience to the gospel is implied in passages that concern sovereignty and citizenship. Paul does *not* say the purpose of the king's death and resurrection is to achieve forgiveness for humans regardless of their bodily activities, but on the contrary so that the Christ "might reign *as Lord* over the dead and the living" (Rom 14:9; cf. Acts 10:42; 1 Pet 4:5). The need for obedience is also why Paul calls the Philippians to "live as citizens" in a manner worthy of "the gospel of the Christ" (Phil 1:27). The purpose of the gospel is allegiant obedience to the king.

8.3. The Restorative Gospel. Paul speaks of the gospel as saving. The gospel is the power of God for salvation (Rom 1:16). Likewise, Ephesians speaks of "the gospel of your salvation," and the gospel is also called the "message of truth" (Eph 1:13). Death is defeated, and life and immortality are brought to light through the gospel (2 Tim 1:10).

The larger aim is a process of rescue. The gospel is one's salvation if one holds fast to it (1 Cor 15:2). Paul's focus is on the collective rescue of the community that continually confesses "Jesus is Lord," for that confession is indicative of the true work of the indwelling Holy Spirit (see 1 Cor 12:3). The gospel is connected to heavenly hope and future glory (e.g., Col 1:5; 2 Thess 2:14).

Salvation through the gospel is not just rescue from a plight but is for the purpose of glory's restoration. Although made in God's image, humanity exchanged God's glory for nonglorious idols (Rom 1:23). The result for humanity is not merely a sin problem but also a lack of glory (Rom 3:23). Creation has been dishonored (Rom 8:21). God's glory—his reputation—has been smeared too (Rom 1:21; 2:23-24).

Paul is not speaking trivially when he calls the good news "the gospel of the glory of the Christ, who is the image of God" (2 Cor 4:4). Through viewing the pristine image of God—Jesus the Christ—right now humanity is in the process of glory restoration (2 Cor 3:18). Creation will be reinvigorated as humans recover and fully distribute God's glory to it afresh (2 Cor 8:21). As humans are transformed into the image of the king, they become fit to reign gloriously over the restored creation alongside the king of kings (2 Tim 2:12). As humanity and creation recover glory, then the God revealed by the gospel—Father, Son, and Holy Spirit—receives the maximum glory too.

The purpose of the gospel is allegiant obedience to Jesus the Christ in every nation. Conformity to the king's pattern of life, death on the cross, resurrection, and enthronement is how glory is being restored for humans, creation, and ultimately God. Jesus is the victorious king. He has conquered sin, evil cosmic powers, and death. As the Christ, Jesus gives his resurrection life and other saving benefits to all those who respond to his kingship with trusting allegiance.

See also CHRIST, MESSIAH; FAITH; GOD; HOLY SPIRIT; JUSTIFICATION; KINGDOM OF GOD/CHRIST; OLD TESTAMENT IN PAUL; RESURRECTION; RIGHTEOUSNESS; SALVATION; SIN, GUILT.

BIBLIOGRAPHY. **M. W. Bates,** *The Hermeneutics of the Apostolic Proclamation: The Center of Paul's Method of Scriptural Interpretation* (Waco, TX: Baylor University Press, 2012); idem, "A Christology of Incarnation and Enthronement: Romans 1:3-4 as Unified, Non-adoptionist, and Non-conciliatory," *CBQ* 77 (2015): 107-27; idem, *Salvation by Allegiance Alone: Rethinking Faith, Works, and the Gospel of Jesus the King* (Grand Rapids, MI: Baker Academic, 2017); idem, *Gospel Allegiance: What Faith in Jesus Misses for Salvation in Christ* (Grand Rapids, MI: Brazos, 2019); **M. F. Bird,** *Introducing Paul: The Man, His Mission, and His Message* (Downers Grove, IL: IVP Academic, 2014); idem, *An Anomalous Jew: Paul Among Jews, Greeks, and Romans* (Grand Rapids, MI: Eerdmans, 2016); **R. Bultmann,** *Theology of the New Testament*, trans. Kendrick Grobel, 2 vols. (New York: Scribners, 1951-1955); **D. A. Campbell,** *The Quest for Paul's Gospel: A Suggested Strategy* (London: T&T Clark, 2005); idem, *The Deliverance of God: An Apocalyptic Rereading of Justification in Paul* (Grand Rapids, MI: Eerdmans, 2009); **D. J. Downs and B. J. Lappenga,** *The Faithfulness of the Risen Christ:* Pistis *and the Exalted Lord in the Pauline Letters* (Waco, TX: Baylor University Press, 2019); **D. B. Garlington,** *"The Obedience of Faith": A Pauline Phrase in Historical Context*, WUNT 38 (Tübingen: Mohr Siebeck, 1991); **B. Gaventa,** *When in Romans: An Invitation to Linger with the Gospel According to Paul* (Grand Rapids, MI: Eerdmans, 2016); **M. J. Gorman,** *The Apostle of the Crucified Lord: A Theological Introduction to Paul and His Letters* (Grand Rapids, MI: Eerdmans, 2004); idem, *Inhabiting the Cruciform God: Kenosis, Justification, and Theosis in Paul's Narrative Soteriology* (Grand Rapids, MI: Eerdmans, 2009); idem, *Becoming the Gospel: Paul, Participation, and Mission* (Grand Rapids, MI: Eerdmans, 2015); **L. W. Hurtado,** "The Doxology at the End of Romans," in *New Testament Textual Criticism: Its Significance for Exegesis; Essays in Honour of Bruce M. Metzger*, ed. E. J. Epp and G. D. Fee (Oxford: Clarendon, 1981), 185-99; **C. L. Irons,** *The Righteousness of God: A Lexical Examination of the Covenant-Faithfulness Interpretation*, WUNT 386 (Tübingen: Mohr Siebeck, 2015); **R. Jewett,** "The Redaction and Use of an Early Christian Confession in Romans 1:3-4," in *The Living Text: Essays in Honor of Ernest W. Saunders*, ed. D. E. Groh and R. Jewett (Lanham, MD: University Press of America, 1985), 99-122; **J. W. Jipp,** "Ancient, Modern, and Future Interpretations of Romans 1:3-4: Reception History and Biblical Interpretation," *JTI* (2009): 241-59; idem, *Christ Is King: Paul's Royal Ideology* (Minneapolis: Fortress, 2015); **E. Käsemann,** *Commentary on Romans*, trans. G. W. Bromiley (Grand Rapids, MI: Eerdmans, 1980); **L. E. Keck,** "Romans 15:4: An Interpolation?," in *Faith and History: Essays in Honor of Paul W. Meyer*, ed. J. T. Carroll, C. H. Cosgrove, and E. E. Johnson (Atlanta: Scholars Press, 1990), 125-36; **R. N. Longenecker,** *Introducing Romans: Critical Issues in Paul's Most*

Famous Letter (Grand Rapids, MI: Eerdmans, 2011); idem, *The Epistle to the Romans: A Commentary on the Greek Text*, NIGTC (Grand Rapids, MI: Eerdmans, 2016); **M. Luther,** *Preface to the Latin Writings*, in *Martin Luther: Selections from His Writings*, ed. J. Dillenberger (Garden City, NY: Anchor, 1961), 19-34; **J. L. Martyn,** *Galatians: A New Translation with Introduction and Commentary*, AB 33A (New York: Doubleday, 1997); **A. E. McGrath,** *Iustitia Dei: A History of the Christian Doctrine of Justification*, 3rd ed. (Cambridge: Cambridge University Press, 2005); **S. McKnight,** *The King Jesus Gospel: The Original Good News Revisited* (Grand Rapids, MI: Zondervan, 2011); idem, *Reading Romans Backwards: A Gospel of Peace in the Midst of Empire* (Waco, TX: Baylor University Press, 2019); **D. J. Moo,** *The Epistle to the Romans*, NICNT (Grand Rapids, MI: Eerdmans, 1996); **M. V. Novenson,** *Christ Among the Messiahs: Christ Language in Paul and Messiah Language in Ancient Judaism* (Oxford: Oxford University Press, 2012); **S. E. Porter and H. T. Ong,** eds., *Is the Gospel Good News?* (Eugene, OR: Pickwick, 2019); **C. D. Stanley,** *Paul and the Language of Scripture: Citation Technique in the Pauline Epistles and Contemporary Literature*, SNTSMS 69 (Cambridge: Cambridge University Press, 1992); **G. Stanton,** "Paul's Gospel," in *The Cambridge Companion to St Paul*, ed. J. D. G. Dunn (Cambridge: Cambridge University Press, 2003), 173-84; **P. Stuhlmacher,** *Das paulinische Evangelium 1: Vorgeschichte*, FRLANT 95 (Gottingen: Vandenhoeck & Ruprecht, 1968); idem, "The Pauline Gospel," in *The Gospel and the Gospels*, ed. P. Stuhlmacher (Grand Rapids, MI: Eerdmans, 1991), 149-72; **G. Twelftree,** *The Gospel According to Paul* (Eugene, OR: Cascade, 2019); **N. T. Wright,** *What Saint Paul Really Said: Was Paul of Tarsus the Real Founder of Christianity?* (Grand Rapids, MI: Eerdmans, 1997); idem, *Paul and the Faithfulness of God*, 2 vols. (Minneapolis: Fortress, 2013); idem, *The Paul Debate: Critical Questions for Understanding the Apostle* (Waco, TX: Baylor University Press, 2015).

M. W. Bates

GOVERNMENT. *See* Church Structure; Political Systems; Politics and Power.

GRACE

The study of grace in the letters of Paul has often focused exclusively on Paul's use of the term *charis.* But that is a mistake on two counts. First, the Greek term *charis* can be used in a variety of senses. For instance, it can mean "gratitude" or "thanks" (e.g., 2 Cor 9:15: "*charis* be to *God for his indescribable gift"), that is, as the return for a gift, not the gift itself. But second, and more importantly, *charis* is only one of a number of terms that Paul uses for the gift or grace of God (and, derivatively, for the gifts given by human beings). Sometimes he piles up a collection of near-synonymous gift terms (e.g., in Rom 5:15-16: *charis, dōrea, dōrēma, charisma*), and sometimes he weaves together a verb meaning "give" with the noun *charis.* Thus, for instance, when he speaks of "the *Son of God, who loved me and gave himself for me" (Gal 2:20 NRSV), he immediately describes this phenomenon as "the *charis* of God" (Gal 2:21). It is clear that if one is going to understand the concept of grace one needs to include the whole set of "gift" language in Paul.

Like the other gift terms used by Paul, *charis* was a normal word for gift or favor, that is, a benefit voluntarily bestowed out of personal goodwill. It was not a uniquely theological word and it did not have the special meaning of "undeserved gift" now associated with the English word *grace.* When gift-terms acquire this sense in Paul, that derives from the context in which they are used and from the whole structure of Paul's thought, not from a particular word. Nonetheless, for Paul, gift-language used in relation to God, and especially with reference to the Christ-event, did acquire special nuances, and it is necessary to investigate carefully what those were.

For Paul, all the gifts of God in *creation and the long history of God's grace to *Israel came to sharpest focus and were given their definitive expression in the gift of God in *Christ: this can be described either as God's gift of Christ (Rom 8:32) or as the self-giving of Christ, who "gave himself for our sins to set us free from the present evil age" (Gal 1:4 NRSV; see Gal 2:20). Thus, grace has a narrative shape in Paul: it refers most often to an act or event, rather than to a quality in God. There are many kinds of gift (both in antiquity and today), and it is necessary to explore what kind of gift was given in Christ. Indeed, gifts can take perfect or ultimate expression in a variety of ways: in their size, for instance, or in their priority (always being given first). Most gifts in antiquity, as today, were given discriminately with reference to the value or worth of the recipient; indeed, that was commonly regarded as one of the hallmarks of a good gift.

In the history of Christian theology, and especially Protestant theology, it has been common to speak of *salvation "by grace alone" and to associate with that phrase the notion of grace as a "free" or "pure" gift. But that could mean two things. Does free grace mean that God's grace is given without any condition or merit, without regard to the worth of the recipient? Or does a free gift mean that it is given without expectation of a subsequent response or return, coming, as we say, "with no strings attached"? These two senses of a "free gift" are importantly different: although they can be combined, what is free of prior conditions is not necessarily also free of expectation that the recipient will make a response. As will become evident, it is central to Paul's grammar of grace that the gift of God is unfitting or incongruous, given without regard to the worth or capacity of the recipient—indeed, in the absence of worth or strength. But the gift does not leave its recipients unaltered: it establishes a relationship with the Giver, together with a new capacity that transforms the recipients of grace and results, necessarily, in a change of values and behavior.

1. The Unconditioned Gift of Christ
2. Grace and Response
3. Grace and Generosity

1. The Unconditioned Gift of Christ. On several occasions Paul speaks of the grace of God in highly personal, autobiographical terms. Reflecting on his prior life, when he persecuted the *church of God, he notes that he was not worthy to be called an *apostle: "But by the grace of God I am what I am, and his grace toward me has not been in vain. On the contrary, I worked harder than any of them—though it was not I, but the grace of God that is with me" (1 Cor 15:10 NRSV). In similar terms, he narrates in Galatians that he had been set apart before he was born and called through God's grace, such that he received a revelation of Christ and a commission to spread the good news among the *Gentiles (Gal 1:15-16). In such passages, it is evident that Paul had received this gift not because of his prior worth (in his *ethnicity, ancestry, or superior education or achievement), indeed, despite his prior unworthiness (in his persecution of the church). Neither positive nor negative worth determined God's choice and calling in grace, which was in this sense entirely unconditioned. Indeed, the absence of worth makes all the clearer the incongruity of grace, the misfit between the gift and its recipient. Despite the normal conventions concerning gifts, and despite a natural expectation that God *should* give gifts only to those worthy of them, Paul experienced a gift that was wholly unconditioned.

In a similar vein, Paul draws attention to his own physical weakness as the opportunity for a display of Christ's grace: when he appealed three times unsuccessfully to have his "thorn in the flesh" removed, he heard from Christ, "My grace is sufficient for you, for power is made perfect in weakness" (2 Cor 12:9 NRSV). It seems that God's grace operates definitively in the absence of human worth, whether defined by ethnicity, upbringing, ancestry, knowledge, gender, or strength (see 1 Cor 1:26-31). The God "who gives life to the dead and calls into existence the things that do not exist" (Rom 4:17 NRSV) is the one who acts in grace, disregarding all human attributes of worth (and worthlessness), and *granting* the only worth that counts, the worth of being found in Christ (Phil 3:9).

What Paul found to be true of himself matches what he discovered in his *mission to Gentiles and was a truth perhaps clarified in that experience. In his traditional Jewish perspective, Gentiles were, by definition, "sinners" (Gal 2:15) and ignorant of God (Gal 4:8). They were hardly to be regarded as fitting recipients of divine gifts, let alone God's definitive gift of grace in Christ. For a Jew like Paul, the lack of *circumcision marked the Gentile male as someone outside the Abrahamic *covenant and therefore beyond the limit of God's promises. But Paul was called to proclaim the good news among the Gentiles (Gal 1:16), and what he found was that they, too, were "called . . . in the grace of Christ" (Gal 1:6 NRSV) and given the associated gift of the Spirit (Gal 3:1-5). Such gifts were given without regard to their ethnic, religious, and moral "inferiority" as Gentiles. The good news turned out to be good, equally and indiscriminately, for the circumcised and the uncircumcised (Gal 2:6-9; 5:6), because it was given independent of traditional norms of evaluation: "there is no longer Jew or Greek, there is no longer *slave or free, there is no longer male and female; for all of you are one in Christ Jesus" (Gal 3:28 NRSV).

In Galatians, one can watch Paul working out the implications of this radical conviction in contrast to opponents who considered that the gift of God in Christ was given within the conditions established by the Mosaic *law. As Paul reports there, he vigorously objected when *Peter withdrew from Gentile believers at meals dedicated to Christ and thereby gave the impression that Gentiles were acceptable only if they "Judaized" (that is, adopted the Jewish way of life, Gal 2:11-14). To condition the good news in that way would be to contradict it and to deny the effect of grace (Gal 2:14, 21). By putting their trust in Christ, believers, both Jewish and non-Jewish, have staked everything on the absolute value of what has been given in the *death and *resurrection of Jesus: they recognize the bankruptcy of any other form of worth, whether ascribed or achieved, whether based on ethnicity or law observance. On these radical terms, Paul created communities that crossed traditional boundaries and mixed people of different ethnicities and social statuses, because all were given their worth on the same terms, on the basis of a single but universal gift: Christ himself.

In Romans, Paul paints this *truth on a larger canvas and brings out still further the mismatch between the grace of God in Christ and the condition or capacities of its human recipients. While all were "under *sin" to a depth that even the law was unable to resolve, "they are now justified by his grace as a gift, through the redemption that is in Christ Jesus" (Rom 3:24 NRSV). This is not a gift to the worthy, to the righteous or the good, for whom one might, perhaps, be prepared to give the costliest gift of one's life. To the contrary, "while we were still weak, at the right time Christ died for the ungodly," and "God proves his *love for us in that while we still were sinners Christ died for us" (Rom 5:6, 8 NRSV). When the trajectory of human history was leading inexorably from sin to death, from transgression to condemnation, God's grace in Christ effected a miraculous countermovement, leading from many sins into *righteousness, out of compound transgression into life (Rom 5:12-21). This creative power of grace, to *establish* what is absent and to create something from nothing, is part of what Paul means by the "abounding" of grace (Rom 5:20): it abounds not only in size but in its power to achieve the impossible (Rom 1:16).

That counterfactual momentum of grace is what Paul finds in the programmatic story of *Abraham, at the founding of the people of Israel (Rom 4). Since the Genesis text speaks of Abraham's great "reward" (Gen 15:1), one might expect to find there what Abraham did, what made him a fitting recipient. But Paul finds only a gap in the *narrative, or rather the revealing statement that "Abraham believed [or better: trusted] God, and it was reckoned to him as righteousness" (Rom 4:3 NRSV, citing Gen 15:6, as does Gal 3:6). Paul takes the Genesis text to point away from the notion of wage or fitting gift and toward the unfitting gift of *forgiveness "to one who without works trusts him who justifies the ungodly" (Rom 4:5 NRSV). If this is the character of the foundational gift to Abraham, it marks him as the father of all who trust in God, that trust being now crystallized as trust in the one who raised Christ from the dead. Whether they are Jew or non-Jew, their trust signals their dependence on the grace of God, which creates "from nothing" and "calls into existence the things that do not exist" (Rom 4:17 NRSV).

In Romans 9–11 Paul mixes the language of gift/grace with that of *mercy and shows how the whole story of Israel, from start (Rom 9:6-13) to end (Rom 11:25-32), depends on the God who acts in unconditioned mercy. God's calling is not conditioned by birth, ancestry, or moral virtue (Rom 9:6-13); he "has mercy on whom [he has] mercy" (Rom 9:15, citing Ex 33:19); he chooses a remnant by grace (and not on the basis of their works, Rom 11:1-6); he sustains the "olive tree" of the people of God by the rich root of his goodness (Rom 11:17-24); his gifts and calling are "irrevocable" (Rom 11:29 NRSV); and he "has imprisoned all in disobedience so that he may be merciful to all" (Rom 11:32 NRSV). This pattern of grace is what brought Israel into being and what explains the oddity of Gentile believers being grafted into a tree that is not their own, at a time when the majority of Paul's fellow Israelites have not yet welcomed their Messiah. But this story also gives Paul hope for the future, that "all Israel will be saved" (Rom 11:26), because the future of Israel is, as ever, in the hands of a merciful God. The extraordinary gift of God to unworthy Gentiles, witnessed in Paul's mission, indicates that no disobedience is strong enough to resist the grace of God, which operates most characteristically in the absence of human worth. That defies standard expectations of cosmic justice, but it gives Paul hope that, just as God brought resurrection out of death in the gift-event of Christ, so God's grace can and will overcome the obstacles of sin, disobedience, and death.

This conviction is continued and given wider application in Ephesians and in the Pastoral Letters. Ephesians speaks effusively of the "riches" of God's grace (Eph 1:7), which are poured out through Christ and given to Gentiles as well as Jews (Eph 2:1-22). Through this grace, those "dead" in sin have been made alive (Eph 2:1-10), and aliens have been made citizens (Eph 2:11-22), and this is a sign that "by grace you have been saved through *faith, and this is not your own doing; it is the gift of God—not the result of works, so that no one may boast" (Eph 2:8-9 NRSV). In 2 Timothy, grace is mapped across the whole span of time, such that "this grace was given to us in Christ Jesus before the ages began, but it has now been revealed through the appearing of our *Savior Jesus Christ" (2 Tim 1:9-10; see Eph 3:7-9). This perspective ensures that grace cannot be limited to a single event in history, as if God's mind had changed or his resolve to be gracious could be dated from the historical coming of Christ. Rather, what the Christ-event reveals is what has been true all along (but true "in Christ Jesus"): that everything in God's relation to the world has been characterized by a self-giving and undeserved love, both inside and outside time, both in creation and in redemption. In other words, "grace" is the name of God's relation to the world and to all humanity, as sealed, revealed, and most fully enacted in Christ.

2. Grace and Response.

Everyone in the ancient world (as in most cultures today) knew that a gift expected a response—at least in gratitude, but usually also in a countergift of some sort. In the Greek and Roman worlds, the "Three Graces" dancing in a circle were a familiar representation of this reciprocity of gift. For a variety of historical, philosophical, and social reasons, modern Western culture has come to idealize the one-way gift—the gift without return—such that we sometimes prefer to give anonymous gifts, where no return is possible. But in Paul's day gifts were given in order to create or sustain a personal relationship, and that could hardly operate well on a unilateral basis. Thus it was common to speak of being obliged or indebted after the receipt of a gift, and friends would seek ways to "repay" the gifts they had been given.

Paul shares this basic assumption about the gifts of God: they are intended to create a relationship and evoke a response. Thus he speaks of the gratitude and *honor due to God from humanity in relation to creation (Rom 1:18-23), and describes the response to the "mercies of God" that is expected from believers: "present your bodies as a living *sacrifice, holy and acceptable to God, which is your spiritual *worship" (Rom 12:1 NRSV). Although God's grace is given freely, in the sense that it is given without prior conditions, it is not cheap in the sense that it expects nothing in return. Paul is aware that his descriptions of the undeserved grace of God might encourage the impression that sin does not matter—that grace, indeed, gives one the license to continue in sin, so that grace may have still wider effect (Rom 6:1). His response is characteristic: "By no means!" (Rom 6:2 NRSV). Grace cannot leave the believer unchanged: it forges a new relationship, under a new Master, Jesus. Paul speaks of being "under grace" (Rom 6:14-15) and even uses the language of slavery to describe the sense of obligation and allegiance that arises from the gift of Christ (Rom 6:15-23).

But he is not speaking of new obligations loaded onto the old, incapable self, or a new set of demands that turn out to be, once again, beyond human capacity. Grace is a relation that is transformative in its effects. The gift of grace is, for Paul, not the gift of a "thing." It is not a commodity passed over into human possession, or even a quality that is infused into the character of the recipient. It is a relationship—the gift, one may say, of Christ in relation to the self, which amounts to saying that it is the gift of a new self: "if anyone is in Christ, there is a new creation" (2 Cor 5:17 NRSV; see Gal 6:15); "it is no longer I who live, but it is Christ who lives in me" (Gal 2:20 NRSV). Trust in Christ entails, for Paul, participation in the event of the death and resurrection of Christ and in the dynamic created by them. *Baptism means the death of the old self, the end of an old form of existence, and at the same time a "newness of life" that is sourced in the resurrection of Jesus (Rom 6:1-11; the idea is developed in Col 2:11-15 and Eph 2:4-6).

Thus the response elicited by grace is the response of a new self, newly capable and newly empowered by the Spirit. Although Paul can speak sternly of the responsibilities of believers and warns them against *apostasy and its dire consequences (Gal 6:7-8), their agency has been itself transformed and not merely supplemented by the assistance of the Spirit. The Spirit constitutes their new life, not to replace their agency but to empower it: "if we live by the Spirit, let us also be guided [or better: walk] by the Spirit" (Gal 5:25 NRSV). The Spirit and the believer are not two competing agencies (the more of one, the less of the other), nor is one simply added to the other. Rather, the believer is energized to "work out your own salvation with *fear and trembling; for it is God who is at work in you, enabling you both to will and to work for his good pleasure" (Phil 2:12-13 NRSV).

Grace is thus transformative at every level. In the individual believer, grace generates new desires, goals, dispositions, and values; in the community of believers, it establishes new patterns of behavior in social relationships. Although Protestant Christianity has focused primarily on the individual (on the "amazing grace" that "saved a wretch like me"), Paul was also concerned to see this grace enacted in community relations, where new patterns of respect and love indicate a community created by grace and endued with grace-shaped values. Although believers are of different ethnicities and continue to inhabit different cultures and customs, they are able to recognize and welcome one another as people "welcomed" by Christ (Rom 14:3; 15:7). At the *Lord's Supper, where the community remembers and is shaped anew by the gift of Christ "for you" (1 Cor 11:23-26), it practices new patterns of mutual honor and care. Paul was furious when these values were denied, when some powerful Corinthian believers denigrated or ignored other participants at their shared meal (1 Cor 11:17-22). That Christ died "for you" is a statement addressed to everyone at the meal, signaling that every member is significant and every life matters (see 1 Cor 8:10; Rom 14:15). But if the community fails to adjust its norms to "the truth of the good news," the grace of God will have been received "in vain" (Gal 2:14; 2 Cor 6:1). In this sense, grace is only fulfilled if it is enacted in social practice.

Paul expects that this transformation of heart and community will be evident at the coming of Christ and the *judgment of all (1 Thess 3:12-13; Rom 2:6-11; 14:10-12; 2 Cor 5:10). That judgment will not allocate a second installment of grace, as if the grace enacted in Christ were only the beginning, designed only to set believers on the road toward an uncertain future. Rather, this judgment "according to works" will recognize and reward the product of the one gift in Christ, which is the gift of eternal life (Rom 6:23). That gift is the source and energy within every form of "good work" that is pleasing to God (Gal 6:7-10). There is therefore no contradiction in Paul's theology between grace and good works: although neither works nor any other form of worth can make a person fit to be given God's grace in Christ, the transformation created by grace is intended to bear fruit in all kinds of socially active forms. "By grace you have been saved . . . for we are what he has made us, created in Christ Jesus for good works, which God prepared beforehand to be our way of life" (Eph 2:8, 10 NRSV).

3. Grace and Generosity.

The gift of God in Christ transforms interpersonal relationships in a variety of ways. Paul speaks of being enriched by "the grace [*charis*] of God that has been given you in Christ Jesus . . . so that you are not lacking in any spiritual gift [*charisma*]" (1 Cor 1:4, 7 NRSV). These *charismata* can take many forms and are described in differing, illustrative lists (1 Cor 12:4-11; Rom 12:6-8; Eph 4:11-13). Their purpose is to distribute the grace of God around the *body of Christ, in the form of capacities and skills that create strong social bonds and equip the church to support one another in serving Christ. It is important for Paul that these gifts are differentially distributed: no member of the body is self-sufficient, and none can be ignored or dishonored as having nothing to contribute to the rest (1 Cor 12:12-26). In this sense, the grace of God creates a community of gift exchange, where each member is equipped both to give and to receive. That is one reason why grace can never be a solo affair: it transforms its recipients into givers, and their fulfilled human capacities can be expressed only in a community of gift and receipt. It is as conjoined "sharers in God's grace" (Phil 1:7) that they enter most deeply into the transformation it effects.

Paul develops the connection between grace and generosity most fully in his appeal to the Corinthians to contribute to the *collection for *Jerusalem (2 Cor 8–9). Here there is a clear link between the *charis* (favor, benefit, gift) of God (2 Cor 8:1) or of "the Lord Jesus Christ" (2 Cor 8:9) and the *charis* (gift) that Paul is trying to elicit for Jerusalem (2 Cor 8:7). But this is not merely a play on words. It is the grace of God that grounds the possibility of human giving (2 Cor 8:1; 9:8, 14), not just as an example to which they aspire but as the motivating force and shaping dynamic in which they give. This comes to clearest expression in the power of the Christ-event: "for you know the generous act [*charis*] of our Lord Jesus Christ, that though [or better: because] he was rich, yet for your sakes he became poor, so that by his poverty you might become rich" (2 Cor 8:9 NRSV). As other verses in this context make clear, Paul uses the language of "*wealth" or "riches" to mean not so much what one has as how one gives: the Macedonians' poverty, for instance, has overflowed in "a wealth of generosity" (2 Cor 8:2 NRSV; see 2 Cor 9:11).

Thus the richness of Jesus is precisely his self-giving love, expressed paradoxically in his self-limitation (becoming poor) in the incarnation. But as he shares in the human condition and redeems it through his death and resurrection, so he enables believers to share in the divine impulse of grace, in their unreserved and wholehearted giving to others. In this process they are not just channels or conduits of divine grace, if that were to suggest a merely mechanical process. Rather, they are themselves transformed by grace into the sort of givers who give in love, not reluctantly but eagerly and willingly (2 Cor 8:8, 10-11; 9:5, 7). In fact, it is not enough just to give. What matters for Paul is that the Corinthians should *want* to do it (2 Cor 8:10; see 1 Cor 13:3), and this heart transformation is what Paul refers to elsewhere as the operation and *fruit of the Spirit (Gal 5:22-23). Thus grace creates not only the practice of generosity but also a quality of person and of relationship that reflects the generosity at the heart of the universe (2 Cor 9:10).

Even this giving will not be one-way. If the Corinthians are to give out of their present abundance, Paul also expects Jerusalem to give, at some time and in some way, out of theirs (2 Cor 8:13-15). *Equality* here means a constant shifting of surplus toward need, and Paul figures this as an enduring process. He is conscious of the ways that giving can create patronizing, one-way relations of power (Rom 1:11-12), and his model for gift-giving is not top-down charity but the reciprocal support effected when believers "bear one another's burdens and so fulfill the *law of Christ" (Gal 6:2).

In giving to "the saints" in Jerusalem, the Corinthians are also, at the same time, offering worship to God and generating thanksgiving (*eucharistia*) that will reverberate back to God from the interaction between human givers and receivers (2 Cor 9:11-15). In this sense, the *charis* that springs from God and circulates among its recipients circles back *to* God in the form of *eucharistia*. Paul is not embarrassed to point toward this return of the gift, as if it would somehow be better if God's grace were only a one-way gift. To the contrary, he celebrates how the grace of God at work among the Macedonians has led them to "give themselves to the *Lord" and to the collection project led by Paul (2 Cor 8:5). This response to God is not to cause detriment to the human partner, as a limitation on their *freedom or an imposition on their wills: it is how their wills become most eager and free (2 Cor 8:16-17) and how they attain their full intended dignity as creatures of God (Rom 1:18-25). As they give more generously than they might imagine possible, they discover resources in the grace of God that enable a blessing and a *fullness they would otherwise not have known (2 Cor 9:6-8). Grace thus effects simultaneously the blessing of humanity, the sharing of gifts (both material and immaterial), and the worship of God, each augmenting the other.

There is a reason that every letter of Paul begins with a reference to the grace (or favor) of God, in the form of the opening blessing, "Grace to you and *peace from God our Father and the Lord Jesus Christ" (e.g., Gal 1:3; 2 Cor 1:2 NRSV). All the letters also end with a grace benediction, some variant of "may the grace of our Lord Jesus Christ be with your spirit" (e.g., Gal 6:18; see 2 Cor 13:13). These are not simply formulaic expressions or versions of the common Greek greeting (*chairete*). They are loaded with theological meaning and frame everything that is said between beginning and end within the gift giving of God.

This theme has caused rich reflection all through Christian history. In the course of the last century, the Lutheran emphasis on the "free" grace of Christ, contrasted with human reliance on "works," influenced the radical emphasis on grace by Karl Barth, whose commentary on Romans depicts God's act of grace in Christ as a crisis for humanity, an "impossible possibility" that bridges the gulf between God and humanity, acting always despite the human condition and never because of it. Rudolf Bultmann developed the Lutheran critique of human self-reliance, taking God's grace to open up a new possibility for human existence, lived in total dependence on God. For Ernst Käsemann, it was crucial to stress that with the gift comes the Giver, whose grace is also an act of power, enlisting believers into a new allegiance and by no means leaving them free to do as they wish ("cheap grace"). In the same line of tradition, J. Louis Martyn insists on the "uncontingent" nature of grace, which "invades" the world in Christ and elicits the faith and action of believers, who are not autonomous but liberated to serve in forms of activity generated by grace.

A very different debate was opened up by the work of E. P. Sanders, who challenged old caricatures of Judaism as a grace-deficient, legalistic religion. He showed through readings of Second Temple Jewish texts that, when analyzed in terms of sequence, grace was always the *prior* act of God: grace in the election of Israel was the means of "getting in," while obedience to the law was required for "staying in." In the wake of his work, the "new perspective on Paul" emphasized that Paul took grace to be open to all, both Gentiles and Jews, but this was an extension rather than a reconfiguration of Jewish views of grace.

The evidence suggests, however, that there was a variety of views about grace in Judaism in Paul's time: grace was everywhere, but not everywhere the same. In particular, the priority of grace (that God gives first) is not the same as its incongruity (that God gives without regard to worth). Paul was not alone in taking God's grace to be incongruous, but he uniquely tied that unconditioned grace to the act of God in Christ and practiced it in his Gentile mission, taking the Jewish theme of grace in new directions, with new results. In fact, his emphasis on the incongruity of grace has inspired radical interpretations of the Christian tradition all the way from Augustine to Martin Luther, and from John Wesley to Martin Luther King. As indicated above, it remains highly relevant to contemporary issues, such as self-worth, race relations, gift reciprocity, and environmental responsibility, and is a central part of the ongoing significance of Paul's theology today.

See also ABRAHAM; CHRISTOLOGY; COVENANT; ELECTION AND PREDESTINATION; ETHICS; FAITH; FORGIVENESS; GALATIANS, LETTER TO THE; HOLY

SPIRIT; MERCY; PATRONAGE; ROMANS, LETTER TO THE; WORKS OF THE LAW.

BIBLIOGRAPHY. **J. M. G. Barclay,** *Paul and the Gift* (Grand Rapids, MI: Eerdmans, 2015); idem, *Paul and the Power of Grace* (Grand Rapids, MI: Eerdmans, 2020); **K. Barth,** *The Epistle to the Romans*, trans. E. C. Hoskyns (London: Oxford University Press, 1933); **R. Bultmann,** *Theology of the New Testament* (London: SCM Press, 1952); **S. J. Chester,** *Reading Paul with the Reformers: Reconciling Old and New Perspectives* (Grand Rapids, MI: Eerdmans, 2017); **D. A. deSilva,** *Honor, Patronage, Kinship & Purity: Unlocking New Testament Culture* (Downers Grove, IL: IVP Academic, 2000); **D. J. Downs,** *The Offering of the Gentiles* (Tübingen: Mohr Siebeck, 2008); **J. R. Harrison,** *Paul's Language of Grace in Its Graeco-Roman Context* (Tübingen: Mohr Siebeck, 2003); **E. Käsemann,** "Justification and Salvation History in the Epistle to the Romans," in *Perspectives on Paul* (Philadelphia: Fortress, 1971), 60-78; **J. L. Linebaugh,** *God, Grace, and Righteousness in Wisdom of Solomon and Paul's Letter to the Romans* (Leiden: Brill, 2013); **J. L. Martyn,** *Theological Issues in the Letters of Paul* (Edinburgh: T&T Clark, 1997); **M. Mauss,** *The Gift*, trans. W. D. Halls (London: Routledge, 1990); **O. McFarland,** *God and Grace in Philo and Paul* (Leiden: Brill, 2015); **G. W. Peterman,** *Paul's Gift from Philippi: Conventions of Gift-Exchange and Christian Giving* (Cambridge: Cambridge University Press, 1997); **E. P. Sanders,** *Paul and Palestinian Judaism* (London: SCM Press, 1977); **M. Volf,** *Free of Charge: Giving and Forgiving in a Culture Stripped of Grace* (Grand Rapids, MI: Zondervan, 2005); **K. B. Wells,** *Grace and Agency in Paul and Second Temple Judaism* (Leiden: Brill, 2014); **D. Zeller,** *Charis bei Philon und Paulus* (Stuttgart: Verlag Katholishes Bibelwerk, 1990).

J. M. G. Barclay

GRECO-ROMAN RELIGIONS. *See* HELLENISM, ROMAN; RELIGIONS, GRECO-ROMAN.

GUILT. *See* ATONEMENT; JUSTIFICATION; SALVATION; SIN, GUILT.

H

HARDENING. *See* Election and Predestination; Israel; Old Testament in Paul.

HARDSHIPS. *See* Suffering.

HEAD

Until recently, biblical resources such as lexicons assumed a restricted meaning for *kephalē* that either referred to a literal head or it had a figurative meaning of authority and/or superior status, similar to one of the meanings of *head* in English. However, it is widely recognized that *kephalē* did not mean "authority" in idiomatic classical or Koine Greek at least until AD 4. Neither the lexicons by ancient Greeks, nor Liddell and Scott (LSJ), nor the recent *Cambridge Greek Lexicon* (Diggle et al., 799) include "leader," "authority," "rule," or "dominion" as one of the meanings of *kephalē* (Payne 2009, 117-37). Paul's use of *kephalē* was unique in describing the relationship between husband and wife, but he draws on the resources of the Greek language in a way that stays close to the cultural view of the physiological function of a head and can be interpreted consistently with the range of meaning of the Greek idiom.

1. The Range of Meaning of *Kephalē in Greek*
2. *Kephalē* in the LXX
3. The Relationship of *Kephalē* to Status
4. *Kephalē* and Reciprocity
5. God as the *Kephalē* of Christ
6. Christ as the *Kephalē* of Every Man
7. Man as the *Kephalē* of Woman
8. Christ as the *Kephalē* of the Church
9. Conclusion

1. The Range of Meaning of *Kephalē* in Greek. The range of figurative or metaphoric meanings of *kephalē* is complex. Liddell and Scott divide the meanings into animate and inanimate categories; the "head" of animate beings (humans and beasts) refers to the literal head, the noblest part/representative of the whole person, and what is typical of life (LSJ). Semantic domain theory is helpful to further nuance the range of meaning of *kephalē* as it relates to "life."

1.1.* Kephalē *and Semantic Domain Theory. Louw and Nida's *Greek-English Lexicon* (L&N) organizes Greek words and idioms in broad domains and subdomains of meaning relative to their range of meaning, which provides a more systematic approach to meaning. This is particularly helpful with words that have literal and figurative meanings such as *kephalē*. However, Louw and Nida's work on *kephalē* needs to be supplemented in light of recent research. They place *kephalē* only in the semantic domains of "Body, Body Parts and Body Products" (L&N 8.10) and supreme or preeminent "Status" (L&N 87.51). R. S. Cervin convincingly argues that the meaning in 87.51 should be "prominence," which is not intrinsically linked with authority," rather than "supreme or pre-eminent" (Cervin 2016). In addition, the status associated with *kephalē* varies, depending on how the referent is evaluated (below). But most importantly, the semantic range of *kephalē* in the Greek language should be expanded to account for other meanings relevant to its uses in the NT. The semantic "Physiological Processes and States" (23) of a head as understood in the Greek culture, and "Kinship Terms" (10), are additional appropriate semantic domains for *kephalē*, and the use of metonymy in which *prosōpon* ("face") and ("image") function figuratively for *kephalē* also plays a role.

1.2. "Physiological Processes and States" (23). Liddell and Scott as well as the *Cambridge Greek Lexicon* list "life" as one of the primary meanings of *kephalē*. According to Aristotle, the head was like a spring as the source of supply for the whole *body (Aristotle, *Probl.* 10 867a), a view many medical writers shared. Philo reflects the influence of Plato and Aristotle when he claims that the head draws on power from heaven and distributes its life force to the whole body (Philo, *Det.* 85). The head can be a "source of life" when it occurs with the supply of nourishment or other things that create or support life. When *kephalē* occurs with *sōma* (body) in a metaphor (1 Cor 12:12-27; Eph 1:22-23; 4:15-16; 5:22; Col 1:18; 2:19), the physiological aspects of the relationship between the head and body, such as life, unity, and interdependency, constrain the meaning.

1.3. "Kinship Terms" (10). The Greek perception of the physiological processes connected with the head is extended metaphorically in the language of kinship, including family, paternity, ancestry, *identity, family resemblance, and familial support. *Kephalē* was used to refer to an ancestor, a parent (mother or father), siblings, and even the children. Progenitors as "head" are the source or origin of a family's life (Philo, *Congr.* 61). Family members draw both life and a family resemblance from their entire family, which is the origin or source of one's identity. This resemblance is associated with the face because the face bears the family identity, which is genetic: "And to imagine that one is beheaded . . . is grievous for those who have parents and those who have children. For the head is like the parents due to its being the cause of life. And it is like children due to its face and its resemblance to them" (Artemidorus Daldianus, *Oneirocritica* 1.36, trans. Harris-McCoy; see also Tob 9:6). This is primarily how Paul uses *kephalē* to refer to God the Father and his Son, Jesus Christ.

2. *Kephalē* in the LXX.

In Hebrew, "head" (*rʾōš*) was a metaphor for authority, so some have argued that Paul's use of *kephalē* is a Hebraism, but Paul demonstrates competency in Greek idioms. Others, such as Wayne Grudem, argue that Paul is influenced by passages in the LXX where *rʾōš* was translated by *kephalē* where it means authority. Out of 171 instances in which *rʾōš* appears to refer to "authority" in the Hebrew Bible, there are only four passages in which it is translated as *kephalē* that do not have variants (2 Sam 22:44; Ps 18:43 [LXX 17:44]; Jer 31:7 [LXX 38:7]; Lam 1:5). The occurrences might be poor translation choices by the LXX translators (Hebraisms), or some may reflect a symbiotic relationship between an ancient king and his people or territory. As Cervin concludes, "The LXX has been overrated as evidence for *kephalē* connoting 'leader' or 'authority'" (Cervin 2016, 14). These four passages have no intertextual or semantic ties with Paul's use of *kephalē*, so Grudem's argument that LXX passages account for Paul use of *kephalē* is not convincing.

3. The Relationship of *Kephalē* to Status.

Kephalē is used as metonymy for the whole person. The kinship metaphor of "head" can be closely related to *patronage, *leadership, and *honor in the Greco-Roman culture, but *kephalē* can similarly be related to shame and dishonor as well as loss of status due to punishment, disaster, or responsibility falling on a person (Diggle et al., 799). The status depends on the evaluation of the referent or the behavior of the referent. *Kephalē* may represent a person who is honored as imminent or supreme, but it may by the same token represent a person who is dishonored by being shamed and punished. Dishonor and shame are linked with *kephalē* in 1 Corinthians 11:2-16 for both men and *women as well as "*glory."

4. *Kephalē* and Reciprocity.

When *kephalē* occurs in the context of how a "head" is a source or origin of life literally or in the provision of resources or services, then reciprocity or obligation could be in view, though it should not be assumed. A parent is the source of a child's life and identity, which creates a costly obligation for children to return the favors bestowed by their parents as long as they live (deSilva, 186). Paul reflects this sense of obligation when he says, "If a widow has children or grandchildren, they should first learn their religious duty to their own family and make some repayment to their parents; for this is pleasing in God's sight" (1 Tim 5:4 NRSV). Therefore, *kephalē* may refer to a leader or authority such as a parent who provides life, but it is important not to confuse a meaning of the term with its referent.

5. God as the *Kephalē* of Christ.

"Head," "face," and "image" are related metaphors. For Paul, Christ's head literally represents *God so that when one sees the face/head of *Christ, one sees God the Father and his glory. This sense of Christ's representation of God's nature, glory, and image is a theme in Paul as it is in John: "The light of the knowledge of the glory of God [is] in the face of Jesus Christ" (2 Cor 4:6 NRSV; see also Phil 2:6; Col 1:15). For Paul, Christ is God's *image in a similar way to how humanity is Adam's image, which corresponds to "sonship," or *sperma*. In this way, Paul has utilized and exploited the Greek concept of "head" to effectively communicate the relationship of Jesus the Son with God the Father. The metaphor of God as head in 1 Corinthians 11:3 therefore corresponds with a kinship register that is used for the relationship between the Father and the Son in early Christian *tradition. God, Christ, and man each function as heads in different ways, but they are all three consistent with the idiom of head as life: God functions as the Father who generates the Son.

6. Christ as the *Kephalē* of Every Man.
In 1 Corinthians 11:3, Paul states that Christ is the head of man, and consequently, in 1 Corinthians 11:7, that man should not cover his head because he is the "image" and glory of God, which alludes to the *creation of humanity in Genesis 1:27. As Paul says in the close context in 1 Corinthians 8:6, Jesus Christ is the one who created and sustains humanity, "through whom are all things and through whom we exist," or as in Colossians 1:15-17, "He is the image of the invisible God, the *firstborn of all creation; for in him all things in heaven and on earth were created, things visible and invisible, whether thrones or dominions or rulers or powers—all things have been created through him and for him. He himself is before all things, and in him all things hold together" (NRSV). Christ is the creator of every man, but he has not assumed authority over men individually, let alone all dominions, rulers, and powers. Paul's statement that Christ is the "head" of every man is followed by the discussion of man's uncovered head in *worship, which associates "head" and "image" with "dishonor" and "glory," forming significant links with not only Genesis 1:27-28 but also Romans 1:18-32 and 2 Corinthians 3:7-18 (see Westfall 2016, 66-70, 91-92). Paul depicts Christ as creator in terms consistent with his function as the head who is the origin and source of life of every man.

7. Man as the *Kephalē* of Woman.
In 1 Corinthians 11:3, Paul goes on to state that man is the head of woman, and in Corinthians 11:8 he indicates that man is woman's head because woman came out of man, an allusion to Genesis 2:21-23. Eve was made in God's image and created by Christ as well, but she received her life, her body, and her identity from *Adam so that she was in his image in a way that was unique. Adam is the source of life for all humanity and for Eve as well. Yet it is a kinship relationship that is comparable to but closer than Adam's relationship with his descendants: she was bone of his bones and *flesh of his flesh (Gen 2:23). According to Paul, all humanity shares a particular relationship with Adam: "We have borne the image of the man of dust" (1 Cor 15:49 NRSV). In this sense, the creation of Eve has something more in common with the rest of humanity than with Adam. Thus, Genesis 2:21-23 inspired Paul to apply the Greek idiom to the relationship between man and woman, and in that relationship he finds that woman has an enhanced glory: she is the image of God, the glory of God, *and* the glory of man. That is the rationale with which Paul supports women wearing veils during worship—the glory of man should be veiled, but the glory of God should not be veiled. Paul depicts man as the material with which God formed Eve: woman came out of man so that he is the source of her life and identity in a way that is consistent with a kinship register.

In Ephesians 5:21-33, the principles of reciprocity and organic unity are at play as Paul exploits the physiological aspects of the relationship between the head and body to explain how a husband and wife can "be subject to one another" (Westfall 2012). A wife was typically dependent on her husband for life support, and a wife's submission was considered an obligation in Greco-Roman culture because of the benefits she received from her husband. Paul briefly reaffirms the principle of reciprocity for the wife by stating that as a benefactor the husband is her head like Christ is the head of the *church. Then he turns to concentrate on how the metaphor of "head" applies to the man modeled by Christ's behavior as head of the church, the literal relationship of the head to the body, and Genesis 2:24. As the head of the church, Jesus is the *Savior through practical actions that are neither authoritative nor high status but expressions of love through low-status service (bathing, sewing, laundry). Then Paul states that if the husband is the wife's head, then she is his body, stressing the organic unity of the metaphor. By loving and treating the wife as he treats himself, a husband pragmatically bestows on the wife male status in their relationship (she is now figuratively a male body) and so fulfills the mutual submission exhorted in Ephesians 5:21. The quotation in Ephesians 5:31 from Genesis 2:24 connects the head-body metaphor to the creation of woman out of man. It elucidates the biblical basis of such a unity between both the man and the wife: "For this reason a man will leave his father and mother and be joined to his wife, and the two will become one flesh" (NRSV).

8. Christ as the *Kephalē* of the Church.
In addition to Ephesians 5:23, there are a few key passages where Christ is the head of the church in which it is thought that head unambiguously means "authority," but in these passages either *kephalē* refers to the organic unity of Christ as the head with

the church as his body, or it refers to Christ as the source of life for believers. In Ephesians 1:22, the organic unity of the head and the body along with the spatial imagery locate the church on the throne with Christ. The church as his *body is raised up with him and seated in the heavenly realms (see Eph 2:6), sharing his authoritative position. All rule and authority and power and dominion are under the feet of his body. In Colossians 1:18, "head" refers to Christ as the source of the church's existence together with his being the beginning and the firstborn from the dead, none of which has the basic meaning of "supremacy" but all of which provide the legitimate basis for Christ's having supremacy in everything. In Colossians 2:19, there is a clear description of the physiological function of *kephalē* reflected in the head-body relationship in terms of unity, nourishment, and growth. Christ is the head "from whom the whole body, nourished and held together by its ligaments and sinews, grows with a growth that is from God" (NRSV). Christ is the source of believers' life and identity as children of God; but that specific function is not synonymous nor interchangeable with his lordship.

In Colossians 2:10, Christ is the *kephalē* of every ruler and authority, but they are not his body, nor has he yet assumed authority over them. Jesus is the origin, basis, or source of every worldly rule and authority: "for in him all things in heaven and on earth were created, things visible and invisible, whether thrones or dominions or rulers or powers—all things have been created through him and for him" (Col 1:16 NRSV). However, Christ "disarmed the rulers and authorities and made a public example of them, triumphing over them in [the *cross]" (Col 2:15 NRSV). Christ did not triumph because he assumed authority over the rulers and authorities but rather through submitting to their oppression to the point of *death on a cross.

9. Conclusion.

The idiom *kephalē* should be understood according to its range of meaning in idiomatic Koine Greek. Paul was a Diaspora Jew from Asia Minor, and he was competent to communicate effectively in idiomatic Greek. The recipients in *Corinth, Colossae, and *Ephesus would have understood his use of *kephalē* as idiomatic Greek. The various ways in which the idiom *kephalē* connoted the origin or source of life provide a coherent understanding of Paul's interpretation of the creation account in Genesis 1–2 as well as explaining Christ's relationship with God the Father, the church, and the rest of creation.

See also ADAM AND CHRIST; CHRISTOLOGY; CHURCH; HONOR/SHAME; KINSHIP LANGUAGE IN PAUL; MAN AND WOMAN; MARRIAGE AND DIVORCE, ADULTERY AND INCEST; SON OF GOD; WOMEN.

BIBLIOGRAPHY. **R. S. Cervin,** "Does κεφαλή Mean 'Source' or 'Authority Over' in Greek Literature? A Rebuttal," *TrinJ* 10 (1989): 85-112; idem, "On the Significance of Kephalē ('head'): A Study of the Abuse of One Greek Word," *PriscPap* 30, no. 2 (2016): 8-20; **D. A. deSilva,** *Honor, Patronage, Kinship & Purity: Unlocking New Testament Culture* (Downers Grove, IL: IVP Academic, 2000); **J. Diggle et al.,** *The Cambridge Greek Lexicon*, vol. 2 (Cambridge: Cambridge University Press, 2021); **J. A. Fitzmyer,** "Another Look at ΚΕΦΑΛΗ in 1 Corinthians 11:3," *NTS* 35 (1989): 503-11; idem, "*Kephalē* in 1 Corinthians 11:3," *Int* 47 (1993): 32-59; **W. Grudem,** "The Meaning of κεφαλή ('Head'): An Evaluation of New Evidence, Real and Alleged," *JETS* 44 (2001): 25-65; **D. E. Harris-McCoy,** *Artemidorus' Oneirocritica: Text, Translation, and Commentary* (Oxford: Oxford University Press, 2012); **C. C. Kroeger,** "Head," *DPL*, 375-77; **B. Mickelsen and A. Mickelsen,** "What Does *Kephalē* Mean in the New Testament?," in *Women, Authority, and the Bible*, ed. A. Mickelsen (Downers Grove, IL: InterVarsity Press, 1986), 97-110; **P. B. Payne,** "What Does *Kephalē* Mean in the New Testament? Response," in *Women, Authority, and the Bible*, ed. A. Mickelsen (Downers Grove, IL: InterVarsity Press, 1986), 118-32; idem, *Man and Woman, One in Christ; An Exegetical and Theological Study of Paul's Letters* (Grand Rapids, MI: Zondervan, 2009); **L. Peppiatt,** *Rediscovering Scripture's Vision for Women: Fresh Perspectives on Disputed Texts* (Downers Grove, IL: IVP Academic, 2019); **C. L. Westfall,** "'This Is a Great Metaphor!' Reciprocity in the Ephesians Household Code," in *Christian Origins and Greco-Roman Culture: Social and Literary Context for the New Testament*, ed. S. E. Porter and A. W. Pitts (Leiden: Brill, 2012), 561-98; idem, *Paul and Gender: Reclaiming the Apostle's Vision for Men and Women in Christ* (Grand Rapids, MI: Baker, 2016).

C. L. Westfall

HEALING, ILLNESS

Paul understands illness and healing in terms of the interplay between the individual and the community (1 Cor 11:27-34; Phil 2:25-30) and between the natural and supranatural (2 Cor 12:7-10). Paul can consider weakness, sickness, and other afflictions as part of the fallen natural order (2 Cor 4:17), as part of his *suffering as a *servant of *Christ (2 Cor 11:23–12:10), as instrumental in bringing the *gospel to the Galatians (Gal 4:13-14), and as a messenger from *Satan (2 Cor 12:7). Sickness is portrayed as *God's *judgment or chastening occasioned by *sin (1 Cor 11:27-32), though Paul never applies this interpretation to his own sickness or suffering. For Paul healing is probably a *charisma* embedded in the essence of the gospel (cf. Rom 15:18-19; 1 Thess 1:5) and part of the ongoing life of the *church (1 Cor 12:8-11; Gal 3:4). He implies that a companion experienced healing (Phil 2:27).

1. Illness as Judgment and Discipline
2. Illness as a Messenger from Satan
3. Illness as Weakness yet Opportunity
4. Healing

1. Illness as Judgment and Discipline.
A direct relationship between illness and sin is well known in Paul's Jewish tradition (Deut 28:2; 2 Kings 19:15-19; 20:3; Tob 1:18; Sir 3:26-27) and among followers of Jesus (Mk 2:1-12; Lk 13:1-5; Jn 5:14; 9:2-3; Acts 5:1-11; 12:23; Jas 5:15-16). Paul attributes "weakness" (*astheneia*), "sickness" (*arrōstos*; in the NT, Mt 14:14 // Mk 6:5, 13; [Mk 16:18]; 1 Cor 11:30) and even death (*koimaō*, "falling asleep"; cf. 1 Cor 7:39) among the Corinthian Christians as God's judgment and discipline (*paideuō*, 1 Cor 11:32) over abuse of the *Lord's Supper (1 Cor 11:30).

Paul does not have in mind any magical effect of the bread and the cup, nor does he indicate that demonic powers are involved in sickness, even though the alternative to drinking the cup of the *Lord is to drink the cup of *demons (1 Cor 10:21). Rather, in a passage where he plays on the root word *judge* (*krin-*), the failure to discern (*diakrinō*) the *body and the blood of the Lord brings divine judgement (*krinō*). The divisive and greedy behavior of the Corinthians (1 Cor 11:18-19) amounts to a disregard of the meaning of the crucifixion. When the Corinthians meet together, they do not eat the Lord's Supper, proclaiming the benefits of his death (1 Cor 11:20, 26). Instead, they proclaim themselves guilty and condemned (*katakrinō*) along with the world (cf. Heb 10:29). The purpose of the judgment in sickness is disciplinary correction so that believers will not end up being condemned (*katakrinō*) along with the world (cf. 1 Cor 12:9-11).

One cannot maintain that Paul considers all sickness and death to be related to the abuse of the Lord's Supper. However, Romans 1:18-32 and 1 Corinthians 10:1-14 may indicate that Paul held to a general principle that sickness was sometimes caused by sin.

2. Illness as a Messenger from Satan.
In 2 Corinthians Paul says that in order to keep him from being too elated by the abundance of revelations, a thorn in the *flesh, a messenger of Satan, was given to him to batter him (2 Cor 12:7).

The nature of this thorn (*skolops*) has been much debated (Thrall, 809-18). As early as Chrysostom (*Hom. 2 Cor.* 26.2) some propounded the view that the thorn is the persecution Paul experienced, including that from his enemies at *Corinth. The thorn is characterized as a "messenger" or "angel" (*angelos*, 2 Cor 12:7) of Satan, implying a person or group (Satan as "angel of light"), and "to batter" (*kolaphizō*, 2 Cor 12:7) is a personal activity. Further, the context of the passage is Paul's struggle with his *opponents (2 Cor 10–13), and Numbers 33:55 (LXX) uses the image of a thorn for enemies of the Israelites. On the other hand, the thorn may have been given to Paul near the time of his *visions and revelations, when he had yet to confront his opponents. The reference to a messenger or angel of Satan does not seem like a reference to a group of opponents, and in 2 Corinthians 11:14-15 his opponents are Satan in disguise as his servants (*diakonoi*) rather than his messengers.

A view from the Middle Ages is that the thorn is every kind of temptation (cf. Calvin) or sexual temptation in particular. But this does not accord with the list of hardships and weaknesses in 2 Corinthians 11:23-29; 12:10, and it requires too narrow a view of "flesh." First Corinthians 7:7 implies that Paul did not struggle with sexual temptation.

The majority of interpreters, from Tertullian onward (*Pud.* 13.15-16), take the thorn to be some form of physical illness. In favor of this view is the metaphor of a thorn, the connection in ancient times between demonic manifestations and physical illness, and the structure of the 2 Corinthians 12:7-10 passage imitating the narratives of a healing miracle.

Due to the scarcity of data, some scholars do not attempt a diagnosis of the illness. Others have suggested epilepsy (as a result of Paul's *conversion experience), hysteria, migraine, depression, severe sciatica, rheumatism, poor hearing, leprosy, stammering, and solar retinus (an inflammation of the retina caused by blinding light at his conversion). R. H. Lightfoot used Galatians 4:13, 14 (see section 3 below) to interpret the meaning of the thorn as an ophthalmic complaint. W. M. Ramsey's view, that Paul contracted recurring malaria fever from the swarming mosquitoes in Pamphylia, is often accepted, since it takes account of the thorn as being a physical disorder, one that is felt continually or often as battering (2 Cor 12:7, *kolaphizē*, present tense) and humiliating while not stopping Paul's rigorous *mission work.

Insofar as Paul intended the thorn in the flesh to denote a physical ailment (*sarx*, "flesh," taken to refer to the physical *body), he expresses a number of his views on illness and healing in this passage. First, the illness humbled Paul, preventing him from becoming conceited. Second, this illness is a messenger from Satan causing pain and humiliation. Third, the use of the passive *edothē* ("was given," 2 Cor 12:7) is a veiled allusion to the illness being given by God. Paul resolves this paradox by saying that the Lord's *grace is shown to be sufficient for him even though his threefold or earnest prayer (cf. Num 6:24-26; 1 Kings 17:21; Euripides, *Hipp.* 46) for the thorn to leave him was not answered as he expected. Fourth, Paul does not view illness as something the Lord always heals. Remaining weak makes the power of Christ more evident in his life to the point of Paul wishing to boast in his weakness (2 Cor 11:30; 12:9-10).

3. Illness as Weakness yet Opportunity.
In Galatians 4:13 Paul makes a direct reference to a bodily weakness or illness of the flesh (*astheneian tēs sarkos*) that he suffered. If this passage is taken as closely resembling 2 Corinthians 12:7, it is not unnatural to suppose the allusion is to the same illness (see section 2 above). Others, noting that "flesh" (*sarx*) is the only word common to both passages, treat them separately.

Paul's saying that the Galatians would have plucked out their eyes and given them to him, and the postscript in his own hand being in large letters (Gal 6:11), has led to the suggestion that Paul's eyesight was bad. But, given that ancient belief held the eyes to be the most delicate and costly human organ (Deut 32:10; Ps 17:8; *Barn.* 19.9), and that gouging out eyes was an act of self-sacrifice (1 Sam 11:2), notably as a demonstration of friendship (Lucian, *Tox.* 40-41), Paul is probably saying no more than that the Galatians were prepared to give their eyes as one would say one was prepared to give one's "right arm" for a friend.

That Paul's condition was a temptation on the part of the Galatians (*hymōn*, "your," rather than *mou*, "my," has the greater textual support) to despise or neglect Paul has been thought to mean that for them his illness was in contrast to the miracles associated with his *ministry (cf. Gal 3:5). While Paul's illness may not have been severe enough to be listed in a catalogue of his trials (2 Cor 11:24-27), it initially caused Paul to bring the gospel to the Galatians, and they received him as Christ (Gal 4:14). Even illness becomes an opportunity for the gospel. This is of a piece with Paul's view of the positive value of suffering (Rom 5:3-5).

4. Healing.
Paul probably experienced healing (2 Cor 1:8-10), but he does not adopt a triumphalist attitude to illness and healing (2 Cor 12:7-10). He is convinced that nothing can separate a person from the love of God (Rom 8:35-39) and that one of the expressions of the presence of the *Holy Spirit is the gift of healing (1 Cor 12:9, 28, 30).

4.1. The Gifts of Healings. The only place Paul refers directly to the healing of illness is when he mentions gifts, or "charismata of healings" (*charismata iamatōn*) in his lists of *gifts of the Spirit (1 Cor 12:9, 28, 30).

Having introduced the theme of *charismata* ("gifts," 1 Cor 12:4), and saying that each one is given an expression of the Spirit's presence, he repeats the word *charismata* (pl.) when mentioning healing and says that an individual person (*allos*, sg.) receives gifts of healings (pl.; cf. 1 Cor 12:28, 30). Paul may be emphasizing that a person does not inherently possess power to heal but is given *charisma* for specific and different occasions of healing. As there is no mention of full-time healers from Paul, and the gift of healing is mentioned only in the context of gifts for the local community of believers, Paul probably does not envisage itinerant healers. Through the use of *charismata* he draws attention to individuals appointed in the church by God with the gift of healing (*charismata iamatōn*, 1 Cor 12:28; cf. 1 Cor 12:30), which in the context (1 Cor 12:27-31) is not for the sick person but for the healing of others. The body metaphor (1 Cor 12:12-26) and the charismatic nature of Pauline churches (1 Cor 14:26-33) suggests that the healings would be of fellow believers, perhaps through *prayer (cf. 2 Cor 12:8) when gathered (cf. 1 Cor 14:26).

4.2. Healing the Demonized. In the undisputed Pauline letters demons are only mentioned in 1 Corinthians 10:20-21 (cf. 1 Tim 4:1) as the gods that pagans worship. Unlike his contemporaries (see Foerster), Paul did not even attribute the troubles of 2 Corinthians 11:24-27 to demons or evil spirits. Only in 2 Corinthians 12:7 (see section 2 above) is it likely that he directly associates sickness with the demonic. In his notion of principalities and powers one can see what Paul thought about evil spiritual beings (Rom 8:38; 1 Cor 15:24; cf. Eph 6:12; Col 1:16).

Paul may be expected to include exorcism as one of the *charismata* ("gifts"). The *charisma* of "workings of powers" (*energēmata dynameōn*, 1 Cor 12:10) could mean the acts of power driving out demons. These *charismata* are all for the benefits of the body (1 Cor 12:7). Since Paul sees all people in relation to either Satan or Christ (2 Cor 6:14-15; cf. Gal 5:16-26), and the believer has passed from darkness to *light (1 Thess 5:5; cf. Col 1:13), it is perhaps not surprising that exorcism does not appear in Paul's lists of *charismata*.

4.3. Professional Healers. Though not divorced from the sacred (Sir 38:1-15), professional medicine was part of Paul's world (Josephus, *Life* 404; *Ant.* 7.343; 19.157; *J.W.* 1.598). In the later Pauline corpus Luke the physician (*ho iatros*) is mentioned (Col 4:14), and wine is recommended for the stomach and frequent ailments (1 Tim 5:23; cf. Plutarch, *Tu. san.* 3.1; Pliny, *Nat.* 23.22). Paul himself makes no mention of such approaches to healing or of herbal medicine (e.g., Pliny, *Nat.* 16.14; 20.2, 39), or of the healing carried out in the popular Asclepian sanctuaries (e.g., Lucian, *Alex.*), including at Corinth (Pausanius, *Descr.* 2.4.5).

4.4. Paul as Healer. In his letters Paul gives no indication that he was a healer. In describing miracles, presumably including healing, he uses the passive, saying miracles "were performed [*kateirgasthē*] among you" (2 Cor 12:12), implying they were directly from God or provided by him (Gal 3:5).

The traditional phrase he uses to describe miracles associated with his work, "*signs and wonders" (*sēmeia kai terata*, Rom 15:18-19; 2 Cor 12:12; cf. 2 Thess 2:9), would have been understood to include healings (cf., e.g., Jn 4:48; Acts 2:22; 5:12). In recalling the miracles of the exodus (cf. Ex 7:3; Deut 6:22; 7:19; 26:8) and associating "power" (*dynamis*) with his "signs and wonders," Paul emphasizes that God is their author. From Paul's perspective these signs and wonders, along with his message, are Christ working through him, and they identify him as an *apostle as well as help to win obedience from the *Gentiles.

4.5. Acts. Luke credits Paul with performing healings (Acts 14:8-18; 19:11-12; 20:9-10; 28:7-10; cf. Acts 15:12) and exorcism (Acts 16:18). Relying on Acts, it is possible to speculate that, like other followers of Jesus may have been doing and certainly did after him (Mk 9:39; [Mk 16:17]), he used the *name of Jesus as the power-authority for an exorcism (Acts 16:18). Luke depicts Paul as the subject of a healing from a deadly snakebite (Acts 28:1-6). Given that from his *call (Gal 1:15-16; Is 49:1-6; Jer 1:5) and the understanding of his mission (Rom 1:1-2; cf. Rom 16:25-26; 1 Thess 2:15) Paul saw himself in the tradition of the great prophets (Rom 10:15; cf. Is 52:7), Luke may credibly describe Paul adopting one of their dramatic methods of healing in restoring Eutychus (Acts 20:7-12; cf. 2 Kings 4:34).

See also Corinthians, First Letter to the; Demons and Exorcism; Ephesians, Letter to the; Forgiveness; Gifts of the Spirit; Grace; Holy Spirit; Opponents of Paul; Satan, Devil; Signs, Wonders, Miracles; Sin, Guilt; Suffering; Visions, Ecstatic Experience.

BIBLIOGRAPHY. **J. Calvin,** *The Second Epistle of Paul the Apostle to the Corinthians and the Epistles to Timothy, Titus, and Philemon*, Calvin's New Testament Commentaries (Grand Rapids, MI: Eerdmans, 1964); **G. D. Fee,** *God's Empowering Presence: The Holy Spirit in the Letters of Paul* (Peabody, MA: Hendrickson, 1994); **W. Foerster,** "δαίμων, κτλ.," *TDNT* 2:1-20; **J. M. Glessner,** "Ethnomedical Anthropology and Paul's 'Thorn' (2 Corinthians 12:7)," *BTB* 47, no. 1 (2017): 15-46; **J. Jervell,** "The Signs of an Apostle," in *The Unknown Paul* (Minneapolis: Augsburg, 1984); **R. H. Lightfoot,** *Saint Paul's Epistle to the Galatians* (London: Macmillan, 1881); **R. P. Martin,** *2 Corinthians*, WBC (Waco, TX: Word, 1986); **A. Oepke,** "ἰάομαι, κτλ.," *TDNT* 3:194-215; **S. M. Praeder,** "Miracle Worker and Missionary: Paul in the Acts of the Apostles," in *SBL 1983 Seminar Papers*, ed. K. H. Richards (Chico, CA: Scholars Press, 1983), 107-29; **I. L. E. Ramelli,** "Spiritual Weakness, Illness, and Death in 1 Corinthians 11:30," *JBL* 130 (2011): 145-63; **W. M. Ramsey,** *St. Paul and the Roman Citizen* (London: Hodder & Stoughton, 1908), 94-97; **M. E. Thrall,** *II Corinthians*, vol. 2, ICC (Edinburgh: T&T Clark, 2000); **G. H. Twelftree,** *Paul and the Miraculous: A Historical Reconstruction* (Grand Rapids, MI: Baker Academic, 2013).

G. H. Twelftree

HEART. *See* Anthropology, Pauline; Ethics.

HEAVEN, HEAVENLIES. *See* Afterlife; Ascension; Cosmology; Principalities and Powers; Triumph.

HEAVENLY CITIZENSHIP. *See* Citizenship.

HELLENISM, ROMAN

The designation "Roman Hellenism" refers to the cultural system that permeated the Mediterranean basin during the period of the early Roman Principate, or the roughly two centuries that followed the fall of the last of the Greek dynasties at the Battle of Actium in 31 BC. The designation defies essentialist definitions of cultures and, though it is seldom used in scholarly literature, appropriately captures the complex relationship that existed between Roman and Greek traditions during this period, as the Hellenized regions that were embraced by the Roman Empire infused in their conquerors an appreciation for Greek institutions, literature, religion, and *philosophy, and as Roman ways in turn penetrated these regions.

1. Hellenism
2. Roman Hellenism
3. Paul and Roman Hellenism
4. Conclusion

1. Hellenism.

Paving the way for this cultural blend was the precipitous conquest of the eastern Mediterranean by the Hellenized Macedonian kings of the fourth century BC. Expanding control eastward, Philip II and his son Alexander accumulated territory into an *empire of unprecedented size. As they infiltrated Asia Minor, Syria-Palestine, Egypt, and Mesopotamia, they introduced the Greek language, Greek institutions, Greek art, Greek literary styles, and Greek philosophy and religion. In the West, Greek settlements had long existed throughout Illyricum and especially in Magna Graecia in southern Italy; in these regions Greek culture influenced the Romans centuries before the expansion that produced the Roman Empire. Resulting from the diffusion of Greek culture East and West was a cultural uniformity across the Mediterranean basin in which a common ingredient was Hellenism.

Despite the synonymy of Hellenism with Greek culture during the period of Macedonian expansion, Hellenism itself absorbed elements from the Eastern cultures with which it interacted. Thus arises in scholarly discourse a second sense of the word *Hellenism*, in which *Hellenism* is understood as a *syncretism* of Greek and Eastern culture and applies to Eastern culture only after Alexander and the struggles of the Diadochoi at the close of the third century BC (Hengel, 3). Similarly, Roman culture prior to Alexander was itself a blend of Latin, Etruscan, and Greek elements with unique features of its own. The resulting "Roman" culture in turn blended with post-Alexander "Hellenism" to create a cultural blend that could be designated "Roman Hellenism."

2. Roman Hellenism.

2.1. The Roman Empire. As Macedonian rule expanded in the East, the power of Rome was building in the West. Gradually Rome's power extended its reach, first encompassing the Italian peninsula; then growing outward, overtaking Corsica, Sicily, Spain, and northern Africa in the West; and Macedonia, Greece, Asia Minor, and Syria and Phoenicia in the East. All this was Rome's by 63 BC. The Ptolemaic dynasty in Egypt, the last of the Greek dynasties, fell in 31 BC, when Octavian defeated Cleopatra VII and Marc Antony at the Battle of Actium.

The acquired territories were annexed to the Roman state as *provinciae* (provinces). These did not remain under the control of local dynasts but were governed by Roman citizens of either equestrian or senatorial rank, who had complete *imperium* within the realm of their provinces. Within the provinces themselves, some cities remained "free" (*civitas libera*) and were able to govern affairs according to their traditional constitutions and under magistrates of their choosing. Other cities had the status of *municipia*—foreign cities incorporated into the Roman body politic. Rome also established colonies (*coloniae*) in the provinces, either superimposing new civic structures on preexisting cities, rehabilitating cities made desolate by war or impoverishment, or else building new cities from the ground up. Other territories, located on the fringes of the empire, retained the status of client kingdoms, whose kings were considered "friends" (*rex sociusque et amicus*) of Rome. Client kingdoms sat outside the ambit of provincial jurisdiction and remained semi-autonomous, although allegiance to Rome was expected.

2.2. Romanization. Rome's domination around the Mediterranean set in motion a process of Romanization, whereby Rome acculturated non-Romans with what could be called *Romanitas* (Romanness). The essence of *Romanitas* is somewhat nebulous; it was defined less by a distinct culture than by political loyalty to the symbolic power of Rome, its rulers, and its gods. Culturally, Rome remained very much indebted to the Greeks (as one Latin poet summarizes well: "conquered Greece took captive its savage conqueror" [Horace, *Ep.* 2.156-157]). Greek remained the *lingua franca* of the empire. Greek institutions, literature, and rhetorical styles were imitated. Greek philosophy was adopted, and Greek religion was fused with traditional Roman religion. Through the geographical scope of its domination and the efficient connectedness of the empire, Rome only helped to strengthen Hellenistic influence across the Mediterranean world.

Romanitas spread in the provinces through various mechanisms. Roman soldiers migrated from Rome to the provinces and from province to province. Rome planted veteran colonies in strategic locations in the East. New *poleis* (Greek cities) were founded under Roman *patronage. The Latin language became familiar through its predominance in both official (inscriptions) and private communications (gravestones, dedications, graffiti). Roman roads increased traffic east and west, north and south.

Stimulating Romanization was Rome's fierce *honor-shame culture, which promised rewards to those who most promoted Rome and its *glory (Hendrix). As Rome was honored, so was the honoree. Expectations of reciprocity stimulated escalating competition to promote Rome and its ways. In the client kingdoms, cities were named after Roman rulers (e.g., Caesarea Maritima in Samaria, Tiberias in Galilee). Provincial cities curried Rome's favor by sponsoring festivals in the emperor's honor, by setting up honorific monuments, or by displaying honorific inscriptions. Cities—primarily those in the Greek East—established cults to the *worship of Roma and its rulers. Cities replicated Roman *temples, theatres, baths, aqueducts, and other features of Roman cityscapes. Cities that were most zealous for Rome were awarded "free" status, earning a right to local autonomy and often tax exemption.

Initiating these honorific campaigns were the cities' local elites, whose efforts were rewarded in the form of *citizenship, administrative positions, and other public honors. During the imperial period members of their cities' decurial boards eventually earned the right to ascend to equestrian and senatorial rank and thus the ability to govern the provinces where they resided. Such individuals functioned as important brokers between their cities and the emperor himself, the ultimate benefactor, to whom the kingdoms and provinces owed their allegiance. Ties would be strengthened by intermarriage between Romans and notable families, and Romanization would advance as they sent their children to Rome to be educated and groomed for leadership.

The extent to which Roman colonization in the East promoted Romanization is disputed. Suetonius claims that Julius Caesar sent eighty thousand "citizens" to overseas colonies (*Jul.* 42.1). Julius Caesar and Augustus together settled some forty colonies in Macedonia, Greece, Asia Minor, and Syria. One reason for colonization may indeed have been a desire to rehabilitate areas that lay desolate or were hurting economically. Undoubtedly another reason was a need to drain off Rome's flooded urban population. Yet, while colonization brought veterans and dispossessed Romans East, primarily it brought Greeks who had been enslaved in Rome back to their homelands. Moreover, in areas where it was deeply entrenched the influence of Hellenism on colonists would be felt intensely.

The city of *Corinth illustrates well the tension of Greek and Roman propensities in the colonies. Destroyed by the Romans in 146 BC, Corinth was refounded as a Roman colony in 44 BC. New Corinth exhibited a complex blend of cultures (Friesen, Schowalter, and Walters 2010). It hosted attractions popular in Rome while also hosting traditional Greek games. Roman cults existed alongside traditional Greek ones, and these were often adaptations of preexisting Greek cults. The Latin language prevailed among the upper classes and in official city business, though Greek and traditional Greek culture prevailed among the lower classes (Millis 2010).

2.3. Greek and Roman Education. With the conquests of Alexander, education was rapidly systematized and standardized across the conquered world, so that it served across the Macedonian Empire to cultivate a ruling class capable of effective administration anywhere and everywhere. School exercises preserved in papyri indicate that all the elements of the system were in place by the mid-third century BC and that this system persisted with astonishing constancy in its essential form and content until the collapse of the Roman Empire, nearly a thousand years after Alexander.

The Roman educational system grew out of contact with the Greek-speaking world in the Macedonian and Achaian wars of the third and second centuries BC and modeled itself after the Greek system in both its form and its content. Thus, a Roman education could rightly be called a Greco-Roman education.

Curriculum progressed, roughly, through three levels (though these stages were not always easily distinguished). For aristocrats, competency in both Greek and Latin was essential. Until the second century BC there was almost no tradition of Latin literature to speak of, and only in the first century BC did Latin literature reach any level of eminence. Roman families often hired Greek tutors for their children. Many Roman men wrote in Greek as opposed to Latin (Cornutus, Musonius Rufus, Marcus Aurelius). At the secondary level, students copied and learned to imitate classic texts, including Greek ones, most of all Homer, and after the first century BC Latin classics such as the works of Cicero and Virgil. Lists of classic authors in literary works largely agree with one another, leaving the impression of a "canon" of approved Greco-Roman authors, although school exercises in the papyri show that in practice students ranged more broadly.

The capstone of the three-tiered system was training in oratory. Latin manuals on rhetoric, prevalent from the first century BC on, were based on Greek rhetorical theory reaching back at least to the days of Plato and Aristotle (see Rhetorica ad Herennium). However, those at leisure to continue in their studies after completing rhetorical training often moved on to the study of philosophy. As there existed no distinctively Roman school of philosophy, the student would study with one of the traditional Greek schools, especially Stoic, Epicurean, or Academic.

2.4. Greek and Roman Religion. By the late Roman Republic, Hellenistic influence on Roman religion was deep and far-reaching. Rome's imperial cult developed on analogy with the ancient Greek ruler cults. The ruler cults arose in the Greek world when the city-states fell under subjection to external rule, losing their autonomy to regional tyrants. When Alexander completed his conquest in Asia Minor, the Ionian cities proclaimed him a god and gave him such honors as a god was due. The Ptolemaic dynasty, after 270 BC, deified each king upon his accession. From the end of the Roman Republic, Rome declared its rulers deities upon death, beginning with the posthumous deification of Julius Caesar by the Senate in 42 BC. In the Eastern provinces, particularly in Asia, ruler cults were established in honor of living emperors. What started as worship of the goddess Roma—the embodiment of Roman greatness—evolved into worship of Rome's rulers themselves.

The deities of local Greek cults of earlier times (normally deified humans) were gradually merged with the twelve Olympian gods, an institution that became standardized in pan-Hellenic mythology as Greeks everywhere made pilgrimage to the sites of famous oracles (at Delphi and throughout Asia Minor) and various pan-Hellenic games (at Olympia, Pythia, Nemea, and Isthmia). The Romans adopted the Greek Olympians into their mythology and assimilated them to traditional Roman equivalents (Jupiter became identified with Zeus, Mars with Ares, etc.), though the chief three of the Italian gods remained Jupiter, Mars, and Quirinus. Roman mythology adopted the Greek myths but integrated these with Roman political propaganda. Rome's mythology, particularly as formalized in Virgil's *Aeneid*, created a foundational narrative that constructed a Roman identity and legitimated Rome's political domination.

Rome often looked askance at the Eastern mystery cults, due to their secrecy and occasional unruliness. The oldest of the mystery religions was that which originated at Eleusis in Attica, that is, the Eleusian Mysteries. Also prominent were the mysteries of the great gods of Samothrace, the mysteries of Dionysius (Greek), the mysteries of Mithras (Persian), and the mysteries of Isis (Egyptian). These cults migrated from location to location and were uniquely modified in each place. Assimilating the Greek god Dionysius to the Roman god Bacchus, the Dionysian cult was taken up in Rome as the "Bacchanalian" cult; once banned (186 BC), it was viewed thereafter as dangerous and potentially seditious.

2.5. Greek and Roman Philosophy. Greek philosophy did not attract attention in Rome until well into the Republican period (third and second centuries BC); and yet, the Romans claimed that philosophy originated with their very own ancestors. It is said that Protagoras (b. mid-sixth century BC), a Greek-speaking native born on the Aegean island of Samos, was the first to claim the title of "philosopher" (Cicero, *Tusc.* 5.3.10). Later a resident of southern Italy, Protagoras was alleged to have been of Trojan (or Roman) descent and was credited with introducing philosophy to Rome's second king, Numa Pompilius (according to legend, ca. 700 BC). However, historical record traces the origins of philosophy to Greek-speaking men from around Sicily and the Aegean during the sixth century BC, and the genesis of the major philosophical schools to Athens in the fourth century BC.

A critical event in Rome's reception of philosophy occurred in 155 BC, when a Peripatetic, an Academic, and a Stoic philosopher traveled to Rome on embassy business and reportedly inspired amazement in the city's youths. Another critical moment occurred in 87 BC, when the Roman general Sulla laid siege to Athens, forcing many, including the philosophers, to scatter. Decentralization of the schools created opportunities for philosophy to take root abroad, and as a result local schools cropped up across the Roman Empire.

By the early first century BC, Romans were doing "Latin philosophy"—philosophy not just translated from Greek into Latin or passively transmitted but philosophy shaped distinctively by Roman institutions and values (Williams and Volk). While Latin philosophy carried about at first as a matter of everyday conversation or general interest, the inception of Latin philosophical *literature* traces to Varro and

Cicero, around the middle of the first century BC. Traveling to Athens, Rhodes, and the Aegean islands, Cicero studied with Greek teachers of all the major philosophical schools. The avowed purpose of his philosophical writings was to make Greek philosophy available in the Latin tongue, basing his works on Greek authorities, from which he borrowed selectively, often translating directly, but calling his philosophy an "imitation" rather than a "copy" of his Greek models (Cicero, *Acad.* 1.10).

Rome adapted Greek philosophy to suit a distinctly Roman ideology. Among the Hellenistic philosophies, by far the most influential for Roman elites was Stoicism. Stoicism envisaged the world as governed by a universal "natural law" and humanity as comprising a single "world community," an ideal now thought to have been fulfilled in the Roman Empire. Adapting the Stoic notion of fate, Stoicized Romans presented Rome's rise as an inevitable consequence of divine decree.

The Roman period was also a time of significant development and increasing eclecticism for philosophy. This tendency is well represented by figures such as Cicero, who by profession was an Academic but who adopted Stoic views on many points, believing that one should not be enslaved to any particular school but receptive of the most "probable" arguments on each particular point (*Tusc.* 4.4.7). The cross-pollination of systems that resulted in philosophical eclecticism led, in more attenuated form, to what can be called popular philosophy, in which the dominant ingredients were Stoic and Cynic. Through the philosophical epitomes, through inscriptions, oral instruction, discussion in public places, the intermingling of social classes, the influence of so-called street preachers, and other forms of interaction, philosophy of the popular variety dispersed widely and percolated deeply into the population, such as philosophy never had before.

3. Paul and Roman Hellenism.

3.1. Paul as Jew, Greek, and Roman. Paul embodied the cultural tapestry that increasingly characterized the Mediterranean world from the time of Alexander. A self-professed Jew (Rom 11:1; Phil 3:5; Acts 21:39; cf. Rom 2:29) tracing his lineage to the tribe of Benjamin (Phil 3:5), he had devoted himself, prior to his Damascus experience, fervently to his Jewish ancestral traditions (Gal 1:14). According to Acts, he was also a Roman citizen (Acts 16:37-38; 22:25-29; 23:27), born in and a citizen of the Hellenistic city of Tarsus (Acts 21:39; 22:3), and had moved early in his life to *Jerusalem, where he was educated as a Pharisee (Acts 26:4) under renowned rabbi Gamaliel I (Acts 22:3).

While Paul's letters do not themselves reveal his place of birth, his own testimony that he returned to Tarsus after his commissioning and visit to Damascus may suggest that Tarsus was indeed his place of origin (Acts 9:30; Gal 1:21). His time spent there, however long, must have acculturated him into the intellectual world of Hellenism. His fluent Greek suggests that, if Greek was not his first language, he was at least bilingual from childhood (and it is not inconceivable that he acquired competency in Latin). That he spent his career evangelizing the Greek-speaking provinces shows that he was very much at home in a Hellenistic environment.

Acts says that Roman citizenship was Paul's by birthright (Acts 23:28). However, the extent of his loyalty to Rome is contested. His apparently unqualified support of the governing authorities in Romans 13:1-6 could be considered pro-Roman; yet, his letters reflect no interest in vaunting his citizenship, no interest in exploiting citizen rights, and a complete lack of zeal to promote Rome and its glory as one might expect of a citizen. Much in his letters, particularly the Thessalonian letters (Harrison), could be considered counterimperial.

Despite his variegated cultural markers, Paul indicates that his turn to *Christ shattered previous markers of his *identity. After his Damascus experience, he found cultural distinctions irrelevant (Rom 6:3; 1 Cor 12:13; Gal 3:27) and rejected all measures of self-identification apart from his being-in-Christ (Gal 2:20). This, however, did not prevent him from making full use of the philosophical, rhetorical, and religious resources that his culture had to offer.

3.2. Paul and His Education. Whether Paul completed his early education in the Jewish or in the Greco-Roman system is a matter of debate. Biographical evidence is limited almost exclusively to Acts. Assuming Luke is reliable, Paul lived for some time in Tarsus before moving to Jerusalem, but how long he lived there is unclear. According to Acts, he was "born [*gegennēmenos*] in Tarsus," but "brought up [*anatethrammenos*]" and "educated [*pepaideumenos*]" by Gamaliel in "this city [sc. Jerusalem?]" (Acts 22:3); and it is said that he spent his life "from youth [*ek neotētos*] from the beginning [*ap' archēs*]" among his people (Acts 26:4). Acts's characterization of him as a Pharisee is explicitly confirmed in his letters (Phil 3:5), although his tutelage under Gamaliel is not. As a Pharisee, he had belonged, if not to the most powerful class, certainly the most learned class within Jewish society and qualified as an expert not only on the written *law but also on the immense oral *tradition.

It should be considered that Luke had reason to accent Paul's connection with Jerusalem and his identity as a Jew (as he does in Acts 25:8, 10; 28:17), but not to accent his connection with Tarsus. Even if Luke does not exaggerate Paul's Jerusalem ties, it is possible to take his meaning in Acts 22:3; 26:4 to be that Paul received at least his early education in Tarsus, prior to being educated in Jerusalem by Gamaliel. Acts 22:3; 26:4 do not rule out secondary, or even tertiary, training in Tarsus. Paul's letters reflect a measure of rhetorical finesse such as could be expected from one trained at the highest levels in the Greco-Roman system. Other characteristics of his letters, however, belie non-Jewish training. For instance, one of the chief school exercises used at the secondary level was the copying and paraphrasing of the maxims of classic authors. Yet, whereas citations from the Jewish Scriptures are ubiquitous in Paul's letters, citations of non-Jewish authors are virtually nonexistent (but see 1 Cor 15:33).

The question of Paul's educational background, however, is moot if the boundary between Jewish and Greek, Palestinian and Hellenistic, is as permeable as is now believed. Even if Paul did not receive a complete Hellenistic education, Jewish education had already become heavily Hellenized (Hengel; Hidary). Moreover, it should not be supposed that after his Damascus experience, and his travels far and wide, Paul did not gain further, even deep, acquaintance with the intellectual currents of the Greco-Roman world. That he was, in his late years, a man of great learning is the impression given in Acts, where this very description is placed on the lips of the Roman governor Festus (Acts 26:24). Both Acts and Paul attest that after his Damascus experience he returned to Tarsus (Acts 9:30; Gal 1:21), a renowned center of intellectual activity. How his time there was spent is unknown, but if his intentions were missional his interactions there must have immersed him further in Greco-Roman intellectual tradition.

3.3. Paul and Rhetoric. While Paul was not an eloquent speaker by reputation (so 2 Cor 10:10, if this is not a *captatio benevolentiae*, or "capturing of goodwill"), success in his career as an evangelist and letter writer—in a world where rhetorical ability was a measure of educational achievement and where public oratory subject to public evaluation was commonplace—depended on some facility in the art of persuasion.

It would not be unjustified to affirm a consensus that Paul had training in Greco-Roman rhetorical techniques at the secondary and possibly also the tertiary level, although the latter is more contested. Philo of Alexandria stands as proof that Jews could and did receive full rhetorical education in the Greco-Roman system. While rhetorical analyses of Paul's letters have had some success in demonstrating their alignment with formal rhetorical theory as taught in the Greco-Roman system, other evidence suggests that if he did have a rhetorical education, it may have been of a more Jewish stamp. Greek rhetorical techniques infiltrated Palestinian education, where it is evident in rabbinic exegesis (Hidary). Whatever the case, an experienced traveler who spent his career engaging the public in the most flourishing urban centers in the empire might be expected to have absorbed the skills of rhetorical technique informally.

While Paul's letters were not speeches, and epistolary theory was never integrated with rhetorical theory in the ancient tradition, Greco-Roman letters did reflect many of the elements taught in the rhetorical handbooks, particularly in the area of style (Brookins 2022). In that respect, Paul's letters closely mirror the conventions that characterized Greco-Roman letters.

3.4. Paul and Greco-Roman Religion. While the older *Religionsgeschichtliche Schule* (history-of-religions school) emphasized the syncretistic nature of Paul's theology, particularly his dependency on the Greco-Roman mystery religions, some of the most basic assumptions of this school, and therefore its conclusions, have since been called into question. The idea of a dying-and-rising god is not as essential to the definition of the mystery religions as was once thought, and in any case too little is known about them to justify detailed comparison. To be sure, the word **mystery* occurs with some frequency in Paul's letters (the noun eight times in Romans and 1 Corinthians together, and thirteen times in the disputed letters; the verb cognate in Phil 4:12). For Paul, however, the "mystery" consisted specifically in what was once hidden but is now revealed *by the Spirit* in eschatological fulfillment of God's pretemporal plans through the Messiah (1 Cor 2:7). In this way Paul's conception of *mystery* is closer to the ideas of Jewish *apocalyptic, with its emphasis on revealed knowledge about the higher world and the new age—often with reference to God's Messiah—than it is to the Greco-Roman mystery religions.

At least superficial similarities are evident between the communities that Paul founded and the Greco-Roman mystery associations: membership in the group was voluntary (*faith); initiates participated in a ceremonial ritual (*baptism); members shared a ceremonial meal (the Eucharist); group identity was protected by clear boundaries (believers vs. nonbelievers). The similarities could indicate a conscious decision to model the *church after these associations. Much of the resemblances, however, could be attributed to parallel development, owing to convergent adaptation to the needs of people in a common cultural environment.

There can be little doubt about Paul's orientation toward Greco-Roman mythology and the state cults. Roman mythical and civil religion were deeply embedded in *politics. Both were driven by the ideal of loyalty to Roman identity and Roman power. Since all religion was tied to the state, one could worship any deity or many deities without offense; religious loyalties could be divided so long as loyalty to Rome was not. As a self-identifying Jew, Paul could not have endorsed religious pluralism, for only the "One God" was worthy of worship (Deut 6:4; 1 Thess 1:9-10; Gal 3:20; see also Rom 3:30). Nor could he have countenanced participation in the state cults, least of all the imperial cult; Jesus Christ, not Caesar, was "*Lord" (1 Cor 12:3).

3.5. *Paul and Philosophy.* The relationship between Paul's theology and Greco-Roman philosophy has been a topic of enduring interest. Modern analyses have focused especially on the Epicureans, the Cynics, and most of all, the Stoics. The Corpus Hellenisticum project carried on comparative work between Paul and the philosophers through much of the twentieth century, focusing mostly on Stoic sources. A tradition of ancient lineage makes Paul an acquaintance of the Roman Stoic Seneca, as depicted in a spurious fourteen-letter correspondence between them (dating to the fourth century AD). There is no direct evidence that Paul knew him, though some of the circumstantial evidence is enticing: while in Achaia Paul stood before the judicial seat of Seneca's brother, Gallio (Acts 18:12-17), and his time in Rome corresponded with Seneca's time there.

Owing to widespread adoption of Stoicism among elites (at least in the areas of ethics and political philosophy) and the diffusion of Stoicism into popular discourse, Paul's interaction with Stoicism must have been unavoidable. Modern studies have assessed his connections with Stoicism both with attention to individual topics (Stoic indifferents, Stoic anthropology, the Stoic conception of law, the Stoic conception of virtue, Stoic views on marriage) and holistically (Stoic ethics, Stoic cosmology). Undeniably, Paul utilizes some recognizably Stoic motifs. Allusions to Stoic ideas occur so often in 1 Corinthians (1 Cor 3:21; 4:8; 6:19; 7:4, 29-34; 11:14-15; 12:4-6, 12-27; 15:28, 31)—tellingly, where he is dealing with a Stoic-influenced audience (Brookins 2014)—that these allusions must have been deliberate. In many if not all instances, such interaction can be considered accommodating (1 Cor 3:21; 7:4; 12:12-27), and in some cases transformative and polemical (1 Cor 4:8; 6:19; 11:14-15), aiming to undercut his audience by using discourse with which they identified to some degree.

The reason for alleged similarities at a macro level is disputed. It has not generally been accepted that Paul studied philosophy firsthand or in any kind of intensive context, although it would be impossible to rule out the possibility entirely. It could be pointed out that even if Paul did complete his education through the Greco-Roman system, interaction with philosophers was minimal at the primary and secondary levels. While literary sources suggest that students interacted with quotations of philosophers at the secondary level, the papyri show that interaction with philosophers at this level was rarer in practice (Morgan, 123). However, such knowledge need not have been acquired through secondary or tertiary education. Paul could have taken up the philosophical epitomes—handbooks that introduced students to the big ideas of the philosophies. Furthermore, Tarsus, where Paul returned after his conversion (see 3.1 above), was a major nerve center for philosophy. The city had to its credit notable Stoic sages (Strabo, *Geogr.* 14.5.14-15), and none other than Chrysippus, the architect of Stoicism as a canonical system, had originated there (Diogenes Laertius, *Vit.* 7.179).

Paul's letters betray enough Stoic resemblances to suggest that he had absorbed Stoicism from somewhere—if from nowhere else, then through everyday social interaction, public discourse, and indirectly through Hellenistic Judaism.

4. Conclusion.

Paul's interaction with Greco-Roman traditions constitutes a typical example of the kind of cultural exchange that characterized virtually the entire Mediterranean world from the time of Alexander the Great. Hellenism and the East, Hellenism and Judaism, Hellenism and Romanism—each did not have its own essence but drew from various streams in ways that are not quantifiable. Cultural ingredients disperse and evolve, and new creation proliferates. What results is family resemblance between entities but not replication of an identical genetic code.

Paul's letters are inevitably written in the language of his times. All attempts to communicate are limited by the scope of a culture's available semiotic resources—the spoken language, the culture's vocabulary, its idioms, its metaphors, its genres, its configurations of verbal register, and so on. It would be unwarranted to assume that Paul's particular mode of expression did not go unaffected by that environment. At the same time, he adapted his material in ways that were unique and distinctive of his views as a Jewish apocalypticist and Christ-believer.

See also APOCALYPTICISM; CHRIST, MESSIAH; CITIZENSHIP; *CURSUS HONORUM*; EMPIRE; HONOR/SHAME; LETTERS, LETTER FORMS; LORD; PATRONAGE; PAUL IN ACTS; PHILOSOPHY; RELIGIONS, GRECO-ROMAN; RHETORICAL CRITICISM.

BIBLIOGRAPHY. **S. E. Alcock,** *Graecia Capta: The Landscapes of Roman Greece* (Cambridge: Cambridge University Press, 1993); **D. E. Aune,** "The World of Roman Hellenism," in *The Blackwell Companion to the New Testament*, ed. D. E. Aune (Chichester, UK: Wiley & Sons, 2010), 15-37; **T. A. Brookins,** *Corinthian Wisdom, Stoic Philosophy, and the Ancient Economy*, SNTSMS 159 (Cambridge: Cambridge University Press, 2014); idem, *Ancient Rhetoric and the Style of Paul's Letters* (Eugene, OR: Cascade, 2022); **W. D. Davies,** *Paul and Rabbinic Judaism: Some Rabbinic Elements in Pauline Theology* (London: SPCK, 1948); **T. Engberg-Pedersen,** *Paul in His Hellenistic Context* (Minneapolis: Fortress, 1994); idem, *Paul Beyond the Judaism/Hellenism Divide* (Louisville, KY: Westminster John Knox, 2001); **L. H. Feldman,** *Judaism and Hellenism Reconsidered* (Leiden: Brill, 2006); **S. J. Friesen, D. N. Schowalter, and J. C. Walters,** eds., *Corinth in Context: Comparative Studies on Religion and Society* (Leiden: Brill, 2010); **J. R. Harrison,** *Paul and the Imperial Authorities at Thessalonica and Rome: A Study in the Conflict of Ideology*, WUNT 273 (Tübingen: Mohr Siebeck, 2011); **H. Hendrix,** "Thessalonicans Honor Romans" (PhD diss., Harvard University, 1984); **M. Hengel,** *Judaism and Hellenism: Studies in Their Encounter in Palestine During the Early Hellenistic Period*, 2nd ed. (Leiden: Brill, 1974); **R. Hidary,** *Rabbis and Classical Rhetoric: Sophistic Education and Oratory in the Talmud and Midrash* (Cambridge: Cambridge University Press, 2017); **R. Hock,** "Paul and Greco-Roman Education," in *Paul in the Greco-Roman World*, ed. J. P. Sampley (New York: Continuum, 2003), 198-227; **H. J. Klauck,** *Ancient Letters and the New Testament: A Guide to Context and Exegesis* (Waco, TX: Baylor University Press, 2006); **L. I. Levine,** *Judaism and Hellenism in Antiquity: Conflict or Confluence* (Seattle: University of Washington Press, 1998); **A. A. Long,** "Roman Philosophy," in *The Cambridge Companion to Greek and Roman Philosophy*, ed. D. N. Sedley (Cambridge: Cambridge University Press, 2003), 184-210; **B. Millis,** "The Social and Ethnic Origins of the Colonists in Early Roman Corinth," in *Corinth in Context: Comparative Studies on Religion and Society*, ed. S. J. Friesen, D. N. Schowalter, and J. C. Walters (Leiden: Brill, 2010), 13-36; **T. Morgan,** *Literate Education in the Hellenistic and Roman Worlds* (Cambridge: Cambridge University Press, 1998); **S. E. Porter,** ed., *Paul: Jew, Greek, and Roman* (Leiden: Brill, 2008); **E. T. Salmon,** *Roman Colonization Under the Republic* (Ithaca, NY: Cornell University Press, 1970); **R. Schellenberg,** *Rethinking Paul's Rhetorical Education: Comparative Rhetoric and 2 Corinthians 10–13* (Atlanta: Society of Biblical Literature, 2013); **D. N. Sedley,** ed., *Cambridge Companion to Greek and Roman Philosophy* (Cambridge: Cambridge University Press, 2003); **W. C. Van Unnik,** *Tarsus or Jerusalem: The City of Paul's Youth* (London: Epworth, 1962); **G. D. Williams and K. Volk,** eds., *Roman Reflections: Studies in Latin Philosophy* (New York: Oxford University Press, 2016).

T. A. Brookins

HELLENISTIC RELIGION. *See* HELLENISM, ROMAN; RELIGIONS, GRECO-ROMAN.

HERMENEUTICS/ INTERPRETING PAUL

The hermeneutics of reading Paul is an expansive area of study. It includes key interpretive facets regarding the way Paul's *letters function as practical theology, the question of the relationship among his letters (including potential development across them), and Paul's extensive use of the OT (his own hermeneutic). Additionally, a number of lenses for reading Paul have gained traction, whether historically or in recent Pauline studies, such as Paul in relation to first-century Judaism or to the Roman Empire, and Paul interpreted through the lenses of gender and *ethnicity.

1. The Pauline Letters as Practical and Pastoral Theology
2. The Relationship Among the Letters

3. Paul's Use of the Old Testament
4. Hermeneutical Lenses for Reading Paul

1. The Pauline Letters as Practical and Pastoral Theology.

The act of interpretation is dependent on determining the nature of what is being studied. To pursue the hermeneutics of Paul's letters is inevitably tied to understandings of what his letters are—their genre, their purposes, their essence.

While scholars can place Paul's various letters on a spectrum from informal letter to treatise-like epistle, all of his letters are *occasional* in nature. That is, Paul writes each of his letters in response to contingencies of a particular congregation, with which he shares an already existing relationship of some kind. These contingent circumstances (i.e., the "occasion" of the letter) bring forth from Paul pastoral and practical reflection drawn from his theological convictions about the *gospel—the story of God's promised redemptive work now enacted in Jesus the Messiah through the presence and agency of the *Holy Spirit. In his letters, Paul affirms that the believers he addresses have been incorporated into that story and that he seeks to "participate with God in effecting the transformation of [Paul's] communities" (Thompson, 20).

As pastoral and practical theology, Paul's letters seldom yield theology in the abstract (Hooker 2008). Instead, they give us a sense of Paul's ways of "theologizing," which is as much a verb as a noun (Dunn 2006). His letters provide his theology *on the ground*, though this does not mean interpreters should "mirror read" Paul's letters (or overread their situation)—finding in the *church being addressed a problem corresponding to virtually every exhortation (Brown 2021). On the other hand, it is just as problematic to underconstruct the original context of the letter by reading Paul's ideas as abstract and untethered theology. The tendency toward the latter is less pronounced in a letter such as Philemon, which in its length and primary audience (Philemon) feels almost entirely occasional in nature. Alternatively, much of the interpretive history of Romans, Paul's longest letter, exhibits a way of reading Paul as systematic theologian, with Romans understood as the culmination of his theology. For example, Brevard Childs, in his canonical approach to reading Paul, suggests that all thirteen Pauline epistles be read with Romans as a hermeneutical key in its "universalizing" of at least some of Paul's earlier formulations (Childs, 254).

Yet contemporary scholarship has offered any number of compelling readings of Romans that straddle an understanding of the letter as both contingent and an illustration of Paul's pastoral theology par excellence. There are clues enough in Romans to suggest that Paul writes to address particular issues of division and privilege between Jewish and *Gentile Christians, potentially arising from the removal and return of Jews from Rome (and so from the Roman house churches) because of Claudius's edict of AD 49 (e.g., McKnight). Because Paul wants to introduce himself to these house churches (Rom 1:8; 15:23-29), he focuses significant attention on elucidating the gospel as worked out in his Gentile *mission. This provides a sense of theological breadth and depth to Romans that has contributed to its reputation as the centerpiece of Pauline theology.

Being attentive to the occasional or contingent nature of Paul's letters complicates the goal of discerning a theological center in Paul's writings, a task that has long occupied Pauline scholars. Chief among the contenders for such a center historically has been *justification by *faith (the traditional Protestant viewpoint) or incorporation into Christ (e.g., Bousset). More recently, quite a variety of suggestions for Paul's theological center have been made, from apocalyptic (Beker; Campbell 2009) to reconciliation (Martin) to *resurrection (Achtemeier calls this the "generative center" of Paul's thought [138]), and from God's *grace in *Christ (Matera; Thielman 2005) to God's *glory in Christ (Schreiner 2020).

Understanding Paul's writings to project a singular theological center can tend toward a static view of Paul's theology (Dunn 2006). Yet Paul's theologizing as experienced in his letters has a dynamic quality to it, given that it arises in response to different communities and over a considerable period of time (Thompson). His theology "covers too much ground" to be reducible to a singular theme as its center (Fee 1994, 12). Acknowledging such complexity does not argue against the coherence of Paul's theology, since "coherence does not require a 'center'" (Anderson, 123). As Paul Achtemeier suggests, Paul's theology may be coherent without one's being able to "deduce [its] coherent central core" from his "situationally-conditioned statements present in his letters" (Achtemeier, 133).

A narrative lens helps conceptually to broaden the task of finding a center for Paul's theology to identify the "narrative substructure" (Hays's term; 1983) of his thought, which allows for the constellation of his theology to emerge. Michael Gorman, for example, suggests twelve Pauline "fundamental convictions" that are essentially *narrative in nature, rather than a single center (e.g., "God's faithfulness to *Israel and *mercy to the Gentiles" and "the revelatory, representative, and reconciling crucifixion of Jesus the Messiah" [Gorman, 134-35]). Accenting the narrative framework of Paul's theology helps to balance coherence and contingency in the theologizing he has left in his letters (Beker, 15-19).

2. The Relationship Among the Letters.
Although each of Paul's letters provides a proper focus for interpretation, a key synthetic issue involves the relationship among Paul's letters. For those wanting to sketch a portrait of Paul and his theology from more than a single letter, this synthetic task is essential. Yet it is fraught with methodological difficulties, including the less than certain dating of Paul's letters relative to one another, the possible development in Paul's thinking over time (so across his letters), and the foundational question of what counts as the authentic Pauline corpus.

2.1. The Dating of Paul's Letters. While the dating of any particular letter of Paul can affect its interpretation (e.g., early and later dates proposed for Galatians tied to whether a South or North Galatian audience is in view), a key hermeneutical consideration is the dating of Paul's letters relative to one another. Sketching a timeline of Paul's letters, however, is no easy task, as no dates mark his letters and there are few clues to external events that could assist in dating. The itinerary of *Paul in Acts has been used for this purpose but is often contested due to questions of the book's historical reliability as well as the (appropriate) impulse to allow Paul's letters to lead the way. Finally, the letters themselves provide some evidence to assist in their temporal ordering (e.g., references to shared phenomena, such as the Jerusalem *collection and placement based on theological development), but the nature of this evidence is fairly subjective, giving rise to differing proposals.

Nonetheless, scholars do make interpretive decisions based on what they understand to be antecedent letters. For example, it is typical to read the opponent group Paul addresses in Philippians 3:2 ("dogs," "evildoers," "mutilators," NIV) through the lens of Galatians (or at least the situation Galatians depicts). This tendency arises from the brief and allusive nature of the Philippians reference in comparison to the extended polemic against Paul's Galatian *opponents, who are explicitly identified in the letter (traditionally identified as "*Judaizers"). Given that Galatians (AD 48 or 52–54) was very likely written before Philippians (AD 60–63 or potentially in the mid-50s), a circumspect use of the earlier letter to illuminate the later one can make hermeneutical sense and does gain traction by interpreters of Philippians. Frank Thielman, for instance, suggests that Philippians was penned shortly after Galatians and 1 Corinthians (all three from Ephesus), and the warnings in Philippians 3:1–4:1 make sense as a cautionary word from Paul "not to succumb to the errors of these other churches" (Thielman 1995, 21).

The dates of Paul's letters in relation to one another are especially significant for illuminating Pauline theology. The progression of Paul's letters bears on the shape of his theology. For instance, he wrote Romans after Galatians, likely somewhere between AD 56 and 58. This can account for what many scholars view as the solidification or amplification of Paul's theology of justification in Romans (along with other theological themes; see Childs). At the very least, Paul in Romans provides a more balanced perspective on key issues such as *circumcision and Torah than in Galatians, where the polemic situation presses for a more uneven emphasis (Moo, 17).

2.2. Development Across Paul's Letters. An issue that has sparked serious debate in Pauline studies (and is tied to dating issues) focuses on the presence of development across Paul's letters. Do his letters provide evidence that Paul changed his thinking or theology in significant ways? Answers given range from seeing any development as slight or insignificant to accusations of full-blown inconsistencies in Pauline thought (understanding development as part of these inconsistencies). Toward the former end of the spectrum, one could note Thomas Schreiner, who argues against the existence of development in Paul's theology—that Paul changed his mind on any particular topic from one letter to another (Schreiner, 2011, 136-40). On the other end, scholars have argued that Paul's letters exhibit a change of mind in some area of theology, leading to inconsistencies in his theological thinking—for example, his views on *eschatology or on Torah (Räisänen).

In between, one can register views that acknowledge significant development without assuming outright change (e.g., J. P. Sanders suggests "organic growth" vs. "retraction" [333-34]). In the area of soteriology (e.g., on justification and *works of the law), Garwood Anderson has argued that Paul's theology is both coherent and shows signs of development (Anderson, 125), which Anderson traces across the entire Pauline corpus. He describes this development as "organic: from seed to flower, from particular to general, from seminal insight to its principled outworking, from ad hoc claim to more settled abstraction, from a case in point to its implicature" (Anderson, 158).

2.3. The Scope of Paul's Correspondence. While thirteen NT letters have Paul's name attached to them as their author, modern scholarship has questioned the authenticity of six of these: Ephesians, Colossians, 2 Thessalonians, 1 and 2 Timothy, and Titus. The reason for this conclusion arises from differences in vocabulary, theology, and context that, for many, have strained the boundaries of what constitutes Pauline thought and style.

Ephesians, Colossians, and 2 Thessalonians, while often contested, are granted Pauline authorship by a substantial number, or even a majority, of scholars (e.g., Gorman; Campbell 2014). First and Second Timothy and Titus (the "Pastorals") are the most contested. The authorship of the Pastorals is usually tied to a second generation of Pauline disciple(s) writing in a time of increasing institutionalization of church offices and structures (e.g., Scholz, 50), though some scholars consider 2 Timothy to have been written by Paul (e.g., Gorman). A minority voice (usually evangelical scholars) argues that the Pastorals (and so all thirteen letters) come from Paul (e.g., Fee 1988; Anderson). A recent proposal by Luke Timothy Johnson accounts for significant differences among the thirteen letters by suggesting that they fall into five discrete clusters, each attributable to a "Pauline school," with Philippians and Philemon as "outliers." Each school was involved in writing letters with Paul, and the stylistic variations in the thirteen letters can be accounted for by this complex social dynamic (e.g., use of a secretary, cosponsored letters, differing use of traditional materials; Johnson, 90-92).

Johnson's proposal raises an important issue that complicates conversations about Pauline authorship—Paul's regular references to cosponsors and, sometimes, an amanuensis (writing assistant). At the conclusion of Romans, Paul's amanuensis, Tertius, writes his own personal greeting to the churches in Rome (Rom 16:22). One is on good grounds to assume the use of an amanuensis for 1 Corinthians (1 Cor 16:21), Colossians (Col 4:18), and 2 Thessalonians (2 Thess 3:17), based on Paul's distinction that he has written the final greeting in his own hand (see Gal 6:11). Paul mentions cosponsor(s) in a number of his letters, although these associates do not seem to function as coauthors (Timothy, Silas, and/or Sosthenes for 1 Corinthians, 2 Corinthians, Philippians, and Colossians).

The various proposals on authorship within the Pauline corpus have a significant impact on any reconstruction of the "historical Paul" as well as particular presentations of his theology. First, taking on the task of determining authentic letters from inauthentic (i.e., pseudonymous) inevitably *centers* some of Paul's letters—Galatians and Romans especially—as the *most* Pauline. These centered letters often function as a lens for determining authenticity and inauthenticity. The question of authenticity also has something of a symbiotic relationship with the conversation about development in Pauline thought (see 2.2 above). If scholars were not committed to a certain consistency in Paul's theology across his letters, they might not move quite as readily to conclusions of pseudonymity (Anderson, 158). In any case, constructions of authorship (along with letter dating and theological development) have significant hermeneutical importance for interpretation of the Pauline corpus.

3. Paul's Use of the Old Testament.

In discussing the hermeneutics of Paul, the apostle's use of the OT—his own interpretive practices—stands at the forefront of interpretive issues. Paul, as a Jewish teacher and writer, refers to his Scriptures regularly, usually following the LXX rather than the Hebrew text. Paul understands the gospel, enacted in the coming of Jesus the Messiah, as the fulfillment of God's promises to Israel. So it is not surprising that Paul's letters routinely assume or provide partial narration of Israel's story, even when there is little textual borrowing evident. Paul is so well acquainted with his Scriptures that this intertextual relationship is readily apparent in most of his letters.

3.1. Intertextuality. Intertextuality refers to the interconnectedness of texts in dialogue with one another, as well as to the study of this textual networking. Texts stand on the shoulders of other texts, and so can be understood in relation to what has already been written. Intertextuality has been an emerging topic of discussion over the last fifty years, finding its start in the work of Julia Kristeva. In NT studies, intertextuality has focused primarily on how its writers use the Jewish Scriptures or other Jewish writings, both in terms of form and purposes.

Paul draws on his Scriptures in a variety of ways and for a range of purposes in his letters, from an impressionistic or evocative use of the OT, to easier-to-recognize allusions, to explicit quotations. These categories of citation, allusion, and echo should not be thought of as fully discrete categories but rather as flexible groupings on a continuum with overlapping boundaries. Generally speaking, a citation shares substantial verbal repetition with the OT text, sometimes involving a full verse or even multiple verses. An allusion tends to share only a few words with the precursor text but usually includes a thematic association that helps the reader confirm its presence. An echo is a much subtler evocation of another text, containing limited verbal or conceptual links but recognizable by its distinctive fit with the themes of the writer.

Paul incorporates themes, stories, and texts from his Scriptures into his letters for a variety of purposes (e.g., to support an argument he is making, to provide an illustration, to show a promise coming to fulfillment) and for a number of emphases (e.g., *Christology, ecclesiology, eschatology). To understand these varied functions holistically, it can be helpful to bring a storied lens to the task of intertextuality. Given Paul's frequent reference to central elements of Israel's story—such as *creation, fall, *covenant (Torah), and *kingdom—it is quite likely that his use of the Scriptures involves storied assumptions. From this perspective, any citation, allusion, or echo can be interpreted in light of the wider story that it evokes (metalepsis; see Brown 2016).

This storied approach is particularly helpful for identifying echoes. In Philippians 2:14, for instance, Paul encourages the Philippians to do everything without *grumbling* or arguing. The word "grumbling" (*goggysmos*) likely echoes Israel's wilderness experience, which was often marked by grumbling and complaining. The identification of this echo receives confirmation from Paul's allusion to Deuteronomy 32:5, 20 in the next verse (Phil 2:15), also reminiscent of Israel's wilderness experience ("a warped and crooked generation," NIV; *geneas skolias kai diestrammenēs*; Deut 32:5 LXX).

3.2. Paul's Interpretation of the Scriptures. Detecting subtle echoes is only one of the challenges associated with Paul's use of the OT. Some of Paul's uses show him to be a creative interpreter of his Scriptures. In fact, scholars have often pointed out a dissonance between the original meaning of an OT passage and how Paul employs the text for his own purposes. Although a storied approach to understanding Paul's interpretive practices mitigates some of these occurrences, accounting for Paul's intentionally creative uses of the OT remains important. According to Richard Hays, Paul sees himself as a prophetic figure in the new messianic movement and proclaims God's word in a way "that reactivated past revelation under new conditions," something that Israel's prophets had always done (Hays 1989, 14).

Given his fresh use of the Scriptures, it is appropriate to see Paul's interpretive practices as both Jewish and Christian. They are *Jewish* in their methods and assumptions. Although Jewish methods in the first century were varied, as were the Jewish groups who interpreted the Scriptures, several of Paul's interpretive moves are unmistakably Jewish. For example, Paul uses *qal wahomer*—reasoning from lesser to greater (e.g., Rom 5:10, 17; 11:15, 17)—and *gezerah shawah*, which involves word linkages (e.g., Rom 4:1-12; 9:28-33; Gal 4:21-31). Both of these are examples of Jewish rabbinic interpretive practices (Avot R. Nat. 37; see Daube). Additionally, Paul seems to reflect common Jewish interpretive traditions about the biblical text, such as angelic oversight of the giving of the law (Gal 3:19) and the rock accompanying the Israelites in the wilderness (1 Cor 10:4; Daube). These features of Paul's hermeneutics should not surprise readers, as they place him firmly within the Judaism of his upbringing and scriptural training.

Yet Paul's use of the OT is also decidedly *Christian*. Paul draws conclusions from his Scriptures that point to Jesus as the Messiah and the fulfillment of Israel's story. Paul understands Jesus to fulfill God's promises to Israel, initiated in the patriarchs and promised and foretold through the prophets—now realized in the life of the church. For instance, in Galatians 4:22-31, Paul uses the example of *Abraham's two sons, Isaac and Ishmael, and their mothers, Sarah and Hagar, to represent two groups: those who are *slaves under the *law and those who are free in Christ. However, in a stunning turn, he equates the Jerusalem circumcision group with Hagar and Ishmael, calling them slaves, and the Galatian Gentiles with Sarah and Isaac, declaring them free. This is a particularly Christian perspective that focuses on divine promise and inclusion of the Gentiles in Christ through the Spirit, rather than through Torah observance (based in Abrahamic ancestry), yet it employs a creative reading of the Jewish Scriptures to get there.

4. Hermeneutical Lenses for Reading Paul. Interpreting Paul is a dynamic enterprise. Historical discoveries, deeper analysis of texts, and new perspectives for interpretation contribute to this hermeneutical dynamism. It is not surprising, then, that conversations about Paul's letters and theology continue to raise fresh insights and new angles for analysis. Some important ongoing areas for study include Paul's relationship to eschatology, to Judaism, to Greek thought, and to the Roman Empire, as well as ethnic and gender considerations. While the first three have a long history of discussion, the latter categories have surfaced more recently.

4.1. Paul and Eschatology. To understand Paul's eschatology, it is important to start with the assumptions about the eschatological views he would have inherited as a Jewish interpreter within Second Temple Judaism. We can then ask about the degree of continuity and discontinuity between Paul's thinking postconversion and these Jewish eschatological beliefs.

Israel's eschatology involved a constellation of expectations, focused on God's return to Zion and restoration for Israel (e.g., Is 40) and including such hopes as the resurrection of the faithful (Dan 12:1-3) and the arrival of the Spirit (Joel 2:28-32). This constellation of events would occur at the turning of the ages, with the arrival of the "age to come." Paul, like other NT writers, understands the final age to be inaugurated at the coming, *death, and resurrection of Jesus. Israel's restoration and its related expectations have arrived. This fulfillment of Jewish hopes suggests continuity between old and new.

However, for Paul the coming of the Messiah has broken open new categories and expectations, as the present age and the age to come commingle in this time of *already and not yet*. For Paul, "the present evil age" still exists but has been robbed of its power in the work of Christ (Gal 1:4 NIV). The more important reality is the arrival in the present time of the age to come, so that Paul can describe believers as those "on whom the culmination of the ages has come" (1 Cor 10:11 NIV). This proleptic arrival of Israel's hopes includes God's sending of the Spirit "as a deposit, guaranteeing what is to come" (2 Cor 1:22; 5:5 NIV), as well as Christ's resurrection as the "firstfruits" of the future resurrection of believers (1 Cor 15:20-23). For Paul, the still-future consummation will occur at the return of Christ, when all contending powers—evil, *sin, and death—will be gone and "*God [will] be all in all" (1 Cor 15:28 NIV).

Pauline interpreters disagree over how to frame Paul's eschatological portrait: Does he understand significant continuity between the hopes developed in the Jewish Scriptures and what God has enacted in Christ? Or should Paul be read as an *apocalyptic thinker, for whom God's revelation in Christ breaks into the world with cataclysmic effects? One frame for this question involves determining whether Paul's eschatology is *prospective*, that is, understanding Jesus to have fulfilled promises made to Israel (even if in some unexpected ways), or *retrospective*. In the latter case, Paul's view of human history has been "reprogrammed . . . such that he interprets the human plight in a radically new way . . . unanticipated in the Jewish Scriptures" (Blackwell, Goodrich, and Maston, 6).

Pauline interpreters who land on the side of continuity, while acknowledging the importance of the category of revelation within Pauline thought, focus on covenantal categories in Paul's Christology and soteriology in line with Jewish expectations (see 4.2 below). Interpreters who align with an apocalyptic reading of Paul, while allowing for covenantal language and ideas, emphasize the newness of God's revelation in Christ (and often find Paul's apocalyptic center in Romans). Beverly Gaventa expresses the relative weighting of these foci in the apocalyptic perspective when she contends that "Romans is . . . about *more than* God's covenant faithfulness with Israel. Romans situates [all people] within a conflict that is nothing less than cosmic in its horizon and its implications" (Gaventa 2005, 53). The apocalyptic schema is clear in Gaventa's reference to "God's revealing invasion in Jesus Christ," which defeats sin and death.

4.2. Paul Within First-Century Judaism. Paul shares with his Jewish brothers and sisters a broad set of core beliefs and practices, even while holding distinct views within these categories because of his conviction that the Messiah had arrived and so the time of new creation had begun.

Core beliefs of Judaism, including its first-century expressions, included creational monotheism and covenant—convictions that (1) Israel's God, Yahweh, was the true God, having created everything; and (2) Yahweh had chosen Israel to be set apart in mission to the nations (e.g., Ex 19:1-6; see Wright 2013, 179-84). The role of the law was understood to be central to that mission to guide Israel's communal life. Central practices included *prayer, *worship (including the offering of *temple *sacrifices), circumcision, adherence to *food and *purity regulations, celebration of prescribed festivals, fasting, and almsgiving. This set of beliefs and practices remained fairly stable, even in the face of important differences and distinctions among various Jewish groups (e.g., Pharisees, Qumran community).

Determining how Paul fits within this Jewish landscape has been an important task for his interpreters. A common way of framing this question involves the nature of Paul's critique of Judaism. Since at least the time of the Reformation, the virtually univocal answer has been that Paul's critique of Judaism was its legalism. Specifically, first-century Jews (if not their ancestors) were attempting to be justified by works focused on adherence to the law. In this scenario, the role of the law was understood as salvific, with Paul vigorously criticizing this "works-righteousness" in his letters (especially Galatians and Romans). From this perspective, Paul's use of "law" (*nomos*) and especially "the works of the law" (*erga nomou*) signals the problem of Jewish legalism. The solution Paul offers is justification as legal declaration through "faith in Christ" (*pistis Christou*; e.g., Gal 2:15-21), a law-free *salvation.

More recently, some Pauline scholars (holding the "new perspective") have criticized this portrait of first-century Judaism. E. P. Sanders takes issue with the diagnosis of legalism in his watershed *Paul and Palestinian Judaism* (1977), arguing that the Judaism of Paul's day was typified by "covenant nomism"—a covenantal or relationship framework for understanding the law. In this framework, Torah obedience (nomism) did not *get one into the covenant* but *kept one in*, presuming God's prior action of choosing and redeeming Israel. Those who have taken up this shift of framework, most notably Dunn and N. T. Wright, have understood Paul's critique of first-century Judaism to be its ethnocentrism rather than its legalism. From this perspective, Paul's reference to "works of the law" in Romans and Galatians stands in for those central Torah commands that most clearly delineate Jews from non-Jews: circumcision, food laws, and Sabbath. Thus, what Paul is arguing against is the use of Jewish "boundary markers" (Dunn's term; 1983) to set up two tiers in the messianic community, with Gentile believers as second class to Jewish and proselyte believers. Paul's gospel announces justification as full inclusion in the people of God through (faith in) Christ's faithfulness, with *pistis Christou* referring to Christ's faithful work as the object of human faith.

Views that mediate the traditional Reformation perspective and the new perspective have also been offered in recent years (e.g., Bird's via media affirming justification as both forensic in nature and covenantal in effect). Anderson suggests that Paul's soteriology develops over time, his earlier view in Galatians resembling the interpretation offered by the new perspective and his later view in Romans (also Philippians and the Pastorals), in which salvation in Christ is contrasted with all human efforts toward self-justification (the Reformation view). John Barclay, in *Paul and the Gift,* has offered a reworking of both Reformation and new perspectives by showing how Paul's understanding of grace given without regard to the recipient's worth reshapes how he views Israel's identity without a necessary critique of Judaism.

A third important lens for understanding how Paul fits within first-century Judaism has been elaborated by those who see much greater continuity between Judaism and Paul. In this set of views, often articulated by Jewish Pauline scholars such as Paula Fredriksen and Mark Nanos, Paul offers little complaint about his Jewish environment. In fact, he himself is Torah observant and fully expects his fellow Jews in Christ to remain so. Paul's focus instead is on the way in which Gentiles (or pagans; *ethnē*) fully participate in the messianic movement. They do so without conversion to Judaism (through circumcision, adherence to food laws, and Sabbath) but solely through their turning from idols to worship Israel's God (1 Thess 1:9). It is this newfound loyalty (*pistis*) to Israel's God revealed in Jesus Christ that Paul requires of "his pagans" and that brings them to salvation and into the eschatological covenantal community, made up distinctly of Jews and Gentiles (Fredriksen). Thus, for Paul, any attempt within the Christian community to compel Gentiles to become Jews ("to Judaize" them; Gal 2:14) is counter to Paul's gospel. It is from this perspective that "works of the law" may be read as "rites of proselyte conversion" (Nanos, 189).

A final observation relates to Paul's use of *pistis*, usually translated "faith" or "belief" in the Pauline writings, highlighting the longstanding influence of the Reformation view. Recent Pauline scholarship has pressed for widening the possibilities for *pistis* to include notions of faithfulness or loyalty (e.g., Gupta), as well as active participation or identification (Hagen Pifer). As Morna Hooker summarizes a both/and approach to the *pistis Christou* debate, "faith/faithfulness is primarily that of Christ, and we share in it only because we are in him" (2016, 62).

4.3. Paul and Greek Culture. *4.3.1. Greco-Roman Philosophy and Values.* Scholars have long compared Pauline thought to that of Greek and Roman philosophers and moralists. The Greek philosophical traditions were highly influential, affecting Roman philosophical discourse as well as public life across the Mediterranean world. So it would not be unusual to hear strains from these philosophical schools in the discourse of first-century writers, even in a Jewish thinker such as Paul. The Stoic philosophical tradition in particular has provided much fodder for interpreting Pauline letters (e.g., Engberg-Pedersen; Dodson and Pitts). For example,

Seneca, a Roman Stoic philosopher, commends the virtue of contentment, which is only possible if one is able to be content with both *wealth and thrift. For Seneca, if one is unable to be content with less, one will not be able to be content with more (*Tranq.* 9). This resonates with Paul's reflections in Philippians 4:10-13 on his own contentment (*autarkeia*), a theme that can be traced back to Aristotle (Engberg-Pedersen, 100-101).

Other features of the Pauline letters that draw from Greco-Roman *philosophy or moral discourse include his use of the genres of *household code and virtue and vice lists. Ancient moralists were interested in ordering the relationships among those in the household and exhorted the male head of the household to use his authority to maintain this order. They used a fairly standard literary form to address the relationship of the householder to wife, to children, and to slaves (e.g., Aristotle, *Pol.* 1.2.1, 1253b; Plato, *Leg.* 11.917a). Two household codes appear in the Pauline corpus: Colossians 3:18–4:1 and Ephesians 5:21–6:9 (see also 1 Tim 6:1-2). While following the pattern of the genre, the Pauline exhortations diverge from it in some noticeable ways. First, unlike household codes outside the NT, exhortations are given not only to the husband (householder) but also to wives (Eph 5:22-24; Col 3:18), children (Eph 6:1-3; Col 3:20), and slaves (Eph 6:5-8; Col 3:22-24; 1 Tim 6:1-2), thereby providing a greater level of agency for those with less power. Second, the authority of the householder is mitigated by the call to love versus rule his wife (Eph 5:25-33; 3:19), the prohibition against embittering his children (Col 3:21), and an implicit theological warning against mistreating his slaves (Eph 6:9; Col 4:1).

Virtue and vice lists are commonplace in Paul, with vice lists (e.g., Rom 1:29-31; 1 Cor 5:10-11; 2 Tim 3:2-5) being more numerous than virtue lists (e.g., 2 Cor 6:6-8; Phil 4:8). As Stanley Porter suggests, these types of lists likely had their origins in Greek philosophy (e.g., Plato), in which a roster of cardinal virtues (e.g., *dikaiosynē*, "justice") and vices (*adikia*, "injustice") proves foundational to moral reflection. Perhaps the best-known Pauline example of both types of lists is found in his cataloging of "the acts of the *flesh" and "the *fruit of the Spirit" in Galatians 5:19-23. Paul provides a decidedly covenantal cast to the two lists, framing them (respectively) as covenant violations and obligations (Gorman, 219). In line with other Jewish authors, Paul also lays emphasis on the communal (not only the individual's) responsibility to live in light of such covenantal virtues (Porter).

4.3.2. Paul and Greek Rhetoric. Greek rhetoric was an essential and culminating part of Hellenistic education and referred to the art of crafting speech for purposes of persuasion. While rhetorical practice focused on oral communication, rhetoric also affected written communication and so has potential application to the study of Paul's letters. While it is debated whether Paul, a tentmaker, was formally trained in Greco-Roman rhetoric, it is generally accepted that his letters show signs of commonplace rhetorical conventions and tools of persuasion.

Ancient authors categorized three kinds of rhetoric: judicial (assessing past facts), deliberative (considering future potential actions), and epideictic (assigning [present] blame or praise; see Kuypers). Determining whether a particular Pauline letter fits one of these three categories has not produced much consensus, as his letters may have multiple purposes. For example, Hans Dieter Betz understands Galatians to be judicial rhetoric, while George Kennedy categories it as deliberative. In addition to potentially aiding with identification of a letter's overarching purpose, rhetoric provides specific parts of a speech that have been correlated with portions of Paul's letters; e.g., *exordium, narratio, propositio, probatio* (applied below).

Three aspects of rhetoric emerge as foundational for persuasion, and these provide helpful angles from which to evaluate Paul's letters: *ethos*, the character and reputation of the speaker; *pathos*, the use of emotion and audience engagement; and *logos*, the internal logic and content of the speech. For example, in 1 Corinthians 9 Paul attempts to convince his audience to give up their rights in service to their fellow believers (the *logos* of 1 Cor 8) by drawing on his *ethos*—emphasizing his apostolic relationship with the Corinthians and his own willingness at every turn to subsume his rights for the good of believers, the gospel, and mission.

Although many (perhaps all) of Paul's letters show signs of rhetorical shaping, Galatians and 1 Thessalonians stand out as having significant rhetorical interest. In Galatians, Paul vigorously argues against his Gentile audience converting to Judaism via circumcision and adherence to the Jewish law. His goal is to persuade them that their experience of Christ and the Spirit demonstrates their full inclusion in the messianic community. Kennedy understands Paul's apologetic to be establishing the ethos of Paul in service of the greater deliberative purpose of the letter. Paul (1) seeks to establish his character and authority as an *apostle (*ethos*) despite his past as an opponent of Christianity (i.e., Gal 1:11–2:10), (2) appeals emotionally to the connection he has with the audience (*pathos*; i.e., Gal 4:12-20), and (3) fashions a detailed argument (*logos*) using the texts and symbols of the Hebrew Scriptures (i.e., Gal 3:5–4:11; 4:21-31). In addition to these broad points of rhetorical analysis, some scholars also see in Galatians the typical structural elements of a crafted speech. Betz, for example, outlines Galatians as follows: (1) epistolary prescript (Gal 1:1-5), (2) *exordium* (Gal 1:6-11), (3) *narratio* (Gal 1:12–2:14), (4) *propositio* (Gal 2:15-21), (5) *probatio* (Gal 3:1–4:31), (6) *exhortatio* (Gal 5:1–6:10), and (7) epistolary postscript/*conclusio* (Gal 6:11-18).

Similarly, 1 Thessalonians contains elements of intentional rhetorical practice, with Paul charging his audience to continue to stand for Christ. Paul establishes *ethos* early in the letter (1 Thess 1:2–2:8), perhaps even specifically contrasting himself (and his companions) with opponents who cover up greed (1 Thess 2:5) and seek praise from people (1 Thess 2:6). The *logos* of the letter begins with a narrative of Paul's *travels and the hardships of both Paul and the Thessalonians (1 Thess 2:9–3:13), followed by addressing concerns of the audience (1 Thess 4:1–5:22). Each of these elements is punctuated with *pathos* (1 Thess 2:10-11, 17-18; 3:6-7, 9-10; 4:9-10).

4.4. Paul and the Roman Empire. Envisioning Paul's contextual backdrop is a crucial part of the interpretive process. While scholarship has always understood first-century Judaism (see 4.2 above) and Greek culture (see 4.3 above) to be significant backgrounds for analysis, some scholars in recent days have argued for the importance of reckoning with the Roman Empire as a key lens for understanding Paul.

4.4.1. Claims of Empire Critique in Paul. Although there have been scattered voices across the twentieth century that have read Paul with Rome in view, the recent turn to empire analysis has been championed by James Scott, Richard Horsley, Neil Elliott, N. T. Wright, Sylvia Keesmaat, and Brian Walsh, among others. These scholars understand Paul to be offering a thoroughgoing critique of Roman power and propaganda, albeit allusively. Scott has offered the language of "hidden transcripts" to identify such allusive messages. Elliott, in his analysis of Paul's letter to the Romans, suggests that Paul engages in "*oblique* commentary" on Roman hegemonic power and that his audience would be attuned to these implicit messages (Elliott, 42), not least because of their familiarity with this type of political subversion from other sectors (e.g., Roman theater). While this hermeneutical approach and set of assumptions has garnered critique (e.g., Barclay 2011), it seems likely that Paul's message about Jesus' universal lordship (e.g., Phil 2:10-11) would have had (and been heard as having) "critical connotations" (Heilig, 90) for Rome's universal claims regarding Caesar as savior and lord. "Maybe it was not Paul's *primary* intention to say something about Caesar, but rather to say something about the Messiah and God, although he was perfectly aware of the critical *implications* these statements had for other competing worldviews" (Heilig, 90).

4.4.2. Evidence of Empire Critique in Paul. Paul's apocalyptic framework (see 4.1 above), along with his thoroughgoing use of certain terms with political resonance (e.g., **Lord*, *justice/*righteousness*), has led some scholars to read much of the Pauline literature as offering, or at least including, imperial critique (in spite of the portrait from Acts of Paul as taking advantage of his Roman *citizenship; e.g., Acts 22:25-26). For example, Paul's ubiquitous identification of Jesus as the *kyrios* ("lord") may be read as an implicit critique: "Jesus is Lord, Caesar is not" (Wright 2009, 69). For purposes of overview, it is helpful to identify a few of the more compelling instances of anti-Rome rhetoric—what one can understand to be oblique yet intentional Pauline references to Roman realities in Thessalonians and Philippians (for Rom 13:1-7 via the lens of imperial critique, see Elliott, 152-56).

At two points in 1 Thessalonians, Paul seems to offer an implicit critique of Roman power. The first (1 Thess 4:13-18) comes in Paul's assurances to Thessalonian believers that those in their community who have died will most certainly experience resurrection at Jesus' coming or *parousia* (1 Thess 4:15; also 1 Thess 2:19; 3:13; 5:23). This term came to be used in some cases with technical meaning for "a visit of a person of high rank, esp. of kings and emperors visiting a province" (BDAG, 780). Supporting this resonance here in 1 Thessalonians 4 is Paul's use of another technical term, *apantēsis* ("to meet," 1 Thess 4:17), used for the meeting between an official city delegation and a ruler or dignitary arriving for an official visit. The combination of these two political terms in reference to Jesus' reappearing, along with the heavy repetition of *kyrios* in 1 Thessalonians 4:15-17—five times in these three verses—suggest Paul is intentionally describing Jesus' coming with the language of the arrival of "an emperor when he comes to visit" (Koester, 160). Jesus is the true Lord who wields authority over death itself (1 Thess 4:16).

Paul's reference to "*peace and security" (*eirēnē kai asphaleia*; 1 Thess 5:3) provides a second potential political allusion, this one to Roman propaganda. Helmut Koester provides evidence that this is a Roman political slogan (versus a Pauline creation or an allusion to Jer 6:14). If this is the case, Paul uses it to turn the hope of the believing community toward the coming "the day of the Lord" (1 Thess 5:2) and the salvation that will be theirs (1 Thess 5:9) and away from trust in the peace of Rome (*pax Romana*).

In Philippians, Paul writes to a church located in a Roman colony (although not all residents of Philippi were Roman citizens). At two points in the letter, he uses language tied to citizenship (Phil 1:27; 3:20) that is virtually unique in his letters (see Eph 2:12). Paul seems to be intentionally using a term from political discourse to call the Philippians to conduct themselves (*politeuomai*) with reference to their true lord (Phil 1:27) and to remind them that their true citizenship (*politeuma*) is in God's kingdom (Phil 3:20). Additionally, Paul concludes that reminder with a depiction of Jesus' reappearing in terms of universal authority, with the power to "bring everything under his control" (Phil 3:21 NIV), and with the titles of "Lord" and "*Savior" (Phil 3:20), both of which Caesar claimed for himself (Oakes, 138-40).

Such textual examples, joined with Paul's Jewish commitment to monotheism and his apocalyptic vision that in Jesus the reign of Israel's God had broken into the present, suggest to a growing number of interpreters that Paul addresses the overreach of Roman power and calls his churches to live out an allegiance to Jesus, not Caesar, as Lord.

4.5. Illuminating Paul Through the Lens of Gender and Ethnicity. Gender and ethnicity studies have been brought to bear on Paul's letters in recent decades, sometimes with an accompanying acknowledgment that most of the voices at the center of Pauline scholarship have been white and male. Gender and ethnicity have often provided the topic of study; for example, what does Paul say about *women (and men)? What does Paul say about ethnicity? In other analyses, gender or ethnicity has been employed as an analytical lens, for example, for the retrieval of Pauline resources that have been minimized in or omitted from past scholarship.

4.5.1. Topics of Gender and Ethnicity in Paul. While discussions of gender have occurred across the history of Pauline interpretation, female voices in this conversation have occurred at the margins until the latter part of the twentieth century (for the recovery of decentered female biblical interpreters across church history, see Taylor and Choi). A recent noteworthy contribution has been offered by Cynthia Westfall, whose *Paul and Gender* comprehensively addresses hermeneutical issues and relevant texts across the Pauline corpus.

To understand Paul's perspective, relevant texts identified for analysis include Romans 16; 1 Corinthians 11; 14; Galatians 3; Ephesians 5 (see Cohick); and 1 Timothy 2, with often noted tensions among them related to the role of women in *leadership in the communities Paul addresses. Navigating these tensions necessarily involves such hermeneutical issues as determining which text(s) provide the lens for understanding others, how the occasioned nature of Paul's letters affects their interpretation, how Paul's teaching compares to his own cultural contexts, and the issue of the scope of the Pauline correspondence (see 2.3 above).

Recent contributions to Paul's perspective on ethnicity have raised questions of how Paul conceptualizes Gentile identity for those incorporated into the Messiah. According to Caroline Johnson Hodge, Paul creatively constructs a lineage for Gentile believers tracing back to Abraham (e.g., Gal 3; Rom 4), solving the theological problem of their alienation from Israel's God. Yet Jews and Gentiles are not collapsed into a single ethnicity. Johnson Hodge argues that Jewish identity remains distinct from that of non-Jews, so that ethnicity remains a relevant and crucial category for Paul. Alternatively, Love Sechrest argues that Paul understands Christians to be a distinct racial group when understood within ancient conceptions of race deeply connected to religion. In this view, Jew, Gentile, and Christian are three races; and Paul no longer understands himself as a Jew but as a Christian.

4.5.2. Gender and Ethnicity as Lens for Reading Paul. While closely related to the questions of Paul's views on gender and ethnicity, the employment of these categories as a lens for reading Paul expands the terrain for analysis beyond these questions. For example, Beverly Gaventa, in *Our Mother Saint Paul*, explores Paul's use of maternal language for himself and his ministry, for example, imagery related to laboring/birthing and to nursing/breastfeeding (1 Thess 2:7; Gal 4:19; 1 Cor 3:1-2; Rom 8:18-23). In an interpretive act of retrieval (one of the goals of feminist criticism), she marshals Paul's own reflections on his ministry to correct and broaden standard readings.

With ethnicity as a lens for analysis and critique, a number of recent works explore the Pauline corpus. Lisa Bowens analyzes African American history of interpretation of Paul in the last three hundred years. In *Onesimus Our Brother*, African American NT scholars give prominence to this short but influential letter, critiquing Western, white readings that have been particularly sympathetic toward Philemon (not Onesimus) and have attempted to make a significant distinction between ancient and modern slavery (see Johnson, Noel, and Williams). Esau McCaulley provides a compelling glimpse of the letter understood from Onesimus's perspective (McCaulley, 151-57). From another angle, scholars such as Johnson Hodge and Paula Fredriksen have critiqued the tendency to minimize the role of ethnicity in Paul: "The longtime myth constructed by Pauline scholars has been that Paul rejects a particularistic Judaism for [an] ethnicity-free and transcendent Christianity" (Johnson Hodge, 152). In this view, reaffirming Paul as (Torah-abiding) Jewish apostle to the Gentiles offers an important corrective (see 4.2).

See also Apocalyptic Paul; Birth Pangs, Maternal Imagery; Ethnicity in Paul's World; Interpretation of Paul; Justification; Letters, Letter Forms; Old Testament in Paul; Paul and Judaism; Paul in Acts; Philemon, Letter to; Pseudepigraphy/Forgery; Rhetorical Criticism; Women.

BIBLIOGRAPHY. **P. J. Achtemeier,** "The Continuing Quest for Coherence in St. Paul," in *Theology and Ethics in Paul and His Interpreters: Essays in Honor of Victor Furnish* (Eugene, OR: Wipf & Stock, 1996), 132-45; **G. P. Anderson,** *Paul's New Perspective: Charting a Soteriological Journey* (Downers Grove, IL: InterVarsity Press, 2016); **J. M. G. Barclay,** *Pauline Churches and Diaspora Jews* (Grand Rapids, MI: Eerdmans, 2011); idem, *Paul and the Gift* (Grand Rapids, MI: Eerdmans, 2015); **J. C. Beker,** *The Triumph of God: The Essence of Paul's Thought* (Minneapolis: Fortress, 1990); **H. D. Betz,** *Galatians* (Minneapolis: Fortress, 1989); **M. F. Bird,** "Justification as Forensic Declaration and Covenant Membership: A *Via Media* Between Reformed and Revisionist Readings of Paul," *TynBul* 57 (2006): 109-30; **B. C. Blackwell, J. K. Goodrich, and J. Maston,** eds., *Paul and the Apocalyptic Imagination* (Minneapolis: Fortress, 2016); **W. Bousset,** *Kyrios Christos: A History of the Belief in Christ from the Beginnings of Christianity to Irenaeus* (Nashville: Abingdon, 1970); **L. M. Bowens,** *African American Readings of Paul: Reception, Resistance and Transformation* (Grand Rapids, MI: Eerdmans, 2020); **J. K. Brown,** "Metalepsis," in *Exploring Intertextuality: Diverse Strategies for New Testament Interpretation of Texts*, ed. B. J. Oropeza and Steve Moyise (Eugene, OR: Cascade, 2016), 29-41; idem, *Scripture as Communication*, 2nd ed. (Grand Rapids, MI: Baker Academic, 2021); **D. A. Campbell,** *The Deliverance of God: An Apocalyptic Rereading of Justification in Paul* (Grand Rapids, MI: Eerdmans, 2009); idem, *Framing Paul: An Epistolary Biography* (Grand Rapids, MI: Eerdmans, 2014); **B. S. Childs,** *The Church's Guide for Reading Paul: The Canonical Shaping of the Pauline Corpus* (Grand Rapids, MI: Eerdmans, 2008); **L. H. Cohick,** *Ephesians*, NICNT (Grand Rapids, MI: Eerdmans, 2020); **D. Daube,** "Rabbinic Methods of Interpretation and Hellenistic Rhetoric," *HUCA* 22 (1949): 239-26; **J. R. Dodson and A. W. Pitts,** *Paul and the Greco-Roman Philosophical Tradition* (London: Bloomsbury T&T Clark, 2017); **J. D. G. Dunn,** "The New Perspective on Paul," *BJRL* 65 (1983): 95-122; idem, *The Theology of Paul the Apostle* (Grand Rapids, MI: Eerdmans, 2006); **N. Elliott,** *The Arrogance of Nations: Reading Romans in the Shadow of Empire* (Minneapolis: Fortress, 2008); **T. Engberg-Pedersen,** *Paul and the Stoics* (Louisville, KY: Westminster John Knox, 2000); **G. D. Fee,** *1 and 2 Timothy, Titus* (Peabody, MA: Hendrickson, 1988); idem, *God's Empowering Presence: The Holy Spirit in the Letters of Paul* (Peabody, MA: Hendrickson, 1994); **P. Fredriksen,** "Judaizing the Nations: The Ritual Demands of Paul's Gospel," *NTS* 56 (2010): 232-52; **B. R. Gaventa,** "The Cosmic Power of Sin in Paul's Letter to the Romans: Toward a Widescreen Edition," *Int* 58 (2004): 229-40; idem, "God Handed Them Over: Reading Romans 1:18-32 Apocalyptically," *Australian Biblical Review* 53 (2005): 42-53; idem, *Our Mother Saint Paul* (Louisville, KY: Westminster John Knox, 2007); **M. J. Gorman,** *Apostle of the Crucified Lord: A Theological Introduction to Paul and His Letters* (Grand Rapids, MI: Eerdmans, 2004); **N. Gupta,** *Paul and the Language of Faith* (Grand Rapids, MI: Eerdmans, 2020); **J. Hagen Pifer,** *Faith as Participation: An Exegetical Study of Some Key Pauline Texts*, WUNT (Tübingen: Mohr Siebeck, 2019); **R. B. Hays,** *The Faith of Jesus Christ: An Investigation of the Narrative Substructure of Galatians 3:1–4:11* (Chico, CA: Scholars Press, 1983); idem, *Echoes of Scripture in the Letters of Paul* (New Haven, CT: Yale University Press, 1989); **C. Heilig,** "Methodological Considerations for the Search of Counter-imperial 'Echoes' in Pauline Literature," in *Reactions to Empire: Sacred Texts in Their Socio-political* Contexts, ed. J. A. Dunne and D. Batovici (Tübingen: Mohr Siebeck, 2014), 73-92; **M. D.**

Hooker, "Paul the Pastor: The Relevance of the Gospel," *PIBA* 31 (2008): 17-31; idem, "Another Look at Πίστις Χριστοῦ," *SJT* 69 (2016): 46-62; **D. G. Horrell,** *An Introduction to the Study of Paul,* 2nd ed. (London: T&T Clark, 2006); **R. A. Horsley,** ed., *Paul and Empire: Religion and Power in Roman Imperial Society* (Harrisburg, PA: Trinity Press International, 1997); **L. T. Johnson,** *Constructing Paul: The Canonical Paul* (Grand Rapids, MI: Eerdmans, 2020); **M. V. Johnson, J. A. Noel, and D. K. Williams,** *Onesimus Our Brother: Reading Religion, Race, and Culture in Philemon* (Minneapolis: Fortress, 2012); **C. Johnson Hodge,** *If Sons, Then Heirs: A Study of Kinship and Ethnicity in the Letters of Paul* (Oxford: Oxford University Press, 2007); **S. C. Keesmaat and B. J. Walsh,** *Romans Disarmed: Resisting Empire, Demanding Justice* (Grand Rapids, MI: Brazos, 2019); **G. A. Kennedy,** *New Testament Interpretation Through Rhetorical Criticism* (Chapel Hill: University of North Carolina Press, 1984); **H. Koester,** "Imperial Ideology and Paul's Eschatology in 1 Thessalonians," in *Paul and Empire: Religion and Power in Roman Imperial Society,* ed. R. A. Horsley (Harrisburg, PA: Trinity Press International, 1997), 158-66; **J. Kristeva,** *Revolution in Poetic Language,* trans. M. Waller (New York: Columbia University Press, 1984); **J. A. Kuypers,** *The Art of Rhetorical Criticism* (Boston: Pearson and Allyn & Bacon, 2005); **B. W. Longenecker and T. D. Still,** *Thinking Through Paul: An Introduction to His Life, Letters, and Theology* (Grand Rapids, MI: Zondervan, 2014); **R. P. Martin,** *Reconciliation: A Study of Paul's Theology* (Louisville, KY: John Knox, 1981); **F. J. Matera,** *God's Saving Grace: A Pauline Theology* (Grand Rapids, MI: Eerdmans, 2012); **E. McCaulley,** *Reading While Black: African American Biblical Interpretation as an Exercise in Hope* (Downers Grove, IL: IVP Academic, 2020); **S. McKnight,** *Reading Romans Backwards: A Gospel of Peace in the Midst of Empire* (Waco, TX: Baylor University Press, 2019); **D. Moo,** *The Epistle to the Romans,* NICNT (Grand Rapids, MI: Eerdmans, 1996); **M. D. Nanos,** "A Jewish View," in *Four Views on The Apostle Paul,* ed. M. Bird (Grand Rapids, MI: Zondervan, 2012) 159-93; **P. Oakes,** *Philippians: From People to Letter,* SNTSMS 110 (Cambridge: Cambridge University Press, 2001); **S. E. Porter,** "Paul, Virtues, Vices, and Household Codes," in *Paul in the Greco-Roman World: A Handbook,* ed. J. Paul Sampley (London: Bloomsbury T&T Clark, 2016), 2:369-90; **H. Räisänen,** *Paul and the Law* (Tubingen: Mohr, 1983); **E. P. Sanders,** *Paul and Palestinian Judaism: A Comparison of Patterns of Religion* (Philadelphia: Fortress, 1977); **J. P. Sanders,** "Did Paul's Theology Develop?," in *The Word Leaps the Gap: Essays on Scripture and Theology in Honor of Richard B. Hays,* ed. J. R. Wagner, C. K. Rowe, and A. K. Grieb (Grand Rapids, MI: Eerdmans, 2008), 325-50; **D. J. Scholz,** *The Pauline Letters* (Winona, MN: Anselm Academic, 2013); **T. R. Schreiner,** *Interpreting the Pauline Epistles,* 2nd ed. (Grand Rapids, MI: Baker Academic, 2011); idem, *Paul, Apostle of God's Glory in Christ: A Pauline Theology,* 2nd ed. (Downers Grove, IL: InterVarsity Press, 2020); **J. C. Scott,** *Domination and the Arts of Resistance: Hidden Transcripts* (New Haven, CT: Yale University Press, 1990); **L. Sechrest,** *A Former Jew: Paul and the Dialectics of Race* (New York: T&T Clark, 2009); **M. A. Taylor and A. Choi,** eds., *Handbook of Women Biblical Interpreters* (Grand Rapids, MI: Baker Academic, 2012); **F. Thielman,** *Philippians,* NIVAC (Grand Rapids, MI: Zondervan, 1995); idem, *Theology of the New Testament: A Canonical and Synthetic Approach* (Grand Rapids, MI: Zondervan, 2005); **J. W. Thompson,** *Pastoral Ministry According to Paul: A Biblical Vision* (Grand Rapids, MI: Baker Academic, 2006); **C. L. Westfall,** *Paul and Gender: Reclaiming the Apostle's Vision for Men and Women in Christ* (Grand Rapids, MI: Baker Academic, 2016); **N. T. Wright,** *Paul in Fresh Perspective* (Minneapolis: Fortress, 2009); idem, *Paul and the Faithfulness of God,* 2 vols. (Minneapolis: Fortress, 2013).

J. K. Brown and N. A. Fox

HISTORICAL JESUS. *See* Christology; Jesus and Paul; Jesus, Sayings of.

HOLINESS, SANCTIFICATION

Holiness in the Pauline corpus, as in the OT, is an irreducible description of the character or essence of Israel's *God and is primarily on display in God's saving actions. But Paul reconfigures holiness through the lens of God's self-revelation in the crucified, risen, and exalted *Lord (Barton). Hence, holiness refers primarily, but not exclusively, to the cruciform pattern of saving activity embodied by this Lord. God sanctifies those he elects by liberating, reconciling, and setting them apart as a distinct people under Christ's lordship. Granting them the status of being devoted to God as holy ones/saints, God calls and enables them to embody a character and pattern of activity analogous to that of the cruciform Lord. Through the enabling Spirit, God continues the transformative process of sanctifying his people as they participate in Christ-like practices that embody fidelity to God and costly, self-giving *love, while avoiding other practices that violate the cruciform Lord's character. In this sanctifying process, they are being shaped more fully into the truly human image of the cruciform Lord, resulting in their being fully restored into the *image of God (i.e., entirely sanctified) in the parousia.

1. Lexical Considerations
2. Holiness/Sanctification and Election
3. Holiness as Corporate and Public: The Body of Christ as Temple of God and New Creation
4. Sanctification and Transformation
5. Holiness, Righteousness, and Participation in God's Mission
6. Holiness and Purity
7. Sanctification and the Parousia: Bodies, Cosmos, and the Triumph of the *Missio Dei*

1. Lexical Considerations.

Although *hosiōs* ("holy") and *hosiotēs* ("holiness") are each used once (1 Thess 2:10; Eph 4:24), the primary terminology associated with holiness/sanctification in the Pauline corpus is from the *hagios* word group: *hagios* ("holy"); *hagiazō* ("sanctify," Rom 15:16; 1 Cor 1:2; 6:11; 7:14 [2×]; 1 Thess 5:23; Eph 5:26; 1 Tim 4:5; 2 Tim 2:21); *hagiasmos* ("sanctification/holiness," Rom 6:19, 22; 1 Cor 1:30; 1 Thess 4:3, 4, 7; 2 Thess 2:13; 1 Tim 2:15); *hagiōsynē* ("holiness," Rom 1:4; 2 Cor 7:1; 1 Thess 3:13). Of these the term Paul uses most often is *hagios* ("holy"). The LXX and other Jewish texts use *hagioi* ("holy ones/saints") in reference to God's people, *Israel, and Paul applies it to believers (25× in the undisputed letters, 15× in the disputed letters). In addition, Paul depicts both the community (1 Cor 3:16-17; 6:19-20; 2 Cor 6:16; cf. Eph 2:19-22) and the individual believer (1 Cor 6:19-20) as God's/the Holy Spirit's (holy) *temple, implying that holiness is an essential characteristic of the church community and *all* its individual members, not just a special class of especially pious Christians who might be designated "saints." Combining these observations with the seemingly offhand way the Pauline letters refer to other things as "holy" (e.g., Torah, writings, commandment, *sacrifice, kiss, and especially, the **Holy* Spirit [16×]) indicates that holiness/sanctification is a preoccupation of the Pauline corpus (Gorman 2007, 149-50).

2. Holiness/Sanctification and Election.

In the OT, God elects Israel corporately by rescuing and setting this people apart from other nations—sanctifying them—because of God's love for them (Deut 7:6; 14:2). The goal of this divine *election was that Israel would become God's missional instrument for displaying God's desire for justice and shalom in order to draw the nations to God (Ps 105:6; Is 41:8-10; 42:1; 49:1-7). Marked out as God's holy ones (sanctified) by God's initial saving action, Israel's task was to become the holy nation God had already made them by displaying God's holy character to the nations, thus "concretiz[ing] the divine life in the world" (Adewuya, 18). Similar conceptuality pervades the Pauline corpus in that God has rescued and marked out those "*in Christ," God's beloved, elect one (Eph 1:4-6). Now located "in Christ," who reveals the holy character of God (1 Cor 1:30), they have been "definitively sanctified" (Peterson). Because the Holy Spirit is working among and in them, they are "holy ones," a distinct people elected/chosen and beloved by God (1 Thess 1:4; 2 Thess 2:13; Rom 1:7). As such, they are located in the sphere where God's *salvation is being worked out (Phil 2:12-13; cf. 1 Cor 1:18, "to us who are being saved") by means of God's sanctifying activity (1 Thess 4:7; 2 Thess 2:13). Hence, God has indeed "definitively sanctified" (*hēgiasmenois*) those "in Christ" (1 Cor 1:2) but continues to call them to become the "holy ones" (*klētois hagiois*) who publicly display God's holy character (1 Cor 1:2; cf. Rom 1:7). Sanctification, then, is the beginning of salvation, its process, and—as will become clear—its culmination.

3. Holiness as Corporate and Public: The Body of Christ as Temple of God and New Creation.

When God "sanctifies" a people, God relocates them in, and as, a new space or sphere that Paul can refer to metaphorically as the *body of *Christ (1 Cor 12:12-27; 6:15; 10:17; Rom 12:4-5; cf. Col 1:18; 3:15; Eph 1:22-23; 2:16; 4:4, 12-16) and/or the temple of God/the Holy Spirit (1 Cor 3:16-17; 6:19; 2 Cor 6:16; cf. Eph 2:19-22) where the coming new *creation is—or ought to be—on display (Gal 6:15; 2 Cor 5:17).

In 1 Thessalonians 1:5-9, one reason Paul says he knows God has elected the Thessalonians is that their corporate life together had become a public model (*typon*, 1 Thess 1:7) with their faithfulness (*pistis*) to God having become known in "every place." Their publicly observable, cruciform pattern of life of fidelity to God and self-giving love for others was analogous to that of the Lord's and Paul's (1 Thess 1:6; see Paul's cruciform life pattern in 1 Thess 2:1-12). This Spirit-enabled life pattern of missional faithfulness is the concrete form of their being "in Christ" as they re-present the life of the cruciform, risen Christ as his body in the world (Johnson, *1 & 2 Thessalonians*, 45-55; Johnson, *Holiness and the* Missio Dei, 132-34). It marks them out as holy and elect since they are thereby "in" Christ—who became holiness/sanctification (*hagiosmos*) for believers (1 Cor 1:30)—living in the sphere of sanctification where God wills to continue his sanctifying activity (1 Thess 4:3, 7). Further, Christ is the image (*eikōn*) of God (2 Cor 2:4; Col 1:15), in whose face God's glory—God's holiness made visible (Lev 10:3; Is 6:3; Hab 3:3; Harrington, 30-31)—becomes manifest (2 Cor 4:6). Hence, the community that forms Christ's visible body is to be where God's *glory/holiness is publicly—albeit partially—on display.

The image of the *church as the temple of God/the Holy Spirit is also connected with the public display of God's divine glory/holiness (Johnson, *Holiness and the* Missio Dei, 134-37). The plethora of temples (*naoi*) and the images (*eikones*) housed in Greco-Roman cities were the primary public faces of the gods/goddesses they represented. Hence, to refer to the church at *Corinth or *Ephesus as the divine temple implied that their life together was to be a public display of the face of Israel's holy God, the place where true divine glory now dwelled (perhaps the long-awaited, returning Shekinah of Ex 40:34-38 and Ezek 43; Wright 2013, 711-17).

In contexts in which Paul uses the temple image, several features of the church's life together set it apart from its surrounding culture and constitute, in part, its holy character. In 2 Corinthians 6:14–7:1, where Paul calls the community "the temple of the living God," he calls for the community's cleansing and for avoiding what is impure or pollutes. Paul is probably referring to avoiding contact with the "superapostles" in 2 Corinthians 10–13, whose behavior reflects their culture's typical striving for status and power. Such noncruciform behavior is characterized by self-love rather than love for others. In 1 Corinthians 3:16-17, Paul warned the Corinthians about similar behavior within their own community that could have deleterious effects on "God's temple," where the Spirit dwells. Such status-seeking, divisive actions are tantamount to defiling (*phtheirei*) God's holy temple (Brower, 62-63). The Corinthians' actions, therefore, violate Paul's new-creation, cross-shaped purity map (i.e., the means by which Paul judges something as pure or impure in the new creation begun in Christ). Its primary coordinates are fidelity (*pistis*) to God and sacrificial love toward others (*agapē*). Hence, the Corinthians' actions "defile/pollute" because they display the opposite of the cruciform nature of God's holy character as revealed by Christ (Johnson, *Holiness and the* Missio Dei, 145-47).

In 1 Corinthians 6:12-20 Paul responds to the practice of some young men in the congregation having sex with prostitutes. Exploiting these women as objects of sexual self-gratification was a common social practice for young Roman males. Since, however, God gives the Holy Spirit to dwell in each individual and among those in the community (see 1 Thess 4:8), Paul asserts that believers no longer belong to themselves but are individually and communally "a temple of the Holy Spirit" (1 Cor 6:19; Johnson, *Holiness and the* Missio Dei, 136; cf. Brower, 63-66; Wright 2013, 712-13). Hence, their proper response should be to "honor [*doxasate*] God" with their body (1 Cor 6:20). Failing to *honor God—a failure to give God the loyalty/*pistis* God is due—by exploiting others, rather than sacrificially loving them, again violates Paul's new-creation, cross-shaped purity map.

Ephesians 2:11-22 emphasizes God's reconciling work through Christ, who "created one new humanity (*anthrōpon*) in himself by making *peace so that he might reconcile both [Jews and the nations] to God in one body through the *cross" (Eph 2:15-16). Reconciled to God and each other, this community "is growing into a holy temple," being built into "a dwelling place of God" (Eph 2:21-22). Such publicly visible reconciliation between groups previously hostile to each other gives witness that the peacemaking, holy God has been at work among them (Rom 5:10-11; 2 Cor 5:19) and now dwells in their midst. As God's holy temple in the Lord, this reconciled new humanity corporately and publicly reflects the face of "the God/Lord of peace/shalom" (1 Thess 5:23; 2 Thess 3:16) and, in doing so, provides a glimpse of the shalom characteristic of the coming new creation (Gal 6:15; 2 Cor 5:17; Johnson, *Holiness and the* Missio Dei, 141-45).

4. Sanctification and Transformation.

4.1. Sanctification as Transformation. Interpreters generally agree that just as God sanctifies Israel when he elects and rescues them, setting them apart as God's people, God sanctifies those in the *ekklēsia* when he elects and transfers them "into Christ" as a consecrated people set apart for God's purposes. David Peterson argues that Paul limits the language of sanctification to this definitive one-time act of consecration—being "possessed by God"—and reserves the language of "renewal" for the Spirit's continuing transformative work (Peterson, e.g., 133). Undoubtedly Paul does use renewal language in reference to the Spirit's transforming work (e.g., Rom 12:2; 2 Cor 4:16; cf. Col 3:10; Titus 3:5). But the goal of that renewal is transformation into the image of Christ (Rom 8:29; 1 Cor 15:49; Phil 3:21), who embodies *hagiosmos* and is the image of the holy God. Hence, as those initially sanctified "in Christ" (1 Cor 1:2) are being renewed, they are in the process of sanctification, of becoming the "holy ones" (*klētois hagiois*) God intends them to become (1 Cor 1:2; cf. Rom 1:7). As the Spirit enables them to embody a pattern of righteous/just activity (see below), God continues the transformative process leading to their sanctification/holiness (*eis hagiosmon*, Rom 6:19, 22), a process culminating in a final divine sanctifying act at the parousia (1 Thess 5:23). Hence, most interpreters maintain that Paul understands sanctification as an initial divine act followed by a transformative (albeit nonlinear) renewing process in which the Spirit transforms individuals and communities into (partial) reflections of the character of the holy God as revealed in the cruciform Christ, a process fully completed in the parousia (1 Thess 5:23).

4.2. Sanctification and Justification. At least since the Reformation, the relationship between sanctification and *justification has been vigorously debated. Since the first edition of the *Dictionary of Paul and His Letters*, Paul's understanding of justification has received much attention, resulting in proposals differing from more traditional Lutheran and Reformed understandings of justification. But even in these proposals, the question of the relationship between sanctification and justification in Paul's letters still generally turns on whether Paul's justification language refers *only* to a change of status via God's forensic declaration (e.g., Wright 2009) or *also* to a transformation of one's nature in which justification and sanctification are two aspects of a single movement, neither chronologically nor qualitatively distinct (e.g., Campbell; Gorman 2009). While this article cannot do justice to the complexities of this debate, the way the next section connects holiness and *righteousness with each other, and connects both with participation in the divine *mission, moves in the direction of the latter view.

5. Holiness/Sanctification, Righteousness, and Participation in God's Mission.

Like Israel in the OT, those "in Christ" neither initiate nor complete their sanctification. They are, however, enabled by the Spirit to engage in a cruciform pattern of reconciling, redemptive activity—which includes taking on some practices and avoiding others—through which God continues the sanctifying process of transforming them into the image of the cruciform Lord.

In Israel's scriptural tradition, God's holiness is closely linked with God's righteousness/justice (e.g., Deut 32:4). In Isaiah 5:16, the prophet claims that "the Holy God displays himself as holy [or "is sanctified"] by his [and his people's] righteousness" (*ṣədāqâ*/*dikaiosynē*; see Moberly, 63). Holiness and righteousness/justice are also closely linked for Paul: Christ, the truly human one, is at once the embodiment of *dikaiosynē* and *hagiasmos* (1 Cor 1:30). Hence, those the Spirit relocates "in Christ" as they participate in Christ's *death and resurrection in *baptism (Rom 6:3-11) have been "justified" (*edikaiōthēte*) and "sanctified" (*hēgiasthēte*) by the Spirit (1 Cor 6:11).

Paul addresses his Roman audience as those who are called to be(come) the holy ones (*klētois hagiois*) God intends (Rom 1:7), and in Romans 3–5 he describes God's gracious act of justification (*dikaiōsis*) by faith/faithfulness. In Romans 6 he defines what that justification entails in the lives of the justified (Gorman 2009, 73-79; cf. Campbell, 825-27). Justified/liberated (*dedikaiōtai*) from the enslaving powers of *Sin and Death (Rom 6:7) and reconciled to God and each other by God's justice-restoring mission (Rom 5:1, 10-11), they share in Christ's story of being brought from death to life (Rom 6:13). Therefore, rather than continuing to present themselves to the power of Sin as "weapons of injustice/unrighteousness [*adikia*]," they are to present themselves and their members as "weapons of saving justice/righteousness [*dikaiosynē*] to God" (Rom 6:13). As such "weapons/*slaves of God's *dikaiosynē*" (Rom 6:13, 19; cf. 2 Cor 5:21), they become instruments for God to shape and use through which his saving justice is channeled. Paul goes on in Romans 6:18-22 to connect this language to the language of holiness/sanctification, affirming in Romans 6:19, 22 that the benefit of this missional pattern of the justified life—this self-presentation as slaves "to God" and "to [God's] saving justice/righteousness [*dikaiosynē*]"—"leads to sanctification/holiness [*eis hagiosmon*]." Specifically, it leads to God continuing his sanctifying activity of shaping them personally and corporately into a human display of God's own holiness (i.e., into the holy ones God has called them to become).

In Romans 12:1, Paul uses language similar to Romans 6, but with a slight nuance that highlights the corporate aspect of holiness; he urges the Roman believers to present their individual bodies as a singular, holy (*hagian*), living sacrifice that is acceptable to God. As the body of Christ (Rom 12:3-8), their corporate life together—characterized especially by the cruciform practices spelled out in the rest of the letter—is this holy sacrifice. As they present their individual bodies as a part of this holy corporate sacrifice, the effects of being handed over to the impurity/chaos of Romans 1:18-32 are reversed. That reversal includes the transforming renewal of their minds *in order that* they can now discern God's will (in contrast to the enslaved condition of Rom 1:28). Their Spirit-enabled presentation of themselves as weapons of God's *dikaiosynē* is concretized by their engaging in a variety of cruciform practices, practices whose essence is sacrificial, self-giving love (*agapē*, Rom 13:8-10).

Engaging in these practices becomes a primary means by which the Spirit continues sanctifying the community and its members, shaping their ecclesial body into the holy, living sacrifice God desires it to become. Indeed, if the cultic language of "the offering of the *Gentiles" in Romans 15:16 refers to the Gentiles themselves (rather than their *collection for the Jerusalem church), Paul is arguably depicting the ecclesial life together of all Gentile assemblies in Rome and elsewhere as his larger priestly sacrificial offering to God. If so, the goal of Paul's entire mission is that these Gentile assemblies would become a single sacrificial offering "sanctified by the Holy Spirit" (Rom 15:16; cf. Eph 5:26-27), faithfully obedient (Rom 15:18) to the God of peace, who reconciled them to himself and to those Jews with whom he hopes they join together in *worship "with one mouth" (Rom 15:6).

First Thessalonians is more focused on holiness/sanctification than any other epistle. As in Romans, Paul connects manifesting God's holy character to embodying righteousness/saving justice by forging a subtle connection between the two (Johnson, *1 & 2 Thessalonians*, 231-36). In 1 Thessalonians 2:10, he describes his actions among the Thessalonians as holy (*hosiōs*) and righteous/just (*dikaios*). These actions simultaneously displayed both fidelity (*pistis*) to God (1 Thess 2:1-6) and cruciform acts of love (*agapē*) toward others (1 Thess 2:7-9), as did Jesus' faithful, loving death on the cross. Paul also expects these sorts of practices to be on display in the lives of those "in Christ Jesus" (see Gal 5:6). In 1 Thessalonians 5:8, Paul envisions the church wearing one singular piece of defensive armor, a "breastplate of *pistis* and *agapē*." Here, he is echoing Isaiah 59:17, where Israel's divine warrior in his rescuing mission dons a "breastplate of righteousness/saving justice [*dikaiosynē*]." The implication is that divine *dikaiosynē* is being humanly embodied by the Thessalonians' fidelity to God and loving cruciform actions for others (1 Thess 1:3; 3:6) in the service of God's reconciling and redeeming mission. Further, the way Paul uses language from Ezekiel 36–37 (LXX) in 1 Thessalonians (Weima, 110-12; Johnson 2007, 278) suggests that God's purpose in rescuing the Thessalonians is similar to his purpose in restoring Israel, that is, so that God might manifest his holiness to the Gentiles/nations by means of their life together. Since God "continues giving the Holy Spirit into [them]" (1 Thess 4:8 // Ezek 37:6, 14), the Thessalonians are enabled to reflect God's righteousness/saving justice through their *pistis* and *agapē* and thus become God's means of revealing his holiness to those who do not acknowledge God (Ezek 36:23; Is 5:16). Hence, they dare not behave like the latter (1 Thess 4:5).

In 1 Thessalonians 3:11-13 Paul explicitly connects holiness and *agapē* in his prayer that the Lord would enable the Thessalonians "to increase and flourish in *agapē* for one another *and for all . . . in order that* [*eis to*] he might strengthen [their] hearts to be blameless in holiness [*hagiōsynē*] . . . in the royal coming of our Lord Jesus." Flourishing in self-giving, loving practices of seeking the good, not just for each other but "for all" (1 Thess 5:15), would be costly indeed for the Thessalonian church since the "all" would most probably have included those persecuting them (1 Thess 3:3-4). Seeking their good would extend the shalom of the God/Lord of peace (1 Thess 5:23; 2 Thess 3:16) even to their enemies, thereby reflecting God's character and his actions on the Thessalonians' behalf to reconcile them to himself when they were his enemies (Rom 5:1, 6-10). The prayer's reciprocal movement *from* their being engaged in such costly, self-giving practices as participants in God's reconciling mission *to* their hearts/imaginations being strengthened to be blameless in holiness in the parousia is important to note. It suggests that *in the context of*, or even *by means of*, the community's own grace-enabled participation in the *missio Dei*, Paul expects the Lord to continue his sanctifying activity that is reshaping them into the *imago Dei*. This process culminates in the parousia, when God fully sanctifies the church's corporate body and the entire self of each of its members (1 Thess 3:13; 5:23), bringing them into full conformity with Christ (see Rom 8:29; Phil 3:21), the image of the holy God (2 Cor 4:4) and the embodiment of God's *dikaiosynē* and *hagiasmos* (1 Cor 1:30).

6. Holiness and Purity.

Just as the nature of holiness has been reconstrued for Paul in light of the cruciform Lord, so have the related concepts of *purity and impurity. In the Pauline corpus, impurity is often closely related to various forms of sexual immorality, and it seems to retain something from its OT character as a dynamic and polluting force that can spread and harmfully affect communities (e.g., 1 Cor 5, esp. 1 Cor 5:7). This is Paul's concern in 1 Thessalonians 4:3-8, where he maintains that God's will for the Thessalonians' continuing sanctification (*hagisomos*, 1 Thess 4:3) is threatened by the possibility of intracommunal sexual immorality, which he explicitly associates with impurity (1 Thess 4:7; Johnson, *1 & 2 Thessalonians*, 107-12). Such activity would wrong or exploit a brother or sister and make the community indistinguishable from the surrounding culture, where free males were understood to have the "right" to sex with various partners. Such exploitative behavior is the antithesis of cruciform love for others, amounting to idolatrous allegiance to one's own sexual fulfillment rather than fidelity to the God who created the exploited sexual partner in God's image. Hence, it violates the cross-shaped structure of Paul's new-creation purity map.

His characterization of such behavior as impurity captures the effect of its destructive consequences: polluting the community's social network by generating pain and broken relationships rather than the shalom God wills for the church (Brower, 103). As demonstrated above, "impurity" for Paul is not limited to sexual offenses (e.g., the status-seeking, divisive actions that defile [*phtheirei*] God's holy temple in 1 Cor 3:16-17), and any such practice that violates his cross-shaped map must be avoided. This is a necessary condition for God's sanctifying work to continue and be brought to completion with the community being "blameless in holiness" (1 Thess 3:13), that is, "blamelessly" displaying the holy character of the cruciform Lord.

Contrary to how impurity was understood to function in the OT and in Second Temple Judaism, however, those who form God's holy temple are not made unclean simply by contact with outsiders who engage in behaviors that violate (sexually or otherwise) Paul's cross-shaped purity map (1 Cor 5:9-10; 1 Cor 7:12-16). Otherwise, participating in God's reconciling, redeeming mission in the world would be impossible. In fact, 1 Corinthians 7:14 seems to suggest that the holiness of individual church members is itself "contagious," having some sort of sanctifying effect on their non-Christian family members (Brower, 105-7).

7. Sanctification and the Parousia: Bodies, Cosmos, and the Triumph of the *Missio Dei*.

God's sanctifying activity culminates at the parousia both for those "in Christ" and for the whole of creation. Being conformed by the Spirit to Christ's risen body of *doxa*/glory at the final *resurrection is a sanctifying cleansing from death's corruption (1 Cor 15:42: "sown in corruption [*phthora*], raised in incorruption [*aphtharsia*]"). Since in Second Temple Judaism the Lord's *doxa*/glory is considered to be a manifestation of his holiness made visible (Harrington, 30-31), being raised and conformed to the Lord's body of *doxa* in his royal coming (Phil 3:20-21; 1 Cor 15:43) completes the sanctification of the whole *ekklēsia* and the whole of every person's *body within it (1 Thess 5:23). Only then will they fully reflect what their Spirit-empowered life together has been in the (sanctifying) process of becoming, that is, blameless in holiness, a truly human reflection of the image of the cruciform Lord (Rom 8:29; 1 Cor 15:49; 2 Cor 4:4; Phil 3:21), and thus the image of the holy God.

The Spirit who transforms human bodies "sown in corruption" (*phthora*, 1 Cor 15:42) will also transform the cosmos by liberating it from its corruption (*phthora*) and making it incorruptible (Rom 8:21). This same life-giving Spirit who totally permeates dead human bodies at the resurrection so that they become a "spiritual body" (*sōma pneumatikon*, 1 Cor 15:44 NRSV) will completely permeate the cosmic body, entirely sanctifying it, making all of it God's cosmic sanctuary where God is finally "all in all" (1 Cor 15:28).

See also BODY OF CHRIST; CRUCIFORMITY; FAITH; GLORY, GLORIFICATION; HOLY SPIRIT; IDENTITY; IN CHRIST; JUSTIFICATION; LOVE; PURITY AND IMPURITY; TEMPLE; THESSALONIANS, LETTERS TO THE.

BIBLIOGRAPHY. **J. A. Adewuya,** *Holiness in the Letters of Paul: The Necessary Response to the Gospel* (Eugene, OR: Cascade, 2016); **S. C. Barton,** "Dislocating and Relocating Holiness: A New Testament Study," in *Holiness Past and Present*, ed. S. C. Barton (London: T&T Clark, 2003), 193-213; **K. Brower,** *Living as God's Holy People: Holiness and Community in Paul* (Milton Keynes, UK: Paternoster, 2010); **K. E. Brower and A. Johnson,** eds., *Holiness and Ecclesiology in the New Testament* (Grand Rapids, MI: Eerdmans, 2007); **D. Campbell,** *The Deliverance of God: An Apocalyptic Rereading of Justification in Paul* (Grand Rapids, MI:

Eerdmans, 2009); **M. J. Gorman,** "'You Shall Be Cruciform for I Am Cruciform': Paul's Trinitarian Reconstruction of Holiness," in *Holiness and Ecclesiology in the New Testament*, ed. K. E. Brower and A. Johnson (Grand Rapids, MI: Eerdmans, 2007), 148-66; idem, *Inhabiting the Cruciform God* (Grand Rapids, MI: Eerdmans, 2009); **H. K. Harrington,** *Holiness: Rabbinic Judaism and the Graeco-Roman World* (New York: Routledge, 2001); **A. Johnson,** "The Sanctification of the Imagination in 1 Thessalonians," in *Holiness and Ecclesiology in the New Testament*, ed. K. E. Brower and A. Johnson (Grand Rapids, MI: Eerdmans, 2007), 275-92; idem, *Holiness and the "Missio Dei"* (Eugene, OR: Cascade, 2016), 127-52; idem, *1 & 2 Thessalonians*, THNTC (Grand Rapids, MI: Eerdmans, 2016); **W. Moberly,** "Whose Justice? Which Righteousness? The Interpretation of Isaiah V 16," *VT* 51 (2001): 55-68; **D. Peterson,** *Possessed by God: A New Testament Theology of Sanctification and Holiness*, NSBT 1 (Downers Grove, IL: InterVarsity Press, 1995); **J. A. D. Weima,** "'How You Must Walk to Please God': Holiness and Discipleship in 1 Thessalonians," in *Patterns of Discipleship in the New Testament*, ed. R. N. Longenecker (Grand Rapids, MI: Eerdmans, 1996), 98-119; **N. T. Wright,** *Justification: God's Plan and Paul's Vision* (Downers Grove, IL: InterVarsity Press, 2009); idem, *Paul and the Faithfulness of God*, vol. 2 (Minneapolis: Fortress, 2013).

A. Johnson

HOLY DAYS. *See* FOOD LAWS AND CUSTOMS, JEWISH AND ROMAN; PAUL AND JUDAISM.

HOLY SPIRIT

The Holy Spirit serves a central role within Pauline thought, and the Holy Spirit's activity was understood to be a cornerstone of ecclesial experience within Pauline communities. While Paul was certainly influenced by conceptions of the Spirit from the OT and the writings of intertestamental Judaism, the contemporary experience of the Holy Spirit by Paul and within the communities he participated in was likewise formative. For Paul, the Holy Spirit was to be equated with God and the activity of Jesus, and yet also differentiated in some way. The Spirit played a foundational role in the life of a Jesus-follower, both birthing new life and empowering believers in the present, and serving as a down payment for the eschatological fulfillment that is yet to come. This activity of and life in the Spirit for Paul is intimately related with the kingdom of God and the experience of kingdom life in present Christian experience.

1. The Sources of Paul's Conception of the Holy Spirit
2. Pauline Usage of *Pneuma*
3. The Identity of the Spirit: God, Jesus, and the Holy Spirit
4. The Activity of the Spirit and the Christian's New Life
5. The Holy Spirit and Eschatology
6. The Holy Spirit and the Kingdom of God

1. The Sources of Paul's Conception of the Holy Spirit.

Paul's conception of the Holy Spirit derived from a variety of sources, but the primary influences were the OT canon, developments of *pneuma* within intertestamental Judaism, and early Christian experience of God's Spirit.

1.1. Old Testament. Preeminent among these influences is certainly the OT canon. The Spirit of *God is often referred to using the term *spirit* (Heb. *rûah*, Gk. *pneuma*) in the OT, and only occasionally identified as "holy" (3×: Is 63:10-11; Ps 51:13). A number of metaphors are invoked when describing the activity of the Spirit through these writings, including but not restricted to fire (Num 9:15), breath (Job 33:4), oil (Is 61:1), and water (Ezek 36:25; 39:29). Repeatedly the Spirit is closely associated with water imagery in the OT, particularly where the life-giving reign of the future Messiah is in view (see Konsmo, 9).

The Spirit is commonly associated with God's power and very presence throughout the OT. Empowerment can come upon people mightily (Judg 14:6, 19; 1 Sam 16:13), and individuals can be empowered to great feats (Judg 3:10; 11:29; 15:14-15). This power is described as clothing some individuals (Judg 6:34) and descending on others (2 Kings 2:9; Is 11:2). It is likewise associated with the office and empowered utterances of the prophets (Num 11:25-27; 1 Sam 18:10; Ezek 3:12; 8:3; 11:1, 24). Such a conception is clearly in view for Paul (e.g., 1 Cor 2:4, 12; 12:1-31; 14:1-40; 2 Tim 1:7). Likewise, the Spirit is identified with God himself and his activity (Is 31:3; 34:16; 40:13). God repeatedly is described as dwelling among his people, whether by tabernacle or *temple (Ex 25:8; 40:34; 1 Kings 6:37-38; 2 Chron 7:1-2). The very conception of a new temple with God dwelling in the midst of his people is at the heart of Jewish *eschatology (Is 2:2-3; Mic 4:1-3; Jer 3:17-18). Paul invokes this temple imagery when he asks the Corinthian congregation, "Do you not know that you are God's temple and that God's Spirit dwells in you?" (1 Cor 3:16 NRSV).

The Spirit is closely associated with *prophecy throughout the OT, and prophets were endowed with the Spirit of God (Num 11:29; 1 Sam 10:6; 19:20-24; Mic 3:8; Ezek 11:5; Joel 2:28-32). Elisha even requested a double portion of Elijah's own empowerment (2 Kings 2:9). A similar close relationship between the Spirit and prophecy is readily apparent in Paul's writings as well (e.g., 1 Thess 5:19-20; 1 Cor 12:17-31). Similar associations between the Spirit and *wisdom are also present (Ex 31:3; 35:31; Num 11:16-17; Job 32:8; Is 11:1; 42:1-4; e.g., 1 Cor 2:10-11).

The Spirit is also portrayed throughout the OT as foundational in the transformation of moral character, the formation of community *identity, and the heart of *covenant life (Is 4:4; 28:5-6; 59:21; 63:10; Ezek 36:26-27; 39:27-29; Ps 51:10-11; 143:10). The pouring out of God's Spirit brings about corporate justice, *peace, and security, along with *judgment of the proud (Is 32:15-20). The Spirit empowers God's people to obey his commands (Ezek 36:26-27) and keep his covenant (Jer 31:31-34). This accords with Paul's understanding of the *circumcision of the heart by the Spirit as the fulfillment of the original intention of the *law (Deut 30:1-6). This renewal of the heart and ultimately the *salvation of the *Lord is tied closely with the activity of the Spirit both corporately (Ezek 11:19-20, 24; 18:31; 36:26-27; 39:29) and individually (Ps 51:10). This is declared by Ezekiel to be nothing short of Israel's *resurrection from the dead (Ezek 37:1-14).

Thus, the spirit in the OT is intimately connected with the eschatological hope of the future messianic age (Is 32:15; 44:3; Ezek 36:25-27; 39:28-29; Joel 2:28-32). The prophets spoke of a future time when the Spirit would be poured out on the people differently than it had in Israel's past (Joel 2:28-32; Jer 31:31-34). The outpouring of the Spirit is similarly connected with the new covenant (Jer 31:31; Ezek 36:27), and the irrevocable covenant promise is God's Spirit (Is 59:21). Gordon Fee identifies the Spirit as the "Holy Spirit of promise" whose purpose was to initiate the eschatological age (Fee 1996, 4). Elsewhere Fee rightly observes, "the Spirit is the evidence that the *eschatological promises of Paul's Jewish heritage have been fulfilled*" (Fee 1994, 808). Ultimately deliverance of the whole nation of Israel will take place by the power of God's Spirit (Is 63:11-14), and it will be the Lord's Spirit-empowered *servant who will extend his rule to the *Gentiles and be a *light to the nations (Is 42:1-7). God's Spirit will be put into his people (Ezek 37:14) and poured out on all *flesh (Joel 2:28-32), which includes Jew and Gentile alike, a reality eminently relevant for Paul's mission to the Gentiles.

1.2. Intertestamental Judaism. The themes and concepts regarding the Spirit found in the OT continued to be developed within intertestamental Judaism and are present in the writings of both Palestinian and Hellenistic Judaism. One of the most significant developments is the close association of the Spirit with prophetic empowerment and divine wisdom, which enables the prophet or sage to fulfill some divinely ordained task. These close associations can be seen in Josephus (*Ant.* 6.166, 222-223; 8.408; 10.266), Philo (*Mos.* 1.277; 2.188, 191; *Her.* 265; *Spec.* 165; 4.49), and even throughout various Palestinian documents (1QS VIII, 15-16; Jub. 25.14; 31.12; 1 En. 91.1). Similar associations are found within early rabbinic literature (see Levison 1997, 246-47) as well, but it is difficult to clearly date these sources, and so caution is warranted in citing these works as sources for Paul's understanding of the Holy Spirit. Max Turner notes that the four primary functions of this prophetic Spirit were charismatic revelation and charismatic wisdom, and (less frequently) invasive prophetic speech and invasive praise (see Turner 2000, 92–101). The collective label for this activity is the Jewish "Spirit of prophecy," a somewhat anachronistic label that pre-Christian Jewish literature did not regularly use (e.g., Jub. 31; Philo uses an analogous "[divine and] prophetic Spirit" [*Fug.* 186; *Mos. 1*]). This phrase is much more explicit and widely used later in the Targums.

While some want to primarily focus on the role of the Spirit as inspiration of the prophetic/oracular speech within this literature, the activity of the Spirit is not so restricted. One such example is the connection between the Spirit and power, where the same Spirit who empowers prophecy and wisdom also works miraculous activity (3 Kgdms 18.12; 4 Kgdms 2.16; Pss Sol. 17.37). Similarly, the empowerment of the spirit is linked with the messianic tradition (1Q28b V, 24-25; 4Q521; 4Q161 7-10 III, 15-23; 11Q13). In 4Q521 specifically, the activity of the Spirit in the messianic age is tied to *healing and resurrection of the dead, which is linked with the release of the captives (echoing Is 61). In other literature (non-Christian redacted sections of 2 *Baruch* and 4 *Ezra*), the Spirit is likewise associated with miraculous works of new *creation and resurrection.

Finally, the Spirit is often linked with purification and ethical renewal and transformation. Neither of the biblical translations (Targums or LXX) attempts to reduce the connections between the Spirit and ethical transformation in their translations. In some instances, such as *Targums Neofiti* and *Pseudo-Jonathan*, the relationship between Spirit and ethical transformation is only reinforced. Philo (*Gig.* 55) suggests the Spirit leads in every right path. Intertestamental Wisdom literature (e.g., Wis 1:5; 7:7; 9:17; Sir 39:6; 48:12, 24) portrays the Spirit as falling within the general characteristics surveyed thus far, and because the Spirit is the source of heavenly wisdom, the Spirit has significance for ethical and religious communal life. Wisdom of Solomon (Wis 9:17-18) reflects a deep pessimism about the possibility of attaining *righteousness or salvation without an individual receiving the gift of the Spirit.

Similarly, the Spirit's ethical influence is seen in later writings such as the *Testaments of the Twelve Patriarchs*, where the presence of the Spirit is linked to Joseph's stellar character (*T. Sim.* 4.4), absence of pollution in his heart, and his ability to resist sexual temptation (*T. Benj.* 8.1–3). Among the *Qumran documents (1QH), the psalmist thanks God for the gift of his Holy Spirit, by which the covenanter is "upheld" so as to not stumble and which is the means by which one expects further purification. Similarly, 1QS suggests God will sprinkle his people with the Holy Spirit and the Spirit of *truth and purify them. In both the Spirit is both revealing God's wisdom and cleansing the covenanter.

1.3. Early Christian and Pauline Experiences. Hermann Gunkel long ago asserted that Paul's theology is "the expression of his experience, not his reading" (Gunkel, 100). While this position may be somewhat extreme given the obvious continuity among Paul, his contemporaries, and the broader thrust of Judaism, it would be a mistake to suggest that Paul is simply a product of his literary environment and social environment in his understanding of the Spirit. Paul's experience of the risen Jesus Christ and God's Spirit clearly shaped his theology deeply, and this can be seen throughout his writings.

The Damascus event for Paul was fundamentally an experience of the Holy Spirit (Dunn 1975, 104-14; see also Fee 1997, 166-83). Paul regularly looks to his own *conversion (1 Cor 1:8-10; Gal 1:13-17; Phil 3:4-11) and teaches out of his experience of life in *Christ (Rom 5:10; 6:3; 8:1-2; 15:16; 2 Cor 5:17; Gal 1:10-24; 2:16; 3:26-27; Phil 3:2-11) throughout his letters. Beyond his own experience, Paul also points his audience to their own conversion experiences or emphasizes the fundamental experience of the Spirit at conversion for believers (1 Cor 2:4-5; 6:11; 2 Cor 1:21; 3:1–4:6; Gal 3:1-5; 4:4-7; 1 Thess 1:4-6, 9-10; 2 Thess 2:13-14). Paul's theology has been deeply informed by his experiences and those of which he was a part, and to miss this is to miss a fundamental influence on Paul's understanding of the Spirit.

2. Pauline Usage of *Pneuma*.

2.1. Pneuma in Paul's Writings. *Pneuma* is the Greek term for "spirit," and it has a breathtaking range of usage in the first century. John Levison rightly summarizes the staggering complexity of *pneuma* in the first century when he notes, "The range of meanings suggested by the single word, *pneuma,* is itself bewildering, encompassing entities as diverse as subterranean vapors, heavenly winds, human attitudes, unpredictable ghosts, and a holy spirit" (Levison, 1). *Pneuma* occurs 145 times in Paul's writings, with an overwhelming majority of these occurrences referring to the Holy Spirit. Of these 145 occurrences, Paul only uses the full term "Holy Spirit" 17 times, although he utilizes equivalent phrases such as "Spirit of God," "Spirit of Christ," and "His Spirit" frequently. While there has been some debate within scholarship on the use of definite articles with "Holy Spirit," Paul's usage can be both arthrous and anarthrous when referring to the Holy Spirit, and such usage is often a function of grammatical appropriateness rather than any specific challenge to the definiteness of the Spirit of God. As Fee observed many years ago, Paul only knows of the Holy Spirit when referring to divine activity (Fee 1994, 24.)

2.2. Pneumatikos. The adjective *pneumatikos* is almost exclusively used by Paul in the NT, with twenty-four of its twenty-six occurrences in Paul's letters, and over half of these occurrences are in 1 Corinthians. For context on broader usage, this term does not occur in the Septuagintal writings (LXX), and the broader classical and Hellenistic usages of this adjective primarily refer to wind and air. As such, there has been much confusion around this word, especially in the English language, where "spiritual" has been the receptor term. In Paul's usage, *pneumatikos* is primarily used as an adjective for the Spirit and is used primarily for "*that which belongs to, or pertains to, the Spirit*" (Fee 1994, 29). This is particularly relevant in 1 Corinthians, where Paul repeatedly uses *pneumatikoi* for God's people and for activities or realities closely associated with the Holy Spirit (1 Cor 2:6–3:1; 12:1–14:40; 15:44-46).

The relevance of this usage should not be missed as, for Paul, *pneumatikoi* does not describe some metaphysical duality with materiality but rather it is used to denote association with the Spirit of God. That is, the very presence of God, the Holy Spirit, is what distinguishes believers from nonbelievers for Paul, so by this they are "spiritual" or Spirit people (*pneumatikos*). Those who are walking/living/being led by the Spirit are *pneumatikos* (1 Cor 12:1; 14:1, 37; Gal 6:1; Rom 1:11; Col 1:9; 3:16; Eph 5:19).

3. The Identity of the Spirit: God, Jesus, and the Holy Spirit.

3.1. The Spirit of God. For Paul, the Holy Spirit brings the power and presence of God himself (Fee 1994, 5-9). The Spirit is clearly God's own Spirit (Rom 8:9; 1 Cor 3:16; 6:11; 12:3; 2 Cor 1:22; 3:3; Eph 4:30; Phil 3:3; 1 Thess 4:8) and thus knows the depths of God (1 Cor 2:10-11; possibly 1 Cor 14:2). Thus, the Spirit whom Christians receive is the Spirit who is from God (1 Cor 2:12; 6:19; Gal 3:5; 4:6) and who dwells in believers (2 Tim 1:14). Paul clearly articulates that it is God who sends for the Spirit of his Son, Jesus, and that the Spirit dwells in our hearts (Gal 4:6). Galatians 4:6 captures the essence of Paul's conception of the Spirit: (1) from God, (2) the Spirit of Jesus is sent (3) to believers. This Spirit is of he who raised Jesus from the dead (Rom 8:11) and is to be understood as distinct from Jesus in some sense.

3.2. The Spirit of Jesus. The Spirit is distinct from Jesus, while occasionally being equated with Jesus. Paul writes about the Spirit empowering Jesus and thus being distinct from him (Rom 1:4). Paul also identifies the Spirit as the Spirit of Jesus himself (Rom 8:9; Phil 1:19) and equates the Spirit with the Lord Jesus in 2 Corinthians (2 Cor 3:17-18). Elsewhere in 2 Corinthians, Paul invokes a metaphor of being a letter of Christ, with the very ink being written by the Spirit of God and written on human hearts (2 Cor 3:3). The Holy Spirit, while being distinct from Christ, "will inspire only Christ-like attitudes and obedience to Christ as practical Lord and Master" (Thiselton, 81).

For Paul, to have Christ in one is to have the Spirit in one (Rom 8:10). Similarly, to be "*in Christ" is equivalent to being anointed or sealed with the Spirit (2 Cor 1:22; Eph 1:13). This phrase "in Christ" is a robust and flexible idiom often used by Paul to discuss various aspects of the Christian life. It occurs 165 times in just Paul's letters alone. It is used to talk about the actions or gifts of God for believers in Christ, including salvation (2 Tim 2:10), redemption and *justification (Rom 3:24), eternal life (Rom 6:23; 2 Tim 1:1), sanctification (1 Cor 1:2), *grace (1 Cor 1:4), *forgiveness (Eph 4:32), reconciliation (2 Cor 5:19; Eph 2:13), and *freedom (Gal 2:4). It is used to talk about the activities of believers, such as truth telling (Rom 9:1; 2 Cor 2:17), encouragement (2 Cor 12:19), and how to generally conduct one's life (1 Cor 4:17). It is also used to talk about characteristics of believers, such as *faith and *love (2 Tim 1:13), grace (2 Tim 2:1), boldness (Philem 8), godly living (2 Tim 3:12), and spiritual maturity (Col 1:28). In some places it is even used like an adjective where one might expect the word *Christian* (Rom 16:9; 1 Cor 3:1). Theologian William Barcley sums it up well when he suggests: "To be 'in Christ' means to belong to, to serve, to be ruled by Christ" (Barcley, 111; for a more recent study, see also Campbell).

3.3. Trinitarian Formulations. There are a number of instances in Paul's letters where he articulates clear trinitarian formulations in which the Spirit is invoked and equated with both the Lord Jesus and God. One of the most profoundly trinitarian formulations in the entire NT occurs in 2 Corinthians 13:14, where the *fellowship of the Holy Spirit is set alongside the grace of the Lord Jesus and the love of God. That is, the Holy Spirit is equated directly with God and Christ in Paul's blessing. A similar articulation is found in 1 Corinthians, where Paul is talking of gifting (1 Cor 12:4-6). A series of grammatically similar clauses is repeated by Paul as he acknowledges varieties of gifts, services, and activities but the same Spirit, Lord, and God. "The Spirit," "Lord," and "God" are grammatically parallel with one another and clearly equated in Paul's articulation.

Other noteworthy trinitarian formulations can be found in Ephesians. In one instance Paul roots the Christian life in the Trinity (Eph 3:14-17). In another Paul uses a similar series of clauses to communicate unity, with there being one Spirit, one Lord, and one God (Eph 4:4-6). What can be said for all of these instances is that Paul viewed the Spirit to be equated both with Lord Jesus and with God, but distinct from these other persons of the Godhead.

4. The Activity of the Spirit and the Christian's New Life.

For Paul, the presence and activity of the Holy Spirit in the life of a believer is foundational to both the believer's personal faith and the believer's participation in the ecclesial community. Paul fundamentally assumes that all believers have the Spirit (Rom 5:5). The Spirit for Paul is received by hearing with faith (Gal 3:2, 5, 14), and having received the Spirit is synonymous with being part of the ecclesial community (Rom 8:15; 1 Cor 2:12; 6:19; Gal 3:5; 4:6; 6:1). It is noteworthy in Galatians 3:14 that Spirit reception is specifically identified as the "promise of the Spirit," which is reminiscent of

Luke's own language concerning Spirit reception in Luke-Acts (Lk 24:49; Acts 2:38-39). This promise language for the Holy Spirit is also found in Ephesians 1:13.

The new life of the Spirit is described as a renewal and may be linked closely with water *baptism (Titus 3:5). Paul articulates that believers are to understand themselves as *slaves in their new life of the Spirit (Rom 7:6). That is, those who have Christ's Spirit belong to him, and consequently those who do not have the Spirit do not belong to him (Rom 8:9). Paul makes it clear that believers are not their own; to have God's Spirit is to belong to and be owned by God (1 Cor 6:19). Being united with Jesus is thus understood as sharing one Spirit (1 Cor 6:17). There is only one Spirit (2 Cor 4:13; Eph 4:4), and he is indeed shared by all (1 Cor 12:4-11; Eph 2:14). For Paul, all were baptized into one *body with one Spirit (1 Cor 12:13).

4.1. Christian Identity as Children of God. Those who are led by the Spirit are children of God (Rom 8:14) and are not subject to the law (Gal 5:18). The Spirit bears witness to the reality that those with the Spirit are heirs of God and joint heirs with Christ (Rom 8:16-17). That is, the Spirit received is a spirit of *adoption (Rom 8:15), and it is through the Spirit that those adopted have access to the Father (Eph 2:18). The Spirit actualizes the sonship of Christ in the believer (Rom 8:14-17).

As noted previously, those who are walking/living/being led by the Spirit are *pneumatikos* (1 Cor 12:1; 14:1, 37; Gal 6:1; Rom 1:11; Col 1:9; 3:16; Eph 5:19)—they are "spiritual" or Spirit-people. In numerous instances, Paul contrasts those with the Spirit to those who are of the flesh (1 Cor 3:1; Gal 4:29). This contrast of flesh and Spirit is consistent throughout Paul (Rom 8:4-6, 9; Gal 5:22-25). For Paul, not only is gratifying the flesh to be contrasted with living by the Spirit, but the Greek construction of Galatians 5:16 suggests that these activities are mutually exclusive. One cannot ever live by the Spirit and also gratify the flesh. Note the subjective emphatic negation here in Galatians 5:16—if one lives by the Spirit, one cannot, nor will one ever, gratify the desires of the flesh.

Paul suggests that those who *worship in the Spirit of God are the people of God (Phil 3:3), and the people of God are God's temple, whom God's Spirit dwells in (1 Cor 3:16). The community itself is identified as both a *household and a temple to the Lord (Eph 2:21). The dwelling of the Spirit in God's people is not only corporate but also individual and personal for each of God's people (1 Cor 6:19).

4.2. Spirit of Life. One of the central characteristics of the Spirit for Paul is his "life-giving" character (Rom 8:2, 10; 2 Cor 3:6). This life-giving character of the Spirit is closely associated with righteousness for Paul (Rom 8:10). John Yates notes that the Spirit is the agent by which new creation is brought about through the resurrection of the dead (1 Cor 15:45; 2 Cor 3:6). The Spirit is the very "vivifying presence of God in new creation" (Yates, 105). It is plain that it was by the power of the Spirit that Jesus himself was raised (Rom 1:4). For Paul, the law of the Spirit of life is set in contrast with the law of *sin and *death (Rom 8:2). To walk according to the Spirit produces life and peace (Rom 8:6; Gal 6:8). Life is contingent on putting to death the deeds of the *body, and this is accomplished by the empowerment of the Spirit (Rom 8:13).

4.3. General Activity of the Spirit. The Holy Spirit has a wide diversity of activities in Paul's writings and is even described to have a *ministry of his own (2 Cor 3:8). Much like the expanded range of activity of the Holy Spirit in intertestamental Judaism, Paul regularly describes the Spirit as revealing divine guidance, giving wisdom, and directing God's people. The prevailing metaphor for this activity in Paul's writings is walking/living/being led by the Spirit (1 Cor 12:1; 14:1, 37; Gal 6:1; Rom 1:11; Col 1:9; 3:16; Eph 5:19). To walk according to the Spirit is antithetical to walking according to the flesh (Rom 8:4-6, 9, 13) for Paul. The Spirit guides God's people (Gal 5:25), teaches them to understand Spirit things (1 Cor 2:13), and helps his people in their weakness by instructing them to pray (Rom 8:26), even going so far as to intercede on their behalf when they do not know what to pray (Rom 8:26-27). Relatedly, the Spirit is also described as revealing truth (Gal 3:5), confirming believers' consciences (Rom 9:1), and revealing wisdom (Eph 1:17). The expansive reach of the Spirit is such that even the depths of God are known (1 Cor 2:10).

4.4. An Empowering Spirit. One of the central ideas for Paul is the empowering character of the Holy Spirit. The range of this empowerment seems to be diverse, including both the internal sanctifying work of the Spirit and the external displays of power associated with the Holy Spirit. Internally, the Spirit is described as closely associated with sanctification (1 Thess 4:8; 2 Thess 2:13) and actively working in God's people to produce liberty/freedom (2 Cor 3:18), unity, and peace (Eph 4:3-4). Paul suggests that one of the roles of the Spirit is to perfect or *complete those the Spirit dwells in (Gal 3:3). The

Spirit brings love (Rom 5:5; 15:30; Col 1:8), *hope (Rom 15:13), and inner strength (Eph 3:16).

The *fruit of the Spirit's activity is love, *joy, peace, patience, kindness, generosity, faithfulness, gentleness, and self-control (Gal 5:22; 1 Thess 1:6). This fruit is set in opposition to traits such as conceit, competition with one another, and envy (Gal 5:26). Relatedly, genitive constructions are often used by Paul to convey a quality or attitude produced by the activity of the Holy Spirit. Examples of this include the Spirit who brings life (Rom 8:2), the Spirit characterized by *holiness (Rom 1:4), the Spirit who brings faith (2 Cor 4:13), the Spirit who gives wisdom and revelation (Eph 1:17), and the Spirit who brings gentleness (1 Cor 4:21).

There is a close association between the presence of the Spirit and the presence of power for Paul (1 Thess 1:5; 1 Cor 2:4; Gal 3:5; Rom 1:4; Eph 3:16; 2 Tim 1:7). James Dunn observes the almost interchangeable use of *Spirit* and *power* at times throughout Paul's writings (Dunn 2014, 851). For Paul, the Spirit empowers the proclamation of the gospel (1 Thess 1:5), as well as other speech (1 Cor 2:4; 2 Tim 1:7), and it is only by the Spirit that one can proclaim "Jesus is Lord" (1 Cor 12:3). F. W. Horn succinctly summarizes Paul's view of the Spirit simply "as the power of proclamation and sanctification" (Horn, "Holy Spirit," *ABD* 3:272).

One of the most distinctive ways the Holy Spirit empowers believers is by the *gifts (*charismata)* God gives by the Spirit (1 Cor 2:12, 14; 12:1). *Charisma* is an almost exclusively Pauline term, with sixteen of the seventeen occurrences in Paul's letters. The most robust treatment of this concept is found in 1 Corinthians 12–14, where Paul provides instruction for the community in the practice and pursuit of gifts. In this well-known passage, Paul describes a variety of gifts that all come from the same Spirit (1 Cor 12:4). The purpose of the gifts is the common good of the community (1 Cor 12:7) and the building up of the body of Christ, the *church (1 Cor 12:12-13). These gifts include wisdom, *knowledge, faith, healing, working of miracles, prophecy, various *tongues, and interpretation of tongues (1 Cor 12:8-10). The same Spirit gives all gifts to individuals as the Spirit chooses (1 Cor 12:11). Paul's rhetorical questions in this section suggest that he assumes that not all receive all gifts or receive the same ecclesial callings (1 Cor 12:29-30). Paul also suggests that particular gifts can and should be desired and that there is some kind of structure or order among the gifts (1 Cor 12:31; 14:1, 5).

Regardless, all gifts must be practiced in love (1 Cor 13:1-13). Paul goes on to note that the nature of gifts suggests that they are temporary, only for a season, and that they are not full revelations of God's will, which will only come at the eschaton (1 Cor 13:8-13). Paul encourages the church to strive to excel at their practice of the gifts (1 Cor 14:12). Paul suggests that some gifts have specific purposes, such that tongues are for nonbelievers and prophecy is for believers (1 Cor 14:22). Paul encourages the orderly practice of such gifts in the worship context (1 Cor 14:26-40). His instruction here aims to curtail the extreme practices on the ends of the spectrum and these address practices that target both believers and nonbelievers, respectively.

5. The Holy Spirit and Eschatology.
Paul's understanding of the Holy Spirit is inherently eschatological. The experience of the Holy Spirit for Paul involves the very inbreaking of the future into the present—both the foretaste of the future and the guarantee of that which is to come. There is a multistage vision of the benefit of the Spirit for Paul in that believers experience the firstfruits in the present, but there will be a future *fullness that is not yet realized (Rom 8:23). The Spirit brings faith to maintain hope in the present for the future (Gal 5:5) and helps bring about the experience of God's new creation in the present.

The three primary metaphors Paul uses to convey his eschatological understanding are that of a down payment, firstfruits, and seal. The down payment (*arrabōn*) metaphor occurs only in Paul's writings, in his letters to the Corinthian (2 Cor 1:21-22; 5:5) and Ephesian (Eph 1:14) communities. This metaphor invokes the commercial concept that includes both a completed initial installment of a contractual obligation and the promise of future final fulfillment. This metaphor invokes the present or "already" aspect of the experience of the Holy Spirit while also acknowledging a future or "not yet" aspect. This tension of the "already" and the "not yet" is explicit in Ephesians 1:14, where God's people have not received the fulfillment of God's promise and are guaranteed their future inheritance.

The firstfruits metaphor is used in Romans 8:23 to refer to the dual realities of the present experience of the Holy Spirit along with the future final adoption, which will be realized with the redemption of believers' bodies. Paul uses this metaphor elsewhere to refer to Christ's resurrection (1 Cor 15:20, 23), and its use of affirming present experience and guaranteeing future realities is also echoed in these parallel usages. Thiselton rightly observes, "It is a pledge of more of the same quality or kind to come" (Thiselton, 73). Like the down payment metaphor, this metaphor references both the "already" and the "not yet" aspects of the Holy Spirit in the believer's contemporary experience.

The final metaphor, the Holy Spirit as a seal, is used by Paul in three instances (2 Cor 1:21-22; Eph 1:13; 4:30). This metaphor invokes the concept of stamping an impression into wax, which inherently communicates ownership, authenticity, and owner security or protection. While this metaphor is not implicitly eschatological, the context of all of these occurrences is clearly so. In 2 Corinthian 1:21-22, Paul uses the metaphor to communicate that the Spirit both declares God's ownership and authentication of the *mission of Paul, Silvanus, and Timothy and serves as a first installment of that which is to come. This concept of God's ownership is also visible in Ephesians 1:13, as Ephesians 1:14 contextually acknowledges both present fulfillment and the guaranteed fulfillment of future inheritance and redemption. Finally, Ephesians 4:30 uses the metaphor and acknowledges the purpose of the deal is specifically for the future day of redemption.

So it is in the activity, formation, and transformation wrought by the Spirit that the community of faith lives the future life of new creation in the present. Thiselton rightly captures this concept when he says, "The Holy Spirit transforms us into our future destiny, into that which God destines us to become" (Thiselton, 73).

6. The Holy Spirit and the Kingdom of God. Paul only sporadically uses the language of *kingdom despite the centrality of the kingdom in Jesus' teachings. Rather than the conclusion that this concept is not central to Paul's theology, as some have suggested (see Walter, 63), Youngmo Cho has shown in his recent study that "for Paul, life in the Spirit becomes his way of speaking about life in the kingdom" (Cho, 108). For Paul, the kingdom of God is both present (1 Cor 4:2; Rom 14:17) and future (1 Thess 2:12; Gal 5:21; 1 Cor 6:9-10; 15:50). It is associated with God's power (1 Cor 4:2), the present shape of which is defined as righteousness, peace, and joy in the Holy Spirit (Rom 14:17).

Through comparisons of Synoptic literature, Cho demonstrates that Paul uses Spirit language to talk about kingdom realities. Where Jesus proclaims new life in the kingdom and connects it closely with the arrival of the kingdom (e.g., Mk 1:15; 10:17-31; Mt 19:16-28; Lk 15:11-32; 18:18-30), Paul connects this new life to the activity and ministry of the Holy Spirit (e.g., Rom 8:2; 2 Cor 3:3-6). The same can be observed with sonship (e.g., Mt 5:9, 45; 6:9-10; 17:25; Lk 6:35; 11:2; Rom 8:14-15, 23; Gal 4:6), the hope of resurrection (e.g., Lk 14:14; 16:17-31; 18:18-30; 20:27-40; Rom 6:4; 8:11, 23; 1 Cor 6:14; 15:44-46), righteousness and justification (Mt 5:10, 20; 6:33; Lk 6:21; 12:31; Rom 8:10; 14:17; 1 Cor 6:11; 2 Cor 3:8-9; Gal 3:14; 5:5), *ethics (Mt 6:10; 22:34-40; Mk 12:28-34; Lk 10:25-37; Rom 5:2, 5; 8:4-5; 13:8-10; Gal 5:21-22) and the eschatological "now and not-yet" character of both the kingdom and the activity of the Holy Spirit (e.g., Mt 12:28; Lk 11:20; 17:21; Gal 3:1-14; 4:4-5; Rom 8:1-30). Cho concludes that "for Paul, life in the Spirit becomes his way of speaking about life in the kingdom" (Cho, 161; for a full treatment of the above comparisons, see 52-109).

N. Q. Hamilton notes that the present experience of the Spirit "produces the effects in the present human life that are appropriate to future life in the kingdom" (Hamilton, 22). Indeed, while it is not appropriate to collapse the activity of the Holy Spirit with the kingdom of God, it should be acknowledged that the kingdom, as the manifest rule and reign of God, is fundamentally related with the person of the Holy Spirit, the manifest presence of God, and that the activity of the Holy Spirit will always be intimately aligned with the reality and experience of the kingdom of God.

See also Baptism; Christ, Messiah; Eschatology; Flesh; Freedom/Liberty; Fruit of the Spirit; Gifts of the Spirit; God; Holiness, Sanctification; Kingdom of God/Christ; Wisdom.

BIBLIOGRAPHY. **W. B. Barcley,** *"Christ in You": A Study of Paul's Theology and Ethics* (Lanham, MD: University Press of America, 1999); **C. R. Campbell,** *Paul and Union with Christ: An Exegetical and Theological Study* (Grand Rapids, MI: Zondervan, 2012); **Y. Cho,** *Spirit and Kingdom in the Writings of Luke and Paul: An Attempt to Reconcile These Concepts*, PBM (Eugene, OR: Wipf & Stock, 2005); **J. D. G. Dunn,** *Jesus and the Spirit: A Study of the Religious and Charismatic* (Philadelphia: Westminster, 1975); idem, *Romans 9–11*, WBC 38B (Grand Rapids, MI: Zondervan, 2014), 851; **G. D. Fee,** *God's Empowering Presence: The Holy Spirit in the Letters of Paul* (Grand Rapids, MI: Baker, 1994); idem, *Paul, the Spirit, and the People of God* (Grand Rapids, MI: Baker, 1996); idem, "Paul's Conversion as Key to His Understanding of the Spirit," in *The Road from Damascus, the Impact of Paul's Conversion on His Life, Thought, and Ministry*, ed. R. N. Longnecker

(Grand Rapids, MI: Eerdmans, 1997), 166-83; **H. Gunkel,** *The Influence of the Holy Spirit*, trans. R. A. Harrisville and P. A. Quanbeck II (Philadelphia: Fortress, 1979); **N. Q. Hamilton,** *The Holy Spirit and Eschatology in Paul*, SJTOP 6 (Edinburgh: Oliver & Boyd, 1957); **F. W. Horn,** "Holy Spirit," *ABD* 3:260-80; **C. S. Keener,** *The Mind of the Spirit: Paul's Approach to Transformed Thinking* (Grand Rapids, MI: Baker, 2016); **E. Konsmo,** *The Pauline Metaphors of the Holy Spirit: The Intangible Spirit's Tangible Presence in the Life of the Christian,* SBL 130 (New York: Peter Lang, 2010); **J. R. Levison,** *The Spirit in First Century Judaism* (Leiden: Brill, 1997); idem, *Filled with the Spirit* (Grand Rapids, MI: Eerdmans, 2009); **R. P. Menzies,** *Empowered for Witness: The Spirit in Luke-Acts* (New York: T&T Clark, 2004); **F. Philip,** *The Origins of Pauline Pneumatology*, WUNT 2/194 (Tübingen: Mohr Siebeck, 2005); **V. Rabens,** *The Holy Spirit and Ethics in Paul,* WUNT 2/283 (Tübingen: Mohr Siebeck, 2010); **E. P. Sanders,** *Paul: The Apostle's Life, Letters, and Thought* (Minneapolis: Fortress, 2015); **A. Thiselton,** *The Holy Spirit—In Biblical Teaching, Through the Centuries, and Today* (Grand Rapids, MI: Eerdmans, 2013); **M. Turner,** *Power from on High: The Spirit in Israel's Restoration and Witness in Luke-Acts,* JPTSup 9 (Eugene, OR: Wipf & Stock, 2000); idem, *The Holy Spirit and Spiritual Gifts* (Peabody, MA: Hendrickson, 2005); **V. D. Verbrugge,** ed., "Pneuma," *NIDNTT*, abridged ed. (Grand Rapids, MI: Zondervan, 2000), 473-79; **N. Walter,** "Paul and the Early Christian Jesus-Tradition," in *Paul and Jesus: Collected Essays,* ed. A. J. M. Wedderbrun, JSNTSup 37 (Sheffield: JSOT Press, 1989), 51-80; **N. T. Wright,** *Paul and the Faithfulness of God,* 2 vols. (Minneapolis: Fortress, 2013); **J. W. Yates,** *The Spirit and Creation in Paul,* WUNT 251 (Tübingen: Mohr Siebeck, 2008).

T. M. Lyons

HOMOSEXUALITY

The apostle Paul mentions same-sex sexual behavior three times in his letters: Romans 1:26-27; 1 Corinthians 6:9; and 1 Timothy 1:10. Paul's words are best understood as one of many early Jewish responses to what was considered a Greco-Roman sexual practice that was incompatible with a Jewish—and now Christian—sexual ethic.

1. Same-Sex Behavior in Greco-Roman Culture
2. Marriage and Sexuality in Judaism
3. Paul's Response to Same-Sex Sexual Behavior
4. Revisiting Paul

1. Same-Sex Behavior in Greco-Roman Culture. Same-sex sexual behavior was widespread in Greco-Roman culture. The most widespread form of same-sex behavior in ancient Greece was pederasty (Gk. *paiderastia*), or "love for boys," where an adult male citizen would have sexual relations with a teenage (typically twelve to eighteen years old) freeborn boy (Dover). These male relations typically maintained a strict "active" and "passive" distinction, the older man being the active partner and the younger boy being the passive partner.

A typical pederastic relationship would discontinue once the younger boy showed signs of adulthood (e.g., growing a beard and developing chest hair), although sometimes the relationship would blossom into a consensual relationship well into adulthood (see Plato, *Symp.* 181-183)—Agathon and Pausanias being a well-known example (Plato, *Symp.* 193B; see also Aelian, *Var. hist.* 2.21; also Parmenides and Zenon; Plato, *Parm.* 127a). There is evidence that same-aged teenagers would also engage in same-sex sexual relations and that on occasion same-status, same-age adults would engage in mutual same-sex relations (Hubbard 2003, 5; 2014). One writer even refers to an older youth with a beard playing the role of the passive partner, while a younger youth is the active partner (Xenophon, *Anab.* 2.6.28; see Scroggs, 34).

There is much less documentation of female same-sex sexual relations in the ancient world. But the documentation there is describes these relationships as quite different from the pederastic relations popular among males. The earliest attestation of female same-sex relations in the Greek period comes from Sappho, who was born on the island of Lesbos in the late seventh century BC. Sappho quite frequently talks about female same-sex relations in consensual terms, quite unlike what one typically sees in descriptions of male same-sex sexual behavior, where the active/passive distinctions were usually maintained (see Sprinkle 2016). Other references to female homoerotic relations included vase paintings, which depict two adult *women engaging in sexual foreplay (see Brooten). While same-sex sexual relationships were well known and widely accepted, there were several dissident voices, such as Plato, who considered same-sex relations to be "unnatural" (*Leg.* 636B-D), as did many later writers from Stoic, Jewish, and Christian traditions.

Same-sex relationships were also widely popular in the Roman world—the historical setting of the NT and the writings of Paul. Pederasty continued to be the primary form of accepted male same-sex sexual practice. However, unlike Greek pederasty, where the teenage boy was a freeborn youth, the passive partner in a Roman pederastic relationship would not have been a freeborn youth but someone of a lower social status, such as a slave or a youth born to noncitizens. On the whole, Romans accepted same-sex sexual relations as long as they maintained strict power differentials between the active and passive partners. That is, a Roman citizen could be the active partner with a slave, male prostitute, or anyone with a lower social status. But the reverse would not typically happen—a male of higher social status playing the passive role in same-sex sexual intercourse.

However, by the first century AD, the nature of same-sex relationships was becoming much more variegated, and strict power differentials were not always maintained. Best known, of course, is Caesar Nero, who played the passive role in two different male same-sex relationships (Sprinkle 2016, 147). Two centuries later, the emperor Elagabalus (AD 218–222) "[indulged] in unnatural vice with men" (*Augustan History* 5.1-2) where he would play the passive role in sexual intercourse with other men. First-century Roman author Petronius portrays two consensual adult lovers, Encolpius and Ascyltos, who were of equal age and status (Petronius, *Satyricon*). It is striking that Petronius does not at all seem troubled by this relationship, which clearly violated the typical codes of social conduct, where power differentials governed who played the active role and who played the passive role in sexual intercourse. But such was not uncommon in first-century Rome, where many traditional sexual practices were being challenged (Dunn, 91-100).

Adult, consensual, same-sex relationships between women were not uncommon in the Roman era. Sometimes these relationships were even called "marriages" by various writers. Iamblichus (second century AD) writes about a "marriage" between two women named Berenike and Mesopotamia (Photius, *Bibliotheke* 94.77a-b). Lucian of Samosata mentions the *marriage of two wealthy women of equal status named Megilla and Demonassa (*Dialogues of the Courtesans* 5.1-3). Clement of Alexandria refers to female same-sex marriage (*Paed.* 3.3.21.3), as does Ptolemy of Alexandria (*Tetrabiblos* 3.14 sect. 172). Several archaeological discoveries testify to mutual love between women, including a funeral relief that dates back to the time of Caesar Augustus, which depicts two women holding hands in a way that resembles "the classic gesture of ancient Roman married couples" (Brooten, 59-60).

In short, while same-sex sexual relations were typically between two people of different social statuses, there were a number of exceptions where two adults would engage in a same-sex romantic relationships. The idea that same-sex *consensual* adult relationships were nonexistent in Paul's day does not correspond to the historical data.

2. Marriage and Sexuality in Judaism.

Jewish responses to same-sex sexual behavior were both unambiguous and widespread. While Jewish writers held to diverse opinions on some matters of sexual ethics (e.g., grounds for divorce), when it came to same-sex sexual relations, there was no diversity of opinion on the matter. Same-sex sexual behavior, whenever it is addressed in Jewish literature, is considered to go against God's design and is therefore deemed to be *sin.

To understand the Jewish context Paul was nurtured in, one must go back to the beginning of the Jewish Scriptures. In Genesis 1–2, God creates humanity in his own *image as "male and female" (Gen 1:27). In Genesis 2, the male and female (i.e., Adam and Eve) come together to form a "one-*flesh union"—a clear reference to marriage (Gen 2:24). Sex difference, in other words, is an essential part of what marriage *is*. Marriage is never considered to be merely a consensual union between two humans, with sex difference becoming one potential form of marriage. Rather, marriage is the coming together of two sexually different persons—male and female. Sex difference is a necessary part of marriage, according to Jewish thought.

References to same-sex behavior occur at various points in the biblical story (e.g., Gen 19:1-10; Judg 19:22-26) and are explicitly prohibited in OT *law (Lev 18:22; 20:13). Leviticus 18:22 in particular harks back to the *creation account, suggesting that male same-sex sexual relations go against the creational design for human sexual expression (Sklar). Leviticus 20:13 expresses a similar view and uses two words translated as *koitē* and *arsēn* ("laying with a male") in Greek translations of the OT, a point that will be important for understanding Paul's statements in 1 Corinthians 6:9 and 1 Timothy 1:10 (see 3.2 and 3.3 below).

In short, the Jewish Scriptures define marriage as a one-flesh union between two sexually different persons and denounce all sexual relations outside this *covenant bond as going against the Creator's design. Among the rather long list of sexual vices (Lev 18:6-23) is same-sex sexual relations.

Early Jewish writers of the Diaspora responded to the variegated forms of same-sex relationships evident in the Greco-Roman world. Pederasty continued to be the primary kind of same-sex behavior that drew Jewish disapproval (Josephus, *Ant.* 1.200-201; *Ag. Ap.* 2.273-275; Philo, *Contempl.* 59-60; *Hypoth.* 7.1; *Spec.* 1.325; 2.50; 3.37-39; *Decal.* 168; *Abr.* 134-137). However, Jewish writers also condemn same-sex relations that are not clearly pederastic in nature. Josephus, for instance, raises the question, "What are our laws about marriage?" His answer: "That law owns no other mixture of sexes but that which [is] according to nature [*kata physin*]" (Josephus, *Ag. Ap.* 2.199). That Josephus frames his response to same-sex sexual relationships in the context of marriage suggests that his critique cannot be limited to pederasty, which was never considered a kind of marriage. Other Jewish writers condemn same-sex relations, or even same-sex passion, without mentioning age distinctions (Ps.-Phoc. 3.190-191; Let. Aris. 152; 2 En. 34.1-2), which shows that pederasty was not the only kind of same-sex relationship that first-century Jews condemned. In short, there is no evidence of debate within Judaism about whether same-sex relations *of any kind* might be considered moral.

Jesus affirms the standard Jewish view of marriage in his debate with the Pharisees over divorce: "'Haven't you read,' he replied, 'that at the beginning the Creator "made them male and female" [quoting Gen 1:27], and said, 'For this reason a man will leave his father and mother and be united to his wife, and the two will become one flesh' [quoting Gen 2:24]?" (Mt 19:4-5 NIV). By splicing together Genesis 1:27 and Genesis 2:24, Jesus upholds the Jewish view of marriage; namely, that marriage is the one-flesh union between male and female—a perspective that, as far as can be determined, was unanimously held by all Jews in Jesus' day.

Jesus never explicitly mentions same-sex sexual relations. However, this is almost certainly because Jews in Jesus' day never questioned whether such relations were sin. There were many ethical beliefs that were debated within first-century Judaism, and Jesus frequently entered into these debates. The morality of same-sex sexual relations was not one of them.

3. Paul's Response to Same-Sex Sexual Behavior. Paul's response to same-sex sexual behavior resonates with his Jewish contemporaries. With Jesus, Paul believes that the creation account is fundamental for both sexual ethics and the meaning of marriage (Eph 5:22-33; 1 Cor 6:12-20). Human marriage, for instance, points to a more profound relationship between *God and his covenant people. In line with the Jewish Scriptures and early Jewish responses, Paul also believed that same-sex sexual relations did not follow God's creational intention for sexual behavior. He makes this clear in the three passages where he explicitly addresses same-sex sexual behavior.

3.1. Romans 1:26-27. Paul's most descriptive statement of same-sex sexual activity occurs in the midst of a lengthy indictment of the sinfulness of humanity, with a special focus on Gentile vices. In this context Paul describes both female and male same-sex sexual behavior: "Because of this, God gave them over to shameful lusts. Even their women exchanged natural sexual relations for unnatural ones. In the same way the men also abandoned natural relations with women and were inflamed with lust for one another. Men committed shameful acts with other men, and received in themselves the due penalty for their error" (Rom 1:26-27 NIV).

Paul's words resonate with first-century Jewish views on same-sex behavior, and they also find parallels in certain Stoic philosophers who also critiqued same-sex behavior. Like the prohibitions in Leviticus, Paul refracts his critique through the lens of the creation account by alluding to several statements in the early chapters of Genesis (see Sprinkle 2015, 91-93). Paul is not just singling out idolatrous forms of same-sex behavior, as if nonidolatrous forms would be morally legitimate. Paul, rather, is saying that all humanity *is* idolatrous based on how it has exchanged God's will for its own, including engaging in same-sex sexual relationships.

Unlike some of his contemporaries who singled out pederasty as the specific vice in view, Paul's words are generic and absolute, referring to same-sex sexual relations irrespective of age or class distinction. If Paul only wanted to condemn pederasty, there were many Greek words for pederasty available to him (*paiderastēs* ["the love of boys"], *paidophthoros* ["corruptor of boys"], *paidophtoreō* ["seducer of boys"]), and Paul chose none of them here. Neither does Paul draw any attention to certain power differentials, as if same-sex behavior were deemed wrong because it constitutes a person of power taking advantage of a person of lower status. Paul's language is strikingly egalitarian, describing relationships that would appear to be mutual and consensual. In Romans 1:27, he describes men who burned with lust "*for one another*," doing shameful things "*with* other men" and "received *in themselves*" the due penalty for "*their* error"—language that reflects mutuality and not power differentials. Paul does not draw attention to social status or active and passive relationships, as if same-sex behavior were deemed wrong "because it degraded the passive partner into acting like a woman" (Brownson, 245). Instead, Paul selects the most basic terms for males (*arsēn*) and females (*thēlys*) drawn from the Genesis creation account (Gen 1:27) to show that same-sex love goes against the fundamental order of creation (Harper, 94-95). Modern (and mostly Western) interpretations of Romans 1 that argue Paul only had certain kinds of same-sex relations in view (pederasty, master/slave, prostitution, etc.) do not square with the actual words of Paul, nor with the historical and cultural context in which he wrote them.

That Paul's words here include all kinds of same-sex sexual behavior is confirmed by Paul's condemnation of *female* same-sex relations in Romans 1:26. As seen above, female same-sex sexual relations were largely between adults of the same social class and were consensual. Pederasty did not exist (as far as is known) between females, and yet Paul leads with a condemnation of female same-sex relations, labeling them "unnatural" (Gk. *para physin*, Rom 1:26).

The phrase *para physin* was often used in other critiques of same-sex love. Plato was the first to use it when he said that "the pleasure enjoyed by males with males and females with females seems to be against nature" (*para physin*; Plato, *Leg.* 636D). *Para physin* became a common way to describe same-sex sexual behavior by later philosophers and writers who were critical of it (see Hays, 197-98; Brooten, 241). Stoic philosophers around the time of Paul often described same-sex behavior as being *para physin*, as did Jewish writers such as Philo (see Sprinkle 2015, 96-97). By the first century, the phrase *para physin* was already a common and recognizable phrase used by writers who were critical of same-sex behavior. When Paul uses it in Romans 1:26, he "is hardly making an original contribution" (Hays, 194).

Some suggest that what Paul finds wrong with same-sex relations is that they are driven by excessive lust (Brownson). But this does not make sense of Paul's use of *para physin* to describe female same-sex relations in Romans 1:26. While Greco-Roman writers often portrayed male same-sex behavior as the result of excessive lust, the same is not true of female same-sex relations, which were often described in terms of mutual love, not excessive lust. The "excessive lust" interpretation also fails to make sense of Paul's language of exchange (see Rom 1:23, 26, 28) woven throughout Romans 1. Paul says humanity "*exchanged* the *glory of the immortal God for images made to look like a mortal human being" (Rom 1:23 NIV), and "exchanged the *truth about God for a lie" (Rom 1:25 NIV). Glory is exchanged for idols; truth exchanged for a lie. Likewise, women "exchanged natural sexual relations for unnatural [*para physin*] ones." Paul does not say that people exchanged nonlustful sexual relations for lustful ones. Rather, he says that they exchanged opposite-sex relations for same-sex relations (see Sprinkle 2015, 98-101).

In short, Paul's critique of same-sex sexual behavior in Romans 1 is best understood as a condemnation of any kind of same-sex sexual relationship, since these relationships intrinsically go against the Creator's design for human sexual expression—an unremarkable claim in first-century Judaism.

3.2. 1 Corinthians 6:9. The second time same-sex behavior is mentioned in the canonical order of Paul's letters is in 1 Corinthians 6:9, toward the end of a list of vices, many of which are sexual: "Or do you not know that wrongdoers will not inherit the *kingdom of God? Do not be deceived: Neither the sexually immoral nor idolaters nor adulterers nor men who have sex with men nor thieves nor the greedy nor drunkards nor slanderers nor swindlers will inherit the kingdom of God" (1 Cor 6:9-10 NIV). The phrase "men who have sex with men" translates two Greek words, *malakos* and *arsenokoitai*. Both have been subject to much dispute among interpreters.

Malakos literally means "soft," "gentle," or "tender" and was sometimes used to describe men who were not masculine by Roman cultural standards. *Malakos* might be used to describe a man who, for instance, dressed in soft clothes, shaved his chest hair, wore perfume, or did anything else that appeared to cross accepted gender boundaries. The term does not have intrinsic sexual connotations. However, the term often occurs in sexual contexts, and when it does, it typically refers to a man who plays the passive role in male same-sex intercourse. Given that *malakos* is used here in the context of sexual immorality, Paul most likely has this sexual meaning in mind in 1 Corinthians 6:9-10. *Malakos* describes a male who is receiving sex from other men. One can assume some level of consensuality here (i.e., the *malakos* was not a victim of rape), since he is listed alongside those who commit other morally culpable sins. It would be strange for Paul to condemn a person for being a victim of someone else's sin.

Arsenokoitai is a more difficult word to translate and has been the subject of much scholarly dispute. The reason is quite simple: this is the first time this word occurs in Greek literature currently available. Yet, a thorough understanding of the word, including its likely derivation from the LXX, reveals a relatively clear meaning.

Arsenokoitai is a compound word that combines two common Greek words: *arsēn* (male) and *koitē* (bed). While the meaning of compound words can be tricky (e.g., *butterfly* has nothing to do with butter), D. F. Wright's thorough research into the meaning of this term suggests that something like "bedding a male" or "sleeping (sexually) with a male" is the best English rendering of the Greek compound term (D. F. Wright 1987). This meaning also pairs well with the meaning of *malakos* as expressed above.

The most persuasive evidence, however, for translating *arsenokoitai* as "one who sleeps with a male" is found in the LXX. While the compound word *arsenokoitai* never occurs in the LXX, the two words that make up the compound word occur side by side in the Greek translation of Leviticus 20:13—one of the two verses in the Jewish Scriptures that condemn same-sex relations. The LXX reads: *kai hos an koimēthē meta arsenos koitēn gynaikos* ("and whoever lies with a male with the lyings of a woman"). Given that *arsēn* and *koitē* occur next to each other, it is likely that Paul created the compound word *arsenokoitai* based on the words *arsenos* and *koitēn* in Leviticus 20:13. If this is the case—and it is very likely that it is—then Paul's intended meaning of *arsenokoitai* is rooted in the Levitical prohibition against male same-sex relations.

Some have argued that Paul only has in mind certain exploitative forms of male same-sex behavior, such as pederasty or prostitution (Scroggs, 106-9), or some other kind of behavior that resulted in economic exploitation (Martin, 37-50). While these kinds of acts might be included in the meaning of *arsenokoitai*, it is difficult to limit its meaning to these exploitative and nonconsensual acts. The very wording and context of Leviticus 20:13 (and the parallel passage in Lev 18:22, where the two terms *arsenos* and *koitēn* also occur) suggest a mutual relationship between two consensual males. After all, Leviticus 20:13 condemns both people involved in the act (i.e., "both of them have done what is detestable," NIV). While it is possible that Paul detached *arsenos* and *koitēn* from their original sense in Leviticus 20, there is no evidence that he did so. Again, both the *arseonokoitai* and the *malakos* are condemned in 1 Corinthians 6, which suggests a consensual relationship. Plus, as pointed out in regards to Romans 1, there were other popular Greek words used to describe pederasty (*paiderastēs* ["the love of boys"], *paidophthoros* ["corruptor of boys"], *paidophtoreō* ["seducer of boys"]). It would be odd for Paul to not use any of these familiar terms if he wanted to condemn only pederasty here.

As far as translations go, the updated NIV is among the most accurate translations of *malokos* and *arsenokoitai*: "men who have sex with men." This interpretation is confirmed by later Coptic, Syriac, and Latin translations, which all render the word as "one who sleeps with males" (Sprinkle 2015, 115). However, this could appear to overlook the culpability of the *malakos*, the passive partner. Perhaps a more accurate translation would be something like "males who have sex with each other" to convey both the lack of interest Paul has in age distinctions (hence the term *male* instead of *men*) and the moral culpability of the sexually passive partner.

Most other translations are inadequate, especially any translation that translates *arsenokoitai* or *malokos* as "homosexuals." The term *homosexual* is a modern one with no Greek equivalent. It refers to a person's sexual orientation, their predisposition to being attracted to someone of the same-sex. But Paul shows no interest in one's predisposition to engage in particular sexual behaviors but the sexual behaviors themselves. Many modern-day Christians could be considered "homosexual" (though they typically prefer the term "gay" or "same-sex attracted") and yet not be engaging in same-sex sexual behavior. They would therefore not at all fit the profile of an *arsenokoitai* or *malakos*—both of which are describing people who are engaging in illicit sexual behavior. While the Bible condemns same-sex sexual behavior, it does not condemn someone who might be tempted in this direction but refuses to act on this temptation.

3.3. 1 Timothy 1:10. The final reference to same-sex behavior comes in another vice list in 1 Timothy 1: "We also know that the law is made not for the righteous but for lawbreakers and rebels, the ungodly and sinful, the unholy and irreligious, for those who kill their fathers or mothers, for murderers, for the sexually immoral, for those practicing homosexuality" (1 Tim 1:9-10 NIV). The word translated "those practicing homosexuality" is *arsenokoitai*, the same word Paul apparently coined in 1 Corinthians 6. The only difference is that in 1 Timothy 1, *arsenokoitai* is not paired with *malakos*, making it a little more difficult to discern its meaning. However, there is no contextual reason for understanding *arsenokoitai* any differently from the meaning suggested in 1 Corinthians 6. The best translation here would be "men who sleep with males." Its meaning here puts the emphasis on the active partner in male same-sex intercourse, and again, it refers explicitly to same-sex sexual behavior, not same-sex sexual temptations or attractions.

*3.4. **Summary.*** Paul's three references to same-sex sexual behavior should be understood within their Jewish context, where sex-difference was an intrinsic part of marriage, sexual relations were believed to be created for the context of marriage, and same-sex sexual relations (among many other kinds of sexual relations) were therefore believed to go against the Creator's design for sexual expression.

Recently, however, some modern (mostly Western and Protestant) interpreters have questioned this historical and global understanding of Paul. This article will briefly examine some of the most salient revised readings of Paul.

4. Revisiting Paul.

So-called revisionist readings of Paul have grown in popularity ever since 1980, sparked in part by the publication of John Boswell's book *Christianity, Social Tolerance, and Homosexuality.* Boswell argues that the Bible does not in fact condemn adult, consensual, same-sex sexual relationships; instead, it only condemns certain exploitative kinds of same-sex unions, pederasty being the most popular. Many other scholars expand on this reading, oftentimes by revisiting the ancient Greco-Roman context for a more nuanced understanding of Paul's context.

One widespread view among Western scholarship throughout the 1980s and into the early 2000s was that Paul's condemnation of same-sex sexual relations cannot be referring to adult, consensual, monogamous unions, since such relationships did not exist in Paul's day. Paul cannot be condemning something he was not aware of. If Paul were around today, it is presumed, he would have no problem with adult, consensual, same-sex love.

This view, however, has fallen out of popularity among most biblical scholars, since, as has been shown repeatedly, consensual same-sex unions did exist in Paul's day—especially among women—and there is nothing in Paul's actual language that limits his description of same-sex unions to nonconsensual or exploitative forms. Several scholars who even affirm the legitimacy of same-sex relationships today say that there is little historical and exegetical credibility to limit Paul's words to nonconsensual same-sex relations (Brooten; Loader; Crompton).

Another revised reading of Paul suggests that his lack of understanding of sexual orientation is what drove him to condemn same-sex sexual relations. Paul, it is argued, probably thought that all people simply chose whom they want to have sex with and were perfectly capable of choosing an opposite-sex partner. But current scientific discoveries have shown that some people desire a same-sex partner because they have a same-sex orientation. That is, they were born (or created by God to be) gay. If Paul had this modern, scientific knowledge, he would not have condemned same-sex sexual behavior.

This "argument from orientation" comes with two questionable assumptions: one about Paul's context and another about Paul's sexual ethic. In terms of Paul's context, ancient theories about what moderns now label as "sexual orientation" did in fact exist in his day. As early as the fifth century BC, a Greek philosopher named Parmenides believed that men who desired to play the passive role in same-sex relations were "generated in the act of conception" (Sprinkle 2015, 59). Aristotle says that some same-sex desires are formed through habit, while others spring from nature. A Greek physician named Soranus, a contemporary of Paul, also believed that there was something in the very nature of men who desired same-sex sexual relations. Bernadette Brooten has documented many references to ancient forms of same-sex orientation in medical, astrological, and magical texts—texts that were widely popular among the masses. One text written around the time of Paul says that if the sun and moon are at a particular location when a woman is born, she "will be a Lesbian, desirous of women, and if the native is a male, he will be desirous of males" (Maternus, *Matheseos libri viii* 7.25.1; see Brooten, 132-37). After working through several other texts, Brooten concludes: "Contrary to the view that the idea of sexual orientation did not develop until the nineteenth century, the astrological sources demonstrate that existence in the Roman world of the concept of lifelong erotic orientation" (Brooten, 140).

Therefore, while twenty-first-century psychologists might have a deeper understanding of sexual orientation than the ancients, it would be historically inaccurate to say that no parallel concept existed in Paul's day.

But even if Paul were unaware of contemporary ancient concepts of sexual orientation, it does not follow that this would reconfigure his sexual ethic, given his theological understanding of desire. Paul believed that sinful acts sprang from innate sinful desires. Sexual ethics for Paul—and for any first-century Jew—was a matter of behavior. The persistent nature of the desire that led to the behavior did not justify the behavior itself, according to Paul's moral framework. Plus, Paul's ethic was fundamentally shaped by the empowering presence of the Spirit, who gifted the believer with the ability to resist sinful behaviors (rooted in desires) and walk in the faithfulness according to God's revealed will (Rom 8:1-11; Gal 5:19-23). One could imagine Paul being introduced to modern perspectives of orientation and shrugging his shoulders. It certainly does not seem likely that Paul would be as impressed by the argument from orientation as some modern, Western interpreters are.

Other attempts to reinterpret Paul's prohibition statements (Rom 1:26-27; 1 Cor 6:9; 1 Tim 1:10) fail to revisit Paul's Jewish understanding of marriage, in which sex difference is an intrinsic part of what marriage is. Underlying Paul's critique of same-sex sexual relationships is the prior biblical assumption (undisputed in Judaism at his time) that marriage constitutes a one-flesh union between two sexually different people. Romance, partnership, companionship, and other modern values might play a role in marriage, but they are not fundamental to it. Marriage, rather, has deeper roots in Genesis 1–2 and God's purpose for creation as a whole. In the words of N. T. Wright, "the coming together of male plus female" in marriage "is itself a signpost pointing to that great complementarity of God's whole creation, of heaven and earth belonging together" (N. T. Wright, 88). This is why Paul views same-sex relations as a departure from God's intent for creation in Romans 1:19-27. Paul's sexual ethic is rooted in creation, which is why Paul considers nonmarital sexual union to be a distortion of the one-flesh union celebrated at the climax of Genesis 2 (1 Cor 6:16, quoting Gen 2:24).

Paul's understanding of marriage not only reaches back to creation but also anticipates *resurrection, which is why Paul views marriage as a shadow of the church's relationship to *Christ—a relationship that Paul maps on the husband-and-wife relationship, where sex difference is essential (Eph 5:22-33). Sexual differentiation not only captures the unity and diversity of creation but also mirrors the unity between Christ and his diverse *body. Marriage is also the place where children are created and raised up in the *Lord, and where sexual desires can be expressed in a mutual and self-giving manner (1 Cor 7:1-7).

Yet marriage is not essential for kingdom work or for living a joy-filled life. Nowhere in Paul (or the NT as a whole) does one see marriage being promoted as an essential good or a necessary part of the *gospel promise. If Paul departs from his Jewish contemporaries in his understanding of marriage, it is not in his definition or ultimate meaning of marriage but in viewing marriage as not essential for human flourishing.

For a revised understanding of Paul to be convincing, one must not only reinterpret the prohibition passages but also reconstruct a certain view of marriage where sex difference plays no essential role—a view that would need to be recognizable to Paul, a first-century Jew.

See also Corinthians, First Letter to the; Covenant; Jesus and Paul; Man and Woman; Marriage and Divorce, Adultery and Incest; Romans, Letter to the; Sexuality, Sexual Ethics.

BIBLIOGRAPHY. **J. Boswell,** *Christianity, Social Tolerance, and Homosexuality* (Chicago: University of Chicago Press, 1980); **B. J. Brooten,** *Love Between Women: Early Christian Responses to Female Homoeroticism* (Chicago: University of Chicago Press, 1996); **J. V. Brownson,** *Bible, Gender, Sexuality* (Grand Rapids, MI: Eerdmans, 2013); **L. Crompton,** *Homosexuality and Civilization* (Cambridge, MA: Harvard University Press, 2003); **K. J. Dover,** *Greek Homosexuality* (Cambridge, MA: Harvard University Press, 1978); **L. A. Dunn,** "The Evolution of Imperial Roman Attitudes Toward Same-Sex Acts" (PhD diss., Miami University, 1998); **K. Harper,** *From Shame to Sin: The Christian Transformation of Sexual Morality in Late Antiquity* (Cambridge, MA: Harvard University Press, 2013); **R. B. Hays,** "Relations Natural and Unnatural: A Response to J. Boswell's Exegesis of Romans 1," *JRE* 14 (1988): 184-215; **T. K. Hubbard,** ed., *Homosexuality in Greece and Rome: A Sourcebook of Basic Documents* (Berkley: University of California Press, 2003); idem, "Peer Homosexuality," in *A Companion to Greek and Roman Sexualities,* ed. T. K. Hubbard (Chichester, UK: Blackwell, 2014), 128-49; **W. M. Loader,** "Homosexuality and the Bible," in *Homosexuality, the Bible, and the Church*, ed. P. M. Sprinkle (Grand Rapids, MI: Zondervan, 2016), 17-48; **D. B. Martin,** *Sex and the Single Savior: Gender and Sexuality in Biblical Interpretation* (Louisville, KY: Westminster John Knox, 2006), 37-50; **R. Scroggs,** *The New Testament and Homosexuality: Contextual Background for Contemporary Debate* (Philadelphia: Fortress, 1983); **J. Sklar,** "The Prohibitions Against Homosexual Sex in Leviticus 18:22 and 20:13: Are They Relevant Today?," *BBR* 28 (2018): 165-98; **P. M. Sprinkle,** "Romans 1 and Homosexuality: A Critical Review of James Brownson's *Bible, Gender, Sexuality*," *BBR* 24 (2014): 515-28; idem, *People to Be Loved: Why Homosexuality Is Not Just an Issue* (Grand Rapids, MI: Zondervan, 2015); idem, "Same-Sex Relations," in *Dictionary of Daily Life in Biblical and Post-biblical*

Antiquity, vol. 4, *O–Z*, ed. E. M. Yamauchi and M. R. Wilson (Peabody, MA: Hendrickson, 2016), 139-52; **D. F. Wright,** "Homosexuals or Prostitutes: The Meaning of *Arsenokoitai* (1 Cor. 6:9; 1 Tim. 1:10)," *VC* 38 (1984): 125-53; idem, "Translating *Arsenokoites* (1 Cor. 6:9; 1 Tim. 1:10," *VC* 41 (1987): 396-98; **N. T. Wright,** "From Genesis to Revelation: An Anglican Perspective," in *Not Just Good but Beautiful: The Complementary Relationship Between Man and Woman*, ed. S. Lopes and H. Alvare (Walden, NY: Plough, 2015), 86-96.

P. M. Sprinkle

HONOR/SHAME

Maintaining or augmenting one's honor (the positive evaluation of one's value by others) and avoiding disgrace (the disaffirmation of one's value) were primary incentives and disincentives to behavior in Paul's world. The bestowal or withholding of esteem by others was thus an important mechanism for enforcing conformity to the convictions and practices that sustained a social body. In a situation of competing definitions of honorable and censurable behavior among different social groups within the matrix of the Roman world, a number of fairly fixed strategies developed by means of which to assist the members of one's own group remain committed to that particular group's valued commitments and practices. These social dynamics and social strategies pervaded the situations of Paul's Christian audiences and his attempts to shape their responses by means of his letters.

1. Honor, Shame, and Sustaining Group Values
2. Competing Definitions of the Honorable and Shameful
3. Honor, Shame, and Paul

1. Honor, Shame, and Sustaining Group Values. Every society has mechanisms of social control at its disposal both to encourage its individual members to orient and invest themselves in all the ways that maintain the institutions and the smooth operation of that particular society, and to discipline those whose views and practices work against the preservation of the same (Berger). The people groups that constituted the Greco-Roman world, including the Jewish ethnos, relied particularly heavily—and rather explicitly—on honor as an incentive and shaming as a disincentive to society-maintaining practices. As the members of each next generation are born, they are groomed, on the one hand, to value being regarded by others as "honorable" as a foundational facet of their own *identity and worth and, on the other hand, to develop a strong aversion to being shamed as a significant threat to their identity and worth. People who develop this aversion are said to have a "sense of shame," while those who do not are "shameless," the ultimate formational and moral failure (see Rom 1:32).

Individuals properly formed in this world will thus be especially susceptible to the opinion that other members of their society will form about them and thereby will be disposed to align themselves with those values and practices that the people around them will affirm as honorable—those same values and practices that the society needs for its members to embrace so as to ensure its own continuity over time. They will regard doing what sustains the structures of their society as the path to their own self-fulfillment. Those born into the elite families of *Ephesus, for example, will by this means be willing to expend large sums from their family estates to repair dilapidated public buildings, fund the construction of new ones, and underwrite expensive religious sacrifices and games, all chiefly for the honor—the public recognition that they have behaved in the manner expected for people of their status—that will accrue to them. One may have self-respect on the basis of one's perception of how fully one has embodied the society's ideals (Williams). That same person has honor on the basis of one's society's recognition of the same (Pitt-Rivers)—and it takes a great deal of intellectual and psychological energy to maintain self-respect without also experiencing the affirmation of one's honor by the group.

At the same time, the members of each next generation are shaped to *participate* in the social control mechanisms of their society. As they learn whom they themselves are obliged to honor (failure in regard to which would often diminish their *own* honor), they become a part of that social mechanism that encourages the other members of the society to continue to invest in society-maintaining attitudes and practices. As they learn whom they themselves ought to despise and what behaviors ought to elicit reproach and ridicule, they become a part of that social mechanism that dissuades and disciplines the society's deviant members.

The prominence of considerations of honor and shame among other possible axes of values can be demonstrated throughout the literature of the period. Seneca, a first-century Roman statesman and philosopher, locates these considerations at the foundation of all deliberations: "the one firm conviction from which we move to the proof of other points is this: that which is honorable is held dear for no other reason than because it is honorable" (*Ben.* 4.16.2 [LCL]). The honorable and the shameful represent determinative and decisive values. Four centuries before, Aristotle spoke of "the honorable" in his treatise on effective persuasion as "that which is desirable in itself" (*Rhet.* 1.9.3 [LCL]). While acknowledging other values—that which is beneficial or harmful and that which is pleasant or painful—alongside the honorable and shameful as incentives and disincentives to action (Aristotle, *Eth. nic.* 2.3.7), the honorable and shameful tend to emerge as the most decisive in multiple discussions of what drives the decision-making process in the people of the Greco-Roman world (see Aristotle, *Rhet.* 1.9.35-36; Quintilian, *Inst.* 3.7.28). Thus while the unknown author of To Demonicus, a collection of advice wrongly attributed to Isocrates, acknowledges that "safety" and "pleasure" are motives alongside "honor," he advises his reader to prioritize "honor" above both (*To Demonicus* 17, 43). Similarly, the author of the handbook on persuasion known as the Rhetorica ad Herennium writes that people tend to consider both the path that leads to honor and the path that leads to safety or security as they choose a course of action (Rhet. Her. 3.2.3). He acknowledges, however, that an audience would rarely choose the path to safety if it is also shown to be dishonorable (Rhet. Her. 3.5.8-9). As the majority of Paul's letters represent attempts to persuade an audience to adopt or to continue in particular orientations and practices, it is not at all surprising to find the *apostle giving significant attention to what will preserve or augment the audience members' honor and what will jeopardize the same as he seeks to position them to accept his guidance.

2. Competing Definitions of the Honorable and Shameful.

The application of honor and shame as mechanisms of social reinforcement and control in the Roman world of the first century, however, was considerably complicated by the fact that there was no monolithic "Roman world." Rather, a person living in any major urban center, for example, was likely to have been aware of different groups living in the same space that held to different values—different definitions of what kind of behaviors were honorable and which were shameful. One could speak of a "dominant culture" shared and promoted by those who represented the machines of Roman imperialism, which would include local elites and even nonelites whose status and prosperity were enhanced by cooperation with the same. Thus, in many settings, the dominant culture overlapped considerably with the majority culture, that is, the values and practices shared by the greatest number of inhabitants of a given location. (In Galilee and Judea, however, it seems more likely that the dominant culture was at odds with the majority culture, particularly in the period of Roman domination.) Substantial Jewish communities in many urban centers constituted a significant ethnic subculture. Voluntary associations (such as the early Christian movement and devotees of particular philosophical schools) constituted a variety of subcultures as well. Members of *all* of these groups would be concerned about preserving or augmenting honor and avoiding disgrace, yet they might diverge widely in their definitions of what practices were honorable and what practices were shameful.

For example, virtually all people in the Roman world would have agreed that piety was an important value and that honorable people were pious people (and vice versa). However, there was significant disagreement concerning what constituted the honorable enacting of piety. For members of the dominant culture and the majority culture outside *Israel, piety meant honoring the *gods* and doing so most frequently in the context of rituals focused on a physical representation of the god or gods (idols). For most members of the Jewish subculture, piety meant honoring *one* *God and avoiding idolatrous rituals of any sort at any cost. The majority of non-Jews who have left written testimony regarded Jews as atheists and thus shamed them for their failure to honor the gods of their city. For most Jews, piety also involved careful alignment of their practices with the stipulations of the *law of Moses, which Jew and *Gentile alike acknowledged resulted in a somewhat insular orientation on the part of the Jewish community. For the Jew, this was an honorable expression of piety; for the non-Jew, it was a disgraceful breach of civic solidarity and a sign of intolerance or disregard for people of other ethnic groups (see, for example, the criticisms leveled in Tacitus, *Hist.* 5.5; Juvenal, *Sat.* 14.100-104, and reported in 3 Macc 3:3-7; Josephus, *Ag. Ap.* 2.121, 258).

In such a setting, both groups needed to develop strategies to insulate themselves against the opinion of the other so as to remain committed to their own group's definitions of honorable and dishonorable practice rather than find themselves being swayed by the alternative group's definitions (and accompanying social pressures). This was, in practice, rarely an issue for the non-Jew. The dominant and majority culture's general scorn for the Jewish subculture sufficiently neutralized any claims the Jewish definitions of honorable and shameful practice might have to validity, save for the most earnest seekers. The Jewish minority culture was more vulnerable—as attested by occasional *apostasy on the part of Jews seeking acceptance and even advancement within the wider society. Thus one finds a variety of strategic safeguards practiced within the Jewish subculture and reflected in its surviving literature.

(1) It was important to define carefully whose opinion of one's honor or lack thereof really mattered. This was generally limited to members of the culture who were themselves committed to the defining convictions and practices of the Jewish subculture and to the one and only God—whose presence in and aligning with this "court of reputation" offset its minority and potentially deviant status (see, e.g., Sir 2:15-17; 23:18-19; Wis 2:12–3:5; 4:16–5:8; 4 Macc 13:3, 17; 17:5). The conviction that the Jews constituted a people "chosen" by this God for a special relationship with the divine and a correspondingly distinctive (if often maligned) way of life also enhanced the value of maintaining the group's social boundaries and its definitions of what was, and was not, honorable.

(2) It was also important to explain why the majority of human beings failed to hold to the same convictions and embrace the same practices. The Gentiles' alienation from the one and only God, their alienation from the *truth (see Wis 1:16–2:24), their (probably exaggerated) widespread commitment to every shameful and perverted vice (see Wis 13:10–14:21), were frequently invoked to this end. There would come a day, however, when the values of the minority culture would be vindicated and their detractors put to shame themselves (see, e.g., Wis 3:1-13; 4:16–5:23; 4 Macc 11:4-6; 12:11-13).

(3) It was useful to have mechanisms in place by which to reinterpret outsiders' disapproval of members of the group in a manner that enhanced the honor of those suffering *and persevering in the face of* such disapproval—even in the extreme form of physical abuse and *death. For example, experiences of being shamed might be cast as athletic contests or military battles to be won (through perseverance) or lost (through capitulation to the pressures; see 4 Macc 11:20; 16:16; 17:11-16).

(4) Group members needed to actively reinforce for one another the nobility of continuing to align one's practice with the practices embraced by the group as honorable, along with the disgrace of failing to do so (or of aligning one's practices with those of other groups where these were in conflict with those embraced by the group). Group members' investment of themselves in one another's lives had to be sufficiently significant and meaningful that their ascriptions of honor and disgrace would carry far more weight than those from people outside the group.

3. Honor, Shame, and Paul.

As one turns to the Pauline letters, one finds significant attention being given to each of the strategies typically employed by leaders within minority cultures to maintain the identity and cohesion of that culture and its membership. Throughout the cities of the Roman world, those who identified themselves with the Christian movement met with disapproval and shame from their neighbors. Non-Christian Gentiles applied negative social pressure to their own, whom they now found denying their formerly shared gods and pious practices while awaiting the day when a crucified rebel would return to upset the Roman *peace on which the welfare of all depended (1 Thess 1:6; 2:14; 3:1-5; note how Paul presents these new convictions positively—and as a source of honor in the eyes of fellow Christians throughout the region—in 1 Thess 1:9-10). Non-Christian Jews were also likely to shame and otherwise treat as deviant their own who proclaimed a crucified blasphemer to be God's anointed agent and who relaxed certain practices of Torah observance as they now mingled more freely with Gentile Christ-followers. After his *conversion, Paul was a frequent object of such shaming tactics (2 Cor 11:24; Gal 5:11; 1 Thess 2:14-16); he suggests that some Jewish Christian teachers, sensitive to such tactics, have altered the genuine *gospel in order to accommodate it to the convictions and practices of non-Christian Jews (Gal 6:12-13).

To help his converts in Thessalonica, for example, withstand the social pressure of shaming, Paul reminds them of the significantly greater honor that they have attained by virtue of their turning to God and their faithful response to God's Anointed. They enjoy esteem throughout Christian communities in Macedonia and Achaia (1 Thess 1:7-10). Their new commitments and social identity are indicators of divine privilege (1 Thess 1:4) and consequences of the divine will (1 Thess 4:3). By giving thanks to God for their new allegiance to *Christ and one another, Paul indirectly affirms that they have become what they now are by God's design and that God approves of their new state (1 Thess 1:2-3; 2:13). If their neighbors regard them as deviants deserving of being shamed, this can be attributed to their neighbors' alienation from God and God's truth as they stumble about like drunken people in their ignorance (1 Thess 5:1-11) and wallow in their own vices (1 Thess 4:5).

Paul also encourages perseverance in the face of shaming and hostility by identifying *Satan as the force behind it. Indeed, it is one more manifestation of Satan's tempting of the believer, to be resisted at all costs (1 Thess 3:5). Their honor will be manifested (and thus vindicated in the eyes of their detractors, who will themselves come to shame) on the day of the Lord's coming, the decisive event that Paul keeps in view from beginning to end of this letter (1 Thess 1:9-10; 2:11-12; 3:12-13; 5:4-10, 23). In the meanwhile, Paul instructs them to continue to strengthen their relationships with one another as they keep one another's hearts and minds focused on that day and on the practices that will lead to honor on that day (1 Thess 3:12; 4:9-10, 18; 5:11, 14-15), and even to apply shaming within the group to draw members back to respectable practice (1 Thess 5:14).

This thumbnail sketch could be deepened significantly in regard to the presence of honor and shame discourse in 1 Thessalonians and broadened significantly to the other Pauline letters (for further discussion, see especially deSilva 1999, 91-143; 2016; Finney; Gosnell; Hellerman; Jewett; Moxnes 1988; Reasoner). Of particular interest are the ways in which Paul works to suppress competition for honor and precedence within Christian communities, using the framework of the family of God to urge cooperation instead and even "outdoing one another in *showing* honor" rather than in *claiming* honor for oneself (Rom 12:10; Phil 2:3-4) after the example of Christ (Phil 2:5-11). The foregoing should suffice, however, to demonstrate that attention to honor-and-shame language offers one important means of excavating Paul's pastoral concerns and pastoral strategy.

See also Ethics; Ethnicity in Paul's World; Gentiles; Philosophy; Social-Scientific Approaches to Paul.

BIBLIOGRAPHY. **A. W. Adkins,** *Merit and Responsibility: A Study in Greek Values* (Oxford: Clarendon, 1960); **P. L. Berger,** *Invitation to Sociology* (Garden City, NY: Doubleday, 1963); **Z. A. Crook,** "Honor, Shame, and Social Status Revisited," *JBL* 128 (2009): 591-611; **D. A. deSilva,** *The Hope of Glory: Honor Discourse and New Testament Interpretation* (Collegeville, MN: Liturgical Press, 1999); idem, *Honor, Patronage, Kinship & Purity: Unlocking New Testament Culture* (Downers Grove, IL: IVP Academic, 2000); idem, "Paul, Honor and Shame," in *Paul in the Greco-Roman World: A Handbook*, ed. J. P. Sampley, 2nd ed. (London: Bloomsbury, 2016), 2:26-47; **E. R. Dodds,** *The Greeks and the Irrational* (Berkeley: University of California Press, 1966); **G. F. Downing,** "'Honor' Among Exegetes," *CBQ* 61 (1999): 53-73; **M. Finney,** *Honour and Conflict in the Ancient World: 1 Corinthians in Its Greco-Roman Social Setting* (Edinburgh: T&T Clark, 2012); **P. W. Gosnell,** "Honor and Shame Rhetoric as a Unifying Motif in Ephesians," *BBR* 16, no. 1 (2006): 105-28; **J. Hellerman,** "Brothers and Friends in Philippi: Family Honor in the Roman World and in Paul's Letter to the Philippians," *BTB* 39 (2009): 15-25; **R. Jewett,** *Saint Paul Returns to the Movies: Triumph over Shame* (Louisville, KY: Westminster John Knox, 1998); **T. Lau,** *Defending Shame: Its Formative Power in Paul's Letters* (Grand Rapids, MI: Baker, 2020); **B. J. Malina and J. H. Neyrey,** "Honor and Shame in Luke–Acts: Pivotal Values of the Mediterranean World," in *The Social World of Luke–Acts: Models for Interpretation*, ed. J. H. Neyrey (Peabody, MA: Hendrickson, 1991), 25-66; idem, *Portraits of Paul: An Archaeology of Ancient Personality* (Louisville, KY: Westminster John Knox, 1996); **H. Moxnes,** "Honour and Righteousness in Romans," *JSNT* 32 (1988): 61-77; idem, "Honor and Shame," *BTB* 23 (1993): 167-76; **J. Pitt-Rivers,** "Honour and Social Status," in *Honour and Shame: The Values of Mediterranean Society*, ed. J. G. Peristiany (London: Weidenfeld and Nicolson, 1965), 21-77; **M. Reasoner,** *The Strong and the Weak: Romans 14.1–15.13 in Context* (Cambridge: Cambridge University Press, 1999); **B. Williams,** *Shame and Necessity* (Berkeley: University of California Press, 1993).

D. A. deSilva

HOPE

Hope is an essential quality in human flourishing. It is the aspiration, expectation, or desire directed toward that which is possible or yet to happen. Hope as a concept derives from and is rooted in precedence reliable enough to anticipate a possible outcome with a high degree of certitude. In Paul, hope is a virtue and disposition anchored in God's promise. The *apostle Paul employs a wide variety of words to convey this concept, including *elpis, elpizō, proelpizō, apekdechomai*, and *apokaradokia*. Each expression of hope is determined by the context in which it occurs. Sometimes Paul appeals to figures and events in the Hebrew Bible as models of hope; hope in this framework is predicated on precedence in God's dealings with *Israel. It is the imagined future that informs present disposition. Apart from its general usage, Paul's hope is grounded in the *gospel and in a relationship with a faithful *God. The notion is rich in what it reveals about virtue, inner strength, and outlook in life. Hope denotes expectation that inspires courage and a positive attitude in the face of adversity. It dispels *fear and energizes believers to endure afflictions (see Bultmann, 319-20).

When an uncertain future commends to Christ-followers the choice between fear of the unknown and hope, hope is the aspiration for good ends. "Hope as expectation of good is closely linked with trust, and expectation is also yearning, in which the element of patient waiting or fleeing for refuge is emphasised" (Bultmann, 522). It injects optimism and dispels hopelessness. As a virtue, it engenders a positive spirit in the way life is lived—as a transitory state en route to a blissful eschatological end.

1. Hope in the Old Testament
2. Hope in the Letters of Paul

1. Hope in the Old Testament.
Paul understood and interpreted events against the backdrop of his Jewish worldview, in which messianic expectations occupied a central place. He shows no direct connection between OT prophetic predictions and pronouncements with Christian eschatological hope, but occasionally he appeals to characters such as *Abraham and Moses analogously as the embodiment of hope that is rooted in *covenant relationship with Yahweh. Unlike today's English, in which expressions of hope can introduce an element of uncertainty or unfounded optimism, in the Hebraic thought hope is instilled with confidence, trust in God (Dunn, 387n217).

The word features mostly in Job (18×) and the Psalms (26×) in the OT. Job posits that the godless assume hope that is placed in futility when they expect God to meet their desires (Job 8:13; 11:18). Conversely, the righteous may garner hope that is informed by the fact that God will always honor his promises to the faithful. The notion of a trustworthy God is always implied. Job indicates that those who are chastened by God for their transgressions may be assured (hope) that God would always be true to his word (see Job 13:15). The psalmist echoes this sentiment and underscores the idea that God could be counted on to fulfill his promises (see Ps 39:7; 42:5, 11; 43:5; 62:5; 71:5; 119:81). The poor and afflicted may also place their hope in God (Ps 9:18). Hope serves as an impetus for resilience amid *suffering—a thought that reverberates in Paul's writings. When the psalmist speaks of hope in God, the names Elohim and Adonai are his preferred designations for God vis-à-vis rare use of Yahweh (Ps 119:166).

In the OT, hope engenders inner felicity, *joy that is not conditioned by external circumstances. The word features as a virtue associated with God and the righteous. For example, Isaiah refers to the *light (of God) that overcomes darkness (*sin) and brings hope to those under exploitation. Jeremiah calls God's people to exercise hope in difficult times (Jer 14:8). Sometimes, the *Lord himself is presented as the embodiment of hope (Jer 17:13); his people are admonished to place their hope in him who has their highest interest at heart (Jer 29:11; 31:17). Similarly, OT notions of hope amid hardships, as a virtue, and hope in God are all found in the writings of Paul.

2. Hope in the Letters of Paul.
Generally, Paul uses *hope* in the sense of future expectation, as a virtue, or a posture of certainty in the fulfillment of God's promise. Hope is a necessary condition to flourish in current Christian living and in an anticipated future with God. Paul uses one noun and one verb most frequently in reference to hope, namely, *elpis* as a noun, appearing thirty-six times (Romans 13×, 1 Corinthians 3×, 2 Corinthians 3×, Galatians 1×, Ephesians 3×, Philippians 1×, Colossians 3×, 1 Thessalonians 4×, 2 Thessalonians 1×, 1 Timothy 1×, Titus 3×) and *elpizo* featuring nineteen times as a verb (Romans 4×, 1 Corinthians 3×, 2 Corinthians 5×, Philippians 2×, 1 Timothy 4×, Philemon 1×). In all instances, the context and subject matter determine the meaning thereof.

2.1. Hope in General Usage. Paul uses *hope* in the general sense to denote a strong desire, wish, or expectation (see 2 Cor 1:7, 10, 13; 5:11; 8:5; 10:15; 13:6). This is at issue when he cites Deuteronomy 25:4 to make an analogy with the expectation of a plowman necessarily aiming to reap from his harvest as compared to compensation for ministers of the gospel (1 Cor 9:10). Paul indicates that it is natural to expect (hope) that workers would reap from their labor (1 Tim 5:18). Widows are entreated to place their hope on God for his care and provision (1 Tim 5:5). Hope thus engenders reasonable disposition and hope-full future in a time of need (1 Tim 6:17; cf. 1 Tim 4:10).

Moreover, Paul uses the word in divulging his intentions for the future in other areas apart from his personal visits (Philem 22). He hopes to send Timothy to Philippi (Phil 2:19, 23) and visit with the believers in Rome (Rom 15:24; cf. 1 Cor 16:7). Similarly, he wishes (hopes) to join his associate later (1 Tim 3:14). The incarcerated Paul hopes to honor Christ in his *body—regardless of judicial determination about his fate in the foreseeable future (Phil 1:20). He is unashamed to face the verdict if it warrants his execution or vindication. His hope is grounded in the Lord Jesus Christ. As a *slave of Christ (Phil 1:1), he desires and expects (hopes) to honor his master even in affliction. Paul does not hesitate to make confident assertion about his hope to boast someday in what has become of Christ-followers in Thessalonica (1 Thess 2:19-20).

2.2. Hope as a Virtue. Hope is a virtue that inspires exemplary demeanor in human interaction. It enables Christ-followers to face hardship in fitting disposition, as they set their gaze on what lies beyond this life with Christ. Abraham and Moses modeled this quality and realized God's faithfulness in the end. Abraham exercised such hope when he held on to the promise for a son, even against the odds of human biology; he "hoped against hope" in God's promise (Rom 4:18). Paul indicates that hope and *faith (see Eph 4:4) are twin virtues that undergirded Abraham's resolve and confident stance with God; he embodied true faith and *righteousness (Rom 4:18). Hope in this sense engenders certitude and zest in the way life is lived. As a virtue, it anticipates a positive future and dispels any sense of hopelessness.

Hope and *love feature together in Paul as virtues (1 Cor 13:7). Love gives impetus for hope inter alia. Hope and love are purported to be essential qualities for constructive exercising of pneumatic gifts in the Corinthian churches (1 Cor 13). Paul underlines hope as one of three abiding virtues (also love and faith; 1 Cor 13:13) that would be useful beyond the parousia since other gifts would have no cause for operation. Hope also begets proclivity for honorable disposition in reaction to hardship. Paul thus entreats believers to exhibit the "hope of righteousness" (Gal 5:5), "hope of *salvation" (1 Thess 5:8), and "steadfastness of hope" (1 Thess 1:3) in Christian living.

Indeed, hope hinges on God's promise (Rom 8:24-25). Salvation is said to be anchored in the hope that God would restore the *glory that was forfeited by the first *Adam (Rom 8:29). Paul prays that "the God of hope" fills Christ-followers with joy and *peace so that they may "abound in hope" by the enabling of the *Holy Spirit (Rom 15:13). In Romans, hope is derived from a personal relationship and trust in the "God of hope" (Rom 15:4, 13). Consequently, those who possess hope in their hearts are inspired to live for the cause of Christ.

2.3. Hope and Suffering. Hope enables Christ-followers to face suffering as part of the transitory conditions of this life. It offers the *grace to endure. Afflictions are inevitable yet unable to break the spirit of the faithful due to their hope in God—the assurance of God's presence is a source of strength. Ample precedence in God's dealing with his people foregrounds belief in his sovereignty and fidelity in this regard. At the macro level, God will ultimately fulfill his promise to David and restore this fallen *creation from the consequences of Adam's transgressions (i.e., suffering).

Access to God and peace brings joy and "hope in the glory of God," even amid suffering (Rom 5:2). Hope sees beyond the current situation to conceive of what lies ahead. Blithe disposition in suffering attests to God's faithfulness—now and in the future. Paul suggests that suffering may even serve as a refining instrument for a virtuous life. For him, suffering builds endurance, character, and hope that is energized by the Holy Spirit. Hope inspires from within and offers grace to lay hold of God's promises ahead (Rom 5:2-5). Suffering may inspire hope and the love of God in "our hearts" by means of the Holy Spirit (Rom 5:4-5). Hope offers courage to the extent that Paul could assert his readiness to be executed for the sake of Christ (Phil 2:19; cf. Phil 1:29-30).

Hope recalls the triumph of Christ over *death in his *resurrection as motivation (Rom 12:2). In Paul, joy and hope are found in proximity when the subject matter is suffering. This paradox is more pronounced in Philippians, where the *prisoner admonishes his readers to rejoice in the Lord always (Phil 4). Incarceration could not suppress the joy of sharing in the suffering of Christ (Phil 3:9-11). For Paul, believers may "rejoice in hope" even under difficult circumstances (Rom 12:12; cf. Rom 5:4). In a nutshell, the power of Christian hope stands antithetical to a life marked by a deep sense of hopelessness.

2.4. Eschatological Hope. In Paul's *already–not yet* eschatological continuum, the hopeless creation will ultimately find redemption in the Son of Man. This eschatological hope conjures images of restoration, bliss, and anticipation of the resurrection of the dead. Christ-followers can expect (hope for) an inheritance with God (Eph 1:18) and complete realization of the redemptive work of Christ. In Romans 8:19-25, Paul declares that the Spirit of God inspires hope, granting eager anticipation shared even by the creation (Rom 8:19, *apokaradokia*, "eager expectation"; Rom 8:19, 23, *apekdechomai*, "look forward with eagerness or awaiting eagerly"), and gives assurance in this regard. Hope provides confidence for all believers to keep their standing as children of God. Paul contends that the resurrection of the dead is certain and pivotal to the Christian faith (1 Cor 15:19). The resurrection of Christ provides a glimpse and guarantees future resurrection of the dead in Christ (1 Thess 4:13; cf. 1 Cor 15:51-52). The resurrection particularly engenders assurance in the realization of this promise (Rom 5:10). Paul had hoped for this to occur in his lifetime (1 Thess 4:17; 1 Cor 15:51).

Thus, hope gives the motivation to endure all that this present life imposes on Christ-followers in view of God's promises. Citing Isaiah, Paul reiterates that the "hope" of *Gentiles rests with the root of Jesse (Rom 15:12). Gentiles are not excluded in God's eschatological community but are equally destined for a place of honor with God (Col 1:27). Those who were without hope—Gentiles—now have hope in Christ (1 Thess 4:13; Eph 2:12-13; 1 Tim 1:1; Col 1:27). Heaven is the ultimate domain where "the hope of glory" will be fully realized (Col 1:5, 27; Rom 5).

2.5. Observations from the Pauline Corpus. A close look at Paul's use of hope reveals no one consistent pattern or theological import, except for some unique features in individual letters. His reference to God as the object of hope with the preposition *on* and his portrait of Christ Jesus as the embodiment of "our hope" (1 Tim 1:1) is unique to 1 Timothy; one finds phrases such as "hope *on* the living God" (1 Tim 4:10) and "hope *on* God" (1 Tim 5:5; 6:17) only in 1 Timothy. The closest parallel one finds elsewhere is in Romans, where "God *of* hope" appears (Rom 15:13). Moreover, the language of the "hope of eternal life" is unique to Titus (Titus 1:2; 3:7), where hope is consistently employed in an eschatological framework, underscoring eager expectation of the appearing of God's glory and "our savior Jesus Christ" (Titus 2:13; cf. 2 Thess 2:8; 1 Tim 6:14; Rom 5:2; Col 1:27). The mention of hope in 2 Corinthians conveys the meaning of hope as expectation or aspiration for the most part (2 Cor 1:7, 10, 13; 5:11; 8:5; 10:15; 13:6). Hope appears only once in Galatians (eagerly waiting for the hope of righteousness) and once in 2 Thessalonians in reference to "good hope" (Gal 5:5; 2 Thess 2:16). It does not feature at all in Philemon and 2 Timothy.

Paul's hope has significant ramifications for daily living. It engenders a positive outlook that is grounded in concrete aspirations. Salvation in Christ has paved the way for Gentiles to become sharers in what was hitherto an inheritance limited to Jews. This shared hope ought to affect interethnic relations and *ethics in the communities of faith. Hope is grounded in faith that enables believers to live (virtue), endure hardship, and remain steadfast in anticipation of the fulfillment of the promises of God. For Paul, the hopeless cannot anticipate a future with God, but the hopeful may draw from faith in Jesus Christ and the Holy Spirit to live, endure hardship, and remain steadfast as they anticipate a blissful future with God.

See also CORINTHIANS, FIRST LETTER TO THE; ESCHATOLOGY; FAITH; JOY, REJOICING; LOVE; PEACE, RECONCILIATION; SUFFERING.

BIBLIOGRAPHY. **R. Bultmann,** *Theology of the New Testament*, 2 vols. (New York: Scribner's, 1951–1955); **J. D. G. Dunn,** *The Theology of Paul the Apostle* (Grand Rapids, MI: Eerdmans, 1998); **K. Hanhart,** "Paul's Hope in the Face of Death," *JBL* 88, no. 4 (1969): 445-57; idem, "Hope in the Face of Death: Preserving the Original Text of 2 Cor 5:3," *Neot* 31, no. 1 (1997): 77-86; **N. Miguez,** *The Practice of Hope: Ideology and Intention in 1 Thessalonians* (Minneapolis: Fortress, 2012); **J. Moltmann,** *Theology of Hope* (repr., Minneapolis: Fortress, 1993); **C. F. D. Moule,** *The Meaning of Hope* (Philadelphia: Fortress, 1963); **T. R. Schreiner,** *Paul, Apostle of God's Glory in Christ: A Pauline Theology*, 2nd ed. (Downers Grove, IL: IVP Academic, 2020); **F. Thielman,** *Theology of the New Testament* (Grand Rapids, MI: Zondervan, 2005); **N. T. Wright,** *Paul and the Faithfulness of God* (Minneapolis: Fortress, 2013), 1061-95.

D. K. Darko

HOSPITALITY

In his letter to the Romans Paul exhorts the Christians in Rome to "pursue hospitality to strangers [*tēn philoxenian*]" and to practice what is good and makes for *peace with all people (Rom 12:13, 17-21). In the *Pastoral Epistles, overseers are expected to excel in showing hospitality to strangers (*philoxenon*; 1 Tim 3:2; Titus 1:7-8). Hospitality is the ancient domestic custom whereby the status of a stranger is transformed into that of guest and/or friend through the kind provisions of *food, drink, and lodging (see Malina, 181-82). As a result, the language and custom of hospitality is generally reserved for the appropriate and kind reception of outsiders, strangers, or persons generally not part of one's family or immediate social network (Denaux, 256-57). The practice of hospitality, then, presumes a relationship between a host and guest, where the host is responsible for dispensing appropriate domestic responsibilities to care for the guest. It is no surprise that hospitality is most frequently, though not exclusively, dispensed within the host's home, where lodging, food, drink, clothing, conversation, and provisions for the guest's continued journeys are offered. Early Christian documentation of the practice requires some contextual knowledge of the protocols, purposes, and common terms in order to identify both the presence and meaning of hospitality.

1. Historical Context and Terminology
2. Hospitality in Paul

1. Historical Context and Terminology.

1.1. Historical Context. The practice of hospitality is virtually ubiquitous in Greek and Roman texts, and it was often prized as a distinctly noble and virtuous Greek practice in contrast to the uncivilized practices of "barbarians," who, it was supposed, treat strangers with *violence and hostility (e.g., Homer, *Od.* 9.266-370). Serious religious sanctions are connected to the treatment of strangers, as hospitality is frequently related to the virtue of piety, and Zeus himself is often referred to as Zeus Xenios, that is, "Zeus the God of Strangers" (e.g., *Od.* 9.172-176). The deep connection between hospitality to strangers and piety was expressed through the popular stories of *theoxenia.* These stories portray the gods often disguising themselves as poor beggars who search out virtuous, hospitable households. Whereas those who shut their doors against, or even seek to do violence to, the disguised gods receive curses; the hospitable are rewarded with divine blessings (e.g., *Od.* 20.287-319; Ovid, *Metam.* 1.163-252; 8.617-724). The formal protocols of hospitality could be used as a means of initiating nonbiological but permanent and hereditary fictive *kinship relations among different families and households (see Herman). This institution, known as ritualized *friendship or guest-friendship (*xenia*), nicely exemplifies the goal of hospitality as that of social incorporation and friendship.

The OT (and related Jewish literature) also places a significant value on the practice of hospitality to strangers. *Abraham is remembered and celebrated for his exemplary hospitality to the divine visitors (Gen 18:1-16; Philo, *Abr.* 107-118; T. Ab. 1.4-9, 19; 20.5-6), whereas the city of Sodom is destroyed for its inhospitality and abuse of strangers (Gen 19:1-11; cf. Josephus, *Ant.* 1.194; T. Ash. 7.1). Likewise, Egypt is often remembered for wicked inhospitality, hatred of strangers, and exploitation of the Israelites who were their guests (Wis 19:13-16; Philo, *Mos.* 1.33-44, 95). The Torah contains frequent exhortations to *Israel to care for, treat with justice, and refuse to exploit sojourners and immigrants who settle in their land. The command to treat the alien with charity and justice is consistently rooted in the character of *God as one who cares for the aliens and in Israel's remembrance of its own experience as exploited guests in the land of Egypt (e.g., Ex 22:21; 23:9; Lev 19:33-34; Deut 10:16-19). Almost certainly standing behind the Torah's legislation that protects aliens and sojourners is the ancient custom of hospitality to strangers (see van Houten).

1.2. Terminology. One can often discern a hospitality scenario through the mention of distinct social groups or individuals sharing food or meeting in one's home (e.g., Mt 10:5-13; Lk 7:36-50; 19:1-10; Acts 10:23-33). Early Christian writings often activate hospitality scenarios through the use of certain lexical indicators that, depending on their context, frequently bear the meaning of "to welcome" or "to extend hospitality"—for example, forms of the following verbs: *lambanō*, "to receive" (Acts 28:2; 2 Jn 10; 3 Jn 8); *dechomai*, "to welcome" (Lk 10:8); *xenizō*, "to extend hospitality" (Acts 10:6, 18, 23, 32; 21:16; 28:7; Heb 13:2); *menō*, "to stay/lodge" (Lk 9:4; 10:7; 19:5; Acts 16:15; 21:7-8); and *propempō*, "to send" (Rom 15:24; 1 Cor 16:6, 11; Titus 3:13-14; 3 Jn 6; see Arterbury, 53-54, 187-88). Hospitality texts are also often marked by references to friendship, love of humanity, and kindness (e.g., Acts 28:2, 7).

2. Hospitality in Paul.

2.1. Hospitality and Mission. Paul's letters testify that his life was consumed with establishing and safeguarding communities of Christ worshipers all over the ancient Mediterranean world. Paul himself testifies that he has taken the *gospel of *Christ all the way from *Jerusalem in the east to Illyricum in the northwest and that he hopes to go as far west as Spain (Rom 15:19; see Marquis, 22-46). An examination of any decent map documenting Paul's journeys rightly impresses that Paul was a traveling man remarkably well acquainted with Roman roads and sea voyages (2 Cor 11:25-26). As a result, he and his *coworkers were dependent on networks of hospitable households that would share with them lodging, food and drink, financial resources, and even their social networks. Paul's letters, along with the Acts of the Apostles, testify that the gospel took root in major urban centers and in households, which served as the primary location for *worship and *mission (Acts 10:23-33; 16:16-40; 17:1-9; 18:1-13; Gehring, 182-85). For example, Paul reminds the Galatians of the remarkably warm, hospitable reception they gave him when he brought the gospel to them with his initial visit, noting they even "welcomed me [*edexasthe me*] as an angel of God" (Gal 4:14).

Paul's frequent use of family metaphors for God, Christ, and his churches demonstrates Paul's conviction that his churches are friends and family together in Christ (e.g., 1 Cor 1:11, 26; 2 Cor 2:12-13; Phil 2:25). Given that hospitality functioned to establish familial and friendship relations, one can see Paul's expectation that all of his churches will extend hospitality to him and one another since they are a community of friends in Christ. This is perhaps most obvious in 1 Corinthians 16:5-12, where Paul informs the Corinthians of his *travel plans so they can be ready to host him when he makes his visit (also 2 Cor 1:15-16). While Paul's letter to the Romans almost certainly has multiple purposes, one of the most obvious reasons for its composition is Paul's hope that the Roman Christians will welcome him, provide financial support, and send him with the provisions he needs to take the gospel westward to Spain (Rom 15:22-25). In the meantime, Paul writes a brief letter of recommendation for "our sister Phoebe" (who is quite likely the carrier of the letter) asking the believers in Rome to "welcome her in the Lord" (*autēn prosdexēsthe en kyriō*) and to provide for all of her needs (Rom 16:1-2; see Malherbe).

While Paul himself communicates his expectation that he will be received hospitably when he is able to make a personal visit to his churches (e.g., 1 Cor 16:5-9; Philem 22; cf. Rom 16:23), one of the ways Paul maintains connections with his churches, shares and receives information, and warns of false teachers is through sending special envoys and coworkers, some of whom are long-term coworkers with Paul, such as Timothy and Titus, and others who are temporarily available to assist Paul in his mission, such as Epaphroditus (see 1 Cor 16:10-12; 2 Cor 7:5-16; Phil 2:19-30). Paul crafts short letters of recommendation to households indicating that he expects the local congregations will hospitably receive his envoys, provide material assistance for their needs, and send them on their way (e.g., Rom 16:1-2; 1 Cor 16:15-18; Phil 2:19-24, 29-30; Col 4:10-11; 1 Thess 5:12-13; see Ellis). The letters of recommendation also protected the receiving house churches from false teachers and the potential of excessive freeloading from the host churches' resources (Gal 2:12; 4:17-20; 2 Jn 9-10; 3 Jn 9; Did. 11.3-6; 12.1-3).

Paul also provides evidence that the earliest Christians, like Jesus and his disciples (e.g., Lk 9:1-6; 10:1-13), shared the gospel with nonbelievers through receiving hospitality in the homes of nonbelievers. In 1 Corinthians 9:19-23 Paul says that he has adapted himself ("I have become. . . .") to a particular group of people in order that he might *gain* said group for the Lord. Paul's claims to change his behavior in varied circumstances make good sense if they are seen as his self-description of how he adapts to his host as a good guest (see Rudolph). Hospitality protocols demanded that guests respectfully receive the hospitality offered them by their hosts. Paul's claim "I have become all things to all people" (1 Cor 9:22) is likely a reflection of his commitment to follow Jesus' hospitality practices as one who proclaimed God's *kingdom by eating with *women, Pharisees, sinners, and tax collectors. Paul's practice also provides the model for the Corinthians as he encourages them to receive the hospitality, the food, and the drink from any nonbelievers who might invite them into their home. The believer should be a good guest by eating the host's food so as not to give offense. The hospitality given and received between Paul, his coworkers, and his local churches was one of the means whereby the gospel spread to new lands, instilled a sense of global partnership for the sake of the gospel among Paul's churches, and took root in hospitable Christian households (Gehring, 185).

2.2. The Hospitable Messiah and Ecclesial Unity. Gathering together for common meals was a frequent practice of ancient worshipers, philosophical groups, and other intentional communities. Plutarch frequently refers to "the friend-making nature of the dinner table" (*Quaest. conv.* 612 D-E). The sharing of meals expressed social bonding, friendship, and group boundaries (see especially Smith). Meals also expressed fellowship with the gods (for polytheists) or the God of Israel (for Jewish worshipers) whereby the worshipers approached the deity through sacrifices and then shared together a festive common meal. Thus, when Paul's churches gathered together in order to share a meal in celebration and remembrance of the Lord Jesus, they were engaging in an act of worship that was common to other ancient worshipers (see Johnson, 137-79). These meals seem to have been incredibly important, as they expressed the earliest Christians' *fellowship both with Jesus *and* with one another. God's act in Christ both establishes a people as his family and friends *and* provides a model of hospitality for his churches. As I have said elsewhere, "Paul sought to inculcate within his churches a new *identity founded upon God's gracious extension of hospitality in the Messiah for all people, a divine hospitality that produces communities of messianic-shaped friendship and loving regard for the other" (Jipp, 53). One can find this dynamic expressed clearly in the three texts where Paul communicates how these shared meals symbolize both the vertical saving act of God's hospitality in Christ *and* the horizontal mandate to extend hospitality, friendship, and loving other-regard to one another.

2.2.1. Galatians 2:11-14. While there is not consensus as to whether Galatians 2:11-14 describes the celebration of the *Lord's Supper, the meal is certainly an important social practice infused with theological meaning as Paul interprets Peter's decision to stop eating (Gal 2:12) with *Gentile Christians in Antioch as a betrayal of the truth of the gospel of Christ (Gal 2:14). Paul's teaching that humans are justified by Christ's faithfulness (Gal 2:16-21) as well as his baptismal proclamation that "there is neither Jew nor Greek, there is neither *slave nor free, there is neither male nor female, for you are all one in Christ Jesus" (Gal 3:28) was tangibly expressed through Jews and Gentiles sharing the meal and eating together (see further Schüssler Fiorenza, 198).The testimony of Acts 13:1-3, with its list of the five leaders of the church in Antioch, confirms the ethnic diversity of the Antiochene community. Paul interpreted Peter's refusal to eat with Gentiles in Christ as a sign that Peter had broken his bonds of friendship with Gentiles in Christ and thereby had failed to act in accordance with the gospel of Christ.

2.2.2. 1 Corinthians 10:1–11:34. In 1 Corinthians 10, Paul depicts Israel's history as one in which the people experienced God's hospitality as he beneficently provided Israel with food and water in the wilderness (1 Cor 10:1-4); nevertheless, Israel rejected God's hospitality in order to eat, drink, and "play" (perhaps cultic sexual activities) in the presence of the golden calf (1 Cor 10:5-7). Paul here draws on Israel's history of *idolatry, which takes place with respect to food and the celebration of sacrificial banquets in the presence of pagan deities instead of the God of Israel. Paul's argument here is in service of his warning to the Corinthians (1 Cor 10:11-13), for when they eat the Lord's meal they have a real "fellowship in the blood of Christ" and "fellowship in the body of Christ" (1 Cor 10:16). Paul reminds the *church that they have an exclusive fellowship with Christ, one that must prevent them from participating in meals celebrated in the presence of other gods (1 Cor 10:19-22).

This fellowship with the risen Christ is what the Corinthians celebrated when they gathered together to eat at the "Lord's table" (1 Cor 10:21), that is, the "the Lord's Supper" (1 Cor 11:20). Paul is emphatic that the risen Lord is the host of the supper, given that Jesus provides his own *body and blood as the food and drink for the meal *and* that the meal functions as a celebration of remembering and proclaiming the saving death of Jesus (1 Cor 11:24-26). But there are significant social entailments for the Corinthian church as they celebrate the Lord's hospitality to them. The Lord's Supper was almost certainly celebrated in the homes of the moderately wealthy homeowners who served as the patrons and hosts of the meal; the host probably provided both the space and the food and drink for the supper (1 Cor 11:22, 33). While the exact historical reconstruction of the situation is impossible, it seems as though certain members of the Corinthian congregation (most likely those with some level of moderate *wealth) are shaming the "have-nots" (1 Cor 11:22) as they either eat the best portions of the meal or consume the meal before the poor can arrive to eat (1 Cor 11:21). And so, their common meal is leading to factions, divisions, and the shaming of the poor. Paul shames them, especially the hosts with the larger resources, by declaring the church's meal to be their "own meals" (1 Cor 11:21) and not "the Lord's meal" (see especially Walters, 643-64). The true character of the Lord's Supper is a celebration of Jesus's merciful, saving hospitality for all kinds of people (see 1 Cor 1:26-31). Thus, Paul's primary exhortation to the church comes in 1 Corinthians 11:33: "so then my brothers and sisters, when you come together to eat, extend hospitality to one another [*allēlous ekdechesthe*]." The Lord's Supper must be practiced in such a way that it functions as a time of unified coming together, as an opportunity for friendship and social bonding for all those who call on the *name of Jesus (see Koenig, 68-70).

2.2.3. Romans 14:1–15:7. Paul too draws on the character of Christ in order to reframe the potential divisions and conflicts with respect to the church's common meal in his letter to the Romans. It is not necessary to determine the exact nature of the dispute in order to see that Paul refers to a conflict between the weak and the *strong over the foodstuffs and the observance of religious holidays. And this conflict is the result of each group judging and looking down on the other (Rom 14:2, 5). Paul's primary concern is easily discerned as he bookends his treatment of the problem with exhortations to show hospitality to one another: "Let us welcome [*proslambanesthe*] anyone who is weak in *faith, and not for the purpose of passing judgments with respect to doubtful matters" (Rom 14:1). Then in Romans 15:7: "So then welcome one another [*proslambanesthe allēlous*], just as the Messiah welcomed you [*proselabeto hymas*] to the *glory of God." For Paul, human hospitality and friendship with one another flows from and is mandated by God's extension of hospitality in the Messiah (Barclay, 512). This shared hospitality will tangibly be seen in refusing to judge, despise, or discriminate against one another (Rom 14:3). Paul peppers his exhortations in this section with the sibling language "brother/sister" (e.g., Rom 14:10, 15) to remind the members of the church that they are fellow family members in Christ. The result of this shared hospitality, Paul expects, will be that the church will be a place of unity that can praise God together "with one voice" (Rom 15:5-6), with the Messiah himself leading the choir in praise to God (Rom 15:9-12).

The ancient practice of extending hospitality to strangers is evident in the Pauline letters as a key practice for facilitating the Pauline mission to the Gentiles as well as for combating ecclesial disunity. In places, Paul even recommends pursuing hospitality among enemies as a means of transforming outsiders into friends. Paul provides the strongest validation for the practice when he grounds human hospitality in the Messiah, who welcomed both Jews and Gentiles into his family.

See also Church; Coworkers, Paul and His; Fellowship, Communion, Sharing; Food Laws and Customs, Jewish and Roman; Friendship; Households and Household Codes; Kinship Language in Paul; Lord's Supper.

BIBLIOGRAPHY. **A. Arterbury,** *Entertaining Angels: Early Christian Hospitality in Its Mediterranean Setting*, NTM 8 (Sheffield: Sheffield Phoenix Press, 2005); **J. M. G. Barclay,** *Paul and the Gift* (Grand Rapids, MI: Eerdmans, 2015); **A. Denaux,** "The Theme of Divine Visits and Human (In)Hospitality in Luke-Acts: Its Old Testament and Graeco-Roman Antecedents," in *The Unity of Luke-Acts*, ed. J. Verheyden, BETL 142 (Leuven: Leuven University Press, 1999), 255-79; **E. E. Ellis,** "Paul and His Coworkers," *NTS* 17 (1970–1971): 437-52; **R. W. Gehring,** *House Church and Mission: The Importance of Household Structures in Early Christianity* (Peabody, MA: Hendrickson, 2009); **G. Herman,** *Ritualised Friendship and the Greek City* (Cambridge: Cambridge University Press, 1987); **C. van Houten,** *The Alien in Israelite Law*, JSOTSup 107 (Sheffield: Sheffield Academic Press, 1991); **J. W. Jipp,** *Saved by Faith and Hospitality* (Grand Rapids, MI: Eerdmans, 2017); **L. T. Johnson,** *Religious Experience in Early Christianity: A Missing Dimension in New Testament Study* (Minneapolis: Fortress, 1998); **H.-J. Klauck,** *Hausgemeinde und Hauskirche im frühen Christentum* (Stuttgart: Katholisches Bibelwerk, 1981); **J. T. Koenig,** *New Testament Hospitality: Partnership with Strangers as Promise and Mission* (Eugene, OR: Wipf & Stock, 2001); **A. J. Malherbe,** *Social Aspects of Early Christianity*, 2nd ed. (Philadelphia: Fortress, 1983), 60-91; **B. J. Malina,** "The Received View and What It Cannot Do: III John and Hospitality," *Semeia* 35 (1986): 171-94; **T. L. Marquis,** *Transient Apostle: Paul, Travel, and the Rhetoric of Empire*, Synkrisis (New Haven, CT: Yale University Press, 2013); **C. D. Pohl,** *Making Room: Recovering Hospitality as a Christian Tradition* (Grand Rapids, MI: Eerdmans, 1999); **D. J. Rudolph,** *A Jew to the Jews: Jewish Contours of Pauline Flexibility in 1 Corinthians 9:19-23*, WUNT 2/304 (Tübingen: Mohr Siebeck, 2011); **E. Schüssler Fiorenza,** *In Memory of Her: A Feminist Theological Reconstruction of Christian Origins* (New York: Crossroad, 1984); **D. E. Smith,** *From Symposium to Eucharist: The Banquet in the Early Christian World* (Minneapolis: Fortress, 2003); **J. C. Walters,** "Paul and the Politics of Meals in Roman Corinth," in *Corinth in Context: Comparative Studies on Religion and Society*, ed. S. J. Friesen, D. N. Schowalter, and J. C. Walters, NovTSup 134 (Leiden: Brill, 2010).

J. W. Jipp

HOUSEHOLDS AND HOUSEHOLD CODES

The household during the early Roman imperial period played a central part in the economic, cultural, political, and religious life of the society. Aristotle's theories of the family and *polis* (*Pol.* 1253b) reflected and shaped social reality, and his ideas, broadly speaking, influenced the Greco-Roman world. Imperial Rome emphasized the Roman family as foundational to the imperial power base. Three pairs of superordinate/subordinate groups formed the theoretical family: husband/wife, father/child, and owner/*slave. The highly stratified culture found representation in the hierarchically ordered family structure that emphasized cohesion, but at the expense of the subordinate members. While *women and freeborn children had some legal protections and agency, slaves lacked social honor and had no legal family or inheritance and few legal protections; their life could be described as "social death" (Patterson, 38).

1. Greco-Roman Households
2. Greco-Roman Household Codes
3. Pauline Household Codes

1. Greco-Roman Households.

Family units included parents and children, and perhaps grandparents, cousins, slaves, and freed men and women. The family revolved around the parents, and even more, the oldest male (father or grandfather). Theoretically, the father had absolute authority over his children, but in practice, social conventions and pressures mitigated this power, except in one important area: the father chose whether to raise a child born to his wife (Cicero, *Att.* 11.9).

Most people married in their late teens or early twenties, were widowed or divorced, and remarried once or twice. Couples hoped for a harmonious relationship. The *marriage was *sine manu*, which meant that authority over the wife was not transferred to the husband by her family, but the latter retained authority (*manus*). The woman brought a dowry to the marriage, which was returned to her if her husband died or they divorced. The wife might have her own sources of *wealth outside of her husband's control. Some households were led by women. If a woman was widowed or divorced, her children were considered part of the husband's family.

Infant mortality was high, with approximately 50 percent of children dying before their tenth birthday (Laes, 26). Children were thought to need strict discipline and training, for they lacked reason. Additionally, their character was established at birth, and circumstances revealed it. About age seven, children began working in shops or fields, although there is also artwork portraying children playing with toys (Laes, 22-49). In their early years, slave and free children were raised together in the home (MacDonald, 36-48). Adult children showed their piety by caring for their aging parents, a duty second only to honoring the gods.

2. Greco-Roman Household Codes.

2.1. Aristotle's Household Structure and Social Hierarchy. The household codes (*Haustafel*, pl. *Haustafeln*) grew out of Aristotle's political theories formed in Athens, which at the time was a slave economy. Reflecting on the ontology or nature of male, female, child, and slave, Aristotle argued that the superordinate member of the pair (male, father, slave master) was by nature superior and better fitted to command (*Pol.* 1.5.1-2). Free men were distinguished by distinct virtues such as courage and self-control (Hering, 206); females were by nature inferior in both the physical and rational sense (*Historia animalium* 2.3.501b19-21; *De partibus animalium* 2.7.653a28-29). Thus, the wife showed courage by submitting to her husband (*Pol.* 1260a). Aristotle posited that some humans were "natural slaves," and since nature is good, therefore the slave and the owner benefit from slavery (*Pol.* 1252a30-34; 1255a28; Garnsey, 108-27). Aristotle did not base his opinions of slavery on race or skin color but viewed his Greek culture as superior and evaluated other ethnic groups as inferior, and thus more likely to be natural slaves. The slave had minimal virtue and lacked reason; therefore, the owner must rule the slave absolutely (*Eth. nic.* 8.11.6-7). Aristotle labeled the slave a human tool whose owner had despotic power. In contrast, the father was to rule his child benevolently (*Pol.* 1278b32-37; *Eth. nic.* 1161a 30-b6).

2.2. Roman Modification to Aristotle's Household Structure. Stoic philosophers of the first century AD focused less on politics and more on *ethics. Musonius Rufus concentrated on the husband/wife pair, urging husbands to use sexual self-control. A husband should promote philosophical learning with his wife, so that she could keep the house, be chaste, and forgo extravagances and passions. Martha Nussbaum cautions that what looks like advocacy for wives in Musonius Rufus neglects the fact that her virtue is shown only in certain areas of life, in the domestic sphere, and not in social, political, and cultural arenas where decisions affecting her would be made (Nussbaum, 302).

Plutarch's treatise *Advice to the Bride and Groom* likewise advocates for wives to be taught *philosophy to mitigate the woman's natural tendency toward irrationality and passions. Plutarch modifies Aristotle's insistence on male superiority and female inferiority but still sees the husband as the superior "soul" and the wife as the inferior "body" in the union. The harmony and affection promoted within the marriage is based on the wife accepting her husband's gods, friends, and goals (Plutarch, *Conjugalia Praecepta*).

Seneca looked at the owner/slave pair. He was most interested in fostering an owner's self-control and spoke metaphorically about the owner enslaved by his passions. Seneca rejected Aristotle's argument of the natural slave and encouraged merciful treatment of slaves to prevent their uprising (*Ben.* 3.20.1-2; *Contr.* 7.6.18; *Ep.* 123.1-4).

The male owner also had sexual privileges over his male and female slave, and owners often prostituted their slaves. Social norms frowned on female owners having sex with their slaves. Slaves might be permitted by their owner to form a marriage of sorts, but the slave "husband" did not have exclusive sexual privilege, for the slave woman was still sexually available to her owner and anyone to whom he gave her. Additionally, any children from the slave marriage were the property of the owner. Owners might use the threat of separation to make the slave couple work harder. Slaves as young as seven, but typically older, could be used sexually. Art and poetry testify to this ubiquitous practice; for example, a slave owner wrote a eulogy to his deceased twelve-year-old slave boy, Glaucias, a sexual favorite, a *delicium* (Laes, 223-30). However, no evidence exists that Jewish families or the Christian communities sexually used slaves (Philo, *Abr.* 133; *Spec.* 3, 37-42; *Contempl.* 60-62; Josephus, *Ant.* 1.200-201; *Ag. Ap.* 2.37 §§273-275; Did. 2.2; *Barn.* 10.8). Scholars debate whether Paul permitted Christian owners sexual access to their slaves (Glancy, 60; Harper, 87-92).

2.3. Freedmen and Freedwomen. An important social and legal category not reflected in the household codes is that of the freed man and woman. Slaves could be manumitted, but the social stain of slavery remained on their character, and they continued to serve their former owner in the capacity of a client to their patron. Slaves might save money (*peculium*) to buy their *freedom, although the money would remain in some sense with the owner, who was now the patron (Mouritsen, 177-80; 1 Cor 7:22). Female slaves were more typically freed through marriage to their owner, and they might earn money from gifts for sexual favors (Pomeroy, 195-98). Rarely were agricultural or mining slaves freed; most died on the job.

2.4. Jewish Authors on Marriage and Slavery. Jewish writers weighed in on marriage and slavery (Hezser, 124-29). Josephus states that Scripture indicates a woman is inferior to her husband in all things (*Ag. Ap.* 2.25 §204). Philo of Alexandria analyzed slavery through the lens of Torah's teaching on the Sabbath. Slaves and owners were of the same nature (*Spec.* 2.69; 3.137), and owners "submitted" to do tasks on Sabbath that were regularly done by the slave, for the slave abstains from work on that day (*Spec.* 2.66-67).

3. Pauline Household Codes.

At least some of Paul's churches met in homes (Adams, 10). For example, Paul addresses Nympha and the Laodicean *church meeting in her home (Col 4:15), and his *coworkers Priscilla and Aquila held church meetings in their home (1 Cor 16:19). Education and training in the *gospel message, along with rites of *baptism and the *Lord's Supper, characterized these meetings. The familial categories of married/single/widowed, freeborn and slave children, slave women and men, freedmen and -women, and slave owners shaped the community as much as their occupational categories or whether they were Jew or *Gentile. For example, when Paul answers the Corinthians' questions about marriage, he also mentions the Jew and Gentile (1 Cor 7:18-20), the slave (1 Cor 7:21-24), and daughters (1 Cor 7:36-38). Paul adds another dimension to the church family, namely, the virgin/celibate adult woman who does not marry but serves the church community (1 Tim 5:3-16).

3.1. The Context of the Household Codes in Ephesians and Colossians. The household code structure occurs most directly in Ephesians and Colossians. Scholars offer several reasons for its inclusion. Some argue the instructions were apologetic, presenting the church as a nonthreatening group that supported the social status quo (Lincoln, 397). This position assumes the content of the instructions are in line with the broader cultural norms. Others suggest the focus is inward as the author instructs the young church in living out the unity in community established in Christ (Gombis, 176). Scholars debate the authorship of both epistles, but to avoid the awkwardness of using "the author" or speaking with the passive voice, this article presents Paul as the author.

Paul introduces his household codes section in Ephesians with a lengthy sentence about being filled with the *Holy Spirit, expressed by singing psalms, giving thanks, and submitting to each other out of reverence or *fear (*phobos*) for *Christ (Eph 5:18-21; see also Col 3:15-17). The reciprocity reflected in the reciprocal pronoun "one another" (*allēlous*) and the insistence on respect being given first to Christ frame the subsequent injunctions for the three pairs within the household structure.

Paul repeats the title "Christ" throughout the codes, reinforcing Christ as the standard by which to understand and emulate reverence, *love, and obedience. Colossians focuses throughout the short letter on Christ as *Lord, with the believer as his *servant (Col 1:7, 23, 25; 4:7, 12). In both letters, the context of the household codes is the church's *worship of God and imitation of Christ's sacrificial love for his church.

Paul addresses the three pairs that make up the Greco-Roman culture's conceptual family structure: husband/wife, parent/child, owner/slave. In each case, he addresses the subordinate member first, perhaps for two reasons. First, Paul signals his respect for them, for these letters were read aloud in the churches. Second, Paul wishes to constrain the superordinate's power given by society. Paul considers an additional pair, Jew/Gentile, included in the familial structure as siblings, adopted children of God, co-heirs together in Christ (Eph 2:15-19; see also Gal 3:28; Braxton, 94).

3.2. Husband and Wife. In Ephesians, Paul's first sentence to wives borrows the participle *submitting* from the preceding verse, thereby linking the two verses. Only two other contemporary examples survive of wives instructed to submit (Plutarch, *Conjugalia Praecepta* 33; Pseudo-Callisthene 1.22.4).

Usually, wives are instructed to obey their husbands. In Colossians, Paul commands wives to submit themselves to their husbands, using the same verb "to submit." Paul draws on the *body metaphor he has used throughout Ephesians to refer to the husband as the *head of his wife. The metaphorical meaning of the Greek term "head" (*kephalē*) is contested. Some argue it reflects "leader" (Grudem, 51). Others suggest "source," such as the headwaters of a river (Fee, 502-3). A third position postulates the noun is best understood as preeminence or as a synecdoche for the whole (Thiselton, 821). A fourth position connects family, ancestry, and *identity within the metaphor (Westfall, 82-84). A fifth position argues that the metaphor focuses on "one flesh" unity (Sumner, 167). In using the head/body figure of speech, Paul opens new ways of understanding Christ and his body, the church, in which a husband can imagine himself not in terms of *leadership but as loving his wife as Christ loves the church.

Paul commands husbands three times to love (*agapaō*) their wives in a self-sacrificial way, imitating Christ's love (Eph 5:2, 25; see also Col 3:19). Paul commands the husband to love his wife as his own body, as he loves himself (Eph 5:28-29; Westfall, 93-94). Such self-sacrifice by the superordinate member of the pair is strongly countercultural and reflects the mutuality of the Genesis quotation that husband and wife become one *flesh (see also 1 Cor 7:2-4). The wife is not subsumed into her husband, but each as individuals join to be one flesh.

*3.3. **Parent and Child.*** The instruction for children to obey parents is qualified as "in the Lord" (Eph 6:1; see Col 3:20). Paul uses a similar phrase when addressing wives, but he does not stipulate that wives obey their husbands. By mentioning the Lord and citing Scripture (Ex 20:21; Deut 5:16), Paul circumscribes obedience to those actions that would honor God; Paul does not condone immoral requests from parents. Musonius Rufus makes a similar distinction; if a father forbids his son to study philosophy, the son must nevertheless pursue study, for such activity obeys the gods, which is the son's higher calling (Musonius Rufus, *Discourses* 16.30-31, 104-106). Slave children attending church would have an owner, not a father per se, and adults in the church would serve the surrogate parental role.

Romans encouraged education, and Christian communities followed suit. In the church, slave children received the same teachings as their free counterparts by fathers, mothers, and surrogate mothers and fathers. Paul commands fathers to not frustrate (*parorgizō*) or provoke (*erethizō*) their children but instruct them (Eph 6:4; Col 3:21). Paul probably highlights fathers because society empowered fathers with extensive control over their children during the father's lifetime. However, the commandment requires children to honor both father and mother, and mothers (and grandmothers) educated children, as in the case of Timothy (2 Tim 1:5).

*3.4. **Owner and Slave.*** The third set within the household codes is the owner/slave pair. Before turning to the text, a brief word must be said about the metaphorical use of "slave" in Paul's letters. Paul refers to himself as a slave of Christ (Rom 1:1; Phil 1:1; Titus 1:1; see also Jas 1:1, 2 Pet 1:1), drawing on OT images of the faithful Israelite serving God (Num 12:7; Jer 25:4; Ezek 38:17). Paul also describes believers as "slaves" of *righteousness, in contrast to those who are slaves of *sin (Rom 6:17-18). The metaphor is limited, in that Paul does not imagine God or Jesus Christ as the typical slave master who is given free rein to dominate their slaves (Harris, 142).

In Ephesians, Paul charges the slave to obey with fear and trembling (Eph 6:5), a phrase that is best understood as respecting or honoring their human master even as all believers honor or fear Christ (Eph 5:21; Col 3:22-25; see also Phil 2:12; 1 Cor 2:3; 2 Cor 7:15; 1 Tim 6:1-2). This verse has been used out of context to condone domestic *violence, much to the church's shame (Fowl, 197). As he does with wives, so too in Ephesians 5:22 Paul adds the phrase "as to Christ" (*hōs tō Christō*) and does not repeat the verb "to obey" before the phrase, although some English translations add the verb. With this phrase, Paul stresses that the slave's actions provide an opportunity to model Christ to the rest of the church, thereby attaining honor. Moreover, the slave will gain a reward from God for the good work done (Eph 6:8; Col 3:24-25; 2 Cor 5:10). Having a reward and gaining an inheritance are remarkable promises available to the Gentile believing slave.

Paul begins his address to the owners in Ephesus with the command to do to slaves the same things (*ta auta*, Eph 6:9), which can be translated "in the same way." Paul could be pointing owners to emulate the slaves' wholehearted service (Eph 6:7) or their good deeds (Eph 6:8). John Chrysostom exegetes the passage as Paul's exhortation that owners serve their slaves (*Hom. Eph.* 6.9; PG 62:157). Similarly, Paul insists to the Colossian owners that they do what is right and equitable (*to dikaion kai tēn isotēta*, Col 4:1) to their slaves, a posture that dignifies the slave in sharp contrast to wider social norms (McKnight).

Not only does the slave represent a model of discipleship for the owner, but the owner's special privilege of domination is taken away in Christ. Paul insists that the owner may not threaten the slave (Eph 6:9). The injunction would include threatening the use of physical force, or the withholding of food, water, or suitable clothing, or separating a mother from her child, or two slaves who love each other. Paul provides no exception to this ruling; even the disobedient slave cannot be threatened. Paul grounds his *teaching in the theological reality that God shows no favoritism (see also Acts 10:34; Gal 2:6; Col 3:25; Jas 2:1). To the Colossians, Paul points to the crucified and risen Lord as the master in heaven, who expects his followers to emulate the self-sacrificial love he displayed on the *cross. Paul lives out these words in his letter to Philemon, wherein he asks that this owner accept his newly converted slave, Onesimus, as a brother/sibling in Christ and no longer as a slave (Philem 15-16).

See also COLOSSIANS, LETTER TO THE; EPHESIANS, LETTER TO THE; HEAD; KINSHIP LANGUAGE IN PAUL; MAN AND WOMAN; MARRIAGE AND DIVORCE, ADULTERY AND INCEST; SEXUALITY, SEXUAL ETHICS; SLAVE, SLAVERY; VIOLENCE.

BIBLIOGRAPHY. **E. Adams,** *The Earliest Christian Meeting Places: Almost Exclusively Houses?*, LNTS 450 (London: Bloomsbury T&T Clark, 2013); **B. R. Braxton,** *No Longer Slaves: Galatians and African American Experience* (Collegeville, MN: Liturgical Press, 2002); **G. D. Fee,** *The First Epistle to the Corinthians*, NICNT (Grand Rapids, MI: Eerdmans, 1987); **S. E. Fowl,** *Ephesians: A Commentary*, NTL (Louisville, KY: Westminster John Knox, 2012); **P. Garnsey,** *Ideas of Slavery from Aristotle to Augustine* (Cambridge: Cambridge University Press, 1996); **J. A. Glancy,** *Slavery in Early Christianity* (Oxford: Oxford University Press, 2002); **T. Gombis,** *The Drama of Ephesians: Participating in the Triumph of God* (Downers Grove, IL: IVP Academic, 2010); **W. Grudem,** "Does κεφαλή ('Head') Mean 'Source' or 'Authority Over' in Greek Literature? A Survey of 2336 Examples," *TrinJ* ns 6.1 (1985): 38-59; **K. Harper,** *From Shame to Sin: The Christian Transformation of Sexual Morality in Late Antiquity* (Cambridge, MA: Harvard University Press, 2013); **M. J. Harris,** *Slave of Christ: A New Testament Metaphor for Total Devotion to Christ* (Downers Grove, IL: InterVarsity Press, 1999); **J. P. Hering,** *The Colossian and Ephesian Haustafeln in Theological Contexts: An Analysis of Their Origins, Relationships, and Message* (New York: Lang, 2007); **C. Hezser,** *Jewish Slavery in Antiquity* (Oxford: Oxford University Press, 2005); **E. Laes,** *Children in the Roman Empire: Outsiders Within* (Cambridge: Cambridge University Press, 2011); **A. T. Lincoln,** *Ephesians*, WBC 42 (Dallas: Word, 1990); **M. Y. MacDonald,** *The Power of Children: The Construction of Families in the Greco-Roman World* (Waco, TX: Baylor University Press, 2014); **S. McKnight,** *The Letter to the Colossians*, NICNT (Grand Rapids, MI: Eerdmans, 2018); **H. Mouritsen,** *The Freedman in the Roman World* (Cambridge: Cambridge University Press, 2011); **M. C. Nussbaum,** "The Incomplete Feminism of Musonius Rufus, Platonist, Stoic, and Roman," in *The Sleep of Reason: Erotic Experience and Sexual Ethics in Ancient Greece*, ed. M. C. Nussbaum and J. Sihvola (Chicago: University of Chicago Press, 2002), 283-325; **O. Patterson,** *Slavery and Social Death: A Comparative Study* (Cambridge, MA: Harvard University Press, 1982); **S. B. Pomeroy,** *Goddesses, Whores, Wives, and Slaves* (New York: Schocken, 1995); **S. Sumner,** *Men and Women in the Church: Building Consensus on Christian Leadership* (Downers Grove, IL: InterVarsity Press, 2003); **A. C. Thiselton,** *The First Epistle to the Corinthians*, NIGTC (Grand Rapids, MI: Eerdmans, 2000); **C. Westfall,** *Paul and Gender: Reclaiming the Apostle's Vision for Men and Women in Christ* (Grand Rapids, MI: Baker Academic, 2016).

L. H. Cohick

HYMNS, HYMN FRAGMENTS, CONFESSIONS

Paul's letters bear witness not only to Paul's own thinking but also to beliefs and ways of understanding the work of Jesus that he received or that were shared more broadly by others who were members of the early Christian communities. Significant among Paul's use of earlier *traditions are his inclusion of hymns, fragments of hymns, and confessions in his *letters. These elements of Paul's letters can be considered under the broader category of liturgical elements since they likely reflect the kinds of expressions used in communal gatherings of early Christian communities, whether for *worship, proclamation of the good news, participation in the *Lord's Supper, *baptism, reading of Scripture, or *prayer. In some cases Paul makes it clear that he is passing on earlier traditions to his readers (e.g., Rom 10:9). At other times Paul's use of earlier tradition is less clear but may be inferred from indicators in the text such as contextual dislocations, changes in address, formulaic expressions, strophic structure, rhythmical arrangement, and use of participial phrases and relative clauses (e.g., Col 1:15-20). In still other instances Paul composes his own liturgically styled passages drawing on forms and expressions used by early Jewish and Christian communities in their worship (Rom 11:33-36).

1. Hymns and Fragments
2. Confessions
3. Function of This Material in Paul
4. Wider Context

1. Hymns and Fragments.

In antiquity a simple definition of a hymn was a song in praise of a god. However, when it comes to understanding the types of compositions that Greeks, Romans, and Jews could refer to by the term *hymnos*, the diversity is surprising. Hymns could be written in metrical verse or prose. Hymns could be sung in honor of gods, heroes, or deified humans. Hymns could even have as their subject inanimate objects or philosophical concepts. In a Greek context the psalms of the Hebrew Bible could also be referred to as hymns. Thus, the question of what constituted a hymn in antiquity is a challenging one, and contemporary readers should be careful not to impose modern notions of hymns as they consider hymnody in the ancient world.

Paul refers to hymns and the practice of singing hymns in several places, suggesting that the singing of hymns was an important dimension of communal worship within the communities that Paul founded (1 Cor 14:26; Col 3:16; Eph 5:19-20). Beyond the explicit mention of hymns, Paul uses language related to singing and glorifying *God to describe the goal of the Christian community (Rom 15:6-11) and of glorifying God more generally (2 Cor 9:13; Gal 1:24). In addition, within Paul's letters are passages that reflect the features of hymns in praise of God and of hymns in praise of *Christ.

1.1. Hymns to God. In the category of hymns in praise of God we may note especially Romans 11:33-36, which is reflective of a Jewish-Christian psalm style. Related to hymns in praise of God are the doxologies in praise of God, which figure prominently in Paul's letters. Doxologies of the "blessed be God" form can be seen in Romans 1:25; 9:5; 2 Corinthians 1:3-11; 11:31; Ephesians 1:3-14. Doxologies of the "to him be *glory forever" form are seen in Romans 11:36; 16:25-27; Galatians 1:5; Philippians 4:20; Ephesians 3:21; 1 Timothy 1:17; 6:16; 2 Timothy 4:18. As the references above suggest, it is not always possible to draw a sharp distinction between these various categories of praise compositions, since doxological formulations can be part of larger hymns and prayers. The hymn to God in Romans 11:33-36 concludes with a doxology of the form "to him be the glory forever." Also related are expressions of thanksgiving to God, as in Colossians 1:12-14.

1.2. Hymns to Christ. The two premier examples of hymns in praise of Christ in Paul's letters are found in Philippians and Colossians. Philippians 2:5-11 has been a focus of scholarly research on hymns in the NT. Its vocabulary, style, and structure have led to many different proposals for its conceptual background and significance both for Paul and for its original author. The passage can be outlined neatly in a series of two- and three-line stanzas. Such an arrangement reveals a clear downward narrative trajectory of emptying for Christ, followed by a focus on his divine exaltation by God. The turning point in the hymn is Christ's death (Phil 2:8). Some scholars argue for Pauline addition in this line, since it aligns so closely with Paul's theology and the hymn might seem to maintain its structure without it. However, such an excision is not necessary since the line does fit structurally and conceptually as a key turning point from humiliation to exaltation. Understood in its Greco-Roman context, such an emphasis on remembering the cross and Christ's gruesome and humiliating death in this hymnic context is a surprising move. It shows one of the ways in which early Christians appropriated the genre of hymn with countercultural notions of what is praiseworthy. As for its significance in the letter, there is debate over whether the hymn is provided as an example for believers to follow (drawing on "your attitude should be the same as that of Christ Jesus," Phil 2:5) or whether it announces the *eschatological arrival of Christ and thereby describes the context of what it means to be "*in Christ Jesus." The two divergent approaches are not necessarily incompatible.

Colossians 1:15-20, the other major hymn in Paul's letters, has a more Asiatic style of Greek. It can also be arranged into strophes, but the strophes of the Colossian hymn have as their focus the supremacy of Christ in *creation and the supremacy of Christ in redemption, calling Christ the "*firstborn" (Col 1:15, 18). While the Philippian hymn may suggest a notion of preexistence, the Colossian hymn explicitly identifies Christ as the agent of God in creation. In this regard it casts a more philosophical emphasis, drawing on early Jewish *wisdom traditions about creation by means of God's word or *logos*. It also explicitly cites the redemptive work of Christ as that of reconciling and making *peace. Like Philippians, it also inscribes crucifixion of Jesus as a key aspect of early Christian memory of Jesus (Col 1:20). As for its function in the letter, in the face of pressures on the Colossian believers to see their *faith in Christ as requiring some additional augmentation, the hymn suggests that Christ is fully sufficient to handle all forces, spiritual and earthly.

*1.3. **Methodological Concerns.*** Given that Paul does not explicitly identify these passages as hymns, scholars debate the validity of identifying these passages as hymns and what significance such an identification may have for understanding the early Christian movement. Form criticism (a type of literary analysis applied to psalms and narratives in the Jewish Scriptures, as well as to the Gospels, and which concerns itself with oral transmission) is one methodological tool used to help identify when Paul may be quoting an earlier source and what that source may have looked like originally. One major issue is the extent to which Paul may adapt, modify, remove words, or add explanatory comments within the text of a particular hymn he may be quoting. Conclusions become increasingly speculative as one is removed one or more levels from the text as we have it in Paul's letter. A more fruitful approach has been to note where materials in Paul's letters reflect themes, vocabulary, stylistic features, or other characteristics associated with hymns in the ancient world. In this way interpreters may consider where Paul may be quoting early Christian hymns or crafting his own language in ways that are influenced by the practices of early Christian worship. Interpreters may then consider how Paul's choice to include a hymn or hymnic passage contributes to the rhetorical purposes of a given letter.

The ways in which hymns convey their meaning is important to consider when interpreting Paul's letters. Hymns, like poetry, use imagery and metaphors to convey their meaning in ways that have not only a cognitive but an affective dimension. The choice of a hymn or hymn-like passage to describe Jesus is suggestive to the reader/hearer due to the elevated nature of hymnic language and its association with the divine. The experiential dimensions of hymns, poems, and songs has become an area of focus as well, looking at how such a composition enables the reader to enter into an experience of what is described through mimetic participation in an imaginal world that is described in the hymn.

Aside from the major hymns identified above, other hymnic passages in Paul include Ephesians 2:14-16 and 1 Timothy 3:16, although these may be better understood as hymn fragments. The challenges noted above with interpreting hymns apply here as well, and drawing firm conclusions about the fragments is even more challenging since there is much less text to work with in terms of identifying a hymnic original context in which the fragment may be understood. These hymnic fragments have features of the longer hymns, including their language, style, contents, and focus on the person and work of Jesus Christ. In the case of Ephesians 2:14-16, if this passage is not a hymn fragment, at the very least it is the case that the language connects with the language of earlier hymns and is perhaps a reflection on those earlier passages. In the same way, 1 Timothy 3:16 may be a fragment of a longer hymn or potentially a hymn in its own right.

2. Confessions.

Confessional statements (from the Greek, *homologia*) in Paul's letters are those single- or multistatement affirmations that reflect on the nature and person of Christ in a concise way and are presented in the context of something that is confessed, delivered, received, or passed on. In his influential study, V. H. Neufeld (20) explains: "The homologia represented the agreement or consensus in which the Christian community was united, that core of essential conviction and belief to which Christians subscribed and openly testified. The homologia was the admission and acknowledgement of the individual's loyalty to Jesus Christ, and as such represented a personal testimony of his faith." Like other liturgical elements, this could be expressed in public worship, *preaching, apologetics, or contexts of controversy.

Features suggesting confessional statements include use of the *homologein-homologia* word group; other verbs of a kerygmatic, didactic, or confessional nature such as "so it says" (*dio legei*, Eph 5:14) or "I received" (*paralambanō*, 1 Cor 15:3); syntactical considerations such as *hoti*, the double accusative, or the infinitive to introduce a quote; and consecutive use of participial phrases or relative clauses.

Neufeld identified three patterns of confessional material in Paul's letters: (1) the basic confession, (2) a two-part creedal statement, and (3) a two-part antithetical formula. The first pattern, the basic confession, was simply *kyrios Iēsous*, "Jesus is *Lord," and may be found on its own as in Romans 10:9 or embedded in a hymn as in Philippians 2:11; 1 Corinthians 12:3. This basic confession in Paul may represent an expansion from an even earlier Jewish Christian confession of *kyrios Christos*, "Jesus is the Christ." The second pattern is a two-part formula similar to a creedal statement that refers to Jesus as Lord and to God as Father. This double statement can be seen in 1 Corinthians 8:5-6; Galatians 3:20; Ephesians 4:5; 1 Timothy 2:5. The bipartite formula is not necessarily a *homologia* in the pure sense; rather, it is an acclamation. The third pattern is another kind of two-part formulation but an antithetical one indicating that Christ both died and rose or was humbled and exalted. These antithetical formulas occur individually or can be embedded in larger passages: Romans 1:3-4; 4:24-25; 8:34; 10:6-13; 2 Corinthians 13:4; 1 Corinthians 15:3-5; Ephesians 4:8-10; 1 Thessalonians 4:14.

3. Function of This Material in Paul.

Taken together, these passages indicate that the earliest Christian gatherings were generative of praise of Christ that reflected common themes and associated Jesus with the divine. When these hymnic and confessional passages are looked at as a whole, the contents of these passages show an interesting variety but also consistency around several themes. A major theme is, of course, Jesus Christ, and especially his life, death, resurrection, and *exaltation. Related is an emphasis on the saving work of Jesus, including his work of redemption, reconciliation, and making peace. Many of the themes connect closely with Jewish theological concepts, including the announcement of eschatological renewal through God's agent. It is easy to recognize that these passages would be at home in settings of worship, public confession of faith, and baptism, as well as in *ethical instruction and apologetics.

4. Wider Context.

Hymns, fragments, and confessions with these themes centered on Jesus are not unique in the writings of Paul. To adequately grapple with their significance they must also be understood within the larger context of the NT as well as other early Jewish and Christian writings. The importance of hymns and hymn fragments may be seen from their inclusion in writings as diverse as Luke (see Lk 1–2), Revelation (see Rev 4–5), Hebrews (see Heb 1:1-3), and 1 Peter (see 1 Pet 3:18-22). And of course, Paul's Jewish background suggests strong connections with the use of hymns and psalms in Jewish tradition. Of particular note are the ways in which Jewish psalmody was used as part of a larger pattern of a strategy of literary resistance against imperial agendas—from the time of the Hebrew Bible through the Second Temple period. Some of the language of the hymns in Paul's letters resonates with language used in praise of the Roman emperor, suggesting that the early Christian hymns may even participate to some extent in this long-standing practice of Jewish resistance poetry. Confessions likewise had wider use outside Paul, and, as noted above, Paul's inclusion of confessional materials appears to show some developments from even earlier confessions. And the confessional materials included by Paul in his letters likewise appear to be part of a trajectory that is reflected in the further developments seen in John's Gospel and letters, the Acts of the Apostles, and the later letters of the NT.

See also COLOSSIANS, LETTER TO THE; GLORY, GLORIFICATION; PHILIPPIANS, LETTER TO THE; PRAYER; TRADITION; WORSHIP.

BIBLIOGRAPHY. **P. Bradshaw,** *The Search for the Origins of Christian Worship* (London: SPCK, 1992); **R. Brucker,** *"Christushymnen" oder "epideiktische Passagen"? Studien zum Stilwechsel im Neuen Testament und seiner Umwelt,* FRLANT 176 (Göttingen: Vandenhoeck & Ruprecht, 1997); **O. Cullmann,** *The Earliest Christian Confessions* (London: Lutterworth, 1949); **R. Deichgräber,** *Gotteshymnus und Christushymnus in der frühen Christenheit* (Göttingen: Vandenhoeck & Ruprecht, 1967); **B. Edsall and J. R. Strawbridge,** "The Songs We Used to Sing? Hymn 'Traditions' and Reception in Pauline Letters," *JSNT* 37 (2015): 290-311; **G. D. Fee,** "Philippians 2:5-11: Hymn or Exalted Pauline Prose?," *BBR* 2 (1992): 29-46; **S. E. Fowl,** *The Story of Christ in the Ethics of Paul,* JSNTSup 36 (Sheffield: Sheffield Academic Press, 1990); **M. E. Gordley,** *The Colossian Hymn in Context: An Exegesis in Light of Jewish and Greco-Roman Hymnic and Epistolary Conventions,* WUNT 2/228 (Tübingen: Mohr Siebeck, 2007); idem, *New Testament Christological Hymns: Exploring Texts, Contexts, and Significance* (Downers Grove, IL: IVP Academic, 2018); **M. Hengel,** "Hymns and Christology," in *Between Jesus and Paul* (London: Fortress, 1983); **L. W. Hurtado,** *Lord Jesus Christ: Devotion to Jesus in Earliest Christianity* (Grand Rapids, MI: Eerdmans, 2003); **E. Käsemann,** "A Critical Analysis of Philippians 2:5-11," *JTC* 5 (1968): 45-88; **E. Krentz,** "Epideiktik and Hymnody: The New Testament and Its World," *BR* 40 (1995): 50-97; **R. N. Longenecker,** *New Wine into Fresh Wineskins: Contextualizing the Early Christian Confessions* (Peabody, MA: Hendrickson, 1999); **R. P. Martin,** *Worship in the Early Church* (Grand Rapids, MI: Eerdmans, 1974); idem, *A Hymn of Christ: Philippians 2:5-11 in Recent Interpretation and in the Setting of Early Christian Worship* (Downers Grove, IL: IVP Academic, 1997); **V. H. Neufeld,** *The Earliest Christian Confessions* (Leiden: Brill, 1963); **J. T. Sanders,** *The New Testament Christological Hymns: Their Historical Religious Background,* SNTSMS 15 (Cambridge: Cambridge University Press, 1971); **N. T. Wright,** "Poetry and Theology in Colossians 1:15-20," *NTS* 36 (1990): 444-68.

M. E. Gordley

I

IDENTITY

The topic of identity is a burgeoning field of research in Pauline studies. It covers a wide range of material and is multidisciplinary in nature, studied from many angles, including *anthropology, *philosophy, psychology, and sociology. Human identity, personal identity, social identity, and Christian identity all fall within its orbit. Investigations of identity seek to answer questions concerning what we are, who we are, whose we are, and who or what defines us as human beings. "Identity is that sense of being and self-understanding that frames our actions, communicates to others who we are, and sets the agenda for our acts" (Snodgrass, 9).

The word *identity* does not appear in English Bibles. However, there are many related terms and concepts. In certain contexts, *zoē* could be translated as "identity" (e.g., Col 3:3) and *psychē* as "person" (BDAG, 1099; L&N, 321). Further, Paul treats questions of race, gender, and *sexuality, subjects central to postmodern discussions of identity. Even if it is not the exclusive focus anywhere in Paul's letters, identity is covered almost everywhere; "theological anthropology is an implicit and derivative doctrine" (Vanhoozer, 180). The broad topic of identity relates to and overlaps with our understanding of Paul's teaching on many other subjects, including *salvation, *ethics, *Christology, *eschatology, and the *church.

Central to Paul's thinking about identity is the idea that humans are social beings and live in shared stories (Bauckham, 138-39). At the heart of Christian identity in Paul's letters lies three overlapping notions that assume the relational and narratival dimensions of identity: union with *Christ, being known by *God, and *adoption into God's family. Before examining them, Paul's understanding of human identity more generally needs to be considered, not least because for Paul Christian identity is a renewal and completion of human identity.

1. The Image of God
2. Anthropological Terms
3. Traditional Identity Markers
4. Paul's Self Understanding
5. Individual and Corporate Identity
6. Naming and Imagery
7. Union with God's Son
8. Known by God as His Child
9. Adoption into God's Family

1. The Image of God.

The declaration that human beings are made in the *image and likeness of God is stated five times in the opening chapters of Genesis (Gen 1:26, 27 [2×]; 5:1; 9:6) and is rightly seen as "foundational to the biblical concept of humanness" (Johnson, 564). Paul uses image-of-God language once in reference to humanity, but more often with reference to Jesus Christ and Christians.

In 1 Corinthians 11:7 Paul speaks of males (*anēr*) as "being" (*hyparchōn*) the image and *glory of God. This suggests to some that Paul understood Adam to be created in the image of God, but not Eve. However, in 1 Corinthians 15:49 he says that "just as we have borne the image of the earthly man, we shall also bear the image of the heavenly one," suggesting he understands all humanity to share (even if imperfectly) in the image of God as it has been passed down to us through Adam. Understanding 1 Corinthians 11:7 in the light of 1 Corinthians 15:49 suggests that, for Paul, Adam was created directly in the image of God and that the rest of us (from Eve on) are made in God's image as we inherit it from Adam and our parents (see Gen. 5:3; 9:6).

The connection between the image of God and sonship is central to Paul's notion of Christian identity. Increasingly, scholars are recognizing that image-of-God language is conceptually familial (see Ortlund, 685; Rosner 2017, 80-85). That the image of God marks human beings as sons or children of God is clear from the usage of "image and likeness" language in Genesis 5:3 to denote a family relationship between Adam and Seth, as well as in the identification of Adam as the son of God in Luke 3:38, and it is implied in Paul's Areopagus speech in Acts 17, where he describes humanity as "the offspring of God." Paul's notion of salvation as adoption into God's family assumes that human beings have lost their full status as God's children. The two notions come together in Romans 8:29, where the purpose of being conformed to the image of God's Son is that Christ might be the *firstborn among many brothers and sisters.

Paul's creation of Christian identity, central to his person and *mission, builds on the essentials of human identity, including the image of God. Our redemption in Christ entails the restoration of God's perfect image in Christ. In Romans 8:29 believers are conformed to the image of God's Son (see also 1 Cor 15:49; 2 Cor 3:18; 4:4; Col 1:15; 3:10): "It is Christ who supplies the pattern for the renewal of the new self" (Moo, 268).

Colossians 3:10 describes Christian believers as the "new humanity" (*ho neos anthrōpos*), being progressively "renewed in the knowledge of the image of its creator." The growth in *knowledge that is both the goal and means of the renewal in question is knowledge of God and of Christ and also knowledge of ourselves in relation to God and Christ. Renewal into the image of God is the outcome of the process, and it is no accident that Paul has already said in the letter that the *Son of God is "the image of God" (Col 1:15).

2. Anthropological Terms.

Anthropological terms, the ways an author refers to the constitution of human beings, are a window into their view of human nature and identity. Paul has more ways of referring to human beings than any other biblical author, including words translated "*body," "*flesh," "soul," "spirit," "mind," "heart," and "inner being" (see Dunn, 51-78; Rosner 2017, 66-74). In line with OT anthropology, these are generally best understood as aspects of a human being rather than parts of a human being. They represent human existence viewed from different angles.

Taking the first six in pairs, from Paul's use of *sōma* we learn that humans are social beings, marked by social interdependence and responsibility, and also fleshly, *sarx*, that is, frail and weak beings (see 2 Cor 4:11), corrupt and hostile toward God (Rom 7:18; Gal 5:24). Humans are rational beings, with a mind, *nous*, capable of soaring to the heights of reflective thought (Rom 12:2), and also experiencing beings, with a heart, *kardia*, capable of emotions (Rom 5:5), thought, and will (1 Cor 7:37). Humans are also living beings, *psychē*, animated by the *mystery of life as a gift (Rom 11:3), and spiritual beings, *pneuma*, with the capacity to relate directly to God (Rom 8:16). Finally, Paul sees humans as whole beings, determined from within; in three places Paul uses the expression, "inner being," *ho esō anthrōpos* (Rom 7:22; 2 Cor 4:16; Eph 3:17).

Paul's anthropological terms highlight the essence, limitations, and potential of human identity. We are more than our bodies, but not less than them. Being embodied, we are social beings, defined by our relationships, and the body also has a place in the age to come (see 1 Cor 15:35-44, where *sōma* occurs 9×). We are also flesh, that is, mortal, and driven by our desires, which are often harmful and in opposition to God. As beings with mind and heart, we are capable of the highest thoughts and the deepest emotions. And as souls and spirits, we are alive and have the capacity to connect with the living God. From our *psychē* we know that we are alive; from our *pneuma* that we can be alive to God. To neglect any one of these dimensions is to distort human identity.

3. Traditional Identity Markers.

For Paul, as a first-century Jew, the world was divided in binary terms, between Jew and *Gentile, male and female, *slave and free, rich and poor. One side or the other of these pairs would have been among the first answers to questions of identity for every person in the ancient world, and each of them made a world of difference.

Paul reflects the Jew/Gentile division at several points in his letters (see the refrain "Jews and Gentiles" in Rom 1:17; 2:9-10; 3:9; 10:12). But in 1 Corinthians 10:31 Paul breaks with this view and introduces a third grouping that supersedes the other two. There he mentions Jews, Greeks (another term for Gentiles), and "the church of God." At root, being a Jew or a Gentile is displaced in importance by a more important identity, that of belonging to the new people of God.

Indeed, at first blush, it would seem that Paul removes any significance to a person's race, *ethnicity, nationality, culture, and even gender in Galatians 3:28, where in Christ Jesus "there is neither Jew nor Gentile, neither slave nor free, nor is there male and female" (NIV; see also Col 3:11). The same goes for marital status, occupation, and possessions in 1 Corinthians 7:29-31, where Paul counsels that believers are to "live as if you were not married, had no dealings with the world, and did not take full possession of anything that you own."

However, in Paul's hands such markers of identity are "neither obsolete nor irrelevant when it comes to real life situations . . . but are relativized by the call of Christ" (Campbell, 93). They all remain important for identity, but none is all-important. Paul's reflections on his own missionary practice in 1 Corinthians 9:20-22 make this clear: "To the Jews I became like a Jew, to win the Jews," and so on. Far from ignoring cultural differences, Paul is willing to surrender his right to live according to his own culture, context, and preferences, and adapt to the realities and ways of those with whom he works and whom he hopes to reach for Christ.

Paul's advice to married men in 1 Corinthians 7:29 to live as if they were not married is not an instruction to neglect their *marriage or to stop sleeping with their spouse, let alone get divorced. Rather, he aims to downgrade the importance of whether a person is married or not in the light of the coming of Christ: for "the time is short" (1 Cor 7:29), and "this world in its present form is passing away" (1 Cor 7:31). Paul is urging those who are married, and those who are single, for that matter, not to define themselves by their marital status.

Paul reasons that since believers know where the world is headed, they are not to allow the world to dictate their identity or existence. The prospect of a new heaven and new earth takes the edge off prevailing troubles on this earth and may even enable a believer to endure a marital or social status they consider unsatisfying or undesirable and still glorify God within it. According to Paul, being married or not is not central to the identity of Christians. Neither is being sad or happy, nor having certain possessions. Paul is not disparaging a full-blooded engagement with the world (see 1 Cor 5:10), but instead wants it to be tempered by a sober assessment of life's ups and downs in the light of something that eclipses them.

A key feature of Paul's view of personal identity is not to regard other people "by what they seem to be" (2 Cor 5:16 CEV). The *gospel, and especially eschatology, lead to "the relativization of all things in Christ" (Campbell, 89): "He sees with utterly differently eyes, from a perspective that radically relativizes, if it does not wholly obliterate, all social and historical categories" (Barclay, 189-90).

4. Paul's Self-Understanding.
Paul embodies much of his teaching on identity and links it to his own story. This is the case with respect to the relativization of traditional identity markers, as well as many other aspects of Christian identity. For instance, Paul's autobiographical statement in Philippians 3:3-7 exhibits the devaluing of his Jewish identity, which he "counts as loss" for the sake of gaining Christ.

Paul's is a paradigmatic story for Christian identity. This is most clear in Galatians 2:20 ("I have been crucified with Christ and I no longer live, but Christ lives in me"), where he depicts a newly constituted self that lives in union with Christ. "When the 'I' is crucified with Christ, the ego is unmoored from any prior sources of identity, worth, and direction, or conversely, all sources of shame, dishonor, and despair; it is severed from the relational matrix shaped by family of origin, social context, economic status, and so forth" (Eastman, 174).

5. Individual and Corporate Identity.
Does Paul think of human beings in individual or corporate terms? Much recent Pauline scholarship argues that Paul is a communal thinker and may not even have a concept of the individual. *Social-scientific approaches argue that in the first-century Mediterranean world "persons considered themselves in terms of the group(s) in which they experienced themselves as inextricably embedded" (Malina, 62). Anti-individualism was also a key driver for the new perspective on Paul, with Paul's doctrine of *justification understood as "primarily oriented toward the interpretation of the people of God" and union with Christ as "a communal concept" (Davies, 716). A third anti-individualist trend in recent Pauline studies is the *apocalyptic understanding of Paul, with its emphasis on the cosmic *triumph of God at the heart of Paul's view of salvation. Martyn (101), for example, argues that "the root antidote to an individual sin is not an individual instance of forgiveness . . . [but rather] vanquishing the enslaving power of Sin."

However, it is more accurate to think of the individual and the community belonging together in Paul's thought. In terms of the history of ideas, Larry Siedentop's tour de force, *Inventing the Individual*, credits Christianity for the concept of ourselves as free agents, an essential notion for the very idea of a personal identity. According to Siedentop, in Paul's hands, "the identity of individuals is no longer exhausted [as it once was] by the social roles they happen to occupy" (Siedentop, 62). Paul had something to do with the very idea of the individual. There is no need to dismiss the importance of the individual in order to note the fundamentally communal context of his letters. While Paul knows nothing of an isolated individualism, his understanding of salvation in Christ is still deeply personal (see, e.g., Rom 9:3; 1 Cor 15:10; Gal 6:17; Phil 3:13-14).

Ben Dunson argues that Paul conceptualizes the individual in a wide variety of ways. In Romans, for instance, there are: *characteristic* individuals, such as the weak and the *strong in Romans 14:1–15:7, which Paul uses to urge individual action; *generic* individuals in Romans 2–3, to underscore the prospect of final *judgment of all people, both Jews and Gentiles, as individuals; *binary* individuals, in Romans 9–11, to stress the centrality of individual *faith (see Rom 10:6-13) for both Jews and Gentiles; *exemplary* individuals, such as David and *Abraham in Romans 4, whose examples of faith are commended; *representative* individuals, such as *Adam and Christ in Romans 5, a sort of corporately determined individuality; *somatic* individuals, the individual embedded within the believing community in Romans 12; and *particular* individuals, in Romans 16, each with their own distinctive identity. For Paul, there is no individual outside community; equally, there is no community without individuals at the heart of its ongoing life. "The individual and the community are two sides of the same coin" (Dunson, 15).

Recent research informed by social identity theory has led to a better understanding of the social nature of identity and its impact on group interaction in Paul's letters (see Tucker and Baker; Tucker and Kuecker). Brian Tucker, for example, examines the nature of Roman civic identities in *Corinth and argues that "some in [the church in] Corinth were continuing to identify primarily with key aspects of their Roman social identity rather than their identity 'in Christ' and that this confusion over identity positions contributed to the problems within the community" (Tucker, 2). Alistair May's examination of sexual identity within 1 Corinthians examines the nature of "criss-crossing social identity" to consider how various categories may overlap and provide nuanced interaction in different areas of identity construction. He concludes that *porneia* creates an identity for the offender that symbolizes their belonging to the group of outsiders, which helps explain Paul's vociferous opposition to sexual immorality.

6. Naming and Imagery.
"Words, including self-designations, have an ability to lead to a radical reinterpretation of identity" (Trebilco, 300). Along with filling out the character of Christian identity, many names for and images of Christians in Paul's letters are both individual and corporate. Paul calls Christians saints, believers, the church, and, most commonly, brothers and sisters (*adelphoi*). Indeed, "the frequency with which the early Christian movement in general, and the apostle Paul in particular, employed this expression [brothers and sisters] is unprecedented" (Burke, 174). Fictive *kinship created a pervasive ethos of *love, mutuality, togetherness, and belonging in Paul's churches, reflecting and enhancing their individual and community identity and cohesion (Trebilco, 65).

The extensive use of the sibling language in the early church stood out in the ancient world, with the one exception of ancient Jews, whose kinship could be traced in general terms through bloodlines (see many examples in 1–2 Maccabees and generally in rabbinic texts). While the language of brother or sister was not unheard of in pagan philosophical circles, groups such as the Epicureans or Cynics preferred the language of *friendship. Paul, on the other hand, avoids calling Christians his friends: "Paul was familiar with the conventional discussions about friendship but studiously avoided using the word itself" (Malherbe, 104). Paul's preference for sibling language points to his concern not just for individual morality but also for the corporate life of God's family: "We cannot begin to understand the process of moral formation [in Paul's letters] until we see that it is inextricable from the process by which distinctive communities were taking shape" (Meeks, 5).

"Metaphors play a significant role in the formation of social identity" (Lim, 48). Along with sibling metaphors, Paul uses *temple, body, and marriage imagery as a means of social identity construction and maintenance, "to restructure the social reality to match the social vision of the gospel and to realign the values of the churches to the foundational beliefs of the gospel" (Lim, 198). Three times in 1 Corinthians, for instance, he tells the church that they are the temple (1 Cor 3:9, 16-17) and once that individual believers are the temple (1 Cor 6:19; Gupta, 74). Many of the moral exhortations in the letter build on the temple imagery, including those associated with *wisdom (1 Cor 1–4), purity (1 Cor 5–7), edification (1 Cor 8–14), and glorifying God (1 Cor 6:19-20; 10:3-31; 15; Rosner 2016).

7. Union with God's Son.
Being "*in Christ" is arguably Paul's most comprehensive answer to the question of Christian identity: "It is 'in Christ' that Christians understand their true self to be found" (Bauckham, 143). The goal of Paul's *ministry is to "present everyone fully mature *in*

Christ" (Col 1:28). Being in Christ is one of his standard ways to describe both himself (e.g., 2 Cor 12:2) and other believers (e.g., Rom 16:7, 11). Paul makes no small claims about it: "If anyone is *in Christ*, the new *creation has come: The old has gone, the new is here!" (2 Cor 5:17).

Christian identity as God's sons and daughters is based on the fact that believers in Jesus Christ are *in* God's Son. In Gal 3:26 (see also Eph 1:3-5) all of those who have faith in Christ become children of God "in Christ Jesus." "Our true identity, our real identity" is "our identity as adopted children in union with Christ" (Billings, 30). The description in Galatians 3:27 of those baptized into Christ being "clothed" with him reflects the extent to which identity of believers is defined by the person of Jesus: "Their identity is derivative of his" (Macaskill, 196-97).

Finding identity in union with God's Son and the language of sonship raises a major problem of interpretation and translation. Are believers in Christ God's sons or his children? Many modern translations, including the NIV, render the Greek *huios* in Galatians 4:7 (and elsewhere) as "child" rather than as "son": "So you are no longer a slave, but God's *child*; and since you are his *child*, God has made you also an heir" (NIV). While *huios* in this verse is clearly generic and includes both genders, there are two possible reasons for retaining "son" in translation. The first is that in Bible times it was the right of the eldest son in the family to be the primary heir (see Deut 21:15-17; Num 27:8; 36:1-12). However, Paul himself does not always insist on using it. In Romans 8:16-17 he discusses Christians being heirs describing believers as God's "children," *tekna*. A second reason for retaining the language of sonship, at least in some contexts, so long as it is understood that the term is gender inclusive, is that it reminds us that we are part of God's family and heirs thanks to the Son of God; we are sons of God precisely because he is the Son of God.

Union with God's Son implies our participation in the major events of Christ's life (see esp. Col 3:1-4): "Paul argues for a new identity in Christ, one defined historically in relation to Christ's death and resurrection and eschatologically in relation to believers' ultimate and completed destiny" (Keener, 53). If the defining events of Christ's life are his *death, *resurrection, and *ascension, it follows for those in Christ that when they were "dead in [their] transgressions and sins," that "God raised [them] up with Christ and seated [them] with him in the heavenly realms *in Christ Jesus*" (Eph 2:1, 6). In Romans 6:4 *baptism reinforces the status of people who find their identity in Christ: "We were therefore buried with him through baptism into death in order that, just as Christ was raised from the dead through the glory of the Father, we too may live a new life" (NIV).

"At the core of Paul's anthropology lies the declaration that in Jesus true humanity is revealed" (Maston, 159). Paul sets the new identity in Christ in contrast to the old identity in Adam, with Adam as the representative of the old humanity. In Romans 5:12-21 and 1 Corinthians 15:21-22 the archetypal problem of *sin introduced into the human race by Adam finds its eschatological resolution through the climactic breakthrough of the resurrection accomplished by Jesus Christ. To be *in Adam* is to be part of the group that finds in Adam its representative and leader and from him derives its identity and destiny. To be *in Christ* is to be part of the group that finds in Christ its representative and leader and derives its identity and destiny in Christ from what he has brought about for his people.

The notion of being in union with Jesus Christ, the Son of God, draws together several threads of Paul's theology of personal identity. If in Adam we lost our status as God's sons and daughters and damaged the image of God, in Christ we are being conformed to and renewed in the image of God's Son (Rom 8:29; Col 3:10). Indeed, it is Christ's purpose "to create *in himself* one new humanity" (Eph 2:15).

8. Known by God as His Child.

As social beings, humans are defined by their relationships, by whom they know and who knows them. In this light, Paul puts a premium on being known by God intimately and personally for personal identity (Gal 4:8-9; cf. 1 Cor 8:3; 13:12; Rosner 2017, 113-24), a notion he connects to adoption into God's family; believers are known by God as a father knows his child. Galatians 4:8-9 is set in the context of Paul's exposition of adoption in Galatians 3:26–4:7, and in Romans 8:28-29 those who are foreknown are conformed to the image of God's Son. On this score, it is significant that in the Gospels and Acts Jesus is himself known by God as God's Son at his baptism (Mk 1:9-10; see also Mt 3:13-17; Lk 3:21-22), transfiguration (Mt 17:1-5; see also Mk 9:2-8; Lk 9:28-36), and resurrection (Acts 13:32-33; see also Rom 1:1-4). The believer's true identity is to be known by God as his child, an identity that is "hidden with Christ in God" (Col 3:3).

9. Adoption into God's Family.

According to Paul, believers in Christ are sons or children of God, loved by God and given full rights of inheritance as heirs of God and co-heirs with

Christ (Gal 4:4-7; see also Eph 5:5; 1 Cor 6:9-10; Titus 3:7), brothers and sisters in God's family, with their big brother Jesus as the model to whom they conform, thereby taking on the family likeness. This identity leads to a host of implications for conduct. God's children imitate their heavenly Father by walking in love (Eph 5:1-2), *light (Eph 5:8), and wisdom (Eph 5:15), and imitate his Son Jesus Christ by living lives of loving *sacrifice and service to others (1 Cor 11:1; Phil 2:5; 1 Thess 1:6). As brothers and sisters, they are to live in harmony and with care for and support of their spiritual siblings (1 Cor 6:5; Gal 6:1-2; Phil 4:1). They expect God their Father's loving discipline (1 Cor 4:14-15; see also Heb 12:7). "Finding our true selves in Christ, we identify with him who loved us, follow his way of self-giving for God and for others, and thus continually find ourselves afresh in him" (Bauckham, 143).

This identity as God's children and the character that goes along with it has a long backstory. It is not as though divine adoption came out of the blue. If Adam was a rebellious son of God and suffered "death" as a result, *Israel proved to be God's wandering son, and David and his dynasty of kings were God's disobedient sons. Only Jesus Christ was God's perfect and well-pleasing Son; and all believers in Christ are sons of God in him. The new identity as God's sons by virtue of being united to God's Son is the true identity of all believers, since being made in the image of God they were made to be God's sons from the very beginning. In Christ, as those known by God as his children, we regain our true selves.

See also ADOPTION; ANTHROPOLOGY, PAULINE; BODY; ETHNICITY IN PAUL'S WORLD; FLESH; HONOR/SHAME; IMAGE OF GOD; IN CHRIST; KINSHIP LANGUAGE IN PAUL; KNOWLEDGE AND MIND; MAN AND WOMAN; SINGLENESS AND CELIBACY; SLAVE, SLAVERY; SON OF GOD; WEALTH AND POVERTY.

BIBLIOGRAPHY. **J. M. G. Barclay,** "Paul's Story: Theology as Testimony," in *Narrative Dynamics in Paul: A Critical Assessment*, ed. B. W. Longenecker (Leiden: Brill, 2002), 171-96; **R. Bauckham,** *The Bible in the Contemporary World: Hermeneutical Ventures* (Grand Rapids, MI: Eerdmans, 2015); **J. T. Billings,** *Union with Christ: Reframing Theology and Ministry for the Church* (Grand Rapids, MI: Baker, 2011); **T. Burke,** *Family Matters: A Socio-historical Study of Kinship Metaphors in 1 Thessalonians* (London: T&T Clark, 2003); **W. S. Campbell,** *Paul and the Creation of Christian Identity*, LNTS 322 (London: T&T Clark, 2006); **J. Canlis,** "The Fatherhood of God and Union with Christ in Calvin," in *"In Christ" in Paul: Explorations in Paul's Theology of Union and Participation*, ed. M. J. Thate, K. J. Vanhoozer, and C. R. Campbell (Tübingen: Mohr Siebeck, 2014), 400-420; **W. D. Davies,** "Paul: From the Jewish Point of View," in *The Cambridge History of Judaism*, vol. 3, *The Early Roman Period*, ed. W. D. Davies (Cambridge: Cambridge University Press, 1999); **J. D. G. Dunn,** *The Theology of Paul the Apostle* (Edinburgh: T&T Clark, 1998); **B. C. Dunson,** *Individual and Community in Paul's Letter to the Romans*, WUNT 2/332 (Tübingen: Mohr Siebeck, 2012); **S. G. Eastman,** *Paul and the Person* (Grand Rapids, MI: Eerdmans, 2017); **N. K. Gupta,** *Worship That Makes Sense to Paul: A New Approach to the Theology and Ethics of Paul's Cultic Metaphors* (Berlin: de Gruyter, 2010); **P. S. Johnston,** "Humanity," in *New Dictionary of Biblical Theology*, ed. T. D. Alexander and B. S. Rosner (Downers Grove, IL: InterVarsity Press, 2000), 564-67; **C. S. Keener,** *The Mind of the Spirit: Paul's Approach to Transformed Thinking* (Grand Rapids, MI: Baker, 2016); **K. Y. Lim,** *Metaphors and Social Identity Formation in Paul's Letters to the Corinthians* (Eugene, OR: Pickwick, 2017); **G. Macaskill,** *Union with Christ in the New Testament* (Oxford: Oxford University Press, 2018); **A. Malherbe,** *Paul and the Thessalonians: The Philosophic Tradition of Pastoral Care* (Philadelphia: Fortress, 1987); **B. Malina,** *The New Testament World: Insights from Cultural Anthropology* (Louisville, KY: Westminster John Knox, 2001); **J. L. Martyn,** *Galatians: A New Translation with Introduction and Commentary*, AB 33A (New York: Doubleday, 1997); **J. Maston,** "Enlivened Slaves: Paul's Christological Anthropology," in *Anthropology and New Testament Theology*, ed. J. Maston and B. E. Reynolds (London: Bloomsbury, 2018), 141-60; **A. May,** *The Body for the Lord: Sex and Identity in 1 Corinthians 5–7* (London: Bloomsbury, 2004); **W. A. Meeks,** *The Origins of Christian Morality: The First Two Centuries* (New Haven, CT: Yale University Press, 1993); **D. J. Moo,** *The Letter of James*, PNTC (Grand Rapids, MI: Eerdmans, 2000); **G. Ortlund,** "Image of Adam, Son of God: Genesis 5:3 and Luke 3:38 in Intercanonical Dialogue," *JETS* 57 (2014): 673-88; **B. S. Rosner,** "The Church as Temple and Moral Exhortation in 1 Corinthians," in *Ecclesia and Ethics: Moral Formation and the Church*, ed. E. A. Jones III et al. (New York: Bloomsbury T&T Clark, 2016), 41-54; idem, *Known by God: A Biblical Theology of Personal Identity* (Grand Rapids, MI: Zondervan, 2017); **L. Siedentop,** *Inventing the Individual* (Cambridge, MA: Harvard University Press, 2014); **K. R. Snodgrass,** *Who God Says You Are* (Grand Rapids, MI: Eerdmans, 2018);

P. Trebilco, *Self-Designations and Group Identity in the New Testament* (Cambridge, Cambridge University Press, 2012); **J. B. Tucker,** *You Belong to Christ: Paul and the Formation of Social Identity in 1 Corinthians 1–4* (Eugene, OR: Wipf & Stock, 2010); **J. B. Tucker and C. A Baker,** eds., *T&T Clark Handbook to Social Identity in the New Testament* (London: T&T Clark, 2014); **J. B. Tucker and A. Kuecker,** eds., *T&T Clark Commentary on Social Identity in the New Testament* (London: T&T Clark, 2020); **K. Vanhoozer,** "Human Being, Individual and Social," in *The Cambridge Companion to Christian Doctrine*, ed. C. E. Gunton (Cambridge: Cambridge University Press, 1997), 155-88.

B. S. Rosner

IDOLATRY

Paul's attitude toward idolatry (*eidōlolatria*) and idols (*eidōla*) is rooted in his Jewish heritage. The first and second commandments infused *Israel with a countercultural and at times anti-imperial vision of divinity, power, and benefaction. Whereas the first commandment (Ex 20:3 = Deut 5:7) proscribed Israel from the worship of "other gods" (monotheism), the second commandment (Ex 20:4-6 = Deut 5:8-10) proscribed Israel from the material representation of the one God with precious materials (aniconicism). In the ancient Near Eastern and Greco-Roman worlds, Israel's aniconic monotheism articulated an alterity and worldview at odds with the *Gentile polytheism that pervaded most of ancient Mediterranean life.

1. Idolatry in the Old Testament
2. Idolatry in Early Judaism
3. Idolatry in Paul's Letters

1. Idolatry in the Old Testament.

Idolatry is most often described as "the *worship of other gods" in the OT (or what the rabbis called *ʿavôdâ zārâ*—"strange worship"). Strange worship occurred in three forms in ancient Judaism: (1) the cultic veneration of other gods, (2) the material representation of false gods' images, and (3) mistaken conceptions of divinity in the mind of the worshiper (Barclay). Two metaphors illuminate the dangers of idolatry. The first is the marital metaphor of idolatry, wherein Israel is portrayed in an exclusive *covenant relationship between Yahweh (the husband) and Israel (the wife). Idolatry occurs when Israel worships another god and thereby fornicates with a "third partner" (Halbertal and Margalit).

The second is the political metaphor of idolatry, which is more complex. Whereas the marital metaphor is binary (and misogynistic), the political metaphor sees the threatening third party as "human political institutions that demand a competing political loyalty from people" (Halbertal and Margalit, 215). The Jewish fight against idolatry, therefore, was equally a struggle to negotiate and at times resist the deification of political objects of power that could stimulate an erroneous perception of *God in the mind of the worshiper. To resist political idolatry, eighth-century BC prophets developed protest literature to polemicize against the idols and hegemonic imperial policies of foreign *empire (e.g., Is 2:7-8; see Weinfeld). The Deuteronomist, on the other hand, proscribes the Israelite king from accumulating weapons, women, and wealth so that he is not found "exalting himself above other members of the community" (Deut 17:20 NRSV). The fight against idolatry, therefore, was inextricably linked to imperial negotiation both internally and externally. Indeed, "End of idolatry is end of empire. Bowing down to idols made out of gold and silver means worshipping the work of one's own hand and is tantamount to prostration and submission to the imperial power" (Weinfeld, 179).

2. Idolatry in Early Judaism.

The struggle for cultural survival during the Second Temple period hinged on Jews' capacity to remain faithful to the first and second commandments. This struggle was especially acute as Jews lived out most of their life together under the vise grip of Gentile warrior kings both at home and in Diaspora. The LXX translation of the second commandment reflects the increasingly polemical nature of Israelite aniconic values during this period. To translate the Hebrew word *pesel* ("sculptured image"), translators avoided conventional Greek words for images (*agalma*, *eikōn*, *xoanon*, et al.) and instead chose the polemical term *eidōlon* (meaning something that "appears" or "seems to be" [Tatum]). With this term, Jews associated Gentile iconic materiality with superstition. So Philo of Alexandria writes: "These are the things which Moses calls idols [*eidōla*], resembling shadows and phantoms" (*Leg.* 1.25 [Sandelin]).

To animate the lifelessness of *eidōla* and thereby resist assimilation to the dominant imperial culture, Jewish literary sophisticates also recontextualized Second Isaiah's icon parodies (Is 40:18-20; 41:5-7, 21-29; 42:8, 17; 45:16-17, 20-21; 46:1-7; 48:5). Isaiah's sixth-century BC anti-idol polemic, reflecting a more exclusive monotheism, provided subordinate Jews with a dynamic literary device for caricaturing Greco-Roman religion. During the Hellenistic period, Jewish authors blended OT icon parodies with contemporary philosophical debates about monotheism to condemn Gentile religiosity and articulate Judaism's superior philosophical consistency (e.g., Epistle of Jeremiah; Bel and the Dragon; 3 Macc 4:16; Wis 13:1–15:19; Philo, *Decal.* 52-81; *Contempl.* 3-9; *Spec.* 1.13-29; 2.255; Let. Aris. 134-138; Sib. Or. 3.29-35, 5.403-407; 1 En. 99.7; Pseudo-Hecataeus 4.2 [Tromp]).

Of particular significance during this period was the emergence of the Hellenistic cult of rulers in the aftermath of Alexander the Great's conquests. As Alexander's successor kings and subsequently Roman emperors were venerated alongside the cultic infrastructure of the traditional gods (with temples, images, and sacrifices), the built environment of Greco-Roman cities became a space to communicate divine honors toward the emperor as "Savior and Benefactor" (Nock). The impact of imperial cult media on urban spaces was profound (Zanker) and created a new interpretive context for understanding the Jewish icon parodies' objects of resistance (Strait). Indeed, when a Jew allusively resisted iconic statuary and images made with precious material, what was the referent—a god, a ruler, or both at the same time? In some cases, such polemic could even censure the imperial cult more explicitly (Wis 14:16-21). While Jewish iconic sensitivities were toward cultic images ("not images in toto" [Ehrenkrook, 97]), imperial cult media—including noncultic media—afforded the ruling power with a tool to occasionally encroach on Jewish autonomy (Bond). Conversely, Jews' refusal to honor Israelite kings and Roman emperors with anthropomorphic statuary could be a source of consternation and even caricature for Roman onlookers (Tacitus, *Hist.* 5.5.4).

3. Idolatry in Paul's Letters.

Paul maintains the aniconic monotheism of his Jewish heritage but reorients it around devotion to *Christ. In Paul's cosmology, gods and deified political authority ("as in fact there are many gods and many lords" [1 Cor 8:5 NRSV]) can represent a competing allegiance to Christ-followers' loyalty to Christ, who is given the *name "*Lord" that is above every name in the cosmic hierarchy (Phil 2:9-11). The impact of the biblical tradition on Paul's language for idolatry is evident in that nineteen of the thirty-two occurrences of the *eidōl-* word family in the NT are found in Paul's undisputed letters (*eidolon* [Rom 2:22; 1 Cor 8:4, 7; 10:19; 12:2; 2 Cor 6:16; 1 Thess 1:9], *eidōleion* [1 Cor 8:10], *eidōlolatria* [1 Cor 10:14; Gal 5:20], *eidōlolatrēs* [1 Cor 5:10, 11; 6:9; 10:7], *eidōlothyton* [1 Cor 8:1, 4, 7, 10; 10:19]). For Paul, idolatry is the root cause of humanity's turning away from God (Rom 1:18-32) and is a type of *sin alongside various other vices (1 Cor 5:1-11; 6:9; Gal 5:20), including the notion of greed (Col 3:5; Eph 5:5 [Rosner]).

Of central importance to Paul's missionary endeavors is that Gentiles "turned to God from idols, to serve a living and true God" (1 Thess 1:9 NRSV; see also Acts 15:20, 29). Elsewhere, Paul speaks of Gentile Christ-followers' former life as one "led astray to idols that could not speak" (1 Cor 12:2 NRSV). That Paul's missionary preaching may have included polemic against idols is evident in Luke's portrayal of Paul preaching the *gospel in Athens (Acts 17:16-34). After being "apprehended" (Acts 17:19) and taken before the famous Areopagus council, Luke's Paul blends the LXX critique of idols with Greco-Roman philosophical reflections on God to condemn Athenian superstition (*deisidaimonesterous*, Acts 17:22), objects of worship (*sebasmata*, Acts 17:23), temples (Acts 17:24), and images cast in precious materials (Acts 17:29). In so doing, Paul shows the philosophical superiority of the Jesus movement (Jipp), along with the incompatibility of Christ worship with divine honors conferred on gods *and* political authority (Strait).

Paul offers a longer excursus on idols only in 1 Corinthians 8–10 (Liong-Seng Phua). The section concerns "*food sacrificed to idols" (*eidōlothytōn*, 1 Cor 8:1). At stake is how Christ-followers negotiate the temple culture of the Greco-Roman city, including the consumption of meat offered to idols in the precincts of a pagan temple (1 Cor 8:10) and in private homes (1 Cor 10:23-30). To map out boundaries, Paul denies the existence of idols (1 Cor 8:4) and recontextualizes the Shema (Deut 6:4) christologically in order to animate the oneness of the Godhead ("there is one God . . . and one Lord" [1 Cor 10:6]). Paul then takes a pastoral tone, encouraging Christ-followers to not allow their *freedom to consume meat to become a "*stumbling block" for weaker believers (1 Cor 8:9). For Paul, Christ-followers must "flee from the worship of idols" (1 Cor 10:14 NRSV) and straddle a narrow ridge between denying other gods' existence and at the same time acknowledging that they are not innocuous beings—in fact, with some internal contradiction, Paul proceeds to attribute the pagan sacrificial system to demonic worship (1 Cor 10:20-21 [Marcus]). Such competing allegiances incite God's "jealousy" (1 Cor 10:22) and co-opt the church's corporate body through union with an idolatrous third partner, rather than union with Christ through *baptism and the *Lord's Supper (Horrell).

See also Corinthians, First Letter to the; Demons and Exorcism; Empire; Faith; Gentiles; Kingdom of God/Christ; Lord; Mission; Religions, Greco-Roman; Strong and Weak; Stumbling Block.

BIBLIOGRAPHY. **J. M. G. Barclay,** "Snarling Sweetly: Josephus on Images and Idolatry," in *Idolatry: False Worship in the Bible, Early Judaism, and Christianity*, ed. S. C. Barton (New York: T&T Clark, 2007), 73-87; **H. K. Bond,** "Standards, Shields, and Coins: Jewish Reactions to Aspects of the Roman Cult in the Time of Pilate," in *Idolatry: False Worship in the Bible, Early Judaism, and Christianity*, ed. S. C. Barton (London: T&T Clark, 2007), 88-106; **J. von Ehrenkrook,** *Sculpting Idolatry in Flavian Rome: (An)Iconic Rhetoric in the Writings of Flavius Josephus*, EJL 33 (Atlanta: Society of Biblical Literature, 2011); **M. Halbertal and A. Margalit,** *Idolatry*, trans. N. Goldblum (Cambridge, MA: Harvard University Press, 1998); **D. G. Horrell,** "Idol-Food, Idolatry and Ethics in Paul," in *Idolatry: False Worship in the Bible, Early Judaism, and Christianity*, ed. S. C. Barton (New York: T&T Clark, 2007), 120-41; **J. Jipp,** "Paul's Areopagus Speech of Acts 17:16-34 as Both Critique and Propaganda," *JBL* 131 (2012): 567-88; **R. Liong-Seng Phua,** *Idolatry and Authority: A Study of 1 Corinthians 8.1–11.1 in the Light of the Jewish Diaspora*, LNTS 299 (London: T&T Clark, 2005); **J. Marcus,** "Idolatry in the New Testament," in *The Word Leaps the Gap: Essays on Scripture and Theology in Honor of Richard B. Hays*, ed. J. Ross Wagner, C. K. Rowe and A. K. Grieb (Grand Rapids, MI: Eerdmans, 2008), 107-31; **A. D. Nock,** "Soter and Euergetes," in *Essays on Religion and the Ancient World II*, ed. Zeph Stewart (Oxford: Oxford University Press, 1972), 720-35; **B. S. Rosner,** *Greed as Idolatry: The Origin and Meaning of a Pauline Metaphor* (Grand Rapids, MI: Eerdmans, 2007); **K.-G. Sandelin,** "The Danger of Idolatry According to Philo of Alexandria (1991)," in *Attraction and Danger of Alien Religion: Studies in Early Judaism and Christianity* (Tübingen: Mohr Siebeck, 2012), 27-59; **D. J. Strait,** *Hidden Criticism of the Angry Tyrant in Early Judaism and the Acts of the Apostles* (Lanham, MD: Lexington/Fortress Academic, 2019); **W. B. Tatum,** "The LXX Version of the Second Commandment (Ex. 20:3-6=Deut. 5:7-10): A Polemic Against Idols, Not Images," *JSJ* 17, no. 2 (1986): 177-95; **J. Tromp,** "The Critique of Idolatry in the Context of Jewish Monotheism," in *Aspects of Religious Contact and Conflict in the Ancient World*, ed. P. W. van der Horst (Utrecht: Utrechtse Theologische Reeks, 1995), 105-20; **M. Weinfeld,** "The Protest Against Imperialism in Ancient Israelite Prophecy," in *The Origins and Diversity of Axial Age Civilizations* (Albany: State University of New York Press, 1986), 169-82; **P. Zanker,** *The Power of Images in the Age of Augustus* (Ann Arbor: University of Michigan Press, 1988).

D. J. Strait

ILLNESS. *See* Healing, Illness.

IMAGE OF GOD

In the Pauline literature, the concept of the image of *God is employed in three contexts: in reference to Jesus *Christ (2 Cor 4:4; Phil 2:6; Col 1:15), in reference to those conformed to Jesus Christ by the *Holy Spirit (Rom 8:29; Col 3:10; Eph 4:24), and in reference to humanity generally (Rom 1:21-23; though 1 Cor 11:7 requires explanation). These three contexts are connected christologically, as explained below. Elsewhere in the NT, the concept is used to refer to Jesus Christ in Hebrews 1:3 and to humanity generally in James 3:9.

1. In Paul's Letters
2. In the Old Testament
3. In Second Temple Jewish Literature

1. In Paul's Letters.

Paul primarily uses the term *eikōn* when referring to the image of God, echoing Genesis 1:26-27 in the LXX. He deploys other terms in related conceptual contexts, such as "form" (*morphē*) in Philippians 2:6 and "created in the likeness of God" (*kata theon ktisthenta*) in Ephesians 4:24. There is a tight connection between *glory (*doxa*) and the image of God throughout the Pauline literature.

1.1. In Reference to Jesus Christ. In Colossians 1:15-19, Paul employs the term *image* to indicate that Jesus Christ is the visible representation of God. "He [the Son] is the image of the invisible God. . . . All things were created through him and for him. And he is before all things, and in him all things hold together. . . . For in him all the *fullness of God was pleased to dwell" (ESV). This text speaks of Jesus Christ's person, status, and work. Regarding his person, Jesus is the divine Son, Creator of all things. He is no creature; rather, he is the origin and telos of *creation (see Jn 1:1-3). He shares the unique divine *identity as Creator of all things. Regarding his status, he is preeminent over all things. Even Jesus' *death and *resurrection establish his preeminence by extending it into every domain. Regarding his work, he is both Creator and Redeemer, establishing and then reconciling all things to God in himself through the *cross. Jesus uses death to reconcile humanity to God and rises from the dead to make humanity new (establishing the "new humanity" referred to in Col 3:10). Thus, in all things Jesus Christ is *Lord and king, *head and *firstborn. The Son's *kingdom of light is the inheritance of the saints (Col 1:12-14). The saints are conformed through union to Christ's person, participating in Christ's status and vocation.

Philippians 2:5-11 moves from the incarnation of Christ Jesus to his exaltation. He "was in the form [*morphē*] of God" (ESV) but took the form (*morphē*) of a human *servant. He humbled himself even further in his crucifixion. "Therefore God has highly exalted him and bestowed on him the name that is above every name," the very *name of God (Phil 2:9 ESV). It is significant that the Father is glorified by the Son's exaltation and lordship as well as by the confession of all that Jesus Christ is Lord. Jesus shares the name and glory of God. Yahweh says in Isaiah 42:8, "I am the Lord; that is my name; my glory I give to no other" (ESV). And when Jesus Christ is glorified, the Father is glorified.

Second Corinthians 4:4 also identifies Jesus Christ as the image of God. Christians see "the *knowledge of the glory of God in the face of Jesus Christ" (2 Cor 4:6 ESV). Jesus Christ is the visible light of the *gospel of God. Since much of this text describes the conformation of Christians to Jesus Christ by the Holy Spirit, this text will receive further attention below. Similarly, in Hebrews 1:3 the author describes Jesus Christ as the "radiance of God's glory and the exact imprint [*charaktēr*] of his nature" (ESV).

1.2. In Reference to Those Conformed to Jesus Christ by the Holy Spirit. In Colossians 3:10, Paul says that Christians "have put on the new humanity, which is being renewed in knowledge after the image of its creator." Whereas Colossians 1:15-18 is focused on the unique identity of the Son as Creator and Redeemer, Colossians 3:10 is focused on the human creature first made, and then remade, through the Son. Fallen humanity participates in the practices of the "old man," *Adam, the sinful man of Genesis 3. Through union with Christ, God's people have put on a "new man" and are being renewed in God's image. These two texts in Colossians are connected, since it is the redemptive work of the divine Son that enables the renewal of the *church. Christ Jesus definitively fulfills human identity, and he establishes a new creation. Participation in this new creation allows humans to fulfill their original identity as God's image as they represent God in the world. So, in Colossians 3:12-15, Paul encourages the church to

> Put on then, as God's chosen ones, holy and beloved, compassionate hearts, kindness, humility, meekness, and patience, bearing with one another and, if one has a complaint against another, forgiving each other; as the Lord has forgiven you, so you also must forgive. And above all these put on *love, which binds everything together in perfect harmony. And let the *peace of Christ rule in your hearts, to which indeed you were called in one *body. (ESV)

Paul describes a life entirely transformed through union with Christ.

Ephesians 4:24 is a parallel text to Colossians 3:10. Paul says here that the *truth in Christ teaches God's people to "put on the new humanity, created after the likeness of God in true *righteousness and *holiness." Here Paul identifies the likeness of God with righteousness and holiness. Paul summarizes the OT revelation of God's character as righteousness and holiness, which is upheld in the NT by the knowledge of God revealed in Christ Jesus.

In 2 Corinthians 3–4, many of the same Pauline themes are present—holiness, righteousness, and the need for knowledge. As noted above, Christ is identified explicitly as the image of God (2 Cor 4:4). The Holy Spirit extends the glory of the image of God to God's people. "Now the Lord is the Spirit, and where the Spirit of the Lord is, there is *freedom. And we all, with unveiled face, beholding the glory of the Lord, are being transformed into the same image from one degree of glory to another. For this comes from the Lord who is the Spirit" (2 Cor 3:17-18 ESV). Paul connects his christological interpretation of the image of God with the whole body of Christ through the work of the Holy Spirit. By grace a human person sees the Lord's glory (*doxa*) and is thereby transformed into the image of that glory. The tighter the conformity, the greater the degree of glory. Once transformed, the glorified status is likewise granted, though it is possessed "in jars of clay, to show that the surpassing power belongs to God and not to us" (2 Cor 4:7 ESV).

Conformation to the image of Jesus Christ is also eschatological. In Romans 8:29, Paul states that God's people will be conformed to the image of God's Son, "in order that he might be the firstborn among many brothers" (ESV). Through the Spirit of *adoption, Christians become sons of God in the *Son of God, receiving a new, exalted status as coheirs of Christ's kingdom and vicegerents of Christ's rule. Likewise, in 1 Corinthians 15:49, Paul proclaims, "Just as we have borne the image of the man of dust, we shall also bear the image of the man of heaven" (ESV). Christians will bear the image of Christ Jesus by being conformed to the state of his resurrected life.

When referring to humans, then, the image of God should be understood as the underlying identity of humanity, which shapes humanity's telos. The realization of this identity occurs in the new humanity, which is being renewed in likeness to Christ Jesus by the Spirit. Because Christ is the image of God, being transformed into Christ's image is being transformed into God's image. This transformation comes on the basis of the knowledge and love of God, which are necessary prerequisites to realizing human identity. For Paul, the image of God is christological because Christ is the beginning and fulfillment of the image of God—the image of God from first to last. Humans are fulfilled as creaturely images of God by being united to Christ.

1.3. In Reference to Humanity Generally. While Paul does not employ the concept of the image of God to say that all humans are made in God's image, he does assume this reality on the basis of Genesis 1–3. Romans 1:22-23 is an inclusive retelling of Genesis 3 in which all are accountable to God because all "exchanged the glory of the immortal God for images of mortal man" and other creatures. People therefore became like the creatures they worshiped and served rather than like God. They remain creatures in God's image, but they have lost the honor and way of life fitting for their human identity. There is a conceptual parallel with Psalm 115:8, which says of idols and idolators, "Those who make them become like them; so do all who trust in them" (ESV). Paul also echoes Psalm 106:20 here: "They exchanged the glory of God for the image of an ox that eats grass" (ESV). Since all humans are meant to image God, that they instead image mortal men and other creatures demonstrates how much all humans other than Jesus Christ have missed the mark.

It has been argued that 1 Corinthians 11:7 speaks of "males generally" as "the image and glory of God, and implies that women are not" (Clines, "Image of God," 427). This is a misreading of Paul's argument when he writes, "For a man ought not to cover his head, since he is the image and glory of God, but woman is the glory of man" (ESV). While man is glorified by woman, woman is not the image of man but of God (Gen 1:27). All humans are from God, and men and women are dependent on one another. "In the Lord woman is not independent of man nor man of woman; for as woman was made from man, so man is now born of woman. And all things are from God" (1 Cor 11:11-12 ESV). However one takes 1 Corinthians 11:2-16, either as Paul's polemical target (Peppiatt) or a more traditional reading, it is clear that both men and women are made in the image of God for Paul.

2. In the Old Testament.

The OT background for Paul's interpretation of the image of God includes references to the image (*ṣelem*) and likeness (*dəmût*) of God in Genesis (Gen 1:26-27; 5:1, 3; 9:6) along with the teaching throughout the OT that humans are meant to represent God in the world, the use of "glory" in Psalm 8 (*doxa* in the LXX), and references to a divinely exalted human in Ezekiel and Daniel.

2.1. In Genesis. In Genesis 1:26-27, the claim that humanity is made in God's image is a theological account of humanity's identity as a creature. God intends humans to represent God in the world, communicating his presence through reflection of God's character in their roles as vicegerents of God's dominion and priests in God's cosmic *temple. In the ancient world, kings were often said to be images of deities. But in Genesis 1 all humans, male and female, are made in God's image.

Genesis 5:1, 3 also use the terms *ṣelem* and *dəmût*. Adam is said to have been made in God's likeness, and Seth is said to be in the likeness and image of Adam. Many commentators suggest that Genesis 5 puts the image of God in a filial context. Adam is God's son, and Seth is Adam's son. However, Adam also passes his own likeness on to Seth such that Seth bears the consequences of *sin and death. This is important to Paul's argument in Romans 5.

In Genesis 9:3, God permits the killing of animals for food, but in Genesis 9:6 it is made clear that such dominion does not extend to humans. While humans have dominion over other creatures, only God has dominion over the lives of those made in his image. It is clear in Genesis 9 that the image of God is still extended to all humans, even after humanity's fall into sin. A similar logic is offered in James 3:9, where any cursing of a human is seen as cursing someone made in God's likeness (*homoiōsis*).

Following on the theme of representation, in the rest of the Hebrew Bible God's people are expected to reflect the character of God—personally, socially, and politically. When they do, God's presence and rule are known. For example, consider the repeated claim in Leviticus: "You shall therefore be holy, for I am holy" (Lev 11:45 ESV) and "You shall be holy, for I the LORD your God am holy" (Lev 19:2 ESV). Yahweh brought *Israel up out of the land of Egypt so that they would be a people dedicated to the Lord, and therefore they should revere their parents, do justice, deal honestly, tell the truth, help sojourners, and love their neighbors as themselves. They should not take advantage of those who are disabled or otherwise disadvantaged (Lev 19:3-18). The fulfillment of humanity's identity as the image of God is embodied representation of God in the world. Paul takes up this connection of conformation to God's character and the embodied representation of God's presence and rule in his understanding of the image of God.

2.2. In Psalm 8. Psalm 8 praises God for God's glory above creation as well as the glory and honor granted to humanity in creation. In the LXX of Psalm 8, the terms are important for Paul's *anthropology: humanity (*anthropos*) is granted glory (*doxa*), honor (*timē*), and dominion over the other living creatures. As in Genesis 1, human dominion is creaturely participation in God's dominion.

2.3. In Ezekiel and Daniel. In Ezekiel 1:26-28, "the likeness of the glory of the LORD" is envisioned as "a likeness with a human appearance" (ESV) seated above a throne. In Daniel 7:13-14, one "like a son of man" is given "everlasting dominion" (ESV), glory, and a permanent kingdom by the Ancient of Days. Paul's understanding of Jesus Christ and his kingdom was informed by these texts and their reception in Jewish literature.

3. In Second Temple Jewish Literature.

References to Adam as the image of God are common in Jewish literature. Key texts that illuminate the various ways Jewish authors combined "image," "glory," and "form" in the context of creation include Sirach 17:3; 2 Esdras 8.44; Wisdom 2:23; Life of Adam and Eve; 2 Enoch 65.2; and 4Q504 8 I, 4.

Philo regularly connects *eikōn* with *logos* (*Spec.* 1.81; 3.83, 207; *Opif.* 25; *Leg.* 3.96; *Her.* 231; *QG* 2.62; *Conf.* 97; 147; *Fug.* 101; *Somn.* 1.239; Kugler). He also draws on the notion of "likeness to God" found in Plato's *Theaetetus*. In Wisdom 7:22-30, *sophia* has similar qualities and is said to be an *eikōn* of God's goodness. Similar themes show up in Paul's references to Jesus Christ as the image of God and also to the likeness of God gained by conformation to Jesus.

Scholars often disagree on whether a specific text ought to be read with an Adam *Christology or a *wisdom Christology in view. Paul affirms both realities—that Jesus Christ is the Word and Wisdom of God incarnate and that he is the fulfillment of human nature. The Holy Spirit unites God's people to Christ and so conforms them to the likeness of God.

See also ADAM AND CHRIST; ADOPTION; ANTHROPOLOGY, PAULINE; CHRIST, MESSIAH; CREATION AND NEW CREATION; HOLINESS, SANCTIFICATION; HOLY SPIRIT; IN CHRIST.

BIBLIOGRAPHY. **J. Barr,** "The Image of God in the Book of Genesis—A Study in Terminology," *BJRL* 51 (1968): 11-26; **R. Bauckham,** *Jesus and the God of Israel* (Grand Rapids, MI: Eerdmans, 2008); **G. C. Berkouwer,** *Man: The Image of God* (Grand Rapids, MI: Eerdmans, 1962); **P. Bird,** "'Male and Female He Created Them': Gen 1:27b in the Context of the Priestly Account of Creation," *HTR* 74 (1981): 129-59; **G. Bray,** "The Significance of God's Image in Man," *TynBul* 42 (1991): 195-225; **D. J. A. Clines,** "The Image of God in Man," *TynBul* 19 (1968): 53-103; idem, "Image of God," in *DPL*, 426-28; **M. Cortez,** *ReSourcing Christological Anthropology* (Grand Rapids, MI: Zondervan, 2017); **E. M. Curtis,** "Image of God (OT)," *ABD* 3:389-91; **J. Farris,** "An Immaterial Substance View: Imago Dei in Creation and Redemption," *HeyJ* 58 (2017): 108-23; **H. G. Jacob,** *Conformed to the Image of His Son* (Downers Grove, IL: InterVarsity Press, 2018); **J. Jervell,** *Imago Dei. Gen. 1,26f. im Spätjudentum, in der Gnosis undin den paulinischen Briefen* (Göttingen: Vandenhoeck & Ruprecht, 1960); **B. F. Jones** and **J. W. Barbeau,** eds., *The Image of God in an Image Driven Age* (Downers Grove, IL: IVP Academic, 2016); **G. A. Jónsson,** *The Image of God: Genesis 1:26-28 in a Century of Old Testament Research*, Coniectanea Biblica: Old Testament Series 26 (Lund: Almqvist & Wiksell, 1988); **J. Kilner,** *Dignity and Destiny* (Grand Rapids, MI: Eerdmans, 2015); **C. Kugler,** *Paul and the Image of God* (London: Lexington/Fortress, 2020); **R. Lints,** *Identity and Idolatry* (Downers Grove, IL: InterVarsity Press, 2015); **V. Lossky,** *In the Image and Likeness of God* (London: Mowbray, 1975); **C. McDowell,** *The Image of God in the Garden of Eden* (Winona Lake, IN: Eisenbrauns, 2015); **J. R. Middleton,** *The Liberating Image* (Grand Rapids, MI: Brazos, 2005); **L. Peppiatt,** *Unveiling Paul's Women* (Eugene, OR: Cascade, 2018); **R. Peterson,** *The Imago Dei as Human Identity* (Winona Lake, IN: Eisenbrauns, 2016); **G. H. Van Kooten,** *Paul's Anthropology in Context: The Image of God, Assimilation to God, and Tripartite Man in Ancient Judaism, Ancient Philosophy, and Early Christianity*, WUNT 232 (Tübingen: Mohr Siebeck, 2008); **J. Walton,** *Old Testament Theology for Christians* (Downers Grove, IL: IVP Academic, 2017); **N. T. Wright,** "Romans," *NIB* 9:317-664; idem, *Paul and the Faithfulness of God*, 2 vols. (Minneapolis: Fortress, 2013).

R. S. Peterson

IMITATION OF PAUL / OF CHRIST

Imitation was a vital pedagogical tool for ancient Mediterranean cultures. Jewish texts and Greco-Roman philosophical traditions relied heavily on emulation. Positive and negative examples were common in oral and written traditions, and disciples were expected to reflect the thoughts and deeds of their teachers who embodied these traditions. The NT reflects this milieu by making use of imitation in every NT book (Hood 2013). Imitation is particularly prominent in Paul's letters. While the *apostle reflects Jewish and Greco-Roman emphases, he is more forceful and confident in presenting himself as an exemplar than the philosophers of his day (Malherbe, 57) and offers his own distinctively Christian approach focused on the Messiah, his *cross, and the Spirit (Thompson).

1. Theological Foundations
2. Romans
3. 1 and 2 Corinthians
4. Galatians and the Prison Epistles
5. 1 and 2 Thessalonians and the Pastoral Epistles
6. Scholarly Attention

1. Theological Foundations.

Paul's theological architecture for imitation is often overlooked but quite significant. The apostle shares the Jewish belief that humans are God's *images. A required response to this image-bearing *identity in both its original and renewed dimensions is the imitation of the divine character as inscribed in OT *law and narrative: *holiness, *mercy, steadfast *love, and faithfulness (Col 3:9-10; Eph 4:24–5:2). Much of Paul's ethical instruction follows the Jewish and early Christian *tradition in treating God's conduct and character as programmatic for God's people. Perhaps the most overlooked facet of imitation is the call to holiness. If Paul never cites "Be holy, because I am holy," as 1 Peter does (1 Pet 1:16 NIV), he nonetheless applies the OT theme of personal and corporate responsibility for *purity and holiness with force (Rom 6:17-22; 12:1-2; 1 Cor 5–6; 2 Cor 6:14–7:1; 1 Thess 4:1-7).

Because humans are made to reflect God, they are called to imitate Jesus, his true image, who embodies the character of *God (2 Cor 3:18; Eph 4:13-16). Paul's goal for the moral and spiritual formation of believers is the formation of Christ in them (Gal 4:19; Eph 4:11-13; Rom 8:17, 29; 13:14; Phil 3:21). The imitation of *cruciform love takes center stage as Paul offers Jesus as a paradigm for the Christian life (Hays; Gorman). Scholars debate the degree of Paul's reliance on Jesus traditions, but Jesus' teaching that discipleship requires self-denial, cross-bearing, and following the pattern of the Messiah's life (Mk 8:33-35) find an obvious echo in Paul's application of the imitation of Jesus. Paul's letters feature imitation of this pattern as a guide for believers, rather than rote copying of, for example, Jesus' diet, singleness, or itinerant ministry.

Paul assumes that believers possess the new-*covenant renewal promised by the prophets that would bring obedience (Jer 31:33; Ezek 36:26-27; Rom 2:14-16, 29). In this renewal the people of God are given the Spirit in order to aid in their ethical development, so that imitation is never merely the work of God's people apart from the power of the Spirit. The new life in which Christians walk is *resurrection life (Rom 6:3-13; Eph 1:17–2:10) and new *creation (Gal 6:15).

Paul himself has successfully taken up the task of imitating the Messiah, not least in *suffering for the sake of others. Other Christians are to imitate Paul because he is imitating the Messiah (1 Cor 11:1). Paul can use others as models for imitation (1 Thess 2:14; 2 Cor 8:1-5) if they are accurately imitating Paul and Jesus (Phil 3:17) or mirroring the faith of their father *Abraham, who believed God could bring life out of what was dead (Rom 4:16-21). Conversely, Paul uses moral failures as negative examples to avoid ("these things occurred as examples," 1 Cor 10:6 NIV).

2. Romans.

Although image bearers should reflect the character of God, *sin has resulted in a catastrophic loss of *glory (Rom 1–3). While Paul presents his *gospel and *justification as God's work rather than human work, it is clear that his gospel envisions moral transformation (sanctification or discipleship). Accordingly, Paul stresses the believers' participation in new life in the resurrected Messiah by the Spirit (Rom 5–8) and the new-covenant gift of obedience from the heart (Rom 5:17). This obedience takes the shape of a cruciform life (Rom 8:17, 34-36) characterized by the groaning of *birth pains (Rom 8:22-23). Even if the destination is vindication, enthronement, and the full *adoption of resurrection as God's royal children (Rom 8:15-17, 23-24), the journey must be characterized by the Messiah's suffering.

Paul's moral instruction in the latter section of the book builds on earlier theological themes and relies on implicit imitation of the life and teachings of Jesus. The thematic statement to present one's *body as a living *sacrifice (Rom 12:1-2) is an imitation of Jesus in light of the call to "suffer with him" (Rom 8:17) and the cultic interpretation of Jesus' death (Rom 3:25;

5:9; 1 Cor 5:7). One sees the imitation of God's love (Rom 5:8; 8:37) and mercy (Rom 11:30-32) in the call to love and be merciful (Rom 12:8-10; 13:8). God in Christ loved us while we were enemies (Rom 5:7-10), and we must love our enemies (Rom 12:19-21). It takes scant familiarity with the early stories of Jesus and no great moral imagination to see the conduct of Jesus in many of Paul's injunctions, such as "Do not repay anyone evil for evil" and "Do not take revenge" (Rom 12:17, 19 NIV).

Paul explicitly applies imitation to the difficulties of living in Christian community with those who disagree over matters of *food, diet, and calendar (Rom 14–15). Just as the Messiah did not please himself, believers are to please their neighbors (Rom 15:1-3). God's treatment with "no distinction" (Rom 10:12 NRSV; cf. Rom 3:22, 29) of the *Gentiles results in Paul's call for the covenant community to do the same: "Welcome one another, therefore, just as Christ has welcomed you" (Rom 15:7 NRSV).

3. 1 and 2 Corinthians.

In the letters to the Corinthians, Paul repeatedly employs his spiritual résumé in an effort to lead the struggling church toward maturity. They are to imitate him and the *Lord in a general cruciform pattern of life (1 Cor 4:8-17). The pattern receives more specificity in the discussion of food sacrificed to *idols (1 Cor 8:1–11:1). He concludes the discussion by highlighting the ethical imperative driving the argument in 1 Corinthians 8–10: "Imitate me as I imitate Messiah" (1 Cor 11:1; see Belleville's study of imitation and discipleship). In the idol-meat discussion, Paul repeatedly illustrates his own commitment to lay aside his rights for the sake of others. Paul's discipline is a model for the Corinthians (1 Cor 9:24-27), and his commitment to avoiding offense is a model for them to follow (1 Cor 10:32-33).

Paul opens 2 Corinthians by noting that Paul and his companions are imitating Jesus by suffering for the Corinthians' *salvation (2 Cor 1:6). The Corinthians should imitate God's commitment to comforting his people in suffering; the Corinthians walk in the path of suffering and divine comfort that Paul and his companions have experienced (2 Cor 1:3-5). Another résumé appears in 2 Corinthians 4:7-10 as Paul presents his suffering as after the pattern of the death and resurrection of Jesus. Paul and his companions participate in the *ministry of reconciliation (2 Cor 5:11-21), working with Jesus himself (2 Cor 6:1) and therefore in a cruciform pattern of suffering, an implicit imitation of the rejection and suffering of Jesus (2 Cor 6:3-10). The generosity of Jesus in his humiliation becomes a model for the Corinthians to imitate (2 Cor 8:9). Paul's citation of Psalm 112:9 (2 Cor 9:9) is in its original context an application of the imitation of God (Ps 112 being paired with Ps 111), for in his care for his creatures, God's *righteousness endures forever. Yet another résumé follows in 2 Corinthians 11:21–12:10 to again contrast Paul's sacrificial, Christ-shaped manner of life with the socially acceptable polish of the so-called apostles favored by the Corinthians. Paul is spending his life (2 Cor 12:5) as a sacrifice for the Corinthians, and though Paul and his companions are weak after the pattern of Jesus' weakness, they are powerful in the strength of the Messiah (2 Cor 13:3-4).

All of these passages should inform one's interpretation of 1 Corinthians 2:2, a veritable summary statement of Paul's life and ministry: he has resolved to know nothing but the Messiah and him crucified. Paul becomes a living testament to the suffering Jesus, choosing ministry methods and a lifestyle that comport with serving the crucified Jesus as Lord.

4. Galatians and the Prison Epistles.

Galatians, Ephesians, Philippians, and Colossians reflect the dying-and-rising pattern and participatory emphasis Paul employs in Romans. The letters stress crucifixion to the world on the one hand (Col 2:20; Gal 6:14), and rising to new life with Messiah to live a life empowered by the Spirit and resurrection power on the other (Gal 6:15; Eph 1:19-22). Believers are taught they have (or should) put on new life and behavior (Gal 3:27; Col 3:10-14; Eph 4:24; 6:10-18). The *gifts and work of the Spirit within believers enable imitation (Col 1:28-29; Eph 4:4-13; Gal 5:22-24).

Such themes connect closely to explicit calls to imitate Jesus and Paul. Paul urges the imitation of Jesus' love in the love of husbands for their wives (Eph 5:25-33) and in kindness and *forgiveness (Eph 4:32–5:2; Col 3:13; on love more generally compare Gal 2:20; 5:13-14). Colossians lays special focus on the salvific role of Paul's cruciform ministry. As the Messiah has reconciled through his death (Col 1:21-23), so Paul continues that saving work: "in my flesh I am completing what is lacking in Christ's afflictions for the sake of his body" (Col 1:24 NRSV). Imitation is particularly appropriate since the goal of formation is Christlikeness (Eph 4:13-16).

In these letters Paul repeatedly refers to his imprisonment or other hardships, such as the marks of Jesus branded on his body (Gal 6:17). There are four references in Ephesians alone to Paul's imprisonment. For the Philippians, Paul affirms the imitation of his suffering and hardship, and presents his own patience, *joy, and contentment in the face of such difficulties as an example (Phil 1:29-30; 2:17-18; 4:10-13). Such autobiographical statements commend Paul's cruciform missionary strategy to believers for imitation (Hafemann). That cruciformity is itself an imitation of the suffering and humiliation of the Messiah. Bearing one another's burdens is a Jesus-shaped, cruciform activity (Gal 6:2). The strategy also extends to his willingness to enter the new eschatological era in a life crucified in Messiah, so that while Paul may or may not keep Torah, he is never its slave. He thus calls the Galatians to imitate this way of life (Gal 4:12).

Recent scholarship has overturned the attempts of previous generations to downplay the significance of imitation in Philippians, particularly regarding the so-called Christ *hymn (Phil 2:5-13; cf. Eastman; Fowl). In that passage Paul teaches the Philippians to pursue unity and humility after the example of the Messiah, who humbled himself and took the form of a *slave. Paul shows them how he has rejected any confidence in race, *flesh, or law keeping in favor of resurrection power and pressing on in the Messiah (Phil 3:2-14); he calls the Philippians to imitate this mindset (Phil 3:15, 17). Finally, Paul includes a general call to imitate excellence wherever one finds it. As their chief exemplar, he highlights his own teaching and life as excellent things to be practiced (Phil 4:8-9).

Philemon also carries the theme forward. Paul portrays his sacrificial willingness to take responsibility for any accumulation of obligation on Onesimus's part (Philem 1:18). This is an imitation of the work of a Messiah whose crucifixion wiped away a record of indebtedness (Col 2:14). It is also intended to provoke a burden-bearing, cross-shaped imitative response from Philemon.

5. 1 and 2 Thessalonians and the Pastoral Epistles.

The Thessalonians are to imitate the love shown by Paul and his associates (1 Thess 3:12). They are commanded to mirror Paul's commitment to humility and diligence, particularly by working with their hands and staying fruitful (1 Thess 2:4-11; 4:9-12; 2 Thess 3:6-12). They follow Jesus and Paul's pattern of suffering (1 Thess 1:6), and Paul commends to them the imitation of Judean churches (1 Thess 2:14-17), not least because it means that they would become an example for other churches to follow (1 Thess 1:7).

In the Pastorals Paul models healthy ministry rather than self-centered *leadership, and Timothy and Titus are instructed to imitate him. Readers of these letters are meant to envision Paul as the first link in a chain of faithful instruction, with the quality in each subsequent link dependent on whether teachers accurately follow the "example of sound words" modeled by a predecessor (2 Tim 1:13 NASB; see also 2 Tim 2:2). Timothy is invited to walk in the way of co-suffering with Paul (2 Tim 1:8; 2:3, 10; 3:10-13; 4:5-8). Because Titus and Timothy faithfully imitate Paul, they are children who share the *faith and character of Paul their "father" (1 Tim 1:2; Titus 1:4; cf. 1 Cor 4:15-16). Leaders must likewise set "an example for the believers in speech, in conduct, in love, in faith and in purity" (1 Tim 4:12 NIV; Titus 2:7). Requirements for leadership are not for leaders alone but for believers, who will imitate their character and conduct (1 Tim 3:1-13; aspects of Titus 1:7-8 are applied to all believers in Titus 2). As they shed the immoral behavior of their culture, they should instead imitate God: Cretans always lie, but God never lies (Titus 1:2, 12).

6. Scholarly Attention.

In the portrait of Paul in Acts, the disputed Pauline epistles, and the early centuries of the early church, imitation is much appreciated and consistently described as an essential mode of Pauline ministry (Acts 20:32 35). But imitation has not always been a prominent theme in more recent Pauline scholarship and has not infrequently been entirely neglected. Scholarship has often failed to coordinate Pauline *ethics with broader biblical ethics and instructional norms in the era in question. Soteriological emphases have sometimes eclipsed ethical or missional concerns, suppressing any emphasis on imitation both in the agenda of the academy and in the *mission of the church (Hood).

Older studies dependent on explicit references to imitation overlooked much relevant Pauline material, for many instances of imitation in the NT do not involve specific vocabulary (such as *mimēsis*). Paul's lifestyle and the nascent stories of Jesus tacitly undergird Paul's ethical teaching. Full consideration of theological themes such as participation (Eastman) and union with Christ (Hood; Macaskill, chap. 7) are required to recapture the vision for imitation in Paul and the rest of the New Testament. A focus on imitation in one particular area (for Burridge, the imitation of inclusive love) can be fruitful but may also lead to myopia if an approach obscures the full-orbed imitation of God and Christ.

Consideration of imitation has also suffered from misunderstandings that arise from the use of imitation language. Imitation is rarely if ever rote copying. Rather, it is the conformity of one's life and character to the love of God in Christ and the cross-shaped service of the Messiah for his people. The overt references to imitation, such as 1 Corinthians 11:1, make this clear. The Messiah gave up his rights, and Paul urges the Corinthians to give up a very different set of rights. It is the character and pattern of the Messiah, who laid aside his rights to die for the sake of others, that Paul has in view, not an exact copying of his activities. "Successful imitation of Jesus does not depend on literal crucifixion, and the Corinthians are not failures if they are never shipwrecked like the apostle" (Hood, 12).

See also CRUCIFORMITY; ETHICS; FAITH; IN CHRIST; MINISTRY; SUFFERING.

BIBLIOGRAPHY. **L. L. Belleville,** "'Imitate Me, Just as I Imitate Christ': Discipleship in the Corinthian Correspondence," in *Patterns of Discipleship in the New Testament*, ed. R. N. Longenecker (Grand Rapids, MI: Eerdmans, 1996), 120-42; **R. Burridge,** *Imitating Jesus: An Inclusive Approach to New Testament Ethics* (Grand Rapids, MI: Eerdmans, 2007); **S. G. Eastman,** "Philippians 2:6-11: Incarnation as Mimetic Participation," *JSPHL* 1, no. 1 (2010): 1-22; **S. Fowl,** *The Story of Christ in the Ethics of Paul*, JSNTSup 36 (Sheffield: JSOT Press, 1990); **M. J. Gorman,** *Cruciformity: Paul's Narrative Spirituality of the Cross* (Grand Rapids, MI: Eerdmans, 2001); **S. Hafemann,** "The Role of Suffering in the Mission of Paul," in *The Mission of the Early Church to Jews and Gentiles*, ed. J. Ådna and H. Kvalbein, WUNT 127 (Tübingen: Mohr Siebeck, 2000), 165-84; **R. B. Hays,** *The Moral Vision of the New Testament: A Contemporary Introduction to New Testament Ethics* (San Francisco: HarperSanFrancisco, 1996); **J. B. Hood,** *Imitating God in Christ: Recapturing a Biblical Pattern* (Downers Grove, IL: IVP Academic, 2013); **G. Macaskill,** *Union with Christ in the New Testament* (Oxford: Oxford University Press, 2013); **A. Malherbe,** *Paul and the Popular Philosophers* (Minneapolis: Fortress, 1989); **J. W. Thompson,** *Moral Formation According to Paul: The Context and Coherence of Pauline Ethics* (Grand Rapids, MI: Baker Academic, 2011); **J. A. D. Weima,** "'How You Must Walk to Please God': Holiness and Discipleship in 1 Thessalonians," in *Patterns of Discipleship in the New Testament*, ed. R. N. Longenecker (Grand Rapids: Eerdmans, 1996), 98-119.

J. B. Hood

IMMORTALITY. *See* AFTERLIFE; DEATH; RESURRECTION.

IMPRISONMENT. *See* PRISON, PRISONER.

IMPURITY. *See* PURITY AND IMPURITY.

IN CHRIST

The language of being "in *Christ" (*en Christō*)—that is, "in the Messiah"—permeates the Pauline correspondence. It expresses the fundamental identity of both the individual believer and the believing community (*ekklēsia,* the *church) as a whole. It also conveys Paul's theology and spirituality of participation and transformation. Being "in Christ" is not a static but a dynamic, relational, and missional way of life.

1. Interest in "In Christ": Participation and Union
2. Paul's "In Christ" Language
3. Paul's "In Christ" Narrative
4. Dimensions of Being in Christ
5. Participation and Justification
6. Origins
7. Conclusion

1. Interest in "In Christ": Participation and Union.

Interest in Paul's "in Christ" language and theology, once labeled "Christ mysticism" but now generally called "participation in Christ" or "union with Christ," has grown exponentially in recent years (C. Campbell, 31-58; Davey 2019a; Macaskill 2013, 17-41). The work of A. Schweitzer and A. Deissmann was followed later in the twentieth century by R. C. Tannehill (focusing on suffering) and especially E. P. Sanders. Sanders's highly influential *Paul and Palestinian Judaism* echoed Schweitzer in finding participation ("participationist *eschatology"), not a forensic notion of *justification, to be the heart of Paul's theology.

Sanders did not fully articulate what participation entails. Subsequently, R. B. Hays proposed four main elements: belonging to a family, being in political or military solidarity with Christ, participating in the *ekklēsia*, and living within the Christ story ("narrative participation"; see Hays 2008). C. Campbell named four dimensions of the "metatheme" of union with Christ: union with Christ itself (union by *faith, mutual indwelling, trinitarian and nuptial themes), participation (sharing in the Christ-story), identification (being in Christ's realm, having allegiance to him as *Lord), and incorporation (being part of

Christ's *body). These should not be seen as discrete experiences but as inseparable aspects of one reality.

An informal and diverse "participationist perspective" in Pauline studies has emerged, including M. J. Gorman, B. C. Blackwell, C. Campbell, Hays, G. Macaskill, and many other scholars cited in this article. Participation also figures centrally in other interpreters from various viewpoints, including J. D. G. Dunn (new perspective) and D. Campbell and S. Eastman (*apocalyptic perspective). A few scholars, however, have raised questions about the language of participation. T. Morgan finds Paul's "in Christ" language to signify living under Christ's protection and power rather than participating in him. While not dismissing participation, J. T. Hewitt highlights Paul's messianic theology of solidarity, inclusion, and instrumentality.

2. Paul's "In Christ" Language.
A form of "in Christ" language, using the Greek preposition *en*, occurs more than 160 times in the Pauline corpus, with about two-thirds in the undisputed letters. The language varies somewhat from letter to letter. The most common phrases are "in Christ Jesus," "in Christ," and "in the Lord"; there are also minor variations as well as the phrases "in him" and "in whom," especially in Colossians and Ephesians. It is important to remember that "in Christ" means "in [the] Messiah" (Hewitt), and it is possible that "in the Lord" suggests a different, though complementary, aspect of believers' relationship to Jesus.

The preposition *en* can signify relations other than location (e.g., instrumentality, agency, close association), but Paul's use in these phrases is normally locative, or spatial. Because Christ is the living Lord, this located-ness in him involves personal participation and covenantal relations.

Closely related to the language of *en Christō*, also expressing participation, are phrases containing the preposition *eis* ("into") and phrases and words containing the preposition *syn* ("with"; "co-"). These phrases indicate entrance *into* Christ (e.g., Gal 3:27) and intimate experience—past, present, and future—*with* him (e.g., Gal 2:19; Rom 8:17; 1 Thess 5:10). (See 3.3; 4.4 below.)

3. Paul's "In Christ" Narrative.
Paul's participationist theology may be construed as a *narrative that gives an account of soteriology in terms of both divine and human participation in particular "locations": humanity outside Christ; God's participation with us in Christ; our initial participation with, and transfer into, Christ; being in and with Christ now; and future existence with Christ (similarly, Sun).

3.1. Humanity Outside Christ. Paul believes all human beings exist "in" something and someone; they are shaped by a power and a person, and also by the narrative that defines each person and corresponding "location." People are either "in *Adam," where they find present and future death, or "in Christ," where they find present and future life (Rom 5:12-21; 1 Cor 15:22). To be in Adam is to be shaped by his story of disobedience and its consequences. People who are in Adam, and therefore outside Christ, live also "in the *flesh" (Rom 7:5), that is, they are dominated by the self and its proclivities rather than by God's Spirit (Rom 8:8-9). Life outside Christ is also life "in Sin" (Rom 6:1), that is, in the realm of human existence, where the cosmic powers of *Sin and Death reign. To live in this realm is to be enslaved to Sin (Rom 7:14).

To be in Sin is simultaneously to have Sin within (Rom 7:17, 20); the external power that dominates human beings is also an internal force that makes pleasing *God by fulfilling covenant obligations impossible. This is a relationship of mutual indwelling, analogous to people breathing in the air that also surrounds them. Paul's notion of indwelling Sin as that which prevents covenant fulfillment is a logical antithesis of the prophetic promise that an internalized *Law and Spirit will enable covenant fulfillment (Jer 31:31-34; Ezek 11:17-20; 36:23-28; 37:21-28). As the Adam texts also indicate, the end result of existence in and enslavement to Sin is death (Rom 6:16, 23; 7:7-13) because Death (the power) is Sin's potent accomplice in the cosmic attack on God's good *creation. Living outside Christ means living in the sphere of hostile powers poised against humanity (Rom 8:38; Eph 6:12; Col 1:13; cf. 1 Cor 15:24). This sphere encompasses the culture of *idolatry and immorality/injustice (Rom 1:18-32) that Paul and many Jews perceived in the Greco-Roman world.

This predicament of oppressive mutual indwelling—Sin in people and people in Sin—and its deadly consequences means that humanity is not *what* it was created to be because it is not *where* it was created to be. Paul expresses the solution to this predicament in what Sanders calls "transfer language": transferal from *outside* Christ to *inside* Christ. But before that can occur, God must—and did—do something.

3.2. God's Gracious Participation with Us in Christ. For Paul, talk of participation in Christ must begin with what God has done to rectify the human predicament (see esp. Eastman) and thus consideration of Paul's properly theological "in Christ" language. "God was in Christ reconciling the world to himself" (2 Cor 5:19) succinctly summarizes this saving work. God's redemption (Rom 3:24), *forgiveness (Eph 4:32), gift of eternal life (Rom 6:23; cf. 1 Cor 15:22), justification (Gal 2:16), blessing of the *Gentiles (Gal 3:14), *calling (Phil 3:14; cf. Eph 1:4), riches (Phil 4:19), *grace (2 Tim 1:9), *wisdom and knowledge (Col 2:3), *truth (Eph 4:21), victory (Col 2:15, translating *autō* as "him"), and *love (Rom 8:39) are all divine saving actions or gifts located in Christ—though Christ is not a passive conduit but is active in this divine love (Rom 8:35; 2 Cor 5:14; Gal 2:20; Eph 3:19). "In Christ" is the place of divine grace (1 Cor 1:4; Eph 2:7; 2 Tim 1:9).

Colossians and Ephesians especially emphasize this saving divine presence in Christ, both past and future: "all the *fullness of God" dwelt in Christ (Col 1:19 NRSV; cf. Col 2:9), who was and is the locus of God's grace (Eph 1:6; 2:7). Moreover, the *mystery of the Father's will was "set forth in Christ . . . to gather up all things in him" (Eph 1:9-10 NRSV), and God's life-giving power was on display in Christ at his *resurrection (Eph 1:20).

Although Paul can express similar thoughts about God's activity with the preposition *dia* ("through") to indicate Christ or Christ's death as the instrument of *salvation (e.g., Rom 5:1, 21; Eph 5:1; Phil 1:11; even 2 Cor 5:18), "in Christ" in the texts just cited indicates something other than mere instrumentality: Christ is the "place" where God and God's gifts are given and experienced. The "in Christ" phrases in these sorts of texts may therefore serve double duty. For example, "the redemption that is in Christ Jesus" (Rom 3:24 NRSV), "eternal life in Christ Jesus our Lord" (Rom 6:23 NRSV), and "the law of the Spirit of life in Christ Jesus" (Rom 8:2 NRSV) may refer to the divine gift in Christ; the human experience, in Christ, of that gift; or both. This overlap of meanings exists because God was in Christ so that humans could be in Christ (2 Cor 5:19, 21). Focusing on Christ's own initiative (e.g., Phil 2:6-8; 2 Cor 8:9), L. R. Hogan refers to this two-way participation as Christ's *kenosis* and *enosis* (dwelling among us) that permits our individual and corporate *enosis*, or dwelling in him (cf. Hooker on "interchange" formulas).

3.3. Initial Participation with, and Transfer into, Christ. For those who respond affirmatively to God's redemption in Christ, the result is transfer from the sphere of Sin, Death, the flesh, and the self into Christ. This is not merely a private mystical experience but movement into a new social, covenantal, and spiritual space—the body of Christ, the people of the new covenant, and the realm of the *Holy Spirit (cf. Macaskill 2013).

This transfer/incorporation into Christ takes place by means of faith and its public expression in *baptism, which is a "relocative act" (Macaskill 2019, 61). People are baptized into Christ (Gal 3:27; Rom 6:3), which necessarily means into his body (1 Cor 12:13; cf. Rom 12:5).

Paul also sees faith as a relocative act; people believe *into* (Gk. *eis*) Christ (Gal 2:16: "we have come to faith that incorporates us into [*eis*] Christ Jesus"; cf. Rom 10:14; Phil 1:29), where justification is found. This liberation from the reign of darkness and transfer into the Messiah's reign (Col 1:13) results in "eccentric participation": living in Christ rather than oneself (Macaskill 2019, 5-8, 133). The relocation involves both divine action, generally expressed by passive verbs in the texts just noted, and human action, represented especially by active verbs.

A third key preposition now emerges that is closely associated with "into" (*eis*): "with" (*syn*). Paul also characterizes both faith and baptism as an experience of dying and rising with Christ; relocation comes by means of complete identification with the saving event, or paschal *mystery. Baptism "into Christ Jesus" is "into his death" (Rom 6:3 NRSV), which includes the co-crucifixion of the "old self . . . with him" (Rom 6:6 NRSV; *synestaurōthē*), union with him in a similar death (*symphytoi*), and being "buried with him" (Rom 6:4 NRSV; *synetaphēmen*). Present co-resurrection *in* the body is implied in the phrase "walk in newness of life" (Rom 6:4 NRSV; cf. *syn*-prefix terms in Col 2:12-13; 3:1; Eph 2:5-6), while future co-resurrection *of* the body is explicit in the phrases "united . . . [*symphytoi*] in a resurrection like his" and "live with him" (*syzēsomen*; Rom 6:5, 8 NRSV; cf. 2 Tim 2:11).

Similarly, writing about justification in Galatians 2:15-21, Paul speaks of death to the law as the means of life "to God," further explicated as being "crucified with Christ" (Gal 2:19 NRSV; *synestaurōthē*) and, implicitly, also being raised with him: "no longer I who live . . . Christ who lives in me" (Gal 2:20 NRSV). For Paul the faith that justifies is not merely intellectual (assent) or emotive (trust) but participatory (Pifer; D. Campbell). Paul understands justification as dying and rising with Christ, such that a new self emerges—a self that is in Christ (Gal 2:16) and is clothed with Christ (Gal 3:27), and in whom Christ lives (Rom 8:10). The mutual indwelling of Sin and humanity has been transformed into a new relationship of mutual indwelling: in Christ and Christ within.

Thus participation is a transformative immersion into a living person and his story. Just as immersion into water is a completely participatory experience, so too baptism—and the faith it embodies—means the fullest possible immersion *into* Christ, beginning a new life both *with* and *in* him. Faith and baptism, as two sides of one coin, constitute the means of entering Christ, who is defined by his story. Paul's summary of that story in four clauses, or dramatic "acts," in 1 Corinthians 15:3-9 is likely the basis of the participatory process of relocation described in Galatians and Romans. Believers enter into the narrative of the Messiah's death, burial, resurrection, and appearances—the last "act" (appearances) corresponding to believers' ongoing life in Christ.

4. Dimensions of Being in Christ.

4.1. Identity. For Paul, being in Christ is the fundamental identity of Christ-followers, both individually and corporately. They are "alive to God in Christ Jesus" (Rom 6:11 NRSV); "if anyone is in Christ, new creation!" (2 Cor 5:17). The phrase "in Christ" or "in the Lord" occurs eleven times in Romans 16, as Paul instinctively refers to both *coworkers and everyday believers (e.g., "Andronicus and Junia . . . were in Christ before I was"; Rom 16:7 NRSV). A "person," "saint," or "brother" is someone in Christ/in the Lord (2 Cor 12:2; Phil 4:21; Philem 16). Similarly, Paul understands the primary location of the *ekklēsia* to be in Christ, no matter its geographical location: "To all the saints in Christ Jesus who are in Philippi" (Phil 1:1 NRSV; cf. 1 Cor 1:2; Gal 1:22; Eph 1:1; Col 1:2; 1 Thess 1:1; 2:14; 2 Thess 1:1). A recently revived translation of Philippians 2:5 recognizes that Paul equates "in you" (plural; *en hymin*) with "in Christ" (*en Christō*): "have this mind in your community, which is a community in Christ" (see Gorman 2019a, 77-95).

Macaskill calls this "incorporated identity"; Galatians 2:20 means that Paul (speaking representatively) "is now Paul-in-Christ; Paul-in-himself is a thing of the past" (see Macaskill 2019, 53). Again speaking for all believers, Paul avers that being found in the Messiah is the essence and goal of his life (Phil 3:9; cf. Col 1:28).

This shared, fundamental identity means that binaries are transcended and divisions broken down; there is no longer "outsider" and "insider," for all are *in*siders. Whether "Jew or Greek . . . slave or free . . . male and female," all who have been baptized into Christ are one in him as God's children (Gal 3:28 NRSV). *Slave and free are siblings in the Lord (Philem 16). Interdependence between *men/husbands and *women/wives is the norm in the Lord (1 Cor 11:11). And "neither *circumcision nor uncircumcision" matters in Christ, only Messiah-shaped faith and love (Gal 5:6), since through his faithful, loving death Christ acted to "create in himself one new humanity in place of the two" (Eph 2:15 NRSV; cf. Eph 3:6, 11-12).

The "in Christ" language in Ephesians suggests additional aspects of the church's identity. While remaining on earth, believers are in some sense "with [Christ] in the heavenly places in Christ Jesus," sharing his victory over the cosmic powers (Eph 2:6). Some interpreters of Ephesians (e.g., Jipp, 197-208) focus on sharing in the blessings of Jesus' resurrection life and royal reign, while others (e.g., Macaskill 2013) emphasize the church as God's *temple "in the Lord" (Eph 2:21).

4.2. The Sphere of "the Lord Jesus Christ." All three elements of the rare but full phrase "in the Lord Jesus Christ" (2 Thess 3:12) are significant. To be in Christ is to be incorporated into the one messianic "seed" (Gk. *sperma*; NRSV "offspring") of *Abraham (Gal 3:6-16), "grafted into" the one "olive tree" that is the people of God (Rom 11:13-24), and transferred into the Son's *kingdom (Col 1:13). As expected of ancient kings, Jesus the Messiah establishes a realm of *righteousness, justice, and *peace; those in Christ participate in that dominion (Jipp).

Thus to be in Christ is to live in the sphere of his lordship, his dominion; the fundamental confession of those in his body is "Jesus is Lord" (1 Cor 12:3). It is, therefore, to be in a place of allegiance and obedience, specifically to *Jesus*—a place where life together is patterned after the story of Jesus (e.g., 2 Cor 4:1-15; Phil 2:1-11). It is to be a people formed by the narrative of Jesus' incarnation, death, and resurrection; by his faithful obedience to God the Father; by his acts of self-giving, life-giving love. It is a place that is kenotic and *cruciform because Jesus was a crucified Messiah and remains a loving Lord. To be in the sphere of Christ's cruciform lordship is also to be under his protection, "in his hands" (Morgan).

4.3. In the Spirit, in God the Father. For Paul, "in Christ" also means "in the Spirit" (Rom 8:9; 1 Cor 6:11; Eph 6:18; Phil 2:1; 3:3; Col 1:2, 8). Christ is present in and among his people by the Spirit, who is the Spirit of the Father and—critically for the subject of participation—of the Son (Rom 8:8-9; Gal 4:6; Phil 1:19). To be in the Spirit is to be bound in

Christlike love to both God and others in the body of Christ (see Eastman).

On two occasions Paul identifies the church as being "in God the Father and the Lord Jesus Christ" (1 Thess 1:1, 2 Thess 1:1; cf. Col 3:3; 1 Thess 2:2). Though unusual, this sentiment is not unexpected, since Paul always names God the Father and Christ as the co-givers of grace and peace in his letters. Moreover, since Christ crucified is the revelation of God's power, wisdom, and other attributes (1 Cor 1:18-31), to be in Christ and be "clothed" with him is to inhabit the cruciform God (Gorman 2009). "Ultimately, being united with Christ is salvific because to share his life is to share in the life of God" (Hays 2002, xxxiii).

4.4. Mutual Indwelling and Close Association. As noted above, the mutual indwelling of Sin and people is replaced by the mutual indwelling of Christ and people (Rom 8:2, 10), which is also the mutual indwelling of the Spirit and people (Rom 8:9). This reality of mutual indwelling is true both of individuals (see Gal 2:20 NRSV, "Christ who lives in me"; Gal 1:16, "reveal his Son in me") and of the community as a whole (see 2 Cor 13:5, "Jesus Christ is among you"; Gal 4:19, "until Christ is formed among you"). Colossians speaks of mutual indwelling too: those who have "received" Christ should continue to walk in him (Col 2:6) and mature in him (Col 1:28; cf. Col 2:10), and Christ in/among them is their "*hope of *glory" (Col 1:27). Similarly, the "in Christ" emphasis of Ephesians contains the prayer that "Christ may dwell in your hearts" (Eph 3:17 NRSV; cf. Col 3:15-16).

The "with/co-" language connected with transfer into Christ persists for Paul in believers' present experience. To be *in* Christ is also to be *with* Christ (1 Thess 5:10). Numerous Greek words, especially nouns, speak of life in Christ as being *with fellow believers* (as coparticipants, coworkers, etc., as in Phil 1:27; 2:2, 17-18, 25; 3:17; 4:3, 14), while others, especially verbs, speak of activity *with Christ* (conformity, co-suffering, etc., as in Rom 8:17, 29; see Dunn, 401-4).

4.5. Life: Salvation and Blessing. "In Christ" is also a place of both present and future salvation and blessing, a place of life and righteousness rather than sin, condemnation, and death (e.g., Rom 8:1-3), where people are "dead to sin and alive to God" (Rom 6:11 NRSV; cf. 2 Tim 1:1). Being in Christ, then, means liberation (see Gal 2:4) and life, hence salvation and spiritual blessing. It is therefore a place of hope in the face of death (1 Cor 15:18-19), for all the dead in Christ will be made alive (1 Cor 15:22; 1 Thess 4:16).

Ephesians provides a summary of the Pauline perspective: God the Father "has blessed us in Christ with every spiritual blessing in the heavenly places" (Eph 1:3 NRSV): present redemption, forgiveness (Eph 1:7; see Col 1:14), and a future inheritance of glory (Eph 1:11-14; cf. 2 Tim 2:10). Colossians offers another angle: just as the fullness of God was in Christ (Col 1:19; 2:9), so also believers "come to fullness in him [Christ]" (Col 2:10 NRSV), in whom they have redemption/forgiveness (Col 1:14).

Being in Christ means also being in the presence of his ongoing faithfulness and love/compassion (Gal 2:20; Phil 2:1-4; 2 Tim 1:13). Because of all the blessings present in Christ, the proper posture for those in the Lord is thanksgiving (1 Thess 5:18) and *joy (Phil 3:1; 4:4, 10) combined with hope and trust (Phil 2:19, 24).

4.6. Transformation. A cosmic rearrangement of reality has occurred by God's action in Christ, and now those who have entered Christ have entered that new creation (2 Cor 5:17), composed of individual, corporate, and eventually cosmic transformation. Because God's righteousness/justice (*dikaiosynē*) was manifested in Christ (Rom 1:17; 3:21-26; 1 Cor 1:30), those who are in Christ will be transformed into people who share in that divine *dikaiosynē* (2 Cor 5:21; see Grieb), becoming like God. Paul echoes the OT call to *holiness (e.g., Lev 19:2) and foreshadows the *patristic theme of deification/theosis (Blackwell; Gorman).

Becoming like God occurs by the work of God's Spirit and means becoming like Christ, the *image of God (2 Cor 3:18; 4:4). Those who have "clothed" themselves with Christ (Gal 3:27) must continue to do so (Rom 13:14). The narrative contained in the Christ-poem in Philippians 2:6-11 becomes the norm for existence in Christ (Phil 2:1, 5). In Philippians 2:6-8 Paul presents a story that can be summarized as "although *x*, not *y* but *z*," meaning "although status, not selfish exploitation but self-giving love." This pattern becomes Paul's own—his "ways in Christ Jesus" (1 Cor 4:17 NRSV; cf. 1 Cor 9; 1 Thess 2:5-9)—and the one he commends to all in Christ (1 Cor 11:1). To be in Christ is to be a living exegesis of the Christ-story of faithfulness and love. This participatory transformation has been variously labeled as Christification, Christosis, Christoformity, and cruciformity or *resurrectional* cruciformity (Gorman 2019a). The final outcome of this conformity *to* Christ by being *in* Christ is eschatological co-resurrection, co-glorification, and eternal presence *with* Christ (e.g., Rom 6:8; 8:17, 29; 2 Cor 4:14; Phil 1:23; 3:20-21; 1 Thess 4:17).

4.7. Activity: Mundane and Missional. Since being in Christ is the fundamental location of the church, even mundane activities such as *marriage and *household life are located in the sphere of the Lord (e.g., 1 Cor 7:39; Col 3:18, 20).

Being in Christ is also being in a place of internal and external *mission. *Hospitality (Rom 16:2), greetings (Rom 16:22; 1 Cor 16:19), and love (1 Cor 16:24) are to be offered in the Lord, even across distances. Paul's ongoing teaching and exhortation are in the Lord/in Christ (2 Cor 2:17; 12:19; 2 Thess 3:12; Philem 8). Paul's colleagues are *servants and coworkers in the Lord (e.g., Rom 16:3-13; 1 Thess 5:12; Eph 6:21; Col 4:7). The Corinthians are Paul's "work in the Lord" (1 Cor 9:1), as he is their "father in the Lord" (1 Cor 4:15).

The missional life of Paul (2 Cor 2:12) and of all believers is work undertaken in the Lord (1 Cor 15:58; Col 4:17), enabled by being in him: "I can do all things in [not through] the one who strengthens me" (Phil 4:13; cf. Eph 6:10). To "stand firm in the Lord" (Phil 4:1; 1 Thess 3:8 NRSV) is to maintain a Christ-shaped life of faithfulness and love (e.g., Col 1:4) in spite of difficulties.

Paul describes his imprisonment as his "imprisonment in [not for] Christ" (Phil 1:13, seen in many older versions; cf. Philem 23; Eph 4:1). His suffering there is a *witness to believers and nonbelievers alike (Phil 1:12-14). Affliction is a natural aspect of being in Christ (2 Tim 3:12); it is to suffer in and with Christ (*sympaschomen*, Rom 8:17; see Tannehill; Davey). All such participatory *suffering is ultimately missional (Kok and Dunne; Gorman 2015, esp. 106-41, 281-85, 299-301).

5. Participation and Justification.

Schweitzer proclaimed, "The doctrine of righteousness by faith is . . . a subsidiary crater, which has formed within the rim of the main crater—the mystical doctrine of redemption through being-in-Christ" (Schweitzer, 225). *Pace* Schweitzer, emphasizing participation should not become a way of separating it from justification and thereby marginalizing justification. Sanders rightly argued that "righteousness by faith and participation in Christ ultimately amount to the same thing" (Sanders, 506). Focusing on participation should, then, result in a revised understanding of justification to include participation (e.g., Gal 2:15-21) and transformation (e.g., 2 Cor 5:21). Paul has but one central, participatory notion of salvation: justification by grace through faith as co-crucifixion and co-resurrection with Christ, which effects entrance into Christ and hence into the divine life (see Gorman 2009, 40-104; see also Macaskill).

6. Origins.

Certainty about the origins of Paul's "in Christ" language is unlikely, and there may be multiple antecedents (brief survey: Snodgrass 2016, 423-26). Proposed pagan sources are unconvincing. A linguistic explanation ("in the hands of"; Morgan) is helpful but insufficient. Various OT sources have been suggested, including especially corporate personality, the temple (e.g., Jackson), covenant (e.g., Macaskill, who also stresses temple and the divine glory/Spirit), the stories of Adam and *Israel (e.g., Sun), the Davidic Messiah (e.g., Jipp), and Abraham's seed plus Daniel's son of man (Hewitt).

Furthermore, Ezekiel, Isaiah, and Joel speak of God's pouring out his Spirit on the people (Is 32:15; Ezek 39:29; Joel 2:28), suggesting immersion in the Spirit. Ezekiel connects cleansing water with God's infusion of the Spirit (Ezek 36:25) and promises that the Spirit will be placed *within* the people (Ezek 36:26-27; 37:1-14). The "liquid" metaphor of pouring and the promise of internalization are robust images of participation, even mutual indwelling. Such prophetic images about the Spirit are adopted by John the Baptist, Jesus, and the earliest Christians (including Paul), and expanded with additional liquid images of filling (e.g., Lk 1:41; 4:14; Acts 2:4), immersion (baptism; e.g., Jn 1:33; Acts 1:5; 1 Cor 12:13), and drinking (Jn 7:37-39; 1 Cor 12:13), portraying believers' absorption into the Spirit's activity.

Jesus used metaphors of liquidity to speak of cruciform discipleship as both drinking his cup of suffering and being baptized into his death (Mark 10:38-39), perhaps anticipating Paul. The association of liquid language with believers' relationship to Christ was likely enhanced by the conviction that the Spirit is the means of Jesus' ongoing, postresurrection presence in the world. To be immersed in the Spirit is to be immersed in Christ.

7. Conclusion.

Paul's theology and spirituality of being in Christ fills the pages of his letters. The divine goal for humanity is that in Christ, by sharing in his death and resurrection, people might become like Christ—and thus both more fully human and more like God. Elsewhere in the NT only John's theology and spirituality of abiding in Christ has a similar shape (see also C. Campbell, 417-19).

See also ADAM AND CHRIST; BAPTISM; BODY OF CHRIST; CHRIST, MESSIAH; CHRISTOLOGY; CHURCH; COLOSSIANS, LETTER TO THE; CRUCIFORMITY; EPHESIANS, LETTER TO THE; FLESH;

HOLINESS, SANCTIFICATION; HOLY SPIRIT; IDENTITY; IMAGE OF GOD; MISSION; PRINCIPALITIES AND POWERS; ROMANS, LETTER TO THE; SALVATION; SIN, GUILT; SPIRITUALITY.

BIBLIOGRAPHY. **J. W. Aernie,** "Participation in Christ: An Analysis of Pauline Soteriology," *HBT* 37 (2015): 50-68; **B. C. Blackwell,** *Christosis: Pauline Soteriology in Light of Deification in Irenaeus and Cyril of Alexandria,* rev. ed. (Grand Rapids, MI: Eerdmans, 2016); **C. R. Campbell,** *Paul and Union with Christ: An Exegetical and Theological Study* (Grand Rapids, MI: Zondervan, 2012); **D. A. Campbell,** "Participation and Faith in Paul," in Thate, Vanhoozer, and Campbell, *"In Christ" in Paul,* 37-60; **W. T. Davey,** "Playing Christ: Participation and Suffering in the Letters of Paul," *CurBR* 17 (2019a): 306-31; idem, *Suffering as Participation with Christ in the Pauline Corpus* (Lanham, MD: Lexington Books/ Fortress Academic, 2019b); **A. Despotis,** ed., *Participation, Justification, and Conversion: Eastern Orthodox Interpretation of Paul and the Debate Between "Old and New Perspectives on Paul,"* WUNT 2/442 (Tübingen: Mohr Siebeck, 2017); **J. D. G. Dunn,** *The Theology of Paul the Apostle* (Grand Rapids, MI: Eerdmans, 1998), esp. 390-412; **S. Eastman,** "Oneself in Another: Participation and the Spirit in Romans 8," in Thate, Vanhoozer, and Campbell, *"In Christ" in Paul,* 103-25; **M. J. Gorman,** *Inhabiting the Cruciform God: Kenosis, Justification, and Theosis in Paul's Narrative Soteriology* (Grand Rapids, MI: Eerdmans, 2009); idem, *Becoming the Gospel: Paul, Participation, and Mission* (Grand Rapids, MI: Eerdmans, 2015); idem, *Participation: Paul's Vision of Life in Christ* (Cambridge: Grove Booklets, 2018); idem, *Participating in Christ: Explorations in Paul's Theology and Spirituality* (Grand Rapids, MI: Baker Academic, 2019a); idem, "Romans and the Participationist Perspective," in *Preaching Romans: Four Perspectives,* ed. S. McKnight and J. B. Modica (Grand Rapids, MI: Eerdmans, 2019b), 59-79; **A. K. Grieb,** "'So That in Him We Might Become the Righteousness of God' (2 Cor 5:21): Some Theological Reflections on the Church Becoming Justice," *Ex Auditu* 22 (2006): 58-80; **R. B. Hays,** *The Faith of Jesus Christ: The Narrative Substructure of Gal 3:1–4:11,* 2nd ed. (Grand Rapids, MI: Eerdmans, 2002); idem, "What Is 'Real Participation in Christ'? A Dialogue with E. P. Sanders on Pauline Soteriology," in *Redefining First-Century Jewish and Christian Identities: Essays in Honor of Ed Parish Sanders,* ed. F. E. Udoh et al. (Notre Dame, IN: University of Notre Dame Press, 2008), 336-51; **J. T. Hewitt,** *Messiah and Scripture: Paul's "In Christ" Idiom in Its Ancient Jewish Context,* WUNT 2/522 (Tübingen: Mohr Siebeck, 2020); **L. R. Hogan,** *I Live, No Longer I: Paul's Spirituality of Suffering, Transformation, and Joy* (Eugene, OR: Wipf & Stock, 2017); **M. D. Hooker,** *From Adam to Christ: Essays on Paul* (Cambridge: Cambridge University Press, 1990); **D. Jackson,** *Glory in the Letters of Paul: Assimilation, Temple, and Participation,* BZNW 240 (Berlin: de Gruyter, 2020); **J. W. Jipp,** *Christ Is King: Paul's Royal Ideology* (Minneapolis: Fortress, 2015), 139-271; **J. Kok and J. A. Dunne,** "Participation in Christ and Missional Dynamics in Galatians," in Despotis, *Participation, Justification, and Conversion,* 59-85; **G. Macaskill,** *Union with Christ in the New Testament* (Oxford: Oxford University Press, 2013); idem, *Living in Union with Christ* (Grand Rapids, MI: Baker Academic, 2019); **T. Morgan,** *Being "in Christ" in the Letters of Paul: Saved Through Christ and in His Hands,* WUNT 449 (Tübingen: Mohr Siebeck, 2020); **J. H. Pifer,** *Faith as Participation: An Exegetical Study of Some Key Pauline Texts,* WUNT 2/486 (Tübingen: Mohr Siebeck, 2019); **D. G. Powers,** *Salvation Through Participation: An Examination of the Notion of the Believers' Corporate Unity with Christ in Early Christian Soteriology,* CBET 29 (Leuven: Peeters, 2001); **E. P. Sanders,** *Paul and Palestinian Judaism: A Comparison of Patterns of Religion,* 40th anniversary ed. (Minneapolis: Fortress, 2017 [Philadelphia: Fortress, 1977]); **A. Schweitzer,** *The Mysticism of Paul the Apostle,* trans. W. Montgomery (Baltimore: Johns Hopkins University Press, 1998 [1930]); **K. Snodgrass,** "The Gospel of Participation," in *Earliest Christianity Within the Boundaries of Judaism: Essays in Honor of Bruce Chilton,* ed. A. J. Avery-Peck, C. A. Evans, and J. Neusner (Boston: Brill, 2016), 413-30; idem, "Baptized into Christ: Romans 6:3-4—*the* Text on Baptism and Participation," in *Cruciform Scripture: Cross, Participation, and Mission,* ed. Nijay K. Gupta et al. (Grand Rapids, MI: Eerdmans, 2020), 106-22; **W. Sun,** *A New People in Christ: Adam, Israel, and Union with Christ in Romans* (Eugene, OR: Pickwick, 2018); **R. C. Tannehill,** *Dying and Rising with Christ: A Study in Pauline Theology,* BZNW 32 (Berlin: de Gruyter, 1967); **M. J. Thate, K. J. Vanhoozer, and C. R. Campbell,** eds., *"In Christ" in Paul: Explorations in Paul's Theology of Union and Participation,* rev. ed. (Grand Rapids, MI: Eerdmans, 2018).

M. J. Gorman

INSPIRED UTTERANCE. *See* GIFTS OF THE SPIRIT; PROPHECY, PROPHESYING; TONGUES.

INTERCESSION. *See* HOLY SPIRIT; PRAYER.

INTERMEDIATE STATE. *See* BODY; ESCHATOLOGY; RESURRECTION.

INTERPRETATION OF PAUL

Over the past few decades, there has developed a surge of interest in the reader as an interpreter of the Pauline *letters. The idea of an objective, neutral, unbiased, or presuppositionless reader is naive, and the notion that bringing one's experiences and culture to the act of reading jeopardizes serious academic engagement is worth questioning. Interpretation through reading involves two horizons (to borrow language from Anthony Thiselton), reflecting a relationship between text and reader that includes both objective and subjective dimensions. Put another way, the reader brings their whole self, their community and culture, their experiences and values to the reading phenomenon, not just one part of their brain.

With this reality in mind, the following set of articles surveys and discusses two types of reception and community conversations in scholarship. One type involves influential interpreters of Paul throughout the years such as Augustine, Martin Luther, and John Calvin. Here also are included formative eras such as the patristic and medieval periods and modern European biblical scholarship. Understanding the past sheds light on Pauline scholarship then and now. A second set of articles looks at certain reading communities and what they bring to the conversation, such as African American and *Latinamente* readings. A reader's living world shapes their reading and interpretation, and all readers can learn from insights and perspectives from other communities.

It will become clear that this set of articles is far from comprehensive. A whole dictionary could easily be filled with fascinating and important historical, contextualized readings. But included here are several key conversations from leading Pauline scholars.

N. K. Gupta

INTERPRETATION: AFRICAN AMERICAN

African American biblical interpretation is a product of resilience, *hope, and resistance in the face of the *violence and discrimination that accompanies life at the bottom of the United States' stratified society. Despite their shared history, African Americans are not monolithic, so there are diverse Christian expressions among African Americans and no single interpretive posture toward the Bible. However, African American biblical interpretations share some common characteristics, which are meant to affirm African American identity, resist racism and other forms of oppression, highlight the presence of Africans in the Scriptures, and offer hope for the continual progress of African Americans in the world (Hunt; Edwards; McCaulley). To some extent, African American biblical interpretation is a rejoinder to oppressive readings of the Bible, including the Pauline corpus, which served to justify the enslavement of Africans by Europeans. African American biblical interpretation, however, is not entirely reactionary but highlights God's justice, liberation, equity, and dignity for all. Europeans established their identity and justified their behavior with the Bible, so African Americans associated the Bible with power and began to engage the Scriptures in a "self-interested, affirming manner" (Wimbush). Consequently, the Bible became a book that spoke to African American realities, revealing a God who hates injustice and liberates the oppressed.

The history of African American biblical interpretation dates back to the early eighteenth century, so only a brief overview appears here, followed by some key aspects of the diverse field. Some of the aims of womanist biblical interpretation—an integral part of African American interpretation—are noted, followed by an analysis of African Americans' ambivalent relationship with the Pauline corpus.

1. Historical Overview of African American Biblical Interpretation
2. Features of African American Biblical Interpretation
3. Womanist Biblical Interpretation
4. African Americans and Pauline Writings

1. Historical Overview of African American Biblical Interpretation.

Upon embracing Christian *faith, African Americans interpreted the Bible through the grid of their own experiences, as do all other Bible readers. African-American biblical interpretation is part of what has been called *postmodern* interpretative practices that take seriously social location and supplement—or sometimes reject—historical-critical methodologies (Edwards). African American biblical interpretation arises out of historical circumstances in the Americas. As Mitzi Smith asserts, "The history of Africans in the New World is marked by the capture and forced exile of Africans from their homeland," so consequently, "the ultimate hermeneutical goal of enslaved Africans was, of course, freedom from bondage" (M. J. Smith, 5). Lisa Bowens, who focuses on Pauline *hermeneutics, offers a perspective that could be applied to biblical interpretation generally: "In a true sense, African American Pauline hermeneutics are intricately tied to *Geschichte*, or history. The two cannot be divorced. . . . The actions of slaveholders and their ministers shaped African American interpretations of Paul, for many blacks saw the hypocrisy in the behavior of whites who loved and preached the apostle" (Bowens, 4).

The Christianity generally practiced by whites in the antebellum South served to justify the enslavement of Africans in the Americas by selectively citing Scripture in support of *slavery and by presenting a perverted picture of God as an enslaver. In the United States, where enslaved people were largely forbidden to learn how to read, the Bible was mediated through white preachers, who typically supported the status quo. In the British West Indies—places including present-day Jamaica, Barbados, and Antigua—missionaries and preachers published a redacted set of Scriptures in 1807 titled *Parts of the Holy Bible, selected for the use of the Negro Slaves, in the British West-India Islands*. This abridged version of the Bible excised passages that could be taken as denouncing the practice of slavery or that might incite rebellion. God was presented as not only allowing the enslavement of Africans but commanding it through the so-called curse of Ham, found in Genesis 9:20-27, which was the most prominent biblical rationale for slavery offered by white Christians of the nineteenth century (Powery and Sadler; Yamauchi). Proponents of the curse-of-Ham perspective viewed Africans as descendants of Noah's son Ham and destined to be enslaved to Europeans.

Despite being bludgeoned by the so-called curse of Ham and the "slaves, obey your masters" passages of the NT (e.g., Col 3:22), African Americans began to see themselves in the Scriptures in increasingly positive ways. The music of Black spirituals demonstrates how enslaved people came to associate their story with that of oppressed yet faithful heroes in the Bible. Enslaved people sang not only of their troubles but also of *joy, resistance, and hope (Cone 1980; Blount 1995; 2005; Sutherland). Enslaved African Americans, in addition to seeing themselves in the Scriptures, came to view God differently from how their enslavers presented him. God was a liberator who brought his people out of bondage. In time, the numbers of enslaved, formerly enslaved, and freeborn African Americans who interpreted Scripture grew. In the eighteenth to nineteenth centuries, several notable preachers and interpreters of Scripture emerged, such as Jupiter Hammon, Lemuel Haynes, Jarena Lee, and Zilpha Elaw (the latter two being woman who expressed their own calls to *ministry by appealing to Paul) (Bowens). African American students of the Bible were eventually able to attend universities and seminaries, and with their formal education helped to describe and employ the hermeneutical lenses that many African Americans bring to the Bible, confronting and sometimes contradicting the approach of many Eurocentric Bible readers.

2. Features of African American Biblical Interpretation.

While African American exegetes naturally employ a variety of methodologies and reach different conclusions, the four following areas receive the greatest amount of attention.

2.1. Liberation. The exodus story of Israel's deliverance from slavery to *freedom became paradigmatic for African American Bible readers. Allen Dwight Callahan describes how influential the exodus was for enslaved Africans (Callahan, 83-137). Anthony Hunt points out that "the exodus motif is reinforced by the famous Lukan text in which Jesus announces his own ministry of liberation (Luke 4:18)" (Hunt, 304). Not only does African American biblical interpretation depict God as liberator, but it also draws on prophetic and other biblical passages that summon God's people to engage in the work of liberation on behalf of others (e.g., Amos 5:24). The prophetic witness of many Black churches throughout US history, notably—but not limited to—the years of the civil rights movement, testifies of a commitment to freedom for oppressed people with the Spirit of God providing guidance through the Bible.

2.2. Resistance. The civil rights movement exemplifies how liberation and resistance are tied together and woven into African American biblical interpretation and ecclesial tradition. As Brian Blount asserts, "At every critical stage in its existence, the Black Church has preoccupied itself with the task of finding a way to respond appropriately to the racially charged context that conceived it and gave it birth" (Blount 2005, 42). The response to injustice has sometimes been resistance, as under Martin Luther King Jr.'s leadership. Blount finds in the hymns of Revelation a theme of resistance that runs parallel to themes within much of African American music—encompassing spirituals, the blues, gospel, and hip-hop (Blount 2005).

The unity of all humanity has long been affirmed by African American interpreters, with Acts 17:26

being a key passage. These words, flowing from the mouth of the *apostle Paul as recorded by Luke, celebrate humanity's shared ancestry. African American Christians, in reading Acts 17:26, saw themselves within God's grand story despite the way many white Christians distorted that story. Bowens observes, "Acts 17:26, in which Paul states that God has made of one blood all the nations of the earth, is the *sine qua non* for many African Americans in their understanding of who Paul is and what he believes" (299). Resistance entails reading passages such as Acts 17:26 or Galatians 3:28 and finding motivation for actively opposing racism and other injustices.

2.3. *African Presence in the Bible.* The early twentieth-century song "Lift Every Voice and Sing," known as the Black national anthem, serves as inspiration for the titles of compendia by African American biblical scholars: *Stony the Road We Trod* (Felder 1991), *Yet with a Steady Beat* (Bailey), *True to Our Native Land* (see Sadler; A. Smith; St. Clair), and *Bitter the Chastening Rod* (Smith, Parker, and Dunbar). Two lines of the song, "True to our God / True to our native land," communicate the desire for African Americans to continuously be mindful of and respectful toward the continent of Africa.

At times it appeared Africa had been nearly deleted from the Scriptures, as white interpreters generally overlooked African presence (see Sadler). Charles Copher is credited as one of the earliest African American scholars to highlight the presence of Africans in the Bible. Hunt frames well some of the questions related to African presence in the Scriptures: "Who were the Cushites, the Nabateans, the Egyptians, and other African peoples in the Bible? Where were Cyrene, Niger, Sheba, and other locations that are mentioned? Who were the Queen of Sheba (1 Kgs 10:1-3) . . . Ebed-melech (Jer 38:7-13), Hagar (Gen 16:1-3), Simon of Cyrene (Mark 15:12), and the Ethiopian eunuch (Acts 8:27-39)?" (Hunt, 301).

Failure to recognize or affirm the presence of Africa and Africans in the Bible diminished the significance of the continent and the people who came from the continent (see Yamauchi 2004). Africana studies, archaeology, and other explorations of the ancient Near East assisted African American biblical scholars to "direct our attention to Africa rather than away from Africa" (M. J. Smith, 36). Writing from historical and missiological perspectives, Vince Bantu looks toward Africa and argues, "The church has two interrelated and indispensable tasks going forward: (1) the deconstruction of the Western, white cultural captivity of the Christian tradition and (2) the elevation of non-Western expressions of Christianity" (Bantu, 6). Bantu approaches those two goals from missiological and historical frameworks, yet Black biblical scholars have essentially the same goals. Biblical exegesis that honors the role of Africans not only increases the Bible's relevance for people of African descent; it also gives a truer picture of the overall biblical story.

2.4. *Affirmation of Black Personhood.* Connected to the African presence in the Bible is the affirmation of Black personhood. The power encompassed by whiteness caused blackness to be associated with negative notions such as physical ugliness, lewd behavior, laziness, and other degrading characteristics (see Byron for analysis of blackness in early Christianity). African American biblical interpreters connect biblical characters and situations to circumstances that many African Americans have had to face. For example, Esau McCaulley explores several issues at the forefront of contemporary African American life, such as political witness and policing. Willie Jennings interprets the entire book of Acts keeping the African American experience in view. Blount does similarly with Revelation and NT ethics (Blount 2001; 2005). James Cone, followed by many other scholars, characterizes Jesus as "Black" largely because of his marginalized existence (Cone 1997; Douglas). These scholars invite African American readers to discover a *Lord in solidarity with them and their plight in society.

3. Womanist Biblical Interpretation.

The distinctive perspective that Black women bring to Scripture includes that of womanists. Nyasha Junior lists three characteristics of womanist biblical interpreters: "First, they critique what is perceived as white feminism's focus on gender to the exclusion of other factors such as race and class and its preoccupation with the particular concerns of white women. Second, they address the simultaneity of multiple and overlapping oppressions, such as racism, classism, and sexism. Third, they foreground the experiences of African American women" (Junior, 15). Clarice Martin's analysis of *doulos* ("slave," "*servant"), especially in Pauline texts, is an example of how womanist scholars critique translations as well as interpretations of the Bible that give justification for oppressive perspectives and practices. Martin explains, "A womanist critical hermeneutics, then, must not only critique the tendencies of the biblical writers and traditioning processes themselves, but must also analyze contemporary scholarly and popular interpretations and appropriations of those traditions, and the underlying theoretical models"

(60). With specific reference to Paul's use of *doulos*, Martin asserts, "A womanist biblical hermeneutic must clarify whether the *doulos* texts, potential 'texts of terror' for black people, can in any way portend new possibilities for our understanding of what actually constitutes the radicality of the Good News of the Gospel" (Martin, 60). Although not all African American women biblical interpreters identify themselves as womanists, Black women bring a distinctive perspective that seeks to promote wholeness without diminishing others (see St. Clair).

4. African Americans and Pauline Writings. Supporters of the 1850 Fugitive Slave Act invoked Paul's letter to Philemon since it urges the return of an enslaved person to his Christian master, even though many interpreters today read Philemon as a challenge to Greco-Roman slavery. Onesimus, who likely was enslaved by Philemon, finds his way to the imprisoned apostle Paul and becomes a follower of Jesus. Paul intends for Onesimus to return to Philemon and in the letter urges Philemon to receive Onesimus, "no longer as a slave but more than a slave, a beloved brother" (Philem 16 NRSV). Some scholars see Paul urging for manumission, while others see Philemon being urged to treat Onesimus as a fellow Jesus-follower regardless of Greco-Roman society's hierarchy.

As numbers of African American biblical scholars increase, so does attention to Paul's letter to Philemon, particularly because of America's history as a nation built on the backs of enslaved people. Interpretive approaches to Philemon are influenced by different perspectives on slavery. Contemporary readers of Scripture, especially among African Americans and other marginalized groups, cannot gloss over the topic of slavery or confine it to a distant past, as some earlier interpreters did. That the apostle Paul never condemns slavery outright—even in his letter to Philemon—is problematic for many interpreters.

African American interactions with Pauline writings have ranged from what Abraham Smith calls "reverential appropriation" to "radical rejection" (A. Smith, 34-46). McCaulley suggests there are three streams of traditional Black biblical interpretation, "revolutionary/nationalistic, reformist/transformist, and conformist," and largely focuses on Pauline writings (McCaulley, 183). Paul is especially problematic because the instructions to enslaved Christian in Colossians 3:22 (along with Eph 6:5 and 1 Pet 2:18—all part of so-called *household codes) were favorites of American enslavers. It is not surprising that African American "slaves and ex-slaves refused to respect texts that justified their exploitation" (Blount 2001, 120). Not all African American readers of Paul throughout history have been suspicious of Paul even though they were suspicious of Paul's white interpreters. However, some African Americans apply a hermeneutic of suspicion with Paul's writings because of the ways his writings were used. It has become commonplace to recount the anecdote from mid-twentieth-century theologian, poet, and mystic Howard Thurman that his grandmother Nancy Ambrose—who had been enslaved—welcomed his reading the Bible to her, but never from any of Paul's writings because of how frequently "slaves, obey your masters" had been preached to her and others.

However, despite the oppressive use of Paul, a significant number of African American Christians find what Blount calls "theology enabling liberating ethics" (Blount 2001, 119-57). For Blount, Pauline theology offers words of liberation—at least sometimes. Blount discovers in Paul boundary-breaking teaching despite seeing problems with Paul and with the interpreters of Paul. With Galatians 3:28 in view, Blount observes, "Paul's theology has as one of its primary goals the breaking down of religious, social, and political boundaries between Jews and Gentiles in the first-century believing communities" (Blount 2001, 123). Lisa Bowens provides a reception history of Paul among African Americans from the early eighteenth through the twenty-first centuries and demonstrates how Paul has not always been met with resistance or suspicion. Bowens follows Vincent Wimbush and Rosamond Rodman and asks, "What happens when African Americans are at the center of Pauline interpretation?" (Bowens, 292). When African Americans place themselves at the center of Pauline interpretation, increasing attention gets paid to issues of justice, equity, unity, and dignity for all of humanity.

See also Freedom/Liberty; Households and Household Codes; Slave, Slavery.

BIBLIOGRAPHY. **R. C. Bailey,** ed., *Yet with a Steady Beat: Contemporary U.S. Afrocentric Biblical Interpretation*, SemeiaSt 42 (Atlanta: Society of Biblical Literature, 2003); **V. L. Bantu,** *A Multitude of All Peoples: Engaging Ancient Christianity's Global Identity* (Downers Grove, IL: IVP Academic, 2020); **B. K. Blount,** *Cultural Interpretation: Reorienting New Testament Criticism* (Minneapolis: Fortress, 1995); idem, *Then the Whisper Put On Flesh: New Testament Ethics in an African American Context* (Nashville: Abingdon, 2001); idem, *Can I Get a Witness? Reading Revelation Through African American*

Culture (Louisville, KY: Westminster John Knox, 2005); **L. M. Bowens,** *African American Readings of Paul: Reception, Resistance, and Transformation* (Grand Rapids, MI: Eerdmans, 2020); **G. L. Byron,** *Symbolic Blackness and Ethnic Difference in Early Christian Literature* (London: Routledge, 2002); **G. L. Byron and V. Lovelace,** "Introduction: Methods and the Making of Womanist Biblical Hermeneutics," in *Womanist Interpretations of the Bible: Expanding the Discourse*, ed. G. L. Byron and V. Lovelace, SemeiaSt (Atlanta: SBL Press, 2016); **A. D. Callahan,** *The Talking Book: African Americans and the Bible* (New Haven, CT: Yale University Press, 2008); **J. H. Cone,** *The Spirituals and the Blues: An Interpretation* (Westport, CT: Greenwood, 1980); idem, *God of the Oppressed* (Maryknoll, NY: Orbis Books, 1997); **C. P. Copher,** "The Black Presence in the Old Testament," in *Stony the Road We Trod: African American Biblical Interpretation*, ed. C. H. Felder (Minneapolis: Fortress, 1991), 146-64; **K. B. Douglas,** *The Black Christ* (Maryknoll, NY: Orbis, 1994); **D. R. Edwards,** "Hermeneutics and Exegesis," in *The State of New Testament Studies: A Survey of Recent Research*, ed. S. McKnight and N. Gupta (Grand Rapids, MI: Baker, 2019), 63-82; **C. H. Felder,** *Troubling Biblical Waters: Race, Class, and Family* (Maryknoll, NY: Orbis Books, 1990); idem, ed., *Stony the Road We Trod: African American Biblical Interpretation* (Minneapolis: Fortress, 1991); **B. L. Fields,** *Introducing Black Theology: Three Crucial Questions for the Evangelical Church* (Grand Rapids, MI: Baker Academic, 2001); **C. A. Hunt,** "African American Biblical Interpretation," in *Scripture and Its Interpretation: A Global, Ecumenical Introduction to the Bible*, annotated ed., ed. M. J. Gorman (Grand Rapids, MI: Baker Academic, 2017), 298-310; **W. J. Jennings,** *Acts: A Theological Commentary on the Bible* (Louisville, KY: Westminster John Knox, 2017); **N. Junior,** *An Introduction to Womanist Biblical Interpretation* (Louisville, KY: Westminster John Knox, 2015); **C. J. Martin,** "Womanist Interpretations of the New Testament: The Quest for Holistic and Inclusive Translation and Interpretation," *JFSR* 6 (1990): 41-61; **E. McCaulley,** *Reading While Black: African American Biblical Interpretation as an Exercise in Hope* (Downers Grove, IL: IVP Academic, 2020); **E. B. Powery and R. S. Sadler Jr.,** *The Genesis of Liberation: Biblical Interpretation in the Antebellum Narratives of the Enslaved* (Louisville, KY: Westminster John Knox, 2016); **R. S. Sadler,** "Africa and African Imagery in the Bible," in *True to Our Native Land: An African American New Testament Commentary*, ed. B. K. Blount, C. H. Felder, C. J. Martin, and E. B. Powery (Minneapolis: Fortress, 2007), 23-30; **A. Smith,** "Paul and African American Biblical Interpretation," in *True to Our Native Land: An African American New Testament Commentary*, ed. B. K. Blount, C. H. Felder, C. J. Martin, and E. B. Powery (Minneapolis: Fortress, 2007), 35-36; **M. J. Smith,** *Insights from African American Interpretation*, Insights: Reading the Bible in the 21st Century (Minneapolis: Fortress, 2017); **M. J. Smith, A. N. Parker, and E. Dunbar,** eds., *Bitter the Chastening Rod: Africana Biblical Interpretation After Stony the Road We Trod in the Age of BLM, Sayhername, and Metoo* (Lanham, MD: Lexington Books, 2022); **R. St. Clair,** "Womanist Biblical Interpretation," in *True to Our Native Land: An African American New Testament Commentary*, ed. B. K. Blount, C. H. Felder, C. J. Martin, and E. B. Powery (Minneapolis: Fortress, 2007), 54-62; **A. Sutherland,** *I Was a Stranger: A Christian Theology of Hospitality* (Nashville: Abingdon, 2006); **V. L. Wimbush,** "The Bible and African Americans: An Outline of an Interpretive History," in *Stony the Road We Trod: African American Biblical Interpretation*, ed. C. H. Felder (Minneapolis: Fortress, 1991), 81-97; **V. L. Wimbush and R. C. Rodman,** eds., *African Americans and the Bible: Sacred Texts and Social Textures* (New York: Continuum, 2000); **E. M. Yamauchi,** *Africa and the Bible* (Grand Rapids, MI: Baker Academic, 2004).

D. R. Edwards

INTERPRETATION: ASIAN AND ASIAN AMERICAN

All who read Paul interpret his letters with their preunderstanding and cultural background. The Asian and Asian American interpretation of Paul is complex and multilayered simply because "Asian" or "Asian American" as a category is itself a complex (and unstable) signifier. Geographically speaking, Asia as a continent covers all the way to Europe and the Middle East. Linguistically, Asia has thousands of different languages. Asia is culturally, socially, and politically diverse. What defines "Asia," then, is indeed a difficult question to answer. According to R. S. Sugirtharajah, Asia is typically divided into four categories: "West Asia (the Arab world), Central Asia (republics of the former Soviet Union), East Asia (extending to the western Pacific nations), and South Asia (sub-Himalayan countries, sometimes referred to as 'the subcontinent')" (Sugirtharajah 2013, 3). Asian hermeneutics, therefore, becomes a site of dialogue for this plurality of perspectives (Lim). These complexities of the Asian contextual condition are reflected in the great variety of readings of Paul.

The same issue also faces Asian Americans. Because of the diversity of experiences of Asian Americans, Tat-siong Benny Liew argues that Asian American biblical hermeneutics has to be in conversation with Asian American studies. It is the task of Asian scholars to "bridge" Asian American studies and biblical scholarship (Liew 2002). For Liew, Asian American hermeneutics is not only about the "who" and the "what," for that risks excluding many people and ideas (Liew 2008, 4). In short, one cannot claim that because one is Asian American one's interpretation is (the) Asian American interpretation. Nor can one say that one cannot do an Asian American reading of Scripture because one is not an Asian American. Not only are such claims exclusionary, but Liew argues that they are also colonial and essentialist (Liew 2008, 5). Asian American biblical interpretation, therefore, becomes complex interdisciplinary work. In the words of Mary Foskett, "Asian American biblical criticism may best be understood as a dynamic network of voices, perspectives, and strategies" (Foskett, 112). This article briefly describes the trends in the interpretation of Paul in Asian and Asian American contexts.

1. Interpretation of Paul in the Asian Context
2. Interpretation of Paul in the Asian American Context

1. Interpretation of Paul in the Asian Context. It is worth noting from the outset that the interpretation of Paul in Asia has been profoundly influenced by Western discourses on Paul. This should not be a surprise because biblical scholarship developed in both Europe and North America has also been transferred to Asia through the internet, education, missionaries, and many other means. The globalization of Western culture, in other words, goes hand in hand with the globalization of Western biblical scholarship. Many Asian scholars are educated in the Western educational system. Many books authored by white male biblical scholars are not only translated into Asian languages but also used as textbooks in biblical studies classes. As Chin Ming Stephen Lim notes, "Many Asian communities are being brought into conversation that may not be of a priority in their own contexts or [indeed] totally irrelevant" (Lim, 29). In other words, there is a gap between Western Pauline scholarship and the life of people in Asia.

Asian reading strategy, according to Sugirtharajah, often takes two forms: metropolitan and vernacular reading. Metropolitan reading refers to a mode of interpretation that engages Western globalized *hermeneutics with a clear goal in mind: "to meet Asian needs" (Sugirtharajah 1994, 252). Vernacular reading, on the other hand, is an effort to look into "Asia's past" and "to reclaim ancient reading theories and methods of story telling" (Sugirtharajah 1994, 253). Pauline scholarship in Asia is often marked by a reaction to the dominance of Western biblical scholarship and methodologies developed in the West. Asian Pauline scholarship, at least the works that are available in the English language, displays a strong metropolitan mode of reading.

Paul and his letters have historically been used in Asia to justify British colonization. In nineteenth-century India, for instance, missionaries used Paul and interpreted his works to support British imperial rule and the establishment of the Church of England in India. Missionaries would identify themselves with Paul and the Indians with the people whom Paul converted. Paul's letter to the Colossians was one of the favorite texts in the writings of the English missionaries (Das). Bengali thinkers, on the other hand, looked to Paul for inspiration to rebel against the British. "Unlike missionary narratives," Shinjini Das explains, "the Bengali renderings emphasized Paul as an anti-imperial character. He was described to be fighting the imperial forces, as much as fighting Judaism, to spread early Christianity" (Das, 126). Paul's letter to the Philippians, recounting his experience as a Roman prisoner, and his letter to Philemon, in which he frees a *slave, became important texts for the Bengali interpreters (Das, 126).

Sugirtharajah's book *The Bible and Asia* devotes an entire chapter to Paul. Sugirtharajah points out that missionaries often used Paul's letters as a guidebook for new converts. Those missionaries regarded his letters as "offering solutions to 'daily difficulties and problems,'" while they dismissed Hindu sacred writings "as 'philosophical disquisitions on the meaning of life,' containing 'ritual directions' and 'hymns which wrestle with the mystery of external nature,' which had 'little relation to the ordinary life'" (Sugirtharajah 2013, 160). Thus Paul became the tool for the civilizing mission in the colonies. Further, pointing to the works of Bernard Lucas, the founder of United Theological College in Bangalore, India, Sugirtharajah argues that Lucas "cast Paul as a person who gave birth to a Christian imperialism" (Sugirtharajah 2013, 163). For missionaries such as

Lucas, Paul's missionary movement did not contradict the Roman Empire at all: Paul was a "an ideal imperial hero, a loyal, nonpolitical citizen of the empire, one to be emulated" (Sugirtharajah 2013, 162). Yet some Indians found Paul unhelpful for their fight against British imperial rule. Sugirtharajah points to the works of J. C. Kumarappa, who thinks that Paul's insistence that government is appointed by *God in Romans 13 is "weak," for if this is the case, no one could do anything about Hitler and Mussolini (Sugirtharajah 2013, 164).

In the Korean context, Jae Won Lee offers a critique of the Western interpretation of Paul's discourse on difference in Galatians 2 and Romans 14–15 as a construction of a universal religion. This universal scope of Christianity is in direct opposition to Jewish particularism. "Western Christianity tactfully employed the Pauline discourse of there being 'no distinction between Jews and Gentiles' as one of the main proof texts for the purposes of its own missionary and imperial universalism" (Lee, 173). In this construction of universalism, Korean identity is erased and subjugated under Western Christian identity. Unfortunately, Lee points out, many Korean Christians have adopted this understanding of Paul as a preacher of universal religion. "It is as if the closer Asian Christians imitate the content and patterns of Western Christianity, the closer they get to the (soteriological) core of the Christian faith. In this way, Korean Christianity is not only fully assimilated to but also deeply colonized by Western cultural imperialism" (Lee, 174). Lee argues that this imperialist understanding of Paul needs to be revisited in light of the experiences of *minjung* (a Korean word meaning "the people"), framing her discussion mainly in postcolonial and feminist terms. *Minjung* thinkers in both North and South Korea, according to Lee, have come to the realization that "the unity of the Korean people and nation cannot be accomplished by the logic of one side absorbing the other—a reunification that would mean sameness—but [by] a new pattern of confederated reunification—equivalent to unity with difference" (Lee, 177).

Among Chinese communities, the issue of filial piety in the form of ancestor veneration has become a serious issue because, as K. K. Yeo points out, "most missionaries, both Protestant and Roman Catholics, prohibited ritualistic practice of ancestor worship on the grounds that ancestor worship is rooted in filial pietism, a religious exercise in which the Chinese are unintentionally offering food to idol-demons instead of to their ancestors" (Yeo, 294). Arguing against missionaries' strict prohibition of ancestor veneration, Yeo then rereads Paul's discussion on idol meat in 1 Corinthians 8, paying a closer attention to its rhetorical strategies. Yeo concludes that at the rhetorical core of Paul's discourse is *knowledge and *love. A yes/no option is not a Pauline way of responding to the issue of idol meat. Therefore, to prohibit ancestor worship/veneration completely is tantamount to "misapproriat(ing) his theology" (Yeo, 311). Because Paul's theology has to be understood through his rhetoric, the appropriation of Paul's *teaching can take different forms in different contexts. In a Chinese context, Yeo proposes that an "interpathic understanding" of Paul's text and Chinese tradition is necessary. "To advise the Chinese not to practice ancestor worship, or not to offer food to ancestors, is implicitly advising them not to be Chinese, not to love their parents, not to practice love, etc." (Yeo, 309).

Menghun Goh, on the other hand, highlights that Western scholars have read the notion of the idol (Gk. *eidōlon*)—particularly in 1 Corinthians 8:4—through the lens of a Cartesian dualistic worldview. Reading this passage from a Chinese nondualistic worldview, Goh argues that "idol" is invented through a communal habitus. That is to say, an object is not ontologically an idol but is made an idol by humans. As such, Paul's discussion has to be understood as his way of asking the Corinthians to rethink, review, and revisit idol food though the lens of "his cross-like experiences" (1 Cor 9:2, 22) so that they can recognize "cross-like events in others, learning from them, magnifying them so that others will see them, and being cross-like to them as well" (Goh, 92).

These are only a few examples of how Paul has been interpreted in Asia. One thing that should be clear is that although Western missionaries have had and continue to have a deep impact and influence on Asian Christianity, Asian readers of Paul often find themselves in conflict with Western missionaries' interpretation of Paul. This shows that Asians are not just passive recipients of missionaries' teachings. They reclaim their agency by offering a contending interpretation of Paul.

2. Interpretation of Paul in the Asian American Context.

The implementation of Asian American hermeneutics in biblical studies has gained momentum in the past two decades. Besides some major monographs published by Asian American scholars (Liew 2008; Choi; Kato), four collaborative volumes have become landmark publications for Asian American biblical scholarship: (1) *The Bible in Asian America* (2002), edited by Tat-siong Benny Liew and Gale A. Yee; (2) *Ways of Being, Ways of Reading: Asian American Biblical Interpretation* (2006), edited by Jeffrey Kah-Jin Kuan and Mary F. Foskett; (3) *The T&T Clark Handbook to Asian American Biblical Hermeneutics* (2019), edited by Uriah Y. Kim and Seung Ai Yang; and (4) the special issue of *The Bible and Critical Theory* journal (2020), edited by Jin Young Choi and Wongi Park. These volumes represent a wide range of topics, texts, diverse ethnic and linguistic backgrounds, and reading strategies.

The interpretation of Paul among Asian American scholars does indeed take different forms, but all are grounded in Asian American experiences. To his reading of Paul's discourse on the body in 1 Corinthians, Liew brings the Asian American embodied experience of being feminized/sexualized and racialized. Heretofore, scholarly attention to the *body in the Corinthian correspondence has been focused mainly on class and status. Liew argues that Asian American experience can bring another dynamic to the interpretation not only of the Corinthian body but also to Paul's body as racialized and feminized bodies. For Liew, the conflicts between the Corinthians and Paul are not just caused by their "well-acknowledged status anxiety" but also the difference in their racialized bodies. Liew argues that the conflict is deeply rooted in what has become a common experience among Asian Americans, namely, "status inversion" (Liew 2008, 75-97; 2011, 128-30). That is, by becoming Christians, the Corinthians are to identify themselves with a colonized Jew, who is a "no-body." Dealing with Paul, a "stigmatized racial/ethnic body as a colonized Jew," causes the Corinthians to feel uncomfortable and anxious, and thus they have to "distance themselves from Paul" (Liew 2011, 130). Paul's defense of his *ministry in 1 Corinthians 1–4 demonstrates that Paul has an "icy relationship" with the Corinthians. So, the conflict or "divisions" described in these first four chapters are not just among the Corinthians but also between Paul and the Corinthians (Liew 2011, 131).

Furthermore, as in Asian American experience, Paul's Jewish body as a racialized body is also directly connected to the sexualization and feminization of his body. "As colonized Jews, however, Jesus' masculinity and Paul's masculinity were culturally suspect" (Liew 2011, 139). This experience of being sexualized/feminized, according to Lew, has caused Paul's attention to the body to have a sexual slant. In 1 Corinthians 5, Paul seems to think that "the mostly Gentile Corinthians are actually the ones who are sexually deviant" (Liew 2011, 141-42). Paul also employs what Liew calls "reverse condemnation"—a Jew condemning Greco-Roman sexually dissident bodies—by which he seems to be defending sexual *purity. By doing so, says Liew, he would look more "Greco-Roman" than Jewish. This is a typical experience of colonized people, which Homi Bhabha describes in his theory of mimicry as the colonized behaving "almost-white-but-not-quite" but ending up "becom(ing) more and more white" (Liew 2011, 142).

Sze-kar Wan's Asian American interpretation of Paul focuses particularly on Galatians. Wan brings two main stereotypes about Asian Americans—the perpetual foreigner and the model minority—to the forefront of his interpretation. Applying "ambivalence as a reading strategy," Wan argues that Paul's conflict with the *Jerusalem church can be explained by Paul's experience as a diasporic Jew, something that in many ways resonates with many Asian Americans (Wan 2006; 2012, 179-80). "Like Asian Americans, Paul was a member of a model minority and a perpetual foreigner in the Roman Empire. He was a high achiever living in the diaspora" (Wan 2012, 182). Although he lived in the Diaspora, he was still a Jew, a colonized person, which made him a perpetual foreigner. What is evident in Galatians is Paul presenting himself as a model minority not to the center of the Roman Empire but to the Jerusalem church, who are themselves a minoritized group. Paul "hope(s) that his success among Gentiles can bring him recognition, status, and power," so that they can acknowledge his authority and ministry among the uncircumcised. The root of the conflict between Paul and the Jerusalem leaders, Wan insists, is that "they never intend to grant Paul the power he is seeking" (Wan 2012, 185). In Galatians 1–2, Paul displays an ambivalent relationship with them. He sees them as "the before-me apostles" (Wan 2012, 186), which leaves an impression that he is like them but different from them. Wan argues that at the end of the day, Paul's interaction with the Jerusalem leaders reinscribes his perpetual-foreigner experience as a diasporic person (see also Wan 2000). "The Jerusalem hierarchy replicated the Empire and ended up treating Paul the same way the Empire had done" (2012, 187).

Ekaputra Tupamahu focuses attention on the linguistic struggle of Asian Americans in his reading of Pauline discourse on *tongue(s) in 1 Corinthians 14. Tupamahu points out that for Asian Americans, "Language . . . often becomes the identifying mark of [their] foreignness in this society" (Tupamahu 2019). The story of Asian immigrants in

America is the story of their struggle with language. Two major Supreme Court cases, 1974 *Law v. Nichols* and 1989 *Asian American Business v. City of Pomona*, mark Asian immigrants' legal and political struggle with the dominance of English (Tupamahu 2019, 384). "This locus experience informs my reading of the issue of tongue(s) in 1 Cor. 14 in a significant way. I identify my experience with the tongue(s) speakers who are being repressed, instead of with Paul who enforces the monolingual policy in this community" (Tupamahu 2019, 385). For Tupamahu, tongue(s) in 1 Corinthians 14 is not an unintelligible utterance phenomenon but a normal multilingual phenomenon (Tupamahu 2019, 386). Therefore, Paul's effort to silence and demand translation of tongue(s) is interpreted as a political move to enforce a monolingual structure to this community (see Tupamahu 2020). Tupamahu concludes, "Just like the tongue(s) speakers in the Corinthian church, Asian Americans (among many other non-natives) are the embodiment of xenophonic disruption in their impreciseness of speech (read: speaking with a foreign accent) that constitutes the multiplicity of competing discourses against the dominant one" (Tupamahu 2019, 192).

Just like Asian readers of Paul, the works of Liew, Wan, and Tupamahu also take seriously the social location and subjective experience of Asian Americans. Although most of these Asian and Asian Americans scholars are educated in the traditional historical-critical approach, they do historical and literary analysis of Paul and his letters with an obvious *slant*, a *slant* decidedly shaped by their Asian and Asian American experiences.

See also Empire; Identity; Idolatry; Interpretation: African American; Mission; Philemon, Letter to; Philippians, Letter to the; Strong and Weak; Stumbling Block; Tongues.

BIBLIOGRAPHY. **J. Y. Choi,** *Postcolonial Discipleship of Embodiment: An Asian and Asian American Feminist Reading of the Gospel of Mark*, Postcolonialism and Religions (New York: Palgrave Macmillan, 2015); **J. Y. Choi and W. Park,** eds., "Special Issue: Asian American Biblical Criticism," *The Bible and Critical Theory* 16 (2020): 1-116; **S. Das,** "An Imperial Apostle? Paul, Protestant Conversion, and South Asian Christianity," *The Historical Journal* 61 (2018): 103-30; **M. F. Foskett,** "Historical Criticism," in *T&T Clark Handbook of Asian American Biblical Hermeneutics*, ed. U. Y. Kim and S. A. Yang (London: T&T Clark, 2019), 107-17; **M. F. Foskett and J. Kah-Jin Kuan,** eds., *Ways of Being, Ways of Reading: Asian American Biblical Interpretation* (St. Louis, MO: Chalice, 2006); **M. Goh,** "The Issue of *Eidōlothyta*: An Inter(con)textual Interpretation of 1 Corinthians 8:1–11:1 and Chinese Ancestor Veneration," in *1 and 2 Corinthians*, T@C (Minneapolis: Fortress, 2013), 79-96; **J.-K. Kato,** *Religious Language and Asian American Hybridity*, Asian Christianity in the Diaspora (New York: Palgrave Macmillan, 2016); **U. Y. Kim and S. A. Yang,** eds., *T&T Clark Handbook of Asian American Biblical Hermeneutics* (London: T&T Clark, 2019); **J. W. Lee,** *Paul and the Politics of Difference: A Contextual Study of the Jewish-Gentile Difference in Galatians and Romans* (Cambridge: Clarke, 2015); **T. B. Liew,** "Introduction: Whose Bible? Which (Asian) America?," *Semeia* 90-91 (2002): 1-27; idem, *What Is Asian American Biblical Hermeneutics? Reading the New Testament*, Intersections: Asian and Pacific American Transcultural Studies (Honolulu: University of Hawai'i Press, 2008); idem, "Redressing Bodies at Corinth: Racial/Ethnic Politics and Religious Difference in the Context of Empire," in *The Colonized Apostle: Paul in Postcolonial Eyes*, ed. C. Stanley (Minneapolis: Fortress, 2011), 127-45; **T. B. Liew and G. A. Yee,** eds., *The Bible in Asian America*, Semeia 90/91 (Atlanta: Society of Biblical Literature, 2002); **C. M. S. Lim,** *Contextual Biblical Hermeneutics as Multicentric Dialogue: Towards a Singaporean Reading of Daniel*, BibInt 175 (Leiden: Brill, 2019); **R. S. Sugirtharajah,** "Introduction, and Some Thoughts on Asian Biblical Hermeneutics," *BibInt* 2 (1994): 251-63; idem, *The Bible and Asia: From the Pre-Christian Era to the Postcolonial Age* (Cambridge, MA: Harvard University Press, 2013); **E. Tupamahu,** "Lost and Silenced in Translation: Reading Pauline Discourse on Language in 1 Cor. 14 from an Asian American Perspective," in *T&T Clark Handbook of Asian American Biblical Hermeneutics*, ed. U. Y. Kim and S. A. Yang (London: T&T Clark, 2019), 383-94; idem, "'I Don't Want to Hear Your Language!' White Social Imagination and the Demography of Roman Corinth," *The Bible and Critical Theory* 16 (2020): 64-91; **S. Wan,** "Does Diaspora Identity Imply Some Sort of Universality?," in *Interpreting Beyond Borders*, ed. F. F. Segovia (Sheffield, UK: Sheffield Academic Press, 2000), 107-33; idem, "Betwixt and Between: Toward Hermeneutics of Hyphenation," in *Ways of Being, Ways of Reading: Asian American Biblical Interpretation*, ed. M. F. Foskett, and J. K.-J. Kuan (St. Louis, MO: Chalice, 2006), 137-229; idem, "Asian American Perspectives: Ambivalence of the Model Minority and Perpetual Foreigner," in *Studying Paul's Letters: Contemporary Perspectives and Methods*, ed. J. A. Marchal (Minneapolis: Fortress, 2012), 175-90; **K. K. Yeo,**

"The Rhetorical Hermeneutic of 1 Corinthians 8 and Chinese Ancestor Worship," *BibInt* 2 (1994): 294-311.

E. Tupamahu

INTERPRETATION: AUGUSTINE

Jaroslav Pelikan writes that the history of Western theology since the sixth-century Council of Orange is essentially "a series of footnotes" to Augustine (Pelikan 1971, 330). Pelikan's claim is sufficiently accurate to be effective hyperbole. Known as the "doctor of *grace," Augustine is, among other things, remembered for successfully refuting the Pelagian doctrine of *salvation, which was later anathematized by church councils. Augustine won this victory in large part due to his use of Paul's letters, which cast Augustine thenceforth as the champion of orthodox interpretation of the apostle's soteriology. It is no wonder, then, that theologians through the ages have cited him in defense of their readings of Paul. For example, in a private letter written in 1531 to John Brenz, Philip Melanchthon acknowledges that, while he departs from Augustine's understanding of the nature of justifying *faith, he nevertheless continues to appeal to the ancient African as an ally of his position "for the sake of the public" (*propter publicum*; Corpus Reformatum 2:502). Augustine represents "the only church father who even today remains an intellectual power" (Pelikan 1999, xiv). Not surprisingly, then, leading contemporary Pauline exegetes have devoted significant attention to this bishop's work (see, e.g., Fredriksen; Barclay, 85-97).

Augustine's extant corpus is voluminous, comprising roughly 5.4 million words (Stump and Meconi, 1), so even a full-length study would struggle to address Augustine's reading of Paul adequately. The focus here, then, is limited to some specific areas that will likely be of special interest to contemporary readers of Paul.

1. The Young Augustine and the Manichean Paul
2. Ambrose, Paul, and Augustine's Biblical Hermeneutics
3. Paul and Augustine's Teaching on the Fall, the Incarnation, and Incorporation into Christ
4. Augustine on Paul's Teaching Regarding Baptism and Eucharist
5. Augustine on Grace, Faith, and Works
6. Justification and Righteousness in Augustine

1. The Young Augustine and the Manichean Paul.

Augustine describes how he first learned about *Christ from his mother, Monica, yet fell away from her faith. He describes how his life took a dramatic turn when he fell in love with *philosophy through reading Cicero's now-lost work *Hortensius* (*Conf.* 3.4.8). He became attracted to the Manicheans, a group he admired for their conviction that pure reason must be prized above all other authorities (*Util. cred.* 1.2). Still, the Manicheans claimed Paul as an advocate of their own beliefs (Fredriksen, 214-20).

The Manicheans held that *God must be recognized as wholly good and therefore could not be the source of evil, which originates from a wicked deity. They observed that *sin was often the result of the desires of the *flesh. Because of this, they believed that the *creation of the grossly material world must be attributed to the evil god. Since Genesis indicates that the God of *Israel created the physical cosmos, the Manicheans argued that the Jews worshiped the evil deity. Christ could not, therefore, be the *Son of the God of Israel.

Augustine's corpus indicates that the Manicheans appealed to Pauline texts in support of their dualism (*Gen. Man.* 1.2.3). According to the Manichean reading, Paul's *teaching in Philippians 2:8 that Christ was born "in the likeness of men" meant that Jesus only "appeared" to take on a human *body (see *Fort.* 7). The Manicheans also exploited Paul's discussion of the perduring conflict between the spirit and the flesh (Gal 5:16-18; see *Commentary on Galatians* 46) and the way he closely associates sin and the flesh: "For I know that nothing good dwells in me, that is, in my flesh" (Rom 7:18 ESV). The apostle's proclamation that Christ has set us free "from the *law of sin and *death" (Rom 8:2 ESV) was seen by the Manicheans as indicating his opposition to the God of the Jews and the law of Moses (see *Faust.* 19.2). In the *Confessions* Augustine relates the appeal of the Manichean perspective. Augustine found solace in the notion that he himself was not responsible for his sinful behavior but that it was due to a "different nature" within him (5.10.18; see also *Exposition on the Psalms* 140.10).

2. Ambrose, Paul, and Augustine's Biblical Hermeneutics.

The preaching of Ambrose, the bishop of Milan, who offered intellectually sophisticated interpretations of the Scriptures of Israel, transformed Augustine's understanding of the Bible. Central for Ambrose's biblical *hermeneutics was Paul's teaching in 2 Corinthians 3:6: "The letter kills, the spirit gives life" (*Conf.* 6.4.6). Augustine became convinced that Christians should read the writings of the Scriptures of Israel in light of Christ, such that the readers might recognize the reciprocal relationships of the

Testaments: "New in Old concealed, Old in New revealed" (*Quaest. Hept.* 2.73 [trans. Cameron, 248]). He points out that Paul himself lists the Scriptures of Israel as one of the divine gifts bestowed on Israel (*Faust.* 12.3, citing Rom 9:4).

Like Ambrose, Augustine anchors his approach to hermeneutics in 2 Corinthians 3 (2 Cor 3:14-16; see *Faust.* 12.11; Fredriksen, 268; Cameron, 134-37). In his later work *On Instructing Beginners*, Augustine cites Paul's teaching in 1 Corinthians 10:6 that the events of the exodus were "written down for our sake" to explain that these events happened figurally (*in figura*) for the sake of believers (3.6). Yet Augustine's hermeneutical principles are not merely rooted in a new commitment to figural interpretation (see below).

3. Paul and Augustine's Teaching on the Fall, the Incarnation, and Incorporation into Christ.

Augustine refuted the Manichean view of Jesus by returning to a passage they themselves used: Philippians 2. Augustine points out that Paul says that Jesus was "in the form of God" and took "the form of a *servant" (Phil 2:6-7 ESV), suggesting the reality of *both* divinity *and* humanity in Christ. Augustine contends that the Manicheans fail to make sense of Paul's teaching (*Faust.* 3.6). By taking on human nature, Christ is "less than the Father" but retains "equality with God" in his divinity (*Trin.* 1.7.14). Augustine insists that Christ is therefore able to be the "one mediator" between God and humanity (1 Tim 2:5) precisely because he is both divine and human (*Trin.* 1.10.20).

Augustine argues that material existence is not inherently evil for Paul. The same God who created the animal body is the one who will give glorified bodies to the saints (1 Cor 15:38-49; *Faust.* 24.1). Sin entered the world not through or as physical flesh as such but through the disobedience of "one man"—namely, *Adam—"and death through sin" (Rom 5:12; see *Trin.* 4.12, 15). Not only has all humanity come under condemnation (Rom 5:18) because of the sin of Adam, but human nature *itself* has also been "corrupted" on account of it (*Nat. grat.* 40.47). Like *Satan before them, Adam and Eve fell because of pride (*Civ.* 14.11; 14.13).

The incarnation solves the problem of sin. The root of sin is pride, but because Christ "humbled himself" (Phil 2:7), there is an antidote for sin: "The way of humility comes from no other source; it comes only from Christ. It is the way originated by him who, though most high, came in humility" (*On Psalms* 31.2.18). Christ is not simply the *model* of humility for Augustine; he is the *way* to salvation. *Augustine's soteriology is thus thoroughly participationist*: "the soul does not become righteous except by participation in him who is better, who justifies the impious" (*Epistula* 140.21). Augustine explains that Christ comes to share in our humanity so that in him believers can share in his divinity: "by uniting the similarity of his own humanity with us, he has taken away the dissimilarity of our iniquity, and having been made a sharer of our mortality, he has made us a sharer of his divinity" (*Trin.* 4.2.4; see also Meconi 2013).

Believers are saved, then, through union with Christ. Yet Augustine does not construe salvation in individualistic terms. Salvation for Augustine is, at heart, an ecclesial reality (Ployd). "Christ" for Augustine denotes not simply Jesus but also his *body, the *church. Together, head and body are members of "the whole Christ" (*Doctr. Chr.* 3.31.44). To be saved is to be incorporated into Christ's body, a theme he develops from Paul. Even the holy men and women prior to the coming of Christ and the good angels are saved by being part of "the whole Christ" (*Serm.* 4.11; *On Psalms* 137.4; Klein; Lee).

4. Augustine on Paul's Teaching Regarding Baptism and Eucharist.

In his refutation of the Manicheans' rejection of the goodness of the world, Augustine highlights the sacraments as evidence of the incarnational dimension of Christian faith. Augustine frequently cites Galatians 3:27-28 ("For as many of you as *were baptized into Christ* have put on Christ . . . for *you are all one in Christ Jesus*," ESV, emphasis added) to uphold *baptism as the means by which believers are "united with the body and members of Christ" (see, e.g., *Peccat. mer.* 3.4.7). Likewise, Augustine often draws on Paul's teaching that believers have a "participation" in the body and blood of Christ through the "one bread" and "one cup" (1 Cor 10:16-17):

> That bread which you can see on the altar, sanctified by the word of God, is the body of Christ. That cup, or rather what the cup contains, sanctified by the word of God, is the blood of Christ. It was by means of these things that the Lord Christ wished to present us with his body and blood, which he shed for our sake for the forgiveness of sins. If you receive them well, you are yourselves what you receive. You see, the apostle says, "We, being many, are one loaf, one body" (1 Cor 10:17). That is how he explained

> the sacrament of the Lord's table; one loaf, one body, is what we all are, many though we be. (*Serm.* 227)

It is through participating in the eucharistic celebration that believers offer themselves up together with the one body of Christ, fulfilling Paul's mandate to "present your bodies as a living *sacrifice, holy and acceptable to God, which is your spiritual *worship" (Rom 12:1 ESV; see *Civ.* 10.6; Lee, 95-122).

5. Augustine on Grace, Faith, and Works. Drawing directly on Paul's teaching in Romans, Augustine insists, "By grace they are, of course, justified gratuitously, that is, without any preceding merits from their own works. 'Otherwise, grace is no longer grace' [Rom 11:6]" (*Spir. et litt.* 10.16). To think as Pelagius did that Adam's sin had no lasting impact on human nature and that grace is simply an external help to salvation fails to grasp Paul's teaching; if human nature *itself* is not in need of Christ, then Christ "died in vain" (*Nat. grat.* 1.1, quoting Gal 2:21). For Augustine, faith itself is the result of grace and divine aid. He quotes from John 6:29 to explain that faith is itself "the work of God" (*Praed.* 7.12). Paul teaches the same: "No one can say 'Jesus is *Lord' except in the *Holy Spirit" (1 Cor 12:3 ESV; see *Serm. Dom.* 2.25.83).

Importantly, *faith* has a range of meanings in Augustine's work. James speaks of a "faith" that is "dead" (Jas 2:17). "Faith alone"—that is, faith that is not "working in *love" (Gal 5:6)—is insufficient for salvation. Even the *demons "believe" (Jas 2:19; see, e.g., *Serm.* 53.10). Augustine therefore warns against "a treacherously false security" that holds that "faith alone is sufficient for salvation" (*Fid. op.* 21). The Catholic Epistles of the NT were written to counter this view, which arose as a misreading of Paul:

> Even in the days of the Apostles certain somewhat obscure statements of the Apostle Paul were misunderstood, and some thought he was saying this: "Let us now do evil that good may come from it" [Rom 3:8] because he said: "Now the law intervened that the offense might abound. But where the offense has abounded, grace has abounded yet more" [Rom 5:20]. . . . Since this problem is by no means new and had already arisen at the time of the Apostles, other apostolic letters of Peter, John, James and Jude are deliberately aimed against the argument I have been refuting and firmly uphold the doctrine that faith does not avail without works. (*Fid. op.* 21; trans. Nienhuis, 2)

What is required is not mere belief but participation in the "faith of Christ" (Rom 3:22), which Augustine identifies as "the faith of Christian grace" (*Fid. op.* 16.27). In his mature works, he comes to distinguish "believing *in* Christ" from merely "believing Christ" (*Serm.* 144.2). Unlike the latter, the former is faith united to love. It is a faith not simply motivated by *fear of punishment, a servile fear, but the faith that desires to be conformed in love to Christ (Sehorn). This saving faith represents the antidote to the source of human fallenness, sin—particularly, pride—since it requires learning humility in Christ (*Trin.* 4.10.13).

6. Justification and Righteousness in Augustine. For Augustine, *justification is understood as involving the transformation of the believer; the believer is "made righteous" (*Spir. et litt.* 26.45). Augustine did not take this view simply because the Latin rendering of Paul's "to justify," *justificare*, appears to connote a factitive meaning, for Augustine's reading has precedent in earlier Greek fathers such as John Chrysostom (McGrath, 36-37). Rather, Augustine's realist account of justification is derived from his broader reading of Pauline texts.

Augustine wholeheartedly affirms the apostle's teaching that God "justifies the ungodly" (Rom 4:5; see *Trin.* 4.3.5; *Faust.* 21.3). Yet Augustine believes that "when they have been incorporated in [Christ] through the Spirit and have become his members, they can, because he gives the increase interiorly [see 1 Cor 3:7], do the works of righteousness" (*Spir. et litt.* 29.50). This is not a "*righteousness" of one's own making (Phil 3:9) but that which comes from Christ (*Grat. Chr.* 13.14). Augustine's reasoning flows out of his reading of passages such as 2 Corinthians 3, which contrasts "the *ministry of death," associated with the law, with the "ministry of righteousness" available in Christ (2 Cor 3:7-9). The law of Moses is identified with "the ministry of death" because, without grace, no one was capable of keeping it, rendering it the "ministry of condemnation" (2 Cor 3:9).

The new covenant heralds the coming of the Spirit and the gift of grace, which empowers believers to do what the law commands: "the law of the New Testament, he calls the ministry of the Spirit and the ministry of righteousness, because through the gift of the Spirit we do the works of righteousness, and we are set free from the condemnation owing to transgression" (*Spir. et litt.* 18.31). By writing the law on believers' hearts, God "justifies from within" (*Spir. et litt.* 17.30). Elsewhere, Augustine writes: "The law, then, was given in order that we would seek after grace; grace was given so that we might fulfill the law" (*Spir. et litt.* 19.34). Augustine also points to Paul's teaching in 2 Corinthians 5:21 that "we might become the righteousness of God" in Christ Jesus, adding, "This is not the righteousness of God by which he himself is righteous, but that by which he makes us righteous" (*Spir. et litt.* 18.31). Likewise, he cites from Romans 5:19 to show that just as many were "made sinners" because of Adam's disobedience, in Christ "the many will be made righteous" (*Peccat. mer.* 1.15.19).

Romans 5:5, "Augustine's most quoted verse" (Ployd, 122), underscores the need for grace. An illustrative example occurs in Augustine's argument that Pelagius and Caelestius—who insisted that children were born unaffected by Adam's sin—had failed to reckon adequately with Paul's teaching on the necessity of grace: "I have never found that they confessed, as one should confess, this grace by which we are justified, that is, by which 'the love of God is poured out in our hearts by the Holy Spirit who has been given to us' [Rom 5:5]" (*C. Jul. op. imp.* 1.38). Here Augustine identifies the Holy Spirit's infusion of love into the hearts of believers with "the grace by which we are justified."

For Augustine, justification in Christ is "greater than [the creation] of heaven and earth" (*Tract. Ev. Jo.* 72.3; trans. Mooney, 7). In justification, Christ comes to make believers like himself. Drawing together 2 Corinthians 4:16 and Colossians 3:10, Augustine writes: "This likeness to him is now beginning to be formed again as human beings are interiorly renewed from day to day 'according to the image of him who created them'" (*Spir. et litt.* 22.37). Quoting Philippians, Augustine holds that believers are truly able to do salvific works because (and only because) their works are the result of Christ working within them: "Though it pertains to a human being to do this [i.e., good works], it is also the gift of God and, hence, you ought not to doubt that it is a work of God. 'It is God, after all, who produces in you,' says the Apostle, 'both the willing and the action in accord with good will'" (*Spir. et litt.* 2.2, quoting Phil 2:13).

Lewis Ayres writes: "The hardest thing for the modern reader to grasp in the account . . . is how Augustine thinks that grace and human freedom intertwine" (Ayres, 350-51; see also Kincaid). While Augustine once thought that divine *election was due to God's ability to foresee who would act righteously (*Notes on Romans* 61.2-3), he changed his view, concluding that grace is first given prior to any human merit, with election remaining mysteriously gratuitous (*To Simplicianus* 1.2,16). Nevertheless, this pivot did not alter his view of the effects of election; while no good work can merit the initial gift of grace that causes the believer to come to justifying faith, once given grace, the believer is empowered to do works that are truly meritorious (*Ep.* 194). The works that are rewarded are ultimately those accomplished by God's grace in believers. Thus, when Paul says, "it is . . . the doers of the law who will be justified" (Rom 2:13 ESV), Augustine explains that Paul is referring to those who have *already* been justified by grace (*Spir. et litt.* 26.45). One is justified first by grace through faith apart from works; however, once given grace, the believer truly grows in righteousness. Augustine writes,

> But the whole thing is from God; not however as though we were asleep, as though we didn't have to make an effort, as though we didn't have to be willing. Without your will, there will be no righteousness of God in you. . . . There can be such a thing as God's righteousness without your will, but it cannot be in you apart from your will. . . . So while he made you without you, he does not justify you without you. (*Serm.* 169.13)

For Augustine, the beginnings of faith, such as those stirred in catechumens seeking baptism, can be described as a kind of "conception" (*To Simplicianus* 1.2.2). Such faith is only possible by the work of the Spirit, who can be received prior to baptism, as in the case of Cornelius in the book of Acts (Acts 10:44-48). Augustine, however, nevertheless insists on the need for baptism. Had Cornelius not needed baptism, he would not have been told to send for *Peter (*Bapt.* 4.21.29). While in certain cases (e.g., the thief crucified with Jesus or martyrs), the graces of baptism can be received spiritually (*Bapt.* 4.23.29-31), incorporation into the body of Christ is identified with this sacrament (*Bapt.* 1.11.16, citing Gal 3:27). Thus, Augustine links baptism to justification (*Peccat. mer.* 1.16.21). He never pits faith against baptism; baptism is efficacious "by believing" (*Peccat. mer.* 1.25.35). Nevertheless, Augustine is adamant that it is the gift of the Spirit that *causes* believing and not the act of believing that causes God to give the gift of the Spirit. He therefore argues that the Pelagians are wrong for rejecting infant baptism (*Peccat. mer.* 3.2.2). Having received righteousness in baptism, believers continue to grow in it through good works such as fasting, *almsgiving, and *prayer, through which believers are perfected (*Perf.* 8.18).

See also ELECTION AND PREDESTINATION; FAITH; GRACE; IN CHRIST; INTERPRETATION: PATRISTIC; JUSTIFICATION; WORKS OF THE LAW.

BIBLIOGRAPHY. **L. Ayres,** "Augustine," in *The Blackwell Companion to Paul*, ed. Stephen Westerholm (Malden, MA: Wiley-Blackwell, 2011), 345-60; **J. M. G. Barclay,** *Paul and the Gift* (Grand Rapids, MI: Eerdmans, 2015); **M. Cameron,** *Christ Meets Me Everywhere: Augustine's Early Figurative Exegesis* (Oxford: Oxford University Press, 2012); **P. Fredriksen,** *Augustine and the Jews: A Christian Defense of Jews and Judaism* (New Haven, CT: Yale University Press, 2008); **J. A. Kincaid,** "New Covenant Righteousness as the Transformation of the Heart: An Augustinian Reading of 2 Corinthians 3" (paper presented at the Annual Meeting of the Society of Biblical Literature, Boston, November 20, 2017); **E. Klein,** *Augustine's Theology of Angels* (Cambridge: Cambridge University Press, 2018); **J. K. Lee,** *Augustine and the Mystery of the Church* (Minneapolis: Fortress, 2017); **A. E. McGrath,** *Iustitia Dei: A History of the Christian Doctrine of Justification*, 4th ed. (Oxford: Oxford University Press, 2020); **S. McKenna, CSSR,** trans., *The Trinity*, FC 45 (Washington, DC: Catholic University of America Press, 1963); **D. V. Meconi, SJ,** *The One Christ: St. Augustine's Theology of Deification* (Washington, DC: Catholic University of America Press, 2013); **C. R. Mooney,** "*Iustitia Fidei:* The Development of Augustine's Account of Justification by Faith" (PhD diss., Notre Dame University, 2021); **D. R. Nienhuis,** *Not by Paul Alone: The Formation of the Catholic Epistle Collection and the Christian Canon* (Waco, TX: Baylor University Press, 2007); **J. Pelikan,** *The Christian Tradition: A History of the Development of Doctrine*, vol. 1, *The Emergence of the Catholic Tradition (100-600)* (Chicago: University of Chicago Press, 1971); idem, "Foreword," in *Augustine Through the Ages: An Encyclopedia*, ed. A. D. Fitzgerald, OSA (Grand Rapids, MI: Eerdmans, 1999), xiii-xiv; **A. Ployd,** *Augustine, the Trinity, and the Church: A Reading of the Anti-Donatist Sermons* (Oxford: Oxford University Press, 2015); **J. Sehorn,** "Threading the Needle: Fear of the Lord and the Incarnation in St. Augustine," in *Saving Fear in Christian Spirituality*, ed. A. W. Astell (Notre Dame, IN: University of Notre Dame Press, 2020), 76-101; **E. Stump and D. Meconi, SJ,** "Introduction," in *The Cambridge Companion to Augustine*, 2nd ed., ed. D. Meconi, SJ, and E. Stump (Cambridge: Cambridge University Press, 2014), 1-13.

M. P. Barber

INTERPRETATION: CALVIN

The influence of Paul's letters, especially Romans, on Calvin's theology and biblical exegesis is well recognized in the field of Calvin studies. Calvin also admired Paul as an exemplar in Christian living and pastoral ministry.

1. The Roman Road to Paul and His Letters
2. Calvin's Biblical Exposition
3. Calvin's Appreciation of Paul
4. Critiquing Paul?
5. Paul Shapes the *Institutes*

1. The Roman Road to Paul and His Letters. During the early modern period, the road to Paul was paved by the epistle to the Romans. Over seventy new biblical commentaries were written and published on Romans alone from 1500–1650 (Adams), and this statistic stands in striking contrast to the previous century, when most new editions were critical reprints of patristic and medieval commentators (Steinmetz, 1). In fact, no other book of the Bible garnered near the same level of attention as Romans during the Reformation period, and this elevation served to promote renewed interest in Pauline thought among both Protestant and Catholic exegetes (e.g., in the latter case of Thomas de Vio Cajetan).

The journey toward a greater emphasis on Pauline texts in early modern exegesis was profoundly shaped by the life, theology, and biblical studies of Martin Luther (1483–1546) just a generation before John Calvin (1509–1564). Luther's reinvigoration of Pauline studies began in his own life while lecturing on Romans (1515–1516; see Malysz), which led to "theological breakthrough" involving Romans 1:17. In 1522, Luther published the first translation of the German NT using the first published Greek NT by Desiderius Erasmus (second edition published 1519). In the first edition of Luther's preface to the NT, he identifies the prolegomena for reading Scripture, which prioritizes John's Gospel, Paul's epistles (especially Romans), and 1 Peter as the "true and noblest books of the New Testament" (WA DB 6:10-11; LW 35:361-62). In Luther's preface to Romans, he famously describes it as "the chief part of the New Testament" and "truly the purest gospel" (Cameron, 464). To Luther, Romans captured the fullness of Pauline thought and indeed "the whole Christian and evangelical doctrine" (Cameron, 479), and this thinking pervaded among the Protestant Reformers. Romans was, without question, the key to the early modern reception of Paul.

2. Calvin's Biblical Exposition.
John Calvin's entrance into the publishing world of biblical exegesis began during a fruitful season of life and *ministry in Strasbourg (1538–1541), which immediately followed an unexpected exile from Geneva due to disagreement with political leadership. In Strasbourg, Calvin served as pastor of a French refugee congregation and began writing his commentary on Romans, the first of many biblical commentaries he published over his lifetime.

Calvin dedicated *Romans* to Simon Grynaeus, whom he likely heard lecture on Romans at Basel in fall 1535. The dedication was the context for Calvin's description of his approach to the genre of biblical commentary, which he describes as "lucid brevity" (*perspicua brevitas*). In this he meant that extended theological commentary should be reserved for theological works, while contemporary application was frequently reserved for the pulpit. Starting with his Romans commentary, Calvin advances a hermeneutical circle, which expects readers to directly engage with Scripture alongside consultation of Calvin's *Institutes of the Christian Religion* for theological insight and biblical commentaries for exegesis (Pitkin, "John Calvin and the Interpretation of the Bible," 350).

Calvin's biblical exegesis employs the tools of Renaissance humanism with attention to philology and grammar. He both practices and promotes the study of the exegetical tradition, and he describes engagement with both ancient and contemporary readings of Scripture as a cultivation of "brotherly discourse." Because Calvin regarded the expositor's duty as to uncover the original intention of the author, he spent time exploring the historical context of the text, and he did not overlook the value of intratextual exegesis (Zachman). For Calvin, the goal of biblical commentary was to advance the edification of the *church according to Scripture's proclamation rather than the expositor's agenda.

3. Calvin's Appreciation of Paul.
By viewing Romans as not only the superior apex of Pauline thought but the lens through which the entirety of Scripture should be interpreted, Calvin mirrored the accepted Protestant thinking of his time (see Ehrensperger and Holder). Both the OT and the NT found their ultimate explanation through Pauline thought in Romans, and not incidentally, Calvin identified the main subject of Romans to be the doctrine of *justification by *faith. In both his summation of the content of Romans for the commentary and in his *Institutes of the Christian Religion* (1.4.1; 1.5.1), Romans 1 provided the pivot for the entire theological narrative of human soteriology; the inexcusability of the human condition due to *sin required adoption from a good Father.

Calvin's appreciation for Paul extended beyond the superiority of his theological teaching to his life and pastoral ministry. Calvin regarded Paul as Christian exemplar, and he stresses in his commentary on 1 Corinthians that it was Paul himself who exhorted the church to imitate him insofar as he imitated Christ (Calvin, *Corinthians*, 349-50). As it stood, Calvin identified with the account of Paul's story as a biblical lens through which he could interpret his own story and *calling (Gordon, 3). Similarly to how Calvin resonated with the exilic dimensions of Abraham and David's stories in light of his own experience as a French refugee, Calvin's commentary draws focus to Paul's calling to preach the *gospel and self-description as "*servant" of *Christ, which Calvin interpreted to mean both minister and *apostle. Importantly, Calvin commented on this text in the same year (1539) that he responded to Cardinal Sadeoleto on behalf of Geneva with assertions of his pastoral authority in spite of being self-trained in theology and without a formal ordination. As Calvin explored the dimensions of Paul's authority in Romans 1, he elevated the necessity of receiving "a special call" in which God alone is the "author" (Calvin, *Corinthians*, 42). Calvin's imitation of Paul extended to the origins and nature of his call to the pastorate in addition to his theological teachings.

4. Critiquing Paul?
Although Calvin overwhelmingly affirmed Paul's teachings in his letters, 1 Corinthians 11 provides an interesting case study of Calvin's discomfort with certain established interpretations of Paul. As Barbara Pitkin's work notes, "Paul for Calvin was not beyond criticism, but he was nevertheless the primary biblical model and authority for Calvin's own program" (Pitkin, "Calvin's Reception of Paul," 296).

In the history of biblical interpretation, 1 Corinthians 11 had been used as the basis for questioning women as made in the *image of *God: "For a man ought not to have his head veiled, since he is the image and reflection of God; but woman is the reflection of man. Indeed, man was not made from woman, but woman from man. Neither was man created for the sake of woman, but woman for the sake of man" (1 Cor 11:7-9 NRSV). Theologically speaking, Calvin regarded humanity's creation in the image of God as crucial to distinguishing humans from animals and affirming equal access to *salvation among the sexes. Consequently, Calvin expresses discomfort, first in his Corinthians commentary (1546) and then in his Genesis commentary (1554), with established interpretations of Paul's teachings that would deny female access to both created dignity and *freedom in Christ.

Calvin grapples with the implications of 1 Corinthians 11 for seeming to teach that man serves as an intermediary for woman, and he questions what Paul could mean in light of Galatians 3:28. Given the Reformation's strong insistence that only Christ is the mediator of human salvation, he writes, "There is somewhat more of difficulty in what follows" (Calvin, *Corinthians*, 353). Furthermore, Calvin also notes the contradictions between Paul forbidding woman to prophesy with her head uncovered "while elsewhere he wholly prohibits women from speaking in the Church (1 Tim. 2:12)." He therefore takes care, even as he interprets the passage to affirm a patriarchal dynamic in *marriage, to stress that "both sexes were created in the image of God, and Paul exhorts women no less than men to be formed anew, according to the image" (Calvin, *Corinthians*, 356-57).

Importantly, Calvin continues to moderate the force of the passage through 1 Corinthians 14:33-35 by noting that necessity may occur requiring *women to speak in the worship assembly (Calvin, *Corinthians*, 468). With this, he recognizes a Huguenot (French Protestant) audience with robust female *leadership in the context of the desert churches. He further moderates the passage by noting that wives may not have competent husbands on these theological understandings and therefore would need to consult the prophets for guidance rather than husbands as Paul directs. Calvin expresses recognition of the fact that Paul was not intending to block women from education, and he determines the passage to be speaking of nonessentials: "the things of which he here treats are intermediate and indifferent, in which there is nothing unlawful, but what is at variance with propriety and edification" (Calvin, *Corinthians*, 469). Here Calvin's basis for the exclusion of female public leadership is rooted in "common sense," historical precedent, and propriety. Paul's direction nonetheless is not eternally mandated.

Nearly a decade later, Calvin continued to grapple with the interpretation that Paul denied the image of God in woman, which was used in late medieval celibacy propaganda to demean the practice of marriage. This time, Calvin explored the question in the context of chapter one of his Genesis commentary: "This difficulty is also to be encountered, namely, why Paul should deny the woman to be the image of God, when Moses honours both indiscriminately, with this title" (Calvin, *Genesis* 1:96). Calvin acknowledged that Moses was being pitted against Paul, so he spent time to reconcile the two seemingly conflicting teachings.

This example illustrates how Calvin brought Paul's teachings to bear even in his interpretations of the OT, thereby indicating how Pauline texts and teachings served as a prominent theological lens for interpreting both testaments of Scripture. Establishing the harmony of Scripture's teachings was consistently one of Calvin's priorities, particularly in cases when hard readings implicated Pauline teachings on soteriology and the doctrine of justification by faith, as seen later in Calvin's James commentary (1550).

5. Paul Shapes the *Institutes*.
Importantly, as Calvin wrote his Romans commentary, he also completed the second edition of his *Institutes of the Christian Religion* (1539). The second edition saw the purpose of the *Institutes* expand (i.e., from seven to seventeen chapters) and shift from providing catechetical exposition of the faith in the structural vein of Luther's catechism to guiding theology students in a survey of biblical and theological themes (Spijker). New chapters explored justification and good works, the relationship between the OT and NT, predestination, providence, and the Christian life. In the end, it was Paul's letter to the Romans that shaped the content and structure of Calvin's most substantial revision of the *Institutes*.

See also INTERPRETATION: LUTHER; ROMANS, LETTER TO THE.

BIBLIOGRAPHY. **G. W. Adams,** "Introduction to Romans 1–8," in *Romans 1–8*, Reformation Commentary on Scripture New Testament 7 (Downers Grove, IL: InterVarsity Press, 2019), xliii-lxviii; **J. Calvin,** *Commentaries on the Epistle of Paul the Apostle to the Romans*, trans. and ed. J. Owen (Grand Rapids, MI: Christian Classics Ethereal Library, n.d.); idem, *Institutes of the Christian Religion*, ed. J. T. McNeill (London: SCM Press, 1961); idem, *Commentaries on the First Book of Moses Called Genesis*, trans. J. King (Grand Rapids, MI: Baker, 2009);

idem, *Commentary on the Epistles of Paul the Apostle to the Corinthians*, trans. J. Pringle (Grand Rapids, MI: Baker, 2009); **E. K. Cameron,** "Preface to the Epistle to the Romans," in *The Interpretation of Scripture*, ed. E. K. Cameron, The Annotated Luther 6 (Minneapolis: Fortress, 2017), 457-80; **K. Ehrensperger and R. W. Holder,** eds., *Reformation Readings of Romans* (New York: T&T Clark, 2008); **A. Ganoczy and S. Scheld,** *Die Hermeneutik Calvins: Geistesgeschichtliche Voraussetzungen und Grundzüge* (Wiesbaden: Steiner, 1983); **B. Gordon,** *Calvin* (New Haven, CT: Yale University Press, 2009); **R. W. Holder,** *A Companion to Paul in the Reformation* (Leiden: Brill, 2009); **P. J. Malysz,** "Lectures on Romans 3:20-27, 1515–1516," in *The Annotated Luther: The Interpretation of Scripture*, ed. E. K. Cameron (Minneapolis: Fortress, 2017), 6:481-500; **B. Pitkin,** "Calvin's Reception of Paul," in *A Companion to Paul in the Reformation*, ed. R. W. Holder (Leiden: Brill, 2009), 267-96; idem, "John Calvin and the Interpretation of the Bible," in *A History of Biblical Interpretation: The Medieval Through the Reformation Periods*, ed. A. J. Hauser and D. Watson (Grand Rapids, MI: Eerdmans, 2009), 341-71; idem, *Calvin, the Bible, and History* (Oxford: Oxford University Press, 2020); **W. V. Spijker,** *Calvin: A Brief Guide to His Life and Thought*, trans. L. D. Bierma (Louisville, KY: Westminster John Knox, 2009); **D. C. Steinmetz,** ed., *The Bible in the Sixteenth Century* (Durham, NC: Duke University Press, 1990); **R. C. Zachman,** "Gathering Meaning from the Context: Calvin's Exegetical Method," *Journal of Religion* 82, no. 1 (January 2002): 1-26.

J. P. McNutt

INTERPRETATION: JEWISH

Although the modern Jewish acceptance of Jesus has tended to take a more positive route, acceptance of Paul, thought at times to be the ultimate apostate, has had a longer and more polemical journey. Despite this, the figure of Paul has brought forth significant reflection and response from the Jewish community.

To study Paul's reception in modern Judaism is in many ways to trace the acceptance and treatment of Jews in the broader Western Christian world. Therefore, this article will be broken up into significant movements, both positive and tragic, of Jewish peoplehood, and with it the place of interreligious dialogue as signaling expansion and development in the discussion of Paul in the Jewish community.

1. The Long Nineteenth Century, the Question of Assimilation, and Religious Identity.

The nineteenth century saw the flowering of the great liberal intellectual movement, beginning in Germany, and with it the development of nationalization in Europe. In the dream of renewed *volks*/nations, religious identity was minimized if not eventually eliminated. Jewish thinkers struggled between the powerful forces of assimilation into their respective nations and retaining their full Jewish identity within. Thus, the struggle between being a *German* Jew and a *German of Mosaic persuasion* began.

1.1. Heinrich Graetz (1817–1891). Graetz, an Orthodox Jewish Polish historian, produced the first scholarly approach to Paul within Judaism in his monumental historical work, *The History of the Jews* (1853). In it he distances Paul from Judaism by pointing out the poor knowledge Paul demonstrates of its basic ideals. For Graetz, Paul devised the connection between the coming of the Messiah (Jesus) and the abrogation of the *law primarily as a form of pragmatics. Paul's motive for teaching such was to bring in the end days more easily and promptly. Paul's message was cloaked in the Hellenistic mythology of his day, which, although pleasing to *Gentile converts, in the end created a new religion separate from Judaism.

1.2. Isaac Mayer Wise (1819–1900). An Austrian-born American Reform rabbi, Wise in a lecture titled "Paul and the Mystics" (1868) heaped praise on Paul, calling him a brilliant star within the history of ideas who brought to a Gentile world what Jewish tradition anticipated and desired. Wise saw Paul as representing the denationalization of Jewish ideas in the universal religious language of a greater humanity. Wise was innovative in seeking Paul in the Talmud. In the writings of the sage called Acher, Wise saw veiled rabbinic commentary on Paul's influence as a heretic. For Wise, Paul was the creator of a distinct "Gentile Christianity" he placed beyond the current Jewish community, preaching a new mythology focusing on vicarious *atonement, bodily *resurrection, and a sacramental system found most clearly in the mystery cults of his day.

1.3. G. F. Montefiore (1858–1938). Montefiore, an English-born liberal Jewish scholar, was prominent in his day for his work in Jewish-Christian relations.

In *Judaism and St. Paul: Two Essays* (1914), Montefiore paved the road for Samuel Sandmel by calling Paul a genius with important things to contribute to humanity (including Jews) in both Paul's time and Montefiore's. In regard to the problem of Paul's polemic against the Judaism of his day, which rippled into attacks on the Judaism of Montefiore's, he delivers an ingenious answer: *Paul did not know the same Judaism as rabbinic Judaism/modern Judaism.* Paul faced and criticized a type of Judaism, found perhaps in Hellenistic and Diaspora areas, that justly needed castigation. Therefore, Paul did not attack the Judaism of the rabbis, and thus modern-day Judaism, but rather a deformed type of it that could equally be rebuked by modern Jews.

2. Zionism, the Crisis of Nazism, and *The Ten Points of Seelisburg.*

With the continuing era of nationalization in the twentieth century came the danger of Nazi ideology and rising anti-Semitism throughout Europe, encapsulated in the Dreyfus Affair (1894–1906), a political scandal centered in France. In the tragedy of the Shoah, both nationalists and Zionists spoke of Paul from the needs of their times. In the ashes of Auschwitz, *The Ten Points of Seelisburg* (1948) was drafted in Switzerland by Christians and Jews, beginning a slow repentance and a turn by European Christians to condemn the "teaching of contempt" and to renew dialogue with Jews as a matter of great importance.

2.1. Joseph Klausner (1874–1968). A Lithuanian-born Jewish historian and significant supporter of the early Zionist cause, Klausner was the first Jewish author to write not only from within the newly formed State of Israel (joining the Hebrew University of Jerusalem) but in Hebrew on the contributions of Paul (*From Jesus to Paul*, 1942). In Paul Klausner finds a figure who in the end must be rejected by Jews but who in general played a crucial role in disseminating the powerful ideas of Jewish ethical monotheism to the world. Klausner notes that, where Jewish ideas have been valued in the world, so has Judaism; therefore, Paul's contribution to world Jewry and its safety should not be understated. Once cleansed of his un-Jewish additions, Paul could eventually be seen by the Jewish community as a preparer of the ways for the Messiah.

2.2. Leo Baeck (1873–1956). Baeck, a German Reform rabbi and scholar who emigrated from Nazi Germany to England, wrote of Paul in two significant essays ("The Faith of Paul" and "Romantic Religion"). Although noting the deep influence of Hellenistic wisdom speculation within Paul, Baeck, similar to Klausner, lifts up the significance of Paul's training as a Pharisee. This training meant that an important byproduct of the Christian *gospel's spread was the promotion of the Hebrew Scriptures to the outside world. Paul's allegiance to his Judaism, and with it the Hebrew Scriptures, never wavered. Baeck also notes that Paul's antinomian approach toward the Jewish law had a transformative effect within Judaism itself, causing it to shift toward full devotion to the Torah.

2.3. Samuel Sandmel (1911–1979). Sandmel was a prolific American Reform scholar of the twentieth century who wrote the provocative and promising book *The Genius of Paul* (1958). He sought to highlight the fruits of comparison between Philo and Paul, saying that one must look to a Grecian Judaism to understand Paul. Sandmel states that Paul's concerns were primarily a result of his individual psychology and experience, unique to his personal struggles and perspective, rather than simply a form of syncretism. Sandmel finds Paul's genius in his rebellion against ossified and institutionalized religion in general. It is from Paul's root that all religious reformers find their inspiration.

3. The State of Israel, *Nostra Aetate*, and the Age of Dialogue.

The birth of the State of Israel (1948) brought a Jewish national presence to the modern world and with it a need for Christian acknowledgment. This came in the groundbreaking Roman Catholic Second Vatican Council (1962–1965) in the encyclical *Nostra Aetate/In Our Time* (1965). This statement acknowledged Jews as older spiritual siblings to Christians, beloved by *God, and deserving of respect and collaboration. With this public statement came a more open and public era of dialogue between Jews (often Orthodox) and Christians.

3.1. Pinchas Lapide (1922–1997). Lapide, a German Orthodox Jew, became a significant dialogue partner with other Christian theologians (Jürgen Moltmann, Karl Rahner, Hans Küng) during this time period. In *Paul, Rabbi and Apostle* (1984), he claims Paul as a Jew in the long tradition of seeking to spread the message of monotheism. Significantly, Lapide posits that Paul's letters were only written to a Gentile audience, leaving Torah-practicing Jews to continue in their fidelity to the law. Lapide also thinks that in the end Paul's attempt to bring *Christ as Messiah to Jews was a failure, whereas his greatest accomplishment was to bring Christ as *Savior to the Gentiles. Lapide urges tolerance regarding the differences between Jews and Christians, seeing a Pauline tolerance of sacred pluralism within his letters (1 Corinthians and Rom 9) that could be fruitfully embraced in the current day.

3.2. Michael Wyschogrod (1928–2015). Wyschogrod, a German American Orthodox thinker, became well known for his writings regarding Christian topics as well as interaction with Swiss theologian Karl Barth. Like Lapide, Wyschogrod sees in Paul's letters advice specifically to Gentile communities. Paul not only thought as a Jewish Pharisee but also allowed for the continuance of Jewish practice among both nonbelieving and Christ-believing Jews. The main conflict between Paul and his Jewish communities, Wyschogrod says, was Paul's postresurrection perspective in contrast to their preresurrection viewpoint; the issue was *not* Judaism itself but rather *timing*. For Paul, the Christ event opened up a way to be "adopted" children of *Israel (a new social category) for Gentiles, while for the Jew, Christ brought forth the mercy of God (*midas horachamin*) rather than the wrath of God (*midas hadin*) in regard to the performance of the law. Wyschogrod provocatively challenged Christians to, like Paul, allow Jewish members in their churches to practice the legal requirements of the Torah as a recognition of Paul's full eschatological view.

4. *Debru Emet*, American Scholarship, and "Paul Within Judaism."

A half century after *Nostra Aetate* and the free and respectful discussion that ensued between Jews and Christians came a Jewish response in the document *Debru Emmet/Speak the Truth* (2000). This statement notes that Nazism was not a Christian phenomenon and that public interaction and dialogue with Christians does not endanger Jewish practice/existence. Alongside this positive stance toward further and deeper dialogue came the emergence of many prominent NT Jewish scholars, with many books and articles regarding the place of Paul, culminating in all of Paul's letters being interpreted from a Jewish point of view in the *Annotated Jewish New Testament* (2011).

4.1. Alan Segal (1945–2011). A professor of religion at Barnard College, Segal raised the question of Paul's *conversion from Judaism in *Paul the Convert* (1992), seeing in Paul's description of apostleship similar rhetoric to the call narratives of the Hebrew prophets. Just as the prophets had a specific calling, so Paul saw himself called, as a Jew, to the Gentiles of his day. Segal brings to light significant sociological work on conversion, explaining Paul's conversion to Christ as more akin to taking on a new role than a new religion. He helpfully examines Paul's love/hate rhetoric regarding Judaism as in line with how a convert to a new religious tradition speaks both positively and negatively of their religion of birth. Paul shows this psychological feature of a Jew converted to a *new form of Jewish orientation* in his letters.

4.2. Mark Nanos (1954–). Nanos is a Jewish scholar known for a theological school called "Paul Within Judaism." For Nanos, the study of Paul using the same Lutheran/polemical *hermeneutics of the past did not contribute to reconciliation between Christians and Jews. So Nanos examines the question, Was Paul an apostate who turned his back on the Jews of his day? In his study of Romans 9–11 Nanos begins a fruitful path forward of construing Paul as speaking from within Judaism, as a faithful Jew, to Jews of his day (1996). In doing so Nanos finds different answers to the question of Paul and Judaism (2017). Even in Paul's seemingly anti-Jewish rhetoric in his correspondence with Galatia, a place where scholarship has long seen a non-Jewish audience, Nanos sees Paul writing within and to a Jewish community (2002). Paul was fully Jewish, even if messianically inclined, and he dealt with and spoke to an as yet undifferentiated Judaism that was able to hold the diversity of opinion Paul exhibits.

4.3. Pamela Eisenbaum. Eisenbaum, an NT scholar at Iliff School of Theology, participates in the late twenty-first-century trend of seeing Paul as fully Jewish (see *Paul Was Not a Christian*, 2010). According to Eisenbaum, Paul never believed that all difference between Jew and Gentile had been abolished. She reconstructs a more thoroughly Jewish schema in Paul's thought, seeking the meaning of the Christ-event for Paul in an authentically Jewish way, as Gentiles ingrafting genealogically into *kinship (via *Abraham) while retaining difference from Jews. For Paul, despite his universal rhetoric, Israel was still Israel, Jews were still Jews, and Gentiles were still Gentiles; they were all part of one family but retained difference. Eisenbaum also stresses the *apocalyptic worldview of Paul in seeing Gentiles as "eschatological pilgrims," which in the Hebrew Scriptures is noted as a sign of the coming of the Messiah. This, for Eisenbaum, explains Paul's insistence in Galatians on Gentiles remaining Gentiles.

4.4. Paula Fredriksen (1951–). A scholar of early Christianity at Boston University, Fredriksen takes a fully Jewish approach to Paul, all the while accounting for the interpretative strategies he used to seek Gentile converts in *Paul the Pagan's Apostle* (2017). She finds room for Paul's worldview within the diversity of Second Temple Judaism and the eschatological traditions it contained. Specifically, Fredriksen finds Paul to be a law-practicing Jew, not abrogating the law but seeking to reach the Gentile populace. She sees Paul as creating a sociological place for eschatological converts in his day (echoing Wyschogrod) not found in either God-fearers or full proselytes. The idea of a third eschatological way was a provocative one that in practice, Fredriksen says, threatened the accepted religious equilibrium between Jews and the Roman hierarchy in many places. Paul's seeking conversion from Gentiles was the reason he was disciplined by the Jewish community. Nonetheless, the disagreement among the Jewish community was over timing and political safety rather than over Judaism as such.

Although unknown to many today, both Jewish and Christian, the writings of Paul have inspired a lively conversation about a number of common philosophical, theological, ethical, and, surprisingly, Jewish issues. Although not seen as offering a viable path for practicing Jews today, Paul is increasingly viewed as representing a respectable and historically recognizable place within the developing myriad of Jewish traditions and expectations now known to both Christians and Jews as Second Temple Judaism.

See also Apocalyptic Paul; Apocalypticism; Christ, Messiah; Conversion and Call of Paul; Eschatology; Ethics; Gentiles; Hellenism, Roman; Israel; Paul and Judaism; Peace, Reconciliation; Works of the Law.

BIBLIOGRAPHY. **L. Baeck,** "The Faith of Paul," in *Judaism and Christianity: Essays by Leo Baeck* (Philadelphia: Jewish Publication Society of America, 1964); **M. Bird and P. Sprinkle,** "Jewish Interpretation of Paul in the Last Thirty Years," *CurBR* 6 (2008): 355-76; **D. Boyarin,** *A Radical Jew: Paul and the Politics of Identity* (Berkeley: University of California Press, 1997); **P. Eisenbaum,** "Paul as the New Abraham," in *Paul and Politics: Ekklesia, Israel, Imperium, Interpretation* (Harrisburg, PA: Trinity Press International, 2000), 130-45; idem, "Following in the Footnotes of Apostle Paul," in *Identity and the Politics of Scholarship in Religion* (London: Routledge, 2006), 77-97; idem, *Paul Was Not a Christian* (New York: HarperOne, 2010); **P. Fredriksen,** "Why Should a 'Law-Free" Mission Mean a "Law-Free" Apostle?," *JBL* 134 (2015): 637-50; idem, "Paul and Judaism," in *The Annotated Jewish New Testament* (Oxford: Oxford University Press, 2017), 633-37; idem, *Paul: The Pagan's Apostle* (New Haven, CT: Yale University Press, 2017); idem, "God Is Jewish, but Gentiles Don't Have to Be," in *The Message of Paul the Apostle Within Second Temple Judaism* (Minneapolis: Fortress Academic, 2020), 3-19; **J. Gager,** "Scholarship as Moral Vision: David Flusser on Jesus, Paul, and the Birth of Christianity," *JQR* 95 (2005): 60-73; **H. Graetz,** *The History of the Jews* (Philadelphia: Jewish Publication Society of America, 1898); **D. Hagner,** "Paul in Modern Jewish Thought," in *Pauline Studies* (Grand Rapids, MI: Eerdmans, 1981), 143-65; **J. Klausner,** *From Jesus to Paul* (Boston: Beacon, 1943); **D. Langton,** *The Apostle Paul in the Jewish Imagination: A Study in Modern Jewish-Christian Relations* (Cambridge: Cambridge University Press, 2010); idem, "Jewish Readings of Paul," in *The Blackwell Companion to Paul* (Hoboken, NJ: Blackwell, 2011), 455-71; **P. Lapide and P. Stuhlmacher,** *Paul, Rabbi and Apostle* (Minneapolis: Augsburg, 1984); **C. G. Montefiore,** *Judaism and St. Paul: Two Essays* (London: Goschen, 1914); **M. Nanos,** *The Mystery of Romans: The Jewish Context of Paul's Letters* (Minneapolis: Fortress, 1996); idem, *The Irony of Galatians: Paul's Letter in First-Century Context* (Minneapolis: Fortress, 2002); idem, *Reading Paul Within Judaism: Collected Essays of Mark D. Nanos* (Eugene, OR: Cascade, 2017); idem, "Paul—Why Bother? A Jewish Perspective," *Svensk Teologisk Kvartalskrift* 4 (2019): 271-87; **J. Neusner,** *Children of the Flesh, Children of the Promise: A Rabbi Talks with Paul* (Cleveland: Pilgrim, 1995); **S. Sandmel,** *The Genius of Paul* (New York: Farrar, Straus & Cudahy, 1958); **H. J. Schoeps,** *The Theology of the Apostle in the Light of Jewish Religious History* (Cambridge: Lutterworth, 1961); **A. Segal,** *Paul the Convert: The Apostolate and Apostasy of Saul the Pharisee* (New Haven, CT: Yale University Press, 1992); idem, "Paul's Religious Experience in the Eyes of Jewish Scholars," in *Israel's God and Rebecca's Children: Christology and Community in Early Judaism and Christianity* (Waco, TX: Baylor University Press, 2008), 321-43; **B. Spinoza,** *Theological-Political Treatise* (New Haven, CT: Yale University Press, 2007); **I. M. Wise,** "Paul and the Mystics," in *Three Lectures on the Origins of Christianity* (Cincinnati: Bloch, 1883); **M. Wyschogrod,** "Paul, Jews, and Gentiles," in *Abraham's Promise: Judaism and Jewish-Christian Relations* (Grand Rapids, MI: Eerdmans, 2004), 188-201.

J. L. Moses

INTERPRETATION: LUTHER

Martin Luther's interpretation of Paul was central to his breach with the Roman church and the ultimate division of Western Christianity into Protestant and Catholic confessions. This explosive impact made him Paul's most enduringly controversial interpreter. Working in the context of Renaissance humanism, Luther criticized medieval scholasticism's emphasis on human cooperation with divine *grace through good works. He instead stressed the effectiveness of *God alone in *salvation and read Paul's statements about *justification by *faith in these terms. In the modern era, Protestant NT scholarship typically regarded Luther as a source of positive trajectories in Pauline interpretation, but in the 1970s and 1980s this evaluation was reversed in the scholarship of the "new perspective on Paul" (especially E. P. Sanders, James Dunn, N. T. Wright, and their forerunner, Krister Stendahl). Luther is here cast as Paul's chief misinterpreter, whose influence must be escaped.

Critics of the new perspective on Paul defend Luther's legacy: "Students who want to understand Paul but feel they have nothing to learn from a Martin Luther should consider a career in metallurgy" (Westerholm 1988, 173). Yet advocates of the new perspective on Paul have responded with equal vigor: "Anyone trying to be a Pauline exegete while still in thrall to Luther should consider a career as a taxidermist" (Wright, 128). The task of evaluating such incompatible conclusions is complicated by Luther's own history of reception. Shortly after the emergence of the new perspective on Paul, new trends also appeared in the interpretation of Luther that emphasized his theology's apocalyptic nature (Oberman) and the importance of union with *Christ (the Finnish school: see Braaten and Jenson; Mannermaa; Vainio). These themes have also been prominent in recent interpretation of Paul, and it remains an open question whether new perspective interpreters reacted against what Luther really held or, in important respects, merely outdated representations of him.

1. Luther's Writings on Paul.

Luther characteristically produced tracts for the times and expositions of Scripture, not systematic statements of his theological and exegetical positions. He was a professor at the University of Wittenberg, and what are termed his "commentaries" are mostly based on notes of his classroom lectures. The only ones dealing with what are today regarded as undisputed letters of Paul are two series on Galatians (1516–1517, publication 1519: *LW* 27; 1531, publication 1535: *LW* 26-27). Luther also gave lectures on Romans (1515–1516: *LW* 25) but these were not published until the twentieth century. Since they predate the beginning of the Reformation, in 1517, there is much debate as to whether they represent Luther's mature perspective on Paul. That there was significant development is evident from comparison of Galatians 1516–1517/1519 with Galatians 1531/1535. In the later lectures some vital themes, perhaps especially that of the nature of faith, enjoy far greater prominence. Luther did not teach Romans again, despite attaching to it great significance as "the chief part of the New Testament" (*LW* 35:365), simply because his younger colleague, Philip Melanchthon (1497–1560), joined the Wittenberg faculty and subsequently taught the book. Luther also published a "commentary" on 1 Corinthians 7 (1523: *LW* 28), written as a wedding gift for a friend, and one on 1 Corinthians 15 (1534: *LW* 28), which originated as a series of sermons.

Any overview of Luther's interpretation of Paul must therefore rely on important but scattered references to Pauline texts in his polemical tracts, on his short prefaces (guides to readers) to Pauline letters included in his translation of the NT into German (first edition: September 1522), on his sermons, and, above all, on the later lectures on Galatians (1531/1535). This "commentary" indisputably represents Luther's mature perspective on Paul.

2. Luther's New Soteriology in Galatians (1531/1535).

In medieval interpretation Paul's statement that justification is not by *works of the *law (Gal 2:16) was understood to apply only to works done before *baptism. Subsequent works of charity were meritorious. Luther regards this as a complete misconstruing of Paul's intention to eliminate any role for works in justification. The proper role of the OT law is not to show what must be done for salvation but to demonstrate human inability to obey God and the need for a savior: "the Law only shows sin, terrifies, and humbles; thus it prepares us for justification and drives us to Christ" (*LW* 26:126). Luther also rejects the medieval idea that justification is a lifelong process in which individuals gradually become more Christlike, with the distance traveled along this pathway of transformation determining whether and how much time in purgatory will be necessary. Rather, believers are judged on the basis of Christ's person and his work on their behalf. The *righteousness of Christ granted to the believer in justification is perfect and cannot be supplemented or completed. It is also alien and remains wholly and entirely that of Christ: "Christian righteousness is, namely, that righteousness by which Christ lives in us, not the righteousness that is in our own person" (*LW* 26:168). This righteousness must be received, not earned, and, in Luther's preface to the commentary, he deploys as an organizing principle the distinction between the "active righteousness" taught by his own opponents and the "passive righteousness" Paul teaches (*LW* 26:4-12).

The means by which passive justifying righteousness is received is faith. At Galatians 3:6, when Paul quotes Genesis 15:6, "Abraham believed God and it was reckoned to him as righteousness" (Gal 3:6 NRSV), Luther understands faith as trust (*fiducia*) in God's promises. *Abraham believed that God would keep his promise that the aged Sarah would have a son. Similarly, Christians are to trust that Christ's saving work has secured forgiveness of sins even while experiencing themselves as sinners: "Christ protects me under the shadow of his wings. . . . This prevents God from seeing the sins that still cling to my flesh. . . . In His sight they are as though they were not sins. This is accomplished by imputation on account of the faith by which I begin to take hold of Christ" (*LW* 26:231-32). The existence of believers therefore has a dual aspect possible only because of divine favor: they are simultaneously justified and sinners. This divine favor is what Paul terms grace.

Although the word *grace* has a wide semantic range and can also refer to God's gifts, in contexts concerning justification Paul uses it as a shorthand for God's desire to forgive sins through Christ. It is not, as in medieval accounts, something infused into people to enable them gradually to change but instead something on which they cast themselves: "The more we work and sweat to extricate ourselves from sin, the worse off we are. For there is no way to remove sin except by grace" (*LW* 26:26-27). Paul directs the attention of the Galatians not to the deeds they must perform in order to be saved but instead to the salvation they already fully possess in Christ. Whereas medieval accounts left final *judgment uncertain, since no person can know how far they have advanced in righteousness, Luther held that reliance on Christ yields complete assurance of salvation. From Luther's perspective his opponents were repeating the error made by Paul's Jewish opponents when they insisted on *circumcision as essential for *Gentile believers (Gal 6:12-13). Both groups were attempting to place human obedience alongside faith in Christ as a cause of salvation. Luther felt that he and Paul were fighting the same battle in different eras.

3. Luther and the New Perspective on Paul: The Introspective Conscience.

In *Paul Among Jews and Gentiles* Stendahl argues that Paul and Luther were not fighting the same battle. Paul's teaching on justification does not answer the human need for *forgiveness but instead explains the calling of the Gentiles into the people of God. Confusion over this arose because "the Pauline awareness of sin has been interpreted in light of Luther's struggles with his conscience" (Stendahl, 12). It was Luther's experiences of guilt and despair (*Anfechtungen*) over what he perceived as his inability to do the good works required for salvation that led to his new soteriology. In Luther's account of his "Reformation breakthrough" to a new interpretation of "the righteousness of God" (Rom 1:17), he emphasizes that he struggled with the text because of his rage with God at his predicament (*LW* 34:336-37). This was Luther's gateway to the discovery of a gracious God. Stendahl suggests that Paul's experience was quite different. Key texts (Gal 1:13-14; Phil 3:6) show that prior to his Damascus road experience, Paul's conscience was robust. Paul did not struggle with guilt as a result of his inability to keep the law and did not formulate his understanding of justification as an answer to a guilty conscience.

Yet while Luther always regarded his struggles as essential to his progress in biblical interpretation, the assumption that Paul suffered from a guilty conscience did not shape his ideas about justification. He even imagines Paul attributing his *sin in persecuting the *church to blind zeal, reporting that "in place of these horrible sins of mine, which I then regarded as a service most pleasing to God, He gave me His grace and called me to be an apostle" (*LW* 26:69). Paul's problem was not a guilty conscience but false confidence that he was fulfilling the law. It is this misplaced confidence in the possession of righteousness that Luther associates with Paul's use of the phrase "works of the law" and that he takes to be typical of Judaism (*LW* 25:241). The theological use of the law to reveal sin is what Luther hears Paul teaching as the law's true salvific purpose, not what he hears Paul saying about the way the law functioned in his own life before the Damascus road. It is a false line of reasoning to suggest that Luther must have misunderstood Paul concerning justification because he projected his own guilty conscience back onto the *apostle. Whether Luther is right about justification must be argued on other grounds, for he regards Paul's conscience as robust (Chester, 121-35).

4. Luther and the New Perspective on Paul: Justification by Faith.

Luther's account of justification has provoked anxiety not only among those concerned to emphasize the significance of Gentile inclusion but also those concerned with Paul's focus on the participation of believers in Christ. Luther's apparently narrowly forensic understanding of justification, in which the righteousness of Christ is transferred to those who believe across the divine courtroom, is held to lack any textual basis in Paul and to propose a fictional righteousness. Believers are left basically unchanged and the close connections drawn by Paul between justification and their transformation obscured. Yet it was not Luther but his colleague Melanchthon who developed a forensic account of justification. While accepting that Paul's imagery is drawn from the law courts, Luther himself rarely describes justification in legal terms. He instead emphasizes that faith unites the believer with Christ: "Faith takes hold of Christ and has him present, enclosing him as the ring encloses the gem" (*LW* 26:132). Responding to Paul's statement that he has been crucified with Christ and that he no longer lives but Christ lives in him (Gal 2:19-20), Luther pictures Paul saying that "this death acquires an alien life for me, namely, the life of Christ, which is not inborn in me, but is granted to me in faith" (*LW* 26:170). When Luther uses the term *imputation* he does not mean that righteousness is transferred from Christ to the believer. As the Finnish school has emphasized, he means that through the presence of Christ in faith believers receive Christ's righteousness as an essential component of their union with his person (Vainio, 138-54). Luther does not partition Paul's themes of justification and participation but integrates them.

It is therefore unsurprising to find Luther emphasizing what faith does: "It is impossible for it not to be doing good works incessantly" (*LW* 35:370). Luther strenuously resists all suggestions that works are an efficient cause of justification. Yet, while works are not meritorious, they are essential to the Christian life, since those who receive the alien righteousness of Christ must also live the alien life of Christ. Luther's description of believers as simultaneously justified and sinners describes not those stalled in an abortive process of change but those engaged in an apocalyptic daily struggle to live from the life of Christ and not from their old selves. It is faith that empowers the Christian in this struggle. Either faith is active or it is not faith. Medieval interpreters typically took Paul's assertion that what counts is faith working through *love (Gal 5:6) to indicate that faith works only when it is formed by love. Apart from love, faith (*fides*) is merely intellectual assent to the *truth of the *gospel that depends on love to vivify it and make it into something active. In contrast, Luther argues that Paul "attributes the working itself to faith. . . . He makes love the tool through which faith works" (*LW* 27:29). It remains controversial among Luther interpreters whether the renewal that faith empowers is an aspect of justification or its consequence. However, it is for Luther indisputably an essential aspect of what it means for believers to live the alien life of Christ.

5. Luther and the New Perspective on Paul: Works of the Law.

If new developments in Luther interpretation have in some areas narrowed the gap with contemporary Pauline interpreters, the same is not true in relation to the nature of Judaism. New perspective scholarship reassessed Second Temple Jewish texts, exposing as unfounded Protestant scholarship's portrayal of Judaism as a legalistic religion of works righteousness (Sanders, 33-430). This made Luther's drawing of an analogy between his own opponents and those of Paul appear exaggerated. It also made it unlikely that Paul's denials that works of the law justify were targeted against Jewish attempts to earn salvation (Rom 3:20, 27-28; Gal 2:16; 3:2, 5, 10). Dunn proposes that Paul was instead attacking ethnic privilege. The phrase "works of the law" refers primarily to Jewish practices (circumcision, *food laws, Sabbath observance) that served as boundary markers with Gentiles. Paul is stressing that justification does not come through maintaining a Jewish identity in separation from Gentiles (Dunn, 1-97).

At a general level, the new perspective on Paul here represents a welcome advance. While it would be unfair to expect a sixteenth-century interpreter to produce a historically accurate account of Second Temple Judaism, it is undoubtedly Luther's legacy that shaped

Protestant portrayals of Judaism. His vile attacks on supposed Jewish misanthropy in *On the Jews and Their Lies* (1543; *LW* 47:121-306) must be repudiated. Luther also unhelpfully interprets "works of the law" in terms of a general principle of earning salvation abstracted from the realities of Jewish practice. Yet against those contemporaries who argued that "works of the law" refers exclusively to ceremonies, Luther insisted that it refers to everything that the law requires. At this formal level, he and new perspective interpreters are in fact in agreement. The contrast is that Luther interprets all Paul's uses of the phrase exclusively in terms of works righteousness, Dunn in terms of boundary markers. While Luther's account may fail to convince, this exclusive focus on boundary markers is itself vulnerable to criticism. Precisely as boundary markers demarcate a social space for an entire Jewish way of life swathed in divine commandments, they also mark the frontier between *holiness and sinfulness (Gal 2:15). It is possible to regard Paul as warning from the perspective of faith in Christ that ethical achievement under the law does not lead to justification (Rom 4:4-5; 9:10-13; Phil 3:6) without ascribing a general principle of works righteousness to Judaism or distancing Paul's argument from the issue of Jew-Gentile relationships (Westerholm 1988, 142). Although Luther's perspective is no longer persuasive, debate over the meaning of "works of the law" continues.

6. Luther's Legacy and Contemporary Pauline Interpretation.

The rise of reception history is moving appraisal of Luther's Pauline interpretation beyond oversimplified approval or rejection. More major works seek to locate their own contributions in the context of trajectories of interpretation shaped by influential past interpreters, including Luther (e.g., Barclay, 97-115). In some areas, such as the meaning of "works of the law," Luther does not offer a viable alternative perspective but can at least provide a potential corrective to dominant contemporary voices. In other areas, Luther is surprisingly in tune with contemporary concerns. The centrality of union with Christ to his account of justification, so that believers participate in a reality that remains in significant senses external to them, offers a way of integrating fundamental components of Paul's theology. Repristinating Luther's exegesis in very different contemporary contexts would lead only to anachronism, but ignoring him would be to neglect a significant resource.

See also Abraham; Apocalyptic Paul; Covenant; Faith; Forgiveness; Galatians, Letter to the; Grace; Holiness, Sanctification; In Christ; Interpretation: Medieval; Interpretation: New Perspective; Justification; Law; Love; Paul and Judaism; Righteousness; Romans, Letter to the; Salvation; Sin, Guilt; Works of the Law.

BIBLIOGRAPHY. **M. Allen and J. A. Linebaugh,** eds., *Reformation Readings of Paul* (Downers Grove, IL: IVP Academic, 2015); **J. M. G. Barclay,** *Paul and the Gift* (Grand Rapids, MI: Eerdmans, 2015); **C. E. Braaten and R. W. Jenson,** eds., *Union with Christ: The New Finnish Interpretation of Luther* (Grand Rapids, MI: Eerdmans, 1998); **S. J. Chester,** *Reading Paul with the Reformers* (Grand Rapids, MI: Eerdmans, 2017); idem, "Apocalyptic Union: Martin Luther's Account of Faith in Christ," in *In Christ in Paul: Explorations in Paul's Theology of Union and Participation*, ed. M. J. Thate, K. J. Vanhoozer, and C. R. Campbell (Grand Rapids, MI: Eerdmans, 2018); **J. D. G. Dunn,** *The New Perspective on Paul,* rev ed. (Grand Rapids, MI: Eerdmans, 2005); **K. Ehrensperger and R. Ward Holder,** eds., *Reformation Readings of Romans* (New York: T&T Clark, 2008); **K. Hagen,** *Luther's Approach to Scripture as Seen in His "Commentaries" on Galatians* (Tübingen: Mohr Siebeck, 1993); **R. W. Holder,** *A Companion to Paul in the Reformation* (Leiden: Brill, 2009); **R. Kolb, I. Dingel, and L. Batka,** eds., *The Oxford Handbook of Martin Luther's Theology* (Oxford: Oxford University Press, 2014); **J. A. Linebaugh,** "The Christocentrism of Faith in Christ: Martin Luther's Reading of Galatians 2:16, 19-20," in *The Word of the Cross: Reading Paul* (Grand Rapids, MI: Eerdmans, 2022); idem, "Until Christ: Advent Again and Again in Martin Luther's Interpretation of Galatians," in *The Word of the Cross: Reading Paul* (Grand Rapids, MI: Eerdmans, 2022); **T. Mannermaa,** *Christ Present in Faith: Luther's View of Justification* (Minneapolis: Fortress, 2005); **H. Oberman,** *Luther: Man Between God and the Devil* (New York: Image, 1992); **E. Rummel,** *The Humanist-Scholastic Debate in the Renaissance and Reformation* (Cambridge, MA: Harvard University Press, 1995); **E. P. Sanders,** *Paul and Palestinian Judaism* (Minneapolis: Fortress, 1977); **M. Seifrid,** "Paul, Luther, and Justification in Gal 2:15-21," *WTJ* 65 (2003): 215-30; **K. Stendahl,** *Paul Among Jews and Gentiles* (Philadelphia: Fortress, 1976); **O. P. Vainio,** ed., *Engaging Luther: A (New) Theological Assessment* (Eugene, OR: Cascade, 2010); **S. Westerholm,** *Israel's Law and the Church's Faith: Paul and His Recent Interpreters* (Grand Rapids, MI: Eerdmans, 1988); idem, *Perspectives Old and New on Paul: The "Lutheran" Paul and His Critics* (Grand Rapids, MI: Eerdmans, 2004); **N. T. Wright,**

Paul and His Recent Interpreters: Some Contemporary Debates (Minneapolis: Augsburg Fortress, 2015).

S. J. Chester

INTERPRETATION: MEDIEVAL

During the Middle Ages in the Latin West (600–1500), the interpretation of St. Paul's epistles was mediated largely through Augustine and, before him, Origen. Many other scholars, however, also commented on these epistles, which were generally understood to comprise the fourteen *letters found in the NT authored by or ascribed to Paul, including the letter to the Hebrews. Commentaries on some or all of Paul's epistles were written by Marius Victorinus, Ambrosiaster, John Chrysostom, Pelagius, Jerome, Theodore of Mopsuestia, Cyril of Alexandria, and Theodoret of Cyrus, but many medieval exegetes in the Latin West often followed Augustine in identifying the key themes in Paul's writings. These themes included the relations among the trinitarian persons, the *salvation offered by Jesus *Christ by his death and *resurrection, the role of *grace in justifying the believing members of the *church, actual and original *sin, predestination and free will, *faith and *works of the *law, the relationship between *Israel and the church, the sacraments, and *eschatology. This article will sketch the medieval development of Pauline exegesis in the Latin West from Augustine and other patristic authors through the monasteries and cathedral schools of the early Middle Ages to representatives of scholastic exegesis in high and late medieval universities.

1. Patristic Foundation
2. Carolingian Period
3. Eleventh and Twelfth Centuries
4. Thirteenth Century: Thomas Aquinas
5. Late Middle Ages: Nicholas of Lyra
6. Conclusion

1. Patristic Foundation.

Particularly important in medieval exegesis was Paul's teaching on *election, grace, and works. Origen and Pelagius had interpreted Paul's emphasis on the primacy of grace and opposition to works of the law (see Rom 3:20, 28) to mean that faith precludes only works of the old law and not postbaptismal moral works of justice, which are necessary for Christians according to James 2:24. This interpretation was generally accepted in the Middle Ages. On this issue of election and predestination, early Christian exegesis tended to interpret Paul's use of those phrases (see Rom 8:29; 9:11; 11:5) to mean that God elected by means of his *foreknowledge of faith and merit on the part of the believer. Augustine, in his early commentaries on Romans and Galatians (written between 394 and 396), holds that God's grace is found in the call to faith and that one's response to that call is the basis for election or reprobation. Nevertheless, he later believed that not only does God foreknow responses of faith and good works, but he also graciously gives the *gifts that allow humans to respond in faith. Particularly important in this regard is Augustine's deeper appreciation of Romans 9:16, "So it depends not upon man's will or exertion, but upon God's *mercy" (RSV). Augustine found that this verse from Paul prioritized divine sovereignty over human agency (*De natura et gratia* 231-99; *De praedestinatione*, 959-92; *De dono perseverantiae*, 993-1034).

Augustine also appropriated Paul to develop his doctrine of original sin. Although Augustine expressed admiration for Pelagius's commentary on Romans, he found Pelagius's interpretation of Romans 5:12 to be dissatisfying. When Paul says, "Therefore as sin came into the world through one man and death through sin, and so death spread to all men because all men sinned" (RSV), Pelagius understood that teaching to mean that sin entered the world by means of people imitating Adam's example of disobedience. Augustine believed that sin was transmitted not merely by people imitating a bad example but rather through propagation (*De natura et gratia*, 238-39).

The Second Council of Orange in 529 vindicated Augustine's theology against what was later called semi-Pelagianism, and it did so by drawing directly from Augustine and other important passages in the Pauline corpus. For example, in order to establish the doctrine of original sin, the council cites Romans 5:12 and Romans 6:16 ("Do you not know that if you yield yourselves to any one as obedient *slaves, you are slaves of the one whom you obey, either of sin, which leads to death, or of obedience, which leads to *righteousness?" RSV). Emphasizing the priority of grace, the council cites Philippians 2:13: "God is at work in you, both to will and to work for his good pleasure" (RSV). Paul also says that the God "who began a good work in you will bring it to completion at the day of Jesus Christ" (Phil 1:6 RSV); this passage shows that even the beginning of faith has its source in divine grace, as does 1 Corinthians 4:7 ("What have you that you did not receive?" RSV). Nonetheless, the council also condemns predestination to evil, a position Augustine was accused of holding on account of his belief that reprobation occurs because God withholds efficacious grace from some people according to his inscrutable *wisdom (de Clercq, 55-63). In his response to Pelagian critics, Augustine maintained the priority of grace, the unmerited nature of predestination, and human *freedom, which can be empowered by God to respond freely in faith (*De praedestinatione sanctorum*, 964-69; *De dono perseverantiae*, 1013-34). In these matters pertaining to grace and free will and in the interpretation of Augustine's thought by the Second Council of Orange, Paul's writings were foundational.

2. Carolingian Period.

In the early Middle Ages, the reception of St. Paul in both Latin and Byzantine cultures occurred primarily, at least at first, through elaborate compilations of scriptural exegesis from the church fathers. In his commentary on the Pauline epistles, for example, Rabanus Maurus compiles interpretations from the Fathers and includes few of his own opinions, and Florus of Lyons draws from a wide variety of Augustinian passages in his own commentary.

Eventually, in the Carolingian period (ca. 750–ca. 900), a number of scholars, still drawing heavily from patristic exegesis, began to include more of their personal insights. Claudius of Turin, although having compiled numerous passages from the Fathers, especially Jerome, to apply to his commentaries on the Pauline epistles, nevertheless offers his own interpretations as well. Sedulius Scottus generally follows Augustine and Jerome in his commentaries but is also attentive to the original languages of the Bible and emphasizes the literal sense. He links predestination with God's foreknowledge and emphasizes that grace and free will must work together.

The Pauline commentaries of Haimo of Auxerre were particularly influential in the Middle Ages. They began as a homiliary and exerted significant influence on later medieval exegesis. Haimo makes annotations between the words of the scriptural text, anticipating the interlinear comments of the twelfth-century *Glossa ordinaria* (a collection of scriptural commentaries associated with the cathedral school of Laon). Many passages from his commentaries, including patristic citations, became part of the marginal glosses of the *Glossa ordinaria*. Haimo's Pauline commentaries manifest a profound interest in trinitarian doctrine. According to Haimo, the "*knowledge of the *truth" mentioned in 1 Timothy 2:4 and Titus 1:1 (RSV) refers to belief in the Trinity (*In epistolam I ad Timotheum*, 788-90; *In epistolam ad Titum*, 809-11). The "word of Christ" dwelling "in all wisdom" (Col 3:16 RSV) is also trinitarian doctrine (*In epistolam ad Colossenses*, 761-62). It is the Trinity who makes sinners just through "the righteousness of God" (Rom 1:17 RSV; *In epistolam ad Romanos*, 372-74). *Justification occurs freely, without preceding merits, but Christ communicates the effects of his passion and death by means of the church's sacraments and their reception in faith. Haimo's doctrine of predestination involves more than divine foreknowledge. Those "whom he foreknew" (Rom 8:29 RSV) are those whom God foresaw would have faith, but God gives the faithful both their ability to will the good and their perseverance in faith (*In epistolam ad Romanos*, 436-37). Referring to Paul's juxtaposition of Jacob and Esau in Romans 9:13 ("As it is written, 'Jacob I loved, but Esau I hated,'" RSV), Haimo claims that Jacob's election originated in God's mercy and not in his good works and that Esau was hated apart from evil works. Paul's statement in Romans 9:14 that Esau's disfavor is not the result of divine injustice confirms God's righteousness, but only God knows why Jacob was elected mercifully and why Esau was rejected justly (*In epistolam ad Romanos*, 442-43).

The Carolingian commentaries on Paul were valuable not only on account of their careful textual analysis. The scholars of the eighth and ninth centuries extracted numerous passages from patristic commentaries to augment their own interpretations of the letters of Paul. This process of editing and collating has been dismissed as unoriginal, but recent scholarship has begun to realize not only the immense amount of work that was necessary to produce these commentaries but also more precisely how influential they were later in the Middle Ages.

3. Eleventh and Twelfth Centuries.

The practice of glossing in the Carolingian period became more popular in the eleventh and twelfth centuries. It also became more common for the scriptural text to be located in a central column or columns, with annotations and commentary written in interlinear spaces and in the margins of the manuscript. Pauline commentaries attributed to such authors as Lanfranc of Bec and Bruno the Carthusian were influential for the authors of the *Glossa ordinaria* and other twelfth-century commentators. Lanfranc in particular is careful to examine the syntax of Paul's letters, and Berengar of Tours calls the reader's attention to the patterns of Paul's expressions. Lanfranc and Berengar also happen to have differing approaches to scriptural exegesis and to Paul's account of the Eucharist in 1 Corinthians 11. Lanfranc finds the authority of Scripture superior to the liberal arts and the exegete's interpretative abilities, while Berengar has greater use for the skill and learning of the commentator. Before the doctrinal debates surrounding the Eucharist in the 1050s, commentaries on 1 Corinthians 11 displayed an interest in that chapter's sacramental teaching but focused on the liturgy, ecclesiastical *discipline, and the real presence of Christ in the Eucharist. After Berengar's theology of the Eucharist was condemned, on account of its emphasis on the symbolic nature of the bread and wine and its denial of transubstantiation, commentaries on 1 Corinthians attributed to Bruno the Carthusian and Manegold of Lautenbach incorporate terms and philosophical distinctions that developed to affirm both the identity of Christ's *body in the Eucharist and the *flesh he assumed at the incarnation, and the substantial conversion from bread and wine to Christ's body and blood.

Twelfth-century interpretations of Paul developed the interpretations and exegetical methodologies of earlier centuries. The *Glossa ordinaria* uses both interlinear and marginal glosses, sometimes from the church fathers and Carolingian exegetes, and sometimes from the scholars from the school of Laon who compiled the text. Anonymous comments are included. The Romans commentary of William of St. Thierry applies Augustinian categories of grace to Paul's description of grace in Romans 5–8. For William, Paul was a master of Christian meditation and contemplation, and he finds in Romans a series of stages by which the Christian progresses through the struggle with sin to the experience of a relative *peace granted by God, and finally to the filial *adoption mentioned by Paul in Romans 8:14, which is granted by the *Holy Spirit (*Expositio super Epistolam ad Romanos*, 114). If William's emphases are monastic and contemplative, Peter Abelard's Romans commentary is written in a more critical and analytical style. Peter was accused by William of Pelagianism on account of his position that the will alone can respond to God's offer of grace. This position seemed to deny the necessity of the helping grace needed to respond to God's prevenient grace. Regarding soteriology, Peter in his comments on Romans 3:26 rejects the ransom theory of *atonement and claims that Christ's *sufferings and death kindle in the believer the *love that reconciles the sinner to God (*Expositio in Epistolam*, 2:280-90).

4. Thirteenth Century: Thomas Aquinas. In the thirteenth century, Thomas Aquinas read attentively and commented at length on the Pauline epistles. In addition to using Paul's works extensively in his theological treatises, such as the *Compendium theologiae* and the *Summa theologiae*, Thomas devoted much time in commenting on the Pauline corpus. Treating the Pauline epistles as a single body of literature, Thomas divides the Pauline corpus into numerous subdivisions.

Eschewing a more traditional division of the text that explains the fourteen books as symbolizing the four Gospels added onto the Ten Commandments, as one finds in the *Glossa ordinaria*, Peter Lombard, and Hugh of Saint-Cher, Thomas offers a more complex *divisio textus*. Thomas says that Paul's letters explain the power of grace, whose origin is described in the Gospels' account of Jesus. In Thomas's prologue to his commentary on the Pauline epistles, he explains how each epistle manifests a particular aspect of Christ's grace. Grace can be considered in the *head of the church, in the principal members of the church, and in the mystical body of Christ, which is the church (*Super epistolas S. Pauli lectura*, 1:3). Insofar as grace is in Christ, the head of the church, one can find that treated in Hebrews. Insofar as grace is in the prelates of the church, who are the church's principal members, one can find that treated in 1 Timothy (emphasizing ecclesial unity), 2 Timothy (exhorting resistance against persecutors), Titus (defending against heretics), and Philemon (counseling temporal rulers). Finally, the letters to the *Gentile communities express grace insofar as it is in the mystical body of Christ, which is the church. Christ's grace can be considered in three ways. First, Paul writes about grace as it is in itself in Romans. Second, he discusses grace as it is in the sacraments in 1 Corinthians (the sacraments themselves), 2 Corinthians (the dignity of the ministers of the sacraments), and Galatians (the superfluity of the old sacraments). Third, Paul treats grace insofar as it produces unity in the church in Ephesians (the establishment of ecclesial unity), Philippians (the strengthening and progress of ecclesial unity), Colossians (defense against certain errors), 1 Thessalonians (defense against current persecutions), and 2 Thessalonians (defense against future persecutions).

Thomas offers this *divisio textus* of the Pauline corpus not only because he viewed Paul as a wise *teacher communicating divinely revealed truths in a fitting order, as recognized in the church's liturgical use of these texts, but also because God, as their primary author, communicated the message of the *gospel through them as part of a larger, suitably ordered canon of Scripture. The Gospels portray the origin of Christ's grace. The power of Christ's grace is the overarching theme of the Pauline corpus, and reading it prepares one to appreciate the exercise of the power of Christ's grace depicted in the remainder of the NT canon (*De commendatione*, 439).

5. Late Middle Ages: Nicholas of Lyra.

One of the last major medieval Pauline commentators was Nicholas of Lyra, an early fourteenth-century Franciscan scholar who was outstanding in the Middle Ages for his knowledge of Hebrew, rabbinic sources, and the church fathers. In the prologue to his commentary on the Pauline epistles, Nicholas claims that the material cause, that is, the subject matter of the epistles, is Christ crucified; and that the purpose, that is, the formal cause, is to benefit the church by calling to mind the life of grace in the present and the future *glory of heaven. Nicholas also notes that each epistle is typically divided into three sections, namely, a preface, an explanation, and a conclusion.

Several of Nicholas's interpretations, especially of Romans, address themes important in late medieval and early modern soteriology. For example, when Paul says that in the gospel, "the righteousness of God is revealed through faith for faith" (Rom 1:17 RSV), Nicholas interprets that to mean that there is a transition from unformed faith (faith without charity) to formed faith (faith formed by charity). In his discussion of justification, as mentioned in Romans 5:1, Nicholas distinguishes between two kinds of justification, namely, justification as a state of glorification, such as the first parents had in their state of innocence, and justification as movement from guilt toward righteousness, such as obtains by God's grace in a postlapsarian state. Nicholas says that this latter form of justification merits its name on account of the true justice that is the conclusion of the process and not the guilt from which it begins. Regarding predestination, as found in Romans 8:29, Nicholas claims that one should not contrast it with divine foreknowledge. Predestination from all eternity takes effect by grace in time. The grace is such that it makes the believer pleasing to God apart from any preceding merits, but human cooperation, enabled by grace, is required to maintain sanctity and grow in *holiness (*Postilla super Totam Bibliam*).

6. Conclusion.

The reception of Paul in the Middle Ages occurred through constant exposure to his letters in the divine office and in Mass, in *lectio divina*, and in academic study. Theologians and exegetes returned constantly to the exegesis of previous centuries, both to confirm and at times criticize the interpretations of earlier commentators. Over time, newer methods of exegesis developed, and newer insights tended to occur more in schools and universities than in monasteries. Nonetheless, since the writings of Paul contained such a broad array of topics, they proved to be an inexhaustible source for reflection and debate, regardless of the doctrinal, liturgical, or ecclesiastical crises that pertained to each century. In their ceaseless engagement with the *apostle to the Gentiles, medieval theologians transmitted to future generations not only the fruits of their prayerful study, but also a history of exegesis that shaped the life of the church.

See also ELECTION AND PREDESTINATION; FAITH; GRACE; HEAD; HERMENEUTICS/INTERPRETING PAUL; INTERPRETATION: AUGUSTINE; INTERPRETATION: PATRISTIC; LORD'S SUPPER; RIGHTEOUSNESS; ROMANS, LETTER TO THE; SIN, GUILT; WORKS OF THE LAW.

BIBLIOGRAPHY. ***Primary sources:*** **Peter Abelard,** *Expositio in Epistolam ad Romanos/Römerbriefkommentar*, ed. Rolf Peppermuller, 3 vols., Fontes Christiani 26/1-3 (Freiburg: Herder, 2000); **Augustine,** *De natura et gratia*, ed. C. F. Vrba and J. Zycha, CSEL 60 (Vienna, 1913); idem, *De praedestinatione sanctorum*, PL 44:959-992; idem, *De dono perseverantiae*, PL 45:993-1034; idem, *Epistulae ad Galatas expositio*, ed. J. Divjak, CSEL 84 (Vienna, 1971); idem, *Epistulae ad Romanos inchoata expositio*, ed. J. Divjak, CSEL 84 (Vienna, 1971); idem, *Expositio quarumdam propositionum ex epistula ad Romanos*, ed. J. Divjak, CSEL 84 (Vienna, 1971); **C. de Clercq,** ed., *Concilia Galliae, A. 511–A. 695*, CCSL 148A (Turnhout: Brepols, 1963); **Haimo of Auxerre,** *Expositio in epistolas Pauli*, PL 117:361-938; **Lanfranc of Bec,** *Commentarii in omnes epistolas Sancti Pauli*, PL 150:101–405; **Nicholas of Lyra,** *Postilla super Totam Bibliam*, 4 vols. (Strassburg, 1492; repr., Frankfurt am Main, 1971); **Origen,** *Der Römerbriefkommentar des Origenes: Kritische Ausgabe der Übersetzung Rufins*, ed. C. P. Hammond Bammel, 3 vols. (Freiburg im Breisgau: Herder, 1990–1998); **A. Rusch,** ed., *Biblia Latina cum Glossa ordinaria*, 4 vols. (Turnhout: Brepols, 1992); **Thomas Aquinas,** *De commendatione et partitione sacrae Scripturae*, ed. R. A. Verardo, in *Opuscula theologica*, vol. 1 (Turin: Marietti, 1954); idem, *Super epistolas S. Pauli lectura*, ed. Raffaele Cai, 2 vols. (Turin: Marietti, 1953); **William of St. Thierry,** *Expositio super Epistolam ad Romanos*, ed. Paul Verdeyen, CCCM 86 (Turnhout: Brepols, 1989).

Secondary sources: **S. R. Cartwright,** ed., *A Companion to St. Paul in the Middle Ages* (Leiden: Brill, 2013); **C. Chazelle and B. Van Name Edwards,** eds., *The Study of the Bible in the Carolingian Era* (Turnhout: Brepols, 2003); **G. Dahan,** *L'exégèse chrétienne de la Bible en Occident médiéval, XIIe-XIVe siècle* (Paris: Cerf, 1999); idem, *Lire la Bible au Moyen Âge: Essais d'hermeneutique médiévale* (Geneva: Droz, 2009); **M. T. Gibson,** *The Bible in the Latin West* (Notre Dame, IN: University of Notre Dame Press, 1993); **A.-M. La Bonnardière,** ed., *Saint Augustin et la Bible* (Paris: Beauchesne, 1986); **I. C. Levy,** *Holy Scripture and the Quest for Authority at the End of the Middle Ages* (Notre Dame, IN: University of Notre Dame Press, 2012); idem, *Introducing Medieval Biblical Interpretation: The Senses of Scripture in Premodern Exegesis* (Grand Rapids, MI: Baker Academic, 2018); **G. Lobrichon,** *La Bible au Moyen Age* (Paris: Picard, 2003); **H. de Lubac,** *Exégèse médiévale. Les quatre sens de l'Écriture*, 2 vols. (Paris: Aubier, 1959–1964); **B. de Margerie,** *Introduction à l'histoire de l'exégèse*, 2nd ed., 4 vols. (Paris: Cerf, 2009); **R. Marsden and E. A. Matter,** eds., *The New Cambridge History of the Bible: From 600 to 1450* (Cambridge: Cambridge University Press, 2012); **R. E. McNally,** *The Bible in the Early Middle Ages* (Westminster, MN: Newman, 1959); **P. Riché and G. Lobrichon,** eds., *Le Moyen Age et la Bible* (Paris: Beauchesne, 1984); **B. Smalley,** *The Study of the Bible in the Middle Ages*, 3rd ed. (Notre Dame, IN: University of Notre Dame Press, 1964); **C. Spicq,** *Esquisse d'une histoire de l'exégèse latine au Moyen Age* (Paris: J. Vrin, 1944); **D. Thomas,** ed., *The Bible in Arab Christianity* (Leiden: Brill, 2005); **F. Van Liere,** *An Introduction to the Medieval Bible* (New York: Cambridge University Press, 2014); **I. Van 't Spijker,** ed., *The Multiple Meaning of Scripture: The Role of Exegesis in Early-Christian and Medieval Culture* (Leiden: Brill, 2009).

A. Canty

INTERPRETATION: MODERN EUROPEAN

Modern European interpretation of Paul began with the realization that the image of Paul in the Acts of the Apostles and the self-portrayal of the apostle in his letters show tensions. This was followed by the insight that some of the letters that Paul was named as the author of could hardly be authored by himself. These two distinctions, between (a) the Paul of Acts and the Paul of the epistles and (b) within the Pauline epistles between authentic and pseudepigraphic letters, were the basis for critical modern European interpretation of Paul. The results of this research enabled further historical and theological studies to present Paul's theology in its particular individuality and to make it fruitful for contemporary theological questions.

1. Precritical Scholarship
2. The Basis of Critical Pauline Research
3. Conservative Historicism
4. The History-of-Religions School
5. The Rediscovery of Eschatology
6. Dialectical Theology and Existentialistic Exegesis
7. Apocalypticism in Paul
8. Conclusion

1. Precritical Scholarship.

In the seventeenth and eighteenth centuries, Dutch, Scandinavian, and English scholars shaped NT research. They were primarily interested in reconstructing the text of the NT and followed the antiquarian-historical method of evaluating the internal testimony of the NT uncritically. Despite excellent language skills and a specific understanding of methodological research, great scholars as Joseph Justus Scaliger (1540–1609), Richard Bentley (1662–1742), Johann Albrecht Bengel (1687–1752), and Johann Jakob Wettstein (1693–1754) mostly collected information based on secondary literature or printed editions of ancient sources and had only accidental access to manuscripts. The interpretation of Paul of this time was not yet able to grasp the individuality of Paul's theology and the peculiarity of his position as a Jew educated by Pharisees and a Jewish *apostle for the *Gentiles.

German scholars made the epistemological shift toward critical research. According to the judgment of Jewish-German classical philologist Jacob Bernays (1824–1881), they introduced "a new, perfect art of criticism" (Bernays, 33). Whereas the scholarly elites of the eighteenth century in England, France, and the Netherlands were distracted by archaeological colonial expeditions, German scholars of the NT remained in their offices and libraries.

2. The Basis of Critical Pauline Research.

The connection of biblical exegesis to classical and oriental philology promoted the objectivity and methodical precision of the research. Rationalist Johann Philipp Gabler (1753–1826) had freed historical research into the NT from the task of providing references ("loci") for dogmatic theology. Instead, biblical theology aimed to separate the "purely human" from the "truly divine" through historical analysis to work out the "general," the "universal," which is at the same time the "divine." Friedrich Schleiermacher (1768–1834) also stated that understanding and interpreting biblical texts did not require particular theological *hermeneutics. Scholars of the NT should follow general hermeneutics used for all phenomena in human culture and intellectual history. Schleiermacher saw the goal of the interpretation in capturing the individuality and unmistakable character of the historical object. He concluded that the "language-forming power of Christianity" had created something "new" compared to Judaism and *Hellenism (Schleiermacher, 124). In doing so, Schleiermacher also laid the foundation for a tradition of the interpretation of Paul, which sought to distinguish the new Christian in Paul sharply from the Jewish and Hellenistic through detailed philological work. Schleiermacher concluded that Paul could not have written 1 Timothy since this *letter lacked the skillful "didactic" argumentation he valued in Paul (Schleiermacher, 144-45). Schleiermacher and Gabler emphasized the priority of philological and historical analysis against theological interpretation.

Ferdinand Christian Baur (1792–1860) was the first to energetically and consistently apply these fundamental insights into critical research. Through a careful grammatical, stylistic, and conceptual analysis, he distinguished the individuality of the Pauline letters from the other writings of the NT. He also found that the letters attributed to Paul differed so clearly from each other stylistically and theologically that they could not have come from the same author. In the history of early Christianity, inspired by Hegel's philosophy of history, Baur also discovered two antagonistic forces: "Christianity" profiled in "Paulinism," which was defined by a consistent doctrine of *justification and an unlimited universalism, and "Judaism," which in Christianity was determined by the Jewish Christianity and "Petrinism" represented and not yet wholly overcome. He then related these criteria to the Pauline letters and concluded that only four represented "Paulinism" ultimately and were genuine: Romans, both Corinthians, and Galatians. Baur further deprived the Acts of the Apostles of credibility by defining it as a product of the apologetic synthesis between "Paulinism" and "Petrinism." He also interpreted the theology of Paul in Hegelian categories: in *faith, the spirit of the Christian becomes "identical" with the spirit of *God and thus receives "absolutely free" self-confidence (Baur, 139).

As a result of the consistent historical method introduced by Baur in NT exegesis, numerous studies, some of which are still fundamental today, have been carried out on the question of the authenticity and historicity of the epistles of Paul and the Acts of the Apostles. At the same time, Baur's speculative construction of history applied a Hegelian philosophy of history, with the effect of distorting the history of early Christianity. This stimulated both speculative exaggerations among Baur's students, the so-called Tübingen school, and sharp critics. European exegesis outside Germany, such as that represented by Joseph Barber Lightfoot (1828–1889), Fenton John Anthony Hort (1828–1901), or Brooke Foss Westcott (1825–1901), looked with astonishment at these hypothetical highlights but also saw in them fatal aberrations of the German NT biblical criticism, which was from then on considered radical.

While David Friedrich Strauss (1808–1874) dealt primarily with Jesus, his central thesis, that the NT only contains "myth" in the sense of legend and not "history" in the sense of reliable historical information, also had an impact on Paul's research. The Acts of the Apostles came under increasing criticism for the miracles it contains. Comparison with the authentic Pauline letters also revealed more and more clearly that their presentation sometimes deviated considerably from the Pauline one. In connection with Baur's theological criticism, the Acts of the Apostles represented a synthesis of Paulinism and Petrinism, that is, of the doctrine of justification and obedience to the *law; thus the only historical overall narrative of the early *church became the object of historical criticism.

These observations cleared the way for controversial interpretations of Paul. Ernst Renan (1823–1892) described the missionary Paul as an "intruder" who was inferior to Jesus and the circle of the first disciples. Paul followed an "illusion" and, as an apostle of vengeance, proclaimed the opposite of what Jesus preached. Renan also influenced Friedrich Nietzsche's (1844–1900) negative image of Paul. In Paul's "doctrine of sin," he saw the continued effect of Jewish "slave morality" in Christianity. European anti-Semitism took up both authors' views and used them for polemics against what they identified as Jewish in Christianity.

3. Conservative Historicism.

Pauline scholarship did not dismiss the importance of the Acts of the Apostles as a source for Paul's life ultimately. Adolf von Harnack (1851–1930) mostly followed critical research but insisted on the traditional authorship of the Acts of the Apostles. The author was "Luke the physician," a travel companion of Paul with a high level of education. In particular, Theodor von Zahn (1838–1933) stepped into the first row of those who held on to the authenticity of the corpus Paulinum from Romans to 2 Timothy and also considered the historical value of the Acts of the Apostles to be high. Due to his impressive knowledge of the sources and his astute talent for combination, Zahn brought together many historical details into a comprehensive interpretation of Paul. Zahn's canonical-synthetic image of Paul saw the apostle, in agreement with Jesus and the other apostles, as the preacher of the one *gospel of the facticity of *salvation history, particularly the *resurrection and the repeal of the law for non-Jewish Christians. Based on this commonality, which also encompassed the doctrine of *righteousness through faith, Paul developed a "peculiar theology" made up of "intricate and extensive lines of thought" as an "empirical doctrine" that was not "popular" in early Christianity (Zahn, 83).

A group of conservative scholars, Hermann Cremer (1834–1903), Adolf Schlatter (1852–1938), Julius Kögel (1871–1928), and Gerhard Kittel (1888–1948), the latter the editor of the *Theological Dictionary of the New Testament* (1932–1979), followed an interpretation of the language of the NT in the tradition of sacred lexicography (Lat. *lexicographia sacra*). They considered the new and unique NT linguistic usage by differentiating it from the Jewish and the Hellenistic as their research goal. They followed up Schleiermacher's mandate of the "language-forming power of Christianity" and represented the idea that the old Greek words in the NT received an entirely new meaning: "The old words and yet completely new words!" (Kögel, X-XI). This assumption led to a great interest in Judaism, as reflected, for example, in the *Commentary on the New Testament from the Talmud and Midrash* by Paul Billerbeck (1853–1932). Scholars used the knowledge of Judaism to delimit Christianity from it sharply and invented or reproduced often anti-Judaic prejudices and even anti-Semitic stereotypes. The image of Paul from this research tradition highlighted Paul's break with Judaism and the new christological foundation of Pauline theology. The most eminent Christian experts researched Judaism to precisely grasp Paul's difference and uniqueness. As a result of this line of interpretation, Paul was interpreted even more clearly than Jesus of Nazareth as the first Christian theologian and fundamental overcomer of Judaism.

4. The History-of-Religions School.

Researchers who felt they belonged to the history-of-religions school chose a significantly different research approach. William Wrede (1859–1906) identified Paul as a religious man who started from the fundamental insight "Jesus is the Messiah." Everything else, including his doctrine of redemption and justification as an argumentative "battle doctrine," are the conclusions that Paul had to draw mentally to defend this religious experience against attacks (Wrede, 48). Paul's achievement was to make Christianity the religion of salvation. The insight of Paul as the "second founder of Christianity" (Wrede, 104) moved a question of Paul's interpretation that no scholar had ever asked before to the center: What was the actual relationship between Jesus and Paul, between Jesus' proclamation of the *kingdom of God and the Pauline doctrine of redemption? Wrede intensified this question to the radical alternative "either Jesus or Paul" (106).

Wilhelm Bousset (1865–1920) used the Pauline letters to analyze the early Christian religion. The first communities with predominantly Hellenistic and non-Jewish members, influenced by ancient mystery cults, understood themselves as a cult community of *Kyrios Christos* (Bousset, 91). Richard Reitzenstein (1861–1931) followed this assessment but set Paul apart as a "pneumatic." Paul sought to confront the "Hellenistic new-Christians" in *Corinth influenced by *Gnosticism, who transformed Christianity into a mystery religion (Reitzenstein, 390). Albert Eichhorn (1856–1926) interpreted the *Lord's Supper as a sacramental "cult meal" without lineage to either the OT or the teaching of Jesus (Eichhorn, 30). Finally, Wilhelm Heitmüller (1869–1926) attributed *baptism and the Lord's Supper to the syncretistic milieu of paganism and Judaism. He understood them as a cultic practice that conveyed the "primitive animistic-spiritualistic" experience of "Christ mysticism" (Heitmüller, 335-36).

Adolf Deißmann (1866–1937) linked the history-of-religions school with social-scientific research by recognizing the increasing importance of nonliterary papyri, which became more and more accessible to researchers in the course of the colonial-archaeological expeditions. With their help, Deißmann released the analysis of Paul's language from what he saw as its one-sided ties to the LXX. He succeeded in relating the language of Paul's letters to the "popular language" of the lower and middle classes as well as to the economic, legal, and political terminology of Roman Hellenism of the first century (e.g., *euangelion*). The papyri have been extensively considered in the revision of Erwin Preuschen's (1867–1920) *Lexicon of the New Testament and Other Early Christian Literature* by Walter Bauer (1877–1960). In his epochal study of orthodoxy and heresy in early Christianity, Bauer concluded that Paul's theology had sunk into insignificance due to the dominance of the apostolic tradition (Bauer 1934, 229-30).

Martin Dibelius (1883–1947) continued Deißmann's linguistic and sociohistorical questions and entrusted Heinz-Dietrich Wendland (1900–1992) with writing a social history of Christianity. This approach ended in the time of German National Socialism. Scholars only took it up again in the 1970s.

5. The Rediscovery of Eschatology.

Heinrich Julius Holtzmann (1832–1910) had combined the research results of the nineteenth century into a liberal-psychological picture of Paul. Ironically, his student Albert Schweitzer (1875–1965) became his harshest critic. In 1911 he analyzed the Pauline research of the nineteenth century. Analogous to his much better-known criticism of the quest of the historical Jesus, Schweitzer accused Pauline research of the nineteenth century of not having taken into account the fundamental importance of *eschatology for Paul, which alone could determine the unity of Pauline theology (Schweitzer 1911, 187-88). He published his consistent eschatological interpretation of Paul in 1930. He harshly rejected the idea of Paul's closeness to the Hellenistic mystery religions. For Schweitzer, Paul's thoughts were within the Judaism of his time, namely, Jewish *apocalypticism. Through the collective experience of the connection with the "mystical *body of Christ," the new Christian entered the status of "being *in Christ" (*en Christō*; Schweitzer 1930, 123).

Charles Harold Dodd (1884–1973) also placed eschatology at the center of his interpretation of Paul. Analogous to his famous analysis of the parables of Jesus, he found "realized eschatology" in Paul's theology. Paul's futuristic statements are to be understood symbolically and are already part of the present determined by the *cross and resurrection of Jesus.

6. Dialectical Theology and Existentialistic Exegesis.

Karl Barth (1886–1968) criticized the neglect of the theology of Paul by liberal and conservative Pauline scholarship with his commentary on the epistle to the Romans. Barth made little contribution to the historical knowledge of Paul. He brought Paul's theology back into the center of scholarly debate. At the same time, he insisted that Christianity could not be based on past events and related alleged facts of faith. It has to engage with Paul's constructive and provocative theology, again and again, to gain confidence in itself—or speak, in Barth's sense: the gospel of the infinite difference between God and humanity and its overcoming is always anew to be achieved through the theology of Paul.

Rudolf Bultmann (1884–1976) followed Barth's view. Bultmann called for a theological interpretation of the NT Scriptures. Paul's theology has an "existential character," and one must therefore admit "that Paul's world-historical significance is nowhere other than that he was a theologian" (Bultmann 1929, 337). Bultmann succeeded in taking up the results of critical research and continuing them in some places: He consistently stuck to Schleiermacher's insight to base NT research on the "general hermeneutics" applicable to all phenomena of humanities. He took up the alternative "either Jesus or Paul" suggested by Wrede and decided consistently against Jesus. His *preaching could not be part of a theology of the NT since Jesus only preached the kingdom of God and the coming of the Son of Man. A theology must be based on God's eschatological act of salvation in the death and resurrection of Jesus.

Bultmann followed up on Bousset by stating that Paul had taken over the confession "Christ is *Lord" from the pre-Pauline congregation. He also followed up on Heitmüller and Eichhorn's work on baptism and the Lord's Supper as cultic practices. He also accepted Schweitzer's insistence on consistent eschatology in an adapted way. Bultmann placed the relevant results of critical research under an interpretative principle that the Marburgian scholar had already discovered in Baur: the human self. Additionally, he gave this principle a decisive turn through the concept of understanding of existence adopted from Søren Kierkegaard (1813–1855) and Martin Heidegger (1889–1976): The theology of Paul has to be analyzed and interpreted in terms of the human understanding of existence expressed in it. Only this, and not the theological concepts and statements in their plain meaning or factual content, is theologically relevant since "Paul's theology is at the same time anthropology" (Bultmann 1948, 187).

Bultmann had carried out these points of view exegetically in numerous articles written for the *Theological Dictionary of the New Testament* since 1929. He took over, among others, the articles on *alētheia*, *ginōskō*, *eleos*, *elpis*, *zoē*, *thanatos*, and *pistis*. He placed the latter term at the center of his presentation of Paul's theology. He developed this as *anthropology that distinguished between humanity "prior to the revelation of *pistis*" and that "under *pistis*." At its core, Paul's theology thematizes Christian existence as an eschatological existence characterized by absolute distance to the world's demands (*Entweltlichung*) and the ability to act freely in *love. Bultmann also emphasized that this Christian existence is not realized other than in present acts of life "here and now" and provides "an opportunity of understanding ourselves." Therefore, any real futuristic statement of the NT should be dropped and questioned in terms of the understanding of existence expressed in it, that is, interpreted "existentially." Bultmann thus linked the theology of the NT to Heidegger's ontology. He understood this to be the best scientific way to speak about humans and did not see that he was also adopting Heidegger's lack of moral responsibility with his existential analysis. For Bultmann, the NT had a clear answer to the ethical question in the love command. But he did not realize that following Heidegger made it impossible for him to give the NT's demand for love an appropriate place in his theology.

7. Apocalypticism in Paul.
Bultmann's presentation of the theology of Paul reached the status of a comprehensive interpretation of Paul that had taken into account the most important results of critical research and consistently developed previous insights. Any further research could only position itself in demarcation or approval of Bultmann. Bultmann received the sharpest criticism from two of his most talented students, Günter Bornkamm (1905–1990) and Ernst Käsemann (1906–1998). Both rejected Bultmann's excessive delimitation of the preaching of Jesus from the theology of the NT since the reconstruction of the preaching of Jesus is reliable and a representation of his theology is possible. Nor could they follow the teacher in saying that an interpretation of Paul should aim exclusively at the underlying understanding of existence. Bornkamm stuck to the relevance of the factual futuristic statements since Paul's theology's cosmological and political claims would be missed.

At this point, Käsemann continued the criticism: The Pauline *dikaiosynē theou* is not a concept of existence but of power that encompasses the legal demand of the Creator to the world and not only to the individual. Paul was an apocalyptic, just as apocalypticism became the mother of all Christian theology. Käsemann also deepened his Bultmann criticism by attesting naive docetism and sectarian *ethics to the Gospel of John, which was so crucial for his teacher. On the other hand, Paul's theology tears people out of their false religious and social self-certainty and inevitably confronts them as part of the whole of humanity with the legal demand of the one and only God and Creator of the world. Käsemann's emphasis on "apocalyptic as the mother of all Christian theology" influenced J. Louis Martyn (1925–2015) and his students for the so-called apocalyptic interpretation of Paul. This approach was very different from that of Martin Hengel (1926–2009), one of the most influential German NT scholars in the English-speaking world, who insisted on the importance of chronology and on the continuity between Jesus' self-understanding and the *Christology of the first church of Jerusalem (*Urgemeinde*) as well as Paul's.

8. Conclusion.
The interpretation of Paul in Europe posed many fundamental questions. It also produced significant results: the authenticity of the Pauline letters, the historical reliability of the Acts of the Apostles, the relationship between the preaching of Jesus and the theology of Paul, the position of Paul in the circle of the apostles, the distinction between Pauline theology and pre-Pauline community practice, the influence of early Christian religiosity and cult through Hellenism and Judaism, the importance of the doctrine of justification, and finally the goal of the Pauline gospel in the individual and *creation. To this day, a description of Paul's theology has to provide answers to these questions, which had to do justice to the level of reflection reached in the primarily German European interpretation of Paul presented here.

See also Apocalyptic Paul; Apocalypticism; Eschatology; Hermeneutics/Interpreting Paul; Jesus and Paul; Justification; Paul in Acts; Pseudepigraphy/Forgery; Social-Scientific Approaches to Paul.

BIBLIOGRAPHY. **K. Barth,** *Der Römerbrief*, 2nd ed. (Munich: Kaiser, 1922); **W. Bauer,** *Griechisch-deutsches Wörterbuch zu den Schriften des Neuen Testaments und der übrigen urchristlichen Literatur* (Gießen: Töpelmann, 1928); idem, *Rechtgläubigkeit und Ketzerei im ältesten Christentum* (Tübingen: Mohr, 1934); **F. C. Baur,** *Paulus, der Apostel Jesu Christi* (Stuttgart: Becher & Müller, 1845); **M. Bauspiess, C. Landmesser, and D. Lincicum,** eds., *Ferdinand Christian Baur and the History of Early Christianity* (Oxford: Oxford University Press, 2017); **J. Bernays,** *Geschichte der Klassischen Philologie*

(Hildesheim: Olms, 2008); **P. Billerbeck,** *Kommentar zum Neuen Testament aus Talmud und Midrasch,* vol. 3, *Die Briefe des Neuen Testaments und die Offenbarung Johannis* (Munich: Beck, 1926); **L. Bormann,** *Theologie des Neuen Testaments: Grundlinien und wichtigste Ergebnisse der internationalen Forschung* (Göttingen: Vandenhoeck & Ruprecht, 2017); idem, "Das Theologische Wörterbuch zum Neuen Testament im 21. Jahrhundert. Überlegungen zu seiner Geschichte und heutigen Benutzung," in *Theologisches Wörterbuch zum Neuen Testament,* ed. G. Kittel and G. Friedrich (Darmstadt: WBG Academic, 2019), v-xxii; idem, "Rudolf Bultmann und das Theologische Wörterbuch zum Neuen Testament. Eine Neubewertung," *ZTK* 118 (2021): 21-54; **G. Bornkamm,** "Art. Paulus," in *Religion in Geschichte und Gegenwart,* 3rd ed. (Tübingen: Mohr, 1961), 5:166-90; idem, *Paulus* (Stuttgart: Kohlhammer, 1969); **W. Bousset,** *Kyrios Christos. Geschichte des Christusglaubens von den Anfängen des Christentums bis Irenäus* (Göttingen: Vandenhoeck & Ruprecht, 1913); **R. Bultmann,** "Zur Geschichte der Paulus-Forschung," *Theologische Rundschau* 1 (1929): 26-59; idem, "Art. Paulus," in *Religion in Geschichte und Gegenwart,* 2nd ed. (Tübingen: Mohr, 1930), 4:1019-45; idem, *Theologie des Neuen Testaments* (Tübingen: Mohr, 1948–1953); **A. Deissmann,** *Paulus* (Tübingen: Mohr, 1911); **M. Dibelius,** *Paulus* (Berlin: de Gruyter, 1951); **C. H. Dodd,** *The Apostolic Preaching and Its Developments* (London: Hodder & Stoughton, 1936); **A. Eichhorn,** *Das Abendmahl im Neuen Testament* (Leipzig: Mohr, 1898); **J. Ph. Gabler,** "De iusto discrimine biblicae et dogmaticae regundisque recte utriusque finibus 1787," in *Biblische Theologie des Neuen Testaments in ihrer Anfangszeit,* ed. O. Merk (Marburg: Elwert, 1972); **A. von Harnack,** *Lukas der Arzt. Der Verfasser des dritten Evangeliums und der Apostelgeschichte* (Leipzig: Hinrichs, 1906); **W. Heitmüller,** *Taufe und Abendmahl im Urchristentum* (Tübingen: Mohr, 1911); **M. Hengel,** *Between Jesus and Paul: Studies in the Earliest History of Christianity* (Philadelphia: Fortress, 1983); **H. J. Holtzmann,** *Lehrbuch der neutestamentlichen Theologie,* vol. 2 (Freiburg: Mohr, 1897); **E. Käsemann,** "Die Anfänge christlicher Theologie," *ZTK* 57 (1960): 162-85; idem, "Gottesgerechtigkeit bei Paulus," *ZTK* 58 (1961): 367-78; **B. N. Kayne,** "Lightfoot and Baur on Early Christianity," *NovT* 26 (1984): 193-224; **J. Kögel,** ed., *Biblisch-theologisches Wörterbuch der neutestamentlichen Gräzität von Hermann Cremer,* 10th ed. (Gotha: Perthes, 1915); **W. G. Kümmel,** *The New Testament: The History of the Investigations of Its Problems* (Nashville: Abingdon, 1972); **F. Nietzsche,** *Zur Genealogie der Moral* (Leipzig: Naumann, 1887); **F. Regner,** *"Paulus und Jesus" im neunzehnten Jahrhundert* (Göttingen: Vandenhoeck & Ruprecht, 1977); **R. Reitzenstein,** *Die hellenistischen Mysterienreligionen* (Leipzig: Teubner, 1910); **E. Renan,** *Saint Paul* (Paris: Lévy, 1869); **K. H. Rengstorf,** ed., *Das Paulusbild in der neueren deutschen Forschung* (Darmstadt: WBG, 1964); **A. Schlatter,** *Der Glaube im Neuen Testament* (Leiden: Brill, 1885); **F. D. E. Schleiermacher,** *Kritische Gesamtausgabe Teil: Abt. 2, Vorlesungen / Bd. 4., Vorlesungen zur Hermeneutik und Kritik* (Berlin: de Gruyter, 2012); **A. Schweitzer,** *Geschichte der paulinischen Forschung von der Reformation bis auf die Gegenwart* (Tübingen: Mohr, 1911); idem, *Die Mystik des Apostels Paulus* (Tübingen: Mohr, 1930); **D. F. Strauss,** *Das Leben Jesu kritisch bearbeitet* (Tübingen: Osiander, 1835); **G. R. Treloar,** *Lightfoot the Historian: The Nature and Role of History in the Life and Thought of J. B. Lightfoot (1828–1889) as Churchman and Scholar* (Tübingen: Mohr Siebeck, 1998); **W. Wrede,** *Paulus* (Tübingen: Mohr, 1905); **W. Zager,** *Liberale Exegese des Neuen Testaments. David Friedrich Strauss—William Wrede—Albert Schweitzer—Rudolf Bultmann* (Neukirchen-Vluyn: Neukirchener, 2004); **T. von Zahn,** "Art. Paulus," in *Realencyklopädie für protestantische Theologie und Kirche* (Leipzig: Hinrichs, 1904), 15:61-88.

L. Bormann

INTERPRETATION: NEW PERSPECTIVE

The "new perspective on Paul" seeks to interpret the apostle's writings in greater continuity with his Jewish heritage than has typically been the case in NT studies, and it understands that heritage in light of the complete reevaluation of Judaism in works such as those by E. P. Sanders. To varying degrees, traditional Pauline interpretation understood him to be moving away from his Jewishness. The Paul of the new perspective is more at home in his Jewishness. He not only *was* a Jew and a Pharisee but in many ways *remained so* as a follower of Messiah Jesus.

1. Origin of the New Perspective.
From fairly early on, Christian interpreters viewed Paul as having turned away from Judaism, instead embracing *Christ and Christianity at his *conversion on the road to Damascus. As they saw matters, the impossible and legalistic demands of the Jewish *law ("do this and live") could lead only to Paul's anguished cry in Romans 7:19, "For I do not do the good I want, but the evil I do not want is what I do." In Christ's *gospel Paul received *salvation as an unearned gift rather than as a reward to the meritorious. Christian *faith replaced Jewish works. *Grace replaced law.

Of course, Jewish scholars had long decried this legalistic and graceless caricature of their own religious tradition—for example, S. Schechter and C. G. Montefiore. Occasional Christian voices had echoed the Jewish complaint—for example, Moore, Munck, and Davies—but the first real crack in this almost monolithic Christian view of Paul *against Judaism* came with Krister Stendahl's "The Apostle Paul and the Introspective Conscience of the West." Rather than laboring under a conscience burdened by failure to keep the law's onerous demands, Stendahl's Paul was robustly confident ("as to *righteousness under the law, blameless," Phil 3:6). Instead of converting to Christianity, Paul saw himself called as a Jewish "prophet to the nations" (Jer 1:5; cf. Gal 1:15-16), not as the propagator of a radically new religious *tradition.

Thus, the first step toward a new perspective on Paul was to develop a new perspective on Judaism, a step taken decisively for biblical scholarship by Sanders in *Paul and Palestinian Judaism*. Here the caricature of legalistic Judaism was laid to rest. In its place Sanders portrayed a Jewish soteriology, a "pattern of religion" he labeled "covenantal nomism." Salvation in Jewish thought was based on unearned divine grace, sustained by *forgiveness and *atonement (i.e., the *covenant) and maintained by faithful human obedience to God's ways (nomism). Interestingly, Sanders himself did not think Paul's pattern of religion was a continuation of this Jewish pattern.

It was James Dunn who made that final step and termed it a "new perspective on Paul." He built on Sanders's paradigm-changing new perspective on Judaism but faulted him for failing to see how remarkably similar Paul's own soteriology actually was to the covenantal nomism of Sanders's Judaism. In both, the individual enters the realm of salvation by an act of divine initiative, by grace; and in both, the individual is then expected to maintain this salvation by faithful obedience, to live a life of substantial conformity to the divine expectations, to be holy. If Paul's words can no longer be understood as reacting to and opposing legalistic Judaism or some form of works-righteousness, one needs to reexamine many of Paul's foundational words and concepts.

Galatians 2:16 formed Dunn's test case: "yet we know that a person is justified not by the *works of the law but through faith in Jesus Christ." Traditional exegesis saw here a striking contrast with Judaism. Instead of sinners being justified by their own efforts ("works of the law"), *God now declares them to be righteous by simple faith in Christ. But if Sanders was right, this can hardly be Paul's meaning. Jews never thought they could be justified by their own efforts. The key for Dunn lay in the phrase "works of the law" (*erga nomou*). Instead of suggesting legalism, works-righteousness, or meritorious human effort, these *erga nomou* are the characteristic observable behaviors that mark the social boundary between Jew and *Gentile. In the context of Galatians 2 these refer to *circumcision and *food laws, but they ultimately include Sabbath keeping and any other Torah commands that distinguished Jews from non-Jews. They are badges of identity, markers of Jewishness in the ancient world vis-à-vis all non-Jewish peoples. One can recognize who is a Jew by looking for practices such as circumcision, observance of food laws, keeping of Sabbath, and so on.

Thus, in rejecting "works of law," Paul was opposing not legalism but reliance on Jewish *identity. Gentiles who wish to belong to the righteous, the justified since Christ's advent need not become Jewish but align themselves with Messiah Jesus. In the post-*cross era, all are justified, both Jews and non-Jews, by adherence to Messiah, not by Jewish identity. In a further departure from traditional Protestant interpretation, *justification in Paul was now taken to mean primarily identification as a covenant member, not imputation of flawless law keeping on the heavenly books.

2. Distinctives of the New Perspective.
Many Pauline scholars adopted the more positive view of Judaism espoused by Sanders and explored what a more Jewish Paul might look like. They still differed widely in their interpretations of specific passages. Various proponents of the new perspective interpreted Romans 7, for instance, quite differently, some allowing (Dunn) and some rejecting (Wright) an autobiographical reading. Some understood *pistis Christou* to refer to Christ's own faithfulness (Hays), while others took it more traditionally as the believer's faith (Gupta). Nor did the new perspective

dictate a particular theological orientation. Some understood their new perspective stance to imply the overthrow of Lutheran justification teaching (Campbell), while others thought them compatible (Garlington). Some thought Paul's gospel called both Jews and Gentiles to faith in Messiah Jesus equally (Dunn); others saw primarily a Gentile target audience (Nanos).

Thus, the new perspective is more of a general attitude toward how to relate Paul with his Jewish heritage (i.e., with more continuity than a law-versus-gospel contrast tends to imply) than a commitment to a set of interpretations of specific passages. This exegetical and theological diversity has led to the suggestion that there are numerous new *perspectives* (plural) rather any single new perspective. However, even with this considerable diversity in details, there remains a fairly unified perspective vis-à-vis the following distinctives:

- views Paul's Jewish theological environment more in terms of covenantal nomism than legalism
- finds Paul in substantial agreement with his Jewish heritage rather than opposing or rejecting it
- views faith and works as two sides of the same theological coin rather than as opposing principles
- interprets *erga nomou* as marks of social identity rather than as efforts to earn divine approval
- sees the generative issue for Paul's gospel not as individual salvation (i.e., how can a sinful individual be saved?) but as missiology—that is, how are Gentiles to be brought into the *worship of the one true God? Will it be through adopting Jewish identity ("works of the law") or through becoming Gentile followers of the Jewish Messiah ("faith in Christ")?

This favoring of Jewish continuity also differentiates the new perspective from other approaches to interpreting Paul. This is already evident in the case of more traditional Lutheran interpretation. It also differentiates the new perspective from the apocalyptic interpretation of Martyn and others. For Martyn the discontinuities dominate. The Christ event is not the climax to a long development in Israel's story—that might make Christ but a subplot in the story of God's work with *Israel—but an explosive invasion of something brand new. It is a "new *creation," not simply a redemption or reworking of the old. The new perspective, while recognizing the two-age dialectic of Jewish apocalyptic, sees this inbreaking of the divine rule within an overarching salvation history with less disjunction and more continuity.

3. Subsequent Developments of the New Perspective.

One of the most prolific early proponents of the new perspective, N. T. Wright, has continued to develop his own perspective, which he at one point dubbed a "fresh perspective" on Paul (2005, 5). He has, in particular, championed a more narrative reading of the apostle's *letters and thought as well as a more empire-critical reading. As to the first, this means Paul viewed the gospel of Christ primarily within the larger story of God and Israel. Christ is the "climax of the [Jewish] covenant." The "plight" from which God in Christ has rescued Israel was its continuing exile under Roman domination. This led to Wright's second development: Paul wrote with an eye toward Rome. If Christ is *Lord, then Caesar is not. Like other empire-critical interpreters, Wright sees here a way forward in applying Paul to the modern day. The church is to be a critical actor in the social-political realm.

Another early advocate, Richard Hays, launched a major debate over the meaning of *pistis Christou* in texts such as Galatians 2:16, "a person is justified not by the works of the law but through *pisteōs Iēsou Christou*." Did Paul replace "works of law" with human faith in Jesus (objective genitive) or with Christ's own faithfulness on the cross (subjective genitive)? Should *pistis Christou* be translated "faith in Christ" or "the faith(fulness) of Christ"? New perspective–friendly authors will be found on both sides of this particular exegetical divide. While not unimportant, neither is a decision one way or the other distinctive of the new perspective.

Further Pauline scholars picked up this Sanders-Dunn-Wright trajectory of a more Judaism-friendly Paul and explored various aspects of Pauline theology from this perspective. Don Garlington explored Paul's "obedience of faith" (Rom 1:5; 16:26), concluding that it testifies to the marriage of faith and works in Paul's thought, rather than to a tension or contrast. Terence Donaldson focused on Paul's concern for Gentiles and found the apostle shared this concern with other Jewish thinkers but reconfigured it around Christ rather than Torah. Kent Yinger found in Paul's use of the "*judgment according to deeds" motif a continuation of Jewish soteriological principles.

Dunn himself continued as the most notable proponent of the new perspective, responding to critics and supplying additional clarification and evidence. Against those who accused him of reducing "works of the law" to a few select marks (circumcision, Sabbath, and food laws), he clarified that he had always meant to include all of Torah as it marked out Israel's path of life from the non-Jewish nations. Key passages such as Galatians 3:10-14 and Philippians 3:2-14 received in-depth treatment, and he applied the new perspective in his major commentary on Romans (Dunn 1988) and *Theology of Paul the Apostle* (Dunn 1998).

Since the originating work of Dunn and others, several authors have sought to synthesize the new perspective on Paul with more traditional Reformed and Lutheran interpretation. Michael Bird, for example, wants to "effect reconciliation between the traditional Reformed view of Paul and that espoused in the New Perspectives on Paul" (2007, xiv). In particular, he wants to hold together what he thinks these two interpretive traditions have held apart, namely, the vertical (soteriological) aspect of justification (so the "old" perspective) and the horizontal (social).

Although the new perspective is more Judaism-friendly than most previous interpretations of Paul, for one group of Pauline scholars it did not go nearly far enough. This "radical new perspective" argues that Paul did not break with his Judaism at all. He remained *within Judaism*, ever a Torah-keeping, synagogue-attending follower of the God of Israel. As Pamela Eisenbaum provocatively proclaims, *Paul was not a Christian*. Texts that might be taken as negative toward Torah or Judaism ("you are not under law but under grace," Rom 6:14) should be understood as spoken only to Gentiles. They should remain non-Jews and not come "under law," that is, not obligate themselves to full Jewish identity and lifestyle. For these interpreters, even the new perspective charge of "Jewish ethnocentrism" is too anti-Jewish in tone and betrays the Christian bias of much new perspective interpretation. Rather than seeking to establish separate Christian churches (*ekklēsiai*), perhaps Paul's letters are aimed at helping Gentile converts successfully integrate into Jewish synagogue life (Nanos).

4. Criticisms of the New Perspective.

If Sanders's view of first-century Judaism was wrong, then, obviously, the new perspective would be equally off track. Thus, some fault Sanders and the new perspective for ignoring the diversity of Jewish views (Carson et al.). Even if they were correct that many, or even most, Jews were not legalists, they glossed over the others who leaned toward legalism. Maybe Paul was responding to a minority position within Judaism that did hold to some form of works-righteousness. For others (Das), Sanders may have been accurate regarding the nonlegalistic nature of Second Temple Judaism, but he and the new perspective have missed the legalism that remains in Paul's reading of the OT. In the light of Christ Paul now sees Jewish obedience to commandments as nothing other than works-righteousness. Even if Second Temple Jews did not see it that way (so Sanders), logically they should have.

Others faulted Sanders for a too-benign view of Judaism. Just because Jews spoke of grace does not mean they meant it in the same way as Paul. Grace in Judaism was more synergistic, giving more emphasis to the actions of the human agent, while Paul was more monergistic, thus Luther's *sola gratia* (Gundry; Schreiner). John Barclay contends that this whole discussion of grace lacks sufficient nuance. While Sanders correctly noted the priority of divine grace in both Paul and Judaism (i.e., given prior to human action), he failed to note the diversity in matters such as incongruity (grace given to the unworthy) or efficacy (grace achieves its aim unilaterally).

Another major point of criticism stems from the perception that the new perspective undercuts the Reformation and Luther's doctrine of justification by faith alone (Westerholm). The new perspective's more positive take on "works" and "works of law" sounds to some like a return to Roman Catholic works-righteousness, or at least to some form of divine-human synergism (with the accompanying pastoral implications such as loss of personal assurance of salvation). New perspective supporters acknowledge their heightened appreciation of "good works" in Pauline literature and theology. It was Paul, after all, who pleaded with his hearers to "lead a life worthy" of God and to "bear fruit in every good work" (1 Thess 2:12; Col 1:10). Such good works do not earn divine favor but are simply the path of life expected and required of those who confess allegiance to the true God, which is exactly what Paul had learned from his Jewish upbringing.

For other critics, the new perspective seems to downplay far too much the "newness" or uniqueness of the gospel and of Christ. Sanders's grace-filled Judaism hardly cried out for some bold new solution to the human dilemma—it seemed to work pretty well (see on Paul's robust conscience above). If Judaism already had solutions for human *sin in the form of *sacrifice and repentance, why was the cross even necessary?

New perspective supporters have varied responses to this critique. Some see the cosmic power of Sin as the problem that Torah could not solve and that cried out for Christ and the cross. Others see the primary dilemma as Israel's rebellion and continuing exile. For yet others, the new perspective has not gone far enough regarding continuity with Judaism (see section 3 above on "Paul within Judaism"). Too much anti-Judaism still lurks within Dunn's charge of "ethnocentrism" or Wright's "national righteousness." For still others (Gorman), the new perspective remains too stuck in the past and fails to address the needs of today's church; it should focus more on justification as "participatory transformation" than on first-century debates over Gentiles.

5. Conclusion.

The heyday of focus on this new perspective now lies in the past. Everything new in scholarship becomes old at some point. Thus, some writers can speak of it as passé. More important, however, than counting who still does or does not call themselves proponents of the new perspective would be to recognize the permanent influence of this approach on the way nearly all students of the NT now examine Pauline texts.

A more robust and positive, less caricatured portrait of Second Temple Judaism must form the backdrop of NT studies.

- It can no longer be taken for granted that Paul was against Judaism, Torah, obedience to commandments, and so on. The issue of his continuity with his own Jewish heritage is more alive than ever.
- The meaning of key Pauline theological concepts such as grace, faith, justification, works, and salvation must now be carefully reanalyzed.
- The understanding of Paul's aims must be broadened beyond the justification/salvation of individual sinners to include (potentially) Christ's lordship over evil (political) powers, the reconciliation of peoples, and the healing of creation.
- Whether the new perspective remains an important interpretive movement or not, it has left all readers of the NT with a Paul who looks and sounds very much more at home in his Jewish skin.

See also Christ, Messiah; Covenant; Faith; Faith of Christ; Gentiles; Grace; Holiness, Sanctification; Interpretation: Jewish; Justification; Law; Paul and Judaism; Salvation; Works of the Law.

BIBLIOGRAPHY. **J. M. G. Barclay,** *Paul and the Gift* (Grand Rapids, MI: Eerdmans, 2015); **M. F. Bird,** *The Saving Righteousness of God: Studies on Paul, Justification and the New Perspective,* PBM (Eugene, OR: Wipf & Stock, 2007); idem, *An Anomalous Jew: Paul Among Jews, Greeks, and Romans* (Grand Rapids, MI: Eerdmans, 2016); **D. A. Campbell,** *The Deliverance of God: An Apocalyptic Rereading of Justification in Paul* (Grand Rapids, MI: Eerdmans, 2009); **D. A. Carson et al.,** eds., *Justification and Variegated Nomism,* vol. 1, *The Complexities of Second Temple Judaism*; vol. 2, *The Paradoxes of Paul* (Grand Rapids, MI: Baker Academic, 2001, 2004); **A. A. Das,** *Paul, the Law and the Covenant* (Peabody, MA: Hendrickson, 2001); **T. L. Donaldson,** *Paul and the Gentiles: Remapping the Apostle's Convictional World* (Minneapolis: Fortress, 1997); **J. D. G. Dunn,** *Romans,* WBC 38A-38B (Dallas: Word, 1988); idem, *The Theology of Paul the Apostle* (Grand Rapids, MI: Eerdmans, 1998); idem, *The New Perspective on Paul,* rev. ed. (Grand Rapids, MI: Eerdmans, 2008); **P. M. Eisenbaum,** *Paul Was Not a Christian: The Original Message of a Misunderstood Apostle* (New York: HarperOne, 2009); **D. B. Garlington,** *The Obedience of Faith: A Pauline Phrase in Historical Context,* WUNT 2/38 (Tübingen: Mohr Siebeck, 1991); **M. J. Gorman,** *Participating in Christ: Explorations in Paul's Theology and Spirituality* (Grand Rapids, MI: Baker, 2019); **R. H. Gundry,** "Grace, Works, and Staying Saved in Paul," *Bib* 66 (1985): 1-38; **N. K. Gupta,** *Paul and the Language of Faith* (Grand Rapids, MI: Eerdmans, 2020); **R. B. Hays,** *The Faith of Jesus Christ: The Narrative Substructure of Galatians 3:1–4:11,* 2nd ed., Biblical Resource Series (Grand Rapids, MI: Eerdmans, 2002); **J. L. Martyn,** *Galatians: A New Translation with Introduction and Commentary,* AB 33A (New York: Doubleday, 1997); **S. McKnight and B. J. Oropeza,** eds., *Perspectives on Paul: Five Views* (Grand Rapids, MI: Baker Academic, 2020); **M. D. Nanos and M. Zetterholm,** eds., *Paul Within Judaism: Restoring the First-Century Context to the Apostle* (Minneapolis: Fortress, 2015); **E. P. Sanders,** *Paul and Palestinian Judaism: A Comparison of Patterns of Religion* (Philadelphia: Fortress, 1977); **T. R. Schreiner,** *The Law and Its Fulfillment: A Pauline Theology of Law* (Grand Rapids, MI: Baker, 1993); **K. Stendahl,** "The Apostle Paul and the Introspective Conscience of the West," in *Paul Among Jews and Gentiles* (Philadelphia: Fortress, 1976), 78-96; **F. Watson,** *Paul, Judaism, and the Gentiles: Beyond the New Perspective,* rev. and exp. ed. (Grand Rapids, MI: Eerdmans, 2007); **S. Westerholm,** *Perspectives Old and New on Paul: The "Lutheran" Paul and His Critics* (Grand Rapids, MI: Eerdmans, 2004); **N. T. Wright,** *The Climax of the Covenant: Christ and the Law in Pauline Theology* (Minneapolis: Fortress,

1993); idem, *Paul: In Fresh Perspective* (Minneapolis: Fortress, 2005); idem, *Paul and the Faithfulness of God*, 2 vols. (Minneapolis: Fortress, 2013); **K. L. Yinger,** *Paul, Judaism, and Judgment According to Deeds*, SNTSMS 105 (New York: Cambridge, 1999); idem, *The New Perspective on Paul: An Introduction* (Eugene, OR: Cascade, 2011).

K. L. Yinger

INTERPRETATION: PATRISTIC

Due to his central role in the NT, Paul has captured the imagination of Christians throughout history. Some have argued that Paul's theology was almost lost and not recovered until the Reformation, apart from being glimpsed by Augustine along the way. However, the *church never lost interest in Paul, and he was central to earlier discussions and developments, not least to those in the patristic era, where he is known as "the *apostle." (*Patristic* here refers to the time frame from the beginning of second century [ca. AD 100] to end of fifth century [ca. AD 500], roughly from the completion of the NT to the final fall of Rome, in 476.) During this period Christianity evolved from a Jewish sect to the dominant religion in the ancient Mediterranean. With his role in embodying and communicating the *faith of *Christ to the Greco-Roman world in the first century, Paul's life and teaching proved especially influential for the patristic church.

1. Reception History
2. Across the Patristic Era
3. Interpretive Diversity
4. Select Distinctive Issues

1. Reception History.

The reception of Paul occurs in a variety of ways. Beyond direct citations and allusions, one also encounters engagement with Pauline topics. Whether a particular topic is specifically Pauline is often a matter of dispute, and reception history includes disagreement or modification and not just repetition or extension. In contrast to the modern focus on the undisputed letters, the early church engaged the canonical Paul—the Paul in the thirteen self-attributed letters, the narrative of Acts, and Hebrews, since this was also considered Pauline. The wide use of his letters shows that a functional *canon (of the thirteen letters) existed from the earliest stages of patristic theology. Other "Pauline" literature arose, and some of it became influential, but the canonical Paul is central to patristic theology.

As scriptural writings, Paul's letters, Acts, and Hebrews are given special authority since these pastoral documents were inspired by *God. Patristic interpreters do not highlight the distinctions between Paul and other parts of the canon as strongly as modern scholarship, but neither do they simply flatten out all the differences. As these interpreters were influenced by their particular contexts, the theological controversies of their times help shape the topics that capture their attention. Occasionally, contemporary scholars critique patristic interpreters for not simply repeating Paul or for emphasizing an aspect of Pauline theology that they find central today (or from the Reformation). Yet, contemporary interpreters have the challenge of discerning the coherent (the common uniting themes) and the contingent (the diverse message due to the specific situation) aspects of Paul's letters, and one should afford the same interpretive hospitality to diverse patristic methods and purposes as one does for those today.

2. Across the Patristic Era.

Prior scholarship taught that Paul initially fell out of favor in the church, being promoted primarily by unorthodox preachers (e.g., Marcion). Eventually, as the argument goes, the burgeoning orthodox church reclaimed Paul and engrafted him into its teaching. This was partially stimulated by the Protestant critique of "early Catholicism" supposedly evident in the deutero-Paulines but also by the idea that patristic interpreters had to mute Paul's apocalyptic fervor in their assimilation (see Elliott). This assessment has been thoroughly overturned due to reconsiderations of the diversity of topics addressed by Paul and the variety of patristic approaches to Paul over the course of the second to fifth centuries.

Paul's life and letters directly influenced several apostolic fathers (late first to mid-second century), who encourage Christians to remain faithful in the face of persecution, *apostasy, and division. Some show no evidence of engaging Paul, while others display direct and indirect interactions with him (especially Clement, Ignatius, and Polycarp). For example, Paul's letters and his patient endurance of *suffering for Christ serve as a model for believers (see *1 Clem.* 5.2-7; 47.1-4; Ign. *Eph.* 12.1-2; Pol. *Phil.* 3.1-3; 9.1). The apologists (mid-second to early third century) were more focused on addressing concerns raised by those outside the faith, and they provided a philosophical and legal defense of Christianity. Interestingly, Paul plays almost no direct role with some (e.g., Justin Martyr, especially given his Christian-Jewish dialogue) but is more central to others (e.g., Theophilus of Antioch).

In the late second century and onward, antiheretical treatises that addressed Marcionism, Valentinianism, and the like became a more popular genre of literature. In these contexts, one finds a close reading of particular controversial Pauline passages (e.g., Irenaeus, *Haer.* 5 [esp. 5.6-14], which is focused primarily on 1 Cor 15; and Tertullian, *Marc.* 5, which addresses the main Pauline letters more widely). In the third century, commentaries and homilies on particular Pauline texts join the topical theological works, though few of these early commentaries are extant. It was in the fourth and fifth centuries when commentaries flowered and became a distinctive genre. For example, John Chrysostom has over 250 homilies covering all the Pauline letters. As the Greek and Latin patristic traditions begin to form increasingly distinct identities, one sees this reflected in readings of Paul: "With the 3rd c. it happened that the Pauline tradition followed divergent paths in the Eastern and in the Western church. . . . The East propagated the Paul of 1 and 2 Corinthians, the West that of Romans" (Dassmann, 657).

3. Interpretive Diversity.

Though the reception of Paul is often focused on well-known patristic interpreters, such as Irenaeus, Cyril of Alexandria, and Augustine, the patristic era contains a diverse engagement with Paul.

3.1. Apocryphal Texts. Perhaps the most direct way that Paul's identity and theology was received, outside his letters themselves, was through a variety of texts that purport to be written by Paul or give a narrative account of Paul's experiences. As a part of what is considered the NT Apocrypha, this extension of Paul's legacy reflects similar attention given to other apostolic figures.

In addition to the canonical letters, several other letters are attributed to Paul. The Letter to the Laodiceans (noted in Col 4:16) was part of the (no longer extant) Marcionite canon. A Latin edition of a letter under this title is extant, but it is widely seen as a later creation, and the relationship to the Marcionite version is disputed. As part of the Acts of Paul, 3 Corinthians is a short pseudepigraphical letter from the second century commending an orthodox position on the *resurrection of the *flesh. Arising centuries later, the Letters of Paul and Seneca contains a pseudepigraphical exchange between Paul and the Roman philosopher.

There are a number of narrative descriptions of Paul's life and *ministry. Central among these is the Acts of Paul (see also the Acts of Peter and Paul), a now fragmentary account from the late second century that traces the ministry travels of Paul to Rome, similar to the canonical Acts. Some aspects, such as his teachings that encourage virginity, extend aspects one sees in his letters (e.g., 1 Cor 7), whereas other aspects are more fantastical, such as his *baptism of a lion. The concluding narration of his martyrdom before Nero, the Martyrdom of Paul, is the earliest description of his *death. In addition to the Martyrdom, the Acts of Paul includes other sections that also circulated independently, including 3 Corinthians and the well-known Acts of Paul and Thecla. Paul's apocalyptic experience of a heavenly journey is central to two texts, the (Coptic) Apocalypse of Paul in the Nag Hammadi library (see also the Prayer of Paul) and the Apocalypse of Paul, known through its Latin edition as the *Visio Pauli*, which ultimately influenced Dante's eschatological narrative, *The Divine Comedy*.

3.2. Heterodox Readers. Tertullian famously describes Paul as the "apostle of the heretics" (*Marc.* 3.5.4), not because he thought Paul was heretical but because heretical leaders liked to (over) extend themes from Paul's letters and engage Paul as a (functional) canon within the canon. The main groups addressed here include Jewish-Christian anti-Paulinism, Marcion, and Gnostic traditions.

3.2.1. Jewish-Christian Anti-Paulinism. Paul was seen as a threat to Judaism in his own lifetime, as evidenced by trouble at the hands of synagogue leaders, and his writings were later rejected by various Jewish-Christian groups. These groups are often combined under the moniker of the Ebionites, and among their other teachings, the Ebionites are noted to have rejected Paul (see Irenaeus, *Haer.* 1.26.2; Origen, *Cels.* 5.65; Epiphanius, *Pan.* 30.16.8-9; 30.25.1-14). The Pseudo-Clementine writings are Jewish-Christian texts that possibly reflect anti-Paulinism. Among these, three passages address Paul, though indirectly: Recognitions 1.27-71; Homilies 17.13-19; and Epistula Petri 2.3 (see also Kerygmata Petrou 2.16-17). Given the indirect references, the nature of the anti-Paulinism is disputed, but others see them as essential for reconstructing attitudes in the first and second centuries.

3.2.2. Marcion. Marcion agreed with those who saw Paul as critical of Jewish practice, but in contrast to those sects that rejected Paul, Marcion promoted him. His canon included modified forms of the Gospel of Luke and the Pauline letters (though without the Pastorals). Extending Pauline antitheses such as faith and *works of the *law, Marcion promoted a radical disjunction not merely between the salvation-historical progression of the OT and the NT but even between the Gods reflected in these two economies. The true God represented by Jesus Christ was a God of *grace who redeemed people from the *curse of the law from the God of the OT, who was motivated by justice and *judgment (see also Gal 3:13). Without promoting Marcion, this antithesis between law and grace continues to shape many traditions through today, particularly by concentration on grace as singular (focused on benevolence as God's singular motivation to the exclusion of judgment).

3.2.3. Gnostic Traditions. Similar to Marcion, wider Gnostic traditions are characterized by their distinction between the most high God and the Demiurge (the "Creator" God), though often with a number of intermediaries in between. Rather than being driven by the dualism of law and grace, wider Gnostic traditions were motivated by a cosmological dualism, particularly between the spiritual and the material. Valentinus is an influential figure, but **Gnosticism* is a generic term that captures a diverse array of traditions. For example, earlier Gnostic traditions are represented by the Nag Hammadi codices, and Manicheism represents a later form. While Paul was not the only scriptural source for these traditions, a distinctive reading of Paul's letters provided a hermeneutical key to understand authoritative texts. Some texts are focused on Paul directly, as with the (Coptic) Apocalypse of Paul, but more often Pauline texts and themes are employed to make sense of other ideas, as exemplified in the Gospel of Truth. As part of its cosmological dualism, Gnostic traditions famously question a future bodily resurrection (see also Epistle of Rheginos 45.15, 25-28). Patristic theologians especially criticize Gnostics as promoting a soteriological determinism, separating between the pneumatic and the psychic/sarkic (see 1 Cor 3:1; 15:44-49).

Marcionism and Gnosticism remained influential for centuries, even if indirectly. They were appealing because they extended inclinations already prevalent among many Christians, particularly those influenced by Hellenistic *philosophy. Though rejecting the foundational premises of the pagan philosophers regarding the nature of God and of *creation, patristic Christians also appreciated and appropriated aspects of ancient ontology, especially as mediated by (neo) Platonic philosophy, though with varying levels of interaction. For instance, one sees cosmological hierarchies expressed in considerations of *anthropology (e.g., soul over body) as well as ecclesiology (e.g., bishops over priests, and the role of obedience in monasteries).

4. Select Distinctive Issues.

The reception of Paul as "the apostle" among patristic theologians is as diverse as theology as a whole in the patristic period. That diversity is beyond the scope of this article, but it will briefly address illustrative issues.

4.1. Spiritual Theology. In contrast to modern academic approaches, patristic interpreters engage Paul in the context of spiritual theology, theology within and for the church, because Paul witnesses to pastoral concerns about living faithfully and blamelessly in a pagan world. Because they integrated doctrinal teaching with *spirituality, dogmatic discussions, such as that concerning the divine and human natures in Christ, are also grounded in the spiritual life of the church (e.g., see Cyril of Alexandria's repeated engagement with Phil 2 in his *Unity of Christ*). Likewise, one sees great attention to Pauline themes related to the nature of spirituality, particularly in more ascetic approaches with calls to embody chastity and virginity (e.g., Acts of Paul and Thecla and Chrysostom's *On Virginity*). Though some "encratic" positions (devoted to sometimes extreme asceticism) were critiqued by the orthodox theologians, an emphasis on a holy life devoted to God was widely valorized, and even more so with the rise of monasticism. In contrast to later approaches, especially in the Reformation, which highlight ordinary flourishing as embodied realities (*marriage, work, etc.), patristic interpreters also strongly emphasize extraordinary flourishing (fasting, solitude, etc.), which lead to purification of the soul through mastery of the passions. In this way, noetic aspects of Paul's theology are emphasized.

4.2. Salvation Economy. As seen above with heterodox debates, Paul's voice was often strong in discussions related to the relationship of Christianity and Judaism. This included issues related to the parting(s) of the ways, but also to the nature of the *salvation economy, which raised many questions: In what ways does the work of Jesus represent (dis)continuity with the OT? Do the discontinuities between the OT and NT reflect cosmological discontinuities between creation and new creation? Critiques of wider cosmic dualism were widespread in patristic Christianity, based on an emphasis on one God and one salvation economy, evidenced by the unity of divine and human in the incarnate Christ. This sense of unity helped undergird later trinitarian arguments. However, patristic approaches to the nature of that salvation economy and the integration with the OT and NT are varied, as is their appropriation of Paul to narrate them. (One sees similarly diverse approaches within modern scholarship by apocalyptic and "new perspective" readings.) In many cases, the rule of faith provided grounds for a theology of continuity but by means of a retrospective epistemology. These theologians read Paul in concert with the rest of the Bible, similar to how the NT writers use the OT. Thus, the early church found not only the interpretive conclusions of Paul as normative but also his interpretive practices.

When considering the nature of the salvation economy, individual salvation played an important role. In contrast to some Gnostic traditions that emphasized the present reality of an immaterial resurrection, many patristic theologians defended a future resurrection of the *body, even resurrection of the flesh. That said, some orthodox interpreters within a more mystical tradition give less attention to the body while not degrading it (e.g., Clement of Alexandria, Gregory of Nyssa). Across the tradition more widely, interpreters of Paul highlight theosis, or participation in divine life through union with God, as the new creation fulfillment of God's creational intention for humanity. Resurrection was not simply a point of doctrine but fit within a wider framework of creational restoration (see Rom 8:17-30). With the problem of determinism associated with Gnostic traditions, patristic theologians gave strong place to human *freedom and cooperation in the spiritual life based on a theology of participation. With the rise of the Pelagian controversy in the West (ca. AD 400), Augustine and interpreters of Paul who followed him came to reconsider the relationship of divine and human agency. At this juncture *justification became more of interest to Pauline interpreters (see Augustine's *Spir. et litt.*; cf. Cyril of Alexandria's *Adoration and Worship in Spirit and in Truth* 2–3).

See also Apocryphal Pauline Literature; Canon of Paul's Letters; Gnosis, Gnosticism; Interpretation: Augustine; Interpretation: Medieval; Paul and Judaism; Salvation; Spirituality.

BIBLIOGRAPHY. **W. S. Babcock**, ed., *Paul and the Legacies of Paul* (Dallas: SMU Press, 1990); **E. A. Clark,** *Reading Renunciation: Asceticism and Scripture in Early Christianity* (Princeton, NJ: Princeton University Press, 1999); **M. F. Bird and J. R. Dodson,** *Paul and the Second Century*, LNTS 412 (New York: T&T Clark, 2011); **E. Dassmann,** "Paulinism," in *Encyclopedia of the Early Church*, ed. A. di Berardino (New York: Oxford University Press, 1992), 2:657-58; **M. W. Elliott**, "The Triumph of Paulinism by the Mid-third Century," in *Paul and the Second Century*, ed. M. F. Bird and J. R. Dodson LNTS 412 (New York: T&T Clark, 2011), 244-56; **A. Lindemann,** *Paulus, Apostel und Lehrer der Kirche* (Tübingen: Mohr Siebeck, 1999); **D. Marguerat,** "Paul After Paul: A (Hi)story of Reception," in *Paul in Acts and Paul in His Letters*, WUNT 310 (Tübingen: Mohr Siebeck, 2013), 1-21; **M. M. Mitchell,** *The Heavenly Trumpet: John Chrysostom and the Art of Pauline Interpretation* (Louisville, KY: Westminster John Knox, 2002); **R. I. Pervo,** *The Making of Paul: Constructions of the Apostle in Early Christianity Paperback* (Minneapolis: Fortress, 2010); **J. Schröter, S. Butticaz, and A. Dettwiler,** eds., *Receptions of Paul in Early Christianity: The Person of Paul and His Writings Through the Eyes of His Early Interpreters*, BZNW 234 (Berlin: de Gruyter, 2018); **T. D. Still and D. E. Wilhite,** eds., *Tertullian and Paul*, PPSD (London: T&T Clark, 2013), idem, *The Apostolic Fathers and Paul*, PPSD (London: T&T Clark, 2017); idem, *Irenaeus and Paul*, PPSD (London: T&T Clark, (2020); **J. Strawbridge,** *Paul and Patristics Database*, https://paulandpatristics.web.ox.ac.uk; **M. F. Wiles,** *The Divine Apostle: The Interpretation of St. Paul's Epistles in the Early Church* (Cambridge: Cambridge University Press, 1967).

B. C. Blackwell

INTERPRETATION: POSTCOLONIAL

In the 1955 Asian-African conference in Bandung, Indonesia, representatives from twenty-nine countries gathered to discuss the reality of their postindependence, postcolonial world. In his opening address, the first president of Indonesia, Sukarno, challenged the idea that "Colonialism is dead." He declared:

> I beg of you[,] do not think of colonialism only in the classic form which we of Indonesia, and our brothers in different parts of Asia and Africa, knew. Colonialism has also its modern dress, in the form of economic control, intellectual control, actual physical control by a small but alien community within a nation. It is a skillful and determined enemy, and it appears in many guises. It does not give up its loot easily.

The postcolonial world indeed still wrestles not only with the legacy of colonialism but with the many guises of colonialism. The reality of independence is really a condition of being "in-dependence" or continuous dependence, as Robert Young points out (Young 2020, 3). Postcolonial theory interrogates this continuous relation of dependence and subordination between the colonizers and colonized.

1. Overview of Postcolonial Theory
2. Postcolonial Theory in Pauline Studies
3. Conclusion

1. Overview of Postcolonial Theory.

The early development of postcolonial studies was rooted in the works of anticolonial intellectuals, particularly in the aftermath of World War II. The early works of Frantz Fanon, Albert Memmi, and Aimé Césaire, among others, paved the way for a more robust critique of colonialism in later times (Young 2001). Postcolonial theory in its current shape is primarily an intellectual movement. The resistance to colonialism is performed not by weapons, nor any physical means, but by intellectual activism, philosophical arguments, and cultural critique. It is no surprise that postcolonial theory originated in and flourished at the center of intellectual life in both North America and Europe. The three major thinkers who are often described as the "trinity" of postcolonial studies—Edward Said, Gayatri Chakravorty Spivak, and Homi Bhabha—are all professors at elite universities in the United States. All of them are literary scholars. Most of the works of postcolonial theory revolve around literary analysis, production, and criticism.

Said argues that knowledge production about the "Orient" (particularly the Arabs) by the "Occident" (European intellectuals and writers) is not neutral at all. Rather, employing Michel Foucault's notion of the interconnectedness of power and knowledge, Said insists that Occidental literature is constructed in complex colonial relations of power. Such writings are not separated or detached from colonialism but thoroughly enmeshed in it. Small wonder, then, that most of the production of knowledge in the West aimed to solidify colonial rule over the Orient. Said calls this Western intellectual enterprise that *speaks for* and *talks about* the Orient "Orientalism."

Bhabha and Spivak pushed the discussion further by complexifying the relationship between the colonizers and the colonized. Bhabha maintains that there is no clear-cut binary separation between the West and the East, or the colonizer and the colonized. Postcolonial theory has to move beyond the simplistic dichotomy or binary of the West and the East. Engaging a wide range of discourses including psychoanalysis, philosophy, Marxism, history, and theory of nationalism, Bhabha introduces concepts such as hybridity, mimicry, ambivalence, and so on in his seminal collection of essays, *The Location of Culture*. Spivak also pays close attention to the subjectivity and agency of the subaltern. In her groundbreaking 1985 essay, "Can the Subaltern Speak?," Spivak discusses the silencing force of the epistemic violence the subaltern subject experiences. The act of *speaking for* the subaltern is problematic because it silences them. Spivak unsurprisingly answers negatively the question she proposes in the title of the article. The politics of representation, she notes, makes it impossible for the subaltern to speak. While Said, on the one hand, focuses on the analysis of the wealth of literature produced in the West about the Orient, Bhabha and Spivak, on the other hand, deal with the theoretical aspects of postcolonialism, particularly by engaging the French poststructuralist tradition.

It is worth noting that Said, Bhabha, and Spivak are not by any means the only scholars of postcoloniality. Scholars such as Dipesh Chakrabarty, Mary Louis Pratt, Rey Chow, Ngũgĩ wa Thiong'o, Chinua Achebe, Robert Young, and many others have also contributed significantly to the discussion of postcolonial theory. Works about other forms of colonization have also begun to surface in postcolonial studies (e.g., among others, Srinivas Aravamudan's *Guru English*, Kuan-Hsing Chen's *Asia as Method*).

As a literary strategy, postcolonial criticism can generally be understood as a critique of representation. This strategy of reading emerges from the poststructuralist tendency to see language and textuality as the ground for any knowledge production. As Stephen Moore puts it, postcolonialism is, "for the most part, poststructuralist through and through" (Moore, 312). Understood this way, reality does not come to a reader as naked or brute facts but already filtered through language and the web of textuality. Thus, language re-creates, re-produces, and re-represents reality—often a colonial reality (Chow; Clark). Not only does it focus on the problem of representation, but it pays a closer attention also to the power relations of the characters depicted in the texts, the author, and the readers of the texts, its history of reception.

2. Postcolonial Theory in Pauline Studies.

Postcolonial studies made its way into biblical scholarship in the 1990s through the works of, among others, Fernando Segovia, R. S. Sugirtharajah, Kwok Pui-Lan, and Stephen Moore (see Moore and Segovia). It came as a breath of fresh air because it gave scholars from the colonized world a critical language with which to integrate their experience both of reading the biblical texts and of resisting the domination of colonial imagination in biblical scholarship. It empowered such scholars to speak from their positionality as the colonized people. In other words, it brought the subjectivity of readers—the flesh-and-blood readers, as Segovia puts it—to the forefront. Postcolonial criticism, therefore, resists a European scholarly tendency to pretend that readers can detach themselves from the text and that they need to remove their subjective experience from the process of reading. Postcolonial criticism rejects such a white scholarly nostalgia of objectivity. By doing so, the postcolonial approach pays a closer attention to the role of ideology and power relations, both in the texts themselves and in the interpretations of those texts.

Postcolonial criticism has influenced almost every aspect of biblical scholarship from the Hebrew Bible to NT studies. The publication of an edited volume, *The Colonized Apostle*, in 2011 marks an important development in postcolonialism in Pauline scholarship. Instead of simply repeating the content of that book here, it is much more useful to highlight three important features that postcolonial scholars have discussed in the past few decades: (1) Roman imperialism, (2) gender and *sexuality, and (3) race and ethnicity. These are not by any means the only features of Pauline postcolonial scholarship. However, they are the major trends in the postcolonial conversation of Pauline texts.

2.1. Roman Imperialism. As R. S. Sugirtharajah points out, one of the contributions of postcolonial studies is "unveiling biblical and modern empires and their impact" (Sugirtharajah 2012, 2-3). This inquiry into the *empire and imperial structure in postcolonial studies has a rather different slant from empire studies in Pauline scholarship, particularly works by white male scholars such as Robert Jewett, N. T. Wright, Richard Horsley, John Dominic Crossan, Warren Carter, and many others. Postcolonial scholars are in conversation with these empire studies scholars because both of them read the Pauline texts mainly from a political point of view, as opposed to the traditional theological reading. However, empire studies has depicted Paul almost exclusively as an anti-imperial figure (Liew 2018).

Postcolonial scholarship acknowledges the anti-imperial tendency of Pauline texts. Abraham Smith, for instance, argues that 1 Thessalonians 2:13-16; 5:1-11 contain a strong political critique of the Roman imperial order. The declaration that Jesus is *Lord and *Son of *God, according to Smith, is "in pointed contrast to the visible signs of the 'lordship' and 'divine sonship' of the emperor in Thessalonica" (Smith 2004, 60; see also 2009). Paul's establishment of *ekklēsia* as an alternative network of community is also a politically anti-imperial gesture against the Roman Empire. Likewise, by grounding his work in Puerto Rican experience as a "Latino 'child of colonialism,'" Efrain Agosto argues that Paul's political message of good news (*euangelion*) about the coming of a *kyrios* in his letter to the Philippians is a subversive move against the Roman Empire. Paul, in other words, challenges the Philippians' "loyalty to Caesar *Kurios*" (Agosto 2002; see also 2009).

Postcolonial scholarship pushes the discussion further. Paul is not *only* an anti-imperial figure. Postcolonialism also further complexifies the relationship between Paul, his churches, and the Roman Empire. Jeremy Punt's works have contributed significantly to this conversation. Employing postcolonial theoretical frameworks such as mimicry and hybridity, Punt argues that "Pauline rhetoric of weakness (e.g., Phil 2:5-11, 2 Cor 10–13) as well as a rhetoric of foolishness (1 Cor 1–4), served both as a challenge to imperial discourse and as authority and sanction for securing his own discourse of power" (Punt 2015, 133; see also Punt 2010; 2011). Tat-siong Benny Liew's recent article ably captures the hybridity of Paul's relationship with the Roman Empire as a colonized subject. As a subject who lived under "the haunting (omni) presence of the Roman empire," Paul's letters contain both his critiques of the Roman Empire and his "mirroring" of that Empire. In Liew's words, Paul "seems to serve a God who is both a rival and a mirror of the Roman Emperor and [his] service to God both causes Paul great problems with the Empire and gives Paul wonderful opportunities to build up his own imperialistic network and authority" (Liew 2018, 17).

In other words, Paul mimics the imperial strategies in his relationship with the local church communities. Paul is not just a colonized subject; he is also a mimic of the empire. As a hybrid colonized subject, Paul is "a subject of a difference that is almost the same, but not quite"—to borrow an expression from Homi Bhabha (122).

2.2. Gender and Sexuality. Another prominent aspect in postcolonial studies of Paul is the attention given to gender and sexuality. In particular, the works of Musa Dube and Kwok Pui-Lan have been quite significant in this inquiry. Dube's book *Postcolonial Feminist Interpretation of the Bible* launches a strong critique of white feminism—particularly of Elisabeth Schüssler Fiorenza's work—for overlooking the non-Western female experience under the regime of imperialism (Dube, 23-43). African women, or women in the colonized world, experience "double or triple oppression" (Dube, 43). White feminists cannot speak for every woman in the world. Kwok Pui-Lan, attempting to bridge Schüssler Fiorenza and Dube, argues that postcolonial feminist scholars can learn from white feminists because many liberation theologians and postcolonial scholars tend to ignore feminine experience in the colonized world (Pui-lan 2009; see also Schüssler Fiorenza, 111-48).

In Pauline studies, Kwok notes that not only is Paul anti-imperial or perpetuating imperialism, but that her postcolonial sensibility brings the voices of colonized women into conversation. The picture of Paul becomes "more complicated." Bringing gender to the discussion, Kwok argues that Paul also "supported the subordination of women to men (1 Cor 11:2-16; 14:33b-36, though some consider the latter as Deutero-Pauline)." Paul operated with a "double standard" by transforming the Jew-Gentile relationship but "not challeng[ing] gender roles and sexual relationship[s]" (Pui-lan 2005, 90-91).

Kwok's analysis of Paul along with that of Dube provides a substantive theoretical foundation for Joseph Marchal's works on postcolonial feminist interpretation of Paul. Marchal focuses mainly on Paul's letter to the Philippians. Marchal argues that Paul's statement that his parousia in Philippians 1:26 could ring a bell for the Philippians as "a term describing the arrival of a victorious emperor or the visit of an imperial administrator" (Marchal 2006, 20; see also Marchal 2008) and that his message of expecting his audience to be "blameless and pure" can be read as a form of civilizing mission through "adhering purely to Paul's exclusive, absolutist vision" (Marchal 2006, 24). Then Marchal pushes his analysis further by pointing out that Paul's rhetoric of hierarchy throughout his letter to the Philippians also "reflect[s] hierarchical gender dynamics." Paul's statement that "we ourselves are the circumcision" (Phil 3:3) is "phallocentric." Arguing that Paul is from a higher social status, Marchal insists that Paul constructs this hierarchical relationship on the basis of his own experience and status. A particularly vivid example of Paul's gendered hierarchical arrangement in Philippians is when he deals with two *women in that church, namely, Euodia and Syntyche, in Philippians 4:2-3. For Marchal, the argument in Philippians 4 "is most likely [about] his effort to convince them [i.e., Euodia and Syntyche] to adopt his imperially gendered mind-set, accept his authority within a subordinating chain of models, and be on the 'right' side of this *kyrios*" (Marchal 2006, 29).

While Marchal is critical of the Pauline rhetoric of subordination, Jennifer Bird argues that Paul's texts have long been used by biblical scholars "for programs of colonization, domination, and control," particularly in subjugating women (Bird, 175). Combining both feminist and postcolonial analyses, Bird critically examines Paul's rhetoric in 1 Corinthians 11 and its implication for gendered space as contested space. For Bird, the debates on the meaning of this passage actually concern a political struggle. "The struggle over this passage is ultimately about controlling meaning, which in turn 'controls' lives" (Bird, 181). Since Pauline texts have authority over the *church today, Bird argues that these texts have power to shape and form "the identities and practices of faith communities." It is no surprise, then, that both Pauline texts and their interpretations have been used to colonize female bodies. "I suggest that Pauline scholars would do well to attend more carefully to the ethics and politics of their own interpretations." Why? Because "this is truly a matter of life and death that affects the well-being of all members of faith communities that embrace passages such as 1 Corinthians 11" (Bird, 185).

Marchal and Punt have also explored the interconnection between postcolonial theory and queer theory (Marchal 2015; Punt 2008; 2018). Queer theory is suspicious of any claim of normativity, or normality, while postcolonial theory is suspicious of any claim of authority. Both question the binary way of social analysis, here in particular of the male-female and colonized-colonizer binaries. In this inquiry, it is about the construction of gender difference by the colonial power in order to serve the colonial desire, aspiration, and control. As Marchal puts it, "ruling groups construct different definitions of sexual propriety in order to claim their exceptionally superior status" (Marchal 2019, 162). In this sense, gender becomes an unstable construction in a politically and colonially bounded social reality.

2.3. Race and Ethnicity. Postcolonial theory is profoundly connected to the issues of race and ethnicity. The works of early decolonial thinkers such as Frantz Fanon, Albert Memmi, and many others have already shown that colonial rule works through the construction of racial difference. Race/ethnicity, therefore, becomes a crucial site of postcolonial analysis. This racial approach to the Bible typically combines two levels of analysis: the texts and the readers (Liew 2007). That is to say, postcolonial scholars pay attention to the racial construction in the ancient text and how racial struggle in the modern world influence the interpretation of the text. Oftentimes, these two levels are simultaneously engaged in the analysis of Pauline texts. Regarding the combination of these two levels, Segovia calls it a "minority biblical criticism" (Segovia 2000; 2010). Postcolonial theory pays closer attention to the subjectivity of readers. These two aspects are, in other words, a call to return home. Sugirtharajah argues that there are three trends in biblical studies today that postcolonialism challenges:

Europeanization, racialization, and the negation of the "other" (Sugirtharajah 2003). By decentering Europe and the European discourses, postcolonialism opens a space for a colonized reader to speak, to read, and to interpret.

Liew grounds his reading of 1 Corinthians on Asian American bodies that have been constructed as racial others, foreigners, insufficient, and weak. Bodies, in other words, are the marker of their racial differences. Liew challenges Dale Martin's reading of Corinthian bodies as signifying the social status, arguing that Martin has overlooked the importance of the reality of colonized body in Paul's interaction with the Corinthians. This colonized body, according to Liew, is not only racialized but also feminized and sexualized. "As one rightfully critiques Paul's marginalization of women and sexual dissidents in 1 Corinthians, one must also not fail to account for the absent presence of Roman colonization and racialization of Jews like Paul" (Liew 2007, 145).

Likewise, Sze-kar Wan advances the idea that Paul's cultural identity can to be understood through an Asian American diasporic experience. In his reading of Galatians, Wan argues that Paul is not necessarily erasing ethnic or racial difference; he is instead "combining these differences into a hybrid existence" (Wan, 126). This diasporic hybridity is the "universality" in Pauline theology. Expanding Wan's project, Roland Charles's extensive research in *Paul and the Politics of Diaspora* highlights Paul's life as a Diaspora person. Framing his discussion primarily in diaspora studies combined with postcolonial categories such as hybridity, in-betweenness, and so on, Charles discusses the debates in Antioch, Paul's gender and ethnic constructions, and his collection project.

Allen Dwight Callahan brings African American experience in the United States to his reading of Philemon (Callahan 2008). He challenges the long history of the interpretation of this letter, beginning from John Chrysostom's homily to white settlers' interpretation in the new world. For Callahan, this reading is imperialist through and through and has been used as a tool for subjugating Black bodies as slaves under the rule of whites (Callahan 2009). Callahan argues that Onesimus was not a runaway *slave at all but an alienated brother (Callahan 1997).

3. Conclusion.

As a form of political reading of the text, postcolonial criticism prioritizes the analysis of the existing power differential in both texts and readers. As Steed Davidson puts it:

> Done well, postcolonial biblical criticism invokes wide-ranging histories and identities marginalized by western knowledge dominance, reassesses normative methodologies of textual interpretation, challenges interpretive output, and expands the range of texts either seen as biblical or privileged within discussions of the Bible as the means towards dismantling oppressive afterlives of the Bible and its texts or breathing liberating power within those texts among those who live in or through postcoloniality. (Davidson, 6)

Postcolonialism places the question of power at the center of texts' readings because it is grounded in the liberation vision of biblical scholarship. It aims to open more space for voices from the margins of the empire to speak.

See also Empire; Ethnicity in Paul's World; Philemon, Letter to; Politics and Power; Sexuality, Sexual Ethics; Women.

BIBLIOGRAPHY. **E. Agosto,** "Paul vs. Empire: A Postcolonial and Latino Reading of Philippians," *Perspectivas: Hispanic Theological Initiative Occasional Paper Series* 6 (Fall 2002): 37-56; idem, "The Letter to the Philippians," in *A Postcolonial Commentary on the New Testament Writings*, ed. F. F. Segovia and R. S. Sugirtharajah (London: T&T Clark, 2009), 281-93; **H. K. Bhabha,** *The Location of Culture* (New York: Routledge, 1994); **J. G. Bird,** "To What End? Revisiting the Gendered Space of 1 Corinthians 11:2-16 from a Feminist Postcolonial Perspective," in *The Colonized Apostle: Paul in Postcolonial Eyes*, ed. C. Stanley (Minneapolis: Fortress, 2012), 175-85; **R. Broadbent,** "Postcolonial Biblical Studies in Action: Origins and Trajectories," in *Exploring Postcolonial Biblical Criticism: History, Method, Practice*, by R. S. Sugirtharajah (West Sussex, UK: Wiley-Blackwell, 2012), 57-93; **A. D. Callahan,** *Embassy of Onesimus: The Letter of Paul to Philemon* (Valley Forge, PA: Trinity Press International, 1997); idem, *The Talking Book: African Americans and the Bible* (New Haven, CT: Yale University Press, 2008); idem, "The Letter to the Philemon," in *A Postcolonial Commentary on the New Testament Writings*, ed. F. F. Segovia and R. S. Sugirtharajah (London: T&T Clark, 2009), 329-37; **R. Charles,** *Paul and the Politics of Diaspora* (Minneapolis: Fortress, 2014); **R. Chow,** "The Interruption of Referentiality: Poststructuralism and the Conundrum of Critical Multiculturalism," *The South Atlantic Quarterly* 101 (2002): 171-86; **E. A. Clark,** *History, Theory, Text* (Cambridge, MA: Harvard University Press, 2009); **S. V. Davidson,** *Writing/Reading the Bible in Postcolonial Perspective* (Leiden: Brill, 2017); **M. W. Dube,**

Postcolonial Feminist Interpretation of the Bible (St. Louis, MO: Chalice, 2000); **T. B. Liew,** "Margins and (Cutting-)Edges: On the (Il)Legitimate and Intersections of Race, Ethnicity, and (Post)Colonialism," in *Postcolonial Biblical Criticism: Interdisciplinary Intersections*, ed. F. F. Segovia and S. D. Moore (New York: Bloomsbury T&T Clark, 2007), 114-65; idem, "Roman Empire in Paul's Letters," in *The Oxford Handbook of Postcolonial Biblical Criticism*, ed. R. S. Sugirtharajah (Oxford: Oxford University Press, 2018), 1-26; **J. A. Marchal,** "Imperial Intersections and Initial Inquiries: Toward a Feminist, Postcolonial Analysis of Philippians," *JFSR* 22 (2006): 5-32; idem, *The Politics of Heaven: Women, Gender, and Empire in the Study of Paul* (Minneapolis: Fortress, 2008); idem, "The Exceptional Proves Who Rules: Imperial Sexual Exceptionalism in and Around Paul's Letters," *Journal of Early Christian History* 5 (January 2015): 87-115; idem, *Appalling Bodies: Queer Figures Before and After Paul's Letters* (New York: Oxford University Press, 2020); **S. D. Moore,** *The Bible in Theory: Critical and Postcritical Essays* (Atlanta: Society of Biblical Literature, 2010); **S. D. Moore and F. F. Segovia,** "Postcolonial Biblical Criticism: Beginnings, Trajectories, Intersections," in *Postcolonial Biblical Criticism: Interdisciplinary Intersections*, ed. F. F. Segovia and S. D. Moore (New York: Bloomsbury T&T Clark, 2007), 1-22; **K. Pui-lan,** *Postcolonial Imagination and Feminist Theology* (Louisville, KY: Westminster John Knox, 2005); idem, "Elisabeth Schüssler Fiorenza and Postcolonial Studies," *JFSR* 25 (2009): 191-97; **J. Punt,** "Intersections in Queer Theory and Postcolonial Theory, and Hermeneutical Spin-Offs," *The Bible and Critical Theory* 4 (2008): 1-16; idem, "Empire as Material Setting and Heuristic Grid for New Testament Interpretation: Comments on the Value of Postcolonial Criticism," *TS* 66 (2010): 1-7; idem, "Pauline Agency in Postcolonial Perspective: Subverter of or Agent for Empire?," in *The Colonized Apostle: Paul in Postcolonial Eyes*, ed. C. Stanley (Minneapolis: Fortress, 2011), 53-61; idem, *Postcolonial Biblical Interpretation: Reframing Paul* (Leiden: Brill, 2015); idem, "Postcolonial Biblical Criticism and Queer Studies," in *The Oxford Handbook of Postcolonial Biblical Criticism*, ed. R. S. Sugirtharajah (Oxford: Oxford University Press, 2018), 1-32; **E. W. Said,** *Orientalism* (New York: Penguin Books, 2003); **E. Schüssler Fiorenza,** *The Power of the Word: Scripture and the Rhetoric of Empire* (Minneapolis: Fortress, 2007); **F. F. Segovia,** *Decolonizing Biblical Studies: A View from the Margins* (Maryknoll, NY: Orbis Books, 2000); idem, "Poetics of Minority Biblical Criticism: Identification and Theorization," in *Prejudice and Christian Beginnings: Investigating Race, Gender, and Ethnicity in Early Christianity*, ed. L. Nasrallah and E. Schüssler Fiorenza (Minneapolis: Fortress, 2010), 279-312; **A. Smith,** "'Unmasking the Powers': Toward a Postcolonial Analysis of 1 Thessalonians," in *Paul and the Roman Imperial Order*, ed. R. A. Horsley (Harrisburg, PA: Trinity Press International, 2004), 47-66; idem, "The First and Second Letter to the Thessalonians," in *A Postcolonial Commentary on the New Testament Writings*, ed. F. F. Segovia and R. S. Sugirtharajah (London: T&T Clark, 2009), 304-22; **G. C. Spivak,** "Can the Subaltern Speak?," in *Marxism and the Interpretation of Culture*, ed. C. Nelson and L. Grossberg (Urbana: University of Illinois Press, 1988), 271-313; **R. S. Sugirtharajah,** *Postcolonial Reconfigurations: An Alternative Way of Reading the Bible and Doing Theology* (London: SCM Press, 2003); idem, *Exploring Postcolonial Biblical Criticism: History, Method, Practice* (West Sussex, UK: Wiley-Blackwell, 2012); **Sukarno,** "President Sukarno of Indonesia: Speech at the Opening of the Bandung Conference, April 18 1955," Internet History Sourcebooks, accessed February 2, 2021, sourcebooks.fordham.edu/mod/1955sukarno-bandong.asp; **S. Wan,** "Does Diaspora Identity Imply Some Sort of Universality?," in *Interpreting Beyond Borders*, ed. F. F. Segovia (Sheffield: Sheffield Academic Press, 2000), 107-31; **R. J. C. Young,** *Postcolonialism: An Historical Introduction* (Oxford: Blackwell, 2001); idem, *Postcolonialism: A Very Short Introduction*, 2nd ed. (New York: Oxford University Press, 2020).

E. Tupamahu

INTERPRETATION: READING PAUL *LATINAMENTE*

The relatively recent emphasis in biblical *hermeneutics on how the social location of an interpreter influences the interpreter's readings of texts has allowed traditionally marginalized minority groups to join scholarly conversations about biblical interpretation and to revitalize the academic study of the NT. Among those groups, those reading Scripture *Latinamente* are particularly relevant due to their demographics in the United States. Although the designation *Latinamente* is often controversial, it is used here in reference to a diversity of interpreters who read Paul in light of their experiences as part of a nonmajority group in the United States with rich Latin American cultural heritages.

Those type of interpretations are largely preserved orally in communities that read, preach, and interpret Paul's letters in weekly gatherings. A systematic study of the diverse oral hermeneutics of this community remains a desideratum. The following survey provides general observations and brief descriptions that illustrate some of the approaches and topics prominent in the publications of those interpreters who explicitly join the larger academic discourse on Paul.

1. Approaches
2. Topics
3. Challenges

1. Approaches.

Scholars who interpret Paul *Latinamente* offer a *relectura* of his letters. Critically engaging the best of traditional Pauline scholarship, they read Paul in light of and for the benefit of the communities they represent. These interpreters consciously use their social, cultural, and historical context in their interpretations of Paul. The goal is to understand him in his first-century context by reading his letters from the edges of society and to appropriate his message in order to respond to issues their communities face in their daily life.

The particular perspective that scholars adopt is *desde la periferia*, "from the periphery." The experiences of marginalization and even oppression that many of them suffer on a daily basis is taken as a privileged place that resonates with the contextual circumstances of Paul's churches. Many early Christians who were the first readers of Paul's letters experienced social exclusion, discrimination, and injustice. The Roman Empire pushed many of them (e.g., *women, children, *slaves) to the margins of society. Those interpreting Paul *Latinamente* read his letters as a reflection of their own struggles, hopes, and beliefs.

These scholars also approach Paul as a *persona bicultural*, "bicultural figure." On the one hand, he was of the people of *Israel, lived righteously under the *law, offered *sacrifices in the *temple, quoted from the OT, and likely spoke Aramaic. On the other hand, he was a missionary to the *Gentiles, became as one outside the law, debated with pagans in marketplaces and the Areopagus, quoted pagan authors in his *preaching, and penned all his letters in Greek. His biculturalism left a noticeable imprint in his letters because it deeply influenced his theology. This bicultural experience resonates with a majority of interpreters who were born in Spanish-speaking contexts but live in a predominantly English-speaking environment. They see Paul as model and inspiration for their *ministry among their communities.

Although Latino and Latina scholars interpret Paul using different approaches, and they seldom use only one particular method to read his letters, the three characteristics mentioned above are found implicitly or explicitly in several of their publications. Furthermore, the individual characteristics of these approaches might not be completely original, but taken collectively they form a distinctive way of reading Paul's letters.

2. Topics.

Interpreters who read Paul *Latinamente* highlight the rich cultural diversity of Paul's churches. The original recipients of his letters were, for example, Jews and Gentiles, women and men, free people and slaves. This diversity created tensions, which Paul addressed through the articulation of theology and through specific commandments and prohibitions. Christian doctrine reflected in his letters is intended to shape the social relationships of this new multicultural community. It is difficult to properly understand Paul's theology without reference to this larger social context. For example, the oppression and exclusion that the poor were suffering in cultic contexts such as the *Lord's Supper properly frame Paul's instructions and theology about *worship.

Paul's life and ministry are also read as a paradigm for church *leadership development in multicultural settings. Scholars observe that Paul's church-planting strategies privileged *urban contexts and that he selected urban centers of the Roman provinces to evangelize and train leaders. Currently the communities of those who read Paul *Latinamente* are mainly found in metropolitan areas. Therefore, Paul becomes a natural source of reflection about the preaching of the *gospel, evangelism, discipleship, and leadership training in those contexts. Although scholars recognize significant differences between the first-century Roman Empire and modern societies, they attempt to contextualize Paul's example and theology to current life and global society.

Those interpreting Paul *Latinamente* also highlight the topic of *hospitality. Experiences of hospitality and inhospitality are common among their communities. Many have faced pressures to be assimilated into the majority culture or have been excluded for refusing to assimilate. This experience is used heuristically to read important sections of Paul's letters. One example that illustrates this point is Paul's encounter with Cephas in Galatians 2. Paul experienced hospitality by the Galatians because they received him as an angel of *God, and he instructs his audience to love their neighbor and to do good to all people (Gal 5:14; 6:10). However, the letter also includes the story of Cephas's incomplete hospitality toward Gentiles in the context of table *fellowship. Paul questions Cephas's hypocrisy, reflected in his refusal to consistently follow Christian conventions concerning hospitality.

*Identity is another important topic found in these readings of Paul. There is wide discussion about the cultural shape of the communities of those who read Paul *Latinamente*. The issue of identity is of particular importance for those who arrive in the United States from other American countries. Their first language is not often English, and their primary culture is Latin American. However, they are now living in a different country. Each person negotiates this identity issue in different ways: How much of their Latin American identity will they give up? How much of the new culture will they embrace? What aspects of the new culture do they want to transform? Scholars use these questions heuristically to read Paul. They observe that as a racial-ethnic minority person in the Roman Empire, Paul can provide theological perspectives that may help Christians navigate those important cultural questions.

3. Challenges.

The specific and unique contribution of these interpreters is becoming a challenge for traditional scholars. Some of them wonder whether these readings are only valid for a minority group in the United States that suffers alienation and marginalization. They question whether these readings actually contribute to a proper historical understanding of Paul and whether their interpretations are applicable to other groups of Christians with different experiences. Since experiences of injustice, racism, diaspora, and poverty are often caused by majority groups that practice social injustice and oppression, and global marginalization that pushes others to migrate, majority scholars should attentively engage those readings. The particular experiences of those interpreting Paul *Latinamente* are intertwining with the experiences of those who belong to majority cultures. Therefore, their interpretations have a wider application beyond the specific minority group that they belong to.

Another challenge that will continue to generate debate among scholars is the influence and integration of Latin American theology in what is called *Latinamente*. Often, there are topics developed in, for example, Latin American liberation theology that are appropriated by those who read Paul *Latinamente*. However, liberation theology is not the only theology that has grown in Latin American soil. How, for example, do Latin American evangelical theologies of *mission shape readings of Paul done *Latinamente*?

Given the particular circumstances of those who interpret Paul *Latinamente*, access to formal theological training is still a challenge. This situation creates a perceived distinction between popular readings of Paul and academic interpretations of his letters. The question remains how accurately academic interpretations of Paul reflect the daily use of his letters in worship contexts by scholars. Related to this question, one might also ask whether those few who have access to the highest level of theological training are effectively interpreting Paul for the benefit of the communities they represent.

See also EMPIRE; HERMENEUTICS/INTERPRETING PAUL; HOSPITALITY; IDENTITY; LORD'S SUPPER; MINISTRY; MISSION; PASTOR, PAUL AS; URBAN SETTING OF PAUL'S CHURCHES; WEALTH AND POVERTY; WORSHIP.

BIBLIOGRAPHY. **E. Agosto,** "Paul, Leadership, and the Hispanic Church," in *Seek the Peace of the City: Reflections on Urban Ministry,* ed. E. Villafañe (Grand Rapids, MI: Eerdmans, 1995), 103-22; idem, "Paul vs. Empire: A Postcolonial and Latino Reading of Philippians," *Perspectivas: Hispanic Theological Initiative Occasional Papers* 6 (2002): 37-56; idem, *1 y 2 Corintios,* Conozca su Biblia (Minneapolis: Augsburg Fortress, 2008); idem, *Servant Leadership: Jesus and Paul* (St. Louis, MO: Chalice, 2005); idem, "Reading the Word in America: US Latino/a Religious Communities and Their Scriptures," in *Misreading America: Scriptures and Difference*, ed. V. L. Wimbush with Lalruatkima and M. R. Reid (Oxford: Oxford University Press, 2013), 117-64; idem, "Confronting Empire: The Apostle Paul & Pedro Albizu Campos, the Apostle of Puerto Rican Independence," *Apuntes* 35 (2015): 118-33; **M. D. Carroll R.,** "Latino/Latina Biblical Interpretation," in *Scripture and Its Interpretation: A Global, Ecumenical Introduction to the Bible*, ed. M. J. Gorman (Grand Rapids, MI: Baker Academic, 2017), 311-23; **E. Conde-Frazier,** "*Evangélicas* Reading Scripture: Readings from Within and Beyond the Tradition," in *Latina Evangélicas: A Theological Survey from the Margins*, ed. L. I. Martell-Otero, Z. Maldonado Pérez, and E. Conde-Frazier (Eugene, OR: Cascade, 2013), 73-89; **D. Cortés Fuentes,** "El mensaje apocalíptico de Pablo en Primera de Tesalonicenses como un medio de esperanza," *Apuntes* 13 (1993): 190-97; **J. L. González,** "Reading the Bible in Spanish," *Apuntes* 9 (1989): 39-46; idem, *Santa Biblia: The Bible Through Hispanic Eyes* (Nashville: Abingdon, 1996); idem, "Reading the Bible from the Edges of Society," *Apuntes* 35 (2015): 38-53; **L. A. Guardiola-Sáenz,** "Latina/o Interpretation," in *The Oxford Encyclopedia of Biblical Interpretation*, ed. S. L. McKenzie (Oxford: Oxford University Press, 2013), 1:483-91; **P. A. Jiménez,** "Creando una nueva humanidad: Reflexión sobre la tarea educativa de la Iglesia basada en Efesios 4:17-32," *Apuntes* 11 (1991): 75-80; idem, "The Bible: A Hispanic

Perspective," in *Teología en conjunto: A Collaborative Hispanic Protestant Theology*, ed. J. D. Rodríguez and L. I. Martell-Otero (Louisville, KY: Westminster John Knox, 1997), 66-79; idem, "From Text to Sermon with Philippians 1:1-6: A Hispanic Perspective," *Apuntes* 17 (1997): 35-40; **F. Lozada Jr.,** *Toward a Latino/a Biblical Interpretation*, RBS 91 (Atlanta: SBL Press, 2017); **F. Lozada Jr. and F. F. Segovia,** eds., *Latino/a Biblical Hermeneutics: Problematics, Objectives, Strategies*, SemeiaSt 68 (Atlanta: SBL Press, 2014); **A. E. Martínez,** "El apóstol Pablo y la comunidad de Tesalónica: Leceiones [*sic*] sobre el uso del poder," *Apuntes* 15 (1995): 3-13; idem, "Filipenses 3:4-11 y la conversión de Pablo como preceso de resocialización," *Apuntes* 22 (2002): 44-63; idem, *Después de Damasco: El Apóstol Pablo desde una perspectiva latina* (Nashville: Abingdon, 2003); idem, "The Immigration Controversy and Romans 13:1-7," *Apuntes* 27 (2007): 124-44; idem, "Pablo, el obrero: Oficio y opción a favor de 'los trabajadores,'" *Apuntes* 23 (2007): 44-64; idem, *Interpretación bíblica con sabor latino: Una invitación al diálogo desde la diáspora* (Caracas: Acción Ecuménica, 2012); **J. E. Mulligan,** "The Good News According to Paul: An Invitation to Community," *Apuntes* 3 (1983): 15-20; **A. L. Nieves, A. Padilla, C. F. Pozzi, and A. B. Spencer,** *The Latino Heritage Bible* (Iowa Falls, IA: World Bible, 2003); **F. F. Segovia,** "Toward Latino/a American Biblical Criticism: Latin(o/a)ness as Problematic," in *They Were All Together in One Place? Toward Minority Biblical Criticism*, ed. R. C. Bailey, T. B. Liew, and F. F. Segovia, SemeiaSt 57 (Atlanta: Society of Biblical Literature, 2009), 193-223; **A. B. Spencer,** "God the Stranger: An Intercultural Hispanic American Perspective," in *The Global God: Multicultural Evangelical Views of God*, ed. A. B. Spencer and W. D. Spencer (Grand Rapids, MI: Baker, 1998), 89-103.

C. R. Sosa Siliezar

ISRAEL

In readers' first encounter with Israel within the canon of Paul's writings, the *apostle states that "not all who are from Israel are Israel" (Rom 9:6), perhaps signaling for the reader that defining Paul's understanding of this term may be a complex undertaking. Indeed, Paul's conception of Israel has proven to be a highly contested question, not least within debates regarding *supersessionism and the relation of the *church to the Jewish people. Within historic discussions on this question, readers on one end of the spectrum have assumed Israel in Paul's thought to simply be the church of the *Gentiles, a "new Israel" that has now replaced ethnic Israel as the *covenant people of *God. At the other end, some readers have rejected any sense in which the church can be called Israel, insisting instead that Paul simply refers to the ethnic Jewish people by use of this term.

This article will begin with a brief introduction to Israel in early Jewish contexts and the NT, and then proceed to an overview of the uses of *Israel* in the Pauline corpus. It will then synthesize this Pauline material by seeking to answer major questions in current debates related to Paul's understanding of this term. It will become clear that Paul identifies Israel as the covenant people of God, both throughout history and continuing in his own day. For Paul, Israel is made up of the promised descendants of *Abraham, who have been and continue to be characterized by God's calling and the response of *faith rather than simply physical descent.

1. Israel in Paul's Context
2. Israel in Paul
3. Disputed Questions on Paul and Israel

1. Israel in Paul's Context.

It may be surprising to learn that Jews in Paul's time held to competing conceptions of what constituted Israel, but the extant evidence indeed suggests this to be the case. Within the Jewish Scriptures, *Israel* is used to describe (1) the patriarch Jacob after seeing God at Peniel and being renamed Israel (Gen 32:28-30); (2) the twelve-tribe covenant people of God that are traced back to Jacob/Israel's sons, who are identified as God's own *firstborn and called to be a kingdom of priests (see Ex 4:22; 19:5-6); (3) the ten-tribe northern kingdom of Israel, which separated from the southern kingdom of Judah under Jeroboam and was conquered and dispersed among the nations by the Assyrians; (4) the returnees from the Babylonian exile, who, though living in the territory of the former southern kingdom, nevertheless are sometimes referred to as Israel (see Ezra, Nehemiah; similarly later in 1 Maccabees); and (5) the land itself where the tribes of Israel have historically dwelt.

Paul's contemporary Philo is well-known for defining Israel as those who see God, which is drawn from the term's first usage, when Jacob sees God and becomes Israel (see Philo, *Fug.* 208). Interestingly, Israel for Philo does not seem to be either an identical category with the Jewish people or one that is strictly limited to Jews, as he sometimes uses the term more generically to describe those who reach perfection in virtue (*Mut.* 12.81-82; *Ebr.* 20.80-84) and likewise praises the sect of the Therapeutae, which he attests to have Greeks and barbarians among their membership, as constantly seeing God (*Contempl.* 2.10-12; 3.21). *Israel* is thus a term descriptive of those who reach the height of philosophic virtue, to which Philo's own Jewish people have privileged—though perhaps not exclusive—access from their possession of divine revelation.

Josephus uses *Israel* in the second and third senses, referring to the full twelve-tribe nation and the northern kingdom after the division from Judah, which he distinguishes terminologically from "Jews," the name used for the people after the return from Babylon due to the prominence of the tribe of Judah (*Ant.* 11.173). The authors of the Dead Sea Scrolls use various forms of *Israel* as their preferred term for self-identification (such as "the repentant of Israel"), which contrasts with the near-absence of the term *Jew* to describe their members. Interestingly, in scrolls such as the Damascus Document, *Israel* is used as the term to describe both the unrepentant and fallen nation in general *and* the righteous remnant that shares in the renewed covenant (e.g., CD III, 13-14).

While *Israelite* and *Jew* were closely related terms in antiquity, with Jews indeed understanding themselves as representing the ongoing heritage of Israel, recent scholarship has emphasized how the two terms were not strictly synonymous but rather related to each other as a set and subset. This can be witnessed by the example of the Samaritans, who similarly claimed to be Israelites, as the partial remnant of the ten northern tribes, but nevertheless were clearly distinct from the Jews (see Justin, *1 Apol.* 53.4). Indeed, some recent scholarship has contended that "Judeans" is a more appropriate translation for *Ioudaioi* than "Jews" in antiquity, arguing that the term's primary sense signified those from the region of Judea more so than a distinct religious and ethnic identity in this period (see Mason 2007). While this interpretative move may go too far (Josephus's comment that the region was named after the people when they returned from Babylon interestingly seems to argue against the idea), the debate serves well to illustrate how *Jew* often carried more specific associations with Judea and the tribe of Judah rather than the full twelve-tribe body of Israel.

In the NT writings, *Israel* is frequently used in the Gospels in the geographic sense (i.e., "land of Israel"). Many usages of the term do not clearly distinguish between the people and the land (such as Jesus not finding such faith as the centurion's in Israel, Mt 8:10), and in others the patriarch himself may also be in view (such as in the phrases "house of Israel" and "God of Israel"). This polyphonic quality is unsurprising given the history of the term, which originated first with the patriarch Jacob/Israel, then was used derivatively for the various groups of his descendants throughout history and the land they inhabited.

The book of Acts also contains a number of references to Israel that are relevant to Paul's own case. In the first example, Ananias is told that Paul is a chosen vessel to bear God's *name "before the Gentiles and kings and sons of Israel" (Acts 9:15). The second instance is Paul's first recorded sermon on his inaugural missionary journey, addressed to the "men of Israel" and those fearing God at the synagogue of Pisidian Antioch (Acts 13:16). Paul traces the story of God's dealings with "this people Israel" (Acts 13:17), culminating with John the Baptist proclaiming a *baptism of repentance "to all the people of Israel" and God bringing Israel a savior from David's seed (Acts 13:23-24). Finally, at the conclusion of Acts, Paul identifies himself as chained "for the sake of the *hope of Israel" before the Jewish leaders in Rome (Acts 28:20). In each of these usages related to Paul in Acts, it is the covenant people that derives from the patriarch that is referred to by use of the term.

2. Israel in Paul.

Within the Pauline corpus itself the word *Israel* is found seventeen times, with by far the highest density of references occurring in Romans 9–11, where Paul follows his enigmatic introduction to the identity of Israel in Romans 9:6 with eleven usages in the next three chapters. Given the diverse employment of the term *Israel* elsewhere, it should not be surprising to find variation in Pauline usage as well. From his first use of the term in Romans 9, however, what is striking is how Paul is not simply making use of the term's polyphonic quality but rather attempting to distinguish what makes one truly Israel. This parallels Paul's earlier discussion of what makes one truly a Jew in Romans 2, which he concludes by stating, "For one is not a Jew by what is visible, nor is *circumcision by what is visible in the *flesh; but one is a Jew by what is hidden, and circumcision is of the heart in the spirit, not the letter" (Rom 2:28-29).

2.1. Romans. Paul begins Romans 9 by lamenting the situation of his brothers and relatives according to the flesh, whom he identifies as "Israelites" and heirs of God's sonship, *glory, covenants, legislation, *ministry, and promises, as well as the fathers and even *Christ himself. Their situation, however, does not mean that God's word has failed (see Is 40:6-8); rather, it reflects the fact that "not all they who are from Israel are Israel" (*ou gar pantes hoi ex Israēl houtoi Israēl*), just as not all of Abraham's children were his "seed," but rather his seed would be called in Isaac rather than Ishmael (Rom 9:6-7; cf. Gen 21:12). This means that it is not simply fleshly descent that determines the children of God (see Ex 4:22; Jer 31:9), but rather the children of the promise are accounted as this "seed" (Rom 9:8). Paul then gives the example of the children of "our father Isaac" to demonstrate this principle, as Jacob too was chosen rather than Esau based not on any prior deeds but rather on God's *calling (Rom 9:10-12). As Paul summarizes in 9:16, to share in Israel's divine sonship is thus based neither on one's desire nor on striving and instead on God's *mercy.

Paul's image of the potter and the clay in Romans 9:18-24 is also relevant to the question of the *identity of Israel, though the connection is sometimes missed. While also evoking similar imagery found in Isaiah 29 and 45, the strongest biblical echoes for Paul's imagery are from God's revelation to Jeremiah at the potter's house, which is precisely a story of the making and remaking of *Israel* (Jer 18:1-6). Jeremiah is sent to the potter's house to witness how he can shape and remake a vessel according to his good pleasure, and after seeing the vessel spoiled in the potter's hand and remade into another, God speaks to Jeremiah: "'Can I not do with you, O house of Israel, just as this potter has done?' says the Lord. 'Just like the clay in the potter's hand, so are you in my hand, O house of Israel'" (Jer 18:6). God continues by calling all to repentance, as those nations for whom God has prepared destruction will be saved if they repent, while those for whom God has prepared blessing will not be saved if they turn away from him (Jer 18:7-10). Like the potter in Jeremiah, Paul writes that God has shown great patience in now preparing some vessels for destruction and others for glory, the latter of which he has called not just from the Jews but also from the Gentiles (Rom 9:24).

Paul substantiates his assertion by citing Hosea, who prophesied that those called "not my people" would be called "sons of the living God" (Rom 9:25; cf. Hos 1:10; 2:23), and then Isaiah, who cried out concerning Israel that even if the number of the sons of Israel should be like the sand of the sea, the remnant would be saved (Rom 9:27; cf. Is 10:22). Paul then contrasts Israel with the Gentiles; while the nations attained the *righteousness of faith without pursuing it, Israel pursued instead a law of righteousness and did not reach it, since it did so by relying on the law's works rather on the faith on which it was based (Rom 9:31-32).

In Romans 10:19, Paul asks whether Israel did not know how God would act and counters that God clearly foretold through Moses what would take place: "I will make you jealous with what is no nation; with a foolish nation I will provoke you" (Deut 32:21). In this case, Israel is clearly distinct from the "no nation" that God is using to provoke it. This contrast between the two peoples continues in Romans 10:21, where Paul recounts how Isaiah boldly states that God was found by those not seeking him, whereas to Israel he says, "all day I stretch out my hands to a disobedient and contradictory people" (Is 65:2 LXX).

In Romans 11:1-6, Paul states that God has not abandoned the people that he foreknew, which he demonstrates with his own example ("for indeed I am an Israelite") and that of Elijah: when the prophet was appealing to God against the unfaithful nation, God revealed that there were seven thousand who had not turned away from him (see 1 Kings 19). Here the principle appears to be that while many may be outwardly Israel, only a portion of them are inwardly—a reality that may not be easily discernible, even for a prophet! For Paul, this gracious preservation of a faithful, select Israelite remnant in Elijah's day offers the precedent for understanding God's dealings with his people in the present.

In Romans 11:7, Paul continues by commenting that "what Israel seeks, it did not attain, but the remnant did; the rest were hardened," which he illustrates by citing testimonies on Israel's blindness and deafness from Deuteronomy, Isaiah, and the Psalms (Deut 29:4; Is 6:9; 29:10; Ps 69:22-23; 35:8). Paul's last usages of *Israel* in this section come in Romans 11:25-26, where he describes the *mystery that "a partial hardening has come over Israel until the *fullness of the Gentiles should come in." Paul continues: "And thus all Israel will be saved, just as it is written: 'the rescuer will come from Zion, he will turn away impiety from Jacob.'" The identity of "all Israel" is examined in greater detail below, but in this preliminary survey, it appears less likely that Paul is now referring to every individual ethnic Israelite (given Paul's citations of Isaiah in Rom 9:27-29 regarding a remnant and seed of Israel being saved) and more likely that his focus is on the faithful remnant.

2.2. The Corinthian Correspondence. Turning to 1 Corinthians, one finds Paul's one usage of *Israel* to be his command for his readers to consider "Israel according to the flesh" in matters of cultic participation (1 Cor 10:18). Paul's specification seems to require that ethnic Israel is not the only sense of the term. What is the implied contrast? Israel according to the Spirit? This is a possible inference, but Paul does not say so explicitly (as this is the only use of *Israel* in 1 Corinthians). Nevertheless, there are indications throughout the *letter that Paul regards his Corinthian audience as now sharing in Israel's identity. For example, in 1 Corinthians 10:1, those who passed through the Red Sea and the desert are identified as "our fathers," and in 1 Corinthians 12:2 he speaks of how his audience previously were Gentiles (*hote ethnē ēte*). As Richard Hays (2005, 9) comments:

> This formulation implies that he considers them *ethnē* no longer. Within Paul's symbolic world, they are no longer among the *goyim*, because they have been taken up in to the story of Israel. It should be noted that Paul is not trying to convince his Gentile readers to accept this identity description as a novel claim; rather, he assumes their identification with Israel as a given and tries to reshape their behavior in light of this identification.

In 2 Corinthians, Paul twice comments regarding the "sons of Israel" who could not look at Moses' face because of the glory (2 Cor 3:7, 13), recounting the events of Exodus 34. While these sons remain veiled today when Moses is read, when they turn to the *Lord this veil is taken away, and they behold God's own transforming glory (2 Cor 3:15-18).

2.3. Galatians, Ephesians, and Philippians. In Galatians 6:16, Paul closes his letter by writing that "as many as will adhere to this standard, *peace upon them and mercy, and upon the Israel of God." This usage of *Israel* is a particularly enigmatic one. By the end of the epistle, it seems unlikely that this refers to Israel in a straightforward ethnic sense, given Paul's prior comments (such as those of the "present *Jerusalem" descended from the slave woman not inheriting with the free, Gal 4:25, 30). Israel corresponds not with the descendants of Ishmael but those of Isaac, who are equated with his audience in Galatians 4:28: "But you, brothers, are children of promise in accordance with Isaac." The likeliest conclusion is that Israel is the people of Christ in Galatians 3:28, which is confirmed by Galatians 3:29: "And if you are of Christ, then you are Abraham's seed, heirs according to the promise."

In Ephesians 2:12, Paul addresses his audience who once were Gentiles in the flesh, called uncircumcision by those called circumcision in a manmade, fleshly sense (Eph 2:11). Paul reminds them that they were previously "without Christ, estranged from the *citizenship of Israel and aliens of the covenants of the promise, having no hope and without God in the world," conditions that have all now been reversed in Christ.

Finally, the last Pauline instance of *Israel* is in Philippians 3:5, which is preceded by Paul's statement that he and the Philippian believers are actually "the circumcision" (rather than "the mutilation" who put confidence in the flesh, ostensibly Paul's Judaizing *opponents, Phil 3:2-3). Paul recounts his own previous fleshly credentials, which are now surpassed by the *knowledge of Christ: "circumcised on the eighth day, from the people of Israel, tribe of Benjamin, a Hebrew of the Hebrews, with respect to the law a Pharisee" (Phil 3:5).

3. Disputed Questions on Paul and Israel. Having briefly examined each use of *Israel* in the Pauline corpus, this article is now in position to engage some of the main disputed questions related to Paul's use of the term.

3.1. Does* Israel *Always Carry the Same Meaning in Paul's Writings? *Israel* is employed in more than one way in the Pauline writings, which is seen from his use of the word at Romans 9:6: if not all those from Israel are Israel, it is evident that there is an authentic sense of Israel and another that is only apparent. This can be similarly observed from 1 Corinthians 10:18, where Paul tells the Corinthians to consider "Israel according to the flesh," a specification that seems intelligible only if Israel can be understood in a distinct nonphysical sense as well.

Like the practice noted in the Dead Sea Scrolls, Israel in Paul at times identifies the largely disobedient physical descendants of Abraham (Rom 9:27; 10:21; 11:2) and at others the continuing faithful heritage (Rom 11:26; Gal 6:16; Eph 2:12). The former group is sometimes specified as those of the flesh (Rom 9:3, 8), with the faithful party variously identified as the "children of promise," "remnant," or "select" (Rom 9:8, 27; 11:7). Though *Israel* is not used in the immediate context of Galatians 4, one can also note the close parallels with Romans 9:6-13 in Galatians 4:21-31, which contrasts Abraham's two sons and the two covenants: one is the fleshly son of the slave woman Hagar, corresponding with the present Jerusalem and the old covenant; the other is the spiritual son of the promise through the free woman, corresponding with the Jerusalem above and the Galatian brethren, who are the new covenant's children in accordance with Isaac.

If Jeremiah 18 indeed lies behind Paul's image of the potter and the clay in Romans 9, then perhaps it should be unsurprising if *Israel* at times seems like a term under construction for Paul, since it is precisely the case that God's reconstruction of the vessel of Israel is now taking place in Christ. Indeed, it is Christ himself who inaugurates the renewal of Israel, beginning with his choice of twelve disciples as a symbol of the restoration of Israel's twelve tribes and culminating with his sending of the apostles to all nations in fulfillment of the universal Abrahamic blessing. For Paul, Christ is the promised descendant of

Abraham par excellence (Gal 3:16), and those in him have a share in Abraham's heritage (Gal 3:29).

3.2. *Are* Israel *and* Jew *Equivalent Terms for Paul?* While closely related, *Israel* and *Jew* nevertheless appear to be distinct terms in Paul's writings (as indeed elsewhere in ancient literature). To employ a familiar analogy, one might take the case of crocodiles and alligators, where all alligators (i.e., Jews) are in the broader category of crocodiles, but not all crocodiles (i.e., Israelites) are in the subcategory of alligators. (The difficulty, of course, is that Paul continues by saying that not all those who are crocodiles are actually crocodiles!) Paul's distinction between *Israel* and *Jew* can be observed from Galatians 3:28; 6:16: while there is no longer Jew nor Greek in Christ, there is still an "Israel of God," on which Paul wishes peace.

Paul recognizes the way that *Jew* can stand as a *pars pro toto* (part for the whole) of Israel, which is evident in passages such as Romans 2:25-29, where the dialogue regarding what makes one truly a Jew has close parallels to Paul's discussions of Israel in Romans 9–11. Nevertheless, while Paul's statements regarding identification as a Jew are ambivalent, Israel as the broader covenant people of God is more consistently affirmed in his writings. For example, while Paul agrees with Peter in identifying as a Jew by nature in Galatians 2:15, in the next chapter he writes that this identification is now made relative in Christ (Gal 3:28; cf. Rom 10:12; 1 Cor 12:13; Col 3:11). Indeed, in 1 Corinthians 9:20 Paul writes that to the Jews he became like a Jew in order to win them—as a Jew by nature, how could he now "become like a Jew," unless he no longer regarded this identifier as binding? This principle can also be witnessed from the outset of 1 Corinthians, where Paul contrasts those in Christ as a third party who are distinct from Jews and Greeks (see 1 Cor 1:22-23; similarly 2 Cor 5:16).

While Paul recognizes more than one sense of *Israel* (with many uses in Rom 9–11 relating to the failures of those according to the flesh), his identification with this term is nevertheless more clear and positive. In Romans 11:1, Paul presents himself as exhibit A that God has not abandoned Israel ("for I myself am an Israelite, from the seed of Abraham, of the tribe of Benjamin"), and he similarly identifies himself unequivocally as an Israelite in 2 Corinthians 11:22. When Paul wishes peace on "the Israel of God" in Galatians 6:16, he offers no further modifier for the term, while in the closest parallel usage of the term *Jew*, Paul distinguishes between the visible Jew, with fleshly circumcision, and the hidden Jew, with circumcision of the heart, the latter of which is validated by praise from God (Rom 2:28-29).

One can summarize the matter in this way: while there is now no distinction between Jew and Greek, Paul continues to identify with Israel as the designation for God's covenant people.

3.3. Does Paul Believe That Gentiles Who Are in Christ Become Part of Israel? This matter is one of some controversy, though it seems difficult to avoid the conclusion that Paul regards such Gentiles as indeed now a part of Israel. The most explicit testimony is Ephesians 2:11-13, where the Ephesians are reminded that they were once Gentiles in the flesh and called "uncircumcision" by the so-called circumcision, which was handmade in the flesh. "At that time, you were without Christ, estranged from the citizenship of Israel [*tēs politeias tou Israēl*] and foreigners to the covenants of promise, having no hope and without God in the world. But now in Christ Jesus you who were once far off have become close by the blood of Christ" (Eph 2:12-13). Just as these former (!) Gentiles in Christ are now with God, with hope, and members of the covenants, so too have they now been made partakers of Israel's citizenship.

This passage is closely parallel with Paul's image of the olive tree in Romans 11:16-24, where Paul tells his readers from the Gentiles that they have been grafted in and made fellow sharers in Israel's rich root. This also provides the likeliest answer to the question of what Paul is referring to in the next verse when he says that Israel is partially hardened until "the fullness of the Gentiles should come in" (*to plērōma tōn ethnōn eiselthē*, Rom 11:25). Paul's verb "come in" notably lacks an object, and while commentators have suggested many possibilities for what precisely the Gentiles are entering into (such as the *kingdom of God or Jerusalem), the most contextually probable solution is that Paul is still talking about Israel, which is the subject under discussion both in the broader and immediate context. (This would produce the following reading: "a partial hardening has come to Israel, until the fullness of the Gentiles should come in [i.e., to Israel], and thus all Israel shall be saved.") As James Dunn summarizes on this section: "Strictly speaking, it is not possible to include 'Greeks' within 'Jews'; that is simply a confusion of identifiers. But it might be possible to include 'Gentiles' within 'Israel.' And this is in effect what Paul attempts to do in Romans 9–11" (506).

This picture is further substantiated by Pauline testimony elsewhere. For example, in Philippians 3, Paul writes to a congregation of largely Gentile background—recall the absence of a Philippian synagogue in Acts 16:12-13—that "we are the circumcision, who are worshiping by the spirit of God and boasting in

Christ Jesus" (Phil 3:3; cf. Col 2:11-12). For Paul, this sign of Abraham's covenant relationship with God properly belongs not to those who rely on physical circumcision and fleshly Israelite lineage but rather to those who minister by the spirit of God (see the similar contrast between visible fleshly circumcision and the spiritual circumcision of the heart in Rom 2:28-29).

This reading of Paul is confirmed by the imprint left by his teaching in the earliest Christian communities, in which it appears to be taken for granted that those in Christ who are from Gentile backgrounds have been grafted into Israel. This can be clearly witnessed in *1 Clement*, which is written from the Roman church to that of Corinth in the latter first century (ca. AD 69–95) and which early testimony attributes to Paul's own coworker (Phil 4:3). This letter was written to resolve a schism in the Corinthian church, and the influence of Paul is pervasive in it, with Clement going so far as to explicitly tell the Corinthians to "take up the epistle [i.e., 1 Corinthians] of the blessed apostle Paul" in *1 Clement* 47.1. What is striking within this context is how, much like Paul and his audience in 1 Corinthians, the various conflicted parties all take for granted as a point of commonality that they participate in Israel. This identification is implicitly assumed by Clement's calling both Jacob and Abraham "our father" in *1 Clement* 4.8 and 31.2, and explicitly stated in *1 Clement* 29.1-3, where Clement praises God for graciously choosing him and the Corinthian recipients by citing Deuteronomy 32:8-9 ("when God divided the nations . . . the allotment of his inheritance was Israel"). Further, neither Clement nor his readers show any indication of continued identification as Gentiles, and on the rare occasions that Clement makes appeal to non-Israelite examples, he specifies them as "examples from the Gentiles" without identifying them as forefathers, like he does the Israelites Abraham and Jacob (see *1 Clem.* 55.1). Hays's observations on Paul and the Corinthians apply here as well: rather than trying to convince his audience of their identification with Israel, Clement—following Paul—can already assume it as a given.

This early self-understanding of Christians can be similarly witnessed in Justin Martyr's mid-second-century *Dialogue with Trypho*, a text that likewise shows strong evidence of influence from Paul's epistles. Justin is a fascinating witness to the development of early Christian theology, as he openly acknowledges when Christians hold to differing opinions on disputed questions, such as whether it is licit for Jewish Christians to continue practicing the Mosaic law (see *Dial.* 45–47). No such controversy is attested on the question of whether Christians are truly Israel, however, with Justin consistently testifying to Trypho that this is indeed the case.

While Justin is sometimes characterized as holding to a supersessionist theology whereby the (Gentile) church is a replacement for (Jewish) Israel, this is a misconception, as Justin indeed argues directly against replacement theology when Trypho asks whether he holds that "none of us Jews will inherit anything on the holy mountain of God" (*Dial.* 25.6). Justin makes clear that he rejects this idea, "but I do say that those who have persecuted Christ in the past and still do, and do not repent, shall not inherit anything on the holy mountain, unless they repent. Whereas, the Gentiles who believe in Christ and are sorry for their sins shall receive the inheritance, along with the patriarchs, the prophets, and every just descendant of Jacob" (*Dial.* 26.1; cf. Jer 18:7-10). Because Christ is the fulfillment of the promises to Abraham to which Jacob's righteous descendants have all looked forward, and indeed is Israel himself in the fullest sense (see Is 42:1-4; Gal 3:16), it is one's relation to him—whether Jew or Gentile—that determines one's participation in Israel and inheritance with God.

Should such an engrafting of Gentiles into Israel be a surprise? In one sense, yes—after all, Paul himself describes it as a mystery only now revealed that the Gentiles should share in the body and promises of Israel as co-heirs in Christ (Eph 3:3-6)—but it is not a surprise entirely without precedent. Consider the nation as it began the exodus, with a mixed multitude of foreigners joined with Israel, who likewise experienced God's saving acts (Ex 12:38). The principle of grafting in and breaking off is as old as Israel's existence in the promised land: the allegiance of Rahab and her Canaanite family grafts them in, while the faithlessness of Achan and his Israelite *household cuts them off (Josh 6:25; 7:22-26). The vision of Isaiah, so important in Paul's theology, culminates with those from among the Gentiles becoming priests and Levites and the nations flooding into Jerusalem (Is 66:18-23). If even David himself comes from Ruth, a Moabite grafted into Israel, perhaps it should not be astonishing to find the Son of David grafting those from the Gentiles into Israel's rich root—an incorporation not now effected by fleshly assimilation but by the power of the Spirit (see Eph 2:16-22). For Paul, such Gentiles are true children of Isaac (Rom 9:10), who are generated not by natural means, like Ishmael, but miraculously in accordance with God's promise (Gal 4:28-29).

3.4. Whom Does Paul Identify as "All Israel" That Will Be Saved in Romans 11:26? It is difficult to briefly engage such a historically disputed question, and one easily sympathizes with Origen, who wrote on the identity of "all Israel" in his Romans commentary (ca. AD 240) that "only God knows and his only-begotten and perhaps anyone who are his friends." Nevertheless, at this point in the analysis one can briefly state three parties that would seem to be included in "all Israel" for Paul.

First are those believing Israelites who, like Paul, have now received Abraham's promises in Christ. Second are those in Christ from the Gentiles who are now grafted into Israel. (As recent scholarship has suggested, these may also include those of Israelite lineage from the northern tribes that had been dispersed among the nations and so functionally had become indistinguishable from the Gentiles. Interestingly, this suggestion would mean that the calling of the Gentiles simultaneously effects the restoration of Israel's lost tribes in the process, coinciding with Isaiah's closing vision of the nations carrying back Israel's dispersed brethren in Is 66:18-20.) Third are those among Israel according to the flesh who have been broken off for infidelity but whom God will restore and regraft when they are provoked to jealousy, as Moses promised (Deut 32:21; cf. Rom 10:19; 11:11, 14, 23-24).

3.5. What Hope Does Paul Have for Those of Ethnic Israel Who Have Rejected Christ? If Paul is unambiguous that *salvation is only in Christ, who fulfills the Abrahamic promises, and that those who reject Christ thus cut themselves off from the Abrahamic heritage, he is also unambiguous in his hope that those cut off can be restored. It is true that such a restoration would appear as nothing short of life from the dead, an idea that Paul happily embraces (he is into this sort of thing). It seems unlikely that Paul's biography is far from the surface here: as an ethnic Israelite who had not only rejected but actively waged war against Christ, Paul has no shortage of confidence that God can effect restoration in others as well. For Paul, it seems that it is precisely the Gentile *mission and engrafting into Israel that he expects to provoke his brethren to salvation (see Moses in Deut 32:21), which would provide an explanation for why he follows his statement that "thus all Israel will be saved" by citing Isaiah 59:20, which he appears to have altered from "the rescuer shall come to Zion" (MT) or "on behalf of Zion" (LXX) to "the rescuer shall come *from* Zion." This is indeed the essence of the mystery: that the Messiah's coming from Zion to the nations will actually be the means of drawing rebellious ethnic Israel to salvation.

Does this mean Paul believes each individual ethnic Israelite will be saved? This would appear to go beyond the evidence: interestingly, the rabbis themselves did not seem to identify "all Israel" as every single Israelite (see m. Sanh. 10.1-3), and as Paul writes in Romans 11:14, his hope is that by the magnification of his ministry to the Gentiles his flesh (Israel) will be made jealous, and *some* of them will be saved.

See also Abraham; Circumcision; Corinthians, First Letter to the; Covenant; Election and Predestination; Faith; Gentiles; Interpretation: Patristic; Paul and Judaism; Romans, Letter to the; Supersessionism.

BIBLIOGRAPHY. **Augustine,** "Epistle 196," in *The Works of St. Augustine: Letters 156–210*, ed. B. Ramsey, trans. R. Teske (Hyde Park, NY: New City, 2004), 310-19; **J. S. Bergsma,** "Qumran Self-Identity: 'Israel' or 'Judah'?," *DSD* 15 (2008): 172-89; **Clement of Rome,** "1 Clement," in *The Apostolic Fathers*, ed. M. Holmes (Grand Rapids, MI: Baker Academic, 2007), 33-131; **J. D. G. Dunn,** *The Theology of Paul the Apostle* (Grand Rapids, MI: Eerdmans, 1998); **S. G. Eastman,** "Israel and the Mercy of God: A Re-reading of Galatians 6.16 and Romans 9–11," *NTS* 56, no. 3 (2010): 367-95; **O. J. Filtvedt,** "'God's Israel' in Galatians 6.16: An Overview and Assessment of the Key Arguments," *CurBR* 15, no. 1 (2016): 123-40; **R. B. Hays,** *Echoes of Scripture in the Letters of Paul* (New Haven, CT: Yale University Press, 1989); idem, *The Conversion of the Imagination: Paul as Interpreter of Israel's Scripture* (Grand Rapids, MI: Eerdmans, 2005); idem, "Hope for What We Do Not Yet See: The Salvation of All Israel in Romans 11.25-27," in *One God, One People, One Future: Essays in Honor of N. T. Wright*, ed. J. A. Dunne and E. Lewellen (Minneapolis: Fortress, 2019), 545-71; **Justin Martyr,** *Dialogue with Trypho*, ed. T. P. Halton, trans. T. B. Falls (Washington, DC: Catholic University of America Press, 2003); **S. Mason,** "Jews, Judaeans, Judaizing, Judaism: Problems of Categorization in Ancient History," *JSJ* 38 (2007): 457-512; **Origen,** *Commentary on the Epistle to the Romans Books 6–10*, ed. T. P. Halton, trans. T. P. Scheck (Washington, DC: Catholic University of America, 2001); **J. M. Scott,** "'And Then All Israel Will Be Saved' (Rom 11:26)," in *Restoration: Old Testament, Jewish and Christian Conceptions*, ed. J. M. Scott, JSJSup 72 (Leiden: Brill, 2001), 490-527; **J. A. Staples,** "What Do the Gentiles Have to Do with 'All Israel'? A Fresh Look at Romans 11:25-27," *JBL* 130, no. 2 (2011): 371-90; idem, *The Idea of Israel in Second Temple Judaism* (Cambridge: Cambridge University Press, 2021); **N. T. Wright,** "The Letter to the Romans: Introduction, Commentary, and Reflections," *NIB* 10:393-770; idem, *Paul and the Faithfulness of God* (London: SPCK, 2013).

M. J. Thomas

J

JAMES AND PAUL

It did not take long for the *church to notice that James's words—"*faith by itself, if it has no works, is dead" and "You see that a person is justified by works and not by faith alone" (Jas 2:17, 24)—create not a little tension with Paul's well-known "we know that a person is justified not by the *works of the *law but through faith in Jesus *Christ" (Gal 2:16; also Gal 3:11; Rom 3:20, 24, 26, 28; 5:1; Allison, 444-57). Not only was this tension apparent already in the apostolic church, but it has been a serious theological threshold from the days of Augustine on (e.g., the common response to D. Bonhoeffer by the Lutheran establishment was that works featured too prominently in his understanding of the proper Christian response to *God in Christ; see Bonhoeffer). Roman Catholics and the Eastern Orthodox have also argued consistently and at times polemically against Protestants on this very issue ever since the Council of Trent and the Orthodox responses to the Reformation teachings. James 2:14-26 often emerges as the defining battleground (Allison, 434-36). On the Reformation side, the Anabaptists disagreed fiercely with Lutherans over the place of works in one's understanding of faith (Simons, 333-34). Modern debates over the issues here have diminished significantly (Lutheran World Federation and Roman Catholic Church), not least because of a deeper embrace of the ethical demand of Jesus in the Sermon on the Mount.

1. The Problem
2. The Proposals
3. Works
4. Faith
5. Justification

1. The Problem.

That Galatians-Romans and James are undeniably related at the level of terms (Allison, 445-46) and that Paul and James clearly had met one another (according to Acts 15; 21:17-26; Gal 1:18-24; 2:9, 12) complicate the tension, leaving the reader of these two authors with many questions unanswered. Add to this the strong teachings of *sola fide* flowing from Augustine and the Reformation (e.g., *Articles of Religion* 11-14), absorbed as these teachings are into the very bones of global evangelicalism, and one has the makings of a rejection of James altogether, not least among those in the wake of Luther (Hengel; Stuhlmacher, 495-502). Far more often one encounters a rather casual dismissal of James as but a minor voice in the NT and Christian theology, though some see Paul as incoherent (Räisänen). So, how does one explain a James who believed "faith alone" is not enough and a Paul who pushes hard against faith "without works"? The explanations are beyond summary or even counting (Allison, 426), but J. Dunn is correct to observe that there is a "Paul-fixation" that often distorts James (Dunn 2009, 1142). Nonetheless, a consensus view is that James corrects a "defective opinion" (Allison, 448).

2. The Proposals.

There are roughly four types of proposals to resolve the (apparent) tension between Paul and James (Davids, 457-58; McKnight, 259-64; Allison, 426-34).

2.1. Independence. Some contend James and Paul are writing without regard to the other and are using the same early Christian and Jewish terms but with different meanings (Martin, 81) or come out of differing contexts and have different strategies (McCartney, 154-75, 272-79). That is, James is speaking of works after faith while Paul of works before faith; or faith for Paul would include some kind of good works, while James erases all works from how he uses faith; or James's concern is sanctification and Paul's initial justification; or the problem being addressed (legalism versus easy believism, or nonbelievers who need to hear of faith versus believers who are soft in Christoformity) was sufficiently different that similar language emerges with different intentions (Allison, 429-32). Others have anchored their independence in their particular biographies: Paul discovered sheer, magnificent, and undeserving *grace after his reckless opposition to Christ, while James saw no need to diminish the significance of Torah observance as he came to faith in Jesus.

2.2. James Responding to Paul. Some think James is responding to Paul's theology of *justification by faith and is at some level in tension with Paul, perhaps because of James's *leadership in *Jerusalem. The tension bubbling to the surface is over Paul's *mission to include *Gentiles in the people of God with no or little respect for Torah observance. Perhaps James has heard about Paul from a distant connection or even distortion of Paul, something on this order: "Paul demands only faith and not obedience or works." So, it is conjectured, James pushes hard for a stronger sense of faith as allegiance (Dunn 2009, 1142-44; Bates). Others think James thinks Paul got it wrong and so is in strong opposition (Hengel; Stuhlmacher, 498-99: "emphatically contradicted"; Allison, 455), but this surely does push hard against the obvious lack of tension in the decision in Acts 15, which is led by James. Other passages in James have been suggested as anti-Pauline as well (Jas 1:19-20 with Phil 3:2; Jas 4:13-16 with Rom 16:3-5; Jas 5:12 with Gal 1:8, 20). One can argue, too, that at the least James points out possible problems in how Paul frames the human response (Stuhlmacher, 502).

2.3. Paul Responding to James. Depending on the dating of James (for discussion of options, see Allison, 3-32) and assuming a late date for James, one could argue Paul's constant pressing of the necessity only of faith for justification simultaneously engages the Jerusalem leaders' hesitations about Paul with James at the center. This, too, presses against what seems to be the consensus judgment of the *Jerusalem Council in Acts 15.

2.4. James Responding to a Distortion of Paul. The apparent consensus opinion of Acts 15 influences enough scholars for them to argue that James is actually responding to Paul but not to Paul's mature statements of justification by faith. Instead, James responds to an earlier version of Pauline theology or, even better, James is responding to some who have taken Paul's by-faith-alone theology and distorted it into easy believism (Davids, 458; Moo, 121; McKnight, 259-64). One needs reminding at times that opponents often do not understand the other well and some do not even attempt to do so.

It seems reasonable, then, to pose a biographical element as well: Paul's *conversion and early expressions of theology before writing either Galatians or Romans (AD 33–48), followed by James's response to what he was hearing about Paul from especially those very concerned about Paul's *teachings (ca. AD 45; see Gal 2:12), a public discussion with James (Gal 2:9) along with the Jerusalem Council (Acts 15), and then Paul's own later articulations with nuances following many conversations and debates with fellow Judeans (Romans; McKnight, 259-63).

3. Works.

The issue of which "lexicon" James and Paul were using matters immensely. James uses the Greek *ergon* a dozen times (Jas 1:4, 25; 2:14, 17, 18, 20-26; 3:13). In James 1:4 it is used generally for the *impact* of "endurance." In James 1:25 it is used for the one who does the works of the Torah, but Torah is defined here as "the law of liberty," which most likely is the "royal law" in James 2:8, where it is defined as loving one's poor neighbor (McKnight, 153-61, 205-9). Back to James 1:25: "works" refers to the control of tongue and even more to caring for orphans and widows (Jas 1:26-27). Something similar is found in James 2:14-17, where *ergon* means caring for those who lack clothes and food. The concrete illustrations of *ergon* in James 2:18-26 are the Aqedah of *Abraham (Gen 22) and the *hospitality of Rahab. In James 3:13 the use of *works* is general: *erga* manifests "one's beautiful behavior" (*ek tēs kalēs anastrophēs*), in which case *erga* are actions done in public. In short, James's view of *erga* is entirely in the realm of publicly visible, moral conduct, with *love for others being the chief virtue (Davids, 458; McCartney, 156: "faith-deeds"; also 272-79; Allison, 460; Blomberg and Kovalishyn, 132).

The apostle Paul's sixty-three uses of *erga* cannot be assumed to be the same as James's. Scholars have reached a reasonable consensus that the expression "works of the law" in Paul (e.g., Gal 2:16; 3:2, 5, 10) has the sense of referring to Torah observance in general (Dunn 1998, 354-55; Barclay, 374). The operative idea in much of Protestant thinking, that "works of the law" refers to human attempts to merit *righteousness before God, has been successfully defeated (but see Rom 4:4-5; Eph 2:8-9; Dunn 1998, 366-71). Torah observance is not, however, an abstraction in any form of Judaism or Judean Christianity. Observance is always hermeneutically based and formed in community, so that what one considers Torah observance—say, among the Essenes (e.g., 4QMMT [4Q394-399])—another—say, among the

Sadducees—does not. The "new perspective" contribution appears precisely here: that Torah observance for Paul as expressed in "works of the law" had particular connotations when Paul used it for those who opposed his mission. No one questioned the Torah about murder or adultery, but the points of contention were over what Dunn repeatedly calls "boundary markers," that is, those observances of Torah that distinguished Jews from Gentiles especially in Diaspora contexts—which means *circumcision, Sabbath observance, and *food laws (Dunn 1998, 355-59). Notice how close Barclay (374) gets to this, seeing Paul's "works of the law" as "the authoritative cultural frame," terms that suggest something like ethnic, elective claims to privilege. These precise observances are the points of contention in Paul's mission churches (Gal 2:1-21; Rom 14:1–15:13; Col 2:16). Yet, Paul has a powerful sense of the believer being a person of good works (Eph 2:8-9), most especially as one filled with the Spirit (Gal 5:6, 16, 22-26).

Accordingly, when the apostle Paul contends justification is by faith and not by "works of the law," he has this sense in mind—not works as moral virtue as in James but Torah observance as manifested in the particular context of the tension between Judean and Gentile believers in the churches of Paul. The concrete manifestations there are circumcision (e.g., Rom 4), food laws (Rom 14:1–15:13), and Sabbath (Col 2:16; Dunn 1998, 359-66; 2009, 1144). In the case of "works," then, James and Paul are independent of each other. James thinks faith is to be accompanied by good behaviors, which is as Pauline as it is Jakobite (see 2 Cor 5:10), but James is saying nothing about the common sense of boundary markers that vexed the Pauline mission so much. In this case, either James misunderstood what Paul was saying or—and this is far more accurate—James is responding to some who have taken Paul's teachings and either purposefully distorted them or misunderstood them, but James in both of these cases is not responding to what Paul actually taught.

4. Faith.

Faith is defined in Paul on a spectrum from initial (saving) trust in Christ through faithfulness, to faith over time or allegiance, to faith as the deposit of orthodox beliefs. It is one of the core terms for Paul's evangelism and theology (Dunn 1998, 371-85; Bates; Gupta). Exegesis then pushes the reader to ponder which of the three or a combination of them best fits in each usage. Paul's emphasis is often faith as trust, or at least as the distinguishing disposition toward Christ, and this evidently caused concerns for those who emphasized faith more as allegiance in a Judean context as Torah observance.

The Pauline sense of faith is clear, so I concentrate here on James, who uses the term a dozen times (Jas 1:3, 6; 2:1, 5, 14, 17, 18-26; 5:15). In James 1:3 the sense is allegiance (trust over time), while James 1:6 is more of a case-specific expression of faith by one who is already a believer (also Jas 5:15). James 2:1 refers to "the faith" and points to what Judean believers in Jesus considered properly basic. The poor who trust in Jesus are those who are "rich in faith" (Jas 2:5) in the sense that they are allegiant. When the *locus classicus* (Jas 2:14-26) uses *faith*, one should almost certainly think of it here as either initial trust or as properly basic, as in "faith by itself" in James 2:17 and "you believe that God is one" in James 2:19, or as ongoing trust in Jesus that does not manifest itself in the kinds of works that are consistent with that trust. James's harsh judgment is famous: such a kind of trust/faith (no more than the basic act of trust) is unable to save (Jas 2:14) because it is "dead" (Jas 2:17, 26) and "barren" (Jas 2:20). James believes true faith is "brought to completion by the works" (Jas 2:22) because one is not justified "by faith alone" (Jas 2:24), this latter verse referring to the kind of faith that trusts Jesus but does not become manifest in moral virtue ("by the works" in Jas 2:22; see Mussner, 133-36).

5. Justification.

Justification is sometimes translated "rectification" to avoid the seemingly endless theological wrangling since the Reformation of its meaning and implications ("infused," "imparted," "imputed"). The terms behind *justify* and *justification* translate the *dikai-* word group, which has a deep history in the OT and Judaism (Hebrew *ṣdq*). The Greek word group is found in James 1:20; 2:21, 23, 24-25; 3:18; 5:6, 16.

It should be observed that the characteristic Pauline usage, where *justification* means declaring right apart from "works of the law" and without merit or status, is particular to Paul and not characteristic of Judaism. In Judaism this word group largely describes those whose behavior is consistent with the will of God expressed in Torah and then later in the Judean observance traditions (*halakot*; Przybylski). *Justification* is thus a relational term. To be sure, it can mean God's act of making things right in the sense that God is faithful to his own *covenant with *Israel. That is, it can refer to God's great acts of redemption. Paul moves from this latter sense to his sense of justification (or right-making, or righting). For him, justification is an act of God to declare a person fit for divine presence. In his Christian worldview this word group will inevitably connote an efficacious act by God that prompts a person to do the will of God as taught by Jesus and as one empowered by the *Holy Spirit (Rom 8:4; Dunn 1998, 334-89; Allison, 485).

God's own righteousness in James 1:20, which does not derive from human *wrath, has the sense of God's act of redemptive *judgment. The "harvest of righteousness" in James 3:18 fits with James 1:20: peacemakers effect redemptive conditions. There is dispute over who it is who is "righteous" in James 5:6, but the term has implications for the unjustly treated poor, while the "prayer of the righteous" in James 5:16 points to the person whose life is consistent with divine will.

This leaves the crucial sense of justification in James 2:18-26. Abraham's justification includes the Aqedah with his son (Jas 2:21-24; cf. 1 Macc 2:52), so one is now one step removed from the Pauline notion that justification occurs solely on the basis of God's redemptive decision accompanied by the singular, initial human act of trust. Some opt here for a "demonstrative" sense of justification, that is, that this act proves that Abraham was (already) justified (Davids, 459-60; Blomberg and Kovalishyn, 136-37; McCartney, 162-71). When James then cites Genesis 15:6 in James 2:23, he includes the Aqedah of Genesis 22 as the operative act along with the act of trust in Genesis 15:6. More or less the same point is made about Rahab, whose justification is rooted in her hospitality to the "messengers" (Jas 2:25). Faith for James must be finished off with works of love (Jas 2:8). That James has the demonstrative view in mind is doubtful. The question "Can faith *save* you?" in James 2:14 pushes hard against the demonstrative view (Moo, 135).

In summary, the view that James and Paul are independent has some elements in its favor because there is so much between these two authors that does not overlap, but that both Paul and James are so fastened on Genesis 15:6 and on Abraham and on the terms *faith* and *justification* and *by faith alone* and *works*—this all requires that James has heard some distortions of Paul (see Acts 21:21) and sets about to correct them as a kind of mediator (Dunn 2009, 1144; Mussner, 146-50, James's emphases make the church healthier). Where James finishes is consistent with the *apostle's own general framework of a grace that transforms the unworthy person into an agent of works.

See also Abraham; Ethics; Faith; Freedom/Liberty; Holiness, Sanctification; Interpretation: Luther; Interpretation: New Perspective; Jerusalem, Council of; Justification; Righteousness; Works of the Law.

BIBLIOGRAPHY. **D. C. Allison Jr.,** *A Critical and Exegetical Commentary on the Epistle of James*, ICC (New York: Bloomsbury, 2013); **J. M. G. Barclay,** *Paul and the Gift* (Grand Rapids, MI: Eerdmans, 2015); **M. W. Bates,** *Salvation by Allegiance Alone: Rethinking Faith, Works, and the Gospel of Jesus the King* (Grand Rapids, MI: Baker Academic, 2017); **C. L. Blomberg and M. J. Kovalishyn,** *James*, ZECNT 16 (Grand Rapids, MI: Zondervan Academic, 2008); **D. Bonhoeffer,** *Discipleship*, DBWE 4 (Minneapolis: Fortress, 2001); **P. H. Davids,** "James and Paul," *DPL*, 457-61; **J. D. G. Dunn,** *The Theology of Paul the Apostle* (Grand Rapids, MI: Eerdmans, 1998); idem, *Beginning from Jerusalem*, CIM 2 (Grand Rapids, MI: Eerdmans, 2009); **N. K. Gupta,** *Paul and the Language of Faith* (Grand Rapids, MI: Eerdmans, 2019); **M. Hengel,** "Der Jakobusbrief als antipaulinische Polemik," in *Tradition and Interpretation in the New Testament: Essays in Honor of E. Earle Ellis for His Sixtieth Birthday*, ed. G. F. Hawthorne and O. Betz (Grand Rapids, MI: Eerdmans, 1987), 248-78; **Lutheran World Federation and Roman Catholic Church,** *Joint Declaration on the Doctrine of Justification* (Grand Rapids, MI: Eerdmans, 2000); **R. P. Martin,** *James*, WBC 48 (Grand Rapids, MI: Zondervan, 1988); **D. G. McCartney,** *James*, BECNT (Grand Rapids, MI: Baker Academic, 2009); **S. McKnight,** *The Letter of James*, NICNT (Grand Rapids, MI: Eerdmans, 2011); **D. J. Moo,** *The Letter of James*, PNTC (Grand Rapids, MI: Eerdmans, 2000); **F. Mussner,** *Der Jakobusbrief: Auslegung*, HThKNT (Freiburg: Herder, 1987); **B. Przybylski,** *Righteousness in Matthew and His World of Thought*, SNTSMS 41 (Cambridge: Cambridge University Press, 1981); **H. Räisänen,** *Paul and the Law*, 2nd ed., WUNT (Tübingen: Mohr Siebeck, 1987); **M. Simons,** *The Complete Writings of Menno Simons*, trans. L. Verduin, ed. J. C. Wenger (Scottdale, PA: Herald Press, 1984); **P. Stuhlmacher,** *Biblical Theology of the New Testament*, ed. D. P. Bailey and J. Ådna, trans. D. P. Bailey (Grand Rapids, MI: Eerdmans, 2018).

S. McKnight

JEALOUSY, ZEAL. *See* Israel; Paul and Judaism.

JERUSALEM APOSTLES. *See* Jerusalem, Council of; Judaizers; Opponents of Paul.

JERUSALEM, CITY OF

Though the nature of Paul's Jewish *identity after his *conversion is debated in NT scholarship, it seems clear from the NT record that Paul's view of Jerusalem, and his relationship with it, became increasingly eschatological as Saul the Pharisee became Paul the *apostle proclaiming Jesus *Christ as the risen *Lord.

Indeed, Paul could speak of two Jerusalems: "the present Jerusalem" (*tē nyn Ierousalēm*, Gal 4:25) represented the historical, physical city and life under the Mosaic law, and "the Jerusalem above" (*hē anō Ierousalēm*, Gal 4:26) represented a new era of salvation history in which a lasting Jerusalem would be composed of people from all nations. Paul describes this superior iteration of Jerusalem as those justified, redeemed, and adopted by God through Christ's redemptive work on the cross (see also Is 60–62; Zech 12; Gal 3:10-14; 4:25-27). Though the manifestation of God's one, eternal people awaits Christ's return, Paul recognizes the citizens of this better Jerusalem are those who belong to Christ's *church, which he elsewhere calls the "*household of God," the "holy *temple," and the "dwelling place for God by the Spirit" (Eph 2:19-22 ESV).

In order to understand both senses of Jerusalem, it is also necessary to grasp the way in which this transition took place for Paul. It reflected Paul's expanded appreciation for God's use of Israel's institutions to reveal his greater soteriological, ecclesiological, and eschatological purposes for his people. For just as new wine would require new wineskins, and just as Jesus said the hour would come when "neither on this mountain nor in Jerusalem will you *worship the Father" (Jn 4:21 ESV), so in one sense the significance of physical Jerusalem would be superseded, yet its role expanded in another. For Christians it became a shadow, yet one that directed their gaze to the glorious reality of the eternal city.

Thus, along with many other old *covenant institutions and signs, such as kingship and *sacrifice, the present Jerusalem's significance would be seen with new eschatological eyes with Christ's coming. The city became an analogical aid to grasp a greater reality, yet provided the necessary temporal, physical arena in which the world would comprehend God's revelational and salvific purposes in the person of Jesus. The Holy Messiah of Israel would be crowned and crucified in the obstinate yet Holy City, in order that he be recognized as the King and Savior not only of *Israel but of all nations (Rom 15:8-13, 18-20). In this way, Jerusalem has a critical place in the life of Israel and in the understanding of the OT. This history, accessible in the Scriptures, provides the hermeneutical lens with which the world comprehends and receives its sacrificial Savior and eternal King (e.g., Rom 1:1-5; 3:19-26).

1. The Present Jerusalem.

It is difficult to overstate the theological and religious significance of Jerusalem in the minds and hearts of Jews, even Diaspora Jews, prior to its destruction along with the temple in AD 70. Although only one of many biblical and extrabiblical sources, Paul's testimony about Jerusalem contributes a rich and insightful witness to its significance.

1.1. Jerusalem in the Old Testament. The earliest biblical references to Jerusalem may be to Salem, where King Melchizedek, referred to as "priest of God Most High," ruled during the lifetime of *Abraham (Gen 14:18; see also Ps 76:2). Later, after conquering what was then called Jebus, King David brought the ark of the covenant into Jerusalem (2 Sam 6), where his son King Solomon would build the temple. Jerusalem (also called "the City of David" or "Zion," after the name of the southeast hill) thus became the political and religious capital of Israel, with the twelve tribes united under David's rule (2 Sam 5:6-10).

Jerusalem was unlike any other city in the world—Israel considered it nothing less than "the city of God, the holy habitation of the Most High" (Ps 46:4 ESV; see 1 Kings 8:48; 9:3; Ps 87:1-3). The Prophets and Psalms convey the deep affection Israel had for its holy city as well as the grief endured when Jerusalem was captured (597 BC) and destroyed (587/586 BC) by the Babylonians (see Ps 137; Lamentations).

From the time the remnant returned to Jerusalem and its walls were repaired in the mid-fifth century BC, along with the rebuilding of the temple (Ezra 1–3), the second iteration of nationhood, city, and dwelling place of God never matched the first. What was previously a united nation of Israel had become numerous dispersed Jewish communities in the neighboring lands—more Jews lived in Egypt and Babylon than in Judea. For Jews outside Judea and Palestine there was a diminished though residual connection to Jerusalem through pilgrimages, festivals, and the annual temple tax. As one example, Philo Judaeus (ca. 50 BC–ca. AD 20) had some allegiance to his own city of Alexandria yet called

Jerusalem "my native country, and the capital, not only of the one country of Judea, but also of many" cities and colonies of the Jewish dispersion (Philo, *Leg.* 281).

The temple was restored to a scale and *glory beyond that of the Solomonic original during the reign of Herod the Great (37–4 BC). The NT provides a sense of the temple's splendor and Jerusalem's spiritual and religious significance for Jews and God-fearers in Paul's lifetime. Matthew, for instance, refers to Jerusalem as "the holy city" (Mt 4:5; 27:53). Though synagogues were numerous, Jerusalem remained the destination for festivals and the central place for *prayer, worship, and priestly service, as well as the seat of Israel's spiritual authority through the high priest, Sanhedrin, and Pharisees.

1.2. Jerusalem's Saul and Saul's Jerusalem. None of Paul's epistles discloses his place of birth, but the book of Acts describes "a man of Tarsus named Saul" (Acts 9:11 ESV). He introduces himself by declaring, "I am a Jew, from Tarsus in Cilicia, a citizen of no obscure city" (Acts 21:39 ESV). Elsewhere he expresses his affinity for Jerusalem when saying, "I am a Jew, born in Tarsus in Cilicia, but brought up [*anatephō*] in this city, educated [*paideuō*] at the feet of Gamaliel, according to the strict manner of the law of our fathers, being zealous for God as all of you are this day" (Acts 22:3 ESV).

Saul's Jerusalem was not merely a place but a community. He learned from the highly respected Pharisaic rabbi Gamaliel and was known by the priests and all the elders (Acts 22:5). He had relatives also dwelling in Jerusalem (Acts 23:16). Though not born in Jerusalem, it was in Jerusalem that Saul was forged to become "a Hebrew of Hebrews; as to the law, a Pharisee; as to zeal, a persecutor of the church; as to *righteousness under the *law, blameless" (Phil 3:5-6 ESV).

When Saul later wrote as the apostle Paul, he considers these gains cultivated in Jerusalem not as reason for boasting but as loss "because of the surpassing worth of knowing Christ Jesus" his Lord (Phil 3:7 ESV). He expresses remorse for his "former life in Judaism" as he advanced beyond his peers in his zeal for the traditions of his fathers (Gal 1:13 ESV). For, as a consequence of his misplaced zeal, he "persecuted the church of God violently and tried to destroy it" (Gal 1:13 ESV; cf. 1 Cor 15:9). He recognizes the Jerusalem *leadership was complicit in his own shameful actions—the *letters he carried were from Jerusalem's high priests and elders, giving him the authority to bring the followers of Jesus "in bonds to Jerusalem to be punished" (Acts 22:5 ESV).

Saul's murderous threats and approval of Christian executions beyond Jerusalem are said to be in addition to the "much evil he has done to [the Lord's] saints at Jerusalem" (Acts 9:13 ESV). He and Jerusalem's chief priests who authorized the Christians' capture (Acts 9:13-14) would further fulfill what was both a historic observation and proleptic *prophecy not fully satisfied even by the execution of Israel's Messiah: "O Jerusalem, Jerusalem, the city that kills the prophets and stones those who are sent to it!" (Mt 23:37; Lk 13:34).

Later, despite the prophetic warnings about the dangers he would himself face in Jerusalem (Acts 21:10-11), the apostle Paul received Jerusalem's mistreatment in a way resembling the OT prophets, John the Baptist, Jesus the Messiah, other apostles, and the early church. Paul too was beaten, condemned, and arrested in Jerusalem, and this precipitated his imprisonment (Acts 21:27-36) and execution.

Saul's former way of life and then his own experience of Jerusalem's persecution reflect the NT's portrayal of the broader culpability of Jerusalem's leaders and Israel for failing to be their Lord's fruitful vineyard. Jerusalem's hostility toward Israel's Messiah and God's Son (see Ps 2; Is 2; cf. Acts 4:23-28) are a fall from the lofty heights of Israel's worship mandate and experience (e.g., the Songs of Ascent in Ps 120–134).

The apostle Paul was presumably very aware of Jesus' warnings to Jerusalem, which were delivered clearly and repeatedly: he overturned the temple tables, prophesied of Jerusalem's rejection of him (e.g., Mt 16:21; 20:17-19) and its destruction (Mk 13:1-31; Mt 24:1-35), and alluded to it in parables (e.g., Mt 21:33-46). Jesus the Jew, Paul's Lord, lamented Jerusalem's shameful past and culpability in the present:

> for it cannot be that a prophet should perish away from Jerusalem. O Jerusalem, Jerusalem, the city that kills the prophets and stones those who are sent to it! How often would I have gathered your children together as a hen gathers her brood under her wings, and you were not willing! Behold, your house is forsaken. And I tell you, you will not see me until you say, "Blessed is he who comes in the *name of the Lord!" (Lk 13:33-35 ESV; cf. Mt 23:37-38)

In fulfillment of Jesus' prophetic warnings, Jerusalem's and the temple's destruction followed soon after, in AD 70 (see Josephus, *Jewish War*), and the Jews were further humiliated and even banished from Jerusalem, renamed Aelia Capitolina by Hadrian, following the Bar Kokhba revolt of 132–135.

This erasure of Jerusalem affected both Jewish and Christian attitudes to Jerusalem in the first two centuries AD. Estranged from their mother city, Jewish communities (large ones in places such as Babylon, Alexandria, and Antioch) continued to gather in synagogues, centered on the Torah. Christians, however, recognized the destruction was in fulfillment of Christ's prophecies and had likely benefited from Paul's shift of attention from the temple to Christ himself, now risen in glory. Christians, corporately and individually, were to see themselves as God's holy dwelling place (1 Cor 3:16-17; 6:18-19). They could draw consolation from Paul's insistence that the Jerusalem of lasting significance was "Jerusalem above" (discussed further below).

1.3. The Apostle Paul's Ministry Engagement with Jerusalem. With letters from the high priest, Saul left Jerusalem "breathing threats and murder against the disciples of the Lord" (Acts 9:1 ESV). He planned to return soon with Christian captives from Damascus (Acts 9:2). After being confronted by the risen Lord Jesus, however, a chastened Saul was led by the hand to Damascus and did not return to Jerusalem for some years. Scholars are divided as to how Paul's two visits to Jerusalem described in Galatians relate to the timing of the visits recorded in Acts (see Stein, 465-68).

The visits recorded in the book of Acts reflect Luke's literary purpose and are several: (1) three years after Paul's conversion (Acts 9:26-28; cf. Gal. 1:18), (2) from Antioch to bring relief during the famine to "the brothers living in Judea" (Acts 11:29-30; 12:25 ESV), (3) to the *Jerusalem Council to affirm *Gentile inclusion (Acts 15:6, 12, 22), (4) after his second missionary journey (Acts 18:22), and (5) after his third missionary journey, bringing a financial offering from Gentile churches for the Jerusalem church. On this visit he was arrested, imprisoned, and thence appealed to Rome (Acts 21:17–25:12).

Turning to Galatians, according to Galatians 1:17-18, it was three years after meeting the Lord Jesus on the Damascus road that Paul returned from Damascus and Arabia to Jerusalem. His purpose was "to visit Cephas," who presumably shared information about the Lord Jesus' earthly life, teachings, *death, and *resurrection. Paul reports that he made a second visit to Jerusalem "after fourteen years" (Gal 2:1), the time reckoned either from the date of his conversion or from his first visit. Paul's purpose this time, in his own words, was "because of a revelation" that led him to "set before them . . . the gospel . . . in order to make sure I was not running or had not run in vain" (Gal 2:2 ESV). The account in Galatians 2 reveals a tense atmosphere in Jerusalem—false teachers "slipped in to spy out" and to challenge Paul's Christian *freedom (Gal 2:4-6 ESV), but James, Cephas, and John, "who seemed to be pillars," perceived the *grace given to Paul and gave him the right hand of *fellowship (Gal 2:9 ESV). Thus, in his letter to the Galatians Paul stresses Jerusalem is not the place he became *qualified* to be Christ's apostle; rather, it is the place his apostleship was *recognized.* The "right hand of fellowship" (Gal 2:9 ESV) offered during this visit to Jerusalem by Jesus' inner-circle apostles served to unify the church (e.g., 1 Cor 1:10-13).

Moreover, it was during this visit to Jerusalem that Christ's commission of Paul to "go to the Gentiles" was recognized and endorsed by the apostles (Gal 2:9; cf. Acts 9:15; 26:17-18; Rom 15:15-21). Paul's burden that the nations hear the *gospel did not preclude his loving engagement with Jews, nor his witness in Jerusalem and even at the temple—Paul was "ready not only to be imprisoned but even to die in Jerusalem for the name of the Lord Jesus" (Acts 21:13). Despite his message being met with shouting and *violence, in Acts 21-23 Paul earnestly attempted in the Hebrew language to reach Jews in Jerusalem, as he sought to do also in synagogues elsewhere (e.g., Acts 17:1-3), that they might be saved (Rom 9:1-3; 10:1-4).

2. The Jerusalem Above.

Saul's relationship with Jerusalem and Judaism more broadly was radically transformed by his encounter with the risen Lord Jesus. Indeed, in Galatians Paul contrasts the two Jerusalems to express the movement from bondage under the law as sinners (Gal 3:10-15) into the righteousness, freedom, and spiritual empowerment (Gal 5:16-25) of those who are Christ's by faith. "The first is an era of slavery under the law, in which the heirs of God are held in bondage, awaiting their promised redemption. The second is an era of freedom in which God's heirs are enabled to embrace their sonship and their inheritance as God's children" (Campbell, 82). In Paul's analogy, the two Jerusalems represent two covenants. The "present Jerusalem" (*nyn Ierousalēm*) corresponds with categories such as *slavery, Hagar and the *flesh, Mount Sinai in Arabia (Gal 4:22-25), existence "under the law" (Gal 4:21), and the mark of *circumcision (Gal 5:2-6). But the "Jerusalem above" (*anō Ierousalēm*) represents a superior sphere of life and freedom in the Spirit, owing to Christ's redeeming death and resurrection (Gal 3:13-15, 23-29; 5:1)—in Paul's words, "the Jerusalem above is free [*eleutheros*], and she is our mother [*mētēr*]" (Gal 4:26 ESV).

This spiritual, eschatological Jerusalem is bound up therefore with the risen Lord Jesus and his Spirit's presence in the hearts of Christ's people (Gal 4:4-6). A place in this Jerusalem implies *adoption and inheritance as God's sons (Gal 4:7), the rejoicing foreseen by Isaiah as promises for Zion are fulfilled (Gal 4:27-28), and "the *hope of righteousness" (Gal 5:5). In this way, the new Jerusalem is for Paul an integral image reflecting believers' new status as heirs with Christ and anticipating life in the new *creation (see also Heb 12:22-24; Rev 3:12; 21).

3. Conclusion.

It may be reductionistic to say that Saul the Jew identified with the earthly cities of Tarsus and Jerusalem, while Paul the Christian identified only with "Jerusalem above." For Paul the present Jerusalem was the divinely appointed, highly symbolic venue God chose to exalt his Son, the world's true King, who purchased salvation on the *cross, so that sinners of all nations might enter the Jerusalem of lasting significance.

The church as a whole was "the new temple" raised with Christ in the heavenly places, the new household in whom God dwelled by his Spirit (Eph 2:22). As believers are citizens of heaven (Phil 3:20-21), Paul's "Jerusalem from above" contributes to anticipation for the coming ages, when God will "show the immeasurable riches of his grace in kindness toward us in *Christ Jesus" (Eph 2:7 ESV).

See also CHRIST, MESSIAH; CONVERSION AND CALL OF PAUL; ISRAEL; JERUSALEM, COUNCIL OF; TEMPLE.

BIBLIOGRAPHY. **T. D. Alexander,** *From Eden to the New Jerusalem: An Introduction to Biblical Theology* (Grand Rapids, MI: Kregel, 2008); **J. M. G. Barclay,** *Pauline Churches and Diaspora Jews* (Tübingen: Mohr Siebeck, 2011); **G. K. Beale,** *The Temple and the Church's Mission: A Biblical Theology of the Dwelling Place of God*, NSBT (Downers Grove, IL: IVP Academic, 2004); **F. F. Bruce,** *Paul: Apostle of the Heart Set Free* (Grand Rapids, MI: Eerdmans, 1977); **C. R. Campbell,** *Paul and the Hope of Glory: An Exegetical and Theological Study* (Grand Rapids, MI: Zondervan, 2020); **R. Charles,** *Paul and the Politics of Diaspora* (Minneapolis: Fortress, 2014); **M. Hengel and A. M. Schwemer,** *Paul Between Damascus and Antioch: The Unknown Years* (Grand Rapids, MI: Eerdmans, 1997); **P. McKechnie,** "Paul Among the Jews," in *All Things to All Cultures: Paul Among Jews, Greeks, and Romans*, ed. M. Harding and A. Nobbs (Grand Rapids, MI: Eerdmans, 2013), 103-23; **R. L. Reymond,** *Paul, Missionary Theologian: A Survey of His Missionary Labours and Theology* (Fearn, UK: Christian Focus, 2002); **R. H. Stein,** "Jerusalem," *DPL*; **N. T. Wright,** "Jerusalem in the New Testament," in *Jerusalem: Past and Present in the Purposes of God*, ed. P. W. L. Walker (Cambridge: Tyndale House, 1992), 53-77.

D. K. Burge

JERUSALEM, COUNCIL OF

The episode in Acts 15:1-33 in which Luke reports the events surrounding what is commonly called "the Apostles' Council" or "the Council of Jerusalem" established for the early *church that male *Gentiles who come to *faith in Jesus Messiah must not be pressured to be circumcised and keep the entirety of the Mosaic *law.

1. Historical Context
2. Sequence of Events
3. The Reports of Peter, Barnabas, and Paul
4. The Speech of James
5. The Decision and the Letter
6. The Aftermath: Paul and the Apostolic Decree

1. Historical Context.

The interpretation of the Council of Jerusalem is connected with the question of whether Acts 15 should be correlated with Galatians 2:1-10, which has been the majority view (see Barrett), leading scholars to date Paul's confrontation with *Peter in Antioch (the so-called Antioch incident) to a time after the Council of Jerusalem and to posit a complete break between Paul and Peter (see Dunn 2009). Some think that Acts 15 conflates sources that reported two separate incidents when the church in Antioch consulted the leaders of the Jerusalem church: a consultation at which *circumcision and the obligation of Gentile Christians to observe the Mosaic law was discussed (Gal 2:1-10), and a later consultation at which matters of diet and marital unions were decided (Acts 15; see Fitzmyer). Some suggest that the decree that addresses matters of diet and immorality (Acts 15:16-20) originated in the Antioch church (see Slee).

It should be noted, however, that the correlation of Acts 15 with Galatians 2:1-10 involves several problems: (1) Galatians 2 reports a private meeting of Paul and Titus with the "pillar apostles," whereas Acts 15 reports a public convocation of

Paul, Barnabas, and other delegates of the church in Antioch with the apostles and the elders of the church in *Jerusalem; (2) in the meeting of Galatians 2 the subject matter is Paul and the *gospel he proclaims, whereas the meeting of Acts 15 discusses circumcision and other matters related to the Mosaic law, including *food. If Galatians 2 is correlated with Acts 15, Paul fails to mention the famine-relief visit to Jerusalem in his account of his Jerusalem visits in Galatians 1:18–2:1, which is not plausible. Paul does not mention the decision of the Council of Jerusalem in his letter to the believers in Galatia, even though the agreement of Peter and James would have been an important argument in the discussion about the legitimacy of the gospel that Paul proclaimed, a discussion in which Paul deems the chronological sequence of important events to be important (Gal 1:11–2:10). Paul's silence suggests that the consultation in Jerusalem described in Galatians 2:1-10 took place before the events described in Acts 15 (see Bock). The consultation of Galatians 2:1-10 is most plausibly correlated with the famine-relief visit of Paul and Barnabas (Acts 11:27-30; see Bauckham 2005; Zeigan; Moo).

2. Sequence of Events.
Luke reports the prehistory of the Council in Acts 15:1-3. Unidentified believers from Judea had traveled to Antioch (Syria) and taught the Gentile believers that their *salvation depended on being circumcised according to the custom of Moses, effectively demanding that they undergo circumcision and become proselytes. They were confronted by Paul and Barnabas, who disagreed with this demand and disputed the merits of their argument. It was the Antiochene church (rather than "those who had come from Jerusalem," as Codex D surmises) who sent Paul and Barnabas and other believers to Jerusalem for a decision in this "controversial matter" (*zētēma*). The delegation reported in a meeting of the Jerusalem church "all that God had accomplished through them" in Antioch, Cyprus, Galatia, and Pamphylia. After they had finished their report, believers "who belonged to the party of the Pharisees" stood and demanded that the Gentiles who had come to faith in Jesus "must be circumcised and ordered to keep the law of Moses" (Acts 15:5).

Luke recounts the events of the council in terms of seven incidents.

- Convocation of a meeting of the apostles and elders with the Antiochene delegation (Acts 15:6; the presence of the Antiochene delegation can be inferred from what follows), for the purpose of discussing the status of converted Gentiles, the necessity of their circumcision, and their obligation to keep the Mosaic law
- Extensive debate about the matter (Acts 15:7); it is unclear whether the converted Pharisees mentioned in Acts 15:5 were present or whether their position was represented among the apostles and elders
- Report by Peter (Acts 15:7b-12a)
- Report by Barnabas and Paul (Acts 15:12b-e)
- Speech by James (Acts 15:13-21)
- Decision and letter to the churches (Acts 15:22-29)
- Aftermath in Antioch (Acts 15:30-35)

Incidents 3 to 7 will be discussed in more detail below. In Luke's telling, the council focused on establishing a theological solution (Acts 15:7-19) before providing practical guidance for Gentile believers and their interaction with Jewish believers (Acts 15:20-21), expressed in a pastoral letter to the churches outside Palestine (Acts 15:22-29).

3. The Reports of Peter, Barnabas, and Paul.
Peter's speech (Acts 15:7-11) has two parts. First, he reviews developments in the past, when God established a precedent regarding the status of Gentile believers in Jesus (Acts 15:7-9). He reminds the audience that God chose him from among the apostles to proclaim the gospel to "the Gentiles," a fact that establishes his privileged right to be heard in the deliberations about the status of Gentile believers. The confirmation that God accepted these Gentiles, that is, the Roman Cornelius and his relatives and friends who believed in the gospel of Jesus Messiah that Peter had proclaimed to them, was that God gave them the *Holy Spirit "just as he did to us," which suggests that these Gentile believers miraculously spoke in unlearned human languages (see Acts 10:44-47). Peter made the same argument earlier in Jerusalem when he defended his behavior in Caesarea (Acts 11:15-17). As God had cleansed the hearts of the apostles and elders in Jerusalem by faith in Jesus Messiah, so he cleansed the hearts of the Gentiles in Caesarea by faith in Jesus Messiah, without making a distinction between Jews and Gentiles (Acts 15:9).

Second, Peter infers from the Caesarea revelation that salvation is conveyed to both Jews and Gentiles by the *grace of the *Lord Jesus, not through circumcision and obedience to the Mosaic law

(Acts 15:10-11). The believers who demand circumcision of believing Gentiles demonstrate unbelief regarding the revelation that God gave to Peter in Caesarea, and unbelief regarding the Holy Spirit, whom God gave to Cornelius and his friends. Peter's reference to the "yoke" that the stipulations of the law represent, and that Jews have not been able to bear, can hardly mean that the Mosaic law could not be kept and was regarded as a burden; pious Israelites and Jews believed that the law was a good and precious gift from God, and that the obligation to obey the law was a privilege, a joy, and a blessing (see Ex 19:5; 24:7-8; Lev 18:1-5; Deut 4:7-18, 32-40; Ps 19; see also Mt 5:17; Rom 7:12; Phil 3:6). Since it was Pharisaic believers who were insisting that Gentile believers should keep the law, it is possible that the "yoke" refers to the halakic interpretations of various commandments of the law in the Pharisaic traditions, perhaps the extension of *purity requirements for priests to ordinary working-class Jews (Witherington). Peter argues that the presence of the law did not bring the experience of messianic salvation to the Jews as now faith in Jesus does (Nolland). The reaction to Peter's speech is stunned silence (Acts 15:12), presumably because the audience realizes that Peter agrees with the practice of Paul, who does not circumcise Gentiles who have come to faith in Jesus Messiah.

The speeches of Barnabas and Paul are summarized in the briefest of terms (Acts 15:12). Luke notes that the apostles and elders "listened" to Barnabas and Paul. An extensive report of the events in Salamis and Paphos (Cyprus), in Pisidian Antioch, Iconium, Lystra, and Derbe (Galatia), and in Perga (Pamphylia) is unnecessary given the details in Luke's report in Acts 13:4–14:26. Luke highlights the miraculous events "among the Gentiles" that happened in the course of the missionary work of Barnabas and Paul (see Acts 13:11; 14:3, 8-10). These "*signs and wonders" God performed through Barnabas and Paul authenticate their missionary work among Gentiles. Given that Barnabas and Paul do not require Gentile believers in Jesus to be circumcised and become Jewish proselytes, God's approval of their missionary work validates the argument that Gentile believers in Jesus should not be circumcised and made to submit to the entirety of the law.

4. The Speech of James.

James explains his missionary-theological position in Acts 15:13-18 with Amos 9:11-12, a text that speaks of Yahweh's return to "rebuild the fallen tent of David," which will be restored "so that the rest of humanity may seek the Lord, even all the Gentiles over whom my name is invoked, says the Lord." James explains the Amos prophecy in the context of Hosea 3:5; Jeremiah 12:15; and Isaiah 45:21 in order to facilitate the interpretation of the Amos text in terms of the eschatological *temple of the messianic period (for details see Bauckham 1995; also Ådna). The Hosea text speaks of the restoration of the temple and links "seeking the Lord" with the restoration of Davidic rule. The Jeremiah text also refers to the conversion of the nations in the last days, and it also uses the metaphor of a building: the Gentile nations who learn from Israel will "dwell [be built] in the midst of my people" (LXX); that is, the converted Gentiles, together with the people of *Israel, constitute the eschatological temple to which Amos 9:11 refers. The Isaiah text to which the end of James's quotation alludes prophesies that the nations will turn to Israel's *God and receive salvation; the allusion to this text gives the phrase "who does these things" (*poiōn tauta*) a different meaning: James emphasizes that God's intention to integrate Gentiles into his people in the last days is older than these prophecies.

By linking these texts, James interprets the "tent of David" in the prophecy of Amos as the messianic temple mentioned in Israel's prophetic traditions, which he identifies with the community of all believers in Jesus Messiah. James argues that the Gentiles who have come to worship Israel's God as they have come to faith in Jesus Messiah are integrated into the eschatological, messianic people of God *as Gentiles*, without having to become Jews by circumcision and wholesale submission to the law.

5. The Decision and the Letter.

According to Luke's report, James agreed with Peter, Paul, and Barnabas *not* to demand circumcision and wholesale submission to the Mosaic law. He argued that one request should be made of the Gentile believers: they should "abstain" (*apechesthai*) from four things—food polluted by idols, sexual immorality, food from animals that have been strangled, and blood (Acts 15:19-20). The first prohibition concerns *idolatry: Gentile believers must not attend sacrificial ceremonies in pagan temples nor banquets held in pagan temples, where they would be eating meat of animals slaughtered on altars devoted to pagan deities. The prohibition of eating food polluted by idols relates to the first commandment of the Decalogue not to have any other God besides

Israel's God (Ex 20:3), and to the commandment not to make a *covenant with Gentile people who sacrifice to other gods (Ex 34:15). The second prohibition refers to unsanctioned sexual intercourse, which from an OT and Jewish perspective included adultery, that is, intercourse with a married person other than one's spouse (Lev 20:20; Deut 22:22); prostitution (Lev 19:29; Deut 23:18; prostitution was apparently tolerated; see Lev 21:7, 14; 1 Kings 3:16, although with contempt; see 1 Kings 22:38; Jer 3:3; Amos 7:17); bestiality (Ex 21:19; Lev 18:23; 20:11-16), homosexual relationships (Lev 18:22, 29; 20:13), and incest, that is, *marriage within close degrees of kinship prohibited by the law (Lev 18:6-18).

The third prohibition alludes to Leviticus 17:15 (see Gen 9:4; Ex 22:31); meat from strangled animals, that is, from animals that were not slaughtered according to *kashrut* laws, contained blood. The fourth prohibition ("blood") could refer to the spilling of blood, that is, murder, but it is more plausibly taken to refer to eating food made from the blood of animals, for example, blood pudding, which the Mosaic law prohibits (Lev 17:10-11; see Lev 3:17; 7:26-27). This is inferred from the principle that "blood is life," which explains why "human blood may not be spilled and animal blood may not be ingested. . . . Jew and non-Jew are bound by a single prohibition, to abstain from blood. The rationale is now clear. The human being must never lose sight of the fundamental tenet for a viable human society. Life is inviolable; it may not be treated lightly" (Milgrom, 1:713). The last two prohibitions could be easily followed by Gentile believers: they could avoid food items made from blood, and they could purchase any meat they ate from Jewish butchers, which did not contain blood.

These four prohibitions were included in the letter that was drafted at the council by "the apostles and elders" and sent to "the Gentile believers in Antioch, Syria, and Cilicia" (Acts 15:23-29). The rationale for the stipulations of the four prohibitions is disputed. Six interpretations have been suggested; the last two are the most likely (see Schnabel 2012):

- The stipulations of the Apostles' Council are practical measures designed to facilitate the (table) *fellowship between Jewish Christians and Gentile Christians as "*ad hoc* advice on how not to offend certain Jews" (Turner, 114). However, since the abandonment of idolatry and pagan illicit sexual conduct was a basic requirement when Gentiles committed to faith in Yahweh and his Messiah, this explanation is difficult. The suggestion that the four stipulations reflect the ethos of "sensitivity about that which may cause offense" and "respecting the practices of others and not forcing oneself on another because of such views" (Bock, 507) does not explain the prohibition of idolatry and immorality.
- The stipulations of the Apostles' Council correspond to the Noachian commandments, which Jews regarded as normative behavior for both Jews and Gentiles (Bockmuehl). The correspondence is only partial, however: the relevant lists also mention blasphemy, murder, stealing, and perverting justice (see Jub. 7.20-21; t. Abod. Zar. 8:4; b. Sanh. 56a).
- The four prohibitions correspond to the cardinal sins that Jews must avoid under any circumstances, that is, idolatry, fornication, and murder (see Sifre Devarim 41.85; b. Qidd. 40b; b. Sanh. 74a; y. Sanh. 3.21b; 4.35a). This explanation cannot account for the council's prohibition of eating "what is strangled" (which is omitted in the Western text of Acts).
- The prohibitions are derived from the catalogs of vices and virtues that Jews used in teaching Gentiles before they were accepted as proselytes: the council removed circumcision but kept the other requirements (Borgen). This explanation cannot explain the prohibition of "what has been strangled," and its focus on Jewish proselyte traditions goes beyond the dispute about the law and its application to Gentile believers in Jesus, which was the point of dispute at the council.
- The prohibitions reflect the context of the Jewish Diaspora and the OT polemic against idolatry: the council directs Gentile believers in Jesus Messiah to refrain from participating in pagan cults and other pagan practices (Wilson). However, the regulations regarding strangled animals and blood cannot be associated with practices in pagan temples; if the main concern was idolatry, this could have been formulated in a much more straightforward manner, without the use of rare Greek words (e.g., *ta alisgēmata*, "polluted things"; *to pnikton*, "what has been strangled").
- The prohibitions can be understood in terms of the regulations formulated in Leviticus 17–18 for Gentiles who live in the land of Israel as resident aliens (Wehnert). Leviticus 17–18 prohibits sacrifices not offered on the altar at the tabernacle, which means that the consumption of meat sacrificed to idols in pagan

temples is prohibited (Lev 17:8-9); immorality, specifically sexual relations between blood relatives (Lev 17:10, 12); eating meat from animals that have been strangled and from animals that have a defect (Lev 17:13); and eating blood (Lev 18:26).

It has been plausibly suggested that the four stipulations the council requests Gentile believers should follow are specifically based on Leviticus 17–18 because they are connected by the phrase "in the midst of them" (Heb. *bətôk*; Lev 17:8-9, 10-14; 18:26). These stipulations for resident aliens who live among the Israelites are also linked by this catchphrase with the prophecies in Jeremiah 12:16 and Zechariah 2:11 concerning Gentiles who join the people of God and who live "in the midst of them" (Bauckham 1996). These provisions do thus not constitute an arbitrary qualification of the admission of Gentile believers in Jesus Messiah into the people of God without the requirement to become Jewish proselytes through circumcision and complete commitment to the Mosaic law; rather, the prohibitions of the council follow with exegetical logic from the Amos text interpreted in the context of Israel's prophetic tradition: "If Gentile Christians are the Gentiles to whom the prophecies conflated in Acts 15.16-18 refer, then they are also the Gentiles of Jer 12.16; Zech 2.11/15, and therefore the part of the law of Moses which applies to them is Leviticus 17–18" (Bauckham 1996, 177). This interpretation has been criticized with the argument that Leviticus formulates more requirements for resident aliens living in Israel than these four stipulations (Blomberg). Yet this objection vanishes if one accepts that the phrase "in the midst of" was deliberately chosen as the principle that decided which stipulations should be selected and which stipulations should be omitted (such as the Sabbath commandment); the four prohibitions the council formulated were particularly relevant in pagan religious contexts and were thus a likely source of defilement for Jewish believers.

6. The Aftermath: Paul and the Apostolic Decree.

Luke relates that Judas Barsabbas and Silas, leaders in the Jerusalem church, accompanied Paul and Barnabas to Antioch, where they delivered the letter to the believers, who rejoiced in the outcome of the discussion in Jerusalem (Acts 15:22, 25, 30-31). According to Luke, when Paul set out with Silas, they visited churches in Syria and Cilicia (Acts 15:41), evidently communicating the decision at the council whose letter was specifically addressed to them (Acts 15:23).

Some argue that Paul could not have accepted the rules of the Council of Jerusalem as narrated by Luke (Hill, 108). This is not convincing: (1) Paul argues that Gentile believers should not attend banquets in pagan temples or in private settings where it would be public knowledge that they were eating meat from animals sacrificed to idols (1 Cor 10:1–11:1); (2) he categorically and unconditionally opposes sexual immorality, specifically incest, visiting prostitutes, adultery, and *homosexuality (1 Cor 5:1-13; 6:12-20; 7:2; 10:8; Rom 1:26-27; 13:9, 13; Gal 5:19); and (3) the matter of eating food items made from blood and meat from strangled animals that contained blood is not explicitly mentioned in Paul's letters but is probably the background of the practice of some believers in the churches in the city of Rome to refrain from eating any meat (Rom 14:1-23), a practice that Paul argues should be respected. Some suggest that Paul's silence concerning the consumption of blood is perhaps accidental and that Paul probably did not tolerate the consumption of blood (Bockmuehl).

Richard Bauckham's explanation of the rationale of the four prohibitions can be taken to mean that the two prohibitions related to eating meat containing blood and blood products specifically apply to Gentile believers who *worship and eat with Jewish Christians, that is, who live "in Israel," in predominantly Jewish Christian congregations such as Antioch. That is, Gentile believers in predominantly Gentile congregations (such as the church in Rome, after Claudius's edict of AD 49 evicting the Jews from the city of Rome) could dispense with the stipulations regarding blood, allowing members of the congregation to decide whether they consumed blood (Rom 14:1–15:13), while the stipulations regarding idolatry and immorality of course remained valid. The deciding factor was not simply ecclesial and missionary strategy (Keener, 2290) but indeed principle: the biblical principle of injunctions that apply to Gentiles living "in the midst of" Israel.

See also CIRCUMCISION; COLLECTION FOR THE SAINTS; FELLOWSHIP, COMMUNION, SHARING; FOOD LAWS AND CUSTOMS, JEWISH AND ROMAN; GENTILES; ISRAEL; JERUSALEM, CITY OF; LAW; PAUL AND JUDAISM; PAUL IN ACTS; PETER.

BIBLIOGRAPHY. **J. Ådna,** "Die Heilige Schrift als Zeuge der Heidenmission. Die Rezeption von Amos 9,11-12 in Apg 15,16-18," in *Evangelium – Schriftauslegung – Kirche*, ed. J. Ådna et al. (Göttingen: Vandenhoeck & Ruprecht, 1997), 1-23; **L. C. A.**

Alexander, "Community and Canon: Reflections on the Ecclesiology of Acts," in *Einheit der Kirche im Neuen Testament*, ed. A. A. Alexeev et al., WUNT 218 (Tübingen: Mohr Siebeck, 2008), 45-78; **C. K. Barrett,** *The Acts of the Apostles*, ICC (Edinburgh: T&T Clark, 1994–1998); **R. J. Bauckham,** "James and the Jerusalem Church," in *The Book of Acts in Its Palestinian Setting*, ed. R. J. Bauckham (Exeter, UK: Paternoster, 1995), 415-80; idem, "James and the Gentiles (Acts 15.13-21)," in *History, Literature, and Society in the Book of Acts*, ed. B. Witherington (Cambridge: Cambridge University Press, 1996), 154-84; idem, "James, Peter, and the Gentiles," in *The Missions of James, Peter, and Paul: Tensions in Early Christianity*, ed. B. D. Chilton and C. A. Evans, NovTSup 115 (Leiden: Brill, 2005), 91-142; **C. L. Blomberg,** "The Christian and the Law of Moses," in *Witness to the Gospel: The Theology of Acts*, ed. I. H. Marshall and D. Peterson (Grand Rapids, MI: Eerdmans, 1998), 397-416; **D. L. Bock,** *Acts*, BECNT (Grand Rapids, MI: Baker, 2007); **M. Bockmuehl,** *Jewish Law in Gentile Churches: Halakhah and the Beginning of Christian Public Ethics* (repr., Grand Rapids, MI: Baker, 2003); **P. Borgen,** "Catalogues of Vices, the Apostolic Decree, and the Jerusalem Meeting," in *Early Christianity and Hellenistic Judaism* (Edinburgh: T&T Clark, 1996), 233-51; **D. R. Catchpole,** "Paul, James, and the Apostolic Decree," *NTS* 23 (1977): 428-44; **R. Deines,** "Das Aposteldekret – Halacha für Heidenchristen oder christliche Rücksichtnahme auf jüdische Tabus?," in *Jewish Identity in the Greco-Roman World*, ed. J. Frey et al. (Leiden: Brill, 2007), 323-95; **M. Dibelius,** "Das Apostelkonzil," in *Aufsätze zur Apostelgeschichte*, ed. H. Greeven, FRLANT 60 (Göttingen: Vandenhoeck & Ruprecht, 1951–1968), 84-90; **J. D. G. Dunn,** *The Partings of the Ways: Between Christianity and Judaism and Their Significance for the Character of Christianity* (repr., Philadelphia: Trinity Press International, 1996); idem, *Beginning from Jerusalem* (Grand Rapids, MI: Eerdmans, 2009); **J. A. Fitzmyer,** *The Acts of the Apostles*, AB 31 (New York: Doubleday, 1998); **C. C. Hill,** *Hellenists and Hebrews: Reappraising Division Within the Earliest Church* (Minneapolis: Fortress, 1992); **D. Instone-Brewer,** "Infanticide and the Apostolic Decree in Acts 15," *JETS* 52 (2009): 301-21; **C. S. Keener,** *Acts: An Exegetical Commentary*, 4 vols. (Grand Rapids, MI: Baker, 2012–2015); **M. Klinghardt,** *Gesetz und Volk Gottes. Das lukanische Verständnis des Gesetzes nach Herkunft, Funktion und seinem Ort in der Geschichte des Urchristentums*, WUNT 2/32 (Tübingen: Mohr Siebeck, 1988); **J. Milgrom,** *Leviticus*, AB (New York: Doubleday, 1991–2001); **D. J. Moo,** *Galatians*, BECNT (Grand Rapids, MI: Baker, 2013); **J. Nolland,** "A Fresh Look at Acts 15:10," *NTS* 27 (1980): 105-15; **H. D. Park,** "Drawing Ethical Principles from the Process of the Jerusalem Council: A New Approach to Acts 15:4-29," *TynBul* 61 (2010): 271-92; **P.-A. Paulo,** *Le problème ecclésial des Actes à la lumière des deux prophéties d'Amos* (Paris: Cerf, 1985); **F. Refoulé,** "Le discours de Pierre à l'assemblée de Jérusalem," *RB* 100 (1993): 239-51; **B. Rost,** "Das Aposteldekret im Verhältnis zur Mosetora: Ein Beitrag zum Gottesvolk-Verständnis in der Apostelgeschichte," in *Die Apostelgeschichte im Kontext antiker und frühchristlicher Historiographie*, ed. J. Frey et al., BZNW 162 (Berlin: de Gruyter, 2009), 563-604; **K. Salo,** *Luke's Treatment of the Law: A Redaction-Critical Investigation* (Helsinki: Suomalainen Tiedeakatemia, 1991); **A. Schmidt,** "Das historische Datum des Apostelkonzils," *ZNW* 81 (1990): 122-31; **J. Schmidt,** *Gesetzesfreie Heilsverkündigung im Evangelium nach Matthaus. Das Apostelkonzil (Apg 15) als historischer und theologischer Bezugspunkt fur die Theologie des Matthausevangeliums*, FzB 113 (Würzburg: Echter, 2007); **W. Schmithals,** "Probleme des 'Apostelkonzils' (Gal 2,1-10) [1997]," in *Paulus, die Evangelien, und das Urchristentum. Beiträge von und zu Walter Schmithals*, ed. C. Breytenbach, AGJU 54 (Leiden: Brill, 2004), 5-38; **E. J. Schnabel,** *Early Christian Mission*, 2 vols. (Downers Grove, IL: InterVarsity Press, 2004); idem, *Acts*, expanded digital ed., ZECNT 5 (Grand Rapids, MI: Zondervan, 2012); idem, *Jesus in Jerusalem: The Last Days* (Grand Rapids, MI: Eerdmans, 2018); **J. M. Scott,** *Paul and the Nations*, WUNT 84 (repr., Tübingen: Mohr Siebeck, 2002); **M. Slee,** *The Church in Antioch in the First Century CE: Communion and Conflict*, JSNTSup 244 (London: Sheffield Academic Press, 2003); **M. M. B. Turner,** "The Sabbath, Sunday, and the Law in Luke/Acts," in *From Sabbath to Lord's Day: A Biblical, Historical, and Theological Investigation*, ed. D. A. Carson (Grand Rapids, MI: Zondervan, 1982), 99-157; **J. Wehnert,** *Die Reinheit des 'christlichen Gottesvolkes' aus Juden und Heiden. Studien zum historischen und theologischen Hintergrund des sogenannten Aposteldekrets*, FRLANT 173 (Göttingen: Vandenhoeck & Ruprecht, 1997); **A. Weiser,** "Das 'Apostelkonzil' (Apg 15,1–35): Ereignis, Überlieferung, lukanische Deutung," *BZ* 28 (1984): 145-67; **D. Wenham,** "From Jesus to Paul—via Luke," in *The Gospel to the Nations: Perspectives on Paul's Mission*, ed. P. Bolt and M. Thompson (Downers Grove, IL: InterVarsity Press, 2000), 83-97; **T. Wiarda,** "The Jerusalem Council and the Theological Task," *JETS* 46

(2003): 233-48; **S. G. Wilson,** *Luke and the Law*, SNTSMS 50 (Cambridge: Cambridge University Press, 1983); **H. Zeigan,** *Aposteltreffen in Jerusalem. Eine forschungsgeschichtliche Studie zu Galater 2,1-10 und den möglichen lukanischen Parallelen* (Leipzig: Evangelische Verlagsanstalt, 2005).

E. J. Schnabel

JESUS, SAYINGS OF

In the past two centuries of biblical criticism, Paul has often been called the true founder of Christianity as it now exists (or at least the second founder, after Jesus of Nazareth). A cursory reading of both the Gospels and the letters of Paul discloses many differences in the teachings and actions of these two men. Of numerous surprises is the absence of quotations of Jesus in Paul's epistles. Various scholars have claimed that Paul must have learned very little about what the historical Jesus taught. R. Bultmann famously insisted that this was because Paul, as a Christian, had learned not to put his hope in historical evidences. Second Corinthians 5:16 declares that he knows no person "according to the *flesh" (ESV), so that even though he once knew Jesus that way, he no longer does. For Bultmann, the focus was to be on the risen *Christ rather than the historical Jesus. Today it is widely recognized that this interpretation misses Paul's point, which is that Christians do not view Jesus in the same way that non-Christians do. The absence of quotations of Jesus in Paul cannot be explained by this verse. Indeed, in the past half-century, a discrete subdiscipline of Pauline studies has focused on identifying traces of Jesus' teachings in Paul's letters, with varying results.

1. One Quotation.

In his discussion of the Corinthian abuses of the *Lord's Supper, Paul lapses into a full-fledged quotation of parts of Jesus' teaching about the new significance with which he was investing the bread and wine of the Passover meal he celebrated with his disciples the night before his crucifixion (1 Cor 11:23-26). Quotations in a world without quotation marks or any felt need for them did not necessarily reproduce long strings of words verbatim. First Corinthians 11:24b-25 still closely enough resembles Jesus' words in Matthew 26:26-28; Mark 14:22-24; and Luke 22:19-20 to refer to them as a quotation. Paul's version is closest of all to Luke's, as each has Jesus declare, "This is my *body . . . for you; do this in remembrance of me," along with "This cup is the new *covenant in my blood . . ." (NIV). Luke adds "given" and "which is poured out for you" in the ellipses above but lacks several distinctives that Mark and Matthew share, most notably "my blood of the covenant" (without explicitly saying "new covenant") and "for many" (hinting at substitution). Studies of Luke's distinctives in his passion narrative have often attributed them to a very early L-source that may have predated Mark's Gospel, so Paul may be in touch with the oldest circulating form of the Jesus *tradition.

As with all of the sayings discussed here, Paul could not have learned of them from the finished form of the Gospels, since the Synoptics did not appear until the 60s at the earliest, while Paul penned all of his undisputed letters between the late 40s and the very early 60s. The language of receiving and delivering in 1 Corinthians 11:23 nevertheless speaks against the notion that Paul received these words by direct revelation, as well as the idea that he knew them simply from the church's liturgy, because these two verbs, especially when paired, regularly referred to the faithful transmission of oral tradition. Paul had learned, at the very least, what the historical Jesus taught at his last meal with his followers.

2. Ten Probable Allusions.

No hard and fast criteria exist for separating an allusion from a quotation. Allusions typically involve a greater degree of uncertainty as to whether a source has been used and a smaller amount of a saying that is reproduced. The following ten passages in Paul, presented in canonical sequence, contain the most frequently cited allusions among the past half-century of scholarship.

2.1. Romans 12:14, 17, 21. All three verses appear in Paul's discussion of loving one's enemies. Romans 12:14 commands believers to bless and not curse their persecutors; Romans 12:17, not to repay anyone evil for evil; and Romans 12:21, to overcome evil with good. Both Matthew's Sermon on the Mount and Luke's Sermon on the Plain contain parallel instructions. Matthew 5:44 enjoins the disciples to *love their enemies and pray for those who persecute them, while Luke 6:27-28 contains a longer and closer parallel to Paul's sentiments, insisting, "Love your enemies, do good to those who hate you, bless those who curse you, pray for those who mistreat you" (NIV). Luke 6:35 repeats, "love your enemies, do good to them" (NIV). The parable of the good Samaritan, found only in Luke (Lk 10:29-37), forms Jesus' classic illustration of this principle. First Corinthians 4:11-13 and 1 Thessalonians 5:15 likewise stress repaying good for evil.

Of course, one can attribute these varying remarks to the influence of the proverbs (Prov 25:21-22) Paul quotes in Romans 12:20. The idea of returning good for evil, however, was almost nonexistent in his world, while the OT text is quite distinctive within that corpus's teaching. So it seems more likely that Paul would have understood the generalized concept of enemy love from Jesus' own teaching. Once again, Paul knows the older form of the tradition (Luke's Sermon on the Plain), and he appears to know at least one entire segment of that sermon since the verses alluded to are not all consecutive.

2.2. Romans 13:7. Here Paul alludes to the saying of Jesus found in Mark 12:17 and parallels: "Give back to Caesar what is Caesar's and to God what is God's" (NIV). The saying is essentially the same in all three Synoptics. Only one word is exactly parallel in Paul, but it is from the rare compound verb *apodidōmi*, meaning "to repay," and the context is identical in both instances—the payment of taxes. The teaching in the Gospels is widely held, even by otherwise more skeptical scholars, to be an exact reproduction of Jesus' authentic teaching. It forms part of a group of passages about questions and traps set for Jesus on his last day of teaching in the *temple precincts and is not the only allusion to that material (see 2.3 below). Again, this makes one wonder whether Paul was aware of a larger unit of material of Jesus' words than just the individual sayings he explicitly uses. Especially after Paul's use of the countercultural commands about enemy love, his much more conventional injunction to pay one's taxes is surprising until one realizes that Jesus surprised his audiences with his Catch-22 teaching as well.

2.3. Romans 13:8-10. The very next paragraph in Romans returns to the topic that introduced the section beginning in Romans 12:9—love in action. Now Paul explicitly labels love as the fulfillment of the *law. He itemizes four commandments from the Decalogue and then generalizes to include "whatever other command there may be," declaring them to be fulfilled in the law of loving one's neighbor as oneself. Of course, this law comes from the OT (Lev 19:18), but it also forms half of Jesus' famous double love command in Mark 12:30-31 and parallels. It is possible that Paul had in mind the first half about loving *God with all one's being, when he penned Romans 12:1-2 about complete transformation of *body and mind. At any rate, it is striking that Jesus speaks of all the Law and the Prophets being summed up in treating others as one would want to be treated (Mt 7:12), a virtual paraphrase of loving one's neighbor as oneself. And Paul has already used the same language that Jesus does earlier in his great sermon when he says he has come "to fulfill" the Law and the Prophets.

Numerous other rabbis debated how to boil down all of the laws of Torah into a handful of concepts, but they did not use the language of fulfillment. Neither, for that matter, was anyone else besides Jesus ever seen as personally fulfilling the Hebrew Scriptures, so it is natural to assume that Paul learned this from the oral Jesus tradition. In addition, Paul lists several of the identical commands Jesus gave the rich young ruler (not to murder, commit adultery, steal, etc.—Mk 10:19 and pars.) before summing up the Torah in neighbor love, just as Jesus followed up his conversation with the specific instruction for the rich man to sell his possessions and give to the poor, a consummate act of loving one's neighbor. When it becomes clear how distinctive this answer was to the question about the greatest commandment, it is natural to expect Paul to have gotten this cluster of concepts from Jesus' teaching. Paul reuses them again in Galatians 5:14.

2.4. Romans 14:14, 20. Another highly distinctive position that both Paul and Jesus adopt deals with the dietary laws. Paul makes the astonishing claims, in the context of discussing *food and drink, that "nothing is unclean in itself" and "all food is clean" (Rom 14:14, 20 NIV). To be sure, by this time the events of Acts 10, involving the *vision commanding Peter to eat unclean food (Acts 10:9-16) and its implications for *fellowship with *Gentiles (Acts 10:28, 34-35), have already occurred. Paul would have learned of this at the latest during the *Jerusalem Council of Acts 15 (Acts 15:7-11; no later than AD 49). But the language in Romans is linked to Mark 7:15 by the use of the *koin-* root, as Mark translates Jesus' words about nothing going into a person from outside being able to "defile" them with the same term for making "unclean" as in Romans. By this time, Peter would have recognized what Mark adds parenthetically in Mark 7:19 (no doubt derived from Peter himself) that God was declaring all foods clean. The very difficulty of imagining Jesus' treatment of clean and unclean having such sweeping implications makes it all the more unlikely that neither he nor Paul could have come to the views they finally held unless they believed that the historical Jesus had himself authorized this change.

2.5. 1 Corinthians 7:10-11. The concern for ethics that dominated Romans' allusions to the Jesus tradition continues in 1 Corinthians. The teaching on divorce and remarriage provides the first example of Paul referring specifically to what the *Lord has commanded (1 Cor 7:10). Curiously, in 1 Corinthians 7:12, he then mentions what he and not the Lord was saying. Is this some admission that he senses divine inspiration for only part of his teaching? This seems hardly plausible, given that in 1 Corinthians 7:25 he again has "no command from the Lord" but gives "a judgment as one who by the Lord's *mercy is trustworthy" (NIV), while in 1 Corinthians 7:40 he believes he too has the Lord's Spirit, despite some in *Corinth apparently claiming exclusive access. Much more probably, Paul is distinguishing between when he can allude to a teaching of the historical Jesus and when he has to rely on how the Spirit is guiding him more directly. This also fits the fact that Jesus gave the general prohibition of divorce in Mark 10:11-12 and parallels, to which Paul refers in 1 Corinthians 7:10, whereas Jesus never addressed the situation of a nonbeliever wanting to leave a believing spouse (1 Cor 7:12-16). That Paul uses an unusual verb for "divorce" (*chōrizomai*, "separate") four times in 1 Corinthians 7:12-15, rather than the more common one (*apoluō*, "release from"), just as Mark 10:9 and parallel do, further supports a direct link between the two traditions. Even though many assume Mark's shorter version is more original, Matthew's additions of the exception clause (Mt 19:9) and Jesus' teaching on celibacy (Mt 19:10-12) are particularly appropriate in a Jewish context and may be authentic. Paul's possible recognition of these elements of the Jesus tradition (1 Cor 7:7, 32-35 and 1 Cor 7:2, respectively) reinforces this suggestion. In any case, at least Paul's use of Genesis 2:24 in the immediately preceding context of 1 Corinthians 6:16 suggests he knows even more of Jesus' teaching on the topic (cf. Mk 10:8 and par.).

2.6. 1 Corinthians 9:14. Once again, Paul refers to a command of the Lord, that "those who preach the *gospel should receive their living from the gospel" (NIV). The teaching in question appears to be that recorded in Luke 10:7, as Jesus sends out the seventy(-two), where "the worker deserves his wages" (NIV). Matthew's parallel, in the sending of the Twelve, has "the worker is worth his keep" (Mt 10:10 NIV; *trophēs*, "food"). Paul probably followed the Lukan form, since he uses the term for "wages" (*misthos*). First Timothy 5:18 contains a more direct quotation of this Lukan form. A double uncertainty surrounds exegesis here. First is the question of authorship and date. If 1 Timothy is post-Pauline, the author could easily have been quoting the Gospel of Luke. Yet if Paul is the author, he is more likely indebted to the Jesus tradition. Second is that 1 Timothy 5:18 prefaces the reference to Jesus' teaching with a quotation of Deuteronomy 25:4, "For Scripture says, 'Do not muzzle an ox while it is treading out grain' and 'The worker deserves his wages'" (NIV). Is the writer of 1 Timothy implying that he is quoting Luke as Scripture? The answer is not at all clear, but these two issues are a reminder that one should probably not use 1 Timothy to draw any firm conclusions about Paul's use of the Jesus tradition.

2.7. 1 Thessalonians 2:14-16. Turning to the Thessalonian epistles, one finds Paul alluding to Jesus' teaching on *eschatology and not just *ethics. The least secure but still frequently mentioned allusion involves Paul's summary of the *suffering of the Jerusalem Christians at the hands of those "who killed the Lord Jesus and the prophets" and who "displease God and are hostile to everyone" (1 Thess 2:14-15 NIV). Paul continues, "In this way they always heap up their sins to the limit. The *wrath of God has come upon them at last" (1 Thess 2:16 NIV). The language he uses seems to allude to phraseology from Matthew 23:32-36; Luke 11:48-51 about certain religious leaders repeating the deeds of their ancestors in persecuting the prophets and killing and even crucifying certain messengers, so that all the righteous blood shed on earth comes on this generation. The language of constantly filling up the measure of their sins also recurs, even if not verbatim. The teaching of Luke 21:23 may likewise form the background for Paul's statement about God's wrath coming on these persecutors. By themselves, these verses in 1 Thessalonians 2 might not seem to allude to Jesus' teaching, but once one observes other clearer allusions in 1–2 Thessalonians the case grows stronger.

2.8. 1 Thessalonians 4:15-17. Here is another explicit "word of the Lord" (1 Thess 4:15). As a result, some have postulated this to be the teaching of a Christian prophet. The parallels in the Jesus tradition, however, suggest otherwise. Paul is maintaining that those who die before the parousia are in no way disadvantaged from those living at its time (1 Thess 4:15). He then goes on, "For the Lord himself will come down from heaven, with a loud command, with the voice of the archangel and with the trumpet call of God. And the dead in Christ will rise first" (1 Thess 4:16 NIV). After that, living believers "will be caught up together with them in the clouds to meet the Lord in the air" (1 Thess 4:17 NIV). Because the language used for the meeting (*apantēsis*) often refers to a welcoming party that escorts a visiting dignitary back to the city to which he is traveling, it seems better to views this as a gathering to welcome Jesus down to earth when he returns. This corresponds at several points to the language of Mark 13:26-27 and parallels of Jesus returning on the clouds and sending out his angels to gather his elect from the four winds. The unique detail in Matthew's account (Mt 24:31) about a loud trumpet call creates a further link both with Paul's words here in 1 Thessalonians and with his teaching about believers' *resurrection in 1 Corinthians 15:51-52.

2.9. 1 Thessalonians 5:2. This verse contains one of the clearest allusions to Jesus' teaching in all of Paul. The introductory clause, "for you know very well" (NIV), shows that Paul is not introducing new teaching here but is referring back to what the Thessalonian church has already learned. This would be something he taught them on his second missionary journey, when he first evangelized Thessalonica (Acts 17:1-9). The word itself explains that "the day of the Lord will come like a thief in the night" (1 Thess 5:2 NIV). That the saying is something Paul taught his addressees early on does not by itself prove an origin in Jesus' teaching, but the image is so striking and so easily misunderstood as something negative (what is it Jesus has come to steal?) that it is hard to imagine anyone other than Jesus inventing it. Of course, it is the surprise factor of the timing of the parousia to which Jesus and Paul are pointing, which is the theme of the longer sequence of parables in Matthew 24:42–25:13, in which Matthew 24:43 is embedded (cf. the role of the parallel in Lk 12:39 within Lk 12:38-48). As is clear elsewhere, Paul seems to know multiple parts of larger discourses of Jesus rather than just isolated, individual sayings.

2.10. 2 Thessalonians 2:3-4. This is another possible allusion, like 1 Thessalonians 2:14-16, that is a little less secure but still commonly suggested. The enigmatic reference in 2 Thessalonians to a "*man of lawlessness," who is "doomed to destruction" (2 Thess 2:3 NIV) but who will be revealed when he sets himself up in God's holy temple and masquerading as God himself, vividly calls to mind Jesus' teaching about the abomination of desolation "standing where it does not belong" (Mk 13:14 NIV). Given that this desolating sacrilege comes from Daniel 9:27; 11:31, where it too was to be set up in the temple, and given that many Jews initially believed it to have been fulfilled by Antiochus Epiphanes's desecration in 1 Maccabees 1:54 (cf. 1 Macc 6:7), it is almost certain that Paul is referring back to this specific prediction, which was further fulfilled by Rome in AD 70 (cf. Lk 21:20, 24). With each successive allusion, Paul is showing that he knows a large swath of Jesus' eschatological discourse. Because there is evidence that perhaps all three Synoptic Gospels drew on an original discourse larger than any of the ones preserved, when there are allusions to distinctives in Matthew or Luke it is better not to discount them but to see them as support for Paul knowing bedrock, early Jesus tradition.

3. Additional Possible Allusions or Echoes. Occasionally, scholars have been carried away in their search for echoes in Paul of the Jesus tradition and cited huge numbers of parallels linked only by a single word, not necessarily used in at all the same way. Others have abandoned the quest because of the lack of substantial controls in the process or criteria for identifying further examples. R. B. Hays's seven famous criteria for discerning echoes in Paul of OT texts may be applied, nevertheless, with some profit to the question of Paul's use of the Jesus tradition. These are: (1) "availability" (is Paul likely to have known the teaching?), (2) "volume" (how explicitly are words or syntactical patterns repeated?), (3) "recurrence" (does Paul use the possible echo elsewhere?), (4) "thematic coherence" (does such an echo fit well with Paul's main points in its immediate context?), (5) "historical plausibility" (could Paul have understood it as Jesus used it?), (6) "history of interpretation" (have others made the same suggestion?), and (7) "satisfaction" (does the proposed echo make the text at hand more meaningful?; Hays, 29-32).

Applying these criteria in an admittedly subjective enterprise yields the following probable echoes. Not being ashamed of the gospel (Rom 1:16) may show awareness of Jesus' words in Mark 8:38; 9:26. Romans 12:18 may allude to Jesus' beatitude on peacemaking (Mt 5:9). The warnings against not judging fellow Christians (Rom 14:10-13) could allude to Matthew 7:1; Luke 6:37. Romans 16:19 on being wise regarding the good but innocent concerning evil may echo Matthew 10:16. Various references on the foolishness of God's *wisdom and his revealing himself to those not wise by worldly standards in 1 Corinthians 1:18–2:16 may hark back to Matthew 11:25-27 and parallel. First Corinthians 3:5-9 with its planting and harvesting metaphors recalls Jesus' seed parables in Mark 4:1-34 and parallels. First Corinthians 4:1-5 on stewards recalls portions of several of Jesus' parables of stewardship, especially Luke 12:42; 16:1, 3, 8. The procedures for church *discipline in 1 Corinthians 5:3-5 may presuppose Matthew 18:15-18. In 1 Corinthians 8:13 "*stumbling block" (cf. also 2 Cor 11:29) may echo Mark 9:42 and parallel. The saying about *faith that can move mountains in 1 Corinthians 13:2 likely alludes to Jesus' similar words (Mk 11:23 and par.) Second Corinthians 1:17 alludes to Jesus' commands on giving a simple yes or no rather than taking oaths (Mt 5:37). Philippians 2:15 could echo Jesus' calling his disciples the "*light of the world" (Mt 5:14). Philippians 3:7-8 uses the language of "gain" and "loss" in the identical fashion as Mark 8:36 and parallel. Many other suggestions have been made, but these seem the most probable.

4. Reasons for Believing Paul Knew Even More Sayings.

The clearest allusions and echoes to Jesus' teaching tend to fall in clusters, linking Paul with larger discourses of Jesus and suggesting that he may have known larger portions of those "sermons." This is particularly obvious with the Sermon on the Mount/ Plain (Mt 5–7; Lk 6:20-49) and the Olivet discourse (esp. Mt 24–25; Mk 13), but the principle could extend to Jesus' missionary discourse (Mt 10 and pars.), his teaching on the dietary laws (Mk 7:1-23 and pars.), and even scattered teachings on finances (brought together in 2 Cor 8–9). There are numerous topics that Jesus and Paul also share, even if at times in different proportions, which would have led Paul to learn about Jesus' specific teachings on them, even if it is not possible to isolate specific allusions or echoes:

- the already-but-not-yet kingdom of *God
- *righteousness*/justification (the same word, *dikaiosynē*, lies behind both concepts)
- a combination of apocalyptic and salvation-historical understandings of the arrival of the new age
- *salvation by *grace
- good news to the poor
- *ministry to the outcasts as preparation for ministry to the Gentiles, especially via table fellowship
- participation with Christ in suffering
- countercultural if not entirely egalitarian attitudes toward *women
- the importance of miracles
- certain consistent but creative uses of the OT
- a lot of implicit with occasionally more explicit *Christology

Knowledge of events in Jesus' life, especially in the passion narrative, suggests awareness of accounts that would have included whatever sayings of Jesus were preserved from those periods. Simply in order to tell the gospel story in the first place, Paul would have needed to learn a basic core of the teachings recorded in the Gospels, first no doubt from Ananias and his companions in Damascus (Acts 9:17-19) and later from his fifteen-day meeting with Peter and James (perhaps as early as AD 35) in *Jerusalem, which would have given those key leaders ample opportunity to instruct him (Gal 1:18-19). Galatians 1:11-12, 22 refer to the basics of the gospel, which he learned and deduced from his Damascus road vision of the risen Lord. Those verses do not preclude Paul from having learned a lot of supplementary information about Jesus from others. It is even possible, though perhaps not too likely, that Saul of Tarsus met Jesus in Jerusalem and learned something of his teachings before his *conversion. (His presence at Stephen's trial [Acts 7:58; 8:1] was more likely to have afforded him a chance to learn more about what Jesus taught.)

5. Reasons for the Remaining Silence.

Even if all the allusions and echoes suggested here proved genuine, there would still be large stretches of Paul's letters where he appears never to reference anything Jesus taught. At least six factors come into play to help explain this remaining silence. First, Paul's letters do not represent evangelistic preaching. He is writing to Christians who already know a lot about Jesus, even though there are certain things Paul must emphasize about the gospel or explain by way of correction. Second, none of the other NT letter writers cites or alludes to Jesus more unambiguously, and the one writer, John, who probably could have mined his own Gospel for Jesus' teachings when he wrote his later epistles, never does so. Paul is scarcely unique in this respect. Third, as a result, it would appear that the genre of early Christian letter writing was simply not the form used to transmit detailed information about Jesus' sayings. Fourth, early Christianity certainly believed that Jesus' death and resurrection were the most important facets of his life and ministry rather than his teachings per se. Fifth, the very conviction that Paul was being guided or inspired by the Holy Spirit would have given him great freedom to put Jesus' sayings in his own words. Even authors without a belief in any divine influence regularly reworded source material as a way of owning it for themselves. Finally, Paul frequently had to defend his apostolic legitimacy and authority over against claims by teachers supposedly representing the Jerusalem *apostles that he was not as directly in touch with Jesus as they. Perhaps they were the ones regularly but selectively quoting the Jesus tradition so that Paul felt he had to stress more his direct, divine encounter with the risen Lord.

6. Conclusions.

Paul almost certainly knew a considerable number of Jesus' sayings. Of these, he quoted, alluded to, or echoed a smaller percentage. Many allusions have been suggested that seem unlikely, but there remain plenty that appear more probable than not. The largest clusters of these come in his undisputed letters, so one does not have to worry whether only a pseudepigrapher quoted Jesus after the Gospels were in written form. There are differences in emphasis between Jesus and Paul in their use of various sayings, but overall they complement each other well. A larger study comparing and contrasting the theologies of Paul and Jesus is needed before coming to firm conclusions, but even based just on an examination of Jesus' teachings in the Gospels and in Paul's letters, it is possible to be confident that Paul was neither the real nor the second founder of Christianity.

See also ESCHATOLOGY; ETHICS; JESUS AND PAUL; KINGDOM OF GOD/CHRIST; LORD'S SUPPER; LOVE; OLD TESTAMENT IN PAUL; WEALTH AND POVERTY.

BIBLIOGRAPHY. **D. H. Akenson,** *Saint Saul: A Skeleton Key to the Historical Jesus* (Oxford: Oxford University Press, 2002); **D. C. Allison Jr.,** "The Pauline Epistles and the Synoptic Gospels: The Pattern of the Parallels," *NTS* 28 (1982): 1-32; **C. L. Blomberg,** *Making Sense of the New Testament: Three Crucial Questions* (Grand Rapids, MI: Baker, 2004), 71-103; idem, "Quotations, Allusions, and Echoes of Jesus in Paul," in *Studies in the Pauline Epistles: Essays in Honor of Douglas J. Moo* (Grand Rapids, MI: Zondervan, 2014), 129-43; **F. F. Bruce,** *Paul and Jesus* (Grand Rapids, MI: Baker, 1974); **R. Bultmann,** *Existence and Faith* (New York: Meridian, 1960), 183-201; **C. L. Carter,** *The Great Sermon Tradition as a Fiscal Framework in 1 Corinthians: Toward a Pauline Theology of Material Possessions* (London: T&T Clark, 2010); **D. L. Dungan,** *The Sayings of Jesus in the Churches of Paul* (Philadelphia: Fortress, 1971); **D. A. Fiensy,** "The Synoptic Logia of Jesus in the Ethical Teachings of Paul," *SCJ* 13 (2010): 87-98; **B. Fjärstadt,** *Synoptic Tradition in 1 Corinthians* (Uppsala: Teologiska Institutionen, 1974); **V. P. Furnish,** *Jesus According to Paul* (Cambridge: Cambridge University Press, 1993); **S. Gathercole,** "The Historical and Human Existence of Jesus in Paul's Letters," *JSHJ* 16 (2018): 183-212; **D. Haüsser,** *Christusbekenntnis und Jesusüberlieferung bei Paulus* (Tübingen: Mohr Siebeck, 2006); **R. B. Hays,** *Echoes of Scripture in the Letters of Paul* (New Haven, CT: Yale University Press, 1989); **H. Hiestermann,** *Paul and the Synoptic Jesus Tradition* (Leipzig: Evangelische Verlagsanstalt, 2017); **C. Jacobi,** *Jesusüberlieferung bei Paulus? Analogien zwischen den echten Paulus-briefen und synoptischen Evangelien* (Berlin: de Gruyter, 2015); **S. Kim,** "Jesus, Sayings of Paul," *DPL*, 474-92; **Y. Lee,** *Paul, Scribe of Old and New: Intertextual Insights for the Jesus-Paul Debate* (London: Bloomsbury T&T Clark, 2015); **S. E. Porter,** *When Paul Met Jesus: How an Idea Got Lost in History* (Cambridge: Cambridge University Press, 2016); **P. Richardson,** "The Thunderbolt in Q and the Wise Man in Corinth," in *From Jesus to Paul: Studies in Honour of F. W. Beare* (Waterloo, ON: Wilfrid Laurier University, 1984), 91-111; **H. Ridderbos,** *Paul and Jesus* (Grand Rapids, MI: Baker, 1958); **R. Riesner,** "Paulus und die Jesus Überlieferung," in *Evangelium, Schriftauslege, Kirche* (Göttingen: Vandenhoeck & Ruprecht, 1997), 356-65; **M. A. Robinson,** "SPERMOLOGOS: Did Paul Preach from Jesus' Parables?," *Bib* 56 (1975): 231-40; **G. Schoberg,** *Perspectives of Jesus in the Writings of Paul: A Historical Examination of Shared Core Commitments with a View to Determining the Extent of Paul's Dependence on Jesus* (Eugene, OR: Pickwick, 2013); **H. Stettler,** "Did Paul Invent Justification by Faith?," *TynBul* 66 (2015): 161-96; **T. D. Still,** ed., *Jesus and Paul Reconnected: Fresh Pathways into an Old Debate* (Grand Rapids, MI: Eerdmans, 2007); **M. Thompson,** *Clothed with Christ: The Example and Teaching of Jesus in Romans 12.1–15.13* (Sheffield: JSOT Press, 1991); **A. J. M. Wedderburn,** "Paul and Jesus: Similarity and Continuity," *NTS* 34 (1988): 161-82; **D. Wenham,** *The Rediscovery of Jesus' Eschatological Discourse* (Sheffield: JSOT Press, 1984); idem, *Paul: Follower of Jesus or Founder of Christianity?* (Grand Rapids, MI: Eerdmans, 1995); **C. Wolff,** "Niedrigkeit und Verzicht in Wort und Weg Jesu und in der apostolischen Existenz des Paulus," *NTS* 34 (1988): 183-96; **E. K. C. Wong,** "The De-radicalization of Jesus' Ethical Sayings in Romans," *NovT* 43 (2001): 245-63; idem, "The De-radicalization of Jesus' Ethical Sayings in 1 Corinthians," *NTS* 48 (2002): 181-94; **M. W. Yeung,** *Faith in Jesus and Paul: A Comparison with Special Reference to "Faith That Can Remove*

Mountains" and "Your Faith Has Healed/Saved You" (Tübingen: Mohr Siebeck, 2002).

C. L. Blomberg

JESUS AND PAUL

The relationship between Jesus and Paul poses both historical and theological questions concerning the coherence of Christianity. Is the theology of Paul in tune with the message of Jesus, or does it diverge significantly by placing Jesus' life and *death in a new, alien framework? Was Paul, in fact, the "second founder" of the Christian *tradition? Since Paul speaks of Jesus from the perspective of *faith, is there an unbridgeable gulf between "the historical Jesus" and "the Christ of faith," or is that a modern, false dichotomy? For all these interconnected questions the stakes are high.

1. History of the Debate
2. Reframing the Issues
3. Paul's Encounter with Jesus
4. Paul and Jesus' Life
5. Paul and Jesus' Teaching
6. The Significance of Jesus for Paul

1. History of the Debate.

1.1. Late Nineteenth and Early Twentieth Centuries. When F. C. Baur opened the modern era of historical criticism in the nineteenth century, he placed Paul's life and theology on a trajectory that led away from the original Jewish context of Jesus' *ministry and of his Jerusalem-based *apostles. On philosophical-theological grounds, Baur acclaimed Paul for breaking "free" of the Jewish "constraints" of Jesus' horizons. Where Jesus spoke of "the *kingdom of God," Paul's theology recognized in Jesus the absoluteness of the Spirit. Leaving behind the "national" messianic identity of Jesus, Paul conducted his *mission to the *Gentiles on the basis that Jesus is *Lord of all the world. Baur's historical method encouraged critics to envision competing trends in the early Christian movement, raising the possibility that Paul represented just one, and perhaps an extreme, wing of Christianity. That created a lively debate about the relationship between Jesus and Paul, which came to a head in the twenty years before the First World War. Whereas liberal Protestantism depended on a synthesis of the teaching of Jesus and Paul, radical historical critics posited a gulf between them, with a preference (contrary to Baur) for returning "back from Paul to Jesus."

This "Jesus and Paul" controversy was sharply focused in the publication (in 1904) of W. Wrede's popular book *Paul.* Wrede argued that Paul's theology represented a religion of redemption whose centerpiece was the notion of a superhuman figure (the *Son of God) who entered the world to break the hold of the powers that keep it in *slavery. Paul inherited this system of ideas preformed, from apocalyptic Judaism, and merged it with the story of the death and *resurrection of Jesus. What was significant to Paul was not the life and *teaching of Jesus, but only the fact that Jesus was a man, that he died, and that he was raised. As a representative of humanity, Christ effected an "objective" *salvation, mediated to those who take part in the sacraments.

Wrede argued that this thought structure was altogether different from the simple, prophetic style of Jesus and the pure moral truths he had pronounced. Paul's *conversion took place through an encounter with the risen Christ, not the earthly Jesus; in fact, he could describe Christ as a heavenly, divine figure only because he had never known the human Jesus. Thus Paul was not deeply influenced either by the personality of Jesus or by the spirit of his thought. On this basis, Wrede reached his oft-quoted conclusion that "Paul is to be regarded as the second-founder of Christianity" (Wrede, 179). Paul rescued the Christian faith from "pining away as a Jewish sect," but only by transforming it. The theological dynamite packed into this conclusion is clear in Wrede's observation: "This second founder of Christianity has even, compared with the first, exercised beyond all doubt the stronger—not the better—influence" (180).

The response to such views was vigorous, both from liberal German theologians (A. von Harnack, A. Jülicher, A. Resch) and from more conservative scholars in the English-speaking world (J. Moffatt, C. A. A. Scott, J. G. Machen). It was commonly argued that (1) Paul knew a lot more of the teaching of Jesus than we have acknowledged and alludes to it often; (2) although Paul's letters contain few references to the life of Jesus, he must have talked about Jesus in his missionary preaching; (3) the supposed gulf between Jesus and Paul has been greatly exaggerated: Jesus was just as critical of the *law as was Paul, and the implicit *Christology in Jesus' teaching is not remote from the divine roles and titles explicitly accorded him by Paul; and (4) despite external differences, Jesus and Paul were one at the kernel of their thought (e.g., with regard to the fatherly *love of *God and the primacy of the love command).

In this period of historical research into the religious context of early Christianity (the time of the "history of religions" school), two differing configurations of the relation between Jesus and Paul achieved some prominence just before the First World War. W. Heitmüller drew attention to the Hellenistic Christian circles in which Paul was nurtured in his allegiance to Christ, and from whom he derived the creeds or confessions that we find in such passages as Philippians 2:6-11 and 1 Corinthians 15:3-7. Such Hellenized believers emphasized the risen Lord rather than the earthly Jesus, using categories of salvation derived from Hellenistic religions such as the mystery cults. On this picture, Paul was not an isolated "second founder" of Christianity, but his theology was still very far from the Palestinian Judaism of Jesus. By contrast, A. Schweitzer, in his *Paul and His Interpreters* (followed up in *The Mysticism of Paul the Apostle*), identified Jewish *apocalypticism as the shared framework for the theology of both Jesus and Paul. Instead of a gulf between a Jewish Jesus and a Hellenized Paul, Schweitzer suggested that both Jesus and Paul thought in terms derived from apocalyptic Judaism and were distinguished only by the fact that the eschatological events that Jesus anticipated were viewed by Paul as having already begun in the resurrection of the Messiah in union with his elect.

This debate indicated that any comparison between Jesus and Paul depends on establishing a clear picture of the two parties. At the end of the nineteenth century a liberal-theological consensus regarding Jesus was challenged by historical research, from which emerged different Jesus figures, even where it was agreed that the best historical information could be gleaned from the Synoptic Gospels (not John). At the same time, a variety of "Pauls" were propounded, even where it was agreed that, for historical purposes, the picture of Paul in Acts and in the Pastoral Epistles should be discounted. But if reconstructions of Jesus and Paul are unstable, there can be no agreement concerning their connection or comparison. That problem persisted throughout the twentieth century and has acquired new forms of complexity today.

1.2. Rudolf Bultmann. In the next phase of the discussion (from the First World War to the 1950s), Bultmann's contributions were of decisive significance in two respects. First, he drew an important distinction between historical *continuity* (how much Paul knew about Jesus and quoted his teaching) and theological *congruity* (how far, in their essence, the messages of Jesus and Paul were agreed). If we allow this distinction, it might be possible to judge that, at the core of their message, Jesus and Paul were at one, even if Paul had limited access to what Jesus said and cited little of it. Second, Bultmann propounded an influential stance on the relationship between the historical Jesus and the understanding of history implied by faith.

1.2.1. Continuity or Congruity? Bultmann's distinction between continuity and congruity enabled him to take what might seem a surprising stand on the Jesus-Paul question. On the one hand, he saw very little historical connection between Jesus and Paul. He emphasized how little Paul quotes of the words of Jesus and argued that any possible allusions affect only Paul's *ethics: "It is most obvious that he does not appeal to the words of the Lord in support of his strictly theological, anthropological and soteriological views," in which are contained "the essentially Pauline conceptions" (Bultmann 1966, 223). Justification by faith, the critique of "*works of the law," the *church as *body of Christ, salvation and reconciliation through the death and resurrection of Christ—all that, Bultmann argued, is worked out by Paul without reference to the teaching of Jesus or stories of his miraculous works.

On the other hand, Bultmann detected a close match between the core demand in the preaching of Jesus and the central thrust of Paul's theology. Building on the work of Weiss and Schweitzer, Bultmann insisted that Jesus taught an apocalyptic message about a national and cosmic crisis, in which he demanded total (not just partial or external) submission to the authority of God (the kingdom of God). In response to this absolute demand, the individual surrenders their previous self-satisfaction and self-reliance. Likewise, at the center of Paul's theology, in his critique of the law and in his theology of the *cross, was an attack on Jewish "legalism" and on any attempt to secure salvation from purely human resources. "The real *sin of man is that he himself takes his will and his life into his own hands, makes himself secure and so has his self-confidence, his 'boast'" (Bultmann 1966, 228). What Paul demanded was the surrender of this self, in total dependence on the *grace of God enacted in the death and resurrection of Jesus. This interpretation of Jesus and Paul, derived from an amalgam of Lutheran theology and existentialist *philosophy, identified a point of deep correspondence between Jesus' teaching and Paul's theology. They differed only in that what Jesus proclaimed in anticipation of an imminent, world-changing act of God, Paul preached as an (at least partially) accomplished fact.

1.2.2. History and Faith. Bultmann's second contribution to the Jesus-Paul debate lay in the field of *hermeneutics. In his form-critical work on the Gospels, Bultmann insisted that stories about Jesus were circulated from the perspective of faith and with regard to the needs of the earliest churches or the special interests of the Evangelists. This historical conclusion matched what he found in Paul: what mattered for Paul and for his preaching was not **knowledge about* Jesus (whether Jesus did or said this or that), but that Jesus, the crucified one, had been raised by God and is to be *acknowledged as Lord*. Apart from the fact that Jesus had been crucified, everything that was important about Jesus theologically—that he was the incarnate Son of God, that he died "for us," that he is the Lord of the cosmos—was established by the resurrection and in the preaching of the church, not by the accumulation of historical facts. In Paul's theology "one does not acquire knowledge about the Messiah: one either acknowledges him or repudiates him" (Bultmann 1966, 236). Thus one cannot and theologically *should not* go "back to Jesus from Paul." "All that one can do is go to Jesus through Paul: i.e., one is asked by Paul whether one is willing to understand God's act in Christ as the event that has decided and now decides with respect both to the world and to us" (Bultmann 1961, 201).

Bultmann's stance here fitted his hermeneutical conviction that one cannot study history—any history—without being to some extent involved; there is no "objective history," undertaken without presuppositions, since history is only meaningful if interpreters find some contemporary significance in what they study. But that matched his theological conviction that for Christian faith Jesus can never merely be an object of historical study—with its limited and uncertain results—but the focus of self-involving faith: to believe in Christ is not to believe certain things *about* him, but to be confronted by God's challenge to one's self-understanding, one's confidence, hopes, and fears. Thus Christian faith cannot be authentic if it operates in a two-stage process: first determining what is historically plausible, and then deciding whether this is a truth decisive for you. Bultmann thus challenged the historicist assumptions of his predecessors and made the theological question first and foremost not "Who was Jesus?" but "Who is Jesus, now, for you?"

1.3. The Landscape Since Bultmann. The topic "Jesus and Paul" presupposes that one can compare, and perhaps connect, two figures about whom something definite can be said. Since the 1960s, NT scholarship has had much to say on both figures, but with increasing degrees of uncertainty regarding "the historical Jesus," and large areas of disagreement concerning Paul. But if we have many varieties of Jesus and Paul, the relation between them becomes uncertain, and it is not clear that the old questions about Jesus and Paul are answerable, at least as previously posed.

1.3.1. Jesus in Recent Decades. The 1960s saw a renewed interest in the "quest for the historical Jesus," even among Bultmann's pupils (E. Käsemann, E. Fuchs), who warned against the dangers of docetism if the Christ preached in the *gospel is not firmly linked to the historical realities of the life of Jesus. This new interest gained momentum with the discovery and publication of the Dead Sea Scrolls (since 1947), which occasioned a new effort to understand Jesus within his Jewish context. The title of G. Vermes's book *Jesus the Jew* represents the focus of this scholarly endeavor, which was conducted on "purely" historical terms: books by A. E. Harvey, J. Riches, E. P Sanders, G. Theissen and A. Merz, N. T. Wright, J. P. Meier, D. C. Allison Jr., and J. D. G. Dunn have variously reconstructed Jesus as a Jewish figure best understood with the social, political, and religious environment of his day. However, the historical method of enquiry requires some agreement about sources and their reliability, and the past few decades have witnessed increasing uncertainty, even skepticism on this score. Confident reconstructions of a Q source have given way to dispute about the nature of this source, even doubt concerning its existence, while the "criteria for authenticity" typically used in judging the historical reliability of Jesus material have been criticized as inadequate or loaded. While a few historians have questioned whether Jesus ever existed, the vast majority affirm his historical existence. But they have presented him variously as a *wisdom teacher, a prophet, an apocalyptic seer, a charismatic wonder-worker, or a self-conscious bearer of the divine presence. With this degree of uncertainty concerning Jesus, the historical connection between Jesus and Paul is increasingly hard to reconstruct.

1.3.2. Paul in Recent Decades. With Paul we are on firmer historical ground, even if some dispute continues about which letters to consider authentic. With the waning of Bultmann's theology, new readings of Paul have placed him in fuller and more accurate comparison with his fellow Jews. E. P. Sanders's analysis of Second Temple Judaism undermined the Protestant antithesis between Pauline grace and Jewish "works-righteousness," so that it was possible to ask in new ways (in "the new perspective on Paul") how Paul's Gentile mission related to his Jewish matrix. Did Paul shift the Jesus movement beyond the traditional boundaries of the Jewish tradition, or did he remain (in some senses) "within

Judaism"? Were Jesus and Paul "marginal" or "anomalous" Jews, and if so, in similar or in different ways? It is clear from Paul's letters (e.g., Galatians) that he was in dispute with other Jewish Christ-followers and was a controversial figure among Jews who did not believe in Christ, but the reasons for this controversy are still disputed among scholars. Plotting Paul's place in the trajectories of development in early Christianity has become an uncertain business, but older theories that Paul "hellenized" the Christian movement or became the "second founder" of Christianity are no longer in vogue.

1.3.3. Tracing the Connecting Links. There have been continuing efforts to trace how the material in Paul's letters relates to the early traditions concerning Jesus. Most scholars acknowledge that Paul's contact with the disciples of Jesus in the Palestinian churches was not extensive, although he must have gleaned something from his meeting with *Peter (Gal 1:18). Some argue that Paul created a fundamental split in the early Christian movement, but his continued commitment to the believers in *Jerusalem (evidenced in the *collection; see Rom 15:25-32) does not justify such a radical conclusion. In tracing lines of tradition from Jesus to Paul, special interest has focused on the "Hellenists," the Greek-speaking group of Jewish Christ-believers (such as Stephen and Barnabas; Acts 6–7). These may have been the target of Paul's persecution of "the church of God" (Gal 1:13 NRSV), and, after his call/conversion, they may have influenced the development of his theology. If there is a "bridge" between Jesus and Paul, it might lie here (Wedderburn). Unfortunately, our knowledge of this group remains frustratingly thin and insecure.

Research has continued to probe overlaps between material found in the Gospels and in the letters of Paul. Similarities with Jesus' teaching (e.g., on the priority of love and kindness to enemies) have led some to propose that "Paul is steeped in the mind and the words of his Lord" (Davies, 140). Paul rarely cites Jesus explicitly, but D. L. Dungan concludes from 1 Corinthians 7:10; 9:14 that the Corinthians were familiar with such material, which must have circulated in his churches. New work on the identification of echoes and allusions has highlighted connections not only in ethical but also in eschatological material (e.g., 1 Thess 4:13–5:10), with particularly strong links to certain blocks of material in the Synoptic Gospels (Wenham 1995; 2002).

At the popular level (both inside and outside churches), there remains a prevailing perception of a fundamental difference between Jesus and Paul, with an implicit value judgment: Jesus seems to many more accessible and more attractive, while Paul has a reputation for being convoluted, aggressive, and patriarchal. Thus, Wrede's judgment on Paul as "the stronger, not the better" influence on the Christian tradition finds parallels today, at least outside academic circles.

2. Reframing the Issues.

A number of shifts in NT scholarship, together with new, postmodern approaches to history and historiography make it possible now to conduct the "Jesus and Paul" debate on different terms. The traditional debate operated on the assumption that, using historical tools, one could establish an agreed, factual account of Jesus and could then decide on the degree of continuity (or congruity) between Paul and "the historical Jesus." It was presumed that historical truths about Jesus could be distinguished from later interpretations, such that one could "peel off" the overlay of interpretation and return to the original facts. Behind the Synoptics, beneath the redactional layers introduced by their authors, and underneath layers of interpretation that took place in the oral tradition, it was possible to discover the authentic, uninterpreted Jesus—the original words he spoke and the bare facticity of the things he did or suffered. After returning to this Jesus, one could then determine how far Paul had (or had not) deviated from him. However, recent intellectual shifts have changed the terms of this discussion in three significant ways.

2.1. Jesus and the Mediation of Memory. It has long been recognized that the earliest stages of transmission of the Jesus tradition were oral, as reports about Jesus and accounts of his words were passed down by word of mouth. Although some have viewed those who transmitted these traditions as conservative and passive, recent studies of memory and of the social processes of memorialization have indicated that even the process of committing something to memory involves active steps of selection and interpretation (Allison 2010). When this memory making takes places within social settings, the environment, interests, and needs of those who perpetuate these memories play a significant role in shaping (and reshaping) what is remembered. In other words, memory is far more than recollection: it frames and molds what is remembered in light of what is considered significant. Thus, relevant questions concern not just the accuracy of memories but also their purpose, individual and social. Nothing that Jesus said or did could be passed down in a mode free of interpretation. From the very beginning, indeed at the very moment when Jesus said or did anything, the facts were filtered, selected, and framed in the memories of the eyewitnesses and auditors, and this process continued in the telling and retelling conducted by subsequent bearers of those memories. In this sense, we can never have unmediated access to Jesus; we have only "Jesus-in-the-memory" of those who spoke about him. There was never a singular, original version of these memories: like any figure who made an impact on his contemporaries, Jesus was understood and interpreted in diverse ways from the very beginning.

2.2. New Approaches to Historiography. Recent decades have seen a turn away from older, "positivist" approaches to history, which regarded good historiography as the pursuit of ever-more-accurate accounts of the "bare" facts, recounted with impartial objectivity. Without abandoning the distinction between fact and fiction, recent understandings of historiography emphasize that, in telling history, no facts are simply "bare": they are all inevitably clothed with the significance accorded by the historian. In selecting, prioritizing, and framing the material—all of which are acts of interpretation—the historian is not just *discovering* but also *creating* the historical record, and this active process of reception is what makes history meaningful and significant. Thus, it is, in principle, impossible to give an account of Jesus (or Paul) that is not also, at the same time, an *interpretation* of what is recounted: the interpretation is part of the facticity of Jesus. Where two scholars of differing perspectives agree on this or that fact about Jesus, that is not proof that they have reached "pure" objectivity: it is an indication that *at that point* (if not at others) they share a matrix of interpretation. It is simply impossible to talk about Jesus without also, at the same time, interpreting who he was—and the same is true of every historical person. Thus the question is not whether Paul was in tune with the original, "real," uninterpreted Jesus, but how his historical interpretation of Jesus compares with other historical interpretations of Jesus that were active from the lifetime of Jesus onward.

2.3. History and Theology. Since the Enlightenment, Western scholarship has developed a dichotomy between "history" and "faith," such that the realm of "empirical" historical fact is sharply distinguished from discourse that accords agency to God or other supernatural forces. History, so defined, cannot include theological statements, especially those that have "God" as the subject of a verb. But this is a modern phenomenon, and it is a mistake to retroject it onto the past. Although some ancient historians were uncertain how to integrate divine and human agency in their account of events, it is clear that Jesus and his Jewish contemporaries interpreted all events with reference to God, whom they took to be operative through history, through Scripture, and in present circumstances. In that sense, all interpretations of Jesus, from the very beginning, were theological. Some of his contemporaries may have considered Jesus mistaken, even an agent of diabolical forces (see Mk 3:22), but, whether in approval or disapproval, the default assumption was to interpret Jesus' words and actions within a frame of divine (or antidivine) activity. Their historical frame of interpretation was always, at the same time, an expression of faith.

For those who considered Jesus an agent of the God of *Israel, the frame of interpretation was hugely enhanced, indeed transformed, by the resurrection. There is no shift here from "the Jesus of history" to "the Christ of faith." Rather, the faith interpretation of Jesus took on a new shape when it was believed that Jesus had been raised by God and installed as Lord of the cosmos, as the inauguration of the eschatological events. This belief was not a departure from history (unless our definition of history excludes the belief that God raised Jesus), but it framed anew all the historical events of Jesus' life and death. Those who believed in and experienced the living, risen Jesus now recounted all that happened before that point anew: they "saw" in the history of Jesus what they had not fully seen before.

Paul was at one with all those who believed in the resurrection of Jesus, and, like them, he viewed the whole life and death of Jesus through this resurrection lens. All the canonical Gospels share this perspective; in fact, we have no early accounts of Jesus that are not written from this angle. The important distinction is not between Paul and other early believers, but between those who believed in the resurrection and those (outside the church) who did not. For those who did believe, no account of Jesus that failed to read his life and death from the perspective of the resurrection could be adequate.

This changes the debate on Jesus and Paul in significant ways. The question is not how much Paul knew about, and was in continuity with the "historical" Jesus (in the sense of an uninterpreted Jesus), but how his representation of Jesus relates to other versions of the remembered Jesus, and in particular to other faith interpretations of the life and death of Jesus. For Paul, and for all fellow believers, there was no possibility of going back "behind" the resurrection to some earlier interpretation of Jesus, and no point in doing so: Why evoke a half-perception when the fullness was now possible? There was nothing "better" or more "objective" about reading the story of Jesus as if the resurrection had not happened: that would simply refuse the proper interpretation of the whole.

One must still ask, of course, how Paul's reading of the life, death, and resurrection of Jesus compares to other readings of the same. Paul is our earliest written source for these matters, since his letters were written before any of our Gospels took written form, but he indicates in 1 Corinthians 15:3-5 that he had received a creedal formula that already framed what had happened in Jesus by reference to the Scriptures, with special focus on his death, burial, and resurrection. That does not preclude interest in what Jesus said and did before he was crucified, but it indicates a very early (pre-Pauline) effort to understand the whole life of Christ from the perspective of the cross and the resurrection. In this regard, both Paul and this creed share points in common with the earliest written Gospel, the Gospel of Mark, which gives disproportionate space to the end of Jesus' life and is significantly shaped in thought and structure by his death and resurrection. Paul had his own reading of the significance of Jesus, with his own theological emphases, but as far as we know he was at one with other Christ-followers in interpreting the life, actions, and sayings of Jesus through the lens of faith in the resurrection and through the experience of the risen, living Lord. That is a far more significant point of similarity than whether he had access to the same quantity of information about the deeds and sayings of Jesus. The distinction is not between "historical" accounts that contain lots of stories of Jesus and "faith" accounts that focus on Jesus' death and resurrection. It is only a difference in degrees of detail about the precrucifixion life of Jesus among accounts that are all forms of theologically interpreted, resurrection-shaped history.

Our question now is: How, specifically, did Paul interpret Jesus? We will begin by examining what he says about his encounter with Jesus (§3), before surveying what he says (or gestures toward) concerning the life and the teaching of Jesus (§§4 and 5). What matters most is how he interprets the whole Jesus event, and here we can trace how his reading of Jesus encapsulates much that might also be derived from the individual stories and sayings that circulated in the memory of the early believers (§6).

3. Paul's Encounter with Jesus.

It would be impossible to divorce Paul's interpretation of the Christ event from his own, personal experience of Christ, in what he terms his "calling." We will confine our attention to his own descriptions of this event in Galatians 1:13-17 and 1 Corinthians 15:8-10 (cf. 1 Cor 9:1; 2 Cor 4:4-6). These passages are brief, but they contain four essential clues to the frame in which Paul interpreted everything he knew about Jesus.

In the first place, it was important to Paul that he encountered the risen Jesus *directly and personally* in a "revelation" granted specifically to him (Gal 1:16); he had "seen" Christ (1 Cor 9:1), who appeared, last in the line, to him (1 Cor 15:8). This gave Paul the confidence to speak about the significance of Christ, a confidence not dependent on the memories of those who had witnessed Jesus' preresurrection life. Feeling himself on a par with other apostles, Paul was entitled to interpret Christ with no less authority (Gal 1:1, 11-12). This did not mean that he was uninterested in the memories passed on by disciples such as Peter. But he was confident that he knew what was good about the good news directly and authoritatively, and within that frame passed on what he had received concerning events in Jesus' life (1 Cor 11:23) or ways of summarizing its significance (1 Cor 15:3-5). Thus, revelation and tradition are not binary alternatives: Paul's revelation frames how he hears, interprets, and passes on the memories contained in the tradition. When he says that he no longer knows Christ *kata sarka* (in a merely human way; 2 Cor 5:16), that does not mean that he has no interest in what might be known about the life of Jesus. But everything must now be placed within the frame of the death and resurrection of Christ, the inauguration of the "new *creation" (2 Cor 5:17). Within that hermeneutical frame, everything is received "from the Lord" (1 Cor 11:23 NRSV): all knowledge is filtered through the risen Christ, who is present and active in the church.

Second, Paul's encounter was with the *risen* Christ (1 Cor 15:8); his perspective on all reality was shaped by that radically new moment in the history of the cosmos. For Paul, the resurrection of Jesus was not a one-off, freak event, but the firstfruits of the resurrection in general (1 Cor 15:20), the beginning of the new creation in which God's purposes for all humanity and for all creation would be fulfilled. Thus, the resurrection of Jesus was not just one additional event in the life of Jesus; it was *the* defining moment in history, for Jesus, for history, and for the world (Phil 2:6-11). This helps us understand why the resurrection dominates Paul's mental landscape. The good news that he proclaims is not primarily that Jesus healed this or that person, or spoke this or that moral wisdom, but that God has changed the condition of the world, and the parameters of the possible, through raising the crucified Jesus from the dead. Given the urgency of this new eschatological moment, the most important thing for Paul to communicate to his Gentile hearers was to react quickly, before it was too late. Whatever else they heard about Jesus, the essential thing was to turn "to God from idols, to serve a living and true God, and to wait for his Son from heaven, whom he raised from the dead—Jesus, who rescues us from the *wrath that is coming" (1 Thess 1:9-10 NRSV).

Third, Paul encountered the risen Christ as *Lord* of the world, installed as *kyrios* by God to subjugate all counter-God forces (1 Cor 15:20-28; Phil 2:6-11). The stance to adopt to this Lord/Master is submission or *service. Those who show allegiance to Jesus are best described as slaves, not disciples; their primary task is to obey, not to learn (Rom 6:15-23; 14:1-12). Paul could never be content with an interpretation of Jesus as a teacher who issued wisdom about this or that topic: even where he alludes to memories of Jesus' teaching about *purity (Rom 14:14), he attributes this to "the Lord Jesus." Jesus, for Paul, does not merely teach about things: he demands loyalty and obedience, issuing instructions as Lord.

Fourth, and crucially, Paul encountered Jesus as *the bearer of grace*. His revelation, he says, was given as a result of the fact that "God . . . had set me apart before I was born and called me through his grace" (Gal 1:15 NRSV), a grace given despite his previous persecution of "the church of God" (Gal 1:13 NRSV). Elsewhere, he reflects on this further: "For I am the least of the apostles, unfit to be called an apostle, because I persecuted the church of God. But by the grace of God I am what I am, and his grace toward me has not been in vain" (1 Cor 15:9-10 NRSV). This grace shaped Paul's whole life and thought, such that he viewed the life, death, and resurrection of Christ as a gift, the climactic act of divine benevolence directed toward a world that was alienated from God, sinful and weak (Rom 5:6-8). At a personal level, Paul could declare, "I live by faith in the Son of God, who loved me and gave himself for me" (Gal 2:20 NRSV). But what he experienced himself was true for all: "If the many died through the one man's trespass, much more surely have the grace of God and the free gift in the grace of the one man, Jesus Christ, abounded for the many" (Rom 5:15 NRSV; cf. 2 Cor 5:14-15). Thus, Paul's account of Jesus could never be confined to particular incidents or sayings: the whole story of the coming, life, death, and resurrection of Jesus was a divine gift given "for us," and was to be viewed first and foremost through that lens (2 Cor 8:9).

4. Paul and Jesus' Life.

There are very many details in the life of Jesus recounted in the Gospels that we do not hear about from Paul, despite the fact that he is our earliest Christian source: the circumstances of Jesus' birth; the places he was associated with; his *baptism, temptation, and transfiguration; his *healings and exorcisms; his followers and opponents; his arrest; and his trials. All Paul recounts of Jesus' family is that he was "born of a woman" (Gal 4:4) and had brothers, including James (1 Cor 9:5; Gal 1:19). The only incident in Jesus' life before his crucifixion mentioned by Paul is the supper on the night he was handed over (1 Cor 11:23-25). These are enough to indicate that Paul knew something about Jesus as a historical figure (against those who have argued that Jesus is a mythical invention). Of course, it is possible that Paul knew a lot more than he recounted, especially after staying with Peter in Jerusalem for two weeks (Gal 1:18). But what is important for Paul is not individual incidents in the life of Jesus but the shape of the whole event, and not so much what happened in the past for individuals who encountered Jesus in Galilee or Jerusalem but what Jesus means for all people, everywhere, now.

That wide-screen picture is summarized in Galatians 4:4-5: "But when the fullness of time had come, God sent his Son, born of a woman, born under the law, in order to redeem those who were under the law, so that we might receive *adoption as children" (NRSV). There are two things about the life of Jesus that seem important here: his human nature ("born of a woman") and his Jewish identity ("born under the law"). Jesus' human, Adamic nature is crucial to Paul's theology. As he puts it in Philippians, Christ "emptied himself" (of power; NRSV), took the form of a slave, was found in human form, humbled himself, and was obedient to the point of death, even death on a cross (Phil 2:7-8). Here the whole life-and-death of Jesus is summarized in a form that emphasizes the limitations, humiliations, and vulnerabilities of Christ's human condition. That humanity is the basis for the comparison between *Adam and Christ in Rom 5:12-21, where Adam's disobedience is contrasted with Christ's obedience—that is, his whole-life stance of alignment with the purpose of

God. Jesus' refusal of sin (2 Cor 5:21), even while living "in the likeness of sinful *flesh" (Rom 8:3 NRSV), is what enabled him to condemn "sin in the flesh" (Rom 8:3 NRSV). Jesus identified with the depths of the human condition (becoming "sin" and "a *curse," 2 Cor 5:21; Gal 3:13 NRSV) in order to redeem humanity, both in his death and in his resurrection. Thus, by a human being (Adam) came death, and by a human being (Jesus) came also the resurrection of the dead (1 Cor 15:21). In that sense, the human life of Jesus matters hugely to Paul, but its details (when, where, with whom) are subordinated to the significance of the whole.

Jesus' Jewish identity is also crucial. As the seed of *Abraham, Jesus is the definitive recipient of the Abrahamic promises (Gal 3:16, 19), and his primary life orientation was as "a servant of the circumcised on behalf of the *truth of God in order that he might confirm the promises given to the patriarchs" (Rom 15:8 NRSV). As one "born under the law," he came to redeem those "under the law" (Gal 4:4 NRSV), because the purposes of God cannot be completed without the redemption of Israel. In particular, as the Davidic Messiah (Rom 1:3; 9:5; 15:12), Jesus brings Israel's destiny to completion and, even though he was killed by Jews/Judeans (1 Thess 2:14-15), his universal reign, established at the resurrection, enables him to unite both Jews and non-Jews (Rom 15:8-12). This Jewish particularity in the life of Jesus is by no means a historical residue that can be left behind in Paul's Gentile mission, because neither Scripture nor history can make sense for Paul without the irrevocable *election of Israel (Rom 11:28-29), and Jesus is installed as universal Lord precisely because he is the Messiah of Israel. The details of how Jesus operated as Messiah (and was or was not recognized as such) are submerged under the all-embracing fact that that is who he is.

Paul's theology is thus structured around a narrative of participation: as Jesus participates in the Jewish story and in the story of all humanity, so Jews and all human beings can participate in Jesus' life and power, which bring the destiny of Israel, humanity, and creation to its fulfillment. Being rich (in the self-giving love of God), he became poor (limited by the vulnerabilities of the human condition), so that by his poverty those who participate in Christ might become rich (2 Cor 8:9). The gift of God in Christ, by which Jesus was handed over to the human condition (Rom 8:32), is a gift of love for humanity (and through humans, for creation, Rom 8:19-23). Self-giving love is the hallmark of this narrative and shapes the ethos of those caught up in its momentum. Humility, gentleness, and sharing in the needs of others are the characteristics of the Christ story and therefore of those who share in this grace (2 Cor 10:1; Phil 2:3-5; Rom 15:3). Imitation of Christ thus takes on precisely this form for those empowered by him (1 Cor 10:31–11:1), while love is the essence of "the law of Christ" (Gal 6:2 NRSV).

The cross and the resurrection are for Paul the focal point of the life of Jesus, but only as summing up the meaning of the whole. At the cross Christ identifies most fully with the *suffering, sin, poverty, weakness, and curse of the human condition (2 Cor 1:5; 5:21; 8:9; 13:4; Gal 3:13), and at the cross it becomes most apparent that his life is given in love (Gal 2:19-20; Rom 5:8). Accordingly, the Last Supper narrative recounted by Paul highlights Jesus' potent words concerning the gift of his life "for you" (1 Cor 11:24). Because this life-and-death is a gift, Jesus' resurrection occurs not just for him but for the benefit of all, as the firstfruits of the resurrection (1 Cor 15:20-22). Without this larger frame of interpretation, the individual acts and events of Jesus' life remain isolated and ambiguous, incidents of the past without contemporary significance for all. In common with other early believers, Paul sees the whole story of Jesus through the lens of his death and resurrection, but his focus rests on those events to a remarkable degree. It is likely that Paul's theology influenced the Gospel of Mark, where the death of Jesus is given disproportionate space and emphasis. But whereas Mark uses the death of Jesus to interpret and frame a narrative with many individual scenes, Paul abbreviates the Jesus story to the few things necessary for grasping the meaning of the whole and places it in the still larger context of God's purposes for Israel, for humanity, and for the cosmos.

5. Paul and Jesus' Teaching.

We can only touch here on the long debate concerning the extent to which Paul used the teaching of Jesus. There is little dispute about the occasions on which Paul explicitly cites the words of Jesus (e.g., 1 Cor 7:10; 9:14; 11:23; 1 Thess 4:15; probably Rom 14:14). The question is whether Paul alludes to Jesus tradition in other places where we can detect parallels in the Gospels, even where he does not trace the material to Jesus. That these are clustered in certain places (Rom 12–14; 1 Thess 4:13–5:10; cf. Col 3–4), which also match blocks of Jesus material, might suggest that Paul draws on precollected material (Allison 1982; Thompson; Wenham 1995). But because his letters predate the written Gospels it is impossible to trace now the processes of transmission by which this material ended up both in Paul's letters (unattributed to Jesus) and in the Gospels, attached to the memory of Jesus. If Paul knew that this material could be traced to Jesus, it is striking that he did not think it necessary to point this out. Even where Paul does cite a saying from Jesus, it seems open to adaptation, even selective disqualification, in the circumstances of Paul's mission (1 Cor 7:10-16; 9:3-18; Rom 14:13-15). That suggests that the teaching of Jesus is not an independent source of authority for Paul but is to be used only within the larger framework of the whole Christ event. For the same reason, while Paul sometimes uses the phrase "the kingdom of God" (e.g., Rom 14:19; 1 Thess 2:12; Gal 5:21; 1 Cor 4:20; 6:9), it does not feature in his letters as a central motif in the way we might expect after reading Jesus' language in the Synoptic Gospels. That is because Paul reads all language of sovereignty and rule from the perspective of the resurrection, at which Jesus was installed as Lord (Phil 2:6-11). From this angle of vision, the present is the time of Jesus' reign, when all powers are being put "under his feet" (1 Cor 15:27 NRSV), though ultimately his reign is subordinate to God, who will be "all in all" (1 Cor 15:28 NRSV). While the end vision is the same as in the Synoptic material, the lived experience of the resurrection makes it impossible for Paul to speak of this matter without reference to Jesus as the present exalted Lord.

6. The Significance of Jesus for Paul.

It is unlikely that Paul knew nothing about Jesus when he persecuted his followers before his calling (Gal 1:13). At that point, he may have viewed Jesus as a false prophet and a convicted criminal whose crucifixion brought him, scandalously, under the curse of God (Gal 3:13; 5:11). After his calling, Paul probably learned something about the life and acts of Jesus from the apostles in Jerusalem, who knew Jesus personally. But for Paul there is a distinction between knowing *about* Jesus and knowing him because that direct, self-involving knowledge required submission to his authority: what counts is not the quantity of information gleaned at second hand, but "the surpassing value of knowing Christ Jesus my Lord" (Phil 3:8 NRSV). Thus, "though we once knew Christ from a human point of view [*kata sarka*], we know him no longer in that way" (2 Cor 5:16 NRSV). That does not mean that Paul was uninterested in the life and acts of Jesus, or that he diminished the importance of "the historical Jesus" in favor of the "cosmic Christ." But it does mean that everything that could be said about the birth, life, miracles, parables, instructions, controversies, and trials of Jesus had to be placed in a *theological* frame (what God was doing in and through this life and death) and specifically in a *postresurrection* frame (how God had changed the conditions of existence through the life, death, and resurrection of Jesus). All the traditions in our canonical Gospels remember Jesus in the light of the resurrection, and the Gospel narratives are shaped accordingly, on the basis of faith. But it was incumbent on Paul, in his pioneering Gentile mission, to explain why all this mattered; it was necessary to paint with a broad brush, at the cost of particular details. For Paul, the human presence of Jesus, his Jewish identity, his cross, and his resurrection encapsulated all that needed to be said for the sake of this big picture. Nonetheless, Paul's summary statements resonate closely with the memory of Jesus preserved in the Gospels, in at least three ways.

6.1. Jesus and the Fulfillment of the Destiny of Israel. The Gospel materials place Jesus, in multiple ways, at the climax of Israel's history, as the fulfillment of God's purposes for his people. John the Baptist prepares the way for this eschatological exodus, the twelve disciples evoke the gathering of the twelve tribes, the miracles of Jesus replay and transcend themes from Israel's history, and throughout the narrative the Scriptures of Israel, cited or echoed, provide the framework for understanding the significance of Jesus. As the Messiah of Israel, Jesus completes the destiny of his people, while the controversies that surround him, and his eventual rejection, play out the trauma of a fulfillment largely unrecognized or misunderstood. The Gospels also gesture to a wider horizon: narratives (e.g., the Syro-Phoenician woman), parables (e.g., the good Samaritan), and sayings (e.g., Mk 14:9) indicate that the good news of Israel's Messiah will bring blessing to all the nations—a perspective developed in the birth and resurrection narratives of Matthew and Luke.

As we have seen (§4 above), it is crucial for Paul that Jesus "confirm[s] the promises given to the patriarchs" as the "servant of the circumcised" (Rom 15:8 NRSV), and in Paul's fullest analysis of Israel's story (Rom 9–11), Jesus, as Messiah and Redeemer from Zion, plays a central role (Rom 9:5; 11:25-27). Here also, Israel's Scriptures are the foundation of Paul's theology, repeatedly cited, paraphrased, and interpreted by reference to Jesus. Paul's vocation as apostle to the Gentiles makes central what is suggested in the Gospels, that Jesus' (contested) fulfillment of Israel's history brings salvation to the nations (Gal 3:6–4:8; Rom 11:11-16). Writing in a different genre and with distinctive accents, Paul makes explicit the larger narrative to which the Gospels gesture.

6.2. Jesus and the Birth of the New Creation. The Jesus remembered in faith in the early traditions also confronted, in the *name of God, the powers that limit and oppress humanity, opening the possibility of a mode of life that signaled the beginning of a new world. In healing the sick, the demon-possessed, and the impure, and in pronouncing the *forgiveness of sins, Jesus was remembered as confronting and overcoming the powers that hold humanity captive, whether external forces, the inner corruptions of the heart, or the ever-pressing menace of death. In healing and in nature miracles, Jesus is remembered as heralding the inbreaking of the kingdom of God, a power supreme over nature and over the constraints of the present human condition; indeed, he commands his followers to adopt a new orientation that breaks with the normal structures of family, *wealth, and self-protection. The power of the kingdom is accompanied by rejection and suffering, and, as its representative, Jesus is reduced to the humiliation of the cross, which is the site of God's ultimate gift in the overcoming of death. Called to take up the cross, Jesus' followers are led into a radical new allegiance, breaking with family and with the security of property and embracing the new world promised by Jesus and guaranteed by his resurrection.

Paul summarizes this whole trajectory in the twin moments of Jesus' crucifixion and resurrection, where the meaning of Jesus' coming reaches its climax and comes to its clearest expression. The powers that limit and enslave humanity are identified by Paul as Sin and Death: forgiveness of sins is effected through Christ's death as part of the larger drama whereby Christ condemns Sin (Rom 8:3), while believers, in baptism, die to it (Rom 6:1-6). The individual stories of the Jesus traditions find their counterpart in the grand narrative of the reconciliation of the world (2 Cor 5:19-21), while the resurrection opens the final stage of God's combat with the *principalities and powers (1 Cor 15:20-28). For Paul, the gift of the Spirit makes present the power of the new creation, which enters into conflict with the flesh and the "present evil age" (Gal 1:4 NRSV; see Gal 5:17). The new allegiance to Jesus is not encased within family ties, and that opens the possibility of celibacy as a sign that "the present form of this world is passing away" (1 Cor 7:25-31 NRSV). Shaped by the narrative of the cross, believers can break with the wisdom of the world and the standards of power that govern social and political behavior (1 Cor 1:18–2:5). Like those who "take up their cross" and "lose their life" in order to save it (Mk 8:34-35 NRSV), believers live a paradoxical existence, "always carrying in the *body the death of Jesus, so that the life of Jesus may also be made visible in our bodies" (2 Cor 4:10 NRSV). This is what "knowing Christ" means for Paul (Phil 3:10 NRSV): the world-breaking and world-recreating event of Christ takes place not just in the history of Jesus, but in the present bodily reality of life "*in Christ." As in the Gospels, the ultimate horizon is God's purpose in Christ to liberate the cosmos and to bring it to its goal (Rom 8:18-23).

6.3. Jesus and the Incongruous Generosity of God. What gives this narrative its shape and inner rationale is the way it enacts the mercy and incongruous grace of God. The traditions in which Jesus was remembered contain a striking emphasis on his scandalous actions and words, which seemed to prioritize those least fitting to be the recipients of God's grace. Jesus was remembered as a friend of "tax collectors and sinners" (Mt 11:19 NRSV), that is, persistent law-breakers whose manner of life brought dishonor or hardship on fellow Jews through sexual, financial, or political compromise of Israel's traditions. Jesus welcomed such as these to the meal table, as a foretaste of the eschatological banquet (Mk 2:16; Lk 15:1-2; 19:1-10). The beneficiaries of his healing included non-Jews who were manifestly unworthy of such gifts (Mk 5:1-20; 7:24-30). Sayings of Jesus were passed down that gave special attention to "little ones," children, widows, and the poor; his love command extended beyond circles of guaranteed reciprocity to enemies and persecutors, mirroring the unlimited generosity of God (Mt 5:38-48). As the shepherd seeking the lost sheep (Mt 15:24; Lk 15:3-7) or the doctor prioritizing the sick (Mk 2:17), Jesus represented the unconditioned *mercy of God, gathering the lost and repentant into the restored house of Israel.

This memory is most clearly crystallized in the parables of Jesus, such as the parable of the prodigal son (Lk 15:11-32). Here the son who had shamed the family and squandered its property is welcomed home by the father, who refuses to let him take the role of hired worker but reinstates him as son and celebrates his return with a feast: "for this son of mine was dead and is alive again; he was lost and is found" (Lk 15:24 NRSV). For the older brother, such generosity to an unworthy sibling is hard to accept: it challenges deep-rooted notions of fitting reward, the just principles by which gifts are normally and properly distributed. The father's gift is not just excessive; it is undeserved and unfitting, honoring the son who should be hiding his head in shame. In this sense, the grace that Jesus speaks about is subversive, both liberating and caustic, both welcoming and threatening to normal, stabilizing notions of justice.

At this point there is a deep congruity between the memories of Jesus and the theology and practice of Paul. Paul sees the history of Israel as being directed, from the start, by the unconditioned mercy of God—enacted in the election of the patriarchs, operative throughout history, and climaxing in the "richness" of Christ; this is a mercy accorded to the disobedient and without regard to worth, and it will finally envelop "all Israel" (Rom 9:6-18; 10:12-13; 11:17-32). Because this grace is given without condition, it extends to all, including all nations, whose previous sinful *idolatry does not disqualify them from the gracious initiative of God in Christ (Gal 1:6; 4:8-10). Thus Paul's Gentile mission, to which he was called in grace, is interpreted as a large-scale enactment of the grace of God (Gal 1:3-6; 2:7-10, 21), which has flooded the world with a power that matches and overcomes the power of Sin (Rom 5:12-21). This grace was at work in the programmatic story of Abraham and is extended to all the nations (Rom 4:1-25); it is given without regard to work or worth (Rom 4:3-8) and therefore to all. This is the logic of *justification in Paul's theology, which is applied not, as one would expect, to those considered righteous and fitting, but is at work, paradoxically, in the justification of *the ungodly* (Rom 4:5; 5:6). One would expect a good gift to be given to the righteous, especially a gift as costly as the life of Christ: "Rarely will anyone die for a righteous person—though perhaps for a good person someone might actually dare to die. But God proves his love for us in that while we were still sinners Christ died for us" (Rom 5:7-8 NRSV). That extraordinary, incongruous grace is what undergirds hope for the future, despite the disobedience that might reasonably make God turn away from the world (Rom 11:28-32).

As in the stories told about Jesus, this liberating grace entails the prioritization of those who would normally be considered unworthy or insignificant. "Consider your own call, brothers and sisters: not many of you were wise by human standards, not many were powerful, not many were of noble birth" (1 Cor 1:26 NRSV). That God has acted in Christ without regard to the normal hierarchies of value is demonstrated in baptism, where "there is no longer Jew or Greek, there is no longer slave or free, there is no longer male and female; for all of you are one in Christ Jesus" (Gal 3:28 NRSV). Paul's communities demonstrated an innovative, boundary-breaking capacity, cutting across ethnic, social, gender, and *household lines, because the new worth accorded to each was founded not on natural capacity, nor on social esteem, but on the unconditioned fact of the death of Christ "for you" (1 Cor 11:24; cf. 1 Cor 8:11; Rom 14:15). In this sense, Paul sums up all the traditions of the acts, sayings, and parables of Jesus in the one great act of his death. The giving of God's only Son is the definitive enactment of God's love toward the world (Rom 8:31-39). This is the "indescribable gift" (2 Cor 9:15 NRSV) by which Paul sums up the meaning of Christ, who "though [or because] he was rich, yet for your sakes he became poor, so that by his poverty you might become rich" (2 Cor 8:9 NRSV). That is the metanarrative within which all the individual narratives of Jesus' meals and parables could be best understood. Whether or not Paul knew those individual stories, there is here, at their central point, a deep congruence between the dynamic of the Gospel traditions and the enactment of the good news in the mission and theology of Paul.

On all these grounds the traditional divide between the Gospels and Paul is a gross exaggeration, for all their differences in genre and idiom. Across early Christianity, Jesus was remembered in faith and in the light of the resurrection, and we have no reliable access to a Jesus remembered in any other terms. This resurrection faith was not a departure from "history," but it framed all the historical traditions about Jesus by reference to their significance within the cosmic purposes of God. Paul's broad-brush depiction of those purposes, and his reduction of focus to the human nature, the Jewish *identity, and the death and resurrection of Jesus, is, in theological terms, both a strength and a weakness: it gets to the essentials but omits nearly all the concrete details by which these truths were enacted in the human realities of Jesus' life and death. Fortunately, the NT canon allows Paul's letters to be complemented by the Gospels, and the four Gospels to complement each other. That allows a rich diversity in understanding the identity of Jesus (Gaventa and Hays), while at the same time reinforcing that there is no significant distinction between Jesus and Paul.

See also ADAM AND CHRIST; CHRIST, MESSIAH; CHRISTOLOGY; CONVERSION AND CALL OF PAUL; CREATION AND NEW CREATION; CROSS; ESCHATOLOGY; ETHICS; GRACE; HERMENEUTICS/

Interpreting Paul; In Christ; Interpretation: New Perspective; Israel; Jesus, Sayings of; Kingdom of God/Christ; Law; Lord; Paul and Judaism; Resurrection; Sin, Guilt; Tradition.

BIBLIOGRAPHY. **D. C. Allison Jr.,** "The Pauline Epistles and the Synoptic Gospels: The Pattern of the Parallels," *NTS* 28 (1982): 1-32; idem, *Constructing Jesus: Memory, Imagination, and History* (Grand Rapids, MI: Baker Academic, 2010); **J. M. G. Barclay,** "'Offensive and Uncanny': Jesus and Paul on the Caustic Grace of God," in *Jesus and Paul Reconnected*, ed. T. D. Still (Grand Rapids, MI: Eerdmans, 2007); idem, *Paul and the Gift* (Grand Rapids, MI: Eerdmans, 2015); **R. Bultmann,** "Jesus and Paul," in *Existence and Faith* (London: Hodder and Stoughton, 1961) 183-201; idem, "The Primitive Christian Kerygma and the Historical Jesus," in *The Historical Jesus and the Kerygmatic Christ*, ed. C. E. Braaten and R. A. Harrisville (Nashville: Abingdon, 1964), 15-42; idem, "The Significance of the Historical Jesus for the Theology of Paul," in *Faith and Understanding I* (New York: Harper & Row, 1966), 220-46; **W. D. Davies,** *Paul and Rabbinic Judaism* (Philadelphia: Fortress, 1948); **D. L. Dungan,** *The Sayings of Jesus in the Churches of Paul* (Oxford: Blackwell, 1971); **J. D. G. Dunn,** *Jesus Remembered* (Grand Rapids, MI: Eerdmans, 2003); **C. Evans and A. White,** *Who Created Christianity? Fresh Approaches to the Relationship Between Jesus and Paul* (Peabody, MA: Hendrickson, 2020); **V. P. Furnish,** "The Jesus-Paul Debate: From Baur to Bultmann," *BJRL* 47 (1965): 342-81; **B. Gaventa and R. B. Hays,** eds., *Seeking the Identity of Jesus* (Grand Rapids, MI: Eerdmans, 2008); **W. Heitmüller,** "Zum Problem Paulus und Jesus," *ZNW* 13 (1912): 320-37; **E. Käsemann,** "The Problem of the Historical Jesus," in *Essays on New Testament Themes* (London: SCM Press, 1964); idem, *On Being a Disciple of the Crucified Jesus* (Grand Rapids, MI: Eerdmans, 2010); **A. Kirk,** *Memory and the Jesus Tradition* (London: T&T Clark, 2019); **A. Le Donne,** *Historical Jesus: What Can We Know and How Can We Know It?* (Grand Rapids, MI: Eerdmans, 2011); **E. P. Sanders,** *Paul and Palestinian Judaism* (Philadelphia: Fortress, 1977); idem, *Jesus and Judaism* (Philadelphia: Fortress, 1985); **A. Schweitzer,** *Paul and His Interpreters* (London: A&C Black, 1912); idem, *The Mysticism of Paul the Apostle* (London: A&C Black, 1930); **T. D. Still,** *Jesus and Paul Reconnected* (Grand Rapids, MI: Eerdmans, 2007); **J. D. Tabor,** *Paul and Jesus: How the Apostle Transformed Christianity* (New York: Simon & Schuster, 2013); **M. B. Thompson,** *Clothed with Christ: The Example and Teaching of Jesus in Romans 12.1–15.13* (Sheffield: *JSNT* Press, 1991); **G. Vermes,** *Jesus the Jew* (London: Collins, 1973); **A. J. M. Wedderburn,** ed., *Paul and Jesus: Collected Essays* (Sheffield: *JSNT* Press, 1989); **D. Wenham,** *Paul: Follower of Jesus or Founder of Christianity?* (Grand Rapids, MI: Eerdmans, 1995); idem, *Paul and Jesus: The True Story* (London: SPCK, 2002); **S. G. Wilson,** "From Jesus to Paul: The Contours and Consequences of a Debate," in *From Jesus to Paul*, ed. P. Richardson and J. C. Hurd (Waterloo, ON: Wilfrid Laurier University Press, 1984); **W. Wrede,** *Paul* (London: Philip Green, 1907); **N. T. Wright,** *Jesus and the Victory of God* (London: SPCK, 1996).

J. M. G. Barclay

JEW, PAUL THE. *See* Conversion and Call of Paul; Paul and Judaism.

JEWISH EXEGESIS. *See* Interpretation: Jewish; Old Testament in Paul; Paul and Judaism.

JEWISH GNOSTICISM. *See* Gnosis, Gnosticism; Opponents of Paul.

JOURNEYS. *See* Chronology of Paul; Paul in Acts; Travel and Itinerary Plans.

JOY, REJOICING

For Paul, joy (or rejoicing) is a product of redemption, a divine perspective that situates the present and all it contains (good or ill) in the purview of eternity. Joy does not wish away the present moment or cling to it but embraces the *knowledge of *God, revealed in the *cross of *Christ, that either extreme—*suffering or comfort—offers the same opportunity: redemption.

1. Jewish Background
2. Context
3. Theological Relationship
4. Definition
5. Result
6. Conclusion

1. Jewish Background.

Joy and rejoicing in Jewish literature are rooted in God's favor (Is 44:23; cf. Is 35:2). The establishment of new kings (1 Kings 1:40), the reception of military victories and riches (Ps 21:2; see also Deut 12:7; 33:18), and even mundane daily tasks (Eccles 3:22; cf. Eccles 11:8) merit joyous exultation, since all are understood as expressions of God's favor.

Tension increases, however, when God's favor is brought into question leading up to and during the exile. The prophets express "shouts of joy" at visions of the restoration of Israel's relationship with God (Jer 31:7; Is 12:6; 49:11; Zeph 3:14), a coming time where the exile will cease and glory will return to Zion (Is 54:1; cf. Zech 2:10). This joyous restoration, though, necessitates the destruction of Israel's enemies (Is 34:1–35:6; Jer 31:11-12; 51:48; cf. Is 35:2). Indeed, exilic imagery depicts Israel's enemies as gloating over the fallen nation (Mic 7:8; Ps 137:3, 6; cf. Ps 35:19, 24)—a malicious rejoicing, for which they will be judged (Ezek 25:6; cf. Ps 35:15). Thus, the dominant context for joy and rejoicing in Jewish literature is the annihilation of the enemies of God (Is 24:14; 65:14; cf. 1 Sam 2:1; 18:6; Ps 9:2; 35:27; 48:12; Prov 29:6; Is 9:2), prompting creation itself to joyously gloat over the fall of Israel's enemies (Is 14:8).

In Jewish literature, then, joy and rejoicing replace affliction and suffering (Ps 90:14) since the latter is birthed from unrighteous acts that remove God's favor and blessing (see Ps 32:11; cf. Lev 9:24). This context of joy and rejoicing is inherited and recrafted by Paul in light of the revelation of Christ's crucifixion.

2. Context.

Typically, in Paul, joy and rejoicing appear in contexts of suffering, whether physical or nonphysical. So in 2 Corinthians 6:3-10 Paul defends his *ministry by listing a litany of hardships endured, such as beatings, defamation, imprisonment, and loss of *honor. The list climaxes with "grieving, yet always rejoicing [*chairontes*]" (2 Cor 6:10; cf. 1 Thess 2:17-20; 3:7-9). Even regarding the joy of others, suffering provides the framework: "During a severe test of affliction, [the Macedonian church's] immense joy [*charas*] and their excessive poverty overflowed into rich generosity" (2 Cor 8:2; cf. 1 Thess 1:6-8).

3. Theological Relationship.

Joy is not, however, wed with suffering arbitrarily. Joy and suffering are united by the cross. In redemption, the believer's inheritance of Christ's story includes Christ's suffering, a progression Paul highlights.

In Colossians 1, "the inheritance of the saints" is defined as "joyfully [*charas*] giving thanks to the Father" as they "endure everything with patience" (Col 1:11-14). Joy amid opposition is secured through God's redemption, which "rescued us from the dominion of darkness and transformed us into the kingdom of his beloved Son" (Col 1:14). In Colossians 1:15-23, Paul recounts "the *gospel" (Col 1:23), emphasizing Christ's suffering (Col 1:20, 22), which reconciled "all things . . . through the blood of his cross" (Col 1:20; cf. Col 1:21-22). In Colossians 1:24, Paul does not just proclaim the gospel but himself transforms into the story of Christ: "Now I rejoice [*chairō*] in my sufferings on your behalf, and in my *flesh I make complete what lacks in Christ's sufferings on behalf of his *body, who is the church" (Col 1:24).

Redemption unites the believer with Christ in his *glory and in his suffering. Philippians 1:29 makes this clear: "For it was generously bestowed to you on behalf of Christ not only to believe in him but also to suffer on behalf of him." Such an inheritance compels Paul to replace *fear of mortality with rejoicing in Philippians 2:17, "But even if I am being poured out as a libation on the *sacrifice . . . I rejoice [*chairō*]."

Redemption, then, transforms the enemy of God (Col 1:21) into the story of God (Gal 2:20), resulting indeed in suffering, but more importantly one who, like Christ and Paul, *rejoices* amid suffering (Phil 2:18). Joy is an outworking of union with the crucified Christ.

4. Definition.

Joy is not defined as merely "being happy" during times of misery or a denial of reality, as if the suffering were miraculously transformed into a happy predicament despite the evidence. Joy is a shift in gaze, a move from beholding what is right in front of a person (positive or negative) to beholding what is beyond (God himself).

Following the model of Jesus in Gethsemane (Lk 22:42), suffering is not denied but fully understood and lamented. Yet Christ's redemption through his suffering on the cross reveals "the knowledge of God" (Col 1:9-10) and a divine perspective that no longer laments what is present, for whatever may come—positive or negative—reconciliation and transformation arise (Phil 4:10-13). Joy is the state of complete acceptance of this divine perspective. Joy is a *fruit of the Spirit (Gal 5:22) that offers the believer resolute insight flowing from the knowledge of God that, in Christ, all things, including all suffering, are ingredients for redemption.

5. Result.

Joy, then, is not the result of suffering, even if it is most starkly seen in contexts of suffering. Joy is the divine perspective that precedes all contexts, anchoring Christians to Christ so that, come what may, the divine knowledge remains unmoved. This explains why Paul ignites exhortations against anxiety

(Phil 4:6) and "all forms of evil" (1 Thess 5:22) with the command, "Rejoice in the Lord always. Again, I will say: Rejoice!" (Phil 4:4; see also Phil 3:1; 1 Thess 5:16). Joy secures the divine perspective that redemption wastes nothing—good or ill. Thus, joy liberates Christ-followers from "selfish ambition or vain conceit" (Phil 2:3) to be, like Christ (Phil 2:5) and Paul (Phil 2:2), "rejoicing in *hope, enduring in affliction, remaining constant in *prayer" (Rom 12:12; see Rom 15:13).

Naturally, joy's divine perspective leads to sharing all with fellow Christians who have need (2 Cor 9:7), for union with Christ naturally results in union with the *body* of Christ, whether in suffering or in honor (1 Cor 12:26). Joy, then, is not just an inner virtue but an external outworking of union with Christ that extends even to enemies who cause suffering (Rom 12:14; 1 Thess 5:15).

6. Conclusion.

With joy fully engaged, eternity displaces mortality, allowing the *fullness of God to transfer one's gaze from the immediate to the infinite. As such, worries fade, vengeance subsides, and the Spirit begins to produce its treasured fruit: *love. In Christ, if the present moment is filled with persecution or prosperity, the same opportunity for redemption persists, for suffering can be repurposed for redemption just as easily as comfort. Such a shift not only corrects believers' actions but anchors them in the heavenlies as they traverse the perils of earth with the knowledge of God untainted by *sin and in no way beholden to *death, otherwise known as joy.

See also Colossians, Letter to the; Corinthians, Second Letter to the; Fruit of the Spirit; Suffering.

BIBLIOGRAPHY. **E. Beyreuther and G. Finkenrath,** "Joy, Rejoice," *NIDNTT* 4:644-49; **M. Bouttier,** *Christianity According to Paul*, trans. Frank Clarke, SBT 49 (London: SCM Press, 1966); **H. Conzelmann,** "χαίρω, χαρά, συγκαίρω," *TDNT* 9:359-72; **M. J. Gorman,** *Participating in Christ: Explorations in Paul's Theology and Spirituality* (Grand Rapids, MI: Baker, 2109); **W. G. Morrice,** *Joy in the New Testament* (Grand Rapids, MI: Eerdmans, 1984); **E. A. C. Pretorius,** "A Key to the Literature on Philippians," *Neot* 23 (1989): 125-53; **S. Voorwinde,** "Paul's Joy in Philippians," *RTR* 76 (December 2017): 145-71; **N. T. Wright,** *Paul and the Faithfulness of God*, vol. 1 (Minneapolis: Fortress, 2013).

S. J. Wood

JUDAISM. *See* Israel; Paul and Judaism.

JUDAIZERS

The term *Judaizer* is by all accounts the most convenient label that scholars have given to a supposed group of Jewish Christians who chased after Paul's *Gentile *mission to advocate Jewish practice over against his law-free *gospel. This understanding, or slight variations of it, has dominated the landscape of Pauline scholarship since the time of F. C. Baur in the mid-1800s (see Dunn; Goulder). In the past two decades, however, scholars (e.g., Bauckham) have rightly challenged both the appropriateness of the label Judaizer and its concomitant historical reconstructions that derive from a supposed conflict between Paul and the *church in *Jerusalem.

It is beyond the scope of this short piece to trace the remarkable afterlife of Baur's reconstruction of earliest Christianity (see Bauspiess, Landmesser, and Lincicum; cf. Nanos, 110-92). Instead, the aim of this discussion is (1) to define the misleading appellation *Judaizer*, (2) to assess the most significant alternative labels, and (3) to summarize a way forward after revisiting the biblical evidence.

1. The Term *Judaizer* and Its Problems
2. Assessing Alternative Labels: Opponents, Teachers, and Influencers
3. Plotting a Way Forward: The Agitators from Galatia

1. The Term *Judaizer* and Its Problems.

The term *Judaizer* is derived from the verb *ioudaizein* (to judaize/live as a Jew), which is used only once in the NT (see also Josephus, *J.W.* 2.454, 463). It appears in Paul's letter to the Galatian churches, when he recounts his public rebuke of Peter at *Syrian Antioch: "But when I saw that they were not walking in step with the truth of the good news, I said to Cephas in front of everyone, 'If you—being a Jew—live as gentiles and not as Jews, how is it that you are compelling gentiles to live as Jews [*ioudaizein*]?'" (Gal 2:14). In this infamous "Antioch incident," Paul recalls that after certain men from James arrived, Peter suddenly withdrew table *fellowship from Gentile believers because he feared the ones from *circumcision (Gal 2:12). Peter's hypocrisy triggered a massive fissure between Jewish and Gentile believers in Antioch when other Jews joined in his hypocrisy, even Barnabas (Gal 2:13). Paul's mention of Barnabas is significant for two reasons. First, if one accepts the South Galatian theory, the Galatians would likely have known him personally (see Acts 13:42-50; 14:1-3, 12, 20). Second, if one also accepts the evidence in Acts 11:22-26, Barnabas represented Jerusalem's approval of Gentile inclusion in

Antioch and even recruited Saul from Tarsus to serve in Antioch's Jewish-Gentile mission. Thus, Peter's shift in policy and Barnabas's bombshell defection critically destabilized the very headquarters of the Gentile mission.

It is in this context that one must understand the meaning of the term *ioudaizein*. Three salient features emerge from this narrative retelling in Galatians. First, someone who "judaizes" is technically a Gentile who lives as a Jew, *not* a Jew who forces Gentiles to live as Jews (on this point, see esp. Novenson, following Mason). Second, Paul accuses Peter, *not* the ones who had come from James, of compelling Gentiles to "judaize." Third, the context is Jewish and Gentile table fellowship, which confirms that "judaizing" pertains to the application of the good news, *not* to a supposed "rival gospel" over against "Paul's gospel." The evidence in Galatians, in other words, does not require one to conjure up a party of Jewish Christian legalists who challenged Paul's mission with a competing gospel. For these reasons, the label *Judaizer* should, at the very least, be dropped from the reconstructed story of Paul's *ministry adventures with respect to any of his supposed rivals or opponents. Whatever one posits about the "false brothers" in 2 Corinthians 11:26 or the "dogs" in Philippians 3:2, one must not assume they belong to an organized anti-Paul movement (see further Grindheim).

2. Assessing Alternative Labels: Opponents, Teachers, and Influencers.

If the term *Judaizer* is a misapplied tag, a number of scholars have sought an alternative label for the ones who were confusing the Galatian believers. These must now be assessed briefly.

2.1. Opponents. In the 1970s, Hans Dieter Betz broke new ground in studies on Galatians by comparing its literary style with the ancient rhetorical conventions of the Greco-Roman world. Betz categorized this *letter (especially Gal 1–2) as judicial rhetoric, which confirmed the view that Paul was defending himself from opponents who were maligning his apostolic status and his Gentile mission. Although widely influential, Betz's conclusions have been met with serious critique. First, the rest of Galatians does not easily fit into the mold of judicial rhetoric, and other scholars have demonstrated that Galatians (including Gal 1–2) shares features with deliberative and epideictic rhetoric (e.g., Hall; Smit; Hester). Second, in a careful methodological study, Philip Kern rightly questions whether Galatians conforms to ancient rhetorical handbooks at all, which in any case were used for public declamations, not epistolary literature.

In more recent studies on Galatians, scholars have rightly sought to read Galatians in the light of Greco-Roman epistolary conventions. Mark Nanos, for example, has convincingly argued that Galatians is a letter of rebuke, which is signaled with the rebuke formula ("I am amazed") that launches into a right scolding of the Galatian churches for giving ear to those who were compelling them to get circumcised: "I am amazed [*thaumazō*] that you are so quickly turning away from the One who called you by the grace of Messiah, to a different 'good news'—not that there is another, but only some who are confusing you and want to distort the Good News of Messiah" (Gal 1:6-7 TLV). Although *opponents of Paul may still lurk in the dark alleys of Galatians, it is by no means apparent from the literary structure of the letter. To arrive at that conclusion, one must mirror read Paul's statements in Galatians (e.g. Paul asserts his apostleship is from God because some are questioning his apostolic status), a technique that crumbles under the heavy methodological weight placed on such readings (see Hardin, "Galatians 1–2 Without a Mirror"; Barclay).

2.2. Teachers. In his creative reconstruction on the crisis in Galatia, J. Louis Martyn seeks to rehabilitate the aims and motives of those whom Paul opposes in Galatians. Martyn uses the neutral term *teachers* and concludes that this group was not seeking to destroy Paul's mission. They simply had their own law-observant mission, against which Paul reacts. Martyn's detailed reconstruction, however ingenious, only works if one completely excludes Paul's autographed finale in Galatians 6:11-18. In those verses, Paul reveals the self-preserving motives of those who were compelling the Galatian Gentiles to get circumcised. Martyn, however, dismisses this unsavory description as nothing more than unreliable exaggerations of an irritated *apostle (Martyn, 317; see also Sumney, 134-59). Martyn therefore misses the important point that Paul's accusations in Galatians 6:12-17 are best understood within his wider strategy of contrasting his own God-pleasing motives with the people-pleasing motives of those confusing them (for further elaboration, see below and Hardin, "Galatians 1–2 Without a Mirror," 296-303; cf. Hardin 2008, 94-102). Throwing out these concluding verses would undermine not only Paul's rhetorical strategy but also the very moral high ground he was seeking to establish throughout the letter, especially when one reckons that the "teachers" would have been poised to defend themselves against trumped-up accusations.

2.3. *Influencers.* In his groundbreaking work on Galatians, Nanos also suggests a neutral label, but he prefers the term *influencers* because of their clear influence on the Galatian congregations (Nanos, 193-99). In his wider thesis, Nanos is probably correct that this group did not actually come from Jerusalem (or anywhere else) but were from Galatia (159-83; see also Hardin 2008, 92-94). But his argument that they were not themselves Jesus-followers stretches the slender evidence in Galatians to its breaking point. This conclusion, for example, depends on an ironical understanding of the phrase *heteron euangelion* (Gal 1:6), which he argues had nothing to do with Messiah Jesus. This reading is unconvincing, not least because it lacks any markers of irony and runs against the natural understanding of the surrounding context of Galatians 1:6-9 (Nanos, 296-97). It also falls aground when one considers the entire autobiographical narrative is to demonstrate a similar scenario where the gospel of Messiah was perverted, not absent altogether.

Nanos also suggests the influencers may have been Gentile proselytes from the local community (Nanos, 234-44; cf. Munck). But again, this theory puts too much burden on the translation of the singular participle in Galatians 6:13 (*hoi peritemnomenoi*, which also has a significant textual variant). Despite these shortcomings, Nanos has paved new ground both in reading Galatians as a letter of rebuke and in understanding Paul's Gentile mission *within* the bounds of Judaism (see also Soulen; Rudolph; Nanos and Zetterholm; Hardin 2013).

3. Plotting a Way Forward: The Agitators from Galatia.

If these aforementioned labels are inadequate, the best way forward is to take one's cue from Paul's own descriptions within the letter. Paul refers to this group in four major sections (Gal 1:6-9; 4:13-17; 5:7-12; 6:12-17), each time contrasting their aims with his own (Hardin, "Galatians 1–2 Without a Mirror," 296-98; 2013, 160-61):

> Gal 1:7 Some are agitating [*tarassontes*] you and who are wanting to distort [*metastrepsai*] the gospel of Messiah.

> Gal 4:17 They are zealous for you—not in a good way—but they are wanting to shut you out [*ekkleisai*] so you would seek them.

> Gal 5:10-12 The one who is agitating [*tarassōn*] you will be bear the penalty. . . . Indeed, I wish the ones upsetting [*anastatountes*] you would castrate themselves.

> Gal 6:12 The ones wanting to make a good showing [*euprosōpēsai*] in the flesh are compelling [*anankazousin*] you to be circumcised, only that they would not be persecuted because of the cross of Messiah.

Paul also asks two rhetorical questions to the Galatians that further illuminate his thinking:

> Gal 3:1 Who has bewitched you?

> Gal 5:7 Who hindered you from obeying the truth?

If these claims about this group in any way match up with the actual situation on the ground, then one can move the discussion forward in at least two ways. First, one can make a strong case for using the appellation *agitators*, since Paul himself uses it twice (Gal 1:6; 5:10; Muddiman; Hardin 2014). Second, from these verses one can begin to piece together who these agitators were and what motivated them. Without unpacking the detailed arguments to sustain them, the following three theses will conclude this discussion (see further Hardin 2014). First, the agitators were local to Galatia (see above). Second, they were Jewish believers in Messiah Jesus who were compelling Gentiles to be circumcised and to live as Jews. Third, they were motivated not by nomistic or anti-Pauline convictions but—as was Peter in Antioch—by expediency (avoiding persecution). If the agitators themselves were worried about being persecuted, this raises an immediate question: Persecution from whom? In the wake of the older theory that they were concerned with Judean zealots (Jewett), scholars have provided wide-ranging answers to this question, including the civic authorities for not participating in the imperial cult (Winter), local Jewish communities (Nanos), "a fanatical Diaspora brand of Pharisaism" (Muddiman, 260), or a combination of these scenarios (Hardin 2008, 110-14). Seeking to answer that question, however, falls beyond the purview of this essay.

If the above discussion is on the right track, then it is time to bury the label *Judaizers* as a descriptor for a supposed group of Jewish Christian missionaries who opposed or challenged Paul's credentials or Gentile mission. As shocking as it might sound to those still under the sway of Baur's historical reconstruction of early Christianity, the Judaizers never existed. They are but an apparition of the enlightened Pauline imagination.

See also Galatians, Letter to the; Opponents of Paul; Paul and Judaism.

BIBLIOGRAPHY. **J. M. G. Barclay,** "Mirror-Reading a Polemical Letter: Galatians as a Test Case," *JSNT* 31 (1987): 73-93; **R. Bauckham,** "James, Peter, and the Gentiles," in *The Missions of James, Peter, and Paul: Tensions in Early Christianity*, ed. B. Chilton and C. A. Evans, NovTSup 115 (Leiden: Brill, 2005), 91-142; **M. Bauspiess, C. Landmesser, and D. Lincicum,** eds., *Ferdinand Christian Baur and the History of Early Christianity*, trans. R. F. Brown and P. C. Hodgson (Oxford: Oxford University Press, 2017); **H. D. Betz,** "The Literary Composition and Function of Paul's Letter to the Galatians." *NTS* 21 (1975): 353-79; idem, *Galatians: A Commentary on Paul's Letter to the Churches in Galatia*, Hermeneia (Philadelphia: Fortress, 1979); **J. D. G. Dunn,** "The Relationship Between Paul and Jerusalem According to Galatians 1 and 2," *NTS* 28, no. 4 (1982): 461-78; **M. D. Goulder,** *A Tale of Two Missions* (London: SCM Press, 1994); **S. Grindheim,** *The Crux of Election: Paul's Critique of the Jewish Confidence in the Election of Israel*, WUNT 2/202 (Tübingen: Mohr Siebeck, 2005); **R. G. Hall,** "The Rhetorical Outline for Galatians: A Reconsideration," *JBL* 106 (1987): 277-87; **J. K. Hardin,** *Galatians and the Imperial Cult: A Critical Analysis of the First-Century Social Context of Paul's Letter*, WUNT 2/237 (Tubingen: Mohr Siebeck, 2008); idem, "'If I Still Proclaim Circumcision' (Gal 5.11a): Paul, the Law, and Gentile Circumcision," *JSPHL* 3 (2013): 17-36; idem, "Galatians 1–2 Without a Mirror: Reflections on Paul's Conflict with the Agitators," *TynBul* 65, no. 2 (2014): 275-303; **J. D. Hester,** "Epideictic Rhetoric and Persona in Galatians 1 and 2," in *The Galatians Debate: Contemporary Issues in Rhetorical and Historical Interpretation*, ed. M. D. Nanos (Peabody, MA: Hendrickson, 2002), 181-96; **R. Jewett,** "The Agitators and the Galatian Congregation," *NTS* 17 (1971): 198-212; **P. H. Kern,** *Rhetoric and Galatians: Assessing an Approach to Paul's Epistle*, SNTSMS 101 (Cambridge: Cambridge University Press, 1998); **J. L. Martyn,** "A Law-Observant Mission to Gentiles: The Background of Galatians," *SJT* 38, no. 3 (1985): 307-24; **S. Mason,** "Jews, Judaeans, Judaizing, Judaism: Problems of Categorization in Ancient History," *JSJ* 38 (2007): 457-512; **J. Muddiman,** "An Anatomy of Galatians," in *Crossing the Boundaries: Essays in Biblical Interpretation in Honour of Michael D. Goulder*, ed. S. E. Porter, P. Joyce, and D. E. Orton (Leiden: Brill, 1994), 257-70; **J. Munck,** *Paul and the Salvation of Mankind*, trans. Frank Clarke (London: SCM Press, 1959); **M. D. Nanos,** *The Irony of Galatians: Paul's Letter in First-Century Context* (Minneapolis: Fortress, 2002); **M. D. Nanos and M. Zetterholm,** eds., *Paul Within Judaism: Restoring the First-Century Context to the Apostle* (Minneapolis: Fortress, 2015); **M. V. Novenson,** "Paul's Former Occupation in Ioudaismos," in *The Epistle to the Galatians and Christian Theology*, ed. N. T. Wright, M. W. Elliott, and S. J. Hafemann (Grand Rapids, MI: Baker, 2014), 24-39; **D. J. Rudolph,** *A Jew to the Jews: Jewish Contours of Pauline Flexibility in 1 Corinthians 9:19-23*, WUNT 2/304 (Tübingen: Mohr Siebeck, 2011); **J. F. M. Smit,** "The Letter of Paul to the Galatians: A Deliberative Speech," *NTS* 35 (1989): 1-26; **R. K. Soulen,** *The God of Israel and Christian Theology* (Minneapolis: Fortress, 1996); **J. L. Sumney,** *"Servants of Satan," "False Brothers," and Other Opponents of Paul*, JSNTSup 188 (Sheffield: Sheffield Academic Press, 1999); **B. W. Winter,** "Civic Obligations: Galatians 6:11-18," in *Seek the Welfare of the City: Christians as Benefactors and Citizens*, First Century Christians in the Graeco-Roman World (Grand Rapids, MI: Eerdmans, 1994), 123-44.

J. K. Hardin

JUDGE. *See* God; Judgment.

JUDGMENT

Within Paul's occasional *letters, judgment is embedded within the story of God's redeeming plan in the world through Messiah Jesus. For this reason, one cannot possibly speak of judgment apart from his message of *salvation, which began with Adam and Eve in the garden, was enshrined in the covenant promises to *Abraham and David, and was anticipated both in the Mosaic *covenant and in the prophetic messages of *hope for future salvation. This promise of redemption was fulfilled in Messiah Jesus through his redeeming work on the *cross and in the *resurrection. Messiah Jesus inaugurated God's Spirit-filled covenant community, who now experience "new *creation" (2 Cor 5:17) and eagerly anticipate his parousia (appearing), when he will judge all things and bring final restoration to the world and to his people. Paul's understanding of judgment thus belongs to the broader contours of God's faithfulness to redeem his people and the world from the curse of *sin and *death.

At the same time, one cannot hope to be exhaustive or definitive in piecing together Paul's understanding of judgment. First, God's final judgment is still a future event. Paul's letters are therefore intended not to reveal every little detail but to encourage and to challenge his congregations to persevere in their *faith. Second, Paul's letters are situational. As Paul corresponds with his congregations, one is limited to a fractional glimpse of Paul's understanding of judgment. Having made these qualifications, one can confidently detect at least four aspects of Paul's theologizing on judgment.

1. Judgment and the Scriptural Story
2. Judgment and Justification Through Messiah Jesus
3. Judgment and God's Spirit-Filled Community
4. Judgment and Tomorrow

1. Judgment and the Scriptural Story.
As a Pharisee, Paul's understanding of judgment is fused to his reading of God's story. First, *God alone is creator and judge. Paul reflects theologically on God's creative acts in Genesis 1–3 (Rom 5–8; 1 Cor 15). The first human couple is distinct and set apart from all creation, but they are nevertheless mortal and fleshly (1 Cor 15:35-57). Adam experiences these limitations par excellence when he sins against God's *law in the garden and receives the punishment of death (Rom 5:12-21; 7:7-12; 1 Cor 15:20-22, 45-49). At the same time, God springs into action a magnificent rescue plan that began before the foundation of the world (Eph 1:4). From this story, Paul concludes that all humans stand in a long line of sinners, who follow in Adam's footsteps (Rom 5:12). Even creation experiences the destructive afterlife of Adam's sin (Rom 8:19-22). Thus, Genesis 1–3 is the source and origin for the story of judgment and redemption.

Second, God's covenant promises reveal his plan to redeem all creation through his righteous judgments. According to Paul, God's covenant with Abraham not only points to the *forgiveness of sins through Abraham's descendant (Gal 3:16) but also models the appropriate response of faith for both Jew and *Gentile (Rom 4; Gal 3). Paul furthermore draws from the Mosaic covenant, namely that God's people (redeemed from Egyptian *slavery) must worship the one true God (1 Cor 8:4-6; Deut 6:4-6) and keep his commands. Their response would activate God's concomitant covenant blessings for obedience or curses for rebellion (Deut 27–30; Gal 3:10-14). Tragically, God's people had overwhelmingly abandoned God and therefore experienced judgment (Rom 2:1–3:20; 5:21; 7:1-25; Gal 3:10-14; 1 Cor 15:56). For Paul, however, this dire situation is not final. He points to the covenant with David (see section 2) and draws deeply from the Jewish *hope in a new covenant through Messiah Jesus and the Spirit (see section 3). In this way, God's people look forward to a future judgment when God will redeem his people and set the world to rights.

The building blocks of Paul's understanding of judgment are therefore found in the grand story of God as revealed in the Scriptures. To sever judgment from this larger story would be to misappropriate the themes of judgment found in Paul's letters.

2. Judgment and Justification Through Messiah Jesus.
Within this grand story, Paul believes that all people, both Jew and Gentile, are equally accountable to God, who does not show partiality (Rom 2:6-11; Gal 2:6; Thielman). For Jews, the basis of this judgment is seen most clearly through their response to God. This is both an individualistic calling to covenant faithfulness and, vitally, a corporate calling for the entire covenant community. Paul points to a common pattern of sin–exile–restoration and concludes that, before Messiah Jesus, God's people were still living in "exile," awaiting ultimate restoration (Rom 9:30–10:21). For Gentiles, the basis of this judgment begins with their response to (or perversion of) God's special gift of creation. Paul notes that Gentiles are subject to the gods of this world, who pervert God's creation by worshiping it instead of him as Creator and Judge (Rom 1:18-32). Gentiles who are not in Messiah are therefore perishing and are under his righteous judgment (Rom 1:18-32; Gal 4:8-10; Eph 2:1-3; 4:17-19; 1 Thess 1:9). The sober verdict is that all people are enemies of God (Rom 5:6-10), are guilty of God's righteous judgment (Rom 1:18–3:20), and experience judgment (death), in and with Adam (Rom 5:12).

Against this backdrop, Paul introduces the "good news" (*euangelion*) of the Lord Messiah Jesus, who is the climactic fulfillment of God's covenant promises to redeem the world from sin and judgment. One can highlight at least four aspects of these covenant promises. First, Messiah Jesus fulfills the promise to David. Paul's ubiquitous use of the honorific title Messiah (*Christos*) indicates that Jesus is the promised "son of David" (Rom 1:3; 2 Tim 2:8), who has been given authority to rule over (i.e, judge) all things (1 Cor 15:24-28, 50-57; Eph 1:19-23; Phil 2:9-11; Col 1:15-20). Second, Messiah Jesus is the promised seed of Abraham (Gal 3:16), who justifies the ungodly through faith in Jesus (Rom 4:1-8).

Third, and in fulfillment of these twin promises, God sent his Son, born of a woman, born under the law's *curses, to redeem his people through his perfect *sacrifice (substitution) on the cross (Rom 5:12-21; 8:1-4; 1 Cor 15:3-4; Gal 3:10-14; 4:4-5). But that is not all; one can also observe how Paul artfully interlaces these twin promises ("son of David" and "son of Abraham") in his exposition of the Abraham story in Romans 4. A key word in this chapter is the accounting term *reckoning* (Gk. *logizomai*), which Paul draws both from Abraham's faith confession (Gen 15:6) and from David's sin confession (Ps 32:8). Paul's language of *justification in Romans 4 is therefore linked to both faith and forgiveness. Justification through Messiah Jesus (by faith) is the antidote to judgment from sin. It is therefore fitting that Paul concludes by confessing "our Lord Jesus" (Rom 4:24), who is Abraham's "seed" (Gal 3:16) and the promised Davidic "Messiah" Jesus.

Fourth, Messiah Jesus brings restoration from judgment by establishing his promised Spirit-filled community (2 Cor 3:7-18). The *Holy Spirit guarantees the inheritance of God's children (Eph 1:13-14), empowers a life of obedience to God (Gal 5:16-18; Rom 8:1-17), and equips God's new covenant community (1 Cor 12–14). The age of the Spirit has thus broken into the present, signaling that God's covenant promise of salvation from judgment has already been inaugurated (but not fully realized).

3. Judgment and God's Spirit-Filled Community.
Interpreters of Paul have long debated how this salvation from judgment through the gospel of Messiah Jesus squares with Paul's statements on the divine judgment of those *within* God's Spirit-filled community. To resolve this tension, one can make the following observations. First, Paul's vision of salvation from judgment is robustly set out in Romans 8. He begins emphatically that "there is now no condemnation for those who are in Messiah" because Messiah has condemned sin in the *flesh. Furthermore, the Holy Spirit (1) assures God's people that they belong to his family (calling him "Abba, Father"), (2) guides them in the ways of *righteousness, and (3) even intercedes for them as they await final redemption. Paul's thinking is decisive: those who are found in Messiah (who also intercedes for Paul himself) will never be condemned and will never be separated from the *love of God.

Second, as believers eagerly await their final redemption in the future, Paul calls them in the present to be led by the Spirit in the "present evil age" (Gal 1:4; 5:13–6:10). This Spirit-renewed life of faith results in godly character (Rom 5:1-5; Gal 5:22-26) and enables believers in Messiah to fulfill God's law through love as they (super)naturally produce the fruits of righteousness. By contrast, Paul holds out the sober reality that believers might continue to gratify their fleshly cravings and thus be subject to God's judgment (Gal 5:19-21). Paul therefore finds no contradiction in asserting that all believers will receive recompense for the things they have done, whether good or bad (2 Cor 5:10).

Third, Paul's letters are a living testimony that God's people were at times woefully imperfect and that they continued to contend with sin and immaturity and even to flirt dangerously with God's judgment. As a test case to this struggle, one needs only consider the laundry list of Corinthian dysfunctions. To the community that has allowed a grievous sexual sin to grow up among the weeds of their disunity, Paul casts judgment on the guilty man in the name of Messiah and by his Spirit and calls on the congregation to do the same. Still, this is no punitive "away with him" declaration but an urgent call to repent and therefore to be saved on the final day of judgment (1 Cor 5:1-13). More than this, Paul is concerned that the community, as a whole, has failed to live as God's redeemed people: "The Church must do *in the present* among its own membership what the one God will do *in the future* in relation to the rest of the world" (Wright 2013, 978). To those who think it is their right to go to Gentile temple feasts, Paul responds with a resounding, "No, you may not!" This is not only because they might lure a brother or sister back into *idolatry and thus thrust them into the sphere of God's judgment (1 Cor 8:1-13) but also because they themselves might fall into sin and therefore perish in the desert, like their ancestors (1 Cor 10:1-13). To those who make a mockery of the Lord's Table by arranging themselves according to *wealth and power, Paul declares that they eat and drink judgment on themselves—some have even gotten sick and died (1 Cor 11:17-34). The irony of this catalogue of catastrophes is that the Corinthians were judging *Paul* for his lack of eloquence in public speaking (2 Cor 10:10), and yet they should have been preparing to judge the world and even angels (1 Cor 6:2)!

Fourth, Paul's letters reveal his conviction that, at the final judgment, *servants of the *gospel message (Paul himself included) will be accountable for their work. Again, Paul's Corinthian correspondence is instructive. God's servants will be judged (1) by their labors as his field hands (1 Cor 3:1-9), (2) by their methods as his builders (1 Cor 3:10-17), and (3) by their secret motives as his household workers (1 Cor 4:1-5). Paul holds out the possibility that their work might even be burned up in judgment before their very own singed eyelashes. This perspective explains Paul's own abandonment of his apostolic rights (*marriage, salary) and his accommodation to all people in proclaiming the gospel (1 Cor 9:1-23). At the end of his life, this also explains his remark to Timothy that he has "finished the race" (2 Tim 4:6-8).

Fifth, in Romans Paul explains that his "to the Jew first" principle applies not only to matters of salvation (Rom 1:16) but also to matters of judgment (Rom 2:9-10). This is because God's people have been given the privileges of being his people, from whom the Messiah has come (Rom 9:1-5). Thus, even in judgment Paul is thinking in terms of God's covenant promises and their fulfillment.

In summary, while Paul looks forward to the promise of final redemption from judgment, he simultaneously calls the Spirit-filled community of believers in Messiah Jesus to live a life of obedience today on the basis of the (sure) hope of their redemption tomorrow.

4. Judgment and Tomorrow.

As seen in the above discussion, Paul's whole cosmic landscape is predicated on salvation from final judgment, which will be revealed at the parousia of Messiah. From his letters, however, one can observe at least three further aspects of this final judgment with respect to its execution. First, God will vindicate his people. Paul encourages the persecuted Thessalonians with this message by declaring that the day of the Lord will come as a thief in the night to sweep away all those who oppose God's people, including the *"man of lawlessness" (1 Thess 5:1-11; 2 Thess 1:5-6; 2:1-12).

Second, the dead in Messiah (participation) will be raised to new life and thus gloriously delivered from judgment. In his stirring defense of the bodily resurrection, Paul explains that Messiah is the firstfruits of the resurrection and that all those "in Messiah" will be raised with imperishable *bodies as his fully redeemed people (see 2 Cor 4:17–5:10).

Third, Messiah Jesus will establish his *kingdom through the defeat of all his enemies, including Death (and its stinger, Sin). God has in fact appointed Messiah Jesus to be the rightful king over all his enemies (Paul carefully draws on the messianic promises in Ps 8; 110).

Fourth, God will establish new creation when his people and all creation enjoy life and liberation from sin and death. Paul speaks of this future with the particular Jewish terms "the *Jerusalem above" (Gal 4:26), "new creation" (Gal 6:15; 2 Cor 5:17), and "kingdom of God" (1 Cor 15:24, 50). Seen in this way, judgment is a positive thing for God's people: "'Judgment' is thus the other end of the long outer narrative from 'good creation' itself . . . good news for all who long to see creation restored" (Wright 2013, 482).

In summary, Paul points forward to a grand assize, when God will judge all people and powers and fully establish the kingdom of God (1 Cor 15:24-28, 50-57). The good news of Jesus contains both elements of deliverance (for faith) and judgment (for disbelief). Paul's concept of judgment is therefore rooted in a robust Jewish understanding that God has promised to reverse the curse of sin and has all authority to judge all things. In the resurrection and ascension of Jesus, God has given this authority to the *Lord Jesus. In this context of hope for the future and perseverance for today Paul utters his eschatological call, *Marana tha* ("Come, O Lord!"; 1 Cor 16:22).

See also ESCHATOLOGY; JUSTIFICATION; SALVATION; SIN, GUILT; TRIUMPH; WRATH, DESTRUCTION.

BIBLIOGRAPHY. **J. M. G. Barclay,** *Paul and the Gift* (Grand Rapids, MI: Eerdmans, 2015); **M. F. Bird,** "Judgment and Justification in Paul: A Review Article," *BBR* 18 (2008): 299-313; **A. B. Caneday,** "Judgment, Behavior, and Justification According to Paul's Gospel in Romans 2," *JSPHL* 1 (2011): 153-92; **D. A. Carson, P. T. O'Brien, and M. A. Seifrid,** eds., *Justification and Variegated Nomism,* vol. 1, *The Complexities of Second Temple Judaism* (Grand Rapids, MI: Baker Academic, 2001); idem, *Justification and Variegated Nomism,* vol. 2, *The Paradoxes of Paul* (Grand Rapids, MI: Baker Academic, 2004); **J. R. Coulson,** *The Righteous Judgment of God: Aspects of Judgment in Paul's Letters* (Eugene, OR: Wipf & Stock, 2016); **J. D. G. Dunn,** *The Theology of Paul the Apostle* (Grand Rapids, MI: Eerdmans, 1998); **D. W. Kuck,** *Judgment and Community Conflict: Paul's Use of Apocalyptic Judgment Language in 1 Corinthians 3:5–4:5,* NovTSup 66 (Leiden: Brill, 1992); **D. R. Rudolph,** "'To the Jew First': Paul's Vision for the Priority of Israel in the Life of the Church," *Kesher: A Journal of Messianic Judaism* (2020): 11-25; **C. Stettler,** "Paul, the Law and Judgement by Works," *EvQ* 76 (2004): 195-215; **F. Thielman,** "God's Righteousness as God's Fairness in Romans 1:17: An Ancient Perspective on a Significant Phrase," *JETS* 54 (2011): 35-48; **S. H. Travis,** *Christ and the Judgement of God: The Limits of Divine Retribution in New Testament*

Thought (Peabody, MA: Hendrickson, 2009); **N. T. Wright,** *Paul and the Faithfulness of God*, 2 vols., COQG (London: SPCK, 2013); idem, "Justification by (Covenantal) Faith to the (Covenantal) Doers: Romans 2 Within the Argument of the Letter," *The Covenant Quarterly* 72 (2014): 95-108.

J. K. Hardin

JUSTICE. *See* God; Judgment; Justification; Righteousness.

JUSTIFICATION

Justification is God's powerful action to declare or set right humans in relation to himself. Debates over justification in Paul have ebbed and flowed since the Reformation, and they have been reignited in the wake of the renewed interest since the 1970s in Pauline texts that shed light on Paul's relationship to his Jewish heritage. Particular attention has been paid to passages in which Paul discusses justification, raising many issues, such as how Paul's "doctrine" of justification relates to contemporary Jewish teaching, the relationship of human and divine action, the contrast between *faith and works, and the place of justification within Paul's theology.

Protestant exegesis since the Reformation, because of post-Reformation dogmatic and theological developments, generally regards justification in forensic terms. By virtue of their faith in *Christ, *God declared repentant sinners no longer guilty of the penalty for their *sin. Because of the *death of Christ, God could forgive sinners and declare them righteous. Many, if not most, Protestant interpreters go further to note that this declaration of *righteousness was due to the imputation of Christ's righteousness. Another general observation about Protestant exegesis, across most dogmatic traditions and systems of theology, is that it associates justification with the event that occurs at conversion. That is, justification sets right the sinner's relation to God, sanctification describes the sinner's gradual growth in *holiness, and glorification is the full transformation of justified sinners.

This scenario held sway until late into the twentieth century. Until that time, debates over justification were dominated by German scholars who were focused on identifying the place and significance of justification—understood in forensic terms—in Paul's theology. The dominant position had been that justification by faith was the center of Paul's theological vision, the substance of his *gospel *preaching. An exception was William Wrede, who denied that the message of justification by faith was what Paul preached during his *ministry. It was, rather, only a polemical rhetorical tool he used to address the churches in Rome and Galatia that were struggling with unifying as communities across ethnic lines. Albert Schweitzer also departed from the consensus, arguing that justification was "a subsidiary crater" within the larger theological concern of being mystically (or spiritually) united to Christ. Schweitzer envisioned Paul's theology in cosmic terms and, perhaps because he was working with an understanding of justification common in his day, saw Paul's doctrine of righteousness by faith in individual rather than in cosmic terms. For him, approaching Paul's theology through the lens of justification obscured nearly the whole of Paul's theological vision.

Since the late 1970s, scholars in the English-speaking world have reevaluated the very character of justification. Ernst Käsemann, the father of the *apocalyptic school of Pauline interpretation, stressed the cosmic dimensions of the righteousness of God and therefore of justification. He maintained that the matter must be understood against the backdrop of contested cosmic fields of power, with hostile cosmic forces holding humanity enslaved and contesting the sovereignty of God. The righteousness of God is his saving power to reassert his kingship and authority over *creation. For Käsemann, then, justification is the manifestation of the righteousness of God and is the claim on humanity made by the sovereign God.

Another development, and certainly the most critical one for determining the landscape of Pauline studies since, is the work of E. P. Sanders, who reevaluated the place of righteousness in the Judaism(s) of Paul's day. His most lasting contribution was breaking the hold that a certain conception of justification in Paul over against Judaism had attained in Protestant exegesis. Broadly speaking, interpreters had long read Paul's negative statements in Romans and Galatians that justification did not come about by "*works of *law" to indicate the legalism of Judaism. From this perspective, Paul portrayed Judaism as a religion of "works-righteousness" that required the accumulation of merit through good works in order to present to God a claim for *salvation on the last day. This was an impossible task, according to this vision of Paul, since no one could perfectly obey the Mosaic law or render to God the life of moral perfection God required.

Sanders's work profoundly challenged this consensus by demonstrating that the varieties of first-century Judaism were not legalistic and that this was a Christian theological imposition of a way of thinking theologically that did not rightly regard the priority of Israel's *election and the gracious dimensions of "covenantal nomism." Sanders's work sparked new research avenues into Paul and his relation to Judaism, along with more intense investigation of Judaism and Jewish history and *identity. With regard to justification, however, Sanders's work bore fruit in that it provoked a reevaluation of Paul's negative statements about justification in Romans and Galatians—that justification did not come about by works of law. Scholars took up the questions of whether and why Paul portrayed Judaism as legalistic if Jewish texts did not indicate that righteousness came by legalism. That is, reevaluations of the nature of justification were to a great extent driven by Paul's negative statements regarding justification in Romans and Galatians, and not necessarily his positive ones.

In the wake of Sanders's work, several proposals for configuring the nature of justification have emerged. N. T. Wright has argued against justification understood as righteousness imputed to sinners (among many others who have objected to this notion; see also Dunn). Wright claims that justification belongs within a law-court scenario, though imputation gets the metaphor wrong. Rather than righteousness being transferred from one party in the courtroom to another, the law court has to do with vindication of righteousness. Because the righteousness of God (*dikaiosynē theou*) has to do with God's faithfulness to his promises to set creation right and redeem his people, justification (*dikaiosynē*) has to do with vindicating or demonstrating those who belong to God's *covenant people. Justification is the eschatological declaration of the status of being rightly related to God brought forward into the present.

For apocalyptic interpreters of Paul, following Käsemann, justification has more to do with deliverance (de Boer; D. Campbell 2009; Martyn). It is usually rendered "rectification," which has to do not so much with a legal declaration at one's conversion but with liberation from the realm of the present evil age, held enslaved by hostile cosmic powers, and transfer into the new creation, which is the presence of the future *kingdom of God by the power of the Spirit.

A number of interpreters maintain that justification has merely to do with the forensic declaration of *forgiveness and the imputation of righteousness to repentant sinners (Schreiner; Vickers; Westerholm). While justification is doubtless related to other aspects of God's work of redemption for Paul, justification as such must be understood in a more limited sense.

1. The Language of Justification
2. Righteousness in the Old Testament
3. Contexts of Justification
4. Justification and Works of Law
5. Justification by Faith
6. Justification "in Christ"
7. Justification as Rectification
8. Present and Future Justification
9. Paul and James on Justification

1. The Language of Justification.

Paul's language for justification involves the *dik-* word group, which holds together a complex of thought that English does not capture well. The verb *dikaioō* is often translated as "to justify" but could also be translated as "to set right, to vindicate, to rectify." The noun *dikaiosynē* is often translated as "righteousness" but could also be translated as "justice" or "justification." The adjective *dikaios* means "righteous" but also "just." The noun *dikaiōma* means "righteous judgment" or "righteous act."

Justification, then, is closely related to God's justice/righteousness. Justification represents God's action on humans to bring about a condition of righteousness, and this is the connection that translation into English obscures. Scholars have proposed various ways of translating the verb *dikaioō* to represent the way this language works in the Bible, such as "to right-wise" or "to rectify," though to date no major English translation works this out in full. Understanding justification in Paul, however, requires that the manner in which the language works in the OT and the manner in which it works in Paul be held together.

2. Righteousness in the Old Testament.

Dikaiosynē appears throughout the LXX for the Hebrew term *ṣədāqâ*, indicating faithful adherence to the terms of a covenant. In response to the promise of God to give him an heir, Abram (later *Abraham) trusted God's promise, and God "reckoned it to him as righteousness [*dikaiosynē*]" (Gen 15:6 NIV), indicating Abram's faithful covenant partnership. The term is also used in law-court scenarios, indicating that a person is in the right. In the narrative of Genesis 38, Judah accuses Tamar of prostitution and produces Judah's seal, cord, and staff, proving that her pregnancy is the result of an encounter with him. Judah states that "she is more righteous [*dikaioō*] than I," vindicating her innocence of the charge (Gen 38:26 NIV). Relative to Tamar's behavior,

Judah has not been "righteous" in that he did not give Tamar his next available son as husband but rather told her to go back to her father's household to live as a widow, in violation of his covenant obligations (Deut 25:5-10).

The God of *Israel is a faithful covenant partner who delivers Israel and righteous individuals from their enemies. In a number of psalms, righteous Israelites call on God to deliver them according to the terms of the covenant and his character as *dikaios*. Psalm 71 (Ps 70 LXX) brings together notions of deliverance and God's righteousness in several places: "In your righteousness [*dikaiosynē*], rescue me and deliver me" (Ps 71:2 NIV). "My mouth will tell of your righteous [*dikaiosynē*] deeds, of your saving acts all day long—though I know not how to relate them all. I will come and proclaim your mighty acts, Sovereign LORD; I will proclaim your righteous [*dikaiosynē*] deeds, yours alone" (Ps 71:15-16 NIV; see also Ps 31:1; 143:1). The psalmist's call for God to rescue him also indicates that the *dik-* word group points to notions of vindication, pleading for rescue because of the sufferer's character as *dikaios*. Furthermore, God's character as *dikaios* is closely linked with his salvation of Israel in the sight of the nations: "The LORD has made his salvation known and revealed his righteousness [*dikaiosynē*] to the nations" (Ps 98:2 NIV).

God's righteousness as his covenant faithfulness to Israel will be demonstrated by his deliverance of Israel from the crisis of exile, prominently displayed in the promises of restoration in Isaiah: "Listen to me, my people; hear me, my nation: instruction will go out from me; my justice will become a light to the nations. My righteousness [*dikaiosynē*] draws near speedily, my salvation is on the way, and my arm will bring justice to the nations" (Is 51:4-5 NIV). While much more can be said about appearances of the *dik-* word group in the OT, this background is particularly important for understanding how Paul uses this language to speak of justification in terms of God's deliverance and vindication of his people.

3. Contexts of Justification.

Paul refers to justification mainly in Romans and Galatians (letters in which *dik-* words also appear most frequently). He addressed these letters to churches that were fracturing over the issue of whether and under what conditions non-Jews could be included in God's work of salvation accomplished in Christ. This reality has provided fodder for the view that justification is a polemical doctrine—that is, that justification was not a central theme in Paul's theology and that he only deployed it to address the unity of God's people (Wrede). While there is some merit to this conviction, it simplifies things too much, for Paul does indeed use *dik-* language to speak of justification in other letters and in less polemical contexts.

He writes to the Corinthians that Christ has become for us "*wisdom from God—that is, our righteousness [*dikaiosynē*], holiness and redemption" (1 Cor 1:30 NIV). Later he reminds the Corinthians that "you were sanctified, you were justified [*dikaioō*] in the name of the Lord Jesus Christ and by the Spirit of our God" (1 Cor 6:11 NIV). In 2 Corinthians 5:21, in what may have been an early Christian confessional formula, he states that "God made him who had no sin to be sin for us, so that in him we might become the righteousness of God [*dikaiosynē theou*]" (NIV).

Another important text for understanding justification is Philippians 3:3-11, which is not a polemic involving a church fracturing along ethnic lines. Rather, Paul here clarifies the identity of the true people of God—those who can expect to be vindicated as righteous at the day of Christ. Rather than putting confidence in a range of earthly credentials, even those garnered within a cultural context shaped by Torah, the true people of God "serve God by his Spirit" and "boast in Christ Jesus" (Phil 3:3 NIV). For Paul, this involves forsaking his Torah-based, socially impressive credentials in his quest to be conformed to the *sufferings of Christ so that at the day of Christ he may be found with "the righteousness [*dikaiosynē*] that comes from God on the basis of faith" (Phil 3:9 NIV).

The notion of vindication is likely present with the appearance of the verb *dikaioō* in 1 Timothy 3:16. There Paul cites a confessional formula about Jesus Christ, that "he appeared in the *flesh, was vindicated [*dikaioō*] by the Spirit" (NIV). This vindication is closely related to Paul's statement in Romans 1:3-4 that Christ was from the seed of David according to the flesh and that he "through the Spirit of holiness was appointed the *Son of God in power" (NIV).

In the end, then, it is an overstatement that justification in Paul is merely a polemical doctrine, though because it has to do with vindicating God's righteous people, it was a particularly useful tool Paul could use to clarify in Romans and Galatians that God justifies all humans on the same basis, without regard to social status, gender, or *ethnic identity. At the same time, there is not enough evidence to conclude that justification is the center of

Paul's theology or that it was the core content of his preaching. His literary legacy consists of occasional letters from which interpreters must draw conclusions about the shape of his theology.

4. Justification and Works of Law.

In several places, Paul makes negative and positive statements about justification, clarifying that *dikaiosynē* (righteousness/justification) does not come about by works of law but by the faithfulness of Christ/faith in Christ (Rom 3:20-26; Gal 2:16; see also Phil 3:9). In the dominant tradition of Protestant interpretation, these oppositional statements were long interpreted as pitting the legalism of "works-righteousness" (i.e., works or works of law) against human passive reception of God's gift of righteousness (i.e., faith). Protestant interpreters until late into the twentieth century understood Paul as reacting to Judaism as a religion of works-righteousness—the conviction that in order to be righteous before God one had to meticulously obey the Mosaic law. According to this perspective, Paul argued that justification could not come through legalistic striving in obedience to the Mosaic law because the law demanded perfect obedience, and no one was able to fulfill this requirement since all were born in sin and inevitably fall short of perfection.

While occasionally over the last few centuries scholars had questioned whether Judaism was rightly regarded as a legalistic religion, it was not until the work of Sanders in 1977 that this scenario was seriously questioned. His research into the character of first-century Judaism demonstrated that it could not rightly be understood in this way. While Sanders concluded that Paul did not faithfully represent Jewish convictions, few scholars followed his lead, choosing rather to reevaluate what Paul meant when he used the expression "works of law." While some interpreters still maintain that the expression involves Paul's critique of legalistic striving, a new consensus has emerged that Paul had in mind Jewish identity rather than legalism. This conclusion is based on the fact that the contexts in which "works" and "works of law" appear, Paul is making reference to Torah-based deeds that constitute a Jewish identity. This is clear from an examination of Romans and Galatians.

*4.1. **Romans.*** After stating in Romans 3:20 that "no one will be justified [*dikaioō*] in God's sight by the works of the law" (NIV), Paul expresses this opposition in Romans 3:28: "For we maintain that a person is justified [*dikaioō*] by faith apart from the works of the law" (NIV). Paul makes these statements within a larger argument that Jewish identity does not give anyone priority among the people of God. Paul's burden in Romans 2:1–5:11 is to unite all believers in Rome together as a singular social unit. One group ("the weak") is passing judgment on another ("the *strong") over practices that constitute a Jewish identity (see Rom 14:1–15:13). Paul does not accept the assertions of the weak but rather condemns them for passing *judgment (Rom 2:1-16) and questions their claims to a Jewish identity (Rom 2:17-29), condemning them as transgressors of the Mosaic law, to which they are looking to bolster their claims. He then lumps all believers together as sinners (Rom 3:9, 23) before noting that God has justified (*dikaioō*) them all on the same basis (Rom 3:24).

Just after his summary statement that "a person is justified by faith apart from the works of the law" (Rom 3:28), he notes that restricting justification only to ethnic Jews turns God into a mere tribal deity (Rom 3:29). If only Jews are acceptable to God, then God is indeed the God of Jews only. But this runs directly counter to the central Jewish confession. In the *Shema* (the Jewish confession that the God of Israel is the one true God; see Deut 6:4-9), Jews confess the singularity of God as the great King who rules over all nations. Paul's negative statement, then, that justification does not come about by "works of law" has to do with his assertion that a Jewish identity is irrelevant when it comes to justification.

In Romans 4:1-6, Paul uses only the term *works*, rather than "works of law," on which basis some argue that he is referring to good works in general rather than the deeds that constitute a Jewish identity. But his discussion of Abraham in Romans 4:1-25 is replete with the distinction between Jews and non-Jews. He refers to the circumcised and uncircumcised in Romans 4:9-12, and distinguishes those who have a relation to the law (i.e., Jews) in Romans 4:13-17. The thrust of his argument in this chapter is to unite the factions in the Roman churches together, regardless of ethnic identity. Both Jewish and non-Jewish believers have Abraham as their forefather, and the promise belongs to all, "not only to those who are of the law but also to those who have the faith of Abraham. He is the father of us all" (Rom 4:16 NIV).

*4.2. **Galatians.*** Paul's use of the expression "works of law" has the same significance in Galatians. In Galatians 2:15-21 Paul continues his report of his confrontation of *Peter when the latter visited the church in Antioch. Peter had enjoyed table *fellowship with non-Jews in order to embody the unity of Jew and non-Jew in Christ. He later withdrew from the *Gentiles, however, with the arrival of some visitors from the *Jerusalem church. Paul confronted Peter because his action signaled a division in the unified people of God, which crosses ethnic lines (Gal 2:11-14).

He reveals his logic for doing so in Galatians 2:15-21. After identifying his and Peter's shared Jewish identity in Galatians 2:15 and their distinction from "sinful Gentiles," he stated the common Christian conviction that "a person is not justified by the works of the law, but by faith in Jesus Christ" (Gal 2:16 NIV). He repeats this opposition twice more, noting that because of the singular basis of justification, both he and Peter, along with Gentiles, have needed to believe in Christ for justification. This context is a clear indication that Paul's polemic with regard to works of law is directed against any implicit notions that Gentiles must become Jews (and vice versa) in order to be justified, or that Jewish Christians have a priority with God over against non-Jewish believers.

Paul's negative statements about justification—that God does not justify a person based on works of law—have to do with the reality that God does not justify a person because of their ethnic identity as Jewish. God has united Jews and non-Jews into one *body of people in Christ. For Paul, this unity must be publicly displayed through the church's gathering together across ethnic lines and its participation in a common meal, as was seen in Antioch and which Peter had initially demonstrated.

Paul's negative statements about justification do not have to do with anything inherently deficient in the Mosaic law. The law was God's good gift (Rom 7:13-16; see Deut 4:5-8; Ps 119), his covenant with Israel and the instruction for them to walk within his *love and maintain their faithfulness so that they could enjoy his blessing. The law was never intended to function in the same way for non-Jewish people. Rather, non-Jews could come to know the God of Israel and how to live in obedience to him as non-Jews by hearing from the law and observing the corporate life of the nation of Israel. For Paul, now that God is including all ethnicities into one new people in Christ, the law can be read in the same way as Scripture, rather than as commending that all ethnicities be absorbed into a singular Jewish ethnic identity.

Further, Paul's negative statements about justification do not have to do with human inability to perfectly keep the law. The law did not demand perfect obedience but made provisions for forgiveness and atonement. While Paul would have denied that legalistic striving was a possible pathway to justification, this was not the problem he confronted in his letters. The specific problem he addresses in Romans and Galatians is that non-Jews are being pressured to become Jewish in order to enjoy salvation in Christ. This explains his polemical statements.

One text in which Paul appears to set the Mosaic law in opposition to faith is Galatians 3:12, where he states that "the law is not based on faith." Protestant interpretation has typically read this to mean that the Mosaic law had a dynamic of "doing," or encouraged a legalistic striving, while Paul's gospel commended faith, understood as passive reception. But this is not an abstract assertion about the character of the Mosaic law in general. It is, rather, a polemical statement in a highly charged rhetorical letter in which Paul seeks to persuade the Galatian Gentiles not to submit to *circumcision, which is the rite of initiation into a Jewish identity. It is more likely that Paul is using theological shorthand to refer to the *teaching to which the Galatians are being tempted to submit when he refers to "the law." This statement is better understood to mean that the teaching that Gentiles must submit to the law and be circumcised to become Jews is not based on faith.

5. Justification by Faith.

In two strategic texts in which Paul asserts that justification is by faith and not by works of law, he states the matter with somewhat greater complexity than is represented in many English translations. In Romans 3:22 and Galatians 2:16 he writes that justification is *dia pisteōs Iēsou Christou*, a phrase that may be variously translated. Some interpreters claim that it ought to be understood as a subjective genitive, indicating "through the faithfulness of Jesus Christ." On this view, Paul is pointing to the covenant fidelity of Jesus Christ to God in both his life and death on the *cross as the mode whereby justification takes place. Alternatively, it could be translated as an objective genitive, stressing the obedient human response to the gospel: "by faith in Jesus Christ." Still other interpreters claim that the phrase is deliberately ambiguous, pointing to both the fidelity of Jesus Christ to God and the response of faith/faithfulness for which the gospel calls.

In Galatians 2:15-21 Paul repeats this expression several times. In Galatians 2:16 Paul states that a person is justified *dia pisteōs Iēsou Christou*, and he explains what he means by this in Galatians 2:20. Paul has been crucified together with Christ—crucified to "the world" (Gal 6:14) and delivered out of the present evil age (Gal 1:4). He has been raised together with Christ so that now his life is conjoined with Christ as "Christ lives in me" (Gal 2:20). Paul now lives "by the faithfulness of the Son of God" (Gal 2:20, *en pistei zō tē tou huiou tou theou*). The expression *pisteōs Iēsou Christou* is best understood, then, as a subjective genitive, referring to "the faithfulness of Jesus Christ," and Paul is underscoring that justification is made effective by Jesus Christ and his faithful obedience to God. It is effective for all those whom God has joined together with the dying of Jesus Christ, along with his resurrection and current life toward God.

Paul also includes the necessity of human trust in God for justification when he states that because he and Peter know that "a person is not justified by the works of the law," but *dia pisteōs Iēsou Christou* (Gal 2:16, "through the faithfulness of Jesus Christ"), they have both put their "faith in Christ Jesus" (Gal 2:16, *eis Christon Iēsoun episteusamen*). With these two expressions, Paul captures both the work of God through the faithfulness of Jesus Christ, through whom justification comes, and the human response required.

This same twofold emphasis is found in Romans 3:22. Paul writes that justification comes about *dia pisteōs Iēsou Christou, eis pantas tous pisteuontas* ("through the faithfulness of Jesus Christ for all who believe/trust"). The expression *dia pisteōs Iēsou Christou* more likely does not refer to human faith or trust, because that is the referent in the expression that immediately follows (*eis pantas tous pisteuontas*, "for all who believe"). That is, Paul is emphasizing that the mode of justification comes through the faithfulness of Jesus Christ rather than taking on a Jewish identity. "The faithfulness of Jesus Christ" refers to the life of obedience to God rendered by Jesus Christ to God the Father, an obedience that took him to the point of death on the cross.

The thrust of what Paul is getting at here is clarified in Romans 3:28 when he refers to the justified person as "the one who is of the faithfulness of Jesus" (*ek pisteōs Iēsou*). That is, God justifies the person who participates in an identity wrapped up into the faithfulness of Jesus Christ.

6. Justification "in Christ."
In addition to Romans 3 and Galatians 2, several other texts indicate that justification comes about by God's joining of believers with the dying and rising of Jesus Christ, brought about by the *Holy Spirit. In 1 Corinthians 1:30, Paul tells the Corinthians that "you are all in Christ Jesus" (*hymeis este en Christō Iēsou*), "who has become for us wisdom from God—that is, our righteousness [*dikaiosynē*], holiness and redemption" (NIV). The "in Christ' relationship is the reality that effects justification/righteousness. In 2 Corinthians 5:21, Paul states that God made Christ "to be sin for us, so that *in him* we might become the righteousness of God" (NIV). The transformation of believers into "the righteousness of God" is a reality that comes about "in him"—that is, by believers being joined together with Christ.

In relaying his personal quest to leave behind his impressive Torah-based credentials and identify with the humiliation and suffering of Christ to the Philippians, Paul notes that he does this "that I may gain Christ and be found *in him*" (Phil 3:8-9 NIV). He is referring to the eschatological dimension of justification—the verdict of "righteous" that God will render on all those who are "*in Christ" at the day of Christ. On that day, Paul aims not to have "a righteousness of my own that comes from the law," by which he indicates his former understanding that his impressive Torah-based credentials would somehow secure for him eschatological justification/righteousness. Rather, he aims to be found in Christ so that he will have a righteousness "which is through the faithfulness of Christ [*tēn dia pisteōs Christou*], the righteousness of God which is by faith" (Phil 3:9). Paul reveals here that righteousness/justification comes to all those who are joined together with Christ, and this incorporation into Christ comes about by faith.

7. Justification as Rectification.
Paul portrays justification in Romans and Galatians in terms of deliverance and transformation. Regarding justification as merely a legal pronouncement does not do full justice to Paul's complex portrayal of the problem that justification addresses. It is not only that humanity is guilty and in need of forgiveness; they are, rather, in a condition of "unrighteousness" (*adikia*), have become something other than the image of God, are enslaved within the present evil age, and are dominated by the cosmic power of Sin. Justification is God's powerful act to liberate humanity from this complex condition and so is better understood as "rectification"—God's setting humans right by delivering them from cosmic enslavement and transforming them into the image of God.

*7.1. **Romans.*** Paul states in Romans 1:16-17 that the gospel "is the power of God that brings salvation," for in it "the righteousness of God [*dikaiosynē theou*] is revealed" (NIV). He associates the righteousness of God with God's saving action of deliverance, drawing on the OT texts that make this same connection (e.g., Ps 71:2, 15-16; 98:2; Is 51:4-5).

The problem that justification solves also indicates that it has to do with deliverance and transformation. In Romans 1:18-32, Paul writes that what is wrong with humanity is that it has "changed" or "exchanged" its role as the *image of God within creation. Rather than ruling creation on behalf of the one true creator God, humans have become in the image of something within creation (Rom 1:23). They have "changed" or "exchanged" "the *truth of God" (Rom 1:25), which here refers to God's creational intentions that God's faithfulness to his creation be manifested by humans ruling it on God's behalf. Humanity bought the lie that they were not God's image but rather the image of some created thing. (In systematic-theological terms, humanity remains "the image of God." This is merely Paul's way of portraying humanity's corrupted condition that its disobedience caused.)

Because of its rebellion humanity is now filled with *adikia* (unrighteousness/injustice; Rom 1:29). God is *dikaios* ("righteous"), and God's righteous character was to be displayed within creation through humanity, but with humanity mired in *adikia*, this cannot happen. Paul asks rhetorically in Romans 3:5, "If our unrighteousness [*adikia*] brings out God's righteousness [*dikaiosynē theou*] more clearly, what shall we say? That God is unjust [*adikia*] in bringing his wrath on us?" (NIV). He emphatically rejects this question. God must bring about a transformation of this situation in order to set right his creation and humanity's appointed role within it.

In addition to this, Paul says that all humanity is enslaved under the cosmic power of Sin (Rom 3:9) and subject to God's judgment (Rom 3:19). Humanity is in need, then, of having its full humanity as God's image restored, of being freed from the cosmic power of Sin, and being transformed from being filled with *adikia*. Paul summarizes the complex problem that justification solves in Romans 3:23: humans have sinned and thus are enslaved to the cosmic power of Sin. They lack "the glory of God"—that is, their *adikia* prevents them from faithfully being the image of God within creation.

This twofold condition affected all the Roman Christians, and they were all "justified as a gift by his *grace" (Rom 3:24). Justification here should be understood in the sense of rectification, for God transformed the Roman Christians from the condition of *adikia* into *dikaios*. This is not simply a declaration of a new legal status before God, nor is it merely the forgiveness of their guilt. Justification has everything to do with their condition as humans within God's creation, their being image bearers within the creation that is God's *temple.

The final clause in Romans 3:24 reveals that this act of God also involved their liberation from enslavement to the cosmic power of Sin. Justification took place "through the redemption which is in Christ Jesus." Just as God delivered (redeemed) Israel from slavery to Egypt, God delivered believers from cosmic enslavement to Sin. Paul again articulates justification as deliverance from Sin in Romans 6:5-8, when he notes that those who have been joined together with Christ's crucifixion are no longer slaves to Sin, since they have been "justified [*dikaioō*] from Sin." In this context he also associates justification with the future *resurrection (Rom 6:5, 7) and the present enjoyment of resurrection life that flows from union with Christ (Rom 6:11), a connection he already made in Romans 4:25: Christ "was delivered over to death for our sins and was raised to life for our justification" (NIV).

Paul describes the results of justification in Romans 5:1-11. Believers now together have "*peace with God," which has to do with their participation in the *shalom* of God—the human experience of inhabiting creation as God intended. They are transformed as creatures within God's good creation. They have been brought into "this grace in which we stand" (Rom 5:1-2). That is, justification effects the relocation of believers into new cosmic space, delivered from enslavement under the cosmic power of Sin into the new creation reality that is present in time even while they await the final transformation of their bodies and creation itself at the future day of Christ.

7.2. Galatians. Paul depicts a similar scenario in Galatians, indicating that justification solves the problem not only of human sin but of cosmic enslavement. In the opening of the letter, Paul states that Christ "gave himself for our sins to rescue us from the present evil age" (Gal 1:4 NIV). Apart from Christ, believers were formerly under bondage to Sin (3:22) and enslaved to hostile cosmic forces (Gal 4:8-9). In Galatians 2:15-21, Paul connects justification with being raised together with Christ and the present experience of resurrection life. Because God has united Paul together with the death and resurrection of Christ, Paul has died "so that I might live for God" (Gal 2:19 NIV). His current life, which is a participation in "the faithfulness of the Son of God," is his experience of righteousness, as he indicates in Galatians 3:21. This close association of resurrection life with righteousness is clear in Galatians 3:21, where Paul states that "if a law had been given that could impart life, then righteousness [*dikaiosynē*] would certainly have come by the law" (NIV). Justification/righteousness for Paul in Galatians, then, is the impartation of eschatological life through the deliverance from the present evil age.

*7.3. **Philippians.*** In Philippians 3:9-11, Paul associates *dikaiosynē* with the present experience of Christ's resurrection power and the future resurrection at the day of Christ. He has left behind his privileges, his Torah-based credentials he formerly thought would bring him resurrection life at the eschatological day (Phil 3:4-6). He now considers them "garbage, that I may gain Christ and be found in him" (Phil 3:8-9 NIV). Rather than his credentials giving him a claim to righteousness at the day of resurrection, Paul knows now that only "participation in [Christ's] sufferings, becoming like him in his death" is how he participates in the faithfulness of Christ (Phil 3:10 NIV). It is this being joined with Christ by faith that brings "the righteousness that comes from God" (Phil 3:9 NIV).

Justification, then, has to do with transformation, resurrection, and deliverance. Because of this, the term *rectification*—making right—captures the reality that for Paul, justification is God's act to liberate humans from enslavement to the present evil age and hostile cosmic powers, and to bring them into the cosmic space Paul calls "the new creation" and "in Christ."

8. Present and Future Justification.
While Paul refers to believers as having already been justified (Rom 5:1), he also portrays *dikaiosynē* as happening in the future, at the day of Christ. Romans 2:13 points to both the present and future aspects of justification when he writes, "It is not those who hear the law who are righteous/just [*dikaios*] in God's sight, but it is those who obey the law who will be justified/rectified [*dikaioō*]." Paul contrasts a purported identity as Jewish with genuine obedience to the law, noting that the truly obedient (referring to the Jewish and non-Jewish believers in the Roman churches) can be confident that they are righteous/just now and will be rectified/justified at the day of Christ. Paul represents both present and future aspects in Galatians too. Having referred to the status of Christians as justified already in Galatians 2:16, Paul writes in Galatians 5:5 that "through the Spirit we eagerly await by faith the righteousness [*dikaiosynē*] for which we hope" (NIV).

While typical dogmatic or doctrinal constructions of justification associate it with the moment of conversion, referring to final salvation as glorification, it is important to keep in mind that Paul does not have this conception of justification, sanctification, and glorification. He can speak of each of these as having already happened in the past (Rom 8:30), of sanctification as what God does to believers at the moment of conversion (1 Cor 6:11), and of justification as the final transformation of believers into their full humanity for participation in the new creation.

9. Paul and James on Justification.
Interpreters have long detected a tension between Paul and *James on justification. Whereas Paul states that God justifies a person by faith apart from works of the law, James contends that "a person is justified by works and not by faith alone" (Jas 2:24 NRSV). Paul and James cite Abraham in apparently contradictory ways. Paul cites Abraham as an example of someone who was justified by faith and not by works (Rom 4:2-4), while James looks to Abraham as one who was justified by works (Jas 2:21).

One line of interpretation claims that James wrote his letter to quell antinomianism in the churches planted by Paul. His teaching on justification by faith had led to Christian communities that were disregarding God's commands through immorality. James wrote to remind these communities that obedience to God was a critical matter.

But understanding Paul's formulation of justification by faith apart from works of the law settles any apparent discrepancy between James and him. James wrote to Christian communities to correct many of the same corporate dysfunctions that Paul confronted in his letters—various forms of conflict across socioeconomic lines, such as favoritism and the rich exploiting the poor (Jas 2:1-12; 5:1-6; see 1 Cor 11:17-34). James addresses a situation in which church members confess the faith, but their lives do not match their confession. Such faith, he writes, is dead (Jas 2:20). True faith is demonstrated in action, a conviction with which Paul would heartily agree (2 Cor 13:5). Paul, on the other hand, addresses situations in which non-Jews are being pressured to become Jewish in order to enjoy salvation. When he states that God justifies a person without reference to works of law, he is not referring to good works in general but to Torah-oriented works that mark a person as having a Jewish identity. Ultimately, Paul and James agree that genuine faith is demonstrated through good works (see Gal 5:6).

See also FAITH; FAITH OF CHRIST; GALATIANS, LETTER TO THE; IN CHRIST; INTERPRETATION: LUTHER; INTERPRETATION: NEW PERSPECTIVE; ISRAEL; JAMES AND PAUL; JUDGMENT; RIGHTEOUSNESS; ROMANS, LETTER TO THE; WORKS OF THE LAW.

BIBLIOGRAPHY. **J. M. G. Barclay,** *Paul and the Gift* (Grand Rapids, MI: Eerdmans, 2015); **M. F. Bird,** *The Saving Righteousness of God: Studies on Paul, Justification, and the New Perspective*, PBM (Eugene, OR: Wipf & Stock, 2007); **M. C. de Boer,** *Galatians: A Commentary*, NTL (Louisville, KY: Westminster John Knox, 2011); **C. R. Campbell,** *Paul and Union with Christ: An Exegetical and Theological Study* (Grand Rapids, MI: Zondervan, 2012); **D. A. Campbell,** *The Deliverance of God: An Apocalyptic Rereading of Justification in Paul* (Grand Rapids, MI: Eerdmans, 2009); idem, *Pauline Dogmatics: The Triumph of God's Love* (Grand Rapids, MI: Eerdmans, 2020); **D. A. Carson,** "The Vindication of Imputation: On Fields of Discourse and Semantic Fields," in *Justification: What's at Stake in the Current Debates?*, ed. M. Husbands and D. J. Treier (Downers Grove, IL: InterVarsity Press, 2004), 46-78; **C. H. Cosgrove,** "Justification in Paul: A Linguistic and Theological Reflection," *JBL* 106 (1987): 653-70; **J. D. G. Dunn,** *The Theology of Paul the Apostle* (Grand Rapids, MI: Eerdmans, 2006); **S. J. Gathercole,** "Justified by Faith, Justified by His Blood: The Evidence of Romans 3:21–4:25," in *Justification and Variegated Nomism*, vol. 2, *The Paradoxes of Paul*, ed. D. A. Carson, P. T. O'Brien, and M. A. Seifrid (Grand Rapids, MI: Baker Academic, 2004), 147-84; **M. J. Gorman,** *Inhabiting the Cruciform God: Kenosis, Justification, and Theosis in Paul's Narrative Spirituality* (Grand Rapids, MI: Eerdmans, 2009); idem, *Participating in Christ: Explorations in Paul's Theology and Spirituality* (Grand Rapids, MI: Baker Academic, 2019); **R. B. Hays,** "Justification," *ABD* 3:1129-33; idem, "The Letter to the Galatians," *NIB* 11:181-348; **M. Horton,** *Justification*, 2 vols. (Grand Rapids, MI: Zondervan, 2018); **E. Käsemann,** "'The Righteousness of God' in Paul," in *New Testament Questions of Today* (Philadelphia: Fortress, 1969), 168-82; idem, *Commentary on Romans*, trans. G. W. Bromiley (Grand Rapids, MI: Eerdmans, 1980); **J. Linebaugh,** "Righteousness Revealed: The Death of Christ as the Definition of the Righteousness of God in Romans 3:21-26," in *Paul and the Apocalyptic Imagination*, ed. B. Blackwell, J. Goodrich, and J. Maston (Minneapolis: Fortress, 2016), 219-37; **J. L. Martyn,** *Galatians*, AB 33A (New Haven, CT: Yale University Press, 1997); **A. McGrath,** *Iustitia Dei: A History of the Christian Doctrine of Justification*, 4th ed. (Cambridge: Cambridge University Press, 2020); **H. Ridderbos,** *Paul: An Outline of His Theology*, trans. J. R. De Witt (Grand Rapids, MI: Eerdmans, 1975); **E. P. Sanders,** *Paul and Palestinian Judaism* (Philadelphia: Fortress, 1977); **T. R. Schreiner,** *New Testament Theology: Magnifying God in Christ* (Grand Rapids, MI: Baker Academic, 2008); **A. Schweitzer,** *The Mysticism of Paul the Apostle*, trans. W. Montgomery (Baltimore: Johns Hopkins University Press, 1953); **M. A. Seifrid,** *Justification by Faith: The Origin and Development of a Central Pauline Theme*, NovTSup 68 (Leiden: Brill, 1992); idem, *Christ, Our Righteousness: Paul's Theology of Justification*, NSBT (Downers Grove, IL: InterVarsity Press, 2000); **T. D. Stegman,** "Paul's Use of *DIKAIO-* Terminology: Moving Beyond N. T. Wright's Forensic Interpretation," *TS* 72 (2011): 496-524; **K. Stendahl,** *Paul Among Jews and Gentiles* (Philadelphia: Fortress, 1976); **P. Stuhlmacher,** "The Apostle Paul's View of Righteousness," in *Reconciliation, Law, and Righteousness: Essays in Biblical Theology* (Philadelphia: Fortress, 1986), 68-93; **B. Vickers,** *Jesus' Blood and Righteousness: Paul's Theology of Imputation* (Wheaton, IL: Crossway, 2006); **S. Westerholm,** *Justification Reconsidered: Rethinking a Pauline Theme* (Grand Rapids, MI: Eerdmans, 2013); **S. K. Williams,** "The 'Righteousness of God' in Romans," *JBL* 99 (1980): 241-90; **M. Wolter,** *Paul: An Outline of His Theology*, trans. R. L. Brawley (Waco, TX: Baylor University Press, 2014); **W. Wrede,** *Paul*, trans. E. Lummis (London: Philip Green, 1907); **N. T. Wright,** *Paul and the Faithfulness of God*, COQG 4 (Minneapolis: Fortress, 2013); idem, *Justification: God's Plan and Paul's Vision*, 2nd ed. (Downers Grove, IL: IVP Academic, 2016).

T. Gombis

K

KERYGMA. *See* PREACHING, FIRST-CENTURY.

KINGDOM OF GOD/CHRIST

The claim that Jesus of Nazareth's primary message, at least as presented in the Synoptic Gospels, consisted in the proclamation of the kingdom of *God is largely uncontroversial. The fourteen occurrences of "kingdom of God/*Christ" in the Pauline epistles look remarkably meager in comparison to the approximately eighty references in the Synoptics (including references to the "kingdom of heaven" in Matthew). As a result, scholarly studies on Paul's kingdom language have almost invariably centered on its relationship to the Jesus *tradition, matters related to the timing and *eschatology of the kingdom, and offering explanations for why Paul supposedly minimizes the theme of the kingdom of God. In other words, despite making valuable historical contributions, a majority of scholarship examines and evaluates Paul's kingdom language by accounting for what is *not* in the text rather than taking seriously the fact that Paul does employ kingdom language for his own particular ends. While much can indeed be learned from the admittedly well-worn prior discussion of kingdom language in Paul (see section 1 below), this article will set forth a robust, albeit brief, study of kingdom language in Paul that takes its point of departure from *Paul's own emphases* (section 2). Paul's kingdom language is best interpreted in its epistolary context and as signifying his royal-messianic discourse.

1. Paul's Kingdom of God/Christ Language and Jesus of Nazareth
2. The Kingdom of God/Christ and Paul's Royal-Messianic Theology

1. Paul's Kingdom of God/Christ Language and Jesus of Nazareth.

1.1. Paul and the Jesus Tradition. Studies on Paul's teaching of the kingdom of God are almost singularly and invariably focused on explaining its continuity or discontinuity with Jesus' proclamation of the kingdom. Paul refers to the kingdom of God on eight occasions in the undisputed epistles (Rom 14:17; 1 Cor 4:20; 6:9-10; 15:24, 50; Gal 5:21; 1 Thess 2:12). There are six references to kingdom language in the disputed epistles. In addition to "the kingdom of God" (Eph 5:5; Col 4:11; 2 Thess 1:5; 2 Tim 4:1, 18), there are references to the kingdom as also belonging to Christ (Eph 5:5; Col 1:13; 2 Tim 4:1 disputed). There are, indeed, good (though by no means indisputable) reasons for supposing that Paul's use of the phrase demonstrates familiarity with the sayings of Jesus of Nazareth, who repeatedly and uniquely proclaimed the presence and coming of the eschatological kingdom of God (e.g., Mt 4:17, 23; 8:11; 9:35; Mk 3:24; 4:11; Lk 17:20; Jn 3:3, 5). First, Paul uses the phrase in a conventional, formulaic manner, which suggests his audience's familiarity with the theme as he refrains from any detailed development of its meaning (1 Cor 4:20; 1 Thess 2:12; see Donfried). Second, on occasion Paul himself hints that his references to the kingdom of God are connected to prior teaching or tradition (Gal 5:19-21; Eph 5:5). In one instance, the language of "kingdom of God" is connected to the rite of *baptism, thereby further suggesting the likelihood that Paul himself taught his churches about the kingdom of God (1 Cor 6:9-10; cf. 1 Cor 1:11-17; 12:13). Third, some have seen thematic connections between Paul and Jesus with respect to the kingdom of God: for example, the notion of inheriting the kingdom of God power and eschatological *judgment (e.g., 1 Cor 15:24, 50 with Lk 11:20), discipleship (Mt 4:18-22; 5:10-11 with 1 Thess 2:12; 2 Thess 1:4-5), and *peace and *righteousness (Mt 5:20; 10:7, 13 with Rom 14:17).

1.2. Kingdom and Eschatology. One of the central preoccupations of nineteenth- and twentieth-century scholarship on the Gospels (and quests for the historical Jesus) centered on eschatology and specifically whether Jesus proclaimed the imminence of the kingdom of God or an inaugurated kingdom (the kingdom as both *already* present and *not yet* consummated). Scholars often took up the question of whether there was any continuity between Jesus and Paul with respect to the timing of the kingdom (see Kümmel; Witherington). Not unlike Jesus in the Gospels, Paul speaks of the kingdom as an already present reality (e.g., Rom 14:17; 1 Cor 4:20). The effects or foretastes of the future kingdom are present in the church's experience of divine power and peace, *joy, and righteousness. But Paul primarily speaks of the kingdom as an eschatological expectation that will be inherited once Christ has defeated all of his enemies (e.g., 1 Cor 6:9-11; 15:23-28, 50; Gal 5:21). While many of these references describe a realm that one enters or inherits, it is also clear that Paul often assumes the present reality of God and Christ's reign (so Carr, 453-54). God has raised Christ from the dead as his messianic king, and he is enthroned at God's right hand, and yet the *church waits for his return, when he will transform his people to fully share in his kingdom. Despite Paul's insistence that the believers await the consummation of the kingdom, it is precisely his emphasis on the powerful dynamic of the kingdom at work in the church and the believer that has led some to see Paul as using alternative metaphors and concepts to describe what Jesus referred to as the kingdom of God.

1.3. Paul's Supposed Avoidance of Kingdom Language. For those who argue that Paul's kingdom language demonstrates some awareness of traditional sayings of Jesus, most are compelled to explain why he draws on kingdom language so infrequently (again, *when* compared with Jesus). Some have argued that Paul's Greek-speaking *Gentile audiences would have misunderstood its meaning and might have interpreted it in a political, revolutionary sense (e.g., Wedderburn, 112). Perhaps some of Paul's opponents had co-opted the phrase "kingdom of God" (e.g., 1 Cor 4:8) to articulate an overly realized eschatology, which Paul found problematic (see Wenham, 78-80). Those concerned with the question of continuity between Paul and Jesus have, therefore, often argued that Paul replaces Jesus' kingdom language with another term or concept. Popular Pauline replacement terms and themes for Jesus' kingdom-of-God teaching have included, for example, righteousness (see Wenham; Dunn, 80, 822) and life in the Spirit (see Cho).

2. The Kingdom of God/Christ and Paul's Royal-Messianic Theology.

While it is perfectly legitimate to compare and contrast Paul with Jesus, it is more profitable to study and examine, at least in the first instance, Paul's kingdom language on its own terms (see Jipp 2015; 2020). Only when one has a sense of what *Paul* was communicating with his teaching on the kingdom of God can one properly engage in comparative analysis. Further, focused attention on individual Pauline epistles and the literary context within which kingdom language occurs, rather than immediately moving to an overarching Pauline synthesis of each occurrence of "the kingdom of God," enables interpreters to see how Paul's kingdom language occurs within a cluster of related terms and themes (see Carr, 449-52). In other words, Paul's kingdom-of-God language makes good sense when one recognizes it is related to other terms and themes such as Messiah, *Lord, divine power, *resurrection and enthronement, and *triumph over *principalities and dominions (see Cerfaux, 92-106). While it would be overly simplistic to give a singular definition, the kingdom of God/Christ centers on God's establishment of a saving messianic reign over his people by means of resurrecting his royal *Son from the dead and exalting him to a position of powerful rule from heaven. God's kingdom is experienced through the liberation of his people from the rule of other powers and authorities, and through empowering his people's moral behavior and preserving the quality of their social relationships.

2.1. 1 Corinthians. Paul refers to God's *basileia* on five occasions in 1 Corinthians (1 Cor 4:20; 6:9, 10; 15:24, 50); as such, it makes sense to give some detailed attention to the themes and literary context of this epistle. As already noted, Paul draws on different metaphors, concepts, and clusters of terms to describe the fundamental reality of God's kingdom inaugurated through the present reign of Christ (see Carr, 452-54). Paul speaks repeatedly of the church as sharing in the saving rule, triumph, and judgment of the resurrected and enthroned Christ.

In his first letter to the Corinthians, Paul repeatedly reminds the church that they belong to and have fellowship with God's "Son, Jesus Christ our Lord" (1 Cor 1:9). Paul even declares that the church shares in Messiah Jesus' sovereign lordship when he reminds them: "*all things are yours*, whether Paul or Apollos or Cephas, whether the world or life or death, whether things present or things to come; *all things belong to you*" (1 Cor 3:21-22). Paul's claim that all things belong to the Corinthians stems from his conviction that "you belong to the Messiah, and the Messiah to God" (1 Cor 3:23). Thus, Paul's sarcasm in 1 Corinthians 4:8-9 is not based on the Corinthian expectation that they reign but that they are already reigning apart from Paul. Paul's hope, in fact, is that the Corinthians "might reign [*ebasileusate]* so that we might reign with you *[symbasileusōmen]*" (1 Cor 4:8).

This provides some important context for Paul's explicit occurrences of "the kingdom of God." In 1 Corinthians 4:20 Paul states: "For the kingdom of God does not consist in word but in power." The claim supports his warning to the Corinthians that, should they continue in their pride and arrogance, Paul—as an agent of the kingdom of God—will come to them with displays of power (1 Cor 4:18-19). This statement recalls Paul's earlier reminder to the Corinthians that his initial proclamation of the *gospel did not come through clever speech but through "the demonstration of the Spirit and power" (1 Cor 2:4). Paul is emphatic that the Corinthians'* faith rests on God's power, not human *wisdom or speech, and this divine power has been revealed in the crucified Messiah (1 Cor 1:18, 23-25). God's power, the crucified and resurrected Messiah, and the Spirit, as we see here, are interconnected. For Paul, this is almost certainly due to his conviction that the resurrected and enthroned Christ is the one who dispenses the Spirit: "So it is written, 'The first man, *Adam, became a living being, the last Adam has become a life-giving Spirit" (1 Cor 15:45). Thus, Paul argues that both Christ and the Spirit are present within, and give life to, the Corinthian community. F. Carr states it well: "The Spirit's empowerment is, therefore, a mediation of the enthroned Christ's present rule" (Carr, 458).

Paul further expands on the kingdom of God in 1 Corinthians 6:1-11, where he twice speaks of Christ's sovereign lordship as the basis for the church's moral behavior. First, Paul declares that the church should not take one another to the law courts since "they will judge the world" (1 Cor 6:2) and "will judge angels" (1 Cor 6:3; cf. Dan 7:22 LXX). Second, Christ's saving work and transformation of the moral lives of the Corinthians ensures that they will not be among those who "do not inherit the kingdom of God [*theou basileian*]" (1 Cor 6:9). Paul's conviction that the Corinthians share the very same "Spirit" of the resurrected and enthroned Messiah undergirds his claim that the Corinthians will inherit the kingdom of God. Again, this claim depends on the premise that the Corinthian church participates in Christ because they share the *same Spirit* that the Messiah received when he was raised from the dead (see 1 Cor 6:13; 15:45). By virtue of sharing Christ's Spirit, the Corinthians too are joined to the Lord (1 Cor 6:14, 17; 12:11-13, 27). Given their participation in Christ, their reception of the Spirit, and eschatological expectation of sharing in the kingdom of God, Paul calls them to reject sinful vices (1 Cor 6:9-10) and to live as holy saints (1 Cor 6:1-2).

The Corinthians' promised hope of inheriting the kingdom of God is predicated on the *apocalyptic scenario set out in 1 Corinthians 15:20-28, a schema that takes its bearings from the resurrection and enthronement of the Messiah and his promised return. The present and future aspects of the kingdom are thus made clear here by Paul as the risen and enthroned Christ has already subjected his enemies to his authority *even as* the Corinthians are called on to wait for Christ's ultimate subjection of *all things* to God. In this text, both the present and future connotations of the kingdom of God are discernible. In 1 Corinthians 15:25, for example, Paul draws on Psalm 110:1 to show that currently the Messiah is now reigning even as he waits for all things to be subjected to his authority. Similarly, in 1 Corinthians 15:27 Paul quotes Psalm 8:6 to show that "all things have been subjected underneath his feet." At the end, the Messiah's primary activity will be one of triumph by means of destruction of his cosmic-political powers (1 Cor 15:24). As such, God will be "all in all" (1 Cor 15:28). Paul's depiction of Christ's victory resonates strongly with Daniel's Son of Man figure, who receives from God a kingdom, a rule, and an authority that also results in the subjection of God's enemies (Dan 7:13-14, 27; see Novenson; Kreitzer, 144-48; 131-64). When the Messiah defeats his enemies, then will he "hand over the kingdom to God the Father" (1 Cor 15:24). In this scenario, the messianic king is the enthroned Lord who rules and defeats God's enemies (Ps 109:1 LXX in 1 Cor 15:25), the foremost of which is the final enemy, Death (1 Cor 15:24, 26). This defeat of Death calls the reader back to Paul's argument in 1 Corinthians 15:20-22, where he claims that all who are in Adam will die, whereas all those who are "in [the already resurrected] Christ will be made alive" (1 Cor 15:22). The destruction of Adam's kingdom of death has taken place through the Messiah's resurrection from the dead, even as the Corinthians await their full experience of resurrection with Christ (1 Cor 15:20-21). Thus, sharing in Christ's resurrection is a requirement for the eschatological inheritance of God's kingdom (1 Cor 15:50). Paul's christological participatory statements (e.g., 1 Cor 15:21, 23), the promises of sharing in Christ's sovereignty over all things (1 Cor 3:21-23; 4:8-9; 6:2-3), and eschatological hope for inheriting the kingdom of God (1 Cor 6:9-11; 15:50) show that Paul's language about the kingdom of God is a complicated metaphor for articulating how God, through his enthroned messianic king, accomplishes his saving purposes for humanity and the world.

2.2. Romans. Only once does Paul refer to "the kingdom of God" in his letter to the Romans (Rom 14:17). Yet, as in 1 Corinthians, Paul repeatedly uses royal language to describe the identity of the Messiah (Rom 1:1-4), Adam and Christ as sharing in dominions (Rom 5:12-21), *Sin and Death as over-*lords* (Rom 6:9, 12, 14), humanity awaiting judgment or condemnation (Rom 8:1, 33-34), humanity's redemption through Christ's regal-filial status (Rom 8:15, 29), and echoes of the Messiah's enthronement to lordship through resurrection (Rom 8:9-17, 33-34).

Especially throughout Romans 5–8, Paul portrays believers as sharing in the rule of the enthroned Messiah and thereby experiencing the benefits of reigning over sin and death (see Jipp 2015; Grindheim, 72-90, 179-90). As a result, believers experience peace and reconciliation with God (Rom 5:1, 10-11). For example, Paul uses the language of *basileuō* on three occasions to describe Sin and Death ruling through Adam (Rom 5:14, 17, 21). Sin and Death take root in the flesh of unredeemed humanity, and so Paul commands believers not to let sin "reign" in their *bodies (Rom 6:12). In addition to the language of reigning, Paul repeatedly uses regal and military language to describe Sin and Death as having a "lordship" (*kyrieuō*; Rom 6:6, 9, 14), "enslavement" (*doulos* and *douloō*, Rom 6:15-22), and "waging of war and imprisonment" (Rom 7:23). Sin's reign of death over humanity results in a situation of moral and ethical incapacity, thereby leading to death (Rom 6:21-23; 7:4-6, 21-24). God's messianic ruler, through his crucifixion, resurrection, and enthronement to God's right hand, releases humanity from this tyrannical reign of Sin and Death. As a result, freed humanity shares in Christ's sonship as children of God (Rom 8:14-17, 19-23, 29). They share the Spirit of the Son, which ensures their future resurrection from the dead (Rom 8:9-15). Paul also notes that the enthroned Christ has all authority and power over their enemies and, as such, redeemed humanity experiences peace instead of fear (see esp. Rom 8:35-39).

One of the primary effects for persons-in-Christ sharing in Christ's rule is the transformation of their moral agency; this reality is on display as they are now empowered to triumph over sin. This interpretation makes good sense of the only explicit occurrence of "the kingdom of God" in Romans 14:17—"For the kingdom of God is not about *food and drink but righteousness and peace and joy in the Holy Spirit." Sharing in the kingdom of God is not about selfish bodily pleasures associated with food and drink; rather, believers participate in God's kingdom when they love their fellow brothers and sisters and seek their edification (Rom 14:8-12). This is, after all, how the messianic king of the kingdom has acted, namely, as one who did not please himself but rather embodied a life of love for others (esp. Rom 15:1-8). S. Grindheim shows that Paul has repeatedly, and in significant sections of his argument, associated the new realities of righteousness, peace, and joy with God's gospel of Messiah Jesus (e.g., Rom 1:17; 3:21-22; 5:1; 15:13; Grindheim, 88-89). Paul's singular reference to "the kingdom of God" (Rom 14:17) should thereby be understood as a pithy shorthand for communicating the revelation of God's gospel and kingship in his messianic Son.

2.3. Galatians and Ephesians. Paul's claim in 1 Corinthians 6:9-11 that the immoral will not inherit the kingdom of God is repeated in remarkably similar fashion in both Galatians and Ephesians. In his letter to the Galatians, Paul contrasts life in the *flesh with life in the Spirit. Those who are marked by "the works of the flesh" and practice the vices of "fornication, impurity, licentiousness, *idolatry, sorcery, enmities, strife, jealousy, anger, quarrels, dissensions, factions, envy, drunkenness, carousing, and other such things" are those who "will not inherit the kingdom of God" (Gal 5:19-21). Paul does not engage here in a detailed explanation of what the kingdom of God might mean here, but its association here with virtues, the Spirit, and sharing in Christ's *cross suggests that the kingdom of God is on display in the transformed moral agency of those who share the Spirit of Christ. Similarly, Paul states in Ephesians 5:5 that the immoral will have no "inheritance in the kingdom of the Messiah and of God." While this is the only occurrence of kingdom language in Ephesians, Paul repeatedly portrays Christ as a royal-messianic figure who mediates God's saving benefits to his people, not the least of which is their transformation into a people marked by peace, good works, and transformed moral agency (Eph 2:1-10, 14-18; 4:20-32; see Jipp 2014).

2.4. Colossians. While most have seen Colossians 1:15-20 as indebted to categories of personified Wisdom, the immediate referent of the pronouns in the *hymn is clearly stated as "the son of his [i.e., God's] *love" (Col 1:13). This son is spoken of as a royal figure who has his own kingdom, where his rescued people reside as ones who have been "delivered from the dominion of darkness" (Col 1:13) and from their "sins" (Col 1:14). The language of "father" (Col 1:12), "kingdom" (Col 1:13), and "the son of his love" echoes 2 Samuel 7 (and related Davidic traditions) whereby God makes a *covenant with the house of David: "I will be a father to him, and he will be a son to me" (2 Sam 7:14; also Ps 2; 89; 132; Pss. Sol. 17). Paul later also refers to his *ministry partners as those who labor together with him "for the kingdom of God" (Col 4:11). Paul does not provide the kind of definition we might want for the meaning of *kingdom*, but, similar to what we have already seen, Paul does consistently portray Christ as a royal figure who enables his people to share in and benefit from his rule. As Christ is "the *image of the invisible God" (Col 1:15), so are his people in the process of being renewed "according to the image of the one creating it" (Col 3:10). The Colossians have been *filled in Christ,* who is the *head of all things (Col 2:10), and this results in their ability to share in Christ's victory over the rebellious cosmic powers and authorities (Col 2:14-15). Just as Christ is "the head of the body" (Col 1:18), so the Colossians receive nourishment, growth, and good from their head (Col 2:19). Christ is the resurrected and enthroned-in-heaven messianic ruler, and as such his people share in the Messiah's resurrection and enthronement (Col 1:18; 2:12-13; 3:1-4).

2.5. 2 *Thessalonians and 2 Timothy.* Briefly, one can note here that, whether Pauline or Deutero-Pauline, the author of 2 Thessalonians 1:5-10 offers an apocalyptic scenario whereby judgment of the wicked, particularly those persecuting the Thessalonian Christians, plays a significant role in God's establishment of the kingdom. Paul states that the Thessalonians are currently *suffering so that they might be "considered worthy of the kingdom of God" (2 Thess 1:5). Paul argues that "when the revelation of Lord Jesus" takes place God will "pay back" the wicked with final judgment (2 Thess 1:6-7); and those who faithfully suffering now can expect God's establishment of them within his kingdom.

In 2 Timothy Paul speaks of the exalted Christ as the one who can guard Paul's deposit safely until the day of judgment (2 Tim 1:12). Paul exhorts Timothy to encourage others to have the same confidence (2 Tim 1:13-14). The statement fits neatly with Paul's concluding words in 2 Timothy 4:18, where he expresses his confidence that "the Lord will rescue me from every evil work and will save me for his heavenly kingdom [*eis tēn basileian autou tēn epouranion*]." A few verses earlier, Paul spoke of Christ Jesus as the one entrusted with the task of judging the living and the dead in light of his future "appearing and his kingdom [*tēn basileian autou*]" (2 Tim 4:1). Christ's powerful ability to protect his people *and* the expectation that he will appear as Lord and Judge of his kingdom is built on a messianic structure (see Downs and Lappenga, 10). The basis of Paul's confidence is expressed in 2 Timothy 2:8-13 and centers on Jesus' messianic identity *and* the promise of sharing in his messianic rule. Herein Jesus is described as both "the ultimate example of endurance amongst suffering, [and] as the resurrected and living Davidic messiah-king, whose faithfulness to believers allows them to participate in the salvific reign of his victory over death" (Marossy). Paul here reminds Timothy of the gospel and its saving implications: "Remember Messiah Jesus, raised from the dead, from the seed of David, according to my gospel" (2 Tim 2:8). Paul emphasizes the resurrection as a means of countering potential shame at Paul's sufferings and imprisonment. Furthermore, Paul argues that his suffering is a result of his commitment to the gospel he proclaims and that his faithfulness in the midst of his incarceration is a participation in the Messiah's sufferings (2 Tim 2:9-11). Those who faithfully share in the sufferings of the Messiah have the hope of sharing in the Messiah's resurrection life and reigning together with him. "The saying is trustworthy: For if we die together with him, we will also live with him; if we endure, we will also reign together with him" (*ei gar synapethanomen, kai syzēsomen, ei hypomenomen, kai symbasileusomen,* 2 Tim 2:11-12). The *syn-* prefixes serve to emphasize Paul's creative application of the saving events of the messianic king's narrative to his people, namely, death, resurrection life, and enthronement. Paul concludes with the promise that the resurrected messianic king has the power to protect and safeguard those who remain faithful to Messiah Jesus, *for the risen Christ himself is faithful* even when humans are faithless (2 Tim 2:12-13; cf. 2 Tim 1:10-12; see Downs and Lappenga, 3-10). This is stated well by D. Downs and B. Lappenga: "To the extent that those in Christ *have died* and *will live* and *reign* with him, the risen and exalted Christ will remain faithful to them, for his faithfulness to those who participate in his own *cruciform, resurrected, and kingly existence is actually faithfulness to himself" (Downs and Lappenga, 9).

This royal-messianic theology helps us understand the two meanings of kingdom language in 2 Timothy. As the "Righteous Judge," Jesus is the faithful one who is able to give the "the crown of righteousness" both to Paul and "to all those who love his appearing" (2 Tim 4:8). The risen and enthroned Davidic Messiah is able to protect his people and sustain their faith so that they will be brought safely into Christ's heavenly kingdom when he returns (2 Tim 4:1, 18).

See also CHRIST, MESSIAH; ESCHATOLOGY; JESUS, SAYINGS OF; JESUS AND PAUL; LORD.

BIBLIOGRAPHY. **F. D. Carr,** "Beginning at the End: The Kingdom of God in 1 Corinthians," *CBQ* 81 (2019): 449-69; **L. Cerfaux,** *Christ in the Theology of St. Paul* (New York: Herder and Herder, 1966); **Y. Cho,** *Spirit and Kingdom in the Writings of Luke and Paul: An Attempt to Reconcile These Concepts,* PBM (Eugene, OR: Wipf & Stock, 2005), 52-109; **K. P. Donfried,** "Paul and the Kingdom of God," in *Paul, Thessalonica, and Early Christianity* (Grand Rapids, MI: Eerdmans, 2002), 233-52; **D. J. Downs and B. J. Lappenga,** *The Faithfulness of the Risen Christ: Pistis and the Exalted Lord in Paul* (Waco, TX: Baylor University Press, 2019); **J. D. G. Dunn,** *Romans 9–16,* WBC 38B (Dallas: Nelson, 1988); **S. Grindheim,** "The Kingdom of God in Romans," *Bib* 98 (2017): 72-90; **J. W. Jipp,** "Sharing in the Heavenly Rule of Christ the King: Paul's Royal Participatory Language in Ephesians," in *"In Christ" in Paul: Explorations in Paul's Theology of Union and Participation,* ed. M. J. Thate et. al., WUNT 2/384 (Tübingen: Mohr Siebeck, 2014), 251-79; idem, *Christ Is King: Paul's Royal Ideology* (Minneapolis: Fortress, 2015); idem, *The Messianic Theology of the New Testament* (Grand Rapids, MI: Eerdmans, 2020); **L. J. Kreitzer,** *Jesus and God in Paul's Eschatology,* JSNTSup 19 (Sheffield: JSOT Press, 1987), 131-64; **W. G. Kümmel,** "Jesus und Paulus," in *Heilsgeschehen und Geschichte* (Marburg: N. G. Elwert, 1965), 439-56; **M. Marossy,** "The Rule of the Resurrected Messiah: Kingship Discourse in 2 Timothy 2:8-13," *CBQ* 82 (2020): 84-100; **M. V. Novenson,** *Christ Among the Messiahs: Christ Language in Paul and Messiah Language in Ancient Judaism* (Oxford: Oxford University Press, 2012); **A. J. M. Wedderburn,** "Paul and Jesus: The Problem of Continuity," in *Paul and Jesus: Collected Essays,* ed. A. J. M. Wedderburn, JSNTSup 37 (Sheffield: Sheffield Academic Press, 1989), 99-116; **D. Wenham,** *Paul: Follower of Jesus or Founder of Christianity?* (Grand Rapids, MI: Eerdmans, 1995); **B. Witherington,** *Jesus, Paul and the End of the World: A Comparative Study in New Testament Eschatology* (Downers Grove, IL: InterVarsity Press, 1992).

J. W. Jipp

KINSHIP LANGUAGE IN PAUL

Paul is no paper *apostle who can be confined to the pages of the NT; rather, he was a real, historical individual who lived and moved in a particular period and particular social context of his day. It is only when one grapples with the social and cultural contexts of the first-century Mediterranean world that one can begin to understand the many kinship terms Paul employed in his letters and the roles, responsibilities, and expectations of the individuals who composed his communities.

1. Kinship Matters: Putting Paul in His Place
2. Kinship and Identity: The Community and the Individual in Symbiotic Relationship
3. Social Values and Expectations of Kinship Group Members in Antiquity
4. Kin (the Language of Belonging) and Nonkin (the Language of Separation)
5. Kinship and Honor
6. Kinship and Ethics
7. Sibling Relations: A Test Case of Early Christian Origins?

1. Kinship Matters: Putting Paul in His Place. In Paul's (and Jesus') time, there were only two social institutions of note and concern to people: government/politics and kinship/family. Religion and economics were important and substantive institutions embedded in government (political religion and political economy) and kinship (domestic religion and domestic economy). Kinship (or better kinship *group*) itself is not a biological but a social construct, affecting virtually every other aspect of life and social domain in the ancient world. The kinship group was the most important foundational structure, centered on fathers as the head of the family. Unlike the twenty-first-century Western understanding of family as a nuclear unit (two adults, two children), the ancient family was much larger, comprising a father, mother, children (including adopted children), *slaves, and retainers. Within this kinship group, a person was related to parents and through them to aunts, uncles, siblings, and cousins.

While there were many groups in existence in the first century (e.g., trade associations, synagogues, voluntary associations, and philosophical schools; Ascough, 11-94), the kinship group/family was the most basic social structure underpinning ancient society. It is precisely because the bonds of kinship and family were so powerful and pervasive in Paul's day that they became for him a potent set of metaphors by which to describe God's new kinship family—"the household of *faith" (*oikeious tēs pisteōs*, Gal 6:10).

2. Kinship and Identity: The Community and the Individual in Symbiotic Relationship.
The ancients were much more communally oriented than twenty-first-century Western individuals today. Not only was the kinship group the basic community to which a person belonged, its importance was such that it would have been inconceivable for an ancient person to understand who they were apart from it. First-century persons were collectivist personalities—that is, they needed other persons as a means of determining who they were (Malina, 3). This is also known as a dyadic personality, where a person's lineage situated them in a specific location and their *identity was traced back to their parents in general and the father in particular.

The priority of the group over the individual in the ancient world has long been recognized by Pauline interpreters. After all, Paul wrote more letters to communities than he did to individuals. However, the importance of the latter ought not to be downplayed, for there is a synergy between the community and the individual. Moreover, Richard Bauckham observes: "the claim that ancient people perceived the self in relational terms, as essentially related to others or to the group, rather than as autonomous and atomized individuals that modern individualism envisages, presupposes selves that were distinguishable, however closely related" (3).

Identity concerns the way in which people both individually and collectively as members of a group understand themselves in relation to one another, to the society in which they live and move, and to those they perceive on the periphery of their community (i.e., outsiders). Paul's churches consisted of individual people in community with each other, and it is within this context that Christian identity was forged and understood. The twin notions of identity and belongingness are evident in the Gospel narratives, for example, where people are known by their linkage to their father's name—James, one of the Twelve, is specifically identified as the "son of Zebedee" (Mt 4:21), Simon as "son of Jonah" (Mt 16:17), and Bartimaeus "son of Timaeus" (Mk 10:46). Paul demonstrates a similar awareness when he traces his origins, that is, who he is, ascribed to him by birth and the importance of belonging to the group: "of the people of Israel, of the tribe of Benjamin, a Hebrew of the Hebrews . . . a Pharisee" (Phil 3:5).

3. Social Values and Expectations of Kinship Group Members in Antiquity.
When Paul employs kinship expressions in his *letters, what lies behind his usage of such terms? One must consider the Greco-Roman context (e.g., the gods and emperor as "father") and especially the Hebrew Scriptures, where God is Father and Israel/ites are his children (e.g., Ex 4:22; Deut 14:1-2; 32:8; 2 Sam 7:14; Is 1:2-4; Jer 31:9; Hos 11:1-11). *Israel itself is also designated as a community of siblings (e.g., Lev 25:35, 46; Amos 1:9). This kinship term is found throughout the books of the OT, where the Hebrew term for "brothers and sisters" (often translated as "fellow Israelite/s") is found in the historical (e.g., Deut 1:16), Wisdom (e.g., Ps 133:1), and prophetic literature, both Major (e.g., Is 66:5) and Minor Prophets (e.g., Mal 2:10).

Kinship terms are also evident in sources (Jewish and non-Jewish) contemporaneous to Paul's day, where there is a general consensus among scholars that he is drawing on the ideals and social norms of the kinship group/family of the period (e.g., Moxnes, 28-31). Terms such as *father*, *mother*, *children*, *sister*, and *brother* are used by Paul because there is "a range of shared understandings and values . . . that require reader alert before the message comes properly into focus" (Bossman, 164). Paul frequently refers to God as "Father" (e.g., Gal 1:1), believers as his "children" (e.g., Rom 8:16), and Christians as "brothers and sisters" (e.g., 1 Cor 1:10), so it would be instructive to provide a brief sample of stereotypical attitudes of real parent-child and sibling relations from Greco-Roman and Jewish sources of the period (deSilva, 185-90, 165-73; Burke, *Family Matters*, 36-127).

3.1. Parents and Children. The parent-child relationship was both a structured and a reciprocal one, with the father as the head of the *household: "parents belong to the superior class . . . which comprises seniors, rulers . . . and masters, while children occupy the lower position with juniors" (Philo, *Spec.* 2.226-227, LCL). Parents bring their children into the world and are responsible for their nurture and care, "sparing nothing . . . profitable for their . . . welfare" (Josephus, *Ant.* 4.261, LCL). If the first gift a mother gives to her child is birth, the second is "the afflux of milk [that] flows gently fostering . . . tender growth" (Philo, *Virt.* 130). Indeed, to separate a mother from her newborn infant can have catastrophic effects—it is "brutal" and causes "mothers . . . great distress . . . because of the maternal affection natural to them" (Philo, *Virt.* 128). Parents were responsible for exercising authority over their children and administering discipline (e.g., Philo,

Spec. 2.233; Sir 3:2, 6-7) but were exhorted "not to be harsh . . . but gentle" (Ps.-Phoc. 8, LCL).

Fathers and mothers both clearly loved their offspring, though they demonstrated this in different ways: "The father orders his children to be aroused from sleep in order that they may start early upon their pursuits, even on holidays he does not permit them to be idle, and he draws from them sweat and sometimes tears." On the other hand, "the mother fondles them in her lap, wishes them out of the sun, wishes them never to be unhappy, never to cry, never to toil" (see Seneca, *Prov.* 2.5; Philo, *Spec.* 2.240, LCL). Moreover, "parental affection is stronger in the mother" because "parenthood costs the mother more trouble" (Aristotle, *Eth. nic.* 8.12.3; 8.7.7, LCL).

A father was expected to provide an *example* for his offspring to follow (Isocrates, *Dem.* 4:11; Sir 3:1), which included teaching children their religious traditions and observances (Sir 41:14). According to Jewish *tradition, children are "taught . . . from their swaddling-clothes by their parents" (Philo, *Legat.* 31, LCL) and expected to "hearken to their [parents'] commands and obey them in everything" (e.g., Philo, *Spec.* 2.236; Aristotle, *Eth. nic.* 9.2.1). By obeying, children were giving *honor—the foundational social value of the ancient Mediterranean world of the first century—to their parents, since an honorable child brings honor to them and vice versa (Sir 3:2, 6-7). Failing to honor one's parents not only was detrimental to internal kinship relations (Philo, *Spec.* 2.235) but also affected adversely those outside the family: "children . . . are to honor them [parents] not only by trying to be good [but] . . . for the worth and the praise of those around you" (Philo, *Spec.* 2.235). In return, children reciprocated the *love shown to them by their parents (Philo, *Spec.* 2.240; Josephus, *Ant.* 1.222) and were to imitate their father's example: "by looking at their father's lives as at a mirror [they] may be deterred from disgraceful deeds and words" (Plutarch, *De liberis educandis* 20/14B).

3.2. Siblings. The relationship between siblings in antiquity was even closer than that between parents and children because siblings will outlive parents, share a common nature, and were born of the one womb. Because of this and according to Paul's closest contemporary, siblings were expected to love one another: "brothers love [*philountes*] and feel affection for each other" (Plutarch, *Frat. Amor.* 5/480B, LCL). Siblings were also to demonstrate solidarity and cooperation: "since nature from one seed and source has produced a paradigm for how brothers are to live and *work together*" (*Frat. amor.* 2/478E). Most importantly, sibling relations were to be marked by unity and agreement: "the concord of brothers . . . [is] sound and flourish[es] . . . like a harmonious choir [they] neither . . . say, nor think, anything discordant" (*Frat. amor.* 2/479A; Musonius Rufus, *Frag.* 15.100.6).

What is less appreciated, however, is that sibling relations in antiquity were not absolutely egalitarian (i.e., equal): rather, the relationship was characterized by asymmetry (e.g., Burke, *Family Matters*, 244, 256; Aasgaard, 307; Trebilco, 37). Plutarch, for example, states that "it is impossible for them [i.e., siblings] to be equal in all respects" (*Frat. amor.* 12/484C). Siblings also differed with regard to age, and so "the older [brother] should be solicitous about the younger [brother] and should lead him" (*Frat. amor.* 16/487B). Moreover, a younger brother is charged with the responsibility "to honor and emulate and follow an older [brother]" (*Frat. amor.* 16/487C). This characteristic is also evident in Jewish literature of the period, where "among brothers, their leader is worthy of honor" (Sir 10:20). Siblings also differed in relation to role: "it is fitting that the older [brother] should *admonish* the younger [brother]" (*Frat. amor.* 16/487B).

In addition to the scriptural resonances noted at the beginning of this section, these social values and stereotypical assumptions about kinship relationships in Paul's day will prove useful when read alongside a number of key Pauline texts, including 1 Corinthians 4:14-21; 5:1-12; 6:1-11; 1 Thessalonians 2:7-12; 4:3-12; 5:12-15; Romans 8:12-17, 18-23; 14:10-23; Galatians 4:1-7; Ephesians 6:1-4; Philippians 2:19-24; Philemon 1-25.

4. Kin (the Language of Belonging) and Nonkin (the Language of Separation).
Paul employs a raft of kinship terms in his letters, which Wayne Meeks describes as the "language of belonging" over against those who do not belong (nonkin), the "language of separation" (Meeks, 85-96).

4.1. Kin—the Language of Belonging. God is frequently designated as "Father" (36×), particularly at the beginning of Paul's letters (e.g., Gal 1:1, 3-4), and Jesus is designated as "Son" (22×), most notably in two capital epistles, Romans (e.g., Rom 1:3-4, 9; 8:3) and Galatians (e.g., Gal 1:16; 2:20; 4:4). Believers are variously named as "children [*tekna*] of God" (e.g., Rom 8:16), "sons [*huioi*] of God" (Rom 8:14), "daughters" (*thygateras*, 2 Cor 6:18), and "adopted children" (*huiothesia*), a complex term unique to the corpus Paulinum (see Rom 8:15, 23; 9:4; Gal 4:5; Eph 1:5). In relation to the latter, Paul strikes a clear christological note in that Jesus, God's eternal and unique *Son, is the broker on his Father's behalf because the believer's sonship only and always takes place through him: "God sent his Son . . . in order to redeem . . . in order that we might receive *adoption to sonship*" (Gal 4:5). Here also it is most important to note that Christ is never spoken of in adoptive terms (*huiothesia*), an expression used by Paul only of believers (Gal 4:5; Rom 8:15, 23; Eph 1:5) and the Israelites (Rom 9:4). Elsewhere, Paul describes Christians both positively and pejoratively as "infants" (see 1 Cor 14:20; 3:1). A variation on the filial designation is the description "children of the light" and "children of the day" (1 Thess 5:5), where kinship language is used in the context of the eschaton and provides a moral thrust to live appropriately as "children *characterized* by light" (Wallace, 81n27).

It is particularly noteworthy how Paul also describes *himself* using paternal ("father," 1 Thess 2:11; 1 Cor 4:15) *and* maternal ("nursing-mother," 1 Thess 2:7) language and describes his converts as *his* spiritual offspring ("children," 1 Thess 2:7, 11; Phil 2:22; see Burke 2012). Referring to his converts (e.g., Philem 10) and his communities (e.g., 1 Cor 4:14) as his spiritual progeny is significant for "when Paul speaks in unambiguous *paternal language*, he does so with reference *to the origin of faith in the life of a person or a group*" (Gaventa 1998, 33; emphasis added). Moreover, there is no contradiction regarding God's paternal and Paul's paternal roles because on the matter of instruction, for example, "what Paul taught . . . was God's own teaching and word (see 1 Thess 2.2-9)" (Witherington 2006, 120). Paul in one letter even appears to invert his parental roles (1 Thess 2:7, 11) by describing himself as an "infant" (1 Thess 2:7) and "orphan" (1 Thess 2:17). Assuming such vulnerable kinship roles as these may be an indication Paul's authority is not under threat from anyone within this nascent (Thessalonian) community, which he helped to establish and from which he had been so suddenly and forcibly separated (see Acts 17:1-9; Burke, *Family Matters*, 154-60).

By far, however, Paul's favorite kinship term for Christians is "brothers and sisters" (*adelphoi*), which is ubiquitous throughout his letters (Burke, *Family Matters*, 163-67; Aasgaard, 267-72). While this article is concerned with Paul's use of this term, it is worth noting in passing how the book of Acts records that the first words Paul heard immediately after his *conversion were those of fraternal welcome, "Brother Saul!" (*Saoul adelphe*, Acts 9:17). In Paul's letters, the term *adelphoi* itself is a generic expression that includes both men *and* women, as Philippians 4:1-2 makes clear: Paul begins, "Therefore my brothers and sisters" (*adelphoi*, Phil 4:1), which is immediately followed by, "I plead with Euodia and I plead with Syntyche" (Phil 4:2).

Paul most frequently employs the sibling metaphor in the plural form as a nominative (or vocative) of address (*adelphoi*) in a number of ways: (1) to emotively connect with his communities (e.g., Phil 4:1); (2) to call believers to action (e.g., Rom 12:1); (3) to complete the Christians' *knowledge (e.g., Gal 1:11); and (4) to exhort communities toward particular conduct (e.g., Phil 3:1; see Trebilco, 25-28). Paul also employs the sibling metaphor in other ways: for example, he combines the terms "brother" and "love" to form the composite expression *philadelphia* ("brotherly love"), thereby intensifying fraternal relations within the community (e.g., Rom 12:10; 1 Thess 4:9).

On other occasions, Paul places this expression at the center of a discourse and in the singular form (*adelphos*, 1 Thess 4:6) to sound a warning about sexual morality within the community (e.g., 1 Thess 4:3-8). Elsewhere sibling language is repeatedly used by Paul to address division in the *church (e.g., Rom 14:1-23; see Rom 14:10 [2×], 13, 15, 21). In Romans 14, the contention concerns the consumption of certain foods that divided the so-called weak and *strong, where Paul concludes by reminding the Roman Christians that the *kingdom of God (Rom 14:17) is not only about what one *eats* but how one *treats* another brother or sister in *Christ (Rom 14:21). Significant, too, are the times when Paul employs the nominative (vocative) of address in its singular form (*adelphe*) at a strategic point in a letter; for example, it is used in the thanksgiving section, in respect to Philemon (Philem 7), to which he returns in the main body (*adelphe*, Philem 20), a linguistic and rhetorical move given that a sibling relationship is what he wants to see being brought about between Philemon and Onesimus (*adelphon*, Philem 16). Rarer, but no less significant, is Paul's use of "sister" (*adelphē*) to identify a female member of a Christian community, two of whom are named (Phoebe, a deacon in the church of Cenchreae, Rom 16:1; and Apphia, Philem 2; cf. 1 Cor 7:15; 9:5; 1 Tim 5:2).

Two other points are worth noting in respect of Paul's use of sibling language: first, while believers are most often spoken of as siblings, Paul in Romans 8:29 also describes Christ in this way: "For those whom he foreknew he also predestined to be conformed to the image of his Son, in order that he might be the *firstborn among many brothers and sisters" (*adelphoi*). In this verse Paul also describes

Jesus as "Son" where one might have expected him to conclude that the believers' conformity to Christ is as his "co-children," thereby linking his sonship with that of the believers ("children/sons," Rom 8:16-17). However, the phrase "firstborn *among many* siblings" suggests that Christians are not only "children of God" but are also siblings of Christ. More than that, the theological implication (and logical implication that Paul's first readers would have made) is that believers are also siblings *of one another*.

Second, E. Earle Ellis claims that the plural form "the brothers" (*hoi adelphoi*) in Paul's letters is a title or office in a community used to describe a limited group of workers who were full time in *ministry (447). This is unlikely given Paul's diverse use of this kinship expression to describe Christians: for example, Phoebe is described as a "sister" as well as a "deacon" (Rom 16:1) where the latter indicates her office, not the kinship term.

4.2. Nonkin—the Language of Separation. Paul also employs a wide variety of expressions to describe nonkin as those who are of the "world" (e.g., 1 Cor 1:20-28), "those who do not know God" (1 Thess 4:5), "outsiders" (e.g., 1 Cor 5:12; 1 Thess 4:12), "the rest who have no *hope" (1 Thess 4:13), "[those who are] of the night" (1 Thess 5:5), "nonbelievers" (1 Cor 6:6), "ungodly" (1 Cor 6:1), "those . . . scorned in the church" (1 Cor 6:4), "false brothers and sisters" (*pseudadelphous*, Gal 2:4; cf. 2 Cor 11:26), "sons [*huioi*] of disobedience" (Eph 2:2), and "children [*tekna*] of *wrath" (Eph 2:3). The latter two designations are sometimes paraphrased by Bible translations (e.g., NIV) and merely viewed as a Hebraism, but such terminology should probably be retained and rendered literally (see ESV, NASB), for it stands in contrast to other filial language used earlier in Ephesians for the believer (i.e., "adopted son," Eph 1:5) and therefore describes two very different identities, relationships, and belonging.

In light of all this, Paul's kinship language invites several observations. First, the relative frequency of the terms "Father" (God) and "Son" (Jesus) describe a God who is relentlessly relational in nature: "God reveals himself in personal relationship and only in personal relationship. . . . God is triply personal, emphatically personal, unrelentingly personal" (Peterson, 86-87, 198).

Second, kinship language is fundamental to Paul's understanding of soteriology (Burke 2006, 37-45; 2008). For example, when Paul describes the believer as an "adopted son" (*huiothesia*, e.g., Rom 8:15), he is (in part) drawing from the Roman socio-legal context of his day (see also Ex 4:22; Deut 14:1-2; 32:6, 7; 2 Sam 7:14; Is 1:2-4; 64:8; Jer 31:9-10, 20; Hos 11:1, 4, 10), where an adult son was *transferred* from his old family into a new one with all its attending privileges (e.g., a new name and status) and responsibilities (e.g., sons were not to besmirch the name of the father or his household). In this case, *salvation, as expressed by Paul's metaphor of adoption, is the taking of an outsider—one who does not belong—and bringing them into the security of a new family, "the household of faith" (Gal 6:10).

Third, kinship language aptly describes the believers' new identity as God's sons and daughters who through union with Jesus Christ now belong in the community of faith. Thus, kinship terminology is one way by which Paul talks about *ecclesiology*, that is, a community or new church family that is countercultural to the surrounding society. It is no surprise, then, that the house church (*kat' oikon*, see Rom 16:5; 1 Cor 16:19; Philem 2) became such an important locus where the early Christians met for *worship, as Peter Lampe observes: "in the first and second centuries the church existed not *beside* the Christians' private households, it existed exclusively *in* them" (8).

5. Kinship and Honor.

Ancient society was an agonistic culture where people sought to outdo one another in terms of honor. "In the honor-shame culture of the Roman world, one's goal was undoubtedly to obtain the largest possible share of creditable attention (honor) while avoiding the least possible experience of discreditable attention (shame)" (Lau, 136). Most importantly, in regard to honor and dishonor, ancient people were focused and oriented toward the approval or disapproval of others in the group. Thus, there were two kinds of honor: first, *achieved* honor, which was earned, for example, by winning a battle; and second, *acquired* honor, the honor with which a person was born and that traced back to one's parents.

For Paul the latter was always more important than the former (see Phil 3:5), and this is patently obvious in terms of the salvific blessings experienced by the believer. For example, adoption practices in the ancient Roman world of the first century demonstrate that Octavian, later Emperor Augustus, had honor ascribed to him later in life through being adopted into a more honorable family. Given that "a person's honor comes from his father" (Sir 3:11), the believer receives such honor by virtue of being adopted by a no less distinguished Father, the God of the universe, enabling them to address God as intimately as Jesus himself did, "*Abba*, Father" (see Mk 14:36; Rom 8:15; Gal 4:6). God ascribes the honor of his household to the adopted child. Accordingly, God's spiritual offspring are given the honorable mark of belonging to him, "the Spirit of adoption" (Rom 8:15).

Here also status inconsistency comes into play, for while Christians on the one hand are already God's adopted children and enjoy the honor of belonging to him (Rom 8:15), on the other hand their adoption has yet to be fully realized (Rom 8:23). In the intervening period between the "now" (Rom 8:14) and the "not-yet" (Rom 8:23) God's children experience dishonor, reproach, and persecution from those outside because of who they are and by virtue of their weakened human condition as they groan their way to the "*glory [*doxa*] to be revealed in us" (Rom 8:18, 23; Burke 2006, 152-76).

Honor also plays a key role vis-à-vis sibling relationships: in 1 Corinthians 6:1-11, Paul is seeking to resolve a judicial case between Christians whom he repeatedly identifies as "brothers/sisters" (1 Cor 6:5, 6 [2×], 8)—the sibling expression plays a major role in the discourse of relations. Church members, that is, siblings in Christ, were taking one another to the local court (i.e., to outsiders) rather than resolving the problem among themselves (i.e., insiders). As a result, they were risking their share in the inheritance of the kingdom of God (1 Cor 6:9). Paul confronts them head on and directly with the first of two shaming terms: "I say this to *shame* [*entropēn*] you. . . . One brother takes another to court—and this in front of unbelievers!" (1 Cor 6:5-6 NIV).

Additionally, Paul poses a number of rhetorical questions that are part of his shaming strategy (1 Cor 6:1, 2, 3, 4), climaxing in 1 Corinthians 6:5: "Is it possible that nobody among you is wise enough to judge a dispute between *brothers and sisters*?" A second shaming term follows in 1 Corinthians 6:7: "The very fact you have lawsuits among you means you have been completely *defeated* [*hēttēma*] already" (NIV), that is, (they are) "a moral failure" (Thiselton, 436). As noted earlier, siblings of the period were not to do or say anything that would cause discord and bring the father's name or his household into disrepute. Thus, when these siblings in Christ proceeded to wash their dirty linen in such a public manner (before outsiders), those on the periphery would rightly question the virtue and value of the Corinthian community that calls itself family.

6. Kinship and Ethics.

The dictum "like father, like son" was etched into the psyche of the ancients, since all kin were expected to live in such a way as not to tarnish the father's good name or that of the household. Indeed, "nothing seems to drive New Testament ethics quite so much as kinship" language (deSilva, 143). *Ethics and sonship are two sides of the same coin in Paul's thinking. This is evident in Romans 8:12-17, a key text considered by the overwhelming majority of commentators (e.g., Dunn; Schreiner) and Bible translations (e.g., ESV, NRSV) as a single unit where Paul twice links the believer's filial identity to the Spirit: "those led by the Spirit . . . are the sons of God" (*gar pneumati . . . agontai houtoi huioi tou theou*, Rom 8:14) and "you received the Spirit of adoption" (*elabete pneuma huiothesias*, Rom 8:15). The latter expression is important and best understood as "the Spirit that 'goes with' *huiothesia*" (Byrne, 100; Scott, 261n143). This reading is supported by the parallel passage in Galatians, where Paul connects the sonship of Christ with the Spirit ("the Spirit of his Son," Gal 4:6) to stress that just as it is inconceivable to think of Christ's sonship without the Spirit, so it is equally inconceivable to think of the adoptive sonship of believers without that same Spirit. Christ's sonship and the believers' adoptive sonship belong together, and both are endtime gifts. So, when Paul states "we have an obligation" (Rom 8:12), it is a moral obligation or responsibility that he has in view.

Paul further adds that "all who are led by the Spirit are the sons of God" (Rom 8:14), a leading that is not simply guidance per se but that is understood retrospectively with a clear moral focus, namely, "to put to death the misdeeds of the *body" (Rom 8:13; Kruse, 337). This is only done "by the Spirit" (v. 13b), where God's adopted children must demonstrate a ruthlessness toward all *sin by killing it off continually. When Romans 8:12-17 is viewed as a unit of discourse, rather than with verses 12-13 isolated (see NIV), fresh insights into Paul's kinship expressions, and adoption in particular, emerge. Moreover, Paul's first-century readers would have been aware of the moral responsibilities to which he refers, given that all children were expected to live in such a way as not to bring social opprobrium on their father or the family. In short, "the ethical responsibility for God's sons to live circumspectly pervades Paul's thesis of adoption" (Burke 1995, 64; 2006, 140-47; see Cranfield, 395).

The same moral responsibilities are at play and reinforce the ethos of sibling relations. In the paraenetic section of his letter to the church in Rome (Rom 12–15) Paul writes, "Therefore, . . . brothers and sisters [*adelphoi*], in view of God's mercy . . . offer your bodies as a living *sacrifice, holy and pleasing to God. . . . Do not conform to the pattern of this world, but be transformed by the renewing of your mind" (Rom 12:1-2 NIV). Here Paul's opening appeal to the whole church is the moral imperative for them to live appropriately as members of God's new household.

Elsewhere, Paul situates sibling language at the heart of a discourse (e.g., 1 Thess 4:6, *ton adelphon autou*, "a brother or sister," NRSV) together with a heavy preponderance of *holiness language (see 1 Thess 4:3, 4, 7-8). This is a call for believers to take a wife or control one's body (depending on one's understanding of *skeuos*, "wife," "body," or "male sex organ") and not to wrong or take advantage of a brother or a sister (1 Thess 4:4-6). Whatever meaning is given to *skeuos*, Paul's linking of sibling and moral language, coupled with his use of honor terminology (*timē*, 1 Thess 4:4) and his drawing of the boundary lines between those "inside" ("the brother or sister," 1 Thess 4:6) and those on the periphery ("the pagans who do not know God," 1 Thess 4:5), is a warning shot across the bow for these siblings in Christ to live morally distinct and different lives to the rest of society.

7. Sibling Relations: A Test Case of Early Christian Origins?

It has long been argued that the kinship expression *adelphoi* in the NT indicates that sibling relations were essentially egalitarian in nature (e.g., Jewett, 30). According to this view, the Jesus movement and the early Christian communities show a level playing field composed of brothers and sisters. Over time, it is argued, this ideal degenerated as the early Christian communities became more rigid and structured, as evidenced in the Pastoral Epistles. We earlier noted how some sources contemporaneous with Paul show sibling relations as asymmetrical. Of course, Christian brothers and sisters in Paul's communities were all equal as far as their being the recipients of the saving benefits of Christ's *death, burial and *resurrection (see Gal 3:28). But does Paul's use of sibling language demonstrate any differentiation in seniority and *role* within his communities?

First Thessalonians 5:12-13 is an important test case, where Paul writes, "we appeal to you, brothers and sisters, to respect those who labor among you and have charge of you in the Lord and admonish you; esteem them very highly in love because of their work" (NRSV). Paul begins by addressing the whole community, "brothers and sisters" (*adelphoi*, 1 Thess 5:12), who are to acknowledge those who have "charge of you" (NRSV, *proistamenous hymōn*, 1 Thess 5:12), indicating some form of *leadership. But, most importantly, these leaders are also included among the brothers and sisters, given that Paul repeatedly addresses the entire community as *adelphoi* on no fewer than seventeen occasions in 1 Thessalonians (e.g., 1:4; 2:1, 17; 3:7; 4:1; 5:27). That is, there are some *adelphoi* who were tasked with leading and others who are led, but they are all *adelphoi* in Christ.

Karl Donfried speaks for the majority of scholars (and with due recognition of the kinship language in the letter): "from these verses it is apparent that there was leadership in this Thessalonian church, whatever form it may have taken, and that it is leadership 'in the Lord'" (155). Note that Paul here is not describing "elders," for this is too early, nor is he thinking of a title; rather, his language denotes a leadership that tends toward or is perhaps on the cusp of constituting an office. It suggests some degree of structure or order within the Thessalonian siblingship where specific *adelphoi* are endorsed as leaders imbued with authority because of their role (e.g., Collins, 297; Clarke; Boring, 191). Of this language Paul Ellingworth points out: "The New Testament church . . . was a closely knit community of . . . brothers and sisters. But it was not an egalitarian community in which all hierarchical structures were abolished or transcended" (137; cf. Horrell, 303; Witherington 1995, 453).

Of course, unlike Plutarch, for example, who talks of siblings as "inferior" or "superior," Paul views the leading siblings in Christ as doing so because of their devoted service and work in the Lord (1 Thess 5:13). Nonetheless, a comparison with sources contemporaneous with Paul (see section 3) shows a number of striking similarities in that the leading siblings were expected to (1) lead (1 Thess 5:12), (2) be honored/respected (1 Thess 5:13), and (3) admonish (1 Thess 5:12). If so, the view that the Jesus movement and the earliest Christian communities began life as a siblingship of equals is more complex and requires some nuancing.

Moreover, given that Paul in 1 Thessalonians assumes the elevated roles of "nursing mother" (1 Thess 2:7) and "father" (1 Thess 2:11) toward his Thessalonian "children," this coupled with some differentiation in role among the siblings in this community (1 Thess 5:12-13) could have profound ramifications for the question of Christian origins. Rather than thinking that the earliest Christian communities were exclusively egalitarian, only to become more rigid and organized later, as in the Pastoral Epistles, the church in Thessalonica, which was Paul's earliest extant community, suggests there was some degree of leadership structure from their earliest inception (Burke, *Family Matters*, 230-35, 248; see also 1 Cor 16:15-16).

See also ADOPTION; BIRTH PANGS, MATERNAL IMAGERY; CHURCH; CORINTHIANS, FIRST LETTER TO THE; ETHICS; FIRSTBORN; HONOR/SHAME; IDENTITY; ROMANS, LETTER TO THE; THESSALONIANS, LETTERS TO THE; WOMEN.

BIBLIOGRAPHY. **R. Aasgaard,** *"My Beloved Brothers and Sisters!" Christian Siblingship in Paul*, JSNTSup 265 (London: T&T Clark, 2004); **R. S. Ascough,** *What Are They Saying About the Formation of the Pauline Churches?* (New York: Paulist, 1998); **R. Bauckham,** *Gospel of Glory: Major Themes in Johannine Theology* (Grand Rapids, MI: Eerdmans, 2015); **E. M. Boring,** *I & II Thessalonians: A Commentary* (Louisville, KY: Westminster John Knox, 2015); **D. M. Bossman,** "Paul's Fictive Kinship Movement," *BTB* 26 (1996): 163-71; **T. J. Burke,** "The Characteristics of Paul's Adoptive Sonship (HUIOTHESIA) Motif," *Irish Biblical Studies* 17 (1995): 62-74; idem, *Family Matters: A Socio-historical Study of Kinship Metaphors in 1 Thessalonians*, JSNTSup 247 (London: T&T Clark, 2003); idem, "Paul's Role as 'Father' to His Corinthian 'Children' in Socio-historical Context (1 Cor. 4:14-21)," in *Paul and the Corinthians: A Community in Conflict; Essays in Honor of Margaret Thrall*, ed. T. J. Burke and J. K. Elliott, NovTSup 109 (Leiden: Brill, 2003), 95-113; idem, *Adopted into God's Family: Exploring a Pauline Metaphor*, NSBT 22 (Nottingham, UK: Apollos, 2006); idem, "Adopted as Sons (ΥΙΟΘΕΣΙΑ): The Missing Piece in Pauline Soteriology," in *Paul: Jew, Greek, Roman*, ed. S. E. Porter, Pauline Studies 5 (Leiden: Brill, 2008), 259-87; idem, *The Message of Sonship: At Home in God's Household* (Nottingham, UK: Inter-Varsity Press, 2011); idem, "*Paul's* New Family in Thessalonica," *NovT* 54 (2012): 269-87; idem, "Mother, Father, Infant, Orphan, Brother: Paul's Variegated Pastoral Strategy Towards His Thessalonian Church-Family," in *Paul as Pastor*, ed. B. S. Rosner, A. Malone, and T. J. Burke (London: T&T Clark, 2018), 123-42; idem, "Social Relations," in *The Pauline Mind*, ed. S. E. Porter and D. I. Yoon, Routledge Religious Minds (New York: Routledge, forthcoming); **B. Byrne,** *"Sons of God"—"Seed of Abraham": A Study of the Idea of the Sonship of God of All Christians in Paul Against the Jewish Background*, AnBib 83 (Rome: Biblical Institute, 1979); **A. D. Clarke,** "Equality or Mutuality? Paul's Use of 'Brother' Language," in *The New Testament in Its First-Century Setting: Essays on Context and Background in Honour of B. W. Winter on His 65th Birthday*, ed. P. J. Williams et al. (Grand Rapids, MI: Eerdmans, 2004), 151-64; **R. F. Collins,** "The Church of the Thessalonians," in *Studies on the First Letter to the Thessalonians* (Leuven: Leuven University Press, 1984), 285-98; **C. E. B. Cranfield,** *The Epistle to the Romans*, vol. 1, ICC (London: T&T Clark, 2010); **D. A. deSilva,** *Honor, Patronage, Kinship & Purity: Unlocking New Testament Culture* (Downers Grove, IL: IVP Academic, 2000); **K. P. Donfried,** *Paul, Thessalonica, and Early Christianity* (Grand Rapids, MI: Eerdmans, 2002); **J. D. G. Dunn,** *Romans 1–8*, WBC 38A (Nashville: Thomas Nelson, 1988); **P. Ellingworth,** "Translating the Language of Leadership," *BT* 49 (1998): 126-38; **J. H. Elliott,** "The Jesus-Movement Was Not Egalitarian but Family-Oriented," *Biblical Illustrator* 11 (2003): 173-210; **E. E. Ellis,** "Paul and His Co-workers," *NTS* 17 (1970–1971): 437-52; **B. R. Gaventa,** *First and Second Thessalonians* (Louisville, KY: John Knox, 1998); idem, *Our Mother Saint Paul* (Louisville, KY: Westminster John Knox, 2007); **J. H. Hellerman,** *The Ancient Church as Family* (Minneapolis: Fortress 2001); **D. G. Horrell,** "From ἀδελφοί to οἶκος θεοῦ: Social Transformation in Pauline Christianity," *JBL* 120 (2001): 293-311; **R. Jewett,** "Tenement Churches and Communal Meals in the Early Church: The Implications of a Form-Critical Analysis of 2 Thessalonians 3:10," *BR* 38 (1993): 23-43; **C. G. Kruse,** *Paul's Letter to the Romans*, PNTC (Grand Rapids, MI: Eerdmans, 2012); **P. Lampe,** "'Family' in Church and Society of New Testament Times," *Affirmation* 5 (1992): 1-20; **T.-L. Lau,** *Defending Shame: Its Formative Power in Paul's Letters* (Grand Rapids, MI: Baker Academic, 2020); **B. J. Malina,** *Timothy: Paul's Closest Associate* (Collegeville, MN: Liturgical Press, 2008); **J. H. McNeel,** *Paul as Infant and Nursing Mother: Metaphor, Rhetoric, and Identity in 1 Thessalonians 2:5-8*, ECL 12 (Atlanta: SBL Press, 2014); **W. A. Meeks,** *The First Urban Christians: The Social World of the Apostle Paul* (New Haven, CT: Yale University Press, 1983); **A. M. Mengestu,** *God as Father in Paul: Kinship Language and Identity Formation in Early Christianity* (Eugene, OR: Wipf & Stock, 2013); **H. Moxnes,** "What Is Family? Problems in Constructing Early Christian Families," in *Constructing Early Christian Families: Family as Metaphor and Social Reality*, ed.

H. Moxnes (London: Routledge, 1997), 13-41; **E. H. Peterson,** *Practice Resurrection: A Conversation on Growing Up in Christ* (Grand Rapids, MI: Eerdmans, 2010); **T. R. Schreiner,** *Romans*, 2nd ed. (Grand Rapids, MI: Baker Academic, 2018); **E. Schüssler Fiorenza,** *In Memory of Her: A Feminist Theological Reconstruction of Christian Origins* (London: SCM Press, 1983); **J. M. Scott,** *Adoption as Sons of God: An Investigation into the Background of HUIOTHESIA*, WUNT 2/48 (Tübingen: Mohr Siebeck, 1992); **A. C. Thiselton,** *The First Epistle to the Corinthians*, NIGTC (Grand Rapids, MI: Eerdmans, 2000); **P. Trebilco,** *Self-Designations and Group Identity in the New Testament* (Cambridge: Cambridge University Press, 2012); **D. B. Wallace,** *Greek Grammar Beyond the Basics: An Exegetical Syntax of the New Testament* (Grand Rapids, MI: Zondervan, 1996); **B. Witherington,** *Conflict and Community in Corinth: A Socio-rhetorical Commentary on 1 and 2 Corinthians* (Grand Rapids, MI: Eerdmans, 1995); idem, *1 and 2 Thessalonians: A Socio-rhetorical Commentary* (Grand Rapids, MI: Eerdmans, 2006).

T. J. Burke

KNOWLEDGE AND MIND

Epistemology has generally referred to the study of knowing and knowledge, but it overlaps with fields such as *hermeneutics, cognitive linguistics, *philosophy of mind, historiography, scientific method, and wisdom studies. These explorations could be clustered together under the umbrella *attempts to know or understand something with a reasonably higher degree of confidence than can be achieved in the unexamined life.* When discussing Paul's epistemology, *wisdom is a key feature, though its meaning in scholarly discourse has ranged from mystical insight to the practical application of factual knowledge. Similarly, metadisciplines such as epistemology and philosophy acquire various meanings, especially in relation to Paul (where they are hardly considered). A key task in examining Paul's epistemology is grasping that the *apostle, along with the OT authors, conceives of knowledge in a manner that does not cleanly fit most modern paradigms.

The basic question, covering all epistemological pursuits, might be posed as follows: *Who knows what, and how do they know it?* To answer this question, one must think of "knowledge" as ranging from the basic ability to recognize something (e.g., "that is a table") all the way to nuanced discernment (e.g., "that is a nineteenth-century cherry wood Shaker table, and here is how I know that"). The OT authors generally depict the former in terms of "seeing" or "knowing," and the latter in terms of "wisdom" (*ḥokmâ*) and its various Hebrew synonyms (e.g., *bîn, mûsār, tābûn, ʿārûm*). But such terms are elastic and are used interchangeably at points. Paul avails himself of similar terms referring broadly to knowledge and wisdom, such as *sophia, synesis, gnōsis*, and semantically related terms such as *didaskō/didaskalia*.

But a focus on Paul's terminology alone is insufficient given that his writings sit at the confluence of several intellectual currents that include the epistemologies depicted in the Hebrew Bible, the Hebraic wisdom genre that pervades Scripture, and the Romanized *Hellenism of Second Temple Judaism. Understanding the epistemology revealed in Paul's writings requires a brief summary of the intellectual world of the Hebrew Bible, from which Paul funds much of his thinking. Paul's strategic employment of Hebrew epistemology in Greco-Roman rhetorical packages shows his conversance with the logic of Hellenism while simultaneously possessing different strategies and goals from the usual topics and methods of Hellenistic thought.

1. The Intellectual World of Paul's Scriptures
2. Modern Scholarship on Paul
3. Knowing in the Old Testament and Paul
4. The Pursuit of Wisdom in Paul

1. The Intellectual World of Paul's Scriptures. Though the narrow study of epistemology is relatively recent (ca. seventeenth-century Europe), some have argued that the exploration of the question "Who can know what and how?" can be traced back to the Hebrew Bible (Gericke; Hazony; Johnson 2017). Some Assyriologists go back further in time to detect epistemologies in the Babylonian lexical lists and omenology, parts of which date three thousand years prior to the Greeks (Van De Mieroop). Egyptologists have also creatively reconstructed the Egyptian intellectual environment and the key elements of their epistemology (Assmann 1996; 2008).

In the mid-twentieth century, several of the University of Chicago's ancient Near Eastern scholars observed that, compared to the intellectual worlds of Mesopotamia and Egypt, the Hebrew Bible contained a distinctive "skeptical method" and "critical intellectualism." This distinct form of thinking fit more appropriately with the intellectual world of the Greeks than with the literatures of the ancient Fertile Crescent (Wilson). These conclusions, which must be held in tension with their progressivist ideology, still hold some sway with Egyptologists and Assyriologists. Specifically, the Hebrew intellectual tradition that spans the OT was remarkably untethered from the mythopoeic foundations that are thought to have restrained intellectualism in the ancient Near East.

More recently, scholars have argued that discourses on epistemology have an early predecessor in the Hebrew Bible (Carasik 2005; Hazony; Healy; Johnson 2013; 2017; 2021; O'Dowd 2009). These interpreters contend that, in the OT, one finds a sustained argument across narratives, legal traditions, and poetry about the nature and kinds of knowing and the kinds of errors that distort understanding.

These examinations of Hebrew epistemologies have been well received in biblical studies, yet their incorporation into theology or NT scholarship, save for a few works, has been slow (Healy; Scott 2008). In Anglophone scholarship, the Greek philosophical style permeates later medieval theology, which then persisted into the Enlightenment, where it has been retrieved in sectors of modern theology. With their focus ultimately trained on ancient Greece as the source of philosophy, scholars have often determined what counted as epistemology proper according to a singular Aegean standard.

Some might claim that the Platonic literature defines epistemological tradition: how one knows confidently and what is the nature of that secured knowledge. Others might situate epistemology as properly beginning in the seventeenth century with René Descartes's *Meditations*. Rooting epistemology in either intellectual tradition might only reveal a preference for a particular style of discourse, where the author overtly informs the audience about what is being discussed and why. Most philosophers in the Anglo-American tradition, for example, conclude that some story of the intellectual worlds of Greece and Europe constitutes good philosophical discourse.

Viewing Hebrew narrative, poetry, and legal texts as philosophical discourse has been regarded with some skepticism in the Anglo-American world (though less so for the same view of epistolary works). Nonetheless, several volumes have demonstrated that ancient narratives, prophetic texts, ritual instruction, legal materials, and even lists can be employed as philosophical analysis, though these represent an entirely different style of examination compared to that of classical Greek philosophers (Dietrich; Hazony; Gericke; Johnson 2016; 2021; Van de Mieroop; Müller-Wille and Charmantier; Neusner).

2. Modern Scholarship on Paul.

When NT scholars do consider Paul's views in a philosophical light, they typically deal with Paul's place at the intersection of the Hebraic and Hellenic traditions. They puzzle about what his corresponding philosophical inclinations and rhetorical style might be. Is Paul a Hellenistic Jew reorganizing his thought in Stoic concepts and rhetoric? Or does Paul reflect the deep-seated history and narratives of the Hebrew Scriptures dressed up in different rhetorical packages for communities across the Greco-Roman world? Abraham Malherbe captures the tension in this way: "Paul was part of all that he had met," yet "the differences are greater than the similarities" (Malherbe 2014, 67, 729). In short, a decision to place Paul *exclusively* in one camp or another will usually be fraught with generalizations and oversimplifications.

Nonetheless, modern interpreters have drawn the lines rather sharply in these debates. One can group them loosely as those who rate Paul's acquiescence to Hellenistic thought, specifically Stoics such as Seneca, Epictetus, and Marcus Aurelius (Huttunen; Engberg-Pedersen; etc.), and those who see a consistently Jewish Paul who engages Hellenistic audiences while anchored in Hebraic thought (Rowe; Wright; etc.)—with some in moderating positions (Barclay; Martyn; Malherbe; etc.).

N. T. Wright claims that the organizing features of Paul's thinking find their roots in the Hebrew Scriptures but that Paul would see them as directly relevant to the classical tripartite division of philosophy (physics, logic, and *ethics): "The many parallels here would only be surprising to someone who supposed that Paul derived everything from Torah on the one hand and the teaching of Jesus on the other, and indeed that those two sources would themselves be completely discontinuous with pagan moralism" (Wright, 1376). Hence, if one takes the physics, logic, and ethics of the Torah seriously, then Paul's letters will have purchase with his disparate audiences.

C. Kavin Rowe has pushed even further to claim that the traditions of Stoicism and Christianity are incommensurable rivals. They may invoke the same language, causing some scholars to weigh their contents with the same scales of judgment, but this does not constitute substantial similarity. Rowe employs Alasdair MacIntyre's notion of tradition to argue that even the word *god* (Gk. *theos*) gets packaged so differently in the traditions of Stoicism versus that of the early Jesus movement that its meaning within each *tradition is mutually exclusive of the other. Hence, "different traditions can both be speaking

Greek, but effectively speaking different languages" (Rowe, 226).

Some scholars have been skeptical of Paul's acquiescence to Hellenistic philosophy. They argue that, because Paul viewed the Torah and Prophets as a complete, sufficient, and robust philosophical system of thought, he can then translate its content into the philosophical *lingua franca* and according to the needs of his audiences. Recent examinations of Paul's rhetoric have noted modest parallels with several Roman rhetorical forms, including the philosophical *letters of Plato and Aristotle. However, these also conclude that Paul's rhetoric does not categorically fit within any particular Roman school of rhetoric (Parsons and Martin; Scott 2008; Spencer; Thompson). On most occasions, Paul alludes to, cites, and employs the intellectual tradition that he sees as primarily shaping his own thought—the Hebraic tradition—while sometimes adopting certain modes of Hellenism and other times flagging its problematic features.

Paul appears fully aware of the two intellectual traditions in which he lives: Hellenistic and Hebrew. The OT is not a "religious" book for him but a rigorous and sometimes rival intellectual tradition that can therefore be put in conversation with contemporary intellectual voices. Living with and writing to Hellenistic Jews and *Gentiles, he uses Greek terms and concepts to share what he thinks is most important for that community. The OT is his Scripture, Second Temple Judaism is his culture, and he is speaking to people with varying awareness of these influences in whatever way he deems suited to his main task: guiding others to know the *kingdom of *God as it is now revealed through this Jesus from Nazareth.

3. Knowing in the Old Testament and Paul. Guided by the paradigm of "who knows what and how," one finds three epistemological pillars that recur throughout the OT, the Gospels, and Paul's thinking:

1. Knowing is guided.
2. Knowing is interdependent on ethics and rituals.
3. Knowing is contingent on God's revealing through rationality.

3.1. Knowing Is Guided. If knowledge is framed in terms of discernment rather than as acquiring chunks of information, then becoming wise by means of guidance is the final goal of knowing in the Pentateuch (O'Dowd; Johnson 2013). This makes sense of the many occurrences of "listen" (*šāmaʿ*), where the voice to whom one listens guides one to proper discernment.

In some of the most renowned scenes of the Pentateuch, the voice guides toward knowledge. The prudent (*ʿārûm*) serpent's voice guides the first couple to know (Gen 3:1-7, 11, 17) just as Moses guides Israel and Pharaoh in scenes punctuated with "you shall know" (e.g., Ex 7:17; 8:10, 22; 9:14, 29; 16:6; Num 16:28; etc.), which the texts connect to "listening to the voice." This conflict of guidance in order to know at the center of Israel's seminal stories creates the dilemma of authority. The biblical authors paint both the serpent and Moses as discerning, yet the former should not be listened to and the latter should. To resolve this dilemma, the Pentateuch establishes rubrics for assessing one's allegiance to a particular voice.

Deuteronomy 13; 18 make specific what has already been depicted in several prophetic authentication scenes in Numbers 12; 16. In each case, discernment beyond mere knowledge of facts is required to properly heed the prophets. God promises to raise up and authenticate future prophets but then to cause them to mislead *Israel in order to test its discernment (see Deut 13:1-5; 18:15-22). Hence, "seeing" a prophet's *signs and wonders is merely an entrée to discerning whether to listen to that prophet's voice. In other words, not everything that proceeds from a prophet will truly guide Israel to know.

This same emphasis on guidance from authenticated knowers who have been measured against the Pentateuch can be seen in Paul's synagogue interactions. Luke depicts this framework of authentication and testing in Paul's visit to Berea, highlighting the eager hearing given to Paul (Acts 17:10-15) alongside the prudent scrutiny of everything he said according to the "Scriptures" (*graphē*). Within his corpus, Paul may highlight his authentication as a guide to the growing Jesus movement, but he does not proffer his *teaching as exempt from the scrutiny of scriptural orthodoxy (see Rom 1:1-5; 1 Cor 1:1; 2 Cor 1:1; Gal 1:1; Eph 1:1; Col 1:1; 1 Tim 1:1; 2 Tim 1:1; Titus 1:1-3).

In fact, Paul suggests a cascade of epistemological authentication: God has guided Paul to discernment (Eph 3:3) so that the *church can be made to know mysteries that were once hidden (Eph 3:10). This structure appears to parallel Jesus' self-ascribed role as guide to the "mysteries of the kingdom" with his disciples (Mk 4:10-12), with the aim of revealing what was previously hidden (Mk 4:22). Paul often appeals not to his authoritative understanding but to his authentication to guide the churches to discern what he is showing them (e.g., 1 Cor 11:23;

1 Thess 1–2; Titus 1:1-3)—that is, to see the same data differently. The seminal events in his authentication are his Damascus road experience—"I did not receive [my *gospel] from any man, nor was I taught it; rather, I received it by revelation from Jesus *Christ" (Gal 1:12 NIV)—and his acceptance by the apostles at the *Jerusalem Council (Acts 15). Paul's instruction aims at helping the church to discern beyond the superficial features of culturally constructed values: the frailty of human political structures (1 Cor 1:26-29; Phil 1:9-10; Col 2:15), the flimsiness of "philosophies" (1 Cor 1:20-25; Gal 4; Col 2:8) the upside-down nature of strength (2 Cor 12:9-10), the vapidity of eloquent rhetoric (1 Cor 1:17; Col 2:4), the beauty of humiliation (Phil 2:1-11), and so on. This also makes sense of Paul's metaphor of maturity in wisdom, knowledge to be grown into by the church through his guidance (1 Cor 14:20; Eph 4:13; Col 1:28).

How does Paul use his epistles to guide his audiences to proper knowing? Paul's use of *narrative in the *law and in his reasoning suggests reliance on Hebrew forms of rhetoric alongside Hellenistic forms. First, scholars have noted the distinct literary form of laws in the Hebrew Bible as opposed to the same legal content found elsewhere in the ancient Near East. Where one might expect laws to be formed in plain conditionals (e.g., "If X, then Y"), instead, one finds laws that include characters, setting, plot, and resolution (Bartor). Rather than "a stray animal must be returned," one finds "when you see the donkey of one who hates you lying under its burden and you would hold back from setting it free, you must help to set it free" (Ex 23:5 NRSV). The legal code exhorts the hearer with reference to a particular place, with a perspective on an unfolding drama, one that has important relational and societal implications.

This narrative repackaging of laws undercuts the rule-following (statutory) mode as the reigning legal paradigm in Paul's Scriptures, even if rule following was practiced widely in his day. Paul uses this same narrative technique to situate his Corinthian audience in a drama that requires shrewd *judgment. Paul does not categorically instruct the Corinthians to avoid meat sacrificed to idols; rather, he guides them to be discerning through narrative (1 Cor 10:23-33). He initiates this section of teaching with an epistemological problem: "I do not want you to be unknowing [*agnoein*], brothers and sisters" (1 Cor 10:1). Paul then limits his discussion of the facts and focuses on the fundamental problem: the facts did not help Israel to discern what was good when put to the test by God in the wilderness (see 1 Cor 10:2-8; Rom 11:25).

Like Israel's law, Paul frames his guidance narratologically: setting (invited dinner party), characters (hosts and guests), conflict (knowledge of meat used in pagan *worship). The rest of his instruction aims at resolving the conflict of this microdrama. He even visualizes the Corinthians' perspective on the scene: "Eat whatever is *set before you*" (1 Cor 10:27 NRSV). By means of a *narrative* description, the conflict intuitively demands a resolution to the drama, as opposed to rhetoric that treats the law as statute: "do this" or "don't do that." Paul's instruction, and his presumption that the whole process is guided by the Spirit, places the Corinthians in a conflicted narrative matrix where wisdom, not juridical knowledge, is required to alleviate the tension.

One of the most comprehensive examinations of Paul's epistemology finds that his "theological knowledge is structured as a narrative" (Scott 2008, 278). Mirroring his own thinking, Paul reconfigures the master narratives of Scripture in light of Christ and rhetorically plants his audience in this reconfigured arc (Scott). This might explain some affinity between Paul's letters and Roman *narratio* rhetoric (Parsons and Martin, 98-99).

Paul overtly takes on the mantle as the guide to this burgeoning new "Israel of God," claiming a *call to the task and, like Moses, guarding against anyone who might come and teach "another gospel" (2 Cor 11:4). In the vein of Deuteronomy (Deut 4:33-40), no one, not even a "messenger from heaven," can teach a different gospel (Gal 1:8; Col 1:23). Why not? Because of the historically unique and personally witnessed events of the first *preaching, which is recalled in the tone of Deuteronomy's account of Sinai: "*before your eyes* that Jesus Christ was publicly portrayed as crucified" (Gal 3:1; see Deut 29:2). Paul's inescapable call, like Jeremiah's, was set *in utero*, "before I was born" (see Jer 1:4-5; Gal 1:15).

In conclusion, Paul sees himself as one who has been taught to see and know the mysteries revealed by God. Anything that can be considered true knowledge must be properly authenticated by the Spirit, particularly in relation to the Hebrew Scriptures and the Christ-event. Paul understands himself as an authenticated figure, guiding other believers in their ability to know and see what he has experienced himself. This cooperative approach to knowing requires both Paul's instruction and the inner workings of the Spirit (Rom 1:9; 1 Cor 2:4, 10;

2 Cor 3:3; Eph 1:13; 1 Tim 3:16; etc.), and mirrors what one finds in Paul's Scriptures.

3.2. Knowing Is Interdependent on Ethics and Rituals. Hebrew Scripture and Hellenistic Jewish texts both connect ethical behaviors with Israel's rituals and ability to know (see Ex 12:24-28; Lev 23:42-43; Josh 4:6-7; Johnson 2016), but with different emphases. Wisdom of Solomon and Philo, among others, connect epistemic blindness to the *idolatry of created things and its related "fornications." But these critiques appear to differ from the ethical concerns stated in the Pentateuch and Prophets, where impoverished understanding leads to the exploitation of the vulnerable. How one treats one's children, the impoverished, widows, orphans, visitors, foreigners, and animals determines whether one's *sacrifices are fragrant or foul before Yahweh (see Ex 23; Lev 19; Amos; Mic; Is 3:13-26; Jer 7:5-20).

Exploitative practices and fornication are the invisible aspects that the Hebrews brought to their visible ritual lives, as can be seen in the infamous rhetoric of Amos against those who "oppress the poor and crush the needy." God is repulsed by their sacrifices (Amos 4:1-5).

Faithful participation in the life of the community makes rituals efficacious and revealing (O'Dowd; Culp; Johnson 2013). Those who are recalcitrant to the Pentateuch's guidance cut off their access to such understanding through a distorted ethical life that ultimately numbs and dumbs them to these mysteries now being revealed.

Like the discourses of Jesus in the Gospels, and the Hebrew Scriptures that preceded them (see Gen 2:17; Deut 28; Hos 4:6), authors tied knowing both to embodying God's guidance and to warnings of his coming judgment. Jesus' hearers, blinded by their maintenance of status quo behaviors (Mt 24:36-42; Lk 17:22-37), fail to discern the times and the certainty of a coming judgment mediated by who knows whom and how (see Jer 31:34; Mt 7:22-23). Above all other implications that one might draw from such a pairing—knowing and judgment—it signals the intimate connection between ethics and epistemology. Skilled discernment gained from participation in the cult and the ordinary affairs of life has implications for wisdom. Israel's ritual participation can yield knowing that is presumed to be transferrable for understanding the eschatological impact of current events.

Paul plays up this same connection among ethics, rituals, and knowing most prominently in 1 Corinthians. He famously critiques the Corinthians for their faulty practice of Communion while also developing wisdom in them about *food sacrificed to idols (1 Cor 8). For the sake of their community, Paul concludes that eating idol food might be an unwise action (1 Cor 8:13). When it pertains to the ritualized food of Communion, Paul insists that ethical behavior prior to the meal mediates one's participation in the meal (1 Cor 11:17). Why is their ritual meal counterproductive? It is because of the divisions and strife (1 Cor 11:18), sexual immorality (1 Cor 5:1-13), and abuse of the sacrifice (i.e., bread and wine) itself (1 Cor 11:20-22).

For Paul, their ritual preparation begins in an individual ethic (i.e., sexual immorality and idol food) that extends through the community (i.e., divisions and strife). This scheme is not distant from Hellenistic ideals of the philosophers: a life that fully integrates ethics and logic based on the metaphysics of the cosmos. Likely aware of this, Paul shies away from the Roman target of tranquility of one's soul and aims his ethical instruction at the health of the community of God's people and its extension into its locale (Hadot).

The entire epistle sets forth a program by which they are to develop this wisdom through Paul's guidance, ethical practices, and epistemological rituals that both correctly remember and proclaim. From its introduction to its repetitious "do you not know" questions throughout, 1 Corinthians exhibits what appears to be largely programmatic for Paul: ritual and ethical guidance foster knowledge and wisdom. In this way, Paul methodologically diverges from other Hellenistic Jewish texts and the Roman philosophies *du jour*. To know properly, one must *heed* and *do* what Paul prescribes within an ethical matrix that includes the daily and cultic life of individuals and communities.

3.3. Knowing Is Contingent on God's Revealing Through Rationality. Deuteronomy 29 examines God's role in revealing "the hidden" to bear on the enigma of Israel's hardened hearts. They witnessed the exodus and Sinai wonders "before your eyes," yet many did not understand that they were performed by Yahweh with obligated responses (Deut 29:2-4). Why not? Yahweh has not "given a heart to know, eyes to see, ears to listen," an exclusive triplet repeated in this form only in Isaiah 6:9-10.

The *covenant renewal then goes on to separate out "the hidden" (LXX: *ta krypta*) from "the revealed" (LXX: *ta phanera*), where the hidden things are "to Yahweh" and the revealed are "to us and our children that we may do all the word of this *torah*" (Deut 29:29 [MT 29:28]). Mark's Gospel alone employs both the Deuteronomic juxtaposition of hidden and revealed, and intensified repetitions of Deuteronomy's phrasing of "ears to listen" (*ōta akouein*, Deut 29:3 LXX).

Several recent works have demonstrated Paul's dependence on the Deuteronomic language and logic (Deut 27–30) in his emphasis on revelation (Lincicum; Wells). Regarding the blurring of moral and epistemological development in Paul's thinking, Kyle Wells concludes that Paul roots his epistemology in the same Deuteronomic triplet: "Bereft of eyes that see, ears that hear, or understanding hearts, they lack the faculties to respond to God effectively" (Wells, 294). Conversely, Paul faults a lack of epistemic humility that leans on visions without cause/reason for their misunderstanding (Col 2:18).

Of course, Paul is willing to seek and communicate knowledge through seemingly superrational means, including divine revelations (2 Cor 12:5-7) and speaking in heavenly *tongues (1 Cor 14:18). However, he explicitly prefers intelligible words (1 Cor 14:19), and even his charismatic experiences require a reasoned framework in which to understand them. This follows from Peter's attempt to grasp the significance of Pentecost by interpreting it in light of the history of Israel and the expectations of the prophets (Acts 2). Likewise, Paul discourages naiveté about spiritual power and its manifestations (e.g., 2 Cor 11:13–12:10) and exhorts his audience to look for the presence of the Spirit in tangible actions of *love, *joy, and *peace (Gal 5:22-23). In other words, rationality foregrounds and pervades his charismatic experience.

In fact, even Paul's rhetorical style, sometimes in perfunctory Greco-Roman packaging, demands that rationality play a key role in understanding, even in those things that seem plainly revealed. Paul himself says that he was a great learner (Gal 1:14), and he calls his readers to be "transformed by the renewing of your mind [*nous*]" (Rom 12:2 NIV). In brief, Paul inhabited the intellectual world of Scripture, including its love of reason within a larger supernatural framework. As one study of Paul's rhetoric concludes, "'Moses,' not 'Homer,' was the 'Bible'—the source of authority . . . even if that faith and practice were communicated through thoroughly Hellenized rhetorical devices" (Parsons and Martin, 9).

Paul felt free to "engage in the kind of logical argument which characterized the philosophers of his day" (Wright, 1365) but also to diverge from it for the sake of orienting his hearers to the true source of wisdom being revealed to them. This dualism in Paul of divine revelation and rationalism reflects a through line persistent in Deuteronomy, if not the whole of Paul's Scripture.

4. The Pursuit of Wisdom in Paul.

Paul's concept of wisdom derives from the heart of his gospel, specifically his understanding of the Christ-event, which he calls the "wisdom of God" (e.g., 1 Cor 2:1-5, 7). In different places, this wisdom can adopt, reorient, or flatly contradict "human wisdom" (1 Cor 1:25; 2:1, 5, 13). Research in this area began with Eduard Grafe (1892), and it has swelled since the "new perspective" on Paul as interpreters increasingly read Paul's letters in relation to Second Temple Judaism and the broader Hebraic tradition, including its wisdom literature.

4.1. What Is "Wisdom" in Paul's Scriptures? The pursuit of knowledge in the OT is guided by an authenticated authority who prescribes ethically prepared rituals meant to produce bare knowledge (seeing what was always there) and ultimately wisdom (nuanced discernment that can lead others to see). Hence, wisdom refers to those "who . . . are 'competent,' 'skilled.' It can be used even of manual workers or sailors" (von Rad, 20).

Proverbs says the beginning of wisdom is reverence for Yahweh and his commands (Prov 9:10). Wisdom is personified as a feminine figure who preaches in the streets and makes her instruction known to a busy or uninterested world (Prov 8:1-36). Elsewhere wisdom is both "an associate in God's works" (Wis 8:4; also Ps 1:1-3) and attainable through reason and experience (e.g., Eccl 2:3; 7:25; Prov 6:6-8). In other words, wisdom is a matter of divine revelation—even finding it in *creation requires divine aid (e.g., Job 38–39)—but it is arguably acquired more often through simple observations over a lifetime (e.g., Eccl 12:9-14).

The content of wisdom includes use of one's words, heart attitudes, sexual ethics, use of money and alcohol, relationships with family and friends, and approach to vocation and work.

4.2. Wisdom Material in Paul's Letters. Paul quotes directly from Proverbs (Rom 2:6; 12:20; 2 Cor 9:7), Job (Rom 11:35; 1 Cor 3:19), and Ecclesiastes (Rom 3:10); however, allusions and echoes relating to Wisdom literature can be detected in a variety of texts attributed to Paul, including, but certainly not limited to Romans 1:19-21; Ephesians 5:18; and 2 Corinthians 10:7. The traditional Pauline corpus also adopts wisdom forms, such as aphorisms (e.g., Gal 4:16, 18; 5:9), exhortations (e.g., Rom 12–13), and *household codes (e.g., Col 3:18-25).

There is growing recognition, especially in Romans, of conceptual connections to wisdom material outside the Hebrew Bible. For instance, Linebaugh argues that Wisdom of Solomon not only foregrounds Paul's approach to creation but also offers a shared theological lexicon in which Paul understands the law and the relationship between the righteous and the unrighteous. However, there is certainly more difference than similarity between the two documents.

Any inquiry into the relationship between a wisdom tradition and Paul should consider the best practices for comparisons generally (Barclay 2020): (1) make a legitimate comparison (historically or analogically), (2) select focus texts from each source that are representative of the whole, (3) create a framework for the comparison, (4) determine the purpose, and (5) measure degrees of similarity and difference.

4.3. Christology and Dialectical Wisdom. In 1 Corinthians 1–4, and especially in 1 Corinthians 1, the central element in Paul's approach to wisdom is his understanding of Jesus, whose *ministry involved elements of wisdom teaching, including revealing divine knowledge and speaking in parables. For Paul, however, it is Jesus' *death and, specifically, the mode of death—crucifixion—that most inform wisdom's theological and ethical content. This crucified Jesus "has become for us wisdom from God" (1 Cor 1:30 NIV) because he represents God's redemptive program: to use "the foolish things of the world to shame the wise" and to use "the weak things of the world to shame the *strong" (1 Cor 1:27 NIV; see Is 29:14). The dialectic is as follows: that although believers appear foolish according to certain cultural standards—and may, in fact, be of humble origin and have little knowledge (1 Cor 1:26)—they nonetheless possess the apostolic proclamation, Christ himself, who is the "foolishness of God" that is "wiser than human wisdom" (1 Cor 1:25 NIV).

Paul's rhetoric about cruciform wisdom does not form a hard paradox. Paul maintains that wisdom is distinct from foolishness, but they are interchangeable if one holds two perspectives in mind at the same time. The first is, of course, Paul's own perspective (i.e., assumed to be divine wisdom), and the second is "worldly" wisdom. Given the predominantly Gentile community at Corinth, interpreters have tended to locate the latter, contrasting perspective in the broad Greco-Roman tradition: typically the style of the rhetors and sophists (e.g., Conzelmann) or, more recently, the larger phenomenon of "higher education" (e.g., White). Yet even within this milieu, and notwithstanding his eschatological emphasis, Paul reverts to reasoned conscience on secondary or less certain issues (e.g., 1 Cor 7:25).

4.4. Ethics. Like other ancient thinkers, Paul was concerned with the connection between his thought world and the decisions and actions of everyday life. In 1 Corinthians, he moves from his opening discourse on the wisdom of the crucified Jesus to a series of arguments that discourage division and outline his view of the apostleship (e.g., 1 Cor 3:5-15; 4:1-13), all of which are shaped by the humility and sacrifice of the *cross. Elsewhere Paul issues exhortations that are more typical of wisdom discourse, such as the call to be renewed in one's mind (Rom 12:2), and thus bear resemblance to the Stoic emphasis on rational choice. Eckhard Schnabel rightly notes that, nonetheless, the Stoics emphasized the autonomy of the human being, whereas Paul prefers divine *grace and location within the community as sources of wisdom. In this sense, Paul inhabits the theocentric tradition of wisdom native to Second Temple Judaism. But given the dialectic he advances in 1 Corinthians 1, he also differs in certain ways from this tradition, too, and the precise divide is the Christ event and its accompanying implications.

See also CHRISTOLOGY; ETHICS; PHILOSOPHY; WISDOM.

BIBLIOGRAPHY. **J. Assmann,** *The Mind of Egypt: History and Meaning in the Time of the Pharaohs,* trans. Andrew Jenkins (New York: Metropolitan Books, 1996); idem, *God and Gods: Egypt, Israel, and the Rise of Monotheism* (Madison: University of Wisconsin Press, 2008); **J. M. G. Barclay,** *Paul and the Gift* (Grand Rapids, MI: Eerdmans, 2015); idem, "'O wad some Pow'r the giftie gie us, To see oursels as others see us': Method and Purpose in Comparing the New Testament," in *The New Testament in Comparison: Validity, Method, and Purpose in Comparing Traditions,* ed. J. M. G. Barclay and B. G. White (London: T&T Clark, 2020), 9-22; **A. Bartor,** *Reading Law as Narrative: A Study in the Casuistic Laws of the Pentateuch,* AIL 5 (Atlanta: Society of Biblical Literature, 2010); **M. Carasik,** *Theologies of the Mind in Biblical Israel* (Bern: Peter, 2005); **H. Conzelmann,** *1 Corinthians* (Philadelphia: Fortress, 1975); **A. J. Culp,** *Memoir of Moses: The Literary Creation of Covenantal Memory in Deuteronomy* (Minneapolis: Fortress Academic, 2019); **J. Dietrich,** "Empiricism or Rationalism in the Hebrew Bible? Some Thoughts About Ancient Foxes and Hedgehogs," in *Sounding Sensory Profiles in the Ancient Near East,* ed. A. Schellenberg and T. Krüger, ANEM 25 (Atlanta: SBL Press, 2019), 57-68; **T. Engberg-Pedersen,** *Paul and the Stoics* (Louisville: Westminster John Knox, 2000); **J. Gericke,** *The Hebrew Bible* *and Philosophy of Religion* (Atlanta: Society of Biblical Literature, 2013); **E. Grafe,** "Das Verhältnis der paulinischen Schriften zur Sapientia Salomonis," in *Theologische Abhandlungen* (Freiburg, 1892), 251-86; **P. Hadot,** *What Is Ancient Philosophy?*, trans. M. Chase (Cambridge, MA: Harvard University Press, 2002); **Y. Hazony,** *The Philosophy of Hebrew Scripture* (New York: Cambridge University Press, 2012); **M. Healy,** "Knowledge of the Mystery: A Study of Pauline Epistemology," in *The Bible and Epistemology: Biblical Soundings on the Knowledge of God*, ed. M. Healy and R. Parry (Milton Keynes, UK: Paternoster, 2007); **N. Huttunen,** *Paul and Epictetus on Law: A Comparison*, LNTS 405 (New York: T&T Clark, 2009); **D. Johnson,** *Biblical Knowing: A Scriptural Epistemology of Error* (Eugene, OR: Cascade, 2013); idem, *Knowledge by Ritual: A Biblical Prolegomenon to Sacramental Theology* (Winona Lake, IN: Eisenbrauns, 2016); idem, *Epistemology and Biblical Theology: From the Pentateuch to Mark's Gospel* (New York: Routledge, 2017); idem, *Biblical Philosophy: An Hebraic Approach to the Old and New Testaments* (New York: Cambridge University Press, 2021); **C. S. Keener,** *The Mind of the Spirit: Paul's Approach to Transformed Thinking* (Grand Rapids, MI: Baker, 2016); **D. Lincicum,** "Paul's Engagement with Deuteronomy: Snapshots and Signposts," *CurBR* 7, no. 37 (2008): 37-67; idem, *Paul and the Early Jewish Encounter with Deuteronomy* (Grand Rapids, MI: Baker Academic, 2013); **J. A. Linebaugh,** *God, Grace, and Righteousness in Wisdom of Solomon and Paul's Letter to the Romans*, NovTSup 152 (Leiden: Brill, 2013); **A. Malherbe,** *Paul and the Popular Philosophers* (Minneapolis: Fortress, 1989); idem, *Light from the Gentiles: Hellenistic Philosophy and Early Christianity; Collected Essays, 1959–2012*, 2 vols. (Leiden: Brill, 2014); **J. L. Martyn,** *Galatians: A New Translation with Introduction and Commentary*, AB 33A (New York: Doubleday, 1997); idem, "De-apocalypticizing Paul: An Essay Focused on *Paul and the Stoics* by Troels Engberg-Pedersen," *JSNT* 86 (2002): 61-102; **S. Müller-Wille and I. Charmantier,** "Lists as Research Technologies," *Isis* 103, no. 4 (2012): 743-52; **J. Neusner,** "The Mishnah's Generative Mode of Thought: *Listenwissenschaft* and Analogical Contrastive Reasoning," *JAOS* 110, no. 2 (1990): 317-21; **R. O'Dowd,** *The Wisdom of Torah: Epistemology in Deuteronomy and the Wisdom Literature* (Göttingen: Vandenhoeck & Ruprecht, 2009); **M. C. Parsons and M. W. Martin,** *Ancient Rhetoric and the New Testament: The Influence of Elementary Greek Composition* (Waco, TX: Baylor University Press, 2018); **G. von Rad,** *Wisdom in Israel*, trans. J. D. Martin (Nashville: Abingdon, 1986); **C. K. Rowe,** *One True Life: The Argument of Rival Traditions* (New Haven, CT: Yale University Press, 2016); **E. J. Schnabel,** "Wisdom," in *DPL*, 967-73; **I. W. Scott,** *Implicit Epistemology in the Letters of Paul: Story, Experience and the Spirit*, WUNT (Tübingen: Mohr Siebeck, 2006); idem, *Paul's Way of Knowing: Story, Experience, and the Spirit* (Grand Rapids, MI: Baker Academic, 2008); **A. B. Spencer,** *Paul's Literary Style: A Stylistic and Historical Comparison of II Corinthians 11:16–12:13, Romans 8:9-39, and Philippians 3:2–4:13* (New York: University Press of America, 1998); **J. W. Thompson,** *Apostle of Persuasion: Theology and Rhetoric in the Pauline Letters* (Grand Rapids, MI: Baker Academic, 2020); **M. Van de Mieroop,** *Philosophy Before the Greeks: The Pursuit of Truth in Ancient Babylonia* (New York: Oxford University Press, 2017); **K. B. Wells,** *Grace and Agency in Paul and Second Temple Judaism: Interpreting the Transformation of the Heart*, NovTSup 157 (Leiden: Brill, 2014); **A. G. White,** *Where Is the Wise Man? Graeco-Roman Education as a Background to Divisions in 1 Corinthians 1–4* (London: T&T Clark, 2015); **J. A Wilson,** "The Nature of the Universe," in *The Intellectual Adventure of Ancient Man: An Essay on Speculative Thought in the Ancient Near East*, ed. H. Frankfort et al. (Chicago: University of Chicago Press, 1977); **N. T. Wright,** *Paul and the Faithfulness of God*, 2 vols. (Minneapolis: Fortress, 2013).

D. Johnson and B. G. White

KNOWLEDGE, GIFT OF. *See* Gifts of the Spirit.

KOINONIA. *See* Fellowship, Communion, Sharing; Lord's Supper.

KYRIOS. *See* Christology; Lord.

L

LAW

Paul's treatment of the Jewish law lies near the center of his christologically redefined vision for a renewed *Israel. For this reason, it also occasioned much controversy and apparent confusion during Paul's historical *ministry, in the subsequent interpretation of his letters, and to the present day. Since adherence to the law of Moses was constituent of Jewish praxis and *identity, the question of law observance for *Gentile converts almost immediately became primitive Christianity's first defining controversy, with Paul's missionary efforts and subsequent theological justification being the eye of the storm. His sometimes polemical, sometimes measured, sometimes oblique discourse around this topic has challenged interpreters for centuries.

1. Terminology and Use in Paul
2. The Law and Pauline Biography
3. *Law* in Paul's Letters
4. Toward a Pauline Synthesis
5. The Law and the Christian Moral Life

1. Terminology and Use in Paul.

The letters attributed to Paul refer to "law" (*nomos*) 121 times. The vast majority of Paul's discourse concerning law is found in Romans (74×) and Galatians (32×), with brief but significant discussions scattered elsewhere, especially in the Corinthian correspondence and Philippians, but with only three such references found among the disputed letters (Eph 2:15; 1 Tim 1:8-9).

Paul's customary use of the term is consistent with the LXX, where *nomos* characteristically translates *tôrâ* and is the default referent of the Hebrew term. Although through a series of translations, the Hebrew *tôrâ* came increasingly to be understood as an exclusively legal category (Gk. *nomos*; Lat. *lex*; English *law*), Hebrew lexicography agrees that its original sense is more inclusive: "instruction," which, depending on context, may bear a legal frame of reference, but not necessarily or exclusively so. Thus, *tôrâ* is not first a legal system calling for obedience or mere compliance but is indicative more broadly of the way one is to "walk" (*halakh*; e.g., Ex 18:20; Lev 18:4; 26:3; Deut 8:6; 28:9; 30:16). While it is true that Israel's civil life and disputes are addressed in *tôrâ*, this is not the whole of the instruction; daily, moral, legal, cultic, and ritual life are all included.

The Greek term is likewise flexible in its extrabiblical use, including a "custom," "rule," or "norm," on the one hand, or codified ordinances or statutes on the other, or the collective reference to either. BDAG notes that, while the term may also reference a legal tradition or fixed ordinance, *nomos* is a veritable synonym for *ēthos* ("habit, custom, way of being"), invoking this caution: "A special semantic problem for modern readers encountering the term [*nomos*] is the general tendency to confine the usage of the term 'law' to codified statutes. Such limitation has led to much fruitless debate in the history of NT interpretation" (BDAG, 67). Although the opportunity is long since passed, the more polysemous English word *rule* might better carry the range of *nomos* than "law," allowing for its various overlapping senses.

***1.1. Paul's Use of* Nomos.** Paul's particular uses of *nomos* can be summarized across four categories:

- *Nomos*[1]: *tôrâ* directives, the law of Moses. Most frequently for Paul, *nomos* refers to the "law of Moses," the moral, legal, and cultic directives found in the Pentateuch, given to Israel, either considered individually or, more often, taken as a whole—the *tôrâ* (instruction) *within* the Torah (Pentateuch). Understood this way, *nomos* is understood as that which is to be "done" (*poieō*) or "kept" (*phylassō*) or, alternatively, that which can be "transgressed." It is "the doers [*hoi poiētai*] of the law who will be justified" (Rom 2:13 NRSV; cf. Rom 10:5; Gal 3:10, 12; 5:3). It is this subset of the Pentateuch, associated with Moses at Sinai, rather than the Torah as a whole, to which Paul most frequently refers. A paradigmatic reference in this respect is Galatians 3:17, in which Paul describes the *nomos* given through Moses at Sinai coming 430 years after the promise made to *Abraham. Paul considers this law to have been "added" (*prosetethē*, Gal 3:19) or to have "slipped in" (*pareisēlthen*, Rom 5:20); thus it is clear that Paul can think of this subset of Pentateuch as its own body of material, located within but not coextensive with the canonical division. The exceptions to this predominant use of *nomos* are noted below.

- *Nomos*[2]: Pentateuch. Again, following LXX use, *nomos* can also refer to the Pentateuch as a whole, as the first and foundational division of the Jewish Scripture (Rom 3:19a; 1 Cor 9:8, 9; 14:34; Gal 3:10 [Deut 27:26]; 4:21b).
- *Nomos*[3]: Scripture. By way of synecdoche, the "law" can refer to Jewish Scripture as a whole, through reference to its most prominent subdivision (Rom 3:19a, 21b, 31; 1 Cor 14:21, 34; cf. Gal 3:22).
- *Nomos*[4]: "rule" or "principle." Some interpreters regard certain uses of *nomos* as generic, rhetorical, or even ironic, as a "principle" or a "rule" (e.g., Rom 3:27; 7:21, 23; 8:2b; Gal 3:21; 5:23), while others dispute this, arguing that a reference to torah is always intended by *nomos* in Paul. Yet this more generic sense may well be intended, especially when Paul refers to *nomos* in relationship to a qualifying genitive ("of works," "of faith," Rom 3:27; "of the husband" [= marriage], Rom 7:2; "of my mind," Rom 7:23; "of *sin," Rom 7:23, 25; "of the Spirit of life," Rom 8:2; "of sin and *death," Rom 8:2; "of righteousness," Rom 9:31). Meanwhile the expression "law of *God" seems to point to the Mosaic law but in its most idealized sense, as the law of which God is the source and that expresses the mind of God (Rom 7:22, 25; 8:7). For the expression "*law of Christ" (Gal 6:2; 1 Cor 9:21), see 4.1.2 below.

The recognition of the above distinctions is essential for a competent reading of Paul's approach to law because these multiple senses of *nomos* become a key feature in his nuanced arguments. For Paul, the legal demands of torah are in a certain tension with the narrative testimony of Torah (see especially Watson). Not infrequently, Paul will play these senses over against each other in near collocation. For example, a righteousness of God is manifested apart from the law (*nomos*[1]), though the law (*nomos*[2]) and prophets bear *witness to it (Rom 3:21). Likewise, "Tell me, you who desire to be subject to the law [*nomos*[1]], will you not listen to the law [*nomos*[2]]?" (Gal 4:21 NRSV), after which Paul goes on to rehearse a creative retelling of the narrative of Sarah and Hagar from Genesis. By the same token, Paul may use *nomos*[4] as a sort of wordplay to explicate his claims about *nomos*[1] (e.g., Rom 3:27).

***1.2. Synonyms for* Law.** As elsewhere in biblical literature, the Pauline corpus employs a variety of synonyms to describe the law in its various aspects. Recognition of these synonyms is important not only for determining the extent of Paul's discourse on law but also because of nuances that, attached in certain instances, suggest a purposeful word choice.

- "commandment" (*entolē*). Since Paul's characteristic use of *nomos* is as a singular collective, the law as a whole, "commandment" will sometimes function to refer to a specific or representative directive. So, for example, Romans 13:9 refers to instructions from the second table of the Decalogue as "commandments." Likewise, Ephesians 6:2 refers to the decalogue's "first commandment with a promise," "honor your father and mother" (NRSV). The language of commandment also plays an important illustrative role in the argument of Romans 7:7-13, where "commandment" refers specifically to the prohibition of covetousness and functions not only as a specification but as though a personified agent of the law. This part-to-whole relationship is evidenced also in Ephesians 2:15, the "law [consisting] of commandments." However, the presumption that *entolē* carries a more legalistic connotation, natural to the English *commandment*, is not verified by Pauline use (e.g., 1 Cor 14:37; Col 4:10; Titus 1:14).
- "letter" or "written code" (*gramma*). Besides its literal use (Gal 6:11; 2 Cor 3:7) and reference to Scripture as "sacred writings" (*hiera grammata*, 2 Tim 3:15 NRSV), *gramma* as "written code" occupies an important polemical function in Paul's discussion of the law. Described as "letter," mere writing, the law is characterized with respect to its static and inert character, capable only of codifying righteousness but not of enabling it. Thus, in Romans 7:6, Paul contrasts "the new way of the Spirit" with "the old way of the written code" (ESV; see also 3.3.2 below).

- "ordinance" or "legal demand" (*dogma*). Used only in the parallel passages of Colossians 2:14 and Ephesians 2:15, the "legal demands" are depicted as the law arrayed antagonistically against transgressors, thus needing to be overcome—"canceled" and "abolished," respectively.
- "the oracles of God" (*ta logia tou theou*). Found only in Romans 3:2 (NRSV), this may simply be a general reference to Scripture or even the speech of God more generally. But a more specific reference to the law is contextually probable in answer to the rhetorical question, "Then what advantage has the Jew?" (Rom 3:1 NRSV), given the Jewish sentiment that the gift of the law is a unique privilege of Israel (Deut 4:8; Ps 147:19-20).

As it concerns patterns of terminology, two related observations are apposite. First, attempts to track a pattern in Paul's use of *law* distinguished by the presence or absence of the definite article do not bear up under close scrutiny and have thus proven unconvincing to most interpreters. References to *the* law are not uniformly distinguishable in use from references to *a* law. Indeed, some uses of *nomos* with the article are generic in character and arguably not referencing the Mosaic law, and not infrequently context shows that an anarthrous *nomos* is both definite and can only refer to the Mosaic commandments. It is true that, on occasion, Paul will make generic or even ironic references to law (*nomos*[4]), but it is not the absence of the article that reliably signals this distinction.

Second, to adhere closely to Pauline use, it bears noting that the Pauline corpus is absent the sense of *law* that became prominent in later Christian discourse. In no undisputed case does Paul use *law* (*nomos*) as shorthand for the sum of divinely ordered moral requirements in general terms, irrespective of salvation-historical particularities. While Paul can summarize the requirements of the law, it is their manifold particularity that is encapsulated under the second commandment, "You shall love your neighbor as yourself" (Gal 5:14 NRSV, from Lev 19:18; see also Rom 13:9). Thus, the Mosaic law has an integrative principle, but this is not to be mistaken for an abstract or genericizing reference to law.

Although one may regard this later generic or even hermeneutical use as a natural theological extension of Pauline use, it confounds the interpretation of Paul's discourse when this anachronism is read into his writings, as became the case within certain influential interpretive schemes. In particular, the famous Reformed and especially Lutheran "law and *gospel" dichotomy, whatever its other merits, is not so much incompatible with Paul as it is an alien terminological framework, born of a different set of concerns from Paul's. Nor is there in Paul advocacy for the tactic of law as proto-evangelical—the preaching of the law creating a sense of conviction for which the gospel, God's provision of *grace, is the remediation (see Campbell). Likewise, whatever its distinguished pedigree, the traditional Catholic framework of natural and revealed law bears no precise intrinsic relationship to Paul's Jewish-particular concerns. In short, Paul's notion of law is Pentateuch-specific, with a particular accent on Sinai and its Deuteronomic reiteration.

2. The Law and Pauline Biography.

Paul's torah-observant life until the fateful event on the road to Damascus is beyond any serious dispute. Even allowing for a skeptical approach to the details of Paul's early life as narrated in Acts (e.g., Acts 22:3-4; 26:4-7), the same general picture, absent some details, is evident from his letters. With respect to the law, Paul describes his prior relationship to the law as "a Pharisee" (Phil 3:5), supposing membership in that sect to speak for itself, being "far more zealous for the traditions of my ancestors" than others (Gal 1:14 NRSV), and, "as to righteousness under the law, blameless" (Phil 3:6 NRSV). Paul epitomizes his zeal as "a persecutor of the *church" (Phil 3:6 NRSV; cf. Gal 1:13), suggesting that this also was part and parcel of his torah fealty. It is a fair surmise that Paul was not only personally observant but preached and prosecuted an enforcement of faithful law observance. Paul's claim that he no longer preaches *circumcision (Gal 5:11) naturally implies that he had done so earlier.

While debate continues about whether and in what sense Paul's transition to Christ-allegiance is to be considered a *conversion, it is clear—being multiply attested both in his letters and in Acts (Gal 1:13-14; 5:12; Phil 3:3-6; Acts 8:1-3; 9:1-2; 22:3-5; 26:9-11)—that the Damascus road encounter led to a thoroughgoing reestimation of the law. Whereas Paul had been zealously torah-observant to the point of persecuting the church for a perceived torah infidelity prior to that event, following his "conversion," Paul no longer advocated a torah-centered renewal for Israel. It is not entirely obvious by what process or reasoning Paul reached this radically new understanding (on the transition, see especially Donaldson), nor is it necessary that the reason be singular, nor that Paul's first impulse be his last or only. Surely near the center of his reasoning is an argument (or intuition) stemming from the necessity of the Messiah's crucifixion: if it was necessary that the *Christ should be crucified, it follows that the law never had the capacity to save (Gal 2:21; cf. Gal 3:21; 5:4). Likewise, as is frequently noted, every account of Paul's transition to Christ-fidelity is depicted as most fundamentally a call to Gentile *mission. Although there is no direct evidence that Paul understood that divine summons itself as a law-free gospel, it is a fair surmise that he understood the implications of his call accordingly. Correspondingly, the advent of the empowering, guiding, and indwelling Spirit both points to a turn of the ages and highlights the limitations of the law as mere "written code" (*gramma*).

Thus, the functions the law served in Paul's prior salvation-economy were supplanted by alternatives. Faith in Christ—and thus union with Christ—not obedience to the law, became the marker of the elect community. The abiding influence of the *Holy Spirit became both the moral criterion and the empowerment for behaviors and dispositions congruent with the will of God. Likewise, the Spirit became the eschatological foretaste (*arrabōn*; 2 Cor 1:22; 5:5; Eph 1:14) of a new age, thus the manifestations and *fruit of the Spirit supplanted "*works of the law" as the markers of *covenant membership and eschatological destiny.

It is more difficult to determine whether Paul's thinking on the law evidences a traceable development. In one sense, it is antecedently improbable that Paul's thinking on this and any number of issues would not have developed (see, e.g., Sanders 2008; Anderson). Although there is no consensus as to the relative dating of Galatians and Romans, there is general agreement that the latter represents, among other things, a more measured and nuanced account of the law. It is less clear whether the difference is best accounted for as a correction, a clarification responding to misunderstanding, a development of his thought, or simply a difference born of rhetorical occasion. For such questions, the data may prove insufficient.

Not all contemporary interpreters of Paul affirm that Paul's "conversion" marks a radical departure as regards his view of the law. Strands of recent Pauline scholarship have stressed Paul's continuity with torah-observant Judaism, arguing that the radical break with his torah-observant past has been overstated, having been pressed into service for Christian (especially Protestant) theological claims and too often exploited toward anti-Semitic ends. The argument of this "Paul within Judaism" school goes beyond locating Paul with respect to his Jewish roots. It notes that once Paul's favorable regard for the law is duly noted and the narrow polemical purposes of his dispute with Christian nomists are given their due, the picture of a torah-disparaging and nonobservant Paul has been overdrawn (e.g., Nanos; Nanos and Zetterholm; Fredriksen; Gager; Thiessen). Bearing significant weight in this argument is the observation that all of Paul's discourse decentering the law is addressed to Gentiles for the express purpose of dissuading them from coming under a law that was never their burden to bear and that would stymie the Gentile mission.

It is true that one does not have all the evidence one might wish. In particular, Paul's letters—all addressed to primarily ethnic Gentiles—offer only hints as to how Jewish Christians within Paul's ambit were continuing to practice torah observance, and presumably that was not uniform. For a variety of reasons, Paul seems to have exercised a high level of tolerance, falling short of endorsement, as it concerned Jewish-Christian torah observance. In the first place, he considers the law and its observance as intrinsically moral, the commandment being "holy and just and good" (Rom 7:12 NRSV). He also places a premium on the conscience as a personal moral criterion, such that obedience conforming to the conscience is necessary even if he regards the action itself as objectively unnecessary (1 Cor 8:7, 12; 10:28-29; cf. Rom 14:5, 14, 23). Thus, the category of *adiaphora* (matters of indifference) enjoys a wide berth in Paul's moral imagination as a means of mutual tolerance. Even if he himself is persuaded that "nothing is unclean in itself," he would be willing to observe the law so as to win those "under the law," but he would not consider himself for that reason to be obliged to the law, save for "Christ's law" (1 Cor 9:20-21 NRSV). Thus, it seems clear that Paul understood the socially distinguishing dictates of the Mosaic law as *adiaphora*: on the one hand, harmless for Jews to continue unless imposed on Gentiles as requirements, while compulsory if dictated by conscience, even if objectively unnecessary.

3. *Law* in Paul's Letters.

3.1. Thessalonian Correspondence. The word *law* does not occur in the Thessalonian correspondence, nor does the topic seem to have been a site of controversy. There is no evidence of a controversy surrounding the function of the law soteriologically or toward community *ethics. The basis of Gentile adherents into covenant membership seems to have been *faith broadly defined as allegiance to Israel's God, evidenced by a turn from *idolatry (1 Thess 1:9-10) and from base Gentile mores, especially sexual profligacy (1 Thess 4:2-8), with an adoption of moral patterns commended and exemplified by Paul and his associates. Although Paul refers to "instructions" (*parangelia*, 1 Thess 4:2 NRSV) given to the Thessalonians "through the Lord Jesus," there is no indication that these were specifically rooted in the law as such, being more likely the transmission of the Jesuanic traditions (see esp. 1 Thess 4:15). Likewise, in 2 Thessalonians, the object of "obedience" is the gospel itself (2 Thess 1:8) and the instruction of the *apostle himself (2 Thess 3:14). In both letters, there is a presumption that this elect community—predominantly Gentile—be distinguished in its behavior as a sanctified people, distinct from their past and morally differentiated from fellow ethnic Gentiles. Although the emphasis on sexual *purity harks broadly to the torah's own such emphasis (Deidun), neither the moral nor cultic peculiarities of the law seem to form the specific basis for this called-for differentiation.

In short, the testimony of the Thessalonian correspondence demonstrates that, although prominent in certain letters, controversy over the law was not intrinsic to the original Pauline proclamation as such, but the eventual result of a torah-free inclusivity perceived as too lax or generous to sustain a cultural differentiation or a moral framework on the part of the new adherents.

3.2. Galatians. It is with his letter to the Galatians that Paul's unsettling and profound reevaluation of the law comes to the fore. Whether the letter is dated relatively early (allowed by the so-called South Galatian hypothesis) or later (required by the so-called North Galatian hypothesis), Galatians marks an intense storm center in the Pauline corpus, untempered by the later subtleties characteristic of Romans.

Although the reconstruction of the details is elusive, the precipitating cause of this letter is generally accepted. Paul having successfully gained Gentile adherents to messianic Judaism among the "Galatians," teachers or countermissionaries from Judea infiltrated the community to rectify, as they saw it, defects of Paul's *teaching—chiefly that Paul had offered covenant membership through faith in Jesus the Messiah and apart from circumcision and concomitant torah observance for the Gentile converts. The position of the nomistic missionaries, in whatever forms the Galatians encountered it, unsettled the new converts and provoked Paul's most polemical extant letter. A challenge in interpreting Paul's letter is assessing to what degree Paul is countering the claims of his opponents as opposed to building his own argument from the ground up. In the nature of the case, this is hard to discern, but there are reasons to believe Paul engages in a certain amount of counteroffensive, not least as concerns the law and his engagement with critical prooftexts.

Paul's broadside against the law is multifaceted and, given the context of his torah-observant training and heritage, novel. Paul's marginalization of the law in the economy of *salvation can be summarized under four interwoven themes in the central section of the letter.

1. Paul's initial salvo is practical and experiential—that the Spirit had already manifested among the Galatians apart from "works of the law." The claim of Paul's missionary antagonists that torah observance is a necessity is rendered dubious already from the first experience of the Gentile converts. Apparently, the Galatians' reception of the gospel was accompanied by evident experiences of the Spirit, including "miracles" and presumably other manifestations (Gal 3:2-5). But since these experiences were apart from and preceded any proffered conversion to torah observance, the law is shown to be otiose. The Spirit, marking the turn of the ages and the covenantal inclusion of the Gentiles, was manifested not "by works of the law" (ESV, *ex ergōn nomou*) but "by hearing with faith" (ESV) or a "message eliciting faith" (*hē ex akoēs pisteōs*; Gal 3:2, 5).

As becomes evident later in the letter, this argument is not merely an ad hoc appeal to experience. The advent of the Spirit marked a new era, and the Galatians' encounter with the Spirit marked them accordingly (Gal 3:14; 4:6; 5:5). The Spirit undertook and fulfilled the law's functions of moral direction, enabling human obedience (Gal 5:18, 22-23, 25). Indeed, perhaps the most positive treatment of the law in Galatians is Paul's affirmation of the law's divine intent, not as it is accomplished in the law itself but by virtue of its fulfillment in Christ and the Spirit.

2. The second and dominant theme is Paul's extended salvation-historical reading of the law in Israel's history. The point, made in a variety of ways, is that the original covenantal promise made to Abraham long preceded the giving of the law through Moses. Indeed, the law given to Israel followed the promise by 430 years (Gal 3:17), and the prior promise made to Abraham was *already* inclusive of Gentiles apart from any law: "All the Gentiles shall be blessed in you" (Gal 3:8 NRSV; Gen 12:3). Thus, capitalizing on the secular sense of "covenant" (*diathēkē*)

as "will," Paul insists that to hope in the law is to emphasize what is later and secondary as if an added codicil (Mosaic law) superseded the original will (covenantal promise to Abraham; Gal 3:15-18).

But the law's temporary and thus secondary status is amply asserted in Galatians. Against traditional Jewish presumption of the law's eternality (e.g., Sir 24:9; 2 Esd 9:37; 1 En. 99.2; Philo, *Mos.* 2.13-16), Paul asserts that it was "added" (*prosetethē*; Gal 3:19), on the one hand, and that it has a terminus, on the other (Gal 3:19, 23, 24; cf. Gal 4:2). That terminus, though variously described ("offspring," Gal 3:19; "faith," Gal 3:23, 25; "Christ," Gal 3:24), is identified with the advent of Christ and the Spirit.

The temporary character of the law does not render it in opposition to promise, much less the purposes, of God: "Is the law then opposed to the promises of God?" (Gal 3:21 NRSV). Of course, the answer is, "Certainly not" (*mē genoito*), yet a more favorable account of the law does not follow. Thus, Galatians will claim that, while the law has a certain purpose in the divine economy, distinct from but not opposed to the promises of God fulfilled in the seed of Abraham, there is nothing in this dissuasive to commend the law to his readers. Were one to judge from Galatians alone, there would be no grounds for assuming that Paul envisioned an ongoing function for the law among his Gentile converts.

3. A theme already present in Galatians that becomes more prominent in Romans is the soteriological impotence of the law. Whatever its divine purposes, the law has not succeeded in rendering humans righteous: "if *justification comes through the law, then Christ died for nothing" (Gal 2:21 NRSV). Likewise, in Galatians 3:21, "For if a law had been given that could make alive, then righteousness would indeed come through the law" (NRSV), a scenario Paul presents as a contrary-to-fact conditional.

Paul's most detailed argument toward this end is found in a dense soteriological argument (Gal 3:10-13), the precise interpretation of which is contested. The core of the argument rests with a catena of four OT citations woven into a new argument.

- "Cursed is everyone who does not observe and obey all the things written in the book of the law" (Gal 3:10 NRSV, citing Deut 27:26).
- "The one who is righteous will live by faith" (Gal 3:11 NRSV, citing Hab 2:4).
- "Whoever does the works of the law will live by them" (Gal 3:12 NRSV, citing Lev 18:5).
- "Cursed is everyone who hangs on a tree" (Gal 3:13 NRSV, citing Deut 21:23).

While the interpretation of this passage has yielded little consensus in recent years with respect to the details, the broad contours are clearer. Paul understands the law and faith as alternative paths to righteousness and eschatological life. The law expects and requires obedience, and to fail in that obedience is to be under a *curse (however understood). Meanwhile, as Habakkuk 2:4 testifies and Paul argues elsewhere (Gal 3:2, 5-9, 24, 26; 5:6), righteousness is not a matter of doing but of faith. Interpreters divide over whether Paul's precise reasoning includes an unstated minor premise—"No one keeps the law perfectly"—but there can be little question in the context that Paul deprecates the law for its inability to save.

4. Perhaps the most controversial dimension of Paul's argument is a certain polemicism as concerns the origins of the law at Sinai and, in turn, the status of the law. It is a notorious feature of Paul's rhetoric in Galatians that even his "rehabilitation" of the law comes as a damning by faint praise. To be sure, the law has an essential function in the divine economy, but not such that Gentiles should yield to its thrall. Lest Paul seem to disparage the law wholesale, he offers a divine purpose. In a diatribe rhetorical style anticipating Romans, Paul asks "Why then the law?" (Gal 3:19 NRSV). Paul's initial answer, that it "was added because of [*charin*] transgressions" (Gal 3:19 NRSV), is ambiguous. While it may fit Paul's more general claim that the law makes sin or a misdeed into a "transgression" (*parabasis*) by rendering it an express violation of a known norm (see, e.g., Rom 5:12-14, 20), this may freight the preposition beyond what it ought to bear.

More likely, Paul intends that the law's function was to ameliorate, in some unspecified way, what the law would show to be "transgression"—perhaps to curb or restrain, perhaps to atone (the sacrificial system was itself a prominent feature of the law), less likely to provoke (although Paul makes this claim in Romans). In any case, less important for Paul than the reason that the law was given are the circumstances and temporary character. What might elsewhere have been the law's splendor, the presence of angels with the prophet Moses on Sinai is not regarded so here (see Heb 2:2; Acts 7:58; cf. LXX Deut 33:2; Jub. 1.29; Philo, *Somn.* 1.141-143; Josephus, *Ant.* 15.136). Although it probably goes too far to claim with some that the angels imply a nondivine origin of the law or that the "angels" are depicted as malevolent, the law's mediated character points to its secondary status in comparison to the direct character of the unmediated promise made to Abraham.

Likewise, by means of a provocative salvation-historical reading of the Torah, Paul stresses the secondary and temporary character of its embedded torah. According to the law of Moses, the law given to Moses at Sinai was preceded by the promise made to Abraham by 430 years (Gal 3:16-17; see Gen 12:7; 13:5; 17:7-8). Paul thus characterizes the law as an addendum to a "will" (*diathēkē*, i.e., also "covenant"). The original will (or covenant) having already been made with Abraham, the subsequent addition of the law through Moses "does not annul a covenant previously ratified by God" (Gal 3:17 NRSV). For Paul, not only is the law a late addition to the covenantal promise, but its function is also impermanent. Under related metaphors, Paul asserts that the law exercised a custodial function for Israel as long as the people were, as it were, minors: "Now *before faith came*, we were imprisoned and guarded under the law until faith would be revealed. Therefore the law was our disciplinarian [*paidagōgos*] *until Christ came*, so that we might be justified by faith. But now that faith has come, we are *no longer* subject to a disciplinarian" (Gal 3:23-25 NRSV). Extending the image in Galatians 4:1-6, Paul reinforces the claim by asserting that children while minors are tantamount to slaves, "under guardians and trustees until the date set by the father" (Gal 4:2 NRSV). Now, however, "in the fullness of time," God has adopted the heirs as children (lit. "sons"): "So you are no longer a slave but a child, and if a child then also an heir, through God" (Gal 4:7 NRSV).

3.3. Corinthian Correspondence. The themes of law, works of the law, and justification do not preoccupy either of the extant letters to the Corinthians as they do Galatians and Romans. The Corinthian correspondence represents an incidental, oblique, yet important testimony, showing that the law is not merely a matter of polemical interest for Paul but that it became central to his overall theological vision.

3.3.1. 1 Corinthians. The law does not dominate the discourse of 1 Corinthians, a letter apparently written in response to concerns raised by the Corinthians themselves. Yet here readers are given some of the most illuminating insights into the place of the law in Paul's theology and missionary endeavors (Rosner 1999; 2013).

First Corinthians includes several examples in which Paul uses *law* to refer to the text of the first division of the Hebrew canon. Under the moniker "law of Moses," he cites Deuteronomy 25:4 (1 Cor 9:8, 9; cf. 1 Tim 5:18, where the reference is to "scripture"). Extending beyond the Pentateuch in 1 Corinthians 14:21, Paul refers to the law when he cites Isaiah 28:11-12. The most controversial and uncertain such reference in the Pauline corpus is found in 1 Corinthians 14:34, which appeals to the "law" to enjoin the silence of *women in the assembly: "For they are not permitted to speak, but should be subordinate, as the law also says" (NRSV). Given that there is no direct allusion to a known OT text, some of have inferred that Paul is generalizing about role differentiation on men and women found therein, with perhaps a particular recalling of the *creation narratives, while others see this as among the evidence of a post-Pauline interpolation (see Payne).

In one of the more intriguing excerpts of the letter, Paul engages the status of circumcision for his predominantly Gentile readers. Unsurprisingly, Paul treats circumcision as a matter of indifference: "Was anyone at the time of his call already circumcised? Let him not seek to remove the marks of circumcision [*mē epispasthō*]. Was anyone at the time of his call already uncircumcised? Let him not seek circumcision [*mē peritemnesthō*]. Circumcision is nothing, and uncircumcision is nothing; but obeying the commandments of God is everything" (1 Cor 7:18-19 NRSV). Paul's indifference to circumcision is hardly surprising given his parallel statements on the matter (e.g., Gal 5:6; 6:15; Rom 2:25-29; Col 2:11-12; 3:11), though his tone here is less polemical than the forbidding admonitions of Galatians (Gal 5:2-3). Curiously, he contrasts circumcision with the "commands of God," even though, by any account, circumcision is also a command from God (Gen 17:10-14, 23-27; Lev 12:3). But, as in the case of Romans 2:25-29, it is conceivable that circumcised persons may not keep the commandments of God more generally and that the uncircumcised, in this general sense, do keep the commandments. Here "commands of God," like "law of God" (Rom 7:22, 25; 8:7), is to be taken as a broad gesture to the moral requirements of God, albeit without specificity. Thus, Paul's indifference to this (and other) torah-required observance(s) does not signal an indifference to moral probity itself but dissociates those moral standards from the particularities of the "written code" in favor of a Christ-ethic inspired of the Spirit.

This subtle distinction is borne out a few chapters later when Paul speaks of his choosing to be as one "outside the law" for the sake of those outside the law, while quickly rejoining, "though I am not free from God's law but am under Christ's law" (1 Cor 9:21 NRSV). Thus, Paul can imagine a law-lessness that is nonetheless a fulfillment of the will of God as revealed in Christ and the gospel. What is most telling in this excerpt is Paul's indifference to the law when his object is the missionary spread of the gospel to both those having and those apart from the law. The radicality of Paul's position is evident in the claim, "To the Jews I became *as* a Jew, in order to win Jews. To those under the law I became as one under the law (though I myself am not under the law) so that I might win those under the law" (1 Cor 9:20 NRSV). But, of course Paul *was* a Jew, and if he "became" (*egenomēn*) *as* a Jew and *as* one under the law, it can only mean that he had relativized that identity and those practices such that they became elective and subservient to his larger mission project, that torah fidelity had become an *adiaphoron*. Contrary to the impression one might receive from Galatians alone, Paul did not disparage torah observance as unfaithfulness; it had only become elective and contextually determined in his own practice. Paul's own apparent flexibility on this matter surely confounded his contemporaries, presumably on all sides.

Theologically, a most telling statement with respect to the law is found in Paul's epigram of 1 Corinthians 15:56, entering somewhat unanticipated at the conclusion of Paul's discourse concerning the resurrection: "The sting of death is sin, and the power of sin is the law" (NRSV). Anticipating the more extended arguments of 2 Corinthians 3 and especially Romans, Paul makes the provocative and counterintuitive claim that the law is in league with sin—its "power"—though here without any explanation of how that is so.

3.3.2. *2 Corinthians.* Even though there is no use of *nomos* in 2 Corinthians, Paul's treatment of the law in covenantal terms in 2 Corinthians 3 offers crucial insight (Hafemann). Here Paul refers to the law by means of a rhetorically charged synonym, "the letter" (or "written code"; *gramma*), which "kills" and is contrasted with the Spirit, who "gives life" (2 Cor 3:6 NRSV). That Paul intends especially a reference to the Sinaiatic law is indicated by his reference to a "letter . . . inscribed" [*epistolē . . . engegrammenē*] by the Spirit on "tablets of fleshly hearts," not on "*tablets of stone*," the latter an unmistakable reference to Sinai (2 Cor 3:3; cf. Ex 24:12; 31:18; 32:16).

He develops this theme more explicitly in 2 Corinthians 3:7, characterizing the Mosaic economy as "the ministry of death, chiseled in letters on stone" (NRSV; *hē diakonia tou thanatou en grammasin entetupōmenē lithois*). Here as elsewhere (e.g., Rom 7:6), characterization of the law, contrasted to the Spirit, as mere "letter" draws attention to the law in its inert writtenness, its incapacity to enable the obedience it demands, and its limitations as a source of moral guidance. As a result, the "ministry" (*diakonia*) of the letter was, according to Paul, a "ministry of condemnation" in contrast to the new covenant's "ministry of righteousness." This stark contrast demonstrates that, whatever else Paul might say about the law, he understands it to have an objectively condemnatory function, anticipating themes taken up later in Romans.

Nonetheless, the law as "letter," even in its "ministry of condemnation," is still a dispensation of "*glory." Yet the argument is a fortiori. By means of an inferred analogy to the iterative fading of Moses' face (Ex 34), the law's glory was a "fading" glory, the law's dispensation coming to naught (*katargeō*, 2 Cor 3:7, 11) in the light of the surpassing glory of the new covenant.

3.4. Romans. Romans stands out among Paul's letters as the most thorough and nuanced treatment of the law. While this letter stands in general congruity with the critique of the law found in Galatians, in Romans Paul makes such claims less polemically and with more balance. Whereas it would be possible to read Galatians such that the law is viewed as only a nemesis, in Romans, Paul goes to lengths to exonerate the law, without reversing his earlier claims regarding the law's impotence to save or empower the moral life. In short, Romans argues that the insufficiency and impotence of the law are due not to flaws intrinsic to the law itself but are owed to fallen and incapacitated humanity, which, in collaboration with the power of sin, frustrates the law's own good purposes.

Although perhaps implicit elsewhere, only in Romans does Paul explore the claim that the law functions as a standard of judgment to reveal misdoing as sin: "through the law comes the *knowledge of sin" (Rom 3:20 NRSV; cf. Rom 2:12; 4:15; 5:13; 7:7). But, for Paul, this is an especially important element in his overall argument, showing that the law has a particular function of defining culpability. "All who have sinned apart from the law will also perish apart from the law, and all who have sinned under the law will be judged by the law" (Rom 2:12 NRSV). Thus, the law does not create the human dilemma but reveals it more starkly and holds humanity accountable for its misdoings: "If it had not been for the law, I would not have known sin. I would not have known what it is to covet if the law had not said, 'You shall not covet'" (Rom 7:7 NRSV). As Paul reasons, the law's righteous function of exposing and naming sin is ultimately a bane for sinful humanity. The law's trustworthy guidance into what is right has the corollary of demonstrating culpability for the law's trespass (*paraptōma*) or transgression (*parabasis*).

More provocatively, Paul indicates that the law not only reveals but increases transgression. Not only does the law cast sinful behavior into bold relief against a divine righteous standard, but Paul asserts that the righteous standard serves also to incite its transgression. The law "insinuated itself [*pareiserchomai*] in order to increase the trespass" (Rom 5:20). How this is so is suggested later in Romans 7, where one finds that sin lies dormant but is awakened or provoked by the commandment—as illustrated in the prohibition of coveting (Rom 7:7-11).

It is not quite possible to understand this aspect of Paul's treatment of the law without grasping the basic contours of his *anthropology, especially the toxic combination of sin, *flesh, and law. Sin is understood by Paul both as individual misdeed and as a reified power. In the former sense, sin as the individual misdeed long preexisted the giving of the law, but the giving of the law showed those same sins to be trespass or transgression. In the latter sense, sin (or perhaps Sin) is understood as a force active in the world, personified as an antagonist. This Sin conspires with the law and the flesh, frustrating the human attainment of righteousness and creating a cycle of futility in which the weakness of the flesh is exploited by the opportunism of Sin, exacerbated by the condemnatory leverage of the law. Paul sees this as a vicious cycle, which renders the law not merely a nonsolution, but its entry into the world an exacerbation rather than alleviation of the human dilemma of sinfulness.

The condemnation and futility wrought by the law is not, however, to be taken as a disparagement of the law itself. In itself, the law, Paul is at pains to say, is "holy, and the commandment is holy and just and good" (Rom 7:12); the law is "spiritual" (Rom 7:14). What may seem to be the law's failure is rather the law's exposure of human incapacity and malformation. The law, good in itself, drives humans who are under sin's thrall (Rom 6:12-23) and "weakened by the flesh" (Rom 8:3 NRSV) into frustration and futility, unable to fulfill its own telos. For all its virtues as divine revelation and instrument, the law does not come equipped with its own potency to accomplish its ends.

Yet, for Paul, this does not mean that the law is to be discarded, abolished, or otherwise circumvented: "Do we then overthrow [*katargeō*] the law by this faith? By no means! On the contrary, we uphold the law" (Rom 3:31 NRSV). The dilemma of condemnation imposed by the law in Romans 2–3 is ameliorated by a newly disclosed "righteousness of God apart from the law [*nomos*[1]]," nonetheless to which "the law [*nomos*[2]] and prophets bear witness" (Rom 3:21). Likewise, the dilemma of malformation characterized by the "flesh" in weakness and at enmity toward God, especially outlined in Romans 6–7, is ameliorated expressly by the Spirit in Romans 8. "For God has done what the law, weakened by the flesh, could not do: by sending his own Son in the likeness of sinful flesh, and to deal with sin, he condemned sin in the flesh, so that the just requirement of the law might be fulfilled in us, who walk not according to the flesh but according to the Spirit" (Rom 8:3-4 NRSV). This righteousness—both the extrinsically granted release from condemnation (Rom 5:1; 8:1) and the internally wrought transformation by the Spirit—fulfills the telos of the law. "Christ is the end [*telos*] of the law so that there may be righteousness for all who believe" (Rom 10:4 NRSV).

3.5. Philippians. Paul's reflection on the law in this letter is limited to an important polemical section of the third chapter. In an apparent counterpoise to an actual or anticipated incursion of a "circumcision group," Paul appeals autobiographically over against those who would impose torah observance, being himself the paragon of Jewish identity ("circumcised on the eighth day, a member of the people of Israel, of the tribe of Benjamin, a Hebrew born of Hebrews") and torah observance ("as to the law, a Pharisee; as to zeal, a persecutor of the church; as to righteousness under the law, blameless"; Phil 3:5-6 NRSV). But these credentials are not only of no value to Paul; he counts them as metaphorical debits (*zēmia*) and "rubbish" (*skybala*), compared to "the surpassing value of knowing Christ Jesus my *Lord" (Phil 3:8 NRSV).

Autobiographically, this text demonstrates that Paul's own pre-Damascus experience with the law seems not to have been that of existential condemnation; he regarded himself as "blameless" (*amemptos*). Thus, Paul's subsequent claims about the law's condemning function seem not to flow from his experience but are best understood as a retrospective and objective account (see, e.g., Chester 2003). In any case, from this vantage Paul does not regard his zealous and blameless relationship to the law as a Pharisee to have been productive of an adequate righteousness. Rather, his had been "a righteousness of my own that comes from the law" (*emēn dikaiosynēn tēn ek nomou*), which is inferior to a righteousness "that comes through faith in Christ, the righteousness from God based on faith" (Phil 3:9 NRSV; *tēn dia pisteōs Christou tēn ek theou dikaiosynēn epi tē[i] pistei*). Here Paul's concern is not so much the impossibility of keeping the law (as in Romans and perhaps Galatians) as it is the intrinsic inadequacy of a righteousness that depends on torah observance when compared to a "from-God" (*ek theou*) righteousness that comes as gift rather than achievement.

3.6. Disputed Letters. The following text briefly considers letters that are ascribed to Paul, the authenticity of which is disputed. If regarded as authentic, these—presumably later—letters suggest that Paul never ceased reckoning with the question of the relevance and application of the law in his communities, even if the theme (or threat) is not as prominent on these occasions.

3.6.1. Colossians. As in other of Paul's letters, Colossians describes the failure to conform to the divine commands as "trespasses" (*paraptōmata*) in need of *forgiveness (Col 2:13). In Colossians 2:14-15 the law's "legal demands" (*dogmata*) are collectively depicted as a ledger of indebtedness, now canceled and nailed to the *cross. Thus, in Colossians, the law is an antagonist whose charge against humanity needs to be defeated and broken. The degree to which the rest of Colossians speaks to the law depends significantly on the reconstruction of the circumstances in Colossae that Paul addresses. If, as many contend, the Colossian "heresy" is Jewish and nomistic in character, even if syncretized with other influences, there is evidence of Paul's (assuming authenticity) opposition to a basis of rectitude codified by Jewish law or its appropriations. Paul marginalizes physical circumcision by reference to its spiritual antitype in Christ (Col 2:11), and he relegates "*food and drink" and participations in feasts, a new moon, or the Sabbath as *adiaphora*.

3.6.2. Ephesians. Ephesians contains only one reference to *nomos*: "the law with its commandments and ordinances" (Eph 2:15 NRSV, *ton nomon tōn entolōn en dogmasin*). The language and depiction of Judaism's legal requirements is similar to Colossians: disobedience has rendered humanity dead in "trespasses and sins" (Eph 2:1 NRSV; cf. Eph 2:5) such that only Christ's intervention can save.

But the treatment of the law in Ephesians renders another, more sociological, dimension to the law. The law's "commandments and ordinances" function as a "dividing wall of hostility" between Jew and Gentile. That the law functioned so historically is verified by numerous studies stressing the law's political function of social differentiation given Judaism's Hellenized environment (Barclay 1996). Christ has "broken down" (*lysas*) this dividing wall by abolishing the "law with respect to its commandments and regulations" in his flesh. Thus, Ephesians 2 depicts the law as a standard condemning sinners, on the one hand, and as a barrier prohibiting Jew and Gentile fellowship, on the other. While the claim that Paul has "abolished" (*katargeō*) the law sits awkwardly with the explicit claim to the contrary elsewhere (Rom 3:31), here it is the law considered less holistically, only with respect to its at once condemning and dividing legal demands (*entolōn en dogmasin*).

3.6.3. Pastoral Epistles. Reference to the law in the Pastorals is limited to 1 Timothy 1:8-9. In a play on words, the author affirms that "the law is good" (NRSV; see Rom 7:12) provided it is used "lawfully" (*nomimōs*; 1 Tim 1:8). The next verse suggests what might be entailed by "lawfully." The "law is not laid down for the just person [*dikaiō[i]*] but for the lawless and disobedient [*anomois . . . kai anypotaktois*]" (1 Tim 1:9), followed by a list of self-evidently egregious violators. The point seems to be a discouragement from using the law for the definition and enforcement of Christian righteousness, reserving it exclusively for its condemnatory aspect for violators. Irrespective of the question of authenticity, this text provides corroboration for an early Christian disinclination from nomism as ground for the moral life.

4. Toward a Pauline Synthesis.

The task of constructing a Pauline view of the law has vexed interpreters throughout the critical era. Although not mutually exclusive, three general approaches have prevailed. (1) Some scholars have kept a sharp focus on the rhetorical occasion of the individual writings and the particularity of the perspectives therein (e.g., Thielman 1994). At the far end of that spectrum the approach may eventuate into an argument for incoherence (Räisänen 1983). (2) Others have advocated a developmental scheme (e.g., Hübner; Drane), in which typically the earlier polemicism of especially Galatians is rounded out into the more mature and nuanced synthesis of Romans. A sharper-edged variant of this approach has subsequent letters functioning as actual correctives of earlier letters, for example Romans correcting Galatians (Tobin; see Hurd for a similar tack). (3) Without disputing the diversity of Paul's witness to the law, numerous scholars maintain that a coherent synthesis is possible without charging the apostle with contradiction.

On balance, it seems appropriate to presuppose an underlying, if not immediately apparent, coherence. J. D. G. Dunn says it well: "Basic to good exegesis is respect for the integrity of the text and, in the case of Paul, respect for his intellectual calibre and theological competence. Such respect includes the possibility or indeed likelihood that the situations confronting Paul were more complex than we can now be aware of, or include important aspects which are now invisible to us" (Dunn 2008, 121).

4.1. Leading Motifs. *4.1.1. "Not Under Law."* That those now *in Christ are "not under law" (*ou[ch] hypo nomon*; Rom 6:14, 15; 1 Cor 9:20; Gal 3:23; 4:5, 21; 5:18; see *en tō[i] nomō[i]* in Rom 2:12; 3:19; Phil 3:6) is a Pauline refrain. To be "under law" is, for Paul, either a former condition (Gal 3:23; 4:5) or an ill-advised and unnecessary elective stance (1 Cor 9:20; Gal 4:21), but Paul's normative claim is that those in Christ are "not under law" (Rom 6:14, 15; 1 Cor 9:20; Gal 5:18). The implication of this repeated claim may be understood as twofold. Those under law are subject to the law's *judgment and condemnation, a condition relieved by Christ's own curse-bearing crucifixion. Thus, to be not under law in that sense is to be justified by faith. The alternative to not under law is under grace (Rom 6:14-15).

But Paul's claim that Christians are not under law extends beyond a forensic status; it also describes a freedom for obedience that is conditioned by grace, liberated from both the objective sentence and existential angst of the law's condemnation: "For sin will have no dominion over you, since you are not under law but under grace" (Rom 6:14 NRSV). Paul maintains that this release from the law, far from being a permission for licentiousness (Rom 6:15; cf. Rom 6:1), is a precondition for the surpassing of the law's particulars by a life "led by the Spirit" (Gal 5:18 NRSV), under the "Christ's law" (1 Cor 9:21 NRSV), "not under the old written code but in the new life of the Spirit" (Rom 7:6 NRSV).

4.1.2. The Fulfillment of the Law. Paul depicts the law in terms of impotence and incompleteness. This is less a disparagement than a characterization of the law in terms of its context in salvation history and in a larger economy of salvation. The law's function is not only to make people righteous but also to create a righteous people, holy to the God of the covenant. Already within the narration of Israel's history, the law did not characteristically produce the obedience it commanded, hence the prophetic call for a *new* covenant (Jer 31:31-34; Ezek 36:25-27) that would effect change within persons to interiorize the law such that they would become capable of keeping and propagating it.

While Paul also understands the law's paramount demand for obedience, it is not finally or merely obedience to the law that he advocates, but rather a multidimensional fulfillment of the law by which the law's intent to produce righteous persons formed into a holy people comes to fruition. Paul's understanding of the law's fulfillment is multidimensional. Whereas with respect to its discrete commandments, the law is meant to be "done" (*poieō*) or "kept" (*phylassō*), in Christ, Paul considers the law in more holistic terms with respect to its telos or fulfillment. While Paul affirms that persons outside Christ under the law will fail to keep it and experience a futility in their best efforts, those in Christ *fulfill* rather than *keep* the law per se.

Thus, Paul famously summarizes the law by means of the *love of neighbor (Rom 13:8-10; Gal 5:14), specifically Leviticus 19:18, "You shall love your neighbor as yourself" (NRSV). The language of "fulfillment" in these passages is significant, pointing to a realization of the law's intent that is not strictly identified with the performance of discrete commands but by behaviors thoroughly conditioned by love.

Similarly, Paul describes those who "walk with the Spirit" as fulfilling what the law demands as though a matter of course, as a formerly antagonistic relationship to the law is transformed into a synergistic relationship in which one "keep[s] in step with [*stoicheō*] the Spirit" (Gal 5:25; cf. Gal 5:16). Even more dramatically, in Romans 8:3-4, Paul asserts that what the law, "weakened by the flesh," was incapable of accomplishing is fulfilled in the atoning work of Christ (Rom 8:3) and in the fulfillment of the law's "just requirement" (*dikaiōma*) by those "who walk not according to the flesh but according to the Spirit" (Rom 8:4 NRSV). Thus, Paul envisions not only a satisfaction of a legal claim against transgressors (Rom 8:3) but also the transformation wrought by the Spirit whereby those in Christ fulfill the law's intent.

Finally, in Romans 10:4, Paul famously declares that "Christ is the end [*telos*] of the law" (NRSV). The Greek *telos* is, like the English "end," susceptible to a double meaning: goal and terminus. Both senses of *telos* are well-attested in Paul (Rom 6:21, 22; 2 Cor 11:15; Phil 3:19; 1 Tim 1:5 and 1 Cor 15:24; 2 Cor 3:13, respectively), and, while various interpreters will wish to place the accent on one or the other meaning, both fit the immediate context and indeed cohere with the other. In the divine economy, the law seeks a fulfillment beyond itself, which, in the nature of the case, will also be its termination, just as an athlete reaching the goal of a race also completes the race.

Thus, Paul's language points consistently to a relationship with the law that fulfills its intent and arguably transcends the letter of its demands, with believers empowered by the Spirit and thoroughly conditioned by love. For this reason, Paul could not advocate an ethical recourse to the law for Christians. Paul thus confronts his readers with a paradox that has confounded them through the ages: although the discrete commands of the law confront the unredeemed as an unkeepable and oppressive burden, they constitute a standard too low for those walking with the Spirit, characterized by the fruit of the Spirit (Gal 5:22-23) and conditioned by divine love.

4.1.3. The Law of Christ. In only two tantalizing references, Paul refers to the "law of Christ" (Gal 6:2; 1 Cor 9:21). Although the precise meaning of the phrase is elusive given its limited use, this has not deterred interpretive suggestions. The relatively minimal appeal in Pauline writings to Jesus traditions makes it unlikely that the phrase is to be taken as the law *that was given by Christ* (a subjective genitive), that is, his moral teachings. In a similar but more explicit vein, others have suggested that the "law of Christ" refers to Paul's summary of the law by means of the command to love neighbor (Gal 5:14; Rom 13:9; see Lev 19:18), which is arguably derived from Jesus' "second" great commandment, which epitomized the law by means of Leviticus 19:18 (Mk 12:31; Mt 22:39; cf. Lk 10:27). While Paul's invocation of Leviticus 19:18 is likely derived from Jesus, that the "law of Christ" intends this degree of specificity is more difficult to prove, although it is impossible that the phrase could intend anything less than that.

Given the cleverness of his discourse around this theme, it would not be impossible for Paul to use the phrase in a more paradoxical manner: *the law that is Christ himself* (an epexegetic genitive), but this must remain only a possibility. More probably, Paul intends the phrase in a more general sense: *the law as conditioned by Christ* (a descriptive genitive). This use fits a more general pattern by which Paul supplies genitive modifiers to *nomos* to refer to the law variously qualified ("of faith," "of sin," "of sin and death," "of righteousness"; see 1.1, point 4, above), the law in relation to something else or viewed with respect to something.

Tempting though it may be, there is simply not a broad enough basis from Pauline usage (or the NT more generally) to claim that this phrase served itself as a new watchword for Christian ethics. Nonetheless, it is clear that Paul's employment of the phrase confirms that he cannot be regarded as antinomian, on the one hand, and that the law's relevance is radically conditioned by Christ, on the other. While Paul is not under the law, as a *slave of Christ, neither he nor his followers can be said to be "without a law."

4.2. Synthesis. Paul's approach to the Mosaic law may finally be synthesized under a series of claims that (it is hoped) would commend the apostle's assent (see Westerholm).

- The law of Moses is a true revelation from the God of Israel, expressing his will for his elect people. It is scarcely possible that Paul could think otherwise than this, given his torah-observant life as a Pharisee, and no apparent disparagement of the law contradicts this claim, though there are several ways in which it could be qualified. Whatever else might be said, in itself "the law is holy, and the commandment is holy and just and good" (Rom 7:12 NRSV).
- The law's chief functions, however, are not in themselves saving or even redemptive. The law functions to reveal sin as transgression, the express violation of a public and explicit norm. As such, the law exacerbates the culpability of the offender, exposing the consciousness and willfulness of the wrongdoing. Moreover, Paul understands that this very phenomenon not only increases culpability but further incites rebellion against the divine will by placing constraints on the appetitive and autonomous human. The law thus not only shows persons to be unrighteous but also functions to make them more unrighteous.
- Therefore, paradoxically, the law is impotent to accomplish its putative end of producing righteous human persons and a righteous covenant community; indeed, the law's purposes are destined to futility if the law itself is viewed as the means of accomplishing its own ends. The law is not defective, but it engages defective and malformed persons under the sway of sin and incapacitated by the corrupting influence of the "flesh." Only the person in union with Christ, reconstituted in the Spirit, participating in the age to come will have the capacity both to will and to do the moral requirements of the law. The law itself cannot so empower.
- The incapacity of the law to produce lawkeepers is understood by Paul to have necessitated

the saving intervention of God through Jesus Christ. If persons could have been saved or justified through the law, then Christ died for no purpose (Gal 2:21; 3:21). In this soteriological sense, the law's function is satiated in the atoning death and saving resurrection of Jesus Christ, whose verdict of vindication is commuted to those who by faith are in a saving union with him.

- Nonetheless, the telos of the law never ceases to be important to Paul, being fulfilled in its intent by the work of the Spirit in the human person under the lordship of Christ. Paul's treatment of the law is finally not that it is abolished or discarded as a misstep or false start of a bygone era or another people, but that its divine purposes, if often frustrated, were never abandoned but brought to fruition in a redeemed and holy people incorporated into the Messiah Jesus.
- As a means for forming righteous and virtuous persons, the law is deficient; toward those ends it has been transcended by the work of the Spirit. As written code, the law is fundamentally inert, and from the vantage of Pauline anthropology, the law is incapacitated by the thrall of sin and the "weakness of the flesh," unable of itself to generate righteous behavior. For this, only the transforming work of the Spirit will suffice.
- To the possible charge (Marcionite in character) that the law was a divine failure, Paul rejoins that the law itself (*nomos*[2] and *nomos*[3]) had already borne witness to the provisional character of *nomos*[1]. The temporary character of the law is intrinsic to the narration of the OT, Sinai following centuries after the call of Abraham, and even the mark of circumcision (Gen 17) following as but a sign of the more original declaration that "Abraham believed God and it was reckoned to him as righteousness" (Gen 15:6 LXX; Gal 3:6; Rom 4:3, 9, 22).

5. The Law and the Christian Moral Life. Christian theological debates subsequent to the NT have not infrequently confounded the reading of Paul, not only by drawing him into controversies not of his own time but also by laying hold of law in a generalized sense as the moral demands of God, whereas Paul's use is characteristically specific to the Jewish-particular directives inscribed in the Torah. To be clear, Paul could no more be considered an antinomian (as the term is customarily understood) than he could be considered a nomist. That Christians are "not under law" (see 4.1.1) does not make them "without a law of God" (1 Cor 9:21). Permitting a neologism, Paul would be best understood as a "supranomian." The law's expectations are not invalidated by the end of the ages but are met and transcended by those "guided by [*stoicheō*] the Spirit" (Gal 5:25 NRSV; cf. Gal 5:16, 22-23; 2 Cor 3:6; Rom 7:6; 8:3). The Christian tradition has labored with varying success to represent this Pauline paradox toward the end of Christian moral guidance, understanding at once the value and necessity of moral codifications while also acknowledging their insufficiency.

A protracted and lively debate has carried on for centuries within Reformation strands of Christianity concerning the so-called third use of the law. In this scheme, the "first use" (*usus politicus*) is the law's function as a restraint of evil in human society, the application of "special revelation" toward the ends of common grace; the "second use" (*usus elenchticus*) is the specific function of the law to convict sinners of their guilt and drive them to Christ for salvation. Both of these uses of the law are widely accepted by heirs of the Reformation. The "third use" (*usus normativus*) describes the alleged function of the law as a guide to moral living for the Christian. Here Calvinistic and Lutheran understandings depart from each other, with the former characteristically affirming the third use and the latter rejecting it.

To bring Paul into this dispute is to invite him into a debate in which the terms and context have been changed from his own. Inasmuch as Paul regarded the law as divine revelation, he might ambivalently affirm the first use, but he could only be pessimistic for its success. As for the second use, Paul's claim that the law identifies the objective guilt of all humans does not necessarily entail that he would understand the preaching of law toward conviction as a kerygmatic strategy. "Lutheran" and revivalist enthusiasm for the second use of the law does not find direct support in Paul. As for the so-called third use of the law, it would have been impossible for Paul to affirm the *Mosaic* law as a basis for the Christian moral life, for while he viewed the law as a true revelation of the will of God, he regarded the pursuit of Christian morality by means of the Mosaic law as an exercise in futility and a moral standard too low for the Spirit-endowed Christian. Paul could not endorse this Calvinistic use of the law without a terminological sleight of hand that substitutes reference to the Mosaic law for a moral code otherwise derived and defined.

The "end" of the torah is not its replacement with updated behavioral codifications but with a new principle and the extrinsic energy of the Spirit for the righteousness to which the law aspired. Thus, Paul regarded the law as a moral floor too high for the unregenerate by their own efforts, and a moral ceiling too low for those being remade into the image of Christ (Rom 8:29; 2 Cor 3:18; 1 Cor 15:29; cf. Col 3:10; Eph 4:24). Here Franz Overbeck's frequently cited quip applies, "[Paul] has but one student of the second century who understood him—Marcion!—and he misunderstood him!" (218-19).

The venerable, ubiquitous, and expedient subdivision of the law of Moses into three categories—civil, ceremonial, and moral (e.g., Aquinas, *Summa theologiae* 2a, q. 99; John Calvin, *Institutes of the Christian Religion* 4.20.14-15; Thirty-Nine Articles of Religion, VII)—runs afoul of both the Pentateuch's self-presentation and Paul's understanding of the law as an indissoluble whole (e.g., Gal 5:3; Rom 2:25-29; cf. Jas 2:10-11) and stumbles at such points as so-called civil and ceremonial or civil and moral overlap. Nonetheless, as a subsequent and analytic classification of Torah materials, the subdivision has enjoyed sufficient assent as to be serviceable. Moreover, to the extent that Paul himself reaffirms the moral substance of the law, whether as the law of love or the law of Christ or as that which is "holy, righteous and good," and understands the Christian *ekklēsia* as a nontheocratic, ethnically inclusive entity, the scheme is not entirely alien and without utility. One can be reasonably assured, however, that Paul would balk at this as a strategy for supporting a third use of the law, if by *law* was meant the ordinances given to Moses.

See also Conversion and Call of Paul; Faith; Flesh; Gentiles; Justification; Law of Christ; Old Testament in Paul; Paul and Judaism; Righteousness; Sin, Guilt; Works of the Law.

BIBLIOGRAPHY. **G. P. Anderson,** *Paul's New Perspective: Charting a Soteriological Journey* (Downers Grove, IL: IVP Academic, 2016); **J. M. G. Barclay,** *Obeying the Truth: A Study of Paul's Ethics in Galatians* (Edinburgh: T&T Clark, 1988); idem, *Jews in the Mediterranean Diaspora: From Alexander to Trajan (323 BCE—117 CE)* (Edinburgh: T&T Clark, 1996); **M. N. A. Bockmuehl,** *Jewish Law in Gentile Churches: Halakhah and the Beginning of Christian Public Ethics* (Edinburgh: T&T Clark, 2000); **D. A. Campbell,** *The Deliverance of God: An Apocalyptic Rereading of Justification in Paul* (Grand Rapids, MI: Eerdmans, 2009); **D. A. Carson, P. T. O'Brien, and M. A. Seifrid,** eds., *Justification and Variegated Nomism: The Paradoxes of Paul*, vol. 2, WUNT 181 (Grand Rapids, MI: Baker Academic, 2004); **S. J. Chester,** *Conversion at Corinth: Perspectives on Conversion in Paul's Theology and the Corinthian Church* (New York: T&T Clark, 2003); idem, *Reading Paul with the Reformers: Reconciling Old and New Perspectives* (Grand Rapids, MI: Eerdmans, 2017); **C. E. B. Cranfield,** "St Paul and the Law," *SJT* 17 (1964): 43-68; idem, "'The Works of the Law' in the Epistle to the Romans," *JSNT*, no. 43 (1991): 89-101; **A. A. Das,** *Paul, the Law, and the Covenant* (Peabody, MA: Hendrickson, 2001); **T. J. Deidun,** *New Covenant Morality in Paul*, AnBib 89 (Rome: Pontifical Biblical Institute, 1981); **T. L. Donaldson,** *Paul and the Gentiles: Remapping the Apostle's Convictional World* (Minneapolis: Fortress, 1997); **J. W. Drane,** *Paul, Libertine or Legalist? A Study in the Theology of the Major Pauline Epistles* (London: SPCK, 1975); **J. D. G. Dunn,** *Jesus, Paul, and the Law: Studies in Mark and Galatians* (Louisville, KY: Westminster John Knox, 1990); idem, *The Theology of Paul the Apostle* (Grand Rapids, MI: Eerdmans, 1998); idem, ed., *Paul and the Mosaic Law* (Grand Rapids, MI: Eerdmans, 2001); idem, *The New Perspective on Paul* (Grand Rapids, MI: Eerdmans, 2008); **P. Fredriksen,** *Paul: The Pagans' Apostle* (New Haven, CT: Yale University Press, 2017); **J. G. Gager,** *Who Made Early Christianity? The Jewish Lives of the Apostle Paul*, American Lectures on the History of Religions 18 (New York: Columbia University Press, 2017); **L. Gaston,** *Paul and the Torah* (Vancouver: University of British Columbia Press, 1987); **S. J. Hafemann,** *Paul, Moses, and the History of Israel*, WUNT (Tübingen: Mohr Siebeck, 1995); **R. B. Hays,** "Three Dramatic Roles: The Law in Romans 3–4," in *Paul and the Mosaic Law*, ed. J. D. G. Dunn, WUNT (Tübingen: Mohr Siebeck, 1996), 151-64; **H. Hübner,** *Law in Paul's Thought: A Contribution to the Development of Pauline Theology*, trans. J. C. G. Greig (Edinburgh: T&T Clark, 1984); **A. J. Hultgren,** "Paul and the Law," in *The Blackwell Companion to Paul*, ed. Stephen Westerholm (Malden, MA: Wiley-Blackwell, 2011), 202-15; **J. C. Hurd,** *The Origin of I Corinthians* (New York: Seabury, 1965); **V. Koperski,** *What Are They Saying About Paul and the Law?* (New York: Paulist, 2001); **C. G. Kruse,** *Paul, the Law, and Justification* (Peabody, MA: Hendrickson, 1997); **D. J. Moo,** "Israel and the Law in Romans 5–11: Interaction with the New Perspective," in *Justification and Variegated Nomism: The Paradoxes of Paul*, ed. D. A. Carson, P. T. O'Brien, and M. A. Seifrid, WUNT 181 (Grand Rapids, MI: Baker Academic, 2004), 2:185-216;

M. D. Nanos, *Reading Paul Within Judaism* (Eugene, OR: Wipf & Stock, 2017); **M. D. Nanos and M. Zetterholm,** eds., *Paul Within Judaism: Restoring the First-Century Context to the Apostle* (Minneapolis: Fortress, 2015); **F. Overbeck,** *Christentum und Kultur* (Basel: B. Schwabe, 1919); **P. B. Payne,** *Man and Woman, One in Christ: An Exegetical and Theological Study of Paul's Letters* (Grand Rapids, MI: Zondervan, 2009); **H. Räisänen,** *Paul and the Law*, WUNT 29 (Tübingen: Mohr, 1983); idem, "Paul's Word-Play on Nomos: A Linguistic Study," in *Jesus, Paul and Torah: Collected Essays*, ed. H. Räisänen (Sheffield: JSOT Press, 1992), 69-94; **B. S. Rosner,** *Paul, Scripture, and Ethics: A Study of 1 Corinthians 5–7* (Grand Rapids, MI: Baker, 1999); idem, "Paul and the Law: What He Does Not Say," *JSNT* 32 (2010): 405-19; idem, *Paul and the Law: Keeping the Commandments of God*, NSBT 31 (Downers Grove, IL: InterVarsity Press, 2013); **E. P. Sanders,** *Paul, the Law, and the Jewish People* (Philadelphia: Fortress, 1983); idem, "Did Paul's Theology Develop?," in *The Word Leaps the Gap: Essays on Scripture and Theology in Honor of Richard B. Hays*, ed. J. R. Wagner et al. (Grand Rapids, MI: Eerdmans, 2008), 325-50; **E. J. Schnabel,** *Law and Wisdom from Ben Sira to Paul: A Tradition Historical Enquiry into the Relation of Law, Wisdom, and Ethics*, WUNT 2/16 (Tübingen: Mohr Siebeck, 1985); **T. R. Schreiner,** *The Law and Its Fulfillment: A Pauline Theology of Law* (Grand Rapids, MI: Baker, 1993); **F. Thielman,** *From Plight to Solution: A Jewish Framework to Understanding Paul's View of the Law in Galatians and Romans*, NovTSup (New York: Brill, 1989); idem, *Paul and the Law: A Contextual Approach* (Downers Grove, IL: InterVarsity Press, 1994); **M. Thiessen,** *Paul and the Gentile Problem* (New York: Oxford University Press, 2016); **L. Thurén,** *Derhetorizing Paul: A Dynamic Perspective on Pauline Theology and the Law*, WUNT 124 (Tübingen: Mohr Siebeck, 2000); **T. H. Tobin,** *Paul's Rhetoric in Its Contexts: The Argument of Romans* (Peabody, MA: Hendrickson, 2004); **P. J. Tomson,** *Paul and the Jewish Law: Halakha in the Letters of the Apostle to the Gentiles* (Minneapolis: Fortress, 1990); **F. Watson,** *Paul and the Hermeneutics of Faith* (London: T&T Clark, 2004); **S. Westerholm,** *Perspectives Old and New on Paul: The "Lutheran" Paul and His Critics* (Grand Rapids, MI: Eerdmans, 2004); **N. T. Wright,** "Christ, the Law, and 'Pauline Theology,'" in *The Climax of the Covenant: Christ and the Law in Pauline Theology* (Edinburgh: T&T Clark, 1991), 1-17.

G. P. Anderson

LAW OF CHRIST

Nearly three centuries ago Johann Albrecht Bengel referred to Paul's "*law of *Christ" as "a rare appellation" (Bengel, 738). Recent interpreters, however, have not felt the need to be so discreet. The "law of Christ" has been dubbed "arresting" (Cole, 225), "strange" (Betz, 299), "striking" (Stanton, 116), "extremely baffling" (Hong, 173), "doubly astonishing" (Barclay, 126), indeed "a phrase more likely to mislead than to instruct" (Winger, 545).

But why such astonishment over what appears to be a relatively straightforward expression? Perhaps the simplest answer is also the one with a good deal of explanatory power: many interpreters find the expression "law of Christ" singularly ill-suited for the argument and theology of Galatians. In Galatians, Paul's polemic against the law climaxes with what appears to be an outright antithesis between Christ and law. A positive reference to believers fulfilling the law of Christ is therefore highly paradoxical, if not completely bewildering.

As a result, scholars tend to view the law of Christ as an anomaly within Galatians because it fails, on the surface, to harmonize with the rest of the letter. It introduces serious cognitive dissonance and disrupts perceived theological patterns, not to mention that it seems to run contrary to several rather stark-sounding statements about the temporality of the law (Gal 3:22-25; 4:1-7) and its irrelevance for *justification (Gal 2:15-16; 5:5-6). The phrase is therefore often adapted to fit with the rest of what Paul says about the law in Galatians, that is, with his more paradigmatic insights about the law, which are to be derived from elsewhere in the letter (i.e., Gal 2–4).

There are signs, however, that things may be changing for the "law of Christ." While the phrase has traditionally been harmonized with Paul's negative portrayal of the law by treating the expression either as a circumlocution for Christian living or as a reference to some other law, a growing number of interpreters want to treat the law of Christ as a reference to the *law of Moses*. This is not to suggest, of course, that these scholars agree on either the precise sense of the expression or on how exactly it was that Paul could claim that uncircumcised *Gentiles "fulfill" the law of Moses (Gal 5:14; 6:2), only that an increasing number of interpreters are persuaded that the expression itself somehow refers to the law of Moses.

Before turning to the history of interpretation, a summary of the ways in which the law of Christ has been interpreted by scholars will be helpful. There are basically two views: (1) the law of Christ refers to a new law that somehow replaces the law of Moses, and (2) the law of Christ refers to the law of Moses interpreted or embodied by Christ.

1. History of Interpretation
2. The Phrase in Galatians
3. Conclusion

1. History of Interpretation.
It may come as something of a surprise to learn that within the history of interpretation, the expression "law of Christ" has seldom been taken as a reference to the law of Moses. While it may not be entirely unprecedented, prior to the late twentieth century it certainly would have been difficult to find anyone stating explicitly and unambiguously that with the expression "law of Christ" Paul intended to refer to the law of Moses. The near-universal view has been that with this expression Paul refers to that which *replaces* the law of Moses. Often this has meant taking "law of Christ" to be a reference to some kind of *nova lex* for Christians (Thielman, 142). While the exact character of this new law has been understood in different ways by different interpreters in different traditions, the basic outlook appears to be the same: just as the *church has superseded *Israel, so also the law of Christ has replaced the law of Moses (see Esler).

This way of understanding the law of Christ, however, began to be seriously called into question with the work of E. P. Sanders and the larger Copernican shift in Pauline studies conveniently dubbed the "new perspective" (Hagner, 111-12). Following a century or more of German-Lutheran predominance in NT studies (1830s–1960s), the emergence of the new perspective in the 1970s–1980s has, among other things, helped to make the world of Pauline studies much more hospitable to positive references to the Jewish Torah from the *apostle to the Gentiles. From another angle, one could just as well say that by presenting a serious challenge to, and in some ways undoing, the hegemony of the Reformation law-*gospel contrast as the framework for understanding Paul's view of the law, the new perspective has promoted an atmosphere in which it is far easier for exegetes to *hear* positive affirmations of the law in the *letters of Paul.

Another feature of the broader exegetical and theological milieu helping to give rise to this recent trend in interpretation is, ironically enough, the perceived failure within the guild of twentieth-century attempts to identify a convincing Jewish background for the interpretation of the law of Christ. Largely missing from the first nineteen centuries of the interpretation of this expression are proposals of possible linguistic or conceptual parallels from *outside* the NT. The twentieth century, of course, did much to redress this, yet overall these efforts appear to have found few supporters and to have generated little consensus (Davies).

For nearly a century, immense energy was devoted to finding within Christianity's Jewish matrix a hermeneutical key to unlock Paul's law of Christ. Overall, however, this quest is perceived at least to be something of a failure. Either the required evidence has been found wanting, or the connection to Paul's actual use of the phrase in Galatians is deemed too tenuous. For the interpretation of the law of Christ, then, the upshot has been to return attention to the primary context of Paul's letters, not least Galatians itself.

2. The Phrase in Galatians.
Since at least the 1970s, NT scholars have increasingly shied away from writing the grand syntheses of Pauline theology characteristic of earlier generations and instead have focused attention more on the distinctive contributions of each of Paul's letters. This methodological reorientation has obvious implications for the interpretation of "law of Christ." While it was not at all uncommon to find patristic commentators explaining the law of Christ by readily appealing to the record of Jesus' teaching of a "new commandment" in John 13:34-35 (e.g., Theodoret, Jerome, Pelagius; cf. Aquinas), or an earlier generation of interpreters happily turning to similar phraseology in Paul's other letters (see Rom 3:27; 8:2; 1 Cor 9:21), scholars are now content to advise that the phrase is best interpreted in the immediate context of Galatians.

Consequently, the context within which one can make sense of Paul's law of Christ appears to have narrowed considerably in recent years. Now scholars offer interpretations that begin and end, as it were, with Galatians itself. Importantly, what this has done is give ascendancy to Galatians 5:13-14 as *the primary datum* for interpreting the law of Christ, thus dislodging John 13:34-35; Romans 3:27; 8:2; or 1 Corinthians 9:21 from the pride of place. And once the link between Galatians 6:2 and Galatians 5:13-14, with its clear reference to the law of Moses, has been firmly established in the mind of the exegete, it becomes far easier to begin to *see* Paul referring to the law of Moses in both places.

There are several reasons for interpreting "law of Christ" as a reference to the law of Moses. First, the terminological and conceptual parallels between

Galatians 6:2 and Galatians 5:13-14, with its clear reference to the law of Moses, argue in favor of seeing "law of Christ" as a reference to the law of Moses. Second, the proximity of Galatians 5:13-14 and Galatians 6:2 within the epistle makes it unlikely that Paul would have intended to refer to something other than the law of Moses in Galatians 6:2, when he has just said virtually the exact same thing a few verses earlier (Gal 5:13-14). Third, there is the sheer consistency of Paul's usage of *nomos* in Galatians (let alone in his other epistles). The appearance of *nomos* in Galatians 6:2 is the thirty-first in the epistle, and in each previous instance it is a reference to the law of Moses (Martyn, 555). There is no indication that Paul means anything other than the law of Moses when he uses *nomos*. A fourth and admittedly more speculative point is that if Paul has in fact picked up the expression from his opponents, who certainly would have meant it as a reference to the law of Moses, it makes sense for him transpose the phrase into a new context but preserve its original reference to the law of Moses (Hong, 177; Longenecker, 86).

Taking "law of Christ" to be a reference to the law of Moses, however, raises an important question: Why the "*of Christ*"? Explaining the precise significance of the "of Christ" gives rise to a diversity of opinions, even among those who want to treat the expression as a reference to the law of Moses. One line of approach would be to argue that Paul was at this point in conscious dependence on Jesus' own summary of the law in terms of the love command, a tradition of which there is little reason to doubt he was aware (Wenham, 256-59). Perhaps the "of Christ" is intended to signify that the expression refers to the law of Moses as taught and exemplified by Christ (Dunn 1993, 322-23). More easily demonstrated from the text of Galatians, however, would be the claim that Paul added the "of Christ" because he saw an inextricable link between *love (i.e., burden bearing) and Christ as the example par excellence of love (Gal 2:20; cf. Rom 15:1-3; Barclay 1988, 132-33). On this reading, to fulfill the law of Christ would be to fulfill the law of Moses in a Christlike way, that is, through lovingly bearing burdens, as did Christ himself.

3. Conclusion.

Despite growing scholarly consensus that the "law of Christ" does in fact refer to the law of Moses, many important questions remain. How, for example, can Paul affirm that uncircumcised Gentiles fulfill the law of Christ when it is understood as a reference to the law of Moses? Or how should one understand the relationship between the law of Christ, understood as a reference to the law of Moses, and Paul's sharp polemic against the law elsewhere in Galatians? Or how important is the law of Christ to Paul's own thinking about the law? Or is it merely a clever rhetorical device he uses to score some important rhetorical points?

More importantly, questions remain as to whether Paul envisioned an abiding presence for Torah in the life of the Christian. If the law of Christ is something of an anomaly in Paul's thinking, then scholars will look elsewhere for Paul's more fundamental teaching about the law. But should this recent trend sustain itself exegetically, something that is yet to be seen, it might serve to call into question the somewhat neglected status of this striking expression and perhaps provide grounds for moving the law of Christ from the periphery of discussions of Paul and the law closer to the center. This could in turn have far-reaching consequences for Pauline theology.

See also GALATIANS, LETTER TO THE; GENTILES; INTERPRETATION: NEW PERSPECTIVE; LAW.

BIBLIOGRAPHY. **J. M. G. Barclay,** *Obeying the Truth: A Study of Paul's Ethics in Galatians* (Edinburgh: T&T Clark, 1988); **J. A. Bengel,** *Gnomon Novi Testamenti, in Quo ex Nativa Verborum VI*, 3rd ed. (Stuttgart: Steinkopf, 1860 [1st ed. 1742]); **H. D. Betz,** *Galatians: A Commentary on Paul's Letter to the Churches in Galatia* (Philadelphia: Fortress, 1979); **R. A. Cole,** *The Letter of Paul to the Galatians*, 2nd ed., TNTC 9 (Grand Rapids, MI: Eerdmans, 1989); **W. D. Davies,** *Torah in the Messianic Age and/or the Age to Come* (Philadelphia: Society of Biblical Literature, 1952); **J. D. G. Dunn,** *The Theology of Paul's Letter to the Galatians* (Grand Rapids, MI: Eerdmans, 1993); idem, *The Theology of Paul the Apostle* (Grand Rapids, MI: Eerdmans, 1998); **P. F. Esler,** *Galatians* (London: Routledge, 1998); **D. Hagner,** "Paul and Judaism: The Jewish Matrix of Early Christianity: Issues in the Current Debate," *CurBR* 3, no. 1 (1993); **R. B. Hays,** "Christology and Ethics in Galatians: The Law of Christ," *CBQ* 49 (1987): 268-90; **I.-G. Hong,** *The Law in Galatians* (Sheffield: JSOT Press, 1993); **B. W. Longenecker,** *The Triumph of Abraham's God: The Transformation of Identity in Galatians* (Edinburgh: T&T Clark, 1998); **J. L. Martyn,** *Galatians: A New Translation with Introduction and Commentary* (New York: Doubleday, 1997); **E. P. Sanders,** *Paul, the Law, and the Jewish People* (Philadelphia: Fortress, 1983); **T. R. Schreiner,** *The Law and Its Fulfillment: A Pauline Theology of Law* (Grand Rapids, MI: Baker, 1993);

G. N. Stanton, "The Law of Moses and the Law of Christ—Galatians 3.1–6.2," in *Paul and the Mosaic Law*, ed. J. D. G. Dunn (Tübingen: Mohr, 1996), 99-116; **F. Thielman,** *Paul and the Law: A Contextual Approach* (Downers Grove, IL: InterVarsity Press, 1994); **D. Wenham,** *Paul: Follower of Jesus or Founder of Christianity?* (Grand Rapids, MI: Eerdmans, 1995); **T. Wilson,** "The Law of Christ and the Law of Moses: Reflections on a Recent Trend in Interpretation," *CurBR* 5, no. 1 (2006): 123-44; **M. Winger,** "The Law of Christ," *NTS* 46 (2000): 537-46.

T. Wilson

LAWSUIT. *See* Corinthians, First Letter to the; Legal System, Roman.

LEADERSHIP

The Greek language of the first century has a flexible and widely used word for "leader" (*archōn*). However, this word is never applied in the NT to Christian leadership roles. Rather, it is commonly used in the Gospels and Acts, often disparagingly, to refer to political, judicial, and Jewish religious authorities, including synagogue leaders (Mt 20:25; Lk 8:41; 12:58; 23:13; Acts 3:17; 16:19). Across the NT letters, only Paul uses this term, and he does so exclusively in reference to nonhuman, spiritual powers (Rom 13:3; 1 Cor 2:6, 8; Eph 2:2). Paul does not make wide use of any single equivalent to the generic English word *leader* as a class description of those recognized and appointed to lead a local community of believers or direct an area of *church *ministry.

However, Paul does use a range of verbs in respect to the function of leading figures within local and wider church contexts. These verbs are often used prescriptively, rather than descriptively. In other words, they frame what ought to have happened and not necessarily what was happening. Indeed, much of what can be determined about church leadership from Paul's letters is corrective (Clarke 2008, 11-16).

These verbs are not the equivalent of job titles; neither are they narrow role descriptions. Rather, they frame some of the functions that are expected in regard to local church leaders (*proistēmi*, "be in a position of leadership," Rom 12:8; 1 Tim 3:4-5, 12; *noutheteō*, "warn/admonish," 1 Thess 5:12; *kopiaō*, "work hard," Rom 16:6, 12; 1 Cor 16:16; 1 Thess 5:12; 1 Tim 5:17; *paramytheomai*, "console," 1 Thess 2:12; *parakaleō*, "encourage," 1 Tim 6:2; 2 Tim 4:2; *oikodomeō*, "build up," 1 Cor 14:4; *didaskō*, "teach," 2 Tim 2:2; see also *hypotassō*, "be submissive or subject to," 1 Cor 16:16, as an appropriate, respectful response to church leaders).

In one particular list of functions, Paul selects a range of verbs to reflect a distribution of spiritual *gifts, almost all of which might be regarded as tasks of leadership (Rom 12:6-8: prophesying, serving/ministering, *teaching, exhorting, contributing, leading, laboring, showing *mercy). It is significant that these activities are not combined as the particular responsibility of a single individual, nor even distributed across a team of leaders. Indeed, all of the believers in Rome are urged not to think of themselves as superior to each other (Rom 12:3; see also Phil 2:3). Rather, these gifts are distributed by *God across the whole community (Rom 12:3-5).

This dynamic, whereby characteristic actions, skills, or responsibilities of leaders are also expected of all others in a church community, is repeatedly reflected across the Pauline letters. The tasks and qualities of leaders are to be exercised and fulfilled by all, sometimes in mutual ways and sometimes in an inverted fashion so that, for example, members of a church might expect to see leaders submitting to them, or they might note that the *apostles have been placed at the end of the line and are serving as *slaves to the *body of *Christ (1 Cor 3:20-23; 4:9; 2 Cor 4:5; see also Rom 15:14; 2 Cor 1:4; 13:11; Eph 5:21; Col 3:16; 1 Thess 4:18; 5:11, 14). Similarly, Christ's distribution of leadership gifts in Ephesians 4:11-16 is specifically in order that the work of ministry is actually carried out, not simply by the leaders but by all members of the body of Christ. It is the sanctified believers who are together equipped to build each other up in *love and are thereby not dependent on their leaders for ministry.

This reciprocity and inversion appear to downplay but not dissolve qualitative and status distinctions between leaders and others in Paul's injunctions. Rather than presupposing or exercising a power differential, leaders are to be characterized by humility and engaged in empowering and equipping all others.

1. Titles of Leaders
2. Leaders as Models
3. Leadership by Persuasion
4. Leadership and the Cosmic Plan of God

1. Titles of Leaders.

Paul also uses specific titles for three discrete church offices, although only in a very few chapters as references to appointed leaders (predominantly 1 Tim 3; 5; Titus 1; see also Acts 14:23; 20:17, 28). These titles of overseer, deacon, and elder have had a disproportionate significance in reconstructions of leadership in the NT churches, which has displaced other important evidence about leaders (Clarke 2008, 42-78). Although each of the titles finds a continuing place in a number of subsequent church denominations, it is important to recognize how specific and different was the first-century context in which they served.

It is noticeable that these three Pauline titles differ from the significantly more prestigious titles of officers in Jewish synagogues of the time. Since the late nineteenth century, the majority of scholars have noted that the Pauline titles are concentrated in the later NT texts. References in the Pastoral Epistles to a protocol of selecting, appointing, and disciplining elders, overseers, and deacons have been taken to be evidence by this time of a greater level of organization and an already clearly established and normative hierarchy of governance. This long-standing academic consensus held that this structural pattern reflected early signs of the inevitable institutionalization of church authority. In turn, this has also been regarded as a corroborating indication that these particular letters must reflect a later period and therefore are quite possibly not be Pauline in origin. This trajectory of increasing institutionalization and hierarchy is further justified by its apparent continuity and development through subsequent centuries. The consensus has also regarded the contrasting general absence of titles for church leaders in the earlier Pauline letters as evidence of a pattern of primitive egalitarian communities, in which whole communities were instead led by the Spirit. In these small, simple, and apparently ideal settings, there was no obvious need for a recognized group of trained, appointed, and authorized leaders. These early years of the church were characterized instead by the involvement of all rather than the professionalized ministry of a few.

This view has been largely refuted since the late twentieth century, as it has become recognized that the Pauline letters do not present the inclusion or omission of different titles in clearly and consistently differentiated ways. Neither is it the case that these descriptors are obviously restricted only to the later Pauline epistles (see Phil 1:1; Rom 16:1-2). Further, there is overwhelming evidence in other vocabulary that leadership was being exercised from the outset (1 Thess 5:12-13). Finally, Greco-Roman society was fundamentally stratified, with clearly and universally recognized distinctions of status and rank. This was apparent not only in the public sphere but also in private dwellings (as evidenced in the mistreatment of the disadvantaged in the practice of the *Lord's Supper in *Corinth, 1 Cor 11:17-34). While Paul is clear that the *gospel of Christ is extended to all, irrespective of social status, gender, or nationality (Gal 3:28; Col 3:11), there is no extant record of the early Pauline communities radically and widely implementing nonhierarchical structures, which would have supplanted these particular cultural norms that were so deeply embedded in society. Structural equality was never a widespread and inherent characteristic of these communities.

A new scholarly consensus recognizes that the settings for meetings of the early church communities changed little during the entire postascension period of the NT. These predominantly remained small spaces, where hosting was normally by a head of *household (not infrequently a married couple or a single, perhaps slave-owning, woman; Acts 16:14-15; Rom 16:3-5; 1 Cor 16:19; Col 4:15). Common social and cultural practice would have recognized the inherent authority of householders within their own private spaces, and this, together with the comparatively small size of groups, should have mitigated, although not removed, any sense of dominant, externally imposed, institutional authority.

The description of an overseer (*episkopos*) in 1 Timothy 3:1-7 (see also Phil 1:1) may presuppose that this occasionally used title was normally applied to householders who were leading a church community in their own home (Clarke 2008, 47-52). The dynamic of the domestic and family context is here to the fore (1 Tim 3:4-5), and the dominant responsibilities within this setting concern caring for the community and teaching (1 Tim 3:2, 5). The qualifications for a deacon (*diakonos*) are juxtaposed here (1 Tim 3:8-13; see also Phil 1:1; Clarke 2008, 60-71). The related word group has a very wide application, and its uses and contexts elsewhere in the NT are too varied to provide a clear and consistent role description for deacons as a church appointment. In particular, the Acts 6:1-6 distinction between serving the word and serving at tables is an inadequate and likely irrelevant basis for establishing a standard role for those called deacons in the Pauline communities. Paul expects that deacons, like overseers, would need to have the character and essential skills necessary to manage a household in a godly fashion (the dominant context for church meetings); but there does not seem to be the same expectation, as for overseers, that they would have a responsibility to teach (1 Tim 3:8-13).

A third title, again only occasionally used by Paul in the context of a church appointment, is that of elder (*presbyteros*, 1 Tim 5:17-20; Titus 1:5-9; Clarke 2008, 52-60; Campbell). Just as the term *diakonos* did not most commonly refer to a church deacon, so also the terms *presbyteros* and *presbytis* often referred in first-century times simply to an older man or woman (see the distinctions in 1 Tim 5:1-2). In this sense, Paul described himself as an old man, *presbytēs*, in Philemon 9. Indeed, it may be that Acts 14:23 reflects a situation in which Paul and Barnabas identified which of the older individuals (i.e., elders) were most respected within that community and then duly appointed these to positions of leadership. If so, elders would have been the pool from which leaders were being recognized and then selected by the apostles.

Many have identified an overlap in usage between elder and overseer and concluded that these were interchangeable terms or roles. A more likely interpretation is that, where a single overseer served in the context of an individual church meeting (as head of a household), *elders* was a much older and typically plural term (see the collective word *presbyterion*, "eldership" or "council of elders," 1 Tim 4:14). One reconstruction is that, where someone might have been an overseer in their own home, they might also have been one of the elders by virtue of age and maturity, and consequently respected across all the believers in a town. In this sense, elders might have acted together, as a council, in some aspects of community-wide judging or decision making. This overlap in personnel but distinction in jurisdiction might explain why the qualifications for both the singular overseer and the plural eldership are similar, and why a number of individual overseers, who would have been responsible for teaching the believers who met within their own homes, might together have been known as elders (see Acts 20:17, 28; 1 Tim 5:17; Titus 1:5).

It is not possible to determine a singular and widespread blueprint for church governance from these very few references to church titles. Although Paul does draw attention to certain doctrines or matters that he speaks of as relevant to all churches (1 Cor 4:17; 7:17; 11:16; 14:33; 16:1), neither a complex nor a particular structure for church leadership is promoted by the apostle.

2. Leaders as Models.

Jesus, John the Baptist, and other Jewish rabbis called their own followers or disciples (Mt 4:19-20, 22, 25; 9:14; 11:2; 23:6-9; Jn 3:25-26; 4:1). By contrast, Paul rebukes those who would identify themselves as the followers of particular church leaders (1 Cor 1:10-17). The universal headship of Christ over his own body makes such a dynamic of human headship entirely anomalous (Eph 1:22; Col 1:18; 2:19).

Church leaders, like the apostle, are instead to exercise influence by means of modeling (Clarke 2008, 173-82; Barentsen, 112-40). Using the words *mimētēs*, *mimeomai* (imitate, emulate), and *typos* (model/pattern/example), Paul repeatedly emphasizes that learning and formation are achieved by close observation of good and bad examples (Acts 20:18; 1 Cor 4:16; 11:1; Phil 3:7; 1 Thess 1:6-7; 2:15; 2 Thess 3:7-9; 1 Tim 4:12; Titus 2:7). In recounting their *mission to the people of Thessalonica, Paul draws attention specifically to the ways in which he and his fellow apostles made their impact, not simply as a consequence of the message they delivered and through powerful acts of the Spirit but also by clearly observable evidence of their life and character. Their apostolic ministry was characterized not by greed, flattery, or boastfulness but by the intimate, costly, and parental qualities of gentleness, affection, and urgent encouragement (1 Thess 2:5-12). The Thessalonian believers then had a subsequent and consequent impact, not only across their own region but also further afield through their own example (1 Thess 1:5-8; 2:13-14).

This presumption that leaders should lead by example is consistent with Paul's catalogs of qualifications for local church leaders (1 Tim 3:1-13; Titus 1:5–2:15). Across the period reflected by the Pauline letters, the dominant setting for meetings of believing communities was the private home (Gehring, 119-228). Other locations may sometimes have served in a minority of localities, but these are most likely to have been occasionally rented spaces that at other times fulfilled a different purpose (e.g., taverns; see Adams). There is no evidence of large, nondomestic meeting spaces that were exclusively for the purposes of church meetings.

These small and predominantly domestic settings constrain a number of important and interrelated assumptions about gatherings of early Christ-followers: their size, their activities, the complexity of any organizational or authority structures, and the nature, training, tasks and expectations of any leadership. Consistent with these cultural influences and physical constraints, it becomes immediately transparent why Paul's emphasis lies not on the character of leaders in their private lives, or their hidden qualities, but on how leaders live in full view of others, day by day and in proximity with a small number of fellow community members. In particular, a focus on how church leaders manage their own households is not simply that these qualities are usefully transferable also to a church context or that a disrupted domestic background might distract a leader from their spiritual duties elsewhere. Rather, the context in which local leadership is exercised is precisely in the home, alongside one's spouse and children, under the daily scrutiny of one's neighbors (1 Tim 3:4-5, 7, 11-12).

It follows that another implicit qualification of most church leaders was that they were householders, who would have been in a position to host a relatively small gathering of believers, whether in a rented or owned house or apartment. Leading was typically mediated, therefore, through the culturally widespread custom of extending *hospitality (1 Tim 3:2; Titus 1:8; see also Rom 12:13). By contrast, missional leaders typically pursued their ministry as the vulnerable and grateful recipients of hospitality (Acts 16:15, 34; 20:20; 21:8, 16; 28:23). Consequently, it can be presumed that Paul expected leaders to exercise influence by means of the accessible model of their lived lives, more than by the institutional authority of their appointment.

3. Leadership by Persuasion.
It is also clearly the case that Paul expected leaders of small church communities to exercise influence by persuasion more than by command or imposition (Clarke 2008, 159-72). Negotiated appeal is a dominant motif, reflected across Paul's writings. The apostle's own attempts to persuade are moderated by the nature of the specific relationship he has with his readers, including whether they are individuals or churches. In particular, he is significantly more circumspect in his exhortation when he is addressing a community he has not himself founded or fathered as an apostle of Christ Jesus (1 Cor 4:14-21, although even here he recognizes that the house churches in Corinth could point to a number of spiritual father figures).

Paul's extensive use of verbs of persuasion ranges in strength and force. As an apostle, he is at his most blunt only when he is encountering opposition to the content and supremacy of the gospel (see Gal 1:6-9). More typically, he urges formation in the *faith through encouragement and appeal more than imposition.

There is little evidence to suggest that local church leaders normally taught by means of a structured monologue to a regular and large congregation. On the contrary, the predominantly small contexts for meeting enabled Paul to invite or engage in discussion and debate and even submit himself to questioning (1 Cor 9:3). This is also likely to have been in mind when he urged local church leaders (not least Timothy and Titus) to give attention to teaching. While Paul embraces opportunities for reasoning, defense, and the expression of doubt (Rom 2:15; 14:1), it is clear that, at times, this medium of interactive learning descended inappropriately into quarrelling, controversy, contentiousness, strife, and dissension. Paul urges that this dynamic should be avoided (1 Cor 10:27; Phil 2:14; 1 Tim 2:8; 6:4; Titus 3:9). As with other aspects of leadership, an important feature of these interactive contexts for formation is that much of the engagement is handled mutually and not exclusively directed by those who were recognized as leaders ("able to instruct one another," Rom 15:14; "comfort one another, agree with one another," 2 Cor 13:11; "addressing one another," Eph 5:19; "teaching and admonishing one another in all *wisdom," Col 3:16; "encourage one another and build one another up," 1 Thess 5:11; see also 1 Thess 4:18).

4. Leadership and the Cosmic Plan of God.
This nuanced and at times almost contradictory tension in Paul's expectations that church leaders should be those who cede authority and who empower others may have roots in his wider understanding of the place and purpose of human leadership within the cosmic plan of God.

Paul may well have been influenced by the tradition of Jesus' teaching that the mission of the Son of God was to serve and that his followers were similarly to avoid exercising power over others (Lk 22:24-27; Mk 10:42-45; see also Rom 15:9, where Paul describes Christ as a *servant). The accounts in the OT of how priests, judges, and kings exercised governance over the people of God and the surrounding nations are consistently problematic (see 1 Cor 10:1-13). Genesis 1–2 reveals the *call and appointment of human beings to cooperate in subduing and having dominion over only "the fish of the sea and the birds of the skies and every animal that moves on the earth" (Gen 1:28; see Gen 2:19-21). The *curse on the *man and woman, following their disobedience, includes an expectation that human beings will engage in rule and subordination in relation to one another. This clearly arises as a consequence of the pain, struggle, toil, scarcity, and conflict that are to be faced by them as they are expelled from the garden in Eden (Gen 3:14-19). The authority of one person over another was not, therefore, God's original intention but became an inevitability.

The OT reflects a repeated theme of a human desire for leadership (1 Sam 8:6), a repeated failure of leadership (Ezek 34:1-10), and a rejection of leadership (Judg 17:6; 21:25).

God, however, remains the one who is sovereign over all earthly and spiritual beings. In this regard, Paul understands that all human, governing authorities are fundamentally appointed by God and should not be resisted (Rom 13:1-7). However, these local and national authorities should understand that they are finally answerable to God. In tension with this, believers, as those who have the wisdom of God, should not unnecessarily turn to judicial authorities to resolve their own minor, interpersonal differences (1 Cor 6:1-8). It is the faithful, after all, who will ultimately rule over angels and all spiritual powers. At this point, the leadership of humans over each other will again be unnecessary. In the meantime, God's people have the necessary means to resist and exercise authority over the cosmic powers (Eph 6:10-20).

See also CHURCH; CHURCH STRUCTURE; ETHICS; GIFTS OF THE SPIRIT; HOLINESS, SANCTIFICATION; HOUSEHOLDS AND HOUSEHOLD CODES; PASTOR, PAUL AS; SERVANT, SERVICE.

BIBLIOGRAPHY. **E. Adams,** *The Earliest Christian Meeting Places: Almost Exclusively Houses?* (London: T&T Clark, 2013); **J. Barentsen,** *Emerging Leadership in the Pauline Mission: A Social Identity Perspective on Local Leadership Development in Corinth and Ephesus* (Eugene, OR: Pickwick, 2011); **J. T. Burtchaell,** *From Synagogue to Church: Public Services and Offices in the Earliest Christian Communities* (Cambridge: Cambridge University Press, 1992); **R. A. Campbell,** *The Elders: Seniority Within Earliest Christianity* (Edinburgh: T&T Clark, 1994); **A. D. Clarke,** *Serve the Community of the Church: Christians as Leaders and Ministers* (Grand Rapids, MI: Eerdmans, 2000); idem, *A Pauline Theology of Church Leadership* (London: T&T Clark, 2008); **R. W. Gehring,** *House Church and Mission: The Importance of Household Structures in Early Christianity* (Peabody, MA: Hendrickson, 2004); **C. S. Smith,** *Pauline Communities as "Scholastic Communities": A Study of the Vocabulary of "Teaching" in 1 Corinthians, 1 and 2 Timothy and Titus* (Tübingen: Mohr Siebeck, 2012).

A. Clarke

LEGAL SYSTEM, ROMAN

Rome began as a small settlement on the banks of the Tiber in the eighth century BC. It grew to command an *empire with vast territories and a diverse, stratified population of millions. Its legal system, beginning as a "primitive customary law" (Lyall, 192), flexed and changed in response.

Paul's life and writing stood within and beneath the arc of Rome's dominion and judicial arrangements. Acts attests to and Paul's *letters intimate the apostle's privilege in law as a born Roman citizen. He appeared before magistrates, receiving the approbation of some and experiencing the coercive disciplines and restraints of others. The documents indicate his extensive travels through provinces, visits to towns and cities, and *ministry and instruction to people who themselves stood under various arrangements in relation to Roman law and governance.

1. The Legal System of Rome
2. Roman Law and Christian Experience: Provinces, Cities, and Rome
3. Roman Law in Direct Pauline Instruction and Experience
4. Roman Legal Metaphors in Paul's Letters

1. The Legal System of Rome.

1.1. Early Republic (450 BC–200 BC). Honoré indicates that Rome's legal history is generally divided into four periods ("Law and Procedure, Roman," 827-29). The first follows the expulsion of King Tarquin and his replacement by two chief magistrates (*consuls*) chosen from the nobility (*patricii*), who governed the state for a year, including administering the Roman civil law (*ius civile*). The great body of commoners (*plebs*), though free citizens, struggled for legal rights under the dominance of the nobility and their priestly advisers (*pontifices*). Intense plebeian agitation eventually gave them both more effective recourse to the law and increased representation among its councils (*pontifices*), chief magistrates (*consuls*), and magistrates (*praetors*). The earliest system of proceedings, called the *legis actio* (Gaius, *Inst.* 4.11-19, 30), offered a limited number of actions, was restrictive in its formalism, and offered only modest scope for development in civil and criminal law (Honoré, "Law and Procedure, Roman," 828; cf. Lyall, 192-93).

Rome's *legis actio*, moreover, was for citizens and did not service Rome's growing interchange and commerce with foreigners (*peregrini*). This problem was significantly addressed by a magistracy, the *praetor peregrinus*, tasked to develop more flexible, written formulas in pursuit of the principle of a law common to all states (*ius* [*omnium*] *gentium*; Gaius, in Justinian, *Digest* 1.1.9; Berger, 528-29), including Rome. The "formulary system," giving new remedies, creating efficiencies, and achieving greater equity, eventually replaced the older *legis actio* (Gaius, *Inst.* 4.30-31).

1.2. Late Republic (200 BC–31 BC). Significant developments in the period of the late republic were the emergence of an independent legal profession and the formation of standing criminal jury courts (*quaestiones perpetua*). Whereas advice on points of law was at first sought from the college of priests, over time jurists (*iuris consulti* or "lawyers") who were not members of the college began to be influential. They advised out of their own legal experience, reflection, and writing and gave instruction (Honoré, "Lawyers, Roman," 835; Lyall, 199).

Criminal law was not a standing body, but rather a patchwork of laws by which to prosecute very powerful individuals for overstepping in publicly damaging ways and others who had committed egregious individual acts. Earliest criminal procedure was inquisitorial and conducted by a magistrate (*tribunus plebis*). It was a one- to three-step process before the citizen assembly (*iudicium populi*). If a defendant confessed, he was punished. If he was convicted, the magistrate referred him for a hearing (*quarto accusatio*) and vote before one of two assemblies, depending on whether his crime was capital or monetary. Criminal prosecution also took place through ad hoc "jury courts" (*quaestiones*). Given a number of spectacular instances of their ineffectiveness, however, standing jury courts (*quaestiones perpetua*) were set up, each to prosecute a specific type of crime (e.g., treason) and without recourse to appeal. The fix was partial. The list of crimes was still limited, the courts operated only in Rome, and they could try only Roman men.

1.3. Classical Period (31 BC–AD 235). The violence of social conflict, the rise of dictators, and the eruption of civil wars in the late republic culminated in the concentration of powers in the victorious Augustus. While Augustus made a "serious attempt to adhere to republican forms of legislation (*lex, plebiscitum*)," his successors did not (Honoré, "Law and Procedure, Roman," 828). As *princeps* ("first [citizen]"), the emperor was formally the leading member of the senate. Augustus's legislative powers "were at first conceived as modeled on those of republican magistrates" (Honoré, "Law and Procedure, Roman," 828). The progressive aggregation of powers to him rankled some with strong republican convictions (Garnsey et al., 8-10); many others, fearing a return to earlier *violence, accommodated.

The great innovation of the Augustan principate was a new form of legal proceeding called *cognitio extra ordinem* or *cognitio extraordinaria*. It was based on the principle that "the administration of justice is *a function of the state*, while in the previous forms of proceedings the trial was *dominated by the parties* under the moderation and supervision of the magistrate" (Berger, 394, italics added). The magistrate, "acting as a delegate for the emperor or high functionary" (Berger, 394), personally conducted the trial from start to finish. Augustus's grant of *imperium* allowed discretion in the definition of crimes and the scale of punishments in the conduct of *cognitio*. It also created new imperial agents and jurisdictions, making Augustus and his successors the ultimate source of law-making, interpretation, and enforcement.

Jurists in this period became directly influential with the emperor and his magistrates, which caused them to be even more broadly attended to throughout the legal system. Aware of this increased influence and that not all were entirely supportive of him, Augustus and his successors deftly controlled them by a process of preferment (Honoré, "Lawyers, Roman," 836; Augustus, *Res gestae* 6).

1.4. Postclassical Period (AD 235–Emperor Justinian). The final period reflects the efforts of Constantine I and his successors to introduce "important reforms in public and procedural law and in the religious life of the empire" (Honoré, "Law and Procedure, Roman," 827). The most significant of the surviving documents of Roman law in this period are the three volumes of the Corpus Iuris Civilis of Justinian I (AD 527–565). The *Code* (AD 534) is a compilation of imperial legal enactments, including those parts of earlier codes that were still in effect (Gregorius, Hermogenianus, and Theodosius I). The *Digest*, or *Pandects* (AD 533), brings together excerpts from the most important classical juristic writing up to AD 300, including liberal citations from Ulpian and Iulius Paulus. The *Institutions* (AD 533), which served as a kind of primer on Roman law, draw heavily on the *Institutes* of Gaius (AD 161). Gaius's work was only known in its expurgated version in the *Institutions*. In 1816, a largely intact copy of the *Institutes*, replete with historical comment, was discovered. It illuminates much about Roman law and puts readers nearer in time to the NT.

2. Roman Law and Christian Experience: Provinces, Cities, and Rome.

2.1. Provinces. The Roman interest in the provinces was to dominate and profit by them (Brunt 1997), not to make them Roman or enfranchise their populations. The characteristics of a province were "permanent military occupation, regular taxation, and Roman supervision of public order, including jurisdiction and municipal government"

(Sherwin-White, 12). Oversight was pragmatic and selectively efficient, the object being to undergovern foreigners by granting the right "to continue organizing their legal life according to their own laws" (Honoré, "Law and Procedure, Roman," 829) so long as this did not imperil the peace of the province (*quies provinciae*) or intrude on Rome's financial interests (Lyall, 211-12). "Provincial governors may not have exercised criminal jurisdiction from the first, when their task was chiefly military and their subjects were predominantly foreign. But in time, probably by the late Republic, they performed as civil and criminal judges" (Garnsey 1968, 59). Provincials with rights as Roman citizens or special privileges, such as citizens of free cities and those honored for services rendered, "had a choice of courts. The latter could choose between local courts and laws, and those presided over by Roman administrators. Roman citizens, except where they were subject to local laws, were able to claim trial by Roman judges. With the coming of the empire, there was yet another alternative, the court of the emperor" (Garnsey 1966, 183).

Provinces were either senatorial or imperial from the time of Augustus. Largely pacified provinces were senatorial. Their governors were former consuls (*pro consule*) and praetors (*pro praetore*) whose magisterial power had been extended for them to govern for a one-year, renewable term. They had enough troops for general policing. Strategic or unstable larger provinces needing a stronger military presence were under the emperor as commander (*Imperator*). They were governed by trusted senatorial legionaries of consular rank called legates (*legati Augusti/Caesaris pro praetore*). Egypt and provinces considered too small to merit a legate were governed by praesidial equestrian *procuratores* (originally called *praefecti*) with *imperium* at the emperor's behest.

Sent with imperial instructions (*mandata principum*) and issuing edicts announcing the priorities of their administration, governors had military and fiscal control and exercised full civil and criminal jurisdiction. They had discretion to use the older, more restrictive procedures and remedies of civil and criminal Roman law or the creative and flexible arrangements of *cognitio extra ordinem*. The governor's *imperium* was extensive and nontransferable. He had the right physically to compel compliance (*coercitio*) with his orders and decrees and to punish broadly and to the fullest extent (*ius gladii*: cf. Cassius Dio, *Hist.* 52.22; 53.13.6-7; 53.14.5; cf. Rom 13:4). Hopeful Roman citizens might appeal (*provocatio*) to the emperor as ultimate holder of tribunician power and source of a governor's *imperium* against summary punishment. In this instance, the grant of appeal was at the discretion of the governor (Garnsey 1966). Foreign provincials, however, stood fully exposed to the powers of the governor as magistrate, excepting where the prospect of the latter's prosecution in Rome for provincial maladministration at the end of his term of office might serve caution to predatory action (Sherwin-White, 1).

How well did the above arrangements work? Proconsuls and legates had experience with the law in Rome, but the provincial context was complicating. Praesidial equestrian procurators without experience administering the law were amateurs (Brunt 1975, 134). The relative rank and status of plaintiffs and defendants necessarily influenced the conduct of civil and criminal litigation (Garnsey 1970; Rapske, 37-62, 442 fig. 9). Magistrates and juries could be swayed by favor, influence, and money (*gratia, potentia, pecunia*). Not a few governors vested with *imperium* in provinces far from Rome found the temptation to abuse their powers irresistible (Brunt 1961; 1975; Rapske, 62-70 and sources).

2.2. Cities. Believers in cities and towns where Paul founded churches and to whom he wrote letters had a varied exposure to and experience of Roman law. Philippi, *Corinth, and several of the cities of Galatia were colonies.

2.2.1. Colonies. Philippi came under general Roman rule in 167 BC. Because the kingdom of Macedon, of which it was part, and its neighbors were unstable, it was made a province in 148 BC governed by a *praetor* or *pro praetor* with legionary forces. In 42 BC, Antony established Philippi as a military veteran colony (Strabo, *Geogr.* 7, frag. 41; Pliny, *Nat.* 4.42). Further veteran settlement followed (Cassius Dio, *Hist.* 51.4.6), and in 27 BC Augustus made Macedonia a senatorial province, reorganizing and naming Philippi *Colonia Iulia Augusta Philippensium* (Augustus, *Res Gestae* 28.1).

Philippi's Roman citizens (*coloni*) had the same legal privileges as those living on Italian soil (*ius italicum*; Justinian, *Digest* 50.15.6; 50.15.8.8), including the right of self-government structured and operated according to Roman law, land ownership, and freedom from tribute and land taxes. Its two colonial magistrates (*archontes/strategoi*, Acts 16:19-20, 22, 36, 38 [= *praetor*]; Cicero, *Leg.* 2.93) were called *duoviri* and their attendants *lictores* (*rhabdouchoi*, Acts 16:35, 38). Latin was the official language, but Greek was predominant. Farmland was distributed to Roman colonists on a centuriated grid. This displaced the local Thracian and Greek farmers. The former resettled on further outlying territory; the latter moved into the city. The minority Roman population retained a tight and exclusive hold on power in Philippi for three centuries from its colonial beginning (Brélaz; Oakes 2001; 2018).

The Roman complaint against Paul and Silas of Jewish proselytizing and their experience of magisterial *coercitio* (Acts 16:16-40; Rapske, 115-34; cf. 1 Thess 2:2), the names of known Philippian believers (Brélaz, 163-66; Oakes 2018), and the strong theme of Philippian *suffering in Paul's letters (esp. Phil 1:27-30; 2:30; 3:18-21; 4:5-6, 16, 18-19; cf. 2 Cor 8:1-2) all suggest a predominantly Hellenistic Christian community having if anything a nominal Jewish and Roman presence. This belies notions of a *church filled with Roman citizens. Most Philippian believers would have known Roman law and life, but "from the outside and below."

Roman Corinth was a little over a century old in Paul's day. It became a colony in 44 BC and, eventually, the capital of the senatorial province of Achaia. The Augustan *rostrum* (*bēma*, Acts 18:12, 16, 17) from which the proconsul Gallio heard Paul's case can still be seen. It was "a city with an entrenched elite, a political oligarchy that perpetuated itself over generations by its control of wealth, office, and honor" (Welborn, 58-59). Freedmen could hold office, unlike elsewhere (Welborn, 64). At the same time, there was grinding poverty and hunger (Welborn, 56-57, 61). Paul's description of the congregation as having "not many" wise, influential, or nobly born but many foolish, lowly, and despised members by contemporary societal standards (1 Cor 1:26-28; 11:20-22) is "a mirror and microcosm of the city itself" (Welborn, 73).

The biblical record shows believers' negative experience with Roman law at the church's founding (Acts 18:12-17). Litigious disputes between believers before colonial magistrates were a blight on the church's later life (1 Cor 6:1-11), contradicting Paul's declaration that the damaging potentials of difference in the congregation, summarized in the oppositional binaries Jew and Greek and slave and free, have been rendered harmless by *God in practice (1 Cor 12:13).

Paul wrote a letter to the Galatians. The client kingdom of Galatia came into Rome's provincial system in 25 BC. M. Lollius governed it as praetorian legate (*legatus pro praetor*; cf. Eutropius, *Breviarium ab urbe condita* 7.10; Strabo, *Geogr.* 12.5.1). He established veteran colonies at Pisidian Antioch, Iconium, and Lystra (Hansen, 382, 387-89; Keener 2012–2015, 2036-37, 2110, 2120-21, 2129, 2178). Iconium was a "double community" consisting of a Greek city (*polis*) and a *colonia* (see Mitchell). The foreign population paid Roman tribute and taxes and, if residents of a Greek *polis*, were governed by indigenous assemblies and magistrates according to local law. Colonies self-governed to the rights that their status conferred (see Philippi above). It was the governor's responsibility "to preside over all matters of jurisdiction. In practice, however, he passed most minor matters to the local courts and to judges appointed by him. Roman citizens had the right to appeal decisions made by local courts to the governor and finally to the Emperor himself" (Hansen, 388). The later Pauline correspondence reflects on and reminds of Paul's legal troubles there (2 Tim 3:10-11; cf. Acts 16:1-2).

There was strong official Jewish opposition to Paul's *preaching in Pisidian Antioch. It consisted in levering the power of prominent God-fearing women associated with the synagogue to influence the Roman ruling elites (*prōtoi*, Acts 13:50; cf. Pliny, *Ep.* 3.2.2 [*princeps*]; Keener 2012–2015, 2103-5) to act against them. The harsh treatment and expulsion from the colony's borders expressed duoviral *coercitio*.

Ministry in Iconium sparked similar hostility. The plan of the Jews and Greeks (*Hellēnes*) together with their leaders (*archoi*, Acts 14:5) had a lethal intent. Stoning was a Jewish capital punishment for blasphemy (Acts 14:5; cf. Mt 23:37; Lk 13:34; Jn 10:32; 11:8; Acts 7:58-59; m. Sanh. 6:1–7:10). The terms noted above suggest that the magistrates of the Greek city and not the colony were involved.

The preaching in Lystra was to the poorer local Anatolian population, a crowd (*ochlos*, Acts 14:11, 13, 14, 19) who acclaimed the apostles as Greek gods (Acts 14:12; cf. Gal 4:14; Keener 2012–2015, 2143) in the Lycaonian language (Acts 14:11). Later incitement to stone Paul equated to mob justice (Acts 14:19; Keener 2012–2015, 2173).

The Galatian Christian communities, as at Philippi and Corinth, probably reflected the makeup and proportions of their broader respective communities, including Jews and Greeks, slaves and free persons, and men and women (Gal 3:28). Believers were still mindful of the secular social and legal distinctions. But Paul taught that their enfranchisement in Christ had brought a unity with eternal and present transformative impact.

2.2.2. Free Cities. Below a *colonia*, *municipium*, and *civitas foederata* (a city having special treaty with Rome) was a *civitas sine foedere immunis et libera*—a technically free city not having treaty

(Lyall, 211). Thessalonica, Ephesus, and probably Colossae were free cities.

Thessalonica, an administrative center of one of the four regions of Macedonia in the Roman annexation of 167 BC (Strabo, *Geogr.* 7, frag. 41; Livy, *Hist.* 45.29), became a free city in 42 BC (Pliny, *Nat.* 4.36), as demonstrated by its minting of both imperial and autonomous coinage. It was the capital of proconsular Macedonia in Paul's day and governed itself according to the Greek model. Citizens (*politai*) were divided into tribes (*phylai*) whose representatives populated its assembly of the people (*ekklēsia tou dēmou*) and governing council (*boulē*). The city was administered by five or six senior officers called politarchs (*politarchai*) who served a one-year renewable term. They convened meetings, introduced motions, and confirmed, recorded, and acted on the decisions of council and assembly (Horsley). They also served as magistrates (Acts 17:6, 8).

Preaching in the synagogue among Jews, God-fearing Greeks, and a few prominent (*tōn prōtōn*) women inflamed Jewish "zeal" (*zēloō*) to stop the apostles (Acts 17:4-5; cf. 1 Thess 2:2, 16; Levinskaya, 154-57). Jewish action coincided with the meeting of the assembly. Loafers (*agoraioi*) in the agora were coopted to create a disturbance. Not finding the apostles at the house of Jason (Keener 2012–2015, 2550 and n2532), they dragged him and other "brothers" before the politarchs in the assembly (*dēmos*, Acts 17:5; BDAG, 223). The apostles were accused as troublemakers (cf. Suetonius, *Claud.* 25.4; Acts 18:2) who defied the "decrees of Caesar" (*dogmata Kaisaros*, Acts 17:7) by preaching another king.

Edicts prohibited predictions of the imperial succession (Augustus, AD 11: Cassius Dio, *Hist.* 56.25.5-6; Tiberius, AD 16: Cassius Dio, *Hist.* 57.15.8; cf. Paulus, *Sententiae* 5.21), and Paul's *teaching could have been so construed (1 Thess 1:9-10; 2:12, 19; 4:2-3, 15-16; 5:1-3; 2 Thess 2:3-5, 8, 15). The politarchs would have had to address the accusation of a violation of Caesar's decrees (Acts 17:7-8). Loyalty oaths to the emperor administered to all called for oath takers to report violators (Paphlagonian Oath); they were equatable to "decrees of Caesar" (Cypriot oath); and local magistrates were responsible for administering them (Samos inscription) (Judge 1971, 5-7).

As Thessalonian believers' means were limited (1 Thess 2:9; 4:11-12; 2 Thess 3:7-10; cf. Phil 4:16; 2 Cor 8:1-2), the requirement that Jason and the others post a bond (*labontes to hikanon*, Acts 17:9 [= Latin *satis accipere*]) could have proven devastating if accusations were sustained. The apostles left the city (Acts 17:10, 13-14; 1 Thess 2:17-18). Consistent with Acts, Paul's letters to the Thessalonians suggest a largely Hellenistic congregation (*hypo tōn idiōn symphyletōn*, 1 Thess 2:14) whose members continued to have legal trouble (1 Thess 1:6; 2:14-15, 18; 3:2-5, 8; 4:13-15; 5:15; 2 Thess 1:4-7; 2:15; 3:3).

*Ephesus became a free city in 133 BC, lost the status in 84 BC (Appian, *Mithraditic Wars* 48), and regained it in 47 BC. Octavian reaffirmed its position as free and the capital of provincial Asia (Plutarch, *Ant.* 24.4; Appian, *Bell. civ.* 5.6; Trebilco, 12-13). The local elites of Ephesus were organized into five tribes (Augustus added a sixth) from which were drawn the members of the council (*boulē*) and assembly of the people (*ekklēsia tou dēmou*). Membership in the latter required a property qualification. Each body was presided over by a chief executive official (*grammateus*; BDAG, 206). The *grammateus* of the assembly sometimes also discharged the civic administrative office of "Asiarch" (*asiarchēs*, Acts 19:31-35; Josephus, *Ant.* 14.225, 230; Kearsley). The players, the legal and economic business, and the form of its conduct were Greek. But everything tilted to the Roman requirements (Murphy-O'Connor, 33-35; cf. Acts 19:38-40). Ephesus was also the center of an assize district (*conventus*) where the Roman proconsul or one of his legates regularly heard cases (Trebilco, 18; cf. Acts 19:38).

A city of 200,000 to 250,000 inhabitants, Ephesus had a significant and favored Jewish community (Josephus, *Ant.* 14.234, 236-240, 262-264; Trebilco, 37-51; Levinskaya, 143-46). Paul's proclamation in synagogue and lecture hall (*scholē*, Acts 19:8-9), together with other powerful ministry, resulted in the conversion of many Jews and Greeks in Ephesus and throughout the province (Acts 19:10, 17-20, 26). It early garnered the benign official notice of the "Asiarchs," leading to their becoming Paul's "friends" (*philoi*, Acts 19:31, 37; Trebilco, 166-67; Kearsley; cf. Keener 2012–2015, 2908-18; were they patrons?). It also adversely affected the *worship of Artemis, depressing the market in small silver temple shrines (Keener 2012–2015, 2880-87; Trebilco, 25-26, 157). Local agitation caused an unruly gathering in the theater, the usual meeting place of the *dēmos* (Murphy-O'Connor, 34).

The warning of the *grammateus* that the disturbance might read as "insurrection" (*stasis*, Acts 19:40) would likely have sent a chill into the crowd given Ephesus's history (Trebilco, 161-63n27). So too notice that the fame of Artemis and Ephesus was undeniable (*anantirrētos*) and the accusation *already* known to be without cause (Acts 19:35-37). The *grammateus* gave two options: either the accusers could lodge formal complaint (*logos*) and delate it (*enkaleō*) at the assize (*agoraioi*) of the proconsul (*anthypatoi* [pl.]), or they could bring the matter before a "lawfully" (*ennomos*; BDAG, 337-38) convened meeting of the *dēmos* (Acts 19:38-39).

The witness of Paul's letters generally corroborates the Lukan intimations of a predominantly Greek congregation. Arguably, three Pauline letters are destined for Ephesus (Eph 1:1; 1 Tim 1:3; 2 Tim 1:16-18; 4:12, 19). The letter addressed to the Ephesians intimates a majority of *Gentile over Jewish addressees (*ethnē*, Eph 2:11; 3:1, 6, 8; 4:17 and the Gentile perspective in the unity language at Eph 2:14-15; 3:6; 4:4-6). The presence of Ephesian élites in the church may be suggested when Timothy is instructed that aspiring leaders not be lovers of money (*aischrokerdeis*, 1 Tim 3:8; *aphilargyron*, 1 Tim 3:3; cf. 1 Tim 6:3-10; 2 Tim 3:2), that those with riches be generous (1 Tim 5:8, 16-17; 6:17-18), and that Timothy not show favoritism (1 Tim 5:21). Perhaps reflecting on past troubles in Ephesus, Paul urges that prayers be offered for all persons in authority, including the emperor and his regents (*basileis* [pl.]) and their administrative officials (*hyperochē*, 1 Tim 2:1-2), so that Christians might live peaceful, quiet, spiritually fruitful lives.

First Corinthians was sent from the Ephesian house church of Prisca and Aquila (further below). It serves notice of both opportunity and continuing trouble in Ephesus and carries greetings from "the churches of Asia" (1 Cor 16: 8-9, 19-20; cf. 1 Cor 15:32). Included among those churches would have been Colossae.

Once deemed a large city (*megas*; Herodotus, *Hist.* 7.30; Xenophon, *Anab.* 1.2.6), Colossae was surpassed in the Hellenistic foundation by Laodicea as the central metropolis of the Lycus Valley (Huttner, 35). It was a "town" (Strabo, *Geogr.* 12.8.13; Pliny, *Nat.* 5.41) and not a large/famous "city" (Strabo, *Geogr.* 12.18.13; Tacitus, *Ann.* 14:27). Despite this, Colossae thrived and grew after a fashion through the first and second centuries AD. The coins in the later period bear the authorization of Colossae's citizens (*dēmos*), but more often a civic officer, identified as "leader" (*archōn*), "town clerk" (*grammateus*), or "magistrate" (*stephanēphoros*), sometimes also carrying the name of a local benefactor (Standhartinger, 244-45).

Jewish settlement in the Lycus Valley had been a Seleucid strategy (Josephus, *Ant.* 12.147-153), and the community later figured in Rome's foreign policy (1 Macc 15:16-24; Cicero, *Flac.* 67-68; Josephus, *Ant.* 14.237-243). The epigraphic record suggests a symbiosis of Jews and Greeks in the imperial period and an influential Jewish population of something less than 5 percent in the Lycus Valley (Huttner, 69-79).

The Colossian church's beginning was Greek and not Jewish, given the name (Philem 23; Col 4:12-13; cf. Col 2:1) and ethnicity (Col 4:10-11) of its founder, Epaphras. That he served on behalf of believers in Colossae, Laodicea, and Hierapolis gives further pause (Col 4:13-14, 16; Huttner, 87-92), and so does the fact that, while "the *philosophy" (Col 2:8) addressed in the Colossian letter carries Jewish threads, the syncretistic weave appears to have drawn heavily on local Phrygian-Lydian beliefs and practices (Arnold).

The discovery of a large first- to second-century AD pedestal near the ancient site of Colossae also suggests strong Greek sensibilities. It was dedicated by thirty of Colossae's elites in honor of Korymbos. The pattern of the names and genealogies suggests a striking desire to eschew Roman in favor of Greek identity (Cadwallader and Harrison, 13). A like sense of Colossian priority to Greek identity may account for the word "Greek" appearing before "Jew" (Cadwallader and Harrison, 13-14) and the presence of the binary "barbarian, Scythian" at Colossians 3:11. The teaching of the verse in its context is essentially the same as 1 Corinthians 12:13 and Galatians 3:28 in theirs, but it is "tuned" for the Lycus Valley.

The Greek names of Colossian believers (Philem 1-2; 10; Col 4:9, 17) are consistent with the above indications, as is Philemon's significant *patronage (Huttner, 86-87). Born out of a predominantly and proudly indigenous Greek community in a town where the structures of local society, law, and governance were Greek, the church, transformed by Christ who "is all, and in all" (Col 3:11), was taught to embody, serve in, and proclaim the *gospel without harm across the normally damaging barriers.

2.3. Rome. Paul had planned to visit Rome (Rom 15:23; cf. Rom 1:9-13; Acts 19:21) to fulfill his broad gospel obligation. His commission to the Gentiles (*ethnē*, Rom 1:13) would begin with first preaching to Jews (Rom 1:16; Acts *passim*) and run from the most cultured Greek and Latin speakers (*Hellēnes*) to those decidedly not so (*barbaroi*), from educated sophisticates (*sophoi*) to unlearned rustics (*anoētois*, Rom 1:14). Roman legal action was a continual risk. Paul acknowledges this to the believers of Rome and celebrates at Romans 16 some who, along with him, had steeled themselves to both the prospect and the reality.

Of the million inhabitants of Rome in Paul's day, about 4 to 5 percent were Jews. Settled in several districts, many were descendants of Jews brought to Rome as slaves (Josephus, *Ant.* 14.78-79; Plutarch, *Pomp.* 45.1-2; Appian, *Mithraditic Wars* 117.571-573) and eventually freed and given *citizenship by their owners (Philo, *Legat.* 155). Early imperial patronage fostered religious identity and encouraged growth (Philo, *Legat.* 156-158; Josephus, *Ant.* 16.162-165). There is evidence for at least eleven synagogues in the city, of which four date to the early empire (Levinskaya, 168-70, 182-93).

Later imperial edicts, however, resulted in the expulsion of Jews from Rome under Tiberius (AD 19: Tacitus, *Ann.* 2.85.4; Suetonius, *Tib.* 36.1; Josephus, *Ant.* 18.83-84; Cassius Dio, *Hist.* 57.18.5a) and Claudius (AD 49: Suetonius, *Claud.* 25.4; Acts 18:2). In the latter case, the stated cause was disturbances over an individual named Chrestus, possibly a reference to Jewish Christian preaching (Levinskaya, 28-31, 167-82). Suetonius reports that Jews were expelled and Luke that "all the Jews" had to leave. Given this was an imperial edict, Jews, whether slaves, *peregrini*, *Latini Iuniani*, or citizens, were bound to comply. The logistics, as much as the motives and effects, would have been complex (Rutgers; Van der Lans).

Paul's extensive and quite carefully structured greeting list at Romans 16:3-16 gives some insight into the church's experience of and stance toward the law in several cases. Significant first mention is to the freeborn Roman Jew Prisca and her lower-status husband Aquila at Romans 16:3-5 (Jewett, 955; cf. Judge 2008, 143nn18, 20). Expelled from Rome by Claudius (Acts 18:2), they continued to devote their resources to gospel witness and "risked their necks" for Paul (*ton heautōn trachēlon hypethēkan*, Rom 16:4; cf. Diogenes Laertius, *Vit.* 4.11). Evoking the image of trial, conviction, and execution of a Roman citizen by decapitation, Paul speaks of significant legal peril. It might be asked whether the risk was shared by others in their house church (perhaps those mentioned at Rom 16:5-6; see Dunn, 893).

Romans 16:7 may reflect a second Roman house church earlier disrupted by the Claudian edict. The greetings to Andronicus and Junia are as extensive as for Prisca and Aquila. Their names are Greek and Latin respectively. Both names have slave and free currency, but Junia may indicate Roman citizenship (Judge, 2008, 143n18). Paul identifies them as fellow Jews (*syngeneis*; BDAG, 950; cf. Rom 16:11-12), noting that they were believers before he was (ca. AD 34). As Paul's "fellow *prisoners of war" (*synaichmalōtous mou*; cf. Philem 23; Col 4:10) they too had braved legal peril in supporting him (Rapske, 381-92).

Paul's greetings commend believers whom he may largely have come to know because of their expulsion from Rome. Christian courage and generosity in face of the threat of legal trouble only continued in Paul's presence and on their return. While Paul asserts the ultimate vindication of the heavenly assize, he does so by means of a standing contrast to the court of a Roman magistrate with *imperium*. Suffering for their faith (Rom 5:3; 8:18), they may be brought up on charges/impeached (*egkalesei . . . kata*, Rom 8:33) and "condemned" (*katakrinōn*, Rom 8:34). If they should die by the executioner's sword (*machaira*, Rom 8:35), they must remember that this cannot separate them from the *love of God in Christ Jesus.

3. Roman Law in Direct Pauline Instruction and Experience.

3.1. Romans 13:1-7. Paul calls for informed Christian thinking about and behavior toward those who have charge of the legal system. The essential command applies to "every soul" (*pasa psychē*, Rom 13:1), a Semitic expression inclusive of all those greeted at Romans 16:3-16 irrespective of their station or circumstances. Paul calls for "submission" (*hypotassō*, Rom 13:1, 5) to "governing authorities [pl.]" (*exousiai hyperechousai*, Rom 13:1; cf. *exousia*, Rom 13:1-2; *archontos*, Rom 13:3), the agents having "political and civic authority as it would actually bear upon his readers" (Dunn, 759). The expressions of submission due to Roman magistrates and other officials in view, called "good/lawful behavior" (*ergon agathon*, Rom 13:3), are broadly illustrated: dutiful payment of tribute (*phoros*) and taxes/tolls (*teleō*) levied, affirming jurisdiction by showing proper reverence/respect (*phobos*), and giving rightful honor (*timē*) for services rendered (Rom 13:6-7). Resistance (*antitassomai*, *anthistēmi*, Rom 13:2), called "evil/unlawful behavior" (*to kakon prassonti*, Rom 13:3-4), would be the opposite: tax evasion/revolt, repudiation of jurisdiction, and dishonor of the powers.

The motivations for submission over resistance made at Romans 13:1-4 are summarized succinctly at Romans 13:5 in the words "because of *wrath" (*dia tēn orgēn*) and "because of conscience" (*dia tēn syneidēsis*). The pragmatic (*ou monon*, Rom 13:5a) motivation is that officials are set not only to praise good behavior (*hexeis epainon*, Rom 13:3; Winter, 25-40), but also to punish bad (*krima*, Rom 13:2;

ekdikos eis orgēn, Rom 13:4). The military short sword (*machaira*, Rom 13:4; cf. Rom 8:35), a symbol of magisterial power to punish to the extreme, is not carried to no purpose (*ou . . . eikē*), Paul reminds his readers, allowing them to cherish "no illusion about the fate of evildoers" (Jewett, 795). Compelling as this is, Paul encourages that in addition (*alla kai*) his readers should submit owing to *knowledge of the ultimate source of the magistrate's power and duty. Reflecting deeply held Jewish conviction (e.g., Jer 27:5-6; Dan 4:17, 25, 32; 5:21), Paul argues that all authority and every particular authority is "ordained by God" (*hypo theou tetagmenai*, Rom 13:1; cf. *diatagē*, Rom 13:2). Magistrates and officials are "God's *servants" (*theou diakonos*, Rom 13:4; *leitourgoi . . . theou*, Rom 13:6) for the believer's good and for the punishment of the evildoer. As such, their time and labor is rendered to God so that a recompense is owed (*apodote pasin tas opheilas*, Rom 13:7) by those who benefit.

Astute Pauline insight into the varied contexts of ministry, careful missional calculation, and painful experience argues caution to ideas that the teaching of Romans 13:1-7 is subversive, quietist, naive, or ironic. Its breathtaking view of the mandates and limits of magisterial power and the consequent responsibility of the faithful under law resonates with the *tradition of Jesus' instruction (Mk 12:17; Jn 19:10-11).

3.2. 1 Corinthians 6:1-11. Paul forbade Christian recourse to Corinthian law courts to settle their disputes. His incredulous question at 1 Corinthians 6:1 lays out the circumstances. One believer has "brought a lawsuit" (*pragma echōn*; Fee 1987, 231; cf. *krinō*, 1 Cor 6:6) against another. The matter is civil rather than criminal, and context suggests it is financial (*adikeō* with *apostereō*, 1 Cor 6:8; BDAG, 20, 121; Winter, 107 and n7). The notice of "judgments/lawsuits [pl.]" (*krimata echete*, 1 Cor 6:7) may indicate a pattern of litigiousness in the congregation.

"If the defendant was a parent, a patron, a magistrate, or a person of high rank, then charges could not be brought by children, freedmen, private citizens and men of lower rank respectively" (Winter, 107-8). Prosecution was generally "matched" or "downward" (Winter, 108). An action in a colony such as Corinth would have begun with one of the *duoviri*. David Gill surmises, "Paul is referring to cases brought by members of the social elite against other elite families: the δυνατοί of chapter 1" (Gill, 330). The biting use of *sophos* at 1 Corinthians 6:5 confirms (cf. 1 Cor 1:26).

Paul identifies two compelling reasons why litigation in a court should never occur. The first relates to competency. Magistrates in Roman courts are nonbelievers (*apistōn*, 1 Cor 6:6) and unrighteous/unjust (*adikōn*, 1 Cor 6:1, 9; Winter, 109-11). "In Roman society legal and political capacity depended, not only upon the *persona* or character of the individual as defined or recognized by the civil law (free or slave, citizen or alien), but also upon his background or status" (Garnsey 1970, 271). "Judges and juries (where there were juries) were easily impressed by qualities such as social prominence, wealth and good character, and this was thought perfectly proper" (Garnsey 1970, 148; Pliny, *Ep.* 9.5; cf. Cicero, *Rep.* 1.34.53). More sinister were the influences a litigant might be tempted to employ to ensure consideration from the magistrate (cf. Acts 24:26; Winter, 111-13). Moreover, the process was fractious and damaging to all parties, energizing lasting, bitter hostility (Winter, 113-15).

Paul advises that if there are disputes they must only ever come "before the saints" (*epi tōn hagiōn*, 1 Cor 6:1-2). The Corinthian believers' present superior competency (*axios/anaxios*; BDAG, 69, 93-94), beyond that of any magistrate, is confirmed by the eschatological task the former will have to judge the world and angelic beings (1 Cor 6:2-3). A just verdict in mundane present matters (*biōtikos*) that have so little relative consequence (*elachistos*) is assured and should make the choice obvious (1 Cor 6:3-4). Shaming them, Paul challenges the feuding elites to affirm this truth by daring to appoint their lowliest brothers (*exouthenēmenous*, 1 Cor 6:4; cf. 1 Cor 1:28) to decide their case (*kathizō*, 1 Cor 6:4; Josephus, *Ant.* 13.75; Cassius Dio, *Hist.* 37.27.1).

Paul notes an even greater problem. All thought of ecclesial arbitration aside, the believing disputants have suffered a complete moral defeat (*holōs hēttēma*, 1 Cor 6:7). Believing defendants are defeated for acting like the unrighteous (*adikoi*) whose behaviors exclude them from inheritance of the *kingdom (1 Cor 6:9-10). Believing plaintiffs are defeated for preferring aggressive litigation before nonbelieving magistrates over nonretaliation (1 Cor 6:7). Such behaviors were characteristic of what some of the believing Corinthians once were; they should *not* characterize them now (1 Cor 6:11)!

3.3. 2 Timothy 4:16-18. Where other captivity letters are tight-lipped about Paul's legal circumstances, 2 Timothy 4 stands as a tantalizing exception. It describes the circumstances of his "first defense" (*tē prōtē apologia*, 2 Tim 4:16). Some think this is a reference to an earlier trial, perhaps related to Jerusalem and Caesarea (Acts 23–26) or his first imprisonment in Rome (Acts 28; Riesner, 398-400), but texts and contexts resist such identifications (Marshall, 823; Kelly, 217-18; Herzer, 422).

Alternately, the first defense is identified with a second Roman imprisonment, what Marshall calls "the so-called *prima actio*, the first hearing in a two-part trial, the preliminary investigation of the case." In that phase, he continues, "the verdict could be *Non liquet* or *Amplius*" (823)—"Not clear/No verdict" or "Further hearing required," respectively. Tajra, citing Acts 23:34 as a parallel, describes the *prima actio* as given over to judicial "information gathering" related to the defendant's identity and a home province and a review of the indictment (88-89). Others characterize it as "not the trial proper" (Kelly, 218) or argue that the *secunda actio* was "the actual trial" (Fee 1988, 296). These characterizations of the *prōtē apologia* raise significant questions.

Regarding Tajra's supposed parallel, does not the notice that the accused *and* plaintiffs must be present for a trial to occur (Acts 23:35; cf. Acts 25:5, 7-8, 16-18) rule out his comparison of the *prōtē apologia* here with Acts 23:34 (87)? Moreover, if the first part of the trial is preliminary or merely informational, any discussion of a verdict of *Non liquet* or *Ampliatio* makes no sense unless there is the real prospect of a finding of guilt (*condemno*) or innocence (*absolvo*) here.

Context makes clear that Paul's *prōtē apologia* is hardly preliminary or safe. He reports intense despair that ministry colleagues have completely abandoned him (*oudeis moi paregeneto*, 2 Tim 4:16; Kelly, 219; *pace* Herzer, 420-21). He had wanted the support of their physical presence and social standing in the courtroom (for pattern, see Cicero, *Pro Sulla* 4-5) in answer to the plaintiffs' counterdemonstration (for pattern, see Acts 24:1, 9; 25:7). The abandonment of his associates is a *sin that Paul asks God to forgive (2 Tim 4:16; see esp. Lk 23:34; Acts 7:60). Moreover, Paul writes that at his *prōtē apologia* he was delivered from the lion's mouth (2 Tim 4:17), a metaphor (Ps 22:21 [LXX 21:22]; Marshall, 825 and n43) surely indicating true mortal peril: Paul had escaped a sentence of *death.

The attempt to align Paul's *prōtē apologia* in its NT context to the dynamics of the *prima actio* of an earlier Roman trial form (Whittuck; Ramsay and Lanciani, 342-44; Berger, Nicholas, and Lintott) is complicated and uncertain, which probably accounts for Marshall's wise regret that Paul's *prōtē apologia* was not discussed in A. N. Sherwin-White's *Roman Society and Roman Law in the New Testament* (823n36).

One might better think of a Roman magistrate with *imperium* conducting a criminal trial with a *concilium* at 2 Timothy 4. He has absolute discretion in matters of process and outcome in keeping with *cognitio extra ordinem*. The trials before Felix (Acts 24:1-22) and Festus (Acts 25:1-12) provide better comparison, particularly the full judicial engagement by all parties under Felix, who, instead of rendering a verdict, "adjourns" the proceedings to await "further information" (*anaballomai*, Acts 24:22; BDAG, 58-59; but see Acts 24:26-27; Rapske, 317-20, on trial delays). The trial before Festus compares in its earlier part, though its finish raises significant questions (Acts 25:9-12; Garnsey 1966, esp. 182-85 on *reiectio*).

If colleagues had deserted Paul at his first defense, the *Lord did not. Paul attests to Christ's own presence, standing with and empowering him (*paristēmi*, *endynamoō*) so that he made a full gospel proclamation in the imperial courtroom, a venue effectively reflecting the Gentile world (*panta ta ethnē*, 2 Tim 4:17; Herzer, 422-23; Karakolis, 516). Awaiting the next phase of his trial, Paul expresses confidence that, whatever the earthly verdict, he will ultimately be preserved from every wicked act against him and granted safe conduct to God's heavenly kingdom (2 Tim 4:18).

4. Roman Legal Metaphors in Paul's Letters. It remains to ask whether Roman law is the legitimate or even necessary background to grasp Paul's instruction in other matters of theology and praxis where legal metaphors are in play. There is much debate in this regard. First is to acknowledge, in principle, the potential relevance of a Roman nexus where Paul uses legal metaphor in the teaching of his letters. Paul is a Jew who bears a message from the heart of Judaism, but he preaches it to a world that "was first Hellenized and then Romanized" (Sampley, 4). Consequently, it will not do to privilege or disqualify out of hand the Jewish, Greek, or Roman background from consideration. Each must be considered.

Second, the complexity of Paul's own *identity argues for consideration of Roman law as a potential clarifying factor within the teaching of his letters. To be sure, Paul had impeccable Pharisaic Jewish birth and educational credentials, earlier sustained influential religio-political connections to official Judaism, and found in Jesus the fulfillment of the *hope of *Israel. But he also qualified for, possessed, and actively maintained his citizenship status in Tarsus, a Hellenistic city having received from the Romans free status and immunity from tribute (Appian, *Bell. civ.* 5.30; Dio Chrysostom, *2 Tars.* 34.8; cf. Gal 1:21). Paul was, besides, a born Roman citizen (Acts 22:28 *et passim*; Rapske, 71-112). This suggests, at least, facility with law in the three realms, but likely something more.

Third, one should not forget Paul's missionary commitment. It is succinctly expressed at 1 Corinthians 9:19-23: "Though I am free and belong to no one, I have made myself a slave to everyone, to win as many as possible" (1 Cor 9:19 NIV). Paul's slavery consists in "becoming as" (*egenomēn hōs*, 1 Cor 9:20), reflecting a deliberate, deeply principled adaptability for interchange with "all" nonbelievers (*pasin*, 1 Cor 9:19, 22). Paul illustrates the "all" as Jews, non-Jews, and persons despised for their humble circumstances (*asthenēs*, 1 Cor 9:22; cf. 1 Cor 1:26-29; Fee 1987, 427; Rapske, 110-12). His object is their salvation (*kerdainō*, 1 Cor 9:19, 20 [*bis*], 21, 22a = *sōzō*, 22b). Those with Roman rights in law would figure in either of the first two groups. This certainly suggests Roman legal metaphor as a potential expression of adaptability in preaching and teaching. The prospect of subsequent reminder and development in later letters to churches would not be out of the question.

The above points secure the theoretical prospect of Paul's use of Roman law in the context of his letters. Whether a Pauline legal metaphor is actually Jewish, Greek or Roman, or perhaps some amalgam, however, will ultimately depend on (1) what is known of the city and its population, (2) the mix of the congregation, and (3) an actual analysis of the use of legal metaphor against the candidate legal backdrops as they are presently known. A priority of the last element will be to look not only for the degree of consonance but also for dissonance with the principle and practice of law. It is often in the latter that the Pauline teaching is most powerfully laid out (Sampley, 6-7). A helpful demonstration of this in relation to adoption can be seen in Keener (2019, 340-45), Kim, and Walters.

The range for fruitful consideration of Roman law in the legal metaphors of Paul's letters is extensive. It includes family and household; the position of a father as *paterfamilias*; *marriage, divorce, and adultery; *adoption and inheritance; slavery and freedom; alienage and citizenship; patron and client relations; and the use of courtroom and commercial contract terminology (Sampley; Williams; Lyall).

See also Citizenship; Corinth; Corinthians, First Letter to the; Empire; Ephesus; Pastoral Epistles; Paul in Acts; Political Systems; Politics and Power; Prison, Prisoner; Romans, Letter to the; Slave, Slavery.

BIBLIOGRAPHY. **C. E. Arnold,** *The Colossian Syncretism: The Interface Between Christianity and Folk Belief at Colossae* (Grand Rapids, MI: Baker, 1996); **A. Berger,** *Encyclopedic Dictionary of Roman Law*, Transactions of the American Philosophical Society NS 43.2 (1953; repr., Philadelphia: American Philosophical Society, 1991); **A. Berger, B. Nicholas, and A. W. Lintott,** "Ampliatio," *OCD*, 78; **C. Brélaz,** "First-Century Philippi: Contextualizing Paul's Visit," in *The First Urban Churches 4: Roman Philippi*, ed. J. R. Harrison and L. L. Welborn, WGRWSup 13 (Atlanta: SBL Press, 2018), 153-88; **P. A. Brunt,** "Charges of Provincial Maladministration Under the Early Principate," *Historia* 10 (1961): 189-227; idem, "The Administrators of Roman Egypt," *JRS* 65 (1975): 124-47; idem, "Laus Imperii," in *Paul and Empire: Religion and Power in Roman Imperial Society*, ed. R. A. Horsley (Harrisburg, PA: Trinity Press International, 1997), 25-35; **A. W. Cadwallader and J. R. Harrison,** "Perspectives on the Lycus Valley: An Inscriptional, Archaeological, Numismatic, and Iconographic Approach," in *The First Urban Churches 5: Colossae, Hierapolis, and Laodicea*, ed. J. R. Harrison and L. L. Welborn, WGRWSup 16 (Atlanta: SBL Press, 2019), 3-70; **R. Canavan,** "A Woman, a Coin and the Prosperity of Colossae," *Australian Biblical Review* 67 (2019): 1-16; **K. P. Donfried,** *Paul, Thessalonica, and Early Christianity* (Grand Rapids, MI: Eerdmans, 2002); **J. D. G. Dunn,** *Romans*, WBC (Dallas: Word, 1988); **G. D. Fee,** *The First Epistle to the Corinthians*, NICNT (Grand Rapids, MI: Eerdmans, 1987); idem, *1 and 2 Timothy, Titus*, rev. ed., New International Bible Commentary (Peabody, MA: Hendrickson, 1988); **P. Garnsey,** "The *Lex Iulia* and Appeal Under the Empire," *JRS* 56, nos. 1-2 (1966): 167-89; idem, "The Criminal Jurisdiction of Governors," *JRS* 85, nos. 1-2 (1968): 51-59; idem, *Social Status and Legal Privilege in the Roman Empire* (Oxford: Clarendon, 1970); **P. Garnsey et al.,** eds., *The Roman Empire: Economy, Society and Culture*, 2nd ed. (Oakland: University of California Press, 2015); **D. W. J. Gill,** "In Search of the Social Elite in the Corinthian Church," *TynBul* 44, no. 2 (1993): 323-37; **G. W. Hansen,** "Galatia," in *The Book of Acts in Its First Century Setting*, vol. 2, *Graeco-Roman Setting*, ed. D. W. J. Gill and C. Gempf (Grand Rapids, MI: Eerdmans, 1994), 377-95; **J. Herzer,** "The Mission and the End of Paul Between Strategy and Reality: A Response to Rainer Riesner," in *The Last Years of Paul*, ed. A. Puig i Tàrrech et al., WUNT 352 (Tübingen: Mohr Siebeck, 2015), 411-31; **T. Honoré,** "Law and Procedure, Roman: 1. Civil Law," *OCD*,

827-29; idem, "Lawyers, Roman," *OCD*, 835-36; **G. H. R. Horsley,** "The Politarchs," in *The Book of Acts in Its First Century Setting*, vol. 2, *Graeco-Roman Setting*, ed. D. W. J. Gill and C. Gempf (Grand Rapids, MI: Eerdmans, 1994), 419-31; **U. Huttner,** *Early Christianity in the Lycus Valley*, AJEC 85 (Boston: Brill, 2013); **P. Jewett,** *Romans*, Hermeneia (Minneapolis: Fortress, 2007); **E. A. Judge,** "The Decrees of Caesar at Thessalonica," *RTR* 30 (1971): 1-7; idem, *Social Distinctives of the Christians in the First Century: Pivotal Essays by E. A. Judge*, ed. D. M. Scholer (Peabody, MA: Hendrickson, 2008); **C. Karakolis,** "Paul's Mission to Hispania: Some Critical Observations," in *The Last Years of Paul*, ed. A. Puig i Tàrrech et al., WUNT 352 (Tübingen: Mohr Siebeck, 2015), 507-19; **R. A. Kearsley,** "The Asiarchs," in *The Book of Acts in Its First Century Setting*, vol. 2, *Graeco-Roman Setting*, ed. D. W. J. Gill and C. Gempf (Grand Rapids, MI: Eerdmans, 1994), 363-76; **C. S. Keener,** *Acts: An Exegetical Commentary*, 4 vols. (Grand Rapids, MI: Baker Academic, 2012–2015); idem, *Galatians: A Commentary* (Grand Rapids, MI: Baker Academic, 2019); **J. N. D. Kelly,** *The Pastoral Epistles: I & II Timothy, Titus*, BNTC (London: Black, 1963); **K. S. Kim,** "Another Look at Adoption in Romans 8:15 in Light of Roman Social Practices and Legal Rules," *BTB* 44, no. 3 (2014): 133-43; **I. Levinskaya,** *The Book of Acts in Its First Century Setting*, vol. 5, *Diaspora Setting* (Grand Rapids, MI: Eerdmans, 1996); **F. Lyall,** *Slaves, Citizens, Sons: Legal Metaphors in the Epistles* (Grand Rapids, MI: Zondervan, 1984); **I. H. Marshall,** *The Pastoral Epistles*, ICC (London: T&T Clark, 1999); **S. Mitchell,** "Two Double Communities in Roman Asia Minor," *Historia* 28, no. 4 (1979): 409-38; **J. Murphy-O'Connor,** *St. Paul's Ephesus: Texts and Archaeology* (Collegeville, MN: Liturgical Press, 2008); **P. Oakes,** *Philippians: From People to Letter*, SNTSMS 110 (Cambridge: Cambridge University Press, 2001); idem, "The Imperial Authorities in Paul's Letter to Predominantly Greek Hearers in the Roman Colony of Philippi," in *The First Urban Churches 4: Roman Philippi*, ed. J. R. Harrison and L. L. Welborn, WGRWSup 13 (Atlanta: SBL Press, 2018), 221-38; **W. Ramsay and R. Lanciani,** *A Manual of Roman Antiquities*, rev. ed. (London: Charles Griffin, 1894); **B. M. Rapske,** *The Book of Acts in Its First Century Setting*, vol. 3, *Paul in Roman Custody* (Grand Rapids, MI: Eerdmans, 1994); **R. Riesner,** "Paul's Trial and End According to Second Timothy, *1 Clement*, the Canon Muratori, and the Apocryphal Acts," in *The Last Years of Paul*, ed. A. Puig i Tàrrech et al., WUNT 352 (Tübingen: Mohr Siebeck, 2015), 391-409; **J. L. Rife,** "Religion and Society in Roman Kenchreai," in *Corinth in Context: Comparative Studies on Religion and Society*, ed. S. J. Friesen et al., NovTSup 134 (Boston: Brill, 2010), 391-432; **L. V. Rutgers,** "Roman Policy Toward the Jews: Expulsions from the City of Rome During the First Century C.E.," *Classical Antiquity* 13, no. 1 (1994): 56-74; **J. P. Sampley,** ed., *Paul in the Greco-Roman World: A Handbook* (Harrisburg, PA: Trinity Press International, 2003); **A. N. Sherwin-White,** *Roman Society and Roman Law in the New Testament*, Sarum Lectures 1960/61 (repr., Grand Rapids, MI: Baker, 1978); **A. Standhartinger,** "A City with a Message: Colossae and Colossians," in *The First Urban Churches 5: Colossae, Hierapolis, and Laodicea*, ed. J. R. Harrison and L. L. Welborn, WGRWSup 13 (Atlanta: SBL Press, 2019), 239-56; **H. W. Tajra,** *The Martyrdom of St. Paul: Historical and Judicial Context, Traditions, and Legends* (repr., Eugene, OR: Wipf & Stock, 2010); **P. Trebilco,** *The Early Christians in Ephesus from Paul to Ignatius* (Grand Rapids, MI: Eerdmans, 2004); **B. Van der Lans,** "The Politics of Exclusion: Expulsions of Jews and Others from Rome," in *People Under Power: Early Jewish and Christian Responses to the Roman Empire*, ed. M. Labalm and O. Lehtipuu (Amsterdam: Amsterdam University Press, 2015), 33-78; **J. C. Walters,** "Paul, Adoption, and Inheritance," in *Paul in the Greco-Roman World: A Handbook*, ed. J. P. Sampley (Harrisburg, PA: Trinity Press International, 2003), 42-76; **L. L. Welborn,** "Inequality in Roman Corinth: Evidence from Diverse Sources Evaluated by a Neo-Ricardian Model," in *The First Urban Churches 2: Roman Corinth*, ed. J. R. Harrison and L. L. Welborn, WGRWSup 8 (Atlanta: SBL Press, 2016), 47-84; **E. A. Whittuck,** "Judex, Judicium," in *Dictionary of Greek and Roman Antiquities*, ed. W. Smith et al. (London: John Murray, 1890), 1:1026-31; **D. J. Williams,** *Paul's Metaphors: Their Context and Character* (Peabody, MA: Hendrickson, 1999); **B. W. Winter,** *Seek the Welfare of the City: Christians as Benefactors and Citizens* (Grand Rapids, MI: Eerdmans, 1994).

B. M. Rapske

LEGALISM. *See* INTERPRETATION: NEW PERSPECTIVE; LAW; WORKS OF THE LAW.

LETTERS, LETTER FORMS

The first-century Mediterranean world loved letter writing. Papyrus or parchment letters needed to stay continuously dry to survive for two thousand years. Similarly, letters on wooden or leaf tablets needed to be discarded in a place that stayed moist continuously. Few places in the ancient Roman world met such rigorous climate standards: the deserts of Egypt, the ravines of Judea, or the bogs of England. In every such place, archaeologists have uncovered thousands of everyday letters from ordinary people. Surely these were not the only regions that wrote or received letters. Rather, in the centuries around the NT, it appears letters were crisscrossing the Roman *Empire.

1. Greco-Roman Letters
2. Letter Writing
3. Writing as a Community
4. Dispatching
5. Length and Cost

1. Greco-Roman Letters.

Paul stands solidly within the Greco-Roman letter tradition. Our knowledge of ancient Mediterranean letters comes from two quite different sources: (1) manuscripts of the collected letters of famed rhetoricians of antiquity, copied through the centuries, and (2) original letters uncovered by archaeologists. The Roman Empire (and the Greeks previously) created great commonality in letter-writing customs. From Egypt to England, letters shared the same format, language, and usually even diction and *rhetoric. While some subcultures such as the Jews retained their local languages, they still followed the basic format of the Greco-Roman letter (Wise, 213).

1.1. Form and Structure. Greco-Roman letters followed the structure of opening, body, and closing. The briefer, everyday letters usually stuck more rigidly to this format. Skilled rhetoricians brought more variety and complexity to their letters. Nonetheless, there was amazing conformity. The typical letter opening was sender to recipient, greeting: "Antimenes to Zenon, greetings" (P.Zen. 10). The infinitive (*chairein*, to rejoice) was used for greeting, probably arising from "Sender [tells] to recipient to rejoice (at receiving a letter)" (Klauck, 18). Paul plays on greetings (*chairein*) with "grace" (*charis*). Jewish letters often began with variations of the traditional Jewish greeting, "*Peace to you." Paul combined the two greetings, producing what becomes his characteristic opening, "*Grace and peace to you." Elaboration of the recipient and of the sender were often added: "Sempronius Clemens to his most esteemed Apollinarius, greetings" (P.Mich. 8.486). Similarly, Paul: "Paul, a *servant of Jesus *Christ, called to be an *apostle . . . to all in Rome who are loved by *God . . . Grace and peace to you" (Rom 1:1, 7 NIV).

Tripartite Roman names comprised a given name (*praenomen*), a clan/ancestral name (*nomen*), and a family/tribe name (*cognomen*). Contrary perhaps to modern custom, Romans customarily used only their family name in letters (see Tab. Vindol. 291). Given names were so limited and common, they were often just written as an initial. Thus, famous orator M. (Marcus) Tullius Cicero referred to himself as Cicero in his letters. Paul's Roman name was likely [Something] Saul Paul.

The letter opening was commonly followed by wishes or prayers for the recipient's health, "Before all else I wish you good health and make obeisance on your behalf to all the gods" (P.Mich. 8.491). Paul occasionally noted prayers for the recipients (Eph 1:17; Col 1:3), but he preferred the far less common thanksgiving. There seem to be no other ancient letter writers with such extended thanksgivings, and Paul often used the thanksgiving section to preview the contents of the letter (e.g., 1 Cor 1:4-7).

The letter body follows the opening prayer or thanksgiving or health-wish. Most everyday letters functioned primarily to indicate the sender was alive and well and to maintain friendships (P.Mich. 8.495; P.Oxy. 1666), but most letters also addressed a bit of news or business. Fewer letter writers included extended content in the letter body, but Paul was one of them.

Most Greco-Roman (but not Aramaic or Hebrew) letters ended with lists of greetings, as do most of Paul's letters. Paul did use generic greetings (e.g., Phil 4:21; 1 Thess 5:26) but normally named ones (e.g., Col 4:10). Romans contains all three types of greetings: first person, "I, Tertius, who down wrote this letter, greet you"; second person, "Greet Priscilla and Aquila"; and third person, "All the churches of Christ send greetings" (Rom 16:22, 3, 16 NIV).

Following closing greetings, letters often had another brief health-wish, such as "Farewell," and often an authenticating postscript. Rather than "signing" their names, senders wrote the final phrase in their own handwriting (see below). Paul desired the Thessalonians to learn his handwriting: "I, Paul, write this greeting in my own hand, which is the distinguishing mark in all my letters. This is how I write" (2 Thess 3:17 NIV). He follows with his version of closing health-wish: "The grace of our Lord Jesus Christ be with you all" (2 Thess 3:18 NIV).

1.2. Formulas and Rhetoric. Modern letters share certain standard diction, "Dear So-and-So," even when they are not that dear to us. Ancient letters were far more standardized, both in the content (stereotyped formulas) and method (epistolary rhetoric).

1.2.1. Stereotyped Formulas. Greek has flexibility in the word order, so it is more remarkable the word order for these standardized phrases was very fixed. Familiar phrases aided the reader and listener. The disclosure formula, "I want you to know, Clemens, that . . . ," alerted Clemens. Standardized phrases indicated tone (formal, friendly, displeased). Besides greetings and disclosure, other common formulas were appeal (petition), astonishment (likely indicating displeasure), compliance, rebuke, report, thanksgiving, and transitions. When Paul writes, "I am astonished" (Gal 1:6 NIV), the point is not that Paul is surprised. The point is to note his displeasure and why.

1.2.2. Epistolary Rhetoric. Ancients valued expressing an idea well. Paul may not have had a pleasing appearance for public speaking (or this may have been rhetoric), but even Paul's opponents conceded his skills in epistolary rhetoric (2 Cor 10:10). It is unlikely Paul received advanced training in rhetoric; rather, he likely learned it by observation. Famed philosopher Epictetus used a rhetorical device termed "an imaginary interlocutor," where the letter asks an abrupt question as if interrupted by someone. The interjection represents a question the writer assumes his hearers/readers are thinking, providing the opportunity to respond. Thus, Epictetus seems to interrupt himself with a question: "What then [*ti oun*], would anybody have you dress out to the utmost? By no means [*mē genoito*], except . . ." (Arrian, *Epistula* 4.11.5 LCL). Likewise, Paul: "What then [*ti oun*]? Shall we sin because we are not under the law but under grace? By no means [*mē genoito*]! Don't you know . . ." (Rom 6:15-16 NIV). The standardized rhetoric prepared the reader for something they were likely pondering and provided a lively dialogical rhetoric.

Chiasm was a popular rhetorical device in generations before Paul, but Paul seemed to love it, using it much more often than his contemporaries. In a chiastic structure, statements build toward a main point. After the main point, the argument backs away, restating each point in reverse order. An untrained reader may see a rambling or redundant argument, but ancients saw clever poetry, such as confess-mouth-believe-heart-*saved*-heart-believe-mouth-confess in Romans 10:9-10. The main point is seen at the center of the chiasm.

One last example of epistolary rhetoric: Paul included inordinately large amounts of parenesis, material that exhorts the reader to socially acceptable behavior. Catechesis instructs the proper content (what to believe); parenesis encourages proper action (how to behave). Paul's letters contain more parenesis than those of any other ancient writer. Moreover, his letters often flowed from catechesis to parenesis, from "the indicative to the imperative," from the "you are" to the "you ought." The transition is often marked by "Therefore . . ."

Parenesis included some standardized structure. For example, parenesis often cited (in lists of five) virtues to imitate and vices to avoid (see Col 3:5-7, 9, 12). In such lists, the point is not that Paul lists five (or even that there is a list at all), but rather which virtues and vices Paul cites compared to what his culture valued.

2. Letter Writing.

Discussions of Paul's letters often use "Paul wrote." While this is accurate, one should not read modern individualist culture back into the ancient Mediterranean collectivist world. Paul was the author, but almost every aspect of ancient letter writing differed from our own. The mediating impact of secretaries, input from ever-present colleagues, and in Paul's case often a co-sender all could and did influence the final product.

2.1. Literacy. The Roman world readily sent and retained written documents, but this does not mean most people read well. Although a 10 percent literacy rate is commonly cited for Paul's world (see Harris, Hezser), this is likely too low (Schnelle). Ancient references to *Acta* (a sort of *Roman Daily News*), tablets, and ostraca all suggest (basic) literacy even in the lower classes was more common than is often conceded today. Graffiti in Pompeii demonstrates at least some soldiers, weavers, and barmaids were able to read and write at least a little. Perhaps 10 to 15 percent of the Mediterranean population could read with any proficiency. Italy and some groups (such as Jews and Christians) probably had higher reading rates.

Literacy is often understood to mean the ability to both read and write. The expression "reading and writing" attests that these skills are commonly connected, but these are not merely two sides of the same coin. Ancient literacy was the ability to read. Writing was a practiced skill. Writing large, clumsy letters (Gal 6:11) was not a sign of poor literacy but rather an unpracticed hand. Someone who could read probably was able to scratch out letters (write). Nonetheless, a quite literate person might still handwrite poorly, much as most of us when writing with the opposite hand. Even for those with the skills to write well, writing was tedious and time consuming. Like most letter writers of his day, Paul used a secretary.

2.2. Secretaries. More so than perhaps today, ancients valued beautiful handwriting—similar to calligraphy today. Crafting an appropriate letter required more than penmanship; professional scribes marked and scored the lines, mixed ink, cut reed pens, and wrote on the rough, fibrous surface. Most senders needed secretarial help, so usually the sender contracted a secretary from a shop in the market. Such shops maintained rolls (*charta*) of paper (usually papyrus or parchment) from which to cut off the necessary length.

Letters had set structure (rhetoric) and stereotyped expressions, often determined by the occasion, but the average person (then and now) was not trained in this; secretaries were. Using an inappropriate formula or rhetorical approach implies a certain ignorance or incompetence. Secretaries protected a sender. Even Cicero, who was highly skilled, noted (privately) that Tiro, his secretary, provided "assistance" (*Fam.* 16.4.3; 11.1).

2.2.1. Uses. Secretaries could be used in several ways. Secretaries composed most routine, brief correspondence. For example, the sender described the letter he wanted, such as "I arrived without incident on the sixth day before the December kalends. I sold the goods for the price we wanted. I am remaining here for the festival and then will return. Greet my father and mother." The secretary made notes and then prepared a nice letter with all the proper pleasantries, titles, a health-wish, and so on. He used the appropriate formulas, such as disclosure. He even added personal greetings. At the opposite extreme, a secretary could merely transcribe, as the author dictated. When Cicero fretted over a composition to a respected colleague, he chose to dictate it carefully, "syllable-by-syllable" (*Att.* 13.25.3 LCL), because he wanted the document *precisely* as he intended.

Most preferred not to dictate, because secretaries were better trained in letter writing. A main reason for hiring a secretary was to leave such details to the expert. Even the better-trained author preferred not to dictate the letter, being too slow to dictate at the speed of writing, "Paul [pause] called [pause] an apostle [pause] of Christ Jesus." Likely, dictating 1 Corinthians to a normal secretary would have taken two full days (see Richards 2004, 163-65). In Paul's time, secretaries trained to take shorthand existed in select areas. Most senders did not have access to—nor could afford—tachygraphists (rapid writers). There is no evidence Paul dictated his letters word-for-word to his secretary, whether rapidly to a tachygraphist or painfully slowly to a transcriber.

Aside from brief letters, most secretaries were not given free rein, nor did they take precise dictation, but typically somewhere between. The sender gave detailed instructions, perhaps even dictating the exact wording of some key passages, and the secretary took notes, usually on stacks of reusable wax tablets or the recent innovation of washable parchment notebooks (*membranae*; 2 Tim 4:13). Returning when a draft was ready, the author listened to the draft read aloud, interrupting for corrections and additions. The secretary left to prepare the revised draft, repeating the process until the author was completely satisfied. Since secretaries charged by the line (*stichos*), a less literate writer (or a less important letter) might stop with one draft, but for a secretary, more drafts meant more pay. It is likely Paul used as many drafts and revisions as necessary, since he considered his letters important. Paul expended much energy on his letters and valued them (Col 4:16; see sections 3-4 below).

2.2.2. Effects. Secretaries influenced the content of letters, primarily wording. For example, two letters (P.Mich. 8.490, 491) by Apollinarius clearly used two different secretaries (as seen by handwriting). The letters differ significantly in style and spelling. It has long been noted Cicero's letters varied considerably in style and vocabulary, with some of his letters closer in style to letters of others than to his own (Tyrrell and Purser, 2:lxix-lxx). That Paul uses *dōrea* for "gift" (Rom 5:15, 17; 2 Cor 9:15) but *dōron* for "gift" in Ephesians 2:8 (a word he never uses elsewhere) should not be evidence that Ephesians is pseudonymous, but rather that a different secretary wrote *doron* and Paul did not bother to correct it in a revision, since it is a synonym. Letters varied in style and diction because secretaries varied. Since secretaries often caused minor stylistic differences between letters, as classical scholars have long allowed (Tyrrell and Purser, 2:lxvii), this is expected in Paul.

2.2.3. Responsibility. Writers did not abandon control of the letter to the secretary (except for the briefest of letters by the illiterate). There are no examples of ancient authors blaming the secretary for poor wording, grammar, or content in a letter. In the politics of the Roman republic, when a letter was intercepted and the author needed to discount something written, he did not claim a secretary misrecorded what he said. Rather, he claimed the entire letter was a forgery. Ancient authors were held responsible for everything, every phrase and nuance, in a letter (Richards 2004, 30, 81-84). For this reason, authors carefully checked the final draft, meaning that although Paul used a secretary, he remains the author.

3. Writing as a Community.

3.1. Team Input. Paul was the author, but perhaps not in the sense many of us imagine as modern individualists. The first-century Mediterranean world was collectivist, thinking in terms of "we" not "me." One should not superimpose modern values on Paul's culture (see Richards and James). The Paul seen both in his letters and in Acts shows a collectivist, a leader of a community, a team. Paul did not choose to use a team approach; it would not have occurred to him to do otherwise.

Before contracting a secretary, Paul likely discussed with his team what the letter needed to say. Likely, it was rehearsed in teaching settings. Collectivists would not draft and revise in a private room—only a sleeping room (*cubiculum*) was really private—but likely in one of the common rooms. Ancient philosophers and writers are described as working in the open-air colonnaded garden (*peristylium*). Cicero and his peers often read parts of letters in the dining area (*triclinium*) as part of a meal. Team members probably had comments. That dialogue was a regular part of the letter-writing process should be assumed. Perhaps 1 Corinthians 10:1-22 was a midrash by Sosthenes against idols, or 2 Corinthians 6:14–7:1 was from Timothy. Both letters (as well as at least four others) specifically name co-senders (coauthors?). Paul was not merely mentioning those who were in the room when he wrote. In fact, letters with co-senders also mention the presence of others who were not named as co-senders. For example, the letter to Philemon is co-sent (coauthored?) by Paul and Timothy; yet five other named individuals send greetings at the end of the letter. While it is still being debated, there is little or no evidence this was merely a sign of courtesy or humility. Why would Paul have humility in 2 Corinthians (2 Cor 1:1) and not in Romans (Rom 1:1)? Timothy was with him both times (Rom 16:21). These co-senders were in some way coauthors.

3.2. Preformed Traditions. In addition to input from his team, Paul included material in his letters that had been composed on an earlier occasion, often termed "preformed." Some *tradition is non-Pauline, meaning that the tradition originated from someone other than Paul. Scripture, for instance, is a common type of preformed material quoted by Paul but not originating with him. When Paul exhorts the Philippians to humility, many scholars think Paul quoted preformed material, perhaps a *hymn that emphasized Christ's humble nature (Phil 2:6-11). When citing something preformed, whether an OT quotation, early Christian hymn or creed, or clever chiasm, it was not necessary to cite it to the secretary. The material could be handed to the secretary to be copied into the next draft. The secretary would note where to place it, and Paul would move on. For this reason, Paul's text often reads rather smoothly if such preformed material is pulled out. Careful study often reveals telltale signs of such interpolation (insertion of "foreign" material). While scholars usually assume all interpolations are postdispatch (material added by others after Paul's time, and thus needing extraction), an interpolation could be predispatch (foreign material inserted into the letter during composition and with Paul's approval).

A preformed tradition may come from the author himself. Good authors rework and reuse material they have found effective (Cicero, *Att.* 13.29). Atticus included a cleverly written passage about his sister in letters to two different people (13.29). Cicero kept a notebook of prefaces from which he selected (16.6). A *church question or issue was perhaps routine enough that Paul may have answered it in the synagogue or at dinner banquets numerous times. Romans 13 is a series of three sermonettes, perhaps preformed material he used many times and included to illustrate his point of overcoming evil with good (Rom 12:21). Regardless of who originally composed it, that Paul decided to include a particular preformed tradition in his letter meant he stood in full agreement with its teaching.

While a modern individualist might prefer an unmediated Paul (the individual) as the ideal, one should not imagine Paul as struggling to free himself from his *coworkers' (or his secretary's) influence. Paul's "we" was not just empty rhetoric (1 Thess 1:1-6). Nonetheless, the commonality among Paul's letters shows he was the dominant force. He controlled the message. For Paul, the letter was not finished until he agreed with all of its content, because Paul was the head of his team and accountable for the letter.

4. Dispatching.

Ancient rhetoricians considered appearance to be an integral part of rhetoric. Thus, Paul's opponents ridiculed his appearance (2 Cor 10:10). It is unlikely a letter hastily scrawled across papyrus would have been considered "weighty and strong." Or at the very least, Paul's opponents would have added the insult of ridiculing the letter's appearance. One should not assume Paul merely signed the last working draft. His letters do not evidence such casualness. "Even people who could read and write did not think of submitting their readers to unprofessional penmanship. It was probably not even a concern for legibility, but rather a concern for beauty, or at least for neatness" (McKenzie, 14). When an ancient wished his letter to be well received, he used a good pen and nice paper (Cicero, *Quint. fratr.* 2.15b.1) and even a different secretary whose handwriting was more beautiful (Cicero, *Att.* 13.14-25). When a polished draft was prepared—and checked—and ready for dispatch, Paul added a final postscript.

4.1. Postscript. Once the dispatch copy was prepared, the sender usually added a summary comment and/or greeting in his own hand. In a letter found in Egypt, dated the fourteenth year of Tiberius (AD 54) the fifteenth day of Caesareus, Ammonius sold a loom to Tryphon, listing a description of the loom (by size and elements), the kind of coinage for payment, the bank, default penalty, and so on. Then a postscript that summarized: "[2nd hand] I, Ammonius, son of Ammonius, have sold the loom, and have received the price of 20 drachmae of silver and will guarantee the sale as aforesaid. I, Heraclides, son of Dionysius, wrote for him as he was illiterate" (P.Oxy. 264). Paul uses such a summary postscript: "I, Paul, am writing this with my own hand. I will pay it back" (Philem 19 NIV). If the sender were unable and the letter was official, then another person attested for the authenticity of the letter's content and the sender with an illiteracy formula (as Heraclides did).

The sender's handwriting authenticated the letter, the ancient equivalent of our signature. These changes are evident in handwriting in two ways. Original letters discovered by archaeologists (as the example above) clearly show what the original recipient would have seen, the change in handwriting, indicated by modern editors with [2nd hand]. Those writers who expected copies to be made of their letters, where copies no longer show the handwriting change, explicitly noted it: "Greetings to Pilia and Atticus. . . . The rest I write to you in my own hand" (Cicero, *Att.* 12.32.1 LCL). Since Paul expected copying of his letters (Col 4:16), he made similar comments: "I, Paul, write this greeting in my own hand" (1 Cor 16:21 NIV; see also Gal 6:11; Col 4:18; 2 Thess 3:17; Philem 19).

While a mere word of farewell (*errōso*, often abbreviated *err*) sometimes with a date concluded many ancient letters, more official and business letters used a summary of the key point or points as a means of confirming in the sender's hand. Paul sometimes summarized, such as the postscript in Galatians, returning to the issue of *circumcision (Gal 6:11-18), or Philemon's indebtedness to Paul (Philem 19-25). Most postscripts were brief, but in the earlier example, Cicero concludes with a postscript in his own hand five times the length of the part written by the secretary (Cicero, *Att.* 12.32.1).

Similarly, in the time lapse between composing and delivery of the secretary's final draft, sudden news or a changing situation could cause the author's opinion to shift or to need to modify or clarify. The sender might not wish to delay dispatch (or to pay to prepare a new draft). In a letter home to his mother, a soldier had stated he did not yet know his final assignment, but the postscript added, "Know that I have been assigned to Misenum, for I learned it later" (P.Mich. 8.490). The wealthy Atticus dashed a postscript caused by a sudden shift in political allegiance, "Curio is now defending Caesar" (Cicero, *Fam.* 2.13.3 LCL). A softening (or stiffening) of tone might be merited in light of some new information: "Just as I was in the act of folding this letter, there came letter-carriers from you and Caesar. . . . How distressed I was!" (Cicero, *Quint. fratr.* 3.1.17 LCL). Second Corinthians 10–13 has been suggested as a postscript in Paul's own hand (so Dibelius and others), perhaps caused by Paul receiving new information (so Munck and others) or by a sleepless night (so Lietzmann) or by a sudden questioning of their repentance (so Guthrie). (See the discussion in Richards 1991, 180-81.) An author repeating his name (2 Cor 10:1) to start a postscript is seen elsewhere (P.Oxy. 264).

4.2. Sending. After checking the letter and adding any closing remarks, the letter was folded with a string tied around (and sometimes sealed over the knot). The purpose was the same as today, to keep out prying eyes: "There are very few who can carry a letter of weight without lightening it by a perusal" (Cicero, *Att.* 1.13 LCL). Most of Paul's letters, however, were much too long to fold in the normal fashion. They were rolled into a scroll (technically, scrolled into a roll) and tied.

Much like the Pony Express of the American West, Romans had an imperial postal service, but only for official use. Paul like everyone else had two choices for carrying a letter: asking someone traveling that way or sending someone. Most writers likely used a happenstance carrier, someone traveling to that locale or at least in that general direction: "Having had the luck to find someone going up to you, I felt obliged to [send a letter]" (P.Oxy. 123). Because these are happenstance, writers often mentioned other letters to check whether they arrived. "I rejoiced greatly on receiving your letter which was given to me by the cutler, though I have not yet received the one which you say you have sent me by Platon the dancer's son" (P.Oxy. 1676). It appears the cutler was more reliable than the dancer's son. Paul likely used happenstance carriers to deliver his early letters. The cities of southern Galatia, Thessalonica, and *Corinth were stops along the main roads, providing many travelers to deliver his letters. Paul likely saw no reason for the expense to send his own carrier.

Time demonstrated, however, advantages to sending a trusted carrier, who could improve chances of the letter's safe arrival (for a lost letter, see Cicero, *Fam.* 7.25.1) and authenticate his letters against forgeries (2 Thess 2:2; 3:17). Recipients appear to have often misunderstood Paul's earlier letters, for example, 1 Corinthians 5:9-13. Forgeries and misinterpretations perhaps prompted Paul to switch to private carriers, a trusted associate who could assure authenticity and interpret Paul's intent.

*4.3. **Reading and Performing.*** Ancient letters were from the viewpoint of the reader. Paul wrote "I sent him" (Epaphroditus), which is translated "I am sending him" (Phil 2:28). Pliny noted that his uncle the Elder (*Ep.* 3.5) and he himself (*Ep.* 8.1) used a reader (*lector*), even though they were highly literate and trained speakers. The letter had not truly arrived until it was heard. The words of the sender then arrived. The recipient did not smile at the greeting until he heard the reader say, "I greet my father" (P.Tebt. 415).

Ancients valued the *performance of a reading, including intonation, cadence, gestures, and so on, as essential aspects of communication. Since Paul spent so much effort (and cost) on the letter, one may assume Paul also planned, when he could, who might best deliver (read/perform) it. A reader who knew Paul's letter and intent could much more effectively read the letter. Quite possibly the carrier heard it before carrying it. In at least some situations, Paul deliberately picked someone to carry the letter who could give a trustworthy elaboration, noting he expected the carrier/lector to share additional information: "Tychicus will tell you all the news about me. . . . I am sending him to you for the express purpose that you may know about our circumstances" (Col 4:7-8 NIV).

5. Length and Cost.

Unlike today, the cost of writing (and rewriting) was not insignificant. Like anyone whose income relies on billing, secretaries kept count of how many lines (*stichos*) they wrote each time. It is not possible to know the exact cost charged Paul for making the various drafts and the polished letter, but it is possible to offer some educated calculations. Commonly a denarius is described as a day's wage, but the *only* basis for this is Jesus' parable (Mt 20:1-15), where he is describing a generous master. A half-denarius was standard pay for a day laborer. Using that rate, one can estimate (very conservatively) the cost in today's dollars to prepare Paul's letters (Richards 2004, 165-69).

Table 1. Costs to Prepare Paul's Letters

	Number of Lines	**Estimated Equivalent in US$**
Romans	979	$2,275
1 Corinthians	908	$2,108
2 Corinthians	607	$1,408
Galatians	311	$722
Philippians	221	$515
2 Thessalonians	111	$255
Philemon	44	$101

Why so expensive? Paul's letters were inordinately long. Rather than short, Paul's letter to Philemon was a trifle longer than a typical letter. Paul's letters were even longer than those considered the great Roman letter writers, Cicero and Seneca.

Table 2. Length of Letters Compared

Number of Words	**Typical Papyrus Letter**	**Cicero**	**Seneca**	**Paul**
Shortest	18	22	149	335
Longest	209	2,530	4,134	7,114
Average	87	295	995	2,495

Many of Paul's letters were so long that they had to be rolled like a book (scroll). The Corinthians were likely shocked initially not over the contents but over its length. His *opponents were making a double-edged jab at Paul when they said his letters were "weighty" (2 Cor 10:10).

Paul stands in the tradition as one of the great letter writers of the Greco-Roman age, writing during a time when the use of private letters was undergoing change. The brief occasioned letter was being commandeered by a few (Cicero, Seneca, Pliny) and transformed into a means for propagating philosophies (see Richards 2019, 90-91). Paul joined the movement, using letters as part of his *mission.

BIBLIOGRAPHY. **H. Y. Gamble,** *Books and Readers in the Early Church: A History of Early Christian Texts* (New Haven, CT: Yale University Press, 1997); **W. H. Harris,** *Ancient Literacy*

(Cambridge: Harvard University Press, 1989); **P. Head,** "Named Letter-Carriers Among the Oxyrhynchus Papyri," *JSNT* 31, no. 3 (2009): 279-99; **C. Hezser,** *Jewish Literacy in Roman Palestine*, TSAJ 81 (Tübingen: Mohr Siebeck, 2001); **H.-J. Klauck,** *Ancient Letters and the New Testament: A Guide to Context and Exegesis* (Waco, TX: Baylor University Press, 2006); **J. McKenzie,** *Light on the Epistles: A Reader's Guide* (Chicago: Thomas More, 1975); **T. Y. Mullins,** "Formulas in New Testament Epistles," *JBL* 91 (1972): 380-90; **Jerome Murphy-O'Connor,** *Paul the Letter-Writer: His World, His Options, His Skills*, GNS 41 (Collegeville, MN: Liturgical Press, 1995); **E. R. Richards,** *The Secretary in the Letters of Paul*, WUNT 2/42 (Tübingen: Mohr Siebeck, 1991); idem, *Paul and First-Century Letter Writing* (Downers Grove, IL: InterVarsity Press, 2004); idem, "When Is a Letter Not a Letter? Paul, Cicero and Seneca as Letter Writers," in *Paul and the Giants of Philosophy*, ed. J. Dodson and D. Briones (Downers Grove, IL: InterVarsity Press, 2019), 86-94; **E. R. Richards and R. James,** *Misreading Scripture with Individualist Eyes* (Downers Grove, IL: InterVarsity Press, 2020); **U. Schnelle,** "Das frühe Christentum und die Bildung," *NTS* 61, no. 2 (2015): 113-43; **R. Y. Tyrrell and L. C. Purser,** *The Correspondence of M. Tullius Cicero* (Dublin: Hodges & Figgis, 1915); **J. D. Weima,** *Paul the Ancient Letter Writer: An Introduction to Epistolary Analysis* (Grand Rapids, MI: Baker, 2016); **M. O. Wise,** *Language and Literacy in Roman Judaea: A Study of the Bar Kokhba Documents*, AYBRL (New Haven, CT: Yale University Press, 2015).

E. R. Richards

LIBERTY. *See* FREEDOM/LIBERTY.

LIGHT AND DARKNESS

Light (*phōs*) and darkness (*skotos*) are both created by *God. They are fundamental to the rhythm and reality of life. Like all things in *creation, they are "good," and they are referred to often in the Bible. Yet light and darkness are also often used as contrasting symbols in Scripture. Given the frequent use of the metaphor of light and darkness in Scripture, especially in the teaching of Jesus (e.g., John's Gospel), Paul, unsurprisingly, also uses these images regularly in his letters.

1. Background
2. Light/Darkness Language in Paul
3. The Light of God and the Powers of Darkness
4. Walking as Children of Light

1. Background.

In the first act of creation, God creates light (Heb. *ʾôr*), separates it from the darkness (Heb. *ḥōšek*), and calls it "good" (Gen 1:3-5; see Is 45:7). Light and darkness were not often used symbolically in the ancient cultures (e.g., Egyptian, Sumerian, Babylonian, and Assyrian) surrounding *Israel. The Greeks, however, were interested in light and darkness as metaphors. While they tended to associate light/darkness with *knowledge/ignorance and only secondarily with good/evil, the biblical tradition tended to prioritize them in the opposite order (Medill, 18, 22). God's light, as goodness and *truth, is expressive of God's presence and character (Ps 27:1; 104:2). Yet even darkness is useful for God (see Gen 15:12; Deut 5:22; 2 Sam 22:12; Ps 18:11; 97:2; 139:11). Still, in the majority of instances, the metaphorical usage of darkness in Scripture is associated with gloom, disorder, suffering, *judgment, evil, and *death, especially in Job (Job 10:21-22; 30:26; 38:17; etc.). Isaiah acknowledges this as he surveys the land of Israel (Is 5:20, 30) and yet looks for hopeful light even for those who walk and dwell in darkness (Is 9:2; 42:7, 16; 60:2; 61:1). For humans, God's light is truth and *wisdom (Ps 119:105, 130; Is 2:3, 5), and light is where God's *righteousness is "seen" (Mic 7:9; see Ps 36:9), while darkness veils wisdom and leads to ignorance and willful disobedience of God and his word (Job 24:16; Ps 74:20; 107:10-11; Prov 2:13).

2. Light/Darkness Language in Paul.

The primary usage of light/darkness language in Paul is symbolic. Still, Paul notes the physical reality and rhythm of light/darkness as indicated by his "night and day" labors and prayers for others (1 Thess 2:9; 3:10; 2 Thess 3:8; 2 Cor 11:25; 2 Tim 1:3). The order in which Paul refers to these quotidian realities (i.e., night followed by day) is likely shaped by the creational reference to "evening and morning" (Gen 1:5, 8, 11, etc.). Paul extends the light/darkness metaphor by connecting night and day to different contexts in which practices reflect the image. Illicit deeds of darkness occur in the "night" (e.g., 1 Thess 5:7; Rom 13:12) whereas *faith, *love, *hope, and honorable living belong to the "day" (1 Thess 5:8; Rom 13:13).

Paul often uses verbal and adjectival "light" (*phōtizō, phainō, phaneros*) language to express what can be known/shown/declared/revealed (e.g., 1 Cor 3:13; 4:5; 14:25; 2 Cor 2:14; 3:3; 4:2, 10-11; Rom 1:19; 3:21; 16:26; Eph 3:9; Col 1:26; 1 Tim 3:16; Titus 1:3; etc.). Like the broader Greek usage of "light" language, this relates to enlightening knowledge and/or truth, but in Paul's case it is not abstract truth that is illuminated—it is the personal knowledge of God revealed in the *gospel. Less frequently, "darkness" (*skotos, skotizō*) language refers to disobedient, "darkened" hearts (Rom 1:21) or minds (Eph 4:18).

3. The Light of God and the Powers of Darkness.

Paul's dependence on the symbolic usage of light/darkness language is rooted in the creation account of Genesis. Since God dwells in glorious, "unapproachable light" (1 Tim 6:16 NIV) and created light and darkness (Gen 1:3), he can also create "light" in human hearts—as a "new creation"—so that people can know God's luminous *glory in the face of *Christ (2 Cor 4:6). The "light of the gospel" is revealed in Christ, the "icon/image" of God (2 Cor 4:4; see 2 Tim 1:10). Without this illumination, the human heart remains darkened in *sin (Rom 1:21) and captive to the powers of darkness (Eph 6:12), personified in *Satan, who masquerades as an "angel of light" (2 Cor 11:4). The two spheres are exclusive (see 2 Cor 6:14): one is either held captive by the *dominion* of darkness (Col 1:13; see Acts 26:19) or rescued and transferred into the *kingdom* of God's beloved Son so as to share in the inheritance of the saints in light (Col 1:12-13).

4. Walking as Children of Light.

Foundational in the biblical tradition is the clear distinction between two ways of living, expressed variously as life or death, blessing or *curse, light or darkness. In step with other contemporary Jewish traditions following this "two way" tradition (see T. Levi 19; 1QS III, 13–IV, 26; see also 1QS I, 19; II, 16; 1QM [War Scroll] XIII, 5, 9-16), Paul describes the conduct of believers as reflecting their *identity as "children of light" (1 Thess 5:5; Eph 5:8; see also Eph 1:18; 1QM I, 1-11). One's state of being/identity, as darkness or light, is inextricably linked to one's conduct in deeds of darkness or light (Stenschke, 128). Children of the day "put aside" their deeds of darkness and "put on" the armor of light (Rom 13:11-12; see also 1 Thess 5:8; Eph 6:13) and thus "shine" like the stars in the midst of this crooked and twisted generation (Phil 2:15).

Paul employs light and darkness imagery extensively in Ephesians as he describes believers' "walk" with Christ (Eph 4–6). Believers are to "walk" (*peripateō*) worthy of their calling (Eph 4:1) and no longer "walk" (*peripateō*, Eph 4:17) as unbelieving "*Gentiles" in a futile and "darkened" understanding about God (Eph 4:18). As those transferred from darkness to light—"you *were* darkness" (Eph 5:8 NRSV)—believers must have no part in the disobedient and "fruitless" deeds of darkness (Eph 5:6-11). Instead, as those who are "light in the *Lord," believers must "walk [*peripateō*] as children of light" (Eph 5:8), reflected in lives filled with goodness, righteousness, and truth (Eph 5:9). Dark deeds may at present seem hidden in secret, but they will in the future be exposed by the light of Christ (Eph 5:12-14). In the meantime, the children of light struggle against the powers of the darkened world (Eph 6:12) equipped with the whole armor of God (Eph 6:13-17).

See also CREATION AND NEW CREATION; ETHICS; IMAGE OF GOD; SATAN, DEVIL; TRUTH.

BIBLIOGRAPHY. **C. E. Arnold,** *Powers of Darkness: Principles and Powers in Paul's Letters* (Downers Grove, IL: IVP Academic, 1992); **H. Conzelmann,** "σκότος, κτλ.," *TDNT* 7:423-45; idem, "φῶς, κτλ.," *TDNT* 9:310-58; **B. R. Gaventa,** *From Darkness to Light: Aspects of Conversion in the New Testament* (Philadelphia: Fortress, 1986); **K. Medill,** "Light and Darkness: Sectarian Rhetoric in Qumran and the New Testament," *Indiana University Linguistics Club Working Papers Online* 14 (2014): 1-49; **C. W. Stenschke,** "Once You Were in Darkness: The Past of the Readers of Ephesus," *European Journal of Theology* 23 (2014): 123-39; **A. Stewart,** *On the Two Ways—Life or Death, Light or Darkness: Foundational Texts in the Tradition* (Yonkers, NY: St. Vladimir's Seminary Press, 2011).

D. Pinter

LITURGICAL ELEMENTS. *See* HYMNS, HYMN FRAGMENTS, CONFESSIONS; PRAYER; WORSHIP.

LORD

Lord is one of the major christological titles in Paul's letters. It occurs nearly two hundred times in reference to Jesus, but the range of meaning for the word allows him to use it for both divine and human referents. Depending on the translation, "Master" or "master" may be employed especially when the governing context involves social relationships.

The English word *Lord* or *lord* in Paul's writings translates two Greek words. In some versions the Greek *despotēs* is rendered "lord" or "master" when referring to slave owners (1 Tim 6:1-2; Titus 2:9) or the owner of a house (2 Tim 2:21); but scholars dispute whether and to what extent Paul may have authored these letters. Overwhelmingly the word translated "Lord" or "lord" in Paul's undisputed letters and the rest of the NT is *kyrios*. The central meaning behind both Greek words is the recognition that a person or deity stands in authority over others, who are considered the *servants/*slaves of the superior. To express this relational, religious, and/or social reality Paul turns more often to *kyrios* than any other term.

As the rest of the NT demonstrates, Paul's use of Lord (*kyrios*) as a christological title does not appear to have been unique or necessarily innovative; it is likely to have been a title used frequently by those who were "*in Christ" before him. Central questions around this title have had to do with the sociolinguistic and historical background, the forces and factors that led to this title being applied to Jesus, and its use and significance in Paul as a christological title.

1. Background
2. Paul's Use of Lord/*Kyrios*
3. Context of Paul's Use of *Lord* for Jesus
4. *Kyrios*/Lord and Monotheism
5. *Kyrios* as Counterimperial Rhetoric

1. Background.

In Greco-Roman antiquity *kyrios* is used in a variety of ways: (1) as a form of polite address, similar to "sir"; (2) as a way to designate people in authority or ownership over land, businesses, and slaves; (3) as an expression of loyalty and devotion to rulers who claimed divine status; and (4) as a descriptive title of or address to gods and goddesses in various *religions. Paul and the rest of the NT reflect similar patterns of use with one exception: Jews and Christians refused to acknowledge Caesar as Lord (*kyrios*). According to reports from the historian Josephus, faithful Jews avoided the acclamation "Caesar is *kyrios*" because of the word's close association with the name of *God (Josephus, *J.W.* 7.10.1). Likewise, early Christians refused to recognize the emperor as *kyrios* or Lord likely because of their commitment to the creed: "Jesus is Lord" (Rom 10:9).

Overall, the Greco-Roman pattern of usage is consistent with the Greek version of the Hebrew Scriptures, where *kyrios* designates referents both human (e.g., heads of families, husbands of wives, owners of property, and kings) and divine. In the Septuagint *kyrios* translates several Hebrew words that refer to the one God of *Israel (e.g., *ʾădōnāy* and *ʾĕlōhîm*) and the divine name (Yahweh, over 6000×). Scholars have debated whether Paul's christological use of *kyrios* derives its significance more from a Greco-Roman or Hellenistic-Jewish context (see below). The emerging consensus is that the forces and factors most influential on Paul's theology and letters arise from his Jewish context (Fletcher-Louis).

The twentieth century witnessed a vigorous debate among scholars regarding when the *kyrios* title was used first in reference to Jesus, where it occurred, and what the faithful meant when they called Jesus "Lord." In Germany the history-of-religions school addressed these questions primarily as matters of history and not as dogma. In his classic book *Kyrios Christos* (German, 1913; English, 1970), W. Bousset made the case that it was not until the Jesus movement slipped away from a Jewish environment that *Gentile Christians would have first applied the title *kyrios* to Jesus. Jewish monotheism, he thought, would have precluded the confession among the earliest Palestinian Christ-believers because of the word's close association with God and the divine name. In a Hellenistic context such as Syria there were many gods addressed by the title *kyrios*, so it was a designation ready for application to Jesus. Therefore, pagan usage determined what Hellenistic Christians meant when they called Jesus Lord/*kyrios*. Although some scholars immediately pushed back on Bousset's reconstruction, for decades others accepted it with little modification.

After the Holocaust and World War II, historians and theologians undertook a fresh assessment of Second Temple Judaism and early Christianity based in part on discoveries such as the Dead Sea Scrolls. W. D. Davies, M. Hengel, and others proposed that one could explain Christian origins by means of Jewish beliefs and practices rather than pagan; this would include christological beliefs and practices including the confession "Jesus is Lord."

L. Hurtado (1998; 2003) made the case that it was possible to account for the christological use of *kyrios* and religious devotion to *Christ by appealing to Jewish notions of divine agency reshaped by powerful religious experiences. These encounters convinced Aramaic-speaking believers in Palestine that Jesus had conquered *death and was now enthroned in divine *glory. For Hurtado, Christ-devotion and the application of *kyrios* to Jesus did not require an explanation away from Jewish Palestine. In particular, the *maranatha* invocation ("Our Lord, come," 1 Cor 16:22 NRSV; cf. Rev 22:20; Did. 10.6) demonstrated that Aramaic-speaking Christians addressed Jesus as "Lord" either as an appeal for his presence in *worship or as a *prayer for his return.

2. Paul's Use of Lord/*Kyrios*.

In his letters Paul uses *kyrios* in a variety of ways. First, he uses the term *kyrios* in reference to people in authority (masters over slaves, Col 3:22-24; owner of an estate, Gal 4:1). But he situates those relationships over against the ultimate claim of Jesus as *kyrios* (e.g., Col 3:22-24; Eph 6:5-9). Second, rhetorically, Paul gives lip service to the so-called gods and lords of the nations (1 Cor 8:4-6); but he regards them as inconsequential compared to the "one God, the Father" and "one Lord, Jesus Christ" (NRSV). Third, Paul predominantly treats *kyrios*/Lord as a theological and christological word. He employs it in reference to God (e.g., Rom 4:7-8; 11:34; 2 Cor 6:17-18), the Lord Jesus (approximately 200×), and perhaps the *Holy Spirit (2 Cor 3:18). Thus, in a few instances Paul employs *kyrios* for humans in authority and pagan gods; in a few others he predicates it to the one God of Israel. Yet in the vast majority of occurrences the *apostle employs *kyrios*/Lord as a christological title. Other than *Christos* (Christ/Messiah), *kyrios* is the most frequently attested christological title in Paul's letters.

2.1. The Risen Jesus as Lord. Paul's letters are the earliest witness to the church's address and description of Jesus as *kyrios*: he uses it over two hundred times in his letters in a variety of places and contexts. It is found in combination with other titles and names that often appear formulaic: "Lord Jesus" (e.g., Rom 14:14; 2 Cor 8:9), "Jesus Christ our Lord" (e.g., Rom 1:4; 1 Cor 1:9), "Lord Jesus Christ" (e.g., Rom 5:1; 1 Cor 1:2-3; Gal 6:14), "Christ Jesus our Lord" (e.g., Rom 6:23; 1 Cor 15:31; Col 2:6), and "Jesus our Lord" (e.g., Rom 4:24; 1 Cor 9:1). It is also found alone about one hundred times in the undisputed letters as a title for Jesus (Rom 14:6, 8; 1 Cor 3:5; 4:4-5; 1 Thess 3:8; 4:16; Phil 3:1, 5). Among other things, this suggests that *kyrios* had become a routine way of referring to Jesus without any other identifying terms.

The apostle was not the first to acclaim Jesus as "Lord," *kyrios*. The *maranatha* invocation (1 Cor 16:22) provides clear evidence that the earliest, Aramaic-speaking churches in and around Palestine referred to Jesus as *mareh*, an Aramaic word with a semantic field roughly equivalent to *kyrios*. Coming as it does in the setting of worship, *maranatha* may be taken as a prayerful appeal for the risen Jesus/Lord to come again. Additionally, Paul's letters appear to be punctuated with *hymns and creedal statements he inherited from other Christians; in many of these preformed traditions *kyrios* plays a vital role as a christological title (e.g., Rom 10:9; Phil 2:9-11). Paul never makes the case that Jesus is "Lord"; the churches he writes seem familiar with the term already. For him it seems part of the common language of what it means to be a Christ-follower.

For the apostle the *resurrection of Jesus is closely allied with the title *kyrios* and the confession "Jesus is Lord" (e.g., Rom 10:9-13; 1 Cor 12:3). The conviction that the crucified, dead, and buried Messiah has conquered death and is now enthroned in lordly glory is a regular feature of Paul's letters, particularly in strategic places (Rom 1:3-4; 14:8-9; Phil 2:9-11). While it is possible for Paul to refer to the earthly Jesus as "Lord," it is primarily the risen Jesus, seated at the right hand of the Father (1 Cor 15:25, from Ps 110), who is so addressed and acclaimed (see Acts 2:32-36).

Paul begins his Roman letter by linking together resurrection, lordship, and *gospel (Rom 1:3-4). Many scholars believe he has adopted a preformed *tradition that declares the heart of the gospel as the arrival of "his [God's] *Son." The sonship is then explicated in two stages: first, the Son is the royal Messiah by virtue of his ancestor David (literally "seed of David"); and second, the sonship of Jesus is raised to a whole new level by virtue of the resurrection, that is, the Son of God empowered (literally, "in power") according to the Spirit of *holiness. For the apostle, there is a close connection between Spirit and power (e.g., Rom 15:18-19; 2 Cor 6:6-7; Gal 3:5). Paul adds his own postscript to the tradition: "Jesus Christ our Lord." Thus, under one gospel-oriented theme, he brings together three key titles: Christ (= Messiah), Son, and Lord.

The acclamation of Jesus as Lord, for Paul, transcends time and location. It expresses universal and cosmic themes. It begins with the first *creation and continues through the new. In recasting Israel's central creed, the Shema (Deut 6:4), the apostle places "one God, the Father" parallel to "one Lord, Jesus Christ" (1 Cor 8:6 NRSV). Both God the Father and the Lord Jesus have key roles to play in the dramas of creation and redemption. Through the one Lord/*kyrios* "all things" have come into existence, and Christ-believers ("we") are redeemed through him. The Lord Jesus has a mediatorial role in creation and redemption, which some scholars propose is based on understanding Jesus as a manifestation of divine *Wisdom (e.g., Prov 8:22-29). Still, to be a coworker with God in creation meant that the one called "Lord" had to be present when the all things were made (see Col 1:15-20). Thus, preexistence must be predicated by virtue of the Lord Jesus' role in creation (Bauckham).

The cosmic significance of the "Lord Jesus" is likewise a key aspect of Paul's theology of the cross and resurrection. For him, Jesus' death and resurrection established him as Lord over the living and the dead (Rom 14:8-9). Intrinsic to this claim is the conviction that the risen Jesus has dominion (lordship) over creation. To be Lord over the realm of the dead and living is a cosmic position (Moule). Another christologically rich passage, known as the Philippian hymn or Christ hymn (Phil 2:6-11), presents an eschatological scene in which every creature—in heaven, on earth, and below—bends the knee before the humble, crucified, superexalted Jesus and confesses "Jesus Christ is Lord" to the glory of God the Father (Phil 2:9-11 NRSV). The cosmic scope of this passage is self-evident (Gorman). In the resurrection, the Father grants to the risen one "the name above every name." While some argue that the *name is "Jesus," it is best taken as a possessive, that is, the name that belongs to Jesus. The name is revealed at the climax of the hymn, "Jesus the Messiah is Lord [*kyrios*]." While *kyrios* can be a title, it should here be taken as a common surrogate for the name, referring to God's unique *covenant name, Yahweh. Texts such as these clearly demonstrate how the title/name *kyrios* is associated with the universal and cosmic significance of Jesus.

2.2. The Earthly Jesus as Lord. Not only does Paul describe the resurrected Jesus as *kyrios*, but he is also able to speak of Jesus during his earthly career as "Lord." For example, Paul claims to have received his account of the *Lord's Supper "from the Lord" and handed it on to the Corinthians (1 Cor 11:23-24). Part of that traditional narrative states that on the night of his betrayal the "Lord Jesus" instituted the actions and sayings of the Lord's Supper, a sacrament the church has passed on and imitated for two thousand years. On both accounts, by "Lord Jesus" Paul has in mind Jesus prior to his death and resurrection. A similar tendency could be reflected in Paul's manner of referring to members of Jesus' family as "brothers of the Lord" (1 Cor 9:5) and particularly James, "the Lord's brother" (Gal 1:19). While the phrase could mean "the brothers of the risen Lord," it is more natural to take these as references to his earthly family. We should also note the occasions on which Paul appeals to a "word of the Lord" (1 Cor 7:10, 25; 9:14; 1 Thess 4:15). Certainty is not possible, but these teachings could be Paul's distillation of sayings he received from the earthly *ministry of Jesus. Some sayings could have been incorporated into the four NT Gospels; others remained part of the oral tradition or *agrapha* (unwritten sayings). The sharp distinction the apostle draws between his own words and the words "of the Lord" make it clear that he considered these teachings as having unusual authority.

2.3. Scriptural Quotations and Allusions. A unique class of Paul's use of Lord/*kyrios* appears when the apostle quotes from or alludes to a passage from the Hebrew Bible that contains the divine name. Since Paul wrote to his churches in Greek and since the divine name had been rendered *kyrios* in many Greek versions of the Tanakh, his application of these YHWH/*kyrios* texts has received special attention. Not long ago it was held that *kyrios* in Paul's letters refers to Jesus except in OT quotations. This conclusion, however, was not based on a contextual analysis of Paul's texts or letters. Now it has become commonplace for scholars to recognize that Paul occasionally refers to Jesus using scriptural texts where the Greek *kyrios* stands for the divine name, Yahweh (Wright).

God the Father appears as the referent in the following Pauline texts where *kyrios* translates the divine name in the Hebrew text of Scripture: Romans 4:8 (Ps 32:1-2); Romans 9:28-29 (Is 28:22; 1:9); Romans 10:16 (Is 53:1); Romans 11:34 (Is 40:13); Romans 15:11 (Ps 117:1); 1 Corinthians 3:20 (Ps 94:11); and 2 Corinthians 6:17-18 (Is 52:11; 2 Sam 7:14). We should note as well several passages where Paul inserts *kyrios* into a scriptural quotation where the divine name does not occur: Romans 11:3 (1 Kings 19:10); Romans 12:19 (Deut 32:35); and 1 Cor 14:21 (Is 28:11).

Jesus the Messiah appears as the referent in the following Pauline texts where *kyrios* translates the divine name in the Hebrew text of Scripture: Romans 10:13 (Joel 2:32); Romans 14:11 (Is 45:23); 1 Corinthians 1:31 (Jer 9:23-24); 1 Corinthians 2:16 (Is 40:13); 1 Corinthians 10:26 (Ps 24:1); and 2 Corinthians 10:17 (Jer 9:23-24). We should also consider a number of allusions Paul makes to Yahweh texts with Christ as referent: 1 Corinthians 10:21-22 (Mal 1:7, 12; Deut 32:21); 2 Corinthians 3:16 (Ex 34:34); 1 Thessalonians 3:13 (Zech 14:15); 1 Thessalonians 4:6 (Ps 94:2); 2 Thessalonians 1:7-8 (Is 66:15); 2 Thessalonians 1:9 (Is 2:10, 19, 21); and 2 Thessalonians 1:12 (Is 66:5). Among this latter group, the most striking example of an OT YHWH/*kyrios* text applied to Jesus is found in Philippians 2:10-11. Many scholars regard this as a preformed hymn that Paul incorporates into his letter because he agrees with its implicit claims. What is remarkable about this language is that words of monotheistic import regarding Yahweh

(Is 45:23-25) have been applied so readily to an eschatological scene where Christ is universally hailed as "Lord," and this "to the glory of God the Father" (Phil 2:10-11 NRSV).

While not all scholars agree on the classification of each passage above, there are sufficient examples so that the weight of evidence is unmistakable; Paul applies passages containing the divine name to Christ under the title "Lord." In itself this is a remarkable exegetical maneuver made by an early Jewish follower of Jesus. This practice appears unprecedented (contra Kirk); it suggests that Paul links Jesus with God in truly remarkable ways and includes Jesus within the name, dignity, and unique *identity of Israel's God. Along with other patterns of religious devotion to Christ, Paul's christological exegesis points to a high *Christology in the earliest moments of the Jesus movement.

3. Context of Paul's Use of *Lord* for Jesus. The undisputed letters of Paul demonstrate that the apostle and his coauthors tend to use names and christological titles in particular contexts. They are not randomly sprinkled through his letters. As a result, each title comes with a set of associations the apostle wants to develop. A close reading of Paul's letters demonstrates that Paul prefers to use the *kyrios* title for Jesus in three contexts: ethical, eschatological, and liturgical.

3.1. Ethical Context. While Paul employs the title *Lord* for Jesus throughout his letters, the title appears most prominent in his ethical sections, that is, matters dealing with the prescribed conduct and practices of believers in his churches. The idea appears to be that the people of God, constituted by the confession "Jesus is Lord," ought to live according to his example and by his teaching (Capes 2018). Thus, Paul affirms the Thessalonian believers for becoming imitators of the apostles and of the Lord (1 Thess 1:6) and condemns troublemakers because they do not serve the Lord Christ (Rom 16:18). In matters of *sexual ethics, the *body is meant for the Lord and not immorality; after all, he is Lord over the body (1 Cor 6:13). To the unmarried Paul promotes the undivided attention of a single life so that a person might be fully devoted to the Lord (1 Cor 7:32-35). Widows are free to marry if they wish, but only in the Lord (1 Cor 7:39-40).

The frequent use of the phrase "in the Lord" demonstrates the close connection between Jesus as Lord and how his servants ought to walk: "in the Lord" believers are to stand firm (Phil 4:1), rejoice (Phil 4:4), exchange greetings (Rom 16; 1 Cor 16:19), receive one another (Rom 16:2), be faithful (1 Cor 4:17), and maintain confidence (Gal 5:10). But Paul's instruction to his churches about what they should do is not limited to any formula. For instance, with the reputation of the *church on the line, Paul passes *judgment on the incestuous man in Corinth and instructs the church to exercise his oversight as their apostle with a threefold appeal to their Master and Lord, Jesus (1 Cor 5:1-5). When addressing the disaffection between "the weak" and "the *strong" in the Roman church, the apostle urges them to recognize they live and die to the Lord; indeed, they belong to the Lord. Thus, they must refrain from passing judgment on each other (Rom 14:5-9). Seven times in the *household code in Colossians (Col 3:18–4:1) Paul appeals to Jesus' authority as *kyrios* as the basis for a wife's respectful conduct before her husband, children's obedience to their parents, slaves' service to their earthly masters, and masters' just treatment of their slaves. Properly understood, all of life is lived "in the Lord."

The apostle grounds these ethical teachings on the finished work of God in the Messiah. As *kyrios*, the risen Jesus is authorized to command and order the lives of Christ-followers. He has the ability to do so because of what he has done for them through his death, burial, resurrection, and ascension to the right hand of the Father. The redemption won by his sacrifice and death gives him an exclusive status as *head of the church (the body of Christ). Believers, as servants of the Lord, ought to be prepared to live in obedience to him, seeing their bodies and their entire lives ultimately as his.

As the *kyrios* Jesus stands in the same kind of relation to the church/individual believers as Yahweh/*kyrios* stands in relation to Israel/individual Jews. C. Tilling makes the case that this "Christ-relation" is key to understanding Paul's divine Christology. Thus, Jesus' example and teaching form the basis of Christian *ethics according to the pattern established in the OT, as Yahweh's example and commandments shape Jewish ethics or *halakah* (e.g., Ex 20; Lev 17–26; Deut 5).

3.2. Eschatological Context. For Paul, *eschatology informs many aspects of his pastoral counsel in his letters. Eschatology has to do with last or ultimate realities such as death, resurrection, the end of the age, and (final) judgment. Properly understood, Paul's eschatology is not just future-oriented: it addresses past, present, and future. It stretches back in time to the resurrection of Jesus, when the end of the age invaded the middle of history. It looks to the future, when God will act decisively to right wrongs and fill the new creation full. But in anticipation of that day, Christ-followers are to live uprightly so that they can stand blameless in the judgment (e.g., 1 Thess 5:2-11; 2 Cor 1:14). In passages that deal with Christ's role in this drama, Paul prefers "Lord" over other christological titles.

In large measure Paul's eschatology is derived from the Hebrew Scriptures, but is attenuated by his experiences with the risen Jesus. One of the themes Paul adapts from the prophets is "the day of the LORD" (Yahweh/*kyrios*). According to Israel's seers, a day of judgment was coming when Yahweh would intrude dramatically in history; he would judge evil and right wrongs, even if those wrongs were found among his people. Cosmic disturbances would accompany God's invasive actions (Joel 2:1-2; Zeph 1:14-15). While generalizations are never completely accurate, the preexilic prophets speak of the day of Yahweh primarily as a day of destruction and disaster for Israel (e.g., Amos 5:18-20; Is 2:11-17). Exilic and postexilic prophets see in the day a ray of *hope as God will step in to punish Israel's enemies and rescue his people from the nations (e.g., Ezek 37; cf. Is 65). In some cases, the threat is enough to induce repentance. The full phrase "the day of the Lord" is not necessary to evoke the image; often the prophets shorten it to "the day," perhaps in keeping with their poetic interests. Rebirth (Is 66:7-17) and resuscitation (Ezek 37) are other expressions of the prophetic imagination about Israel's restoration.

In the phrase "the day of the Lord," the word *Lord* translates the divine name, Yahweh. This is both a pertinent and extraordinary observation, because for Paul the day of the Lord has become "the day of our Lord Jesus Christ" (1 Cor 1:8 NRSV; cf. 1 Thess 5:2, "the day of the Lord"; 2 Cor 1:14 NRSV, "the day of the Lord Jesus"). Here is yet another example of the apostle's willingness to situate the "Lord" Jesus within an OT reference to Yahweh. In keeping with OT motifs, the day will come unexpectedly and will mean sudden destruction for some (1 Thess 5:2-3) and *salvation for others (1 Thess 5:9). In Philippians Paul clarifies the phrase to ensure that his hearers understand the christological connection: "the day of Christ Jesus" (Phil 1:6 NIV) and "the day of Christ" (Phil 1:10; 2:16 NIV). The apostle embraces the threat/hope of "the day of Yahweh" from his Bible and transfers that hope to the Lord Jesus.

In Paul's way of thinking, "the day of the Lord" is inaugurated by the coming of the Lord Jesus. The language he employs to portray this singular event is similar to OT theophanic visions and descriptions of God's entrance into the world. Creation gives way to the irresistible might of the Creator, who comes to judge the wicked, rescue the righteous, and establish his reign (e.g., Is 40; Hab 3:3-6, 13; Ps 68:7-8). Similarly, the apostle envisions the coming (parousia) of the Lord Jesus amid fantastic phenomena: the dead rising, the living transformed, and a gathering of the faithful in the air (1 Thess 4:13-18; cf. 1 Cor 15:23-28). With mighty angels and flaming fire, the Lord Jesus will be revealed (*apokalypsis*) from heaven to relieve the afflicted and inflict vengeance on those who do not follow the gospel (2 Thess 1:5-12). For Paul, the coming appears imminent ("The Lord is near," Phil 4:5 NIV), and the Corinthians are described as patiently waiting for the eschatological revelation of the day of the Lord Jesus Christ (1 Cor 1:7-8). In passages such as these there is a close connection between the one who comes and the title "Lord."

For Paul, the day of the Lord, the second coming and the final judgment appear to form a pattern of related, however distinct, events. History is moving toward a grand finale, inaugurated by the other world-shattering event of the *cross, burial, and resurrection of Jesus. So, it is natural for Paul to use the *kyrios* title for Jesus in matters related to his role in executing final judgment (e.g., 1 Cor 4:4-5; 5:3-5; 1 Thess 4:6). Some of the imagery he uses is appropriated from the OT and other contemporary Jewish texts that speak of Yahweh coming as ruler and judge. In Paul's letters, a referential shift takes place where the promise/threat of God's arrival in the world to right wrongs and rescue his people is applied to Jesus. Under the *kyrios*/Lord title the apostle has deliberately applied to Christ OT actions expected of Yahweh; it is not that God does not do them, but God does so personally in the Messiah. L. J. Kreitzer describes a "conceptual overlap" in Paul's letters between God and Jesus, with only a fluid boundary separating them. But Paul was convinced that such ideas were already present in Judaism—particularly in the pseudepigraphic literature—before the Christian movement. In particular, divine agents (e.g., principal angels and the Messiah) were expected to execute final judgment on God's behalf. Similarly, L. Hurtado makes the case that divine agents provided some important categories for early Christians to think about Christ's significance; but it ultimately took powerful religious experiences for Jesus' followers to convince them that Jesus occupied those roles originally reserved for Yahweh (Hurtado 2003).

3.3. Liturgical Context. Occasionally in his letters Paul alludes to various practices and challenges related to his churches as worshiping communities. He addresses the Corinthians as "those who in every place call on the name of our Lord Jesus Christ, both their Lord and ours" (1 Cor 1:2 NRSV). The apostle identifies the church in *Corinth and other locations by a cultic action, "calling on the name of the Lord Jesus Christ." That phrase echoes Joel 2:32 (Joel 3:5 LXX): "everyone who calls on the name of the LORD shall be saved" (NRSV). Typically, in the Hebrew Bible calling on the name of the Lord is a shorthand way of describing ritual words and actions that accompany *temple *sacrifices. Since the word *Lord* translates the divine name (Yahweh/*kyrios*], Paul's application of that language to the "Lord" Jesus signifies that he has become a rightful recipient of worship in the churches. Furthermore, when the people gather, Paul writes, they do so "in the name of [our] Lord Jesus" (1 Cor 5:4-5). The apostle clearly gives the *kyrios* title priority when addressing Christ's role as an appropriate object of worship.

The proper response to Jesus' resurrection and now-exalted status is *faith and the confession "Jesus is Lord" (Rom 10:9-13; cf. 1 Cor 12:3). Those who confess and so believe are assured of salvation regardless of their ethnic identity. Again, Paul marshals Joel 2:32 (Joel 3:5 LXX) to encourage everyone—Jew and non-Jew—to call on the name of the Lord Jesus to be saved. The closest analogue to calling on the name of the Lord Jesus must be the invocation of Yahweh in temple sacrifices.

The Lord's Supper offers a special case for how Paul employs the *kyrios*/Lord title. While it is known today by a variety of names—the Eucharist, Holy Communion—Paul refers to the practice as the Lord's Supper (1 Cor 11:20), a tradition he himself says he received "from the Lord Jesus." The actions and words of institution he relates are remarkably close to the Gospel accounts (e.g., Lk 22:19-20; Mt 26:26-29; Mk 14:22-25), so they likely proceed from the earthly Jesus, not a later revelation. Still, Paul's pastoral interpretation of the event is unique: "For as often as you eat this bread and drink the cup, you proclaim the Lord's death until he comes" (1 Cor 11:26 NRSV). What is unusual about the phrase "the Lord's death" is that Paul typically refers to Jesus' death by the title "Christ," not "Lord" (e.g., Rom 5:6-8; 1 Cor 1:23-24; 2:2; 15:3-5; Gal 2:19-20). The lordly association of the Supper is strengthened by Paul's references to various aspects of the custom, for example, "the cup of the Lord" and "the table of the Lord" (1 Cor 10:21 NRSV). Those who partake of "the cup of the Lord" unworthily, he writes, profane "the body and blood of the Lord" (1 Cor 11:27 NRSV). Thus, in relating the traditions associated with the Lord's Supper, Paul prefers to cite Jesus' role as the *kyrios* (Kramer).

Another aspect of the early churches' liturgy deserves comment. There is good evidence to suggest that the apostle expected his *letters to be read aloud when Christ-believers gathered to worship (e.g., Col 4:16). If so, then the form and content of the letters themselves would necessarily participate in their worship even as they instructed in matters of belief and practice. Thus, the formula "*Grace to you and *peace from God our Father and the Lord Jesus Christ" becomes a stereotypical part of Paul's initial greetings to several of his churches (e.g., Rom 1:7; 1 Cor 1:3; Gal 1:2; Phil 1:2). United in purpose and function, God the Father and the Lord Jesus are the source of grace and peace for the churches. The binitarian formula demonstrates how closely Paul associates the Father and the Lord, yet the two figures remain distinct; for in the formula the Father always precedes the Lord. Furthermore, Jesus is never referred to as the Father (Ehrman). While the thanksgivings of Paul's letters are less fixed, they often contain a binitarian reference: "Blessed be the God and Father of our Lord Jesus Christ" (2 Cor 1:3 NRSV; see 1 Thess 1:2-3). Benedictions, hymns, and doxologies referencing God the Father and the Lord Jesus also punctuate Paul's letters (e.g., 1 Thess 3:11-13; 2 Cor 11:31; Phil 2:6-11). In saying farewell at the end of his letters, Paul has a different practice: he typically refers to "the grace of the Lord Jesus" (e.g., 1 Cor 16:23; Gal 6:18; 1 Thess 5:28) without reference to God the Father (see 2 Cor 13:13).

A stunning example of the binitarian formula comes with Paul's adaptation of the Shema (Deut 6:4): "Hear, O Israel: The Lord [Yahweh/*kyrios*] our God, the Lord [Yahweh/*kyrios*] is one" (NIV). During the Second Temple period this prayer had become a regular feature of synagogue life and personal devotion. At the heart of it is a declaration of absolute allegiance to Israel's God (Wright), not an abstract statement about the nature of monotheism. Paul takes the Greek version of the Shema, revamps it, and expands it to include Jesus (1 Cor 8:6):

> for us [Christ believers] there is one God, the Father,
> from whom are all things and for whom we exist,

> and one Lord, Jesus Christ,
> through whom are all things and through whom we exist. (NRSV)

The doubling of the term *one* in his revised Shema is not additive (1 + 1 = 2) but inclusive. For Paul there is no second God; however, he includes "the Lord/*kyrios* Jesus Christ" within the identity of the one God (Bauckham). If Paul were in the habit of *preaching or reciting this revised form of the Shema with its bold references to God the Father and the Lord Jesus Christ, we might expect that such phrases would surface, almost unconsciously, at key moments in his correspondences.

The title *Christ* often appears in these stereotypical formulas, but not all; yet the designation *Lord* is always linked with the personal name *Jesus* in binitarian formulas. For Paul the *kyrios* title holds great significance in matters of worship.

4. *Kyrios*/Lord and Monotheism.

Paul's use of *kyrios*/Lord for Jesus and the way he associates him with the divine name constitute a remarkable feature of the early Jesus movement. Given the Jewishness of this movement, scholars have engaged a lively debate over the nature of pre-Christian monotheism. At the heart of the matter is the question: What kind of monotheism would have accommodated calling Jesus "Lord," associating him with the divine name, and acknowledging him as the rightful recipient of worship? One answer has been to retire the use of the word *monotheism* altogether from any description of Second Temple Judaism and early Christianity. Fredriksen makes the case that (1) the term is anachronistic and (2) it is not descriptive of the reality of these faiths (Fredriksen 2007). Other scholars want to retain the term *monotheism* because of its utility, but they disagree over how "strict" or "exclusive" Jewish and Christian practices were at the time.

In the middle of the last century A. R. Johnson made the case that the Israelite conception of the human provided the most appropriate analogue for thinking about God. In imagining "What is a human being?" he proposed that ancient Jews conceived of the human as having an indefinable extension to one's personality, so that a person was more than individual; one had a corporate identity/personality (which included other people and possessions). When applied to God, this conception allowed for the one God to be treated as having similar extensions and multiple manifestations (e.g., Spirit, Wisdom, Name). According to Johnson, this conceptual framework would have permitted early Christians to designate Jesus as "Lord" and offer him religious devotion along with God the Father (Johnson 1942).

Hurtado offers a different proposal. He argues for what he describes as the "binitarian/dyadic shape" of Christian devotion in the early years of the movement (Hurtado 1998). Jewish Christians, however, had not abandoned their monotheistic roots in order to assign to Jesus so lofty a status. This was made possible because of (1) the divine-agency category in Second Temple Judaism and (2) powerful religious experiences that reshaped monotheistic beliefs and practices among early Jesus followers. Among these agents were divine attributes (e.g., Wisdom and Word), exalted patriarchs (e.g., Enoch and Moses), and principal angels (e.g., Michael and Yahoel). These agents carry out divine actions by creating, sustaining, and superintending the world in accord with God's will. For Hurtado, regardless of how close these agents may have been to God and divine power, they never posed a threat to Jewish monotheism because they were never worshiped. Yet, the earliest evidence (Paul's letters) describes Jesus in terms of divine agency (e.g., 1 Cor 8:6; Col 1:15-20), assigns him an exalted status as risen Lord, and endorses his worship (e.g., Phil 2:9-11). Among the catalysts for this innovation were (1) the influence Jesus had on his followers, (2) the conviction that God had raised Jesus from the dead to inhabit divine glory, and (3) refinements that came amid the churches' *mission.

Not every scholar, however, regards the divine-agency concept as playing such a catalytic role in the early movement. R. Bauckham proposes a new conceptual category: divine identity. Properly understood, divine identity has to do with God as a relational and active being, a God who acts, speaks, knows, and can be known. Identity distinguishes God from everything that is not God. Traditionally, God's identity has been understood as revealed through the Scriptures of Israel. Accordingly, God stands in relation to creation as Creator, Judge, and Ruler of all things; and God stands in relation to Israel as a covenant partner who has acted and will act decisively in history. For Bauckham, Second Temple Judaism was strictly monotheistic and drew hard lines of distinction between God and everything that was not God. Therefore, in understanding Christology, including Paul's claim that Jesus is "Lord," Bauckham advocates that early Christians included Jesus within the unique identity of the one God of Israel (Bauckham 2008). As a result, early Christian texts routinely regard Jesus on the same relational terms as Creator, sovereign Lord, and the embodiment of the covenant-making and covenant-keeping God of Israel. "Christological monotheism," a phrase used to describe this perspective, was indeed an innovation, but it developed out of Jewish monotheism; it was not a violation of it, nor was it an imposition by pagans. Such theological innovations emerged as early Christians engaged in creative readings of Scripture. In particular, Psalm 110 offered early Christians an image of the risen Jesus as Lord, seated on the throne and exercising divine rule.

Another proposal centers on the identity of the one, true God and his promise to return one day to Zion. Many Second Temple Jews were convinced that Israel's God had abandoned Jerusalem and its temple prior to its destruction (sixth century BC); but the same God had also promised to return again to his people one day in person and in glory. To put it simply, YHWH would return to be King/Lord. According to N. T. Wright, this return-to-Zion theology was the origin of Christology, for it explained how early Christians such as Paul considered that Israel's God had returned to his people personally in and as Jesus the Messiah. If this is the correct conceptual framework, then language about God and texts that refer to Jesus as *kyrios* could be applied liberally to Jesus. For Wright, this innovation happened before Paul wrote any of his letters and represented an authentically Jewish response to the crucified, risen Lord. In the end, the exalted status granted to Jesus did not violate God's oneness.

Each of these proposals has merit, for they can and do explain key aspects of early Christian faith and practice. Given the complexities of history and the vast distances between us and the early tradents, we are unlikely to gain complete clarity on the nature of pre-Christian Jewish monotheism and how the first Jesus followers came to regard him as Lord/*kyrios*. What seems clear, however, is that the language Paul applied to Christ and the devotional posture he advocated toward him meant that Jesus enjoyed an unprecedented status among the churches, equal to God, yet distinct from him.

5. *Kyrios* as Counterimperial Rhetoric.

Over the last three decades Pauline scholars and historians have made the case that Paul's rhetoric about Jesus' lordship emerged as the churches' counterimperial propaganda. The confession "Jesus is Lord" was the churches' answer to the pagan claim "Caesar is Lord." By Paul's day there is considerable evidence that the ruler cult was well established, particularly in the East, and was one of the means by which Rome governed the remote provinces. Most of the apostle's Gentile mission would have been carried out against the backdrop of Rome's unrelenting presence. In his day, religion and politics were not discrete spheres of life, as they are for the post-Enlightenment West; thus, Paul's claim that Jesus, not Caesar, is Lord has political overtones and calls for absolute loyalty to Jesus, not Rome. Christians, including Paul, would have benefited from Roman peace, Roman roads, local acts of *patronage, and at times even Roman justice. But, for Paul, Caesar's empire was a dimly burning wick compared to the glorious light of the gospel and the world's true King, Jesus the Messiah.

Observant Jews rejected and mocked any ultimate claim made by Rome or any of its functionaries. The Shema (Deut 6:4) stands in absolute opposition to any other than God who claim the title "Lord." For Paul and his churches, the slain Messiah has been vindicated by God in the resurrection and shown to be the rightful Lord of all things. Paul's clearest anti-imperial rhetoric professes that believers' citizenship is in heaven, and it is from there that they await "a Savior, the Lord Jesus Christ" (Phil 3:20 NRSV). "Savior," "Lord," and "Christ/Messiah" (King) were titles regularly claimed by Caesar, now predicated to Jesus. Thus, in Paul's way of thinking, the world is ruled from heaven and not Rome. True citizenship and absolute allegiance lie above even as believers await Jesus' parousia. But it is unlikely that the Christian claims made about Jesus and his lordship are merely responses to counterimperial claims. Indeed, Paul's Christology is inherently and radically counterimperial, but it unlikely to be the reason that early Christians declared him "Lord" in the first place. Rather, the confession is rooted in the churches' extraordinary experiences with the risen Jesus and Spirit-inspired exegesis of the Hebrew Scriptures that associated the crucified, resurrected Messiah squarely with the God of Israel.

See also CHRIST, MESSIAH; CHRISTOLOGY; CORINTHIANS, FIRST LETTER TO THE; CREATION AND NEW CREATION; CROSS; ESCHATOLOGY; ETHICS; FELLOWSHIP, COMMUNION, SHARING; GOD; HEAD; HOLY SPIRIT; HOUSEHOLDS AND HOUSEHOLD CODES; HYMNS, HYMN FRAGMENTS, CONFESSIONS; JUDGMENT; LORD'S SUPPER; NAME; OLD TESTAMENT IN PAUL; PAUL AND JUDAISM; RESURRECTION; ROMANS, LETTER TO THE; SON OF GOD; TRADITION; WORSHIP.

BIBLIOGRAPHY. **R. Bauckham,** *Jesus and the God of Israel* (Grand Rapids, MI: Eerdmans, 2008); **W. Bousset,** *Kyrios Christos* (Nashville: Abingdon, 1970); **D. B. Capes,** *Old Testament Yahweh Texts in Paul's Christology,* WUNT 2/47 (Tubingen: Mohr,

1992); idem, *The Divine Christ: Paul, the Lord Jesus, and the Scriptures of Israel* (Grand Rapids, MI: Baker, 2018); **D. B. Capes, A. D. DeConick, H. K. Bond, and T. A. Miller,** *Israel's God and Rebecca's Children: Christology and Community in Early Judaism and Christianity* (Waco, TX: Baylor University Press, 2007); **M. Casey,** *From Jewish Prophet to Gentile God: The Origins and Development of New Testament Christology* (Louisville: Westminster John Knox, 1991); **L. Cerfaux,** "Kyrios dans les citations pauliniennes de l'Ancien Testament," in *Receueil Lucien Cerfaux: Études d'exégèse et d'historie religieuse de Monseigneur Cerfaux* (Gembloux: Duculot, 1954), 1:173-88; **W. D. Davies,** *Paul and Rabbinic Judaism: Some Rabbinic Elements in Pauline Theology*, 4th ed. (Philadelphia: Fortress, 1980); **J. D. G. Dunn,** *The Theology of Paul the Apostle* (Grand Rapids, MI: Eerdmans, 1998); **B. Ehrman,** *How Jesus Became God: The Exaltation of a Jewish Preacher from Galilee* (San Francisco: HarperOne, 2014); **G. Fee,** *Pauline Christology: An Exegetical-Theological Study* (Peabody, MA: Hendrickson, 2007); **J. A. Fitzmyer,** "The Semitic Background of the New Testament Kyrios-Title," in *A Wandering Aramean: Collected Aramaic Essays*, SBLMS 25 (Missoula, MT: Scholars Press, 1979) 115-42; **C. Fletcher-Louis,** *Jesus Monotheism*, vol. 1, *Christological Origins: The Emerging Consensus and Beyond* (Eugene, OR: Cascade, 2015); **W. Foerster and G. Quell,** "κυριος, κτλ.," *TDNT* 3:1039-98; **P. Fredriksen,** "Mandatory Retirement: Ideas in the Study of Christian Origins Whose Time Has Come to Go," in *Israel's God and Rebecca's Children: Christology and Community in Early Judaism and Christianity*, ed. D. B. Capes et al. (Waco, TX: Baylor University Press, 2007), 25-38; **M. J. Gorman,** *Apostle of the Crucified Lord*, 2nd ed. (Grand Rapids, MI: Eerdmans, 2016); **R. B. Hays,** *Echoes of Scripture in the Letters of Paul* (New Haven, CT: Yale University Press, 1989); **M. Hengel,** *Judaism and Hellenism: Studies in Their Encounter in Palestine During the Early Hellenistic Period*, trans. John Bowden, 2 vols. (Philadelphia: Fortress, 1974); **R. Horsley,** ed., *Paul and Politics: Ekklesia, Israel, Imperium, Interpretation; Essays in Honor of Krister Stendahl* (Harrisburg, PA: Trinity Press International, 2000); **L. W. Hurtado,** *One God, One Lord: Early Christian Devotion and Ancient Jewish Monotheism*, 2nd ed. (London: T&T Clark, 1998); idem, *Lord Jesus Christ: Devotion to Jesus in Earliest Christianity* (Grand Rapids, MI: Eerdmans, 2003); **A. R. Johnson,** *The One and the Many in the Israelite Conception of God* (Cardiff, UK: University of Wales Press, 1942); **D. Juel,** *Messianic Exegesis: Christological Interpretation of the Old Testament in Early Christianity* (Philadelphia: Fortress, 1988); **D. Kirk,** *A Man Attested by God: The Human Jesus of the Synoptic Gospels* (Grand Rapids, MI: Eerdmans, 2016); **W. Kramer,** *Christ, Lord, Son of God*, SBT 50 (London: SCM Press, 1966); **L. J. Kreitzer,** *Jesus and God in Paul's Eschatology*, JSNTSup 19 (Sheffield: JSOT Press, 1987); **A. T. E. Loke,** *The Origin of Divine Christology*, SNTSMS 169 (Cambridge: Cambridge University Press, 2017); **C. F. D. Moule,** *The Origin of Paul's Christology* (Cambridge: Cambridge University Press, 1977); **C. Newman,** *Paul's Glory Christology: Tradition and Rhetoric*, NovTSup 69 (Leiden: Brill, 1992); **J. T. Sanders,** *The New Testament Christological Hymns: Their Historical Religious Background* (Cambridge: Cambridge University Press, 1971); **C. Tilling,** *Paul's Divine Christology*, WUNT 2/323 (Tubingen: Mohr Siebeck, 2012); **N. T. Wright,** *Paul and the Faithfulness of God*, 2 vols. (Minneapolis: Fortress, 2013).

D. B. Capes

LORD'S SUPPER

Almost the entirety of contemporary knowledge of Paul's understanding of the Lord's Supper or Eucharist is a result of problems in the Corinthian body surrounding *food and meals. Many of the problems surrounding meals in *Corinth were related to issues of social status and divisions between the rich and the poor. Greco-Roman dining practices created a context in which the divisions in the ancient world were uncritically accepted by the Corinthian assemblies and led Paul to offer a corrective to refocus the meal as a place of *love, equity, and unity.

1. Dining and Meals in the Ancient World
2. The Source of the Problem in Corinth
3. The Meal in Corinth and Paul's Response
4. Paul's Knowledge of Other Traditions
5. Conclusion

1. Dining and Meals in the Ancient World.

1.1. The Architecture of Dining in Corinth. Eating is a central part of human life, as it is critical to human existence, and eating with others comes with the territory. Meals were important in the Greco-Roman world and affected both Jews and *Gentiles. Like all things in the ancient world, these were both social and religious events ("Meals," *OCD*, 942). Practically speaking, a dining room in Latin was called a *triclinium*, referring to a three-couch arrangement in a U-shaped pattern ("Dining-Rooms," *OCD*, 469). In this arrangement, a table was placed at the end of one of the couches or in the middle, between all three. Those dining would recline on their left elbow and reach with the other hand for food. Social meals were sometimes referred to as *convivium*, and guests were known as *convivae*. Such meals and arrangements were typical of the upper classes and those who (1) owned a home and (2) had the room for the dining experience. Most people, in contrast, would eat their meals on the street or at one of the outdoor venues known as a *caupona*, *popina*, or *taverna*. Such places offered food for purchase if one could afford it. In the Greco-Roman context, a wealthy benefactor could increase their status by providing a public meal in a city center for a wide variety of friends and guests. They would also dictate the seating arrangements and food offered.

The situation in Corinth is debated. Gerd Thiessen, Jerome Murphy-O'Connor, Bruce Winter, and others have argued that an upper-class home is the best explanation for the context for the Corinthian meals. They have proposed that the villa at Anaploga (discovered in the late 1970s) suggests the sort of setting that would have produced the type of divisions in Corinth. The villa would have allowed for around forty to fifty people to gather at once provided that the atrium was used for overflow. The high-status and wealthy friends of a homeowner such as Stephanas (1 Cor 16:15) would have dined with him in the *triclinium*, while those of lesser status would have resided in the atrium.

Justin Meggitt and David Horrell vigorously disagree with this assessment and argue that the proposals of an atrium and *triclinium* are misplaced in positing the situation that Paul's communities faced in Corinth. They propose a more modest area of Corinth known as East Street, which has smaller one- to two-room homes or workshops, as a more likely model (Horrell, 360-68). Although most people in the first century who were poor resided in tenement apartments and lacked the space and lighting to host an early Christian meal, this was probably less of an issue in Corinth since overpopulation was not as severe as in Rome. However, much of their proposal underdetermines the evidence available at Corinth, and there is no need to pit one view against another. One can easily imagine multiple house *churches in Corinth and a variety of places and spaces for Christian gathering(s). The existing evidence must be taken into consideration.

1.2. Greco-Roman Group Meals. It was not just Pauline communities that gathered to eat together in a religious context. A variety of groups gathered for shared meals in religious settings, since all activity in the ancient world was to some extent religious activity. Groups known as *collegia* or associations included everything from religions (Judaism was considered a *collegia*) to various trade guilds that had deities as their founding patrons. Meals were one of the most consistent activities of these gatherings (see Kloppenborg, 209; Ascough, Harland, and Kloppenborg). These meals were elective in that one chose to be there instead of eating in one's home or on the street (Baumgarten, 97). First Corinthians shows that religious meals were on offer in Corinth, and so much so that a debate arose concerning whether Jesus-followers could partake. The Pauline communities that also gathered for meals participated in a common ancient activity—hence how easily confusion could arise.

1.3. Meals in a Jewish Context. It was not just Greco-Roman *collegia* or *religions that had sacred meals. The Jewish calendar was filled with feast days to commemorate, celebrate, and participate in the communal life of God's people. Judaism was formally categorized as a *collegia* from a Roman perspective and appears to have been organized similarly to Roman associations (Baumgarten, 97-98). Jewish meals had features that were both similar to and distinct from Greco-Roman practices (Smith). Obvious differences included how food defined the community and the exemption from eating certain foods, such as pork and other items (Lev 11:1-47; Deut 14:3-21). The dietary restrictions made table *fellowship with Gentiles difficult and are addressed in both Jewish literature and Greco-Roman authors (see 1 Macc 1:62-63; Tacitus, *Hist.* 5.4-5; Plutarch, *Quaest. conv.* 669-671).

*Purity concerns affected nearly all Jewish groups, even if they did not affect them the same way (Meyers). Not all Jewish groups practiced meals the same way. According to Philo, the Essenes ate only with other members, and their meals were not open to the public due to purity concerns (*Hypoth.* 11.5; Baumgarten, 97-98). Likewise, Diaspora Jews faced different challenges and had varying degrees of assimilation and accommodation (Barclay, 434-37). Some Jewish groups, such as the Therapeutae in Egypt, were distinguished by their practices from the lavish and scandalous Greek *symposia* (Smith). There was also considerable overlap in key behaviors between Greco-Roman banquets and Jewish dining. Conversations surrounding such meals were commonplace, but Jews would focus on philosophical topics, including matters such as the *law or biblical passages related to the festival (such as the exodus at Passover). The setting would also be similar, including a shared full meal, reclining around tables, a master of the ceremony to preside over the dinner, music, and *prayer for a meal (Smith). These practices certainly informed Paul's understanding of the eucharistic meal.

1.4. Meals as Social Contests. Meals also provided an opportunity for status display and acquisition, as dining crossed multiple social strata, since not everyone invited to a meal shared the same social location. A meal hosted by an upper-class person would include a wide range of social statuses: from the host, to high-status patrons, to lower-status clients, and of course to *slaves, who would serve the food. The dynamics of *honor, shame, and status were all at play in the activity of eating together. Several ancient authors comment on the treatment of various persons in the dining experience (Pliny, *Ep.* 2.6; Martial, *Epig.* 4.85). One was sat according to one's status, with the most desired location being near the host or other higher-status patrons. If one's status was not very high, one might be sat farther down or even in another room entirely. Location was not the only way to differentiate status. The best food and wine were served to those further up the social ladder, while those of lower honor were served lesser food and cheaper wine. Securing an invitation (or the lack thereof) to a party could increase one's status in the ancient world. Parallels appear in the Corinthian house churches.

2. The Source of the Problem in Corinth. Scholars generally espouse one of three proposals for how these meals operated in the Corinthian churches: the *patronage model, group model, or some combination of these two models. The patronage model argues that the wealthy elite members of the house churches provided the weekly (or monthly) meals for the members in their homes. Alternatively, the group model asserts that each member brought their own food to eat, either on their own or as a contribution to a larger meal. Finally, some argue for a modified version that combines elements of each. Complicating understanding of the situation is that Paul does not discuss the practical matters of how these meals were funded.

2.1. The Patronage Model. Theissen argues that the problem in Corinth was rooted in wealthy members who brought their private meals and then consumed them early in the service so when other, poorer members arrived later, the food was mostly if not entirely gone. In another version of this position, based on the Roman dining experiences described above, richer members would bring their meals and then allocate lesser-quality foods and portions to lower-status members, thus reinforcing ancient social scripts in terms of status and honor. Paul is therefore critical of these practices as ostentatious displays of *wealth and as reinscribing social boundaries he is seeking to deconstruct. This view is not without its weaknesses, and two main critiques have been put forward.

First, in light of the available data, it does not appear that a patron of a *collegia* would have funded every meal that the patron's group consumed. These were often one-time donations or at most a few meals out of the year. Therefore it should not be assumed that the owner of the house church was responsible for providing or even likely to have provided every meal for the Christian community in their home (Kloppenborg, 210-25). Second, even when meals were doled out according to status, the inequality was not excessive, sometimes just a double or third portion more given to persons of higher status (Kloppenborg, 227-28). However, this idea seems to fail to account then for Paul's assessment that some are "going hungry" and not receiving anything at all (1 Cor 11:21).

Mitigating these criticisms is that the house churches, although very similar to associations, were not identical to them. For example, associations often met in locations such as rooms attached to a temple, outdoor venues, or taverns. They were in public spaces, as they were performative social contests. With few exceptions, Paul's communities met in homes, not public spaces. It was the home that provided a new social challenge, as homes had homeowners. Would the role of a homeowner have differed from that of a public benefactor to a *collegia*? Were there more or fewer responsibilities for the provision of food? Others have argued that the home setting of a meal crossed several social boundaries as well but also might have included persons of higher status than the homeowner (Oakes). If homeowners did have more responsibility for the provision of food, then perhaps a scalable offering of food based on status would have helped alleviate some of the homeowner's costs around the meal.

Not all are persuaded by this model, as it seems unsustainable for one person to have provided a year's worth of meals to a small community. Other models (see below) have thus evolved to take the strengths of the patron/benefactor model and offset its weaknesses.

2.2. The Group Model. In this envisioning of the early Christian meal, each member coming to the gathering would bring food with them and either eat by themselves or contribute to a larger communal meal—something akin to a potluck. If there were a potluck, this might explain why issues surrounding food became so controversial (see Gal 2:11-14; Rom 14:1-23; 1 Cor 10:23-33). The wealthy would have brought more food and perhaps more extravagant food, while the poorer members of the community might not have had anything to bring at all. Hence Paul's critique is that some are overindulgent on various items such as wine (1 Cor 11:21). These group meals could have consisted of the contribution of actual food or of resources to purchase food (Kloppenborg, 228). Once the food was acquired, then it was handed out based on status, and again one sees the problem at work in the community.

Complicating this approach is that John Kloppenborg argues that associations often sought to mitigate this problem by having rules for apportionments, and more importantly "no other associations of the early Roman period are known to have engaged in the . . . practice" (230). A similar concern as with the patronage model plagues this interpretive option as well. The association bylaws that Kloppenborg mentions may have had no basis in a house-church community that was not identical to a *collegia*.

2.3. The Patronage-Group Model. Given the weaknesses of both the patronage and group models, some have sought to combine them creatively. Thus it has been proposed that the Pauline communities shared the responsibility to provide the meal by means of several of high-status persons as well as member contributions—thus addressing the concern of the lone benefactor in the patronage model. In other associations, meals were provided through a combination of leaders within the communities and member contributions. A financial tithe in a house community may have been different from a member-initiation fee or association dues in Greco-Roman associations.

Kloppenborg rightly notes that there is no extant evidence from Paul's letters of *how* the communities funded the meals of their gatherings, but given the extant evidence from Greco-Roman associations it would have been anomalous to have had either a purely benefaction model or exclusively member contributions (Kloppenborg, 235). Given the nature of Paul's ad hoc documents, one should not expect to find such detail on how the meals were secured. Such practical concerns remain out of view of his correspondences even while the practice of meals is documented within the *letters. Out of this evidence, then, it seems most likely that the Pauline communities practiced some modified form of donations and contributions to secure their meals.

3. The Meal in Corinth and Paul's Response. In 1 Corinthians 11:18, Paul refers to oral reports (as in 1 Cor 1:10–4:21 and 1 Cor 5:1-13) about divisions around the assembling of the Corinthian house churches and especially the Lord's Supper (1 Cor 11:20). This is the third reference to a schismatic issue within the Corinthian body (1 Cor 1:10; 12:25). Censure of the practices in Corinth is clear, especially when one notes that in the same chapter Paul commends them for maintaining *traditions (compare 1 Cor 11:2 and 1 Cor 11:17, 22). Although much of 1 Corinthians 7–11 is based on questions from the Corinthians to Paul, he interrupts this section with this report. The following three-part structure is helpful to see Paul's rhetorical argument at work.

3.1. Report and Diagnosis of the Problem (1 Cor 11:18-22). Paul diagnoses the problem with a description of the oral report. The main problem revolves around eating and drinking, with terms related to eating and drinking referenced seven times in five verses: eating (1 Cor 11:20, 21, 22), drinking (1 Cor 11:22), supper (1 Cor 11:21), hungry (1 Cor 11:21), drunk (1 Cor 11:21). Paul focuses on their "assembling together" and the "meal" they undertake. His initial assessment is negative, that these meals do more harm than good, and although his information is coming from a report, he is inclined to believe it (1 Cor 11:17-18). The meal has devolved from what should have been the Lord's meal to something entirely different. Hence Paul's indictment, "It is not the Lord's supper you eat."

Debate arises over the verb *prolambanō* in verse 21 and whether it means "goes ahead with" or is an intensive form of *lambanō*, which can mean "devour" or "consume." At issue is whether the problem in Corinth is that the rich are eating ahead of the poor or that the style of eating is greedy or selfish. The first view (temporal) is predicated on an assumption that the poor are arriving late and thus all the food is gone. Such a view is misleading, as there is no reason to suppose it is the poor who were arriving late rather than the rich. Modern presuppositions about workdays inhibit a more complex view of the ancient world (Kloppenborg, 239-42). Following others, it is *how* the Corinthians are eating, not the timing, that is the problem (although timing is not entirely ruled out; see Thiselton, 863). Thus Paul critiques the practices that constitute the manner of eating.

Devouring or selfishly consuming meals (1 Cor 11:21) when some in the community have nothing to eat is what provokes Paul's shock and anger. Such habits have turned the Lord's meal from communal participation in *salvation with thanksgiving into an individual encounter for selfish consumption. The Lord's meal has been inverted in the Corinthian context. The effects of this disastrous eating shame those who do not have enough and show contempt for God's church (1 Cor 11:22). Shame (*kataischynō*) is an important term in 1 Corinthians as it is directly linked to God's activity in Christ (the same term is used in 1 Cor 1:27) and the choosing of the Corinthians (1 Cor 1:26-28), and thus the shaming done in 1 Corinthians 11:22 reveals a world shaped not by the *cross but by Roman honor and power. These decisions stand in direct contrast to the activity of *God in 1 Corinthians.

At the center of the problem is the nature and purpose of the Lord's Supper, namely, to incorporate in participation all who have benefited from Christ's life, *death, and *resurrection. The Corinthians, by their exclusive dining, have subversively transformed the Lord's meal into their own private experience, contra Paul's stress of unity in 1 Corinthians 10:16-17. Paul repeats that this is not something he can express approval of but rather must censure. The Lord's Supper ought to invite participation in subverting the ancient practice of *household-based power by reordering the social relations in the community (Batron, 239). What has unfolded in Corinth is a meal of self-satisfaction rather than self-giving for the sake of others.

3.2. Remembrance of the Gospel Meal (1 Cor 11:23-26). Paul appeals to the Corinthians in light of a pre-Pauline tradition they presumably know that began with Jesus and was "handed on" to Paul and subsequently to them (1 Cor 11:23). This is the earliest account of the liturgy around the Lord's Supper, and it is rooted in tradition that is inaccessible today (Fitzmyer, 429). Paul's account is similar to the accounts found in the Synoptic Gospels (Mk 14:22-24; Mt 26:26-28; Lk 22:17-20; see below) as he rehearses the episode of that last fateful night of Jesus.

Opinions diverge on whether Jesus was "handed over" or "betrayed" with the translation of *paradidomai.* At debate is whether Paul is referring to (1) the handing over of Jesus to death by God or (2) the betrayal of Judas. Richard Hays convincingly argues that the term *paradidomai* is at once a play on words from the "handing on of the tradition" in the first half of 1 Corinthians 11:23 and an allusion to Isaiah 53:6 (LXX), where "the Lord *gave him up for our sins*" (Hays, 198). The tradition was handed on that Jesus was handed over. Paul's terminology specifically envisages a delivering up unto his death that was for the reconciliation of God and humanity as well as Jesus' self-renunciation of his status and privilege for the sake of others. Paul's use of this "handing over" language, then, is directly related to the problem in Corinth and why the meal should not just proclaim a general sense of Jesus' death but a specific type or manner of death that is an antidote to the Corinthians' posture.

In 1 Corinthians 11:24, Paul reminds the Corinthians that on his last night with his disciples, Jesus took the bread and cup and "blessed" them or gave thanks for them. From the plural participle *eucharistēsas* (having given praise or blessing) comes the word *Eucharist.* This thanksgiving is communal, and this is again at odds with the Corinthians' current eating practices. The singular bread and cup also communicate the sense of unity currently lacking in the Corinthian context (see also 1 Cor 10:16-17). Similarly, the notion of the bread as Jesus' *body being broken signals the sacrificial and self-giving elements of the meal, which Paul intends the Corinthians to emulate.

Likewise, the twice-repeated "in remembrance of me" (1 Cor 11:24-25) is also related to the nature of Jesus' death, which is "for you," raising the other-centered approach of the meal. Remembrance (*anamnēsis*) in this sense is not just memory but active, obedient participation in the living out the cruciform story of Jesus. By remembering this together, the Corinthians form a new *identity together around this sacred meal. Such a remembrance brings together the past event of the meal, the present practice of it, and the future consummation it entails, thus transforming these ordinary elements of foodstuffs and the setting of the meal into something more than memory. This eating is more than a historic memorial or consumption of food; for Paul, it is an eschatological proclamation of the cruciform *gospel (1 Cor 11:26) that shapes all reality, both now and in the future.

*3.3. **Reevaluating the Corinthian Meal (1 Cor 11:27-34).*** Having reframed the Lord's meal around communal and sacrificial sharing, Paul offers a new, stark reminder of the importance of this meal in 1 Corinthians 11:27-32. Paul contrasts the previous, unexamined meal with the examined partaking of the Lord's bread and cup. This eating is consequential. Paul elevates the meal: not only are the bread and cup "of the Lord," but also it is the *Lord to whom the Corinthians will be answerable. An unworthy partaking of the meal affirms that one's outlook and activity are not conforming to the reality of the meal in both redemptive and social terms (Thiselton, 891). For Paul, one cannot take the body of Christ without taking stock of the treatment of Christ's body, the church. Self-examination or genuineness in this context is the conformity of one's life and conduct to the selflessness of Jesus in redemption. Hays shows that in light of Paul's use of *judgment language elsewhere in 1 Corinthians (1 Cor 6:5; 14:29) this is not an individualized self-assessment but a call to communal discernment (Hays, 202). Examination or judging is key to the section, although this is muddied in English translations. Paul employs various forms of the verb *krinō* throughout the passage: *krima*, "judgment," and *mē diakrinōn*, "not acknowledging" (1 Cor 11:29); *diekrinomen*, "we were to evaluate," and *ekrinometha*, "we would be subject to judgment" (1 Cor 11:31); *krinomenoi*, "being judged," and *katakrithōmen*, "we may be condemned" (1 Cor 11:32); and *eis krima*, "to judgment" (1 Cor 11:34; Fitzmyer, 446-47).

Debate surrounds the meaning of the phrase "discerning the body" and its referent in 1 Corinthians 11:29. Is it the body of Christ in the form of the bread, or the communal body, that is, the Corinthian assembly? Anthony Thiselton offers an excellent summary of the views (Thiselton, 891-94). Since Augustine, some have interpreted this as a reference to discerning the sacred bread from other, ordinary bread. More recent interpretations focus on the body as the social community as the body of the Lord. This interpretive tradition appeals to Paul's reference to bread in 1 Corinthians 10:17 and the "one loaf" theme. Rather than holding these options in an antithesis, it is best to see them as mutually interpretive of each other. The ambiguity of Paul in the word *body* accomplishes several rhetorical purposes. As the term *body* is reflexive in this context, when the Corinthians participate in the meal as a body, they reflect on Christ's body, so that they may image the body of Christ toward one another.

Any misgivings the Corinthians may have had about their conduct in 1 Corinthians 11:17-22 are now recast in the starkest theological terms (1 Cor 11:29-30). Paul's warning is to not minimize the "sacral power of the Eucharist" (Mitchell, 265). Such power is

Table 1. Comparison of Lord's Supper Passages

1 Cor 11:23-25 NRSV	Mk 14:22-25 NRSV	Mt 26:26-29 NRSV	Lk 22:15-21 NRSV
For I received from the Lord what I also handed on to you, that the Lord Jesus on the night when he was betrayed **took a loaf of bread, and when he had given thanks, he broke it and said, "This is my body *that is for you. Do this in remembrance of me.*"** In the same way **he took the cup** also, **after supper, saying, "This cup is the *new* covenant in my blood. *Do this*,** as often as you drink it, ***in remembrance of me.*"**	While they were eating, **he took a loaf of bread, and after blessing it he broke it, gave it to them, and said, "Take; this is my body."** Then **he took a cup,** and after giving thanks he gave it to them, and all of them drank from it. He said to them, **"This is my blood of the covenant,** *which is poured out for many.* Truly I tell you, I will never again drink of the fruit of the vine until that day when I drink it new in the kingdom of God."	While they were eating, Jesus **took a loaf of bread, and after blessing it he broke it,** gave it to the disciples, and said, **"Take,** eat; **this is my body."** Then **he took a cup,** and after giving thanks he gave it to them, saying, "Drink from it, all of you, for **this is my blood of the covenant,** *which is poured out for* many for the forgiveness of sins. I tell you, I will never again drink of this fruit of the vine until that day when I drink it new with you in my Father's kingdom."	He said to them, "I have eagerly desired to eat this Passover with you before I suffer, for I tell you, I will not eat it until it is fulfilled in the kingdom of God." Then he took a cup, and after giving thanks he said, "Take this and divide it among yourselves, for I tell you that from now on I will not drink of the fruit of the vine until the kingdom of God comes." Then he **took a loaf of bread, and when he had given thanks he broke it and gave it to them, saying, "This is my body, *which is given for you. Do this in remembrance of me.*"** And he did the same with **the cup after supper, saying, "This cup** *that is poured out for you* **is the *new* covenant in my blood."**

communicated through the eschatological judgment that permeates the section. Since *eschatology dominated the earlier section on the sacrament (1 Cor 11:26), it should not be surprising to see it resurface in a judgment theme in 1 Corinthians 11:29-32 (Moule).

After delineating the consequential meal, Paul sets the scene for how to eat rightly in light of the Lord. Linking the beginning and end of the section is Paul's use of "come together" (*synerchomai*) in 1 Corinthians 11:17, 33. Now when they come together, they should wait for one another. To "wait" (*ekdechomai*) solves the practical issue specified earlier wherein patience was not exercised, resulting in some going hungry (1 Cor 11:21). Paul only uses the term *wait* one other place in his letters (1 Cor 16:11), but in the LXX and papyri literature, this term conveys the sense of hospitality or receiving one another (Winter, 151). In some sense, this command of Paul is close to his appeal to the divided community in Rome, where he encourages them to "welcome one another" (Rom 15:7).

That those who are hungry in 1 Corinthians 11:34 are not the same group as the hungry mentioned in 1 Corinthians 11:21 is evidenced from the logic of the entire section, though not as clear in a surface reading. The group criticized in 1 Corinthians 11:21-22 was also driven by hunger when they devoured their food before others, resulting in those without resources remaining hungry. The higher-status group resurfaces here at the end of Paul's instructions, where they are instructed to eat at home if they are hungry so that when they come for the meal they will not go ahead before others to devour their food. Rather, with their stomachs filled, they will be able to share communally and avoid condemnation from the Lord (1 Cor 11:34). To equate the hungry in 1 Corinthians 11:34 with the hungry in 1 Corinthians 11:21 would certainly be a callous move by Paul and contradict (in literary ways) not only his concern not to humiliate those who have nothing but also his theology of the Lord's Table as communal sharing (1 Cor 10:16-17).

4. Paul's Knowledge of Other Traditions.

Amid the problems surrounding the Corinthian meal and celebration of the Lord's Supper, Paul reminds the Corinthians of a tradition that he has received that he is authoritatively passing on to them (1 Cor 11:23). The question is, To what tradition(s) does Paul refer, and where do they come from? At the end of Jesus' life, he shares a Passover meal with his disciples and uses this as an opportunity to discuss his impending death. As a Passover meal, bread and wine constituted part of the celebration. Jesus transforms these elements to speak of his body and his blood. As one reads the Synoptic accounts and compares them with 1 Corinthians 11, the similarities emerge easily. The question arises as to the historical relationship between these traditions.

Complicating the issue is Paul's phrase "I received from the Lord" and whether this Lord's Supper tradition is a direct revelation from Christ to Paul. Few argue that this is a tradition mediated by a revelatory *vision from *Christ to Paul (Watson). Scholars are nearly unanimous that Paul has some form of either an oral or a written Jesus tradition (Dunn, 599-623). Viewing the entire scenario as the creation of the early church and completely devoid of any historical elements is not a viable option. A comparison of the Corinthians passage with the relevant pericopes in the Synoptics (see table 1) shows the degree of similarity and difference.

Paul's construction is neither entirely similar to nor entirely different from the Synoptics. At issue is which tradition is oldest, Paul or Mark. It is clear, however, that Paul shares the most unique similarities with Luke's account. The most striking are the phrases "do this in remembrance of me" (1 Cor 11:24, 25; Lk 22:19) and the addition of the word *new* to the *covenant language (1 Cor 11:25; Lk 22:20). Differences appear as well with Jesus' words concerning the bread; Mark and Matthew have Jesus "blessing" the bread (*eulogēsas* in Mk 14:22; Mt 26:26), and both Paul and Luke have Jesus "giving thanks" for the bread (*eucharistēsas* in 1 Cor 11:24; Lk 22:19). Though the terms are not entirely unrelated, much should not be made of this difference, as Mark uses *eucharistēsas* in Mark 14:23 for the cup. What is common to both traditions is that Jesus consecrates the bread. Unique to Paul is both what is present and absent in his handing over of the tradition. The twelve are noticeably absent in Paul's account, as is the Passover setting of the Synoptics. Likewise, Paul has introduced the liturgical elements to the passage in the words "as often as you drink it" (1 Cor 11:25), indicating the regular and habitual celebration of the meal in the early Christian gatherings.

5. Conclusion.

The problematic situation in Corinth allows Paul to clarify the nature and purpose of the Lord's Supper and reveal a robust *Christology, ecclesiology, and eschatology. All three are intertwined in Paul's exposition and explanation of the eucharistic meal. This celebration was a meal meant to unite the community around their common connection and participation in the life of Christ. The meal was transformative of the social relationships and a proclamation of the rule and reign of Christ as the Corinthians awaited his return.

See also Body of Christ; Corinthians, First Letter to the; Fellowship, Communion, Sharing; Food Laws and Customs, Jewish and Roman; Honor/Shame; Judgment; Love; Patronage; Tradition; Wealth and Poverty.

BIBLIOGRAPHY. **R. S. Ascough, P. A. Harland, and J. S. Kloppenborg,** eds., *Associations in the Greco-Roman World: A Sourcebook* (Waco, TX: Baylor University Press, 2012); **J. M. G. Barclay,** *Jews in the Mediterranean Diaspora: From Alexander to Trajan (323 BCE–117 CE)* (Berkeley: University of California Press, 1996); **S. C. Batron,** "Paul's Sense of Place: An Anthropological Approach to Community Formation in Corinth," *NTS* 32 (1986): 225-46; **A. Baumgarten,** "Graeco-Roman Voluntary Associations and Ancient Jewish Sects," in *Jews in a Graceo-Roman World*, ed. M. Goodman (New York: Oxford University Press, 1998), 93-112; **J. D. G. Dunn,** *The Theology of the Apostle Paul* (Grand Rapids, MI: Eerdmans, 1998); **J. A. Fitzmyer,** *1 Corinthians* (New Haven, CT: Yale University Press, 2008); **R. B. Hays,** *1 Corinthians* (Louisville, KY: Westminster John Knox, 1997); **D. G. Horrell,** "Domestic Space and Christian Meetings at Corinth: Imagining New Contexts and the Buildings East of the Theatre," *NTS* 50 (2004): 349-69; **J. Jeremias,** *The Eucharistic Words of Jesus* (New York: Scribner, 1966); **J. S. Kloppenborg,** *Christ's Associations: Connecting and Belonging in the Ancient City* (New Haven, CT: Yale University Press, 2019); **J. J. Meggitt,** *Paul, Poverty and Survival* (Edinburgh: T&T Clark, 2000); **E. M. Meyers,** "Purity Concerns and Common Judaism in Light of Archaeology," in *The Pharisees*, ed. J. Sievers and A.-J. Levine (Grand Rapids, MI: Eerdmans, 2021), 43; **M. M. Mitchell,** *Paul and the Rhetoric of Reconciliation* (Louisville, KY: Westminster John Knox, 1992); **C. F. D. Moule,** "The Judgment Theme in the Sacraments," in *The Background of the New Testament and Its Eschatology: Studies in Honour of C. H. Dodd*, ed. W. D. Davies and D. Daube (Cambridge: Cambridge University Press, 1956), 464-81; **J. Murphy-O'Connor,** *St. Paul's Corinth: Texts and Archaeology* (Collegeville, MN: Liturgical Press, 2002); **P. Oakes,** *Empire, Economics, and the New Testament* (Grand Rapids, MI: Eerdmans, 2020); **D. E. Smith,** "Meals," in *The Eerdmans Dictionary of Early Judaism*, ed. J. J. Collins and D. C. Harlow (Grand Rapids, MI: Eerdmans, 2010), 925; **G. Theissen,** *The Social Setting of Pauline Christianity: Essays on Corinth* (Philadelphia: Fortress, 1982); **A. C. Thiselton,** *The First Epistle to the Corinthians* (Grand Rapids, MI: Eerdmans, 2000); **F. Watson,** "'I Received from the Lord . . .': Paul, Jesus, and the Last Supper," in *Jesus and Paul Reconnected: Fresh Pathways into an Old Debate*, ed. T. D. Still (Grand Rapids, MI: Eerdmans, 2007), 103-24; **B. Winter,** *After Paul Left Corinth: The Influence of Secular Ethics and Social Change* (Grand Rapids, MI: Eerdmans, 2001).

J. A. Myers

LOVE

While it is an overstatement to say that love encapsulates the core of NT *ethics, a good case can be made that it does so for those of Paul. The significance of love in Paul is evidenced in its integral role within his soteriology, pneumatology, ecclesiology, and *eschatology. It appears that the apostle's prior conception of divine love is revolutionized in light of the sacrificial death of Israel's Messiah. *Cruciform love gives shape to the entirety of the Christian life. The Spirit of unity empowers believers to love one another, and the *apostle prioritizes love as critical to the integrity of the first Christian communities. Paul's focus on moral transformation is framed within his inaugurated eschatology—love in the present is a foretaste of a perfected future (1 Cor 13).

1. Terminology and Meaning.

The frequent use of the noun *agapē* (love, 75×), verb *agapaō* (to love, 34×), and adjective *agapētos* (beloved, 27×) across the Pauline corpus indicates the importance of the concept. This total of 136 occurrences of love language comprises 42.5 percent of the 320 uses in the NT as a whole (Morris). While statistics are a blunt tool by which to evaluate the significance of an idea, in this case they point to how pivotal love is within Paul's life and thought. Of note is how the use of *agapē* in Paul and elsewhere is always constructive; it is a word intimately connected with the goodness of *God—his love for others, believers' love for him, and their love for one another within a community formed and inhabited by God's Spirit. Love therefore is parallel to concepts such as *faith, *righteousness, and *grace, as all having a single point of origin in God alone (Silva). This is not to say that Paul understands love to be the sole property of Christian communities. Love was a familiar and important concept in both Greek and Jewish thought, and Paul's theology of love fits within recognizable parameters of both, particularly the latter (see section 3 below). However, it is to say that love in Paul takes a unique form.

The other Greek word for love in Paul, used much less frequently, is *phileō* (to love, 2×) and its numerous cognates. R. Mohrlang lists them: *aphilargyros* (no lover of money, 1×), *philagathos* (lover of good, 1×), *philadelphia* (brotherly or familial love, 2×), *philandros* (lover of one's husband, 1×), *philanthrōpia* (love for people, 1×), *philēma* (kiss, 4×), *philotheos* (lover of God, 1×), *philoxenia* (*hospitality, 1×), *philoxenos* (hospitable person, 2×), *philostorgos* (devoted, 1×), and *philoteknos* (lover of children, 1×). *Phileō* is never used to refer to divine love or human love for God. The one appearance of *philotheos* in 2 Timothy 3:4 is a negative comparison with *philedonos* (lover of pleasure).

Other Greek words for love such as *storgē* (affection) and *erōs* (passion) do not appear in Paul, or other NT authors, at all. Care is needed not to make arguments from silence. For example, A. Nygren's extremely influential 1930 work *Agape and Eros: The Christian Idea of Love* drew a sharp contrast between *agapē* and *erōs*, the latter being viewed in very negative terms. The remarkable dominance of *agapē* in Paul, and the rest of the NT, neither necessarily entails a negative attitude toward *storgē* or *eros* nor is conclusive evidence that *agapē* was understood as a higher form of love than *philia*. Nevertheless, the prominence of *agapē* and its cognates raises the question of why this word became virtually the apostle's default choice when talking about love.

The verb *agapaō*, which appears regularly in classic Greek literature, has a flexible range of usage, not dissimilar to the way *love* is used within contemporary English. It can mean to value particular things highly or to behave toward or view certain people with affection. Occasionally it refers to *sexual love, and sometimes it denotes the love of a god for a specific individual (Silva). In contrast, *agapē* is a late development, appearing for the first time in the LXX and only once outside the Bible (Brown).

In the LXX, *agapaō* becomes the translators' primary choice for rendering multiple Hebrew words for love. The verb appears about 250 times, most often representing *ʾāhab*, the central Hebrew word for "love" (ca. 170×). In contrast, *phileō* occurs much less frequently (ca. 30×), usually for *friendship love, and translates *ʾāhab* only ten times. The reasons for *agapaō* becoming the default word for love in LXX are debated, but its prominence is likely a factor behind the emergence of the noun *agapē* within LXX. The latter is still relatively marginal considering the central place it would take in the NT. It occurs eighteen times, none of which refer to God's love, the majority appearing in the Song of Songs (10×), denoting sexual love.

This brings us back to why *agapē* became Paul's (and the other NT authors') default word for love. While it cannot be proven, and therefore caution is required, it may be that Paul's reconfigured understanding of love led to the use of an effectively new term with which he was familiar from the LXX—*agapē*. In this account, perhaps Paul and first Christians deliberately chose a new noun, obviously associated with *agapaō* but relatively free to be filled with specific meaning: a love seen in elective love of God for Jews and *Gentiles, particularly in the death of Jesus; in believers' response of love to God's prior love; and in communities called to love one another as they had been loved by God.

2. Background Influences.

Beyond the OT and LXX, it is uncertain what influence contemporary understandings of love had on Paul's own innovations concerning love. Certainly he exemplifies a very different theology from that of *Qumran sectarianism: "love everyone whom God elects, hate everyone he hates" (1QS 1, 3-4, quoted in Silva, 106). Nor do Hellenistic and rabbinic Judaism offer a likely source of theological novelty. Love had become the central motif for understanding God's relationship with his people, but, despite some influence from Greek and ancient Near Eastern mysticism, it retained core OT themes such as God's unbreakable *covenant love, the Torah as his supreme gift to this people, love for God displayed in obedience to his commands, and loving one's neighbor as the pinnacle of Jewish piety (Silva).

Some have argued that Paul was indebted to Stoic *philosophy and its focus on moral enlightenment, virtue, *wisdom, and self-control, among other themes (Engberg-Pedersen 2000). There are parallels, including the apostle's teaching on love, goodness, and virtue in texts such as Philippians 4:8 and Romans 12:9-21, and the apostle can sound Stoic in his willingness to endure *suffering and hardship (Bird 2019). However, while Paul was at home within *Hellenism and engages in high-level philosophical argument and *rhetoric worthy of a Greek intellectual, he does so out of a profoundly different perspective from Stoicism (Rowe). Love is located within a messianic narrative in which believers are conformed to *Christ in and through the transformative presence of the Spirit.

The extent to which Paul was influenced directly by the teaching of Jesus is debated. J. D. G. Dunn (1993) suggests that Paul's summary of the *law in terms of neighbor love (Gal 5:14; see Rom 13:8-10) and bearing of each other's burdens (Gal 6:2) might derive from Jesus' interpretation of the law. Yet Paul neither makes any reference to Jesus' teaching nor ever connects love of God with love of neighbor. In addition, given deep-rooted continuity between Paul and Jewish conceptions of love (see below), it is impossible to trace with any certainty Paul's linkage of love and fulfillment of the law specifically with the teaching of Jesus.

3. Continuity and Discontinuity.

While multifaceted, three great love themes run through the Hebrew Scriptures: the elective, saving love of Yahweh for his chosen people; Israel's response to God's redemptive action; and a horizontal dimension—how love is to characterize the life of *Israel. Of the three, elective love towers over the other two. Within the OT, there is a chasm between divine and human love. In contrast to Greek thought, humans can never ascend to God to some form of mystical union with the gods: instead, the only way humans can know and experience God is in humble response to his prior revelation.

Unsurprisingly Paul's theology of love stands squarely in continuity with each of these three categories. However, if Paul maintains fidelity to established Jewish conceptions of love, he does so with considerable creativity. The question of just how radical is the apostle's discontinuity with Judaism ties in to wider debates concerning "old" and "new" perspectives on Paul and *apocalyptic and narrative interpretations of Paul. A helpful way to view this development is to see Paul as an "anomalous Jew" (Barclay; Bird), navigating a complex path between Jewish identity, beliefs, and praxis and the radical impact of God's *apokalypsis* (revelation) of his Messiah, Jesus. In regard to love, this *christological anomaly leads to a radical new social praxis (Thompson).

3.1. God's Elective and Saving Love. If divine love in Paul remains elective and gracious, it is reframed in light of Jesus Christ. Two examples illustrate this transfiguration.

3.1.1. Election. Second Thessalonians 2:13 combines believers being loved by the *Lord and chosen (*haireō*, to choose) by God for *salvation. In two places in Romans the "*called" (*kletoi*, chosen) are also described as loved (Rom 1:7; 8:28). While Romans 9–11 is a notoriously complex argument, J. R. Wagner makes a case that a hermeneutical key to the mind of Paul is the utter reliability of the love of God for Israel, despite its rejection of the *gospel (Rom 9:1-5). Paul frequently uses the adjective *agapētos* in an elective sense of being chosen. An example is Romans 11:28-29, where, talking primarily to Gentile believers about ethnic Israel's resistance to the gospel, the apostle links elective themes with God's unbreakable love. Significantly, the beloved *elect now constitute all who love God (Rom 8:28), including Gentiles, a claim made explicit in the striking intertextuality of Romans 9:25-26 with Hosea. Formerly "not my people," God has now made known "the riches of his *glory" (Rom 9:23 NRSV) in enabling them to become beloved "children of the living God" (Rom 9:26 NRSV). In Ephesians God chooses believers (*eklegō*, to select) before the *creation of the world to be his *holy people and in love predestines them for *adoption to sonship (Eph 1:4-5).

3.1.2. The Cross. Unconditioned divine love is the motive for the *cross, which liberates believers from a destructive cycle of *sin, *wrath, and *judgment. However the "I" of Galatians 2:20 is interpreted, it is clear that the self-giving death of Christ is an act of sacrificial salvific love. In Romans 5:6-11 recipients of God's saving love are "weak," "ungodly," "sinners," "enemies" who face his wrath (NRSV). But due to God's grace (Rom 5:2), through justifying faith, believers now have "*peace with God through our Lord Jesus Christ" (Rom 5:1 NRSV). The result is reconciliation through the death of Christ (Rom 5:10-11). The cross for Paul is therefore the supreme demonstration of God's love (Rom 5:8). Parallel themes of sinners being "dead," under the power of the *flesh, and facing wrath appear in Ephesians 2:1-3 with an added *cosmology, being under the influence of the world (*kosmos*) and the "ruler of the power of the air" (NRSV). Again, divine love is salvific; it is out of his "great love," "*mercy," and "grace" that believers are made alive and are raised up with him within a new eschatological existence "in Christ Jesus" (Eph 2:4-7).

3.2. Human Response to God's Love. If divine love in the OT is unconditioned, it is not unconditional. Since Yahweh is the one, true, and all-powerful God who graciously loves, the appropriate response within the covenant community is humility, reverent obedience, and heartfelt *worship. Love in this holistic sense is about faithfulness and practical obedience. The opposite of love so understood is not hate but *idolatry—allegiance to something or someone other than God. Such themes continue in Paul but are comprehensively reshaped in light of the Christ event.

3.2.1. Obedient Love. The OT emphasis on faithful obedience perhaps sheds light on the intriguing fact that the apostle rarely, if ever, exhorts believers to love God. The great first commandment is nowhere cited (the second great commandment is referenced twice; Rom 13:9; Gal 5:14), and most texts within the Pauline corpus that talk of love for God tend to assume its existence rather than specifically encourage its practice (Rom 8:28; 1 Cor 2:9; 8:3; 16:22; Eph 6:24; 2 Tim 3:4). A possible exception is 2 Thessalonians 3:5, but its meaning is ambiguous. Rather, Paul's pastoral concern is that a deep experience of divine love will lead to a life of obedience to Christ characterized by love for others, particularly within the covenant community (see 3.3 below). This is a theme of particular importance in Romans: Paul understands his apostolic mission in terms of bringing about the "obedience of faith" among the Gentiles (Rom 1:5; 6:16; 15:18; 16:19, 26 NRSV). Misdirected love of money as a form of idolatry leading to disobedience is later developed in the Pastoral Epistles (1 Tim 6:9-10).

The close relationship between love and obedience sheds light on how, while the Torah is uncompromisingly rejected by Paul as a means of salvation for Jews or Gentiles, it continues to play a major role in framing his moral and ethical vision of new-creation life (Rosner). Love lies at the heart of how the Torah applies to the social life of Paul's churches. In Galatians 5:6, "the only thing that counts is faith working through love" (NRSV). *Freedom in Christ leads to a paradoxical imperative: "through love become *slaves to one another" (Gal 5:13 NRSV). Leviticus 19:18 is reapplied in Romans 13:8-10 and Galatians 5:14: love of neighbor, not Torah obedience, fulfills the law. Bearing one another's burdens fulfills the *law of Christ (Gal 6:2). In effect, the law finds its true purpose in relationships of self-giving love within a community of believers who are being transformed by the Spirit according to the character of their Lord.

3.2.2. Experience of God's Love. God's people are loved by God (1 Thess 1:4; 2 Thess 2:13, 16; Rom 1:7; 2 Cor 13:11, 14; Eph 1:4-5; 2:4; 3:17-19; 5:1-2; 6:23; Col 3:12), a fact for Paul that has profound experiential implications. The motive or impulse for obedient love is personal experience of God's elective love in Jesus Christ. By grace believers are brought into the sphere of God's love, an experience that leads to joyful response. In Romans 5 all believers experience God's love being poured into their hearts (the seat of *identity) through the Spirit (Rom 5:5, taking love here as referring to God's love for us rather than our love for God, contra Wright). In relation to the theme of boasting in Romans, believers have nothing to boast about except their shared experience of the love of God conveyed by the gift of the Spirit (Jewett). The "us" and "our" language employed by Paul is suggestive; it is likely he is speaking autobiographically.

Such is the depth and irrevocable nature of God's elective love that later in Romans (Rom 8:35-39) Paul can ask rhetorically whether any difficulty, opposition, death itself, or nonhuman power can separate believers "from the love of God in Christ Jesus our Lord" (Rom 8:39 NRSV; see 1 Cor 15:57-58). Of note here, and elsewhere in Paul, is that there is no innate conflict between suffering, persecution, hardship, and even martyrdom and being loved by God. There are parallels to OT Wisdom literature here in the immeasurable disparity between divine and human love (e.g., Job 2:10). Paul neither attempts to answer the question "Why suffering?" nor promises any *quid pro quo* rewards for loving God. Rather, love for God means trusting in him in the face of whatever affliction comes the believer's way while awaiting a future eternal glory (2 Cor 4:17).

Such is the importance of love for the Christian life that Paul prays that believers under his care will continue to know the love of God in their communal life together (2 Cor 13:11, 14). Love is of particular importance in Ephesians (Heil; Hoehner), with *agapaō* and *agapē* both appearing ten times, the latter six times within the construction *en agapē,* which occurs at key points of the letter (see 3.3.3 below). The apostle's prayer to the Father that he may strengthen all believers, through his Spirit, to grasp "the breadth and length and height and depth" of the love of Christ (Eph 3:18 NRSV) illustrates Pauline christological innovation. Experience of messianic love leads to being filled with all the *fullness of God (Eph 3:19). These sorts of integral connections between Father, Spirit, and Messiah represent significant theological development in how God's love is understood.

3.2.3. Love, Faith, the Spirit, and Union with Christ. Love for Paul is never simply a natural human virtue. The gospel calls for a response of faith, which results in believers being joined together "*in Christ." Within Paul's inaugurated eschatological framework, those in Christ belong to God's new creation (Gal 6:14-15; 2 Cor 5:14, 17), are *baptized into Christ's death and *resurrection, and enjoy new life in the Spirit. It is the Spirit through whom God's love is poured out into believers' hearts (Rom 5:5) and through whom God is known (1 Cor 8:3; Eph 3:19). Indeed, faith and love are often mentioned alongside each other (Eph 6:23; 1 Thess 1:3; 3:6; 5:8; 1 Tim 1:14). The primary evidence of the empowering presence of the Spirit is love (Gal 5:6, 13).

How exactly experience of divine love transforms believers to love one another is not spelled out by the apostle, and an area of recent interest in Pauline studies is exploring implicit contours of Paul's thought around moral transformation, particularly its relationship to union in Christ. M. J. Gorman lists examples: participation, incorporation, identification, (mutual) indwelling, and even (Christ-)mysticism. Some scholars have examined the dynamics of transformation in more detail. Examples include V. Rabens, on the relational and transformative work of the Spirit; C. S. Keener (2016) on Paul and the transformation of the mind; S. Harding on Paul's eschatological *anthropology and the dynamics of human transformation; J. P. Sampley on the shaping force of Paul's christological narrative theology in guiding believers as they walk in love with God, with Christ, and with one another; and S. G. Eastman on Paul's participatory anthropology. A sustained treatment of the role of love in moral transformation is D. A. Campbell's *Pauline Dogmatics: The Triumph of God's Love*, which devotes five chapters to love within the theme of formation. For Campbell, "agapeism" (that love explains everything important about Pauline ethics) is evident in Paul and derives from his understanding of the loving relationality of the Trinity as revealed in Jesus. Other virtues can be interpreted as particular expressions of love in specific circumstances—self-sacrificial giving, faithfulness, peacemaking, and enjoying.

At least two points are important to note. First, love for Paul is a thoroughly corporate enterprise (see 3.3 below). Second, love in Paul is much more than a virtue by which to live a good life. Not only is love central to Paul's ethics (Rom 13:8-10; 1 Cor 13; Col 3:12), but it can be seen as pivotal within an eschatological conflict between forces belonging to the old age and the new. In 1 Corinthians 13:8-13 love is both the goal of God's salvation and an eschatological foretaste of God's new creation in the present. Within the present believers are to "pursue love" and are later exhorted "Let all that you do be done in love" (1 Cor 14:1; 16:14 NRSV). In Galatians love grows and matures in opposition to attitudes, desires, and actions that belong to the "present evil age" (Gal 1:4 NRSV) or *kosmos* (world). It is only the empowering presence of the Spirit that can transform uncontrolled "desires of the flesh" (*epithymia*, "desire"), which lead to destructive "works of the flesh" (Gal 5:16, 19 NRSV). In contrast, "those who belong to Christ Jesus have crucified the flesh with its passions [*pathēma*, 'passion'] and desires" (Gal 5:24 NRSV). In the ancient world it was not unusual for the passions to be seen as obstacles to a virtuous life (Thompson). What is exceptional in Paul is his rejection of both Greek (reason, education) and Jewish (Torah obedience) solutions to the problem of damaging human desires in favor of self-giving love. Love in this eschatological perspective is God's weapon in a cosmic battle against destructive forces opposed to his good purposes (Longenecker).

3.3. *Communal Love.* The third strand of OT love is horizontal—how love is to characterize the social life of the covenant community (Lev 19:18). Such love speaks of communal solidarity in contrast to the morality and ethics of the surrounding nations. Similarly, in Paul the great majority of love language relates to the love within the community of God's people, the *church (*ekklēsia*).

Paul's agapeism has a missional focus in that he understands well that love is essential for the health and *witness of his Christian communities, composed as they are of individuals from across the profound religious, gender, socioeconomic status, and *ethnic divisions of the ancient world. Believers now have a new primary identity in Christ as brothers and sisters (*adelphoi*) within God's *household. In this vein, coming from a *social-scientific angle, D. G. Horrell has made a strong case that the primary moral value in Paul is the construction of a corporate solidarity that acts to heal innercommunal conflict and draws strength from a vocation to holiness within an immoral world. Previous identities are relativized, not erased. In this perspective, love is not an end in itself. Rather, it plays a central role in defining the corporate life of the first Christian converts in their God-given vocation of living together under the lordship of Jesus Christ within a world that is "passing away" (1 Cor 7:31 NRSV).

The principle of cruciform love is applied by Paul to a multiplicity of situations and contexts (Mitchel 2016). Repeated appeals to maintain unity (Rom 12:16; 14:1–15:7; 1 Cor 1:10; 12:21-27; 14:12; Gal 6:10; Eph 4:1-3; Phil 2:1-2; Col 3:12-13; 1 Thess 5:12-15; Titus 3:1-2, 8) sit alongside caution against any divisive attitudes or behavior (1 Cor 3:1-4, 16-17; 6:1-11; 8:9-13; 10:24, 31-33; 11:17-34; 2 Cor 12:19-20; Gal 5:15; 6:3-4; Eph 4:25-32; Phil 2:3, 14-15; Col 3:5-9; 1 Thess 4:3-6; 1 Tim 6:2-10;

2 Tim 2:23; 3:1-5; Titus 3:9-11). Converts to Christ are to act in love for each other (1 Thess 4:9; Rom 12:9-10; 14:15; 1 Cor 8:1; Eph 4:2, 15-16; Phil 2:1-2; Col 2:2). Famously, in 1 Corinthians 13:1-3, all Christian life and *ministry is of no value at all if it is not done in love (see 3.3.1 below). The Colossians are encouraged to clothe themselves with love on top of a list of other virtues (Col 3:14), and in 1 Thessalonians 5:8 Paul includes himself in an exhortation to put on the breastplate of faith and love. Paul prays that believers' love would grow as they await the coming of the Lord (1 Thess 3:12; Phil 1:9) and is glad to hear of a church's love (e.g., 1 Thess 3:6; 2 Thess 1:3). He is thankful when Christ is preached "out of love" (Phil 1:16). He rejoices when he hears of believers' love for God's people (Col 1:4; Philem 5, 7) and encourages the Corinthians to show the genuineness of their love by giving *financial help for brothers and sisters in need (2 Cor 8:8, 24). Rather than use *apostolic authority, he prefers to appeal to Philemon about Onesimus "on the basis of love" (Philem 9 NRSV). It is noteworthy how often Paul expresses his deep love for the communities to which he ministers (e.g., 1 Thess 2:8; 3:12; 1 Cor 4:21; 16:24; 2 Cor 2:4; 8:7; 11:11; Phil 4:1).

3.3.1. The Shape of Love: The Imitation of Christ. When it comes to what love looks like in practice, the apostle's previous Jewish conception of love is reimagined christologically. The ultimate goal of a life pleasing to God is one in which Christ is formed (Gal 4:19)—a text framed by the eschatological imagery of childbirth. Such future-oriented ethics based on transformation into the *image of Christ become more explicit in other texts (Rom 8:29; 1 Cor 15:49; 2 Cor 3:18; see Col 3:10). In this vein, Paul can exhort believers to *imitate him and his coworkers as they imitate Christ (1 Thess 1:6; 2 Thess 3:7, 9; 1 Cor 4:16; 11:1; Phil 3:17; see Phil 4:9; Gal 4:12). Of these texts only 1 Thessalonians 1:6 and 1 Corinthians 11:1 explicitly mention imitation of the Lord. Sometimes the imitation is of God, which takes the form of self-giving love, as demonstrated by Christ's sacrificial death (Eph 5:1-2). Elsewhere the imitation is of churches and their willingness to suffer as Christ did (1 Thess 2:14-15). The relative paucity of texts calling for imitation of Christ means that any argument that this is a significant theme in Pauline ethics, or that other-regard has a christological basis, needs to be rooted in broader argument (Horrell). This argument can be made. Imitation is located within a wider theology in which Paul holds up Jesus Christ as the paradigm of selfless other-regard to be imitated by all believers.

One example is Romans 15:1-3; pleasing one's neighbor is based on Christ's refusal to please himself. A few verses later welcoming one another imitates how "Christ has welcomed you" (Rom 15:7 NRSV; see Col 3:13). Probably the most important is Philippians 2:5-11, where Paul's encouragement to humble other-regard is rooted in the story of Christ's voluntary descent to death on a cross, which precedes resurrection glory. *Agapē* is mentioned twice in Philippians 2:1-4 within an appeal for Christian unity. Paul goes on to outline his own narrative of giving up previous status and identity for the sake of the Philippians (Phil 3:2-16), an example he calls them to imitate (Phil 3:17). Other texts of significance include 1 Corinthians 9:14-15 (giving up of rights); 2 Corinthians 8:9 (costly self-giving); and Galatians 6:2 (where fulfilling "the law of Christ" [NRSV] includes reference to Jesus' example of bearing burdens for the good of others). Within *marriage, husbands are to love their wives "just as Christ loved the church and gave himself up for her" (Eph 5:25 NRSV; see Col 3:19).

This description of the Christian life as imitation of Jesus is virtually synonymous with the apostle's most sustained explanation of love, in 1 Corinthians 13. First Corinthians 13:1-3 summarizes the absolute necessity of love. *Gifts particularly admired by the Corinthians—inspired speech, *prophetic powers, *knowledge, and faith—are rendered utterly redundant without love (1 Cor 13:1-2). First Corinthians 13:3 echoes the self-giving example of Jesus: even unlimited giving—whether all one owns or even of one's own body—gains nothing without love. In the description of love and its antithesis that follows, fifteen examples are given, eight negatives and seven positives. Each is a verb in the present continuous tense indicating how love is an active choice, characteristic of a way of life consistent with faith in Jesus the Lord. While not explicit, it is clear that such love imitates the love of God in Christ—a relentless commitment to act for the good of others above the good of the self, exemplified in being patient and kind, and rejoicing in the truth. The final four positives are each accompanied by an "all things" (*panta*), indicative of Paul's joyful celebration of the unlimited power of love. Love so defined builds relationship and community regardless of opposition, in sharp contrast to the destructive self-interest being displayed by the Corinthians.

3.3.2. Love for Outsiders. It is a matter of debate the extent to which the apostle's overwhelming focus on love within Christian communities leaves room to include much, if anything, about love for outsiders. Voices such as T. Engberg-Pedersen (2000; 2006) and R. Thorsteinsson (2006; 2010), focusing particularly on Romans 12:9-21, contend that love in Paul is restricted to believers only. While he encourages those in Christ to treat others well, he does not specifically exhort them to love everyone, including their enemies. Love, in this perspective, is an "in-group" ethic, characteristic of the family of faith, called to live in sharp contradistinction from the world. As such it stands in marked contrast with the universal scope of Stoic ethics. Yet the evidence is thin for such a sharply defined dual ethic in Paul (Hubbard). Positive instruction to love fellow believers is not synonymous with teaching not to love outsiders. Texts such as 1 Corinthians 16:14 and 1 Thessalonians 3:12 (see 1 Thess 5:15); Philippians 4:5; Galatians 6:10 exemplify an impulse to extend love to all, while texts such as Romans 12:14 and 2 Corinthians 6:3-10 strongly suggest love of enemies. At a broader level, framing love within the imitation of Christ (see 3.3.1) includes a life characterized by self-sacrificial love of the other, including enemies (see Rom 5:8). Horrell argues it is possible to see in Paul some universal ethical norms, such as a shared recognition of the good (e.g., Phil 4:8). Such concerns have a missiological aspect: avoiding unnecessary conflict may help to win outsiders to Christ, and the apostle's instructions to do good to all, including opponents, is an extension of the positive Christian obligation to love one another. This vocation to be a peaceable, nonviolent community in a world ruled by *empire resonates with a Hauerwasian perspective (e.g., Hauerwas). Yet this dominant theme in Paul needs to be held in tandem with a lesser, yet persistent, concern for the good of all people. Not insignificant in this discussion is how "the love of Christ" propels Paul's *mission since "one has died for all" (2 Cor 5:14 NRSV). Paul's self-giving attitude and actions within his mission to the Gentiles flow from Christ's prior love for him (Martin).

At a macro scale lies the question of how inclusively Paul's understanding of God's love in Christ can be interpreted. For example, while acknowledging that Paul unambiguously holds to an eschatological future in which all humanity belonging to realms opposed to God (e.g., world, flesh) will perish, Campbell proposes that Paul was an implicit universalist. If Romans 9–11 tells a story of divine benevolence overcoming human recalcitrance (all Israel will be saved), then there is no good reason why God's love will not triumph in regard to humanity in general. Such *universalism requires substantial reinterpretation of Pauline judgment texts and will therefore likely remain a lively and controversial area of debate within NT scholarship.

4. Conclusion.

S. E. Porter rightly comments that theology often overwhelms ethics in Pauline studies. An important step in readdressing this imbalance is to recognize how love in Paul should be central to any analysis of the apostle's own experience, mission, and thought. It embraces his christologically transformed understanding of God; the motive for the cross; the dynamics of personal transformation into the image of Christ through the Spirit; fulfillment of the law; the paradoxical nature of Christian freedom; *joy and Christian worship; the cosmic conflict between the realm of the flesh and the Spirit; the difficult realities of corporate life within diverse church communities and the apostle's pastoral response; the countercultural witness of those communities within stratified cultures of hierarchy and power; financial aid to fellow believers in need; a Christian response to suffering, persecution, and death; the motive for mission; attitudes to the wider world; and the character of eschatological hope.

See also CORINTHIANS, FIRST LETTER TO THE; COVENANT; CROSS; CRUCIFORMITY; ELECTION AND PREDESTINATION; ESCHATOLOGY; ETHICS; FELLOWSHIP, COMMUNION, SHARING; FRUIT OF THE SPIRIT; GOD; IMITATION OF PAUL / OF CHRIST; MERCY.

BIBLIOGRAPHY. **J. M. G. Barclay,** "Paul Among Diaspora Jews: Anomaly or Apostate?," *JSNT* 60 (1995): 89–120; **M. J. Bird,** *Paul: An Anomalous Jew: Paul Among Jews, Greeks and Romans* (Grand Rapids, MI: Eerdmans, 2016); idem, "Paul, a Jew Among Jews, Greeks and Romans," in *The State of New Testament Studies: A Survey of Contemporary Research*, ed. S. McKnight and N. K. Gupta (Grand Rapids, MI: Baker Academic, 2019), 182-96; **C. Brown,** ed., "Love," *NIDNTT* 2:538-51; **D. A. Campbell,** *Pauline Dogmatics: The Triumph of God's Love* (Grand Rapids, MI: Eerdmans, 2020); **J. D. G. Dunn,** *The Theology of Paul's Letter to the Galatians*, NTT (Cambridge: Cambridge University Press, 1993); idem, *The Theology of Paul the Apostle* (Grand Rapids, MI: Eerdmans, 1998); **S. G. Eastman,** *Paul and the Person: Reframing Paul's Anthropology* (Grand Rapids, MI: Eerdmans, 2017); **T. Engberg-Pedersen,** *Paul and the Stoics* (Edinburgh: T&T Clark, 2000); idem, "Paul's Stoicizing Politics in Romans 12–13: The Role of 13:1-10 in the Argument," *JSNT* 29 (2006): 163-72; **G. D. Fee,** *God's Empowering Presence: The Holy*

Spirit in the Letters of Paul (Peabody, MA: Hendrickson, 1994); **V. P. Furnish,** *The Love Command of the New Testament* (London: SCM Press, 1973); idem, "Living to God, Walking in Love: Theology and Ethics in Romans," in *Reading Paul's Letter to the Romans,* ed. J. L. Sumney (Atlanta: Society of Biblical Literature, 2012), 187-202; **M. J. Gorman,** "'Pauline Theology: Perspectives, Perennial Topics, and Prospects," in *The State of New Testament Studies: A Survey of Recent Research,* ed. S. McKnight and N. K. Gupta (Grand Rapids, MI: Baker Academic, 2019), 197-223; **S. Harding,** *Paul's Eschatological Anthropology: The Dynamics of Human Transformation,* ES (Minneapolis: Fortress, 2015); **S. Hauerwas,** *The Peaceable Kingdom: A Primer in Christian Ethics* (Notre Dame, IN: University of Notre Dame Press, 1983); **J. P. Heil,** *Ephesians: Empowerment to Walk in Love for the Unity of All in Christ* (Atlanta: Society of Biblical Literature, 2007); **H. W. Hoehner,** *Ephesians: An Exegetical Commentary* (Grand Rapids, MI: Baker, 2002); **D. G. Horrell,** *Solidarity and Difference: A Contemporary Reading of Paul's Ethics,* 2nd ed. (London: Bloomsbury T&T Clark, 2016); **M. V. Hubbard,** "Enemy Love in Paul: Probing the Engberg-Pedersen and Thorsteinsson Thesis," *JSPHL* 6, no. 1 (2016): 115-35; **R. Jewett,** *Romans: A Commentary,* Hermeneia (Minneapolis: Fortress, 2007); **C. S. Keener,** *The Mind of the Spirit: Paul's Approach to Transformed Thinking* (Grand Rapids, MI: Baker Academic, 2016); **B. W. Longenecker,** "Faith, Works and Worship: Torah Observance in Paul's Theological Perspective," in *The Apostle Paul and the Christian Life: Ethical and Missional Implications of the New Perspective,* ed. S. McKnight and J. Modica (Grand Rapids, MI: Baker Academic, 2016), 47-70; **R. P. Martin,** *2 Corinthians,* 2nd ed., WBC 40 (Grand Rapids, MI: Zondervan, 2014); **S. McKnight and N. K. Gupta,** eds., *The State of New Testament Studies: A Survey of Recent Research* (Grand Rapids, MI: Baker Academic, 2019); **P. Mitchel,** "The New Perspective and the Christian Life: Solus Spiritus," in *The Apostle Paul and the Christian Life: Ethical and Missional Implications of the New Perspective,* ed. S. McKnight and J. Modica (Grand Rapids, MI: Baker Academic, 2016), 71-102; idem, "New Testament Eschatologies," in *The State of New Testament Studies: A Survey of Contemporary Research,* ed. S. McKnight and N. K. Gupta (Grand Rapids, MI: Baker Academic, 2019), 224-52; **R. Mohrlang,** "Love," *DPL,* 575-78; **L. L. Morris,** *Testaments of Love: A Study of Love in the Bible* (Grand Rapids, MI: Eerdmans, 1981); **A. Nygren,** *Agape and Eros: The Christian Idea of Love,* trans. P. S. Watson (Chicago: University of Chicago Press, 1982); **S. E. Porter,** *The Apostle Paul: His Life, Thought, and Letters* (Grand Rapids, MI: Eerdmans, 2016); **V. Rabens,** *The Holy Spirit and Ethics in Paul: Transformation and Empowering for Religious-Ethical Life,* 2nd rev. ed. (Minneapolis: Fortress, 2014); **B. S. Rosner,** *Paul and The Law: Keeping the Commandments of God,* NSBT (Downers Grove, IL: IVP Academic, 2013); **C. K. Rowe,** *One True Life: The Stoics and Early Christians as Rival Traditions* (New Haven, CT: Yale University Press, 2016); **J. P. Sampley,** *Walking in Love: Moral Progress and Spiritual Growth with the Apostle Paul* (Minneapolis: Fortress, 2016); **M. Silva,** ed., "Agapaō," *NIDNTT* 1:103-14; **C. Spicq,** *Agape in the New Testament,* vol. 2, *Agape in the Epistles of St. Paul, the Acts of the Apostles and the Epistles of St. James, St. Peter, and St. Jude,* trans. Sister M. A. McNamara and Sister M. H. Richter (Eugene, OR: Wipf & Stock, 1964); **J. A. Thompson,** *Moral Formation According to Paul: The Context and Coherence of Pauline Ethics* (Grand Rapids, MI: Baker Academic, 2011); **R. Thorsteinsson,** "Paul and Roman Stoicism: Romans 12 and Contemporary Stoic Ethics," *JSNT* 29 (2006): 139-61; idem, *Roman Christianity and Roman Stoicism: A Comparative Study of Ancient Morality* (Oxford: Oxford University Press, 2010); **J. R. Wagner,** "'Enemies' yet 'Beloved' Still: Election and the Love of God in Romans 9–11," in *God and Israel: Providence and Purpose in Romans 9–11,* ed. T. D. Still (Waco, TX: Baylor University Press, 2017); **N. T. Wright,** *Paul and the Faithfulness of God,* 2 vols., COQG (Minneapolis: Fortress, 2013).

P. Mitchel

M

MAGIC

Magic commonly refers to a ritual means of acquiring spiritual power to coerce gods, *demons, spirits, and other supernatural beings to accomplish something on behalf of the person invoking them. These powers could bring *healing, protection, dream revelations, and assistance, or they could be compelled to bring harm or even *death to an opponent. The practice of magic often carried with it the promise of guaranteed results if the ritual was carried out precisely. Magic was less concerned about a relationship with a deity and more interested in what could be gained from a god. Magic also assumed the principle of cosmic sympathy—that the microcosm is bound to the macrocosm in a system of correspondences.

Because magic was "omnipresent in classical antiquity" (Graf, 1), many people who became Christians would have had some experience with magic. As they joined the early Christian communities, they would have been tempted to bring their magical beliefs and practices with them, as one sees in the Acts account of an incident in *Ephesus (Acts 19:18-19). These people needed perspective on their past and a changed attitude toward it in the light of Paul's interpretation of the *gospel. Some of Paul's theological accents can be explained by his efforts to meet this discipleship need.

1. Definition of Magic
2. Sources and the Issue of Dating
3. Magic and the Spirit World
4. The Uses for Magic
5. Jewish Magic
6. Paul and Magic in Acts
7. Paul and Magic in the Letters

1. Definition of Magic.

The precise definition of magic and its relationship to the traditional Greek, Roman, and Egyptian cults is highly contested in the academic literature. Some have emphasized a sociological approach to the definition of magic by observing that magic was illegal in the Roman *Empire and regarded as socially deviant, outside the boundaries of acceptable religious practice. Accusing a person or group of practicing magic was a powerful tool of social dominance in the ancient world. Others, however, have emphasized an emic perspective—an ethnographic perspective from an insider's point of view. This approach often sees magic positively and not in conflict with religion. It could be viewed as an autonomous domain or a substructure to an established cult. Magicians or shamans would not have seen themselves as acting outside the boundaries of the cult.

When one looks at the primary source documents, however, one sees a common set of characteristics that brings coherence to the category and justifies some differentiation from religion. Some of these include an individual orientation and focus on individual goals, a common set of purposes for its use, the prominence of rituals of power, a disregard for the will of the deity combined with a tendency to coerce or manipulate the god, the regular use of words and symbols of power, and distinct focus on the end results, which are guaranteed if the spell is done properly. Nevertheless, the categories of religion and magic are overlapping, and to some extent magic can be described as a substructure to religion.

2. Sources and the Issue of Dating.

The most important witnesses for understanding magical beliefs and practices are a collection of nearly 250 papyrus documents originally discovered in Egypt. Most are written in Greek, but some are in Coptic. The Greek texts have been published in a critical edition edited by K. Preisendanz (abbreviated *PGM*) and translated into English in a volume edited by H. D. Betz that also includes the Coptic texts. Many of these papyri date to the third and fourth centuries AD (although a few date as early as the first century BC).

Over fifteen hundred curse tablets (*defixiones*) have also been discovered in tombs and water wells, and at archaeological sites throughout the Mediterranean world. The preferred writing material was thin lead sheets, but some are inscribed on tin, other metals, and ostraca. These date as early as the fifth century BC, with a few dating as late as the sixth century AD. They uniformly invoke spirits to come and cause harm or kill.

In addition, hundreds of magical amulets have been discovered from every corner of the ancient world. These were created to counter and ward off attacks from evil spirits. These protective spells were inscribed on gems and lamellae (thin metal sheets) and often worn on the person seeking protection. Although notoriously difficulty to date, they are common throughout the entire Roman era.

Finally, the understanding of magic is also enhanced by the many Greek and Roman authors who describe the practice (see Luck, 3-131). Magic was employed by all levels of society, even by the emperor himself. Cassius Dio reports that Tiberius made use of the art every day, assisted by a magician he employed named Thrasyllus (Cassius Dio, *Hist.* 57.15.7).

Some NT scholars have expressed a reticence to use magical texts, especially the Greek magical papyri, for illuminating the NT text because so many of these documents date later than the NT era. Yet this hesitation should be alleviated by the fact that it is known that the practice of magic existed for centuries before the NT era, that numerous texts date prior to the NT, and that the contents of many of the later magical papyri contain traditions that reflect the way magic was practiced during Paul's time and earlier. Yet caution needs to be exercised, especially in attempting to root the background of a lexical item in a later text.

3. Magic and the Spirit World.

The wearing of amulets, recitation of magical formulas, and performance of magical rites were carried out in the belief that these words and actions could exert a compelling influence over one or more spirits. Practitioners would try to "conjure" (*orkizō*) well-known deities (e.g., Mithras, Isis, Helios), but more often the "angels" (*angeloi*) or "assistants" (*paredroi*) of the gods. Note the following magical formula in a recipe that reputedly "accomplishes anything":

> I call upon you, holy, very powerful . . . assistants of the great god, the powerful chief daimons, you who are inhabitants of Chaos, of Erebos, of the abyss . . . dwelling in the recesses of heaven, lurking in the nooks and crannies of houses . . . leaders of those in the underworld, administrators of the infinite, wielding power over earth . . . lords of Fate . . . rulers of daimons . . . do the matter [which I demand]. (*PGM* IV. 1345-75)

This formula is to be recited after performing an elaborate rite using, among other things, some fat and hairs from an ass, a female goat, and a black bull. The person who performed the rite and uttered the formula would expect the spirits to fulfill the demand if the recipe was followed in precise detail.

Magic also drew on nonpersonal powers and forces for its purposes. What affects one part affects the other in this integrated whole of life forces. The magician would therefore make use of animal viscera, plants, herbs, precious stones, and metals, believing that there was a cosmic correspondence.

4. The Uses for Magic.

People who used magic generally sought self-serving aims. There are no extant examples of people using magic to accomplish the will of a deity. Rather, magic was used precisely to influence the will of a deity or spirit. But magicians may also have attempted to serve their community as wise men (or shamans) to provide spells that would ward off spirits or bring healing or supernatual assistance in a variety of ways.

4.1. To Bring Harm on Someone. Putting a *curse on a person was a common use of magic and is reflected in the numerous lead curse tablets (*defixiones*) that have been discovered. Some of the papyri give instructions on the proper rituals to be used in the creation of such a tablet.

4.2. To Provide Protection from Spirits. Living in fear of being cursed and getting help to counteract a curse was part of life in the Roman world. Consequently, one of the primary uses of magic in everyday life was for protection. In a world thought to be populated by hordes of evil spirits bent on bringing harm in every conceivable way, people sought supernatural protection. This was perhaps the chief use of the magical amulets, which frequently bore the inscription "Protect me!," "Save me!," or simply, "Help!" Many recipes for constructing these kinds of amulets appear in the magical papyri.

4.3. Love Spells of Attraction. Another widely attested use for magic was to compel the physical attraction of another person (aphrodisiacs). Invoking spirits to accomplish this was central to the performance. One text, after listing numerous magical names, contains this invocation: "I adjure you by the twelve elements [*stoicheia*] of heaven and the twenty-four elements [*stoicheia*] of the world, that you attract Herakles whom Taaipis bore, to me, to Allous, whom Alexandria bore, immediately, immediately; quickly, quickly" (*PGM* XXIX. 1-21).

4.4. Other Uses. There were numerous other uses for magic—some for honorable purposes, but many for less honorable. Some sought to heal various kinds of illnesses, to solicit an appearance from a deity who could reveal special *knowledge, to acquire a divine assistant, to alter cosmic fate, or to aid in childbirth and contraception. Others were for gaining favor and influence with people, winning at dice, winning a race, catching a thief, and a wide variety of other purposes.

5. Jewish Magic.

Magic was by no means practiced only by pagans. Jewish magic flourished in antiquity (Alexander 1986, 342). There are many testimonies to Jewish involvement in magical practice in apocrypha, pseudepigrapha, *Qumran, Josephus, the earliest traditions within the Talmud and the midrashim, early Christian writings, pagan authors, and even in the NT itself (Acts 19:13-20, "certain itinerant Jewish exorcists"). The Greek magical papyri also contain many magical formulas of probable Jewish origin.

An interesting example of Jewish magic is the Testament of Solomon (first to third centuries AD). Essentially a manual of magical formulas, the testament ostensibly records how Solomon directed demons to build the *temple at Jerusalem by manipulating them through magical means. Another important early Jewish book of magic, translated into English and published under the title *Sepher ha-Razim* (*Book of Mysteries*), probably comes from the fourth century AD. However, the book likely contains traditions and reflects the magical practices of certain segments of Judaism dating to the first century AD.

6. Paul and Magic in Acts.

Luke records one incident in which Paul was confronted with a magician (Acts 13:4-12). This magician was Jewish and yet was attached to the *Gentile proconsul of Cyprus. Paul encountered him on the island at the outset of his first missionary outreach. When the proconsul showed interest in the gospel Paul preached, Elymas (the magician) strongly opposed Paul. According to Luke, Paul denounced Elymas as a pawn of the devil, and the *Lord immediately struck the magician with blindness.

Acts recounts another dramatic episode that occurred during Paul's Ephesian *ministry (Acts 19:13-20). Luke narrates a situation involving itinerant Jewish exorcists who invoked the *name of Jesus as part of their magical rite for exorcism. On one occasion they were tragically unsuccessful as they applied this method to a demon-possessed man. Luke says they were physically assaulted by the man and forced to flee the house naked and bleeding. As word spread among Christians about this incident, those who continued to practice magic came under strong conviction. Gathering all of their expensive books of magical formulas and incantations, they burned them. This account reinforces the reputation of Ephesus as being something of a center for magical practices during the first century. It is also important for understanding the pre-Christian background of many of Paul's converts. Early Christians faced a strong temptation to combine their magical beliefs and practices with their Christianity. It is clear that Luke regards magic as evil and the domain of the devil (see Garrett, 101-9). In this respect, he also accurately reflects the convictions of Paul.

7. Paul and Magic in the Letters.

Very little has been written on the theme of magic in relation to Paul's *letters. This is probably due to the fact that he explicitly mentions it only once (Gal 5:20) in his undisputed letters. Furthermore, his theology betrays nothing of a magical worldview.

7.1. "Witchcraft" (Gal 5:20). If Galatians 5:20 is any indication of Paul's overall attitude toward magic, one can conclude that he believed it to be inconsistent with life in the Spirit. He roundly condemns "magic" (*pharmakeia*) in Galatians 5:20 as on the same level as *idolatry; both are acts of the "*flesh," which should have no part in the life of a believer (see Rev 21:8, where it is said that those who practice magic will experience the "second death").

7.2. "Magicians" (2 Tim 3:13). The text of 2 Timothy 3:13 predicts that "evil men and impostors [*goētes*] will go from bad to worse, deceiving and being deceived" (NIV). The term *goēs* is commonly used in literature as a derogatory reference to a magician—a person who is a charlatan or a swindler. Although it is possible that 2 Timothy 3:13 uses the term in a general sense, it is more likely that a magician is in mind, perhaps of the same sort as Apollonius of Tyana (Philostratus, *Vita Apollonii*). This interpretation is rendered more likely because the deceivers are compared in 2 Timothy 3:8 with magicians who opposed Moses (Jannes and Jambres). Here again, the practice of magic is viewed in the worst possible light.

*7.3. **Principalities and Powers.*** Practitioners of magic were obsessively interested in supernatural powers for utilitarian reasons. Paul's letters, especially Colossians and Ephesians, provide his readers with a new outlook on the spirit realm. Paul never denies the real existence of evil spirits (but see 1 Cor 8:4); rather, he is careful to describe them as minions under the control of the prince of evil, *Satan (e.g., Eph 2:2). Most importantly, *Christ has defeated all these forces by his work on the *cross (Col 2:15) and is now exalted far above them to a position of sovereignty (Eph 1:20-22). Nevertheless, the powers still exert their influence and are hostile to the *church. Christ's parousia will bring an end to their tyranny over the world (1 Cor 15:24; Eph 1:10; Col 1:20). Because of their dangerous hostility to the church, these powers are not to be invoked or manipulated by Christians but rather resisted through the power of *God (Eph 6:10-20).

The terms Paul uses for the powers reflect the wide array of vocabulary shared by people of all religious traditions during the NT era. Some of these terms are used in magical texts (e.g., *dynameis, kosmokratores, thronoi*), although his vocabulary for the powers more closely reflects the angelology and demonology of Second Temple Judaism. Paul draws on this reservoir of terminology with which his readers would be familiar, lumping together all manner of spirits when he speaks of the supernatural realm of evil.

*7.4. **The "Elemental Spirits."*** It is possible that Paul's terminology for "elemental spirits of the world" (*stoicheia tou kosmou*, Gal 4:3, 9; Col 2:8, 20) comes from a background of usage in astrology and magic (of course, it is also possible that the meaning "elementary principles" is more appropriate to these contexts). The expression appears, for instance, in the astrological section of the Testament of Solomon (T. Sol. 18.1-2; see also 8.1-4), a portion that probably had an independent existence and use as early as the first century BC. It is used there to refer to the astral decans, thirty-six spirits controlling every ten degrees of the heavenly sphere. The expression is used similarly in the magical papyri (*PGM* XXXIX. 18-21). If Paul was drawing the phrase *stoicheia tou kosmou* from the tradition represented in this literature, he did so strictly because it was part of the wide array of vocabulary shared by Jew and Gentile alike to refer to the spirit world. In this case, he may have chosen this particular expression for the powers because it was well known to the readers of Galatians and Colossians. Paul does not necessarily give credence to the notion that astral spirits hold the keys of fate; rather, he is more concerned to subsume them under the category of the demonic and assert that by participation in Christ's death, believers have died to their enslaving influence.

*7.5. **Addressing a Magical Worldview (Ephesians).*** Many aspects of the teaching of Ephesians about divine power and supernatural spirits seem particularly appropriate for people who have come to Christ from a background of involvement in magical practices (Arnold 1989, esp. 167-72; see also now Darko). That such people were entering the churches is certain because of the widespread use of magic at the time. This is corroborated by Luke's account of the burning of the magical books at Ephesus (Acts 19:18-19), which is especially relevant for understanding the struggles of the Asia Minor churches.

In Ephesians Paul declares the superiority of the power of God and the supremacy of Christ over all spiritual powers, indeed, over "every name that is named" (Eph 1:19-23; 4:8-10). For those who lived in constant fear of the dreadful workings of evil spirits, this would have provided much comfort. Fate is not in the hands of capricious powers but rather is determined by the loving Father, who "chose us in him before the *creation of the world" (Eph 1:3 NIV). The will and purpose of this benevolent heavenly Father is being worked out in history (Eph 1:5, 9-11; 2:10); he is not a deity to be manipulated according to one's carnal whims. One approaches God with humility and thankfulness, and prays according to his will (Eph 3:14-19; cf. Eph 1:15-19). In contrast to the self-serving attempts to use divine power in magic, Ephesians stresses the believer's reception of divine power to manifest *love to other people in a selfless manner (Eph 3:16-17; 5:2). The letter also gives a new perspective on the powers by highlighting their collusion with the devil and exposing their objective of attacking the church (Eph 2:2; 4:27; 6:12). Ephesians assures believers of the availability of God's power for resisting these forces. God's power, according to Paul, is not obtained through incantations and formulae but by virtue of a close union with the resurrected Christ (Eph 2:5-6; 6:10).

*7.6. **Addressing Shamanistic Practices in the Local Church (Colossians).*** Although a precise identification of the nature of the oppositional *teaching at Colossae is debated, a strong case can be made that it was a form of magic and shamanism (Arnold 2012). The descriptive phrase "*worship of angels" is best interpreted as ritual invocation of angels for help and deliverance. There are many angel inscriptions from western Asia Minor that attest this practice. The principal factional teacher at Colossae may very well have been a Sceva-like figure who served the community as a spiritual healer and advocated rituals, taboos, and practices to assist them in dealing with the harmful impact of spiritual forces. Paul counters this influence by pointing to the supremacy of Christ over all creation (including all principalities, authorities, thrones, and dominions), stressing the union of all believers with Christ in his *resurrection and enthronement, and urging all believers to resist the spiritualistic practices of the so-called *philosophy and to hold tightly to Christ, who is their *head (Col 2:19).

See also Cosmology; Curse, Accursed, Anathema; Demons and Exorcism; Ephesians, Letter to the; Paul in Acts; Principalities and Powers; Religions, Greco-Roman; Satan, Devil; Triumph.

BIBLIOGRAPHY. **P. S. Alexander,** "Incantations and Books of Magic," in *The History of the Jewish People in the Age of Jesus Christ (175 B.C.–A.D. 135)*, rev. and ed. G. Vermes, F. Millar, and M. Goodman (Edinburgh: T&T Clark, 1986), 3:342-79; idem, "'Wrestling Against Wickedness in High Places': Magic in the Worldview of the Qumran Community," in *The Scrolls and the Scriptures: Qumran Fifty Years After*, ed. S. E. Porter and C. A. Evans, JSPSup 26 (Sheffield: Sheffield Academic Press, 1997), 318-37; **C. E. Arnold,** *Ephesians: Power and Magic*, SNTSMS 63 (Cambridge: Cambridge University Press, 1989); idem, *The Colossian Syncretism*, WUNT 2/77 (Tübingen: Mohr Siebeck, 1995); idem, "Sceva, Solomon, and Shamanism: The Jewish Roots of the Problem at Colossae," *JETS* 55 (2012): 7-26; **D. Aune,** "Magic in Early Christianity," *ANRW* 2.23.2:1507-57; idem, "'Magic' in Early Christianity and Its Ancient Mediterranean Context: A Survey of Some Recent Scholarship," *Annali di storia dell'esegesi* 24 (2007): 229-94; **M. Aydas,** "New Inscriptions from Asia Minor," *Epigraphica Anatolica* 37 (2004): 121-25; **H. D. Betz,** ed., "Magic and Mystery in the Greek Magical Papyri," in *Hellenismus und Urchristentum: Gesammelte Aufsätze I* (Tübingen: Mohr, 1990), 209-29; idem, *The Greek Magical Papyri in Translation*, vol. 1, *Text*, 2nd ed. (Chicago: University of Chicago Press, 1992); **P. Busch,** *Magie in neutestamentlicher Zeit*, FRLANT 218 (Göttingen: Vandenhoeck & Ruprecht, 2006); **D. K. Darko,** *Against Principalities and Powers: Spiritual Beings in Relation to Communal Identity and the Moral Discourse of Ephesians* (Carlisle, UK: Langham HippoBooks, 2020); **M. W. Dickie,** *Magic and Magicians in the Greco-Roman World* (New York: Routledge, 2001); **C. A. Faraone and D. Obbink,** eds., *Magika Hiera: Ancient Greek Magic and Religion* (New York: Oxford University Press, 1991); **J. G. Gager,** *Curse Tablets and Binding Spells from the Ancient World* (New York: Oxford University Press, 1992); **D. Frankfurter,** ed., *Guide to the Study of Ancient Magic*, RGRW 189 (Leiden: Brill, 2019); **S. R. Garrett,** *The Demise of the Devil: Magic and the Demonic in Luke's Writings* (Minneapolis: Fortress, 1989); **F. Graf,** *Magic in the Ancient World* (Cambridge, MA: Harvard University Press, 1994); **E. R. Goodenough,** *Jewish Symbols in the Greco-Roman Period*, vol. 2, *The Archaeological Evidence from the Diaspora* (New York: Bollingen Foundation, 1953); **S. Johnson,** *Restless Dead: Encounters Between the Living and the Dead in Ancient Greece* (Berkeley: University of California Press, 1999); **R. Kotansky,** *Greek Magical Amulets: The Inscribed God, Silver, Copper, and Bronze Lamellae*, part 1, *Published Texts of Known Provenance*, ANWAW, Sonderreihe Papyrologica Coloniensia 22/1 (Opladen: Wesdeutscher Verlag, 1994); **T. Laus,** "Paul and 'Magic,'" in *Magic in the Biblical World: From the Rod of Aaron to the Ring of Solomon*, ed. T. Klutz, JSNTSup (London: T&T Clark, 2003), 140-56; **G. Luck,** *Arcana Mundi* (Baltimore: Johns Hopkins University Press, 1985); **M. W. Meyer and R. Smith,** *Ancient Christian Magic: Coptic Texts of Ritual Power* (San Francisco: Harper, 1994); **P. Schäfer,** "Magic and Religion in Ancient Judaism," *in Envisioning Magic: A Princeton Seminar and Symposium*, ed. P. Schäfer and H. G. Kippenberger (Leiden: Brill, 1997), 19-44; **L. C. Watson,** *Magic in Ancient Greece and Rome* (New York: Bloomsbury, 2019).

C. E. Arnold

MAN AND WOMAN

The discussion of Paul's view of man and woman often focuses on the apostle's view of *women, such as whether it is liberating, traditional, misogynistic, and so on, or on the differences between men and women. However, it may be more meaningful to consider how Paul views man and woman according to God's purpose in *creation, especially how they are to come together as one even as they are different. Therefore, man and woman in Paul's *letters must be understood as a relational category.

In this light, this article will examine Paul's view through two lenses: (1) man and woman and creation, that is, Paul's understanding of the Genesis *narrative;

and (2) man and woman and new creation, that is, the eschatological significance of their new life in *Christ in light of the Genesis narrative. Questions about *marriage, *ministry, and *sexuality can then be viewed from this more overarching perspective.

Genesis 1:27 declares that man and woman were created as distinct beings, made in God's *image as male and female. Genesis 2:18-27 presents more detail. God created *Adam from the dust from the ground (Gen 2:7). He then formed Eve from the man and for the purpose of being his "helper" because it was not good for Adam to be alone. One also learns that the man and woman were to become "one *flesh" (Gen 2:24).

Therefore, from the beginning there is both an implicit unity and a differentiation. Eve is from Adam, not from the dust as he is. It is as two distinct persons that they are then called to become "one flesh," a term that implies not merely a sexual union but a spiritual and emotional intimacy, perhaps even a kinship relationship usually extended to blood relations (Wenham, 71). In discussing man and woman, Paul applies both the creation differences between Adam and Eve and their intended unity.

Furthermore, he sees their unity as a possibility only in Christ, as those who participate in God's renewing activity inaugurated in Christ. Though the specific phrase "new creation" itself occurs only in 2 Corinthians 5:17 and Galatians 6:15, it is commonly understood to refer to the new era begun through Christ's *death and *resurrection, which carries implications for the believer as well as the transformed universe (Moo, 42). In Paul's new creation thought, the believer is transformed, and yet the original creation account remains foundationally relevant.

For example, in 1 Corinthians 11:8-9 and 1 Timothy 2:13-14 Paul uses the Genesis creation account, and in particular the creation of Adam first, as the basis for his instructions. However, elsewhere he speaks of "neither male nor female" in Christ (Gal 3:28). Gender is in some way transcended as all Christ's followers are united in the one Spirit into his *body (1 Cor 12:12-13). Consequently, one must consider both creation distinctions and new creation unity for understanding male and female in Paul's thought.

1. The Foundation of Creation Distinctions. In the gender debate, discussion tends to fall rather predictably around whether men have a particular *leadership role and authority in the *church and marriage, or whether men and woman have equal opportunity in ministry and shared decision-making in marriage. However, in focusing on issues such as authority and equality, one may be missing more profound implications of seeing the continuing relevance of creation differences in light of new existence in Christ—in other words, how the coming of Christ informs the goal of man and woman living together before *God.

One of the most disputed passages regarding men and women is 1 Timothy 2:8-15. Paul says women are not allowed to teach or "have/exercise authority" or "domineer" over men (for a comprehensive bibliography on the discussion, see Westfall, 290-91). Instead of these activities, they are to "remain quiet." Debate about this difficult passage has largely become mired in whether Paul's commands are universal or situational, including how he uses the references to Adam and Eve to support his instructions. But this focus on the specifics of *teaching, authority, and silence often overshadows a vital aspect of Paul's use of the creation references—the basic question of why he would continue to see the significance of the creation distinctions at all when he also says that male and female are transcended in Christ (Gal 3:28).

So, while this article cannot discuss every aspect of this complex passage, it can make observations on how Paul views the fundamental importance of God's creation of humanity as man and woman. Was Paul proposing a universal principle prohibiting women from teaching and being in authority over men? Or was he dealing with a unique situation, perhaps involving the infiltration of false teachers into the community? In the latter view, Paul's instructions, including his references to Adam and Eve, are especially intended for that particular situation. What is generally overlooked is the simple yet foundational observation that Paul sees a continuing relevance for Eve's creation after and for Adam (1 Tim 2:13) in a community in which there is "neither male nor female."

Part of the difficulty in interpreting the passage comes from the way in which the apostle's instructions seem to conflict with other Pauline references. For example, the references to Adam and Eve support the idea that Paul is presenting a universal principle, particularly since Paul's use of "for" in 1 Timothy 2:13 indicates that this is the reason for the prohibition. That Paul considers Adam in particular as having representative status is seen elsewhere, such as in his appeal in 1 Corinthians 11, which will be discussed in more detail below, as well as other passages, such as 1 Corinthians 15:45-49 and Romans 5:12-21. In these latter passages, Paul describes Adam as the "first" and earthly man, the one because of whom *sin and death entered the world, and who brings condemnation to all people.

Alternatively, some counter that the seemingly broad and overarching nature of the prohibition conflicts with the robust ministry of women in the rest of the Pauline *mission and instructions. Although Paul says women are to be silent (1 Tim 2:11-12; also 1 Cor 14:34, where he instructs women to be "silent in the churches"), he clearly allows for women to speak by prophesying in the assembly in 1 Corinthians 11:2-16, giving instructions regarding only the manner of their activity. While 1 Timothy 2 says women are not to teach men, Priscilla appears several times as an example of a woman teacher, as she and Aquila together instruct Apollos (Acts 18:18, 26; Rom 16:3). In four out of the six times she is mentioned with her husband, she is listed first (Acts 18:18; 26; Rom 16:3; 2 Tim 4:19), which may reflect her greater prominence in the community.

The intractable nature of the debate may indicate that the current framework itself is inadequate for explaining Paul's instructions, and so it may be helpful to look at more fundamental themes. One should not overlook the way in which Paul's instructions are built on the belief that there are real and meaningful differences between men and women. When examining the larger cultural context, one discovers a concern for the need to distinguish male and female and for each to act accordingly. Paul shares this concern, which he grounds in creation.

Scholars have long looked at the possible cultural situation behind the passage. One influential proposal was that in 1 Timothy 2 Paul was responding to a particular situation in which he was combating a heresy that encouraged a type of ancient feminism and was perhaps associated with Artemis, the patron goddess of *Ephesus (Kroeger and Kroeger). However, S. M. Baugh has shown that Ephesus was a fairly typical Hellenistic city in this regard, making it harder to see Paul's injunctions as uniquely aimed at a specific situation in the church.

Even if Paul's instructions were not motivated by a specific heresy, there has been much research on what might have been happening in Ephesus within a framework of larger movements in the greater Greco-Roman context. Bruce Winter explores the expectation for women's proper behavior, arguing that Paul's writings may reflect the impact of the "new" Roman woman, whose influence would have reached into Ephesus (Winter 2003, 97-122). Mostly wealthy women, they were characterized by their lavish hairstyles, ostentatious adornment, immodest dress, and rejection of sexual mores. The extent to which the new women could upset the status quo was so concerning that Augustus instituted new legislation in order to curb their behavior and encourage marriage and having children (Winter 2003, 39-58). First Timothy 2:8-15 may then be contrasting the wife's virtues to the dress of the new woman and her alternative lifestyle identified by her dress. Paul may be trying to avoid a situation in which the Christian women were being misidentified with the arrogant and promiscuous new woman.

Some have pointed out that one may apply cultural observations without having to be so precise. According to Alicia Batten, Paul's instructions may simply reflect a continuing concern for female modesty and emphasis on women's position in the domestic sphere (Batten, 497). Lynn Cohick argues that the construct of the new woman was more a political tool than a historical fact, a critique by men because of the increased involvement of women in the public sphere due to greater *wealth, political instability, and a relaxing of social norms (72-78).

Whether Paul's instructions over women's dress came about because of the new woman or reflect a more general concern over women's modesty, the social context reflects an overall regard for women's dress as indicative of appropriate behavior and her personal conduct as representative of her virtue. Such a concern would not have been unusual, as the ancient moralists commonly spoke of a woman's character as reflecting her true beauty, stating that this quality should also be represented in her modest dress (Keener 1992, 103-7).

In light of the prominence of concerns related to appearance and virtue, it is noteworthy that Paul begins and ends his instructions to the women with references to self-control in 1 Timothy 2:9, 15. Self-control (*sōphrosynē*) was considered one of the four cardinal virtues identified by philosophers such as Plato, Aristotle, and Cicero, and was associated with the virtuous woman and her dress. In this way Paul speaks in the context of the proper adornment of the virtuous Roman wife (Winter 2003, 60-62, 101-2). Christian women are to display appropriate dress as well as attitudes and behavior, as is fitting for their gender.

Maintaining the proper distinction between male and female was a prominent concern during the Roman era during which Paul wrote. It was also central in Judaism (Lev 20:13; Deut 22:5). While there is still debate today as to the proper nature and form of women's conduct, Paul's use of the Genesis story demonstrates a concern for gender that is very much grounded in the creation narrative and emphasizes the distinctiveness of male and female. In the ancient context, women honored this distinction in their dress and moral conduct. However, before reflexively moving on to the specifics of what that might look like in a contemporary context, as is often done, it is vital to ask why it was so important for Paul to ground his instructions in creation distinctions and why these remain relevant to those who are made new in Christ.

2. 1 Corinthians 11 and the Intersection of Creation and New Creation.

First Timothy 2 is not the only Pauline passage that asserts the foundational value of the Genesis account in understanding the significance of male/female distinctions. In 1 Corinthians 11, another key passage in the gender debate, Paul discusses male and female not only in the context of creation but also in terms of the intersection of these creation differences and the believers' new creation existence.

In 1 Corinthians 11 Paul addresses the issue of women prophesying in the Corinthian assembly, stating it is shameful for them to prophesy with their heads uncovered. As Gordon Fee points out, it is extremely difficult to say with certainty what *tradition Paul is referencing since in antiquity there was a wide range of traditions, which would necessitate making distinctions between Greek, Roman, and Jewish customs, public versus private occasions, and differences between rich and poor (Fee, 560-63). Still, despite this limitation, one can draw important observations for Paul's larger theological concerns as he appeals to their identities derived from the Genesis creation account.

One of the main issues is the significance of Paul's identification of the man as the "*head" of the woman. Although scholars debate whether Paul is referring to husbands and wives or men and women in a broader sense, in the end there may not be an essential difference since the basic principles underlying a marriage relationship reflected how men and women in general were to relate (Ciampa and Rosner, 508).

Paul uses a play on words as he instructs the woman to cover her physical head during *worship to avoid shaming her husband, who is her metaphorical head (1 Cor 11:3-5). He compares the woman's lack of a covering to having her head shaved or cut short (1 Cor 11:5-6), which would represent the loss of her femininity and would have been considered dishonoring to her husband. Some also argue the absence of a covering was associated with the shame of a woman publicly exposed as an adulteress and with prostitutes (Winter 2001, 128). In connecting the lack of a head covering with a shaved head, Paul's argument is a *reductio ad absurdum*, in which he is essentially saying, "If you want to be uncovered, why don't you go all the way with it?" (Keener, "Man and Woman," 585).

The need for the woman to honor her husband is established from the beginning of the section, where Paul identifies the man as the "head" (*kephalē*) of the woman, set in the context of Christ as the head of man and God as the head of Christ (1 Cor 11:3). The meaning of *kephalē* has been heavily debated, and prominent suggestions include "authority" (Grudem), "source" (Kroeger, 268; Payne, 113-37), and "preeminent" (Cervin).

As will be presented in more detail below, the "head" metaphor was informed by the physiological understanding of the *body, as metaphors were commonly drawn from observations from the physical world. In this view, the head represented the position at the top of the body and so was considered the leading and guiding member of the body. Examining the ancient medical literature reveals that the head was thought to unify and coordinate the other members of the body and was thought to be the source of provision to the body as a whole (Arnold 1994).

The body metaphor was a popular analogy, particularly in speeches that emphasized the unity and proper functioning of a group. The idea of the head of the body could be used in a variety of ways depending on the context, with the possible applications deriving from its overarching placement and function as the highest and most important member due to its guiding function. (See Lee 2006 for more on the general body metaphor in antiquity.)

For Paul, the husband's headship relates to the creation account in that the woman was created "from" and "for" man (1 Cor 11:7-9). Whether or not this entails a particular leadership role for the man, the direct reason for Eve's creation was so Adam would have a suitable companion, a helper who was like him (Gen 2:18-25). He is not complete without her, and together they fulfill the mandate to have dominion over the earth (Gen 1:28).

Paul also explains that the reason the woman and not the man should be covered is that she is his "glory," as the man is the *glory of God (1 Cor 11:7). In the ancient context, the image of a god would reflect or represent the god's glory. Image bearers also caused the admiration of the one whose glory they reflected. Paul wants the glory of God to be uncovered in worship, and the glory of man, who is the woman, to be covered. Paul appears to be instructing the woman, as the glory of man, to have a head covering in worship in order to avoid distracting from the worship of God (Ciampa and Rosner, 525-33).

But at the same time that Paul posits gender distinctions as relevant to the worship of God, he also takes care to ensure that the creation implications are not misunderstood. Following his initial remarks on the creation of Eve for and from Adam, he talks about the interdependence of man and woman: "Nevertheless, in the Lord woman is not independent of man nor man of woman; for as woman was made from man, so man is now born of woman" (1 Cor 11:11-12 ESV). That these verses are likely Paul's attempt to mitigate any potential misunderstandings about the creation order and purpose is evident through Paul's use of "nevertheless" to introduce the thought. This indicates it is a qualification but not rejection of his previous statements. Although Eve was created for and from Adam, men cannot consider themselves to be superior to women. Rather, they must recognize their interdependence, since after Adam all men are born from women (1 Cor 11:12). In this Paul seems to follow rabbinic tradition, in which one may obtain some principles from the creation of the first man and woman while also understanding that the creation was unique and that other principles may apply based on the creation of men and women since the first man and woman (Ciampa and Rosner, 534).

Even more importantly, though, Paul prefaces the statement with "in the *Lord." While the phrase is somewhat puzzling in its immediate context since the interdependence of man and woman through birth certainly applies to all humanity, the addition here indicates he also sees this interdependence as an implication of their new creation life. In this way, Paul uses creation as the basis for his instructions for men and women in worship but also makes clear that in Christ's community all members must recognize their interdependence.

Finally, Lucy Peppiatt argues that 1 Corinthians 11:7-10 represents phraseology from the Corinthians rather than Paul. This would include the statements about woman being the glory of man and being created "for" man, while Paul affirms woman's origin from man in 1 Corinthians 11:12 (Peppiatt 2015, 139-40). Peppiatt's proposal would put further focus on interdependence being a primary concern of the passage, situated within the context of the man being the head of the woman.

Overall, there is an essential distinction as well as an interdependence between male and female. Whether or not one concludes that the Genesis references support a transcultural principle of male leadership, the identification of a general pattern of Paul's concern that men and women conduct themselves in a manner that reflects their gender is significant, for it illustrates an underlying principle in his letters that the proper distinction between male and female is critical for humanity's worship of God as the Creator. In considering the two aspects of creation and new creation, one does not override the other, but both affect the worshiping community. The followers of Jesus are to remember that man was created first and woman was created from man, although they are also interdependent.

3. Galatians 3:28 and New Creation.

The implications of new creation must still be integrated with the continuing significance of God's creation of male and female. Galatians 3:28 has traditionally been at the heart of the gender debate, revolving around the question of whether there is still a special leadership role for men in the new era in which there is "neither male and female." However, one may learn more by noting a more fundamental purpose of the passage, which is to state the oneness of the Christian community made up of different members. In particular Paul describes three pairs of opposites, who would traditionally be divided from or antagonistic to one another. In Galatians 3:28 these three pairs—Jew/*Gentile, *slave/free, and male/female—represent some of the leading ways people were separated from one another, but Paul concludes the statement by saying, "for you are all one in Christ" (ESV). The significance of the pairs is that they now form a unity. The threefold formula in Galatians 3:28 follows a similar pattern elsewhere in Paul and in other cases also includes references to oneness (1 Cor 12:12-13; Col 3:11-15), reflecting the centrality of unification in the presentation of opposites through this formula.

This oneness does not preclude distinction but *depends* on distinctions. For example, although Paul says there is "neither Jew nor Greek," he elsewhere speaks of a continuing role for the Jews (Rom 1:16; 2:9-10; 11:1-31). Elsewhere he speaks of the "*mystery of Christ" being the inclusion of Gentiles into the one body of Christ. The result of their inclusion is reconciliation and *peace between the two (Eph 2:13-16), not the abolishing of distinctions. This point is particularly important for the relational implications of the oneness of Galatians 3:28.

The establishment of peace between Jews and Gentiles presupposes hostility. The two groups were characterized by a mutual animosity as the *law separated them, leading to Jewish contempt for Gentiles and Gentile suspicion of the Jews. However, Christ has now broken down the dividing wall to reconcile both to God. Instead of animosity and estrangement, *love is to be a defining feature of the one body of Christ (Eph 4:16).

Consequently, the question of whether Galatians 3:28 implies a functional equality should not overshadow the critical implications of the relational unity that seem to lie at the heart of Paul's declaration. The role of gender distinctions must be seen within the context of the unity of the new creation community. God has brought together those who were once separated from one another, not to abolish the differences between them but for them to live in unity and love one another.

Gender, therefore, not only remains relevant but also assumes a transcendent purpose. Differences are not abolished but become a key component in unity. Perhaps one might say the overcoming of differences as differences is itself what makes their unity particularly profound. As they are one in Christ, they can overcome their respective prejudices that prevent them from having table *fellowship together (Gal 2:12). Instead of being antagonistic toward those who are different, they are to be united in the "same mind" and in the "same love" by following the selfless example of Christ in their relationships with each other (Phil 2:1-11).

The eschatological quality to this unity is further seen in the presence and work of the Spirit, highlighting the interdependence and a certain transcendence of gender distinctions. Their unity is that of the one body of Christ brought about by the Spirit (1 Cor 12:12-13), who also gives spiritual manifestations to everyone for the common good (1 Cor 12:7). In the giving of gifts, the Holy Spirit transcends gender, as well as other distinctions such as age and race, for the purpose of accomplishing the church's mission. Paul states that spiritual manifestations are for the building up of the body (e.g., 1 Cor 14:5, 12, 26) and that they are given to "all" (1 Cor 12:7).

In this way, Paul reflects the understanding in Acts of the *Holy Spirit coming on all believers for the purpose of ministry. In Acts 2 one learns that in contrast to the Holy Spirit's coming on God's people temporarily and for a specific task, as in the OT (e.g., Ex 31:2-5; Num 11:25-26; Judg 6:34; 1 Sam 10:10), now the Spirit will indwell the believers. The coming of the Spirit is in fulfillment of Joel's *prophecy (Joel 2:28-32) and Jesus' promise in Acts 1:5 and Luke 24:49.

The coming of the Spirit in Acts has sometimes been interpreted as indicating that now the "highest levels of ministry" are open to women. However, this is not the primary purpose of the passage. The leadership the prophets exhibited was still subject to the authority of the elders (e.g., Acts 15:28; 21:10-14), and the prophecies themselves were to be judged by the community (1 Cor 14:29; 1 Thess 5:21). In addition, women such as Huldah (2 Kings 22:14-20; 2 Chron 34:22-28) and Miriam (Ex 15:20) were accepted as prophets in the OT, indicating that this was not primarily a new opening of ministry for women.

A more crucial contribution of the passage is to make a statement about the universality of ministry for all believers, including women. All of God's people, including women, as well as young and old, slave and free, Jew and Gentile, are empowered by the Spirit for God's purposes. Any newness of women's ministry must be understood in the context of the newness of ministry for all in the eschatological age. Pentecost is the beginning of the age of the Spirit and the last days. In this way, the coming of the Spirit marks the beginning of the fulfillment of God's eschatological goal of gathering his people into the *kingdom. Women are equally included in this outpouring, although the purpose is not to make a statement about rights or ministry opportunities. Instead, the focus is on the participation and inclusion of all in the kingdom blessings and the mission of the church.

Nevertheless, the nature of this inclusion does not mean that distinctions associated with the old age are rendered irrelevant—for example, the abovementioned continued relevance of Jew and Gentile (e.g., Rom 1:6-17). Elsewhere Paul exhorts the community to show proper respect to older men and women (1 Tim 5:1-2; Titus 2:2-3). In 1 Corinthians 11, women may prophesy but must do so in a manner that honors their husbands, as grounded in creation. To recognize the new era is to recognize the contribution all make to the new community through the Spirit. At the same time, women's prophesying is done in a context in which particular distinctions are honored. In this way, the one body of Christ is unified and built up in the Spirit and in love (Eph 4:16).

4. Man and Woman in Marriage.

Paul's discussion of marriage also reflects the significance of this intersection between the implications of creation and new creation. Again, he emphasizes the basic creation distinction of male and female at the same time that he sees the ramifications for their new life in Christ.

In Romans 1, in line with Jewish thought (e.g., Lev 18:22; 20:13), Paul sees marriage as between man and woman, as first outlined in Genesis. In Romans 1–3, Paul confronts people for failing to honor God properly (Rom 1:21) and falling short of his glory (Rom 3:23). Part of their failure is their acceptance of "unnatural" relationships of men with men and women with women (Rom 1:26-27). What is particularly striking about Paul's discussion is his many allusions to the Genesis creation account. Among other connections, he refers to God as the "Creator" in Romans 1:25, who has been revealing himself "since the creation of the world" (Rom 1:20 ESV). In Romans 1:26-27 he uses the same terms to describe the genders—*arsēn* (male) and *thelys* (female)—as in the LXX translation of Genesis 1:27. Preston Sprinkle concludes that Paul in Romans is purposefully drawing attention to God's creation of humanity into two distinct sexes. The actions in Romans 1:26-27 go against God's intent for the creation of male and female (2015, 91-93).

However, Paul draws additional implications for marriage for those who are made new in Christ. Although complementarians and egalitarians have argued about whether men have a particular authority over women in marriage, that the discussion has remained so intractable may itself be an indication that the full answer lies elsewhere. From the perspective of the intersection of creation and new creation, one may see the significance of Paul's instructions for marriage in a different light, in that they evidence both a mutuality and an asymmetrical relationship between husband and wife.

In 1 Corinthians 7 Paul appears to be addressing a misunderstanding of the implications of the Corinthian believers' new life in Christ related to marriage and marital relations. In regard to spousal rights to intimacy, both husband and wife have a respective duty to each other, and each has "authority" over the body of the other (1 Cor 7:2-4). The reciprocal nature of the duties stands in contrast to some Jewish texts and general Greek culture (Keener, "Man and Woman," 584). Throughout the passage, Paul speaks in balanced pairs, addressing both husbands and wives, including 1 Corinthians 7:10-11, where Paul says that the woman must not divorce her husband, and the husband must not divorce his wife. This passage is particularly noteworthy since Paul's instructions for wives stand in contrast to the Jewish understanding, in which divorce was considered the man's prerogative, although Greco-Roman women did on occasion divorce their husbands (Fee, 325).

But while Paul illustrates a mutuality in marriage in 1 Corinthians 7, he also speaks of the headship of the husband in regard to the wife in Ephesians 5:21-33 as well as 1 Corinthians 11. It is important, therefore, to consider what headship entails. As discussed above, the identification of the husband as the head would traditionally correspond to the head's position as the leading member of the body. What is remarkable, however, is how Paul develops the metaphor.

Although debate has generally revolved around the question of whether the husband's headship is permanent and transcultural, the more relevant point may be how Paul redefines headship according to kingdom principles. Paul's support of the idea by appealing to Christ's headship over the church seems to indicate a transcendent principle.

The head-body metaphor was commonly used in antiquity to illustrate various aspects of unity and diversity of a particular entity or group. Within this understanding, individual parts might be singled out to illustrate a particular contribution to the body. As the head occupied the highest point in the physical body, this corresponded to its position as the superior and leading part, the most critical one for the overall well-being of the body. For example, the head or brain was important because it coordinated the functioning of the other members (e.g., Hippocrates, *De morbo sacro* 20.27-29; Plato, *Tim.* 44d; Philo, *QG* 2.9). When applied politically, the metaphor emphasized the head's power and authority, as, for example, an emperor, a general, or a king (e.g., Seneca, *Clem.* 1.4.3; Plutarch, *Galb.* 4.3; Philo, *Mos.* 2.30).

The head's prominent position also led naturally to certain privileges. Since the head was the most vital part for the overall functioning of the body, the rest of the body was to protect it at all costs for the survival of the whole. At times, this would mean the other members of the body should be willing to sacrifice themselves in order to protect it (e.g., Seneca, *Clem.* 1.3.4). Indeed, the head's responsibility was to ensure its own survival if it was to do what was best for the whole body (e.g., Plutarch, *Pel.* 2.1-2). Not surprisingly, then, the head was the body part most deserving of love, to which in return it did not give love but *mercy (Seneca, *Clem.* 1.5.1-2; Aristotle, *Ethica eudemia* 7.3.4).

In Ephesians, Paul appears to use the metaphor in line with this popular conception at the same time as he radically modifies it to communicate kingdom values. In particular, he uses the metaphor to illustrate a startling reversal of expectations. Instead of having the body sacrifice to protect the head, Paul says that the head, the husband, should sacrifice himself for the body (Eph 5:25). To the ancient mind, this would be incomprehensible. It would be a foolish and suicidal action that would result in the destruction of the entire body for the leading member to sacrifice itself. Furthermore, it would be offensive in an *honor/shame society, as the head would be taking on the duty of the lesser member. The head would bring additional shame on itself by being the one to love rather than receive love (Eph 5:26).

But the critical point is that Paul's instructions do not bring about the destruction of the body but the opposite. To describe the result of the husband's actions, Paul returns to Genesis and the account of the first man and woman: "Therefore a man shall leave his father and mother and hold fast to his wife, and the two shall become one flesh" (Eph 5:31 ESV; see Gen 2:24). In other words, the husband's sacrificial actions result in the intended unity between man and woman.

Two important points need to be made here. First, the idea that the husband's sacrifice paradoxically leads not to shame and the destruction of the whole but rather the fulfillment of God's intention for unity seems to fit with an overarching scriptural paradigm. Throughout the Bible, God works through a reversal of the expectations of the world to show that his ways are not humanity's ways (Is 55:8-9). This is seen in areas such as God's choice of the elder Esau to serve the younger Jacob (Gen 25:23), the selection of David as the Lord's anointed over his older brothers (1 Sam 16:7), or the news of the birth of the Messiah given not to kings but to lowly shepherds (Lk 2:8-20). Most pointedly, the crucifixion is the ultimate demonstration of how God operates in ways that are confounding to humans. In particular, the sacrifice of his *Son leads to life for those who belong to him (1 Cor 1:18–2:16).

Second, the actions of the husband carry a particular eschatological significance, for it is only by acting like Christ that the intended unity is achieved. In this way, Paul sees the marriage relationship as a focal point of creation and new creation. As Eve was created from Adam, the two were separate and yet to become one flesh. However, this aspect of their intended union occurs only through Christ.

In this light, possible ideas of authority or equality seem less central to the point of the passage than achieving this unity. The passage does not explicitly speak of the husband exerting authority over the wife, nor does it emphasize their equality. Rather, the passage is shaped through a different set of lenses: the leading member—the head, or husband—sacrifices himself for the sake of the body, the wife, in order to bring about the fulfillment of God's intention for the oneness of male and female as stated from the beginning of creation.

Significantly, the relationship between God and Israel in the OT was also described as an intimate marital relationship, with a special focus on the husband's actions. Particularly in Hosea, "husband" is a metaphor signifying intimacy. The idea that *Israel will "know the Lord" (Hos 2:20 ESV; see Ex 6:2-7) applies a term that is used metaphorically for intimacy in a covenantal sense. The expression "I will speak to her heart" (Hos 2:14) is from the language of courtship and seeks to overcome estrangement and produce union. Overall, the image of the husband highlights the love and trust between God and his people more than any other metaphor, including God as Father or Shepherd (Lee-Barnewall, 160-61; citing Stienstra, 96).

The OT depiction of the relationship between Yahweh and his people provides important background for the relationship between Christ and his people in the NT. Clinton Arnold contends that the comparison between the husband-wife and Christ-church relationship goes beyond analogy to describe a new eschatological reality. In this way it is a typological relationship in which the union of husband and wife prefigures that of Christ and the church (Arnold 2010, 395-96).

If true, this highlights the importance of Paul's understanding of marriage. Comprehending the significance of male and female in marriage entails understanding that Paul sees the simultaneous existence of both creation and new creation aspects in this union. As God created Eve from Adam and Adam was to bring unity from their separateness, now in Christ, the husband can accomplish what Adam could not. It is the believers' new creation existence that enables the fulfillment of their creation purposes.

5. Creation and New Creation.

As one considers both creation and new creation principles in Paul's discussions on man and woman, one must further note that there is a certain tension characterizing the apostle's thought. On the one hand, Paul sees the need to protect the separation and distinction between the two. On the other hand, the *apostle can say that in their oneness in Christ, there is "neither" male and female. To understand oneness, one must see that it does not equate to sameness, and if anything, differentiation is *essential* for fulfilling the implications of their unity. The body is one in Christ, so there is neither Jew nor Gentile and male nor female at the same time that there remains a profound significance to Jew and Gentile and male and female. In marriage, the two become one flesh at the same time that there is a very real and necessary distinction between man and woman. Indeed, the unity in marriage is dependent on that distinction.

The significance of this tension between creation distinctions for man and woman and their new creation oneness becomes clearer when contrasting Paul's thought with that expressed in the apocryphal text Gospel of Thomas, whose proposed dating varies from around the time of Jesus to the latter part of the second century AD. The work is a collection of sayings attributed to Jesus, some of which are found in the canonical Gospels and others of which reveal essential Gnostic influence. Seeing how unity and difference between men and women are treated in a noncanonical text can help one to understand and appreciate the uniqueness of Paul's vision for God's intent for man and woman.

In stark contrast to Paul's belief that the unity of husband and wife is achieved by the particular role of the husband in relation to the wife, one saying in Thomas reveals the belief that the unity of male and female takes place when there is no longer any distinctiveness between the two: "When you make male and female into a single one, so that the male will not be male nor the female be female" (Logion 22; translation from Miller). An additional saying in Thomas states that the female must become male for this to happen: "For every female who makes herself male will enter the domain of Heaven" (Logion 114). Not only does the Gospel of Thomas assert that the male/female distinction is not necessary, but elsewhere it holds that only male existence ultimately matters.

The Thomas sayings are revealing for their commentary on the creation account in Genesis. Where humanity was initially one but then became two as the woman was created from the man, there is ultimately a return to the one, the original male. This contrasting text makes Paul's understanding of the relationship between creation and new creation all the more remarkable. Paul sees a unity, but one that maintains the essential creation distinctions of male and female rather than a merging of the two and abolishing of the distinctions or making woman become man.

Moreover, for Paul the distinctions are central to the unity, for it is the asymmetrical relationship of the husband as head and wife as body that enables the fulfillment of Genesis 2:24. The eschatological key to the fulfillment of Genesis 2:24 is the husband's following of Christ's example, in which he loves as Christ loved and sacrificed for the church, not the merging of the woman back into the man.

The contrast with the Thomas passages highlights the significance of Paul's insistence that the Christian community recognize and honor the distinctions between man and woman even as they are all one in Christ. In contrast to the Gnostic influence in Thomas, which prioritizes the spiritual aspect and disdains the body, Paul identifies the continuing relevance of the creation differences that pertain to their bodily existence. Their separateness, which begins from their creation and is maintained in their continued bodily existence, is absolutely essential to their oneness, for it is the actions of the husband toward the one who was created from him that lead to the intimate "one flesh" union.

Key to understanding Paul, therefore, is the way he sees the integration of and continuity between the believers' creation and new creation existence. The latter does not supersede the former and make it irrelevant; rather, in Christian marriage, husbands and wives fulfill what was intended in Genesis. Creation differences are maintained, but the intended unity of male and female can only happen in their new creation life, in which the husband is like Christ.

6. Conclusion.

Although discussions of man and woman in Paul have often been dominated by questions about authority and equality, other areas such as unity and the significance of humanity's creation/new creation existence may go further for understanding how Paul sees the relationship between man and woman.

For example, focusing on the inclusion of formerly separated and hostile groups into the promises of God may be a more accurate characterization of the new community than the equality of the members. The concept of equality evokes more contemporary political concerns over rights and opportunities than salvation-history implications of the unity of all God's people (Lee-Barnewall, 83-101).

On the other hand, the prominence of Genesis 2:24 would seem to indicate that if any type of authority for the husband is found in Ephesians 5, it must be understood in the larger context of the goal of unity. That authority may not be the most accurate way to describe the husband's role in marriage is further seen in the emphasis on mutuality in regard to sexual relations in 1 Corinthians 7.

Instead of concerns over authority and equality, Paul's more foundational beliefs may instead be grounded in the honoring of God as the Creator, who made humanity as male and female and also declared them to be one in Christ. In this, Paul's reliance on and vision for the fulfillment of the Genesis account provide the keys to his understanding of man and woman. Genesis describes how the world was founded on God's creation of order from chaos (Gen 1:2). Within this order, humanity is the apex, the point toward which Genesis 1 moves (Wenham, 36-40). Consequently, it should not be surprising that Paul prioritizes the preservation of the order recounted in Genesis. Within this order, the separate and sequential creation of male and female provides the basis for Paul's instructions in both the worshiping community and marriage.

The intersection of creation and new creation thus appears to be predicated on the continued existence of humanity as male and female in creation along with the transcendent, unifying work of the Spirit for those made new in Christ. The coming of the Spirit does not negate the importance of humanity's existence as male and female. Rather, Paul sees the separate and yet intertwined existence of man and woman as created by God as essential to their eschatological destiny.

As a result, Paul exhorts the believers to consider the implications of their bodily, separated existence as male and female as they live out their eschatological oneness in Christ and in the Spirit. Their distinctions are an indispensable aspect in the goal of eschatological unity. In the beginning God created man and woman, and now believers are to continue to live accordingly and move toward true unity in love as they await Christ's final coming.

See also Adam and Christ; Corinthians, First Letter to the; Creation and New Creation; Galatians, Letter to the; Head; Marriage and Divorce, Adultery and Incest; Pastoral Epistles; Women.

BIBLIOGRAPHY. **C. E. Arnold,** "Jesus Christ: 'Head' of the Church (Colossians and Ephesians)," in *Jesus of Nazareth: Lord and Christ*, ed. J. B. Green and M. Turner (Grand Rapids, MI: Eerdmans, 1994), 346-66; idem, *Ephesians*, ZECNT (Grand Rapids, MI: Zondervan, 2010); **A. J. Batten,** "Neither God nor Braided Hair (1 Timothy 2:9; 1 Peter 3:3): Adornment, Gender and Honour in Antiquity," *NTS* 55 (2009): 484-501; **S. M. Baugh,** "A Foreign World: Ephesus in the First Century," in *Women in the Church: An Interpretation and Application of 1 Timothy 2:9-15*, 3rd ed., ed. A. J. Köstenberger and T. R. Schreiner (Wheaton, IL: Crossway, 2016), 25-64; **J. R. Beck,** ed., *Two Views on Women in Ministry* (Grand Rapids, MI: Zondervan, 2005); **J. K. Beilby and P. R. Eddy,** *Understanding Transgender Identities: Four Views* (Grand Rapids, MI: Baker, 2019); **R. Cervin,** "Does *Kephalē* ('Head') Mean 'Source' or 'Authority over' in Greek Literature: A Rebuttal," *TrinJ* 10 (Spring 1989): 85-112; **R. E. Ciampa and B. S. Rosner,** *The First Epistle to the Corinthians*, PNTC (Grand Rapids, MI: Eerdmans, 2010); **L. H. Cohick,** *Women in the World of the Earliest Christians: Illuminating Ancient Ways of Life* (Grand Rapids, MI: Baker, 2009); **G. D. Fee,** *The First Epistle to the Corinthians*, rev. ed. (Grand Rapids, MI: Eerdmans, 2014); **W. Grudem,** "Does Κεφαλη ('Head') Mean 'Source' or 'Authority over' in Greek Literature? A Survey of 2,336 Examples," *TrinJ* 6 (1985): 38-59; idem, "The Meaning of *Kephalē* ('Head'): A Response to Recent Studies," in *Recovering Biblical Manhood and Womanhood: A Response to Evangelical Feminism*, ed. J. Piper and W. Grudem (Wheaton, IL: Crossway, 1991), 425-68; **C. S. Keener,** *Paul, Women and Wives: Marriage and Women's Ministry in the Letters of Paul* (Peabody, MA: Hendrickson, 1992); idem, "Man and Woman," *DPL*, 583-92; **A. J. Köstenberger and T. R. Schreiner,** *Women in the Church: An Interpretation and Application of 1 Timothy 2:9-15*, 3rd ed. (Wheaton, IL: Crossway, 2016); **C. C. Kroeger,** "The Classical Concept of *Head* as 'Source,'" in *Equal to Serve*, ed. G. G. Hull (Grand Rapids, MI: Baker, 1991), 267-83; **R. C. Kroeger and C. C. Kroeger,** *I Suffer Not a Woman: Rethinking 1 Timothy 2:11-15 in Light of Ancient Evidence* (Grand Rapids, MI: Baker, 1992); **M. V. Lee,** *Paul, the Stoics, and the Body of Christ*, SNTSMS 137 (Cambridge: Cambridge University Press, 2006); **M. Lee-Barnewall,** *Neither Complementarian nor Egalitarian: A Kingdom Corrective to the Evangelical Gender Debate* (Grand Rapids, MI: Baker, 2016); **W. A. Meeks,** "The Image of the Androgyne: Some Uses of a Symbol in Earliest Christianity," *History of Religions* 13 (1974): 165-208; **R. J. Miller,** ed., *The Complete Gospels* (Sonoma, CA: Polebridge, 1994); **D. J. Moo,** "Creation and New Creation," *BBR* 20 (2010): 39-60;

P. B. Payne, *Man and Woman: One in Christ: An Exegetical and Theological Study of Paul's Letters* (Grand Rapids, MI: Zondervan, 2009); **L. Peppiatt,** *Women and Worship at Corinth: Paul's Rhetorical Arguments in 1 Corinthians* (Eugene, OR: Cascade Books, 2015); idem, *Rediscovering Scripture's Vision for Women: Fresh Perspectives on Disputed Texts* (Downers Grove, IL: IVP Academic, 2019); **R. Pierce,** "First Corinthians 7: Paul's Neglected Treatise on Gender," *PriscPap* 23 (2009): 8-13; **R. W. Pierce and R. M. Groothius,** eds., *Discovering Biblical Equality* (Downers Grove, IL: InterVarsity Press, 2005); **J. Piper and W. Grudem,** eds., *Recovering Biblical Manhood and Womanhood: A Response to Evangelical Feminism* (Wheaton, IL: Crossway, 1991); **R. L. Saucy and J. K. TenElshof,** eds., *Women and Men in Ministry* (Chicago: Moody, 2001); **T. R. Schreiner,** "Head Coverings, Prophecy, and the Trinity," in *Recovering Biblical Manhood and Womanhood: A Response to Evangelical Feminism*, ed. J. Piper and W. Grudem (Wheaton, IL: Crossway, 2012), 124-53; **P. Sprinkle,** *People to Be Loved: Why Homosexuality Is Not Just an Issue* (Grand Rapids, MI: Zondervan, 2015); idem, ed., *Two Views of Homosexuality, the Bible, and the Church* (Grand Rapids, MI: Zondervan, 2016); **N. Stienstra,** *YHWH Is the Husband of His People* (Kampen: Kok Pharos, 1993); **M. Vines,** *God and the Gay Christian* (New York: Convergent Books, 2014); **G. Wenham,** *Genesis 1–15*, WBC 1 (Nashville: Thomas Nelson, 1987); **C. L. Westfall,** *Paul and Gender: Reclaiming the Apostle's Vision for Men and Women in Christ* (Grand Rapids, MI: Baker, 2016); **B. W. Winter,** *After Paul Left Corinth: The Influence of Secular Ethics and Social Change* (Grand Rapids, MI: Eerdmans, 2001); idem, *Roman Wives, Roman Widows: The Appearance of New Women and the Pauline Communities* (Grand Rapids, MI: Eerdmans, 2003).

M. Lee-Barnewall

MAN OF LAWLESSNESS AND RESTRAINING POWER

In 2 Thessalonians Paul writes to combat the misunderstanding that the day of the *Lord has already occurred (2 Thess 2:2). He reminds the Thessalonians how he told them that prior to the Lord's coming, the man of lawlessness who opposes *God will set himself in the *temple as God (2 Thess 2:4). Yet he also reminds them that this mysterious figure is being restrained and that they know "what is holding him back, so that he may be revealed at the proper time" (2 Thess 2:6 NIV).

Paul's terminology and thinking here are probably influenced by texts such as Psalm 88:23 LXX (Ps 89:22), which uses the phrase "son of lawlessness" to describe the enemies of David. Similarly, the Psalms of Solomon (17.11-20) labeled the Roman general Pompey "lawless" after his desecration of the temple in 63 BC. Added to these is the tradition whereby those who stood in opposition to God by declaring themselves to be a god were brought down by God (Dan 11:36; Ezek 28:2; Is 14:13-14). Paul reminds the Thessalonians that the lawless one will be brought down by the Lord Jesus (2 Thess 2:8). Since *apostasy and lawlessness are wedded in 2 Thessalonians, Paul probably envisioned the man of lawlessness as someone such as Antiochus Epiphanius during the Maccabean period. This history and imagery would have been particularly pertinent in light of Caligula's claims of divinity and attempt to set up his own image in the *Jerusalem temple in AD 41 (Josephus, *Ant.* 18.8.2).

Whoever or whatever is restraining the man of lawlessness was known well enough by the Thessalonians that Paul did not feel the need to fully explain. Compounding the interpretive challenge is that "restrainer" in Greek can be either neuter (2 Thess 2:6) or masculine (2 Thess 2:7), so it is unclear whether it is someone or something holding back the appearance of the lawless one. Some early church fathers, such as Tertullian (*Res.* 24), Hippolytus (*Comm. Dan.* 4.21), and John Chrysostom (*Hom. 2 Thess.* 4) thought the "restrainer" was the Roman emperor or the empire. Others, such as John Calvin, suggested it was the *apostle Paul and his preaching of the *gospel. Saint Augustine spoke for many when he said, "I frankly confess I do not know what he means" (*Civ.* 20.19). Yet ancient and modern commentators have surmised, probably correctly, that it is God's sovereign hand, through the *Holy Spirit, that restrains evil in the world and the final arrival of the lawless one. Although evil is already at work in the world, it is only by the power and grace of God that good is not completely overwhelmed by evil.

Despite whatever or whoever is holding back the lawless one, Paul warns that the "secret" power of lawlessness is already at work. Paul uses *mystērion*, which probably means "hidden" in the context of the man of lawlessness being "revealed" (2 Thess 2:6, 8). But what exactly he means is unclear. The most one should probably conclude is that Paul is convinced that although the power of evil is already at work in the world, so also is the one who restrains it.

See also SATAN, DEVIL; THESSALONIANS, LETTERS TO THE.

BIBLIOGRAPHY. **C. R. Nicholl,** *From Hope to Despair in Thessalonica* (New York: Cambridge University Press, 2004), 225-49; **N. K. Gupta,** *1 & 2 Thessalonians* (Grand Rapids, MI: Zondervan, 2019).

J. Byron

MANUSCRIPTS. *See* TEXTUAL CRITICISM.

MARCION. *See* CANON OF PAUL'S LETTERS; INTERPRETATION: PATRISTIC.

MARRIAGE AND DIVORCE, ADULTERY AND INCEST

A comprehensive survey of modern studies on this topic and its background in rabbinic studies can be found in Thomas Kazen, while Andrew Naselli gives a clear survey of the implications for the interpretation of various NT passages as a result of different approaches. Such surveys tend to ignore the use of Exodus 21:10-11, which is key for understanding Jewish marriage vows in Paul and in the marriage contracts of his day. For this, William Luck and David Instone-Brewer (2002) are the best sources.

1. Background
2. Marriage
3. Divorce
4. Incest and Conclusions

1. Background.

1.1. Old Testament. The OT has no definition of marriage, so the use of this term and the nature of the institution has to be inferred somewhat from the cultures of the time. Ancient Near Eastern laws said that a wife (unlike a concubine) exchanged vows publicly with her husband (Roth, e.g., nos. 2, 25). This concurs with the concept of a marriage covenant (Ezek 16:8, 59-62; Mal 2:14), which by the time of Paul was a written document.

Adultery in the OT was punished by *death if there were two witnesses. Otherwise, a suspected woman was subjected to the rite of *sotah*: drinking water mixed with dust from the sanctuary floor, which would (it was believed) result in a prolapsed womb if she were guilty (Num 5:11-28).

Polygamy was allowed and even demanded in the case of a childless widow who had a married brother-in-law. He was instructed to marry her to produce a son who would inherit the family estate. Similar levirate marriages were known in other ancient Near Eastern laws, but these required that she marry a father-in-law or nephew if no male of her own age was available.

1.2. Greco-Roman World. Before the first century AD, most Roman marriages were with *manus* ("hand")—which meant the property of the woman transferred from the control of her father to her husband—and divorces were rare. By the first century, fewer marriages were with *manus*, and women could spend their money or divorce their husbands without permission from a male relative. Divorce was enacted by either partner by simply separating from the other, without the need for any document or other legal action.

Polygamy was strictly forbidden except in Palestine, but a husband's use of mistresses or brothels was permitted, though some exceptional marriage contracts specifically forbade this.

1.3. First-Century Judaism. Marriage contracts that have survived from the first and early second centuries AD (e.g., in Lewis et al.) all refer to vows concerning faithfulness and neglect. The usual wording is somewhat euphemistic; for example: "[1] Be my wife according to the law of Moses and the Judeans and [2] I will feed you and [3] clothe you and [4] I will bring you into my house" (numbers added).

The first vow refers to sexual faithfulness and the last refers to conjugal rights, in language suitable for reading out at the wedding, as was customary. Adultery no longer resulted in judicial death (Jn 18:31; see Aus), so divorce occurred instead.

The final three vows were derived from Exodus 21:10-11, on the assumption that if a slave wife had rights to food, clothing and love, then a free man and woman also had these rights. Hillelite and Shammaite rabbis in the early first century debated about the minimum amount of food and clothing that a husband had to supply and that a wife had to prepare, and also the minimum frequency of conjugation (m. Ketub. 5:5-8). These debates indicate that both groups still accepted neglect of these as a ground for divorce by men or women, and there is no record of any group that did not recognize them.

The contract also specified the amount of money payable to the woman on divorce or death of her husband. This was a minimum of two hundred denarii (about a year's wage for day laborers) but was usually considerably more. This payment was called her *ketubah*, and it was so important that the marriage contract tended to be called the *ketubah*. If the wife were guilty of breaking her vows, she would be divorced without her *ketubah* payment, and if the man were guilty, she would receive this payment when she divorced him. In theory, the man had to be willing to initiate the divorce, but if the court decided against him, "They compel him until he says: I will it" (m. ʿArak. 5:6).

By the early first century, Hillelite rabbis had introduced a new form of divorce for "any cause" (m. Giṭ. 9:10; y. Sotah 1.1, 1a; Sifre Deut. 269; Josephus, *Ant.* 4.8.23; Philo, *Spec.* 3.2.304; cf. Mt 19:3). This no-fault divorce was popular with men because they did not need to present embarrassing proof to a court. Women could not use this ground for divorce, but in recompense they always received their *ketubah* divorce payment because no fault had been proved against them.

The scriptural foundation came from the phrase "a thing of indecency" (*ʿerwat dābār*, Deut 24:1). The Hillelites interpreted the first word, "indecency," as adultery, and the second word, "a thing," as anything else or "any cause." A cause as minor as a burned meal could be cited (m. Giṭ. 9:10), so it was effectively a no-fault divorce. This interpretation was disputed by Shammaite rabbis, who said this phrase referred to "nothing but adultery"—a conclusion that Jesus may have cited (Mt 5:32; 19:9). Opposition to this form of divorce ended when the Shammaite leaders all perished at the destruction of *Jerusalem in AD 70.

2. Marriage.

2.1. Paul Affirms Roman Structures Within Marriage. Paul cites a formula summarizing the threefold Aristotelian structure of *households that was followed by Romans: submission of a wife to her husband, submission of children to their father, submission of *slaves to their master. This is cited or alluded to in a wide spectrum of Pauline literature (Col 3:18–4:1; Eph 5:22–6:9; 1 Tim 2:9–3:7; 6:1-2; Titus 2:3-10) and also by other Jews of the time (1 Pet 2:18–3:7; cf. Philo, *Hypoth.* 7.3, 14; Josephus, *Ag. Ap.* 2.201-215).

Paul and these others refer to Aristotle's structure with some diffidence, adding caveats such as "Husbands, love your wives and do not be harsh with them" (Col 3:19 NIV); "just as *Christ loved the *church" (Eph 5:25 NIV). Paul's reason given for commending this moral code is evangelistic: "[wives must] be subject to their husbands, so that no one will malign the word of *God" (Titus 2:5 NIV). The caveats expressed by Philo and Josephus are both contained in apologetic works, so their motives may be similar.

Paul commends the Roman system of morality even in a detail that was not subsequently emulated by later Christians. Although in public the man was the "ruler of the house" (*oikodespotēs*), in the privacy of home a Roman wife commanded slaves, made purchases, and generally "ruled the house" (*oikodespoteō*). Paul counsels wives to fulfill this role of household *leadership "to give the enemy no opportunity for slander" (1 Tim 5:14 NIV)—that is, to fit in with Roman expectations of morality.

2.2. Paul Affirms Jewish Marriage Vows. Paul agrees with the three marriage vows based on Exodus 21:11, which required married couples to give themselves sexually to each other (1 Cor 7:2-5) and to supply and prepare physical necessities such as food and clothing (1 Cor 7:28-34). In Ephesians 5:25, 29 these activities are referred to in euphemistic language with regard to Christ and his bride, whom he "loves," "nourishes," and "cherishes" (i.e., keeps warm).

2.3. Paul Condemns Adultery. Paul regarded activity at brothels as "sexual immorality" (*porneia*), consistent with Jewish views but contrary to the attitude of most Romans. He teaches that husbands should remain "one body" with their wives instead of with prostitutes (1 Cor 6:16), contrary to the former practice of many converts (1 Cor 6:11).

Leaders are to set an example by being "a man of one woman" and a "woman of one man"—often translated as "husband of one wife" and "wife of one husband" (1 Tim 3:2, 12; 5:9; Titus 1:16). This phrase may be a Greek form of Latin *univira*, which commonly describes faithful wives on tombstones.

Some interpreters regard "man of one woman" as a command that all leaders should be married, but "woman of one man" could not mean this because it is used of widows. Others regard these phrases as a prohibition of bigamy, but this was already strictly prohibited under Roman law.

2.4. Paul Both Condemns and Affirms Mixed Marriages. Judaism condemned marriages to non-Jews, and Romans insisted that a wife worship the gods of her husband (Plutarch, *Mor.* 140D). In spite of this, Paul regards nonbelieving spouses of converts to be "sanctified" (1 Cor 7:14). However, when believers have a choice about who to marry, he tells widows that the one they marry "must belong to the *Lord" (1 Cor 7:39 NIV) and tells others to not be "unequally yoked" (2 Cor 6:14—"unyoking" was a Greek term for divorce; see Instone-Brewer 2001).

3. Divorce.

3.1. Paul Rejects Roman Divorce-by-Separation. Paul tells a woman who had separated from her husband to remain unmarried and attempt reconciliation, and he tells the man to not to divorce her (1 Cor 7:10-12). He says that she should not "separate" (Gk. *chōrizō*, "to leave") and that he should not "divorce" (*aphiēmi*, "to send"). Both of these words refer to "divorce" in the Greek world (Instone-Brewer 2001) and in the NT (*chōrizō* at Mt 19:6; Mk 10:9; *aphiēmi* at 1 Cor 7:12-13). The difference may relate to the fact that men would usually own the house, so divorce entailed a woman leaving the marital home, whereas a men sent away his wife.

There is a curious asymmetry in these verses in that the woman is instructed to seek reconciliation, but the man is not. This is especially significant in the context of 1 Corinthians 7, which is extremely careful to express equal instructions to men and women throughout, even to the point of sounding repetitious (see 1 Cor 7:3, 12-14, 16, 27-28, 32-34). This asymmetry has three possible explanations.

First, if Paul is thinking in terms of Jewish *law, a woman could not change her mind after a divorce (Deut 24:1-4), so this asymmetry would be an affirmation that only a man can actually initiate a divorce. That is, he would be saying that a woman getting divorced would not be legally valid, so she should be reconciled to the man who is still her husband. Even if the woman had valid grounds for a divorce, due to her husband's broken marriage vows, he still had to initiate it by writing the divorce certificate—though in Paul's day a court could still force him to do this (m. ʿArak. 5:6). However, if Paul were thinking in terms of Jewish law, why did Paul instruct such women to not remarry? Under Jewish law they would not be able to remarry because they were still married.

Second, if Paul is thinking in terms of Roman law, he is telling women not to carry out a Roman divorce-by-separation. This enabled either partner to leave a marriage with the unspoken intention of enacting a divorce. The divorce became legally complete as soon as their intention was clear, without needing any further legal process, and they would both be free to remarry. Therefore, Paul tells such a woman not to make her unspoken intention legally clear by remarrying. However, if Paul is thinking in terms of Roman law, the man's remarriage would transform the separation into a legally binding divorce just like his wife's. So why does Paul not tell the man not to remarry?

The third possibility is that Paul is mixing Roman and Jewish law in terms of an actual case occurring in the Corinthian church. The woman had walked out on her husband, so, by Roman law, she had divorced him and was free to remarry. Paul points out that she could nevertheless show that she had not intended to enact a divorce by initiating a reconciliation with her husband; he tells them both to ensure they do not make such reconciliation impossible. She could make it impossible by getting remarried—which would confirm that she had intended to divorce him. And he could make reconciliation impossible by divorcing her.

The asymmetry—telling her but not him to attempt reconciliation—is explained by Jewish law. When the wife left, she was breaking her marriage vows to prepare food and clothing and exchange love with him (based on Ex 21:10-11). As an abandoned partner, her husband could divorce her on these three grounds of neglect, or he could accept her back if she repented. The divorce would not be final in Jewish terms until he has done this. As the victim of these broken marriage vows, the choice is his to make, so Paul tells him to not divorce her. Paul did not tell him to initiate reconciliation, because that was up to his wife, the partner who had abandoned the marriage; the victim could then decide whether to accept that reconciliation.

This passage makes sense, therefore, if Paul and his congregations were following the Jewish understanding of divorce in the OT. However, at this point Paul introduces a specifically Christian element.

3.2. A Command from "the Lord" About Divorce. Paul cites a command from "the Lord" when telling the woman not to end her marriage (1 Cor 7:10). This is generally recognized as a reference to a Jesus *tradition that is similar or identical to that found in the Gospels. It is possible that Paul also applies this tradition when he subsequently tells a man not to divorce his wife (1 Cor 7:11), though Paul does not actually state that it does apply to him. However, in 1 Corinthians 7:12-14, where he tells Christians not to divorce a non-Christian partner, he specifically states that the Jesus tradition does not cover this situation because he has to rely on teaching from "I, not the Lord" (1 Cor 7:12 NIV). Paul would not need to say this if the Jesus tradition included a prohibition against believers divorcing their nonbelieving partners.

This tells something about the Jesus tradition that Paul had: it prohibited divorce for the woman who had no apparent grounds for divorce, and possibly prohibited it for the man who had been abandoned by her, but it did not prohibit divorcing a nonbelieving husband or wife.

There are various Jesus traditions in the Gospels that Paul may be referring to: (1) "the two will become one *flesh" (Mt 19:5-6; Mk 10:8 NIV); (2) "a man will . . . be united to his wife" (Mt 19:5; Mk 10:7 NIV); (3) "what God has joined together, let no one separate" (Mt 19:6; Mk 10:9 NIV); (4) "anyone who divorce his wife and marries another commits adultery" (Mk 10:11; Lk 16:18 NIV); (5) "if she divorces her husband and marries another man, she commits adultery" (Mk 10:12 NIV); (6) number 4 with the addition of "except for sexual immorality" (Mt 5:32; 19:9 NIV).

The first three are commands or injunctions against divorce in general, and the last three state that remarriage after at least some divorces is equivalent to adultery in some way. None of these sayings is limited to divorcing believers, so they do not explain why Paul needed to add teaching on his own authority to prohibit divorcing nonbelievers.

Perhaps the limitation is found in their interpretation. These sayings have been interpreted in four main ways: (1) prohibiting all divorces (the view of Catholic interpreters and some Protestants such as Wenham and Piper); (2) prohibiting divorce except for adultery (the view of most Protestants); (3) prohibiting divorce except for anything that can be interpreted as "sexual immorality" (*porneia*), which is used in Greek literature and the NT for incest, premarital sex, adultery, visiting prostitutes, and so on, but is extended by some modern interpreters to include viewing pornography or anything that corrupts the marriage (e.g., Clark; Atkinson); (4) prohibiting the any-cause divorce because it is not an OT ground for divorce (Instone-Brewer 2002).

The first interpretation prohibits all divorces, so this would not be limited to divorcing believers. The next two give various exceptions, but none depend on whether the spouse is a believer. The last one regards Jesus' teaching as a reply to the specific question about the new Hillelite divorce for any cause based on subdividing a phrase in Deuteronomy 24:1. According to their critics the Shammaites, this phrase referred to "nothing except adultery," though both groups recognized that neglect was also a ground for divorce (see above).

Jesus' teaching in the fourth interpretation is, in effect, an affirmation of the OT grounds for divorce. In this view Jesus confirms that Deuteronomy 24:1 allows divorce for adultery (and for nothing else). He is not asked about divorce for neglect, and he does not offer any teaching on this.

Modern readers might regard it as strange that there is no Jesus tradition on these other important grounds. However, no Jews at the time denied what was stated in every marriage contract—that divorce was possible if the marriage vows based on Exodus 21:10-11 were broken. So, for early readers, these grounds for divorce were as universally accepted as the laws against rape—on which there is also no recorded Jesus tradition.

In this interpretation, the essence of Jesus' teaching is that any divorce carried out using the grounds of "any cause" was invalid. Unfortunately, it appears that this form of divorce was already overwhelmingly popular, because Jesus is able to summarize his teaching simply as "Anyone who has divorced and remarried commits adultery." This assumes they had all used the any-cause no-fault divorce—so Jesus says they were not actually divorced at all; they were still married to their former partner and therefore committing adultery. This interpretation implies that Jesus allowed divorce only for biblical grounds such as adultery or neglect.

The woman in 1 Corinthians 7:10 was likely divorcing without any biblical grounds because she appears to be using a Roman divorce-by-separation instead of a divorce based on OT grounds. Jewish "any cause" divorce was very similar to a Roman divorce-by-separation, because in both cases no grounds for divorce needed to exist and there was no need to appear before a court. Paul could therefore apply Jesus' teaching directly to this woman's situation, telling her that Jesus' teaching condemns her action.

The couples in 1 Corinthians 7:12-13 are different: they have grounds for divorce that most Jews would have accepted, because after returning from the exile, Jews did not regard a marriage to a nonbeliever to be valid (Neh 13:27). This was universally agreed on by Jews. Even Paul agreed with this principle with regard to non-Christians (see above regarding mixed marriages). There is no recorded tradition by Jesus on this point, so this would explain why Paul cannot apply Jesus tradition to divorcing nonbelievers.

This situation required a Christian ruling because, although most Jews were agreed, the OT is not clear. Marriage to nonbelievers was avoided but recognized—for example, Isaac to Rebekah, who still honored her family gods (Gen 24:3-4, 29; 31:19); Moses to the daughter of a Midianite priest (Ex 2:16-22); Esther to a non-Jewish king (Esther 2:5-7, 16-17). Some of these may have converted, but it is significant that this is not mentioned. However, Ezra campaigned (by a public prayer) for Jews to divorce non-Jews (Ezra 9), thereby establishing a new principle. Paul reasoned that the nonbeliever becomes holy through marriage to a believer, and his clinching proof (the meaning of which is uncertain) is that their children are not made unclean by the nonbeliever (1 Cor 7:14).

3.3. *When Nonbelieving Partners Divorced Believers.* Although Paul could instruct believers to remain married to nonbelievers, he could not instruct nonbelievers to likewise remain in the marriage. It is likely that many divorces occurred when a Greek or Roman became a Christian and their partner did not. Christians who refused to worship the emperor or other gods would likely be divorced by a Roman spouse, who would want to avoid the disdain or dangerous accusations of their neighbors.

Jay Adams argues that nowadays this reasoning about mixed marriage can be applied to a believer married to someone who does not *behave* like a Christian, in that (unlike believers in ancient Corinth) they do not obey Paul's instruction to remain married.

What should a believer do if their partner divorces them against their will when they have not broken any marriage vows? Should they remain unmarried and wait for their former partner to offer reconciliation, as Paul instructs the woman in 1 Corinthians 7:10? In this situation Paul gives a different instruction, in 1 Corinthians 7:15: "the [Christian] brother or sister is not bound [*douloō*]" (NIV)—though this word is surprising, because it normally refers to *freedom from slavery.

What is this slavery that such believers were no longer "bound" to? Those who regard divorce as impossible interpret this as freedom to separate from the spouse but not to divorce—the marriage continues, so one cannot remarry. Those who allow divorce but not remarriage interpret this as freedom to divorce. However, these two views would make no sense to the original readers because Paul is writing to believers who had already been left by their spouse, so he would be granting them no additional freedom.

Catholic interpreters add that this may refer to the marriage being annulled, meaning that legally it had never happened, because the nonbeliever failed to take the marriage vows seriously. In that case this phrase marks the believer's freedom to remarry. Some Protestant interpreters also regard this as freedom to remarry, by recognizing their right to divorce. This fits the circumstances of the original readers who were legally divorced in Roman law but who could not remarry unless the marriage was declared ended under Jewish (or Christian) law. This interpretation also helps explain the curious terminology, because the wording of Jewish divorce certificates was specifically based on the wording of a certificate of emancipation from slavery (m. Giṭ. 9:3).

3.4. *Paul Recognizes Neglect as an Old Testament Ground for Divorce.* How does Paul allow remarriage when divorce is initiated by a nonbeliever (1 Cor 7:15)? Under Roman law, when the nonbelieving partner left, the marriage had ended in a legal divorce. Under OT law, however, a divorce could occur for one of a limited number of grounds, and if these grounds were not met, the divorce could not happen. And by the Jesus tradition Paul appeals to (in 1 Cor 7:10), divorce in these circumstances may also have been forbidden.

There are (mainly) four possible interpretations of Jesus' teaching on divorce in the Gospels, as outlined above (see 3.2 above). Of these, the first disallows all divorce, the second allows divorce only for adultery, and the third interprets "sexual immorality" as a broad category—though not broad enough to include nonbelief by a spouse. The fourth interprets Jesus as affirming OT grounds for divorce—specifically adultery—without mentioning other OT grounds.

If Paul likewise affirmed OT grounds for divorce, specifically including the vows based on Exodus 21:10-11 (see 2.2 above), this would explain why he could grant the right of remarriage for those who had been abandoned by their nonbelieving partners. Their partners were no longer supplying or preparing food and clothing or joining in sexual activity, which was the definition of these grounds for neglect (based on Ex 21:10-11).

3.5. *Remarriage Is Allowed After Death or Divorce.* Marriage self-evidently ended with death as well as divorce, so both Roman and Jewish law allowed remarriage after either. Actually, under Roman law, remarriage was mandated for citizens within a period of eighteen months after a divorce or twenty-four months after bereavement, if the person could still be expected to be fertile (Augustine's laws, the *lex Julia de maritandis de ordinibus* and *lex Papia Poppaea nuptialis*). Similarly, Jews regarded "Be fruitful and increase" (Gen 1:28 NIV) as a most important commandment because it is the first in Scripture. Therefore, they regarded it as a moral duty for men to remarry after divorce or bereavement if they were still fertile (see m. Giṭ. 4:8).

This means that if Paul intended to forbid remarriage, he would have had to state this very clearly, because failure to remarry was regarded as impious in Jewish society and opened one to the possibility of legal prosecution in Roman society. If he says nothing, his followers would have assumed they should follow Jewish norms and Roman law by getting remarried.

The only comments that Paul makes concerning remarriage are in 1 Corinthians 7:11, 15 (as discussed above), and possibly also allowing it in 1 Corinthians 7:27—if "free from such a commitment" (NIV) means the end of a marriage rather than the end of a betrothal, as the context suggests. Some interpreters conclude that Paul allows a woman to remarry only after her husband's death, because "A woman is bound to her husband as long as he lives" (1 Cor 7:39 NIV) and "a married woman is bound to her husband as long as he is alive" (Rom 7:2 NIV).

Outside their contexts, these two verses do appear to say that the only way a woman can be released for remarriage is by death. However, this is based on the lack of a statement that a woman is also free to remarry after divorce, so one has to consider whether this silence is significant. In neither case would a mention of divorce be appropriate in the context, because the first instance relates to widows and the second to a Jew's metaphorical marriage to the law. Romans 7 describes a new believer as wishing to be married to Christ, but they cannot because they are married to the law. Unless the law broke a marriage vow—which would never happen—a divorce is impossible. So the only possible means of release is death—and Paul says that the believer dies with Christ, thus ending the marriage (Rom 7:3-4).

Confirmation that Paul agrees with the right of divorcées to remarry is found when he cites, with approval, the wording of the Jewish divorce certificate that grants the right to remarry—see the following section.

3.6. Levirate Marriages Are Ended. Paul's teaching to widows is very significant because he finds a way to abrogate the OT requirement that they marry a brother-in-law if there is no male heir. He tells a widow that "she is free to marry anyone she wishes, but he must belong to the Lord" (1 Cor 7:39 NIV).

This is effectively a quote from the core wording of a Jewish divorce certificate ("You are free to marry any man you wish," m. Giṭ. 9:3). Rabbis discussed whether the husband was allowed to add constraints concerning whom she might marry. They concluded that the only permitted constraint was "any Jewish man," because marriage outside the faith was not permitted (m. Giṭ. 9:3). Paul adds an equivalent Christian constraint: "he must belong to the Lord." The similarity of this addition helps to confirm that Paul has in mind the wording of the divorce certificate.

But why quote a divorce certificate to a widow? Gordon Fee points out that the casuistic argument in Paul's mind was likely to be this: A widow's marriage is ended by God, whereas a divorcée's marriage is ended by the *sin of one partner. Therefore, if a divorcée has a right under the law, a widow should certainly also have this right. This logic based on *a fortiori* ("from the stronger") is found in almost all legal systems and was used by Jews in the first century (Instone-Brewer 1992, 17-18). Rabbi Ashi used this same reasoning in the fifth century to end levirate marriages in Judaism.

3.7. Paul Does Not Mention Divorce for Adultery. One cannot argue from Paul's silence that he does not allow divorce for adultery, which was allowed by all Jews and by all Romans. In the same way, one cannot argue from silence in the Gospels that Jesus does not allow divorce for neglect of food, clothing, and love, which was allowed by all known Jewish groups and is referred to in Jewish marriage contracts, as well as being assumed in Pauline writings (see above).

If it is allowed that the Gospels and Pauline literature do not each provide exhaustive teaching on this topic, these two sources can be in agreement. In that case, both bodies of teaching are based on the OT and reject no-fault divorce. However, if both bodies of teaching are regarded as exhaustive, the Gospels allow divorce either not at all or only for adultery, while Pauline literature allows it only when enacted by a nonbeliever.

4. Incest and Conclusions.

Paul criticizes the man sleeping with his father's wife as something "even pagans do not tolerate" (1 Cor 5:1 NIV). This assumes that his readers recognize an unnamed moral standard higher than that of their current culture—which is presumably that of Judaism.

This implies that Paul and his church regarded OT teaching on sexual and family morals as an authoritative foundation. Paul added adaptations as necessary: affirming existing marriages to nonbelievers, adding Greco-Roman family structures, assuming the rights in Exodus 21:10-11 and divorces based on neglect of them, and releasing widows from levirate marriage. One can therefore assume he would have affirmed most, if not all, other laws about topics such as rape and degrees of relationships prohibited for marriage, including incest.

See also CORINTHIANS, FIRST LETTER TO THE; ETHICS; HOUSEHOLDS AND HOUSEHOLD CODES; JESUS AND PAUL; MAN AND WOMAN; SEXUALITY, SEXUAL ETHICS; WOMEN.

BIBLIOGRAPHY. **J. E. Adams,** *Marriage, Divorce and Remarriage in the Bible* (Phillipsburg, NJ: Presbyterian and Reformed, 1980); **D. W. Amram,** *The Jewish Law of Divorce According to Bible and Talmud* (repr., New York: Sepher-Hermon, 1975); **L. J. Archer,** *Her Price Is Beyond Rubies: The Jewish Woman in Greco-Roman Palestine*, JSOTSup 60 (Sheffield: Sheffield Academic, 1990); **D. Atkinson,** *To Have and to Hold: The Marriage Covenant and the Discipline of Divorce* (London: Colins, 1979); **R. D. Aus,** *"Caught in the Act," Walking on the Sea, and the Release of Barabbas Revisited*, South Florida Studies in the History of Judaism 157 (Atlanta: Scholars Press, 1997); **S. Clark,** *Putting Asunder: Divorce and Remarriage in Biblical and Pastoral Perspective* (Bridgend, UK: Brynterion, 1999); **J. J. Collins,** "Marriage, Divorce and Family in Second Temple Judaism," in *Families in Ancient Israel*, ed. L. G. Perdue et al. (Louisville, KY: Westminster John Knox, 1997), 104-62; **A. Cornes,** *Divorce and Remarriage: Biblical Principles and Pastoral Practice* (London: Hodder & Stoughton, 1993); **S. Dixon,** *The Roman Family* (Baltimore: Johns Hopkins University Press, 1992); **L. M. Epstein,** *Marriage Laws in the Bible and Talmud*, The Harvard Semitic Series 12 (Cambridge, MA: Harvard University Press, 1942); **G. D. Fee,** *The First Epistle to the Corinthians*, NICNT (Grand Rapids, MI: Eerdmans, 1987); **J. A. Fitzmyer,** "Divorce Among First-Century Palestinian Jews," *Eretz-Israel* 14 (1978): 103-10; **W. A. Heth,** "Jesus on Divorce: How My Mind Has Changed," *The Southern Baptist Journal of Theology* 6 (2002): 4-29; **D. Instone-Brewer,** *Techniques and Assumptions in Jewish Exegesis Before 70 CE*, TSAJ 30 (Tübingen: Mohr Siebeck, 1992); idem, "Jewish Women Divorcing Their Husbands in Early Judaism: The Background to Papyrus Se'elim 13," *HTR* 92 (1999): 349-57; idem, "1 Corinthians 7 in the Light of the Graeco-Roman Marriage and Divorce Papyri," *TynBul* 52 (2001): 101-16; idem, *Divorce and Remarriage in the Bible: The Social and Literary Context* (Grand Rapids, MI: Eerdmans, 2002); **T. Kazen,** *Scripture, Interpretation, or Authority? Motives and Arguments in Jesus' Halakic Conflicts*, WUNT 320 (Tübingen: Mohr Siebeck, 2013); **C. S. Keener,** *. . . And Marries Another: Divorce and Remarriage in the Teaching of the New Testament* (Peabody, MA: Hendrickson, 1991); idem, *Paul, Women and Wives: Marriage and Women's Ministry in the Letters of Paul* (Peabody, MA: Hendrickson, 1992); **N. Lewis, Y. Yadin, and J. C. Greenfield,** eds., *The Documents from the Bar Kokhba Period in the Cave of Letters: Greek Papyri* (Jerusalem: Israel Exploration Society; Hebrew University of Jerusalem: Shrine of the Book, 1989); **W. F. Luck,** *Divorce and Remarriage: Recovering the Biblical View* (San Francisco: Harper & Row, 1987); **J. Murphy-O'Conner,** "The Divorced Woman in 1 Cor. 7.10-11," *JBL* 100 (1981): 601-6; **A. D. Naselli,** "What the New Testament Teaches About Divorce and Remarriage," *Detroit Baptist Seminary Journal* 24 (2019): 3-44; **S. M. Paul,** "Exod. 21:10: A Threefold Maintenance Clause," *Journal of Near Eastern Studies* 28 (1969): 48-53; **J. Piper,** "Divorce & Remarriage: A Position Paper," Desiring God, July 21, 1986, www.desiringgod.org/articles/divorce-and-remarriage-a-position-paper; **M. T. Roth,** *Babylonian Marriage Agreements 7th–3rd Centuries B.C.* (Neukirchen-Vluyn: Neukirchener Verlag, 1989); **M. L. Satlow,** *Tasting the Dish: Rabbinic Rhetorics of Sexuality*, BJS 303 (Atlanta: Scholars Press, 1995); **S. Treggiari,** "Divorce Roman Style: How Easy and How Frequent Was It?," in *Marriage, Divorce and Children in Ancient Rome*, ed. B. Rawson (Oxford: Clarendon, 1991), 31-46; **J. R. Wegner,** *Chattel or Person? The Status of Women in the Mishnah* (Oxford: Oxford University Press, 1988); **G. J. Wenham and W. A. Heth,** *Jesus and Divorce: Towards an Evangelical Understanding of New Testament Teaching*, 2nd ed. (Carlisle, UK: Paternoster, 1997).

D. Instone-Brewer

MARS HILL/AREOPAGUS. *See* PAUL IN ACTS; PHILOSOPHY.

MATURE. *See* COMPLETE, MATURE (PERFECT).

MEALS, RELIGIOUS. *See* FOOD LAWS AND CUSTOMS, JEWISH AND ROMAN; LORD'S SUPPER.

MERCY

The nature of *God is to be gracious and merciful. In a sense, *grace and mercy are "sibling" characteristics of God. For Paul, God is rich in mercy to all alike, to Jews *and* to *Gentiles; indeed, God is the father of compassion and intends that his people reflect and embody his recreative mercy in their lives. While God's mercy has a passive dimension to it—that is, God does *not* deal with people according to their sins—it is more than a preservative withholding of *judgment or restorative *forgiveness. It is also a creative or recreative *active agent* that enlivens *Israel and is the *hope of all the earth (see Barclay). This kind of generative mercy is the basis and source for Paul's *mission and *service.

1. Background
2. The "Mercy" Word Group in Paul
3. God's Mercy to All—Both Jew and Gentile
4. The Re-creative Power of Mercy

1. Background.
In the Greco-Roman world, *mercy* was a technical term for the closing defense speech in a court of law (Bultmann, "ἔλεος, κτλ.," 478; Silva, 168). It was also one of the primary virtues characterizing the emperor's expression of power toward his subjects (see Seneca, *De Clementia*). It is the world of Scripture, however, that primarily shaped Paul's imagination and theology.

In the LXX, the Greek word *eleos* is normally used to translate the Hebrew word *ḥesed,* while the Greek verb *eleeō* occurs often for the Hebrew *ḥānan*. In Scripture, the content of God's *ḥesed* includes God's steadfast, loving, *covenant commitment to Israel and the notion of merciful *love in action (Ryliškytė, 100). God's mercy is expressed throughout Scripture, especially the Psalms. Arguably the most extensive self-revelation of God as the God of mercy occurs in Exodus (Barclay, 84-85). In response to Moses' request for God to "teach me your ways" and "show me your *glory" (Ex 33:13, 18 NIV), God promises to cause all his goodness to pass in front of Moses and proclaim the name, "the LORD (YHWH)," to Moses. He defines himself as the one who "will have mercy [*eleeō*] on whom I will have mercy [*eleeō*], and I will have compassion [*oiktirō*] on whom I will have compassion [*oiktirō*]" (Ex 33:19 NIV; see also Ex 3:14-15). With the scene set, God renews the covenant and proclaims himself to be "The LORD, the LORD, the compassionate [*oiktirmōn*] and merciful [*eleēmōn*] God, slow to anger, and abounding in steadfast love, maintaining steadfast love to thousands of generations" (Ex 34:6-7).

Mercy and compassion, often linked together, are characteristic of who God *is*. Mercy is expressed not only as self-revelatory of who God *is* but as an action of what God *does* in mercy by forgiving *sin (e.g., Ps 51:1) and by rescuing his people when they are endangered, enslaved, or in exile (e.g., Is 63:15; see Gupta). Mercy is active. God "does" mercy (Deut 5:10; 13:17), and his people reflect this by also doing mercy (e.g., Ruth 1:8; 3:10; 1 Sam 15:6). Mercy, on God's part, is an expression of his *abundant* love (e.g., Ex 34:6; Num 14:18; Ps 51:3; 68:14; 86:5, 15; 103:8; Jon 4:2), which extends through the generations (e.g., Ex 20:6; 34:7; Deut 5:10; 1 Chron 16:34; 2 Chron 7:3; Ps 100:5; 103:17; 118:1-2)—even unto the heavens (e.g., Ps 36:5; 57:10).

2. The "Mercy" Word Group in Paul.
In Paul, the mercy word group includes the following: nine uses of the noun *eleos*, fourteen uses of the verb *eleeō*, one occurrence of the adjective *eleeinos*, two uses of the noun *oiktirmos*, and four uses of the verb *oiktirō*. The words in this group are commonly translated as "mercy," "compassion," "kindness," or "pity."

3. God's Mercy to All—Both Jew and Gentile.
The disclosure of God's merciful identity in Exodus 32–34 ripples throughout Scripture and continues to resonate in Paul's understanding of divine mercy. It undergirds his references to God, who is "rich in mercy" (Eph 2:4) and is in fact "the father of mercies" (2 Cor 1:3). It is not surprising, then, that in Romans 9–11, where the most concentrated cluster of "mercy" language occurs (eleven times in Rom 9:15, 16, 18, 23; 11:30, 31, 32), Paul quotes from Exodus 33:19 and uses it as a platform to explain how God both keeps his promises to Israel and, in *Christ, extends his mercy mission to the world. "For Paul divine mercy is itself the creative agent in Israel's history, not its restorative assistant" (Barclay, 98). Israel is not restored by mercy so much as it is rooted in it and, because mercy is the enlivening power for them (see Ex 32–34), mercy offers hope not only for the future of Israel but for "the nations" of the world as well (Barclay, 98). Further, mercy both establishes relationships between God and people and is the agent of reconciliation between people whereby divisions (ethnic or otherwise) are undone. Important as mercy is for Paul's argument in Romans 9–11, it may be the key thematic undercurrent for the entire letter (see Gupta; Ryliškytė). God's recreative and loving mercy, manifest for both Jews and Gentiles, is the basis for a holistic response to God in all of life, from embodied *worship (Rom 12:1) to cheerful work (Rom 12:8) and welcoming *witness to the world (Rom 15:9).

4. The Re-creative Power of Mercy.
While the bulk of Paul's mercy language occurs in Romans, it also emerges in other letters. He opens (e.g., 1 Tim 1:2; 2 Tim 1:2) and closes (Gal 6:16) letters with references to mercy. Paul's own identity as a servant and *apostle of Jesus Christ is shaped by God's forgiving and restorative mercy. That is, he has a *ministry to others because he has received mercy (1 Cor 7:25; 2 Cor 4:1; 1 Tim 1:13, 16). Even though he understands God's merciful commission on his life, Paul asserts that God's recreative ("rebirth" and "renewal") *salvation in Christ by the *Holy Spirit is

not the result of human effort or human worth but "because of [God's] mercy" (Titus 3:5).

Paul acknowledges that the experienced reality of re-creative mercy/compassion through union with Christ and the *fellowship of the Spirit (Phil 2:1) empowers believers to think appropriately (Phil 2:2, 5). Mercy/compassion is a constituent part of a believer's baptismal "wardrobe" (Col 3:12) at the beginning of their new life in Christ, and mercy is a believer's eschatological hope at the end when the day of the Lord occurs (2 Tim 1:18). "In other words, the whole history of salvation . . . can be contracted into one word: *eleos*" (Ryliškytė, 104).

See also Grace; Israel; Lord; Love; Ministry; Mission; Old Testament in Paul; Romans, Letter to the; Servant, Service.

BIBLIOGRAPHY. **J. M. G. Barclay,** "'I Will Have Mercy on Whom I Have Mercy': The Golden Calf and Divine Mercy in Romans 9–11 and Second Temple Judaism," *EC* 1 (2010): 82-106; **R. Bultmann,** "ἔλεος, κτλ.," *TNDT* 2:477-87; idem, "οἰκτιρμός, κτλ.," *TNDT* 5:159-61; **S. Eastman,** "Israel and the Mercy of God: A Re-reading of Galatians 6:1 and Romans 9–11," *NTS* 56 (2010): 367-95; **H. H. Esser,** "Mercy, Compassion," *NIDNTT* 2:593-601; **N. Gupta,** "What 'Mercies of God'? *Oiktirmos* in Romans 12:1 Against Its Septuagintal Background," *BBR* 22 (2012): 81-96; **L. Ryliškytė,** "God's Mercy: The Key Thematic Undercurrent of Paul's Letter to the Romans," *CBQ* 81 (2019): 85-105; **M. Silva,** "ἔλεος," *NIDNTT* 2:167-72; **F. Staudinger,** "ἔλεος, κτλ.," *EDNT* 1:429-31.

D. Pinter

MERCY SEAT. *See* Atonement; Romans, Letter to the.

MERIT. *See* Justification; Law; Works of the Law.

MIDRASH. *See* Old Testament in Paul; Paul and Judaism.

MIND. *See* Anthropology, Pauline; Knowledge and Mind.

MINISTRY

According to Paul, ministry is *service rendered to *God for the benefit of others. Since God has appointed believers to do the work of ministry (Eph 3:7; Col 4:17), serving others is the result of their divine gifting and empowerment (1 Cor 12:28), especially to the *church (Eph 4:11-12). The term Paul used most often to refer to ministry is *diakonia*, "service." He refers not only to his ministry as *diakonia* (Rom 11:13), but also to the ministry of the Spirit (2 Cor 3:8), the ministry of Stephanus's house church (1 Cor 16:15), and the ministry of reconciliation (2 Cor 5:18), as well as the ministry of *death and condemnation—the old *covenant (2 Cor 3:7, 9).

So it is not surprising that Paul would call himself a *diakonos*, "servant/deacon" (Col 1:23), as well as *Christ (Rom 15:8), his co-laborers (1 Cor 3:5; 2 Cor 6:4), and letter carriers such as Phoebe (Rom 16:1) and Tychichus (Eph 6:21). Paul even uses the term to refer to government officials (Rom 13:4) and to his *opponents, claiming they are Satan's agents who "disguise themselves as ministers of *righteousness" (2 Cor 11:15 NRSV). On a few occasions, Paul uses priestly language to describe his ministry. He calls himself a "minister of Christ Jesus" (*leitourgon*, from which comes the word *liturgy*) "in priestly service [*hierourgounta*] of the *gospel of God" when he presents the "offering of the *Gentiles" during his visit to *Jerusalem (Rom 15:16 NRSV). When he preaches the gospel, Paul says he "serves God" (*latreuō*) in his spirit (Rom 1:9)—the same word he uses to describe those who "worship in the Spirit of God" (Phil 3:3 NRSV), offering themselves as a "living *sacrifice" in "spiritual *worship" (Rom 12:1 NRSV). So Paul refers to the ministry of all members, not just himself and his coworkers. Ministry was not only something Paul did but also what he expected his churches to do.

1. Paul's Ministry: What He Did
2. Church Ministry: What Paul Expected
3. Paul's Theology of Ministry

1. Paul's Ministry: What He Did.

From beginning to end, Paul attributes his ministry to God. Paul did not start a ministry and then ask God for his blessing. Rather, Paul claims he became a minister of the gospel of Jesus Christ because God took the initiative and graced him to do it (Rom 15:15-16; Eph 3:7-8). It all started when God called him to be the *apostle to the Gentiles. The resurrected Christ appeared to Paul and commissioned him to preach the gospel to Gentiles (Gal 1:15-16), empowering him to perform "the *signs of a true apostle" (2 Cor 12:12 NRSV). The Christophany not only marked the beginning of his ministry but was also the basis of his authority (1 Cor 9:1-2). He was Christ's emissary to the uncircumcised, compelled "not of my own will" to preach the gospel (1 Cor 9:17).

Pressed into the service of God's ministry of reconciliation through Christ (2 Cor 5:18), Paul turned enemies of God—Gentiles who once served dead and dumb idols (1 Cor 12:2; 1 Thess 1:9)—into children of God, adopted into Abraham's family by *faith in Christ (Gal 4:5-7). Paul not only claimed to be the apostle to Gentiles but also the family father of his Gentile converts, requiring their obedience to his paternal guidance and Christ's commands (1 Cor 4:14-21). Paul also saw himself as a *slave of Christ, serving his master by doing everything the *Lord commanded (1 Cor 9:16-23). As a priest of Christ Jesus, Paul claimed his gospel ministry among the profaned Gentiles was an "acceptable" offering to God, a sacred service of *temple worship sanctified by the Spirit (Rom 15:16). Indeed, the way Paul saw himself—apostle, parent, slave, and priest—reveals how he conceived of his ministry: a work that started with God and will end in praise to God when Paul presents his converts to Christ on the last day, his crowning achievement (1 Thess 2:19-20).

1.1. As an Apostle. To preach the gospel of Jesus Christ to Gentiles was the primary purpose of Paul's ministry as an apostle. Describing the Christophany in prophetic terms, Paul believed he was called not only to deliver the gospel message to godless idolators but also to reveal the *truth of the gospel in his life. Like the prophets of old, Paul claims God "set me apart even from my mother's womb" in order to "reveal His Son in me" (Gal 1:15-16 NASB). Apostolic *preaching was an embodied ministry. The people would not only hear the gospel message, "Christ crucified" (1 Cor 2:1-2); his converts were supposed to see the *cross of Jesus incarnated in their apostle (Gal 2:20–3:1; 6:17). Through all his weaknesses—his deficiencies as a public speaker (1 Cor 2:3-4), the hardship he endured as a missionary (2 Cor 11:23-33), his afflictions (Gal 4:13-15; 2 Cor 12:7-10), his poverty (1 Cor 4:11)—Paul believed the cross of Jesus Christ was most clearly seen in believers "always carrying in the *body the death of Jesus, so that the life of Jesus may also be made visible in our bodies" (2 Cor 4:10 NRSV). This was good news: being "crucified with Christ" meant that death brought life (Gal 2:20), loss was gain (Phil 3:7-8), strength was perfected in weakness (2 Cor 12:9), proving that "God chose what is foolish in the world to shame the wise" (1 Cor 1:27 NRSV). Indeed, as Christ's apostle to the Gentiles Paul was God's fool, "content with weaknesses, insults, hardships, persecutions, and calamities for the sake of Christ" (2 Cor 12:10 NRSV). Paul admits he is "the least of the apostles, unfit to be called an apostle, because I persecuted the church of God" (1 Cor 15:9 NRSV). Yet, what looked like failure in ministry was actually the evidence of Paul's apostleship, a revelation of God's work in the world that could only be spiritually discerned (1 Cor 2:15).

An itinerant preacher, Paul traveled the world to start churches in places where Christ had not "already been named" (Rom 15:20 NRSV). Unlike wandering prophets known for delivering their message and moving onto the next town (Mt 10:41; Did. 11.3-12), Paul sought to establish long-term relationships with his converts. To him, preaching the gospel was just the beginning of the work of an apostle. He believed it was his responsibility to teach his converts how to grow in their faith. That these converts gathered weekly to worship God, forming a community of faith to support one another throughout the week, proved that Paul had "laid a foundation" of the new temple as Christ's apostle (1 Cor 3:10, 16; Eph 2:20). Founding churches was the "seal" of his apostleship (1 Cor 9:2), a Pauline letter of Christ written on "tablets of human hearts" (2 Cor 3).

Even though he was compelled to leave these new churches in order to preach the gospel in new frontiers (often forced out of town, sometimes departing on his own accord), Paul maintained contact with his converts through follow-up visits and written correspondence. Even though Paul recognizes that outsiders will build on his foundational work as an apostle (1 Cor 3:11-15), he wants his authoritative voice to guide the churches in their life together, whether through his *coworkers, sent to "remind you of my ways in Christ Jesus, as I teach them everywhere in every church" (1 Cor 4:17 NRSV), or via his letters, "for we write you nothing other than what you can read and also understand" (2 Cor 1:13 NRSV). Paul puts a lot of stock in his letters (not to mention a lot of time and money). In fact, it could be said that Paul's letter writing is the clearest sign of his understanding of apostolic authority. For he believes not only that he offers sage advice that his converts need to follow when dealing with the pressures of life (1 Cor 7:25, 40). Paul claims he issues the Lord's commandments (1 Cor 14:37; 2 Thess 3:6, 12), proof to his converts that "Christ is speaking in me" (2 Cor 13:3 NRSV). He indicates often that he prefers to deal with church problems "face to face" (1 Cor 4:19-21; 2 Cor 13:2; Gal 4:20; Phil 2:24; 1 Thess 2:17-18) but resorts to sending letters when absent in order to "win obedience from the Gentiles, by word and deed" (Rom 15:18 NRSV; see 2 Cor 13:10; Phil 2:12).

A part of his apostolic ministry, Paul performed miracles—what he refers to as "signs and wonders and mighty works" (2 Cor 12:12 NRSV; see Rom 15:19). Miracles were supposed to be another bit of evidence proving to his converts that he was a "true apostle"

(2 Cor 12:12). Even though the apostle never describes in his letters any of the miracles he performed, Acts includes dramatic accounts of Paul healing the infirmed, cursing his opponents, exorcizing demons, and raising the dead (Acts 13:9-11; 14:8-10; 16:16-18; 19:11-12; 20:9-12; 28:3-6). Paul does, however, mention the time he traveled to the third heaven/paradise and "heard things that are not to be told"—a miraculous experience he could have boasted about but is reticent to talk about, recalling the dramatic event in the third person (2 Cor 12:4 NRSV).

Apparently for Paul, then, describing the details of these apostolic signs and wonders is unnecessary (perhaps even counterproductive to his ministry), as he prefers to boast about his weaknesses instead "so that no one may think better of me than what is seen in me or heard from me" (2 Cor 12:6 NRSV; see 2 Cor 11:23-33). Besides, performing miracles was not supposed to be unique to apostolic ministry, for the Spirit gifted members of churches to work miracles too (1 Cor 12:10, 27).

1.2. As a Parent. It is telling that Paul never mentions any members of his immediate Jewish family in his letters, people he refers to as "my kindred according to the flesh" (Rom 9:3 NRSV). Echoing the sentiment of Jesus (Mt 12:46-50), Paul has found a new family *"in Christ," boasting that his new-creation identity is mutually exclusive to finding any "confidence in the flesh" (Phil 3:4 NRSV). Like his Gentile converts who discovered they had a spiritual father and mother in *Abraham and Sarah (Gal 4:28-29), Paul found another mother, different brothers and sisters, and even sons and daughters "in the Lord" (Rom 16:7, 13; 1 Cor 4:17; Philem 1, 2, 10, 16). Paul is quick to point out that, even though his converts will have many tutors to teach them about their faith in Christ, they only have one father (1 Cor 4:15). Paul is their *paterfamilias*, and they are his "beloved children."

As children replicate the qualities of their parents, Paul expects his gospel children to "imitate" him (1 Cor 14:16) just as he imitates Christ (1 Cor 11:1). Paul was crucified, buried, and raised with Christ (Rom 6:3-11; Gal 2:19–3:1)—a narrative model for their spiritual formation too (Col 2:11–3:11). Paul appeals to their shared experience of the Spirit to convince them he taught them well (Gal 3:2-5). When outsiders questioned his devotion to them, they should have defended him—like children sticking up for their parents (2 Cor 12:11-19; Gal 4:12-20). When they misbehave, he scolds them—like a father threatening corporal punishment when he got home (1 Cor 4:14-21; 2 Cor 13:2-10). Yet, his paternal role in their spiritual growth is also supposed to foster fond feelings between them, "like a father with his children, urging and encouraging you and pleading that you lead a life worthy of God" (1 Thess 2:11-12 NRSV). Their response to his fatherly advice determines whether he will need to play the part of a strict disciplinarian ("Am I to come to you with a stick") or doting father ("or with *love in a spirit of gentleness?" 1 Cor 4:21 NRSV).

Passing down the teachings of the fathers was constitutive of Paul's religious experience in Judaism, traditions he used to guard zealously (Gal 1:13-14). But when it comes to the gospel of Jesus Christ, Paul claims he "did not receive it from a human source, nor was I taught it, but I received it through a revelation of Jesus Christ" (Gal 1:12 NRSV). Even the few details about Jesus' life that show up in Paul's letters, such as the night Jesus was betrayed and instituted the *Lord's Supper, Paul claims to have "received from the Lord" (1 Cor 11:23). Yet, at other times Paul affirms the importance of handing down traditions he received from the apostles (1 Cor 15:3-6), saying he is eager to do what they asked of him (Gal 2:10). Paul is the paternal source of Christian traditions for his children, handing down what he received from Christ and the apostles. As a loving father, he expects his children to "maintain the traditions just as I handed them on to you" (1 Cor 11:2 NRSV).

As their disciplinarian, Paul wants his children to not only do what he says but also do what he does, modeling what it means to imitate Christ (1 Cor 11:1). Giving fatherly instructions, he teaches them how to pray in the Spirit (Rom 8:15-16, 26-27; Eph 6:18-20), how to interpret the Scriptures (1 Cor 4:6; 2 Cor 3:6, 12-17; Gal 3:6-22; 4:21–5:1), and how to live holy lives in a pagan world (1 Thess 4:1-8). Like a working father, he expects his children to imitate him by getting jobs and to "not eat anyone's bread without paying for it" (2 Thess 3:7-8 NRSV). He hopes they will follow his lead and not get married (1 Cor 7:7-8), not eat idol meat in front of "the weak" (1 Cor 8:11-13), and not observe certain holy days (Gal 4:10-12). When opponents question Paul's authority, he is quick to remind his children that he is their gospel source. "Indeed, in Christ Jesus I became your father through the gospel" (1 Cor 4:15 NRSV). It was because of Paul, and the sacrifices he made preaching the gospel, that they became children of God (1 Cor 3:5, 10; 4:7-14; 1 Thess 2:1-13).

Paul also played a maternal role in the maturation of his converts. Exasperated by their childish behavior, Paul muses that he has to treat them like infants needing breast milk because they are not ready for "solid food" (1 Cor 3:1-3). When the opinion of outsiders causes a rift between Paul and his children, he reminds them of the *birth pangs he experienced, wondering when they will finally grow up—when "Christ is formed in you" (Gal 4:19 NRSV). He never makes selfish demands of them, nurturing them instead like a nursing mother caring for her own children (1 Thess 2:7). His affection for them makes him vulnerable to their restrained response, forcing uncomfortable confrontations when he is forced to bare his heart to them, hoping they will reciprocate: "There is no restriction in our affections, but only in yours. In return—I speak as to children—open wide your hearts also" (2 Cor 6:12 NRSV).

To Paul, then, ministry was as much about having healthy relationships with members as doing meaningful work in the church. Therefore, like a parent, it rattled Paul when his children fought with each other. He not only wants them to get along with one another; he wants them to love one another, constantly reminding his converts of their family loyalties. Rather than fight and bicker, they are supposed to help one another, take care of one another, looking "not to your own interests, but to the interests of others" (Phil 2:4 NRSV)—just like Christ, just like Paul. A divided family threatens the integrity of the singular *body of Christ (1 Cor 1:10-13). Their inability to "have the same mind" and settle their own disputes causes them to air their dirty laundry before nonbelievers (1 Cor 6:1-8). Family feuds keep Paul awake at night as he longs for reconciliation, wondering whether his letters will make things better or worse (2 Cor 7:5-13). The risk of a vain labor is constantly hanging over his head, driving him to work harder than any apostle (1 Cor 15:10; 2 Cor 11:23, 28).

1.3. As a Slave. Even though Paul preferred sending his letters as the "apostle of Christ Jesus," a few times he addresses his readers as Christ's slave (Rom 1:1; Phil 1:1; Titus 1:1). In a revealing (and somewhat surprising) comment, Paul claims he did not preach the gospel voluntarily. Rather, the "obligation" to preach the gospel was laid on him against his will (1 Cor 9:16-17). Enslaved to Christ, Paul sees himself as his master's house manager (1 Cor 9:17)—the servant of Christ charged with running the *household of Christ (Eph 3:2; Col 1:25)—and he very much wants his converts to "think of us in this way" (1 Cor 4:1 NRSV). Since "it is required of stewards that they may be found trustworthy" (1 Cor 4:2 NRSV), Paul shows no hesitation in bringing order to Christ's household. He sets down rules for orderly worship (1 Cor 14:26-40). He challenges Roman table customs that are "unworthy of the Lord," ordering proper conduct when his converts ate together (1 Cor 11:17-34). He instructs husbands and wives on how they are to behave toward each other when they gather in house churches as brothers and sisters in Christ (Eph 5:21-33). He tells men and *women what clothing to wear and how to wear their hair (1 Cor 11:4-16; 1 Tim 2:9).

When it comes to religious *identity, he encourages his converts to "follow this rule": "neither *circumcision nor uncircumcision is anything" (Gal 6:15-16 NRSV). When the "weak" and the "*strong" are contemptuous of one another over holy days and eating meat, Paul says they have no business judging "servants of another," for "it is before their own lord that they stand or fall" (Rom 14:4 NRSV). Indeed, Paul claims to be a "slave of Christ" who pleases only God and not people (Gal 1:10). Therefore, he refuses to listen to those who would judge him—not even trusting his own judgment as to whether he will be found "trustworthy" as Christ's house manager. On the last day, "it is the Lord who judges me" (1 Cor 4:4 NRSV).

Even though Paul does not expect his converts to imitate him by becoming an apostle or act like a father to new converts, he does claim they have become slaves of Christ just like him. Whether slave or free, they all became slaves of Christ because they were "bought with a price," their bodies owned by Christ (1 Cor 6:19-20; 7:22-23). Previously enslaved to *sin, they were set free by God to become slaves of righteousness (Rom 6:16-18). Since the salient feature of slavery is obedience, Paul devotes a lot of attention in his letters instructing his fellow slaves to obey their common master. "To win obedience from the Gentiles, by word and deed" is crucial to the success of his ministry as Christ's steward (Rom 15:18 NRSV).

"Because Christ Jesus has made me his own," Paul tries to inspire his converts to imitate him and suffer "the loss of all things" in order to "gain Christ" (Phil 3:8, 12 NRSV). For, just as Christ "emptied himself, taking the form of a slave," becoming "obedient to the point of death—even death on a cross," Paul wants his converts to be of the "same mind" (Phil 2:5, 7-8 NRSV), following the same example (Phil 3:17). Since Christ became a servant of all to save all (Rom 15:8-12), Paul makes himself a slave to all people "that I might by all means save some" (1 Cor 9:22 NRSV). To him, leaving behind the malevolent master of sin that leads to death in order to serve a good Lord with complete devotion is a no-brainer (Rom 6:15-21): "The advantage you get is sanctification. The end is eternal life" (Rom 6:22 NRSV). Obedience to Christ is liberating to Paul the slave.

1.4. As a Priest. Paul is inclined to use priestly language when he talks about how church members are devoted to the Lord. He encourages them to "present your bodies as a living sacrifice, holy and acceptable to God, which is your spiritual worship" (Rom 12:1 NRSV). They are to think of themselves as "God's temple"—holy vessels—knowing that "God's Spirit dwells in you" (1 Cor 3:16 NRSV). Even though *prayer is not unique to priestly service, Paul uses Levitical imagery to describe his ministry of serving God by preaching the gospel and praying for the church in Rome (Rom 1:9). In fact, praying for the churches is a significant part of Paul's ministry, as he often relays to his readers the content of his prayers at the beginning of his letters (Rom 1:10; 1 Cor 1:4-9; Eph 1:16-19; Phil 1:3-6, 9-11; Col 1:3-6, 9-14; 1 Thess 1:2-3; 2 Thess 1:3, 11-12; 2 Tim 1:3-5; Philem 4-6).

Paul's description of his ministry as a priest shows up even more clearly when he writes about the relief offering he collected from his converts for the church in Jerusalem (Rom 15:28). As a "minister [*leitourgon*] of Christ Jesus," he hopes his "priestly service" (*hierourgounta*) of presenting the "offering [*prosphora*] of the Gentiles" to the saints in Jerusalem will be acceptable (Rom 15:16 NRSV). Relying on the principle of reciprocity (2 Cor 8:14), where spiritual benefactors receive material blessings from their beneficiaries, Paul describes the relief offering as *leitourgēsai*, a term often used of priestly service (Rom 15:27, the same word he uses for the relief offering in 2 Cor 9:12). This sacrificial gift will have the desired liturgical effect. Not only meeting the needs of the poor in Jerusalem, the offering will also inspire people to worship God, producing "thanksgiving to God" (2 Cor 9:11-12). By collecting money from his converts and delivering the gift to Jerusalem, Paul believes his priestly service to God will vindicate his gospel ministry, proving "what Christ has accomplished through me" (Rom 15:18 NRSV; see 2 Cor 9:13). Having laid the foundation of the temple, Paul expects others to bring only the best materials to build it up (1 Cor 3:10-16).

2. Church Ministry: What Paul Expected. Paul sent letters to churches to persuade them to join him in ministry, reminding them of what they should already be doing, teaching them to do for themselves what he had done for them. To be sure, Paul expected his converts to depend on him for instruction, for encouragement, for direction, for help. But several times Paul puts the onus on his churches to sort out their own problems (1 Cor 6:1-8), to hold each other accountable (1 Cor 11:13-16), to be able to recognize false teachers (Gal 1:8-9), and to infer from his example what they are supposed to do (2 Thess 3:7-11).

Yet, it is apparent that Paul does not expect his converts to do everything he does in ministry. For example, nowhere in Paul's letters does he encourage his converts to start other churches. He never expects members to leave their homes, become missionaries, and evangelize other parts of the world. In fact, Paul never tries to persuade his converts to preach the gospel to outsiders in their own town. Paul never encourages members to organize the collection of a relief offering for the poor in other cities. Nor does he expect churches to send letters of encouragement or share written advice with other congregations other than his correspondence (Col 4:16). Paul tries to strike a delicate balance: wanting his converts to be loyal to him, holding true to the gospel he preached, but also expecting them to minister to each other in his absence, proving they are growing in Christ by their dependency on the Spirit.

Paul anticipates the day when he will be "poured out as a libation" (Phil 2:17 NRSV), no longer with them "in the flesh [, which] is more necessary for you" (Phil 1:24 NRSV). By remaining faithful to Christ in his absence, they will prove that Paul did not labor in vain (Phil 2:16). This is why he works so hard, why he suffers so much, why he travels so far, why he gave his life to Christ. To Paul, the ministry of a growing, holy, flourishing, and confident church is the hope of the world in Christ Jesus (Col 1:24-29). As the body of Christ, the temple of the Spirit, the family of God, and a colony of heaven, the church is the only *witness to the truth of the gospel of Jesus Christ.

2.1. The Body of Christ. Paul's favorite metaphor for the church may reveal his primary focus of ministry: the *ekklēsia* is a diverse group of people united as one body in Christ to serve one another. When it comes to church ministry, Paul has more of an inward than outward focus. Rather than train his converts' eyes on the world and its needs, Paul spends most of his time in his letters trying to get members of churches to minister to each other. They are mutually dependent, needing every member to use their spiritual gifts for the common good (1 Cor 12:7-11). Composed of many parts, every member plays a crucial role in the health of their singular body (1 Cor 12:12-17). God set it up this way so that church members would always look to one another for help: the sick need healers, the ignorant need teachers, the confused need prophets, the weak need miracle-workers (1 Cor 12:18-31).

Some gifts may appear more important to some and more desirable to others (1 Cor 12:22-25, 28-31). But Paul believes the church needs every member to exercise their spiritual gifts to build up the whole body of Christ "until all of us come to the unity of the faith and of the *knowledge of the *Son of God, to maturity, to the measure of the full stature of Christ" (Eph 4:13 NRSV). No individual member can reveal all that Christ is to the world (Eph 4:15-16). Christ conquered the world, distributing the booty of war as gifts to the church, so that the *fullness of Christ's powerful love would be evident to the world through his body (Eph 4:7-10; 1 Cor 13:1-10). It takes the whole church, then, to bear witness to nonbelievers, speaking truth to neighbors and living as "children of *light" in order to "expose" the "unfruitful deeds of darkness" (Eph 5:8-11 NRSV; see Eph 4:17-25).

Although Christ is the *head of the body, God gifted certain members to help lead the church: "first apostles, second prophets, third teachers," then other high-profile gifts with different forms of *leadership (1 Cor 12:28 NRSV). Paul encourages the church to recognize these spiritually endowed leaders who "have charge of you in the Lord and admonish you" (1 Thess 5:12 NRSV). He relies on them to keep order in worship (1 Cor 14:37-40), to restore sinners (Gal 6:1), and to supply "what was lacking" from the rest of the membership (1 Cor 16:17). Because these leaders "devoted themselves to the service of the saints" (1 Cor 16:15 NRSV), Paul encourages members to "put yourselves at service of such people, and of everyone who works and toils with them" (1 Cor 16:16 NRSV). That would include, of course, Paul's coworkers whom he sent to minister to his converts as well as other leaders (patrons, overseers, elders, and deacons) who were either appointed by Paul or set apart by the local church. It is difficult to know whether leaders such as Stephanus (1 Cor 16:15-16) and Archippus (Col 4:17) were established by Paul or installed by members of the church—or perhaps even both. Regardless, Paul recognizes the Lord's hand in raising up leaders within the congregation, attributing their giftedness to the work of the Spirit (Rom 12:8; 1 Cor 12:28). Therefore, he expects members to submit to their leadership and support them financially (1 Cor 9:8-12; 16:16; Gal 6:6; 1 Thess 5:12).

Some scholars have tried to pit Paul's early charismatic view of church leadership against later developments of institutional hegemony in Paulinism, even suggesting Pauline churches started out as egalitarian congregations that eventually became hierarchical much later. The problem, of course, is that Paul relied on hierarchical structures early on to get his converts to obey him, either appealing to his God-given authority (1 Cor 14:37-38) or to recognized hierarchies embedded in their culture (1 Cor 11:3-16). There were times when Paul could have exerted his apostolic authority to get his converts to do what he wanted but chooses instead to appeal to their conscience to do the right thing, confident they will even go beyond what he asked (Philem 8-14, 21). When he encourages his converts to contribute to the relief offering, he wants them to "make up your mind, not reluctantly or under compulsion, for God loves a cheerful giver" (2 Cor 9:7 NRSV). Then he will be able to boast in their obedience, generated by God's *grace in them and in him (2 Cor 7:4; 8:7-8; 9:8; 10:15). Paul writes about ministry as if human and divine agency were indivisible. So, whether by Paul's commands or the Spirit's prompting, the apostle attributes all ministry in churches to what one might call "charismatic leadership"—even when he tells Timothy and Titus what to look for in overseers, deacons, and elders (1 Tim 3:1-15; Titus 1:5-9).

It is not clear whether there were overseers and deacons at the beginning of Paul's ministry—leaders that are mentioned only in later Pauline letters (Rom 16:1; Phil 1:1; 1 Tim 3:1-15; Titus 1:5-9) and featured in early patristic literature (*1 Clem.* 42.1-5; Ign. *Eph.* 3.2–6.1). But it cannot be inferred that Paul was reluctant to foster local leadership to keep his converts completely reliant on him. Even though he hoped his voice would rise above the rest, Paul knew leaders would play a significant role in church ministry, whether they came from within or without (Rom 16:1-4, 7, 12; 1 Cor 3:5-10; 4:6, 17; 16:15-18; 2 Cor 10:12-18; Gal 2:5-13; 5:7-12; Phil 2:19-30; 4:2-3; 1 Thess 5:12-13; 1 Tim 3:1-13; 5:17-22). It would be up to the churches to test Paul, test leaders, test themselves, indeed "test everything" in order to "hold fast to what is good" (1 Thess 5:20-21 NRSV; see 2 Cor 13:3-7; Gal 1:7-10; 6:4-5). For Paul the locus of gospel ministry is found only in the body of Christ.

2.2. Temple of the Indwelling Spirit. Paul wants the church to see themselves as the temple of God so that they will live in *purity. Since the church is where the *Holy Spirit dwells, they are supposed to be a holy people (1 Cor 3:16). Whether he is dealing with sexual immorality in the church (1 Cor 5:1-13; 6:15-20) or warning his converts about dining with *demons in the idol's temple (1 Cor 10:20-22; 2 Cor 6:14-16), Paul calls out the church: "Come out from them, and be separate from them" (2 Cor 6:17 NRSV, quoting Is 52:11). They are to hold each other accountable to live holy lives (1 Thess 4:1-8), distinct from unbelievers, whose sins remind them of the way they used to be: "fornicators, idolaters, adulterers, male prostitutes, sodomites, thieves, the greedy, drunkards, revilers, robbers" (1 Cor 6:9-11 NRSV). If they give in to lustful desires to which they were once enslaved, not only will they quench the Spirit, but their sin will harm one another (Eph 4:17-32). By walking in the Spirit, Paul's converts will learn how to control the desires of the flesh and overcome sin that pollutes and destroys God's temple—individually and corporately (1 Cor 6:16-20; Gal 5:16-26). And anyone who "destroys God's temple, God will destroy that person" (1 Cor 3:17 NRSV). "The Lord is an avenger in all these things" (1 Thess 4:6 NRSV). The pursuit of holiness is crucial to their ministry of loving one another and honoring God (Gal 5:13-15; 1 Thess 4:7-10).

Since temples were where sacrifices were offered to worship God/the gods, Paul encourages Christ-believers to present themselves as holy sacrifices that are "acceptable to God," no longer being "conformed to this world" but "transformed by the renewing of your minds" (Rom 12:1-2 NRSV). Such a mental transformation will happen by the power of the indwelling Spirit, who enables them to "discern all things" because they have "the mind of Christ" (1 Cor 2:15-16 NRSV). Since "Christ did not please himself" (Rom 15:3 NRSV), setting aside divine privileges as "he humbled himself and became obedient to the point of death—even death on a cross," Paul encourages his converts to have "the same mind" and "do nothing from selfish ambition or conceit, but in humility regard others as better than yourselves" (Phil 2:3-8 NRSV). When that happens, there will be no food fights because the weak and the strong will encourage each other (Rom 14:1–15:6; 1 Cor 8:7-13). There will be no ethnic hatred because Jews and Gentiles will welcome one another (Rom 15:7-13; Eph 2:11-22). Having the mind of Christ, they will "work for the good of all, and especially for those of the family of faith" (Gal 6:10 NRSV).

2.3. *The Family of God.* Paul's vision of the church as God's family is beautiful. Imagine how important it was for Gentiles who left behind their ancestral religion and patron gods, giving up their "social security" in such a risky world, to be baptized into a new family of brothers and sisters who would care for them until they died. Indeed, for Paul, *baptism is an exit ritual from the world and entry rite into the church: buried with Christ through baptism, having cast off their old garments and clothed themselves "with Christ"—what Paul called "the new self"—believers are brought out of the water by their new brothers and sisters, raised from the dead as adopted children of God to walk in Christ's *resurrection power through the Spirit until the last day (Rom 6:3-5; 8:11; Gal 3:26-27; Eph 4:24; Col 2:11-15). That baptism proves to be divisive among his converts frustrates Paul (1 Cor 1:10-17). Rather than quarrel with one another, brothers and sisters are supposed to be "united in the same mind and the same purpose" (1 Cor 1:10 NRSV), "one Lord, one faith, one baptism" (Eph 4:5 NRSV).

The same is true for the Lord's Supper. One family, gathered around the Lord's table, all partaking of one loaf of bread (1 Cor 10:17), should reveal their unity in Christ. But when house churches in Corinth come together to celebrate communion, "it is not for the better but for the worse"; the fissures of their *fellowship are revealed (1 Cor 11:17 NRSV; see 1 Cor 11:18-22). The issues that divide them in the world—gender, social status, ethnic identity—are even more evident when they eat the Lord's Supper, inviting God's *judgment (1 Cor 11:27-32). Regardless of their worldly identity, all Christ-believers are supposed to treat one another as brothers and sisters: "For in the one Spirit we were all baptized into one body—Jews or Greeks, slaves or free—and we were all made to drink of one Spirit" (1 Cor 12:13 NRSV). A church that gathers in a house is supposed to be home for the *whole* family of God, "for God shows no partiality" (Rom 2:11 NRSV).

When a husband and wife come to a house church to worship God, they enter as brother and sister in Christ. When a master and his slave join the family table to eat the Lord's Supper, they serve each other as equals. When Jews and Gentiles sing praises to the Lord from the Psalter, they glorify God with one voice as a "new *creation" of the *Israel of God (Rom 15:9-13; Gal 6:15-16). Since the same Spirit gifted all members, whether male or female, Jew or Gentile, slave or free, a woman does not need to claim a man's role when she prophesies and prays (1 Cor 11:5-16). Her veiled hair helps maintain her identity in Christ. A Gentile man does not need to get circumcised to become a child of Abraham (Gal 4:28–5:6). His foreskin helps maintain his identity in Christ. A slave does not need to become a freedman to be received by his master as a brother (Philem 16). His slave name helps maintain his identity in Christ (Philem 10-11). People never lose their identity when they join the family of God.

So, Paul believes a married sister in Christ should still submit to her husband (Eph 5:22-24), Gentile

Christ-believers should still recognize they are unnatural branches grafted into the Jewish tree (Rom 11:17-24), and slaves of the Lord Jesus should still obey their masters (Eph 5:22). But being a woman or a Gentile or a slave does not prevent people from serving the Lord as ministers of the gospel of Jesus Christ in the family of God. In fact, their identity as brothers and sisters in Christ proves they are equally endowed by the same Spirit. That is why Paul tells wives they should not usurp authority over their husbands (1 Tim 2:12), the strong should not eat idol meat in front of the weak (1 Cor 8:13; Rom 14:13-21), and runaway slaves must return to their masters (Philem 12-14). In deference to one another, they are supposed to reveal what sets Christians apart from the world: they love each other as family, especially evident when husbands love their wives like Christ loves the church, the circumcised welcome the uncircumcised as children of Abraham, and masters treat their slaves like brothers.

2.4. A Colony of Heaven. In a letter to Roman colonists, Paul reminds his converts that "our citizenship is in heaven" (Phil 3:20 NRSV). When he writes, "*live your life* in a manner worthy of the gospel of Christ," he uses a political term (*politeuesthe*) to describe their witness to the world, "in no way intimidated by your opponents" (Phil 1:27-28 NRSV). Like an imperial colony that advertised the Roman way of life (Acts 16:21), Paul sees the church as a colony of heaven, an embodied politic that stands against the world, putting on display the "Christ way of life" on earth: love, compassion, sympathy, humility, *joy (Phil 1:29–2:12). As "blameless and innocent, children of God," believers would "shine like stars in the world," a prophetic witness in the "midst of a crooked and perverse generation" (Phil 2:15 NRSV). Paul's evangelistic strategy, then, is thoroughly ecclesial: the reputation of the gospel rests on the shoulders of the entire body of Christ. Their life together testifies to the "truth of the gospel" (Gal 2:14).

That is why Paul becomes so angry with his converts when they fight: their social problems ruin their witness to the world. The church is supposed to be a place where people find the justice of God (1 Cor 6:1-11), where the *peace of Christ destroys ethnic hatred (Gal 2:11-21; Eph 2:11-22), and where the love of God covers a multitude of sin (2 Cor 5:14-21). Paul expects Christ-believers not only to "contribute to the needs of the saints" so that they will not need any help from nonbelievers—what Paul refers to as behaving "properly toward outsiders" and being "dependent on no one" (Rom 12:13; 1 Thess 4:12 NRSV). He also encourages the church to feed their enemies, help the poor, bless their persecutors, offer *hospitality, and never take revenge (Rom 12:13-21; Gal 2:10). By overcoming evil with good, Christ's ambassadors will be his peacemakers in a world filled with *violence and corruption (Rom 12:17-19). Christians do not judge outsiders for being worldly; it is God who judges the wicked (Rom 12:19; 1 Cor 5:12-13). Instead, wearing the light of Christ like body armor, the church wars against evil powers, knowing that "our struggle is not against enemies of blood and flesh" (Eph 6:17 NRSV; see Eph 6:10-16; Rom 13:12-14).

3. Paul's Theology of Ministry.

Paul believes he and his converts are witnessing the beginning of the end: "the night is far gone, the day is near" (Rom 13:12 NRSV). They are the generation "on whom the ends of the ages have come" (1 Cor 10:11 NRSV). Anticipating the imminent appearance of Jesus Christ on the last day, Paul believes he has only so much time to prepare his converts for the day of the Lord (Rom 13:11-14; 1 Thess 2:17-20; 5:2-11). Indeed, Paul's ministry is heavily influenced by his eschatological outlook. Since the end is near, Paul ministers like a man possessed with fulfilling his divine calling as he watches the last grains of sand pass through the hourglass. So much to do, so little time.

Like a father who has arranged his daughter's *marriage, Paul tells his converts, "I promised you in marriage to one husband, to present you as a chaste virgin to Christ" (2 Cor 11:2 NRSV), to be "kept sound and blameless at the coming of our Lord Jesus Christ" (1 Thess 5:23 NRSV). His mission to bring about the "obedience of the Gentiles" will not only "glorify" his ministry, adding the "full number of Gentiles" to Abraham's family (Rom 11:13, 25 NRSV). Paul hopes it will also provoke his kinsmen to believe the gospel, potentially triggering the resurrection at the end of time (Rom 11:14-15). From start to finish, Paul conceives of ministry as an eschatological mission.

3.1. Ministry at the End of Time. When the messianic age dawned on Israel, the *salvation of the Lord would extend to the ends of the earth; the whole world would see the *glory of God (Is 49:1-6; 56:4-8; 60:1-9; 66:18-24). With the crucifixion, burial, resurrection, and *ascension of Christ, Paul believed the messianic age had begun, that the old age was passing away (1 Cor 7:31), and that he was the herald of the good news (Is 53:1; Rom 10:16). Christ inaugurated his end-of-the-world *kingdom on earth, reigning through the church as believers realize his victory over the law of sin and death. Since the age to come is already being played out in history through the work of Christ in his body, Paul wants his converts to live as if the end of the old age has already come: old things have passed away, everything becomes new in Christ (2 Cor 5:17). Getting his converts to see it, believe it, and live it was the hard part.

Indeed, in Paul's ministry the obedience of the Gentiles is a sentient matter. He writes letters "so that, with the eyes of your heart enlightened, you may know what is the *hope to which he has called you" (Eph 1:18 NRSV). If they can see that Christ fulfilled Jewish *law, then they will live in *freedom to serve the *law of Christ in the Spirit (Gal 4:1-7; 5:1, 13-16; 6:2). If they can see that they have already died to sin through Christ's death, then they will live rightly, justly—individually and corporately—the righteousness of God that comes through Jesus Christ, empowered by the Holy Spirit. If they can see the power of Christ's resurrection in their lives, then they will persevere in the face of evil and *suffering, groaning prayers in the Spirit, knowing "that all things work together for good for those who love God, who are called according to his purpose" (Rom 8:28 NRSV). The Spirit is God's end-of-the-world work in Christ, empowering believers to walk in confident faithfulness (Rom 8:9-17; 2 Cor 1:20-22). As believers are already crucified with Christ, already buried with him, already raised to walk in new life, throughout his letters Paul's advice follows the same cadence: become what you are in Christ.

Paul is convinced "that the one who began a good work among you will bring it to completion by the day of Jesus Christ" (Phil 1:6 NRSV). That God was not finished with his new creation on earth was obvious: believers still struggled with sin (Rom 6:12-19), creation still groaned for redemption (Rom 8:19-22), death was still regnant (1 Cor 15:20-26), the devil still incited rebellion (Eph 2:1-2; 2 Thess 2:7-12). So, Paul constantly reminds his converts of the coming day of the Lord, when Christ will return to earth and put "all his enemies under his feet. The last enemy to be destroyed is death" (1 Cor 15:25-26 NRSV). Because Christ was raised from the dead, the firstfruits of the resurrection (1 Cor 15:20-23), the *firstborn of the family of God (Rom 8:29), Paul claims all Christ-believers will be raised from the dead too: "If the Spirit of him who raised Jesus from the dead dwells in you, he who raised Christ from the dead will give life to your mortal bodies also through his Spirit that dwells in you" (Rom 8:11 NRSV). That is why Christ-believers grieve with hope (1 Thess 4:13-14), knowing that "this mortal body must put on immortality" (1 Cor 15:53 NRSV). That will be the end (1 Cor 15:24), when "death has been swallowed up in victory" (1 Cor 15:54 NRSV).

The "redemption of our bodies" will be the last sign of believers' *adoption into God's family (Rom 8:23 NRSV). "Creation itself will be set free from its bondage to decay and will obtain the freedom of the glory of the children of God" (Rom 8:21 NRSV). All of this was more than theological talk for Paul. He believed the hope of Christ's resurrection would comfort his converts, regardless of whether they lived to see the last day or not (1 Thess 4:15-17). Indeed, he counted on them to minister to each other in the face of death, encouraging "one another with these words" (1 Thess 4:18 NRSV), remaining "steadfast, immovable, always excelling in the work of the Lord" until the end (1 Cor 15:58).

3.2. Heavenly Ministry. Even though some were saying "the day of the Lord is already here" (2 Thess 2:2 NRSV), Paul reminds his converts that, before the end of the world, Christ will destroy "with the breath of his mouth, annihilating . . . by the manifestation of his coming" "the lawless one" and the works of *Satan (2 Thess 2:8-10 NRSV). Paul sees the return of Christ as a cosmic invasion, where the ruler of heaven will conquer the "ruler of the power of the air" (Eph 2:2 NRSV) and reclaim earth for heaven's purpose at the end of time. Yet, Paul does not believe his converts have to wait until the last day to live in victory over the devil and his army. For, just as Paul sees a temporal overlap between the old age and the age to come, he also claims a spatial overlap, the place where heaven has already invaded earth—the church. Since "God put this power to work in Christ when he raised him from the dead and seated him at his right hand in the heavenly places, far above all rule and authority and power and dominion," having "put all things under his feet" as the head of the body (the church), God has put all things under the feet of the church too (Eph 1:20-23 NRSV). Christ-believers reign with him in heaven over all things, seated "in the heavenly places in Christ Jesus" (Eph 2:6 NRSV).

Paul never mentions exorcism as a way to combat malevolent powers on earth. Instead, he encourages his converts to wear Christ like body armor as they wage war against the devil, remaining strong in their victorious faith, fighting "against the cosmic powers of this present darkness, against the spiritual forces of evil in the heavenly places" (Eph 6:12 NRSV; see Rom 13:12-14; Eph 6:10-17). Ministry is war, a constant battle over evil powers in heaven and on earth, a reclamation of all things that God has created. The church stands, therefore, as a powerful witness against evil and suffering, claiming heaven's victory on earth through Christ's resurrection. It is just a matter of time until the devil and his minions are pushed out and destroyed because Christ is taking back everything God has made—the church's steadfast faith proves it. That is why, according to Paul, "every knee should bend, in heaven on earth and under the earth, and every tongue should confess that Jesus is Lord, to the glory of God the Father" (Phil 2:10-11 NRSV). Paul believes the end is near, and ministry is doing something about it in the meantime.

See also APOSTLE; BIRTH PANGS, MATERNAL IMAGERY; BODY OF CHRIST; CHURCH; FINANCIAL SUPPORT; GIFTS OF THE SPIRIT; HOLY SPIRIT; LEADERSHIP; PASTOR, PAUL AS; PEACE, RECONCILIATION; PRAYER; SERVANT, SERVICE; SIGNS, WONDERS, MIRACLES.

BIBLIOGRAPHY. **R. J. Banks,** *Paul's Idea of Community: The Early House Churches in Their Cultural Setting* (Peabody, MA: Hendrickson, 1994); **A. D. Clarke,** *A Pauline Theology of Church Leadership*, LNTS 362 (London: Bloomsbury, 2008); **D. J. Downs,** *The Offering of the Gentiles: Paul's Collection for Jerusalem in Its Chronological, Cultural, and Cultic Contexts* (Grand Rapids, MI: Eerdmans, 2016); **E. E. Ellis,** *Pauline Theology: Ministry and Society* (Grand Rapids, MI: Eerdmans, 1989); **B. R. Gaventa,** *Our Mother Saint Paul* (Louisville, KY: Westminster John Knox, 2007); **M. J. Gorman,** *Becoming the Gospel: Paul, Participation, and Mission* (Grand Rapids, MI: Eerdmans, 2015); **C. Kruse,** *New Testament Models for Ministry: Jesus and Paul* (Nashville: Thomas Nelson, 1985); **B. W. Longenecker,** *Remember the Poor: Paul, Poverty, and the Greco Roman World* (Grand Rapids, MI: Eerdmans, 2010); **M. Y. MacDonald,** *The Pauline Churches: A Socio-historical Study of Institutionalization in the Pauline and Deutero-Pauline Writings* (Cambridge: Cambridge University Press, 1988); **D. B. Martin,** *Slavery as Salvation: The Metaphor of Slavery in Pauline Christianity* (New Haven, CT: Yale University Press, 1990); **S. McKnight,** *Pastor Paul: Nurturing a Culture of Christoformity in the Church* (Grand Rapids, MI: Brazos, 2019); **W. A. Meeks,** *The First Urban Christians: The Social World of the Apostle Paul* (New Haven, CT: Yale University Press, 1983); **B. S. Rosner, A. S. Malone, and T. J. Burke,** eds., *Paul as Pastor* (London: T&T Clark, 2018); **E. J. Schnabel,** *Paul the Missionary: Realities, Strategies, and Methods* (Downers Grove, IL: IVP Academic, 2008); **J. W. Thompson,** *Pastoral Ministry According to Paul: A Biblical Vision* (Grand Rapids, MI: Baker Academic, 2006); **C. L. Westfall,** *Paul and Gender: Reclaiming the Apostle's Vision for Men and Women in Christ* (Grand Rapids, MI: Baker Academic, 2016).

R. Reeves

MIRACLES. *See* GIFTS OF THE SPIRIT; SIGNS, WONDERS, MIRACLES.

MISSION

First and foremost, Paul was not a theologian who circulated his ideas or a *pastor who cared for local congregations but a missionary who was caught up in God's saving activity in the world. This fundamental reality is crucial for understanding both Paul the man and the message of his *letters. Although long neglected by Pauline scholars, interest in mission as a key to Paul's thought has accelerated in recent decades (e.g., Barram 2006; Bosch, 123-78; Gorman 2015; Schnabel 2008; Schreiner). The question remains open, however, as to what mission means in relation to Paul and his writings, and this is where the article begins. It then considers the apostle's own mission consciousness and activity, the place of mission in Paul's thinking, and, finally, how Paul's churches participate in *God's mission.

1. What Is Mission?
2. Paul's Mission Consciousness
3. Paul's Mission Practice
4. Paul's Mission Theology
5. The Church's Role in the *Missio Dei*
6. Conclusion

1. What Is Mission?

It is difficult to find consensus about Paul's understanding of mission, both at a scholarly and a popular level. This owes in part to the varied use of the language of *mission/missionary* in contemporary circles, as well as to the reality that Paul himself does not use the terminology. Paul's closest equivalent is the term *apostle, derived from the Greek verb *apostellō*, "to send." But whereas the language of *apostle* and *apostolic* is appropriate for describing Paul's vocation, it is less applicable to the missional calling of Paul's churches (Barram 2006, 178).

Many interpreters of Paul take the apostle's understanding of mission in a relatively narrow sense, focusing particularly on the activities of initial evangelism through proclaiming the *gospel and planting churches (e.g., Schnabel 2008; Dickson; Plummer; Ware; Marshall 2008). Mission, from this perspective, comprises one part of the *church's *calling, is primarily carried out by a group of called and sent individuals, and seeks to lead outsiders to *faith in *Christ and establish them in Christian communities. Those who adhere to such narrower definitions of mission often limit discussions of mission in Paul to texts that deal with Paul's evangelistic activity among non-Christians (e.g., Rom 10:8-18; 15; 1 Cor 9:19-23; Gal 1–2; Eph 3:1-13).

Other interpreters, however, approach Paul's letters in light of a more comprehensive meaning of mission (see C. J. H. Wright; Barram 2006; N. T. Wright, 436-37, 1484-1504; Gorman 2015; Flemming 2015). From this perspective, a biblical understanding of mission begins not with the activities of the church or of a group of missionaries, but with the mission of the triune God, the *missio Dei*. Mission, then, is about God's sweeping purpose to bring *fullness and restoration to the entire *creation, especially people from every nation, as well as what God's people are called to be, do, and say in connection with the divine purpose. Although attention to the *missio Dei* is nothing new, it has gained momentum in recent decades with the burgeoning interest in missional *hermeneutics among biblical scholars and missiologists (see Goheen; Hunsberger). Such missional readings of Paul shift the focus from the various outreach *activities* of Paul and his converts to the wider concern for how Paul and his churches participate in the comprehensive mission of God. At the same time, Paul's gospel mission carries not only an *outward* focus—preaching to non-Christians and bringing them to faith in Christ—but also an *inward* concern for transforming Christian communities to reflect the character of Christ and to bear *witness to God's saving purposes in the world (Gorman 2015, 19). Reading Paul missionally, therefore, moves from combing Paul's writings for a prescribed set of *mission texts* to reading Paul's letters as *missional documents*.

Both the traditional and emerging paradigms for discerning mission in Paul contribute to our grasp of the apostle's missional vocation and thought, and there is considerable overlap between them. This article explores *both* Paul's mission toward people outside the faith community *and* his wider concern to engage in God's redemptive purpose for the whole creation and to shape Christian communities that embody the gospel in the world. Using the language of *mission* as a principal category for understanding Paul's thought has nothing to do with dominant groups coercing less powerful people to accept their beliefs or cultures. Mission in Paul is about getting caught up in God's liberating, reconciling purposes in the world.

2. Paul's Mission Consciousness.

To grasp Paul's mission theology, we must come to terms with his missional *identity. First and foremost, Paul understands himself as one "called to be an apostle of Christ" (1 Cor 1:1 NRSV; see, e.g., Rom 1:1; 2 Cor 1:1; Col 1:1). Specifically, he is "apostle to the *Gentiles" (Rom 11:13 NRSV), someone commissioned to extend God's good news to the nations of the world. Since Paul never fully lays out what that apostleship means for him, we must discover clues within his contextual arguments.

2.1. Paul's Calling and Transformation. Paul's mission begins with his Damascus road revelation. Without it, there would be no apostle Paul and no Pauline mission. Both Paul's understanding of his apostleship and his missional theology find their wellspring in this event. Not only does Luke recount Paul's Damascus road Christophany three times (Acts 9; 22; 26), but Paul repeatedly points back to it, directly or indirectly, in his letters (Gal 1:11-17; 1 Cor 9:1-2; 15:8-10; Phil 3:4-11; 2 Cor 4:4-6; see Fringer).

First, Paul considers this vision of the risen Christ as the source of his calling to participate in a divine, boundary-breaking mission. While defending the divine origin of his call and his gospel, Paul states the purpose of God's revealing his Son in him: "so that I might proclaim him among the Gentiles" (Gal 1:16 NRSV). Although Paul shares with the other apostles a visible encounter with the resurrected Christ (1 Cor 9:1; 15:8), his commission as apostle to the Gentile nations was unique. Paul describes that calling in *prophetic language. Like Jeremiah and the Servant in Isaiah, God set Paul apart before he was born (Gal 1:15; Jer 1:5; Is 49:1, 5). There is wide agreement that Paul saw his missional vocation as a continuation of the work of Isaiah's Servant. Paul does not claim to be a new Servant of Yahweh; rather, he participates in the *ministry of the Servant, who was given as a light to the nations to bring God's *salvation to the end of the earth (Is 49:6; see Is 42:6).

Second, in addition to his missional calling, Paul experienced a life-altering transformation on the Damascus road. Was this a "*conversion" experience? In a classic essay, K. Stendahl argues that Paul's Damascus encounter brought a vocational calling but not a personal conversion (Stendahl, 7-23). Stendahl rightly grasps that many interpreters have read Paul's experience through modern Western lenses, in terms of God's rescue of an individual from a guilt-ridden conscience or as a change in religions from Judaism to Christianity. But Stendahl overplays his hand in limiting Paul's Christophany to a change in vocations. Paul experienced a world-altering encounter that radically transformed his values, commitments, self-identity, and life direction (Phil 3:7-9). Moreover, what transpired on the Damascus road was not simply about Paul's personal experience but also about what has happened to the whole world through the death and *resurrection of Christ. The transforming work that God did *in* Paul through his Damascus road encounter God was now doing *through* Paul as he fulfilled his apostolic mission to the nations (N. T. Wright, 1426).

Third, Paul claims that he received the gospel he proclaimed through "a revelation of Jesus Christ" on the Damascus road (Gal 1:12 NRSV). This phrase focuses primarily on the *content* of that revelation—Christ—and not merely its source. S. Kim argues convincingly that key elements of Paul's gospel find their origin in Paul's Damascus Christophany, even if he overstates how much of Paul's theology derives from that event (e.g., Kim, 31). Paul likely grasped the full implications of his gospel and apostleship only through later reflection on Scripture and in the course of his missionary work. Nevertheless, Paul's transforming vision on the Damascus road certainly convinced him that the crucified Jesus was the risen *Lord, the *Son of God (Gal 1:16), and the Messiah of *Israel, and that what God had done in Jesus' death and resurrection opened up a new time of salvation that embraced Gentiles as well as Jews. Paul's gospel, and consequently his missional theology, are anchored in that event.

2.2. Paul's Apostolic Identity. Paul uses various metaphors to describe his apostolic identity and mission. He pictures himself as a **servant* (*diakonos*) of God and the gospel, and, through God's commission, a servant of the church (1 Cor 3:5; Eph 3:7; Col 1:23, 25). Even more striking is Paul's embracing the identity of a **slave* (*doulos*) of Christ (Rom 1:1; Phil 1:1; see Titus 1:1), a term that in Paul's world signaled humility, submission, and ownership. In Philippians, that language points to Paul adopting the attitude of Christ, who took "the form of a slave" (Phil 2:7 NRSV) in loving service to others.

In Romans, Paul draws on cultic language to envision his ministry as a "priestly service of the gospel of God" (Rom 15:16 NRSV). The goal of Paul's mission as *priest* is that the Gentiles might become an acceptable offering to God as a result of Paul's gospel ministry. Further, apostles are *stewards* of God's message (1 Cor 4:1), accountable to God alone for faithful service (1 Cor 4:2). They are *ambassadors* of Christ, agents of God's reconciling work in the world (2 Cor 5:18-20), and the *aroma* of Christ among those who are saved (2 Cor 2:15). In addition, apostles function as *parents* who give birth to, care for, discipline, encourage, and model before their children (1 Cor 4:14-21; Gal 4:19-20; 1 Thess 2:7-12).

At the heart of Paul's apostolic identity lies his calling and sending to proclaim the good news of Christ (1 Cor 1:17). He fulfills this vocation eagerly (Rom 1:15) as someone under joyful obligation to God (1 Cor 9:16). But Paul not only *speaks* the gospel; he also *embodies* it. Accused by some of impure motives in his apostolic conduct, Paul assures the Thessalonians that out of deep *love, he shares with them not only the gospel but also his own life (1 Thess 2:8). Paul recognizes that if he is discredited, so is the gospel he proclaims and the mission he fulfills.

Paul's personal identification with the gospel leads him to refuse the rights of an apostle to *financial support (1 Cor 9:12, 15; 1 Thess 2:9-12). Out of love, he chooses instead to work long hours with his own hands—a socially demeaning activity in the Greco-Roman world—so that his acceptance of support will not prove an obstacle to the gospel (1 Cor 9:12). Indeed, Paul, like his Lord, makes himself "a slave to all" in order to win others to Christ (1 Cor 9:19 NRSV; see Phil 2:7).

Further, although Paul sees his apostolic mission as directed especially toward the Gentiles (Rom 1:5; 11:13; 15:16; Eph 3:1-2, 8), he never abandons his passion that his fellow Jews might be saved (Rom 10:1). Paul understands the gospel to be the power of salvation for *everyone* (Rom 1:16-17). There is "no distinction" between Jew and Gentile; consequently, Paul envisions himself (and other apostles) as messengers who herald God's saving good news to Jews and Gentiles alike (Rom 10:12-15; see Is 40:9; 52:7; 61:1-3).

2.3. Missional Suffering. Nowhere does the intersection between the life Paul lives and the gospel he proclaims display more visibly than in his apostolic *suffering. S. Hafemann calls it the glue that unites Paul's life, his message, and his mission (140). To be an apostle means to share in the destiny of Jesus, as someone scorned and rejected, sentenced to death and treated like refuse by the world (1 Cor 4:9-13). So close is that connection that Paul can claim, "I carry the marks of Jesus branded on my body" (Gal 6:17 NRSV; see Col 1:24).

The bond between suffering and mission comes to center stage in 2 Corinthians, where Paul's opponents charge that his afflictions and weakness disqualify him as a true apostle. His critics boast in their mighty works (2 Cor 12:12), but Paul chooses to boast in his weaknesses (2 Cor 12:8-10). He carries the gospel treasure in the "clay pot" of his afflicted body so that the world might see that the gospel's power for salvation belongs to God, not the messenger (2 Cor 4:7). Paul *lives* the *cross of Christ. *His* story of suffering and divine power embodies the story of Jesus' death and resurrection that he proclaims (2 Cor 4:10-11). God therefore uses apostolic suffering as a vehicle of mission to bring life to others (2 Cor 1:6; 4:12). Paul conceives of his own sufferings as a participation in the sufferings of Christ (2 Cor 1:5; Phil 3:10; Col 1:24). But those very weaknesses, paradoxically, become a living demonstration of God's resurrection power in his ministry (2 Cor 12:9-10). Weakness, then, lies at the heart of both Paul's gospel and his mission.

2.4. Motivations and Goals. What motivated Paul to "spend and be spent" for others (2 Cor 12:15 NRSV; see Bosch, 133-39)? Paul's motivation as a missionary no doubt rested on various elements. These include his apostolic commission (Gal 1:15-16), his deep concern for people who face God's *judgment apart from salvation in Christ (see Rom 2:8, 16; 1 Cor 1:18; 1 Thess 1:10), and the character of the gospel itself as the power of God for salvation (Rom 1:16; 1 Cor 1:18). Paul testifies that he carries a sense of God-given obligation toward Greeks and barbarians, wise and foolish (Rom 1:14). He is compelled by God to proclaim the good news (1 Cor 9:16) so that all people might be saved (1 Cor 9:19-23; 10:33).

Yet at the deepest level, Paul's motivation for mission surely flows from the transforming love of God, demonstrated in the cross of Christ. "The love of Christ urges us on," Paul attests, "because we are convinced that one has died for all; therefore all have died" (2 Cor 5:14 NRSV; see Rom 5:8; Gal 2:20). Paul's missionary work flows naturally out of his experience of God's love and *grace, displayed in the cross.

As for the goals of Paul's cruciform mission, he seeks to spread the powerful word of God to Gentiles and Jews alike in order to establish mature, multicultural communities of believers. Twice in Romans, Paul affirms that the aim of his apostleship is "to bring about the obedience of faith" among the Gentiles (Rom 1:5; 16:26 NRSV), which includes the life of obedience that grows out of faith in Jesus the Messiah. Paul proclaims and teaches the gospel in order to "present everyone mature in Christ" (Col 1:28 NRSV; see Col 1:15-29). He anticipates that his converts will stand firm on the last day, showing that he has not run in vain (Gal 2:2; Phil 2:16).

From a broader perspective, Paul understands his apostolic work as part of God's purpose to establish the Messiah's rule over the whole world, realizing its goal when at last God becomes "all in all" (1 Cor 15:28 NRSV; N. T. Wright, 449-50). Paul engages in mission so that ultimately all creation might bow in *worship, bringing total *glory to God (Rom 16:27; Phil 2:10-11; 4:20).

3. Paul's Mission Practice.

What did Paul's participation in the mission of God look like in practice? Any attempt to answer that question leads to two main sources: Luke's narrative of Paul's missionary career in Acts and Paul's letters themselves. Although some scholars have questioned the historical reliability of Luke's accounts, in reality, "the record available in Acts is found to be in fairly close and sometimes quite precise accord with the letters" (Bowers 1993, 609). This article focuses primarily on Paul's own testimony to his mission strategy and practice in his letters.

3.1. The Scope of Paul's Missionary Activity. Unlike Acts, Paul nowhere offers a detailed narrative of his mission practice. He does, however, allude to that activity on various occasions. Above all, Paul's missionary vocation focused on three interrelated practices: (1) primary evangelization, (2) founding new congregations, and (3) nurturing Christian communities.

First, Paul's apostolic calling compelled him to proclaim the good news (1 Cor 1:17; 9:16) so that he might "win" followers of Jesus the Messiah and Lord among both Jews and Gentiles (1 Cor 9:19-21). According to Acts, that ministry often happened in public settings, such as a Jewish synagogue, a marketplace, or a rented hall. But Paul also used his trade as an evangelistic occasion, proclaiming the gospel while working "night and day" as a *tentmaker (1 Thess 2:9; 2 Thess 3:8 NRSV). Even his imprisonment resulted in the gospel spreading "throughout the whole imperial guard," the emperor's elite troops (Phil 1:12-13 NRSV). Repeatedly, Paul's letters recall his initial telling of the good news in mission contexts (see 1 Cor 2:1-5; 4:15; Gal 4:13; 1 Thess 2:2, 13, 16). Paul's distinctive vocation was not to build on another's foundation but to spread the gospel in places where Christ had not yet been named (Rom 15:20; see 2 Cor 10:16).

Second, Paul's pioneer mission work involved not only winning individual converts but founding and establishing new communities of faith. As God's servant, he "plants" churches and lays the "foundation" as a skilled master builder (1 Cor 3:7-10 NRSV). The very existence of these congregations authenticates his apostleship (1 Cor 9:1-2; 2 Cor 3:1-3).

Third, Paul's calling was in no sense limited to primary evangelism and church planting. The ongoing nurture of Christian communities became just as vital to Paul's missionary work as giving birth to them in the first place (see Barram 2006; Bowers 1987). To that end, Paul's ministry of the gospel was not only directed to nonbelievers but also to Christians. Early in Romans, Paul declares his eagerness "to proclaim the gospel to you also who are in Rome" (Rom 1:15 NRSV). This surely refers to Paul's ministry of teaching and edifying the Roman Christians (see Col 1:25-28). Paul's willingness to adjust his personal conduct on behalf of different groups of people in order to "win" them (1 Cor 9:19-23) speaks of more than gaining converts. He desires to "win the weak," which involves bringing weak Christians to full maturity in Christ. Likewise, Paul models a lifestyle of giving no offense to Jews, Gentiles, or "the church of God . . . so that they may be saved" (1 Cor 10:32-33 NRSV). The aim of Paul's missional behavior is a comprehensive salvation that only is completed when the church stands before Christ on the final day (see 1 Cor 9:22; Rom 5:9-10; 1 Thess 2:19).

Christian nurture, then, is not peripheral but central to Paul's missional practice. Not only does Acts describe Paul's ongoing residential ministry in places such as *Corinth and *Ephesus, but Paul also recalls "urging and encouraging" believers to "lead a life worthy of God" (1 Thess 2:12 NRSV).

3.2. Paul's Letters as Missional Documents. Paul's letters form a crucial component of his mission practice. As the *product* of Paul's mission, they address issues that arise out of his missionary work. Letters function as "apostleship by proxy" (Gorman 2008, 27), substituting for what Paul would have said in person. Further, Paul's letters *bear witness* to God's mission, expressing the good news of Jesus Christ and its ramifications, from which Christian mission flows. They enable the gospel to speak into the concrete problems and circumstances faced by his churches.

Finally, Paul's letters function as *instruments* of mission. They work to shape and establish young congregations into mature Christian communities that are conformed to the likeness of Christ, communities that embody an alternative to the other *political and religious assemblies in the ancient world. Paul's mission could not succeed if congregations failed to continue in Christ (Phil 2:16; 1 Thess 3:1-10). What is more, Paul writes to congregations that are already engaged in the mission of God (Phil 1:5). He seeks to energize and equip faithful missional communities that by word and deed participate in the ongoing story of God's loving mission in the world. Paul's letters, then, do not merely inject the *theme* of mission from time to time; they are missional texts, from start to finish. Paul's writings are birthed by mission, articulate God's mission, and promote the divine mission in the lives of concrete churches.

3.3. Mission Strategy. To what extent did Paul's ministry follow a deliberate mission strategy? First, Paul's mission work focused on cities rather than villages or rural areas. Cities represented cosmopolitan, culture-forming places, which held the greatest concentration of both Jews and Gentiles. Some interpreters argue that Paul followed a conscious "*urban strategy," planting churches in certain strategic centers, from which he intended the gospel to radiate to surrounding towns and rural communities (Allen, 12; Bosch, 129-31). But according to Acts, not all the cities Paul visited were major commercial and political centers (e.g., Iconium, Lystra, Derbe), and it is possible to overstate Paul's use of a "grand strategy" in selecting urban centers for church planting (Schnabel 2008, 282-84, 287). Nevertheless, Paul surely was aware that cities such as Corinth, Ephesus, and Thessalonica lay on international roads and trade routes, where God's word could "sound forth" in the neighboring regions (see 1 Thess 1:8).

Second, Paul's apostolic mission featured a striking geographical dimension. Paul testifies "that from *Jerusalem and as far around as Illyricum I have fully proclaimed [literally 'fulfilled'] the good news of Christ" (Rom 15:19 NRSV). Paul "fulfilled" the gospel not merely in discharging his apostolic task of *preaching and planting new churches in the eastern Mediterranean world but also by accomplishing the full scope of his missionary calling. This involved establishing strong and strategic missional communities in those regions (Bowers 1987). Having "no further place" to work in those territories, Paul can now shift his focus westward to Rome, the imperial capital, and to Spain (Rom 15:22-24 NRSV). Why Spain? In the ancient world, Spain was thought to lie at the "end of the earth" (Schnabel 2004, 1271-73). Paul's geographical strategy ranges from east to west in the Roman world. In part, this made pragmatic sense, since Paul, a Roman *citizen, could *travel freely within the empire. But Paul also may have intentionally established congregations that revered Christ as Lord in cities where another ruler, Caesar, was worshiped as lord (N. T. Wright, 1503).

Third, Paul modeled flexibility and identification for the sake of mission. In a classic expression of that practice, Paul testifies that he became "as a Jew" to Jews, "as one outside the *law" to Gentiles, and "weak" to the weak. In short, he became "all things to all people" in order to bring Jews, Gentiles, and weak Christians to the fullness of salvation (1 Cor 9:19-23 NRSV). Paul shows a willingness to forgo his personal freedom and rights, to "contextualize" his cultural and social practice, for the greater good of the gospel (see Flemming 2005, 193-99). This contextualization principle likely extended beyond Paul's personal behavior to his communication of the gospel to various groups of people. Acts narrates that Paul adapted his evangelistic preaching to fit Jewish and Gentile audiences and different social groups (Acts 13:13-41; 14:15-17; 17:16-34). Further, his letters articulate the gospel and its implications in various ways, addressing the specific needs and circumstances of his churches. In both cases, however, Paul's identification with his audience reaches limits. Paul was not "an *idolater to the idolaters," nor could he water down his message to suit people's tastes. Both his conduct and his communication had to be consistent with the gospel in its saving power and *cruciform content (1 Cor 9:23; 10:33–11:1).

Does Paul's willingness to contextualize his words and walk for Gentiles mean that he was a "crosscultural missionary"? Not in the modern sense. Although Paul's primary identity and worldview remained Jewish, as a Diaspora Jew from Tarsus, he was fluent in both cultural worlds. Paul encountered both Jewish and Gentile audiences from an insider's perspective.

*3.4. **Paul's Coworkers.*** Paul's mission work was anything but a solo enterprise. Paul committed himself to a shared mission, along with a team of colleagues. They served as fellow evangelists and church founders, representatives to and from local congregations, co-senders of letters, and secretaries. They functioned not merely as assistants but as full participants in Paul's mission work. Frequently, Paul sent his closest colleagues, such as Timothy and Titus, as envoys, substituting for the apostle's own presence (1 Cor 4:17; 16:10-11; 2 Cor 7:6-7, 15). Other *coworkers, such as Epaphras, fulfilled ongoing ministries in local churches and established new congregations in the surrounding regions (Col 1:7-8; 4:12; see 1 Cor 16:15-16).

It is notable that *women played a significant role in Paul's mission. In Romans 16, Paul names seven women with specific ministry roles, including Phoebe as deacon, Junia as apostle, Priscilla as coworker, and several other females who work in the Roman church. Euodia and Syntyche shared in Paul's pioneer evangelistic mission in Philippi, "struggled beside [him] in the work of the gospel," and later they presumably fulfilled more settled congregational leadership functions (Phil 4:2-3 NRSV). Nothing in these references suggests that women were restricted to certain roles in the Pauline mission, differentiated from men (Marshall 2008, 119).

*3.5. **Compassion, Power, and Prayer.*** Three further aspects of Paul's mission practice deserve attention. First, Paul made the *collection for the needy believers in Jerusalem a ministry priority (Rom 15:25-31; 1 Cor 16:1-4; 2 Cor 8–9; Gal 2:10). He devoted considerable effort to gather the offering from Gentile churches and even delayed his intended visit to Rome and mission to Spain so that he could first deliver the collection in Jerusalem (Rom 15:23-25). Reasons for Paul's passion for the collection include (1) it represented a compassionate response to the concrete needs of an impoverished Christian community, a service to others (Rom 15:25-26, 2 Cor 9:12-13); (2) it demonstrated the unity of Jewish and Gentile Christians, enabling Diaspora Gentile churches to show their debt of gratitude to Jewish believers for their spiritual heritage (Rom 15:27); and (3) it provided a concrete opportunity to live out the gospel of God's grace in Christ (1 Cor 16:3; 2 Cor 8:6-7, 19). Far from a second-tier distraction from Paul's evangelistic ministry, the collection put hands and feet on Paul's gospel of grace.

Second, Paul's apostolic mission demonstrated acts of miraculous power (Rom 15:18-19; 2 Cor 12:12; Gal 3:5). Paul does not spotlight this dimension of his ministry. Nevertheless, he testifies that Christ brought about obedience from the Gentiles "by word and deed, by the power of *signs and wonders, by the power of the Spirit of God" (Rom 15:18-19 NRSV). Third, *prayer was indispensable to Paul's apostolic mission (Carson). On one occasion, Paul expresses his earnest prayer for the salvation of his fellow Jews (Rom 10:1). Surely Paul also offered such evangelistically oriented prayers on behalf of the Gentiles to whom he was called. Moreover, if Paul's mission sought to establish mature Christian communities, then his constant prayers (Phil 1:4) for the Christian formation of his converts (e.g., Phil 1:9-11; Eph 3:14-21; Col 1:9-14; 1 Thess 3:10-13) were integral to that ministry. At the same time, Paul relied on the intercessory prayer of his churches in order to faithfully carry out his own gospel mission (2 Cor 1:11; Eph 6:19-20; Col 4:2-4; 2 Thess 3:1).

4. Paul's Mission Theology.

Paul's interpreters often have shortchanged his theology of mission, presumably because *mission* is restricted to what Paul says about proclaiming the gospel to nonbelievers (Barram 2006, 38). If, however, we anchor Paul's mission theology in the comprehensive *missio Dei*, then Paul's understanding of mission becomes a key to his entire life and thought. Indeed, Paul's theology, at its heart, is a *mission theology*.

4.1. The Divine Mission. For Paul, mission begins with God. The apostle's missional calling and that of the church only have meaning as they participate in God's loving, reconciling purposes for the world. According to Paul, God is on a mission to bring salvation to the world (Rom 1:16), to liberate all people and the whole creation from the powers of *sin and death (Rom 8:2, 21; Gorman 2015, 23-24). Such a comprehensive vision challenges some Western, individualistic readings of Paul that focus almost exclusively on God's desire to save individuals from the guilt of their sins. Paul views the *missio Dei* from a cosmic perspective. Its goal is to reconcile all things in heaven and on earth in Christ (Col 1:20; see Eph 1:9-10; 3:10) so that ultimately every facet of creation acknowledges Christ's lordship and gives glory to God (Phil 2:10-11). The fullness of God's new creation, promised by the prophets, lies in the future. God's people, along with creation itself, anticipate that reality with longing and *hope (Rom 8:18-25). Yet Paul is convinced that God's saving power is already at work, that God is actively restoring and reconciling the world. God does this primarily by creating a new humanity, made up of Jews and Gentiles, who bear witness to the liberating purposes of God by their life together in the world (Eph 2:15-16; 3:9-11). These transformed communities embody God's new creation now (2 Cor 5:17; Gal 6:15) in an incomplete sense, living as a sneak preview of the *eschatological fullness to come. For Paul, *the church* is not the goal of God's mission. The church participates in and bears witness to God's plan to transform and unite everything in heaven and earth in Christ (Eph 1:10).

4.2. The Gospel Paul Proclaims. Paul's missional identity is caught up in the gospel, for which God set him apart to proclaim and serve (Rom 1:1; 15:16; Eph 3:7; Col 1:23). Gospel language pervades Paul's letters, and the gospel lies at the heart of his thought. But what is the good news Paul heralds and teaches? This is not a simple question to answer, since Paul never lays out a full definition of it. Occasionally, Paul offers brief gospel summaries in the course of his arguments (e.g., Rom 1:3-4; 1 Cor 15:1-5; Gal 4:4-7; 1 Thess 1:9-10), but no two of them are alike. Paul's understanding of the gospel is far more comprehensive than any gospel sound bite could capture. Paul's letters reveal, however, several key dimensions of the gospel (see Flemming 2013, 163-71).

First, the gospel is not a set of propositions but tells the story of God's loving and redeeming mission in Christ. It is the gospel *from* God (Rom 1:1; 15:16; 2 Cor 11:7; 1 Thess 2:2, 8) and *about* Christ ("the good news of Christ," Rom 15:19 NRSV; see 2 Cor 9:13; Gal 1:7), particularly Jesus' death and resurrection as saving events (Rom 1:3-4; 4:24-25; 1 Cor 1:23; 15:1-5). This story comes to magnificent expression in Philippians 2:6-11, which narrates "Jesus' faithfulness to the point of death in self-giving love for others and God's subsequent vindication of him as the world's true Lord" (Johnson, 129). This story does not stand on its own but is part of a larger story of God's restoring mission promised in Scripture (Rom 1:2; 1 Cor 15:3-4). Paul can even claim that the gospel was "declared . . . beforehand" to *Abraham (Gal 3:8 NRSV); Paul's gospel fulfills God's ancient promise to bless all nations through his people Israel.

Second, the gospel is God's transforming power unleashed in the world by the Spirit. According to Paul, the gospel is "the power of God for salvation to everyone who has faith" (Rom 1:16 NRSV; see 1 Cor 1:18-25; 1 Thess 1:5). The good news proclaimed becomes the means by which God brings about change, at a personal, corporate, and cosmic level. Paul speaks of the gospel as something that pulsates with life—growing, spreading, and bearing fruit throughout the world (Col 1:5-6; 2 Thess 3:1). Further, if the good news "has been proclaimed to every creature under heaven" (Col 1:23 NRSV), the gospel carries transforming effects for the entire *cosmos.

Third, the gospel is *truth to be embraced and guarded. In Galatians, Paul defends "the truth of the gospel" (Gal 2:5, 14 NRSV) against those who would distort it and replace it with a bogus version of the good news (Gal 1:6-7; see 2 Cor 4:2-3). The gospel, then, confronts as well as announces. It collides with competing stories, taking "every thought captive to obey Christ" (2 Cor 10:5 NRSV). In the context of the Roman world, this gospel represents a public announcement that challenges the *empire's version of good news. It summons people into a new relationship with God and others that excludes all other religious and political allegiances.

Fourth, the gospel constitutes a norm for Christian conduct. Even as Paul's mission embraces Christian formation as well as evangelistic proclamation, Paul's gospel must not only be believed but also obeyed (Rom 10:16; 16:25-26; 2 Thess 1:8) and embodied (Phil 1:27). For Paul, the story of Jesus' self-giving love at the heart of the gospel must shape the lifestyle and relationships of his followers, so that, by the Spirit's enabling, they reenact that story in their public world (Phil 2:5-11). This all suggests that if Paul's gospel is comprehensive and multidimensional, then so is Paul's understanding of mission.

4.3. God's Saving Mission. Paul's mission rests on his unshakable confidence that the gospel is God's power "for salvation," that God has acted graciously in Christ "for us" (Rom 1:16; 8:31 NRSV). Paul expresses that salvation in various ways. These include God's act of **justification*, language that has sparked considerable debate among Paul's interpreters. Fundamentally, God's justifying work springs from God's *covenant love and faithfulness and seeks to put right everything that is wrong—individuals, society, the entire cosmos—through what God has done in the death and resurrection of Christ (Rom 3:21-26; see N. T. Wright, 925-1032). God's saving *righteousness (the "righteousness of God"; e.g., Rom 1:17; 3:21-22; 2 Cor 5:21) not only brings sinful people the assurance of vindication on the last day but also transforms them in the present so that they can live righteously and practice covenant love and justice toward others (Marshall 2004, 438-40; Gorman 2015, 212-96).

Drawing on exodus language, Paul also pictures God's saving mission as *redemption* from the law's curse (Gal 3:13; 4:4-6) and from the power of darkness (Col 1:3-14). Romans depicts God's purpose for humanity as a rescue from the enslaving powers of sin and death, which can only come from the outside, accomplished by Christ's dying and rising (Rom 5:12-21; 6:12-23; 7:1-25; 8:1-2; see 1 Cor 6:20; 7:23; Gaventa, 73-74).

Particularly important for Paul's theology of mission is God's work of *reconciliation* (2 Cor 5:18-21; Rom 5:10-11). Some interpreters judge this theme to offer a key to Paul's vision of God's mission in the world (Porter; N. T. Wright, 1487-95; Martin; Constantineanu). God's reconciling action establishes *peace between enemies (Rom 5:10) and restores right relationships. Ultimately God seeks to heal and reconcile "all things" through Christ's death (Col 1:20 NRSV), whether a broken creation, a sinful humanity, or alienated peoples, such as Jews and Gentiles (Eph 2:13-18; see Okure, 66-72). Second Corinthians 5:18-21 forges a strong link between God's work of reconciling "us" to himself and the "ministry of reconciliation" God gave "us" (2 Cor 5:18 NRSV). This likely refers not simply to Paul and his coworkers but to all those God has reconciled and now called to become agents of God's reconciling mission in the world (Porter, 173). In this way, the Corinthians "*become* the righteousness of God" (2 Cor 5:21 NRSV); that is, they participate in God's mission as "the embodiment of God's saving, reconciling, restorative justice in the world" (Gorman 2015, 249).

4.4. Paul's Universal Gospel. Paul was captivated by the conviction that the gospel of God's salvation is for *all*, that "there is no distinction between Jew and Greek" in their access to God's grace (Rom 10:12-13 NRSV; see Rom 1:16). This means that former barriers dividing Jews and Gentiles were demolished by the cross, creating a new humanity in which the *shalom* of Christ rules (Eph 2:13-22). Paul situates the social division between Jews and Gentiles in their enmity against God; they must be reconciled to God to experience peace with one another (Schreiner, 56-57). God's eternal purpose to embrace Gentiles as co-heirs with Israel, members of the one *body of Christ, is a "*mystery," something formerly hidden but now revealed in the mission of the Messiah (Eph 3:5-6; see Eph 3:1-13; Col 1:24–2:5). Paul radically reconfigures the prophets' end-time hope of Gentile nations streaming to Jerusalem to serve Israel's God (e.g., Is 2:2-4; 60:1-7; Mic 4:1-3). Instead, God's eschatological reign over the Gentiles is inaugurated *now* as salvation moves *from* Zion *to* the nations (Rom 10:14-18; N. T. Wright, 1250-51).

In Romans 9–11, Paul piles up arguments and draws on massive scriptural support to show that the inclusion of the Gentiles does not signal the abandonment of God's promise to Israel but rather its fulfillment (C. J. H. Wright, 528). Gentiles currently are being grafted in the one olive tree. Paul, however, envisions that "the ingathering of the Gentiles will cause such jealousy among the currently unbelieving branches that even they will come to repentance, faith, and regrafting" (C. J. H. Wright, 528; Rom 11:23-24). "And so all Israel will be saved" (Rom 11:26 NRSV), Paul concludes. Interpreters disagree over the meaning of "all Israel" and precisely how and when Paul expects that will happen (see Bosch, 162-65). Nevertheless, Paul offers little support for the notion that Jews follow a separate path to salvation from Gentiles (see Schnabel's discussion, 2004, 1309-19). Jews and Gentiles comprise one people of God, joined on the same basis of faith in the Messiah, Jesus (Rom 11:23). Consequently, Christian heralds engage in God's mission by proclaiming the gospel to "everyone," both Jews and Gentiles (Rom 10:12-15; see Rom 10:1), even "to the ends of the world" (Rom 10:18 NRSV).

At the same time, if the death of Christ the peacemaker reconciles the two groups not only *vertically* to God but *horizontally* to each other (Eph 2:1-22), then God's people must also share in Christ's peace-making mission. The church embodies and practices that mission as a renewed humanity in which divisions of religion, *ethnicity, social status, culture, or gender no longer apply (Gal 3:28; Col 3:10-11). Moreover, when Paul urges Roman Christians not to repay evil for evil, but to "live peaceably with all" (Rom 12:17-18 NRSV), he presents rejecting *violence and making peace "as mandates to the church for its life in the world of unbelievers" (Gorman 2015, 256).

5. The Church's Role in the *Missio Dei.*
For Paul, mission was not only the calling of an apostle such as himself but also the vocation of the congregations he cared for. They, too, engaged in the *missio Dei* by being, doing, and telling the good news.

*5.1. **Embodying the Gospel.*** Paul perceives mission not simply as something the church *does* but what the church *is*. He pictures the Christian community as a living **temple* (1 Cor 3:16-17; 2 Cor 6:16; Eph 2:21), filled with God's presence and making God's glory visible in the Roman world (N. T. Wright, 437; Johnson, 134-35). The church is to *be* the new creation in the world (2 Cor 5:17; Gal 6:15), the arena where God's reconciling purposes for humanity go on public display. Christians must not only embrace the gospel but embody it, through their unity, their holiness, and their cruciform love (Phil 2:1-9, 14-15). The self-giving mindset of Christ that led Jesus even to "death on a cross" must shape both the church's gathered life in community and its scattered witness in the world (Phil 2:5-11 NRSV; Flemming 2015, 87). Paul models this missional mindset for his converts in 1 Corinthians 10:31–11:1. He calls on the Corinthians to *imitate his attitude and conduct as he imitates Christ (1 Cor 11:1). Like Paul, they are not to seek their own advantage but rather the good of others, "so that they may be saved," in a holistic sense (1 Cor 10:33 NRSV). Whether in relation to Jews, pagans, or fellow Christians (1 Cor 10:32), they are to develop a "missional consciousness" in every dimension of their lives (Barram 2011, 236).

*5.2. **Practicing the Gospel.*** Near the beginning of Philippians, Paul thanks God for the church's "partnership in the gospel" (Phil 1:5 NIV). This refers especially to the Philippians' active sharing with Paul in the ministry and advance of the good news. The congregation's partnership with Paul means a participation in God's mission, which takes concrete form in their missional lifestyle and practices. Later in the same chapter, the apostle urges the Philippians, "Live out your citizenship" (*politeuesthe*)—your public, corporate life—"in a manner worthy of the gospel of Christ" (Phil 1:27). "Paul's political language (see Phil 3:20) reminds the church that although they conduct their visible, common life in the setting of a Roman colony, they must do so according to a higher loyalty and a different set of practices" (Flemming 2011, 12).

For Paul, a gospel-worthy lifestyle has both a positive and a negative side. Positively, Christians should live public lives that are attractive and winsome to outsiders (Titus 2:9-10). They are to abound in love for all (1 Thess 3:12), let their gentleness and obedience be known to all (Phil 4:5; Rom 16:19), and seek to "do good" to all, including those who seek to do harm to them (1 Thess 5:15 NRSV). Such actions visibly display the love of a God who reconciles enemies (Rom 5:10). If Christians live *holy and blameless lives within a corrupt environment, they will carry a light-bearing testimony to the surrounding culture (Phil 2:15; see Is 42:6; Dan 12:3). On the negative side, a pattern of grumbling and arguing could injure their public witness (Phil 2:14). Behavior inconsistent with the gospel has the potential to discredit the word of God (Titus 2:3-5; see Titus 2:8). When Christians practice and condone immorality that "is not found even among pagans" (1 Cor 5:1-5 NRSV) or when they take one another to court "before unbelievers" (1 Cor 6:6 NRSV), they risk sabotaging the church's testimony before a watching world.

Paul pictures Christians practicing their "partnership in the gospel" in other concrete ways. In Philippians, that includes providing Paul with financial and material support through their representative, Epaphroditus (Phil 4:10-20). Local churches also help to send him on his way (Rom 15:24; 1 Cor 16:6; 2 Cor 1:16), supplying practical resources for his missionary travels. Congregations participate in God's mission through intercessory prayer for Paul's ministry and that of his coworkers (Rom 15:30-32; Eph 6:19; Col 4:3-4; 1 Thess 5:25; 2 Thess 3:1), as well as for those outside the church (1 Tim 2:1-4). They contribute to Paul's mission through mutual encouragement (Rom 1:11-12), and they suffer along with Paul for the gospel's sake (2 Cor 1:6-7; Phil 1:30; 4:14). The church's worship also can serve as an occasion for witness to nonbelievers. Christians in Corinth must exercise self-restraint in their practice of spiritual *gifts, in part, so that when visiting outsiders hear the intelligible words of Christian prophecy, they will be cut to the heart with conviction. As a result, they "will bow down before God and worship him" (1 Cor 14:25 NRSV).

Paul does not encourage Christians to sever relationships with nonbelievers (1 Cor 5:9-10). Rather, he expects Christian communities to engage their world in transforming ways. On one occasion he lists virtues that Christians should dwell on (Phil 4:8), all of which were widely valued in the Greco-Roman world. Instead of rejecting such publicly recognized values, he affirms them as points of contact with the wider culture, as long as they are consistent with the cruciform pattern of Christ (see Phil 4:9; Flemming 2011, 15).

5.3. Narrating the Gospel. Did Paul envision churches participating in God's mission by actively proclaiming the good news like he did? Paul says less on that subject than might be expected. Nowhere does he direct his congregations to join him in bearing witness to non-Christians or pray that they might do so. This leads some scholars to conclude that preaching the gospel was the task of authorized individuals, such as missionaries and evangelists, *not* the church as a whole (Bosch, 137-38, 168-70; Bowers 1991; Dickson; Peterson). Other Pauline interpreters, however, contend that Paul did indeed expect churches to follow his lead in evangelizing through gospel proclamation, finding support in a number of Pauline texts (e.g., 1 Thess 1:7-8; Eph 6:15, 17; Phil 2:16; Plummer; Schnabel 2004, 1459-65; Ware).

Although local congregations probably were not engaged in public preaching like he was, Paul's letters suggest that they were narrating the good news to outsiders. The Thessalonians, Paul recalls, became an example to others because "the word of the Lord has sounded forth," in the surrounding provinces and beyond (1 Thess 1:7-8 NRSV). Presumably, the gospel rang out in all directions largely through the oral witness of Christians. Elsewhere, God's provision of spiritual armor to meet the attacks of evil powers includes shoes fit "with the readiness of the gospel of peace" (Eph 6:15), which probably signifies the church's active preparedness to share the good news of peace (see Is 52:7; Eph 6:17).

The church's verbal witness takes various forms. Paul urges the Colossians to speak graciously as they "answer everyone" (Col 4:6 NRSV). Here Paul sees attractive speech happening less as intentional proclamation than as a response to nonbelievers' questions or objections in the course of daily interactions. *Marriage provides another scenario for gospel witness. Paul imagines Christian husbands and wives "saving" their pagan marriage partners (1 Cor 7:16) through word and deed.

Philippians, in particular, highlights the church's verbal witness. One reason that Paul narrates his persistence to "proclaim Christ," despite personal attacks, is so that the Philippians might also make Christ known in their context (Phil 1:15-18 NRSV). What is more, Paul draws attention to the bold witness of the Roman Christians in part as an example for the Philippians to follow (Phil 1:14).

Most notably, Paul envisions Christians shining like *lights in a dark world by "holding out the word of life" (Phil 2:16). Linguistically, the verb *epechō* can mean either "hold fast" or "hold forth," with commentators split over the issue. J. P. Ware advocates the latter (256-84), citing, among other reasons, that the "word of life" refers to the gospel, which imparts life to the hearers. Even if, however, Paul exhorts the Philippians to hold firmly *to* the gospel, this still includes a missional focus. Faithfulness to the gospel implies narrating the life-giving word when the opportunity comes. M. J. Gorman questions whether it is plausible to picture the Philippians regularly worshiping Jesus as Lord, refusing to sacrifice to the gods that protect the empire, or living a countercultural lifestyle without ever explaining their unusual behavior to others or introducing their pagan compatriots to their community's Lord. Further, would they encounter such stiff opposition if they were silent about their faith? (Phil 1:28-29; Gorman 2015, 127, 290). For Paul, speaking the gospel cannot be isolated from embodying the gospel in every aspect of life (Col 4:5-6).

6. Conclusion.

Paul was a person obsessed by Christ and captured by a vision of God's saving, reconciling purposes for the world. Commissioned by Christ himself as apostle to the Gentiles, Paul's whole life and identity were caught up in advancing the gospel, proclaiming the gospel, suffering for the gospel, and living the gospel, with the goal of establishing mature, multiethnic communities of Christians. Paul's mission activity was anchored in an expansive understanding of the mission of God. Although no consensus has yet emerged about how to define *mission* in Paul, increasingly Paul's interpreters see mission as central to his entire theology. For Paul the gospel bears witness to God's sweeping purpose to bring all people and all of creation under the lordship of Jesus the Messiah. Paul wanted churches to participate in God's mission with a seamless witness of both word and life. By living in a manner worthy of the gospel (Phil 1:27), they put on display the transforming power of God, by the Spirit's enabling, before a watching world. This remains Paul's missional challenge to Christian communities in their various global contexts today.

See also Apostle; Chronology of Paul; Church; Collection for the Saints; Conversion and Call of Paul; Coworkers, Paul and His; Cruciformity; Ecological Paul; Ephesus; Eschatology; Ethics; Financial Support; Gentiles; Gospel; Hermeneutics/Interpreting Paul; Jerusalem, City of; Love; Ministry; Opponents of Paul; Paul and Judaism; Paul in Acts; Peace, Reconciliation; Salvation; Suffering; Tentmaking; Travel and Itinerary Plans; Universalism; Urban Setting of Paul's Churches; Witness.

BIBLIOGRAPHY. **R. Allen,** *Missionary Methods: St. Paul's or Ours? A Study of the Church in the Four Provinces* (London: World Dominion, 1912); **M. Barram,** *Mission and Moral Reflection in Paul,* SBL 75 (New York: Lang, 2006); idem, "Pauline Mission as Salvific Intentionality: Fostering a Missional Consciousness in 1 Corinthians 9.19-23 and 10.31–11.1," in *Paul as Missionary: Identity, Activity, Theology, and Practice*, ed. T. J. Burke and B. S. Rosner, LNTS 420 (London: T&T Clark, 2011), 234-46; **P. Bolt and M. Thompson,** eds., *The Gospel to the Nations: Perspectives on Paul's Mission* (Downers Grove, IL: InterVarsity Press, 2000); **D. J. Bosch,** *Transforming Mission: Paradigm Shifts in Theology of Mission* (Maryknoll, NY: Orbis, 1991); **P. Bowers,** "Fulfilling the Gospel: The Scope of the Pauline Mission," *JETS* 30 (1987): 185-98; idem, "Church and Mission in Paul," *JSNT* 44 (1991): 89-111; idem, "Mission," *DPL,* 608-19; **T. J. Burke and B. S. Rosner,** eds., *Paul as Missionary: Identity, Activity, Theology, and Practice,* LNTS 420 (London: T&T Clark, 2011); **D. A. Carson,** "Paul's Mission and Prayer," in *The Gospel to the Nations: Perspectives on Paul's Mission,* ed. P. Bolt and M. Thompson (Downers Grove, IL: InterVarsity Press, 2000), 175-84; **C. Constantineanu,** "Reconciliation as a Missiological Category for Social Engagement: A Pauline Perspective from Romans 12:1-21," in *Bible and Mission: A Conversation Between Biblical Studies and Missiology,* ed. R. G. Grams et al. (Schwarzenfeld: Neufeld, 2008), 132-59; **J. P. Dickson,** *Mission-Commitment in Ancient Judaism and in the Pauline Communities: The Shape, Extent and Background of Early Christian Mission,* WUNT 2/159 (Tübingen: Mohr Siebeck, 2003); **D. Flemming,** *Contextualization in the New Testament: Patterns for Theology and Mission* (Downers Grove, IL: IVP Academic, 2005); idem, "Exploring a Missional Reading of Scripture: Philippians as a Case Study," *EvQ* 83 (2011): 3-18; idem, *Recovering the Full Mission of God: A Biblical Perspective on Being, Doing and Telling* (Downers Grove, IL: IVP Academic, 2013); idem, *Why Mission?* (Nashville: Abingdon, 2015); **R. A. Fringer,** *Paul's Corporate Christophany: An Evaluation of Paul's Christophanic References in Their Epistolary Contexts* (Eugene, OR: Pickwick, 2019); **B. R. Gaventa,** "The Mission of God in Paul's Letter to the Romans," in *Paul as Missionary: Identity, Activity, Theology, and Practice,* ed. T. J. Burke and B. S. Rosner, LNTS 420 (London: T&T Clark, 2011), 65-75; **M. W. Goheen,** ed., *Reading the Bible Missionally* (Grand Rapids, MI: Eerdmans, 2016); **M. J. Gorman,** *Apostle of the Crucified Lord: A Theological Introduction to Paul and His Letters* (Grand Rapids, MI: Eerdmans, 2004); idem, *Reading Paul* (Eugene, OR: Cascade, 2008); idem, *Becoming the Gospel: Paul, Participation, and Mission* (Grand Rapids, MI: Eerdmans, 2015); **S. Hafemann,** "'Because of Weakness' (Galatians 4:13): The Role of Suffering in the Mission of Paul," in *The Gospel to the Nations,* ed. P. Bolt and M. Thompson (Downers Grove, IL: InterVarsity Press, 2000), 131-46; **G. R. Hunsberger,** "Proposals for a Missional Hermeneutic: Mapping the Conversation," *Missiology* 39 (2011): 309-21; **A. Johnson,** *Holiness and the Missio Dei* (Eugene, OR: Cascade, 2016); **S. Kim,** *The Origin of Paul's Gospel* (Tübingen: Mohr Siebeck, 1981); **J. C. Laansma, G. Osborne, and R. Van Neste,** eds., *New Testament Theology in Light of the Church's Mission: Essays in Honor of I. Howard Marshall* (Eugene, OR: Cascade, 2011); **I. H. Marshall,** *New Testament Theology* (Downers Grove, IL: IVP Academic, 2004); idem, "Paul's Mission According to Romans," in *Bible and Mission: A Conversation Between Biblical Studies and Missiology,* ed. R. G. Grams et al. (Schwarzenfeld: Neufeld, 2008), 96-130; **R. P. Martin,** *Reconciliation: A Study in Paul's Theology* (Atlanta: John Knox, 1981); **T. Okure,** "'In Him All Things Hold Together': A Missiological Reading of Colossians 1:15-20," *IRM* 91 (2002): 62-72; **B. K. Peterson,** "Being the Church in Philippi," *HBT* 30 (2008): 163-78; **R. L. Plummer,** *Paul's Understanding of the Church's Mission: Did the Apostle Paul Expect the Early Christian Communities to Evangelize?,* PBM (Milton Keynes, UK: Paternoster, 2006); **R. L. Plummer and J. M. Terry,** eds., *Paul's Missionary Methods: In His Time and Ours* (Downers Grove, IL: IVP Academic, 2012); **S. E. Porter,** "Reconciliation as the Heart of Paul's Missionary Theology," in *Paul as Missionary: Identity, Activity, Theology, and Practice,* ed. T. J. Burke and B. S. Rosner, LNTS 420 (London: T&T Clark, 2011), 169-79; **E. J. Schnabel,** *Early Christian Mission: Paul and the Early Church,* vol. 2 (Downers Grove, IL: IVP Academic, 2004); idem, *Paul the Missionary: Realities, Strategies and Methods* (Downers Grove, IL: IVP

Academic, 2008); **T. R. Schreiner,** *Paul: Apostle of God's Glory in Christ* (Downers Grove, IL: IVP Academic, 2001); **K. Stendahl,** *Paul Among Jews and Gentiles* (Philadelphia: Fortress, 1976); **J. P. Ware,** *Paul and the Mission of the Church: Philippians in Ancient Jewish Context* (Grand Rapids, MI: Baker Academic, 2011); **C. J. H. Wright,** *The Mission of God: Unlocking the Bible's Grand Narrative* (Downers Grove, IL: IVP Academic, 2006); **N. T. Wright,** *Paul and the Faithfulness of God*, 2 vols., COQG 4 (Minneapolis: Fortress, 2013); **J. Wu,** *Reading Romans with Eastern Eyes: Honor and Shame in Paul's Message and Mission* (Downers Grove, IL: IVP Academic, 2019).

D. Flemming

MISSIONARY JOURNEYS. *See* CHRONOLOGY OF PAUL; PAUL IN ACTS; TRAVEL AND ITINERARY PLANS.

MONEY. *See* COLLECTION FOR THE SAINTS; FINANCIAL SUPPORT; TENTMAKING; WEALTH AND POVERTY.

MONOTHEISM. *See* CHRISTOLOGY; GOD.

MORTALITY. *See* DEATH; RESURRECTION; SUFFERING.

MOSES. *See* COVENANT; LAW; OLD TESTAMENT IN PAUL.

MYSTERY

The English word *mystery* (or sometimes *secret*) translates the Greek word *mystērion* in the NT and Greek versions of the OT, as well as in other ancient Greek writings (Lang). *Mystērion* itself translates the Aramaic word *rāz* and occasionally the Hebrew *sôd* in biblical and other Jewish literature (Bockmuehl; Thomas). Both of these biblical words express concealment, or a "secret," as *rāz* is often rendered. In subsequent Christian literature, Paul's *mystērion* is translated from Greek into Latin by two words: *sacramentum* and the cognate *mysterium*. Later Christian liturgical language associates these two Latin words with the Eucharist—hence, *sacraments* or *mysteries* became technical terms for the eucharistic elements of bread and wine. This association is fitting insofar as the elements of bread and wine veil what they most truly are for believers who receive them—the *body and blood of Jesus. This interplay of veiling and unveiling is vital for understanding what Paul means by "mystery."

It is critical to remember: Paul's use of *mystērion* does not convey common meanings associated with the English word *mystery*. *Mystērion* is not a word for inscrutable puzzles or perplexing ideas. Contrary to the use of the word *mystery* in much contemporary theological discourse, Paul does not apply *mystērion* to things he does not understand. *Mystery* is Paul's word for information that has been revealed to him by *God. A revealed mystery may be of inexhaustible profundity, but if revealed, it is known and so no longer mysterious.

The hidden/revealed dynamic involves two factors: *interpersonal* and *temporal* (Wolter). Interpersonally, a mystery may be revealed to some but not to others. Temporally, a mystery may be previously hidden and then later revealed ("once hidden/now revealed"). These scenarios also intersect. A mystery may have been concealed absolutely in the past and then subsequently revealed to only some people. Or it may have been concealed from some people in the past and then subsequently revealed to all people. Other interpersonal and temporal arrangements are possible.

1. Ancient Context
2. "Mystery" and Revelation in Paul

1. Ancient Context.

The language of mystery entered Greek literature as a technical term for various cultic groups associated with miscellaneous ancient gods. Such cults were named "the mysteries." Central to these associations were secretive rites and sacred teachings into which initiates were inducted (Bremmer; Burkert). "The mysteries" thus refer, with respect to outsiders, to *hidden* rites and ideas and, with respect to insiders, to *revealed* rites and ideas. Throughout antiquity, *mystērion* (usually in the plural) retained this dynamic of *hidden* and *revealed* divine information. Even as Plato extended the religious vocabulary of "the mysteries" to the domain of *philosophy, his use of *mystērion* maintained the sense of initiation into newly revealed sacred information (e.g., *Meno* 76E; *Theaetetus* 155C-156A; *Euthyd.* 277D; *Gorgias* 497C; *Phaedr.* 249C-250C; *Symp.* 209E-210A).

In Greek versions of the Protestant OT, *mystērion* only appears in translations of the Aramaic portions of Daniel (Dan 2:18-19, 27-30, 47; 4:9), though it does occur in other ancient Jewish literature (Bockmuehl). The usage in Daniel coheres with the key points already identified. A mystery is something hidden or perhaps revealed. To reveal a mystery is to disclose that previously hidden information. In the case of Daniel, the competence to reveal mysteries—for him, the content and meaning of a king's distressing dream—only occurs through divide aid. As the king exclaims in response to Daniel's revelation, "Truly, your God is God of gods and Lord of kings and a revealer of mysteries, for you have been able to reveal this mystery!" (Dan 2:47 NRSV).

In the NT, *mystērion* occurs twenty-eight times. Three of the occurrences are in one synoptic pericope. Jesus describes knowledge of the mystery of God's *kingdom as granted to some but not to others, thus emphasizing the interpersonal dynamic (Mt 13:11//Mk 4:11//Lk 8:10). The word also appears four times in Revelation (Rev 1:20; 10:7; 17:5, 7), where it again involves the disclosure of coded information (akin to Daniel).

This leaves the Pauline letters with twenty-one of the twenty-eight NT occurrences. Paul is *the* Christian theologian of mystery.

2. "Mystery" and Revelation in Paul.

Modern research on "mystery" in Paul has been dominated by questions of backgrounds to his thought (Brown). Is the background for Paul's use of the word *mystērion* Hellenistic or is it purely Jewish—and so innocent of "pagan" influence? This question, and the Judaism/*Hellenism dichotomy it reifies, disfigures history (Smith). These two cultural domains cannot be so neatly disentangled. Early Christianity, like early Judaism, was a Hellenistic religion. (The NT is, in fact, written in Greek!) It is therefore essential to consider the relevance of all contextual information—Jewish and non-Jewish. Arguments for an unalloyed Jewish background to which Paul "purely" belongs are erroneous. Paul's total world—Jewish and *Gentile—is the context of his words, and his words mean and intervene within that total world.

The Pauline use of *mystērion* can be divided into two subsets. Whether this division has chronological significance or contributes to questions of the authenticity of various letters is ultimately not determinable, but the division does mostly lie along the lines of the so-called undisputed and disputed letters (Lang).

The first subset speaks of mystery in varying ways, sometimes generically, sometimes interpersonally, and sometimes in the plural. *The second subset* consistently applies the "revealed mystery" discourse temporally, and specifically in relation to the inclusion of Gentiles into the promises of God, and always in the plural. In both subsets, the dynamic of hiddenness and revelation is essential for any presentation of a Pauline theology of mystery.

2.1. The First Subset. This subset includes Romans 11:25; 1 Corinthians 2:1, 7; 4:1; 13:2; 14:2; 15:51; 2 Thessalonians 2:7; Romans 11:25. Three of these are undefined and plural. Paul writes of "administrators of the mysteries of God" (1 Cor 4:1), an understanding of "mysteries" that corresponds to prophetic powers and exceptional *knowledge (1 Cor 13:2), and "mysteries in the Spirit" that are communicated via glossolalia (1 Cor 14:2 NRSV). The precise content of these plural "mysteries" is not defined. The remainder of occurrences in this subset are singular and linked to assorted eschatological events. In 2 Thessalonians 2:7, Paul refers to "the mystery of lawlessness," which is indefinite but relates to an unfolding eschatological crisis associated with a certain *"man of lawlessness" (2 Thess 2:3-12). The usage in Romans 11:25 also relates to a unfolding eschatological scenario: the interconnected hardening of *Israel, inclusion of Gentiles, and ultimate *salvation of "all Israel." This association of a revealed mystery and Gentile inclusion anticipates the consistent usage in the second subset. Eschatological information is again labeled a mystery in 1 Corinthians 15:51. But here the *mystērion* concerns how earthly bodies will be transformed "at the last trumpet" and so obtain imperishable (or "spiritual") bodies.

Perhaps most important for the second Pauline subset (and subsequent Christian usage) are the two occurrences in 1 Corinthians 2. Paul recalls his initial proclamation of "the mystery of God" in *Corinth (1 Cor 2:1) and how he and his entourage "speak in a mystery" about the previously hidden but newly revealed *wisdom of God (1 Cor 2:7). In both cases, the announced mystery refers to the surprising power of God disclosed in Christ's *cross. But, in contrast to later usage, the emphasis throughout 1 Corinthians 2:6–3:1 is more on the interpersonal arrangement of the hidden/revealed dynamic ("revealed to some/not to others") than on the temporal ("once hidden/now revealed"). There is unquestionably a temporal element in the revealed mystery (see 1 Cor 2:9-10), but the accent in 1 Corinthians 2:6–3:1 is on the current interpersonal play of concealment and revelation. This differs from the second subset.

2.2. The Second Subset. This subset includes Ephesians 1:9; 3:3-4, 9; 5:32; 6:19; Colossians 1:26, 27; 2:2; 4:3; 1 Timothy 3:9, 16. The use of *mystērion* in the second subset (often viewed as comprising "disputed" or deutero-Pauline writings) is consistent across the set. *Mystērion* is always singular. It always underscores a temporal arrangement ("once hidden/now revealed"). Perhaps most importantly, it always applies to Gentiles as new and equal members of

God's people vis-à-vis *Christ. In Colossians, the "secret" (*mystērion*) is the long-hidden but newly revealed fact that now among the Gentiles are "the riches of the *glory of this mystery, which is Christ in you [i.e., Gentiles], the *hope of glory" (Col 1:26-27). So also in Ephesians, the "mystery of Christ," which has been made known to Paul by revelation, is that "the Gentiles are co-heirs, co-members, and co-partakers of the promise in Christ Jesus through the Gospel" (Eph 3:1-13).

The association of the "once hidden/now revealed" mystery of Gentile inclusion is again highlighted in 1 Timothy. The phrases "mystery of the *faith" (1 Tim 3:9) and "mystery of devotion" are explicitly aligned with the proclamation of Christ's story among the Gentiles (1 Tim 3:16). The same alignment of mystery with newly revealed facts related to Gentiles occurs in the concluding doxology of Romans 16:25-27. This passage is almost certainly a much later editorial amendment to prior letter forms of Romans. But it is perhaps the clearest and most developed expression of the "once hidden/now revealed" mystery schema of Gentile inclusion. It is a fitting final word and segue to subsequent Christian usage:

> Now to the God who is able to strengthen you according to my *gospel and the proclamation of Jesus Christ, according to the revelation of the mystery that has been kept silent for eternal ages but now has been disclosed, and through the prophetic writings made known, according to the command of the eternal God for the obedience of faith for all the Gentiles, to the only wise God, through Jesus Christ, to whom is the glory into the ages. Amen. (Rom 16:25-27)

See also ESCHATOLOGY; GENTILES; ISRAEL; LORD'S SUPPER.

BIBLIOGRAPHY. **M. N. A. Bockmuehl,** *Revelation and Mystery in Ancient Judaism and Pauline Christianity,* WUNT 2/2 (Tübingen: Mohr Siebeck, 1990); **G. Bornkamm,** "μυστήριον, μυέω," *TDNT* 4:802-28; **J. N. Bremmer,** *Initiation into the Mysteries of the Ancient World,* Mūchner Vorlesungen Zu Antiken Welten 1 (New York: de Gruyter, 2014); **R. E. Brown,** *The Semitic Background of the Term "Mystery" in the New Testament* (Philadelphia: Fortress, 1968); **W. Burkert,** *Ancient Mystery Cults* (Cambridge, MA: Harvard University Press: 1987); **B. L. Gladd,** *Revealing the "Mysterion": The Use of Mystery in Daniel and Second Temple Judaism with Its Bearing on First Corinthians,* BZNW 160 (New York: de Gruyter, 2008); **T. J. Lang,** *Mystery and the Making of a Christian Historical Consciousness: From Paul to the Second Century,* BZNW 219 (New York: de Gruyter, 2015); **J. Z. Smith,** *Drudgery Divine: On the Comparison of Early Christianities and the Religions of Late Antiquity* (Chicago: University Chicago Press, 1990); **S. I. Thomas,** *The "Mysteries" of Qumran: Mystery, Secrecy, and Esotericism in the Dead Sea Scrolls,* EJL 25 (Boston: Brill, 2009); **M. Wolter,** "Verborgene Weisheit und Heil für die Heiden: Zur Traditionsgeschichte und Intention des 'Revelationsschema,'" *ZTK* 84 (1987): 297-319.

T. J. Lang

MYSTERY RELIGIONS. *See* MYSTERY; RELIGIONS, GRECO-ROMAN.

MYSTICISM. *See* QUMRAN AND PAUL; VISIONS, ECSTATIC EXPERIENCE.

N

NAME

Of the 230 NT occurrences of the noun *name* (*onoma*), twenty-one of those appear in the letters of Paul. The verb "to name" (*onomazō*) is used only ten times, but six of those occur in Paul. In the biblical tradition, name and person are often interchangeable—especially when it comes to the divine name. To call on the divine name is to call on the divine person. In continuity with Scripture, Paul employs "name" as something beyond a descriptive marker to denote the personal identity, reputation, or even sovereignty of the one being named. The startling theological significance of this is clear when he names Jesus as the "*Lord," the one and only *God of *Israel.

1. Background
2. Name and Humans
3. God's Name
4. The Name of Our Lord Jesus Christ

1. Background.
"Name" (*šēm*) is used frequently in Scripture to designate a person, place, or thing and, by extension, to refer to the fame or reputation associated with a name. "The name of the Lord/YHWH" is an important recurring phrase throughout Scripture (e.g., Gen 4:26; 12:8; 26:25; 1 Sam 17:45; 1 Kings 18:32; Job 1:21; Ps 20:7; 113:1-3; Prov 18:10; Is 18:7; 59:19; Jer 3:17; Joel 2:32; Mic 4:5; Zeph 3:9, 12). When God discloses himself personally to his *servants and people, it is his "name" that he reveals (Ex 3:13-15; 6:3; 33:19; 34:5-7; Is 42:8). God chooses *Jerusalem as the city to place his name (1 Kings 11:36; Ezra 5:1; Neh 1:9; cf. Deut 12:11, 21, 26; 14:23-24; 16:2, 6, 11; 17:8, 10; 26:2) and the *temple within it is the "house" for "the name of the Lord" (1 Kings 3:2; 5:5; 8:16-20, 27, 29, 33, 35, 43-44, 48; cf. 2 Kings 23:27). Help (Ps 124:8), blessing (1 Chron 16:2, 8, 10, 29, 35; cf. Ps 118:26), promise (2 Chron 7:17, 16, 20), and *salvation are available to all who call on the name of the Lord (Joel 2:32; cf. Is 12:1-4; 43:1-7).

2. Name and Humans.
Paul infrequently employs "name" or "to name" in relationship to humans. He is assured that the names of his friends in Philippi are contained in "the register of citizens of the heavenly commonwealth" (Fee, 397); in fact, every family in heaven or on earth derives its "name," its fundamental identity, from God (Eph 3:15; see Is 40:26). Paul is concerned that unbecoming conduct not be named among believers (1 Cor 5:11; Eph 5:3). Because Christian *identity and unity is rooted in *Christ, he is appalled that divisions have formed in the *church in *Corinth over the names of Paul, Cephas, and Apollos. After all, believers are not baptized in the name of Paul (1 Cor 1:13, 15; cf. Mt 28:19; Acts 8:16; Gal 3:27).

3. God's Name.
On four occasions, three times in Romans (Rom 2:24; 9:17; 15:9) and once in 1 Timothy (1 Tim 6:1), Paul makes explicit reference to "God's name" in support of the *mission to the *Gentile world. Interestingly, all three of the occurrences in Romans are quotations from Scripture (i.e., Is 52:5; Ex 9:16; Ps 18:49//2 Sam 22:50, respectively). While the goal is proclamation and praise of God's name, Paul also recognizes that God's name (i.e., reputation) can be marred by both Jews and Gentiles.

4. The Name of Our Lord Jesus Christ.
The theological richness of Paul's use of the word *name* occurs in relationship to Christ. Reminiscent of the usage of the biblical phrase "the name of the Lord," Paul appeals on nine occasions to "the name of the Lord Jesus Christ" (2 Thess 3:6; 1 Cor 1:2, 10; 6:11; Eph 5:20), sometimes shortening it to "the name of the Lord Jesus" (2 Thess 1:12; 1 Cor 5:4; Col 3:17) or "the name of the Lord" (2 Tim 2:19). In contrast to Acts, where Luke frequently refers to "the name of *Jesus*" (e.g., Acts 2:38; 3:6; 4:10, 12, 30; 8:16; 9:27; 10:48; etc.), in Paul it is

always "the name of the *Lord*." Even when the exact phrase does not occur, it is the name of the *Lord* Jesus Christ that is the foundation of Paul's proclamation (Rom 1:5; 15:20), the source of salvation (1 Cor 1:2; 6:11), and the locus of authority (Eph 1:21). Nothing, in fact, that is said or done escapes the lordship of Jesus (Col 3:17). Whereas the appeal in Deuteronomy (see above) is made to the place (i.e., Jerusalem in general or the temple in particular) where the Lord God chose to have his name called on, now, in every place, it is the person of Jesus who is called on.

It is the identification of Jesus as "the Lord" that reveals Paul's remarkable "christological theology" (Rowe). In Scripture, to call on the name of the Lord is to acknowledge exclusive devotion to the one God of Israel, in contrast to the nations, who called on many gods. In what can only be explained as a dramatic paradigm shift in Paul's thinking, derived from his own experience of the risen Jesus, Paul decidedly uses "the name of the Lord" to refer to Jesus when he connects the quotation from Joel (Joel 2:32 [LXX 3:5]) with Jesus (Rom 10:13; see Acts 2:21).

> The name which *is* the God of Israel alone, is now the name which *is* [emphasis his] Jesus. The saving name in its original context was YHWH, now the saving name is Christ's. In Joel the Israelites would have called out "YHWH" to be saved, and now in Romans, all would call out "Jesus." "The name of the Lord" = YHWH has become, through Paul's OT citation, "the name of the Lord" = Jesus. (Rowe, 160)

This is highlighted climactically in Philippians (Phil 2:9-11; see Is 45:23), where Paul describes God giving to Jesus "the name that is above every name" so that "at the name of Jesus every knee should bow . . . and every tongue confess that Jesus Christ is Lord" (ESV). In this intimate union, there are no varying levels of divinity between Father and Son. God reveals himself as a crucified and glorified human being.

See also Christology; Lord; Old Testament in Paul.

BIBLIOGRAPHY. **R. Abba,** "Name," *IDB* 3:506-8; **T. G. Allen,** "God the Namer: A Note on Ephesians 1.21b," *NTS* 32 (July 1986): 472-73; **R. J. Bauckham,** "The Worship of Jesus in Philippians 2:9-11," in *Where Christology Began: Essays on Philippians 2*, ed. R. P. Martin and B. J. Dodd (Louisville, KY: Westminster John Knox, 1998); **H. Bietenhard,** "Name," *NIDNTT* 2:648-56; idem, "ὄνομα, κτλ.," *TDNT* 5:270-83; **D. B. Capes,** *Old Testament Yahweh Texts in Paul's Christology*, WUNT 2/47 (Tübingen: Mohr Siebeck, 1992); **C. J. David,** *The Name and Way of the Lord: Old Testament Themes, New Testament Christology*, JSNTSup 129 (Sheffield: Sheffield Academic Press, 1996); **J. D. Estes,** "'Calling on the Name of the Lord': The Meaning and Significance of *Epikaleo* in Romans 10:13," *Themelios* 41 (April 2016): 20-36; **G. D. Fee,** *Paul's Letter to the Philippians*, NICNT (Grand Rapids, MI: Eerdmans, 1995); **L. Hartman,** "Into the Name of Jesus: A Suggestion Concerning the Earliest Meaning of the Phrase," *NTS* 20 (1974): 432-40; idem, "ὄνομα," *EDNT* 2:519-22; **C. K. Rowe,** "Romans 10:13: What Is the Name of the Lord?," *HBT* 22 (2000): 135-73; **B. Witherington III and G. F. Wessels,** "Do Everything in the Name of the Lord: Ethics and Ethos in Colossians," in *Identity, Ethics, and Ethos in the New Testament*, ed. J. G. Van der Watt, *BZNW* 141 (Berlin: de Gruyter, 2006), 303-33.

D. Pinter

NARRATIVE

Paul authored *letters and not narratives. Yet the last decades of the twentieth century witnessed the pioneering of narratival analysis. Twentieth-century cognitive scientists recognized how stories are the mind's organizing principle (Turner). Narrative theology emerged as a formal discipline (Stroup). Paul's thought began to be viewed as a storied understanding of reality.

The watershed in Pauline studies was Richard Hays's *The Faith of Jesus Christ*, which promised in its subtitle *An Investigation of the Narrative Substructure of Galatians 3:1–4:11* (see Hays's intellectual autobiography: 2001, xxv-xxvi). Formative for his thinking was the work of Hans Frei, who pointed to the modern loss (since the eighteenth century) of Scripture's narratival sense. An underlying story poses constraints on Paul's reflection and argument (Hays 2001, 21). Hays appreciated Northrop Frye's distinction between mythos, the plotted sequence of events, and *dianoia*, the meaning of that sequence. Underlying stories—a narratival substructure—configure patterns of thought that are then restated in nonnarratival language (Hays 2001, 28). Subsequent scholarship identified several of these patterns. Some insisted on a *single* narratival substructure. Still others developed Hays's groundbreaking work on scriptural echoes (1989) in a narratival direction.

1. Narratival Substructures to Paul's Thought. Since structuralism remained in vogue at the time Hays began his labors, he applied the "actantial" method of A. J. Greimas, who supposed that narratives have their own syntactical laws and grammar (Hays 2001, 82-95). Although Hays found the methodology helpful, he abandoned it after publication of *The Faith of Jesus Christ*. Other scholars did not rush to the method. James Dunn complains that when he sees scholars drawing on actantial terminology and Greimasian diagrams, he inwardly groans (Dunn 2002, 220-21). Hays expresses sympathy (2001, xxvii), reaffirming simply the narratival substructure of Paul's thought (see also Wright, 69-77).

In the explosion of narratival approaches in the wake of Hays's work, Norman Petersen analyzed Philemon's "story elements"—its point of view, plot (expressed and implied), and closure—comparing its referential (reconstituted chronological) sequence with the poetic sequence of events as narrated by Paul (for rhetorical effect). The apostle even, later in the poetic sequence, extends the story backward to incorporate Philemon's personal debt, thus refocusing the story on the slave's owner. Petersen drew the literary results into a conversation with social-anthropological analysis of the letter.

N. T. Wright followed Hays's lead and distinguished "the symbolic universe" or precognitive "worldview" from its theological articulations (Wright, 38, 122-37). The worldview takes shape through the stories by which people interpret reality. The stories generate and support the overlying beliefs and convictions. Paul's thought therefore presupposes a story and symbolic universe (Wright, 405). As with Wright's tripartite scheme, Ben Witherington III distinguished Paul's symbolic universe from his narrative thought world, and that from his theological articulations as the discourse emerges from an underlying story (Witherington, 2, 4, 6). For Witherington, *all* Paul's thought results from underlying stories: (1) the story of a world gone wrong, (2) the story of *Israel in that world, (3) the story of *Christ, and (4) the story of Christians.

Many have, like Witherington, identified multiple narratives that underlie Paul's thinking. Bruce Longenecker edited *Narrative Dynamics in Paul*, in which Pauline scholars explore *five* stories: *God and *creation, Israel, Jesus, Paul, and predecessors and inheritors in Paul's communities. Dunn and Francis Watson provide summaries within the volume evaluating the project. Unfortunately, the notion of a coherent narrative behind Paul's letters does not fulfill its promise. First, the contributors are not clear *where* the narrative is to be located—whether within the text, behind the text (informing and enriching it), or in front of the text (as constructed by the reader, irrespective of Paul's intent) (Dunn 2002, 219-20). Second, Paul's letters may be forced into a preconceived narratival mold, for example, a Greimasian diagram. Are the stories behind Paul's letters necessarily linear? For instance, *Abraham may be an element in Israel's story but also in Paul's. What of apocalyptic invasions of the story (Dunn 2002, 220-21)? Third, the stability of a story should not be assumed. Paul may narrate the story of Israel to the Galatians very differently from his rivals. Did Paul subvert the story or just the rivals' *version* of the story? Perhaps the story gets reshaped in its retelling and does not function as a textual artifact (Dunn 2002, 222-24). Fourth, is there a *single* story that underlies Paul's reasoning? The story of Christ is the leading candidate, but it is not clear whether the story of Israel may be subsumed into Christ's story or whether Christ's story is overwriting Israel's. These questions assume that one can identify all the *sub*elements of that larger story (Dunn 2002, 224-26).

Francis Watson questioned whether God's vertical, invasive activity in *salvation is reducible to a horizontal narrative (232). Paul may interpret scriptural stories of creation and Israel, but his *gospel of Jesus Christ does not easily lend itself to a linear narrative (233-38). Paul appeals to individual scriptural stories but does not identify a single scriptural narrative. Watson throws down the gauntlet in his conclusion: "The only 'narrative substructure' in Paul is the scriptural narrative collection from which he draws in order to elucidate an essentially nonnarratable gospel" (239).

2. *The* Narrative Behind Paul's Letters. The skeptics did not deter Hays and Wright from striving to identify a *single* underlying narrative behind Paul's letters. In an essay in *The Forgotten God*, Hays (2002) traces the story that Paul explicitly refers to in his letters to the Galatians and Romans. The most panoramic sketch of that story is in Romans: Paul begins with creation (Rom 1:20, 25; 3:30; 4:17; 11:26) and God's plan for humanity and God's own people (Rom 8:21, 29-30) in the face of *wrath because of human *sin since *Adam (Rom 1:18-32; 5:12-21). God promised already to Abraham in Scripture a rescue operation targeting God's elect (Rom 4:13, 17; 9:6-24, 33; 10:19-21), a necessary operation since God's *law had proven ineffectual (Rom 3:2, 19; 7:12-24). God's faithfulness and *identity (Rom 3:21-26; 5:8; 8:31-35; 9:5) were ultimately revealed through the *Son, who suffered *death (Rom 3:25; 4:25; 5:8; 7:24-25; 8:32; 14:15). The resurrection of the Son of God with power bears implications for God's own (Rom 1:4; 4:17, 25; 6:4-5; 8:34; 10:9-13; 14:9). God calls *Gentiles (Rom 1:17; 3:29-30; 4:5; 9:23-24; 15:9-12) and temporarily hardens Israel (Rom 3:3-4; 11:1-28). Ultimately, the faithful God will judge the world and be glorified (Rom 5:9; 8:18, 31-39; 12:19; 14:10-12; 15:9-12). Hays's sketch of that narrative as it appears in Galatians is summarized in Das (2016, 1-2). The foundational story acts as a constraining factor and renders Paul's reasoning intelligible (Hays 1989, 21-22). Where Adam failed, the protagonist Jesus was obedient to the point of death in order to deliver humanity from sin's power (Hays 2002, 210-11). The believer is justified and *participates* in the crucified, justified Messiah, "whose destiny embodies theirs" (211-12). In short, the believer joins the story.

Building on Hays, N. T. Wright describes "a larger implicit narrative"—a "story-world" and the "symbolic universe that accompanies it"—that stands behind Paul's letters (405). Humanity's identity, situation, and ultimate destiny are embedded within stories that serve as the foundation for beliefs and convictions (79). Compressed within a single story of Jesus Christ, for Paul, is the Creator's intervention to restore a fallen humanity, both Israel and the world (407). In tracing the central story explicitly mentioned, Hays and Wright were trailblazers in the narratival logic of the corpus. Hays has continued to write about "Paul's foundational story," "Paul's gospel story," and "the dramatic events of Jesus' death and its immediate consequences" (2001, xxxv, xl; see also Dunn 1998, 17-18; Matera, 83-88).

3. Grand Thematic Narratives.

The Paul and Scripture Group of the Society of Biblical Literature (which concluded its work in 2011) began with Hays's seminal *Echoes of Scripture* methodology for recognizing and classifying the use of Scripture in Paul. Stanley Porter parsed Hays's various "echoes" but went further to identify another category, which he called "grand thematic narratives" (102-3). This is not the central narrative that Paul explicitly outlines in his letters that those such as Hays and Wright strove to identify. Rather, Porter drew attention to foundational stories or overarching traditions within the Scriptures that Paul draws on *implicitly* in his letters but that come to the surface in allusions and echoes. G. K. Beale included Porter's category in his textbook on the New Testament's use of the Scriptures: "Sometimes a NT author takes over a large OT context as a model after which to creatively pattern a segment in his own writing" (80; also 88-89).

Sylvia Keesmaat in *Paul and His Story*, for instance, detects a narratival "exodus tradition" providing the shape for Romans 8:14-17, 18-39 and Galatians 4:1-7. In Romans 8:14-17, the Spirit "leads" (*agō*) God's "sons" (*huioi*) to enjoy "sonship" (*prōtotokos*). This is the same combination of motifs in Deuteronomy 32; Isaiah 63; and Jeremiah 38 (31 MT) that derive from the exodus (e.g., Deut 32:12; Is 63:14; Jer 38:8-9—note the new "Passover"; Keesmaat 1999, 55-65). The Spirit leads "sons" out of "bondage" (*douleias*) as they "cry out" (*krazō*) to God, even as the Israelites "cry out" to God in Exodus 5:14; 13:18 (Keesmaat, 66-68, 74-75). Israel's exodus thus foreshadowed and inspired God's *adoption and deliverance of Christ's followers from captivity to sin, the new creation, the Spirit's leading through trial and *suffering, the believer's crying out to God, and the subsequent inheritance. Keesmaat's proposal was reviewed by Das (2020). For critical assessments of several other grand thematic narratives, see Das 2016.

Methodologically, Porter maintained that grand thematic narratives are anchored in concrete quotations, allusions, and even echoes (102-3). Hays's *Echoes of Scripture* suggests criteria for the detection of Paul's appropriation of Scripture, which should apply to the identification of grand thematic narratives as well. One critique of proposed grand thematic narratives questions whether proposals *unanchored* in such critically discernible ties may only be present in the eye of the beholder (Das 2016, 28-30, 218-20). For instance, the pattern of God's salvation of Israel resulting in a Gentile influx into Zion (Is 2:2-4; 25:6-10; 45:20-23; 56:6-8; Mic 4:1-2) has been detected in Galatians 3:10-14; 3:23-26; 4:3-5 even though the scriptural texts are not cited or alluded to by Paul. An unanchored proposal is likely illusory (Das 2016, 33-63). Should a grand thematic narrative be based on a series of *weaker* echoes—for instance, shared words that are not particularly unique or decisive—then an interpreter may be reading an OT narrative *into* a NT context in an intertextual version of what linguists call "illegitimate totality transfer" (Barr, 218, 221-22; also Cotterell and Turner, 122-23; Silva, 25-26, 61). Another question is whether the ancient audience, let alone the modern skeptic, may be expected to recognize these narratives. To what extent, for instance, would the Gentile Galatian audience detect Keesmaat's exodus narratival pattern in Galatians 4:1-7?

Second Temple trajectories of narratives require attention as well. Second Temple authors reflected, for instance, on the relational element in biblical covenants, as well as on the requirement to obey covenantal commands. Second Temple appropriations may play a role in how a narratival pattern functions (Das 2016, 65-92). Paul may even be *subverting* a pattern, as appears to be the case in his appropriation of Isaac's near sacrifice in Genesis 22. (Paul passes over Isaac to Christ as Abraham's seed in Gal 3:15-18; see Das 2016, 93-124.)

In his presidential address to the Society of Biblical Literature over fifty years ago, Samuel Sandmel warned against "parallelomania," the craze to detect sources or, in this case, narratives behind Paul's thought. Ultimately, the interpreter must guard against overenthusiasm for a particular narratival pattern. In exercising due methodological control, the plausibility of the proposed pattern becomes clearer. Narratives are functioning in Paul's letters and thought on several levels, but caution is in order. Hays's reflections on his former application of the Greimasian methodology are worth considering as scholars reappropriate the narratival elements of Paul's thought (2001, xxvi): The method is only an instrument to recover the story; what matters is the story.

See also Hermeneutics/Interpreting Paul; Old Testament in Paul.

BIBLIOGRAPHY. **J. Barr,** *The Semantics of Biblical Language* (Oxford: Oxford University Press, 1961); **G. K. Beale,** *Handbook on the New Testament Use of the Old Testament* (Grand Rapids, MI: Baker, 2012); **P. Cotterell and M. Turner,** *Linguistics and Biblical Interpretation* (Downers Grove, IL: InterVarsity Press, 1989); **A. A. Das,** *Paul and the Stories of Israel: Grand Thematic Narratives in Galatians* (Minneapolis: Fortress, 2016); idem, "Israel's Exodus Outside Paul's Corinthian Correspondence," in *Paul and Moses*, ed. F. Wilk, SERAPHMIE (Tübingen: Mohr Siebeck, 2020); **J. D. G. Dunn,** *The Theology of Paul the Apostle* (Grand Rapids, MI: Eerdmans, 1998); idem, "The Narrative Approach to Paul: Whose Story?," in *Narrative Dynamics in Paul: A Critical Assessment*, ed. B. W. Longenecker (Louisville, KY: Westminster John Knox, 2002), 217-30; **H. Frei,** *The Eclipse of Biblical Narrative: A Study in Eighteenth and Nineteenth Century Hermeneutics* (New Haven, CT: Yale University Press, 1974); **R. B. Hays,** *Echoes of Scripture in the Letters of Paul* (New Haven, CT: Yale University Press, 1989); idem, *The Faith of Jesus Christ: An Investigation of the Narrative Substructure of Galatians 3:1–4:11*, 2nd ed. (Grand Rapids, MI: Eerdmans, 2001); idem, "The God of Mercy Who Rescues Us from the Present Evil Age: Romans and Galatians," in *The Forgotten God: Perspectives in Biblical Theology*, ed. A. A. Das and F. J. Matera (Louisville, KY: Westminster John Knox, 2002), 123-42; **S. C. Keesmaat,** *Paul and His Story: (Re)Interpreting the Exodus Tradition*, JSNTSup 181 (Sheffield: Sheffield Academic Press, 1999); **B. W. Longenecker,** ed., *Narrative Dynamics in Paul: A Critical Assessment* (Louisville, KY: Westminster John Knox, 2002); **F. J. Matera,** *New Testament Christology* (Louisville, KY: Westminster John Knox, 1999), 83-88; **N. R. Petersen,** *Rediscovering Paul: Philemon and the Sociology of Paul's Narrative World* (Philadelphia: Fortress, 1985); **S. E. Porter,** "Further Comments on the Use of the Old Testament in the New Testament," in *the Intertextuality of the Epistles: Explorations of Theory and Practice*, ed. T. L. Brodie, D. R. MacDonald, and S. E. Porter, NTM 16 (Sheffield: Sheffield Phoenix, 2007), 98-110; **S. Sandmel,** "Parallelomania," *JBL* 81 (1962): 1-13; **M. Silva,** *Biblical Words and Their Meanings: An Introduction to Lexical Semantics*, rev. ed. (Grand Rapids, MI: Zondervan, 1994); **G. W. Stroup,** *The Promise of Narrative Theology* (London: SCM Press, 1981); **M. Turner,** *The Literary Mind: The Origins of Thought and Language* (Oxford: Oxford University Press, 1996); **F. Watson,** "Is There a Story in These Texts?," in *Narrative Dynamics in Paul: A Critical Assessment*, ed. B. W. Longenecker (Louisville, KY: Westminster John Knox, 2002), 231-39; **B. Witherington III,** *Paul's Narrative Thought World: The Tapestry of Tragedy and Triumph* (Louisville, KY: Westminster John Knox, 1994); **N. T. Wright,** *The New Testament and the People of God* (Minneapolis: Fortress, 1992).

A. A. Das

NARRATIVE TRADITION. *See* Jesus, Sayings of.

NEW COVENANT. *See* Atonement; Covenant; Israel.

NEW CREATION. *See* Creation and New Creation; Ecological Paul.

NEW ISRAEL. *See* Israel; Supersessionism.

NEW NATURE AND OLD NATURE.
See Anthropology, Pauline; Ethics; Flesh; Romans, Letter to the.

NEW PERSPECTIVE ON PAUL.
See Interpretation: New Perspective; Romans, Letter to the.

O

OBEDIENCE. *See* ABRAHAM; ADAM AND CHRIST; ETHICS; FAITH; JAMES AND PAUL; JUSTIFICATION; LAW; WORKS OF THE LAW.

OFFERING. *See* ATONEMENT; SACRIFICE, OFFERING; TEMPLE.

OLD TESTAMENT IN PAUL

Like many Jews in the first century, Paul originally saw the Christian *gospel as antithetical to Jewish *identity and convictions. He tells his readers that he was once a Pharisee and that in his zeal he persecuted the *church. Acts 6:11-14 suggests early Christians were persecuted due to what were perceived to be blasphemous views of Moses/the *law, the *temple, and *God. One might presume that Paul had settled views on the law of Moses. Although one cannot know what biblical texts and interpretations of them played prominent roles in his thinking before his encounter with *Christ, it may be that some of the biblical arguments he engages in his letters were aimed not only at views held by latter *opponents but also interpretations of texts he held when he was persecuting Christians. For example, Paul's citation of Deuteronomy 27:26; Leviticus 18:5; and Deuteronomy 21:23 in Galatians 3:10-13 may have informed his previous view that followers of Christ were under a *curse (and could not have found life) for not holding strictly to the law and for claiming that someone who was cursed by God was God's Messiah. Paul's knowledge of Scripture and of common interpretations of it would have been quite strong well before he became known as the *apostle to the *Gentiles.

Once Paul encountered Christ, it is clear that his interpretations of biblical texts became largely governed by his newfound knowledge of Jesus' messianic identity and his own related *mission, and the core teachings of early Christians, the *kērygma*.

The question of Paul's use of the OT raises the related question of what books he assumed to be inspired Scripture. In cases where Paul provides a quotation formula, one may be confident that the cited text was understood to be inspired Scripture. Books of the Hebrew Bible (and Protestant OT, but counting Samuel, Kings, and the Book of the Twelve [minor] prophets as one book each) that Paul does not cite include Joshua (but see 1 Cor 5:13), Judges, Ruth, Chronicles (are there allusions in 1 Cor 15:58; Rom 2:11; Eph 6:9; and/or Col 3:25?), Ezra, Nehemiah (is there an allusion in Rom 11:16?), Esther, Ecclesiastes (are there allusions in Rom 3:10-12; 8:20; 1 Tim 6:7; and/or 2 Cor 5:10?), and the Song of Songs/Solomon. That he does not quote from them does not necessarily mean he rejects them as Scripture, which means one also has to refrain from declaring Paul's view of other books that were later contested.

Decisions about texts to which Paul alludes are much more subjective. For example, most scholars recognize that in parts of his letter to the Romans Paul reflects the influence of the Wisdom of Solomon (e.g., Rom 1:18-23 and Wis 13:1-17), and in 1 Corinthians 6:18 he seems to allude to *Testament of Reuben* 5.5. Scholars have pointed to possible allusions or parallels to Baruch in 1 Corinthians 10:20, to Enoch in Colossians 2:3, to 1 Maccabees in 2 Timothy 4:17, to 2 Maccabees in 1 Timothy 6:15, to 3 Maccabees in 1 Timothy 6:15, to 4 Maccabees in Romans 7:7, to Sirach in 1 Corinthians 2:9; 6:12; 1 Thessalonians 4:6; Romans 2:6; 2 Corinthians 7:10; Galatians 3:8, to Wisdom in Romans 9:20-21, 31; 1 Corinthians 6:2; 11:7; Ephesians 1:17; 6:14; 1 Thessalonians 5:8.

Paul might have found such texts to be insightful and edifying without *necessarily* believing them to be Scripture. But there is no way to be certain, and the centuries-long early Christian ambiguity regarding the limits of the canon suggest the necessity to leave this as an open question. One should probably also avoid the assumption that Paul himself had a clear conviction about some of the books that would be historically contested. He may have been more comfortable with ambiguity and uncertainty than many modern people are.

1. Diverse Types of Scriptural Presence in Paul's Letters.
Paul's *letters are marked by biblical quotations, allusions, and more subtle echoes, as well as references to people, ideas, and things that are mentioned in the Scriptures and concepts (such as the Messiah) that are understood to reflect interpretations of various biblical texts and traditions. Although it can be difficult if not impossible in some cases, to decide which usages belong in which categories, it is helpful to keep in mind that each type has a somewhat different rhetorical function in a discourse. Each of these categories merits some attention, even if they are not always clearly distinguished.

1.1. Citations. Citations or quotations are typically described as marked or unmarked. Marked quotations are introduced by some sort of quotation formula or other statement that explicitly identifies the text for the readers as a quotation of Scripture. This is often, "[just] as it is written," *kathōs gegraptai*, but ad hoc citation markers are also common. Examples of the latter include "as it also says in Hosea" (Rom 9:25) and "Isaiah cries out concerning *Israel" (Rom 9:27 NRSV). At times an explicit citation may be introduced simply with "because" (*hoti*), although this is potentially ambiguous.

Unmarked quotations (a debated category) lack any linguistic quotation marker and are identified merely by the presence of sufficient verbal agreement with a biblical text to be considered a citation. Like marked quotations, unmarked quotations may be analyzed in terms of their source text, or *Vorlage* (e.g., does it reflect a LXX text or something found in Hebrew texts?) and signs of revision (has the text been modified by the author, whether intentionally or accidentally, etc.?). Unmarked quotations, however, function rhetorically like more subtle allusions in that in both cases the usage depends on readers' ability to recognize the allusion for themselves. By suggesting readers are able to do so on their own, the author reinforces the perception that he and the readers share certain background information that others could not be expected to share and thus reinforces a kind of group bond. Marked quotations and more subtle allusions fall on either side of such allusions, with the former suggesting the possibility that the text might not be recognized without a citation formula, or stressing the authority of the text and its argumentative importance. Of course, by citing a scriptural text that is presumed to be authoritative for his readers as well as himself, Paul (like anyone else doing the same) reinforces a sense of solidarity between himself and his readers as they take the same Scriptures to be authoritative.

While some aspects of Paul's interpretation of Scripture can be assessed by looking at his quotations in isolation from their contexts in his letters, some cannot. Often Paul's many scattered citations are gathered together from their widely distributed literary locations in order to be examined side-by-side either according to their canonical order of appearance or according to the particular categories of usage that the investigator is interested in examining. However, one must not overlook questions such as, Why is there a series of explicit citations *here* (e.g., in Gal 3–4 or Rom 3–4) and not *there* (e.g., Gal 1–2 or Rom 5–8)? And if one excises the citations from their contexts to analyze them by themselves, one may not pay sufficient attention to how the argument leading up to and immediately following the citation(s) reflect the language and thought of the cited passage—for example, the appearance of *ek pisteōs* before its appearance in the citation of Habakkuk 2:4 in Romans 1:17, or the occurrence of the same expression in Galatians both before (Gal 2:16; 3:7-9) and after (Gal 3:12, 22, 24; 5:5) it is cited in Galatians 3:11. Understanding the relationship between citations, allusions, and more subtle echoes, and the rhetorical reasons for the employment of one or the other, or combinations of both, is a crucial issue for understanding Paul's use of the OT.

B. J. Oropeza (19-20) suggests the following possible reasons for an author to use explicit quotations in their writings:

> (1) Quotations of biblical Scripture establish the authority of the communicated words, since God or esteemed persons of the past are thought to be the originator of the words. (2) The author is able to deflect some responsibility for what is quoted since God or esteemed persons of the past are the ones speaking. (3) Quotations of biblical Scripture are used to support the fulfillment of

prophecy. (4) Quotations validate the author as a credible and competent writer and teacher of the traditions cited. (5) Quotations provide a sense of continuity between the author and the *tradition cited. (6) Quotations strengthen the solidarity of the author and the community addressed since they share the same traditions. (7) They support and fill in the author's words, whether arguments, teachings, narratives, exhortations, speeches, analogies, prophecies, or foreshadowing. (8) They add stylistic variation and decoration to the author's words. (9) They may help structure the composition of the writing.

When Paul did cite biblical texts, he followed the norms and conventions that prevailed within Second Temple Judaism. In contrast to modern Western culture, words could be modified, substituted, or omitted (for example, by changing third-person forms to second-person forms, or omitting parts of the text that might distract from the point of the person quoting the text). A text could be quoted with much less precision than would be expected today (although today one could use ellipses and brackets to indicate modifications, resources that were not available to Paul and his contemporaries), as long as its basic sense was presumed to remain intact (see Stanley 1992).

Paul's quotations from Scripture are not found equally distributed throughout his letters. In fact, his explicit citations are found mainly in Romans and Galatians, with a few also found in 1 and 2 Corinthians. Ephesians, 1 Timothy, and 2 Timothy only have one biblical citation each, while Philippians, Philemon, Titus, 1 Thessalonians, Colossians, and 2 Thessalonians do not have any explicit scriptural citations. When Paul does quote Scripture, those quotations tend to be clumped together in sections where a variety of scriptural texts are drawn together and interpreted in light of each other.

Quotations occur in a variety of patterns. Sometimes they seem to be lone references to Scripture in their context (e.g., Rom 1:17; Gal 5:14). Sometimes a single quotation occurs in a context with one or several allusions (but no other quotations) in the surrounding context (e.g., 1 Cor 10:1-10). Often separate quotations appear in series with brief intervening comments that weave them into an argument (e.g., Gal 3:10-13; in Gal 4:21-31 Paul includes two citations [from Is 54:1 and Gen 21:10] in the midst of his condensed, allegorized paraphrase of Gen 21). Sometimes they come in chained quotations, that is, quotations connected by simple conjunctions or other minimalistic linguistic markers linking a series of citations. Sometimes they appear as extended conflated or composite citations, where quotations from multiple sources are strung together without clear linguistic indications of transitions from one citation to another, so that readers unfamiliar with the texts may think they are being presented with one extended citation from a single source. Chain-linked or clustered citations entail "disclosed" combinations of citations, while conflated or combined citations entail "undisclosed" combinations of citations (Adams and Ehorn, 224). In fact, Paul's uses of Scripture present themselves in so many different ways that one may wonder whether the more important thing to observe would be each of the different scenarios and how they differ, or simply that Paul uses whatever combination seems intuitively useful and does not think in terms of set categories from which he is choosing (even if each presentation reflects careful composition).

In a number of cases where several citations are woven together into an argument (as separate or as conflated citations), it is difficult or impossible to discern whether or not Paul has inserted into his letter preformed interpretive material, from a source book or *testimonia* collection that he has previously created or acquired; or material he has developed in the past and memorized in the course of his in-person *ministry work, or that someone else developed and that he is borrowing; or material that has been composed specifically for and in the process of writing the particular letter in which it is found. It is important to note that although Paul does cite some of the same texts in more than one letter (e.g., Gen 15:6 and Hab 2:4 in Galatians and Romans), one never finds any interpretive material in the same form in more than one letter. There are many similarities between Galatians and Romans, between 1 Thessalonians and 2 Thessalonians, between Colossians and Ephesians and between Titus and 1 Timothy, but one does not find any close duplication of interpretive arguments in multiple letters (as might be expected if Paul worked with a preformed *testimonia* collection).

In cases where multiple biblical texts (citations or allusions) are woven into an argument (whether as separate or conflated citations), there are almost always clear lexical and thematic links between the texts that may have suggested that there would be rhetorical and argumentative advantage to using them together. This, and other features, will be pointed out in brief comments about some of the various types of scriptural presentation one finds in the Pauline letters.

1.1.1. The Vorlage *(Source) of Paul's Citations.* One of the constant questions about Paul's interpretation of Scripture has to do with the sources from which he drew his citations and on the basis of which he formed his interpretations. It would not have been feasible to own or carry scrolls with all of the Scriptures with him in his traveling ministry. Did Paul own and carry scrolls of some books of Scripture? Did he keep notebooks with key scriptural passages in them and perhaps add to them when he visited a synagogue or found other access to scrolls? If so, did he always take note of what book the citation was found in? Did he hear or read and record quotations of Scripture that had already been joined together along the lines of some of the combined or conjoined citations found in his letters? Did he study Scripture mainly in Hebrew or in Greek, and how often did he quote biblical texts from memory rather than with a written source at hand?

It is not certain whether Paul always knew or remembered the precise sources of his citations, or whether he was always familiar with their original literary contexts. Certainly, in some cases he shows that he is well aware of the context. It is very important to him that *Abraham was reckoned righteous (Gen 15) before he was circumcised (Gen 17). He clearly knew the key lines of the Genesis narrative and (one presumes) the story of Israel quite well. Sometimes he explicitly identifies a text as coming from Isaiah, or Hosea, or Moses, and other times he does not. Does his vagueness in some cases reflect imprecision in his memory of the textual source or the voice attributed in the original context?

It is not possible to answer all of these questions. One can observe that the vast majority of his biblical quotations seem to follow the Greek text found in LXX manuscripts, even if they are modified in some ways. In the few cases where quotations differ from extant texts of the LXX and seem to have more in common with Hebrew texts, it remains unclear whether Paul reflects reading or memory (and self-translation) of the Hebrew texts, or whether, as usually seems more likely, the text had already been rendered by someone into Greek in a way that reflected a proto-Masoretic text.

Paul's quotations of Habakkuk 2:4 provides an interesting test case. Scholars have differed on whether Paul's citations of Habakkuk 2:4 are dependent on his familiarity with a proto-Masoretic text or the LXX. The Hebrew text reads, "the righteous, by *his* faith[fulness] will live," while the LXX texts read, "the righteous, by *my* faith[fulness] [or, possibly, 'by faith *in me*': *ek pisteōs mou*] will live." Paul's quotation of Habakkuk 2:4 lacks any pronoun (whether "his" or "my"). Some think the result has more in common with the Hebrew/MT text, as it is the righteous person's *faith/*pistis* that is stressed. For several reasons, however, Paul's use of *ek pisteōs* ("by faith"), where the Hebrew text has *beʾemûnātô*, clearly seems to suggest he is offering a modified version of the LXX text. In fact, *ek pisteōs* seems to be a telltale sign marker of the LXX of Habakkuk 2:4.

First of all, *ek* is not the most natural translation for the Hebrew preposition *bə*. In other cases where the preposition modifies the same Hebrew noun, the combination is usually translated *en pistei* (as in 4 Kgdms 12:16; 22:7; Hos 2:22; Ps 33:4). In fact, the translation *ek pisteōs* was unexpected enough (or was thought to be opaque enough) that manuscripts sometimes changed it to *pistei* or *en pistei.* Both the Greek Minor Prophets Scroll from Naḥal Ḥever (8ḤevXII gr) and Aquila rewrote *ek pisteōs* (or retranslated the Hebrew) as *en pistei,* and Symmachus renders the same expression simply as *pistei.* Even authors who cite Habakkuk 2:4 following the LXX (with *ek pisteōs*) often go on to rewrite it as *pistei* or *dia pisteōs* (as did the author of Hebrews and Paul himself; see Ciampa 2021). A search of Greek papyri, inscriptions, and literature shows that the expression *ek pisteōs* never occurred until Habakkuk 2:4 was translated into Greek, and then the expression only became common thereafter in Christian texts that are indebted to the NT and its citation of Habakkuk 2:4 in Greek. In fact, it may be that wherever Paul uses the expression *ek pisteōs* it should be taken as a snippet quotation of Habakkuk 2:4 (even more certainly whenever the expression is found together with any word of the Greek *dikai-* [righteous] word group) (see Ciampa 2021). In the inventory of citations that follows, all occurrences of *ek pisteōs* are noted but are not included in the formal counting of citations.

1.1.2. A Single Quotation in the Midst of Multiple Allusions. In 1 Corinthians 10:1-10 Paul strings together a series of allusions to Israel's exodus and wilderness experience, expressed in terms intended to suggest they were analogous to the Corinthians' experience of *baptism and the *Lord's Supper (1 Cor 10:1-5). Paul argues that Israel's experience "occurred as examples for us, so that we might not desire evil as they did" (1 Cor 10:6 NRSV). This is followed by a citation of Exodus 32:6 and a series of allusions to judgments suffered by Israel in the wilderness. As Gary Collier has pointed out, what could appear to be a random series of vices (*idolatry, sexual immorality/harlotry, testing, and grumbling) are actually thematically related by their associations with eating and drinking. Note that in the quotation from Exodus 32:6 the harlotry (1 Cor 10:8) took place when "the people 'ate the [Moabite] sacrifices and worshipped their idols'" (Num 25:1-2), and the testing took place when "the people said, 'there is no food or water'" (Num 21:4-7), and the grumbling probably refers to Numbers 11:1-4, where Israel's complaining is related to its "insatiable (and deadly) craving for meat" (Collier, 66). So Israel's experience is presented by Paul as a pattern and a warning that they must be careful to avoid repeating.

1.1.3. Separate Quotations Woven into an Argument with Brief Intervening Comments. In Galatians 3:10-14 Paul weaves together an argument out of four texts in a chiastic structure. The outside texts are both texts in Deuteronomy that talk about curses (Deut 27:26 in Gal 3:10, and Deut 21:23 in Gal 3:13), while the two citations in the middle both mention the condition(s) in which one "will live" (Hab 2:4 in Gal 3:11, and Lev 18:5 in Gal 3:12). The second of the middle citations (Lev 18:5 in Gal 3:12) also ties back to the first citation about the curse (Deut 27:26 in Gal 3:10), as they both refer to the requirement to "do them" (namely, the things written in the law). Two scriptural promises about finding "life" are set against each other, with the approach based on faith being opposed to and required rather than the approach based on doing everything stipulated in the law. Paul's references to the two texts about curses argue that Christ's suffering of a curse through his crucifixion provide those who have faith (in Christ) redemption from the curse for failing to keep all of the law.

Table 1. Old Testament Citations in Paul's Letters

Adapted from Silva. *Note:* All OT references are keyed to the chapter/verse numbers of the English Bible. In the Psalms, the Hebrew and the English are frequently off by one or two verses; beginning with Psalm 10, the Hebrew and the LXX are off by one chapter, so that, for example, Psalm 24 in the Hebrew and English is Psalm 25 in the LXX. Discrepancies of the sort outside the Psalms are noted in parentheses.

1. Rom 1:17	Hab 2:4	Paul = LXX ≠ MT
2. Rom 2:6	Ps 62:12	Paul = LXX = MT
3. Rom 2:24	Is 52:5	Paul = LXX ≠ MT
4. Rom 3:4	Ps 51:4	Paul = LXX = MT
5. Rom 3:10-12	Ps 14:1-3 (cf. Ps 53:1-3)	Paul ≠ LXX ≠ MT
6. Rom 3:13a	Ps 5:9	Paul = LXX = MT
7. Rom 3:13b	Ps 140:3	Paul = LXX = MT
8. Rom 3:14	Ps 10:7 (LXX 9:28)	Paul = LXX ≠ MT
9. Rom 3:15-17	Is 59:7-8	Paul ≠ LXX ≠ MT
10. Rom 3:18	Ps 36:1	Paul = LXX = MT
11. Rom 3:20	Ps 143:2	Debated
· Rom 3:26	Hab 2:4 [*ek pisteōs*]	Paul = LXX ≠ MT
· Rom 3:30	Hab 2:4 [*ek pisteōs*]	Paul = LXX ≠ MT
12. Rom 4:3 (9, 22)	Gen 15:6	Paul = LXX ≠ MT
13. Rom 4:7-8	Ps 32:1-2	Paul = LXX ≠ MT
· Rom 4:16 (x2)	Hab 2:4 [*ek pisteōs*]	Paul = LXX ≠ MT
14. Rom 4:17	Gen 17:5	Paul = LXX = MT
15. Rom 4:18	Gen 15:5	Paul = LXX = MT
· Rom 5:1	Hab 2:4 [*ek pisteōs*]	Paul = LXX ≠ MT

16. Rom 7:7	Ex 20:17 (= Deut 5:21)	Paul = LXX = MT
17. Rom 8:36	Ps 44:22	Paul = LXX = MT
18. Rom 9:7	Gen 21:12	Paul = LXX = MT
19. Rom 9:9	Gen 18:10, 14	Paul ≠ LXX ≠ MT
20. Rom 9:12	Gen 25:23	Paul = LXX = MT
21. Rom 9:13	Mal 1:2-3	Paul = LXX = MT
22. Rom 9:15	Ex 33:19	Paul = LXX = MT
23. Rom 9:17	Ex 9:16	Paul ≠ LXX ≠ MT
24. Rom 9:20	Is 29:16 (45:9)	Debated
25. Rom 9:25	Hos 2:23 (25)	Paul ≠ LXX ≠ MT
26. Rom 9:26	Hos 1:10 (2:1)	Paul = LXX = MT
27. Rom 9:27-28	Is 10:22-23 (+ Is 29:10)	Paul ≠ LXX ≠ MT
28. Rom 9:29	Is 1:9	Paul = LXX ≠ MT
· Rom 9:30	Hab 2:4 [*ek pisteōs*]	Paul = LXX ≠ MT
· Rom 9:32	Hab 2:4 [*ek pisteōs*]	Paul = LXX ≠ MT
29. Rom 9:33	Is 8:14 + 28:16	Paul ≠ LXX ≠ MT
30. Rom 10:5	Lev 18:5	Paul = LXX = MT
· Rom 10:6	Hab 2:4 [*ek pisteōs*]	Paul = LXX ≠ MT
31. Rom 10:6-8	Deut 9:4 + 30:12-14 (cf. Ps 107:26)	Paul ≠ LXX ≠ MT
32. Rom 10:11	Is 28:16	Paul ≠ LXX ≠ MT
33. Rom 10:13	Joel 2:32 (3:5)	Paul = LXX = MT
34. Rom 10:15	Is 52:7	Paul ≠ LXX ≠ MT
35. Rom 10:16	Is 53:1	Paul = LXX ≠ MT
36. Rom 10:18	Ps 19:4	Paul = LXX ≠ MT
37. Rom 10:19	Deut 32:21	Paul = LXX = MT
38. Rom 10:20-21	Is 65:1-2	Paul = LXX ≠ MT
39. Rom 11:1-2	Ps 94:14	Debated
40. Rom 11:3	1 Kings 19:10 (cf. v. 14)	Paul ≠ LXX ≠ MT
41. Rom 11:4	1 Kings 19:18	Paul = MT ≠ LXX
42. Rom 11:8	Deut 9:4 (+ Is 29:10)	Paul ≠ LXX ≠ MT
43. Rom 11:9-10	Ps 69:22-23	Paul ≠ LXX ≠ MT
44. Rom 11:26-27a	Is 59:20-21	Paul ≠ LXX ≠ MT
45. Rom 11:27b	Is 27:9	Paul ≠ LXX ≠ MT
46. Rom 11:34	Is 40:13	Paul = LXX ≠ MT
47. Rom 11:35	Job 41:11 (?)	Paul ≠ MT ≠ LXX
48. Rom 12:16-17	Prov 3:7	Debated
49. Rom 12:19	Deut 32:35	Paul = MT ≠ LXX

50. Rom 12:20	Prov 25:21-22	Paul = LXX ≠ MT
51. Rom 13:9a	Deut 5:17-21 (cf. Ex 20:13-17)	Paul = LXX = MT
52. Rom 13:9b	Lev 19:18	Paul = LXX = MT
53. Rom 14:11	Is 45:23 (+ 49:18?)	Paul = LXX ≠ MT
· Rom 14:23 (x2)	Hab 2:4 [*ek pisteōs*]	Paul = LXX ≠ MT
54. Rom 15:3	Ps 69:9	Paul = LXX = MT
55. Rom 15:9	Ps 18:49 (cf. 2 Sam 22:50)	Paul = LXX = MT
56. Rom 15:10	Deut 32:43	Paul = LXX ≠ MT
57. Rom 15:11	Ps 117:1	Paul = LXX = MT
58. Rom 15:12	Is 11:10	Paul = LXX ≠ MT
59. Rom 15:21	Is 52:15	Paul = LXX = MT
60. 1 Cor 1:19	Is 29:14	Paul ≠ LXX ≠ MT
61. 1 Cor 1:31	Jer 9:24 (23)	Paul ≠ LXX ≠ MT
62. 1 Cor 2:9	(Is 64:4 + 65:16?)	Debated
63. 1 Cor 2:16	Is 40:13	Paul ≠ LXX ≠ MT
64. 1 Cor 3:19	Job 5:13	Paul = MT ≠ LXX
65. 1 Cor 3:20	Ps 94:11	Paul = LXX = MT
66. 1 Cor 5:13	Deut 17:7 et al.	Paul = LXX = MT
67. 1 Cor 6:16	Gen 2:24	Paul = LXX ≠ MT
68. 1 Cor 9:9	Deut 25:4	Paul ≠ LXX ≠ MT
69. 1 Cor 10:7	Ex 32:6	Paul = LXX = MT
70. 1 Cor 10:26	Ps 24:1	Paul = LXX = MT
71. 1 Cor 14:21	Is 28:11-12	Paul ≠ LXX ≠ MT
72. 1 Cor 15:25	Ps 110:1	Debated
73. 1 Cor 15:27	Ps 8:6	Paul = LXX = MT
74. 1 Cor 15:32	Is 22:13	Paul = LXX = MT
75. 1 Cor 15:45	Gen 2:7	Paul = LXX = MT
76. 1 Cor 15:54	Is 25:8	Paul ≠ LXX ≠ MT
77. 1 Cor 15:55	Hos 13:14	Paul ≠ LXX ≠ MT
78. 2 Cor 3:16	Ex 34:34	Paul ≠ LXX ≠ MT
79. 2 Cor 4:13	Ps 116:10 (LXX 115:1)	Paul = LXX = MT
80. 2 Cor 6:2	Is 49:8	Paul = LXX = MT
81. 2 Cor 6:16	Lev 26:12 (cf. Ezek 20:37)	Paul = LXX = MT
82. 2 Cor 6:17	Is 52:11 + Ezek 20:34	Paul = LXX = MT
83. 2 Cor 6:18	2 Sam 7:14 (+ v. 8; cf. 1 Chron 17:13)	Paul ≠ LXX ≠ MT
84. 2 Cor 8:15	Ex 16:18	Paul = LXX = MT
85. 2 Cor 8:21	Prov 3:4	Debated

86. 2 Cor 9:7	Prov 22:8 (LXX only)	Paul ≠ LXX ≠ MT
87. 2 Cor 9:9	Ps 112:9	Paul = LXX = MT
88. 2 Cor 9:10	Is 55:10 + Hos 10:12	Debated
89. 2 Cor 10:17	Jer 9:24	Paul ≠ LXX ≠ MT
90. 2 Cor 13:1	Deut 19:15	Paul = LXX ≠ MT
· Gal 2:16	Hab 2:4 [*ek pisteōs*]	Paul = LXX ≠ MT
91. Gal 2:16	Ps 143:2	Debated
92. Gal 3:6	Gen 15:6	Paul = LXX ≠ MT
· Gal 3:7	Hab 2:4 [*ek pisteōs*]	Paul = LXX ≠ MT
· Gal 3:8	Hab 2:4 [*ek pisteōs*]	Paul = LXX ≠ MT
93. Gal 3:8	Gen 12:3 + 18:18	Paul = LXX = MT
· Gal 3:9	Hab 2:4 [*ek pisteōs*]	Paul = LXX ≠ MT
94. Gal 3:10	Deut 27:26	Paul ≠ LXX ≠ MT
95. Gal 3:11	Hab 2:4	Paul = LXX ≠ MT
· Gal 3:12	Hab 2:4 [*ek pisteōs*]	Paul = LXX ≠ MT
96. Gal 3:12	Lev 18:5	Paul = LXX = MT
97. Gal 3:13	Deut 21:23	Paul ≠ LXX ≠ MT
98. Gal 3:16	Gen 13:15 (cf. Gen 12:7; 17:7; 22:18)	Paul = LXX = MT
· Gal 3:22	Hab 2:4 [*ek pisteōs*]	Paul = LXX ≠ MT
· Gal 3:24	Hab 2:4 [*ek pisteōs*]	Paul = LXX ≠ MT
99. Gal 4:27	Is 54:1	Paul = LXX ≠ MT
100. Gal 4:30	Gen 21:10	Paul = LXX = MT
· Gal 5:5	Hab 2:4 [*ek pisteōs*]	Paul = LXX ≠ MT
101. Gal 5:14	Lev 19:18	Paul = LXX = MT
102. Eph 4:8	Ps 68:18	Paul ≠ LXX ≠ MT
103. Eph 5:31	Gen 2:24	Paul ≠ LXX ≠ MT
104. Eph 6:2-3	Ex 20:12 (cf. Deut 5:16)	Paul ≠ LXX ≠ MT
105. 1 Tim 5:18a	Deut 25:4	Paul = LXX = MT
106. 2 Tim 2:19a	Num 16:5	Paul = MT ≠ LXX
107. 2 Tim 2:19b	Is 26:13? (+ Sir 35:3?)	Debated

One wonders whether Paul had understood some or all of these texts rather differently before he came to faith in Christ. Perhaps previously he thought of the followers of Christ as cursed for their perceived lack of commitment to the law of Moses (Deut 27:26). This would have left them disqualified to receive life through the law (Lev 18:5) or on the basis of faith reflected in loyalty to the law (Hab 2:4). Certainly that Christ was hung on the *cross would have confirmed to Paul/Saul and his colleagues that he could not have been the Messiah, as he was clearly cursed by God. But for Paul the tables have been turned. Those he previously condemned are now understood to be redeemed through faith in Christ, and those who oppose that faith are understood to be the ones remaining in need of redemption.

In Galatians 4:21-31 Paul includes two citations (from Is 54:1 and Gen 21:10) in the midst of his condensed, allegorized paraphrase of Genesis 21.

1.1.4. Composite Citations. While Paul often brings different texts into conversation with each other in his arguments, he usually presents them in a way where the individual citations are distinguishable. But, as was also common citation practice in his time, Paul sometimes presents composite or conflated citations, where multiple texts are brought together in such a way that only a reader/hearer who was familiar with one or more of the conflated texts would necessarily recognize that he had brought together multiple texts rather than citing one more complex text. By one estimate (Adams and Ehorn, 209) about 19.3 percent of Paul's citations are found in composite citations (including combined, conflated, and condensed citations in this larger category). Examples of various types will aid in the recognition of similarities and differences between the various interpretations and their presentations.

1.1.4.1. Chain-Link or Clustered Citations (Disclosed Combinations). In Romans 15:8-12 Paul introduces a citation of Psalm 17:50 LXX (18:50 MT; 18:49 ET, which finds a close parallel in 2 Sam 22:50) with the formula "as it is written" (*kathōs gegraptai*), after which he introduces a citation from Deuteronomy 32:43 LXX with the words "and again he/it says" (*kai palin legei*). That is immediately followed by a citation from Psalm 117:1 (116:1 LXX), which is simply introduced by "and again" (*kai palin*). The final citation in the series is the only one to be identified with a particular book of Scripture. It is a citation of Isaiah 11:10 LXX, introduced with the words "and again, Isaiah says" (*kai palin Ēsaias legei*). There are no intervening comments or arguments between the citations. Readers may or may not know where the first three citations came from or whether they are all from the same source or different sources (or whether they are also cited from Isaiah, like the final one of the list). The whole catena of citations is introduced by Paul's statement that Christ had come "so that the Gentiles might glorify God for his *mercy" (Rom 15:9). Each of the cited texts was clearly selected and added to the others because it depicts the Gentiles (*ta ethnē*) glorifying God in one way or another (confessing and singing along with the speaker [Christ?] in Rom 15:9, rejoicing with God's people in Rom 15:10, praising the *Lord in Rom 15:11, and hoping in God's appointed ruler in Rom 15:12). As a group these texts paint a picture of God's intention for Gentiles to glorify and *worship God together with Jews.

1.1.4.2. Conflated or Combined Citations (Undisclosed Combinations). In Romans 3:9-20 Paul introduces an extended conflated (or combined) citation that includes parts of Psalm 14:1-3 (= 53:1-3); Psalm 5:10 LXX; Psalm 140:3 LXX; Psalm 10:7 LXX; Isaiah 59:7-8; and Psalm 36:1. The combined citation is introduced with the formula "just as it is written" (*kathōs gegraptai hoti*), and there are no linguistic indications of when one citation ends and another is beginning. The citation from Psalm 14:1-3 (found in Rom 3:10-12) introduces the citation as a whole as complaint about the complete absence of righteous people. It repeats "no one" (*ouk estin*) four times (or five, depending on a textual variant), declaring that people who are righteous, understanding, or seeking God are not to be found (just before the final "no one" Paul writes, "everyone has turned aside"). The citation from Psalm 5:10 LXX says "their throat is an opened grave; with their tongues they would practice deceit" (NETS). The reader or hearer who does not recognize the text will assume the pronouns ("their"/"they") refer to the same people who turned aside in the previous line. Each of the following cited texts continues to use similar pronouns, and together they paint a picture of a group of people who share all of the listed characteristics.

All the citation fragments share several attributes. They are complaints about wicked people (presumably wicked Israelites) who act in harmful ways toward others. Each identifies a different body part that participates in the evildoing, and each refers to that part as "theirs" (their throats, their tongues, their lips, their mouths, their feet, their eyes) in a way that makes it easy to stitch them together into one combined description of wicked people. These people described have not one but all of these body parts engaged in wickedness. Paul's commentary is provided before and after the combined citation, not in its midst. In Romans 3:9 he affirms that both Jews and Greeks are under sin's power. In Romans 3:19-20 he argues that inasmuch as these are indictments found in the law, they address those who are under the law (that is, Israelites or Jews) and so establish that not even Jews, with their possession of the law, are free from condemnation, and so Jews as well as Gentiles are in need of Christ's redemption.

The method behind the selection of texts and the purpose of joining them together to form the powerful indictment that Paul presents seems clear. The actual concerns the complaints raise in their original context (that the world is full of wicked people doing wicked things and God needs to intervene to bring about a different reality) do not seem to be addressed in this particular context but are addressed by the time Paul finishes Romans 8 (and Rom 15) with the transformational redemption of individuals, communities, and of all of *creation, and a world of redeemed Jews and Gentiles glorifying God together (Ciampa 2019).

As a second example of a conflated or combined citation (marked by undisclosed combinations), in 2 Corinthians 6:15-18, Paul introduces a combined citation of Leviticus 26:11-12//Ezekiel 37:27; Isaiah 52:11; Ezekiel 20:34; 2 Kingdoms 7:14; 2 Kingdoms 7:8. Within the passage there are three citation formulae: "just as God said" (*kathōs eipen ho theos hoti*) at the start, in 2 Corinthians 6:16; "says the Lord" (*legei kyrios*) in the middle of 2 Corinthians 6:17; and "says the Lord Almighty" (*legei kyrios pantokratōr*) at the very end of 2 Corinthians 6:18. The passage is a carefully designed rhetorical piece and not something quickly put together. All of the texts are presented as direct address from God to his people.

The citation is filled with a series of conjunctions, some of which appear between material from different sources. If readers/hearers were familiar with the source texts, they might have recognized some of the conjunctions as markers of changed source texts. However, anyone who did not already know the texts well would not have been able to discern from Paul's presentation whether this was the citation of one extended text or, if it consisted of multiple texts, where the seams were between them. The cited texts have been altered in a variety of ways (see Ciampa 2018 for details).

The conflated citation reflects a chiastic structure (Webb). There is a promise of God's presence and of relationship with God (with the *covenant formula) in the opening and closing citations. At the beginning one finds, "I will live in them and walk among them" (God's presence) and "I will be their God, and they shall be my people" (relationship, covenant formula) in the citations of Leviticus 26:11-12// Ezekiel 37:27. At the end one finds, "then I will welcome you" (God's presence), in the citation of Ezekiel 20:34, and "I will be your father, and you shall be my sons and daughters" (relationship, covenant formula) in the citation of 2 Kingdoms 7:14. In the middle of the conflated citation one finds two imperatives of separation: "Therefore come out from them, and be separate from them," followed by "and touch nothing unclean" (both from Is 52:11). The conflated citation begins and ends with citation formulae: "as God said" at the beginning, and "says the Lord Almighty" from 2 Kingdoms 7:8 at the end.

The combination provides a focused redeployment of scriptural new covenant and second exodus/return traditions with the requirement to separate from wicked people. The condition for the fulfillment of God's promises to restore Israel to its land is now being redeployed to urge the Corinthians, as participants in God's new covenant, to separate themselves from those who are misleading them and to be reconciled.

After surveying the wide range of ways in which Paul cites Scripture, including the various patterns described above, it may seem the most pertinent observation is that no two cases are alike. One might prefer to point out that no two cases are quite alike. Each one is about as unique as a human fingerprint.

1.1.4.3. Condensed Citations. Rather than drawing together two or more different texts into one citation, a condensed citation works by shortening or summarizing a single text. It can function as "a sort of summarizing quotation format" (Reasoner, 150). Romans 13:9 is a condensed composite quotation of phrases from Deuteronomy 5:17-21 LXX or Exodus 20:13-17 LXX (probably the former, given the order of the LXX text), created by skipping from the prohibition against stealing to that against coveting (thus omitting the prohibition of false *witness).

1.2. Allusions. The rhetorical function of allusions and unmarked quotations is different from that of more subtle echoes and from that of marked quotations (for one approach to distinguishing different kinds of allusions, see S. Smith, 150). More subtle echoes may only be recognized by those most familiar with particular texts, and in some cases the author himself may not even have been conscious of the fact that his wording was indebted to a particular scriptural subtext. Thus, even if the author's thought was based on or informed by a particular scriptural intertext, these instances do not need readers to recognize that such was the case for the statements to have their intended argumentative and rhetorical effect. While the rhetorical difference between intended allusions and other usages (including marked citations and more subtle echoes) is significant, one's ability to distinguish between intentional allusions and more subtle echoes is limited, given the inability to know Paul's own perception of where the line dividing between them would be for the readers of his various letters.

When Paul refers to the "gospel concerning [God's] Son, who was descended from David according to the flesh and was declared to be *Son of God" (Rom 1:3-4 NRSV), it seems clear that he has the promise found in 2 Samuel 7:12-16 in mind. In Romans 5:12-21 Paul clearly alludes to Genesis 3 and

Adam's trespass that brought *sin into the world. The way Paul weaves the story of Adam's sin together with references to a reign or dominion of sin (and *righteousness) in Romans 5–6 may suggest that he means to allude not only to Adam's sin in Genesis 3 but also to the reign or dominion spoken of in Genesis 1:26-28 (see Ciampa 2013).

In 1 Corinthians 10:1-10 one finds one marked citation (Ex 32:6 in 1 Cor 10:7) amid a series of allusions. The statement that the fathers were "under the cloud" (1 Cor 10:1) alludes to Exodus 14:24, when God "looked down" from the pillar of fire and cloud on the Egyptians trailing the Israelites (see also Ex 13:21-22; Num 9:15-23; 14:14; Deut 1:33; Ps 78:14). In mentioning that the Israelites passed through the midst of the sea (1 Cor 10:1), Paul alludes to Exodus 14:22, 29 (or the event described in those verses). Paul's reference to "spiritual food" alludes to the divine provision of quail and manna in Exodus 16 and Numbers 11, and celebrated in Deuteronomy 8:3, 16; Nehemiah 9:20; Psalm 78:24; 105:40. The water from the rock (1 Cor 10:4) is mentioned in Exodus 17:6 and Numbers 20:8-11, and then celebrated in a series of texts, including Deuteronomy 8:15; Nehemiah 9:15; Psalm 78:20; 105:41; 114:8; Isaiah 48:21.

In 1 Corinthians 10:8 Paul alludes to the incident in Numbers 25:1-9, where the first verse refers to Israel's participation in gross sexual immorality (LXX: *ekporneuō*) with Moabite women, and the last verse refers to the consequential death of twenty-four thousand.

Paul highlights the Israelites' involvement in sexual immorality associated with an idolatrous meal. Numbers 25:2 indicates that the incident began when Israelites, having been invited by Moabites to the sacrifices to their gods, ate the *sacrifices and then bowed down to those gods/idols. Thus idolatry and sexual immorality are tied together in both Numbers 25:1-2 and 1 Corinthians 10:8 (see further in Ciampa and Rosner 2007, 726). In 1 Corinthians 10:9, Paul's reference to destruction by serpents alludes to Numbers 21:5-6, where the Israelites spoke against God, complaining about a lack of food and water. Numbers 21:5-6 probably is being read in the light of Psalm 78:18, where the incident is related to craving food—a theme found throughout this passage (see Hays 1997, 164; Collier). When God's people test his patience by insisting on things that they crave rather than what he provides, such insolence can expect to be met with judgment.

There is no agreement on what passage(s) Paul is alluding to in 1 Corinthians 10:10. It could be Numbers 11; 14; or Psalm 106. Numbers 11 begins, "And the people were grumbling," while Numbers 11:33-34 describes the plague of the Lord, which "takes place in the context of rampant *epithumia* [craving] . . . described as an insatiable (and deadly) craving for meat" (Collier, 66). Psalm 106 shares several lexical and conceptual links with this passage, including "craving," "testing God," "grumbling," spiritual "adultery," and "destruction." Thiselton affirms that the reference to grumbling serves as a general allusion to the various pentateuchal texts that cite Israel's guilt in this area (Thiselton 2000, 742-43).

In 2 Corinthians 3:7-14 Paul alludes to the story of Moses putting a veil over his face in Exodus 34:33-35. In Philippians 2:10-11 Paul alludes to Isaiah 45:23. In describing his own apostolic *calling in Galatians 1:15-16, Paul alludes to Jeremiah 1:5 and/or Isaiah 49:1-6. In Romans 5:12, in stating that "sin came into the world through one man, and *death came through sin," Paul alludes to Genesis 3. Paul's statement that "death exercised dominion from *Adam to Moses" (Rom 5:14) may entail an allusion to both Genesis 1 and Genesis 3, with the dominion promised to humanity in Genesis 1:26, 28 being turned into a dominion of death due to the entrance of sin in Genesis 3 (see Ciampa 2013).

1.3. Echoes. The term *echoes* has been used in more than one way by various scholars, sometimes being used to refer to citations as well as clear or subtle allusions or minimal traces of a biblical intertext. A number of scholars, however, use the term exclusively for subtler traces of an intertext, ones that the author may or may not have been conscious of and that typical readers or hearers would not be required or expected to recognize. Because they tend to be more ambiguous and debatable, scholars have tried to develop criteria to justify their identification. Richard Hays opened up the area of focused study on echoes of Scripture in the NT and proposed seven criteria for identifying such echoes:

1. *Availability*: "Was the proposed source of the echo available to the author and/or original readers?"
2. *Volume*: "The volume of an echo is determined primarily by the degree of explicit repetition of words or syntactical patterns, but other factors may also be relevant: how distinctive or prominent is the precursor text within Scripture, and how much rhetorical stress does the echo receive in Paul's discourse?"
3. *Recurrence*: "How often does Paul elsewhere cite or allude to the same scriptural passage?"

4. *Thematic coherence*: "How well does the alleged echo fit into the line of argument Paul is developing?"
5. *Historical plausibility*: "Could Paul have intended the alleged meaning effect? Could his readers have understood it?"
6. *History of interpretation*: "Have other readers, both critical and pre-critical, heard the same echoes?"
7. *Satisfaction*: "[Does] the proposed reading make sense? Does it illuminate the surrounding discourse? Does it produce for the reader a satisfying account of the effect of the intertextual relation?" (Hays 1989, 29-32)

These criteria have been used by a number of scholars, while others have offered critiques or modifications, finding value in three or five of them or finding the whole project problematic (see Allen). Most concede that the identification of echoes entails more of a subjective assessment than one based on objective criteria, even if it is helpful to consider some or all of those proposed by Hays. Does Paul's use in Philippians 1:19 of the words "this will turn out for my deliverance," which are found in Job 13:16, reflect a deliberate echo? Does one find an echo of Habakkuk 2:4 in the reference to "living by faith" in Galatians 2:20? When Paul speaks of the Corinthians being among "all those who in every place call on the *name of our Lord Jesus Christ," is there an echo of Malachi 1:11, with its expectation that incense would be offered to the Lord "in every place"? Does the *anathema* that Paul says should be applied to those seeking to seduce the Galatians to *apostasy reflect an echo of the anathema found in Deuteronomy 13:16 LXX (such people are to be "*anathematized* with the *anathema*")? When Paul says that God "did not spare his only son," should one detect an echo of Abraham's offering of his only son in Genesis 22? These are just a few of the innumerable echoes that have been proposed in Paul's letters.

1.4. Scriptural Language and Ideas. Even when Paul does not echo, allude to, or quote specific biblical texts, he may often be understood to be employing biblical language and ideas. Even Paul's "diction is scripture-shaped" (Johnson, 194; see his survey of examples from 1 Thessalonians, 194-95). This is consistent with the literary concept of intertextuality, which affirms that *all* discourse is intertextual inasmuch as it always reflects engagement with previous discourse(s) in any number of ways. No text is written in a vacuum. Paul's interpretations of Scripture take place in a context of a long history of prior biblical interpretation, and it is not always possible to distinguish when Paul's thought is directly informed by biblical texts themselves and when it is informed indirectly through the influence of early Jewish scriptural interpretations as reflected in Second Temple literature (for discussion of possible criteria and further examples, see Ciampa 2008; cf. Rosner).

Some of those concepts that Paul probably would have conceived of as biblical can be identified by the fact that in one place or another in Paul's writings he quotes or alludes to one or more biblical texts when expounding on the subject. His quotations are often focused on topics such as the goodness of creation, the Ten Commandments, the law's promise of life, the sinfulness of human beings (or of Jews and Gentiles in particular), God's promises to Abraham and David, the *salvation of the Gentiles, *justification by faith, Israel's history and problems with idolatry, or the reign of Christ. Where Paul addresses any of these topics elsewhere, one may still assume that he understands himself to be discussing biblical concepts even if he does not quote or allude to any biblical texts while doing so.

Some ideas seem to have distinctive roots in the Scriptures of Israel and are introduced as "known" concepts in Jewish settings. So when, in Romans 9:4-5, Paul lists things that belong to the Israelites, including, "*the* *adoption, *the* *glory, *the* covenants, *the* giving of the law, *the* worship, and *the* promises, . . . *the* patriarchs . . . , and from them . . . *the* Messiah," its seems clear that he expects his readers or hearers to know which adoption, glory, covenants, and so on he has in mind, based on their presumed presence in biblical texts and Jewish traditions about them (Ciampa 2008, 49). Of course, there were almost always postbiblical developments in how these were conceived, and Paul's readers probably would not have always known *precisely* what texts (or constellation of texts) he had in mind in referencing these ideas.

It seems clear that many aspects of the distinctly Jewish (and biblical) understanding of God are reflected in Paul's thought. Similarly, offhand references to characters or promises found in the Scriptures, or to God's prophets (in general or specific prophets), or to God's plans for Israel, or to the significance of Abrahamic descent or sonship, or references to the "day of the Lord" or to eschatological judgment, among others, may often be indicators that Paul is referring to what he perceives to be a biblical idea or concept (see Ciampa, 2008, 55, for further examples).

In one sense, Scripture is being "used" whenever it is invoked. For example, in Romans 1:2 Paul says that the good news about God's Son was "promised beforehand through his prophets in the holy scriptures" (NRSV). In 1 Corinthians 15:3-4 Paul says Christ's death and *resurrection both took place "according to the Scriptures." Readers are left to guess what biblical texts Paul might have had in mind, and it seems likely that he was often alluding to constellations of biblical texts and interpretations rather than to specific individual texts.

2. Hermeneutical Framework and Interpretive Practices.

In many ways, Paul followed interpretive practices that were familiar to him and to his contemporaries. One must avoid the anachronistic tendency to expect that he should and would interpret the biblical text as post-Enlightenment interpreters do, with an implicit commitment to the re-creation of the "original" historical meaning of the text. In fact, one must beware of the culturally rooted assumption that one's hermeneutical competency would have been judged by one's faithfulness to a historically reconstructed meaning. Philo, Qumran's Teacher of Righteousness, Hillel, and other ancient interpreters were not concerned that someone might look over their shoulder and detect that they were incompetent interpreters because their allegorical or pesher interpretations did not hold up under the light of historical interpretive methods. In fact, it seems that nearly the opposite was true of the hermeneutical culture of Paul's environment: the ability to see things in Scripture that others had not seen, to suggest connections between biblical texts that others had not made, and to find relevance in biblical texts through a variety of creative interpretive moves were the marks of inspired genius, not of interpretive malpractice, as long as the interpretive result did not contradict key convictions and values of the community. For Paul and many of his contemporary biblical interpreters, the ability to find relevance in texts that others might miss and to see potentially relevant connections between texts that could illuminate a current situation was part of what it meant to have the Spirit open up mysteries in the biblical texts that had been waiting for this moment to be revealed.

Modern interpreters tend to prefer to interpret texts in isolation from each other (with the exception of earlier intertexts), as though one's interpretation of a given text should not be "contaminated" by the influence of a historically unrelated text. But, like ancient Jewish writers, Paul tended to find new insights by bringing different texts into conversation with each other. So, in Galatians 3:5-9 Paul's argument reflects reading Genesis 15:6 and Genesis 12:3 together, and in Galatians 3:10-13, Paul starts and ends with two different texts that refer to people being cursed (Deut 27:26 and Deut 21:23), and in the middle he plays two texts that suggest alternative ways of finding "life" against each other (Hab 2:4 and Lev 18:5). In Galatians 3:14 he brings the conversation back to Abraham's blessing (Gen 12:3). Of course, at times he seems to have just one particular text in mind (e.g., Hab 2:4 in Rom 1:17, although even there he may have other OT passages about God's righteousness in mind, e.g., Ps 98:2-3), but that seems to be the exception rather than the rule.

Much scholarly attention has been dedicated to the question of the extent to which Paul "respected" the contexts from which his citations were taken and the extent to which his readers or hearers were expected to know the sources and contexts of the biblical texts quoted by Paul. Was Paul familiar with the contexts of the texts that he quoted, and did it matter whether his readers were familiar with those contexts? It is certainly always worth reviewing the contexts from which any quotation has been taken to see whether there is clear (or ambiguous) evidence that Paul's argument is informed by other material in or the thrust of the near context of the quoted material. The verdict should not be prejudged before the investigation is undertaken. If other material in the literary context of the quoted material seems to have informed Paul's argument, one may then seek to discern whether familiarity with that contextual material was essential to following Paul's argument (see Abasciano; Keefer; Stanley 2004; 2008).

2.1. Paul's Narrative-Theological Framework. Philo "knew" the Scriptures would contain the best of all Greek *wisdom and *philosophy once allegorically interpreted, and he interpreted them accordingly. The Teacher of Righteousness and others in *Qumran "knew" the Scriptures were speaking about their own community and their eschatological moment, and they interpreted them accordingly. Hillel "knew" that once the right interpretive rules were applied the Jewish community could discern the proper application of the law for Jewish living despite gaps and a failure to explicitly address all of the situations that required some guidance, and he interpreted them accordingly. What was it that guided Paul's interpretations?

Paul read the Scriptures in light of a Messianic Jewish restorationist-apocalyptic story that centered on Christ and the redefinition of God's people accomplished through his death and resurrection and the pouring out of the *Holy Spirit on those who respond to Christ in faith. This Christ-centered narrative unlocked interpretive insights in the Scriptures for Paul. He knew that the end or culmination of the ages had come (1 Cor 10:11) with the coming of Jesus the Messiah, the Son of God, with whom the prophets had associated the coming of good news (Rom 1:1-4) and the revelation of mysteries long awaited (Rom 16:25-26), and whose death and resurrection were the keys to God's redemptive purposes, with the resurrection declaring him to be the Son of God in power (Rom 1:4). He understood that all of God's redemptive promises were being or would be fulfilled through Christ, who was setting right all things that were corrupted by sin from the beginning (Rom 5–6). For Paul God's intent was to justify both Jews and Gentiles on the basis of faith in the Messiah rather than seeing them separated by the requirements of the law of Moses and needing to base their relationship with God on keeping it (which Israel had failed to do over the centuries as a nation). Paul reflects different facets of his understanding of the governing narrative according to the needs of his arguments in each letter.

2.2. Gezerah Shawah. In many cases the texts that Paul brings together contain common terms or expressions, as was common in the Jewish technique that came to be referred to as *gezerah shawah,* which proposes that texts containing common terms or expressions can or should be read as mutually interpreting, understanding that aspects pertaining to one of the texts can be appropriately attributed to the other as well. This is one of the two first interpretive principles that were historically attributed to the first-century Pharisee Hillel. In Romans 4:3-9 Paul reads Genesis 15:6 and Psalm 32:1-2 as mutually interpreting, as they both contain the language of "accounting" or "accrediting" (the accrediting of righteousness in Genesis and refraining from accrediting sin in the psalm). In Galatians 3:10-13, Paul creates a stronger sense of *gezerah shawah* by substituting the word for "cursed" used in Deuteronomy 21:23 with the one used in Deuteronomy 27:26, taking advantage of the more flexible norm for quotations mentioned above. In doing so he indicates even more clearly his understanding that the two Deuteronomic texts were to be understood as theologically related.

2.3. Qal Wahomer. *Qal wahomer* ("light to heavy") is the other of the first two interpretive principles attributed to Hillel. This is also known as *a minore ad maius,* meaning that what applies in a less important case will certainly apply (or apply all the more) in a more important case. This type of biblical argumentation shows up several times in Paul's letters. For example, in Romans 5:15-19, Paul argues, on the basis of the superiority of Christ compared to Adam, that if Adam's transgression (Gen 3) brought consequences (condemnation) for all people, certainly Christ's obedience (given its role in God's redemptive plan) also brought consequences (justification and life) for all. In Romans 11:11-12, Paul argues (with Deut 32:19-43 in the background) that if salvation has come to Gentiles even as a consequence of Israel's stumbling in failing (in the majority) to believe in Christ, certainly the redemption of Israel will also bring (even greater) salvation to the Gentiles. In 2 Corinthians 3:7-11 Paul argues that since the ministry of Moses (which brought death) was marked by glory, so also the ministry of Christ (the one whose ministry brings life) will also be marked by (even greater) glory. A similar argument may be at work when Paul quotes Deuteronomy 25:4 ("You shall not muzzle an ox while it is treading out the grain," NRSV) to argue in favor of apostles' receiving support for their work (1 Cor 9:6-11).

2.4. Interpretation by Gloss. Interpretation by gloss entails providing a snippet annotation, commentary, or explanation of a word or expression in a marginal or interlinear style (equivalent to parenthetical clarifications in modern writing). In Romans 10:6-8 Paul provides a series of glosses to interpret lines he cites from Deuteronomy 30:12-14. "Who will ascend into heaven?" is glossed as "that is, to bring Christ down," and "Who will descend into the abyss?" is glossed as "that is, to bring Christ up from the dead" (NRSV). The expression from Deuteronomy 30:14, "The word is near you, on your lips and in your heart," is glossed as "that is, the word of faith that we proclaim" (Rom 10:8 NRSV). In 1 Corinthians 8:6 Paul provides two glosses to interpret the key expression of the Shema (from Deut 6:4, "the Lord our God, the Lord is one"). He explains that the reference to "one God" is to be understood as a reference to "the Father, from whom are all things and for whom we exist," and the reference to "one Lord" is to be understood as referring to "Jesus Christ, through whom are all things and through whom we exist" (NRSV), thus embedding Christ within the identity of God found in Israel's key confession. In 2 Corinthians 3:15-17 Paul alludes to Exodus 34:34, which says that whenever Moses went in to the Lord he removed his veil, saying "but when one turns to the Lord, the veil is removed" (2 Cor 3:16 NRSV). The next line (2 Cor 3:17) seems to be a gloss interpreting the meaning of "the Lord" in Exodus 34:34: "Now 'the Lord' is the Spirit." Ephesians 4:8-10 provides an interpretation by gloss of the part of the quotation from Psalm 67:19 LXX that says "he ascended on high": "When it says, 'He ascended,' what does it mean but that he had also descended into the lower parts of the earth? He who descended is the same one who ascended far above all the heavens, so that he might fill all things" (NRSV). Note that each of these glosses suggests a Christotelic reading of the OT passages, as they interpret these passages as referring to Christ or the Spirit.

2.5. Figural or Typological Interpretation. By "typological interpretation" is meant interpretation where people or events in the world of the NT are interpreted as conforming (or potentially conforming) to a pattern found in the OT. Typological identifications could be made prospectively (in anticipation of the recurrence of the pattern) or reflectively (in recognizing the recurrence of a pattern after it has appeared). The prophet of the OT looked forward to a new or second exodus in anticipation of the end of Israel's exile. While others have argued that Paul worked with a Christocentric hermeneutic (predominantly finding testimonies about Christ in the OT), Hays argues that Paul worked primarily with an ecclesiocentric hermeneutic, predominantly finding in Scripture prefigurations of the church as God's people (Hays 1989). This can be seen in Paul's treatment of the exodus and wilderness wandering texts in 1 Corinthians 10:1-12, in his glossing of Deuteronomy 30:12-14, and in his biblical exposition of Gentiles worshiping together with Jews in Romans 15:8-12, as well as many other texts.

When Paul looks in the Bible to understand the church, he finds his understanding in what the Bible says about (eschatological) Israel. But there is more. When Paul looked in the Bible to understand Jesus, he found his understanding in the Bible's promises of a Davidic king, Son of God (Rom 1:3-4; 1 Cor 15:25-28), and Suffering Servant (among other concepts). When Paul looked in the Bible to understand himself, he found his understanding in the picture of a prophet called to preach good news in the last days (Gal 1:15-16). As the next section will illustrate, when Paul looked in the Scriptures he also found prefigurations of his theological opponents (Gal 4:21-31).

What Paul saw prefigured in Scripture depended on where he read and what he understood to be happening in the churches to which he wrote. In this and many other cases it bears keeping in mind that Paul was involved in a project that had as much to do with helping his readers interpret their own situation as it did with helping them interpret the Scriptures. The interpretation of Scripture was not carried out for its own sake but in order to better interpret and respond to the circumstances in which the churches found themselves.

2.6. Allegorical Interpretation. There is only one explicitly allegorical interpretation in Paul's letters. Even there he does not engage in the kind of running allegorical interpretation for which Philo and other interpreters were known. While much allegorical interpretation in Paul's world (including for Philo) was about finding the best Greek philosophy in narrative texts, Paul's interpretation is grounded in his understanding of OT covenants and their application to believers in Christ. In Galatians 4:21-31, as he interprets the Genesis story of Sarah and Hagar and their two sons, he provides what he explicitly calls an allegorical interpretation of the text (or, possibly, suggests the text itself is meant as an allegory, "they are *allēgoroumena*"). He breaks down the text into a series of oppositions or dualisms (two women, two sons, two covenants, two Jerusalems), with a good side (free mother [Sarah], free son, born supernaturally, who is picked on by the other [Isaac], Abrahamic covenant, *Jerusalem above) and a bad side (*slave mother [Hagar], enslaved son, born naturally, who picks on the other [Ishmael], Mosaic law, present Jerusalem). His ultimate goal is to establish that the Galatian Gentile believers have more in common with Isaac and those pressuring them to be circumcised have more in common with Ishmael. This allegorical interpretation also reflects an ecclesiocentric interpretation in that Paul finds in the Genesis narrative prefigurations of the Galatian believers (and those seeking to impose *circumcision on them).

2.7. Prosopological Interpretation: Scriptural Voices in Paul's Citations. Paul attributes his scriptural quotations to a diverse set of voices. At times texts are attributed to the presumed or explicitly identified human authors or speakers in the OT texts, such as when one reads "Isaiah says" (Rom 10:20; 15:12) or "Moses says" (Rom 10:19). At other times Paul identifies God as the speaker in the OT text, as in "God says" (Rom 9:15, 25) or "the Lord says" (Rom 12:19). It is worth pointing out that Paul does not always point out that God is the speaker of the text when that is the case. For instance, in Romans 10:20, where Paul says, "Isaiah says," God is the speaker in the Isaianic text ("I have been found by those who did not seek me; I have shown myself to those who did not ask for me," NRSV). But in this case Paul identifies the book where God is quoted. In other cases Paul merely points out that God is the speaker. In still other cases Paul simply says "the law says" (Rom 3:12; 4:21; or "it is written in the law" [1 Cor 9:9; 14:21]) or "Scripture says" (Rom 9:17; 10:11; 11:2). Elsewhere, the subject of the verb is indefinite, so that it could be understood as "he says" or "it [the text] says" (Rom 15:10; 1 Cor 9:10; 15:27; 2 Cor 6:2). It is not clear whether Paul has criteria other than his unconscious rhetorical intuition to determine what voice, if any, is identified as the voice of any particular citation.

Prosopological interpretation or exegesis is the term used when someone citing a biblical text attributes its speech (explicitly or implicitly) to a person or character (*prosōpon*) who is not clearly identified in the biblical text as its speaker (Bates 2012, 183). Paul sometimes attributes his citations to some unexpected sources or voices, as when Paul identifies part of Genesis 12:3 ("in you shall all the Gentiles be blessed") as something that "Scripture" declared to Abraham, having foreseen God's plan (Gal 3:8). Paul identifies part of Deuteronomy 30:12 as something spoken by "the righteousness that is by faith" (Rom 10:6), and immediately after identifies Leviticus 18:5 as something that "Moses writes" (Rom 10:5).

In some cases, it seems Paul may understand biblical texts to represent the voice of Christ, mediated through the original speaker. So, in Romans 15:3 many scholars think Paul takes Psalm 69:9 to represent Christ speaking through the mouth of the prophet when he says, "The insults of those who insult you have fallen on me" (NRSV). Even in cases where Paul identifies a biblical text as originating from a biblical author, some have argued that the biblical author might still be understood to serve as the mouthpiece of Christ himself (see Bates 2012 on Rom 10:16 and the possibility that Christ, rather than Isaiah, should be understood to be the ultimate speaker of Is 53:1; see also the discussion in Scott 2014).

3. Conclusion.

Matthew 13:52 reports Jesus saying "every scribe who has been trained for the kingdom of heaven is like the master of a *household who brings out of his treasure what is new and what is old" (NRSV). Every time an interpreter takes a text that was written for a previous occasion and inserts it into a new context to speak to a different audience, it communicates meaning in its new setting, which includes both old and new elements. Whether Paul cites, alludes to, or echoes an individual text or composes a text out of number of citations or allusions, he (explicitly or not) brings remnants of old meanings into conversation with each other and with the new context(s) into which they are to speak once again. In the composition of combined conflated (undisclosed) citations, he is creating new biblical texts out of old ones. But in recognizing the canon of the NT, the Christian church has affirmed that the NT authors were creating new biblical texts whether they were building them out of earlier biblical texts or not.

Paul "inhabits a scripturally defined world" and views "reality from within the symbols given by Scripture" (Johnson, 192). He is one of those who "wrote with scripture, shaping a distinctive idiom of discourse in so doing. They turned to scripture not for proof texts, let alone for pretexts, to say whatever they wanted, anyhow, to say. They used scripture as an artist uses the colors on the palette, expressing ideas through and with scripture as the artist paints with those colors and no others" (Neusner, 4). Thus he wrote with Scripture in light of his *knowledge of Christ and under the conviction that the biblical texts "were written down to instruct us, on whom the ends of the ages have come" (1 Cor 10:11 NRSV), "so that by steadfastness and by the encouragement of the scriptures we might have *hope" (Rom 15:4 NRSV). The diversity and subtlety of ways in which Paul interpreted the Scriptures and wove biblical texts together to communicate their meaning and relevance for his churches reveals his remarkable interpretive and rhetorical abilities.

See also ABRAHAM; HERMENEUTICS/INTERPRETING PAUL; HOLY SPIRIT; INTERPRETATION: PATRISTIC; ISRAEL; LAW; NARRATIVE; PAUL AND JUDAISM; PREACHING FROM PAUL TODAY; QUMRAN AND PAUL.

BIBLIOGRAPHY. **B. J. Abasciano,** "Diamonds in the Rough: A Reply to Christopher Stanley Concerning the Reader Competency of Paul's Original Audiences," *NovT* 49 (2007): 153-83; **S. A. Adams and S. M. Ehorn,** "Composite Citations in Antiquity: A Conclusion," in *Composite Citations in Antiquity*, vol. 2, *New Testament Uses*, ed. S. A. Adams and S. M. Ehorn, LNTS (London: Bloomsbury T&T Clark, 2018), 208-48; **D. Allen,** "The Use of Criteria: The State of the Question," in *Methodology in the Use of the Old Testament in the New*, ed. D. Allen and S. Smith, LNTS 579 (New York: T&T Clark, 2019), 129-41; **D. Allen and S. Smith,** eds., *Methodology in the Use of the Old Testament in the New: Context and Criteria*, LNTS 579 (New York: T&T Clark, 2019); **M. W. Bates,** *The Hermeneutics of the Apostolic Proclamation: The Center of Paul's Method of Scriptural Interpretation* (Waco, TX: Baylor University Press,

2012); idem, *The Birth of the Trinity: Jesus, God, and Spirit in New Testament and Early Christian Interpretations of the Old Testament* (Oxford: Oxford University Press, 2015); **G. K. Beale and D. A. Carson,** eds., *Commentary on the New Testament Use of the Old Testament* (Grand Rapids, MI: Baker Academic, 2007); **R. E. Ciampa,** "Scriptural Language and Ideas," in *As It Is Written: Studying Paul's Use of Scripture,* ed. S. N. Porter and C. D. Stanley, SymS 50 (Atlanta: Society of Biblical Literature, 2008), 41-57; idem, "Genesis 1–3 and Paul's Theology of Adam's Dominion in Romans 5–6," in *From Creation to New Creation: Essays on Biblical Theology and Exegesis,* ed. D. M. Gurtner and B. L. Gladd (Peabody, MA: Hendrickson, 2013), 103-22; idem, "Composite Citations in 1–2 Corinthians and in Galatians," in *Composite Citations in Antiquity,* vol. 2, *New Testament Uses,* ed. S. A. Adams and S. M. Ehorn, LNTS (London: Bloomsbury T&T Clark, 2018), 159-89; idem, "Suffering in Romans 1–8 in Light of Paul's Key Scriptural Intertexts," in *Suffering in Paul,* ed. S. F. Wu (Eugene, OR: Pickwick, 2019), 7-28; idem, "Habakkuk 2:4 in Romans: Echoes, Allusions, and Rewriting," in *Scripture, Texts, and Tracings in Romans*, ed. A. Das and L. Belleville (Philadelphia: Lexington/Fortress Academic, 2021), 11-29; **R. E. Ciampa and B. S. Rosner,** "1 Corinthians," in *Commentary on the New Testament Use of the Old Testament*, ed. G. K. Beale and D. A. Carson (Grand Rapids, MI: Baker Academic, 2007), 695-752; **G. D. Collier,** "'That We Might Not Crave Evil': The Structure and Argument of 1 Corinthians 10:1-13," *JSNT* 55 (1994): 55-75; **C. H. Dodd,** *According to the Scriptures: The Sub-structure of New Testament Theology* (London: Fontana, 1952); **L. Goppelt,** *Typos: The Typological Interpretation of the Old Testament in the New* (Grand Rapids, MI: Eerdmans, 1982); **R. B. Hays,** *Echoes of Scripture in the Letters of Paul* (New Haven, CT: Yale University Press, 1989); idem, *First Corinthians* (Louisville, KY: John Knox, 1997); idem, *The Conversion of the Imagination: Paul as Interpreter of Israel's Scripture* (Grand Rapids, MI: Eerdmans, 2005); **R. B. Hays, S. Alkier, and L. A. Huizenga,** eds., *Reading the Bible Intertextually* (Waco, TX: Baylor University Press, 2009); **H. Hübner,** *Gottes Ich und Israel. Zum Schriftgebrauch des Paulus in Römer 9–11,* FRLANT 136 (Göttingen: Vandenhoeck & Ruprecht, 1984); **L. T. Johnson,** *Constructing Paul: The Canonical Paul* (Grand Rapids, MI: Eerdmans, 2020); **A. Keefer,** "The Meaning and Place of Old Testament Context in OT/NT Methodology," in *Methodology in the Use of the Old Testament in the New*, ed. D. Allen and S. Smith, LNTS 579 (New York: T&T Clark, 2019), 73-85; **D.-A. Koch,** *Die Schrift als Zeuge des Evangeliums. Untersuchungen zur Verwendung und zum Verständnis der Schrift bei Paulus*, BHT 69 (Tübingen: Mohr, 1986); **M. J. Lee and B. J. Oropeza,** eds., *Practicing Intertextuality: Ancient Jewish and Greco-Roman Exegetical Techniques in the New Testament* (Eugene, OR: Cascade, 2021); **B. Lindars,** *New Testament Apologetic: The Doctrinal Significance of the Old Testament Quotations* (Philadelphia: Westminster, 1961); **S. Moyise,** *Paul and Scripture* (Grand Rapids, MI: Baker Academic, 2010); **J. Neusner and W. S. Green,** *Writing with Scripture: The Authority and Uses of the Hebrew Bible in the Torah of Formative Judaism* (Atlanta: Scholars Press, 1993); **B. J. Oropeza,** "Quotations, Allusions, and Echoes: Their Meanings in Relation to Biblical Interpretation," in *Practicing Intertextuality: Ancient Jewish and Greco-Roman Exegetical Techniques in the New Testament,* ed. M. J. Lee and B. J. Oropeza (Eugene, OR: Cascade, 2021), 17-26; **S. N. Porter and C. D. Stanley,** eds., *As It Is Written: Studying Paul's Use of Scripture,* SymS 50 (Atlanta: Society of Biblical Literature, 2008); **M. Reasoner,** "'Promised Beforehand Through His Prophets in the Holy Scriptures': Composite Citations in Romans," in *Composite Citations in Antiquity,* vol. 2, *New Testament Uses, ed.* S. A. Adams and S. M. Ehorn, LNTS (London: Bloomsbury T&T Clark, 2018), 128-58; **B. S. Rosner,** *Paul, Scripture, and Ethics: A Study of 1 Corinthians 5–7,* AGJU 22 (Leiden: Brill, 1994); **M. Scott,** *The Hermeneutics of Christological Psalmody in Paul: An Intertextual Enquiry*, SNTSMS 158 (Cambridge: Cambridge University Press, 2014); **M. Silva,** "Old Testament in Paul," in *DPL*, 630-42; **D. M. Smith,** "The Pauline Literature," in *It Is Written: Scripture Citing Scripture; Essays in Honour of Barnabas Lindars, SSF*, ed. D. A. Carson and H. G. M. Williamson (Cambridge: Cambridge University Press, 1988), 265-91; **S. Smith,** "The Use of Criteria: A Proposal from Relevance Theory," in *Methodology in the Use of the Old Testament in the New*, ed. D. Allen and S. Smith, LNTS 579 (New York: T&T Clark, 2019), 142-54; **C. D. Stanley,** *Paul and the Language of Scripture: Citation Technique in the Pauline Epistles and Contemporary Literature*, SNTSMS 69 (Cambridge: Cambridge University Press, 1992); idem, *Arguing with Scripture: The Rhetoric of Quotations in the Letters of Paul* (New York: T&T Clark International, 2004); idem, "Paul's 'Use' of Scripture: Why the Audience Matters," in *As It Is Written: Studying Paul's Use of Scripture*, ed. S. E. Porter and C. D. Stanley, SymS 50 (Atlanta: Society of Biblical Literature, 2008), 125-55;

idem, ed., *Paul and Scripture: Extending the Conversation*, ECL 9 (Atlanta: Society of Biblical Literature, 2012); **A. C. Thiselton,** *The First Epistle to the Corinthians: A Commentary on the Greek Text* (Grand Rapids, MI: Eerdmans, 2000); **F. Watson,** *Paul and the Hermeneutics of Faith* (New York: T&T Clark International, 2005); **W. J. Webb,** *Returning Home: New Covenant and Second Exodus as the Context for 2 Corinthians 6.14–7.1* (Sheffield: JSOT Press, 1993).

R. E. Ciampa

ONESIMUS. *See* PHILEMON, LETTER TO; SLAVE, SLAVERY.

OPPONENTS OF PAUL

Interpreters have been assigning identities to those Paul opposes in his *letters from at least as early as Tertullian. In the earliest times, authors identified their own opponents with the opponents Paul opposed in his letters (e.g., Tertullian, *Praescr.* 5-6). Such practices continued into the time of the Reformation. But as interpreters increasingly gave attention to setting the Pauline letters in their original context, they began giving more attention to the original *identity of his opponents. The early historical-critical discussion of Paul's opponents was dominated by F. C. Baur's thesis. Baur identified Paul's opponents as Jewish *church members who argued that *Gentiles must be fully Torah observant to be saved. They argued this in opposition to Paul's teaching that Gentiles must remain Gentiles. (These opponents have often been called *Judaizers, but that name was intended as a value judgment about them. It also fails to recognize that the church was fully Jewish at its beginning.) Baur presupposed Hegel's understanding of history. Thus, the "Jewish Christianity" Paul faced was a thesis, while Paul and "Gentile Christianity" was the antithesis. Those two came together in the second century to form the synthesis of "catholic Christianity." It, in turn, became the next thesis. This historical scheme left no room for diversity among the groups that opposed Paul. Thus, all Paul's letters opposed this same theological position, even when there was no evidence they held this position, because Baur presupposed there was only one group of opponents.

Nearly all interpreters now reject such a strict Hegelian view of history. Yet hypotheses that assert that all Paul's letters address the same kind of opponent remain. Some even contend that Baur identified them correctly (Barrett; Goulder). Walter Schmithals began his search for Paul's opponents with 1 Corinthians, assuming that the opponents he found there would be the opponents Paul faced everywhere. Since *knowledge is an important topic of 1 Corinthians, Schmithals identified those opponents as Gnostics. If there were Gnostics in *Corinth, he assumed that the opponents in all of Paul's letters must be Gnostics. When a letter did not seem to oppose *Gnosticism, Schmithals argued that Paul had failed to understand that they were Gnostics.

There were voices that spoke against this dominant pattern. J. B. Lightfoot saw more diversity within those Paul opposed and refused to see them as a single movement. Wilhelm Lütgert also rejected the single-type hypothesis and found multiple types of opponents in the letters. More broadly, Walter Bauer argued that the church was a much more diverse movement than Baur's thesis could accommodate. Interpreters who worked on identifying the opponents of a single letter were often less constrained by the single-type-of-opponent thesis (e.g., Georgi).

1. A Method for Identifying Opponents
2. Identifying the Opponents in the Letters
3. Conclusion

1. A Method for Identifying Opponents.

Rejecting the notion that there can be only one type of opponent allows for numerous hypotheses about their identity. In fact, there are multiple proposals about opponents for nearly every Pauline letter. Yet few interpreters have given attention to developing a method for identifying them. Exceptions to this tendency include Nils Dahl, Klaus Berger, John Barclay, and Mark Nanos. This essay will identify the opponents using the method devised by Jerry Sumney. This method privileges explicit statements about opponents over allusions and allows affirmations about beliefs or rejections of practices to count as evidence about their identity only if the topic has been raised in explicit statements and allusions. Further, the method finds statements that appear in polemical sections less likely to be evenhanded descriptions of the opposed teachings than statements that appear in more didactic and apologetic sections. At times comments in polemical sections even seem to be shaped by the methods of anti-Sophistic polemic (Becker). In addition, the method limits one's initial inquiry about the opponents to the letter being examined. Only after one's basic understanding of them is formed should one admit outside information to clarify their identity.

2. Identifying the Opponents in the Letters.

This article will examine the letters in roughly chronological order (assuming a later date for Galatians). It will not discuss Philemon because its occasion does not include opposition to Paul. It will review proposed hypotheses about the opponents and use the method described above to identify them. The primary meaning of the term *opponents* here is that they are people or groups within the church who oppose Paul's *teaching or apostleship.

2.1. 1 Thessalonians. Some interpreters see members of this church questioning the *leadership of both Paul and local leaders because Paul seems to defend his ministry in 1 Thessalonians 2:1-14. But most interpreters find no opponents in the sense of opposition to Paul's teaching or apostleship from within the church. Indeed, there are no explicit statements about such opposition, even as he clarifies some instructions about the parousia. Readers do hear that both Paul and the Thessalonians face opposition from outside the church (1 Thess 1:6-7, 9-10; 3:3), but not from within. Thus, it seems that responding to opponents is not a part of this letter's occasion.

2.2. 1 Corinthians. Most interpreters think the problems 1 Corinthians addresses come from within this church rather than being introduced by teachers from outside. Of course, Baur finds traveling Jewish teachers who want Gentile church members to keep the *law in the same way Jews do, and Schmithals finds Gnostics. Others contend that outsiders started the "Cephas party" (1 Cor 1:12-13) but left before Paul wrote 1 Corinthians. This party is often said to have demanded that Gentile members keep the Torah as Jews kept it. That would have included being circumcised and observing the Sabbath and Mosaic *food laws. This party, then, opposed Paul's teaching about Gentiles' place in the church. Others see the "Apollos party" (1 Cor 1:12-13) as an opposition group that was started by Apollos and questioned Paul's standing. While most interpreters find none of these intruders as the problem, some Corinthians were raising questions about Paul's authority and teaching.

The first explicit statement that suggests opposition to Paul is 1 Corinthians 1:12-13, where he says people are saying that they belong to Cephas, Apollos, Paul, or *Christ. These are probably not labels the Corinthians have adopted because Paul begins this sentence saying, "I say this" or "What I mean is" (NRSV). This phrase suggests he is interpreting the report from Chloe's people (1 Cor 1:11) rather than quoting it. Some interpreters have picked one of these names as the source of the real problem at Corinth and identified a particular kind of theology it represents. But when Paul concludes his discussion of this matter, he names only himself and Apollos, noting that he has applied what he is saying to them so that it is obvious that the problem is not about the named leaders (1 Cor 3:1-23).

Another explicit statement about the Corinthians, not opposition groups, is that they are still "of the flesh" rather than maturing spiritually (1 Cor 3:3). Paul also tells them not to boast in any human leader (1 Cor 3:21-21). And when Paul speaks of some who are puffed up about leaders (1 Cor 4:6-7), it does suggest that there is at least some questioning of his authority. Paul even notes that some have challenged his authority (1 Cor 4:18-19). They do not appear to have formed a group that wants to oust Paul, but they are evaluating his authority and teaching (1 Cor 4:3). His defense of refusing money from the Corinthians suggests that it is one of the things that some Corinthians raise questions about (1 Cor 9:3-6, 12).

There is, then, some challenge to Paul's authority. It seems related to tendencies to favor other leaders. While Paul names some famous ones, the leaders questioning his authority are probably members of the Corinthian church. It could even be the case that there is competition between congregations about who has the best leader. But they have not gone as far as rejecting Paul's claim to be an *apostle. The only aspect of his apostolic behavior mentioned explicitly as problematic is his refusal to accept pay. Thus, there is some questioning of his authority but no opponents in the sense of an organized competing *ministry.

2.3. 2 Corinthians. Questions about the literary integrity of 2 Corinthians complicate attempts to identify the opponents Paul is responding to. But however many letters make up 2 Corinthians, there is a clear continuity across them in the kind of opposition to Paul they address. These opponents have been identified as a group that demands the same Torah observance of Jews and Gentiles, Gnostics, divine men, and pneumatics. Those who find Gnostics point to verbal parallels between 2 Corinthians and later Gnostic writings. But Gnostic thought did not coalesce into an organized system before the end of the first century AD. Dieter Georgi argues that the opponents of 2 Corinthians were Hellenistic Jewish propagandists who exercised extraordinary powers from the Spirit to show that they were apostles. They saw themselves and Jesus as divine men, as was Moses. For them, Christ's coming was not an eschatological event, just another instance of the appearance of a divine man. But much of Georgi's reconstruction of these divine men is dependent on Hellenistic Judaism rather than

2 Corinthians. Ernst Käsemann identifies the Spirit as the central issue, with the opponents claiming that the Spirit makes them powerful speakers. They said the Spirit also gave them powerful personalities and authority that the church must submit to.

It makes sense to begin by looking at these opponents as they appear in 2 Corinthians 1–9 since at least 2 Corinthians 10–13 could be a separate letter. In 2 Corinthians 2:17 Paul seems to accuse them of being hucksters. This suggests that they accept pay for their ministerial work. They commend themselves and bring letters of recommendation (2 Cor 3:1). These teachers present their qualifications to the Corinthians in a way Paul thinks is inappropriate (2 Cor 5:12). What Paul calls "boasting," the opponents see as the proper telling of how God's power is seen in the exercise of their own power. The Corinthians have begun evaluating Paul's behavior as an apostle (2 Cor 1:12-14, 17). His rejection of self-commendation indicates that they are asking for Paul's credentials in the wake of the teachers who tout theirs (2 Cor 3:1; 2:16). Paul acknowledges that the Corinthians have misunderstood his ministry, suggesting that he is even accused of deceitfulness (2 Cor 4:2-3). After all, he promised to return after a painful incident that led him to leave, but he did not. Instead he sent a harsh letter (2 Cor 1:15–2:4). Some Corinthians, perhaps with the help of the opponents, have interpreted this as deceitfulness and cowardice (2 Cor 1:17-22; 2:17; 5:11).

The focus of the criticism is Paul's weakness, his life of apostolic *suffering for his churches (2 Cor 4:7–5:2). The discussions about his weakness allude to questions about his sufficiency for apostleship. Some argue that his sufferings disqualify him from being an apostle because his life is not a manifestation of God's power. Paul argues that the opponents and the Corinthians who accept them evaluate ministries by appearances (2 Cor 5:12) and by earthly standards rather than by the standards of the eschatological era (2 Cor 5:16-17).

Some interpreters use 2 Corinthians 3:7-18 to reconstruct the opponents as a group that demands that Gentiles keep the law as Jews do (Lüdemann; Hafemann). Others see it connecting covenant renewal, possession of the Spirit, and Torah observance (Blanton). But since there is no discussion of Torah observance in any explicit statements about the opponents, there is insufficient reason to see this discussion of Moses' ministry as evidence of demands about Torah observance. Instead, this text is an explication of the gloriousness of the new covenant's ministry (2 Cor 3:6).

The tone of 2 Corinthians 10–13 is more polemical, and Paul's comments about the opponents are more direct. The main issue in these chapters is the appropriate manner of life for apostles. Paul calls the teachers who claim to be apostles "false apostles" (2 Cor 11:13), and he chides them with the title "super-apostles" (2 Cor 11:5; 12:12-13). They also call themselves "servants [*diakonoi*] of Christ" and "workers" (*ergatai*, 2 Cor 11:12-13), titles Paul uses elsewhere for people in ministry.

These opponents claim that apostles should have powerful and obviously successful lives (2 Cor 12:1-13) and argue that Paul's "weakness" shows that he is not an apostle. Paul calls their claims to be powerful "boasting" and "boasting according to the *flesh" (2 Cor 11:18). They call for comparisons of ministries as proof of apostolic status (2 Cor 10:12-18) and say God's power should come to expression in demanding deference and submission (2 Cor 11:20-21). Some Corinthians want Paul to provide the same kind of proof that Christ speaks through him (2 Cor 13:2-3).

The opponents argue that the powerful lives of apostles must include being powerful speakers (2 Cor 11:6). They say that Paul's letters seem to exert the right kind of power, but then his presence, his demeanor, and his speaking ability are weak and contemptible (2 Cor 10:10-11). They use this contrast as evidence of a deceitful inconsistency. They assert further that apostles accept pay for their ministry. Thus, Paul's refusal of pay suggests that even he knows he is not a real apostle (2 Cor 11:7-15). They add the accusation of deceitfulness in financial matters to these claims, probably saying that Paul takes money from the *collection for Jerusalem (2 Cor 12:15-18). *Visions and revelations are also evidence of their powerful apostolic lives (2 Cor 12:1-10). The combination of the mighty works they perform (2 Cor 12:12) and such visionary experiences indicates that these opponents claim a measure of the Spirit that bestows these powers.

These opponents also claim to be "Hebrews," "Israelites," and "seed of *Abraham" (2 Cor 11:23). Some have seen a reference to Jerusalem or the Jerusalem apostles in these ways to claim to be thoroughly Jewish, but Paul makes no such connection. Since Jews were raised with knowledge of *God, they were often granted authority in predominantly Gentile churches. These opponents draw on that advantage to claim authority. Interpreters have seized on Paul's chiding of the Corinthians for accepting anyone who comes to them with a different Jesus, Spirit, or *gospel (2 Cor 11:4) to identify the primary theological concern of the opponents. But Paul's other descriptions of these opponents do not support making christological or pneumatological teachings or Torah observance as issues they raise. Paul is reprimanding the readers for being gullible enough to accept anything, not describing the alternative teaching. The closest connection to any of these matters seems to be that Paul rejects their understanding of the way the Spirit is manifested in apostles' lives.

The same evaluations of Paul's ministry and the demands for evidence of apostolic status that were evident in 2 Corinthians 1–9 are also central in 2 Corinthians 10–13. This continuity in subject and demands show that the same opponents are in view in both. These opponents claim a superior measure of the Spirit as the basis for their power and apostleship. They claim further that Paul is not a genuine apostle because he lacks these.

2.4. Galatians. Throughout the nineteenth and most of the twentieth century, nearly all interpreters identified the opponents of Galatians as emissaries of the *Jerusalem church who rejected Paul's apostleship and required Gentiles to keep the law as Jews keep it. Most argued that these intruders said such law observance was necessary for *salvation or to achieve perfection. They were nearly always characterized as legalists. As most late twentieth- and early twenty-first-century interpreters came to recognize that first century Judaism was not legalistic, many have also refrained from seeing the Galatian opponents as legalists.

Most interpreters think these opponents say Gentile church members must adopt the central identity markers of Judaism (*circumcision, Sabbath, and food laws) to fully join the people of God (e.g., Dunn). Some still see them as emissaries of the Jerusalem church (Watson). Other interpreters frame the issue as eschatological: Paul claims that Gentiles are fully part of the eschatological people of God in the present without those signs of Jewish identity, but the opponents say that the eschatological moment has not arrived. They contend that in the time before the final eschatological event, all of God's people must take on these identity markers (Martyn). Recently, some argue that these opponents are Jews outside the church who want to bring these Gentiles fully into the Jewish community (Walter; Nanos). While all of these interpreters see these teachers as opposing Paul's teaching, George Howard argues that they think their teaching is consistent with Paul's, in part because Paul denies that he preaches circumcision (Gal 5:11).

Much of what Paul says about the teachers in Galatia is evaluative rather than straightforwardly descriptive. He says they are a disruptive presence (Gal 5:7-12), even bewitching the church (Gal 3:1). Their message is so problematic that it will sever their relationship with him (Gal 4:17) and with Christ (Gal 5:2). They clearly urge Gentile believers to be circumcised (Gal 6:12-13). Paul describes their teaching as wanting to be "under the law" and as calling the Gentiles to observe "the *works of the law" (Gal 2:15-16). These works of the law include the keeping of Jewish religious festivals (Gal 4:8-10), and since the Antioch incident involved division over food laws (Gal 2:11-14), these teachers probably want the Gentiles to adopt the law's dietary regulations.

Paul's discussion of his relationship with the Jerusalem apostles does not show that the teachers he opposes in Galatians are from that church, as some have argued. Not only is such an identification missing in the text, but Paul also has the Jerusalem apostles affirm his mission in those stories. These contacts with Jerusalem establish his ethos as one who stands for the gospel. His report of the Antioch incident further shows him to be one who stands for the *truth, in all circumstances (Gal 2:11-14). He seems to emphasize this aspect of his character because the Galatians are being told that Paul does require Gentile converts to be circumcised. He at least feels it is necessary to deny that he teaches this (Gal 5:11). This denial suggests that these teachers do not know they are contradicting what Paul teaches. This mischaracterization may be why he tells the Galatians not to believe even him if he preaches something other than what he taught on his initial visit (Gal 1:8-10).

It remains unclear how much of the law the other teachers want the Galatian Gentiles to adopt. They clearly want them to accept circumcision and observe religious festivals and perhaps the food laws. But twice Paul warns the Galatians that if they accept circumcision they will be required to observe the whole law (Gal 5:2-6; 3:10). This seems to be news to them, news that Paul thinks will help dissuade them from listening to these teachers. It is also unclear what the teachers say the Galatians gain by adopting these aspects of the law. Paul makes it a matter of salvation, but this does not mean the other teachers did. It may be that the teachers see their plan as a way to help the Gentiles fit into the larger Jewish community (Lategan).

Most interpreters remain convinced that these teachers are intentionally opposing Paul's teaching about Gentile Torah observance. Most also remain convinced that they argue that Gentiles are not saved or are not fully members of the people of God without observing these commands.

2.5. Romans. Romans was written to a church that Paul did not establish and had never visited. It introduces him both as the apostle to the Gentiles and as a missionary who wants this church's support for a *mission to Spain. This occasion suggests that there is no great opposition to him there. In addition, there is no explicit reference to opposition to him there. His fuller claim to the apostolic office in Romans 1:1-7 is not evidence that some at Rome question his apostleship but serves to introduce him to this church.

There are places, however, that indicate that his teaching has been misrepresented. In Romans 3:7-8, Paul says he has been slandered by people who say he teaches that people should do evil so that God's goodness will abound. This interpretation of his teaching probably comes from those who oppose his teaching on how Gentiles relate to the law. His repetition of this matter suggests that the Romans have heard this charge (Rom 6:1, 15). Such mischaracterization may also be at the root of the questions of whether the law is *sin (Rom 7:7) and of whether his teaching annuls the law (Rom 3:31). Thus, Paul recognizes that some know these questions have been raised and perhaps have these questions themselves. It does not seem these questionings quite amount to opposition, but he suspects they are strong enough that he needs to address them.

2.6. Philippians. Paul's harsh words in Philippians 3:2-4 convince many interpreters that this letter combats teachers who demand that Gentile believers keep the law in the same ways Jews keep it. Helmut Koester argues that the goal of this Torah observance is gaining full possession of the Spirit. Others understand Paul's comments about perfection (Phil 3:12-16) to show that these are the same kind of opponents Paul battles in 2 Corinthians, teachers who say they have reached perfection and thus have visionary experiences. Paul's comments about those who are "enemies of the *cross" (Phil 3:18-19) lead others to identify them as Gnostic libertines (Schmithals; R. P. Martin). Still others find both libertines and a group that demands the same kind of Torah observance for Jews and Gentiles (Jewett).

Paul mentions multiple kinds of opponents in Philippians. In Philippians 1:28 he speaks of people outside the church who persecute the Philippians and are headed for destruction. Then in Philippians 1:15-18 he mentions some who preach the gospel to cause him grief, but he is happy to have them continue to preach. They do not like Paul, but he does not find their teaching objectionable. But in Philippians 3 Paul rejects the teachings of some within the church. He warns the readers about people he calls "dogs," "evil workers," and "mutilators." These invectives alone do not reveal what they teach, but Paul next claims the identity of "the circumcision" for the church (Phil 3:3). This indicates that these opponents require Gentile believers to be circumcised and that the label "mutilators" alludes to that demand. Paul's comparison of his Jewish credentials with those of other teachers shows that they use their Jewishness to convince Gentiles to accept circumcision. Paul, then, is warning the Philippians about Jewish believers in Christ who urge circumcision and some Torah observance for Gentiles that Paul says they should not take up. It is unknown what they said was gained by this observance. It might be salvation, full membership in the people of God, or something else.

The epithets "enemies of the cross" whose "god is their belly" and who "glory in shame" (Phil 3:18-19) are not descriptions of the opponents' teachings but polemical accusations intended to make them despicable. This kind of invective is typical of ancient polemic and appears elsewhere in Paul (e.g., Gal 5:12). Paul gives no further description of these characters. In a letter that relies heavily on the use of good and bad examples to make its argument, these people (whoever they are) simply serve as bad examples.

In Philippians, then, Paul mentions three kinds of people causing trouble: nonbelievers who persecute the Philippians, believers who preach the gospel but try to grieve Paul, and teachers who urge Gentiles to take on fuller Torah observance. If Paul has a specific group in mind when he mentions "enemies of the cross," the Philippians may know who they are, but there is no way of knowing anything specific about them. It seems that neither those who require different Torah observance nor the "enemies of the cross" are actually present in Philippi. Paul tells the Philippians to watch out for the former group and reminds them that he had earlier spoken of the latter. Still, Paul feels the need to warn them against the appearance of at least those who want different Torah observance. This suggests that there is a group that opposes Paul's teaching about Gentiles' observance of the law that travels to his churches urging them to reject that element of Paul's teaching.

2.7. Colossians. A majority of interpreters argue that the opponents of the Colossians were urging church members to worship angels and to take up some ascetic practices taken from Judaism. Some, however, see the teaching as more syncretistic, bringing in the *worship of beings worshiped in mystery cults (Arnold). Still others associate the ascetic practices and mystical experiences with some form of Hellenistic philosophy (Schweizer; DeMaris; T. Martin). Yet other interpreters argue that the opponents claim that their ascetic practices help believers worship with angels rather than offering worship to angels (Francis; Sappington; Sumney). Bandstra argues that they say that attaining these mystic flights means they do not need Christ as a mediator in their relationship with God.

Some interpreters have argued that the teachers opposed are Jews who are not within the church. They reject the church's claims to participate in the blessings of Israel by rejecting what the church teaches about Christ and thus assert that the believers in Christ have no relationship with God (Dunn; Wright). We should expect there are Jews in Colossae who hold that position. There were, after all, Jews who rejected the church's claims about what Christ did for Gentiles in every city where Paul founded a church. But the Jewish elements of the teaching Colossians opposes are mixed with non-Jewish elements. Further, the emphasis in Colossians's description of the work of Christ is on forgiveness, not on claiming a place in Israel's heritage as the means of a relationship with God. In addition, this view must ignore the centrality of ascetic elements in the description of the other teaching by seeing it as an ironic way to refer to the Mosaic law (Wright). Finally, this view relies on some traditional but very questionable renderings of the language of Colossians 2:14-15 and other terminology in the letter (e.g., a more specific use of *philosophy* than is warranted by its first-century usage).

Some aspects of the teaching that Colossians opposes are clear. The opponents certainly pass *judgment against church members who do not follow their commands (Col 2:16, 18). The book's emphasis on the security of believers' relationship with God, and especially on the *forgiveness of sin, suggests that this is its central reason for rejecting this teaching. The quoted liturgical poem of Colossians 1:15-20 is both introduced and followed by declarations of forgiveness (Col 1:12-14, 22-23). Thus, the liturgy's reminder of the exalted place of Christ serves to assure readers that they have forgiveness through the one who holds the highest place in heaven. Forgiveness of sins is also stressed as the meaning of *baptism (Col 2:13-15).

The regulations the opponents demand include food regulations and observance of holy days that are, at least in part, taken from the Mosaic law (Col 2:16, 21). They go beyond the usual observance of these matters because the practices can be referred to as "severity to the *body" (Col 2:23). The goal of these mildly ascetic practices is attaining visions (Col 2:18). The opponents tell of their experiences and engage in worship practices that go beyond those the rest of the church performs. The author calls these practices "will-worship" (Col 2:23).

Most interpreters argue that these visionary experiences include worshiping angels with the teachers claiming that these angels are so highly placed that they can interfere with a person's relationship with God. But if worshiping angels is involved, it is strange that Colossians never tells the readers to stop worshiping beings other than God. Colossians 2:18 says that the opponents condemn the readers on the basis of "humility and worship of angels." While most take this to mean that they worship angels, *humility* and *worship* are governed by the same preposition. This makes it more likely that "of angels" applies to both terms. A clearer translation, then, is "angelic humility and worship." If this is correct, the opponents participate in the angelic worship in their visions. They then demand that elements of that worship be incorporated into the church's worship and that others have these visionary experiences.

Colossians does not oppose having visions, only making them a requirement for salvation. Colossians responds to this teaching by asserting that believers in Christ have forgiveness and possess all the spiritual *wisdom available (Col 1:9-10). This letter argues that such visions bring no closer relationship with God because believers are already in Christ and he is "the *fullness of deity" (Col 1:19; 2:2-3, 9-10).

2.8. Ephesians. Few interpreters think Ephesians was written to respond to opponents. Still, a few have found Gnostic opponents (R. P. Martin). But there is no refutation of specifically Gnostic teachings in the letter. Michael Goulder sees it opposing Jewish visionaries who claim they have been admitted into God's presence. But Ephesians mentions false teaching only once in a rather general, even if strong, warning about avoiding it (Eph 4:14). This letter addresses the relationship between Jews and Gentiles in the church but not in response to a group that rejects Paul's teaching.

2.9. 2 Thessalonians. Most interpreters identify the group 2 Thessalonians opposes as teachers who have quit their jobs to await the imminent day of the *Lord. Many draw on the problems of expecting an imminent end in 1 Thessalonians to identify the problem in 2 Thessalonians because people are quitting their jobs in both letters. This view of the opposed eschatology faces the difficult task of interpreting the letter's citation of what the opponents teach. In 2 Thessalonians 2:2 readers are told that they say, "The Day of the Lord has come." This "has come" is in the perfect tense, meaning that it has already happened. Some interpreters have argued that the opponents say that the day of the Lord has begun and that its completion is imminent. But this does not give full weight to this statement. Beginning in the mid-twentieth century, more interpreters attribute an overrealized *eschatology to these teachers (Malherbe). Willi Marxsen and Schmithals argue that their overrealized eschatology shows they are Gnostics. But the letter refutes no other characteristics of Gnostics. Robert Jewett argues that the opponents' eschatology has led them to claim superior spiritual *gifts and to reject both Paul's authority and traditional morality. Other interpreters argue that there are no opponents in the sense of a group that intentionally opposes Paul. Rather than opposing Paul, they have misunderstood his statements about the imminence of the day of the Lord in 1 Thessalonians (Holland). A few interpreters see the group that propounds the overrealized eschatology as separate from the people who have quit their jobs (Russell), but this seems unlikely.

The teachers causing the problems that 2 Thessalonians addresses first appear in 2 Thessalonians 2:2-3, which tells the readers not to be disturbed by any teaching that supposedly comes from Paul that claims "the Day of the Lord has come" (2 Thess 2:2). As noted, the tense of the verb here shows that some are claiming that the parousia has already happened. Since they draw on Paul's authority to assert this, they do not see themselves as his opponents. They have individualized and spiritualized the day of the Lord. They emphasize the present reality of some blessings that they received by participating in the second coming, an experience that only some have had. They may claim that their spiritual gifts lift them above the persecution the rest of the church is enduring (2 Thess 1:4-5).

In 2 Thessalonians 3:6 the Thessalonians are ordered to stay away from every "brother" who lives in a "disorderly" way and does not follow the *tradition Paul gave them. While nearly every English translation renders *ataktōs* as "idle," that is not the meaning of the word. It is rendered "idle" because the tradition that they do not adhere to is that Paul worked while he brought the gospel to them. Interpreters usually assert that quitting their jobs means they are doing nothing, are idle. But the writer defines their disorderliness by saying they are not working but are busybodies (2 Thess 3:11). The problem is not just that they have quit their jobs but that they are involved in church affairs in harmful ways. If the analogy of Paul's plying a trade while establishing their church applies directly to this situation, it suggests that these teachers have quit their jobs to devote themselves to church work full time. Paul's ministry was not "disorderly" precisely because he worked while he preached (2 Thess 3:7-9). Since these teachers are involved in ministry, they are not loafers or unemployed. Rather, as those who have experienced the parousia, they are the people best suited to lead the church and to expect a salary from it. They impose their ministerial services on the church because of their superior spiritual experiences. While few interpreters have adopted this view, it holds together the two issues the letter raises about them in a more coherent fashion than other hypotheses.

2.10. 1 Timothy. While interpreters have often dealt with the opponents of the Pastorals as a single group, this article will examine each letter individually before deciding whether they oppose a single group. Those who identify the Pastorals' opponents as a single group often identify them as adherents to a type of Gnosticism that incorporated aspects of Judaism (Haufe; Oberlinner). Other interpreters identify the opponents of 1 Timothy and Titus together because issues of interpreting the law are present in both (Murphy-O'Connor; Müller). Yet others combine 1 and 2 Timothy to find elders who possess an overrealized eschatology and urge ascetic practices related to the law (Fee). Those who confine their investigation to 1 Timothy find different opponents. Some find libertines who disparage the law (McEleney), while others see ascetics who claim esoteric knowledge (Johnson). Yet others find an overrealized eschatology that prohibits *marriage because the end has come and there is to be no marriage in the final age (Lane).

When 1 Timothy speaks of opponents, it often employs stock polemical characterizations (1 Tim 1:4, 19-20; 6:3-5). Still, readers do get some description of them. The central problem is the way they interpret the law (1 Tim 1:6-7). The letter rejects their reading of it but affirms the value of the law (1 Tim 1:8). The only objectionable teaching that 1 Timothy mentions explicitly is that they forbid marriage (1 Tim 4:1-3). They may interpret the law in a way that prohibits it, but that remains unclear. One cannot assume that they forbid it out of an asceticism based on a devaluation of the world, though that is possible. Yet even 1 Timothy says that those who have once committed themselves to be widows cannot marry (1 Tim 5:11). Given that interpretation of the law is a central issue, the affirmation that all created things can be eaten in 1 Timothy 4:4-5 suggests that they require observance of Mosaic dietary laws. Describing their teaching as myths (1 Tim 1:3-4; 4:7-8) does not clarify the content of the teaching because this is a well-known trope to denigrate the position of one's opponents. Further, that they refer to their teaching as "knowledge" (1 Tim 6:20-21) is not an indication that they are Gnostics because many groups identified their teaching in this way.

Perhaps surprisingly, the letter makes no connection between the false teachers and the "widows" the letter gives instruction about (1 Tim 5:3-16). The only common issue is marriage. Since those enrolled as widows vow not to marry (1 Tim 5:11-12), this could be the prohibition against marriage that is mentioned in 1 Timothy 4:1-3. But when he goes on to say what might happen if younger women are enrolled, he mentions only gossiping and being busybodies, not spreading false teaching. Given the emphatic assertion of Paul's mission to Gentiles and the allusion to dietary rules, these teachers are opponents because they require Gentiles to observe more of the law than 1 Timothy thinks they should. They also urge people not to marry, but it remains unclear whether this is related to their interpretation of the law.

2.11. 2 Timothy. Some interpreters find 2 Timothy rejecting opponents who have an overrealized eschatology. Some contend that this eschatology includes seeing the material world as evil and so rejecting the *resurrection of the body. Others propose that their overrealized eschatology led them to advocate emancipation for *women (Müller). Luke Timothy Johnson, on the other hand, argues that the opponents are simply a foil the author uses to clarify his image of the ideal minister.

In 2 Timothy 2:16-18, the author describes people who quarrel about words and say that the resurrection has already happened, but the author does not say what they claim to experience in this resurrection. Even if this is the author's interpretation of what they claim, it shows they have an overrealized eschatology. Other comments about these opponents mention their quarreling about words but also leave an opening for them to repent (2 Tim 2:23-26). The letter's use of stock polemical charges does not allow for adding other features to their teaching. Even the comment that they are influential among women is a stock accusation (2 Tim 3:6) that appears in a list of such stock characterizations. One is left, then, being able to say that they advocate an overrealized eschatology and seem to engage in quarrelsome debate about it.

2.12. Titus. Interpreters who do not assume the same identity for the opponents of all the Pastorals consistently see the opponents of Titus advocating that Gentiles take up parts of the law that the author thinks they must not (Fee). Walter Lock argues that they require observance of the Mosaic food and *purity laws but not circumcision. He adds that they live immoral lives. Johnson contends that those advocating additional Torah observance are not church members but members of the Jewish community seeking converts to their synagogues.

Titus identifies the teachers it rejects as "the circumcision" (Titus 1:10-12). This shows that they are Jews. It then warns against talking about Jewish myths and obeying human commands. The only hint about the content of these commands is the assertion that all things are clean to those who are clean (Titus 1:15). The mention of "the circumcision" in the context indicates that these teachers urge the church to adopt purity regulations from the law. This paragraph also identifies these teachers are Cretans, so they are local teachers rather than part of a traveling group that opposes Paul's teaching. Further, Titus is told to rebuke them with the goal of making their teaching healthy (Titus 1:13; 3:10). This suggests that they are church members. The only other direct statements about these teachers also associate them with arguments about the law (Titus 3:9-11) and warn against disputes about genealogies. While some have taken this to refer to the genealogies of heavenly beings that appear in some Gnostic texts (Hanson), no other elements of Gnosticism are opposed in the letter. These disputes seem rather to be related to interpreting the law. The opponents of this letter are local teachers who urge all believers to adopt some purity regulations from the Mosaic law. Thus, they are not part of a common opponent that all the Pastorals oppose, even if there are commonalities between them and the opponents of 1 Timothy.

3. Conclusion.

This survey of the Pauline letters indicates that there were two anti-Pauline movements: one that advocated that Gentiles observe the law more as Jews do, including being circumcised and keeping the Sabbath and food laws; and one that rejected the form of Paul's apostleship and argued that the lives of apostles should appear powerful to be demonstrations of the Spirit's power. Those who urge different Torah observance appear in Galatians and Philippians 3; those with a different understanding of apostleship appear in 2 Corinthians. While other letters address a range of problems, including some that touch on some of the same issues as these movements, the advocates of the alternative teachings in them do not seem to be part of an anti-Pauline movement. Their teaching arises from their attempts to understand and practice the faith. Thus the Pauline letters oppose them, even when they do not intend to oppose Paul's teaching. Still, Paul saw their teaching as harmful to the church and so urged his churches to reject them.

See also APOSTLE; CIRCUMCISION; COLOSSIANS, LETTER TO THE; CORINTHIANS, SECOND LETTER TO THE; GALATIANS, LETTER TO THE; GENTILES; GNOSIS, GNOSTICISM; JUDAIZERS; LAW; PASTORAL EPISTLES; PHILIPPIANS, LETTER TO THE; THESSALONIANS, LETTERS TO THE.

BIBLIOGRAPHY. **C. E. Arnold,** *The Colossian Syncretism: The Interface Between Christianity and Folk Belief at Colossae* (Grand Rapids, MI: Baker, 1996); **A. J. Bandstra,** "Did the Colossian Errorists Need a Mediator?," in *New Dimensions in New Testament Study*, ed. R. N. Longenecker and M. C. Tenney (Grand Rapids, MI: Zondervan, 1974), 329-43; **J. M. G. Barclay,** "Mirror-Reading a Polemical Letter: Galatians as a Test Case," *JSNT* 31 (1987): 73-93; **C. K. Barrett,** "Paul's Opponents in 2 Corinthians," *NTS* 17 (1971): 233-54; **J. W. Barrier,** "Visions of Weakness: Apocalyptic Genre and the Identification of Paul's Opponents in 2 Corinthians 12:1-6," *ResQ* 47 (2005): 33-42; **W. Bauer,** *Rechtgläubigkeit und Ketzerei im Ältesten Christentum* (Tübingen: Mohr, 1934); **F. C. Baur,** *Paul, The Apostle of Jesus Christ—His Life and Work, His Epistles and Doctrine*, 2nd ed., trans. E. Zeller, 2 vols. (1876; repr., Peabody, MA: Hendrickson, 2003); **M. Becker,** "A Template for Picturing Rivals? Paul's Depictions of Opponents and the Elements of Anti-Sophistic Polemic," *Biblische Notizen* 180 (2019): 105-29; **K. Berger,** "Die implitzen Gegner: zur Methode des Erschliessens von 'Gegner' in neutestamentlichen Texten," in *Kirche*, ed. D. Lührmann and G. Strecker (Tübingen: Mohr Siebeck, 1980), 372-400; **T. R. Blanton IV,** "Spirit and Covenant Renewal: A Theologoumenon of Paul's Opponents in 2 Corinthians," *JBL* 129 (2010): 129-51; **N. Dahl,** "Paul and the Church at Corinth According to 1 Corinthians 1:10–4:21," in *Christian History and Interpretation*, ed. W. R. Farmer, C. F. D. Moule, and R. Niehbuhr (Cambridge: Cambridge University Press, 1967), 313-35; **R. E. DeMaris,** *The Colossian Controversy: Wisdom in Dispute at Colossae*, JSNTSup 96 (Sheffield: Sheffield Academic Press, 1994); **P. B. Duff,** "Paul's Elusive Opponents: Reading 2 Cor 3 Without the 'False Apostles' of 2 Cor 11:13," *BR* 54 (2009): 37-59; **J. D. G. Dunn,** "Works of the Law and the Curse of the Law (Gal 3:10-14)," *NTS* 31 (1985): 523-42; idem, "The Colossian Philosophy: A Confident Jewish Apologia," *Bib* 76 (1995): 153-81; **G. Fee,** *1 and 2 Timothy, Titus*, rev. ed., NIBC (Peabody, MA: Hendrickson, 1988); **F. O. Francis,** "Humility and Angelic Worship in Col 2:18," in *Conflict at Colossae: A Problem in the Interpretation of Early Christianity Illustrated by Selected Modern Studies*, ed. W. A. Meeks and F. O. Francis, Sources for Biblical Study 4 (Missoula, MT: Scholars Press, 1973), 163-96; **D. Georgi,** *The Opponents of Paul in Second Corinthians*, trans. H. Attridge et al. (Philadelphia: Fortress, 1986); **M. Goulder,** "The Visionaries of Laodicea," *JSNT* 43 (1991): 15-39; idem, *St. Paul Versus St. Peter: A Tale of Two Missions* (Louisville, KY: Westminster, 1994); **S. Hafemann,** *Suffering and the Spirit: An Exegetical Study of II Cor. 2:14–3:3 Within the Context of the Corinthian Correspondence*, WUNT (Tübingen: Mohr, 1986); **A. T. Hanson,** *The Pastoral Epistles*, New Century Bible Commentary (Grand Rapids, MI: Eerdmans, 1982); **G. Haufe,** "Gnostische Irrlehre und ihre Abwehr in den Pastoralbriefen," in *Gnosis und Neues Testament: Studien aus Religionswissenschaft und Theologie*, ed. K.-W. Tröger (Gutersloher: Gerd Mohn, 1973), 325-39; **G. Holland,** *The Tradition That You Received from Us: 2 Thessalonians in the Pauline Tradition*, HUT 2 (Tübingen: Mohr Siebeck, 1988); **G. Howard,** *Crisis in Galatia*, 2nd ed., SNTSMS 3 (Cambridge: Cambridge University Press, 1990); **R. Jewett,** "The Agitators and the Galatian Congregation," *NTS* 17 (1971): 198-212; idem, *The Thessalonian Correspondence: Pauline Rhetoric and Millenarian Piety* (Philadelphia: Fortress, 1986); **L. T. Johnson,** *The Writings of the New Testament*, rev. ed. (Philadelphia: Fortress, 1999); **E. Käsemann,** "Die Legitimität des Apostels: Eine Untersuchung zu 2 Korinther 10-13," *ZNW* 41 (1942): 33-71; **H. Koester,** "The Purpose of the Polemic of a Pauline Fragment (Philippians III)," *NTS* 8 (1961–1962): 317-32; **W. L. Lane,** "1 Tim IV.1-3: An Early Instance of Over-realized Eschatology?," *NTS* 11 (1965): 164-67; **B. C. Lategan,** "The Argumentative Situation of Galatians," in *The Galatians Debate: Contemporary Issues in*

Rhetorical and Historical Interpretation, ed. M. D. Nanos (Peabody, MA: Hendrickson, 2002), 383-95; **J. B. Lightfoot,** *Saint Paul's Epistle to the Galatians* (London: Macmillan, 1865); **W. Lock,** *A Critical and Exegetical Commentary on the Pastoral Epistles*, ICC (New York: Scribner's, 1924); **G. Lüdemann,** *Opposition to Paul in Jewish Christianity* (Minneapolis: Fortress, 1989); **W. Lütgert,** *Freiheitspredigt und Schwarmgeister in Korinth: Ein Beitrag zur Charakteristik der Christuspartei*, BFCT (Gütersloh: C. Bertelsmann, 1908); **A. J. Malherbe,** "'Gentle as a Nurse': The Cynic Background to 1 Thessalonians ii," *NovT* 12 (1970): 203-17; idem, *The Letters to the Thessalonians: A New Translation with Introduction and Commentary*, AB (New York: Doubleday, 2000); **R. P. Martin,** *Ephesians, Colossians, and Philemon*, Interpretation (Atlanta: John Knox, 1991); **T. Martin,** *By Philosophy and Vain Deceit: Colossians as a Response to a Cynic Critique*, JSNTSup 118 (Sheffield: Sheffield Academic Press, 1996); **J. L. Martyn,** "Apocalyptic Antinomies in Paul's Letter to the Galatians," *NTS* 31 (1985): 410-24; idem, "A Law-Observant Mission to Gentiles: The Background of Galatians," *SJT* 38 (1985): 307-24; **W. Marxsen,** *Der zweite Thessalonicherbrief*, ZBK (Zürich: Theologischer Verlag, 1982); **N. J. McEleney,** "Vice Lists of the Pastoral Epistles," *CBQ* 36 (1974): 205-10; **U. Müller,** *Zur frühchristlichen Theologiegeschichte* (Gütersloher: Gerd Mohn, 1976); **J. Murphy-O'Connor,** "2 Timothy Contrasted with 1 Timothy and Titus," *RB* 98 (1991): 403-18; **M. Nanos,** "The Inter- and Intra-Jewish Political Context of Paul's Letter to the Galatians," in *The Galatians Debate: Contemporary Issues in Rhetorical and Historical Interpretation*, ed. M. D. Nanos (Peabody, MA: Hendrickson, 2002), 146-59; **L. Oberlinner,** *Die Pastoralbriefe*, vol. 1, HThKNT 11/2 (Freiburg: Herder, 1988); **B. J. Oropeza,** *Apostasy in the New Testament Communities*, vol. 2, *Jews, Gentiles, and the Opponents of Paul: The Pauline Letters* (Eugene, OR: Cascade, 2012); **S. E. Porter,** ed., *Paul and His Opponents*, Pauline Studies 2 (Leiden: Brill, 2005); **B. Reicke,** *Diakonie, Festfreude und Zelos in Verbingung mit der altchristlichen Agapenfeier* (Uppsala: Lundequistska, 1951); **R. Russell,** "The Idle in 2 Thessalonians 3:6-12: An Eschatological or Social Problem?," *NTS* 34 (1988): 105-19; **T. J. Sappington,** *Revelation and Redemption at Colossae*, JSNTSup 53 (Sheffield: JSOT Press, 1991); **W. Schmithals,** *Gnosticism in Corinth* (Nashville: Abingdon, 1971); idem, *Paul and the Gnostics* (Nashville: Abingdon, 1972); **E. Schweizer,** "Die 'Elemente der Welt' Gal 4,3. 9; Kol 2,8. 20," in *Verborum Veritas*, ed. O. Böcher and K. Haacker (Wuppertal: Theologischer Verlag Rolf Brockhaus, 1970), 245-59; **J. L. Sumney,** *"Servants of Satan," "False Brothers," and Other Opponents of Paul*, JSNTSup 188 (Sheffield: Sheffield Academic Press, 1999); idem, "Studying Paul's Opponents: Advances and Challenges," in *Paul and His Opponents*, ed. S. Porter, Pauline Studies 2 (Leiden: Brill, 2005), 7-58; **N. Walter,** "Paulus und die Gegner des Christus-evangeliums in Galatien," in *L'Apôtre Paul: personnalité, style, et conception du ministère*, ed. A. Vanhoye (Leuven: Leuven University Press, 1986), 351-56; **F. Watson,** *Paul, Judaism, and the Gentiles: Beyond the New Perspective*, 2nd ed. (Grand Rapids, MI: Eerdmans, 2007); **N. T. Wright,** *Colossians and Philemon*, TNTC (Downers Grove, IL: IVP Academic, 2008).

J. L. Sumney

ORDER. *See* CHURCH STRUCTURE; MINISTRY.

ORDINATION. *See* CHURCH STRUCTURE; TEACHING, TEACHERS.

P

PAGANISM. *See* IDOLATRY; RELIGIONS, GRECO-ROMAN; URBAN SETTING OF PAUL'S CHURCHES.

PAROUSIA. *See* CHRISTOLOGY; ESCHATOLOGY.

PARTICULARISM. *See* ELECTION AND PREDESTINATION; UNIVERSALISM.

PASSOVER. *See* LORD'S SUPPER; SACRIFICE, OFFERING.

PASTOR, PAUL AS

Given the *apostle Paul's care for churches and efforts to help them grow in *Christ, it seems obvious that Paul was a pastor. But Paul's pastoral efforts were distinctive. They were not exactly like what a parish pastor is expected to do today. Nevertheless, what Paul did to express his care for churches, combined with how he describes his work with churches and the purpose of his apostolic *ministry, make it clear that Paul served as a pastor in an innovative and uncommon way in response to the particular needs of the geographically scattered churches and individuals entrusted to his care.

1. Was Paul a Pastor?
2. What Did Paul Do as a Pastor?
3. How Did Paul Talk About His Pastoral Work?
4. Why Was Paul a Pastor?

1. Was Paul a Pastor?

The apostle Paul had pastoral relationships with the churches he had planted as well as some that had been founded by others (Rome, for example). He demonstrated heartfelt care for churches as he sought to help them grow in Christ. Were it not for his pastoral concern for churches, it is doubtful that much would be known about Paul apart from Acts, since his *letters were written for pastoral purposes. Thus, it is tempting to call Paul a pastor without qualification.

But that identification is not as obvious as it might seem. For one thing, Paul never refers to himself as a pastor by using the Greek word *poimēn*, which literally means "shepherd." In Ephesians 4:11 Paul does use *poimēn* in the phrase "pastors and teachers." In 1 Corinthians 9:7 he speaks of one who tends a flock, but in a literal sense. Otherwise, the only place in the NT where Paul uses explicit shepherding language is in Acts 20, in his farewell speech to the Ephesian elders (Acts 20:17-38). He urges the elders to keep watch over the "flock" and to "shepherd the *church of *God" (Acts 20:28). Yet, he says this work is what the elders do as "overseers," not pastors.

Scholars refer to three letters attributed to Paul as "Pastoral Epistles." Yet, 1 Timothy, 2 Timothy, and Titus are not so much letters in which Paul is pastoring churches as they are guidance for two of Paul's pastoral protégés. Today one might call those letters "coaching epistles" or "mentoring epistles." If one is interested in how and why Paul served as a pastor to churches, the Pastoral Epistles are not nearly as helpful as the other Pauline letters.

When one calls Paul a pastor, one is applying a term from experience that Paul did not use for himself. This is not necessarily wrong, since one can also call Paul a theologian, a missionary, and a church planter. Paul did not use any of those titles either. But one must be aware of what is meant by the word *pastor* and how the present meaning might be both similar to and different from how Paul actually functioned in his pastoral role. For example, one might envision pastoring as focused mainly on individuals who need "pastoral care." Yet, while Paul surely attended to people in a personal way (see, e.g., Phil 2:25-30), his version of pastoral care was mainly focused on churches and their cultures. Similarly, for people today the word *pastor* usually identifies someone who serves in one particular church, often for an extended period of time. Paul, on the contrary, did not spend long periods of time in single churches and functioned in a pastoral role to many churches at once, some he had founded (Thessalonians, Corinthians) and some he had not (Colossians, Romans). One could even say without exaggeration that Paul was the original multisite pastor.

So, if one wants to understand Paul as a pastor, one must pay close attention to what he actually did as a pastor, how he talked about his pastoral work, and why he believed pastoring was an essential element of his apostolic ministry.

2. What Did Paul Do as a Pastor?

It is helpful to think of Paul's pastoral work in light of what he did while physically present with churches and what he did when he was separated from them by distance.

2.1. Pastoring in Person. There is not a detailed description of Paul's in-person pastoral efforts. One can glean bits and pieces from Acts, though the focus there is on Paul as a traveling missionary preacher. From Paul's letters one can sometimes find references to his in-person care for his churches.

The most extensive description of Paul's on-site pastoral work comes in 1 Thessalonians, where he reports on what he did when he was present with his converts in Thessalonica. Part of this autobiographical report focuses on his evangelistic efforts (for example, 1 Thess 1:5, 9; 2:3-7), but it also points to ways Paul cared for to the Thessalonians after they had welcomed the *gospel. These include not making apostolic demands but being gentle as a nursing mother (1 Thess 2:7), sharing not only the gospel but also Paul's own soul with those who had become dear to him (1 Thess 2:8), working hard both at his day job (*tentmaking) and in his church-planting task (1 Thess 2:9), exemplifying right living (1 Thess 2:10), urging and encouraging his converts like a father (1 Thess 2:11), and giving theological/ethical instruction (1 Thess 4:2).

Paul's description of his evangelistic and pastoral work with the Thessalonians is shaped by his awareness of others in the Greco-Roman world who did things that were similar to his apostolic efforts. A. J. Malherbe has shown that, in particular, Paul interacts with ideas and practices associated with contemporaneous popular philosophers. Paul presents himself in a way that is similar to the ideal Cynic philosopher, who acts with integrity to improve the lives of those to whom he preaches (see Dio Chrysostom, *Alex.* 11-12). Yet Paul also distinguishes himself even from the Cynic ideal. His open confession of deep *love for the Thessalonian Christians, for example, is something that the Cynics would have avoided because, in their view, such affection would keep a philosopher from saying the hard things that needed to be said to those who needed to hear them. Paul's love for his converts does not seem to have squelched his ability to say difficult things, however (see Galatians, for example).

That Paul highly valued his in-person pastoral interactions with churches is clear in his letters. Sometimes he mentions specific plans to visit his churches (1 Cor 16:5-7; 2 Cor 12:14; Philem 22). More often he speaks of his *hope or longing to see people (Rom 1:11-14; 15:22-24; Phil 2:24; 1 Thess 2:18; 3:6). Paul even shares his earnest *prayer that he might see his converts "face to face" (1 Thess 3:10).

2.2. Pastoring from a Distance. When Paul left one of the churches he had founded, he did not assume that his work with them was done. On the contrary, he continued to have pastoral relationships with his own churches and even added to those relationships churches he had never visited.

2.2.1. Sending Emissaries. One of the chief ways Paul pastored churches was by sending emissaries who represented him and his interests (1 Cor 4:17; 2 Cor 9:3; 1 Thess 3:2). These *coworkers would also report back to Paul on what they had found in the churches to which they were sent (1 Thess 3:6). They could implement specific projects of Paul, such as raising funds for the *collection for *Jerusalem (2 Cor 8:6), but they also acted in pastoral roles as they sought to "strengthen and exhort" church members "for the sake of [their] *faith" (1 Thess 3:2). While some have argued that Paul's representatives were an inferior substitute for his personal presence, given the function and esteem of envoys in the Greco-Roman world as well as Paul's high regard for his coworkers, it seems likely that Paul's emissaries were received by his churches as respected representatives of Paul and trusted pastors in their own right (Mitchell).

2.2.2. Supporting Local Leaders. Through his letters, Paul does acknowledge local leaders in churches, supporting them and their work (Rom 16:3-16; 1 Cor 16:15-18; Phil 4:2-3). In 1 Thessalonians he urges his converts to respect and esteem "those who labor among you and who are leading you in the *Lord" (1 Thess 5:12-13). Yet there is no certain evidence that Paul himself established local leaders in the Thessalonian church when he was there (or in any other church he planted). Moreover, much of what one today would identify as pastoral work Paul assigned to the whole community, not just to its leaders. All the "brothers and sisters" in Thessalonica were to "admonish the disorderly, comfort the discouraged, and help the weak" (1 Thess 5:14). Reading between the lines, one senses that when present with his churches, Paul taught their members to exercise shared *leadership and mutual care as they were gifted by the *Holy Spirit (see 1 Cor 12–14).

2.2.3. Praying. Paul's letters repeatedly refer to his prayers for churches, including those he planted (1 Thess 1:2; 3:11-13) and those he did not (Rom 1:8; Col 1:3-14). His prayers incorporate consistent thanksgiving (Eph 1:16; Phil 1:3; 1 Thess 1:2) and intentional intercession (2 Cor 13:7-9; Eph 1:16-19; 3:18-19). Paul may have regarded his prayers as the most powerful and effective tool he had for pastoring at a distance because he knew that the health and growth of a church was ultimately God's responsibility (1 Cor 1:4-9; 1 Thess 3:11-13; see also Wiles). Paul was not so much on a *mission from God as he was participating in God's mission (McKnight).

2.2.4. Writing Letters. It would be easy to take for granted that Paul pastored churches through writing letters. But in doing so one would miss the extraordinary technological innovation employed by this distant pastor. There was little or no precedent in the Greco-Roman world for Paul's use of personal letters for community organizing. Yet he creatively used the cutting-edge technology of his day, including writing tools and materials as well as the extensive Roman transportation system, to exercise his pastoral concern from a distance. While relying heavily on this technology-based solution, Paul recognized its limitations, which helps to explain why his letters often referred to plans for future in-person visits (Rom 1:9-15; 1 Thess 3:10-11).

All of Paul's letters might be called pastoral epistles since all were written as an expression of his care for churches, except, ironically, the so-called Pastoral Epistles (1 Timothy, 2 Timothy, Titus), which are addressed to individuals who served in pastoral roles. The letter to Philemon is addressed to one individual but also to "the church in [Philemon's] house" (Philem 1-2).

Paul's letters are situational in that they were written in response to particular situations faced by churches. They are not theological tractates so much as pastorally shaped communications that focus on the needs, crises, challenges, and opportunities faced by churches. The one possible exception to this rule is Ephesians, which was probably written as a circular letter to several churches (Roberts 1992). On at least one occasion, Paul received a letter from one of his churches, which enabled him to respond to the various challenges they faced (1 Cor 7:1).

2.2.5. Being Spiritually Present Though Physically Absent. In writing to the Corinthians, Paul claims that though he is "absent in *body" he is "present in spirit" (1 Cor 5:3). Thus, when the Christians in Corinth are assembled Paul can say, "my spirit is present with the power of our Lord Jesus" (1 Cor 5:4). This means more than when someone says, "You're in my thoughts" (Wiles; Fee). Though Paul does not explain how exactly this happens, he does believe that he can be spiritually present with churches through the medium of the Holy Spirit and the power of the Lord Jesus.

3. How Did Paul Talk About His Pastoral Work?

Paul did not use the title of pastor for himself, even when he was doing what one would call pastoral work with his churches. He preferred other ways of talking about how he functioned in a pastoral way and how he thought of himself as he did so. The most significant of these titles are drawn from the family, in that Paul portrayed himself as a father, mother, brother, and even a child. His use of family imagery not only shaped his pastoral role with his people but also helped to nurture their growth as cultures of Christlikeness.

3.1. Paul as Father. In 1 Thessalonians 2:11-12 Paul describes his pastoral work while in Thessalonica by using the analogy of a father: "As you know, we treated each one of you like a father with his own children, exhorting, encouraging, and urging that you walk worthy of God, who is calling you into his own *kingdom and *glory." As in the Greco-Roman world, where a father was primarily responsible for the instruction and moral upbringing of his children, Paul accepted this responsibility as the spiritual father of the Thessalonians.

As father to his converts, Paul regards them as children in need of nurture and instruction (1 Cor 3:1-3; 1 Thess 2:11-12). He became their father "through the gospel," that is, through *preaching that led to conversion (1 Cor 4:15). For this reason, Paul claims to have a unique relationship with his children in Christ, one that gives him the *freedom to admonish them and gives them the obligation to imitate him, just like Roman children were expected to imitate their own fathers (1 Cor 4:16). As Paul pictured his pastoral/parental relationship with his converts, *imitation was an essential element. He did not just instruct them with words but also with the model of his life (1 Thess 1:3-6; 2:10-12). Yet, for Paul, the imitation expected of his spiritual children was qualified by their primary relationship with Christ (Williams). Thus, he writes that the Thessalonians "became imitators of us and of the Lord" (1 Thess 1:6). He urges the Corinthians to be "imitators of me, as I am of Christ" (1 Cor 11:1). In Ephesians, which was to be read in several churches Paul did not plant and therefore for whom he was not their father, he writes, "Therefore be imitators of God, as beloved children" (Eph 5:1). He does not in this case call people to imitate him.

Paul thinks of himself as father not only of churches he planted but also of individuals whom he led to Christ and/or with whom he had a deep personal relationship, including Timothy (1 Cor 4:17), Titus (Titus 1:4), and Onesimus (Philem 10).

*3.2. **Paul as Mother.*** Paul also adopts motherly images to describe his pastoral relationships with his churches. In 1 Corinthians 3:1-2, for example, he speaks of feeding his "infants in Christ" with milk, which in the ancient world was something a wet nurse or mother would do. Paul tells the Galatians that he is "again having labor pains until Christ is formed in you" (Gal 4:19). The most striking use of mothering imagery appears in 1 Thessalonians, where Paul begins by saying that he did not exercise the heavy authority of an apostle. Rather, "we were gentle among you, like a nursing mother cherishing her own children" (1 Thess 2:7). As a spiritual mother to the Thessalonians, Paul was not only gentle and nurturing but also vulnerable and loving: "Caring for you so much, we were pleased to share with you not only the gospel of God, but also our own souls, because you had become beloved to us" (1 Thess 2:8). Popular philosophers in Paul's day sometimes used the image of the nurse in their discussions of how best to serve people (Malherbe). But they insisting on balancing gentleness with harshness. Paul's unabashed use of mothering imagery, emphasizing both tender care and personal vulnerability, was exceptional (Roberts 1992).

*3.3. **Paul as Brother.*** Sixty-nine times in his letters Paul addresses his recipients as "brothers and sisters" (*adelphoi*). This is by far the most common way for Paul to identify those to whom he is writing. It is also a way of qualifying Paul's paternal relationship with his converts. On the one hand, as their parent he has a unique responsibility for instructing, nurturing, and loving his children in Christ. On the other hand, as their brother, Paul understands their relationship as one of shared experience as well as mutual edification and care. Paul's brothers and sisters, for example, are encouraged to pray for him (Rom 15:30; 2 Thess 3:1), to admonish one another (Rom 15:14; 1 Thess 5:14), to minister to each other through spiritual *gifts (Rom 1:11-13; 1 Cor 14:26), and to know about Paul's struggles and vulnerability (2 Cor 1:8; 1 Thess 2:17-18). Even as Paul loved his brothers and sisters in Christ (Phil 4:1), so they loved him (1 Thess 3:6-8).

Yet, for Paul, the loving relationship he had with his siblings in Christ was second in importance to the loving relationship they had with God. In the opening verses of 1 Thessalonians, Paul addresses his recipients as "brothers and sisters beloved by God" (1 Thess 1:4; see also 2 Thess 2:13). It is striking that Paul did not refer to them as "my beloved brothers and sisters." The love of God, their truest Father, matters more than all human loves. Paul the pastor is committed to helping his people know the love of God most of all. He is seeking to encourage among his churches a culture of mutuality and maturity, in which his brothers and sisters see themselves most of all as children of God through Christ.

*3.4. **Paul as Child.*** Though a few commentators and translations (NIV, NLT) believe Paul refers to himself as a young child in 1 Thessalonians 2:7, the reading "we were gentle among you" is preferable to "we were infants among you" (see Malherbe 2000). Yet, no matter how one translates 1 Thessalonians 2:7, only ten verses later Paul does speak as if he were a child, an orphaned child at that: "Brothers and sisters, having been orphaned from you for a while, in person, not in heart, we longed most eagerly to see your face" (1 Thess 2:17). In the previous verses Paul portrays himself as a mother and father to the Thessalonians. Why this sudden and surprising shift to "orphan"? On the one hand, he uses this unexpected language to emphasize his feelings of helplessness and vulnerability in being separated from his converts against his will (1 Thess 2:17-20). On the other hand, the familial sense of the verb "to be orphaned" strengthens the emotional bond between Paul and the Thessalonians, who now play the role of Paul's parents. Like children separated from their actual parents, Paul's heart remains connected to those for whom he longs with great eagerness. The vulnerability of Paul and his dependence on the Thessalonians is reiterated several verses later when he writes, "For now we live, if you are standing firm in the Lord" (1 Thess 3:8).

Paul's self-portrait as an orphaned child accentuates the tensions between the various family images that convey Paul's pastoral self-understanding, shape his relationships with churches, and, indeed, help to shape the cultures of these churches. Paul as father accepts responsibility and authority to instruct, admonish, and mold his churches. Paul as mother does this work with gentleness and self-giving love. Paul as brother nurtures mutuality with his converts, helping them to live as beloved children of God who serve and care for each other in the power of the Spirit. Paul as child is dependent on his churches emotionally and vocationally. Even his ultimate success as a pastor hinges on their faithfulness and growth in Christ (1 Thess 2:19-20; 3:5, 8-13; 5:23).

3.5. Paul as Builder. In addition to family language, Paul also talks about his work in terms of building. In 1 Corinthians 3 he refers to the Corinthian church as "God's building" (1 Cor 3:9). From this metaphor Paul launches into a brief description of his work as a "wise, expert builder" who "laid a foundation" for the church (1 Cor 3:10). That foundation is none other than "Jesus Christ" (1 Cor 3:11). Anyone who builds on the foundation, such as others who exercise a pastoral role in a church, will have their work evaluated in that future day when God judges all things (1 Cor 3:12-15). Presumably that will include the pastoral work Paul did when building on foundations, both the ones he laid and those laid by others. Though in his church-planting strategy Paul seeks not to build on the foundations laid by others (Rom 15:20), he has no hesitation about building by letter in churches founded by other people (Rome, Colossae).

According to Paul, the Lord gave him authority for "building up" his churches, not for tearing them down (2 Cor 10:8). One way Paul did this was by teaching and encouraging the members of the churches to build up each other. He affirms the Thessalonians for encouraging and edifying each other (1 Thess 5:11). To the Romans he writes, "Let us seek after the things that make for *peace and mutual upbuilding" (Rom 14:19). In Ephesians, Paul explains that the work of church leaders, including "pastors and teachers," is "to equip the saints for the work of ministry, for building up the *body of Christ" (Eph 4:11-12). The church, as the body of Christ, will only grow up to be like Christ "as each part is working properly," which will enable the body to "build itself up in love" (Eph 4:15-16). Thus Paul is not just the builder of churches. He is also the building expert who trains and encourages others to build as well.

3.6. Paul as Farmer. In 1 Corinthians 3, before using building imagery to describe his pastoral work, Paul portrays himself as a farmer. More specifically, he is the one who planted. Apollos, another first-century servant of Christ, is watering the seeds Paul planted (1 Cor 3:6). Paul's point is that neither the planter nor the waterer counts for much since God alone makes the seeds grow (1 Cor 3:7). Those who work on God's farm should be seen as co-laboring servants (1 Cor 3:9).

3.7. Paul as Teacher. Only twice in his letters does Paul refer to himself as a teacher, in both cases associating his teaching effort with his appointment as a "preacher" and an "apostle" (1 Tim 2:7; 2 Tim 1:11). Yet Paul clearly functioned as a teacher of churches. This is evident not only from the extent to which teaching fills his letters but also in how he describes his work. He teaches his "ways in Christ Jesus . . . everywhere in every church" (1 Cor 4:17). He teaches "everyone in all *wisdom" (Col 1:28) and offers ample "instructions" (1 Cor 11:17; 1 Thess 4:2). Paul teaches not only through his content but also through his personal example. Imitation is central to his teaching strategy (Williams). Moreover, as in the case of Paul the builder, he is not only a teacher but also a trainer of teachers. All Christians should aspire to "teach and admonish each other in all wisdom" (Col 3:16) as they are inspired by the Spirit (1 Cor 14:26). Paul does not envision his churches as forever dependent on him as their only or primary teacher. God will teach them and empower them to teach each other through the power of the Spirit (1 Thess 4:10; 1 Cor 12:28; 14:12, 26).

3.8. Paul as Apostle. Paul understood himself to be "an apostle of Christ Jesus by the will of God" (1 Cor 1:1). He had been set apart by the Lord "for the gospel of God," which he preached in order "to bring about the obedience of faith among all the *Gentiles" (Rom 1:1, 5). Whatever Paul did that one would call pastoral was an essential element of his apostolic ministry. Because Paul was an apostle, he was therefore a pastor.

Yet, it has been common, both in the academy and in the church, to see Paul's apostolic calling as mainly evangelistic. He was called, after all, to preach the gospel. Because the gospel not only saved individuals but also immersed them in the church, Paul was secondarily a church planter. Exercising pastoral care for churches has been seen as a minor aspect of Paul's apostolic work. Of course, scholars have been enthusiastic about Paul's theological efforts, though often ignoring the extent to which the letters that contain Paul's theology are profoundly pastoral in their purpose and content. In order better to grasp the extent to which pastoral work was, in Paul's understanding, an absolutely essential part of his apostolic *calling, one needs to consider the question, Why was Paul a pastor?

4. Why Was Paul a Pastor?

If pastoring is about caring for people who have already accepted the gospel, if it is a matter of helping both individuals and churches to be formed in Christ, then there is little doubt that Paul was a pastor, even though his particular practice of multisite pastoring differed in several ways from what most pastors do today. Yet, since Paul talked about his apostolic mission primarily as preaching the gospel, and since he was eager to preach throughout the Roman world rather than settling down in one particular church or region (Rom 15:18-20, 23-24), one may wonder why he valued pastoral work with existing churches. Why, for example, did Paul feel "daily pressure, namely [his] care for all the churches" (2 Cor 11:28)? Why did he not simply move on after planting a church and leave that church in God's capable hands?

Paul embraced his pastoral responsibility because he believed that in fact God had entrusted churches into Paul's capable hands. Just because his preaching led to converts who gathered as a church did not mean Paul's work in a given city was done. This is clear from what Paul writes in several of his letters. For example, he explains to the Thessalonians that he sent Timothy to "find out about your faith; I was afraid that somehow the tempter had tempted you and that our labor had been in vain" (1 Thess 3:5). So, even though Paul had been successful in evangelism and church planting, if the church he left behind did not thrive, then Paul's work would have been in vain.

As Paul was writing to the Thessalonians, he admitted, "For now we live, if you stand firm in the Lord" (1 Thess 3:8). His current well-being was dependent on the continued existence and thriving of the church. But Paul did not see his pastoral efforts only in terms of their present-day flourishing. Rather, he looked ahead to the day when the Lord would come again. At that future moment the Thessalonian church would be Paul's "hope or *joy or crown of boasting" and his "glory and joy" (1 Thess 2:19-20). For this reason, he prayed that the Lord would "so strengthen" the hearts of his converts "in *holiness so that [they] might be blameless before God" when Jesus comes (1 Thess 3:13).

Part of pastoring churches so that they might become fully holy is helping both individual Christians and whole churches to become mature. In his letter to the Colossians Paul explains his ministry in this way: "We proclaim Christ, warning every person and teaching every person with all wisdom, in order that we might present every person mature in Christ. To this end I labor and struggle with his energy that is energizing me powerfully" (Col 1:28-29). Here Paul's pastoral concern is with the maturity of every individual believer. Notice that his energy goes not just to getting people to be in Christ but mainly getting them to be mature in Christ. That requires vigorous pastoral work.

Pastors, according to Paul, are also responsible for the maturity of the body of Christ, not just individuals. This is seen most clearly in Ephesians, where Christ gives gifts of servant leaders to the church, including "pastors and teachers." These pastor-teachers are to "equip the saints for the work of ministry, for building up the body of Christ" (Eph 4:11-12). Notice that it is the church as the body of Christ that is built up in this context, not primarily individual Christians. The corporate dimension of maturity is underscored in what follows, where "all of us [together] reach the unity of the faith and the *knowledge of the *Son of God, the perfect man, and the measure of the stature of the *fullness of Christ" (Eph 4:13). Though commentators debate the intricacies of this verse, it surely points to the maturity of the church, a maturity that is defined and measured by the stature of Christ himself, who is the "perfect man" (Roberts 2016). The growth of the body does not happen only by the work of pastor-teachers. Rather, the body will grow to maturity from Christ only "according to the working of each member" (Eph 4:16). Then and only then will the body grow up in Christlike love.

So, in the only place where Paul mentions the work of pastors, their primary responsibility is to equip the members of the church for their ministry, which is necessary if the church is going to grow in unity, stature, and maturity. Though Paul does not refer explicitly to his own pastoral efforts in Ephesians 4, his understanding of pastoral work must have informed what he did in relationship to his churches. As seen in previous discussions of Paul as builder and teacher, he was consistently working to equip church members for mutual ministry. Thus, he was exemplifying the kind of work he commends in Ephesians 4. Whether Paul was functioning as an apostle, a prophet, an evangelist, or a pastor-teacher, he sought to equip churches to grow up into Christ.

Or, Paul could say, he sought to have Christ formed in them. He uses this language when expressing his perplexity over his converts in Galatia: "My little children, with whom I am once again having labor pains until Christ is formed in you, I wish I were present with you" (Gal 4:19). Here Paul envisions Christ taking form not just in individual believers but in the church as a whole.

Such formation is not something that happens only on the inside as an invisible work of the Spirit. It is also something that occurs as Christians in community model their lives on Christ. For example, Paul urges the Philippians, "Do nothing from selfish ambition or conceit, but with humility think of others as better than yourselves" (Phil 1:3). They should care not for their own good but for the good of others (Phil 1:4). They are to do this by letting the "mind of Christ" live within them (Phil 1:5). What reveals Christ's mind? Paul continues speaking about Christ Jesus, "who, though he was in the form of God, did not regard equality with God as a matter of seizing the advantage. Rather, he emptied himself, taking the form of a *slave, taking on human likeness. He humbled himself, becoming obedient to *death, death on a *cross" (Phil 2:6-8). At the center of the gospel, at the center of Christlikeness, one finds the cross. To act like Christ, to have Christ formed in one, is to imitate his self-giving *sacrifice. It is, to borrow a word popularized by Michael Gorman, an experience of *cruciformity.

Pastors help both the individuals and the churches entrusted to their care to grow to maturity in Christ, to have Christ formed in them, and to imitate Christ. There is no doubt that Paul sought to do this with churches he planted as well as others. Therefore, though he speaks of his apostolic calling in terms of preaching, and though his commitment to geographically broad evangelization and church planting kept Paul from spending long periods of time in individual churches, there is little doubt that Paul was what one would call a pastor. The work of shepherding churches, helping them to grow in Christ and to have Christ formed in them, was an essential aspect of his apostolic mission. Paul's ultimate success as an apostle would be measured not by the number of people he converted or the number of churches he planted but by the perseverance of those churches and by their growth to full maturity in Christ.

See also Apostle; Birth Pangs, Maternal Imagery; Body of Christ; Church; Cruciformity; Imitation of Paul / of Christ; Kinship Language in Paul; Letters, Letter Forms; Love; Ministry; Mission; Prayer; Thessalonians, Letters to the.

BIBLIOGRAPHY. **E. Best,** *Paul and His Converts* (Edinburgh: T&T Clark, 1988); **G. Fee,** *The First Epistle to the Corinthians*, rev. ed., NICNT (Grand Rapids, MI: Eerdmans, 2014); **M. Gorman,** *Cruciformity: Paul's Narrative Spirituality of the Cross* (Grand Rapids, MI: Eerdmans, 2001); **A. J. Malherbe,** "Gentle as a Nurse: The Gnostic Background to 1 Thess 2," *NovT* 12 (1970): 203-17; idem, *Paul and the Thessalonians: The Philosophic Tradition of Pastoral Care* (Philadelphia: Fortress, 1987); idem, *The Letters to the Thessalonians: A New Translation with Introduction and Commentary*, AB 32B (New York: Doubleday, 2000); **S. McKnight,** *Pastor Paul: Nurturing a Culture of Christoformity in the Church*, TECC (Grand Rapids, MI: Brazos, 2019); **M. Mitchell,** "New Testament Envoys in the Context of Greco-Roman Diplomatic and Epistolary Conventions: The Example of Timothy and Titus," *JBL* 111, no. 4 (1992): 641-62; **M. Roberts,** "Images of Paul and the Thessalonians" (PhD diss., Harvard University, 1992); idem, *Ephesians*, SGBC (Grand Rapids, MI: Zondervan, 2016); **B. Rosner, A. Malone, and T. Burke,** eds., *Paul as Pastor* (Edinburgh: T&T Clark, 2017); **E. Schnabel,** *Paul the Missionary: Realities, Strategies, and Methods* (Downers Grove, IL: IVP Academic, 2008); **J. W. Thompson,** *Pastoral Ministry According to Paul: A Biblical Vision* (Grand Rapids, MI: Baker, 2006); **G. Wiles,** *Paul's Intercessory Prayers: The Significance of the Intercessory Prayer Passages in the Letters of St Paul*, SNTSMS 24 (Cambridge: Cambridge University Press, 1974); **D. Williams,** "The Imitation of Christ in Paul with Special Reference to Paul as Teacher" (PhD diss., Columbia University, 1967).

M. D. Roberts

PASTORAL EPISTLES

The term *pastoral* for the *letters of Paul to Timothy and Titus can be traced back to Thomas Aquinas (1274), who wrote in his commentary on 1 Timothy, *est haec epistola quasi pastoralis regula* ("this letter is like a pastoral rule"; cited in Harrison, 13). He describes 2 Timothy in a similar manner. The modern use of the term dates to Paul Anton, who, in a series of lectures in 1726–1727, described a number of passages in the NT as "pastoral" or useful in the preparation for *ministry; however, the letters to Timothy and Titus he regarded as *pastoral Scripta par excellence*. They were "supreme examples of writings serviceable to those who seek preparation for, and guidance in, the Christian ministry" (Harrison, 14). Percy Harrison (1921) observed that the reference to these letters as "Pastoral Epistles" became firmly established in Germany between

Anton's lectures and their publication in 1753–1755. While some thought that this term reflected their purpose, others, such as August Heydenreich (1826), thought it inadequate to think of these letters as a "compendium" of pastoral instruction since they fail "to include all the occupations and duties which fall to a teacher of Christianity. . . . There is much in them that refers to purely local circumstances" (Harrison, 15). So the term "Pastoral Epistles" came to be accepted as a matter of convenience, but not necessarily as a descriptor of their contents. Certainly, a number of German scholars preferred the term *sogenannten Pastoralbriefe* (so-called Pastoral Epistles).

1. Attestations
2. Authorship and Letter Collections
3. Historical Background
4. Asia Minor as the Background
5. Genre
6. Significant Studies on the Pastoral Epistles
7. Studies on Individual Letters
8. Theological Themes
9. Research Directions

1. Attestations.
The oldest surviving attestation of the Pastoral Epistles is to Titus, preserved on a fragment from a papyrus codex called P[32] (P.Ryl. 1.5). Based on the style of the script, this papyrus fragment has been dated by some to the second century AD (Bell and Skeat; Aland). However, recent considerations based on placing the script style within its historical "graphic stream" and on the original size of the fragment suggest that it is dated to the third century AD (Gathergood, 591). The fragment is written on both sides, which indicates that it is from a codex; further, the placement of the text on the page suggests that there was a document before and one following Titus. It is tempting to suggest that Titus is placed between 2 Timothy and Philemon, as it is in Codex Sinaiticus (fourth century AD), which is the earliest manuscript to preserve these letters. However, eclectic collections of the Scriptures from the third century rule out any assured confidence.

Attestation of the Pastoral Epistles also occurs in the writings of the early church fathers. There are some verbal similarities between the Pastoral Epistles and the letter of Clement (ca. AD 96) and the letters of Ignatius of Antioch (ca. AD 110–117), which "may show some dependence" (Berding, 143). The near consensus is that Polycarp in his letter to the Philadelphians (ca. AD 120–135) is the first to quote 1 and 2 Timothy. Not much later, Justin Martyr (ca. AD 140) seems to show some familiarity with them. However, it is Irenaeus (ca. AD 188) who makes a clear connection between the Pastoral Epistles and Paul. Kenneth Berding (2002) investigated whether Polycarp quotes the Pastoral Epistles because he considered them to be Pauline. He found that Polycarp does cluster Pauline citations around Paul's name and that these include citations from 1 Timothy 6:7, 10 and 2 Timothy 4:10. He concludes by saying, "Polycarp becomes the earliest external witness to the belief in the early church that Paul was the author of the Pastoral Epistles" (Berding, 155).

1.1. Inclusion of the Pastoral Epistles into Letter Collections on Papyrus. There has been considerable debate about the incorporation of the Pastoral Epistles into the Pauline letter collection before the fourth century AD. The question revolves around the inclusion of the Pastoral Epistles into the incomplete Chester Beatty codex (P[46]), which dates to about AD 200. This codex preserves most of Romans, Hebrews, 1–2 Corinthians, Ephesians, Galatians, Philippians, Colossians, and 1 Thessalonians, but there are pages missing at the end of the codex. The last surviving page breaks off at 1 Thessalonians 5:28, and the original editor, Frederic Kenyon (1934; 1936), inferred from the page numbers that there were seven pages missing from the end of the manuscript, not enough to contain 2 Thessalonians, the Pastoral Epistles, and Philemon. The possibility that additional pages were added was considered but ruled out by Kenyon, and this judgement is followed by Bruce Metzger (1981) and Eldon Jay Epp (1997; 2002).

However, Jeremy Duff (1998) argues that the scribe was compressing his script as he neared the end of the codex to fit in the necessary amount of text he was copying; his conclusion is that the scribe had intended to fit in the Pastoral Epistles and Philemon. Duff suggests that the scribe either left the manuscript incomplete or added pages, a practice found in Nag Hammadi codex 1 (587). If this is the case, then the Pastoral Epistles were considered a part of the Pauline *canon by the beginning of the third century. However, Edgar Ebojo has argued that the increasing number of the characters in the second half of the codex should not be taken as a scribal intention to include the Pastoral Epistles and Philemon. Ebojo convincingly argues that there are only six sheets (twelve pages) missing and that four of these would have included 2 Thessalonians, beginning at 2 Thessalonians 1:9b, and a blank back cover page. The remaining seven pages do not have enough space for the missing Pastoral Epistles and Philemon. Further, as Epp (2002) points out, given the variety of Christian material in the papyrus collections, there are any number of options that may have concluded P[46]. Epp concludes, "Our understanding of the nature of the Pastoral Epistles and of their place in early collections of Pauline Letters and, consequently, their place in the early New Testament canon, is not dependent on whether P[46] did or did not contain them"; rather, it will be determined primarily by external evidence on one hand and the internal evidence of the letters themselves on the other hand (2002, 502).

1.2. A Separate Letter Collection. Based on Kenyon's earlier proposal that P[46] does not include the Pastoral Epistles, Jerome Quinn (1974) argued that the Pastoral Epistles and Philemon had circulated as a separate collection of Pauline letters to individuals, while P[46] was a collection of letters to churches. While not relying on P[32] as a letter collection containing the Pastoral Epistles, he took this papyrus as suggestive evidence along with the evidence of Tertullian (AD 207–208), who seems to presuppose a collection of letters to individuals. Writing to refute the heretic Marcion, Tertullian takes issue with his *Apostolicon*. Marcion seems to have left the Pastoral Epistles out because they were short and directed at individuals but in contradiction to this rule includes Philemon. This seems to presuppose a letter collection to individuals, which Quinn goes on to argue explains the "seam" in every Pauline letter collection (382).

In his later commentary on Titus, Quinn (1990) adds to this argument by pointing to the arrangement of the Pauline letters to churches by length, while the Pastoral Epistles mark "a new beginning," since 1 Timothy is longer than 2 Thessalonians (3). That the Pastoral Epistles along with Philemon circulated as a separate collection from the Pauline letters to churches does not imply that they were not considered authoritative in the early *church. The Muratorian fragment (early third century AD) concludes its authoritative list with Philemon, Titus, and "two to Timothy," and "these are held sacred in the esteem of the Church catholic for the regulation of ecclesiastical discipline" (61-63; trans. Metzger 1987). Whether the addition of Philemon and the Pastorals after Revelation indicates a separate collection is difficult to judge, but the order here, which reflects the order in the Latin commentary of Ambrosiaster, is also suggestive.

2. Authorship and Letter Collections.

The discussion of authorship is one of the enduring features of scholarship regarding the Pastoral Epistles. One could say that modern scholarship of the Pastoral Epistles was birthed by the question of authorship when German scholars Johann Schmidt and Friedrich Schleiermacher raised questions about the vocabulary and the syntactical structures of 1 Timothy in comparison with the other Pauline epistles. Not long after, others, including Ferdinand C. Baur (1835) and Heinrich J. Holtzmann (1880), noted the similarities of vocabulary and themes between 1 Timothy and the two other related letters, 2 Timothy and Titus, and made the case that all three letters were written by the same author and therefore were written pseudonymously. Thus these three letters came to be treated as a corpus within the NT, and the author was identified as a second-generation Christian pastor.

In German scholarship, these results tended to be taken as assured. In English-speaking scholarship the idea of pseudonymous authorship was championed by Harrison in his 1921 study. His method was to compare the vocabulary of the Pastoral Epistles with the other Pauline epistles, noting the differences per page. He claimed that by this method he had shown that the writer of the Pastoral Epistles not only varied in the vocabulary of significant words but also in the use of smaller words and phrases. From this study, he argued that a secretary took genuine Pauline fragments and wove them together into three letters. While many scholars were sympathetic to his argument, his idiosyncratic methodology was not convincing. However, Harrison's approach spawned a significant strand of research focused on the statistical differences between the Pastoral Epistles and those epistles now identified as authentic to Paul.

Yet the similarity between the three letters has meant that scholars, no matter their views on authorship, continue to treat them as a unique corpus. Some scholars, observing that Titus occurs first in some lists, have argued that either Titus introduces the new program or that 2 Timothy is the concluding letter. Peter Trummer and Jürgen Roloff argue that the letters were conceived as a unit. Roloff argues that the problems on the ecclesiastical horizon do not change from letter to letter and proposes a double purpose for the corpus: first, to make Paul's authority usable for a contemporary crisis facing the church, and second, to reinforce the apostle's authority in general. As I. Howard Marshall highlights, the question is, Why a corpus is needed at all when this aim could be achieved with one letter? Certainly, by the beginning of the twenty-first century this debate had reached a stalemate, and new possibilities needed to be explored. Jens Herzer (2017) argues that the Pastoral Epistles should be interpreted separately since it is possible that 2 Timothy or Titus could be authentic letters of Paul. Herzer's aim is to probe the emergence of the corpus.

However, differences between the vocabulary and syntax of the Pastoral Epistles and the authentic Pauline epistles are not the only reasons scholars have proposed a pseudonymous author. Reconstructing a historical timeline for Paul's life from the Pastoral Epistles is another problem.

3. Historical Background.
For those who argue that the Pastoral Epistles are pseudonymous, the audience to which these letters are directed becomes difficult to pinpoint. John Marshall points to not only a fictive writer but a fictive audience, arguing that the "real" audience is the same for all three letters (784). However, like many, he identifies the intended audience as a congregation in Asia Minor, perhaps *Ephesus. Quinn (1990), noting that the point of origin of 2 Timothy is Rome, hypothesizes that the Roman church is the audience and the writer was attempting to rehabilitate the martyred *apostle.

3.1. Historical Reconstruction of a Pauline Authorship. Those who argue that Pastoral Epistles were written by Paul situate the audience of 1–2 Timothy in Ephesus and Titus on Crete. All scholars take the view that while Timothy and Titus are the nominated addressees, there is a church congregation in the background "looking over the shoulder of the addressee as he reads" (Kidson, *Persuading*, 45). Paul is taken to have been somewhere in Macedonia when he wrote 1 Timothy (1 Tim 1:3), in Nicopolis (or traveling there) when he wrote Titus (Titus 3:12), and finally in Rome when he wrote 2 Timothy.

Those who argue for Pauline authorship of the letters are faced with two difficulties. First is the difficulty of reconciling the plans of 1 Timothy with the *travel itinerary of Acts. In 1 Timothy 1:3 Paul travels to Macedonia, leaving Timothy in Ephesus. In Acts 20 Paul leaves Ephesus for Macedonia, but there is no mention of leaving Timothy behind nor suggestion of conflict with *opponents. The plan in 1 Timothy is that Paul will return (1 Tim 4:13), whereas in Acts he decides to sail past Ephesus and calls into Miletus (Acts 20:15-16). In 2 Corinthians, Paul leaves Titus in Troas and returns to Macedonia, although he does not visit *Corinth, thus the letter (2 Cor 1:15-17; 2:1-4, 12-13). The most significant problem in reconciling these accounts is the dramatic difference in style between the correspondence of 2 Corinthians and 1 Timothy.

The second problem is locating Paul's missionary trip to Crete within the framework of Acts. One solution is to posit an unmentioned trip to Crete before the Roman imprisonment. Jakob van Bruggen (1981) argues that a gap exists between Acts 19:20 and Acts 19:21 and inserts a yearlong trip. He sees the "third" visit mentioned in 2 Corinthians 12:14; 13:1 as suggesting a second visit. Yet van Bruggen has to forfeit Paul's actual visit to Crete and proposes that Paul instead dispatched Titus before he left. But as Philip Towner (2006) points out, Titus 1:5 implies that Paul was in Crete with Titus. This historical construction relies on making an argument from silence (Silva).

The second solution is to posit that Paul was released from *prison and made another missionary journey to the East: a trip not recorded in Acts (Fee 1988). After this, he was imprisoned again in Rome, which is why this is called "the second imprisonment theory" (Towner 2006, 11-12). This historical construction has the support of tradition; *1 Clement* 5.7, the Muratorian canon, and Acts of Peter all mention that Paul traveled to Spain, which implies a release from the Roman imprisonment in Acts. Eusebius claims that Paul was released from Roman imprisonment, only to be imprisoned again, and died at the hands of Nero (*Hist. eccl.* 2.22). These mentions could be nothing more than attempted reconstructions based on Paul's aspiration to travel to Spain (Rom 15:24). Even if these mentions are based on a reliable tradition of a Pauline journey to Spain, this does not solve the problem of the missionary journey to Crete. Jerome Murphy-O'Connor therefore proposes that Paul traveled both to Spain and then made a trip through Macedonia to Asia. This suffers from the same lack of evidence as the previously proposed construction.

Despite these attempts, it would seem that the evidence of Paul's life is too ambiguous to reconstruct (Hopkins); in relation to the writing of the Pastoral Epistles, the evidence is so lean that it is impossible to locate with any certainty the date that they were written. Further, no reconstruction of Paul's life nor proposed dating of the Pastoral Epistles overcomes the significant problem of the difference in style between the Pastoral Epistles and Paul's correspondence to Macedonia and Greece.

3.2. Historical Reconstruction Focused on the Audience. A more positive and reliable historical construction is needed that does not rely on the identification of an author or an audience at a particular place or time. Some scholars have found that much can be achieved by researching the Pastoral Epistles against a more general historical background of the church in the first and second centuries.

Martin Dibelius began to probe the historical circumstances of the Pastoral Epistles. He argued that throughout the Pastoral Epistles there was a change in the approach to the Christian life from Paul's "end of the age" radicalism to a *bürgerlich* (bourgeois) lifestyle. He believed it was necessary for the church to settle into the world because of the delay in the parousia. This settling into the world brought about an internal development in the church that saw debate reduce to an assertion of opinion and a propensity to categorize other Christian groups as orthodox or heretical. Not that these elements were not already present in Paul's paraenesis, but they were being consolidated into the life of the church. While a number of scholars have taken issue with Dibelius for characterizing the citizenship motif of the Pastoral Epistles as bourgeois, his methodological approach to the letters opened up fresh avenues of investigation.

Reggie Kidd took this approach in his investigation of *wealth, beneficence, and the church in the Pastoral Epistles. He found that, while the writer of the Pastoral Epistles interacts with the language and ideals of benefaction at large in the Greco-Roman social setting, he was at pains to adapt this cultural model for his own needs. In countering the idea of cultural accommodation proposed by Dibelius that the Pastoral Epistles are "bourgeois" he says, "No one should suggest that the Pastorals' answers are scandalously radical. Divestment is not demanded of wealthy Christians. . . . All the same, the conclusion that the Pastorals' approach is but an uncritical accepting of contemporary *bürgerlich* or even 'aristocratic' values is vacuous" (Kidd 1990, 157).

Similarly, David Verner, in his study of the social world of the Pastoral Epistles, had taken issue with Dibelius's gentrification model of the emerging church in the later first and early second centuries, saying that it obscured the social realities of the urban Hellenistic society. Starting with the view of E. A. Judge (1960) and others that Christianity drew its leadership from the urban upper strata from the beginning, he argues that the image of the *household of *God in 1 Timothy 3:14 shaped the author's conception of the social structure of the church. Verner finds that the author used this image for prescriptive purposes, suggesting that "authority is properly concentrated in the hands of an official leadership that is expected to govern effectively and to represent the church to the world. As in the household, women, slaves, children and young men properly belong to subordinate stations" (Verner 1983, 182).

4. Asia Minor as the Background.

Many scholars, such as Veneer and Kidd, are at pains to use the social conditions of Asia Minor to reconstruct the historical conditions of the church that stands behind the Pastoral Epistles. This approach has an advantage in that it allows the researcher to take seriously the location of the church as suggested by the writer of the Pastoral Epistles, at least for 1–2 Timothy. As has become apparent in recent research, regional differences within the Roman Empire need to be taken into account when studying the literature of this era. Greco-Roman culture was not monolithic (Goldhill).

4.1. The Social and Intellectual Background. Asia Minor was a culturally and intellectually energetic region in the early Roman imperial period. Many of its cities were not only administrative centers; they were also centers of educational and intellectual pursuits. Throughout the first and second centuries, cities such as Ephesus, Sardis, Philadelphia, Pergamum, and Smyrna grew in prosperity and numbers. Not only did the local elites grow wealthier, but there was also a migration of the very wealthy into these cities. These wealthy elites cultivated a high standard of culture, both publicly and privately. They were patrons of *teachers, philosophers, rhetoricians, writers and poets, musicians, associations, and various cults (Kidson, *Persuading*, 14).

The elite, as Kidd rightly points out, become benefactors in their cities, not only maintaining city infrastructure but supporting cultural activities. These people were honored by city councils with statues and inscriptions extolling their benevolence and personal qualities (Kidson, *Persuading*, 15). However, in the first and second centuries, political and social dynamics were changing within Asia Minor. Older scholarship had seen Hellenistic and Roman imperial rule as a political force that led to a consolidation of power into the hands of a few elite families in each city. However, more recent scholarship has come to appreciate the fluid and volatile social dynamics within cities. While there was a movement toward a consolidation of power, just who made up this elite was not as stable as their inscribed accolades would imply (Zuiderhoek). Work done by Arjan Zuiderhoek demonstrates that there was competition at a subelite level by families wishing to improve their social standing within their communities. Lyn Kidson has argued that

Zuiderhoek's work on these subelites potentially identifies candidates for Kidd's "rich" benefactors in Christian communities (*Persuading*, 21).

4.2. The Early Christian Church as an Intellectual Community and Paul the Letter Writer. It is in this social world that historical Paul's activities as a letter writer should be seen. Judge argued that the activities of the early Christians should be seen as "scholastic" (1960–1961). Yet Judge (1960) shrinks away from the term *bourgeois*. He argues that although the original Jewish Christianity may have started out as a movement for the ordinary person (cf. Deissmann), it soon attracted priests and Pharisees; one of those was Paul himself. While there had been questions about Paul's educational level, it is now without question that he was writing letters to communities dominated by an educated hierarchy, at least by a group of relatively wealthy and pretentious patrons (cf. Hoag). Paul and other Christian preachers were aided by these wealthier householders; hence the Christian movement had parallels to philosophical movements within the Roman Empire. As Judge points out, the very act of writing paraenetic letters is a scholastic activity. Thus those who argue that the writer of the Pastoral Epistles is pseudonymous see a continuation of this letter-writing activity as a feature of the scholastic or intellectual nature of the Christian community.

5. Genre.

The question of the genre of the individual letters almost ceases to be salient if the Pastoral Epistles are seen as written as a unified corpus. As discussed above, this might be claiming too much, and thus there is a shift toward interpreting each letter on its own terms (Herzer 2017). Identifying the genre of each letter is an important first step in interpretation as it provides the reader with "ready-made strategies for reading" (Rabinowitz, 177). All three Pastoral Epistles have the generic markers that identify them as letters—the A to B formula: the sender to the recipient (Doty).

Scholars have noted generic similarities between 1 Timothy and Titus. Second Timothy appears to have a *testamentarischen Charakter* ("testamental character"; Herzer 2017, 441). Kidson (2014) observes that 1 Timothy appears to owe something to administrative correspondence that is found in the bureaucracies of the Hellenistic and Roman periods. Donelson concludes that the Pastoral Epistles are "fine examples of the pseudepigraphical letter genre" (66) even though the pseudepigraphical letter is not a genre in any formal sense. However, Kidson (2014) argues that the underlying motivation of the writer cannot be ascertained and therefore cannot be used as a generic marker. Similarly, Deissmann's category of public and private letters suffers from the same lack of observable evidence because it locates decisions about the literature in long-dead authors. Kidson (2014) argues that the best way forward is to compare the letter under study with existent contemporary letters.

Many scholars have taken up the idea that 1 Timothy has a "mandate" character. However, Margaret Mitchell demonstrates that this identification of 1 Timothy with a Roman imperial mandate is based on a confusion of genres, from one era to another. Ceslas Spicq, in his commentary on the Pastoral Epistles, comments that the relationship between a superior official and his newly appointed subordinate in the Ptolemaic memorandum (P.Tebt. 703) bears some similarity to the relationship between Paul and Timothy in 1 Timothy. He does not suggest any generic parallels since his thesis is that the Pastoral Epistles are a type of *logos protreptikos* (a word of encouragement). Sometime later, Benjamin Fiore in his dissertation noted the possibility that the superior was setting an example for the junior official in Tebtunis Papyrus 703. Luke Timothy Johnson, seemingly inspired by Fiore's comment, claims that 1 Timothy is a Roman appointment charter (*mandata principis*) and that an "almost perfect example is the Tebtunis Papyrus 703" (Johnson, 140). Fiore, in his later commentary, goes a step further, saying, "Reference to this sort official memorandum letter or appointment charter helps readers of the Pastoral Epistles make sense of the anomaly that the letters contain commands and duties that presumably would have been covered by Paul in meetings with Timothy and Titus before he left them in charge" (2007, 10).

Mitchell is roundly critical of this slide into generic confusion by these NT scholars, saying that the *mandata principis* introduced by Augustus may owe something to the Ptolemaic memorandum, as the translator of Tebtunis Papyrus 703 suggests, but this is a far cry from conflating the two. As Mitchell notes, "to name our 3rd C. BCE papyrus an 'almost perfect example' of a Roman administrative invention of the first princeps Augustus has a troublingly anachronistic ring to it" (362). Mitchell concludes by saying,

> PTebt 703, in the final analysis, does not in and of itself contribute a great deal to the question of the genre and authenticity of 1 Timothy. What it does show is an affinity in language and, as

Wolter [1988] has nicely put it, "communicative structure" between the Pastoral Epistles and a wide range (as richly illustrated by Spicq) of ancient Hellenistic and Roman administrative and diplomatic correspondence. (368)

6. Significant Studies on the Pastoral Epistles.

6.1. Robert Karris. In 1973 Robert Karris published "The Background and Significance of the Polemic of the Pastoral Epistles." He noted that the author only once (1 Tim 4:1-5) argues against his opponents by "picking up their themes and debating with them theologically," even though this tactic is a feature of the genuine Pauline Epistles (549). Karris notes that strategies such as name-calling belonged to a long tradition of polemical argument. In order to uncover the unique elements of the opponents' teaching, his method was to establish the traditional polemical elements to see whether the author had added any new elements. Primarily, the author of the Pastoral Epistles employs a "philosophers against the sophists" polemic, which was used by philosophers such as Plato, Aristotle, Dio Chrysostom, Maximus of Tyre, the Jewish writer Philo of Alexandria, and a number of early Christian writers. Plato had originally attacked the innovative education of sophists because they "claimed to impart wisdom to youth by means of rhetoric and because they accepted money for their instruction" (Karris, 551). Karris argues that there are two facets to the polemic; on one hand, it has "stock" rhetorical features, and on the other, there are glimpses into the teaching of the opponents. He concludes that the opponents were "Jewish Christians," teaching "Jewish myths" and genealogies (562-63). He says they forbade *marriage and enjoined abstinence from food, taught that the *resurrection had already occurred, and may have had "significant success among the womenfolk" (563).

6.2. Abraham Malherbe. Abraham Malherbe published "Medical Imagery in the Pastoral Epistles" first in 1980, then subsequently in 1989 in *Paul and the Popular Philosophers.* He notes that the Pastoral Epistles make "frequent use of the language of health and disease in polemic leveled at false teachers and their followers" (19). Others had touched on this theme but argued either that the non-Christian material was utilized in a cursory manner (Michaelis; Luck) or that the scholar resorted to lists of parallels (Dibelius; Spicq). Malherbe is particularly critical of Karris, who, although he had gathered parallels to support his thesis, "studiously avoided dealing with the terms describing health and disease" (20). These motifs operate in two directions, argues Malherbe; on the positive side, "'the sound words' are thought to form a pattern received from Paul." On the negative side, the author uses this terminology not to describe the content of the heretic's teaching but to direct it at their demeanor. He says the details given about the heretics are "not isolated bits of polemic" but form, in the author's perception, a major feature of their character and their preaching method. Thus he says that the author urges his readers, "in explicitly antithetic form," to "the exact opposite mien and method" (21).

Malherbe compares the polemic of the Pastoral Epistles with the non-Christian material to gain some insight into the medical imagery of the Pastoral Epistles. He finds that the description of human vices and passions as diseases was widespread; for instance, when passion in "the soul rages savagely," it "produces itching and ticklings which arise from lust and indulgence" (24). This disease of the soul can be treated with an effective therapy based on reason and frank speech. The one giving such therapy was described as a "physician for the soul": Dio Chrysostom (*Invid.* 77/78) alludes to frank speech as surgery. The philosopher/physician is "one who is sound in words and deeds" (Malherbe, 25). Similarly, Plutarch in *How to Tell a Flatterer from a Friend* describes frankness as "a potent medicine, when used in moderation." Flattery, he says, is insidious and can take the form of specious frankness. Plutarch argues that the flatterer himself is diseased and needs remedies because he is not deterred that his flattery becomes "a pestilence in society." His frankness "merely titillates and tickles" (Malherbe, 29).

Malherbe concludes that the author of the Pastoral Epistles accused the heretics of being diseased in their minds and morals. Their verbal battles, he says, did not eliminate disease in others but were "products of their own disease," which infected others who listened to them with itching ears, "which wait only to be tickled" (30). While Malherbe finds that medical imagery is being used in a polemical fashion, he argues that, unlike the moral philosophers, who cured a person by reason, the author believed it was the "apostolic tradition" that would restore the health of the reader.

6.3. Lewis Donelson. Lewis Donelson begins his 1986 study *Pseudepigraphy and Ethical Argument in the Pastoral Epistles* with three postulates: the Pastoral Epistles are pseudepigraphical; the author is "creating logical interdependencies" much as any Greco-Roman ethicist would, which explains the apparent disorganized appearance; and this author is best understood as a Greco-Roman ethicist (3). He begins his study by discussing the convention of pseudepigraphical letter writing in the Greco-Roman world in comparison with the Pastoral Epistles. A significant contribution that Donelson makes is his development of Karris's study on varying types of argument. Particularly helpful is his description of the enthymeme and the paradigm in Aristotle's *The Art of Rhetoric* and their application by the author of Pastoral Epistles to build a case against the opponents and to promote his view of *Christology and *ethics. Building on this, Donelson makes the case that there are cosmological links that, when traced, give insight into the author's ethical system: "his concept of who God is, who Jesus is, what they have done and will do, determine . . . the lifestyle of the Christian" (135).

6.4. Mark Harding. Mark Harding in his study *Tradition and Rhetoric in the Pastoral Epistles* (1998) investigates the use of rhetoric in ancient philosophical letters. He stresses that since they are letters of moral instruction, they cannot be classified using the Aristotelian scheme of forensic, deliberative, or epideictic speeches. Still, he finds that the writer employs some persuasive strategies drawn from Aristotle's three proofs: logical deduction, induction through the use of paradigms and examples, and appeals based on pathos. In summing up, Harding concludes that "the Pastoral Epistles are best characterized as letters standing self-consciously in the Pauline tradition and in the Greco-Roman tradition of moral exhortation" (1998, 232). The writer, he argues, has utilized epistolary, philosophical, and rhetorical conventions, adapting them to his own purposes in preserving the Pauline *tradition.

6.5. Michael Goulder. Michael Goulder, in "The Pastor's Wolves: Jewish Christian Visionaries Behind the Pastoral Epistles," takes a similar approach to Karris, although more in debt to Martin Dibelius and Hans Conzelmann for his argument that the polemic in the Pastoral Epistles is aimed at Jewish-Christian visionaries. Unlike Karris, who saw all of the polemical devices as "stock," Goulder argues that these polemical devices are aimed at rebuffing the visionaries' asceticism and their observance of the Jewish *food laws. Moving away from this line of exploration, he then argues that these Jewish visionaries are related to Irenaeus's Gnostics. He suggests that they claimed two bases of authority: "rulings of wisdom of the Jewish sages" and rulings of "knowledge" derived from their "firsthand experience of the heavenly world" (249). He also makes the case that the central hymn of 1 Timothy 3:16 is aimed at the incorrect teaching on the incarnation and the resurrection.

While Goulder does not in the end offer a convincing argument that some Ebionites (Christians who kept the Jewish *law) were also Gnostic, as Irenaeus describes, his observation that the polemic in the Pastoral Epistles was constructed with the view to countering the teaching of the opponents has moved the understanding of the polemic devices beyond Karris's observation that they belong to the polemicists' stock in trade.

6.6. Lloyd Pietersen. Lloyd Pietersen's sociological study of the use of the polemic in the Pastoral Epistles, *The Polemic of the Pastorals: A Sociological Examination of the Development of Pauline Christianity*, provides a controlled and methodological approach to understanding the conflict behind the letters. He criticizes Karris's method of setting aside the stock polemic to reveal the unique polemical features, which in the end reveals little. Unlike Goulder, he begins by saying that there "are real problems with viewing the opponents as Gnostics and that the view they represent 'a Gnosticizing form of Jewish Christianity' is far too vague" (Pietersen, 2). He goes on to make the case that a modified Weber model of charismatic groups can be used to explore "the power struggle taking place in the immediate post-Pauline communities between factions with competing memories of Paul" (35-36). He makes the case that there were sociological changes in the Christian groups after the death of their charismatic leader, Paul, which led to both institutionalization and the intensification of thaumaturgical demand—that is, a demand for miracles and oracles.

Pietersen concludes by saying that the writer adopts a multiprong approach to dealing with the factionalism caused by these sociological changes, including stereotypical language to describe the opponents, a focus on character rather than charismatic gifting in the selection of leaders, directions to women who are vulnerable to the opponents' teaching, and placing boundaries around charismatic phenomenon. The writer places an emphasis on sobriety, moderation, and soundness of mind; presents Paul as the model teacher; and, last, emphasizes the Pauline tradition and Timothy and Titus's role as tradition bearers.

6.7. Annette Huizenga. Annette Huizenga begins her study *Moral Education for Women in the Pastoral and Pythagorean Letters: Philosophers of the Household* by first looking at the Pythagorean letters and discourses, pseudonymously written by women to women. Most of these texts "specifically address social expectations for women in their roles as wife, mother, and mistress" as they preside over their *slaves and households (12). She notes that the texts deal predominantly with women's household roles and moral behavior. They use an "unusual strategy" involving "the production of texts ascribed to female authors writing to female recipients on women's subjects. The literary gendering of virtue and of the philosophical life [has] reached a well-defined position within the Pythagorean text collection, supporting the notion of moral women as 'philosophers of the household'" (15).

Huizenga observes that the Pastoral Epistles have a similar vocabulary, literary character, and subject matter as ancient philosophical ethics texts. This makes the Pastoral Epistles participants in "the ongoing philosophical discussion of women's moral formation but from an early Christian perspective" (18). Huizenga argues that the author offers sex-specific teachings because he believes that there are essential differences between males and females. He prescribes, she says, "not simply wifely submission to a husband (Titus 2:5), but the total fulfillment of the three socially approved female domestic roles of wife, mother, and mistress of the household (1 Tim 2:15; 5:9, 14; 2 Tim 1:5; Titus 2:4-5)." She concludes that "any believing woman who adopted this approach to developing her virtue would become the Pastorals' version of a 'philosopher of the household'" (19).

Huizenga concludes that a similar perspective of gender permeates the educational curriculum in both the Pythagorean women's letters and the Pastoral Epistles. Both suppose that "women, as well as men, can be taught by means of instructional letters that employ pedagogical techniques of paraenesis, rebuke, and antithetical argumentation." Yet both believe that the "moral education of women requires female teachers, especially to serve as examples of feminine virtue." However, despite the similarities between them, Huizenga finds that the Pastoral Epistles and Pythagorean letters differ significantly. While "the Pythagorean women's letters emerge from the intellectual milieu of popular moral philosophy," the author of the Pastoral Epistles "constructs a curriculum for Christian women that makes use of two strands of ancient thought: the popular philosophical, and the Pauline traditions" (365).

7. Studies on Individual Letters.

7.1. 1 Timothy. In his study *Jesus as Mediator: Politics and Polemic in 1 Timothy 2:1-7*, Malcolm Gill argues that it is essential to read 1 Timothy against the political and cultural background of Asia Minor in the first century. His particular focus is on the relationship of the church with the imperial cult. He argues that in 1 Timothy 2:1-7 the author presents Jesus *Christ as the unique mediator between God and humanity. This, he says, "contains polemical overtones easily identifiable by his original audience" (163). In this way 1 Timothy presents "a unique Christian perspective on mediation that stands in direct contrast to the notions found in the Asian context, where the emperor, or various priests within the imperial cult, offered mediation between humanity and the gods" (163).

Similarly, Kidson, in her study *Persuading Shipwrecked Men: The Rhetorical Strategies of 1 Timothy 1*, reads 1 Timothy against the educational background of Asia Minor. Like Donelson, she argues that the author and his reader were familiar with the conventions of rhetoric. The rhetorical devices were used within the context of the epistolary genre. Unlike Donelson, she does not think that the pseudepigraphical nature of the letter contributes significantly to its interpretation. She finds that the letter stands closer to administrative letters, which were a subgenre of personal and business letters in antiquity. This leads her to argue that the purpose of the letter was to persuade "certain men" (1 Tim 1:3) to give up their other educational program and return to Paul's "sound teaching" (138). The "certain men" could be saved from an arrogant superiority they found in their other educational program through the same means as Paul, which was the acceptance of Christ's *mercy (1 Tim 1:16).

7.2. 1 Timothy 2. There has been a lot of scholarship produced on 1 Timothy 2. A significant amount of this has focused on the 1 Timothy 2:8-15; however, little research has gone into studying this chapter in the context of the letter as a whole, as Kidson (*Persuading*) does for 1 Timothy 1, or against the political and religious background of Asia Minor, as Gill does for 1 Timothy 2:1-7.

Kidson argues in her article "Fasting, Bodily Care, and the Widows of 1 Timothy 5:3-15" that the instructions of 1 Timothy 2 should be seen as the implementation of the opening command of the letter that "certain people" should not teach the other instruction or educational program (*mē heterodidaskalein*); rather, they are to busy themselves with God's household management (1 Tim 1:3-4). As opposed to the other educational program, which causes various maladies (Malherbe) such as "controversies and quarrels about words which result in envy, strife, malicious talk, evil suspicions and constant friction between men of corrupt mind" (1 Tim 6:4-5), the healthy, good, and holy (1 Tim 1:10; 4:6; 6:3) educational program that they are to attend to comes from Jesus Christ (1 Tim 6:3). The other educational program is an ascetic one, which uses diets to control sexual desires.

In a recent Society of Biblical Literature paper (2019), Kidson argued, based on the research of Judith Gundry on sexual asceticism in 1 Corinthians 7, that the nub of the problem in 1 Timothy 2:12-5 is that wives were attempting to persuade their husbands to abandon sexual relations, that is, to have a spiritual marriage. Based on the observation that Timothy will save his hearers if he sets a good example by attending to himself and the educational program (*tē didaskalia*; 1 Tim 4:11-16), Kidson argues that the wife of 1 Timothy 2 will be saved from the ill effects of the opponents teaching by submission to Jesus Christ's educational program (1 Tim 2:10, 12). This is because she will conduct herself in a manner fitting a married, godly woman (1 Tim 2:10) and have intercourse with her husband, which of course will lead to childbearing. Therefore, the childbearing will in effect save the wife, if they, that is, she and her husband, remain (*ean meinōsin*) in "*faith, *love and *holiness" (1 Tim 2:15), just as Timothy is commanded to persevere (*epimene*) in attending to himself and Jesus Christ's educational program (1 Tim 4:16).

7.3. 2 Timothy. There have been few independent studies of 2 Timothy. While there is a general consensus that the letter in style owes much to the farewell discourse or a testamentary letter, Michael Prior argues in his *Paul the Letter-Writer and the Second Letter to Timothy* that 2 Timothy 4:6-8 does not refer to Paul's impending *death but to his hoped-for release from prison. Prior's overall research goal was to demonstrate that 2 Timothy belongs to a series of genuine personal letters from the apostle Paul.

Dillon Thornton in his *Hostility in the House of God: An Investigation of the Opponents in 1 and 2 Timothy* begins by identifying four problems with Karris's "stock character of the polemic." He is critical of Karris's claim that the interpreter can "spot the places where Paul echoes his opponents' language" and that Paul was willing to reuse their language (Thornton, 15). Thornton argues that Karris does not give a satisfactory reason for using the sophists' schema, that he gives too much weight to individual words alone (e.g., *myths, deceivers*), and, last, that "it is unreasonable simply to assume that a secular philosopher and an early Christian writer will use a set of terms or phrases in the exact same way" (16). He then critiques other methods that have been employed to study the opponents in 1 and 2 Timothy and in so doing formulates these two questions: "What doctrines and practices set the opponents apart from the faithful Christian community?" and "How does/should the Christian community respond to them?" (29). His method progresses through three stages, exegeting the units he identifies as containing explicit language, that is, those he believes give clear and certain reference to the opponents and the doctrines and practices they promulgate; then he analyzes the discourse units that probably have references to the opponents; and last he brings together the data to draw his conclusions.

Through this method Thornton finds that the opponents came from within the Pauline community in Ephesus: "they once were considered to be in good standing within the community; they now have in Paul's view revealed their true nature as spiritual outsiders, though probably they continue to identify themselves as insiders" (237-38). Breaking from a general consensus, he finds no evidence to suggest that for the opponents' *gnosis was based on Gnostic views of the world or *creation. Neither were they involved in *aeon* and *archon* speculation. Their gnosis, asceticism, and "myths and genealogies" were connected to an erroneous eschatological position. The lack of engagement with the opponents Thornton puts down to Paul cutting "to the chase" with Timothy (275).

Similarly, Seán Martin in his *Pauli Testamentum: 2 Timothy and the Last Words of Moses* begins with Karris's polemic but makes the point that if the problem for churches in the latter half of the first century is the lapse of authority, then the "solution for those churches must also involve a claim to authority" (12). His thesis is that Paul is a figure of authority to be reclaimed, as Moses was for the writer of the Testament of Moses and for Philo in his *Life of Moses*, as well as Pseudo-Philo and Josephus. All these writers retold the story of Moses in order to "let the great Mediator of the Torah speak to their contemporaries, so too, does the Pastor bring back Paul from the dead, and permit him to speak again to another generation" (Martin, 15). An important feature of his approach is that Martin studies 2 Timothy "in its own right" (16), although not going as far as Prior and Murphy-O'Connor, who argue for a literary independence between 2 Timothy and the other Pastoral Epistles.

7.4. Titus. Titus has had even less research attention given to it. Quinn's commentary appears to be the only one devoted to Titus alone, which allows him to go into a great deal of detail about its grammar and unique vocabulary. Both David Gill, "A Saviour for the Cities of Crete: The Roman Background to the Epistle to Titus," and George Wieland, "Roman Crete and the Letter to Titus," investigate the cities of Crete as a plausible background to the letter. An interesting study focusing on ethics in Titus is Dogara Manomi's *Virtue Ethics in the Letter to Titus*. This is an interdisciplinary study examining biblical ethics using virtue ethics theory. His primary goal is to identify explicit and implicit ethical norms in Titus; in particular, self-control, *righteousness, piety, good works, and the household codes. He concludes that the virtue-ethical perspectives of Titus correlate significantly with a sense of a moral telos that leads to human flourishing. There is also an emphasis on character, habits, and inner dispositions, and a focus on the morality of persons more than the morality of actions.

8. Theological Themes.

After surveying the arguments for the unity of the Pastoral Epistles, Herzer proposes that the scholarly consensus for their unity be suspended so that "we can reach a more appropriate understanding of these three small letters within the Pauline tradition, their social setting, and theological profile" (Herzer 2022, 286; cf. Towner 2006, 88-89). This would make for a radical departure, as most studies of the theology of the Pastoral Epistles take it for granted that the theological themes are unified across all three letters. Three intensive studies on the theological themes in the Pastoral Epistles have been conducted by Lewis Donelson, Towner (1989), and Hanna Stettler. As these scholars found in their studies, the three epistles share a lot of common themes. The danger is, as Herzer points out, that the commonalities can overshadow the differences between the letters. This need not be an either-or situation, but rather a consideration of the interplay between the Pastoral Epistles is needed since each letter has its own genre and purpose, as Kidson's study of 1 Timothy suggests (*Persuading*).

8.1. The Cosmological Framework. Donelson begins his discussion on Christology by pushing back against the idea that "the author of the Pastorals had no theology of his own" (Hanson, 110). Even those who hold to a Pauline authorship see Paul "as perhaps debilitated by a faded intensity" (Donelson, 129). Those who hold to a non-Pauline view see "a churchman" piecing together materials "resulting in an unsystematic collage of liturgy, hymns, misapprehended Paulinisms, and Greek ethics" (129). The object of such analysis was to determine what was borrowed from tradition rather than taking the writer's theology on his own terms. Donelson's argument is that once the "enthymematic and paradigmatic logic" of the letters is taken into account, it is possible to discern the author's theological system (133). The author of the Pastoral Epistles, observes Donelson, has a cosmological framework. First Timothy 1:3-4 introduces a contrast between God's plan for *salvation and the empty speculation of the opponents: "οἰκονομία . . . means both to have a plan and to execute it" (133). Thus, the "οἰκονομία θεοῦ is God's pre-existent plan of salvation for creation which has now been revealed" (134). This plan of salvation has two elements: first, it is carried out through Jesus, second, the epiphany of Jesus is a key historical moment of the plan. The cosmological origins of God's plan issue into historical dimensions by "moving through Jesus into Paul and his traditions" (135).

8.2. Salvation and Savior. Although Towner's study (1989) is slightly later than Donelson's, his approach is not as nuanced as Donelson's study in terms of its sensitivity to the rhetorical devices used by the author. Towner's method is to survey the theological themes across the letters, gathering data strata-like. Using this method, Towner finds that the idea of salvation in the Pastoral Epistles does not diverge greatly from other works in the NT: "Salvation is a present reality made possible by a past event" (2 Tim 1:9; Titus 2:11; 3; cf. 1 Tim 1:15; Towner 1989, 75). Salvation has, says Towner, "a future orientation which suggests that the 'present' commodity is somehow incomplete" (1 Tim 2:15; 4:16; Towner 1989, 75). The use of the word **savior* to designate both God and Christ appears to be a development in the latter NT. The use of *savior* for Christ may be related to the ruler cult, which suggests "the competing claims and pressure leveled upon the Christian communities by the Imperial religion" (Towner 1989, 77). As Towner notes, four of the six instances of *God* identify God as the originator of the plan of salvation (1 Tim 2:3; Titus 1:3; 2:10; 3:4; cf. 1 Tim 1:1; 4:10). Salvation is a matter of God's will (1 Tim 2:4; 2 Tim 1:9). God made salvation available through the appearance and death of Christ (2 Tim 1:9-10; Titus 1:3). Titus 2:11-14; 3:6 connect similar thoughts, as it is clear that Christ's redemptive death procured salvation. In Titus 2:13 the final accomplishment of salvation is connected with the final appearance of the Savior, and this "past Christ-event forms the basis of that future event" (Towner 1989, 77). From his investigation, Towner finds that "the theme of salvation is central to the author's message" (118).

8.3. Incarnation. Stettler, in her study, seeks to bring the Christology of the Pastoral Epistles into conversation with the Christology of other Testament works. She finds five dimensions: the preexistence of Jesus, Christ as a *servant, Christ as Son, the Christ of proclamation, and Jesus revealed in the *flesh (328-44). Stettler describes the epiphany of Jesus as the fulfilment of God's purpose (2 Tim 1:9), which makes it clear that this is the whole revelation of God, apart from which there is no other. Jesus, as the son, is unified with the father while at the same time subordinated. Stettler concludes by saying that it is to the merit of the author that he has preserved the message of the past in new linguistic forms in a new situation and "den von Häresie bedrohten Gemeinden in einprägsamen Formeln übermittelt zu haben" (to have transmitted [this message] to communities threatened by heresies by using memorable phrases) (344).

8.4. House of God. Herzer, in his recent study *Die Pastoralbriefe und das Vermächtnis des Paulus: Studien zu den Briefen an Timotheus und Titus* (2022), challenges this stratified method of theological investigation into the Pastoral Epistles. As a case in point, he focuses on the overreliance on "the lexeme οἶκος θεοῦ 'House of God,'" which appears "only once within the Pastoral Epistles in 1 Tim 3:15" (279). Yet, says Herzer, scholars have chosen this one lexeme as a general characteristic of the Pastorals' ecclesiology. In reviewing the scholarship, Herzer finds that viewing all three Pastoral Epistles through the lens of "house of God" has led to the conclusion "that the church has already become an institution, solidly grounded in the truth" (280). Rather than seeing the *oikos theou* as a type of household code, Herzer argues that it is best to see that the metaphor "primarily evokes the idea of the congregation as God's temple" (282). This better fits the author's concern for the *oikonomia theou* (1 Tim 1:4), or "salvation plan of God," to put it in Donelson's terms. In this perspective, says Herzer, "the congregation represents the house of God—a new kind of spiritual temple, which should be solid and strong, a fortification to preserve and keep the truth of the faith" (283).

On the other hand, the ecclesiological concerns of Titus and 2 Timothy are somewhat different. In Titus, the author is primarily concerned with the behavior of the young and old people (Titus 2:1-8) and admonishing slaves (Titus 2:9-10), suggesting he is concerned about social relations. Further, it may seem that 2 Timothy relies on the metaphor of "house"; however, the term used is *oikia*, which varies from 1 Timothy. This suggests, says Herzer, that *oikia* "serves as an illustration of the argument that not everyone in the congregation contributes positively to its growth (cf. [2 Tim 2]:16-19)—it is not a metaphor identifying the church as οἶκος θεοῦ" (285). These observations by Herzer potentially open new approaches to the study of the theology of the Pastoral Epistles.

9. Research Directions.
Since Karris published his study on the polemic in the Pastoral Epistles in 1973, numerous new avenues for research have opened up. Certainly, the refining of Karris's observations by Harding and Donelson has opened up new investigative leads into the rhetoric of the letters. Yet Harding offers a reminder that the Pastoral Epistles generically are letters, and certainly this epistolary aspect, especially in relation to 2 Timothy and Titus, needs further investigation. That they both present as everyday letters (Kidson 2014) yet stand in the philosophical letter tradition (Huizenga) points to the importance of a synthetic investigation.

In a recent thematic study, *Civilized Piety*, T. Christopher Hoklotubbe explores "piety" or "godliness" in the Pastoral Epistles. Piety, he says, is presented as comprising an ideal way of life (1 Tim 2:2; 4:7; 2 Tim 3:12; Titus 2:12) that is in line with proper "instruction" (1 Tim 6:3) and the "truth" (Titus 1:1). He concludes that the Pastoral Epistles' rhetoric of piety is "informed by and evoked contemporaneous appeals to *pietas* and εὐσέβεια operative in intersecting and mutually informing imperial, civic, and philosophical cultural domains" (205). What is significant about Hoklotubbe's study is that he details how appeals to piety advanced sociopolitical aims, reinforced cultural values, and ideological assumptions in order to better understand what the claims to piety were achieving in the Pastoral Epistles. This functional aspect of the theme provides greater insight into the purpose of these letters. As Harding observes in his review, Hoklotubbe makes a persuasive case that the author is aligning Christian behavior with "popular notions of proper filial piety and reverence directed towards the Roman emperor," which are "essential strategies if the Christian community is to deflect prejudice and claim cultural legitimacy and institutional conformity" (2018, 345). This kind of study could also achieve significant results for other themes present in the Pastoral Epistles.

See also CANON OF PAUL'S LETTERS; ETHICS; GNOSIS, GNOSTICISM; LETTERS, LETTER FORMS;

Opponents of Paul; Paul in Acts; Pseudepigraphy/Forgery; Rhetorical Criticism; Roman Christianity; Salvation; Savior; Travel and Itinerary Plans; Urban Setting of Paul's Churches; Women.

BIBLIOGRAPHY. ***Commentaries:*** **M. Dibelius,** *Die Pastoralbriefe* (Tübingen: Mohr, 1955); **G. D. Fee,** *1 and 2 Timothy*, NIBC (Peabody, MA: Hendrickson, 1988); **B. Fiore,** *The Pastoral Epistles: First Timothy, Second Timothy, Titus*, SP 12 (Collegeville, MN: Liturgical Press, 2007); **A. L. C. Heydenreich,** *Die Pastoralbriefe Pauli* (Hadamar: Verlag der neuen Gelehrten-Buchhandlung, 1826); **C. R. Hutson,** *First and Second Timothy and Titus*, Paideia (Grand Rapids, MI: Baker, 2019); **L. T. Johnson,** *The First and Second Letters to Timothy*, AB (New York: Doubleday, 2001); **I. Howard Marshall,** *A Critical and Exegetical Commentary on the Pastoral Epistles*, ICC (Edinburgh: T&T Clark, 1999); **J. Quinn,** *The Letter to Titus*, AB (New York: Doubleday, 1990); **J. D. Quinn and W. C. Wacker,** *The First and Second Letters to Timothy*, Eerdmans Critical Commentary (Grand Rapids, MI: Eerdmans, 2000); **J. Roloff,** *Der Erste Brief an Timotheus*, EKKNT (Neukirchen-Vluyn: Neukirchener Verlag, 1988); **C. Spicq,** *Saint Paul: Les Épitres Pastorales*, 4th ed., 2 vols., Études Bibliques (Paris: J. Gabalda et Cie, 1969); **P. H. Towner,** *The Letters to Timothy and Titus*, NICNT (Grand Rapids, MI: Eerdmans, 2006).

Studies: **K. Aland,** *Repertorium der griechischen christlichen Papyri*, vol. 1, *Biblische Papyri*, Patristische Texte und Studien 18 (Münster: de Gruyter, 1976); **F. C. Baur,** *Die sogenannten Pastoralbriefe des Apostels Paulus aufs neue kritisch untersucht* (Tübingen: Stuttgart, 1835); **H. I. Bell and T. C. Skeat,** *Fragments of an Unknown Gospel and Other Early Christian Papyri* (London: Trustees of the British Museum; Oxford University, 1935); **K. Berding,** *Polycarp and Paul: An Analysis of Their Literary and Theological Relationship in Light of Polycarp's Use of Biblical and Extra-biblical Literature* (Boston: Brill, 2002); **J. van Bruggen,** *Die geschichtliche Einordnung der Pastoralbriefe* (Wuppertal: Brockhaus, 1981); **G. A. Deissmann,** *Light from the Ancient East: The New Testament Illustrated by Recently Discovered Texts of the Graeco-Roman World*, trans. L. R. M. Strachan (1927; repr., Grand Rapids, MI: Baker, 1980); **L. R. Donelson,** *Pseudepigraphy and Ethical Argument in the Pastoral Epistles* (Tübingen: Mohr, 1986); **W. G. Doty,** *Letters in Primitive Christianity* (Philadelphia: Fortress, 1973); **J. Duff,** "P46 and the Pastorals: A Misleading Consensus?," *NTS* 44, no. 4 (1998): 578-90; **E. B. Ebojo,** "A Scribe and His Manuscript: An Investigation into the Scribal Habits of Papyrus 46 (P. Chester Beatty II–P. Mich. Inv. 6238)" (PhD diss., University of Birmingham, 2014); **E. J. Epp,** "Textual Criticism in the Exegesis of the New Testament, with an Excursus on Canon," in *Handbook to Exegesis of the New Testament*, ed. S. E. Porter, New Testament Tools and Studies 25 (Leiden: Brill, 1997), 45-97; idem, "Issues in the Interrelation of New Testament Textual Criticism and Canon," in *The Canon Debate*, ed. L. M. McDonald and J. A. Sanders (Peabody, MA: Hendrickson, 2002), 485-515; **B. Fiore,** *The Function of Personal Example in the Socratic and Pastoral Epistles* (Rome: Biblical Institute, 1986); **E. Gathergood,** "Papyrus 32 (Titus) as a Multi-text Codex: A New Reconstruction," *NTS* 59, no. 4 (2013): 588-606; **D. W. Gill,** "A Saviour for the Cities of Crete: The Roman Background to the Epistle to Titus," in *The New Testament in Its First Century Setting: Essays on Context and Background in Honour of B. W. Winter on His 65th Birthday*, ed. P. J. Williams et al. (Grand Rapids, MI: Eerdmans, 2004), 220-30; **M. Gill,** *Jesus as Mediator: Politics and Polemic in 1 Timothy 2:1-7* (Oxford: Lang, 2008); **S. Goldhill,** "What Is Local Identity? The Politics of Cultural Mapping," in *Local Knowledge and Microidentities in the Imperial Greek World*, ed. Tim Whitmarsh (Cambridge: Cambridge University Press, 2010), 46-68; **M. D. Goulder,** "The Pastor's Wolves: Jewish Christian Visionaries Behind the Pastoral Epistles," *NovT* 38, no. 3 (1996): 242-56; **J. Gundry-Volf,** "Controlling the Bodies: A Theological Profile of the Corinthians Sexual Ascetics (1 Cor 7)," in *The Corinthian Correspondence*, ed. R. Bieringer (Leuven: Leuven University Press, 1996), 519-41; **A. T. Hanson,** *Studies in the Pastoral Epistles* (London: SPCK, 1968); **M. Harding,** *Tradition and Rhetoric in the Pastoral Epistles* (New York: Lang, 1998); idem, *What Are They Saying About the Pastoral Epistles?* (New York: Paulist Press, 2001); idem, review of *Civilized Piety: The Rhetoric of Pietas in the Pastoral Epistles and the Roman Empire*, by T. Christopher Hoklotubbe, *Review of Biblical Literature* (2018); **P. N. Harrison,** *The Problem of the Pastoral Epistles* (Humphrey Milford: Oxford University Press, 1921); **J. Herzer,** "Zwischen Mythos und Wahrheit: Neue Perspektiven auf die Sogenannten Pastoralbriefe," *NTS* 63, no. 3 (2017): 428-50; idem, *Die Pastoralbriefe und das Vermächtnis des Paulus: Studien zu den Briefen an Timotheus und Titus*, WUNT 476 (Tübingen: Mohr Siebeck, 2022); **G. G. Hoag,** *Wealth in Ancient Ephesus and the First Letter to Timothy: Fresh Insights from Ephesiaca by Xenophon of Ephesus*, BBR Supplement 11 (Winona Lake:

Eisenbrauns, 2015); **T. C. Hoklotubbe,** *Civilized Piety: The Rhetoric of Pietas in the Pastoral Epistles and the Roman Empire* (Waco, TX: Baylor University Press, 2017); **H. J. Holtzmann**, *Die Pastoralbriefe, kritisch und exegetisch behandelt* (Leipzig: Engelmann, 1880); **K. Hopkins,** "Half-Resurrection Man," review of *Paul: A Critical Life*, by J. Murphy-O'Connor, and *Paul: The Mind of the Apostle*, by A. N. Wilson, *London Review of Books* 19, no. 12 (1997): 14-15; **A. B. Huizenga,** *Moral Education for Women in the Pastoral and Pythagorean Letters: Philosophers of the Household* (Boston: Brill, 2013); **E. A. Judge,** *The Social Pattern of Christian Groups in the First Century* (London: Tyndale, 1960); idem, "The Early Christians as a Scholastic Community," *JRH* 1 (1960–1961): 4-15, 125-37; **R. J. Karris,** "The Background and Significance of the Polemic of the Pastoral Epistles," *JBL* 92 (1973): 549-64; **F. G. Kenyon,** *Chester Beatty Biblical Papyri, Fasciculus III, Pauline Epistles and Revelation* (London: Emery Walker, 1934); idem, *Chester Beatty Biblical Papyri, Fasciculus III Supplement, Pauline Epistles, Text* (London: Emery Walker, 1936); **R. M. Kidd,** *Wealth and Beneficence in the Pastoral Epistles: A "Bourgeois" Form of Early Christianity?* (Atlanta: Duke University Press, 1990); **L. M. Kidson,** "1 Timothy: An Administrative Letter," *EC* 5 (2014): 97-116; idem, "Saving the Woman in 1 Timothy 2: Childbirth, Women's Bodies, and the 'Other Instruction'" (paper presented at the Annual Meeting of the Society for Biblical Literature, San Diego, November 23, 2019); idem, "Fasting, Bodily Care, and the Widows of 1 Timothy 5:3-15," *EC* 11, no. 2 (2020): 191-205; idem, *Persuading Shipwrecked Men: The Rhetorical Strategies of 1 Timothy 1*, WUNT 526 (Tübingen: Mohr Siebeck, 2020); **A. J. Köstenberger and T. L. Wilder,** eds., *Entrusted with the Gospel: Paul's Theology in the Pastoral Epistles* (Nashville: B&H Academic, 2010); **U. Luck,** "ὑγιής, ὑγιαίνω," *TDNT* 8:312; **A. J. Malherbe,** "Medical Imagery in the Pastoral Epistles," in *Texts and Testaments: Critical Essays on the Bible and Early Church Fathers; A Volume in Honor of Stuart Dickson Currie*, ed. W. E. March (San Antonio, TX: Trinity University Press, 1980), 19-35; also *Paul and the Popular Philosophers* (Minneapolis: Fortress Press, 1981), 121-136; also *Light from the Gentiles: Hellenistic Philosophy and Early Christianity: Collected Essays, 1959-2012* (Leiden: Brill, 2014), 117-134; **D. I. Manomi,** *Virtue Ethics in the Letter to Titus: An Interdisciplinary Study*, WUNT 526 (Tübingen: Mohr Siebeck, 2021); **J. W. Marshall,** "'I Left You in Crete': Narrative Deception and Social Hierarchy in the Letter to Titus," *JBL* 127, no. 4 (2008): 781-803; **S. C. Martin,** *Pauli Testamentum: 2 Timothy and the Last Words of Moses* (Rome: Gregorian University Press, 1997); **B. M. Metzger,** *Manuscripts of the Greek Bible: An Introduction to Greek Palaeography* (Oxford: Oxford University Press, 1981); idem, *The Canon of the New Testament: Its Origin, Development, and Significance* (Oxford: Clarendon, 1987); **W. Michaelis,** *Pastoralbriefe und Gefangenschaftsbriefe: Zur Echtheitsfrage der Pastoralbriefe* (Gütersloh: "Der Rufer" Evangelischer Verlag, 1930); **M. Mitchell,** "PTebt 703 and the Genre of 1 Timothy: The Curious Career of a Ptolemaic Papyrus in Pauline Scholarship," *NovT* 44 (2002): 344-70; **J. Murphy-O'Connor,** *Paul: A Critical Life* (Oxford: Clarendon, 1996); **L. K. Pietersen,** *The Polemic of the Pastorals: A Sociological Examination of the Development of Pauline Christianity*, JSNTSup (New York: T&T Clark, 2004); **M. Prior**, *Paul the Letter-Writer and the Second Letter to Timothy*, JSNTSup 23 (Sheffield: JSOT Press, 1989); **J. Quinn,** "P46—the Pauline Canon?," *CBQ* 36, no. 3 (1974): 379-85; **P. J. Rabinowitz,** *Before Reading: Narrative Conventions and the Politics of Interpretation* (Columbus: Ohio State University Press, 1987); **F. D. E. Schleiermacher,** *Ueber den Sogenannten ersten Brief des Paulos an den Timotheos*, ed. J. C. Gass (Berlin: In der Realschulbuchhandlung, 1807); **J. E. C. Schmidt,** *Historisch-kritische Einleitung in's Neue Testament* (Gießen: Tasché und Müller, 1804); **M. Silva,** Review of *Die geschichtliche Einordnung der Pastoralbriefe*, by J. van Bruggen, *JETS* 25, no. 3 (1982): 381-82; **H. Stettler,** *Die Christologie der Pastoralbriefe*, WUNT 105 (Tübingen: Mohr Siebeck, 1998); **D. Thornton,** *Hostility in the House of God: An Investigation of the Opponents in 1 and 2 Timothy* (Winona Lake, IN: Eisenbrauns, 2016); **P. H. Towner,** *The Goal of Our Instruction*, JSNTSup 34 (Sheffield: Sheffield Academic, 1989); **P. Trummer,** *Die Paulustradition der Pastoralbriefe*, Beiträge zur biblischen Exegese und Theologie 8 (Frankfurt: Lang, 1978); **D. C. Verner,** *The Household of God: The Social World of the Pastoral Epistles* (Chico, CA: Scholars Press, 1983); **G. M. Wieland,** "Roman Crete and the Letter to Titus," *NTS* 55, no. 3 (2009): 338-54; **B. Witherington III,** *Letters and Homilies for Hellenized Christians*, vol. 1 (Downers Grove, IL: IVP Academic, 2006); **M. Wolter,** *Die Pastoralbriefe als Paulustradition*, FRLANT 146 (Göttingen: Vandenhoeck & Ruprecht, 1988); **A. Zuiderhoek,** "Oligarchs and Benefactors. Elite Demography and Euergetism in the Greek East of the Roman Empire," in *Political Culture in the Greek City After the*

Classical Age, ed. O. van Nijf and R. Alston (Leuven: Peeters, 2011), 185-95.

L. M. Kidson

PATRONAGE

Foundational cultural systems, such as patronage, usually went without being said. Paul's world functioned through gifts and gratitude, the reciprocal exchange of patronage. When Pliny (*Ep.* 1.19 LCL) cautions, "The length of our *friendship pledges you not to forget this gift," he means patronage and all its obligations, but he does not have to say so. Ancient patronage encompassed a wide range of asymmetrical, reciprocal relationships, broader than the Latin terms *patronus, cliens,* and *patrocinium* (see Marshall, 6). The web of mutually dependent relationships created by patronage interconnected the community, usually under the generic terms *friend* or *kinsman*. Patrons and clients were "friends," albeit socially and/or economically lopsided (see Pitt-Rivers, 140).

1. Lopsided Friendships
2. Strings Attached
3. Reciprocity
4. Gifts and Gratitude
5. Patronage in Paul
6. Grace, Faith, and Patronage

1. Lopsided Friendships.

Inequality permeated the Greco-Roman world (so Friesen, James, and Schowalter, 2). One's groups determined one's opportunities. Social systems are often better explained by illustration. Let us suppose Belen owns a family bakery in first-century Philippi. A fire destroys his bakery. What does Belen do? Relationship. Every morning, Diocles's "friends" line up at this wealthy benefactor's door to see whether Diocles needs anything done that day, to make any requests for help, and to receive any benefits he wished to give. These friends all have established relationships with Diocles as their patron. Belen joins the end of the line. He explains his problem and asks for help rebuilding his bakery. Diocles is not required (socially or morally) to help Belen (Seneca, *Ben.* 1.1.2), but he does help, likely through a mix of benefits. Seneca (*Ben.* 1.2.4 LCL) advises, "Help one person with money, another with credit, another with influence, another with advice, another with sound precepts" (see deSilva 2000, 97). Perhaps Diocles, drawing on the resources of his extended household, asks a brickmaker friend and a woodcutter friend to provide supplies, and another friend loans *slaves. Belen obviously has not earned this gift and will not be able to repay, but he will be expected to reciprocate by showing gratitude in more than words. Henceforth, Belen bakes bread for the people in Diocles's household. Belen wants to; he is grateful. Likewise, Diocles will ensure Belen receives a fair price for his bread. Now, Belen also lines up every morning at Diocles's house. The community would have seen the fire and knows Belen's plight. All know Diocles has helped the baker, and many will give Diocles *honor for it—a purpose of benefaction. Belen will boast of his patron's goodness (Seneca, *Ben.* 4.10.4-5; for much of this paragraph, see Richards and James).

2. Strings Attached.

Patronage often flourishes in cultures with higher levels of inequality and lower levels of governance. Those who controlled access to resources functioned as doorways for others. Those who had more were considered virtuous when they gave benefaction to others. Seneca (*Ben.* 1.3) allegorizes benefaction as throwing a ball back and forth and also (perhaps better) as three young maidens dancing in a circle. Patronage starts with giving a gift, but there must be reciprocity for it to work. It was a circle. Individualists often criticize this as gifts with strings attached. Ancients would agree but say it in a positive way: they hold hands.

3. Reciprocity.

Clients reciprocated to their patron, not usually with financial gifts, but with gratitude, meaning honoring, obeying, and being loyal to the patron (Cicero, *Fam.* 10.24). Politicians were not above using the strings of patronage to obligate clients to vote for them; Cicero's brother purportedly urged it (Q. Cicero, *Comm. Pet.* 4). The greatest wrong clients could commit was to be ungrateful to their patrons for their gifts. Seneca notes, "homicides, tyrants, thieves, adulterers, robbers, sacrilegious men, and traitors there always will be; but worse than all these is the crime of ingratitude" (*Ben.* 1.10.4 LCL; also Virgil, *Aen.* 6.609). A patron complains to his clients that they are being ungrateful: "You have received many favors . . . from us, and I am exceedingly amazed that you remember none of them but speak badly of us. For the ungrateful . . . forget noble men" (Pseudo-Libanius, *Ep. St.* 64 LCL; see Harrison, 71).

A teaching of Jesus is sometimes used to reject reciprocity (Lk 14:12-14). Jesus rejects shallow motives, urging us to invite the disempowered, thus giving a gift to God, who will reciprocate to us

(Lk 14:14). Granted, Jesus' teachings here are radical, as they are elsewhere, but his teachings about guarding our motives are not a wholesale rejection of reciprocity, any more than he rejected praying or fasting. Collectivists disapproved when gifts had no strings attached, for it meant no bonds, no lifelong friendships, no patrons or protectors (Seneca, *Ben.* 6.41.2; see deSilva 2017, 153). In Paul's world, gifts created relationship; they were supposed to have strings. Likely Paul hoped the strings of the Jerusalem offering would tie the Jewish to the *Gentile churches (2 Cor 9). Proverbs means it positively when it advises, "Everyone is the friend of one who gives gifts" (Prov 19:6 NIV).

4. Gifts and Gratitude.
Unlike modern (Western) individualism, the ancient Mediterranean world believed people were born into and also joined collective groups. Someone in need would turn to a friend (usually within the group) for help (Lk 11:5-6) and would later reciprocate. In Paul's world people gave to others and expected others to give to them. Even *God participated in this reciprocity: "Do good to the devout, and you will be repaid—if not by them, certainly by the Most High" (Sir 12:1-2 NRSV; see Crook, 81). Gratitude and loyalty maintained patronage, rather than legal documents. Although there were no contracts, both patrons and clients knew they were under obligation, a moral duty, to continue the relationship. They trusted the other party would give when they were in need, as seen in *letters acknowledging this sense of obligation to one another, expressing gratitude, and asking for favors (Barclay, 27). Gifts and gratitude was the air they breathed, the grease of society. In a Corinthian inscription replete with patronage language, Junia Theodora is called a "benefactress," praised for her "patronage" (*prostasian*) to Lycian travelers, for being a "generous" patron who "benefits" many citizens and does so because of her "goodwill" and who acts on any "favor" asked of her. Her benefaction is reciprocated by the "gratitude" and "loyalty" of all the Lycians (Murphy-O'Connor, 82-83).

5. Patronage in Paul.
Paul commends Phoebe (Rom 16:1-2) as a *prostatis* (benefactor), a cognate of *prostasian* (patronage) used in the Corinthian inscription. When the Jewish leadership brought their charges against Paul before Felix, their lawyer used a common approach, praising their patron's prowess and knowledge, rehearsing all the ways the patron had benefited them in the past, culminating in expressing their profound gratitude to the patron (Harrison, 68). Repeating the patronage history reinforced the strings attached between them before the client made a request (Acts 24:2-4). We see the dynamics of patronage used (and abused) throughout this story. As their patron, Felix would be looking for ways to do favors as part of the reciprocal process of binding the Jewish leadership as his loyal clients. Ultimately, though, Felix does not act in the genuine interests of the Jews but simply in his own interests—the worst behavior of a patron. He does not use his imbalanced power to serve the communities who are dependent on him but rather to benefit himself (see Ezek 34). Seneca would have been appalled, as Luke likely expected us to be.

Paul had patrons. Staying in the home of an influential person often meant receiving their patronage. *Wealthy benefactors often hosted guests, clients, and other friends passing through. The inscription for Junia notes how her benefaction involved hosting. Likely Lydia acted as a patron for Paul (Acts 16:14-15). Paul later mentions that he was *financially supported by the Philippian church, probably meaning Lydia and/or the jailer (2 Cor 11:8; Phil 4:18-19). This makes it more striking Paul refuses to accept gifts from the Corinthian church (1 Cor 9), probably because the church in Corinth is torn by factions (1 Cor 1). If Paul accepts financial support from any patrons in these factions, he will become indebted—tied—to that faction of the church. Paul does not allow them to gain control of him through their patronage. Was it hypocrisy for Paul to accept the patronage in Philippi and not in Corinth? Paul understood all gifts have strings attached, so it depended on what *kind* of strings were attached.

6. Grace, Faith, and Patronage.
One of the most common Greek terms in patronage was *charis* (Harrison, 2). It meant the way a patron benefited a client but also could mean the gift itself. But it could also refer to the way clients reciprocated with gratitude (deSilva 2000, 104-5). Thus, *charis* could refer to the giver's generosity, the gift, and the recipient's gratitude (Georges, 98-99). Thus, the NT can speak of the **grace* (*charis*) of God (Lk 2:40), sending a *gift* (*charis*) to *Jerusalem (1 Cor 16:3), and being *grateful* (*charis*) to God (Rom 7:25). This makes more sense when we remember Seneca describes benefaction (*charis*) as constantly flowing between the three dancers.

Another common term in patronage was *pistis* (Latin: *fides*) to describe how clients *trusted* their patron (deSilva 2000, 115). The client was loyal (1 Cor 4:2) and did not seek others to provide. *Pistis* also was used for the way a patron was loyal in acting to benefit their clients (Heen, 728). Thus, according to Seneca, the proper response to a gift is *fides* (trustworthiness) by the receiver, fulfilling "the trust (*fides*) placed in the receiver by the giver" (Engberg-Pedersen, 40, on Seneca, *Ben.* 1.1.3). Like *charis, pistis* is also part of the dance of giving and receiving and giving back. When talking about patron-client relationships, *pistis* could be translated into English as "trust," "loyalty," "*faith," or "faithfulness" depending on the context.

Paul commandeered everyday terms Mediterranean people used to talk about patronage, *charis* and *pistis,* to explain the mysterious *salvation (*sōteria*) of God (Eph 1:7-8, 13): the proper response to God lavishing *charis* (grace) is for the Christian to respond with *pistis* (faith), "new patterns of loyalty and behavior" (Barclay, 444). Paul used *charis* to describe both God's generosity and the gift (Rom 5:15). Similarly, like a patron is faithful to care for and protect their clients, so Paul uses *pistis* to describe God's faithfulness (Rom 3:3) and also to illustrate the way Christians trust in God alone: "to the one who does not work but trusts [*pisteuonti*] God who justifies the ungodly, their faith [*pistis*] is credited as *righteousness" (Rom 4:5 NIV).

Paul's understanding of *pistis* and *charis,* like his other theological ideas, is complex and influenced by Israel's Scriptures (Dunn, 321-22; see Oropeza); nonetheless, the basic context is patronage. A client's faith (*pistis*) was not believing a list of concepts about the patron but trusting in the patron. The effect of this trust was to bind the client to the patron. J. Georges notes, "Israel's 'faith' was not a set of cognitive ideas *about* God but an embodied allegiance *to* God as their sovereign. In this view, the opposite of faith/faithfulness would be treason and disloyalty (not intellectual doubt or atheism)" (102). Talking about faith as allegiance can be overplayed (see Bates). In ancient patronage, a client trusted in facts/ideas about the patron and was loyal to the patron. It is a false dichotomy to ask, Are we saved by assenting to ideas about Jesus or by loyalty to Jesus? A client *believed* certain things about the patron, and so too did the followers of *Christ (1 Cor 15:3-5). Trusting these things are true about the patron leads to allegiance. One's life now revolves around a new lord and benefactor. The common English translations of "faith" and "believe" can suggest an individualized intellectual decision about facts, but *pistis* (faith) was "not primarily internal emotions or cognitive assent, but a sense of covenantal loyalty and allegiance" (Georges, 102).

In the first century, patrons were criticized for not giving benefits to those they could and for stopping if people were not grateful and deserving clients. Such actions did not describe an ideal patron (Seneca, *Ben.* 2.1.2; 1.1.3). Paul would have agreed in at least two ways. First, while as clients we are no better (and sometimes worse) than a typical client, God is not like the typical patron, who only gives to the grateful: "But God demonstrates his own *love for us in this: While we were still sinners, Christ died for us" (Rom 5:8 NIV). Second, anyone who trusts in God's offer of patronage—who accepts the *charis*—enters into a relationship with him. Likely, this was part of Paul's purpose in choosing the patronage metaphor. Patronage began with trust in an unmerited gift of benefaction, but it continued in an ongoing relationship. *Patronage brings one into the *household.* For Paul, I am not primarily called to be loyal to and to trust in Jesus individually. Grace and faith is not about having an individual, isolated relationship with God. By God's grace (benefaction), I have been made part of God's household (Eph 2:19) and should behave like it (1 Tim 3:15). Like an ancient client, I should begin every day by receiving his daily benefaction and by asking my patron, my father, what he needs of me this day.

See also Faith; Financial Support; Friendship; Grace; Hospitality; Kinship Language in Paul.

BIBLIOGRAPHY. **G. R. Anderson,** *Charity* (New Haven, CT: Yale University Press, 2013); **J. M. G. Barclay,** *Paul and the Gift* (Grand Rapids, MI: Eerdmans, 2015); **M. Bates,** *Salvation by Allegiance Alone* (Grand Rapids, MI: Baker Academic, 2017); **Z. A. Crook,** "Reciprocity: Covenantal Exchange as a Test Case," in *Ancient Israel: The Old Testament in Its Social Context,* ed. P. F. Esler (Minneapolis: Fortress, 2006), 78-91; **D. A. deSilva,** *Honor, Patronage, Kinship & Purity: Unlocking New Testament Culture* (Downers Grove, IL: IVP Academic, 2000); idem, "We Are Debtors," in *Paul and Seneca in Dialogue,* ed. J. Dodson and D. Briones (Leiden: Brill, 2017); **J. D. G. Dunn,** *Theology of Paul the Apostle* (Grand Rapids, MI: Eerdmans, 1998); **T. Engberg-Pedersen,** "Gift-Giving and Friendship: Seneca and Paul in Romans 1–8 on the Logic of God's χαρις and Its Human Response," *HTR* 101 (2008): 15-44; **S. J. Friesen, S. A. James, and D. N. Schowalter,** "Inequality in Corinth," in *Corinth in Contrast: Studies in Inequality,* ed. D. N. Schowalter, S. J. Friesen, and S. A. James, NovTSup 155 (Leiden: Brill, 2014), 1-16; **J. Georges,** *Ministering in Patronage Cultures*

(Downers Grove, IL: InterVarsity Press, 2019); **J. R. Harrison,** *Paul's Language of Grace in Its Greco-Roman Context* (Eugene, OR: Wipf & Stock, 2017); **E. Heen,** "Pistis," in *Routledge Encyclopedia of Ancient Religions,* ed. E. Orlin (New York: Routledge, 2016), 728-29; **J. Marshall,** *Jesus, Patrons, and Benefactors: Roman Palestine and the Gospel of Luke,* WUNT 2/259 (Tübingen: Mohr Siebeck, 2009); **J. Murphy-O'Connor,** *St. Paul's Corinth: Texts and Archaeology,* 3rd ed. (Collegeville, MN: Liturgical Press, 2002); **B. J. Oropeza,** "The Expectation of Grace: Paul on Benefaction and the Corinthians' Ingratitude (2 Corinthians 6:1)," *BBR* 24 (2014): 207-26; **J. Pitt-Rivers,** *The People of the Sierra* (London: Weidenfield and Nicholson, 1954); **E. R. Richards and R. James,** *Misreading Scripture with Individualist Eyes: Patronage, Honor, and Shame in the Biblical World* (Downers Grove, IL: InterVarsity Press, 2020).

E. R. Richards

PAUL AND HIS INTERPRETERS. *See articles under* INTERPRETATION.

PAUL AND JUDAISM

The *apostle to the *Gentiles was born a Jew. Judaism in Paul's day included allegiance to the Jerusalem *temple, the house of the one, true *God, who had called a people unto himself. Jews were monotheists who followed their ancient Scripture. Three specific practices distinguished Jews from their Gentile, pagan neighbors: *circumcision, *food laws, and Sabbath rest. The relationship of Paul's calling to his Judaism, and thus the *gospel message to the Torah/*law, was controversial even in his own lifetime.

1. Brief Biography of Paul
2. Judaism and the Law
3. Paul Against Judaism
4. Paul Alongside Judaism
5. Paul Within Judaism
6. Paul According to Jewish Scholars
7. Conclusion

1. Brief Biography of Paul.

Paul identifies himself as a Hebrew and as an Israelite, labels that draw on the history of God's people found in Jewish Scripture (2 Cor 11:21-22; Phil 3:5). The book of Acts tells us that Paul was a Diaspora Jew, born in Tarsus, a large, thriving Greco-Roman city on the transportation route between Asia Minor and Syria. In Paul's world, "Jew" and "Gentile" were persistent religious, social, and ethnic categories that were continually negotiated, sometimes with violent results (Acts 16:19-23; 17; 19:23-41; Josephus, *J.W.* 7.3.3-4). Paul trained in Jerusalem under a well-respected Jewish teacher, Gamaliel (Acts 5:33-39; 22:3). Paul speaks of having *knowledge and zeal far beyond what was typical among his peers (Gal 1:13-14). He identifies as a Pharisee (Phil 3:5).

This composite picture of Paul demonstrates the ways Jews negotiated their cultural milieu. J. Barclay (1999) helpfully suggests three basic options chosen by Jews as they expressed their identity: assimilate, acculturate, accommodate. These categories are important as we explore Paul and Judaism, because they highlight that Jews themselves came to different conclusions and responded in a variety of ways to the realities of the Greco-Roman world. Paul moderately assimilated as he worked in cities throughout the Roman *Empire. He acculturated to the Greek language (he wrote his letters in Greek), even as he probably was familiar with Hebrew and Aramaic. Paul did not accommodate but rather rejected explicit pagan religious expressions such as idols and temples.

S. Cohen provides another useful way to think about Jewish identity, arguing that it centered on (1) religious, cultural, and political affiliation, and (2) *ethnicity and geography. Paul's Jewish contemporaries thought of their Jewish ethnicity as a status granted at birth, and their religious identity the result of choices they made with respect to the law. Paul was Jewish by birth, and he chose the religious identity of Pharisee. Paul's Gentile contemporaries also valued their own ethnicity. The Gentile believers were not a homogeneous ethnic group that represented a universal culture; D. K. Buell reminds us that we should not imagine that Jews were the only group that had an ethnicity.

1.1. Paul's "Conversion." It is common to think of Paul as having converted from Judaism to Christianity, but the situation is more complicated. Paul describes a vibrant, zealous religious life as a Pharisee before he believed in Jesus *Christ as *Lord (Phil 3:4-6), not a life of fear or dread before God. He contrasts that time with his work as an apostle to the Gentiles as before and after his encounter with Christ Jesus. Thus if *convert* means "change belief about Jesus as Messiah," then Paul converted. S. McKnight explains, "His radical change in his view of Jesus created a radical change in Paul's life" (140). However, because Paul continued to embrace the Jewish Scriptures, to participate in synagogue *worship, and to self-identify as a Jew, we should not conclude that Paul "converted" to Christianity as if he left Judaism altogether. Instead, it is better to think about Paul testifying to a new *identity, that is, "*in Christ," that involved a new *mission (*witness to Gentiles) and a new community (congregations that confess Jesus as Lord). This point becomes important in looking at Paul and Judaism, as the greater the historical distance one places between Paul and his Jewish heritage, the greater the theological distance tends to be between his gospel and the Torah/law.

1.2. Evidence of Paul and Judaism from Paul's Letters. Paul speaks of the time before he was called as an apostle to the Gentiles as one of great zeal for God (Gal 1:13-14). He outlines his heritage as being of the tribe of Benjamin and describes pursuing Pharisaic teachings with dedication (Phil 3:5-6). He acknowledges Andronicus and Junia as "fellow Jews" in ministry with him, including imprisonments (Rom 16:7). He lived with Aquila and Priscilla, Jews who settled in *Corinth after fleeing Rome (Acts 18:1-3); this shows that he regularly fellowshipped with Jews who were believers in Jesus Messiah.

1.3. Evidence of Paul and Judaism from Acts. Paul regularly attended synagogue and spoke to groups gathered there (Acts 17:2, 10; 18:4; see also 2 Cor 11:24). He participated in the *Jerusalem Council, which discussed his gospel and the role of circumcision and law obedience for Gentile converts (Acts 12:12). Paul fulfilled a purification rite at the Jerusalem temple and paid for four other men to do likewise (Acts 21:23-26; 24:18). Paul declares that he believes the Law and the Prophets, and in the *resurrection, even as many Jews of his day did (Acts 24:10-16; 28:17-23). He speaks of the *hope he has that God will fulfill his promise to Paul's ancestors (Acts 26:5-8).

2. Judaism and the Law.

One of the defining features of ancient Judaism is the law, which stands alongside monotheism, *election of *Israel as a people, and a single cult site, the temple in Jerusalem. Paul uses the term *law* (Gk. *nomos*) with a range of nuance in his letters, using the term 118 times in four of the seven undisputed letters, predominantly in Romans (74) and Galatians (32; Soards, 255). In later Christian writings, the terms *Judaism* and *law* are used interchangeably. Often the one is defined by the other: Judaism is law, therefore Judaism is "legalistic." Because the two concepts are interwoven in Christian writings, it is important to highlight key Christian historical figures' views on Judaism and the law.

Generally speaking, the ancient *church, which by the second century included an overwhelming majority of Gentiles, viewed Judaism as a failing religion. Its Jerusalem temple was in ruins, its population scattered throughout the Roman Empire (although with a growing population in Babylon, part of the Persian Empire). Jews were harassed, their property vandalized, and the gospel's account of Christ's crucifixion laid at the entire community's feet. An influential voice was that of Augustine, bishop of the North African city of Hippo (354–430). He knew only a few Jews but used Judaism as a concept to argue with Manicheans and Pelagians. In a letter to his contemporary Jerome, Augustine declares, based on Galatians 2:14, that Paul was a Jew, and even after he followed Christ, Paul continued to observe Jewish rites (*Letter 40*, 4.4). This behavior of following the law, however, held only for the apostolic period. Augustine defended himself against Manichaeans and their strong dualism by stressing that the law was good and literally true, although Christians benefited from it most through allegorical readings. On this basis, Augustine held that Jews benefit society for two reasons: first, they show that the ancient Scriptures are not false, and second, their current misery demonstrates their failure to recognize Jesus as Messiah (Nirenberg, 129). They are doomed to roam the earth, much as was Cain. Augustine's views guided the political policies of the Middle Ages and informed Martin Luther's theology.

The Reformation included rising antagonism toward Jews, with Martin Luther's words having a lasting impact on the Protestant views of Jews and Judaism. Like Augustine, Luther stressed the literal meaning of Scripture, but he argued that the Jewish Scripture had Jesus Christ as its focus. For example, while Augustine heard King David's voice in the Psalms, Luther heard Jesus' voice—for all prophets and prophecies are of Jesus Christ. In Psalm 1, the wicked and scoffers are Jews who taunted Jesus, according to Luther (WA 3:11).

Luther promoted a strong contrast between "*grace" and "works," with the former accepted "by *faith alone." This contrasted with the current teachings of the church, which he complained focused on grace received through sacraments and merits as well. For example, Luther understood 2 Corinthians 3:6 through his argument with the Catholic Church (WA 22:219.31-38). The papists adhered to the spiritual reading, he argued, but in their hands, it was no more than elevating human reason and allegorical readings. Luther condemned this as relying on merit for *salvation. He concluded that "Paul's 'killing letter' is not the literal sense of Scripture, but rather the law itself" (Nirenberg, 258). This hermeneutical move on

Luther's part erased the positive role that Jews played in society in Augustine.

In 1543 Luther wrote *Von den Jüden und ihren Lügen* ("The Jews and Their Lies"; WA 50:330.5-6), a strongly anti-Jewish tract used by Adolf Hitler centuries later in his *Mein Kampf.* Jewish proselytism toward Christians was Luther's asserted motivation, but historical evidence supporting this claim is thin. Existing stereotypes of Jews as Luther found them in the church and wider European culture are found throughout his writings. Luther distinguished between biblical Jews such as Moses who looked forward to the Messiah, and Jews of the Gospels and later who rejected Jesus as Messiah. We must note that Luther wrote a theological evaluation of law and grace, with his signature claim "*justification by faith alone"; he did not offer a historical exploration into Second Temple Judaism itself (Bird 2009, 115).

Luther's writings have a lasting influence in Western Christian thought. His words were preserved in Theodor Fritsch's *Catechism for Antisemites* (1887), later published as *Handbook on the Jewish Question: The Most Important Facts Necessary for Judgement of the Jewish People* (1907). The twentieth century was arguably the bloodiest time in world history. The Holocaust was fueled in part by anti-Semitic Christian rhetoric that included words of Luther, transposed into a Nazi and German Christian (Deutschen Christen) key. S. Heschel observes that Jewish teachings and the Jewish identity of Jesus, Paul, and the other apostles created problems for Christian Nazis, who wanted to erase all traces of Judaism and Jewishness from the NT witness. She concludes, "Through the various methods, Jesus was transformed from a Jew prefigured by the Old Testament into an anti-Semite and a proto-Nazi" (Heschel, 26-27).

Modern scholars tend to fall into three camps when approaching Paul and Judaism, arguing that Paul and his gospel stand against Judaism, alongside Judaism, or within Judaism.

3. Paul Against Judaism.

This view asserts that Paul spoke against the Judaism of his day, which was a works-righteousness religion. That is, Jews sought to gain salvation, or God's favor, by meritorious works that would tip the divine scales in their favor. This posture is generalized as a human stance of pride and self-righteousness over against God's grace. The position that Judaism is legalistic has enjoyed strong support among scholars and the church down through the centuries. For example, F. Weber wrote *System der altsynagogalen palästinischen Theologie aus Targum, Midrasch und Talmud* (1880) and viewed his Jewish sources through a lens of nineteenth-century Protestant theology. He concluded that Judaism promoted a distant God and an empty, external shell of religious rites, in contrast to Christianity's rich inner life of faith. E. Schürer followed Weber's views on Judaism as legalistic in *The History of the Jewish People in the Age of Christ* (1897; 1973–1987). H. Strack and P. Billerbeck published a multivolume commentary on the NT from the Mishnah and Talmud (1922–1961) that included numerous Jewish stereotypes. So too W. Bousset, whose *Die Religion des Judentums im neutestamentlichen Zeitalter* offered a negative portrait of Judaism. Bousset was part of the "history of religions" school and held that religion moved from primitive to mature expressions. He described Second Temple Judaism as preliminary to Christianity. His student, R. Bultmann (1884–1976), went on to greatly influence twentieth-century NT studies with a similarly disapproving view of Judaism.

In the early and mid-twentieth century, Bultmann's view of Paul's gospel was widely followed. Bultmann claims that Paul exposed the universal human condition of striving for autonomy, boasting before God. Bultmann's existentialist worldview contributed to his framing of Paul, and he assumed that the Jew in Paul's letters was legalistic and self-righteous. For Bultmann, the worst *sin was self-righteousness. His work *Theologie des Neuen Testaments* (*Theology of the New Testament*, 1948) argues that Paul did not view humanity in two camps—Jew and non-Jew—but rather as a single whole. From this, Bultmann asserts that Paul viewed the law as leading to sin, based on his reading of Romans 3:20. This theme continued in his student E. Käsemann (1906–1998), who speaks negatively of the "hidden Jew in all of us" (Käsemann 1969, 186), a phrase used positively by Paul in Romans 2:29. "Jew" is generalized to any person who vindicates himself before God. Käsemann spoke against K. Stendahl's views (see below), arguing that they diminish the centrality of the *righteousness of God and justification by faith, considered to be Paul's central position. He was a member of the German confessing church, and Bultmann supported the confessing church during Nazi rule.

Both scholars are heirs to F. C. Baur (1792–1860) and the Tübingen school. Baur published *Paulus, der Apostel Jesu Christi* (1845; ET, *Paul, the Apostle of Jesus Christ*, 1876), arguing that Christianity represents universal religious endeavor, and Judaism is particularistic. Baur relied on Hegel's *philosophy and developed a view of history that requires thesis and antithesis. Judaism provided the antithesis, for it was inferior in its particularism. In all three cases, Baur, Bultmann, and Käsemann drew, perhaps unwittingly, from Luther's antithesis of Judaism (legalistic/inferior) and Christianity (faith-based/superior).

Recent proponents of a Paul-against-Judaism view include S. Westerholm, who follows a traditional reading of Paul, with the caveat that ancient Judaism was not legalistic. Reflecting on Romans 3:20, he writes that the verse's "denial that the law's requirements can serve as the path to righteousness is based rather on a more radical perception of human sinfulness than that held by most Jews" (Westerholm, 97-98). He concludes that Paul's doctrine of justification expresses Paul's interest in distinguishing grace and works.

F. Watson shares some similarities with Luther's theological views but disagrees with Luther's "essentially allegorical interpretation of Paul's critique of works" (Watson, 25). He argues that Paul parted from Judaism but qualifies this in important ways. First, Paul's congregations were a sectarian group separating from the parent group. Second, the separation was "in the form of an ongoing argument about scriptural interpretation, an attempt to show that the true sense of scripture—the one that attests the truth of the gospel—belongs to 'us' rather than to 'them'" (21-22). He holds that "works of the law" communicates any aspect of the Jewish way of life, not merely boundary markers such as circumcision, food laws, and Sabbath practices. Watson adds that Paul stresses divine agency to a greater degree than did contemporary Jews.

Some scholars who identify with the apocalyptic Paul view share similar ideas about the role of law and Judaism within Paul's thought, although they argue from a different angle. Here the emphasis is on the break with Judaism and any earlier religions, and the newness of Christ's redemption over against the *covenant of the law. Käsemann's commentary on Romans highlights aspects of this view. He focuses on dichotomies of sin/grace, law/gospel, Jew/Gentile, and *Adam/Christ. His apocalyptic focus can be seen in his insistence that until the revealing of Christ by God, no one could know that the law convicts of sin. He argues that "the signature of *cosmology may be perceived in *anthropology" (Käsemann 1980, 52). J. L. Martyn's commentary on Galatians (1997) promotes an apocalyptic reading of Paul's gospel as an unanticipated but welcomed inbreaking of God into human history with Christ's *death on the *cross. The contrast is not between works and faith but between human and divine actions, the faithfulness of Christ who died for the world.

D. Campbell affirms Martyn's *hermeneutics and affirms Sanders's position (see below) that Jews in Paul's day were not legalists. Campbell focuses on Romans 1–4, arguing against an interpretation that sees Paul moving from universal plight in Romans 1 to solution in Romans 3–4. Instead, Campbell suggests that Paul's Jewish Christian missionary interlocutor presents a (false) version of the gospel that includes Gentile conversion to Judaism. Romans 1:18-32 does not represent Paul's thought, but is his presentation of his Jewish opponent's views.

M. C. de Boer focuses on the cosmic dimension of Adam's sin and Christ's redemption, and the two ages represented by them. Sin and Death are personified, alien forces that enslave humans, and only Christ defeats them. The law is irrelevant to such a situation, to obtaining righteousness. Paul's position is at odds, de Boer argues, with two contemporary apocalypses (4 Ezra, 2 Baruch) that put confidence in law observance as the solution to sin and death. As a final example of this view, B. Gaventa examines Romans 9–11 and concludes that the revealing of Christ uncovers the identity of Israel. She explains that Romans 10:4-13 shows that "Christ has, in effect, displaced the law" (Gaventa, 251). She insists that Paul did not cease to be a Jew, nor cease thinking of himself as a Jew.

I include here the Catholic post-Holocaust position, expressed in the Second Vatican Council's document *Nostra Aetate* (1962–1965). This document asserts that the passion of Christ must not be laid at all Jews' feet. It continues, "Although the Church is the new people of God, the Jews should not be presented as rejected or accursed by God, as if this followed from the Holy Scriptures" (4.13). It affirms that "God holds the Jews most dear for the sake of their Fathers; He does not repent of the gifts He makes or of the calls he issues—such is the witness of the Apostle" (4.10). Here the document makes an implied reference to Romans 11:28-29.

4. Paul Alongside Judaism.

This position places Paul within the milieu of Second Temple Judaism and asserts that Paul's gospel reimagines the fulfillment of God's promised Messiah. Some expressions of the new perspective on Paul fit here. The new perspective on Paul began with a reexamination of Second Temple Judaism after World War II. The "new" in the title reflects a contrast with the traditional picture of Judaism as legalistic and a works-righteousness religion that sought favor with God by earning merit through good works. The argument asserts that Jews did not try to earn salvation but were elected as God's people and obeyed the law as a faithful, covenant response. N. T. Wright summarizes, "The 'new perspective' contained elements of a *Reformed* protest (Judaism and the Law as positive and God-given) against a *Lutheran* theology (Judaism as the wrong sort of religion, the Law as negative" (Wright, 369).

One of the earliest arguments challenging the traditional view came from K. Stendahl (1921–2008). His 1963 article, "The Apostle Paul and the Introspective Conscience of the West," broke new ground in arguing that Paul did not experience the law as burdensome; instead, Paul had a "robust conscience" (see Phil 3:6). Stendahl contrasts Paul's views with Luther's position and adds that Luther had a troubled conscience, based on his late medieval context. Stendahl focuses on Paul's work with Gentiles, who were not obliged to keep the law in their life in Christ. He also argues that Paul did not convert to Christianity but should be understood in a similar fashion to the ancient Israelite prophets who were called by God to preach a message to a people (Gal 1:13-16).

The ideas of the new perspective on Paul coalesced with E. P. Sanders, who coined the phrase "covenantal nomism" to describe the Jewish belief that they are elected as God's people by God's covenant and follow the law (*nomos*) as obedient people. He argues that Judaism is a religion of grace. Sanders looks for patterns of religion, ascertaining the function of getting in and staying in as members of the religious group. Paul saw nothing inherently wrong with Judaism, except that it did not accept Jesus as the Messiah, according to Sanders. Sanders's covenantal nomism spawned four movements in Pauline studies: the new perspective on Paul, the apocalyptic Paul (noted above), the participationist Paul, and Paul within Judaism.

Continuing in the new perspective on Paul, J. D. G. Dunn puts forward that Paul had in mind ethnic boundary markers in his critique of *works of the law. These markers included circumcision, food laws, and Sabbath rites, and were best put aside by Gentile members of the congregation, although Jewish members could continue to follow Torah observance as an expression of ethnic identity. N. T. Wright focuses on covenant and exile in developing his understanding of Judaism in Paul's milieu. B. Pitre, M. P. Barber, and J. A. Kincaid coined the phrase "new covenant Jew" to represent Paul's relationship within Judaism. Paul's message is described as "*new covenantal nomism*—that is, as a system whereby one 'gets in' to the new covenant through the grace of faith and *baptism, and 'stays in' by fidelity and fulfilling 'the *law of Christ'" (Pitre, Barber, and Kincaid, 74). These Roman Catholic authors stress the Jewish cultic and sacrificial foundations of Paul's new-covenant understanding of the *Lord's Supper and baptism. Participation in Christ through the Eucharist brings unity to his *body, the members of the new covenant.

J. Barclay develops a second trajectory, attending to the various understandings of grace in Second Temple Judaism. He builds on the fact that *charis* can be translated as "gift" or "grace." "Grace is everywhere in the theology of Second Temple Judaism, but not everywhere the same" (Barclay 2015, 565). He presents six perceptions (he calls them perfections) of grace: superabundance, singularity, priority, efficacy, incongruity, and noncircularity. Incongruity refers to a gift given without regard to the recipient's worthiness to receive it. Paul argues that the gift of the gospel is given without condition. Noncircularity refers to a gift having no necessary reciprocity. Paul commanded believers to live lives worthy of the gospel (Eph 4:1), and in this way, he understood the gospel gift to have circularity or reciprocity.

5. Paul Within Judaism.

This position starts with Paul as a Jew and not as a believer in Jesus as Messiah. It addresses Paul's vocation as an apostle *to the Gentiles*. S. K. Stowers's *A Rereading of Romans* forged a new path from Sanders's initial observations. Stowers argues that Paul's implied audience in his Romans epistle is Gentile believers. He proposes that Paul used speech-in-character (*prosōpopoiia*) to identify a boastful Gentile in Romans 2:1-16, and a Jewish teacher of Gentiles in Romans 2:17–4:22. Stowers remarks, "The readers thus overhear a debate between Paul and his Jewish competitors for gentile hearts and minds" (Stowers, 37). R. Thorsteinsson builds on Stowers's argument. Focusing on the phrase "if you call yourself a Jew" (Rom 2:17), he concludes that Paul's intended or implied audience was Gentiles and presents his chief interlocutor as a Judaizing *Gentile* missionary. Thorsteinsson's reading of Romans 2 rejects the traditional reading that Paul criticizes Judaism and Jews as hypocrites, temple thieves, adulterers, and the like. R. Rodriguez and M. Thiessen engage these questions further in a collection of essays, *The So-Called Jew in Paul's Letters to the Romans*.

M. Nanos argues that Paul incorporated his belief in Jesus as Messiah into his Jewish way of life. "Paul saw himself wholly within Judaism, as one who was assigned a special role in the restoration of Israel and the nations (Rom 11:1-15; Gal 1:13-16)" (2011, 552). As such, Paul continued to follow Jewish rites and sought to convince his fellow Jews to follow Jesus as Messiah even as they continued to observe Torah. Nanos contends that Paul's letter to the Romans concentrates on Gentile believers' arrogance and sense of privilege. Paul does not dismiss or disregard the law (Rom 3:31). His concern with the law centers on Gentile circumcision, not the entire law (Gal 2:16).

Others allege that Paul spoke the gospel only to Gentiles because Paul was convinced that the Jewish covenant remains in place for Jews. This position, often referred to as *Sonderweg*, or "two paths," insists that Jesus is the savior of Gentiles only. L. Gaston maintains that Paul has no concerns with Judaism but that he disagreed with his fellow Jews about the salvation of the nations in Christ Jesus. Thus, when Paul critiques the law, it is in relation to non-Jews. To avoid the *curse of the law, Gentiles must enter the covenant through Christ. J. Gager finds Paul to be strongly supportive of Israel and reasons that his target audience is Gentiles, not Jews. Gager resists reading Paul as speaking in universal terms and insists that he is interested only in the particular situation of Gentiles not doing the law. For Paul, the law condemns Gentiles, not Jews.

6. Paul According to Jewish Scholars.

Few Jewish scholars take up the task of exploring the life and thought of the apostle Paul. Jewish scholars often attributed the perceived anti-Jewish rhetoric in Paul as rooted in his Diaspora setting, infused with Hellenistic religions and Gnostic views (Hagner). C. Montefiore published *Judaism and St. Paul* (1914), wherein he argued that Paul's Hellenistic Jewish background was vastly different from rabbinic Judaism. So too K. Kohler and J. Klausner, who determined that Paul's views of Judaism were influenced or infected with *Hellenism. These scholars concluded that whatever Paul argued against, it was not rabbinic Judaism. Most scholars in the late nineteenth and early twentieth centuries had a higher trust in the value of rabbinic literature for historical reconstruction than is evident in scholarship today.

S. Sandmel's *The Genius of Paul: A Study in History* (1958) emphasizes Paul's apocalyptic views and his context as a Hellenistic Jew. A. Segal concludes in *Paul the Convert* (1990) that Paul's vision of the crucified and risen Christ best explains his relationship with Judaism. Paul "converted" from Pharisaic Judaism to a new, Gentile community transformed by the spirit through faith in Christ. "Paul's constant theme of the opposition of faith and law is a social and political justification for a new variety of community" (Segal, 122). Paul understands the value of the Torah as a sacred story of Israel's past but minimizes the observance of Torah in creating community identity. Segal understands Romans 7 to be Paul's argument as one sort of Jewish Christian who seeks to convince other Jewish Christians on the superior value of faith (228).

D. Boyarin's *A Radical Jew: Paul and the Politics of Identity* (1994) explores Paul's letters from the vantage point of a "talmudist and postmodern Jewish cultural critic" (Boyarin, 1). Boyarin brackets rabbinic Judaism as a second-century movement and observes that, as such, it grew in a milieu that included Pauline thought. He sees in Paul a first-century Jewish cultural critic who desired to transform or reform his society. Paul's letters reveal his self-identification as a Jew and self-understanding as "everyman" (3). Boyarin makes a case for a central *universalism in Paul's thought, the goal of which is for all humanity to be unified under the one true God.

A diametrically opposite opinion on the value of Paul's thought comes in Rabbi J. Sacks's *One People?* (1993). Sacks explores Jewish identity and thought in an effort to reach Jewish unity. He rejects the concept of an exclusive, saved remnant, as seen in the Qumran sect and the followers of Bar Kokhba and, most critically, in the apostle Paul's works. Sacks understands Paul to state that Torah law is repealed, and God's relationship with Israel is broken. "No doctrine has cost more Jewish lives. Pauline theology demonstrates to the full how remote from and catastrophic to Judaism is the doctrine of a second choice, a new election" (Sacks, 206-7). D. Langton echoes Sacks's conclusion, "The Jewish relationship with the apostle to the Gentiles has been, and remains, a bitter one" (Langton, 587), and contrasts it with the generally positive view of Jesus held by many Jews.

Recently, P. Fredriksen paints a less fearsome portrait of the apostle, demonstrating the commonalities Paul shares with his Jewish compatriots. Paul is not against Jewish Torah observance. The novelty, she concludes, is with Paul's opponents who insist on Gentile circumcision. She observes that in the first century, synagogues made a place for interested Gentiles, although there was no concerted effort to evangelize them. She notes that Gentiles were welcome in the outer temple precincts, and proximity to Gentiles did not generate Jewish anxiety about impurity. The presenting issue for Paul's communities was table *fellowship, eating in a Gentile believer's home or drinking their (nonkosher) wine. Fredriksen asserts that Paul did not promote "Law-freeness" over against Judaism's works of the law (Fredriksen, 110). Paul's gospel promoted an undifferentiated Gentile group that, together with Israel, would know the one God through Christ. Fredriksen argues that Romans 7 is best read through the rhetorical lens of *prosōpopoiia*, reflecting Gentile struggles to break from *idolatry—they cannot do so outside Christ.

7. Conclusion.

The apostle Paul was a Jew who engaged in conversations about the law and the Messiah that marked his Jewish community. The apocalyptic thought that characterized much of Second Temple Judaism found expression in his thoughts, as did the realities of Diaspora life and the prevalence of Gentiles among Jews in their towns and cities. Paul's comments about Judaism and the law are embedded in occasional documents, namely, his letters written to specific churches reflecting pertinent issues. Some scholars find discordant notes about the value and purpose of the law in Paul's letters, while others see an overall positive view of law and Judaism. There is no doubt but that Paul's writings have been used to justify anti-Semitic actions. Interpreting Paul's views on Judaism and the law carries a great responsibility to be faithful to the apostle's call to live at *peace with everyone (Rom 12:18).

See also Apocalypticism; Christ, Messiah; Circumcision; Conversion and Call of Paul; Covenant; Ethnicity in Paul's World; Food Laws and Customs, Jewish and Roman; Gentiles; Gospel; Hellenism, Roman; Interpretation: Jewish; Interpretation: Luther; Interpretation: New Perspective; Israel; Jerusalem, Council of; Law; Old Testament in Paul; Salvation; Works of the Law.

BIBLIOGRAPHY. **J. M. G. Barclay,** *Jews in the Mediterranean Diaspora: From Alexander to Trajan* (Berkeley: University of California Press, 1999); idem, *Paul and the Gift* (Grand Rapids, MI: Eerdmans, 2015); **M. F. Bird,** "What if Martin Luther Had Read the Dead Sea Scrolls? Historical Particularity and Theological Interpretation in Pauline Theology: Galatians as a Test Case," *JTI* 3, no. 1 (2009): 107-25; idem, *An Anomalous Jew: Paul Among Jews, Greeks and Romans* (Grand Rapids, MI: Eerdmans, 2016); **W. Bousset,** *Die Religion des Judentums im neutestamentlichen Zeitalter* (Berlin: Verlag von Reuther & Reichard, 1903); **D. Boyarin,** *A Radical Jew: Paul and the Politics of Identity* (Berkeley: University of California Press, 1994); **D. K. Buell,** *Why This New Race: Ethnic Reasoning in Early Christianity* (New York: Columbia University Press, 2005); **D. Campbell,** "An Apocalyptic Rereading of 'Justification' in Paul: Or, an Overview of the Argument of Douglas Campbell's *The Deliverance of God*—by Douglas Campbell," *ExpTim* 123 (8): 382-93; **S. J. Chester,** *Reading Paul with the Reformers: Reconciling Old and New Perspectives* (Grand Rapids, MI: Eerdmans, 2017); **S. J. D. Cohen,** *The Beginnings of Jewishness: Boundaries, Varieties, Uncertainties* (Berkeley: University of California Press, 1999); **J. D. G. Dunn,** *The New Perspective on Paul*, rev. ed. (Grand Rapids, MI: Eerdmans, 2008); **P. Fredriksen,** *Paul: The Pagan's Apostle* (New Haven, CT: Yale University Press, 2017); **J. G. Gager,** *Reinventing Paul* (Oxford: Oxford University Press, 2000); **L. Gaston,** *Paul and the Torah* (Eugene, OR: Wipf & Stock, 2006); **B. Gaventa,** "Thinking from Christ to Israel: Romans 9–11 in Apocalyptic Context," in *Paul and the Apocalyptic Imagination*, ed. B. C. Blackwell, J. K. Goodrich, and J. Maston (Minneapolis: Augsburg Fortress, 2016), 239-56; **D. A. Hagner,** "Paul in Modern Jewish Thought," in *Pauline Studies: Essays Presented to Professor F. F. Bruce on His 70th Birthday*, ed. D. A. Hagner and M. J. Harris (Grand Rapids, MI: Eerdmans, 1980), 143-65; **S. Heschel,** *The Aryan Jesus: Christian Theologians and the Bible in Nazi Germany* (Princeton, NJ: Princeton University Press, 2008); **E. Käsemann,** "Paul and Israel," in *New Testament Questions of Today* (Philadelphia: Fortress, 1969), 182-87; idem, *Commentary on Romans*, trans. G. W. Bromiley (Grand Rapids, MI: Eerdmans, 1980); **D. R. Langton,** "Paul in Jewish Thought," in *The Jewish Annotated New Testament*, ed. A.-J. Levine and M. Z. Brettler (Oxford: Oxford University Press, 2011), 585-87; **J. L. Martyn,** *Galatians*, AB (New York: Doubleday, 1997); **S. McKnight,** *Pastor Paul: Nurturing a Culture of Christoformity in the Church* (Grand Rapids, MI: Brazos, 2019); **M. D. Nanos,** *The Mystery of Romans: The Jewish Context of Paul's Letter* (Minneapolis: Fortress, 1996); idem, "Paul and Judaism," in *The Jewish Annotated New Testament*, ed. A.-J. Levine and M. Z. Brettler (Oxford: Oxford University Press, 2011), 551-54; **D. Nirenberg,** *Anti-Judaism: The Western Tradition* (New York: Norton, 2013); **B. Pitre, M. P. Barber, and J. A. Kincaid,** *Paul a New Covenant Jew: Rethinking Pauline Theology* (Grand Rapids, MI: Eerdmans, 2019); **R. Rodriguez and M.**

Thiessen, eds., *The So-Called Jew in Paul's Letter to the Romans* (Minneapolis: Fortress, 2016); **E. P. Sanders,** *Paul and Palestinian Judaism*, 40th anniversary ed. (Minneapolis: Fortress, 2017); **S. Sandmel,** *The Genius of Paul: A Study in History* (New York: Farrar, Straus & Cudahy, 1958); idem, *Paul, the Law and the Jewish People* (Minneapolis: Fortress, 1983); **A. F. Segal,** *Paul the Convert: The Apostolate and Apostasy of Saul the Pharisee* (New Haven, CT: Yale University Press, 1990); **M. L. Soards,** "Following Paul Along the Way of the Parting of Judaism and Christianity," *Bib* 100, no. 2 (2019): 249-71; **K. Stendahl,** "The Apostle Paul and the Introspective Conscience of the West," *HTR* 56, no. 3 (1963): 199-215; **S. K. Stowers,** *A Rereading of Romans: Justice, Jews, and Gentiles* (New Haven, CT: Yale University Press, 1994); **H. L. von Strack and P. Billerbeck,** *Kommentar zum Neuen Testament aus Talmud und Midrasch* (Munich: Beck, 1922–1961); **F. Watson,** *Paul, Judaism, and the Gentiles: Beyond the New Perspective* (Grand Rapids, MI: Eerdmans, 2007); **S. Westerholm,** *Justification Reconsidered: Rethinking a Pauline Theme* (Grand Rapids, MI: Eerdmans, 2013); **N. T. Wright,** "Paul in Current Anglophone Scholarship," *ExpTim* 123, no. 8 (2012): 367-81.

L. H. Cohick

PAUL IN ACTS

There has been much scholarly discussion of the portrait of Paul in Acts, particularly how well and how far it fits with the portrait of Paul derived from his (undisputed) letters. Perhaps the majority scholarly view is that the two portraits are, at least at some points, incompatible; a significant minority (including the present author) thinks otherwise. This article lays out the data of the Lukan portrait of Paul, noting places of compatibility or tension with the "Paul of the letters" (which usually means the undisputed letters) in engagement with scholarship. This article generally follows the nomenclature of Acts for Saul/Paul by using "Saul" for his life up to his travels in Cyprus, and "Paul" for his life thereafter, including his letters.

Methodologically, many scholars assert that the portrait derived from the letters is "primary" and that from Acts is "secondary," which is frequently linked to the view that Acts is biased and unreliable. They thus downplay Acts in discussing Paul. However, there is no reason to regard another person's portrait as necessarily more or less reliable than a self-portrait: both are looking at the subject from their own angle. For example, Paul's portrait of the teachers he opposes in Galatians is likely to be different to their self-presentation, but we do not have access to writings by these teachers. In the case of Paul himself, we have access to his letters and Acts, and thus have two sources of information to use in constructing an historical portrait of Paul. Both sources should be used with discernment, bearing in mind the authors' understanding and purpose(s) in writing.

1. The Pre-Christian Saul/Paul
2. The Damascus Road Experience and Its Aftermath
3. Paul as Believer
4. Paul as Collaborator
5. Paul as Evangelist and Church Planter
6. Paul as Controversialist
7. Paul as Pastor
8. Paul as Missionary-Prisoner

1. The Pre-Christian Saul/Paul.

Saul was born in Tarsus in Cilicia and educated as a Pharisee under Gamaliel in *Jerusalem (Acts 22:3; 26:5). The young Saul was a devout Jew, deeply opposed to the followers of Jesus: he supported those stoning Stephen to death (Acts 7:58; 8:1) and took believers in Jerusalem off to prison (Acts 8:3). His persecution extended wider as he gained letters from the high priest to Jews in Damascus to seek and bind believers and take them to Jerusalem (Acts 9:1-2; 22:5; 26:12). He later described himself as "zealous [*zēlōtēs*] for God," a zeal that led him to persecute believers violently (Acts 22:3-4; also Acts 26:9-11). He may have served on the supreme Sanhedrin, which condemned believers to death (Acts 26:10), although this could be figurative language simply signaling his support, since the Sanhedrin had no right to put people to death (John 18:31; Keener, 45-47).

The lines of this portrait resonate well with the letters (Hengel and Deines). Paul writes of his persecution of the believing assembly in order to destroy it, his precociousness in his ancestral faith, including that he was "zealous" (*zēlōtēs*), and a Pharisee (Gal 1:13-14; Phil 3:5-6). Looking back, he considers himself "the least of the *apostles" because he persecuted the assembly of God (1 Cor 15:9; see 1 Tim 1:15). This regret is not explicit in Acts—it takes Paul himself to speak so bluntly about his past life.

2. The Damascus Road Experience and Its Aftermath.

Acts tells the story of Saul's transformative experience on the road to Damascus three times (Acts 9:1-22; 22:3-21; 26:2-23); the first is in the narrator's voice, and the others on the lips of Paul. These events are also mentioned in the letters (Gal 1:13-20; 1 Cor 9:1; 15:18; 2 Cor 11:32-33; 1 Thess 2:15), and the relationship of the various accounts is much debated.

2.1. Acts. There is a *common core* to the Acts accounts: Saul persecutes believers (Acts 9:1; 22:3-4; 26:4-5, 9-11); the high priest authorizes Saul to seek and arrest believers (Acts 9:1-2; 22:5; 26:10, 12); Saul travels to Damascus for this purpose (Acts 9:2; 22:5; 26:11-12); close to Damascus, a bright light shines (Acts 9:3-4; 22:6-7; 26:13-14); Saul hears Jesus speak (Acts 9:4-5; 22:7-8; 26:14-15), telling Saul he is persecuting Jesus (Acts 9:5; 22:8; 16:25); Saul receives instructions (Acts 9:6; 22:10; 26:16-18); Saul cannot see (Acts 9:8-9; 22:11); Ananias meets Saul after the *Lord visits Ananias (Acts 9:10-19; 22:12-16); Saul proclaims Jesus in Damascus (Acts 9:20-22; 26:19-20) and Jerusalem (Acts 9:26-27; 22:17-21; 26:20).

There are *distinctive features* in each of the Acts accounts that supplement the other accounts. In Acts 9:1-31: the dialogue between Ananias and the Lord (Acts 9:11-16), which is unsurprisingly absent from the other accounts told from Saul's perspective; a Jewish conspiracy in Damascus to kill Saul and his escape through the wall (Acts 9:23-25), again unsurprisingly absent from Paul's later accounts, which are to audiences that are either Jewish or sympathetic to Judaism—there, he would not wish to imply that Jewish people opposed him; Saul's journey to Tarsus (Acts 9:31). In Acts 22:3-21: Paul's zeal and study under Gamaliel (Acts 22:3; see Acts 26:4-5), which signal his loyalty to Judaism, appropriately in the temple setting; the mention of Ananias's Jewish devotion (Acts 22:12), also natural in addressing a hostile crowd that believes Paul is not a loyal Jew (Acts 21:28); Paul's encounter with Ananias is told from Paul's perspective rather than the narrator's (Acts 22:13-16; see Acts 9:10-19); Paul's *vision of the Lord in the temple instructing him to leave and go to the *Gentiles (Acts 22:17-21). In Acts 26:2-23: Paul casts his vote against believers (Acts 26:10); Jesus' *call to Paul to *mission among the Gentiles happens during the Damascus road experience (Acts 26:16-18); focus on the *resurrection of Jesus (Acts 26:8, 23), which is (from Paul's perspective) the major issue in the trial, for it bespeaks the exalted status of Jesus.

There are a very few *apparent inconsistencies* among the Acts accounts: whether Saul receives his call to Gentile mission from Ananias or Jesus (Acts 9:15-16; 22:13-16; 26:16-18)—it is, of course, possible that both took place; and what Saul's companions saw and heard, and their physical reaction (Acts 9:7; 22:9; 26:14). However, ancient historians did not have the same concern for small points of detail that moderns do (Witherington, 311).

Recent *narrative studies read each account in its literary setting, and the three show progression and development (e.g., Marguerat, 179-204). This approach illuminates how Luke leads readers to understand the story. Marguerat notices *amplifications*: Paul as Pharisee is first mentioned in Acts 26:4-8; Paul's persecution of believers grows from Acts 9:1-2 to Acts 22:3-5; 26:9-11; *suppressions*: Ananias is a key character in Acts 9:10-17, is mentioned more briefly in Acts 22:12-16 and not at all in Acts 26; Saul is persecuted in Acts 9:23-25, 29-30, but this is not mentioned in Acts 22; 26; and an *interpolation*: Paul's call to mission among Gentiles is part of the Damascus road experience in Acts 26:16-18 and appears to happen later in Acts 9:15-16, where readers might assume that Ananias relayed this call to Saul, and Acts 22:17-21, where Saul hears this call in a vision in the temple. Luke's presentation of Saul's companions goes through suppression (their role reduces from Acts 9:6-8 through Acts 22:9, 11 to Acts 26:14), interpolation (Luke mentions them before Jesus and Saul's conversation [Acts 26:14], during that conversation [Acts 22:9-10], and afterwards [Acts 9:7-8]), and transformation (they hear without seeing [Acts 9:7]; they see without hearing [Acts 22:9]; they stand speechless [Acts 9:7], they fall to the ground with Paul [Acts 26:14], and their posture is not mentioned in Acts 22).

What readers experience are different perspectives appropriate to different narrators and situations, and the later accounts are "retrospective readings" of the event (Marguerat, 187; Kurz, 125-31). Seen from this perspective, Acts 9 tells the story, surrounded by conversions of other "outsiders": the Samaritans, the Ethiopian eunuch, and the *household of the centurion Cornelius (Acts 8:4-25, 26-40; 10:1-48). Acts 22 has Paul present himself to fellow Jews as a godly, traditional Jew whose life direction was changed by encountering Jesus—Paul is defending himself against the charge of "teaching everyone everywhere against our people, our law, and this place [the temple]" (Acts 21:28). In Acts 26 Paul speaks to Gentiles and focuses on the resurrection of Jesus as a matter of internal Jewish controversy—and thus it need not concern Festus and Agrippa (Acts 26:19-23). In light of these settings, the focus on Jewish matters in the temple (Acts 22) makes good sense: it is here that Jesus is "the Nazarene" (Acts 22:8), a phrase used with Jewish audiences (Luke 18:36; Acts 2:2; 3:6; 4:10; 6:14; 22:8; 24:5; 26:9).

The compression involved in Acts 26 makes sense of Paul saying Jesus told him on the Damascus road to go to Gentiles (Acts 26:16-18), for it allows Paul to highlight the heart of his testimony to Agrippa, the resurrection of Jesus as the fulfillment of Scripture (Acts 26:8, 22-23). The story of Paul's encounter(s) with Jesus is cut to the minimum—noticeably, neither Acts 9 nor Acts 22 states that Jesus did *not* call Saul to Gentile mission on the Damascus road. It is possible that Paul received his call to Gentiles there but that Luke reveals this only at the climax of the three tellings (Churchill, 227-28). If so, Ananias confirms what Jesus says in the Damascus road encounter (Acts 22:14-15), and the temple vision underlines that mission among Gentiles will be Paul's *primary* focus (Acts 22:17-21). Alternatively, events may be being telescoped for the setting before Agrippa.

The "increasing sequence" of the three accounts is striking: Paul's persecuting efforts grow (Acts 9:1; 22:4; 26:9-11), the light is ever brighter (Acts 9:3; 22:6; 26:13) and spreads more widely (Acts 9:3; 22:6; 26:13), and the response to the light is more marked (Acts 9:7; 22:7; 26:14; Churchill, 226). In particular, Jesus and Paul's conversation develops: Jesus's message begins as a directive to wait to learn what to do, in response to an implied, but unanswered, question (Acts 9:6); in the temple, Paul makes the question explicit (Acts 22:10), but Jesus only tells Paul that he will learn in Damascus what to do; finally, on trial, Jesus tells Paul his calling explicitly without Paul asking at all (Acts 26:16-18). Luke uses literary techniques to engage readers by (1) suspense, gradually opening readers' eyes to the nature of Paul's call through the three accounts; (2) curiosity, provoking readers to reflect by the relation of (unasked) question and answer in the accounts; and (3) reversal of expectations, as the initial impression of Paul's call to Gentile mission is that Ananias was its vehicle (Acts 9:15-16) is shifted to the temple vision as its means (Acts 22:17-21), and finally the Damascus road encounter itself is the time when this call occurred (26:16-18; Churchill, 228; Hedrick, 427). Ananias's conversation with Jesus (Acts 9:15-16) thus functions as a key signal *to readers* that Saul is called to Gentile mission.

After Saul leaves Jerusalem for Tarsus (Acts 9:30), Acts is silent about him until Barnabas goes to Tarsus to fetch him to help in teaching the new, and controversial, mixed Jew-plus-Gentile believing community in *Syrian Antioch (Acts 11:19-26).

2.2. Acts and Paul's Letters. There are several agreements between Acts and the letters concerning Paul and his Damascus road experience: (1) Paul persecutes the *church (1 Cor 15:9; Gal 1:13; Acts 9:1-2, 21; 22:3-4; 26:9-11); (2) the exalted Jesus appears to Paul (1 Cor 9:1; 15:8; Acts 9:4-6; 22:7-8; 26:14-15), and his behavior changes suddenly and dramatically as he begins following Jesus (Gal 1:13, 23; Phil 3:7; Acts 9:20-22; 26:19-20); (3) a strong light shines (2 Cor 4:6; Acts 9:3-4; 22:6-7; 26:13-14); (4) God revealing his *Son to Paul is closely linked to Paul's call to be apostle to the Gentiles (Gal 1:16; Acts 26:16); (5) the incident is near Damascus (Gal 1:17; Acts 9:3; 22:6; 26:12-13; Lohfink, 21-24; Lyons, 146-52; Kim, 5-8).

There are also some apparent differences between Acts and the letters (for many of these points, see Lohfink, 24-30).

1. The letters do not tell the story of Paul's calling as in Acts 22; 26 but mention it only briefly and in passing. This raises the question whether Paul reported the details of his experience to others. However, S. Kim shows that there are clear allusions to the Damascus road encounter in Paul's letters, although Paul writes relatively briefly about his personal experience of Jesus (e.g., 2 Cor 12:1-4, taking that to be Paul's own experience). He would not need to write at length if he had previously told his converts about the Damascus road encounter in person; rather, he could briefly allude to the story to evoke the memory of his converts.

2. "I have seen the Lord" (1 Cor 9:1) seems to contrast with Acts 9:17, 27; 22:14; 26:13-16, which focus on Paul *seeing* light and *hearing* the Lord. However, Acts 22:14 has Ananias say that God appointed Saul "*to see* the righteous one," Acts 9:17 has Ananias speak of "the Lord Jesus who *was seen* by you on the road," Acts 9:27 has Barnabas reporting that on the journey Saul "*had seen* the Lord," and Acts 26:16 has the Lord himself telling Saul that he is to be a *witness "of the events in which *you saw* [me]." In each Acts telling there is a clear statement that Saul saw the exalted Jesus.

3. For Paul the Damascus road encounter is part of the sequence of Easter resurrection appearances (1 Cor 15:3-9), but Luke's description (Acts 1:3, 9-11) suggests that those appearances last for forty days and end with Jesus' *ascension. Further, Acts 13:31-33 seems to place Paul outside the circle of "witnesses"—he simply brings the good news. Nevertheless, Paul's reporting of the resurrection appearances is not as straightforward as may appear, for it is widely recognized that he is passing on a traditional summary in 1 Corinthians 15:3-7—the uses of the language of *tradition ("I passed on," "you received," 1 Cor 15:3) imply this, as does the

way Paul demarcates his experience as "as to one born in an untimely way" (1 Cor 15:8), and the phrasing of 1 Corinthians 15:8 implies that this appearance is not straightforwardly part of the same series as the appearances in 1 Corinthians 15:5-7 (Thiselton, 1186-89). Further, Luke uses *witness* (both verb and noun) as a semitechnical term for those who are eye- and ear-witnesses to Jesus' resurrection (note Acts 1:21-22); thus, according to Luke, Paul *is* a witness (Acts 22:14-15; 26:16). Paul uses *witness* less and treats as witnesses the broad group who presently give testimony to Jesus as witnesses (e.g., 1 Cor 15:15) or who speak in Jesus' *name (e.g., Gal 5:3; 2 Thess 1:10). Thus Luke's usage is consistent with that found in Acts 13:31-33 and is compatible with Paul's less technical usage.

4. Paul considered himself an apostle on the basis of the Damascus road encounter (1 Cor 9:1), but Luke reserves the designation "apostle" for the Twelve. On this view, Acts 14:4, 14 are nonspecific uses of *apostles*, identifying Barnabas and Paul as envoys sent by the church in Antioch (Acts 13:1-3; Haenchen, 114-15). It is true that Luke generally reserves *apostles* for the Twelve, and Acts 14:4, 14 is a significant exception. That said, the quotation of Isaiah 49:6 applied to Paul and Barnabas's work is nearby (Acts 13:47), and that quotation echoes Acts 1:8 (which itself alludes to Is 49:6). Paul and Barnabas are thus participating in the same mission promised to the Eleven. Further, they perform "*signs and wonders done through their hands" (Acts 14:3), a strong parallel to the work of the Jerusalem apostles (Acts 5:12). These features suggest that Luke saw Paul and Barnabas as fulfilling a role like that of the Twelve (Clark, 182-85).

5. Paul is sure he received his call and *gospel directly from God (Gal 1:1-2, 11-12), whereas in Acts, Paul learns what he is to do through Ananias (Conzelmann, 71). Indeed, reading Acts 9 alone could produce the impression that Saul received his commission secondhand through Ananias, but as noted above, the sequence of the three accounts of the Damascus road encounter in Acts builds up information. This buildup invites careful readers to recognize that Paul receives his initial commission to mission among Gentiles on the Damascus road, in tune with Paul's own description (Gal 1:1-2, 11-12).

6. After Saul's time in Damascus, he spends time in "Arabia" (Gal 1:17), whereas Luke has him travel to Jerusalem (Acts 9:26), although Paul denies that he visited Jerusalem until "after three years" (Acts 1:18). However, the time notices in Acts 9 are vague: Saul spends "some days" (Acts 9:19) with the Damascene disciples, and it was after "many days" (Acts 9:23) that Saul's Jewish opponents plotted against him. This certainly allows for a period between these two periods sufficient to cover a visit to "Arabia" (which could have been fairly brief) followed by a return to Damascus (Gal 1:17).

7. Acts 9:27-29 gives the impression that Saul was well-known among the Jerusalem believers, whereas Paul himself says he met only Cephas (*Peter) and *James the Lord's brother (Gal 1:18-19) and was unknown in person to the believers in Judea, even though they heard what he was doing (Gal 1:22-23). Reading Acts 9 alone might suggest that Saul met more "apostles" than Peter and James (Gal 1:18-19) on his visit to Jerusalem and that he became quite well-known among the Jerusalem believers (Acts 9:27-29). However, Luke is making a general, rather than precise, statement and not aiming to offer exact information—and thus contrasts with Galatians, where Paul is defending the independence of his call. During this visit, Luke makes no suggestion that Saul left Jerusalem, and so Paul's statement that he was unknown among the "churches of Judea" (Gal 1:22) may mean "Judea outside Jerusalem" or simply that he was not well-known among Judean believers (Wenham, 224-25). Paul indicates that this visit to Jerusalem was brief—fifteen days (Gal 1:18)—which limits how much Saul could get to know the Jerusalem believers, let alone those in wider Judea.

In sum, while Luke does not give us all the information that we can glean from Paul's letters about this period, Luke's summarized account, which focuses on essentials, is compatible with the extra information we have from Paul, even though in places, if we read Acts alone, we might gain a less-than-complete impression.

3. Paul as Believer.

Acts presents a huge shift in Paul's engagement with Yahweh, for Paul encounters Israel's God through Jesus on the Damascus road. After that experience, much changes in Paul's life, although some things remain constant.

There is real continuity in Paul's Jewish devotion, according to Acts: he continues to attend synagogues (Acts 13:5; 14:1; 17:1-4, 10-12, 17; 18:4), and this seems unlikely to be merely "strategic," to gain a hearing for the gospel; he is willing to *circumcise Timothy (Acts 16:1-3); he wants to be in Jerusalem for the festival of Pentecost (Acts 20:16); and he consents, apparently willingly, to demonstrate his Jewish loyalty by participating in and funding a vow (Acts 21:23-26).

Regarding the letters, by contrast with study in the mid-twentieth century, when the Greco-Roman world was considered the major influence on Paul (and Paul was seen through deeply Lutheran spectacles), recent study highlights Paul's devotion to Israel's God as now known in Jesus, including: his strategy of going "to the Jew first" (Rom 1:16); his readiness to be like Jews to win Jews (1 Cor 9:20), a likely explanation of his circumcision of Timothy; his constant use of Scripture as speaking about the renewed people of God constituted by Jesus (e.g., 1 Cor 10:1-11: note the repeated "These things happened as examples for us" [1 Cor 10:6, 11]); and his mentions of Jewish festivals and *sacrifices (Passover [1 Cor 5:7-8], firstfruits [Rom 11:16; 16:5; 1 Cor 15:20, 23; 16:15], the sin offering [Rom 3:25; 8:3; 2 Cor 5:21]). In the letters Paul instructs believing communities, and it is thus unsurprising that we hear more of the communities' inner life in the letters than in Acts, for in Acts, Paul's speeches are primarily evangelistic or forensic.

Nevertheless, it is clear in both Acts and the letters that the driver and dynamic of Paul's life post–Damascus road is his relationship with *Christ. Encountering Jesus in person changes him (Acts 9:5-6; 22:7-8; 26:14-15; see 1 Cor 9:1) and initiates him into a new relationship with Jesus, whom he previously opposed. Jesus "the Lord" appears to him to encourage him in Corinth and Jerusalem (Acts 18:9-10; 23:11), and an angel appears during the voyage to Rome (Acts 27:23-26). This new relationship is facilitated and experienced through the *Holy Spirit, received at Paul's *baptism (Acts 9:17), an experience that the letters expect to be normal among believers (Rom 8:9; see Acts 19:1-7). The Spirit directs and empowers Paul's *ministry by directing him (Acts 13:2, 4, 9; 19:21; 20:22) or, on occasion, preventing him (Acts 16:6-8). Paul also knows by the Spirit that he is to suffer in Jerusalem (Acts 20:22-23) and thus is unwilling to accept well-intended directions by believers not to go there, even though they also understand by the Spirit that he will suffer (Acts 21:4, 10-14 seems to be compressed versions of such conversations; Rapske, 406-7). Paul prays alone (Acts 9:11; 22:17) and with others (Acts 13:2-3; 16:13, 25; 28:8), sometimes—unusually for a Jew—kneeling, suggesting some intensity in the praying (Acts 20:36; 21:5).

The letters contain much more than Acts about the content of Paul's *prayer life, for in his letters Paul regularly asks for prayer (e.g., Rom 15:30-32; 2 Thess 3:1-2; 2 Cor 1:8-11) and frequently records his prayers for believing communities (e.g., Rom 15:5-6, 13; 1 Thess 3:11-13; 5:23-24; 2 Thess 2:16-17; 3:5) as well as his thanksgiving for them (e.g., Rom 1:8-15; 1 Thess 1:2-10; 2 Thess 1:3-12). The Spirit's work in Paul and his communities is essential to their experience of God-in-Christ (Rom 8:9), producing *fruit in changed relationships and attitudes (Gal 5:22-24) and releasing *gifts in the assemblies (1 Cor 12–14). Paul characterizes the Christian life as walking in, being led by, or living by the Spirit (Gal 5:16, 18, 25). Again, it is natural that the letters fill out the picture of Acts, since the letters focus more on the inner life of the assemblies. For example, *prophecy, giving direction to believers (1 Cor 14:1-6, 29-33), illuminates Paul's experience in Acts by suggesting the probable means by which the *Spirit directed or informed him (Acts 13:2; 16:6-8; 20:22).

4. Paul as Collaborator.

In Acts Paul works with others consistently, including a number of named *coworkers: Barnabas (and John Mark; Acts 13–14); Silas (Acts 15:22-41; 16:19, 25, 29; 17:4, 10, 14-15; 18:5); Timothy (Acts 16:1-3; 17:14-15; 18:5); Aquila and Priscilla (Acts 18:2-3, 18, 26); and the character who writes of "we" (Acts 16:10-17; 20:5-15; 21:1-18; 27:1–28:16; Phillips, 167-78). In places it is apparent that a character is present during episodes where they are not named, such as Timothy, who is present in Philippi and Thessalonica and Berea, since he is one of "they" who travel through Phrygia, Galatia, and Asia to Troas (Acts 16:4-8), and he is present in Berea, for Paul leaves him there (Acts 17:14) before Timothy eventually rejoins Paul in Corinth (Acts 18:5). Acts does not say whether Paul collaborated with Apollos or ever met him (Acts 18:24–19:1). Gaps like these make tracking Paul's relationships with his coworkers complicated.

Barnabas has a particular role in supporting Saul in Saul's early days as a believer, introducing and commending Saul on his first visit to Jerusalem (Acts 9:26-28). Barnabas enables Saul to have a wider ministry by fetching him from Tarsus to Syrian Antioch to teach the new Jew-plus-Gentile assembly there (Acts 11:25-26), and the church there sends the two men to Jerusalem with a contribution of aid for the famine (Acts 11:29-30). In response to the Spirit's call, the Antiochene community sets Barnabas and Saul apart to travel as gospel agents (Acts 13:1-4). During these travels, Saul becomes known as Paul (Acts 13:9), and he is named first, thus acting as leader of the team, which includes more than Barnabas (Acts 13:13, 42, 46; 14:1). Paul also becomes the primary speaker (Acts 13:16-41; 14:9, 12). Nevertheless, the relationship breaks down because of Barnabas's desire to take John Mark on a second trip, which Paul resists because John Mark abandoned them on the previous trip. The outcome is that Paul takes Silas with him, and Barnabas takes John Mark (Acts 15:36-41). Paul's relationships with colleagues could thus be fractious. Silas, who disappears from Acts in Corinth (last mention: Acts 18:5), may be another example: Phillips (169-71) speculates that Silas disagreed with Paul about mission among Gentiles.

The letters offer a similar picture of Paul working with others: other than Romans and Galatians, the undisputed letters are sent by Paul with at least one co-sender (1 Cor 1:1; 2 Cor 1:1; Phil 1:1; 1 Thess 1:1; cf. 2 Thess 1:1; Col 1:1). In the Thessalonian letters, the team that Acts presents as planting this church is named as co-senders (Acts 17:1; note the evidence above that Timothy was present). There is a significant overlap of personnel between the letters and Acts, including: Prisc(ill)a and Aquila (Rom 16:13), Timothy (Rom 16:21; 1 Cor 4:17; 2 Cor 1:1; Phil 1:1; 2:19-24; 1 Thess 1:1; 3:4-6; Philem 1), [John] Mark (Philem 24), Silvanus/Silas (1 Thess 1:1), and Barnabas (1 Cor 9:6; Gal 2:1-13). Barnabas is evidently more prominent in Acts, and Timothy in the letters. The locations within which these people engage with Paul generally mesh well. For example, Silas/Silvanus is with Paul in Thessalonica and is a co-sender of the letters to that church (Acts 17:4, 10; 1 Thess 1:1; 2 Thess 1:1). Similarly, Prisc(ill)a and Aquila move with Paul from Corinth to *Ephesus (Acts 18:18, 26), and Paul sends greetings from them from "Asia," where Ephesus is, to the Corinthians (1 Cor 16:19). Paul later sends greetings to them in Rome, where they now host a church, and from whence they originally came (Rom 16:3-5; Acts 18:2).

The letters mention a wider group of coworkers (notably in Rom 16), including Titus, who was evidently a significant Pauline emissary in his difficult relationship with the Corinthians (e.g., 2 Cor 8:16-23); Epaphroditus, apparently a Philippian believer (Phil 2:24-29; 4:18); and some who had been in prison with him (Rom 16:7; Philem 23). Apollos is mentioned only in 1 Corinthians (1 Cor 3:4-6, 22; 4:6; 16:12), where Paul regards him as a gospel coworker (1 Cor 3:5-6). Paul says he urged Apollos to visit Corinth (1 Cor 16:12), which may mean that they met, although the urging could be through an intermediary or letter.

Acts 13–20 centers on Paul's ministry of evangelism and church planting, and it is in this part of Acts that most of Paul's companions are mentioned (for Paul is in custody from there on). The significant overlap of names between Acts 13–20 and the letters, combined with the distinctive information and the differences in emphasis in each, suggests that Luke is not using the letters in compiling Acts—for had Luke done so, we might have expected to hear in Acts about Titus and to learn more about Timothy's role. Such independence underlines the quality of the shared information.

5. Paul as Evangelist and Church Planter. In Acts, Paul is preeminently a missionary who begins and supports new groups of believers in cities of the Roman *empire. Acts is silent on his activities in Tarsus (Acts 9:30), although Barnabas's going there to fetch Paul to Antioch suggests that Paul had continued to be an effective evangelist and teacher (Acts 11:25-26; see Acts 9:27-29). Their yearlong ministry in Antioch, followed by their visit to Jerusalem (Acts 11:26-30), brings them to prominence among the five prophets and teachers in Antioch (Acts 13:1). Paul knows already that he is to be a missionary among Gentiles, via Ananias (Acts 9:15; 22:14-15) and through a vision (Acts 22:17-21), and so the meaning of the Spirit's call "to the work to which I have called them" (Acts 13:2) would be clear to him—Paul is called to a wider ministry among Gentiles. The Antioch community recognizes this call and commissions the pair through prayer and laying on hands (Acts 13:3).

Thus begins Paul's traveling ministry, which will take him through most of the region from Palestine through Syria into Cyprus, and into Cilicia, Pamphylia, Galatia and Asia, Macedonia, and Achaia. His travels are often characterized as three "missionary journeys," although it seems unlikely that Luke or Paul conceived them that way, for they seem not to be planned in advance.

5.1. Paul's Strategy in Cities. Paul's mission is conducted primarily in *urban settings, which are often multicultural places. He has a consistent approach, engaging first with the Jewish community for as long as he is welcomed there, and then, when division occurs among the Jews (as it inevitably does), he forms a believing community that includes both Jews and Gentiles. Thus in Pisidian Antioch and Corinth he first goes to the synagogue (Acts 13:14-15; 18:4; see Acts 19:8) and speaks after the Scripture readings. Conversation in the synagogue could go on for several Sabbaths. In Corinth, Paul works with Aquila and Priscilla to support himself during this period (Acts 18:2-3) until Timothy and Silas arrive bringing *financial support from the churches of Macedonia, which frees him to engage full time in evangelism (Acts 18:5). In Antioch, typically, Paul's message divides the Jewish community: some wish to hear more (Acts 13:42-43), but others reject his message, particularly because they recognize that Paul's teaching that the Messiah is Jesus entails the inclusion of Gentiles in the believing community (Acts 13:44-45; in Corinth, see Acts 18:5-6). Paul then proclaims the gospel message among Gentiles, as well as Jews and God-fearers who will listen (Acts 13:46-48), and a mixed community of believers forms: in Corinth, Paul's base becomes the home of one of the new believers, and this may be typical (Acts 18:7-8; although see Adams for evidence that the believers in Acts may have met in places other than homes, such as Aquila and Priscilla's workshop).

Paul stays in a place as long as possible, to enable the new believers to become rooted in their faith in Jesus (Acts 13:51-52; 18:11, 18): there are notable longer residences in Philippi, Corinth, and Ephesus (Acts 16:11-40; 18:1-18; 19:1-41). The impact of Paul's mission in a city includes the gospel being received by visitors from the surrounding countryside, so that a whole region hears the message (Acts 13:49; 19:10). Overall, this is very much the picture we see in the letters, where Paul gives priority to evangelism among Jews (Rom 1:16; 2:10) and also writes of evangelism among Gentiles (1 Thess 1:9 indicates that many of the believers in Thessalonica were not Jewish). Paul is also insistent about the equal standing of Jewish and Gentile believers before God and within the believing communities (Rom 2:11; 3:29-30; Gal 2:11-21; 3:28).

A second phase of Paul's relationship with the communities he plants is to return when he is able. After reaching Derbe and evangelizing there (Acts 14:20-21), Paul and Barnabas return through the cities they previously visited, Lystra, Iconium, and Pisidian Antioch (Acts 14:21-23). Paul later revisits those communities with Silas (Acts 15:36, 41; 16:1). These visits are times for encouraging, teaching, and further evangelism (Acts 14:21-23; 16:5; 18:23). Paul's desire to visit his communities shines through his letters too (e.g., 1 Cor 16:5-7; 2 Cor 13:1); when he cannot visit, he sends Timothy as his substitute to find out what is going on in Thessalonica and Philippi (1 Thess 3:1-6; Phil 2:19-24). Indeed, the letters themselves are part of the maintenance of Paul's relationship with his assemblies—although Acts does not mention them.

Paul's travels in Acts are built around three key points. First, Syrian Antioch, where he teaches alongside Barnabas, serves as a base for much of his travels. That is where he and Barnabas are first called to travel (Acts 13:1-3), and they return there after this initial trip (Acts 14:26-28). After the Jerusalem meeting, Paul and Barnabas return again to Antioch accompanied by Judas and Silas, and evidently spend some time there (Acts 15:30-35). On Paul's landing at Caesarea Maritima, he briefly "greets the church" (i.e., in Jerusalem) before traveling north to Antioch (Acts 18:22). It is only later that he sets his sights on Rome (Acts 19:21) and thus tells the Ephesian elders that he does expect to see them again (Acts 20:25; this expresses Paul's expectation at the time, rather than being an implicit statement that Paul had died by the time Luke wrote; Walton 2000).

Second, Paul often travels along Roman roads, which facilitate speedy journeys (by first-century standards; for what follows, see French). These well-built roads were designed to allow troop movements to be carried out efficiently, as well as enabling rapid dissemination of decrees and news, and were as straight as possible in order to take the shortest journey between two cities (for estimated travel times, see Thompson). When Paul and Barnabas land on the southern Asian coast, most probably at Attalia (Acts 13:13), they would take a paved road to Perga (Acts 13:13), the main city of Pamphylia, which is a little inland. The Via Sebaste, built in 6 BC, would then take them to Pisidian Antioch and on to Iconium, and probably to Lystra—all three cities were Roman colonies (Acts 13:14, 51; 14:6). At a later date, Paul uses part of the very long Via Egnetia to travel from Philippi via Amphipolis and Apollonia to Thessalonica (Acts 16:40–17:1).

Third, Paul goes to regional centers and spends as much time there as possible, notably Philippi, Corinth, and Ephesus (Acts 16:11-40; 18:1-18; 19:1-41). Because people come from the countryside and from smaller towns into these cities, Paul's evangelism has effects far beyond the city itself: with understandable hyperbole, Luke says that, over a two-year period, the whole province of Asia hears the word while Paul is in Ephesus (Acts 19:10; compare Pisidian Antioch [Acts 13:49]). The believing community in Colossae is an example, where the founder seems to be Epaphras, an inhabitant of that city (Col 1:7-8; 4:12): he most probably became a Jesus-follower in Ephesus during Paul's time there.

5.2. Paul's Mission Among Jews. When Paul evangelizes Jewish people, he focuses on showing Jesus to be Israel's Messiah. This entails arguments from Scripture, demonstrating that Jesus is the one to whom Scripture points, and, especially, showing that Jesus' death and resurrection fulfill Scripture. The latter point is vital, since our extant documents give no indication that first-century Jews were expecting a crucified Messiah—rather the reverse, as messianic expectation ranged from a military leader, through priestly and prophetic figures, to a teacher ("Messianism," *DNTB*, 698-707). Thus the early believers face a major apologetic task in claiming Jesus to be Messiah (Green).

Paul's speech in Pisidian Antioch is a typical synagogue presentation of the gospel among Jews (Acts 13:16-41)—as often, Luke provides a long speech in one setting to imply that Paul spoke similarly in similar settings (see Acts 13:5; 14:1; 17:1-4, 10-12, 17; 18:4). The key elements are: (1) Jesus' ministry is the fulfillment of the story of *Israel in Scripture (Acts 13:17-23); (2) John the Baptizer prepared the way for Jesus by his baptism and his preaching (Acts 13:24-25); (3) Jesus was unjustly crucified by Pilate and the Romans at the instigation of the Jewish leaders and the Jerusalemites (Acts 13:27-29); (4) God raised Jesus from the dead, and Jesus was seen by those who are now his authorized witnesses (Acts 13:30-31); (5) Scripture testifies to Jesus' resurrection (Acts 13:32-37, citing Ps 2:7; 16:10; Is 55:3); (6) *forgiveness of sins is available to the hearers through Jesus and, if that offer is declined, God will reject those who decline (Acts 13:38-41, 46). Thus the answer to the question whether the Messiah could be crucified is that God vindicated Jesus by raising him from the dead and that Jesus is now God's agent in the offer of forgiveness. When Paul himself outlines his gospel message, many of these elements are also present (1 Cor 15:1-11; 1 Thess 1:9-10), although, understandably, the fulfillment of Scripture and John the Baptizer's ministry are less prominent in Gentile settings.

In synagogues, God-fearers would also be present (Acts 13:16; 14:1-2), and the indications are that the gospel found particularly fertile soil among such people. God-fearers were deeply sympathetic to Judaism, sharing its monotheism and *ethical imperatives and often participating in *almsgiving, although the men had not been circumcised (e.g., Cornelius, Acts 10:2; see "Proselytism and Godfearers," *DNTB*, esp. 846-47). Paul's announcement that Jesus as Messiah embraced Gentiles without requiring full adherence to Jewish customs and practices would be very attractive to God-fearers, not least men. Lydia and her household may have been God-fearers, for Paul finds them at a place of prayer by the river in Philippi, a city without a synagogue (Acts 16:13-15). There was clearly controversy over this, and Acts does not hide that, as we shall see (section 6 below).

The closing scene of Acts has Paul engaging in discussion with Jews in Rome (Acts 28:17-28), highlighting that he never ceases to evangelize Jewish people. There also, his teaching focuses on showing from Scripture that the Messiah is Jesus (Acts 28:23; see Acts 28:30), and Luke's mention of "the *kingdom of God" as part of the substance of his proclamation (Acts 28:23, 30) implies that he said much on the teaching and ministry of Jesus.

5.3. Paul's Mission Among Gentiles. Paul's evangelism among Gentiles who were not God-fearers faced different challenges to his evangelism among Jews, for the culture was predominantly polytheistic and included a variety of beliefs about the gods (see, e.g., Cicero, *Nat. d.*; "Polytheism, Greco-Roman," *DNTB*, 815-18). Luke presents a shift in Paul's evangelism in a city, from focusing on Jews and God-fearers to engaging with Gentiles, at the point when the synagogue community ejects or rejects him and his message. This happens for the first time in Pisidian Antioch (Acts 13:46), and Paul and Barnabas justify their turning to Gentiles from Scripture (Acts 13:47, quoting Is 49:6)—Luke regards it as vital that the Gentile mission is seen to be scriptural.

Two key speeches show Paul engaging with Gentiles: in Lystra (Acts 14:15-17) and Athens (Acts 17:22-31). Both are responses to misunderstandings in the setting. In Lystra, Barnabas and Paul respond with great concern to the priest of Zeus's attempt to offer sacrifice to them as gods, as a result of Paul's part in a man's *healing (Acts 14:8-14; see Gempf 1995). The likely background is the story of a visit of Zeus and Hermes to this part of Asia Minor, a visit that led to the gods destroying the neighborhood (Ovid, *Metam.* 7.624-674); the Lystrans would not be anxious to have a repeat of such events and so offered *worship to their visitors. This speech is apologetic, for it critiques and corrects this idolatrous misunderstanding. Paul's earlier preaching (Acts 14:9) would certainly concern Jesus, and thus the brief speech is a corrective rather than the entire substance of Paul's evangelistic message in Lystra. It highlights Barnabas and Paul's mortal nature (compare Peter's response to the Roman centurion Cornelius [Acts 10:25-26]), and insists that the true God is the world's creator and the provider of rains and crops. There are some converts in Lystra ("the disciples," Acts 14:20), but not the large numbers at Pentecost (Acts 2:41).

In Athens, Paul debates in the synagogue (Acts 17:17) and in the marketplace with the populace, including Epicurean and Stoic *philosophers

(Acts 17:17-18). These conversations lead to him being summoned to the Areopagus, the city council, which has wide powers (Winter). Notably, the Areopagus controls the recognition of new gods and sects in the city. To recommend official recognition to the citizen assembly (which normally rubber-stamps the Areopagus's recommendation), they require evidence of an epiphany or revelation of the god; sufficient followers of the god to sustain financially and practically the building and maintenance of a temple, including creating a statue of the god and holding festival days; plus the required priests to offer sacrifices to the god and administer the cult. The council's questions are focused on Paul's "new teaching" about "foreign deities" (Acts 17:18-19), and their request is best translated, "We therefore wish to make a judgment on what is being claimed these things are" (Acts 17:20). Paul's speech is thus not a general apologetic speech in a polytheistic setting but a response to the Athenian requirements for a new god's recognition. Paul critiques the assumptions of their requests, for there is already an altar to the one true God, although labeled as "unknown" (Acts 17:23), so a new one is not required; this God does not need a temple, since he is the creator (Acts 17:24); neither does this God need priests and others—rather than needing to receive sustenance from humans, this God gives generously in sustaining the world and humanity (Acts 17:25-28); moreover, no statue of this God is required, for *humans* are his *image bearers (Acts 17:29). Thus people need to turn from their misguided beliefs and concomitant lifestyles and turn to this God, for they will face Jesus in judgement (Acts 17:30-31). Paul's basis for the last claim is that God raised Jesus from the dead (Acts 17:31), thus aligning the central point of his announcement of Jesus in Athens with that of his synagogue proclamation.

The Athens speech echoes Paul's summary of the initial evangelization of Thessalonica, which highlights that believers turned from *idolatry to the true God (thus showing that they are predominantly Gentile), having recognized that they must answer to Jesus in judgment, for he is the one who delivers from God's coming *wrath (1 Thess 1:9-10). Some argue that Paul's analysis of pagan idolatry and lifestyle in Romans 1:18-32 contrasts with the Athens speech: they read the Athens speech as implying that worship of other gods provides a preparation for the gospel, since it corrects ignorance of the true God rather than stating that Gentiles are culpable for their false worship; by contrast, they see Romans as only critiquing such worship (e.g., Vielhauer; Dibelius, 26-78). However, the speech is not simply addressing the question of whether Gentiles are guilty or innocent in relation to the true God but provides a critique of their present beliefs and practices, and is then future focused in giving them the opportunity to change. Paul's observation that God's ordering of the world was designed so that people would seek God is heavily qualified by "and perhaps—although this is unlikely—grope after him and find him" (Acts 17:27). The optative verbs *psēlaphēseian* ("grope after") and *heuroien* ("find") express an unlikely-to-be-fulfilled incomplete condition. Romans, likewise, treats the worship of idols as foolish (Acts 1:22-23)—and thus people should turn from it. In neither passage is there a "natural" experiential *knowledge of God available outside Jesus, although in both passages, *creation is designed to call people to seek God (Gempf 1993).

As well as spoken engagement, "wonders and signs" seen in the Jerusalem community continue in Paul's ministry (Acts 15:12; 19:11-12; 28:3-6; see earlier Acts 2:43; 4:30; 5:12; 6:8). These include healing (Acts 14:8-10; 19:11-12; 28:7-9), raising from the dead (Acts 20:9-12), deliverance (Acts 16:16-18; 19:11-16), and even a *curse that causes blindness (Acts 13:6-12). Paul's long ministry in Ephesus brings issues concerning *magic and spells to the fore in a city famous for its magical practices (Acts 19:11-19; Walton 2016). Each of these activities is intrinsic to Paul's gospel proclamation, since they demonstrate that Jesus is Lord of the world, even though that world is out of kilter with its creator's purposes. Paul speaks of such events in his ministry: his initial evangelization of the cities of southern Galatia featured remarkable events along these lines (Gal 3:3-5), as was true elsewhere (Rom 15:19; 2 Cor 12:12; probably also 1 Thess 1:5). At this point, Paul's letters and Acts are united.

In two Gentile contexts, Luke portrays the financial impact of Paul's ministry on other belief systems. In Philippi, Paul delivers a *slave girl from *demon possession (Acts 16:16-18), and this provokes the girl's owners, who make money from her fortune telling, to bring Paul and Silas to the city authorities. Luke says their motivation is financial (Acts 16:19), but they present their case as advocating Jewish customs in this Roman colony (Acts 16:20-21). In Ephesus, Paul's ministry damages the trade in silver models of the Artemis shrine, provoking Demetrius to gather his fellow silversmiths to oppose Paul (Acts 19:24-27). Again, Luke presents their motivation as financial (Acts 19:24-27), but the silversmiths accuse Paul of attacking the goddess

Artemis, leading to a riot (Acts 19:27-29). Both stories are historically plausible, for each features a key point where the gospel clashes with the worship of Greco-Roman gods, and that clash was central to the gospel's impact (Hurtado). Although Paul in his letters says a little about *wealth and poverty, notably in relation to his *collection for the Jerusalem believers (Rom 15:25-28, 31; 1 Cor 16:1-4; 2 Cor 8–9), Acts here adds something distinctive to our understanding of the impact of Paul's ministry. It is unsurprising that Paul himself does not mention these things explicitly in his letter, for his letters are addressing believers and say little directly about evangelism and its results. However, he is advising his believers how to live godly lives in a polytheistic context, and in places the tensions that arise come to the surface, such as in his advice on eating (or not) meat offered in temples (1 Cor 8). Thus encounters such as those in Acts 16; 18 may well be manifestations of these tensions boiling over.

5.4. Suffering as Intrinsic to Paul's Mission. When Saul becomes a Jesus-follower, Ananias is told that his missionary vocation integrally includes suffering for Jesus (Acts 9:15-16), and this saying is programmatic for Saul's ministry (Tabb, 152-53). He faces physical attacks, both actual and planned (Acts 14:5, 19-20; 16:19-24; 17:5-10, 13; 21:27-28; 22:22-24; 23:9-10, 12-24), and other forms of persecution, including being brought to the Roman court in Corinth (Acts 18:12-18), and the riot in Ephesus (Acts 19:23-41). Paul knows by the Spirit that he faces suffering on his last visit to Jerusalem and expresses willingness to meet it in order to complete the work Jesus has given him to do, and he therefore resists well-meaning believers who wish to turn him from that path (Acts 20:22-24; 21:13). Acts does not theologize explicitly much about Paul's suffering; the picture in the letters both agrees that Paul *suffers in his ministry and offers greater theological reflection on this fact. As part of his "fools' speech," Paul highlights how much he suffers in his apostolic ministry (2 Cor 11:23-29), listing far more examples of suffering than Acts describes. That said, he includes imprisonment, beating with rods, stoning, shipwreck, and dangers from fellow Jews, all of which Acts reports (respectively, Acts 16:24; 16:22-23; 14:19; 27:39-44; 18:12-13).

Acts adds a dimension to the letters in reporting Paul's Roman *citizenship at key points in relation to suffering (Acts 16:35-39; 22:24-29; 25:7-12), something Paul himself never mentions. Paul announces his Roman citizenship to prevent further mistreatment of him by Roman authorities in Philippi and Jerusalem. Some scholars doubt that Paul was a Roman citizen, particularly because of evident tensions between Jewish and Roman citizenship (Stegemann). However, some men held both citizenships in Rome (Philo, *Legat.* 155-157), and some Jewish freedmen relocated to Judea and lived there as Roman citizens (Hengel and Deines).

6. Paul as Controversialist.

The admission of Gentiles to the believing communities is central to Paul's ministry in Acts, and this is deeply controversial, particularly among some Jewish believers. Paul becomes convinced during his ministry that God's purpose is that the believing community should include Jews and Gentiles on an equal footing, that is, that Gentiles do not need to accept the Jewish law (including circumcision for men) in order to belong to God's people as renewed in Jesus. The dispute becomes sharp after Paul and Barnabas's return to Syrian Antioch (Acts 15:1-2), leading to the Jerusalem meeting, where some Pharisaic believers assert that Gentile believers must accept circumcision and the law (Acts 15:5). In what must have been a long discussion, Luke presents Barnabas and Paul's contribution briefly: they give testimony about their missionary experience of God accepting Gentiles, signaled by "signs and wonders" (Acts 15:12). As Acts presents the event, however, Peter is the major protagonist for not requiring Gentile believers to be Torah observant, including testifying to his own experience of God taking him to Cornelius; it is Peter who states the key theological point, that "it is through the *grace of our Lord Jesus that we [Jews] are saved, just as they [Gentiles] are" (Acts 15:7-11, quoting Acts 11; see Acts 10:1–11:18). After the meeting's conclusion, which accepts the case made by Peter, Barnabas, and Paul, Paul is part of the propagation of the decree (Acts 15:25, 30-31; 16:4).

Paul's letters make clear that this controversy was real and significant. Galatians is Paul's answer to the claim that some teachers are making that Gentile believers must be circumcised and keep the law. Assuming Galatians predates the Jerusalem meeting, the ferocity of Paul's argument is understandable, for the controversy was at its height then (Acts 15:1-2; see Longenecker). Some doubt that the Paul of Galatians could agree to the conditions set by the Acts apostolic decree, since they require Gentiles to eat kosher, at least when eating with Jewish believers (Acts 15:20, 29). However, Paul regards matters of the Jewish law as indifferent for Gentile believers, even including circumcision, which is "nothing"

(Gal 6:15); what he opposes is the requirement that Gentile believers *must* keep the law in order to be part of the people of God, particularly when Jewish believers separated from Gentile believers on that basis (Gal 2:11-21). Paul's regarding circumcision or uncircumcision as a matter of indifference comports well with the Acts record of his having Timothy circumcised (Acts 16:3): the key question in Paul's mind would be what would open the door to the gospel best, a principle he himself expresses (1 Cor 9:19-23).

In Romans, the unity of Jew and Gentile believers is also central, although from a different angle—here, some years later, Gentile believers are suspicious of Jewish believers after Jewish people were first expelled from Rome and later returned (Fitzmyer, 68-85, esp. 77-78). Paul thus needs to argue for his "to the Jew first" model of mission (Rom 1:16; 2:10).

Certainly, the controversy about law-free admission of Gentile believers seems sharper in Paul's letters, and that may reflect that Paul writes in the white heat of debate, whereas Luke writes looking back after the issues have been decided and the churches have adapted to the new normal. Luke is far from covering up the controversy: from one perspective, Acts is an explanation of how a Jewish prophet, Jesus, gave rise to a community that embraced Gentiles apart from the law. The debates around that question rumble on into Paul's final visit to Jerusalem, where he is falsely accused of teaching that Jewish believers should not circumcise their children or keep Jewish customs (Acts 21:21). The Jerusalem elders' speech, which repeats the terms of the Jerusalem meeting's agreement (Acts 21:25), does not imply that Paul did not know of this agreement—on that basis, some claim that Paul was not present in Jerusalem for the meeting. Rather, it is there to remind *readers* of that agreement. Ancient reading was aloud, generally by one person to a group, and so readers would not flip back and forth in a book as we moderns do—they would need to be reminded of things, as Luke does here.

7. Paul as Pastor.
Acts offers relatively little about Paul's pastoral care of his converts—understandably, given its focus on the progress of the *missio Dei* "to the end of the earth" (Acts 1:8). The letters, by contrast, offer many windows into Paul's relationships with his converts, for better and worse. The different foci of the letters and Acts again enable us to interpret their differences of emphasis.

Paul's warm and affectionate relationships with his converts are a feature of his ministry in Acts. Paul both gives and receives considerable care in these relationships, even after a relatively short time. Thus, in Lystra, his converts surround him after his stoning, perhaps in prayer, and certainly in support (Acts 14:20). In Berea, when Jews from Thessalonica come to incite violence against Paul, the believers enable him to travel to the coast and on to Athens, which probably includes paying the cost of his sea voyage (Acts 17:13-15). Paul kneels on the beach to pray with the Ephesian elders and the believers from Tyre (Acts 20:36-38; 21:5-6), and the elders weep, and embrace and kiss Paul, demonstrating their grief at parting from him. Luke uses family language to describe Paul's relationships, such as "brothers and sisters"—and terms such as this appear widely in Acts of the "fictive *kinship" relationships of the believing communities, notably for mixed groups of Jews and Gentiles (Walton 2014, 225-26; Trebilco, 50-53). This affection and care is evident in Paul's letters. As in Acts, "fictive kinship" language is prominent, found over one hundred times in the undisputed letters. The affection associated with this language is particularly clear in 1 Thessalonians, where Paul compares his relationship with the believers to that of both mother and father (1 Thess 2:7, 11), as well as speaking of the believers as "brothers and sisters" some nineteen times in a mere eighty-nine verses (see Philem 1, 7, 16, 20).

Acts 20 offers a series of stories that portray more of Paul's pastoral relationships with his churches than other parts of Acts. Here Paul the teacher engages at (considerable) length with the believers in Troas (Acts 20:7-12) to the extent that Eutychus falls asleep and falls to his death! Even after Paul shows that Eutychus has recovered, he then speaks with the community until dawn (Acts 20:11). In Miletus Paul meets with the Ephesian elders and speaks with them about his and their ministry at length—this is the only substantial speech Paul makes to believers in Acts (Acts 20:18-35). Paul emphasizes his example of faithful *leadership, the suffering he has endured, the importance of rightly handling wealth and work, and the suffering and death of Jesus—all themes that find ready echoes, often with the same vocabulary, in Paul's letters (Walton 2000, 84-93, 157-74).

8. Paul as Missionary-Prisoner.
Paul is a prisoner for about a quarter of Acts, as well as in Philippi (Acts 16:19-34), although it is right to think of him as a missionary-prisoner, for he continues to take every opportunity to call others to follow

Jesus (Rapske; Skinner). Acts here provides much information that the letters do not.

Paul's long imprisonment begins with the riot in Jerusalem caused by false claims that Paul has brought Gentiles into forbidden parts of the temple (Acts 21:27-30). The riot leads to Paul being taken into protective custody by the Romans from the Antonia fortress adjacent to the temple (Acts 21:31-36). Paul's conversation with the tribune in Greek leads to Paul speaking in his defense to the crowd, who listen when he addresses them in Aramaic (Acts 21:40–22:21). Paul's words focus on his encounter with Jesus on the Damascus road, which turned his life around from opposition to the messianic movement to being a great advocate for it, and this emphasis is typical of his speeches during this period. Paul is much more concerned that his hearers respond to Jesus than with what happens to him, for he knows he will suffer for Jesus (see 5.4 above). On hearing that Jesus called Paul to go to Gentiles, the temple crowd turns against Paul again, and the tribune removes him (Acts 22:22-24). Paul avoids standard Roman interrogation by torture by declaring his Roman citizenship (Acts 22:24-29), and so the tribune seeks expert advice from the Sanhedrin (Acts 22:30–23:10). Paul focuses the Sanhedrin's attention on resurrection of the dead as the reason he is on trial, thus dividing Sadducees and Pharisees, for the former reject resurrection and the latter accept it (Acts 23:6-10). The Lord appears to Paul to encourage him that he will give testimony in Rome (Acts 23:11, confirming Paul's hope in Acts 19:21).

Paul's nephew learns of a plot against Paul, and the tribune arranges for Paul to be transferred to Caesarea Maritima, the Roman regional headquarters (Acts 23:12-35). Paul will spend two years here under Felix as governor (Acts 24:27). During this time, Felix conducts an initial hearing, at which the Jewish leaders (primarily through their professional advocate, Tertullus) accuse Paul of profaning the temple (Acts 24:2-9). Paul's response is again to tell his story with a focus on the resurrection (Acts 24:10-21). He denies that he has caused a public disturbance or committed a crime. Felix, under Roman law, requires the eyewitness testimony of the tribune Lysias, who arrested Paul in Jerusalem, before taking the case further (Acts 24:22), and Acts never reports that he received Lysias's testimony. That may be a partial explanation for Paul's long imprisonment. During that period Paul continues to testify about faith in Jesus to Felix, although Felix (not untypically of Roman officials) is rather hoping for a bribe to set Paul free (Acts 24:24-26).

The final stage of Paul's Caesarean imprisonment comes under Festus, the new Roman governor (Acts 24:27). On taking up his post, he naturally desires to build good relationships with the Jewish leaders and meets them in Jerusalem, where they raise Paul's case (Acts 25:1-5). On returning to Caesarea, Festus sends for Paul, and again the Jewish leaders accuse Paul (Acts 25:6-7). Paul denies that he has committed any crime and exercises his right as a Roman citizen to appeal to the emperor, a request that Festus grants (Acts 26:10-12). Festus seeks expert advice on Paul from Agrippa, whose wife, Bernice, is Jewish (Acts 25:13-27), and Paul tells his story, again highlighting his Damascus road encounter with the exalted Jesus (Acts 26:2-23). It is clear that he is seeking to convert Festus (Acts 26:25-29). Agrippa advises Festus that Paul has committed no crime but that Festus is bound by Paul's appeal to Caesar (Acts 26:30-32).

Paul's long and dangerous journey to Rome is described in some detail by Luke: it is one of our longest extant accounts of storm and shipwreck from antiquity and abounds in technical seafaring language (Acts 27:1–28:16). During this journey, Paul is treated well by Roman officials, including the centurion Julius, who permits him to meet other believers in Sidon (Acts 27:3), takes Paul's advice amid the storm (Acts 27:30-32), and effectively allows him to exercise leadership on board by speaking to the crew and passengers (Acts 27:21-26, 33-36). After the shipwreck, Malta's Roman governor, Publius, gives Paul and his company *hospitality (Acts 28:7-10). En route to Rome overland from Puteoli, Paul is allowed to meet with believers there, and also other believers who travel from Rome to accompany him on the last steps of the journey (Acts 28:13-15).

Acts closes with Paul under house arrest in Rome for two years, free to have visitors to whom he speaks the gospel (Acts 28:30-31), including meeting the city's Jewish leaders (Acts 28:17-28).

The picture of Paul's arrest, imprisonment, journey to Rome, and time in Rome is little attested in the letters. Some of the letters are written from prison: among the undisputed letters, Philippians (Phil 1:7, 13-14, 17, 19-24) and Philemon (Philem 1, 9-10); and among the disputed letters, Ephesians (Eph 3:1; 4:1; 6:20), Colossians (Col 4:3, 18), and 2 Timothy (2 Tim 1:8; 2:9). In other places, Paul writes of his imprisonments, which are evidently more numerous than Acts records (2 Cor 6:4-5; 11:23). Scholars debate whether the prison letters were written from Caesarea or Rome, or perhaps Ephesus (since Paul says that he "wrestled with wild animals" there, which some take to hint at imprisonment [1 Cor 15:32]). These hints from the letters certainly show that Paul was quite often imprisoned as a result of his mission work and indicate some of the deprivations involved. The letters are complemented by the picture in Acts, which is more detailed about the imprisonments it reports, while the letters give a greater sense of the extent of Paul's imprisonments.

See also Apostle; Chronology of Paul; Conversion and Call of Paul; Coworkers, Paul and His; Gentiles; Mission; Opponents of Paul; Pastor, Paul as; Paul and Judaism; Prison, Prisoner; Suffering; Travel and Itinerary Plans; Urban Setting of Paul's Churches.

BIBLIOGRAPHY. **E. Adams,** *The Earliest Christian Meeting Places: Almost Exclusively Houses?*, LNTS 450 (London: T&T Clark, 2013); **T. W. R. Churchill,** *Divine Initiative and the Christology of the Damascus Road Encounter* (Eugene, OR: Pickwick, 2010); **A. C. Clark,** "The Role of the Apostles," in *Witness to the Gospel: The Theology of Acts*, ed. I. H. Marshall and D. Peterson (Grand Rapids, MI: Eerdmans, 1998), 169-90; **H. Conzelmann**, *Acts of the Apostles*, Hermeneia (Philadelphia: Fortress, 1987); **M. Dibelius,** *Studies in the Acts of the Apostles* (London: SCM Press, 1956); **J. A. Fitzmyer,** *Romans: A New Translation with Introduction and Commentary*, AB 33 (London: Geoffrey Chapman, 1993); **D. French,** "Acts and the Roman Roads of Asia Minor," in *The Book of Acts in Its Graeco-Roman Setting*, ed. D. W. J. Gill and C. H. Gempf, BAFCS 2 (Grand Rapids, MI: Eerdmans, 1994), 49-58; **C. H. Gempf,** "Athens, Paul at," *DPL*, 51-54; idem, "Mission and Misunderstanding: Paul and Barnabas in Lystra (Acts 14:8-20)," in *Mission and Meaning*, ed. A. Billington, M. M. B. Turner, and T. Lane (Carlisle, UK: Paternoster, 1995), 56-69; **M. Green,** *Evangelism in the Early Church* (London: Hodder & Stoughton, 1970); **E. Haenchen,** *The Acts of the Apostles* (Oxford: Blackwell, 1971); **C. W. Hedrick,** "Paul's Conversion/Call: A Comparative Analysis of the Three Reports in Acts," *JBL* 100 (1981): 415-32; **M. Hengel and R. Deines**, *The Pre-Christian Paul* (Philadelphia: Trinity Press International, 1991); **L. W. Hurtado,** *Destroyer of the Gods: Early Christian Distinctiveness in the Roman World* (Waco, TX: Baylor University Press, 2016); **C. S. Keener,** "Three Notes on Figurative Language: Inverted Guilt in Acts 7.55-60, Paul's Figurative Vote in Acts 26.10, Figurative Eyes in Galatians 4.15," *JGRChJ* 5 (2008): 42-50; **S. Kim,** *The Origin of Paul's Gospel*, 2nd ed., WUNT 2/4 (Tübingen: Mohr Siebeck, 1984); **W. S. Kurz,** *Reading Luke-Acts: Dynamics of Biblical Narrative* (Louisville, KY: Westminster John Knox, 1993); **G. Lohfink,** *The Conversion of St Paul: Narrative and History in Acts* (Chicago: Franciscan Herald, 1976); **R. N. Longenecker,** *Galatians*, WBC 41 (Dallas: Word, 1990); **G. Lyons,** *Pauline Autobiography: Towards a New Understanding*, SBLDS 73 (Atlanta: Scholars Press, 1985); **D. Marguerat,** *The First Christian Historian: Writing the "Acts of the Apostles,"* SNTSMS 121 (Cambridge: Cambridge University Press, 2002); **T. E. Phillips,** *Paul, His Letters, and Acts* (Peabody, MA: Hendrickson, 2009); **B. M. Rapske,** *The Book of Acts and Paul in Roman Custody*, BAFCS 3 (Grand Rapids, MI: Eerdmans, 1994); **M. L. Skinner,** *Locating Paul: Places of Custody as Narrative Settings in Acts 21–28*, AcBib 13 (Atlanta: Society of Biblical Literature, 2003); **W. Stegemann,** "War der Apostel Paulus ein römischer Bürger?," *ZNW* 78 (1987): 200-229; **B. J. Tabb,** *Suffering in Ancient Worldview: Luke, Seneca and 4 Maccabees in Dialogue*, LNTS 569 (London: Bloomsbury T&T Clark, 2017); **A. C. Thiselton,** *The First Epistle to the Corinthians*, NIGTC (Grand Rapids, MI: Eerdmans, 2000); **M. B. Thompson,** "The Holy Internet: Communication Between Churches in the First Christian Generation," in *The Gospels for All Christians: Rethinking the Gospel Audiences*, ed. R. Bauckham (Edinburgh: T&T Clark, 1998), 49-70; **P. R. Trebilco,** *Self-Designations and Group Identity in the New Testament* (Cambridge: Cambridge University Press, 2012); **P. Vielhauer,** "On the Paulinism of Acts," in *Studies in Luke-Acts*, ed. L. E. Keck and J. L. Martyn (London: SPCK, 1968), 33-50; **S. Walton,** *Leadership and Lifestyle: The Portrait of Paul in the Miletus Speech and 1 Thessalonians*, SNTSMS 108 (Cambridge: Cambridge University Press, 2000); idem, "Calling the Church Names: Learning About Christian Identity from Acts," *PRSt* 41 (2014): 223-41; idem, "Evil in Ephesus: Acts 19:8-40," in *Evil in Second Temple Judaism and Early Christianity*, ed. C. Keith and L. T. Stuckenbruck, WUNT 2/417 (Tübingen: Mohr Siebeck, 2016), 224-34; **D. Wenham,** "Acts and the Pauline Corpus II. The Evidence of Parallels," in *The Book of Acts in Its Ancient Literary Setting*, ed. B. W. Winter and A. D. Clarke, BAFCS 1 (Grand Rapids, MI: Eerdmans, 1993), 215-58; **B. W. Winter,** "On Introducing Gods to Athens: An Alternative Reading of Acts 17:18-20," *TynBul* 47 (1996): 71-90; **B. Witherington III,** *The Acts of the Apostles: A Socio-Rhetorical Commentary* (Grand Rapids, MI: Eerdmans, 1998).

S. Walton

PEACE, RECONCILIATION

In Pauline literature *peace* and *reconciliation* are theopolitical terms that represent the in-breaking of God's messianic age of justice and peace through the life, *death, and *resurrection of Israel's Messiah—Jesus *Christ, the "*Lord of peace" (2 Thess 3:16). Paul's grammar of peace and reconciliation represents a social reality and ethical distinctive in Pauline Christianity, along with a controlling metaphor that becomes a dimension of major Pauline topics such as *justification, *righteousness/justice, *faith, *grace, *love, participatory soteriology, and ethnic reasoning. As Willard Swartley observes, "Paul, more than any other writer in the NT canon, makes peace, peacemaking, and peace-building central to his theological reflection and moral admonition" (2006, 190). Although one cannot reduce Paul's understanding of peace and reconciliation to word occurrences alone, it is significant that the word "peace" (*eirēnē*) occurs forty-four times in Pauline (and deutero-Pauline literature), along with its cognates "to live in peace" (*eirēneuō*) three times and "to make peace" (*eirēnopoieō*) one time. Terms for "reconciliation" (*katallagē*), or "to reconcile" (*katallassō, apokatallassō*), on the other hand, occur thirteen times and are employed exclusively by Paul among NT authors.

For Paul, peace and reconciliation are interrelated and overlapping concepts that animate the whole Jesus event, wherein the *God of peace has climactically made peace between humans and God (vertical dimensions of peace) and humans and one another (social or horizontal dimensions of peace). Peace can also refer to the church as an alternative community of new *creation, the sociopolitical nature of Christ's peaceable *kingdom, cosmic dimensions of Christ reconciling the *whole* created order, and the inner flourishing of human *spirituality (Swartley 2014).

Underlying Paul's vertical and social interpretation of peace is the inner- and interpersonal nature of shalom in the OT, a concept rooted in the wholeness and the vitality of human flourishing with God, with fellow humans, and with the cosmic order (Yoder). While Paul does not explicitly quote the shalom texts of the OT, he constructs a "*shalom*-collage" of intertextual allusions (Gorman 2014). Paul's interpretation of peace and reconciliation is eschatological and cosmic in that it is not yet fully realized. It is covenantal and thereby existential insofar as a messianic age of shalom, rooted in the OT prophets, has arrived in the form of a "new *covenant of peace" (Ezek 34:25; 37:26; Is 54:10, see Gorman 2014). But peace is also an ecclesial habit and vital character trait of the church's public *witness, an invitation for disciples to bear witness to Christ the peacemaker by participating in "the *ministry of reconciliation" (2 Cor 5:18).

1. Peace Under Imperial Rome
2. Paul's Conversion and Enemy Love
3. Vertical Dimensions of Peace and Reconciliation
4. Social Dimensions of Peace and Reconciliation

1. Peace Under Imperial Rome.

In classical Greece, *eirēnē* was understood as the absence of enmity between warring nations. Indeed, it was "a quiet period in respect to military conflict" (Plato, *Def.* 413a6). The conquests of Alexander the Great amplified this emphasis around the Hellenistic warrior king, who became a superhuman vehicle for military domination of distant peoples for personal enrichment. Indeed, Alexander even claimed to be "reconciler [*diallaktēs*] for the whole world" (Plutarch, *Alex. fort.* 1.6). This emphasis was intensified under imperial Rome when Caesar Augustus politicized *pax* (Latin for peace) as a metonym for imperialism. In Augustus's own words, "peace had been achieved by victories on land and sea throughout the whole empire of the Roman people" (*Res gestae divi Augusti* 13, trans. Cooley). *Pax* was transformed from reconciling agreements (*pactum, pactio*) between enemies under the Roman republic to pacification of the globe (Cornwell). Augustus's peace propaganda articulated his role as peacemaker (*eirēnopoios/pacificator*) over the *empire—an imperial ideology now called the *pax Romana* ("Roman peace").

Three metaphors fueled the *pax Romana* and Rome's expansionist ambitions: military domination, enslavement, and the purported inferiority of distant peoples. Together, these metaphors, articulated especially through material culture, both justified and legitimated Rome's violent pacification of subordinate subjects throughout the Mediterranean. Although subjects could eulogize the emperor for bringing peace to the known world (Horace, *Carm.* 4.15.4-24; Suetonius, *Aug.* 98.1; Philo, *Legat.* 143-153), Rome's pacification program was hardly devoid of *violence (Tacitus, *Agr.* 30; Virgil, *Aen.* 6.851-853), a point foregrounded by Rome's widespread use of crucifixion to police the dissident voice (Josephus, *J.W.* 2.75, 241; 5.449-451; *Ant.* 17.295). The emperor's role as peacemaker, then, monumentalized two realities: Rome brought peace to sea and land, but Rome could simultaneously flex its policing power to *make* the known world peaceful if subordinates chose to rebel.

With this context in mind, Paul's peace theology redefines power, reorients allegiances, and challenges agency. For Paul, *eirēnē/pax* is not through coercion; rather, it is God's gift through Christ crucified and raised, who pacifies human enmity with God, neighbor, and the cosmic order paradoxically "by making peace [*eirēnopoiēsas*] through the blood of his *cross" (Col 1:20 NRSV). Indeed, imperial Rome's offer of "peace and security" (1 Thess 5:3)—a phrase proliferated on imperial coinage and inscriptions—was, for Paul, ephemeral compared to the peace and *salvation offered through the *pax Christi* (Weima).

2. Paul's Conversion and Enemy Love.

Paul's understanding of peace and reconciliation cannot be understood apart from his *call and commission, or what one may cautiously call his "*conversion" to Messiah Jesus (Gal 1:15-16; 1 Cor 15:8-10; Phil 3:4-11). Paul himself acknowledges that he persecuted (*diōkō*) and tried to destroy (*portheō*) the *church (Gal 1:13, 23; Phil 3:6; 1 Cor 15:9); the potential for violence in these verbs is corroborated by Luke (Acts 7:58–8:3; 9:1-2; 22:3-5; 26:9-12). While Paul may have been exposed to nonretaliatory *ethics in early Jewish sources (Zerbe 1993), it is clear that Paul's paradigm shift from persecutor to nonviolent peacemaker was initiated by an "apocalypse/revelation of Jesus Christ" (Gal 1:12). In Paul's own words, "I have been crucified with Christ" (Gal 2:19 NRSV). The result of Paul's co-crucifixion on the road to Damascus was that "the violent Paul died when Christ was apocalypsed in him; now Christ-in-Paul shapes Paul's life in the flesh into a cruciform existence" (Gabrielson, 95).

In Paul's post-Damascus world, Christ's pattern of faithfulness became Paul's own. This remarkable transformation hinged on Christ's resurrection and Paul's enlivenment by the Spirit, which vindicated and validated not only Jesus' messianic *identity but also Jesus' way of peace, enemy love, and nonretaliation (Gorman, 2009, 129-60). Paul's call or commission, then, was not only about soteriology; it also articulated Paul's transformation in Christ to a messianic ethic that was Christocentric, cruciform, and shalom-centric. Paul, then, was called and commissioned by the risen Christ; consequently, he *converted*, ethically speaking, to Christ's way of peace and nonviolence.

In Paul's apocalyptic, Christ-oriented *cosmology, Christ crucified was no longer an oxymoronic caricature of messianic divine power. Rather, Christ humiliated and Christ exalted was a mimetic paradigm of discipleship, a template for life *in Christ* to be imitated (1 Cor 4:16; 11:1; Phil 2:1-11). Paul appeals to churches to embody this pattern of peace and nonretaliation through moral exhortation (Rom 12:14, 17-21; 1 Cor 4:12-13; 1 Thess 5:13-15; Col 3:12-15) but also through the example of Paul's sufferings he bears in his own body as a persecuted *apostle (2 Cor 6:4-10; 11:23-25; Gal 5:11; 6:17). Paul's sufferings remind readers that the teachings of Jesus and Jesus' way of peace were authoritative for Paul in *this* life (and not relegated to an esoteric eschatological future reality). While the transmission of dominical sayings of *Jesus through Paul's *letters is highly disputed, there is striking continuity between the memory of a nonviolent Jesus in the Synoptic Gospels and Paul's letters (Gabrielson, 55-78).

The impact of Paul's call and conversion on Paul's peace ethic is also felt in his language of reconciliation. Like *eirēnē* in the Greco-Roman context, *katallassō/katallagē* was used predominantly at the level of Hellenistic diplomacy and interpersonal relationships to signify peace between political enemies and the restoration of *friendship (Fitzgerald, 259; *katallassō* = "change a person from enmity to friendship" [*LSJ*]). In the Hellenistic Jewish context, on the other hand, reconciliation reflected God's reconciliation with God's apostate people (2 Macc 1:5; 5:20; 7:33; 8:29; Marshall). Paul nuances the secular and early Jewish understandings of reconciliation, reorienting the object of reconciliation to human beings' reconciliation with God through Christ's initiative (rather than God to humans or between political parties). The interpretive move is significant and may reflect the violent Paul's own experience of reconciliation with God on the Damascus road. To be sure, the pronouns "we" and "us" in Paul's earliest extended reflection on reconciliation in 2 Corinthians 5:11-21 can be interpreted as a first-person apologetic defense of Paul's call and conversion, wherein Paul is legitimately a "new creation" (2 Cor 5:17), "reconciled to God" (2 Cor 5:18), and divinely commissioned with a "ministry of reconciliation" (2 Cor 5:19; see Kim). With echoes of Paul's personal experience of reconciliation with God—and Isaiah's eschatological vision of restorative justice and new creation (Is 65:17-25)—Paul's call and conversion become a paradigmatic example of Christ's embrace of an enemy and the transformation of an enemy to a friend.

3. Vertical Dimensions of Peace and Reconciliation.

In Paul's letters, there is only one direct reference to *eirēnē* between humans and God (Rom 5:1; Klassen, "Peace"). The forty-three other occurrences of *eirēnē* surface in contexts that illuminate a divine attribute and social, cosmic, political, ecclesial, and inner-spiritual realities. When discussing vertical dimensions of soteriology, Paul prefers the reconciliation word family (Rom 5:10-11; 2 Cor 5:18-20; Eph 2:16; Col 1:20, 22), but he nuances this language for the postresurrection world. For example, Paul is the first Jewish-Christian to merge OT theology of atonement with reconciliation to map the divine-human relationship, but he flips the paradigm: instead of the offending party taking initiative by offering *sacrifice at the altar to atone for *sin, God, the offended party, takes initiative by offering sacrifice *through* Christ to restore peace and friendship—to reconcile humans to God (Fitzgerald).

Paul also flips the secular paradigm of reconciliation in Hellenistic diplomacy and interpersonal relations, wherein the offending party was expected to take initiative in restoring peace with the offended party (Fitzgerald). The Jewish and Hellenistic backdrop animates the profundity of God's graceful initiative: even while humans were "sinners" (Rom 5:8) and "enemies" (Rom 5:10), *through* Christ God restored estranged humans' friendship and peace with God. For Paul, then, reconciliation and peace with God are bound up with justification (Rom 5:1, 9), whereby Christ's faithfulness to the point of death restored and redefined friendship between God and neighbor. Reconciliation, therefore, is "the joyous result of a series of initiatives begun and sustained by God. . . . God is the One who makes friends of his human adversaries. The friendship of the Christian community is thus grounded in its members' friendship with God" (Fitzgerald, 259).

The restoration of humans' friendship and peace with God is rooted in Paul's perception of God's character, a concept captured through Paul's use of the appellation "God of peace." In continuity with OT appellations ("God of *truth," Is 65:16; "God of *glory," Ps 29:3; etc.), Paul formulates the peace epithet in benedictions (Rom 15:33; Phil 4:9; 1 Thess 5:23; 2 Thess 3:16), promise or prediction (Rom 16:20; 1 Cor 14:33), moral pronouncement (2 Cor 13:11), and as "Lord of peace" (Swartley 2006). Strikingly, the appellation only occurs once elsewhere in the NT (Heb 13:20) and once in early Jewish literature (T. Dan 5.2), illuminating its significance for Paul's thought. To be sure, in Paul's letters, "God of *hope" occurs once (Rom 15:13) and "God of love" once (2 Cor 13:11). Notably, Paul nowhere speaks of a God of war, God of *wrath, or God of *judgment—"God of peace" best captures God's character and incarnational purposes in Christ (Mauser, 106).

4. Social Dimensions of Peace and Reconciliation.

The social significance of Paul's ethic of peace and reconciliation was largely overlooked by NT scholars until recent years (Constantineanu). Paul's social vision is rooted in the conviction that humanity is enslaved to sin and that humanity's collective sins emerge in the form of Sin—fallen suprahuman powers that perpetuate systems of division, violence, and domination (Croasmun). Paul illumines the harmful effects of violence and the absence of peace amid human community: "Their feet are swift to shed blood; ruin and misery are in their paths, and the way of peace [*eirēnēs*] they have not known" (Rom 3:15-17 NRSV). Paul's solution to human retaliatory impulses can be summarized thus: God interrupts Sin and its spiral of violence through Christ's faithfulness, thereby inviting those who are *in Christ* to become participants in pacifying divine-human *and* intra-human enmity by participating in Christ's faith, or faithfulness. The logic here is significant: peace *through* Christ (divine-human pacification), which, in turn, transforms and empowers those *in* Christ to become God's peace on earth (human-human pacification). The vertical and social dimensions of soteriology and divine pacification, for Paul, are inseparable.

Paul's social vision of peace and reconciliation has two foci: an internal focus (inner-personal and intra-believer peace) and an external focus (peacemaking toward enemies and ethnic enmity). The former is amplified through emphasis on peace as a *"fruit of the spirit" (Gal 5:22) and God's gift of peace under anxiety (Phil 4:7; Rom 8:6-13; 2 Thess 3:16; Col 3:15; see de Villiers, 19), along with sixteen epistolary greetings (Rom 1:7; 1 Cor 1:3; 2 Cor 1:2; Gal 1:3; Eph 1:2; Phil 1:2; Col 1:2; 1 Thess 1:1; 2 Thess 1:2; Philem 3) and benedictions (Rom 15:13, 33; 2 Cor 13:11; Eph 6:23; 1 Thess 5:23; 2 Thess 3:16) that extend the benefit of peace—often preceded with "grace"—to assemblies of Christ-believers through Paul's apostolic authority (Lieu).

The inner-personal and intra-believer benefits of peace do not result in solipsism, a point made most vividly in Romans 12:14-21, where Paul's exhortation to "live peaceably [*eirēneuontes*] with all" (Rom 12:18 NRSV) extends outwardly to persecutors

(Rom 12:14) and enemies (Rom 12:20). Far from a call to passive deference toward evil, Paul invites Roman believers to nonretaliatory active resistance: to bless, to do good, to be at peace, to pursue noble conduct, and to provide *hospitality to enemies (Rom 12:20//Prov 25:21); the result is that vengeance and just judgment are deferred and remain God's prerogative (Rom 12:19-20; Klassen 1984). Believers are thereby empowered with a theodicy to disorient enmity with acts of love and to "overcome evil with good" (Rom 12:21 NRSV; Zerbe 2012).

Christ's pacification of enmity is also felt in Paul's ethnic reasoning. Whereas Rome pacified ethnic enmity through militarized coercion and imposed cultural homogeneity (Pliny, *Nat.* 3.39), Paul understands the Christ event as God's apocalyptic-peacemaking-disruption of ethno-racial enmity and invitation to embrace human difference rather than fear it. Although the authorship is disputed, this ethnic reasoning is especially at work in Ephesians 2:14-17, where Christ serves as God's agent to pacify the "dividing walls" and "hostilities" that exacerbate ethnic enmity and ethno-racial binaries. With allusions to Isaiah ("How beautiful upon the mountains are the feet of the messenger who announces peace, who brings good news" [Is 52:7 NRSV] and "Peace, peace, to the far and the near" [Is 57:19 NRSV]), the author of Ephesians acclaims that Christ is our peace (Eph 2:14), Christ brings peace (Eph 2:15), Christ reconciles enemies in one *body with God (Eph 2:16), and Christ proclaims peace to those on the periphery and at the center (Eph 2:17). Thus, Christ is the incarnation of the gospel of peace and proclaims himself as peace (Dinkler, 96). Moreover, those *far off* (*Gentiles) and *those near* (Jews) have become one through the peace of Christ (Eph 2:17; Swartley 2006, 200).

The cumulative impact of Paul's ethnic reasoning is that human allegiances to racialized state power and racialized supremacy are thrown off-kilter, wherein loyalty to Christ, the cosmic peacemaker, supersedes loyalties to one's culture, ethno-racial group, or nation (Volf, 159). Such reorientation of allegiances, however, does not result in a new *non-ethnic* baptismal identity, imposed cultural homogeneity, racial colorblindness, or the segregation of ethnic difference (Buell and Hodge). In Christ, the peace and justice of God liberate the weak and reorient the power of the strong (Rom 14:1–15:13) to form peaceable and just multicultural communities of *fellowship—spaces where ethno-racial particularities are maintained while in friendship with God and the other. In this messianic economy of human difference, Christ-believers are habituated into a shared mission of *just peace* or *peacemaking* that interrupts domination systems (military, enslavement, and xenophobia) through a shared ministry of reconciliation that is restorative, reparative, transformative, and justice-making among formerly alienated peoples (De Gruchy).

See also CONVERSION AND CALL OF PAUL; EMPIRE; ETHNICITY IN PAUL'S WORLD; FELLOWSHIP, COMMUNION, SHARING; FORGIVENESS; LOVE; VIOLENCE.

BIBLIOGRAPHY. **D. K. Buell and C. J. Hodge,** "The Politics of Interpretation: The Rhetoric of Race and Ethnicity in Paul," *JBL* 123, no. 2 (2004): 235-51; **C. Constantineanu,** *The Social Significance of Reconciliation in Paul's Theology*, LNTS 421 (New York: T&T Clark, 2010); **H. Cornwell,** *Pax and the Politics of Peace: Republic to Principate* (Oxford: Oxford University Press, 2017); **A. E. Cooley,** *Res Gestae Divi Augusti: Text, Translation, and Commentary* (Cambridge: Cambridge University Press, 2009); **M. Croasmun,** *The Emergence of Sin: The Cosmic Tyrant in Romans* (Oxford: Oxford University Press, 2019); **J. W. De Gruchy,** *Reconciliation: Restoring Justice* (Minneapolis: Fortress, 2002); **E. Dinkler,** "*Eirene*—the Early Christian Concept of Peace," in *The Meaning of Peace*, ed. P. B. Yoder and W. M. Swartley (Elkhart, IN: Institute of Mennonite Studies, 1992), 71-120; **J. T. Fitzgerald,** "Paul and Paradigm Shifts: Reconciliation and Its Linkage Group," in *Paul Beyond the Judaism/Hellenism Divide*, ed. T. Engberg-Pedersen (Louisville, KY: Westminster John Knox, 2001), 241-62; **J. Gabrielson,** *Paul's Nonviolent Gospel: The Theological Politics of Peace in Paul's Life and Letters* (Eugene, OR: Pickwick, 2013); **M. Gorman,** *Inhabiting the Cruciform God: Kenosis, Justification, and Theosis in Paul's Narrative Soteriology* (Grand Rapids, MI: Eerdmans, 2009); idem, *The Death of the Messiah and the Birth of the New Covenant* (Eugene, OR: Cascade, 2014); idem, *Becoming the Gospel: Paul, Participation, and Mission* (Grand Rapids, MI: Eerdmans, 2015); **S. Kim,** "God Reconciled His Enemy to Himself: The Origin of Paul's Concept of Reconciliation," in *The Road from Damascus: The Impact of Paul's Conversion on His Life, Thought, and Ministry* (Grand Rapids, MI: Eerdmans, 1997), 102-24; **W. Klassen,** "Peace," *ABD* 5:206-12; idem, *Love of Enemies: The Way of Peace* (Minneapolis: Fortress, 1984); **J. Lieu,** "'Grace To You and Peace': The Apostolic Greeting," *BJRL* 68, no. 1 (1985): 161-78; **H. Marshall,** "The Meaning of 'Reconciliation,'" in *Unity and Diversity in New Testament Theology*, ed. R. Guelich (Grand Rapids, MI: Eerdmans, 1978); **R. P. Martin,** *Reconciliation: A*

Study of Paul's Theology (Atlanta: John Knox, 1981); **U. Mauser,** *The Gospel of Peace* (Louisville, KY: Westminster John Knox, 1992); **W. M. Swartley,** *Covenant of Peace: The Missing Peace in New Testament Theology and Ethics* (Grand Rapids, MI: Eerdmans, 2006); idem, "Peace and Violence in the New Testament: Definition and Methodology," in *Struggles for Shalom: Peace and Violence Across the Testaments*, ed. L. L. Brenneman and B. D. Schantz (Eugene, OR: Wipf & Stock, 2014), 141-54; **P. G. R. de Villiers,** "Peace in the Pauline Letters: A Perspective on Biblical Spirituality," *Neot* 43 (2009): 1-26; **M. Volf,** "The Social Meaning of Reconciliation," *Int* 54 (2000): 158-72; **J. A. D. Weima,** "'Peace and Security' (1 Thess. 5.3): Prophetic Warning or Political Propaganda?," *NTS* 58 (2012): 331-59; **P. B. Yoder,** *Shalom: The Bible's Word for Salvation, Peace and Justice* (Nappanee, IN: Evangel, 1997); **G. Zerbe,** *Non-retaliation in Early Jewish and New Testament Texts: Ethical Themes in Social Contexts*, JSPSup 13 (Sheffield: Sheffield Academic Press, 1993); idem, *Citizenship: Paul on Peace and Politics* (Winnipeg: CMU Press, 2012).

D. J. Strait

PERFECT, PERFECTION. *See* COMPLETE, MATURE (PERFECT); ETHICS.

PERFORMANCE

Performance is the oral delivery and reception of texts, speeches, and sermons. Paul preached and communicated to congregations using the same media as other ancient orators. He employed the conventions of the ancient world to communicate to crowds and congregations. In Acts, Luke portrays Paul as an orator familiar with Jewish and Greco-Roman conventions of rhetoric. In public and private settings, crowds respond similarly to how they reacted to famous speakers such as Demosthenes, Quintilian, and Cicero. To communicate across congregations, Paul deployed a trained lector, usually the scribe or courier, to read aloud to an engaged audience (1 Thess 5:27; Col 4:16). They would respond personally to the message, engage the speaker, and form a common identity with each other (Shiell 2011, 59-61).

A template for Paul's performances comes from 1 Timothy 4:13-16. Paul instructs Timothy to devote himself to the public reading of Scripture, exhortation/*preaching, and *teaching. This threefold practice will "save both yourself and your hearers." In this case a reader/lector named Timothy was also a pastor. He was to perform the Scriptures publicly; the audience would observe his progress in reading, preaching, and teaching. Both Timothy and the audience would be "saved" or trained in the process. They would also be "saved" from those who were sowing discord among the emerging followers of Jesus and those outside the congregation testing their loyalty to Jesus. This example of a public performance of Scripture reflects the widespread practice of oral reading, delivery, and reception of epistles and other media in the ancient world. The passage also reveals an important dynamic in early Christian *paideia* (education). Performance events mark the progress of the performer and the audience (Shiell 2011, 53).

1. Performance of Texts in the Ancient World
2. Performance in Christian Contexts
3. Practices in Pauline Circles
4. Significance of Pauline Performance

1. Performance of Texts in the Ancient World. Communication in the first-century Mediterranean world came primarily through oral-aural media. If there was a text, it was usually communicated orally to groups rather than distributed to be read silently by each person (Livy, *Hist.* 6.25.9; Polybius *Historiae* 6.38.4.4; Seneca, *Ep.* 75.1; 40.10; 64.2; Dio Chrysostom, *Virt.* 8.9; *Dei cogn.* 5; Ex 24:3-8; Neh 8:1-18). Most listeners were not scribal literate, but they listened well, responded verbally to performances, and developed strong memories (Botha, 40). Texts were not as widely published or affordable in the first century. Writing merely reinforced the more reliable oral *tradition. The Greeks preferred oral to written records because the written records were cumbersome and accessible only to trained scribal-literate persons (Achtemeier, 9-10; Plato, *Phaedr.* 274c-277a; Eusebius, *Hist. eccl.* 3.39.4). People read with their ears as well as their eyes (Yaghjian, 207).

Communication began in the early stages of writing and transmission. Authors maintained a close connection to the scribe and the courier, who were at times the same person (Cicero, *Quint. fratr.* 3.1.23; 3.7.1). The author dictated letters to the scribe, and the scribe/lector read it back to the author for editing (Cicero, *Orat.* 1.30.136). Some scribes also served as couriers and were considered more reliable than the letter itself (Cicero, *Fam.* 5.4.1; 5.6.1). The courier often functioned as the lector, delivering a recitation of the text as well as sharing additional information from the sender (Shiell 2004, 126-27; Xenophon, *Hell.* 7.1.39; Stirewalt, 16).

Orators and trained lectors, usually *slaves and freedmen, spoke and read orally at festivals, funerals, and homes. A *recitare* featured an author performing his own works. A *cantare* was a "full scale reenactment" conducted by a trained lector in a style appropriate to the stage (Quinn, 86-87). Authors also used elite reading circles known as *amici* and used lectors to deliver to home audiences at symposia following the meal (Quintilian, *Inst.* 1.11-14; Pliny, *Ep.* 1.9; 3.1.4-5; 34; Nepos, *Atticus* 14.1; Gellius, *Noctes atticae* 2.22.1; on *amici* see Johnson, 55-56; on symposia see Starr, 341). In ancient Judaism, the community participated in similar reading circles (Philo, *Somn.* 2.127; *QE* 2.34; 1QS VI, 6-8; CD XIII, 2-4). Readers were not required to recite texts verbatim. They prepared their recitation by retaining the content in their memories and often paraphrased the text for their audiences (Snyder, 156; Jub. 13.10-15; Theon, *Progymnasmata* 66-67; Hermogenes, *Progymnasmata* 4-6).

Hellenistic Jewish education taught students to perform using Greco-Roman conventions. The rabbinic schools used the *chreia* to teach students how to expand on texts. They bonded in *love through their education, which included reading aloud sacred texts as well as community meals that reflected the influence of symposia recitations. In liturgical settings, such as the synagogue or at *Qumran, the reader took on a prophetic presence within the community. They reenacted events and embodied the emotions in their performance (4 Macc 13:22-26; Sir 24:30; 30:1; Let. Aris. 287; Jaffee, 37, 138, 447; see Harkins, 94, on the performance of the Hodayot scroll at Qumran).

In the performance event, scribes/readers read the text aloud, the audience responded, and the readers elaborated on the meaning extemporaneously (see Neh 8:1-12 LXX; 1 Macc 14:1-38; Lk 4:16-21). For a visual analogue, see the painting from the House of the Tragic Poet in Pompeii (Ling, 125, fig. 127), which dates from the first century BC to the first century AD. A slave reader sits in the foreground with an open scroll reading aloud to six persons. For an ancient Jewish setting, see the Ezra painting in the synagogue at Dura Europos. Performances were also common at funerals to commemorate the deceased's life. Funerals dramatically combined recitation, music, and art (Weitzmann and Kessler; Cassius Dio, *Hist.* 75.4-5).

First- and second-century audiences participated in performances (Haines-Eitzen, 58). Audience responses were not only included in the story (the story audience) but also were part of the living formation of the community (the performance audience). The hearers not only listened to a text; they also identified with the characters as they were discussed (Dewey, 155). The process of listening, retaining, correcting, and retelling was part of memorization and formation in a community. Memorization was more than rote repetition of words. The discipline involved paraphrasing, visualizing, and participating in the story. The speaker was given the freedom to elaborate on the text or omit sections depending on the setting or his purpose (Shiell 2011, 22, 73). Hellenistic Jews used performance to preserve their distinctive Jewish *identity around Torah (4 Macc 13:22-26).

Readers were also interpreters. They responded to their audiences as they delivered messages and explained the meaning of the message to their listeners. For example, in the second century, Aristedes moved Marcus Aurelius to tears by recounting the destroyed city of Smyrna. The emperor responded by sending aid to the city (Aelius Aristides, *Or.* 19.2-3; Philostratus, *Vit. soph.* 582; Shiell 2011, 36).

2. Performance in Christian Contexts.

The conventions of ancient performance were widely known in Christian settings. Readers are presumed in epistolary, apocalyptic, and gospel genres. For example, Philip hears the Ethiopian eunuch reading the text of Isaiah aloud (Acts 8:15). The Antioch *church follows the practice of reading texts aloud (Acts 15:31). Revelation 1:3 provides a *makarism* (blessing) for both reader and hearer: "Blessed is the one who reads aloud the words of the *prophecy, and blessed are those who hear and who keep what is written in it" (NRSV). Matthew and Mark include an aside: "Let the reader understand" (Mk 13:14//Mt 24:15).

Other early Christian writings provide even more instructions for or comments about the reader. The letter of 2 Clement echo the instructions to Timothy: "Pay attention to that which is written, that you may both save yourselves and him who is the reader among you" (2 *Clem.* 19.1 [LCL]). The audience corrects one another (*1 Clem.* 35.5-8). In the context of a diatribe against heretics, Tertullian notes how quickly the catechumens move from being a deacon one day to a reader the next (*Praescr.* 41). Eusebius cites readers in a list of other offices of the church (*Hist. eccl.* 6.43.11; Hippolytus, *Trad. ap.* 1.12). By the fourth century, the church recognized the lector as a minor office and formally ordained individuals who had this charism (Apostolic Constitutions 8.22; Nässelqvist, 110-16).

Like the ancient world, early Christians also relied on memory in their performances. Clement of Alexandria refers to a "true tradition preserved in memory" (Eusebius, *Hist. eccl.* 3.23.6 [trans. Bockmuehl, 346]). Their performances required the audience to listen, recall previous information, forget past mistakes, practice what they heard, and paraphrase other texts. The performance linked the audience with events and figures of the past and connected them to their present issues. In Hebrews 10:32, the writer challenges the listeners to recall previous good efforts as a way of motivating and inspiring the audience (Thompson, 221). In 2 Peter 1:12-15, memory is used as a way to arouse the listener once the speaker has departed. The recipient knows the information but needs a reminder. The writer helps the audience visualize the "sacred mountain" of the transfiguration and the scene by imaginatively hearing the "living voice" of *God over the audience (Bockmuehl, 346; Porphyry, *Vita Plotini* 14-15).

Early Christian texts provide evidence of widespread audience participation within both the story itself and its reception. A crowd interrupts Peter's sermon in Acts 2 with a question: "What shall we do?" (Acts 2:37). The Ephesians respond to Demetrius with an acclamation: "Great is Artemis of the Ephesians" (Acts 19:28). Festus interrupts Paul's defense before Agrippa in Acts 26:24. Through performance of the texts, the community was bound by a common identity around the memory of Jesus (Tertullian, *Praescr.* 41; Eusebius, *Hist. eccl.* 6.43.11; Hippolytus, *Trad. ap.* 1.12).

3. Practices in Pauline Circles.

Paul prepared his letters anticipating that they would be read aloud in multiple congregations. In addition to the reference from 1 Timothy, Paul requests that his *letters be read aloud to other churches. Paul states in 1 Thessalonians 5:27, "I solemnly command you by the *Lord that this letter be read to all of them" (NRSV). Colossians 4:16 assumes multiple locations for readers: "And when this letter has been read among you, have it read also in the church of the Laodiceans; and see that you read also the letter from Laodicea" (NRSV). Although a specific reader is not mentioned, the letters themselves suggest widespread presentation and distribution orally (Stirewalt, 17). Couriers such as Epaphroditus (Philippians), Tychicus (Ephesians, Colossians, Philemon, and Philippians), and Onesimus (Philemon) served as lectors. Phoebe the deacon likely performed Romans (McKnight 2019, 3-5). Such practices presumably created challenges for Paul. In Galatians 4:20, Paul laments his absence and wishes that he "could change his tone [of voice]" in the reading of the epistle.

3.1. Performance of Paul's Letters. Based on archaeological evidence from homes in Pompeii, readings of Paul's letters likely occurred in groups no larger than fifty persons (Oakes, 30). Lectors read the letter aloud, interpreted the message, gave personal information about the condition of Paul, and responded to the audience. In Ephesians and Colossians, Tychicus in his reading will supply personal information and elaborate on the interpretation of the letter to the Ephesians, Colossians, and presumably Philemon. "Tychicus will tell you everything you need to know" (Col 4:7).

As the letters were performed, audiences engaged and participated. In his letter to the Galatians, Paul references an oral confrontation with Cephas where they debated, corrected, and confronted each other like an ancient audience (Gal 2:11-12). The audience recalls previous communication (2 Tim 2:8, 14; Acts 20:31; Bauckham, 196) and remembers Paul's instructions in light of Jesus' Last Supper with his disciples (1 Cor 11:23). They remember the oral traditions of their *faith handed down from previous generations, commemorated by the ritual gesture of the laying on of hands (2 Tim 1:1-14).

As the letter was performed, the audience was instructed to avoid godless chatter (2 Tim 2:16). They corrected each other (2 Tim 3:16). They rebuked one another (1 Tim 5:20) and confronted disagreements (Gal 2:11). They spoke psalms and sang *hymns to one another (Eph 5:19; Col 3:16) and greeted one another with a holy kiss (Rom 16:16; 1 Cor 16:20; 2 Cor 13:12; 1 Thess 5:26). In Philippians 4:2-3, Paul through the reader singles out three members of the audience in the letter—Euodia, Syntyche, and Syzygus/"loyal companion"—to learn to work together. He directly addresses Archippus (Col 4:17) to complete the task and to Philemon to prepare a room for him (Philem 22).

3.2. Communal Memory and Identity Formation. Oral performances trained listeners in Christian *paideia*. Through the lector, Paul took on the role of instructor with *coworkers (Rom 16:3, 21; 1 Cor 3:9). The listeners were bound to God, Paul, and one another through the performance. The reader performed scriptures from the Hebrew Bible that were also suitable for instruction in Christian brotherhood (2 Tim 3:16). The performances commended persons to the recipients and facilitated reconciliation among the listeners and in some cases the sender (2 Cor 3:1-3; Titus 2:11; 2 Tim 2:25; Stirewalt, 94).

The listeners in turn were accountable to help those personally addressed to carry out the instructions (Col 4:17; Phil 4:2-3; Oestreich, 107).

4. Significance of Pauline Performance. Studying Paul in light of performance has implications for interpretation.

4.1. Personal and Communal Formation. Performance saves readers and listeners. Just as Timothy is presented as a lector being trained for the work of public reading of Scripture (1 Tim 4:13-16), so the oral performance of Paul forms the reader and audience today. The audience was able to see the reader's progress, and the audience was trained by participating in the process. The performance created a mutual accountability to the message. Teaching and way of life were the tests of a reader's faithfulness and the basis of their credibility (Gloer, 179). The reader mirrored back to the audience how they should view their lives. The reader's *ethos* was connected to their reception. The reader's character mattered as much as the performance itself (Witherington, 341).

4.2. Participatory Interpretation. Silent reading of the text distances the reader from the ancient audience, privatizes study, and focuses attention solely on the person of Paul. Such methods ignore the communication process and the significant roles of the courier, reader, and recipients. Because these letters were presented for house churches, they required oral interpretation in groups of listeners. Rather than reading and studying texts silently, performance suggests that Paul must be read dynamically, with people prompted to respond. A study of Philemon requires attention to the presence of Tychicus, Onesimus, and Philemon (McKnight 2017, 85-88).

4.3. Embodied Reconciliation. As evidenced in Galatia, *Ephesus, and Rome in Paul's letters, and in Jerusalem in Acts 15, Jewish and Gentile believers were divided against one another. The oral (not written) performance and communication event unified congregations and helped them be reconciled to *Christ and thus to one another across racial, gender, and ethnic lines. The oral performance invited the audience to engage immediately in the work of reconciliation by participating with the drama of characters such as Euodia, Syntyche, and Syzygus. The reading and response of the audience provided opportunities for audiences to enter the story and participate in the drama.

See also Letters, Letter Forms; Rhetorical Criticism; Teaching, Teachers.

BIBLIOGRAPHY. **P. J. Achtemeier,** "*Omne Verbum Sonat:* The New Testament and the Oral Environment of Late Western Antiquity," *JBL* 109 (1990): 3-27; **R. J. Bauckham,** *Jesus and the Eyewitnesses: The Gospels as Eyewitness Testimony* (Grand Rapids, MI: Eerdmans, 2006); **M. Bockmuehl,** "New Testament Wirkungsgeschichte and the Early Christian Appeal to Living Memory," in *Memory in the Bible and Antiquity: The Fifth Durham-Tübingen Research Symposium*, ed. S. C. Barton, L. T. Stuckenbruck, and B. G. Wold, WUNT 212 (Tübingen: Mohr Siebeck, 2007), 341-68; **P. J. J. Botha,** "Mute Manuscripts: Analysing a Neglected Aspect of Ancient Communication," *Theologica Evangelica* 23, no. 3 (1990): 35-47; **J. Dewey,** "The Gospel of Mark as an Oral-Aural Event: Implications for Interpretation," in *The New Literary Criticism and the New Testament*, ed. E. S. Malbon and E. V. McKnight, JSNTSup 109 (Sheffield: Sheffield Academic Press, 1994), 145-63; **H. Gloer,** *1 & 2 Timothy–Titus*, SHBC (Macon, GA: Smyth & Helwys, 2010); **K. Haines-Eitzen,** *Guardians of Letters: Literacy, Power, and the Transmitters of Early Christian Literature* (New York: Oxford University Press, 2000); **A. K. Harkins,** *Reading with an "I: to the Heavens: Looking at the Qumran Hodayot Through the Lens of Visionary Traditions*, Ekstasis: Relgious Experience from Antiquity to the Middle Ages 3 (Boston: de Gruyter, 2018); **M. S. Jaffee,** *Torah in the Mouth: Writing and Oral Tradition in Palestinian Judaism 200 BCE–400 CE* (New York: Oxford University Press, 2001); **W. A. Johnson,** *Readers and Reading Culture in the High Roman Empire: A Study of Elite Communities*, Classical Culture and Society (Oxford: Oxford University Press, 2010); **C. H. Kraeling,** *The Synagogue*, Final Report 8, part 1, Excavations at Dura-Europos (New Haven, CT: Yale University Press, 1956); **R. Ling,** *Roman Painting* (Cambridge: Cambridge University Press, 1995); **S. McKnight,** *The Letter to Philemon*, NICNT (Grand Rapids, MI: Eerdmans, 2017); idem, *Reading Romans Backwards: A Gospel of Peace in the Midst of Empire* (Waco, TX: Baylor University Press, 2019); **D. Nässelqvist,** *Public Reading in Early Christianity: Lectors, Manuscripts, and Sound in the Oral Delivery of John 1-4*, NovTSup 163 (Leiden: Brill, 2016); **P. Oakes,** *Reading Romans in Pompeii: Paul's Letter at Ground Level* (Minneapolis: Fortress, 2009); **B. Oestreich,** *Performance Criticism of the Pauline Letters*, Biblical Performance Criticism Series 14 (Eugene, OR: Cascade, 2016); **K. L. Quinn,** "The Poet and His Audience in the Augustan Age," *ANRW* 30.1:76-180; **D. Rhoads,** "Performance Criticism," in *The Dictionary of the Bible and Ancient Media*, ed. T. Thatcher,

C. Keith, R. F. Person, E. R. Stern, and J. Odor (London: Bloomsbury, 2017), 281-88; **W. D. Shiell,** *Reading Acts: The Lector and the Early Christian Audience*, BibInt 70 (Leiden: Brill Academic, 2004); idem, *Delivering from Memory: The Effect of Performance on the Early Christian Audience* (Eugene, OR: Pickwick, 2011); **H. G. Snyder,** *Teachers and Texts in the Ancient World: Philosophers, Jews, and Christians* (London: Routledge, 2000); **R. J. Starr,** "Reading Aloud: *Lectores* and Roman Reading," *Classical Journal* 86 (1991): 337-43; **M. L. Stirewalt,** *Paul, the Letter Writer* (Grand Rapids, MI: Eerdmans, 2003); **J. W. Thompson,** *Hebrews*, Paideia (Grand Rapids, MI: Baker Academic, 2008); **R. F. Ward and D. J. Trobisch,** *Bringing the Word to Life: Engaging the New Testament Through Performing It* (Grand Rapids, MI: Eerdmans, 2013); **B. Witherington III,** *A Socio-Rhetorical Commentary on Titus, 1–2 Timothy, and 1–3 John*, Letters and Homilies for Hellenized Christians 1 (Downers Grove, IL: IVP Academic, 2006); **K. Weitzmann and H. L. Kessler,** *The Frescoes of the Dura Synagogue and Christian Art* (Washington, DC: Dumbarton Oaks Research Library and Collection, 1990); **L. B. Yaghjian,** "Ancient Reading," in *The Social Sciences and New Testament Interpretation*, ed. R. Rohrbaugh (Peabody, MA: Hendrickson, 1996), 206-30.

W. D. Shiell

PERSECUTION. *See* Suffering; Violence.

PERSECUTOR, PAUL AS. *See* Conversion and Call of Paul; Paul in Acts.

PERSEVERANCE. *See* Apostasy; Faith.

PERSON, THE. *See* Anthropology, Pauline; Flesh; Identity.

PETER

Simon Peter was called from his fishing nets to "fish" for people in the earliest days of Jesus' public *ministry (Mk 1:16-18; Mt 4:18-20). He was the first to verbalize that Jesus was the *Christ (Mk 8:27-30; Mt 16:13-20; Lk 9:18-22; Jn 6:66-69) and was one of Jesus' three closest disciples, who experienced the transfiguration (Mk 9:2-8; Mt 17:1-8; Lk 9:28-36). He resisted Jesus' attempt to wash his feet (Jn 13:2-11) and defended, but then denied, Jesus at his arrest (Mk 14:54, 66-72; Mt 26:58, 69-75; Lk 22:54-62; Jn 18:10-18, 25-27). Peter was the first to enter Jesus' empty tomb (Lk 24:12; Jn 20:2-10), and despite his failures was forgiven and reinstated to his apostolic calling by the resurrected Christ (Jn 21:1-23). Because of his personal relationship with Jesus, Peter may have been perceived by many to have an advantage of *knowledge and authority over the apostle Paul.

1. Peter's Name
2. Peter's Ministry
3. Peter's Conflict with Paul

1. Peter's Name.

The name *Peter* was not a common name in the first century prior to its occurrence in the NT. The apostle's given name was Simon bar Jonah (Mt 4:18; 10:2; Lk 6:14; Jn 1:42; Gk. *Simōn* in the Gospels or *Symeōn* in Acts 15:14 and the probable original reading of 2 Pet 1:1). Jesus gave Simon the nickname *Petros* ("rock"; Aram. *Cephas*; Mt 16:16-20; Lk 6:14), later anglicized as *Peter*. The Aramaic form *kēphas* (Cephas, "rock"; Jn 1:42) was the name favored by the apostle Paul, who uses it several times in 1 Corinthians 1:12; 3:22; 9:5; 15:5; Galatians 1:18; 2:9, 11, 14. Paul only twice uses the name *Peter*, when he refers to the "*apostle to the circumcised" (Gal 2:8 NIV).

2. Peter's Ministry.

Luke refers to the apostle only as *Peter* in his Gospel and Acts, and documents Peter's prominent *leadership in the earliest days of the *Jerusalem church until he was forced by persecution to leave "for another place" (Acts 12:17 NIV). Some time later Peter addressed the *Jerusalem Council (Acts 15:7), debated the controversial issue of whether *Gentiles needed *circumcision for admission into the *church, and described himself as the one whom God chose that the Gentiles might hear and believe the *gospel (Acts 15:7) after the Gentile Cornelius came to *faith through Peter's message (Acts 10). Nevertheless, after the Jerusalem Council Paul designated him as the apostle "to the circumcised" (Gal 2:7-8 NIV). Peter, James, and Paul agreed that the Gentiles must not be forced to become Jews through circumcision, but that Jewish Christians could continue to practice the Jewish way of life. Strong and early church traditions preserved by Clement of Rome, Ignatius, Irenaeus, Eusebius, Tertullian, and Jerome identify Peter as a leader of the church in both Antioch and Rome. It is believed he was martyred in Rome during the reign of Emperor Nero (AD 64–68) and was buried in the area now encompassed by the Vatican.

Peter's following in *Corinth is an indication of the reach of his ministry from Jerusalem to Rome (1 Cor 1:12). In 1 Corinthians, Paul refers to him four times using the Greek transliteration of the Aramaic nickname *kēphas* (Cephas, "rock"). Paul does not take issue with Cephas personally but calls for unity in Corinth based on following Christ alone in response to factious quarrels among those who followed Paul, Cephas, or Apollos (1 Cor 1:10-17). Paul also acknowledged Cephas had the right to take a believing wife along on *mission journeys, indicating that Peter was married (1 Cor 9:5; cf. Mt 8:14; Mk 1:30; Lk 4:38). In 1 Corinthians 15:5-9 Paul aligns himself with the chain of witnesses to Christ's *resurrection, naming Cephas, the Twelve, the five hundred, and James, to indicate a unity of *witness underlying the gospel message.

3. Peter's Conflict with Paul.

The entailments of the gospel were subject to debate as it crossed geopolitical and cultural boundaries, requiring in this case interpretation of the agreement reached at the Jerusalem Council (Acts 15), which later came into sharp focus in the church at Antioch.

Luke reports that the Jerusalem Council decided not to require Gentile circumcision for admission to the Christian church (Acts 15:1-35). When Paul learned that the question of Gentile circumcision for *salvation was being raised in Galatia, he responded with revealing autobiographical information intended to establish his authority independently from Peter and the Jerusalem apostles while asserting their agreement with the gospel he preached (Gal 2:1-10). Paul recounted a sharp conflict with Peter in Antioch in which he asserted the authority to confront Peter, whom he believed had reneged on the Jerusalem agreement and was jeopardizing the *truth of the gospel. Consistent with the *vision of unclean animals (Acts 10:9-16; 11:1-18), Peter had joined the Jewish and Gentile Christians in Antioch eating together (see Acts 10:9–11:3). But when some men from *James arrived in Antioch, Peter began to separate himself from table *fellowship with the Gentile Christians. Peter's example influenced others, such as Barnabas, to do the same. It is because Paul and Peter agreed in principle that he was able to point out that Peter's behavior was inconsistent with his principles, unintentionally jeopardizing the truth of the gospel and the unity of the church.

Peter's behavior in Antioch has often been construed as hypocritical, but this may be a rush to judgment when his motives are unknown. Peter, we may assume, had good reasons for his actions that could appear to Paul as hypocrisy (Dunn 1993, 125-26). At least three pressures seem to have been in play: (1) misunderstandings or conflicting interpretations of the Jerusalem agreement, (2) a shift in authority and power in the Jerusalem church focusing on James, and (3) a volatile political situation characterized by outbreaks of nationalistic violence (Dunn 1993, 122-23).

Peter and other Jewish Christians may have withdrawn from mixed table fellowship to extend *hospitality to the brothers from Jerusalem, who most likely observed a Jewish way of life and were not accustomed to a strong Gentile presence in their church fellowship. Or perhaps James had requested that Peter and the Jewish believers at Antioch help mitigate the increasing danger of persecution by the Jewish establishment in Judea or in Antioch by aligning more closely to Jewish practices. It cannot be known with certainty. Nevertheless, as Paul sharply points out, Peter's behavior, regardless of his motive, violated the unity of the church and was "not acting in line with the truth of the gospel" (Gal 2:14 NIV), for it implicitly pressured the Gentiles in Antioch to Judaize.

This incident in Antioch contributed to Paul's breach with Judaism, with Barnabas, and with the church at Antioch, which he visited only once more (Acts 18:22; Dunn 1993, 130). The extent of a subsequent reconciliation, if any, is unknown (Bond and Hurtado 2015, 10). Peter's canonical writings mention Paul only once, as "our dear brother" who writes with *wisdom and authority (2 Pet 3:15-16).

See also CORINTH; GALATIANS, LETTER TO THE; JAMES AND PAUL; JERUSALEM, COUNCIL OF; SYRIAN ANTIOCH.

BIBLIOGRAPHY. **M. Bockmuehl,** *Simon Peter in Scripture and Memory: The New Testament Apostle in the Early Church* (Grand Rapids, MI: Baker Academic, 2012); **H. K. Bond and L. W. Hurtado,** eds., *Peter in Early Christianity* (Grand Rapids, MI: Eerdmans, 2015); **J. D. G. Dunn,** *The Epistle to the Galatians*, BNTC (Peabody, MA: Hendrickson, 1993); **L. R. Helyer,** *The Life and Witness of Peter* (Downers Grove, IL: IVP Academic, 2012); **M. Hengel,** *Saint Peter: The Underestimated Apostle* (Grand Rapids, MI: Eerdmans, 2006).

K. H. Jobes

PHARISEES. *See* PAUL AND JUDAISM.

PHILEMON, LETTER TO

With only 335 words in Greek, Philemon is the shortest of the Pauline corpus while at the same time the most personal. The letter is an appeal to Paul's associate Philemon, requesting that he welcome back his formerly unconverted *slave, Onesimus, who is carrying the *letter with him ahead of Paul's anticipated arrival as a guest in Philemon's home. The letter is short not only on words but on details. Readers are left to speculate on the location of Paul's imprisonment, the reasons for Onesimus's separation from Philemon, how Onesimus came to meet Paul in *prison, and the outcome between Onesimus and Philemon. Scholarly interest has been out of proportion to the letter's size and has generated a variety of clever and influential reconstructions.

1. Authorship
2. Historical Context
3. Philemon and Onesimus
4. Structure of the Letter
5. History of Interpretation
6. Theological Significance

1. Authorship.

Few have questioned Paul's authorship of this letter. The close connection between Philemon and Colossians has sometimes been noted by those who question the latter's authenticity and suggest that if Colossians is a post-Pauline creation, then Philemon must also be later. Enough evidence, however, can be garnered to support the authenticity of Colossians and, by extension, Philemon. The author identifies himself as Paul three times (Philem 1, 9, 19) and all evidence indicates that Philemon was included in the earliest collections of Paul's letters, including Marcion and the Muratorian Canon.

2. Historical Context.

Paul does not offer any geographical or chronological clues that help to pinpoint a location for Philemon on his *ministry timeline. An apparent affinity between Colossians and Philemon suggests that, although the content and length of the two letters noticeably differs, they are uniquely connected. Both were written while Paul was in prison. Colossians refers to Paul's bonds (Col 4:3) and Aristarchus his "fellow prisoner" (Col 4:10 NRSV), while Philemon twice refers to his chains/imprisonment (Philem 1:1, 10). Both speak to the slave-master relationship, albeit in different ways. Colossians addresses slaves and masters through the *household code (Col 3:22–4:1), while in Philemon it is part of Paul's appeal for Onesimus. The names of eight different persons are mentioned by Paul in both letters (Timothy, Archippus, Onesimus, Epaphras, Mark, Aristarchus, Demas, and Luke). Moreover, the only other mention of an Onesimus in the NT is in Colossians 4:9, where he is identified as a member of the Colossian *church returning there to report on what is happening with Paul. All of this makes a strong case for concluding that the two letters share a common author and a common destination.

Although Paul says he is a prisoner, he fails to mention the location. Rome is the traditional location (Acts 28:16, 30; Phil 1:13-14), but *Ephesus is probably a better candidate. Possible allusions to an Ephesian imprisonment may be found in 2 Corinthians, which mentions hardships Paul experienced in Asia (2 Cor 1:8) and his claim to have been imprisoned far more than his *opponents (2 Cor 11:23). The theological themes present in Colossians could suggest a time later in Paul's life, and thus his imprisonment in Rome. But assuming Colossae was destroyed by the earthquake of AD 60–61 means Paul must have written the letters very early on during his time in Rome. The proximity of Ephesus to Colossae (120 miles) means Onesimus could reach Paul in about a week, while the distance between Colossae and Rome (1,200 miles) would have required several weeks to months and the navigation of various roads and sea crossings. Added to this is Paul's request that Philemon prepare a guest room for him (Philem 22). If Paul were in Rome and hoping to visit Spain (Rom 15:28), a trip to Colossae first seems less likely. Another piece of evidence is found in Marcion's prologue to Colossians, which identifies the place of writing as Ephesus. If Paul was imprisoned in Ephesus, one can assume a date of AD 53–55. If imprisoned in Rome, one can assume a date of AD 58–60.

3. Philemon and Onesimus.

While a focus on authorship, date, and provenance is helpful, it can distract from important information about the object and recipient of the letter, Onesimus and Philemon, respectively. A close reading of the letter reveals important details about these two individuals that add to the understanding of the situation.

*3.1. **Philemon.*** He was probably a wealthy individual who owned a house large enough to host a local Christian assembly (Philem 2) and provide guest room(s) for travelers (Philem 22). He owned at least one slave, but the size of his household implies he owned multiple slaves. He had a reputation as one who "refreshed the hearts of the saints" (Philem 7), which probably extended to both spiritual and physical necessities. Evocative commercial language used by Paul (Philem 17-18) suggests Philemon was a successful businessman. He was probably converted under Paul's ministry (Philem 19) but met the *apostle some place other than Colossae since neither Acts nor Colossians offers any evidence that Paul ever traveled there. Paul calls him a "fellow worker" (Philem 2 ESV), which places him among a small group of people who took an active part in Paul's ministry (Rom 16:3, 9, 21; 1 Thess 3:2; 1 Cor 3:9; 2 Cor 1:24; 8:23; Phil 2:25; 4:3; Col 4:11; Philem 24). Paul's use of *koinōnia* ("partner," ESV) in Philemon 17 suggests that Philemon not only had *fellowship with Paul in the *Lord but was a partner with him in the Lord's work. Consequently, Philemon was not an obscure figure but a prominent member of the Lycus Valley church and a vital part of Paul's ministry. Paul was not writing to a stranger but a friend and ministry partner.

3.2. Onesimus. Although Onesimus is the object of the letter, very little about him is revealed in it. He was a slave (Philem 16), though apparently not a very useful one (Philem 11). He was converted by Paul, became close to the imprisoned apostle (Philem 10), and was sent back to Philemon carrying a letter announcing his conversion and requesting that he be treated as a "beloved brother" (Philem 16 NRSV). If Onesimus was a fugitive, Paul never mentions it, nor does he indicate whether he had expressed regret or remorse for any wrongdoing. It is also unknown whether Onesimus's return put him in danger of being punished. The closest Paul gets to suggesting Onesimus is guilty of an infraction is his promise to cover any financial restitution that may be required (Philem 18).

Lurking in the background is the question of how Onesimus remained unconverted while part of a household owned by a prominent local believer who hosted the church in his home. As a household movement, early Christians sought the conversion of the heads of households, whose dependents joined them in the new faith, a pattern illustrated several times in Acts (Acts 10:2, 24, 44-48; 16:14-15, 31-34; 18:18). The Greco-Roman household included not only family but also slaves, as reflected in the way the household codes address not only family members but also slaves and masters in an almost seamless fashion (Eph 5:22–6:9; Col 3:18–4:1; 1 Pet 2:18; 3:7). As a member of Philemon's household, one would anticipate that Onesimus's conversion would have followed Philemon's own conversion. It is possible Onesimus was initiated into the church as part of Philemon's household but never fully embraced the Christian faith. However, Paul's request for Philemon to welcome Onesimus as a beloved brother suggests this is something Philemon had failed to do. Thus, even if Onesimus had not "fully converted," Philemon, for his part, had failed to fully include Onesimus as part of his household family.

4. Structure of the Letter.

Philemon follows the standard Greco-Roman letter format. Paul adapts the structure to fit his own needs and takes every opportunity to remind readers of the work of *God in their lives.

4.1. Opening Greeting (Philemon 1-3). The opening reveals the public/private nature of the letter. Although a personal letter to Philemon, the greeting includes others. Apphia is either a fellow believer or even Philemon's wife, while Archippus is most likely a local Christian leader (Col 4:17). The mention of "the church that meets in your home" (Philem 2 NIV) emphasizes the letter's public nature. Although the situation is between slave and master, it affects all of Philemon's household and the church.

4.2. Thanksgiving (Philemon 4-7). Paul expands the standard wish greeting to include a description of Philemon's reputation among the saints (Philem 5). Even here Paul connects Philemon to his activity within the church. Paul's mention of "partnership" connects Philemon's ministry in Colossae to the wider ministry of Paul and Timothy. Philemon's ministry to the saints is described as refreshment, which will be important later in his appeal for Onesimus (Philem 7).

4.3. Body (Philemon 8-22). Paul sets up the request so that Philemon will respond positively while appearing to do so voluntarily. His tactic is to intertwine Philemon's well-known ministry with the situation of Onesimus. He announces Onesimus's conversion as a birthing process, with himself as the parent and Onesimus the child. As such, Onesimus has an identity outside slavery and within the ministry of the apostle and the *body of Christ. Paul emphasizes this new status by referring to Onesimus as "my own heart" (Philem 12 NRSV), which connects Onesimus back to Philemon's ministry of refreshing "the hearts of the saints" (Philem 7). By describing Onesimus this way, it is as if Paul has appeared in the person of Onesimus. The letter climaxes with Paul declaring Onesimus as "more than a slave, a beloved brother" (Philem 16 NRSV), which places Onesimus on the same level as Philemon (Philem 7). Although part of Philemon's household, he was never really part of Philemon's family. With conversion everything has changed. Philemon may be Onesimus's owner, but Paul is the spiritual father to both Philemon and Onesimus; they are children of the same man. Paul makes a final request—"refresh my heart in *Christ" (Philem 20 NRSV; see Philem 7, 12). Paul wants Philemon to do for Onesimus what he is so well known for, refreshing the saints, in other words, by treating him as a fellow saint. Philemon's response will have consequences not only for himself but also for Paul and the Lycus Valley church. A request for lodgings at some undetermined future date adds further to the appeal by suggesting Paul plans to ensure compliance in person.

4.4. Closing (Philemon 23-25). The closing follows the conventional Greco-Roman formula of well-wishes and greetings from others. Of particular interest is the way that the closing mirrors that of Colossians (Col 4:12-18). Many of those who send greetings in Philemon do the same in Colossians.

5. History of Interpretation.

5.1. Traditional Interpretation. Since at least John Chrysostom, Philemon has been interpreted as Paul interceding on behalf of Onesimus, a runaway slave, to his owner, Philemon. J. B. Lightfoot outlines the situation as follows. Onesimus, a slave owned by Philemon, ran away, funding himself at his master's expense, and fled to Rome. While there, Onesimus encountered the imprisoned apostle and was converted. Although Onesimus was beloved to Paul, the apostle recognized the need for both repentance and restitution. Paul sent Onesimus back to Philemon, with Tychicus, carrying a letter in which he asks Philemon to forgive the truant slave and to consider him no longer a slave but a beloved brother.

5.2. Challenges to the Traditional Interpretation. Despite its longevity, the traditional interpretation has been reexamined numerous times. F. C. Baur argues Philemon is a second-century, pseudonymous work written to influence Christian attitudes toward slavery while emphasizing reconciliation. While few have followed Baur's lead, his interpretation represents an attempt to explain gaps in the letter by stressing a theological rather than historical interpretation.

Erwin Goodenough notes how Athenian law permitted slaves to seek asylum at a *temple, altar, or family hearth. Its influence on Roman law, he surmises, made it applicable to Onesimus who, caught stealing from his master, sought asylum with Paul and requested his intercession. Since a prison cell did not qualify as a place of asylum, Goodenough suggests the phrase "prisoner of Christ Jesus" (Philem 1 NRSV) be interpreted metaphorically since Paul clearly planned to visit Philemon later (Philem 22) and was, therefore, not a prisoner when Onesimus sought his intercession. Similarly, F. F. Bruce suggests that if Paul was under house arrest in his own lodgings, the location might have qualified as a place of asylum.

John Knox is unconvinced Onesimus was a fugitive because Paul includes no explicit statement in Philemon indicating such. Comparing Philemon with Pliny's letter to Sabinianus, Knox notes that Pliny is direct, mentions the freedman's penitence, and requests leniency and clemency. Paul, on the other hand, says nothing about Onesimus's repentance, nor does he make an explicit appeal for *forgiveness. Knox proposes that Philemon is not about the return of an errant slave but a request to a friend. Paul wanted Onesimus released to him so he could assist in the work of the ministry. Knox further suggests that Archippus, not Philemon, was Onesimus's master. Based on the close relationship between Philemon and Colossians, Knox hypothesizes the Laodicean letter mentioned in Colossians 4:16 is the letter to a church overseer named Philemon, whom Paul wanted to oversee the reconciliation between slave and master by ensuring Archippus treated Onesimus as a brother. Knox goes on to suggest that Onesimus was released, returned to serve Paul, and eventually became the second-century bishop of Ephesus about whom Ignatius writes in his letter to the Ephesians.

While Knox's overall hypothesis won few adherents, it cast a long shadow over Philemon studies. J. L. Houlden argues Onesimus had not run away but was "lent out." Similarly, Sara Winter and Craig Wansink propose Onesimus was sent to Paul as an emissary to aid in the ministry of the *gospel. J. Albert Harrill compares Philemon with journeyman apprentice contracts and suggests Paul wanted Onesimus to serve him as an apprentice in the gospel, while Scott Elliot considers Onesimus to be a gift of *patronage from Philemon, which Paul rejects.

Nonetheless, the traditional interpretation has remained resilient. John Barclay notes that one of the major drawbacks to the emissary hypothesis is the suggestion that an unconverted slave with a reputation for being useless would be sent to minister to Paul. Similarly, John Nordling surveys the problem of fugitive slaves in antiquity and the laws that allowed owners to recoup and punish slaves, which would have hindered Paul from mentioning Onesimus's fugitive status and alerting authorities.

More recently, Scot McKnight restates the argument in favor of the traditional interpretation, while at the same time establishing the enduring value of the epistle to the church. He demonstrates that the story of Philemon is relevant to understanding not just Greco-Roman or North American antebellum slavery but the ongoing modern scourge of slavery manifest in human trafficking. McKnight suggests that churches not simply read Philemon but "perform it." Just as the first readers would have heard the letter performed in their congregational setting, today's readers should experience the letter physically as well as verbally and thus discover a window into the world of enslaved people all around them.

*5.3. **Legal Interpretations.*** Some turn to Roman law to assist with interpreting Philemon. Peter Lampe argues that a slave was considered a fugitive not based on absence but rather the intention behind the absence. A slave who knew the master wanted to physically harm him was not a fugitive if he fled seeking someone to intercede on his behalf. Such a legal interpretation could explain how Onesimus met Paul in prison and why there is no direct mention of his flight. Onesimus did not abscond to escape slavery but to obtain the intercession of Philemon's friend Paul.

Lampe's interpretation provided interpreters a more plausible solution to interpreting Philemon than that of Knox and others. Brian Rapske notes that one significant obstacle to interpreting Philemon has been explaining why a runaway slave would willingly go to Paul's prison cell and how the apostle could send Onesimus back to his master carrying a letter without running afoul of the legal authorities. Lampe's thesis explains how Onesimus knew the location and circumstances of Paul. Onesimus was not running away but seeking intercession from his master's friend.

Harrill brings a helpful corrective to this interpretive trajectory by questioning the use of legal texts for interpreting Philemon (Harrill 1999). Jurists frequently disagreed, and their rulings were often based on hypothetical rather than the actual cases. Laws are not necessarily indicative of social practice and can only provide inexact knowledge about the past and a potentially misleading picture of slavery. Scholars run the risk of buying into the ideology of the slaveholder.

*5.4. **Sociorhetorical Interpretations of Philemon.*** The late twentieth century witnessed a growing interest in and development of sociorhetorical interpretive methods. In the case of Philemon, sociorhetorical methods focused less on Onesimus and the questions surrounding his legal status and instead on how Paul brought pressure to bear on Philemon.

Using the traditional interpretation, Forrester Church demonstrates how Paul frames his appeal to Philemon using deliberative rhetoric. Paul addresses Onesimus's situation by establishing Philemon's *honor while at the same time convincing him to fulfill the request (i.e., forgive Onesimus). Although it concerns a private matter between a slave and a master, Philemon is also a public letter. Onesimus is the subject of Paul's appeal, but its objects are *love and brotherhood, and Paul uses the opportunity to instruct the community about the practice of Christian love.

Norman Petersen suggests the most important idea in Philemon is indebtedness. Paul considers Philemon indebted to him, which allows him to request repayment. Philemon could either fulfill Paul's request or jeopardize his status both with Paul and the church. Onesimus's new status as a brother places the slave in the position of playing two roles. In the social structures of the world, he is Philemon's slave, but in the church, he is a brother. If the church emphasizes equality, how could Philemon maintain his role as master? Prevailing social pressure would expect Philemon to punish Onesimus. But Paul presses Philemon to treat Onesimus as a Christian brother and thus calls into question the social structure of the master/slave relationship.

Clarice Martin notes how the commercial language in Philemon 18 is often interpreted as a promise by Paul to repay Philemon and seen as evidence of Onesimus's thievery. She argues, however, that Paul's use of the rhetorical device of anticipation suggests that his promise to repay is only for argument's sake and not necessarily because an actual theft occurred or debt was owed. The combination of this rhetorical promissory note combined with the reminder to Philemon about his debt to the apostle mitigates suggestions that Onesimus had committed a crime and shifts the focus onto the request Paul is making of Philemon.

While some emphasize the social pressure brought to bear on Philemon, others, such as Andrew Wilson, highlight how Paul avoids alienating Philemon. By identifying himself as "prisoner" rather than "apostle," Paul reduces the appearance of his authority over Philemon while creating social solidarity between him and the slave Onesimus. At the same time, Paul uses familial language that connect him to Philemon and Onesimus in a way that creates a bond between all three. The lack of an explicit request for Onesimus's forgiveness and *freedom is part of Paul's strategy, since indirectness avoids alienating Philemon since nothing has been put on record. Paul's promise to repay any debts, request for a room, and expectation that Philemon will "do even more than I ask" are not meant to threaten or alienate Philemon. Rather, they provide evidence of Paul's quiet confidence in his friend.

Others observe that Onesimus was an unconverted slave, living in the home of a prominent Christian leader, and wonder whether some early Christian congregations willfully excluded slaves. Noting that the church was the primary means of socialization for its members, Nicholas Taylor concludes Onesimus's conversion was either incomplete or had somehow lapsed. But with his conversion confirmed under Paul's oversight, Onesimus was sent back to be reinstated in Philemon's home and complete the socialization process.

By declaring Onesimus to be a brother, Karl Sandnes argues, Paul challenged the autonomy and sovereignty of the slave master in a Christian fellowship. By asking him to welcome Onesimus back, Paul encourages a symbolic unity that promotes egalitarianism while challenging the socially acceptable structure of the household. Sandnes concedes, however, that this new relationship may not work out in practical terms, and the easiest way for this equality to be put into practice is for Onesimus to return and work with Paul.

Not everyone has been convinced that Paul's household rhetoric would have brought about equality in the church. Craig de Vos points out that the Mediterranean world determined self-identity by sociological, rather than psychological, terms. The understanding of gender, *kinship, and class were all part of one's self-identity. Related to this is the patriarchal system, in which males sought to dominate through the patron-client relationship. In the case of slaves, de Vos argues, this would be even more pronounced. With the structures of the slavery system moving slaves to the status of freed, there would be no major shift in attitude or habit. Lingering legal obligations after manumission would not have changed the situation very much. This evidenced in Pliny's letter, in which the freedman, although no longer a slave, was still obligated to the former master and could expect similar treatment as if he were still a slave. Considering the social realities of the day, the best that Paul could hope for was a perceptual shift rather than a structural one.

5.5. African American Responses. There is no doubt Philemon has had a long and often devastating impact on African Americans. It was used to support the Fugitive Slave Law of 1850 and the Supreme Court's 1857 Dred Scott decision. Frederick Douglass looked forward to the day when "Doctors of Divinity shall find . . . better employment for their time and talents than in finding analogies between Paul's Epistle to Philemon and the slave-catching bill of Millard Fillmore." Itinerant plantation preachers related the sometimes-strong reactions they received from slaves when Philemon was the basis of a Sunday sermon. Howard Thurman's grandmother famously refused to listen to any of Paul's epistles due to her experience as a slave.

Admitting that Paul has been "more bane than blessing" for African Americans, Lloyd Lewis uses Galatians as the interpretive key to Philemon. When Paul used familial language in Galatians 3:1–4:7 to define the church as a pseudo-household/family, everyone understood what it meant to be called "brother." Paul's decision, therefore, to call Onesimus a "brother" (Philem 16) would have strongly suggested the kind of relationship he wanted Philemon to have with his formerly unconverted slave. Prior to conversion, Onesimus was not a member of the church/family. But upon entering the pseudo-house of the church, Onesimus collided with Philemon. Both were now brothers in the church and, according to the familial langue of the church and Galatians 3:28, could no longer be slave and master. All three—Paul, Onesimus, and Philemon—were brothers in the same pseudo-household.

Noting that the letter does not explicitly say that Onesimus was a runaway slave, Allen Dwight Callahan proposes that he was not a runaway or, for that matter, even enslaved. Callahan does not consider Paul's request that he be welcomed back "no longer as a slave but more than a slave" as sufficient evidence that Onesimus was a slave. Noting that this comparative construction also appears in Philemon 17 about Paul, Callahan argues that Philemon was to accept Onesimus as if he were accepting the apostle himself. Thus, Onesimus was not a returning fugitive but a minister coming to minister on behalf of the imprisoned apostle. Moreover, the terms "beloved brother" and the phrase "both in the *flesh and in the Lord" link Philemon and Onesimus not only as Christian brothers but as kinsmen. The problem being addressed in Philemon, then, is not whether Onesimus was a real slave or even Philemon's brother, but that he was not Philemon's "beloved brother." Paul was writing a letter to defuse a family quarrel that could possibly jeopardize the apostolic ministry provided through Onesimus.

Cain Hope Felder argues that, although antislavery, Paul "was astute enough to recognize that the role of a pronounced abolitionist would . . . have been disastrous to the nascent Christian missionary movement" (887). He thinks that 1 Corinthians 7:21 explains why Paul sent Onesimus back.

It underscores the personhood of the slave and provides a fresh socioeconomic perspective of the master/slave relationship. Thus, "when Paul made his plea to Philemon to receive Onesimus [now converted] back no longer as a slave but more than a slave, a beloved brother, it should be forcefully clear that Paul wanted Philemon to honor their new tie as Christians above and beyond any legal demands. Their relationship was to be conditioned by love, not law, now they were linked by faith not fealty" (Felder, 901).

In a volume dedicated to interpreting Philemon within the African American experience and legacy of slavery, Demetrius Williams offers an overview and analysis of reading strategies (see Johnson, Noel, and Williams). He acknowledges that there is a wide variety of marginal and other interpretative possibilities, apart from the traditional interpretation. But he also notes that these are sometimes critiqued for failing to take history seriously. Some, such as Williams, would respond that it is not only the experience of the first reader that matters but also the readers who interpret today. Such approaches allow for liberative readings, even in the context of the traditional framework of slavery.

6. Theological Significance.

Although short on words and details, Philemon offers interpreters much to consider. It is a window into the early house-church movement and the role of slaves within that movement. It demonstrates the honor-shame culture of the Mediterranean world that Paul carefully brings to bear on the situation, and it is invaluable for understanding the conventions of ancient rhetoric and letter writing. Yet, while all of these are important aspects that cannot be overlooked, one could be in danger of overlooking the letter's most important purpose, which is pastoral.

Philemon provides a window into Paul's practice of ministry. It shows the relationship between two church leaders as they grapple with a personal issue that has wider consequences and complications within the church and society. The ultimate value of this letter to the church is found in understanding Paul's strategy as *pastor (Byron 2009).

The letter demonstrates Paul creating family ties where none previously existed. Although Onesimus was, and still is, known as the slave of Philemon, his slavery was subverted by his conversion. Paul has given birth to Onesimus, which makes him his spiritual child. At the same time, Paul is also Philemon's spiritual father, making slave and master brothers in the Lord. Based on this new reality, Paul encourages Philemon to treat Onesimus the same way he does all the saints, by refreshing Onesimus's heart. The outcome of Paul's request is unknown. But if Philemon followed through with Paul's wishes, the structures of slavery would have been undermined.

Interpreters sometimes lament what they see as Paul's missed opportunity to offer a more robust critique of slavery. But they may be overlooking his most significant critique. The new family ties within the body of Christ replaced those created by slavery. Paul papers over the circumstances that led to Philemon and Onesimus's separation by focusing on Onesimus's conversion. Paul's strategy as pastor is to forge new ties of kinship.

See also Church; Colossians, Letter to the; Ephesus; Ethics; Honor/Shame; Households and Household Codes; Interpretation: African American; Kinship Language in Paul; Letters, Letter Forms; Ministry; Pastor, Paul as; Patronage; Rhetorical Criticism; Slave, Slavery; Urban Setting of Paul's Churches.

BIBLIOGRAPHY. ***Commentaries:*** **F. F. Bruce,** *Epistles to Colossians, Philemon, and to the Ephesians*, NICNT (Grand Rapids, MI: Eerdmans, 1984); **J. B. Lightfoot,** *Saint Paul's Epistles to the Colossians and to Philemon*, 5th ed. (London: Macmillan, 1880); **S. McKnight,** *The Letter to Philemon*, NICNT (Grand Rapids, MI: Eerdmans, 2017).

Studies: **J. M. G. Barclay,** "Paul, Philemon, and the Dilemma of Christian Slave Ownership," *NTS* 37 (1991): 161-86; **F. C. Baur,** *Paul the Apostle of Jesus Christ: His Life and Work, His Epistles and His Doctrine* (London: Williams & Norgate, 1875); **J. Byron,** *Recent Research on Paul and Slavery* (Sheffield: Sheffield Phoenix, 2008); idem, "The Epistle to Philemon: Paul's Strategy for Forging the Ties of Kinship," in *Jesus and Paul: Global Perspectives in Honor of James D. G. Dunn for His 70th Birthday*, LNTS (Edinburgh: T&T Clark, 2009), 205-16; **A. D. Callahan,** "Paul's Epistle to Philemon: Toward an Alternative Argumentum," *HTR* 86 (1993): 357-76; **F. F. Church,** "Rhetorical Structure and Design in Paul's Letter to Philemon," *HTR* 71 (1978): 17-33; **S. S. Elliot,** "'Thanks, but No Thanks': Tact, Persuasion and the Negotiation of Power in Paul's Letter to Philemon," *NTS* 57 (2011): 51-64; **C. H. Felder,** "Philemon," *NIB* 10:463-80; **E. R. Goodenough,** "Paul and Onesimus," *HTR* 22 (1929): 181-83; **J. A. Harrill,** "Using the Roman Jurists to Interpret Philemon," *ZNW* 90 (1999): 135-38; idem, *Slaves in the New Testament* (Minneapolis: Fortress, 2006); **J. L. Houlden,** *Paul's Letters from Prison* (Philadelphia: Westminster,

1970); **M. V. Johnson, J. Noel, and D. K. Williams,** eds., *Onesimus Our Brother: Reading Religion, Race, and Culture in Philemon* (Minneapolis: Fortress, 2012); **J. Knox,** *Philemon Among the Letters of Paul: A New View of Its Place and Importance*, rev. ed. (New York: Abingdon, 1959); **P. Lampe,** "Keine 'sklavenflucht' des Onesimus," *ZNW* 76 (1985): 133-37; **L. Lewis,** "An African American Appraisal of the Philemon-Paul-Onesimus Triangle," in *Stony the Road We Trod: African American Biblical Scholarship*, ed. C. H. Felder (Minneapolis: Fortress, 1991), 232-46; **C. J. Martin,** "Commercial Language in Philemon (v.18)," in *Persuasive Artistry: Studies in New Testament Rhetoric in Honor of George A. Kennedy*, ed. D. F. Watson, JSNTSup 50 (Sheffield: Sheffield Academic Press, 1991), 321-37; **J. G. Nordling,** "Onesimus Fugitivus: A Defense of the Runaway Slave Hypothesis in Philemon," *JSNT* 41 (1991): 97-119; **N. R. Petersen,** *Rediscovering Paul: Philemon and the Sociology of Paul's Narrative Thought World* (Philadelphia: Fortress, 1985); **B. M. Rapske,** "The Prisoner Paul in the Eyes of Onesimus," *NTS* 37 (1991): 187-203; **K. O. Sandnes,** "Equality Within Patriarchal Structures," in *Constructing Early Christian Families: Family as Reality and Metaphor*, ed. H. Moxnes (New York: Routledge, 1997), 150-65; **N. H. Taylor,** "Onesimus: A Case Study of Slave Conversion in Early Christianity," *R&T* 3 (1996): 259-81; **C. S. de Vos,** "Once a Slave, Always a Slave? Slavery, Manumission and Relational Patterns in Paul's Letter to Philemon," *JSNT* 82 (2001): 89-105; **C. S. Wansink,** *Chained in Christ: The Experience and Rhetoric of Paul's Imprisonments*, JSNTSup 130 (Sheffield: Sheffield Academic Press, 1996); **A. Wilson,** "The Pragmatics of Politeness and Pauline Epistolography: A Case Study of the Letter to Philemon," *JSNT* 48 (1992): 107-19; **S. C. Winter,** "Paul's Letter to Philemon," *NTS* 33 (1987): 1-15.

J. Byron

PHILIPPIANS, LETTER TO THE

Philippians is a warmhearted letter of gratitude and comfort from Paul to a church he was instrumental in founding. In the letter, Paul assures these believers that his *ministry and *joy are unhindered even though he is in *prison, and he exhorts the church toward unity especially as they navigate any *suffering arising from their singular allegiance to Jesus as *Lord. Across the letter, Paul provides a number of exemplars for the church, with Jesus as supreme example of one who renounced status prerogatives to care for the interests of others. Philippians provides a rich tapestry of Pauline theological motifs that encourage his audience to take on the mindset and habits of Christ.

1. Historical Situation and Questions
2. Literary Shape and Analysis
3. Theological Messages and Themes

1. Historical Situation and Questions.

1.1. Author. Paul is the declared author of the letter to the Philippians (Phil 1:1). While Timothy is mentioned alongside Paul in the introduction to the letter (Phil 1:1), the letter itself uses singular, first-person language throughout. Additionally, Paul references Timothy in the third person, mentions his desire to send Timothy to the Philippian church, and commends Timothy to the church (Phil 2:19-23). So, Paul has authored the letter, and Timothy can be considered its cosponsor. Pauline authorship of Philippians is not contested, and it sits among the seven authentic letters of Paul affirmed within contemporary scholarship.

One tool for understanding authorship is the concept of the implied author, which can help illumine Paul's persona that emerges specifically from this letter—the portrait of Paul gained from Philippians without recourse to his other letters. Through this lens, the letter of Philippians provides a portrait of Paul deeply and warmly engaged with one of his churches. This tone is evident in his affectionate language for them (e.g., Phil 1:3-8; 4:1); in his concern for their well-being (e.g., Phil 1:24-26; 3:1; 4:19) and their sensibilities and emotional state (e.g., Phil 2:28; 4:6-7); and in the reassurance that he is all right, even joyful, in his present situation (e.g., Phil 1:12; 2:17-18; 4:18).

1.2. Audience. A historical reconstruction of the recipients of Paul's letter builds on knowledge of the city of Philippi and its inhabitants as well as on information from the letter itself and from the book of Acts, which records Paul's founding of the church at Philippi.

1.2.1. The City of Philippi. The city that came to be known as Philippi was first settled (and named Krenides) by Greeks from the island of Thasos around 360 BC. Philip of Macedon, the father of Alexander the Great, subjugated the city shortly thereafter (356 BC) and named it after himself. The Romans conquered and claimed the city in 168 BC, creating from it and its environs a Roman province (Macedonia; see Phil 4:15; Acts 16:12). The city was resettled as a Roman military colony in 42 BC; and in 30 BC Octavian again granted land and citizenship to war veterans, this time to those who had opposed him (under Mark Antony), thereby building a loyal citizenry in Philippi (Fee, 25-26). Philippi was a desirable conquest for a number of reasons: it was located in a fertile farming region that made it an agricultural center, it sat along a major trade route, and it was only about ten miles from Neapolis, which offered seaport access.

As a Roman colony, Philippi "carried the status of a city on Italian soil" (Cohick, 16). As such, its residents (even the many without *Roman citizenship) would have felt the presence of Rome in daily and significant ways (see Acts 16:21)—through the local power exerted by Roman citizens who had been resettled in the city and surrounding countryside, through the city's various Roman institutions (e.g., the forum), and through the use of Latin by the ruling class. As P. Oakes suggests, in Philippi "Romans owned almost all the land. Romans had all the *political control in the city. Romans largely monopolized *wealth and high status" (Oakes, 74).

The presence of the imperial cult would have been felt in Philippi, as it was across the Roman empire. From inscriptional evidence, it seems that two temples in Philippi's forum were devoted to the imperial cult, that is, worship and veneration of the Caesars and their family members (Cohick, 18). Although not legally mandatory, social and political pressure ensured that participating in the imperial cult was considered normative (Nikki, 66).

1.2.2. The Church at Philippi. Paul writes to a church with whom he shares deep connection; that much is clear from the tone and content of the letter itself (e.g., Phil 1:7-8; 2:17-18; 4:1). In it, he commends the church's commitment from the earliest days of their relationship, and specifically the choice of the Philippians to contribute to Paul's ministry even after he left the province (Phil 4:15-16). Acts 16 provides a narration of these early days, as Paul, Silas, and Timothy arrive in Philippi, where the *gospel both finds traction and garners opposition (Acts 16:11-40; see Phil 1:28).

Leading with evidence from the letter itself, with Acts functioning in a corroborating role, we can note a number of points of coherence between the two, including positive welcome and hostile reception of Paul and his message (Acts 16:14, 22-24, 30; Phil 1:28; see 1 Thess 2:2), the generosity of the new believers toward Paul (Acts 16:15, 34; Phil 4:10-20), and reference to Paul's imprisonments (Acts 16:23-24; Phil 1:12-13, 30; Fowl, 13). To these we can add an emphasis on Roman sensibilities or features (Acts 16:21, 37; Phil 1:13, 27; 3:20; 4:22) and the prominence of *women in the church—Lydia and a female slave (Acts 16:13-18, 40) and Euodia and Syntyche (Phil 4:2-3). Additionally, there is little in the letter itself to suggest any significant Jewish contingent in the Philippian church (coupled with the lack of a synagogue within the city of Philippi; see Acts 16:16). Likewise, the four names attributed to church members at Philippians 2:25; 4:2-3 are either Greek or Roman, and Paul's scant use of the Jewish Scriptures may also point toward a primarily non-Jewish audience.

From these shared features of Philippians and Acts 16, we can offer the following sketch of Paul's audience. The church seems to be (primarily) non-Jewish, with a likelihood of significant female leadership within the Philippian house church(es) (e.g., Thurston and Ryan; Keown). Although it has often been assumed that the Philippian church consisted primarily of veterans who had been given land and granted Roman citizenship by Octavian (see 1.2.1 above), Oakes argues convincingly that the Philippian church would have consisted of a broad social spectrum. Oakes's modeling of first-century Philippi, and more particularly the church there, suggests that only about one-third of the church might have been Roman (and about two-thirds Greek). He further proposes significant social diversity in the church reflecting the social diversity of Philippi, including colonist farmers, *slaves, those living in poverty, people involved in service (e.g., trades), and (potentially) a small percentage of elite Romans (Oakes, 61). Envisioning such diversity in the church illuminates various features of the letter, including its themes of suffering, unity, and status renunciation.

1.3. Date and Provenance. Paul's location when writing the letter correlates with the date of writing. While Paul makes it clear that he is in prison as he writes (Phil 1:12-14, 17), the location of his imprisonment is not specified. The author of Acts provides evidence of two lengthier Pauline imprisonments—Caesarea and Rome (Acts 24:23-27; 28:16-31, respectively)—both of which have been suggested as the provenance of Paul's prison letters, including Philippians. Scholars have also suggested *Ephesus as a possible location (e.g., Thielman; Osiek; Bird and Gupta). Traditionally, Paul was assumed to be in a Roman prison, which would date the letter to some point between AD 60 and 63. The strength of this proposal is that it most naturally accounts for Paul's references to the *praetorium* or "palace guard" (*praitōrion*; Phil 1:13 NIV) and to Caesar's household (Phil 4:22). Although the term *praetorium* could be used to refer to a provincial governor's residence (with its attending guard; see Acts 23:35) as well as to the imperial guard in Rome, there is no direct evidence of a *praetorium* in Ephesus.

Those who question Roman provenance raise two primary difficulties. First, Paul mentions in Romans (AD 56–58) his intention to *travel westward to Spain rather than return to previous areas of *mission in the east (Rom 15:23-24), which would contradict his plan expressed in Philippians 1:26; 2:24 to return to the Philippian church, if Philippians was written after Romans. Second, the distance between Rome and Philippi (about 800 miles, requiring at least a month of travel) seems problematic when coupled with the number of trips back and forth mentioned or assumed in the letter itself (Phil 2:25-30; 4:18), making Roman provenance less likely and giving rise to the proposal of Ephesus (about 300 miles from Philippi). A provenance of Ephesus would also more readily place the writing of Philippians earlier in Paul's ministry (ca. AD 52–55) and eastward of Philippi, addressing the purported difficulty of Paul's plans for westward mission.

There is no need, however, to hold Paul to his intentions stated in Romans 15 for mission westward in lieu of a return to the east. After writing of this plan and as he endured imprisonment, he might have discerned a need to return to some of his churches in the east (Phil 1:25-26; Fee, 36) before going westward. Furthermore, the argument based on the distance between Rome and Philippi is only problematic if we assume from Philippians 2:25-30 multiple trips between Paul and the Philippian church (four to five errands) within a relatively brief span of time. Yet Acts attests to at least a two-year Roman imprisonment (Acts 28:30; on the type of imprisonment envisioned in Acts compare to Phil 1:12-26; see Keown, 32-33), and Philippians 2:25-27 may not imply as many trips between Paul and the church as is often suggested (see Fee, 277-78).

1.4. Occasion and Purposes. Although a relatively brief letter, Philippians gives evidence of a number of reasons for its existence. One primary "occasion" of the letter is the return of Epaphroditus to Philippi and to the church there: "I think it is necessary to send [him] back to you" (Phil 2:25 NIV). The Philippian church had sent Epaphroditus to Paul as their "messenger" (Phil 2:25) to function as their representative, in order to provide assistance and support ("gifts") to Paul in his imprisonment (Phil 4:15). Sometime on his way or after arrival, Epaphroditus falls gravely ill. Once he is recovered, Paul moves quickly to send him back to Philippi, both to lessen the anxiety the church is experiencing at the prospect of the death of their coworker (Phil 2:28) and to acknowledge the gifts that they sent to Paul through Epaphroditus (Phil 4:10-20).

In the first-century world, *letters were a primary form of communication across spans of distance. If someone, such as Epaphroditus, were traveling some distance, it would be routine, even expected, for him to carry letter(s) from person(s) he would know at the point of departure to those they wanted to communicate with at the destination. In this sense, a traveler was a ready-made mail carrier. The return of Epaphroditus was a prime opportunity for Paul to communicate with his beloved community at Philippi any number of other things that were on his mind and were for their benefit. These include assurances about Paul's own situation in prison and a number of warnings about certain threats to their growth in *faith.

Paul first addresses his own situation of being in prison ("in chains," Phil 1:13 NIV). He is keen to let his Philippians friends know that they need not worry about him. Instead, they can rejoice because his imprisonment is, somewhat surprisingly, helping the spread of the gospel about Jesus the Messiah. The next textual clue that provides a glimpse into his purposes for writing comes in the first exhortation (Phil 1:27-30). Paul's central call to the Philippian church is to live as a community in line with their allegiance to the gospel, even as they experience opposition and suffering. While the source of the opposition is left unstated, it seems likely that it comes from outsiders in Philippi. As Oakes has suggested, the Philippian believers are likely experiencing social ostracization arising from their singular allegiance to Jesus. Such singular loyalty would involve a rejection of all other deities and would curtail their temple involvement and all the benefits (religious, social, and economic) arising from that involvement (Oakes).

A key purpose of Paul in Philippians 1:27–2:4 is to encourage unity among the Philippian church as a way for the community to stand firm together in the face of this opposition. Given this pronounced call to unity, it seems likely then that the church at Philippi is struggling with some amount of disunity. This becomes clear with an issue of disunity directly addressed in Philippians 4:2-3, where Paul calls for Euodia and Syntyche to embrace the same mindset across their differences.

Finally, there seem to be a number of at least potential threats to the well-being of the Philippian church that Paul wants to address in the letter, although such external hazards are not the primary occasion of the letter (Flemming). In addition to the *opponents mentioned in Philippians 1:28 (nonbelievers in Philippi opposing the church's loyalties), Paul warns the church against one or more groups, internal or external to them (although, e.g., Silva and Nikki argue that Paul's multiple and varied descriptions of opponents across the letter refer to a single group). At the beginning of Philippians 3, Paul warns of "the dogs, those evildoers, those mutilators of the flesh" (Phil 3:2 NIV). Later in the chapter, he refers to those who are "enemies of the cross of Christ . . . [whose] destiny is destruction, their god is their stomach, and their glory is in their shame [with] their mind . . . set on earthly things" (Phil 3:18-19 NIV). Scholars debate whether Paul refers to one group or two as well as whether he describes believers in Jesus, former believers, or nonbelievers with these vivid descriptors. Some have also suggested that those described in Philippians 3:2, 18-19 function as foils for Paul's positive example emphasized in Philippians 3:4-21, rather than illuminate real dangers to the Philippian church (Stowers). It is likely, given the language of Philippians 3:2, that the first group consists of Jewish Christians whose goal is to persuade *Gentile believers to convert to Judaism so as to participate fully in the new messianic community (see *Judaizers). Yet there is little in the letter itself to suggest that this group is currently present within the Philippian church. More likely, since the Judaizing impulse seems to have been common enough among Jewish Christians (and proselytes to Judaism who had become Christians), Paul is warning his Gentile audience against this potential threat and provides a counterexample in his own focus on boasting in and knowing Christ alone (Phil 3:4-11; Holloway).

Those who are (or have become) "enemies of the *cross" (Phil 3:18 NIV) might be a group distinct from the Judaizers (though, e.g., Osiek; Cohick argue otherwise), but it is difficult to create a clear profile of this group due to the strong *rhetoric and the lack of specificity (e.g., what does "their god is their stomach" signal?). Some have argued these are Christians with strong libertine sensibilities in the Philippian church (e.g., Fee; Bockmuehl). Alternatively, it is possible that Paul is referring to some among the Philippians believers attempting to avoid the social ostracization that has come from their allegiance to Christ (Oakes), and Paul uses language of *idolatry to frame their attempts at straddling their former and present loyalties.

2. Literary Shape and Analysis.

2.1. Genre. Scholars have analyzed ancient letters and noted that they range from more formal epistles functioning like treatises (and intended for a wide readership) to personal letters, often very brief and covering various mundane subjects. Philippians sits somewhere midway on this spectrum, given its strongly relational and fairly informal qualities coupled with the identity of its audience—an entire church community in a specific city. The basic structure of an ancient letter is apparent in Philippians: identification of writer and recipient (Phil 1:1), greeting (Phil 1:2), *prayer and/or thanksgiving (Phil 1:3-11), body (Phil 1:12–4:20), and personal news, greetings, and well-wishes (Phil 4:21-23).

While formal rhetoric practices could be used in first-century epistles, the application of rhetorical analysis for understanding the structure of Paul's letters, including Philippians, has yielded little consensus. For example, Philippians 1:27-30 is often identified as the *propositio* (or *partitio*) of Paul's discourse—which, in ancient rhetoric, provided the introductory thesis of a speech. Without recourse to these categories, however, commentators have routinely noted that Philippians 1:27-30 contains the letter's first imperative and so introduces and prepares for Paul's many exhortations to follow. Additionally, much of the rest of Philippians defies simple classification using rhetorical categories (e.g., *exordium, narratio, confirmatio, peroratio*). What can be helpful for interpreting Philippians is attention to the rhetorical strategies Paul marshals, such as his use of exemplars (*exempla*) to shape his audience (Smit) and his intentional use of *ethos* and *pathos* (in addition to his arguments—his *logos*) to persuade his audience to follow his guidance and to remain loyal to Jesus their Lord.

Further specification of the genre of Philippians has garnered little consensus. The most common argument is that Philippians is a letter of *friendship (e.g., Stowers; Fee), a particular form mentioned in contemporaneous pedagogical manuals. Other suggestions of a subgenre of letter include P. A. Holloway's proposal that Philippians resembles Greco-Roman "consolations," and the consolatory letter specifically. In this genre, the author seeks to assuage his recipient's grief through rational argument. L. Alexander has argued that Philippians fits the genre of a family letter, given certain structural and thematic features of Philippians that also typify this kind of ancient letter. Those who have come to these conclusions bring their generic understanding to bear interpretively on the letter's structure and substance (e.g., Fee, 3; Holloway, 161-64). Yet most scholars, while granting the influence of language and themes from these various ancient *topoi*, do not find adequate internal evidence to qualify Philippians as one of these particular subgenres. (On the theme of friendship in Philippians, see 3.3 below.)

2.2. Integrity of the Letter. In the recent history of interpretation, the unity or integrity of the letter to the Philippians has sometimes been questioned. The assumption by some that the canonical Philippians contains two or more Pauline letters brought together arises primarily from the fairly abrupt change of direction and tone between Philippians 3:1a and Philippians 3:1b-2, along with the delay of Paul's expression of gratitude for the Philippians' gift until the end of the letter. The basic proposal is that Paul wrote a number of shorter letters (two or three) to the church at Philippi that then were assembled, and not all that carefully, by a later editor.

Both of these literary features, however, can be explained fairly well by the aural nature of the letter—the reality that it would have been read aloud to the Philippian church (on Phil 3:1-2, see Achtemeier, 26; on Phil 4:10-20, see Fee, 17). Additionally, S. E. Fowl notes the numerous literary connections between Philippians 1:3-11 and Philippians 4:10-20 that suggest these opening and closing sections function together as "a well-crafted frame" and so support the letter's unity (Fowl, 192).

2.3. Structure and Movement of Thought. The following outline of Philippians highlights the role of exemplars and exhortations in an alternating pattern in the rhetorical flow of the letter.

1:1-2	Introductory Greeting
1:3-11	Thanksgiving and Prayer
1:12-26	Paul's Situation and Perspective vis-à-vis the Gospel
1:27–2:4	Exhortations: To Singular Loyalty and Resilient Unity in Suffering
2:5-11	Jesus as Exemplar: The Ultimate Servant
2:12-18	Exhortations: To Obedience, Unity, *Witness, and Joy
2:19-30	Timothy and Epaphroditus as Exemplars: *Service to Others
3:1–4:1	Paul as Exemplar: A Contrast to Opponents of the Gospel and the Cross
4:2-9	Summative Exhortations: To Unity, Joy, *Peace, and *Imitation
4:10-20	Paul's Situation and Perspective vis-à-vis the Philippians' Gift
4:21-23	Concluding Greetings

After a standard introductory greeting (which includes specific attention to the leaders of the Philippian church), Paul gives thanks to God for the recipients and prays for their growth in *knowledge and *love, discernment and righteousness.

The body of the letter (Phil 1:12–4:20) is framed by Paul's communication about his own situation and his words of encouragement to and affirmation for the Philippians (Phil 1:12-26; 4:10-20). He begins by assuring the church that his own imprisonment has contributed to, and not hindered, the spread of the gospel. He also expresses confidence that his imprisonment will not end in his death but in his release, so that he will again be able to minister among them (Phil 1:19-26; see Phil 2:24).

As Paul turns to the parenetic needs of the Philippian church, he alternates between giving explicit exhortation and highlighting role models or exemplars for them. Both rhetorical strategies are aimed at shaping his audience toward greater alignment with the gospel and to conformity with their Lord.

His first (and headlining) exhortation calls for complete allegiance to the gospel: "Whatever happens, live in singular loyalty to the gospel of Christ" (Phil 1:27). In Philippi as a Roman colony with its heightened attention to fidelity to Rome, Paul uses language that would evoke living as a citizen. Yet he focuses that language on the believer's true allegiance. Paul takes pains to exhort the church in Philippi to conduct itself with reference to its true sovereign, *Christ, and its true citizenship in the *kingdom of God (see Phil 3:20). Paul trusts that such allegiance will cause the church to stand firm with a united front in relation to opposition and suffering (Phil 1:28-30). He continues calling them to unity and to a shared mindset, which will allow them to be other-oriented rather than self-focused (Phil 2:1-4).

Paul's first exemplar is Jesus, who provides the prototype mindset for believers (Phil 2:5-11). Potentially adapting an early christological *hymn, Paul provides a poetic portrait of Christ relinquishing divine prerogatives and status to take on humanity's form and plight, even enduring the most contemptible form of death in the Roman world—death by crucifixion. The story of Christ's "downward mobility" (Eastman) is followed by an acclamation of his exaltation by God to the highest place of lordship, echoing Isaiah 45 in its reference to universal submission to Israel's God, now granted to Jesus.

In Philippians 2:12-18, Paul indicates that this christological reality empowers Christian obedience, especially in light of God's initiating work among the Christian community. Paul again calls for unity (eschewing grumbling and arguing) for the purpose of mission to the surrounding world. He provides a potent image comparing his self-giving vocation to being a drink offering, which is mingled with their own service, pictured as a *sacrifice presented to God. This specter of their co-laboring should lead them to a mutual joy.

Paul returns to providing exemplars for the community (Phil 2:19-30), first by highlighting Timothy's sacrificial service and active concern for the Philippian church. Paul hopes to send Timothy to them soon and even speaks of his confidence that he himself might soon be able to see them. He commends Epaphroditus upon his return (with letter in hand) and shares that he knows Epaphroditus's return will relieve their anxieties about his recent serious illness. He calls for honor to be given to Epaphroditus because of his role as intermediary and his willingness to die "for the work of Christ" (Phil 2:30 NIV).

The tone of the letter turns to warning at Philippians 3:1-2. To safeguard the believers in Philippi (Phil 3:1), Paul draws on a counterexample of those he vividly describes as "those dogs, those evildoers, those mutilators of the flesh" (Phil 3:2 NIV). Likely describing Jewish Christians who press their Gentile counterparts to convert to Judaism for full inclusion into the messianic community, Paul affirms instead that the (primarily) Gentile church at Philippi—as Christocentric and Spirit-empowered—is the true "*circumcision" (Phil 3:3). Paul then gives his own example of knowing Christ and participating in his death and *resurrection as the highest value, which causes all identity markers and accomplishments to pale by comparison (Phil 3:4-11).

Highlighting the goal of final resurrection leads Paul to commend his own example of living *eschatologically—acknowledging that this final perfection has not arrived, while still pursuing it with all the energy he has (Phil 3:12-17). Imitating such an eschatological mindset will protect the Philippian church from following those who, regardless of their professed allegiance, have become "enemies of the cross" by focusing their attention and their craving on present comforts (Phil 3:18 NIV). In contrast, Paul affirms the church's true citizenship in God's kingdom and its true savior, Jesus, whose resurrected *body holds the promise for believers' resurrection upon his return (Phil 3:20-21). Concluding his exhortations and examples begun in Philippians 1:27, Paul reiterates the call to "stand firm" (Phil 4:1 NIV; see Phil 1:27).

Paul makes a plea for two of his *coworkers in the gospel to be like-minded (Phil 4:2-3), before providing concluding exhortations to rejoice, to pray when anxious, to discern the good, and to imitate his example (Phil 4:4-10). The basis for such exhortations is the (eschatological) nearness of the Lord (Phil 4:5), and a promised result is God's peace (Phil 4:7, 9). In the final turn of the letter, Paul shares his gratitude for the gift the Philippians sent to him through Epaphroditus, emphasizing themes of contentment, participation, and God's ongoing provision (Phil 4:10-20) before offering concluding greetings (Phil 4:21-23).

2.4. Use of the Old Testament. There is minimal use of the Jewish Scriptures in Philippians, especially when compared to Galatians, the Corinthian correspondence, and Romans. While Paul nowhere explicitly quotes the Scriptures in Philippians, he does allude to various OT texts (from the LXX). Most clearly, he draws on Isaiah 45:23 at the climax of the "Christ hymn" (Phil 2:9-11) to affirm the exaltation of Jesus and his inclusion in the divine identity and sovereignty (Bauckham). Other recognizable allusions or potential echoes include (1) Job 13:16 at Philippians 1:19; (2) Deuteronomy 32:5; Daniel 12:3; Isaiah 49:4 at Philippians 2:14-15 (McAuley); (3) Psalm 22:16 at Philippians 3:2 (suggested by Henderson); (4) Psalm 69:28 at Philippians 4:3; and (5) Psalm 145:18 at Philippians 4:5 (Keown).

Whether or not Paul expects his primarily Gentile audience to catch each of these brief allusions, his communicative intentions can often be more clearly understood by attending to the way he uses and adapts the echoed OT text. For example, at Philippians 2:14-15, Paul alludes to Deuteronomy 32:5, where *Israel of the wilderness years is described as a warped and crooked generation and is even distanced from Yahweh because of their *sin ("not his children"). Paul uses this indictment of the wilderness generation as a contrast to the Philippian believers, who are to live blamelessly as "children of God . . . in a warped and crooked generation" (Phil 2:15 NIV). The language of "generation" no longer describes God's wayward people, as in Deuteronomy; instead, it describes the society in which the church lives out its missional mandate ("shin[ing] among them like stars," Phil 2:15 NIV). Believers are also to avoid "grumbling" (Phil 2:14), an additional hint that Israel's situation during their wilderness wanderings is being used as a counterexample for Paul's audience (see Deut 1:27).

2.5. The Christ Hymn (Phil 2:6-11). A crucial and much-discussed passage in Philippians is what has been called the "Christ hymn"—the story of Christ's emptying and exaltation (Phil 2:6-11). A few key literary issues receive ongoing attention: the form or genre of Philippians 2:6-11 and whether it is Pauline or pre-Pauline, the use of the christological hymn within Philippians 1:27–2:30, and its background and associations.

The poetic and rhythmic qualities of Philippians 2:6-11 are indisputable, even as scholars suggest a range of appropriate descriptions—running from elevated prose to possessing significant poetic qualities to full-blown poetry that includes meter, stanzas, and a lyrical mode. In the latter category, it has been described as a hymn, a poem, a liturgy. A difficulty in assigning it to the genre of poem or hymn is a lack of consensus on how to divide it into lines and stanzas.

Those who consider Philippians 2:6-11 pre-Pauline typically suggest it functioned in the early church as a christological hymn, which Paul then took up and likely adapted for use in the letter. Form-critical questions involve the meaning and use of the hymn in its pre-Pauline form. For the purposes of its function in Philippians, Flemming notes that "*in the setting of the letter,* these are the apostle's words and thoughts" (106). A number of scholars argue that Paul himself authored this more poetic section of Philippians (see 1 Cor 13) and so look no further than the Pauline intentions of Philippians 2:6-11 (e.g., Fee; Oakes; Thielman).

In either case, an important determination for Paul's use of this passage has been framed in terms of either a kerygmatic or an *ethical usage. Paul's introduction to the poem in Philippians 2:5 is quite compact: "Have this mindset [or, 'consider this'] among yourselves, which also in Christ Jesus." Two different readings are possible, depending on how the two clauses are connected; that is, how the *also* (*kai*) functions and what verb should be implied in the second clause. The *also* might connect the mindset to be pursued with what believers already possess "*in Christ," resulting in a kerygmatic reading: "which you also have in Christ Jesus." Alternatively, and more likely, the *also* might connect the mindset to be pursued with Christ's own mindset of humility, issuing in an ethical reading: "which Christ Jesus also had/has."

A final formal issue involves the background and associations of the poem. Although E. Käsemann suggested its background was a *Gnostic hymn, more recent work has leaned toward Jewish antecedents for the poem's contents, whether in the Jewish personification of *Wisdom, an *Adam *Christology (see 3.1 below), or through allusion to the suffering servant of Isaiah 53. It has also been suggested that the poem has imperial associations, in which case it offers a contrast between Christ as Lord and the emperor (Oakes).

3. Theological Messages and Themes.
Paul communicates any number of prominent themes in his letter to the Philippians, some of them shared in common with other of his letters (e.g., the centrality of the gospel) and some fairly distinctive (e.g., joy). These themes are interwoven with one another across the discourse of the letter, so it can be helpful to consider the clustering and overlapping of motifs within core thematic and theological emphases, delineated here as Christology, eschatology, friendship, communal discernment, unity and resilience in response to suffering, and Christian imitation.

3.1. Christology. The centerpiece of Christology in Philippians comes in the Christ hymn at Philippians 2:6-11. Whether this poetic ovation to Christ is an adapted preexistent hymn or of Pauline construction (see 2.5 above), it provides a distinctive offering for Pauline Christology, especially as it highlights the preexistent Christ. The first movement of the poem traces Christ surrendering the advantage of equality with God to embrace humanity's desperate condition (Phil 2:6-8). A key interpretive issue involves whether to read the participle of Philippians 2:6 as concessive ("*although* being in very nature God") or causal ("*because*"), raising the theological question of God in relation to power and weakness (Gorman). Some have read Philippians 2:6 as describing Christ's Adamic identity (prefall) and so dispute that the hymn identifies Christ's preexistence. Yet it is more likely that Christ's association with Adam comes in the second movement of the hymn (Eastman), in which Christ takes on the form of a slave, "being made in human likeness [*homoiōmati anthrōpōn*]" (Phil 2:7 NIV). It is not until this point in the hymn that echoes of Genesis occur (see LXX Gen 1:26). Key to this downward movement is the divine Christ humbly taking the nature or form of a slave (*doulos*), a person of very lowest status. Such *kenosis* (*kenoō*; Phil 2:7) is the defining shape of Pauline Christology in Philippians and is marshaled to inform and infuse the way the Philippians believers are to live. They are to "value others above" self, without retaining or grasping for status (Phil 2:3 NIV). In this connection between Christology and ethics, the gospel exposes false ideas of power, what M. J. Keown refers to as "the kenotic ethic of the gospel" (Keown, 67).

The second half of the Christ hymn (Phil 2:9-11) illumines the lordship Christology of Philippians. God's exaltation of Jesus after his self-humbling puts him in the "highest place" with "the *name . . . above every name" (Phil 2:9 NIV). This phrase references the divine name of Isaiah 45:18-24 heard via the allusion to Isaiah 45:23 in Philippians 2:10-11 and in the explicit affirmation "Jesus Christ is Lord [*kyrios*]" (Phil 2:11 NIV). Lordship, through this intertext, speaks not only to universal acknowledgment but also to Christ's participation in "the divine sovereignty" (Bauckham, 200). Christ's exaltation has practical implications for the Philippian believers. It is the exalted and ruling Christ who "will transform our lowly bodies . . . [to] be like his glorious body" (Phil 3:21 NIV). His exaltation in resurrection makes possible their own resurrection (Phil 3:10-11).

Christ's exaltation to universal lordship also presses against false claims of lordship that would have been ubiquitous in Philippi—in its temples and in its Roman-saturated culture. If Jesus is *the* exalted Lord, then Caesar is not (note Paul's consistent use of *kyrios* to describe Jesus; e.g., Phil 1:2; 2:11, 19; 3:8, 20; 4:23). An implicit critique of imperial power may also sit behind Paul's language of *sōtēr* (Phil 3:20), especially given his sparse use of the term elsewhere (outside the Pastorals, it only occurs here and in Eph 5:23) and its regular use in Roman imperial claims (e.g., Josephus, *J.W.* 7.4.1; additional examples in Oakes, 138-40).

Paul's Christology in Philippians is profoundly relational. Not only is Christ the exemplar par excellence for the mindset believers are to hold (Phil 2:5), but "knowing Christ" is Paul's greatest desire and focus (implying the same should be true for all believers; Phil 3:7-11). Paul can also speak of Christ's affection or compassion, which enlivens his own (Phil 1:8); Christ's love, which brings the greatest comfort (Phil 2:1); his nearness to believers (Phil 4:5, if indicating the presence of Christ); and the *grace he gives (Phil 4:23; see Phil 1:2).

3.2. Eschatology. Paul's already-not yet eschatology is on full display in Philippians, especially in Philippians 3:7-21, a section of the letter focused on Paul's own experience of Christ. He compares what he had previously found valuable in his heritage and religious practice (Phil 3:4-6) to his present experience of knowing Christ and participating in Christ's sufferings and death (Phil 3:7-10). For Paul, there is no comparison; all else is worthless when compared to "the surpassing worth of knowing Christ Jesus my Lord" (Phil 3:8 NIV). This present reality of knowing Christ also sets on course the future possibility of "attaining to the resurrection from the dead" (Phil 3:11 NIV). In this way, Paul, along with all believers, participates in Christ's story of humbling to exaltation (Phil 2:5-11), now mapped onto the eschatological terrain of *already* (participating in the current realities of the time of the Messiah) and *not yet* (waiting for the general resurrection in the final day).

Paul promotes a finely tuned balance between already and not yet in Philippians 3:12-14. Conceding that he has not yet obtained resurrection with all its benefits, Paul lives in a way that presses with abandon toward that final goal, and he exhorts the Philippians to live in a way that is consistent with what they "have already attained" (Phil 3:16 NIV). This eschatological mindset is a key sign of Christian maturity (Phil 3:15).

Paul's discourse then turns to a warning about some, likely (former) believers, who "live as enemies of the cross" (Phil 3:18 NIV). His further description signals that this group has abandoned the eschatological mindset he has just painstakingly described. "Their mind is set on earthly things" (Phil 3:19 NIV). In contrast, Paul calls the Philippians to embrace their true eschatological identity ("our citizenship is in heaven," Phil 3:20 NIV) and to keep their eyes on the final-day arrival of Jesus and their own final-day resurrection (Phil 3:21).

Paul's recurring language of the "day of Christ [Jesus]" across the early part of Philippians highlights Paul's eschatological mindset, which he commends to these believers (Phil 1:6, 10; 2:16). This language coheres with Paul's similar (and varied) language elsewhere to indicate the future arrival of eschatological salvation for believers (e.g., 1 Cor 1:8; 5:5; 1 Thess 5:2; Rom 2:5, 16) and resonates conceptually with the "day of the Lord" motif that emerges in Jewish prophetic literature to signal a future day when Israel's God will bring restoration and *judgment (e.g., Joel 2:31; 3:14; Zech 1:14; 14:1). Paul particularizes the language of the "day of the Lord" from the prophets to reflect his conviction that in Messiah Jesus God's final restoration has already begun and it will be completed on that final day—"the day of Christ Jesus" (Phil 1:6 NIV). In light of this certain future reality, believers can look ahead to their *salvation (Phil 1:28) without fearing death (Phil 1:21-23).

3.3. Friendship. Scholars often point to elements of Philippians that correspond to the Greco-Roman *topos* of friendship (see 2.1 above). For example, Paul frequently draws on the language of *koinōnia* ("participation"; Phil 1:5; 2:1; 3:10) and its cognates *sygkoinōnos* (Phil 1:7), *sygkoinōneō* (Phil 4:14), and *koinōneō* (Phil 4:15) in Philippians. He does so to highlight the significant and reciprocal relationship he shares with the Philippians (Phil 1:5, 7; 4:14, 15), grounded in the participation they all experience in Christ (Phil 3:10) and through the Spirit (Phil 2:1). Friendship with fellow believers is predicated on believers' friendship with God received in the representative work and example of Christ (Phil 2:5-11; Fowl). This union with Christ is also signaled in Philippians by Paul's language of being "in Christ" (*en Christō*; e.g., Phil 1:1; 2:1; 3:14; 4:7, 21) and by his own deep desire to "know Christ" (Phil 3:8-10).

Language of affection and longing also permeates the letter (Phil 1:7-8; 2:26; 4:1), along with Paul's consistent expressions of joy at the thought of his spiritual siblings in Philippi (Phil 1:4; 2:17; 4:1, 10) and his frequent prompts toward rejoicing on their side of the friendship (Phil 2:18, 29; 3:1; 4:4). For Paul, "the proper working of Christian friendship" produces joy (Fowl, 209).

Though not as often recognized, Paul's references to his own anxiety in Philippians 2:25-30 also nest within this category of friendship expressed in the letter. His depth of relationship with the Philippian believers brings about a kind of relational anxiety arising from his concern for their well-being, including their emotional welfare. Paul also refers to the distress or anxiety of Epaphroditus upon knowing his own community has heard he has been ill (Phil 2:26). Paul then speaks of God's *mercy in sparing Epaphroditus's life "to spare me sorrow upon sorrow" (Phil 2:27 NIV). Paul is earnest for them to hear the good news from Epaphroditus himself, which will in turn relieve Paul's anxiety (Phil 2:28). The warmth of their relationship brings with it the probability, indeed the inevitability, of concern for the circumstances and well-being of the other.

3.4. Communal Discernment. In Philippians, Paul exhorts his audience to discern and to cultivate gospel-centered dispositions and a shared mindset, which involves both thinking and action (Fee). We see this theme already in Paul's opening prayer that the Philippians will "discern what is best" (Phil 1:10 NIV; Holloway). Contributing to this theme of discernment is a term that is particularly prominent in Philippians, *phroneō*, which is frequently used to identify the shared mindset Paul desires for the Philippian church (e.g., Phil 2:2, 5; 3:15a; 4:2). S. E. Fowl suggests the language of "practical reasoning" for *phroneō* and describes it especially in Philippians 2 as a "pattern of practical reasoning involv[ing] a common perspective on their situation and how it fits into the divine economy and the practical implications of that perspective" (Fowl, 90).

Two other terms in Philippians contribute to this constellation around the concept of discernment. At Philippians 4:8, Paul calls the Philippians to a posture of discernment related to "the good" and uses the verb *logizomai* (also used at Phil 3:13), for the activity of evaluating or weighing what is esteemed in their cultural context in light of the gospel (Phil 4:8-9; Fee, 416). Paul also uses *hēgeomai* (often, "consider") in reference to discernment and specifically to viewing a situation from a lens informed by the gospel. Such a perspective should inform how believers view each other (Phil 2:3; as more valuable than self) and how they view Christ (as supremely valuable compared to all else; Phil 3:7-8). Christ provides the cardinal example of such a discerning mindset, as he considered taking on human likeness more valuable than using his own divine prerogative for advantage (Phil 2:6-7).

Paul's emphasis on discernment is decidedly communal—the Philippians are to discern together God's wisdom and direction for them. They are to pursue a shared mindset in the midst of their differences or disputes (Phil 2:2; 4:2) that comes from reflection on Christ's story and mindset (Phil 2:5). And Paul trusts that God will bring clarity to the community toward this shared mindset as individuals grow in maturity (Phil 3:15).

3.5. Unity and Resilience in Suffering. The shared mindset, which Paul exhorts the Philippians to pursue and which arises from the communal discernment (see 3.4 above), points to the prominent theme of unity. At the onset, this theme is coupled with resilience in suffering, described in Philippians 1:27-28 as "stand[ing] firm in one spirit, striving together as one . . . without being frightened . . . by those who oppose you" (NIV). Paul reiterates the importance of unity in Philippians 2:1-4, where he calls for unity of mindset, affections, and purpose (Phil 2:2) and provides particular guidance for pursuing this unity (Phil 2:3-4). Their shared mindset (*to auto phronēte*; Phil 2:2) is based on their imitation of Christ Jesus (Phil 2:5-11). Paul uses the same language (*to auto phronēte*) at Philippians 4:2, where he implores Euodia and Syntyche toward a shared mindset "in the Lord."

Though Paul only explicitly mentions suffering at Philippians 1:29 (in conjunction with those who are opposing the Philippian church; Phil 1:28), the theme emerges at a number of additional points in the letter: (1) in Paul's struggle that mirrors that of the Philippians (Phil 1:30), (2) in the image of Paul's ministry as a drink offering being poured "on the sacrifice and service coming from [the church's] faith" (Phil 2:17 NIV), and (3) in the negative example of those who seem to eschew suffering for the gospel. Paul describes the latter as "enemies of the cross" whose "god is their stomach" (Phil 3:18-19 NIV)—an image of an indulgent and insatiable appetite that contrasts with the ideal of contentment (Phil 4:10-13). What emerges in Philippians is a portrait of a church being encouraged to suffer, when necessary, to remain true to the gospel and to Christ, who himself provides an example of suffering that the Philippians are to emulate (Phil 2:8). Moreover, they are to follow Paul's own example of participation (*koinōnia*) in Christ's sufferings (Phil 3:10). With this mindset, the Philippians believers will be able to "stand firm in the Lord" (Phil 4:1 NIV).

3.6. Christian Imitation. The theme of imitation fits comfortably within both the Greco-Roman and Jewish ethical contexts of which Paul was a part (Osiek). Noteworthy in Philippians is Paul's use of exemplars to shape the dispositions and practices of his audience. Not only does he expressly call the Philippians to imitation (Phil 3:17; 4:9), but he implicitly does so by providing a series of exemplars, beginning with the model par excellence, Christ Jesus (Phil 2:5-11). His use of exemplars extends to Timothy, Epaphroditus (Phil 2:19-30), and Paul himself (Phil 3:4-21), along with those who show a similar commitment to living out the pattern of Christ (Phil 2:30; 3:17). In Philippians, the grounding of all such imitation is Christ's own movement to imitate humanity, by taking up the human condition (Phil 2:7-8; see 3.1 above). In the hymn of Philippians 2:5-11, we see Christ "shar[ing] fully in the desperate contingency, suffering, and death of Adam's heirs" (Eastman, 445). Because of this identification, believers are incorporated into Christ's own story of humility and exaltation.

See also CHRISTOLOGY; CHRONOLOGY OF PAUL; COWORKERS, PAUL AND HIS; CRUCIFORMITY; ESCHATOLOGY; FRIENDSHIP; HYMNS, HYMN FRAGMENTS, CONFESSIONS; IMITATION OF PAUL / OF CHRIST; JOY, REJOICING; LETTERS, LETTER FORMS; LORD; PRISON, PRISONER; SLAVE, SLAVERY; SUFFERING; TRAVEL AND ITINERARY PLANS.

BIBLIOGRAPHY. ***Commentaries:*** **M. Bird and N. Gupta,** *Philippians*, NCBC (Cambridge: Cambridge University Press, 2020); **M. Bockmuehl,** *The Epistle to the Philippians*, BNTC (London: A&C Black, 1997); **J. K. Brown,** *Philippians*, TNTC (Downers Grove, IL: IVP Academic, 2022); **L. H. Cohick,** *Philippians*, SGBC (Grand Rapids, MI: Zondervan, 2013); **G. D. Fee,** *Paul's Letter to the Philippians*, NICNT (Grand Rapids, MI: Eerdmans, 1995); **D. Flemming,** *Philippians: A Commentary in the Wesleyan Tradition* (Kansas City, MO: Beacon Hill, 2009); **S. E. Fowl,** *Philippians*, THNTC (Grand Rapids, MI: Eerdmans, 2005); **G. F. Hawthorne and R. P. Marn,** *Philippians*, rev. ed., WBC (Grand Rapids, MI: Zondervan, 2004); **P. A. Holloway,** *Philippians*, Hermeneia (Minneapolis: Fortress, 2017); **M. J. Keown,** *Philippians*, EEC (Bellingham, WA: Lexham, 2017); **R. P. Martin,** *The Epistle of Paul to the Philippians*, TNTC (Grand Rapids, MI: Eerdmans, 1959); **C. Osiek,** *Philippians, Philemon*, ANTC (Nashville: Abingdon, 2000); **J. Reumann,** *Philippians: A New Translation with Introduction and Commentary*, AB (New Haven, CT: Yale University Press, 2008); **M. Silva,** *Philippians*, WEC (Chicago: Moody, 1988); idem, *Philippians*, 2nd ed., BECNT (Grand Rapids, MI: Baker, 2005); **F. Thielman,** *Philippians*, NIVAC (Grand Rapids, MI: Zondervan, 1995); **B. Thurston and J. M. Ryan,** *Philippians and Philemon*, SP (Collegeville, MN: Liturgical Press, 2005).

Studies: **P. J. Achtemeier,** "*Omne Verbum Sonat*: The New Testament and the Oral Environment of Late Western Antiquity," *JBL* 109, no. 1 (1990): 3-27; **L. Alexander,** "Hellenistic Letter-Forms and the Structure of Philippians," *JSNT* 37 (1989); 87-101; **R. Bauckham,** *Jesus and the God of Israel* (Grand Rapids, MI: Eerdmans, 2008); **S. Eastman,** "Imitating Christ Imitating Us: Paul's Educational Project in Philippians," in *The Word Leaps the Gap: Essays in Scripture and Theology in Honor of Richard B. Hays*, ed. J. R. Wagner, C. K. Rowe, and A. K. Grieb (Grand Rapids, MI: Eerdmans, 2008), 427-51; **J. Fitzgerald,** ed., *Friendship, Flattery, and Frankness of Speech: Studies on Friendship in the New Testament World*, NovTSup 82 (Leiden: Brill, 1996); **M. J. Gorman,** "'Although/Because He Was in the Form of God': The Theological Significance of Paul's Master Story (Phil 2:6-11)," *JTI* 1, no. 2 (2007): 147-69; **T. Henderson,** "Beware of Overlooked Allusions: A New Proposal for Intertextuality in Philippians 3" (paper presented at Annual Meeting of the Upper Midwest Region of the Society of Biblical Literature, St. Paul, MN, April 10, 2010); **P. A. Holloway,** *Consolation in Philippians: Philosophical Sources and Rhetorical Strategy*, SNTSMS 112 (New York: Cambridge University Press, 2001); **E. Käsemann,** "A Critical Analysis of Philippians 2:5-11," *JTC* 5 (1968): 45-88; **D. McAuley,** *Paul's Covert Use of Scripture:*

Intertextuality and Rhetorical Situation in Philippians 2:10-16 (Eugene, OR: Pickwick, 2015); **N. Nikki,** *Opponents and Identity in Philippi*, NovTSup (Leiden: Brill, 2019); **P. Oakes,** *Philippians: From People to Letter*, SNTSMS 110 (Cambridge: Cambridge University Press, 2001); **P. Smit,** *Paradigms of Being in Christ: A Study of the Epistle of Philippians*, LNTS 476 (London: Bloomsbury T&T Clark, 2013); **S. Stowers,** "Friends and Enemies in the Politics of Heaven," in *Pauline Theology*, ed. J. M. Bassler (Minneapolis: Fortress, 1991), 1:105-21.

J. K. Brown

PHILOSOPHY

As a "Hebrew of Hebrews," Paul, the *apostle to the *Gentiles, was a Roman citizen who wrote in Greek and ministered to a Mediterranean world teeming with philosophical notions from philosophical schools whose spirited competition was plain as the sun. Within this setting, the apostle—according to his own words—became all things to all those around him. For Luke, this included Paul facing off against the best philosophers of his day, citing their sources, and even convincing some of them to follow his *Christ (Acts 17:16-34). Most scholars similarly find in Paul's *letters a borrowing, modifying, upstaging, and/or correcting of popular philosophical teachings. For example, according to Max Lee, "Paul certainly employed language that had philosophical origins, that was in use among different schools of philosophy in his day, and which filtered into a wider linguistic currency as part of the cultural environment of the Greco-Roman world" (26). Additionally, many of Paul's pagan contemporaries would have seen him and his churches as a school of philosophy, especially with its promotion of a society without walls of race, class, and gender (Gal 3:28). Even so, the apostle actually only uses the word *philosophy* once in his letters, where he rails against a hollow *wisdom based on human *tradition that ensnares the *church and puffs up its pupils with pride (Col 2:8). Elsewhere, Paul also distinguishes divine wisdom from worldly wisdom and clarifies that the "wise man" who considers the message of the *cross "foolishness" finds no point of harmonization with the wisdom that comes from *God (1 Cor 1:18-25).

To understand the apostle more fully, it is important to view him in light of this cultural context, so deeply marked by Greco-Roman philosophy. With this aim, this article will cover (1) the general background of Greco-Roman philosophy and (2) its influence on Judaism before (3) honing in on Paul's possible allusions to and specific comments about philosophy in a sampling of his letters. The final section (4) will make some concluding comments with respect to comparing Paul with the philosophers.

1. General Background
2. The Influence of Philosophy on Judaism
3. Paul and Philosophy
4. Final Comments

1. General Background.

1.1. Definition. One first-century writer boils ancient philosophy down to discovering the *truth about things human and divine so as to rid oneself of moral filth by achieving a pure mind resulting in virtuous action (Seneca, *Ep.* 90.3). More generally, ancient philosophy can be defined as the search to discern the mysteries of life and *death, the intricacies of the *body and soul, and the nature of good and evil. It searched for the meaning of space and time, the beginning and ending of *creation, and—related to all of the above—the social contract of humans with one another, the state, and the divine. In many ways, there was an overlap between philosophy and religion in the ancient world, particularly since many philosophers rejected the capricious mythological gods—notorious for quarreling with one another and copulating with mortals—and endorsed instead a supreme, righteous being who, as an "all-glorious parent," governed the world with providence and care (Seneca, *Prov.* 1.1–2.9).

Ancient philosophy was divided into logic, *ethics, and physics (which included metaphysics). One burning question for the philosopher concerned how a person could moderate, control, or overcome desires such as anger, vainglory, greed, and lust. Various philosophers aimed for their sermons to induce a deep conviction in their audience so that when people received wisdom into their hearts, they would experience a radical conversion, transforming them into a new creation marked with spiritual *freedom, moral renewal, and personal virtue (Valerius Maximus, *Fact. dict.* 3.3.1; Horace, *Ep.* 1.1.33-37). These converts were known to abandon their old lives, give away their worldly possessions, and then submit to a process of rehabilitation, which trained them for prudence, courage, justice, and self-control. Therefore, rather than an unbiased, dispassionate field of study, the intellectual explorations of ancient philosophy were tied to the strict indoctrination of personal practices and habits as prescribed by the tradition to which a disciple belonged. This philosophy was not for individual *knowledge for knowledge's sake but for group comprehension so that a community could walk in the way of the truth they promulgated.

1.2. The Famous Founders of Philosophy: Socrates, Plato, and Aristotle. Despite obvious differences, Socrates could be described as the Jesus of the Greeks. Like the Messiah, the humbly born philosopher lived a meager life, endured insults by the establishment, and calmly submitted to an execution in the wake of a kangaroo court. Socrates's verdict resulted from his challenging religious leaders and undermining their misconstrued conceptions of divinity, justice, and truth. He broke new ground from the philosophers who came before him (to the extent that those philosophers were henceforth referred to as the *pre*-Socratics). According to Cicero, Socrates brought divine wisdom down from heaven to usher her into private homes and public streets so that she could help ordinary people discern between good and evil and to understand truths about morality and life (Cicero, *Tusc.* 5.10).

For Socrates, the truth that sets one free from a life in shadow begins with humility and leads to the meticulous scrutiny of everything, including cherished traditions and beliefs. For many, Socrates stood as the world's wisest and most righteous man, who served as the paradigm for how people should live and die. Since Socrates himself left no writings, his followers published accounts of his life and redactions of his teachings. Consequently, all extant information about Socrates is secondary, and much of it disputed. The story of Socrates's trial and death is nonetheless the founding event of Greco-Roman philosophy, and his influence has been felt in every age, far and beyond philosophy itself.

Plato served as Socrates's beloved disciple, his John. In a famous line Plato reflects: "I thank God that I was born Greek and not barbarian, free and not slave, male and not female; but above all, that I was born in the age of Socrates" (see Gal 3:28; Col 3:11). Due to Plato's sweeping influence on the Greco-Roman philosophical traditions, Ralph Waldo Emerson reasoned, "Plato is philosophy, and philosophy Plato." If N. T. Wright is correct in saying Plato's writings served as the NT of the Greeks, then *The Republic* would be Plato's Romans, about which Emerson quipped: "Burn the libraries; for their value is in this book." Plato's popularity led him to start his own school called the Academy, where he guided his acolytes in the nurturing of their souls and in living a life that pleases god. For Plato, the righteous person does so by training the inner man who delights in justice to tame his *flesh despite being trapped in a tarnished body (*Phaedr.* 270E-271D; *Resp.* 9.588-589; cf. 2 Cor 4:16–5:10; Rom 7:1-25). A truly righteous person, Plato illustrates, would be one falsely accused of doing wrong throughout his life to the point of being scourged, racked, and bound before finally being impaled (*Resp.* 2:361-362; cf. Lk 23:47). According to his *Republic*, there were surpassing rewards for the just in the *afterlife, in which the virtuous souls go to paradise for a thousand years to experience inexpressible delights. During this same time, the wicked suffer infernal torments as they repay tenfold the sins they committed in this life (*Resp.* 10.614d-619b; cf. Mt 25:31-33). Regarding god, the Academy stressed divine transcendence—a celestial being far removed from the material world who avoided sullied flesh by enacting his will through lesser powers. Therefore, what matters most to the wise man is the unseen rather than what is seen and what is above rather than what is below (cf. Mt 6:19-21; Col 3:1-2).

Aristotle was Plato's top disciple. In addition to being the tutor of Alexander the Great, Aristotle is known for founding his school of Peripatetics and for being remarkably prolific. His work constitutes a significant development in logic and ethics. He taught his students to pursue *eudaimonia*—a happy, flourishing life—which results from employing reason, practicing moderation, and avoiding extremes (i.e., the "golden mean"). He argued that what separates virtuous from fools regards the former's attempt to pay back the endless debt of gratitude they owe god for the gift of life (*Eth. nic.* 8.14.1; 1163b15-18; cf. Rom 1:21). Aristotle is esteemed for his systematic logic, which stresses the syllogism. For example, "All men are mortal. Socrates is a man. Therefore, Socrates is mortal." (Syllogisms appear in Paul's letters. For example, in Rom 6, Paul argues that Jesus died to *sin. Believers died with Jesus through *baptism. Therefore, believers are dead to sin.)

Even though Socrates, Plato, and Aristotle died centuries before Paul, the major philosophical schools active in the first century stemmed from their teachings. The next section will introduce some of these traditions that plausibly served as contexts for Paul's churches and letters: the Sophists, the Cynics, the Epicureans, and the Stoics.

1.3. The Sophists. Protagoras was the first philosopher to claim the title Sophist. He developed techniques for arguing, likened the craft to wrestling, and established rhetorical grappling matches, of which he was a celebrated champion (Plato, *Prot.* 335a; Diogenes Laertius, *Vit.* 9.52). For the Sophists, then, rhetoric became the mother of all the arts, which led the school to focus on teaching oratory skill to young men entering into politics (Philodemus, *De Rhetorica*). The first half of the first century experienced a Sophist revival despite the blistering attacks it absorbed from other philosophers—possibly including Paul (see below). The perennial complaint against the Sophists was that their words were aimed at tickling people's ears in order to line their own pockets (cf. 2 Tim 4:3). They were also eviscerated as self-absorbed blowhards boasting about being stout, sleek, rich, and robust, while their sermons advised others how to live when they themselves had no clue how to do so themselves (Dio Chrysostom, *4 Regn.* 35; 28.35; Philo, *Det.* 33-34; *Leg.* 3.232; *Contempl.* 31; *Post.* 86; *Migr.* 72).

1.4. The Cynics. Diogenes, the most popular of the Cynics, gained the school its name because he lived like a dog (*kyon*), veritably barking at anything he deemed excess (Epictetus, *Diatr.* 3.22.9-10). He rejected luxurious living and chose homelessness over common social norms so that his extreme asceticism would serve as a visible affront to the status quo. The Cynics believed freedom entailed being untethered from fleshly lusts, from worries about what they would eat and what they would wear (cf. Mt 6:25-34), as well from the concerns associated with family, customs, and the state. Most of their writings are no longer extant, and the sayings attributed to them are largely unreliable. Even so, more than by a central body of teaching or an established school, Cynics were identified by their simple lifestyle and its resulting appearance—a tattered cloak, messy hair, and a leather pouch (cf. Mt 10:9-10). The Cynics did still use words, though, employing numerous tropes and tailoring their speeches in light of their audiences, speaking to children as if they were a child and to governors as if a governor. Although Cynics were often viewed in a pejorative light, Dio Chrysostom argues that the ideal Cynic sought to rescue people from folly by using bold persuasion and open rebuke: gentle words when possible but harsh ones when necessary.

1.5. The Epicureans. According to Epicurus, pleasure is humanity's ultimate aim and highest good, and the purest form of pleasure is the absence of pain. The philosopher must therefore employ reason to avoid *suffering as well as to set aside superstition and *fear. The Epicureans stressed human agency more than divine sovereignty—especially since, for them, the events of life came from the random collisions of atoms. Despite how the term is used today, an ancient Epicurean was a person who pursued spiritual rather than worldly pleasures and who considered the best life one of simplicity and moderation. Despite this, Epicurus's later followers still became known as carousers shackled to self-indulgence and sexual desire. Their conviction that god had forsaken humanity to their own devices and their disbelief in an afterlife provided no lasting motivation to pursue virtue.

1.6. The Stoics. The Stoic father Zeno met with his disciples under a porch (stoa), hence the name "Stoics." Although Zeno founded the school, it was Chrysippus who established it as a great tradition. Having been influenced by the Cynics, the Stoics in many ways could be considered kinder, gentler Cynics in that they were less belligerent to others and more open to material possessions. The school also drew heavily from Aristotle—so much so that Cicero concluded the difference between the two schools was of words more than principles (*Fin.* 3.6–4.7). Nonetheless, Stoicism came to be the most favored philosophy in the *empire, and by the time of Paul it pervaded the Roman world. Over against the Platonic emphasis of a transcendent deity, the Stoics underlined the immanence of god, present with humanity through his logos and world soul. In further contrast to Plato's theological conception, the Stoics considered god a spirit with a body composed of fiery, celestial matter. For them, god's spirit was seated in people's minds, which enabled them to worship him. Genuine *worship, therefore, consisted in having a correct knowledge of god, who possesses all things, allots all things, and bestows all things to all people without price. For the Stoics, this proper religious understanding leads people to discard burdensome superstitions, since god does not desire human rituals or seek anyone to serve him in a manmade *temple. Rather, the worship god requires is for his followers to imitate him by living a virtuous life and being kind to others (Seneca, *Ep.* 95).

The Roman Stoics centered their attention on the pursuit of virtue, arguing that the value of character surpasses that of passing *wealth, health, fame, and beauty (Cicero, *Fin.* 3.13.45). This virtue ensued from people living according to the divine pattern established at creation, which helped them gain incremental freedom from sinful passions, discover the secret to contentment, and attain self-sufficiency (*autarkeia, autarkes*; cf. 2 Cor 8:9; Phil 4:11). For the Stoics, compared to this tranquil independence nothing else mattered: neither death nor life, not even family relationships (e.g., Epictetus, *Diatr.* 3.3.5; cf. 1 Cor 7:32-35; Mk 3:33; Lk 14:26). Once this mindset is achieved, even when in chains the Stoic can boast that his choice, will, and moral purpose remain unfettered (*Diatr.* 1.1.23; cf. Acts 28:31).

In contrast to the modern use of the word *stoic*, the ancient Stoics were not unfeeling robots. According to Seneca, they too mourned, just within moderation and with reason, and they—as a matter of fact—considered *joy serious business. For them, a person's mind kept feelings in line and inspired the individual, in the face of those feelings, to yawn at torture, suffering, exile, and execution (for wisdom teaches that there is nothing to fear in affliction but the fear of affliction). Therefore, the Stoic sage was not impeded when confined, not stuck down when flung down, not tortured when on the rack, not injured when mutilated, and not constrained when a *slave (Plutarch, *Mor.* 1057d-e; cf. 2 Cor 4:8). Nevertheless, there would be a time, they believed, when suffering would cease: at the termination of a person's life or the end of the world. Regarding the latter, the Stoics believed the cosmos would come to a sudden close by flood and fire through cataclysm and conflagration. At this time, humanity and wickedness will be blotted out, and Death will defeat the powers and *principalities before ending his own life (Seneca, *Herc. Ot.*, 1102-17; cf. 1 Cor 15:24-28). After that, nature will rest, and god will retire into himself and become all in all. Meanwhile the righteous souls will wait for god to reboot the cosmos to repeat the cycle again (Seneca, *Nat.* 3.3.27-30).

Many Stoic concepts seem to overlap with Paul's (see below). While Stoicism would have been best known by the educated minority in Rome, its widespread popularity makes it probable that its teaching influenced the lower classes as well. Therefore, N. T. Wright concludes Paul likely expected his audience to recognize basic concepts of Stoicism so as to be able to read some passages in his letters within that context (2013, 2:1384).

2. The Influence of Philosophy on Judaism.

There was no great divide between Greco-Roman philosophy and Jewish thought—as if these two were clear-cut, unvariegated traditions standing against each other in a zero-sum game. Nor did, as John Barclay concludes, any assimilation of philosophy by the Jews constitute a diminution or dilution of their thought. Rather, to various degrees, Jewish writers employed philosophical themes to extol their God and way of life. That most Jews in the Diaspora only read the Hebrew Bible in Greek doubtlessly added to this scheme. The parade example is Philo of Alexandria, the most prolific Jewish philosopher, who—to buttress his Hebraic *faith—brings together biblical stories with philosophy, Homeric epic, and Hellenistic commonplaces. From this vantage point, Philo interprets the Pentateuch, often with an allegorical reading similar to those in Galatians 4:21-31 and 1 Corinthians 10:1-10. This sort of Jewish philosophy may provide a window into the heresy many scholars believe Paul opposed in Colossians: that is, philosophical teachings propagated by Jewish apologists particularly related to strict ascetic rules regarding diets, Sabbaths, and festival days.

3. Paul and Philosophy.

When Rome captured Athens in 86 BC, philosophers dispersed to find new accommodations. One key city that became a hub for these exiles was Tarsus in Cilicia, Paul's hometown. As a result, Paul's city became esteemed for its notable philosophers and prominent schools. Although the apostle eventually moved to *Jerusalem, he spent enough time in Cilicia to be identified as Paul of Tarsus. Since he also returned to the area after his *conversion, he was likely there long enough to be familiar with the fundamental questions and discussions in the Cilician air (Acts 9:30; 22:3; Gal 1:21). In fact, on Mars Hill, Paul even cites a Stoic line from one of his fellow Tarsians (Acts 17:28).

Taking into account the apostle's background as a Second Temple Jew from Greco-Roman Tarsus, it is unsurprising to see notes of philosophy in his letters—even if his ability to adapt to these specific contexts keeps one from categorizing what he wrote into a single mold. That is to say, Paul was not *either* a Jewish rabbi *or* a Greek philosopher, nor was he merely *both* rabbi *and* philosopher: rather, he was *both/and-more than* them both. Therefore, to borrow from Margaret Mitchell, instead of scholars lobbing missiles of parallel Jewish and philosophical texts from opposing trenches, it is better to plod into the murky middle to see within Paul's letters a complicated amalgam of Judaism and Hellenism.

Paul's life fell within a transitional period for philosophy that focused on how to attain virtue and avoid vice. It was also an age of eclecticism and syncretism, in which the picking and choosing from an intellectual smorgasbord caused school lines to blur. These boundaries became increasingly smudged as philosophers attacked other traditions while at the same time appropriating their ideas. Nevertheless, what mattered most was a basic allegiance to one's own school. Once this loyalty was established, the sage had a flexibility to absorb and assimilate notions from rival academies. If Paul was a man of his time who followed the patterns of his period, he had the license to borrow from various philosophical traditions (incorporating and redefining certain philosophical thoughts) in order to bolster and articulate his theology even while denouncing those schools. Any use of these philosophical expressions would have mostly been in the service of his proclaiming Christ as *Lord in an attempt to win over a crowd already bombarded with other philosophers struggling to convert them as well.

The following section will highlight some of the resonances in a handful of Paul's letters to provide a sampling of his engagement with philosophy: Romans, 1 Corinthians, and 1 Thessalonians.

3.1. The Role of Philosophy in Romans. Commentators often highlight parallels in Romans with passages from various philosophers. They tend to note, for example, how Romans 1:18-32 is replete with resonances from Stoicism, especially with the school's penchant for vice lists and its complaint about humanity's rejection of the divine design clearly displayed in creation (see Rom 1:20). Moreover, scholars point out that in Romans 1:26, 28 the phrases "against nature" (*para physin*) and "which are not proper" (*ta mē kathēkonta*) were technical expressions for the Stoics. Ben Witherington goes so far as to conclude that Paul may have fashioned his critique of pagan culture to have contact with similar versions by Seneca. For instance, in *Epistle* 95, Seneca gives an exposé of the empire by recounting its descent into depravity. According to the Stoic, divine reason was therefore the single hope for his soul-rusted society marked by theological foolishness and shame. Similar to Romans 1:26-27, Seneca illustrates this moral topsy-turvy by lamenting how men's abandonment of the divine design led to their women's contravening (what he considers) their sexual nature—not to mention males who exploit children and violate slaves (*Ep.* 95.13-33).

Additionally, the imaginary dialogue partner Paul introduces in Romans 2:1 follows the practice of Stoic preachers. Moreover, though debated, some scholars take Paul's reference to the Gentiles "who have the *law in themselves" (Rom 2:14-15) as referring to moral philosophers and as cohering with the Stoic dictum regarding how a person can live according to the law by nature without a written code. While N. T. Wright concludes that these law-keeping Gentiles in Romans 2 refer to non-Jewish Christians instead, he argues that Paul still provides clear echoes here of Stoicism to use the same language of the pagan moralist whom the apostle has been addressing since Romans 2:1 (Wright 2013, 2:1088, 1381). There are also parallels with philosophy in the second half of Romans. For instance, Paul's "For from him [God] and through him and for him are all things" stands close to the Stoic phrase "All things are from god, in god and for god" (Rom 11:36 NIV; Marcus Aurelius, *Comm.* 4.23).

Moreover, Paul's word for "spiritual" (*logikēn*) worship in Romans 12 smacks of the Stoic notion of worship seen, for example, in Epictetus's exhortation: "If, indeed, I were a nightingale, I would sing as a nightingale; if a swan, as a swan. But as it is, I am a rational being [*logikos*], therefore I must be singing hymns of praise to god" (*Diatr.* 1.16.20-21 [LCL]). For the Stoics, then, the service god desires is *not* found in animal *sacrifices or cultic rituals but in imitating god, resulting in an upright heart and a reverent life (Seneca, *Ep.* 115.5). Furthermore, just as Paul goes on to appeal to the body metaphor to call the church to be unified (Rom 12:4-5), Seneca uses the same metaphor to instantiate how people are born for *fellowship and mutual protection: "What if the hand should desire to harm the feet, or the eyes the hand? All the members of the body are in harmony with another because it is to the advantage of the whole body" (*De ira* 2.31.7). And while Paul commands his audience to be devoted to brotherly *love (Rom 12:10), Seneca proclaims to his disciples that they must live for others if they would live for themselves (*Ep.* 95.51-52; 48.2).

Additionally, related to Romans 12:14-21, the Stoics also stressed nonretaliation. For example, Epictetus calls for his followers to love those who persecute them so that even when they are being flogged like an ass, they should love those who flog them like a brother (*Diatr.* 3.22.54). Rather than with retaliation, the wise man wins over wrongdoers with persistent kindness: graciously calling them back into reconciliation rather than doggedly hunting them down (Seneca, *Ben.* 7.31.1; *De ira* 2.10.6-7; cf. Rom 2:4). These parallels and more cause Runar Thorsteinsson to conclude that even if every detail in Paul's letter may not be interpreted in Roman Stoic fashion, there is enough to suggest that the basic framework of it and many details in it may have been seen in a Stoic light.

3.2. The Role of Philosophy and the Corinthians. Scholars tend to agree that the Corinthians' understanding of wisdom led to the disunity menacing the church. Some have argued that Paul directs his critique toward (1) a rhetorical emphasis from the Sophists, (2) a Christian adaptation of Stoicism, or (3) an eclectic body of popular philosophical thought.

3.2.1. The Sophists and the Corinthians. According to Bruce Winter and Johannes Munck, the Corinthians compared Paul with the Sophists so that, in response, the apostle employs terms and makes allusions to Sophist teaching in a strategy to refute and evacuate their expressions so that the church will put its hope in the saving power of God rather than in sophistry and rhetoric. Paul also seems to underline how different his *ministry is from the Sophists. Whereas they were known for entering into the city seeking personal *glory by flaunting their charm, Paul insists that he came to the church in weakness, trembling, and fear (1 Cor 2:3).

Furthermore, while the Sophists charged fees and boasted about how well they eschewed manual labor, Paul highlights rolling up his sleeves and working with his hands in order to offer his *gospel for free (cf. Musonius Rufus, *Fragment* 11). Because of the tuition paid to their philosophers, the Sophists claimed to belong to their particular teacher. Paul, however, turns this notion on its head by declaring that in the *body of Christ it is the teacher who belongs to the people. Moreover, in contradistinction to the Sophists' reputation of adapting their messages to their audiences in the pursuit of wealth and glory, Paul admits to becoming all things to all people to save them from their sins (not to bleed them of their money). Finally, in further juxtaposition, whereas the Sophists mocked those who trained their bodies for virtue and were themselves scorned for being "degenerate athletes" who "fight in the shade," "punch the air," and refuse to enter the stadium, Paul announces that he beats his body and makes it his slave so that he does not run aimlessly or box the air—hoping that in his contest for the church he might receive a lasting prize (1 Cor 9:24-27).

3.2.2. The Stoics and the Corinthians. Rather than a refutation of Sophist rhetoric, Timothy Brookins (2014) argues the Corinthian problem is best understood as the church's adaptation of Stoic philosophy. In addition to the school having pride of place in the first century, "the wise man" whom Paul refutes in 1 Corinthians 1:20 was chiefly associated with the Stoics, so much so that the tradition boasted exclusive right to the term. Further, similar to Paul's profession in 1 Corinthians 3:21 that all things belong to the Corinthians, the Stoics bragged that all things belonged to their wise man, who was noble, mature, honorable, and strong. Consequently, the Stoic sage alone was ruler and king, he alone powerful and rich, he alone prudent and free (Stoicorum Veterum Fragmenta 3.613; 3.655; Cicero, *Fin.* 3.75). Such claims ring familiar when placed beside Paul's rebuke of the Corinthian believers: "Already you have become rich! Quite apart from us you have become kings! . . . We are weak, but you are strong. You are held in honor, but we in disrepute" (1 Cor 4:8-10 NRSV). There is also a similar resonance with 1 Corinthians 15:28 and the Stoic belief that at the end of the world "all would be in Zeus and Zeus will be in all" (Stoicorum Veterum Fragmenta 2.596-632; 3.302). Brookins takes this as an immediate challenge to the Stoics: it is the God of Jesus Christ (not Jupiter or Zeus) who will become "all in all."

Though this point is contested, Troels Engberg-Pedersen (2010) goes so far as to argue that Paul's understanding of the *resurrection in 1 Corinthians 15 has similarities with the Stoic idea of the afterlife to the point that the apostle's conception of spiritual bodies presupposes a Stoic *cosmology. For example, according to Engberg-Pedersen, both Paul and the Stoics construed individuals as living beyond this world in a tangible state likened to the stuff of stars (see 1 Cor 15:40-54; Phil 2:14-16). Engberg-Pedersen concludes that whereas the Stoics depicted this as a *separation* of the material spirit from the earthly body, the apostle sees it as the *transformation* of the physical body into a spiritual body, which despite the nuance was the same final state of the righteous conceived by the Stoics.

3.2.3. Popular Philosophy and the Corinthians. According to Dale Martin, the educated elite in Rome sought to display their knowledge of catchphrases from a variety of schools. Eclecticism was the goal of the learned, and to be committed too strictly to one tradition was considered too eccentric or extreme. Therefore, Martin concludes, the philosophy Paul counters in *Corinth was more likely a mixed bag from various traditions rather than a specifically Sophist or Stoic philosophy. According to Richard Horsley, though, this was not a purely Hellenistic hodgepodge but a Jewish assimilation of that hodgepodge, reworked to articulate their own devotion to God, which closely associated eloquent speech with wisdom and which related devotion to Lady Wisdom (see Prov 8; Wis 7:7–8:1) with achieving a royal status of being noble, powerful, rich, and wise (Horsley, 47).

3.3. The Role of Philosophy in 1 Thessalonians. Abraham Malherbe points out similarities between Paul's construal of his ministry in 1 Thessalonians with Dio's depiction of the good Cynic. For instance, Dio places his sage who speaks with frankness (*parresia*) and without flattery in juxtaposition to those fecal philosophers who spoke with guile and an impure mind. Likewise, Paul stresses that he spoke openly (*e parresia smetha*) to the Thessalonians, not sweet-talking the believers or seeking their praise (1 Thess 2:5-6). What is more, Dio also insists that good philosophers will not always be harsh with their hearers but at times will be as tender as a father and, like gentle nurses, provide bitter pills with a spoon full of sugar to ameliorate the unpleasant taste (*Discourse* 33.10). Likewise, Paul argues that although he could have been harsh with the congregation, he was instead as gentle as a nurse and as encouraging as a father (1 Thess 2:1-12).

Further, the good Cynic stood out from those who refused to enter into the good fight (*agōn*) because these second-ranked philosophers feared the opinion of man and the *violence (*hybris*) of the crowds. In comparison, Paul proclaims that even though he had been ill-treated (*hybristhentes*) by the mob, he still spoke frankly to the church as he participated in the great struggle (*agōn*) for them (1 Thess 2:2). Similarly, Dio depicts the true Cynic as divinely directed to speak for the benefit of the people and not for the sake of personal glory or gain. Dio considers himself that philosopher: not out of his own choosing, mind you, but out of his obedience to the divine will (Epictetus, *Diatr.* 32.11-12). Likewise, Paul ensures the church that he has been approved by God and that his words are not of human origin but from the *Holy Spirit, along with the Spirit's power and conviction.

4. Final Comments.
As seen from the above examples, scholars have found value in placing Paul and the philosophers side by side. Due to the abuse of past comparisons, however, scholars are becoming more careful to approach such enterprises *not* for apologetic assertions, nor for arguing for the dependence of one author on the other, nor in committing "parallelomania" (taking passages out of context and exaggerating the similarities). Kavin Rowe, however, has recently challenged all such comparisons, arguing that Christianity and rival traditions are altogether incommensurable and fundamentally untranslatable. Although Rowe's thesis has not yet been widely accepted among scholars, it helps one find a point between the opposite poles of this pendulum. Here, without dismissing the enterprise outright, the proper comparison seeks to elicit a mutually illuminating conversation between embodied, historically embedded voices in order to elucidate Paul's thoughts in fresh ways. It also distinguishes between derivation and confrontation, realizing that just because the apostle used alien categories and phrases from philosophical schools does not mean he endorsed them or that his allusion was directly derivative of them. When Paul employed philosophical expressions, it is likely he did so to contest, reframe, or redefine their typical conclusions.

Finally, any dialogue that is set up between the apostle and the philosophers should underscore that Paul's belief regarding salvation as resting on a Jewish carpenter would have bewildered the scholars of his day. Likewise, the apostle's conviction that God's ultimate revelation was manifest in the crucifixion of God's Son, "a Nazarian hick," would have been altogether foolish to the educated elite. Therefore, no matter how much it may seem Paul was in lockstep with a particular philosopher or philosophical school, the decisive point of departure is at the very start of Paul's gospel: the apocalyptic death and bodily resurrection of Jesus Christ.

See also Body; Corinthians, First Letter to the; Creation and New Creation; Ethics; Flesh; Preaching, First-Century; Romans, Letter to the; Thessalonians, Letters to the.

BIBLIOGRAPHY. **D. E. Aune,** "The Problem of the Passions in Cynicism," in *Passions and Moral Progress in Greco-Roman Thought*, ed. J. T. Fitzgerald (London: Routledge, 2008), 48-66; **J. M. G. Barclay,** *Jews in the Mediterranean Diaspora: From Alexander to Trajan* (Berkeley: University of California Press, 1996); **J. M. G. Barclay and B. G. White,** eds., *The New Testament in Comparison: Validity, Method, and Purpose in Comparing Traditions*, LNTS 600 (London: Bloomsbury, 2020); **T. Brookins,** *Corinthian Wisdom, Stoic Philosophy, and the Ancient Economy*, SNTSMS 159 (Cambridge: Cambridge University Press, 2014); idem, *Christianity and Stoicism Through the Centuries*, Perspectives in Religious Studies 45 (Waco, TX: Baylor University Press, 2018); **A. Carr,** "St. Paul's Attitude Towards Greek Philosophy," *The Expositor* 9 (1899): 372-78; **D. A. deSilva,** *Fourth Maccabees and the Promotion of the Jewish Philosophy* (Eugene, OR: Cascade, 2021); **J. R. Dodson,** "The Transcendence of Death and Heavenly Ascent in the Apocalyptic Paul and the Stoics," in *Paul and the Apocalyptic Imagination*, ed. B. Blackwell, J. Goodrich, and J. Maston (Minneapolis: Fortress, 2016), 157-76; idem, "The Fall of Men and the Lust of Women in Seneca's *Epistle 95* and Paul's Letter to the Romans," *NovT* 59 (2017), 355-65; **J. R. Dodson and D. E. Briones,** eds., *Paul and Seneca in Dialogue* (Leiden: Brill, 2017); **J. R. Dodson and A. W. Pitts,** *Paul and the Greco-Roman Philosophical Tradition*, LNTS 527 (London:

Bloomsbury, 2017); **S. G. Eastman,** *Paul and the Person: Reframing Paul's Anthropology* (Grand Rapids, MI: Eerdmans, 2017); **T. Engberg-Pedersen,** *Paul and the Stoics* (Edinburgh: T&T Clark, 2000); idem, *Cosmology and Self in the Apostle Paul: The Material Spirit* (Oxford: Oxford University Press, 2010); **D. Fredrickson,** "Natural and Unnatural Use in Romans 1:24-27: Paul and the Philosophical Critique of Eros," in *Homosexuality, Science, and the "Plain Sense" of Scripture* (Louisville, KY: Westminster John Knox, 1999) 197-222; **V. P. Furnish,** *The Moral Teaching of Paul*, 2nd ed. (Nashville: Abingdon, 1986), 52-82; **P. Hadot,** *What Is Ancient Philosophy?* (Cambridge, MA: Harvard University Press, 2004); **A. M. Holowchak,** *The Stoics* (London: Continuum, 2008); **R. A. Horsley,** *1 Corinthians*, ANTC (Nashville: Abingdon, 2011); **M. V. Hubbard,** *Christianity in the Greco-Roman World* (Grand Rapids, MI: Baker, 2010); **M. J. Lee,** *Moral Transformation in Greco-Roman Philosophy of Mind*, WUNT 515 (Tübingen: Mohr Siebeck, 2020); **A. J. Malherbe,** *Paul and the Popular Philosophers* (Minneapolis: Fortress, 1989); **J. W. Martens,** "Romans 2.14-16: A Stoic Reading," *NTS* 40, no. 1 (1994): 55-67; **D. B. Martin,** *The Corinthian Body* (New Haven, CT: Yale University Press, 1999); **W. A. Meeks,** "Judaism, Hellenism, and the Birth of Christianity," in *Beyond the Judaism/Hellenism Divide*, ed. T. Engberg-Pedersen (Louisville, KY: Westminster John Knox, 2001), 17-27; **M. M. Mitchell,** "Pauline Accommodation and 'Condescension': 1 Cor 9:19-23 and the History of Influence," in *Beyond the Judaism/Hellenism Divide*, ed. T. Engberg-Pedersen (Louisville, KY: Westminster John Knox, 2001); **J. Munck,** *Paul and the Salvation of Mankind* (Louisville, KY: Westminster John Knox, 1977); **J. T. Pennington,** *Jesus the Great Philosopher: Rediscovering the Wisdom Needed for the Good Life* (Grand Rapids, MI: Brazos, 2020); **T. Rasimus et al.,** *Stoicism in Early Christianity* (Grand Rapids, MI: Baker, 2010); **C. K. Rowe,** *One True Life: The Stoics and Early Christians as Rival Traditions* (Oxford: Oxford University Press, 2016); **A. Setaioli,** "Physics III: Theology," in *Brill's Companion to Seneca*, ed. G. Damschen and A. Heil (Leiden: Brill, 2014), 379-95; **J. Z. Smith,** *Drudgery Divine* (Chicago: University of Chicago Press, 1990); **D. Swancutt,** "Sexy Stoics and the Rereading of Romans 1.18–2.16," in *A Feminist Companion to Paul*, ed. A.-J. Levine (London: Continuum, 2004), 42-73; **C. H. Talbert,** *Romans* (Macon, GA: Smyth & Helwys, 2002); **R. M. Thorsteinsson,** *Roman Christianity and Roman Stoicism: A Comparative Study of Ancient Morality* (Oxford: Oxford University Press, 2013); **P. Vining,** "Comparing Seneca's Ethics in *Epistulae Morales* to Those of Paul in Romans," *ResQ* 47, no. 2 (2005): 83-104; **Bruce W. Winter,** *Philo and Paul Among the Sophists: Alexandrian and Corinthian Responses to a Julio-Claudian Movement*, 2nd ed (Grand Rapids, MI: Eerdmans, 2002); **B. Witherington III,** *Paul's Letter to the Romans: A Socio-Rhetorical Commentary* (Grand Rapids, MI: Eerdmans, 2004); **N. T. Wright,** *Paul and the Faithfulness of God*, 2 vols. (Minneapolis: Fortress, 2013); idem, *Interpreting Paul: Essays on the Apostle and His Letters* (Grand Rapids, MI: Zondervan, 2020).

J. R. Dodson

POLITICAL SYSTEMS

Paul the Hebrew of Hebrews (Phil 3:5) and the Roman citizen (Acts 16:37-38; 22:25-29; 25:7-12) lived within both the Jewish and Roman political systems. Paul's doctrine that one should be obedient to earthly authorities as to *God (Rom 13:1-7) indicates that he held himself accountable to both Jewish and Roman political systems.

1. Jewish Political System
2. Roman Political System

1. Jewish Political System.

While the Mediterranean world was under Roman rule and Paul called himself a missionary to the *Gentiles, Paul himself was a member of the Jewish Diaspora and worked in dialogue with the Jewish population. The Mishnah gives evidence of a hierarchy from synagogue cantor up to the high priest at the *temple, but it is unclear whether this hierarchy extended to all or most synagogues in the Diaspora (m. Sotah 7:7; m. Yoma 7:1). Any political connection between *Jerusalem leaders and Diaspora Jewry was weakened after 70 CE, when the temple was destroyed.

While the Second Temple stood, some sort of political system may have monitored synagogues within Palestine and the Diaspora and also served to collect the half-shekel temple tax required of some Mediterranean Jewry. This quasi-political hierarchy linking local synagogue to Jerusalem temple was at least imagined by the author of Acts, who portrays Paul as bearing *letters from the high priest to the synagogues of Damascus, authorizing Paul to arrest believers, and such a hierarchy is also assumed when Paul receives warnings that the Jews in Jerusalem will hold him accountable for his *mission work in the Diaspora (Acts 9:1-2; 21:4, 10-11). The tax-collecting function of the Jewish political system was guaranteed by Augustus's edict in 12 BCE that the Jews could send money to Jerusalem. This support for the Jerusalem temple provides the ideological background for Paul's own *collection for the Jewish Christians in Jerusalem (2 Cor 8–9; Rom 15:25-31). As Sara Mandell effectively shows, it was probably only the Pharisaic Jews who were expected to pay the temple tax, and when the temple was destroyed at the end of the First Jewish War, Rome required them to pay the *didrachmon* tax as a war indemnity.

1.1. Synagogues and Synagogue Rulers. As communities with official recognition by the municipal and provincial authorities, Jewish residents were fully under the secular political system. There is record of the Jewish communities in Alexandria and Sardis being called *politeuma* in the first century BCE, the term for an organized body of citizens within a Hellenistic city. In Alexandria this *politeuma* was governed by a council called the *gerousia*. For the most part, however, the political matters unique to Diaspora Jews were conducted through the local synagogue. While synagogues were not accorded the sanctity of the Jerusalem temple, inscriptions related to a number of them show that they were regarded as holy places, and during the time of Paul's *ministry synagogues retained the status of *aedes sacrae* (sacred buildings) in Roman law. Lee Levine notes that terms such as *hieros* were used for a synagogue, and some inscriptions assert a synagogue's orientation to *worship of "the most high God." Terms such as *temenos* or *hieros peribolos* were used to designate the synagogue's land as a sacred area.

Synagogues without a permanent fixture for the Torah ark could function as meeting houses of the Jewish community for nonreligious matters. Here thefts would be reported, *slaves would be released, the poor would be fed, and decisions about community life would be made. Many synagogues also functioned as schools for the religious education of the Jewish youth. The synagogue ruler (*archisynagōgos* in the NT) could function as a local political ruler with regard to Jewish affairs, though as Tessa Rajak and David Noy show, the title could also recognize a benefactor and/or patron of the synagogue community. There were a number of synagogue rulers for each synagogue (ten according to an inscription dating from 56 CE in Cyrene; see *SEG* 17.823).

According to Acts, Paul habitually began his mission outreach in any Hellenistic city by preaching in the synagogue (Acts 9:20-22; 13:5, 14; 14:1; 17:1-3). In Acts 13:15 one sees the synagogue rulers asking Paul and Barnabas whether they would like to speak. Acts 18:8, 17 seems to indicate that two synagogue rulers in *Corinth (Crispus and Sosthenes) believed in Christ (see 1 Cor 1:1).

1.2. Sanhedrin. The Sanhedrin (*synedrion* in the NT) in Paul's day was composed of seventy-one men and included the high priest (Acts 23:1-5; Josephus, *Ant.* 4.8.14 §218). James VanderKam concludes his monograph on the high priesthood of the Second Temple period by calling the office "rich in sacerdotal and political associations," and the same can be said for the Sanhedrin as a whole, that is, it functioned as both a political and religious authority. In light of the link made by Tannaitic rabbis between the Sanhedrin and the seventy elders who worshiped God at Sinai with Moses (Ex 24:1, 9-11; t. Sanh. 1.6), to stand before the Sanhedrin was not a small matter (cf. Mt 5:22).

While the Talmud allowed for Jewish councils in cities outside Jerusalem (t. Sanh. 1.6; e.g., Josephus, *J.W.* 2.20.5 §§570-571), in the biblical record Paul does not stand trial before any except the Jerusalem Sanhedrin. This Sanhedrin included both a priestly component and a component of scribes, or teachers of Torah. The former were Sadducean in orientation, and the latter were primarily Pharisees. This accounts for Paul's ploy of splitting the council on the issue of the *resurrection, a point of disagreement between the two groups (Acts 23:6-9).

A third component within the Sanhedrin were the "elders," prominent men who were respected as leaders, though they were not of religious vocation (Mk 15:1; Acts 4:5, 8, 27-28; 23:14; 24:1; 25:15). Acts first presents Paul as a passive but approving accomplice of the Sanhedrin-led stoning of Stephen (Acts 6:12; 7:58; 8:1). It was after years of ministry that he was then a defendant before the Sanhedrin (Acts 22:30–23:9) and later sought to avoid a death plot in which the Sanhedrin was implicated (Acts 23:12-22).

1.3. High Priest. The high priesthood secured for itself a political function during the Maccabean period. From this time and throughout the ministry of Paul, the high priests were Sadducees. Yet Pharisees also continued to wield considerable influence. For example, VanderKam notes that though the Pharisees do not appear in Josephus's account of the long high priesthood of Hyrcanus II, they very likely influenced this high priest. The influence that a high priest (*archiereus* in the NT) held in Diaspora communities can be seen by Josephus's account (*Ant.* 14.10.20 §§241-242), in which it is evident that the high priest in Jerusalem sent documents on behalf of Jews in Laodicea so that they would be able to observe the Sabbath and live out their Jewish *identity in the Lycus Valley. Acts confirms such influence of the high priest outside Palestine, for Acts 9:1-2 describes how Paul had received arrest warrants for Jewish Christians in Damascus from the high priest. Acts 23:1-5; 25:2 show an older Paul, after years of Christian ministry, on the other side of the high priest's favor.

2. Roman Political System.

Officially still a republic, though referred to now as the early *empire, or the *principate*, first-century CE Rome ruled its provinces with a strong hand. Many provinces were ruled by the senatorial order, which provided proconsuls to adjudicate legal cases and maintain Rome's interests. Especially unstable provinces, such as Judea, or resource-rich provinces, such as Egypt, were identified as imperial provinces, over which the emperor's hand-picked representatives from the equestrian order ruled. Though *tradition indicates that Paul was executed by the Romans, Acts presents the Roman political system as identifying Paul as a just man. Acts typically describes the Romans rescuing Paul from Jewish hands, thus allowing him to continue his *witness (Acts 18:12-17; 21:27-40; 23:12-24). Also, it is at Roman expense that Paul the prisoner travels to Rome, a trip he had long anticipated (Rom 1:11-13; Acts 27:1–28:16). But this is not the whole story in the book of Acts. As Kavin Rowe so helpfully argues, Acts portrays the formation of an apocalyptic community that challenges the Greco-Roman status quo, including its political institutions.

2.1. Native Rulers. Rome's political efficiency during Paul's lifetime meant that it did not maintain a standardized bureaucracy with each province. Instead it typically ruled through the agency of native rulers of various cities and provinces who had pledged loyalty to Rome. Because of this one sees a variety of offices that correspond with the NT record of Paul's ministry.

2.1.1. City Magistrates. Unnamed city officials (*archontes*) appear in the Acts record of Paul's ministry. The rulers of Philippi handed Paul and Silas over for imprisonment after the latter pair had deprived some citizens of their means of livelihood by exorcizing a demon from their fortune-telling slave girl (Acts 16:16-24). City rulers (*politarchēs*) who were troubled by the disturbance raised in opposition to Paul's ministry are also mentioned in the account of Paul's visit to Thessalonica (Acts 17:8-9). "Some of the Asiarchs" are mentioned in Acts 19:31, counseling Paul not to appear before the violent Ephesian mob. These Asiarchs were probably native rulers of that area of Asia Minor, Greeks from the Hellenistic period who were entrusted by the Romans to rule it.

As Steven Friesen has indicated, the title "Asiarch" was probably used interchangeably with *agonothete*, an official of games of the period. The clerk (*grammateus*) of the Ephesian assembly is described in Acts 19:35-40 as talking his fellow citizens of the city out of mob *violence against Paul. Because this was a thoroughly Hellenized area of the empire, the Asiarchs conducted all their business of government in the Greek language. (See the commentaries for local background to these titles, accurately reproduced in Acts.)

2.1.2. Ethnarch of Aretas. The Nabataean ruler Aretas IV was ruling Damascus around the time of Paul's conversion. Herod Antipas married Aretas's daughter but later divorced her. The latter action led to Aretas's impulsive attack on Perea and defeat of Antipas. A Roman force under L. Vitellius was preparing to counterattack Aretas for this strike, but it withdrew at the news of Tiberius's death in March of 37 CE. It was Gaius Caligula, the next emperor, who gave Aretas jurisdiction over Damascus. Paul's description in 2 Corinthians 11:32 indicates that Aretas's deputy in charge (*ethnarchēs*) of the Jewish community there was poised to arrest Paul. (See 2 Corinthians commentaries by Furnish and Matera for the portrait of this ethnarch as an official under King Aretas, delegated to rule the Jewish population in or near Damascus.) This attempt to arrest him led to Paul's escape over the wall of Damascus (Acts 9:23-25).

2.1.3. Agrippa II. Marcus Julius Agrippa II lived in the court of Emperor Claudius until around 49 CE. At this time he was made the king of Chalcis (*Ituraea*). Then, in 53 CE, Agrippa's rule was moved to the territory formerly ruled by Herod Philip: Auranitis, Trachonitis, Batanaea, Gaulanitis, and Paneas. Abilene and Arcene were added at that time, and later Nero added parts of Galilee and Perea to his rule. Agrippa's capital was Caesarea Philippi, though he called it Neronias in honor of the emperor. Agrippa maintained a close working relationship with the Jewish leaders, since it was his responsibility to appoint the high priest and oversee the Jerusalem temple's finances. His position as native ruler in that region, a member of the Herodian dynasty, explains how he came to visit the Roman procurator Festus (Acts 25:13). Agrippa may have helped Festus draft the legal brief that was sent with Paul to Rome. His familiarity with Judaism accounts for Paul's appeal to Agrippa's belief in the OT prophets and Agrippa's sympathetic response to Paul (Acts 26:27-32).

2.2. Centurion. This military officer (*hekatontarchēs* in the NT) served to enforce Rome's political rule in the provinces. There were five or six centurions per cohort. (Each cohort contained from five hundred to one thousand men; there were ten cohorts per legion.) Some men rose to the post of centurion after serving in the legion as *principalis* or as a junior officer. Other centurions were promoted from the praetorian guard, either during their active service or after the retirement that followed sixteen years of service in the guard. Finally, some equestrians or city leaders (such as decurions) could be appointed to the post of centurion. Against the stereotype that the centurion rose from within the legion's ranks, the first of the three paths just mentioned, Adrian Goldsworthy leans toward the last path—appointment from the outside—as the most common route to the post.

Whatever the path to centurion, men were attracted to the post because of its high salary and retirement benefits. In the NT record of Paul's travels, centurions appear as favorable officers who rescue Paul from the mob (Acts 21:32), help him escape beating (Acts 22:25-26), guard him (Acts 24:23), and take him to Rome (Acts 27:1). The only centurion named is Julius of the Sebastian cohort (Acts 27:1), which probably indicates that he was from an auxiliary cohort with the honorific title *Augusta.* Paul must have come into frequent contact with centurions during his imprisonments (Phil 1:13-14).

2.3. Military Tribune. The *tribunus militum* (*chiliarchos* in the NT) served as leader of a Roman legion. There were usually six tribunes per legion. During Paul's time these officers were taken from either senatorial or equestrian orders. Acts shows a tribune rescuing Paul from a mob (Acts 21:31-33; 24:7), respecting Paul's *citizenship (Acts 22:29), listening readily to the report of a plot against Paul (Acts 23:18-22), and attending Paul's speech before Festus and Agrippa (Acts 25:23). The only tribune named in the NT record about Paul is Claudius Lysias (Acts 23:26; 24:7, 22). The exchange he has with Paul about citizenship (Acts 22:26-28) indicates that he was a freedman of the emperor Claudius who had been granted equestrian status. The "large amount of money" (Acts 22:28) does not refer to a price he paid for his *freedom but rather a bribe to officials in Caesar's bureaucracy or the provincial government, who put his name on the list of people to be granted citizenship. Indeed, the demand for Roman citizenship and its privileges led to a lucrative business for some imperial officials (Tacitus, *Ann.* 14.50.1). The importance of the tribune's office is seen by Felix's comment that he will wait until Lysias the tribune arrives to pass judgment on Paul's case (Acts 24:22).

2.4. Proconsul. Both the titles of proconsul (*anthypatos* in the NT) and procurator (see 2.5 below) designate officials who functioned as governors of Roman provinces. The proconsuls functioned as independent administrators of Roman provinces under the Senate's rule in one-year terms of office. Selected by lot, proconsuls in the republic and principate were typically ex-consuls or ex-praetors, therefore of the senatorial order. As representative of the consuls, this post was officially under authority of the Roman senate rather than the emperor, at least through Paul's lifetime.

But this in no way means that the proconsuls functioned as deputies of the senate. Their appointment as proconsuls gave them *imperium*, or ultimate administrative power, including the power to inflict capital punishment. Invested with *imperium*, the proconsul had no obligation to consult with the Roman senate for his decisions. Practically, as long as he did not offend the wealthy citizens in his province, he had no worries about censure from Rome. Indeed, the common provincial had little recourse in the face of a proconsular decision. The only legal constraints on a proconsul's decisions in the first century were laws against extortion and treason and part of the *lex Iulia* that protected citizens from undeserved execution. The proconsul's influence over the provincials was also limited by the manner in which his yearlong administration of a province was conducted. Proconsuls typically moved on a circuit of the major cities in their provinces to hear litigants. This meant that there was no center for efficient administration of the whole province.

Paul's appearance before Gallio, proconsul of Achaia (Acts 18:12), shows that the plaintiffs were sufficient in number or persistence to get a hearing. This is noted because there was no guarantee that litigants' cases would be heard, given the proconsul's itinerant court that could move on to the next judicial center before all of one city's cases were heard. Besides their judicial function, proconsuls also inspected public buildings for needed repairs, maintained the water supply for the province through aqueducts or other means, and participated in municipal governance when they wanted. Both proconsuls mentioned in Acts are portrayed as positive influences in the spread of the *gospel.

2.4.1. Sergius Paulus. Sergius Paulus is the proconsul of Cyprus described in the record of Paul's first missionary journey (Acts 13:6-7). This proconsul is not attested in pagan literature, but one does find his name on ancient coins of Cyprus (*Catalogue of the Greek Coins of Cyprus*, 119-21). The Soloi inscription, found on Cyprus, provides evidence that a Sergius Paulus was active there in 54 CE (*IGRR* 3.930). Inscriptions from Rome mention a Sergius Paulus as responsible for the Tiber River during the reign of Claudius, and someone by the same name as consul in the year 70 CE (CIL 6.31545; 6.253). William Ramsay and J. G. C. Anderson found an inscription near Psidian Antioch that identifies a son of Sergius Paulus as tribune of Legio VI Ferrata. The Sergii Pauli were a senatorial family of the first century; the name therefore fits one of consular status. The account in Acts says that this proconsul believed the message of Paul and Barnabas after seeing the divine *judgment Paul brought against Elymas the magician. It has been suggested that Sergius Paulus adopted Saul and that this accounts for the apostle's name change from Saul to Paul after a description of the proconsul's conversion in Acts 13:12-13.

2.4.2. *Gallio.* Lucius Annaeus Novatus Gallio was a proconsul of Achaia, the province that included Corinth. The brother of Seneca the philosopher, Gallio had been adopted by the senator Lucius Junius Gallio and therefore took his patron's name. After Seneca's political ruin, Gallio of necessity committed suicide. Paul's appearance before Gallio (Acts 18:12-17) has been a crucial starting point for some who construct a *chronology of his ministry, since the letter in the Gallio inscription can be dated between January 25 and July 31 in 52 CE (SIG 2.801). Gallio is amply attested in pagan literature (Cassius Dio, *Hist.* 61.35.2-4; 62.20.1; Seneca, *Ep.* 104.1; Tacitus, *Ann.* 15.73.4). Some, including Klaus Haacker (in *ABD*), do not think that Seneca's reference to Gallio as proconsul refers to his service in that office in either 51–52 or 52–53 CE.

2.5. Procurator. This title (*hēgemōn* in the NT) designates a post in the lesser Roman provinces equivalent to that of governor. The title had been used earlier of financial administrators in provinces under senatorial rule, but its use as the title for governor is the only way it is used in the NT. The procurator was normally of the equestrian order and directly appointed by the emperor to rule as his agent in the province for as long as the emperor wished.

2.5.1. *Felix.* Marcus Antonius Felix was procurator of Judea when Paul stood trial before him (Acts 24:1-21). Felix agreed to try Paul even though Paul was not from the geographical area under Felix's responsibility (Acts 23:34-35) because it was probably under the imperial legate of Syria, who did not need to be bothered by an individual's case. Also, Paul's home city of Tarsus was considered a free city, which meant that its citizens were not required to stand trial in their own provincial courts.

A freedman of Emperor Claudius's mother, Antonia, Felix may have come to Samaria in 52 CE as procurator. Felix's brother Pallas was in charge of the emperor's financial accounts and managed to obtain equestrian ranking for his brother and positions normally held by this order, such as procurator. This promotion of a freedman to the equestrian order and appointment to posts in the normal equestrian career was scandalous in the highly stratified Roman society (Suetonius, *Claud.* 25.1.28) and illustrates how easily Claudius was influenced by those in the imperial household. Like Paul, Felix was also accused by the Jews of wrongdoing. He was appointed procurator for Judea, but social upheaval increased during his tenure, and he was replaced by Festus in 59 CE.

2.5.2. *Festus.* Porcius Festus took over from Felix the responsibility for Paul's trial (Acts 25:1-8) when he relieved the latter of his post as procurator of Judea. His plan to try Paul in Jerusalem formed the pretext for Paul's appeal for trial before Caesar (Acts 25:9-12). Festus led battles against militant Jewish opposition and took part in a dispute between King Agrippa II and Jewish leaders. He died in 62 CE; his position as procurator of Judea was then filled by Albinus.

2.6. Praetorians. From the time of Sejanus's consolidation of the praetorian guard in a single, established base on the eastern side of Rome in 23 CE, the praetorians became a political force in Roman life. In 41 CE, after the murder of Gaius, it was the praetorians who saluted Claudius as emperor while the senate was considering reinstatement of the republic. By this action they ensured that the principate would continue and that Claudius would be the next emperor. Elite soldiers who were paid very well, the praetorians served for terms of sixteen years. The praetorians guarded the emperor and his family members in Rome and abroad. Paul's statement that the cause of his imprisonment was well known throughout the whole praetorian guard (Phil 1:13) is strong but not by itself sufficient evidence for the Roman provenance of Philippians.

The leader of the praetorian guard, the praetorian prefect, had a great deal of political power. Since Nero had announced at the beginning of his reign that he would not judge cases personally (Tacitus, *Ann.* 13.4.2), it is thought that the praetorian prefect took this responsibility. If Paul appeared in Caesar's court for trial soon after the time period covered in Acts, it is very likely that the praetorian prefect was his actual judge.

2.7. Caesar's Household. This term designates the slaves and freedmen who served in both personal and political capacities for the imperial family. There was a significant distinction in status within this *household; slaves or freed persons entrusted with financial matters held highest status and exercised significant power. From the reign of Augustus these slaves and freed persons were entrusted with power previously reserved for men of equestrian or senatorial orders. The resulting status dissonance disturbed Roman nobility and began undermining the highly structured Roman social order. Caesar's household thus constituted the elite civil service, as is shown by the phenomenon that freeborn women would marry men of servile classes in this household. Indeed, Weaver's study of imperial slaves and freedmen reveals that two-thirds or higher of their marriages were to freeborn women. While the partners would not hold the right of *conubium*, these marriages across class lines to imperial slaves at times were accorded legal recognition because of the status and political power of the imperial slaves and freedmen.

Paul's mention of Caesar's household in Philippians 4:22 is another piece of evidence for the Roman provenance of the letter, though members of the imperial household did serve in other cities of the empire. It also shows that the Christian message had made significant inroads into the imperial court. At least two groups mentioned in Romans 16 may designate members of the imperial household. "Those of Aristobulus" (Rom 16:10) might refer to the former slaves of Aristobulus, the younger brother of Agrippa I. Since he was a member of the Herodian family and the immediately preceding name is Herodion, this identification is quite likely. Aristobulus lived in Rome and was a friend of Claudius (Josephus, *Ant.* 18.5.4 §§133, 135). If he passed on his property to the emperor, his slaves would have been members of Caesar's household when Paul wrote Romans. "Those of Narcissus who are in the Lord" (Rom 16:11) may signify the family of Tiberius Claudius Narcissus, a rich freedman who wielded much influence in Claudius's imperial household. Nero executed Narcissus shortly after he came to power (Tacitus, *Ann.* 13.1.4; Cassius Dio, *Hist.* 60.34), but his slaves would still have remained in Caesar's household.

2.8. Caesars. Four emperors reigned during Paul's lifetime. He was born during the reign of Tiberius (14–37 CE), called to be an *apostle of *Christ to the nations probably during the reign of Gaius Caligula (37–41 CE), and ministered mostly during the reigns of Claudius (41–54 CE) and Nero (54–68 CE). By the time of Paul the office of emperor (*kaisar* in the NT) was not simply "first among equals" but dictator. Claudius and Nero are the emperors most significant in the consideration of Paul's ministry and letters.

2.8.1. Claudius. Tiberius Claudius Nero Germanicus (10 BCE–54 CE) received little notice in the reigns of Augustus or Tiberius. While alternate consul with his nephew, Gaius Caligula, the latter did not mark him as successor. His accession in 41 CE was therefore a surprise, brought on by the political muscle of the praetorians (see 2.6 above). Claudius's daughter Octavia was Nero's first wife. Claudius was known for being easily swayed by his wives and those closest to him in the imperial household (Suetonius, *Claud.* 25, 29).

Paul met Priscilla and Aquila as a result of Claudius's edict that expelled Jews from Rome (49 CE; Acts 18:1-2). While this edict might be partially due to Claudius's love of Roman traditions and religion, one must note that Claudius exerted significant effort to end the social upheavals in Alexandria and Judea resulting from Gaius's anti-Semitism. Paul's missionary effort (Rom 15:17-24) may have been influenced by Claudius's expansionistic drive, which resulted in adding provinces and extending citizenship. In any event, Paul at least uses language of Roman military policy when he describes his apostolic commission in his letter to the Romans (see Rom 1:5; 15:18; 16:26; *Res Gestae Divi Augusti* §26.1).

2.8.2. Nero. Nero Claudius Caesar (37–68 CE) is the emperor first known to have persecuted Christians (Tacitus, *Ann.* 15.44) and was reigning at the time of Paul's execution. When Nero acceded to the throne in 54 CE, he was under the influence of his powerful mother, Agrippina. Seneca and the praetorian prefect Burrus did much to lead the empire during the first five years of his reign. Helpful legislation was enacted (Tacitus, *Ann.* 13.51), and competent governors were appointed. It must be noted that Paul wrote Romans 13:4 in the context of his directives on civil obedience during this period of Nero's reign.

But in 59 CE, after his matricide of Agrippina, the death of Burrus and Seneca's retirement, Nero began to lead as he wished, establishing games, founding a *gymnasium*, and singing in public. Those closest to him were of low birth or freedmen of Greek or Asian descent. They were known for their arrogance. Nero's lavish spending on himself and the cost of wars in Armenia and Britain induced him to take money from the rich. By 62 CE people at a variety of levels in Roman society hated him. In 64 Nero was suspected of starting the great fire in Rome in order to build a bigger palace and gain more land for his gardens. He blamed the fire on Christians and began executing them (Tacitus, *Ann.* 15.44). It is probable that Paul was executed circa 64–65 CE, after trial in Nero's court.

Then a conspiracy to assassinate Nero and install Calpurnius Piso as emperor was discovered in 65 CE, and Nero executed all who were implicated. Paranoid of rebellion from this time on, he killed anyone whom he suspected. In 67 Nero toured Greece, granting it tax immunity. He was summoned back to Rome after the city had experienced famine and there was increasing dissatisfaction with his reign. Arriving in Rome in January of 68, he was unable to reverse the political tide. Beginning in March, three officials in various parts of the empire revolted. When the praetorians removed their support from Nero, he left Rome on June 9, 68 CE, and committed suicide. Paul's martyrdom in Nero's court was certainly tragic in its time, though T. R. Glover's comment that the day would come when men would name their sons Paul and their dogs Nero shows the justice that the passage of time brings.

See also CITIZENSHIP; EMPIRE; LEGAL SYSTEM, ROMAN; PAUL AND JUDAISM; PAUL IN ACTS; POLITICS AND POWER.

BIBLIOGRAPHY. **F. F. Bruce,** *Paul: Apostle of the Heart Set Free* (Grand Rapids, MI: Eerdmans, 1977); **P. A. Brunt,** "Procuratorial Jurisdiction," *Latomus* 25 (1966): 461-89; **G. P. Burton,** "Proconsuls, Assizes and the Administration of Justice Under the Empire," *JRS* 65 (1975): 92-106; **T. W. Davis,** "New Testament Archaeology Beyond the Gospels," in *The Oxford Handbook of Early Christian Archaeology*, ed. D. K. Pettegrew, W. R. Caraher, and T. W. David (New York: Oxford University Press, 2019), 47-66; **S. J. Friesen,** "Asiarchs," *Zeitschrift für Papyrologie und Epigraphik* 126 (1999): 275-90; **V. P. Furnish,** *II Corinthians*, AB 32A (Garden City, NY: Doubleday, 1984); **P. Garnsey and R. Saller,** *The Roman Empire: Economy, Society and Culture* (Berkeley: University of California, 1987); **A. Goldsworthy,** *The Complete Roman Army* (London: Thames & Hudson, 2003); **K. Haacker,** "Die Gallio-Episode und die paulinische Chronologie," *BZ* 16 (1972): 252-55; idem, "Gallio," *ABD* 2:901-3; **S. Hornblower and A. Spawforth,** eds., *Oxford Classical Dictionary*, 3rd rev. ed. (Oxford: Oxford University Press, 2003); **L. Levine,** *The Ancient Synagogue: The First Thousand Years*, 2nd ed. (New Haven, CT: Yale University Press, 2005); **E. Lohse,** "συνέδριον," *TDNT* 7:860-71; **S. Mandell,** "Who Paid the Temple Tax When the Jews Were Under Roman Rule?," *HTR* 77 (1984): 223-32; **F. J. Matera,** *II Corinthians: A Commentary*, NTL (Louisville: Westminster John Knox, 2003); **F. Millar,** "The Emperor, the Senate and the Provinces," *JRS* 56 (1966) 156-66; **A. Momigliano,** *Claudius: The Emperor and His Achievement* (Oxford: Clarendon, 1934); **A. M. Rabello,** "The Legal Condition of the Jews in the Roman Empire," *ANRW* 2/13:662-762; **T. Rajak and D. Noy,** "*Archisynagogi*: Office, Title and Social Status in the Greco-Jewish Synagogue," *JRS* 83 (1993): 75-95; **C. K. Rowe,** *World Upside Down: Reading Acts in the Graeco-Roman Age* (New York: Oxford University Press, 2009); **S. Safrai and M. Stern,** eds., *The Jewish People in the First Century*, vol. 1, Compendia Rerum Iudaicarum ad Novum Testamentum (Philadelphia: Fortress, 1974); **A. N. Sherwin-White,** *Roman Society and Roman Law in the New Testament: The Sarum Lectures 1960–1961* (repr., Grand Rapids, MI: Baker, 1978); **J. C. VanderKam,** *From Joshua to Caiaphas: High Priests After the Exile* (Minneapolis: Fortress, 2004); **P. R. C. Weaver,** *Familia Caesaris: A Social Study of the Emperor's Freedmen and Slaves* (Cambridge: Cambridge University Press, 1972).

M. Reasoner

POLITICS AND POWER

While scholars sift Paul's writings for evidence of imperial struggle, Paul targets *Satan with his *ministry of reconciliation. Indeed, conflict with *empire occurs, but the *cross of *Christ clarifies the true enemy and the definition of power: *replacing *death with life*. Indeed, Paul's *conversion and subsequent *mission to the *Gentiles embody this cruciform paradigm. His life imitated Christ, and his writings call the *church to do the same.

1. Imperial Inquiry
2. Imperial Interaction
3. Clarifying the Enemy
4. The Paradigm of Christ's Cross
5. The Definition of Power
6. Christ's Power in Paul's Politics
7. The Politics of God's People
8. Conclusion

1. Imperial Inquiry.

In the late twentieth and early twenty-first centuries, empire studies emerged in NT scholarship with force. While scholarship in this field existed earlier (e.g., Deissmann), a distinct shift is evident in more recent projects, with meticulous and persistent probing of individual verses for power dynamics and political insights. From Gospel studies to the book of Revelation, scholars such as Richard Horsley, Warren Carter, and Neil Elliott, among many others, focus on questions of empire, providing fresh interpretations of familiar texts. This empire-centered hermeneutic uses interdisciplinary approaches to examine the text from the perspective of an imperial subject with the purpose of resurrecting the marginalized voice.

During this time scholarly projects on power and politics in Paul have predominantly centered on various iterations of "How does Paul *interact* with the Roman Empire?" Unfortunately, as empire studies has progressed, in Pauline literature and elsewhere, the question has begun to morph into "How does Paul *subvert* the Roman Empire?" Such a shift has real consequences for historical inquiry and exegetical integrity.

When subversion becomes the *only* option for the exegete, the voice of the subject becomes marginalized once again. Imperial inquiry in a text must allow for acquiescence as well as resistance to empire. As the work of James Scott and postcolonial critics has uncovered (e.g., Homi Bhabha, Fernando Segovia, R. S. Sugirtharajah), those who are subjected to an empire are far more complex than the clear-cut categories of for or against. Analysis of a subject text must allow for nuance and ambivalence regarding the empire. Interpreters must allow for resistance, compliance, both, or neither to adequately answer the question, "How does Paul *interact* with the Roman Empire?" Without the full range of options, exegetes ironically suppress the very voices they intend to resurrect.

2. Imperial Interaction.
Studies of empire in Paul's letters have yielded discordant results. Both acquiescent *and* anti-imperial elements are present in Paul's writings. At times Paul seems unconcerned or unmoved by the Roman Empire altogether, as if his gaze were somewhere else entirely. Such variety creates further intrigue around the question, "How does Paul *interact* with the Roman Empire?"

Anti-imperial elements are present throughout Paul's writings in varied degrees. For example, in 1 Thessalonians 5:3 Paul writes, "While some are proclaiming, 'Peace and security,' suddenly destruction overtakes them, just as labor pains in pregnancy, and they absolutely will not escape." While scholars squabble over whether *pax et securitas* ("*peace and security") is in fact a Roman slogan, the text's target is clear: the Roman Empire. This verse directly follows the depiction of Christ's future royal procession (1 Thess 4:13-18) and directly precedes imagery and exhortations centered on military armor (1 Thess 5:8). This is a subject text situated in an empire whose message—emblazoned on coins, architecture, and dinnerware, and enacted in public rituals—declared worldwide dominance through which *pax* was secured, offering divine protection and prosperity to those aligned with Rome (Wood, 77-109). In such a context, "peace and security" conjures connections to Rome in the same way "pledge of allegiance" invokes parallels to America. Thus, in 1 Thessalonians 5:3, Paul envisions the destruction of the Roman Empire at the coming of Christ, a proclamation impossible to confuse as compliant from a sovereign or a subject's perspective.

Yet Paul also exhorts Christians to actions and dispositions of imperial compliance. For example, in Titus 3:1-2, Paul admonishes Titus to "remind the people to submit to rulers [*archais*] and authorities [*exousiais*]," specifying that they are "to slander no one" and at all times show "gentleness to all people"—a sentiment reminiscent of Romans 13:1-5. While it is irresponsible to consider these passages "pro-Roman" endorsements (Elliott 1997, 184-204), the commands and contexts hardly portray a call to arms against the empire. In 1 Timothy 2:1-4 Paul instructs Timothy to offer "pleas, prayers, intercessions, and thanksgivings" to the Lord on behalf of "all people," even specifying "for kings and all those in high positions." Such prayers, according to 1 Timothy 2:3-4, "please *God our *savior" because God "desires all humanity to be saved," which, in context, includes the emperor.

Therefore, to properly assess the query "How does Paul *interact* with the Roman Empire?" one must resist the temptation to alter it to "How does Paul *subvert* the Roman Empire?" Predisposing Paul's relation to power and politics with anti-imperial intent distorts the tension present in his writings, at times resistant to empire and at others compliant, and many commentators tend to obscure this tension. Instead of alleviating the tension between resistance and compliance in Paul's writings, what is needed is a paradigm through which both elements are not incidental but essential—the natural outworking of Paul's political perspective.

3. Clarifying the Enemy.
When scholars reduce Paul's relation to power and politics to "interaction with the Roman Empire," the

evidence is distorted by limiting its scope. Rome is indeed present in the discourse, but Paul consistently situates the conflict on a cosmic scale that *includes* Rome while *superseding* Rome's reach.

In Ephesians 6:10-17 Paul issues a call to arms, encouraging the church to assemble the appropriate "weapons and armor" (Eph 6:13) to fight the true enemy at hand: "the devil" (Eph 6:11). To dispel any confusion, Paul in Ephesians 6:12 stresses the identity of the primary adversary with vivid detail: "Our fight is not against blood and *flesh, but against the powers, against the authorities, against the cosmic rulers of this darkness, against the spiritual forces of evil in the heavenlies." The military garb that follows is only rendered sensible if "the devil" is the primary target: "Because of this [enemy], take up all the weapons and armor of God . . . the belt of *truth . . . the breastplate of righteousness . . . the shield of *faith . . . the helmet of *salvation . . . the sword of the Spirit" (Eph 6:13-17). If Rome is Paul's primary adversary, he advocates for a decidedly ineffective assault. Yet if Paul's target is cosmic in nature, the weapons are remarkably poised for warfare.

The "spiritual forces of evil in the heavenlies" in Ephesians 6 are the same satanic enemy identified throughout Pauline literature with various descriptions that follow the same trajectory: "the ruler [*archonta*] of the power of the air, the spirit now operating in the sons of disobedience" (Eph 2:2; see 1 Cor 2:6-8; Col 1:15-16); "the dominion of darkness" (Col 1:13); "the adversary" (*Satanas*—1 Tim 5:15; 1 Cor 7:5; 2 Cor 2:11; 11:14). Time and again, Paul identifies the true enemy as "not blood and flesh," yet nevertheless potent and worthy of confrontation.

Even when human enemies are identified, Paul typically telescopes the *narrative to unveil the primary adversary: Satan. So, in 1 Thessalonians 2:14-16, Jewish hostiles "pursued and drove out [*ekdiōxantōn*]" Paul and his companions from Thessalonica. Nevertheless, Paul characterizes the separation as the work of spiritual forces of evil, emphatically concluding: "*Satan* blocked us" (1 Thess 2:18; see also 2 Cor 12:7). For Paul, even in the face of tangible conflict, Eden clarifies the true enemy. So, in the concluding lines of his letter to the Romans, with edenic undertones, Paul pronounces, "the God of peace will soon crush the adversary [*Satanan*] under your feet" (Rom 16:20).

Clarifying the enemy provides an entry point to Paul's paradigm of power and politics. For Paul, the Roman Empire is the tangible manifestation of a far grander narrative, centered on war "not against blood and flesh" but against "the dominion of darkness." This does not mean Rome is ignored or bypassed in the assault. Paul's target *includes* Rome even if it cannot be *summarized* by Rome. A depiction of Rome's utter destruction (1 Thess 5:3), then, is merely an image of collateral damage in a much larger war. Even if Rome provides the grammar for the conflict (e.g., Col 2:15-16), Eden provides the target.

To reduce power and politics in Paul down to interaction with the Roman Empire is to regionalize a conversation that for Paul is cosmic. Paul is not disinterested in the empire; Rome is simply too small a target. Paul is not affirming the empire's politics; Rome just does not matter as much as the empire presumes. Paul's paradigm of power and politics is not governed by the Roman Empire but by the cross of Christ.

4. The Paradigm of Christ's Cross.

In 1 Corinthians 1:18-30 Paul unveils "Christ crucified" (1 Cor 1:23) as the "power [*dynamin*] of God and *wisdom [*sophian*] of God" (1 Cor 1:24). This revelation offers a lens through which all definitions of power, victory, politics, enemies, *suffering, mission, and ministry can be seen. Christ's cross discloses a "*mystery that has been hidden" since Eden yet written "before time began" (1 Cor 2:7; see Rom 16:25; Rev 13:8).

In 1 Corinthians 1:18, Paul juxtaposes two perspectives that define the cross with stark contrast. For "those who are spiritually lost" (*apollymenois*) the cross is "foolishness" (*mōria*); for "those who are being saved" (*sōzomenois*), the cross is the "power [*dynamis*] of God." This ideological collision over the cross is understandable. Crucifixion was a Roman tool of torture and execution typically reserved for political revolutionaries; it declared Roman supremacy over its subjects. Paul, though, classifies it here and elsewhere as a paragon of victory, where God "disarmed the rulers [*archas*] and authorities [*exousias*]" and "exposed them in a public spectacle, leading them in a triumphal procession [*thriambeusas*] by the cross" (Col 2:15).

If Rome is the chief enemy, Paul's perspective borders on disingenuous, rendering the previous verse and others like it nonsensical or even foolish. Yet Paul preaches that, through the cross of Christ, redemption is found, victory secured, and the true enemy unveiled *and* plundered: "For [God] has *rescued us* from the *dominion of darkness* and transformed us into the kingdom of the Son he loves, in whom we have redemption, the *forgiveness of sins" (Col 1:13-14; see Rom 5:9). The cross as Christ's point of victory confirms the cosmic, satanic kingdom as the primary adversary and unveils the power and wisdom of God that transforms Christ's death into an empty tomb.

Indeed, Christ's *resurrection converts the defeat of the cross into the moment of his royal coronation. As Paul explains, when God's "power" (*kratous*) raised "Christ from the dead," Jesus ascended to the throne of sovereignty, seated "at [God's] right hand in the heavenlies, far above all rule [*archēs*] and authority [*exousias*], power [*dynameōs*] and dominion, and every name invoked, not only in this age but also in the one to come" (Eph 1:19-21). Coupled with the empty tomb, the cross clarifies and secures God's sovereignty, supreme authority over things seen and unseen, over Rome and the dominion of darkness.

Paul, then, embraces the cross as not just salvation but the revelation of God's power and wisdom, shattering all earlier understandings of power and wisdom. Foolishness is frustrated through God's victory on the cross; intellect is overcome by the crucified king (1 Cor 1:19). The cross of Christ contained a divine mystery (1 Cor 2:7) unveiled by the resurrection. Indeed, "none of the rulers of this age had comprehended" this cruciform wisdom, "for had they understood, they would not have crucified the Lord of *glory" (1 Cor 2:8). Yet they did crucify him, and Paul celebrates this paradoxical paradigm of power and politics "taught by the Spirit" to those with "the mind of Christ" (1 Cor 2:9-17).

The mystery of Christ's victory on the cross clarifies how God's *kingdom now advances on earth: by loving enemies instead of annihilating them. On the cross, in the face of the sneers and jeers of Jews and Gentiles alike, Jesus cried out, "Father, forgive them; for they do not know what they are doing" (Lk 23:34). In this moment, the divine mystery and methodology were on full display: on the cross, God targeted his enemies with peace and reconciliation. As Paul reveals, "For God was pleased to have all his *fullness dwell in him, and through him to reconcile to himself all things, whether things on earth or things in heaven, by making peace through his blood, shed on the cross" (Col 1:19-20 NIV). Whereas the dominion of darkness works to obliterate its enemies, the cruciform wisdom works to convert enemies into co-heirs with Christ (Rom 8:12-17). The power of the cross works to transform *all* (Col 1:21-23; 2:13-14; see also Rom 3:25; 5:10; Eph 1:7), so that those who "were far away" from God, ensnared by the adversary, can now be "brought near by the blood of Christ" (Eph 2:13; see also Rom 12:14-21).

Thus, for Paul, Christ is "*head over every power and authority" (Col 2:10) precisely *because* he was executed on a Roman cross on behalf of his enemies. This cruciform inversion is not just blind optimism reinventing a bad situation as good. It is the pinnacle of scholarly pursuits (1 Cor 1:20), the zenith of philosophical inquiry (1 Cor 1:20), the treasure sought by the Jews, who "plead for signs," and the Greeks, who "search for wisdom" (1 Cor 1:22). Christ crucified, while "scandalous to the Jews" and "foolishness to the Gentiles" (1 Cor 1:23), unveils a divine paradigm through which power, weakness, nobility, and insignificance are redefined from a divine perspective. This is why Paul's epiphany of "Christ crucified" in 1 Corinthians 1:18-25 climaxes with a cruciform appraisal of the Corinthian church:

> Consider your own *calling, brothers and sisters: not many of you were wise [*sophoi*] according to human standards, not many powerful [*dynatoi*], not many noble-born. Yet God chose the foolish things of the world to shame the wise; God chose the weak things of the world to shame the strong; God chose the ignoble-born of the world and the contemptible things—the things that are not, in order to render powerless [*katargēsē*] the things that are. (1 Cor 1:26-28)

If the cross secures victory over Satan, then it transforms how one sees and engages all things, including the empire and even one's self.

The paradigm of the cross reorients everything seen and unseen through "the power of God and wisdom of God" (1 Cor 1:24). Yes, Christ was "crucified in weakness, yet he lives by God's power" (*dynameōs*, 2 Cor 13:4). Thus "Christ crucified" (1 Cor 1:23; see 1 Cor 2:2) contains a revelation and a definition of power undiscovered by the politics of Rome and unappreciated by the dominion of darkness.

5. The Definition of Power.

Contained in the cross-centered paradigm is Paul's definition of power. This definition governs Paul's politics and organizes the actions, mission, and ministry of those who follow Christ.

Power appears in a variety of contexts throughout Paul's writings, but a common theme is discernible: *creation. The act of creation (or God as "creator") is the *foundation* for Paul's definition of power. In Romans 1:20, Paul writes, "For from the creation [*ktiseōs*] of the world, God's unseen qualities [*aorata*] are seen clearly, being understood from what was made—both his eternal power [*dynamis*] and divine nature." Like the cross, creation reveals God's power and sovereignty.

With similar language, in Colossians 1:15-20 Paul describes Jesus as "the image of the unseen [*aoratou*]

God" (Col 1:15), who is sovereign over creation because of his role as Creator: "For in him all things were created [*ektisthē*] in the heavens and on the earth, the seen [*orata*] and the unseen [*aorata*]—whether thrones or sovereign powers or rulers [*archai*] or authorities [*exousiai*]—all things have been created [*ektistai*] through him and for him" (Col 1:16). Paul extends the discourse on Christ's power beyond creation to redemption—or *re*-creation through the cross: "For God was pleased to have all his fullness dwell in him, and through him to reconcile to himself all things, whether things on earth or things in heaven, by making peace through his blood, shed on the cross" (Col 1:19-20 NIV). The cross's ability to "make peace" demonstrates its power to restore creation, to set the wrongs of Eden right, to create anew what was distorted by *sin and death. Additionally, Paul celebrates this power of *re*-creation in the life of the Christian who was "buried together with Christ in *baptism" only to be "raised to life together with him" (Col 2:12). Indeed, "you were dead in your sins," yet, through the power of the cross, "God made you alive together with [Jesus]" (Col 2:13).

For Paul, then, power is defined by the act of creation or *re*-creation. Power is "giving life," as God did in Genesis 1; power is "replacing death with life," as Christ did on the cross. For example, in the description of *Abraham and Sarah in Romans 4:19-21, the "deadness [*nekrōsin*] of Sara's womb" (Rom 4:19b) prohibited the "promise of God" from bearing fruit through Abraham's line. But Abraham's faith did not waver. He was "fully persuaded that God had power [*dynatos*] to do what he had promised" (Rom 4:21)—to replace death with life.

Instead of the "ability to take life" (as Satan and the Roman Empire do), Paul defines power as "the ability to give life" (as creation and the cross do). In Romans 5, Paul contrasts these two definitions through two figures representing two regimes: *Adam—the "reign of death" (Rom 5:12-14, 17); Jesus—the "reign of life" (Rom 5:15-17). Each kingdom defines power differently. "The reign of death" uses power to destroy, to take life, to attempt *un*-creation; "the reign of life" uses power to restore, to give life, to accomplish *re*-creation. These two kingdom powers collide in the crucifixion. Christ's power on the cross *re*-creates death itself, repurposing it to *give* life instead of *take* it: "We know this: that our old self was crucified with him so that the body ruled by sin might cease to be, that we might no longer be slaves to sin. For anyone who has died has been set free from sin. But if we died with Christ, we trust that we will also live together with him" (Rom 6:6-9). Christ's life-giving power transforms death itself, since through *his* death, the dead in Christ are resurrected, no longer imprisoned by death as *slaves to sin.

In Paul, power is "replacing death with life." This is why Paul describes the *law as "powerless [*adynaton*]," for it was incapable of producing life (Rom 8:3). In contrast, the Spirit of God, who "lives in you" (Rom 8:9), works to "make you alive" (Rom 8:11)—*re*-creating believers as "children of God" who are "led by the Spirit of God" (Rom 8:14).

6. Christ's Power in Paul's Politics.

At its core, politics is the organization of a group of people, directing decisions, values, actions, power, conflict, conduct. To articulate a group's politics can prove difficult since it is all-encompassing. Many methods and measurements exist, but how a group treats those outside its community (how the group uses its power) provides significant insight into its overall allegiance (its politics). The kingdom of death uses its power to destroy, while the kingdom of Christ uses its power to reconcile. The respective definitions of power are embodied in the actions of the followers of each regime. Thus, in death, like the law, humans do not produce life, for death destroys and takes life. In Christ, through the Spirit, humans are agents of life, for Christ replaces death with life and *re*-creates the sinner as a saint (Rom 5:12-17). Paul's conversion provides a dramatic contrast between these competing paradigms of power and politics.

Before Paul's conversion to the kingdom of Christ, his ministry was quite different. As a Pharisee and "Hebrew of Hebrews" (Phil 3:5), Paul was "violently persecuting the church of God and trying to destroy it" (Gal 1:13). Why? To preserve the *purity and integrity of God and his law (Phil 3:6). Yet after encountering the risen Christ (1 Cor 15:8; also Gal 1:12), Paul's paradigm strikingly shifted. Instead of being a persecutor of Christians and an enemy to Gentiles, Paul pursued *all* with *grace, life, and *love.

Paul's conversion shifted his paradigm of power and politics from that of the kingdom of death to that of the kingdom of Christ, significantly affecting how he treated his enemies. Instead of obliterating enemies, as the kingdom of death does, the kingdom of Christ transforms enemies into friends. Once again, the cross provides the paradigm: "While we were still sinners [or enemies], Christ died on our behalf" (Rom 5:8). The conduct of a Christian, Paul included, is governed by the cruciform definition of power: giving life. Even to enemies.

This explains Paul's conversion and subsequent mission to the Gentiles. Paul declares in Romans 15:15-16 that due to "the grace of God" (Rom 15:15) he was transformed into "a minister of Christ Jesus to the Gentiles, serving as a priest the good news of God" (Rom 15:16). The shift in paradigm is evident in the next phrase, heralding Paul's priestly purpose: "so that the Gentiles might become an offering acceptable to God, having been made holy by the *Holy Spirit" (Rom 15:16). Paul's work targeted enemies of the cross with the same grace God used to transform him, the self-declared "chief of sinners" (1 Tim 1:15-16), into a member of "the *household of God" (Eph 2:19). Paul's passion for persecuting enemies of God was repurposed in Christ to pursue them with transformational *mercy.

Paul's ministry to the Gentiles, therefore, is not just a subpoint to one's understanding of his power and politics; it is the natural outworking of the cruciform paradigm. The "mystery" of the cross (1 Cor 2:1; see also 1 Cor 4:1) *contains* the "mystery" of Gentile inclusion. In Ephesians 3:1-6, Paul confirms that "the mystery of Christ" (Eph 3:4) heretofore concealed "in other generations" has now been "unveiled by the Spirit" (Eph 3:5). The mystery proclaims: "the Gentiles are co-heirs, co-members of the same body, and co-partakers of the promise in Christ Jesus through the *gospel" (Eph 3:6; see Eph 3:7-13). Christ's defeat of the true enemy by the cross revealed to Paul God's political plan for all humanity: to make two people groups one, to reconcile "both groups [Jew and Gentile] to God in one body through the cross, eradicating their hostility in him" (Eph 2:15-16). Consequently, Christ's power in Paul's politics centered on *reconciliation*. Paul's ministry eradicated hostility by making peace between warring groups, as exemplified on the cross.

7. The Politics of God's People.

Paul organizes Christ's *polis* (the church) in the same way he organizes his own ministry: around the cruciform definition of power found in Christ Jesus. The cross clarifies the enemy, defines power, and directs God's politics for the citizens of heaven. Indeed, Paul's cruciform life (Gal 2:20) is a pattern for the church to emulate as members of God's household.

Consider Philippians. With their "*citizenship [*politeuma*] in heaven" (Phil 3:20), Paul exhorts the Philippian church to "live life as citizens [*politeuesthe*] worthy of the gospel of Christ" (Phil 1:27). This admonition comes in the context of Paul's imprisonment (Phil 1:7, 12-14), which, due to Paul's cruciform paradigm, he celebrates: "what has happened to me has actually helped spread the gospel" (Phil 1:12 NRSV). He reports that fellow prisoners and even the "whole praetorian guard" has heard the "good news" (Phil 1:13) because of his chains. What governs Paul's ministry to the Philippian church and to the praetorian guard, to friends and to enemies, is the definition of power and wisdom unveiled at the cross. Paul admonishes the Philippian church to submit to the same cross-centered politics.

Paul's life, then, becomes a pattern through which the mystery of Christ's cross takes shape. Paul's life is the exemplar for the politics of God's people: his transition from the kingdom of death to the kingdom of Christ, his subsequent shift in his primary enemy, and his new way of living through the wisdom and power of God revealed in the cross. Because this transformation is a result of God's work and not his own (Eph 2:8-10; 1 Cor 1:29-31; 2 Tim 1:9-10), Paul, free from pride, can exclaim: "Become imitators of me just as I am of Christ" (1 Cor 11:1).

Paul's life was redefined by the cross, allowing him to view all things seen and unseen with divine insight. For example, in violation of conventional wisdom, Paul considers his suffering and weakness as emblems of victory: "I delight in weaknesses, in abuses, in distress, in persecutions, and anguish for the sake of Christ, for when I am weak then I am strong [*dynatos*]" (2 Cor 12:10). This is not perverse optimism or a form of Stockholm syndrome. Instead, it is divine insight into power and victory. Christ's cross repurposes suffering as a conduit through which the kingdom advances. Thus Paul understands his suffering as not a defeat to be ashamed of but as a unique opportunity to unite with "the power [*dynamis*] of Christ" (2 Cor 12:9).

This is why, in chains, Paul calls for Timothy to "not be ashamed of the testimony of our Lord or of me his prisoner" (2 Tim 1:8a). Instead, he directs Timothy to "join [Paul] in suffering for the gospel" by fully embracing "the power [*dynamin*] of God" (2 Tim 1:8) revealed in Christ's cross and exemplified in Paul's life. Paul unashamedly boasts in his suffering (2 Tim 1:12) not out of self-hate but out of love for all, even his enemies. Through the cross, suffering is discipled by Christ's power. Victory is unveiled by Christ's crucifixion, where he "destroyed death and brought life and immortality to light through the gospel" (2 Tim 1:10). God's politics, then, does not necessitate self-preservation, as in other empires. Consequently, Christ's sacrifice on the cross secured sovereignty and redefined victory in this life and in the age to come.

Paul embraced this divine mystery in faith, sometimes while he was in chains (Col 4:18). His writings summon the church to do the same. His writings call the church to lay down their lives for the gospel, for their enemies, offering reconciliation through the power unleashed on Christ's cross that replaces death with life and understands self-sacrifice as God's path to victory over the dominion of darkness.

8. Conclusion.

Power and politics in Paul are typically limited by scholars to the query, "How does Paul interact with the Roman Empire?" Some scholars suggest subversion, while others argue for compliance. Paul's writings, though, demonstrate that the inquiry is too limited in scope, for Rome is too small of a target for Paul's ministry and Christ's *sacrifice. The true enemy is not "blood and flesh" (Eph 6:12) but the satanic adversary that *uses* Rome for its ends—that is, death and destruction—but whose means stretches far beyond any empire. Such an enemy demands a power superior to conventional weapons of war (2 Cor 10:3): the cross of Christ. Paul's paradigm of power is defined by Christ's purpose on the cross: to *give* life to all, to replace death with life.

This explains Paul's conversion from killer of Christians to Christ's minister to the Gentiles, a mission empowered by the cross and distinguished by Paul's boasts in weakness and suffering. Why? Because Paul is not at war with Rome but with the "dominion of darkness" (Col 1:14). Conflict with empire occurs, but Paul's cruciform definition of power necessitates *conversion* of the enemy and not *annihilation*, even if the enemy's transformation results, as it did for Christ, in Paul's suffering. The cross reveals not just the primary adversary but the definition of "power" itself: not the ability to *take life* (*un*-creation) but the ability to *give life* to all (*re*-creation). The politics of Paul's kingdom message is one of reconciliation, one that replaces death with life, one that gives mercy to all, enemies included. This is the means through which the satanic kingdom is plundered.

Paul's life and ministry imitate Christ, providing a pattern for the church to follow (1 Cor 11:1). Paul's writings organize God's people around the cruciform ministry of reconciliation. This is a ministry of peace and restoration unleashed by the unveiling of the divine mystery in the cross, the "wisdom and power of God" (1 Cor 1:24), a ministry that wages war against the dominion of darkness with a sacrificial love that startles the satanic and confounds the empire. Through the church, death is replaced with life, quarreling with mercy, and grasping at authority with boasts of weakness. This is a power and politics found in Christ alone.

See also CONVERSION AND CALL OF PAUL; CREATION AND NEW CREATION; CROSS; CRUCIFORMITY; DEATH; EMPIRE; MISSION; MYSTERY; POLITICAL SYSTEMS; PRINCIPALITIES AND POWERS; SATAN, DEVIL; SUFFERING.

BIBLIOGRAPHY. **J. M. G. Barclay,** *Pauline Churches and Diaspora Jews* (Grand Rapids, MI: Eerdmans, 2011); **W. Carter,** *Matthew and Empire* (Harrisburg, PA: Trinity Press International, 2001); **J. D. Crossan,** *In Search of Paul: How Jesus' Apostle Opposed Rome's Empire with God's Kingdom* (New York: Harper, 2004); **A. Deissmann,** *Light from the Ancient East,* trans. L. R. M. Strachan (repr., Grand Rapids, MI: Baker, 1978); **J. A. Dunne and D. Batovici,** eds., *Reactions to Empire: Sacred Texts in Their Socio-political Contexts,* WUNT 2/372 (Tübingen: Mohr Siebeck, 2014); **N. Elliott,** *Liberating Paul: The Justice of God and the Politics of the Apostle* (Maryknoll, NY: Orbis, 1994); idem, "Romans 13:1-7 in the Context of Imperial Propaganda," in *Paul and Empire: Religion and Power in Roman Imperial Society,* ed. R. A. Horsley (Harrisburg, PA: Trinity Press International, 1997), 184-207; **R. A. Horsley,** ed., *Paul and Empire: Religion and Power in Roman Imperial Society* (Harrisburg, PA: Trinity Press International, 1997); idem, "Submerged Biblical Histories and Imperial Biblical Studies," in *The Postcolonial Bible,* ed. R. S. Sugirtharajah (Sheffield: Sheffield Academic Press, 1998), 152-73; idem, ed., *Paul and Politics* (Harrisburg, PA: Trinity Press International, 2000); idem, ed., *Paul and the Roman Imperial Order* (Harrisburg, PA: Trinity Press International, 2004); idem, ed., *In the Shadow of Empire: Reclaiming the Bible as a History of Faithful Resistance* (Louisville, KY: Westminster John Knox, 2008); **S. Kim,** *Christ and Caesar: The Gospel and the Roman Empire in the Writings of Paul and Luke* (Grand Rapids, MI: Eerdmans, 2008); **S. McKnight and J. B. Modica,** eds., *Jesus Is Lord, Caesar Is Not: Evaluating Empire in New Testament Studies* (Downers Grove, IL: InterVarsity Press, 2013); **S. D. Moore,** *Empire and Apocalypse: Postcolonialism and the New Testament* (Sheffield: Sheffield Academic Press, 2006); **P. Oakes,** "Re-mapping the Universe: Paul and the

Emperor in 1 Thessalonians and Philippians," *JSNT* 27 (2005): 301-22; **A. E. Portier-Young,** *Apocalypse Against Empire: Theologies of Resistance in Early Judaism* (Grand Rapids, MI: Eerdmans, 2011); **J. C. Scott,** *Domination and the Arts of Resistance: Hidden Transcripts* (New Haven, CT: Yale University Press, 1990); **B. J. Walsh and S. C. Keesmaat,** *Colossians Remixed: Subverting the Empire* (Downers Grove, IL: InterVarsity Press, 2004); **K. Wengst,** *Pax Romana and the Peace of Jesus Christ*, trans. J. Bowden (Philadelphia: Fortress, 1987); **L. Williamson,** "Led in Triumph: Paul's Use of Thriambeuo," *Int* 22 (1968): 317-22; **S. J. Wood,** *The Alter-Imperial Paradigm: Empire Studies and the Book of Revelation*, BibInt 140 (Leiden: Brill, 2016).

S. J. Wood

POOR. *See* Collection for the Saints; Urban Setting of Paul's Churches; Wealth and Poverty.

POVERTY. *See* Wealth and Poverty.

POWER. *See* Cross; Holy Spirit; Magic; Politics and Power; Principalities and Powers.

POWERS. *See* Apocalyptic Paul; Magic; Principalities and Powers; Triumph.

PRAISE. *See* Hymns, Hymn Fragments, Confessions; Prayer; Worship.

PRAYER

"Prayer is the Christian's vital breath, the Christian's native air." This key line from the 1818 hymn by James Montgomery captures an important reality in the life of Paul: prayer was for the apostle's spiritual existence and well-being as crucial as oxygen and as ordinary as the act of breathing. This essential yet commonplace aspect of prayer can be seen in both Paul's life and his *letters.

1. Prayer in Paul's Life
2. Prayer in Paul's Letters

1. Prayer in Paul's Life.

1.1. The Evidence of Paul's Jewish Background. The importance of prayer in Paul's life as a follower of Jesus is a natural extension of his preconversion life as a member of the Jewish *faith. Paul was privileged to study at the Harvard school of Judaism: he was a pupil of the renowned rabbi Gamaliel in *Jerusalem, where he was "thoroughly trained in the *law of our ancestors" (Acts 22:3 NIV; see also Acts 5:34). Paul was a member of an extremely conservative Jewish party not merely in name only; those who knew him for a long time could testify that his life "conformed to the strictest sect of our religion, living as a Pharisee" (Acts 26:5 NIV). Paul's own self-assessment about his pre-Christian life within Judaism is that he was "extremely zealous for the traditions of my fathers" (Gal 1:14 NIV), that his "zeal" for the Jewish faith was evident in his persecution of the *church (Phil 3:6; also Gal 1:13, 23; 1 Tim 1:13), and that with regard to a *righteousness based on the Jewish law he was "blameless" (Phil 3:6). The apostle's indebtedness to his Jewish upbringing can be additionally seen in the multiple citations of and allusions to the OT found scattered throughout his letters. All this strongly suggests that Paul's understanding and practice of prayer were heavily influenced by his Jewish background.

Paul would have known well and been powerfully affected by not only the prayers of praise and lament of his Jewish people that had long ago been recorded in the Psalter but also the numerous stories of individuals praying in the OT. His understanding of prayer would have ranged from the earliest days of Enosh, when "people began to call upon the *name of the *Lord" (Gen 4:26) to the prayers connected with key figures among God's *covenant people (e.g., Job, Moses, Hannah, Elijah, Elisha, David, Daniel, Hezekiah, etc.) throughout Israelite history (see the survey of prayer in the OT by Balentine; Seitz, 3-22). But the Judaism of Paul's day also featured prayer at the center of its faith and practice in both public and private life.

Public prayer was such an integral part of the offered *sacrifices that the *temple in Jerusalem was called a "house of prayer" (Lk 1:10; Sir 50:19; Josephus, *Ag. Ap.* 2.196), and the time when morning and afternoon sacrifices were given was called "the hour of prayer" (Acts 3:1). Public prayer was just one of the diverse activities that took place in a synagogue (in addition to *worship, there was also education of the youth, adjudication of internal conflicts among members, *hospitality to travelers), but it was an important and frequent enough activity that a synagogue too was sometimes referred to as a "house of prayer" (Josephus, *Ag. Ap.* 2.10; *Life* 277; see Acts 16:13). The central feature in the daily worship services held in the synagogue included the Shemoneh Esreh or "Eighteen Benedictions," designated in the Talmud as Tefillah, which means "intercession" and serves as the basic prayer to be followed by all Jews. The first three benedictions of the Shemoneh Esreh consist of prayers of praise directed to *God, the next twelve involve prayers of petitions dealing with the needs of the Jewish community of faith, and the last three comprise prayers of thanksgiving.

Prayer also functioned as a major part of Jews' private life. Pious Jews such as Paul would recite the Shema ("Hear, O Israel: The LORD our God, the LORD is one," Deut 6:4 NIV; 11:13-21) at the end and beginning of each day, thereby fulfilling the scriptural command to affirm the commandments of God "when you lie down and when you get up" (Deut 6:7; 11:19 NIV). They typically opened their meals with a prayer of thanks to God and often repeated this prayer of thanks when they had finished eating their food (Deut 8:10; 1QS VI, 4-5; Josephus, *J. W.* 2.131; m. Ber. 6:1–8:8; see Mt 14:19; 15:35; 26:26; Acts 27:35; 1 Cor 11:24). Private prayers were uttered in everyday life situations such as when a traveler was going through a dangerous place (m. Ber. 4:4) or when a rabbi entered a synagogue to teach the Torah (m. Ber. 4:2).

Paul's Jewish background of prayer, therefore, "provided him with an understanding that in responding to God's mercy and grace, one was both (1) to affirm one's faith in God's creation, revelation, and redemption (as in the Shema), and (2) to pray to God in adoration, petition and thanksgiving (as in the *Shemoneh Esreh*). All these matters seem to have been intertwined in Paul's Jewish prayer experience" (Longenecker, 212).

1.2. The Evidence of Acts. The book of Acts reveals that every major event in Paul's life—his *conversion, commission, *baptism, missionary work—happened in the context of prayer (Hunter, 725-26). The first time that the future apostle makes an appearance in the story line of Acts records him guarding the clothes of those stoning Stephen and approving of their action, which happens in the context of Stephen offering a prayer to the Lord Jesus (Acts 7:60–8:1; 22:20). After meeting the risen Jesus on the road to Damascus, Paul is blinded and spends three days not only fasting and reflecting on this divine encounter with *Christ but also praying (Acts 9:9, 11). Paul then experiences three dramatic events all at the same time through the *ministry of Ananias: his eyesight is restored, he is commissioned to be Christ's *witness to all people, and he is baptized while "calling on his [Jesus'] name" in prayer (Acts 22:13-16). After Paul ultimately returns to Jerusalem, now as a Christ-follower, he is "praying at the temple" when he falls into a trance, through which Jesus gives him instructions to leave the city and shift his ministry from the Jewish community to the *Gentiles (Acts 22:17; see Acts 9:26-30).

Paul's first missionary journey begins and ends with prayer. The church in *Syrian Antioch "fasted and prayed" before sending Barnabas and Paul off to preach the *gospel (Acts 13:3). After a difficult but successful missionary tour, the two evangelists retraced their steps to the newly established churches of Lystra, Iconium, and Pisidian Antioch, appointing elders and committing them to the Lord through "prayer and fasting" (Acts 14:23). Paul's second missionary journey describes the conversion of Lydia just outside the city of Philippi at "a place of prayer" (Acts 16:13). The apostle's ministry in Philippi also involves the dramatic exorcism of the python-possessed female *slave who predicted the future—an episode that takes place while Paul and his fellow missionaries "were going to the place of prayer" (Acts 16:16). After Paul and Silas are physically beaten and thrown into *prison in Philippi, the missionaries respond to their unjust treatment by spending their evening in jail "praying and singing *hymns to God" (Acts 16:25). On the return leg of his third missionary journey, Paul summons the elders from Ephesus to join him in Miletus, where, after sharing with them his emotional words of farewell, "he knelt down with all of them and prayed" (Acts 20:36 NIV). Another poignant scene of farewell takes place in the port city of Tyre, where not just the elders but all the believers, including wives and children, accompany Paul and his fellow travelers outside the city, where "there on the beach we knelt to pray" (Acts 21:5 NIV).

Prayer was an important component of Paul's life during his two-year incarceration in Caesarea Maritima. After the local governor Felix was replaced by Festus, Paul met before the new Roman representative, as well as the Jewish king Agrippa and his sister, Bernice. In this meeting the *apostle reveals his ongoing prayers for the conversion of those with whom he has an opportunity to share the gospel: "I pray to God that not only you but all who are listening to me today may become what I am, except for these chains" (Acts 26:29 NIV). Prayer continued to be part of Paul's life and ministry during his prison journey to Rome. After fourteen anxious and foodless days during which Paul and the other 275 people on his ship were driven across the Adriatic Sea by a storm, the apostle exhorts everyone to eat something and then "took some bread and gave thanks to God [in prayer] in front of them all" (Acts 27:35 NIV). After everyone survives the shipwreck by making it ashore on the island of Malta, the father of Publius, the chief official of the island, is sick, and it is "after prayer" that Paul places his hands on him and heals him, as well as many others who are ill (Acts 28:8-9).

A survey of these texts leads Richard Longenecker to conclude: "Indeed, throughout Luke's Gospel and Acts, to be an apostle of Jesus, as was Paul—or, to be a follower of Jesus, as are all those who claim Christ's name—is to be a person of prayer" (203).

1.3. The Evidence of Paul's Letters. The essential yet commonplace aspect of prayer in Paul's life is also evident in his letters, where "Pauline prayer vocabulary is the richest in the NT, and the apostle uses prayer terms more frequently than any other writer" (Hunter, 729; see also Cullmann 1995, 70; Longenecker, 204-5). Paul's most recurrent and thus preferred words for prayer include the following: the verb "to pray" (*proseuchomai*), which occurs nineteen times (Rom 8:26; 1 Cor 11:4, 5, 13; 14:13, 14 [2×], 15 [2×]; Eph 6:18; Phil 1:9; Col 1:3, 9; 4:3; 1 Thess 5:17, 25; 2 Thess 1:11; 3:1; 1 Tim 2:8); the cognate noun "prayer" (*proseuchē*), which occurs fourteen times (Rom 1:10; 12:12; 15:30; 1 Cor 7:5; Eph 1:16; 6:18; Phil 4:6; Col 4:2, 12; 1 Thess 1:2; 1 Tim 2:1; 5:5; Philem 4, 22); the noun "request" (*deēsis*), which has twelve occurrences (Rom 10:1; 2 Cor 1:11; 9:14; Eph 6:18 [2×]; Phil 1:4 [2×], 19; 4:6; 1 Tim 2:1; 5:5; 2 Tim 1:3); and the compound verb "call upon" (*epikaleō*), which occurs six times (Rom 10:12, 13, 14; 1 Cor 1:2; 2 Cor 1:23; 2 Tim 2:22; note also the related compound verb *parakaleō* in 2 Cor 12:8).

It would be wrong, however, to limit Paul's prayers only to those texts where these terms are found. The letters of the apostle also contain many passages that do not make use of explicit prayer vocabulary but nevertheless in terms of their form ought to be classified as prayers. In fact, in each of the four major sections of his letters—the opening, thanksgiving, body, and closing—either one or more prayers is included (some of which are referred to by scholars as "prayer wishes," "prayer reports" or "benedictions") or prayer plays a key formal element in an epistolary convention within that major section. Since this prayer material is not part of Paul's private worship but is incorporated by the apostle into his letters, he has adapted these prayers to fit more appropriately in an epistolary genre. Therefore, these prayers are not addressed directly to God but to the readers, and the prayers do not typically contain a word-for-word recording of Paul's actual prayers but a summary of the content of the apostle's prayers to God concerning his readers.

2. Prayer in Paul's Letters.

Most studies of prayer in Paul's letters seek to help the modern reader better make sense of the large volume of the apostle's prayer material by classifying the relevant texts into various categories. Some classify the apostle's prayer material on the basis of content. David Crump, for example, categorizes the pertinent passages into four types: Paul's general exhortations to pray, his own prayers for himself, his requests to others to pray for him and his ministry, and his intercessory prayers for others (Crump, 212-46). Although classifications such as this based on content are helpful, they typically overlook material where prayer vocabulary is missing but where the relatively fixed and repeated form of these passages reveal that they too ought to be identified as prayer material. What follows below, therefore, is an introduction and analysis of the many formal prayers found in each of the four major sections of a Pauline letter.

2.1. Letter Opening. Paul's letter opening always ends with a greeting formula that exhibits a very fixed form: "*Grace to you and *peace from God our Father and the Lord Jesus Christ." Although modern readers may not immediately recognize it as such, this greeting formula ought to be viewed as a prayer of Paul. The apostle calls on God and Christ to grant grace and peace to his readers—a fact that leads G. P. Wiles to include these opening greetings in the category of "wish-prayers." Although the verb in these opening greetings is omitted, the use of the optative mood—the mood commonly used in a wish or prayer or utterance directed to God—in the opening greetings of other NT letters (1 Pet 1:2; 2 Pet 1:2; Jude 2) suggests that the same mood is implied here, which in turn further supports classifying this opening formula as a prayer.

The greeting prayer "Grace to you and peace" would have sounded unfamiliar and unique to both Paul's Gentile Christian readers and his Jewish Christian readers. The standard greeting of contemporary Greek letters was the simple infinitive *chairein*, meaning literally "to rejoice" but with the idiomatic sense of "Greetings!" (for examples in Greek papyrus letters, see Exler 1923, 24-40, 42-44, 50-56; for examples in the NT, see Acts 15:23; 23:26; Jas 1:1; 2 Jn 10-11). Paul's greeting prayer also differs from the opening greeting found in the few Jewish letters that survive from that time period (see Weima 2014, 70-71). Many commentators believe that the apostle appropriated the *chairein* greeting from Greek letters and transformed it into a Christian greeting, using the related word *charis*, "grace." Paul then added the expected Jewish greeting "peace." The combining of "grace and peace" resulted, therefore, in a new and distinctive greeting prayer that would be familiar and noteworthy for both Gentiles and Jews in the churches to which he was writing.

With this subtle but significant change of the secular "Greetings" (Gk. *chairein*) to the Christianized new salutation "Grace" (Gk. *charis*), Paul infuses an important theological point into this greeting. This new grace greeting functions as a prayer, underscoring God's initiative in salvation. Because of their union with Christ, readers receive God's grace, his undeserved favor, apart from their own merit. The Jewish greeting "Peace" performs a similar function, suggesting God's great achievement in the lives of the readers. For Paul peace is not simply a static thing, as in the lack of strife or conflict; rather, peace points to shalom, completeness, the fullness of humanity's communion with God and all the world in its edenic state (see Rom 2:10; 8:6; 14:17; Eph 6:15; Foerster). By combining the old Greek revised greeting with the Jewish, Paul thus shows his letter-writing skill and ingenuity, creating new forms out of current epistolary conventions. Paul's clever revision of the traditional greeting formula results in "as rich a greeting as can be imagined: a prayer which recognizes God as the source of the enabling ('grace') to live in mutually productive and beneficial harmony ('peace')" (Dunn 1993, 23).

Paul also adds to his new greeting prayer the divine source of grace and peace: "from God our Father and the Lord Jesus Christ." This supplementary clause reflects the apostle's theological perspective, acknowledging the primacy of divine action by the Father and Christ, not just in providing the gifts of grace and peace to the readers but in being the ultimate cause of their salvation. This juxtaposition of "the Lord Jesus Christ" and "God our Father" also reflects Paul's high *Christology, which was central to his *preaching and presumably embraced by those to whom he was writing.

One opening greeting prayer stands out from the others because of the way Paul has greatly expanded it. In Galatians 1:3-5, after the expected words "Grace and peace to you from God our Father and the Lord Jesus Christ," the apostle adds the following: "who gave himself for our sins to rescue us from the present evil age, according to the will of our God and Father; to whom be *glory for ever and ever. Amen" (NIV). This expansion is hardly fortuitous but instead stems from a conscious attempt on Paul's part not just to prepare his Galatian readers for key arguments that he will make in the body of the letter but also to win their acceptance of these key arguments. For example, the reference to the *death of Christ ("who gave himself") foreshadows the central role that the topic of Christ's crucifixion plays throughout the Galatian letter. The added mention of God's divine will and fatherhood ("according to the will of our God and Father") is a not-so-subtle reminder to the Galatian readers that their rejection of Paul and his gospel is tantamount to acting against the will of God and also refusing to submit to the divine authority of God as their Father (see fuller discussion in Weima 2016, 44-50).

2.2. Thanksgiving. The second major section of a Pauline letter is the thanksgiving, and prayer plays an important part in both the form and function of this epistolary unit.

2.2.1. Form. The thanksgiving sections of Paul's surviving letters exhibit a common form that typically consists of five distinct units.

1. Statement of thanksgiving: The thanksgiving opens with the main verb "I/we give thanks" and the identification of the one to whom thanksgiving is directed: "to [my] God." Paul explicitly directs this thanksgiving to God, the one whom he views as the ultimate source of the spiritual gifts evidenced in the lives of his readers.
2. Manner of thanksgiving: Paul's preferred manner of expressing thanksgiving to God is through prayer. Thus his thanksgivings typically contain some reference to "remembering/making mention of you all in my prayers."
3. Cause of thanksgiving: Every thanksgiving includes one or more causal constructions (often involving verbs of "hearing" or "learning") that give the reason for Paul's thanksgiving. Although Paul's theocentric perspective requires him to direct his thanksgiving to God, the apostle is not hesitant to acknowledge the praiseworthy actions of his readers.
4. Explanation: This section usually modifies the preceding causal unit and so serves either to explain more fully the just-stated cause for Paul's thanksgiving or to provide additional reasons for giving thanks.
5. Prayer report: Paul sometimes concludes his thanksgiving with a report of what he specifically prays for regarding his addressees. In contrast to the second unit, which shares with the readers simply the fact of Paul praying for them, this fifth unit lets the readers know very clearly what particular

things the apostle is praying will happen in their lives.

The thanksgiving section of Philippians 1:3-11 illustrates well all five of the units typically found in this epistolary convention: (1) statement of thanksgiving: "I give thanks to my God" (Phil 1:3a); (2) manner of thanksgiving: "in every remembrance of you, always in every prayer of mine for you all, making my prayer with *joy" (Phil 1:3b-4); (3) cause of thanksgiving: "because of your partnership in the gospel" (Phil 1:5-6); (4) explanation: "It is right for me to feel this way about all of you, because . . ." (Phil 1:7-8); (5) prayer report: "And this is my prayer: that . . ." (Phil 1:9-11). Not all of Paul's thanksgivings, of course, follow this five-part structure perfectly; some of them, in fact, deviate from this structure in significant ways. It would be wrong, therefore, to conclude that Paul had a form of the thanksgiving fixed firmly in his mind and that he slavishly followed this form in all his letters. As David Pao observes: "Paul is not a prisoner to an epistolary form, even a form that he himself creates" (119). Nevertheless, the *freedom with which Paul expresses his thanksgiving to God is not a random or unreflective process. The fivefold structure of the Pauline thanksgiving is sufficiently established with the result that, when one or more of these formal units is missing or altered in a significant manner, such a change in the expected form is likely due to the specific epistolary situation and reflects Paul's particular purposes at work in the letter.

2.2.2. Function. Virtually all ancient letters move directly from the opening to the body. The question naturally arises as to why Paul does not follow this pattern but chooses instead to preface this material with an expression of thanks to God about his readers. The answer to this question lies in recognizing three important functions of Pauline thanksgivings that support his broader persuasive strategy.

2.2.2.1. Pastoral Function. The thanksgiving has a pastoral function: it reestablishes Paul's relationship with his readers by means of a positive expression of gratitude to God for their faith, *hope, and *love. The letter is typically the first communication that Paul has had with a given church since his original mission-founding ministry among them. It is important, therefore, for the apostle to reconnect with his readers, if he wants them not only to accept his letter but also to obey his exhortations contained in it. The thanksgiving also reveals Paul's deep pastoral concern for his readers as evidenced by his comments in units two (the manner of thanksgiving) and five (the prayer report) that he regularly prays for them. It is harder for the apostle's readers to dismiss his exhortations when they have an image of "Pastor Paul" on his knees praying on their behalf (see Eph 3:14, "I kneel in prayer to the Father"). But Paul's reason for including a thanksgiving is not merely to enhance the persuasive force of his letter. He did so because he also genuinely cared about his spiritual children and prayed to God about them. As Paul himself observed, even more difficult for him than the physical sufferings he endured because of his ministry—the imprisonments, floggings, stonings, shipwrecks, robberies, sleeplessness, hunger, thirst—was his "anxiety for all the churches" (2 Cor 11:28). The thanksgiving, especially with its expressed references to his prayers, allows Paul the pastor to convey in a powerful way to his readers his deep gratitude to God for them as well as his genuine care and deep affection for them.

2.2.2.2. Exhortative Function. The thanksgiving has an exhortative function: even though Paul is expressing his thankfulness to God, there is an implicit, or at times even an explicit, challenge for the letter recipients to live up to the praise the apostle is giving them in his words of gratitude (Schubert states that the Pauline thanksgiving is "implicitly or explicitly paraenetic": 26, 89; also O'Brien, 141-44, 165, 262-63). This function involves persuasion through praise, since people typically respond to the praise that others have of them by desiring to live up to that praise. Thus, for example, when Paul gives thanks to God for the Christians in Philippi "because of your partnership in the gospel from the first day until now" (Phil 1:5 NIV), this not only expresses his gratitude to the Philippian believers for their active support of his ministry in the past (see Phil 4:15-19) but also implicitly puts pressure on them to continue their support of him in the future. In those thanksgivings where Paul includes the fifth and final formal unit—the prayer report (2 Thess 1:11-12; Phil 1:9-11; Col 1:9-14; also Rom 1:10)—the challenge is no longer implicit but explicit, since his readers know from the content of the apostle's prayer for them exactly what he expects from them. There is nothing subtle or hidden about Paul's desires for the Philippian church when he closes his thanksgiving to this church with the following prayer report: "And this is my prayer: that your love may overflow more and more with knowledge and full insight to help you to determine what is best, so that in the day of Christ you may be pure and blameless, having produced the harvest of righteousness that comes from Jesus Christ for the glory and praise of God" (Phil 1:9-11).

2.2.2.3. *Foreshadowing Function.* The thanksgiving, third, has a foreshadowing function: it looks ahead to the main topics that will be taken up in the body of the letter. Paul is an extremely skilled letter writer who knows ahead of time the issues that he will be addressing in the body of the letter and who thus effectively foreshadows those issues already in the thanksgiving section. The thanksgiving, however, anticipates not only the central themes and key issues to be developed in the body of the letter but also the nature of the relationship that exists between Paul and the church as well as the overall tone of his correspondence to them. As Paul Schubert recognizes in his groundbreaking study: "Each thanksgiving not only announces clearly the subject matter of the letter, but also foreshadows unmistakably its stylistic qualities, the degrees of intimacy and other important characteristics" (77). The thanksgiving reveals whether Paul enjoys a "warm and fuzzy" relationship with his readers (1–2 Thessalonians, Philippians) or whether feelings between the apostle and his readers are cool (1 Corinthians) or even downright frosty (Galatians). Such knowledge of the letter's context revealed in its form (in this case, the thanksgiving section) is crucial to an accurate interpretation of the letter's content.

2.3. *Body.* In light of the important role that prayer plays in the opening and thanksgiving sections of Paul's letters, it is not surprising to find six actual prayers of the apostle in the body of his correspondence (Rom 15:5-6; 15:13; 1 Thess 3:11, 12-13; 2 Thess 2:16-17; 3:5).

2.3.1. *Form.* These six "body prayers," or as they are more often identified, "benedictions" (Champion, 29-30; Jewett; Mullins; Weima 1994, 101-4), have a common structure consisting of five basic elements: (1) the adversative particle "but" (*de*), which sets the prayer apart from the preceding material in the letter; (2) the divine source of the prayer, either God and/or the Lord, along with a noun or participial clause that provides a further description of these persons; (3) the wish or content of the prayer expressed in the main verb (normally expressed in the optative mood); (4) the recipient of the prayer, involving in every instance except one some form of the personal pronoun "you"; and (5) the purpose of the prayer, expressed by either a *hina* or *eis* clause ("so that"). This fivefold structure can be seen, for example, in Paul's prayer in Romans 15:5-6: "(1) But (2) may the God of endurance and comfort (3) give the same attitude of mind toward each other that Christ Jesus had (4) to you (5) so that together you may with one voice glorify the God and Father of our Lord Jesus Christ."

2.3.2. *Function.* These body prayers possess a summarizing function: Paul adapts the conventional elements of the prayers such that they recapitulate and place the spotlight on the letter's major concerns and themes (Jewett, 24; Wiles, 68; Weima 2016, 136-38; Crump, 233). This summarizing function can be seen, for example, in the prayer of Romans 15:5-6 cited above: Paul echoes his extended treatment of the division between the "*strong" and the "weak" in the house churches of Rome (Rom 14:1–15:6) with a prayer for unity, specifically that God would give to this divided Christian community "the same attitude" of concern for others exemplified in Christ's life so that "together" and "with one voice" both groups may glorify God. Yet, as noted above in the survey of the different functions of the thanksgiving section, these body prayers also have an exhortative function. By sharing with his readers the specific content of his prayer to God for them, Paul not so subtly also lets them know what he hopes and even expects them to do in their lives.

2.4. *Letter Closing.* Two types of prayers of Paul also appear in the letter closing in the form of what is typically referred to as a "peace benediction" and a "grace benediction." The location of these two formally distinct prayers in the first position in the letter closing (the peace benediction) and the last position (the grace benediction) with the remaining items of a closing section (the hortatory section, greetings, autograph) placed between them stems from the chiasm that Paul creates between the opening prayer greeting ("Grace to you and peace from God the Father and the Lord Jesus Christ") and the closing peace and grace benedictions.

2.4.1. *Peace Benediction.* Paul's prayer that his readers receive peace from God ends six of his thirteen letters (Rom 15:33; 16:20; 2 Cor 13:11; Gal 6:16; Phil 4:9; 1 Thess 5:23; 2 Thess 3:16). The similarities of each occurrence reveal that four formal features can be ascribed to Paul's peace benediction.

The adversative particle "but" (*de*) that introduces the prayer sets the letter closing apart from the preceding letter body (Rom 15:33; 1 Thess 5:23; 2 Thess 3:16; see Rom 16:20). In some letter closings, however, the peace benediction is preceded by another closing convention (2 Cor 13:11; Gal 6:16; Phil 4:9) and then this adversative particle is appropriately replaced with the connecting conjunction "and" (*kai*).

Next is the divine giver of peace, whom Paul usually identifies as God (see, though, 2 Thess 3:16). Paul's order in the letter closing of beginning with the peace benediction and concluding with the grace benediction reverses the sequence found in the letter opening with the "grace and peace" greeting and reveals yet again Paul's careful attention to the form of his letters. Just as the apostle identifies God as the origin and bestower of peace, so he identifies Christ as the origin and bestower of grace in the grace benediction. In the letter opening, the "grace and peace" greeting prayer is complemented by both God and Christ, thereby forming a chiasm in which grace is connected to Christ and peace is connected to God. God is the "God of peace," an unusual moniker for God in early Judaism and early Christianity (cf. T. Dan 5.2; Heb 13:20). For Paul God is the origin, the source, the dispenser of peace, of shalom, restoring the relationship that was broken by *sin.

The third element of the peace benediction is its content, where Paul states what he hopes the God of peace may do or, more confidently, what the God of peace will do. This formal feature is not as uniform as the others. Sometimes Paul uses a being verb ("May the God of peace *be* with you"), explicitly or implicitly (Rom 15:33; 2 Cor 13:11; Gal 6:16; Phil 4:9), while at other times he says "sanctify" (1 Thess 5:23), "give" (2 Thess 3:16), or "crush" (Rom 16:20). In either case, it is the God of peace whose presence gives peace or who acts to give peace to his people.

The last element of the peace benediction is the wish-recipient: those who receive God's peace. The recipient involves, with one important exception, some form of the personal pronoun "you."

The typical or expected form of Paul's peace benediction, therefore, exhibits the following basic form: "But may the God of peace be with you."

As observed above, in the prayers found in the opening, thanksgiving, and body sections of Paul's letters, the apostle frequently adapts and expands the standard form of these prayers so that they more directly relate to the specific epistolary situation and reflect Paul's particular purposes at work in the letter. The same phenomenon occurs in the closing prayer for peace. The peace benediction in 1 Thessalonians 5:23, for example, reads: "But may the God of peace himself sanctify you completely, and may your whole spirit and soul and *body be preserved blamelessly at the coming of our Lord Jesus Christ." Here Paul adds to the content of the prayer (the third formal element) material that harks back to issues he dealt with previously in the letter body (see the fuller discussion in Weima 2016, 168-71). First, Paul incorporates his concern for *holiness with the two main verbs of the prayer: "may he sanctify" and "may it [your whole spirit and soul and body] be preserved blamelessly." Although the concern with holy living manifests itself in the thanksgiving (1 Thess 1:2-10) and the first half of the letter (1 Thess 2:1–3:13), the second half (1 Thess 4:1–5:22), with its exhortative focus, throws a spotlight on this theme (see esp. 1 Thess 4:3-8, where the key word *holy* occurs four times). The second theme, the comfort the Thessalonians have in light of Christ's parousia or return, appears in the closing prayer by means of the addendum, "at the coming of our Lord Jesus Christ," included in no other peace benediction. References to Christ's return are found not only throughout the letter (1 Thess 1:3, 10; 2:19; 3:13; 4:6) but in two lengthy paragraphs (1 Thess 4:13-18; 5:1-11).

2.4.2. Grace Benediction. As might be expected, given the apostle's skillful letter-writing habits and the contemporary epistolary canons, Paul ends his letters with his own personal touch. Greco-Roman letters often ended with "Be strong!" (*errōso*, Acts 15:29; 23:30 *v.l.*) or "Prosper!" (*eutychei*). As seen with his Christianizing of the opening greeting, Paul's new identity in Christ causes him similarly to conclude his letters in a uniquely Christian way: "May the grace of our Lord Jesus Christ be with you." This grace benediction, as it has come to be called, ends all of Paul letters and displays an almost rigid, formal consistency, unlike the peace benediction. The grace benediction is made up of three parts.

The first part of the grace benediction consists of the simple prayer for grace. Rather than praying for health or strength or good fortune to be given to his readers, Paul asks that Christ himself might grant the recipients of his letters what they need most in the Christian life: grace. As noted above, the closing grace benediction and the peace benediction invert the opening "Grace and peace" greeting, thereby creating a chiasm, bookending the letter body with prayers for divine favor and spiritual shalom.

Paul next identifies the origin of grace with the genitive phrase "of our Lord Jesus Christ," referring to the grace that Jesus Christ has and gives to his followers. In Paul's letters generally, divine grace comes from both God and Christ. In his letter endings, however, Paul is keen to emphasize the central role that Christ has in the Christian life, which by definition is lived out by grace alone.

Finally, Paul prays that the grace of Jesus Christ be given to a particular recipient, using the phrase "with you" or "with your spirit." These two phrases are synonymous. By "spirit" Paul simply means one's person.

Unlike the peace benediction, which may use an implied or explicit being verb or alternatively a transitive verb, the grace benediction never contains an explicit verb, transitive or otherwise. This means that Paul has in mind an implied being verb. That is clear enough. There is some ambiguity, though, in determining the mood of the verb. There are three options, all of which have some merit. The implied verb may be in the indicative mood, expressing the reality that "The grace of our Lord Jesus Christ *is* with you." Or it could be imperative, in which Paul is commanding Christ to give grace to the readers: "The grace of our Lord Jesus Christ *be* with you." A third and most likely option is the optative mood, conveying a reverent prayer: "*May* the grace of our Lord Jesus Christ be with you." Other benedictions in Paul's letters often but not always use the optative (see Rom 15:5-6, 13; 1 Thess 3:11, 12-13; 5:23; 2 Thess 2:16-17; 3:5, 16), as do the letter openings of non-Pauline NT letters (1 Pet 1:2; 2 Pet 1:2; Jude 2), suggesting a similar mood for the implied "to be" verb in the grace benedictions.

As Paul adapts other epistolary conventions for his letter writing purposes, so he also amends his grace benediction in order to link it closely with important themes and issues discussed previously in the letter body. Second Corinthians 13:13 is an example of this: "May the grace of the Lord Jesus Christ, and the love of God, and the *fellowship of the *Holy Spirit be with you all" (NIV). The expansions are seen clearly with the last two phrases: "the love of God" and "the fellowship of the Holy Spirit." Paul incorporates here two additional wishes, "love" and "fellowship," along with their respective divine origins, "God," and, "the Holy Spirit." These are not innocuous additions. Instead, both call to mind and summarize well the overarching concern of Paul throughout this letter, namely, the unity and mutual love that ought to characterize relationships within the Corinthian church.

See also LETTERS, LETTER FORMS; PASTOR, PAUL AS; PAUL AND JUDAISM; PAUL IN ACTS; SPIRITUALITY.

BIBLIOGRAPHY. **S. E. Balentine,** *Prayer in the Hebrew Bible: The Drama of Divine-Human Dialogue* (Minneapolis: Fortress, 1993); **L. G. Champion,** *Benedictions and Doxologies in the Epistles of Paul* (Oxford: Kemp Hall, 1934); **D. Crump,** *Knocking on Heaven's Door: A New Testament Theology of Petitionary Prayer* (Grand Rapids, MI: Baker, 2006); **O. Cullmann,** *Prayer in the New Testament* (Minneapolis: Fortress, 1995); **J. D. G. Dunn,** *The Epistle to the Galatians*, BNTC (Peabody, MA: Hendrickson, 1993); **F. X. J. Exler,** "The Form of the Ancient Greek Letter: A Study in Greek Epistolography" (PhD diss., Catholic University of America, 1923); **W. Foerster,** "εἰρήνη," *TDNT* 2:400-417; **W. B. Hunter,** "Prayer," *DPL*, 725-34; **R. Jewett,** "Form and Function of the Homiletic Benediction," *AThR* 51 (1969): 18-34; **R. N. Longenecker,** "Prayer in the Pauline Letters," in *Into God's Presence: Prayer in the New Testament* (Grand Rapids, MI: Eerdmans, 2001), 203-27; **T. Y. Mullins,** "Benediction as a New Testament Form," *AUSS* 15 (1977): 59-64; **P. O'Brien,** *Introductory Thanksgivings in the Letters of Paul* (Leiden: Brill, 1977); **D. W. Pao,** "Gospel Within the Constraints of an Epistolary Form: Pauline Introductory Thanksgiving and Paul's Theology of Thanksgiving," in *Paul and the Ancient Letter Form*, ed. S. E. Porter and S. A. Adams (Leiden: Brill, 2010), 101-27; **P. Schubert,** *Form and Function of the Pauline Thanksgivings* (Berlin: Töpelmann, 1939); **C. R. Seitz,** "Prayer in the Old Testament or Hebrew Bible," in *Into God's Presence: Prayer in the New Testament*, ed. R. N. Longenecker (Grand Rapids, MI: Eerdmans, 2001), 3-22; **J. A. D. Weima,** *Neglected Endings: The Significance of the Pauline Letter Closings* (Sheffield: JSOT Press, 1994); idem, *1–2 Thessalonians*, BNTC (Grand Rapids, MI: Baker, 2014); idem, *Paul the Ancient Letter Writer: An Introduction to Epistolary Analysis* (Grand Rapids, MI: Baker 2016); **G. P. Wiles,** *Paul's Intercessory Prayers: The Significance of the Intercessory Prayer Passages in the Letters of St. Paul* (Cambridge: Cambridge University Press, 1974).

J. A. D. Weima

PREACHING, FIRST-CENTURY

First-century preaching was oratory for believers to announce, encourage, reenact, and deliberate the *gospel of Jesus *Christ. One could preach for good or ill. A sermon's success rested on the character (not sex) of the preacher, the Spirit's presence, the content of the sermon, and the audience's response. From Paul's perspective, an effective sermon might result in conversions, deepened discipleship in Jesus Christ, personal *suffering for the preacher, or all three.

Preachers followed Hellenistic Jewish and Greco-Roman rhetorical conventions from the first and second centuries BC through the third century AD. Paul would have first preached in Pharisaical training, and most ancient audiences would have been familiar with this medium and would have listened to sermons with similar expectations. In the NT, Paul's kerygma, or topic of his preaching, was the "gospel of *God" (1 Thess 2:9; Acts 17:18-28). The *death and *resurrection of Jesus Christ, the *Son of God, validated him as reigning *Lord and required a decision from the audience. Paul adapted this theme depending on the needs of his listeners. As Paul preached, audiences participated with one another in the sermons. Audiences that responded negatively often beat or imprisoned the preacher. Churches that responded positively claimed an *identity as siblings of the Lord Jesus Christ.

1. Preaching in the Ancient World
2. Preaching in Early Christian Settings
3. Paul's Preaching
4. Implications

1. Preaching in the Ancient World.

Preaching began as a form of communication in the Hellenistic Jewish and Greco-Roman world in religious and panegyric settings. Borrowing from ancient rhetorical categories, Hellenistic Jewish and Greco-Roman speakers delivered religious and panegyric speeches using the epideictic and deliberative genres of ancient rhetoric. They based their arguments on the speaker's character (*ethos*), used emotional appeals (*pathos*), and reached logical conclusions (*logos*) (Aristotle, *Rhet.* 2.1.2-3). In most cases, religious oratory addressed an issue or *stasis* that arose in the group (Quintilian, *Inst.* 3.6.1-2). They employed two of the three styles of oratory, attic and sophistic, depending on the audience and the nature of the speech. Orators spoke in an attic style for simple topics. They followed a simple structure and employed three figures of speech: antithesis, parallelism in sound, and parallelism in structure (Cicero, *Brut.* 23.79; 24.82; *Orat.* 25.84; Shiell 2004, 45). Orators used the middle or conversational style to charm an audience and convey a moral tone (Dionysius of Halicarnassus, *De Demosthene* 15; Cicero, *Brut.* 28.96, 99). They rarely read an ancient text and offered commentary. Most speakers improvised, speaking from memory on sacred topics, and referenced oral and scripted *tradition from philosophical and religious writings as they spoke. Judicial speeches were rarely sermons. Epideictic speeches encouraged the audience to imitate the central figure or honor their memory (in the case of a funeral) with their behavior. Deliberative speeches taught an audience how to apply the speaker's message to their circumstances and provoked or encouraged a call to a decision.

1.1. Terms for Preaching. The English words *preaching* and *sermon* are anachronistic in attempting to understand the context of the ancient world. Orators used eight terms to describe religious oratory, and their sermons or messages followed four distinct arrangements. It is first necessary to define the terms associated with preaching within the wider context of Paul's world.

Apangellō. A verb associated with a messenger who spoke with a moral purpose (Aristotle, *Rhet.* 1417b8-10), often used in connection with a report from a military messenger. In religious oratory, this report came in the form of a dream interpretation (Gen 41:8 LXX) or a riddle (Judg 14:12 LXX).

Euangelizō. A verb carrying the sense of good news, as in a report of the good news of God's favor. For example, Joshua reported "good tidings" after the walls of Jericho fell (Josephus, *Ant.* 5.23; Pss. Sol. 11.1 LXX; Is 61:1-3 LXX; Ps 39:10; 67:12 LXX).

Katangellō. A verb often used in the sense of "announce" or "proclaim," which could refer to a verbal or nonverbal proclamation of an authority figure in a sacred setting. For instance, with a gesture to the crowd, Pyrrhus dedicated his spoils of battle in the *temple of Athena Itonis (Plutarch, *Pyrrhus* 26.3-5; negatively in reference to Antiochus in 2 Macc 8:36–9:17).

Kērygma and *kēryx.* A noun carrying the sense "proclamation" that could be used of a ruler's message being announced or amplified. This word is associated with *kēryx*, or "herald." Jonah proclaimed a message of repentance to the Ninevites (Jon 3:4 LXX; Lk 11:32; Xenophon, *Hell.* 2.4.20; Philostratus, *Vit. soph.* 2.33.4; Siegert, 427).

Kēryssō. A verb related to *kērygma* and sometimes used in the sense of heralding or proclaiming. In some contexts it was closely associated with prophets who preached (Epictetus, *Diatr.* 3.13; Mic 3:5; Is 61:1 LXX). For instance, a prophet such as Jeremiah proclaimed from *prison (Josephus, *Ant.* 10.117). Lady Wisdom preaches on the streets (Prov 1:21; 8:1; Pss. Sol. 11.1 LXX; see also 1 Esd 2:1; Jon 1:2; 3:2 LXX).

Homileō. A verb sometimes used in the sense of "speaking" or "addressing," such as in moral discourse or diatribe, usually among philosophers and students for instruction or changing the student's behavior (Josephus, *Life* 222; Xenophon, *Mem.* 1.2.6).

Paraklēsis. A noun often used in the sense of "exhortation" or "encouragement" toward sound moral judgment (Demosthenes, *On the Crown* 18.185; Isocrates, *To Nicocles* 2.14; 3.12; 1 Macc 13:3; 2 Macc 2:3; 6:12).

1.2. Arrangement of "Sermons." Just as there were many words for what is called preaching today, a sermon took on four forms in public speaking. Preachers adapted the sermon's arrangement to fit the need of the audience and the setting of the sermon, whether liturgical or public.

1.2.1. Pesher Interpretation. In Hellenistic Judaism a teacher read or paraphrased Scripture and interpreted the text for their community. In Nehemiah 8:7-9 LXX, Ezra read the text aloud, and a group of interpreters around Ezra "gave the sense" or literally "defined the knowledge." The interpreters explained what they heard and helped the people understand or synthesize the Scriptures. The emphasis was on the role of the group to enable understanding. In the Pesher Scroll of Habakkuk, a Teacher of Righteousness received an interpretation of a text from divine revelation and explained the text to his community (1QpHab VII, 1-12; see also 4Q252; Bruce, 6).

1.2.2. Homily. Greco-Roman philosophers used the homily to instruct students. Students dialogued with their instructors (Aelian, *Var. hist.* 3.19; Xenophon, *Mem.* 1.2.6, 15). In Hellenistic Judaism, teachers used homilies to interpret sacred texts and paraphrase stories (Let. Aris. 128-171).

The homily was the predominant form of preaching in first-century BC synagogues. Preachers improvised an interpretation of a sacred text in conversation with an audience. The group's size could be large or small; the setting was often inside a house or a large room; and the homily could extend for two hours or more.

The oldest extant Jewish homilies are two Armenian translations of Jewish homilies, one on Jonah and one on Samson, from sometime between the second century BC and the fourth century AD. Neither one began with a reading from a text. Instead, the preacher paraphrased a story from Scripture, expanding significantly on the text and adding details for rhetorical flourish. Both appear to have been written after the sermons were delivered. *On Samson* is a retelling of Samson's life with personal and practical reflections interspersed throughout the sermon on the theme of Samson's strength (*On Samson* 2.2). The preacher addressed the audience directly as "Beloved" (*On Samson* 10.1) and engaged in a dialogue with the audience (*On Samson* 25-26, 38, "a listener would perhaps say"). The sermon did not end with a call to decision but a conclusion of the story. *On Jonah* is similar in length. After a short preamble, the sermon did not make any overt references to the audience but followed a similar pattern to *On Samson*. The sermon's theme is the metaphor of God as a ship's pilot steering Jonah and Nineveh toward *salvation (Muradyan and Topchyan, 750-51).

1.2.3. Word of Exhortation. A word of exhortation used either epideictic or deliberative rhetoric to persuade the audience (Plato, *Menex.* 236d-237a; Quintilian, *Inst.* 4.2.21, 31) in four parts.

- Opening introduction with a gesture to mark the beginning of the speech
- Statement of the background information related to the case (Quintilian, *Inst.* 4.2.1-3, 31-52, 123; Cicero, *Inv.* 1.20.28-21.30). Here the speech could respond to the audience's attentiveness and the "demands of the occasion" or *stasis* (Quintilian, *Inst.* 4.2.64, 76, 119)
- Scriptural example, positive or negative (T. Reu. 4.1–6.1; 1 Macc 2:50-68; T. Jos. 2.4-11.1) (Stewart-Sykes, 33)
- Concluding exhortation/paraenetic section (Black, 3)

1.2.4. Declamation. The declamation was a form of public address that could be adapted for religious use in a sermon (Philostratus, *Vit. soph.* 579-580). With one day's notice, an orator prepared a speech on a familiar topic. He wrote the speech, memorized it, and delivered the speech extemporaneously. The audience circulated copies of the speech in the city (Russell, 78-80; Schnabel, 176).

In summary, ancient religious speeches proclaimed, reported, or dialogued about a message from an authoritative religious figure. They arranged their speeches in four ways. Each responded to an issue that the audience needed to address. Most did not depend primarily on a written text but could be adapted to their audiences. They focused on retelling a story, announcing a proclamation, provoking a call to action, or imitating a prominent figure. Orators spoke directly to and involved the audience, often in dialogue. Most messages were extemporaneous, delivered without notes on themes with which the speaker was familiar.

2. Preaching in Early Christian Settings.

Early Christians followed some of these patterns from the ancient world of religious oratory. Christian preachers adapted their delivery from the categories of ancient rhetoric. Sermons were epideictic or deliberative. Like their Greco-Roman and Hellenistic Jewish counterparts, they argued from *ethos*, *pathos*, and *logos*. However, the preacher's *ethos* played the most significant role of the three. The sermon often shaped their character along with the audience (Shiell 2011, 53). For instance, in Paul's instructions to Timothy (1 Tim 4:13-16), preaching, *teaching, and public reading saved Timothy and the audience. This mutual character formation was significant in early Christian preaching (Heb 10–13; Herm. *Visions* 2; Pss. Sol. 3–16; Acts 7:2-60;

Lk 24:13-34). They preached in a sophistic and plain style. For instance, a sermon by Melito of Sardis and Hebrews represents a middle style, a more sophisticated rhetoric yet not overbearing (*Peri Pascha*; Heb 6:7; 12:5). Other sermons reflect a simple, conversational tone designed for extempore topics or long, unscripted conversations (short: Lk 4:16-30; long: Origen, *Homily on 1 Kings 28*). Christians used similar terms to describe their preaching and followed the same four arrangements. However, unlike their ancient counterparts, women also preached in early Christian settings (Lk 24:9; Acts of Thecla 39, 42; Martyrdom of Perpetua 5.4).

2.1. Terms for Preaching in Early Christianity. Christians used eight terms to describe their preaching, but they often used these terms interchangeably.

Apangellō. A verb that refers to the preacher as an eyewitness responsible to report and retell the events he has experienced. Jesus commands the *women at the tomb to preach to the disciples following the resurrection (Mt 28:9-10), and they do so in Luke (Lk 24:9). First John is an eyewitness sermon (1 Jn 1:2-3).

Euangelizō. A verb for preaching good news of rest and deliverance, especially to the marginalized. This form of preaching was connected to Jesus' sermons and to Isaianic prophetic preaching (Lk 4:18, citing Is 61:1 LXX; also Mt 11:5; Lk 7:22; Heb 4:2; Luke 16:16; 20:1; Acts 10:36; Rev 10:7). This form was used in itinerant sermons (Lk 4:43; 8:1; 9:6; Acts 5:42; Philip in Acts 8:4, 12, 25, 35, 40; Acts 11:20; 1 Pet 1:12, 25; 4:6; Rev 14:6).

Katangellō. A verb carrying the sense of prophetic preaching of the gospel foretelling Jesus (Acts 3:24–4:2; Ign. *Phld.* 5:2) or the apostolic preaching of the gospel in continuity with prophetic preaching (Pol. *Phil.* 6.2).

Kēryx and Kēryssō. Two terms (the first a noun, the second a verb) used to refer to preaching to amplify a message or to make a formal announcement. They are used with *euangelizomai* in Luke and Acts (Lk 4:18-19; 8:1; Acts 8:5) and *apangellō* in 1 Peter (1 Pet 3:19). The words connect John and Jesus' prophetic proclamation (Mt 3:1, 4:17). A woman who sacrifices her ointment and anoints Jesus is an example in this preaching (Mk 14:9; see also Acts 10:37-42).

Kērygma. A noun describing the content of the proclamation in reference to Jonah's sermon (Mt 12:41; Lk 11:32) as well as the preaching of apostles and teachers to persons who sinned after *baptism (Herm. *Similitudes* 9.6.15-16).

Homileō. A verb carrying the sense of an extended conversation and dialogue with a small group conversation (Luke 24:14-15). The journey to Emmaus formed the background of many early Christian *worship services.

Paraklēsis. A noun describing an exhortation that provoked a decision or call to action, often engaging persons in the crowd. For instance, John exhorts and proclaims in Luke 3:18; Hebrews 12:6. Acts 15 contains a recitation of a letter that functions as a sermon. Barnabas was the son of exhortation/preaching (Acts 4:32).

2.2. Arrangement of Sermons. Early Christian sermons followed the same four patterns of ancient religious oratory.

2.2.1. Pesher Interpretation. A preacher utilized the pesher interpretation method to explain OT testimonia from either a text or memory. This type of sermon emphasized instruction more than persuasion. The best-known example comes from Luke 4. Jesus reads the lection of Isaiah 61:1-4 LXX, sits, and interprets the meaning for the synagogue audience. Cyprian's sermon in Carthage *Adverus Iudaeos,* a mid-third-century sermon, contains a long list of testimonia from the OT Scriptures with an interpretation designed to shape the narrative against Judaism. Second Clement and the epistle of James fit this pattern (see, for example, in continuity with Ps 110:1: Acts 2:34-35; Heb 1:13; Dodd, 15).

2.2.2. Word of Exhortation. The word of exhortation was a formal, structured version of a pesher that provoked a decision. The sermon had three parts: an example, a thesis statement, and a concluding exhortation or provocation anticipating a decision from the audience (Heb 3:1; Wills, 299; Black, 5). This form is suggested by Justin (*1 Apol.* 67) when he mentions the "exhortations" after a reading in early Christian worship. For example, see one of the earliest extant sermons outside the NT, Cyprian's *Adversus Aleatores* (*Against Dice Players;* Siegert, 439). The bishop preached to elders to address a situation in the flock regarding gambling. There is a clear *propositio*; narration and retelling of Scripture; *probatio* of the problem of gambling as a spiritual battle; discussion of *Gentiles, who are welcome in the *church but should not gamble; and a closing exhortation to trust in the Lord (Siegert, 439; see also Acts of Peter 20; Stewart-Sykes, 257). This form was not limited to Christian preaching, of course, in Christian texts. The town clerk exhorts the Ephesians in Acts 19:35-40, and the Jerusalem elders charge Paul in Acts 21:20-25.

2.2.3. Homily. The Christian homily was a long sermon that included dialogue or direct address to the audience and multiple references to or paraphrases of Scripture (Hebrews; Ign. *Pol.* 5.1; Clement of Alexandria, *Strom.* 6.6.52.3). As mentioned previously, Jesus homilies the disciples on the road to Emmaus in Luke 24. Clement's late second- to early third-century sermon *Quis dives salvetur* ("Who Is the Rich Man That Shall Be Saved?") was thirty pages, with rhetorical questions and asides to the audience. The sermon reads like a "running diatribe." In Origen's *Homily on 1 Kings 28* (homily on the witch of Endor), the homily came after several texts were read. Origen asks the bishop which one he should address. In his sermon, Origen refers to a verse, improvises an explanation, and then moves to another topic (Siegert, 443; see also Tertullian, *Apol.* 39).

2.2.4. Declamation. A declamation was a sermon on a theme suitable for multiple occasions and adapted to different audiences. For instance, Melito, the second-century bishop of Sardis, used Exodus 12 as a sketch of Jesus' death to address Marcionite controversies in his congregation (Cohick, 371; Wifstrand, 219).

Pseudo-Hippolytus's sermon on Jesus' baptism is also a declamation (*On the Epiphany*). After a paraphrased retelling of Jesus' baptism, the preacher spoke directly to the audience and invited them to wash away their sins (Siegert, 439). First John functioned as a declamation. He preached from an eyewitness report, similar to the women's sermon following the resurrection. This epideictic sermon invited believers to follow Jesus' life in community with others (see also the fragment of a sermon in Letter of Diognetus 11-12).

2.3. Delivering Sermons in Worship. Other than the evidence from Acts, Christians did not deliver many sermons publicly through the third century AD. They did, however, preach in house churches following a consistent pattern. Early Christians viewed preaching as a declaration of the word of God. When they preached, the sermons became the word of God (Heb 1:1-4, 13; Griffiths, 108).

Before the sermon, a lector read the Scriptures (Melito, *Peri Pascha* 1; Acts of Peter 20), likely in the original language, and then translated the text for the audience (Zuntz, 300; Melito, *Peri Pascha* 1). Following the reading, the president or leader preached. The congregation interrupted and asked questions. Then they rose together, prayed, and partook of bread and wine. They kissed each other and distributed the leftover meal to those who were not present (Justin, *1 Apol.* 67).

3. Paul's Preaching.

In light of the evidence from the ancient world and early Christian congregations, one now can see how Paul's preaching fits these patterns. The sources for Paul's sermons include those recorded by Luke in Acts and the discussion and reminders of his preaching to his recipients in his letters ("as you know" in 1 Thess 1:5; 2:1, 5, 11; 3:3-4; 4:2). In 1 Corinthians, Paul reminds them of the gospel he preached to them (1 Cor 15:1-7; Cho, 30).

What he reminded his audience of and solidified in communicating through the letter, he previously introduced in sermons. The letters functioned as prompts to continue the preaching event. His sermons addressed an issue or *stasis* in the congregation (Thompson 2020, 129). Since a lector or courier read his letter for gathered Christians in worship, the reader could highlight the sermon material and jog their memories of Paul's oral presentation. What worked to explain how Paul's letters are read also helps in understanding how the audience responded to or retained the sermons (Shiell 2004, 145-48).

Paul preached like a parent addressing problems his spiritual children faced (Shiell 2011, 65). He addresses them in a sophistic style in Acts, and his letters indicate that he preached in churches in an attic style (2 Cor 2:1-5). Despite Paul's claim that he lacked rhetorical expertise (2 Cor 2:4; 11:6), his letters reflect knowledge and facility with rhetoric as the art of persuasion, including Greek and rhetorical categories (Braxton, 8).

While preaching, like a parent, he corrected, rebuked, and taught the audience patiently (2 Tim 4:2; Griffiths, 56). His arguments are based on similar categories to ancient rhetoric, but he relies less on appeals to character than other early Christian preachers. He emphasizes the character of Jesus over his own. Paul knew that the content of Jesus' story could not be separated from his character (Thompson 2001, 121). He notes how God in Jesus Christ changed his character, appealing to his weakness and humility (1 Cor 2:1-5; 4:6-13). In a "reverse ethos," Paul uses the categories of training as a Pharisee, normally to establish credibility, to validate Jesus' work in him (2 Cor 1:12–2:13; 7:5-16; Young and Ford, 37-39). He says that the foolishness of the *cross determines conduct, not *ethnicity or education (2 Cor 2:4–4:6; Thompson 2001, 121). He reflects on his condition as a prisoner and leverages his distance and suffering to provide a model to the Philippians to emulate (Thompson 2018, 239). When he could not be physically present, he appointed authoritative representatives such as Phoebe, Epaphroditus, and Timothy to represent his character and presence to the people (Griffiths, 55).

Paul uses several emotional appeals. He speaks in the first-person plural to connect to the audience (1 Thess 2:1-12). He expresses vulnerability to the Corinthians when he says that "our heart is open to you" (2 Cor 6:11-12) and uses familial language to the Galatians and Thessalonians, addressing them as a parent (Gal 4:19; 1 Thess 2:11-12), and then the Thessalonians and Philippians as siblings (1 Thess 2:1; Phil 1:12). Paul also does not hesitate to warn them of impending *judgment (Thompson 2001, 41).

He logically reasons by basing his sermons not on his expertise but on a received tradition passed down from Jesus to the *apostles to himself (1 Cor 15). He uses examples from the past and connects his story to the gospel (1 Cor 8:6; 9:1-23; 11:23-26; 15:1-3; Gal 1:10–2:21; Phil 3:2-16). In deliberative sermons he exhorts his audience to make expedient decisions, that is, to act on what is most advantageous in the present (1 Cor 6:13; 10:23; 2 Cor 8:10; 12:1; Thompson 2001, 41; Mitchell, 37-38).

Paul adapts a theme that he broadly calls "the gospel of God" and appropriates this theme in his sermons. God has entrusted a message or "word of *faith" to him that God passed down from Jesus, the apostles, himself, and now to his listeners. This word of faith is available freely to everyone because God created all persons, and everyone descends from this bloodline (Acts 17:26). Jesus of Nazareth, the crucified and resurrected Son of God, King, and Lord, revealed and validated God's work and now reigns. Through preaching, Paul announces his reign, subverts structures that opposed his reign, and overturns unjust systems that oppress people. God "rendered ineffective" the world's systems (1 Cor 1:28) and proclaims a new age that offers *forgiveness, *wisdom, reconciliation, restoration, and life. This new age demands a response because God's judgment is coming, and the end is near (1 Thess 1:9-10; Dodd, 12). Believers appropriate this reign, but not through human strength, pedigree, ingenuity, or skill. God no longer requires Gentiles and Jews to participate in *circumcision. Persons access this gift of *grace from Jesus Christ through repentance and turning from their idols (Munck, 101). They surrender to his reign in weakness and dependency through faith and obedience to him and join a new community related spiritually through *adoption. These new siblings in Jesus Christ still face difficulty because they live in the old era while simultaneously participating in the new. They need to continually depend on the Spirit's power as they participate in the new age in their daily lives (Braxton, 50-56).

3.1. Terms for Paul's Preaching. Paul uses eight terms to describe his preaching.

Apangellō. In Acts 26, Paul is an eyewitness with a responsibility to report events (Acts 26:20).

Euangelizō. Paul "proclaims good news" fifty-four times (e.g., Rom 1:15; 10:15; 15:20; 1 Cor 9:16; 15:3; 2 Cor 10:16; 11:7) and "declares the gospel of God" (1 Thess 2:2). He describes his *call to preach using this language (Gal 1:16; Griffiths, 20).

Katangellō. Paul uses this word for preaching eighteen times. Like Plutarch's description of Pyrrhus's sacrifice, this preaching was personal and collective, verbal and nonverbal. The people participated in the sermon in the *Lord's Supper (1 Cor 11:26; see also 1 Cor 2:1; Phil 1:18; Griffiths, 25). *Opponents in Philippi preached this way with impure motives (Phil 1:17).

Kērygma and *kēryx.* The core content of Paul's preaching is *kērygma*, but he rarely uses this word (Rom 16:25; 1 Cor 1:21; 2:4; 15:14; 2 Tim 4:17; Titus 1:3; Thompson 2001, 43). He also refers to himself only once as a *kēryx* (1 Tim 2:7).

Kēryssō. Instead of the noun *kērygma*, Paul prefers the verb *kēryssō*, which refers to Paul's message, delivered itinerantly (Acts 20:25) and at home (Acts 28:31). He uses this word fifty-nine times. This word describes the mission and content of his preaching, which include Jesus Christ as Lord (2 Cor 4:5), Son of God Jesus Christ (2 Cor 1:19), gospel of God (1 Thess 2:9), word of faith (Rom 10:8; Thompson 2018, 236; Griffiths, 27).

Homileō. Paul preaches a homily in two significant places, both of which occur in Acts. The first was in Troas during the night of preaching when Eutychus fell from the window. His sermon was likely a similar length as *On Samson* or the Emmaus homily. Paul uses a homily in his discussion in the middle of his defense with Agrippa (Acts 24:26). If Paul preached here, he would be unique among orators to preach in a judicial setting. He fulfills Jesus' admonition in Luke to be prepared for such occasion and trusts that the *Holy Spirit will give him the words to preach extemporaneously.

Paraklēsis. Paul equates the spiritual gift of *prophecy with preaching as exhortation (1 Cor 14:3). He uses the Scriptures as a basis for his exhortations (Rom 15:4-5) and charges Timothy to give attention to this kind of preaching (1 Tim 4:14; see also 1 Thess 2:3; Philem 8; Rom 12:1; 1 Cor 1:10; 2 Cor 5:20; 10:1; 1 Thess 4:1; Bowens, 91).

3.2. Arrangement of Paul's Sermons. As stated above, Paul preaches a homily in Acts 20. There are also scriptural examples of Paul's use of the three other kinds of sermons from the ancient world and early Christian settings.

3.2.1. *Word of Exhortation.* As noted previously, these sermons contained three distinct parts: an example, thesis, and concluding exhortation. In Acts 13:13-41, Paul preaches a "word of exhortation" in synagogues, like a Hellenistic Jewish orator (Acts 13:5). This form of preaching demanded a response (1 Thess 1:5–2:12; Thompson 2020, 84-85).

Paul marks the beginning of the speech with a gesture (Acts 13:16). Part two was the narration/*narratio* (Acts 13:17-25). This section provided the background example and statement of facts. God's faithfulness to the tribe of Benjamin has brought the audience to this moment. Paul retells the history of *Israel through the line of Benjamin. Both Paul and King Saul were Benjamites.

The thesis or *propositio* (Acts 13:26) of his argument is in Acts 13:26. The same faithful promise God made to *Abraham has now been given to all, followed by evidence or proofs why this promise matters to them (Acts 13:27-37). Jesus fulfilled God's faithful promise. His death was not a failure but the result of people's ignorance in collaboration with the Romans. Jesus remained faithful to the *mission, and God has vindicated Jesus and confirmed his work by raising him from the dead.

The word *therefore* marks the concluding exhortation, which is a call to action (Acts 13:38-41). Paul calls them to believe in Jesus to be liberated from their sins in ways that the *law of Moses cannot. They are warned not to scoff, lest they miss out on the new beginning (Shiell 2017, 106).

3.2.2. *Pesher Interpretation.* Paul uses the pesher arrangement in his reflection on preaching in Romans 10:11-17. He inserts his interpretation of Deuteronomy 30:12-14 and Isaiah 52:7 LXX between his citations of these scriptures. He says "the scripture says" in Romans 10:11, explains the scripture, and cites other scriptures to support his case. As Griffiths notes, "Just as the Israelites in the wilderness were given God's word through Moses the great prophet and leader, so now the people of God are given his word through the apostle as representative Christian preacher" (Griffiths 69-70; Seifrid, 35).

3.2.3. *Declamation.* Paul uses a declamation in Athens. After being asked to speak with one day's notice, Paul could have distributed notes to the audience. His chosen theme required little preparation (Acts 17:18-19; Schnabel, 176).

The Athenians accuse Paul of proclaiming "foreign deities." Paul responds with an epideictic sermon on a familiar theme: the importance of repenting and turning to the one true God. He uses the rhetorical device of inflection on the word *God*, highlighting the theme (Shiell 2017, 141).

Introduction/*Captatio benevolentiae* (Acts 17:22-23): Paul greets the audience and establishes common ground with them. They, like him, are religious.

Thesis (Acts 17:23b): What they worship as unknown is now known. Paul preached to inform them who this unknown God is and what God has done.

Proofs (Acts 17:24-29):

- God has created everything.
- Diverse nations originated from one person (Acts 17:26).
- Seasons, boundaries, and places are evidence of God's existence (Acts 17:26-27).
- Our quest for God is evidence that God exists (Acts 17:27-28).
- Even the philosopher Aratus agrees that humans come from the same God (Acts 17:28).

Conclusion/call to action: Paul calls the Athenians to repent because the time of the end has arrived. The resurrection confirms the appointed time and assures them that this will come to pass. Therefore, the Athenians must repent from idols (Shiell 2017, 143).

3.3. ***Paul's Delivery.*** Paul preached occasionally in public using the declamation (Acts 17) and anticipated a response from the crowd. He primarily preached in a house church or synagogue setting using short words of exhortation, pesher messages, or homilies in the night (Stowers, 80-81).

In a liturgical setting, Paul likely delivered his sermon this way:

- Paul offered an opening greeting of grace and *peace (Rom 1:7; 1 Cor 1:3; 2 Cor 1:2; Gal 1:3; Eph 1:2; Phil 1:2; Philem 3; "Grace to you and peace from God the Father and the Lord Jesus Christ"; Thompson 2001, 80-81; Cho, 28).
- A reading of the Scripture preceded the sermon.
- Paul preached in one of four arrangements, sometimes through the night.
- The church continued the sermon by participating in the Eucharist. By sharing the meal, they too were "proclaiming the Lord's death until he comes" (1 Cor 11:26; Knowles, 20).
- Paul provided a closing benediction: "Grace to you and peace" or "The grace of the Lord Jesus be with you." The benediction and likely the

*prayer were in the optative mood (Rom 15:33; 16:20; 2 Cor 13:11; Gal 6:16; Phil 4:9b; 1 Thess 5:23; 2 Thess 3:16; Thompson 2018, 242; Collins, 53).

- The audience followed with a response. There were times when the audience responded favorably to Paul's message. They engaged his teaching throughout the sermon, asked questions, and participated publicly in the sermon. At other times, the audience responded with mocking, beating, and imprisonment (2 Cor 11:24-27; Knowles, 11-12).

Paul's letters and reminders of his sermons were delivered in absentia in worship by a lector who performed the letter. Afterward, the audience kissed each other, demonstrating their "communal unity, love, fellowship, and reconciliation" (Heil, 60).

4. Implications.

Despite Paul's comments in 1–2 Corinthians, the early church through Luke, *1 Clement* 5.5-6, and later the Acts of Paul and Thecla and Acts of Titus present Paul as an effective preacher. Even today, Paul's call to preach and subsequent messages have had a profound effect on preachers (Bowens, 155). He valued preaching so much he considered it to be a type of work, similar to military service, farming, or temple service (1 Cor 9:14; Griffiths, 79).

Paul's expansive *knowledge of God from his Pharisaical training and familiarity with rhetoric placed him in the tradition of Hellenistic Jewish and Greco-Roman religious orators. Taught by the religious leaders to preach into the night, Paul could converse with the philosophers in Athens as well as believers in Troas. He leveraged this training to communicate to his audiences.

Paul preached like a parent to children. He focused on more than just "the facts of Jesus' death and resurrection in an eschatological setting" (Dodd, 13). Paul improvised, adapting a *narrative to fit the *stasis* or issue the people faced. He did not preach off the cuff. He worked from a standard set of themes and used the rhetorical cues he learned. As William Willimon writes, "The oratorical skill of Paul cannot remove the offense of the gospel—in fact, it accentuates it" (Willimon, 164). Paul preached in a conversational, simple style that would connect to his audience. He rarely preached verse by verse but paraphrased testimonia from the OT and relied on the audience's memories of sacred texts to participate in the delivery.

The arrangement of the sermon corresponded to the *stasis* of the audience and Paul's goals in communication. When preaching a pesher interpretation, Paul connected his work to the prophecies from the LXX. When preaching a word of exhortation or declamation, Paul challenged the listeners' worldview and story and called for the audience to turn away from their mental model of how the world works and surrender to Jesus (Thompson 2001, 47). Paul assumed an imminent return of Jesus and preached with that urgency (Still, 12). When preaching a homily, Paul dialogued with the audience for instruction and conversion. The audience participated verbally and nonverbally in his sermons—during the preached word and in the meal that followed the sermon. The meal was an important part of the message.

Contemporary preaching that aspires to replicating first-century methods would follow a similar unscripted pattern. Thus preachers would not assume that one sermon arrangement fits all or presuppose "a call to decision" for every sermon. Rather, preachers would adapt core content for the occasion, focusing less on a new sermon for every Sunday and more on the issues in the congregation that arise from Sunday to Sunday. A preacher would anticipate a variety of responses, from rejection and accusations to conversion and reconciliation. The sermon's effectiveness would not be judged on the listener's positive response but on the participation of the listener in the death and resurrection of Jesus Christ. In the Pauline tradition, both preacher and congregation will suffer together personally and publicly. As they do, people will surrender their lives, turn from their idols, and identify with Jesus Christ as Lord.

See also Gospel; Performance; Preaching from Paul Today; Rhetorical Criticism; Teaching, Teachers; Worship.

BIBLIOGRAPHY. **C. C. Black,** "The Rhetorical Form of the Hellenistic Jewish and Early Christian Sermon: A Response to Lawrence Wills," *HTR* 81, no. 1 (1988): 1-18; **L. M. Bowens,** *African American Readings of Paul: Reception, Resistance, and Transformation* (Grand Rapids, MI: Eerdmans, 2020); **B. R. Braxton,** *Preaching Paul* (Nashville: Abingdon, 2004); **F. F. Bruce,** *Biblical Exegesis in the Qumran Texts* (London: Tyndale, 1960); **K. Cho,** *Paul's Community Formation Preaching in 1 Thessalonians: An Alternative to the New Homiletic* (Bern: Lang, 2017); **L. Cohick,** "Melito of Sardis's Peri Pascha and Its 'Israel,'" *HTR* 91, no. 4 (1998): 351-72; **R. F. Collins,** "1 Thes and the Liturgy of the Early Church," *BTB* 10, no. 2 (1980): 51-64; **C. H. Dodd,** *The Apostolic Preaching and Its Developments: Three Lectures with an Appendix on Eschatology and History* (New York:

Harper & Brothers, 1936); **J. I. Griffiths,** *Preaching in the New Testament: An Exegetical and Biblical-Theological Study,* NSBT 42 (Downers Grove, IL: InterVarsity Press, 2017); **J. P. Heil,** *The Letters of Paul as Rituals of Worship* (Eugene, OR: Cascade, 2011); **M. P. Knowles,** "Preaching Like Paul? Lessons from Ancient Corinth," *McMaster Journal of Theology and Mission* 11 (2009–2010): 3-27; **M. M. Mitchell,** *Paul and the Rhetoric of Reconciliation: An Exegetical Investigation of the Language and Composition of 1 Corinthians 10,* 2nd ed. (Louisville, KY: Westminster John Knox, 1991); **J. Munck,** "1 Thess. 1.9-10 and the Missionary Preaching of Paul: Textual Exegesis and Hermeneutic Reflections," *NTS* 9 (1963): 95-110; **G. Muradyan and A. Topychan,** "Pseudo-Philo, On Samson and On Jonah," in *Outside the Bible: Ancient Jewish Writings Related to Scripture,* ed. L. H. Feldman, J. L. Kugel, and L. H. Schiffman (Lincoln: University of Nebraska Press, 2013), 750-803; **D. A. Russell,** *Greek Declamation* (Cambridge: Cambridge University Press, 1983); **E. J. Schnabel,** "Contextualizing Paul in Athens: The Proclamation of the Gospel Before Pagan Audiences in the Graeco-Roman World," *R&T* 12, no. 2 (2005): 172-90; **M. A. Seifrid,** "Paul's Approach to the Old Testament in Rom 10:6-8," *TrinJ* 6, no. 1 (1985): 3-37; **W. D. Shiell,** *Reading Acts: The Lector and the Early Christian Audience,* BibInt 70 (Leiden: Brill Academic, 2004); idem, *Delivering from Memory: The Effect of Performance on the Early Christian Audience* (Eugene, OR: Pickwick, 2011); idem, *Acts: Preaching the Word* (Macon, GA: Smyth & Helwys, 2017); **F. Siegert,** "Homily and Panegyrical Sermons," in *Handbook of Classical Rhetoric in the Hellenistic Period 330 B.C.–A.D. 400,* ed. S. E. Porter (Leiden: Brill, 1997), 421-44; **A. Stewart Sykes,** *From Prophecy to Preaching: A Search for the Origins of the Christian Homily,* VCSup 59 (Leiden: Brill Academic, 2001); **T. D. Still,** "'Since We Believe That Jesus Died and Rose Again': The Gospel Paul Preached in Thessalonica as Evidenced by 1 Thessalonians," *ResQ* 54, no. 1 (2012): 7-18; **S. K. Stowers,** "Social Status, Public Speaking and Private Teaching: The Circumstances of Paul's Preaching Activity," *NovT* 26, no. 1 (1984): 59-82; **J. W. Thompson,** *Preaching Like Paul: Homiletical Wisdom for Today* (Louisville, KY: Westminster John Knox, 2001); idem, "The Grammar of Preaching," *RQ* 60, no. 4 (2018): 235-43; idem, *Apostle of Persuasion: Theology and Rhetoric in the Pauline Letters* (Grand Rapids, MI: Baker Academic, 2020); **A. Wifstrand,** "The Homily of Melito on the Passion," *VC* 2, no. 4 (1948): 201-23; **W. H. Willimon,** "'Eyewitnesses and Ministers of the Word': Preaching in Acts," *Int* 42, no. 2 (1988): 158-70; **F. M. Young and D. Ford,** *Meaning and Truth in 2 Corinthians* (Eugene, OR: Wipf & Stock, 2008); **G. Zuntz,** "On the Opening Sentence of Melito's Pascal Homily," *HTR* 36, no. 4 (1943): 299-315.

W. D. Shiell

PREACHING FROM PAUL TODAY

Preaching from Paul's writings requires awareness of a range of factors associated with his letters, with his preaching, and with our perception of him as a person. M. M. Mitchell, noting John Chrysostom's fascination with the *apostle Paul, comments that throughout time "exegesis is inherently interwoven with portraiture" (409). To some degree, our debates surrounding Paul relate to the mental images we have inherited or created of the apostle. Paul's *identity as *pastor, preacher, and disciple maker informs our pastoral work, including preaching. Our perceptions of Paul and his *ministry can prompt creativity and flexibility regarding how to communicate Paul's teachings.

1. Challenges to Preaching Paul
2. Paul as Model
3. Communicating Paul's Writings

1. Challenges to Preaching Paul.

Throughout the centuries, preachers have discovered the truth of this early testimony concerning Paul's letters: "There are some things in them hard to understand, which the ignorant and unstable twist to their own destruction, as they do the other scriptures" (2 Pet 3:16 NRSV). Misunderstanding, misuse, and possible destruction have perpetually plagued preachers of Paul's letters. The challenges associated with preaching from the Pauline corpus are theological, historical, *hermeneutical, and methodological.

1.1. Theological Challenges. There are ongoing debates concerning the apostle Paul's theological framework. For example, M. J. Gorman (2016) sketches ten distinct, even if at times overlapping, perspectives on Paul and his writings. The theological challenges include interpreting several key words and expressions that are central to Paul's arguments, especially in Romans and Galatians. For example, in Romans 3:21-26, one finds "*righteousness of God," "*faith in (faithfulness of) Jesus Christ," and "*justify" (Rom 3:21-22, 24, 26 NRSV). Those terms appear in Galatians, along with another contested term, "*works of the law" (Gal 2:16 NRSV). Furthermore, several scholarly books are devoted entirely to the concepts of *salvation, *gospel, and faith in

Paul's writings—ideas that many preachers may have thought they had already grasped.

In their attempts to construct Paul's religious outlook as well as his ministry strategy, scholars examine the meaning of the aforementioned words and phrases, resulting in various perspectives on Paul. Pastors, as well as other teachers and preachers, may find the amount of secondary literature on Paul's life and theology to be limitless. Consequently, wading through the scholarly discussions can be overwhelming, especially for pastors with a myriad of other duties to perform. Even so, as faithful practitioners who strive to accurately explain the Scriptures (see 2 Tim 2:15), preachers and teachers do well to reconsider prior theological assumptions (Edwards 2020). Our understanding of Paul's theology, through the vocabulary he uses to explain it, requires exploration of Second Temple Judaism, as well as Greco-Roman history. Discovering as much as we can of Paul's historical context enhances our preaching and teaching.

1.2. Historical Challenges. Knowing some of the issues facing the addressees of Paul's letters allows us to find analogues for contemporary audiences. Analogies are necessary elements for crafting relevant sermons and other teaching events that help listeners to discern how biblical texts might pertain to present-day predicaments. Paul's letters are occasional, which is to say they are written to specific audiences to address particular issues. Discerning details about the audiences and issues behind Paul's writings requires attention to the religious and geopolitical landscape of the first century CE.

Insights may be gained through mirror reading, an exercise in reconstructing the issues facing the addresses even though we do not hear directly from them. J. M. G. Barclay points out the polemical nature of much of the NT, while noting the "essential and extremely problematic" practice of mirror reading, since we only have access to the "thoughts and identities" of the writers' (or community's) opponents through the NT documents (Barclay, 367-68). Even with its limitations, mirror reading may illuminate some of the historical circumstances behind Paul's writings, which helps in addressing hermeneutical challenges. For example, through mirror reading, McKnight (2019) connects the "weak" and "*strong" in Romans to contemporary issues of power and privilege within Christian communities. Navigating issues of power and privilege are among the hermeneutical challenges facing contemporary preachers, especially with society's tendency toward polarization.

1.3. Hermeneutical Challenges. Hermeneutical questions linger, especially surrounding Paul's parenetical material. For example, arguments concerning gender, *sexual identity, and *marriage persist, often with Paul's writings central in the discussions. The *Haustafeln* (*household codes, in Paul and elsewhere) played a key role in the subjugation of *women as well as the enslavement of Africans in the New World. The NT household codes are approached by many with a hermeneutic of suspicion. Those who affirm the full participation of women in every aspect of Christian ministry appeal to Paul's writings, as do those who restrict the role of women. Increasing numbers of women scholars, as well as those of non-European background, bring their social locations to shed light on some of these persistent hermeneutical questions (Edwards 2019). As Christians who have been marginalized (such as women and ethnic minorities) find and raise their voices, we discover increasingly diverse ways that Paul's teachings are communicated in contemporary society.

1.4. Methodological Challenges. Teaching and preaching from the Pauline corpus touches on the form of delivery as well as the content. There is an interplay of written and spoken word in the development and delivery of sermons. Preachers write sermons to be delivered orally (primarily) from written material that was first delivered in oral form but served as a stand-in for the writer's physical presence. Furthermore, communication is a competitive sport. In the Greco-Roman world, public speakers were judged for their *rhetorical skills, while today communicators compete for attention and affirmation in a variety of settings. Social media offers nonstop access to all manner of information designed to persuade and exhort. Consumers are constantly bombarded with written and spoken words. The Covid-19 pandemic created unprecedented challenges for Christians to communicate Scripture teaching because in many places throughout the world, congregations could not gather in person. Yet, even as the logistics of preaching change over time, we can learn from the way Paul viewed his own oral communication. Paul's expressed motivation for preaching, along with his resultant expectations, can inform modern-day preachers and teachers.

2. Paul as Model.

Aristotle (*Poet.* 4) asserts that human beings learn their first lessons by imitation. With Paul being the patron saint of missionaries, evangelists, writers, and public workers, he has been—apart from Jesus—the preeminent model for Christian leaders. Chrysostom and Augustine developed different portraits of Paul, yet both modeled their thinking and writing after the apostle (Mitchell). Paul's ministerial identity and practices can inform our current preaching and teaching strategies. As Thompson suggests, Paul's "preaching in a pre-Christian age has much to tell preachers who live in a post-Christian age" (2000, 19). Investigating Paul as preacher, writer, and pastor shapes our communication of Paul's written ideas.

*2.1. **Paul the Preacher.*** Our image of Paul is constructed primarily from Luke's portrayal in Acts and from the writings that bear the apostle's name (including the disputed letters). Paul was a preacher of the gospel of Jesus *Christ, yet we must avoid casting Paul in our own image, portraying him as an American tent-meeting revivalist, television evangelist, megachurch pastor, or motivational speaker. While Paul was a *witness (*martys*) who spoke from his own experiences (e.g., Acts 16:16), he primarily envisioned himself as a herald (*kēryx*), a messenger, in the vein of OT prophets. Being sent as an apostle of Christ Jesus (e.g., Rom 1:1; 1 Cor 1:1; 2 Cor 1:1; Gal 1:1), Paul was entrusted to convey what *God had given to him (see 1 Cor 9:17; Gal 2:7; 1 Thess 2:4; 1 Tim 1:11; 2:7; 2 Tim 1:11). Following Isaiah (see Is 52:7; 61:1), Paul preached God's good news of Jesus Christ, with the goal of developing mature followers of Jesus.

Paul's most forthright presentation of his preaching ministry is found in his Corinthian correspondence. The apostle writes to Christians in a city that appreciated the performative and competitive nature of public speaking and ironically focuses on his own ministry of proclamation (1 Cor 1:17). Paul tells the Corinthians that he does not communicate with the rhetorical artistry of skilled orators (e.g., 1 Cor 1:17; 2:1, 4; 2 Cor 11:6). Some scholars, noting Paul's skill in letter writing, suggest that the apostle's self-deprecating words are a rhetorical ploy, designed to disarm his opponents. However, A. D. Litfin, M. F. Bird, and J. W. Thompson are among those scholars who take the apostle's words at face value, asserting that Paul purposely contrasted himself with the polished orators of the Greco-Roman world.

Throughout his writings, Paul presented himself as a simple herald rather than as a professional persuader. For Paul, the human wisdom of the world cannot communicate the message of the *cross, which prompts faith in Jesus Christ, being accompanied by the *Holy Spirit's power (e.g., 1 Cor 2:4-5, 13; 3:19-20; 1 Thess 1:5). Although Paul sought to persuade his listeners (see Acts 18:4; 19:8), he relied on the power of God rather than skillful oration. Preaching should not be boring, but according to Paul, it should demonstrate dependence on the power of God more than on impressive speaking ability.

*2.2. **Paul the Writer.*** Paul's written work was an extension of his public presence. Ancient *letters, including Paul's, were dictated to a secretary (amanuensis), and read aloud to the recipients. Scholars debate, however, to what extent Paul incorporated the conventions of skilled oration in his letters. On the one hand, some scholars consider Paul's letters to be essentially written speeches, reflecting the same conventions of Greco-Roman oration. *Rhetorical criticism has made students of the NT aware of Latin terms such as *exordium* (introduction), *narratio* (brief recounting of events), *partitio* (outline of what follows), *confirmatio* (the main body of the speech with an appeal to logic), *refutatio* (answers to counterarguments), and *peroratio* (the emotional appeal), derived from ancient rhetorical handbooks. Speeches fell into three basic categories, according to Aristotle (*Rhet.* 1.3.3): (1) forensic (to accuse or defend), (2) epideictic (to offer praise or assign blame), and (3) deliberative (to persuade). Paul's letters primarily employ deliberative rhetoric as the apostle directs readers toward right decisions and actions.

Paul's letters, on the other hand, while deliberative in nature, do not fit neatly into the categories of ancient rhetoric found in the handbooks. Written communication is a substitute for face-to-face interaction but is not exactly the same as a speech. While Paul's writing style does make use of creative devices, such as chiasm, parallelism, repetition, and diatribe, he employs what Bird calls "*functional* rhetoric" as opposed to *formal* rhetoric (Bird, 379). This is to say that Paul makes use of some rhetorical conventions, along with philosophical and epistolary practices, but does not write as one schooled in the Hellenistic art of public speaking.

Even if lacking the formal qualities of speech, Paul's letters were designed to communicate his apostolic authority as well as his pastoral concern. Consider, for example, his emotional appeal to the Philippians to "fulfill my *joy" (Phil 2:2 NKJV), and his subtle exercise of authority when exhorting Philemon, not by commanding, even though the apostle possessed that prerogative (Philem 8). Through letters, Paul exercised power and influence in various Christian communities. For the contemporary preacher and teacher, greater attention to function over form may help our communication. Paul's words had impact and were worth preserving because he was God's herald, and his presence—in word even if not in person—was helpful for the Christian community. Our preaching should reflect the God who calls us and simultaneously convey our pastoral concern.

2.3. *Paul the Pastor.* Paul was a pastor, and his writing is prompted by pastoral concerns. Indeed, the churches were constantly on Paul's mind. In 2 Corinthians 11:28, after rehearsing a litany of horrendous and painful experiences, such as being beaten, pummeled with stones, shipwrecked, hungry, and destitute, Paul says, "And, besides other things, I am under daily pressure because of my anxiety for all the churches" (NRSV). In addition to his role as herald and his experience as a writer, Paul was fundamentally a shepherd responsible for nurturing disciples of Jesus Christ.

Nurturing believers as a pastor meant that Paul took on a parental role. At times his parenting is described in maternal terms. For example, he tells the Galatians, "My little children, for whom I am again in the pain of childbirth until Christ is formed in you, I wish I were present with you now and could change my tone, for I am perplexed about you" (Gal 4:19-20 NRSV). In 1 Thessalonians 2:7 Paul likens himself to a *trophos* ("nursing mother") in describing his love and care to the converts in Thessalonica. Interestingly, a few verses later, Paul describes his ministry in paternal terms: "As you know, we dealt with each one of you like a father with his children, urging and encouraging you and pleading that you lead a life worthy of God, who calls you into his own kingdom and glory" (1 Thess 2:11-12 NRSV).

Even though Paul presented himself in parental terms at points, he typically referred to the recipients of his letters as his siblings (*adelphoi*, "brothers and sisters"). Part of Paul's pastoral identity included a posture of mutuality, where he notes his dependence on the communities to which he writes (Gombis). Mutuality is evident in Paul's frequent use of the language of sharing or *fellowship (e.g., *koinōnia* and its cognates). Some of the benefits Paul received from his relationship with churches included encouragement (e.g., Rom 1:11-12), joy (e.g., Phil 1:3; 2:2), and prayerful support (e.g., Eph 6:18-20).

As a pastor, Paul offered himself as a model for others to follow: "Be imitators of me, as I am of Christ" (1 Cor 11:1 NRSV; see Gal 4:12; 2 Thess 3:7, 9). Paul instructs his protégé, Timothy, to pass on to faithful people whatever he heard from his mentor (2 Tim 2:2). McKnight (2019b) describes the pastoral task as nurturing a culture of *Christoformity*, where the *church, the community of Christ-followers, is continually conformed to Christ. Christoformity, according to McKnight, has at least seven associated themes that are demonstrated in Paul's ministry: (1) a culture of *friendship, (2) a culture of siblings, (3) a culture of generosity, (4) a culture of storytellers, (5) a culture of witness, (6) a culture of world subversion, and (7) a culture of *wisdom. Paul as a pastor demonstrated how the gospel is believed and also embodied (Gorman 2015).

3. Communicating Paul's Writings.
Not all preaching or teaching looks the same, as communication is a function of cultural practices. For example, some churches are culturally conditioned to hearing a homily of twenty minutes or less during the worship service, while other congregations expect sermons approaching forty-five minutes to one hour in length. Bible instruction, such as what might take place in a study group, also varies in length and level of detail. The preacher's setting is sometimes an overlooked factor, as homileticians typically give instructions with their own contexts in view.

Classical rhetoric influenced Paul as a letter writer even though he did not slavishly adhere to rhetorical devices. The greater impact on Paul's writing came from his and his recipients' setting and issues rather than from formal rhetorical training. Paul's style and vocabulary are a function of the circumstances facing him and his addressees. Similarly, textbooks on homiletics guide contemporary preachers, yet those preachers may veer from standard practices based on their relationship with their listeners. Visiting preachers or new pastors, for example, may take fewer liberties in public communication than pastors who have served the same congregation for several years. Even though preacher-scholars offer practical guidance for preaching Pauline texts, the art and skill of communication is more about connecting with listeners than about rhetorical structure.

3.1. *Preparing Sermons and Lessons.* To best reflect Paul's writings, preachers and teachers should choose passages that are literary units, as opposed to individual words or phrases, in an attempt to give context to the apostle's message. The lectionary readings offer guidance in selecting passages, but it is also possible to choose literary units for a series of messages based on a theme or an entire Pauline letter. Exegetical work reveals Paul's likely reasons for writing, and those reasons should be stated in the sermon. Preachers help to bridge the ancient and modern contexts by connecting Paul's goals for his addressees to the concerns of contemporary listeners.

In addition to exegetical work, preachers and teachers engage in spiritual work. This is to say that, prior to delivery, preparation should include prayer along with personal reflection on the passage under consideration. Preachers are careful to practice what they preach, striving, like Paul, to avoid hypocrisy (see 1 Cor 9:27). As the transforming work of the Holy Spirit is consciously acknowledged by the communicator, the message can be delivered with greater conviction and confidence.

Preparation also includes a plan to invite a variety of responses. In some traditions, sermons end with an invitation for personal commitment to Jesus (i.e., the altar call), with the Eucharist, or with both. Other creative responses may involve more of the physical senses. Responses might include inviting listeners to write, to draw, to sing, to make a craft, or to simply to reflect in silence.

Allowing others to help imagine creative responses to messages is an opportunity to appreciate how aspects of preaching and teaching can reflect communal effort. We often picture the apostle Paul as a loner, traveling by himself, or perhaps sitting alone in *prison. However, the NT picture shows the apostle accompanied by fellow workers (e.g., Priscilla and Aquila in Rom 16:3; Urbanus in Rom 16:9; Justus in Col 4:11), fellow soldiers (e.g., Epaphroditus in Phil 2:25 and Archippus in Philem 2), and fellow *slaves (Epaphras in Col 1:7 and Tychicus in Col 4:7). Paul does not write his letters alone. Timothy is a frequent fellow author (2 Cor 1:1; Phil 1:1; 1 Thess 1:1; 2 Thess 1:1; Philem 1:1). Other fellow letter senders include Sosthenes (1 Cor 1:1) and Silvanus (1 Thess 1:1; 2 Thess 1:1). Paul's canonical letters were not private communications, and our sermons and lessons, while flowing from our personal study and prayer, can find ways to include others in the preparation, delivery, and response, demonstrating the communal nature of Christian faith and practice.

3.2. Performance Criticism. Performance criticism is an emerging discipline within biblical studies and is relevant to the topic of preaching Paul. Performance criticism seeks to take seriously the oral culture in which the NT emerged. The NT is a collection of written documents, but they were dictated, carried by hand, then read to listeners. Performance critics assert that the reading was actually a *performance, conveying emotion, using gestures, and otherwise emphasizing particular topics according to the author's concerns. Consider, for example, Philippians 3:2 and the repetition of *blepete* ("beware"): "Beware of the dogs, beware of the evil workers, before of those who mutilate the *flesh!" (NRSV). Some translations do not translate *blepete* three times. For example, the NIV reads, "Watch out for those dogs, those evildoers, those mutilators of the flesh." No repetition appears in the NIV, as it is not necessary from a grammatical standpoint. However, from a performative standpoint, one can imagine Epaphroditus gesturing in order to emphasize the three warnings. Similarly, in Philippians 4:2, Paul pleads with Euodia and Syntyche using *parakalō* twice when only once would suffice. Perhaps Epaphroditus fixed his eyes on Euodia with the first mention of *parakalō* and then searched across the room to fix his eyes on her rival, Syntyche, with the second mention.

Ancient rhetoricians had five tasks in the preparation of speeches: (1) *inventio* (what arguments will be used), (2) *disposition* (arrangement of the arguments), (3) *elocutio* (style of the speech), (4) *memoria* (memorization), and (5) *pronuntiatio* or *actio* (presentation of the speech). Performance critics point out that of these five areas, rhetorical critics primarily focus on the first three. Performance criticism gives attention to the latter two items on the list, as it attempts to reconstruct likely models of the original performance situation. Oral retelling of a written work is meant to demonstrate how texts functioned in an orality-based culture. D. Rhoads and B. Oestreich delineate seven aspects of the performance event:

1. Performance, being a holistic event, includes not only language but also articulation with voice and gestures.
2. The content presented is not generated directly by the written words but is a bodily interpretation of the text.
3. The presenter, engaging his or her entire being, embodies the text with its values and perceptions.
4. Listeners/observers, as a community, actively influence the presentation.
5. The location and physical context of the performance influence the presentation.
6. Details of the text will generate new meanings given the respective historical and social situation in which the performance takes place.
7. The text being presented influences ideas, perceptions, and values, changes relationships, and provokes actions.

"Performance criticism is concerned not only with what the text means but also with the effect it achieves and how that happens" (Oestreich, chap. 1). Some contemporary preachers and teachers may find ways to incorporate performance criticism as an aid to biblical interpretation. At the very least, this emerging discipline highlights the importance of giving an engaging presentation, as well as the powerful influence that listeners possess.

In some African American churches, for example, listeners play an active role with the preacher in the call-and-response. The back and forth between congregation and preacher gives prominence to the two-way nature of communication and its function in the context of biblical teaching. Call-and-response also respects the power that listeners have to influence the presentation. Enthusiastic responses energize the preacher, while lackluster responses might result in the preacher taking a seat earlier than anticipated. Other traditions have ways of actively including listeners. Some Anabaptists, for example, engage in some form or another of *Zeugnis* (German for "testimony" or "evidence"), where listeners give responses to the message in an attempt to be a hermeneutical community, working together with the Holy Spirit to discern the meaning of biblical texts for their setting.

*3.3. **Facing the Difficulties.*** It takes concerted effort to confront the difficulties associated with preaching and teaching Paul in our time. Seven of the eleven NT occurrences of *spoudazō* (suggesting haste, diligence, and conscientious effort) appear in letters attributed to Paul (Gal 2:10; Eph 4:3; 1 Thess 2:17; 2 Tim 2:15; 4:9, 21; Titus 3:12; see Heb 4:11; 2 Pet 1:10, 15; 3:14). As a command, it is often translated, "do your best" or "make every effort." Most preachers likely embrace the concept of *spoudazō* found in 2 Timothy 2:15, "*Do your best* to present yourself to God as one approved by him, a worker who has no need to be ashamed, rightly explaining the word of *truth" (NRSV). Part of doing our best in communicating Paul's writings means wrestling with and refining our understanding of the debated aspects of Paul's theology, even if such wrestling produces some angst. Coming to terms with theological difficulties will always require study ("study" is the KJV translation of *spoudazō* in that 2 Tim 2:15 passage).

Addressing historical concerns involves appreciating the diversity of Pauline congregations. The early house churches consisted of the extended family of the *paterfamilias* (head of the household), including craftspeople, enslaved people, freed people, migrant workers, and possibly tenants (McKnight 2015; Oakes). Coming to grips with the early church's diversity should influence our preaching and teaching. The "homogenous unit principle" touted during the church-growth movement long held sway in how congregations developed and functioned. Preaching may be perceived as easier when church attendees are essentially homogeneous, but preaching becomes more poignant when congregations grow in diversity. Indeed, increasing numbers of congregations perceive diversity as a value and are eager to embrace economic, sexual, racial, and generational differences. To preach Paul means consciously acknowledging and celebrating the diversity of Christian community.

Christians throughout the centuries have addressed various hermeneutical challenges that Paul's letters present. For example, enslaved as well as free African Americans of the eighteenth and nineteenth centuries challenged the way the household codes and other biblical passages were used to subjugate and dehumanize them. Many African Americans who became Christians countered oppressive uses of the Bible with biblical arguments of their own. By bringing tensions in Paul's writings to the forefront, African Americans were able to interpret the Bible as a means of their survival (Powery and Sadler). Preaching Paul today involves heeding the voices of Christians from among marginalized communities, who counter colonial, patriarchal, and racist readings of Scripture.

Allowing Paul to serve as a model will help in communicating Paul's writings in preaching and teaching in our contemporary settings. His ministry posture, as preacher, writer, and pastor, along with the historical situation of his diverse readers, sheds light on our own communication challenges. Viewing Paul as a herald of God's word rather than as a professionally trained communicator might relieve us of some pressure to perform in the pulpit or classroom. This is not to bless boring presentations but to shift more responsibility onto the Holy Spirit, which Paul seemed to do. He proclaimed Christ crucified, "a *stumbling block to Jews and foolishness to *Gentiles" (1 Cor 1:23 NRSV), and his teachings were to be "spiritually discerned" (1 Cor 2:14 NRSV). Paul's preaching depended on the power of God rather than clever argumentation.

As a writer, Paul addressed specific situations, even with the book of Romans. Paul's letter to the Romans had long been viewed by some as the apostle's theological treatise, a *magnum opus* of sorts, where he shared his general theological ideas.

However, increasing numbers of scholars point out how Romans is an occasional document, addressing issues within the community. Similarly, to the extent that we are sensitive to the specific experiences of our Christian communities, our preaching and teaching becomes increasingly pertinent. Current events do not necessarily determine our messages but should surely influence them. Theoretical presentations about lofty theological ideas are not helpful for most local congregations. Current events are not only stories relayed from news outlets, but more so the situations facing the local congregation. The closing of a local farm, store, or factory may influence a sermon in a way that general economic news might not.

An old adage serves as a warning for preachers eager to share what they have learned about Scripture passages and how they might apply to their listeners' lives: "They won't care how much you know till they know how much you care." Paul's pastoral identity must inform our preaching and teaching. Our preaching is an extension of pastoral ministry and can enhance the familial bonds between congregants as well as communicate positively to nonbelieving onlookers.

See also Gospel; Hermeneutics/Interpreting Paul; Imitation of Paul / of Christ; Letters, Letter Forms; Pastor, Paul as; Performance; Rhetorical Criticism.

BIBLIOGRAPHY. **J. M. G. Barclay,** "Mirror-Reading a Polemical Letter: Galatians as a Test Case," in *The Galatians Debate: Contemporary Issues in Rhetorical and Historical Interpretation*, ed. M. D. Nanos (Peabody, MA: Hendrickson, 2002), 367-82; **M. F. Bird,** "Reassessing a Rhetorical Approach to Paul's Letters," *ExpTim* 119, no. 8 (2008): 374-79; **P. J. J. Botha,** *Orality and Literacy in Early Christianity*, BPC 5 (Eugene, OR: Cascade Books, 2012); **B. R. Braxton,** *Preaching Paul* (Nashville: Abingdon, 2004); **P. R. Burroughs,** ed., *Practicing with Paul: Reflections on Paul and the Practices of Ministry in Honor of Susan G. Eastman* (Eugene, OR: Cascade Books, 2018); **C. J. Classen,** "St. Paul's Epistles and Ancient Greek and Roman Rhetoric," *Rhetorica* 10, no. 4 (Autumn 1992): 319-44; **D. R. Edwards,** "Hermeneutics and Exegesis," in *The State of New Testament Studies: A Survey of Recent Research*, ed. S. McKnight and N. Gupta (Grand Rapids, MI: Baker Academic, 2019), 63-82; idem, "Pastoral Reflections on *Perspectives on Paul: Five Views*," in *Perspectives on Paul: Five Views*, ed. S. McKnight and B. J. Oropeza (Grand Rapids, MI: Baker Academic, 2020), 259-66; **T. J. Gombis,** *Power in Weakness: Paul's Transformed Vision for Ministry* (Grand Rapids, MI: Eerdmans, 2021); **M. J. Gorman,** *Becoming the Gospel: Paul, Participation, and Mission*, GOC (Grand Rapids, MI: Eerdmans, 2015); idem, *Apostle of the Crucified Lord: A Theological Introduction to Paul and His Letters*, 2nd ed. (Grand Rapids, MI: Eerdmans, 2016); **S. Greidanus,** "Preaching from Paul Today," in *DPL*, ed. G. F. Hawthorne, R. P. Martin, and D. G. Reid (Downers Grove, IL: IVP Academic, 1993); **N. L. Gross,** *If You Cannot Preach Like Paul* (Grand Rapids, MI: Eerdmans, 2002); **L. T. Johnson,** *Constructing Paul: The Canonical Paul* (Grand Rapids, MI: Eerdmans, 2020); **A. D. Litfin,** *Paul's Theology of Preaching: The Apostle's Challenge to the Art of Persuasion in Ancient Corinth*, rev. and exp. ed. (Downers Grove, IL: IVP Academic, 2015); **F. J. Matera,** *Strategies for Preaching Paul* (Collegeville, MN: Liturgical Press, 2001); **S. McKnight,** *A Fellowship of Differents: Showing the World God's Design for Life Together* (Grand Rapids, MI: Zondervan, 2015); idem, *Reading Romans Backwards: A Gospel of Peace in the Midst of Empire* (Waco, TX: Baylor University Press, 2019); idem, *Pastor Paul: Nurturing a Culture of Christoformity in the Church*, TECC (Grand Rapids, MI: Brazos, 2019); **S. McKnight and J. B. Modica,** eds., *Preaching Romans: Four Perspectives* (Grand Rapids, MI: Eerdmans, 2019); **M. M. Mitchell,** *The Heavenly Trumpet: John Chrysostom and the Art of Pauline Interpretation*, HUT 40 (Tübingen: Mohr Siebeck, 2000); **P. Oakes,** *Reading Romans in Pompeii: Paul's Letter at Ground Level* (Minneapolis: Fortress, 2013); **B. Oestreich,** *Performance Criticism of the Pauline Letters*, BPC 14 (Eugene, OR: Cascade Books, 2016); **E. Powery and R. Sadler,** *The Genesis of Liberation: Biblical Interpretation in the Antebellum Narratives of the Enslaved* (Louisville, KY: Westminster John Knox, 2016); **D. Rhoads,** "Performance Criticism: An Emerging Methodology on Biblical Studies," *BTB* 36 (2006): 118-33, 164-84; **B. S. Rosner, A. S. Malone, and T. J. Burke,** eds., *Paul as Pastor* (New York: T&T Clark, 2018); **J. W. Thompson,** *Preaching Like Paul: Homiletical Wisdom for Today* (Louisville: Westminster John Knox, 2000); idem, *Apostle of Persuasion: Theology and Rhetoric in the Pauline Letters* (Grand Rapids, MI: Baker Academic, 2020); **C. S. Works,** *The Least of These: Paul and the Marginalized* (Grand Rapids, MI: Eerdmans, 2020).

D. R. Edwards

PREDESTINATION. *See* Election and Predestination.

PRE-EXISTENCE. *See* CHRISTOLOGY; GOD.

PRINCIPALITIES AND POWERS

The terms *principalities* and *powers* are among those used in English Bibles for Greek words Paul used to speak of supernatural powers who opposed God's plan of *salvation through *Christ, as well as the ongoing sanctification of believers and the ongoing Great Commission. Related terms include *rulers, authorities, dominions, lords,* and *thrones.* Collectively these English words gloss a range of Greek lemmas, or lexical forms: *archōn, archontes, archai, exousiai, dynameis, kosmokratores, kyriotētes, thronoi.*

The meaning of Paul's vocabulary has been debated by scholars for some time, particularly since the terms in question are also used of human powers in certain NT passages. Few scholars question that Paul used these terms to describe evil supernatural powers. One example is Wesley Carr, who concludes that all the powers mentioned by Paul should be viewed as good, not evil. His work subsequently received devastating critique (Arnold 1987). Walter Wink's effort to navigate between demythologizing of the powers as social structures and actual entities is also "seriously flawed" (Arnold 1989, 50). While offering structural insights on the symbiotic relationship of human and supernatural powers, Wink is unable to show from the primary source material how the powers were *not* regarded as entities in first-century thinking.

Paul's theology of principalities and powers derives from vocabulary found in the Hebrew Bible contextualized by the conceptual worldview of its authors, the development of that worldview in Second Temple Jewish literature, and the translation of that vocabulary in the LXX. In all these sources, terms for human rulers are used to describe supernatural opposition to *God and his people. The conceptual worldview of the Hebrew Bible, where the nations of the world were "allotted" to supernatural beings, was part of Second Temple Judaism. Further, that allotment worldview was also part of the Greco-Roman religious outlook, of which Paul was certainly knowledgeable.

1. Context and Background
2. Paul and the Powers

1. Context and Background.

1.1. Hebrew Bible. A convenient entry point in the discussion is the term "prince" (*śar*; pl. *śārîm*). There are many obvious instances where *śar* identifies human authority figures (Gen 21:22, 32; 26:26; Num 21:18; 22:8; Judg 4:2, 7; 1 Chron 21:2; Neh 2:9). Equally evident instances where a supernatural figure is in view are also found. In Joshua 5:14-15, Joshua encounters "the commander [*śar*] of the LORD's army [*ṣabaʾ*]" (ESV). The same terms found in the Joshua episode are found in Daniel 8:11, where a supernatural "Prince [*śar*] of the host [*ṣabaʾ*]" of heaven is mentioned in Daniel's vision. Daniel 10:13, 21; 12:1 describe the angel Michael, "one of the chief princes [*śārîm*]." Michael is one of a supernatural class of beings ("chief princes") in the heavenly host hierarchy. Michael is thus not to be confused with his superior, the "Prince of the host" of Daniel 8:11, though he holds the high office of "great prince [*śar*]" of Israel (Bampfylde).

Daniel 10 also reveals that the nations of the world were governed by supernatural princes. Israel and her "great prince" (Michael) battle against "princes" over Persia and Greece (*śar* in each instance; Dan 10:13, 20). The origin of this worldview comes from earlier biblical material, namely, Deuteronomy 32:8-9, a passage that, referencing the division of the nations at Babel, notes that those nations were distributed "according to the number of the sons of God" (reading Deut 32:8 with the LXX and *Qumran; Heiser 2001, 52-59; Tigay, 513-16). Deuteronomy 4:19-20, a parallel to Deuteronomy 32:8-9, has the nations "allotted" (*ḥālaq*) to members of the heavenly host, identified elsewhere in Deuteronomy as supernatural beings (*ʾəlôhîm*; Deut 17:1-3; 29:23-26; 32:17; Hannah, 417). This allotment occurred when the nations were divided and their borders established, a circumstance brought about in the Tower of Babel event (Gen 11:1-9). Since the Table of Nations in Genesis 10 is intimately related to the division of the nations at Babel, the "number of the sons of God" was thought to be seventy, since that is the number of the listed nations (Tigay, 302, 514-15; the number is seventy-two in the LXX).

The concept of divine rulership over geographical territory is consistent with wider ancient Near Eastern religious ideology about the relationship between deities and nations, regions, or city-states. Rulership was not merely a human enterprise. The gods were thought to have territorial claim on nations by allotment (Block, 21-34). Kings in Mesopotamia were frequently referred to as a deity's coregent or vicar (e.g., *iššiak Aššur*, "Assur's vicar") since they were believed to be ruling over land that belonged to the god. The king "administered the god's territory and his people, [and so] the people of the nation were subjects of the god and lived in his *baʿūlatum*, 'dominion'" (Ahlström, 2-3). Pharaohs in New Kingdom Egypt could be titled "deputy regent" (*idnw*) of his god (Murnane, 59). A city's *temple was viewed as the god's estate in his land. At Ugarit multiple human rulers (*mlkm*) in hierarchy mirrored the divine sphere (Handy, 58-59), where the high god, El, was over patron deities and city rulers, all of whom bore the same name (*mlk*). Hence the gods and their chosen human agents were perceived as simultaneously ruling nations, regions, and cities.

As noted above, Hebrew *śar* is also used of military figures in tandem with "host" (*ṣaba'*) terminology (Josh 5:14; Dan 8:11). "Host of heaven" (*ṣeba' haššamayim*) occurs in several passages as a description of spiritual entities (Deut 4:19-20 [see Deut 17:3; 29:26; 32:8 LXX, Qumran]; 1 Kings 22:19-23). "Hosts" occurs in parallel to "angels" in Psalms 103:21-22; 148:2. The overlap of celestial language for inhabitants of the spiritual world is perhaps seen more readily in Job 38:7, where the "sons of God" that witness the earth's *creation are referred to as the "stars of God/El" (see Is 14:13).

God's host of "holy ones" is cast as a heavenly army in several passages (Deut 33:1-2; Joel 2:9-11; Is 13:1-5; Zech 14:5). The military context should be no surprise given the familiar *YHWH ṣeba'ôt* (traditionally, "Lord of hosts"), which occurs 284 times in the Hebrew Bible. The epithet is a royal one to paint the portrait of Yahweh as king and divine warrior, leader of heavenly armies. As such, it is no surprise that Yahweh's supernatural warriors are referred to with celestial terminology ("hosts"). For example, the seven occurrences of the specific phrase "their host" (*ṣebā'ām*) refer unambiguously to the starry heavens, not human armies (Gen 2:1; Ps 33:6; Is 34:2, 4; 40:26; 45:12; Neh 9:6). Isaiah 34:4 is of specific interest, as "their host" (*ṣebā'ām*) occurs two verses earlier (Is 34:2 ESV) to inform readers that "the LORD is enraged against all the nations, and furious against all their host; he has devoted them to destruction, has given them over for slaughter." The point must not be missed: human armies are described as functioning in tandem with supernatural warriors in opposition to Yahweh's will, a conception that aligns with Daniel's theology of supernatural princes over the nations who have opposed and will oppose the true God and his people.

1.2. Septuagint (LXX). LXX translators rendered the vocabulary of the Hebrew Bible with Greek terms (lemmas) that would later be used by Paul. The heavenly "prince" of Daniel 8:11 is also *archistratēgos*. The "prince" terminology of Daniel 10 is variously rendered with the lemmas *stratēgos* ("commander"; Dan 10:13, 20) and *archōn* (active participle of *archō*, "to begin, be first [in rank], be leader, govern, rule"; Silva 1:412; Dan 10:13) and *angelos* ("angel"; Dan 10:21). The LXX text of Theodotion translates all the occurrences of Hebrew *śar* with *archōn* (Dan 10:13 [3×], 20 [2×], 21) and casts Michael as the great *archōn* ("commander").

Greek *dynameis* ("powers") was a frequent LXX translation choice for the supernatural heavenly host armies of God. In LXX Joshua 5:14-15, the supernatural figure is "commander in chief" (*archistratēgos*) of God's heavenly "army" (*dynameōs*). The lemma is utilized where "their host" (*ṣebā'ām*) refers to God's heavenly armies (Ps 33:6 [32:6 LXX]; Is 34:4). "*Lord of hosts" is rendered as "God/Lord of the powers [*dynameis*]" in many passages (e.g., Ps 84:1, 3, 8 [83:2, 4, 9 LXX]; Ps 89:8 [88:8 LXX]; Ps 103:21 [102:21 LXX]; Ps 148:2; Jer 40:12; Zeph 2:9). If LXX Daniel 8:10 and Isaiah 34:4 are read together, the powers (*dynameis*) are stars from heaven, suggesting their supernatural nature.

Occasionally the gods (*'ĕlōhîm*) allotted to the nations are rendered with *daimonion*, the word in the NT for "*demons" (Deut 32:17; Ps 96:5; cf. Deut 17:3; 29:23-26). Greek *daimonion* is actually a neutral term with broad usage for supernatural powers (Rexine). That is, it may be used for good or evil beings. These LXX passages are obviously negative, a factor in Paul's use of *daimonion* in 1 Corinthians 10:21-22 (below), in which he alludes to Deuteronomy 32:17. Last, the LXX sparingly employs *exousia* for supernatural figures, but as a function, not an identification of a class. Positively, there is personified Wisdom, who has *exousia* (Sir 24:11). Daniel 7:12 LXX has the human tyrants whose power is later linked with supernatural princes as losing *exousia* to the kingship of the son of man (Dan 7:14). The term is, however, used of a class of supernatural power in Second Temple Jewish works.

1.3. Second Temple Jewish Literature. Other Jewish works contemporary with the LXX utilize Greek terminology later found in Paul's writings to describe evil supernatural beings. While not common, "there is still clear evidence to suggest that such usage was current at the time of Paul" (Williams, 128).

In the Testament of Solomon, written as early as the first century AD (Duling, 1:940), Solomon exorcises a demon and asks, "Tell me, then, how you, being demons, are able to ascend into heaven." The demon replies, "Whatever things are accomplished in heaven (are accomplished) in the same way also on earth; for the principalities [*archai*] and authorities [*exousiai*] and powers [*dynameis*] above fly around and are considered worthy of entering heaven" (T. Sol. 20:15; Duling, 1:983). Philo (*Migr.* 181) and the writer of Jubilees (Jub. 1.29) use *dynameis* to refer to supernatural powers. The wording of 2 Maccabees 3:24, where God is described as "the Lord of the spirits and every authority [*exousias*]," is nearly identical to Pauline usage (1 Cor 15:24; Eph 1:21; Col 1:16; 2:10, 15; 1 Pet 3:22), where the referents are supernatural powers and authorities (Williams, 131). In Testament of Levi 3.7-8 "authorities" (*exousiai*) and "thrones" (*thronoi*) are in the Lord's presence praising him for eternity. In 1 Enoch 61.10 (Ethiopic) one encounters "angels of power, and all the angels of principalities" (Greek text not extant).

While used in various passages for human rulers (e.g., Sib. Or. 8.112; 11.275; 12.274; 3 Bar. 6.12; Apoc. Dan. 2.15; 3.4, 16; 5.14), *archōn* and *archai* are used interchangeably in 1 Enoch 6.3, 7-8 to describe the named transgressing Watchers listed in 1 Enoch's expanded account of the biblical flood narrative (see Gen 6:1-4). Other passages in 1 Enoch evince the same vocabulary for evil supernatural beings (1 En. 8.1; 15.9). In Testament of Simeon 2.7 and Testament of Judah 19.4 readers encounter the "Prince [*archōn*] of Error," a reference to Satan (Twelftree, 176), who is elsewhere referred to as *archōn* (T. Dan 5.5-6; see Jn 16:11). The identification is found elsewhere. Beelzeboul is the "Prince of Demons" (*archōn tōn daimoniōn*) and "ruler [*archōn*] Beelzeboul" (T. Sol. 6.1; 16.5; see T. Sol. 3.5; Mt 9:34; Lk 11:15). Mastema, another name for *Satan in this literature, is called *archōn* in Jubilees 17.16. Still another name for the Devil, Beliar, is paired with *archōn* in Ascension of Isaiah 4.4. More positively, Philo uses *archōn* to describe God (*Opif.* 100; *Cher.* 29, 82; *Conf.* 170; *Mut.* 128; *Spec.* 1.307; *Prob.* 19). In a parallel to Daniel 10:13, 21; 12:1, Michael is "prince" (*archōn*) in Ascension of Isaiah 3.16; 4.4.

Several Jewish texts from the mid-second century BC specifically affirm the worldview of Deuteronomy 32:8, where supernatural beings are "patron angels" of the nations. Ben Sira labels Israel as God's "portion," in contrast to the other nations, over each of which God assigned a ruler (Sir 17:17), an "exact parallel" to Deuteronomy 32:8 (Hannah, 418). In the book of Jubilees, Israel's *election (Deut 32:9) is contrasted with God's allotment of the nations to supernatural rulers. In this text the writer adds the idea that God did so punitively to lead the nations astray (Jub. 50.30-32). Despite the absence of such a motive in biblical material, the theology of Sirach 17:17 and Jubilees 50.30-32 derives from Deuteronomy 32:8 (Michalak, 102-3; VanderKam, 1:53, 523; cf. Jub. 15.11-34).

The same worldview is behind 1 Enoch 89.59–90.19, also known as the Animal Apocalypse, an apocalyptic allegory. In 1 Enoch 89.59-60 the allegory has God summoning seventy shepherds to whom God has decided to hand over the sheep for destruction (see Ezek 34:28). Some scholars take the seventy shepherds to be pagan human rulers. Others disagree sharply, arguing that "their heavenly nature seems certain" (Nickelsburg, 390) and that the shepherds are the seventy supernatural rulers of the nations (Michalak, 145-46; Davidson, 107-8; Hannah, 420-21), turned against the people of God at the end of days (see Rev 20:7-9). First Enoch 56.5-6 has "angels" (not extant in Greek) fomenting the assault of the Parthians and the Medes against *Israel.

In another second-century BC text, an angel tells the patriarch Levi, "I am the angel who makes intercession for the nation Israel, that they might not be beaten" (T. Levi 5.6). The later (medieval) Hebrew text of the second-century BC Testament of Naphtali has seventy angels descending at Babel to teach the seventy nations (T. Naph. 8.1-6; Caird, 6).

The War Scroll (1QM) from Qumran is famous for its portrayal of the final conflict as a war involving both human and supernatural armies. While this scroll nowhere explicitly references the forces of Belial/Mastema as the supernatural princes of the nations, such a reading is conceptually possible (Michalak, 149-55; Davidson, 108-9). It is interesting that one passage apparently references the Babel event when the battle lines are being drawn (1QM X, 9-15), but the text is too fragmentary to draw any conclusions.

Writing later in the first century AD, Philo quotes Deuteronomy 32:8 with respect to the allotment of the nations to supernatural rulers: "Ask thy father, and he will tell thee; ask thy elders, and they will make it known to thee, how the Most High, when he divided the nations, dispersed the sons of Adam, and fixed the boundaries of the nations according to the number of the angels of God. And the portion of the Lord was his people Jacob, the limitation of the inheritance of Israel" (Philo, *Post.* 89, in Yonge, 141; see further *Post.* 91-92; Runia, 32, 40). Elsewhere Philo asserts that "the Gentiles have wrongly made gods from the powers [*dynameis*]," an allusion that points to the gods of the nations of Deuteronomy 32 (Williams, 129). The same theology surfaces in rabbinic writings, though as a warning: "These texts presuppose a function of angels as guardians of or advocates for the Gentile nations, which is analogous to the role ascribed to many national deities in the ancient Near East" (Stuckenbruck, 30).

1.4. Greco-Roman Thought Before the New Testament. Given the religious and cultural influence of the ancient Near East on the Aegean world (West), it is not surprising that early classical writers had their own conception of nations and city-states being allotted by and to the gods. For example, the Spartan poet Tyrtaeus (seventh century BC) writes that Zeus "hath given this city to the children of Heracles" (*Orderliness* 2.12). The thought of one passage from Plato aligns closely with the biblical worldview that nations had been allotted to supernatural beings: "In the days of old, the gods had the whole earth distributed among them by allotment. . . . They all of them by just apportionment obtained what they wanted, and peopled their own districts; and when they had peopled them they tended us, their nurselings and possessions" (Plato, *Critias* 109; trans. Jowett, 3:529-30). As noted earlier, in the LXX the patron deities over the nations of the Hebrew Bible were at times rendered with *daimonion.* Plato's writings include this term in the context of geographical rule: "In *Symp.* 202D-203A, Plato speaks of the *daimones* as intermediaries between God and man. . . . Plato's *daimones* as guardians of cities (*Leg.* 4.713C ff., 5.738D) has something in common with the angelic viceroys who rule over pagan nations in Deut 32:8 (LXX); cf. Deut 4:19; 17:2-7" (Lee, 23n63).

2. Paul and the Powers.

Given these contextual data, it is no surprise that Paul could and did use terms that speak of both heavenly and earthly authorities and rulers. Nevertheless, many past studies of Paul's principalities and powers by NT scholars neglect the foundational points of his *teaching in this regard. This is due in part to the recency of the discovery of the Dead Sea Scroll fragment of Deuteronomy 32:8, which clearly informs the reader that God allotted the nations to members of his heavenly host, the sons of God. The same notion is paralleled by other portions of Deuteronomy (Deut 4:19-20; 17:1-3; 29:23-36).

G. B. Caird was an exception to this oversight. Writing before the publication of the Qumran fragment of Deuteronomy 32:8, Caird discerned, largely on the basis of LXX vocabulary, Psalm 82, Deuteronomy 4:19-20, and Second Temple sources, that each nation "had its own angelic ruler and guardian . . . allotted to them by God." He was equally clear in his assessment of Daniel 10 in this regard. The princes of Persia and Greece in that passage "are the angelic guardians of the two nations" (Caird, 5-6).

Paul's vocabulary for supernatural geographical powers is variegated but consistent. His terms are all found in the LXX and other Greek texts for geographical rulership and dominion. These word choices (as opposed to opting for a sweeping term such as *daimonion,* "demon") arise from his knowledge of the OT concept of *Gentile geography being under supernatural dominion.

2.1.* Archontōn *and* archai *(Rulers). Paul uses *archai* or another plural of the lemma *archē* in a number of his *letters (Rom 8:38; 1 Cor 15:24; Eph 1:21; 3:10; 6:12; Col 1:16; 2:10, 15). Most of these passages are not disputed as to the supernatural nature of these rulers. Paul uses a singular form of the lemma as a collective in reference to hostile supernatural opponents in Ephesians 1:21 and 1 Corinthians 15:24. Some scholars have argued the latter reference speaks only of human rulers. This seems dubious since the combination of terms used in 1 Corinthians 15:24 is also used by Paul in Ephesians 1:20-21 along with *pas* ("all"). In Ephesians 1:20-21 Christ is seated in the heavenly places ruling over "all" rulers, authorities, powers, and dominions. The same wording appears in 1 Corinthians 15:24. The comprehensive language ("all") does not allow interpreters to exclude spiritual rulers from the declaration.

One finds Paul using *archontōn* in 1 Corinthians 2:6, 8. Though the passage is controversial, it is difficult to ascertain how the "rulers of this age" (*archontōn tou aiōnos toutou*) could be mere mortals. Why would Paul think that any mortal ruler who clearly understood that the crucifixion of Jesus would result in the reconciliation of Israel and all nations back to the God who created them would oppose that outcome? This opposition is quite comprehensible, though, if the rulers of this world were supernatural agents in rebellion against God and his plan to save humanity.

Nevertheless, Gordon Fee contends that "the term *archontes* is never equated with the *archai* of Col 1:16 and Eph 6:12 . . . [and] there is no evidence of any kind, either in Jewish or Christian writings until the second century, that the term was used of demons" (Fee, 104n24). Separation of *archontōn* from *archai* is a distinction without a difference. Recent scholarship has concluded that *archōn* and *archē* "are related and perhaps not always to be distinguished," with *archōn* "more clearly a proper angelic term" (Williams, 130-31). Fee's argument is seriously flawed in other respects. As noted earlier, *archōn* in the plural is used interchangeably with *archai* in 1 Enoch 6.7-8 to describe the fallen Watchers. The evil Watchers are identified with both singular and plural forms in 1 Enoch 8.1. In addition, Michael is one of the plural *archontōn* in Daniel 10:13 (Theod.).

If it is clear that the princes of Persia and Greece, counterpart rivals to Michael, are supernatural beings, and those beings are referred to by the singular *archōn* (Theod.), and Michael is likewise one of many *archontōn* in the same passage, it is incoherent to suggest that the supernatural princes of Persia and Greece cannot be construed together as *archontōn*. In regard to these sources, though some scholars push the date for Theodotion to the late second century AD, experts in the matter date the text to pre-Christian times (Di Lella, 596-97; Marcos, 148-52). Likewise, the Greek text of 1 Enoch was extant at the *latest* by the end of the first century and was most likely produced at the beginning of the Common Era (Nickelsburg, 14).

There are positive exegetical cues in 1 Corinthians 2:6-8 that point to a supernatural context for Paul's *archontōn*. The *archontōn* of 1 Corinthians 2:6, 8 are characterized as being of "this (present) age" and ignorant of God's salvation plan "decreed before the ages." This criticism would be meaningless if the rulers were human, as Paul's point about their ignorance would hardly need attention. Most telling is that the verb used in 1 Corinthians 2:6 (*katargeō*, "doomed to pass away") is employed in the same letter (1 Cor 15:24) in reference to the eschatological destruction of supernatural powers by Christ. In 1 Corinthians 2:6, however, these rulers "are presently being destroyed" (present passive participle). The characterization has been regarded as an absurdity if it refers to Pilate or Herod (Williams, 137) but is quite coherent if the rulers are supernatural beings whose status and destiny are part of Paul's "already but not yet" eschatological framework (see below).

***2.2. Dynameis** (Powers).* The terminology occurs in Romans 8:38; Ephesians 1:21; 1 Corinthians 15:24; 2 Thessalonians 1:7. These instances are in contexts that include angels, the spiritual world ("heavenlies"), rulers (*archai*), and the final eschatological judgement that includes *every* power, not merely human ones. Only 2 Thessalonians 1:7 is questionable. The phrase *met' angelōn dynameōs autou*, usually translated "with his powerful angels," could identify a class of supernatural being ("his angels of power"). A parallel to this latter possibility is 1 Enoch 61.10 ("angels of governance"), but this is inconclusive.

***2.3. Kyriotētes** (Lords).* This lemma occurs twice in Paul's writings (Col 1:16; Eph 1:21). The supernatural context of Ephesians 1:21 was noted earlier. Spiritual beings cannot be coherently excluded in Colossians 1:16, for Paul is referencing the creation of "all things visible and invisible, whether thrones [*thronoi*] or dominions [*kyriotētes*] or rulers [*archai*] or authorities [*exousiai*]." On the basis of Paul's phrase "domain of darkness" (*tēs exousias tou skotous*) in the near context (Col 1:13), scholars have proposed that "the Hebrew term *memšelet*, used of the dominion of Belial in 1 QS 1:18; 2:19; 1QM 14:9; 18:1; 4Q 286-287, is the equivalent of *kyriotēs*" (Reid, 749). The suggestion may be bolstered by the use of *archē* and *exousia* in the LXX for celestial *memšalâ* in the Hebrew Bible (Gen 1:16; Ps 136:8-9) rather than *kyriotētes*.

***2.4. Daimoniōn** (Demons).* A related trajectory regarding *kyriotēs* is to follow Paul's use of *kyrioi* in 1 Corinthians 8:5 to "many gods and many lords." The subject matter of Paul's comment there is continued into 1 Corinthians 10:20, where Paul references these other gods and lords as "demons" (*daimoniōn*). Scholars have noted that Deuteronomy 32:17 is Paul's point of reference (Waters, 133-36, 140-42). That verse, which presumes the worldview of Deuteronomy 32:8, where the territories outside Israel are under the dominion of supernatural powers, labels those powers as *shēdîm* and *ʾəlōhîm*. Paul uses *theoi* in 1 Corinthians 8:5, which corresponds to LXX rendering of *ʾəlōhîm* in Deuteronomy 32:17. The LXX translates *shēdîm* with *daimonion*. The use of *kyriotētes* in 1 Corinthians 8:5, linked as it is by Paul with Deuteronomy 32:17 later in 1 Corinthians 10:20, effectively defines these *kyriotētes* as hostile supernatural powers.

While the gods of 1 Corinthians 8:5 are referred to pejoratively ("so called"), this is not a statement of nonexistence. Paul's language reflects contempt. Very similar expressions are employed by other Second Temple writers who elsewhere affirm the reality of the other gods (Williams, 147; Burnett, 197). Paul embraces the reality of the dangerous *shēdîm/ʾəlōhîm* put forth in Deuteronomy 32:17 (Heiser 2008).

***2.5. Thronoi** (Thrones).* Paul uses this term in Colossians 1:16. As Daniel Reid notes, it is used in Daniel 7:9 LXX to describe "the thrones set in place in the heavenly tribunal of the Ancient of Days, clearly indicating positions of transcendent authority" (749). The term in Daniel is positive (see 1 En. 61.10; 2 En. 20.1; T. Levi 3.8), for the meeting is one of God's council to determine the fate of his enemies, symbolized by the four beasts earlier in the vision (Dan 7:1-8). The terms among which *thronoi* appears in Colossians 1:16 are used negatively elsewhere, but this cannot be taken as though the powers he has in mind are exclusively supernatural or negative. Paul is speaking of all these powers "visible and invisible," and so all supernatural ruling powers, including those not hostile to God and believers, are logically included in the description.

2.6. Exousiai *(Authorities).* This is the term most frequently used by Paul for supernatural powers, often in tandem with other terms already discussed (1 Cor 15:24; Eph 1:21; 2:2; 3:10; 6:12; Col 1:16; 2:10, 15). Paul also uses it of human authorities (Rom 13:1-3). As noted above, Testament of Levi 3.8 has *exousiai* (along with *thronoi*) in the presence of God, who delegates authority to members of his host (see 1 En. 61.10; 2 Bar 12.3). God also delegates *exousia* ("authority") to angels in the NT (Rev 6:8; 9:3, 10, 19). Given this delegation language and that Daniel 7; 10 LXX intertwine human and supernatural powers, scholars propose that Paul's choice of the term more often than other Second Temple writers reflects the worldview of Qumran, where the Satan figure Belial grants authority to "the spirits of his lot" (1QM IV, 2; XIII, 2-5, 12).

2.7. Kosmokratores Tou Skotous Toutou *(Cosmic Rulers of This Darkness).* Generally, *kosmokratores* is used to describe "world ruling gods" or "spirit beings who have parts of the cosmos under their control" (BDAG, 561). It also occurs in Testament of Solomon 8.2; 18.2 of demons. Paul's employment of the term (Eph 6:12) in conjunction with plural *archas* and *exousias* would reflect the OT notion that the world was under dominion of hostile gods allotted to the nations.

2.8. Nullification of the Powers. An intriguing component of Paul's teaching about the supernatural powers is his connection of the *resurrection with the nullification of their authority (Eph 1:15-23; Col 2:8-15; 1 Cor 15:20-24, 39-57; see 1 Pet 3:14-22). This nullification is an aspect of Paul's inaugurated ("already but not yet") *eschatology. For Paul, the *death of Jesus and his subsequent resurrection and *ascension stripped away the authority of the hostile supernatural powers over the nations. The Most High, who assigned this authority as a *judgment at Babel (Deut 32:8-9), became a man, died, and rose again, and then sat down at the right hand of God as Lord of the nations. This development was intrinsic to the Great Commission (Mt 28:18-20) and served as a central focus of Paul's role as *apostle to the nations.

Hebrew Bible scholars have long recognized that the judgment of the sons of God allotted to the nations (Deut 4:19-20; 32:8) is described in Psalm 82 (Parker). The Table of Nations, deriving from this judgment, has been recognized as part of biblical eschatology (Scott, 10-12, 135-80). Caird was among the first NT scholars to discern the link between the Deuteronomy 32 worldview and Paul's apostolic *mission: "If the earthly kingdoms were tainted with evil, the angelic rulers could hardly be acquitted of the responsibility for sins committed under their supervision. This theme is strikingly illustrated in Psalm 82, which pictures God standing in the heavenly court, accusing his heavenly entourage of acquiescing in human injustice" (Caird, 8-9). After aligning Psalm 82 with the apocalyptic outlook of Isaiah 24:21-23; 34:2-4 and the day of the Lord, Caird observes, "The classic expression of this hope is found in the book of Daniel. . . . And the angelic princes of Persia, Greece, and Israel mentioned later in the book of Daniel become *archontes,* the rulers of this age" (Caird, 10-11).

More recent scholars have contributed to the fullness of this eschatological picture, noting the use of the important resurrection lemmas (*anistēmi, anastasis*) in LXX of Psalm 82:8; Isaiah 11:10-12; and Zephaniah 3:8, all of which connect the "rising up" of God or the Davidic Messiah with the resurrection of Jesus and the removal of the ruling authority of the powers (Rom 15:8-12; 1 Cor 15:20-28; Burnett, 193-203). For Paul, the powers, the gods of the nations, are already defeated, yet believers are in spiritual conflict with their desperate attempts to forestall the success of the Great Commission, the *fullness of the Gentiles, which precedes the end of days (Eph 6:12-20; Rom 9:22-28; 11:25-27).

See also APOCALYPTIC PAUL; APOCALYPTICISM; COSMOLOGY; DEATH; DEMONS AND EXORCISM; ESCHATOLOGY; IDOLATRY; TRIUMPH.

BIBLIOGRAPHY. **G. W. Ahlström,** *Royal Administration and National Religion in Ancient Palestine*, Studies in the History of the Ancient Near East 1 (Leiden: Brill, 1982); **C. E. Arnold,** "The 'Exorcism' of Ephesians 6.12 in Recent Research: A Critique of Wesley Carr's View of the Role of Evil Powers in First-Century AD Belief," *JSNT* 30 (1987): 71-87; idem, *Power and Magic: The Concept of Power in Ephesians* (1989; repr., Eugene, OR: Wipf & Stock, 2001); **G. Bampfylde,** "The Prince of the Host in the Book of Daniel and the Dead Sea Scrolls," *JSJ* 14, no. 2 (1983): 129-34; **D. I. Block,** *The Gods of the Nations: Studies in Ancient Near Eastern National Theology*, 2nd ed. (Eugene, OR: Wipf & Stock, 1988); **D. A.**

Burnett, "A Neglected Deuteronomic Scriptural Matrix for the Nature of the Resurrection Body in 1 Corinthians 15:39-42," in *Scripture, Texts, and Tracings in 1 Corinthians*, ed. L. L. Belleville and B. J. Oropeza (Minneapolis: Fortress Academic, 2019), 187-212; **G. B. Caird**, *Principalities and Powers: A Study in Pauline Theology* (Eugene, OR: Wipf & Stock, 2003); **W. Carr,** *Angels and Principalities: The Background, Meaning, and Development of the Pauline Phrase HAI ARCHAI KAI HAI EXOUSIAI*, SNTSMS 42 (Cambridge: Cambridge University Press, 1981); **M. J. Davidson,** *Angels at Qumran: A Comparative Study of 1 Enoch 1–36; 72–108 and Sectarian Writings from Qumran*, JSPSup 11 (Sheffield: JSOT Press, 1992); **A. A. Di Lella,** "The Textual History of Septuagint Daniel and Theodotion Daniel," in *The Book of Daniel: Composition and Reception*, ed. J. J. Collins and P. W. Flint (Leiden: Brill, 2002), 2:586-607; **D. C. Duling,** "Testament of Solomon," in *OTP* 1:935-88; **G. D. Fee,** *The First Epistle to the Corinthians*, NICNT (Grand Rapids, MI: Eerdmans, 1987); **L. K. Handy,** "A Solution for Many *mlkm*," *Ugarit-Forschungen* 20 (1988): 57-59; **D. D. Hannah,** "Guardian Angels and Angelic National Patrons in Second Temple Judaism and Early Christianity," in *Angels: The Concept of Celestial Beings—Origins, Development and Reception*, ed. F. V. Reiterer, T. Nicklas, and K. Schöpflin (Berlin: de Gruyter, 2007), 413-35; **M. S. Heiser,** "Deuteronomy 32:8 and the Sons of God," *BSac* 158 (January–March 2001): 52-74; idem, "Does Deuteronomy 32.17 Assume or Deny the Reality of other Gods?," *BT* 59, no. 3 (2008): 137-45; **B. Jowett,** *The Dialogues of Plato: Translated into English with Analyses and Introductions* (Oxford: Oxford University Press, 1892); **S. M. Lee,** *The Cosmic Drama of Salvation: A Study of Paul's Undisputed Writings from Anthropological and Cosmological Perspectives*, WUNT 276 (Tübingen: Mohr Siebeck, 2010); **N. F. Marcos,** *The Septuagint in Context: Introduction to the Greek Version of the Bible*, trans. W. G. E. Watson (Leiden: Brill, 2000); **A. R. Michalak,** *Angels as Warriors in Late Second Temple Jewish Literature*, WUNT 330 (Tübingen: Mohr Siebeck, 2012); **W. J. Murnane,** *Ancient Egyptian Coregencies: Studies in Ancient Oriental Civilization*, Studies in Ancient Oriental Civilizations 40 (Chicago: Oriental Institute, 1977); **G. W. E. Nickelsburg,** *1 Enoch: A Commentary on the Book of 1 Enoch*, ed. K. Baltzer, Hermeneia (Minneapolis: Fortress, 2001); **S. B. Parker,** "The Beginning of the Reign of God—Psalm 82 as Myth and Liturgy," *RB* 102, no. 4 (1995): 532-59; **D. G. Reid,** "Principalities and Powers," in *DPL*, 746-52; **J. E. Rexine,** "*Daimōn* in Classical Greek Literature," *Greek Orthodox Theological Review* 30, no. 3 (1985): 335-61; **D. T. Runia,** "Philo and the Gentiles," in *Attitudes to Gentiles in Ancient Judaism and Early Christianity*, ed. D. C. Sim and J. S. McLaren, LNTS 499 (London: Bloomsbury, 2013); **J. M. Scott,** *Paul and the Nations: The Old Testament and Jewish Background of Paul's Mission to the Nations with Special Reference to the Destination of Galatians*, WUNT 84 (Tübingen: Mohr Siebeck, 1995); **M. Silva,** ed., "ἀρχή," in *New International Dictionary of New Testament Theology and Exegesis*, 2nd ed. (Grand Rapids, MI: Zondervan, 2014), 1:412-18; **L. T. Stuckenbruck,** "Angels of the Nations," in *DNTB*, 29-31; **J. H. Tigay,** *Deuteronomy*, JPS Torah Commentary (Philadelphia: Jewish Publication Society of America, 1996); **G. H. Twelftree,** "Exorcism and the Defeat of Beliar in the Testaments of the Twelve Patriarchs," *VC* 65, no. 2 (2011): 170-88; **J. C. VanderKam,** *Jubilees: A Commentary on the Book of Jubilees, Chapters 1–50*, ed. S. W. Crawford, Hermeneia (Minneapolis: Fortress, 2018); **G. P. Waters,** *The End of Deuteronomy in the Epistles of Paul*, WUNT 221 (Tübingen: Mohr Siebeck, 2006); **M. L. West,** *The East Face of Helicon: West Asiatic Elements in Greek Poetry and Myth* (Oxford: Clarendon, 1997); **G. Williams,** *The Spirit World in the Letters of Paul the Apostle: A Critical Examination of the Role of Spiritual Beings in the Authentic Pauline Epistles* (Göttingen: Vandenhoeck & Ruprecht, 2009); **W. Wink,** *Naming the Powers: The Language of Power in the New Testament* (Philadelphia: Fortress, 1984); **C. D. Yonge**, trans., *The Works of Philo: Complete and Unabridged* (Peabody, MA: Hendrickson, 1995).

M. S. Heiser

PRISON, PRISONER

It was not a surprise to earliest believers that a man like Saul of Tarsus would become a violent persecutor of believers. Jesus' *prophecy had promised as much (Mt 10:17-22; Mk 13:9-13; Lk 21:12-19). That Saul would become thereafter arguably the early church's most ardent and frequent prisoner *witness to Jesus and the *gospel was astonishing (Gal 1:23). Paul's frequent troubles and the powerful shame associations of bonds and imprisonment did raise the question of whether he and his gospel had thereby been disqualified. The *letters that bear Paul's name—and particularly the "captivity epistles"—are alive to the question.

This article canvasses the canonical Paulines against the backdrop of antiquity for their account of Paul's imprisoning activity, his own experience of imprisonment, and how being chained and confined made sense in his *ministry. For discussion of the provenance of the captivity epistles, see the articles on Philemon, Colossians, Ephesians, Philippians, and 2 Timothy (in "Pastoral Epistles").

1. Saul the Persecutor
2. Paul the Prisoner
3. The Shame of Imprisonment and Ministry

1. Saul the Persecutor.

1.1. Harming the Church. The nonbelieving Saul counted himself a more extreme advocate of the ancestral traditions (*perissoterōs zēlōtēs*, Gal 1:14) than any of his contemporaries. "Zeal" (*zēlos*, Phil 3:6) for him meant leveraging all his influence to force Jews away from Jesus and back to the traditions. In short, he persecuted (*diōkō*, Gal 1:13, 23; 1 Cor 15:9; Phil 3:6; cf. 1 Tim 1:13; Eph 3:8) the *church with great intensity (*hyperbolē*, Gal 1:13). The church in *Jerusalem and throughout Judea (Gal 1:22; see 1 Thess 2:14-16) first knew Saul as the man wreaking havoc on them to eradicate the *faith (*portheō*, Gal 1:13, 23).

1.2. Imprisoning Believers. Saul's own account of his Damascus escape (2 Cor 11:32-33) correlates well enough with Acts (Acts 9:1-2, 23-25) to give comfort of Luke's accuracy on the pattern of Saul's imprisoning Jewish believers. Saul's possession of letters from the high priest and Sanhedrin to "their brothers" in Damascus (Acts 9:2; 22:5; 26:12) instructing them to bind (*deō*) and extradite Jesus' followers (Acts 9:2; 22:4; cf. Acts 8:3) suggests an official process. The Sanhedrin could expect cooperation in places such as Damascus, where there were connections to a large Jewish population (Josephus, *Ant.* 20.20.2 §561; 7.8.7 §368; cf. m. Mak. 1.10) with "rights to practice their own customs as ethnic conclaves" (Keener, 2:1625 and n260) and where an ethnarch (*ethnarchēs*, 2 Cor 11:32; cf. Josephus, *Ant.* 14.7.2 §117; *J.W.* 2.6.3 §93) was cooperative. Believers were kept in prison (*eis phylakas* [pl.], Acts 22:4; 26:10; cf. Acts 4:3; 5:18, 19, 21-23; 8:3) pending final disposition of their cases. "The prison of the Sanhedrin in Jerusalem is likely to have been either in the Temple, or in, probably below, the Gazith" (Lake, 478). Greco-Roman prison environments generally created terrible physical and psychological distress, particularly for women awaiting trial, sentence, or execution who were pregnant, very young, guarded by male jailers, or placed in prison with men (Wansink, 44-58; Rapske, 196-225, 279-80). Saul's imprisoning actions, while constrained by Jewish law, caught up and terrorized both men and women (Acts 8:3; 9:2; 22:4). As a convert, Paul abandoned his persecutions. Others, however, continued to trouble the church (1 Thess 2:14-15; 2 Cor 11:32-33).

2. Paul the Prisoner.

2.1. Prisoner of the Jews. It is a puzzle that Paul indicates at 2 Corinthians 11:23 that he had been in prisons "more frequently" (NIV, *perissoterōs*; see also 2 Cor 6:5) than his *opponents, when Luke records for the same period but a single imprisonment (Acts 16:23-40; see 1 Thess 2:2; Phil 1:30). Why are other imprisonments not noted in Luke's record? Paul's practice described in Acts of imprisoning (*phylakōn*; BDAG, 1068) and beating (*derōn*) Jewish believers "from one synagogue to another" (NIV, *kata tas synagōgas*, Acts 22:19) admits the category of *synagogue* imprisonments (see Marshall 1980, 357; Keener, 3:3238). Such may account for what he says at 2 Corinthians 11:23. Confinement could run from arrest to trial; conviction would result in public binding, stripping, and beating (Josephus, *Ant.* 4.8.21 §238; m. Mak. 3:12-13; Gallas, 182). The number of Paul's synagogue imprisonments could equate to at least the five times he experienced the forty lashes minus one (2 Cor 11:24; m. Mak. 1-3; Gallas) and possibly more, as trial might not always have led to conviction. Paul held himself under authority to Judaism (1 Cor 9:19-23)—including its right to confine and punish—for the opportunity to evangelize his own people (Rom 1:16; 9:3-4; see Acts 17:2 and throughout). Luke notes Paul's imprisoning activities but features only Paul's experience of Roman imprisonments, apparently passing over Jewish imprisonments for other expressions of Jewish "zeal" (*zēlos*, Acts 13:45; *zēloō*, Acts 17:5; *zēlōtēs*, Acts 21:20-21; 22:3-5).

2.2. Prisoner of the Romans. Roman custodial arrangements took into account points of law and matters of personal identity. Charges could be serious or deemed so based on status differences between accuser and accused (Rapske, 41-46). Distinctions between free and *slave and citizen and alien mattered greatly, but these were cut across by factors such as honorable status, *wealth, presumed innocence, and rank relative to others (Ulpian in Justinian, *Digesta* 48.3.1; see also Pliny, *Ep.* 9.5; 10.96; Garnsey). The above and judicial corruption (Justinian, *Digesta* 48.11.7 *prol.*; Pliny, *Ep.* 2.11; Brunt; and see Josephus, *Ant.* 20.21.5 §215; *J.W.* 2.14.1 §273; 2.14.4-9 §§284-308) could undermine legal protections of and due process for Roman citizens (Livy, *Hist.* 10.9.3-5; Cicero, *Verr.* 2.5.170; Justinian, *Digesta* 48.6.7-8; Paulus, *Sentences* 5.26.1-2).

Custodial options from most to least severe were prison (*carcer*), military custody (*custodia militaris*), entrustment to sureties (*fideiusoribus committenda*), or release on one's own recognizances (*etiam sibi*)

(Ulpian in Justinian, *Digesta* 48.3.1). Custody was used to prevent flight, to protect, or to secure an accused before ratification or execution of sentence. It was a means of extrajudicial coercion (*coercitio*), but never intended in Roman law to be a punishment in itself. Delays caused by difficult cases, choked trial calendars, and exploitation of custody's punitive potentials, however, added to prisoners' misery (Rapske, 10-20).

Paul reminds the Thessalonian believers of the harsh judicial action he and Silas had suffered in the Roman colony of Philippi (1 Thess 1:1; 2:2). He reminds the Philippians that they had *seen* it, and it matched to their knowledge of his *present* circumstances (Phil 1:30). The Philippian letter's reference to "chains" (*desmoi*, Phil 1:7, 13, 14, 17), use of juridical vocabulary (Phil 1:7, 16) and notice of an uncertain legal outcome (Phil 1:20-30; 2:17, 23), together with mention of the Praetorian Guard (Phil 1:13) and Caesar's *household (Phil 4:22) indicate earlier and later Roman confinements.

Paul says the Philippian magistrates had "shamefully treated" them (ESV, *hybrizō*, 1 Thess 2:2); they had violated the apostles' dignity against an expectation of better treatment in Roman law. Paul's sketch essentially reflects Acts 16:16-40. Presumed Jews without Roman legal standing, they were publicly stripped, severely beaten (see Seneca, *Const. sap.* 9.2.21 and notes there in LCL edition; Rapske, 123-27), and chained in the inner cell of Philippi's prison. The Roman beating is one of three to which Paul attests (2 Cor 11:25); the jailing, one of his many imprisonments (*en phylakais perissoterōs*, 2 Cor 11:23). That Paul was beaten and imprisoned indicates his refusal publicly to claim Roman rights where this might betray his essential identity as a follower of Jesus the Messiah or his *mission (see Rapske, 133-34, 139-43).

The Philippi imprisonment equates to a severe form of Roman *carcer*. The Roman imprisonment from which Paul later wrote Philippians, including notice of a largely affirming local Christian community and support from nearby ministry associates (Phil 1:1, 14; 2:19-22, 25-30; 4:18), as well as multiple communications between Paul and the church, suggests an extended, lighter form of *custodia militaris*.

Paul uses "prisoner of war" (*aichmalō-*) terms positively of the work of *Christ (Eph 4:8; see Ps 68:18) and *apostles (2 Cor 10:5), and negatively of the work of the *law (Gal 3:23; Rom 7:23) and false teachers (2 Tim 3:6). At Philemon and Colossians, however, he characterizes certain associates with him as "my fellow prisoner of war" (*ho synaichmalōtos mou*, Philem 23; Col 4:10), evoking the image of capture in pitched military conflict and custody. In Philemon, the Gentile Epaphras heads the greeting list as Paul's "fellow prisoner of war in Christ" (Philem 23); the Jewish Aristarchus appears further down the list as "fellow worker" (*synergos*, Philem 24). In Colossians, Aristarchus heads the list as "fellow prisoner of war" (Col 4:10) and Epaphras follows as "*servant of Christ" (*doulos Christou*, Col 4:12; see also Col 1:7). The hypothesis of actual arrests and releases to account for the switch seems strained. More likely, "fellow prisoner of war" is a functional honorific given to individuals who, beyond other service (Aristarchus also continues as *synergos* at Col 4:11), arranged to actually spend time with Paul in his confinement (Wansink, 78-84; Rapske, 378-83; see Heb 13:3). This may be how the Jewish couple Andronicus and Junia are counted Paul's fellow prisoners of war at Romans 16:7, given his strategic mention of celebrated collaborations in ministry and help from others whom he greets.

The use of military honorifics (see also Archippus, "our fellow soldier," *systratiōtēs hēmōn*, Philem 2), overlapping greetings lists and other names, and indications of the passage of time suggest that Philemon and Colossians were written in a lighter *custodia militaris*.

Romans 16:7 likely indicates a Roman imprisonment. But it is too brief for certainty of its conditions.

In Ephesians Paul is identified as a "prisoner" (*desmios*, Eph 3:1; 4:1) and an "ambassador in a chain" (*presbeuō en halysei*, Eph 6:20). The latter image evokes an embassy to a hostile state that has gone wrong. The extended military metaphor at Ephesians 6:10-20 may be partly inspired by the kit of a Roman legionary (see Arnold, 436; Lincoln, 435-38). Tychicus is identified as the letter carrier (Eph 6:21; see Col 4:7; 2 Tim 4:12), but no other *coworkers are explicitly noted. The above suggests *custodia militaris*.

Finally, 2 Timothy indicates Paul wears a chain (*halysis*, 2 Tim 1:16; *desmoi*, 2 Tim 2:9) and, though earlier "often refreshed" (2 Tim 1:16-17), he is concerned for necessities (2 Tim 4:13, 21). There is presently help, and he can correspond (2 Tim 4:9, 11-13, 21), but those from provincial Asia have abandoned him (2 Tim 1:15), among his associates only Luke is with him (2 Tim 4:10, 11), and he stands damaged (2 Tim 4:14) and legally unsupported (2 Tim 4:16-18). The above together with notice that the Ephesian Onesiphorus insistently sought out the apostle "in Rome" (*en Rhōmē*, 2 Tim 1:16-17) suggests a particularly distressing imprisonment in the imperial capital.

3. The Shame of Imprisonment and Ministry.

3.1. The Shame of Imprisonment. The drive to attain honor and avoid shame created a constant push and pull in ancient Mediterranean society. Imprisonment and chains decisively occupied the shame side of the ledger (Plutarch, *Solon* 15.2-3; Pausanias, *Descr.* 6.13.1; Cicero, *Verr.* 2.5.148; *Pro Caecina* 100; Arrian, *Epict. diss.* 1.4.23-24; 2.1.35; 2.6.25; Seneca, *Lucil.* 85.41). Suetonius wondered at the depth to which the emperor Vitellius had fallen that he should beg to be "confined for a time, even in the prison" (Suetonius, *Vit.* 7.17.1). Prison was for despicable miscreants, and those conducted there in bonds, whether deserving or not, were intended to be seen as going dishonorably into dishonor and shame (Dio Cassius, *Hist.* 58.11.1-4; Seneca, *Contr.* 9.4.20-21; 9.1.7; Apuleius, *Metam.* 3.2; Ovid, *Con. Liv.* 271-276; Suetonius, *Nero* 6.12.3; *Vit.* 7.17.1; *Vesp.* 8.5.6; Tacitus, *Hist.* 3.12; Philostratus, *Vit. Apoll.* 7.34; Josephus, *J.W.* 4.10.7 §628-629; *Ant.* 18.6.6 §189-190; 18.6.10 §237; see Rapske, 288-91). Revulsion attached to a prisoner even after release (Philostratus, *Vit. Apoll.* 7.34-37; cf. Antiophon, *De caede Herodis* 18; Demosthenes, *Timocr.* 115). The higher one's status and dignity, the more profound the shame of imprisonment. The danger of associating with a prisoner also damaged relationships. Friends might desert "at the first rattle of the chain" (Seneca, *Lucil.* 9.9; see also Lucian, *Tox.* 18, 28-29). The philosopher Apollonius's students shrank in number from thirty-four to eight at his imprisonment (Philostratus, *Vit. Apoll.* 4.37).

3.2. Imprisonment and Paul's Ministry. Paul resists the negative impact of chains and custody on his ministry by setting them in theological perspective, showing their true values and advantages. The most economical apologetic against shame and disqualification is in the phrases "prisoner *of Christ Jesus*" (Philem 1, 9; Eph 3:1; see also "prisoner *of him*," 2 Tim 1:8) and "prisoner *in the *Lord*" (Eph 4:1). Paul is not detained *by* Christ as though Christ were his jailer (*contra* Reitzenstein). Rather, his actual imprisonment is defined *in relation to* Christ (Kittel, *TDNT* 2:43)—fulfilling his calling in obedience to Christ, he has been chained; kept in chains, he continues faithful and obedient to Christ. The same dynamics hold in Philemon: he is "in chains for the gospel" (NIV, *en tois desmois tou euangeliou*, Philem 13; see O'Brien, 294, on the genitive). In Philippians his bonds are revealed to be *"in Christ" (*en Christō*, Phil 1:13, 16), and in Colossians he asks *prayer that he would continue to proclaim the *mystery of Christ on account of which he has been bound (*di' ho kai dedemai*, Col 4:3). The self-designation "ambassador in a chain" (*presbeuō en halysei*, Eph 6:20) suggests an embassy earlier conducted freely but now carried forward *in extremis.* Second Timothy 2:9 declares that Paul has suffered for the gospel "to the point of being chained like a criminal" (NIV, *mechri desmōn hōs kakourgos*), though God's word is "not chained" (NIV, *ou dedetai*).

Paul also makes his case against shame and disqualification on the basis of effects. Chains and imprisonment are a divinely appointed means for the gospel's advance (*eis prokopēn tou euangeliou*, Phil 1:12), he tells the Philippians. The whole *praetorian* guard and many others besides know that he wears chains (*desmoi*) for preaching Christ (*en Christō*, Phil 1:13). Most believers, knowing that Paul has been divinely "posted" (*keimai*, Phil 1:16; Hawthorne and Martin, 46) in chains to defend the gospel, dare more fearlessly to bear witness. Others see him only as a disqualified rival and preach to make his imprisonment more difficult (Phil 1:17; see Rapske, 206-9, on the physical damage of extended chaining). He exults in the increased proclamation and is unconcerned about what others think of him (Phil 1:18). But he is grateful for the Philippians' prayers that he will "in no way be ashamed" (NIV, *en oudeni aischynthēsomai*) but rather, with all boldness (*en pasē parrēsia*), exalt Christ no matter what the outcome (Phil 1:20).

Paul advises the Colossians that his sufferings (Col 1:24; see 2 Cor 11:23-33), including imprisonment (Col 4:3, 10, 18), are "for you" (*hyper hymōn*) and "for the sake of his [Christ's] *body, which is the church" (NIV, *hyper tou sōmatos autou, ho estin hē ekklēsia*, Col 1:24). Paul says of the benefit: "I fill up in my *flesh what is still lacking in regard to Christ's afflictions" (NIV, Col 1:24). Context makes clear that there is no deficiency in Christ's atonement (see Col 1:12-14, 19-22; 2:9-15). Rather, Paul sees his bodily *suffering as "en-fleshing the ministry of Christ in his apostolic mission for the em-bodied body of Christ" (McKnight 2018, 190-91). With the words "Remember my chains" (*mnēmoneuete mou tōn desmōn*, Col 4:18), Paul solicits Colossian support and prayer in his purposeful suffering.

In Ephesians, Paul characterizes himself as the prisoner of Christ "for you Gentiles" (*hyper hymōn tōn ethnōn*, Eph 3:1) precisely because he has powerfully preached the mystery of God's work in Christ that unites believing *Gentiles and Jews. The Ephesians are not to be disheartened by his troubles (*en tais thlipsesin*); as the sign of his faithful proclamation, they "are your *glory" (*estin doxa hymōn*, Eph 3:13). That he twice asks for prayer that his proclamation would be "fearless" (*parrēsia/parrēsiasōmai*, Eph 6:19-20) admits to real shame potentials.

Paul says at 2 Timothy 1:11-12 that he "was appointed" (*etethēn*, the aorist passive clearly recalling God's agency on the Damascus road [see Acts 9; Gal 1:1, 11-17]; see Wallace, 437-38, on the so-called "divine passive") to proclaim the gospel as herald, apostle, and teacher and that his present suffering (*tauta paschō*) is "inherent in the role" (Marshall 1999, 708; cf. Acts 9:15-16). Against imprisonment and Christian abandonment, he declares, "I am not ashamed" (*ouk epaischynomai*, 2 Tim 1:12). He endures everything "for the sake of the elect" (*dia tous eklektous*) and their *salvation (2 Tim 2:10).

3.3. Imprisonment and the Church's Help. The Philippian church's "*fellowship/partnership" (*koinōnia*) with Paul in the gospel (Phil 1:5) includes sharing with (*synkoinōnous*) him in the *grace (*charis*) of his chains and defense of the gospel (Phil 1:7; see Phil 4:14-15). It is a divinely given privilege (*echaristhē*, passive; see above on 2 Tim 1:11-12) for them to believe and suffer "on behalf of Christ" (*hyper Christou/autou*, Phil 1:29; see comment on Phil 3:10; Col 1:24). Paul speaks at Philippians 2:17-18 of his imprisonment and their own material *sacrifice and service coming together "just as a libation completes any offering made to God" (Hawthorne and Martin, 149; Phil 4:18; see 2 Tim 4:6). In his imprisonment Paul aspires to know Christ in his *resurrection power and the *koinōnia* of his sufferings (Phil 3:10). The Philippians' *koinōnia* is also actualized in the supplemental help of Epaphroditus (Phil 2:25-30). Paul covers Epaphroditus with five epithets of approbation (Phil 2:25), equating his hazarding his own life to help Paul with doing "the work of Christ" (*to ergon Christou*) and calling the church to esteem (*entimous*) him and his like (Phil 2:29-30).

Koinōnia also forms "the basis of the Pauline exhortation" to Philemon regarding Onesimus (McKnight 2017, 70). Paul lays out its dynamics and expression in faith with reference to his imprisonment and chains. His prayer that the *koinōnia* of Philemon's faith would become more active (Philem 6) prepares for his request of a demonstration that Philemon considers Paul a "partner" (*koinōnos*, Philem 17).

Consistent with what he knows of Philemon (Philem 5, 7; Wansink, 193-96), Paul sets aside top-down boldness to "order" (*epitassō*, Philem 8) Philemon and makes instead a self-humbling "appeal" (*parakaleō*, Philem 9) upward for love. He pleads the pathos of his vulnerability and dependency as an "old man" (*presbytēs*; Wansink, 157-64; *pace* Petersen, 125-28), now become a "prisoner of Christ Jesus" (*desmios tou Christou Iēsou:* see Philem 1), who has spiritually fathered (*gennaō*; BDAG, 193-94) an infant while in chains (Philem 9-10; see Wansink, 56). This prepares for his request that Philemon receive Onesimus, who is now Paul's "very heart" (*ta ema splanchna*, Philem 12; cf. Philem 7), and thus refresh Paul's heart in Christ (Philem 20; cf. Philem 17).

The implied request at Philemon 13 that Philemon return Onesimus to serve (*diakoneō*, see Col 4:7) the prisoner Paul "taking your place" (*hyper sou*), if embraced, would confirm Philemon a "fellow prisoner of war" by surrogacy beyond his being a "dear friend" and "fellow worker" (Philem 1). The personal greeting to Philemon from his fellow Colossian Epaphras, whom Paul identifies as "fellow prisoner of war for Christ Jesus" (Philem 23; cf. Col 4:12-13), seems strategic.

Other associates in the captivity letters are recognized for bravely standing with the apostle and helping him against the pressure of his chains. To the Philippians, Paul writes that he has no one more devoted than Timothy at his side (Phil 2:19-24). The extremity of Paul's circumstances described at 2 Timothy, however, leads Paul to exhort Timothy that he "not be ashamed of the testimony about our Lord or of me his prisoner" (NIV, 2 Tim 1:8-9). The Ephesian Onesiphorus and his household are commended to God's *mercy for often physically "refreshing" (*anapsychō*) the prisoner Paul without shame (*ouk epaischynthē*) on account of his chain (*halysis*, 2 Tim 1:16-17; cf. 2 Tim 1:8, 12).

Associates are gratefully acknowledged by honorifics of solidarity in relationship and service (Philem 23-24; Col 4:7, 9-11, 14; Eph 6:21-22), or simply mentioned by name (Col 4:14; 2 Tim 4:21). Paul serves notice of some who remove to other ministry locations without apparent criticism (2 Tim 4:10-12). These support him, co-labor with him, and stand by him. To Paul's distress, however, not all do (Phil 2:21; 2 Tim 1:15; 4:10, 16, 14).

See also COLOSSIANS, LETTER TO THE; COWORKERS, PAUL AND HIS; EPHESIANS, LETTER TO THE; FELLOWSHIP, COMMUNION, SHARING; GOSPEL; HONOR/SHAME; LEGAL SYSTEM, ROMAN; PASTORAL EPISTLES; PAUL IN ACTS; PHILEMON, LETTER TO; PHILIPPIANS, LETTER TO THE; SUFFERING.

BIBLIOGRAPHY. **C. E. Arnold,** *Ephesians*, ZECNT 10 (Grand Rapids, MI: Zondervan, 2010); **P. A. Brunt,** "Charges of Provincial Maladministration Under the Early Principate," *Historia* 10 (1961): 189-227; **R. J. Cassidy,** *Paul in Chains: Roman Imprisonment and the Letters of St. Paul* (New York:

Crossroad, 2001); **S. Gallas,** "Fünfmal vierzig weniger einen . . . Die an Paulus vollzogenen Synagogalstrafen nach 2 Kor 11,24," *ZNW* 81 (1990): 178-91; **P. Garnsey,** *Social Status and Legal Privilege in the Roman Empire* (Oxford: Clarendon, 1970); **G. F. Hawthorne and R. P. Martin,** *Philippians*, rev. ed., WBC 43 (Nashville: Nelson Reference and Electronic, 2004); **C. S. Keener,** *Acts: An Exegetical Commentary*, 4 vols. (Grand Rapids, MI: Baker Academic, 2012–2015); **G. Kittel,** "αἰχμάλωτον, κτλ.," *TDNT* 1:195-97; idem, "δεσμόν, δεσμιόν," *TDNT* 2:43; **K. Lake,** "Note 35: Localities in and near Jerusalem Mentioned in Acts," in *The Acts of the Apostles*, vol. 5, *Additional Notes to the Commentary*, ed. F. J. Foakes Jackson and K. Lake, Beginnings of Christianity (repr., Grand Rapids, MI: Baker, 1979), 474-86; **A. T. Lincoln,** *Ephesians*, WBC 42 (Dallas: Word, 1990); **I. H. Marshall,** *Acts*, TNTC 5 (Downers Grove, IL: IVP Academic, 1980); idem, *The Pastoral Epistles*, ICC (New York: T&T Clark, 1999); **S. McKnight,** *The Letter to Philemon*, NICNT (Grand Rapids, MI: Eerdmans, 2017); idem, *The Letter to the Colossians*, NICNT (Grand Rapids, MI: Eerdmans, 2018); **P. T. O'Brien,** *Colossians, Philemon*, WBC (Milton Keynes, UK: Word, 1987); **N. R. Petersen,** *Rediscovering Paul: Philemon and the Sociology of Paul's Narrative Worlds* (Philadelphia: Fortress, 1985); **B. Rapske**, *The Book of Acts and Paul in Roman Custody*, BAFCS 3 (Grand Rapids, MI: Eerdmans, 1994); **R. Reitzenstein,** *Hellenistic Mystery-Religions: Their Basic Ideas and Significance*, trans. J. E. Steely (Pittsburg: Pickwick, 1978); **F. Staudinger,** "δεσμόν," *EDNT* 1:288-90; **D. B. Wallace,** *Greek Grammar Beyond the Basics* (Grand Rapids, MI: Zondervan, 1996); **C. S. Wansink,** *Chained in Christ: The Experience and Rhetoric of Paul's Imprisonments*, JSNTSup 130 (Sheffield: Sheffield Academic Press, 1996).

B. M. Rapske

PROMISE AND FULFILLMENT. *See* Abraham; Israel; Law; Old Testament in Paul.

PROPHECY, PROPHESYING

Paul's sole *knowledge of the *faith was prophetic and charismatic from start to finish. For example, his apostolic calling came by way of supernatural revelation on the Damascus road (Acts 9:1-5). Shortly after, Paul received a *vision that a disciple named Ananias would come and lay hands on him in *prayer so that he might see again and receive the *Holy Spirit (Acts 9:10-18). Paul later took part in the charismatically empowered, multiracial *church in Antioch of Syria. It was here that the Holy Spirit inspired prophets and teachers to commission Paul's special *ministry to the *Gentiles (Acts 13:1-2). Furthermore, Paul is careful to note that his *gospel was not of human origin. On the contrary, he received it by divine revelation (Gal 1:1, 11-16). He claims that his proclamation of the good news was not in word only, but in *signs and wonders wrought by the power of the Holy Spirit (1 Cor 2:4; Rom 15:18-19). All of this means that for Paul, Christianity is supernatural and charismatic through and through and that prophecy and prophesying occupied a special place in his theology and religious experience.

1. Paul's Religious Heritage, Personal Experience, and Apostolic Role
2. Prophet and Prophecy in Paul
3. Was Paul a Prophet?
4. Prophecy for Today?

1. Paul's Religious Heritage, Personal Experience, and Apostolic Role.

Prophecy and prophesying were not at all foreign to Paul's world, both the Greco-Roman world and that of Judaism. For example, the famed Oracle of Delphi, located at the foot of Mount Olympus, was the home of Greek prophetesses and priests. Here the Pythia, as early as 1400 BC, would prophesy for a fee, wielding considerable influence over commoners and kings alike. In like manner, as many as ten sybils would prophesy throughout the Mediterranean world. These prophetesses, in their journey to the spirit world, were known to enter wild frenzies only to culminate in a trancelike state and prophesy. Additionally, the imperial cult of the caesars had no lack of priests, sacrifices, and soothsayers. Thus, prophets, prophetesses, oracles, and divination were common throughout the first-century world.

Nevertheless, when speaking of prophecy and prophesying in Paul, one should start with his personal religious heritage in Judaism. Here one can speak of three distinct loci: his life as a Jew, his practice as a Pharisee, and his *identity as an *apostle of *Christ.

As a practicing Jew of the first century, Paul would have been very familiar with the prophets of old. Prophets and prophesying were part and parcel with Judaism from the beginning (Gen 20:7; Ex 7:1; Num 11:25-29). Many, if not most, of the Jews of Paul's day revered the ancient prophets (Mt 1:22; 2:1-6). The devout prayerfully waited for *the* Prophet, the promised Messiah of God (Jn 6:14; 7:40). The Gospels repeatedly identify Jesus as that prophet (Mt 21:11; Mk 6:15; Lk 7:16; 24:19) who fulfilled all the messianic prophecies (Mt 26:56;

Lk 1:70). Last, Jesus self-identified as a prophet (Mt 13:57; Mk 6:4). The point here is that Paul, and his newfound faith in Christianity, were immersed in a religious context defined by the prophets and prophesying. Furthermore, all of this would have been amenable to Paul's pre-Christian life as a Pharisee.

Like his father before him, Paul was a Pharisee, one of the strictest sects in Judaism (Phil 3:3-6; Acts 23:6). His life as a Pharisee became the hermeneutical lens through which he viewed *God and the Scriptures. For example, in contrast to the Sadducees, who accepted only the Pentateuch as authoritative, the Pharisees embraced the full range of Scripture, from Genesis to Malachi, as the word of God. So, from Enoch to Abraham (Jude 14; Ex 33:1) and from Moses to Malachi (Deut 34:10; Mal 1:1), the ministry and message of the prophets informed the religious heritage of Paul. It follows that for him, the promise of the gospel came by way of the prophets (Rom 1:2). Indeed, Paul claims that the law *and the prophets* testify to the *righteousness of God revealed in the gospel (Rom 3:21).

However, Paul's life as a Pharisee was open to an even more expansive understanding of prophecy. For Pharisees, the work of God that defined the prophet in the Scriptures was not confined to the Scriptures. For them, divine revelation did not end with pen strokes on parchment. Unlike the Sadducees, who viewed the universe as "closed," the Pharisees believed that the Spirit of prophecy was still active among God's people (Acts 23:6-9). Thus, when Nicodemus, also a Pharisee, comes to inquire of Jesus by night, Jesus speaks about the sovereign work of the Holy Spirit (Jn 3:8). For Pharisees, the Spirit still spoke to those who had ears to hear. In the same way, Paul believed that the Spirit of prophecy and revelation (1 Cor 14:1) was an ongoing religious phenomenon for his time. It was this kind of openness to the voice of God that prepared Paul to receive the greatest revelation of all: the revelation that would make him an apostle of Christ.

All of this means that, from beginning to end, God used prophets and prophecy to direct and inform the apostle Paul (Acts 13:1-2; 21:10). Not only this, but Paul evidenced prophetic gifts in his own ministry, mentored prophets and prophesied throughout the church, and established authoritative *teaching on prophecy for the ages (Rom 15:18-19). Indeed, Paul would go on to pen more on the gifts of the Spirit and prophecy than any other writer in the New Testament (1 Cor 12–14).

For all these reasons, the subjects of prophets and prophecy form an important part of Paul's life and *letters.

2. Prophet and Prophecy in Paul.

The English words *prophet* and *prophecy* are derived from Greek. Both are compound words consisting of the prefix *pro-* and the ancient Greek root *pha. Pro* can be understood temporally, as in "prior to" or "in advance," yet can also have a directional meaning, as in "forth." The root *pha* originally meant "to shine" or "to bring to light" but in time came to mean "to speak" (Krämer, 6:783n7). In summary, a prophet was one who not only revealed God's will *in advance* but also *spoke forth* God's word in the present. Paul masterfully employs all these meanings, with some form of the noun "prophet" (*prophētēs*) or "prophecy" (*prophēteia*) appearing twenty-three times in his letters and the verb "prophesy" (*prophēteuō*) eleven times.

For Paul, God's promise of the gospel came by way of the prophets of old (Rom 1:2; 11:3; 16:26). Paul teaches that the prophets testified to a righteousness of God that did not depend on the *law (Rom 3:21). Also, as was the case with Jesus, Paul notes that the prophets suffered unto *death for their prophetic word (1 Thess 2:15).

Yet Paul also speaks of charismatically empowered prophets in the church. Such persons are gifts of Christ (Eph 4:11), ordered by God (1 Cor 12:28) and graced by the Spirit (1 Cor 12:10; 14:37). They are second only to the apostles (1 Cor 12:29) and are recipients of divine revelation through the Spirit. As such, they are foundational for the faith (1 Cor 12:29; Eph 3:5).

Nearly two-thirds of Paul's use of prophet/prophesy words are linked to *gifts of the Holy Spirit. Well over a third of these references mentions prophecy and speaking in *tongues (*glossolalia*) in the same verse (1 Cor 12:10, 28; 13:8; 14:4-6, 22, 39). Finally, all these usages occur within the context of corporate *worship.

For Paul, prophecy is numbered among the *charismata* and is a sign for believers (Rom 12:6; 1 Cor 12:10; 13:8; 14:22, 39). For him, prophecy is preferable to speaking in tongues, except if the latter are interpreted (1 Cor 14:5). Indeed, regarding the value of spiritual gifts, Paul entertains a kind of hierarchy, with *love trumping all the gifts (1 Cor 13:1-2, 13). Paul asserts that all may prophesy, both men and *women, but they cannot all prophesy at the same time (1 Cor 11:4-5; 14:23-26, 31). Even though the gifts originate from and are distributed by the Holy Spirit, the faithful can control the expression of the gifts (1 Cor 12:4-11; 14:32). This fact allows Paul to give directives for the orderly use of gifts in the church, including the gift of prophecy (1 Cor 14:27-29).

Paul's counsel here strikes a note of caution. Where there is power, there is also the abuse of power. The same holds true for prophecy. There were false prophets in first-century Judaism (Acts 8:9-24; 13:6), and Jesus repeatedly warns against false prophets and prophecy (Mt 7:15; Mk 13:22; Lk 6:26). Although Paul never explicitly addresses the issue of false prophets in the church, he does admonish believers to be vigilant. No one can say, "Jesus is cursed," by the Holy Spirit (1 Cor 12:3). Also, the church is to test prophecies to see whether they are good (1 Thess 5:20-21).

Although the manifestation of gifts proved problematic at times, in the end Paul endorsed, encouraged, and protected the gift of prophets and prophecy in the church (1 Cor 14:1, 39; 1 Thess 5:20). In fact, Paul elevates prophets second only to the apostles (1 Cor 12:28; Eph 2:20; 3:5; 4:11). Similarly, Paul exhorts believers to zealously pursue all the gifts of the Spirit yet gives priority to prophecy (1 Cor 14:1).

Yet Paul admits that the value and tenure of prophecy are limited. Prophetic revelation in the church is partial when compared to the full revelation of Christ that is to come (1 Cor 13:8-9). The obscurity inherent to a fallen world inhibits prophecy (1 Cor 13:12). In fact, all the spiritual gifts, whether tongues, prophecy, or the gift of knowledge, will have run their course when believers see Jesus face to face (1 Cor 13:2, 8, 12).

3. Was Paul a Prophet?

Linguistically, Paul never explicitly refers to himself as a *prophet. His preferred self-designations are "apostle" and "*servant" (Rom 1:1; Gal 1:1). In addition, he calls himself a preacher and a teacher (2 Tim 1:11), but never a prophet. Yet if one asks whether Paul functioned as a prophet in the church, the evidence points in another direction (Witherington, 1998, 130-31). For example, when describing his *calling, the apostle states that God separated him from his mother's womb (Gal 1:15), a phrase reminiscent of the great prophets of old (Jer 1:5; Is 49:1). He understands that he alone is God's mouthpiece to make known one of the greatest revelations of all time, that is, that uncircumcised Gentiles can now be counted among the people of God (Rom 16:25; Eph 3:8-9). He prophesies about the end time in terms that are uniquely his own (1 Cor 15:51-55; 1 Thess 4:15-18; 2 Thess 2:1-12). On the other hand, Paul carries forward the jargon of the ancient prophets, frequently speaking of "the day of the Lord" (1 Thess 5:2; 2 Thess 2:1-2; 1 Cor 1:8; 5:5; Phil 1:6, 9-10). Paul's prophetic contribution here is that "the Lord" in the phrase "the day of the Lord" is Jesus, thus making Jesus equivalent to YHWH (Fee, 140). On the order of Elijah, Paul's ministry was confirmed with signs and wonders and miracles (Rom 15:18-19; 2 Cor 12:12), even raising the dead (Acts 20:9-10). Like Elijah, Paul was caught up into heaven. Yet unlike Elijah, Paul came back (2 Cor 12:2-4)! He has all confidence that divine visions and revelations will come to him as a matter of course (2 Cor 12:1). He writes the commandments of the Lord, and any true prophet will acknowledge this (1 Cor 14:37). In summary, there can be little doubt that Paul was indeed a prophet. Moreover, he was an apostolic leader of the prophets in the church, and he spoke forth directives that they were to obey (1 Cor 14:29).

4. Prophecy for Today?

Paul has provided a richly textured portrait of prophets and prophecy in the early church. The critical question is whether this portrait is applicable to the church today. One view is that prophecy ceased by the end of the apostolic era. It is argued that once the apostles have passed from the scene, the canon has closed because "that which is perfect" has come (1 Cor 13:10). Consequently, according to this view, every partial revelation, whether tongues or prophecy, has come to an end. Yet this view has rightly been criticized as anachronistic. Paul, as well as the other writers of the NT, were not aware of composing the canon. Moreover, it is generally agreed that the phrase "when that which is perfect has come" is an eschatological expression referring to the second coming of Christ and not the close of the canon (1 Cor 13:12; see also Porter, 267).

Another view is that prophecy in Paul is the same thing as *preaching. It is contended that prophecy is simply the intelligible proclamation of the gospel that conveys the foundation of the faith by way of theological discourse (Gillespie, 165, 198, 263). Yet some have challenged the conflation of prophecy and preaching in Paul on linguistic and methodological grounds (Witherington 1998, 130-35). For example, Paul employs distinct jargon for preachers and prophets and never conflates the two. For Paul, the preacher (*kēryx*, Rom 10:14; 1 Tim 2:7; 2 Tim 1:11) preaches (*kēryssō*, Rom 10:15; 1 Cor 9:27) the message (*kerygma*) of Christ. In no instance in Paul is the preacher said to be prophesying. By comparison, the prophet (*prophētēs*) prophesies (*prophēteuō*,

1 Cor 14:5) prophecy (*prophēteia*, 1 Cor 12:10) and, as such, is not described as preaching. No doubt some preachers prophesied in the church and some prophets preached the gospel, but to say that preaching and prophecy are the same thing is untenable.

Most scholars acknowledge that prophecy in Paul is not a sermon prepared in advance but rather a spontaneous gift of the Holy Spirit expressed in corporate worship (Schreiner, 360-61). Prophecy for Paul is a supernatural revelation, granted by the Spirit, that he has personally experienced and that he affirms in the lives of fellow believers (Fee, 140-41; Witherington 1992, 82). Finally, the thought that the sovereign gifts of the Spirit would come to an end at his death is not found in Paul.

What then can be said about prophecy and the contemporary church? Pentecostals and charismatics, the fastest-growing sector in Christendom, assert that all the gifts of the Spirit are for the church today (see Johnson and Zurlo, 26, 936). For them, miracles, revelations, and supernatural gifts that were so evident in the church then are simply part and parcel with normal Christian life now (Keener, 162-63). It should be remembered, however, that an important aspect of the *charismata* for Paul is "exhortation" (Rom 12:8; 1 Cor 14:3). To that end, Paul exhorts that the gifts of the Spirit should promote unity, edify the church, and bring glory to God (1 Cor 10:31; 12:1-11; 14:3, 12, 16). Paul continues that even when there is a dramatic operation of the gifts in the church, unless they are infused with the authentic love of God, they amount to nothing (1 Cor 13:1-3; Bailey, 347-65).

See also Apostle; Gifts of the Spirit; Preaching, First-Century; Prophet, Paul as; Tongues; Visions, Ecstatic Experience; Worship.

BIBLIOGRAPHY. **J. W. Aernie,** *Is Paul Also Among the Prophets? An Examination of the Relationship Between Paul and the Old Testament Prophetic Tradition in 2 Corinthians*, LNTS 467 (London: Bloomsbury, 2012); **D. E. Aune,** *Prophecy in Early Christianity and the Ancient Mediterranean World* (Grand Rapids, MI: Eerdmans, 1983); **K. E. Bailey,** *Paul Through Mediterranean Eyes: Cultural Studies in 1 Corinthians* (Downers Grove, IL: IVP Academic, 2011); **L. S. Cook,** *On the Question of the "Cessation of Prophecy" in Ancient Judaism*, TSAJ 145 (Tübingen: Mohr Siebeck, 2011); **S. G. Eastman,** *Recovering Paul's Mother Tongue: Language and Theology in Galatians* (Grand Rapids, MI: Eerdmans, 2007); **G. D. Fee,** *Jesus the Lord According to Paul the Apostle: A Concise Introduction* (Grand Rapids, MI: Baker Academic, 2018); **T. W. Gillespie,** *The First Theologians: A Study in Early Christian Prophecy* (Grand Rapids, MI: Eerdmans, 1994); **T. Johnson and G. Zurlo,** *World Christian Encyclopedia*, 3rd ed., vol. 3 (Edinburgh: Edinburgh University Press, 2020); **C. Keener,** *Spirit Hermeneutics: Reading Scripture in Light of Pentecost* (Grand Rapids, MI: Eerdmans, 2016); **H. Krämer,** "προφήτης," *TDNT* 6:783-96; **S. E. Porter,** *The Apostle Paul: His Life, Thought, and Letters* (Grand Rapids, MI: Eerdmans, 2016); **K. O. Sandnes,** *Paul—One of the Prophets? A Contribution to the Apostle's Self-Understanding*, WUNT 2/43 (Tübingen: Mohr Siebeck, 1991); **T. R. Schreiner,** *Paul: Apostle of God's Glory in Christ* (Downers Grove, IL: IVP Academic, 2001); **A. C. Thiselton,** *The Living Paul: An Introduction to the Apostle's Life and Thought* (Downers Grove, IL: IVP Academic, 2009); **B. Witherington III,** *Jesus, Paul, and the End of the World: A Comparative Study in New Testament Eschatology* (Downers Grove, IL: IVP Academic, 1992); idem, *The Paul Quest: The Renewed Search for the Jew of Tarsus* (Downers Grove, IL: IVP Academic, 1998).

W. A. Simmons

PROPHET, PAUL AS

Paul never explicitly identifies himself as a prophet, yet his language, hermeneutics, and self-description suggest that in some sense Paul understood his apostleship in terms of the OT prophetic tradition. Scholars have debated which of the major prophets—Isaiah (Holtz) or Jeremiah (Rengstorf, 439-40)—served as Paul's principal template. Both prophets have contributed significantly to Paul's thinking (Doering).

1. Relationship Between Apostle and Prophet
2. Prophetic Call
3. Prophetic Gospel
4. Prophetic Comparison
5. Prophetic Criticism

1. Relationship Between Apostle and Prophet. Recent research has rightly recognized the close relationship between *apostle and prophet (Aernie; Agnew, 90-96; Evans 1999; Rugg; Sandnes, 17-20). By definition, prophets are those who have been "sent" (Heb. *šālaḥ*; Gk. *apostellō*) by Yahweh. Isaiah, Jeremiah, and Ezekiel are "sent" by *God to the people of *Israel (Is 6:8; Jer 1:7; Ezek 2:3; see Rengstorf, 419). Throughout Israel's history God has sent his "servants the prophets to them" (Jer 7:25). Malachi prophesies that God will "send [his] messenger" (Mal 3:1) and "will send Elijah the prophet" (Mal 4:5). Similar language is employed in the NT, in reference both to OT prophets and to Jesus' disciples/apostles

(Mt 23:37; Mk 1:2; Lk 9:2; 10:3; 13:34; 22:35; Jn 1:6; 3:28; Rom 10:15). In later traditions, the prophets are called "apostles" (see Mek. on Ex 12:1 [Pisḥa §1], where God says to Jonah: "I have other apostles [*šelûḥîn*] like you"). The great lawgiver and prophet Moses is "sent" (Ex 3:10, 12-15; 4:28; 7:16; Deut 34:11). In later Jewish and Samaritan traditions Moses is also called a *šālîaḥ* (Mek. Rabbi Simon Yohai on Ex 3:10-11; Avot R. Nat. A §1; Ex Rab. 3.4 [on 3:12]; 3.14 [on 4:10]; Memar Marqa 5:3; 6:3).

2. Prophetic Call.

In Galatians Paul adopts prophetic language in describing his apostolic calling. His reference to God, "who set me apart from my mother's womb and called me through his *grace . . . that I might preach him among the *Gentiles" (Gal 1:15-16), is clearly reminiscent of the call of Jeremiah (Jer 1:5: "Before I formed you in the womb I knew you. . . . I appointed you a prophet to the Gentiles") and of the language found in Isaiah (Is 49:1, 5: "He called my name from my mother's womb . . . to gather Jacob and Israel to him"). Even Paul's criticism of his Galatian *opponents (Gal 1:7-8: "there are some who trouble you and wish to distort the *gospel of *Christ. But even if we, or an angel from heaven, should preach to you a gospel contrary to that which we preached to you, let him be accursed") likely echoes biblical language employed against false prophets and others who would encourage God's people to worship false gods (Deut 13:12-13, 15 LXX: "And if . . . evil men in one of your cities . . . say, 'Let us go and worship other gods . . . ,' you will curse it"; see also Deut 13:1-5, 6-11; 20:17-18). Prophetic language is also found in Paul's description before Herod Agrippa II of his Damascus road experience (compare Acts 26:16-17 with LXX Jer 1:7-8; Ezek 2:1-3). Although the speech is a Lukan composition, the language may accurately reflect Paul's sense of a prophetic *call.

There is evidence, moreover, that prior to the Galatian crisis Paul understood himself as a prophet and that he did not adopt this vocabulary ad hoc to deal with the problem he faced in the churches of Galatia. His language in 1 Thessalonians, which is probably his earliest extant epistle, suggests that Paul's prophetic self-understanding originated with his apostolic calling. His expression of sincerity (1 Thess 2:4: "even as we have been tested by God . . . to please God who tests our hearts") echoes the words of Jeremiah (Jer 11:20 LXX: "Lord, who judges justly, testing the reins and the hearts . . ."). Both Paul and Jeremiah uttered these words in the face of opposition (compare 1 Thess 2:2 with Jer 11:19). Later Paul again takes up the theme of persecution (1 Thess 3:4: "For when we were with you, we told you beforehand that we were to suffer affliction, just as it has come to pass"; cf. 2 Cor 11:23-27), which recalls the *tradition of the suffering and persecuted prophet (see Lk 13:33-34; Pesiq. Rab. 26.2: "Jeremiah said, 'Master of the universe, I cannot prophesy to them. What prophet ever came forth to them whom they did not wish to slay?'"). Paul's eschatological warning (1 Thess 5:3: "When people say, 'There is *peace and safety,' then sudden destruction will come upon them as travail comes upon a woman with child") echoes similar solemn warnings found in the OT prophets (see Jer 6:14, 24; 8:11, 21; 14:13-14; Ezek 13:10, 16; Hos 14:1). The prophetic tradition "was active in shaping Paul's presentation of himself with respect to the Christian community of Corinth" (Aernie, 112). Paul is compelled to proclaim the gospel; failure to do so will bring *judgment (1 Cor 9:16; see Jer 20:9; Stuhlmacher, 152).

Finally, it is important to observe that the very nature of Paul's *conversion invites comparison with the prophets. Just as the prophets received revelations and *visions of God and/or heaven, particularly in connection with their call to prophetic office (Is 1:1; 6:1-13; Ezek 1:1; 8:4; Obad 1; Nah 1:1; Hab 2:2), so also Paul received revelations and visions (1 Cor 15:8; 2 Cor 12:1-4; Gal 1:12, 16; 2:2; cf. Acts 9:3-9; 22:6-11; 26:13-20).

3. Prophetic Gospel.

Paul's understanding of the apostolic obligation to proclaim the gospel is informed by the words of Isaiah 52:7: "And how can men preach unless they are sent? As it is written, 'How beautiful are the feet of those who preach good news'" (Rom 10:15; see Is 53:1; Dinter, 48). Moreover, when Paul says, "Woe to me, if I should not preach the gospel" (1 Cor 9:16), he echoes the exclamations of the OT prophets (Is 24:16; Jer 13:27; Hos 9:12). Paul's anguish (Rom 9:2: "I have great sorrow and unceasing anguish in my heart"; Rom 11:1: "Has God rejected his people?") also is reminiscent of prophetic anguish: "Hast thou utterly rejected Judah?" (Jer 14:19).

Paul's allusion to and application of Isaiah 64:3 in 1 Corinthians 2:9 ("what eye has not seen") coheres with rabbinic discussion of the divine source of the prophetic message: "No eye has seen what God . . . will work for him who waits for Him" (b. Abod. Zar. 65a). "All the prophets prophesied only for the messianic age, but in the world to come the eye has not seen, O Lord, beside you [what he has prepared for him who waits on him]" (b. Shabb. 63a).

4. Prophetic Comparison.
Despite the fact that relatively few Israelites had responded in faith to the Christian message, Paul was convinced that God had not rejected Israel (Rom 11:1-2). He grounds this conviction on the example of Elijah (Rom 11:3-4; see 1 Kings 19:10, 18) and on Isaiah's remnant theology (Rom 9:27-29; 11:5; see Is 1:9; 10:22). What is interesting here is Paul's comparison with Elijah. Evidently the apostle saw himself very much like Elijah of old, who felt alone and threatened. Just as God had preserved a remnant of the faithful in Elijah's time, so now in the eschatological period God once again has preserved a faithful remnant.

It is important to note too that Paul did not regard himself as an apostate from Judaism (Rom 11:1: "I myself am an Israelite, a descendant of *Abraham, a member of the tribe of Benjamin") but rather as an apostle (and prophet) to an apostate Israel, even as Elijah the prophet had been sent to an apostate Israel.

5. Prophetic Criticism.
Paul's application of Scripture to his own generation is similar to the hermeneutics of prophetic criticism employed by the true prophets of the OT (Evans 1984). "True prophecy," as J. A. Sanders has explained, is theocentric, not ethnocentric. Unlike most of the "false prophets," who prophesied peace and safety, the true prophet understood sacred tradition and history from the divine point of view. Nowhere can this be seen more clearly than in the prophets' respective interpretations of Israel's sacred tradition. Ezekiel warns his contemporaries not to assume, as false prophets would have them believe, that since "Abraham was only one man, yet he got possession of the land, [then] we [who] are many" will surely be able to possess the land (Ezek 33:24). Jeremiah tells his contemporaries not to listen to the false prophets who assure the inhabitants of *Jerusalem that there is nothing to fear because of the presence of the *temple: "Do not trust in these deceptive words: 'This is the Temple of the *Lord'" (Jer 7:4); "No evil shall come upon you" (Jer 23:17).

One of the most startling examples comes from Isaiah, who alludes to two of David's great victories over the Philistines: "The Lord will rise up as on Mount Perazim [see 2 Sam 5:17-21], he will be wroth as in the valley of Gibeon [see 2 Sam 5:22-25]; to do his deed—strange is his deed! and to work his work—alien is his work!" (Is 28:21; Evans 1986, 96-97). But unlike the false prophets, Isaiah does not find in these victories assurance that Israel will once again be victorious against her enemies. On the contrary, Isaiah has "heard a decree of destruction from the Lord God of hosts" (Is 28:22). God is angry and ready to defeat sinners on the field of battle; only this time the sinners are the Israelites, not their enemies.

"Paul's understanding of God's continuing activity was prophetic and dynamic. God could, as in the days of Isaiah, do a 'new thing'" (Is 43:19; Dinter, 52). The new thing that God was doing in Paul's time was to take a noncovenant people and make a people of God out of them (Rom 9:25-26; see Hos 1:10; 2:23). Imprecations originally uttered against Israel's enemies are applied against Israel herself: "Let their table become a snare and a trap, a pitfall and a retribution for them" (Rom 11:9; see Ps 69:22-23; Evans 1984, 567-68). This remarkable application of the sacred tradition is not anti-Jewish—for Paul is a loyal Jew (see Rom 9:1-5; 11:1-2)—but rather prophetic in the same sense as what one sees in prophets such as Isaiah, Jeremiah, and Ezekiel. Paul is no more anti-Jewish than were these great prophets of old. If Paul's interpretation and application of the Scripture of Israel are to be properly understood, it will be necessary to take into account the apostle's prophetic self-understanding.

See also Apostle; Conversion and Call of Paul; Gospel; Prophecy, Prophesying.

BIBLIOGRAPHY. **J. W. Aernie,** *Is Paul Also Among the Prophets? An Examination of the Relationship Between Paul and the Old Testament Prophetic Tradition in 2 Corinthians*, LNTS 467 (London: Bloomsbury, 2012); **F. H. Agnew,** "The Origin of the NT Apostle-Concept: A Review of Research," *JBL* 105 (1986): 75-96; **P. Dinter,** "Paul and the Prophet Isaiah," *BTB* 13 (1983): 48-52; **L. Doering,** "The Commissioning of Paul: Light from the Prophet Jeremiah or the Self-Understanding of the Apostle?," in *Jeremiah's Scriptures: Production, Reception, Interactions, and Transformation*, ed. H. Najman and K. Schmid, JSJSup 173 (Leiden: Brill, 2016), 546-65; **S. G. Eastman,** *Recovering Paul's Mother Tongue: Language and Theology in Galatians* (Grand Rapids, MI: Eerdmans, 2007); **C. A. Evans,** "Paul and the Hermeneutics of 'True Prophecy': A Study of Romans 9–11," *Bib* 65 (1984): 560-70; idem, "Isaiah's Use of Israel's Sacred Tradition," *BZ* 30 (1986): 92-99; idem, "Paul and the Prophets: Prophetic Criticism in the Epistle to the Romans," in *Romans and the People of God: Essays in Honor of Gordon D. Fee on the Occasion of His 65th Birthday*, ed. S. Soderlund and N. T. Wright (Grand Rapids, MI: Eerdmans, 1999), 115-28; **T. W. Gillespie,** "A Pattern of Prophetic Speech in First Corinthians," *JBL* 97 (1978):

74-95; **S. Grindheim,** "Apostate Turned Prophet: Paul's Prophetic Self-Understanding and Prophetic Hermeneutic with Special Reference to Galatians 3.10-12," *NTS* 53 (2007): 545-65; **T. Holtz,** "Zum Selbstverständnis des Apostels Paulus," *TLZ* 91 (1966): cols. 321-30; **J. M. Myers and E. D. Freed,** "Is Paul Also Among the Prophets?," *Int* 20 (1966): 40-53; **T. Nicklas,** "Paulus—der Apostel als Prophet," in *Prophets and Prophecy in Jewish and Early Christian Literature*, ed. J. Verheyden et al., WUNT 2/286 (Tübingen: Mohr Siebeck, 2010), 77-110; **K. H. Rengstorf,** "ἀποστέλλω, κτλ.," *TDNT* 1:398-447; **S. P. Rugg,** "The Prophet in the Apostle: Paul's Self-Understanding and the Letter to the Romans" (PhD diss., Boston College, 2017); **J. A. Sanders,** "Hermeneutics in True and False Prophecy," in *From Sacred Story to Sacred Text* (Philadelphia: Fortress, 1987), 87-105; **K. O. Sandnes,** *Paul—One of the Prophets? A Contribution to the Apostle's Self-Understanding*, WUNT 2/43 (Tübingen: Mohr Siebeck, 1991); **P. Stuhlmacher,** "The Pauline Gospel," in *The Gospel and the Gospels*, ed. P. Stuhlmacher (Grand Rapids, MI: Eerdmans, 1991), 149-72.

C. A. Evans

PROPITIATION. *See* ATONEMENT; ROMANS, LETTER TO THE; SACRIFICE, OFFERING.

PSEUDEPIGRAPHY/FORGERY

Thirteen of the twenty-seven NT books were published under the name of Paul. How many of them are pseudepigraphic (falsely ascribed to Paul by another author) is controversial. While some church fathers also regarded the letter to the Hebrews as Pauline, because of its anonymity the problem of pseudepigraphy does not apply.

In addition, about one-third of the speech material in the book of Acts is attributed to Paul. The extent to which these speeches are pseudonymous (falsely attributed to Paul) is also the subject of much debate (Gleich).

Other ancient texts composed under the name of Paul were not accepted into the NT canon, among them the Epistle to the Laodiceans, the Epistle to the Alexandrians, the Epistles of Paul to Seneca, and the Apocalypse of Paul. It is generally agreed that all of them are pseudepigraphic.

The apocryphal Acts of Paul contains a narrative about Paul's *ministry, but the book may have been distributed anonymously. However, Paul's Third Epistle to the Corinthians and the Pauline speeches it contains are also generally regarded as pseudonymous.

1. Anonymity, Orthonymity, Pseudonymity, and Allonymity.

In discussions of ancient texts with false authorial attributions, four technical terms are relevant.

A text without an authorial attribution is called "anonymous" (from *anōnymos* = "without name" [*LSJ*, *s.v.*]). A text with a correct attribution is called "orthonymous" (from *orthōnymos* = "rightly named" [*LSJ*, *s.v.*]).

In contrast, a falsely attributed text is called "pseudonymous" (from *pseudōnymos* = "under a false name" [*LSJ*, *s.v.*]). An alternative designation for a pseudonymous text is "pseudepigraphic" (from *pseudepigraphos* = "with false superscription or title" [*LSJ*, *s.v.*]). A pseudepigraphon is an ancient text that was not written by the author to whom it is attributed in its title. An alternative designation is "literary forgery." The terms *pseudepigraphy*, *pseudonymity*, and *literary forgery* designate the use of a false authorial attribution or the state of a text that carries a false authorial attribution.

Since *pseudepigraphy* is, as a rule, used for a false attribution with deceptive intent, the modern term *allonymity* has been coined to designate a false attribution irrespective of its deceptive or nondeceptive intent (see Marshall, 84).

The word *pseudepigraphon* must not be confused with *apocryphon*. An *apocryphon* is a writing for which canonical status was claimed but which was not received into the biblical canon. Apocrypha could be anonymous (such as perhaps the Acts of Paul) or pseudepigraphic (such as the Apocalypse of Paul). Pseudepigrapha (such as the Epistle to the Alexandrians) could in principle be regarded as apocryphal or as canonical.

2. Different Kinds of False Attribution.

Three kinds of false attribution are closely related but must be carefully distinguished: primary false attribution, secondary false attribution, and literary borrowing.

First, an author could publish his own complete text under someone else's name. This is primary complete false attribution (as in the Apocalypse of Paul). Second, an author could publish someone else's complete text under another name (as happened with medical texts that were falsely ascribed to Hippocrates). This is secondary complete false attribution. Third, an author could publish someone else's complete text under his own name (as happened to some of Galen's texts). This is complete literary borrowing.

Each kind of false attribution can be applied not only to complete but also to embedded texts. First, an author could compose a falsely attributed speech or *letter and embed it into his narrative (as the author of the Acts of Paul did with 3 Corinthians). This is primary embedded false attribution. Second, an author could interpolate a passage from one author into the text of another author (as, according to some, a reader of 1 Corinthians did in 1 Cor 14:33b-35). This is secondary embedded false attribution. Third, an author could insert passages from someone else's work into his own text (as, according to some, the author of Ephesians did with passages from Colossians). This is partial literary borrowing.

Table 1. Different Kinds of False Attribution

	by publishing one's own text under someone else's name	by publishing someone else's text under another name	by publishing someone else's text under one's own name
as independent text	Primary complete false attribution (Apocalypse of Paul)	Secondary complete false attribution (some Pseudo-Hippocratica)	Complete literary borrowing (some of Galen's texts)
as embedded text	Primary embedded false attribution (3 Corinthians)	Secondary embedded false attribution (1 Cor 14:33b-35)	Partial literary borrowing (Ephesians/Colossians)

3. False Attribution with Deceptive Intent. For the ancient texts that are ascribed to Paul, it is controversial not only how many of them are falsely ascribed but also whether the false attributions were deceptive. Regarding this second question, the ancient evidence is quite clear that the concept of intellectual and literary property was already known in antiquity (Blum; Schickert; Mülke).

According to the ancient sources (see the collection in Baum 2013), primary complete false attribution was usually not practiced as transparent literary fiction (without deceptive intent) but as literary forgery (with the intention to deceive). Motives for the writing of pseudepigraphic texts varied; the sources mention profit seeking, the intention to discredit opponents, and the concern to increase the effectiveness of a text. Such motives presuppose a deceptive intent (Baum 2001).

Literary analogies point in the same direction: that some ancient historians (such as Duris of Samos) put unhistorical speeches into the mouths of their protagonists was considered inadmissible (as primary embedded pseudepigraphy) by Polybius and many others (Baum 2001). Interpolators (such as Onomakritos) were regarded as forgers, against whose manipulations authors sought to protect their works (Mülke). Galen denounced readers who distributed his texts under their names. Pliny and Vitruvius considered partial borrowing from technical treatises theft (*klopē* or *furtum*) of intellectual property, that is, plagiarism (Stemplinger; Janßen 2016). These analogies confirm the conclusion that the composition of pseudepigraphic writings was generally regarded as literary forgery.

Table 2. Different Kinds of Deceptive False Attribution (Forgery)

	by publishing one's own text under someone else's name	by publishing someone else's text under another name	by publishing someone else's text under one's own name
as independent text	Primary complete pseudepigraphy		Complete plagiarism
as embedded text	Primary embedded pseudepigraphy	(Secondary) interpolation	Partial plagiarism

Ancient authenticity criticism identified pseudepigrapha (as well as invented historical speeches, interpolations, and plagiarism) based on internal and external criteria. Critics evaluated external historical testimonies about the origin of a given text and compared its style and content with the genuine writings of the alleged author (Speyer; Blum).

In ancient authenticity criticism, a text's authenticity was not assessed based on its wording (thus Ehrman). Rather, its authorial attribution was regarded as correct and nondeceptive if its content (and not necessarily its wording) could be traced back to the author whose name it carried (Baum 2017; Gleich).

Table 3. Criteria of Ancient Criticism

		Style	
		from the author	from someone else
Content	from the author	authentic	authentic
	from someone else	forged	forged

4. False Attribution Without Deceptive Intent.

Secondary false attribution of independent medical and philosophical texts usually happened by mistake. Secondary false attribution of embedded texts (interpolation) could also occur erroneously.

While most ancient texts that were falsely ascribed by their authors were literary forgeries, this is not true for all categories of false authorial attributions.

- A clear exception was falsely ascribed texts that were written as rhetorical exercises (Sint; Brox). An important piece of evidence is a text by a certain Mithridates in which he tells his readers that he composed historically plausible letters under different names. This is a case not of (deceptive) primary complete pseudepigraphy but of (transparent) primary complete allonymity.
- A second exception is ancient epics and novels in which authors such as Homer or Apuleius put freely invented speeches into the mouths of their characters without deceptive intent. These false attributions were not primary embedded pseudepigraphy but primary embedded allonymity.
- A third exception is literary borrowing in poetry that could be regarded as transparent artistic imitation of great models, in both independent and embedded texts (Janßen 2016).

Table 4. Different Kinds of Transparent False Attribution

	by publishing one's own text under someone else's name	by publishing someone else's text under one's own name
as independent text	Primary complete allonymity (in stylistic exercises)	Transparent full borrowing (in poetic imitation)
as embedded text	Primary embedded allonymity (in novels)	Transparent partial borrowing (in poetic imitation)

Some scholars have identified other areas of ancient literature in which nondeceptive false attribution was acceptable, but these are controversial. Among them are the following:

- Some scholars believe that false attribution in medical and philosophical schools, where pupils composed their own texts under the names of their famous teachers, was transparent (Speyer; Brox; Wilder), while others regard it as deceptive (Donelson; Baum 2001; Ehrman).
- Some scholars believe that false attributions in letters and letter collections that were attributed to famous persons of the past were transparent (Schmidt; Wilder), while others regard them as deceptive (Sint; Donelson).
- Some scholars believe that in early Jewish apocalypses and related texts the attributions to famous men of the biblical past were transparent (Sint; Speyer; Brox; Meade; Najman; Dobroruka), while others regard them as deceptive (Donelson; Baum 2001; Van der Toorn).

5. The Deceptive Intent of False Attribution in Early Christianity.

Apocryphal texts that were composed under the name of Paul (the Epistle to the Laodiceans, the Epistle to the Alexandrians, the Epistles of Paul to

Seneca, and the Apocalypse of Paul) are generally regarded as pseudepigrapha or literary forgeries. The same holds true for the Pauline speeches and Paul's Third Epistle to the Corinthians, which are contained in the apocryphal Acts of Paul.

The question whether and to what extent NT or early Christian pseudepigrapha were meant to deceive their readers is answered differently. In textbooks, nondeceptive NT pseudepigraphy is assumed more often than in research monographs on the subject (Janßen 2003).

- Some researchers believe that all NT pseudepigrapha were transparent fictions (Kiley; Meade; possibly Riedl).
- Others believe that some NT pseudepigrapha were transparent fictions (Brox; Frey, Herzer, et al.; Schmidt as a possibility).
- A third group believes that no NT pseudepigraphon was a transparent fiction (Speyer; Donelson; Duff; Baum 2001; Frenschkowski; Wilder; Ehrman; Lüdemann).

6. The Moral Evaluation of Literary Forgery by Its Authors.

Ancient forgers rarely attempted to justify their activities or explicitly stated whether they acted with a clear conscience.

Indirect insights into the self-justification of ancient forgers are provided by literary forgeries (such as the Apostolic Constitutions) that warn against literary forgeries. Their ethical stance is clear: they considered forgeries in favor of their own theological convictions to be legitimate and only forgeries in favor of opposing positions to be reprehensible. Early Christian forgers considered themselves justified in writing under the names of recognized authors of the past if doing so served the cause of what they considered to be the *truth.

This self-justification must be viewed in the context of numerous statements from pre-Christian and Christian antiquity that declare a useful, salutary, or pious lie to be legitimate. The authors of literary forgeries applied this general justification of deception to the production of their texts (Speyer; Brox; Donelson; Baum 2001; Lüdemann).

7. Roman Catholic Coping Strategies for Canonical Pseudepigraphy.

The Christian churches agree that the biblical canon is the normative basis of Christian *faith and practice. In academic theology, different strategies are pursued to cope with canonical pseudepigraphy. Some authors combine several arguments. Overall, Protestant theologians have more options at their disposal than Roman Catholic theologians.

Roman Catholic (and some Protestant) exegetes presume that the *church has made a definitive dogmatic delimitation of the biblical canon of Scripture (Schelkle) and interpret canonical pseudepigraphy on this basis:

1. False author attributions were not intended to deceive and therefore do not represent a moral problem (Kiley; Meade; possibly Riedl).—This argumentation can hardly be reconciled with the historical evidence in the ancient source texts (see sections 3-5 above).
2. In the process of canon formation, literary authenticity was not a necessary criterion; therefore, it may not be used as such today (Ohlig; Brox). For the contemporary church, the historical origin of a biblical pseudepigraphon is of secondary importance in comparison to its canonization by the early church and to its ecclesiastical influence (Childs).—The historical argument on which this approach is based cannot be substantiated from the sources. In the early church, literary authenticity was not regarded as a sufficient but as a necessary canon criterion (Baum 2001).
3. NT pseudepigrapha are literary forgeries, which *God accepted in his *mercy, just as he accepted the deceiver Jacob after he had obtained the rights of the *firstborn by deception. Therefore, pseudepigraphy should only be rejected outside the canon (Pokorný).—This distinction between a canonical and an extracanonical morality is not convincing. Moreover, a valid analogy can only be drawn between the cheater Jacob and the forger of a pseudepigraphic text. Just as Jacob (although he had promoted himself as a Pseudo-Esau and had to go into exile for this) did not forfeit the *grace of God, God's grace also remains valid for a Christian forger (who published a text under Paul's name and had therefore been deprived of his office). There is, however, no analogy in the story of Jacob to the question of canonical forgeries (Baum 2001; Lüdemann).

8. Protestant Coping Strategies for Canonical Pseudepigraphy.

For (most) Protestants the assumption of an infallible canon decision of the church is not acceptable. Therefore, they can (in accord with Martin Luther's freedom regarding the canon) change the boundaries of the canon of Scripture, or (going beyond Luther) partially or completely abandon the concept of a binding canon of Scriptures in favor of a "canon in the canon." This leads to further options:

4. Early Christian pseudepigrapha are literary forgeries and cannot have a full canonical but at most a deuterocanonical or apocryphal status. Because of the pious lie (and the associated historical and content-related problems), pseudepigraphic texts cannot serve as theological yardsticks in the same way as orthonymous biblical texts (Baum 2001; Wilder).—One objection to this position is that it leads to a reduced canon of Scriptures (Janßen 2003; Riedl).
5. Literary forgeries can remain in the canon, because it is not the canon of Scripture as a whole that serves as the yardstick for Christian faith and practice but rather a "canon within the canon" (Käsemann). Therefore, a distinction has to be made between normative and nonnormative elements within the canon. Thus it is possible to detach the valuable ethical and theological contents of a biblical book from its deceptive statements (Lindeman).—This position abandons the theological concept that determined the creation of the biblical canon as a collection of normative Scriptures.

Most unproblematic are canonical forgeries for researchers who deny any normativity of the canon:

6. The biblical canon has no normative significance whatsoever since its texts were purely human contributions to the theological and ethical discussions of early Christianity. The deceptive intention of the NT pseudepigrapha corresponds to the fact that all human theology is deficient (Donelson; see Ehrman; Lüdemann).—This position is incompatible with any normative use of the biblical Scriptures.

See also Apocryphal Pauline Literature; Canon of Paul's Letters; Letters, Letter Forms; Pastoral Epistles; Performance.

BIBLIOGRAPHY. **A. D. Baum,** *Pseudepigraphie und literarische Fälschung im frühen Christentum* (Tübingen: Mohr Siebeck, 2001); idem, "A Theological Justification for the Canonical Status of Literary Forgeries," *JETS* 55 (2012): 273-90; idem, "Authorship and Pseudepigraphy in Ancient Christian Literature: A Translation of the Most Important Source Texts and an Annotated Bibliography," in *Paul and Pseudepigraphy*, ed. S. E. Porter and G. P. Fewster (Leiden: Brill, 2013), 11-63; idem, "Content and Form," *JBL* 136 (2017): 381-403; **R. Blum,** *Kallimachos und die Literaturverzeichnung bei den Griechen* (Frankfurt am Main: Buchhändler-Vereinigung, 1977); **N. Brox,** *Falsche Verfasserangaben* (Stuttgart: Katholisches Bibelwerk, 1975); **B. S. Childs,** *The New Testament as Canon* (London: SCM Press, 1984); **V. Dobroruka,** *Second Temple Pseudepigraphy* (Berlin: de Gruyter, 2014); **L. R. Donelson,** *Pseudepigraphy and Ethical Argument in the Pastoral Epistles* (Tübingen: Mohr Siebeck, 1986); **J. Duff,** "A Reconsideration of Pseudepigraphy in Early Christianity" (PhD diss., Oxford University, 1998); **B. D. Ehrman,** *Forgery and Counterforgery* (Oxford: Oxford University Press, 2012); **M. Frenschkowski,** "Pseudepigraphie und Paulusschule," in *Das Ende des Paulus*, ed. F. W. Horn (Berlin: de Gruyter, 2001), 239-72; **J. Frey and J. Herzer et al.,** eds., *Pseudepigraphie und Verfasserfiktion in frühchristlichen Briefen* (Tübingen: Mohr Siebeck, 2009); **D. Gleich,** *Die lukanischen Paulusreden* (Leipzig: Evangelische Verlagsanstalt, 2021); **M. Janßen,** *Unter falschem Namen* (Frankfurt: Lang, 2003); idem, "Plagiat," *Reallexikon für Antike und Christentum*, ed. Georg Schöllgen (Stuttgart: Hiersemann, 2016), 27:811-37; **M. Kiley,** *Colossians as Pseudepigraphy* (Sheffield: JSOT Press, 1986); **E. Käsemann,** ed., *Das Neue Testament als Kanon* (Göttingen: Vandenhoeck, 1970); **A. Lindemann,** *Der Kolosserbrief* (Zürich: Theologischer Verlag, 1983); **G. Lüdemann,** *Die gröbste Fälschung des Neuen Testaments* (Springe: zu Klampen, 2010); **I. H. Marshall,** *A Critical and Exegetical Commentary on the Pastoral Epistles* (Edinburgh: T&T Clark, 1999); **D. G. Meade,** *Pseudonymity and Canon* (Tübingen: Mohr Siebeck, 1986); **M. Mülke,** *Der Autor und sein Text* (Berlin: de Gruyter, 2008); **H. Najman,** *Seconding Sinai* (Leiden: Brill, 2003); **K.-H. Ohlig,** *Die theologische Begründung des neutestamentlichen Kanons in der alten Kirche* (Düsseldorf: Patmos, 1972); **P. Pokorný and U. Heckel,** *Einleitung in das Neue Testament* (Tübingen: Mohr Siebeck, 2007); **H. J. Riedl,** *Anamnese und Apostolizität* (Frankfurt: Lang, 2005); **K. H. Schelkle,** *Die Petrusbriefe. Der Judasbrief* (Freiburg: Herder, 1961); **K. Schickert,** *Der Schutz literarischer Urheberschaft im Rom der klassischen Antike* (Tübingen: Mohr Siebeck, 2005); **K. M. Schmidt,** *Mahnung und Erinnerung im Maskenspiel* (Freiburg: Herder, 2003); **J. A. Sint,** *Pseudonymität im Altertum* (Innsbruck: Wagner, 1960); **W. Speyer,** *Die literarische Fälschung im heidnischen und christlichen Altertum* (München: Beck, 1971); **E. Stemplinger,** *Das Plagiat in der griechischen Literatur* (Leipzig: Teubner, 1912); **K. Van der Toorn,** *Scribal Culture and the Making of* *the Hebrew Bible* (Cambridge, MA: Harvard University Press, 2007); **T. L. Wilder,** *Pseudonymity, the New Testament, and Deception* (Lanham, MD: University Press of America, 2004).

A. D. Baum

PSYCHOLOGY. *See* ANTHROPOLOGY, PAULINE; SOCIAL-SCIENTIFIC APPROACHES TO PAUL.

PURITY AND IMPURITY

Purity is generally understood as that which is clean, clear, or refined; it can also connote things that are simple, without superfluous elements, wholesome, faultless, and correct. In the Hebrew Bible purity is an essential part of the ordering of the world created by *God. Purity and impurity were categories by which *Israel as the people of God, holy and set apart from the nations, was instructed to order its world. The code of purity was particularly focused on the *temple, which portrayed the degrees of holy space surrounding the most holy place of Yahweh's presence in the midst of his people. By the time of Jesus and Paul, the priestly requirements of purity had been adopted by the Pharisees as a code for everyday living. Born and raised as a Pharisaic Jew, the *apostle Paul would have been immersed in the Jewish laws of purity. But as a Christ-follower, his understanding of the *holiness and purity of the people of God was reordered around the risen *Christ.

1. Living Before a Holy God
2. Purity in Second Temple Judaism
3. Purity in the Letters of Paul

1. Living Before a Holy God.

1.1. Old Testament Laws and Regulations. The OT's idea of purity is rooted in God's character, in his holiness and *righteousness. Israel's purity maps "involve persons, places, times, foods, and the physical body of the individual" (deSilva, 256). To be in a covenantal relationship with the holy God meant keeping his *law and requirements of holiness. A holy God established his divine order in the nation of Israel so that his presence might dwell among his people. This particular ordered purity set Israel apart from the other nations of the earth. The whole community of Israel was obligated to adhere to God's commands as a way of learning how to live together in God's ordered world.

On the reverse side, anything that was deemed impure had to be avoided. Defilement was always negative, as it is that which infects or pollutes whatever is normally considered commonplace. Israel was warned not to contaminate what God deemed holy, and there were consequences for disobedience. Pollution of any sort removed the person from the presence of God. Whatever was considered impure was a disruption in God's ordained order, and defilement came from any circumstance that demonstrated the lack of "wholeness" of a person or a creature. As David deSilva observes, to fully grasp the "radical reconfiguring of the Jewish purity system" by the early *church, one must consider the purity laws and the pollution regulations found in the OT (deSilva, 241).

1.2. Holiness and the Common. Israel's life as the people of God was ordered by two categories that separated them from the cultures around them. Their priests, *sacrifices, offerings, and rituals displayed the distinctions between the holy and common and between the clean and unclean (Lev 10:9-11). *Holy* is a term of position, meaning "set apart" or "separated" from the ordinary, everyday things. *Holiness* (Heb. *qādôš*; Gk. *hagios*, "set apart"), or that which is sacred, is perfect, complete, whole, and awe-inspiring. This includes certain objects (i.e., clothing), people, spaces, and times that are set aside for specific purposes. A key theme of Leviticus, holiness was a total consecration to God to be expressed by his people in every aspect of daily life (Lev 11:44-45). It was also any area dedicated to God's presence, such as the tabernacle or the temple. All other space not associated with the sacred was considered "common" (Heb. *ḥōl*; Gk. *koinos*). Common things were also considered to be profane, without a strictly negative connotation. A neutral term, *common* refers to ordinary things in the world that are appropriate for human use (deSilva, 253).

1.3. Clean and Unclean. *Clean* is another neutral term, referring to a normal state of being or existing within the proper boundaries established by God. In Greek, "to make clean or clear" is *katharizō*. People are considered clean and common most of the time but can move between conditions of clean and unclean. Uncleanness, then, designates a position of being defiled (Heb. *ṭāmēʾ*) or in a state of impurity (Heb. *niddâ*; Lev 10:10; 11:4; 17:15; Is 52:11). It denotes that something has gone beyond the mapped boundaries of cleanliness into a dangerous point of pollution. In Greek, to be "unclean" or "impure" is *akatharsia* or *akathartos*, the opposite of *katharos*, "clean" (1 Cor 7:14; 2 Cor 6:17; Eph 5:5). However, there were certain temporary states of being unclean for a period of time that did not involve disgrace or indignity. Disease and childbirth, for example, were temporary states of impurity or uncleanness (Lev 15:19).

There was always a danger of the unclean contaminating that which was clean or holy. Uncleanness could endanger the individual person, the whole Israelite community, or even the land itself (Lev 25:3-12; 26:14-33; Num 19:13). Israel was instructed to keep purity regulations through systematic, ceremonial, and ritual actions, or by waiting for a specified time period. *Sin, burnt, and guilt offerings were among those sacrifices brought to the temple sanctuary that could restore a person to a state of purity. The purpose of such categories and purity laws was to establish boundaries for God's people and to prepare them to live in the presence of a holy and righteous God. To faithfully obey the purity regulations led to the expectation (and the celebration) of God's favor (Ps 18:20) toward the individual and/or the entire nation.

1.4. Purity of Heart. Purity was not simply an external display, for the OT speaks of the outer symbols as representing internal purity. It is associated with the human heart, the center of human emotion, courage, motivations, and actions. A pure heart resulted in pure attitudes, motives, and intentions. The psalmist declares, "Who may ascend the mountain of the LORD? Who may stand in his holy place? The one who has clean hands and a pure heart, who does not trust in an idol or swear by a false god" (Ps 24:3-4 NIV; see also Ps 51:7, 10; Jer 4:14; 17:9). The *Lord says to Ezekiel, "I will give them an undivided heart and put a new spirit in them; I will remove from them their heart of stone and give them a heart of *flesh. Then they will follow my decrees and be careful to keep my laws. They will be my people, and I will be their God" (Ezek 11:19-20 NIV). God was teaching his people about pure righteousness, moral integrity, and faithfulness to him that was from the heart.

2. Purity in Second Temple Judaism.

During the Second Temple period the idea and symbols of purity developed in new ways. This can be observed clearly in the Jewish sect that established the community at *Qumran, near the Dead Sea. In the Dead Sea Scrolls associated with this community there is a great deal of purity language. Having removed themselves from the Jerusalem temple, geographically and ritually, at least some of these sectarians considered their community to be the temple of God, his dwelling place. In their view, neither God nor his angels could inhabit the Jerusalem temple because of its corruption. Sin and impurity had tainted its leadership and the sanctuary. As a holy community of Israel, set apart in the wilderness and awaiting the future restoration of Israel, the Qumran community maintained purity requirements for admission to their assembly as well as for ordering the lives of its members. They made no distinction between moral (ethical) and ritual (cultic) purity; the two areas were so intertwined that they often could not be differentiated.

Less radical than the Qumran sect but with some points of similarity were the Pharisees. Broadly speaking (the Shammaite and Hillelite schools are evidence of diverse emphases among the Pharisees), they were a lay movement that viewed the temple and its *leadership as corrupt. But rather than separating and retreating to the wilderness, they continued to participate in worship at the temple in Jerusalem. Their zeal for restoring Israel led them to apply the priestly codes of ritual purity to domestic life and the study of Torah. This pharisaic approach to Torah and purity seems to have been formative for rabbinic Judaism, evidenced in the later emergence of the Mishnah (ca. AD 200). After the destruction of the Jewish temple in AD 70, with no singular designated holy space for sacrifice and *worship, issues of purity and impurity became central concerns of rabbinic Judaism. The Jewish community itself was to reflect the presence of God (see Wright, 181-209).

3. Purity in the Letters of Paul.

3.1. A New Temple of God. Paul characterizes his former life as a Pharisee as "extremely zealous for the traditions of my fathers" (Gal 1:14 NIV). He was deeply attuned to the biblical link between purity and the presence of God, and the rejection of sin and impurity found a prominent place in his Christian theology. Paul views the church as the "temple of God," and therefore it should be purified "from everything that contaminates *body and spirit, perfecting holiness out of reverence for God" (1 Cor 3:16; 2 Cor 7:1 NIV). Christians are "living sacrifices," surrendering themselves to the Christ they serve (Rom 12:1). Christians believe that Jesus redeemed them "from all wickedness" and that he will "purify for himself a people that are his very own, eager to do what is good" (Titus 2:12-14 NIV).

3.2. Jews, Gentiles, and the Law. Purity codes and taboos were a part of the *Gentile world as well as the Jewish tradition (see deSilva, 249-53). Nevertheless, Jews regarded Gentiles as unruly and immoral because they did not adhere to the laws of the one true God. For Paul, both Jews and Gentiles alike were *slaves to sin and impurity (Rom 3:9; 6:19-21). The law had not eradicated sin and impurity (Rom 2:12-15). In fact, none of the "*works of the law" redeemed them from sin and iniquity (Gal 2:16; 3:2, 5, 10). For Paul, Christ alone redeems people from the bondage of sin (Gal 2:15-16; 3:13-14; 1 Thess 4:3). Christ-followers, then, are "set free from sin and have become slaves to righteousness" and are to "obey from [their] heart" (Rom 6:17-18 NIV modified). God's law is written on human hearts, not on "tablets of stone" (Jer 31:33; Gal 2:15-16; 5:4-5).

Both Jewish and Gentile Christians had to learn a new way of living together "*in Christ" as "one body" (Rom 12:5). The law, with its commandments and ordinances that separated Jew from Gentile, has been abolished in Christ, and one new humanity created from those "who were far away" (Gentiles) and "those who were near" (Jews), together forming a "holy temple" and dwelling place for God (Eph 2:11-22).

3.3. Paul Rewrites the Purity Code. The OT cultic and purity laws were removed in Christ's *death. Christians are not under the OT law, which was fulfilled in Christ (Rom 3:22-25, 28, 31). However, they are still called to "live in order to please God" (1 Thess 4:1 NIV): "God did not call us to be impure, but to live a holy life" (1 Thess 4:7 NIV). Furthermore, Christians are given the gift of the *Holy Spirit, who enables them to live a "holy life" (Gal 5:4-6, 16-26).

Thus Paul calls those in Christ to a purity of heart. In contrast, he condemns contamination within the church, including improper attitudes and behavior (1 Cor 5:6-13). Paul's concern for purity in the church is evidenced in his handling of issues of speech, doctrines, *foods, sacred days, and sexual impurity. Paul assures the Philippians that purity of thoughts leads to purity of speech and actions (Phil 4:8). He warns Timothy about false doctrines in the church, but the goal is "*love, which comes from a pure heart and a good conscience and a sincere *faith" (1 Tim 1:5 NIV). A striking example of Paul's concern for purity is in 1 Corinthians 5:1 (see Newton). A Corinthian man was openly living with "his father's wife," which for Paul was certainly an "uncleanness." Disciplinary action was necessary to protect the whole community from contamination. Instead of "being proud" of "sexually immoral people," Paul told the church to "get rid" of such a person (1 Cor 5:2, 6-7, 13). Sinful behavior and sexual impurity within the church injures corporate unity and blemishes the reputation of Christians. In maintaining its purity, he instructs the church to "judge" the people inside the community; yet ultimately it is God who "judges those outside" the church" (1 Cor 5:12-13).

Paul tells Timothy to "keep yourself pure" as he serves as a minister to others. Church leaders are to "keep pure" in their personal lives and guide God's people in an exemplary fashion. Righteousness comes out of a pure heart, while resentment, quarrels, arguments, and opposition arise from impure, selfish motives (2 Tim 2:22).

Paul also implies that sexual impurity is an expression of selfish gratification, in place of human love, which mirrors the love and sacrifice of Christ. In Ephesians 5:2 Paul instructs his readers to "walk in the way of love, just as Christ loved us" (NIV). In Ephesians 5:3, he turns to condemn "sexual immorality, or . . . any kind of impurity, or . . . greed, because these are improper for God's holy people" (NIV; see also Rom 1:29-32).

3.4. Food Denial and Sacred Days. Paul believed that no food was ceremonially unclean for Christian believers; nor was "one day more sacred than another" (Rom 14:5 NIV). For Paul, all days were to be dedicated to God through holy living and godly *service (Rom 14:5-9). He tells the Galatians that they are "enslaved" to "special days and years," which never in themselves produced redemption or sanctification (Gal 4:8-10). Similarly, to the Colossians he says, "these were a shadow of the things that were to come" (Col 2:17 NIV). Believers are not to judge or reject one another based on ceremonial foods or days, because both the "*strong" in faith and the "weak" should serve God together and be grateful for what they have. One's personal freedoms and rights are not a Christian's only consideration; one must give concern and thoughtfulness to the "good of others" (1 Cor 10:24, 33; Gal 6:2).

Still, Paul forbids believers' consuming food sacrificed to false gods within the context of idol temple worship, for this involves believers in demonic worship (1 Cor 10:19-21). Some Christians felt that it was wrong to eat such meat when it was sold in the market, but Paul reassures them: "Eat anything sold in the meat market without raising questions of conscience, for, 'The earth is the Lord's, and everything in it'" (1 Cor 10:25-26 NIV). That is, impurity does not reside within the essence of a given object, such as meat, but in the concepts and beliefs behind the object. "So," Paul says, "do it all for the *glory of God" (1 Cor 10:31 NIV).

3.5. Toward the Eschaton. In his *letters Paul is concerned about the church maintaining acceptable standards of behavior so as to be ready for the "final days." The words *holy*, *righteous*, and *blameless* (1 Thess 2:10 NIV; see also 1 Thess 3:13) are used in the LXX to describe purified conditions for those who want to enter the temple and offer sacrifices. Paul's vision of the end of the age provides motivation for those in Christ to live pure and godly lives in the present. In this light Paul instructs the Galatians to live by "the *fruit of the Spirit," which is "love, *joy, *peace, forbearance, kindness, goodness, faithfulness, gentleness and self-control. Against such things there is no law" (Gal 5:22-23 NIV).

See also FOOD LAWS AND CUSTOMS, JEWISH AND ROMAN; HOLINESS, SANCTIFICATION; ISRAEL; LAW; QUMRAN AND PAUL; SACRIFICE, OFFERING; SEXUALITY, SEXUAL ETHICS; SIN, GUILT; TEMPLE.

BIBLIOGRAPHY. **G. W. Buchanan,** "The Role of Purity in the Structure of the Essene Sect," *RevQ* 4 (1963): 397-406; **D. A. deSilva,** *Honor, Patronage, Kinship & Purity: Unlocking New Testament Culture* (Downers Grove, IL: IVP Academic, 2000); **M. Douglas,** *Purity and Danger: An Analysis of the Concepts of Pollution and Taboo* (London: Routledge & Kegan Paul, 1966); **H. K. Harrington,** *The Impurity Systems of Qumran and the Rabbis*, SBLDS 143 (Atlanta: Scholars Press, 1993); **W. Houston,** *Purity and Monotheism: Clean and Unclean Animals in Biblical Law*, JSOTSup 140 (Sheffield: Sheffield Academic, 1993); **J. Klawans,** "Methodology and Ideology in the Study of Priestly Ritual," in *Perspectives on Purity and Purification in the Bible*, ed. B. J. Schwartz, D. P. Wright, J. Stackert, and N. S. Meshel (New York: T&T Clark, 2008), 84-95; **J. Milgrom,** "The Dynamics of Purity in the Priestly System," in *Purity and Holiness: The Heritage of Leviticus*, ed. M. Poorthuis and J. Swartz (Leiden: Brill, 2000), 29-32; **M. Newton,** *The Concept of Purity at Qumran and in the Letters of Paul* (Cambridge: Cambridge University Press, 1985); **J. H. Neyrey,** "Body Language in 1 Corinthians: The Use of Anthropological Models for Understanding Paul and His Opponents," *Semeia* 35 (1986): 129-70; idem, *Paul, in Other Words* (Louisville, KY: Westminster John Knox, 1990); **E. Ottenheijm,** "Impurity Between Intention and Deed: Purity Disputes in First Century Judaism and in the New Testament," in *Purity and Holiness: The Heritage of Leviticus*, ed. M. Poorthuis and J. Swartz (Leiden: Brill, 2000), 129-48; **R. C. T. Parker,** "Sacrifice, Greek," in *The Oxford Companion to Classical Civilization*, ed. S. Hornblower and A. Spawforth (Oxford: Oxford University Press, 1998), 628-69; **M. Poorthuis and J. Swartz,** "Introduction Survey," in *Purity and Holiness: The Heritage of Leviticus*, ed. M. Poorthuis and J. Swartz (Leiden: Brill, 2000), 3-26; **J. Sklar,** "Sin and Impurity: Atoned or Purified? Yes!," in *Perspectives on Purity and Purification in the Bible*, ed. B. J. Schwartz, D. P. Wright, J. Stackert, and N. S. Meshel (New York: T&T Clark, 2008), 18-31; **N. T. Wright,** *The New Testament and the People of God* (Minneapolis: Fortress, 1992).

J. A. Diehl

Q

QUMRAN AND PAUL

The scrolls of Qumran, found in eleven caves near the Dead Sea in the Judean wilderness in 1947–1956, shed light on Paul and his letters at many points (Fitzmyer).

1. Ecclesiastical Terminology
2. Theological Terminology
3. Paul and "Works of Law"
4. Paul and Ascent into Heaven

1. Ecclesiastical Terminology.

The Qumran scrolls clarify some of Paul's ecclesiastical terminology, especially with reference to *leadership and community structure (Kuhn).

1.1. The Many. In a context of *discipline Paul speaks of the "punishment by the majority" (2 Cor 2:6 NRSV). What the RSV translates as "by the majority" is literally "by the many" (*hypo tōn pleionōn*), which closely corresponds to Qumran's references to "the many" (*rabbîm*), as in the Rule Scroll (1QS), which provides guidelines as to how one addresses "the many" or "the general membership" (e.g., 1QS VI, 8-23). These guidelines approximate those Paul recommends to the *church at *Corinth: "When you come together, each one has a *hymn, a lesson, a revelation, a *tongue, or an interpretation. Let all things be done for building up . . . each in turn. . . . If there is no one to interpret, let them be silent in church. . . . All things should be done decently and in order" (1 Cor 14:26-28, 40 NRSV). Likewise, the Rule Scroll requires that "each man be in his proper place," where "each man may state his opinion to the Council of the Community. None should interrupt the words of his comrade, speaking before his brother finishes what he has to say. Neither should anyone speak before another of higher rank. Only the man being questioned shall speak in his turn" (1QS VI, 9-11).

1.2. Leadership. In this context there is also reference to the "Inspector" (*məbaqqer*):

> During the session of the Many [*rabbîm*] no man should say anything except by the permission of the Many [*rabbîm*], or more particularly, of the man who is the Inspector [*məbaqqer*] of the Many [*rabbîm*]. . . . If anyone of Israel volunteers for enrollment in the party of the Community, the man appointed as Overseer [*paqîd*] of the Many [*rabbîm*] shall examine him regarding his understanding and works. (1QS VI, 11-14)

Qumran's *məbaqqer* and *paqîd* approximate Paul's *episkopos* ("overseer" or "bishop"; see Phil 1:1 NRSV, "to those who are in Philippi, with the bishops [*episkopoi*] and deacons"; cf. Judg 9:28 [Heb. *paqîd* = Gk. *episkopos]*; Lev 13:36; Ezek 34:11 [Heb. *bqr* = Gk. *episkeptesthai]*). Also, Paul's "deacons" or "ministers" (*diakonoi*) may find an equivalent in Qumran's *meshartîm* (see 1QM II, 1; 1QH[a] XIII, 23; XXIII, 34; XV, 29; cf. Esther 1:10 [Heb. *məšartîm* = Gk. *diakonoi]*). Paul also tells the Corinthians that *God provides the church with gifted *didaskaloi*, "teachers" (1 Cor 12:28). Similarly, the *Rule Scroll* speaks of a *maskîl*, "instructor" or "teacher," who instructs the community (1QS I, 1; III, 13; IX, 12, 16, 21).

1.3. Assembly. Furthermore, Qumran sometimes refers to its congregation of the faithful as the *qāhāl*, "assemby" (CD VII, 17; XII, 6; 1QSa II, 4), or *qāhāl ʾēl*, "assembly of God" (1QM IV, 10). Likewise Paul calls the Christian congregation the *ekklēsia*, "assembly" (1 Cor 4:17; 6:4; 7:17; 2 Cor 8:1; Phil 3:6; 4:15), or *ekklēsia tou theou*, "assembly of God" (1 Cor 1:2; 2 Cor 1:1; Gal 1:13; 1 Thess 2:14). This language, of course, is derived from OT Scripture (e.g., Deut 9:10 [Heb. *qāhāl* = Gk. *ekklēsia*]; Neh 13:1 [Heb. *qāhāl ʾelōhîm* = Gk. *ekklēsia theou*]; cf. Judg 20:2 [Heb. *qāhāl ʿam hāʾelōhîm* = Gk. *ekklēsia tou laou tou theou*, "assembly of the people of God"]).

Paul reminds the Corinthian Christians that they are the "*temple [*naos*] of the living God" (2 Cor 6:16 NRSV). Similarly the Essenes think of themselves as "a temple [*qōdeš*] for Israel, and—mystery!—a Holy of Holies for Aaron" (1QS VIII, 5-6); and, again, as "the holy house [*bēit qōdeš*] of Aaron uniting as a Holy of Holies, and the synagogue of Israel as those who walk blamelessly" (IX, 6).

1.4. Sons of Light. It should also be noted that Qumran calls its members "Sons of Light": "The Instructor should enlighten and teach all the Sons of Light [*benei ʾōr*] about the character and fate of humanity" (1QS III, 13). Qumran's "Sons of Light" are sometimes explicitly contrasted with their opponents, the "Sons of Darkness": "The first attack of the Sons of Light [*benei ʾōr*] shall be undertaken against the forces of the Sons of Darkness [*benei ḥōšek*], the army of Belial" (1QM I, 1). Paul describes Christians the same way: "for you are all sons of *light [*huioi phōtos*] and sons of the day; we are not of the night or of darkness [*skotos*]" (1 Thess 5:5 RSV; see Eph 5:8 NRSV, "For once you were darkness [*skotos*], but now in the *Lord you are light [*phōs*]. Live as children of light [*tekna phōtos*]"). In the context of Paul's contrast of believers with nonbelievers, one also finds reference to Belial (or Beliar): "What agreement does *Christ have with Beliar? Or what does a believer share with an unbeliever?" (2 Cor 6:15 NRSV).

2. Theological Terminology.

Qumran offers several important parallels to Pauline theology (Fitzmyer, 614-16; Kuhn).

2.1. New Covenant. In 2 Corinthians 3:6 Paul says God has made him and the other leaders of the church "ministers of a new *covenant" (NRSV). This "new covenant" (*kainē diathēkē*) stands in contrast with the old (Sinai) covenant, "chiseled in letters on stone," as Paul puts it (2 Cor 3:7 NRSV). The adjective *new* also appears in Paul's version of the words of institution: "This cup is the new covenant [*hē kainē diathēkē*] in my blood" (1 Cor 11:25 NRSV; see Lk 22:20). Four times in the *Damascus Covenant* readers hear of the *bərît ḥădāšâ*, "new covenant" (CD VI, 19 [= 4Q269 4 II, 1]; VIII, 21; XIX, 33-34; XX, 12; cf. 1QpHab II, 3). Readers also hear of the covenant "renewed" (1Q34bis 3 II; 4Q509 97-98 I, 8). The language of "new covenant" harks back to the *prophecy of Jeremiah: "Behold, the days are coming, says the LORD, when I will make a new covenant [*bərît ḥădāšâ / diathēkē kainē*] with the house of *Israel and the house of Judah" (Jer 31:31 RSV = LXX 38:31). Jesus and his followers, no doubt guided by Jeremiah's qualification, "not like the covenant that I made with their ancestors when I took them by the hand to bring them out of the land of Egypt" (Jer 31:32 NRSV), envisioned a truly new covenant, a covenant ratified by the blood of Jesus, not the blood of an animal. But the men of Qumran understood Jeremiah's new covenant as the old covenant *renewed*.

2.2. Righteousness of God. Several times Paul makes reference to the *dikaiosynē theou*, "*righteousness of God" (Rom 1:17; 3:21-22; 10:3; 2 Cor 5:21; Phil 3:9), a divine virtue that is clearly revealed in the *gospel of Jesus the Messiah. At Qumran one hears of *tsidəqōt ʾēl*, "righteous (acts) of God" (1QS I, 21; X, 23), *tsidəqat ʾēl*, "righteousness of God" (X, 25; XI, 12), and *tsedeq ʾēl*, "righteousness of God" (1QM IV, 6). Sometimes the Rule Scroll sounds a very Pauline note: "Through his love He has brought me near; by his loving-kindness shall he provide my justification. By his righteous truth has he justified me; and through his exceeding goodness shall he atone for all my sins. By his righteousness shall he cleanse me of human defilement and the sin of humankind—to the end that I praise God for his righteousness" (XI, 14-15).

Paul also speaks of the *dikaiokrisia tou theou*, "righteous *judgment of God" (Rom 2:5), which has a counterpart in the Scrolls: *mišpətē tsdəqkāh*, "righteous judgments" (1QH IX, 32; *olim* I, 30; see also IX, 25; *olim* I, 23).

2.3. Grace of God. Paul frequently speaks of the *charis tou theou*, "*grace of God" (Rom 5:15; 1 Cor 1:4; 3:10; 2 Cor 1:12; 6:1; 8:1; Gal 2:21). Paul views the grace of God as the ultimate gift (Rom 3:24), whereby human *sin is freely forgiven. It must be this way, Paul argues, for "no *flesh [*sarx*] will be justified in his sight by *works of the *law" (Rom 3:20); and it cannot be, for flesh is sinful (Rom 8:3, *sarkos hamartias*). The Rule Scroll approximates these ideas when its sectarian author confesses, "As for me, if I stumble, the grace of God [*ḥasdei ʾēl*] forever shall save me. If through sin of the flesh [*ʿāûn bāśār*] I fall, my justification will be by the righteousness of God which endures for all time" (1QS XI, 11-12; 1QM XIV, 8, "Blessed is your name, O God of lovingkindnesses [*ʾēl haḥăsādîm*]"; cf. Esth 2:9, 17; Sir 7:33; 40:17, where *charis* translates *ḥesed*).

2.4. Flesh and Spirit. Paul sometimes contrasts flesh (*sarx*) with spirit (*pneuma*). The former is weak and sinful, unable to fulfill the law of God: "We know that the law is spiritual; but I am carnal, sold under sin. . . . For I know that nothing good dwells within me, that is, in my flesh [*sarx*]. I can will what is right, but I cannot do it" (Rom 7:14, 18 RSV). The law can be fulfilled, says Paul, if the believer walks "not according to the flesh [*sarx*] but according to the Spirit [*pneuma*]" (Rom 8:4 RSV). The *apostle adds: "For those who live according to the flesh [*sarx*] set their minds on the things of the flesh, but those who live according to the Spirit [*pneuma*] set their minds on the things of the Spirit" (Rom 8:5 RSV). One finds a similar anthropology in the *Rule Scroll*: "By his truth God shall then purify all human deeds, and refine some of humanity so as to extinguish every perverse spirit from the inward parts of his flesh [*bāśār*], cleansing from every wicked deed by a holy spirit [*rûaḥ qōdeš*]. Like purifying waters, he shall sprinkle each with a spirit of truth, effectual against all the abominations of lying" (1QS IV, 20-21).

2.5. Mystery. Most of the occurrences of **mystery* or *secret* (*mystērion*) in the NT occur in the writings of Paul. The apostle says the gospel is "according to the revelation of the mystery [*mystērion*] that was kept secret for long ages" (Rom 16:25 NRSV). Elsewhere Paul describes the gospel as the "mystery [*mystērion*] of God" (1 Cor 2:1; see 1 Cor 2:7; 4:1, "Think of us . . . as *servants of Christ and stewards of the mysteries [*mystēria*] of God" [RSV]). Similarly the Qumran Scrolls speak of God's mysteries (*rāzîm*) that have been revealed in recent times (1QS XI, 19; 1QM III, 9; 1QpHab VII, 4-5, where God is praised for having disclosed "all the mysteries of the words of the prophets" to the Teacher of Righteousness).

3. Paul and "Works of Law."

The Qumran Scrolls have been especially helpful in clarifying the meaning of Paul's *teaching regarding "works of the law" that cannot justify a human being (Fitzmyer, 605-9).

3.1. General Meaning. The importance of "works of law" is made clear in the Rule Scroll in reference to one who wishes to join the community: "When he has passed a full year in the Community, the Majority shall inquire into the details of his understanding and observance of the law [*maʿaśāw batōrâ*]" (1QS VI, 18; cf. V, 21, "his understanding and practice of the law"). In these texts "observance" and "practice" translate *maʿăśeh*, "work." Similarly Paul speaks of the "work of law" (*ergon nomou*) written on the hearts of even pagans, which informs their conscience in evaluating their behavior (Rom 2:13-15).

3.2. Relation to Food and Purity. Where Qumran has been especially helpful is in clarifying the context in which Paul speaks of "works of law." Paul emphatically states that "we know that a person is justified not by the works of the law [*ex ergōn nomou*] but through *faith in Jesus Christ. And we have come to believe in Christ Jesus, so that we might be justified by faith in Christ, and not by doing the works of the law [*ex ergōn nomou*], because no one will be justified by the works of the law [*ex ergōn nomou ou dikaiōthēsetai*]" (Gal 2:16 NRSV; see Gal 3:2, 5, 10; Rom 3:20, 27-28). For scriptural support of this position Paul appeals to the faith of *Abraham: "Just as Abraham 'believed God, and it was reckoned to him as righteousness [*elogisthē autō eis dikaiosynēn*]'" (Gal 3:6 NRSV, quoting Gen 15:6; see Rom 4:1-5).

Qumran's Halakhic Letter (4QMMT), of which there are six fragmentary copies (4Q394–399), sheds a great deal of light on Paul's argument (Dunn). It also clarifies the parallels with the discussion of works and faith in James 2. After a description of some twenty "works of the law," the letter concludes:

> Now, we have written to you some of the works of the Law [*miqṣat maʿăśe hatōrâ*], those which we determined would be beneficial for you and your people, because we have seen that you possess insight and knowledge of the Law. Understand all these things and beseech Him to set your counsel straight and so keep you away from evil thoughts and the counsel of Belial. Then you shall rejoice at the end time when you find the essence of our words to be true. And "it will be reckoned to you as righteousness," in that you have done what is right and good before Him, to your own benefit and to that of Israel. (4Q398 14-17 II, 2-8 = 4Q399 1 I, 10-11 + II, 1-5)

The words "it will be reckoned to you as righteousness" in line 7 allude either to Genesis 15:6 (Abraham "believed the LORD; and the LORD reckoned it to him as righteousness" [NRSV]) or Psalm 106:30-31 ("Phinehas stood up and interposed, and the plague was stayed. And that has been reckoned to him as righteousness from generation to generation for ever" [RSV]). Although it is possible that the author of the Halakhic Letter had both passages in mind, the passage from Psalm 106 offers a better match. The verb "will be reckoned" (*tēḥāšeb*) in the letter is a *niphal*, which agrees with the *niphal* in Psalm 106:31, not with the *qal* in Genesis 15:6. More importantly, however, is the context. Psalm 106 sings the praises of the priest Phinehas (Num 25:6-9), whose piety and zeal for God and his law the men of Qumran would have found worthy of emulation (see 1 Macc 2:49-54, where the zeal of Phinehas is cited as a role model).

The Halakhic Letter makes it clear that in speaking of "works of law" Paul refers to *purity, especially as it relates to *food. Among the "works of law" in the Halakhic Letter are prohibitions against mixing Gentile grain with pure grain (4Q394 3-7 I, 6-8; see 4Q258 4 IX, 8-9, "be separated from all the unrighteous men . . . and do not eat with them"). This prohibition sheds light on Peter's refusal to eat with *Gentiles (Gal 2:11-13), which also clarifies why in rebuking *Peter (Gal 2:14) Paul speaks of "works of law" that cannot make one righteous (Gal 2:15-16).

*3.3. **Faith and Works in James.*** The Halakhic Letter also helps interpreters make better sense of the apparent discrepancy in the respective understandings of "works" in the writings of Paul and James. The "works" in James 2, which must be done to show that one's faith is genuine and thereby of saving value, relate to deeds of compassion that are in keeping with Jesus' command to love one's neighbor (Lev 19:18; see Mk 12:28-34; Lk 10:25-28). It is not enough, says James, to confess that "God is one" (Jas 2:18-19; see Deut 6:4-5); one must also have compassion on the person in need. Confessions and platitudes, such as "Go in *peace, be warmed and filled" (Jas 2:15-17 RSV), are insufficient. Abraham "believed" God and then showed that his faith was genuine when he obeyed God (Jas 2:21-24). Purity and food are not at issue in James. Given the tenor of his argument, one should assume that James would have agreed with Paul that avoidance of impure food would not provide grounds for being "reckoned as righteousness."

4. Paul and Ascent into Heaven.

Forced to disclose an impressive experience, Paul describes his ascent into heaven (2 Cor 12:1-12; Abegg; Angel; Litwa; O'Neill; Wise). Speaking of himself in the third person, Paul says, "This man was caught up into Paradise—whether in the *body or out of the body I do not know, God knows—and he heard things that cannot be told, which man may not utter" (2 Cor 12:3-4 RSV). A number of studies point to parallels with Jewish *merkavah* ("chariot") mysticism, in which the mystic after a period of intense *prayer and fasting ascends into heaven and gazes on the chariot throne of God (Ezek 1; Dan 7).

These parallels could be helpful, but they are found in late sources. More helpful is the description of ascent into heaven found in a few texts recovered from Qumran's Caves 1 and 4. In these texts an unidentified speaker asks, "Who compares with me? I have never been taught, but no teaching compares with my teaching. For I have dwelt on high . . . in the heavens. Who is like me among the angels? Who shall assault me when I open my mouth? Who can endure the utterance of my lips? Who with the tongue will challenge me and compare with my judgment?" (4Q427 frag. 7, lines 7-10, with restorations; see 4Q471b frags. 1-3, lines 3-6; 4Q491c frag. 11, lines 6-11; 1QH^{a} XXVI, 6-8). It has been proposed that Michael the archangel is speaking, but a boastful angel seems out of place. It is better to think an exalted human is in view, who has entered heaven and has learned things that no one can challenge. This seems roughly to parallel Paul's experience. While in heaven, or paradise, the apostle has "heard things that cannot be told, which man may not utter." Presumably these are things that if uttered could not be challenged or contradicted. In other words, they were things akin to what the mystic in the Qumran scrolls is expressing.

See also CHURCH; CHURCH STRUCTURE; COVENANT; FLESH; FOOD LAWS AND CUSTOMS, JEWISH AND ROMAN; GRACE; JAMES AND PAUL; LAW; LEADERSHIP; MYSTERY; PURITY AND IMPURITY; RIGHTEOUSNESS; VISIONS, ECSTATIC EXPERIENCE; WORKS OF THE LAW; WORSHIP.

BIBLIOGRAPHY. **M. G. Abegg Jr.,** "Who Ascended to Heaven? 4Q491, 4Q427, and the Teacher of Righteousness," in *Eschatology, Messianism, and the Dead Sea Scrolls*, ed. C. A. Evans and P. W. Flint (Grand Rapids, MI: Eerdmans, 1997), 61-73; **J. Angel,** "The Liturgical-Eschatological Priest of the *Self-Glorification Hymn*," *RevQ* 24 (2010): 585-605; **J. D. G. Dunn,** "4QMMT and Galatians," *NTS* 43 (1997): 147-53; **J. A. Fitzmyer,** "Paul and the Dead Sea Scrolls," in *The Dead Sea Scrolls After Fifty Years: A Comprehensive Assessment*, ed. P. W. Flint and J. C. VanderKam (Leiden: Brill, 1998–1999), 2:599-621; **H.-W. Kuhn,** "The Impact of the Qumran Scrolls on the Understanding of Paul," in *The Dead Sea Scrolls: Forty Years of Research*, ed. D. Dimant and U. Rappaport, STDJ 10 (Leiden: Brill, 1992), 327-39; **M. D. Litwa,** "Paul's Mosaic Ascent: An Interpretation of 2 Corinthians 12.7-9," *NTS* 57 (2011): 238-57; **J. C. O'Neill,** "'Who Is Comparable to Me in My Glory?' 4Q491 Fragment 11 (4Q491C) and the New Testament," *NovT* 42 (2000): 24-38; **S. Pfann,** "Abducted by God? The Process of Heavenly Ascent in Jewish Tradition, from Enoch to Paul, from Paul to Akiva," *Henoch* 33 (2011): 113-28; **E. Qimron and J. Strugnell,** *Qumran Cave 4: V. Miqṣat Maʿaśe Ha-Torah*, Discoveries in the Judaean Desert 10 (Oxford: Clarendon, 1994), 62-63; **P. A. de Souza Nogueira,** "Ecstatic Worship in the Self-Glorification Hymn (4Q471B, 4Q427, 4Q491C): Implications for the Understanding of an Ancient Jewish and Early Christian Phenomenon," in *Wisdom and Apocalypticism in the Dead Sea Scrolls and in the Biblical Tradition*, ed. F. García Martínez, BETL 168 (Leuven: Peeters, 2003), 385-93; **M. O. Wise,** "מי כמוני באלים, A Study of 4Q491c, 4Q471b, 4Q427 7 and 1QH A 25:35–26:10," *DSD* 7 (2000): 173-219.

C. A. Evans

R

RABBINIC BACKGROUND. *See* Paul and Judaism.

RECONCILIATION. *See* Atonement; Peace, Reconciliation.

REDEMPTION. *See* Atonement; Salvation.

RELIGIONS, GRECO-ROMAN

The peoples of the ancient Mediterranean world were deeply religious. Evidence of their religiosity confronts the modern observer on virtually every type of media recovered from antiquity: coinage, utensils, graffiti, artwork, literature, and of course shrines and *temples. This material reveals a myriad of deities and beliefs, yet also attests to a dominant religious ethos permeating the major and minor religious groups of this era, an ethos characterized by a concern to appease divine *wrath and procure divine blessing. The hyphenated adjective "Greco-Roman" likewise suggests both complexity and syncretism, while also gesturing toward the larger geopolitical drama that had unfolded in the centuries before the birth of *Christ. The conquests of Alexander the Great (334-323 BC) led to a notable expansion of traditional Greek religious conceptions throughout the Mediterranean, yet without suppressing regional deities, local mythologies, and indigenous folk practices. The ascendency of Rome—itself enthusiastic for Greek culture and tolerant of religious diversity—maintained the religious status quo; eventually the traditional gods of Rome merged with the classical pantheon of Athens. Against this backdrop of cross-fertilization and hybridity, firm distinctions between native Greek religion (*thrēskeia*, *eusebeia*) and traditional Roman religion (*religio*, *pietas*) become difficult to sustain, especially in describing the first-century religious environment in which the *apostle Paul primarily worked, in Greek or Hellenic cities within Roman provinces.

1. Disambiguating "Religion"
2. Sources for Greco-Roman Religion
3. Sources for Understanding Paul's Engagement with Greco-Roman Religiosity
4. The Divine Cosmos
5. Public Expressions of Religion
6. Domestic Expressions of Religion
7. Individual Expressions of Religion
8. Mystery Religions
9. Philosophy as Religion
10. The Afterlife
11. Engaging Greco-Roman Religion

1. Disambiguating "Religion."

Contemporary readers inevitably bring with them assumptions about "religion" that may be at variance with ancient notions of religion. It will be useful to first disambiguate this term by clarifying what Greco-Roman religion was *not*. Greco-Roman religion was not practiced in an exclusive manner. Many divinities could be worshiped and many superstitions could be practiced by an individual; this was considered appropriate and beneficial. Following from this, there was no emphasis on conversion from one faith or god to another and no evangelistic tendencies. Greco-Roman religion was little concerned with *ethics, *sin, or how one "ought" to live. Rather, it focused on procedures to avoid the gods' displeasure and to secure material blessings. With the exception of some mystery cults, Greco-Roman religion was not experienced as a personal *faith, nor was it concerned with psychological wholeness or the character formation of the worshiper. There was no centralized cult or leadership with translocal jurisdiction. The priests of the temple of Mars in Rome, for example, had no authority over the priests of Mars in Corinth. Further, there was no separation of religion and state. On the contrary, the state and the municipality had a vested interest in ensuring that the traditional gods were appropriately honored. Finally, Greco-Roman religions were not "book" religions. There were no sacred texts to study for training in "orthodox" dogma. Denizens of the ancient world learned about the gods from their mother's knees; they visited local shrines, considered the mythological scenes depicted on art and decor, retold fables, participated in civic festivals, and acquired a sufficient grasp of the divine world to negotiate the expectations of family, city, and state.

2. Sources for Greco-Roman Religion. Historians rely on a variety of sources for reconstructing religious beliefs prevalent in the Greco-Roman world—literary, archaeological, and epigraphic. Literary works include the classic poets and playwrights, popular humorists, and philosophers, but also private works, such as personal letters and magical papyri. Archaeological sources include any artifact of material culture, ranging from grand temples to the realia of everyday life—vases, jewelry, lamps. Epigraphic evidence refers to inscriptions, whether official engravings on public monuments or graffiti scratched on an alley wall. This classification is important both for organizing the data and for capturing the full breadth of religious beliefs during this period. Homer and the tragic poets, for example, portray the gods as petty, vindictive, supersized humans, interested in mortals only as pawns in their own squabbles or for satiating their lusts. Philosophers of every school contested these "demented myths" (Cicero, *Nat. d.* 1.16) as nonsense. They preferred to recast the gods according to their own high-minded ideals of perfection, resulting in a divine college of beneficent, aloof intellectuals, or a single, all-permeating rationality. Nonliterary sources—inscriptions, letters, amulets, incantations—reveal the grimy underside of popular religiosity. Here one learns of witches telling fortunes from the grit of a wine goblet, spirits summoned to curse or to infatuate, the malevolent potential of an inopportune sneeze, the protective power of the phallus, and so much more. This bird's-eye survey should alert one to the danger of oversimplification, particularly through focusing on one type of source material to the exclusion of others. Equally important, it should give one at least an initial sense of the complex, intricate, wildly variegated, and expansive mosaic of religious beliefs in this period.

3. Sources for Understanding Paul's Engagement with Greco-Roman Religiosity. Paul's letters and the Acts of the Apostles constitute the most important sources for understanding how the apostle Paul navigated the religious environment of the first-century Mediterranean world. Paul's letters represent a primary source, while Acts can be reasonably considered a "secondhand primary source" (Johnson 2010, 216). The narrative contains first-person reminiscences of some of the events described (the "we" sections: Acts 16:10-17; 20:5-15; 21:1-18; 27:1-37; 28:1-16), indicating that the author/compiler of Acts was either a participant in these events (Keener, 402-16) or had access to notes taken by one of Paul's traveling companions (Ehrman, 158-60). While the Acts of the Apostles is formally anonymous, ancient ecclesiastical testimony connects the Gospel of Luke and the book of Acts ("Luke-Acts," using the modern idiom) to Luke (Barrett, 30-48), a companion of Paul referenced in both undisputed (Philem 24) and disputed letters (Col 4:14; 2 Tim 4:11). The narrative itself presents readers with nothing implausible or out of character with what is known from other sources concerning the religious sensibilities of the period, which is in keeping with the author's claim to have "carefully investigated everything" before setting out his own account (Lk 1:1-3 NIV). The book of Acts represents a credible account of Paul's travels, conveying reliable information on the events and interactions it describes, and can be used with reasonable confidence in sketching a portrait of Paul's engagement with pagan belief systems in this period.

4. The Divine Cosmos. The most fundamental reality of Greco-Roman religion was polytheism. This is not an acknowledgment simply that there were multiple gods, but that there were innumerable gods and their presence was pervasive. There were gods for every activity and interest one could name: gods for bakers, gods for sailors, gods for poets, gods for litigators, gods for lovers. There were divinities that protected the hinges on your door, watched over your beehives, helped in the spreading of manure, cured hangovers, kept other divinities from harming you, and on it goes. The fragmentary and incomplete evidence surviving from *Corinth identifies more than fifty deities in the area, some known from only a single inscription. Writing in the early second century, Juvenal bemoans the "mob of deities" that congested the streets of Rome in his day (*Sat.* 13.34). The situation did not improve, and a few decades later the satirist Lucian penned *The Parliament of the Gods*. Here one finds Zeus addressing the heavenly population explosion by summoning a parliament, checking divine credentials, and expelling a multitude of pretenders. Of course, not all gods were equally important or widely worshiped.

4.1. The Olympic Deities. The traditional pantheon of Greece, often in Roman guise by the first century, was worshiped in one form or another throughout the Greco-Roman world. In epic literature they are depicted as dwelling on Mount Olympus (the Olympians) or in the underworld (the chthonic deities), but in popular writings, inscriptions, and epigraphy, they are usually represented as dwelling in the temples dedicated to their *worship. This group is sometimes reduced to twelve, though the actual number varied. These gods were eternal and ageless but not self-existent. Each came into being at a particular point of time, usually born from other gods, and remained in the state of their original creation: Zeus was forever middle-aged and bearded, Apollo remained a beardless youth, Persephone a young maiden, and so on. They maintained their immortality through consuming ambrosia, a nectar (or food) that rendered them deathless. Although Zeus (Jupiter) was the king of the gods and father to many of the Olympians, neither he nor the others were omnipotent or omniscient. Stories abound of one god being thwarted or tricked by another. Each god was associated with a particular talent or sphere of authority (see table), though these attributes varied considerably from region to region. Their portrayal in art and literature was highly anthropomorphic. In physique they were represented as the epitome of masculine virility or womanly beauty, but in character and temperament, they were deeply flawed.

Table 1. Principal Greco-Roman Deities

Greek (Roman) Name	Principal Attributes
Aphrodite (Venus)	Goddess of beauty, sexual love, and fertility
Apollo (Apollo)	God of music, prophecy, healing, and archery
Ares (Mars)	God of war
Artemis (Diana)	Goddess of fertility, the wilderness, and hunting
Asclepius (Aesculapius)	God of healing
Athena (Minerva)	Patron deity of Athens; goddess of wisdom, arts and crafts, and war; helper of heroes
Demeter (Ceres)	Goddess of grain
Dionysus/Bacchus (Liber)	God of wine, merriment, and nature
Eros (Cupid)	God of love
Hades (Pluto)	God of the underworld and the dead
Hecate (Trivia)	Goddess of the underworld and sorcery; also associated with crossroads
Hephaestus (Vulcan)	God of fire; blacksmith of the gods; disfigured and banished from Olympus
Hera (Juno)	Goddess of marriage; wife of Zeus
Hermes (Mercury)	Messenger of the gods; helper of travelers and merchants
Hestia (Vesta)	Goddess of hearth and home
Persephone/Kore (Proserpina)	Daughter of Zeus and Demeter; queen of the underworld; associated with spring and the fruits of the field
Poseidon (Neptune)	God of the sea and earthquakes
Uranus (Caelus)	God of the sky; father of the Titans
Zeus (Jupiter)	Ruler of the gods

These principal deities appear in countless inflections throughout the Greek- and Roman-influenced world. Quite commonly an epithet is attached to a deity's name, resembling a surname. This phenomenon is not fully understood, but often these epithets function almost as nicknames, connecting the god to a particular locale or highlighting a specific attribute. For example, in Corinth, where tradition holds that Athena assisted local hero Bellerophon in taming Pegasus, the goddess is honored as Athena Chalinitis, "the Bridler." Zeus Leminoskopos, "Watcher of Havens," was invoked by sailors praying for a safe voyage. On the Island of Samos one finds Apollo Epactaeus, "worshiped on the coast."

4.2. Regional Deities. The Greco-Roman world of the first century was composed of scores of people groups spread over several continents, each with their own long and deeply held religious traditions. Although the advance of *Hellenism and the later hegemony of Rome did nothing to stifle indigenous cults, local gods were commonly drafted into the ranks of the Greco-Roman pantheon, particularly where there were shared characteristics. So, one finds Zeus-Serapis in North Africa and Mars-Cocidius in Britain. Of the thousands of regional deities that have been cataloged, two examples relevant to Paul's *ministry can be mentioned. The god Theos Hypsistos ("Most High God"), whose cult was widespread in Macedonia, is encountered in Philippi (Acts 16:16-18). Understanding this as a regional deity, as opposed to a reference to the *God of the OT (see Gen 14:18; Ps 78:35), helps us understand Paul's adverse reaction to the herald of this deity (Acts 16:18). The territorial gods of Galatia and Phrygia (Men Axiottenos, Ainatas, Meter Taszene, and others) were known to exact severe punishment for even minor ritual infractions, making obedience to cultic stipulations an urgent concern. This religious mindset may well have predisposed residents of Galatia to accept the message of the Jewish-Christian missionaries that they needed to undergo *circumcision and submit to other requirements of Torah to be legitimate members of Abraham's family (Arnold).

*4.3. **Lesser Divinities.*** Rounding out the roll call of the gods would be a host of lesser deities—nymphs, personifications, and heroes. Nymphs were a large class of divine beings presiding over all manner of natural phenomena—woods, springs, caverns, clouds, streams, breezes, and so forth. They were not as powerful as the Olympian deities, and some expired when the element of nature they represented ceased, as when a tree withered or a stream dried up. Paul very likely refreshed himself at the Spring of Pirene, the mourning nymph, whose fountain was a prominent attraction in Corinth. Equally abundant were divine personifications, whereby virtues, emotions, or activities would assume divine garb and be worshiped as a deity: Persuasion (Peithō), Love (Eros), Health (Hygeia), Wisdom (Sophia), Justice (Dikē), Trust (Pistis), and many others. In the Roman era, these divine personifications were increasingly conscripted as couriers of imperial propaganda and deployed to declare the blessing of imperial rule. Coins of this period regularly depicted the ruling emperor on the obverse, with deities such as Peace (Pax), Security (Securitas), Hope (Spes), Stability (Constantia), Grain (Annona), and Abundance (Abundentia) on the reverse.

Heroes—a peculiarly Greek phenomenon—represent a class of "divine mortals," humans who attained divine status through legendary feats undertaken during this life. While a few gained Panhellenic status (e.g., Perseus, Heracles, Theseus), most were known only in a particular locale—and every locality boasted several homegrown heroes (e.g., Palaimon, Archemoros, and Belerophon in Corinth). Their shrines were commonly built near tombs, and their cult resembled the worship of chthonic deities. In the later Hellenistic and Roman eras, their exceptional status became somewhat degraded, as the burial rites and funerary markers of ordinary folk took on heroic overtones. Gravestones outside Philippi frequently contain greetings to the heroes, as if the deceased were joining that throng, and even occasionally proclaim, "I am a hero!" (Pilhofer, no. 547; see also Dio Chrysostom, *3 Regn.* 54).

*4.4. **Daimones.*** Hovering between the gods and mortals was another vast assemblage of spiritual beings whose presence was ubiquitous in the Greco-Roman world, the *daimones,* "spirits." The *daimones* had a long and evolving history in the ancient world. In earlier writers, *daimones* are sometimes described as the spirits of the noble dead (Hesiod, *Op.* 107, 235). In other ancient writers the *daimones* are understood to be guardian spirits assigned to protect and guide an individual (Pindar, *Pyth.* 3.108; Plato, *Phaedr.* 107d). Increasingly, however, the *daimones* came to be perceived as capricious and dangerous. In later writers, the *daimones* are commonly regarded as "the most harmful beings in the universe" (Plutarch, *Mor.* 153). They figured prominently in popular superstition and *magic as malevolent beings that could be invoked to harm others. In the NT and early Christian literature, the *daimones* are consistently presented as evil spirits, "*demons." In Paul's view, the *Gentiles unwittingly worship demons in their temples (1 Cor 10:20-21), and this perspective is shared by other Jewish writers (see 1 En. 19; 2Q23 1 7; L.A.B. 25.9; Ps 95:5 LXX).

*4.5. **The Imperial Cult.*** The Roman emperor was a latecomer on the celestial stage but became an increasingly important divine figure in the first-century Mediterranean world. Emperor worship began in earnest after the posthumous deification of Julius Caesar by the Roman senate in 42 BC, and by the beginning of the second century AD the imperial family was worshiped in temples and shrines in every significant city and township throughout the Roman-influenced world. Augustus (Octavian), Julius Caesar's adopted son, was then able to claim the title "son of [a] god" (*Divi Filius*), a practice his successors happily continued. The accumulation of divine ascriptions also continued, and expressions such as, "Lord," "God," "Savior of all People," and

"Ruler of the World" became part of the established nomenclature to refer to the ruling emperor.

The worship of the emperor was not simply, or even primarily, an expression of religious piety but was undertaken for political and economic advantage as well. Imperial priesthoods became important appointments for those intent on working their way up the sociopolitical hierarchy. Gaining the favor of the imperial family meant tangible financial and political benefit for a region, which left local municipalities scrambling to demonstrate their devotion to Caesar. Temples were built, artwork and statuary commissioned, athletic competitions were hosted in his honor, annual oaths of allegiance were administered, and the ruling emperor's birthday was celebrated with feasting and sacrifices. Not all of these were instituted everywhere, but a sociopolitical climate was cultivated that took seriously the community's responsibility to revere the emperor, and equally seriously any perceived neglect of that duty.

5. Public Expressions of Religion.

5.1. Temples and Shrines. Temples were the most obvious visible expression of religious devotion in antiquity. These edifices represent a significant expenditure for a local community (even though most were of modest proportion) and are evidence of how seriously the ancients took their duty to the gods. Every municipality would have several significant temple structures as well as numerous smaller shrines and sanctuaries. The city center of first-century Thessalonica boasted major temples to the imperial cult, the Egyptian gods (Isis and Serapis), Dionysus, Kabirus (a regional deity), a Nymphaeum, and others. The book of Acts's description of Paul's extreme discomfort as he strolled about Athens and observed that the city was "full of idols" (Acts 17:16) should probably be understood as a common reaction by the apostle during his travels.

Temples were not used for regular, gathered worship in the modern sense but for sacrificial rites, civic ceremonies, and various social functions. Temples would house statuary of the god, display artwork depicting mythological scenes associated with the god (Pausanias, *Descr.* 1.21.4; 4.31.1; Pliny, *Nat.* 35.17; Dio Chrysostom, *Dei cogn.* 44), post regulations relating to ritual requirements (Pausanias, *Descr.* 5.13.3-4; Pliny, *Ep.* 8.8.5-8), and provide facilities for sacrifice. Animal *sacrifices are regularly pictured in art, but offerings of grain, fruit, and votive offerings were probably more typical for the average worshiper. Portions of the sacrificial animal were burned as an offering to the god, while other portions were distributed among the participants and temple functionaries or sold in the public market (1 Cor 10:25-30; Pliny, *Ep.* 10.96.9-10). Patrons of temples generally paid to perform rites; collection boxes could be found within the temple precincts. Sacrifices and offerings were made for four primary reasons: (1) to honor the god (perhaps on the occasion of a festival), (2) to give thanks to the god for a tangible benefit (a good harvest, recovery from a sickness, a safe journey), (3) to appease the god in the case of a ritual infraction or a perceived punishment from the god, and (4) to secure help from the god.

Temples were staffed by local citizens of rank, elected or chosen by lot. In general, male officiants served male deities, female officiants served female deities. Many priesthoods were considered politically advantageous and were jealously sought after by those eager to ascend the social hierarchy in a city or province. Roman magistrates regularly boasted of their priestly appointments alongside their magistracies in their publicly displayed **cursus honorum* (ladder of offices). Secular and religious service were not separate spheres; both were expected of aspiring citizens. Priestly honors often came with the expectation of financially supporting the upkeep and activities of the temple. Priests would be called on to officiate at important ceremonies but otherwise would continue in their civilian activities.

It is important to emphasize that temples were not simply the locus of religious observance but the social hub and economic fulcrum of a city in Greco-Roman antiquity. Many temples had extensive dining facilities that were used by voluntary associations, guilds, and other civic groups (Aelius Aristides, *Orationes* 8.54.1; Plutarch, *Mor.* 146D; see 1 Cor 8:10). Important family rituals and rites of passage involved temple ceremonies (Pausanias, *Descr.* 2.32.1; Lucian, *Syr. d.* 60). The artwork and statuary of a temple were intended to attract visitors, as were sacred groves (Horace, *Ars* 14-20), libraries (Apuleius, *Metam.* 11.7; Aelius Aristides, *Orationes* 8.54; Horace, *Ep.* 1.3.15-16), and theaters. The temple of Demeter and Kore in Corinth had a small amphitheater attached that seated about one hundred. Larger temples would employ troupes of dancers and singers for special religious ceremonies (Cynic Epistles; Diogenes Laertius, *Vit.* 32.3; Lucian, *Salt.* 16). The worshipers, tourists, and patrons of a temple kept vendors and craftsmen gainfully employed (Acts 19:24-25). Farms supplied grain and livestock for sacrifices, inns provided rooms for pilgrims, and so on.

Mention should also be made of the numerous smaller shrines and sacred memorials that lined the curbsides and dotted the countryside. Altars to major and minor deities could be spotted from any vantage point in a typical city, and there would be hardly any crossroad without a shrine to Hecate (chthonic goddess of liminality) or the *lares compitales* (gods of the crossroads). References to wayside shrines along the roads for travelers are commonplace (Dio Chrysostom, *1 Regn.* 52; Martial, *Epig.* 7.15; Greek Anthology 4.10.12). Pausanias's hike up the Acrocorinth (the rocky butte overlooking Corinth) to the temple of Aphrodite at the top led him past nearly a dozen minor shrines and sacred porticoes (Pausanias, *Descr.* 2.4.5-6).

5.2. Festivals. Religion in antiquity was decidedly more communal in orientation and practice than in modern Western societies, and this is particularly evident in the numerous religious festivals observed in cities and townships throughout the Greco-Roman world. State and local magistrates understood that they were charged with ensuring that the ancient contract with the gods—whereby safety and prosperity were promised to the community for proper worship of the gods—was faithfully executed. Each city had a festal calendar specifying the dates on which various gods would be celebrated; most on an annual basis, but some monthly. The festal calendar of Rome was notoriously packed with holidays devoted to honoring the gods (Ovid, *Fasti*), but Athens was little different, with some sixty days designated for festal veneration.

While most of these would involve a simple sacrifice at the temple, major festivals could last several days and involve grand processions, banquets, and sporting competitions, attracting tourists from far and wide. Plutarch describes such festal days and associated temple banquets as "the most pleasant events that people enjoy" (*Mor.* 169D), while Dio Chrysostom gives a glimpse into the bustle and commerce they produced: "Many bring in merchandise of all sorts. . . . Some display their own arts and crafts while others show off their accomplishments, declaiming poems, tragedies, epics, and prose works as well" (*Compot.* 6 [LCL]). Further, it is important to bear in mind that virtually every public event—a sporting event, theatrical exhibition, installing a magistrate—would involve some type of religious ceremony, however perfunctory, be it a libation, a sacrifice, or a toast to the patron deity at the banquet of civic association.

The most important point to grasp in this brief synopsis of public religiosity is that religion, *politics, society, and economy were tightly intertwined, mutually sustaining, and inextricably connected to the local network of temples. This issue becomes particularly salient in the Corinthian correspondence (1 Cor 8; 10:14-30; 2 Cor 6:14–7:2; see 11.3 below). As Plutarch observed, a traveler may find a city without walls or a gymnasium, "but a city without holy places and gods, without any observance of prayers, oaths, oracles, sacrifices for blessings received or rites to avoid evils, no traveler has ever seen" (*Adv. Col.* 22 [LCL]).

6. Domestic Expressions of Religion.

Cicero observes that no place is more sacred (*sanctius*) than the Roman home, because here the entire spectrum of piety finds expression: "In this dwelling one finds altars, hearths, household gods, sacred rites, religious ceremonies and domestic rituals—a holy sanctuary" (*Dom.* 41.109). This would be equally true of the Greek *household, as the ideal home was considered a microcosm of the larger society—well ordered, religiously scrupulous, and divinely favored (Aristotle, *Ath. Pol.* 55.3). Every Greek or Roman domicile, from grand villa to one-room flat, would have at least some space devoted to the worship of traditional household deities. Vesta and Hestia were the goddesses of the hearth, the symbolic center of the home. The Penates were gods associated with the pantry and food supply. The Lares and Genii were protective spirits, sometimes associated with deceased ancestors, and in many Roman homes worshiped at a small shrine, a *lararia*. The Agathos Daimon (Good Spirit) was another protective spirit, often depicted as a snake painted on inner walls of the home or within the *lararia*.

The outer precincts of the home were also well guarded. Zeus Herkeios ("of the fence") and Apollo Agyieus ("of the street") might be stationed at the gate or entryway, warding off intruders. Zeus Ktesios ("of the property") kept the domestic holdings intact. To these more or less universal domestic deities one could add scores of other gods, varying from city to city or region to region. For example, altars to Liber and Libera were common in *insulae* in Philippi (Pilhofer, nos. 332, 338-40). The Cynic Epistles report that thresholds in Cyzicus (northern Asia Minor) invoked the might of Heracles: "The triumphant son of Zeus, Herakles, lives here. Let no evil enter" (Diogenes Laertius, *Vit.* 36.1).

Rituals were routinely performed to honor these deities throughout the day, principally libations, offerings, and prayers. The morning would begin with the matron of the house offering a *prayer and grain offering at the *lararia;* libations would begin meals, toasts to the gods would conclude meals; token portions of meals would be burned in the hearth in gratitude, and so on. Every significant family event was commemorated religiously and carefully ritualized to ensure the blessing of the gods. Ceremonies of inclusion were particularly important for incorporating new members into the household structure and procuring acceptance of the domestic gods, for example, a new baby, a bride, or a purchased *slave.

Often overlooked in discussions of domestic expressions of religion is the extent to which the home would mirror the mythology of the broader culture in its décor and furnishings. Upper-class homes in particular would be decorated with murals, frescoes, and elaborate tiled floor mosaics depicting scenes of the gods' antics from literature and mythology. A typical Greek or Roman home might contain vases relating the labors of Heracles, cabinets featuring Pan and the wood nymphs, a wall painting of Mars fondling Venus, brushes and combs bearing Athena's likeness, oil lamps with a phallic design, and serving utensils etched with magical symbols, to name some common examples. This observation becomes more relevant when one remembers that the primitive Jesus movement, Paul's assemblies in particular, was centered in the home and spread through multiplying household assemblies (Acts 8:1-3; 20:20; Rom 16:3-5; 1 Cor 16:19; Col 4:15; Philem 2).

7. Individual Expressions of Religion.
While the broad contours of civic and domestic religion are easily sketched and likely familiar to most readers, more difficult to depict—yet arguably more important for the ancients themselves—were the myriad of activities voluntarily undertaken by individuals to ward off evil, secure blessings, and obtain *knowledge concerning the future.

7.1. Divination and Dreams. Divination was an established institution of Roman civic religion and assisted the ruling authorities in discerning the disposition of the gods toward important matters, particularly military endeavors (Cicero, *De divinatione*; Valerius Maximus, *Fact. Dict.* 1.4-6). Its principal forms were augury (studying the flight patterns and eating habits of birds), haruspicy (examining the entrails of animals), astrology (discerning one's future from the position and movement of celestial bodies), and observing unusual cosmological phenomena (lightning, eclipses, earthquakes). Yet when Epictetus queries his audience, "What induces us to such constant use of divination?" (*Diatr.* 2.7.9), he is not referring to the venerable traditions of Roman statecraft but to the mediums, seers, and street-corner psychics whose ubiquitous presence is amply attested throughout the literature and artwork from this period. Patrons of these clairvoyants would pay a fee to receive insight concerning the future and plan accordingly. Oracles were another popular form of divination, and these also had a more respectable form in the ancient oracular shrines of the Greek East: Delphi (honoring Apollo), Dodona (honoring Zeus and Dione), Epidaurus (honoring Asklepios), and Corinth (honoring Apollo). Pilgrims would visit these shrines, perform the (sometimes lengthy) rites of purification, and receive a reply from the officiating priest or sibyl, all for a fee, of course. A sampling of such questions has been uncovered from Oxyrhynchus: "Will I be sold? Shall I become a senator? Is the one who left home alive? Will I receive the inheritance?" (P.Oxy. 1477). *Travel to distant shrines, however, was not typical, as marketplace diviners could forecast the future easily enough.

Certainly, the most universally accepted form of preternatural knowledge was dreams, "the most ancient and respected form of divination," according to Plutarch (*Mor.* 159A [LCL]). References to nocturnal *visions congest the ancient sources, from passing references (Horace, *Sat.* 1.10; Martial, *Epig.* 11.49-50; Petronius, *Satyricon* 17), to academic treatises (Artemedorus, *Oneriocritica*; Philo, *Somn.*). The Homeric dictum "Dreams come from Zeus" (*Il.* 1.63) became established doctrine on the topic (see Pliny, *Ep.* 1.18.1), so much so that Tertullian could claim that "nearly all people learn what they know about God from dreams" (*An.* 47.2). Paul, too, was the recipient of several revelatory dreams that altered the course of his ministry (Acts 16:9-10; 18:10; 23:11).

7.2. Superstition and Magic. Less amenable to delineation and classification are the incohesive assortment of practices loosely gathered under the label "superstition and magic." While temple priests punctiliously performed time-honored rites and while philosophers opined confidently on the dignity and perfection of the gods, the baker scratched a curse in lead on his rival, the farmer trembled at a donkey braying in the distance, a mother with a dying child purchased an incantation guaranteed to cure, a courtesan buried a frog at an intersection to prevent fever, a seafaring merchant consulted a prophetess to obtain the precise timing of the next winter squall. As noted above, the Greco-Roman world was brimming with gods and spirits, and the common religious disposition was oriented toward procuring their aid and avoiding their displeasure. This temperament spawned a prolific industry of charms, talismans, amulets, and incantations, together with soothsayers and sorcerers who trafficked in the dark arts.

This industry thrived because the average person in this period was deeply superstitious—fearful of unwanted attention from the gods and wary of the capricious antics of the *daimones*. The principal forms of magic in antiquity were protective magic (from enemies, illness, evil spirits), imprecatory magic (invoking a *curse on a foe or rival), and love magic (compelling affection in another). The sordid prescriptions of religious charlatans and the pitiable state of their often-desperate clientele are best depicted by Plutarch's masterful *On Superstition*. Plutarch compares the ignorant atheist with the gullible superstitious person and, while rejecting both, considers the person gripped by superstitious *fear to be in a far worse condition.

8. Mystery Cults.

The mystery cults provided an alternative form of religion, one that offered a more personal experience for the devotee, held out hope for a blissful *afterlife, and in some manifestations evinced a communal dynamic. Ancient Greece was the home to several important mystery cults, including Orphism, the Cabiri at Samothrace, the Andanian Mysteries, and most importantly the Eleusian Mysteries (at Eleusis, near Athens). As the name implies, the mystery cults employed secret rites of initiation, which remain obscure, although it is known they involved rituals of purification (ceremonial washings), sacrifices, recitation of oaths, vows of silence, and (perhaps) ceremonies symbolizing the *death and rebirth of the initiate. Although the history-of-religions school postulated a generative connection between the rituals and beliefs of the mystery cults and primitive Christianity, particularly its Hellenistic (Pauline) expression (e.g., Bousset; Bultmann), subsequent scholarship has rejected this claim (e.g., Wagner; Wedderburn; Bremmer).

The most readily available primary sources discussing the mysteries include the "Homeric" Hymn to Demeter (sixth century BC), Plutarch's *Isis and Osiris* (late first century AD) and Apuleius's *Metamorphosis* (second century AD). The lengthy Andania Inscription, dated somewhere between 91 BC and AD 24, provides tantalizing details of the social organization of an active mystery cult bordering the NT era. In it one finds rules concerning orderly behavior during worship and punishment of the disorderly (39-45); the requirement of marital faithfulness for female initiates (7-9); appropriate ceremonial apparel for each social class, including proscriptions against extravagant dress, jewelry, and braided hair for *women (13-27); details of the sacred procession, which included dancers and musicians (29-34, 74-75); the collection and administration of fees (45-64, 90-94); the requirement of harsher punishment for slaves than for free persons (75-78); instructions for observing the sacred meal (95-99); and the selection and disciplining of *leadership (119-75). This text invites comparison and contrast with Paul's guidelines to his assemblies, where many of the same issues are addressed.

By the NT era, the influence of the ancient Greek mystery cults had waned, and attention became focused on mysteries of Egyptian (Isis) or Persian (Mithras) origin. The Egyptian goddess Isis, whose iconography frequently depicted her as a nursing mother (Isis Lactans), was conceived as more personal and affectionate than the traditional gods of Greece and Rome (see Apuleius, *Metam.* 11). Historians speculate that this attribute may have contributed to the growing popularity of her cult in the Greco-Roman world.

9. Philosophy as Religion.

Conversion, character formation, and ethics seem intrinsically connected to religion in the modern setting, yet these were not constituents of conventional Greco-Roman religion. Rather, these were the domain of *philosophy, particularly Stoicism and Cynicism. Increasingly, contemporary scholarship has come to recognize the religious dimension of Roman-era philosophical discourse (e.g., Johnson 2009). Philosophical conversion narratives follow a standard format: moral exhortation (*preaching) that induced psychological trauma (guilt), which led to an existential crisis and a radical change of lifestyle (repentance). This radical change was characterized by moral renewal and the pursuit of virtue; in plain language, conversion.

The writings of Dio Chrysostom, Epictetus, and Musonius Rufus provide numerous examples of this kind of Stoic-Cynic preaching. Lucian poignantly relates the effect of one such philosopher-evangelist on him: "When he stopped speaking . . . I dripped with sweat, I stumbled . . . my voice failed, my tongue faltered, and finally I began to cry in embarrassment; for the effect he produced in me was not superficial or casual. My wound was deep and vital;

his words carved my soul in two" (*Nig.* 35 [LCL]). Descriptions of the inner renewal and recreation (Horace, *Ep.* 1.1.33-36) that come from "accepting philosophy into your heart" (Valerius Maximus, *Fact. Dict.* 3.3.1 [LCL]) punctuate the writings of these moral philosophers, as Seneca illustrates, "I am not only being reformed, but transformed" (*Ep.* 6.1). Seneca's writings provide the fullest exposition of moral formation from the Stoic perspective and echo many themes in Paul's letters, particularly the importance of hardship in developing character. So similar are Paul and Seneca on this subject that many in the early church believed that Seneca must have been converted by Paul during his imprisonment in Rome (Jerome, *Jov.* 1.49).

10. The Afterlife.
There was no consensus among Greeks and Romans on what, if anything, lay beyond this life. Philosophers, priests, and the unlettered masses entertained a variety of disparate views on the afterlife, a situation that is entirely predictable given that there were no "canonical" texts to guide and control speculation on any point. From Homer on one reads of the dreary underworld of Hades, to which all mortals were destined. Plato's happier Elysian Fields is the hope of the philosophers (*Phaedo*; Cynic Epistles; Diogenes Laertius, *Vit.* 14.6-7) and emperors (Martial, *Epigr.* 11.5). With less precision are depictions on funerary monuments containing symbols of new life or images of Thracian rider gods escorting the deceased to the undefined beyond (Pilhofer, no. 029). Notions of astral immortality are broadly attested (Cynic Epistles; Juvenal, *Sat.* 13.34; Cicero, *Nat. d.* 39-40), as is the belief that the spirit of the deceased somehow lived on in the tomb (Petronius, *Satyricon* 71; Philodemus, *Epigrams* 3). Followers of Epicurus were notable for their belief in the complete extinction of all existence at death, material and immaterial (Epicurus, *Principal Doctrines* 2). This belief was held beyond Epicurean circles and is expressed in the common funerary epitaph "I was not, I am not, I care not." Notions of transmigration, joining the heroes, harsh punishments for the wicked, and other such beliefs could be catalogued, but the general picture should be clear enough. Amid this cacophony of voices, Pliny's inconsolable grief at death of his friend appears entirely justified: "What I need is something new and effective which I have never heard or read about before. For everything I have heard or read . . . is powerless against grief like this" (*Ep.* 1.12.13 [LCL]).

On one issue, however, there was near unanimity: the denial of a bodily *resurrection. This peculiar conception, where it did surface, was roundly rejected (Pliny, *Nat.* 7.189-90; Acts 17:32).

11. Engaging Greco-Roman Religion.
Paul was a culturally and religiously complex individual. He was a Diaspora Jew but educated in the Jewish heartland under one of the leading rabbis of his day (Acts 22:3). He was a Roman citizen (Acts 22:25-29), yet a member of "the strictest sect" of Judaism, the Pharisees (Acts 26:5; Phil 3:6). He was conversant in Hebrew, Aramaic, and Greek, and in all probability Latin as well. He taught in Jewish synagogues (Acts 9:20; 13:5; 14:1, etc.) and Greek lecture halls (Acts 19:9). He was Jewish to the core, yet he traveled extensively and lived perceptively in the broader Mediterranean world, a world populated by numerous ethnic groups and dominated by Rome.

In his mission to proclaim to the Gentiles the "good news" of the death, resurrection, and return of Jesus, Paul regularly engaged with the religious conceptions of the people among whom he lived and preached. A partial record of this interaction is found in the book of Acts and the letters of Paul that have survived. In general, Acts reflects more of a public, outward-facing posture toward the pagan belief systems Paul encountered; there is little invective, and the apostle's primary *modus operandi* is persuasive engagement. Paul's letters, on the other hand, which were internal communications with his communities and coworkers, reflect an inward-facing posture. Here we see polemic and denunciation of pagan religiosity. Paul's personal disposition versus his missional approach is especially evident in Luke's record of the apostle's visit to Athens (Acts 17:16-34, discussed below).

11.1. Acts. One can take for granted that Paul's travels through Anatolia and Europe brought him into daily contact with virtually every dimension of religious activity outlined above. Luke, the narrator of Acts, highlights only those encounters that he deems significant for depicting the spread of the primitive Jesus movement through Paul's work in the Aegean basin.

The prominence of *divination* is illustrated in two confrontations Luke relates. The first occurs on Cyprus, where Paul meets a well-connected diviner (*magos*) by the name of Elymas, or Bar-Jesus (Acts 13:6-8), in the entourage of the Roman governor. His Jewish extraction, in conjunction with his soothsaying, earns him the epithet "false prophet" from Luke. When he attempts to turn the governor from the faith, Paul utters an imprecation that blinds him, preventing him from seeing the sun (Acts 13:11). This unusually specific pronouncement may indicate that the primary means of Elymas's divination was astrology, where calculations based on the position of the sun, moon, and stars were crucial. The second encounter occurs in Philippi, where Paul meets a slave girl with, literally, "a python spirit." The python was associated with Apollo's oracular shrine in Delphi, and this expression is understood to mean "a spirit of divination" (BDAG, 896). Luke's comment that she netted her owners "a great deal of income" (Acts 16:16) betrays the popular demand of such diviners, and when the spirit is expelled, the local magistrates get involved, and Paul and Silas are thrown into *prison (Acts 16:19-24).

The widespread practice of *sorcery* takes center stage in Luke's account of the magical bonfire in Ephesus in Acts 19:17-20. In a fascinating series of events, Luke relates how a revival grips the *Christian community* in Ephesus, and they proceed to bring forth a monumental amount of magical scrolls and paraphernalia in repentance—worth fifty thousand drachmas in Luke's estimation. The material is burned publicly as a demonstration of their sincerity. In order to account for such a colossal figure, one must conclude that the number of believers in Ephesus who continued their involvement in the dark arts was substantial and their monetary investment enormous.

These accounts also foreground the delicate interdependence of *cult and the economy* in the ancient world (see section 5 above). There was money to be made in religion, and when religious enterprise was threatened, riots ensued and the local authorities took notice. This is epitomized in the riot of the silversmiths in Ephesus, which Luke relates just after the incident of the bonfire (Acts 19:23-41). The primary instigation for the disturbance was the loss of income that the local guild of silversmiths incurred because of the expanse of Christianity in the region (Acts 19:24-27); nobody was buying their handcrafted images of Artemis anymore, and other merchants were affected as well (Acts 9:25). As this episode illustrates, temples were vital organs of the local economy, providing income for merchants, artisans, innkeepers, food vendors, and others. When religious devotion waned, the financial stability of the city was imperiled. Hence, following his suppression of Christianity in Bithynia at the turn of the second century, Pliny, the Roman governor, was able to boast to the emperor, "the flesh of sacrificial meat is being sold everywhere again, which until recently no one was buying" (Pliny, *Ep. Tra.* 10.96.10). As Christianity advanced, the massive economic edifice of paganism crumbled, and that collapse entailed substantial collateral damage.

Moderns might be tempted to question how seriously the ancients took the religious conceptions outlined above. However, the *vibrancy of religious belief* in this period is evident throughout the primary sources and is underscored by Luke's portrayal of the residents of Lystra and Malta. In Lystra, Paul's *healing of a man lame from birth prompts the Lystrans to proclaim, "the gods have come down to us in human form" (Acts 14:11 NRSV). They identify Barnabas as Zeus and Paul as Hermes, and attempt to offer bulls in a spontaneous sacrifice to the apostles (Acts 19:12-13). Shipwrecked on Malta, Paul is bitten by a snake, and the islanders draw the only reasonable conclusion: "He must be a murderer; for he escaped from the sea but Justice [Dikē] has not permitted him to live" (Acts 28:4). The goddess Dikē, the Greco-Roman personification of Justice (see 4.3 above), was particularly known for pursuing the guilty and avenging crimes. The islanders' immediate appeal to Dikē to explain this misfortune betrays a worldview in which the gods are active participants in human affairs, causative agents effecting their purposes among mortals.

Paul's experience in Athens, as mediated by Luke, illustrates several facets of Greco-Roman religiosity sketched above, including the abundance of gods (Acts 17:16, 23) and the prevailing skepticism concerning a bodily resurrection (Acts 17:32). More importantly, however, Luke highlights Paul's *missional strategy* in engaging belief systems completely contrary to his own. Luke notes that, while touring Athens and observing that the city was "full of idols," Paul became "greatly distressed" (Acts 17:16 NIV). Yet far from berating the Athenian intellectuals on their *idolatry, Paul makes it a point to compliment them on their religiosity: "People of Athens, I see that in every way you are very religious" (Acts 17:22 NIV). Paul proceeds to use one of their own altars, to an "unknown god" (see Pausanias, *Descr.* 1.1.4; 5.14.8; Diogenes Laertius, *Vit.* 1.110), as the launching point for his proclamation of the true God "who made the world and everything in it" (Acts 17:24 NIV). While Paul's personal disposition and theological convictions were strongly opposed to the polytheist framework of the Athenians, Luke emphasizes Paul's use of winsome persuasion as a means of opening a door for his message among a skeptical audience.

Paul's letters to his assemblies, on the other hand, provide his candid "insider" perspective on the travesty and tragedy of worshiping other gods. While each of Paul's letters addresses various aspects of Greco-Roman religiosity, three notable examples are worth brief comment.

*11.2. **Romans.*** In the opening chapter of Romans Paul offers his most comprehensive assessment of the dire state of humanity apart from Christ, focusing particularly on the religious beliefs of Gentiles (Rom 1:18-32). Paul understands the Gentile world to be living under God's wrath due to its intentional suppression of what the created order allows all people to intuit concerning his divine nature (Rom 1:18-20). This has resulted in a darkened understanding (Rom 1:21-22), rampant idolatry (Rom 1:23), and all manner of depravity and vice (Rom 1:24-32).

*11.3. 1–2 **Corinthians.*** The Corinthian correspondence underscores how difficult it was for Gentile converts to separate themselves from the socioreligious structures that surrounded them and how slow they were to relinquish certain deeply ingrained religious beliefs. In terms of social separation, this article noted earlier the diverse functions of temples in a local community (see section 5 above), one of which was to provide dining facilities for various community groups. Members of the Corinthian assembly had a difficult time completely recusing themselves from such activities, quite possibly because a guild or civic organization they were involved in used these temple facilities for their gatherings. Paul patiently makes his case against such participation in 1 Corinthians 8:1-13; 10:14-30, but when the problem persists, his patience grows thin, resulting in a more confrontational approach in 2 Corinthians (2 Cor 6:14–7:1).

Two foundational Christian beliefs that some believers in Corinth struggled to fully embrace were *monotheism* and the notion of a *physical, bodily resurrection.* This should not be surprising, as these were distinctive Christian doctrines, virtually without parallel among Greco-Roman religious systems. Reticence in comprehending monotheism is addressed in 1 Corinthians 8:1-14, where one learns that those who lack adequate "knowledge" that there is only one God (1 Cor 8:4-6) are actually believers whose "weak" faith is dealt a serious blow by the "*strong," who continue to dine in pagan temples, knowing that these gods are not gods at all (1 Cor 8:7-13). Interestingly, Paul does not focus on correcting the weak (although his argument assumes that their knowledge is incomplete and their developing faith was not where it should be) but rather the strong, whose callous behavior is spiritually detrimental to their weaker brothers and sisters. Those believers who continue to doubt the resurrection are vigorously taken to task in 1 Corinthians 15, where Paul goes to great lengths to refute their claim that "There is no resurrection of the dead" (1 Cor 15:12 NRSV).

*11.4. 1–2 **Thessalonians.*** In 1 Thessalonians Paul is responding to a report from Timothy (1 Thess 3:6) that includes the information that members of the Christian community in Thessalonica had died and others were genuinely distressed concerning the ultimate state of their deceased friends. Paul realizes that they need further instruction regarding key elements of *eschatology, and he provides this so that the Thessalonian believers "will not grieve like those who have no *hope" (1 Thess 4:13). This cannot be understood to mean that there was no hope for an afterlife among Greeks and Romans, as the evidence overwhelmingly contradicts this interpretation. Rather, as Pliny's experience cited above illustrates (see section 10 above), the myriad of conflicting opinions on what, if anything, lay beyond this life left the grieving individual drowning in a sea of uncertainty. Paul's unflinching proclamation of the resurrection of Jesus and the future resurrection of believers provides certainty amid the chaos of contradiction and offers genuine hope for those in despair (1 Thess 4:18; 5:11).

*11.5. **Paul and the Imperial Cult.*** In recent decades, the NT writings have been explored from the perspective of *empire criticism. Scholars working within this framework examine domination and oppression from the vantage point of the dominated and oppressed. Artifacts of culture—literary works in particular—are scrutinized to detect any subversive, counterimperial themes that may lie beneath the surface, encrypted in terminology and symbols recognizable to those in the know but not necessarily to outsiders. Applied to Paul's letters, this approach identifies camouflaged expressions and imagery that function as anti-imperial rhetoric. Acknowledging, with most NT scholarship, the pervasive influence of Rome's empire, this school of thought sees Paul's letters as coded attacks against emperor worship and the imperial gospel. The "imperial gospel" was not a formally articulated dogma but widely disseminated propaganda that the emperor (and Rome) ruled the world by the authority of the gods and brought *peace and blessing to all who submitted to his rule. From the perspective of empire criticism, the affirmation "Jesus is *Lord" necessarily entails the corresponding claim, "Caesar is not."

While the proposals and exegesis of empire critics need to be evaluated on a case-by-case basis—as does the methodological assumption of argument by double entendre—two plausible examples can be noted. Each phrase of the exaltation portion of the Christ *hymn in Philippians 2:9-11 can be paired with strikingly similar visual images from imperial statuary, coinage, and reliefs that depict the exaltation of the emperor (Phil 2:9), prostration of enemies (Phil 2:10a), and the emperor's dominion over the cosmos (Phil 2:10b), with accompanying acclamations of lordship (Phil 2:11).

In a similar way, in 1 Thessalonians Paul names Jesus as "Lord" (seventeen times) and *"Son of God" (1 Thess 1:9-10), and describes his impending visitation using terminology (*parousia*, 2:19; 3:13; 4:15; 5:23; *apantēsis*, 1 Thess 4:17) and imagery (heralds, proclamations, trumpets in 1 Thess 4:16-17) commonly associated with the visitation of a royal dignitary. This visitation will bring "*salvation" (1 Thess 5:8-9) for those who are called to God's "*kingdom" (1 Thess 2:12) and swift destruction to the current heralds of "peace and security" (1 Thess 5:3). This language, particularly the denunciation of peace and security—stock slogans of imperial propaganda (see 4.3 above)—would surely have sounded provocative to Roman ears. It is possible, of course, that Paul did not intend any allusion to the imperial order and the imperial gospel. It can be easily understood, however, how elements of his message could have been interpreted this way, as had already occurred (according to Luke) on his first visit to Thessalonica: "These men . . . are defying Caesar's decree, claiming that there is another king, called Jesus" (Acts 17:6-7). Whatever Paul's intention, the beliefs of the early Christians set them on a collision course with Rome, and by the early second century Christians were routinely executed for refusing to pay homage to the emperor (Pliny, *Ep.* 10.96).

See also AFTERLIFE; COSMOLOGY; EMPIRE; ESCHATOLOGY; HELLENISM, ROMAN; IDOLATRY; LORD; MAGIC; MISSION; PAUL IN ACTS; PHILOSOPHY; POLITICS AND POWER; RESURRECTION; SACRIFICE, OFFERING; STRONG AND WEAK; TEMPLE; URBAN SETTING OF PAUL'S CHURCHES; WORSHIP.

BIBLIOGRAPHY. **C. E. Arnold,** "'I Am Astonished That You Are So Quickly Turning Away!' (Gal 1.6): Paul and Anatolian Folk Belief," *NTS* 51 (2005): 429-49; **J. M. G. Barclay,** "Why the Roman Empire Was Insignificant to Paul," in *Pauline Churches and Diaspora Jews* (Grand Rapids, MI: Eerdmans, 2016), 363-87; **C. K. Barrett,** *The Acts of the Apostles,* vol. 1 (New York: T&T Clark, 1994); **M. Beard, J. North, and S. R. F. Price,** *Religions of Rome* (Cambridge: Cambridge University Press, 1998); **W. Bousset,** *Kyrios Christos: A History of Belief in Christ from the Beginnings of Christianity to Irenaeus* (Waco, TX: Baylor University Press, 2013); **J. R. Brandt and J. W. Iddeng,** *Greek and Roman Festivals: Content, Meaning, and Practice* (Oxford: Oxford University Press, 2012); **J. Bremmer,** *Initiation into the Mysteries of the Ancient World* (Berlin: de Gruyter, 2014); **R. Bultmann,** *Primitive Christianity in Its Contemporary Setting* (London: Thames & Hudson, 1956); **W. Burkert,** *Ancient Mystery Cults* (Cambridge, MA: Harvard University Press, 1987); **R. G. Edmonds,** *Drawing Down the Moon: Magic in the Ancient Greco-Roman World* (Princeton, NJ: Princeton University Press, 2019); **B. D. Ehrman,** *The New Testament: A Historical Introduction to the Early Christian Writings,* 4th ed. (New York: Oxford University Press, 2009); **E. Ferguson,** *Backgrounds of Early Christianity,* 3rd ed. (Grand Rapids, MI: Eerdmans, 2003); **D. Frankfurter,** *Guide to the Study of Ancient Magic* (Leiden: Brill, 2019); **R. A. Horsley,** ed., *Paul and Empire: Religion and Power in Roman Imperial Society* (Harrisburg, PA: Trinity Press International, 1997); **M. V. Hubbard,** *Christianity in the Greco-Roman World: A Narrative Introduction* (Grand Rapids, MI: Baker, 2010); **L. W. Hurtado,** *Destroyer of the Gods: Early Christian Distinctiveness in the Roman World* (Waco, TX: Baylor University Press, 2016); **L. T. Johnson,** *Among the Gentiles: Greco-Roman Religion and Christianity* (New Haven, CT: Yale University Press, 2009); idem, *The Writings of the New Testament: An Interpretation,* 3rd ed. (Minneapolis: Fortress, 2010); **C. S. Keener,** *Acts: An Exegetical Commentary: Introduction and 1:1–2:47* (Grand Rapids, MI: Baker, 2012); **H.-J. Klauck,** *The Religious Context of Early Christianity: A Guide to Graeco-Roman Religions* (Minneapolis: Fortress, 2003); **R. MacMullen,** *Paganism in the Roman Empire* (New Haven, CT: Yale University Press, 1981); **S. McKnight and J. B. Modica,** eds., *Jesus Is Lord, Caesar Is Not: Evaluating Empire in New Testament Studies* (Downers Grove, IL: IVP Academic, 2013); **J. D. Mikalson,** *Ancient Greek Religion* (Malden, MA: Wiley-Blackwell, 2011); **P. Pilhofer,** *Philippi: Katalog Der Inschriften von Philippi,* vol. 2 (Tübingen: Mohr Siebeck, 2000); **G. Wagner,** *Pauline Baptism and the Pagan Mysteries: The Problem of the Pauline Doctrine of Baptism in Romans 6, 1-11* (London: Oliver & Boyd, 1967); **J. M. Wedderburn,** *Baptism and Resurrection: Studies in Pauline Theology Against Its Graeco-Roman Background,* WUNT 44 (Tübingen: Mohr, 1987); **B. W. Winter,** *Divine*

Honours for the Caesars: The First Christians' Responses (Grand Rapids, MI: Eerdmans, 2015).

M. V. Hubbard

RESTORATION OF ISRAEL. *See* ISRAEL; SUPERSESSIONISM.

RESTRAINING POWER. *See* MAN OF LAWLESSNESS AND RESTRAINING POWER.

RESURRECTION

It is difficult to overstate the importance of Jesus' resurrection for the Christian *faith. The *apostle Paul writes that the hope of eternal life is worthless if Jesus did not rise from the dead (1 Cor 15:17-19). Pieter Craffert comments, "There is probably no other topic in Jesus research that creates such controversy and inspires more seminars than that of Jesus's resurrection" (Craffert, 383). Along with Pontius Pilate and the Jewish authorities, one would anticipate that Jesus' *death by crucifixion should have brought about the end of the movement Jesus had started. Instead, that movement not only survived but flourished and became the world's largest religion because Jesus' disciples and many others came to believe that Jesus had risen from the dead and had appeared to them. But what brought about that belief? Dale Allison answers, "The question holds its proud place as the prize puzzle of New Testament research" (Allison 2005, 200).

1. Paul as Eyewitness of the Resurrected Jesus
2. Why Paul's View of Resurrection Is Important
3. Pauline Texts That Have Led to Debate
4. Paul's Conversion Experience Described in Acts
5. Pauline Texts That Provide Clearer Insights on How He Imagined Resurrection
6. Paul as Pathway to the Apostles' Belief About Jesus' Resurrection
7. The Value of Paul for Answering the Question "Did Jesus Rise from the Dead?"
8. Summary

1. Paul as Eyewitness of the Resurrected Jesus. According to Paul's own accounts, he aggressively persecuted the Christian *church until he had an experience he interpreted as the resurrected Jesus appearing to him. This experience radically transformed his life. He became a follower of Jesus and claimed to work harder than the rest of the apostles to spread the message about him (1 Cor 15:8-9; Gal 1:22-23). Jesus' appearance to Paul is narrated in Acts 9:1-9 and described in Acts 22:6-11 and Acts 26:12-18. A slight majority of English-speaking scholars think that the author of Acts was a traveling companion of Paul (Keener 2012, 1:407). If these scholars are correct, the author of Acts probably received this information from Paul. After his *conversion, Paul zealously proclaimed the message of Jesus and his resurrection, despite enduring great and repeated sufferings and eventually martyrdom as a result (1 Thess 2:2; 1 Cor 15:30-32; 2 Cor 11:23-28; Phil 1:12-13, 29; 3:8-10; Acts 14:4-6, 19; 16:22-24; 17:5-9, 13-15; 19:23-41; 20:3; 21:27–28:10; *1 Clem.* 5.2-7; Pol. *Phil.* 9.2; Ign. *Smyrn.* 3.2, 3.4; Tertullian, *Scorp.* 15; Origen and Dionysius of Corinth, quoted in Eusebius, *Hist. eccl.* 2.25.8; 3.1).

2. Why Paul's View of Resurrection Is Important. The resurrection narratives in the Gospels clearly present Jesus' resurrection in a manner indicating that his physical *body was raised and transformed. The risen Jesus left behind an empty tomb (Mk 16; Mt 28; Lk 24; Jn 20–21). He can eat (Lk 24:41-43) and be touched (Mt 28:9; Jn 20:17, 27). He can appear as a normal human (Lk 24:15-31; Jn 20:14-15), and his transformed body can appear and disappear at will (Lk 24:30-36; Jn 20:19).

However, there are a few texts in Paul's letters and the book of Acts that can give the impression that Paul thought of resurrection as something *spiritual* (i.e., immaterial) in nature rather than *physical* (e.g., Gal 1:11-16, esp. Gal 1:12, 16; 1 Cor 15:5-8, 42-44, 50; Acts 9:3-20; 22:6-16; 26:12-18). Since Paul's letters are typically thought to predate the Gospels, some have posited that Paul provides the original view of resurrection, whereas the Gospels present a later and different view. Is Paul's view of resurrection fundamentally different from the one presented in the Gospels?

3. Pauline Texts That Have Led to Debate.

3.1. Galatians 1:11-16.

> For I make known to you, brothers, that the *gospel being preached by me is not according to man. For neither from man did I receive it or was taught it, but through a revelation of Jesus *Christ. . . . But when the one who set me apart from my mother's womb and called [me] through his *grace was pleased to reveal his son in me, in order that I might proclaim him among the *Gentiles [*or* nations], I did not consult immediately with *flesh and blood.

Most scholars think Paul had his conversion experience in mind here. Some go further and suggest that he was speaking entirely of an internal experience—perhaps a subjective *vision or an epiphany not involving an external appearance of the resurrected Jesus (Carnley, 209; Segal, 407). In support, these scholars appeal to Paul's use of the term *revelation* (Gk. *apokalypsis*) in Galatians 1:12 when describing how he received the gospel message he had been preaching and his statement in Galatians 1:16 that God "was pleased to reveal his son *in me* [Gk. *en emoi*]."

Such readings of Galatians 1:12, 16 are plausible. However, given the ambiguity of these terms, it is far from clear that they should be understood in this manner. The term *apokalypsis* refers to a physical revealing on at least three occasions in the Pauline corpus and perhaps four (Rom 8:19; 1 Cor 1:7; 2 Thess 1:7; Rom 2:5 [possible]). In 2 Corinthians 12:1, Paul mentions "visions and revelations [*apokalypseis*] of the Lord" he received. He then claims to have been taken to heaven on one occasion and says he does not know whether he was in or out of his body at the time (1 Cor 12:2-4).

The *en emoi* of Galatians 1:16 can be translated in a number of ways. Many scholars render it "in me" (Bruce 2000, 75; Dunn, 857, 873; Longenecker, 30; Morris, 55-56; Patterson 1994, 145; NASB, NET, NIV, NJB, WEB), while others prefer "to me" or "through me" (Allison 2005, 264; Arichea and Nida, 22; Boers, 117; Borg and Crossan, 206; Ehrman, 301; Wright, 380; CEB, ESV, NABRE, NLT, NRSV, RSV). Here is how the phrase is used elsewhere in the Pauline corpus:

> Galatians 1:24: "they were glorifying *God *in me*" (i.e., because of me)
>
> Galatians 2:20: "Christ lives *in me*"
>
> 1 Corinthians 9:15: Having mentioned his right to receive financial and material support from the Corinthian church, as well as to take along a Christian wife on his journeys, Paul says that he has chosen not to do so and that he does not mention these things in order that "it may be [this way] *in me*" (i.e., for me; in other words, he is not laying the ground that he might start claiming these rights).
>
> 1 Corinthians 14:11: Paul says that it is not beneficial for believers to speak in *tongues to one another, for if Paul cannot understand what is being said, "I will be a foreigner to the one speaking and the one speaking a foreigner *in me*" (i.e., to me).
>
> 2 Corinthians 11:10: "the *truth of Christ is *in me*" (i.e., I am telling you the truth of Christ)
>
> 2 Corinthians 13:3: "since you are seeking proof of the one speaking *in me*: Christ, who is not weak toward you, but powerful in you"
>
> Romans 7:8: "through the commandment *sin produced *in me* all kinds of wrong desires"
>
> Romans 7:17, 20: "sin which lives *in me*"
>
> Romans 7:18: "for I know that nothing good lives *in me*"
>
> Philippians 1:26: "your proud confidence *in me*"
>
> Philippians 1:30: "having the same conflict which you saw *in me*" (i.e., you saw me experiencing), "and now hear [to be] *in me*" (i.e., you hear that I am experiencing)
>
> Philippians 4:9: "practice the things you have learned and received and heard and seen *in me*"
>
> Colossians 1:29: "his working that works powerfully *in me*"
>
> 1 Timothy 1:16: "But because of this, I received *mercy, so that *in me* as the foremost, Christ Jesus might display perfect patience, making an example of those about to believe in him unto eternal life."

Although every occurrence has been rendered "in me," readers will notice a variety of meanings *en emoi* carries. With equal plausibility the phrase can be rendered as either "to reveal his son *in me*" or "to reveal his son *to me*." Moreover, a number of commentators interpret Paul in a sense whereby he has both meanings in mind, so that in Galatians 1:16 he is referring to the inward illumination that coincided with his external experience (Bruce 1982, 92; Byrskog, 227; Craig, 81; Hendriksen, 53; Longenecker, 30; Witherington, 314).

In Galatians 1:11-16, it is not clear whether Paul was revealing his thoughts on the nature of the appearance of the risen Jesus to him. If he was, the ambiguity of the text prevents any sure conclusion based on this text alone. Therefore, the reader should look to other Pauline texts where his view of resurrection is stated more clearly and interpret Galatians 1:16 in light of those texts.

3.2. 1 Corinthians 15:5-8. Most critical scholars agree that in 1 Corinthians 15:3-7, Paul was drawing from very early oral *tradition that he had received from others (Licona, 229-35). Having mentioned Jesus' death, burial, and resurrection, Paul follows with "and that he appeared to Cephas, then to the Twelve, then he appeared to more than five hundred brothers at one time, among whom most remain until now, but some have died, then he appeared to James, then to all the apostles. And last of all, as to one untimely born, he appeared also to me" (1 Cor 15:5-8). The term for "appeared" is *ōphthē*, from the verb *horaō* and the noun *horama*. With its cognates, the term carries a number of meanings, including reference to a vision outside space-time (e.g., Acts 10:9-17; 11:5; 16:9; Col 2:18). Some have, therefore, claimed that the postresurrection appearances of Jesus likely occurred in visions rather than in space-time, such as those one finds narrated in the Gospels. However, *ōphthē* and its cognates refer more often to physical sight (e.g., Acts 7:2, 30; 1 Cor 2:9; 8:10; 16:7; Licona, 330-33). Therefore, this text is also ambiguous as far as the nature of the appearances is concerned.

3.3. 1 Corinthians 15:42-44. Paul was addressing the implied questions asked by the Corinthian Christians: "How are the dead raised, and with what kind of body do they come?" (1 Cor 15:35). He answers that after a seed is planted, it does not produce another seed but something different, such as wheat. He continues, "So also is the resurrection of the dead. It is sown in corruption. It is raised in incorruption. It is sown in dishonor. It is raised in *glory. It is sown in weakness. It is raised in power. It is sown a natural body. It is raised a spiritual body. If there is a natural body, there is also a spiritual [body]" (1 Cor 15:42-44). The difficulty with how to understand Paul properly here comes from two terms in 1 Corinthians 15:44: "natural" (Gk. *psychikos*) and "spiritual" (Gk. *pneumatikos*). The root of *psychikos* is *psychē* ("soul"). Thus, in its rudimentary form, *psychikos* means "soulish." A number of scholars have translated *psychikos* as "physical" (BDAG, s.v. "ψυχικός," 1a, 100; Friberg, Friberg, and Miller, 414; Newman, 201; Smith, 28; L&N 1:693; RSV, NRSV, REB, GNT, CEB, Amplified Bible; for a more comprehensive listing, see Licona, 412n454). Many of these scholars understand "spiritual" in this context to mean "immaterial." Translated and understood in these senses, Paul is saying in 1 Corinthians 15:44, 46 that one's present body is *physical* but that the one to which it will be transformed at the parousia is *immaterial*. But is this the correct way of defining the terms in this context?

There are 846 occurrences of *psychikos* in the extant Greek literature written between the eighth century BC and the third century AD, only five of which appear before the fourth century BC. But none of the 846 carries the meaning of "physical." Of interest, *psychikos* is often contrasted with *sōmatos* ("body") and *physikos* ("natural, physical"). *Daimōnia* ("*demons") are described as *psychikos*. (Note: Outside Judaism and Christianity, *daimōnia* could have referred to the spirits of the dead who had returned to earth or to any divine being. Although they did not carry the same negative connotation as they do in Christianity, they were feared.) One also finds an interesting combination of terms in which *psychikos* is an adjective describing *pneuma* (spirit): *psychikon pneuma*, *pneumatos psychikou*, *psychikou pneumatos*, and *to pneuma to psychikon* (see Chrysippus, *Fragmenta logica et physica* 716.2, 722.2, 781.3, 783.2, 870.2; Alexander of Aphrodisias, *Probl.* 2.64.28, 2.67.40; Cassius Iatrosophista, *Quaestiones medicae et problemata physica* 52.3; 72.9; Vettius Valens, *Anthologiarum libri ix* 109.13). If *psychikos* is understood as "physical" and *pneuma* as "immaterial," this would suggest that there are immaterial things that are physical, which would be a contradiction of concepts.

Psychikos appears only once in the LXX: "Of desires, some are *psychikai*, others are *sōmatikai* [bodily, physical], and reason appears to rule over both of these" (4 Macc 1:32). *Psychikos* appears six times in the NT, four of which are in 1 Corinthians. Three of these are in the texts being examined: 1 Corinthians 15:44 (2×) and 1 Corinthians 15:46. The other appears in 1 Corinthians 2:14-15, where Paul contrasts *psychikos* and *pneumatikos*: "But the *psychikos* man does not accept the things of the Spirit of God, for they are foolishness to him. And he is unable to understand them because they are *pneumatikōs* [spiritually] examined. Now *ho pneumatikos* [the spiritual person] examines all things, but he is examined by no one." In this context, it is obvious that *psychikos* does not mean "physical," and *pneumatikos* does not mean "immaterial." In James 3:15, bitter envy and selfish ambition (Jas 3:14) are said to be "earthly" (*psychikē*) and "demonic." Jude 19 refers to those persons causing divisions as *psychikoi* and "not having the Spirit." In none of these occurrences does *psychikos* carry the meaning "physical." In summary, if one brackets the three occurrences of *psychikos* in 1 Corinthians 15:44, 46, of the remaining 843 occurrences of *psychikos* in the extant literature written between the eighth century BC and the third century AD, the term never carries the meaning of "physical"; this is true also of the way it is used elsewhere in 1 Corinthians.

There are 1,131 occurrences of *pneumatikos* in the same Greek literature, first appearing in the sixth century BC. Although the term often carries the idea of an *immaterial* consistency (i.e., ethereal), there are a robust number of exceptions. Zeno describes those who enjoy Stoic teachings as *hoi pneumatikoi* (spiritual ones; Zeno, *Testimonia et fragmenta* 33.2). Especially of interest is Chrysippus, who writes that bodies (*sōmatikōn*) have a spiritual (*pneumatikē*) essence (Chrysippus, *Fragmenta logica et physica* 389.5). He later makes mention of a *sōma pneumatikon kai aitherōdes* (a body that is spiritual and ethereal; Chrysippus, *Fragmenta logica et physica* 1054.13). Thus, material objects can be *pneumatikos*. Democritus (*Testimonia* 140.2), Straton (*Fragmenta* 94.2), Comarius (*De lapide philosophorum* 2.290.28), Clement of Alexandria (*Ecl.* 55.1.1), and Pseudo-Plutarch (*De placita philosophorum* 905.B.7) also speak of a spiritual body. However, none of them appears to be referring to an immaterial body. Although *pneumatikos* can mean "immaterial," that is not the only meaning of the term.

Pneumatikos is absent from the LXX but appears twenty-six times in the NT, with only two occurring outside Paul's letters. In 1 Peter 2:5, believers are told to allow themselves to be built into an "*oikos pneumatikos* [spiritual house], to be a holy priesthood, to offer *pneumatikas thysias* [spiritual *sacrifices] acceptable to God through Jesus Christ." *Pneumatikas* carries a number of meanings in Paul's letters, where it refers to spiritual maturity (1 Cor 2:15; 3:1; 14:37; Gal 6:1); spiritual *wisdom (1 Cor 2:13; Col 1:9); spiritual blessings (1 Cor 9:11; Rom 15:27; Eph 1:3); spiritual food and drink in the wilderness, that is, physical food provided by God (1 Cor 10:3-4); spiritual *gifts (1 Cor 12:1; 14:1; Rom 1:11); the *law being spiritual (Rom 7:14); and spiritual songs (Eph 5:19; Col 3:16). Note also that spiritual forces of evil in the heavenlies are contrasted with "blood and flesh" (Eph 6:12). The related adverb *pneumatikōs* appears in 1 Corinthians 2:14 and Revelation 11:8. In the latter, one reads about "the great city, which is *spiritually* [i.e., figuratively] called Sodom and Egypt where also their Lord was crucified." In summary, if one brackets the four occurrences of *pneumatikos* in 1 Corinthians 15:44, 46, one observes the term carrying a variety of meanings in the remaining 1,127 times it appears in the extant Greek literature spanning from the eighth century BC through the third century AD. In the NT, aside from those four occurrences in dispute (1 Cor 15:44, 46), only in Ephesians 6:12 may *pneumatikos* be seen as referring to the immaterial or ethereal consistency of a being.

What then does Paul mean when he says, "It is sown a natural body. It is raised a spiritual body" (1 Cor 15:44)? There is no reason to think *psychikos* carries the meaning of "physical," since it never does elsewhere. Moreover, had Paul wanted to contrast a physical body with an immaterial one, he had a better term than *psychikos* at hand, one he had already used only a few chapters earlier and when also using the analogy of a seed. In 1 Corinthians 9:11, Paul writes, "If we sowed *spiritual things* [*ta pneumatika*] in you, is it too much if we reap *material things* [*ta sarkika*] from you?" In 1 Corinthians 15:44, Paul could have used *sarkika* if he meant to describe the body that is buried as being physical.

Elsewhere in Paul's letters and in the NT, *psychikos* is not a positive characteristic. Outside the NT, it carries a number of different meanings. When Paul uses the term earlier in 1 Corinthians 2:14-15, he is describing those who live by their fleshly and sinful desires and who think in accordance with the world's wisdom. In fact, the NRSV, which translates *psychikos* as "physical" in 1 Corinthians 15:44, translates the same word as "unspiritual" in 1 Corinthians 2:14. What then does Paul mean when he says in 1 Corinthians 15:44 that bodies are buried *psychikon* but raised *pneumatikon*? Paul is claiming that the *psychikos* body is buried, having lived with this-worldly appetites (e.g., food, water, sleep, sex) and weaknesses (e.g., emotional, mental, diseases, sinful desires), and will be raised and transformed into a *pneumatikos* body with spiritual appetites and qualities. Paul may also have in mind the power that animates the body. Modern machines are powered by steam, electricity, fossil fuels, and nuclear energy. The *psychikos* body is animated by a heart, lungs, and other organs. But the *pneumatikos* body will be animated by God's Spirit.

Thus, in the context of 1 Corinthians 15, most scholars have correctly understood *psychikos* to mean "natural." Paul is not drawing a contrast between believers' present physical bodies and future immaterial ones (Ackerman, 96; Barnett, 9; Barrett, 373; Bostock, 271; Brodeur, 122; Collins, 567; Conzelmann, 290; Fee, 788-89; Gundry, 165-66; Harris, 118; Hays, 272; Héring, 176-77; Hurtado, 170-71n29; Johnson, 304-5; Kistemaker, 573; most English Bible translations; for a more comprehensive listing, see Licona, 412n454).

3.4. 1 Corinthians 15:50. Continuing to contrast the present *psychikos body* with the *pneumatikos body* believers will have when Christ returns, Paul writes in 1 Corinthians 15:50, "*Flesh and blood* cannot inherit the *kingdom of God. Neither is the perishable able to inherit the imperishable." Some scholars have contended that Paul's statement stands in tension with Luke 24:39, where the resurrected Jesus appears to a group of his male disciples for the first time and says, "See my hands and my feet, that it is me! Touch me and see! For a spirit does not have *flesh and bone* as you see me having" (see Brown 1973, 87; Patterson 2004, 114-15).

Most scholars think that "flesh and blood" is a figure of speech (whereas "flesh and bone" is not), probably a Semitism, referring to humans as mortal beings (Jeremias; Carson, 367; Collins, 579; Conzelmann, 289-90; Gundry, 166; Keener 2005, 133; for a more comprehensive list, see Licona, 417-18n465). In this sense, Paul is stating in effect, "*The living* [in their present condition] cannot inherit the kingdom of God." Their bodies must be transformed (Allison 2021, 131).

3.5. 2 Corinthians 5:1-8.

> For we know that if our earthly house of dwelling is destroyed, we have a building from God, a house made without hands eternal in the heavens. For even in this we groan, longing to be further clothed by our heavenly dwelling. If indeed, even having taken it off, we will not be found naked. For indeed we groan, being burdened while in this house, because we do not desire to be unclothed but to be further clothed in order that the mortal may be swallowed up by life. God is the one who prepared us for this very thing, who gave his Spirit to us as a deposit. Therefore, we are confident always and know that to be at home in the body is to be absent from the Lord. For we walk by faith, not by sight. And we are confident and rather pleased to be absent from the body and to be at home with the Lord.

There is no standard position taken by scholars regarding how this text is best interpreted. However, most interpretations can be placed in one of three general categories (Gillman): (1) since writing 1 Corinthians, Paul changed his mind about postmortem existence and is now saying that believers will receive their new body at death; (2) consistent with what he wrote in 1 Corinthians, Paul is speaking of the resurrection of the body at the parousia; (3) Paul is speaking of a different matter than he was in 1 Corinthians 15: the intermediate state of believers between death and the parousia.

At the forefront of the confusion is a textual discrepancy in 2 Corinthians 5:3. Is Paul saying "having taken it off" (*ekdysamenoi*) or "having put it on" (*endysamenoi*)? The difference rests in a single Greek letter. If the former is correct, Paul is saying, "If indeed, even *having taken it off*, we will not be found naked." In other words, having shed the earthly body at death, believers will immediately put on a resurrection body so that their spirits will never be naked. This understanding of the text fits best with John Gillman's first category. However, if the latter is correct, Paul is saying, "If indeed, even *having put it on*, we will not be found naked." In other words, when believers put on a resurrection body, their spirits will not be naked. This understanding of the text fits best with Gillman's second and third categories.

This text is relevant to how Paul thought of Jesus' resurrection, because he believed that Christians would be raised, as Christ was (1 Cor 15:20, 23). Thus, if Paul thought believers abandon their bodies at death and immediately put on resurrection bodies in heaven (i.e., category 1 above), resurrection is not something that involves the corpse. This would mean that Paul had changed his mind and now thought the resurrection of Jesus did not involve his corpse.

The twenty-eighth edition of the Nestle-Aland critical Greek NT prefers "having taken it off" (*ekdysamenoi*) because it creates a nice paradox (i.e., even after removing the clothing [that is, the body], one's spirit will not be naked) and avoids being bland and tautologous (e.g., it is so self-evident that it need not be stated that one is not naked when one puts on clothing). However, Paul is painfully redundant in 1 Corinthians 15:53-54, to the point of being nearly tautologous while writing on the same subject as he does in 2 Corinthians 5:1-8. This observation greatly reduces the force of tautology, leaving the paradoxical element as the only positive reason for preferring *ekdysamenoi*.

The critical Greek NTs produced by the Society of Biblical Literature and Tyndale House Cambridge, followed by the vast majority of English Bible translations, prefer "having put it on" (*endysamenoi*), against "having taken it off" (*ekdysamenoi*) in Nestle-Aland, because the reading enjoys superior manuscript support. Moreover, the term *ependysasthai* ("to be further clothed," as when one puts a coat over one's clothing) in the verse that follows (2 Cor 5:4) fits far more comfortably with "having put it on" (*endysamenoi*) than "having taken it off" (*ekdysamenoi*) in 2 Corinthians 5:3. It also supports a transformation of the present body, which is what Paul had in mind in 1 Corinthians 15:52-54.

Although more can be said, it seems most likely that in 2 Corinthians 5:1-8 Paul primarily had in mind both the parousia and an intermediate state. Believers will be transformed at the parousia. However, Paul was uncomfortable with the thought of existing as a disembodied spirit if he were to die prior to the parousia. But he took comfort in the thought that, if he were absent from his body, he would be present with the Lord until he received his resurrected body at the parousia. This interpretation is consistent with Paul's thoughts elsewhere (1 Cor 15:42-44; Phil 1:21-24; 1 Thess 4:16-18; Rom 8:11-25).

4. Paul's Conversion Experience Described in Acts.
In his letters, Paul never describes his experience of the resurrected Jesus appearing to him. However, it is described on three occasions in Acts (Acts 9:1-9; 22:6-11; 26:12-18). Paul is en route to Damascus to arrest Christians there when a *light with immense brightness shines on him and his traveling companions. They fall to the ground. Paul then hears a voice that asks him why he is persecuting him. When Paul asks who it is, the voice answers that it is Jesus and tells Paul that he is appointing him to be his *servant. Paul then has to be assisted because he has been blinded by the light.

Why was Jesus' appearance to Paul in Acts of a different nature from the appearances reported in the Gospels? What is one to make of this? It is germane that Jesus appeared to Paul after his *ascension. Thus, Jesus appeared to Paul in his glorified state. Moreover, elsewhere in Acts 2:27-32 (see also Acts 13:35-37), Paul speaks of Jesus' resurrection as an event that involved his corpse. He mentions Jesus' resurrection and then cites the words of David in Psalm 16:8-11. Psalm 16:10 is of special importance: "For you will not abandon my soul to Hades nor allow your holy one to experience decay." In Acts 2:29-32, Paul continues,

> Men! Brothers! I can say to you with confidence concerning the patriarch David that he both died and was buried and his tomb is with us until this day. Therefore, being a prophet and knowing that God had sworn to him with an oath to set one of his descendants on his throne, having foreseen, he spoke of the resurrection of the Christ, that he was neither abandoned to Hades nor did his flesh experience decay. God raised this Jesus of whom we are all witnesses.

This text could not be clearer. David died and his body decayed. Jesus died and his body did not decay because God raised him. Regardless of the nature of Jesus' appearance to Paul, Paul taught that Jesus had been raised bodily. One could suggest that Paul is being misrepresented in Acts. But one must then provide reasons for holding that position, since none of the Pauline texts examined thus far clearly favors it.

In summary, none of the above texts clearly suggests that Paul thought of *resurrection* as ethereal disembodiment.

5. Pauline Texts That Provide Clearer Insights on How He Imagined Resurrection.
Paul imagined that followers of Jesus go to be with him immediately upon death and exist in a disembodied state. When Paul wrote to the church in Philippi, he was facing possible execution. In Philippians 1:21-24, Paul tells them he prefers to die and be with Christ. For such would be to his advantage. However, he recognized that it would be to their advantage if he were to remain alive, since he could continue his *ministry with them. If Paul had envisioned death resulting in soul sleep until the parousia, his death would have been of no advantage to him, since he would not have been with Christ in the interim. Nor would he have had reason to prefer soul sleep over remaining alive and carrying on his apostolic ministry.

Paul says something quite similar in 2 Corinthians 5:6-8: "Therefore, we are confident always and know that to be at home in the body is to be absent from the *Lord. For we walk by faith, not by sight. And we are confident and rather pleased to be absent from the body and to be at home with the Lord." In 1 Thessalonians 4:13-17, Paul speaks about the general resurrection in order to comfort those who have loved ones who have died. They are not forever lost. God will bring them with him when he returns.

Paul imagined that corpses would be raised and then transformed at the parousia. When Christ returns, God will bring with him those who have died in Christ. Then the trumpet will sound and the dead in Christ will be raised (1 Thess 4:13-17). But how can this be, since they are already returning with God? Paul envisioned believers in their disembodied state accompanying Christ at the parousia. They will then be returned to their corpses, which will be raised and transformed. For a similar view of resurrection, see 2 Baruch 49–51. In Romans 8:11, 23, Paul says that the same Spirit of God who raised Jesus will likewise give life to believers' mortal bodies when they are redeemed at the parousia. In 1 Corinthians 6:12-20, Paul instructs believers to glorify God with their bodies. In the context of this instruction, Paul says that God raised Jesus and will also raise Christians, implying that resurrection involves their bodies. Otherwise, 1 Corinthians 6:14 would be a random statement. In 1 Corinthians 15:52-54, Paul says that the dead will be raised imperishable at the last trumpet. The body that is perishable and mortal will clothe itself with imperishability and immortality.

Paul imagined that the resurrection of believers would be as Christ's was. In 1 Corinthians 15:20-23, Paul says that Christ is the first to be raised in the general resurrection and that all others will follow at the parousia. He then goes on to describe how believers will be raised. As noted above, this involves the corpse being raised and transformed. Although Paul does not describe the nature of Jesus' resurrection directly, he does so indirectly. For if the body will be raised and transformed in resurrection, so was Christ's body in his resurrection. In Philippians 3:20-21, Paul says that at the parousia, Christ will transform believers' humble bodies to be conformed to that of his glorious body.

Paul imagined Jesus' resurrection as having been a historical event. In 1 Corinthians 15:29-32, Paul says that there is no need for the practice of baptizing for the dead or for him and the other apostles to subject themselves to continuous hardships, persecution, and threats to their lives if the dead will not be resurrected and this life is all there is. When considered along with 15:20-23, one may formulate Paul's argument as follows: If Christ was not raised, believers will not be raised. In that case, the Christian life is not worth living. However, Christ has been raised. Therefore, believers will be raised. Therefore, the Christian life is worth living. This argument makes sense only if Paul regarded Jesus' resurrection as a historical event.

6. Paul as Pathway to the Apostles' Belief About Jesus' Resurrection.

NT scholars disagree on many topics. For example, they have different views on the authorship of the canonical Gospels, ranging from accepting the traditional authorship of all four (Blomberg, 138-40, 153-56, 173-74, 197-201) to asserting that it is not possible to have any idea who wrote them (Ehrman, 66-67). However, it is extremely rare to find a scholar who does not think Paul knew the lead apostles in Jerusalem.

Paul tells his readers that he met with Peter in *Jerusalem for fifteen days. It is very likely that *Peter informed Paul extensively about Jesus at that time (Gal 1:18-19). Paul then says that he met with Peter, James, and John fourteen years later. In order to ensure that he was on message with what they were proclaiming, he presented before them the gospel message he had been preaching. He tells his readers that Peter, James, and John certified that his gospel message was the same as their own (Gal 2:1-10). Elsewhere, Paul provides an outline of his gospel message, which included Jesus' death, burial, resurrection, and appearances to Peter, James, the Twelve, all of the apostles, and more than five hundred people at one time. He then claims that the other apostles were preaching the same message he was preaching (1 Cor 15:1-7, 11-12).

Two leaders in the early Christian church, named Clement of Rome and Polycarp, use very positive terms when speaking of Paul. Clement places Paul on par with Peter (*1 Clem.* 5; writing ca. AD 95–97, although a number of scholars prefer ca. AD 64–70s), while Polycarp (Pol. *Phil.* 3:2; writing ca. AD 110–120) comments that the "glorious Paul . . . taught the message about the truth, accurately and reliably." This is relevant because some early church tradition claims that Clement and Polycarp were associates of the apostles Peter and John, respectively (Licona, 250-56). If this is correct, one would not expect Clement and Polycarp to have referred to Paul using such positive terms if he had been preaching a gospel that was fundamentally different from what Peter and John had preached.

One also observes Paul being careful not to comingle traditions of Jesus' authentic teachings with his own apostolic opinion and ruling, when doing so would have been to his advantage, adding to his perceived authority (1 Cor 7:1-17). Accordingly, there are good reasons to think that Paul's gospel message was very closely aligned with the one proclaimed by the apostolic leadership in Jerusalem. Consequently, when one reads Paul's gospel message, one can have confidence that one is likewise hearing the voice of the Jerusalem apostles. However, this does not guarantee that Paul and the apostles always agreed theologically on everything outside the gospel message (Gal 2:11-14; Acts 15:1-7).

7. The Value of Paul for Answering the Question "Did Jesus Rise from the Dead?"

Data from Paul's letters allow historians to recognize a number of facts they must consider when answering the question of whether the resurrection of Jesus was a historical event. These facts include that (1) Paul persecuted the Christian church until he had an experience he was firmly convinced was the risen Jesus appearing to him. This experience resulted in Paul's becoming a follower of Jesus. (2) Paul zealously proclaimed the message of Jesus and his resurrection, despite enduring great hardships, much persecution, and eventually martyrdom.

(3) Paul thought of resurrection as an event whereby God brings a corpse back to life and transforms it into a body that is incorruptible and immortal. (4) The apostles proclaimed Jesus' resurrection very soon after his death. (5) The Jerusalem apostles proclaimed Jesus' resurrection in the same sense as Paul: Jesus' body was raised and transformed. (6) The oral tradition in 1 Corinthians 15:3-7 informs readers that the apostles were claiming Jesus had appeared to groups of them.

These six facts allow one to rule out the following hypotheses that offer an alternative explanation to resurrection.

*7.1. **Hallucinations.*** This is the most popular naturalistic hypothesis that scholars today offer (Habermas, 12). That Jesus' disciples experienced hallucinations of the risen Jesus seems entirely plausible at first, since after Jesus' sudden and brutal execution they were undoubtedly in a state of immense grief and stress. Distress, grief, and a lack of sleep over the previous few days would have created conditions favorable for the disciples to experience hallucinations.

A hallucination is a false sensory perception of something not actually present. Hallucinations can be experienced in a number of modes: auditory, visual, olfactory, kinesthetic (e.g., the sensation of movement, such as falling off a building), gustatory, and tactile (e.g., of touch or being touched). Hallucinations generally occur in a single mode. However, percipients may experience multimode hallucinations, such as when one involves both visual and auditory components (Aleman and Larøi, 25-46). However, these are extremely rare outside those already experiencing an altered state of consciousness resulting from drugs or alcohol and those suffering from schizophrenia (Aleman and Larøi, 25-46, esp. 46). Senior adults who are bereaving the very recent loss of a loved one are among those most likely to experience a hallucination: roughly 50 percent (Aleman and Larøi, 67-69). Yet, only 14 percent of these (or 7 percent of all bereaving senior adults surveyed) were visual in nature. Since hallucinations are mental events having no external reality, one cannot share in the hallucination of another. In this sense, hallucinations are similar to dreams. One cannot join another person in the dream they are experiencing at that moment.

How likely is it that Jesus' disciples experienced hallucinations of the risen Jesus that resulted from their deep grief over his sudden and brutal execution? To answer, consider the following: despite the fact that visual hallucinations are experienced by roughly 7 percent of those most likely to experience them, an incredible 100 percent of the Twelve would have had to experience a visual hallucination of the risen Jesus (rather than something else, such as guards coming to arrest them), and do so simultaneously on several occasions. Moreover, when the group experiences occurred, what group members experienced individually on that occasion would have to have been so similar as to be virtually indistinguishable. It would be an understatement to suggest that such a proposal bears only a very thin possibility of reflecting what actually occurred.

The hallucination hypothesis does not accommodate Paul's experience well, since there is no reason to think he was in a state of grief over Jesus' execution. After all, Paul was in the midst of his attempts to destroy the movement Jesus had started. He regarded Jesus as a false prophet and failed messiah. So Jesus would have been the last person in the world Paul would have expected to see or have even wanted to see. If anything, hallucinations would most likely have convinced some percipients that Jesus' spirit had appeared to them. They would not have accounted for the beliefs of Paul and the other apostles that Jesus had been raised physically. And if one grants that Jesus' tomb was found empty on the first Easter morning, hallucinations do not account for how it became empty.

*7.2. **Metaphor.*** Some scholars have asserted that the earliest Christians used *resurrection* as a metaphor. However, the metaphor's referent often differs among these scholars. To say that Jesus has risen means that people are experiencing God's power through Jesus' continuing perceived presence—that he is alive again (Crossan, quoted in Halstead, 521). Or does *resurrection* refer to the early Christians' belief that God had vindicated the righteous Jesus, who had suffered martyrdom (Patterson 2004, 106-21)?

On a few occasions, Paul uses *resurrection* as a metaphor. He speaks of the persecutions and afflictions he suffered in the cause of Christ, along with the power of God manifested in them as carrying in his body the death and life of Jesus (2 Cor 4:7-12). *Baptism is an act by which believers are forsaking a life of following their sinful inclinations and receiving new life in Christ, by which they are also participating in Jesus' death, burial, and resurrection (Col 2:11-13; see also Eph 5:14).

As discussed above, Paul also uses *resurrection* to refer to Jesus' return to life after having been executed. So one can be certain that Paul and the apostolic leaders in Jerusalem believed that Jesus had been raised physically. Consider how Paul argues in 1 Corinthians 15 as discussed above: if Christ was not raised, believers will not be raised. In that case, the Christian life is not worth living. However, Christ has been raised. Therefore, believers will be raised. Therefore, the Christian life is worth living. Paul's argument becomes incoherent when resurrection in that context is understood metaphorically. However, it is perfectly coherent when resurrection in that context is understood as an actual event.

Furthermore, Matthew suggests that the Jewish leadership at the time of Jesus' crucifixion and those up to the time he wrote were claiming that the cause of the empty tomb was Jesus' disciples having stolen his body (Mt 28:11-15). Justin Martyr says that the Jewish leadership was still telling this story when he was writing (*Dial.* 108; ca. AD 150). Tertullian also makes note of the claim but does not attribute its origin to the Jewish leaders. He also notes that some were circulating the story that a gardener had reburied Jesus' corpse in order to avoid having his lettuce trampled on by those coming to see where Jesus had been buried (*Spect.* 30; ca. AD 180–220). In the final third of the second century, a harsh critic of Christianity, Celsus, suggested that Jesus may have used tricks and *magic to fake his death and resurrection (Origen, *Cels.* 2.56). So it appears that many of Christianity's critics interpreted the Christians as having claimed that Jesus' resurrection was a historical event. When Christians responded in writing to the charges of their critics, they defended the historical nature of Jesus' resurrection rather than claiming that their critics had misinterpreted their use of metaphor as historical claims.

*7.3. **Theft/Reburial.*** That Jesus' disciples stole his corpse is rarely, if ever, proposed by scholars today, since the data strongly suggests that those disciples sincerely believed that their Lord had risen from the dead and appeared to them. However, in 2007 two popular writers argued that Jesus had been reburied by family members in their family tomb (Jacobovici and Pellegrino). This scenario is likewise implausible for the same reason. That someone else reburied or stole Jesus' corpse is unlikely. For if the resurrection narratives preserve at least a historical core, neither Jesus' women followers nor any of his disciples, except the Beloved Disciple (Jn 20:8), came to believe that Jesus had been raised solely upon seeing an empty tomb. It was the appearances that led to their belief in Jesus' resurrection. Moreover, upon hearing the report that Jesus had been raised, one of Paul's first thoughts would doubtless have been that Jesus' body had been relocated, whether legitimately or by theft. It was an experience he understood as the risen Jesus appearing to him later on that led to his conversion to Christianity.

*7.4. **Later Development.*** Also rare today is a scholar who would suggest that reports of the resurrection of Jesus were a later development and were not part of the oldest reports of what happened to Jesus. Burton Mack is an exception. He claims that the hypothetical Q source belongs to the earliest traditions about Jesus and is the best record of him (Mack, 245). He also asserts that, since Jesus' crucifixion as king of the Jews and the resurrection narratives are absent from Q, they resulted from mythmaking and thereby "have no claim as historical accounts" (Mack, 247). A number of observations can be made in reply. There are a number of reasons one may posit for why the Q material does not contain Jesus' resurrection: (1) Many scholars contend that the Q material is better explained by Luke's borrowing from Matthew (Greisbach hypothesis) or vice versa. (2) Q was a collection of Jesus' teachings composed during his lifetime. His crucifixion and resurrection are not mentioned because they had not occurred at the time of composition. Moreover, to report them would have been outside the genre of sayings literature. (3) Q originally contained a resurrection narrative that Matthew used, while Luke preferred other sources. (4) Many Q specialists acknowledge that not all of Q is extant. Therefore, it is possible that Q contained a resurrection narrative but the Gospels preferred other sources.

Although the accuracy of any of these proposed reasons cannot be confirmed, they are less speculative than Mack's contentions regarding Q. Most damaging to Mack's hypothesis is the observation above that one can get back to the apostolic preaching via Paul. That preaching certainly included the resurrection of Jesus and his postresurrection appearances to others. In contrast, it is unclear who may have been behind Q. Why then would the prudent historian prefer Mack's highly speculative understanding of Q to what can be known of the apostolic preaching?

8. Summary.

Paul's letters provide very early testimony from someone who claimed to be an eyewitness of the risen Jesus. That Paul was not a follower of Jesus when he had the experience increases the value of his testimony, since one can hardly accuse Paul of having been a biased Christian at the time. Paul knew the Jerusalem apostles, and it can be shown that he very likely preached the same message about Jesus' resurrection that the Jerusalem apostles were preaching. This provides a window through which historians may peer and see what the leading apostles in Jerusalem were preaching about Jesus' resurrection. Paul's letters speak of resurrection being a bodily event, that is, something that involves the corpse. Accordingly, Paul's view of resurrection is consistent not only with what the Jerusalem apostles were preaching but also with how the canonical Gospels portray the nature of Jesus' resurrection body. Thus, when one is reading Paul on Jesus' resurrection, one is likewise hearing the voice of the Jerusalem apostles.

See also Body; Christology; Conversion and Call of Paul; Corinthians, First Letter to the; Death; Eschatology; Flesh; Gospel; Paul in Acts; Visions, Ecstatic Experience.

BIBLIOGRAPHY. **D. A. Ackerman,** *Lo, I Tell You a Mystery: Cross, Resurrection, and Paraenesis in the Rhetoric of 1 Corinthians* (Eugene, OR: Pickwick, 2006); **A. Aleman and F. Larøi,** *Hallucinations: The Science of Idiosyncratic Perception* (Washington, DC: American Psychological Association, 2008); **D. C. Allison Jr.,** *Resurrecting Jesus: The Earliest Christian Tradition and Its Interpreters* (New York: T&T Clark, 2005); idem, *The Resurrection of Jesus: Apologetics, Polemics, History* (New York: T&T Clark, 2021); **D. C. Arichea and E. A. Nida,** *A Handbook on Paul's Letter to the Galatians* (New York: United Bible Societies, 1993); **P. Barnett,** "The Apostle Paul, the Bishop of Newark, and the Resurrection of Jesus," *Crux* 30 (1994): 2-11; **C. K. Barrett,** *A Commentary on the First Epistle to the Corinthians* (New York: Harper & Row, 1968); **C. L. Blomberg,** *Jesus and the Gospels: An Introduction and Survey*, 2nd ed. (Nashville: B&H Academic, 2009); **H. Boers,** "The Meaning of Christ's Resurrection in Paul," in *Resurrection: The Origin and Future of a Biblical Doctrine*, ed. J. H. Charlesworth with C. D. Elledge, J. L. Crenshaw, H. Boers, and W. W. Willis Jr. (New York: T&T Clark, 2006), 104-38; **M. J. Borg and J. D. Crossan,** *The Last Week: What the Gospels Really Teach About Jesus's Final Days in Jerusalem* (San Francisco: HarperSanFrancisco, 2006); **G. Bostock,** "Osiris and the Resurrection of Christ," *ExpTim* 112, no. 8 (2001): 265-71; **S. Brodeur,** *The Holy Spirit's Agency in the Resurrection of the Dead: An Exegetico-Theological Study of 1 Corinthians 15,44b-49 and Romans 8,9-13* (Rome: Gregorian University Press, 1996); **R. E. Brown,** *The Virginal Conception and Bodily Resurrection of Jesus* (New York: Paulist Press, 1973); **F. F. Bruce,** *The Epistle to the Galatians: A Commentary on the Greek Text* (Grand Rapids, MI: Eerdmans, 1982); idem, *Paul: Apostle of the Heart Set Free* (Grand Rapids, MI: Eerdmans, 2000); **S. Byrskog,** *Story as History—History as Story: The Gospel Tradition in the Context of Ancient Oral History*, WUNT 123 (Boston: Brill Academic, 2002); **P. Carnley,** *The Structure of Resurrection Belief* (New York: Oxford University Press, 1987); **D. A. Carson,** "Matthew, Mark, Luke," in *Expositor's Bible Commentary*, ed. F. E. Gaebelein (Grand Rapids, MI: Zondervan, 1984), 8:1-599; **R. F. Collins,** *First Corinthians*, SP 7 (Collegeville, MN: Liturgical Press, 1999); **H. Conzelmann,** *1 Corinthians*, trans. J. W. Leitch, Hermeneia (Philadelphia: Fortress, 1975); **P. F. Craffert,** *The Life of a Galilean Shaman: Jesus of Nazareth in Anthropological-Historical Perspective* (Cambridge: Clarke, 2008); **W. L. Craig,** *Assessing the New Testament Evidence for the Historicity of the Resurrection of Jesus* (New York: Mellen, 1989); **J. D. G. Dunn,** *Jesus Remembered* (Grand Rapids, MI: Eerdmans, 2003); **B. D. Ehrman,** *The New Testament: A Historical Introduction to the Early Christian Writings*, 4th ed. (New York: Oxford University Press, 2008); **G. D. Fee,** *The First Epistle to the Corinthians* (Grand Rapids, MI: Eerdmans, 1987); **T. Friberg, B. Friberg, and N. F. Miller,** *Analytical Lexicon of the Greek New Testament* (Grand Rapids, MI: Baker Books, 2000); **J. Gillman,** "A Thematic Comparison: 1 Cor 15:50-57 and 2 Cor 5:1-5," *JBL* 107 (1988): 439-54; **R. H. Gundry,** *Sōma in Biblical Theology with Emphasis on Pauline Anthropology* (New York: Cambridge University Press, 1976); **G. Habermas,** *The Risen Jesus and Future Hope* (Lanham, MD: Rowman & Littlefield, 2003); **J. Halstead,** "The Orthodox Unorthodoxy of John Dominic Crossan: An Interview," *Cross Currents* 45, no. 4 (1995–1996): 510-30; **M. J. Harris,** *Raised Immortal: Resurrection and Immortality in the New Testament* (Grand Rapids, MI: Eerdmans, 1985); **R. B. Hays,** *First Corinthians, Int* (Louisville, KY: John Knox, 1997); **W. Hendriksen,** *Exposition of Galatians*, Baker New Testament Commentary (Grand Rapids, MI: Baker, 1995); **J. Héring,** *The First Epistle of Saint Paul to the Corinthians* (London: Epworth, 1962); **L. W. Hurtado,** *Lord Jesus Christ: Devotion to Jesus in Earliest Christianity* (Grand Rapids, MI: Eerdmans, 2003); **S. Jacobovici and C. Pellegrino,** *The Jesus Family Tomb: The Discovery, the Investigation, and the Evidence That Could Change History* (San Francisco: HarperSanFrancisco, 2007); **J. Jeremias,** "'Flesh and Blood Cannot Inherit the Kingdom of God' (1 Cor. XV.50)," *NTS* 2 (1955–1956): 151-59; **A. F. Johnson,** *1 Corinthians*, IVPNTC 7 (Downers

Grove, IL: InterVarsity Press, 2004); **C. S. Keener,** *1–2 Corinthians*, NCBC (New York: Cambridge University Press, 2005); idem, *Acts: An Exegetical Commentary*, vol. 1, *Introduction and 1:1–2:47* (Grand Rapids, MI: Baker Academic, 2012); **S. J. Kistemaker,** *Exposition of the First Epistle to the Corinthians* (Grand Rapids, MI: Baker, 1993); **M. R. Licona,** *The Resurrection of Jesus: A New Historiographical Approach* (Downers Grove, IL: IVP Academic, 2010); **R. N. Longenecker,** *Galatians*, WBC 41 (Dallas: Word, 1990); **B. L. Mack,** *The Lost Gospel: The Book of Q and Christian Origins* (San Francisco: HarperCollins, 1993); **L. Morris,** *Galatians: Paul's Charter of Christian Freedom* (Downers Grove, IL: InterVarsity Press, 1996); **B. M. Newman,** *Concise Greek-English Dictionary of the New Testament* (New York: United Bible Societies, 1993); **S. J. Patterson,** "Why Did Christians Say: 'God Raised Jesus from the Dead'? 1 Cor 15 and the Origins of the Resurrection Tradition," *Forum* 10, nos. 3-4 (1994): 135-60; idem, *Beyond the Passion: Rethinking the Death and Life of Jesus* (Minneapolis: Fortress, 2004); **A. F. Segal,** *Life After Death: A History of the Afterlife in Western Religion* (New York: Doubleday, 2004); **D. A. Smith,** *Revisiting the Empty Tomb: The Early History of Easter* (Minneapolis: Fortress, 2010); **B. Witherington III,** *The Acts of the Apostles: A Socio-Rhetorical Commentary* (Grand Rapids, MI: Eerdmans, 1998); **N. T. Wright,** *The Resurrection of the Son of God* (Minneapolis: Fortress, 2003).

M. R. Licona

REVELATION. *See* CONVERSION AND CALL OF PAUL; JESUS, SAYINGS OF; JESUS AND PAUL; MYSTERY; PROPHECY.

REVERENCE. *See* FEAR, REVERENCE.

RHETORIC. *See* PREACHING, FIRST-CENTURY; PREACHING FROM PAUL TODAY; RHETORICAL CRITICISM.

RHETORICAL CRITICISM

Paul lived in an oral and aural world that was formed by rhetoric. Rhetoric, or the art of speaking well, communicated with a majority of an ancient audience that was mostly illiterate and where speaking was the primary means of communication and persuasion. Paul's context in communities of moral discourse and persuasion inherently inclined them toward rhetoric. Given practical requirements, Paul sends "*letters" to his communities, but these were read aloud and thus had to be shaped with how they would be heard by his community. Hence rhetoric was a necessary aspect of Paul's pastoral strategy.

1. Greco-Roman Rhetoric
2. Rhetorical Methodology
3. Paul and Rhetoric
4. Conclusion

1. Greco-Roman Rhetoric.

1.1. Rhetorical Theory. The foundational work for rhetoric is Aristotle's fourth-century BC treatise *The Art of Rhetoric.* Aristotle's summation and advancement of rhetorical theory continued to hold sway on the development of rhetoric. Rhetorical theory is ultimately traced back to development after Aristotle's *Rhetorica.* The work of Aristotle reemerged in the first century by Andronicus of Rhodes (Kennedy, 63). Not many works by Greek rhetoricians survive, only a few handbooks and fragments, but much of Greek rhetorical theory was translated and preserved in Latin. Several notable works of rhetoric exist, such as that of Dionysius of Halicarnassus. From the first century BC, there is the anonymous Rhetorica ad Herennium along with Cicero's many works (*On Invention, Topics, Oratory*), and from the later first century Quintilian's *On the Education of the Orator.* The goal of these handbooks is setting out the parameters of rhetoric and the training of rhetoricians both before and after the first century; they thus reflect both theory and practice. These handbooks provide the most significant insight into how Paul might have organized and arranged his correspondences and offer the modern interpreter of Paul the categories and definitions of essential aspects of rhetorical theory.

Notable interpreters to use these handbooks in the interpretation of Paul are Hans Dieter Betz, George Kennedy, Robert Jewett, and Ben Witherington III. The comparison of Paul's letters and the rhetorical handbooks showcases the vast overlap between them and indicates that Paul used ancient rhetoric to communicate with his communities. The handbooks must be used with caution as they inform only of general practice within the first century. One should not imagine Paul sitting down with one of the handbooks and using it to write a letter. As one steeped in rhetoric, Paul considered how best to identify, create, and arrange his arguments. One must allow for Paul's creativity in the use, adaptation, and execution of rhetoric in his work, as all rhetoricians did.

1.2. Rhetorical Foundations and Concepts. The main outline of rhetorical theory was invention, arrangement, style, memorization, and delivery. The first three areas were the primary focus of the handbooks. Invention was close to the ancient Greek idea of "research," where the speaker planned the discourse and after analysis chose the best arguments for that discourse (Steel 2009, 80). Proofs (*pisteis*) or arguments were meant to convince an audience to trust the conclusion of the rhetor. Cicero considers this the most crucial section (*Inv.* 1.7). According to Aristotle, there were two types of proofs: artificial and inartificial (*Rhet.* 2.2.3-7). Artificial proofs were those created by the rhetor, and there were three subtypes: pathos, ethos, and logos. Ethos was a way to establish one's character with one's audience and something internal to the speech. Pathos existed in the audience and was the emotional reaction that the hearer underwent. Logos was the logical argument found in the discourse. Cicero relates these three proofs to the duties of the orator—to teach, to please, and to move (*Opt. gen.* 1.3). Paul's use of artificial proofs is abundant in his letters, as his primary mode of discourse is argumentation. This is what one is looking at when reading one of his letters. Notable examples would include 1 Corinthians 9:24-27.

Inartificial proofs or external proofs were those outside the author, or the proofs that the author did not invent, such as witnesses or documents. Within Paul's letters, these are usually references to miracles, naming of witnesses, and quotations from the OT. For example, Galatians 3:5-8 combines miracles and a reference to the story of *Abraham. Many rhetoricians practiced how to compose arguments at an early age through composition exercises known as the *progymnasmata* or "elementary exercises" that comprised educational practices across the Roman Empire. These practices provided a method for working out common types of discourse. They included various exercises in

- creation of narratives, as in Galatians 4:1-7;
- encomium, or a short speech of praise, such as Philippians 2:5-11;
- *synkrisis*, or a comparison of two figures, such as *Adam and Christ in Romans 5–6;
- *ekphrasis*, or vivid description, such as Galatians 4:15; 5:12; and
- *prosopoeia*, or speech in character—see the use of "I" in Romans 7:7-25.

1.3. Types of Rhetoric. Aristotle defines the three types of rhetoric: forensic, deliberative, and epideictic (Aristotle, *Rhet.* 1.3; Cicero, *Inv.* 1.9; Quintilian, *Inst.* 3.4, Rhetorica ad Herennium 3.2-4). As part of the stage of invention, the rhetorician needed to determine the aim, scope, and focus of their speech. Each domain had a setting, a goal, and an outcome. Forensic rhetoric was the rhetoric associated with judicial settings and the law court and tried to accuse or defend a person. It strived to convince judges whether or not an action had happened. This type of rhetoric focused on things done in the past with the subject matter of right or wrong, and the goal of this type of rhetoric was justice. Betz famously argues that Galatians is a forensic document, though many scholars today are not convinced (Betz, 14-25). Some have argued 2 Corinthians is a forensic argument (Kennedy, 87-91; Witherington 1995, 333-34) where Paul is seeking to defend himself for his past actions and relationship with the Corinthian community.

The second type of rhetoric was deliberative, and this was the rhetoric of the assembly. Harking back to the democracy of Athens, a truly free body of citizens needed to be persuaded or dissuaded from courses of action that were either advantageous or not advantageous. Deliberative rhetoric focused on activities in the future. This type of rhetoric typically invoked *honor and shame language. The end of this type of rhetoric was the expedient or what was useful for a community. One finds this type of rhetoric at work frequently in Paul, who is attempting to persuade his audiences to take particular courses of action. At a macro-rhetoric level, the following letters can be categorized in deliberative rhetoric category: 1 Corinthians, Romans, and Galatians, just to name a few examples. Margaret Mitchell provides an excellent study of 1 Corinthians along these lines, arguing that Paul is seeking to quell discord and argue for reconciliation in the community.

The final type of rhetoric was epideictic. Although this typically functioned as a catchall category, it was mainly used in funerary orations and encomiums and was the rhetoric of praise and blame, with its subject of honor or dishonor. It was focused primarily on the present time and frequently used amplification in argumentation. Unlike deliberative rhetoric, epideictic rhetoric sought to ingrain existing positions rather than argue for change. Epideictic has been the most problematic category, as it is usually invoked as a general category when speeches do not fit into forensic or deliberative. The categories were not inflexible or static. The issue of mixed genres was considered in antiquity, with Pseudo-Aristedes showing that the speeches of Demosthenes were a mixture of all three categories. The essential element in determining the type of rhetoric is the setting. Scholars do not think Paul used this type of rhetoric at a macro level, although there might be epideictic pieces embedded within Paul's letters that are arranged according to another category—most famously 1 Corinthians 13 and a speech in praise of *love (Witherington 2008, 14).

1.4. Rhetoric Building Blocks. The next step in rhetorical development was the arrangement of one's speech into parts to produce a persuasive argument. Aristotle held that there were four parts of a speech, but by the time of Cicero this could be expanded to six sections: *exordium*, *narratio*, *propositio*, *probatio*, *refutatio*, and *peroratio*. Complete agreement on the order, terminology, or definition of parts eluded ancient rhetorical theory. Depending on the species of rhetoric employed, various parts could be omitted or rearranged. *Exordium* is the Latin name for the beginning section of a speech. It was one of the most critical sections, as many rhetoricians talk about adjusting one's speech to the audience. One of the goals of this section was to put the audience in the right position to hear the argument (Cicero, *Inv.* 1.15). If the audience was hostile to the rhetorician's view, the rhetorician would need to engender goodwill or sympathy before advancing to their main argument. This section also included the list of topics to be covered in the speech and functioned somewhat as an oral table of contents for the audience, highlighting for them issues to appear later in the speech. Some also recommended that the character or aptitude of the speaker is established in this section. Examples of this in Paul include Galatians 1:6-12, where Paul establishes his authority.

The next section, the *narratio*, was a "statement of facts" or the establishment of a *narrative. Young students were trained in the *progymnasmata* to create these. One can understand the importance of such a section in a forensic speech, where one establishes a chronology of supposed events. A *narratio* could be omitted or moved to another section if deemed more efficient by the rhetorician. The *narratio* was supposed to be brief and precise. A great example of a *narratio* is in Galatians 1:13–2:14, where Paul rehearses a chronology of events (also 2 Cor 1:8–2:14).

The third section was the *propositio*, or thesis statement. Depending on the rhetorician, this could come before or after the *narratio*. The thesis statement in a forensic argument would focus on the innocence or guilt of the party, whereas in a deliberative speech it would focus on the issue argued for or against. One of the most famous examples of the *propositio* is Romans 1:16-17.

The thesis statement set up the next section(s), known as the *probatio*, where one found the actual argument in support of the thesis. The *probatio* was one of the most extended parts of any speech and was where the rhetorician made their case (Phil 2:1–4; Rom 1:18–8:39). In this section a rhetorician made use of what was called in Greek *topos*, originally referring to theme stock arguments on various topics (i.e., bravery, love, *friendship). Aristotle innovated on this aspect, and *topoi* came to refer to some type of argumentative structure, such as arguments from the lesser to the greater, "if X, then Y." The use of *topoi* was quite beneficial in this section.

Often, but not always, the *probatio* would be followed by a *refutatio*, although this was omitted if need be. A skilled rhetor would anticipate the objections to their argument and offer a rebuttal in advance of the opposition to undercut their argument and bolster their own. One clear example of this in Paul is Romans 9:1–11:36, where it seems he addresses objections to the argument just made in Romans 1:18–8:39.

The final section of any speech was the *peroratio*. After one's case, one repeated the main points of the speech to refresh the memory of the audience and to make one final appeal. This section tended to be highly emotive, and according to Quintilian (*Inst.* 6.1.52), one would let loose with one's eloquence (Aune, *Rhetoric*, 347). Examples include Galatians 6:12-17; Philippians 4:4-20; 2 Corinthians 13:5-10.

2. Rhetorical Methodology.

The use of rhetorical study in NT studies (see Martin) is often attributed to the influential work of Kennedy, who outlines a five-stage analytical structure (Kennedy, 33-38). First is to determine the rhetorical unit to be analyzed. The unit can be understood in a macro sense as the letter as a whole or as a subunit (e.g., Rom 5–8). Once the unit has been delineated, the second stage is to define the rhetorical situation, or in other words, the *Sitz im Leben*—the events, persons, and problems of the audience and the author. What gives rise to the need for Paul to respond? One needs to determine the fundamental issue at stake or problem. One also needs to note whether the issue is a past, present, or future problem, as the species of rhetoric used by Paul (forensic, deliberative, or epideictic) is defined at this stage. Third is the observation of how the rhetorical unit is arranged—analyzing the flow of the argument, breaking it down into subdivisions. Following this, the fourth stage is paying attention to the elements within the unit, such as repetition or enthymemes (an argument in which one premise is not explicitly stated), or other rhetorical features, such as *synkrisis* (comparisons, as in Rom 5, with Adam and Christ), and *prosopopoeia* (speech in character, such as the "I" in Rom 7:7-25). Finally, at the fifth stage, one surveys the entire rhetorical unity in light of the rhetorical situation and sees whether any illumination of the text occurred or whether new insights have been gleaned.

Interpreters will disagree on the precise nature and function of various rhetorical sections in Paul, but such disagreement was evident in the ancient discussion of rhetoric itself.

3. Rhetoric at Work in Paul.

3.1. Does Paul Use Rhetoric? What is one to make of Paul? Did Paul knowingly use the procedures/theory of rhetorical handbooks? At the heart of this disagreement is perhaps the a priori consideration of whether Paul's letters are well-thought-out and structured arguments or whether Paul's letters are too impulsive and off the cuff to adhere to a structure. Opinions diverge, but it is agreed that Paul uses micro-rhetoric—comparisons, metaphor, rhetorical questions, enthymemes, and personification, among other micro-rhetoric examples. The broader debate attends to the question of whether Paul used macro-rhetoric in the composition of his letters—species of rhetoric and rhetorical categories from the handbooks. Not all are convinced that he did (Stanley 2016). Disagreement about Paul's rhetorical education stems from the level and location of Paul's education. Ancient educational practices had local variations but were fairly standardized throughout the *empire (Morgan 1999). Rhetoric was part of each level of ancient education, and it appears that Paul was highly educated for an ancient person. The dispute about Paul's rhetorical education concerns whether his advanced education included rhetoric or was primarily early rabbinic studies. Such bifurcation blurs the fluidity of the stages of rhetorical education practice in the ancient world. There was debate in the first century concerning the overlapping domains of the *grammaticus* and the rhetor. Quintilian criticizes grammar teachers who overtake the role of rhetoricians (Quintilian, *Inst.* 2.1.1-3; Maurice 2013) and introduce rhetoric at earlier stages.

Further objections point to Paul himself, where he appears to distance himself from rhetoric (1 Cor 2:1-4). Missing from the discussion is that downplaying one's rhetorical ability was a known rhetorical strategy, according to Quintilian (*Inst.* 4.1.8-11; 11.1.15), and Paul may be employing it in 1 Corinthians in contrast to other more exaggerated or sophistic forms of rhetoric (Keener 2005, 34). Others suggest epistolary theory is a better strategy for understanding Paul (Weima). In contrast to the long history of rhetoric in the Greco-Roman world and the schools dedicated to teaching rhetoric, letter writing was a more recent development in the early part of the first century BC, with Cicero and epistolary theory not part of ancient educational practices (Witherington and Myers forthcoming). Epistolary theory cannot explain the largest sections of Paul's letters—what it calls the "body"—and offers only limited insights to the beginning and ending features of Paul's letters, which were necessary for the sending of the document to its recipients. Other than Philemon, none of Paul's letters bears resemblance to ancient letters in terms of size. More insight is gained from the practice of rhetorical theory and its categories for examining Paul's correspondences in the NT.

3.2. Rhetoric in Paul. The book of Galatians provides an excellent entry into rhetoric in Paul. One may begin by noting that the overall aim of Paul in Galatians is to persuade his *Gentile congregants to not be circumcised (Gal 5:2-6). In terms of category of rhetoric, this is a future decision that the Gentiles have not yet made. Thus it falls in the domain of deliberative rhetoric. As one dives into the early part of the correspondence, one finds the epistolary prescript in Galatians 1:1-5, which is then followed by the *exordium* (Gal 1:6-10), which introduces Paul's main themes, related to summarizing the singular *gospel for the singular people of *God. This is followed by a *narratio* (Gal 1:12–2:14), or statement of facts, where Paul walks his audience through a review of past events, including his own biographical components and, more recently, events in Antioch that spurred the writing of the letter. Next is the *propositio*, or thesis statement of the letter, in Galatians 2:15-21, that inclusion in God's people is by God's *grace alone and not by the *works of the *law.

The *probatio*, or main arguments, of Galatians then comprise the bulk of the letter, in Galatians 3:1–6:10. Broadly speaking, Galatians 3 is an inartificial proof from the story of Abraham, followed by an artificial proof on the nature of *covenant making in Galatians 4. These sections are full of *synkrisis*, such as the two sons in Galatians 4:21-31, and vivid speech, such as Galatians 4:15 referring to tearing out one's eyes, to name just a couple of examples of micro-rhetoric. The more exhortatory sections of Galatians 5:1–6:10 are actually arguments assisted by exhortations (Witherington 1998, 33). Finally, there is an emotional and rousing *peroratio*, or conclusion, in Galatians 6:11-18. Attention to the rhetorical features helps to interpret the particular elements therein.

Likewise, 1 Corinthians is an excellent example of deliberative rhetoric as well, with its themes of unity and concord (1 Cor 1:10; see Mitchell, 25-32). Deliberative rhetoric often included an appeal to the advantage or benefit of a community to pursue a set of actions. Paul uses such advantageous or beneficial language five times in the letter (1 Cor 6:12; 7:35; 10:23, 33; 12:7). This can be lurking in the background of English translations that render these terms differently:

> **1 Corinthians 6:12:** "All things are lawful for me," but not all things are **beneficial**. "All things are lawful for me," but I will not be dominated by anything. (NRSV)

> **1 Corinthians 7:35:** I say this for your own **benefit**, not to put any restraint upon you, but to promote good order and unhindered devotion to the Lord. (NRSV)

> **1 Corinthians 10:33:** just as I try to please everyone in everything I do, not seeking my own **advantage**, but that of many, so that they may be saved. (NRSV)

> **1 Corinthians 12:7:** To each is given the manifestation of the Spirit for the common **good**. (NRSV)

The NRSV renders the same root terms for "benefit" and "advantage" (the verb *sympherō* and the adjective *symphoros*) in multiple ways: "beneficial," "benefit," "advantage," or even "good." According to Aristotle, the end goal of deliberative rhetoric is the advantageous. The term "advantageous" in Aristotle is the same term, *sympherō*. He along with numerous other ancient authors regarded this as a chief end of deliberative rhetoric. Finally, divisions and factionalism were key points of discussion within the domain of deliberative rhetoric. The answer for factions is unity, and thus it should not be surprising that the thesis or *propositio* of 1 Corinthians is 1 Corinthians 1:10, where Paul appeals to the Corinthians to be not divided but united.

Micro-rhetoric also helps one to understand Paul elsewhere as well. One might also look to one of Paul's most famous letters and most famous sections, the "I" of Romans 7:7-25. The "I" in this section has proved problematic and confusing for many readers of Paul. However, if one understands the ancient rhetorical practice of *prosopopoeia*, or speech in character, the section is illumined, allowing one to realize that Paul is in character. The question then becomes, What character is Paul using? Previously Romans 5–6 used the two characters of Adam and Christ, and it becomes clearer that Romans 7:7-25 sounds a lot more like the character of Adam than it does the person of Christ.

4. Conclusion.

The Pauline correspondences are replete with examples of rhetoric, and the study of Paul's letters is illuminated with a comparison to the ancient rhetorical handbooks. Due attention to the study of rhetoric in Paul yields incredible insights, from the understanding of the themes and purposes of letters as a whole to further clarity on specific details of Paul's arguments. Certainly one of the features that made Paul such a persuasive writer, both then and now, was his ability to command the rhetorical skills and arguments necessary to persuade even the most ardent of opponents.

See also GALATIANS, LETTER TO THE; HELLENISM, ROMAN; LETTERS, LETTER FORMS; PHILOSOPHY.

BIBLIOGRAPHY. **D. E. Aune,** *The Westminster Dictionary of New Testament and Early Christian Literature and Rhetoric* (Louisville, KY: Westminster John Knox, 2003); **H. D. Betz,** *Galatians,* Hermeneia (Philadelphia: Fortress, 1979); **C. J. Classen,** *Rhetorical Criticism of the New Testament* (Boston: Brill, 2000); **W. Dominick and J. Hall,** *A Companion to Roman Rhetoric* (Malden, MA: Wiley-Blackwell, 2010); **E. Gunderson,** ed., *The Cambridge Companion to Ancient Rhetoric* (New York: Cambridge University Press, 2009); **R. Jewett,** *Romans,* Hermeneia (Philadelphia: Fortress, 2006); **C. Keener,** *1–2 Corinthians* (New York: Cambridge University Press, 2005); **G. A. Kennedy,** *New Testament Interpretation Through Rhetorical Criticism* (Chapel Hill: University of North Carolina Press, 1984); **T. W. Martin,** ed., *Genealogies of New Testament Rhetorical Criticism* (Minneapolis: Fortress, 2014); **L. Maurice,** *The Teacher in Ancient Rome: The Magister and His World* (New York: Lexington Books, 2013); **M. M. Mitchell,** *Paul and the Rhetoric of Reconciliation* (Louisville, KY: Westminster John Knox, 1991); **T. Morgan,** *Literate Education in the Hellenistic and Roman Worlds* (New York: Cambridge University Press); **J. Murphy,** ed., *A Synoptic History of Classical Rhetoric* (Mahwah, NJ: Hermagoras, 2003); **S. Porter and B. E. Dyer,** eds., *Paul and Ancient Rhetoric: Theory and Practice in the Hellenistic Context* (Cambridge, Cambridge University Press; 2016); **E. Schüssler Fiorenza,** "Rhetorical Situation and Historical Reconstruction in 1 Corinthians," *NTS* 33 (1987): 386-403; **C. Steele,** "Divisions of Speech," in *The Cambridge Companion to Ancient Rhetoric*, ed.

E. Gunderson (New York: Cambridge University Press, 2009), 77-91; **L. Thurén,** *Derhetorizing Paul: A Dynamic Perspective on Pauline Theology and the Law* (Harrisburg, PA: Trinity Press International, 2000); **D. F. Watson,** "The New Testament and Greco-Roman Rhetoric: A Bibliography," *JETS* 31 (1988): 465-72; idem, "A Rhetorical Analysis of Philippians and Its Implications for the Unity Question," *NovT* 39 (1988): 57-88; idem, "1 Corinthians 10:23–11:1 in the Light of Greco-Roman Rhetoric: The Role of Rhetorical Questions," *JBL* 108 (1989): 301-18; idem, ed., *Persuasive Artistry: Studies in New Testament Rhetoric in Honor of George A. Kennedy,* JSNTSup 50 (Sheffield: Sheffield Academic Press, 1991); **J. A. D. Weima,** *Paul the Ancient Letter Writer: An Introduction to Epistolary Analysis* (Grand Rapids, MI: Baker, 2016); **A. C. Wire,** *The Corinthian Women Prophets: A Reconstruction Through Paul's Rhetoric* (Minneapolis: Fortress, 1990); **B. Witherington III,** *Conflict and Community in Corinth: A Socio-rhetorical Commentary on 1 and 2 Corinthians* (Grand Rapids, MI: Eerdmans, 1995); idem, *Grace in Galatia: A Commentary on Paul's Letter to the Galatians* (Grand Rapids, MI: Eerdmans, 1998); idem, *New Testament Rhetoric: An Introductory Guide to the Art of Persuasion in and of the New Testament* (Eugene, OR: Cascade, 2008); **B. Witherington III and J. A. Myers,** *New Testament Rhetoric: An Introductory Guide to the Art of Persuasion in and of the New Testament,* 2nd ed. (Eugene, OR: Cascade, 2022); **I. Worthington,** *A Companion to Greek Rhetoric* (Malden, MA: Wiley-Blackwell, 2010); **W. Wuellner,** "Paul as Pastor: The Function of Rhetorical Questions in First Corinthians," in *L'Apôtre Paul: Personnalité, style et conception du ministère,* ed. A. Vanhoye, BETL 73 (Leuven: Leuven University Press, 1986).

J. A. Myers

RIGHTEOUSNESS

Paul's letters contain a significant number of references to righteousness (*dikaiosynē*) in relation to *God, believers, *salvation, *ethics, and *church life. In addition, Paul frequently makes mention of the righteousness of God (*dikaiosynē theou*) at key points when discussing the theocentric framework of salvation (see Rom 1:17; 3:5, 21-22, 25-26; 10:3; 2 Cor 5:21; Phil 3:9). Because of the prominence of the phrase in the Pauline letters and its salience for mapping Paul's theology, the meaning of the righteousness of God has been heavily disputed since the Reformation. Debate has been particularly acute on how the righteousness of God relates to a Pauline doctrine of *justification by *faith, orbited around lexical matters, background, exegetical meaning, and the overall significance of the righteousness of God in Paul's thought.

1. Lexical and Linguistic Issues
2. Jewish Background to Paul's "Righteousness of God" Language
3. Patristic, Medieval, and Reformed Interpretation
4. Contemporary Scholarship
5. Key Pauline Texts
6. Conclusion

1. Lexical and Linguistic Issues.

Paul was a Hellenistic Jew immersed in the Jewish traditions of the Diaspora and Judea, and simultaneously conversant with wider Greco-Roman culture. As such, Paul's references to the righteousness of God must be situated in relation to the Hebrew Scriptures and Hellenistic language. Paul's discourse about the righteousness of God is thoroughly indebted to the Hebrew Scriptures with its specific conception of Yahweh's rightness and deliverance. In addition, the Greek Scriptures (or Septuagint) are equally significant as the literary corpus where Hebrew words for "righteousness" were translated into Greek, and the Greek Scriptures constitute the primary intertext that Paul utilizes in his letters.

When discussing the righteousness of God, a few caveats are required in order to avoid linguistic fallacies. First, the English distinctions between *righteousness, justice,* and *justification* do not necessarily correspond to analogous Hebrew and Greek words, which often sustain a wider semantic range of ideas (e.g., one cannot assume that the noun *dikaiosynē* always denotes ethical righteousness, while the verb *dikaioō* always pertains to a forensic righteousness; context decides). Second, one should be wary of positing an erroneous dichotomy between Hebrew and Greek in their language-concept distinctions (i.e., wrongly supposing that Hebrew words are concrete and relational, whereas Greek words are more abstract and static). The differences between Hebrew and Greek words for righteousness will not be at the abstract level but in semantic domains and in the specific discourses that those words are used in. Third, additional fallacies include trying to reduce righteousness language to a single concept (i.e., whether "*covenant faithfulness" or "distributive justice"), or engaging in an illegitimate totality transfer (i.e., all possible uses of a word are present in a given instance). There are differences between lexicography (identifying the band of meaning for words), mapping semantic domains (grouping words with associated meanings), and theological word description (unpacking how biblical words are used in relation to God).

1.1. Hebrew. The Hebrew words deriving from the *ṣdq* root pertain to adherence to a norm with the norm provided by social, familial, and covenantal relationships or else by abstract entities such as *truth and *wisdom. For example, in Genesis 38:26, Judah says of Tamar, "She [Tamar] is more righteous than I" because Tamar, through prostitution, finds a way to raise up offspring for her late husband when her father-in-law Judah refuses to help her, reflecting the norms of ancient of Near Eastern cultures and the later levirate *law given in Deuteronomy 25:5-10.

The words *ṣedeq* (justness, rightness) and *ṣədāqâ* (justice, blamelessness) pertain to Yahweh's character and requirements (e.g., Gen 18:19; Deut 6:25; Ps 11:7; 119:137) and are frequently used in forensic, punitive, ethical, or salvific senses. These words are regularly put in parallel with Yahweh's *mišpāṭ* (*judgment), *ʾəmet* (firmness, faithfulness, truthfulness), *ḥesed* (faithfulness, kindness, *mercy), and *yeshûâ* (salvation; see, e.g., Deut 33:21; Ps 143:1, 11-12; Is 46:13; 51:1-8; 56:1; 63:1). Also, Yahweh, as maker and lord of creation, is bound to judge the world in righteousness and to establish justice throughout *creation (Gen 18:25; Ps 9:8; 96:13; 98:9; Is 11:4; 26:9). Similarly, Yahweh's righteousness is also his faithfulness to the covenant, demonstrated in contending against the injustice of Israel's oppressors and even establishing the righteousness of the people (Deut 32:4; Is 61:8-11; Ps 50:1-6; 89:14; 111:1-10; 143:1-3; Zech 8:8; Hos 2:16-20; Neh 9:32-33; Dan 9:4-7). Thus, in scriptural narration, *mišpāṭ* and *ṣədāqâ* suggest the faithful exercise of Yahweh's power across creation and in his covenant *love with *Israel (Goldingay, 21). The creational and covenantal aspects of Yahweh's righteousness dovetail in Psalm 98:2-3: "The *Lord has made known his salvation; he has revealed his righteousness in the sight of the nations. He has remembered his covenant love and faithfulness to the house of Israel. All the ends of the earth have seen the salvation of our God." Importantly, the plural of *ṣədāqâ* is used to describe the "victories of Yahweh" (Judg 5:11), the "deliverance of Yahweh" (1 Sam 12:7; Mic 6:5), the "vindication of Yahweh" (Ps 103:6), and Yahweh's "righteous acts" (Dan 9:16), and is an obvious precursor to Paul's usage of *dikaiosynē theou*.

Accordingly, in the Hebrew Bible, Yahweh's righteousness is a dynamic series of concepts, a divine attribute, married to Yahweh's ruling and judging in justice, an explanation for Yahweh's acts on behalf of his people, and Yahweh's covenant-keeping fidelity to Israel.

1.2. Greek. In ancient Greek, the noun *dikaiosynē* and the adjective *dikaios* are associated with justice, equity, fairness, rectitude, and rightness (GE; L&N 88.13; *GELS*; Thielman; Irons, 84-107), specifically the quality, characteristic, and standard of right behavior (BDAG; *NIDNTT*).

In Greek literature going as far back as Homer, *dikaiosynē* was associated with justice, virtue, civility, and piety. Plato defined *dikaiosynē* as "the state that distributes to each person according to what is deserved; the state on account of which its possessor chooses what appears to him to be just; the state underlying a law abiding way of life; social equality; the state of obedience to the laws" (*Def.* 411d-e). Book 5 of Aristotle's *Nicomachean Ethics* is an exposition of *dikaiosynē*. Aristotle acknowledged the diverse usages of *dikaiosynē* and centers it on what is equal, lawful, and fair (*Eth. nic.* 5.1.8), and contends that *dikaiosynē* is the most perfect and sublime of virtues (5.1.15). Elsewhere Aristotle connects *dikaiosynē* with distributive justice, truthfulness, fidelity, and duty:

> To righteousness it belongs to be ready to distribute according to desert, and to preserve ancestral customs and institutions and the established laws and to tell the truth when interest is at stake, and to keep agreements. First among the claims of righteousness are our duties to the gods. Then our duties to the spirits, then those to country and parents, then those to the departed; and among these claims is piety. . . . Righteousness is also accompanied by holiness and truth and loyalty and hatred of wickedness. (*Virt. vit.* 5.2-3)

The Greek Scriptures deploy *dikaiosynē* over three hundred times, predominantly in the Psalms, Isaiah, and Proverbs, normally to translate the Hebrew words *ṣedeq* and *ṣədāqâ*, but sometimes other words too such as *mišpāṭ* (judgment), *ʾəmet* (faithfulness), and *ḥesed* (covenant love). In addition, the Greek Scriptures, including writings contained in the so-called Apocrypha, frequently associate Israel's Lord with the *dik-* word group in regard to the Lord's upright character, decrees, justice, and judgment (e.g., Pss. Sol. 9:2-4; Wis 15:3; Tob 3:2; Sir 18:2; Bar 5:9; 2 Macc 1:25). Specific instances make mention of the "justice of the Lord" (*dikaiosynēn kyrios*) concerning what Gad executed for Israel (Deut 33:21). The "righteousness of the Lord" (*dikaiosynēn kyriou*) describes "all the things he [God] has done for you and your fathers" by delivering them from Egypt (1 Sam 12:7 LXX). Similarly, there is "the righteousness of the Lord" (*hē dikaiosynē tou kyriou*) equated with the prior saving deeds of the Lord in Israel's covenant history (Mic 6:5 LXX). Tobit blesses "the Lord of righteousness" (*ton kyrion tēs dikaiosynēs*) for his regal qualities and redemptive acts (Tob 13:7 LXX). A salvific sense is further underscored when the Lord's *dikaiosynē* (righteousness) is closely related to redemption (*lytroomai*), mercy (*eleos*), deliverance (*rhuomai*, *exaireō*), and salvation (*sōtēria*; see, e.g., Ex 15:13; Ps 50:16 [ET 51:14]; 142:1-12 [ET 143:1-12]; Is 45:8; 46:13; 51:5; 63:1).

Whereas Greek notions of *dikaiosynē* are related to the laws of nature and exercising justice in the *polis*, Hebrew notions are bound up with God and his workings (Seifrid 2004, 43-44). So, on the one hand, the translation of Hebrew words into a Greek equivalent meant that *dikaiosynē* acquired Hebraic associations with God's mercy and fidelity (Hill, 109) and designated conformity to the strictures of Israel's ancestral way of life (GELS). Thus, the Greek Scriptures do mediate Hebraic semantic content, especially when righteousness (*ṣədāqâ*) is translated as mercy (*eleos*) or when covenant love (*ḥesed*) is translated as righteousness (*dikaiosynē*), but not without escaping influence from Hellenistic conceptions of righteousness. That is because, on the other hand, the switch from Hebrew to Greek also meant that Hellenistic translators, readers, and auditors of Scripture were prone to import Greek notions of justice into their appropriation of Israel's Scriptures (Olley). There are Greek-Hebrew congruities on righteousness, demonstrated in the Hebrew Scripture's notion of God's punitive justice (e.g., Ps 50:6; 96:10-13; Is 59:16-21), which is not far removed from the Greek notion of distributive justice. Similarly, there are Hebrew-Greek contrasts on righteousness, for although the Greek translators of the Hebrew Scriptures never reduced *dikaiosynē* to a single concept such as "salvation"—the tendency was in fact to ethicize and judicialize the scriptural idioms—nonetheless, the salvific connotations of *dikaiosynē* were still preserved when context mediated it (Seifrid 2004, 51-52; Irons, 108-93). So rather than posit a stark contrast between Hebrew and Greek terms for righteousness (Dunn 1998, 341), it is more proper to say that the Greek Scriptures contain Greek words with possible Hebrew resonances (Irons, 75).

Coming to Hellenistic Jewish authors, Philo deploys *dikaiosynē* in a fundamentally ethical sense with connotations of justice and equality (*Her.* 162-63; *Mut.* 153; *Aet.* 108; *Mos.* 2.9). Justice is the most excellent human virtue, and it comes from the most excellent being, that is, God (*Spec.* 1.277). God is the chief source of virtue, with righteousness classified as one of the highest of virtues that avails before him (*Opif.* 81; *Mut.* 197; *Somn.* 1.179). Moses, says Philo, commanded the Israelites to practice justice, goodness, and virtue so that God might save them in their hour of need (*Virt.* 47). The Mosaic legislation calls for judges who rule in justice and "justice to assign to each according to his deserts" (*Spec.* 4.57). Noah avoided unrighteousness and by doing righteousness obtained divine favor (*Leg.* 3.77-78). For Philo, humans owe God *holiness and all people righteousness (*Abr.* 208; *Spec.* 2.63; 4.134; *Praem.* 162). At one point, Philo equates Israel's God with the actions of *Dikē*, the Greek goddess of justice (see Acts 28:4). Philo narrates how Flaccus, anti-Jewish Roman prefect of Egypt, was overthrown by *Dikē* because she was the "defender of the wronged." Speaking of Flaccus's assassination, Philo says that *Dikē* decreed in fairness that Flaccus should receive the same number of blows as Jews he had illegally put to death, which Philo furnished as proof that God had not deprived the Jews of his help (*Flacc.* 104, 189, 191).

Josephus too uses *dikaiosynē* predominantly in an ethical sense of virtue (*Ant.* 4.223), yet he also utilizes the *dik-* root words to accent punitive judicial measures far more than biblical accounts (e.g., *Ant.* 4.278 = Ex 21:22-23). Josephus connects *dikaiosynē* closely to God's character when he says that judges should judge justly because "God's strength is his justice" (*Ant.* 4.217) and describes Abel as a "lover of righteousness" who believed that "God was present in all of his virtuous acts" (*Ant.* 1.53). According to Josephus, God loved Noah because of his righteousness and despised others because of their wickedness (*Ant.* 1.75, 99). Reminiscent of Philo, Josephus places *dikaiosynē* in parallel to piety (*eusebeia*; *Ant.* 6.160, 265; 7.341; 8.120-121, 314; 10.50; 12.43). For Josephus, pious worship before God and doing justice before others (*Ant.* 15.376; 18.117; *Ag. Ap.* 2.291) is how one becomes "worthy of his providence" (*Ant.* 7.338) and obtains God's favor (*Ant.* 9.182; 11.139, 169). In one instance, Josephus makes a clear reversion to the Hebraic background when narrating Nicholas of Damascus's speech before Agrippa on behalf of the Ionian Jews: "And none of our customs is hateful to the human race. They are all pious and consecrated together with saving righteousness [*sōzousē dikaiosynē*]." The assertion is that Jewish practices are salvific in the sense that they contribute to the benefit of a city (*Ant.* 16.42).

In the NT, God's *dikaiosynē* is cognate with God's *dikaiōma* (righteous act, regulation, decree), *dikaiokrisia* (righteous judgment), and the role of someone as *dikaiosynos* (guardian of justice; BDAG; GE; outside Paul's letters, see Mt 6:33; Jas 1:20; 2 Pet 1:1). When Paul places *dikaiosynē* in relation to God, either syntactically or contextually, *dikaiosynē* pertains to the divine quality of righteousness, the rightness of a divine redemptive action, and its rectifying effect for believers (Rom 1:17; 3:21-26; 10:9-11; 1 Cor 1:30; 2 Cor 5:21; Phil 3:9). God's *dikaiosynē* expresses the exercise of executive privilege in conferring a salvific dividend on believers and the inherent rightness of God doing so (BDAG). Understood this way, God's *dikaiosynē* combines God's reputation for rightness with his redemptive plan to put persons right (Rom 3:21-26). To experience God's *dikaiosynē* is to be *edikaiōsen* (righteoused or justified) and means participating in *dikaiōsin* (justification or rectification), which is the opposite of *katakrima* (condemnation; Rom 3:24; 5:1, 15-19; 8:1, 30-34; 2 Cor 3:9). More precisely, when *dikaiosynē* is closely aligned with God it can describe a divine action characterized by the dispensing of the divine attribute of righteousness to believers who are thereafter considered righteous before God through union with Christ (Rom 3:22-24; 5:17; Phil 3:9; 2 Cor 5:21; Gal 2:17).

2. Jewish Background to Paul's "Righteousness of God" Language.

Paul's account of the righteousness of God is best related to the salvific sense of righteousness present in Jewish sources where there are discreet connections between God's saving activity and God's righteousness. That is not to make *righteousness* a mere synonym for *salvation*; more likely, God's salvation is an instance of God's righteousness (Ziesler, 41-42). Still, Paul's discussion of the righteousness of God is always nested in soteriological discourses and belongs to the semantics of salvation. That is valid given that, first, Pauline usage resonates closely with notions of Yahweh's victories, deliverance, and vindication manifested in scriptural accounts (Judg 5:11; 1 Sam 12:7; Mic 6:5; Ps 103:6; Dan 9:16). Second, there is the close parallel drawn between righteousness and deliverance in several texts in Isaiah, the Psalms, and postbiblical literature:

> Deliver me from bloodguilt, O God, O God of my salvation, and my tongue will sing aloud of your righteousness. (Ps 51:14)
>
> The LORD has made known his salvation, he has revealed his righteousness in the sight of the nations. He has remembered his mercy to Jacob, and his truth to the house of Israel; all the ends of the earth have seen the salvation of our God. (Ps 98:2-3)
>
> Hear my prayer, O LORD; give ear to my supplications in your faithfulness; answer me in your righteousness. Do not enter into judgment with your servant, for no one living is righteous before you. (Ps 143:1-2)
>
> Maintain justice and do what is right, for my salvation is close at hand and my righteousness will soon be revealed. (Is 56:1)
>
> As for me, if I stumble, the mercies of God shall be my eternal salvation. If I stagger because of the *sin of the *flesh, my justification shall be by the righteousness of God which endures forever. . . . He will draw me near by his *grace, and by his mercy will he bring my justification. He will judge me in the righteousness of his truth and in the greatness of his goodness and he will pardon all my sins. Through his righteousness he will cleanse me of all the uncleanness of man and of the sins of the children of men. (1QS XI, 11-15)
>
> For in this, O Lord, your righteousness and goodness will be declared, when you are merciful to those who have no store of good works. (2 Esd 8:36)

Evidently, then, righteousness is sometimes a description of God's salvation, but elsewhere righteousness is the basis for his salvation, and elsewhere again righteousness is the result of his salvation (see, e.g., Ps 31:1; 36:6; 72:2; 89:16; 103:17; 111:3; 119:40; 143:1, 11; 145:7; Is 42:21). In addition, there are other contexts where the righteousness of God takes on a punitive function (Seifrid 2001, 429-30; 2004, 58), so that the righteousness of God is expressed in enacting salvation for Israel by executing judgment against those who oppress Israel (Ex 9:27; Ps 98:9; 129:4; Is 1:27-28; 28:17; 59:16-21) or else in bringing judgment on Israel because of its unrighteousness and unfaithfulness (e.g., Ps 7:10-12; 50:6; 51:4; 143:2; Is 5:15-16; 10:22; Dan 9:7, 14). Thus, the Jewish tradition presents the righteousness of God within a web of associations connected to God's salvation and bound up with God's character, judgments, and justice. To speak of the righteousness of God in Jewish coordinates familiar to Paul is to say something about the righteousness of God's character and how he demonstrates his character as the judge of all the earth and in his faithfulness toward Israel. The righteousness of God becomes the character of God embodied and enacted in his saving actions, which means vindication for Israel and condemnation for the wicked (Bird, 15).

3. Patristic, Medieval, and Reformed Interpretation.

Patristic and medieval sources regarded the righteousness of God (*iustitia Dei* in Latin) as either a divine attribute (Ambrosiaster, Anselm) or a righteousness given to the believer (Augustine, Chrysostom). Though for Pelagius the righteousness of God was God's example of righteousness, Pseudo-Jerome and Julian of Eclanum designated the righteousness of God as God's distributive justice enabling the righteous to be rewarded, and Peter Abelard identified the righteousness of God as God's righteous recompense. Additionally, patristic and medieval scholars did not separate the remission of sins from sanctification; justification was a God-given gift and process to make the unrighteous become righteous. The medieval tradition also distinguished operative and cooperative grace, connected justification to a grace infused into the communicant through the sacraments to make them righteous, traded in notions of merit, insisted that final judgment was determined by works of charity, and left the faithful without a sense of assurance. Justification was both a communication of righteousness and the gradual conforming to righteousness (McGrath, 82-102; Fitzmyer, 259-63; Irons, 10-19).

German Reformer Martin Luther initially regarded the righteousness of God as God's distributive justice, a view popular among philosophical nominalists of the time. But in the course of preparing lectures of Romans, Luther came to the profound insight that the righteousness of God was in fact God's gracious provision of righteousness for sinners:

> I hated the expression "righteousness of God," for through the tradition and practice of all the doctors I had been taught to understand it philosophically, as the so-called "formal"—or, to us another word, "active"—righteousness through which God is just and punishes sinners and the unjust. But I could not love the righteous God, the God who punishes. I hated him. . . . I pondered incessantly, day and night, until I gave heed to the context of the words, namely: "for in the Gospel is the righteousness of God revealed, as it is written: the just shall live by faith." Then I began to understand the righteousness of God as a righteousness by which a just man lives as by a gift of God, that means by faith. I realized that it was to be understood this way: the righteousness of God is revealed through the Gospel, namely the so-called "passive" righteousness we receive, through which god justifies us by faith through grace and mercy. . . . Here I felt that I was altogether born again and had entered paradise itself through open gates. (*LW* 34:336-37, cited in George, 112-13)

Luther's breakthrough was a retrieval of Paul's *gospel, resourced in Augustinian tradition, and explained why the gospel was genuinely good news for sinners. Justification for Luther was not an internal renewal toward righteousness, but an alien righteousness imputed to the believer in Christ. Luther grasped Paul's anthropological pessimism with human slavery to sin, the distinction between a forensic justification and a separate moral transformation, and affirmed the believer's assurance. Even so, Luther's reading of Paul was often marked by a mixture of exegetical wisdom and tendentious anachronism. Subsequent Protestant theology with its emphasis on the gift of righteousness bruised the nerve that connected faith and obedience (Seifrid 2000, 175). Protestant commentators did not adequately grasp the social horizon where justification by faith was argued by Paul precisely to ensure that *Gentiles did not have to become Jews in order to become Christians and so safeguarded the unity of multiethnic churches. Subsequent Protestant articulations of the righteousness of God gradually became unmoored from Pauline harbors and drifted into systematic discussions about the relationship between justification, sanctification, and *election; a tripartite covenant structure; law versus gospel; Christ's active and passive obedience; the antitheses between faith and *works; and anti-Catholic polemics. Protestant articulations of the righteousness of God were mainly then concerned with connecting justification into a wider web of Protestant dogmatics rather than with a retrieval of Paul's teaching in its original setting.

4. Contemporary Scholarship.

In scholarship there are several perspectives for describing the righteousness of God and its meaning within Paul's letters.

4.1. Divine Attribute. The righteousness of God has often been regarded as God's own righteousness, while for some this implies too God's demonstration of his righteous character in his judgment, fidelity, and salvation. Here the righteousness of God is somewhere between a divine quality and a divine distribution of justice. This resonates with scriptural descriptions of God as righteous (e.g., Ps 11:7; 116:5) and with the medieval tradition's interpretation of the righteousness of God with God's upright character as umbilically related to his truthfulness and faithfulness. What is perhaps problematic here is that the righteousness of God is often regarded as the cause of justification by faith rather than its actual content.

4.2. Divine Gift. The predominant Protestant view has regarded the righteousness of God as the gift of righteousness given to the believer. The righteousness in the righteousness of God is a righteousness that avails before God, something given by God, and apprehended by faith. The righteousness of God is manifested as the validation of God's own righteousness and the vindicating status of righteousness that God graciously gifts to those with faith (Baur, 135-36; Bultmann; Seifrid 2000, 37-66; Westerholm, 284-86; Wolter, 334-37; Watson 2016, 43-47; Irons, 311-29; Schreiner, 66-78). Treating the righteousness of God as an objective genitive (i.e., a righteousness that enables one to stand before God) or a genitive of source (i.e., righteousness from God given to believers) is credible given

1. scriptural and Second Temple references to righteousness as something given or bestowed (Ps 106:31; Is 61:10; Jer 33:16; Bar 5:2, 9; Wis 12:16; Let. Aris. 280; Jub. 1.16; 16.26; 1QH IV, 17-23; XII, 37; XIV, 1-19);
2. Paul mentions a righteousness given explicitly *from* (*ek or apo*) God (Phil 3:9; 1 Cor 1:30);
3. he refers to being "freely justified" (Rom 3:24) and the "gift of righteousness" (Rom 5:15-17);
4. Paul talks of being righteous or justified *before* God (Gal 3:11; Rom 2:13; 3:20); and
5. the righteousness of God is either synonymous with or closely aligned with the "righteousness of faith" (Rom 4:11, 13; 9:30; 10:6; Phil 3:9).

In effect, then, the righteousness of God is a divinely approved righteousness that comes as a gift from God and makes one righteous before God. The righteousness of God means *homo iustificatus*, a person righteous before God (Wilckens, 204-5). The problem with this view is twofold. (1) There is the dilemma of how one shifts from God's punitive righteousness (*iustitia distributiva*; Rom 1:18; 3:5, 25-26) to righteousness as a gift (*homo iustificatus*; Rom 3:24; 5:18) without righteousness as salvation in Christ's *cross and *resurrection (*iustitia salutifera*; Rom 1:17; 3:21). (2) The righteousness of God as a gift becomes reducible to righteousness received by faith, that is, justification. Yet in some places where Paul mentions the righteousness of God he does not refer to "faith" (2 Cor 5:21), nor the language of "gift" (Rom 1:17), or else the righteousness of God is a mixture of divine power and authority in salvation (Rom 10:3). In addition, Paul's discourse about the righteousness of God incorporates a wider suite of motifs beyond justification by faith, including *peace, reconciliation, life, *forgiveness, transformation, and liberation. According to J. Dunn (1988, 386): "The 'righteousness of God' is nowhere conceived as a single, once-for-all action of God, but as his accepting, sustaining, and finally vindicating grace." While the righteousness of God is not less than justification by faith, it is certainly more than justification by faith.

4.3. Covenant Faithfulness. H. Cremer popularized the view that Paul's righteousness of God equates to God's covenant faithfulness. For Cremer, "righteousness" in Hebraic thought was a relational concept, not an abstract one, and God's righteousness stood in parallel to God's faithfulness (Ziesler, 36-43; Hill, 88-89, 93-98; Dunn, 1998, 342-44). The righteousness of God is God's covenant faithfulness to his promises and to Israel revealed in the gospel. In support of this view, Yahweh is righteous when he is true to himself, true to his covenant people, and delivers them as he promised to (Deut 32:4; Ps 89:14, 49; 96:13; 119:38; 143:1; Hos 2:19-20; Zech 8:8; *Jub.* 1.5-6). In Isaiah, the new David (Is 11:5), King Cyrus (Is 45:8, 13, 19), and the Servant of the Lord (Is 42:6) express God's faithfulness as chosen deliverers. Plus, *pistis* can be a specific instance of *dikaiosynē* in extra-Greek usage (e.g., Herodotus, *Hist.* 2.151; see Irons, 105-6). Paul does place the righteousness of God in proximity to God's faithfulness (Rom 3:3, 5), and God's faithfulness to his promises to the patriarchs is central to his gospel (Rom 15:8). There is also a long history of locating the righteousness of God amid God's faithfulness, including Ambrosiaster, Thomas Aquinas, Erasmus, Johannes Oecolampadius, English Puritan George Joye, Genevan theologian Jean-Alphonse Turretin, Swiss theologian K. Barth, and J. Dunn and N. T. Wright among scholars of the new perspective on Paul. New England pastor-theologian Jonathan Edwards commented: "God's righteousness here [Is 51:8], is meant his faithfulness in fulfilling his covenant promises to his church, or his faithfulness towards his church and people, in bestowing the benefits of the covenant of grace upon them" (*History of Redemption*, introduction 2.1).

Criticisms do abound (Westerholm, 286-96):

1. Seifrid observes that in the OT the words for "righteousness" (*ṣədāqâ*) and "covenant" (*berith*) rarely occur together (Is 42:6; 61:8-11; Hos 2:16-20; Ps 50:1-6; 111:1-10; Dan 9:4-7; Neh 9:32-33). More properly, someone keeps, remembers, establishes, forgets, or forsakes a covenant; someone is never said to act righteously toward it. Even if all covenant keeping is righteousness, not all righteousness is covenant keeping (Seifrid 2001, 423-24).
2. In addition, righteousness is not a relational concept (*Verhältnisbegriff*), nor reducible to the single idea of faithfulness to a community (*Gemeinschaftstreue*) or to the covenant (*Bundestreue*; Seifrid 2004, 43). Irons (106) rightly points to differentiating between lexis and discourse, so that righteousness does not mean faithfulness, as much as faithfulness can sometimes be a specific instance of righteousness (cf. Seifrid 2000, 40; Campbell 2013, 700-702; Schreiner, 75).
3. When Paul refers to God's fidelity he normally speaks of God's truthfulness (*alētheia*), faithfulness (*pistis*), or reliability (*bebaioō*), not *dikaiosynē*. Plus, in the one place where Paul does link *pistis* and *dikaiosynē* (Rom 3:3-5), it is connected to God's punitive judgment, so God is faithful in exercising justice rather than salvific righteousness (Irons, 273-79, 339).

4.4. Divine Saving Action. In the early twentieth century many scholars located the righteousness of God within biblical narrations of salvation, recognizing the righteousness of God as a "saving righteousness" (*iustitia salutifera*). J. Ropes identified the righteousness of God against a background in Isaiah, pertaining to God's vindicating power on behalf of the oppressed, rendering the righteousness of God as a divine attribute displayed in divine power for salvation. Similar perspectives were given by Dodd ("God vindicating the right, redressing wrong, and delivering men from the power of evil" [13]), Schlatter ("An act of God that reveals what God does for the believer and what God makes him to be" [21]), and Gorman ("saving and restorative justice of God . . . covenant faithfulness and saving power" [168]). This view trades in the Hebrew Scripture's periodic yet overwhelmingly salvific sense attributed to *ṣədāqâ*, which carries over to usage of *dikaiosynē* in the Greek Scripture, and is amplified when *ṣədāqâ* is translated in terms of divine mercy (*eleēmosynē* and *eleos* in Deut 6:25; 24:13; Ps 23:5; 102:6; Is 1:27; 56:1; 59:16 LXX). A salvific and spiritual sense of righteousness is replete across the Dead Sea Scrolls. The righteousness of God in Romans 1:17 is undoubtedly a subjective genitive, proximate to God's power (Rom 1:16), wrath (Rom 1:18), judgment (Rom 2:2-3, 5), kindness (Rom 2:4), faithfulness (Rom 3:5), and "truthfulness" (Rom 3:7); at the same time, the righteousness of God is something revealed by God in delivering persons, chiefly by bestowing them with a righteous status. This explains why Paul frequently parallels the righteousness of God with God's "salvation" and "power" (Rom 1:16-17; 10:9-11), "redemption" and "justification" (Rom 3:21-24), "reconciliation" (2 Cor 5:18-21), and participating in Christ and the resurrection (Phil 3:9-11). The righteousness of God, especially in Romans, perhaps echoing Ps 98:2; 143:2 (Hays; Campbell 2008), refers to God's saving action and its accompanying effect of giving the status of righteousness to believers (Rom 3:21-26; 4:1-8; 5:17-18; 10:9-10). The righteousness of God becomes the experience and effect of God's righteous character in action (Ziesler, 186-89; Fitzmyer, 257, 262; Bird, 15-16; Moo, 77-78).

There is room to dispute this view:

1. While righteousness and salvation overlap, they are not necessarily the same thing, both in the OT and in Paul (Westerholm, 284-86; Irons, 131-62).
2. When the OT speaks of God's saving righteousness, even that is an instance of God's judicial activity, with punitive and forensic connotations (Seifrid 2000, 43).
3. In Romans 1:17, though salvation and power stand behind the righteousness of God, they are not on the same semantic plane (Irons, 299-300).
4. When Paul ties the righteousness of God to Scripture, his go-to text is not Psalm 98:2, nor Isaiah 56:1, but Habakkuk 2:4, with righteousness mediated by faith (Watson 2016, 43-45).

4.5. Apocalyptic Deliverance. A variation of the saving-righteousness position are those scholars who specify the righteousness of God as denoting an *apocalyptic act of deliverance. The righteousness of God is something "revealed" (Rom 1:17), "made known" (Rom 3:21), an invasive cosmic act of rectification (Moore; Keck; Gaventa). E. Käsemann advocated that the righteousness of God was a technical term in apocalyptic texts designating God's salvation-creating power (see Deut 33:20; Is 26:10; Dan 9:16; T. Dan 6.10; 1QS X, 25; XI, 12-15; 1QM IV, 6; 1 En. 71.14; 99.10; 101.3; Bar 5.2, 9; 4 Ezra 8.36; T. Jud. 22.1-2). Where Paul differs from Judaism is that he invests the righteousness of God with a Christocentric focus, so that for Käsemann the righteousness of God is the gift and power of Christ's lordship over the believer, resulting in both justification from sin's penalty and liberation from sin's power (cf. Kertelge; Stuhlmacher 1965; Schreiner, 58-76). The righteousness of God "denotes God's activity of creating salvation and well-being for people," says Stuhlmacher, "God's own activity and the result of that activity" (2018, 369). Similarly, for D. Campbell the righteousness of God is a singular, eschatological, saving, liberating, and life-giving event whereby Christ is the definitive disclosure of God's righteousness and simultaneously the righteousness from God given to the believer (Campbell 2013, 667-711).

In criticism: (1) It is generally agreed that the righteousness of God was not a technical term in Jewish apocalyptic texts. (2) This view blurs the distinction between a forensic justification and a subsequent moral transformation. M. Seifrid (2004, 74) believes that justification and transformation are linked logically but not conceptually. Even if *marriage is a transformative union and more than just a legal status, it cannot happen without a legal status.

Not all commentators fit neatly into the above categories. Identifying the righteousness of God as a divine attribute, action, or status, seeing the righteousness of God related to creational justice, covenantal faithfulness, or cosmic rectification, are often combined in different schemes.

A. K. Grieb plots the righteousness of God in relation to God as Creator, God's covenant faithfulness to Israel, God's judgment to put things right for the poor, and God's saving faithfulness to restore all things in the end time (Grieb, 12, 19-25). Hence: "God's demonstration that the crucified Jesus of Nazareth is the risen Lord was the apocalyptic event in which the veil separating heaven from earth is torn in two or pulled aside, so that God's saving justice is evident to the whole world" (25).

For Seifrid, Paul's articulation of the righteousness of God refers to the event of Christ's cross and resurrection whereby the contention between the Creator and the fallen creature is decided in the Creator's favor and yet savingly resolved on the creature's behalf (Seifrid 2000, 63-66; 2004, 59, 63). For Seifrid, the righteousness of God is revealed in justification by faith, and justification is no mere verdict but is the execution of actual justice in Christ's cross and resurrection.

F. Thielman contends that Paul's use of the righteousness of God in Romans 1:17 displays God's intention to make salvation equally available to every ethnic group—Greeks, Jews, and barbarians—on the condition of faith. However, in Romans 1:18–3:5, Paul deploys righteousness language to demonstrate God's impartiality in judging all people on the basis of their deeds. Then, in Romans 3:21-26, the righteousness of God is both the righteous character of God and a powerful activity God whereby he bestows the gift of righteousness on the one who has faith. It is Christ's atoning death that bridges the gap between the pervasiveness of human wickedness and the declaration that such people are now righteous before God.

According to E. P. Sanders, the righteousness of God is Paul's assertion of God's uprightness that slides into the claim that God provides righteousness for people who put faith in Christ (Sanders, 609-11, 624-25, 672-73). The righteousness of God is a new and universal dispensation of pardoning where God "righteouses" believers. The problem with the Torah was that it does not lead to salvation through faith in Christ and being in Christ, which alone provides a new form of righteousness from God.

N. T. Wright affirms the covenant-faithfulness position: "'God's righteousness' referred to the great, deep plans which the God of the Old Testament had always cherished, the through-Israel-for-the-world plans, plans to rescue and restore his wonderful creation itself, and, more especially, to God's faithfulness to those great plans" (Wright 2009, 178). Yet in his broader exposition, Wright connects the righteousness of God to broader biblical depictions of right behavior, the law court, the covenant, and cosmic rectification (2013, 796-804, 1053-56).

U. Schnelle treats the righteousness of God as both a universal-forensic concept in the disclosure of God's eschatological saving justice (Rom 1:17; 3:5, 21, 25; 10:3) and expressing participation in the gift of righteousness (2 Cor 5:21; Rom 3:22; Phil 3:9; Schnelle, 318-21). The righteousness of God is simultaneously a "revelatory act and the act of the believer's incorporation and participation in God's justifying/rightwising act in Jesus Christ" (320).

5. Key Pauline Texts.
Discussion of the righteousness of God in Pauline thought cannot escape a close reading of his letters, which reveals the precise meaning of the phrase in Paul's specific arguments.

5.1. Romans 1:16-17. The central thesis of Romans is that gospel is God's power for salvation because the gospel is the divine unveiling of the righteousness of God for Jew and Greek, received by faith, in accordance with Habakkuk 2:4: "The righteous will live by faith." Here the righteousness of God is a subjective genitive; it is something belonging to God, parallel to God's "power" (Rom 1:16), "wrath" (Rom 1:18; 3:5), "judgment" (Rom 2:2-3, 5), "goodness" (Rom 2:4), "truthfulness" (Rom 3:7), and "faithfulness" (Rom 3:3). At the same time, Paul segues from God's own righteousness to a righteousness given from God, with the Habakkuk 2:4 citation stressing faith as the instrument for obtaining this righteousness (Campbell 2013, 683; Watson 2016, 43-47). Hence, the righteousness of God is a divine attribute and action, while humanly apprehended by faith. The righteousness of God signifies the fidelity and justice of God's character and how God demonstrates his character in the powerful saving event narrated in the gospel. The righteousness of God, then, is the character of God embodied and enacted in his saving actions and appropriated by faith. As John Chrysostom writes: "[This] righteousness, not thine own, but that of God; hinting also the abundance of it and the facility. For you do not achieve it by toilings and labors, but you receive it by a gift from above, contributing one thing only from your own store, 'believing'" (*Hom. Rom.* 2 [*NPNF*[1] 11:349]).

*5.2. **Romans 3:21-26.*** Paul exposits the proposition set forth in Romans 1:16-17 and brings resolution to his simultaneous affirmations of God's wrath against pagan *idolatry and immorality, God's impartiality in judging Jews and Gentiles, God's faithfulness to Israel, and God's salvation revealed singularly in Christ and not through Torah. In contrast to the unrighteousness of Gentiles and Jews (Rom 1:18, 29; 2:8; 3:5), God reveals his righteousness without requiring Torah observance even while the Torah and prophets prefigure it (e.g., Gen 15:6; Hab 2:4). The righteousness of God is revealed specifically through the "faith of Christ," that is, "the faith that pertains to God's saving action in Christ—originating in it, participating in it, and orientated towards it" (Watson 2007, 225). The saving event embodied in Christ comes to all believers without discrimination. This salvation is depicted using a courtroom metaphor (justification), a cultic metaphor (propitiation or mercy seat), and a commercial metaphor (redemption). The delay in the righteousness of God was not God's fickleness but his forbearance. In any case, the righteousness of God is shown now in God's prosecution of his contention against human sin in Christ's cross, which has the dual effect of vindicating God's just character and justifying those who put faith in Christ because Christ carries their sins away.

*5.3. **Romans 10:3-4, 9-11.*** Paul reasons that Israel's error lies in ignoring how the righteousness of God is manifested in Christ and how they improperly try to establish a righteous standing that avails before God based on their own Torah keeping, cultus, *purity, and *identity, whereas what they really need is the righteous status that God freely bestows by faith. The righteousness of God is posed here not as something gifted—one receives a gift; one does not submit to it—so the righteousness of God signifies God's own authority and action. The great tragedy is that Israel, despite its inherited privileges and notwithstanding its zeal for God, has become like the nations who "do not know God" because it did not submit to the righteousness of God in the Messiah. In this context *dikaiosynē* is repeatedly put in parallel with *sōtēria* (Rom 10:1, 3, 9-10) and connected to *pistis/pisteuō* (Rom 10:4-11).

*5.4. **2 Corinthians 5:21.*** Paul, defending his *ministry to the Corinthians, explains that his vocation as Christ's ambassador entails urgent kerygmatic and pastoral tasks, proclaiming reconciliation and new creation, and urging congregations to keep themselves in amicable relations with God. While God is reconciling the world to himself by not counting people's sins against them (2 Cor 5:19), the Corinthians, on account of their estrangement from Paul and the fractures among themselves, need to again be reconciled to God (2 Cor 5:20). Paul thus reminds them of what God has done for them: "For our benefit, he [God] made him [Christ] to be sin who knew no sin, so that in him we might become the righteousness of God" (2 Cor 5:21). In an instance of parallelism, Paul declares that Jesus was made to identify with what was alien to him (i.e., sin) so that we might identify with what is alien to us (i.e., righteousness). It is "in him," that is, *in Christ, that there is an "interchange" (Hooker) so that Christ is identified with human sin, and we are identified with the righteousness of God. The penalty of sin is borne away, and a status of righteousness is given to those who seek reconciliation with God. Here the righteousness of God is tantamount to either God's saving action or being declared righteous.

*5.5. **Philippians 3:9.*** Paul, in the midst of a section that is highly polemical against Jewish Christ-believing proselytizers, and yet intensely autobiographical too, contrasts a false righteousness attained from the Torah with a better righteousness attained in union with Christ (Phil 3:1-11). He says that to "gain Christ" is to "be in him" and to apprehend "a righteousness that is not my own and that does not come from the Torah but comes rather through the faithfulness of Christ, the righteousness from God that is based on faith" (Phil 3:9). Paul narrates how participation in Christ, as opposed to performance of Torah, is the pathway to receiving a right standing with God and righteous status from God. Paul narrates how Jesus' messianic fidelity (see Phil 2:8) reconstitutes a new people within himself, a people who participate in his death and resurrection and who receive righteousness (Phil 3:9) ahead of resurrection (Phil 3:10). This righteousness from God is received by entrusting oneself to Jesus' messianic faithfulness.

6. Conclusion.

Barclay notes how Pauline scholars can explain the righteousness of God in relation to diverse conceptual frames related to gift, power, promise, covenant, and apocalypse (Barclay, 474n65). Barclay is right that the righteousness of God is a "polyvalent phrase" that cannot be "given a single meaning or fitted into any one conceptual matrix" (cf. Ziesler, 186; Thielman, 47-48; Moo, 75; Schnelle, 318; Wright 2013, 802; Stuhlmacher 2018, 369). Though one may cautiously conclude that Paul's articulation of the righteousness of God is broadly that of a saving event, it is a saving righteousness demonstrated in Jesus' death and resurrection, expressive of God's own rightness and justice, which results in believers declared to be righteous in Christ. Beyond that one can observe that Paul's discourses involving the righteousness of God incorporate several motifs touching on God's attributes, saving actions, covenant faithfulness, justice, a gift, and the status of righteousness; the prominence of any one or more of these concepts will depend on the given literary context, any intertexts cited or alluded to, and the preunderstanding of readers. Scholars will continue to debate whether the righteousness of God encompasses the whole of Paul's theology (Stuhlmacher 2018, 371) or is central only in Romans (Schnelle, 321).

See also CORINTHIANS, SECOND LETTER TO THE; COVENANT; FAITH; GOD; JUDGMENT; JUSTIFICATION; PHILIPPIANS, LETTER TO THE; ROMANS, LETTER TO THE; SALVATION.

BIBLIOGRAPHY. **J. M. G. Barclay,** *Paul and the Gift* (Grand Rapids, MI: Eerdmans, 2017); **F. C. Baur,** *Paul, Apostle of Jesus Christ: His Life and Works, Epistles and Teachings* (Peabody, MA: Hendrickson, 2003); **M. F. Bird,** *The Saving Righteousness of God: Studies on Paul, Justification, and the New Perspective* (Milton Keynes, UK: Paternoster, 2007); **R. Bultmann,** "Dikaiosyne Theou," *JBL* 83 (1964): 12-16; **D. Burk,** "The Righteousness of God (*Dikaiosunē Theou*) and Verbal Genitives: A Grammatical Clarification," *JSNT* 34 (1964): 346-60; **D. A. Campbell,** "The Meaning of δικαιοσύνη γὰρ θεοῦ in Romans: An Intertextual Suggestion," in *As It Is Written: Studying Paul's Use of Scripture*, ed. S. E. Porter and C. D. Stanley (Atlanta: Society of Biblical Literature, 2008), 189-212; idem, *The Deliverance of God: An Apocalyptic Rereading of Justification in Paul* (Grand Rapids, MI: Eerdmans, 2013); **H. Cremer,** *Die Paulinische Rechtfertigungslehre im Zusammenhange ihrer geschicthlichen Voraussetzungen*, 2nd ed. (Gütersloh: Bertelsmann, 1900); **C. H. Dodd,** *The Epistle of Paul to the Romans* (London: Hodder & Stoughton, 1932); **J. D. G. Dunn,** *Romans 1–8* (Dallas: Word, 1988); idem, *The Theology of Paul the Apostle* (Edinburgh: T&T Clark, 1998); **J. A. Fitzmyer,** *Romans: A New Translation with Introduction and Commentary*, AB (New York: Doubleday, 1993); **B. R. Gaventa,** *When in Romans: An Invitation to Linger with the Gospel According to Paul* (Grand Rapids, MI: Baker, 2016); **T. George,** "Martin Luther," in *Reading Romans Through the Centuries: From the Early Church to Karl Barth*, ed. J. P. Greenman and T. Larsen (Grand Rapids, MI: Brazos, 2005), 101-19; **J. Goldingay,** *The Theology of the Book of Isaiah* (Downers Grove, IL: InterVarsity Press, 2011); **M. J. Gorman,** *Apostle of the Crucified Lord: A Theological Introduction to Paul and His Letters*, 2nd ed. (Grand Rapids, MI: Eerdmans, 2017); **A. K. Grieb,** *The Story of Romans: A Narrative Defense of God's Righteousness* (Louisville: Westminster John Knox, 2002); **R. B. Hays,** "Psalm 143 and the Logic of Romans 3," *JBL* 99 (1980): 107-15; **M. D. Hooker,** "On Becoming the Righteousness of God: Another Look at 2 Corinthians 5:21," *NovT* 50 (2008): 358-75; **D. Hill,** *Greek Words and Hebrew Meanings: Studies in the Semantics of Soteriological Terms* (Cambridge: Cambridge University Press, 1967); **C. L. Irons,** *The Righteousness of God: A Lexical Examination of the Covenant-Faithfulness Interpretation*, WUNT 2/386 (Tübingen: Mohr Siebeck, 2015); **E. Käsemann,** "'The Righteousness of God' in Paul," in *New Testament Questions of Today* (Philadelphia: Fortress, 1969), 168-82; **L. E. Keck,** *Paul and His Letters* (Philadelphia: Fortress, 1979); **K. Kertelge,** *Rechtfertigung bei Paulus* (Münster: Aschendorff, 1967); **A. McGrath,** *Iustitia Dei: A History of the Christian Doctrine of Justification*, 4th ed. (Cambridge: Cambridge University Press, 2019); **D. J. Moo,** *The Letter to the Romans*, 2nd ed. (Grand Rapids, MI: Eerdmans, 2019); **R. K. Moore,** *Paul's Concept of Justification: God's Gift of a Right Relationship* (Eugene, OR: Wipf & Stock, 2015); **J. W. Olley,**

Righteousness in the Septuagint of Isaiah: A Contextual Study (Missoula, MT: Scholars Press, 1979); **J. H. Ropes,** "'Righteousness' and 'the Righteousness of God' in the Old Testament and in St. Paul," *JBL* 22 (1903): 211-27; **E. P. Sanders,** *Paul: The Apostle's Life, Letters, and Thought* (Minneapolis: Fortress, 2015); **A. Schlatter,** *Romans: The Righteousness of God* (Peabody, MA: Hendrickson, 1995); **U. Schnelle,** Apostle Paul: His Life and Theology (Grand Rapids, MI: Baker, 2005); **T. R. Schreiner,** *Romans,* 2nd ed. (Grand Rapids, MI: Baker, 2018); **M. A. Seifrid,** *Christ, Our Righteousness: Paul's Theology of Justification* (Downers Grove, IL: InterVarsity Press, 2000); idem, "Righteousness Language in the Hebrew Scriptures," in *Justification and Variegated Nomism,* vol. 1, *The Complexities of Second Temple Judaism,* ed. D. A. Carson, P. T. O'Brien, and M. A. Seifrid (Grand Rapids, MI: Baker, 2001), 415-42; idem, "Paul's Use of Righteousness Language Against Its Hellenistic Background," in *Justification and Variegated Nomism,* vol. 2, *The Paradoxes of Paul,* ed. D. A. Carson, P. T. O'Brien, and M. A. Seifrid (Grand Rapids, MI: Baker, 2004), 39-74; **D. Southall,** *Rediscovering Righteousness in Romans: Personified Dikaiosynē Within Metaphoric and Narratorial Settings* (Tübingen: Mohr Siebeck, 2008); **P. Stuhlmacher,** *Gerechtigkeit Gottes bei Paulus* (Göttingen: Vandenhoeck & Ruprecht, 1965); idem, *Biblical Theology of the New Testament* (Grand Rapids, MI: Eerdmans, 2018); **F. Thielman,** "God's Righteousness as God's Fairness in Romans 1:17: An Ancient Perspective of a Significant Phrase," *JETS* 54 (2011): 35-48; **F. Watson,** *Paul, Judaism, and the Gentiles: Beyond the New Perspective* (Grand Rapids, MI: Eerdmans, 2007); idem, *Paul and the Hermeneutics of Faith,* 2nd ed. (London: T&T Clark, 2016); **S. Westerholm,** *Perspectives Old and New on Paul: The "Lutheran" Paul and His Critics* (Grand Rapids, MI: Eerdmans, 2004); **U. Wilckens,** *Der Brief an die Römer* (Neukirchen-Vluyn: Neukirchener Verlag, 1978); **M. Wolter,** *Paul: An Outline of His Theology* (Waco, TX: Baylor University Press, 2015); **N. T. Wright,** *Justification: God's Plan and Paul's Vision* (Downers Grove, IL: InterVarsity Press, 2009); idem, *Paul and the Faithfulness of God* (London: SPCK, 2013); **J. A. Ziesler,** *The Meaning of Righteousness in Paul* (Cambridge: Cambridge University Press, 1972).

M. F. Bird

RISING WITH CHRIST. *See* Baptism; Cruciformity; In Christ; Resurrection; Spirituality.

ROADS AND HIGHWAYS. *See* Travel in the Roman World.

ROMAN CHRISTIANITY

Consideration of how Rome in the republic and early principate sought to regulate foreign cult is useful for helping us understand the challenges Paul and the house churches in Rome faced as they worshiped the God of Israel and this God's Messiah. Paul's description of how the Roman churches' faith is known throughout the world and his references to what the Roman believers were initially taught indicate that Christianity in Rome probably had a distinct character (Rom 1:8; 6:17; 16:17). It is thus worth investigating and learning as much as possible about Roman Christianity, in order to understand what in Paul's letter to the Romans is integral to his gospel and what is adapted or added to communicate effectively with believers in the capital of the empire.

1. Roman Policies and Attitudes to Foreign Religions
2. Roman Christianity

1. Roman Policies and Attitudes to Foreign Religions.

As one of the later foreign religions to seek entrance into Rome, Christianity inherited stereotypes and government policies developed from past encounters between the Roman government and foreign religions. Any study of church-state relations not only must begin with the state cult of Rome but also must include the reception Rome gave to the foreign cult that antedated Christianity.

1.1. Introduction of Foreign Cults into Republican Rome. It is first of all necessary to make clear that foreign cults could not be introduced in Rome without official approval from the senate. In the late republic and early *empire, Rome viewed the worship of the gods as a concern of the state. Since the late republic, Rome looked at all foreign cults with suspicion. At the same time, it was ready to attempt the introduction of foreign cult when it perceived that such cult offered a solution to an unmet need in Rome. For example, the Asclepius cult (known in Rome as Aesculapius) was brought from Epidaurus to Rome when in 293 BCE the priests who kept the Sibylline Books called for its introduction to quell a plague in Rome. Its temple on the island of Tiber was dedicated on January 1, 291 BCE. The minor deity Hygieia was also worshiped there, to whom the Romans later attached the name of their Italian goddess, Salus.

The official importation of new cult did not mean that state cult was somehow abandoned. There was actually no mechanism in Roman government or its established priesthoods for abolishing any traditional practice. Rather, new cults were brought to Rome and new interpretations of state cult were made as history progressed. Exclusive *worship of only one deity, such as was found in Judaism and Christianity, was therefore unheard of to the traditional Roman. In 186 BCE the Roman senate acted to forbid the practice of the Dionysian *orgia*, or *bacchanalia*, as they are called in Latin. This cult had entered Rome from Campanian Italy. In response to the senate's measures (CIL 1:196; ILS 18), the people of Rome reacted violently, and an outbreak of crime spread through the city (Livy, *Hist.* 39.8-18). This incident, known now as the Bacchanalia, helped shape the Roman stereotype that foreign cult would be likely to bring disorder. It stands to reason, then, that when Christianity entered Rome it was viewed with suspicion.

1.2. Judaism in Rome. Judaism had been treated as a legal cult (*religio licita*) by Julius Caesar and then Augustus. This meant that the Jewish people were given permission to meet for religious purposes in their synagogues, and the Jews' observance of the Sabbath could not be used to their disadvantage. It is true that Jews were expelled from Rome in 139 BCE (Valerius Maximus, *Fact. dict.* 1.3.2), in 19 CE (Josephus, *Ant.* 18.3.5 §§81-84; Tacitus, *Ann.* 2.85.5; Suetonius, *Tib.* 36; Cassius Dio, *Hist.* 57.18.5), and in 49 CE (Suetonius, *Claud.* 25.4; Acts 18:1-2). The first two cases were probably a Roman response to active proselytizing by the Jews; the third was probably due to unrest within the Jewish community about Christianity (on the basis of Suetonius's "at the instigation of Chrestus" [*impulsore Chresto*]). But these expulsions were not permanent measures and at least in the latter two cases probably did not apply to Jews who were Roman citizens.

It is also necessary to realize that some of the synagogues in Rome were closely tied to Judaism and to Jews with political authority in *Jerusalem. Around 140 BCE the high priests in Jerusalem had sent emissaries to Rome in order to offset the power of the Seleucid Empire. Later, ruling priests in the first century BCE politically endorsed Julius Caesar (and not Pompey, who had entered the *temple in 63 BCE), and Herod the Great was in political alliance with Augustus. In the first century CE princes in the family of Herod such as Agrippa II (who would later hold the rights of appointing high priests in Jerusalem) were raised in Rome under imperial patronage. At least one or more forms of Judaism in Rome therefore at different times had close ties with cultic and political leaders in Jerusalem. And it was within the synagogues of Rome that Christianity first gained its inroads in the imperial capital.

2. Roman Christianity.

Although Christianity first appeared as a sect of Judaism, the Roman *church by the time of Paul's initial visit (ca. 60 CE) was beginning to make the break with Judaism, a break that must have been complete by 64 CE, when Nero focused persecution on Christians. The churches in Rome represented a body of Christianity that Paul could not ignore. Their strategic potential came from their close connection with Jerusalem, their location in the world capital, and their connections with the rest of the empire through people groups represented in Rome's congregations.

2.1. Origins. The connection between the Jews in Rome and Jerusalem and the Jewish element within early Roman Christianity lead to the probable conclusion that Christianity was brought to Rome by Jewish Christians from Palestine. This is supported by the note that Jews from Rome were in Peter's audience in Jerusalem at Pentecost (Acts 2:10). Jewish Christians most probably entered into dialogue with fellow Jews, and this resulted in tumultuous encounters and some conversions. One such encounter occurred in 49 CE, when Claudius expelled the Jews from Rome. Suetonius's brief description of this event (see 1.2 above) is generally taken to mean that the Jews were arguing among themselves about *Christ. The identification of Priscilla and Aquila as Jewish Christians who left Italy when Claudius expelled the Jews from Rome supports this reconstruction (Acts 18:2).

It is generally accepted that Christianity in Rome arose not in a single church but in a plurality of house churches. The Jewish component in early Roman Christianity suggests that these house churches may have developed in association with various synagogues. Evidence for this plurality of churches comes from Paul's greeting given not to a church (see 1 Cor 1:2; 2 Cor 1:1) but to "all those who are in Rome, beloved of God, chosen saints" (Rom 1:7). Peter Lampe's focus on "the fractionation of Roman Christianity" (Lampe, 357-408) ignores the pluriform beginnings of what is now called Christianity in Rome. Since Christianity probably entered Rome through some of its synagogues and by apostolic *witness, the question is not how Christianity could stay unified within second-century Rome, but how an established church emerged from the various Jewish and *Gentile assemblies in Rome that called on the *name of Jesus.

2.2. Characteristics. The Jewish presence in the Roman church and its ascetic element (see 2.2.3 below) presented both challenges and opportunities for Paul. The *slaves who made up part of this church did not deter him from scaling theological heights in the presentation of his *gospel, since Paul held that in Christ there is no slave or free (Gal 3:28) and considered himself bound to communicate his gospel to all (Rom 1:14-15).

2.2.1. Jewish Presence. Because of its likely origin in the synagogues of Rome, Jewish Christianity retained a close connection with its Jewish roots in Jerusalem. Paul's letter to the church is evidence for this (Rom 1:16; 3:1-30; 9–11). Half a century later, when Tacitus describes Christianity, he links it to Judea (Tacitus, *Ann.* 15.44.2). Roman Christianity must have included a distinctly Jewish element. Theologically, such a presence within the churches most representative of the world's peoples forced Paul to outline his gospel in a manner that accounted for God's dealings with all people (Rom 2:1-16; 15:7-13). Apologetically, a letter and visit to this church provided opportunities for Paul to defend himself to people with close ties to the groups that most criticized and resisted Paul's *ministry, the Judaism and Christianity of Jerusalem. Thus one sees Paul working to defend before the Romans his theology (Rom 6:1-2) and mission strategy (Rom 15:14-24). His upcoming visit to Jerusalem is explained and addressed to them as a worthwhile and spiritual endeavor (Rom 15:25-32). While Roman Christianity was primarily composed of Gentiles, as Paul's letter shows, it is probable that there was an ethnically Jewish presence in the Roman churches.

2.2.2. Servile Presence. Since many Jews first came to Rome as slaves, it is likely that some of the Jews within the Roman churches were of the servile classes (either slaves or freedmen and freedwomen). The slaves in Rome were primarily of foreign origin in the first century of the principate. While there were certainly some freeborn foreigners in Rome, the possibility that many were servile foreigners fits with Suetonius's conviction that Nero administered Roman law properly when crucifying Christians (Suetonius, *Nero* 16.2; 19.3), since Roman law prohibited crucifixion of its citizens. Further evidence for the servile nature of the Roman church is the references to those of certain "*households" (Rom 16:10-11), a standard euphemism for the slaves and former slaves of a Roman *domus*.

2.2.3. Asceticism. Giorgio La Piana suggests an ascetic element within the first-century Roman church. This seems fully in accord with extrabiblical evidence and indications in Paul's letter to the Romans. Vegetarianism was taught in the school of Quintus Sextius in the early first century. The philosopher Sotion led Seneca to practice vegetarianism for a time (Seneca, *Ep.* 108.22). Another philosopher who was very influential during the reign of Nero, Musonius Rufus, also taught vegetarianism (*Peri Trophēs*). Vegetarianism is reflected in *1 Clement* 20.4, while asceticism in dress is mentioned in 17.1 of the same letter. Biblical evidence for asceticism in Roman Christianity comes from Hebrews 13:9 and Romans 14:1-3, 21. In the latter reference the "*strong" and "weak" are differentiated within the Roman church by different postures toward ascetic practice. The mind/*body dualism common to ascetics is found in Romans 1:24; 6:19; 7:23-24; 12:1-2. Later one sees the ascetic tendencies of Roman Christianity worked out in one of its leaders, Tatian (flor. in Rome ca. 160–172 CE). The ascetic movement within the Roman church at the time Paul wrote his letter prompted him to delineate an ethic of responsibility in which the "strong" in conscience was to respect the "weak," more ascetic, Christian (Rom 14:14-17; 15:1-3).

2.3. Influence. By the time Paul wrote Romans, it is clear that the Roman church was ascendant in influence among churches of the Mediterranean world. Paul's uncharacteristic desire to visit the church in Rome that he had not founded is evidence of this (Rom 1:9-13; see Rom 15:20). His desire for the Roman church's endorsement and support (Rom 15:22-24) can be interpreted as a response to the influence that this church carried in the Mediterranean world. Extrabiblical evidence for the influence of Rome comes as early as 96 CE, when a letter from the church at Rome to the church at Corinth, *1 Clement*, was written. In this letter one sees the Roman church expecting its directives to its sister church in *Corinth to be followed (*1 Clem.* 7.1-3; 62.1-3; 65.1, cf. Ign. *Rom.*, introduction).

2.4. Paul's Relationship with Roman Christianity. Though the church in Rome was not founded by an *apostle, Paul is associated with its early history. As apostle to the Gentiles, he considered this within his sphere of ministry (Rom 1:11-15). His relationship with Roman Christianity certainly bore fruit from his presence there and continues to do so through his letter to the Romans.

2.4.1. Before 60 CE. One's understanding of the relationship that Paul had with Roman Christianity before his visit in 60 CE affects not only one's conception of early church history but also one's interpretation of the letter to the Romans. For if Paul knew some of the Roman Christians and the circumstances of the churches there, his letter must be read not simply as a general theological treatise but as an occasional letter to a particular body of believers. While it is true that Romans is the most systematic of Paul's letters, its occasional nature cannot be denied. The influence that Roman Christianity enjoyed likely meant that Christians throughout the empire knew something about the Roman churches. Paul's statement "Your *faith is announced throughout the whole world" (Rom 1:8) is certainly more than epistolary flattery. Paul met Christians from Rome at least by 50 CE, after Aquila and Priscilla had come to Corinth from Rome (Acts 18:1-2; see Rom 16:3-5). Christians in Pauline circles no doubt had associations with other Christians in Rome. The best evidence for this is Romans 16. While this chapter has been assigned an Ephesian destination by T. W. Manson, later works by Harry Gamble, Peter Lampe, and Wolf-Henning Ollrog have conclusively demonstrated the integrity of this chapter as a part of the original letter. On the basis of Romans 16, then, it is most probable that Paul knew a number of people in Rome. The letter was written in order to strengthen an already existing relationship.

2.4.2. After 60 CE. Paul arrived in Rome circa 60 CE (Acts 28:14-16) in order to stand trial before Nero's representative, the Praetorian prefect. By the time Paul arrived in Rome, Nero had murdered his mother, his adviser Burrus had died, and Seneca had retired. The imperial government was not as stable as in the earlier part of Nero's reign. According to *tradition, Paul was freed after his first trial. From *1 Clement*'s testimony that Paul "reached the limits of the West" (*1 Clem.* 5.7), it is possible that Paul then reached Spain as intended (Rom 15:24). It is then most likely that Paul was arrested and imprisoned again at Rome, where he was executed sometime between 64 and 67 CE. *First Clement* 5.2-5, in citing "pillars of the church," mentions *Peter first and then Paul as examples of endurance under *suffering. Today one can see a carving of both apostles baptizing their jailers in the Mamertine Prison (Rome's state prison), another testimony to the tradition that both men suffered for their faith in Rome. The details of Paul's second trial (if he had one) and martyrdom are unknown. Tradition says that he was beheaded on the Ostian Way at about the same time and place as Peter (Eusebius, *Hist. eccl.* 2.25.7-8). While the account of milk spurting out of his beheaded body is obviously legendary (Acts of Paul 11.5), Paul's association with Roman Christianity continues to provide both milk and solid food (1 Cor 3:2) for Christians throughout the world.

See also CITIZENSHIP; EMPIRE; HOUSEHOLDS AND HOUSEHOLD CODES; LEGAL SYSTEM, ROMAN; PASTORAL EPISTLES; POLITICAL SYSTEMS; RELIGIONS, GRECO-ROMAN; ROMANS, LETTER TO THE.

BIBLIOGRAPHY. **M. Beard and M. Crawford,** *Rome in the Late Republic* (London: Duckworth, 1985), 25-39; **R. E. Brown and J. P. Meier,** *Antioch and Rome: New Testament Cradles of Catholic Christianity* (New York: Paulist, 1983); **F. L. Cross and E. A. Livingstone,** eds., "Tatian," in *Oxford Dictionary of the Christian Church*, 3rd ed. (Oxford: Oxford University Press, 1997), 1579; **H. Gamble Jr.,** *The Textual History of the Letter to the Romans* (Grand Rapids, MI: Eerdmans, 1977); **P. Garnsey and R. Saller,** *The Roman Empire: Economy, Society and Culture* (Berkeley: University of California Press, 1987); **G. La Piana,** "La primitiva communitá cristiana di Roma e l'epistola ai Romani," *Ricerche Religiose* 1 (1925): 209-26, 305-26; idem, "Foreign Groups in Rome During the First Centuries of the Empire," *HTR* 20 (1927): 183-403; **P. Lampe,** *From Paul to Valentinus: Christians at Rome in the First Two Centuries*, trans. M. Steinhauser (Minneapolis: Fortress, 2003); **H. J. Leon,** *The Jews of Ancient Rome* (Philadelphia: Jewish Publication Society of America, 1960); **T. W. Manson,** "St. Paul's Letter to the Romans—and Others," in *The Romans Debate*, ed. K. P. Donfried (Minneapolis: Augsburg, 1978), 1-16; **J. A. North,** "Conservatism and Change in Roman Religion," *Papers of the British School at Rome* 44 (1976): 1-12; idem, "Religion in Republican Rome," in *Cambridge Ancient History*, vol. 7.2, *The Rise of Rome to 220 B.C.* (Cambridge: Cambridge University Press, 1990), 573-624; **W.-H. Ollrog,** "Die Abfassungsverhältnisse von Röm 16," in *Kirche*, ed. D. Lührmann and G. Strecker (Tübingen: Mohr, 1980), 221-44.

M. Reasoner

ROMAN CITIZENSHIP. *See* CITIZENSHIP.

ROMAN LEGAL SYSTEM. *See* LEGAL SYSTEM, ROMAN.

ROMAN POLITICAL SYSTEM. *See* EMPIRE; POLITICAL SYSTEMS; POLITICS AND POWER.

ROMAN RELIGION. *See* RELIGIONS, GRECO-ROMAN.

ROMANS, LETTER TO THE

Paul's letter to the Romans is the most influential biblical text in the history of Christian theology, shaping the theologies of the Cappadocians,

Augustine, Aquinas, Luther, Calvin, the Anabaptists, Wesley, Edwards, Hodge, and Barth. All Pauline theology is more or less a theology of Romans (Dunn 1998; Wright 2013; Gorman, "Pauline Theology"), most *gospel preaching and evangelism are rooted in Romans, most church statements of *faith and confessions are formed from Romans, and the theology of Romans is what many congregants hear from the pulpit. Much of these various audiences remain oblivious to the intense debates about Romans today (Donfried; McKnight, "Paul and Romans"; McKnight and Modica; Bowens, McKnight, and Modica).

1. Author, Date, and Audience
2. Purpose
3. Contemporary Discussions
4. Context
5. The Letter

1. Author, Date, and Audience.

1.1. Authorship. One of the rare indisputables in Pauline studies is that Paul wrote Romans (Rom 1:1), though this letter also states that it was Tertius who actually inscribed the letter (Rom 16:22). Paul inscribed none of his *letters, though at times he did pick up the pen and write a few lines (Philem 19; Richards).

1.2. Date. Paul's letters, combined with the Acts of the Apostles, have enough details to piece together a reasonable sketch of the life of Paul, though debates lead most of the conclusions to be held with less than certainty (Riesner 1997; 2011). Use of the Acts of the Apostles is disputed, so some concentrate only on the Pauline letters (Campbell 2014). One makes cases for dates or conclusions about the following (as outlined by careful methodological scholar R. Riesner in his 2011 work):

1. the date of Jesus' crucifixion (AD 30);
2. the experience of Saul on the road to Damascus (AD 31/32);
3. the flight from Damascus and the mentioning of King Aretas IV, who died in AD 40 (2 Cor 11:32; Hengel and Schwemer);
4. Agrippa I's persecutions of followers of the Way (Acts 12:1-2; ca. AD 41/42);
5. the famine under Claudius (AD 44-46);
6. the Cypriot proconsul of Sergius Paulus (Acts 13:6-12; Riesner 2011, 12-13);
7. Claudius's edict to expel Judeans (or Judean Christians) from Rome in what appears to be AD 49 (Acts 18:2; Suetonius, *Claud.* 25.4), while Dio Cassius places perhaps an earlier expulsion in 41 (*Hist.* 60.6.6);
8. Gallio's proconsulship in AD 51 (Acts 18:12-17);
9. Paul's time in *Ephesus, where the term *anthypatoi*, a general term for a proconsul-like authority, is used (Acts 19:38), perhaps indicating the lack of a clear appointment after the death of Claudius in AD 54 and the murder of Silanus (Riesner 2011, 14-15), and where Paul probably was imprisoned (Rom 16:4, 7; 2 Cor 1:8-10; Trebilco, 83-87);
10. the trip to *Jerusalem and trials under Felix and then Festus (AD 59); and
11. a mixture of details from his letters and the Acts of the Apostles (Riesner 2011, 10-22), including the details of Galatians 1–2 as well as what is found in 1–2 Corinthians and Romans 15. One needs to examine with care 1 Corinthians 16:1-4; 2 Corinthians 8–9; Romans 13:6-7; 15:25-32 to date these letters.

Here is my reconstruction, a slight modification of Riesner, of the order and dates of Paul's letters:

1. 1–2 Thessalonians (ca. AD 50)
2. 1 Corinthians (AD 54, from Ephesus)
3. letters from the *prison time in Ephesus in circa AD 53–55 (Philippians, Philemon, Colossians, perhaps Ephesians)
4. 2 Corinthians (AD 55–56 from Macedonia)
5. Romans (AD 57 from Cenchreae; after 2 Corinthians because of Rom 15:25-32; Longenecker 2011, 46-51)

One needs then to add to these Paul's arrest in Jerusalem (AD 57), imprisonment in Caesarea Maritima (AD 57–59), travel to Rome (AD 59), imprisonment in Rome in AD 60–62, travel to Spain (?), and in about AD 63–64 rearrest, trials, and martyrdom, or perhaps release and the Pastoral Epistles in the mid-60s AD.

1.3. Audience. Was Romans sent to a mixed set of assemblies in Rome, to mostly Judean Christians of Rome, or mostly (or even only) to the *Gentile assemblies in Rome? Christianity was established in Rome among Judean believers, and they were active in gospeling in the synagogues, probably in poorer sections of Rome (today's Trastevere, along the Via Appia, perhaps on the Aventine, Mars Field, and Via Lata/Flaminia; Lampe). That Judean believers were in the audience of this letter makes best sense of "to the Judean first" theme (Rom 1:16) and Paul's "I am speaking to those who know the *law" in Romans 7:1; his pastoral emotion for Judeans (Rom 9:1-5; 10:1-4); the potency of his interrogations in Romans 2–4; 9–11; and his extensive use of the OT in those six chapters (Longenecker 2011, 75-78). Yet, it is clear, too, that he speaks to Gentile believers, especially in Romans 11:13, "Now I am speaking to you Gentiles," and in Romans 1:5, "among all the Gentiles." This is followed up in Romans 1:6 with "including yourselves" (also Rom 15:7-12). It is hard to make sense of an expulsion of Judean Christians from Rome and there being Christians in Rome after it—assuming there were—without the Gentile believers then becoming the leaders. (I use the term *Judean* because the Greek term is *Ioudaios* and refers to a person from the area called Judea.)

Some of these conclusions have led a school of thought to argue the entire letter was sent to Gentile believers, some of whom had become convinced of their so-called Judeanness because they were as committed to Torah observance as nonbelieving observant Judeans (Nanos 1996; 2018; Rodriguez; Rodriguez and Thiessen). Most noticeable is the back and forth between *strong and weak in Romans 14:1–15:13, which on nearly all accounts is about both Gentile and Judean believers (Dunn 2015; *contra* Longenecker 2011, 75-91, 141-47). This indicates that Romans was sent to both Judean and Gentile believers. Scholars differ on whether it has more of a Judean or Gentile makeup, but the view that it had a synagogue origin and then shifted to a Gentile flavor after the expulsion of Claudius still makes most sense (Wiefel; Longenecker 2011). (See more below in section 4.)

2. Purpose.

The array of apparent purposes, some of which are mentioned immediately below, makes one wary about narrowing Romans to one purpose, as some have done. A. Wedderburn's informed analysis admits it is an "enigma" and that there is "no consensus" (1) and wisely concludes that there is more than one reason for the letter: "The reasons for Romans are thus a cluster of different interlocking factors: the presence of both Judaizing and law-free Christians in the church there, the present situation of the church in Rome and the present situation of Paul, the visit to Jerusalem now being undertaken and the prospect of a future visit to Rome" (142). Yet, there might be a gradation of levels for the multitude of proposals for the purpose of the letter (esp. Longenecker 2011, 92-166; Donfried). Tied into purpose is the genre of the letter, though scholarship simply has not come to anything resembling a consensus on genre (Aune).

The letter is loaded with (1) theology, (2) constructed opponents, (3) responses to their constructed questions, and (4) the (assumed) history of the apostle's engagement with challenges to his apostolic *mission to the Gentiles (Rom 1:8-16; 11:13-15, 25-26; 15:18-24, 28), which created churches without regard to status or gender or *ethnicity (Gal 3:28). As such, the letter is a real letter sent by a real *apostle to a real church with real problems. Thus, it is wisest to see the letter as having at least the following general purposes: theological, pastoral (Rom 1:8-15; 12; 14:1–15:13; 15:14–16:27), missionary (Rom 15:24, 28), apologetic (Rom 1:16; 3:8), and polemical (Rom 2–4; 9–11; 16:17-20). One is hard-pressed to read Romans 2–4 or Romans 9–11 without thinking Paul is laying out what he has heard in his missionary work and responding now with his best answers (e.g., Dunn 2015; Campbell 2013; contra Stowers). Those challenges revolved around *God's *election of Israel, the *Ioudaioi* (Judeans), the history of God's work with Israel, the inevitable boasting it promoted, and the place of *Abraham and the centrality of faith. Each of these are challenges to his Gentile mission without requiring strict Torah observance, and for each challenge and more he has biblically grounded and theologically extrapolated responses. This is level one, the most general purpose of Romans. Even if delineation of a specific kind of letter (ambassadorial, etc.) is indetectable, the genre of Romans *as a letter* matters as well to reading Romans well (Jervis; Weima). One must be careful neither to ignore the opening and closing of the letter nor to exaggerate what one finds there—all the key themes of the purpose of the letter (as Longenecker 2011, 128-30, 136-60).

Level two of the purpose of Romans can get more specific. Some (Martin Luther, John Calvin) have contended the letter is a rather timeless dogmatics in outline for a church Paul has not yet visited, and it would be accurate to summarize most of its use in theological history as "the first systematic theology" (Longenecker 2011, 95). Yet, there are too many themes in Paul's own theology that are either unmentioned or undeveloped to see Romans as an abstract of his theology (future *eschatology; *Christology, as one finds in Phil 2:6-11 or Col 1:15-20; Eucharist; *resurrection). The suggestion that Romans is Paul's last will and testament or précis of his apology when on trial in either Jerusalem or Caesarea falls short for the same reason (Bornkamm; Jervell), though one needs to recognize that this letter does bundle some of the most important elements in Paul's theology. Too many proposals for the purpose of Romans mistakenly argue that Paul was unknown in Rome and would have needed to introduce his theology. Two of his closest friends and *coworkers, Priscilla and Aquila, appear to be pastors of the leading house church (Rom 16:3-4) and would themselves, ignoring here the rest of those known by Paul (Rom 16:3-16), have disseminated his theology.

The pervasive presence of questions and Paul's responses, which occupy Romans 2–4 and Romans 9–11, must be considered at least relevant in adjudicating the purpose of Romans. These interrogations cohere with the lengthy address to the weak and strong in Romans 14:1–15:13 (Minear; Wiefel; Watson 1991; 2007, 163-91; Longenecker 2011, 133-36; McKnight, *Reading Romans*). The question then becomes just how polemical this letter is: Is it a strong critique, like Galatians even if from a different angle, of those who impose Torah observance on Gentiles? Many today would answer this question with a firm "No!" but their firmness does not wash the evidence into the gutter, and a yes answer deserves serious consideration (Dunn 2015; Wedderburn; D. A. Campbell 2013; McKnight, *Reading Romans*). The contested points of Romans 14–15 are indicators of how serious the tensions are over whether Gentile believers are to practice Torah observance.

Level three of Paul's purpose in the letter gets even more specific. Emphasizing the missionary nature of Paul's life, one suggestion is that Romans is an "ambassadorial letter," raising support for Paul's mission to Spain after time in Rome (Rom 15:24; Jewett). This suggestion is weakened by being too narrow in orientation, while the theological self-introduction that begins Romans would not be comprehensive enough and unnecessary if this were the case. That Paul, however, wanted support for his mission to Spain is clear enough ("to be sent" in Rom 15:24 indicates so), and raising funds is one of the most common features of Paul's mission (Downs; McKnight, *Pastor Paul*, 79-101). How important is Romans 13:1-7, especially the verses on taxation, to the purpose of Romans? The singular nature of the theme along with the probable rise of tension of taxation in Rome at the time of this letter suggests Paul felt obligated to give his point of view (Longenecker 2011, 121-22). Yet, one should not raise taxation in Rome to anything other than a live issue in Rome.

Longenecker has the most extensive discussion of the purpose of Romans to date, and he postulates the following more complex set of purposes: Romans was written for two primary reasons: (1) to give some spiritual gift for mutual encouragement (Rom 1:11-12) and (2) to acquire support for his mission to Spain (Rom 15:24). But at a second level Paul writes to clarify the theological agreements he has with the Roman Christians, the gospel he gospels among the Gentiles, and how his gospeling connects with the story of Israel's election. At a third level he (3) defends himself, (4) addresses in a secondary way the tensions in the churches of Rome (Rom 14:1–15:13), and (5) deals with how to relate with civil authorities in Rome (Rom 13:1-7; Longenecker 2011, 147-60). His mission to the Gentiles, however, is more central than what Longenecker posits as the first two purposes and reshapes both (Barclay 2015, 457-59).

3. Contemporary Discussions.

To discuss scholarship on Romans is to discuss scholarship on Paul, and that means the history of theology and *hermeneutics. One must at least recognize the traditional, Reformation (i.e., "old") perspective on Paul, the "new" perspective with the "early" perspective, the apocalyptic perspective, the participationist perspective, the Paul-within-Judaism perspective, the gift perspective, and the hermeneutics of socio-pragmatic and liberationist approaches. At least in the latter Paul is often *the* problem to be solved (Gray). Each of the above affects one's reading of Romans. The following can be little more than sampling of studies, with an imbalance toward theological readings.

The Reformation, Lutheran view of Paul emphasizes that in God's eyes everyone is a sinner and condemned, that no one is capable of being accounted righteous before God on the basis of deeds, that God redeems sinners from their unrighteousness on the basis of the redemptive work of *Christ, and that this is all by *grace through faith so that boasting is erased (Westerholm). Romans, read through such a set of factors, is about a vertical, personal, individualistic redemption on the basis of Christ's death and God's grace through faith for anyone who believes, a grace that compels the believer to be marked by doing good (also see Das 2006; 2016).

E. P. Sanders gets the credit for the turn against the Reformation perspective as an imposition of Reformation categories onto first-century Judaism and Paul (Sanders 2016; 2017). His fundamental argument is that Judaism was a covenant-based, not a works-based *righteousness, religion, and that works were how one maintained one's relationship in the *covenant not how one entered into the covenant. He calls this construct "covenant nomism": a covenant-based requirement for those in the covenant to follow the Torah (Greek *nomos*). Sanders's contribution was a destruction of the Protestant theory of Judaism, a theory, especially of "*works of the *law," needed at times to prop up the Reformation perspective. His view of Judaism unleashed reactions, renewals, and reformulations, all developments in Pauline studies since his original volume on Paul.

The first development has been called the "new" perspective and was framed on the basis of Sanders's view of Judaism and a new reading of Paul by J. D. G. Dunn (Dunn 2008; McKnight, "New Perspective"). If Judaism was not a works-righteousness religion, then Paul's "works of the law" was not about merit-seeking behaviors but about boundary-making behaviors by Judeans that separated them from Gentiles. Thus, Dunn's famous works on Romans (Dunn 2015) and Paul (Dunn 1998) worked out his thesis extensively to show that the problem Paul faced among his churches, not least in Galatia and Rome, was not merit-seeking individual behaviors but an ethnic elective privilege that sought Gentile conversion to Judaism. Others have developed Sanders in a similar direction, including especially N. T. Wright (Wright 2002; 2013; 2015). The new perspective, then, is more about the horizontal relationship both of Israel to the church and of the individual Christian to others in the church. Dispute arose early against both Sanders's view of Judaism and the development of the new perspective by Dunn and Wright (Carson, O'Brien, and Seifrid). However, a breakthrough has recently occurred in M. Thomas demonstrating that the interpretation of "works of the law" in second-century Christian theology was very much along the line of Dunn and Wright. Hence, he dubs his view not the "new" but the "early," with the early perspective preceding then the "old" perspective (Thomas).

One line of thinking that became noticeable after Sanders's destruction of the works-righteousness frame of much Protestant thinking has been called an *apocalyptic approach to Paul. This approach that owes some of its origins to E. Käsemann, J. Beker, J. L. Martyn, and B. Gaventa, but its most complete thinker today is probably D. Campbell (Käsemann; Beker; Martyn; D. Campbell 2013). While there are features of D. Campbell's theory of Romans that are unlike others, the foundational lines of his thinking begin with epistemology, an epistemology that begins with God's grace and love to us in Christ's life, death, burial, resurrection, and *ascension. On the basis of this all can be known, and nothing else is knowable (D. Campbell 2019; 2020). Once one knows God in the face of Christ, one learns to tell the story of God's redemption in a completely new way, shattering all other storytellings, and this story to be told begins with Christ and works backwards. That is, it moves from solution to problem (as Sanders had argued). D. Campbell's focus for reading Romans is Romans 5–8. He sees a polemical tone in the earlier chapters: he once called the theology at work "justification theory," which is a contractual relationship with God (do this and you will be saved), while Romans 5–8 has an unconditional, redemptive covenant in view. God's *love is revealed in sending the *Son, the Spirit incorporates all humans in Christ, the Christian life is one of transformation in the Spirit *"in Christ," and it is essentially communal and relational. What is radically distinct about D. Campbell's reading of Romans is that he sees so much of especially Romans 1–3 as the *teaching of a false teacher, whom he at times calls "the Teacher." The apocalyptic approach to Paul is reshaping Pauline studies as well as Romans.

Another view emerging in the aftermath of the Sanders's new perspective on Judaism can be found in M. Gorman's participationist approach to Paul. The glue to his theology of Paul is the term **cruciformity*, by which he means redemptive, transformative participation "in" Christ to embody Christ in word and deed and mission. Paul's narratival, apocalyptic, and theopolitical gospel shows continuity with Israel and is in serious tension with Rome's imperial ideology. That gospel is about the crucified and exalted Messiah, a gospel that inaugurated the new *creation for all those who through "self-abandoning and self-committing faith" participate in Christ and so are restored to a right relation with God and others and adopted into God's family, the *church. Such persons are "infused both individually and corporately by the Spirit," so these new-creation people can live "bifocal" lives—focused back on Christ's first coming and forward to his future coming. They live a cruciform life of faithfulness, *hope, and love, and so *witness in word and deed to the lordship of Jesus—in mission, reconciliation, justice, and *peace (Gorman 2015, 302; 2016, 183; *Participating*). Gorman reads Romans thoroughly with this category of participation (Gorman, "Participationist Perspective"; also C. Campbell 2012; 2020).

The new perspective awakened NT scholars and theologians to a view of Judaism that itself provoked anti-Semitism. The consequence of Sanders's efforts was to compel Christian scholars to study Judean literature and beliefs with greater sensitivity, which led to various versions of the new perspective as well as to other perspectives mentioned below. A radicalizing of the new perspective turned the tables to argue that Paul never broke with "Judaism" but instead remained "within" Judaism (Zetterholm). The conflict model operative in the pre-Sanders era of Christian scholarship, a conflict between Judaism and Christianity, gives way here to a more continuous view of Paul and Judaism. Paul remained a Judean (or Jew) and observant of the Torah. His mission calling was to non-Judean Gentiles to bring them into the one people of God, but Judeans and believers did not thereby cease their covenant relation or with one another in Torah observance. For some in this approach there are thus two ways of *salvation, one for Judeans and one for Gentiles. What is undeniable to the Paul-within-Judaism approach is the inviolability of God's covenant with Israel while also finding a way to bring Gentiles into the covenant as well.

Yet another approach is that of J. Barclay, which can be called the gift perspective (Barclay, "Gift Perspective"). This approach takes none other than a, if not *the*, central term *grace* as the lens through which to see Paul's mission and theology. It places Paul within Judaism in a way that expands on the central contributions of Sanders, and it draws themes from both the old and new perspectives on Paul and thus effects some reconciliation between the two. It respects the history of Pauline theology from Ephesians to the Pastorals in church history, where grace (e.g., the Pelagian controversy with Augustine, the debate of Catholicism with Luther and Calvin) has been played out more completely. Further, it has angles on social and church concerns of our day. (On grace as here defined, see 5.4 below.) The emphasis in Pauline theology is the incongruity of grace, but this sense of grace extends as well into Christian ethics in the practices of grace (Barclay, *Paul and the Power*).

Less theological but influential in modern studies of Romans have been those examining the socio-historical context of Rome and the makeup of the Pauline (mostly) house churches (Meeks; Esler; Adams). A particular analysis of the location of the synagogues and then earliest churches in the earliest history of the church in Rome has also contributed to readings of Romans (Wiefel; Lampe). Included in such contextual studies now are examinations of Paul's letters as performance by Phoebe (Jewett; Finger; Shiell; McKnight, *Reading Romans*; Agnew) and the significance of the number of *women (Lampe; Jewett; Mathew). One must imagine one's way into hearing Phoebe both read this letter and answer questions about what Romans means and what is going on in Paul's life.

Alongside these more traditional—mostly white, mostly male, mostly historical-critical—approaches to Paul but with a different, potent hermeneutical orientation are what can be called socio-pragmatic and liberationist (feminist, womanist, Asian, Latinx, brown, Black) readings of Paul and Romans (Braxton). Each hermeneutic, not least each of the preceding approaches to Paul and Romans, is anchored in a particular context, which can at times radically shape what one sees. Liberationists read Paul or Romans in order to retrieve what is retrievable or to resist what they deem needing resistance (hermeneutics of suspicion)—all for the sake of establishing justice and liberation (Patte and Grenholm). In these readings, what Romans *meant* in its context is used in order to examine its ideological underpinnings, and then made use of for justice in various contemporary contexts (e.g., Blount; Bowens). From a slightly different angle one also observes the flourishing of political and systematic approaches to Paul (and therefore Romans; Odell-Scott).

4. Context.

Paul provides helpful insight on the context of the letter to the Romans in Romans 14:1–15:13 as well as in Romans 16:1-16. Paul is addressing groups called—perhaps by themselves, perhaps by others, perhaps by Paul (see 1 Cor 8–10)—"strong" and "weak." While some think the correlation of *strong* with Gentile and *weak* with Judeans is inaccurate (Longenecker 2011, 133-36), the majority still see the strong as Gentile believers, perhaps now in the majority because of the expulsion of Claudius and only recently returned to Rome, and the weak as Judeans (Wiefel; Watson 2007, 163-91; McKnight, *Reading Romans*, 3-23). Barclay tosses dust in the eyes of much of this orientation (Barclay 2015).

We can begin with two observations: that the weak were a real group among Roman Christians and that their distinguishing mark was scrupulous observance of the Torah. Everywhere Paul went, beginning as he did in synagogues, opposition to his acceptance of Gentile believers without *circumcision caused a brouhaha (see Gal 2:11-14; Acts 10:13-16; 11:3; 15:19-21; probably Col 2:16–3:4). There are a number of names in Romans 16 that are Jewish (e.g., Mary), and Judeans in Rome were known for kosher *food observance (e.g., Juvenal, *Sat.* 14.96-99). The dynamic of the letter is an interplay between Gentile and Judean believers (esp. Rom 1–4; 9–11), but it is terms such as *unclean* food (Rom 14:14, i.e., *kosher*) and *clean* (Rom 14:20) and sacred days (Rom 14:5-6), along with *circumcision* (Rom 15:8; 3:1-20), that lead the majority to connect the weak to Judeans. The strong, on the other hand, inasmuch as this party is over against the weak, seem to be (at least mostly) Gentile, and their characteristic feature is liberation from Torah observance, that is, they eat what they want (Rom 14:2, 15, 20-23). This view has then much to commend it.

It is noticeable, too, that the fierce rhetoric of Romans 2–4 is matched by the fierce descriptions Paul uses of how the strong and weak speak to one another. If the strong "disdain" (Rom 14:3, 10), the weak call out the strong in terms of *judgment (Rom 14:3-4, 5, 10, 13, 22), and such language is used too in Romans 2 of someone called "the Judge" (Rom 2:1, 3, 27). It is difficult to know whom Paul disapproves the most, but it is clear this language is tantamount to saying they are claiming the role of God.

The terms *strong* and *weak* are customary for a more theological understanding of the tension between the two, but there is a social edge to these terms. Notice Romans 15:1, which can be translated, "We, the powerful, ought to carry the weaknesses of the powerless, and not to please ourselves." (Thus, in Greek the contrast is between the *dynatoi* and the *adynatoi*.) It appears the strong or the powerful are people of high social status, while the weak are people of lower or even no status, and this mattered in Rome and the *empire because status was everything. The issue at hand then is not simply, or even primarily, theology, but status and power. Yet, the weak have their own claims of privilege, if not also status of a different order. They are the elect of God, the people of the Torah, the people of the Messiah (Rom 9:1-5). One then suspects that the return of the Judeans to Rome during Nero's reign led to this tension: the returning Judeans evidently believed they, as God's covenant people, had privilege, while the Gentiles, now in the majority and now in charge, had another kind of privilege called status and power.

The issue among the Roman Christians then was a battle of privilege and power, and the point of entry for unity for Paul was that they were to learn to welcome one another as Christ had welcomed them (Rom 14:1; 15:1, 7).

Romans 16, too, opens another window on the house churches (or tenement churches) of Rome. There were probably five house churches in Rome: the *household of Prisca and Aquila (Rom 16:3-5); the residences of Aristobulus (Rom 16:10), Narcissus (Rom 16:11), Asyncritus and others (Rom 16:14); and Philologus, Julia, and others (Rom 16:15). From research into evidence of names in first-century Rome, one can infer too that a number of the names mentioned in Romans 16 are those of *slaves; there are Jewish and Latin and Greek names; and there is a sizable presence of women (Mathew). One can infer that the households are possible indicators of *leadership in the Roman assemblies.

The preeminent place of Phoebe (Rom 16:1-2) is an indicator of the Pauline mission as well as of the ministries of women in the Pauline mission churches. She is a sibling in Christ; she is a "deacon of the church at Cenchreae," the harbor port for Corinth. One should think here first of a leadership position in the church (Phil 1:1; 1 Tim 3:8-13). She is to be received with warm *hospitality, and this is yet another indicator, along with the position in the letter in which we find Phoebe, that she was the letter courier. The courier often enough read the letter, or at least saw to it that it was read properly, and answered questions about Paul's condition as well as the contents of the letter (Shiell). Finally, Phoebe is a "benefactor," a term indicating someone whose *wealth was used for the public good and given public honors. Phoebe's benefactions support "many" as well as Paul's mission. Her "public *honor" is now found in hospitality among the Christians in Rome and the *glory given to God (not to her).

5. The Letter.

5.1. Lived Theology Aiming at Peace Among the Siblings (Rom 12–16). The above-sketched context adds sharpness to our reading of Romans 1–11, but we begin with locating a thematic statement in the letter. Many have rightly considered Romans 1:16-17 to be programmatic for the letter, but one can also argue that the aim of this letter is beyond the articulation of theology. The aim is "lived theology" (Marsh, Slade, and Azaransky). Lived theology is theology embodied in the life of the community as well as in an individual, but the embodiment transcends the idea and makes it incarnate expression. Lived theology, then, is not simply application or practice of an idea but a way of life that *is* theology. In Romans 12:1-2, the expressions "living *sacrifice" and not being "conformed to this world" and "transformed by the renewing of your minds" bring into expression that kind of lived theology. Perhaps the best expression of lived theology in all of Paul, however, is "predestined to be conformed to the *image of his Son" in Romans 8:29. Christoformity and cruciformity are other ways of expressing this and are the programmatic expression of the entire letter. The tension between the strong and the weak in Rome can only be resolved when Christoformity is the embodied way of life for the Christians. Such Christoformity entails embodied sacrifice (Rom 12:1-2), prayer (Rom 15:13; 16:20, 25-27), a life in the *body of Christ (Rom 12:3-8), generosity (Rom 15:15-16), a unity in peace among one another (Rom 12:9-21), a remarkably modern sense of toleration (Rom 14:1–15:13), welcoming one another to one another's table (Rom 14:1; 15:1, 7), a love for all (Rom 12:9; 13:8-10; 14:15; 15:30) and a life of public goodness (Rom 13:1-7). Everything in the letter is oriented toward this assortment of components in Christoformity, and a lived theology like this transcends the articulations of theology.

5.2. The Opening (Rom 1:1-17). A powerful statement of God's gospel opens Romans (Rom 1:1-4), defining it as Israel's story fulfilled in God's Son, a Davidide in flesh and God's Son "in the spirit of *holiness" (perhaps the *Holy Spirit) by the resurrection. Through this Son Paul has received the commission to gospel the Gentiles (Bates 2012). A thanksgiving that is highly personal (notice the use of "I") follows seamlessly into a statement of his mission to the Gentiles (Rom 1:14-15). Then comes a rather abrupt "I am not ashamed of the gospel" statement (Rom 1:16-17), which brings to the surface major terms at work in Romans, in Paul's mission, and in arguments with his contemporary Judean opponents: *gospel*, *salvation*, *everyone*, *faith*, with "through faith for faith" and "righteousness of God."

The gospel is the story of Israel come to fulfillment in King Jesus (Bates 2017; McKnight 2015), while faith in Paul expresses a spectrum from trust to allegiance and obedience to the system of faith/belief (Gupta; Morgan). The category of salvation encompasses a number of words about the impact and benefits Christ brings (reconciliation, *justification, redemption, etc.) through his life, death, burial, resurrection, ascension, and return. These themes are prominent in Romans 3–8, but the heart of Paul's theology of redemption is to be found Romans 5–8 especially, and the means of that redemption finds a golden key in Romans 3:21-26. At the heart of the gospel mission is offering it first to the Jew and then to the Greek. This means Romans 1:16-17 already sets tones for the weak-and-strong tension in Rome as well as the various people groups found in Romans 16. Paul makes clear in this statement that all are saved by faith, and the meaning of *all* is made clear in Galatians 3:28—Judean, Gentile, slave, free, male and female.

When it comes to "God's righteousness," a hornet's nest is disturbed (Dunn 1998, 334-89; Wright 2013, 795-804; D. Campbell 2013, 677-714). The Greek term *dikaiosynē* translates the Hebrew *ṣedeq*, a term that in the Judean world most often referred to moral behavior that conformed to the Torah, God's standard for the covenant people (Przybylski). One sees such a sense in Matthew 1:19. When used of God, the term evokes an attribute of God that compels God out of love and covenant to act for the redemption of creation as a gift. This gift makes those unworthy become fit for the presence of God. Paul, however, comprehended this term as both an attribute of God (God's own faithfulness to God's own standard, which is God's own being) and as the act of God's power in redemption and rectification, and these two senses are added to the standard Judean sense of conformity to God's standard. So, when Paul speaks of "God's righteousness" a given usage will be on the spectrum from God's own attribute, God's gift, and human conformity to that attribute. Thus, to be "justified" or to "be righted" or "made right" or "declared right" will inevitably mean at some level a transformation of a person in Christ to conform to God's standard, which in the new covenant is Christoformity through life in the Spirit and participation in Christ (Gorman 2015).

5.3. A Torah-Disrupting Peace (Rom 1:18–4:25). A soteriological reading, which emphasizes individual redemption, contends Paul is arguing from Romans 1:18–3:20 that all humans (Gentiles in Rom 1:18-32, Judeans in Rom 2:1–3:8, and all in Rom 3:9-20) are sinners and need the redemption that is provided by Christ (Rom 3:21-26). Further, such a redemption is apart from works and privilege and is by faith alone (Rom 3:27–4:25). Such an approach to reading Romans makes sense, but one needs also to consider the context of Romans.

In fact, the language of Romans 1:18-32 is not as generic or *universal as some have argued, for Paul never quite says what this typical reading says he is saying. Rather, his indictment here borrows a Judean stereotype of the godless idolater of the Gentile world, and it shows significant parallel to Wisdom of Solomon 13–14. These lines in Romans 1:18-32, then, are not even a good summary of the typical Gentile sinner but of a specific kind of Gentile. One may suggest that the "weak" at this point were nodding in agreement, but it is Romans 2 that disrupts the nodding into a stunning awareness of an indictment. "The judge" (or in NRSV, "whoever you are, when you judge others" in Rom 2:1, the very term used in Rom 14:3-5, 10, 13, 22 of the weak) is now on trial for the very indictment he was using of the Gentile idolater. This rhetorical move in Romans 2:1-16 makes clear that Romans 1:18-32 was a rhetorical setup rather than a simplistic, universal indictment of Gentiles as sinners. As such, we are hearing opening forays into the problem of the strong and weak in Romans 14–15.

In Romans 2 we learn that this judge, who embodies the position of the weak's own judgment of the strong's disregard of Torah observance, "presumes God will judge such Gentiles, relies on the Torah, boasts in his relationship with God, knows the divine will, is instructed in the Torah, is a guide to the blind (Gentiles) because he is a *light in the world's darkness, is a corrector of the foolish, is a teacher of children, and knows the Torah and so teaches others the Torah" (McKnight, *Reading Romans*, 109). These terms are what Paul has observed in his opponents throughout his mission to include Gentiles without requiring circumcision and Torah observance. Paul's strong indictment of the judge continues by raising the Gentiles to the level of the Judeans in Romans 2:12-16. He does this by appealing to God's utterly impartial judgment of all on the basis of deeds (Rom 2:6, 11, 12-16). This upends what circumcision actually indicates—not the removal of a portion of male flesh but the heart relation to God (Rom 2:17–3:8). Nothing in the radicality of Paul's theology would have been more confounding to the Torah observant than Romans 2:25-26, 29: "Circumcision indeed is of value if you obey the law; but if you break the law, your circumcision has become uncircumcision. So, if those who are uncircumcised keep the requirements of the law, will not their uncircumcision be regarded as circumcision? . . . Rather, a person is a Jew who is one inwardly, and real circumcision is a matter of the heart—it is spiritual and not literal."

Paul asks a number of questions in Romans 2–4, which some do not notice but were surely nothing short of a nuisance to the first hearers of this letter. The passage becomes nothing less than a somewhat aggressive interrogation of the judge. If the reader of Romans performed this letter well, the reader would have paused after each question long enough for the audience to respond either silently or aloud. There are three primary issues/questions at work: the question about Judean elective privilege (Rom 3:1-20), the question about boasting (Rom 3:27-31), and the question about Abraham (Rom 4:1-25). But these three primary questions are among a total of twenty-seven questions from Romans 2:22–4:10.

The first primary question, *the question about elective privilege* (Rom 3:1-20), is one about advantage for those who first were in the covenant. Yes, in fact, there is an advantage because they have the Torah (Rom 3:2; cf. Rom 9:4-5), but they will be judged as the Gentiles are judged—on the basis of works—and so their elective privilege is erased if they are unfaithful (Rom 3:9-20). (It does not appear that Paul moves from a Judean indictment in Romans 3:8 to a universal indictment in Rom 3:9-20, as often presented in individual soteriological readings of these chapters. At least, he does not move to a universal reading completely, for he still has the Judeans in mind ["deeds prescribed by the law"] in Rom 3:19-20.)

In using "deeds prescribed by the law," or as the NIV has it, "works of the law" (Rom 3:20), we land on another minefield in Pauline studies. Is Paul speaking here of the universal quest of humans to justify themselves before God on the basis of their works, their deeds, their acts of public benevolence and compassion? Or is Paul speaking here of those singular "works" prescribed or at least derived from the Torah that create boundaries between Judeans and Gentiles, especially as noticed in the Diaspora? The recent study by M. Thomas demonstrates that in the second century the expression "works of the law" most often pointed to Sabbath, food laws, and circumcision—those border-defining Judean observances (Thomas; Dunn 2008). What is most important here is not to exaggerate, for there is here, too, a spectrum from boundary markers to an anthropocentricity that assumes one can justify oneself before God on the basis of behaviors. It is noticeable, however, in the letters of Paul "boundary markers" are far more prominent. If one considers Romans 14–15, the issue there is not the Decalogue in general but food laws and sacred days, that is, boundary markers.

One of Paul's most well-known passages is Romans 3:21-26. Justification, or God's gracious righting of humans, occurs solely through the redemptive death of Jesus Christ, and this very claim destroys the privileges of the weak. God's righteousness is revealed not in the Torah but "through faith in Jesus Christ" (Rom 3:22 NRSV) or, better yet, "through the faithfulness of Jesus Christ" himself (Hays). This righteousness is for anyone who believes. Jesus Christ is here presented as the mercy seat, the place of redemption and expiation, and in so revealing God's righteousness in the Christ of the *cross God revealed both his patience with Israel's sinfulness and his fidelity to his righteousness in the faithfulness of Jesus Christ.

Not as extensive is the second question, *the question about boasting* (Rom 3:27-31). The soteriological, individual approach focuses here on humans boasting before God on the basis of their meritorious works. The issue in this section is not, however, narrowly shaped by personal final redemption but by the relationship of Judeans and Gentiles in the one family of God. If Paul is right about not requiring Gentiles to observe Torah, what then of the advantage, the very advantage that led to boasting? Boasting, however, needs context as well. Boasting in one's advantage or accomplishments was the honorable way of life in the empire, and the weak (like no doubt the strong, for other reasons) had assimilated boasting into elective privilege. Thus, in Romans 2 the judge boasts in his (or her) relation to God as a Judean and in having and knowing the Torah (Rom 2:17, 23). This is the boasting of which Paul disapproves, and the proper response makes room for Gentiles who are allegiant to King Jesus. The boast ends when one admits into the center of the room the "Torah of faith" (NRSV has "law of faith"; Rom 3:27). Notice that the immediate consequence in this paragraph is to deny elective privilege on the basis solely of ethnic heritage (Rom 3:29-31).

The question about Abraham has formed the heart of Protestant theology's understanding of "faith apart from works" (Rom 4:1-25). In that soteriological reading of Romans, with universal sinfulness proven and the effective redemption of Christ on the cross and the annihilation of self-absorbed boasting established, the gospel's proper response of faith alone is now launched. One need not question the central elements of this soteriology to see the question about Abraham addressed as a more pastoral, ecclesial understanding. Each of the three questions in Romans 3–4 has a similar aim: to eliminate the privilege of the weak in its claim to election and covenant status. Further, these questions and Paul's answers simultaneously demonstrate the redemption of faith alone apart from the necessity of Torah observance for all, Judean or Greek. This leads to Paul's vision of lived theology of reconciliation of both groups in Rome.

Abraham in Romans 4 is both a paradigm of the proper response (faith, allegiance) and therefore also the father of both the weak and the strong. In the world in which Paul was nurtured Abraham was a believer (Gen 15:6), to be sure, but his faith was demonstrated in the Aqedah of Genesis 22, the binding of Isaac. For Paul, however, Genesis 15 contains it all. A *chronological* account of Abraham's faith-status demonstrates that he was "righted" with God not on the basis of Genesis 17 (circumcision) nor on the basis of the Aqedah (Gen 22), but because he trusted the promissory word of Yahweh (Gen 15). Because Paul seemingly has no concern in Romans 4 with the Aqedah, his argument is simple: since Abraham was made right with God by faith (Gen 15), circumcision (Gen 17) had nothing to do with it—it was a seal of the rightness he already had by faith—and, therefore, it is not needed for the Gentile (the strong). The promise comes to Abraham (Rom 4:12-25) by faith (Rom 4:1-8), not the observance of the Torah of circumcision (Rom 4:9-12). The beginning theme and final theme is the same: faith led to being made right with God (Rom 4:3, 22).

The advantage question that opens the chapter (Rom 4:1) can be translated, then, as follows: "Therefore, what do we say Abraham, our first father consistent with flesh [= Judean, = weak], has found [with respect to favor with God? Was it by works, by the act of circumcision]?" Since 4:2 immediately raises the issue of "works" and "a boast," it is clear too that favor in Romans 4:1 is about finding favor on the basis of his Judean heritage and observance. Thus, "For if Abraham was righted from works, he has a boast but not with God" (Rom 4:2).

In Romans 1:18–4:25, then, the apostle's argument is with the place the Torah is to play in both determining who the true people of God are (ethnic Israel or an expanded Israel according to Rom 11:11-36) and how the community of King Jesus is to observe the Torah (or not, and if so, by whom?). Those who impose Torah observance (the weak) on Gentiles (the strong), then, are disrupting the unity that is found through the Spirit in Christ by faith alone (not by following the Torah). Within, but only within, that argument the soteriology of the apostle Paul becomes clear: one is made right by grace through faith—by Christ alone.

5.4. A Spirit-Creating Peace (Rom 5–8). The solution to the problem of tension between the strong with their claims to superior status and the weak is to be found in the power of the Spirit (Rom 5:5; 7:6; 8:2, 4, 9-11, 13-16, 23, 26-27) to transform Christians through Christoformity (Rom 8:29). There is a noticeably flexible use of personal pronouns in Romans 5–8 (e.g., *I*, *we*, *all*). When scrutinized, however, they share a very similar map for resolving the tensions in Rome. The pronouns are generic plural ("all"; Rom 5:12-21; 8:1-8), *you* (Rom 6:11-23; 8:9-15), *we* (Rom 5:1-11; 6:1-10; 7:1-6; 8:16-17, 18-39), and *I* (Rom 7:7-25).

Since it would be redundant to cover the same basic theology (the map) by going passage by passage, in what follows I provide a thematic approach. The paradigmatic passage is Romans 5:12-21, where we encounter the major terms and impulses, not least *sin and death as agents or cultures acting to conform humans to their ways (Croasmun) or, in other terms, recognizing that no human is isolated from other humans as one forms an *identity (Eastman). That passage sets in motion the terms that not only have become operatives in Christian theology but are the very terms that anchor Paul's theology of transformation (Jacob). There are, Paul contends, two maps for life—the map of *Adam and the map of Christ.

The map of Adam is nothing less than a *body of sin*, and it operates in the sphere of the *flesh (an agent). The *determinative act* on this map is the act of sin, first by Adam and then by all humans, and this sin can be called trespass or disobedience or a mind set on flesh or being hostile to God or sin becoming Sin (Agent Sin). The ones who sin have a *status*, which can be called sinners or being in the flesh. The *means of knowing God* in the map of Adam is distorted and incapable of its aim because it involves the Torah captured by sin and the flesh, because it is weakened by the flesh, because it is the Torah of sin and death, and because it has minds set on the flesh. This map of Adam with its sin, flesh, and death patterns fully established leads to a *divine decision*: judgment or condemnation. The *consequence*, therefore, is final, eternal death. Who travels on the map of Adam? The *parameters* are stated: "many," understood as "all" (Rom 5:12, 15, 18-19). Those who follow the map of Adam in this body of sin are the ones accountable for the disunity and lack of peace in the heart of the empire's assemblies in Rome.

The map of Christ both mirrors the map of Adam and transcends it in the power of God's unfathomable grace of conquering death and glorifying the objects of grace. The *body of Christ* is all in the Spirit and through God's grace. Grace is the

> sphere *of voluntary, personal relations, characterized by goodwill in the giving of benefit or favor, and eliciting some form of reciprocal return that is both voluntary and necessary for the continuation of the relationship*. In accord with the anthropology of gift, its scope includes various forms of kindness, favor, generosity, or compassion enacted in diverse services and benefits, with the expectation of some reciprocating gratitude or counter-gift. (Barclay 2015, 575)

Grace as gift can be "perfected" or led to its thematic fullness in (1) superabundance, (2) singularity, (3) priority, (4) incongruity, (5) efficacy, or (6) noncircularity (Barclay 2015, 185). Not all of these themes are present for each appearance in Paul, but neither should any of them be ignored when reading Romans. One needs to ask

- whether grace is present in supreme measure
- whether the gift-giver is solely marked by giving
- whether a gift is given prior to a receiver's prompting it
- whether the gift is given against or regardless of the person's lack of deserving, status, or worth
- whether the gift's emphasis is that it has transforming power
- whether the gift expects reciprocation

Paul's theology is a theology of grace (Barclay, "Gift Perspective").

Powered by Spirit and grace, the *determinative act* for following the roads on the map of Christ is the obedience of Christ, a reception of grace and the sending of the Son. His redemptive act radically alters the *status* of those formerly walking along the map of Adam so they become righteous and no longer condemned. They now live through the Spirit the true observance of Torah. That status entails a new *means of knowing God's will* through the Torah of the Spirit or the Torah of Christ, through the gift of righteousness, through a Torah of the Spirit of life in Christ, and through having minds on the Spirit. The *divine decision* through this act of God in the map of Christ is redemption, salvation, and liberation of all creation—redemption is cosmic in Romans 8—as well as a justification that condemns sin in the flesh. The manifold *consequences*, like the theme of grace, are life, eternal life, peace, reconciliation now and in the age to come, unity, love, welcoming of one another, a fictive but transcending sibling relation with all others in Christ, a liberation, a glorification, and entering into God's *kingdom. Like the *parameters* of the map of Adam, in the map of Christ "all" or "many" are brought into God's redemptive orbit.

The map of Christ thus transcends in all ways the map of Adam by slaying death and bringing new and eternal life for those formerly strapped to the flesh and trapped in death. This is all done by God through Christ in the Spirit for those who participate in Christ through faith. For Paul those who participate in Christ are called to a life of peace with one another solely on the basis of their grace-shaped status in Christ.

5.5. A Narrative Leading to Peace (Rom 9–11). Narrative theology is in, which is good, but how does one form a narrative? How does one form a *narrative that is not quite formed the way we modern readers might form one? Is such a constructed narrative imposing on an author such as Paul, who does not ever quite give such a narrative?

The place to begin to answer such questions is with names, events, and texts from the OT being used and with how interactive is Paul with other literature (Judean or Greco-Roman). Along with this it is vital to know other narrations of the story of Israel to see what concerns Paul might have in comparison. Once again the soteriological story has been used to form a narrative that is not expansive enough (Piper) to cover what Paul says here. A noticeable feature of Romans 9–11 is the abundance of interrogation questions in Romans 9:1–11:11, and these questions are much on the order of those in Romans 2–4. So much are these alike that it is reasonable to think the two parts of Romans are addressed to the same audience, namely, the weak. But Paul speaks to both sides: to the weak in Romans 9:1–11:10 and to the strong in Romans 11:11-36. Once again, we need to ponder whether the points argued in these three chapters are not once again evidence of the sorts of combative debates he had with his Judean contemporaries who struggled with his seeming laxity over Torah observance for Gentiles now in the covenant God made with Abraham (and Moses).

5.5.1. To the Weak (Rom 9:1–11:10). Paul dashes into the importance of the salvation-historical privilege of election for the Judeans (Rom 9:1-5) while dashing in and out of several other themes: the surprising nature of God's covenant acts of election, which dispel any shock over including Gentiles without Torah observance (Rom 9:6–10:4); the importance once again of covenant status on the basis of faith (Rom 9:30–10:21); a new covenant renewal (Rom 10:5-13) and the mission to Gentiles that follows (Rom 10:13-21), emphasizing all along that a Judean remnant remains (Rom 11:1-10). God remains faithful, God is sovereign, but God's ways are not the ways of the weak or the strong. This new-covenant status is shaped by grace not by one's observance of the Torah or social status.

5.5.2. To the Strong (Rom 11:11-36). There is a subtle change in these verses in toning down the more aggressive interrogation of Rom 9:1–11:10, but Paul does not go easy on the strong either. Several themes operate in the words to the strong in Romans 11:

1. the jealousy of the Israelites over Gentile inclusion (Rom 11:11, 13-14)
2. a significant appeal to the correlation of Gentile pagan disobedience and Judean faithfulness as well as a Judean unfaithfulness and disobedience with Gentile faith and obedience and redemption (Rom 11:11-12, 16, 23-24, 26, 28, 30-31)
3. an expansion of Israel to include Gentile believers in Jesus the Messiah, along with a warning that what happened to Israelites who did not obey can happen just as well to Gentiles who walk away from the Messiah (Rom 11:17-24)
4. that unbelief is temporary (Rom 11:25, 30-31)
5. the hopeful and undeniable future redemption of Israel (Rom 11:12, 14, 15, 16, 23-24, 26) because of the faithfulness of God (Rom 11:29)

Once again, if these are gospel truths, the weak and the strong are siblings by faith in Christ, and through the Spirit they are to welcome one another. This leads us back to the vision of community and public life in Romans 12–16, which is the lived-theology aim of everything written from Romans 1–11.

See also ABRAHAM; ADAM AND CHRIST; APOCALYPTIC PAUL; CHRONOLOGY OF PAUL; COVENANT; COWORKERS, PAUL AND HIS; CRUCIFORMITY; ELECTION AND PREDESTINATION; FAITH; FLESH; GENTILES; GOD; GOSPEL; GRACE; HERMENEUTICS/ INTERPRETING PAUL; HOLY SPIRIT; INTERPRETATION: LUTHERAN; INTERPRETATION: NEW PERSPECTIVE; ISRAEL; JUDGMENT; JUSTIFICATION; KINSHIP LANGUAGE IN PAUL; LAW; MISSION; OLD TESTAMENT IN PAUL; PAUL AND JUDAISM; RIGHTEOUSNESS; ROMAN CHRISTIANITY; SALVATION; SIN, GUILT; STRONG AND WEAK; WOMEN NAMED IN PAUL; WORKS OF THE LAW.

BIBLIOGRAPHY. **E. Adams,** *The Earliest Christian Meeting Places: Almost Exclusively Houses?*, rev. ed. (New York: Bloomsbury T&T Clark, 2015); **S. Agnew,** *Embodied Performance: Mutuality, Embrace, and the Letter to Rome* (Eugene, OR: Pickwick, 2020); **D. E. Aune,** "Romans as *Logos Protreptikos,*" in *The Romans Debate*, ed. K. P. Donfried, rev. ed. (Grand Rapids, MI: Baker Academic, 1991), 278-96; **J. M. G. Barclay,** *Paul and the Gift* (Grand Rapids, MI: Eerdmans, 2015); idem, "The Gift Perspective on Paul," in *Perspectives on Paul: Five Views*, ed. S. McKnight and B. J. Oropeza (Grand Rapids, MI: Baker Academic, 2020), 219-36; idem, *Paul and the Power of Grace* (Grand Rapids, MI: Eerdmans, 2020); **M. W. Bates,** *The Hermeneutics of the Apostolic Proclamation: The Center of Paul's Method of Scriptural Interpretation* (Waco, TX: Baylor University Press, 2012); idem, *Salvation by Allegiance Alone: Rethinking Faith, Works, and the Gospel of Jesus the King* (Grand Rapids, MI: Baker Academic, 2017); **J. C. Beker,** *Paul the Apostle: The Triumph of God in Life and Thought* (Philadelphia: Fortress, 1980); **B. Blackwell,** ed., *Reading Romans in Context: Paul and Second Temple Judaism* (Grand Rapids, MI: Zondervan, 2015); **B. K. Blount,** *Then the Whisper Put On Flesh: New Testament Ethics in an African*

American Context (Nashville: Abingdon, 2001); **B. K. Blount, C. H. Felder, C. J. Martin, and E. B. Powery,** eds., *True to Our Native Land: An African American New Testament Commentary* (Minneapolis: Fortress, 2007); **G. Bornkamm,** "The Letter to the Romans as Paul's Last Will and Testament," in *The Romans Debate*, ed. K. P. Donfried, rev. ed. (Grand Rapids, MI: Baker Academic, 1991), 16-28; **L. M. Bowens,** *African American Readings of Paul: Reception, Resistance, and Transformation* (Grand Rapids, MI: Eerdmans, 2020); **L. M. Bowens, S. McKnight, and J. B. Modica,** eds., *Romans in the Pew* (Eugene, OR: Cascade, 2022); **B. R. Braxton,** *Preaching Paul* (Nashville: Abingdon, 2004); **C. Campbell,** *Paul and Union with Christ: An Exegetical and Theological Study* (Grand Rapids, MI: Zondervan, 2012); idem, *Paul and the Hope of Glory: An Exegetical and Theological Study* (Grand Rapids, MI: Zondervan Academic, 2020); **D. A. Campbell,** *The Deliverance of God: An Apocalyptic Rereading of Justification in Paul* (Grand Rapids, MI: Eerdmans, 2013); idem, *Framing Paul: An Epistolary Biography* (Grand Rapids, MI: Eerdmans, 2014); idem, "Romans and the Apocalyptic Reading of Paul," in *Preaching Paul: Four Perspectives*, ed. S. McKnight and J. B. Modica (Grand Rapids, MI: Eerdmans, 2019), 40-58; idem, *Pauline Dogmatics: The Triumph of God's Love* (Grand Rapids, MI: Eerdmans, 2020); **D. A. Carson, P. T. O'Brien, and M. A. Seifrid,** eds., *Justification and Variegated Judaism, vol. 1, The Complexities of Second Temple Judaism, vol. 2, The Paradoxes of Paul* (Grand Rapids, MI: Baker Academic, 2001); **M. Croasmun,** *The Emergence of Sin: The Cosmic Tyrant in Romans* (New York: Oxford University Press, 2017); **A. A. Das,** *Solving the Romans Debate* (Minneapolis: Fortress, 2006); idem, *Paul and the Stories of Israel: Grand Thematic Narratives in Galatians* (Minneapolis: Fortress, 2016); **K. P. Donfried,** ed., *The Romans Debate*, 2nd ed. (Grand Rapids, MI: Baker Academic, 1991); **D. J. Downs,** *The Offering of the Gentiles: Paul's Collection for Jerusalem in Its Chronological, Cultural, and Cultic Contexts* (Grand Rapids, MI: Eerdmans, 2016); **J. D. G. Dunn,** *The Theology of Paul the Apostle* (Grand Rapids, MI: Eerdmans, 1998); idem, *The New Perspective on Paul*, rev. ed. (Grand Rapids, MI: Eerdmans, 2008); idem, *Romans*, 2 vols., WBC 38 (Grand Rapids, MI: Zondervan, 2015); **S. G. Eastman,** *Paul and the Person: Reframing Paul's Anthropology* (Grand Rapids, MI: Eerdmans, 2017); **P. F. Esler,** *Conflict and Identity in Romans: The Social Setting of Paul's Letter* (Minneapolis: Fortress Press, 2003); **R. H. Finger,** *Roman House Churches for Today: A Practical Guide for Small Groups* (Grand Rapids, MI: Eerdmans, 2007); **B. Gaventa,** *When in Romans: An Invitation to Linger with the Gospel According to Paul* (Grand Rapids, MI: Baker Academic, 2018); **M. J. Gorman,** *Becoming the Gospel: Paul, Participation, and Mission* (Grand Rapids, MI: Eerdmans, 2015); idem, *Apostle of the Crucified Lord: A Theological Introduction to Paul and His Letters,* 2nd ed. (Grand Rapids, MI: Eerdmans, 2016); idem, *Participating in Christ: Explorations in Paul's Theology and Spirituality* (Grand Rapids, MI: Eerdmans, 2019); idem, "Pauline Theology: Perspectives, Perennial Topics, and Prospects," in *The State of New Testament Studies: A Survey of Recent Research*, ed. S. McKnight and N. K. Gupta (Grand Rapids, MI: Baker Academic, 2019), 197-223; idem, "Romans and the Participationist Perspective," in *Preaching Romans: Four Perspectives*, ed. S. McKnight and J. B. Modica (Grand Rapids, MI: Eerdmans, 2019), 59-79; **P. Gray,** *Paul as a Problem in History and Culture: The Apostle and His Critics Through the Centuries* (Grand Rapids, MI: Baker Academic, 2016); **N. K. Gupta,** *Paul and the Language of Faith* (Grand Rapids, MI: Eerdmans, 2019); **R. B. Hays,** *The Faith of Jesus Christ: The Narrative Substructure of Galatians 3:1–4:11*, 2nd ed. (Grand Rapids, MI: Eerdmans, 2002); **M. Hengel,** *The Pre-Christian Paul*, trans. J. Bowden (Philadelphia: Trinity Press International, 1991); **M. Hengel and A. M. Schwemer,** *Paul Between Damascus and Antioch: The Unknown Years*, trans. J. Bowden (Louisville: Westminster John Knox, 1997); **H. G. Jacob,** *Conformed to the Image of His Son: Reconsidering Paul's Theology of Glory in Romans* (Downers Grove, IL: IVP Academic, 2018); **J. Jervell,** "The Letter to Jerusalem," in *The Romans Debate*, ed. K. P. Donfried, rev. ed. (Grand Rapids, MI: Baker Academic, 1991), 53-64; **L. A. Jervis,** *Purpose of Romans: A Comparative Letter Structure Investigation*, LNTS 55 (Sheffield: Sheffield Academic Press, 1991); **R. Jewett,** *Romans: A Commentary*, Hermeneia (Minneapolis: Fortress, 2007); **E. Käsemann,** *Commentary on Romans* (Grand Rapids, MI: Eerdmans, 1980); **P. Lampe,** *From Paul to Valentinus: Christians at Rome in the First Two Centuries*, trans. M. Steinhauser, ed. M. D. Johnson (Minneapolis: Fortress, 2003); **R. N. Longenecker,** *Introducing Romans: Critical Issues in Paul's Most Famous Letter* (Grand Rapids, MI: Eerdmans, 2011); idem, *The Epistle to the Romans* (Grand Rapids, MI: Eerdmans, 2016); **C. Marsh, P. Slade, and S. Azaransky,** eds., *Lived Theology: New Perspectives on Method, Style, and Pedagogy* (New York: Oxford University Press, 2016); **J. L. Martyn,** "The Apocalyptic Gospel in Galatians,"

Int 54 (2000): 246-66; **S. Mathew,** *Women in the Greetings of Romans 16.1-16: A Study of Mutuality and Women's Ministry in the Letter to the Romans,* LNTS 471 (London: T&T Clark, 2014); **S. McKnight,** *The King Jesus Gospel: The Original Good News Revisited,* 2nd ed. (Grand Rapids, MI: Zondervan, 2015); idem, *Pastor Paul: Nurturing a Culture of Christoformity in the Church,* Theological Explorations for the Church Catholic (Grand Rapids, MI: Brazos, 2019); idem, "Paul and Romans," in *The State of New Testament Studies: A Survey of Recent Research,* ed. S. McKnight and N. K. Gupta (Grand Rapids, MI: Baker Academic, 2019), 368-88; idem, *Reading Romans Backwards: The Gospel of Peace in the Midst of Empire* (Waco, TX: Baylor University Press, 2019); idem, "Romans and the New Perspective," in *Preaching Romans: Four Perspectives,* ed. S. McKnight and J. B. Modica (Grand Rapids, MI: Eerdmans, 2019), 20-39; **S. McKnight and J. B. Modica,** eds., *Preaching Romans: Four Perspectives* (Grand Rapids, MI: Eerdmans, 2019); **S. McKnight and B. J. Oropeza,** eds., *Perspectives on Paul: Five Views* (Grand Rapids, MI: Baker Academic, 2020); **W. A. Meeks,** *The First Urban Christians: The Social World of the Apostle Paul,* 2nd ed. (New Haven, CT: Yale University Press, 2003); **P. S. Minear,** *The Obedience of Faith: The Purposes of Paul in the Epistle to the Romans,* SBT 2/19 (London: SCM Press, 1971); **T. Morgan,** *Roman Faith and Christian Faith: Pistis and Fides in the Early Roman Empire and Early Churches* (New York: Oxford University Press, 2015); **M. D. Nanos,** *The Mystery of Romans: The Jewish Context of Paul's Letters* (Minneapolis: Fortress, 1996); idem, *Reading Romans Within Judaism: Collected Essays of Mark D. Nanos* (Eugene, OR: Cascade, 2018); **P. Oakes,** *Reading Romans in Pompeii: Paul's Letter at Ground Level* (Minneapolis: Fortress, 2009); **D. Odell-Scott,** ed., *Reading Romans with Contemporary Philosophers and Theologians* (New York: T&T Clark, 2007); **D. Patte and C. Grenholm,** eds., *Modern Interpretations of Romans: Tracking Their Hermeneutical/Theological Trajectory* (London: T&T Clark, 2013); **J. Piper,** *The Justification of God: An Exegetical and Theological Study of Romans 9:1-23,* 2nd ed. (Grand Rapids, MI: Baker Academic, 1993); **B. Przybylski,** *Righteousness in Matthew and His World of Thought,* SNTSMS 41 (Cambridge: Cambridge University Press, 1981); **M. Reasoner,** *Romans in Full Circle: A History of Interpretation* (Minneapolis: Fortress, 2005); **E. R. Richards,** *The Secretary in the Letters of Paul,* WUNT 2/42 (Tübingen: Mohr Siebeck, 1991); **R. Riesner,** *Paul's Early Period: Chronology, Mission Strategy, Theology,* trans. D. W. Stott (Grand Rapids, MI: Eerdmans, 1997); idem, "Pauline Chronology," in *The Blackwell Companion to Paul* (Chichester, UK: Wiley-Blackwell, 2011), 9-29; **R. Rodriguez,** *If You Call Yourself a Jew: Reappraising Paul's Letter to the Romans* (Eugene, OR: Cascade, 2014); **R. Rodriguez and M. Thiessen,** eds., *The So-Called Jew in Paul's Letter to the Romans* (Minneapolis: Fortress, 2016); **E. P. Sanders,** *Judaism: Practice and Belief, 63 BCE–66 CE* (Minneapolis: Fortress, 2016); idem, *Paul and Palestinian Judaism: A Comparison of Patterns of Religion* (repr., Philadelphia: Fortress, 2017); **W. D. Shiell,** *Delivering from Memory: The Effect of Performance on the Early Christian Audience* (Eugene, OR: Pickwick, 2011); **S. K. Stowers,** *A Rereading of Romans: Justice, Jews, and Gentiles* (New Haven, CT: Yale University Press, 1994); **M. Thomas,** *Paul's "Works of the Law" in the Perspective of Second-Century Reception* (Downers Grove, IL: IVP Academic, 2020); **P. Trebilco,** *The Early Christians in Ephesus from Paul to Ignatius* (Grand Rapids, MI: Eerdmans, 2007); **F. Watson,** "The Two Roman Congregations: Romans 14:1–15:13," in *The Romans Debate,* ed. K. P. Donfried, rev. ed. (Grand Rapids, MI: Baker Academic, 1991), 203-15; idem, *Paul, Judaism, and the Gentiles: Beyond the New Perspective,* 2nd ed. (Grand Rapids, MI: Eerdmans, 2007); **A. J. M. Wedderburn,** *The Reasons for Romans* (Minneapolis: Fortress, 1991); **W. Wiefel,** "The Jewish Community in Ancient Rome and the Origins of Roman Christianity," in *The Romans Debate,* ed. K. P. Donfried, rev. ed. (Grand Rapids, MI: Baker Academic, 1991), 85-101; **J. A. D. Weima,** *Neglected Endings: The Significance of Pauline Letter Closings,* JSNTSup 101 (Sheffield: JSOT Press, 1994); **S. Westerholm,** "Romans and the 'Lutheran' Paul," in *Preaching Romans: Four Perspectives,* ed. S. McKnight and J. B. Modica (Grand Rapids, MI: Eerdmans, 2019), 3-19; **N. T. Wright,** "The Letter to the Romans," *NIB* 10:393–770; idem, *Paul and the Faithfulness of God,* 2 vols., COQG 4 (Minneapolis: Fortress, 2013); idem, *Paul and His Recent Interpreters* (Minneapolis: Fortress, 2015); **M. Zetterholm,** "The Paul Within Judaism Perspective," in *Perspectives on Paul: Five Views,* ed. S. McKnight and B. J. Oropeza (Grand Rapids, MI: Baker Academic, 2020), 171-93.

S. McKnight

RULERS. *See* Empire; Political Systems; Politics and Power; Principalities and Powers.

S

SACRIFICE, OFFERING

Religious sacrifices were common in Judaism and throughout the Greco-Roman sociocultural and religious milieu in which Paul lived, labored, and ministered. As such, a choice for the background of Paul's imagery or his use of sacrificial language in specific passages, although useful, should be considered only as necessary. Nevertheless, Paul's use of the sacrifice imagery often hews closely to that of the OT because the religious importance of the sacrificial system among the Israelites gave them a distinct and unique concept of sacrifice deeper than those of the surrounding cultures.

1. Old Testament Background
2. The Sacrifice of Christ
3. Sacrifice and Christian Living
4. Paul's Use of the Sacrificial Language of *Osmēn Euōdias*

1. Old Testament Background.

The OT Scriptures are replete with examples of sacrifice, some of which are often considered typological or allusions to the sacrificial *death of *Christ. Paul draws out the implications of some of OT passages for Christian living (compare Ex 12:1-11 with 1 Cor 5; 7; Deut 21:23 with Gal 3:13).

2. The Sacrifice of Christ.

Throughout his letters, Paul in various ways interweaves sacrifice imagery with the person and the work of Christ. Romans 3:21-26, especially Romans 3:25, presents the clearest example of Paul's discussion of the sacrifice of Christ, particularly in his use of the term *hilastērion*. Although the meaning of the word in its relation to Christ's atoning work as either expiation or propitiation remains unresolved, it is nonetheless agreed that the atonement emphasizes where *God deals with the problem of human *sin but not how. Avoiding the hermeneutical dichotomy, some recent translations, such as the NIV and NRSV, translate the term neutrally, as "sacrifice of atonement." As such, Paul hints that the death of Jesus was the great Day of Atonement. God made the death of Jesus "the new place of atonement, epiphany, and divine presence," the new means of access to God open to all (Jewett, 287).

In Romans 5:5-10, Paul shows why the sacrificial death of Christ is so important. He died at the right time, when humanity was helpless and ungodly. The result of this is threefold: (1) believers are justified by his blood (Rom 5:9a), (2) they are saved by him (Rom 5:9b, 10c), and (3) the *wrath of God was satisfied (Rom 5:9c). In the same vein, Paul argues that God sent Jesus to deal with the problem of sin, *peri hamartias* (Rom 8:3); there is no more condemnation for those who are in Jesus (see Rom 8:1-4) since Christ is the atoning sacrifice. Paul argues that Christ died for believers while they were still sinners. Paul refers to Christ as the Passover Lamb in 1 Corinthians 5:8, thus reminding the Corinthians of Exodus 12:5-6 and the deliverance of the Israelites out of Egypt. Several other passages in the Pauline corpus contain either direct references or allusions to the sacrificial death of Christ (see Rom 8:32).

3. Sacrifice and Christian Living.

Paul employs the terminology of sacrifice to teach important truths about Christian living. In Romans 15:15-16, Paul uses several terms that are common to the OT cultus: *present*, *sacrifice*, *holy*, and *acceptable*. Paul uses these terms as expressive of the believer's new relationship with Christ. He speaks of himself as a priest of the *gospel, bringing the offering of the *Gentiles to *Jerusalem (see also 1 Cor 9:13-14). He uses the language of sacrifice in Romans 12:1-2 to state the ethical response which the Christian is to make to God in view of God's mercies, which is to present oneself as a living sacrifice. This is to let Christians know that, unlike some Greek philosophers who opined that *worship consisted only in the offering up of the human spirit to God, they must worship God in their bodies, that is, in all the activities of *body and mind in daily life. They must do so by carefully considering what sort of behavior conforms with God's will. Christian worship must be a continual offering and presentation of heart and life.

4. Paul's Use of the Sacrificial Language of *Osmēn Euōdias*.
In the LXX, these words first occur together in Genesis 8:21. Noah has built an altar to God on which he offers sacrifices. The *Lord smells the "soothing aroma" (LXX, *osmēn euōdias*) of Noah's sacrifice. The phrase implies that Noah's sacrifice appeased God's wrath. Paul portrays himself and his fellow workers as those who attest to God the efficacy of Christ's sacrifice. It is striking that here the fragrance goes out. Paul and his *coworkers are the ones in a triumphal procession who are responsible for the incense. In other words, they spread the *knowledge of Christ everywhere. As priests, then, Paul and fellow workers offer up a sacrifice that is pleasing to the Lord. In the same vein, Paul's sacrificial language is evident in 2 Corinthians 4:7-12, especially 2 Corinthians 4:11. Paul presents himself as a "living martyr" for the sake of the *church, who, instead of dying in his letter, continues to live. As such, his sacrifice is ongoing, showing that a sacrificial life is needed to enable the hearers of the gospel to share in the life abundant that Jesus came to bring.

In Philippians 2:17-18, reflecting on his situation as a prisoner, with execution a hovering possibility (Phil 1:12-26), Paul switches to a sacrificial metaphor. He would gladly pour himself out, even to the point of martyrdom, to make the Philippians' service acceptable to God (see Ex 29:38-41; Num 15:1-10; 28:1-15). The focus of Paul's vivid metaphor is not on martyrdom itself. Instead, Paul is willing to be poured out to complete his friends' sacrifice at Philippi, whatever that might involve. He also uses the sacrifice imagery to describe the monetary gift from the Philippians in Philippians 4:18. Taken together, Paul's use of the sacrifice imagery admits of broad interpretation, including the Christian life of *faith and their whole life of obedience, humility, *holiness, and *witness that is the fruit of faith.

See also ATONEMENT; ETHICS; JUSTIFICATION; OLD TESTAMENT IN PAUL; SIN, GUILT; TEMPLE; TRIUMPH; WRATH, DESTRUCTION.

BIBLIOGRAPHY. **J. A. Adewuya,** "The Sacrificial-Missiological Function of Paul's Sufferings in the Context of 2 Corinthians," in *Paul as Missionary: Identity, Activity, Theology, and Practice*, LNTS 420 (London: T&T Clark, 2011), 88-98; idem, *Holiness in the Letters of Paul: A Necessary Response to the Gospel* (Eugene, OR: Cascade Books, 2016); **J. Bassler,** "The Passion of Christ in the Letters of Paul," in *Engaging the Passion: Perspectives on the Death of Jesus*, ed. O. L. Yarbrough (Philadelphia: Fortress, 2015); **R. H. Bell,** "Sacrifice and Christology in Paul," *JTS* 53, no. 1 (April 2002): 1-27; **M. J. Boda,** *A Severe Mercy: Sin and Its Remedy in the Old Testament* (Minneapolis: Fortress, 2009); **C. B. Cousar,** *A Theology of the Cross: The Death of Jesus in the Pauline Letters*, OBT 24 (Minneapolis: Fortress, 1990); **X. DeBroeck,** "Becoming a Priestly People: A Biblical Theology of Liturgical Sacrifice as Spiritual Formation" (PhD diss., Duquesne University, 2017); **C. A. Eberhart,** *The Sacrifice of Jesus: Understanding Atonement Biblically* (Minneapolis: Fortress, 2011); **S. Finlan,** *The Background and Content of Paul's Cultic Atonement Metaphors* (Leiden: Brill, 2004); idem, "Spiritualization of Sacrifice in Paul and Hebrews," in *Ritual and Metaphor: Sacrifice in the Bible* (Atlanta: Society of Biblical Literature, 2011), 83-97; **N. K. Gupta,** *Worship That Makes Sense to Paul*, BZNW (New York: de Gruyter, 2010); **R. Jewett,** *Romans*, Hermeneia (Minneapolis: Augsburg Fortress, 2006); **J. L. Patterson,** *Keeping the Feast: Metaphors of Sacrifice in 1 Corinthians and Philippians* (Atlanta: SBL Press, 2015); **M. Vahrenhorst,** *Kultische Sprache in Den Paulusbriefen*, WUNT (Tübingen: Mohr Siebeck 2008).

J. A. Adewuya

SALVATION

In the Pauline corpus the terminology of salvation is frequent. The verb *sōzō* ("to save") occurs twenty-nine times (Rom 5:9, 10; 8:24; 9:27; 10:9, 13; 11:14, 26; 1 Cor 1:18, 21; 3:15; 5:5; 7:16 [2×]; 9:22; 10:33; 15:2; 2 Cor 2:15; Eph 2:5, 8; 1 Thess 2:16; 2 Thess 2:10; 1 Tim 1:15; 2:4, 15; 4:16; 2 Tim 1:9; 4:18; Titus 3:5); the noun *sōtēria* ("salvation") eighteen times (Rom 1:16; 10:1, 10; 11:11; 13:11; 2 Cor 1:6; 6:2 [2×]; 7:10; Eph 1:13; Phil 1:19, 28; 2:12; 1 Thess 5:8, 9; 2 Thess 2:13; 2 Tim 2:10; 3:15). In their general usage, both terms denote deliverance or a secured state of safety. One of the distinctive features of salvation in the Hebrew Scriptures is its consistently theocentric character: Yahweh is almost always the saving agent and is emphatically declared to be the unique *savior. Like the other NT writers, Paul picks up on this universe of discourse, though with a christological inflection: in his thought it is now the crucified and risen Jesus *Christ who has become the sole author of salvation.

In the apostle's narrower usage, salvation refers to a specific future, end-time event in which *God decisively saves the elect from divine *judgment and/or hostile forces. But because this eschatological event presupposes a complex of prior events (regeneration, reconciliation, *justification, *forgiveness, etc.), *sōzō* and *sōtēria* can serve as a synecdoche (a part standing in for a larger whole) for the range of God's saving activities. In this case, Paul's salvation serves as an umbrella term, marking off a larger semantic category under which more specific soteriological terms, including *justification*, are subsumed. In providing an overview of Paul's concept of salvation, then, it will be important to attend not only to usages of *sōzō* and *sōtēria* as they occur in the Pauline and deutero-Pauline letters (this article will assume Paul as the author without prejudice to the issue of pseudonymity) but also to the concept of salvation developed in his writings.

1. The Meaning of Salvation Prior to Paul
2. Salvation in Paul's Early Letters
3. Salvation in Paul's Later Letters
4. Conclusion

1. The Meaning of Salvation Prior to Paul.

The term *sōzō*, together with its cognate *sōtēria*, is employed in various contexts in ancient Greek and Hebrew literature. In the broader corpus, terms of saving are most frequently associated with deliverance, not uncommonly rescue from military threat or disaster at sea. In other contexts, salvation refers to a forensic intervention, where the saving act is tantamount to vindication, or to a medical intervention, where the saving act is tantamount to *healing (as in the Gospels). A not uncommon occurrence of the former usage relates to a king or other political authority granting a pardon (e.g. Plutarch, *Cat. Min.* 69). The noun *sōtēria* and its verbal cognate also came to be applied to civic fruitfulness, wholeness, blessing, and *peace (SIG 2:589). In the Hellenistic period, it fell to kings to ensure the continued *sōtēria* of their people. In this case, salvation carries a certain political or ideological freight, referring to the positive outcome of a powerful ruler's actions, whether in response to external threats or as part of a well-functioning administration.

In the LXX tradition, the Greek verb *sōzō* is most frequently correlated with the Hebrew verb *yšʿ*. Not surprisingly, in both the LXX and the Hebrew Scriptures, terms of saving show considerable semantic overlap with nonbiblical uses. Yet as noted above, in the scriptural tradition, terms of salvation invariably retain a theocentric cast. Yahweh is the one who saves, and the righteous are the beneficiaries of this divine salvation. As a corollary, because the God of *Israel is the one and only savior (Is 43:11), idols are useless to save (Is 45:20; 46:7; Jer 2:27; 3:23; 11:12; Hos 14:4). Yahweh's role as savior cannot be abstracted from his role as the *covenant-making God. This is in part evidenced by the fact that in covenantal relationships between human political leaders, the weaker vassal's bid for help was sometimes framed as requests for salvation (e.g., 2 Kings 16:7). Nor can Yahweh's saving activity be finally separated either from his primordial defeat of chaos at *creation (Ps 74:12-13) or from his identity as king (Is 33:22; Ps 44:3-4). On any account of the Jewish scriptural tradition prior to Paul, Yahweh's identity as savior is situated within a larger monotheistic framework that took for granted God's covenant-making purposes. In working out a christologically reformulated concept of salvation in his epistles, the *apostle builds on this framework.

2. Salvation in Paul's Early Letters.

2.1. Galatians. In his greeting to the Galatians, Paul reflects on the saving action of Jesus Christ, "who gave himself for our *sin to rescue [*exelētai*] us from the present evil age" (Gal 1:4 NIV). The clause anticipates two of the epistle's leading themes: the contrast between the law's inability and Christ's effectiveness in achieving redemption (Gal 2:18-21), and the epic conflict between the spheres of *law/*flesh, on the one side, and *faith/Spirit, on the other (Gal 5:16-26). In expounding on this cosmic struggle and its stakeholders, Paul identifies "those of the law" with the Mosaic covenant, originating at Sinai, while "those of faith" are linked with the present-day trajectory of the *Abraham covenant, situated in the eschatological *Jerusalem (Gal 4:21-31). Those who submit to the law, including those who insist on *Gentile *circumcision, risk being subject to the *curse of the law. By contrast, those who side with the "of faith" party are poised to experience Christ's redemption, which had been achieved by his absorbing the law's curse through crucifixion (Gal 3:13).

Through Christ's *death and the giving of the Spirit, then, the impartation of the Abrahamic blessing (Gen 12:1-3) to the Gentiles is now made possible (Gal 3:14). In reverting to the law, the Galatians are in danger of being enslaved by the elemental powers that impose their yoke through the law (Gal 4:3, 8; 5:1). Those among the Galatians who continue down this path, the apostle warns, would forfeit the prospect of divine *adoption, together with its entailments of future inheritance and the present experience of the Spirt (Gal 4:6-7).

Given this overview of the concept of salvation as presented in Galatians, one may surmise no fewer than five significant points. First, though the apostle's account of salvation clearly has implications for the individual believer (Gal 2:20), these personal aspects are clearly subordinate to concerns of a more cosmic scope, involving the real-time transfer of humanity from an economy of law to a life of faith in the Spirit. Second, Christ's salvation grants deliverance not only from the legal consequences of sin (Gal 2:15-21; 5:1-4; see Rom 3:23) but also from sin's power (Gal 5:13-26). Third, among the benefits of salvation is humanity's release from a specific redemptive-historical trajectory, corresponding to a belief system and way of life, summarily designated as "the law." As a result of Christ's redemption, the law has become an outmoded basis for covenantal blessing and eschatological hope (Gal 3:10-14; see Rom 3:9; 8:32). The redemptive-historical shift from a *temple-based economy, along with its markers of circumcision and dietary protocols, to a Spirit-based economy, with its own set of markers, has signaled not only a qualitatively better salvation than that which was formerly available under the law but also a more inclusive one. Fourth, in whatever sense those who have been justified by faith are saved in the present, such salvation includes their participation in the liberating experience of the Spirit (Gal 4:4-7; see Rom 8:9-11; 2 Cor 5:15). To be saved in this last sense is not only to delivered *from* the flesh and the law, but also to be saved *to and for* the pneumatic experience of sonship (see Rom 8:9-11; 1 Cor 12:4-6; 2 Cor 13:13). Fifth and finally, Christ's saving death is a necessary condition for *mission to the Gentiles (Gal 3:14, 29; see Rom 3:3-4, 21-26). Christ's death and the granting of the Spirit have now made salvation possible for Jew and Gentile alike. In summary, Paul would have his Galatian readers know that Christ's salvation has implications with respect to their objective legal status before God, their experience of power over sin, their eschatological hope, their enjoyment of the Spirit, and the scope of their missionary aspirations.

2.2. Thessalonian Correspondence. In contrast to Galatians, where Paul concentrates on God's saving activity in the past and in the present, 1 and 2 Thessalonians focus on future salvation as a future event. This future event is one and the same as the parousia (1 Thess 4:15), that is, the coming of Christ as the reigning **Lord* (1 Thess 2:19; 4:15; 5:23; see 1 Cor 12:3; Phil 2:9-11). Within this context, the "*hope of salvation" (1 Thess 5:8; see Job 2:9 LXX; 4 Macc 11:7; T. Job 24.1; 1 En. 98.14) refers to the expectation of, in the first place, escaping from an oppressive and morally compromised existence, and, in the second place, entering into the dominion of Christ. By bundling together salvation, parousia, and Christ's universal reign, Paul implies that salvation means nothing less than the arrival of the *kingdom of God with Christ as its rightful *head.

For the apostle, the emphatically futuristic quality of salvation takes nothing away from its present-day practical relevance to ethical living. This is apparent in the very opening of 1 Thessalonians, where the apostle recalls the evidence of God's work among the Thessalonian believers, not least their tangible expressions of faith, *love, and hope (1 Thess 1:3). Paul exhorts his hearers to grasp their future salvation firmly, if only to bring its significance to bear on their struggle with Roman and synagogue-sponsored persecution (1 Thess 1:4-9). The expectation of future salvation is likewise a motivation for the Thessalonians' continuing commitment to *holiness and *purity (1 Thess 3:13; 5:23; see 1 Cor 3:10-17; 6:12-20; Phil 3:20), especially sexual purity (1 Thess 4:3-8). Neither acts of repentance nor concrete demonstrations of loyalty to Christ are material causes of salvation but its fruit. This future salvation, ultimately the outworking of God's prior elective activity (1 Thess 4:15; 5:9), functions as the true north, as it were, of the believers' moral compass. In cultivating hope of salvation through right living, the Thessalonian believers only further confirm their hope of receiving deliverance them "from the *wrath to come" (1 Thess 1:10).

All the while, Paul draws his key soteriological terms from familiar scriptural narratives. For example, in reflecting on his offer of "salvation" to "Gentiles" (1 Thess 2:16), the apostle is inviting the more well-versed of his readers to associate his *ministry with the scriptural promises relating to the eschatological salvation of the nations (Gen 12:13; Ps 22:7; Zech 2:11; 14:16; Mal 1:11; etc.). This is one and the same with the salvation anticipated by Isaiah (Is 42:4; 49:6; 56:7; 60:1-3), as the prophet looked forward to the coming of Yahweh's kingdom (Is 40–55) and the concomitant subjugation of the Gentiles (Is 41:11-13; 45:14; 49:23-26; 51:22-23; 54:15-17; 60:3-5; etc.). Here salvation implies the reversal of Israel's grim political fortunes through the long-awaited return from exile, as well as a renewed creation through the power of the Spirit.

If, in the Thessalonian correspondence, Paul presents salvation in Christ as the fulfillment of the prophetic *visions, he also leverages this and other soteriological terms in dialogue with the religio-political claims of Rome. Because Caesar's devotees in Thessaloniki and across the span of the *empire would have regarded the emperor as their *sōtēr*, and the effects of his rule as *sōtēria*, the apostle's references to Christ's lordship and kingdom would have been understood as a response to emperor *worship, not to mention an oblique challenge to the claims made on Caesar's behalf. The same rhetorical strategy comes into play in Paul's account of the *parousia* ("coming," 1 Thess 4:13-18), where the apostle invites comparison between Christ's coming and the ritual of parousia as it was practiced by imperial visitors (for examples see Harrison).

Similarly, when Paul states that believers who are still alive will join the resurrected dead for a "meeting" (*apantēsin*) with the Lord in the air (1 Thess 4:16-17), the word choice gestures toward a Hellenistic practice whereby visiting dignitaries would be dutifully greeted by the leading citizens outside the city limits only to be led back to town. What is more, ancient usage attests to instances in which *apantēsis* refers not simply to the visit of a passing dignitary but to the grand entrance of a conquering general (e.g., Cicero [*Att.* 16.11.6] in reference to Octavian; Josephus [*J.W.* 7.100] in reference to Titus). Once consideration of such intertextualities in 1 Thessalonians is combined with the not uncommon judgment that the *"man of lawlessness" (2 Thess 2:1-12) is a cipher for a Roman political figure, an unmistakable pattern begins to emerge. By explicating salvation with reference to practices and notions derived from imperial ideology, Paul implies that the benefits of Christ's *sōtēria* are far superior to whatever benefits may be promised by the narratives of Roman propagandists.

Like other Pauline and Jewish texts, 2 Thessalonians affirms that future salvation depends on human agency, including the exercise of proper judgments and existential commitments. Scholars who grant the authenticity of 2 Thessalonians generally maintain that Paul wrote this letter in order to respond to questions or misunderstandings occasioned by the reception of 1 Thessalonians. One such misunderstanding, current among at least some of the Thessalonian believers, seems to have been the notion that the day of the Lord had already come (2 Thess 2:2). Toward clarifying matters, Paul fills out certain details of the eschatological scenario, beginning with the so-called man of lawlessness, who, after perpetrating his deceptions, would be vanquished by Christ at the parousia (2 Thess 2:8). Those seduced by the man of lawlessness would be culpable because "they refused to love the *truth and so be saved" (2 Thess 2:10 NIV), suggesting that an honest desire for truth is a necessary condition for salvation. Similarly, when Paul expresses his confidence that the Thessalonian believers would be among those "to be saved," he adds that this salvation will be accomplished "through the sanctifying work of the Spirit and through belief in the truth" (2 Thess 2:13 NIV). Given the instrumental role of cognition and sanctification in salvation, it becomes clear that for Paul, ordinarily speaking, salvation is operationalized through the channels of either rational thought or ethical decision-making. In short, God's salvation in Christ demands appropriate human response.

2.3. Corinthian Correspondence. Within the scope of the Pauline corpus, the Corinthian correspondence is an exceptional source for illustrating the multifaceted nature of Paul's salvation. For example, in identifying the risen Christ as the believer's *righteousness, holiness, and redemption (1 Cor 1:30), Paul implies that the whole range of soteriological benefits bound up in Christ, however notionally discrete, are logically inseparable. Likewise, when he asserts that the Corinthian believers have been washed, sanctified, and justified (1 Cor 5:11), these perfected divine actions are to be understood as concurrent aspects of one and the same salvation. In this connection, one cannot overlook Paul's introduction of his doctrine of reconciliation (2 Cor 5:11–6:2), which, like justification, sanctification, and redemption, speaks to a specific aspect of God's saving act in Christ. Such data points warn against any attempt to lay inordinate weight to any one of salvation's subcategories over against the others. A truly Pauline account of salvation cannot reduce salvation to one of its constituent aspects but rather must embrace the sum of them.

In 1 and 2 Corinthians, the timing of salvation verges on the paradoxical, whereby the terms *sōtēria* and *sōzō* come to possess an already-but-not-yet quality. For example, in stating that God used the "foolishness of what was preached to save those who believe" (1 Cor 1:21 NIV), the infinitive "to save" virtually functions as a circumlocution for God's activity of regeneration or the divine effecting of conversion. Likewise, in 2 Corinthians 2:15, Paul appears to envision salvation as an unfolding process in the time-space continuum: "For we are to God the pleasing aroma of Christ among *those who are being saved* [*tois sōzomenois*] and those who are perishing" (NIV). Yet if such statements seem to frame salvation as a presently unfolding process, these have to be read against the weightier instances where salvation is decidedly future (1 Cor 3:15; 5:5; 7:16; 10:33; 15:2). In the Corinthian letters, the realities signified by terms such as *sōtēria* and *sōzō* have a present quality to them but are nevertheless incorrigibly eschatological. In the Corinthian letters, as in the Thessalonian correspondence, the apostle locates God's salvation at the climax of redemptive history.

In writing the Corinthians, Paul makes much of the fact that the chief means of achieving salvation is the apostolic *preaching of the *gospel, the essential outline of which is unequivocally stated in 1 Corinthians 15:1-8. According to Paul, the outline of this gospel includes three key reported events: (1) Christ's death according to the Scriptures, (2) his burial, and (3) his *resurrection, supported by numerous appearances. Not only does the rehearsal of these events, the irreducible content of the gospel, make salvation possible; it is equally true that the believer's salvation crucially depends on being persuaded on these points (1 Cor 1:21; 15:1-2). To recite these points faithfully is to preach the *cross, the means by which God's saving power is revealed (1 Cor 1:22-25). The message of the gospel narrative is the basis for salvation.

At the same time, Paul insists that believers will be saved not through artistic rhetoric but through "the foolishness of what was preached" (1 Cor 1:21 NIV; see 1 Cor 15:1-2). This is by divine design, so that faith, together with salvation, may come to rest on a manifestation of divine power through the Spirit (1 Cor 2:5). God's self-revelation in the person of the Spirit makes salvation possible. This has a democraticizing effect, for though the proclamation of salvation is clearly a special purview of the apostles, the Spirit's activity is by no means limited to the office. Paul expects the Corinthians to engage in the process of "saving" others, including their nonbelieving spouses (1 Cor 7:16). In the apostolic *modus operandi*, therefore, effective preaching unto salvation is achieved through the convergence of propositional revelation and pneumatic power.

Given the all-surpassing value of salvation and the critical importance of the gospel as a means of salvation, the preaching of the gospel is for Paul a matter of paramount importance. This in turn exerts a strong shaping influence on the apostle's *ethics. With a view to saving some, the apostle willingly sits loose to his rights and even his socioreligious *identity (1 Cor 9:22). When taking up the contentious issue of meat eating, he closes out the discussion by pointing to the importance of pleasing others rather than oneself so that those same individuals might be saved (1 Cor 10:23–11:1). This point is not unrelated Paul's recurring claim that his apostolic vocation of *suffering has been divinely harnessed for the salvation of others (2 Cor 1:6), all in keeping with his insistence that the power of the Spirit is supremely manifest in human weakness (2 Cor 4:1–6:11; 11:1–12:10). In discharging his vocation of bringing salvation to the Gentiles, the apostle submits to a mysterious economy in which self-abnegation and death to self give rise to salvation for others.

The mysterious quality of God's redemptive plan helps explain why Paul has been so badly misunderstood by his Corinthian readers. In setting the record straight, he argues that "the message of the cross is foolishness to those who are perishing . . . to us who are being saved it is the power of God" (1 Cor 1:18 NIV). Those who perish, including the rulers of this age, are destined for destruction simply because they have not availed themselves of the Spirit's insight (1 Cor 2:6-16). This is why, according to Paul, his gospel message lends itself so easily to misapprehension and rejection. Those who are perishing will perceive Paul's preaching "as an aroma that brings death," while to "those who are being saved" the proclamation is "aroma of life" (2 Cor 2:15-16). The Spirit's necessary role in illuminating the truth of the gospel message speaks to the elective nature of salvation.

Though Paul's theology consistently maintains a clear distinction between the saved and the perishing, this does not rule out, as far as the former category is concerned, degrees of felicity and infelicity. In the Corinthian correspondence, evidence for relative reward within the sphere of salvation presents itself on Paul's warning that "we must all" (*pantas hēmas*) appear before the judgment seat of Christ, in order to receive what is due for deeds done in the *body, whether good or bad (2 Cor 5:10). Because the "we" here presumably includes the Corinthians believers no less than the apostle himself, it would seem to follow that salvation, already tightly correlated with final judgment, neither exempts the elect from judgment (Gathercole, 266) nor precludes recognition of relative merit or demerit. The same eschatological scenario is implied in Paul's warning that Christian believers "build" carefully (1 Cor 3). Only if what is built survives, the apostle warns, will there be reward (1 Cor 3:14). On the other hand, if it is consumed, "the builder will suffer loss but yet will be saved—even though only as one escaping through the flames" (1 Cor 3:15 NIV). Unless such sentiments are mere rhetorical window-dressing, Paul is exhorting the Corinthian believers to holy living by appealing to the future judgment and the variable degrees of postmortem felicity.

3. Salvation in Paul's Later Letters.

*3.1. **Prison Epistles.*** One of the four so-called prison epistles, Paul's letter to the Ephesians is introduced with an extended crescendo of praise, landing final emphasis on salvation as the divine reconfiguration of creation. Here the Ephesian believers are reminded that the spiritual blessings that accrue to them are the result of the Father's elective purposes, securing them an adoptive status (Eph 1:3-5). Furthermore, by virtue of their participation in Christ, they have experienced divine redemption, which is equivalent to forgiveness (Eph 1:7). As important as these redemptive acts are within the "gospel of your salvation" (Eph 1:13), these are only tending toward a cosmic-wide unification of "all things in heaven and on earth" (Eph 1:10 NIV), occurring, as the rest of the letter spells out, on a vertical level (between angelic beings in the invisible realm) as well as on a horizontal level (between Jew and Gentile in the visible realm). Viewed from this aspect, the Pauline concept of salvation refers to God's decisive action in the context of "God's restorative justice for the whole of creation" (Wright, 165).

Written either shortly before or shortly after Ephesians, Colossians together with its companion epistle makes for an interesting study of contrasts, not least in their respective treatment of kingdom. Whereas in Ephesians 5:5 Paul aligns the kingdom with the future eschatological inheritance (see 1 Cor 6:9-10; 15:24, 50; Gal 5:21; 1 Thess 2:12; 2 Thess 1:5; 2 Tim 4:1, 8), in Colossians the kingdom is a present (perfective) reality: "For he has rescued us from the dominion of darkness and brought us into the kingdom of the Son he loves" (Col 1:13 NIV). Paul's appeal to kingdom language in describing salvation is of course reminiscent of certain Jesus traditions relating to the kingdom. Whether and to what extent these dominical traditions (in their oral form) directly influenced Paul is difficult to assess. In any case, such traditions would not be necessary to explain Paul's use of kingdom language, since Paul made direct use of the story where the concept of kingdom is central (Dan 2; 7; Gladd). In any case, in Colossians the fluid movement from "*in Christ" categories to the kingdom implies that for Paul to be in Christ (the King) is to be in the kingdom—and vice versa. In this light, it once again appears that salvation is tantamount to participation in and submission to Christ's rule.

Both Ephesians and Colossians allude to the reconciling work of Christ, driven home in both texts through the metaphor of the body. The crucified and risen *body of Christ is the newly reconstituted humanity, effecting reconciliation between Jews and Gentiles (Eph 2:15). Christ established this reconciliation "by making peace through his blood, shed on the cross" (Col 1:20). Paul's presentation of salvation in these terms speaks, as noted above, to his conviction that divine salvation culminates with all things on heaven and on earth coming into complete unity. At the same time, the parallel between Paul's description of Christ's pacifying act of *triumph and contemporaneous accounts of politico-military "reconciliations" celebrated in contemporary assertions of royal ideology (Jipp, 122-27) invites comparison of the two spheres. If powerful kings were wont to reconcile with their foes through military victory, then Paul's use of reconciliation language speaks both to Christ's legitimacy as the true world savior and to the lasting effects of his salvation.

Nor is it easy to miss, either in Ephesians or in Colossians, Paul's depiction of the triumphant Jesus as *Christus Victor*. In Ephesians, Jesus is presented as the one who, on account of his death and resurrection, has ascended far above every ruler and authority, angelic and earthly—all in order to be the head of creation (Eph 1:15-23). In Colossians, themes of combat and victory, juxtaposed effortlessly with forensic terms, emerge in the apostle's attempt to tease out the implications of Christ's saving death (Col 2:14-15). Combining key terms from Genesis 1; Psalm 8; and *wisdom traditions, Paul in Colossians seeks to render Christ's redeeming work in both sapiential and creational terms (Col 1:15-20). A robust reading of these data points would suggest that for Paul Christ's salvation is the climax of the primordial *Chaoskampf* (struggle against chaos), initiated at creation between the Creator God and his opposers (Gen 1). If so, this would not be an unprecedented notion in early Christianity, since this paradigm for describing Christ's saving act takes its place alongside similar sentiments expressed by other NT writers (e.g., Mk 3:23-39 pars; 1 Pet 3:18-22; Rev 19:11-21).

In Ephesians and Colossians, individual and ecclesial maturity are significant outcomes of salvation. In writing the Colossians, Paul expresses his goal of presenting everyone "perfect in Christ" (*teleion in Christō*, Col 1:28). Along with his *coworkers, Paul prays that the believers at Colossae "stand firm in the will of God, mature [*teleioi*] and fully assured" (Col 4:12 NIV). Transposing the same point into corporate terms, the apostle anticipates the day when, upon attaining unity in faith and in *knowledge, believers together become "the mature man" (*eis andra teleion*), the Adamic body of Christ. This maturity is achieved not just through the proclamation of the gospel but through the exercise of spiritual *gifts, which allows the church to grow out into ever increasing mutual interdependency (Eph 4:11-16).

In both prison epistles, the gratuitous character of salvation comes to the foreground, especially given the conjoining of redemption, forgiveness, *grace, and new life. In Ephesians, Paul lays repeated emphasis on the association between salvation and grace (Eph 2:5, 8), whereby the latter functions as the precipitating cause of the former. Salvation, then, is extrinsic to human works, though it is much debated among Pauline scholars whether salvation is monergistic (purely an act of God) or synergistic (cooperative; on this topic, see Watson; Barclay and Gathercole; Maston; Sprinkle). In both texts, where he depends on metaphors of death and resurrection, Paul conceives of salvation as a totalizing transfer from one sphere of reality (death) to another (life; Eph 2:8-9; Col 2:13).

In Philippians, Paul once again emphasizes the futurity of salvation, this time linking it more explicitly with resurrection. Here the imprisoned apostle rejoices in the knowledge that through the Philippians' prayers and through the power of the Spirit "what has happened to me will turn out for my deliverance [*eis sōtērian*]" (Phil 1:19 NIV). While some commentators take this deliverance to refer to a release from prison, the echoes with Job 13:16 LXX, which anticipates a transcendent vindication (Job 19:25-27), would seem to indicate that a postmortem hope is in view. Paul rests in the confidence that all such setbacks will contribute to the *glory of his everlasting state, one and the same as salvation.

This aspiration takes on slightly different form in Paul's wish to "know the power of his resurrection and participation in his sufferings . . . and so, somehow, attaining to the resurrection from the dead" (Phil 3:10-11 NIV). In the fuller context of Philippians, then, salvation is future resurrection. At first blush, this inference seems to be belied by Paul's instruction that the Philippians "work out" (*katergazesthe*) their "own [*heautōn*] salvation in fear and trembling" (Phil 2:12), as such a command might intimate that salvation is a present possession that takes on fuller form through human volition and actions. On this approach, to "work out" is sometimes taken to mean to "tease out the implications of" or to "complete." But given the fairly obvious comparison between the Philippians' "own salvation" and the salvation obtained by the self-humbling Christ (Phil 2:6-11), a more convincing approach would be to interpret *katergazesthe* as "lay hold of" or something to that effect (Anderson, 304-5). After all, in order for the implied comparison to be effective, the Philippians' salvation must be analogous to the eschatological salvation experienced by Christ at his resurrection and *ascension (Phil 2:9).

3.2. *Romans.* Paul's thematization of salvation in Romans is signaled no later than the epistle's programmatic sixteenth verse: "For I am not ashamed of the gospel, because it is the power of God that brings *salvation* to everyone who believes: first to the Jew, then to the Gentile" (Rom 1:16 NIV). Though the apostle has already expounded on belief as the sole basis for justification in his earlier writings, in this epistle one finds his most extensive treatment of the topic as a component within the larger discussion of salvation. This elaboration occupies the better part of Romans 1–4. First, in Romans 1:18–3:20, Paul undertakes to show that Jew and Gentile alike stand under the condemnation of sin. Sin has leveled the playing field, and the key criterion at the eschatological judgment, Paul insists, will not be ethnic identity but obedience to the law (Rom 2:13-14). In the case of Gentile law-keepers (at least as many commentators read the passage), this obedience is made possible through the empowering presence of the Spirit, which is the law written on their hearts (Rom 2:15). That ability to keep the law and participate in the Spirit, for the Gentile no less than the Jew, is dependent on availing oneself of the righteousness of God through faith (Rom 3:22).

In Romans 4, Paul closes out this portion of his argument by showing that Abraham was credited with righteousness before receiving circumcision and thus had obtained a righteousness apart from the law. Justification by faith is logically prior to but inseparable from salvation (Rom 5:9-10). Paul later reasserts the same point when he states that it is through belief that one is justified and through confession that one is saved (Rom 10:9-12). Justification is God's eschatological juridical act brought forward into present experience, whereas salvation (in its narrow eschatological sense) describes both the future event of vindication and the ongoing ensuring conditions resulting from it.

A second major theme in Romans, embedded in Paul's exposition of justification by faith and also anticipated in Romans 1:16, is the universality of salvation: "first to the Jew, then to the Gentile." Again, the redemptive-historical failure of Jews to keep the law means that they, like the Gentiles, are without excuse (Rom 2:1-4). Insofar as Paul's argument in Romans 1:18–3:20 seeks to establish the inefficacy of the law in affording salvation, the same line of reasoning has immediate implications regarding the futility of Jewish boasting (Rom 3:27-28). At the same time, Paul will later warn that any attempt on the Gentiles' part to exult in their obedience to the gospel (in contrast to the Jews) is misguided, for the Gentiles had been unnaturally grafted in (Rom 11:13-24). Paul anticipates a *fullness of Gentiles coming until "all Israel" might be "saved" (Rom 11:26). Exactly what the apostle intends by this phrase has been much debated, but for the purposes of this article it need only be observed that though tribal identity (Jew or Gentile) provides no advantage to the individual's quest for salvation, this principle does not exclude the possibility of salvation being selectively granted to or withheld from certain ethnic groups.

Building on his argument in Romans 9–11, Paul eventually turns to the issue of meat eating (Rom 14:1–15:7). Whatever personal habits Paul's hearers might adopt when it comes to consuming meat purchased from pagan temples, and wherever they might fall in relation to his categories of "weak" or "*strong," Paul admonishes the Roman believers to think and act in light Christ's final judgment (Rom 14:10-11). The universality of salvation and its progressive unfolding, first for the Jew and then for Gentile, undergirds virtually every aspect of Paul's overall argument in Romans.

In Romans 5:12-20, Paul seeks to convey the prodigiousness of salvation by reflecting on a typological correspondence between *Adam and Christ. Whereas the first man trespassed, thereby ushering death into the world, it would be through the obedience of a kind of second Adam that righteousness would reverse the effects of the first man's sin. More than that, those who avail themselves of this grace would be poised to reign in life through Christ, thereby recapitulating the Adam's role as vice-gerent. The identification of Christ as an antitype of Adam in Romans 5 (see 1 Cor 15; Phil 2:6-11 [?]) not only underscores salvation as having a creational scope (see Rom 8:18-25) but also gives credence to a view that considers Pauline redemption to be not just the canceling out of the fall but the full outworking of creation.

Whereas Paul's earlier letters are strewn with isolated pneumatological reflections (e.g., Gal 3:13-16; 2 Cor 5:15), Romans 6–8 makes up the apostle's most extended treatment of the Spirit's paramount role in salvation. According to Paul, those who fail to rely on the Spirit will remain powerless to obey, enslaved by the Adamic flesh, while those who were set free by the Spirit have died to sin and are made alive to obedience. Furthermore, the Spirit enlivens the believers' cognizance of their adoption before God and their shared identity as heirs of salvation (Rom 8:14-17). That adoption is only fully *complete on the redemption of the believers' bodies, at the resurrection (Rom 8:23). The ultimate goal of this redemption is glorification (Rom 8:29-30), restoring humanity to the glory it had once had in Adam (Rom 3:23). The Spirit is also the means by which the love of God is made palpable (Rom 5:5; 8:26-39). Because this hope of adoption and the power of the Spirit are necessary conditions for salvation (Rom 8:24), it stands to reason that the indwelling of the Spirit is not just evidence of salvation (Gal 3:1-5) but its necessary condition. In contrast to at least some Jews of his day, Paul regarded possession of the Spirit as a nonnegotiable for salvation.

In the letter's paraenetic section (Rom 12:1–15:13), Paul characteristically points to the parousia as the motivating basis for believers' ethical behavior (see 1 Thess 5:1-11). This is demonstrable from an analysis of the structure of Romans 12–13—more exactly, the observation that the string of imperatives contained in Romans 12:3–13:10 is to be carried out with an understanding of the present hour and the nearness of salvation (Rom 13:11; Kim, 117-18). In Romans 13–14, as noted above, Paul's exhortation that the weak and strong accept one another is supported by a reminder of the eschatological judgment awaiting believers (Rom 14:10). Once again, twin prospects of salvation and judgment underwrite the apostle's ethical teaching.

3.3. Pastoral Epistles. The so-called Pastoral Epistles employ language of salvation with relative frequency. Beginning with 1 Timothy, one notes an emphasis on the democratic nature of salvation, that is, its breadth of scope across the register of humanity. In reflecting on his own salvation, Paul considers the sharp contrast between the grace poured out on himself and his own worthiness: "Christ Jesus came into the world to save sinners—of whom I am the worst" (1 Tim 1:15 NIV). Paul's moral self-assessment is meant to back up his earlier insistence that the law (and by extension the gospel of salvation) is intended not for the righteous but for corrupt sinners (1 Tim 1:8-10).

On a related note, the apostle also urges intercession be made "for all people" (*hyper pantōn anthrōpōn*, 1 Tim 2:1), including kings and others in authority. Such prayers, Paul continues, please "God our Savior, who wants all people to be saved" (1 Tim 2:3-4 NIV). The phrase "all people" seems to refer not to the full set of all human persons everywhere but rather to the full range of social and political stations, including, perhaps surprisingly, pagan rulers. If in Romans Paul takes pains to argue that salvation is for both Jew and Gentile, in 1 Timothy he is now concerned to stress that the same salvation provides opportunity for all kinds of individuals, no matter their moral or societal standing.

Whatever one's judgments regarding the authorship of 1 Timothy and 2 Timothy, it is of no small interest that both epistles have something to say regarding the practical value of right living when it comes to saving others. In the former epistle, Paul exhorts: "Watch your life and doctrine closely. Persevere in them, because if you do, you will save both yourself and your hearers" (1 Tim 4:16 NIV). Though the point can be overstated, the apostle posits a logical connection between believers' unstinting attentiveness to their behavior and belief, on the one side, and salvation for themselves and others, on the other. The assertion is akin to Paul's disclosure that he endures his chains and in fact "everything for the sake of the elect, that they too may obtain the salvation that is in Christ Jesus" (2 Tim 2:10 NIV). Paul hopes not simply for his physical survival but for a demonstration of virtues consistent with any believer's vocation (2 Tim 2:1-6).

In this connection, the apostle invites Timothy to co-participate alongside with him in the sufferings of Christ (2 Tim 2:11-13), with the promise that his protégé's endurance would guarantee his reigning with Christ (2 Tim 2:11). Conversely, should Timothy waver in his *calling, he stands to forfeit salvation. This context is also likely relevant to Paul's passing remark on the Scriptures, that they "are able to make you wise for salvation through faith in Christ Jesus [*eis sōtērian dia pisteōs tēs en Christō Iēsou*]" (2 Tim 3:15 NIV). Though the construction may be understood as an objective genitive ("faith in Christ Jesus"), it is equally if not more possible that Paul's point is that salvation is predicated on the faithfulness of Christ (see 2 Tim 3:13; Downs). On this reading, the path to salvation is at least a path characterized by an ongoing *imitatio Christi*.

In Titus 3:5-8 Paul emphasizes both the gratuitousness and dynamism of salvation. Precisely as "the Savior" (Titus 3:4, 6), Christ saves not because of righteous deeds done but because of his *mercy (Titus 3:5a). Moreover, this salvation comes "through the washing of rebirth [*dia loutrou palingenesias*] and renewal [*anakainōseōs*] by the *Holy Spirit" (Titus 3:5b NIV). Arguably drawing on *palingenesia* in its Stoic sense (so Zimmerman), Paul implies that the renewal (*anakainōsis*) of human individuals helps explain the nature of the cosmic renewal intimated by *palingenesia*. Such a fluid movement between individual and cosmic categories would certainly be consistent with earlier Pauline thought.

A final word is in order regarding the notoriously difficult statement that *women will be saved through childbearing (1 Tim 2:12). As to what this means, no less than seven interpretations have been proffered in the contemporary discussion (Köstenberger). Of these, three are especially prominent. First, the messianic interpretation posits that the childbearing in question is Eve's giving birth to the seed, which would of course eventually redeem humanity (e.g., August). A second reading holds that Paul is promising that women will be kept physically safe through literal childbearing, provided they continued in good stead through their faithful life (e.g., Hutson). A third interpretation understands "childbearing" as a synecdoche for raising children (e.g., Kostenberger). Given various factors, not least Paul's interest in refuting false teachings that forbid people to marry (1 Tim 4:3), this final reading is perhaps most likely. In this case, Paul's point is that married women would do well to dedicate themselves to the domestic sphere and thereby save themselves from being beguiled by *Satan, as Eve was (2 Tim 2:14).

4. Conclusion.

In Paul's writing the concept of salvation recurs frequently and is in fact fundamental to his thought. According to the apostle, Jesus Christ is the only Savior, and it is by participating in this death and resurrection that salvation—palpable through the experience of the Spirit and divine forgiveness—is made possible. The verb of saving is used in relation to the past and present, so that there is a sense in in which believers can rightfully be said to have been saved while also being saved. However, strictly speaking, the term is future oriented, referring to the end-of-time scenario ushered in with the parousia. Salvation includes not just a deliverance from the wrath threatening to befall an unbelieving world but also entrance into a sphere of existence firmly under Christ's reign. Having both individual and corporate dimensions, this salvation extends beyond Israel but includes Gentiles and in fact the whole cosmos. Salvation is, therefore, a renewal of creation, providing closure to the account begun in Genesis 1.

See also Atonement; Eschatology; Gospel; Justification; Law; Peace, Reconciliation; Romans, Letter to the; Savior; Sin, Guilt.

BIBLIOGRAPHY. **G. P. Anderson,** *Paul's New Perspective: Charting a Soteriological Journey* (Downers Grove, IL: InterVarsity Press, 2016); **J. M. August,** "What Must She Do to Be Saved? A Theological Analysis of 1 Timothy 2:15," *Themelios* 45 (2020): 84-97; **J. M. G. Barclay,** *Paul and the Gift* (Grand Rapids, MI: Eerdmans, 2015); **J. M. G. Barclay and S. J. Gathercole,** eds., *Divine and Human Agency in Paul and His Cultural Environment* (London: T&T Clark, 2006); **J. C. Beker,** *The Triumph of God: The Essence of Paul's Thought* (Minneapolis: Fortress, 1990); **M. F. Bird,** *The Saving Righteousness of God: Studies on Paul, Justification, and the New Perspective* (Eugene, OR: Wipf & Stock, 2007); **C. R. Campbell,** *Paul and the Hope of Glory: An Exegetical and Theological Study* (Grand Rapids, MI: Zondervan, 2020); **D. A. Campbell,** *The Deliverance of God: An Apocalyptic Rereading of Justification in Paul* (Grand Rapids, MI: Eerdmans, 2009); **D. J. Downs,** "Faith(fulness) in Christ Jesus in 2 Timothy 3:15," *JBL* 131 (2012): 143-60; **G. D. Fee,** *God's Empowering Presence: The Holy Spirit in the Letters of Paul* (Grand Rapids, MI: Baker, 2009); **W. Foerster and G. Fohrer,** "σῴζω, σωτηρία, σωτήρ, σωτήριος," *TDNT* 7:965-1024; **S. J. Gathercole,** *Where Is Boasting? Early Jewish Soteriology and Paul's Response in Romans 1–5* (Grand Rapids, MI: Eerdmans, 2002); **B. R. Gaventa,** *When in Romans: An Invitation to Linger with the Gospel According to Paul* (Grand Rapids, MI: Baker, 2018); **B. L. Gladd,** *Revealing the* Mysterion*: The Use of Mystery in Daniel in Second Temple Judaism with Its Bearing on First Corinthians*, BZNW 160 (Berlin: de Gruyter, 2008); **M. L. Gorman,** *Inhabiting the Cruciform God: Kenosis, Justification, and Theosis in Paul's Narrative Soteriology* (Grand Rapids, MI: Eerdmans, 2009); **J. B. Green,** *Salvation* (St. Louis, MO: Chalice, 2003); **K. Grieb,** *The Story of Romans: A Narrative Defense of God's Righteousness* (Louisville, KY: Westminster John Knox, 2002); **J. R. Harrison,** "Paul and the Imperial Gospel at Thessaloniki," *JSNT* 25 (2002): 71-96; **C. Hutson,** "Saved Through Childbearing: The Jewish Context of 1 Timothy 2:15," *NovT* 56 (2014): 392-410; **J. W. Jipp,** *Christ Is King: Paul's Royal Ideology* (Minneapolis: Fortress, 2015); **S. Kim,** "Paul's Common Paraenesis (1 Thess. 4–5; Phil. 2–4; and Rom. 12–13): The Correspondence Between Romans 1:18-32 and 12:1-2, and the Unity of Romans 12–13," *TynBul* 62 (2011): 109-21; **A. J. Köstenberger,** "Ascertaining Women's God-Ordained Roles: An Interpretation of 1 Timothy 2:15," *BBR* 7 (1997): 107-44; **A. T. Lincoln,** *Paradise Now and Not Yet: Studies in the Role of the Heavenly Dimension in Paul's Thought with Special Reference to His Eschatology* (Grand Rapids, MI: Baker, 1991); **G. Macaskill,** *Union with Christ in the New Testament* (Oxford: Oxford University Press, 2013); **J. Maston,** *Divine and Human Agency in Second Temple Judaism and Paul: A Comparative Study*, WUNT 2/297 (Tübingen, Mohr Siebeck, 2010); **D. G. Powers,** *Salvation Through Participation: An Examination of the Notion of the Believers' Corporate Unity with Christ in Early Christian Soteriology*, CBET 29 (Leuven: Peeters, 2001); **B. D. Smith,** *What Must I Do to Be Saved? Paul Parts Company with His Jewish Heritage* (Sheffield: Sheffield Phoenix, 2007); **P. M. Sprinkle,** *Paul and Judaism Revisited: A Study of Divine and Human Agency in Salvation* (Downers Grove, IL: InterVarsity Press, 2013); **D. F. Tolmie,** "Salvation as Redemption: The Use of 'Redemption' Metaphors in Pauline Literature," in *Salvation in the New Testament: Perspectives on Soteriology*, ed. J. G. Van der Watt, NovTSup 121 (Leiden: Brill, 2005), 247-69; **F. Watson,** *Paul and the Hermeneutics of Faith* (New York: T&T Clark, 2004); **N. T. Wright,** *Paul and the Faithfulness of God*, COQG 4 (Minneapolis: Fortress: 2013); **C. Zimmermann,** "Wiederentstehung und Erneuerung (Tit 3:5): Zu einem erhaltenswerten Aspekt der Soteriologie des Titusbriefs," *NovT* 51 (2009): 272-95.

N. Perrin

SANCTIFICATION. *See* Complete, Mature (Perfect); Holiness, Sanctification; Spirituality.

SANHEDRIN. *See* Political Systems.

SATAN, DEVIL

Paul refers to a personal and evil spiritual being whose purposes are opposed to God, God's people, and God's created order. While *Satan* and *devil* are the most common terms for personal evil in the Pauline corpus, a range of terminology is used, and it is grounded in the OT and Second Temple Judaism. But specific Pauline usages are calibrated to the contours of the *gospel and apostolic *ministry.

1. Background
2. Pauline Terminology
3. Satan's Activity
4. A Conquered Enemy

1. Background.

In the OT the Hebrew noun *śāṭān*, "accuser" (with nuances of "adversary" or "slanderer" in certain contexts), is used of both human (see 1 Sam 29:4; 1 Kings 11:14, 23, 25) and transcendent beings (Job 1–2; 1 Chron 21:1 [cf. 2 Sam 24:1]; Zech 3:1-2). In Job and Zechariah, the "satan" is a court functionary (see Walton). In none of these cases is there a clearly defined cosmic evil adversary. But these three canonical contexts lay a foundation for later developments in Jewish thought in which an evil, transcendent spiritual being, known by various names, maintains a spiritual kingdom that is opposed, but ultimately subject, to God.

Within this worldview, intelligent beings, whether physical or spiritual, were ultimately aligned with either *God or Satan, *light or darkness, good or evil (1QS IV, 15-16). Whereas in the OT *Israel was often juxtaposed against the nations, a deeper dimension of reality was now in view (canonically evidenced in Daniel's visions; see Dan 10:1-11:1). Behind the story of Israel and the nations a transcendent drama was unfurled, in which God and angels were set over against Satan and his minions. Battle lines now ran through individuals' hearts as well as between children of light and children of darkness (1QS IV, 22-24). A mythology now accounted for the origin of *demons (Jub. 5.1-11; 10.1-14; 1 En. 15.8-9; cf. Gen 6:1-5), so that Israel's history could be retold, set off in relief by a host of spiritual forces (e.g., Jub. 48.9-12).

Satan was understood as a personal spiritual being of the highest order (*LAE* 12.1), originally created by God for good purposes (but see 1QM XIII, 11), but now the fallen leader of a cosmic rebellion (*LAE* 12–16). Second Temple literature offers a number of alternative titles: "the enemy" (*T. Job* 47.10); Belial (1QM XIII, 11; XIV, 9) or Beliar (*T. Levi* 3.3; 18.12; 19.1); Azazel (*1 En.* 8.1; 10.4; *Apoc. Ab.* 13.6-14; cf. Lev 16:8); Mastema ("hatred," "enmity"; Jub. 10.8; 11.5; 17.16; 19.28); "the spirit" or "angel of darkness" (1QS III, 20-24). The Gospels speak of "Beelzebul," "the ruler of the demons" (Mt 12:24 and par.).

2. Pauline Terminology.

Within the Pauline corpus there is also an array of names, descriptive titles, and phrases referring to this archenemy.

2.1. Satan. "Satan" (*ho satanas*, Rom 16:20; 1 Cor 5:5; 7:5; 2 Cor 2:11; 11:14; 12:7; 1 Thess 2:18; 2 Thess 2:9; cf. 1 Tim 1:20; 5:15), a Greek transliteration of the Hebrew *śāṭān* (e.g., Job 1:6-8, 12; 2:1-7; Zech 3:1, 2), is the term most commonly found.

2.2. Devil. In the contested Pauline letters, *diabolos*, "devil," is found in Ephesians 4:27; 6:11, and is used with some frequency in the Pastorals (1 Tim 3:6-7; 2 Tim 2:26; 3:3; Titus 2:3). Meaning "slanderer" or "adversary," *diabolos* in the LXX translates the Hebrew *śāṭān*. But the term *diabolos* can be used in more than one sense. In 1 Timothy 3, while the devil is presented as one who condemns and ensnares *church leaders (1 Tim 3:6-7), one reads that *women deacons "must be serious, not slanderers [*diabolous]*" (1 Tim 3:11). The Pastorals also refer to "Satan" (1 Tim 1:20; 5:15) and once to "the enemy" (*antikeimenos*, 1 Tim 5:14), evidencing an interchangeability of the names "Satan" and "devil" among early Christians (see Mt 4:1, 5, 8, 10-11; Mk 4:15; Lk 8:12; cf. Revelation: *satanas* 8×; *diabolos* 5×).

2.3. Other Terms. Outside Ephesians and the Pastorals, Satan is alluded to as "Beliar" (2 Cor 6:15), or "the god of this age" (2 Cor 4:4; cf. Acts 26:18), who blinds unbelievers to the "light of the *glory of the gospel of *Christ" (NRSV). He is also called the "serpent" (*ophis*, 2 Cor 11:3; cf. 1 En. 69.6; 2 En. 31.6; Apoc. Ab. 23; LAE 9; Apoc. Mos. 17), "the tempter" (*ho peirazōn*, 1 Thess 3:5; cf. Mt 4:3) and "the evil one" (*ho ponēros*, 2 Thess 3:3; cf. Eph 6:16 and, e.g., Mt 5:37; 13:19, 38). In Colossians he is perhaps implied as controlling the "power of darkness" (Col 1:13), in contrast with "the holy ones in the light" (Col 1:12; cf., e.g., Rom 13:12; 1 Thess 5:4-5). Satan is not always easily identified, for he may surface amid God's people disguised as an "angel of light" (2 Cor 11:14; cf. Apoc. Mos. 17.1; *LAE* 9.1). Ephesians offers a particularly rich selection of descriptive titles: "the prince [or 'ruler,' *archōn*] of the power of the air" (Eph 2:2 NASB; cf., e.g., Jn 16:11); the "spirit that is now at work among those who are disobedient" (Eph 2:2 NRSV); the "evil one" (Eph 6:16; cf. 2 Thess 3:3); and "the devil" (Eph 4:27; 6:11).

3. Satan's Activity.

While Pauline vocabulary resonates with the common terminology of Judaism, it is transposed into a Christian framework.

3.1. The God of This Age. Paul distinguishes between two kingdoms in the present age: the *kingdom of Christ and the kingdom of Satan. The "god of this age [*aiōn*]" keeps "unbelievers" (*hoi apistoi*) from the gospel by blinding them from seeing "the revealed splendor of the gospel of the glory of Christ who is the *image of God" (2 Cor 4:4). "Unbelievers" (2 Cor 4:4) may include false teachers who carry out Satan's work (see 2 Cor 11:13-15). Satan's sovereignty is ultimately limited but powerful, compelling, and opposed to the work of God in Christ. In 2 Corinthians 6:15 Paul warns the Corinthians not to be yoked with unbelievers, for "what agreement does Christ have with Beliar?" (NRSV). This passage (2 Cor 6:14–7:1), with its series of contrasts, resonates with language found in the Qumran scrolls. The distinction between the two realms is also reflected in Colossians and Ephesians. In Colossians 1:13 the dominion (*exousia*) of darkness (implied to be Satan's) is contrasted with the kingdom of Christ. In language echoing the exodus, believers are rescued from the authority of darkness and delivered into the kingdom of God's *Son. In Ephesians 2:2 the arch-ruler of this age is called "the ruler of the power [or realm, *tēs exousias*] of the air, the spirit that is now at work among those who are disobedient" (NRSV). Believers addressed here were once slaves to the world order of this age, "dead" in their trespasses and *sins (see Col 1:13-14). But in Ephesians the devil (see Eph 4:27; 6:11) is associated with the "air" and called a "prince" or "ruler" (*archōn*). The "air" may refer to the lower reaches of the heavens (see *2 En.* 29.4-5). This lower atmosphere seems to be related to the "heavenly realms" which, in Ephesians 3:10; 6:12, are inhabited by the *principalities and powers, who are in a power alliance with the devil (Eph 6:11-12; see Lincoln 1990).

Finally, in Romans 8:19-23 the created order is subjected to "futility" (or "vanity," *mataiotēs*, Rom 8:20) and the "bondage of decay" (Rom 8:21), in which it "groans in labor pains" (Rom 8:22) as it awaits its liberation. Is Paul here alluding to the created order's subjection to the power of Satan as the "god of this age"? In support of this, Paul ends with a confident statement that no power of the cosmos can keep believers from the *love of God in Christ (Rom 8:37-39), and in Romans 16:20 he looks forward to the defeat of Satan in terms clearly echoing Genesis 3:15.

3.2. Satan the Aggressor. Satan strives to hold humans in his thrall, attempts to regain those he has lost to Christ, and resists Paul's apostolic battle for human lives.

Among believers one finds that Satan brings sexual temptation (1 Cor 7:5) and outwits believers and leaders by taking advantage of unforgiving attitudes and discord in the community (2 Cor 2:11). Just as the serpent deceived Eve, Satan cunningly leads believers astray from a pure devotion to Christ by introducing "another gospel" (2 Cor 11:3) and disguising himself as an angel of light (see Gal 1:8; *LAE* 9.1; *T. Job* 6.4). Paul's opponents at Corinth disguised themselves as ministers of *righteousness when they were in fact false apostles and ministers of Satan (2 Cor 11:15). Paul never speaks of Satan "entering" someone (see Lk 22:3; Jn 13:27). On the other hand, trouble may arise in persecution inflicted from outside the community, and the *apostle fears that in his absence new believers will be shaken by such events (1 Thess 3:1-4). This too is attributed to the work of Satan, as the tempter (*peirazōn*) who might render gospel labors "in vain" (1 Thess 3:5). It was Satan who repeatedly thwarted Paul's plans to return to Thessalonica (1 Thess 2:18).

In Ephesians and the Pastorals many of the same concerns come to the fore. The stratagems of the devil must be resisted by divine armor (Eph 6:11). Anger and an unrepentant or unforgiving spirit are a foothold for the devil (Eph 4:27). Believers, and particularly church leaders, must be on the lookout for the "snare [*pagis*] of the devil" (1 Tim 3:7; 2 Tim 2:26 NRSV). For an *episkopos* who is a recent convert, conceit can lead to condemnation by the devil (1 Tim 3:6). Some, perhaps Hymenaeus and Philetus (2 Tim 2:18), have already fallen into that snare and have been held captive (2 Tim 2:26). Young widows should marry so as to close a door of opportunity for the adversary to do his work (1 Tim 5:14). But "some have already turned away to follow Satan" (1 Tim 5:15 NRSV).

Finally, Paul tells the Thessalonians that prior to the parousia of the Lord an eschatological rebellion, led by the "*man of lawlessness," will occur in accord with the working of Satan (2 Thess 2:9). The "mystery of lawlessness" is already at work (2 Thess 2:7), but in its final crystallization of evil it will be accompanied by "power, signs, lying wonders, and every kind of wicked deception" (2 Thess 2:9-10 NRSV).

3.3. Satan, an Instrument of Divine Will. Satan's opposition is carried out under the sovereignty of God. Paul speaks of a "thorn in the flesh," a messenger (*angelos*) of Satan, which was permitted by God to afflict him (2 Cor 12:7 NASB). Despite Paul's fervent prayers, the afflictions were allowed (*edothē*, "given") under God's providence and are emblematic of Paul's theology of the *cross: God's power made perfect in weakness. Satan also plays a role in community *discipline. A man at Corinth, guilty of incest, is to be delivered over "to Satan for the destruction of his *flesh, so that his spirit may be saved in the day of the *Lord" (1 Cor 5:5 NRSV). Whether remedial, with the expectation of repentance, or intended that his *death would be his *salvation (see Roetzel), the individual is to be excommunicated from the community "gathered in the *name of the Lord" (1 Cor 5:4) and sent into the domain of Satan. Perhaps like ancient Israel, cut off from the blessings of the land of promise, this individual's flesh (e.g., his propensity for sin) would through suffering be destroyed, and thus he would be saved on the day of the Lord. Similarly, in 1 Timothy 1:20 Hymenaeus and Alexander have been turned over to Satan so that they may learn not to blaspheme.

4. A Conquered Enemy.

In Romans, Paul is confident that "the God of *peace will soon crush Satan under your feet" (Rom 16:20 NIV). The phrasing "under your feet" suggests a melding of Genesis 3:15 with Psalm 110:1 and/or Psalm 8:6. The latter text speaks of God placing the created order under the superintendence of humankind. On this reading, Paul would be saying that in defeating Satan, God restores the children of the last *Adam (the "seed of the woman," Gen 3:15) to their role of dominion and eschatological shalom. That this will happen "soon" (*en tachei*) may be an indication of Paul's confidence in the coming *triumph of God. But it may also arise from confidence that Roman believers will soon experience divine victory over the present threat of "those who cause dissensions and offenses" and "deceive the hearts of the simple-minded" (Rom 16:17-19 NRSV).

Paul looks back to Christ's triumph at the cross over the "principalities and powers" (Col 2:15 KJV; cf. 1 Cor 2:6-8). This suggests a proleptic triumph over Satan, parallel with the defeat of the personified powers of sin, death, flesh, and the *law. Texts such as Galatians 1:4 and Colossians 1:12 imply a defeat of satanic power reminiscent of the exodus. But Satan is still a potent and aggressive force seeking to thwart the work of God in Christ, and believers are to rely on God's faithfulness and power (2 Thess 3:3).

In Ephesians 6:10-16 the imagery of divine weaponry (see 1 Thess 5:8; Rom 13:12) is developed. The church's enemies are not "flesh and blood." God's people are engaged with principalities, powers, and "the spiritual forces of evil in the heavenly realms" (Eph 6:12 NIV). These powers are directed by "the devil," whose schemes these powers carry out. The church is outfitted with spiritual weaponry and finds strength in its Lord and in the power of his might (Eph 6:10). With the "shield of faith" believers can "quench all the flaming arrows of the evil one" (Eph 6:16 NRSV).

See also APOCALYPTIC PAUL; COSMOLOGY; DEMONS AND EXORCISM; EPHESIANS; ESCHATOLOGY; FLESH; KINGDOM OF GOD/CHRIST; LIGHT AND DARKNESS; PRINCIPALITIES AND POWERS; QUMRAN AND PAUL; SIN, GUILT; TRIUMPH.

BIBLIOGRAPHY. **C. E. Arnold,** *Ephesians: Power and Magic,* SNTSMS 63 (Cambridge: Cambridge University Press, 1989); **R. H. Bell,** "Demon, Devil, Satan," *DJG*[2], 193-202; **P. L. Day,** *An Adversary in Heaven: Satan in the Hebrew Bible,* HSM 43 (Atlanta: Scholars Press, 1987); **M. Dibelius,** *Die Geisterwelt im Glauben des Paulus* (Göttingen: Vandenhoeck & Ruprecht, 1909); **T. Elgvin,** "Belial, Beliar, Devil, Satan," *DNTB,* 153-57; **N. Forsyth,** *The Old Enemy: Satan and the Combat Myth* (Princeton, NJ: Princeton University Press, 1987); **M. S. Heiser,** *The Unseen Realm* (Bellingham, WA: Lexham, 2015); **A. T. Lincoln,** *Paradise Now and Not Yet,* SNTSMS 43 (Cambridge: University Press, 1981); idem, *Ephesians,* WBC 42 (Dallas: Word, 1990); **S. H. T. Page,** *Powers of Evil: A Biblical Study of Satan and Demons* (Grand Rapids, MI: Baker, 1995); **C. J. Roetzel,** *Judgement in the Community: A Study of the Relationship Between Eschatology and Ecclesiology in Paul,* NovTSup (Leiden: Brill, 1972); **J. B. Russell,** *The Devil: Perceptions of Evil from Antiquity to Primitive Christianity* (Ithaca, NY: Cornell University Press, 1977); idem, *Satan: The Early Christian Tradition* (Ithaca, NY: Cornell University Press, 1981); **K. van der Toorn** et al., eds., *Dictionary of Deities and Demons in the Bible,* 2nd ed. (Leiden: Brill, 1999); **J. H. Walton,** "Satan," *DOTWPW,* 714-17; **R. Yates,** "The Powers of Evil in the NT," *EvQ* 52 (1980) 97-111.

D. G. Reid

SAVIOR

Savior (*sōtēr*) appears twenty-four times in the NT, twelve of which occur in the Pauline corpus. *Sōtēr* conveys the meaning of "one who rescues, saves, delivers, or preserves." Throughout the NT, the term generally refers to God's rescuing of his people from the final *judgment through Jesus' redemptive *death and *resurrection. It holds important implications for how Christ-followers live ethically in the present, embodied moment. *Sōtēr* is absent in Mark and Matthew and occurs only once in John, wherein some Samaritans of Sychar declare Jesus the "Savior of the world" (Jn 4:42; see Jn 3:17; 12:47). Thus, Luke is distinctive among the canonical Gospels for describing Jesus four times as *sōtēr*, three of which refer to his role as the messianic king in the line of David (Lk 1:47; 2:22; 13:23; cf. Lk 5:30). It is possible that Luke's use of *sōtēr* reflects his attempt to describe Jesus' significance in both a biblical and universally (Hellenistic) familiar manner (Schnackenburg).

While only occurring once in Philippians 3:20 and in Ephesians 5:23, both in reference to Jesus, "Savior" is used much more frequently in the letters to Timothy and Titus. Only in the letters to Timothy and Titus is *God called Savior among NT writings ascribed to Paul—otherwise God is called Savior in Mary's Magnificat in Luke 1:47 (with respect to God's concern for the lowly over against the oppressive powerful and rich) and in the doxology of Jude 25. In Titus alone, "Savior" occurs six times to describe both God and Jesus—a frequency that is comparable to the five times it occurs in another often presumably late NT writing, 2 Peter.

1. Savior in Judean, Greek, and Roman Cultures
2. Savior in Philippians and Ephesians
3. Savior in the Letters to Timothy and Titus

1. Savior in Judean, Greek, and Roman Cultures. *Sōtēr* occurs thirty-eight times in the LXX, often in translation of the Hebrew nouns *yēšûa*ʿ ("salvation") and *yēšaʿ* ("deliverance, rescue") and the participle *māšîaḥ* ("savior"). While the God of *Israel is the primary designate of the title savior (34×), on four occasions God's human agents are also called saviors for carrying out God's rescuing deeds, including Othniel (Judg 3:9), Ehud (Judg 3:15), and Mordecai (Esth 16:13; see also Neh 9:27). In contrast to the NT, God's work as Savior in the LXX primarily concerns the Lord's deliverance of God's people from their enemies. God is praised nine times in the Psalms as "our Savior" (Ps 64:6 [MT 65:5]) who is mercifully benevolent to his people (Ps 23:5 [MT 24:5]), whose protection dispels fear (Ps 26:1 [MT 27:1]), since God is a fortress (Ps 61:3, 7 [MT 62:2, 6]) and is called on (Ps 78:9 [MT 79:9]) and praised for rescue (Ps 94:1/95:1). The next highest frequency of the term is found in Isaiah, wherein God is celebrated as a righteous Savior, like whom there is no other (Is 45:21), who will rescue his people from all idolaters through his anointed Cyrus (Is 45:15; see also Is 12:2; 17:10; 62:11). In the LXX, *Savior* never explicitly references an anointed figure in the line of David—although Zechariah describes such a figure as "saving" (*sōzōn*, Zech 9:9). Also, Isaiah refers to the ambiguous Servant of the Lord as Israel's *sōtēr* (Is 62:11).

Jewish writings composed during the Hellenistic and Roman periods continue to make use of *sōtēr* primarily to describe the God of Israel's past and present actions to preserve his people (Add Esth 15:2; 16:13; Judg 9:11; 1 Macc 4:30; 3 Macc 6:29, 32; 7:16; Odes Sol. 2.15; 4.81; 9.47; Wis 16:7; Sir 51:1; Pss. Sol. 3.6; 8.33; 16.4; 17.3; Bar 4:22). However, there seems to be no equivalent to *sōtēr* applied in the Dead Sea Scrolls, Ethiopic Enoch, and Jubilees (Foerster and Fohrer). Philo of Alexandria applies the epithets "savior and benefactor" to both the Creator (*Opif.* 169; *Leg.* 2.56; *Sobr.* 55) and Caesar Augustus (*Flacc.* 74). In resonance with what one sees in the letters to Timothy and Titus, Philo speaks of God as the "Savior of all" (*sōtēr tou pantos*; *Deus* 156; *Fug.* 162), who is the "the only Savior" (*monos sōtēr; Conf.* 93) and whose saving benefactions compel people to live ethical lives in control of their passions in a posture of gratitude (*Migr.* 25). And among Josephus's writings, the appellation of "savior" is not applied to God but to human deliverers, including Joseph (*Ant.* 2.94) Jonathan (*Ant.* 6.240), Mordecai (*Ant.* 11.278); Vespasian (*J.W.* 71), and even himself, as he was celebrated as a "benefactor and savior" of the land by Judeans during Roman revolt (*Life* 244, 259).

Some of the earliest designations of Jesus as Savior may have originated as an etymological breakdown of his personal *name. "Jesus" (Gk. *Iēsous*, Heb. *yhwš[w]*ʿ) was short for "Joshua" (*yəhôšua*ʿ in Hebrew), which meant "the salvation of the Lord" (Quinn). Joshua, who led the Israelites into the Promised Land, was remembered to have lived up to his name as bringing the Lord's *salvation, as evidenced in Sirach 46:1 and by Philo (*Iēsous de sōtēria kyriou* in *Mut.* 121). This etymological recognition may be underneath the mockery of the crucified Jesus as being unable to "save" himself in Mark 15:30-31 and the explanation of Jesus' name in Matthew 1:21. In the mid-second century, Justin Martyr makes this etymological connection (*1 Apol.* 33; *2 Apol.* 6).

In the surrounding Hellenistic world, *sōtēr* could mean "savior, deliverer, preserver." It was also used as an honorific title, often paired with *euergetēs* ("benefactor") in recognition of the life-preserving benefaction and/or military victory of generous donors, philosophers, public officials, governors, emperors, and divine beings (Foerster and Fohrer; Wendland). For example, the title *sōtēr* was applied to members of the Ptolemaic and Seleucid dynasties within the context of the Hellenistic ruler cult. A third-century BC inscription honors "Ptolemy, the Savior and God" (*Ptolemaiou tou sōtēros kai theou*; IBM 4.1:906, 2f). In the Priene Calendar Inscription, Augustus is celebrated as a savior sent by Providence to act as a benefactor surpassing all others in his benefactions to humanity (OGI 458; 9 BC).

Savior was also applied as an epithet to such divine figures as Zeus Soter, Artemis Soteira, Asclepius (esp. for healing), Apollo, the Dioscori (esp. for rescue from perils at sea), Isis, Athena (esp. as protector against political trouble), and Sandon-Heracles (revered in Paul's hometown of Tarsus) (Graf). Such gods, most frequently Zeus Soter, were honored through *sacrifices, *sōtēria* festivals, and dedicatory statues and inscriptions for their protection of both rulers and their subjects in times of war, political crises, and natural disasters and threats, both past and potential future (Graf). Insofar as the appellation of *sōtēr* was common in discourses around benefaction, applying the epithet *sōtēr* to a benefactor functioned to honor benefactors, to express and encourage a posture of gratitude among recipients of the benefactions, to elicit further philanthropic generosity from patrons and protectors, and even to spur on other potential patrons to act similarly.

Monumental inscriptions honoring divine and human benefactors as saviors marked the cities pertinent to the study of letters ascribed to Paul, including Crete and Ephesus. On the island of Crete, an inscription on a dedicatory statue base, possibly dating to the second century CE and found at the temple of Asclepius near the Cretan provincial capital of Gortyn, honors this god as "Savior" for restoring the dedicator's eyesight (Gill). In another dedicatory inscription found at the Roman colony of Knossos on Crete, Zeus is also honored as "Savior" (Gill). In Ephesus, inscriptions celebrated the emperors Augustus, Hadrian, and Antoninus Pius as saviors, honored Artemis Soteira and Zeus Soter, and recognized the saving benefactions of provincial proconsuls and local patrons. Of note is an inscription found on what was likely a statue base honoring Julius Caesar as the "the manifest [*epiphanē*] god (sprung) from Ares and Aphrodite, and universal savior of human life" (*SIG* 347, 760; Baugh). It is plausible to imagine such monumental honorary inscriptions informing how the author(s) and ancient audiences interpreted the meaning and cultural significance of designating the God of Israel or Jesus *Christ as *sōtēr.*

In the second century AD, *sōtēr* was used predominantly as a title for Jesus. Only once is the appellation applied to God, as found in a prayer in *1 Clement* 59.3. Justin frequently describes the Lord Jesus Christ as "Savior" with respect to the Savior's sayings, advent, and saving work (e.g., *Dial.* 8, 18, 93, 110; *1 Apol.* 33, 61, 66, 67; *2 Apol.* 6). Ignatius of Antioch too speaks of "Jesus Christ our Savior" (Ign. *Eph.* 1.1; Ign. *Magn.* pref.) and applies the appellation with regard to Christ's advent (Ign. *Phld.* 9.2) and his saving work memorialized in the Eucharist (Ign. *Smyrn.* 7.1). Otherwise among proto-Orthodox writings, *sōtēr* only occurs once in the Epistle of Polycarp (prologue), the Martyrdom of Polycarp (19.2), Epistle to Diogenes (9.6), and *2 Clement* (20.5), and is absent from the Didache, the Epistle of Barnabas, and the Shepherd of Hermas. "Savior" seems to have been a preferred epithet for Christ among texts associated with Valentinus and his students, as attested by Irenaeus (*Haer.* 1.3) and evidenced throughout Ptolemy's *Letter to Flora*, Excerpts of Theodotus, the Treatise of the Resurrection, and the Tripartite Tractate.

References to Jesus as "savior" also occur in the fragmentary, so-called Gospel of the Savior and among a number of other second-century early Christian writings that have been preserved in the Nag Hammadi codices. For example, Jesus is "Savior of the World" in the Epistle of Peter to Philip (VIII, 2.132.18-19) and is recognized as Savior in the Gospel of Truth for his "redemption of those who were ignorant of the Father" through his enlightening *teaching (I, 3.16:38-39). "Savior" is the primary or among the preferred references for Jesus Christ in the Apocryphon of John, the Gospel of Mary, the Sophia of Jesus Christ, and the so-called Dialogue of the Savior.

2. Savior in Philippians and Ephesians. Among the undisputed Pauline letters, *sōtēr* only appears in Philippians 3:20 in the context of Paul's eschatological expectation of Christ's return from heaven. Paul describes "the *Lord Christ Jesus" as Savior while encouraging his readers to consider their true *citizenship as belonging to heaven, from which the Savior shall come to transform their earthly *bodies into glorious, renewed bodies (Phil 3:21). In light of the previous passage emphasizing the coming destruction of those who live as "enemies of the *cross of Christ" (Phil 3:18), it seems that Christ is described as Savior for saving Christ-followers from God's *wrath on the day of judgment (see 1 Thess 1:10). When ancient audiences heard Paul's reference to Christ as Savior in proximity to his encouragement to his audience to remember their heavenly citizenship, some may have contrasted Christ's protection over his heavenly citizens with Caesar's subordinate rule. Yet it is unlikely that Paul's rhetorical aim here is to polemicize against the Roman emperor or to denigrate the concept of Roman citizenship in absolute terms or with explicitly political or revolutionary implications (Cohick; Reumann). The epithet "savior" was not viewed as exclusive to the emperors, nor did the ideology of the imperial cult hold that any of the emperor's saving benefactions had any implications for the *afterlife. Rather, Paul's immediate concern are those who live as "enemies of the cross of the Christ" (Phil 3:18), whose focus on earthly concerns, status, and pleasures contrasts with Paul's eschatological *hope and orientation of his values.

In Ephesians 5:23, "Paul" describes Christ as the "*head of the *church, the body of which he is the Savior" as a model for the role a husband should live as the "head" of his wife.

3. Savior in the Letters to Timothy and Titus. In 1 Timothy, "Paul" opens the letter referring to God as Savior, by whose command Paul has been commissioned as an *apostle of Jesus Christ (1 Tim 1:1). The author describes God as Savior twice more (1 Tim 2:3; 4:10), both times in reference to the universal salvation God offers as one "who desires everyone to be saved and to come to the *knowledge of the *truth" (1 Tim 2:3-4 NRSV). Furthermore, "God our Savior" is described as welcoming prayers on behalf of "kings and all who are in high places" (1 Tim 2:2-3 NRSV), which recognizes the proper subordination of earthly rulers to the kingship of God. Two thematic questions arise here that also concern other occurrences of *sōtēr* in the letters to Timothy and Titus: (1) Does God's identity as a universal Savior entail the eventual salvation of all people or only those who believe? (2) Was the identification of God as Savior intended or interpreted as a critique of Caesar's honorific title as Savior?

Although the author of 1 Timothy does not seem to expect an imminent return of Christ, the author nevertheless understands himself as living in the "later times" (1 Tim 4:1) and is missionally motivated by the eschatological hope of being rescued at the final judgment by Christ. It is within this framework that the author has set his hope on the "living God, who is the Savior of all people, especially of those who believe" (1 Tim 4:10 NRSV). Some have advocated that this passage along with 1 Timothy 2:3-4 indicates not only God's *desire* but also God's eventual plan—for what *desire* of God can go unfulfilled?—to save *everyone*, with believers representing a privileged but not an exclusive subset of "all people." However, it is likely that the author is being ebullient in his expression to emphasize the universality and magnitude of God's saving benefaction that is intended for all kinds of people but is namely (*malista*) received by those who believe or have committed their faithfulness to God.

It remains ambiguous what the author's use of *sōtēr* in 1 Timothy 2:1-4 might indicate about his attitude toward the Roman imperial order, in particular, the imperial cult. The author seems to tacitly endorse an idea at home within the ideology of the Roman imperial cult, namely, that it is important to pray for the *salus* ("well-being" or even "salvation") of the emperor, who is due pious deference and whose own prayers to the gods in his capacity of *pontifex maximus* secure the conditions for his subjects' *peace and prosperity. The recognition that the emperor secures *salus* for the human race was promoted in prayers associated with the imperial cult, celebrated in *sōtēria* festivals, and minted on coins. Annual prayers (*vota*) on behalf of the *salus* of the emperor began under Augustus and by the beginning of the second century AD were a regular facet of everyday life across the Roman provinces, wherein provincial subjects publicly performed their loyalty to the emperor (Moralee). Pliny, the governor of Bithynia in northwestern Asia Minor (modern Turkey), writes to the Emperor Trajan in AD 112 to inform the emperor that he has overseen the fulfillment of the New Year public vows (*vota*) on behalf of the emperor's "safety" (*incolumitas*) in order to guarantee the "salvation" or "welfare" (*salus*) of the state (*Ep.* 10.35). In reply, Trajan thanks Pliny for his prayers to the immortal gods "on behalf of my welfare/salvation and safety" (*pro mea salute et incolumitate*; *Ep.* 10.36). Trajan's reign was further celebrated as bringing salvation to the human race (*salus generis humanis*) in both public prayers (*Ep.* 10.52) and coins minted around AD 111 (*BMCRE* 3:410, p. 87; Moralee). Thus, it is plausible to read 1 Timothy 2:1-2 (as well as Titus 3:1) as encouraging a public posture of loyalty to the emperor and his provincial administration that may reflect the author's concern to promote social integration and a recognizably civilized and respectable attitude toward those in political authority in order to possibly soften the suspicions of outsiders toward Christ-followers (Hoklotubbe; Zamfir).

Granting that the author of 1 Timothy 2:1-4 does not offer a direct or explicit criticism of imperial power, it is possible that the reference to God as "Savior" (and later "only sovereign" in 1 Tim 6:16) in such proximity to references to ruling authorities was interpreted by some early Christians as a sly correction to imperial ideology. Implied in the author's affirmation of the oneness of God and Christ Jesus as the one mediator between God and humanity (1 Tim 2:5) is the recognition that God and Christ are to be credited as the ultimate and universal benefactors for any peace and prosperity that is enjoyed—not the Roman gods nor the emperor. Certainly, it is a common tactic among dominated classes negotiating an imperial or colonial system to offer ambiguous and veiled criticisms of the dominant power. But this difference in theological ideology is still a step away from what seems to have been interpreted by Roman authorities as "anti-Roman," namely, the "obstinate" refusal to offer sacrifices to the imperial *genus* and the traditional gods as a sign of civic loyalty when publicly called on (Pliny, *Ep.* 10.96-97). In the end, the author's designation of God as *sōtēr* at least reflects the author's desire to dignify God with a title of great authority and cultural prestige (Zamfir). It may even be that the author is little concerned with offering any critique of the imperial cult and instead encourages his audience to imagine themselves as participants in the civil order as Christ-followers (Maier).

In 2 Timothy 1:10, the author calls Christ Jesus "our Savior," whose benefaction entails abolishing death and bringing "life and immorality to light through the *gospel" (NRSV). It is possible that some among the earliest audiences of this passage interpreted the author's emphasis on the "appearing" (*epiphaneia*) of the Savior Christ Jesus as a subtle contrast or challenge to an imperial ideology that celebrated the epiphany of the Savior Augustus. But then again, it also could have been that whatever resonances the author hoped his audience would hear between the epiphany of Christ the Savior and the past epiphany of Augustus, such terminology served as linguistic bridges that helped the author communicate his gospel in a recognizable manner that was compelling to Greek and Roman "outsiders."

Among letters attributed to Paul, "Savior" occurs most frequently in the letter to Titus. Similar to 1 Timothy, the authority and mission of "Paul" is authenticated by "God our Savior," by whose command the apostle has been entrusted with proclamation of the gospel (Titus 1:3). In contrast to 1 Timothy and similar to 2 Timothy, the author also describes Christ Jesus as "our Savior" (Titus 1:4). In Titus, the life-giving and life-preserving benefactions of "God our Savior" (Titus 1:10) and "our God and Savior, Jesus Christ" (Titus 2:13) consist in believers' redemption from iniquity and purification that animates a zeal for good deeds. In resonance with Philo (*Migr.* 25; see section 1 above), the evocation of Jesus' philanthropic benefaction functions to inspire an attitude of gratitude that manifests in renouncing the passions and embodying the virtues of self-control, justice, and piety (Titus 2:11). In language reminiscent of Ephesians, the author adds that God has saved believers not because of "any works of *righteousness," "but according to his *mercy" (Titus 3:5 NRSV). These "good deeds" can look like embodying principles of the *household codes. Thus, the author invites *slaves to imagine themselves as "an ornament of the teaching of God our Savior" (Titus 2:10) as they submit themselves to their masters, giving their masters satisfaction in every respect. Whether Christ-following slaves agreed with the author's invitation is up to one's historical-ethical imagination.

Similar to 2 Timothy, the terminology of "appearing" (*epiphaneia*) occurs together with the appellative "Savior" in Titus 2:13; 3:4-6. In Titus 3:4-6, the "goodness" (*chrēstotēs*) and "lovingkindness" (*philanthrōpia*) of "God our Savior" has "appeared" (*epiphainō*). Given that across 1–2 Timothy and Titus, the appearance of Jesus Christ is referenced (1 Tim 6:14; 2 Tim 1:10; 4:1, 8; Titus 2:13; see also 2 Thess 2:8), it seems to be the case that the author of Titus understands Jesus Christ to be the personification or hypostatizing of the "goodness and lovingkindness" (Titus 3:4), "grace" (Titus 2:11), and even "*glory" (Titus 2:13) of "God our Savior" (Towner). Or it may just be that the author of Titus explicitly designates Jesus Christ as "our great God and Savior" here in Titus 2:13 (Quinn). Whatever the case, the author of Titus sees the redeeming work of God the Father and Jesus Christ as Saviors as so interconnected that he can breathlessly shift from the appearance and actions of God to that of Christ in describing the salvation of Christ-followers.

Indeed, it is worth observing that each case of epiphany terminology in 1–2 Timothy and Titus occurs in close proximity to an identification of God or Jesus Christ as "Savior" with respect to the past or future work of salvation materialized in Christ's having abolished death through his own death and resurrection and the pouring out of the *Holy Spirit (2 Tim 1:10; Titus 3:4-6) or his future judgment over the nations (1 Tim 6:13; 2 Tim 4:1, 8; Titus 2:10-13). Again, while there are parallels in the terms used here and those found in the Roman imperial cult, it is not necessary to conclude that the author intends to offer a direct polemic against Caesar being identified as a savior. Rather, it may simply reflect the author's attempt to describe both God and Jesus in a dignified and culturally familiar manner that may have been compelling to his audience or useful for his audience to frame their own understanding of the nature of God to their neighbors.

Last, in Titus, the recognition of God and Jesus Christ as Savior is closely linked to the blessed hope of eternal life (Titus 1:2-3; 2:13; 3:6-7). "The saying is sure," the author of Titus underscores, that "God our Savior" has poured out his Holy Spirit on believers "through Jesus Christ our Savior, so that, having been justified by his *grace, we might become heirs according to the hope of eternal life" (Titus 3:6-7 NRSV). This theme of hope is also closely related to God's identity as Savior in 1 Timothy 1:1; 4:10. Whatever the ambiguous and multiple rhetorical aims of the author of 1 Timothy and Titus to identify God and Christ Jesus as Savior, it is clear that he aims to affirm and encourage hope in his audience(s) as they navigate the challenges of daily life in the ancient Mediterranean, discerning what is right among rival interpretations of the *faith and negotiating a culture and society that is potentially hostile to or at least suspicious of them.

See also Christology; Empire; Ephesians, Letter to the; Lord; Pastoral Epistles; Peace, Reconciliation; Philippians, Letter to the; Religions, Greco-Roman; Salvation; Son of God.

BIBLIOGRAPHY. **S. M. Baugh,** "'Savior of All People': 1 Tim 4:10 in Context," *WTJ* 54, no. 2 (1992): 331-40; **L. H. Cohick,** "Citizenship and Empire: Paul's Letter to the Philippians and Eric Liddell's Work in China," *JSPHL* 1, no. 2 (2011): 137-52; **W. Foerster and G. Fohrer,** "σῴζω, κτλ," *TDNT* 7:965-1024; **D. W. J. Gill,** "A Saviour for the Cities of Crete: The Roman Background to the Epistle to Titus," in *The New Testament in Its First Century Setting*, ed. P. J. Williams et. al. (Grand Rapids, MI: Eerdmans, 2004), 220-30; **F. Graf,** "Theoi Soteres," *ARel* 18, no. 1 (2017): 239-54; **T. C. Hoklotubbe,** *Civilized Piety: The Rhetoric of Pietas in the Pastoral Epistles and the Roman Empire* (Waco, TX: Baylor University Press, 2017), 68-79; **H. O. Maier,** *Picturing Paul in Empire* (London: Bloomsbury, 2013); **J. Moralee,** *"For Salvation's Sake": Provincial Loyalty, Personal Religion, and Epigraphic Production in the Roman and Late Antique Near East* (New York: Routledge, 1994), 17-29; **J. D. Quinn,** *The Letter to Titus*, AB (New York: Doubleday, 1990); **J. Reumann,** *Philippians*, AB 33B (New Haven, CT: Yale University Press, 2008); **R. Schnackenburg,** *Jesus in the Gospels*, trans. O. C. Cean Jr. (Louisville, KY: Westminster John Knox, 1995); **P. H. Towner,** *The Letters to Timothy and Titus*, NICNT (Grant Rapids, MI: Eerdmans, 2006); **P. Wendland,** "Σωτήρ," *ZNW* 5 (1904): 335-53; **G. Wieland,** *The Significance of Salvation: A Study of Salvation Language in the Pastoral Epistles* (Carlisle, UK: Paternoster, 2006); **K. Zamfir,** "Eusebeia, Sōtēra and Civic Loyalty in the Pastoral Epistles," in *Make Disciples of All Nations: The Appeal and Authority of Christian Faith in Hellenistic-Roman Times*, ed. L. T. Stuckenbruck, B. Langstaff, and M. Tilly (Tübingen: Mohr Siebeck, 2019), 121-41.

T. C. Hoklotubbe

SEED. *See* Abraham.

SENDING. *See* Christology; Mission; Son of God.

SERVANT, SERVICE

Three broad-ranging yet overlapping categories of servant/service/serve, *slave/slavery/enslave, and minister/*ministry are widely used by Paul and in very different contexts. These include service as domestic slaves; ministry in and for the *church, particularly by leaders; the humble state of believers in their relationship to *Christ Jesus as *Lord; and metaphorical bondage to certain good or evil powers, including *sin, *righteousness, the *law, and the way of the Spirit.

This range of Greek vocabulary and diversity of usage raise particular challenges for interpreters of Paul's *letters in English. They raise historical, social, cultural, ethical, linguistic, literary, and theological questions.

1. Terminology
2. Translation
3. Literal and Metaphorical
4. The Slave/Servant as Church Leader
5. Slavery and Abolitionism

1. Terminology.

The dominant, relevant terminology occurs across two Greek word groups: (1) *diakonos* (servant/minister), *diakoneō* (serve/minister), *diakonia* (service/ministry); and (2) *doulos* (slave), *douleuō* (be a slave), *douleia* (slavery), and *douloō* (enslave). Paul occasionally uses a third Greek word group: (3) *leitourgos* (servant/minister), *leitourgia* (service/ministry), and *leitourgeō* (serve/minister), especially in reference to aspects of service in the church community or between churches (2 Cor 9:11) or to the state (Rom 13:6). Other, less frequent—but more specific and technical—terms for particular kinds of domestic or religious service also occur in Paul's letters.

2. Translation.

A substantial challenge is posed by many English translations in the varied and sometimes inconsistent, even opaque, ways in which these different Greek words map onto the distinct categories of slavery, domestic service, and church ministry. In particular, it is often unclear whether the word *servant* is being used to translate *diakonos* or *doulos*; whether the word *minister* is being used to translate *diakonos* or *leitourgos*; or why the word *diakonos* is being translated "servant," "minister," or "deacon" in a particular context.

The source of the translation difficulty arises as early as the first English version of the Bible (Wycliffe Bible, 1382/1395), which is a rendering of the Latin Vulgate rather than a translation of the earlier original language manuscripts. The Latin noun *servus* may refer to either a servant or a slave, depending on context (see also the Latin verb *servire*, either "to serve" or "to be a slave"). Where the underlying Greek text of the NT specifically references slavery (as distinct, for example, from hired servants [*misthios*, Lk 15:17, 19]), the earliest English translations nonetheless tended to adopt the words *servant* and *serve*, following the lettering of the Latin stem *serv-*. This set a precedent for the majority of subsequent English translations. It also avoided a later difficulty when societies increasingly came to regard slavery in their own time as universally oppressive and exploitative. In this context it is problematic to reflect Paul's use of slavery language in regard to Jesus' incarnation (Phil 2:7), a believer's submission to Christ Jesus (Rom 1:1), and even an apostle's position in relation to a church (2 Cor 4:5). In these instances, the word *servant* raises fewer ethical challenges than the word *slave* but introduces a lack of transparency.

In the Vulgate of Paul's letters, a second Latin root, *minister/ministro/ministerium/ministratio*, typically translates the Greek noun *diakonos* (servant) and verb *diakoneō* (serve), but sometimes also *leitourgos* (minister, Rom 13:6), *hypēretēs* (assistant, 1 Cor 4:1), even *synergos* (fellow worker, 1 Thess 3:2). In English this Latin word group tends to be rendered as "servant" when referring to domestic staff and "minister/ministry" when referring to church roles; for example, a servant/minister of *God (see Rom 13:4; contrast "a slave of Christ Jesus" in Rom 1:1). Subsequent ecclesiastical usage has similarly preferred the terms *minister* and *ministry* over *servant* or *service* in these contexts.

Accordingly, the Greek word *diakonos* may be rendered "deacon" in some Pauline contexts (Phil 1:1; 1 Tim 3:8, 10, 12-13), "minister" in others (Eph 3:7; 6:21), or "servant" in still others (1 Tim 4:6). Furthermore, the English word *servant* may instead be translating the Greek word for slave (see Col 1:7, "a servant [*diakonos*] of Christ," and Phil 1:1, "slaves [*douloi*] of Christ"; yet contrast also Phil 1:1, "overseers and deacons/servants [*diakonoi*]").

3. Literal and Metaphorical.

This lack of transparency in many English translations is further complicated by other contrasting ways in which Paul uses these terms—sometimes literally and sometimes metaphorically, sometimes negatively and sometimes positively, sometimes with a servile connotation and sometimes conveying significant reflected authority.

In addition to the literal use of this language, as in Paul's dealings with the slave Onesimus (Philemon) or his guidance to slaves and masters (Eph 6:5-9; Col 4:1), Paul also uses slavery language metaphorically. For example, he can describe the state of the nonbeliever as slavery, in contrast to sonship (see Rom 8:12-17, 21-23; Gal 4:1-9, 24-25). Indeed, this language can metaphorically express any relationship of unconditional obedience, whether positively to Christ Jesus or to righteousness, or negatively to *death or sin (Rom 6:18-19). In this way, a person can be freed from slavery to sin (Rom 6:6-7). Ambiguously, this transition may be framed either as *adoption to sonship ("no longer a slave," Gal 4:7; Rom 8:15), or as unconditional obedience to a new master ("slaves of God," Rom 6:22; or "slaves of righteousness," Rom 6:18), or as a transition from *freedom to worship idols to enslavement to the living and true God, who offers deliverance from bondage (1 Thess 1:9-10).

In this way, a slave who is called in the Lord metaphorically becomes a freedperson in the Lord, though remaining a slave in society (1 Cor 7:21-23); and Paul, who is himself both free and a Roman citizen (Acts 22:25-29; 1 Cor 9:1, 19), nonetheless embraces, without irony, the metaphorical idea of being a slave of God (Titus 1:1), of the *gospel (Eph 3:7), of a new *covenant (2 Cor 3:6), of righteousness (2 Cor 11:14), "enslaved in . . . the Spirit" (Rom 7:6), and "enslaved to the law" (Rom 7:25). Conversely, as a free man Paul warns against the trap of being bound in other ways: a slave of *Satan (2 Cor 11:14-15) or of sin (Gal 2:17; Rom 6:6, 17, 20; cf. Rom 7:25). There are, therefore, mutually incompatible metaphors of salvation whether as transition from slavery either to liberty (the Lord's freedperson), or to adoption to sonship, or the upwardly mobile transition from slavery to one master to higher-status bondage and obedience to a more powerful master (Rom 12:11).

4. The Slave/Servant as Church Leader. Counterintuitively, this metaphorical usage of slave or servant language is also widely applied as a way of framing *leadership within the people of God, whether as a consequence of being appointed as Christ's *apostle and slave (*doulos*, Phil 1:1), or as a recognized servant/deacon (*diakonos*) within a community of believers (also Phil 1:1). In this way, the slave/servant terminology frames the leader both in relation to God and to the church. The leader may be the one who presides over a community (1 Thess 5:12) but is also their slave (*doulos*, 2 Cor 4:5; *douloō*, 1 Cor 9:19) and may carry the title of deacon (*diakonos*, Phil 1:1; 1 Tim 3:8, 10, 12-13). Simultaneously, members of the *body of Christ are to be subject to their leaders, that is, to those who are devoted to their service (*diakonia*, 1 Cor 16:15-16).

Paul is indebted to depictions of a number of the prophets in the Jewish Scriptures (Josh 14:7; Amos 3:7) for this notion of leadership as a posture of slavery, in humble service, whether of God or of a people. The Jewish Scriptures widely frame *worship of the God of *Israel in language of service (see Byron). Similarly, in some contexts Greek usage of the term *diakonos* may refer to a high-ranking intermediary, with all the authority of the one that they are representing (see Collins).

More recent representations of church leadership as servant leadership are consequently unhelpful, in that servant leadership neither fully recognizes a slave's subservience and complete absence of rights nor adequately captures that God's appointed slave holds extraordinary, representative authority as his servant.

5. Slavery and Abolitionism. On the vexing issue of human slavery, Paul Ellingworth, following Scott Bartchy, notes that associations with New World slavery in the seventeenth through nineteenth centuries have hindered interpreters in accurately conveying Paul's presentation of slavery, whether literal or metaphorical. The word *servant* conveys certain things within an entrenched slave economy (as in the Roman *Empire, at the time of Paul's writing), while it has other associations in a setting where paid servants are widely employed as domestic staff (as at the time of the earliest English translations of the Bible), and still other connotations are carried in those political contexts that are avowedly abolitionist (as at the time of many of the later English translations). Even among Paul's contemporaries, Jews, Greeks, and Romans had quite varied, dominant attitudes toward slavery.

Paul is not significantly a social reformer, and he does not uniformly weigh in on the evils of Greco-Roman slavery. It is clear that he is negatively disposed toward some aspects of slavery. He recognizes that bondage induces *fear (Rom 8:15), and he appeals to slaves that they seek to obtain their freedom, if they can, and avoid entering into slavery where possible (1 Cor 7:21, 23). Yet, he also urges slaves to be obedient, wholehearted, and sincere, as if they were instead enslaved to and fearful of Christ (Eph 6:5-8; Col 3:22-24; Titus 2:9). On the other hand, Paul does urge believing masters to treat their slaves compassionately, justly, fairly, and without threats (Eph 6:9; Col 4:1). In terms of salvation, there is no difference between slaves and masters (Gal 3:28; Col 3:11). Accordingly, in the church also, slaves and masters are to coexist in mutual respect, forbearance, submission, and compassion (Col 3:5-17). Paul urges Philemon not simply to take back his slave Onesimus but to treat him instead as a brother and no different from how one would treat Paul (Philem 8-17).

Rather than overturn an integral element in the Greco-Roman economy and social order, Paul urges believers to accept their position and act appropriately within it; slaves should embrace their role submissively, while masters should treat their subjects moderately.

See also Households and Household Codes; Leadership; Ministry; Philemon, Letter to; Slave, Slavery.

BIBLIOGRAPHY. **S. S. Bartchy,** *Mallon Chresai: First-Century Slavery and the Interpretation of 1 Corinthians 7:21*, SBLDS 11 (Missoula, MT: Scholars Press, 1973); **J. Byron,** "Paul and the Background of Slavery: The Status Quaestionis in New Testament Scholarship," *CurBR* 3 (2004): 116-39; **J. N. Collins,** *Diakonia: Re-interpreting the Ancient Sources* (Oxford: Oxford University Press, 1990); **P. Ellingworth,** "Servant, Slave, or What?," *BT* 49 (1998): 123-26; **M. J. Harris,** *Slave of Christ: A New Testament Metaphor for Total Devotion to Christ* (Downers Grove, IL: InterVarsity Press, 1999); **D. B. Martin,** *Slavery as Salvation: The Metaphor of Slavery in Pauline Christianity* (New Haven, CT: Yale University Press, 1990).

A. D. Clarke

SERVICE. *See* Ministry; Servant, Service.

SEXUALITY, SEXUAL ETHICS

There are few things in life that are more personal than sexuality. Yet, by its nature, sexual activity is always a social reality because it requires another person in order to come to fulfillment, whether as performance, pleasure, or procreation. Greco-Roman and Jewish communities placed on their members many expectations related to sex. These differed from person to person depending on numerous factors, but chiefly bodily sex and status determined all other options. The ways these expectations were expressed related to the underlying beliefs and practices of the person's particular community. Paul was raised in the Greco-Roman city of Tarsus, but within a family that encouraged and supported his dedication to the Jewish community's beliefs and practices according to the strictures of Pharisaism. Paul's Jewish beliefs provided strong theological ways of navigating the issues of sexuality within *Gentile cultures from a scriptural perspective. It is, therefore, important to understand the common Greco-Roman and Second Temple Jewish beliefs about sex, sexuality, and sexual ethics since Paul knew them and taught about them in the churches he founded in the Mediterranean world. Paul's primary goal when teaching on sexuality and sex ethics was to offer a theology of sexuality that encouraged Christians to live a holy and transformed communal life that reflected the *gospel.

1. Greco-Roman Backgrounds
2. Second Temple Jewish Backgrounds
3. Paul

1. Greco-Roman Backgrounds.

1.1. Greco-Roman Theological Anthropology. A considerable amount of conversation surrounds sexuality in classical literary, medical, and philosophical treatises. These wide-ranging thoughts seek to locate the sex act's place within the cosmos (Aristotle, *Pol.* 1.1259b-1260b; Lakey, 151). Overall, Hellenistic and Roman cultures largely held to a number of similar basic concepts concerning the sexes and sexuality (Harper, 9).

In contrast to late modern sensibilities, Greco-Roman sexual thought had one fundamental anthropological assumption: all humans were male, though some suffered from deformations of the *body resulting in being disabled, feminine, or female (Plato, *Tim.* 41e-42d, 90e-91a; Martin, 32-33; Loader 2013, 35). Male semen was considered a piece of the soul, a pure divine essence torn from the male body (Galen, *De Semine* 1.16; Harper, 58), which fused to the deformed "fleshy semen" of the female body by the heat of sexual orgasm, especially if simultaneous (Soranus, *Gynaecia* 1.12.44; Brown, 9-10, 17-19; cf. Tertullian, *An.* 27). Once the divine seminal essence of the male was trapped in the bodily matter of the female, it would develop into a new child's body (Hippocrates, *On Generation* 1-5; Loader 2012, 98-99). The best child was a son nearly the clone of his father, an almost exact imprint, barely blemished by the body of the mother. A healthy male child who looked more like his mother was less desirable but good. Sickly sons and those who exhibited feminine characteristics were disappointing. Regard was then given to beautiful, healthy, and intelligent daughters, whose female genitalia and organs were interpreted as an unfortunate inversion of male sex organs (Loader 2012, 86). Last, disabled infants and unwanted daughters suffered infanticide by exposure, as they were considered worthless to both family and society (note the priority of Hippocrates, *On Generation* 6-11).

Because of this fundamental theological *anthropology, several assumptions about the sexes permeated Roman Hellenistic society. The female and the feminine were assumed to be constitutionally inferior, meant to be sexually penetrated, to live in passive submission, and to be provided for (Plato, *Tim.* 50c-51b; Martin, 34; Watson, 65). Conversely, the male and the masculine were constitutionally superior, meant to sexually penetrate, to live in active dominance over others, and to provide (Harper, 32-33).

The classical world's medical assessments of sex were supported by cosmological and philosophical rationalizations (Aretaeus, *causis et signis acutorum morborum* 2.5). It was believed that the movement of the celestial bodies revealed how nature constitutionally produced children (Brown, xlv-xlvi), imbuing male and female bodies with more or less masculinity or femininity, which would later manifest through behavior, particularly sexual desires (Claudius Ptolemy, *Tetrabiblos* 3.6; Lakey, 124-25; Martin, 18). Plato's philosophical musings speak about how common sexual desires, both heterosexual and homosexual eroticism, reveal the way the gods formed humanity. One of his etiologies (*Symp.* 189-193) is a depiction of the gods splitting men and *women from a set of primal bodies. Some men were split from a male body and so desire sexual union with another male. Similarly, some women were split from a female body and so desire sexual union with a female. Yet, Plato considered that most people were derived from a male body producing both males and females, engendering desire for the opposite sex.

1.2. Greco-Roman Sexual Ethics and Society. Greco-Roman sexuality was complex, and sexual ethics varied in many ways, but there were a few central tenets. Roman society's legislation of sexual ethics reflects some of these beliefs as they sought to create stability for *marriages and *households within the general sexual chaos of Greco-Roman culture. The first tenet is that men were sexually uncontrollable and insatiable. This assumption generated a primary virtue of sexuality for each sex. For women, this virtue was modesty, as an attempt to mitigate men's sexual desire. For men, it was self-control, which meant moderation rather than chastity or monogamy (Harper, 41, 56; Hoklotubbe, 85). The second tenet, which reinforced the first, was that a person's sexual life must be lived according to their status. Each person's status placed them somewhere within the active-passive and dominance-submission matrix of Greco-Roman sexual expectations. Each member of society was honor bound to live according to these sexual ethics for the good of their household.

Greco-Roman sexual ethics provided libertine allowances for free men, harshly legislated protections for the honor of free men's children, and the exploitation of *slaves (Brown, 23). While there was liberal allowance for generally persistent sexual behaviors considered improprieties and perversities, if a person were to flagrantly disregard sexual norms, they would bring immense public shame on themselves and their household. According to their sexual norms, the Greeks had developed a system of pederasty, but such sexual acts required explicit consent by the "beloved" boys in the grooming process. Hellenistic practices of pederasty held the young male body to be the pinnacle of human beauty, normalizing a desire for boys and young men. Some men did not escape their habits of pederasty, even though such behavior was publicly denounced for men who had entered into marriage (Suetonius, *The Twelve Caesars* 7.22; Sanders, 728-36; Loader 2012, 83-84).

Moving into the Roman era, pederasty was mostly replaced with the sexual exploitation of slaves (Harper, 26). The use of slaves for sexual pleasure was so prevalent there was almost no concept of masturbation mentioned in Roman society (Harper, 27, 60). While rich men often made use of their household slaves, the common man had to avail himself of prostitutes, usually cheap brothel slaves. The harsh, short life of the prostitute was considered most dishonorable, and she was often likened to little more than a corpse. Even still, Roman culture believed prostitution was essential for social order as it diverted the seemingly uncontrollable sexual desires of men away from pursuing the children of free men or from committing adultery with married women (Dio Chrysostom, *Ven.* 139-140; Harper, 46-49). Adultery was seen as the theft of a husband's honor and so carried the threat of legal punishment. It could also possibly taint the husband's household with illegitimate children (Harper, 43; Loader 2012, 76). A primary purpose of marriage as a legal convention was for protecting the procreative rights of legal spouses and the inheritance rights of legitimate heirs. Households enhanced their social status by contributing to society through strategic marriages and childbearing; therefore, marriage formed the foundation of a Roman sexual ethic (Dio Cassius, *Hist.* 54.16.1-2; Whang, 88).

2. Second Temple Jewish Backgrounds.

2.1. Jewish Theological Anthropology. For Jews of the Second Temple era, sex held an important cosmological and theological position within God's good *creation. *God created woman as the sexual companion of man to save him from being the "only one" (Gen 2:18) by becoming the "two in one *flesh" (Gen 2:24) through the gift of marriage's erotic union (Loader 2004, 42; Watson, 63). The theological oneness of sexual identity, borne in the interpenetrating bodies of husband and wife, is also depicted in how the male and female body together bear the *image of God, particularly as procreation enables humanity to expand and rule over creation (Gen 1:26-28; Loader 2004, 27-29; O'Reilly, 203). As in Greco-Roman culture, procreation was recognized as the purpose of marriage's sexual union (Satlow, 20; Loader 2013, 108), but it was also perceived to be an intimate co-creative participation with God in creation (Gen 4:1; Farris, 212-14).

Proper or improper sexual behavior was understood to influence the character of one's children, which continued into future generations as offspring developed into nations (Gen 9:20-27; 19:30-38; see 1 En. 85–90); therefore, sexual immorality is explicitly expounded on for the people of God (Lev 18). God's involvement in the procreative process was essential for Israel's *election, both in the collective memory of the promised sons to barren matriarchs (Gen 21:12; 25:21-23; 30:22-24; cf. Gal 4:21-31) and in the one Creator God's desire to procreate more offspring in *Israel by continually pouring his creating Spirit into their marital unions (Mal 2:14-15).

2.2. Jewish Sexual Ethics. The sexual *ethics generated in Second Temple Judaism by the belief that God's good creational order is embodied within a husband and wife's sexual union (see Mt 19:6) resulted in a number of nuanced beliefs, some similar to surrounding cultures and some extremely distinct. First, a romantic theme celebrated God's provision of sexual oneness to overcome the loneliness of life. This is seen in Ruth, Song of Songs, and Tobit (Loader 2013, 15-16; von Thaden, 131-32). The role of women in such romance was sexual *purity and fidelity to their husbands, families, and people to ensure proper procreation, as Josephus's retelling of the Ruth narrative emphasizes (Levinson). Second, the Mosaic *law forbids any sexual behavior that cannot or should not result in procreation by deeming it sinful and unnatural. This includes sex during menstruation, adultery, homosexual behavior, or sex acts with animals (see Gen 38:9). The condemnation of infanticide at the center of these rejected forms of sex indicates it is the pinnacle of rebellion against God's good order for creation and emphasizes this procreative reasoning (Lev 18:19-23; 20:13; Loader 2012, 32-33).

Third, similar to Greco-Romans, adultery was considered an act of theft against the husband and household to which the wife had been joined because it placed the lineage of children and inheritance in jeopardy (Sir 23:22-25; Wis 3:16-19; 4:3-6; Josephus, *Ant.* 3.12.1). When adultery was publicly known, punishment was often demanded by the Jewish community (see Mt 1:19): divorce at minimum and execution when possible (Loader 2012, 8; see Jn 8:3-5). Adultery, as any sexual act outside marriage by either husband or wife, severed the oneness of marriage and forced a certificate of divorce (Loader 2013, 68-74). Fourth, husbands alone had the right to divorce, though wives could request one from a husband (Loader 2012, 80), and there were differing opinions about what granted the Mosaic allowance for divorce (Deut 24:1; Fee, 325). Some thought any disagreeable pretense given by a husband made divorce justified (Philo, *Spec.* 3.30; Josephus, *Ant.* 4.253; Sir 7:26; 25:26; Mt 19:3), while others argued that sexual immorality was the only legitimate indecency (Giṭ. 90; Mt 5:31-32; 19:3-9). Since women existed to fulfill the dual purpose of companionship through sexual comfort and procreation, the romantic search for the "perfect" wife provided by God (Sir 7:19, 26; cf. Tob 8:4-8, 17) led to divorce becoming a widespread practice within Jewish communities (Loader 2013, 72-73).

Last, there developed an expectation that Jewish men and women would marry exclusively within the Jewish community (Ezra 9:1-3; Philo, *Spec.* 3.29; Josephus, *Ant.* 8.191). Intermarriage with Gentiles was incompatible with God's election, thus bringing impurity into Israel (Ezra 9:10-15; Philo, *Mos.* 1.302-305; Satlow, chap. 3; Southwood) and *judgment to the people of God (Josh 23:12-13; Jub. 30.7-17). The primary dangers of intermarriages were the temptation to be drawn into *idolatry (Ex 34:13-16; Deut 7:3-4; Josephus, *Ant.* 8.192) and the procreation of "mixed" children (Ezra 10:2-3; Mal 2:10-15; Gruen, 96-97; Ben-Eliyahu, 36).

3. Paul.

3.1. A Pauline Theology of Sex. Paul's texts regularly provide teachings on sexual desire and behavior. Only five letters lack an explicit statement on the topic, but even still it is likely three of these (Philippians, 2 Timothy, Titus) implicitly hint at sexuality in terms of modesty and self-control (Westfall, 190; Hoklotubbe, 101-2), which leaves only 2 Thessalonians and Philemon without any reference.

Three frameworks undergird Paul's conversation about sexual desire and behavior. The first is the Jewish creation narrative of Genesis. The narrative provides Paul a basic structure for a theological anthropology based on the Creator's desire for an ordered creation, specifically how humanity might live righteously with God. The second framework is Paul's belief that wherever the *churches reside their communal existence enacts a holy *temple life. This life provides participants with *identity boundary markers, a scriptural logic for *discipline, and sexual expectations within the churches. The last framework depicts marriage as the most intimately embodied revelation of Christ's union with the church. The institution's public, "external" form is generated to protect and respect the private, "internal" act of sex between husband and wife, which transforms key aspects of a person's identity in relation to God and *Christ, the community of *faith, and their spouse.

Paul's frameworks for sex have some major defining characteristics. Foremost is that these frameworks are inherently theological. Paul reworks his Second Temple Jewish creation theology through the crucible of his apostolic gospel, thus reforging it with christological meaning. Next, these frameworks are conceptually interlocked and interdependent. The *truth of one framework often references the others, and in turn they reinforce each other. Such coherence attempts to provide a comprehensive theology concerning sex, providing a fundamental logic to address any ad hoc situation the churches might face. Last, Paul has an order of development for his theology of sex: (1) a general anthropology within creation, (2) expectations particularly for the community of faith, and (3) the personal intimacy of a specific male-female sexual union in marriage. Each layer stacks on the other, arranging a creational order rooted in relation, which is reflected in Paul's assumed theological tiers of Creator, Christ, and husband (1 Cor 11:3; Loader 2004, 100-101; Lakey, 128-29). This order then becomes an entry point to explore a Pauline theology of sexuality and sex ethics.

3.2. Pauline Theological Anthropology. The first framework for a theology of sex draws on Second Temple Jewish creation theology and recognizes that the sex act is a moment embodying the person's place within the cosmic reality of God's creation (see Farris, 218-21). Paul assumes a three-tiered relational structure to God's created anthropological nature: God related to Christ, Christ related to every man, man related to woman (1 Cor 11:3; Barrett; Collins and Harrington, 405-6). While there is debate over what "*head" means between man and woman in 1 Corinthians 11:2-16, Paul's assumed theology about sex is clearer. Drawing on Genesis, Paul believes sex reveals the interdependence of men and women (Peeler, 158; Westfall, 99) because (1) woman was created from man for his good, likely referring to sexual union (1 Cor 11:8-9, 12; Fee), and (2) man only exists by procreation through the woman as the good fulfillment of sexual union (1 Cor 11:12; Gen 4:1; cf. 1 Tim 4:3-4), therefore (3) men and women exist together only through the necessity of sexual union under Christ's lordship and by God's design (1 Cor 11:11-12; Barrett). Erotic desire between the male and female reveals this contingent relationship.

Further, the male-female bodily distinction allows man and woman to form their own self-reflective personal identities (Gen 2:23-24; Watson, 57-61). Unlike Philo (*Cher.* 48-50), Paul's anthropology uses Jewish theology to reject some Greco-Roman anthropological ideas, such as the claim that all humans are male, a common spiritual androgyny in humanity, or any devaluation of female distinction (Gal 3:15-29; Collins, 408; Uzukwu, 177-79). Thereby Paul abolishes any barrier for the female body to fully participate in *salvation (Gal 3:28; Hays, "Galatians"; Dunn, 593; Boles, 97-98). Humanity's corruption of God's good and ordered creation is also part of Paul's Jewish creation theology. He believes sexuality has been deeply warped by *sin. Paul links such disorder in sexual behaviors and desires to idolatry (Rom 1:24-25; Farris, 219). In fact, through immoral sex acts humans actively reject God in two ways: by the corruption, or giving up, of the image of God and by the idolatrous *worship of created bodies (Rom 1:23).

3.2.1. Sexuality and the Image of God. Paul connects sexual immorality to the destructive alteration, if not complete loss, of humanity's bearing the image of God (O'Reilly, 206-7). In Romans, God's giving of humanity over to its impure sexual desires in the body is expressed by terms of alteration, change, or exchange (*allassō*, *metallassō*, Rom 1:23-26; Cranfield, 125). There is a perceivable fall from being good to sinful on account of these exchanges (Wright, 349-51). Therefore, Paul's anthropology expresses three basic alterations to humanity's created nature: (1) from bearers of the immortal image of God *into* bearers of the mortal image of created bodies (see 1 Cor 15:49), (2) from worshipers of the creator God *into* idolatrous worshipers of created bodies, and (3) from bodily participants with God in the pure, honorable, and natural procreative sexual order of creation (Westfall, 195) *into* bodily participants of sexual acts against the good ordering of God's creation, particularly typified in the unnatural (non-procreative) condition of homosexual behavior (Harper, 94; O'Reilly, 208).

In Colossians, Paul's admonition for living the gospel in the body means putting to *death sexual immorality foremost (Col 3:5; Harper, 91). Sexual self-control is a prime indicator someone has become a new person in Christ Jesus, allowing the Christian's renewal to include bearing the image of God (Col 3:9-10)—the image being Christ embodied (Col 1:15; 2:20; 3:1, 11). Similarly, Paul encourages the Ephesians to be renewed by the truth of Christ Jesus and become a new humanity bearing the image of God (Eph 4:21-24; Cohick), emphasizing that imitating God through Christ Jesus means bodily *sacrifice and that the antithesis to this gospel embodiment is sexual immorality (Eph 5:1-6). There are also parallel warnings that shameful, sexually immoral behavior is a quality of those who are lost in the darkness of separation from God (see Eph 5:7-16; Rom 13:11-14) and a decisive occasion for God's judgment and *wrath on humanity (Rom 1:18, 27, 32; Eph 5:5-6; Col 3:5-6). Paul's theological anthropology perceives that humanity's failure to properly bear the image of God is concurrent with humanity's participation in the creational disorder through sexual immorality.

3.2.2. Sex and Desire. Paul uses the language of desire in Romans, particularly *epithymia*, to note the connection between sexual immorality and idolatry. For many Second Temple Jews *epithymia* regularly referred to sexual desire (Dunn, 92; Watson, 154).

The LXX's intentional move of "do not desire your neighbor's wife" to be the initial phrase in the tenth commandment (Ex 20:17 LXX), possibly in order to match Deuteronomy 5:21, supports this inclination that the sexual nuance of *epithymia* was primary for many Second Temple Jews (see 4 Macc 2:1-6; Wright, 473). Paul's own use of *epithymia* connects sexual immorality and the tenth commandment (Rom 7:7-8; 13:9, 13-14; cf. Eph 5:3, 5; Col 3:5; Watson, 152-55). Paul believes sin energizes (*katergazomai*; see Rom 1:27) the body toward death along the pathways of bodily desire (Rom 7:8, 13-20; Dunn, 119). Only the Spirit living in the Christian's mortal body overcomes Sin's power in the body. The Spirit energizes the human body toward *righteousness, *resurrection, and the obedience of faith (Rom 8:9-11; 15:18; cf. Rom 1:5-6). The rule over human bodies, by either Sin or the Spirit, is revealed in a person's righteous or unrighteous living (Rom 6:12-14; Gal 5:16-25).

Sexual immorality is often the preeminent marker in Paul's vice lists for recognizing which dominion a person is allegiant to and thereby whether one is energized by Sin or the Spirit (Rom 13:13; 1 Cor 5:10, 11; 6:9-10; 2 Cor 12:21; Gal 5:19; Eph 5:5; Col 3:5). Since Paul's Jewish creation theology believes sex is for procreative participation with God, he depicts homosexual behavior as the pinnacle example of an anthropology ruled by Sin through corrupt sexual desire. The sinful sexual passions of humanity result in homosexual acts that invert God's created order, cultivating and manifesting in the present the body's ultimate shameful fruit—death (Rom 1:26-27; 7:5; cf. 1 Cor 6:18). Immoral sex acts are the idolatrous worship of other created bodies. Therefore, sexually immoral desires refuse to join in God's work within creation and are oriented toward death. In contrast, a person's sexuality could reveal an embodied participation with God in his good creation through sex acts that are pure, honorable, and naturally procreative, which is proper for the people of God as they conform to their Spirit-filled bodily life in Christ Jesus—the renewed humanity bearing God's image (Rom 8:11, 23, 29; Col 3:9-10).

3.3. Sex and Christian Communal Life. Paul draws deeply on the same themes of creation, worship, and the Spirit's presence that he used in his theological anthropology (Collins and Harrington, 241-43) to integrate and develop his second framework of a communal and holy temple life. But this second framework for Paul's theology of sex requires an approach more exclusive to the people of God as communities of the faith among the nations. Congruous with his Jewish theology and practice (Sanders, 335), Paul made sexual ethics a severe boundary marker for anyone desiring to identify as a member of the Christian community (1 Cor 5:11-12; Furnish, 51). Paul is unequivocal to the Corinthians: those who intentionally participate in sexually immoral practices will not inherit the *kingdom of God because they are not members of God's holy family under the lordship of Christ Jesus, and they lack the Spirit's work in their bodies (1 Cor 6:9-11; Hays 2011; cf. Eph 5:5). Sexual ethics is a matter of participating in the holy temple life of God's people, who embody the Spirit of God on the earth (1 Cor 3:16; 6:18-19; Barrett). This theological reality removes sexuality from the realm of personal preference because "for Paul, sexual morality was a communal property" (Harper, 100). Therefore, sex functions as a boundary marker to appropriate the Christian identity. Sexual behavior is a juncture in which a person either gives their body to be joined (*kollōmenos*) with Sin-filled humanity through sexual immorality or gives their body through sexual *holiness to be submissively and gloriously joined (*kollōmenos*) to Christ Jesus by the embodiment of the *Holy Spirit (1 Cor 6:12-20; Horsley).

3.3.1. Sexual Immorality, Excommunication, and Condemnation. There is a dire warning for those who would slight Paul's teachings about sexuality: Paul's sexual ethics are truly the commands of Christ Jesus, who will punish anyone disregarding them because to do so is to reject God's Spirit, given to empower the people to live in holiness (1 Thess 4:2-8). Latent in Paul's description of Christ Jesus as the righteous avenger is the assumption that sexual immorality invariably creates victims who must be avenged, particularly within the community of faith, where holy ethics and brotherly love should abound (1 Thess 4:1, 7, 9). This victimhood includes sexual self-harm against one's own body. Paul dismisses any claims that consent to sexual immorality negates the harm of those who participate in it (1 Cor 6:18; Hays 2011). He does not believe receiving spiritual gifts from God through Christ will make up for, cover up, or outweigh continued sexual immorality by the person attempting to also participate in the holy temple life of a church. He makes an example of those Israelites after the exodus who were spiritually baptized in the Red Sea and received spiritual food and drink in the wilderness but were still consigned to death for displeasing God in sexual immorality mixed with idolatry (1 Cor 10:1-8; Barrett). Those participants in the churches who follow the ancient Israelites in sexual immorality will also be judged by

Christ, even if they attempt to live as a member of the people of God (1 Cor 10:7-10; Barrett).

According to this holy temple life, Paul demands the Corinthian church excommunicate the person among them who had participated in sexual immorality (1 Cor 5:1-5, 11-13). For guidance on how to address future participants who indulge in sexual immorality, he admonishes them to disassociate with anyone who claims a Christian identity but persists in their sins, sexual immorality foremost among them (1 Cor 5:9-13; Hays 2011). Later, Paul was particularly worried about coming to the Corinthians a third time on account of their disordered communal life. He feared Christ's judgment might be adjudicated against them through his apostolic authority for their lack of communal repentance and transformation concerning sexual immorality (2 Cor 12:21–13:10).

3.3.2. Sex and Church Leaders. Paul particularly expects two groups within the churches to perform the holy social boundaries of sexual embodiment: leaders and the married. Christian leaders must lead holy sexual lives within their households and the household of God (1 Tim 3:2, 12; 4:12; 5:2). Since they teach the law in accordance with the gospel, they are expected to embody the behaviors and practices proper to the holy life of the church. The law condemns as disobedient, ungodly, and unholy the sexually immoral in general, with an emphasis on those practicing homosexual behavior (1 Tim 1:8-11; Towner).

The language of self-control carried heavy undertones of sexual moderation and prudence in first century Greco-Roman and Jewish cultures (Harper, 53). While he expects sexual self-control of Christians in general (1 Cor 7:5, 9; Gal 5:23; 1 Tim 2:9; Titus 2:2, 5, 6, 11), Paul especially demands it from church leaders (1 Tim 3:2; 2 Tim 1:7; Titus 1:8). He rejects the false teachers in Ephesus because they personally lack self-control (2 Tim 3:3) but they teach others to abstain from God's good creations of marriage and certain foods. Instead, Paul encourages participants in the church's holy temple life to prayerfully enjoy God's good creations of sex and food in their proper order and in holiness (1 Tim 4:1-5; Towner).

3.3.3. Christian Marriage and Non-Christians. One reason marital union is a stark boundary marker of holy temple life is that the community of faith should not be mixing with other communities dedicated to other gods (2 Cor 6:14-16). God's people sexually "mixing" with the nations was a concept long despised by Second Temple Jews, typified by Ezra's sorrow and enforced reform against those who had intermarried and procreated with Gentile women (Ezra 9:2, 12; Southwood). Paul's concern follows suit; God's presence among the churches should result in a rejection of sexually joining Christian families to non-Christian families in marriage. The public sexual life of the community of faith must accord to God's temple presence in holy fear (2 Cor 6:16–7:1), though this does not justify divorce if a convert's spouse remains a non-Christian (see below).

3.4. Christian Marriage. The final framework for a Pauline theology of sex means focusing the conversation on the most intimate human relationship: marriage.

3.4.1. Christian Marriage with a Non-Christian Spouse. As above, Paul expects the joining and continuing of Christian families to be formed exclusively within the community of faith (2 Cor 6:14). Still, in the early days of a conversion-based community there were many participants whose spouses were not converted, so Paul instructs Christians to base marriage on the consent of their spouse. A believing spouse must stay within a marriage if the nonbelieving spouse consents (Thiselton, 527). However, if the nonbeliever abandons the marriage on account of their spouse's Christian faith, then the believer's faith does not demand the believer to use marital rights to procure damages from their abandoning spouse or force them to stay married (1 Cor 7:12-13, 15).

Paul offers two theological reasons for the obligation to stay in a "mixed" marriage: the holiness granted to the nonbelieving spouse on account of the believing spouse, which affects procreated children, and the possibility of saving the nonbelieving spouse through eventual conversion (1 Cor 7:14, 16; Thiselton). While conversion is a recognizable idea, a Pauline theology of sex provides the logic for how a nonbelieving spouse is made holy in and through their believing spouse. The anthropological nature of the believing spouse has been transformed by the removal of sin in Christ Jesus, and their body is now energized by the Holy Spirit's presence (1 Cor 1:2; 6:11; Sanders, 292-94). Paul's Jewish theology of sex recognizes that God's Spirit is poured into a marriage's sexual union to procreate godly children, generating more people of God to redeem God's good and ordered creation through a communally holy life (Gen 2:24; 4:1; Mal 2:15-16; Ho, 213). Christ Jesus seems to reference a similar theology of sex when he says men should not tear apart what God has joined together in sexual oneness. It is the Spirit's creative personal presence that imbues sex with its spiritual reality, making it more than merely an act of biological process (Mt 19:4-5; Westfall, 193).

Paul's teaching to the Corinthians assumes the Spirit is the agent of sanctification (1 Cor 6:9-11; cf. Rom 1:4-5; 15:16) and therefore the one whose embodied presence in the Christian spouse during sex purifies the marriage's sexual oneness. This Spirit-sanctified sex allows children even from mixed parentage to be considered holy and grants them access to the life of God's people (Loader 2005, 169-70). This is a substantial change from the Second Temple Jewish perspective, where children born of mixed marriages were considered ungodly or unholy. Paul seems to cohere his sexual and missional theologies: there is no inherent rejection of Gentiles by God in Christ Jesus. Theological and social barriers should inhibit a marriage between a believer and a nonbeliever, but there is no necessary rejection of a nonbelieving spouse when a person converts to be a part of the community of faith similar to Ezra's intermarriage reformation. There is only a hope-filled, holy invitation into salvation (Hays 2011, 122). Therefore, for the Christian, sex within marriage, even marriage to a nonbeliever, is a rightly ordered and good anthropological act by which men and women join into God's procreative act.

3.4.2. Christian Marriage and Celibacy Overcome Sexual Immorality. For Paul, the Spirit's presence in sex also offers married Christians an active practice to overcome sinful sexual desires (von Thaden, 263-92). Husbands and wives are called to give their bodies to one another based on the sexual needs of their spouse. Christians do not merely fulfill the sexual rights and responsibilities protected and expected of marriage but recognize that sex helps stave off sinful temptations that might overwhelm either spouse (1 Cor 7:2-5; Harper, 92). Paul encourages Christians to marry so they might practice holy sex when sexual desires cannot be controlled (1 Cor 7:8-9, 36).

Along this line, he sees holy sex in marriage as a gift from God juxtaposed with the gift of self-control (1 Cor 7:7; cf. 1 Tim 4:3-4). Exercising the gift of sexual self-control in celibacy is a gift with a particular goal in mind, and in Paul's sexual ethics, that goal is the full dedication of oneself in *service to the *Lord (Paul's own reason for relinquishment of rights: 1 Cor 4:16; 7:7; 9:1-27; Ellis, 150; Cohick, 159). Thus, the gift of sexual self-control is a corollary to holy sex within a Pauline theology of sexuality. Such celibacy overcomes sin and allows the Christian to limitlessly contribute their entire self to serving the Lord in the goodness of the renewed creation, especially since the present age's social structures are coming to their eschatological end (1 Cor 7:17-36; Loader 2005, 162). Paul's third framework, holy sex within marriage, becomes a practice channeling sexual desires in a sinless way and participating in the redeemed goodness of the created order. Holy sex still naturally includes all the practical anxieties of a married life, which form limitations for service to the Lord according to the expectations, rights, and responsibilities of family creation (1 Cor 7:33-34; 1 Tim 2:15; 5:14; Titus 2:4-5). Therefore, Paul points to the other sexual gift, celibacy, which frees the Christian of marital anxieties to accomplish even more good service for the Lord (1 Cor 7:36-38; Ho, 182).

3.4.3. Holy Sex as Embodied Metaphor of the Gospel. The final aspect of a Pauline framework of sex is that the male-female sexual union of the Christian husband and wife reflects the union of Christ Jesus and the church (Eph 5:29-32; Whang, 99), which leans heavily on the creational and anthropological framework (Gen 2:24; Loader 2004, 108-10). Paul's depiction of a betrothed wife made holy and prepared through her husband's self-giving, ready to present herself for sexual union on the wedding night, echoes the second framework of a purified holy temple life of the community of faith. Christ has given himself, and further has given spiritual gifts, so the church might present herself holy and faithful at his coming (Eph 5:25-28; Cohick; cf. Eph 4:1-16; 2 Cor 11:2-3; Mt 25:1-13; Rev 21:9-27; 22:12-20). Here Paul emphasizes the sheer theological magnitude of sex. The mutual self-giving of holy sex, emanating outward to create and infuse the institution of marriage with submission and self-sacrificial provision, is an embodied expression of the gospel itself (Eph 5:22-33; Watson, 236; Westfall, 95). This theological oneness of sex rejects divorce as a theological option except for the anticreational inversion of holy sex through sexual immorality (1 Cor 7:10-11; see Mt 5:32; 19:9).

Paul's theology of sexual union also guides Christian marital practice toward monogamy. The total self-giving required of the husband and wife in Paul's sexual ethic leaves nothing to legitimately offer another spouse because Christ gives his whole self to the church alone, and the church fully submits to him alone in responsive *love (O'Reilly, 210; Boles, 319-20). This is another Christian theological development for Paul about marriage because, while Second Temple Jewish sexual theology confessed the presence of God's oneness in sexual union, it still allowed polygyny (Loader 2012, 80). This Pauline christological reframing of monotheism, especially the recognition of Christ's relationship with the church, has historically given theological weight to male-female monogamy being the proper public expression of holy sexuality for Christian communal life (see Mal 2:14-15; Mt 19:4-6; Eph 5:28-33), which agrees with Paul's exemplar expectation of monogamy by church leaders (1 Tim 3:2, 12; 5:9; Titus 1:6). This final framework reveals that through holy sex married Christians submissively align their bodies in accordance with God's redeemed and procreative anthropological order, participate within the holy temple life of the church, and become empowered by the Spirit's presence to embody the gospel as a triumph of holiness over sin. For Paul, good and holy sexuality is the gospel embodied and salvation enacted.

See also ANTHROPOLOGY, PAULINE; CORINTHIANS, FIRST LETTER TO THE; CREATION AND NEW CREATION; DISCIPLINE, CHURCH; FLESH; HOLINESS, SANCTIFICATION; HOMOSEXUALITY; HOUSEHOLDS AND HOUSEHOLD CODES; IMAGE OF GOD; MAN AND WOMAN; MARRIAGE AND DIVORCE, ADULTERY AND INCEST; PURITY AND IMPURITY; SINGLENESS AND CELIBACY.

BIBLIOGRAPHY. **C. K. Barrett,** *The First Epistle to the Corinthians*, BNTC (Peabody, MA: Hendrickson, 1993); **E. Ben-Eliyahu,** *Identity and Territory: Jewish Perceptions of Space in Antiquity* (Oakland: University of California Press, 2019); **K. L. Boles,** *Galatians and Ephesians*, College Press NIV Commentary (Joplin, MO: College Press, 1993); **P. Brown,** *The Body and Society: Men, Women, and Sexual Renunciation in Early Christianity*, 20th anniversary ed., Columbia Classics in Religion (New York: Columbia University Press, 2008); **L. H. Cohick,** *The Letter to the Ephesians*, NICNT (Grand Rapids, MI: Eerdmans, 2020); **L. H. Cohick and A. B. Hughes,** *Christian Women in the Patristic World: Their Influence, Authority, and Legacy in the Second Through Fifth Centuries* (Grand Rapids, MI: Baker Academic, 2017); **R. F. Collins and D. J. Harrington,** *First Corinthians*, SP 7 (Collegeville, MN: Liturgical Press, 1999); **C. E. B. Cranfield,** *A Critical and Exegetical Commentary on the Epistle to the Romans*, ICC (London: T&T Clark, 2004); **J. D. G. Dunn,** *The Theology of Paul the Apostle* (Grand Rapids, MI: Eerdmans, 2008); **J. E. Ellis,** *Paul and Ancient Views of Sexual Desire: Paul's Sexual Ethics in 1 Thessalonians 4, 1 Corinthians 7 and Romans 1*, LNTS 354 (London: T&T Clark, 2007); **J. R. Farris,** *An Introduction to Theological Anthropology: Humans, Both Creaturely and Divine* (Grand Rapids, MI: Baker Academic, 2020); **G. D. Fee,** *The First Epistle to the Corinthians*, NICNT (Grand Rapids, MI: Eerdmans, 2014); **V. P. Furnish,** *The Theology of the First Letter to the Corinthians*, NTT (Cambridge: Cambridge University Press, 1999); **E. S. Gruen,** *Constructs of Identity in Hellenistic Judaism: Essays on Early Jewish Literature and History*, Deuterocanonical and Cognate Literature Studies 29 (Boston: de Gruyter, 2016); **K. Harper,** *From Shame to Sin: The Christian Transformation of Sexual Morality in Late Antiquity*, Revealing Antiquity 20 (Cambridge, MA: Harvard University Press, 2013); **R. B. Hays,** *First Corinthians*, IBC (Louisville, KY: Westminster John Knox, 2011); idem, "Galatians," *NIB* 9:1019-1173; **S. D. Ho,** *Paul and the Creation of a Counter-Cultural Community: A Rhetorical Analysis of 1 Cor. 5–11.1 in Light of the Social Lives of the Corinthians*, LNTS 509 (New York: T&T Clark, 2014); **T. C. Hoklotubbe,** *Civilized Piety: The Rhetoric of Pietas in the Pastoral Epistles and the Roman Empire* (Waco, TX: Baylor University Press, 2017); **R. A. Horsley,** *1 Corinthians*, ANTC (Nashville: Abingdon, 1998); **M. J. Lakey,** *Image and Glory of God: 1 Corinthians 11:2-16 as a Case Study in Bible, Gender and Hermeneutics*, LNTS 418 (London: T&T Clark, 2010); **J. Larson,** *Greek and Roman Sexualities: A Sourcebook* (London: Bloomsbury, 2012); **J. R. Levinson,** "Josephus's Version of Ruth," *JSP* 8 (1991): 31-44; **W. R. G. Loader,** *The Septuagint, Sexuality, and the New Testament: Case Studies on the Impact of the LXX in Philo and the New Testament* (Grand Rapids, MI: Eerdmans, 2004); idem, *Sexuality and the Jesus Tradition* (Grand Rapids, MI: Eerdmans, 2005); idem, *The New Testament on Sexuality: Attitudes Towards Sexuality in Judaism and Christianity in the Hellenistic Greco-Roman Era* (Grand Rapids, MI: Eerdmans, 2012); idem, *Making Sense of Sex: Attitudes Towards Sexuality in Early Jewish and Christian Literature* (Grand Rapids, MI: Eerdmans, 2013); **D. B. Martin,** *The Corinthian Body* (New Haven, CT: Yale University Press, 1999); **M. O'Reilly,** "What Makes Sex Beautiful? Marriage, Aesthetics, and the Image of God in Genesis 1–2 and Revelation 21–22," in *Beauty, Order, and Mystery: A Christian Vision of Human Sexuality*, ed. G. Hiestand and T. Wilson (Downers Grove, IL: IVP Academic, 2017), 197-212; **A. Peeler,** "Imaging Glory: 1 Corinthians 11, Gender, and Bodies at Worship," in *Beauty, Order, and Mystery: A Christian Vision of Human Sexuality*, ed. G. Hiestand and T. Wilson (Downers Grove, IL: IVP Academic, 2017), 151-63; **E. P. Sanders,** *Paul: The Apostle's Life, Letters, and Thought* (Minneapolis: Fortress, 2015); **M. L. Satlow,** *Jewish Marriage in Antiquity* (Princeton, NJ: Princeton University Press, 2001);

K. Southwood, "An Ethnic Affair? Ezra's Intermarriage Crisis Against a Context of 'Self-Ascription' and 'Ascription of Others,'" in *Mixed Marriages: Intermarriages and Group Identity in the Second Temple Period*, ed. C. Frevel (London: T&T Clark, 2011), 46-59; **R. H. von Thaden,** *Sex, Christ, and Embodied Cognition: Paul's Wisdom for Corinth* (Atlanta: SBL Press, 2017); **A. C. Thiselton,** *The First Epistle to the Corinthians: A Commentary on the Greek Text*, NIGTC (Grand Rapids, MI: Eerdmans, 2000); **P. H. Towner,** *The Letters to Timothy and Titus*, NICNT (Grand Rapids, MI: Eerdmans, 2006); **G. N. Uzukwu,** *The Unity of Male and Female in Jesus Christ: An Exegetical Study of Galatians 3.28c in Light of Paul's Theology of Promise* (London: Bloomsbury, 2015); **F. Watson,** *Agape, Eros, Gender: Towards a Pauline Sexual Ethic* (Cambridge: Cambridge University Press, 2004); **C. L. Westfall,** *Paul and Gender: Reclaiming the Apostle's Vision for Men and Women in Christ* (Grand Rapids, MI: Baker Academic, 2016); **Y. C. Whang,** "Cohabitation or Conflict: Greek Household Management and Christian Hausafeln," in *Religion and Sexuality*, ed. M. A. Hayes, W. Porter, and D. Tombs (London: Bloomsbury Academic, 2019), 85-100; **N. T. Wright,** "Romans," *NIB* 9:317-664.

J. K. Gill

SHARING. *See* FELLOWSHIP, COMMUNION, SHARING; LORD'S SUPPER.

SIGNS, WONDERS, MIRACLES

According to Acts, in the early *church Paul had a reputation as an exorcist and healer, as well as being involved in miracles. Although at first glance he appears to say little about miracles, on closer examination Paul's testimony is that miracles occurred whenever he brought the good news and that they remained essential to the life of the church.

1. Signs and Wonders
2. Paul's Understanding of Miracles
3. Paul's Experience of Miracles
4. Miracles in Paul's Ministry
5. Paul as Miracle Worker
6. Signs of an Apostle
7. Miracles of Paul in Acts

1. Signs and Wonders.

For Greek writers a "sign" (*sēmeion*) could be, among other things, a ship's ensign (Euripides, *Iph. aul.* 253), a symptom of sickness (Philo, *Det.* 43), or something in which a god was understood to communicate to a person (Plutarch, *Alex.* 25.1). In the LXX *sēmeion* is almost always used of *God showing himself to be the Almighty and *Israel to be his chosen people through the events associated with Moses leading the Israelites out of Egypt (e.g., Deut 26:8; Jer 32:20-21; cf. Philo, *Mos.* 1.210; Josephus, *Ant.* 2.12.3–2.13.1).

A "wonder" (*teras*) was that which caused fear and trembling in people and indicated the proximity of, and human dependence on, the divine (Homer, *Il.* 4.408; Josephus, *J.W.* 4.5.5). For Philo and Josephus wonders, especially those performed by Moses, assisted those who witnessed them in knowing God's sovereignty (e.g., Philo, *Mos.* 1.90, 95; Josephus, *Ant.* 2.13.3). An explanation of a wonder was required to provide correct insight (Philo, *Agr.* 96; Josephus, *J.W.* 6.5.3-4), for charlatans could also perform wonders and mislead people (Josephus, *Ant.* 20.8.6). In the LXX *teras* almost always translates *môpēt*, which meant something extraordinary from God demanding attention (e.g., Ex 7:9; 1 Kings 13:1-5; Ezek 12:1-16) and sometimes revealed God's will (e.g., Ex 7:4). *Teras* became rare in Greek and Jewish literature in the NT period, and the word does not occur in the NT without *sēmeion*. In the NT *dynamis* ("power") seems to replace *teras*, perhaps in order not to compromise the important element of autonomy in the miraculous activity of Jesus and the early Christians (cf., e.g., Lk 24:19).

The phrase "signs and wonders" (*sēmeia kai terata*) is first known in Polybius (*Historiae* 3.112.18) and refers to the superstitious rites of the Romans (cf. Plutarch, *Alex.* 75:1). Plutarch uses the words synonymously (Plutarch, *Mor.* 2.149C; cf. Josephus, *Ant.* 10.2.1). In the LXX the phrase is generally confined to the wonders associated with Moses (e.g., Ex 4:21; 10:1; 11:10; Num 14:11; Ps 104:26-27). Philo only takes up the phrase as a traditional description of miracles in Egypt (e.g., *Spec.* 2.218). Josephus uses the phrase once of God warning and directing his people and once of imposters deceiving people ("wonders and signs," *Ant.* 20.8.6). He more often used "signs" for these latter events (e.g., *Ant.* 2.12.3), probably to dissociate the work of Moses from the suspicion of *magic (cf. *Ant.* 2.13.3).

As Paul and many of his readers would have been most familiar with the phrase "signs and wonders" (Rom 15:19; 2 Cor 12:12 NRSV) from their Scriptures, it is likely a soteriological use of the term that exercised the strongest control over its meaning for him. In one place, adding "and mighty works" (*kai dynamesin*, 2 Cor 12:12 NRSV), Paul deliberately recalls the salvific miracles of Moses. After Paul, in the NT the phrase in various forms is used mainly by Luke

(Mt 24:24; Mk 13:22; Jn 4:48; Acts 2:19, 22, 43; 4:30; 5:12; 6:8; 7:36; 14:3; 15:12; 2 Thess 2:9; Heb 2:4).

2. Paul's Understanding of Miracles.
For the biblical writers a miracle involved no infringement of any laws but was simply a striking or surprising phenomenon that was humanly impossible and thought to be brought about by, and reveal, a god. What could be called *paradoxoi* ("strange," "wonderful," or "remarkable" things, as in Lk 5:26) included a range of the inexplicable: genetic anomalies, strange natural phenomena, and reports of events bringing human health and safety (LXX: Jdt 13:13; 2 Macc 9:24; 4 Macc 2:14; Wis 16:17; 19:5).

For some phenomena that Paul took to be brought about by God and to reveal him (1 Cor 12:5-6, 18, 24, 28) he coined the term *charismata* (Rom 11:29; 12:6; 1 Cor 12:9, 28, 30-31). Particularly from one of his lists of *charismata* (1 Cor 12:8-10) one gains insight into his view of miracles. The close association of extraordinary *faith (1 Cor 13:2), healings, and powers or miracles, with revelatory gifts, shows that Paul saw them as of the same order (1 Cor 12:9-10): healings and miracles, the accomplishment of the impossible, and the experience and assessment of revelation were of a piece for Paul. While one could take this to be critical for Paul's understanding of miracles, his inclusion of helps and administration among the *charismata* (1 Cor 12:28-29) means that his notion of miracle or the miraculous was not governed by their impossibility but their activation by and expression of God's *grace, and by their benefit for the community (1 Cor 12:7). As the differences between his lists of *charismata* also suggest (Rom 12:4-8; 1 Cor 12:8-10, 28-30), miracles could include more than the items he has listed, perhaps also miracles such as exorcism or provision and protection. Therefore, for Paul, not only healings and works of power but any tangible or solidified expression of God's grace (*charis*; Rom 12:6; 1 Cor 12:4, 28, 30-31) would have been judged miraculous.

3. Paul's Experience of Miracles.
Given his understanding of miracles, in a number of places Paul's own experience of them is clear. He has revelatory experiences. In one of the possible accounts of his conversion from Pharisaism (Phil 3:5) to following Jesus, Paul describes a revelatory experience from God that changed his life: "God, who had set me apart before I was born and called me through his grace, was pleased to reveal his *Son to me, so that I might proclaim him among the *Gentiles" (Gal 1:15-16 NRSV; cf. 1 Cor 9:1; 15:8; Phil 3:4-11). Against the backdrop of doubts in *Corinth about his *leadership he asks, "Am I not an *apostle? Have I not seen Jesus our *Lord?" (1 Cor 9:1 NRSV). Again, defending himself, he writes about his "*visions and revelations of the Lord" and being "caught up to the third heaven" (2 Cor 12:1-4 NRSV).

The *charismata* were a regular part of Paul's experience. It is not that he had all the *gifts, as Augustine supposed (*Gest. Pelag.* 32), for that would make nonsense of Paul saying the gifts were distributed variously (1 Cor 12:8-10). Paul claimed to speak in *tongues a great deal (1 Cor 14:18, cf. 1 Cor 14:6, 14). Although he does not claim to be a *prophet, he describes his *conversion as the *call of a prophet (Gal 1:15-16; cf. Is 49:1) and tells the Thessalonians that he has a word from the Lord for them (1 Thess 4:15). Paul implies he has the gifts of *teaching (1 Cor 14:6) and of *wisdom (1 Cor 2:7). Notably, Paul gives no hint of having the gifts of healing, miracles, or exorcism (see section 5 below).

Paul describes a miraculous rescue. He says, "in Asia . . . we were so utterly, unbearably crushed that we despaired of life itself" (2 Cor 1:8 NRSV). He goes on: "We felt that we had received the sentence of death so that we would rely not on ourselves but on God who raises the dead" (2 Cor 1:9 NRSV). Writing as if a miracle is involved, he says that God "rescued" him from a deadly peril (2 Cor 1:10).

Epaphroditus, a companion in *ministry, was healed, having come near to death (Phil 2:27), risking his life (Phil 2:30) in ministry (Phil 2:29). Paul says, "God had *mercy on him" (Phil 2:27 NRSV). For early Christians, God's mercy often referred to God's healing that came as the result of *prayer (Mt 9:27; 15:22; 17:15; 20:30-31; Mk 5:19; 10:47-48; Lk 16:24; 17:13; 18:38-39).

Another side to Paul's experience of the miraculous is his saying to the Galatians, "It was because of a physical sickness [*astheneia*] that I first brought the *gospel to you" (Gal 4:13). It is not clear what was wrong with Paul; it could be the "thorn in the *flesh" (2 Cor 12:7), which is reasonably supposed to be recurrent malaria. Although he did not receive the healing he prayed for in the best and most sincere way he knew (2 Cor 12:8), the Lord's answer ("My grace is enough for you, for my power is made perfect in weakness [*astheneia*]") gave Paul reason to boast in the ongoing experience of Christ's power evident through his weakness (2 Cor 12:9).

4. Miracles in Paul's Ministry.
There are a number of places in Paul's letters where he is clear about the place of the miraculous in his

ministry (Rom 15:18-19; 1 Cor 2:1-5; 4:20; 2 Cor 12:11-13; Gal 3:1-5; 1 Thess 1:5). From his letter to the Thessalonians it is obvious Paul saw that the gospel involved not only his message but also an unhindered miraculous realization of the Spirit (1 Thess 1:5). In Romans he says he was winning the Gentiles "by word and deed, in the power of signs and wonders, in the power of the Spirit of God" (Rom 15:18-19). The miraculous is not something that simply supported or proved the *truth of his message, though it did that. For Paul, the gospel was salvation heard in the words and experienced in the signs and wonders (Rom 15:18-19). Just as the gospel could not be proclaimed without words, so it could not come or be experienced without miracles.

The way Paul writes to the Galatians indicates he assumes the miraculous is an ongoing part of their experience. Turning his question into a statement, he says, "God goes on supplying you with the Spirit and working miracles in you" (Gal 3:5). Paul's discussion of the *charismata* (see section 2 above) only makes sense if the miraculous was an ongoing, important part of the life of the church, possible because of the gracious activity of the Spirit of God in all of the believers (1 Cor 12:7).

The place of miracles in his ministry has probably determined how he understands himself. Paul often describes himself as a preacher (Rom 2:21; 10:8; 1 Cor 1:23; 9:27; 15:11-12; 2 Cor 1:9; 4:5; Gal 5:11; cf. Rom 10:14-15), though only three times he says he preaches the gospel (Gal 2:2; 1 Thess 2:2, 9; cf. 2 Cor 11:4; Phil 1:15-18). Most often, when he refers to his role in promoting the gospel, he simply says he "gospels" (*euangelizō*, Rom 15:20; 1 Cor 1:17; 9:16 [2×], 18; 15:1; cf. Rom 1:15; 10:15; 2 Cor 11:7). Paul understood that he was involved in more than bringing a message; he was involved in both a message and the miraculous.

5. Paul as Miracle Worker.
It is striking that Paul never claims to perform healings, exorcisms, or miracles. Even when his opponents suggest he was rather inferior at miracle working, he does not claim to perform miracles. He simply says that miracles "were performed among you" (2 Cor 12:12 NRSV), using the passive, "were performed" (*kateirgasthē*), as if the miracles simply happened, implying they were from God. Failing to claim that it was he who was performing the miracles is no accidental slip of the mind or pen.

Paul is happy to use the active in talking about his preaching. A number of times he says, "We proclaim *Christ," or something similar (1 Cor 1:23; 2 Cor 4:5; Gal 1:16; 2:2), but he attributes miracles to God. In Romans it is Christ or God who accomplished the miracles (Rom 15:18-19; cf. Gal 3:3-4). In 2 Corinthians the signs were performed "with utmost patience" (2 Cor 12:12 NRSV), calling to mind a characteristic of God (Rom 15:4-5; cf. Col 1:11). Paul writes about his preaching but never about his miracle working. It is reasonable to conclude that miracles took place in the context of his communicating the gospel through preaching in much the same way as Luke describes the miraculous coming of the Spirit on the household of Cornelius when Peter was speaking (Acts 10:43-46).

One can imagine that over the time when the gospel came to Paul's readers they were hearing his message about Jesus and experiencing God's grace in such things as healings, wisdom, *forgiveness, knowledge, compassion, faith, generosity, prophecy, speaking in tongues, helps, leadership, and administration (cf. Rom 12:3-8; 1 Cor 12–14). No doubt, as the book of Acts claims, from time to time Paul was directly involved in healings and exorcism.

6. Signs of an Apostle.
Defending his apostleship Paul says, "the signs [*sēmeia*] of an apostle were performed among you . . . signs and wonders and mighty works [*sēmeiois te kai terasin kai dynamesin*]" (2 Cor 12:12; cf. 2 Cor 13:3; 1 Cor 1:22). The first occurrence of *sēmeia* here probably means "indication" or "confirmation" and encompasses the second use, one of three words (all in the dative) referring to miracles. The phrase "signs of an apostle" may have come from the Corinthians or perhaps from his *opponents.

Paul does not rely entirely on the miracles as evidence of his apostleship and the truth of his message (cf. Rom 15:19; 1 Cor 2:4; 1 Thess 5:9; see section 4 above). Earlier in 2 Corinthians Paul has already based the authenticity of his apostleship on his holy life of dependence on God (2 Cor 5:18-21; cf. 2 Cor 3:1-3), as well as on his own spiritual experience (2 Cor 1:12; 2:17; 4:2; 7:2), his *suffering and weakness through which the power of God is seen (2 Cor 4:7-15; 6:4-10; 11:21-33), and the reconciliation that has taken place between the Corinthians and God (2 Cor 12:1-6). Thus, not only miracles but also his life of patient suffering in proclaiming the gospel, and the experience of the Corinthians, are the proof of his apostleship and the truth of his message, for in all of these the power of God can be seen (2 Cor 12:9).

7. Miracles of Paul in Acts.
A prominent feature of the portrayal of Paul in Acts is the miracle stories associated with him. Luke says the proconsul believed when he saw Elymas the magician temporarily blinded by Paul for opposing him (Acts 13:4-12). As a result of healing a cripple, Paul and Barnabas are hailed as gods in human form and then take the opportunity to speak about the good news (Acts 14:8-18). It is reported that God did signs and wonders through Barnabas and Paul (Acts 15:12). The exorcism of a spirit of divination from a slave girl brought the eventual conversion of the prison warden and his family (Acts 16:16-18). The Ephesians receive the Spirit when Paul lays his hands on them (Acts 19:6). A summary of Paul's ministry mentions his handkerchiefs being taken to the sick so they are healed or freed from evil spirits (Acts 19:11-12). Paul is then associated with exorcism in the story of the sons of Sceva attempting to use his name in an incantation (Acts 19:13). This contributes to the word of the Lord growing and prevailing mightily (Acts 19:20). In the raising of Eutychus from the dead (Acts 20:7-12) Paul is portrayed as a man of God like Elijah (1 Kings 17:17-24) and Elisha (2 Kings 4:32-37). As a result of Paul healing the father of Publius of fever and dysentery, the rest of the people of Malta are reported as bringing their diseased for curing (Acts 28:7-10).

Paul is portrayed as an object of miracles. He has a visionary experience in or near Damascus that involved seeing and hearing the Lord or Jesus identify himself (Acts 9:1-19; 22:6-16; 26:12-18); he is healed from blindness (Acts 9:8, 18; 22:11-13); he experiences a night vision in which he is called to Europe (Acts 16:6-11); he is released from *prison (Acts 16:25-34) and is unharmed by a deadly snake (Acts 28:3-6).

It is also by no means agreed how far the stories in Acts associated with Paul originated in firsthand reports. Nevertheless, Luke's portrait has clear echoes of Paul's own testimony that the miraculous was profoundly important and integral to his life, gospel, and ministry.

See also Apostle; Conversion and Call of Paul; Corinthians, First Letter to the; Demons and Exorcism; Gifts of the Spirit; Healing, Illness; Holy Spirit; Magic; Ministry; Paul in Acts; Suffering; Visions, Ecstatic Experience.

BIBLIOGRAPHY. **C. A. Evans,** "Paul the Exorcist and Healer," in *Paul and His Theology*, ed. S. E. Porter (Leiden: Brill, 2006), 363-79; **J. Eyl,** *Signs, Wonders, and Gifts: Divination in the Letters of Paul* (New York: Oxford University Press, 2019); **J. Jervell,** *The Unknown Paul* (Minneapolis: Augsburg, 1984), 77-95; **B. Kollmann,** "Paulus als Wundertäter," in *Paulinische Christologie: Exegetische Beiträge; Hans Hübner zum 70. Geburtstag*, ed. U. Schnelle, T. Söding, and M. Labahn (Göttingen: Vandenhoeck & Ruprecht, 2000), 76-96; **B. J. Lietaert Peerbolte,** "Paul the Miracle Worker: Development and Background of Pauline Miracle Stories," in *Wonders Never Cease: The Purpose of Narrating Miracle Stories in the New Testament and Its Religious Environment*, ed. M. Labahn and B. J. Lietaert Peerbolte, LNTS 288 (London: T&T Clark, 2006), 180-99; **F. Neirynck,** "The Miracle Stories in the Acts of the Apostles: An Introduction," in *Les Actes des Apôtres: Traditions, Rédaction, Théologie*, ed. J. Kremer (Gembloux: Duculot, 1979), 169-213; **K. H. Rengstorf,** "σημεῖον, κτλ.," *TDNT* 7:200-261; idem, "τέρας," *TDNT* 8:113-26; **S. Schreiber,** *Paulus als Wundertäter: Redaktionsgeschichtliche Untersuchungen zur Apostelgeschichte und den authentischen Paulusbriefen*, BZNW 79 (Berlin: de Gruyter, 1996); **G. H. Twelftree,** *Paul and the Miraculous: A Historical Reconstruction* (Grand Rapids, MI: Baker Academic, 2013); **M. Whitaker,** "'Signs and Wonders': The Pagan Background," *SE* 5 (1968): 155-58.

G. H. Twelftree

SIN, GUILT

Paul's concept of sin is complex, serving as a category to understand individual human behavior, social structures, and superhuman opposition to God's good purposes. This complexity can be daunting and, no doubt, demands care from the reader in parsing Pauline texts. At the same time, this complexity makes Paul's conception of sin a rich theological resource for the *church. Sin and evil in the contemporary world are complex, involving the distorted dispositions and actions of individuals, social patterns of brokenness, and spiritual oppression. Many contemporary challenges—including racism, addiction, suicide, violence, poverty, forced migration, and the whelming ecological crisis—cannot be understood adequately, much less addressed productively, without being able to recognize the overlapping and intermingling impacts of individual behavior and social realities. Much in contemporary politics—and in contemporary churches, whose imaginations are often held captive by one or another political framework—militates against recognizing this complexity, preferring one or another simpler but less honest account of the world as either entirely governed top-down by social structures or shaped only by the free interaction of individual moral agents. Paul's account of sin demands one recognize these as false alternatives and provides a theological framework nuanced enough to begin to understand and engage the complexity of the brokenness all around.

The extent to which Romans looms large when it comes to Paul's discussion of sin cannot be overstated. Of eighty-one instances of *hamartia* ("sin") and cognate words in the undisputed Pauline corpus, fully sixty are in Romans. The other twenty-one instances are not unimportant. Paul's twelve uses of the language of sin in 1 Corinthians warrant particular attention. But it is not going too far to say that a study of Paul's concept of sin is in large part a study of Paul's account of sin *in Romans*.

1. The Act of Sinning
2. Sin and the Social Body
3. Sin the Cosmic Tyrant
4. Defeat of Sin
5. Personal, Social, and Cosmic Sin

1. The Act of Sinning.

1.1. Sinful Behavior. Paul does not offer a straightforward definition of sin. The numerous "vice lists" found in the Pauline corpus enumerate behaviors that would seem to count as sin for Paul. James Dunn catalogs a number of such lists, including Romans 1:29-31; 13:13; 1 Corinthians 5:10-11; 6:9-10, 2 Corinthians 12:20; Galatians 5:19-21 (*Dunn*, 662-33). Such lists were typical in ancient ethical writing, in both Jewish and Greco-Roman authors. Inasmuch as these lists are quite different from one another, it is hard to lean too strongly on the lists themselves to give a systematic account of what sort of behavior counted as sin for Paul. That said, a few generalizations can be ventured. In general, sins are actions contrary to God's good purposes in the world. Central for Paul, among those purposes, is God's work in calling the church (hence the oft-repeated eponym, "the church of *God," in 1 Cor 1:2; 10:32; 11:16, 22; 15:9; 2 Cor 1:1; Gal 1:13; 1 Thess 2:14). For this reason, as Dunn notes, Paul's vice lists give priority to relational sin that opposes God's work in calling the church (Dunn, 124). But other of God's purposes are surely also in view. God's broadest intentions in *creation are invoked prior to the vice list in Romans 1:29-31. The drama of God's work in Paul's particular moment in history is named in Romans 13:11, prior to the vice list in Romans 13:13.

Of course, conflicts about what behavior is appropriate for Christians abound within the Pauline corpus, a number of which are cast in terms of adjudicating and managing the impacts of sin within the church. Paul's heightened concern for the impact of sin on community clearly governs his language. In 1 Corinthians 6:18, Paul's concern for the community pushes him to *sharpen* the way he deploys the category: sin against one's own *body affects the communal body. Just verses later, in 1 Corinthians 7, Paul's concern for the community pushes him in the opposite direction, *deescalating* the conflict in the Corinthian community, marking out the choice between *marriage or *singleness as one that is not a matter of sin (1 Cor 7:28, 36).

Indeed, it is a notable feature of Paul's discussions of potentially sinful behavior that he has an important category for matters of conscience, that is, disputable behavior about which members of Pauline churches are voicing strong opinions, but about which Paul sees no need to establish a community standard. The example of marriage and singleness is one such case. The classic issue, though, is *food sacrificed to idols. In both 1 Corinthians 8 and Romans 14, in discussing this exceedingly practical issue in the lives of his churches, Paul does not invoke "sin" to describe either side of the issue. Rather, *sin* is appropriate language, Paul suggests, for describing how church members navigate the disputable matter. Christians sin when they violate their own conscience, whether or not their behavior is, as it were, objectively sinful (Rom 14:23). More significantly, they sin when they harm other members of the community with whom they disagree (1 Cor 8:12). The possibility of harm (which would be sin) leads Paul to restrict his own *freedom to do what is not otherwise sin (1 Cor 8:13). Such is the centrality of ecclesial unity—and, therefore, relational mutuality and edification—in Paul's understanding of sin.

1.2. Guilt and the Consequences of Sinning. Guilt is a difficult concept to trace in Paul. The common affective sense of the word in contemporary English—guilt as the unpleasant *experience* of knowing oneself as having done wrong—is more or less absent from Paul's letters in their historical context. If there is an *experience* of sin in Paul, it is that of moral impotence (Rom 7) rather than psychological guilt. But, reading theologically across the chasm of history, one might propose that Paul would expect that guilt in this psychological sense would not be a dominant experience of the Christian, for whom there is now no condemnation (Rom 8:1).

Many Christian theologians since the Reformation have proposed that Paul's letters ought to lead readers to think quite a bit about guilt in the juridical sense (especially if *righteousness is to be understood this way). On this point, it seems that indeed all human beings, apart from redemption in Christ, are guilty. Dunn suggests on the basis of Romans 5:13 that, for Paul, guilt does not follow from sin alone but rather strictly only attaches to transgression of divine *law, but the more general pastoral thought still holds: no one is innocent. This ought to be understood as freeing rather than condemning (again, Rom 8:1). Believers may be justified by Christ, but, as sinners all, none have an innocence to defend or to mourn the loss of when their sin is brought to their attention.

When Paul insists that all human beings sin and all human beings bear guilt as a result of sin, he does so not in the mode of a systematic theologian but rather as a pastoral theologian. So, in Romans 1–3, the classic passage supporting this principle, Paul's interest is less in establishing the universality of sin in the abstract than in helping his divided audience come to recognize their own sin and their equal guilt before God. While scholars differ on how to conceive of Paul's audience, the best approach is probably to use Paul's own language in Romans 14:1-2; 15:1 of "*strong" ("progressive" Gentile believers and their Jewish sympathizers) and "weak" ("conservative" Jewish believers and their *Gentile sympathizers) (McKnight). Knowing his letter will be read aloud in front of a church deeply divided along these lines, Paul deftly leads the group to a profound understanding of their sin and their equal guilt before God.

In Romans 1, Paul indicts the sin of Gentiles with whom the strong identify, using rhetoric that would be familiar to the weak (from places such as Wis 13–14). Paul is not indicting Gentiles generically or universally; he is deploying a certain Jewish (weak) stereotype of Gentiles (strong) in order to stir up in the weak what they would consider righteous indignation. Then, in Romans 2, Paul pulls the rhetoric rug out from under the weak. They are judging, Paul says, while being guilty of these same sins (Rom 2:3). Their approval of Paul's judgment in Romans 1 all of the sudden is a sign of a yet more profound sin: hypocritical judgment. God's righteous, impartial *judgment falls on both groups (Rom 2:9-11). Paul's rhetoric continues to catch those confident of their own righteousness. It is a perennial pitfall to use Romans 1 as a tool to shame particular sinners without feeling accountable to Paul's subsequent indictment of hypocritical judgment. Paul's conclusions about "all" humankind (Rom 3:9-18) follow from this very particular unveiling of sinful practices and the sinful hypocritical judgment of those practices within the community he is addressing. All have sinned; even more, all are "under the power of sin" (Rom 3:9 NRSV), about which more below.

The most important consequence of sinning is *death (Rom 5:12). Typical of important lines of Latin American liberationist thinking, Oscar Romero suggested that death is the telltale sign of sin in the world, its characteristic fruit (Romero, 183). Attentiveness to this relationship between sin and death may help one recognize sin to which one might otherwise be blind—which is important, as Paul predicts that one will quite often be blinded *to* sinful conduct and systems *by* sin-the-cosmic-tyrant.

2. Sin and the Social Body.

It is common to think of Paul's usage of sin as more or less falling into two categories: sin-as-behavior and sin-as-a-power. Each of these usages is prevalent (the former is considered above; the latter will be taken up below). But this dichotomy misses a third significant usage that bridges between these two: the operation of sin within the social body.

Modern Protestant reflection on sin and social structures goes back at least as far as Friedrich Schleiermacher and is a strong feature of liberal Protestant conceptions of sin, while evangelicals have tended to be much more skeptical. Whether one can rightly talk about *social sin* was particularly hotly contested in Catholic theology in the 1980s. Before becoming Pope Benedict, Joseph Ratzinger engaged in an extended debate with Latin American theologians about the latter's routine discussion of social sin. In any ecclesial context, the challenges are largely theological rather than exegetical. If social systems can "sin," whom exactly are we to hold accountable? How are social systems to repent and be forgiven? These questions require careful theological reflection but ought not blind one to the exegetical evidence for Paul's concern for sin's operation in social systems.

In line with many of his contemporaries in the philosophical world (notably the Stoics), Paul conceives of human beings not merely as individuals but as members of larger social bodies. This understanding of social solidarity clearly provides background for Paul's account of the *body of Christ in 1 Corinthians 12–14 and Romans 12. But this understanding is also in view for Paul when he thinks about the way that sin operates in communities.

Some of the most striking language in this respect is in Romans 6. In Romans 6:12, Paul advises the Romans "do not let sin reign in your [pl.] mortal body [sg.]" (NIV). The NRSV reads the singular *body* as distributive across the plural *your*, rendering "your mortal bodies," but one need not do so. When Paul does want to talk about multiple mortal bodies, he is happy to use the plural, as in Romans 8:11, "he who raised Christ from the dead will give life to your [pl.] mortal bodies [pl.]" (NRSV). Paul is speaking instead of a single social body in which sin reigns and brings about its characteristic fruit (death, here, in the form of mortality). In Romans 6:13, Paul invokes language familiar from his discussion of the body of Christ, encouraging the Romans not to present the members of this collective body to sin but rather to God. In Romans 6:6, Paul uses exactly the language one might expect to describe this collective social body: "the body of sin" (NRSV). This collective body is destroyed in one's co-crucifixion with Christ, presumably in *baptism (see section 4 below).

Paul describes the consequences of sin's dominion (described in greater detail below) in collective terms. In the account of the typical sins of the "strong" in Romans 1, Paul lists a cascade of consequences, ending with, "God gave them up to a debased mind and to things that should not be done" (Rom 1:28 NRSV). The collective (singular) mind of this group is debased as a consequence of their sin. If one is right to think about the "body of sin" (Rom 6:6) as in some sense a parody of Paul's notion of the body of Christ, then it may be reasonable to think of this debased mind as a parody of the "mind of Christ" suffused throughout the body of Christ (1 Cor 2:16; Phil 2:5).

3. Sin the Cosmic Tyrant.

Sin is not merely a *topic* in Romans. Rather, as Beverly Gaventa notes, "sin has a leading role in the letter to the Romans" (Gaventa, 2004, 230). Especially in Romans 5–8, sin is routinely the subject of active verbs, advancing a cosmic drama: in Romans 5:12, sin "came into the world"; in Romans 5:20, "sin increased," in Romans 7:8, "sin, seizing an opportunity . . . produced"; in Romans 7:9, "sin revived"; in Romans 7:13, sin works death; in Romans 7:17 sin "dwells" (all translations NRSV). In Romans 7:20, dwelling within, sin acts in place of the individual. In short, sin operates as a cosmic tyrant, holding individuals, human communities, and the entire creation under its sway.

3.1. Dominion of Sin. Most importantly, sin *exercises dominion* (Rom 5:21; 6:12, 14). In Romans 5:21, Paul specifies that sin rules "in death," in contradistinction to *grace, which rules "unto eternal life." In this mode (dominant in Romans) in which Paul talks about sin as a cosmic power, sin reigns together with death, which is similarly figured. The two are so closely associated for Paul that, in Romans 5:17, Paul can make death the subject of the same verb, recounting that "death exercised dominion" (NRSV). When Paul speaks of Christ's victory over sin, he speaks in terms of believers' being liberated from sin (Rom 6:14); here, too, he can just as easily express this idea in terms of the end of death's dominion (Rom 6:9).

Paul typically describes sin's dominion in terms of a master-*slave relationship (Rom 6:6, 16-20, 22; 7:25; 8:21). Sin acts as a slave master over the individual (Rom 6:17, 7:25), constraining the moral psychology of the individual, bringing about an ironic "obedience" to sin. In the extreme, sin's dominion is so acute that Paul is willing to say the sin acts in place of the individual, insisting twice that "it is no longer I that do it, but sin that dwells within me" (Rom 7:17, 20 NRSV).

At the social level, sin reigns through the collective debased mind (Rom 1:28), acting as slave master over communal bodies (Rom 6:6, 16-20), conditioning their modes of collective life. Stepping back further, sin holds the entire creation in bondage to decay (Rom 8:21). This paradigm of dominion through subjection to slavery is so prominent in Paul's writings that one probably ought to understand Paul as invoking this paradigm even in the simple phrase "under sin" (Rom 3:9; 7:14; Gal 3:22).

On Paul's account, sin accomplishes this feat of overcoming the will of the individual through stoking "sinful passions" that "bear fruit for death" (Rom 7:5 NRSV). Sin accomplishes this through the usurpation of the law (Rom 7:7-13). Given the pivotal role played by sinful *passions*, it is no coincidence, nor is it simply by way of example, that Paul takes up the commandment against coveting (Rom 7:7-8). Much ancient *philosophy prevalent in Paul's day was dubious about desire entirely. Against this background, and especially given that rough Pauline contemporaries Philo and the author of 4 Maccabees understand this commandment as a prohibition of desire entirely, readers ought to see Paul as understanding the command this way as well (Stowers, 60). But sin, seizing on the commandment not to desire, produces all sorts of desires (Rom 7:8). Paul then follows a line of reasoning that would be familiar to his audience from Stoic and other popularized philosophical sources: overrun by desire, the individual loses mastery of the self, and thus sin, through its passions, acts in place of the self (Rom 7:17, 20).

When Paul writes about law in this context, it is plain that he means Torah (and, even more specifically in Rom 7, the specific prohibition against desiring). However, as one thinks about sin's dominion, one does well to consider the way that sin uses other sorts of law (judicial law, the rules of the market, other cultural norms), intended to do good, in order to bring about death (Támez 1993, 142). In this way, one can understand sin's usurpation of law as an instance of sin's dominion at the social level, mediating its cosmic dominion to the individual level.

3.2. Origin and Transmission of Sin's Dominion. If Paul depicts sin as a cosmic power, it is reasonable to want to know: Where did this power come from? As Rudolf Bultmann says, "sin came into the world by sinning" (Bultmann, 251). The origin of sin's cosmic dominion is in the particularity of human sinning—specifically, *Adam's* sin: "sin came into the world through one man, and death came through sin" (Rom 5:12 NRSV; cf. Rom 5:17). This is important because it means, however realistically one wants to take Paul's language about sin as an agent or as a cosmic power, one needs to somehow reconcile this fact with sin's origin in human behavior. One cannot inflate sin's power, imagining it as a "supernatural" rival to God. For Paul, whose world is divided not between natural and supernatural (these are modern categories) but rather between "creation" and "Creator," sin falls quite clearly on the *creation* side of the ledger, as its dominion is downstream from human sin.

The trouble comes in trying to understand how sin's dominion is transmitted. Paul is clear that Adam's sin had consequences for those who came after him. Death, sin's characteristic fruit, exercises dominion "even over those whose sins were not like the transgression of *Adam" (Rom 5:14 NRSV). Paul then goes onto confirm that "the many died through the one man's trespass" (Rom 5:15 NRSV). This raises thorny questions about justice (is it right that the many should suffer the consequences of the actions of the one?), which are not helped by an obscure prepositional phrase (*eph hō*) at the crucial moment in Romans 5:12. Both the NRSV and NIV translate "*because* all have sinned," and while this is difficult to justify linguistically, it renders a theological idea that seems to lie behind Romans 5:14, which refers to others having sinned. This idea that Adam's sin set a paradigm that all humans imitated finds ancient Jewish support in 2 Baruch 54.19, which suggests that "Adam is, therefore, not the cause, except for himself, but each of us has become our own Adam" (trans. Charlesworth). If Paul had something similar in mind, this would ward off a number of the thorniest theological problems. But it would still invite questions about how Adam set this universal pattern for human behavior: Why has everyone become the Adam of their own soul? On this point, there are two important families of answers.

First, there is the traditional approach, which suggests that everyone literally, materially sinned "in Adam," in a way analogous to the way that Levi pays a tithe to Melchizedek from within the loins of *Abraham, as Hebrews 7:9-10 claims. This view finds in Romans 5:12 the foundation of the classic doctrine of "original sin." Guilt for sin is inherited. On this account, the transmission of sin's dominion follows a biological or, if you will, genetic model. This idea has been taken up by paleontologist Daryl P. Domning, who argues that the stain of original sin is written in human genes' adherence to the selfish laws of evolution (Domning and Hellwig, 118, 149). Many modern theologians prefer a second model, which focuses on *social transmission*. This model finds its clearest exposition in German theologians Friedrich Schleiermacher and Albrecht Ritschl, who insist that much of each generation's sin is conditioned by the generation that came before through the social institutions and patterns they established. It may be possible to synthesize these views, seeing sin as a matter of epigenetic inheritance. Whether one follows the traditional or social-transmission account, one does well to note that the transmission of sin—whether as inherited guilt or learned behavior—underpins the sustained dominion of sin in the world.

4. Defeat of Sin.
The defeat of sin is core to the message of the *gospel as Paul describes it, appearing in multiple Pauline summaries of the gospel. In 1 Corinthians 15:3, Christ's death for humanity's sins stands at the head of what is likely an early Christian creed in 1 Corinthians 15:3-5: "Christ died for our sins in accordance with the scriptures" (NRSV). In Galatians 1:4, sin's role as a power is front and center as Paul glosses the *Lord Jesus Christ as the one who "gave himself for our sins to set us free from the present evil age" (NRSV).

The efficacy of Christ's death for Paul is in Christ's *obedience*. Christ's death on the *cross is the pivotal act of the gospel narrative, and it is significant for Paul as a demonstration of Christ's obedience (Phil 2:8). For Paul, there is a correspondence between Christ's obedience and Adam's disobedience. Both have consequences for "the many," Adam's sin making the many sinners, Christ's obedience making the many righteous (Rom 5:19). It may be that Paul has in mind that Christ is restoring human agency to its proper grounding in obedience to God. On this line of thinking, Adam's sin has dislodged human obedience from its proper grounding in obedience to God, resulting not just in an ironic "obedience" to sin but in a sort of rebellion of the self against one's own will. Down this road, one's very self no longer obeys one (Rom 7:17, 20; cf. Gal 5:17). In contrast, Christ's act of obedience restores human agency (Rom 5:17) and makes possible a new mode of obedience to righteousness (Rom 6:17), which opens the possibility of fulfilling the just requirement of the law (Rom 8:4). In short, Christ's obedience enables believers' obedience. Obedience thus becomes a central category in Paul's ministry (Rom 16:19; 2 Cor 2:9; 7:15; Phil 2:12; Philem 21). The concept is so central for Paul that, in Romans, he three times summarizes his vocation in terms of summoning "the obedience of *faith" among the Gentiles (Rom 1:5; 15:18; 16:26),

The defeat of sin accomplished through Christ's obedience to death on the cross takes hold in believers' lives through their participation in Christ's death in baptism (Rom 6:3). This baptismal participation in Christ's death is at the same time entry into Christ's body (1 Cor 13:13). Membership in Christ's body entails a departure from the body of sin and freedom from the dominion of sin (Rom 6:7; 8:2). The picture Paul paints is of a creeping necrosis within the body of sin. Ultimately, the body of sin comes to nothing (Rom 6:6) as individual members of sin's body enter into Christ's death and rise to new life in the body of Christ (Rom 12; 1 Cor 12–14).

Just as the dominion of sin has a cosmic scope of impact, so, too, does Christ's defeat of sin. Christ Jesus having set believers free from the dominion of sin ("the law of sin and death," Rom 8:2 NRSV), they are free to a new way of life according to the Spirit, which Paul contrasts to life according to the *flesh (Rom 8:1-17; Gal 5:16-17). This life in the Spirit (glossed as "spirit of *adoption") is the life of the children of God (Rom 8:14-17; Gal 4:4-7). The new way of life of the children of God is inextricably intertwined with God's cosmic work of new creation (Rom 8:19-23; 2 Cor 5:17; Gal 6:15). The defeat of sin is not merely a matter of individuals set free to live rightly but of communities reconciled, the social fabric repaired, and the whole world set free from futility. Ultimately, the defeat of sin results in nothing less than the cosmos remade.

5. Personal, Social, and Cosmic Sin.
Paul's discussion of sin consistently ranges across three levels: personal, social, and cosmic. Sin can be, for Paul, the misdeed of individuals, a force distorting social life, and a cosmic tyrant holding the world under its sway. As noted at the outset, these three different levels in Paul's account of sin can be difficult to hold together. Among scholars, there is a tendency to focus exclusively on one at the expense of the others.

This tendency to reduce Paul's language to just one of these three levels is recognizable among some of the luminaries in modern biblical scholarship. Archetypically, the great advocate for the personal level is Bultmann, who, while recognizing quite explicitly Paul's depiction of sin as a cosmic tyrant, wrote off this language as "mythological" personification that the modern interpreter must set aside. Instead, Bultmann argues, the core Pauline concern insight is always about personal responsibility. Bultmann's student Ernst Käsemann stands as fountainhead of a school of "apocalyptic" readers of Paul, who prefer to *center* rather than discard what Bultmann had identified as the mythological stratum of Paul's language about sin. More recent scholars such as J. Louis Martyn and Beverly Gaventa have taken up this "*apocalyptic Paul" and demonstrated how this lens can produce a compelling holistic account of Paul's writings. By and large it has been liberation theologians who have recovered and highlighted the social dimension of Paul's language about sin. Elsa Támez in particular has highlighted this aspect of Paul's discussion of sin.

In the final accounting, Paul's letters make it plain that all three levels exist side-by-side in Paul's thought. Pastoral experience speaks to the fact that all three dynamics are recognizable in our world. Exegetically and pastorally, one needs to be able to hold all three together. Doing so is not only an exegetical challenge but, as Bultmann's concerns highlight, also a philosophical one. Holding together Paul's doctrine of sin in all its complexity demands recourse to a worldview hospitable to conceptions of suprahuman powers (such as the tyrant sin) and able to deal with genuine social realities that are irreducible to (if dependent on) the individuals that comprise them. Emergence theory in philosophy of science offers just such a framework, as Matthew Croasmun has proposed. On this account, the cosmic tyrant, Sin, emerges from complex systems of individual and social sin in ways analogous to the emergence of the mind from the complex neurological structures of the body. Participation in the body of sin, on such an account, is no matter of mere metaphor. Presumably there are and will be developed other such accounts of the world capacious enough to serve the reader of Paul well in holding together Paul's nuanced language.

Holding together these strands of Paul's thought on sin is no mere matter of theological or exegetical precision. Sin that operates at all three levels requires resistance at all three levels. The sin of individuals demands practices of personal discipleship. Social sin demands social action. Sin that operates beyond merely the individual and social realms demands ministries of deliverance that continue seek the Spirit's power to realize—in ways always inchoate and incomplete—the *hope that "the God of *peace will soon crush *Satan under your feet" (Rom 16:20). Because each of these levels is related to the others, so also are the interventions. Social sin demands personal discipleship and spiritual warfare. Individual sin may spur social action and spiritual warfare. Spiritual oppression is also a matter for personal discipleship and social action. Only if one can embrace the full range of Paul's language of sin can one be attuned to and prepared to participate in the full range of God's work in believers' midst.

See also ADAM AND CHRIST; APOCALYPTIC PAUL; APOCALYPTICISM; BAPTISM; BODY OF CHRIST; CORINTHIANS, FIRST LETTER TO THE; DEATH; LAW; ROMANS, LETTER TO THE; SATAN, DEVIL; STRONG AND WEAK.

BIBLIOGRAPHY. **R. Bultmann,** *Theology of the New Testament,* 2 vols. (New York: Scribners, 1951–1957); **M. Croasmun,** *The Emergence of Sin: The Cosmic Tyrant in Romans* (New York: Oxford University Press, 2017); **D. P. Domning and M. K. Hellwig,** *Original Selfishness: Original Sin and Evil in the Light of Evolution* (Hampshire, UK: Ashgate, 2006); **J. D. G. Dunn,** *The Theology of Paul the Apostle* (Grand Rapids, MI: Eerdmans, 1997); **S. Eastman,** *Paul and the Person: Reframing Paul's Anthropology* (Grand Rapids, MI: Eerdmans, 2017); **B. Gaventa,** "The Cosmic Power of Sin in Paul's Letter to the Romans: Toward a Widescreen Edition," *Int* (2004): 229-40; idem, ed., *Apocalyptic Paul: Cosmos and Anthropos in Romans 5–8* (Waco, TX: Baylor University Press, 2013); **N. K. Gupta and J. K. Goodrich,** *Sin and Its Remedy in Paul* (Eugene, OR: Cascade, 2020); **F. Hinkelammert,** *The Ideological Weapons of Death: A Theological Critique of Capitalism* (Maryknoll, NY: Orbis, 1986); **E. Käsemann,** *Commentary on Romans* (Grand Rapids, MI: Eerdmans, 1980); **C. Keener,** *The Mind of the Spirit: Paul's Approach to Transformed Thinking* (Waco, TX: Baylor University Press, 2016); **J. L. Martyn,** *Galatians: A New Translation with Introduction and Commentary* (New York: Doubleday, 1997); idem, *Theological Issues in the Letters of Paul* (Edinburgh: T&T Clark, 1997); **S. McKnight,** *Reading Romans Backwards* (Waco, TX: Baylor University Press, 2019); **D. Nelson,** *What's Wrong with Sin: Sin in Individual and Social Perspective from Schleiermacher to Theologies of Liberation* (New York: T&T Clark, 2009); **A. Ritschl,** *The Christian Doctrine of Justification and Reconciliation: The Positive Development of the Doctrine,* vol. 3 (Edinburgh: T&T Clark, 1900); **O. Romero,** *Voice of the Voiceless: The Four Pastoral Letters and Other Statements,* trans. M. J. Walsh (Maryknoll, NY: Orbis Books, 1985); **F. Schleiermacher,** *The Christian Faith,* ed. H. R. Mackintosh and J. S. Stewart (London: T&T Clark, 1999); **S. Stowers,** *A Rereading of Romans: Justice, Jews, and Gentiles* (New Haven, CT: Yale University Press, 1997); **E. Támez,** *The Amnesty of Grace: Justification by Faith from a Latin American Perspective* (Nashville: Abingdon, 1993); idem, "A Latin American Rereading of Romans 7," in *Translating the New Testament: Text, Translation Theology,* ed. S. Porter and M. Boda (Grand Rapids, MI: Eerdmans, 2009), 290-304.

M. D. Croasmun

SINGLENESS AND CELIBACY

Though Paul's discussion of singleness and celibacy is limited, the lasting impact of his writing on this subject cannot be underestimated. Although the advice he offers on the topic is often directed toward the practical considerations of his first-century audiences, it is in no way divorced from his larger theological enterprise, centered on his redemptive-christological focus.

In modern usage the terms *singleness* and *celibacy* can either function as synonyms or entail completely different meanings. *Singleness* refers to the state of not being married. Traditionally *celibacy,* deriving from the Latin word for "bachelor," *caelebs,* also designated the state of not being married. In modern usage the term *celibacy* has come to more frequently designate the abstention from sexual intercourse irrespective of marital status. This article will assume this latter definition of celibacy.

1. Old Testament Background
2. New Testament Background
3. Paul's Teaching
4. Paul's Legacy

1. Old Testament Background.

The overwhelming emphasis of the OT is on *marriage and procreation as the pattern and expectation for humankind. In the prophetic period, a larger redemptively inclusive vision emerged for those not married with children.

1.1. The Patriarchal and Kingdom Periods. The centrality of marriage and procreation features prominently in the Genesis *creation account in the divine mandate to "be fruitful and multiply" (Gen 1:28 NRSV). Genesis 2 acknowledges, "It is not good for the man to be alone" (Gen 2:18 NIV), as the basis for the establishment of the institution of marriage. The association of divine blessing with being married and procreating offspring also appears prominently in the three major OT covenants. In the Abrahamic *covenant *God promises to multiply *Abraham with offspring as numerous as the "stars in the sky," "sand on the seashore," and "dust of the earth" (Gen 22:17; 13:16 NIV). To David, God promises to establish "a house" and "offspring," with a kingdom that will endure forever (2 Sam 7:11-16). To the Israelite nation God gives his covenant at Sinai with the promise that if they listen to his commands and keep them, he will bless them in the fruit of their womb (Deut 7:12-13). Conversely, God promises *Israel that "none of your men or *women will be childless" (Deut 7:14 NIV).

Each individual Israelite was accountable to the expectations of the Sinai covenant, such that their disobedience to covenant stipulations would make them liable to the be singled out to receive the covenant *curses with the prospect that "the LORD will blot out his [or her] name from under heaven" (Deut 29:20 ESV). Having one's name "blotted out" was the ultimate curse of the covenant, signifying that one had no children to remember their name or carry their name after *death. Because of the direct association between marriage and children with covenant blessing and divine favor, virtually everyone who was able opted to marry and have children. One notable exception was Jephthah's daughter, who spent two months with her companions to mourn her virginity before she died (Judg 11:37-38). The exceptionality of such a life was underscored by the annual four-day vigil in her honor that was subsequently observed by the daughters of Israel.

1.2. The Prophetic Period. The prophets condemn the overall failure of the Jewish nation to keep the Sinai covenant while also proclaiming the faithfulness of God and the *hope of restoration to come. As part of his message of renewal and restoration following the death of the Suffering Servant, Isaiah offers two portraits of hope for the single and childless person. The first is the portrait of the unmarried and barren women (Is 54:1-5), who now sings because though she has never been in labor, with the Lord Almighty as her husband, she will have offspring that possess the nations. Her disgrace and shame will be fully reversed. The second portrait depicts the childless eunuch (Is 56:1-8), to whom God will give in his *temple and its walls a memorial and a name better than sons and daughters. The eunuch who was formally barred from access to the temple (Deut 23:1) is now given restored access to the divine presence and blessed with recognition and status greater than that provided by a legacy of progeny. This dual reversal-of-fortune motif signals the prophetic hope of a coming new work of God in the advent of a new covenant (Jer 31:31).

Perhaps reinforcing this shift, some of the prophets themselves embody various conditions of singleness. Jeremiah remains unmarried as a prophetic sign that children born in the land will die by the sword and famine and will not be lamented (Jer 16:1-4). Ezekiel becomes a widower as a prophetic sign of the impending loss of the temple (Ezek 24:15-24). Hosea divorces an unfaithful whore and then takes her back as a prophetic picture of Israel's unfaithfulness and God's unfailing *love (Hos 1:2; 2:2). Circumstantial evidence (Dan 1:3-20; 2 Kings 20:18) as well as Jewish interpretive tradition (b. Sanh. 93b; Pirqe R. El. 52) suggests that Daniel served as a court eunuch.

2. New Testament Background.

Paul's interaction on topics of singleness and celibacy was part of the larger cultural milieu in which he was corresponding. Various expressions of singleness motivated from both ascetic and nonascetic causes were already present in the surrounding culture.

2.1. Second Temple Judaism. From the OT prophets there is a trajectory of evidence of a more favorable perspective toward celibacy and singleness in Second Temple Judaism. Wisdom of Solomon 3:13-14 offers dual blessings to the barren woman, that she will have "fruit when God examines souls," as well as to the eunuch, who will be shown special favor for his faithfulness. Judith is portrayed as a feminine prophetic figure who, with heightened devotion to God, maintains chastity as a widow despite being pursued by many suitors (Jdt 16:22). The association of abstinence with *holiness before God in the OT (Ex 19:14-15; Deut 23:9-14) is expanded by Philo in suggesting that Moses entered into a permanent state of abstinence in order that as prophet he could be in constant readiness to receive an oracle from the Lord (Philo, *Mos.* 2.68-69).

Philo also extols a version of celibate life in his portrayal of the Therapeutae, a celibate society of both men and women living on the shores of Lake Mareotis (Philo, *Contempl.* 21-22). Whether the community actually existed or was Philo's own construction is unclear, though scholarship leans in favor of an actual community (Diamond, 43). The Therapeutae serve as a model of those who would abandon conventional family life and material possessions for sake of seeking an eschatologically motivated communal existence of contemplation and service (Philo, *Vit. Cont.* 10-13).

Philo, Josephus, and Pliny the Elder all attest to a celibate group of Essenes most likely identified with the community at Qumran described by the Dead Sea Scrolls (Van Der Horst, 394-96; Charlesworth, 65; see Philo, *Hypothetica*, cited in Eusebius, *Praep. ev.* 8.11.14; Josephus, *J.W.* 2.8.2; *Ant.* 18.21; Pliny the Elder, *Nat.* 5.17). Archaeological evidence of human remains confirms a community at Qumran consisting of celibate males (Zias, 253). Their celibate state was motivated by an awareness of being in a constant state of preparedness for eschatological war in keeping with biblical rules (Deut 23:9-14; 1 Sam 21:5) on abstinence in a war situation (1QM XVIII, 1-3; Charlesworth, 64). Moreover, being a community that saw itself as receiving continual divine revelation necessitated permanent separation from all sexual contact with women (Diamond, 46; Vermes, 182).

2.2. *Greco-Roman Perspectives.* In the Greco-Roman world the question of remaining single versus getting married was a major topos of ethical *philosophy. Hesiod's creation account portrays the newly created woman as a moral dilemma for the man (Hesiod, *Theog.* 507-616; *Op.* 47-105), and the question of the wisdom of marriage became a perennial matter of debate through centuries of philosophical discourse (see Danylak 2010, 183-90). Various schools including Plato's Academy, Aristotle's Peripatetic school, and the Stoics were proponents of marriage (Diogenes Laertius, *Vit.* 3.78; 5.31; 6.11). For the Stoics marriage was necessary for the continuation of society. Since it was necessary for society, it was therefore the optimal course of virtue for each individual. Cynics and Epicureans generally advised against marriage (Diogenes Laertius, *Vit.* 6.11; 10.119). The Epicureans believed that as marriage incurred stressful responsibilities, the optimal life was best served by remaining unattached. To guarantee a continued supply of able soldiers, Augustus enacted laws requiring marriage of both men and women throughout the Roman Empire (see Galinsky). In the imperial period assuming the responsibility of marriage and having at least three children was regarded not merely as personal decision but as a political act.

Nevertheless, male singleness was not uncommon in the Roman world, especially in urban centers (Danylak 2011, 44-51). Cassius Dio records an account of a "vast throng" of unmarried knights petitioning Augustus to repeal the marriage legislation (Cassius Dio, *Hist.* 56.1-10). Soldiers were legally prohibited from marrying and were exempt from the marriage legislation (Cassius Dio, *Hist.* 60.24.3), the validity of which was even acknowledged by the Stoics (Epictetus, *Diatr.* 3.22.78-79). There is little evidence that contemporary writers and poets such as Virgil, Horace, Propertius, Martial, Epictetus, Lucretius, Tibullus, Juvenal, Persius, Petronius, and Sulpicia ever assumed the responsibilities of marriage, and from their prevailing disposition on the subject there is basis to conclude that they did not. Among the lower classes, epigraphic evidence of small families among freedmen suggests that marriage may have been often unaffordable or postponed (Treggiari 1969, 214).

Whereas accounts of lifelong bachelors are frequent in the sources, the references to lifelong unmarried women are more exceptional (Treggiari 1991, 83). Most famous was the female priesthood of the six Vestal Virgins, who carried out their duties under the auspices of the emperor as *pontifex maximus*. Though the virgins were eligible to marry after their term of service was completed, few exercised that option (Plutarch, *Numa* 10.1-2). Female sexual asceticism was associated with prophetic inspiration in Greek religion (Gundry-Volf, 110). Pythia at Delphi was a virgin in order to prophesy, and Pausanias describes the female oracle at the temple of Apollo as being debarred from intercourse with a man (*Descr.* 2.24.1).

2.3. *The Gospels and Acts.* Given the presumption of universal marriage in the Torah and the Sinai covenant, it is striking that the two leading protagonists in the Gospel narratives, John the Baptist and Jesus, conduct their entire ministries as unmarried men. Not only does Jesus not adhere himself to the expectations of traditional Jewish patriarchal family life, but on repeated occasions he directly challenges them. Jesus indicates that he has come to bring "a sword" that will set "a man against his father, and a daughter against her mother" (Mt 10:34-36 ESV). He demands allegiance to himself greater than that owed to one's own father and mother (Mt 10:37). Jesus redefines his family, declaring that his true mother, brother, and sister are "whoever does the will of God"

(Mk 3:35 ESV). The priority of allegiance to Jesus means that "no one who has left home or wife or brothers or sisters or parents or children for the sake of the kingdom of God will fail to receive many times as much in this age, and in the age to come eternal life" (Lk 18:29-30 NIV). Jesus' use of such radical language was not to disregard family members and family obligations but rather to inaugurate a new age in which kingdom allegiances would define a spiritual family that would supersede all previous human relationships.

Jesus' only direct teaching on singleness occurs in Matthew 19:10-12 in context of his discussion on divorce with the Pharisees. His conclusions on marriage and divorce lead the incredulous disciples to respond reminiscent of the Greco-Roman marriage debate: "If such is the case of a man with his wife, [maybe] it is better not to marry" (Mt 19:10 NRSV). The shock of Jesus' next response is threefold. First, he appears to affirm rather than deny their statement. Second, he refers to those single as "eunuchs." The eunuch figure, though disparaged by Jews and *Gentiles alike, may have represented the person (male or female) who gave their full allegiance and loyalty to their Lord God and King and fully trusted in him as sufficient to meet all their needs. Jesus then defines three categories of eunuchs. Some are eunuchs because of the nature of how they are born, some because of "men" (i.e., circumstances beyond one's control), and some have voluntarily "made themselves eunuchs" for sake of the kingdom of God. The third shock in Jesus' language is his direct invitation to his hearers to choose to remain single. While not everyone is able to receive (literally "grasp") this teaching, anyone who can receive it should do so! (Mt 19:12).

Luke records an episode affirming the explicit inclusion of single persons in the early *church. Acts 8:26-40 narrates the conversion of the Ethiopian eunuch. His identification as a eunuch is noteworthy in light of both Jesus' use of the figure and Isaiah's use of the figure (Is 56:1-8) as a redemptive figure of blessing. He appears as both a foreigner and a eunuch, who was just returning from worshiping in Jerusalem, where the temple was located. This is a curious detail in light of Isaiah's *prophecy that the eunuch will be given an everlasting *name "in my house and within my walls" (Is 56:5 NRSV), reversing his exclusion of access in Deuteronomy 23:1. Unlike the former Israelite nation, in the new dispensation, both the childless eunuch and the foreigner now experience full inclusion and membership among God's people.

3. Paul's Teaching.

Singleness and celibacy are topics Paul discusses in the context of his occasional writing addressing specific circumstances in his church communities. Paul's most significant extended discussion in 1 Corinthians 7 also appears to show awareness of the Matthean Jesus tradition on the same subject (Wenham, 245-46). Though his discussion is prompted by the circumstances of his readers, Paul's teaching on singleness should not be presumed to be incidental to his larger theological enterprise but rather as a specific application that flows out of his redemptive-christological perspective. For this reason, it is helpful to begin by summarizing how significant features of that larger enterprise inform the logic of Paul's perspective on singleness and celibacy.

3.1. Singleness in the Contours of Paul's Theology. Both the Sinai covenant of the OT and the new covenant instituted by Jesus center on God's blessing through the divine provision of offspring. In Deuteronomy 7:12-13, contingent on their obedience, God blesses the people by blessing the fruit of their womb. As Paul lays out the blessings of new covenant in Ephesians 1:3-14, God has blessed believers with every spiritual blessing in *Christ, the divinely provided beloved offspring (Eph 1:3). In contrast to the conditional requirement of obedience of Sinai, in Christ believers have been granted redemption through his blood for the *forgiveness of *sin by his *grace (Eph 1:7). This vital distinction in the respective covenants defines the shift in perspective on singleness. Whereas marriage was essential for receiving the divine blessing of offspring in the former dispensation, one is fully blessed in the new dispensation through the divinely beloved offspring irrespective of marital status.

In Galatians 4, Paul writes, "But when the *fullness of time had come, God sent forth his Son, born of woman, born under the *law, to redeem those who were under the law, so that we might receive *adoption as sons" (Gal 4:4-5 ESV). Jesus was born in the former dispensation physically of a woman under the law. But now he has redeemed those under the law into a new spiritual adoption of sonship. Paul then goes on to contrast the believing Gentile Galatian Christians with the law-bound ethnic Jews in a narrative allegory (Gal 4:21-31). The Jews are Abraham's offspring born according to the *flesh whereas the Galatian believers are Abraham's offspring in Christ born supernaturally according to the Spirit. To prooftext his whole argument Paul cites the barren woman of Isaiah 54:1 (Gal 4:27). For Paul, the powerful image of this single, barren woman bearing children supernaturally becomes the exemplar figure of the spiritual new birth in Christ. Reproduction and multiplication of the people of God in the new dispensation come not through physical birth necessitated by marriage but through spiritual birth in Christ exemplified by the single, barren woman.

That Paul sees his own *ministry in the paradigm of the barren woman is evidenced in how frequently he describes his own discipling relationships in language of bearing and begetting children. He refers to the Galatians in the same chapter as "my little children, for whom I am again in the anguish of childbirth until Christ is formed in you!" (Gal 4:19 ESV). He declares to the Corinthians, "I begat you in Christ through the *gospel" (1 Cor 4:15). To the Thessalonians he is like a "nursing mother" (1 Thess 2:7). He says he "begat" Onesimus in his imprisonment (Philem 10), and Timothy and Titus are his "lawfully begotten" sons (1 Tim 1:2; Titus 1:4). As a single man himself, Paul never mentions having any physical children, but he constantly refers to his multitudinous spiritual offspring whom he regards as his true spiritual legacy in Christ.

3.2. 1 Corinthians 7. *3.2.1. The Crux Interpretum (1 Cor 7:1-5).* First Corinthians 7 contains Paul's most extended discussion on the topic of singleness and celibacy. With the introductory words, "Now concerning the matters about which you wrote" (NRSV), there is an apparent turn of attention in the letter to a series of matters about which the Corinthians had written to Paul, the first of which appears to have something to do with matters of singleness, celibacy, and marriage, as these subjects dominate his attention in the chapter. The statement in reference to the correspondence that follows, "It is well for a man not to touch a woman" (NRSV), is a very challenging *crux interpretum,* as evidenced by the variety of ways it is translated into English. The traditional view common until the mid-twentieth century sees the statement either as attributed to Paul himself or as a statement of the Corinthians that Paul endorses (e.g., NLT). Because of cases of fornication, Paul concedes marriage, requiring those who do marry to be faithful to conjugal relations. The more recent "consensus" view, endorsed by Gordon Fee and others, attributes the statement as a quotation from the Corinthians' letter that Paul is rebutting in what immediately follows (e.g., NIV; see Fee 2003, 198). In this interpretation, Paul concedes temporary abstinence in marriage to the Corinthian ascetics for the sake of *prayer but insists that it should not become the rule.

The "consensus" views Paul's Corinthian interlocutors as ascetics who were promoting celibacy within marriage. Numerous theories have attempted to account for the nature and provenance of the Corinthian asceticism, from proto-Gnosticism (Schrage, 217-20), to an overrealized *eschatology "informed by an improper understanding of spiritual enthusiasm" (Fee 1980, 313), to influences from Hellenistic Judaism (Rosner, 155), to Egyptian cults (Oster). Theories that they were pneumatic prophets seeking divine inspiration and insight through celibacy, which was necessary for exercising their prophetic gifts, have been popular, envisioning this group either as a mixed one of males and females (Gundry-Volf, 105) or as one of exclusively female prophets (Wire).

Other interpreters have questioned the need for conjecturing a group of Corinthian ascetics at all (Malcolm, 43-56), especially given logical continuity with Paul's previous discussion in 1 Corinthians 5–6, where Paul is clearly addressing a sexually licentious audience over issues of immorality and their solicitation of prostitutes. In this interpretation the 1 Corinthians 7:1 saying is Paul's response to a question the Corinthians had raised. As the Corinthians were philosophically minded seekers of *wisdom (1 Cor 2:6), the Greek marriage debate may have prompted their question (similar to the disciples in Mt 19:10) in light of the circumstances (1 Cor 7:26) they were facing (see Deming; Danylak 2011). Because of the excessive immorality in the church, Paul responds to their question in a manner that acknowledges the legitimacy of singleness as a viable life choice, while simultaneously upholding the expectation of sexual *purity. For Paul singleness and celibacy go together—to not be married necessitates also abstaining from sexual relations ("touching"). Because of the Corinthians' immorality, Paul immediately proceeds to present marriage as an alternative option. In this reading, he exhorts them to be faithful to their *own* spouse *rather* than to the multiple other sexual outlets to which they otherwise had access.

3.2.2. Singleness as a Charisma and a Calling (1 Cor 7:6-24). In 1 Corinthians 7:7 Paul desires that the Corinthians were as he himself is in his own singleness. Here Paul expresses a wish that on the one hand is capable of realization, and *ought* to be realized, namely that "all would be even as I am" (Fitzmyer, 282). But on the other hand, the wish is qualified with "each has his own gift from God, one this and another that," with the implication that the gift of continence necessary to live without marriage is ultimately a provision given by God. The tension is likely resolved in Paul's expectation that some may have such a gift and have simply not yet discerned having it, as well as his expectation that though spiritual *gifts are divine provisions, it is commendable "to strive" for them (1 Cor 12:31). The balance of human and divine engagement corresponds well to Jesus' open invitation to his hearers to "receive" his invitation to be a eunuch for the kingdom, while simultaneously acknowledging that not all will be able to receive it (Mt 19:11-12). In 1 Corinthians 7:8-9 Paul then applies the principle that summarizes his perspective on singleness. It is better for all those who can to remain single and celibate in the model of Paul, but for those who "burn," that is, suffer undue distraction from the innate desires for sex, companionship, or children, it is better for them to marry as opportunity arises.

Amid the general focus on the question of marriage and singleness in 1 Corinthians 7, Paul appears to enter into a rhetorical *digressio* in 1 Corinthians 7:17-24, in which he presents a side topic to enhance his larger discussion on marriage and singleness. The key to the section appears in his dual use of "calling" in 1 Corinthians 7:20: "each is to remain in the *calling* [*klēsis*] in which he/she was *called* [*eklēthē*]." There is the "calling" to Christ common to the whole congregation (1 Cor 1:26) but also types of callings that are specific to the individual. In the Roman world one's race, class, and marital state were all markers of relative status in the social ordering. But for those called to the community of Christ, no such hierarchy exists, and there is therefore no need to seek to change one's state of life for sake of improving one's status within the community of God's people. There was no need therefore for a Greek to be circumcised and become a Jew (1 Cor 7:18), for a *slave to seek manumission and become free (1 Cor 7:21-23), or for those unmarried to become married (1 Cor 7:27-28). Rather, each may "remain" in the calling in which they were called. Paul's point is that singleness and marriage are equal callings in the *body of Christ. Greater status is not afforded to one class over the other. In Christ, believers are all equal members of the same body whether single, married, or single again (1 Cor 12:20-27).

3.2.3. Three Motivations for Remaining Single (1 Cor 7:25-35). In 1 Corinthians 7:25-40 Paul revisits the marriage question in light of the particular circumstances his audience was facing. As the regional imperial center for Achaia, first-century *Corinth would have had a constant demand for physical labor in moving goods and services across the isthmus and to support the plethora of imperial building projects underway, attracting male migrants from the countryside looking for work. This would have likely resulted in a comparative shortage of marriageable women (virgins) for men looking for potential mates (Danylak 2011, 19-54). Further complicating their situation, it is reasonable that the "present crisis" Paul mentions in 1 Corinthians 7:26 was an economic crisis due to the fluctuations of the city grain market, exacerbating the costs associated with raising children in *urban settings (Winter). Amid these and other urban challenges, Paul offers three motivations for his readers to "remain" unmarried.

3.2.3.1. Living a Simpler Life. Following from Paul's principle that race, class, and marital status are not means of advancing one's status with the body of Christ, he addresses the matter at hand. Amid distressed circumstances Paul advises the one who is unmarried to "remain" as they are (1 Cor 7:26-28). If one is bound in marriage, one should remain committed, and if one is free from that commitment, one should remain single. Paul qualifies his statement before offering his reasons. As he is offering advisory opinion, not a command (1 Cor 7:25), he clarifies that the man who marries does not sin, and neither does the virgin who marries. Given that most females would have felt relentless pressure to marry, often feeling that the decision was not theirs to make, by using the active voice ("marries") Paul clearly affirms the woman's choice in the marriage decision as well as the man's. His rationale for remaining single is to spare them "trouble in the flesh" (1 Cor 7:28). Paul affirms that singleness enables both men and woman to live a simpler life spared of the added complications that naturally come with family life. In the new dispensation the mandate of physical procreation has been superseded by the kingdom mandate of disciple making, so Paul is sympathetic toward the perspective that marriage brings pressure of undue stress that might be avoided in remaining single.

3.2.3.2. Living with Eschatological Expectancy. Next Paul moves to two additional reasons that are decidedly kingdom directed. If the Stoics advocated the need to marry for the sake of preserving the social cosmos, in 1 Corinthians 7:29-31 Paul expands the horizon of that *cosmology. The time "has been shortened," and the present form of the world is passing away. The purposes of the present age are subsumed into the purposes of the anticipated kingdom of God. Paul is not denigrating the present world but radically relativizing the current age in light of the age to come. Since Jesus indicates that in the age to come there will be neither marrying nor giving in marriage (Lk 20:35), the proper posture of the married believer now is to live in their relationships with expectancy and anticipation that the new order of the age to come may be consummated at any time. Those who remain single prophetically anticipate the age to come.

3.2.3.3. Living a Life of Service. In 1 Corinthians 7:32-35 Paul moves to a third theme, which is reminiscent of his earlier desire for them to be as he is (1 Cor 7:7). Paul desires them to remain single that they might be free from concern—using language familiar to the Greek marriage debate. Greek playwright Menander intones that having a wife and children "entails many cares in life" (Menander, *Frag.* 649K [LCL]). The Epicureans advocated the avoidance of marriage in order to live a life of optimal tranquility. But Paul responds to the marriage question in language reminiscent of Jesus' reference to eunuchs. For Paul singleness was not simply a *freedom *from* the concerns of caring for a spouse but a freedom *for* dedicated concern for "the things of the *Lord." There is a direct equivalence of language. The good and necessary concern a married *man or woman directs toward their spouse in support of their needs is instead directed toward the concerns of the Lord.

The equivalence of males and females is striking. Unlike Greek philosophers, who invariably directed the ethical marriage question to males, Paul goes out of his way to clarify that the decision to remain single or to marry is equally a decision for females as for males. He adds an extended result clause exclusive to the female, "the unmarried woman or virgin is concerned for the things of the Lord: *that* she might be holy in *body and spirit" (1 Cor 7:34). The holiness she exhibits in her dedication to the things of the Lord is not pristine virginity in the pattern of the Vestals, for Paul includes here *both* virgin and "unmarried" women. The widowed or divorced woman who reserves herself for the concerns of the Lord is equally holy in body and spirit. This is a spiritual holiness out of a life of dedicated service open to virgins and nonvirgins alike.

Paul concludes in 1 Corinthians 7:35 with language again reminiscent of eunuch-like service to the Lord. The word *euparadros*, sometimes translated "devotion" in English, has as its root the notion of "sitting beside" in the sense of a lady in waiting for a queen (*LSJ*). The picture is of one who sits beside the Lord, ready and waiting in his *service. Also notable in his description are the adjectives *euschēmon*, "above reproach," and *aperispastōs*, "without distraction." Paul's vision of living the calling of singleness well is encapsulated here. They are those who are above reproach in their sexual conduct, undistracted by spouse and family, and ready and waiting at the service of their Lord. Paul's depiction of singleness as dedicated service to the Lord has inspired celibate communities and orders in the Roman Catholic and Orthodox traditions and even occasionally among Protestants.

3.2.4. The Betrothed (1 Cor 7:36-38). There have been three major interpretive paradigms for reading 1 Corinthians 7:36-38: as describing (1) a man and his fiancée, (2) a father and his daughter, or (3) a form of early Christian spiritual marriage. Recent scholarship has generally converged on the first of these interpretations (Fee 2014, 285-89). The repeated appearance of the possessive "his" or reflexive "his own" pronouns modifying "virgin" that do not appear earlier (1 Cor 7:25-35) suggests a betrothal relationship is in view. The most plausible reading of 1 Corinthians 7:36-38 is that Paul is applying his "remain as you are" principle to the specific situation of arranged betrothal relationships that were often very long in the Roman world, with fathers sometimes having daughters betrothed even as infants (Treggiari 1991, 153-55). If marriageable females were in high demand in Corinth, instances of such extended betrothals would have been probable. In such cases the potential of proceeding to consummate the betrothal in marriage could be reevaluated with the maturing of both the female and male respectively. Paul appears to offer two conditions necessary to merit proceeding with the marriage, first that the man's passions toward the woman are evident, and second that the female is physically mature for an appropriate sexual relationship (Danylak 2011, 180-83).

3.3. The Pastorals. *3.3.1. 1 Timothy 4:1-3.* In 1 Timothy 4:1-3 Paul warns his readers of false teachings by "hypocritical liars" characterized by an ascetic perspective that includes the forbidding of marriage and eating certain *foods. The asceticism described here may have some similarity to the "Do not handle, Do not taste, Do not touch" asceticism that Paul also calls out in Colossians 2:21-23 (NRSV). In both instances Paul condemns the perspective, describing it in Colossians as having "the appearance of wisdom in self-made religion and humility and severe treatment of the body" (Col 2:23 NASB). What is clear in these passages and consistent through Paul's writings is that Paul was not an ascetic. He never suggests that singleness or celibacy in and of themselves should be imposed on anyone, nor does he promote either as a means to heightened spiritual status. Paul's advocacy of singleness is a testimony to the sufficiency of Christ, and he promotes it for the practical benefits it offers the practitioner both personally and for service in ministry.

3.3.2. 1 Timothy 5:3-16. Paul instructs the church to "honor widows who are truly widows" (1 Tim 5:3 ESV) and to "enroll" (1 Tim 5:9) widows at least sixty years old who possess genuine need and have a good reputation for supplementary care and provision. However, his direction to the young widows in 1 Timothy 5:11-14 appears to contrast the advice to widows in 1 Corinthians 7:8-9 and in 1 Corinthians 7:39-40. In this passage he directly advises them to marry, have children, and manage their households so as not to give "the adversary" an occasion for slander. But as Fee points out (2011, 120), the perspective here is quite in keeping with Paul's advice in 1 Corinthians, where remaining a widow is encouraged but remarriage is conceded. Paul's advice to widows in 1 Corinthians 7:9 is that if they cannot exercise self-control they should marry. In 1 Corinthians 7:39 he allows them freedom to marry with the caveat that they marry "in the Lord." The young widows in 1 Timothy 5:11 are described by the rare word *katastrēniasōsin*, "behaving wantonly," which has no known attestation elsewhere in any literary or nonliterary sources. From related forms of the word and the context, Bruce Winter argues that what is in view is not just strong feelings or even a one-off sexual indiscretion but a promiscuous lifestyle (Winter 2003, 132-33). Moreover, the young women's susceptibility to the influence of false teachers could incur the prospect of marrying a nonbeliever and shipwrecking their own *faith (Towner, 352). Because of their clear propensity toward promiscuity, Paul is advising the young widows to marry in the Lord for the sake of preserving their own spiritual welfare. Paul is consistent in relegating the question of marriage to the circumstances of what is prudent for the individual. Paul's advocacy for widows also reminds us that while singleness can be a chosen vocation, it is not always necessarily voluntary. It may be the result of the death of a spouse, the unavailability of potential spouses, divorce, or one's individual experience such as same-sex orientation. Paul's special attention for widows expresses an imperative for the church to be inclusive of all varieties of singleness, whether voluntary or involuntary.

4. Paul's Legacy.

Peter Brown describes 1 Corinthians 7 as "the one chapter that was to determine all Christian thought on marriage and celibacy for well over a millennium" (Brown, 54). Whereas Paul affirms singleness as practically advantageous in certain circumstances for service to the Lord, the early church moved in a more ascetic direction in affirming celibate singleness as a morally superior lifestyle in general. This article can only afford to touch on a few examples of how that trajectory developed.

Though early interpretations of singleness and marriage in 1 Corinthians 7 were often shaped by the localized ecclesiastical concerns and battles faced by individual commentators, some general trends and patterns emerged. Patristic authors generally agree that the "not touching" of 1 Corinthians 7:1 depicts an ideal, but only certain Christians, the ascetic elite, were able to sustain this level of purity (Clark, 269). Various interpretive approaches were used to sharpen the ascetic edge. "It is good not to touch" was considered Paul's normative viewpoint overruling other statements more sympathetic to marriage. One anonymous Pelagian author denies that Paul could have written that he who marries "does well" (1 Cor 7:38) because it "contradicts" 1 Corinthians 7:1b (cited in Clark, 267).

Another approach was to sharpen logical contrasts. In *Against Jovinian* Jerome concludes from 1 Corinthians 7:1b, if it is good not to touch a woman, it is therefore bad to touch one: "for there is no opposite to goodness but badness" (Jerome, *Jov.* 7.1). Tertullian uses a reverse logic in reference to 1 Corinthians 7:9, "better to marry than to burn," arguing that if a "good" is only better in comparison to an evil, then it is not so much a good as an inferior evil (Tertullian, *Mon.* 3). From Paul's lack of discussion on procreation in the chapter, John Chrysostom concludes that whereas at creation marriage was granted for procreation, in the new dispensation marriage only remains for one reason—the suppression of licentiousness and debauchery (John Chrysostom, *Virginit.* 19.1). Similarly, another anonymous Pelagian author stresses that Paul's admonition in 1 Corinthians 7:29 signals the shift in times from the old dispensation, when married men without sons were believed to be cursed, to the new era, in which the greatest blessing falls on those who "have wives as if not" (Clark, 311). The Acts of Paul and Thecla shows the empowerment of females also in pursuing the ascetic life, but the author also goes so far as to proscribe virginity (or celibacy) as necessary for inheriting the resurrection and salvation itself (Acts of Paul and Thecla 14, 6).

Although patristic interpreters ranged in the degree to which they also affirmed married life as an alternative good option available to the Christian man or woman, the ascetic disposition of the majority of the patristic writers predisposed them to regard Paul's affirmation of singleness as a normative practice proscribed by the apostle for their own ecclesiastical contexts.

See also Abraham; Call, Calling; Corinthians, First Letter to the; Covenant; Gifts of the Spirit; Grace; Honor/Shame; Kinship Language in Paul; Marriage and Divorce, Adultery and Incest; Pastoral Epistles; Sexuality, Sexual Ethics; Sin, Guilt; Women.

BIBLIOGRAPHY. **W. Braun,** "Celibacy in the Greco-Roman World," in *Celibacy and Religious Traditions*, ed. C. Olson (Oxford: Oxford University Press, 2008), 21-40; **P. Brown,** *The Body and Society: Men, Women and Sexual Renunciation in Early Christianity* (New York: Columbia University Press, 1988); **J. H. Charlesworth,** *The Pesharim and Qumran History* (Grand Rapids, MI: Eerdmans, 2002); **E. A. Clark,** "1 Corinthians 7 in Early Christian Exegesis," in *Reading Renunciation: Asceticism and Scripture in Early Christianity* (Princeton, NJ: Princeton University Press, 1999), 259-329; **B. Danylak,** *Redeeming Singleness: How the Storyline of Scripture Affirms the Single Life* (Wheaton, IL: Crossway, 2010); idem, "Secular Singleness and Paul's Response in 1 Corinthians 7" (PhD diss., University of Cambridge, 2011); **W. Deming,** *Paul on Marriage and Celibacy: The Hellenistic Background on 1 Cor 7* (Cambridge: Cambridge University Press, 1995); **E. Diamond,** "'And Jacob Remained Alone': The Jewish Struggle with Celibacy," in *Celibacy and Religious Traditions*, ed. C. Olson (Oxford: Oxford University Press, 2008), 41-64; **G. Fee,** "1 Cor. 7:1 in the NIV," *JETS* 23 (1980): 307-14; idem, "1 Corinthians 7:1-7 Revisited," in *Paul and the Corinthians: Studies on a Community in Conflict*, ed. T. J. Burke and J. K. Elliot (Leiden: Brill, 2003), 197-213; idem, *1 & 2 Timothy, Titus*, Understanding the Bible Commentary Series (Grand Rapids, MI: Baker, 2011); idem, *The First Epistle to the Corinthians*, rev. ed. (Grand Rapids, MI: Eerdmans, 2014); **R. Finn,** *Asceticism in the Graeco-Roman World* (Cambridge: Cambridge University Press, 2009); **J. A. Fitzmyer,** *First Corinthians: A New Translation with Introduction and Commentary* (New Haven, CT: Yale University Press, 2008); **K. Galinsky,** "Augustus' Legislation on Marriage and Morals," *Philologus* 126 (1981): 126-44; **J. M. Gundry-Volf,** "Celibate Pneumatics and Social Power: On the Motivations for Sexual Asceticism in Corinth," *USQR* 48 (1994): 105-26; **M. R. Malcolm,** "The Church Without Ascetics: The Lack of an Ascetic Group in Corinth," *JSPHL* 8 (2018): 43-61; **R. E. Oster,** "Use, Misuse and Neglect of Archaeological Evidence in Some Modern Works on 1 Corinthians (1 Cor 7,1-5, 8,10, 11,2-16, 12,14-26)," *ZNW* 83 (1992): 52-73; **B. S. Rosner,** *Paul, Scripture and Ethics: A Study of 1 Corinthians 5–7* (Leiden: Brill, 1994); **W. Schrage,** "Zur Frontstellung der paulinischen Ehebewertung in 1 Kor 7, 1-7," *ZNW* 67 (1976): 214-34; **P. H. Towner,** *The Letters to Timothy and Titus* (Grand Rapids, MI: Eerdmans, 2006); **S. Treggiari,** *Roman Freedmen During the Late Republic* (Oxford: Clarendon, 1969); idem, *Roman Marriage: Iusti Coniuges from the Time of Cicero to the Time of Ulpian* (Oxford: Clarendon, 1991); **P. W. Van Der Horst,** "Celibacy in Early Judaism," *RB* (2002): 390-402; **G. Vermes,** *The Dead Sea Scrolls: Qumran in Perspective* (Cleveland: Collins & World, 1978); **D. Wenham,** *Paul: Follower of Jesus or Founder of Christianity?* (Grand Rapids, MI: Eerdmans, 1995); **B. Winter,** "Secular and Christian Responses to Corinthian Famines," *TynBul* 40 (1989): 86-106; idem, *Roman Wives, Roman Widows: The Appearance of New Women and the Pauline Communities* (Grand Rapids, MI: Eerdmans, 2003); **A. Wire,** *The Corinthian Woman Prophets: A Reconstruction Through Paul's Rhetoric* (Minneapolis: Augsburg Fortress, 1990); **J. Zias,** "The Cemeteries of Qumran and Celibacy: Confusion Laid to Rest?," *DSD* 7 (2000): 220-53.

B. N. Danylak

SLAVE, SLAVERY

Slavery is inherently a matter of power, permitting some people to exploit others by dehumanizing them and profiting from them. Fundamentally, slavery is a form of social control, defined as "social death" (Patterson). A *slave society* is one where the enslaved make up at least 20 percent of the population and play a critical role in production (Bradley; Joshel). According to this metric, there have been five slave societies throughout history: Athens and Roman Italy (not the entire *empire) in ancient times; and in the modern era, Brazil, the Caribbean, and the United States. Although ancient slavery was different in many respects from slavery practiced in the United States, many Christians justified the latter institution by using the Bible—especially the writings of Paul.

1. Slavery and the Enslaved in the Greco-Roman World
2. Slavery and the Enslaved in Pauline Literature

1. Slavery and the Enslaved in the Greco-Roman World.
The institution of slavery was virtually omnipresent throughout the ancient world. The Greek *doul-* stem is part of several words that denote servitude, and *doulos* (feminine: *doulē*) is the common Greek word for "slave" used in the LXX and NT, although it is sometimes rendered "servant." An enslaved person and a *servant both perform labor, but a slave is chattel. The translation "servant" might obscure some of the harsh realities of the institution of slavery, so careful attention should be paid to context; "slave" may likely be the more accurate translation. A less common term, *oiketēs*, denotes specifically household slaves (Lk 16:3; Acts 10:7; Rom 14:4; 1 Pet 2:18). The practice of referring to a male slave of any age as *pais*, "boy" (e.g., Lk 7:7), and an enslaved woman as *paidiskē*, "girl" (e.g., Gal 4:22), further reinforces the shame associated with slavery.

Slavery describes legal status, not occupation. For Aristotle, the enslaved are property and tools whose usefulness is like that of animals (Aristotle, *Pol.* 1.1-7). Attitudes regarding slavery in the first century AD were essentially the same as Aristotle's. While it is true that first-century AD slaves were "granted many rights" (Rupprecht, 881), enslaved people were continually vulnerable to *violence and physical abuse. However, enslaved members of noteworthy *households could fare better in society than poor freed people, who typically died of destitution. The possibility of manumission served as "powerful incentive for slave obedience" (Harrill 2016, 310). Relatively few slaves were freed, however, and when they were, their new status introduced other societal obligations as the formerly enslaved entered into a patron-client relationship with their former master (Harrill 2016). The former slave, as client, might continue to live in the patron's house, be expected to give some earnings to the former owner, and even have their movements restricted (McKnight 2017, 24-25). Furthermore, an enslaved woman's emancipation might come with the stipulation that she remain sexually submissive to her former owner (Glancy, 53). Owning slaves signaled prominence and status even over economic benefit for ancient Romans—freedpersons might even become slave owners. Because of the abundance of enslaved people and the relatively low cost of ownership, slavery was ubiquitous during the lifetimes of Jesus and all the writers of the NT, including the *apostle Paul.

1.1. The Population and Acquisition of Slaves. Historians estimate that by the end of the first century BC, 33 to 40 percent of the population of ancient Rome was enslaved, with most of that number in Roman Italy. About 250,000 slaves were sold annually in the empire. Ancient Romans enslaved people from all around the Mediterranean world, primarily through military conquest. Artwork from the first century AD depicts Roman armies parading their captives as a spectacle of *triumph (see Col 2:15). Generals awarded soldiers with some of the enslaved captives. The *Digest*, published in AD 533 under the auspices of Emperor Justinian, preserves earlier laws and imperial declarations, and details the objectification of slaves. When presented for sale, the enslaved stood on a raised platform (*catasta*) to be inspected as animals. The laws regulating the sale of slaves also regulated the sale of livestock. Although slavery was not based on race or skin color as in modern slave societies, it did betray ethnic biases, as slaves' personal qualities and temperament were in part judged by their *natio*, national origin.

> Those selling slaves should declare their nationality when making the sale; for the slave's nationality may often induce or deter a purchaser; therefore, we have an interest in knowing the nationality; for there is a presumption that some slaves are good, coming from a race with no bad repute, while others are thought bad, since they come from a notorious people. If, then, the slave's nationality be not declared, an action will be given to the purchaser and to all interested parties whereby the purchaser may return the slave. (*Digest* 21.31.1.21 [trans. Watson])

Slaves were also acquired through natural reproduction since the offspring of slaves belonged to their owners. Additionally, people were enslaved as the result of kidnapping, piracy, infant abandonment, and criminal punishment.

1.2. The Enslaved Within the Social Order. As part of the *familia*, the patriarchal Roman household, slaves were subject to the whims and aspirations of the head of the household, the *paterfamilias*, and the matron of the house might also own slaves apart from her husband. Stripped of their own identity, slaves were given names that reinforced the owners' dominance and projected the owner's expectations or imaginations for the slave. There are names commonly given to slaves throughout the Pauline literature. A few examples include Andronicus, "male victor" (Rom 16:7); Urbanus, "from the city" (Rom 16:9); Fortunatus, "lucky" (1 Cor 16:17); Onesimus, "useful" (Col 4:9; Philem 10).

Slaves performed a wide range of duties, working as miners, farmers, cooks, teachers, physicians, estate managers, artists, and whatever else their owners needed. Most slaves were *rustici*, agricultural workers, whose relatively secluded and subsistent existence revealed an inferior ranking to *urbani*, slaves who maintained households. Above the *urbani* were the emperor's slaves (*familia Caesaris*), who possessed a relative degree of power and privilege. *Rustici* lived in cramped cells (*cellae*, *cellulae*) within a villa or in simple huts (*casae*) near the livestock. Several *urbani* might live together in one room within the owner's house. It was assumed that slaves should eat the cheapest and poorest-quality food in the household.

Although enslaved men and *women could not legally marry, they could form a union called *contubernium* ("living together"; a term also used for the arrangement of animals and soldiers), as opposed to *matrimonium*. Boys and girls born into slavery were expected to work from childhood (starting around five years of age) through adulthood. At a slave's disposal was the *peculium*, which might consist of cash, food, livestock, clothing, or even other slaves but ultimately belonged to the master. Some slaves hoped the *peculium* might be used toward purchasing their freedom, but that was rare (Bradley 1994).

Slave masters expected absolute obedience from their slaves. Consequently, the bodies of enslaved boys, girls, men, and women were vulnerable to sexual and other physical abuse, such as beatings (see Lk 12:42-48). Jennifer Glancy observes that the Greek *sōma*, "*body," functioned as a synonym for *doulos*, "slave" (see Rev 18:13). Glancy argues that slaveholders relied on the bodies of slaves as "surrogate bodies" to carry out "disreputable actions" or to suffer physical injury in the place of their owners (Glancy, 11, 15). Roman law required that the questioning of slaves in court include flogging, burning, or racking the body since slaves were presumed to be inherently untrustworthy. Slaves fought as gladiators, but an AD 79 law placed limits on condemning slaves to fight wild beasts (Joshel).

Scholars note some humanitarian concerns for slaves during the first century AD, even though the institution remained intact. For example, Tacitus recounts the mid-first-century murder of the city prefect, Pedanius Secundus, by an anonymous slave (Tacitus, *Ann.* 14.42-45). The senate demanded the execution of all of Pedanius Secundus's four hundred slaves. Residents of the city, however, protested publicly, expressing pity for the enslaved men, women, and children, most of whom likely had no knowledge of the murder. The protestors formed a dense crowd and threatened to riot with stones and firebrands. Nero reprimanded the crowd and ordered soldiers to march the four hundred slaves to their executions. Stoics, who viewed all humanity as subjects of Fortune, advocated for less cruel treatment of slaves. In a letter to Lucilius, the philosopher Seneca, a slaveowner and contemporary of Paul, congratulates the kindness of a master toward his slaves:

> I am glad to learn, through those who come from you, that you live on friendly terms with your slaves. This befits a sensible and well-educated man like yourself. "They are slaves," people declare. Nay, rather they are men. "Slaves!" No, they are unpretentious friends. "Slaves!" No, they are our fellow-slaves, if one reflects that Fortune has equal rights over slaves and free men alike. (Seneca, *Ep.* 47.1 [LCL])

Even with the threat of riot, or Stoic appeals that the enslaved be treated more humanely, there was nothing akin to an abolitionist movement. The humane treatment of slaves, as well as physical abuse, served a utilitarian purpose: to make slaves "useful," thereby maximizing the owner's investment (Smith).

1.3. Slave Revolts and Fugitive Slaves. S. R. Joshel comments that "the truism of Roman slaveowners was *tot servi, quot hostes*, 'as many enemies as slaves'"(Joshel, 64), a variant of Seneca's *totidem hostes esse quot servos*, "as many enemies as you have slaves" (*Ep.* 47.5). This reveals owners' awareness of slave resentment (also Bradley 1984, 30). Yet, slaves rarely revolted. James Harrill points out, "The absence of slave revolt in the Roman imperial period does not indicate that slavery was then 'humane' or that slaves had 'relative contentment' with their lot" (Harrill 2016, 314). Harrill also observes that imperial Rome "never forgot the legacy of Spartacus" (Harrill 2016, 314). The enslaved gladiator Spartacus led the most famous slave revolt of antiquity in 73 BC. After about three years, Spartacus and his slave army were defeated, and six thousand were crucified along the Via Appia, serving as a warning to other slaves.

Reminiscent of the Underground Railroad in US history, slave rebellion in ancient times more commonly took the form of flight rather than revolution. The fugitive slave even became a trope in ancient literary works (Bradley 1994, 119-20). *Digest* 11.4 is entirely devoted to runaway slaves, indicting as "thief" anyone harboring a slave. When caught, fugitive slaves could be branded or tattooed on the face, or fettered around the neck with a thick metal collar. The use of such collars was common, often inscribed with the abbreviation "TMQF," for *Tene me quia fugio*, "hold on to me since I flee" (Joshel, 120). Glancy, observing that some Christians were slaveholders, points out that most ancient slave collars that have been recovered are post-Constantinian, and many "bear Christian iconography, such as the alpha and the omega or the chi-rho figure" (Glancy, 88). Ironically, the collar may have been perceived as more humane, as Emperor Constantine forbade tattooing or branding on the face.

Some runaway slaves fled abusive treatment seeking intercession from an *amicus domini*, "friend of the master," and may not have been considered fugitives (Fitzmyer). *Digest* 21.1.17.4 describes a truant (*erro*), rather than *fugitivus*, who hid at the home of a friend of his master until the master's anger abated. Scholars debate the intercession versus runaway hypotheses in discussions of how Onesimus was able to meet imprisoned Paul in the letter to Philemon (e.g., McKnight 2017, 37-41; Young, 25-59).

1.4. Manumission. Increasing numbers of scholars question earlier analyses that asserted manumission was relatively frequent in the Roman Empire. Harrill declares that the commonly held view in NT studies that Roman slaves were automatically released after six years of service or at the age of thirty is mistaken, and asserts that "only a fraction of slaves actually were freed in Roman society—most, especially those laboring in agriculture or the mines, never saw freedom" (Harrill 2016, 310; cf. Bradley 1984, 81-112). It is impossible to know the percentage of slaves freed through manumission, which was primarily available to the *urbani* and likely stipulated in a master's will. In some cases, the enslaved were freed for economic reasons and not altruistic ones, since acquiring a new slave could be more cost-efficient than caring for an older, weakened slave. Manumission provided a degree of enfranchisement but was not emancipation—the end of legal subordination. The *paterfamilias* emancipated sons and daughters but manumitted slaves. With manumission, a freed person (*libertus* or *libertinus*) might still be identified as "of" their former owner, having entered a patron-client relationship, and expected to remain continually deferential to their former masters. Legal obligations (*operae*) continued to bind freed people to their patrons.

Under Caesar Augustus, three laws affected the practice of manumission: (1) the *lex Fufia Caninia* (2 BC) set limits on the number of slaves owners could set free, (2) the *lex Aelia Sentia* (AD 4) required slaveowners to be twenty years old and slaves thirty years old (not to be assumed, given the arduous life of a slave) before manumission, (3) the *lex Junia* gave a freed slave new status but not full *citizenship. Even so, some freed persons, especially those of the *familia Caesaris*, rose to positions of relative prominence, such as Governor Felix, a freed slave of Emperor Claudius, who presided over Paul's defense in Caesarea (Acts 23:24).

2. Slavery and the Enslaved in Pauline Literature.

Enslaved as well as freed persons appear frequently in the background and occasionally in the foreground of NT writings, as in the case of the aforementioned Felix. As for Pauline writings, enslaved people appear in the background as parts of households (Greek *oikos* and *oikia* are equivalent to the Latin *familia*). Examples include Chloe's household (1 Cor 1:11), the household of Stephanas (1 Cor 1:16; 16:15), the households of Aristobulus and Narcissus (Rom 16:10-11), and Caesar's household (Phil 4:22). Onesimus, although silent, is an example of a slave in the foreground, as Paul's letter to Philemon addresses the potentially new relationship between Onesimus and Philemon.

The apostle Paul (along with other NT writers) portrays his awareness of slavery while neither endorsing nor condemning the institution. Similarly, there are several parables of Jesus in the Synoptic Gospels that feature slaves without denouncing the system (e.g., Mt 18:23-25; Mk 13:32-37; Lk 17:7-10). This lack of indictment of slavery enabled enslavers in Europe and the New World to offer biblical support for their practices. In the United States, the NT was regularly used in attempts to make enslaved Africans docile or even content with the situation imposed on them.

Perhaps to minimize the potential negative impact of the NT's silence on the institution of slavery, some contemporary scholars argue that Greco-Roman slavery was not as cruel as slavery in the New World. Yet, historians and other scholars have determined that ancient slavery could be extremely cruel. It is true that ancient slavery did not have a racial component that functioned like that of slavery in Europe and the Americas, but the social control of enslaved people is evident in all slave societies. Rather than trying to contrast degrees of injustice, it may be best simply to acknowledge the Bible's silence. Lynn Cohick, however, building from the claim in Ephesians 6:9 that God shows no favoritism, argues that "the biblical case against slavery is strong" (Cohick, 390). Slavery was part of quotidian existence in antiquity, and while often acknowledged, it is not typically explained or otherwise evaluated in the Bible.

As for Paul, it may be that his relative privilege as a Roman citizen (Acts 16:37; 21:39; 22:25-29) disabled him from perceiving the injustice of the institution. Scot McKnight goes so far as to say, "Paul did not so much turn a blind eye to the morality of slavery as he did not realize slavery was an issue of morality. Paul was blind to the immorality of slavery as an institution" (McKnight, 11). Paul focuses instead on the dynamics of an alternative community, the *ekklēsia* ("*church"), where sibling relationships based on *faith in *Christ challenged Rome's emphasis on status.

2.1. Paul's Slavery Imagery. Paul's writings frequently employ the vocabulary of slavery theologically, to refer to followers of Christ or to the benefits associated with faith in Christ. Examples include *doulos* (slave, servant), *lytrōsis* (ransom, redemption), and *eleutheria* (*freedom), along with their cognates. Paul occasionally identifies himself as a "slave of Jesus" (Rom 1:1; Gal 1:10; and along with Timothy in Phil 1:1) or "slave of God" (Titus 1:1; cf. Jas 1:1; 2 Pet 1:1; Jude 1). In Colossians, Tychicus (Col 4:7) and Epaphras (Col 1:4) are each referred to as "fellow slave" (*syndoulos*), with the latter also called "slave of Christ" (Col 4:12). Paul did not conceive of freedom as the absence of any restraint. Freedom from *sin as master (as in Rom 6:5-23, or *stoichea*, "elemental forces," as in Gal 4:3, 9) meant enslavement to a new Master. Being a slave of Christ meant freedom from having sin dominate the physical body's actions (e.g., Rom 6:13). Ransom, the payment that provided freedom, came through Jesus (e.g., Rom 3:24; Col 1:14).

Some scholars see the "servant of God" motif in Jewish literature (e.g., Is 42–53) as primarily the source of Paul's slavery-related language, while others view Paul's theological use of slave imagery as coming from the Greco-Roman world. The Jewish background evokes honor to Jewish minds because OT heroes such as Moses (e.g., Deut 34:5; Neh 10:29; Dan 9:11) were called "slaves of God." Within the Greco-Roman world's social order, the enslaved of a high-ranking official (e.g., those of Caesar's household) held greater status than the slave of someone of lower rank. Likewise, being a "slave of Christ" signaled higher status than "slave of anyone else" (D. B. Martin, xx-xxiii). The slave of Christ/God is entrusted to serve the perfect Master (the NT uses the rare word *despotēs* at times to refer to God, as in Acts 4:24, and twice for Jesus, 2 Pet 2:1; Jude 4; *kyrios*, "lord," is most common).

The Greco-Roman world's practice of slavery seems to provide Paul with a picture of the all-encompassing nature of service. Slaves of Christ are obedient to the *Lord in every way. One need not confine Paul's slavery imagery to one particular aspect of his life. As with other matters related to Paul, it seems likely that his ideas and language were formed by both his Jewish and his Greco-Roman contexts (Goodrich).

2.2. Galatians 3:28; 1 Corinthians 12:13; Colossians 3:11. These three passages include the slave/free and Jew/*Gentile (Greek) antitheses, with Galatians 3:28 including male/female and Colossians 3:11 adding circumcised/uncircumcised along with Barbarian and Scythian. Paul describes his nonhierarchical (anti-imperial) view of Christian relationships, as believers are to be united "*in Christ." As Brad Braxton contends, "Paul pleads for the eradication of *dominance*, not the erasure of *difference*" (340). It is unlikely that the early Christians envisioned a society without distinctions. However, the ethnic, sex, and social-class stratification of the broader culture were not to undermine the oneness of the growing Christian movement. The community's egalitarianism was not solely about status in the eyes of God; it had to affect human interactions in the present. The relationships between Christian siblings were to be characterized by mutuality (Eph 5:21) in order that conflicts, such as those among the Corinthians as well as the Galatians, would disappear. Paul does not advocate for a utopian Roman society but for an altogether new community maintained by *love through the *Holy Spirit (e.g., 1 Cor 13; Gal 5:22). Paul's words in the three passages (and arguably elsewhere) signal equality and enabled enslaved African Americans to see the injustice of their situation (Smith). Slave-owners in the New World, claiming faith in Christ and quoting Scripture, betrayed their hypocrisy by enslaving fellow believers.

2.3. 1 Corinthians 7:20-24. This passage is one of the few places (along with the household codes, discussed below) where Paul addresses enslaved Christians directly. It may also be the closest readers get to Paul's views on manumission (see Philemon discussion below). Paul wrote 1 Corinthians in response to correspondence from *tōn Chloēs*, "those of Chloe," which likely included enslaved Christians (1 Cor 1:11). Commentators address the confusing syntax of 1 Corinthians 7:21, where Paul does not supply an object for the phrase *mallon* *chrēsai*, "all the more make use of." Consequently, the last part of 1 Corinthians 7:21 is literally, "But if you are indeed able to become free, all the more make use of ____." Some scholars suggest Paul points to slaves making use of their enslaved status, whether or not freedom is an option (NRSV: "Even if you can gain your freedom, make use of your present condition now more than ever"). However, most modern scholarship views Paul as urging enslaved Christians who are able to gain their freedom to make the most of that new status (e.g., NIV: "although if you can gain your freedom, do so") (see Byron 2003, 234-57, for a history of interpretation of 1 Cor 7:21).

Despite the exegetical difficulties of 1 Corinthians 7:21, it seems that Paul's overall argument is to place both slave and free within the Lord's household. Slaves should not be concerned that their societal role prevents them from living as a follower of Jesus (Garland). The free person is actually a slave of Christ, while a measure of *honor is conferred on an enslaved person who becomes *apeleutheros*, "a freed person," with the Lord as patron. Yet even as Paul's main argument is theological, focusing on God's calling, he touches on the actual situation of slaves. Paul does not argue for abolition of slavery but acknowledges that manumission should be pursued if possible.

2.4. The Household Codes. The *Haustafeln*, or household codes, appear in letters where Pauline authorship is disputed, Ephesians 5:21–6:9 and Colossians 3:18–4:1 (see also 1 Pet 2:18–3:7). The codes reflect the organization of the *familia* and have proven to be an obstacle for many contemporary readers in light of patriarchal oppression as well as slavery in Europe and the New World. Clarice Martin argues that "the *Haustafeln* in Colossians, Ephesians, and 1 Peter—all written after AD 70—reflect an attempt to restrict the enthusiasm of women and slaves and thus restore order to the patriarchal household" (213). Martin views the household codes as an oppressive corrective to "disruptions" of the typical family in light of the growing Christian movement's liberative message. Assigning the household codes to a time after Paul might allow Bible readers to absolve the apostle of proslavery accusations directed against him, but the presence of the codes in the NT canon remains a hermeneutical challenge.

As part of their strategy of social control, slaveowners in the New World weaponized the household codes' command that slaves obey their masters (Eph 5:5-8; Col 3:22-25; see also 1 Pet 2:18-21), and a similar argument can be made for how commands directed to wives have been used to subjugate women for centuries. However, the NT *Haustafeln* reflect a degree of deviation from typical Roman societal stratification in at least three ways: (1) Those in the subordinate position are to be motivated by the lordship of Christ more so than by societal requirements. For example, the addresses to enslaved Christians in Ephesians 6:5-8 and Colossians 3:22-25 require that service be rendered as if working directly for the Lord Jesus Christ, with the expectation of godly reward, or inheritance. (2) Paul commands those in dominant positions—husbands, fathers, and masters—not solely those in the subordinate roles. Rather than functioning like Roman laws designed to regulate property, the instructions to those in the socially dominant roles urge loving and respectful attitudes as well as behaviors. In Colossians 4:1, for example, earthly masters are told that they have a heavenly Master who can see whether slaves are treated justly (*dikaion*) and equitably (*isotēta*). (3) Those in the subordinate position are addressed alongside those in the dominant position because both groups are fellow members of the Christian community. Whereas Stoics directed their exhortations on slavery to the socially elite, the household codes are directed to the entire church. For NT writers, social standing might remain, but social control must not.

As noted above, Paul (and *Peter, for that matter) may have been blind to slavery's immorality, although Peter could describe slaveowners' actions as unjust (1 Pet 2:19). The household codes apparently functioned in part as sort of a survival manual for early followers of Jesus. It directed the believers to conform to societal norms, at least to some degree, which potentially allowed them to avoid harsh scrutiny from outsiders. Yet they embarked on a journey of reconfiguring the power dynamics within their relationships as they were now sisters and brothers.

2.5. 1 Timothy 1:10; 6:1-2; Titus 2:9-10. These passages within two Pastoral Epistles are often treated separately by scholars from the aforementioned household codes. Slave traders appear in the vice list of 1 Timothy 1:10. People involved in kidnapping and directly peddling human bodies were particularly notorious in the ancient world. Although 1 Timothy 1:10 demonstrates that an aspect of slavery is denounced within the Pauline corpus, the same letter of 1 Timothy includes the admonition for all those "under the yoke of slavery" to honor their masters (1 Tim 6:1-2). The words to Titus similarly include the admonition for enslaved people to be submissive and to avoid stereotypical behaviors associated with slaves: backtalk and thievery. Paul may have lacked the foresight or imagination to envision a society without slavery. His focus is on Christian *kinship (1 Tim 6:1-2) and *gospel *witness (Titus 2:9-10) rather than social position.

2.6. Philemon. John Chrysostom is one of the earliest interpreters to find in Philemon theological legitimacy for slavery. Many interpreters followed Chrysostom and used Philemon to justify slavery. Advocates of America's Fugitive Slave Act of 1850 used Philemon to support their legislation.

Without the voice of Onesimus, scholars largely assume him to be a fugitive and thief (Philem 18) because such behavior was described as characteristic of slaves in the ancient world, even though Paul does not describe Onesimus in such terms. However, with increasing numbers of African American scholars seeking to discern the circumstances surrounding the silent slave Onesimus, there is less dependence on negative stereotypes of enslaved men and women (e.g., Johnson, Noel, and Williams; Brogdon). Instead, more focus is being placed on Philemon as the possible reason why Onesimus came in contact with Paul. Rather than being a fugitive, Onesimus may have been the victim of Philemon's abuse and sought Paul's intercession as *amicus domini* (noted above). It is also possible that Onesimus was sent by Philemon to care for the imprisoned Paul. What becomes clear, however, is Paul's recognition that the relationship between followers of Christ should not reflect Rome's hierarchical patterns.

Some scholars suggest that Paul is directing the manumission of Onesimus, even though the apostle does not say it directly. Manumission, as noted above, could grant Onesimus certain privileges but would not change the fundamental relationship between him and Philemon (Brogdon). Paul appears to be interested in Philemon recognizing that the "*fellowship of the faith" (*hē koinōnia tēs pisteōs* in Philem 6) includes kinship with enslaved believers. Kinship characterizes the Christian community. Onesimus became Paul's "child" through conversion (Philem 10). Philemon is to receive Onesimus no longer as a slave but in a better relationship, that of brother (Philem 17). One is left to imagine the impact of Paul's words on Philemon's entire household, since other slaves surely heard the letter being read or at least knew Onesimus's story.

NT writings emerge from a patriarchal and socially stratified society where slavery was a part of daily life. The Pauline letters attest to the reality of slavery in the Greco-Roman world, sometimes addressing enslaved people directly while at other times mentioning them in passing. Slavery also describes the apostle's self-perception in relationship to Jesus Christ. While Paul does not endorse or challenge the institution of slavery directly, he arguably sows the seeds for its demise by employing his readers to live as members of an egalitarian community of sisters and brothers.

See also EMPIRE; HELLENISM, ROMAN; HOUSEHOLDS AND HOUSEHOLD CODES; INTERPRETATION: AFRICAN AMERICAN; PASTORAL EPISTLES; PHILEMON, LETTER TO; POLITICS AND POWER; URBAN SETTING OF PAUL'S CHURCHES.

BIBLIOGRAPHY. **S. S. Bartchy,** "Slavery (Greco-Roman)," *ABD* 6:58-73; **M. Beard,** *SPQR: A History of Ancient Rome* (New York: Liveright, 2015); **K. R. Bradley,** *Slaves and Masters in the Roman Empire: A Study in Social Control* (New York: Oxford University Press, 1987); idem, *Slavery and Society at Rome*, Key Themes in Ancient History (New York: Cambridge University Press, 1994); **B. R. Braxton,** "Galatians," in *True to Our Native Land: An African-American New Testament Commentary*, ed. B. K. Blount et. al. (Minneapolis: Fortress, 2007), 333-47; **L. Brogdon,** *A Companion to Philemon*, Cascade Companions (Eugene, OR: Cascade Books, 2018); **J. Byron,** *Slavery Metaphors in Early Judaism and Pauline Christianity: A Traditio-Historical and Exegetical Examination*, WUNT 162 (Tübingen: Mohr Siebeck, 2003); idem, *Recent Research on Paul and Slavery*, RRBS 3 (Sheffield: Sheffield Phoenix, 2008); **R. Charles,** *The Silencing of Slaves in Early Jewish and Christian Texts*, RSECW (New York: Routledge, 2019; **L. H. Cohick,** *The Letter to the Ephesians*, NICNT (Grand Rapids, MI: Eerdmans, 2020); **D. B. Davis,** *Inhuman Bondage: The Rise and Fall of Slavery in the New World* (New York: Oxford University Press, 2006); **J. A. Fitzmyer,** *The Letter to Philemon: A New Translation with Introduction and Commentary*, AB 34C (New York: Doubleday, 2000); **D. E. Garland,** *1 Corinthians*, BECNT (Grand Rapids, MI: Baker Academic, 2003); **J. A. Glancy,** *Slavery in Early Christianity* (New York: Oxford University Press, 2002); **J. K. Goodrich,** "From Slaves of Sin to Slaves of God: Reconsidering the Origin of Paul's Slavery Metaphor in Romans 6," *BBR* 23 (2013): 509-30; **J. A. Harrill,** *Slaves in the New Testament: Literary, Social, and Moral Dimensions* (Minneapolis: Fortress, 2006); idem, "Paul and Slavery," in *Paul in the Greco-Roman World: A Handbook*, rev. ed., ed. J. P. Sampley (London: Bloomsbury T&T Clark, 2016), 301-45; **P. Hunt,** *Ancient Greek and Roman Slavery* (Hoboken, NJ: Wiley-Blackwell, 2018); **M. V. Johnson, J. A. Noel, and D. K. Williams,** eds., *Onesimus, Our Brother: Reading Religion, Race, and Culture in Philemon*, Paul in Critical Contexts (Minneapolis: Fortress, 2012); **S. R. Joshel,** *Slavery in the Roman World*, Cambridge Introduction to Roman Civilization (New York: Cambridge University Press, 2010); **C. J. Martin,** "The *Haustafeln* (Household Codes) in African American Interpretation: 'Free Slaves' and 'Subordinate Women,'" in *Stony the Road We Trod: African American Biblical Interpretation*, ed. C. H. Felder (Minneapolis: Fortress, 1991), 206-31; **D. B. Martin,** *Slavery as Salvation: The Metaphor of Slavery in Pauline Christianity* (New Haven, CT: Yale University Press, 1990); **S. McKnight,** *The Letter to Philemon*, NICNT (Grand Rapids, MI: Eerdmans, 2017); **T. Mommsen, P. Krueger, and A. Watson,** eds., *The Digest of Justinian* (Philadelphia: University of Pennsylvania Press, 1985); **O. Patterson,** *Slavery and Social Death: A Comparative Study; With a New Preface* (Cambridge, MA: Harvard University Press, 2018); **A. A. Rupprecht,** "Slave, Slavery," *DPL*, 881-83; **M. Smith,** "Slavery in the Early Church," in *True to Our Native Land: An African-American New Testament Commentary*, ed. B. K. Blount et. al. (Minneapolis: Fortress, 2007), 11-22; **T. E. J. Wiedemann,** "The Regularity of Manumission at Rome," *ClQ* 35 (1985): 162-75; **S. E. Young,** *Our Brother Beloved: Purpose and Community in Paul's Letter to Philemon* (Waco, TX: Baylor University Press, 2021).

D. R. Edwards

SOCIAL INSTITUTIONS. *See* SOCIAL-SCIENTIFIC APPROACHES TO PAUL; URBAN SETTING OF PAUL'S CHURCHES.

SOCIAL SETTING OF MISSION CHURCHES. *See* URBAN SETTING OF PAUL'S CHURCHES.

SOCIAL-SCIENTIFIC APPROACHES TO PAUL

When the first edition of the *Dictionary of Paul and His Letters* was written, social-scientific approaches to the NT were fairly new in biblical studies. It was right therefore for that entry to spend considerable time explaining the approach and presenting the strengths and weaknesses of social-scientific approaches. Those strengths and weaknesses still apply, so revisiting the original entry for that perspective is recommended. Nearly thirty years on, however, the value of social-scientific ways of thinking about NT writings and early Christians is well established and represented broadly in the field.

Social-scientific approaches to the NT are those that draw on anthropological and sociological ways of thinking about people, communities, and texts. These approaches consider issues such as the construction of self and other, *friendship and social interaction, *kinship and *marriage, gender, ritual, education and literacy, economics and exchange, social stratification, elite governance and popular resistance, and more. The root assumption is that the world of the NT is culturally very different from the world of most North American and Western European readers of the NT, something that can be missed when one reads the NT in a modern language. Therefore, understanding the NT requires one to understand the culture behind (as well as in and around) the language of the NT. Put differently, in order to understand the NT, one has to translate not only the words but also the culture, making both language and culture understandable to a modern reader.

The imperative of a culture-rich reading of the NT applies, of course, to reading the letters of Paul as well. Paul was a first-century Mediterranean writing to other first-century Mediterranean persons. This entry will highlight some of the insights into Paul and his associations that have been gained from asking social-scientific questions.

1. Models Versus Description.

When John Elliott wrote *What Is Social-Scientific Criticism?* (1993) he was charting a new course for the study of the social context of ancient Mediterranean texts such as the NT. Elliott (as well as Malina 1981) differentiated between social *description* (reflected in the work of Hock; Holmberg; Meeks; Theissen) and social-scientific criticism based on the explicit use of models. The models in question were drawn from the social sciences and were meant to provide the means for interpreting texts and cultures that avoided ethnocentrism (that is, reading oneself into the texts). Since it is universal to read from one's own cultural location, the use of a model functions like a lens, allowing readers to see things they might otherwise miss—being foreign to the culture they are reading *in* (as opposed to *from*).

This feature was sometimes characterized as *creating evidence* where there was none, but that was a misunderstanding (Horrell, 91). Any cultural production (e.g., language, monuments, social interaction) assumes certain things of the reader or viewer: that one is an insider and does not need *everything* explained or provided. A model developed from data drawn from that or a similar culture provides those things that an insider could be assumed to know. This is how models work, and all readers read through one: the only question is whether the use of that model is implicit or—better—made explicit (Esler 2000). If through the 1990s–2000s the pendulum had swung wholly away from social description to the practice and robust defense of modeling, it could perhaps be described now as having swung to a middle position, in which the explicit use of models and rich social description operate alongside each other in social-scientific approaches to the NT.

2. Paul's Ancient Mediterranean Culture.

The categories below represent a mix of approaches that are foundational to social-scientific ways of thinking about Paul and others that are current and still fruitful, but the categories are not meant to be exhaustive. They ask the question: What might we know or be able to speculate about Paul (or his associations) when we use these categories as heuristic tools?

2.1. Personality. All people are the product of their culture. Even when someone is being *countercultural*, their act of cultural resistance is still only meaningful within that particular cultural setting. This is not to imply that people cannot inhabit several, and sometimes conflicting, cultural groups—such as a first-century Judean (a more accurate rendition of *Ioudaios* than "Jew") like Paul living among Greeks. One amazing feature of culture and cultural difference is that there can be so many variations of it: *Jerusalem Judeans could be quite culturally distinct from Galilean Judeans, and those two from Egyptian Judeans and Asia Minor Judeans. Being "Judean" did not mean one thing, but it did carry a certain set of characteristics to make it feasible to group them all into a single category. Like Judeans, Greeks shared a certain number of characteristics that, at a higher level of abstraction, make it possible to group them all into a single category, despite important regional variations. And similarly with the category Roman. From there, moving to an even higher level of abstraction, one can say that Judeans, Greeks, and Romans all shared some characteristics that make it possible to group them all into a single category: ancient Mediterraneans, distinct culturally (for our purposes) from modern North Americans and Europeans. Thus, it should be possible to see what Judeans, Greeks, and Romans had in common without ignoring what made them different.

Ancient Mediterranean people were enculturated to be collectivistic, while in general North American and Northern European people (by far the global minority) are enculturated to be individualistic (Geertz; Hofstede, Hofstede, and Minkov). These terms—*collectivism* and *individualism*—are relational, in that they refer to how people in collectivistic or individualistic cultures *tend* to imagine themselves *in relation* to others (Triandis). In a collectivistic setting, the needs of the group tend to take precedence over the needs of the individual. A collectivistic person finds value in the group. In an individualistic setting, the needs of the individual tend to take precedence, and one's value comes from within oneself. Put simply, a person enculturated as an individualist might want their parents' approval in their career choice and marriage partner, but fellow individualists would not think less of them for overruling their parents' opinions on these matters. In a collectivistic society, parental/group wishes carry far more weight. It is not that a collectivistic person *cannot* overrule the expectations of the collective—there are many examples of this very thing happening in antiquity, from people becoming Cynics or Christ-followers to patricide, prostitution, and child abandonment (Malina 2010, 23). Rather, it is that the instincts of most collectivistic people are not to overrule the expectations of the collective and to find meeting those expectations personally fulfilling. There were consequences to not fitting in, and one became open to ostracization and labels of deviance. To this end, the famed Greek maxim "Know thyself" thus meant something very different to ancient Greeks than to modern Americans. It likely meant something akin to "Know your place" or "Know your role."

In collectivistic societies, the most basic element of the collective is the family. The individual is—ideally—embedded within a family, which is embedded in a village/city, which is embedded within an *ethnos*, and so on. Paul does not speak of his family directly, but it is surely implied in his claim to be fully embedded in the *ethnos* of *Israel (Phil 3:5), for that was his parents' doing, not his own. On the other hand, Paul does spend considerable time talking about the new family-like units he is organizing. Anthropologists used to call this phenomenon "fictive kinship" but no longer do. This is primarily because the term implies a looser bond between fictive kin than between actual kin, and this is definitely not always the case. "Voluntary collectivism" (Duling and Rohrbaugh) is a better term for it, and its language dominates in Paul's letters. God is referred to as Father twenty-three times in the undisputed letters. Every single letter opening of Paul includes it. He even calls himself the "father" of the Corinthians (1 Cor 4:15), the Thessalonians (1 Thess 2:11), and Timothy (Phil 2:22) and Philemon (Philem 10). But amazingly, Paul addresses the letter recipients (using the vocative) as "brothers" over sixty times. Few people would contest that Christ-following associations represented parallel kinship units to the Greco-Roman family (Elliott 1990).

Another way in which this topic matters for Paul has to do with his so-called *conversion experience. The tendency among modern Western scholars has been to see Paul's conversion as highly emotional and psychologically traumatic. This is in keeping with the modern Western perspective on the self as introspective and emotionally aware (Stendahl) but also on conversion as individualistic and necessarily emotional (going back to William James and Arthur Darby Nock). This, however, does not match the language of ancient Mediterraneans, for whom conversion from one god to another was expressed in the language of divine benefactions and client obligation (Crook, *Reconceptualising Conversion*; de Silva). There may sometimes have been emotion involved, but emotion was not the primary feature of ancient conversion; rather, it was an assessment that one god was more generous or caring than another. The term *charis*, a favorite of Paul (used twenty-nine times in Luke–Acts and John, never in Mark or Matthew, and sixty-five times in the undisputed Pauline letters), has tended to be translated as **grace*. However, the term appears commonly in settings relating to the giving of benefactions from a patron to a client (Harrison). Thus, in 1 Corinthians 3:10 Paul refers to the benefaction that was given to him (referring to the vision of the risen *Christ in Gal 1:15), and in 1 Corinthians 15:10 he refers to executing his appropriate client obligation to *God for that benefaction (Crook 2008).

2.2. Social Interaction. The importance of understanding *honor and shame in the ancient Mediterranean cannot be underestimated (Malina 1981), even if it is no longer a cutting-edge topic. That honor was a highly sought-after and limited good explains many features of the ancient Mediterranean world, including *patronage and the necessity of gratitude, generosity, *hospitality, and *righteousness; the proliferation of honorary inscriptions; gift exchange; dress and gender; and public social interactions. Honor was about a claim to worth, about reputation, and it required a public acceptance of that claim. Honor gained at birth (attributed honor) was reflected in an elite family name, in one's sex, or in one's *citizenship (see Gal 1:14 and Phil 3:5-6 for Paul's ascribed honor). Honor gained (or lost) in daily social interactions (distributed honor) was much more dynamic and required the active participation of the observing public court of reputation (Crook 2009). One sees the face-to-face honor dynamics (known as challenge and riposte) reflected in Paul's recollection of a painful visit to *Corinth (2 Cor 2:1-4) that was enough to make him write the "letter of tears" (which arguably survives in 2 Cor 10–13) and in his challenge to *Peter in Antioch over the applicability of Jewish *law to *Gentile converts (Gal 2:11-14; E. Stewart 2011). Further, at the heart of Paul's theology of the *cross lies the belief that Jesus' shameful *death (Gal 3:13; Phil 2:8) was transformed into something honorable and glorious (Phil 2:9-11).

Patronage and clientage was a key feature of ancient social interaction because there was much honor to be gained through acts of patronage and benefaction (E. Stewart 2010; Wallace-Hadrill; Saller). Patronage and benefaction, though not identical to each other (Joubert), are systems of exchange between parties of unequal status with unequal access to goods: a client is someone in need of something, and someone else becomes a patron when they bestow it. Honor, loyalty (commonly marked by the term *pistis*; see Crook, "BTB Readers' Guide"), and publicly expressed gratitude were the obligation of every client. This human relationship and its language can also be found in writing about human engagement with the gods in Greek, Roman, Judean, and Christ-following literature. Paul, for instance, boasts of the many benefactions (*charis*) his God can give (Harrison; Neyrey 2004). In addition, Paul frames Jesus as broker, that is, as the one who mediates between God the patron and humanity: see especially Romans 1:8; 7:25, but also most of the letter openings (Batten, "Brokerage"), where access to God and benefactions from God pass *dia* (through) Jesus, as with any broker in a relationship of patronage or benefaction. Finally, as appropriate, Paul gives thanks publicly to God the patron (Rom 1:8; 1 Cor 1:4, 14; 14:18; Phil 1:3; 1 Thess 1:2; 2:13; Philem 4).

Bruce Malina claims that honor and shame were gendered, in that honor was the purview of males, and shame of females (Malina 1981). This is accurate in many ways, in that honor could be associated with courage, assertiveness, aggression, and was public, and for a male to be shamed was a terrible thing, while *women embodied shame. While these features of honor and shame are accurate, they do not tell the whole story (Roberts). Shame is not solely a negative feature to be avoided. Shame is the appropriate recognition of a social superior's status, and everyone had to have it, including men. To be "shameless" was as inappropriate for men as it was for women. Conversely, women did participate in public acts of benefaction and patronage and were honored for it (Brooten 1982; Crook 2009). Paul calls Phoebe *prostatis* at Romans 16:2, which explicitly marks her as a woman of means providing patronage to an association of Christ-followers at Cenchreae near Corinth. In addition, Paul receives news of events in Corinth from "Chloe's people" (1 Cor 1:11), suggesting that Chloe had clients to run errands for her. Finally, a dispute between two women in Philippi, Euodia and Syntyche (Phil 4:2-3), was enough of a concern to Paul that he named them and encouraged the group to assist them. If their dispute was a threat to the stability of the group, this could indicate that these were women of prominence and authority. Honor, culture, and gender also intersect in dress and accoutrement (Batten, "BTB Readers' Guide"; Batten and Olson). Clothing and accoutrement (or lack of accoutrement) expressed social standing (status and power), ethnic or communal identity (culture, sectarianism), and appropriate modesty/masculinity (gender).

Finally, one of the most interesting features of ancient Mediterranean social interaction was the prevalence of evil eye belief and practice. Evil eye belief and practice was rooted in envy—not only wanting what others have but wanting it destroyed if you could not have it—and in ancient understandings of the eye, namely that the eye betrays and emits one's true feelings. Because the evil eye could not be controlled, measures had to be taken to protect oneself (e.g., gestures, colors, prophylactics), because the evil eye was dangerous and could not be controlled. Paul accuses his opponents of sneaking into Galatia behind him and undoing all his work there, which they did by casting the evil eye (the verb *baskainō*) on them (Gal 3:1; Elliott, "Paul, Galatians and the Evil Eye"). A common complaint of those interested in social-scientific approaches to the NT is that modern translations too often obscure the socially significant features in the text, and this is an excellent example: "bewitched" (NRSV) sounds more like Hollywood fancies of *magic than serious ancient Mediterranean concerns (Elliott 2016).

2.3. Economic and Social Standing. One of the longest-standing beliefs about the earliest Pauline associations (replicated in modern scholarship by Meggitt 1998) is that their membership was drawn exclusively from the lowest and poorest segments of society. Gerd Theissen, however, claims that 1 Corinthians reveals a greater degree of social and economic diversity than has traditionally been thought. Slowly but surely, scholars have begun to pay more attention to the question of the economic realities of ancient life and how these might have affected the people in Paul's communities (and Paul himself).

Steven Friesen and Bruce Longenecker have contributed the most to the understanding of ancient economic stratification. Friesen began by positing an economic model with seven levels of *wealth/poverty. That he called it a "poverty scale" (PS) reveals much about the ancient world, namely that wealth resided in the hands of very few. For Friesen, subsistence was the measure differentiating the economic strata in the Roman Empire. The levels PS1-3 reflected the elites of society: imperial elites (PS1), regional or provincial elites (PS2), and municipal elites (PS3). These people never had to worry about subsistence; they enjoyed massive surpluses. Together these three strata accounted for not even 3 percent of the population. People in PS4 had a moderate surplus and were likely well-off merchants, traders, artisans, shop owners, farmers, and regular wage earners. Even these people were rare, amounting perhaps to 7 percent of the population (Friesen is clear about how speculative this number in particular is). People in PS5 comprised those who lived just above the level of subsistence but had a reasonable hope of staying above it. Nonetheless, even for these people—also merchants, traders, artisans, shop owners, farmers, and regular wage earners—dipping below subsistence level was always a possibility. People at PS5 comprised approximately 22 percent of the population, Friesen speculates.

Then there was the rest: 68 percent of the population, comprising PS6 (those living sometimes at and often below the level of subsistence: 40 percent of the population) and PS7 (those for whom the level of subsistence was an impossibility: 28 percent of the population). Longenecker (2009) accepts Friesen's ratios for PS1-3, estimates PS4 at 17 percent, PS5 at 25 percent, PS6 at 30 percent, and PS7 at 25 percent (though he renames the tiers "economy scales"). Longenecker (2010) later revised his own estimations, but the effect is much the same: his middling tiers (4 and 5) are a little larger than Friesen's, and his bottom two are a little smaller. In the end, the differences between Friesen and Longenecker are minimal: for both, a tiny percentage of the Roman population lived with a comfortable surplus, and more than 50 percent lived barely at or well below the level of subsistence.

Friesen and Longenecker agree on several other matters. First, no member of the Pauline associations represented the top three tiers. Second, most members of the Pauline associations likely came from the sixth and seventh tiers. Finally, there were *a few* association members who almost certainly came from the fourth and fifth tiers, and these people likely served as association patrons (Erastus, Phoebe, Chloe, Prisca and Aquila, Crispus, and Stephanus). Gaius is commonly listed among these names as an elite figure acting as patron, but Richard Last argues that Gaius was a guest in Corinth, not a host (and therefore he was not likely a patron of a Pauline association).

The question about Paul and economics should not overlook the topic of the *collection. It is interesting that it took so long for interpreters to put together that the fact of the collection meant that the Pauline communities could not have been composed solely of the poorest of the poor. They clearly had *some* disposable income. A second puzzling position on the collection is that Paul's instructions arose from confusion over how to raise and accumulate money. This might make sense if they were the sort of people who were so poor they had no experience with or *knowledge about money, but if they have *any* disposable income, then they know something about money. John Kloppenborg (2017) shows that Paul's comments addressed their concerns about the security and integrity of the collection, concerns that were typical among voluntary associations (see also Downs).

2.4. Social Formations. Edwin Hatch's assessment that the Pauline groups closely resembled Greco-Roman voluntary associations lay dormant for the better part of a century (Kloppenborg 1993; Ascough 2015). Now this is the most fertile area of research on the origins of Pauline Christianity, supplemented by the study of epigraphical remains, since many of the surviving inscriptions came from associations (Ascough, Harland, and Kloppenborg; A. C. Stewart).

Associations were common in the ancient Mediterranean. Associations formed around features held in common among members. The most common of these unifying features were *ethnicity, occupation, and cult. Examples of ethnic associations include immigrants from Asia Minor in Dacia north of Macedonia, immigrants from Sidon in Phoenicia, Egyptians on the Island of Kos, or Syrians on the island of Delos, among many other options. Occupational associations were formed around merchants, shippers, bakers, silversmiths, coppersmiths, purple dyers, garland makers, vegetable sellers, sack weavers, fishers, and so on. Finally, there were cultic associations devoted to Heracles, Dionysus, Zeus, Diana and Antinoüs, Mēn, and the God of Israel, among many others. These categories are not mutually exclusive, of course, for one frequently finds them combined: an association of priests (cultic and occupational), a Judean synagogue in Macedonia (ethnic and cultic), coral craftsmen (occupational) from Smyrna (ethnic) in Lydia, and, combining all three, Kitian (ethnic) merchants (occupational) applying to be allowed to make a shrine to Aphrodite (cultic).

A significant amount about ancient associations is known, but surprisingly little about Pauline groups (owing to the nature of the letters). However, categorizing the Pauline groups as associations opens up a wealth of comparative data. These data reveal that associations shared a number of features and concerns with Pauline associations: they commonly had socioeconomic diversity (1 Cor 1:26) as well as gender diversity (Phil 4:2-3), had free as well as freed members (1 Cor 16:17), were concerned about internal unity (1 Cor 1:10) and decorum (1 Cor 14:16), sought out connections to local civic elites (1 Cor 1:14; Rom 16:23; Acts 13:7-12), and maintained connections to other translocal groups (the collection) (see Ascough 1997; Kloppenborg 2019). This goes as well for Paul's use of the term *ekklēsiai* for his groups, which could also be a term for non-Christ-following associations, including claims that an association had been "called together" by the god of their devotion. In addition, the use of the language of "voluntary collectivism" (or "fictive kinship") is common to Greco-Roman and Pauline associations (Harland 2005; 2007).

Another feature one potentially learns about Pauline associations by comparison to non-Pauline associations concerns size. Cultic associations could be large (with close to 100 members) and very small (4 people). But a sample of 92 cultic association produces a mean of 29 members, a median of 24, but perhaps most tellingly a mode of 15 (Kloppenborg 2019). This might not indicate exactly the size of each or any of the Pauline associations, but it certainly provides limits and at least allows for imagining probabilities.

There are two possible complaints with comparing Pauline *ekklēsiai* to Greco-Roman associations. The first is that the two entities are different. This complaint assumes that Greco-Roman associations were uniform in terms of their form, characteristics, and function. This, however, is not the case. There was considerable variety among associations, such that it might not be a gross overstatement to say that no two were exactly alike. Thus, that there are differences between Pauline and other associations is not grounds for rejecting comparisons between Pauline *ekklēsiai* and other associations.

A second possible complaint is that the closest comparison for anything early Christian is (and must always remain) Judaism, and thus the synagogue is the closest comparison for Paul's associations. This complaint forgets that as little is known about ancient Mediterranean synagogues as about the Pauline groups. But more than that, it misses the point that in fact Judean synagogues *and* Pauline *ekklēsiai* are examples of ethnic and cultic associations. Thus, to compare Paul's *ekklēsiai* to synagogues is to compare them to another form of Greco-Roman cultic association.

2.5. *Ritual.* Surprisingly, given the importance to Paul of the *Lord's Supper and *baptism, ritual was for the longest time understudied and undertheorized in biblical studies. This is even more surprising when one considers that this is decidedly *not* the case for cultural anthropologists, on whom so many biblical scholars have drawn. This has changed recently, however, with Richard DeMaris (2008), Risto Uro (2016), and Jason Lamoreaux (2013) leading the way, as well as those who work on voluntary associations, since communal meals were a significant part of association life. The magisterial handbook from Oxford University Press cannot be missed (Uro et al.).

The most valuable work on ritual in Paul has been influenced by Victor Turner, Catherine Bell, and Ronald Grimes. A number of observations emerge from this work. Baptism can be understood as a ritual of initiation or a rite of passage (Meeks; DeMaris 1999), but it can also and perhaps better be understood as a political ritual. In keeping with the embedded nature of ancient religion in *politics, early Christ-followers used water in a way that set them apart—and against—Roman practices and thus served as a form of political resistance (Choi). More than that, of course, baptism also served a positive function in that it articulated the political unity of the community of Christ-followers, which can of course be said of the eucharistic meal. There is much to be learned by analogizing Pauline meals and Greco-Roman association meals (Vearncombe; Ascough 2019).

The newest addition to ritual studies has been the integration into it of the cognitive sciences. The cognitive sciences relate to how the mind operates and responds to stimuli. The application of the cognitive sciences to the Pauline letters asks one to consider the religious—which is to say, cognitive, psychological, social, and emotional—experiences of those who joined Paul's communities, and even Paul himself. For instance, the cognitive sciences allow one to go beyond the observation that the ritual of baptism represented a meaningful transition from one community to another (which it certainly did) and that the Lord's Supper fostered solidarity in the movement; the cognitive sciences show that rituals with a high cost (joining a minority movement) or high arousal generate trust and emotional bonding in humans (Uro). The cognitive sciences allow one to consider highly charged and emotional religious *experience* on the premise that, while culture has changed significantly between Paul's time and the present, human physiology and the human brain have not. So, discussing the psychological and cognitive aspects and benefits of glossolalia, *prophecy, and ecstatic trance has contributed much to the understanding of Paul's own experiences and those of his converts, by situating references from Paul's letters within cognitive-scientific frameworks (Shantz; Vearncombe).

3. Conclusion.

Paul was a first-century Judean opponent of Christ-followers who had an experience wherein his original loyalty (*pistis*) to Moses and Torah was supplemented or altered (but not replaced!) to include loyalty to Jesus the Messiah. However Paul himself actually experienced this (something one cannot know and which modern-day psychological thinking about conversion cannot indicate), he expressed it explicitly and implicitly in the language and imagery of divine patronage. The benefaction (*charis*) from God the patron that changed everything was a vision of the risen Christ (Gal 1:12; 1 Cor 15:10). Wholly consistent with his cultural location, this placed Paul in the position of client, obligated (1 Cor 9:16; 1 Cor 15:10) to reciprocate, which he exercised by honoring, praising, and giving thanks to God, as well as by expressing loyalty (*pistis*) to Christ and by establishing cultic associations in Greco-Roman cities with loyalty to Christ as their unifying feature. Naturally, this led to tensions (2 Cor 11:24) with his original community, as he founded several new associations where he also had to navigate the complex question of the place of Torah loyalty in these new communities, especially because they contained not only Judeans but Gentiles as well. Like many associations, Paul's association had a spectrum of socioeconomic diversity (in addition to

Judean-versus-Gentile ethnic diversity), resulting in crises to do with diet, meals, ritual, dress and appearance, unity, authority, and Torah observance. His letters and subsequent visits to his associations were his only means for addressing these crises, and without them, far less would be known about the process of this early spread of Christ-confessing associations.

In the first edition of this entry, Barton hoped that future work might be done on the social contexts not merely of Paul but of Paul's interpreters and the history of Pauline interpretation. This has not happened nearly to the extent that it has happened with scholarship on the historical Jesus, but it has begun (Tofighi; Hart). However, this work has emerged not under the auspices of social-scientific criticism but what one might call metacritism or ideological criticism.

Though this survey covers much, there is also much missing, some of which also relates quite obviously to some of the topics above: among others, social memory (Esler 2003; White), spatial theory (Økland; E. Stewart 2012), gossip/deviance/labeling theory (Esler 2004; Bazzana, "Deviance"; Stratton), and religious experience (Shantz; Shantz and Werline; Bazzana, *Having the Spirit of Christ*).

See also ANTHROPOLOGY, PAULINE; COLLECTION FOR THE SAINTS; HONOR/SHAME; HOUSEHOLDS AND HOUSEHOLD CODES; IDENTITY; KINSHIP LANGUAGE IN PAUL; MAGIC; PATRONAGE; PURITY AND IMPURITY; RELIGIONS, GRECO-ROMAN; WEALTH AND POVERTY; WOMEN.

BIBLIOGRAPHY. **R. S. Ascough,** "Translocal Relationships Among Voluntary Associations and Early Christianity," *JECS* 5 (1997): 223-41; idem, "What Are They Now Saying About Christ Groups and Associations?," *CurBR* 13 (2015): 207-44; idem, "Communal Meals," in *The Oxford Handbook of Early Christian Ritual*, ed. R. Uro et al. (Oxford: Oxford University Press, 2019), 204-29; **R. S. Ascough, P. A. Harland, and J. S. Kloppenborg,** *Associations in the Greco-Roman World: A Sourcebook* (Waco, TX: Baylor University Press, 2012); **A. Batten,** "Brokerage," in *Understanding the Social World of the New Testament*, ed. D. Neufeld and R. E. DeMaris (London: Routledge, 2010), 167-77; idem, "BTB Readers' Guide: Clothing and Adornment," *BTB* 40 (2010): 148-59; **A. J. Batten and K. Olson,** eds., *Dress in Mediterranean Antiquity: Greeks, Romans, Jews, Christians* (London: T&T Clark, 2021); **G. Bazzana,** "Deviance," in *The Ancient Mediterranean Social World: A Sourcebook*, ed. Z. A. Crook (Grand Rapids, MI: Eerdmans, 2020), 289-305; idem, *Having the Spirit of Christ: Spirit Possession and Exorcism in the Early Christ Groups* (New Haven, CT: Yale University Press, 2020); **B. J. Brooten,** *Women Leaders in the Ancient Synagogue. Inscriptional Evidence and Background Issues* (Chico, CA: Scholars Press, 1982); **A. Choi,** "Boundary-Crossing in Christian Baptism," in *Early Christian Ritual Life*, ed. R. E. DeMaris, J. T. Lamoreaux, and S. C. Muir (London: Routledge, 2018), 75-91; **Z. A. Crook,** "BTB Readers' Guide: Loyalty," *BTB* 34 (2004): 167-77; idem, *Reconceptualising Conversion: Patronage, Loyalty and Conversion in the Religions of the Ancient Mediterranean* (New York: de Gruyter, 2004); idem, "Grace as Benefaction in Galatians 2:9, 1 Corinthians 3:10, and Romans 12:3; 15:15," in *The Social Sciences and Biblical Translation*, ed. D. Neufeld (Atlanta: Society of Biblical Literature, 2008), 25-38; idem, "Honor, Shame, and Social Status Revisited," *JBL* 128 (2009): 591-611; **R. E. DeMaris,** "Funerals and Baptisms, Ordinary and Otherwise: Ritual Criticism and Corinthian Rites," *BTB* 29 (1999): 23-34; idem, *The New Testament in Its Ritual World* (London: Routledge, 2008); **D. A. de Silva,** *Honor, Patronage, Kinship & Purity: Unlocking New Testament Culture* (Downers Grove, IL: IVP Academic, 2000); **D. J. Downs,** *The Offering of the Gentiles: Paul's Collection for Jerusalem in Its Chronological, Cultural, and Cultic Contexts* (Grand Rapids, MI: Eerdmans, 2016); **D. Duling and R. Rohrbaugh,** "Collectivism," in *The Ancient Mediterranean Social World: A Sourcebook*, ed. Z. A. Crook (Grand Rapids, MI: Eerdmans, 2020), 93-110; **J. H. Elliott,** *A Home for the Homeless: A Social-Scientific Criticism of I Peter, Its Situation and Strategy* (Philadelphia: Augsburg Fortress, 1990); idem, "Paul, Galatians, and the Evil Eye," *CurTM* 17 (1990): 262-73; idem, *What Is Social-Scientific Criticism?* (Minneapolis: Fortress, 1993); idem, *Beware the Evil Eye*, vol. 3, *The Evil Eye in the Bible and the Ancient World* (Eugene, OR: Cascade Books, 2016); **P. F. Esler,** "Models in New Testament Interpretation: A Reply to David Horrell," *JSNT* 78 (2000): 107-13; idem, *Conflict and Identity in Romans: The Social Setting of Paul's Letter* (Minneapolis: Fortress, 2003); idem, "The Sodom Tradition in Romans 1:18-32," *BTB* 34 (2004): 4-16; **S. Friesen,** "Poverty in Pauline Studies: Beyond the So-Called New Consensus," *JSNT* 26 (2004): 323-61; **C. Geertz,** "From the Native's Point of View: On the Nature of Anthropological Understanding," in *Culture Theory: Essays on Mind, Self and Emotion*, ed. R. A. Shweder and R. A. LeVine (Cambridge: Cambridge University Press, 1984), 123-36; **P. A. Harland,** *Associations, Synagogues, and Congregations: Claiming a Place in Ancient*

Mediterranean Society (Minneapolis: Fortress, 2003); idem, "Familial Dimensions of Group Identity: 'Brothers' (ΑΔΕΛΦΟΙ) in Associations of the Greek East," *JBL* 124 (2005): 491-513; idem, "Familial Dimensions of Group Identity (II): 'Mothers' and 'Fathers' in Associations and Synagogues of the Greek World," *JSJ* 38 (2007): 57-79; **J. R. Harrison,** *Paul's Language of Grace in a Graeco-Roman Context* (Tübingen: Mohr Siebeck, 2003); **P. Hart,** *A Prolegomenon to the Study of Paul* (Leiden: Brill, 2020); **R. F. Hock,** *The Social Context of Paul's Ministry: Tentmaking and Apostleship* (Philadelphia: Fortress, 1980); **G. Hofstede, J. Hofstede, and M. Minkov,** *Cultures and Organizations: Software of the Mind,* 3rd ed. (New York: McGraw-Hill, 2010); **B. Holmberg,** *Paul and Power: The Structures of Authority in the Primitive Church as Reflected in the Pauline Epistles* (Philadelphia: Fortress, 1980); **D. Horrell,** "Models and Methods in Social-Scientific Interpretation: A Response to Philip Esler," *JSNT* 78 (2000): 83-105; **S. J. Joubert,** "One Form of Social Exchange or Two? 'Euergetism,' Patronage, and Testament Studies," *BTB* 31 (2001): 17-25; **J. S. Kloppenborg,** "Edwin Hatch, Churches and Collegia," in *Origins and Method: Towards a New Understanding of Judaism and Christianity; Essays in Honour of John C. Hurd,* ed. B. H. McLean (Sheffield: Sheffield Phoenix, 1993), 212-38; idem, "Paul's Collection for Jerusalem and the Financial Practices in Greek Cities," in *Paul and Economics: A Handbook,* ed. T. R. Blanton IV and R. Pickett (Minneapolis: Fortress, 2017), 307-32; idem, *Christ's Associations: Connecting and Belonging in the Ancient City* (New Haven, CT: Yale University Press, 2019); **J. S. Kloppenborg and R. S. Ascough,** *Greco-Roman Associations: Texts, Translations, and Commentary,* vol. 1, *Attica, Central Greece, Macedonia, Thrace* (Berlin: de Gruyter, 2011); **J. T. Lamoreaux,** *Ritual, Women, and Philippi: Reimagining the Early Philippian Community* (Eugene, OR: Cascade Books, 2013); **R. Last,** *The Pauline Church and the Corinthian Ekklēsia* (Cambridge: Cambridge University Press, 2015); **B. W. Longenecker,** "Socio-economic Profiling of the First Urban Christians," in *After the First Urban Christians: The Social-Scientific Study of Pauline Christianity Twenty-Five Years Later,* ed. T. D. Still and D. G. Horrell (London: Continuum, 2009), 36-59; idem, *Remember the Poor: Paul, Poverty, and the Greco-Roman World* (Grand Rapids: Eerdmans, 2010); **B. J. Malina,** *The New Testament World: Insights from Cultural Anthropology* (Atlanta: John Knox, 1981); idem, "Collectivism in Mediterranean Culture," in *Understanding the Social World of the New Testament,* ed. D. Neufeld and R. E. DeMaris (London: Routledge, 2010), 17-28; **W. A. Meeks,** *The First Urban Christians: The Social World of the Apostle Paul* (New Haven, CT: Yale University Press, 1983); **J. J. Meggitt,** *Paul, Poverty, and Survival* (Edinburgh: T&T Clark, 1998); **J. H. Neyrey,** *Render to God: New Testament Understandings of the Divine* (Minneapolis: Fortress, 2004); idem, "God, Benefactor and Patron: The Major Cultural Model for Interpreting the Deity in Greco-Roman Antiquity," *JSNT* 27 (2005): 465-92; **J. Økland,** *Women in Their Place: Paul and the Corinthian Discourse of Gender and Sanctuary Space* (London: T&T Clark, 2004); **R. D. Roberts,** "Shame," in *The Ancient Mediterranean Social World: A Sourcebook,* ed. Z. A. Crook (Grand Rapids, MI: Eerdmans, 2020), 79-92; **R. P. Saller,** *Personal Patronage Under the Early Empire* (New York: Cambridge University Press, 1982); **C. Shantz,** *Paul in Ecstasy: The Neurobiology of the Apostle's Life and Thought* (Cambridge: Cambridge University Press, 2009); **C. Shantz and R. A. Werline,** eds., *Experientia: Linking Text and Experience* (Leiden: Brill Academic, 2012); **K. Stendahl,** "The Apostle Paul and the Introspective Conscience of the West," *HTR* 56 (1963): 199-215; **A. C. Stewart,** *The Original Bishops: Office and Order in the First Christian Communities* (Grand Rapids, MI: Baker Academic, 2014); **E. Stewart,** "Social Stratification and Patronage in Ancient Mediterranean Societies," in *Understanding the Social World of the New Testament,* ed. D. Neufeld and R. E. DeMaris (London: Routledge, 2010), 156-66; idem, "I'm Okay, You're Not Okay: Constancy of Character and Paul's Understanding of Change in His Own and Peter's Behaviour," *TS* 67 (2011): 1-8; idem, "BTB Readers' Guide: New Testament Space/Spatiality," *BTB* 42 (2012): 139-50; **T. D. Still and D. G. Horrell,** eds., *After the First Urban Christians: The Social-Scientific Study of Pauline Christianity Twenty-Five Years Later* (London: T&T Clark, 2009); **K. B. Stratton,** *Naming the Witch: Magic, Ideology, and Stereotype in the Ancient World* (New York: Columbia University Press, 2007); **G. Theissen,** *The Social Setting of Pauline Christianity* (Philadelphia: Fortress, 1982); **F. Tofighi,** *Paul's Letters and the Construction of the European Self* (London: T&T Clark, 2017); **H. C. Triandis,** "Individualism and Collectivism," in *The Handbook of Culture and Psychology,* ed. D. Matsumoto (Oxford: Oxford University Press, 2001), 35-50; **R. Uro,** *Ritual and Christian Beginnings: A Socio-cognitive Analysis* (Oxford: Oxford University Press, 2016); **R. Uro, J. J. Day, R. Roitto, and R. E. DeMaris,** eds., *The Oxford Handbook of Early Christian Ritual* (Oxford:

Oxford University Press, 2018); **E. K. Vearncombe,** "Rituals for Communal Maintenance," in *Early Christian Ritual Life*, ed. R. E. DeMaris, J. T. Lamoreaux, and S. C. Muir (London: Routledge, 2018), 92-111; **A. Wallace-Hadrill,** ed., *Patronage in Ancient Society* (London: Routledge, 1989); **B. L. White,** *Remembering Paul: Ancient and Modern Contests over the Image of the Apostle* (Oxford: Oxford University Press, 2014).

Z. Crook

SON OF GOD

Paul does not use the phrase "Son of God" with great frequency (Rom 1:4; 2 Cor 1:19; Gal 2:20), but the familial relation between Jesus and *God and then between God and Jesus' followers forms one of the regular and vital themes in Paul's writings. Awareness of the various meanings of "Son of God" in the writings of the Jewish people and in the wider Hellenized culture of Paul's time shapes interpreters' ability to hear the powerful claims Paul makes when he uses or evokes this title.

1. Son of God in Greek and Roman Contexts
2. Son of God in Jewish Contexts
3. Son of God in the New Testament
4. Son of God in Paul

1. Son of God in Greek and Roman Contexts.

It was quite common in the ancient world to speak of gods as "Father" (Homer, *Il.* 1.587; 3.365; 4.288; *Od.* 4.341; 7.311; 8.305). The mythology portrays the chief god as the progenitor of many of the other gods, including Apollo, Artemis, Dionysius, and Hermes. Even the Latin name of the god Jupiter is related to the Greek address of the chief god as father: *Zeus pater* (Horace, *Carm.* 3.5.1-5). The fatherhood of the gods did not always connote direct ancestry but dependence on the power of the god (Chen, 59-61). Because the gods provided for the needs of *creation—physical and intellectual—they were addressed as father (Diodorus Siculus, *Bib. hist.* 3.61.1-6; Epictetus, *Diatr.* 1.3.1-3). This general sense of paternity shared by all, however, became more precise for some.

In C. S. Lewis's *Till We Have Faces*, the royal protagonist frequently asserts that she and her sisters have "the blood of the gods." Somewhere in their ancestral line a god had union with a human to create a hybrid lineage. Lewis's myth retold mimics a similar assertion throughout ancient literature. Many prominent figures were said to have descended from a god, either directly or somewhere further back in their ancient history. Alexander the Great was said to be the son of Jupiter (Plutarch, *Alex* 2.4), and Plato the son of Apollo (Plutarch, *Mor.* 9.114-119). Julius Caesar traced his lineage back to Aeneas, who was the son of Venus (Cassius Dio, *Hist.* 41.34.1). The mother of Octavian, who became Caesar Augustus, was said to have been impregnated by Apollo (Suetonius, *Aug.* 94.11; Cassius Dio, *Hist.* 45.2). Whether or not the claim was interpreted as dogma or propaganda is impossible to know (Talbert, 79-86). The frequency of the story means that readers of the NT would have been familiar with the idea that a person could declare to be son of a particular god. The terminology in this instance, however, was different from that in the NT. The deities of this time had names, and so the title employed was typically "Son of Apollo" or "Son of Venus," not "Son of God." That specific title appeared in the social setting of the NT almost exclusively for the emperor.

The title "Son of God" became prominent during the reign of Augustus (27 BC–AD 14). The previous leader, Julius Caesar, had adopted Augustus as his son and heir in his will. When the Roman senate declared Julius Caesar a divinized man (*divus*) after his death, Augustus became *divi filius*, son of a *divus*. The Latin lexical distinction between a god (*dei*) and a divinized man (*divus*) was lost in Greek, where both were translated as *theou huios*, "son of god." Future emperors made the shift from emphasizing their descent from the gods to emphasizing their descent from previous (divinized) emperors. It was more valued to claim that they were directly related to the divine emperor as his son. This divine filial language continued through the dynasties whether the emperor was a natural-born son or an adopted son, since *adoption was so highly valued as a transfer into the adopting family line. The language of divine filiation was so well established that even Vespasian, who began a new dynasty, used it when he ascended to the throne.

The knowledge of this relationship was widespread throughout the empire. From coins that included the title *divi filius* to statues that made the emperors resemble the previous leaders, residents of the realm would know the status and likeness of the son of god at the top of the wide-reaching Roman family. Hence, by the time of the writings of the NT, "son of god" was a title that would evoke the emperor. Hearing it in reference to Jesus, many early Christians who were influenced by the *empire would see him as a competitor to Caesar (Peppard, 46-85).

2. Son of God in Jewish Contexts.

Very rarely will a reader encounter the phrase "Son of God" in the Hebrew and Greek texts of *Israel.

2.1. In Hebrew Texts. Most often the phrase refers to beings in proximity to God, from the enigmatic sons who mate with human women in the antediluvian period (Gen 6:2, 4) to the worshiping sons (Deut 32:43 LXX) who ascribe *glory to God's *name (Ps 28:1). These beings are quite illustrious. They are present with God at the creation of the earth (Job 38:7), given charge over the nations (Deut 32:8 LXX), appear as God's council (Job 1:6; 2:1), and exist in the realm where righteous humans go after *death (Wis 5:5). Nevertheless, the God of Israel stands superior to these sons of God (Ps 89:6). Psalm 82:6, with its reference to "sons of the Most High," might fit here as well, although some interpreters also see this as an ironic reference to humans. By the time of the Greek translations of Daniel and Job, several scribes rendered these sons of God "angels." In these handful of instances, only once does the title "Son of God" appear in the singular, where a son of God appears fortuitously in Daniel alongside Shadrach, Meshach, and Abednego in the fiery furnace (Dan 3:25); all other phrases describe more than one (angelic) son.

The phrase itself appears only once in the Hebrew text with clear reference to humans. Hosea promises that though Israel had heard "you are not my people," they will be called "sons of the living God" (Hos 2:1). In the Greek text Wisdom of Solomon, the unrighteous know the righteous man claims to be a son of God (Wis 2:18), and in Sirach, the just man will be considered like a son, not precisely of God but of the poetic parallel, the Most High (Sir 2:10).

The *idea* of divine sonship appears with more frequency. God instructs Moses to tell Pharaoh that Israel is "my *firstborn son" (Ex 4:22), and Hosea recalls this moment as the redemption of a child (Hos 11:1). In the opening of Moses' speech to the people in Deuteronomy, he recalls how God treated the nation of Israel as one treats a child. The Hebrew has God carrying Israel, and the Greek has God nursing Israel. In both instances, the nation is God's son (Deut 1:31). This identity should shape how Israel lives (Deut 14:1). At the end of the book, God is the father to the nation because of God's role as Creator (Deut 32:5), emphasized with the analogy of a father eagle (Deut 32:11). Malachi makes the same association between creation and fatherhood of the nation (Mal 2:10). The depth of God's sadness over their *sin appears as a charge against the faithless children (Deut 32:6, 19-20). The prophets speak of the familial relationship between God and Israel several times. God proclaims this *identity in the opening speech in Isaiah (Is 1:2, 4) and appeals to it to bring charges against the nation (Is 30:9) and to offer the hope of restoration (Is 43:6; 63:8, 16; 64:8). Jeremiah too bemoans the fact that Israel is faithless even though they are related to God as children (Jer 3:22), and because of this relationship God is moved to bring them back (Jer 31:9, 20).

The one individual most singled out as the recipient and representative of this filial relationship with God (although not the title per se) is the king of Israel. As a play on the word *house*, the prophet Nathan moves David's vision from the building of God's house, the *temple, to God's building of his house, his family dynasty. God promises that David's son will be his son and God will be his father (2 Sam 7:14, repeated in 1 Chron 17:13; see also 1 Chron 22:10-11). Psalm 89 puts to song the royal call to God as Father and God naming of the king as the firstborn (Ps 89:26-27). The king's speech in Psalm 2 recounts when the Lord said to him, "You are my son; today I have begotten you" (Ps 2:7 NRSV). In the Greek version of Psalm 110:3, God brings forth the king from the womb, a possible allusion to God as his Father (Thompson, 35-48).

2.2. In the Apocrypha. Greek texts that appear in the collection that came to be known as the Apocrypha include several references to human sons of God. A chastened king refers to the imprisoned Jews as "sons of the all-conquering, living God of heaven" when he decides to release them (3 Macc 6:28). The unrighteous mock in disbelief the righteous, who are "counted among the sons of God" (Wis 5:5). Even the Egyptians recognize Israel's status as God's Son (Wis 18:13). The Psalms of Solomon notes that the Messiah will know his holy people as sons of God (Pss. Sol. 17.27). At times, an individual does stand as a representative for the whole. The righteous person claims God as his Father (Wis 2:16-17; Sir 23:1, 4, 10).

Outside these texts, multiple Jewish authors appealed to the idea of divine sonship. The History of the Rechabites and Prayer of Joseph join with other texts that designate angels as sons of God (History of the Rechabites 5.4; Prayer of Joseph 1.6, 7), and History of the Rechabites goes on to portray heavenly elders with the same language (6.3). Josephus and Philo assert that God, as creator, is Father of all (Josephus, *Ant.* 1.20, 230; 2.152; 4.262; 5.93; 7.380; Philo, *Deus* 31; *Mut.* 29, 31; *Ebr.* 30; *Opif.* 74, 76, 77; *Fug.* 109; *Spec.* 1.96; *Decal.* 51, 64-65; *Abr.* 58; *Cher.* 49), and Philo highlights individual entities that he calls God's Son. God is the father of laughter, (Philo, *Mut.* 131), of humans who are wise (Philo, *Conf.* 145) and virtuous (Philo, *Legat.* 1.318), including *Abraham (Philo, *Sobr.* 56), Moses (Philo, *Fug.* 109; *Spec.* 1.41), and the high priest (Philo, *Spec.* 1.96). The path to this relationship may not be easy, but difficulty should be viewed as God's paternal training (Philo, *Congr.* 177, reflecting on Prov 3:11-12), similar to what the author of Hebrews says (Heb 12:5-6). If humans cannot yet attain this enviable position, they can pattern themselves off God's firstborn son, the *Logos* (Philo, *Conf.* 62-63, 146; *Agr.* 51; *Somn.* 1.215).

Several times this literature follows the scriptural texts in designating Israel as the child/children of God. Jubilees and Tobit emphasize God's gracious taking of Israel as his children (Jub. 1.24-25, 28; Tob 13:4). In 3 Maccabees, a foreign king realizes the members of that nation are the sons of God (3 Macc 6:28). Psalms of Solomon portrays the messianic king knowing their filial identity (Pss. Sol. 17.27), and the Sibylline Oracles portrays the sons of God peacefully around the temple after the eschatological *judgment (Sib. Or. 3.702).

Finally, several texts lift up one individual to bear this mantle. Multiple times Joseph bears this title in the extended tale of his life, Joseph and Aseneth (6.2, 6; 21.3; 12.8-15). In the Testament of Levi, God takes him as his son, and in turn he will instruct Israel, God's sons (T. Levi 4.2, 4-5). Isaac prays that God will be a father to Jacob and to his son (Jub. 19.39). Third Maccabees portrays the priest Eleazaros praying to God as father (3 Macc 6:3, 8). Some texts, possibly influenced or written by Christians, name a future leader of Israel as the son of God. Fourth Ezra refers to the Davidic Messiah as God's son (4 Ezra 7.28, 29). The Apocalypse of Abraham portrays a son of God who does the judging at the end of all things (12.5), and 4 Baruch notes that one called a son of God chooses twelve disciples (9.21). The designation continues in the rabbinic literature. A heavenly voice calls the sage Hanina "my son" in the Talmud Bavli (b. Ta'an. 24b). "Son of God" would have been a feature of Jewish literature in the first century.

2.3. In the Dead Sea Scrolls. The writings at Qumran show congruence with the theme of divine sonship. Israel stands above all other nations as sons to God (4Q504 1–2 III, 3–7; see also 1QH IX), although "Israel" becomes a designation for their group against other unfaithful in the nation, and individual supplicants can take on this identity for themselves; they can pray in the voice of Joseph (4Q372) or God's *servant (4Q460 5 I, 5). Scrolls exist that invoke God as Father (4Q382 55 II, 1-9; 4Q379 6 I, 1-7). The literature also elevates the king to this status, not a past or present king but one in the future who will be worthy of this title (4Q174 1-3 I, 10-12). At times this figure designated as God's son is also designated as the Messiah or displays features frequently associated with the Messiah (possibly 1QSa II, 11-14; 4Q174 I, 11; 4Q369; 4Q458; 4Q246). Although the condition of the manuscript leads to debate, in that list, the Aramaic Apocryphon of Daniel (4Q246) is the only one to employ, and therefore the oldest Jewish witness to, the singular title "Son of God" (Thompson, 48-55).

3. Son of God in the New Testament.

As Paul was the earliest author in the NT, it is difficult to know for certain which Christian traditions about Jesus' sonship predate Paul. He does not mention it specifically in his recounting of the *gospel about *Christ that was handed to him in 1 Corinthians 15, but in other places he does associate the designation "Christ" with the title "Son of God" (Rom 1:4; 1 Cor 1:9; 2 Cor 1:19; Gal 2:20).

3.1. In the Gospels. A wide spectrum of scholarship has long believed that the historical Jesus spoke of God as a Father, and himself and his followers as sons/children. The prolific appearance of this language in Paul's letters attests to this (Dunn, 33-46).

The Gospels name Jesus as the Son of God over thirty times and speak of his relationship with God the Father hundreds more. Spiritual beings know this to be true of his identity; *demons and *Satan speak it more often (Mk 3:11; 5:7; Mt 4:3, 6; 8:29; Lk 4:3, 9, 41; 8:28) than angels (Lk 1:32, 35). On the human plane the statistics fall in the opposite direction, with disciples confessing this *truth (Mk 1:1; Mt 14:33; 16:16; Lk 22:70; Jn 1:14, 18, 34, 49; 11:27; 20:31) more often than Jesus' enemies (Mt 27:40, 43; Jn 19:7), with the centurion at the *cross standing somewhere between the two (Mk 15:39; Mt 27:54). Jesus says it of himself multiple times (for example, Mk 14:36; Mt 10:32-33; 26:39; Lk 2:49; 10:21-22; 24:49; Jn 2:16; 3:16; 5:17, 19-20, 25; 10:15; 14:2, 7, 10, 20; 15:1, 10, 23; 20:17). The Gospels also claim that other humans can be sons of God (Mt 5:9, 45; Lk 6:35; 20:36), evoking God as their father (Mt 6:9; 23:9; Lk 11:2) and living in such a way that reflects that reality (Mk 11:25; Mt 5:48; 6:1, 4, 6, 8, 14-15, 18, 26, 32; 7:11, 21; 13:43; Lk 6:36; 11:13; 12:30, 32). It is this identity into which the disciples should baptize the nations (Mt 28:19) and the authority by which Jesus sends out his followers (Jn 20:21). While all four Gospels include this relationship, John's Gospel elevates it as one of the central themes. The letters of John continue the prolific use of Father/Son language found in his Gospel (1 Jn 3:8; 4:9-10, 15; 5:5, 9-13, 20; 2 Jn 1:3, 9; Thompson, 133-54).

3.2. In the Rest of the New Testament. In Luke's history of the *church, strikingly, it is Paul who is first to utter this title, he is speaking about Jesus in the synagogues soon after his *conversion (Acts 9:20), and he applies Psalm 2:7 to Jesus on his first missionary journey (Acts 13:33). Peter's second letter makes the same attribution with this psalm (2 Pet 1:17).

Jesus' status as the Son of God is a vital part of the epistle to the Hebrews. It is the first thing the author says about him (Heb 1:2), and he uses this identity to speak of Jesus' kingship (Heb 1) and relate it to his priesthood (Heb 4:14; 5:5; 7:3, 28). It is a title of *honor, showing what a dreadful thing it would be to turn away from this faith (Heb 6:6; 10:29).

At the end of the canon, Revelation names Jesus explicitly as the Son of God in the letter to Thyatira (Rev 2:18), alludes to his royal status as the Son of God with the evocation of Psalm 2 in Revelation 12:5, and grants the status of divine sonship to those who overcome at the end (Rev 21:7).

While particular nuances shape each author's use, the NT stands unified in his claim that Jesus is the Son of God *par excellence*, and those who follow him can stand in the same familial relationship with the God of Israel.

4. Son of God in Paul.

4.1. The Concept as Critical for Paul's Theology. For Paul, sonship and fatherhood are intrinsic to the identity of God in relation to each other, as revealed in the act of *salvation for the world. Paul indicates that the primary definitive counterpart to God as Father is Jesus as God's Son. This theology is evident in Paul's pervasive *kinship language, including references to the Son, many sons and daughters, adoption, and inheritance. Through these themes, Paul disciples the Christian ecclesia to think rightly about God and consequently work out the struggles of uniting such a diverse group, encouraging them to do so in light of the divine familial relations—Father, Son, and Spirit. The self-giving *love shown between the persons of God grounds Paul's ethic of love within the communities (Mengestu, 159-203).

First Corinthians 8 provides an important example, for it shows how Paul's experience of Jesus the Messiah has shaped his view of God. Scholars agree that this is Paul's articulation of the Jewish Shema (Thiselton, 636), the *prayer repeated regularly to affirm Israel's allegiance to one God. Paul agrees that one God stands as the beginning and end of all things, but his definition of the one God includes the Father, who is related to and at work with the one Lord Jesus Christ (1 Cor 8:6). Similarly, in Ephesians 4:6, the singularity of God's sovereignty and providence over all things stands alongside God's identity as Father, alongside the naming of one Spirit and one Lord.

Paul's claims for the sovereignty of the Son of God, that all things will be subjected to him (1 Cor 15:28), show that he is drawing from the royal connotations of sonship. Jesus will reign supreme, as was hoped for the heir of David (Ps 110:1). In Paul's Greco-Roman context, such claims also pit Jesus as a rival to the emperor, who so frequently claimed to be the son of God.

Paul uses the title to extend beyond the political realm, where naming someone "son of God" showed the leader's power by naming his proximity to God, to make claims about Jesus' point of origin. Paul associates sending language with sonship language. God sent his own Son to deal with the problems in creation, sin (Rom 8:3) and imprisonment (Gal 4:4). Interpreters see evidence of the concept of sending also in Romans 1 (Bates, 115-17), where Paul asserts that God's Son descended from the line of David, implying that God sent his Son into a particular family line (Rom 1:3), and Romans 8, where God's not withholding his Son might encompass God's giving of the Son initially in the incarnation, as well as at the cross. These assertions show not only claims of divine paternity in Paul's writings, as was common in the ancient world, but also divine sonship that extends behind the point of birth. If Jesus was the Son of God before he was born, this title then suggests an intimate relationship with God previous to his human existence.

4.2. Son of God in Death and Resurrection. This intimate relationship then shapes how Paul talks about Jesus' death and *resurrection. Romans 5:10 gives evidence that Paul saw God as a Father who gave his Son in death so that reconciliation with humanity could occur. For readers familiar with the story of Israel, this evokes the story of Abraham willingly offering Isaac. This was not a unilateral move by the Father; Paul can also say that the Son willingly gave himself up for others (Gal 2:20), calling on the Suffering Servant of Isaiah, whose suffering restored the conditions for a flourishing *covenant. Paul attends to the actions of both the Father and the Son when he writes that Jesus' self-giving fulfilled the will of the Father to redeem humanity from the present evil age (Gal 1:4).

Paul connects God's fatherhood with the resurrection of the Son more often than he does with the Son's death. This becomes the action Paul uses to identify God the Father, as the one who raised Jesus Christ from the dead (Gal 1:1; 1 Thess 1:10)—or, said differently in Romans, the Son's resurrection happened by the glory of the Father (Rom 6:4). Jesus the Messiah remained Son through his sending and death, but Paul can also say that he was proclaimed Son of God *in power* by resurrection from the dead (Rom 1:8). Just as his resurrection led to an invigorated sense of his sonship, so too does the resurrection contribute to Paul's perception of the glory of the fatherhood of God (Jacob, 223-27).

4.3. Son of God and the Family of God. God is not only "the Father," or even "the Father of the Lord Jesus Christ," but because Paul and his congregations are in Christ, God has also become for them "our Father." Those who accept his message are now caught up into the family, naming God as their Father, as they are in the *fellowship of God's Son (1 Thess 1:1; 1 Cor 1:9) and God's Spirit (Eph 2:18). Paul's initial wishes of *grace and *peace for his congregations almost always come from "our Father" God and the *Lord Jesus Christ (Rom 1:7; 1 Cor 1:3; 2 Cor 1:2; Phil 1:2; Gal 1:3; 2 Thess 1:1-2; Philem 3; Eph 1:2; Col 1:2). He names the recipients of his letters confidently as children of God (Rom 8:14, 19; Gal 3:26) or the adopted of God (Gal 4:5; Eph 1:5) because they are conformed to the *image of God's firstborn Son (Rom 8:29). Several times he makes this pronouncement by citing from the Scriptures of Israel (Rom 9:26//Hos 2:1; 2 Cor 6:18//2 Sam 7:8), and elsewhere he mimics the words of Jesus in his prayer to God as "Abba" (Rom 8:15; Gal 4:6).

His and his communities' membership in the Son in relationship with the Father becomes the stance from which he prays. He blesses and glorifies God the Father (Rom 15:6; 2 Cor 1:3; 11:31; Phil 4:20; Eph 1:3), gives thanks to the Father (Eph 5:20; Col 1:3, 12; 3:17), and invokes the Father to send blessings to his members of the congregations (Phil 1:17; 1 Thess 1:3; 3:11, 13; 2 Thess 2:16; Eph 3:14; 6:23; 2 Tim 1:2; Titus 1:4).

The actions of the familial God are very personal for Paul. Paul lives by *faith in the Son of God, from whom Paul receives love (Gal 2:20). Jesus the Messiah's status as the Son of God defines Paul's gospel, revealed to him and now shared with others, chiefly the *Gentiles (Rom 1:9; Gal 1:16). The content of that gospel is that the Son of God proclaims the divine "yes" (2 Cor 1:19). The correspondence to Ephesians and Colossians continues this theme. The faith of the believers is to have *knowledge of the Son of God (Eph 4:13) because they are now blessed to be members of the Son's *kingdom (Col 1:13).

Their standing as children of God, as evidenced by their changed lives (1 Cor 6:9-10; Gal 5:21; Eph 5:5), opens to them the privilege of being heirs of God (Rom 8:17; Gal 4:7; Eph 1:14, 18; Col 3:24; Titus 3:7). In the end their *bodies too will be "adopted" and changed so that they can fully inherit the kingdom God has promised to them (Rom 8:23; 1 Cor 15:50). Consequently, the Pauline norm is to refer to fellow confessors of Jesus Christ as siblings, nomenclature that occurs 130 times throughout the letters that bear his name (Hellerman, 92-126).

This future inheritance shows that the relation between the Father and the Son serves as the lens through which Paul imagines the end of this present age. He and his congregations are presently awaiting the return of the Son from heaven, who will rescue them from the coming *wrath (1 Thess 1:10). They will then stand before God the Father blameless (1 Thess 3:13). When that end comes and all are subjected to the Son, the Son will hand over the kingdom to the Father, who gave it to him (1 Cor 15:24, 28). When the Son receives the confession of lordship from all beings, his Father will be glorified (Phil 2:11).

Such a catalogue reiterates that kinship language is extremely prevalent in Paul's divine and messianic affirmations. Perceptive critiques have arisen from the fields of previously marginalized theologies, such as feminist, womanist, *mujerista*, Asian, and liberationist theologies, which draw attention to the oppressive applications of such masculine language. At times, the language of fatherhood and sonship has been utilized to keep oppressed people in their oppression, arguing that *suffering is characteristic of Christianity, or it has been used to argue that men are more like God than *women (Brown and Bohn). Without denying the reality and negative influence of these interpretations, when attention is focused on the description and tone Paul conveys about God with this familial language, the data does not support the misuse. When Paul asserts that Jesus is the Son of God the Father, this is *incredibly positive* news in the Pauline texts. Paul's claims for the sonship of Jesus Christ in relation to the God of Israel are the same claims in which he asserts the goodness of God toward humanity, bringing liberation and unparalleled value for all.

See also ADOPTION; CHRIST, MESSIAH; CHRISTOLOGY; EMPIRE; FIRSTBORN; GOD; KINSHIP LANGUAGE IN PAUL; RESURRECTION.

BIBLIOGRAPHY. **G. V. Allen, K. Akagi, P. Sloan, and M. Nevader,** eds., *Son of God: Divine Sonship in Jewish and Christian Antiquity* (Winona Lake, IN: Eisenbrauns, 2019); **M. W. Bates,** "A Christology of Incarnation and Enthronement: Romans 1:3-4 as Unified, Nonadoptionist, and Nonconciliatory," *CBQ* 77 (2015): 107-27; **J. C. Brown and C. R. Bohn,** *Christianity, Patriarchy, and Abuse: A Feminist Critique* (Cleveland: Pilgrim, 1989); **T. Burke,** *Adopted into God's Family: Exploring a Pauline Metaphor* (Downers Grove, IL: IVP Academic, 2006); **B. Byrne,** *"Sons of God"—"Seed of Abraham": A Study of the Idea of the Sonship of God of All Christians in Paul Against the Jewish Background*, AnBib 83 (Rome: Pontificio Istituto Biblico, 1979); **D. G. Chen,** *God as Father in Luke-Acts*, SBL 92 (New York: Lang, 2006); **J. D. G. Dunn,** *Christology in the Making: A New Testament Inquiry into the Origins of the Doctrine of the Incarnation* (Philadelphia: Westminster, 1980); **F. García Martínez,** "Divine Sonship at Qumran: Between the Old and the New Testament," in *Biblical Traditions in Transmission: Essays in Honour of Michael A. Knibb*, ed. C. Hempel and S. N. C. Lieu, JSJSup 111 (Leiden: Brill, 2009), 109-32; **D. B. Garner,** *Sons in the Son: The Riches and Reach of Adoption in Christ* (Phillipsburg, NJ: P&R, 2016); **E. M. Heim,** *Adoption in Galatians and Romans: Contemporary Metaphor Theories and the Pauline Huiothesia Metaphors* (Leiden: Brill, 2017); **J. H. Hellerman,** *Ancient Church as Family* (Minneapolis: Fortress, 2001); **M. Hengel,** *The Son of God: The Origin of Christology and the History of Jewish-Hellenistic Religion* (Philadelphia: Fortress, 1976); **C. J. Hodge,** *If Sons Then Heirs: A Study of Kinship and Ethnicity in the Letters of Paul* (New York: Oxford University Press, 2007); **H. G. Jacob,** *Conformed to the Image of His Son: Reconsidering Paul's Theology of Glory in Romans* (Downers Grove, IL: IVP Academic, 2018); **R. L. Mowery,** "Son of God in Roman Imperial Titles and Matthew," *Bib* 83 (2002): 100-110; **M. Peppard,** *The Son of God in the Roman World: Divine Sonship in Its Social and Political Context* (New York: Oxford University Press, 2011); **J. M. Scott,** *Adoption as Sons of God: An Exegetical Investigation into the Background of Uiothesia in the Pauline Corpus*, WUNT 2/48 (Tubingen: Mohr Siebeck, 1992); **C. H. Talbert,** "Miraculous Conceptions and Births in Mediterranean Antiquity," in *The Historical Jesus in Context*, ed. A.-J. Levine, D. C. Allison Jr., and J. D. Crossan, Princeton Readings in Religions 31 (Princeton, NJ: Princeton University Press, 2006); **A. C. Thiselton,** *The First Epistle to the Corinthians: A Commentary on the Greek Text*, NIGTC (Grand Rapids, MI: Eerdmans, 2000); **M. M. Thompson,** *The Promise of the Father: Jesus and God in the New Testament* (Louisville, KY: Westminster John Knox, 2000); **B. R. Trick,** *Abrahamic Descent, Testamentary Adoption, and the Law in Galatians: Differentiating Abraham's Sons, Seed, and Children of Promise*, NovTSup 169 (Leiden: Brill, 2016); **A. Yarbro Collins,** "Mark and His Readers: The Son of God Among Greeks and Romans," *HTR* 93, no. 2 (April 2000): 85-100; **A. Yarbro Collins and J. J. Collins,** *King and Messiah as Son of God: Divine, Human, and Angelic Messianic Figures in Biblical and Related Literature* (Grand Rapids, MI: Eerdmans, 2008).

A. L. Peeler

SONGS. *See* HYMNS, HYMN FRAGMENTS, CONFESSIONS; WORSHIP.

SONSHIP. *See* ADOPTION; SON OF GOD.

SOUL. *See* ANTHROPOLOGY, PAULINE; BODY; IDENTITY.

SPIRIT (HUMAN). *See* ANTHROPOLOGY, PAULINE; BODY; IDENTITY.

SPIRIT OF GOD. *See* GOD; HOLY SPIRIT.

SPIRIT WORLD. *See* COSMOLOGY; DEMONS AND EXORCISM; HOLY SPIRIT; MAGIC; PRINCIPALITIES AND POWERS.

SPIRITUAL GIFTS. *See* CORINTHIANS, FIRST LETTER TO THE; GIFTS OF THE SPIRIT.

SPIRITUALITY

Paul's spirituality pertains to how the apostle made sense of his experience of the *Holy Spirit, which he also identified as the Spirit of God's *Son (Gal 4:6). Sometimes, Paul describes his spiritual experience as if it were unique to his *calling as an *apostle (Rom 15:18-19; 1 Cor 9:1; 15:8-11; 2 Cor 12:12; Gal 1:15-16). At other times, since he considered himself the "apostle to the *Gentiles," Paul believed his spirituality was prescriptive for his converts (1 Cor 11:1). More than that, he believed his experience of *Christ was paradigmatic for all believers, since his spirituality was predicated on the person and work of Christ (Phil 3:7-17). Indeed, Pauline spirituality and theology are symbiotic. Paul's* Christology, *anthropology, ecclesiology, and *eschatology provided the framework for how the apostle interpreted his spiritual experiences. One cannot understand his theology without considering the influence of his spirituality. The same could be said about Pauline *ethics. Paul's view of the Christian life was informed by his spirituality. He believed that only Spirit-filled people were empowered to do the right thing. That is why the apostle to the Gentiles could not write about the morality of his converts without referring to their past life, when they were enslaved to malevolent powers, before moving on to describe their new life in Christ, empowered by the Spirit. Certainly, Paul's spirituality was constitutive of everything the apostle believed: his theology, his ethics, his worldview, his ministry, his gospel.

1. Early Approaches: Paul's Mysticism
2. Paul's Apostolic Spirituality
3. "Imitate Me"
4. In Christ/Christ in You
5. Life in the Spirit
6. Conclusion

1. Early Approaches: Paul's Mysticism.

For the longest time, Paul's spirituality was seen as ancillary to his theological purpose. Scholars operated with the presumption that Paul's main reason for writing letters was to anchor his advice to the churches with theological arguments derived from the Hebrew Scriptures and the Jesus *tradition. Unpacking the significance of his theology dominated Pauline studies—determining why Paul held to certain doctrines, tracking how he applied his theology to certain situations, establishing what was the organizing structure or center of his thought. Any descriptions of his own religious experiences that Paul happened to offer now and then either were taken as anecdotal illustrations pressed into the service of his theological claims, or they were seen as rhetorical devices designed to appeal to the pathos of his converts.

But after the publication of A. Deissmann's book *Paul: A Study in Social and Religious History in* 1926, some scholars began to turn their attention to the significance of Paul's spirituality on its own terms, comparing his religious experience to the mysticism of the age. For Deissmann had claimed that Paul's experience of Christ—being a "Christ-bearer"—was more important to him than his Christology, evident by Paul's description of the Christophany as the revelation of Christ "in me." The unmediated, nonsacramental, mystical presence of Christ was determinative for the apostle's life and *ministry. To make sense of his experience, Paul relied on a catabatic form of Hellenistic mysticism that emphasized God approaching humanity (rather than humanity approaching God). He realized he could experience communion with God but never direct union with God, which would result in the "loss of the human personality in God" rather than the "sanctification of the personality through the presence of God" (Deissmann, 150-51). This is why the unmediated, nonsacramental, mystical *presence* of Christ was determinative for the apostle's life and ministry. Christ joined God and humankind—Paul's spiritual experience proved it. And so, the Pauline expressions "Christ in me" and "I in Christ" reveal the essence of the apostle's *communio*-mysticism, one of the most important contributions he made to early Christianity.

Whereas Deissmann elevated Paul's spiritual experiences above doctrine and attributed Paul's mysticism to *Hellenism, A. Schweitzer put the apostle's mystical experiences on equal footing with his theology. Indeed, according to Schweitzer, Paul owes his unique "being-in-Christ" spirituality to Jewish eschatology—a linear view of time that ends on the last day. Christ's death and *resurrection marked the beginning of the messianic age. But believers do not realize the benefits of Christ's *kingdom until the last day, when the *body of Christ is raised from the dead. So, how did Paul deal with this eschatological problem—what Schweitzer called the "pre-kingdom" resurrection of Christ before the end of time? He developed a historic-cosmic (versus a mythical) mysticism to explain how believers experience the death and resurrection of Christ in the meantime through *baptism and communion. This is what Paul meant by "being *in Christ": believers enter the messianic kingdom sacramentally through baptism until the last day when they are raised from the dead. In this way, the resurrection power of Christ is already at work in the life of a believer; both the "transient and eternal worlds are intermingled" and the conditions for such a "peculiar mysticism are created" (Schweitzer, 99). For Paul, then, "being in Christ" means believers are living in two worlds at the same time until they finally experience the "beginning of the Messianic *glory" at Christ's *parousia* (Schweitzer, 98, 115-17, 270). Until then, believers experience the dying and rising of Christ through the *Lord's Supper, becoming part of the "mystical corporeity of Christ" embodied in the *church (Schweitzer, 271-83, 286-87).

Following the lead of Deissmann and Schweitzer, a few scholars have explored the background of Paul's mysticism (Wikenhauser; Segal). But there seems to have been more interest among Pauline scholars in determining the relationship between the apostle's spirituality and his theology (Tannehill; Dunn; Fee; Gorman).

2. Paul's Apostolic Spirituality.
Paul attributed some spiritual experiences to his calling as an apostle. For example, he never held up the Christophany as a model for his converts to emulate. Paul didn't expect nonbelievers to come to Christ like he did. Instead, he believed that seeing the resurrected Christ was what set him apart as an apostle (1 Cor 9:1). Even though Christ appeared to him as "one untimely born," Paul numbered himself among "all the apostles," a membership that went beyond the twelve (1 Cor 15:5-8 NASB). To him, the Christophany was a prophetic calling, when the Lord set him apart to preach the *gospel to Gentiles (Gal 1:15-16)—a unique ministry that put him on the same level as Peter and was recognized by the pillars of the church, James and John (Gal 2:7-9). That God used Paul to start churches of Gentile believers was proof of his apostleship (1 Cor 9:1-2). His converts were his "letter of commendation," written by the Spirit, documenting that the apostle had done his job (2 Cor 3:1-3 NASB). That there were believers in Corinth who had received the gospel proved that Paul was Christ's "adequate" emissary (2 Cor 3:4-6 NASB).

Paul also pointed to his ability to perform apostolic *signs and wonders as vindication of his ministry to the Gentiles (Rom 15:19; 2 Cor 12:12). Summing up his itinerant ministry, Paul claimed he preached the gospel from "*Jerusalem and round about as far as Illyricum," emphasizing his work as a pioneer missionary: "to preach the gospel, not where Christ was already named" (Rom 15:20 NASB). Since Paul referenced Isaiah 52:15 (Rom 15:21) as a guiding light for his ministry, it may indicate the apostle's belief that he was fulfilling the role of the herald of the Servant: "Who has believed our report?" (Rom 10:16 NASB; see Is 53:1). Paul believed that Christ spoke through him—in word and deed. When the Corinthians are "seeking for proof of the Christ who speaks in me," their apostle belittles them for not recognizing the "weakness" of Christ's *cross in him (2 Cor 13:3-4 NASB)—something the Galatians had once recognized in Paul. To his converts, Paul was supposed to be more than a mouthpiece who merely delivered the message of Christ. Because of the weakness of his flesh, Paul believed he was the very embodiment of "Christ Jesus Himself" (Gal 4:14 NASB). That's why he decided to refuse to exercise his rights as an apostle. By sacrificing apostolic privileges—not having his converts support him or even a wife financially (1 Cor 9:5-18)—Paul hoped the Corinthians would see the cross of Jesus in him. Since he carried "in the body the dying of Jesus," Paul believed his death would result in life for them—just like Christ (2 Cor 4:10-12 NASB).

Paul's letter writing is another example of his apostolic spirituality. The Corinthians may have sent a letter to him (1 Cor 7:1), but Paul acted like his response was something more than obligatory correspondence. He claimed that what he wrote to them was "the Lord's commandment" (1 Cor 14:37 NASB). To reject his commandments was the same as rejecting the Holy Spirit (1 Thess 4:2, 8). Furthermore, just as Christ had commissioned Paul as his emissary, Paul had his own cadre of messengers (people such as Timothy, Titus, Tychicus, and Phoebe), whom he sent to his churches to pass along further instructions beyond his letters—things he taught "everywhere in every church" (1 Cor 4:17 NASB). These emissaries were Paul's living letters, dispatched to his converts in his absence, sent to remind them of "my ways which are in Christ" until their apostle could deal with them face to face (1 Cor 4:17 NASB). Just as believers were to yearn for Christ's *parousia*, Paul encouraged his converts to long for his coming to them (1 Thess 3:11-13). Even though his letters and co-laborers functioned as provisional apostolic *parousia* during his absence, Paul also believed he could join the assembly "in spirit" to render judgments against "wicked" members (1 Cor 5:3-13) or to encourage his converts through his spiritual presence (Col 2:5). Indeed, in a variety of ways, Paul presented himself as the exemplar of Christ—a model worthy of *imitation (1 Cor 11:1).

3. "Imitate Me."
Because he was a spiritual father to his converts, Paul expected his children to imitate him (1 Cor 4:14-16). But that didn't mean they would mimic him, doing everything he did; for example, he did not want them to be circumcised or live under Jewish *law (Gal 4:21; 5:1-2, 11), he didn't expect them to remain *single (1 Cor 7:7-8), and he never encouraged them to leave their homes and start churches in other cities like he did. In fact, Paul directed young women to "get married, bear children, keep house" (1 Tim 5:14 NASB). And yet, in other ways Paul wanted his converts to imitate him (Phil 4:9). He expected members to work for a living just like he did (2 Thess 3:7-8). Even though he could have exercised his apostolic prerogative, requiring churches to support him financially, Paul worked hard "night and day" so that he would not be "a burden to any of you" (2 Thess 3:8 NASB). Thus their apostle intended to be "a model for you, so that you would follow our example" (2 Thess 3:9 NASB). That idea—sacrificing himself

for them just as Christ sacrificed himself for all—shows up several places in Paul's letters. Paul called it having "the mind of Christ" (1 Cor 2:16 NASB), and he expected his converts to follow this same pattern that they observed in his life (Phil 2:5; 3:17).

For Paul, imitating Christ was more than merely following his example. The apostle to the Gentiles believed he participated in the death, burial, and resurrection of Christ—that somehow Paul was crucified with Christ, buried with Christ, and raised with Christ. This pattern of Christ's death, burial, and resurrection is evident in what Gorman calls the master story of Paul's spirituality: Philippians 2:5-11. Paul tracks the narrative of Christ's descent from heaven to earth, immortalized by his obedient death on the cross, followed by Christ's *ascent to his exalted status, having been given "the *name which is above every name" (Phil 2:9 NASB). Paul's language is poetic: he does not explicitly mention Christ's burial or his resurrection. But the implication is obvious: having the mind of Christ (Phil 2:5) means being conformed to the pattern of Christ's humiliation and exaltation by God. Paul saw the same pattern come true in his life. The apostle emptied himself of his Jewish privileges—what he called having "confidence in the flesh" through *circumcision, ethnic status, and zealous devotion to Jewish law (Phil 3:4 NASB)—in order to gain the exalted status found in Christ. Paul's loss of Jewish *righteousness, being blameless according to Jewish law, was necessary to gain Christ—not only to gain the glory of his resurrection but also the "fellowship of His sufferings" (Phil 3:10 NASB). Loss by cross, "being conformed to His death," would result in Paul's resurrection from the dead (Phil 3:10 NASB)—a glorious power he experienced even during his ministry (2 Cor 3:18; 4:6). And yet, neither the cross of Christ nor his resurrection was perfected in Paul's life (2 Cor 3:12-14). He still faced the daily challenge of crucifying the *flesh (Gal 5:24) and appropriating the power of Christ's resurrection in the darkest of times (2 Cor 1:8-10). And he expected his converts to do the same, to "keep living by that same standard to which we have attained . . . following my example, and observe those who walk according to the pattern you have in us" (Phil 3:16-17 NASB).

3.1. Crucified with Christ. For Paul, the cross of Jesus was not only something that was done for him, but also to him and through him. Sharing in Christ's death meant the world was crucified to Paul ("old things passed away," 2 Cor 5:17 NASB) and he was crucified to the world (sacrificial life, Gal 6:14). To outsiders, the crucified life was foolish. But to Paul, the cross of Christ was both the *wisdom and power of God (1 Cor 1:23-24). That is why he relished boasting in his weaknesses (2 Cor 11:30). For the cross taught Paul that the weakness of God is stronger than any man (1 Cor 1:25). Carrying in his body the dying of Jesus cast a fragrant aroma, revealing the triumph of Christ's death in his life (2 Cor 2:14-16). Even though the cross scarred Paul's body (Gal 6:17)—the weakness of his flesh that made him appear as "Christ Jesus Himself" to the Galatians (Gal 4:14 NASB)—he claimed his cracked pot revealed more clearly the light of Christ's presence (2 Cor 4:7). Since "power is perfected in weakness," Paul was quick to boast in his weaknesses so "that the power of Christ may dwell in me" (2 Cor 12:9 NASB). To Paul, then, being crucified with Christ meant "I die daily" (1 Cor 15:31 NASB), *suffering the same hardships as Christ: abuse, rejection, insults, persecutions, weakness, even death (2 Cor 11:23-27; Phil 1:20-21, 29-30). What looked like the *curse of God—for who would say that God was on Paul's side in light of all the difficulties he experienced taking the gospel to the ends of the earth?—was proof that Paul bore the cross of Jesus Christ (2 Cor 12:10). According to Paul, there can be no *servants of Christ without scars: "For to you it has been granted for Christ's sake, not only to believe in Him, but also to suffer for His sake" (Phil 1:29 NASB).

3.2. Buried with Christ. Paul claimed believers are buried with Christ through baptism (Rom 6:4; Col 2:12). Just as they experience the cross of Jesus, converts share in the burial of Christ. Baptism is the means by which the novitiate first identifies with the death of Jesus (Rom 6:3). Through baptism, believers also affirm their own death in Christ Jesus, "united with Him in the likeness of His death" (Rom 6:5 NASB). Only dead people are buried. Only dead-in-Christ people are baptized. It is their entrance into the crucified-with-Christ community (Rom 6:3)—a passive ritual done to them. Furthermore, Paul seems to link the initial experience of the Spirit to baptism (1 Cor 12:13). Becoming members of the body of Christ means not only being brought into the grave of Christ through baptism but also sharing in the eschatological gift of the Spirit that unifies many different peoples into one divine *household (Gal 3:27-29). Regardless of *ethnicity or status, those baptized into Christ "were all made to drink of one Spirit" (1 Cor 12:13 NASB)—like the children of *Israel who were "baptized into Moses" and "drank the same spiritual drink" (1 Cor 10:2-4 NASB). According to Paul, then, being baptized with water is a shared spiritual experience that signifies God's work of placing buried-with-Christ members into the diverse body of Christ (1 Cor 12:12-18).

3.3. ***Raised with Christ.*** Even though Paul maintained that believers who die in Christ will be raised from the dead on the last day (1 Cor 15:51-55; Phil 3:21; 1 Thess 4:14-16), he also claimed believers experience the resurrection of Christ in the present (Rom 6:4-5). It is by the power of the indwelling Spirit that God will "give life to your mortal bodies" (Rom 8:10-11 NASB)—not only on the last day but in the meantime. Believers experience resurrection power as they overcome the malevolent powers of *sin (Rom 6:5-7, 12-14), the flesh (Rom 7:4-6), spiritual forces of darkness (Eph 1:19-23; 6:10-12), and death (2 Cor 1:8-10). To know Christ is to experience his resurrection power through "the fellowship of His sufferings" (Phil 3:10 NASB). Death must come before resurrection. Therefore, the only way to participate in the resurrection of Christ is to be "conformed to His death" (Phil 3:10 NASB). So, Paul believed that "carrying about in the body the dying of Jesus" resulted in "the life of Jesus" being "manifested in our body" (2 Cor 4:10 NASB). The apostle risked his life for Christ—"being delivered over to death for Jesus' sake"—so that the resurrection power of Christ would be revealed in his "mortal flesh," evidenced by the daily renewal of his "inner man" (2 Cor 4:11, 16 NASB). For those who are "in Christ," then, every life experience was an opportunity to be "conformed to the *image of His son" (Rom 8:29 NASB)—crucified with Christ, buried with Christ, and raised with Christ—the narrative template of Paul's spirituality.

4. In Christ/Christ in You.

Paul divided humanity into two groups: those who are "in *Adam" and those who are "in Christ" (1 Cor 15:22). The in-Adam group is enslaved to the law of sin and death (Rom 5:12-14); they cannot help but do anything other than to serve their lawless, impure desires (Rom 6:19-20). The in-Christ group has been set free from the law of sin and death (Rom 6:17-18); their old Adam-man was crucified with Christ—with a changed heart they are enslaved to God to live righteously (Rom 6:6-7, 17-18, 22). Believers belong to the new Adam-man created in Christ (Col 3:10)—a new *creation where old things pass away (neither Jew nor Gentile, *slave or free, male or female, Gal 3:28; Col 3:11) because the new has come (2 Cor 5:17). To be in Christ means that believers not only share in the status and power of the one who sits at the right hand of God. They are seated in heaven with Christ, having ascended with him through his resurrection (Eph 2:5-6; Col 3:1-3). So, just as Christ embodies the hopes of all humanity, believers are embodied in him. Not only does Christ represent us in heaven; those who are in Christ reign with him in heaven—regnant as his body, having put "all things" under his/our feet (Eph 1:22). To put it devotionally, who he is reveals who we are because we are in him.

Although Paul writes of Christ indwelling the individual believer (Rom 8:9; Gal 2:20; Eph 3:16-17), more often he refers to Christ's presence in the church. Paul's letters are filled with plural pronouns when he speaks of Christ being "in you" (Rom 8:10; 2 Cor 13:5; Col 1:27) or when he refers to the indwelling Spirit (Rom 8:9, 11, 23; 2 Cor 1:22; 5:5; Gal 3:2; 4:6; Eph 2:22; 4:30; 5:18; 1 Thess 4:8). For Paul, the "*hope of glory" is revealed in the diverse-yet-unified body of Christ (Col 1:27 NASB; see 1 Cor 12:12-13; Col 3:11). What causes division in the world—ethnicity, gender, social status—is united in Christ because Christ is "in you" (Gal 3:28; Philem 6, 16). And this is the work of God (Phil 2:13). Since God is in Christ reconciling believers, and Christ is in us performing the work of ministry, then God is working through us to bring about reconciliation (2 Cor 5:18-20). Christ broke down the walls of enmity, uniting many peoples into one family in peace (Eph 2:11-16)—a unity that should be especially evident during the Lord's Supper (1 Cor 11:17-34). Therefore, it is up to the Spirit-indwelled church to preserve the peaceful unity God has created (Eph 4:3).

When an individual internalizes Christ, the believer begins to think like Christ. Unlike nonbelievers, who "set their minds on earthly things," Christians set their minds on "things above" (Phil 3:19; Col 3:2 NASB). Rather than being conformed to worldly thinking, believers are transformed by renewing their minds (Rom 12:2), having the mind of Christ (1 Cor 2:16). To think like Christ means to dwell on what is virtuous (Phil 4:8), to "regard one another as more important than yourselves" (Phil 2:3-4 NASB), and to decide not to "please ourselves" but to "please his neighbor for his good," having the "same mind with one another according to Christ Jesus" (Rom 15:2, 5). Even though Paul never gives his converts mental exercises to develop Christ-mindedness, he believes such an inner transformation—the righteousness of Christ—is outwardly demonstrable. Right thinking results in right behavior. Since the life of the mind is a spiritual reality, believers should look on the physical world with resurrection eyes (2 Cor 4:16-18; Eph 1:18), recognizing that "our struggle is not against flesh and blood" but against spiritual forces (Eph 6:12 NASB). According to Paul, renewing the mind is like putting on new clothes, laying "aside the old self" and "put[ting] on the new self" (Eph 4:22-24 NASB; see Col 3:10). Wearing Christ is like donning battle armor, empowering the believer to overcome unseen forces in dark places (Rom 13:12, 14; Eph 6:11). These things are "spiritually appraised"—the wisdom of the new age revealed by the Spirit of God—something the old Adam-man cannot understand (1 Cor 2:14 NASB).

5. Life in the Spirit.

Paul points to his converts' experience of the Spirit as proof of the truth of his gospel (Rom 8:15, 16; Gal 3:2-5; 4:6; 1 Thess 1:6). Since their life together began "by the Spirit," their shared spiritual experiences should continue to the last day—to do otherwise would be trying to finish "by the flesh" (Gal 3:3 NASB). Paul often contrasts life in the Spirit with life in the flesh (Rom 8:2-27; Gal 5:13–6:8). To succumb to fleshly desires not only means yielding to baser appetites (1 Cor 3:1-3; 5:1-5; Gal 5:19-21) but also trying to please God in the flesh by submitting to circumcision and living under the law—what Paul calls having confidence in the flesh (Gal 4:21–5:2, 16-18; Phil 3:3-6). To live by the Spirit, on the other hand, means *freedom from the law and victory over fleshly desires, "putting to death the deeds of the body" (Rom 8:13 NASB; see Gal 5:1). As the *temple of God, the Spirit inhabits the church like a refining fire to reveal the eternal work of God (gold, silver, jewels), purifying the people with his holy presence, burning away the "wood, hay, straw" (1 Cor 3:12 NASB; see 1 Cor 6:19). Indeed, the only life that pleases God is the believer who is led by the Spirit because the "requirement of the Law" will be fulfilled in them (Rom 8:4 NASB). The one who sows seeds of a fleshly life will reap corruption (Gal 6:8). To make allowances for the flesh—staging opportunities for this hostile power to enslave humans to their own lusts (Rom 7:5; 13:14)—will "bear fruit for death" (Rom 7:5 NASB). Believers who farm the gospel by the power of the Spirit, on the other hand, will yield the *fruit of righteousness and eternal life (Gal 6:8; 2 Cor 9:10-11). According to Paul, then, the Spirit is the *sine qua non* of the Christian life. Without the Spirit, no one can live a Christlike life.

5.1. Walking in the Spirit. Paul put the onus on his converts to live lives that please God, "resulting in the obedience of the Gentiles by word and deed" (Rom 15:18 NASB). Even though believers are empowered by the Spirit, it is still their responsibility to walk in the Spirit (Rom 8:4; Gal 5:16, 25). Indeed, "walking in the Spirit" is Paul's way of describing our ethical response to receiving Christ, probably derived from the Jewish concept of "walking" (*halak*) according to the law. One might expect Paul to use the phrase "walking in the Spirit" to characterize a believer's esoteric experiences, such as the time "a man in Christ" traveled to the "third heaven" and heard "inexpressible words" (2 Cor 12:1-4 NASB). But to walk in the Spirit means that a believer is properly appropriating the Spirit's power to overcome the flesh (Gal 5:13-26). Fleshly members boast about their *worship experiences (Col 2:18) and ministry credentials (2 Cor 11:18-23; Phil 3:2-6), claiming superiority by comparing themselves to other Christians (2 Cor 10:7-12; 11:6), creating strife among the members of the church (Gal 5:15). On the other hand, believers who walk in the Spirit do not "become boastful, challenging one another, envying one another" (Gal 5:26 NASB). They do not grieve the Holy Spirit with "bitterness and wrath and anger and clamor and slander" (Eph 4:30-31 NASB). Instead, they speak edifying words (Eph 5:29), serving one another by keeping the commandment, "You shall love your neighbor as yourself" (Gal 5:13-14 NASB).

The apostle never tells his converts exactly *how* to walk in the Spirit, as if there were step-by-step instructions to guide them during their spiritual journey. He simply assumes they will know that the Spirit is all they need to "work out your *salvation" together (Phil 2:12 NASB), encouraging his converts to "examine everything carefully" in order to discern "that which is good" (1 Thess 5:21 NASB). For Paul, walking in the Spirit is not prescriptive—a list of commandments to keep—but is determinative for their life together. The Spirit enables believers to know what is good (several times Paul expects his converts to make their own judgments; 1 Cor 4:21; 6:5; 10:15; 11:13, 28; 2 Cor 13:5; Phil 3:15; Philem 8-9), and then the Spirit empowers them to do what is good.

5.2. Spiritual Gifts. It is the Spirit who helps believers minister to each other (1 Cor 12:25). He gifts members with different abilities according to the needs of the congregation. Such spiritual abilities are not self-determined. Instead, the Spirit distributes different *gifts to individuals "for the common good" (1 Cor 12:7 NASB), to build up the whole church (1 Cor 14:26). In other words, it is the needs of the congregation that determine the kind of gift each member receives from the Spirit "just as He wills" (1 Cor 12:11 NASB). These spiritual gifts create a healthy codependency, where members learn they need each other to experience the full revelation of the body of Christ (1 Cor 12:20-26). Paul also uses this principle of reciprocity to explain why his Gentile converts need to *financially support Jewish Christians in Jerusalem: those who are blessed spiritually should share their material blessings with their spiritual benefactors (Rom 15:27). Recognizing their mutual support of one another creates equality among the members of the universal church (2 Cor 8:13-15) and discourages certain members from thinking too highly of themselves (Rom 12:3-8), especially those who exhibit high-profile gifts (1 Cor 12:28-31). The church should recognize every gifted believer (1 Cor 12:20-25); each member is responsible for using the spiritual gift properly. The Spirit does not overpower the believer, causing them to lose control of their mind (1 Cor 14:15, 31-33). They should be able to follow directions while exercising their spiritual gifts, maintaining an orderly worship service (1 Cor 14:27-40). More than that, if the beneficiary does not exercise the gift in *love, it is worthless—both to the individual and the church (1 Cor 13:1-3; 14:12-19).

*5.3. **Prayer and Prophecy.*** The ability to pray does not depend on spiritual gifting; all believers are encouraged to "pray without ceasing," to "pray at all times in the Spirit" (1 Thess 5:17; Eph 6:18 NASB). And yet, *prayer doesn't seem to come naturally. Paul constantly reminds his converts to pray, even appealing to them to "devote yourselves to prayer" (Col 4:2 NASB; see Rom 12:12). Paul never gives prayers for recitation—even though there are times when a believer does not know what to pray. Instead, he encourages his converts to trust the Spirit's ability to understand "groanings too deep for words" (Rom 8:26 NASB). To pray using indiscernible words can also happen due to spiritual gifting (1 Cor 14:2-5). But Paul believes praying in *tongues should only happen during corporate worship when the prayer is translated by a gifted interpreter so that the entire church is edified (1 Cor 14:12-17). Even though Paul does not list prayer as part of the armor of God (Eph 6:13-17), he writes about prayer as a way to stay alert during the battle, encouraging his converts to pray for him as he prays for them (Eph 6:18-20; Col 4:2-4). Believers pray to know God's will, to thank him for his gifts, and to petition the Lord for his benefits (Rom 1:9-10; 15:30-31; 1 Cor 1:4-9; 2 Cor 1:11; 13:7; Phil 1:3-11; Eph 1:16-19; Col 1:3, 9-12; 1 Thess 1:2-4; 1 Tim 2:8).

The Spirit inspires *prophecy (1 Cor 14:32), a sign of God's presence for believers and the "ungifted" (1 Cor 14:22-25). Although Paul prefers prophecy to speaking in tongues, he also recognizes other ways speakers edify the church: through a revelation, *knowledge, or a teaching (1 Cor 14:6). The Spirit also enables believers to read the Scriptures so that they do not live according to the letter of the law but by the Spirit of the new *covenant (2 Cor 3:6, 15-17). It is only by the Spirit that believers are liberated from the law, confirming their *adoption as children of God (Rom 8:2, 14-16; Gal 5:1-6). Since children replicate the qualities of their parents, Paul claims his converts please their heavenly Father—even without the law—because the Spirit produces divine fruit in them (and Paul is quick to point out, "against such things there is no law," Gal 5:23 NASB). That is why Paul is convinced the requirement of the law is fulfilled in his converts even though they do not try to keep it (Rom 8:4). The Spirit not only empowers believers to live godly lives without the law but also inspires saints (holy ones) to hold each other accountable to *holiness (Gal 6:1-5; 1 Thess 4:1-8), encouraging them to shun recalcitrant members (1 Cor 5:11; 2 Thess 3:14-15), sometimes turning the rebel over to *Satan to destroy carnal habits and save his spirit (1 Cor 5:5). Because of the Spirit, Paul's law-free gospel does not lead to a lawless life.

6. Conclusion.

Paul's spirituality gives us insight into how the early church understood their life together. Jesus Christ was the center of their shared experience: in worship, in devotion, in daily living. He defined the imitable Christian life. His Spirit, the Holy Spirit, was the generative source of their life—both individually and corporately. Without the Spirit, there would be no church. Empowered by the Spirit, believers embody Christ at the end of the age, revealing that old things have passed away and everything becomes new in Christ. Sealed by the Spirit, believers walk in him until the last day when Christ returns, gathers the faithful, and raises the dead in Christ. Until then, they reign with Christ in heaven, overcoming every power that opposes God.

See also APOSTLE; CROSS; CRUCIFORMITY; ETHICS; GIFTS OF THE SPIRIT; HOLY SPIRIT; IMITATION OF PAUL / OF CHRIST; IN CHRIST; PRAYER.

BIBLIOGRAPHY. **C. R. Campbell,** *Paul and Union with Christ: An Exegetical and Theological Study* (Grand Rapids, MI: Zondervan, 2012); **W. T. Davey,** *Suffering as Participation with Christ* (Minneapolis: Fortress, 2019); **A. Deissmann,** *Paul: A Study in Social and Religious History,* trans. W. E. Wilson (New York: Harper & Row, 1957); **J. D. G. Dunn,** *Baptism in the Holy Spirit* (Philadelphia:

Westminster, 1970); idem, *Jesus and the Spirit: A Study of the Religious and Charismatic Experience of Jesus and the First Christians as Reflected in the New Testament* (Grand Rapids, MI: Eerdmans, 1975); **G. D. Fee,** *God's Empowering Presence: The Holy Spirit in the Letters of Paul* (Peabody, MA: Hendrickson, 1994); **M. J. Gorman,** *Cruciformity: Paul's Narrative Spirituality of the Cross* (Grand Rapids, MI: Eerdmans, 2001); idem, *Participating in Christ: Explorations in Paul's Theology and Spirituality* (Grand Rapids, MI: Baker Academic, 2019); **C. S. Keener,** *The Mind of the Spirit: Paul's Approach to Transformed Thinking* (Grand Rapids, MI: Baker Academic, 2016); **V. Rabens,** *The Holy Spirit and Ethics in Paul: Transformation and Empowering for Religious-Ethical Life*, 2nd ed. (Minneapolis: Fortress, 2014); **R. Reeves,** *Spirituality According to Paul: Imitating the Apostle of Christ* (Downers Grove, IL: IVP Academic, 2011); **A. Schweitzer,** *The Mysticism of Paul the Apostle*, trans. W. Montgomery (New York: Seabury, 1931); **A. F. Segal,** *Paul the Convert: The Apostolate and Apostasy of Saul the Pharisee* (New Haven, CT: Yale University Press, 1990); **R. C. Tannehill,** *Dying and Rising in Christ: A Study in Pauline Theology* (Berlin: Alfred Topelmann, 1966); **A. Wikenhauser,** *Pauline Mysticism: Christ in the Mystical Teaching of St. Paul* (Edinburgh: Nelson, 1960).

R. Reeves

STRENGTH. *See* Politics and Power; Triumph; Strong and Weak.

STRONG AND WEAK

This phrase refers to groups of people in the churches of *Corinth and Rome whom Paul specifically addresses in 1 Corinthians 8:1–11:1 and Romans 14:1–15:6. In 1 Corinthians Paul does not apply the term *strong* to a group in the Corinthian *church, though his rhetorical question in 1 Corinthians 10:22 may indicate that he knew of members who would call themselves "strong." He calls some in Corinth weak in conscience (1 Cor 8:7, 10, 12) and weak in knowledge (1 Cor 8:11). In 1 Corinthians, he specifically refers to *food offered to idols (1 Cor 8:1, 4, 7; 10:19). It seems that the strong in Corinth considered food offered to idols to be an *adiaphoron* (an amoral, ethically indifferent behavior) and consumed such food with no pangs in conscience, while the weak considered such consumption to be sinful.

In his references to strong and weak in Romans 14:1–15:6, Paul does not explicitly refer to food offered to idols or to conscience. He calls those who eat everything the "strong" (Rom 14:2), but because of the way that the words *believe* and **faith* are used (Rom 14:2, 22-23), it seems likely that Paul means that the "strong" are strong in faith, in a way analogous to how he first identifies the abstinent group as "weak in faith" (Rom 14:1). The behaviors that characterize the strong seem to be the consumption of all foods and wine (Rom 14:2, 21), and probably a disregard for the Sabbath day by treating all days of the week as the same (Rom 14:5). The behaviors that characterize the weak seem to be a vegetarian diet (Rom 14:2), abstinence from wine (Rom 14:21), and the observance of one day as significant in their *worship (Rom 14:5-6). Due to the use of the word *koinon* in Romans 14:14, a term used in Hellenistic Judaism to describe things that are "common" or "profane," significant motivation for the weak came from Judaism's prohibition of consuming food or drink offered to idols and its insistence on keeping the Sabbath. The attitudes accompanying the rival behaviors seem to be scorn shown by the strong toward the weak, and *judgment or condemnation by the weak toward the strong (Rom 14:3-4, 10).

Because Paul had not been to Rome when he wrote Romans (Rom 1:10-13), William Sanday and Arthur Headlam, Franz Leenhardt, and Robert Karris have stated that Romans 14:1–15:6 represents only Paul's treatment of an hypothetical situation, based on his knowledge of a real difference among believers in the Corinthian church. But Paul was well-informed about the situation among the Roman believers to whom he wrote (Rom 1:8). It is unlikely that he would address an hypothetical problem in the way that he does, for he risks alienating some members of his audience if he called some in his audience "weak in faith" when the strong-and-weak division did not exist within the Roman churches. Volker Gäckle, who also thinks that Paul addresses an actual situation in the Roman churches, offers another perspective on Paul's use of "weak" terms, emphasizing that Paul does not view weakness in a negative way, since Paul has a supernaturally informed and positive view of weakness (2 Cor 4:7-11; 12:9-10).

Most exegetes understand the difference among the believers in Rome as an actual situation that is similar to the situation in Corinth. In all cities of the first-century Mediterranean world, food markets' supply of meat came from animals sacrificed in pagan cult at local *temples. The OT does not approve of the consumption of this sort of meat (Num 25:2; Ps 106:28) and gives a positive portrait of abstinence from meat and wine in a foreign land for this reason (Dan 1:8). Early Christianity generally prohibited the consumption of food and drink offered to idols

(Acts 15:20, 29; Rev 2:14, 20; *Did.* 6.3). Paul's response to the question of whether his *Gentile converts can consume food or drink offered to idols is anomalous in light of this background. While Paul seems to prohibit any consumption of food offered to idols within a temple (1 Cor 10:14-22), he is more open to the possibility of consumption of such food in a private home (1 Cor 10:25-29). He does not offer an apodictic prohibition of food offered to idols but is instead concerned about the sensitive consciences of those offended by such consumption (Rom 14:14-15; 15:1-3; 1 Cor 10:24, 29).

In Romans, Paul considers the consumption of meat and wine, as well as disregard for a special day each week, to be *adiaphora*, though it is clear that the weak did not share his perspective (Rom 14:5-6, 14). Paul's instructions to the strong and weak in Rome fit both with the social context of Rome, where vegetarianism was practiced by some, and with the context of the whole letter. The strong's scorn for the weak fits with how the educated in the Mediterranean world could caricature certain practices as superstition (*deisidaimonia/superstitio*) and despise them accordingly. Paul's directions for the strong to support the weak fit with the Roman practice of *patronage, in which Roman society was held together in a web of obligation. Gäckle helpfully analyzes strong and weak in relation to Paul's theology of weakness and emphasizes Paul's discourse as a model for resolving ethical disagreements within a church. His work represents the culmination of over 150 years of exegesis on these texts that is informed by a quest for parallels in first-century asceticism.

Paul Minear thinks that Paul's pastoral intervention in the difficulties between strong and weak, coming as it does at the end of the main argument in the letter, is the main purpose of the letter. While Scot McKnight does not follow Minear's ethico-religious taxonomy of five different groups in Rome, McKnight's approach is indebted to Minear, since he also reads the whole letter as Paul's attempt to bring harmony between strong and weak.

Alain Gignac's approach is to bracket the question of motivation behind the abstinence and day observance of the weak and to ask instead how the passages on strong and weak affect the reader. This reader-response exegesis bypasses the historical questions of the motivation behind the weak's abstinence and the historical presence of strong and weak in Rome. Instead, it analyzes how the passage works on readers who might be divided on whether a given behavior is an *adiaphoron* or sinful.

The apostle is certainly trying to bring pastoral counsel to Gentiles unfamiliar with Judaism's outright prohibition of food offered to idols. His texts addressing the strong and weak in Corinth and in Rome continue to serve as models for awareness and receptivity toward others' sensitive consciences in the body of Christ.

See also CORINTHIANS, FIRST LETTER TO THE; ETHICS; FOOD LAWS AND CUSTOMS, JEWISH AND ROMAN; IDOLATRY; ROMANS, LETTER TO THE.

BIBLIOGRAPHY. **V. Gäckle,** *Die Starken und die Schwachen in Korinth und Rom: Zu Herkunft und Funktion der Antithese in 1 Kor 8,1–11,1 und in Röm 14,1–15,13*, WUNT 2/200 (Tübingen: Mohr Siebeck, 2004); **A. Gignac,** *L'épître aux Romains*, Commentaire biblique: Nouveau Testament 6 (Paris: Cerf, 2014); **A. Gignac and A. Gagné,** "N'est pas fort qui croyait l'être, et sa foi n'est pas celle qu'il convenait d'avoir! Ambiguïté discursive et programmation de lecture en Romains 14," *Theoforum* 35 (2004): 21-46; **R. J. Karris,** "Romans 14:1–15:13 and the Occasion of Romans," in *The Romans Debate*, rev. ed., ed. K. P. Donfried (Peabody, MA: Hendrickson, 1991), 65-84; **F. J. Leenhardt,** *The Epistle to the Romans: A Commentary*, trans. H. Knight (London: Lutterworth, 1961); **S. McKnight,** *Reading Romans Backwards: A Gospel of Peace in the Midst of Empire* (Waco, TX: Baylor University Press, 2019); **P. S. Minear,** *The Obedience of Faith: The Purposes of Paul in the Epistle to the Romans*, SBT 2/19 (Naperville, IL: Allenson, 1971); **M. Reasoner,** *The Strong and the Weak: Romans 14.1–15.13 in Context*, SNTSMS 103 (Cambridge: Cambridge University Press, 1999); **W. Sanday and A. C. Headlam,** *A Critical and Exegetical Commentary on the Epistle to the Romans*, 13th ed., ICC 45 (Edinburgh: T&T Clark, 1911).

M. Reasoner

STUMBLING BLOCK

Paul uses two different Greek word groups in his letters that are variously translated as "stumbling block" and "to cause to stumble/take offense." When Paul employs the "stumbling block" image, he develops two different but fundamental dynamics. On the one hand, there is the "stumbling block" of *God, which is unavoidable; on the other hand, there are "stumbling blocks," primarily from humans, which are avoidable (Stählin, *TDNT* 7:352).

1. Background
2. The "Stumbling Block" Word Group in Paul
3. The Unavoidable Stumbling Block
4. The Avoidable Stumbling Blocks

1. Background.
"Rock/stone" is an important and recurring image in Scripture. Metaphorically, God is a "rock" of safety (Deut 32:4, 15, 18; Is 26:4; Ps 18:31; 19:14; etc.), and God's word is a "rock" on which his followers are to build their lives (Mt 7:24). God can also act as the stone over which people stumble, especially in *judgment for disobedience (Is 8:14; Jer 6:21; Ezek 3:20; 7:19). As such, this stumbling can lead either to repentance and new life or to offense and ruin.

"Stumbling blocks" also have a human origin. While God's people are forbidden from placing literal stumbling blocks in front of the blind (Lev 19:14), other dangerous stumbling blocks are the metaphorical traps set by others (1 Sam 18:21; Ps 69:22). Frequently, the most pernicious stumbling block is the "snare" of *idolatry that leads the people of God into ruin (e.g., Ex 23:33; 34:12; Josh 23:13; Judg 2:3; 8:27; Ps 106:36; Ezek 14:3, 7; 18:30; 44:12).

2. The "Stumbling Block" Word Group in Paul.
Paul uses two different Greek word groups—*proskomma/proskopē/proskoptō/aproskopos* and *skandalon/skandalizō*—to convey the biblical "stumbling block" image in his letters. These words are variously translated as "stumbling block/obstacle" or "to cause to stumble/to fall." The word groups occur almost evenly in Paul's corpus of letters. As in the LXX, the words are often interchangeable and almost synonymous in meaning (e.g., Rom 9:33; 14:13).

Paul uses the noun *proskomma* five times (Rom 9:32, 33 [quoting Is 8:14/28:16]; 14:13, 20; 1 Cor 8:9), the verb *proskoptō* twice (Rom 9:32; 14:21), the noun *proskopē* once (2 Cor 6:3), and the adjective *aproskopos*, twice (1 Cor 10:32; Phil 1:10).

The *skandalon/skandalizō* word group, often more difficult to translate into English, occurs with similar frequency and often in conjunction with *proskomma* and others. Paul employs the noun *skandalon* on six occasions (Rom 9:33 [quoting Is 8:14/28:16]; 11:9 [quoting Ps 69:22]; 14:13; 16:17; 1 Cor 1:23; Gal 5:11) and the verb *skandalizō* three times (1 Cor 8:13 [2×]; 2 Cor 11:29).

3. The Unavoidable Stumbling Block.
For Paul, *Christ is often the unavoidable stumbling block or the cause of stumbling. In Romans, Paul writes that *Israel, in pursuing a *righteousness based on the *law rather than on the basis of *faith, has "stumbled" (*proskoptō*) over "the stumbling stone" (*proskomma*) who is Christ (Rom 9:32). Paul substantiates his claim by appealing to Isaiah (a conflation of Is 8:14 and Is 28:16 using both *proskomma* and *skandalon*), which may have been part of a common early Christian *tradition (see 1 Pet 2:6; Jewett, 612), as evidence that this "stumbling" is God's doing. While Israel may yet receive *mercy, the ongoing *skandalon* (Rom 11:9 [quoting Ps 69:22]) for Paul is that the majority of his fellow Israelites repeatedly stumble over the gospel's ongoing fruitfulness among the *Gentiles.

Paul presses home the unavoidable "scandal" that "trips" many of his fellow Jews in 1 Corinthians (1 Cor 1:23) and Galatians (Gal 5:11). In these instances, the stumbling scandal is the fact of Christ crucified. For any biblically literate Jew of Paul's day, this is an unavoidable offense since the Scriptures declare that anyone who is hung on a pole/tree is under God's *curse (Deut 21:23; see Gal 3:13). This explains the deep rage that Paul once had against Jesus and his fellow Jews who followed this "crucified Christ" (Gal 1:13-14; Acts 8:1; 9:1-9). Despite the inevitable stumbling that occurs for many Jews at the proclamation of a crucified Messiah, Paul insists that this message is also the transformative power of God—a blessing available for those whom "God has called, both Jews and Greeks" (1 Cor 1:24 NIV; see Mt 11:6//Lk 7:23; Jn 6:61-64; Fee, 80).

4. The Avoidable Stumbling Blocks.
For Paul, human agents can also be "stumbling blocks" and/or the cause for stumbling/offense. Whereas the proclamation of the *gospel and Christ crucified are *unavoidable* stumbling blocks that lead to either *salvation or perdition, Paul's other references to "stumbling block" are the result of human causation and occasions that can and should be *avoided.* Paul reproaches "*strong" Christians for causing "weaker" Christians to stumble, often over matters related to *food (Rom 14:13, 20-21; 1 Cor 8:9, 13). According to Paul, those who would cause a weaker brother or sister to stumble as a matter of conscience in this regard are no longer acting in *love (Rom 14:15). Paul would have believers follow his example of solidarity with the weak and not be a "scandal" (*skandalizō*, 2 Cor 11:29) to them. Instead, he would have both God's *glory and the future eschatological hope form the basis for avoiding offense (*aproskopos*, 1 Cor 10:32) and the source of "blamelessness" (*aproskopos*, Phil 1:10) that comes from the fruit of righteousness.

In all things Paul desired that his own *ministry should commend Christ and shun anything that would put a "stumbling block" (*proskopē*, 2 Cor 6:3) in anyone's path and thus invalidate God's *grace in

Christ. In fact, he urges the Romans to avoid those who might cause divisions and place "obstacles" (*skandala*, Rom 16:17; see Rev 2:14) in a way that would thwart the *teaching they had received.

See also CHRIST, MESSIAH; CURSE, ACCURSED, ANATHEMA; ISRAEL; JUDGMENT; PAUL AND JUDAISM; STRONG AND WEAK.

BIBLIOGRAPHY. **W. Carter,** "Constructing Images of Jesus from the Hebrew Bible," in *The Blackwell Companion to Jesus*, ed. D. Burkett (Chichester, UK: Wiley Blackwell, 2014), 127-42; **G. D. Fee,** *The First Epistle to the Corinthians,* 2nd ed., NICNT (Grand Rapids, MI: Eerdmans, 2014); **H. Giesen,** "σκανδαλίζω," *EDNT* 3:248; idem, "σκάνδαλον," *EDNT* 3:249-50; **J. Guhrt,** "Offence, Scandal, Stumbling," *NIDNTT* 2:705-10; **R. Jewett,** *Romans* (Minneapolis: Fortress, 2007); **J. S. Sancken,** *Stumbling over the Cross: Preaching the Cross and Resurrection Today* (Eugene, OR: Cascade Books, 2016); **G. Stählin,** "προσκόπτω, κτλ.," *TDNT* 6:745-58; idem, "σκάνδαλον, σκανδαλίζω," *TDNT* 7:339-58.

D. Pinter

SUFFERING

Suffering is a lived experience of most people. But the ancient view of pain and hardship is not identical to ours today, and one must be aware of this when one reads Paul. Different *letters of Paul speak of different aspects of suffering. What undergirds the apostle's understanding of suffering is the *gospel of the crucified *Christ and the risen *Lord.

1. Suffering in the Ancient World
2. Suffering in the Pauline Corpus
3. Suffering in Paul and the Old Testament
4. Suffering and Participation with Christ
5. Conclusion

1. Suffering in the Ancient World.

1.1. Greco-Roman and Jewish Worldviews. *1.1.1. Education, Virtue, and Character.* The educative value of suffering is prominent in both Greco-Roman and Jewish writings. Plato thought that punishment would benefit the wicked (*Resp.* 380b). For Seneca, hardships were not desirable, but endurance in suffering was a virtue and an honorable act. The suffering of a virtuous person set a pattern for others to follow (Seneca, *Ep.* 67.4, 10; *Prov.* 6.3.). Those who suffered from great misfortunes would learn to face them bravely and turn them into honor (*Helv. 13.6*). Epictetus also thought that affliction led to moral transformation (*Diatr.* 3.1.10-15; 3.23.30).

Likewise, in Jewish writings suffering can be a means for *God to train people. The author of Lamentations asks Israelites to test their ways and return to the Lord (Lam 3:40). Eliphaz asks Job to heed God's discipline (Job 5:17). The affliction of the righteous is seen as the testing of God in Wisdom 3:1-5; Psalms of Solomon 16.14-15; Tobit 12:14. Sometimes the Lord can use sickness to turn people from wickedness (Sir 38:9-10).

1.1.2. Retributive Justice. Despite its educative values, suffering was often understood to be retributive or punitive. Within the Greco-Roman worldview, the gods might cause suffering when humans offended them, and when calamities occurred, they would bring deliverance if offerings were made. Prayers and libations were offered to the gods to ensure safe voyages and good harvest.

In Jewish thought, suffering is frequently portrayed as God's punishment. The *curses in Genesis 3 were a result of human rebellion. The blessings and curses in Deuteronomy 28 clearly present the retributive justice of YHWH. Obedience would bring blessings, but disobedience would lead to famine, drought, illness, infertility, military defeats, and exile. The prophets speak of divine retribution for *idolatry and unjust practices.

1.1.3. Suffering of the Righteous. Not every affliction is punitive. As mentioned earlier, afflictions can be training grounds for the virtuous. And there are prominent Jewish voices against the retributive view of suffering.

In the lament psalms one finds complaints and protests for undeserved suffering (e.g., Ps 44:17, 20; 69:7, 9). Job is innocent, although his friends think that his suffering is the result of God's *judgment. Ecclesiastes says that it is absurd for the wicked to have a long life while the righteous perish (Eccles 7:15).

The steadfastness and *sacrifice of the suffering righteous were important for the Jews after the exile. Daniel and his friends remained faithful despite life-threatening oppression. The account of martyrdom in 2 Maccabees 6:1–7:42 reveals the belief that the suffering of the faithful can bring about God's deliverance. Although God disciplines his people with calamities, he will not forsake them (2 Macc 6:16). Martyrdom will bring the *wrath of the Almighty to an end (2 Macc 7:38).

The fourth Servant Song in Isaiah contains the best example of the suffering of the righteous (Is 52:13–53:12). In the midst of prophetic judgment against Israel's unfaithfulness, the song stands against the dominant view of retributive justice.

1.1.4. Cosmic Powers and Suffering. Suffering and cosmic powers are interconnected. In Homer one finds that Zeus has two urns: one of blessings and the other of evils and thus sorrows (*Il.* 24.515-530). Plato thought that god did good to sufferers in punishing them (*Resp.* 380bc). For Seneca, everything happened by the decree of the gods (*Nat.* 3. pref. 11).

Throughout the OT one sees connections between evil powers and suffering. The serpent in Genesis 3 represents an evil figure that causes human disobedience and the subsequent curses. *Satan incites David in 1 Chronicles 21:1, and a plague follows. Satan is also the one who causes Job's suffering. In the so-called messianic woes, unrighteousness and tribulations will increase before the end, and there is nothing humans can do to change that (e.g., 2 Esd 5:1-12).

In the apocalyptic visions in Daniel 7–12, cosmic powers hold sway over the rise and fall of kingdoms. These powers have great influence on the sociopolitical systems of the world as well as the suffering of God's people. But God's eschatological *triumph over evil forces will take place at the coming of a Son of Man (Dan 7:13-14).

Therefore, cosmic powers transcend the whole cosmos, including the individual lives of humans and all social and *political systems. One may therefore say that they are the ultimate forces behind suffering.

1.2. Hardship and Injustice in the Roman Empire. One must note the lived reality of Paul and his audience. It was a world of short life expectancy and high infant mortality, characterized by socioeconomic hardship and religio-political oppression.

1.2.1. Economic Realities. There was big disparity between rich and poor in the cities. The rich lived in mansions, while the poor could be homeless or lived in slums. The majority of the urban population lived at or below subsistence level, and only a small minority belonged to the elite class. For Jesus-followers, about 35 percent lived at subsistence level and 30 percent below it. About 25 percent had minimum economic resources and 10 percent moderate levels of resources, though they were not without economic risk (Longenecker, 295).

1.2.2. Social Hierarchy and Imperial Cult. What fueled the enormous rich-poor disparity was an intensely hierarchical society. The economic and political systems were controlled by those at the top of the social ladder, supported by the military might of the Roman *Empire. The imperial cult affirmed the blessings of the gods on the emperor's supreme rule and ensured that his subjects remained loyal to him. Christ-followers' nonparticipation in cult *worship would result in direct persecution and/or social isolation, which in turn had adverse economic implications. Racial tensions also existed in the urban centers of the empire, which Romans, Greeks, Africans, Jews, and other cultural groups inhabited.

A large portion of the population in the Roman Empire were *slaves or of slave origin. Slavery itself was no benign system. Emotional abuse, physical mistreatment, and sexual exploitation of slaves were commonplace. Many were war captives who had experienced extreme *violence and forced relocation.

1.3. Interlocking Realities. The harsh realities of poverty, slavery, and religious persecution were supported and reinforced by the social, economic, and political systems in Paul's day. The influence of deities on famine, plagues, and political and military powers was never neglected. The Jesus-communities lived within these systems and experienced afflictions commonly found in that world. Their worldview was one that would not separate lived experiences from the impact of cosmic forces, in contrast to people in the West today. In light of this, it pays to read Paul with the recognition that suffering is an integral part of many interlocking realities.

2. Suffering in the Pauline Corpus.

Paul mentions suffering in most of his letters. But the reasons for mentioning it and the manner in which he mentions it differ from letter to letter. Paul's treatment of suffering in Romans is the most comprehensive. The depiction of affliction in the Corinthian correspondences is most intense and detailed. The other letters frequently focus on persecution, often with a deep personal tone. But all in all, Paul's view of suffering centers on Christ and the gospel.

2.1. Romans. *2.1.1. Romans 5:1–8:17.* After an extended discussion on right relationship with God by *pistis* (faith/faithfulness) in the previous chapters, Paul turns to talk about reconciliation in Romans 5:1-11. The educative value of affliction comes to the fore in Romans 5:3-5. Suffering produces endurance, character, and *hope. The themes of suffering and hope of *glory in Romans 5:2-5 will reappear in Romans 8:18-39 in great detail. A brief discussion on Romans 5:12–8:17 is needed in order to understand the theme of suffering in Romans 8:18-39.

*Sin entered the cosmos (*kosmos*), and *death spread to all people because all sinned (Rom 5:12-13). Both sin and death exercise dominion because of the transgression of *Adam (Rom 5:14, 17, 21; cf. Rom 6:9, 14). This invokes the account of Adam and the curses in Genesis 3. The consequences of the curses are wide-ranging. As Terence Fretheim says, "One could speak of humiliation, domination and subordination, conflict, suffering, and struggle. . . . In all these areas, one could speak of death encroaching on life" (Fretheim, 362-63). In light of this, sin and death are cosmic powers that affect all aspects of life, including suffering. But through the work of Christ and the work of the Spirit, sin and death no longer reign over believers—who belong to the new humanity that God has created in Christ out of the humanity in Adam (Rom 5:15, 17, 20-21; 6:6, 9, 14; 8:1-2).

Through the atoning death of the Son, the just requirement of the *law is fulfilled as believers walk by the Spirit and not the *flesh (Rom 8:3-13). All who are led by the Spirit are God's children (Rom 8:14). Then Paul says, "and if children, then heirs—heirs of God and fellow heirs with Christ, provided we suffer with him in order that we may also be glorified with him" (Rom 8:17 ESV). Thus, as Spirit-led children of God, believers are expected—or called—to share in Christ's suffering, with the purpose of being glorified with him. This important verse sets the stage for Paul's extended treatment on suffering in Romans 8:18-39.

2.1.2. Romans 8:18-30. For Paul, the present sufferings are not worth comparing with the glory to be revealed (Rom 8:18). Then Paul mentions the futility of *creation and its longing to be freed from the bondage to decay (Rom 8:19-23). Notably, the experience and destiny of God's children and those of creation are intertwined—which reflects the ancient worldview that lived realities are interconnected. Believers groan as creation groans (Rom 8:22-23), and creation will be set free from its bondage into the *freedom of the glory of God's children (Rom 8:21). This indicates that the suffering of believers is an essential and integral part of God's purpose for humanity and creation, for their faithful participation in Christ's suffering will result in their glorification with Christ (Rom 8:17), and the future renewal of creation is inseparable from their glorification (Rom 8:21).

The liberation of creation from bondage can be viewed as the reversal of the curses in the Genesis account. The effects of sin and death will eventually be fully nullified, and suffering will cease. Meanwhile, believers must wait in hope, and the Spirit will help them in their weakness and groaning (Rom 8:24-27). The encouragement to wait with endurance for the redemption of the *body in Romans 8:23-25 resonates with the faithful endurance and the expectation of the eventual vindication found in Jewish literature (e.g., Dan 9; 2 Macc 6–7).

2.1.3. Romans 8:31-39. The theme of suffering continues in earnest in Romans 8:31-39. God's triumph is a key theme in this passage. God did not spare his own Son but gave him up for all, and he was raised from the dead and is at the right hand of God (Rom 8:32, 34). The rhetorical questions in Romans 8:33-34 ("Who shall bring any charge?" and "Who is to condemn?") suggest that the suffering of God's children is not the direct result of God's punishment or retributive justice, especially given that they are sharing in Christ's suffering (Rom 8:17; contra Rom 2:9).

Nothing can separate believers from the *love of Christ—not affliction, distress, persecution, famine, nakedness, danger, or sword (Rom 8:35). This hardship list includes all kinds of suffering, not only persecution (Moo, 533; Davey, *Suffering as Participation*, 170). This is not surprising given the context of the groaning of creation and the allusion to Genesis 3. Believers are not exempt from the interlocking realities of physical pain, persecution, socioeconomic hardship, and religio-political oppression.

Paul says that believers are more than conquerors and nothing can separate them from the love of God in Christ (Rom 8:37-39). Paradoxically, the faithful endurance of believers in their suffering is the avenue by which they participate in the triumph of God. The suffering of the Spirit-led children of God is essential to their participation in Christ's suffering and glorification, which is an integral part of God's purpose for humanity and the entire creation.

2.1.4. Romans 9:1-3. Immediately following Romans 8 Paul speaks of his great sorrow over *Israel (Rom 9:1-3), which is due to the present hardening of Israel until the *fullness of the *Gentiles has come in (Rom 11:25). Paul's sorrow and anguish in Romans 9:2 echo Jeremiah 4:19-21, where Jeremiah grieves over Israel's suffering. Paul's willingness to be cut off from Christ in Romans 9:3 is resonant with the prayer of Moses in Exodus 32:30-32 (see Xue, 33-35). This prophetic and Moses-like self-sacrificial suffering for the sake of one's kindred is rather unique in Paul. But its sense of solidarity in affliction bears close resemblance to Paul's call for Jesus-followers to share with one another's suffering within their communities.

2.1.5. Romans 12:9-21; 15:3-4. Romans 12:9-21 speaks of a community of solidarity, mutuality, and endurance, where Christ-followers are to love and honor one another. Believers are to be patient in affliction, share in each other's needs, associate with the lowly, and weep with one another (Rom 12:12-13, 15-16). They must bless those who persecute them and overcome evil with good (Rom 12:14, 17-21). Implicit here is that the Christ-followers experience economic hardship, persecution, and probably other forms of oppression. But as a community they are to share each other's pains and put their love into action.

Suffering is implied at the end of the extended exhortation in Romans 12:1–15:13, where Paul mentions the God of endurance (*hypomonē*) and comfort (*paraklēsis*, Rom 15:5). Believers are to please their neighbor and not themselves, for Christ did not please himself (Rom 15:1-3). Hence the community is to follow the model of Jesus. Here Paul cites from a lament psalm: "the insults of those who insult you have fallen on me" (Ps 69:9 in Rom 15:3 NRSV). All four canonical Gospels allude to Psalm 69 when Jesus is at the *cross, being mocked and insulted (Mt 27:34; Mk 15:23; Lk 23:36; Jn 19:29). In view of this, Paul is urging his audience to follow Christ's cruciform pattern as God's people. In the face of affliction, Paul envisions a community made up of Spirit-led love-centered Jesus-followers whose lives are shaped by the self-giving pattern of Christ—because they share in Christ's suffering in anticipation of the final renewal of all things.

2.2. 1 Corinthians. In 1 Corinthians 1:10–4:21 Paul deals with the divisions in the Corinthian house churches. He bases his exhortation on the divine *wisdom in the message of the crucified Christ, which is a *stumbling block to Jews and foolishness to Gentiles (1 Cor 1:18-25). Paul has applied his *teaching on unity to himself and Apollos (1 Cor 4:6). What soon follows is a hardship list (*peristasis* catalog) in 1 Corinthians 4:10-13 to illustrate that God has exhibited the apostles as a spectacle to the world, like people sentenced to death (1 Cor 4:9). The list starts with three antitheses between the apostles and the Corinthians, designed to rebuke the latter for their worldly wisdom in contrast to the divine wisdom of the cross—fools for Christ/wise, weak/*strong, disrepute/*honor (1 Cor 4:10; cf. 1 Cor 1:26-31). This is followed by six afflictions of the apostles: hunger, thirst, poorly clothed, beaten, homeless, and having to labor with their own hands (1 Cor 4:11-12a). The list continues with three contrasting actions: reviled/bless, persecuted/endure, slandered/entreat (1 Cor 4:12b-13a). Then Paul concludes with the degrading description: scum of the world and refuse of all things (1 Cor 4:13b). For Paul, suffering is part and parcel of being people of the crucified Messiah.

2.3. 2 Corinthians. *2.3.1. 2 Corinthians 1:3-11.* In the letter opening Paul speaks of the comfort of God in all affliction, so that he (and his *coworkers) may be able to comfort others who are in any affliction (2 Cor 1:3-4). If he is afflicted, it is for their comfort (2 Cor 1:6). Importantly, the sufferings of Christ abound in him, so that his comfort may abound in the Corinthians (2 Cor 1:5). He and his audience experience the same sufferings (2 Cor 1:6). Indeed, they are sharers (*koinōnoi*) in sufferings (2 Cor 1:7). This notion of shared affliction and comfort highlights Paul's emphasis on solidarity in suffering within the Christ-community. Death is the key motif in 2 Corinthians 1:8-11. God has delivered him from a deadly peril (2 Cor 1:10). Although his affliction in Asia felt like a death sentence, it caused him to rely on the God who raises the dead (2 Cor 1:8-9). This paves the way for much of his rhetoric on suffering, where the identification with Jesus' death and life is often mentioned.

2.3.2. 2 Corinthians 4:7-12. Paul begins 2 Corinthians 4:7-11 with the metaphor "treasure in clay jars" to show that his *ministry (of Christ and the Spirit under the new *covenant) should be characterized by God's surpassing power in human weakness and fragility (2 Cor 4:7). What follows is the first of the four hardship lists (*peristasis* catalogs) in 2 Corinthians (2 Cor 4:8-9). Here Paul contrasts his hardships with the demonstration of God's power (afflicted but not crushed, perplexed but not driven to despair, persecuted but not forsaken, struck down but not destroyed). Importantly, these sufferings are the outworking of the embodiment of the death of Jesus, so that the life of Jesus may be made visible in the mortal flesh (2 Cor 4:10-11) and that life may be at work in the Corinthians (2 Cor 4:12).

2.3.3. 2 Corinthians 6:1-10. In 2 Corinthians 5:11-21 Paul speaks of his ministry of reconciliation, and at the heart of his message is that Christ died for all so that those in him might live for him (2 Cor 5:14-15). The extended hardship list in 2 Corinthians 6:4-10 serves to assert the integrity of his ministry. Although at first glance the catalog may look like the Stoic view of seeing happiness in affliction (e.g., Epictetus, *Diatr.* 2.19.24), Paul does not depict himself as a virtuous sage but as someone deeply affected by his suffering (Lim, 156).

The catalog consists of general hardships (endurance, afflictions, hardships, distresses) and specific ones (beatings, imprisonments, riots, labors, sleepless nights, hunger). It speaks of the qualities of the sufferers (*purity, *knowledge, patience, and kindness) and what empowers those qualities (*Holy Spirit, genuine love, truthful speeches, and the power of God). Significantly, it comprises many antitheses: honor and dishonor, ill and good repute, imposters yet true, unknown yet well known, dying yet alive, punished yet not killed, sorrowful yet always rejoicing, poor yet making many rich, having nothing yet possessing everything. These contrasts highlight the paradoxical nature of Paul's ministry and suffering, echoing the metaphor of treasure in clay jars in 2 Corinthians 4:7. After all, Paul embodies both Jesus' death and life (2 Cor 4:10-11), and it is in participating in Christ's suffering that believers may be glorified with him (Rom 8:17).

2.3.4. 2 Corinthians 11:23-29; 12:10. There are two hardship catalogs (2 Cor 11:23-29; 12:10) in the so-called fool's speech in 2 Corinthians 11:22–12:10. In contrast to other speeches of rhetoricians, where the speakers boast of their ability to endure hardship or bravery in the face of suffering, Paul boasts of his poverty and weakness (2 Cor 11:21, 29-30; 12:5, 9-10). In doing so, he sets himself in sharp contrast to his opponents, the "super-apostles" (2 Cor 11:5; 12:11).

Recognizing the cosmic evil forces against his ministry, he says that Satan disguises himself as an angel of *light and that his *opponents disguise themselves as apostles of Christ (2 Cor 11:3, 13-15). But instead of exercising power to overcome his opponents, Paul validates his ministry with a most intense hardship catalog (2 Cor 11:23-29). He argues that he is a "better" minister of Christ by stating four examples of his "greater" sufferings (far greater labors, far more imprisonments, countless beatings, and often near death). He lists numerous near-death experiences (lashes, beaten with rods, stoning, shipwrecks, adrift at sea), dangers in his travels (rivers, bandits, wilderness, sea, false brothers and sisters, etc.), and other severe hardships (sleepless night, hunger, nakedness, etc.). The last but not least item in the catalog is his daily anxiety for the churches.

Continuing with the theme of weakness, Paul talks about his *visions and revelations, and the thorn that keeps him from becoming conceited (2 Cor 12:1-8). He focuses on God's power in his weakness (2 Cor 12:9). Fittingly, he concludes with a (short) hardship catalog that begins with weakness—weaknesses, insults, hardships, persecutions, and distresses (2 Cor 12:10).

2.4. Philippians. *2.4.1. Philippians 1:12-30.* Paul refers to his chains four times in Philippians (Phil 1:7, 13-14, 17), which resulted from his allegiance to Christ and defense of the gospel. Life in a Roman *prison involved socioeconomic degradation and physical and mental torment. Philippians 1:17, 22-26 indicates that Paul faces the danger of impending death and the hardship that his opponents inflict on him. But Paul understands his suffering in light of Christ and the gospel. Despite his imprisonment, what matters is that the gospel is proclaimed—for which he rejoices (Phil 1:15-18). He wants Christ to be exalted in his body, whether by life or death (Phil 1:20). He urges the Philippians to conduct their lives in a manner worthy of the gospel (Phil 1:27), because they have been granted not only to believe in Christ but also to suffer for him (Phil 1:27, 29). Importantly, Paul and his audience suffer in partnership—they have the same struggle and strive side-by-side for the gospel (Phil 1:28, 30).

2.4.2. Philippians 3:10-11, 21. Paul wants to know Christ, and he regards all things as loss because of the surpassing worth of knowing him (Phil 3:8, 10-11). The knowledge of Christ has to do with sharing in his suffering, being conformed to his death, and attaining his *resurrection. The conformity to (*symmorphizomenos*) Christ's death echoes the language of the Christ-*hymn in Philippians 2:6-11. Jesus was in the form (*morphē*) of God, but he emptied himself to take the form (*morphē*) of a slave and was obedient to the point of dying on a cross. Death on a Roman cross was an extreme form of suffering, characterized by excruciating pain, public shame, and humiliation. To be conformed to Christ's death and sharing in his suffering means participating in his cross-shaped pattern. Yet this participation in his suffering and death coexists with the power of his resurrection (Phil 3:10-11; cf. Phil 3:21). This Christocentric view of suffering is consistent with the suffering for Christ in Philippians 1:29 and the sharing in his suffering in Romans 8:17.

2.5. 1 Thessalonians. *2.5.1. 1 Thessalonians 1:6; 2:14.* The first two mentions of suffering in 1 Thessalonians are found in 1 Thessalonians 1:6 and 1 Thessalonians 2:14, and in both places Paul speaks of imitation. The Thessalonians became imitators of Paul (and his coworkers) and of the Lord when they received the message with *joy in the midst of great affliction (1 Thess 1:6). As a result, they became the model (*typos*) for the believers in Macedonia and Achaia (1 Thess 1:7). In 1 Thessalonians 2:14-15 one finds that the Thessalonians became imitators of the churches in Judea because they suffered from their own compatriots as the Jews from their own people. Therefore, the persecutions experienced by Paul, the Jewish believers, the Thessalonians, and the believers in their surrounding regions are shared experiences by virtue of their imitation and modeling between the believing communities.

2.5.2. 1 Thessalonians 3:3, 4, 7. Paul says in 1 Thessalonians 3:3-4 that the Thessalonians are destined for affliction and that he told them beforehand that they would suffer (see Acts 14:22). Paul sent Timothy to them to encourage them in their *faith so that they would not be shaken by their afflictions (1 Thess 3:2-3). Timothy has since returned to inform Paul of the good news of their faith, and consequently Paul is comforted in his own distress and affliction (1 Thess 3:6-7). Here one sees the mutual encouragement (see the *parakaleō* in 1 Thess 3:2, 7) and solidarity between Paul and the Thessalonians in the midst of persecution.

2.6. 2 Timothy. *2.6.1. 2 Timothy 1:8-14.* Writing from prison, Paul exhorts Timothy not to be ashamed of the Lord or Paul being a prisoner. He urges Timothy to share in suffering for the gospel (2 Tim 1:8; cf. Rom 8:17). It is for the gospel that he was appointed a preacher, *apostle, and teacher (2 Tim 1:11). This is why he suffers as he does, but he is not ashamed, for he knows the one in whom he has put his trust (2 Tim 1:12). It is for the gospel that Paul suffers, and he asks Timothy to share in the same suffering without shame.

2.6.2. 2 Timothy 3:10-12; 4:5. The exhortation in 2 Timothy 3:10-17 begins with what Timothy has observed from Paul: his teaching, conduct, purpose, faith, patience, love, endurance, persecutions, and sufferings (2 Tim 3:10-11a). Paul declares that the Lord has rescued him from all the persecutions he has endured (2 Tim 3:11b). He states clearly that all who want to live a godly life will be persecuted (2 Tim 3:12). Thus, by following Paul's way of life for the sake of the gospel, Timothy is to endure the same hardship for Christ. In this light, it makes perfect sense that Paul includes the imperative to suffer (2 Tim 4:5) in his solemn charge in 2 Timothy 4:1-5. Apparently having his impending death in mind (2 Tim 4:6), Paul prepares Timothy to follow him to be a minister of the gospel, including the necessary imperative to share in the suffering of Christ.

2.7. Other Letters: Galatians, 2 Thessalonians, Ephesians, and Colossians. In Galatians, suffering is intertwined with the cross. Soon after stating that he has been crucified with Christ (Gal 2:19-20), Paul says that it was before the eyes of the Galatians that Christ was publicly exhibited as crucified (Gal 3:1). He argues that their great suffering will be in vain if they think that it is the *works of the law, and not the activities of the Spirit, that mark them out as God's people (Gal 3:2-5). Indeed, if Paul were still preaching *circumcision, he would not be persecuted—for the offense of the cross would have been removed (Gal 5:11). And Paul says that those who force the Galatians to be circumcised do so to avoid being persecuted for the cross (Gal 6:12; cf. Gal 4:29). Persecution is inseparable from the message of the cross.

In 2 Thessalonians one catches a glimpse of Paul's view of suffering and the future parousia. Paul boasts of the Thessalonians' perseverance and faith in their persecutions and afflictions (2 Thess 1:4). This is evidence of God's righteous judgment, so that they may be worthy of the *kingdom of God, for which they are suffering (2 Thess 1:5). The just God will repay those who afflict them with affliction (2 Thess 1:6; cf. 1:8) and give them relief together with Paul when Jesus is revealed from heaven (2 Thess 1:7). For Paul, there will be divine justice at the parousia, and that relief from suffering will be a shared experience between believers.

In Ephesians 3:1-13 Paul talks about his role in God's purpose for the Gentiles. He starts by saying that he is a prisoner of Christ on their behalf (Eph 3:1). Since the Ephesians themselves are the fruit of his ministry to the Gentiles, he exalts them not to lose heart over his sufferings, which are, paradoxically, their glory (Eph 3:13). Noteworthy here is that Paul's suffering is an integral part of his *call to the Gentiles.

Paul was in chains when he wrote to the Colossians (Col 4:18). In a manner echoing Philippians 1:15-18 and 2 Corinthians 1:3-7, Paul says in Colossians 1:24 that he rejoices in his sufferings for the sake of the Colossians—and in his flesh he is filling up what is lacking in Christ's afflictions for the sake of his body. It is difficult to understand the exact meaning of "what is lacking in Christ's afflictions." But what seems clear is that Paul sees that his suffering is for the sake of the *church, which is a continuation of Christ's suffering.

3. Suffering in Paul and the Old Testament. There have been innovative recent studies on the allusion to the OT in suffering in Paul. A brief survey will highlight some interesting findings.

It is not hard to detect the note of lament in Romans. Paul's cry for Israel in Romans 9:3 is a prime example. Siu Fung Wu studies the direct citations of lament psalms in Romans 8:36 and Romans 15:3 (Ps 44:22; 69:9b, respectively) and concludes that they speak of the suffering of the righteous as believers participate in the suffering of Christ. In the case of Romans 15:3, the call is for the believing community to follow the pattern of Christ's cruciform death (Wu, *Suffering in Romans*, 198-207; "Participating in God's Purpose," 8-10, 18-19). Channing Crisler's monograph on lament in Romans says that "divine wrath is the ultimate cause of suffering" (Crisler, 215). The remedy to pain is the *righteousness of God located in the gospel. But it "paradoxically intensifies the pain and cry of the righteous" (Crisler, 218). It is only at the parousia that lament will finally cease.

Scholars have found echoes of Isaiah in Paul, not least the Suffering Servant. John Dunne detects the Isaianic themes of suffering, sonship, and inheritance in the Galatians. He argues that Paul identifies himself as someone indwelt by the Isaianic Servant and expects the Galatians to resist the compulsion to be circumcised (Dunne, 191-92). Wu detects allusions to the third and fourth Isaianic Servant Songs (Is 50:4-11; 52:13–53:12) in Romans 8:31-34, 36. He argues that the evocation of the songs suggests that believers suffer righteously because of their fidelity to God, just as the Servant does in Isaiah (see Wu, *Suffering in Romans*, 207-21).

Kar Yong Lim finds echoes of Isaiah in 2 Corinthians. He argues that the triumphal procession imagery in 2 Corinthians 2:14-16 is best understood in terms of the new exodus motif in Isaiah 40–66. In addition, Lim suggests that "given over to death for Jesus' sake" in 2 Corinthians 4:11 alludes to Isaiah 53:12 LXX, where the Servant was given over for the sins of many. Hence Paul sees his suffering as part of God's plan, just as the suffering of Jesus was (see Lim, 79-86, 114-16). In his essay on Paul's mention of completing what is lacking in Christ's afflictions in Colossians 1:24, Joel White argues that the apostle draws on the Isaianic Servant as a theological underpinning for his unique calling to be the apostle to the Gentiles. This includes being a light to the Gentiles and sharing in the Servant's sufferings in the second and fourth Servant Songs (see White, 198).

These studies provide substantial arguments for Paul's use/allusion to the OT. While individually their findings will not convince everyone, collectively they put forward a strong case that Paul's thought on suffering was influenced in part by his Jewish heritage.

4. Suffering and Participation with Christ. Earlier scholarship was keen to find parallels between Paul and the Greco-Roman philosophers. The studies often focused on the *peristasis* catalogs and the sage's virtuous endurance in suffering (see, e.g., Fitzgerald). Karl Kleinknecht, however, argues that the suffering of the righteous in the OT and Judaism was the backdrop of Paul's view of affliction, which seems to be affirmed by recent scholarship (see above). But Wesley Davey has helpfully highlighted the emerging trend of viewing suffering as participation with Christ. Davey's survey of studies on suffering (e.g., Gorman; Jervis; Lim; Wolter; Wu) shows that the notion of "participatory suffering" is an important interpretive framework (Davey, "Playing Christ," 313-27). As Dunne says regarding Galatians, "to reject sharing in Christ's sufferings is to reject sharing in everything else that has been extended to believers in their union with Christ" (Dunne, 194). Wu says regarding Philippians, 2 Corinthians, and Romans, "Participating in Christ's suffering is an integral part of Christian existence. . . . Sharing in Christ's suffering is the vocation of the believing community and is intrinsically connected with participating in his glory" (Wu, "Participating in Christ's Suffering," 102; cf. Davey, *Suffering as Participation*, 160).

5. Conclusion. Paul and his audience lived in a world different from the West today. Suffering was understood to be integral to the interlocking realities of pain, socioeconomic hardship, and religio-political oppression, all of which are influenced by cosmic powers in some way. One finds parallels between Paul and the ancient views of suffering, not least the Jewish perspectives. They include the educative value of hardship, lament, suffering of the righteous, and faithful endurance in eager expectation of the renewal of creation. As a minister of reconciliation, Paul encourages the believing communities to rejoice and hope as they persevere in suffering for the sake of the gospel and in solidarity with each other. The message of the crucified Messiah shapes his view of suffering. Recognizing that God has defeated the power of sin and death through Christ, Paul invites his audiences—and by implication, believers today—to participate in Christ's triumph by sharing in his suffering.

See also Christ, Messiah; Corinthians, First Letter to the; Corinthians, Second Letter to the; Cosmology; In Christ; Old Testament in Paul; Philosophy; Prison, Prisoner; Romans, Letter to the; Sin, Guilt; Slave, Slavery; Son of God; Wealth and Poverty.

BIBLIOGRAPHY. **J. C. Beker,** *Suffering and Hope* (Grand Rapids, MI: Eerdmans, 1994); **B. T. Clark,** *Completing Christ's Afflictions: Christ, Paul, and the Reconciliation of All Things*, WUNT 2/383 (Tübingen: Mohr Siebeck, 2015); **C. L. Crisler,** *Reading Romans as Lament: Paul's Use of Old Testament Lament in His Most Famous Letter* (Eugene, OR: Pickwick, 2016); **N. C. Croy,** *Endurance in Suffering*, SNTSMS 98 (Cambridge: Cambridge University Press, 1998); **W. T. Davey,** "Playing Christ:

Participation and Suffering in the Letters of Paul," *CurBR* 17, no. 3 (2019): 306-31; idem, *Suffering as Participation with Christ in the Pauline Corpus* (Lanham, MD: Lexington, 2019); **J. A. Dunne,** *Persecution and Participation in Galatians,* WUNT 2/454 (Tübingen: Mohr Siebeck, 2017); **J. T. Fitzgerald,** *Cracks in an Earthen Vessel: An Examination of the Catalogues of Hardships in the Corinthian Correspondences* (Atlanta: Scholars Press, 1988); **D. E. Fredrickson,** "Paul, Hardships, and Suffering," in *Paul in the Greco-Roman World,* ed. J. P. Sampley (Harrisburg, PA: Trinity Press International, 2003), 172-206; **S. Friesen,** "Poverty in Pauline Studies: Beyond the So-Called New Consensus," *JSNT* 26 (2004): 323-61; **T. E. Fretheim,** "Genesis," *NIB* 1:319-674; **M. J. Gorman,** *Cruciformity: Paul's Narrative Spirituality of the Cross* (Grand Rapids, MI: Eerdmans, 2001); **S. J. Hafemann,** *Suffering and the Spirit: An Exegetical Study of 2 Corinthians 2:4–3:3 Within the Context of the Corinthian Correspondence* (Eugene, OR: Wipf & Stock, 2011); **M. D. Hooker,** "Interchange and Suffering," in *Suffering and Martyrdom in the New Testament,* ed. W. Horbury and B. McNeil (Cambridge: Cambridge University Press, 1981), 70-83; **J. S. Jeffers,** *The Greco-Roman World of the New Testament Era* (Downers Grove, IL: InterVarsity Press, 1999); **L. A. Jervis,** *At the Heart of the Gospel: Suffering in the Earliest Christian Message* (Grand Rapids, MI: Eerdmans, 2007); **K. T. Kleinknecht,** *Der leidende Gerechtfertigte. Die alttestamentlich-judische Tradition vom "leidenden Gerechten" und ihre Rezeption bei Paulus,* WUNT 2/13 (Tübingen: Mohr Siebeck, 1984); **K. Y. Lim,** *"The Sufferings of Christ Are Abundant in Us": A Narrative Dynamics Investigation of Paul's Sufferings in 2 Corinthians* (New York: T&T Clark, 2009); **B. W. Longenecker,** *Remember the Poor: Paul, Poverty, and the Greco-Roman World* (Grand Rapids, MI: Eerdmans, 2010); **D. J. Moo,** *The Epistle to the Romans,* NICNT, 2nd ed. (Grand Rapids, MI: Eerdmans, 2018); **U. Schnelle,** *Apostle Paul: His Life and Theology,* trans. M. E. Boring (Grand Rapids, MI: Baker, 2005); **B. D. Smith,** *Paul's Seven Explanations of the Suffering of the Righteous,* SBL 47 (New York: Lang, 2002); **B. J. Tabb,** *Suffering in Ancient Worldview: Luke, Seneca, and 4 Maccabees in Dialogue,* LNTS 569 (London: Bloomsbury, 2017); **C. H. Talbert,** *Learning Through Suffering* (Collegeville, MN: Liturgical Press, 1991); **J. White,** "Paul Completes the Servant's Sufferings (Colossians 1:24)," *JSPHL* 6, no. 2 (2016): 181-98; **M. Wolter,** "Der Apostel und seine Gemeinden als Teilhaber am Leidensgeschick Jesu Christi," *NTS* 36 (1990): 535-57; **S. F. Wu,** "Participating in God's Purpose by Following the Cruciform Pattern of Christ: The Use of Psalm 69:9b in Romans 15:3," *JSPHL* 5, no. 1 (2015): 1-20; idem, *Suffering in Romans* (Eugene, OR: Pickwick, 2015); idem, "Participating in Christ's Suffering and Being Conformed to the Image of the Son," in *Suffering in Paul,* ed. S. F. Wu (Eugene, OR: Pickwick, 2019), 82-105; idem, *Suffering in Paul: Perspectives and Implications* (Eugene, OR: Pickwick, 2019); **X. E. Xue,** "Suffering of Paul in Romans 9–11," in *Suffering in Paul,* ed. S. F. Wu (Eugene, OR: Pickwick, 2019), 29-50.

S. F. Wu

SUFFICIENCY. *See* Galatians, Letter to the; Wealth and Poverty.

SUPER-APOSTLES. *See* Apostle; Corinthians, Second Letter to the; Opponents of Paul.

SUPERSESSIONISM

In discussions of Pauline theology, *supersessionism* pertains to schemes of Christian *identity and scriptural interpretation that result in the *church either eclipsing or replacing *Israel. Christian supersession has been a contributing factor in anti-Jewish polemics and violence in Western history, climaxing in the Holocaust of the twentieth century. At the same time, there are a range of supersessionist readings of Paul based on diverse configurations of his christological commitments, hermeneutical framework, eschatological hopes, and how they posit the relationship between the church and Israel and between Christians and Jews. Not all schemes necessarily arrive at the notion of a replacement of the Jews by Christians even while they maintain the fulfillment of Israel's hopes in Jesus and identify Christians as the vanguard of a renewed Israel. In addition, supersessionism can be detected between Jewish sectarian groups of antiquity as Jews themselves argued over which group was loyal to the *covenant and who were the true inheritors of YHWH's promises to his people. Finally, there are manifold debates about Paul's remarks about "Israel" and how the church relates to ethnic or empirical Israel.

1. Supersessionism as an Ethical Problem
2. Varieties of Supersessionism
3. Supersessionism in Ancient Judaism
4. Paul, Israel, and the Church

1. Supersessionism as an Ethical Problem.

According to Cornelis van der Kooi and Gijsberg van den Brink (338), Israel is the "raw nerve in Christian theology." That is because, if the church is the "new Israel," then Christians have by implication replaced the Jews as God's people. Such a view has led to a denial of the continuing elect status of the Jewish people and has inspired both religious discrimination and state-sponsored violence against the Jews. Given such a history, Christians have a responsibility to understand how supersessionism has contributed to anti-Jewish violence and to actively ensure that it never again can emerge from their own reading of the *apostle Paul.

The onus for much of Christian supersessionism is laid squarely at the feet of the apostle Paul and his account of Christian identity, critique of Jewish unbelief, polemics against Jews and Jewish Christians, and Christocentric way of reading Scripture. Whether Paul believed in the church's wholescale replacement of Israel can be doubted; however, this still leads to the problem of what Paul thought about the church vis-à-vis Israel and how one appropriates such a view for Christian theology. As such, a constellation of approaches have emerged that are committed to decidedly nonsupersessionist readings of Paul. Among those are the diverse schools of thought referred to as "*Paul within Judaism*" and "*after supersessionism*." Indeed, a curious mixture of dispensational, secular, and interfaith scholars have been concerned to retrieve a view of Paul that is explicitly nonsupersessionist.

To read Paul faithfully and responsibly means simultaneously recognizing the violence that happened as a direct result of certain readings of Paul while also seeking to discern how Paul understands Christ-believers in relation to Israel, with "Israel" as both an ethnic and eschatological category of people.

2. Varieties of Supersessionism.
One immediate problem is that there are different ways of defining supersessionism. Some distinguish a "hard" supersessionism whereby the church replaces Israel from a "soft" supersessionism where the church shares in Israel's *election but without supplanting Israel (e.g., Novak, 65-67; Tucker, 65-80). Others prefer a taxonomy of economic, punitive, and structural supersessionisms (Soulen 1996; 2013). N. T. Wright refers to "hard," "sweeping," and "Jewish" versions of supersessionism (Wright, 806). In addition, any view that believes that Paul identifies a deficiency in the practice of Israel's religion regarding the Messiah, the *works of the *law, and the scope of *salvation can also be classified as a type of supersessionism (Longenecker). The problem is that supersessionism can cover a multitude of perspectives, including Israel's expansion, antiquation, representation, replacement, supplementation, succession, inferiority, and superordination, and so on. Thus, Pauline supersession can take a number of forms beside a simple replacement theology.

3. Supersessionism in Ancient Judaism.
Supersessionism was part of the sectarian context of ancient Judaism whereby various groups fought over who were the true heirs of Israel's religious heritage, who spoke for *God, who belonged to God, and who would be saved in an eschatological deliverance. Many groups engaged in brutal denunciations of each other while simultaneously presaging their own claims to be God's elect people.

In the scriptural story Israel is corporately the elect people (e.g., Ex 4:22-23; Ps 135:4; Is 41:8-10), yet in the aftermath of the exile there was to a be a remnant drawn from Israel who would form the nucleus of returned and renewed Israel (e.g., Is 10:19-22; 37:31-32; Jer 23:3; Ezra 9:8-15). The idea of a remnant anticipates a discrimination within Israel between the elect and nonelect. The Qumran community described itself with labels such as "sons of light" (1QM I, 1), "people of God" (1QM I, 5), "sons of righteousness" (1QM I, 8), "diggers at the well" (CD IV, 11), the "congregation of God" (1QS I, 12), those to whom "shall belong all the glory of Adam" (1QS IV, 22-23), "the house of truth in Israel" (1QS V, 6; VIII, 9), "a temple for Israel" (1QS VIII, 5; all trans. Wise, Abegg, and Cook). It is difficult to determine precisely how the sect related to other Judean groups—whether the Qumranites saw themselves as the vanguard of a renewed Israel, the true Israel as opposed to apostates, or merely as the representatives of Israel for the coming age. In any case, the Qumranites regarded themselves as a special group within Israel.

Even the thoroughly Hellenized Philo has a two-tier approach to Israel as both an organic community and as a deeper philosophical entity. For Philo, beside the Hebrew people is the "Israel who sees God" (*Migr.* 113-114 [LCL]; *Conf.* 56; *Her.* 78), which pertains to any ethically upright monotheist. Rabbinic Jews of the second and third centuries understood themselves as the successors of Pharisees, but also supplanting them, and subjected the earlier generations to rigorous critiques.

Jewish sectarian debates borne of the encounter with Hellenism, sociopolitical crises, and furor over cultus and calendar led many Jews to rethink belonging to Israel in light of perceived *apostasies and group differentiation where the language of election was used. As Jon Levenson observes: "The long-standing claim of the Church that it supersedes the

Jews, in large measure continues the old narrative pattern in which a late-born son dislodges his first-born brothers, with varying degrees of success. Nowhere does Christianity betray its indebtedness to Judaism more than in its supersessionism" (Levenson, x). Accordingly, Paul's supersessionism, however one understands it, is largely inherited from his Jewish context.

4. Paul, Israel, and the Church.

There are several important texts that merit discussion in relation to the topic of Paul and supersessionism.

4.1. 1 Corinthians 10:32. Paul writes to the Corinthians, "Give no offense to Jews or to Greeks or to the church of God" (1 Cor 10:32-33 NRSV). Such a short statement is pregnant with amazing significance because for Paul the "church of God" is neither Jewish nor Greek but seems to be something altogether different, something like a "third race" (see Bird 2016, 51-55). In the same letter, Paul can refer to the Corinthians as former pagans/*Gentiles (1 Cor 12:2), but he also treats Israel's sacred history as if it belongs to them and even climaxes on them (1 Cor 10:11). Thus, Paul regards Gentile Christians as a new religio-ethnic entity (see Gal 3:28; Col 3:11) while they concurrently stand in continuity with Israel's sacred heritage and experience the partial realization of Israel's hopes.

4.2. Galatians 6:16. In the closing section of Galatians, Paul writes: "As for those who will follow this rule—*peace be upon them, and *mercy, and upon the Israel of God" (Gal 6:16 NRSV). Interpreters have been befuddled as to whether Paul's reference to the "Israel of God" refers to the Jews or Jewish Christians, or is a circumlocution for the church composed of Jews and Christians.

Many scholars understand the "Israel of God" to be a prestige label for an in-group similar to Philo's "Israel who sees God" or Qumran's "house of truth in Israel." For N. T. Wright, the "noble, evocative word 'Israel' now denotes, however polemically, the entire faith-family of the Messiah defined by 'faith working through love' (5.6) and 'new creation' (6.15)" (Wright, 1043-44). For other scholars, the "Israel of God" is ethnic Israel, just as it is in Romans 9–11. Susan Eastman argues that if Paul wanted to refer to the church as a spiritual Israel it would have been easier to refer to an "Israel of Christ" or "Israel according to the promise." Further, she identifies two distinct blessings given, first, "peace" for those Jewish Christians who walk in step with Paul's teaching about the new *creation; and second, "mercy" for ethnic Israel (i.e., non-Christian Jews) as a way of expressing hope in their eschatological deliverance similar to Romans 11:25-32. "Thus," Eastman argues, "at the end of this letter in which he has declared the obsolescence of the way of the law that his fellow Jews still follow, Paul prays for God's mercy on Israel, that Israel also will be saved only by grace" (Eastman, 389).

There are two problems with treating the Israel of God as ethnic Israel. First, after making an animated argument that Gentiles do not have to convert to Judaism via *circumcision in order to attain a share in messianic salvation, and that there is equality between Jews and Gentiles in the church, Paul would be unlikely to issue a blessing of mercy that applies exclusively to Jews and not to Gentiles, as this would undercut precisely what has been arguing across the letter. Second, Paul consistently regards Gentile Christians as grafted into Israel's election. Throughout Galatians, Paul uses a variety of arguments to assert that Gentile Christians have become "sons of God" (Gal 3:26; 4:5-7), Abraham's "seed" (Gal 3:29), and "children of promise" (Gal 4:28), and belong to the "Jerusalem which is above" (Gal 4:26, 31). This dovetails with what Paul writes in other letters whereby it is possible for Gentiles with circumcised hearts to be Jews inwardly (Rom 2:29), Gentile Christians are the "circumcision" (Phil 3:3), and Jews and Gentiles together are part of the "my people" and "beloved" whom Hosea wrote about (Rom 9:24-26; Hos 1:10; 2:23). In effect, the symbols and language of Israel's election are applied to both Gentile and Jewish Christians based on Christ alone, with no discrimination between circumcised and uncircumcised members of the church (Bird 2016, 163-64).

4.3. Romans 9–11. In Romans 9, Paul argues through a series of densely packed OT citations that the advent of the Messiah has created a rupture within ethnic Israel (see Bird 2022). That division is between those who believe in the Messiah and those who do not, between an Israel according to the *flesh and an Israel according to the promise (Rom 9:6-21). For the promissory Israel, they are composed of a remnant of Jewish Christians (Rom 9:27-29; 11:1-5) and Gentile Christians who have been grafted into promissory Israel's election by *faith (Rom 9:22-26; 10:4-13; 11:20, 24). Yet this leaves fleshly Israel (i.e., ethnic or empirical Israel, that is, Jews who do not believe in Jesus as Messiah) in an ambiguous space.

On the one hand, put negatively, ethnic Israel is made up of objects of "*wrath" (Rom 9:22), because they "stumbled" (Rom 9:32-33; 11:11-12), they fell into "transgression" (Rom 11:11-12), they are "a disobedient and obstinate people" (Rom 10:21; see Rom 11:30-31), they have been "hardened" (Rom 11:7; see also Rom 9:18; 11:25), experienced "rejection" (Rom 11:15), were "broken off because of unbelief" (Rom 11:20), and became "enemies" of the *gospel (Rom 11:28; all translations NIV).

On the other hand, put positively, Israel's disobedience is instrumental to Gentile salvation and will not be final. Israel's misstep over the Messiah was tragic yet necessary as it occasioned Gentile inclusion in salvation (Rom 11:11, 30), understood as bringing "riches" (Rom 11:12) and "reconciliation" to the world (Rom 11:15). Israel's "hardening" was only temporary until the "*fullness of the Gentiles has come in" (Rom 11:25 ESV). In fact, Paul hopes that the Gentile *worship of God will prompt ethnic Israel to "jealousy" (Rom 11:11, 14), so that ethnic Israel can be grafted back into God's purposes (Rom 11:23-24). Paul goes on to affirm that God has "not rejected his people" indefinitely (Rom 11:1-2 NRSV), that Israel is not "beyond recovery" (Rom 11:11 NIV), that God's *love for Israel is immutable (Rom 11:28), and that Israel's election is "irrevocable" (Rom 11:29 NIV). God's purposes for ethnic Israel in the end are their fullness (Rom 11:12), acceptance (Rom 11:15), and *forgiveness (Rom 11:27; Is 27:9; Jer 31:34). Paul promotes a *mission to ethnic Israel (Rom 10:1, 14-15; 11:14) that his fellow Jews might be "saved" in Christ in the present time (Rom 10:13; 11:14) or in an eschatological consummation (Rom 11:26-32).

While Paul's rhetoric sometimes sounds as if ethnic Israel has been rejected, his understanding of God's covenant faithfulness refuses to let him to draw that conclusion. In fact, Paul explicitly rejects any notion of the replacement of Jews by a Gentile church when he attacks the view that "branches were broken off so that I might be grafted in" (Rom 11:19 NRSV). At the same time, Paul does not envisage any salvation for the Jews outside Christ, hence his hope that ethnic Israel will be reconciled to God "if they do not persist in unbelief" (Rom 11:23 NRSV). The dilemma is not whether Israel is elect but how Israel's enduring election and temporary disobedience will be resolved in a future consummation.

In Paul's thinking, God's mercy may appear capricious (Rom 9:15-16, 18, 23) but in the end it is comprehensive, since God's electing mercy for promissory Israel (Rom 9:6-29) will eventually embrace ethnic Israel (Rom 11:30-32). The interlocking destiny of Christians and Jews in God's saving purposes is the "*mystery" of the gospel (Rom 11:25).

See also CORINTHIANS, FIRST LETTER TO THE; COVENANT; GALATIANS, LETTER TO THE; GENTILES; ISRAEL; LAW; PAUL AND JUDAISM; ROMANS, LETTER TO THE.

BIBLIOGRAPHY. **S. D. Aguzzi,** *Israel, the Church, and Millenarianism: A Way Beyond Replacement Theology* (London: Routledge, 2018); **M. F. Bird,** *An Anomalous Jew: Paul Among Jews, Greeks, and Romans* (Grand Rapids, MI: Eerdmans, 2016); *idem*, "N. T. Wright and Paul's Supersessionism: A Response to Kaminsky and Reasoner," *HTR* 113 (2020): 498-512; idem, "Paul's Messianic Eschatology and Supersessionism," in *God's Israel and the Israel of God: Paul and Supersessionism*, ed. M. Bird and S. McKnight (Bellingham, WA: Lexham, 2022); **S. G. Eastman,** "Israel and the Mercy of God: A Re-reading of Galatians 6.16 and Romans 9-11," *NTS* 56 (2010): 367-95; **C. van der Kooi and G. van den Brink,** *Christian Dogmatics: An Introduction* (Grand Rapids, MI: Eerdmans, 2017); **J. D. Levenson,** *The Death and Resurrection of the Beloved Son: The Transformation of Child Sacrifice in Judaism and Christianity* (New Haven, CT: Yale University Press, 1995); **B. Longenecker,** "On Israel's God and God's Israel: Assessing Supersessionism in Paul," *JTS* 58 (2007): 26-44; **D. Novak,** "The Covenant in Rabbinic Thought," in *Two Faiths, One Covenant? Jewish and Christian Identity in the Presence of the Other*, ed. E. B. Korn and J. T. Pawlikowski (Lanham, MD: Sheed & Ward, 2005), 65-80; **R. K. Soulen,** *The God of Israel and Christian Theology* (Minneapolis: Fortress, 1996); idem, "The Standard Canonical Narrative and the Problem of Supersessionism," in *Introduction to Messianic Judaism: Its Ecclesial Context and Biblical Foundations*, ed. David Rudolph and Joel Willitts (Grand Rapids, MI: Zondervan, 2013), 282-91; **J. B. Tucker,** *Reading Romans After Supersessionism: The Continuation of Jewish Covenantal Identity* (Eugene, OR: Wipf & Stock, 2018); **N. T. Wright,** *Paul and the Faithfulness of God* (London: SPCK, 2014).

M. F. Bird

SYNAGOGUE. *See* PAUL AND JUDAISM; POLITICAL SYSTEMS; WORSHIP.

SYRIAN ANTIOCH

Syrian Antioch, today Antakya in southern Turkey, was built by the Syrian king Seleucus I Nicator near the Orontes River in about 300 BC and was named after his father, Antiochus. In 64 BC, the city was conquered by Pompeius, and the Romans made it the capital of the province Syria and a free city. Most of ancient Antioch is buried under the alluvial soil of the river and the buildings of modern Antakya. From the many magnificent buildings known from literary sources (Strabo, *Geogr.* 16.2.4-7; Ptolemy, *Geographia* 5.14.12; Pliny, *Nat.* 5.18.79) only the remains of the city walls, the hippodrome, and aqueducts can still be seen. Many marvelous mosaics (today placed in different museums) testify to great wealth and high culture (see Cicero, *Arch.* 4). In the first century AD, with more than one hundred thousand inhabitants, Antioch was the third biggest city of the Roman Empire (Norris, 265). Zeus, Tyche, Apollon, Artemis, and Isis as well as Roman gods and deified emperors were worshiped in various *temples. The *philosophy of Stoicism (Pliny, *Ep.* 1.10) as well as the practice of *magic was popular (Philostratus, *Vit. Apoll.* 6.38).

Since its founding, Antioch was partly inhabited by an important Jewish minority (Josephus, *J.W.* 7.43; *Ant.* 12.119), which at times was in severe conflict with the remaining population. Between 30 and 20 BC, Herod the Great, in showing his allegiance to Augustus, paved the main street of Antioch with marble (*J.W.* 1.425; *Ant.* 16.148). After the fall of Jerusalem in AD 70, the future emperor Titus had a triumphal entry to Antioch but refused to destroy the Jewish community, an action he could have taken to punish the Jews there for the rebellion in Judea (Josephus, *J.W.* 7.96-111; *Ant.* 12.121-124).

The cosmopolitan city became the focal point for the spreading of the Jesus movement beyond Palestine. Around AD 31/32, after the stoning of Stephen, some Greek-speaking Jewish Christians, the "Hellenists," fled from *Jerusalem to Antioch, first preaching the *gospel to the Jews but then also to "the Greeks" (Acts 11:19-21). Apparently, their *mission was especially successful (see Acts 17:4), because an extremely large number of God-fearing non-Jews was affiliated with the Antiochian synagogues (Josephus, *J.W.* 7.45). Nicolaus, one of the seven leaders of the "Hellenists," was a proselyte from Antioch (Acts 6:5). In Antioch the members of the new mixed community were first called *Christianoi*, as those belonging to *Christ (Acts 11:26). Perhaps this name was created by the Roman authorities as a distinctive mark (Downey 1961, 192-95) relating to a riot around the years 39/41 in which the Jewish community was involved (*Chronicle of John Malalas* 244-245).

The Levite and *apostle Barnabas strengthened the connections between Antioch and the primitive community of Jerusalem, and he engaged Paul for work in Antioch (Acts 11:22-26). The community comprised certain persons of *wealth, for example, Manaen, "a member of the court of Herod [Antipas] the ruler" (Acts 13:1 NRSV). Hence, during a severe famine around the year 44 (Riesner, 125-36), it was possible to send a *collection to the persecuted and impoverished Jesus-believers in Judea (Acts 11:27-30; 12:24-25; see Gal 2:10).

Antioch was caught up in the divisive question of Gentile converts' adherence to Jewish law. After Paul and Barnabas had returned to Antioch following missionary work also to Gentiles in Cyprus and South Galatia (Acts 13:13–14:25), a crisis broke out (Acts 14:26–15:1-2). Around 48/49, the believers in Judea were put under pressure by Zealot disturbances (Josephus, *J.W.* 2.232-246; see 1 Thess 2:14-16), and in Antioch believers were persecuted by the synagogue (*Chronicle of John Malalas* 247). Envoys of James, the brother of Jesus, from Jerusalem convinced Peter and Barnabas to end the table fellowship with Gentile believers in Antioch to protect Jewish Christians from persecution. *Peter was strongly rebuked by Paul (Gal 2:11-16). A council was convened in Jerusalem around 48 to address the thorny issue of Gentile believers and Jewish law. There some Jewish Christians with a Pharisaic background stated their belief that *Gentile Christians needed to be circumcised (Acts 15:5). After discussion, a fundamental decision was reached: the Gentile believers were to remain free from the ritual of *circumcision and other Jewish ritual laws (Acts 15:6-21). Only a few regulations (such as abstaining "from what has been sacrificed to idols," Acts 15:29 RSV) were formulated for the coexistence of Jewish and Gentile believers in mixed communities such as Antioch (Acts 15:23-29). According to this reconstruction Galatians was written before the apostolic council. This minority view makes it possible to combine the descriptions in Galatians and Luke-Acts. Paul remained in touch with the community in Antioch (Acts 15:40; 18:22-23).

It is frequently assumed that, in his early apostolic career, Paul was heavily influenced by a special Antiochian theology stamped by Hellenistic syncretism (e.g., by using concepts from the mystery religions), but in fact the essential traits of his thinking had already been formed before (Hengel and Schwemer, 268-310). From Jerusalem to Antioch, the Hellenists brought along Jesus traditions, which some identify as the so-called Q source or *tradition (Dunn, 308-11). Ancient church tradition connects Luke, the part-time companion of Paul (Philem 24; Col 4:14) and author of Luke–Acts, to Antioch (*Ancient Greek Prologue*; Eusebius, *Hist. eccl.* 3.4, 6; see

Acts 11:28). Indeed, Luke shows a rather detailed knowledge of this community (Fitzmyer, 44-47), where he could have learned the tradition he has in common with Matthew.

See also CHRONOLOGY OF PAUL; COLLECTION FOR THE SAINTS; GALATIANS, LETTER TO THE; GENTILES; HELLENISM, ROMAN; HOLY SPIRIT; JERUSALEM, COUNCIL OF; MAGIC; MISSION; PAUL IN ACTS; PHILOSOPHY; WEALTH AND POVERTY.

BIBLIOGRAPHY. **R. E. Brown and J. P. Meier,** *Antioch and Rome: New Testament Cradles of Catholic Christianity* (New York: Paulist Press, 1983); **G. Downey,** *A History of Antioch in Syria from Seleucus to the Arab Conquest* (Princeton, NJ: Princeton University Press, 1961); idem, *Ancient Antioch* (Princeton, NJ: Princeton University Press, 1963); **J. D. G. Dunn,** *Beginning from Jerusalem,* CIM 2 (Grand Rapids, MI: Eerdmans, 2009); **G. W. Elderkin et al.,** eds., *Antioch on the Orontes: The Excavations,* 5 vols. (Princeton, NJ: Princeton University Press, 1934–1972); **J. A. Fitzmyer,** *The Gospel According to Luke I–IX,* AB 28 (New York: Doubleday, 1981); **M. Hengel and A. M. Schwemer,** *Paul Between Damascus and Antioch: The Unknown Years* (London: SCM Press, 1997); **E. Jeffreys et al.,** *The Chronicle of John Malalas: A Translation,* Byzantina Australensia 4 (Melbourne: Australian Association for Byzantine Studies, 1986); **C. Kondoleon,** ed., *Antioch: The Lost Ancient City* (Princeton, NJ: Princeton University Press, 2000); **W. Meeks and R. Wilken,** *Jews and Christians in Antioch in the First Four Centuries of the Common Era,* SBS 13 (Missoula, MT: Scholars Press, 1978); **F. W. Norris,** "Antioch of Syria," *ABD* 1:265-69; **R. Riesner,** *Paul's Early Period: Chronology, Mission Strategy, Theology* (Grand Rapids, MI: Eerdmans, 1998); **E. J. Schnabel,** *Early Christian Mission,* vol. 1, *Jesus and the Twelve* (Downers Grove, IL: IVP Academic, 2004), 781-97.

R. Riesner

T

TABLE FELLOWSHIP. *See* FELLOWSHIP, COMMUNION, SHARING; FOOD LAWS AND CUSTOMS, JEWISH AND ROMAN; JESUS AND PAUL; LORD'S SUPPER; LOVE.

TARSUS. *See* PAUL AND JUDAISM; PAUL IN ACTS.

TEACHING, TEACHERS

Paul refers in passing to teaching and teachers in most of his undisputed letters and most heavily in the disputed Pastoral Epistles. He assigns teachers an importance just below apostles and prophets. If the apostles were responsible for laying the church's foundation, prophets and teachers worked to build on that foundation (1 Cor 3:5-15; 14:1-5; also Eph 4:11-16). Nowhere does he discuss in detail the nature of the activity or the persons involved, so one must fill out this picture from his environment and the scattered references. Since Jesus was "the teacher" par excellence, there seems to have been some reticence to assign this label to others (Mt 23:8; Jas 3:1), which may explain the relative paucity of Paul's references.

1. Terminology and Background
2. The Nature of Teaching
3. Gift or Office?
4. Paul as Teacher
5. "Sound Teaching" in the Pastorals

1. Terminology and Background.

The *apostle uses a variety of terminology when referring to teaching and teachers. Most often he uses words drawn from the stem *didask-*, including the verb *didaskein* ("to provide instruction," "teach"); the nouns *didaskalos* ("the one who provides instruction," "teacher"), *didaskalia*, and *didachē* ("the content of what is taught," "teaching"); and the adjectives *didaktos* ("instructed, taught") and *didaktikos* ("able to teach"). Other, less frequent, words are *katēcheō* ("to teach in a systematic or detailed manner"), *paideuō* ("to provide instruction, with the intent of forming proper habits of behavior," "educate," "discipline"), *parangellō* ("announcement about something that must be done," "command"), and *paradidōmi* ("to pass on traditional instruction").

In Hellenistic tradition, teaching involved the communication of *knowledge as well as artistic and technical skills. Those who taught ranged from philosophers and elementary tutors to tradesmen and chorus masters, and their aim was to develop the pupil's abilities. Due to the typical master-pupil relationship, teachers carried some inherent authority. Use of the word group was rare in religious contexts or in relation to the activity of the gods, and some philosophers such as Socrates rejected the label since they held that one could not teach virtue.

Teaching (Heb. *lmd*) in Jewish tradition focused on how to live according to the will of *God or Torah. It thus had a stronger focus on *ethics than on theoretical or technical knowledge but was still aimed at developing the learner's abilities or skills, especially skill in living wisely (Prov 1:1-9). Teaching took place in the home, in *temple and synagogues, in small schools of learners, and in groups attached to a teacher. As in other low-literacy cultures, teaching and learning always involved repetition and memorization.

2. The Nature of Teaching.

The content of Paul's teaching to his congregations was his "ways in *Christ Jesus" (1 Cor 4:17), which he could also term absolutely "the teaching" (Rom 16:17; also Rom 6:17; 1 Tim 6:1, 3; Titus 1:9). This involved instructions regarding holy living, which pleased God (1 Thess 4:1-3); *love of the brethren (1 Thess 4:9-12); and other congregational guidance (1 Cor 11:17, 34; 2 Thess 3:4, 10) and commands (1 Cor 7:10). The Pastoral Epistles speak of this as sound or healthy teaching (see below).

For Paul teaching was a fairly broad and fluid concept. It could include what some would call preaching or *kērygma*, which involved the passing along of core *gospel traditions dealing with the *death and *resurrection of Christ (1 Cor 15:1-4) and the *Lord's Supper (1 Cor 11:23). Equally, however, he could use the term for in-group instruction that was more ethical in nature. Scholars such as C. H. Dodd and Martin Dibelius urged a fairly strict distinction between church teaching (*didachē*) and mission-oriented gospel preaching (*kērygma*). While teaching can be generally distinguished from *prophecy and proclamation of the gospel, it is now recognized that the boundaries between these activities are more fluid (Mt 4:23; 9:35; 11:1; Acts 4:2; 5:42; 28:31; Col 1:28; see McDonald). James Dunn may be in broad outline correct that prophecy is "a new word from God" while teaching is "a new insight into an old word from God," but this should not blind one to prophecy's foundation in "old words" or teaching's ability to convey a "new word" (Dunn, 237).

Teaching in the church involved explication of Scripture (OT), which was "written for our instruction" (Rom 15:4; 1 Cor 10:11; also 1 Tim 1:8; 2 Tim 3:15-16). Paul gives an example in 1 Corinthians 10:1-13, where he relates the story of Israel's exodus and wilderness wandering and then draws lessons for the church.

As for the aim of teaching, it involves the transmission of information but goes beyond this in line with its Jewish antecedents. It seeks the formation of the *body of Christ (1 Thess 5:11; 1 Cor 14:12, 26; Eph 4:12) and individually "to present everyone mature in Christ" (Col 1:28 NRSV; also 1 Tim 1:5). This aim can be pursued via the master-apprentice model whereby the pupil learns to follow the ways of the teacher (1 Cor 4:17) and then passes this along to subsequent learners (2 Tim 2:2). It can also take more public or congregational form through communal listening to Scripture and teachers (1 Cor 14:26; Col 3:16; also 1 Tim 4:13).

In 1 Corinthians 12–14 Paul is particularly concerned to commend this edifying ability of teaching and prophecy over ecstatic speech (*tongues). This does not mean, however, that teaching is somehow less Spirit-inspired, that is, simply a product of human intellect and study. Teaching, prophecy, tongues, *healing, and so on are equally expressions of divine *grace (*charismata*) and are "activated by one and the same Spirit" (1 Cor 12:11 NRSV; also Rom 12:7).

3. Gift or Office?

Teaching in the local assembly was apparently an expression of grace (*charisma*) open to believers generally (Rom 15:14; 1 Cor 14:26; Col 3:16), but Paul did not expect that every believer would teach (1 Cor 12:29). Those so prompted by the Spirit could exercise a variety of *ministries (1 Cor 12:7-11).

Alongside this "charismatic" or spontaneous and unregulated teaching, there were also individuals recognized as teachers who exercised such a teaching function more regularly (Acts 13:1). The list in 1 Corinthians 12:28 mentions three such recognized positions ("God has appointed in the church first apostles, second prophets, third teachers" [NRSV]; see also Eph 4:11), apparently in order of importance. These regularly functioning teachers received some voluntary support from the assembly (Gal 6:6; also 1 Tim 5:17). Just how communal recognition of teachers came about is not clear from Paul's undisputed letters, but the beginnings of some sort of ordination can be seen in the Pastorals (1 Tim 5:22).

Teaching in the ancient world normally presumed some modicum of education, which meant teachers were not from the lowest socioeconomic classes. It also connoted some degree of authority. Thus, it occasions no surprise that the circle of those who taught overlapped considerably with the circle of those exercising *leadership in early Pauline churches. This becomes particularly clear in Ephesians and the Pastorals, where "pastor" and "teacher" seem to be flip sides of the same coin (Eph 4:11), and congregational overseers or elders must have the ability to teach (1 Tim 3:2; 5:17; Titus 1:7-9). This connection to education and authority may also explain, at least in part, forbidding *women "to teach and give orders to" men in 1 Timothy 2:12, since elsewhere Paul permits women to teach, prophesy, and lead (1 Cor 11:4-5; Rom 16:1; also Titus 2:3).

This connection of teaching and authority also explains Paul's ongoing concern with false teachers found throughout his letters. It was not merely doctrinal deviation that concerned him but the resulting leading astray of the assembly from his path, in particular regarding requirements for *Gentiles in his churches (esp. Galatians) and issues of morality.

4. Paul as Teacher.

In Jewish circles Paul may have been viewed as a rabbi-teacher. However, since most of his work took place in a non-Jewish environment, he was likely considered a traveling philosopher, who taught his views wherever he could (public and communal venues, homes, open air) and who gathered small groups of adherents to his "philosophy" (Judge). This similarity to other teacher-philosophers sometimes caused confusion (see esp. 1 Cor 1–4).

Paul clearly viewed himself as the founding teacher for his churches, and he expected associates such as Timothy to pass on his teaching (1 Cor 4:17). It was the foundation of the local community, while other teacher-leaders built on that foundation of the good news of Christ he laid (1 Cor 3:1-17). In the Pastorals Paul terms himself a "teacher of nations" (1 Tim 2:7), which is how he was remembered in the later church (Tertullian, *Res.* 23.8; *Pud.* 14.27).

5. "Sound Teaching" in the Pastorals.

These three relatively short letters contain a surprising concentration of teaching terminology (*didaskō* and cognates, 31×). Clearly (false) teaching was an issue. Several times the Pastoral Epistles use the phrase "sound teaching" (*hygiainousē didaskalia*; 1 Tim 1:10; 2 Tim 4:3; Titus 1:9; 2:1) or "sound word(s)" (1 Tim 6:3; 2 Tim 1:13; Titus 2:8). This refers to teaching that accords with the apostle's own doctrine (2 Tim 1:13) and the Jesus tradition (1 Tim 6:3). It leads to *holiness (1 Tim 1:10; 6:3) and is contrasted with the doctrine of false teachers (1 Tim 1:3-11; 2 Tim 4:3; Titus 1:9). The phrase is not found in the undisputed Paulines and seems to function almost as a technical term for a fixed body of traditional correct doctrine. Thus, for many scholars this seemingly un-Pauline technical phrase functions as an indicator of non-Pauline authorship (Dibelius). Others acknowledge the difference in wording but point out that the idea of a fixed body of traditional teaching is not un-Pauline (1 Cor 15:3-11).

See also Apostle; Church Structure; Gifts of the Spirit; Knowledge and Mind; Letters, Letter Forms; Opponents of Paul; Pastoral Epistles; Performance; Preaching, First-Century; Tradition.

BIBLIOGRAPHY. **M. Dibelius**, *The Pastoral Epistles* (Philadelphia: Fortress, 1972); **C. H. Dodd**, *The Apostolic Preaching and Its Developments* (London: Hodder & Stoughton, 1940); **J. Dunn**, *Jesus and the Spirit: A Study of the Religious and Charismatic Experience of Jesus and the First Christians as Reflected in the New Testament* (Philadelphia: Westminster, 1975); **F. Filson,** "The Christian Teacher in the First Century," *JBL* 60 (1941): 317-28; **H. Greeven,** "Propheten, Lehrer, Vorsteher bei Paulus: zur Frage der 'Ämter' im Urchristentum," *ZNW* 44, nos. 1-2 (1952): 1-43; **E. A. Judge,** "Early Christians as a Scholastic Community, Part 2," *JRH* 1, no. 3 (1961): 125-37; **J. McDonald**, *Kergma and Didache: The Articulation and Structure of the Earliest Christian Message*, SNTSMS 37 (Cambridge: Cambridge University Press, 1980); **R. Riesner,** *Jesus als Lehrer*, 3rd ed., WUNT 2/7 (Tübingen: Mohr Siebeck, 1988); **K. Wegenast and D. Fürst,** "Teach, Instruct, etc.," *NIDNTT* 3:759-81; **A. F. Zimmermann,** *Die urchristlichen Lehrer: Studien zum Tradentenkreis der didaskaloi im frühen Urchristentum*, 2nd ed., WUNT 2/12 (Tübingen: Mohr Siebeck, 1988).

K. L. Yinger

TEACHING OF JESUS. *See* Jesus, Sayings of; Jesus and Paul.

TEMPLE

If Torah was ancient Judaism's most important text, the Jerusalem temple was its most important institution. (This is despite the fact that the *Jerusalem site was contested by the Samaritans, who had established their sacred space in Shechem; by certain Egyptian Jews who looked to a Jewish-style cultus in Leontopolis; and by the Qumran community, which identified itself as the present-day eschatological temple.) The temple was the social nerve center of ancient Judaism, the hub of all Jewish religious activity across the Diaspora, and the seat of political power from which the high priest ruled. In any account of pre-AD 70 Jewish life, it would be difficult to overestimate the significance of the temple.

It should therefore come as little surprise that the Jewish cult provided Paul with one of his most important conceptual categories as he worked out issues of soteriology, ecclesiology, and *ethics. In elaborating on this point, it will be helpful to address (1) the basic historical facts regarding the Herodian temple and the apostle's relationship to it, (2) the ancient Jewish understanding of the temple together with Judaism's expectations of a future eschatological temple, and (3) leading examples of temple images in Paul, particularly as these shed light on his assumptions regarding the Jerusalem temple, the *church, and the interrelationship between the two.

1. The Herodian Temple and Paul
2. Perspectives on the Temple in Second Temple Judaism
3. Temple Imagery in Paul
4. Conclusion

1. The Herodian Temple and Paul.

In the winter of 20–19 BC Herod the Great initiated a massive renovation project of the so-called Second Temple, which had been completed in 516 BC under Zerubbabel. Though Herod had successfully rebuilt the housing for the inner sanctuary (*naos*) within some eighteen months, the larger project subsequently stalled. It was not until some eighty-five years later (AD 64) that the Herodian temple was completely finished, only to be destroyed six years later (AD 70) during the First Jewish Revolt. Notwithstanding its halting progress, the Herodian temple, spectacularly beautiful and greatly expanded, was a significant upgrade from its predecessor (Josephus, *J.W.* 1.401-402; b. Sukkah 51b).

Whereas the First Temple only recognized a simple distinction between the laity and priests (1 Kings 8:41-43; 2 Chron 6:32-33), the policies and architectural structure of the Herodian temple were designed to ensure the segregation of various demographic groupings. The temple precinct included the Court of the *Gentiles, which was open to all worshipers; the Court of *Women, open to Jewish women but closed to the Gentiles; and the Court of *Israel, open to Jewish men but closed to women and Gentiles. As documentary and archaeological evidence confirm, Gentiles who trespassed beyond the balustrade and wandered into either of the two inner courts would be immediately subject to the death penalty (Josephus, *Ant.* 15.417; *J.W.* 5.194; 6.125-126; see also Philo, *Legat.* 212; m. Kel. 1:8). The very fact that Judaism's sharp social distinctions were reinforced in the temple's physical layout gives some indication of the difficulties facing Paul as he preached a gospel of "neither Jew nor Greek . . . neither male nor female" (Gal 3:28).

The temple's interior dividing wall separating Jews and Gentiles relates to one particularly harrowing event in the life of Paul. In Acts 21:27-36, Luke recounts a riot at the temple, centered on Paul and triggered by false rumors that he had smuggled the Gentile Trophimus past the balustrade. Given the widely held perception that Paul had spoken against "our *law and this place" (Acts 21:28), the temple authorities found the rumors all too plausible. Later, when the high priest Ananias met Felix at Caesarea to discuss the matter, he accused Paul of attempting to profane the temple (Acts 24:7)—charges the *apostle vigorously denied (Acts 24:11-12). In fact, in Luke's narrative, the apostle not only insists on his adherence to appropriate temple piety (Acts 22:17; 24:17-18; 25:8) but also exhibits such piety at several points (Acts 22:17; 24:17-18). Undoubtedly Luke had a certain apologetic agenda in relating this narrative. But on the assumption that his depiction of Paul is historically trustworthy, it seems that the rumors had gotten it wrong: the apostle regarded himself as a temple devotee in good standing and was willing to submit himself to any necessary ritual protocol in order to maintain that status. As Paul's peers within the Twelve likewise continued to engage in temple piety throughout Acts, his posture toward the cultus does not appear to be inconsistent with the approach of others in the apostolic circle.

2. Perspectives on the Temple in Second Temple Judaism.

Before exploring how Paul reworked temple categories around his christological convictions, a few observations are in order regarding the Hebrew Bible's theology of the temple and its subsequent trajectory in apocalyptic Judaism. In the scriptural imagination, though Yahweh was thought to rule from his throne in heaven, he retained the earthly temple as his footstool (Ps 103:19; 123:1; 132:7; Is 66:1). The temple contained his real presence, and this was signified not least by the visible presence of the divine *glory in the temple (2 Chron 7:1). The God of Israel, then, was thought to occupy heaven and the temple simultaneously. This is not unrelated to the belief that the design of the tabernacle, and subsequently the temple building, was based on a heavenly blueprint for the tabernacle (Ex 25:9, 40; Num 8:4; Acts 7:44; Heb 8:5). Given this correspondence, Second Temple Judaism widely came to consider the earthly temple an imperfect if not provisional analogue of the heavenly throne room.

By the second century BC, as hopes for the arrival of God's *kingdom became more ardent, Judaism became increasingly polarized between those affirming the existing temple (Ben Sira, Wisdom of Solomon, 2 Enoch), on the one side, and those who either relativized the value of the cultus or rejected it altogether, on the other. Tending toward the latter of these two broad options, Jewish *apocalypticism began to nurture expectations that God and/or his Messiah would usher in the true heavenly temple "not made by human hands" (see Ex 15:17-18; Dan 2:34; 7:1-14), causing it either to absorb or to supplant the existing apparatus. (The Messiah's role in the building of the final temple was fundamentally rooted in 2 Sam 7, where it was promised that David's seed would build the temple.) In some cases, the apocalyptic *hope entailed visions of resplendent architecture; in other instances, the core of the temple's structure and operation—its physical fixtures and rituals—were not so much spiritualized or metaphorized (as much early scholarship has described it) but conceptually remapped onto a remnant worshiping community.

A leading example of such a remapped temple was the Qumran community, which saw its members as comprising the segue to the final temple (1QS

VIII, 6-10; 4Q174 1-7; 11Q19 XXIX, 8-10). Although more sympathetic to the Jerusalem cultus than their Qumran counterpart, the author of the second-century BC text of Jubilees held similar hopes of God establishing the final sacred space (Jub. 1.15-18), though—as a point of difference—seemingly in continuity with the existing temple. Writing around the same time as the writer of Jubilees, the author of the Apocalypse of Weeks (1 En. 93.1-10; 91.11-17) set forth a messianic vision that looked forward to time when a "house will be built for the Great King in glory for evermore" (1 En. 91.12-13). In line with other texts (2 Macc 1:27-29; 1 En. 89–90; CD I, 3-11; 1QH[a] XII, 8-9; 1QS VIII, 12-14; IX, 18-20; 1QM I, 3; 4Q177 5-6 I, 7-10; 4Q258 3 III, 4; 4Q259 1 III, 19), the writer of the Apocalypse denies the possibility of a return from exile apart from the construction of this final and perfected temple. The same pattern obtains in the Maccabean-era Book of Dreams (1 En. 83–90), where the seer catches a glimpse of a renewed temple with new ornaments and columns (1 En. 90.29).

Such sects, positing a radical discontinuity between the Second Temple and the final temple, were often highly critical of the Herodian cultus and the moral degradation of its priesthood (Psalms of Solomon; T. Mos. 5.1-6; b. Yebam. 8a-b; Josephus, *Ant.* 20.180-181, 20.204-207). These criticisms in turn frequently went hand in hand with predictions concerning the temple's destruction (e.g., T. Levi 14.1–15.3; T. Jud. 23.11-5; Life of Jonah 10.11). Jesus' traditions reporting his cleansing of the temple and prediction of its destruction (Mk 11:15-17; 13) strongly suggest that the early Jesus movement fit snugly within this stream.

3. Temple Imagery in Paul.

As a Second Temple Jew who in dramatic fashion had become convinced that Jesus was the resurrected Messiah, Paul would have likely interpreted Christ's resurrection as the trigger event for the eschatological temple and the defining factor accounting for its form. In fact, the community of *faith that would later embrace this unlikely convert must have almost certainly drawn the same inference. Narratives surrounding the pre-Pauline church confirm as much, not least Luke's account of Pentecost (Acts 2), where the church's reception of the Spirit marks the fledgling community as a kind of reconstituted temple (Beale, 201-15). That Paul considered his churches to be extensions of the inbreaking eschatological temple can be sustained on a brief overview of the more salient temple-related Pauline texts.

3.1. Galatians. In what may be his earliest preserved letter, Paul describes the apostles *Peter, James, and John as seeming "pillars" (Gal 2:9). Though the metaphor may refer to nothing more than the apostolic troika's special status within the church, many interpreters (e.g., Barrett 1953, 1-19; Bauckham 1995, 441-50) understand it as a well-established epithet alluding to the pillars straddling the entrance to the temple inner court (see also 4Q164). In this case, Galatians 2:9 perhaps stands as the earliest documented evidence that the (pre-Pauline) Palestinian community considered itself a reconstituted temple of *God. Such temple imagery also seems to inform Paul's use of "to build" (*oikodomeō*) not in just Galatians 2:18 but other texts such as 1 Corinthians 8:1; 10:23; 14:4, 17; 1 Thessalonians 5:11 (so, e.g., Dunn 1993, 142; see also 2 Cor 10:8; 12:19; 13:10). Not insignificantly, the same verb occurs in the LXX in connection with the (re)building of the First Temple (2 Sam 7:5; 1 Kings 3:2; 5:3; 6:2; 2 Chron 3:1) and Second Temple (Is 44:28; Ezra 1:2; Hag 1:2; 1 Macc 4:47-78; 5:1), as well as the eschatological temple (Zech 6:12; Tob 1:4; 13:11; 14:5). Because the Jerusalem temple was operative during the apostle's life, Paul's language hints at an understanding of the Christian community as a kind of countertemple community.

3.2. Thessalonian and Corinthian Correspondence. In 1 Thessalonians Paul prays that the Thessalonian believers would be "blameless in *holiness [*amemptous en hagiōsynē*] before God" (1 Thess 3:13). When viewed against the lexical background of the LXX, Paul's choice of terms has clear cultic associations; meanwhile, the phrase "before God" refers to the atoning space (Ex 28:12; 29:11; Lev 10:17; 23:28; etc.). The notion of "continuous *prayer" (1 Thess 1:2; 2:13; 5:17; see also Rom 1:9) naturally invokes the mental image of the uninterrupted *tāmîd* offerings.

Temple imagery occurs in several key passages in 1 Corinthians. In 1 Corinthians 3:9-10, the apostle identifies the Corinthian community as "God's building" (*theou oikodomē*). Whereas some commentators find either no uniquely cultic significance in the phrase or at the most a pagan significance, such approaches struggle to explain why the apostle appends "of God" if he meant just any building or just any pagan temple. Second, if the combination of architectural and horticultural images in this passage seems like a jarring mixing of metaphors to the modern reader, precisely this combination of symbols signals a cultic context in other literature (e.g., 1QS VIII, 4-10). Finally, that the nearby 1 Corinthians 3:16-17 should identify Corinthian believers as a divinely indwelt temple confirms that Paul saw the Corinthians as together compromising a temple of sorts.

That the imagery here is purely metaphorical as opposed to realistic can hardly be assumed. Although some scholars have supported the former possibility, this reading crucially overlooks how some of the key words and phrases in 1 Corinthians 3:11-15 ("gold," "silver," "revealed with fire," and "burned up") derive from Malachi 3–4, a passage that foretells of the Lord's coming to his eschatological temple. Nor, in Paul's catalogue of sound and unsound construction materials, does it go unnoticed that the former category overlaps with the raw materials used for the First Temple (see 1 Chron 29:2; Beale, 246-47). With these considerations in mind, it would be insufficient to claim that Paul saw the Corinthians *as if* they were a temple. Indeed, as far as the apostle was concerned, his Corinthian hearers were the living fulfillment of Malachi 3–4, fellow members of the eschatological temple.

Scriptural circumlocutions for the eschatological temple (Ezek 11:17; 20:34, 41; 37:26-27) also underwrite Paul's identification of the Corinthian believers as members of the "temple of God" in 2 Corinthians 6:14–7:1, where he treats the believers' relationships with those outside the church. Building on Ezekiel's vision of the future glorious temple (Ezek 37–48), Paul's logic assumes that the temple is presently composed of believers. (Of course, an appeal to Ezekiel's exilic theology would have been rhetorically powerful for an audience struggling to stem the toxic tide of the surrounding culture.) Nor is there any reason to force a false dilemma on Paul's transference of the temple concept. If believers together comprise the temple, the individual human body no less than the community as a whole is constitutive of sacred space (Gupta).

3.3. Romans and Philippians. Paul's epistle to the Romans exhibits the same pattern. In describing the execution of his apostleship as a "priestly duty" (Rom 15:16), the apostle sees his kerygmatic *ministry as a kind of building "on a foundation" (*themelios*, Rom 15:20), a term that elsewhere in the Pauline corpus is applied to the temple foundation (1 Cor 3:10-12; Eph 2:20; 1 Tim 6:19; 2 Tim 2:19; see also Heb 6:1; 11:10). In the same vein, Paul exhorts believers to offer themselves as "living *sacrifices to God," which is an act of "spiritual *worship" (Rom 12:1). All this elaborates on Paul's earlier stated conviction (Rom 6–8) that God's presence dwells through the Spirit in the *bodies of the Roman believers. Since Christ is the new *mercy seat where atonement occurs (Rom 3:25), the Jerusalem temple's apparatus of atonement is no longer relevant to the believing community.

In one of his last letters, Philippians, the apostle calls believers to avoid quarrelling "so that you may be *blameless and innocent* [*amemptoi kai akeraioi*]" (Phil 2:15). The cultic connotations of "blameless" have already been treated above. As for the adjective *akeraios*, regularly used to modify pure or unmixed wine, this anticipates Paul's self-comparison with a cultic libation in Philippians 2:17. By the same token, Paul's receipt of financial gifts amount to "a fragrant offering, a sacrifice acceptable and pleasing to God" (Phil 4:18). Indeed, Paul presents himself is a kind of temple sacrifice (Phil 1:20; see Ware, 201-36; Phil 1:28-30). From beginning to end, Paul's reliance on cultic metaphors remains unstinting and theologically rich.

4. Conclusion.
There is considerable evidence that Paul regarded the category of temple as conceptually integral to his thought. Despite this evidence, a somewhat recent line of scholarship (Hogeterp; Horn; Fredriksen; Regev 2010) has sought to refute this point, arguing that Paul's appeals to cultic images are more rhetorical than substantive. While it is certainly not impossible that Paul resorted to cultic imagery merely to "imbue . . . followers with an atmosphere of holiness" (Regev 2018, 627), this approach overlooks early Christianity's apocalyptic milieu (which as a rule anticipated the eventual redundancy of the Second Temple) as well as the close correlation between Pauline soteriology and "temple logic." By all accounts, the apostle's paraenetic program can be accurately described as a "cultic-priestly ethic" (Berger, 160).

For Paul, the *preaching of the *gospel and its concomitant cultic ethic logically followed from Christ's *ascension and the giving of the Spirit at Pentecost, marking a shift from the Herodian temple to the dispersed Christian communities. His reasoning follows, in other words, from the simple scriptural principle that wherever the Spirit dwells, there too is the temple (Lev 9; Num 17:7 [16:42]; 1 Kings 8:11; 2 Chron 5:14; 7:1-3). If on the basis of early Jesus traditions early Christians regarded the transition from one temple economy to another as a gradual shift culminating in the expected destruction of the Jerusalem temple (Mk 13), one might expect the apostolic temple practices to shift incrementally until such a time when such practices were no longer possible (Perrin, 75-77).

See also Church; Eschatology; Jerusalem, City of; Paul and Judaism.

BIBLIOGRAPHY. **C. K. Barrett**, "Paul and the 'Pillar' Apostles," in *Studia Paulina in honorem Johannis de Zwaan, Septuagenarii*, ed. J. N. Sevenster and W. C. van Unnik (Haarlem: Bohn, 1953), 1-19; **R. Bauckham**, "James and the Jerusalem Church," in *The Book of Acts in Its Palestinian Setting*, ed. R. Bauckham (Grand Rapids: Eerdmans, 1995): 415-80; **G. K. Beale**, *The Temple and the Church's Mission*, NSBT (Downers Grove, IL: InterVarsity Press, 2004); **K. Berger,** *Von der Schönheit der Ethik* (Frankfurt am Main: Insel, 2006); **J. D. G. Dunn,** *The Epistle to the Galatians*, BNTC (Peabody, MA: Hendrickson, 1993); **S. Finlan,** *The Background and Content of Paul's Cultic Atonement Metaphors*, AcBib 19 (Atlanta: Society of Biblical Literature, 2004); **P. Fredriksen,** "Judaizing the Nations: The Ritual Demands on Paul's Gospel," *NTS* 56 (2010): 232-52; **N. K. Gupta,** *Worship That Makes Sense to Paul: A New Approach to the Theology and Ethics of Paul's Cultic Metaphors* (Berlin: de Gruyter, 2010); **A. L. A. Hogeterp,** *Paul and God's Temple*, BTS 2 (Leuven: Peeters, 2006); **F. W. Horn,** "Paulus und der herodianische Tempel," *NTS* 53 (2007): 184-203; **S. Hultgren,** "*Hilasterion* (Rom. 3:25) and the Union of Divine Justice and Mercy. Part 1: The Convergence of Temple and Martyrdom Theologies," *JTS* 70 (2019): 69-109; **I. Jolivet,** "The Ethical Instructions in Ephesians as the Unwritten Statutes and Ordinances of God's New Temple in Ezekiel," *ResQ* 48 (2006): 193-210; **C. Keener,** "One New Temple in Christ (Ephesians 2:11-22; Acts 21:27-29; Mark 11:17; John 4:20-24)," *AJPS* 12 (2009): 75-92; **J. R. Lanci,** *A New Temple for Corinth: Rhetorical and Archaeological Approaches to Pauline Imagery*, SBL 1 (New York: Lang, 1997); **N. Perrin,** *Jesus the Temple* (Grand Rapids, MI: Baker Academic, 2010); **E. Regev,** "Temple Concerns and High-Priestly Prosecutions from Peter to James: Between Narrative and History," *NTS* 56 (2010): 64-89; idem, "Community as Temple: Revisiting Cultic Metaphors in Qumran and the New Testament," *BBR* 28 (2018): 604-31; **J. P. Sweeney,** "Jesus, Paul, and the Temple: An Exploration of Some Patterns of Continuity," *JETS* 46 (2003): 605-31; **M. Vahrenhorst,** *Kultische Sprache in den Paulusbriefen*, WUNT 230 (Tübingen: Mohr Siebeck, 2008); **J. P. Ware,** *The Mission of the Church in Paul's Letter to the Philippians in the Context of Ancient Judaism*, NovTSup 120 (Leiden: Brill, 2005).

N. Perrin

TENTMAKING

There are a number of references to Paul working to support himself, both from his own letters (1 Cor 4:12; 9:1-18; 2 Cor 6:5; 11:23, 27; 1 Thess 2:9; 2 Thess 3:8) and from Acts (Acts 18:3; 20:34-35). By so working Paul supported not only himself but also "those who were with [him]" (Acts 20:34).

Only one of these references, however, identifies the nature of Paul's work—tentmaking (Gk. *ēsan . . . skēnopoioi tē technē*, Acts 18:3). The Greek *skēnopoios* literally means "tentmaker" or "leatherworker."

1. The Nature of Tentmaking
2. Paul: Tentmaker and Apostle
3. Paul's Reasons for Working
4. Problems Caused by Paul's Work
5. The Rabbis and Work

1. The Nature of Tentmaking.

Scholars are divided over the kind of material on which Paul worked. Many scholars from earlier generations suggested it was the rough cloth made of goats' hair, known as *cilicium*, which took its name from Paul's native province, Cilicia. Understandably, they have readily connected this local cloth with the Cilician Paul's tentmaking, suggesting he may have learned this trade as a youth in Tarsus.

A majority today, however, noting that *cilicium* was used widely for purposes other than tentmaking and that the patristic interpretations of *skēnopoios* point in the direction of leather goods, believe that tents were generally made of leather (Hock 1980, 20-21). It is now held that the material with which Paul worked was leather. "Tentmaking" may have taken its name from its primary task but have included manufacture and repair of a range of leather and woven goods. A problem with this view, however, is that if the tanning of leather was a despised trade among the Jews (Jeremias, 303-12), would not any kind of leatherworking have shared the same reputation? Moreover, the staining of hands through this work may have rendered Paul unacceptable in the upper-class circles in which he sometimes moved (e.g., Acts 17:12, 19; 19:31; Rom 16:23; but see "these hands" of Acts 20:34).

Aquila and Priscilla, tentmakers recently arrived in *Corinth after Claudius's expulsion of the Jews from Rome, appear to have been entrepreneurial manufacturers and traders in tents and related goods who moved from city to city. At least, so far as the meager evidence about them goes, one sees them first in Rome, next in Corinth, then in *Ephesus, and finally again in Rome (Acts 18:1-3, 26; Rom 16:3-4). Each of the places Paul is known to have worked—Thessalonica, Corinth, or Ephesus—was a great urban center. Why would tents be needed in these well-developed cities? The many travelers to these great cities may have purchased, as well as sought the repair of, tents and similar items as they passed through. Sailors in these port cities would also have lived in tents while on shore. It is possible that "tentmakers" may have manufactured and repaired various kinds of booths, canopies, and awnings for city use.

2. Paul: Tentmaker and Apostle.

It is clear that Paul's work was physical and arduous. Paul writes of "labor and toil . . . we worked night and day" (1 Thess 2:9; see also 2 Thess 3:8; Acts 20:35) and of "working with our own hands" (1 Cor 4:12; see also Acts 20:34). One gains an impression of one whose daily life was characterized by hard physical labor, which began before sunrise.

Ronald Hock has shown that, far from being peripheral to Paul's life, tentmaking was central to it. "More than any of us has supposed, Paul was *Paul the Tentmaker*. His trade occupied much of his time. . . . His life was very much that of the workshop . . . of being bent over a workbench like a slave and of working side by side with slaves" (Hock 1980, 67).

Fundamental to those passages where Paul catalogs his apostolic sufferings, one finds references to Paul's "labor." Comparing himself with the Corinthians, he writes, "We are weak, but you are strong. You are held in *honor, but we in disrepute. To this present hour we hunger and thirst, we are ill clad and buffeted and homeless, and *we labor working with our own hands*" (1 Cor 4:10-12; see also 2 Cor 11:27).

Significantly, Paul connects his work with his *ministry. He reminds the Thessalonians, "Night and day *working* . . . we proclaimed . . . to you the *gospel of *God" (1 Thess 2:9). This probably means that Paul talked to people while he worked and also, almost certainly, that on some days or during part of the day he laid aside his apron and tools and taught the gospel (Acts 19:9-11). His lifestyle was characterized by both work *and* preaching.

3. Paul's Reasons for Working.

Greco-Roman culture was accustomed to traveling philosophers and teachers who would be paid a fee for their efforts or, alternatively, given *hospitality and other benefits by wealthy patrons, sometimes under circumstances that generated scandal. It was not uncommon for itinerant lecturers to earn an evil reputation (Philostratus, *Vit. Apoll.* 1.13; Lucian, *Hermot.* 59; Dio Chrysostom, *Virt.* 8.9). Paul certainly benefited from the *patronage of the wealthy and could easily have sought and received payment (e.g., Acts 17:4, 12; Rom 16:23; 1 Cor 1:14; Acts 19:31).

There are three reasons in particular why Paul worked to support himself.

First, conscious that he may have been perceived as just one of many itinerant lecturers, some of whom were none too scrupulous, Paul may have worked to support himself out of concern lest his ministry and the message of the gospel be associated with other traveling philosophers (see 1 Thess 1:5; 2:3-6; 1 Cor 9:12; Acts 20:33-35). Paul contrasts with himself the newly arrived opponents in Corinth as "those who peddle [*kapēleuontes*] the word of God" (2 Cor 2:17), "[who] tamper [*dolountes*] with God's word" (2 Cor 4:2), and who "prey upon" (*katesthiei*, literally "devour") the Corinthians (2 Cor 11:20). This vocabulary implies the receipt of improper payment, the watering down of the message, and the exploitation of the hearers. For his part Paul was true to the message, working rather than accepting payment for his ministry, and caring for his congregations (see 1 Thess 2:5-10).

Second, Paul regarded idleness, which was endemic in Greco-Roman society, as inappropriate for the Christian believer. So he deliberately set the example of hard work to support himself and called on his converts to imitate him (1 Thess 5:14; 2 Thess 3:6-13). The practical values of life in *Christ were concretely exemplified in his own consciously executed lifestyle, in which he supported himself by work (Eph 4:28; see Acts 20:35).

Third, as one called to be the *apostle to the *Gentiles, Paul had no option but to obey God's *call to preach the gospel. *God* called him, and so Paul made "the gospel free of charge" to the people to whom he came (1 Cor 9:16-18). His obedience to God would have been diminished by receiving payment from others. His pay was to receive no pay. His work was between him and God; he would not be paid for it.

4. Problems Caused by Paul's Work.

Paul's contemporaries generally regarded work as appropriate for *slaves but not for free citizens. Artisans and manual workers were looked down on. Cicero commented that a workshop was no place for a free man (*Off.* 1.150). Members of churches established by Paul would probably have regarded his manual labor as remarkable and quite possibly offensive. There are hints from Paul himself that his work required a degree of condescension and "abasement" (2 Cor 11:7). That he was born as a Roman citizen is usually taken to imply an affluent background in provincial Cilicia (Acts 22:28).

It is evident from 2 Corinthians 11:7-10; 12:14-18 that Paul's defense for working to support himself in 1 Corinthians 9:15-18 had proved unconvincing to the Corinthians. It is probable that by working to support himself Paul had broken the conventions of patronage whereby the wealthy would provide for the visiting lecturer. Paul appears to have been guilty of a serious slight on the Corinthians, for which, throughout the seven years of their active association, they never forgave him. His "*sin" was compounded because he was prepared to receive assistance from the Macedonians (2 Cor 11:9).

5. The Rabbis and Work.

From late Jewish sources one learns that rabbis were expected to support themselves by some form of labor. Rabbi Zadok says, "Make not of the Torah . . . a spade wherewith to dig . . . whosoever derives a profit for himself from the words of the Torah is helping his own destruction" (*Pirqe Avot* 4.7). Rabbi Gamaliel III declares, "An excellent thing is the study of the Torah combined with some secular occupation, for the labor by them both puts sin out of one's mind. All study of the Torah which is not combined with work will ultimately be futile and lead to sin" (*Pirqe Avot* 2.12).

Based on these texts it is possible that Paul learned his tentmaking as a pupil rabbi. Although Hock has questioned this assumption, there is good reason to accept it. Otherwise, how can one explain a member of the provincial elite having such a menial trade?

See also Apostle; Financial Support; Honor/Shame; Suffering; Urban Setting of Paul's Churches.

BIBLIOGRAPHY. **F. Hauck,** "κόπος, κοπιάω," *TDNT* 3:827-30; **R. F. Hock,** "Paul's Tentmaking and the Problem of His Social Class," *JBL* 97 (1978): 555-64; idem, *The Social Context of Paul's Mission* (Philadelphia: Fortress, 1980); **J. Jeremias,** *Jerusalem in the Time of Jesus* (Philadelphia: Fortress, 1969); **P. Lampe,** *Christians at Rome in the First Two Centuries* (London: Continuum, 2006); **P. Marshall,** *Enmity in Corinth: Social Conventions in Paul's Relations with the Corinthians*, WUNT 2/23 (Tübingen: Mohr Siebeck, 1987); **W. Michaelis,** "σκηνοποιός," *TDNT* 7:393-94; **S. Walton,** "Paul, Patronage, and Pay: What Do We Know About the Apostle's Financial Support?," in *Paul as Missionary*, ed. T. J. Burke and B. S. Rosner (London: T&T Clark, 2011), 220-33.

P. W. Barnett

TEXTUAL CRITICISM

Interpreting the text of Paul presupposes a text of Paul to interpret. Since Paul's autographs no longer exist and the extant copies differ in thousands of places, that text must be reconstructed. As a historical enterprise, textual criticism comprises the sensitive application of time-tested principles in order to establish an author's original text as the evidence allows. It benefits from and contributes to a host of sister disciplines including papyrology, paleography, codicology, reception history, and even art history, to name a few. Although a majority of variants in Paul are easily resolved or bear little consequence on interpretation (or both), no careful interpreter can afford to ignore textual criticism for long.

1. Goal of Textual Criticism.

The place to begin a discussion of textual criticism is with its goals. All questions of method naturally flow from this point. The longstanding goal for the NT has been to obtain the author's original (or autographic) text. In centuries past, the lack of early witnesses led some, such as Karl Lachmann, to aim lower (or later) by producing editions they claimed represented the text of the third or fourth century. With the discovery of so many early witnesses in the nineteenth and twentieth centuries, the discipline settled into the confident belief that one should aim for the original, first-century text of the NT.

Today, the consensus is again contested (Holmes, "Original"). Some suggest that the original text is unreachable given the complexity of the *tradition and the sheer amount of variation (Swanson, xxvi). Others have challenged the usefulness of the term *original text* given its multivalent use (Epp 1999). Still others challenge the idea that a single authoritative text ever existed or ever will (Parker, 2012, 24-25; Larsen). This leads some to value textual plurality as such.

A potentially mediating position is the pursuit of the initial text (or *Ausgangstext*, in its original German). Developed as part of the coherence-based genealogical method, the initial text is defined as that text from which the entire extant tradition developed. The key to this definition is that it avoids prejudging whether the initial text, in any given corpus, is the author's text or something later. The major shortcoming of this goal is that, rather than clarifying, it has generated its own misunderstanding (Wasserman and Gurry, 11-13).

In the end, the quest for the original text cannot be severed from interest in Paul himself. As long as there are readers who want to know what St. Paul really said, the traditional goal will remain relevant, however complicated. One thing that is clear is that, in terms of amount and quality of textual evidence, one is at great advantage in the case of Paul's letters.

2. Composition, Collaboration, and Collection.
The question of goal leads directly to a trio of complicating issues involving the composition of Paul's *letters, the literary collaboration involved, and their subsequent collection into a single corpus.

At a number of points, Paul's letters reference collaboration in their production and transmission. This includes the use of an amanuensis (Rom 16:22), his co-senders both named (1 Cor 1:1; 2 Cor 1:1; Col 1:1; 1 Thess 1:1; 2 Thess 1:1; Philem 1) and unnamed (Gal 1:1), and the attention he draws to taking the pen into his own hand (1 Cor 16:21; Gal 6:11; Col 4:18; 2 Thess 3:17; Philem 19). This has led to the suggestion that there may be variants in the Pauline corpus where one has a choice, present from the time of the very first readers, between Paul's dictated text and his collaborators' text (e.g., *echomen* vs. *echōmen* in Rom 5:1). Aside from the difficulty of proving such a distinction in practice, that Paul sometimes draws attention to his "own" words suggests that where he does not do so it is because he sees no daylight between his words and his collaborators'.

A more difficult question is the relationship of composition to collection. The earliest manuscript of any of Paul's letters (P^{46}) is already a collection. Since Paul's letters encouraged the recipients to share them (Col 4:16), it may be that the collection grew naturally as churches aggregated letters from one another. Alternatively, it is possible that Paul, like others in the ancient world, kept copies of his own letters and so produced the first Pauline letter collection (Trobisch).

Finally, at key points, textual criticism cannot be neatly separated from redactional questions. An instructive comparison is the manuscript evidence for Romans versus 2 Corinthians. Whereas the displacement of Romans 16:25-27 and related variants suggests that versions of Romans circulated without Romans 15–16 (Gamble), the opposite is the case for 2 Corinthians, where the manuscript evidence gives no direct support for the view that 2 Corinthians is a composite letter.

3. Method.
The typical text-critical approach used in classical literature is to establish the key manuscript relationships, identify their lost ancestor (the archetype), and then identify and remove any remaining errors to arrive at the author's text. This approach does not work well in a contaminated tradition such as the NT. Instead, NT textual critics have historically tried to study the text's history in more general terms, choosing the original text from among what they identify as the most important witnesses.

The most important development in recent years is the production of a major new critical edition of the NT known as the *Editio Critica Maior*. Leveraging the coherence-based genealogical method to reconstruct the initial text, its scope includes the text's history through the first millennium. To date, work on Paul is underway but not yet published. When finished, it will be indispensable for serious textual work on Paul.

In lieu of that, three main approaches to NT textual criticism deserve mention. The Byzantine priority position, named for the text found in later and more numerous Byzantine manuscripts, holds that a normal transmission process means that the original text is found in a preponderance of witnesses. In practice, this leads to a Byzantine text that requires textual decisions only where there is no clear majority to follow. (Since Byzantine prioritists typically refuse to reject majority readings, they could fairly be called Byzantine exclusivists.) Quite different is the approach of thoroughgoing eclecticism, which holds that present-day knowledge of manuscript relations is so uncertain that no single manuscript, however old, nor any set of manuscripts, however numerous, can be given priority. Instead, variants are approached on their own merits with less regard for the age or supposed quality of the witnesses that attest them.

The dominant view, which stands behind the most important recent hand editions (SBLGNT, NA^{28}/UBS^{5}, Tyndale House Greek New Testament), is known as "reasoned eclecticism." It holds that the NT text has suffered from significant contamination and is thus not "normal." But it also holds that this contamination is not so severe that one cannot say anything positive about manuscript relations or their relative value. As a result, the original text must be identified on a case-by-case basis, sometimes following one witness, sometimes another (hence "eclectic"). It is considered "reasoned" because judgments are based on a balance of both internal and external evidence. Among a set of well-worn criteria, the single most important one is that the reading that best accounts for how the other(s) developed should be preferred (Epp 2011, 93-96).

*3.1. **Internal Evidence.*** Internal evidence weighs each variant reading on its own merits, without regard for which witnesses are involved. It can be helpfully subdivided in two.

In the first case, one considers what *Paul* is likely to have written based on what one knows of his style and theology. This is known as intrinsic probability. For example, a common argument for reading *echomen* rather than *echōmen* in Romans 5:1 is that it is more in keeping with Paul's argument up to that point. The second type of internal evidence takes account of what *scribes* are more likely to have (mis) copied. This is known as transcriptional probability. Here an overarching principle emerges that the more difficult the reading would be to scribes (not to modern people), the more likely it is to be original. This is because scribes are prone to smooth or clarify a text rather than obscure it (the obvious exception being scribal mistakes that result in nonsense.) For example, in Romans 7:3, scribes would naturally add "of the husband" (*tou andros*) to clarify which *law the wife is freed from. The unqualified form is thus the more difficult one and so original. A large number of meaningful variants fall into this category of changes introduced to smooth the syntax, clarify the theology, or make the implicit explicit.

Statistical study shows that the largest category of scribal mistake is the substitution of one word or form for another. This is followed by addition, omission, and then transposition (Gurry, 126-27). Importantly, recent study of scribal habits has challenged the commonly blunt application of the preference for the shorter reading. Traditionally based on the belief that scribes are more likely to add than to omit, it appears that the opposite is the case, at least in the early period (Royse 2008, 705-36).

Other mistakes to which scribes were prone include harmonizing to the immediate context or to parallel passages, skipping words (parablepsis) or doubling them (dittography) because of similar letters, transposing letters within a word (metathesis), changing rare expressions to more common ones, and conflating readings from multiple sources.

*3.2. **External Evidence.*** External evidence takes into account the witnesses in which a given reading is found and ascribes weight based on their age and, above all, their quality. An earlier witness with a worse text is obviously not better than a later witness with a better text. Careful use of external evidence thus requires what Brooke Westcott and Fenton Hort call a "knowledge of documents" (31). In this way, external evidence is partly built on internal evidence. A shorter reading in a manuscript known for accidental omissions, for example, is less significant than it would be otherwise. Reconstructing Paul's text requires the careful use of extant witnesses. In most critical editions, these are listed in the apparatus in order of Greek manuscripts, early versions, and patristic citations.

4. Important Witnesses.

*4.1. **Greek Manuscripts.*** Greek manuscripts constitute the most important category of witnesses. For Paul, their number totals well over seven hundred. They are subdivided—somewhat arbitrarily, it must be said—into papyri, majuscules, minuscules, and lectionaries. The papyri and majuscules are generally more important for their age and overall quality, whereas the minuscules and lectionaries are more numerous.

4.1.1. Papyri. The most important papyri from the first five centuries are given here according to the Gregory-Aland catalogue.

Table 1. Important Papyri of Paul's Letters

Gregory-Aland Number	Date	Contents
P^{10}	4th	Rom 1:1-7
P^{15}	3rd	1 Cor 7:18–8:4
P^{16}	3rd/4th	Phil 3:10-17; 4:2-8
P^{27}	3rd	Rom 8:12-22, 24-27; 8:33–9:3; 9:5-9
P^{30}	3rd	1 Thess 4:12-13, 16-17; 5:3, 8-10, 12-18, 25-28; 2 Thess 1:1-2
P^{32}	3rd	Titus 1:11-15; 2:3-8
P^{40}	3rd	Rom 1:24-27; 1:31–2:3; 3:21–4:8; 6:4-5, 16; 9:16-17, 27
P^{46}	3rd	Rom 5:17–1 Thess 5:28 (with lacunae; includes Hebrews)
P^{49}	3rd	Eph 4:16-29; 4:32–5:13
P^{51}	5th	Gal 1:2-10, 13, 16-20

Gregory-Aland Number	Date	Contents
P^{65}	3rd	1 Thess 1:3–2:1, 6-13
P^{87}	3rd	Philem 13-15, 24-25
P^{92}	3rd/4th	Eph 1:11-13, 19-21; 2 Thess 1:4-5, 11-12
P^{94}	5th/6th	Rom 6:10-13, 19-22
P^{99}	5th	Rom 1:1; 2 Cor 1:3-17, 20-24; 2:1-8, 22; 9:2–11:8; 11:9-23; 11:26–13:11; Gal 1:4-11; 1:9–6:15; 1:14–4:9; Eph 1:2-4, 21; 3:8-6, 24; 3:19–4:9
P^{113}	3rd	Rom 2:12-13, 29
P^{117}	4th/5th	2 Cor 7:6-11
P^{118}	3rd	Rom 15:26-27, 32-33; 16:1, 4-7, 11-12
P^{123}	4th	1 Cor 14:31-34; 15:3-6
P^{129}	2nd	1 Cor 7:32-37; 8:10–9:3, 10-16; 9:27–10:6
P^{131}	3rd	Rom 9:18-23; 9:33–10:4
P^{132}	3rd/4th	Eph 3:21–4:2; 2:14-16
P^{133}	3rd	1 Tim 3:13–4:8
P^{135}	4th/5th	Gal 3:21-22, 28-29; 4:31–5:6; 5:10-15
P^{139}	4th	Philem 6-8, 18-20

It is remarkable that every book except 2 Timothy is attested at least once by the third century. Romans is the best attested, with seven witnesses, compared to only four early papyri for Ephesians, the next closest. The value of these papyri in terms of date is, unfortunately, offset by how fragmentary they are. In fact, P^{10} and P^{99} are a writing exercise and glossary, respectively, and could probably be excluded.

P^{46} stands out as the exception on this list for how much text is preserved. Besides being such an important window into the early text of Paul, it also provides crucial evidence for the Pauline corpus. The extant leaves end at 1 Thessalonians 5:28, but its pagination and single-quire construction allows one to deduce that six or seven folios are lost from beginning and end. What was on the final folios is a matter of debate. The increased lines per page has suggested that the missing leaves, with some added, could have contained not only 2 Thessalonians and Philemon but also the Pastorals (Duff). A more recent and comprehensive study has cast doubt on that conclusion in favor of leaving the question open (Ebojo, 204-35). The placement of Hebrews and Ephesians is unique in P^{46}, probably because the letters were ordered more strictly by length.

In terms of textual quality, P^{46} is generally considered to be a good underlying text copied with many obvious mistakes. A study of those variants unique to P^{46} shows that the scribe was prone to omission and substitution (Royse 2012, 183).

4.1.2. Majuscules. Though not as old as the earliest papyri, the majuscules provide the most important witnesses to Paul because of their unique combination of age, size, and quality. Since the end of the nineteenth century, these witnesses have provided the foundation for most critical editions and thus for English translations as well. The majuscules for the first six centuries are listed here with their Pauline contents.

Table 2. Early Majuscules of Paul's Letters

Gregory-Aland Number	Date	Contents
ℵ 01	4th	Romans–Philemon
A 02	5th	Romans–Philemon
B 03	4th	Romans–2 Thessalonians
C 04	5th	Romans–Philemon (with lacunae, including 2 Thessalonians)
D 06	6th	Romans–Philemon
I 016	5th	1 Corinthians–Philemon (with lacunae)
048	5th	Rom 13:4–15:9; 1 Cor 2:1-3, 11; 4:4-6; 5:5-11; 6:3-11; 12:13-15, 17, 20-27; 2 Cor 4:7–6:8; 8:9-18; 8:21–10:6; Eph 5:8–6:24; Phil 1:8-23; 2:1-4, 6-8; Col 1:20–2:8, 11-14, 22-23; 3:7-8; 3:12–4:18; 1 Thess 1:1, 5-6; 1 Tim 5:5–6:17, 20-21; 2 Tim 1:4-6, 8; 2:2-25; Titus 3:13-15; Philem 1-25

Gregory-Aland Number	Date	Contents
062	5th	Gal 4:15–5:14
088	5th/6th	1 Cor 15:53–16:9; Titus 1:1-13
0172	5th	Rom 1:27-30; 1:32–2:2
0176	5th	Gal 3:16-25
0185	4th	1 Cor 2:6–6:9; 6:13; 3:2-3
0186	5th/6th	2 Cor 4:5-8, 10, 12-13
0198	6th	Col 1:29–2:10; 2:13-14; 1 Thess 2:4-7, 12-17
0219	4th/5th	Rom 2:21-23; 3:8-9, 23-25, 27-30
0220	3rd	Rom 4:23–5:3; 5:8-13
0221	4th	Rom 5:16-17, 19; 5:21–6:3
0222	6th	1 Cor 9:5-7, 10, 12-13
0223	6th	2 Cor 1:17–2:2
0225	6th	2 Cor 5:1-2, 8-9, 14-16, 19-21; 6:1, 3-5; 8:16-24
0226	5th	1 Thess 4:16–5:5
0230	4th	Eph 6:11-12
0240	5th	1 Tim 6:4-13; Titus 1:4-8
0241	5th/6th	1 Tim 3:16–4:3; 4:8-11
0254	5th	Gal 5:13-17
0261	5th	Gal 1:9-12, 19-22; 4:25-31
0270	4th/5th	1 Cor 15:10-15, 19-25
0282	6th	Phil 2:22-24; 3:6-8
0285+081	6th	Rom 5:12, 14; 8:37–9:5; 13:1-4; 13:11–14:3; 1 Cor 4:2-7; 12:16, 18, 21-30; 14:26-33; Eph 3:13-20; 5:28–6:1; 1 Tim 1:1-7
0296	6th	2 Cor 7:3-4, 9-10

Four Greek majuscules are famous because they are pandects (א, A, B, C), meaning they contain both testaments. The text of א and B represented Westcott and Hort's "neutral text," the one they thought was free from recensional changes. Today, though this view is rightly rejected, the agreement of these two manuscripts still makes up the bulk of the text of the critical editions.

Codex Sinaiticus (א) is the work of two pairs of scribes in the NT. The Pauline corpus was copied by scribes designated A and D, with the former copying the bulk of NT and the latter serving as the senior member of the whole team (Parker 2010, 47-48). A study of the unique readings in Paul shows that omissions, substitutions, and harmonizations (in that order) constitute the largest categories of meaningful scribal mistakes (Jongkind 2007, 202-3). One of the most striking features of Sinaiticus is its tens of thousands of corrections—more than any other manuscript (Parker 2012, 3). The process of correcting started before it left the scriptorium and was continued in later centuries by those who sought to conform the text to the maturing Byzantine text. In using Sinaiticus for text-critical purposes, it is essential not to confuse these correctors with the original hands.

Codex Vaticanus (B) is perhaps the most important witness to the text of Paul. Unfortunately, it breaks off at Hebrews 9:14 so that 1 Timothy–Philemon, which it presumably contained originally, are now lost. Its text was also corrected, but unlike Sinaiticus, this was done by later reinking. Any letters or words not to be read were simply left untraced. Two features of Vaticanus deserve special mention in the context of Paul's letters. The first is that the Pauline corpus exhibits a chaptering system that is consecutive through the whole rather than the typical way of restarting with each book. This numbering system derives from an exemplar in which Hebrews must have followed Galatians because the numbers are not consecutive in Vaticanus. The second important feature is the presence of so-called Distigmai or double dots in the margins. There is a general agreement that these mark variants, but debate continues as to whether they derive from the original scriptorium or from Sepulveda in the sixteenth century. The debate has drawn special attention in Paul because of their use at 1 Corinthians 14:34-35.

The other two important pandects are Codex Alexandrinus (A) and the palimpsest Codex Ephraemi Rescriptus (C). Ephraemi was also subject to multiple levels of correction and was scraped in the twelfth century and reused for Ephrem's sermons. (It has been said this was not the last time sermons have clouded the biblical text!) As a result of chemicals used to read the undertext in the nineteenth century, it is now sometimes impossible to read. Codex

Alexandrinus is best known for preserving the earliest Byzantine text of the Gospels, but its Pauline text, where free from obvious error, is almost as valuable as that of ℵ and B.

The last majuscule to deserve special mention is Codex Claromontanus (D), which is the earliest Greek-Latin bilingual witness to Paul. Its text holds a particularly close relationship with two later bilinguals (F/010 and G/012) whose shared ancestor is thought to go back much earlier than Claromontanus. Their shared text, however, shows signs of concerted editing such that their testimony should be approached with caution when isolated.

4.1.3. Minuscules. The minuscules make up the largest category of Pauline manuscripts. The majority of minuscules attest a well-developed and largely standardized Byzantine text. A key point in the dominance of this text was the transition to minuscule script in the ninth century. Though often dismissed in previous generations, today the value of the Byzantine text for recovering the original text is being reevaluated (Wasserman and Gurry, 10-11). Certainly, the Byzantine text should not be dismissed out of hand. Its most important representatives in Paul are 1, 35, 398, 424, 1069, 1617, and 2352 (Houghton, 352). It is important to stress that the Byzantine text, while far more homogenous than other well-known texts such as the so-called Alexandrian or Western, is not a complete monolith. Instead, there are identifiable subgroups within the larger category.

It should also be remembered that Byzantine and minuscule are not coterminous categories. Some of the most important minuscules preserve a good, early text. These include 33, 81, 1739, and 1881. Each is a reminder that late is not necessarily worse when it comes to a witness's value. Minuscule 1739, for example, was copied in the tenth century by the scribe Ephraim, but its colophons appear to come straight from the exemplar, which itself was copied from a "most ancient manuscript" and bears close connections to Origen. Thus, there is evidence in a tenth-century manuscript that leads back to the third century.

4.1.4. Lectionaries. Lectionaries are those manuscripts that contain selections of the NT for public reading and ordered by the church calendar. The bulk of the lectionaries cover readings for the entire year and divide into two types. The Synaxarion gives readings for the movable calendar, starting on the date of Easter, whereas the Menologion provides readings for the fixed calendar, starting on September 1 (the start of the civil year in Byzantium). The lectionaries cited by the NA^{28} in Paul are *l*249, *l*846. The UBS^{5} is more expansive, citing forty more; none predates the ninth century. The large number of lectionaries reinforces the influence that the public reading of Scripture could exert on scribes copying nonlectionary texts. This could take the form of harmonization (e.g., between Ephesians and Colossians) but also the intrusion of readings needed to aid public reading (e.g., the addition of vocatives).

4.2. Versions. The earliest translations of Paul are in Latin, Syriac, and Coptic. Their text-critical value is that they can be located geographically in ways that most Greek manuscripts cannot. Negatively, it is often difficult to identify the precise Greek form behind them. Latin, for example, has no article, like Greek, while Syriac has no case system. Such structural differences along with all manner of idiomatic expressions mean that establishing the Greek behind these witnesses requires great care and caution. Generally, the translation technique tends to move from the less literal to the more literal as time goes on. In addition, translations too suffer from textual corruptions and so require their own textual criticism to be useful.

The earliest Latin translation of Paul is the Old Latin, whose origins may lie in the third century. The Vulgate is a revision of this Old Latin and dates to the fourth century. Though Jerome translated the Gospels, it is uncertain who is responsible for the Vulgate text of Paul. In the Syriac, the earliest translation of Paul is the Peshitta, from the fourth or fifth century. This was revised in AD 616 by Thomas of Harkel, whose colophon says he revised the now-lost Philoxenian translation. The Coptic translation exists in multiple dialects and is thought to go back to the third or fourth century. Later translations include the Ethiopic (or Ge'ez), Armenian, and Georgian.

4.3. Citations. The patristic citations of Paul have further benefits and drawbacks comparable to the versions. Their value lies in the fact that one can often locate them with some precision in time and place. In some cases, they offer the earliest evidence. The drawbacks are somewhat more severe, however, as one must deal with the realities of citation, which naturally allow for greater laxity in detail. For example, citations were often from memory rather than manuscript. Beyond that, writers regularly worked Paul's text into the flow of their own argument rather than given them verbatim. Nor is it uncommon for them to cite the same text two different ways! To this must be added the difficulty of translation issues in the case of Latin and Syriac fathers and that the patristic texts are not always well preserved. At times, one is at the mercy of a few late witnesses.

The most important patristic sources of Paul's text include Irenaeus, Tertullian, Marcion (per Tertullian), Clement of Alexandria, Origen, Athanasius, Ambrosiaster, Jerome, Augustine, and Chrysostom.

5. Examples.

Like exegesis, textual criticism is better caught than taught. The following examples illustrate the process with two variants in Paul that warrant fresh appraisal.

5.1. Philippians 3:12. Philippians 3:12 offers an overlooked variant relevant to Paul's theology of *justification. In the standard critical texts, Paul assures the Philippians that he has not already received *resurrection or reached perfection. But there is a longer form in which Paul also denies having been already justified (*elabon ē ēdē dedikaiōmai ē ēdē teteleiōmai*). This is found in the earliest witness (P[46]), along with D*, F, G, several Old Latins, and early Latin patristic sources (Irenaeus and Ambrosiaster). Aside from P[46], this is not especially weighty evidence, and it seems to be limited to the Latin West. On the other side, there is weighty and widespread evidence in P[16], ℵ, A, B, C[c], 1, 33, 35, 1739, Old Latin manuscripts, the Vulgate, Syriac, and Coptic, as well as in Clement, Tertullian, Origen, and others.

The picture changes when one turns to internal evidence. There is a very good explanation for the shorter reading in parablepsis. Scribes could easily have skipped from the first *ē ēdē* to the second and accidentally left out the phrase in between. At the same time, there is no obvious reason for the phrase to be added, especially given Paul's emphasis elsewhere on justification as a past reality for believers (Rom 5:1, 9; 6:7; 8:30; 1 Cor 6:11; Gal 2:16; Titus 3:7). Intrinsically, Paul does refer to justification as a future reality (Rom 2:13; 3:20, 30; Gal 2:16), and he elsewhere connects justification directly to Jesus' resurrection (Rom 4:25; 1 Tim 3:16), so Paul cannot be ruled out as the source (Griffin).

For most commentators, the external evidence tips the scales decidedly in favor of the shorter reading. But given that the longer reading explains the shorter so much easier than vice versa, this is a variant that deserves more serious consideration from exegetes. (The UBS third edition gave it a "B" rating, but the variant was dropped in the UBS fourth edition.)

5.2. Ephesians 5:22. Another overlooked variation occurs at an important transition point in Ephesians. The *household code starts either with a call to mutual submission in Ephesians 5:21 or with a command for wives to submit to their husbands in Ephesians 5:22. This problem splits commentators, translations, and modern critical editions, with sometimes significant interpretive implications.

At issue is the lack of a verb in Ephesians 5:22 in most editions, making Ephesians 5:22 syntactically dependent on Ephesians 5:21. However, most manuscripts do have a verb at this point, either *hypotassesthōsan* or *hypotassesthe*. The reading without a verb is found in P[46] and B, Clement, and Theodore, and Jerome, whose commentary explicitly indicates that his Greek manuscripts have no verb. The third-person imperative is found in ℵ, A, I, P, (Ψ), 048[vid], 33, 1739, several lectionaries, and much of the Old Latin, Vulgate, and Coptic as well as a second citation in Clement, Origen, Tertullian, Jerome's Latin, and many others. The second-person imperative is found in D, F, G (with some variation), the Byzantine manuscripts, the Harklean Syriac, and Chrysostom. Externally, P[46] and B are significant especially when combined with Jerome's testimony. Better still is the evidence for the third person given that it is found in equally early, important, and also geographically widespread witnesses. The second person is found in the majority of witnesses but not as early as the other two and not as widespread as the third person.

Internally, most commentators find no reason at all why scribes would omit the verb, and thus it is taken as the more difficult reading. The longer readings are then explained as attempts to fill the awkward gap. Although this explanation is almost universally accepted by modern commentators, a better solution presents itself if one resists treating both longer readings together.

One problem with this explanation is that it explains the presence of a second-person plural imperative much better than that of a quite rare and unexpected third-person plural. Giving serious consideration to the third-person form means that the original text read *andrasin hypotassesthōsan*. In that case, the shorter reading can be explained as a simple case of parablepsis caused by the similarity of *-sin* and *-san*. This is just the kind of error one expects from P[46], as noted above. In fact, one finds another omission stemming from this same letter combination in P[46] in 1 Corinthians 8:12. Nor is it surprising that P[46] would share such a simple omission with B (for other shared omissions, see Eph 2:13; 4:28; 5:19; 6:16). If it easily explains the shorter reading, *hypotassesthōsan* also explains *hypotassesthe* as a simple harmonization to the introductory formulas in the rest of the household code (Eph 5:25; 6:1, 4, 5, 9). Finally, the third-person imperative accords best with Paul's style since he elsewhere pairs *idios* with the third-person imperative, not the second-person imperative (Rom 14:5; 1 Cor 7:2; 14:35; Eph 4:28; 1 Tim 3:12; 5:4; 6:1).

These examples show the importance of textual criticism. When practiced well, it requires a careful sensitivity to the text and, in this way, promises rich rewards for those willing to engage it. Beyond being a necessity for exegesis, textual criticism is also a means to better understanding Paul and his reception.

See also CANON OF PAUL'S LETTERS; HERMENEUTICS/INTERPRETING PAUL; LETTERS, LETTER FORMS; PSEUDEPIGRAPHY/FORGERY.

BIBLIOGRAPHY. **A. M. Donaldson,** "Explicit References to New Testament Variant Readings Among Greek and Latin Church Fathers" (PhD diss., Notre Dame University, 2009); **J. Duff,** "P46 and the Pastorals: A Misleading Consensus?," *NTS* 44 (1998): 578-90; **E. B. Ebojo,** "A Scribe and His Manuscript: An Investigation into the Scribal Habits of Papyrus 46 (P. Chester Beatty II—P. Mich. Inv. 6238)" (PhD diss., University of Birmingham, 2014); **E. J. Epp,** "The Multivalence of the Term 'Original Text' in New Testament Textual Criticism," *HTR* 92 (1999): 245-81; idem, "Traditional 'Canons' of New Testament Textual Criticism: Their Value, Validity, and Viability—or Lack Thereof," in *The Textual History of the Greek New Testament: Changing Views in Contemporary Research*, ed. K. Wachtel and M. W. Holmes, Text-Critical Studies 8 (Atlanta: Society of Biblical Literature, 2011), 79-127; **H. Gamble,** *The Textual History of the Letter to the Romans: A Study in Textual and Literary Criticism*, Studies and Documents 42 (Grand Rapids, MI: Eerdmans, 1977); **R. K. Griffin,** "Paul Not Yet Justified? The Text of Philippians 3:12 in P46," *TC Journal* 25 (2020): 37-47. **P. J. Gurry,** *A Critical Examination of the Coherence-Based Genealogical Method in New Testament Textual Criticism* (Leiden: Brill, 2017); **M. W. Holmes,** "From 'Original Text' to 'Initial Text': The Traditional Goal of New Testament Textual Criticism in Contemporary Discussion," in *The Text of the New Testament in Contemporary Research: Essays on the Status Quaestionis*, 2nd ed., ed. B. D. Ehrman and M. W. Holmes, NTTSD 42 (Leiden: Brill, 2013), 637-88; **H. A. G. Houghton,** "An Initial Selection of Manuscripts for the *Editio Critica Maior* of the Pauline Epistles," in *The New Testament in Antiquity and Byzantium: Traditional and Digital Approaches to Its Texts and Editing; A Festschrift for Klaus Wachtel*, ed. H. A. G. Houghton, D. C. Parker, and H. Strutwolf, ANTF 52 (Berlin: de Gruyter, 2019), 343-59; **D. Jongkind,** *Scribal Habits of Codex Sinaiticus*, Texts and Studies (Piscataway, NJ: Gorgias, 2007); idem, "The Text of the Pauline Corpus," in *The Blackwell Companion to Paul*, ed. S. Westerholm (Chichester, UK: Wiley-Blackwell, 2011), 216-31; **M. D. C. Larsen,** "Accidental Publication, Unfinished Texts and the Traditional Goals of New Testament Textual Criticism," *JSNT* 39 (2017): 362-87; **D. C. Parker,** *An Introduction to the New Testament Manuscripts and Their Texts* (Cambridge: Cambridge University Press, 2008); idem, *Codex Sinaiticus: The Story of the World's Oldest Bible* (Peabody, MA: Hendrickson, 2010); idem, *Textual Scholarship and the Making of the New Testament: The Lyell Lectures* (Oxford: Oxford University Press, 2012); **J. R. Royse,** *Scribal Habits in Early Greek New Testament Papyri*, NTTSD 36 (Leiden: Brill, 2008); idem, "The Early Text of Paul (and Hebrews)," in *The Early Text of the New Testament*, ed. C. E. Hill and M. J. Kruger (Oxford: Oxford University Press, 2012); 175-203; **R. Swanson,** ed., *New Testament Manuscripts: Variant Readings Arranged in Horizontal Lines Against Codex Vaticanus; Romans* (Wheaton, IL: Tyndale House, 2001); **D. Trobisch,** *Paul's Letter Collection: Tracing the Origins* (Minneapolis: Fortress, 1994); **T. Wasserman and P. J. Gurry,** *A New Approach to Textual Criticism: An Introduction to the Coherence-Based Genealogical Method*, RBS 80 (Atlanta: SBL Press, 2017); **B. F. Westcott and F. J. A. Hort,** *The New Testament in the Original Greek: Introduction, Appendix*, 2nd ed. (London: Macmillan, 1896).

P. J. Gurry

THANKSGIVING. *See* PRAYER; WORSHIP.

THESSALONIANS, LETTERS TO THE

The Thessalonian correspondence has enjoyed a fresh period of interest in the last few decades. These short letters are widely considered part of Paul's earliest known writings. Throughout history, theologians have turned to 1–2 Thessalonians for insight into Paul's *eschatology and his theology of *suffering and *hope. They also both include instruction on the importance of positive reputation in society for believers and the benefit of good and honest labor.

1. City of Thessalonica
2. Paul in Thessalonica

3. The Situation Behind 1 Thessalonians
4. The Text of 1 Thessalonians
5. Letter Structure and Argument of 1 Thessalonians
6. Theological Themes in 1 Thessalonians
7. 2 Thessalonians: Letter Order and Situation
8. Authorship of 2 Thessalonians
9. The Text of 2 Thessalonians
10. Letter Structure and Argument of 2 Thessalonians
11. Theological Themes in 2 Thessalonians

1. City of Thessalonica.

In 316 BCE, Thessalonica was built in ancient Macedonia. Macedonian general (and later king) Cassander named this port city after his wife. In 168 BCE, Rome seized control over Macedonia and split it up into four districts, and Thessalonica became a capital of its regional district. Thessalonica held importance as a city stop along the Via Egnatia, a roadway that ran east to west connecting the Adriatic and Aegean Seas. Through a series of shrewd political alliances, Thessalonica eventually received the status of "free city" (*civitas libera*) in the Roman *Empire, which afforded it special privileges and partial autonomy. By the time Paul visited Roman Thessalonica, it was a prosperous, cosmopolitan city, "the mother of all Macedonia" (Antipater of Thessalonica, *Palatine Anthology* 4.228).

The Thessalonica of Paul's time was religiously diverse. City inhabitants respected the traditional Greek deities (e.g., Athena, Hermes, Dionysus, Zeus), but Thessalonians also took interest in the cult of Cabirus. Egyptian gods were also worshiped widely in Thessalonica, as evidenced by the discovery of the Sarapeion, a temple dedicated to the worship of Sarapis. Thessalonica honored Roma (the patron goddess of Rome), and the people built a temple for the emperor during Augustus's reign. Because Roman Thessalonica had a substantial Jewish population, the *God of *Israel was also worshiped there.

2. Paul in Thessalonica.

While we can glean a small amount of information about Paul's initial contact with and *ministry to the Thessalonians from 1 Thessalonians, scholars often turn to Acts 16–17 to fill in some gaps and situate these letters within a wider apostolic *mission and ministry (see Gupta, 54-60). According to Acts, Paul received a *vision from a "man of Macedonia" while he was in Troas (Asia Minor). This man begged him to cross over to help his people (Acts 16:9). In response, Paul and Silas immediately sailed to Samothrace and Neapolis to share the *gospel with the Macedonians (Acts 16:10-11). Next, they went to Philippi, where their ministry caused some unrest, and they were brought before the local authorities (Acts 16:12-21). They were beaten and thrown in *prison, but the *Lord delivered them (Acts 16:22-34). Next, they went through Amphipolis and Apollonia and on to Thessalonica (Acts 17:1). First, they visited the Jewish synagogue, where Paul preached about Jesus for several weeks (Acts 17:2-3). According to Luke, "some of them were persuaded and joined Paul and Silas, as did a great many of the devout Greeks and not a few of the leading women" (Acts 17:4 NRSV).

Some Jews who rejected Paul's message incited a mob to turn against Paul. When they could not find him, they dragged new believers to the city leaders, saying, "These people who have been turning the world upside down have come here also, and Jason has entertained them as guests. They are all acting contrary to the decrees of the emperor, saying that there is another king named Jesus" (Acts 17:6-7 NRSV). Paul and Silas fled from Thessalonica to Berea (Acts 17:10). Some Thessalonian Jews came to learn that Paul was in Berea and went there to prevent his ministry from gaining success.

3. The Situation Behind 1 Thessalonians.

When we read 1 Thessalonians with Acts 17 in view, it appears there are three major concerns that Paul had in mind when he wrote this letter to the church in Thessalonica.

3.1. Local Persecution. It is clear that the Thessalonian believers were dealing with local persecution (1 Thess 1:6; 2:14). This would not have been a government-mandated punishing of Christians but rather personal criticism, social harassment, and alienation by neighbors, relatives, coworkers, and community members who would have found their new religious practices foolish and perhaps even dangerous (Barclay, 512-16). Paul taught them to turn from *idols to serve the one true God (1 Thess 1:9-10), something that most *Gentiles found ridiculous and deviant, as this meant withdrawal from local rituals, holidays, and festivals that ensured the blessing and protection of the Greek and Roman patron gods. Paul wrote 1 Thessalonians, then, in part to encourage a weary and troubled church to persevere in the faith.

3.2. Eschatology Questions and Concerns. In 1 Thessalonians 4:13-18 Paul writes at length about "those who sleep in death" (1 Thess 4:13 NIV). It seems to be the case that some Thessalonian believers died, and this caused the church to be troubled. Paul comforts them by explaining that those who have fallen asleep will receive a special honor at the return of the Lord Jesus. Perhaps the Thessalonians thought that no believer would die until Christ's coming. Other scholars believe that the issue was not the shock of believers dying but rather *how* they died—perhaps they were martyred (Donfried, 43). Whatever the case, this caused great anxiety and distress for the church, prompting Paul to write words of comfort and reassurance in view of future eschatological events.

3.3. The Return of the Lord. A third major issue that Paul addresses in this letter is about the timetable of the Lord's return (1 Thess 5:1-11). Paul resists offering times and dates, encouraging instead that they expect him to come unexpectedly (1 Thess 5:2-3). What matters most is not knowing the day or hour but living in a state of faithfulness and vigilance. Somehow, these believers were struck by fear that they were not ready for the end. Paul reassures them that if they hold closely to their *faith in *Christ, they will be saved (1 Thess 5:9).

3.4. Other Possible Concerns. For the three issues noted above, virtually all scholars agree on their relevance and importance for the interpretation of 1 Thessalonians. But there are a few more possible concerns that could be detected in this letter, though the evidence is not as conclusive. First, Paul addresses the need for the Thessalonians to show honor and respect for God by keeping their *bodies pure and *holy (1 Thess 4:3-4). Paul may not, though, have had a particular (local) incident in view. Greek and Roman men lived in a highly permissive *sexual culture where it was not uncommon to have multiple sex partners, even while married to one woman (though the matter was one-sided; married *women* were expected to be chaste and "faithful"). Paul, though, admonishes them to honor one another and God by showing self-control (1 Thess 4:6).

Some scholars also hypothesize that Paul wrote this letter in part as a defense of his own ministry (see Donfried and Beutler). In 1 Thessalonians 2:1-12, Paul writes about his character and integrity at length, denying any deceitfulness or trickery, or that he was a flatterer or motivated by greed. Later, in 1 Thessalonians 3:6, he underscores how he was so concerned for their well-being that he sent Timothy to check on and aid them. It could be that Paul was simply characterizing himself as a model for them to emulate. But the tone of 1 Thessalonians 2:1-12 in particular can be interpreted as self-defensive, as if some Thessalonians (or outsiders?) attacked his character.

Finally, we might detect some community problems in the church in Thessalonica (1 Thess 4:9-11; 5:12-15). For example, Paul briefly refers to some people as *ataktoi*, idle troublemakers (1 Thess 5:14). In 1 Thessalonians, they receive only the shortest rebuke ("warn [them]"). But by the time Paul writes 2 Thessalonians, these *ataktoi* appear to have become a much bigger problem (2 Thess 3:6-12).

In terms of dating of composition, most scholars agree 1 Thessalonians was written somewhere between 49 and 51 CE.

4. The Text of 1 Thessalonians.

How did Paul go about writing this text? It is obviously a letter. But Greco-Roman *letters are somewhat different in style, genre, and form from modern letters. Letters were written for three main reasons in this period: (1) to correspond socially with family or friends, (2) to supply information, and/or (3) to ask for information, goods, or help. The formal features of private letters are few. They contained a prescript, main body of information, and a closing greeting (Stowers, 15-16). Paul's letters, including 1 Thessalonians, include these features. Perhaps the most unique element of Paul's letters is length: his writings overall are far longer than most ancient personal letters. Around the time of the NT, Pseudo-Demetrius outlined over twenty types of letters (e.g., friendly, threatening, blaming, consoling, congratulatory; see Pseudo-Demetrius, *Epistolary Types*). But Paul's letters do not fit any one type neatly. It would seem Paul utilized the basic letter form and purpose but did not follow a rigid type.

Another way that Paul's letters have been analyzed is in terms of ancient categories of *rhetoric (i.e., deliberative, judicial, epideictic). Some have labeled 1 Thessalonians as deliberative (Kennedy), because Paul was trying to convince the Thessalonian believers to think and act in a new way (e.g., 1 Thess 3:8; 4–5). But more commonly 1 Thessalonians has been identified as epideictic (Jewett, 71-72; Lyons, 219-21), as Paul was reinforcing certain Christian values and offering affirmation and encouragement in light of persecution and anxiety. While interest in reading Paul's letters according to classic rhetoric has been on the rise in the last couple of decades, there has also been resistance and pushback. For many, the value of reading 1 Thessalonians primarily as a *letter*, or as a form of *rhetoric*, is in the eye of the interpreter (Weima 2016).

5. Letter Structure and Argument of 1 Thessalonians.

5.1. Thanksgiving for the Thessalonians (1 Thess 1:1-10). In this first section, Paul is generous with praise, thanking God for the Thessalonians' firm commitment to the gospel and their deep conviction in faith. He acknowledges the persecution they are enduring and encourages them by reminding them of their Spirit-filled experience of the one true God. They took the bold step of rejecting idols and turning to this God, and they dare to live by faith, expectantly waiting for the redemptive return of Jesus, who will rescue them from divine *judgment. First Thessalonians 1:9-10 has played an important role in Pauline studies in giving insight into his understanding of Christian conversion and soteriology. Paul has more than one way to express the gospel, but here we find the emphasis on exclusive *worship as well as a focus on the unique role of the *Son of God, Jesus Christ, in redemption.

5.2. Paul's Blameless Ministry and the Thessalonians' Perseverance (1 Thess 2:1-16). As noted above, this section of his letter includes Paul's presentation of his own blameless ministry, namely, that he has behaved as an *apostle with pure motives and personal integrity. In this passage, he appeals to his courage and conviction (1 Thess 2:1-2), his honest motives (1 Thess 2:3-6), his gentleness and genuine concern for their well-being (1 Thess 2:7-9, 10-12), and his honest labor (1 Thess 2:9). Some scholars read this passage as nothing more than a call to imitate the noble character of the apostles (Malherbe 2000). Others, though, believe that the tone and emotional appeal here implies that Paul felt the need to defend his behavior against attacks of his character, wherever that attack may have originated from (Weima; see Donfried and Beutler).

Paul returns again to the matter of the Thessalonians' experience of persecution, connecting their own suffering with Paul's, and also to Jesus and the prophets (1 Thess 2:13-15a). He highlights a certain type of enemy of God who resists God's redemptive purposes (1 Thess 2:15b-16b). While such persecutors seem to find some success in their hostility (by harming, and even killing, God's people), Paul attests that ultimately they will not succeed—they cannot escape divine punishment for their behavior (1 Thess 2:16c).

Because this passage refers to the damnation of *Jews*, there has been a long-standing discussion about its origins and interpretation. One view proposes that this statement is not original to 1 Thessalonians but was added later by some editor. Therefore, it is treated as an interpolation (i.e., a text inserted later and not written by the apostle Paul). It simply appears too hostile toward Jews to be written by a Jew. Therefore, some think it unfathomable that it came from Paul himself (Pearson). Another approach reads this as Paul engaging in hyperbole, assuring the Thessalonians in no uncertain terms (Johnson). Part of the problem involves the English translation. Scholars sometimes refer to the "anti-Semitic comma" (after the word *Jews*) in English translations of 1 Thessalonians 2:15: "for you suffered the same things from your own countrymen as they did from the Jews, who killed both the Lord Jesus and the prophets" (1 Thess 2:14b-15a RSV) or "You suffered from your own people the same things those churches suffered from the Jews who killed the Lord Jesus and the prophets" (1 Thess 2:14b-15a NIV).

Notice the addition of the comma in the RSV after the word *Jews*. From a grammatical standpoint, if the comma is not included, it limits the scope of who these "Jews" are who are facing damnation, that is, only those who acted in a hostile way toward God's messengers. But when the comma *is* included, it refers to the Jewish people as a whole (see Porter, 92-98). The fact of the matter is that most readers of the English text are not going to recognize the subtle nuances of the presence or absence of a comma. Nevertheless, much discussion has taken place among biblical scholars and translators about how narrow or wide of a group Paul had in mind when he wrote this statement (see Gupta, 114-23).

5.3. Paul's Love, Pride, and Concern (1 Thess 2:17–3:13). The second chapter concludes with Paul expressing his concern for the Thessalonians' faith and his desire to see them again (1 Thess 2:17-20). Paul recounts how, as he fled from Thessalonica and stopped in Athens (1 Thess 3:1), he sent Timothy to Thessalonica to bring encouragement to the church there (1 Thess 3:2-5) and also to gauge their attitude toward Paul himself (1 Thess 3:6). In 1 Thessalonians he expresses great *joy at their ongoing concern for Paul as well as their confident faith. It is clear from this section that Paul had a special *friendship with these believers. They were far more than mere converts of his mission or fellow religionists.

Paul ends this section with an extended prayer-wish (1 Thess 3:11-13). He prays that he may visit them again soon, for their *love to grow, and that they may remain blameless until the coming of Jesus. Scholars have pointed out that Paul includes Jesus as a focal point of this prayer-wish ("may our God . . . and our Lord Jesus," 1 Thess 3:11), demonstrating a divine *Christology in one of his earliest extant letters.

5.4. Exhortation to Persevere and Grow in Holiness, Love, and Integrity (1 Thess 4:1-12). First Thessalonians 4 marks a clear transition in the letter toward more direct exhortation. Paul acknowledges that he gave such instruction to them before but offers it again by way of reminder (1 Thess 4:1). Their goal ought to be to live to please God and to obey his will. More specifically, Paul focuses on rejecting *porneia*. They ought to be fully devoted to God in holiness and not live like pagans, who are swayed by their passions in their ignorance of God (1 Thess 4:2-6). Paul also raises the matter of *philadelphia* ("love for siblings"). Paul's use of this Greek word is unprecedented insofar as he employs it in reference to people who are not biologically related. Paul urges the Thessalonians to continue to show sibling-like love for other believers.

He offers additional wisdom for life, including the exhortation to live "quietly" (1 Thess 4:11), that is, to carry out their work in honest labor for the good of society and not simply to draw attention to themselves for the sake of status and social importance. Paul expresses an ultimate concern that Christians have a reputation for moral integrity as well as social and civic responsibility (1 Thess 4:12).

5.5. The Hopeful Fate of the Christian Dead (1 Thess 4:13-18). This is probably the best-known passage of this letter, studied and discussed carefully across Christian history. Paul offers here a corrective teaching about the fate and future of dead believers. He explains that those who have fallen asleep will be raised when the Lord returns, and those who are still alive will follow them into the air (1 Thess 4:16-17). Romans and Greeks had mixed impressions of life after death. For most, there was no concrete hope for bliss or immortality. We cannot be sure exactly what the Thessalonians had believed that caused them additional grief and dismay. Perhaps they had come to the conclusion that if believers died before the Lord returned, they were consigned to the grave and could not experience eternal life. Or if the "thief in the night" (1 Thess 5:2 NRSV) came and went quickly, the dead would miss out. Paul reassures them that death cannot hold believers back from participating in the final victory of God in Christ. Not only will the dead rise, but they will rise first with dignity and honor (1 Thess 4:16). They will be especially honored in the train of ascending believers journeying to meet the Lord in the air.

This section of 1 Thessalonians has sometimes been associated with the rapture doctrine, so it is helpful to devote space to that matter here. In the Latin Vulgate text of 1 Thessalonians 4:17 we find the word *rapiemur* (from *rapere*), referring to believers being caught up or "raptured." The rapture doctrine is a synthetic theory, first developed in the nineteenth century by John Nelson Darby (later reinforced and promoted by the *Scofield Reference Bible* in 1909), that pieces together information from across the NT. It teaches that Christians will be "raptured" away from the earth at a particular point before the final judgment. While the rapture doctrine has enjoyed widespread popularity in recent years in certain sectors of American Christianity, it should be recognized that this is a theory that cannot be explicated or defended solely based on Paul's comments in 1 Thessalonians or his letter corpus (Rossing; Gupta, 164-65).

5.6. The Day of the Lord and Final Exhortations (1 Thess 5:1-28). In 1 Thessalonians 5, Paul continues to discuss eschatological matters, in particular "times and seasons" related to the day of the Lord (1 Thess 5:1). Paul deflects pressures to prognosticate about any such information, as Christian faith should not depend on the calendar, as much as the attitude of eschatological sobriety and vigilance (1 Thess 5:1-3). Paul calls the Thessalonians to be people of "*light" and "day," like faithful and well-trained soldiers who are fully prepared and alert (1 Thess 5:6-8).

The final major portion of 1 Thessalonians (1 Thess 5:12-28) comprises a set of community instructions. Paul begins with an appeal for the church to recognize those who serve them in *leadership (1 Thess 5:12-13). A host of short exhortations peppers the next ten verses: comfort the discouraged, aid the weak, show patience, pursue goodness, and so on (1 Thess 5:14-22). Paul emphasizes living life with a spirit of joy and thanksgiving, and not letting oneself become enamored with problems and fears. Ultimately, Paul explains, one will do what is right by holding to good and setting evil at a distance (1 Thess 5:21-22).

First Thessalonians 5:23-24 offers another prayer-wish (see 1 Thess 3:11-13), again with a view toward sanctity of the whole person in view of the Lord's return. This text, with its reference to body, soul, and spirit, quickly became a passage of interest regarding Christian *anthropology (Tertullian, Origen, Athanasius, Gregory of Nazianzus; Ambrosiaster; see Thiselton, 161-75). Is the person made up of several separate parts (e.g., body and a soul), or are these different ways of thinking and talking about the human as one thing?

6. Theological Themes in 1 Thessalonians.

6.1. Eschatology and Final Things. Certainly 1 Thessalonians contains significant material related to eschatology (esp. 1 Thess 4:13-18; 5:1-11). Contrary to popular assumptions about Christian eschatology today, though, Paul was not interested in sketching out timetables. In fact, he points the Thessalonians away from any talk of "times and seasons" (1 Thess 5:1) and encourages them to be ready at any time because the Lord will return like a thief in the night (1 Thess 5:2). The main reasons that Paul dwells on eschatological matters relate to hope, holiness, vigilance, and divine justice. First, regarding hope, Paul regularly directs their attention, in the midst of suffering and affliction, toward God's final redemption, where troubles will dissolve and shame will turn to vindication (1 Thess 4:18). Eschatology thus becomes a pastoral tool to encourage these beleaguered believers. Second, Paul calls the Thessalonians to be holy and blameless. They ought to be preparing for the parousia with a measure of holy *fear, knowing that they will be examined by the Lord (1 Thess 3:13; 5:23). Therefore, their responses to persecution and other challenges *now* matter greatly in their formation toward that day of the Lord. Third, they are called to be awake and vigilant as they wait for Christ (1 Thess 5:3-11). People who are "day" people, according to Paul, live with their senses fully alive and attuned to their surroundings—they have their wits about them, as it were. Believers must live constantly in such a state that they really think through their decisions, through potential dangers and missteps, knowing the Master holds them accountable. Finally, Paul's eschatological teaching emphasizes that God is a God of justice, and his people can be confident that he will right the wrongs of the world in the end (1 Thess 2:14-16).

6.2. Faith and Loyalty. The language of faith (*pistis*) appears extensively throughout this relatively short Pauline letter. Paul's interest here is not primarily in initial belief, but rather in persevering faith and ongoing loyalty toward Jesus Christ in the face of obstacles and cultural friction. Paul commends them for the bold faith they had shown in the past (1 Thess 1:8) and spurs them on toward ongoing faith despite apprehensiveness in light of troubling circumstances (1 Thess 3:2-10). It is important to recognize that the faith Paul calls for in 1 Thessalonians is not about a set of doctrinal beliefs but deep trust in God that is expressed in obedience and love (1 Thess 5:8).

6.3. Thanksgiving and Joy. It might seem counterintuitive that a situation (behind 1 Thessalonians) fraught with death, suffering, anxiety, and tension would prompt Paul to talk about expressing joy and giving thanks to God, but this is clearly a key motif of this letter. Paul wanted to move them from being swayed by the troubles of the present moment to trusting more completely in the God of their past, present, and future. Thus, he points them in thanksgiving to their history of devotion to the Lord (1 Thess 1:2), he reminds of their exuberance when they first heard the gospel (1 Thess 1:6; 2:13), and he shows them how much joy they bring to him as part of the family of faith (1 Thess 2:19-20; 3:9). In the end section of the letter, he gives the Thessalonians two important commands: "rejoice always" and "give thanks in all circumstances" (1 Thess 5:16, 18 NRSV). While we think of happiness and appreciation today as more spontaneous emotions, Paul treated them as virtues or dispositions. Knowing and trusting God means having a heart full of appreciation for blessings of *fellowship with God and others now, but also the joy of knowing the full redemption of mortals and the *cosmos that is yet ahead.

6.4. Work and Labor. Another theme of 1 Thessalonians involves the value Paul places on honest, productive work. Paul reminds the Thessalonians of his own work, how he labored day and night while he was in Thessalonica so he did not have to stretch them financially when he was there (1 Thess 2:9; see 2 Thess 3:8). While Paul does not write much about this labor side of his life (as a business artisan), we get the impression that he saw this as more than mere wage-earning. First, given his association with Priscilla and Aquila (as fellow "*tentmakers"; Acts 18:2-3), we know that he made significant relationships through his business work. Second, we can also surmise that this was a context for sharing the gospel in the business world. Paul did not encourage believers to recede from public life and separate themselves to purify them from pagan influence. On the contrary, he told them to make positive contributions in work to society, to engage in honest labor with their own hands, and to live peace-filled lives in their communities (1 Thess 4:11). At the end of his letter, he makes a brief comment to the effect that the church should warn anyone who disregards work and promotes disruptive behavior (1 Thess 5:14). This matter is addressed more extensively in 2 Thessalonians, but here it suffices to demonstrate the emphasis Paul placed on productive community contribution and participation through work.

7. 2 Thessalonians: Letter Order and Situation.

7.1. Letter Order. In the NT, we find "1 Thessalonians" preceding "2 Thessalonians," but the NT book ordering is not based on chronological order of composition. For example, most scholars recognize that Galatians was written before Romans, but Romans heads up the Pauline corpus in the NT. The Pauline corpus is primarily ordered by length from longest to shortest (in words/size, not necessarily number of chapters, since Paul did not write using chapter designations). But letters to the same church were paired together (e.g., 1–2 Corinthians, 1–2 Thessalonians), and letters to individuals were put at the end (1–2 Timothy, Titus, Philemon). Because length was a more prominent factor in ordering, 1 Thessalonians appears before 2 Thessalonians. However, the canonical ordering does not, by itself, presume compositional order. While the vast majority of scholars past and present have favored the earlier composition of 1 Thessalonians, there are at least two important dissenting voices (Manson; Wanamaker). The arguments in favor of putting 2 Thessalonians as the earlier letter can be summarized as follows:

- The mention of past persecution in 1 Thessalonians 2:14 could fit with the present persecution mentioned in 2 Thessalonians 1:4-7.
- The problem of idle troublemaking is explained in more detail in 2 Thessalonians 3:11-15 but almost taken for granted in 1 Thessalonians 4:10-12.
- The mention of Paul's authenticating signature in all his letters (2 Thess 3:17) makes sense as a future warning, with 1 Thessalonians coming later.
- When Paul mentions that the Thessalonians need no further teaching (1 Thess 5:1), this could be taken as a reference to his instruction in 2 Thessalonians 2:1-12.
- The teachings in 1 Thessalonians 4:9, 13; 5:1 ("now about . . .") could be interpreted as a reference to earlier instruction given in 2 Thessalonians.

But these arguments only seem to open up the possibility of the priority of 2 Thessalonians; they do not prove it. In favor of the traditional composition-order theory, we have these common arguments:

- Second Thessalonians refers to a previous letter (2 Thess 2:2, 15; 3:17), while 1 Thessalonians does not.
- In 2 Thessalonians 2:15, Paul uses the language of prior teaching in a way that seems to point back to 1 Thessalonians.
- From a logical standpoint, it makes more sense that the second letter (2 Thessalonians) was written later because persecution intensified and eschatological confusion compounded. If 2 Thessalonians was first, why would Paul write another letter (1 Thessalonians) addressing persecution if the problems were lessening?

7.2. Situation. Given the mood and intensity of 2 Thessalonians (and presuming 1 Thessalonians was written first), it would seem that the situation in Thessalonica had worsened for the church. Paul appears to be concerned with three key issues that needed to be addressed. First, there is have the matter of the believers facing more hostile *persecution*. Here he points to hope and future relief from their afflictions, and judgment on the persecutors (2 Thess 1:4-10). Second, Paul engages in further teaching on *eschatology*. We learn from the letter that some believers had come to believe that "the Day of the Lord is already here" (2 Thess 2:2 NRSV). This caused the church great anxiety and concern. There may have been some local group that stoked fears and concerns (2 Thess 2:3). Paul does not shy away from mentioning some harrowing future events (2 Thess 2:3-10) but ultimately aims at comforting them by appeal to Christ's final victory over evil (see 2 Thess 2:8).

A third major matter that appears to relate to the situation in Thessalonica involves some believers who ceased from wage-earning work (see 2 Thess 3:6-12). Paul had already briefly mentioned such people in 1 Thessalonians 5:14, but obviously the circumstances had carried on and probably worsened such that he needed to offer a stronger and more extensive rebuke. The scholarship of a previous generation had argued that these people were "idle" because they had forsaken work in view of the imminent end of the world. But Paul uses more vivid language here (*atakteō*, *ataktōs*) than that of laziness. It is not so much that they were loafing around as that they were forsaking work *and* meddling in the affairs of others (2 Thess 3:11). They were disrupting the life of the church and neglecting Paul's teachings about work and communal life together. One plausible theory is that these troublemakers were concerned about signs of eschatological happenings, abandoned their jobs, and tried to interfere with the leadership of the church out of anxieties and desperation concerning *apocalyptic signs. Paul offers himself as an example of someone who has maintained steady work to provide for his own needs. But he also directly instructs the church to shun any who cause trouble and reject work (2 Thess 3:14). In spite of whatever troubles they were facing, Paul calls for the *peace of God to be with them in all things, including the present circumstances (see 2 Thess 3:16).

8. Authorship of 2 Thessalonians.

Beginning in the early nineteenth century, we find academics who questioned whether Paul was the author of 2 Thessalonians (see Schmidt; Wrede). In the early twentieth century, it became a central conversation point in relation to interpreting this letter. There are many reasons for this debate, but the main concerns that are consistently raised in the scholarship pertain to these areas: literary imitation, writing style, historical implausibility, tone, theological differences, and what we will call pseudepigraphy "tells." (On the matter of NT pseudepigraphy, canonical reception and inclusion of NT texts in early *canon lists has been a consideration, but it is moot in the case of 2 Thessalonians since there was no doubt or question by the early church; see Muratorian canon.)

8.1. Literary Imitation. It is easily noticeable that 2 Thessalonians bears a lot of verbal and structural similarities to 1 Thessalonians. For example, both letters have the same salutation (1 Thess 1:1; 2 Thess 1:1), and both have long initial thanksgivings with a second thanksgiving later on (1 Thess 2:13; 2 Thess 2:13). Some of the repeated wording (such as *kateuthynai*; 1 Thess 3:11; 2 Thess 3:16) is so peculiar as to raise questions about why Paul would do this. Some have wondered, Could it be the work of a "copycat" forger (see Krentz)?

8.2. Writing Style. There is also the matter of the manner or style of writing. It is often mentioned that 2 Thessalonians uses certain expressions (such as "eternal comfort" or "good hope") that are not commonly found in 1 Thessalonians or other letters considered to be genuine (e.g., Romans, Galatians, 1–2 Corinthians). This also includes the connotations or meanings of words (such as *erōtaō*) and the general length of sentences (2 Thessalonians tends to use longer, more complex sentences).

8.3. Historical Implausibility. One factor that weighs into discerning whether a text is authentic is the presence of features in the text that could not fit into the historical context and timeline of the named author. For instance, Paul makes reference to the importance of "*tradition" (2 Thess 2:15; 3:6), which has caused some scholars to wonder whether such tradition could have been in existence in the middle of the first century (Menken, 141-42). Or we could look at the example of the "lawless one" (2 Thess 2:1-12), a figure that seems to resemble Nero. Some have argued that if the lawless one is meant to be Nero come back from the dead, then it must mean that the author knew of Nero's death in 68 CE (Menken, 107). In that case, 2 Thessalonians must have been written far later than Paul's ministry in Thessalonica, and thus was probably not written by Paul at all.

8.4. Tone. It is somewhat common for scholars to mention a difference of "tone" between 1 and 2 Thessalonians (Furnish, 132; Bridges 194-96). To some, 1 Thessalonians carries a warm, personal, and friendly tone, where Paul comes across as pastoral and reassuring. But 2 Thessalonians has more of a cold, distant, and authoritarian tone. Thus, some argue that these seem like two different people.

8.5. Theological Differences. A classic argument against Pauline authorship of 2 Thessalonians involves an appeal to differences in theological perspective when compared and contrasted to 1 Thessalonians. This tends to focus on eschatology in particular. So, some have argued that 1 Thessalonians carries a sense of eschatology urgency (1 Thess 5:1-11), while 2 Thessalonians outlines a series of major events that must precede the end (2 Thess 2:1-12).

8.6. Pseudepigraphy "Tells." The last major factor of the discussion involves pseudepigraphy tells. These are features of a text that appear to (accidentally) give away or unmask the forger. For example, in 2 Thessalonians 3:17 we read "I, Paul, write this greeting in my own hand, which is the distinguishing mark in all my letters. This is how I write" (NIV; see Gal 6:11; 1 Cor 16:21; Col 4:18). It has been argued by some that this appears either to be a forger mimicking 1 Corinthians 16:21 in some way, or simply a forger trying too hard to pretend to be Paul.

8.7. Responses in Favor of Authenticity. Among the Pauline letters whose authorship is disputed in modern scholarship, 2 Thessalonians has much less evidence weighing against authenticity. Those who find authenticity more likely respond to the above factors in this way. When it comes to literary imitation, there is admittedly a bit of awkwardness or clumsiness in 2 Thessalonians, but this does not discount the possibility that Paul wrote both letters (especially when we take into consideration Paul's use of a letter secretary; see below). As far as tone is concerned, virtually all scholars today agree this is a highly subjective category and that one's "tone" is not fixed but changes with the mood of the writer and situation of the text. One of the more objective elements of the discussion is historical (im)plausibility.

But in the case of 2 Thessalonians, there is no obvious anachronistic statement by the author. The link between the lawless one and Nero, for example, is theoretical, not certain. Also, the letter's appeal to tradition is not unprecedented in the undisputed Pauline corpus (see, e.g., 1 Cor 11:2).

In the past, a major factor that seemed to support pseudepigraphy was the perceived theological divergences between 1 and 2 Thessalonians, but now it is widely recognized that the differences have been exaggerated. The eschatology of 1 Thessalonians is not as focused on *immediacy* as it is on the *suddenness* of the parousia and the need for readiness and vigilance. Furthermore, it has become more recognized that eschatological watchfulness (as we find in 1 Thessalonians) and the explication of unfolding events on a cosmic level (as we find in 2 Thessalonians) are *both* common to Jewish apocalyptic discourse. Put another way, while 2 Thessalonians does not repeat the eschatological information of 1 Thessalonians, neither does it contradict it as a matter of fact.

On the matter of pseudepigraphy tells, again this is a subjective factor. And there are strong points against treating 2 Thessalonians 3:17 as a forger feigning authenticity. If this "forger" were apparently relying on 1 Corinthians 16:21, then why did he decide to address the letter to the *Thessalonians*? That is, if he already had become aware of the whole collection of Pauline letters, he would be operating in the second century or later. Thus, he would also know that it is not clear that Paul provided a mark of authentication in all of his letters.

This leads to what is probably the great criticism of a pseudepigraphy approach to 2 Thessalonians. Any scholar who treats 2 Thessalonians as pseudepigraphy is obligated to propose a scenario that explains why this writer (1) wrote an eschatologically oriented letter to the Thessalonians (which would have not been the same historical audience of 1 Thessalonians, as he would be writing several decades later); (2) why he dwells on the *ataktoi* (idle troublemakers; 2 Thess 3:6-12), who were addressed in 1 Thessalonians 5:14; and (3) and why he imitated 1 Thessalonians so rigidly in literary form while seemingly wanting to modify the eschatological perspective offered by Paul in 1 Thessalonians. Finally, we have the issue that the authorship of 2 Thessalonians went unquestioned by readers of Paul's letters for around seventeen hundred years. How did this forger hide his identity and pass for Paul for so long, only to be discovered in modern times?

8.8. Other Authorship Considerations. In a previous era of scholarship on pseudepigraphy, the biblical studies academy operated with a rather simplistic binary of authentic authorship (e.g., by the apostle Paul) or pseudepigraphical authorship (by another person later on). But in the last few decades the nature of ancient communication and production of literature has been investigated more thoroughly, and a more complete and nuanced picture has emerged. One major consideration involves the role of the amanuensis (or letter-secretary). We know that Paul used such professionals (Rom 16:22), and we know they could have been asked to do much more than simply dictate Paul's words. The secretary sometimes may have been more directly involved with the content and style of the letter. Another factor in this discussion is the notion of writing help or collaboration from some of Paul's apostolic associates. Paul mentions Silvanus and Timothy in 2 Thessalonians 1:1, and either or both may have influenced the style or content of the letter. With all these possibilities in play, deciding definitively for or against genuine Pauline authorship of 2 Thessalonians is challenging, perhaps even impossible.

9. The Text of 2 Thessalonians.

When it comes to the textual features of 2 Thessalonians, this letter resembles 1 Thessalonians in many ways. The conversation is slightly more nuanced on the matter of rhetorical analysis. Several scholars have argued that 2 Thessalonians fits the description of "deliberative" rhetoric, since the author appears to be prompting the readers to reconsider their understanding of the final events of history (2 Thess 2:1-12).

10. Letter Structure and Argument of 2 Thessalonians.

10.1. Thanksgiving and Hope (2 Thess 1:1-12). Paul begins, as with 1 Thessalonians, with thanksgiving for the Thessalonians' strong faith and endurance in the face of daunting trials. In 2 Thessalonians 1:5-10, Paul reassures them of the certain demise of their persecutors and the good purposes of God even in this time of difficulty. These tribulations, while not ideal, fortify believers, making them worthy of the *kingdom (2 Thess 1:5). They are encouraged to persevere in expectation of the revealing of the Lord Jesus along with his angelic host. In 1 Thessalonians, the focus of the parousia instruction is on redemption, but in 2 Thessalonians the parousia hope concentrates on vanquishing the wicked by the fiery flame (2 Thess 1:8). Somewhat unusual is the language of "eternal destruction" (2 Thess 1:9 NRSV), a main text used today to support the notion of "annihilation" of the damned (rather than the traditional view of eternal torment). The language here is paradoxical: "destruction" implies complete termination, while "eternal" carries the notion of extended duration. Whatever the case, Paul's point is that the final judgment is final.

10.2. Perseverance and Hope (2 Thess 2:1-17). In 2 Thessalonians 2 Paul gets into the main concerns of his letter: he offers a clear message that the day of the Lord has not come yet, contrary to what the Thessalonian believers have come to believe (2 Thess 2:1-2). The substance of this section (2 Thess 2:3-12) presents a rough sketch of events leading up to the right-wising justice of Christ (2 Thess 2:8). The sequence begins with a rebellion led by the lawless one (also known as "the son of perdition"; 2 Thess 2:3 RSV). Paul does not link this ominous figure with a particular named person. Although he is not identified, he is described with vivid language. He will name himself supreme over all beings (2 Thess 2:4). The features used to fill out his profile seem to evoke the activities and temperaments of several historical tyrants from Israel's history such as Antiochus IV (Epiphanes) and Pompey. Paul also refers to a "mystery of lawlessness" at work in the world, but a certain restrainer holds the forces of evil at bay until it is removed (2 Thess 2:7 NRSV).

There has been significant academic discussion about the nature and identity of this "restrainer" (Is it a person? A being? An impersonal force?). Some early Christian theologians associated the restrainer with the Roman Empire or the way the empire established order and justice as a feature of governance. Throughout the years, many other theories have been suggested, such as Paul (as preacher of the powerful gospel), or God himself (as sovereign over his plans for the world). A widely popular theory at present is that Paul was referring to a heavenly spiritual power as restrainer, such as the archangel Michael (see Dan 12:1; Jude 9; Rev 12:7; see Nicholl).

Paul's concern in this passage is not to offer a complete schedule of eschatology events but rather to paint a picture of a future cosmic showdown involving a nefarious foe.

According to 2 Thessalonians 2:8, the Lord Jesus will ultimately enter the fray and completely wipe out the enemy. The Thessalonians, then, should be encouraged to hold strong and press on in hope and faith (2 Thess 2:13-17).

10.3. Mission and Community (2 Thess 3:1-18). After a short *prayer request (2 Thess 3:1-5), Paul addresses another major concern, namely, the problematic behavior of a group we can refer to as the idle troublemakers (2 Thess 3:6-10). The key words used by Paul here to explicate this group (*ataktōs*, *atakteō*) can be understood to describe either the indolent or rebellious/insubordinate. We learn from 2 Thessalonians 3:6-10 that these *ataktoi* abandoned their wage-earning work (2 Thess 3:10), but why they did this is unclear. One possibility is that they decided to depend on the care and security of *wealthy benefactors in the church and gave up their skilled labor (see Winter). Another scenario involves these people attempting to assume control over the leadership of the church as they discerned matters related to eschatological concerns. They sought to obtain apostle-like privileges and claimed they did not have to work for wages. Whatever the case, Paul writes with a concern that this church recognizes the importance of independent work. Paul points to his own practice of self-sustaining labor (2 Thess 3:7-9). He also repeats an apostolic maxim: "Anyone unwilling to work should not eat" (2 Thess 3:10 NRSV). In the reception of these words throughout history, one reading has taken this to imply rejection of any kind of economic welfare for the unemployed. This may have been fueled by the English translation of the KJV: "if any would not work, neither should he eat." But in 2 Thessalonians, Paul's primary concern in this case was on a specific group who *refused* to work (but presumably *could* work). Paul says nothing whatsoever about adults who cannot work, either temporarily or permanently. Paul criticizes these *ataktoi* for being meddlers and busybodies (2 Thess 3:11), not for being unproductive per se.

Paul ends this letter with a reminder of the work of the God of peace. Rather than being whipped up into a frenzy over frightening events or news, the Thessalonians should keep the faith and rest in the care of the Lord of peace (2 Thess 3:16). Paul mentions that he writes with his own personal handwriting to provide a mark of authenticity (2 Thess 3:17). Some scholars have identified this as a clue that this letter is by someone other than Paul but working hard to pretend to be Paul (see above). Others take this as Paul's legitimate concern that some have been feeding the Thessalonians misinformation, and it may have come in letter form (see 2 Thess 2:2).

11. Theological Themes in 2 Thessalonians.

11.1. Themes Shared with 1 Thessalonians. Because the content of 2 Thessalonians overlaps so much with 1 Thessalonians, it should not be a surprise that some theological themes are repeated but with some small differences of emphasis. For instance, just as 1 Thessalonians underscores the relationship between faith and *works, so too

2 Thessalonians (2 Thess 1:4). In terms of eschatology, both letters give attention to future hope; this is noticeable in 2 Thessalonians in places such as 2 Thessalonians 1:5, 11-12; 2:16. Just as 1 Thessalonians underscores the importance of honest labor, so it is treated in 2 Thessalonians, even more so. Wholesome, productive labor should be carried out in a spirit of humility and independence with a view toward self-dependence where possible (2 Thess 3:12).

11.2. Dignity and Honor. While 2 Thessalonians often is hidden by the shadow of the longer and elder 1 Thessalonians, it does develop some of its own unique themes. For example, part of the solemnity that scholars have noticed that characterizes this letter points to an emphasis on dignity and *honor. This can give the text a bit of a liturgical tone, as we find in 2 Thessalonians 1:3: "We ought always to thank God for you, brothers and sisters, and rightly so, because your faith is growing more and more, and the love all of you have for one another is increasing." Regularly this letter aims to reinforce what is "right" and "good" in the eyes of the Lord (2 Thess 1:5, 11; 2:16-17; 3:13). Presumably, Paul highlights this in order to strengthen the Thessalonians' resolve to stand firm in their faith and do what is proper even in the midst of great opposition.

11.3. Truth and Deception. More than 1 Thessalonians, 2 Thessalonians dwells on *truth and falsehood. Some of this, undoubtedly, has to do with false rumors that the day of the Lord had already come (2 Thess 2:2). But overall Paul is attentive to the way that evil forces deceptively create an alternative truth. This is instantiated in the conniving work of the lawless one (2 Thess 2:8-9). Paul also urges the Thessalonians to test new teachings and *signs according to the traditions he passed down to them (2 Thess 2:15).

11.4. Justice and Peace. Second Thessalonians extensively addresses the matter of the just activity and judgment of God, the one who promises that justice and truth will prevail in the end. In spite of the imbalances and unfairness in the world at present, God will relieve the afflicted and punish the troublemakers (2 Thess 1:6-7). God is the God of vengeance (2 Thess 1:8) because he will see justice is served. But there is also the complementary emphasis on peace in this letter. The final words that Paul gives about the nature of God point to the "Lord of peace," who will "give you peace at all times in all ways" (2 Thess 3:16 NRSV).

See also BODY; CANON OF PAUL'S LETTERS; CHRONOLOGY OF PAUL; COWORKERS, PAUL AND HIS; ESCHATOLOGY; FAITH; HOPE; JOY, REJOICING; LETTERS, LETTER FORMS; MAN OF LAWLESSNESS AND RESTRAINING POWER; OPPONENTS OF PAUL; PAUL IN ACTS; PSEUDEPIGRAPHY/FORGERY; RHETORICAL CRITICISM; SUFFERING; TRAVEL AND ITINERARY PLANS.

BIBLIOGRAPHY. ***Commentaries:*** **M. E. Boring,** *I & II Thessalonians,* NTL (Louisville, KY: Westminster John Knox, 2015); **L. M. Bridges,** *1 & 2 Thessalonians,* SHBC (Macon, GA: Smyth & Helwys, 2008); **F. F. Bruce,** *1 and 2 Thessalonians,* WBC (Waco, TX: Word, 1982); **G. D. Fee,** *The First and Second Letters to the Thessalonians,* NICNT (Grand Rapids, MI: Eerdmans, 2009); **V. P. Furnish,** *1 & 2 Thessalonians,* ANTC (Nashville, TN: Abingdon, 2007); **B. R. Gaventa,** *First and Second Thessalonians,* IBC (Louisville, KY: Westminster John Knox, 1998); **N. K. Gupta,** *1–2 Thessalonians,* ZCINT (Grand Rapids, MI: Zondervan, 2019); **A. Johnson,** *1–2 Thessalonians,* THNTC (Grand Rapids, MI: Eerdmans, 2016); **A. Malherbe,** *The Letters to the Thessalonians,* AYB (New Haven, CT: Yale University Press, 2000); **M. J. J. Menken,** *2 Thessalonians,* NTR (New York: Routledge, 1994); **A. Thiselton,** *1–2 Thessalonians Through the Centuries* (Oxford: Wiley-Blackwell, 2010); **W. Trilling,** *Der zweite Briefe an die Thessalonicher,* EKKNT (Neukirchener-Vluyn: Neukirchener Verlag, 1980); **C. A. Wanamaker,** *The Epistles to the Thessalonians,* NIGTC (Grand Rapids, MI: Eerdmans, 1990); **J. Weima,** *1–2 Thessalonians,* BECNT (Grand Rapids, MI: Baker, 2014).

Studies: **R. S. Ascough,** *Paul's Macedonian Associations,* WUNT 2/161 (Tübingen: Mohr Siebeck, 2003); **J. M. G. Barclay,** "Conflict in Thessalonica," *CBQ* 55 (1993): 512-30; **J. M. Bassler,** ed., *Pauline Theology,* vol. 1, *Thessalonians, Philippians, Galatians, Philemon* (Minneapolis: Fortress, 1991); **R. F. Collins,** *Studies on the First Letter to the Thessalonians,* BETL 66 (Leuven: Peeters, 1984); **K. P. Donfried,** *Paul, Thessalonica, and Early Christianity* (London: T&T Clark, 2002); **K. P. Donfried and J. Beutler,** eds., *The Thessalonians Debate* (Grand Rapids, MI: Eerdmans, 2000); **K. P. Donfried and I. H. Marshall,** *Theology of the Shorter Pauline Letters,* NTT (Cambridge: Cambridge University Press, 1993); **P. Foster,** "The Eschatology of the Thessalonian Correspondence: An Exercise in Pastoral Pedagogy and Constructive Theology," *JSPHL* 1, no. 1 (2011): 57-82; idem, "Who Wrote 2 Thessalonians? A Fresh Look at an Old Problem," *JSNT* 35, no. 2 (2012): 150-75; **D. Grammenos,** ed., *Roman*

Thessaloniki (Thessaloniki: Archaeological Museum of Thessaloniki, 2003); **J. R. Harrison,** *Paul and the Imperial Authorities at Thessalonica and Rome,* WUNT 273 (Tübingen: Mohr Siebeck, 2011); **R. F. Hock,** *The Social Context of Paul's Ministry: Tentmaking and Apostleship* (Philadelphia: Fortress, 1980); **R. Jewett,** *The Thessalonian Correspondence: Pauline Rhetoric and Millenarian Piety* (Philadelphia: Fortress, 1986); **L. T. Johnson,** "The New Testament's Slander and the Conventions of Ancient Polemic," *JBL* 108, no. 3 (1989): 419-41; **G. A. Kennedy,** *Classical Rhetoric and Its Christian and Secular Tradition from Ancient to Modern Times,* 2nd ed. (Chapel Hill: University of North Carolina Press, 1999); **E. Krentz,** "A Stone That Will Not Fit: The Non-Pauline Authorship of 2 Thessalonians," in *Pseudepigraphie und Verfasserfiktion in früchristlichen Briefen,* ed. J. Frey et al., WUNT 256 (Tübingen: Mohr Siebeck, 2009) 456-63; **G. Lyons,** *Pauline Autobiography: Toward a New Understanding,* SBLDS 73 (Atlanta: Scholars Press, 1985); **A. Malherbe,** *Paul and the Thessalonians: The Philosophical Tradition of Pastoral Care* (Philadelphia: Fortress, 1987); **T. W. Manson,** "St. Paul in Greece: The Letters to the Thessalonians," *BJRL* 35 (1953): 428-47; **L. S. Nasrallah, C. Bakirtzis, and S. J. Friesen,** eds., *From Roman to Early Christian Thessalonikē* (Cambridge, MA: Harvard University Press, 2010); **C. R. Nicholl,** *From Hope to Despair in Thessalonica,* SNTSMS (Cambridge: Cambridge University Press, 2004); **B. A. Pearson,** "1 Thessalonians 2:13-16: A Deutero-Pauline Interpolation," *HTR* 64 (1971): 79-94; **S. E. Porter,** "Translation, Exegesis, and 1 Thessalonians 2:14-15," *BT* 64, no. 1 (2013): 82-98; **B. Rossing,** *The Rapture Exposed* (Boulder, CO: Westview, 2004); **J. E. C. Schmidt,** *Vermutungen über die beiden Briefe an die Thessalonicher* (Hadamar: Gelehrtenbuchhandlung, 1801); **T. D. Still,** *Conflict at Thessalonica,* JSNTSup 183 (Sheffield: Sheffield Academic Press, 1999); **S. K. Stowers,** *Letter Writing in Greco-Roman Antiquity* (Philadelphia: Westminster, 1986); **M. Tellbe,** *Paul Between Synagogue and State,* ConBNT 34 (Stockholm: Almqvist & Wiksell, 2001); **J. A. D. Weima,** *Paul the Ancient Letter Writer* (Grand Rapids, MI: Baker, 2016); **B. W. Winter,** "'If a Man Does Not Wish to Work . . .': A Cultural and Historical Setting for 2 Thessalonians 3:6-16," *TynBul* 40, no. 2 (1989): 303-15; **W. Wrede,** *The Authenticity of the Second Letter to the Thessalonians,* trans. R. Rhea (Eugene, OR: Wipf & Stock, 2017).

N. K. Gupta

THESSALONICA. *See* Thessalonians, Letters to the.

THIS AGE. *See* Apocalypticism; Cosmology; Eschatology.

THORN IN THE FLESH. *See* Healing, Illness; Suffering; Visions, Ecstatic Experience.

TIMOTHY, 1 AND 2. *See* Coworkers, Paul and His; Pastoral Epistles.

TITUS. *See* Coworkers, Paul and His; Pastoral Epistles.

TONGUES

The designation *glossolalia* combines the Greek terms *glōssa* (tongue) and *lalein* (to speak). Paul discusses this phenomenon in 1 Corinthians 12–14 along with other *charismata* (*grace *gifts) given by the Spirit (1 Cor 12:10-11, 28). Paul mentions tongues only in 1 Corinthians 12:10, 28, 30; 13:1, 8; 14:2-6, 13-14, 18-23, 26-27, 39. C. K. Barrett argues, based on Paul's personal use of the gift (1 Cor 14:18), "It is difficult . . . to believe that anyone in personal contact with the Pauline mission was unfamiliar with the phenomenon" (Barrett, 116). Even so, Paul only brings the topic to light in response to the abuse of the gift in the Corinthian community.

Other early Christian references appear in Acts 2:4; 10:46; 19:6. Whereas Paul emphasizes tongues as a form of affective *prayer, Luke seems to emphasize its literary function as a sign that *God is empowering his people to speak for him across all cultural barriers (see Acts 1:8; 2:17-18). There may have been different sorts of glossolalic experiences in the first-century *church as there are today (Barrett, 116; for today see also Turner 2005, 32). Still, the parallel descriptions and many similarities suggest that at the root is Spirit-empowered communication (especially to God; see Acts 2:11; 10:46; see extensive discussion in Keener, *Acts* 1:812-16).

1. Ancient Backgrounds.

As with the biblical *tradition, *Gentiles also valued inspired speech. There is not, however, much available evidence that such speech was unintelligible linguistically. Rather, interpretation was needed when the meaning of the speech was obscure or cryptic, as at Delphi. D. E. Aune thus concludes that the Pythia's speech as glossolalia is "a product of modern scholarly imagination" (Aune, 1551; see also Forbes, 7).

OT and Jewish backgrounds also contain examples of inspired speech but do not depict those who speak in other languages under the inspiration of the Spirit. The closest parallel is *Testament of Job* 48–51, of uncertain (possibly second century) date, in which Job's daughters ecstatically speak in an angelic dialect (48.2-3), in the dialect of the heavenly rulers (49.1-3), and in the dialect of the cherubim (50.1-3). Because their *hymns were written down (49.3; 50.3), they may be envisioned as intelligible, despite their angelic beauty. While speaking in other languages under the inspiration of the Spirit is not certain in the Jewish context, Spirit-inspired speech linked with *prophecy does provide a contextual background for the Corinthian experience. For these reasons, some scholars argue that the Corinthian experience of *glossolalia* is a *religious novum* (Turner 1996, 237).

Tongues continued over a wide geographic area throughout early Christianity (Forbes, 75-84; see perhaps Mk 16:17).

2. Scholarly Trends Related to Paul's View of Tongues.

Modern scholarship exhibits a spectrum of views concerning Paul's overarching perception of speaking in tongues. Views range from the perspective that Paul merely tolerates the Corinthians' use of it to the view that Paul appreciates the gift but disapproves the Corinthians' abuse of it (see, e.g., Thiselton, 14-36, for the view that Paul desires the elimination of tongues in public usage, or Hovenden, 105-6, who argues Paul was grateful for it).

2.1. Glossolalia and Corinth's Factions. The Corinthian believers presumably learned about tongues from Paul (1 Cor 14:18), but it became one flashpoint in their many divisions (see, e.g., 1 Cor 1:11-12). Some Corinthians apparently sought to express their spiritual excellence by making others listen to their unintelligible tongues, a practice not edifying to their hearers. Paul must thus situate the gift of tongues in its proper place for the Corinthian community, especially contending that *love must guide the use of all gifts (1 Cor 13:1).

2.2. Glossolalia and the Best Gifts (1 Cor 12–14). As elsewhere in 1 Corinthians (1 Cor 7:1, 25; 8:1; 16:1, 12), Paul begins his new topic in 1 Corinthians 12–14 with *peri de* ("now concerning"). Paul frames his discussion about tongues with the matter of what builds up (see 1 Cor 14:3-5, 12, 17, 26) the church, Christ's *body (1 Cor 12:12-27), loving being central (1 Cor 13:1–14:1). First Corinthians 12:4-11 situates speaking in tongues within a diverse listing of gifts empowered by the Spirit. Paul's listing is ad hoc rather than exhaustive and provides a window into the varieties of gifts relevant for the Corinthian church. Although the Spirit determines the distribution of the gifts (1 Cor 12:4), Paul also urges believers to *seek* edifying gifts (1 Cor 12:31; 14:1, 39). Tongues is probably last in Paul's list (1 Cor 12:10, 28, 30) because the Corinthians had elevated the gift inappropriately, not because he seeks to denigrate a divine gift. All of the gifts are given for "the common good," a prevalent motif in ancient speeches that focus on unity (see Cicero, *Fin.* 3.19.64; Seneca, *Dial.* 8.1.4).

Ancient literature often used body imagery to reconcile a divided state. Paul adapts this imagery to demonstrate that all believers belong to one community, an even more organic *body in which each member is needed. Paul employs a rhetorical device called *prosopopoeia*, where the body parts are each given a mouth to speak. Just as a body is not ideally whole without all its members, believers cannot afford to reject any gifts God has given others. God himself is the one who gives each member a place in Christ's body (1 Cor 12:18). No one has all the gifts, and no gift is practiced in the church by all believers (1 Cor 12:29-30). One should seek the best gifts (1 Cor 12:31; 14:1), though sought and used in love (1 Cor 13:1-3). The gifts, even in their superlative form, are nothing without love (1 Cor 13:1-3); they are temporary, but love is eternal (1 Cor 13:8-13). In the heart of Paul's treatment of gifts is his praise of love—some of which contrasts directly with his earlier depiction of the Corinthians (1 Cor 13:4-7; see 1 Cor 3:3; 4:6-7, 18-19; 5:2; 8:1).

In 1 Corinthians 13:1-3, tongues, prophecy, and self-sacrificial generosity are meaningless without love, but scholars debate why Paul mentions "tongues of angels" in 1 Corinthians 13:1. Many scholars believe that one problem in Corinth was caused by overrealized *eschatology (for a contrary view, see Keener 2019). On this view, some Corinthians viewed themselves as having an angelic and spiritual status that consequently reduced their need for sexual relations (1 Cor 7:1-7) and a *resurrection body (1 Cor 15:1-58), a status reflected by their *worship in angelic dialects (Fee 1987, 631; 1991, 150). Others conclude that Paul uses the phrase "tongues of angels" as hyperbolic ("*even* tongues of angels"; e.g.,

Keener 2005, 108). Some compare many early church fathers' understanding of tongues as ability to speak many earthly languages (de Jager) even though this may be an overreaction to experiences from the Montanist movement. Paul thus frames the use of spiritual gifts with love, the sine qua non for use of the gifts.

Paul regards both tongues and their interpretation as empowered by God's Spirit (1 Cor 12:7-11), but they function differently. Glossolalia is affective prayer, prayer with one's spirit (1 Cor 14:14), whereas interpretation, like prophecy, is cognitive (1 Cor 14:13-15), making the prayer intelligible for others (1 Cor 14:16-19). Because the gifts' purpose is to build up the church, shepherding them to maintain order (1 Cor 14:33, 40) requires interpretation alongside glossolalic utterances intended for the community. If no one is available to interpret, Paul commands those praying in tongues to do so silently or at home (1 Cor 14:28), as Paul apparently does (1 Cor 14:18-19). In contrast to pagan ecstasy (1 Cor 12:2), believers are able to control and manage their inspiration for the greater good (1 Cor 14:32). Paul's concern is audible unintelligibility, not simultaneous, uncoordinated prayer, as was probably practiced in some early Jewish prayer services (see also group prophetic speech in 1 Sam 10:5; 19:20).

Various views exist related to what Paul means by interpretation. While interpretation often involves communicating the sense rather than direct translation, some view Paul's language as urging the Corinthians to move away from inarticulate tongues to exclusive use of articulate speech (see Thiselton 1979, 15). Others respond that this is not the only use of such terminology (Cartledge, 140) and that Paul's coupling of interpretation with tongues contradicts this view (Turner 1996, 227). Like other devotional practices, private devotional use of tongues as described in 1 Corinthians 14:4, 18-19, edifies the person who prays; because it involves *mysteries even to the speaker (1 Cor 14:2, 14), those who pray in tongues might wish at times to interpret as well (1 Cor 14:13-15).

Most contested in Paul's understanding of tongues is his use of Isaiah 28:11 in 1 Corinthians 14:21-22. Isaiah contextually envisions a sign of *judgment, God speaking to his obtuse people through conquering foreigners. Many thus see it here as an appropriate sign of judgment for nonbelievers. Because pagans in antiquity were familiar with prophecy but not with glossolalia, tongues might cause them to stumble. Others, such as Talbert, contend that Paul is quoting from the Corinthians in 1 Corinthians 14:22 and then refuting their view in 1 Corinthians 14:23-25.

Paul summarizes the essence of argument of 1 Corinthians 14 in 1 Corinthians 14:39-40. Prophecy's intelligibility makes it more helpful for the gathered Corinthian assemblies, but glossolalia should not be forbidden in the Corinthian setting.

3. Interdisciplinary Approaches to Understanding Glossolalia.

3.1. Anthropological and Sociological Perspectives. Although not yet demonstrated in ancient paganism, glossolalia today appears in a range of religious contexts; scholars continue to debate the degree to which these are useful analogies to Paul's description of the experience. Some envision it as a release from the unconscious (Thiselton 2000, 984-88). Psychological approaches today have shifted away from earlier models of aberrant psychology or sociological deprivation due to weak evidence in support (Malony and Lovekin, 93). This has opened doors for conversations about tongues speech as religious ritual along with the benefits experienced by participants. Some have recently argued for it as a form of social empowerment (Poloma, 172) or resistance discourse (Smith; see also Tupamahu).

3.2. Linguistic Perspectives. Scholarship lacks consensus concerning how Paul would have perceived glossolalia. The use of the term *glōssa* ("tongue" in the sense of "language"; see 1 Cor 13:1; 14:11) makes it unlikely that Paul understood the experience as nonlinguistic babbling any more than Luke did (Caird, 54; Garland, 584). Some distinguish Paul's understanding of glossolalia from the empirical phenomenon he interpreted (Dunn, 242-43). Views include (1) xenolalia (Green; Davies; Ford; Robertson; Gundry), (2) speaking in heavenly languages (Ellis), (3) a combination of xenolalia and heavenly languages (Banks and Moon; Fee 1997, 32-33; 1991, 197-202), (4) an idiosyncratic language or prayer language (Forbes, 60), (5) unintelligible speech that sometimes uses foreign words (Mills, 69), or (6) a "sub-or-pre-linguistic form of speech" that may convey a meaning (Carson, 84-86, adapting Poythress, 369, 375-76). On the last view, it functions as communication and is partly linguistic, though not in the fullest sense.

Drawing on relevance theory, speech-act theory, and linguistics generally, David Hilborn approaches glossolalia as communication to God that depends on "shared assumptions." This leads him to argue that the translation of tongues utterance is less a matter of vocabulary and grammar than it is of an interaction that involves paralinguistic, sublinguistic, or nonlinguistic forms of communication (Hilborn, 145). Others might find implied meanings even in the sounds, the way that musical rhythm and keys, for example, communicate sentiments in particular contexts.

3.3. Philosophical Perspectives. Some suggest that speech-act theory, based on a philosophy of language, helpfully shifts the discussion from what tongues speech actually *is* to what it intends to *do*. For example, James K. A. Smith draws on semiotics to realize the variety in the purposes of glossolalia (Smith, 85-93). This perspective may illuminate 1 Corinthians 14:2-4, 14-19: while Paul especially urges glossolalia's communicative purpose in a public setting, he also allows for a private usage of the gift for personal edification. In one sense this type of speech is still communicative since God is marked as the hearer.

3.4. Theological Perspectives. Scholars continue to debate whether Paul would recognize modern uses of glossolalia. A strong majority of exegetes recognize that Paul expected the form of glossolalia to which he referred to continue as useful, alongside other representative gifts such as prophecy and *knowledge (probably related to *teaching) until Christ's return. Seeing Christ face to face and knowing perfectly will then supplant partial knowledge and guidance (such as teaching and prophecy; 1 Cor 13:8-12; see also 1 Cor 1:7).

Some theologians contend that the completion of Scripture obviates the need for prophecy, which could risk introducing postbiblical doctrine. Others counter that the present cessation of prophecy, nowhere clearly attested in Scripture, is itself a postbiblical doctrine. They contend that prophecy need not introduce doctrine, a much greater risk for the gift of teaching. Certainly, prophecy was never coextensive with Scripture; many prophesied whose prophecies do not appear in Scripture (e.g., 1 Kings 18:4; 1 Cor 14:29-31), and not all of Scripture (where the most dominant genre is narrative) takes the form of prophecy. One might also ask why glossolalia, which Paul usually treats as a form of prayer, would be affected by an argument about prophecy in any case. Some differentiate "natural" and "supernatural" gifts, contending that the latter have ceased, but Paul recognizes no such distinctions (e.g., Rom 12:6-8; 1 Cor 12:8; Eph 4:11).

See also CORINTHIANS, FIRST LETTER TO THE; GIFTS OF THE SPIRIT; PRAYER; PROPHECY, PROPHESYING; WORSHIP.

BIBLIOGRAPHY. **D. E. Aune,** "Magic in Early Christianity," in *Aufstieg und Niedergang der Römischen Welt,* part 2, *Principat* (Berlin: de Gruyter, 1990), 23:1507-57; **R. Banks and G. Moon,** "Speaking in Tongues," *The Churchman* 80 (1966): 278-94; **C. K. Barrett,** *Acts,* vol. 1, *1-14,* ICC (New York: T&T Clark, 2004); **G. B. Caird,** *The Apostolic Age* (London: Duckworth, 1993); **D. A. Carson,** *Showing the Spirit: A Theological Exposition of 1 Corinthians 12–14* (Grand Rapids, MI: Baker, 1987); **M. J. Cartledge,** "The Nature and Function of New Testament Glossolalia," *EvQ* 72, no. 2 (2000): 135-50; **J. D. Davies,** "Pentecost and Glossolalia," *JTS* 3 (1952): 228-31; **J. D. G. Dunn,** *Jesus and the Spirit: A Study of the Religious and Charismatic Experience of Jesus and the First Christians as Reflected in the New Testament* (Grand Rapids, MI: Eerdmans, 1997); **E. E. Ellis,** "'Spiritual' Gifts in the Pauline Community," *NTS* 20 (1973–1974): 128-44; **G. D. Fee,** *The First Epistle to the Corinthians,* NICNT (Grand Rapids, MI: Eerdmans, 1987); idem, *God's Empowering Presence: The Holy Spirit in the Letters of Paul* (Peabody, MA: Hendrickson, 1991); idem, "Toward a Pauline Theology of Glossolalia," *Pentecostalism in Context* (1997): 24-37; **C. Forbes,** *Prophecy and Inspired Speech in Early Christianity and Its Hellenistic Environment,* WUNT 2/75 (Tübingen: Mohr Siebeck, 1995); **J. M. Ford,** "Toward a Theology of 'Speaking in Tongues,'" *TS* 32 (1971): 3-29; **D. E. Garland,** *1 Corinthians,* BECNT (Grand Rapids, MI: Baker, 2003); **D. Green,** "The Gift of Tongues," *BSac* 22, no. 85 (1865): 99-126; **R. H. Gundry,** "Ecstatic Utterance," *JTS* 17, no. 2 (1966): 299-307; **D. Hilborn,** "Glossolalia as Communication: A Linguistic-Pragmatic Perspective," in *Speaking in Tongues: Multidisciplinary Perspectives,* ed. M. J. Cartledge (Eugene, OR: Wipf & Stock, 2006), 111-46; **G. Hovenden,** *Speaking in Tongues: The New Testament Evidence in Context* (New York: Sheffield Academic Press, 2002); **E. de Jager,** "An Evaluation of Speaking in Tongues as Angelic Language from the Judaean and Early Christian Perspective," *Journal of the South African Theological Seminary* 28 (2019): 35-64; **C. S. Keener,** *1–2 Corinthians* (New York: Cambridge University Press, 2005); idem, *Acts: An Exegetical Commentary,* vol. 1, *Introduction and 1:1–2:47* (Grand Rapids, MI: Baker Academic, 2012); idem, "Overrealized Eschatology or Lack of Eschatology in Corinth?," in *Scripture, Texts, and Tracings in 1 Corinthians,* ed. L. Belleville and B. J. Oropeza (Lanham, MD: Lexington/Fortress, 2019), 43-66; **H. Malony and A. Lovekin,** eds., *Glossolalia—Behavioural Science Perspectives on Speaking in*

Tongues (Oxford: Oxford University Press, 1985); **W. E. Mills,** *A Theological/Exegetical Approach to Glossolalia* (Lanham, MD: University Press of America, 1985); **M. M. Poloma,** "Glossolalia, Liminality, and Empowered Kingdom Building," in *Speaking in Tongues: Multi-disciplinary Perspectives*, ed. M. J. Cartledge (Carlisle, UK: Paternoster, 2006), 147-73; **V. S. Poythress,** "Linguistic and Sociological Analyses of Modern Tongues-Speaking: Their Contribution and Limitations," *WTJ* 42 (1979): 367-88; **C. F. Robertson,** "The Nature of New Testament Glossolalia" (ThD diss., Dallas Theological Seminary, 1975); **J. K. A. Smith,** "Tongues as Resistant Discourse: A Philosophical Perspective," in *Speaking in Tongues: Multi-disciplinary Perspectives*, ed. M. J. Cartledge (Carlisle, UK: Paternoster, 2006), 81-110; **C. Talbert,** *Reading Corinthians* (Macon, GA: Smyth & Helwys, 2002); **A. C. Thiselton,** "Greek Lexicography and the Context of Argument: The 'Interpretation' of Tongues? A New Suggestion in Light of Greek Usage in Philo and Josephus," *JTS* 30 (1979): 15-36; idem, *The First Epistle to the Corinthians*, NIGTC (Grand Rapids, MI: Eerdmans, 2000); **E. Tupamahu,** "Tongues as a Site of Subversion: An Analysis from the Perspective of Postcolonial Politics of Language," *Pneuma* 38 (2016): 293-311; **M. Turner,** *The Holy Spirit and Spiritual Gifts* (Peabody, MA: Hendrickson, 1996); idem, "Early Christian Experience and Theology of 'Tongues'—A New Testament Perspective," in *Speaking in Tongues: Multi-disciplinary Perspectives*, ed. M. J. Cartledge (Carlisle, UK: Paternoster, 2006), 1-33.

C. S. Keener and J. L. Vaughan

TORAH. *See* INTERPRETATION: JEWISH; LAW; PAUL AND JUDAISM; WORKS OF THE LAW.

TRADITION

For Paul, tradition (*paradosis*) ensured the continued vitality of God's *household. Though some post-Reformation translations of his letters suggest that Paul was suspicious of tradition, he distinguishes between human and God-given tradition, whether written or oral (2 Thess 2:15; 1 Cor 11:2, 23; 15:3; Humphrey 2013). Paul does not contrast the *Holy Spirit with tradition per se but corrects skewed versions of the Christian story, temporary traditions made permanent (e.g., kashrut—i.e., food laws—Sabbath, and *circumcision), and enslaving ideas (Rom 16:17; Col 2:8; Gal 1:14; see Mk 7:8-9, 13). God-given tradition involves three parties—those who "tradition" (*paradidōmi*), those who "receive" (*paralambanō*), and the integrating Holy Spirit. Paul honored what he had received from other Christians and the OT, read as warning and typological proclamation of the *gospel. He also refers to Jesus' sayings and actions and to early creeds, *hymns, and catechesis.

1. Tradition and Communal Revelation
2. Use of Tradition

1. Tradition and Communal Revelation.

Paul received revelations from *God concerning Jesus *Christ (Gal 1:11-12, 15-17; 2:2; 2 Cor 12:1-7) but never presents these as foundational. Instead, he insists that the core revelations are communally discerned, for Christians together see God in the face of Jesus (2 Cor 4:6). In response to Judaizing opponents requiring kashrut, circumcision, and Sabbath laws, he insists that he has seen Christ (1 Cor 9:1; Gal 1:12) and so has apostolic authority. At the same time, he works in unity with apostolic teachers (Gal 2:2, 7-10), and transmits traditions he received—the crucifixion, *resurrection appearances, institution of the *Lord's Supper, and *baptism (1 Cor 11; 15; Rom 6:3-4). These traditions are foreshadowed by the OT, made known through Jesus to the whole *church (Rom 16:25-26; 1 Cor 10:1-6, 11; Col 1:26-27; 2:2-3), clarified through *apostles and prophets, and discerned by God's people (1 Cor 14:26-33; see Cullmann). Paul commends his churches for cleaving to traditions that he has given them (2 Thess 2:15; 3:6; 1 Cor 11:2; 1 Thess 4:1; Col 2:6-7). Contemporary Christians may be surprised to see solemn "sure words" in the Pastoral Letters concerning church order and spiritual *discipline as well as theology (1 Tim 1:15; 3:1; 4:8; 2 Tim 2:11; Titus 3:5-7). For some scholars these more mundane concerns reflect a post-Pauline mediocrity, whereas others see them as a continuation of Paul's own practical concerns (Ellis; Humphrey 2013).

2. Use of Tradition.

Paul's use of tradition reflects his rabbinical heritage and understanding of how God works in and among believers. He rarely quotes predecessors beyond the OT and some quotations of Jesus, including one (mediated through Luke) not found elsewhere (Acts 10:35). Paul also uses quasi-rabbinic argumentation (see Kugel), such as the "rock that followed" the Hebrews in the wilderness (1 Cor 10:4), his interpretation of crossing the Jordan as baptism (1 Cor 10:3), and his allegory of Hagar and Sarah (Gal 4:21-31). Such arguments (see below regarding 1 Cor 8:4-13 and Phil 2:5-11) would not have been received had he not been building on traditions shared by his interlocutors.

2.1. Old Testament Traditions. Paul frequently uses the OT in moral *teaching or as exemplary (Gal 5:14; Rom 13:9; 15:4; 1 Cor 10:11). Jesus and the gospel were the measure by which Paul understood the OT (Hays): *Abraham foreshadowed the new *covenant (Gen 15:6; Rom 4; Gal 3), divine *mysteries are surpassed by the "apocalypsed" Messiah (Rom 10:5-9; see Deut 30:11-14), and the prophet's *vision is fulfilled in Christ (2 Cor 3; see Jer 31:31-34, Ezek 36:26-27). Paul's reworking of prophetic monotheism may have begun in early Christian hymnody (Phil 2:5-11; see Is 45:23). Similarly, his reformulation of the Shema in 1 Corinthians 8:6, applying "God" to the Father, and "*Lord" to Jesus, was likely known to the Corinthians or he could not have used this strategy to address eating idol meat. How often Paul is theologizing and how often he passes on early Christian traditions of interpreting the OT is debatable.

2.2. Jesus Traditions. Perhaps because he is not preaching the gospel, Paul does not frequently refer to Jesus' teachings (but see 1 Cor 7:10; 9:14; 11:23-24; 1 Thess 4:15-17). However, his letters allude to Jesus more often than is recognized (1 Thess 5:2-3; 1 Cor 13:2; Rom 12:14; 13:7-10; 14:14). Indeed, Paul distinguished between Jesus' instruction and his own (1 Cor 7:12, 25), treating dominical teaching with solemnity while trying to address the particular situations of his congregations.

2.3. Christian Traditions. One can be certain of Paul's use of early Christian traditions where these overlap with other written sources (1 Cor 11:23-26; see Lk 22:16-20). The detection of traditional oral formulations is more difficult, but many have postulated confessional material (1 Cor 12:3; Phil 2:11; Rom 10:8-9), creedal fragments (1 Cor 15:3-5; Rom 1:3-4; 3:24-26; 4:24-25; 1 Thess 1:9-10; 2 Tim 2:8; see Rom 6:17), and hymns (Phil 2:6-11; Eph 5:14; Col 1:15-20). When Paul teaches on morality and everyday living (Rom 12:1–15:13; Gal 5:1–6:10; 1 Thess 4:1–5:22; Col 3:1–4:6), one can note connections with Cynics, Stoics, and Jewish exhortation, but whether this is coincidence or dependence is uncertain. Some think it more likely that this material is shaped by early Christian catechesis (Selwyn). It is not always certain, when Paul uses such phrases as "the word of the Lord," whether he is referring to traditional dominical teaching (not found elsewhere) or utterances of Christian prophets ratified by the community (e.g., 1 Thess 4:15; 5:20-21; 1 Cor 14:29).

See also ABRAHAM; APOSTLE; DISCIPLINE, CHURCH; HYMNS, HYMN FRAGMENTS, CONFESSIONS; JESUS, SAYINGS OF; JUDAIZERS; OLD TESTAMENT IN PAUL; PASTORAL EPISTLES; TEACHING, TEACHERS.

BIBLIOGRAPHY. **F. F. Bruce,** *Tradition: Old and New* (Exeter, UK: Paternoster, 1970); **K. Chamblin,** "Revelation and Tradition in the Pauline Euangelion," *WTJ* 48 (1986): 1-16; **O. Cullmann,** "The Tradition," in *The Early Church,* ed. A. J. B. Higgins (London: SCM Press, 1956), 59-99; **E. E. Ellis,** "Traditions in I Corinthians," *NTS* 32 (1986): 481-502; **R. B. Hays,** *Reading Backwards: Figural Christology and the Fourfold Gospel Witness* (Grand Rapids, MI: Baker, 2014); **E. M. Humphrey,** "Why Bring the Word Down? The Rhetoric of Demonstration and Disclosure in Romans 9:30–10:13," in *Romans and the People of God; Festschrift for Gordon Fee,* ed. S. Soderlund and N. T. Wright (Grand Rapids, MI: Eerdmans, 1999), 129-48; idem, *Scripture and Tradition: What the Bible Really Says* (Grand Rapids, MI: Baker, 2013); **A. M. Hunter,** *Paul and His Predecessors,* rev. ed. (London: SCM Press, 1961); **A. Kirk,** "Social and Cultural Memory," in *Memory, Tradition and Text: Uses of the Past in Early Christianity,* ed. A. Kirk and T. Thatcher (Atlanta: Society of Biblical Literature, 2005); **J. L. Kugel,** *Traditions of the Bible: A Guide to the Bible as It Was at the Start of the Common Era* (Cambridge, MA: Harvard University Press, 1998); **G. E. Ladd,** "Revelation and Tradition in Paul," in *Apostolic History and the Gospel,* ed. W. W. Gasque and R. P. Martin (Grand Rapids, MI: Eerdmans, 1970), 223-30; **H. de Lubac,** *L'Écriture dans la tradition* (Paris: Aubier Montaigne, 1966). **J. I. H. McDonald,** *Kerygma and Didache: The Articulation and Structure of the Earliest Christian Message,* SNTSMS 37 (Cambridge: Cambridge University Press, 1980), 101-25; **E. G. Selwyn,** "On the Inter-relation of I Peter and Other N.T. Epistles," in *The First Epistle of St Peter* (London: Macmillan, 1946), 365-466; **K. Wegenast,** *Das Verständnis der Tradition bei Paulus und in den Deuteropaulinen,* WMANT 8 (Neukirchen: Neukirchener Verlag, 1962); idem, "Teach," *NIDNTT* 3:759-75.

E. M. Humphrey

TRANSFORMATION. *See* COMPLETE, MATURE (PERFECT); CREATION AND NEW CREATION; HOLINESS, SANCTIFICATION; JUSTIFICATION; SPIRITUALITY.

TRAVEL AND ITINERARY PLANS

Paul traveled extensively in the ancient world in fulfillment of his commission from the risen *Christ to be an *apostle to the *Gentiles. Our sources are sufficient for us to outline much of his itinerary and to discuss motivation for his journeys.

1. Sources
2. The Evidence of Paul's Letters
3. Apostolic Parousia
4. Paul's Motivation for Travel
5. Paul's Itinerary in Acts
6. Integration of the Letters and Acts

1. Sources.
The primary source for Paul's itinerary must be his letters, as these provide firsthand evidence. Since Paul's letters are occasional documents and do not cover all of his career, they do not tell us of all of Paul's travels. On the other hand, Acts, our main secondary source, describes Paul's travels in detail. Methodologically it is important to examine Paul's letters first and ascertain what probable information can be gained from them. Second, we will outline the evidence of Acts, and, finally, we will see to what extent the evidence can be integrated.

2. The Evidence of Paul's Letters.
From Paul's letters, we can establish the following blocks of travel. We should note that the precise order of some of these travels cannot be determined by reference to Paul's letters alone (see Phillips, 51-65).

2.1. The Early Years. The revelation of Christ to Paul occurred in or near Damascus, and from there Paul went into Arabia (Gal 1:16-17), which refers to the kingdom of the Nabataeans. Paul may have gone to Arabia to begin missionary work, or he may have sought a place of solitude to reflect on his encounter with the risen Christ.

Paul then returned to Damascus (Gal 1:17), where he remained until three years after his encounter with Christ (Gal 1:18). At that time he found it necessary to escape from the hands of the provincial governor under King Aretas IV, the ruler of the Nabataean kingdom (2 Cor 11:32-33). He then went to *Jerusalem for fifteen days, but of the apostles he saw only Cephas (*Peter) and *James the brother of Jesus (Gal 1:18-19). Paul then went into the regions of Syria and Cilicia (Gal 1:21). The churches of Judea heard that Paul was preaching the faith he once tried to destroy (Gal 1:23), so we can infer that in Syria and Cilicia he was involved in missionary work.

After fourteen years Paul went up again to Jerusalem with Barnabas and Titus. The fourteen years could be reckoned either from the time of his encounter with Christ or from his first visit to Jerusalem. When in Jerusalem he had a private meeting with James, Cephas, and John, who gave to Paul and Barnabas the right hand of *fellowship and agreed that Paul and Barnabas should go to the Gentiles (Gal 2:1-10). Paul then returned to Antioch, and shortly afterward there occurred the incident in which he accused Cephas and Barnabas of hypocrisy (Gal 2:11-14).

2.2. Founding the Galatian Churches. Paul first preached the *gospel to the Galatians because of an *illness (Gal 4:13). He does not relate this founding visit to any other event, so it is difficult to place chronologically in relation to other visits. That he first visited Galatia before he wrote 1 Corinthians (see 2.4 below) is clear from 1 Corinthians 16:1, but Paul gives us no more information about when this was. It is debated whether Paul visited places such as Ancyra and Pessinus (the North Galatian view) or Pisidian Antioch, Iconium, Lystra, and Derbe (the South Galatian view). Whether *to proteron* (Gal 4:13; "earlier" or "the first time") indicates that Paul made a second visit before he wrote Galatians is also debated.

2.3. Macedonia and Athens. In 1 Thessalonians 2:2 Paul tells us that he went to Philippi first and then went on to Thessalonica; Philippians 4:15-16 also implies this order. Paul seems to have spent quite some time in Thessalonica, long enough for him to receive help from the Philippian Christians "more than once" (Phil 4:16). After leaving Thessalonica, Paul went to Athens. He wanted to return to Thessalonica to visit the church there but was hindered from doing so by *Satan and thus sent Timothy to strengthen the church. Timothy returned to Paul with a positive report (1 Thess 2:17-18; 3:1-6). As Paul wrote 1 Thessalonians, he was praying that he would be able to go to Thessalonica to see the believers there (1 Thess 3:6, 10-11).

2.4. Ministry in Corinth and Ephesus. Second Corinthians 1:19 indicates that Paul, Silvanus, and Timothy were the first to preach the gospel in *Corinth. This probably occurred shortly after the *mission in Macedonia and Athens for two reasons. First, when Paul was in Corinth, his needs were supplied by believers from Macedonia (2 Cor 11:9). Second, Paul had traveled from Philippi to Athens and then sent Timothy from there to Thessalonica; he met Timothy again at the place where 1 Thessalonians was composed (1 Thess 3:1-2). Silvanus probably accompanied Timothy on the return trip, since he joined Paul and Timothy in writing 1 Thessalonians shortly after Timothy returned to Paul (1 Thess 1:1; 3:6; the three share only 1–2 Thessalonians). Thus we know that the three people who first preached the gospel in Corinth (2 Cor 1:19) were together just after the mission in Thessalonica, when they wrote 1 Thessalonians. This suggests they were in Corinth when they wrote and that we should place Paul's first visit to Corinth shortly after his time in Macedonia. It is clearly a good while after this that Paul wrote 1 Corinthians, since much had happened in the intervening period (Lüdemann, 101-3). This, his second letter to Corinth (see the "previous letter" mentioned in 1 Cor 5:9 and now lost), was written from *Ephesus (1 Cor 16:8, 19), so at some point after his time in Corinth he went on to Ephesus, where his stay seems to have been a prolonged one.

Paul outlines his future travel plans in 1 Corinthians 16:1-8. He hoped to go to Corinth in connection with the *collection and may then accompany those carrying it to *Jerusalem (1 Cor 16:3-4; 4:18-19). But first, after Pentecost, he planned to travel from Ephesus to Macedonia and might then spend the winter in Corinth (1 Cor 16:5-6). In the meantime, he sent Timothy to Corinth (1 Cor 4:17; 16:10-11). Timothy seems to have returned to Ephesus with the bad news that neither the letter nor Timothy's presence had healed the rift between Paul and the Corinthians. Paul then made a second, "painful" visit to Corinth (2 Cor 2:1-2; 13:2); he was humiliated before the church and returned to Ephesus in great distress (2 Cor 12:21). He then sent Titus to Corinth with his third, "tearful" letter to the Corinthians (2 Cor 2:3-4, 9; 7:8-12; some scholars think that this was 2 Cor 10–13).

Paul then went to Troas, where he had planned to meet Titus (2 Cor 2:12-13). When he did not find Titus there, he went on to Macedonia (2 Cor 2:13; 7:5). While there, Titus arrived with encouraging news that the Corinthians mourned their wrongs and longed to see Paul (2 Cor 7:6-7). Titus and two others were then sent on ahead to Corinth with Paul's fourth letter (2 Cor 8:16-24), which was probably 2 Corinthians 1–9, a letter of reconciliation. In the letter Paul also explained his change in travel plans (2 Cor 1:15–2:1; see 1 Cor 16:2-4), which had led to the charge that he was vacillating (2 Cor 1:17). Paul himself hoped to follow Titus (2 Cor 9:4-5). He probably then received word that renewed troubles had occurred in Corinth, so he wrote 2 Corinthians 10–13. He was again ready to visit the Corinthians (2 Cor 12:14, 20-21; 13:1-2, 10) for what was his third visit, and it seems he did so (and was presumably well received), since he wrote Romans from Corinth (Rom 16:23; see 1 Cor 1:14) and noted in Romans 15:26 that he had already added contributions to the collection money from churches in Achaia, which would include Corinth.

Before Paul wrote Romans, he had preached the gospel in Illyricum (Rom 15:19). We do not know when this was, although it was probably connected with a period in Macedonia.

2.5. To Jerusalem and Rome. Paul outlines further travel plans in Romans 15:22-31. Rome is neither his immediate nor his long-term goal. From Corinth he plans to travel to Jerusalem; this is the third Jerusalem visit he mentions in his letters (see also 1 Cor 16:1-4; 2 Cor 1:16). He will deliver the collection there (Rom 15:25-27), although he is fearful that he might face trouble from nonbelievers in doing so (Rom 15:31; see 1 Cor 16:3-4). He will then go to Rome, so that he and the Romans may be mutually encouraged by each other's faith (Rom 1:12). But he also notes that since his mission from Jerusalem to Illyricum is complete (Rom 15:19, 23), he plans to go to Spain to begin a new phase of his mission after he has spent some time in Rome. He hopes that the Roman Christians will become partners in his mission to Spain (Rom 15:24, 28).

2.6. Letters from Prison. Paul was in *prison as he wrote Philippians (Phil 1:7, 13), Colossians (Col 4:3, 10, 18), and Philemon (Philem 1). From Philippians 1:27; 2:24 we know that Paul planned a visit to Philippi if or when he was released from prison. As he wrote Philemon, he was looking forward to release from prison and hoped to visit Philemon (Philem 22), who probably lived in the neighborhood of Colossae (Col 4:9). However, the place of Paul's imprisonment is debated for all three letters, with Rome, Ephesus, and Caesarea all being possibilities. This lack of consensus makes it difficult to use them as evidence here, and in any case we do not know whether Paul was released to travel as he had planned.

2.7. The Pastoral Epistles. The Pauline authorship of the Pastorals is debated; those who think these letters are pseudonymous do not seek to reconcile them with Paul's travels as they are known from other evidence. For those who argue that the Pastorals are genuinely Pauline, it seems most likely that they come from a period after Paul's release from prison in Rome (Acts 28; Mounce, lxxxiv-lxxxvi). The most probable order of events portrayed in the Pastoral Epistles is then as follows. Paul and Titus evangelized Crete, where Titus remained (Titus 1:5). Paul then traveled with Timothy to Ephesus, where Timothy stayed to combat false teaching (1 Tim 1:3). Meanwhile, Paul went on to Macedonia (1 Tim 1:3), where he probably wrote both 1 Timothy and Titus. He planned then to travel to Nicopolis for the winter (Titus 3:12). Paul was probably on his way back to Ephesus (1 Tim 3:14) when he was arrested, perhaps at Troas (2 Tim 4:13-15). At some point he also visited Corinth and Miletus (2 Tim 4:20). When he wrote 2 Timothy he was in Rome, where he expected to die (2 Tim 1:16-17; 2:9; 4:6-8, 16-18).

This outline of events requires us to assume that Paul undertook further travels after release from Rome, for which we have no other clear evidence. Further, it is noted that if Paul was released from prison in Rome, his plans were to go west, not east, and that Luke would surely have written of such a release. These factors, along with the denial of Pauline authorship of the Pastorals on other grounds, have led to the view that this evidence for Paul's travels should be discounted. However, one could maintain that Paul could have changed his plans and gone east. If such an argument is accepted, then the travel information given in the Pastoral Epistles is reliable, but the evidence obviously postdates Acts and cannot be integrated with Luke's account.

2.8. Other Travels. On a number of occasions Paul lists some of the hardships he has endured, and often these refer to his experiences while traveling. For example, in 2 Corinthians 11:25-27 he says:

> Three times I was shipwrecked; for a night and a day I was adrift at sea; on frequent journeys, in danger from rivers, danger from bandits, danger from my own people, danger from Gentiles, danger in the city, danger in the wilderness, danger at sea, . . . in toil and hardship, through many a sleepless night, hungry and thirsty, often without food, cold and naked. (NRSV; see also 1 Cor 4:11; 2 Cor 6:4-5)

Since many of these experiences are unknown to us, these passages serve to remind us of how many gaps there are in our knowledge of Paul's life.

2.9. Summary. From Paul's occasional letters, which do not cover all of his career, we are able to arrive at the following blocks of travel, although, as noted above, the exact order of some of these travels cannot be determined from Paul's letters alone. (We have excluded evidence for travel after Paul's Roman imprisonment, since this is debated.) (1) Damascus, Arabia, Damascus, Jerusalem, Syria and Cilicia, Jerusalem, *Syrian Antioch; (2) founding visit to Galatian churches at some point; (3) Philippi, Thessalonica, Athens; (4) Corinth, Ephesus, Corinth, Ephesus, Troas, Macedonia, Corinth, plans to travel to Jerusalem and Rome.

3. Apostolic Parousia.

3.1. Definition. Certain passages in Paul's letters have been identified by R. W. Funk on the basis of their form and content as literary units concerned with the theme of the "apostolic parousia," that is, the presence of apostolic authority and power. In these passages Paul reminds readers of his apostolic authority by making his presence felt through the letter itself, by reference to the visit of an emissary or to Paul's coming visit. The letter and the envoy are anticipatory substitutes for Paul's own personal presence when he cannot travel, but both function as a means of conveying his apostolic presence (see Harmon).

Thus, these apostolic parousia sections remind the readers of Paul's apostolic authority by making his presence felt in these three related ways. The presence of Paul in person was the primary medium by which he made his apostolic authority effective (1 Cor 4:19; Phil 1:24-25), and he would rather have conveyed his information in person than by letter or via an emissary, but these two substitutes were sometimes necessary. An envoy did not have the same power as Paul himself had, as he implies in 1 Corinthians 4:17-20: Timothy would remind them, whereas Paul himself would put their power to the test.

3.2. Form. Funk identifies the following passages as concerned with the apostolic parousia: Romans 1:8-15; 15:14-33; 1 Corinthians 4:14-21; 2 Corinthians 12:14–13:13; Galatians 4:12-20; Philippians 2:19-24; 1 Thessalonians 2:17–3:13; Philemon 21-22. Funk suggested that the apostolic parousia had five formal units; however, L. A. Jervis has since proposed that there are in fact only three functional units of the apostolic parousia (see Funk, 252-53; Jervis, 113-14; see also Weima, 114-15). These concern

1. the letter-writing unit: Paul's writing of the letter (including the manner in which he is writing), a reference to Paul's apostolic authority to write, and an appeal to obey his teaching
2. the sending-of-emissary unit: Paul's dispatch of an emissary, including the credentials of the emissary and what Paul expects the emissary to do
3. the apostolic-visit unit: Paul's visit and its purpose, along with either (a) the announcement of a visit, including Paul's submission to God's will in this matter, or (b) the desire to visit, including his desire and prayer to see his readers, a recognition that he has been hindered from coming and an expression of love or concern for the readers.

Each of these units or subunits need not be present in each passage. In fact, the visit unit is the only one that occurs in every letter, and only 1 Corinthians 4:14-21 contains all three units.

*3.3. **Significance.*** Clearly Paul attached great significance to his presence with his congregations and hence to his visits. This is clear in the content of the apostolic parousia sections and elsewhere. In Galatians 4:20 he writes, "How I wish I were present with you now and could exchange my voice [for this letter]." Paul can also speak of his presence in terms of power. In 1 Corinthians 4:19-21 he writes:

> I will come to you soon, if the Lord wills, and I will find out not the talk of these arrogant people but their power. For the kingdom of God depends not on talk but on power. What would you prefer? Am I to come to you with a stick, or with love in a spirit of gentleness? (NRSV)

In response to the charge that he wrote bold letters but his bodily presence was weak he replies: "Let such people understand that what we say by letter when absent, we will also do when present" (2 Cor 10:11 NRSV; see 2 Cor 13:10). As Funk comments: "Paul's power is bound to the weakness of Christ, it is true, but that power, even in weakness, is capable of making itself felt" (Funk, 265). Hence he promises to show no leniency when he arrives in Corinth for his third visit (2 Cor 13:1-4).

We see then the significance Paul attached to his actual presence and to the oral word. This is one of the reasons he often prays that he may be able to visit (1 Thess 3:10-11; Rom 1:10; 15:30-32). But as J. A. D. Weima notes, "The authoritative function of the apostolic parousia should not be interpreted as a power-hungry ego trip by the apostle but instead as a useful literary means of placing his readers under his authority such that they will obey the content of the letter" (Weima, 115). It is because of his understanding of the significance of his presence to bring about greater Christlikeness and obedience to the gospel that he gathers the items that concern his presence, either in person or via the substitute of a letter or an envoy, into discrete sections in his letters and thus uses the form that has been called the "apostolic parousia."

4. Paul's Motivation for Travel.

As apostle to the Gentiles, Paul traveled to proclaim the gospel. As he writes in 1 Corinthians 9:16, "An obligation is laid on me, and woe to me if I do not proclaim the gospel" (NRSV). This compulsion led Paul to travel across the ancient world to preach the gospel and establish churches (Rom 10:14-15; 11:13; 2 Cor 2:14; 10:14-16; Col 1:25-29), often while enduring great hardship (2 Cor 11:23-27). In fact, Gorman estimates that Paul walked and sailed around ten thousand miles (Gorman, 77).

In Romans 15:19-20 we see the vision that motivated Paul's travels. He has preached from Jerusalem to Illyricum and has followed his policy of preaching only where Christ was not already known and so not building on another's foundation (see also 1 Cor 3:6; 4:15; Gal 4:19). As he wrote Romans, he wanted to continue to fulfill this missionary vision by preaching in Spain (Rom 15:24, 29). Yet Paul also had a more detailed strategy of focusing his work in large cities such as Ephesus and Corinth. He seems to have used these as large centers for regional outreach through fellow workers (e.g., Col 1:7; 4:12).

Yet Paul traveled not only to preach the gospel and establish churches but also to nurture and encourage his churches that they might be firmly established. Paul often expresses his longing to see a congregation that he may, for example, supply what is lacking in their *faith (1 Thess 3:10; see also 1 Cor 16:5-7; 2 Cor 11:28; 13:9-10). This accords well with Acts, where Paul regularly revisits congregations to strengthen and encourage them (Acts 14:21-23; 15:36, 41; 16:1-5; 18:23; 20:1-2). Paul also traveled extensively because of the need to attend to difficult situations in his congregations, particularly at Corinth (e.g., the "painful visit," 2 Cor 2:1-2). Further, Paul wanted to travel to Rome, a congregation he had not founded, since as apostle to the Gentiles he had a responsibility to strengthen and enrich Gentile believers (Rom 1:11-12; 15:15-16) and to work for their "obedience of faith" (Rom 1:5; 16:26).

Paul traveled extensively in connection with the collection, to which he devoted much time and energy (1 Cor 16:1-4; 2 Cor 8–9; Rom 15:25-26). For Paul the collection symbolized the unity of the churches and the validity of the *salvation of the Gentiles. That Paul was willing to risk his life to deliver the collection (Rom 15:31) indicates the strength of his motivation in this regard.

There was a good deal of flexibility and change in Paul's travel plans, sometimes because of necessity. He notes his plans were hindered by Satan (1 Thess 2:17-18) and that he was unable to travel to Rome when he wanted to because of his service in the East (Rom 1:13; 15:22). It was because of an illness that he stopped to preach the gospel to the Galatians (Gal 4:13-16). Paul also changed his travel plans to Corinth (1 Cor 16:2-4; 2 Cor 1:15-16, 23; 2:1), and this caused difficulty (2 Cor 1:17).

Paul knew that his travel plans were subject to God's will. To the Corinthians he says, "I will come to you soon, if the Lord wills" (1 Cor 4:19 NRSV; see 1 Cor 16:7; Rom 1:10; 15:32). In Acts the Spirit guides Paul in various ways in his travels and particularly initiates new phases of mission (Acts 11:27-30; 13:1-3; 16:6-10; 18:9-10).

5. Paul's Itinerary in Acts.

5.1. The Sequence of Paul's Travels in Acts.

1. From Jerusalem to Damascus, encounter with the risen Christ, meeting with Ananias, flight from Damascus (Acts 9:1-25)
2. First Jerusalem visit, introduction to the apostles, preaching in Jerusalem (Acts 9:26-29)
3. To Caesarea, Tarsus (Acts 9:30)
4. To Syrian Antioch with Barnabas (Acts 11:25-26)
5. Famine relief visit to Jerusalem, return to Antioch (Acts 11:29-30; 12:25)
6. "First missionary journey": Antioch, Seleucia, Salamis to Paphos on Cyprus, Perga, Pisidian Antioch (actually in Phrygia), Iconium, Lystra, Derbe, Lystra, Iconium, Pisidian Antioch, Perga, Attalia, Antioch in Syria (Acts 13:1–14:28)
7. Third Jerusalem visit for the *Council; return to Antioch (Acts 15:1-35)
8. "Second missionary journey": Antioch, Syria, Cilicia, Derbe, Lystra, the Phrygic-Galatic territory, opposite Mysia, Troas, Samothrace, Neapolis, Philippi, Amphipolis, Apollonia, Thessalonica, Berea, Athens, Corinth (for eighteen months), Cenchreae, Ephesus, Caesarea, Jerusalem (a visit to Jerusalem [Paul's fourth] is certainly implied in Acts 18:22), Antioch (Acts 15:36–18:22)
9. "Third missionary journey": Antioch, the Phrygic-Galatic territory, Ephesus (for three years), Macedonia, Greece, Philippi, Troas, Assos, Mitylene, Samos, Miletus, Cos, Rhodes, Patara, Tyre, Ptolemais, Caesarea (Acts 18:23–21:14)
10. Fifth Jerusalem visit (Acts 21:15–23:30)
11. Antipatris, Caesarea, Sidon, Myra, Fair Havens, Crete, Malta, Syracuse, Rhegium, Puteoli, Rome (Acts 23:31–28:31)

5.2. Issues Arising from the Account in Acts. Acts is often taken to imply that Paul undertook three "journeys," during which he was continually on the move. However, this is a misleading modern deduction. The account in Acts is too complex to be analyzed simply in terms of three journeys, since Paul actually settles down for an extended period in Corinth and Ephesus, and in some other places (e.g., Philippi) spends only a short time because of opposition. The Acts picture is better thought of as periods of travel and extended periods in which Paul was resident at one place.

Although we cannot go into the debated question of Luke's sources (particularly in the "we" passages), it is clear that Luke had more information for some of Paul's travels than for others. In addition, Paul made journeys about which Luke probably knew nothing (see 2 Cor 11:25-27). Luke also makes no mention of Paul's "painful visit" to Corinth during his Ephesian ministry (2 Cor 2:1; 13:2). Luke's intention was not to provide a continuous "life of Paul" but rather to present selected episodes that furthered the purposes of his narrative.

On some occasions we cannot be certain of Paul's exact route (e.g., Acts 13:14; 15:41–16:1; 17:14-15; 19:1). Acts 16:6-10 creates particular difficulties. Having visited Derbe and Lystra, Paul probably had planned to follow the Via Sebaste westward to Ephesus but was prevented by the Spirit from entering Asia. As a result they traveled through *tēn Phrygian kai Galatikēn chōran* (Acts 16:6). Taking *Phrygian* as a noun, the phrase would mean that they passed through two regions, Phrygia and then the Galatian country. The latter would refer to the northern part of the province of Galatia and could include Ancyra, Pessinus, and Tavium. On the North Galatian view, Paul conducted a mission in these areas at this time. Alternatively, *Phrygian* can be an adjective that, along with *Galatikēn*, delimits *chōran*; two adjectives bound by a common article would denote one entity, the *regio Phrygia Galatica*. This would then be the Phrygian territory incorporated in the south of the province of Galatia and would include Pisidian Antioch, Iconium, Lystra, and Derbe.

Luke tells us that Paul was arrested in Jerusalem and went to Rome for trial. It is debated why Luke ended here; did his source end, or did he choose to conclude at this point? To record Paul's vindication and release would have suited Luke's apologetic purpose; that no release is recorded has suggested to some that Paul was martyred in Rome at the end of this imprisonment (the tradition of the early church is that Paul was eventually martyred in Rome; e.g., Acts of Paul 11.1-7; Eusebius, *Hist. eccl.* 2.25.7-8). The prediction of martyrdom in the farewell speech to the Ephesian elders (Acts 20:25, 38) was perhaps intended to indicate what occurred at the end of the two-year period. In *1 Clement* 5.6-7 (ca. AD 95) it is said that Paul reached "the Limits of the west," which could mean Spain, although this may simply be an inference from Romans 15:24.

6. Integration of the Letters and Acts.
Apart from some omissions (e.g., Acts does not mention Paul's visit to Arabia), there is substantial agreement between Paul's letters and Acts concerning Paul's travels. Most scholars therefore seek to draw on Acts in order to supplement (to the extent that they judge appropriate) the information Paul himself gives, although recently D. Campbell has sought to construct a Pauline chronology "informed only by epistolary data" (D. Campbell, 23). We turn now to the major issue on which the two sources differ.

6.1. Visits to Jerusalem. In his letters Paul speaks of only three visits to *Jerusalem:

1. the acquaintance visit, three years after his conversion (Gal 1:18-20)
2. the conference visit "after fourteen years" (Gal 2:1-10)
3. the collection visit (Rom 15:25-33; 1 Cor 16:1-4; 2 Cor 1:16)

Acts, however, portrays five visits to Jerusalem:

1. the conversion visit (Acts 9:26-30)
2. the famine visit (Acts 11:27-30)
3. the Jerusalem Council (Acts 15:1-30)
4. the hasty visit (Acts 18:22)
5. the collection visit (Acts 21:15-17)

There is general agreement that Galatians 1:18-20 is to be identified with Acts 9:26-30, although there are significant differences between the two accounts. The collection visit planned by Paul in Romans 15:25-33 and the visit in Acts 21:15-17 are clearly identical, although Luke describes this visit without any mention of the collection (its purpose is mentioned, but only incidentally, in Acts 24:17).

The main difficulty, however, concerns Galatians 2:1-10. R. N. Longenecker gives the most prominent solutions to this question (see Longenecker, lxxii-lxxxiii):

> (a) Galatians 2:1-10 is the Jerusalem Council visit of Acts 15:1-30, with the famine visit seen by Paul as unimportant and so not mentioned by him.
>
> (b) Galatians 2:1-10 is the famine visit of Acts 11:27-30, with the Jerusalem Council visit occurring after Paul wrote Galatians.
>
> (c) Galatians 2:1-10 is the Jerusalem Council visit of Acts 15:1-30, which Luke has turned into two visits by misunderstanding the parallel nature of two reports about the council and so fabricating the visit of Acts 11:27-30.
>
> (d) Galatians 2:1-10 is the Jerusalem Council visit of Acts 15:1-30, while Acts 11:27-30 is a misplaced report of the collection visit, which was originally connected with the material of Acts 21:15-17 but which Luke has chosen to place earlier.
>
> (e) Galatians 2:1-10 is the Jerusalem Council visit of Acts 15:1-30, but the council actually took place during the visit of Acts 18:22; Acts 11:27-30 is an invention of Luke's.

Many scholars point out that, for Luke, Jerusalem had a key role in the expansion of the church. Hence, Luke had specific theological reasons for presenting Paul as making five trips to Jerusalem (Jewett, 67, 92-93; Schnelle, 51-52), which for many scholars casts doubt on Luke's historicity at these points. It is argued, therefore, that Paul only made the three visits to Jerusalem mentioned in his letters. However, while Luke's theological and redactional activity has clearly shaped the story he tells, we need to ask whether he has altered the story to the extent that is sometimes claimed. Or did Luke's theology arise in part, at least, out of the actual circumstances of Paul's career and other features of the story of the early church? We must turn then to a brief consideration of Luke as a historian.

6.2. The Historicity of Acts. The historicity of Acts continues to be a matter of much debate. Three broad positions can be discerned (see Gorman, 55-56). The maximalist approach tends to accept all of what is said in Acts as historically reliable. The minimalist approach discounts Acts as unreliable and theologically motivated. This approach would reject anything in Acts involving Paul that is not explicitly or by clear implication spoken of in Paul's letters. A middle position uses Paul's letters as the key source but supplements his letters with information from Acts "to the extent that it does not contradict the letters or clearly represent Luke's alleged distortion of history for theological purposes" (Gorman, 55). Although the minimalist position has recently made an impact, there has also been much work that has argued strongly for the historicity of Acts. In particular, the five-volume work edited by B. Winter, *The Book of Acts in Its First-Century Setting*, and the four-volume commentary by C. Keener have been influential in putting forward the case for the historicity of Acts. As M. J. Gorman writes, after reflecting on this work:

> The present writer has become convinced in recent years that Acts is a much more reliable reflection of first-century realities and the history of early Christianity than many scholars recognize. . . . This conviction leads one to a critical

approach that leans toward the maximalist, rather than the minimalist, end of the spectrum. That is, Acts should be given the benefit of the doubt on the general veracity of its narratives, and we should do everything possible to allow the witness of both Paul and Acts to stand. This position should still be held, however, with due moderation and caution, with an admission that there remain difficulties in the use of Acts and in the correlation of it with the letters. (Gorman, 55-56)

Thus the case that Acts gives a truer historical picture than many have allowed is a strong one. This does not mean that Luke necessarily always got the story exactly right or that he has not given it his own literary and theological shape. Clearly his perspective and purposes were different from Paul's. Further, Luke may have received mistaken or partial information that he could not check, or he may have been affected by conscious or unconscious bias, which led him to overlook some things or present others from a tendentious angle. But given the work of Winter, Keener, and others, we should take the likely historicity of Luke's account of Paul's itinerary seriously.

In attempting to give an outline of Paul's travels we must begin, as we have done, with the evidence of Paul's letters, but then we can carefully assess the Acts evidence and use it in our reconstruction, provided priority is always given to Paul's letters. We return then to the relationship between the Jerusalem visit of Galatians 2 and the Acts account of Paul's visits to Jerusalem.

6.3. Galatians 2:1-10 and the Visits in Acts. We can note that views (a) and (b) (in 6.1 above) accept the historicity of the Acts framework. With views (c) and (d), Acts has less credibility, and with view (e) Acts is seen as unreliable. Apart from the fact that view (b) takes the likely historicity of Acts seriously, a number of points argue strongly in its favor (see Longenecker, lxxvii-lxxxiii; deSilva, 48-58).

6.3.1. Galatians 2 and Acts 15. There are strong similarities between these passages. Both concern a meeting at Jerusalem at which the main participants were Paul, Barnabas, Peter, and James, and which decided in favor of a law-free mission to the Gentiles. However, there are some very significant differences. In Galatians 2 Paul is at the center of the meeting; in Acts 15 he is a minor player. In Galatians 2:2 the visit is in response to a revelation; in Acts 15:1-3 it is at the instigation of the church at Antioch. In Galatians 2:2 the meeting is private, small, and informal; in Acts 15:6, 12 it is a public council resulting in an authoritative decision. In Galatians 2:10 we are told that the meeting resulted in one stipulation being placed on Paul's work—to remember the poor; Luke gives four (different) stipulations that are to be laid on Gentile believers (Acts 15:29). Are these differences the result of different perspectives and purposes on the part of Luke and Paul, or do the two authors describe different occasions?

We might conclude that the differences are the result of different perspectives if it were not for the fact that there are three factors that question the identification of Galatians 2 and Acts 15. First, if we accept the basic reliability of Acts and identify Galatians 2:1-10 with Acts 15:1-30, we must ask why Paul in Galatians 1–2 has omitted reference to the famine visit of Acts 11:27-30. Given his oath that he is telling the truth (Gal 1:20), such an omission would tend to undermine his argument. To argue that Paul regarded this visit as insignificant and hence not worthy of mention is unconvincing, since his opponents would be quick to mention the omission.

Second, again assuming the Acts account is basically reliable, Paul's silence in Galatians about the major decision of the Jerusalem Council argues very strongly against the identification of Galatians 2:1-10 and Acts 15:1-30. Luke (at least) clearly saw the decision as applicable to Gentile believers in general (Acts 16:4; 21:25; see Acts 15:23). While Paul may have been reluctant to accept and advocate the four prohibitions (Acts 15:20, 29), it is extremely difficult to see why, if he was writing to Galatia after the Jerusalem Council, he would remain completely silent about the council's favorable decision which would have clinched his case in the Galatian conflict. This omission strongly suggests that Paul wrote Galatians before the council of Acts 15 and thus that Galatians 2:1-10 is not Paul's account of that council. The only other alternative is that Luke's account in Acts 15 of a decision in Paul's favor in which Paul was involved is unhistorical.

A final point concerns Paul's inclusion of the account of his clash with Peter and Barnabas in Galatians 2:11-14. In the incident Peter and Barnabas's actions favor the position of Paul's *Judaizing opponents in Galatia. Including an account of the incident in a letter written before the council is understandable; doing so after the council, and without reference to it, actually undercuts Paul's whole argument, since the incident shows Paul's recognition of a continuing chasm between himself and the Jerusalem apostles. This suggests Paul wrote Galatians on the eve of the Jerusalem Council, and that the visits described in Galatians 2:1-10 and Acts 15:1-30 are different. Thus, there are significant problems with identifying Galatians 2:1-10 with Acts 15:1-30.

6.3.2. Galatians 2 and Acts 11:27-30. These factors suggest that Galatians 2:1-10 is to be identified with the famine visit of Acts 11:27-30; the following points argue in this direction.

First, the two accounts are clearly written from different perspectives, but there are significant points of contact. Barnabas had been sent to *Antioch because of the conversion of Gentiles there (Acts 11:19-26), so it would have been natural for him to discuss the Gentile mission with the Jerusalem leaders on his return, even if the trip was primarily concerned with the relief of the famine. This sort of discussion accords well with the clearly private nature of the meeting described in Galatians 2:2. The silence of Acts about this does not exclude the possibility that such discussions occurred. Further, the injunction from the Jerusalem leaders, which can be translated as to "continue to remember the poor" (*mnēmoneuōmen*, Gal 2:10), makes good sense in the context of the famine relief visit of Acts 11:27-30.

Second, the most natural reading of Galatians 1:21 is that between his first two Jerusalem visits Paul was only in Syria and Cilicia. This is in accordance with the Galatians 2:1-10 visit being the famine visit and not the Jerusalem Council visit (see 6.3.3 below).

Third, according to Galatians 2:11-14, Barnabas and Peter gave in to the pressure of Jewish Christians from Jerusalem and separated from the Gentile Christians at Antioch. It is very difficult to believe that Barnabas, a pioneer in the Gentile mission, would have done this after the Jerusalem Council, thus undercutting the council's decision, in which he played a significant part according to Acts, and his own mission work. Peter's action is also difficult to explain as having taken place shortly after the council. The incident at Antioch is much easier to understand as taking place at a time before the council when there were no agreed-on guidelines about table fellowship between Jewish and Gentile believers. Again, this suggests Galatians 2:1-14 occurred before the Jerusalem Council. This view presupposes that Barnabas and Paul renewed their friendship after the incident of Galatians 2:11-14, so that they went together to Jerusalem for the council (Acts 15:2).

Identifying Galatians 2:1-10 with the famine visit of Acts 11:27-30 does, however, raise some difficulties. One concerns the time spans of three years and fourteen years of Galatians 1:18; 2:1, which are difficult to fit into the widely accepted chronological framework established by the crucifixion and Paul's Corinthian ministry, which is dated by Gallio's proconsulship (Acts 18:12). To fit them into this time frame involves assuming that the three years and fourteen years are concurrent and not consecutive (i.e., both are to be counted from Paul's conversion). The other main difficulty is that identifying Galatians 2:1-10 and Acts 11:27-30 compresses the "second missionary journey," since it needs to occur between the Acts 15 council (probably in AD 48–49) and the meeting with Gallio in Corinth in AD 51 after eighteen months there. Again, this is not impossible, particularly on a South Galatian view, but some argue against this identification on the basis of this compression (see Jewett, 89-93). An earlier date for the crucifixion would help (AD 30 rather than 33), but only if we ignore the probable date of AD 37 for Paul's escape from Aretas (2 Cor 11:32-33; see Murphy-O'Connor, 7-8), although this is a date on which we should not rely too heavily.

Thus the equation of Galatians 2:1-10 and Acts 11:27-30 requires us to make some chronological assumptions, although these are not at all impossible. Given the arguments presented above for identifying Galatians 2:1-10 with Acts 11:27-30, the necessity for making these assumptions does not undermine this view.

6.3.3. Galatians 2 and Acts 15; 18:22. The other main possibility is that Luke did not have sufficient information to enable him to sequence his material clearly. If this was the case, the true setting for the council of Acts 15 could be the trip to Jerusalem in Acts 18:22, as proponents of view (e) argue, and the visit of Acts 11 would be a tradition that reflected either the council or collection visits. This three-visit hypothesis, which Jewett (95-104) has worked out in detail, eases the crowding involved in Paul's travels that results from view (b). However, this view has at least three weaknesses:

First, in Paul's letters Barnabas is not connected with Paul's ministry in Macedonia and Achaia (1 Cor 9:6 is no real exception), yet this view requires Paul and Barnabas to be together after this ministry when they travel to the Jerusalem conference (Gal 2:1). Galatians 2:1-10 certainly suggests Paul and Barnabas were mission partners up until the time of this meeting.

Second, in Galatians 1:21 Paul says he went to Syria and Cilicia between his first two visits to Jerusalem. However, this view requires that he also undertook an extensive mission in Galatia, Macedonia, and Achaia during this period. This goes against the natural reading of the verse and seems to discredit Paul's claim to be truthful (Gal 1:20). Further, since Paul is stressing his remoteness from Jerusalem, it seems likely that if he had gone beyond Cilicia he would have said so, since it would have further underlined his independence from Jerusalem.

Third, J. Knox (36-42) thought the collection was an obligation laid on Paul at the Jerusalem conference. Yet if the Jerusalem leaders obliged Paul to undertake the collection, Paul's fears about its acceptance (Rom 15:25-32) and its likely rejection (judging from Luke's silence) are hard to explain. It is more probable that the impetus for the collection came from Paul. This would undermine one of Knox's reasons for arguing that the conference had to be late in Paul's career. Thus, as Longenecker (lxxvii) comments:

> It must be concluded that the Knox reconstruction gives a much less satisfactory account of a series of details found in Paul's own letters than does the traditional framework of Acts. . . . It is, therefore, not simple naivete that causes us to prefer Luke's framework in Acts to Knox's reconstruction.

6.3.4. Conclusions. The most likely view, then, is that Galatians 2:1-10 and Acts 11:27-30 concern the same visit. This results in the outline of Jerusalem visits shown in table 1.

Table 1. Paul's Visits to Jerusalem

1. Gal 1:18-20: three years after conversion	Acts 9:26-30 (the conversion visit)
2. Gal 2:1-10: "fourteen years later"	Acts 11:27-30 (the famine visit)
	3. Acts 15:1-30 (the Jerusalem Council)
	4. Acts 18:22 (the hasty visit)
5. Rom 15:25-33; 1 Cor 16:1-4; 2 Cor 1:16	Acts 21:15-17 (the collection visit)

We thus suggest that there were two meetings held to discuss the issue of the place of Gentiles, one that was more informal and private (Gal 2:1-10; Acts 11:27-30) and the other of a more formal nature, probably called to resolve the problem posed by the Antioch incident (Acts 15:1-30). On this view Paul made five visits to Jerusalem but had no reason to mention visits three and four in his occasional letters. If Galatians was written before Acts 15:1-30, then it was before visits three and four had occurred. When Paul writes about the Collection visit, he does not say it was his third visit, and so it could well have been his fifth; Paul certainly says nothing to indicate that there were no other visits (see Knox, 35-40).

6.4. Summary. Table 2 below summarizes the proposed reconstruction of Paul's itinerary, showing how the information in Paul's letters and Acts may be related.

See also APOSTLE; CHRONOLOGY OF PAUL; COLLECTION FOR THE SAINTS; CORINTH; EMPIRE; EPHESUS; GALATIANS, LETTER TO THE; HOSPITALITY; JERUSALEM, CITY OF; MISSION; PASTORAL EPISTLES; PAUL IN ACTS; SYRIAN ANTIOCH.

BIBLIOGRAPHY. **D. A. Campbell**, *Framing Paul: An Epistolary Biography* (Grand Rapids, MI: Eerdmans, 2014); **T. H. Campbell**, "Paul's 'Missionary Journeys' as Reflected in His Letters," *JBL* 74 (1955): 80-87; **D. A. deSilva,** *The Letter to the Galatians*, NICNT (Grand Rapids, MI: Eerdmans, 2018); **J. D. G. Dunn,** *Beginning from Jerusalem*, vol. 2 of *Christianity in the Making* (Grand Rapids, MI: Eerdmans, 2009); **R. W. Funk,** "The Apostolic Parousia: Form and Significance," in *Christian History and Interpretation: Studies Presented to John Knox*, ed. W. R. Farmer, C. F. D. Moule, and R. R. Niebuhr (Cambridge: Cambridge University Press, 1967), 249-68; **M. J. Gorman**, *Apostle of the Crucified Lord: A Theological Introduction to Paul and His Letters*, 2nd ed. (Grand Rapids, MI: Eerdmans, 2017); **M. S. Harmon**, "Letter Carriers and Paul's Use of Scripture," *JSPHL* 4 (2014): 129-48; **D. G. Horrell**, *An Introduction to the Study of Paul*, 3rd ed. (London: Bloomsbury T&T Clark, 2015); **L. A. Jervis**, *The Purpose of Romans: A Comparative Letter Structure Investigation*, JSNTSup 55 (Sheffield: JSOT Press, 1991); **R. Jewett**, *A Chronology of Paul's Life* (Philadelphia: Fortress, 1979); **C. S. Keener**, *Acts: An Exegetical Commentary*, 4 vols. (Grand Rapids, MI: Baker Academic, 2012–2015); **J. Knox**, *Chapters in a Life of Paul*, ed. D. R. A. Hare (Macon, GA: Mercer University Press, 1987); **R. N. Longenecker**, *Galatians*, WBC 41 (Dallas: Word, 1990); **G. Lüdemann**, *Paul, Apostle to the Gentiles: Studies in Chronology* (Philadelphia: Fortress, 1984); **W. D. Mounce**, *Pastoral Epistles*, WBC 46 (Nashville: Thomas Nelson, 2000); **J. Murphy-O'Connor**, *Paul: A Critical Life* (Oxford: Oxford University Press, 1996); **T. E. Phillips,** *Paul, His Letters, and Acts* (Peabody, MA: Hendrickson, 2009); **S. E. Porter,** "The Portrait of Paul in Acts," in *The Blackwell Companion to Paul*, ed. S. Westerholm (Chichester, UK: Wiley Blackwell, 2014), 124-38; idem, *The Apostle Paul: His Life, Thought, and Letters* (Grand Rapids, MI: Eerdmans, 2016); **R. Riesner**, *Paul's Early Period: Chronology, Mission Strategy, Theology* (Grand Rapids, MI: Eerdmans, 1998); **E. J. Schnabel**, *Paul and the Early Church*, vol. 2 of *Early Christian Mission* (Downers Grove, IL: InterVarsity Press, 2004); idem, *Paul the Missionary: Realities, Strategies and Methods* (Downers Grove, IL: InterVarsity Press; 2008); **U. Schnelle**, *Apostle Paul: His Life and Theology* (Grand Rapids, MI: Baker

Academic, 2005); **J. A. D. Weima**, *Paul the Ancient Letter Writer: An Introduction to Epistolary Analysis* (Grand Rapids, MI: Baker Academic, 2016); **B. W. Winter**, ed., *The Book of Acts in Its First-Century Setting*, 5 vols. (Grand Rapids, MI: Eerdmans, 1993–1996); **N. T. Wright**, *Paul: A Biography* (San Francisco: HarperOne, 2018).

P. R. Trebilco

Table 2. Paul's Travel and Itinerary Plans (adapted from T. H. Campbell, 87)

Letters	Acts
Damascus (Gal 1:17)	Damascus (Acts 9:1-22)
Arabia (Gal 1:17)	
Damascus (Gal 1:17; 2 Cor 11:32-33)	Damascus (Acts 9:23-25)
Jerusalem (**VISIT 1**; Gal 1:18)	Jerusalem (Acts 9:26-29)
Syria and Cilicia (Gal 1:21)	Caesarea, Tarsus (Acts 9:30)
	Antioch (Acts 11:26)
Jerusalem (**VISIT 2**; Gal 2:1-10)	Jerusalem (Acts 11:29-30; 12:25)
	Antioch (Acts 13:1-4)
	Cyprus (Acts 13:4-12)
Galatia (Gal 4:13)	South Galatia (Acts 13:13–14:25)
Antioch (Gal 2:11-14)	Antioch (Acts 14:26-28)
	Jerusalem (**VISIT 3**; Acts 15:1-29)
	Antioch (Acts 15:30-35)
	Syria and Cilicia (Acts 15:41)
	Derbe, Lystra (Acts 16:1-5)
	Phrygic-Galatic region (Acts 16:6)
	Mysia, Troas (Acts 16:7-10)
Philippi (1 Thess 2:2)	Philippi (Acts 16:11-40)
Thessalonica (1 Thess 2:2; Phil 4:15-16)	Thessalonica (Acts 17:1-9)
	Berea (Acts 17:10-14)
Athens (1 Thess 3:1)	Athens (Acts 17:15-34)
Corinth (2 Cor 1:19; 11:7-9)	Corinth (Acts 18:1-18; for 18 months)
	Cenchreae (Acts 18:18)
	Ephesus (Acts 18:19-21)
	Caesarea (Acts 18:22)
	Jerusalem (**VISIT 4**; Acts 18:22)
	Antioch (Acts 18:22)
	Phrygic-Galatic region (Acts 18:23)
Ephesus (1 Cor 16:1-8)	Ephesus (Acts 19:1–20:1; for approximately 3 years)
Corinth (2 Cor 2:1; 13:2)	
Return to Ephesus	

Letters	Acts
Troas (2 Cor 2:12)	
Macedonia (2 Cor 2:13; 7:5)	Macedonia (Acts 20:1)
Illyricum (Rom 15:19)?	
Corinth (2 Cor 13:1; Rom 15:26)	Greece (Acts 20:2-3)
	Philippi (Acts 20:3-6)
	Troas (Acts 20:6-12)
	Miletus (Acts 20:15-38)
	Caesarea (Acts 21:8-14)
Plans to visit Jerusalem, Rome, Spain (Rom 15:22-27)	Jerusalem (**VISIT 5**; Acts 21:15–23:30)
	Caesarea (Acts 23:33–26:32)
	Rome (Acts 28:14-31)

TRAVEL IN THE ROMAN WORLD

The ability to travel extensively within the Roman world was one of the hallmarks of the *pax Romana*, that period of relative peace and calm as well as empire expansion that distinguished Rome roughly from the beginning of the reign of Caesar Augustus in 27 BC to the death of Marcus Aurelius in AD 180. Travel was a major factor that unified and advanced the Roman Empire, especially within the first few centuries of the Christian era, and thus supported the spread of Christianity. The Roman Empire, which came to be one of the largest empires of the ancient or modern worlds, encompassed a massive territory that required a means of travel for the sake of military control, transportation, commerce, and communication. The development of both land and sea routes was vital to ensuring that the empire was able to accomplish its purposes despite its immense size and otherwise prohibitive physical limitations, to the point that some ancients enthusiastically praised the ease of possible travel throughout the empire without fear or intimidation (Aelius Aristides, *Orationes* 26 [Eulogy of Rome] 100-101). This acknowledged overstatement, however, reveals how Rome transformed travel from what it had been to what it became under the empire's control—a relatively safe and efficient means of moving from one place to another, to the point where, as one scholar states, "Nowhere was truly isolated in the Roman Empire; everywhere was connected in one way or another" (Price, 9).

Treatment of travel in the Roman empire must address the two major means of travel, by land and by sea, with attention also to Paul the *apostle as a major traveler within this world.

1. Travel by Land
2. Travel by Sea
3. Paul the Traveler

1. Travel by Land.

The size of the Roman Empire at its largest is sometimes difficult to comprehend. According to the Orbis website, an online resource for examining the configuration of the Roman world and travel within it, the empire encompassed one-ninth of the circumference of the earth and ruled over a quarter of the earth's inhabitants, but it also stretched north and south far more than most other empires (Scheidel, 2). The center of this empire was the city of Rome, and being able to travel to and from Rome was one of the most important goals of travel even when one was at the empire's farthest reaches. Rome, however, was a city fifteen miles inland on a river, without a sea port until Ostia at the mouth of the Tiber River was constructed, beginning under the emperor Claudius (hence the use of Puteoli as its major harbor before that). As a result, an empire of such size would require various modes of transportation.

Beginning with Italy in the fourth century BC and growing with the increase in size of its territory, Rome expanded its roadway system as it expanded its empire. The primary reason for the development of the Roman system of roadways was militaristic, as the Romans required a means of moving their armies to all corners of their territory in as safe and expedient a manner as possible, not just for purposes of conquest but for purposes of maintaining control and ensuring Roman domination. Roman soldiers during the time of the empire were often involved in the building of roads as one of their conscripted or otherwise employed duties. Soldiers were also stationed along the major roads as a means of keeping *peace and safety, as well as performing road maintenance.

Although the streets in Rome were generally narrow until Nero widened them when he renovated after the conflagration of AD 64, the Romans had a keen sensitivity to the lay of the land and designed and planned roads whose paths have even persisted to the present. They also developed advanced road-building technology, including establishing minimum widths of roads, means of laying a road's foundations several feet down using various types of materials, systems of drainage, and, at least in cities, a form of pedestrian crossing to avoid walking in the street, some features of which were not surpassed until reasonably modern times. Romans also developed bridge technology using the arch, which has resulted in some Roman bridges and aqueducts remaining standing and functionable until the present. As with Alexander the Great's conquests before the Romans', military conquest brought in its wake numerous other benefits in terms of communication, trade, and social connection. Archaeological discoveries at Hadrian's Wall on the English/Scottish border illustrate how the farthest reaches of the Roman empire were able, through travel and transportation, to attempt to reproduce the niceties of Roman life, including many of the creature comforts.

Major Roman road systems were developed in the third and second centuries BC that extended throughout the empire. In that sense, all roads (as well as waterways) did end up leading to Rome. The major roads in Italy were the Via Aurelia, which went north on the west coast; the Via Salaria, which ran north through the middle of the country; and the Via Flaminia, running north on the east coast (see Ramsay, 391; Quilici). The Via Tiburtina went due east, and the Via Casilino went south along the west coast. The Via Appia, the longest and most important, originally begun in the late fourth century BC, ran southeast along the length of Italy to Capua and then eventually to Brundisium (modern Brindisi) in the heel of Italy on the Mediterranean (a road that can still be traveled on and is still marked with many of the milestone markers erected along its route).

Outside Italy, some of the most important roads were historical ones that had been in place for centuries (Ramsay, 390-91). There were major trade routes in what is now Western Europe, Asia Minor, and Syria. One of the oldest and longest was the old Persian road that ran from Sardis near the western coast of Asia Minor all the way to Susa, a distance of over sixteen hundred miles, and the Syrian trade route, which ran from Ephesus, overlapped with the Persian road until Laodicea, and then went more along the southern part of Asia Minor to Syria. The Romans used both of these and many others. But the best-known of the Roman trade routes was the Via Egnatia, constructed in the mid-second century BC after the Roman conquest of Macedonia, which ran from Dyrrachium (in modern Albania, then Macedonia) across from Brundisium to Thessalonica and then extended through Philippi to Byzantium (later renamed Constantinople). Some estimate there were as many as fifty thousand miles of main roads and two hundred thousand miles of smaller roads (Kreitzer, 945). The road system was of such complexity and development that there apparently were maps and guidebooks available to aid travelers along their way (Ramsay, 398).

Although in theory one could travel by road any time of the year, the reality was that some of the problems of winter weather deterred travelers by land especially from November to March (see Vegetius, *Epitoma rei militaris* 4.39), as well as the couple of months on either side. These factors included shorter days and longer nights (the night was considered a dangerous time, in which evil could be done), and inclement weather such as wind, rain, and snow. One must remember that some of the Roman roads that connected the empire ran through mountainous terrain that would have been subject to cold temperatures, snow, and spring runoff.

There were various means of transportation used on the roads. Travel by foot was the normal and expected means, and a pedestrian could probably walk up to twenty miles in a day, depending on the terrain. Various forms of animals were also used for either human transport or the carriage of goods, whether on the animal's back or by means of cart or carriage. These animals included oxen—the major beast of burden of the Roman world—donkeys, mules, camels in Egypt, and occasionally horses, although horses were not widely used during the early empire other than by those in the cavalry and other military service (see Acts 23:24). Depending on their burden, animals' speed ranged from two miles an hour for an ox to up to four miles an hour for the others, with horses still faster.

Although the roads were much safer under Roman rule than they generally were before, there was still the possibility of being attacked by bandits or robbers (e.g., the parable of the good Samaritan, Lk 10:30-35). As a result, most tried to travel by means of the major roads, as these would be more secure due to the number of travelers, guards stationed along the way, and the chance of meeting and even accompanying officials who were better protected. Those who could afford to often traveled with guards and others accompanying them, and at the least those who traveled on their own attempted to join the company of groups or even governmental detachments.

Along with matters of safety were questions of *hospitality. Travelers along Roman roads had a variety of options for accommodations. Those who had *wealth could travel from one of their own houses to another, thus avoiding the need to be outside one's own environment during the night, when it was dark and bandits and robbers could take advantage of circumstances. Those who held official positions within the empire, including those in the military, could requisition accommodations from the populace. The vast majority, who did not have such opportunities, however, had a number of other, lesser options. These included staying in private homes with friends, acquaintances, or others with whom they might have contact. If one were sufficiently socially connected, one might avail oneself of regularly staying with others. This is one of the reasons that hospitality is such a prized virtue in the ancient world, including in early Christianity, as many people relied on it, and to violate it was to commit a grievous error (see Euripides, *Alcestis*, where Heracles violates the hospitality of his host, who has just lost his wife). The outposts of the official postal system might also have room available for those in transit, although they gave priority to official travelers. Some might choose to camp, especially those who might be traveling with the safety of numbers. There were also hostels or hotels or inns in the ancient world, but their reputations varied considerably. They often had reputations for providing inadequate housing and poor food, as well as opportunities for immoral behavior. It appears that hotels in the eastern part of the empire had a better reputation than those in the west.

There was an official postal system established by Augustus, the cursus publicus, but this was reserved for official correspondence, such as government officials and the military. The system in some ways resembled the US Pony Express, with vehicles carrying goods from outpost to outpost along the route. Only under rare circumstances could a private individual use the postal system for personal matters; Paul almost assuredly sent his *letters by means of private carriers.

2. Travel by Sea.

Although travel by land was hugely important in the Roman Empire, travel by water was the single most important factor that led to the unity of the empire, especially around the Mediterranean Sea. Travel by sea, if it was available, was by far the fastest, most efficient, and most economical means of transportation, especially if large amounts of cargo were involved (see Rickman). The Roman navy became a significant part of Roman government, as the navy was developed in order to protect the seas for commercial purposes.

One of the major uses of sea travel was the transportation of grain from Egypt to Rome. Just as all roads led to Rome, so did all grain ships. The city of Rome was huge by ancient standards, with probably around a million people, both free and *slave, at the turn of the millennium, and it was unable to provide enough food for its inhabitants. Rulers realized early on that the stability of the government of Rome would depend on keeping its occupants fed and entertained. There were many places from which Rome brought food (including Sicily and northern Africa), but the major source for this food was the abundant wheat supply of Egypt (wheat and barley were the two major grains of the Roman world, and wheat seems to have been preferred because of its ability to be made easily into bread).

To transport the required amount of grain mostly by land would have been possible but prohibitively slow and costly. Thus a regular and consistent run of grain ships moved from Rome to Egypt and back, depending on the Nile to provide Rome's food. The fourteen-hundred-mile trip from Rome to Alexandria could take two weeks or less in good conditions; the ships were known for their speed (Philo, *Flacc.* 26-27). The return voyage, against the wind, was up to two hundred miles longer, depending on the route, and could take three weeks or longer.

As a result, there was a wide variety of different kinds of ships built in increasing size, so that the greatest advantage could be taken of an individual trip. Grain ships were often quite large, with some holding as much as twelve hundred or more tons of grain. Commercial ships were powered by sail, even if oars were carried for emergency purposes, while military vessels used banks of oars. The crew of a merchant ship, even up to the rank of captain, may have been slaves, as the slave economy was crucial to the Roman economy. The owner of a ship, called *navicularius*, often accompanied his ship on its journey (see Acts 27:11). There were no passenger ships during this time, so those who wished to travel by sea had to arrange passage on a commercial vessel. Although sailors may have had rudimentary charts and could test water depth, there were no sophisticated navigational tools such as a compass or sextant during these times, so sailors relied on the sky and any land sightings for navigation. This meant that ships often stayed within sight of land so as to chart their course.

There was also a greater chance of a major storm in an open sea than there was closer to land, but dense cloud cover seems to have been one of the major problems with sea navigation, as it hindered sailors from observing the sky or land to get their bearings. Just as roads were also difficult to travel during certain times of the year, later ancient Roman writer Vegetius (*Epitoma rei militaris* 4.39) says that the sea lanes were closed from 11 November to 10 March by tradition and by law for governmental transit (although the period may have been a little shorter), and they were considered dangerous in the two months on either side of these dates (so from September to May) because of factors such as shorter days, clouds, and wind, rain, and snow (quoted in Rapske, 22). This does not mean that there was not sea travel during these times, as various circumstances, such as a lack of grain requiring shipments be made (Suetonius, *Claud.* 18-19), the death of an emperor, or another urgent political matter, might dictate that someone make a journey nonetheless.

The problem of piracy was one that the Romans attempted to solve early on, to the point that sea travel was relatively secure from the mid-first century BC on. In the first century BC, the general Pompey was given a huge force of ships and soldiers and tasked by the Roman senate with eliminating piracy as a major threat. He did so successfully in both the east and the west. Still, ships sometimes traveled together as a means of ensuring strength in numbers, and occasionally pirates were a problem.

3. Paul the Traveler.

Paul is depicted as a seasoned traveler from his youth to the end of his life. From the book of Acts and the letters, one sees that Paul often traveled along the major land and sea thoroughfares while also using some lesser routes. He also regularly traveled with companions. Estimates of the times and distances of the individual journeys can be calculated by means of Orbis (see Scheidel and Meeks; see also the maps in Ramsay) but do not, of course, take into account the possibilities of delays along the way.

Paul was born in Tarsus, but as either a youth or young man (depending on one's interpretation of Acts 22:3) moved to *Jerusalem. This trip may have been made by either road or sea but would have been fastest if traveled primarily by coastal sea route, probably with numerous stops along the way. There is also an ancient road that goes down the coast of Palestine from Antioch to Egypt.

Paul's travels throughout Judea and Syria would have been by land. Most of these trips would have been by foot; there is no record of Paul traveling by animal apart from his trip from Jerusalem to Caesarea under arrest (Acts 23:24). However, one does note that in all three accounts of Paul's trip from Jerusalem to Damascus he is traveling with companions (Acts 9:7-8; 22:9, 11; 26:14). When Acts says that Barnabas found Paul in Tarsus, after his time in Arabia (Acts 11:25), they probably traveled by land from Tarsus to Antioch, although they may have taken a short coastal boat trip. Paul also says that he was in Arabia (probably Nabataea) and then Damascus (Gal 1:17-18), and then went to Jerusalem (Gal 1:18-20; Acts 9:26-29), before returning to Syria and Cilicia (Gal 1:21; Acts 9:30). Paul was then found in Tarsus by Barnabas and brought by him to Antioch (Acts 11:25-26). All of these trips were probably made by land as well. Paul's trips from Antioch to Jerusalem and back (Acts 11:30; 12:25; 15:1, 30) could have been made by either land or sea by traveling along the coast, and again appear to have been in the company of others.

On Paul's missionary journeys, Paul combined land and sea travel. On his first journey, Paul and his companions traveled from Antioch by land to the coast, and then by sea to Cyprus, where they arrived in Salamis and then traveled around Cyprus by land until they left from Paphos, and then traveled by sea past the port city Attalia and went inland to the river port Perga (Acts 13:4-6, 13). Paul took minor roads to Pisidian Antioch but then joined the major Syrian trade route to travel to Iconium, a hub of road travel, with a small diversion to an adjunct road to Lystra and then Derbe (Acts 13:14, 51; 14:1, 6). They then retraced their steps and returned to Antioch by sea from the port city of Attalia (Acts 14:21, 24-26).

On his second journey, Paul took an alternative route to Asia Minor, this time by land through the province of Syria and Cilicia, almost assuredly passing through Tarsus and then the Cilician Gates on the way to Derbe and Lystra (Acts 15:41; 16:1). For this trip, Paul and his companions would again have joined the Syrian trade route before they reached Tarsus, and then followed one of the branches of that route to Derbe, and then with a slight diversion to Lystra before rejoining the route. Paul and his companions were traveling around the region of Phrygian Galatia (e.g., probably Pisidian Antioch and Iconium) but were then forbidden by the *Holy Spirit to speak the word in the province of Asia (Acts 16:6). This also effectively seems to have blocked their traveling to *Ephesus on the west coast. As a result, they would have turned north, but they would have had several options leading to the north. It appears that they were contemplating taking one of these roads into the province of Bithynia, but they were not permitted to do that either (Acts 16:7). They would have then needed to turn west to head toward Troas. Although they may have taken a more western route through Cotiaeum and then headed northwest (see Bruce, 651), it is also possible they took a more eastern route that passed through Dorylaeum and then proceeded below Bithynia and through Mysia to Troas (Acts 16:7-8; see Thompson and Wilson for more detailed discussion of options; Acts 16:6 clearly indicates subsequent prohibition, on grammatical and geographical grounds).

From Troas, Paul and his companions sailed by coastal vessel toward the island of Samothrace and then north to disembark at Neapolis, a journey of two days (Acts 16:11; cf. Acts 20:6). They traveled by land to Philippi, where, after their stay there, they joined the Via Egnatia to travel west through Amphipolis and Apollonia, two cities along the road, to arrive in Thessalonica (Acts 16:12; 17:1). From Thessalonica, Paul traveled by a lesser road to Berea. From Berea (or ancient Veria), Paul was escorted to Athens (Acts 17:10, 15). This trip would have been either a three-day journey by sea or a two-week-plus trip by land, using an inland route that probably passed through Larissa, Lamia, and Delphi. Since Paul ended up waiting in Athens for Silas and Timothy, he probably sailed. Paul then traveled to *Corinth, a day-and-a-half journey by sea or a three-day journey by road (Acts 18:1). In order to return to Antioch, Paul sailed from the Corinthian eastern port city of Cenchreae to Ephesus, and then from Ephesus to Caesarea, where he went by land to Jerusalem before returning to Antioch (Acts 18:18-22). He probably traveled by land to Antioch because of the description of going up to Jerusalem and then down to Antioch (although he could have sailed, as noted above).

The third missionary journey began at Antioch and moved immediately to the region of Phrygian Galatia, probably the cities of Pisidian Antioch and Iconium (Acts 18:23). However, as seen above, Paul had already traveled to this region by two different means, so he could have sailed from Antioch to Attalia or Perga and then traveled inland by road, or he could have traveled the entire journey by road, including taking the major Syrian trade route. In either case it probably was a journey of about three weeks. Paul then traveled west to Ephesus (Acts 19:1). Acts says that Paul traveled through "the upper portions" to arrive at Ephesus. It is unclear whether this means that he descended from mountains to Ephesus (the interior is definitely higher than the coast) or whether he took a northerly route, rather than the main Syrian and eastern trade route. The main trade route went through the Lycus Valley, with Laodicea and Colossae along the route, so some scholars think that Paul did not take this route because he had not visited Colossae (Col 2:1; Bruce, 651). However, Acts 19:10 says that Paul and his companions evangelized Asia, so it is not impossible that Paul himself may have passed through Colossae, and he or others later evangelized that area while he was staying in Ephesus for several years.

After his adventurous time in Ephesus, Paul probably went to Troas (2 Cor 2:12-13), and then to Macedonia and Greece (Acts 20:1-2). The trip from Ephesus to Troas could have been made by land or sea, with land taking about twelve days and sea three days, depending on the time of year. From Troas, Paul probably sailed by way of Samothrace to Neapolis and then by land to Philippi, a trip he had made before, although he could have traveled by road as well. He then probably visited not only Philippi but Thessalonica, possibly Berea, and may even have gone as far as Dalmatia in Illyricum, by taking the Via Egnatia to Dyrrachium on the coast of Macedonia and then either sailing north or traveling by land north into the region (see Rom 15:19). Paul then went to Greece, probably visiting Corinth. If he traveled directly from Macedonia, Paul could have traveled either by land or sea, as he had before.

Because of a plot, Paul did not sail directly back to Antioch but instead retraced his steps through Macedonia, again accompanied by others. They then sailed from Philippi (Neapolis) to Troas, a trip that could have taken only two or three days apparently taking five (Acts 20:6; cf. Acts 16:11, where it took two days). Paul then went by foot (Acts 20:13) to Assos, a short journey of twenty-five miles (a little over a day of travel), where he joined his other companions who had gone by sea. They all then sailed to Mitylene on the island of Lesbos and then passed near to the island of Chios and then the island of Samos before disembarking at Miletus, a city south of Ephesus (Acts 20:14-15). After his meeting with the elders, Paul and his companions sailed by the island of Cos and then Rhodes and disembarked at Patara (Acts 21:1). At Patara, they found probably a small coastal trading ship sailing for Syria that passed by the southern side of Cyprus and disembarked at Tyre, where the ship unloaded its cargo (Acts 21:3). The group then traveled by ship to Ptolemais (Acco), a trip that could have been done by either land or sea, and then proceeded to Caesarea, again by either land or sea, and then went by land up to Jerusalem (Acts 21:7-8, 15-17). Some have thought that Paul made the trip from Caesarea to Jerusalem by horseback (Rapske, 10-11).

Paul was arrested in Jerusalem and then later transported, apparently on horseback in the company of two centurions and their troops (Acts 23:23-24), to Caesarea. Paul's trip to Rome makes use of a number of sea voyages, some of them overlapping with the grain trade in the Mediterranean. Paul was in the company of a centurion named Julius. For the first leg of his journey, Paul sailed on a ship from Adramyttium, on the west coast of Asia Minor near Troas, apparently now on its return voyage. This would not have been a ship engaged in the grain trade but a coastal vessel used for making short trips along the northern and eastern coasts of the Mediterranean. It probably was not a very large vessel but was like many of those that Paul had previously traveled on as he had sailed along the coasts of Asia Minor, Macedonia, and Greece. The first stop of Paul's voyage after leaving Caesarea was Sidon. After a brief stop, they sailed along the lee side of Cyprus, with the winds against the ship, which was typical for those trying to sail west on the Mediterranean. They landed in Myra on the southern coast of Asia Minor, in the province of Lycia, or perhaps rather they landed at Andriake, Myra's port, with Myra a river port upstream.

At this point, Julius and his prisoner and any companions left the coastal vessel and found a ship engaged in the Alexandrian grain trade heading toward Rome (Acts 27:6), laden with grain (Acts 27:38). Myra was a major port involved in the Alexandrian grain trade (Bruce, 651). Acts tells us that the owner of the ship, the *nauklēros* in Greek, was onboard (Acts 27:11). The slowness of the trip reflects the difficulty of the return voyage from Alexandria, as the ship had to sail into the wind, as well as the fact that it was already late in the sailing season before the winter closing, and the weather was clearly adverse to good sailing (Acts 27:7-8, 12). The ship made slow progress past the island of Cnidus and then on the lee side of Crete opposite the city of Salmone and then to a place called Fair Havens, intending to spend the winter (there is speculation as to its exact location near the town of Lasea on the southern side of Crete).

Since the harbor at Fair Havens was not large enough—the ship was apparently quite large, as it had 276 people on board, besides the cargo (Acts 27:36)—they attempted to get to the harbor at Phoenix, further west, to spend the winter (Acts 27:12). However, a large storm arose, not atypical on the Mediterranean at that time of year and something seamen apparently regularly feared (Acts 27:14). The ship was blown about by the wind, and they passed the small island of Cauda and then were blown for a number of days across the sea until they were able to determine that they were in shallower water and nearing land (Acts 27:16, 27; note that they took soundings; Acts 27:28). They eventually ran aground on the island of Malta (Acts 28:1). There is major discussion over whether the Greek term Melitē used in Acts is the island of Malta, Mljet off of Dalmatia in the Adriatic, or Kefalonia off western Greece, but Malta remains the most likely (see Rapske, 37-43). In any event, they were significantly off their course, but at least were further west and in that regard nearer their destination of Rome.

After three months, the rest of the winter break, Paul's retinue joined another Alexandrian grain ship, the Castor and Pollux, that had safely wintered on Malta (Acts 28:11), perhaps having taken the southern route from Alexandria to Rome. This ship had wisely forestalled its journey because of the winter closing for sailing. On this ship, Paul and the others first sailed north to Syracuse on Sicily, then to Rhegium at the tip of Italy, where they passed between the Italian mainland and Sicily, and then proceeded to Puteoli, where the passengers were disembarked. There is some question of whether Ostia was at this time finished as a harbor suitable for unloading passengers and grain (see Meiggs, 56). Paul then traveled by land to Rome by means of the Via Appia (Acts 29:12-14). A journey that should have taken about three weeks but that sometimes took a month or two ended up taking probably about six or seven months from start to finish.

Later Christians, along with others, such as traveling teachers and philosophers, took full advantage of the opportunities for travel as well. The Christian church was able to communicate across vast expanses of territory, thus helping to ensure the transmission of Christian teaching from place to place. Travel and communication became important as a means of creating and maintaining social *identity within the larger Christian community, contributing to the sense that the Christian movement was coequal with the empire itself. As a result, there developed a form of Christian tourism or sight-seeing, as Christians traveled for various purposes throughout the empire, visiting various Christian establishments, and eventually leading, at least for those who were able to afford it, to development of the Christian pilgrimage movement (see Hunt).

See also Chronology of Paul; Corinth; Coworkers, Paul and His; Ephesus; Jerusalem, City of; Paul in Acts; Travel and Itinerary Plans.

BIBLIOGRAPHY. **L. H. Blumell,** "Beware of Bandits! Banditry and Land Travel in the Roman Empire," *Journeys* 8, nos. 1-2 (2007): 1-20; **F. F. Bruce,** "Travel and Communication (The New Testament World)," *ABD* 6:648-53; **L. Casson,** *The Ancient Mariners: Seafarers and Sea Fighters of the Mediterranean in Ancient Times*, 2nd ed. (Princeton, NJ: Princeton University Press, 1991); **R. L. Cioffi,** "Travel in the Roman World," Oxford Handbooks Online (2016), doi: 10.1093/oxfordhb/9780199935390.013.110; **A. Cohen,** "Art, Myth, and Travel in the Hellenistic World," in *Pausanias: Travel and Memory in Roman Greece*, ed. S. E. Alcock, J. F. Cherry, and J. Elsner (Oxford: Oxford University Press, 2001), 93-126; **F. Hooper,** *Roman Realities* (Detroit: Wayne State University Press, 1979); **E. D. Hunt,** "Travel, Tourism and Piety in the Roman Empire: A Context for the Beginnings of Christian Pilgrimage," *Echos de monde Classique: Classical Views* 28 NS 3, no. 3 (1984): 391-417; **L. J. Kreitzer,** "Travel in the Roman World," *DPL*, 945-46; **K. M. McGeough,** *The Romans: An Introduction* (Oxford: Oxford University Press, 2004); **R. Meiggs,** *Roman Ostia*, 2nd ed. (Oxford: Clarendon, 1973); **S. Price,** "Religious Mobility in the Roman Empire," *JRS* 102 (2012): 1-19; **J. L. Quilici,** "Land Transport, Part 1: Roads and Bridges," in *Oxford Handbook of Engineering and Technology in the Classical World*, ed. John Peter Olseson (Oxford: Oxford University Press, 2008), 551-79; **W. M. Ramsay,** "Roads and Travel (in NT)," in *A Dictionary of the Bible: Extra Volume*, ed. J. Hastings with J. A. Selbie (Edinburgh: T&T Clark, 1904), 375-408; **B. M. Rapske,** "Acts, Travel and Shipwreck," in *The Book of Acts in Its First Century Setting*, vol. 2, *Graeco-Roman Setting*, ed. D. W. Gill and C. Gempf (Grand Rapids, MI: Eerdmans, 1994), 1-47; **G. Rickman,** *The Corn Supply of Ancient Rome* (Oxford: Clarendon, 1980); **W. Scheidel,** "The Shape of the Roman World: Modelling Imperial Connectivity," *JRA* 27 (2014): 7-32; **W. Scheidel and E. Meeks,** "Orbis: The Stanford Geospatial Network Model of the Roman World," Stanford University, http://orbis.stanford.edu; **J.-A. Shelton,** *As the Romans Did: A Sourcebook in Roman Social History*, 2nd ed. (Oxford: Oxford University Press, 1998); **G. L. Thompson and M. Wilson,** "The Route of Paul's Second Journey in Asia Minor: In the Steps of Robert Jewett and Beyond," *TynBul* 67, no. 2 (2016): 217-46; **K. Wengst,** *Pax Romana and the Peace of Jesus Christ*, trans. J. Bowden (London: SCM Press, 1987).

S. E. Porter

TRIALS. *See* Suffering.

TRIUMPH

The scriptural image of divine triumph surfaces in Paul's letters in varied contexts. Infused with Roman inflections, it includes a spectrum of metaphors of opposing power and conflict, as well as military imagery.

1. Triumph of the Divine Warrior in the Old Testament and Judaism
2. Triumph over Principalities and Powers
3. Triumph over Sin, Flesh, Law, and Death
4. Triumph at the End of the Age
5. Prisoners and Soldiers of Christ

1. Triumph of the Divine Warrior in the Old Testament and Judaism.

The master image of Yahweh's warfare is the deliverance of *Israel from bondage in Egypt, in which Yahweh triumphs over the imperial forces of Egypt and Egypt's gods. The Song of Moses acclaims, "Yahweh is a warrior!" (Ex 15:3). The OT employs a variety of associated imagery of the divine warrior: Yahweh riding his cloud chariot (e.g., Ps 68:4; 104:3-4; Is 19:1; cf. Dan 7:13); the people of *God as the army of God marching through the wilderness; the ark of the *covenant, as a portable throne of the heavenly warrior king leading Israel to conquest (cf., e.g., Ex 15:17; Num 10:35-36); the wars of faithful Israel (e.g., Deut 20) in which the heavenly army (e.g., 2 Kings 6:17) and even *creation (e.g.,

Josh 10:1-15; Judg 5:19-21) take part, all under divine *leadership (e.g., Gen 14:19-20; 15:1; Josh 10:40; Judg 5:4-5). Yahweh also fights against unfaithful Israel (Lam 2:5; Amos 2:6-16) and in Yahweh's "strange deed" (Is 28:21) defeats Judah and sends her into exile. The prophets' "day of the Lord" is the sovereign warrior's day of conquest, in which Yahweh defeats Israel's enemies (e.g., Assyria, Is 10:5-19). In Isaiah's new exodus (e.g., Is 35; 40:1-5), Yahweh marches on a highway through the wilderness, with a redeemed Israel now passing through the blossoming desert to Zion, with the nations subdued (Is 60–66). Yahweh's universal and glorious sovereignty is visibly manifested (Is 60:1-3; 62:1-2), and all evil subjugated (Is 63:1-6; 66:15-16, 24).

Within the Judaism of Paul's day, Israel could be viewed as paradoxically resident in the land of promise and yet still in exile, under Roman dominion. God's final triumph over Israel's enemies was still awaited. Its resolution was variously understood, whether as the unmediated act of the divine warrior or by the agency of his Messiah, or a principal angel (11QMelch), or by some synergy of agents (e.g., 1QM). But the hope of a future day of divine conquest and vindication of Israel was widely and popularly held (see Wright 2017).

For Paul the *gospel of Jesus the Messiah is the apocalyptic in-breaking of the eschatological *righteousness of God in which God powerfully sets the world right (Rom 1:17).

2. Triumph over Principalities and Powers.
In Paul's story of *salvation the *principalities and powers play a role parallel to the enemy nations of Israel's story, now viewed from the perspective of cosmic conflict. The spiritual powers, or "*demons," that Israel had understood as standing behind the nations and their gods (Deut 32:8-9, 17; Dan 7; cf. Sir 17:17; Jub. 15.31-32) are now conceived as the opponents of *Christ and his people.

2.1. Enemies Under His Feet. Emblematic of Christ's triumph over the powers is the image of a triumphant Davidic king seated at the Lord's right hand, with Israel's flesh-and-blood enemies depicted as a footstool for his feet (Ps 110:1). The triumphant Davidic Messiah of Psalm 110:1 is fused with the reigning "Adam," under whose feet God has placed "all things" (Ps 8:6). As Israel was God's new *Adam (e.g., 1QS IV, 23; CD III, 20; 1QH XVII, 15; see Wright 1992, 23-25), so Christ is the new Adam/Israel of the new creation, with everything under his feet (1 Cor 15:22-28; cf. Eph 1:19-22; Col 3:1-11). Adam's *death is reversed, and a new cosmic order emerges.

2.2. Triumph at the Cross. Colossians 2:15 portrays Christ's triumph over the powers at the cross. Dense with imagery and difficult of solution (see Dodson, "Many Faces"), it is one of two texts (see 2 Cor 2:14) where Paul uses the verb *thriambeuō*. Translated "lead in triumphal procession," *thriambeuō* is the Greek term for a Roman triumphal march (*triumphus*) in which a victorious general or ruler in ceremonial dress drives his captives and the spoils of war before him into Rome (see Beard). Before the procession reached the temple of Jupiter, prominent prisoners were sometimes sent to execution (Beard, 128-39). In the triumph, the glory and power of the Roman imperium were boldly projected (see Josephus, *J.W.* 7.5.6 §§153-155).

While the imagery is Roman, the narrative substructure resonates with the biblical archetype of the divine warrior. If read in company with 1 Corinthians 2:6-8, the "rulers of this age" did not comprehend the wisdom of the *cross and "crucified the Lord of *glory" (NRSV). *Archontes*, "rulers," commonly used of human rulers (Rom 13:3), can also refer to spiritual powers (see Dan 10 LXX) with human counterparts. These hostile spiritual powers were oblivious to the *wisdom of God's plan for the ages (see Eph 3:10). In this reading, their monumental folly also underlies the compressed drama of Colossians 2:14-15, where Christ is the subject and the enemies are now named as "principalities and powers" (KJV; *tas archas kai tas exousias*; see Caird).

A crucial issue in understanding Colossians 2:15 is the meaning of the verb *apekdysamenos* (the aorist participle of *apekdyomai*, "to strip"). If understood as a true middle in voice (the subject acting upon itself), Christ stripped himself of something. Significantly, the verb occurs twice in Colossians, in Colossians 2:15; 3:9. Its related noun, *apekdysis*, occurs once, and that within the immediate context (Col 2:11). These words occur nowhere else in the NT. In Colossians 2:11 the noun *apekdysis* speaks of the believer's *circumcision in the "stripping off [*apekdysis*] of the body of flesh," a metaphorical removal of *flesh, called the "circumcision of Christ." This circumcision likely refers to Christ's death on the cross, in which believers participate by *baptism (Col 2:12). In Colossians 3:9 Paul uses *apekdysamenoi*, clearly as a true middle participle, to refer to something that takes place in the experience of believers: those who are in Christ undergo an ethical renewal (Col 3:8), metaphorically rendered in their having "taken off" their old humanity (*ton palaion anthrōpon*, Col 3:9) and having "put on" (*endysamenoi*) their new humanity in Christ (Col 3:10; cf. *ekdyō* in 2 Cor 5:4 [5:3 in some MSS] used of taking off "this tent" [= body] at death). It is argued that Paul does not use *apekdysamenos* in Colossians 2:15 in the active sense (Christ stripping the powers of weaponry, power, etc.), for then Christ's action on the cross would lose its force as a basis for Paul's appeal in Colossians 3:8-9. In their participation with Christ, believers too have "stripped off" their old humanity (see Reid and Longman, 146-53).

But how could Christ have stripped himself of the powers, as if they were a garment? The answer given is that an unstated premise stands behind this text. It was Christ's *body that was nailed (*prosēloō*, Col 2:14) to the cross. Metaphorically this body is the "handwritten document" (*cheirographon*), the very point at which his divine nature met in solidarity with Adam and was attacked by the powers (Lightfoot, 190; Robinson, 34-48). Nevertheless, many interpreters understand *apekdysamenos* in Colossians 2:15 as active transitive, suggesting that Christ at the cross divested the powers of their authority or weapons.

However one understands *apekdysamenos* and its associated imagery in Colossians 2:15, the reality of Christ's triumph is refracted through a powerful metaphor. J. R. Dodson ("Convict's Gibbet") points out resonances with the well-known legend of Marcus Atilius Regius, the military general of the Second Punic War, whose perseverance in crucifixion was extolled as even greater than riding in the victor's car in triumphal procession (Silius Italicus, *Punica* 6.545). Paul's audience may well have heard in this text a bold, counterimperial claim for the triumph of Christ's *kingdom (Col 1:13). The cross, a cruel and bloody instrument of Roman imperial power, is transformed into an arresting symbol of divine triumph.

3. Triumph over Sin, Flesh, Law, and Death. Paul views the human plight as subject to four personified, or mythologized, powers—*sin, flesh, *law, and death—each with ontological resonance (de Boer; Gaventa, 125-36). Sin entered the world through the first Adam, and death came through sin. The law given at Sinai stirred up and revealed sin in Israel. In the broader panorama of Israel's history, a metaphorical death came as exile from the land and from the divine presence symbolized in the *temple (Wright 1992, 19-80). This story shapes Paul's narrative of sin, flesh, death, and law in Romans 5–7. The reigns of sin and of death are intertwined, with sin reigning in death (Rom 5:21), and sin the "master" over humankind, its "*slave" (Rom 5:6, 14). Sin finds its foothold in the flesh (Rom 6:12; cf. Rom 8:7), which wields "weapons" (*hopla*) of wickedness (Rom 6:13; 2 Cor 6:7). Sin preys on people, awaiting the opportunity to make the law a "bridgehead" (*aphormē* in Rom 7:8, taken in military sense) into humans, and so "wages war" (*antistrateuomai*, Rom 7:23) and "takes prisoners" (*aichmalōtizō*, Rom 7:23). From this bondage issues the cry of lament for deliverance, which is answered through "Jesus Christ our *Lord" (Rom 7:24-25; cf. 1 Cor 15:57). Indeed, those in Christ "are more than conquerors through him who loved us" (Rom 8:37-38).

3.1. Death. The imagery of death as a personified enemy is found in ancient Near Eastern mythology, where death is a hostile cthonic power in the drama of divine conflict. Paul captures an OT allusion to this theme when in 1 Corinthians 15:54-55 he taunts death in lines drawn from Hosea 13:14. He introduces Hosea with a line from Isaiah 25:8: "Death is swallowed up in victory" (1 Cor 15:54 ESV). There an Isaianic hymn of thanksgiving follows a vivid picture of the divine warrior's epiphany on the day of the Lord (Is 24). In Isaiah this follows a description of Yahweh's defeat and punishment of "the powers in the heavens above and the kings on the earth below" (Is 24:21 NIV). Paul's use of Isaiah 25:8 at this point supports his own ordering of eschatological events—the powers will be defeated first (1 Cor 15:24-25), and then the last enemy, death (1 Cor 15:26).

3.2. Law. Though Paul views the law as in itself holy and good (Rom 7:12), from the perspective of the human plight, the law serves and empowers sin (Rom 7:8, 11; 1 Cor 15:56). It increases the consciousness of sin (Rom 3:20), brings *wrath (Rom 4:15), makes sin evident (Rom 5:13) and abundant (Rom 5:20), and provokes further sin (Rom 7:7-25). In Israel it "heaped up" and consolidated sin in one place, where it could be dealt with (Wright 1992, 151-53, 196, 209). Sin perverted the law, and whereas the law was powerless to overcome the flesh, God did so in sending his *Son (Rom 8:3). In Galatians, the law is "added because of transgressions" (Gal 3:19 NIV). It acts as a jailer (Gal 3:22-23) and works its *curse on Israel (Gal 3:10). Such was Israel's history under the law, leading to the curse of exile, in which Israel still languished when God sent his Son. In Galatians 3:13 Paul speaks of Christ's death as bearing the curse of the law. Christ takes on himself the curse of the covenant (Gal 3:13; see Longman and Reid, 162). Galatians 4 employs a new exodus typology. In the *fullness of time God again delivered his people, not from bondage to Egypt but from enslavement to the law and the elemental spirits (Gal 4:3-5; cf. Gal 1:4).

In Ephesians 2:14-15 Christ "destroyed" (*katargeō*) the law, or "rendered it powerless" (see also Rom 3:31). The law is likened to a "barrier," or "dividing wall of hostility," a reference to the role of the law in forming a barrier of racial and ethnic hostility (Eph 2:14, 16) between Jews and *Gentiles (see *Let. Aris.* 139). This dividing wall, the "law of commandments and regulations," Christ "destroyed" (Eph 2:15), "killing" the enmity "in his body" (Eph 2:16). Gentiles, once "separated" from Israel and "aliens" to the covenants (Eph 2:12), are now brought "near" by the blood of Christ (Eph 2:13), who is "our *peace" (Eph 2:14). The result is a new creation, "one new humanity" (*kainos anthrōpos*, Eph 2:15), and the building of God's new temple (Eph 2:19-22). Interestingly, the ancient pattern of conflict, triumph, and temple building is here recapitulated. In Ephesians 4:8-11 Paul employs Psalm 68:18 (a psalm replete with themes of divine warfare) and applies the imagery of the victorious divine warrior's ascent to his mountain sanctuary, with captives in his train, to Christ's victorious ascension to his heavenly home, with captives in his triumphal procession (see Longman and Reid, 162-64).

4. Triumph at the End of the Age.
In speaking of the day of the Lord (e.g., 1 Cor 5:5; 1 Thess 5:2, 4; 2 Thess 1:10; 2:2) Paul employs the imagery of the divine warrior's day of triumph. The parousia, or "arrival," of Christ is a christological rendering of the divine warrior. The Lord Jesus comes as the eschatological agent of divine *judgment (see 1 Cor 15:23-28; 1 Thess 1:10; 4:14, 16; 5:9; but cf. Titus 2:13). The imagery includes annihilating fire (2 Thess 1:7; cf. Ps 104:4; Is 29:6; 30:30; 66:15-16; Dan 7:9); angels, or "holy ones" (1 Thess 3:13; 2 Thess 1:7; cf. Deut 33:2; Zech 14:5; 1 En. 1.9; Jude 14); and clouds, perhaps an allusion to the cloud chariot of the divine warrior (Ps 68:4; Dan 7:13; Mk 13:26; cf. 2 Kings 2:11-12). In the "meeting" (*apantēsis*) the Lord in the air (1 Thess 4:16-17), the arriving warrior is welcomed and escorted in a triumphal approach (see Ps 68:24-35; Mt 25:6). The "loud command," the "call" of the archangel (1 Thess 4:16; cf. Josh 6:5; Judg 7:20; Zeph 1:16; 1 Macc 3:54) and the "trumpet call of God" (1 Cor 15:52; 1 Thess 4:16; cf. Num 10:9; Josh 6:5; Zeph 1:16; 1 Macc 3:54) all reflect a summons to battle. The scene suggests the processional of the divine warrior to his holy mount and temple to reclaim his territory (Deut 33:2; Judg 5:4; Hab 3:3, 6; Is 35).

If 2 Thessalonians 2:3-12 is understood as an extension of this story, Christ finds on his arrival a usurping power seated in the "temple of God" (2 Thess 2:3-4). This "*man of lawlessness," who has led many astray by his counterfeit parousia and is inspired by *Satan (2 Thess 2:9-10), is overthrown (2 Thess 2:8; cf. Is 66:6). In this compressed episode the enemy is "destroyed" (*anaireō*) by "breath"/"spirit" (*tō pneumati*; see 4 Ezra 13.10) and "annihilated" (*katargeō*) by "splendor" (*tē epiphaneia*; see Is 11:4; 1QSb V, 24). Believers await the coming of the Son from heaven, who rescues them from the coming wrath (1 Thess 1:10; see 11QMelch 8-9, 13). Ultimately, it is Satan who stands behind this human opposition, whether it be in ongoing opposition to the gospel (1 Thess 3:5) or in a final revolt (2 Thess 2:9). Paul tells the Romans that God will "soon crush Satan under your feet" (Rom 16:20).

5. Prisoners and Soldiers of Christ.
Paul also applies the image of the Roman triumph to his apostolic *ministry. In 2 Corinthians 2:14 Paul speaks of himself as being led in the triumphal procession of Christ. Here Paul is not one of the high-ranking officers in Christ's army but led in triumph (*thriambeuonti hēmas*) as a former enemy and persecutor of Christ, who has been conquered and is now marched as a captive, being constantly led to his death (see 2 Cor 4:10; Hafemann, 16-34; Duff). He boldly sets forth the paradox of apostolic ministry: in weakness and cruciform *suffering the power of the triumphant Christ is made manifest (2 Cor 12:10). The triumph of God in Christ is a triumph of *grace.

Yet Paul can also speak of himself as engaged in a battle. He fights "in truthful speech and in the power of God; with weapons [*hoplōn*] of righteousness in the right hand and in the left" (2 Cor 6:7 NIV). He wages war (*strateuometha*), but not as the flesh does. The weapons (*hopla*) of his warfare have divine power to demolish strongholds (*ochyrōmatōn*; see Prov 21:22 LXX), arguments, and pretensions, and he takes captive (*aichmalōtizontes*) "every thought to make it obedient to Christ" (2 Cor 10:3-5). At *Ephesus Paul "fought wild beasts" (*ethēriomachēsa*, 1 Cor 15:32 NIV), perhaps an allusion to battle with human opponents of the gospel, behind whom Paul perceives demonic "beasts" (Dan 7; T. Naph. 8.4, 6; T. Jos. 5.2; cf. Ex 23:29; Hanson, 120). Epaphroditus and Archippus are "fellow soldiers" (*systratiōtēs*, Phil 2:25;

Philem 2). Paul's compares his working for a living to someone in military service (*strateuetai*) paying their own expenses (1 Cor 9:7). Timothy is encouraged to "endure hardship . . . like a good soldier of Christ Jesus" (2 Tim 2:3-4). Three times Paul speaks of colleagues as *synaichmalōtous*, "fellow prisoner of war" (Rom 16:7; Col 4:10; Philem 23). The imagery of warfare is applied to all believers: they are to be armed for warfare (1 Thess 5:8), offer their "members" as weapons of righteousness (Rom 6:13, 23), and put on the armor of *light (Rom 13:12). In their conflict with spiritual forces believers are to take on defensive spiritual armor and shield, and the offensive weapon of the "sword of the Spirit" (Eph 6:10-17 NRSV). The language recalls the armor of Yahweh the divine warrior (Eph 6:13; cf. Is 59:16-18; Wis 5:17-20), and the battle is engaged in "his mighty strength" (Eph 6:10).

See also ADAM AND CHRIST; COLOSSIANS, LETTER TO THE; CROSS; DEATH; ESCHATOLOGY; FLESH; LAW; MAN OF LAWLESSNESS AND RESTRAINING POWER; SACRIFICE, OFFERING; SATAN, DEVIL; SIN, GUILT.

BIBLIOGRAPHY. **M. Beard,** *The Roman Triumph* (Cambridge, MA: Harvard University Press, 2007); **J. C. Beker,** *Paul the Apostle: The Triumph of God in Life and Thought* (Philadelphia: Fortress, 1980); **R. H. Bell,** *Deliver Us from Evil: Interpreting Redemption from the Power of Satan in New Testament Theology,* WUNT 216 (Tübingen: Mohr Siebeck, 2007); **M. C. de Boer,** *The Defeat of Death,* JSNTSup 22 (Sheffield: JSOT Press, 1988); idem, "Paul's Mythologizing Program in Romans 5–8," in *Apocalyptic Paul: Cosmos and Anthropos in Romans 5–8,* ed. B. R. Gaventa (Waco, TX: Baylor University Press, 2013): 1-20; **G. B. Caird,** *Principalities and Powers: A Study in Pauline Theology* (Oxford: Clarendon, 1956); **J. R. Dodson,** "The Many Faces of Metaphor in Colossians 2:15," *BBR* 31, no. 4 (2021): 497-515; idem, "The Convict's Gibbet and the Victor's Car: The Triumphal Death of Marcus Atilius Regulus and the Background of Colossians 2:15," *HTR* 114, no. 2 (2021): 182-202; **R. B. Duff,** "Metaphor, Motif and Meaning: The Rhetorical Strategy Behind the Image 'Led in Triumph' in 2 Corinthians 2:14," *CBQ* 53 (1991): 79-92; **R. B. Egan,** "Lexical Evidence on Two Pauline Passages," *NovT* 19 (1977): 34-62; **B. R. Gaventa,** *Our Mother Saint Paul* (Louisville, KY: Westminster John Knox, 2007); **S. J. Hafemann,** *Suffering and Ministry in the Spirit: Paul's Defense of His Ministry in II Corinthians 2:14–3:3* (Grand Rapids, MI: Eerdmans, 1990); **A. T. Hanson,** "Militia Christi," in *The Paradox of the Cross in the Thought of St. Paul,* JSNTSup 17 (Sheffield: JSOT Press, 1987); **C. Heilig,** *Paul's Triumph: Reassessing 2 Corinthians in Its Literary and Historical Context* (Leuven: Peeters, 2017); **J. B. Lightfoot,** *St. Paul's Epistles to the Colossians and Philemon* (London, 1879); **T. Longman III,** "The Divine Warrior: The New Testament Use of an Old Testament Motif," *WTJ* 44 (1982): 290-307; **T. Longman III and D. G. Reid,** *God Is a Warrior* (Grand Rapids, MI: Zondervan, 1995); **J. A. T. Robinson,** *The Body: A Study in Pauline Theology,* SBT 5 (London: SCM Press, 1952); **H. Schlier,** *Principalities and Powers in the New Testament* (New York: Herder & Herder, 1961); **S. Versnel,** *Triumphus* (Leiden: Brill, 1970); **L. Williamson,** "Led in Triumph: Paul's Use of *Thriambeuo,*" *Int* 22 (1968): 317-32; **N. T. Wright,** *The Climax of the Covenant* (Minneapolis: Fortress, 1992); idem, "Yet the Sun Will Rise Again: Reflections on the Exile and Restoration in Second Temple Judaism, Jesus, Paul, and the Church Today," in *Exile: A Conversation with N. T. Wright,* ed. J. M. Scott (Downers Grove, IL: IVP Academic, 2017), 19-80; **R. Yates,** "Colossians 2.15: Christ Triumphant," *NTS* 37 (1991): 573-91.

D. G. Reid

TRUTH

The Greek noun *alētheia,* typically rendered "truth," "truthfulness," or "faithfulness" in English, appears forty-seven times in the thirteen-letter Pauline corpus. There is a comparable concentration of the term in Romans (8×), 2 Corinthians (8×), Ephesians (6×), 1 Timothy (6×), and 2 Timothy (6×). While *alētheia* occurs regularly across the Pauline *canon, related words are far less common. To wit, the verb *alētheuō* ("to tell or speak the truth") is found only twice in Paul. Additionally, the adjective *alēthēs* ("true, honest, genuine") appears but four times, and the adjectives *alēthinos* ("true, genuine") and *alēthōs* ("truly") are each employed but once.

This entry will not examine singly the occurrences of *alētheia* and its cognates in their given literary contexts in the Pauline letters. Rather, based on examination of the fifty-two applicable verses in their respective literary contexts, five summative statements that capture and convey Paul's understanding of and convictions regarding truth will be proffered and considered with the various verses and usages in view. For and in Paul:

1. Truth Exists and Is Knowable
2. People Are Responsible for Their Response to the Truth and Ultimately to a God Who Is True

3. Truth Is Commendable and Is to Be Cultivated and Demonstrated in the Lives of Christ-Followers
4. Truth Is Grounded in God and Centered on Christ and the Gospel
5. God Entrusts People, Including Paul, with the Proclamation of the Truth of the Gospel, Not Least to Gentiles

1. Truth Exists and Is Knowable.
In his letters, unlike various apologists, Paul does not argue for the existence of truth. Neither does he ponder, like Pontius Pilate in the Fourth Gospel, "What is truth?" (so Jn 18:38). Instead, he assumes that truth exists even as *God exists and that both are available and accessible to people (see 1 Tim 4:3-4; 6:5; Titus 1:13).

According to Paul, this is the case, at least in part, because God has revealed as much through both *creation and the *law. Through creation, God has clearly and plainly self-disclosed "his eternal power and divine nature" (i.e., his "invisible qualities") so that people might see him through what he has made and know him as one who is true (note Rom 1:19-20; cf. Rom 3:4; 1 Thess 1:9; 1 Tim 4:4).

Paul also regarded the law as "the embodiment of *knowledge and truth" through which Jews (and earnest others) might know the truth about God and the God who is true (Rom 2:20 NRSV). If Paul polemicized against what he perceived to be distortions of creation (Rom 1:25; cf. 1 Cor 10:24-25; 1 Tim 4:3) and misappropriations of the law (e.g., Gal 2:11-20), he simultaneously recognized the inherent, if limited, good of both.

2. People Are Responsible for Their Response to the Truth and Ultimately to a God Who Is True.
Paul maintains that people are capable of and responsible for embracing, as well as rejecting, truth pertaining to God and the good (see 2 Thess 2:10-12; 2 Tim 2:25; Titus 1:14). Although people are in principle able to persist in doing (the) good (that God and the law require) by seeking "*glory and *honor and immortality" (Rom 2:7 NRSV; cf. Rom 2:10, 14-15), in practice individuals are inclined to suppress, exchange, and reject divine revelation regarding the glory of and truth about God (see Rom 1:18, 23, 25; 2:8-9). Thus, for Paul, all people are sinful (Rom 3:23). Furthermore, they are culpable before and ultimately accountable to God and his *judgment, which is grounded in truth (note Rom 2:2; 3:3-5, 9, 19).

3. Truth Is Commendable and Is to Be Cultivated and Demonstrated in the Lives of Christ-Followers.
In his letters, the *apostle commends "whatever is true" to his recipients (Phil 4:8 NRSV) and contends that *love "rejoices with the truth" (1 Cor 13:6). Indeed, speaking the truth in love and girding oneself with truth enables and exhibits Christian maturity and stability (note, e.g., Rom 9:1; Gal 4:16; 2 Cor 4:2; 6:7; 7:14; 12:6; Eph 4:15; 6:14; Titus 1:13-14). Furthermore, putting on the new self allows one to become more like God "in *righteousness and *holiness of truth" (Eph 4:24; cf. Titus 1:1). As "children of *light," Christ-followers are to produce the "fruit of light," consisting of "goodness, righteousness, and truth" (Eph 5:8-9 NIV).

In extolling and exhorting others unto truth (fulness), Paul regularly contrasts it to wickedness (Rom 1:18), lies (Rom 1:25; 3:4, 7; 9:1; Phil 1:18; Eph 4:25; 1 Tim 2:7; 2 Tim 4:4), evil (Rom 2:8; 1 Cor 13:7), and the like (see too 2 Cor 6:7; 2 Thess 2:10-12; 1 Tim 6:5; 2 Tim 3:6-7; 4:4). Given Christ's sacrificial *death as a paschal lamb, believers are to eschew "malice and wickedness" and embrace "sincerity and truth" (1 Cor 5:7-8 NIV).

4. Truth Is Grounded in God and Centered on Christ and the Gospel.
For Paul, truth is inextricably linked to and based on a truthful, faithful God (see, e.g., Rom 3:4, 7; 15:8; 1 Thess 1:9). Furthermore, the apostle conjoins truth with Christ (Rom 9:1; 2 Cor 11:10; Eph 4:21) and the *gospel/word of God (1 Thess 2:13; Col 1:5; Eph 1:13).

In Paul's fiery letter to the Galatians, he passionately defends Christian *freedom (Gal 2:4; 5:1, 14) and "the truth of the gospel" (Gal 2:5, 14 NIV). The true gospel, Paul propounds and proclaims, is available to all people (Gal 3:28) and is based on the loving, self-giving, redeeming *Son of God, not the (works of the) law (note esp. Gal 2:20-21; 3:13; 4:5). It is this gospel the apostle declares; it is this truth the Galatians (and other Christ-followers) are to embrace and obey (Gal 5:7).

5. God Entrusts People, Including Paul, with the Proclamation of the Truth of the Gospel, Not Least to Gentiles.
For Paul, the truth of gospel was not to be placed under a bushel; rather, it was to be clearly displayed (see Gal 3:1; Phil 2:15-16) and plainly declared to all people (note 2 Cor 4:1-6; 1 Thess 1:8). Although Paul's particular apostolic vocation was to preach the gospel to the nations/uncircumcised (so, e.g., Rom 11:13;

Gal 2:7; 1 Tim 2:7) "so that the *Gentiles might become an offering acceptable to God, sanctified by the *Holy Spirit" (Rom 15:16 NIV; note too Rom 15:7-12), he was convinced and compelled by a conviction, and concomitant commitment, that the truth of Christ and the gospel was for all people (see 2 Cor 5:11–6:2).

In short and in sum, then, Paul worshiped, walked with, and worked for a God whom he knew to be true, who "wants all people to be saved and to come to a knowledge of the truth" (1 Tim 2:4 NIV), and whose *church serves a "pillar and foundation of the truth" (1 Tim 3:15 NIV).

See also FAITH; GOSPEL; LAW; PREACHING, FIRST-CENTURY.

BIBLIOGRAPHY. **J. M. G. Barclay,** *Obeying the Truth: A Study of Paul's Ethics in Galatians* (Edinburgh: T&T Clark, 1988); **P. C. Langerholz,** *Alētheia in the Letters of St. Paul (Rome: Pontificium Athenaeum Antonianum, Facultas Theologica, 1979)*; **J. Murphy-O'Connor,** "Truth: Paul and Qumran," in *Paul and Qumran* (London: Chapman, 1968), 179-230; **D. J. Theron,** "*Alētheia* in the Pauline Corpus," *EvQ* 26 (1954): 3-18; **L. Tichý,** "Apoštol Pavel a 'pravda,'" *ST* 20 (2018): 165-74.

T. D. Still

TYPOLOGY. *See* ADAM AND CHRIST; OLD TESTAMENT IN PAUL.

U

UNCIRCUMCISION. *See* CIRCUMCISION; GENTILES; ISRAEL.

UNCLEAN. *See* FOOD LAWS AND CUSTOMS, JEWISH AND ROMAN; PURITY AND IMPURITY.

UNIVERSALISM

Universalism within Christian theology is most commonly understood as the belief that all of humanity will experience the *salvation of *God and be redeemed in the new *creation. This has been argued on philosophical, theological, and textual grounds, and is found as early as Origen (*Princ.* 1.6.1) and Gregory of Nyssa (*A Treatise on First Corinthians* 15).

Contemporary claims that Paul had a universalist outlook appear to be driven in Western commentary by the cultural offense of particularity in salvation, which differentiates between those who respond to the invitation of God with *faith and those who appear to refuse this invitation. They rely on either a rereading of the key texts in Paul or a dismissal of texts articulating particularity based on a *Sachkritik* ("subject criticism") reading in which Paul's theological position is contradictory and incoherent, so that one selects the views expressed in certain texts and prioritizes those over the theological position of texts that appear to say something different.

The key texts offering a universalistic understanding of salvation are those passages in which Paul refers to "all," including Romans 5:12-21; 11:32; 1 Corinthians 15:20-28; 2 Corinthians 5:19; Philippians 2:5-11; Ephesians 1:9-10; and Colossians 1:20. Additionally, within the Pastoral Epistles there is "all" language in 1 Timothy 2:4, 6; 4:10. This article will consider these texts in turn and locate them within Paul's wider theology. This article makes no differentiation between Paul and so-called deutero-Paul but rather takes the whole corpus of Pauline literature together.

1. Romans 5:12-21
2. Romans 11:32
3. 1 Corinthians 15:20-28
4. 2 Corinthians 5:19
5. Philippians 2:5-11
6. Ephesians 1:9-10 and Colossians 1:20
7. The Pastorals: 1 Timothy 2:4-6; 4:10
8. Resolving the Tension in Paul

1. Romans 5:12-21.

The universalist claim in relation to Romans 5:18 is that, since the scope of *sin reaches to "all" people, the scope and reach of salvation must, in the same way, apply to "all." To assess this, one needs to understand the place of this passage in Romans and the way Paul uses the language of "all."

Romans constitutes Paul's exposition of the *gospel to a mixed Jewish-*Gentile community that he has neither planted nor visited, and the tensions and questions between Jewish and Gentile believers are evident throughout. Romans 1 rehearses classic Jewish condemnations of Gentile culture, demonstrating the need of Gentiles for *forgiveness of sins, and in Romans 2 Paul turns to the Jew who is also in need of forgiveness, for it is clear that the *law alone cannot save. This is demonstrated negatively in Romans 3 by Scripture itself, and positively in Romans 4 by the example of *Abraham, who was justified by faith and so is "the father of us all" (Rom 4:16), both the Jew who sins with the law and the Gentile who sins without it. This is important background to the language of "all" and "many" in Romans 5.

Paul's language of "all" introduces this section, and in Romans 5:12, 18 it functions to offer both a contrast and a parallel. The contrast is in Romans 5:12 between the "one" who brought sin and *death into the world (Adam) and "all" who are affected by death because "all" have sinned. One should note here the similar wording with Romans 3:23, where "all" has the clear emphasis of "both Jew and Gentile." The parallel is then introduced in Romans 3:18: as one trespass (Adam's) brought sin and death to all, so one righteous action (Christ's) has brought forgiveness and life.

Paul fills out the discussion with a switch to the language of "many"; as I. Howard Marshall notes, "many" is used in a Hebrew sense to contrast with "one" and has the same rhetorical force as "all" (Marshall 2004, 61). This can be seen in the close parallels throughout these verses, as shown in table 1.

Table 1

Rom 5:12	**one** person	**all** people
Rom 5:15	**one** trespass **one** person	**many** died abounded for **many**
Rom 5:18	**one** trespass	condemnation for **all**
Rom 5:19	**one** disobedience **one** obedience	**many** sinners **many** made righteous

In this sense, the universalist reading has a strong appeal; Paul is using comprehensive language for the scope of salvation in Jesus. It is not possible to reject this by claiming that "many" is narrower in scope than "all" in this passage.

However, the universalist claim faces serious obstacles.

First, it is clear that Paul is not talking about categories of humanity *simpliciter*. Humanity "in Adam" is not condemned merely on the basis of its status but because "all sinned" (Rom 5:12), which is the means by which death has spread to all. To borrow later theological categories, original sin is for Paul about people being guilty not because of what Adam has done but because of what they too have done. In other words, condemnation and salvation cannot be explained by group categories alone; they are related to responsible action. If death comes through sin, then life comes through repentance and faith at every point in Paul's writings.

Second, the language Paul uses for salvation has a strong sense of present realization. Whether one takes the language of "*justification" as a forensic declaration, in the Lutheran tradition, or as the future verdict brought forward into the present, in line with "new perspective" readings, Paul is clear that justification is a present reality both in theology and experience. How could this justification then be universal, when it is not universally experienced? Those offering a coherent universalist reading (Talbott; MacDonald = Parry 2012) must argue for a postmortem experience of purging, repentance, and forgiveness for which there is simply no evidence in Paul.

Third, in this passage the comparative greatness of forgiveness is not found primarily in its scope but because of its nature: where death was the appropriate recompense for sin, the gift of life is unmerited and undeserved. To express this gift, Paul uses the language of *charisma* and *dōrēma* in Romans 5:15 and Romans 5:16 respectively, but both are related to his central theological idea of *charis*. John Barclay has demonstrated the contrast between Paul's understanding of God's *charis* and contemporary understandings of gift-giving in the first century, in which gifts were given to those who merited them by their worth and in which the conferring of a gift also conferred an obligation. The gift of life in *Christ is offered *without* consideration of merit, which is what makes God's gift/*grace so remarkable. However, Barclay argues, it is not without the obligation of response; God's *charis* is unconditioned, in the sense that there is nothing one can do to merit it, but it is not unconditional, for it requires the response of faith if it is to be received.

Marshall summarizes this vital connection between salvation and faith and the problem it poses for the universalist reading: "So the 'many' and the 'all' are indeed all people, but the gift becomes a reality for them only when they believe. People do not experience the gift of salvation until they become believers; apart from Christ they do not receive the gift of the Spirit, they do not have peace with God, and they do not share in the fellowship of the body" (Marshall 2004, 62).

2. Romans 11:32.
This remarkable summary verse of Paul's argument about *Israel in Romans 11 is another of his uses of "all" language: "For God has bound everyone over to disobedience so that he may have *mercy on them all" (NIV). "In a quite extraordinary way . . . the verse actually sums up the principal themes of the whole letter" (Dunn, 696). The use of "all" as a reference to those who have sinned and, in parallel, those who might be saved matches the use in Romans 5, and the same arguments apply. It is "possible to see here the expression of a hope for universal salvation" (Dunn, 677), until one notices that Paul is speaking in very general terms, and one needs to locate this in the context of the letter as a whole.

The "all" here cannot be disconnected from the much-debated earlier phrase "all Israel will be saved" (Rom 11:26). The common reading that this refers to future, national, ethnic Israel (Moo, 718) might suggest that "all" here refers to every individual. But this cannot be the case if this is taken to refer to a future, historic moment of turning, since it fails to consider the fate of those who have died. And, as David Peterson comments, "Paul does not imply that every Israelite without exception will be saved" (Peterson, 424).

In fact, the phrase *kai houtōs* should be read modally, meaning "in this way," not temporally, "then" (Peterson, 424; Wright, *NIB* 10:689-90). Although Paul does earlier use *Israel* to mean ethnic Jews, he is clearly capable of using it to refer to all believers (Gal 6:16), and this accords with his earlier distinction between being a Jew "inwardly" or "outwardly" (Rom 2:28), in which being part of Israel is not merely a question of *ethnicity. The coming of the promised deliverer, predicted in Isaiah 59:20-21, must refer to Jesus' incarnation and not to his return (Marshall 2004, 65). On this reading "all Israel" correlates with "the *fullness of the Gentiles"; though not all will turn and repent, nevertheless God's generous grace will run its course. "Here in Romans 11:32 the reference in 'all' is doubtless primarily to both Jews and Gentiles and not necessarily to every individual Jew and Gentile" (Marshall 2004, 66).

3. 1 Corinthians 15:20-28.

This passage contains what is often thought to be the most compelling text for a universalist reading in Paul: "As in Adam all die, so in Christ shall all be made alive" (1 Cor 15:22 ESV). This is the text from which both Origen and Gregory of Nyssa took their universalist readings, and it is commonly cited today. However, as Andrew Wilson highlights, there are in fact four elements of this passage that have been used to argue for universal salvation. It is worth noting from the outset the similarities with Romans 5, where there is an implicit contrast between the one progenitor and the universal effects of his action, and the antithetical parallelism between the act of *Adam and the work of Christ.

First, Johannes Weiss argues that the sequence in 1 Corinthians 15:23-24 should be interpreted as Christ first, those who are in Christ second, and then all others, not yet in Christ but who will receive life of God, third. This relies on translating *telos* as meaning "others" rather than "the end," which is not plausible, and assumes that there is some postmortem process by which people can receive the gift of life, which Paul never suggests.

Second, Origen (*Princ.* 1.6.1) argues that the language of "everything being put in subjection to him" (1 Cor 15:28) implies salvation for all. However, subjection is not the same as salvation; Paul depicts this subjection as including "destruction" (in 1 Cor 15:24); and if all God's enemies are subjected to him, and this means salvation, then this implies that the (personified) force of death is also saved—which does not make much sense.

Third, the language of "all" in 1 Corinthians 15:22, if taken to mean "every individual person," would imply universal salvation. As with the "all" passages in Romans 5; 11, the grammar of 1 Corinthians 15:22, taken on its own and out of the context of Paul's argument, looks universal: the "all" who are in Adam are the same "all" who are made alive in Christ. But it is clear, even in the immediately surrounding verses, that Paul's concern here is not with the destiny of all humanity but with the *hope for believers. This section of Paul's rhetoric, from 1 Corinthians 15:20, is a response to the hypothetical counterargument from 1 Corinthians 15:12: if there is no *resurrection, Christ was not raised, your faith is in vain, and those who have died *in Christ* have perished. The response, starting "But in fact" (*nyni de*), relates precisely to the destiny of those who are *"in Christ." Indeed, the whole argument is framed in terms of "the resurrection of the dead," an explicitly apocalyptic framework that, within both Jewish and Christian theology, involves the dead being raised, *judgment, and separation between those who live and those who perish.

The verses that follow run parallel to and offer a commentary on 1 Corinthians 15:22. How will "all in Christ" be made alive? First, Jesus at his (past) resurrection; then, at his return (*en tē parousia*) those who belong to Christ; and then the end. Paul is quite explicit here that it is those who are already "in Christ" who will be raised; this summary statement mentioning only the righteous being raised accords with much OT expectation, though it is a contrast to Daniel 12:2 and Revelation 20:13, in which both righteous and unrighteous are raised, after which judgment divides them. "The implication of v. 23 is that it is those who already are Christ's people who will be resurrected when he comes (cf. 1 Thess 4:14, 16). There is nothing said to imply that some (other) people will become Christ's people after he has come" (Marshall 2004, 69).

Fourth, some have claimed that the language of "death being destroyed" means that all humanity must receive the gift of life in Christ: "the destruction of the 'last' power effects salvation for all human beings, not just some of them" (de Boer, 136). Wilson describes this as "the strongest argument" for seeing universalism in this passage, since it does not depend on a discussion of the scope of the "all" referred to earlier.

One possible reading would be to see Paul as following the *tradition in Daniel 12:2 and Revelation 20:13-14, where (personified) Death and Hades give up their dead and are themselves destroyed, and the dead are then judged. This tradition is also found in other Second Temple texts (1 En. 51.1-2; 4 Ezra 7.31-35; L.A.B. 3.10; 2 Bar. 21.23), none of which has a universalistic outlook. "When set against this backdrop, the destruction of death that Paul refers to in 1 Corinthians 15:26, rather than implying a soteriological universalism, could in fact be a necessary precursor to the divine judgment of all humanity" (Wilson, 810).

But it might be more natural here to note that Paul's concern in these verses is not with the postmortem destiny of any particular group but with the cosmic and magisterial *triumph of God, through the resurrection of Christ, at the parousia. Although most commentators defer consideration of this until the citation in 1 Corinthians 15:54, it is clear that Paul is dependent on the language and ideas of Isaiah 25:6-8. The triumphant hope that God "will swallow up death forever" is a series of "all"s—all peoples, all nations, tears from all faces, all the earth. The LXX expands this to six "all"s, by repeating "all nations" and referring to "all tears from all faces." This looks like just the kind of universalism some read in Paul—yet the immediate context of the preceding and following verses is of God's judgment of Israel's enemies and their complete destruction. If Isaiah's "all"s are universal in their acclaim but not universalistic in their vision of redemption, then one must surely say the same of Paul's language in 1 Corinthians 15. "For Paul, the defeat of death was an essential and climactic part of Christ's cosmological victory, but it did not negate the judgment of all. Thus, while Paul could say with certainty that all who are in Christ will be 'made alive,' he could not (and does not) say the same of every single human being" (Wilson, 812).

4. 2 Corinthians 5:19.

In his exposition of God's reconciling work in Christ, Paul does not use "all" language, but at a critical point he appears to use absolute language about the scope of the work of Christ: "God was in Christ reconciling the world to himself" (ESV). Although the language of reconciliation is not the most common on Paul, there is an argument that it is the central expression of Paul's theological understanding (see I. Paul).

There is a question as to whether "world" (*kosmos*) as used here refers to humanity or all of creation. On the one hand, Paul appears to use it here as a parallel to "creation" (*ktisis*), and he regards this "creation" to have been consigned to "futility" as part of the problem that redemption in Jesus addresses (Rom 8:20). On the other hand, reconciliation takes place when God does not count their "trespasses" against them; this is a reference to human defiance of God's will rather than the futility of creation as a whole.

But the language before and after this phrase again creates serious problems for reading this in a universalistic way. There is again apocalyptic language of "new creation" for those who are "in Christ"; the promised new age of *holiness has broken into this old age of sin, but only for those who are incorporated into Christ through repentance, faith, and the gift of the Spirit. Paul goes on to extend the language of reconciliation to describe the apostolic *ministry that he has been called to and that he invites others to participate in with him, urging those around to accept this offer of reconciliation.

The wider context of Paul confirms this interpretation. The summary term *reconcile* in Ephesians 2:16 is also set in an apocalyptic context, where those who have not yet been reconciled are spiritually dead and enemies of God. But those who have been reconciled have been made alive and changed from enemies to friends with God, and friends with other former enemies who share this change of status. The dominant themes here are those of sin, disobedience, separation, and forgiveness—ideas that are not compatible with the notion of universal salvation.

5. Philippians 2:5-11.

The so-called Christ *hymn in Philippians 2 has been claimed to be an earlier composition that Paul incorporated in his letter, though the evidence for this is disputed. It is consonant with wider themes in Paul and is incorporated fluently within his argument. The key verse for a universal vision of salvation comes at the climax of the hymn, where, at the eschaton, one again finds "all" language: "every knee will bow . . . and every tongue confess that Jesus Christ is *Lord" (*pan gony kampsē . . . kai pasa glōssa exomologēsētai hoti kyrios Iēsous Christos*).

Paul's rhetorical aim in this text is not an exposition of the (numerical) scope of salvation but to persuade his readers that self-emptying and humility before God is the path to *glory. He immediately follows the hymn with an exhortation to obedience and holiness in contrast to the "crooked and twisted generation" (Phil 2:15 ESV) of this world.

A universalist reading claims that the confession in this verse is voluntary and salvific, rather than being forced (Talbott). But this is difficult to reconcile with Paul's language in Philippians 1:28; 3:19, where he talks of the "destruction" of God's enemies, in explicit contrast to "salvation," and the believers' "*citizenship in heaven." Paul's language in Philippians 2:11 comes from Isaiah 45:22-25, where those who do not acknowledge God are "put to shame" in contrast to Israel being exalted, and rival gods (Bel and Nebo) are forced to bow. The focus here is on division and judgment, and the central assertion is that God alone is the source of salvation. There is no reason to suppose that Paul's concerns are any different.

6. Ephesians 1:9-10 and Colossians 1:20. In Paul's dense introductory exposition of the meaning of the gospel in Ephesians 1, one once again encounters "all" language. The redemption of those God has chosen involves a revelation of "the *mystery of his will," which is to "unite all things in heaven and on earth in Christ" (Eph 1:9-10). The verb here is the middle form of *anakephalaioō*; this verb is elsewhere used with a literary sense of "recapitulation," summing up the plot of a narrative, as well as a mathematical sense of summing up the items in a ledger. Its only other occurrence in the NT is in Paul's summing up of the law as "You shall love your neighbor as yourself" (Rom 13:9 ESV).

In seeing Jesus as the summary principle of the whole of creation, there are theological connections with the Johannine notion of Jesus as the *logos*, the rational principle of the universe in Stoic thought, as well as the claim in Hebrews 1:3 that he "upholds all things by the word of his power." Despite the universal nature of the claims in these passages, there is no suggestion of universal salvation. Indeed, the eschatological "all" in Ephesians 1:10 runs as a close parallel to every knee bowing in Philippians 2:9 and all things being put in subjection to him in 1 Corinthians 15:27. As shown, in neither case does the language suggest that all are redeemed, not least because of the close proximity of the language of enemies being "destroyed."

There is a similar eschatological statement in Colossians 1:20, though this time using the more common Pauline language of reconciliation. The statement here is very similar to that found in 2 Corinthians 5:17-20; God's goal for creation is for it to be reconciled through Christ, but that goal is dependent on the response of faith and repentance, hence the appeal for reconciliation needs to be made. Paul goes on immediately to warn his readers, who have experienced this reconciliation, that this will only be realized "if indeed you continue in faith, stable and steadfast" (Col 1:23 ESV). He later talks about the defeat of powers opposed to Christ (Col 2:15) and of the coming *wrath of God against sinners (Col 3:6), statements impossible to harmonize with the idea of universal salvation.

7. The Pastorals: 1 Timothy 2:4-6; 4:10. Within Paul's instructions to Timothy about the conduct of the local congregation, Paul is once more using "all" language. God "wants all people to be saved" through Jesus, "who gave himself as a ransom for all" (1 Tim 2:4-6 ESV). It is striking that, as in Romans 5, one finds the use of "all" juxtaposed with the use of "one"—there is only one God, and only one mediator, and the status of *Savior is applied to both. This is a highly exclusivist claim for Paul to make in the context of the polytheism of the ancient world, but is also polemical in the context of *Ephesus and its cult of Artemis; for the effects of Paul's polemic claims, see the response in Acts 19:34.

Given Paul's stress on his *calling as *apostle to the Gentiles in 1 Timothy 2:7, it is also likely that the threat of *Judaizers, who challenged Paul's claims (mostly clearly expressed in Romans and Galatians) that both Jew and Gentile had equal access to God through faith in Jesus, is behind Paul's "all" language here (Marshall 1999, 425-26). The repeated emphasis in the Pastorals on the decisive importance of faith in response to the offer of salvation (1 Tim 1:16, 19; 2:15; 3:16 and elsewhere) rules out the possibility of universal redemption without exception. "The context shows that the inclusion of Gentiles alongside Jews in salvation is the primary issue here. . . . The emphasis is thus on universal accessibility to God's salvation on the basis of a faith open to all and a gospel preached to all" (Marshall 1999, 427).

The other reference to God as universal savior occurs in 1 Timothy 4:10. Most English translations render this "Savior of all people, *especially* of those who believe" (ESV). This leads to some strained exegesis, as it suggests that there are some who might be saved who do not believe, but that salvation is somehow particularly efficacious for those who do. But the term here, *malista*, can equally well mean "certainly," or "most assuredly"; it is functioning here to assert the clarity of Paul's confidence. "'All' is thus limited here to believers . . . but the universal emphasis remains: all people are potentially believers" (Marshall 1999, 557).

8. Resolving the Tension in Paul.

Those who argue for a universalist position in Paul frequently note that their reading of the more "universal" texts stands in sharp tension with other texts in Paul that talk about judgment and destruction. The most notable explicit examples are 2 Thessalonians 1:9, "They will suffer the punishment of eternal destruction" (ESV), and 2 Thessalonians 2:10, "those who are perishing because they refused to love the *truth and so be saved" (ESV). Yet the theme is deeper than these specific examples; Paul consistently describes the possibility of people perishing without salvation as a motivation for both his missionary *preaching and his concern to protect the gospel from the error of false *teaching. The truth must be preached far and wide in order that as many as possible might be saved, a motivation that makes no sense if Paul believes that salvation is universal regardless of response. Paul's anguish at the situation of his fellow Jews who have not put their faith in Jesus (Rom 9:1-3) only makes sense if their decision had real consequences.

Robin Parry notes this tension:

> Clearly my interpretation is underdetermined by the texts, so I cannot claim that it is obviously the only way to interpret that matter. I am not so much exegeting the texts as trying to draw out the logic of New Testament theology as I understand it and its implications for those texts. In the process I may be offering ways of reading the texts that go beyond what their authors had in mind. (MacDonald, 140)

The question then is how to resolve the apparent contradiction between wider themes in Scripture, or even within Paul, and what particular texts actually say.

Richard Bell is happy to accept that Paul is simply contradictory: in Romans 5 one is offered a vision of universal salvation; then in Romans 11, it is clear that not all Gentiles will be saved, but all Jews will be.

A more philosophical approach is that of *Sachkritik*, as deployed in different ways over the last one hundred years. It involves a critical assessment of what a biblical text actually says in the light of what the critic believes is the overall message of the gospel. Rudolf Bultmann deployed this approach in his discussion of Karl Barth's theological exegesis, and it eventually led to Bultmann's approach of demythologizing the NT to recast it in terms more acceptable to modern presuppositions. Douglas Campbell and others now use it to reject parts of Scripture in the light of their own modern understanding of what the gospel means. "Reception historians can see from these three strategies how all historically critical theologians claim either more or less continuity with their Scriptures while recognizing that much in them is incredible and inapplicable to modern Christian *identity" (Morgan, 175).

Given that this approach makes the assumption both that the NT texts are incoherent (in that their particular details do not accord with their overall message) and that the modern critical interpreter is in a better position than either the writers or the first interpreters to discern what the message of the gospel really is, it cannot escape the criticism of Marshall: "The major weakness in the universalist view is thus that in attempting to explain the few texts which it interprets to refer to the salvation of all people it has to offer an unconvincing reinterpretation of texts about God's judgement and wrath and to postulate an unattested salvific action of God in the future" (Marshall 2004, 72).

It is important to note here that this article has not addressed the debates around the nature of judgment, in particular the question of whether the unsaved experience eternal conscious torment or annihilation. Neither has it addressed the question of the destiny of those who have not heard or had a chance to respond to the gospel, or the belief in the immortality of the soul. Although these issues are often cited as reasons for leading to a universalist position, it does not logically follow. They are distinct issues that need their own discussion.

There is a better way to read Paul and the whole narrative of Scripture: "Biblical 'universalism,' therefore, consists in this, that in Christ God has revealed the one way of salvation for all men alike, irrespective of race, sex, colour or status. This biblical 'universalism' (unlike the other sort) gives the strongest motives for evangelism, namely, the love of God and of men" (Wright 1979, 58).

See also GOSPEL; JUDGMENT; JUSTIFICATION; PEACE, RECONCILIATION; ROMANS, LETTER TO THE; SALVATION; WRATH, DESTRUCTION.

BIBLIOGRAPHY. **J. Barclay,** *Paul and the Gift* (Grand Rapids, MI: Eerdmans 2015); **R. Bell,** "Romans 5.18-19 and Universal Salvation," *NTS* 48 (2002): 417-32; **M. de Boer,** *The Defeat of Death: Apocalyptic Eschatology in 1 Corinthians 15 and Romans 5* (Sheffield: JSOT Press, 1988); **E. Boring,** "The Language of Universal Salvation in Paul," *JBL* 105, no. 2 (1986): 269-92; **J. D. G. Dunn,** *Romans 1–8*,

WBC 38a (Dallas: Word, 1988); **J. Greever,** "Was Paul a Universalist? Reading Texts in Context," *Credo* 9, no. 4 (2019), https://credomag.com/article/was-paul-a-universalist/; **J. M. Gundry-Volf,** *Paul and Perseverance,* WUNT 2/37 (Tübingen: Mohr Siebeck, 1990); **M. Ludlow,** *Universal Salvation: Eschatology in the Thought of Gregory of Nyssa and Karl Rahner* (Oxford: Oxford University Press, 2000); idem, "Universalism in the History of Christianity," in *Universal Salvation? The Current Debate,* ed. R. Parry and C. Partridge (Grand Rapids, MI: Eerdmans, 2004), 191-218; **G. MacDonald [R. Parry],** *The Evangelical Universalist,* 2nd ed. (Eugene, OR: Cascade, 2012); **I. H. Marshall,** *The Pastoral Epistles,* ICC (London: T&T Clark, 1999); idem, "The New Testament Does *Not* Teach Universal Salvation," in *Universal Salvation? The Current Debate,* ed. R. Parry and C. Partridge (Grand Rapids, MI: Eerdmans, 2004), 55-76; **D. Moo,** *The Epistle to the Romans,* NICNT (Grand Rapids, MI: Eerdmans, 1996); **R. Morgan,** "Sachkritik in Reception History," *JSNT* 33, no. 2 (2010):175-90; **I. Paul,** "Reconciled Reconcilers: 'Reconciliation' in the New Testament," in *Good Disagreement,* ed. A. Atherstone and A. Goddard (Oxford: Lion Hudson, 2015); **D. Peterson,** *Romans, Evangelical Biblical Theological Commentary* (Bellingham, WA: Lexham, 2020); **T. Talbott,** "A Pauline Interpretation of Divine Judgement," in *Universal Salvation? The Current Debate,* ed. R. Parry and C. Partridge (Grand Rapids, MI: Eerdmans, 2004), 32-54; **J. Weiss,** *Der erste Korintherbrief* (Göttingen: Vandenhoeck & Ruprecht, 1910); **A. Wilson,** "The Strongest Argument for Universalism in 1 Cor 15.20-28," *JETS* 59, no. 4 (2016): 805-12; **N. T. Wright,** "Towards a Biblical View of Universalism," *Themelios* 4, no. 2 (1979): 54-58; idem, "The Letter to the Romans," *NIB* 10:396-770.

I. B. Paul

URBAN SETTING OF PAUL'S CHURCHES

Descriptions of the city (Gk. *polis,* Latin *civitas*) in antiquity vary. A cultural/architectural description from Pausanias gives one perspective (Pausanias, *Descr.* 10.4.1). He declares that no center could justify calling itself a true city unless it had government buildings, a gymnasium, a theater, a market square, a fountain, and a few large mansions (i.e., an urban elite). On the other hand, those less inclined to glamorize city life said cities were full of noisy, muddy streets, crumbling tenement houses, and dirty people (Seneca, *De ira* 3.35.5; Juvenal, *Sat.* 3.232-238).

The cities were actually all of the above. These features lead one to ask: After one toured the monumental buildings in the urban center, what would one see, hear, and smell in the rest of a city? Where and how did people—rich and poor—live? What sort of people read Paul's letters?

This article will offer an assessment of the cities of the first century Greco-Roman world, focusing on those receiving Pauline letters: Rome, *Corinth, *Ephesus, Philippi, and, to some extent, Thessalonica and Colossae (little is known of them because of lack of excavations), with occasional reference to other contemporaneous cities for comparison. All (probably including Colossae) of the Pauline cities had the items listed above by Pausanias—and undoubtedly the items given by Seneca and Juvenal.

1. Architecture
2. Leadership
3. Entertainment
4. Hygienic Conditions
5. Demographics
6. Social Interaction
7. Labor
8. Religions
9. Conclusion

1. Architecture.

1.1. The Urban Center. Classical Greek cities had established a kind of architectural standard (as Pausanias observes). They would have a marketplace surrounded by stoas, a council house (*bouleuterion*), a city building (*prytaneion*), a theater, a gymnasium, and a stadium. Nearby would also be numerous *temples, especially those dedicated to the city's divine patron. Hellenistic cities, such as Thessalonica, kept these features, adding the Hippodamian orthogonal (checkerboard) grid of city streets.

When the Romans planted colonies in North Africa and the Mediterranean East, they maintained the orthogonal street planning. The north-south streets were called *cardines* ("hinges"); the east-west were *decumani* ("tenths"). The main conjunction of these streets, the *cardo maximus* and the *decumanus maximus,* was where the forum/*agora* (marketplace) was usually located. To the Greek traditional structures, the Romans added commemorative arches, basilicas, baths, Roman-style aqueducts, drainage ditches, and amphitheaters for gladiatorial contests.

The basic part of any first-century city was its central space, the forum or *agora.* Here the great leaders built their impressive religious and governmental buildings and their constructions for entertainment. In Rome, these structures were mostly on the Palatine and Capitoline hills. In Corinth, they were in the city center; in Ephesus, they were east of the harbor; at Philippi, they were mostly south of the Egnatian Way (its *decumanus maximus*), which dissected the city.

1.2. Urban Housing. As a rule, the elites lived near the center of the city, close to the government buildings. In Rome, they erected mansions, such as the House of Augustus, on the hills (especially the Palatine), while the poor lived in the low-lying areas. Some ethnic groups in Rome lived even farther from the city center. The Jews, for example, lived mostly on the other side of the Tiber River (Leon).

In Corinth, the wealthy lived near the center of the city, with the poor in turn encircling them (Engels). In Ephesus, houses of the wealthy have been excavated just south of the Curetes Street on a sloping hill near the city's governmental and cultural structures (Ladstätter et al.).

One can delineate five kinds of housing in Rome and the Eastern cities.

1.2.1. Domus of the Wealthy. First were the residences of the wealthy. In the traditional house styles of the elites, Italian and Greek influences merged to produce structures with peristyle (colonnaded) gardens and an atrium (central hall). Bedrooms ringed three sides of the atrium, with a dining hall (*triclinium*) at the far end of the hall. The Regionary Catalogue from the fourth century AD gives the total number of domiciles in the city of Rome. It is later than this article's period of interest but can serve as a comparative guide. It lists around eighteen hundred *domus* ("houses"; some detached and others embedded in blocks of condominiums; Carcopino; Stambaugh).

Ephesus presents an example of an aristocratic house. This two-story house—residential unit two—one of six in the block called "Terrace House 2," was located south of the Curetes Street. The peristyle house, built in the first century AD, offered twelve rooms on its ground floor. The total ground-floor habitable space was around six thousand square feet. Among the preserved rooms are an atrium, a triclinium, a kitchen, and a toilet with running water. It was decorated with elaborate mosaics and frescoes and had heated rooms (Ladstätter et al.).

1.2.2. Modest Dwellings. Second were apartments/condominiums of modest size. Archaeologists have identified large buildings (one or perhaps two stories) in several cities (e.g., Pompeii, Pergamum, and Delos) divided into varying sizes of residence, as small as two hundred square feet and as large as two thousand (Oakes; Trümper). The varying sizes of the apartments/condominiums demonstrate that not every person from the nonelite classes lived in dire poverty. Some in the lower classes could own or rent comfortable, modest-sized dwellings.

1.2.3. Shop Houses. Third, many working class people lived near their shop. The living quarters of the shop owners could take several forms: (1) a family could live and work in one room, (2) a family could work on the first floor and live on the mezzanine level, or (3) a family could work on the first floor and live in a room in the back. The Italian port city of Ostia can offer perspective. Of the 806 workshops examined there, 464 were one room, 155 had a mezzanine living space, and 141 had back rooms. Thus, most of the shop owners lived in the same room where they worked (Packer). Family privacy under those circumstances would have been minimal.

David Horrell has identified a block of shops in Corinth near the theater. These were small rooms (ca. 250 square feet). Each shop had a room of equal size in the back, evidently living quarters for the family. The presence of ovens and animal bones indicated that they were perhaps *popinae* ("restaurants"; see below) that sold cooked meat. There were two stories above the shops, presumably for other families to inhabit. Paul and his associates may have rented a similar shop for their *tentmaking work in Corinth (Acts 18:3).

1.2.4. Insulae. Fourth were the high-rise apartments. These blocks of apartments—*insulae* ("islands")—could rise to several stories. Augustus had decreed a maximum height for these constructions in Rome, but this limit was sometimes ignored. Those living on the first floor of the apartment blocks were the more comfortable residents. First-floor apartments were not only more convenient (you did not have to climb stairs), but they were also larger.

In another type of the *insula*, the bottom floor was reserved for shops. The shops opened onto the street with folding doors and usually had a room either behind or on a mezzanine level for the family's sleeping quarters. One *insula* excavated in Rome near the Capitoline Hill had shops on the first floor with mezzanine living quarters, two spacious apartments on the second floor, small rooms arranged in rows on the third floor, and the cheap apartments on the fourth floor (Stambaugh).

Those living in the upper floors of the *insulae*—fourth to sixth floors—had much less comfortable living conditions. The attic apartments were grim. Since they had neither water nor toilets, they had either to carry their chamber pots down stairs to empty them or just dump their waste out the window. They had to carry their water upstairs. Since they had no kitchens, they were forced to use braziers to cook meals and heat the room. Their apartments were smaller than those below. They were dark, smoky, smelly, and insect infested.

Insulae of this type were common in Rome and Ostia. Many of the readers of Paul's letter to the Romans no doubt lived in such dwellings. Recently, some have suggested that high-rise *insulae* of the Roman type were increasingly popular elsewhere in the *empire in cities such as Ephesus (Billings).

According to the Regionary Catalogue, Rome had 46,602 *insulae* in the fourth century AD. Since Rome had a larger population then than in the first century, one should estimate the number of tenement buildings somewhat lower (Carcopino suggests by 15 percent).

The dangers of living in the *insulae* were two: fire and suddenly collapsing floors. The structures—usually built cheaply—might fold at any moment, as one Roman satirist complains (Juvenal, *Sat.* 3.190-199).

Most of the *insulae* of Rome were in the valleys between the hills, where the standing water could cause health problems for the residents (see below), or in the slums south and west of the Tiber River. It was perhaps in one of these that the Roman government held Paul captive (Acts 28:30).

1.2.5. Shanties. Finally, there were the shanties. The poorest persons made shelters from scraps of wood and other items. Sometimes they would erect shelters against or on top of public buildings. Some constructed their unstable shanties outside the walls of the city. Other poor persons found shelter in tombs, under a bridge or aqueduct, under the stairs of an *insula*, or under a theater awning (Scobie).

Some had no roof over their heads at all; they slept on the streets or in public buildings. A Christian author from the fourth century AD observed that the open air, the porticoes, and the street corners were the lodgings of the poor (Gregory of Nazianzus, *On Love of the Poor* 1).

One historian estimates that in Ostia (population 27,000), there were two thousand living in *domus*, twenty thousand in *insulae*, and five thousand homeless (Billings). One can only guess at the number of homeless in the large cities of Corinth, Ephesus, Thessalonica, and Rome.

Discovery of these five dwelling types has led to discussion about the physical space where early Christians gathered. Paul's references to churches meeting in people's houses (*oikoi/oikiai*; Rom 16:5; 1 Cor 16:15, 19; Col 4:15; Philem 2) may refer to (1) the houses of the elites, in which congregations of Christians met in the atrium; (2) the small houses of the poor near or in their shops; (3) the tenement apartments of the *insulae*; or (4) neighborhoods (*vici*; see below) where whole blocks or streets would gather (Murphy-O'Connor 2002; Horrell; Billings; Last).

2. Leadership.

2.1. Formal Leadership. Rome developed a complex system of governance over the centuries. Augustus organized the city into fourteen regions, each with a magistrate to preside over it. The emperor/*princeps* assumed power over the whole.

Two Pauline cities were Roman colonies (Corinth and Philippi), which imitated the city government of Rome. These cities were managed by *duoviri* and their assistants, the *aediles*, as inscriptions from both cities indicate. The *duoviri* of Philippi show up in Acts 16:20, 22 (as the Greek equivalent: *stratēgoi*). One of the members of the Corinthian congregation, Erastus (Rom 16:23), Paul calls the "steward" (*oikonomos*) of Corinth, evidently a management position. Later a man by the same name is featured in an inscription and called an *aedile*. It is debated whether the Erastus of Romans and the one in the inscription were the same person.

Acts 19:35 gives a brief speech of the Ephesian *grammateus* (clerk). This title also appears in inscriptions from Ephesus. At this time, the clerk in Eastern cities was invested with increasing power since he had become the leader of the city council (Jones).

The city leaders of Thessalonica (Gk. *politarchai*, "city rulers") are named both in an inscription and in Acts 17:6. It is a term unknown otherwise for city rulers (Finegan).

2.2. Patronage. Formal *leadership was one kind of honor in the ancient cities. But informal leadership, *patronage, was the oil that greased the wheels. It was practiced everywhere in the Greco-Roman world. There is even reference to a female patroness of a *church in the Corinthian region (Rom 16:1-2). A young man would usually ask a respected older man to be his patron. Or, alternatively, a freed *slave would continue to honor a former master, this time in a patron-client relationship. The patron would defend him, recommend him, and occasionally offer money or *food. In turn the patron expected from his client support in an election, homage every morning at his atrium, and walking with him in public to show support. The more clients one had, the greater the *honor.

Sometimes a person would become the patron of an organization (a club or association; see below), like Phoebe's being patroness of the church at Cenchreae. There are other female patronesses of associations documented in the inscriptions and papyri (Kloppenborg). A patron/patroness might pay for a banquet or a rental hall for the association to meet in.

The elites, who erected buildings and paid for games at their own expense, were the patrons of whole cities (Veyne).

3. Entertainment.

Horace wrote, in reference to the attractions of cities, that in the city one finds games, baths, brothels, and greasy restaurants (*popinae*; Horace, *Ep.* 1.14.15-21). Cities were centers of pleasure. For example, people were drawn to Corinth mainly for two reasons: to visit the temple of Asclepius and to attend the Isthmian games in nearby Isthmia, which took place in the spring every two years. They came to Ephesus not only for the temple of Artemis, one of the wonders of the Greco-Roman world, but to attend the Ephesia, the athletic games, and later to view the gladiatorial combats. The cities offered pleasures that the village and countryside could never match.

3.1. Athletic Contests. The athletic contests of the Greeks consisted of throwing, running, and wrestling/boxing events. They also hosted musical contests. These contests remained popular throughout the Eastern empire and even made some inroads—though not with much enthusiasm—into the city of Rome. Paul alludes to these them in several of his letters (e.g., 1 Cor 9:24-27; Phil 3:12-14), indicating that he thought his readers would be familiar with them.

3.2. Drama. Theaters were a common feature of all Greek cities of any size and became so for Roman cities as well, including all the cities receiving Pauline letters (Acts 19:29). Greek and Latin writers produced tragedies, comedies, and mimes, a kind of satire, usually shocking, sometimes obscene or violent. The Romans added a new genre, the pantomimes, a dancing performance. Paul quotes a Greek play (1 Cor 15:33), showing he had some familiarity with the theater. Although some suggest Paul uses the techniques of the mimes in parts of his letters (2 Cor 11:21–12:10), that is by no means certain (Welborn 1999).

3.3. Gladiatorial Games. Gladiatorial combats, originally funeral rites, were developed by the Romans under Etruscan influence. They featured events that included animal hunts (*venationes*), the execution of criminals, and combat between trained fighters. The Romans also invented a new way to view these contests: the amphitheater (two theaters put together). The games in Rome became more and more extravagant, sometimes with thousands of animals (lions, elephants, ostriches, crocodiles, hippopotami, etc.) killed. The Roman taste for bloodshed became a regular feature throughout the empire. Lamps and relief sculptures from the first century (e.g., from Ephesus, Corinth, and Colossae) depict gladiators in combat. The Corinthians especially loved the blood sports (Concannon). They were introduced in Ephesus one hundred years before Paul arrived there. A century after Paul, the Ephesians established a special gladiators' cemetery. At Ephesus, they held the gladiatorial contests in the stadium; Corinth had an amphitheater; Colossae used its theater (Cadwallader; Yamauchi). In Rome, they fought at first in the forum, then in wooden amphitheaters or in the *circus maximus*, the racetrack that could host up to 250,000 people (the Colosseum was not built in Paul's lifetime). Augustus boasted that during his reign ten thousand gladiators fought and thirty-five hundred criminals were killed (Stambaugh). Increasingly, the Romans found the Greek athletic games boring, preferring the bloody struggles of the arena, in their view the perfect display of Roman machismo. Paul perhaps alludes to the *venationes* of Ephesus in 1 Corinthians 15:32, to the execution of criminals in 1 Corinthians 4:9, and possibly to gladiatorial combats in 2 Corinthians 4:8-9 (Concannon).

3.4. Chariot Racing. Another Roman passion was chariot racing. They raced in huge hippodromes or circuses, such as the *circus maximus* in Rome. Ruins of hippodromes are scattered all over the former empire (from Carthage to Corinth to Caesarea in *Israel), showing the popularity of chariot racing. Participants did not live long lives; inscriptions show that many died in their twenties.

Although the stars of the theaters, the gladiatorial combats, and the chariot races were slaves or freed persons—and therefore *infames* (disreputable) by definition—they were heroes to the populace and sometimes became enormously wealthy, like film and sports stars today.

It is questionable that Paul attended either the races or the gladiatorial combats. Christians later prohibited attendance because of the *violence.

4. Hygienic Conditions.

4.1. Baths. Most Greco-Roman cities had public baths. By the mid-first century BC, there were 170 small baths in Rome. By the fourth century AD, there were eleven large imperial bath complexes (*thermae*) plus one thousand public baths. Five baths have been found at Corinth so far, four at Ephesus, and two in Philippi (Finegan). The baths of

Colossae are mentioned in an inscription (Cadwallader and Harrison). Baths were usually maintained by water piped in by aqueducts. The price of admission was low. Slaves could enter the baths if they could pay the small fee. Both men and *women attended them (not always segregated). Many came not just for personal hygiene: some men lingered for hours looking for a sexual partner. Others came for socializing. John Stambaugh observes that the baths offered exercise, swimming, steam baths, saunas, sex, gossip, lectures, and poetry reading.

The sick came for therapy—physicians prescribed bathing for a multitude of illnesses—but often at a different time of day from the healthy. Still, germs and parasites were undoubtedly transmitted by bathing in these facilities (see below).

The nonelites—although allowed to enter the baths for a small fee—bathed less frequently than the elites (see above; the cities were full of "dirty people"), usually at home by pouring a small amount of water over themselves while standing. It was perhaps not so much the price of admission as the time it would take. One required leisure to walk to a bath and spend hours soaking.

The Forum Baths of Pompeii offer an example of how the baths could operate. They had separate bathing facilities for the men and women (each with hot, lukewarm, and cold baths), an exercise area, an area for lectures, and shops. It could be a full afternoon's entertainment.

Would Paul have attended the baths? On the one hand, Christians later condemned them (Veyne); on the other hand, the Jewish rabbis of the second century frequented them (Eliav).

4.2. Sewage. All Greco-Roman cities had public latrines. They have been excavated in Rome, Corinth, Philippi, and Ephesus. Rome had (according to the Regionary Catalogue) 144 latrines for its one million–plus residents in the fourth century AD. The public latrines were not only for the service they offered but evidently for socializing. Roman satirists poked fun at persons hanging around hoping for a dinner invitation.

Many houses of the elites (see Ephesus above) had their own latrine. The elites were in the habit of bribing officials to siphon off some of the water brought in by the aqueducts to flush their private toilets. Some of the *insulae* had latrines on their first floor.

The vast majority of the population lived too far away from the public latrines to use them. Instead, they used chamber pots and disposed of the sewage the best way they could. There were, here and there, large jars for collecting urine (for the tanners and fullers). There were manure gatherers—the lowest of jobs—who carried some of the human waste to the outskirts of the city to use for fertilizer. There were manure piles at the end of alleys (on which one could often find abandoned human infants). Those living in the high-rise tenements in Rome, and undoubtedly in other cities, often dumped their chamber pots out the window at night, at times on the heads of passersby (Juvenal, *Sat.* 3.268-277). The cities were full of animals leaving behind their waste. Consequently, waste materials (rotten food, feces, corpses of animals, and even human corpses) were left everywhere in the cities (Scobie). The streets were sewers. It all created a foul-smelling muck (Phil 3:8).

4.3. Water. Many cities in Paul's time had aqueducts bringing clean water to fountains and baths. By the time Paul arrived in Rome, there were nine aqueducts there (Connolly and Dodge). Ephesus also had aqueducts beginning in the reign of Augustus. In Corinth there were several natural springs, the Peirene and other fountains. But such water sources served the city centers and might be too far to carry water home from them. There were water carriers who would sell a small quantity for a fee. But all ancient cities depended to a great extent on wells and cisterns; many also relied on nearby rivers (Jones). These sources were often contaminated with cholera and typhoid (see 1 Tim 5:23).

4.4. Disease. The cities were petri dishes of infection. The density of the population facilitated their spread. Further, Corinth, Thessalonica, and Ephesus, being port cities, had the additional problem of seafarers' illnesses. The ancient sources list especially tuberculosis, leprosy, dysentery, typhoid, cholera, intestinal parasites, and malaria (Scobie). The last two illnesses have come to light in recent years due to archaeological remains. Infestations of parasites (especially roundworm, tapeworm, and whipworm) happened because of the unsanitary urban conditions —proximity to human and animal feces—and perhaps through visiting the baths. Examination of the remains of ancient latrines in Rome, Gaul, Briton, Germany, Israel, and Greece has led to the conclusion that most ancient Greco-Roman urban dwellers were infected (Mitchel; Fiensy). Intestinal infection did not usually result in death but weakened the immune system, giving opportunity to other infections that could be lethal.

Malaria's spread was due to standing water, breeding places for mosquitoes, like the marshes near Philippi and the low-lying areas in Rome. Rome experienced a "season of death," in late summer when the mosquitoes were active; other cities in the

Mediterranean area did as well (Shaw; Sallares). Malaria was an equal-opportunity disease; every socioeconomic class could catch it. But those living in the lowland marshes of cities—the poor—were most exposed. Malaria causes periodic high fever and general weakness. There were three types of malaria in the Mediterranean region at that time, of which one was often directly lethal; the others in synergy with other illnesses could be lethal. Thus, visitors to Paul's imprisonment in Rome may have become ill due to malaria (Phil 2:25-27). Paul might have contracted this illness himself during his first missionary tour (Gal 4:13).

*4.5. **Mortality.*** These diseases, caused by unsanitary conditions, made life expectancy lower in the cities. For example, in imperial Rome, over half (54 percent) of the children would not live to adulthood. Harry Leon's statistics for the Jews of Rome are similar: 52 percent youth mortality. By comparison, in the Italian countryside, the mortality rate for children was 42 percent, still high but not as high as the city. In the eastern Mediterranean during this period, the youth mortality rate was 47 percent (Fiensy). Paul's letters were sent to churches where the death rate of children—already high—would have been much worse.

5. Demographics.

One can make the following preliminary statements about the ancient Greco-Roman cities: the poor outnumbered the rich; the cities were full of immigrants; there were more men than women; there were fewer children per family than in the rural areas (see above); and people died earlier (see above; Sjoberg; Stambaugh).

*5.1. **Population.*** On the whole, ancient cities had lower populations than what are classified today as cities. The cities that received Pauline letters included Rome (population 1,000,000; Carcopino), Ephesus (200,000; White), Corinth (80,000; Engels), Thessalonica (40,000; Crossan and Reed), Colossae (25,000; Trainor), and Philippi (population unknown; Brélaz). If one accepts the standard conclusion that only about 10 percent of the population of the empire lived in cities, due to a low level of food surplus, and one accepts a total population of fifty to sixty million, one gets around five to six million people living in all of the cities of the Roman Empire in the first century.

*5.2. **Multiethnicity.*** The cities were built by immigration. Mortality rates were too high (see above) for cities to increase by births. Immigration made the cities multiethnic. Consequently, one might hear a number of languages spoken in a given city and encounter persons from many different regions. Inscriptions at Ephesus reveal immigration from all parts of Asia Minor, as well as from Greece, Syria/Judea, Egypt, Italy, and North Africa (White). At Corinth, there were Romans, Italians, Greeks, Jews, Anatolians, and Phoenicians (Engels). At Philippi there were immigrants from Italy, Egypt, and Anatolia (Meeks) as well as native Thracians and "cultural Greeks" (Brélaz). At Thessalonica were immigrants from Egypt and Palestine.

The city of Rome was a huge ethnic mix, with people immigrating to it from all over the empire. There are references to immigrants from Thrace, Pannonia, Sardinia, Judea/Syria, Egypt, Spain, and Asia Minor (Stambaugh).

One way to understand the persistence of cultural/regional heritage is the examination of inscriptions. There were tens of thousands of Jews living in Rome in the first century (although some were expelled under Emperor Claudius, who reigned AD 41–54). Jews did not quickly assimilate to the Latin culture. The catacomb inscriptions of the Jews of Rome show 405 inscriptions in Greek, 123 in Latin, and five in Hebrew/Aramaic (Leon).

In the two Roman colonies receiving Pauline letters, Corinth and Philippi, the official, elite inscriptions in Latin far outnumber the Greek. But the unofficial, nonelite inscriptions (graffiti, tombstones, and artisans' marks on products), at least in Corinth, were mostly in Greek (Engels; Bitner). The working class remained Greek even in a Roman colony such as Corinth. But inscriptions can also be deceiving. At Philippi, the local Thracians, although they still spoke their native tongue, left inscriptions only in Latin or Greek since their language was not written (Brélaz).

These conditions (ethnic mix through immigration) are reflected in Paul's letter to the Romans (e.g., Rom 16:5, 11-13). Of the twenty-six persons listed in Romans 16, fourteen were not born in Rome. Paul names three of the twenty-six as Jews and indicates that four of them hailed from the Eastern part of the empire (Lampe). The Corinthian church was similar: Meeks observes that of the names associated with the church in that city, half are Latin names and the rest Greek. Such a mix could make for tensions among those thrown together from various provinces.

*5.3. **Gender Numbers.*** There were more men than women in the cities. Men came in greater numbers because of lack of inheritance or jobs. Another factor that contributed to fewer women in the cities was the tendency for the poor to "expose" (abandon) girls at birth. In the list of Christian church persons in Romans 16:1-15, there are almost twice as many men (seventeen) as women (nine).

The lack of women in the cities meant that there were fewer females available for marriage to nonelites, consequently encouraging prostitution. Excavators have found in Pompeii (population 20,000) twenty-eight brothels plus nine apartments rented by prostitutes and open for business. Using this as a comparative calculator, there must have been hundreds of brothels in Corinth and Ephesus and over a thousand in Rome. Thus, Paul's frustrations in teaching about sexual morality are understandable (1 Cor 6:15).

5.4. Children. There were fewer children per family in the cities than in the rural areas because of the costs in the city to raise children. Children, especially girls, were more apt to be exposed in the cities than in the countryside. Excavations have revealed that childhood mortality was also greater in the cities (see above).

5.5. Density. The population density in the cities was practically unbearable. It ranged from 150 persons per acre to 200. The concentration of *insulae* may be seen in the count in the "old city" (the ancient boundaries) of Rome. The Regionary Catalogue lists 174 *insulae* per *vicus*, a compact arrangement (Carcopino).

Such crowding led to inevitable social consequences. When night fell, families came inside and locked their doors. The streets were unlit and full of muggers.

5.6. Privacy and Gossip. The nonelites lived outdoors most of the time during the day. Often their shops intruded into the narrow streets. Barbers might be shaving or cutting hair in the middle of the street; butchers might be cutting meat. Vendors sold food and other wares such as clothing. Women hung up their clothes to dry in the street. People played games, especially dice, there. In the nonelite sections of cities, everyone was outside during the day.

Such closeness meant that there was little of what one might consider privacy. In the nonelite sections of a city, one's neighbors heard everything one said and practically everything one did. Everyone knew everyone else's business—and problems. Gossip was rampant (2 Cor 12:20; Rom 1:29; Eph 4:29, 1 Tim 5:13).

But even in the houses of the wealthy elites, privacy was not what modern people expect. In those houses, slaves were everywhere, sleeping everywhere, listening everywhere, watching everywhere. Slaveowners treated them as if they did not exist or were invisible most of the time. But the slaves knew all the family's business and loved to gossip about the events of their houses (Veyne).

5.7. Mobs. Neighborhoods could erupt. Mob violence, such as what happened at Ephesus (Acts 19), was frequent. People would pick up rocks or broken roofing tiles and let them fly when rumors got them riled up. The ancient sources refer to people being stoned in Athens, Lystra (Acts 14:19), Ephesus, Smyrna, Alexandria, Pompeii, and Rome among others. It could be dangerous for someone outside the neighborhood (*vicus*) to venture into a strange zone (MacMullen).

6. Social Interaction.

6.1. Socioeconomic Levels. Social scientists (e.g., Sjoberg) have typically identified three economic levels or classes in the preindustrial cities: the upper class, the lower class, and the outcasts, or, as Florence Dupont phrases it: the rich, the poor, and the wretched. In the past, based on allusions from ancient authors, historians have understood the plight of the working class/lower class as extremely precarious and miserable.

6.1.1. The Middling Level. More recently, however, biblical scholars and classicists have sought to describe the lower class with more nuance. They argue for a middling level (not strictly a middle class) between the categories of rich and poor. Bruce Longenecker sought to understand economic groups based on subsistence (minimum daily calories needed to sustain the body). Walter Scheidel and Steven Friesen's cowritten article—based on calculations of gross domestic product—finds, like Longenecker, a number of the well-to-do among the nonelites (those earning up to ten times subsistence income) and many in the comfortable yet modest range. These three scholars find more *wealth in a middling class than previous historians. Others (Oakes; Wallace-Hadrill; Trümper) have used the archaeological remains from Pompeii, Rome, and Delos to suggest even more subgroups in the nonelite class based on the square footage of their apartments/condominiums (control of urban space). At Pompeii, for example, some craft workers were quite well off (living in 2,000-square-foot to 9,600-square-foot dwellings), while others (slaves?) crowded into much smaller spaces (as small as 100 square feet), but there were many levels in between.

Table 1 is my attempt to translate these three models into an understandable comparison.

Table 1. Three Models of Economic Levels

Wealth/subsistence level	Percentage of population		
	Longenecker (urban population)	Scheidel/Friesen (average of "optimistic" and "pessimistic" calculations for the total population of the empire)	Oakes (based on control of urban space in Pompeii)
Senatorial, equestrian, decurial, and other wealth	3	1.5	2.5
Middling level (from moderate surplus to 10 times subsistence)	15	11.5 (includes military)	19.5
Near subsistence	27	14	11
At or below subsistence	30	57	67
Chronically below subsistence	25	16	

The effect of these studies is to see less economic misery among the nonelites and to create a larger middling group between the wealthy elites and the subsistence-level poor. Thus Paul, as an artisan, could have been economically comfortable (Blanton).

6.1.2. The Poor. But one should not overlook the number of poor persons. The three models in the table above calculate the poor (the bottom three categories) at 78 to 87 percent of the population. Even more disturbing is the percentage of the miserably poor—those living chronically below subsistence. These are the persons described in the literature as drinking filthy water from a mud puddle; rummaging through discarded nut hulls, bean pods, and pomegranate rinds in hope of finding edible bits; eating rotten bread thrown to the dogs; wearing rags; shivering in doorways; and, at their death, fighting off dogs and birds of prey (Martial, *Epig.* 1.92.10; 10.5.3-12, in reference to Rome; Alciphron, *Letters of Parasites* 3.24, in reference to Corinth).

One meets the poor not only in the literature but also in their remains. Near the Esquiline graveyard in Rome excavators found seventy-five burial pits containing a mixture of human corpses, animal corpses, sewage, and garbage (Scobie). Ancient sources report that the poor were dumped into these holes and left to rot, obviously alongside dead animals and other waste (Welborn 2015). Such persons—the outcasts, the wretched—are those Paul refers to in 1 Corinthians 1:27-28.

6.2. Educational/Cultural Differences. There was not only economic distance between the wealthy, the middling group, and the poor but also educational/cultural differences. On the one hand, in the cities, literacy seems to have been higher than in the rural areas. This is evidenced by the graffiti scratched on walls (Crossan and Reed; Stambaugh). Apparently, many could write a little and wanted to leave their words—both the informative and the prurient—for others. But, on the other hand, they did not write the language with the same proficiency as the elites. Their wall-scratches are replete with spelling and grammatical errors. The same is true for the Jewish catacombs in Rome. The inscriptions marking their graves show that most Jews spoke Greek but Greek that was of a lower social level (Leon). One wonders how the recipients—many of them no doubt from the lower classes of society—of Paul's lofty letters understood them.

Some persons in the cities did not know the official language at all—whether Latin or Greek. Others would have spoken it not only ungrammatically but also with different pronunciation and intonation. The elites would have had difficulty comprehending them.

Further, the sense of etiquette would contrast markedly with the leisured upper class. The poor had no time to learn the niceties of fine society. What would have been seen as acceptable behavior among the lower classes might have been considered quite repulsive to the upper classes. In turn, the lower classes might have been puzzled at upper-class conventions (Sjoberg; Stambaugh). Not only ethnic mix but also social mix could have caused tensions in a Christian congregation.

6.3. Associations. The nonelite class formed several types of social associations.

6.3.1. Street Associations. Street associations (*vici*, "neighborhoods") were common. In the time of Augustus, they counted 265 such groups in Rome, each with perhaps five hundred males in them. In first-century Rome, a *vicus* included the main street and the side streets emanating from it and had its own religious shrine. Some neighborhoods were named for their ethnic group, others for a prominent landmark nearby. Most streets, however, had the name of their craft, for example, Glass Street, Incense Street, Jewelers' Street, Wainwrights' Street, Vintners' Street, Cobblers' Street. One knew where to go to shop for goods based on such names (MacMullen). This is undoubtedly how Barnabas found Paul in Antioch (Acts 11:25-26).

Street associations provided *friendship and society for workers of like interests and skills. You knew your neighbors and you understood their work because you were in the same trade. The neighborhoods often sponsored their own religious festivals and games, the sort of games the elites would never consider (e.g., capturing the head of a dead horse; Stambaugh).

6.3.2. Taverns/Restaurants. Another location for nonelite fellowship was the tavern/restaurant (Latin *caupona*, *popina*, *taberna*). Here one could not only drink with friends but get a simple meal. The *caupona* was a regular restaurant with tables and seats. It also usually offered a room for the night (and a prostitute). The *popina* was a greasy restaurant with bad food and a lot of drinking. The term *taberna* could refer to any shop but could also mean a bar where hot meals were not usually served but drinking was featured. Several of these restaurants have been excavated at Pompeii. These establishments usually clustered in certain regions. The Subura district of Rome (the depression between the Quirinal and Viminal hills) was known for its low-life taverns and brothels (Dupont). The elites would not go to these places, considering them gatherings of drunken debauchery.

6.3.3. Clubs. Probably the most important social groups for the nonelites were the clubs, confraternities, or guilds (Latin *collegia*, Gk. *thiasoi*). Nearly every city boasted one or more of them. These could be based on trade, religion, *ethnicity, neighborhoods, or household membership. Those based on trade or craft might boast of several hundred members; those based on devotion to a religion or deity probably only a few score. Their purpose was comradeship and a guaranteed decent burial. Although most members were male, there was a substantial minority of women members in many of the associations. Slaves especially were keen to join to ensure a proper burial rather than being tossed in the street or in a pit (Scobie; see above). As a matter of fact, some clubs appealed mostly to slaves. Dues plus gifts from benefactors enabled the members to host banquets like the elites (Kloppenborg).

Such associations were the center of life for the lower class. There are many references to them in the literature and the inscriptions (Stambaugh; MacMullen). From Ephesus, for example, inscriptions tell of a silversmiths' guild, the same one mentioned in Acts 19. But they also tell of many others, such as the bakers' guild, which also rioted on one occasion (Jones; Billings).

The early churches' organization and activities might have been largely patterned on these associations.

7. Labor.

7.1. Aristocratic and Nonelite Attitudes. The urban elites made up only between 1.5 to 3 percent of the total population of the empire. The rest were in varying levels of the lower class (including a middling class). These differences in economic standing meant also differences in attitude toward common labor. Artisans did not enjoy high regard among either the Greek or the Roman aristocracy (Dio Chrysostom, *Ven.* 110; Lucian, *Fug.* 12-13; Cicero, *Off.* 1.42). The ancient elites valued leisure and avoiding manual labor.

But the lower classes did not feel a sense of shame in their labor. They seem to have been proud of their life's work, no matter how humble. While the elites boasted—in their public inscriptions and statues—of their political offices and military honors, the commoners took pride in their trade. Four examples will illustrate. From Rome is a tombstone that describes the deceased as "litter bearer at the Cloaca Maximus [the ancient sewage drain]." Such tombstones often named not only one's occupation/craft but where in the city one practiced it. Also from Rome is "barber at the *vicus* Scauri." From Ephesus there is "worker on the Poseidon [temple] at the gate" and "hemp worker at the Serbelius portico" (MacMullen). The poor were proud of their labor—and celebrated it on their tombstones—even if the elites thought them horribly common and crude.

The lower classes also probably did not share a sense of civic values with the elites. The elites were encultured in the "small-town values of aristocracy" (Stambaugh), which supported the great and glorious empire. The lower classes were more "cynical and street-smart" (Stambaugh). If one were of the senatorial or equestrian class, the empire was a great thing. If not, it could be oppressive.

*7.2. **Skeletal Remains.*** One meets the working class in their skeletal remains. Examination of 139 individuals buried in the volcanic ash at Herculaneum revealed the physical condition of the working class. Their skeletal structures exhibited excessive development of limited muscle groups (evidently from repetitive activities), poor nutrition (thin bones), pathology (arthrosis and fused thoracic vertebrae), and many broken bones (Welborn 2015). Similar results have been obtained from the skeletal remains of ninety-four persons at Corinth. The bones show that a high proportion of the Corinthian working class was malnourished and did physically stressful work (Welborn 2016). A pathological examination of the skeletal remains of eighty-five individuals of the working class from Judea (Jerusalem, Jericho, and Qumran) showed the same living and working conditions (Fiensy). Even though some artisans prospered, all lived a life of hard labor.

*7.3. **Labor of Women.*** Upper-class women for the most part kept to the Roman stereotype of an obedient wife and mother who remained at home tending to the household. If they exercised any influence, it was through their husbands. Increasingly in the relevant period here, however, upper-class women were standing out in culture and in *politics. Some Roman authors in response wrote angry pieces about aggressive women who wore too much makeup and jewelry and who showed off their learning (Stambaugh).

For the lower-class women, however, the picture was different. Graffiti from Pompeii and tomb inscriptions from Ostia and Rome mention women at work as weavers, dressmakers, copyists, amanuenses, teachers, midwives, physicians, grocers, innkeepers, barmaids, entertainers, and barbers (Carcopino; Stambaugh). Indeed, when one's tiny shop was also to a great extent one's domicile (see above), women could hardly be expected to remain out of the public eye. And when one's income involved doing one of those occupations listed above, all family members had to contribute. One can speculate that with egalitarian work expectations came also egalitarian social expectations among the lower classes.

There were also women who would have been considered lower class who rose in wealth and influence. Inscriptions inform of women who succeeded in business: women in the Eastern empire who dealt in luxury goods (Lydia, Acts 16:14), a woman in Pompeii who owned a brick factory, women who became benefactors of cities (Meeks). More and more women joined the men's associations and even became patronesses of them, as Phoebe did of the church in Cenchreae (Rom 16:1-2; MacMullen; Kloppenborg).

8. Religions.

*8.1. **Civic Religion.*** Each city had its gods. One deity in particular protected it and was owed civic devotion. But every city was also full of temples and shrines (Acts 17:16) devoted to a range of deities. Temples served not only for sacrifices but also for offices of city bureaucrats and for social events such as banquets (1 Cor 10:27). The two Roman colonies receiving Pauline letters, Corinth and Philippi, show a complex religious picture. They had three levels of religious devotion: the deities imported from Italy; the traditional Greek gods, sometimes recast in more Roman form; and the local deities and cults (Brélaz; Bookidis).

*8.2. **Imperial Cult.*** From Augustus's time on, residents of the empire worshiped the goddess Roma and the *genius* (guardian spirit) of the emperor. In the eastern part of the empire, already accustomed to considering Hellenistic kings gods, they hailed Augustus and his successors as "god and savior." There were temples from Gaul in the west to Israel in the east for this *worship. The spread of the imperial cult—an abomination to Jews—was one of the common features of Paul's Mediterranean world. Based on coinage, inscriptions, and other archaeological remains, it is known that the imperial cult manifested itself in Corinth, Thessalonica, Philippi, and Ephesus during Paul's time. Many find allusions to the cult in Paul's letters (Crossan and Reed; Brélaz; Harrison).

*8.3. **Oriental Cults.*** There was also growing devotion to Oriental divinities. Rome, Philippi, Corinth, Thessalonica, and Ephesus had temples and inscriptions dedicated to the Egyptian cults of Isis and Serapis.

Many of these cities (all those featured in this article except Colossae) had Jewish communities. They show up not only in the book of Acts but also in inscriptions and other ancient literature (e.g., Josephus; Philo).

9. Conclusion.

The cities were centers of government, culture, commerce, religion, and entertainment. One may contrast them with the countryside (the small villages) as shown in table 2.

Table 2. Cities Versus Villages

Villages	**Cities**
Most were unwalled	Walled
No formal marketplaces, but open spaces may have served informally	Clearly designated and ornamented marketplaces (forum/*agora*)
Topography determined how the streets were laid out	Increasingly laid out in a Hippodamian grid (Thessalonica, Corinth, Philippi, Ephesus)
Cisterns and wells were the main sources of water	Had aqueducts and fountains, but urban centers could never supply all their needs from them
No architecture for entertainment	Theaters, baths, stadia, hippodromes, and amphitheaters
Seldom large structures for religious cults	A host of temples and shrines
Population tended to be homogeneous, with about the same number of women as men	Population was of mixed ethnicity and origin and had far fewer women than men

See also CORINTH; *CURSUS HONORUM*; EPHESUS; ETHNICITY IN PAUL'S WORLD; HONOR/SHAME; PATRONAGE; RELIGIONS, GRECO-ROMAN; SOCIAL-SCIENTIFIC APPROACHES TO PAUL; WEALTH AND POVERTY.

BIBILIOGRAPHY. **B. Billings,** "From House Church to Tenement Church: Domestic Space and the Development of Early Urban Christianity—The Example of Ephesus," *JTS* 62 (2011): 541-69; **B. J. Bitner,** "Mixed-Language Inscribing at Roman Corinth," in *The First Urban Churches*, vol. 2, *Roman Corinth*, ed. J. R. Harrison and L. L. Welborn (Atlanta: SBL Press, 2016), 185-218; **T. R. Blanton,** "Manual Labor and Sustenance," in *Handbook to the Historical Paul*, ed. R. S. Schellenberg and H. Wendt (London: T&T Clark, 2022); **N. Bookidis,** "Religion in Corinth: 146 B.C.E. to 100 C.E.," in *Urban Religion in Roman Corinth: Interdisciplinary Approaches*, ed. D. N. Schowalter and S. J. Friesen (Cambridge, MA: Harvard University Press, 2005), 141-64; **C. Brélaz,** "First Century Philippi: Contextualizing Paul's Visit," in *The First Urban Churches*, vol. 4, *Roman Philippi*, ed. J. R. Harrison and L. L. Welborn (Atlanta: SBL Press, 2018), 153-88; **A. Cadwallader,** "Assessing the Potential of Archaeological Discoveries for the Interpretation of New Testament Texts: The Case of a Gladiator Fragment from Colossae and the Letter to the Colossians," in *The First Urban Churches*, vol. 1, *Methodological Foundations*, ed. J. R. Harrison and L. L. Welborn (Atlanta: SBL Press, 2015), 41-66; **A. H. Cadwallader and J. R. Harrison,** "Perspective on the Lycus Valley: An Inscriptional, Archaeological, Numismatic, and Iconographic Approach," in *The First Urban Churches*, vol. 5, *Colossae, Hierapolis, and Laodicea*, ed. J. R. Harrison and L. L. Welborn (Atlanta: SBL Press, 2019), 3-70; **J. Carcopino,** *Daily Life in Ancient Rome* (New Haven, CT: Yale University Press, 1968); **C. W. Concannon,** "'Not for an Olive Wreath, but Our Lives': Gladiators, Athletes, and Early Christian Bodies," *JBL* 133 (2014): 193-214; **P. Connolly and H. Dodge,** *The Ancient City: Life in Classical Athens and Rome* (Oxford: Oxford University Press, 1998); **J. D. Crossan and J. L. Reed,** *In Search of Paul: How Jesus's Apostle Opposed Rome's Empire with God's Kingdom* (San Francisco: Harper, 2004); **F. Dupont,** *Daily Life in Ancient Rome* (Oxford: Blackwell, 1992); **Y. Eliav,** "Bathhouses as Places of Social and Cultural Interaction," in *The Oxford Handbook of Jewish Daily Life in Roman Palestine*, ed. C. Hezser (Oxford: Oxford University Press, 2010), 605-22; **D. Engels,** *Roman Corinth: An Alternative Model for the Classical City* (Chicago: University of Chicago Press, 1990); **D. A. Fiensy,** *The Archaeology of Daily Life: Ordinary Persons in Late Second Temple Israel* (Eugene, OR: Cascade, 2020); **J. Finegan,** *The Archaeology of the New Testament: The Mediterranean World of the Early Christian Apostles* (Boulder, CO: Westview, 1981); **J. R. Harrison,** "Paul and the Imperial Gospel," *JSNT* 25 (2002): 71-96; **D. G. Horrell,** "Domestic Space and Christian Meetings at Corinth: Imagining New Contexts and the Buildings East of the Theatre," *NTS* 50 (2004): 349-69; **A. H. M. Jones,** *The Greek City from Alexander to Justinian* (Oxford: Clarendon, 1940); **J. S. Kloppenborg,** *Christ's Associations: Connecting and Belonging in the Ancient City* (New Haven, CT: Yale University Press, 2019); **S. Ladstätter et al.,** *Terrace House 2 in Ephesos: An Archaeological Guide* (Istanbul: Homer Kitabevi ve Yayincilik, 2013); **P. Lampe,** "The Roman Christians of Romans 16," in *The Romans Debate*, ed. K. P. Donfried (Peabody, MA: Hendrickson, 1991), 216-30; **R. Last,** "The Neighborhood (Vicus) of the Corinthian Ekklesia: Beyond Family-Based Descriptions of the First Urban Christ-Believers," *JSNT* 38 (2016): 399-425; **H. J. Leon,** *The Jews of Ancient Rome* (Peabody, MA: Hendrickson, 1960); **B. W. Longenecker,** *Remember the Poor: Paul, Poverty, and the Greco-Roman World* (Grand Rapids, MI: Eerdmans, 2010);

R. MacMullen, *Roman Social Relations 50 B.C. to A.D. 284* (New Haven, CT: Yale University Press, 1974); **W. A. Meeks,** *The First Urban Christians: The Social World of the Apostle Paul* (New Haven, CT: Yale University Press, 1983); **J. J. Meggitt,** *Paul, Poverty, and Survival* (Edinburgh: T&T Clark, 1998); **P. Mitchel,** "Human Parasites in the Roman World: Health Consequences of Conquering an Empire," *Parasitology* 144 (2017): 48-58; **J. Murphy-O'Connor,** *St. Paul's Corinth: Texts and Archaeology* (Collegeville, MN: Liturgical Press, 2002); idem, *St. Paul's Ephesus: Texts and Archaeology* (Collegeville, MN: Liturgical Press, 2008); **P. Oakes,** *Empire, Economics, and the New Testament* (Grand Rapids, MI: Eerdmans, 2020); **J. E. Packer,** "Housing and Population in Imperial Ostia and Rome," *JRS* 57, nos. 1-2 (1967): 80-95; **R. Sallares,** *Malaria and Rome: A History of Malaria in Ancient Italy* (Oxford: Oxford University Press, 2002); **W. Scheidel and S. J. Friesen,** "The Size of the Economy and the Distribution of Income in the Roman Empire," *JRS* 99 (2009): 61-91; **A. Scobie,** "Slums, Sanitation, and Mortality in the Roman World," *Klio* 68 (1986): 399-433; **B. Shaw,** "Seasons of Death: Aspects of Mortality in Imperial Rome," *JRS* 86 (1996): 100-138; **G. Sjoberg,** *The Preindustrial City: Past and Present* (New York: Free Press, 1960); **J. E. Stambaugh,** *The Ancient Roman City* (Baltimore: Johns Hopkins University Press, 1988); **M. Trainor,** "Colossae—Colossal in Name Only?," *BAR* 45 (2019): 44-50; **M. Trümper,** "Material and Social Environment of Greco-Roman Households in the East: The Case of Hellenistic Delos," in *Early Christian Families in Context: An Interdisciplinary Dialogue*, ed. D. L. Balch and C. Osiek (Grand Rapids, MI: Eerdmans, 2003), 19-42; **P. Veyne,** ed., *A History of Private Life*, vol. 1, *From Pagan Rome to Byzantium* (Cambridge, MA: Harvard University Press, 1987); **A. Wallace-Hadrill,** "Archaeology of Domus and Insulae," in *Early Christian Families in Context: An Interdisciplinary Dialogue*, ed. D. L. Balch and C. Osiek (Grand Rapids, MI: Eerdmans, 2003), 3-18; **L. L. Welborn,** "The Runaway Paul," *HTR* 92 (1999): 115-63; idem, "The Polis and the Poor: Reconstructing Social Relations from Different Genres of Evidence," in *The First Urban Churches*, vol. 1, *Methodological Foundations*, ed. J. R. Harrison and L. L. Welborn (Atlanta: SBL Press, 2015), 189-243; idem, "Inequality in Roman Corinth: Evidence from Diverse Sources Evaluated by a Neo-Ricardian Model," in *The First Urban Churches*, vol. 2, *Roman Corinth*, ed. J. R. Harrison and L. L. Welborn (Atlanta: SBL Press, 2016), 47-84; **L. M. White,** "Urban Development and Social Change in Imperial Ephesos," in *Ephesos Metropolis of Asia: An Interdisciplinary Approach to Its Archaeology, Religion, and Culture*, ed. H. Koester (Valley Forge, PA: Trinity Press International, 1995), 27-80; **E. M. Yamauchi,** *New Testament Cities in Western Asia Minor* (Grand Rapids, MI: Baker, 1980).

D. A. Fiensy

V

VIOLENCE

Paul consistently references the crucifixion of Jesus *Christ and the persecution endured by the early followers of Jesus. In addition to these central images of violence, weapons and warfare, verbal threats, physical discipline, and scenes of apocalyptic *judgment also weave through his letters. It is important to recognize the presence of violence and question its significance for Paul's life and theology.

1. Defining Violence
2. Violence in the Roman Empire
3. Violence in the Letters of Paul
4. Interpreting Violence in Paul's Letters
5. Conclusion

1. Defining Violence.

The vocabulary of violence in the Bible most often indicates physical acts that cause harm (for instance, *ḥāmās* and *šōd* in Gen 6:11; Ps 25:19; Prov 21:7; Is 59:6). Speech associated with injustice and, by extension, economic, legal, and political oppression are also identified with violence (Ex 23:1; Ps 140:11; Prov 10:11; Is 53:9; Ezek 18:10-13). Essentially, in the Bible violence means to cause harm or injury of some sort to another being.

Contemporary academic approaches to violence expand on and complexify this simple definition (see Desjardins, 12-13; Kirk-Duggan, 2-5; Neufeld, 1-7). The harm may be intentional or unintentional. That is, an act of violence may be identified as such by its victim, even if the perpetrator did not intend to cause harm. Likewise, an act of violence may be abusive, or it may be legitimate within particular social circumstances (for instance, policing or war). The harm inflicted may be physical, mental, emotional, or spiritual. Violence also incorporates economic, political, racial, and cultural injury. As such, acts of violence can occur in interpersonal, institutional, and social contexts.

Consequently, the concept of violence in contemporary analysis is flexible enough to incorporate domestic abuse, war, racism, the unequal distribution of *wealth, political policies, and more. Violence "diminishes the inherent dignity of the created, denying the imago Dei in humanity" (Kirk-Duggan, 5). This broad understanding of violence makes the analysis of violence in biblical texts, including the letters of Paul, a necessary theological pursuit.

2. Violence in the Roman Empire.

Violence pervaded daily life in the Roman Empire (see especially Carter, 3-12; Punt, 27-32). Interpersonal violence was common. In *households, men and women directed physical and verbal violence against enslaved people and children, and husbands enacted violence against wives (Valerius Maximus, *Fact. dict.* 6.3.6-12; Seneca, *Clem.* 1.14; Juvenal, *Sat.* 6.474-511). Interpersonal violence also occurred in insults and fights in public spaces (Fagan, 231-45). *Teachers whipped their students as part of their education (Suetonius, *Gramm.* 9). The violence of gladiatorial shows and military parades, which might include displays of battle scenes and public executions, entertained the Romans (Josephus, *J.W.* 7.23-24, 37-38; Cassius Dio, *Hist.* 60.13.1-4).

Beyond the interpersonal level, the enactment of violence was a fundamental value of masculinity and therefore of Roman *identity (see, e.g., Polybius, *Hist.* 10.15.4-5; Valerius Maximus, *Fact. dict.* 2.7, preface, 2.7.14). Rome's military might was made visible by soldiers in city streets, the imagery of coins and imperial statues, and inscriptions. Public floggings and crucifixion displayed Roman power, as did the system of *slavery. Slaves were captured in war, chained, beaten, branded, maimed, and raped (Valerius Maximus, *Fact. dict.* 1.7.4; Pliny the Elder, *Nat.* 18.4.21). The centralization of political power and wealth among the Roman elites enabled oppressive social and economic practices that disadvantaged the poor.

Violence was pervasive in the Roman Empire, from the practices of military occupation to the system of slavery to daily life in a household. The sights and sounds of life in Roman cities were marked by violence. The people in Paul's churches lived within this reality, and it is reflected throughout the *letters Paul wrote.

3. Violence in the Letters of Paul.
Paul's letters incorporate a range of examples of violence, including verbal threats, scenes of apocalyptic judgment, and the physical abuse endured by Jesus and his followers.

*3.1. **Violence and Sin.*** Paul includes physical and verbal violence on two vice lists: murder and *hybristēs*, a term that can refer to verbal or physical abuse, in Romans 1:29-30, and a reference to brutality in 2 Timothy 3:1-7. Similarly, in Romans 3:9-17 a string of OT quotations includes bloodshed and verbal abuse as examples of unrighteous, ungodly behaviors. The rule of *sin and *death over the world is expressed in the language of war and enmity in Romans 5:14, 17; 6:12-14; 7:21-24.

*3.2. **Persecution.*** Before his *conversion, Paul persecuted the followers of Jesus (Acts 8:1-3; 9:1-2; 26:9-11). After his conversion, Paul describes his acts as excessive, violent, and destructive expressions of his zeal (Gal 1:13-14; Phil 3:6). The enactment of persecution and the persecution endured by Paul and the other early followers of Jesus included physical, verbal, and legislative violence (1 Cor 15:30-32; 2 Cor 6:3-10; 11:23-27). In 1 Corinthians 4:9-13, Paul says he and the other apostles are exhibited as a "spectacle," a description that reflects the public practices of corporal punishment and execution in the Roman Empire.

Paul experienced his own *suffering as a death sentence (2 Cor 1:8-11). Persecution is part of the Christian life in Romans 8:35-36 and 1 Thessalonians 1:6; 2:1-2, 14. To be like Christ means to share in Christ's suffering (Rom 8:10-11, 17; Gal 1:24; Phil 3:10; Bowens, 295-96).

*3.3. **Crucifixion.*** Crucifixion displayed imperial power over slaves and the peoples conquered by Rome. Paul's reference to the public display of Jesus' crucifixion in Galatians 3:1 reflects this rhetorical function. Likewise, Paul describes the crucifixion as foolish and weak by the standards of the world (1 Cor 1:17-25, 2:1-5; 2 Cor 13:4), as humiliation (Phil 2:8), and as an offense (Gal 5:11), terms that reflect the Roman understanding of this method of execution.

Some of Paul's references to the crucifixion expand on Jesus' experience of physical violence (Rom 4:25; 1 Cor 1:5; Eph 2:16). The merging of crucifixion with sacrificial imagery in Romans 3:25 and Ephesians 5:2 brings the violence of Jesus' death further into focus, comparing Jesus with the animals butchered, bled, and dismembered as part of *worship in *temples from Jerusalem to Rome.

*3.4. **Divine Violence.*** Paul refers somewhat frequently to the *wrath of God. These references tend to be general, but associated words and imagery indicate that violence is part of divine wrath (Rom 1:18; 2:5, 8, 15-16; 3:5-8; 9:22; 11:32; 1 Thess 4:6; Col 3:6). This imagery extends into apocalyptic scenes of the parousia of Jesus and ensuing divine judgment and destruction (1 Cor 15:23-26; 2 Thess 2:8), described as a time of wrath in 1 Thessalonians 1:10, and associated with battle cries and trumpets in 1 Thessalonians 4:16.

*3.5. **Church Discipline.*** Paul uses strong language against his *opponents in Galatians. He pronounces a *curse, anathema, on anyone who preaches a *gospel different from the gospel originally preached by Paul (notably, he includes himself in this judgment; Gal 1:8-9). He also expresses the desire that those who are attempting to convince the *Gentiles of Galatia to be circumcised would emasculate themselves (Gal 5:12).

Paul employs the language, imagery, and threats of violent discipline in 1 and 2 Corinthians. Identifying himself with paternal authority, Paul asks his "children" in Corinth whether he should come to them in *love and gentleness or with a stick to discipline them (1 Cor 4:14-21). He then pronounces judgment on the man who is having sex with his stepmother. The church community must hand the man over to *Satan for the destruction of the *flesh (1 Cor 5:3-5). That is, the community must cut ties with the person (note 1 Cor 5:2, 7, 9-13).

It is possible that handing over to Satan for the purpose of destruction may also involve physical punishment or death as a result of being cut off from the community (compare destruction in 1 Cor 10:10 and 1 Thess 5:5; the connection of sin with disease and death in 1 Cor 11:30; and handing over to Satan for the purpose of *discipline in 1 Tim 1:20). The significance of Paul's instruction in 1 Corinthians 5 is debated (see Reeder, 156-59).

Finally, in 2 Corinthians 10:1-6, Paul claims to be waging war against his opponents in Corinth with divine weapons. He takes thoughts captive and punishes every disobedience. He concludes the letter with a warning that he will not be lenient when he visits *Corinth (2 Cor 13:1-4).

3.6. Systemic Violence. Paul acknowledges and, in some cases, implicitly supports imperial systems of violence. The reference to the authority of the imperial government in Romans 13:1-7 includes examples of physical and economic violence: the sword, wrath, and taxation (see McCaulley, 34-41). The household codes in Ephesians 5:21–6:9 and Colossians 3:18–4:1 recognize the power imbalances of Roman society between husbands and wives, fathers and children, and slave owners and slaves. Paul does not clearly condemn the system of slavery, instead telling enslaved people not to be concerned about their position and returning the slave Onesimus to his owner (1 Cor 7:21; Philem 12-16). The inherent oppression and violence of slavery are represented in the metaphor of enslavement to sin and death in Romans 5–8 and the allegory of Hagar in Galatians 4:21-31 (see Bowens, 297-98).

3.7. Peace and War. War imagery pervades Paul's letters in general (see Gaventa, 62-65). He presents Jesus' crucifixion as divine victory in the war against sin and death, rescuing captives—human beings—from their dominion (Rom 5–8; Col 2:8, 15; Eph 4:8; Gaventa, 70-74). In Romans 8:37, Jesus' followers are conquerors. Christians should put on God's armor to join Jesus' war (Rom 13:12; 2 Cor 6:7; 10:1-6; Eph 6:11-17; 1 Thess 5:8); Paul identifies the followers of Jesus and their leaders as soldiers in Philippians 2:25; 1 Timothy 1:18; 6:12; and 2 Timothy 2:3-4; 4:7.

As already discussed, Paul employs the language of war against his opponents in Corinth in 2 Corinthians 10:1-6. Earlier in the same letter, Paul describes the apostles being led in triumphal procession, a remarkable statement that reflects the victory of God in Christ with the kind of parade used to celebrate Roman military conquest. In the logic of Paul's image, apostles and perhaps all Christians are conquered by God and taken captive, put on display to showcase the power of God. As such, their bodies testify to life in God, but also they reek of death to those who are not part of the procession (2 Cor 2:14-17). This text displays Paul's richly imaginative use of the imagery of violence and the complicated nature of violence in Paul's letters.

Paul's references to *peace can be understood as a counterpart to his imagery of war. In the Bible and across the Roman Empire, one definition of peace correlated it with victory over an enemy (e.g., Is 52:1-10; Zech 9:9-17; Cicero, *Off.* 1.35; Virgil, *Aen.* 6.851-853). Accordingly, the God of peace defeats Satan violently in Romans 16:20. Peace marks the end of hostility with God in Romans 5:1-10 and Colossians 1:20, and the end of hostility between Jew and Gentile in Ephesians 2:13-14.

3.8. Nonviolence. Despite the common use of violent images and words in his letters, Paul proclaims a message of nonviolence and nonretaliation against opponents outside the Christian community (see especially Swartley, 212-15; Gorman, 143-55). In Romans 12:14-21, he instructs the church to bless persecutors, live peaceably with all, leave vengeance to God, and overcome evil with good. Briefer statements in 1 Corinthians 4:12-13 and 1 Thessalonians 5:15 also expect Christians to endure persecution without retaliation, instead doing good to their persecutors.

Paul limits certain expressions of violence that would have been common and acceptable in Roman society. Husbands should not abuse their wives in Colossians 3:19. Fathers should not provoke their children in Ephesians 6:4 and Colossians 3:21. Slave owners are limited from abuse in Ephesians 6:9 and Colossians 4:1. The new life of Christians in Colossians 3:5-10 excludes anger, wrath, and the misuse of speech. Finally, in 1 Timothy 3:3 and Titus 1:7; 3:2, bullying and anger must be replaced with gentleness and kindness to all.

4. Interpreting Violence in Paul's Letters.

John Gager and E. Leigh Gibson describe Paul as a man of violence whose letters are permeated by "a rhetoric of violence" (Gager and Gibson, 17, 19; see also Desjardins, 69-99; Roetzel, 78-79). While Paul's historical situation in the Roman Empire goes some way to explaining his reliance on violent words, imagery, and threats, the task of interpreting such texts remains. In recent years, several hermeneutical frameworks have emerged: Girardian mimetic violence, identity formation, and postcolonialism.

4.1. Mimetic Violence. Robert Hamerton-Kelly adapts René Girard's theory of mimetic violence and scapegoating to the study of Paul's letters. According to Hamerton-Kelly, as a Pharisee Paul practiced mimetic violence against the followers of Jesus. His conversion brought about the realization that violence distorts the message of love in the *law of Moses. Accordingly, the postconversion Paul preaches a message of love and the avoidance of violence (Hamerton-Kelly, 8-10, 63).

Girard's theory of mimetic violence has been critiqued for Christian triumphalism and anti-Semitic, Marcionite tendencies, concerns that are also problematic for Hamerton-Kelly (see Gager and Gibson,

13-15). Moreover, Hamerton-Kelly does not adequately address the continued significance of violence in Paul's postconversion writings. His Girardian analysis of Paul has garnered limited support.

*4.2. **Identity Formation.*** The construction of group identity involves the differentiation between insiders and outsiders. Violence can be a tool in the process of differentiation (see Reeder, 8-9). While Paul does not direct violence against people outside the community, he does use anger, threats, and the potential for physical discipline to develop and protect identity within the community (Desjardins, 69, 77, 100). Jeremy Punt suggests identity formation and "othering," particularly within the context of the Roman Empire, provide useful frameworks for interpreting the violent imagery and rhetoric directed against Paul's opponents (Punt, 30-35).

*4.3. **Postcolonialism.*** In a postcolonial reading, Paul understands the Roman Empire to be under divine judgment. His letters make use of accommodation, imitation, and protest in explaining this judgment, and Christian participation in the *empire and the reign of God (Carter, 25-26, 86). Paul reflects the imperial, systemic violence of slavery, patriarchy, and power (Carter, 92). But he also adapts the language and symbols of the empire in new and unexpected ways. The centrality of the crucifixion in Paul's theology is significant in this respect. By identifying the crucifixion of Jesus as the means of reconciliation with God, Paul subverts a primary symbol of Roman oppression (Carter, 88).

5. Conclusion.

The prevalence of violence in Roman society, rhetoric, and propaganda makes the use of violent images and ideas in Paul's letters somewhat unremarkable; Paul reflects his social context. However, the significance and function of violence in the empire are radically reinterpreted by the crucifixion of Jesus and Christian participation in Jesus' sufferings through believers' own experiences of persecution. Finally, while Paul does not proclaim an end to systemic violence such as slavery and patriarchy, he does critique the excessive violence of Roman daily life, and he rejects violent retribution against enemies. Paul teaches peace, love, and gentleness as ways of life. In these ways, subtly, Paul reframes the discourse of violence in Roman society.

See also CROSS; DISCIPLINE, CHURCH; EMPIRE; HOUSEHOLDS AND HOUSEHOLD CODES; IDENTITY; OPPONENTS OF PAUL; PEACE, RECONCILIATION; ROMAN CHRISTIANITY; SLAVE, SLAVERY; WEALTH AND POVERTY; WRATH, DESTRUCTION.

BIBLIOGRAPHY. **L. M. Bowens,** *African American Readings of Paul: Reception, Resistance and Transformation* (Grand Rapids, MI: Eerdmans, 2020); **W. Carter,** *The Roman Empire and the New Testament: An Essential Guide* (Nashville: Abingdon, 2006); **M. Desjardins,** *Peace, Violence and the New Testament* (Sheffield: Sheffield Academic, 1997); **G. G. Fagan,** "Urban Violence: Street, Forum, Bath, Circus, and Theater," in *The Topography of Violence in the Greco-Roman World*, ed. W. Riess and G. G. Fagan (Ann Arbor: University of Michigan Press, 2016); 231-47; **J. G. Gager and E. L. Gibson,** "Violent Acts and Violent Language in the Apostle Paul," in *Violence in the New Testament*, ed. S. Matthews and E. L. Gibson (New York: T&T Clark, 2005), 13-21; **B. R. Gaventa,** "The Rhetoric of Violence and the God of Peace in Paul's Letter to the Romans," in *Paul, John, and Apocalyptic Eschatology*, ed. J. Krans et al., NovTSup 149 (Leiden: Brill, 2013), 61-75; **M. J. Gorman,** *Inhabiting the Cruciform God: Kenosis, Justification, and Theosis in Paul's Narrative Soteriology* (Grand Rapids, MI: Eerdmans, 2009); **R. G. Hamerton-Kelly,** *Sacred Violence: Paul's Hermeneutic of the Cross* (Minneapolis: Fortress, 1992); **C. A. Kirk-Duggan,** *Violence and Theology*, Horizons in Theology (Nashville: Abingdon, 2006); **E. McCaulley,** *Reading While Black: African American Biblical Interpretation as an Exercise in Hope* (Downers Grove, IL: IVP Academic, 2020); **T. R. Y. Neufeld,** *Killing Enmity: Violence and the New Testament* (Grand Rapids, MI: Baker Academic, 2011); **J. Punt,** "Violence in the New Testament and the Roman Empire: Ambivalence, Othering, Agency," in *Coping with Violence in the New Testament*, ed. P. G. R. de Villiers and J. W. van Henten, Studies in Theology and Religion 16 (Leiden: Brill, 2012), 23-39; **C. A. Reeder,** *The Enemy in the Household: Family Violence in Deuteronomy and Beyond* (Grand Rapids, MI: Baker Academic, 2012); **C. J. Roetzel,** "The Language of War (2 Cor. 10:1-6) and the Language of Weakness (2 Cor. 11:21b-13:10)," in *Violence, Scripture, and Textual Practice in Early Judaism and Christianity*, ed. R. S. Boustan, A. P. Jassen, and C. J. Roetzel (Leiden: Brill, 2009), 77-98; **W. Swartley,** *Covenant of Peace: The Missing Peace in New Testament Theology and Ethics* (Grand Rapids, MI: Eerdmans, 2006).

C. A. Reeder

VIRTUES AND VICES. *See* ETHICS.

VISIONS, ECSTATIC EXPERIENCE

Readers have frequently dismissed Paul's references to vision and ecstasy as marginal, since they are not frequent. However, the letters are studded at key moments by revelations and are founded on the paradigmatic *apocalypse* of Jesus as Lord. Furthermore, there are references to inspired seeing (*horaō*, 1 Cor 9:1) and unveiling (*apokalypsis*) throughout, including Paul's call-vision (1 Cor 1:11-12, 16), which Luke also relates (Acts 9; 22; 26). Paul's attitude toward visions is complicated by claims to authority by opponent visionaries in 2 Corinthians and (if Pauline) Colossians (2 Cor 11:13; Col 2:18).

1. Pauline Visions in Acts
2. Paul's Ambivalent View
3. The Heavenly Journey

1. Pauline Visions in Acts.
Paul's initial vision (*horama*, Acts 9:12; *optasia*, Acts 26:19) is narrated thrice by Luke (Acts 9:1-9; 22:6-11; 26:13-19), once in the third person, and twice by Luke's Paul in self-defense. In Acts, revelations direct Paul's *ministry (Acts 9:12; 16:9-10; 18:9-11; 21:9-11; 22:17-21; 23:11; 27:23-24), and corroborate God's plan as it includes the *Gentiles. Thus, the *Holy Spirit guides early leaders partly by visions during contentious times.

2. Paul's Ambivalent View.
Though Luke and Paul differ in their approach, Paul also understands his inaugural vision as foundational for his ministry. In Galatians, he describes his apostleship as catalyzed by an *apokalypsis* (Gal 1:1, 12), and his *gospel as consonant with that of the Jerusalem *apostles (Gal 2:1-2). Ecstatic, prophetic, or visionary experiences are not self-authenticating but require the judgment of the *church (1 Cor 14:29-30) and must be in line with the received gospel (Gal 1:8). It bears remembering that Jesus' *resurrection itself was verified by coordinated visions (*optanomai, optomai*, 1 Cor 15:6-8) that fulfilled Scripture (Dan 12:2-3). While Paul taught that some have specific revelatory gifts, the "vision" of Jesus as Lord is common to all and transforms the church (2 Cor 3:16-18; 4:6). Paul refers to revelatory experiences when his apostleship is being questioned (Gal 1:12, 16; 2:2; 1 Cor 9:1) and seems conversant with rabbinic mysticism (2 Cor 2:14-16; 12; Rom 10:6-8; see Humphrey 1999; 2007; Scott; Segal). While apostles are characterized by certain signs, including direct sight of the Lord (1 Cor 9:1; 2 Cor 12:12), Paul implicitly contrasts the role of leadership in the old and new *covenants. Thus, in 2 Corinthians 3–4, Paul distinguishes Moses' veiled face and Ezekiel's esoteric vision of the appearance of the likeness of the *glory of *God from open-faced Christians who *together* perceive "the light of the *knowledge of the glory of God in the face of Jesus" (2 Cor 4:6 NRSV).

3. The Heavenly Journey.
Disagreement continues concerning the relationship of the vision in 2 Corinthians 12 to Paul's calling-vision on the road to Damascus. The passage also presents mysteries: Paul's conception of multiple heavens; the actual content of his vision (objective or subjective "visions of the Lord"); the "messenger from *Satan," whether this vision is a Christian variant of rabbinic *merkavah* mysticism (Segal); and which other revelations Paul has in mind (2 Cor 12:1).

3.1. Context. The specific challenge in interpreting this pericope is its context within 2 Corinthians 10–12—a "fool's speech" and reluctant apologia intended to redirect readers (2 Cor 12:19). Paul's purpose is to emphasize the weakness of the *cross, but secondarily to salvage his pastoral role in the face of *opponents. His self-deprecation is not merely a ploy but a model that he commends to the faithful; there is thus both a parodic and earnest aspect to 2 Corinthians 10–12, and to the vision-report in particular.

3.2. Literary Antecedents and Cosmology. Paul does not encourage mystical speculation and so frustrates readerly expectations set up by an introduction promising esoteric detail (2 Cor 12:2-4). Unfortunately, not all have heeded his caution, as we see in the apocryphal Apocalypse of Paul, which sought to supply esoterica where Paul was silent. While heavenly ascent is widely attested in ancient literature, the apparatus of Paul's vision is mostly Jewish, incongruously set as evidence within the classical form of the fool's speech. It recalls Jewish apocalypses and *cosmology, paradise and "the third heaven" (2 En. 8.1-8; Apoc. Mos. 40.2), angelic mediators, and ineffable voices and sights (Bowker; Scott; Segal; Young). Noticing such links does not preclude also seeing contrasts (Humphrey 2007).

3.3. The Thorn in the Flesh. Scholars continue to debate Paul's thorn in the flesh, identifying it with a loss of sight, epilepsy, unimposing public speech (2 Cor 11:6), and even human detractors. In the context of a vision-report, the thorn recalls the danger of ascending to the heavens, while the messenger (*angelos*) recalls the traditional interpreting angel in apocalypses. In the larger context of the fool's speech, the reference becomes ironic, since Paul privileged vision issues in a weakened state. This leads to the recapitulation of Paul's major theme, that believers should boast only in the weakness of Christ (1 Cor 1:17-31) and that (God's) strength can be nurtured in weakness (2 Cor 4:7-12; 12:9-10).

3.4. The Rhetorical Structure and Theology. The vision-report must be read both as a unit and as part of the fool's speech. When 2 Corinthians 12 begins with formal features of the apocalypse, we anticipate a vision, an interpretation, and some parenesis. These expectations are partially met, since the audition (God's word) is interpreted, and the apostle emphasizes what he has learned, which readers should emulate. As part of the fool's speech, the vision also provides a surprise ending. We expect the defense for Paul's authority to be clinched by a supernatural event; instead the rhetoric is reversed, so that the reader is invited to question assumptions regarding true spiritual strength. Paul's complex rhetoric is risky, since the reader must collaborate to grasp his purpose (see Humphrey 2007; Plank). Earlier readers of Paul were distracted by the unseen world, which the apostle declined to describe; contemporary readers may be distracted by Paul's appeal to experience, seeing it as merely a power play, if they refuse to follow Paul's cue and position his speech within the metanarrative of the crucified Lord.

See also APOSTLE; CONVERSION AND CALL OF PAUL; CORINTHIANS, SECOND LETTER TO THE; COSMOLOGY; MINISTRY; OPPONENTS OF PAUL; PAUL AND JUDAISM; PAUL IN ACTS; PROPHET, PAUL AS.

BIBLIOGRAPHY. **W. Baird,** "Visions, Revelation, and Ministry: Reflections on 2 Corinthians 12:1-5 and Galatians 1:11-17," *JBL* 104 (1985): 651-62; **E. Benz,** *Paulus als Visionäer* (Wiesbaden: Steiner, 1952); **H. D. Betz,** *Paul's Apology: II Corinthians 10–13 and the Socratic Tradition* (Berkeley: Center for Hermeneutical Studies in Hellenistic and Modern Culture, 1975); **J. Bowker,** "'Merkabah' Visions and the Visions of Paul," *JSS* 16 (1971): 157-73; **C. Forbes,** "Comparison, Self-Praise and Irony: Paul's Boasting and the Conventions of Hellenistic Rhetoric," *NTS* 32 (1986): 1-30; **E. M. Humphrey,** "Why Bring the Word Down? The Rhetoric of Demonstration and Disclosure in Romans 9:30–10:21," in *Romans and the People of God,* ed. S. K. Soderlund and N. T. Wright (Grand Rapids, MI: Eerdmans, 1999), 129-48; idem, *And I Turned to See the Voice: The Rhetoric of Vision in the New Testament* (Grand Rapids, MI: Baker, 2007), 31-102; **A. T. Lincoln,** "'Paul the Visionary': The Setting and Significance of the Rapture to Paradise in II Corinthians xii.1-10," *NTS* 25 (1979): 206-20; **K. A. Plank,** *Paul and the Irony of Affliction* (Atlanta: Scholars Press, 1987); **H. Saake,** "Paulus als Ekstatiker: Pneumatologische Beobachtung zu 2 Kor. 12, 1-10," *NovT* 15 (1973): 152-60; **P. Schaefer,** "New Testament and *Hekhalot* Literature: The Journey into Heaven in Paul and in Merkevah Mysticism," *JJS* 35 (1984): 19-35; **J. M. Scott,** "The Triumph of God in 2 Cor 2:14," *NTS* 42 (1996): 260-81; **A. F. Segal,** *Paul the Convert: The Apostolate and Apostasy of Saul the Pharisee* (New Haven, CT: Yale University Press, 1990); **R. P. Spittler,** "The Limits of Ecstasy: An Exegesis of 2 Corinthians 12:1-10," in *Current Issues in Biblical and Patristic Interpretations,* ed. G. F. Hawthorne (Grand Rapids, MI: Eerdmans, 1975), 259-66; **J. D. Tabor,** *Things Unutterable: Paul's Ascent to Parades in Its Greco-Roman, Judaic and Early Christian Contexts* (Lanham, MD: University Press of America, 1986); **B. Young,** "The Ascension Motif of 2 Corinthians 12 in Jewish, Christian and Gnostic Texts," *GTJ* 9 (1988): 73-103.

E. M. Humphrey

VISITS TO JERUSALEM. *See* CHRONOLOGY OF PAUL; TRAVEL AND ITINERARY PLANS.

VOLUNTARY ASSOCIATIONS. *See* SOCIAL-SCIENTIFIC APPROACHES TO PAUL; URBAN SETTING OF PAUL'S CHURCHES.

WEAK. *See* ROMANS, LETTER TO THE; STRONG AND WEAK.

WEALTH AND POVERTY

While older scholarship noted Paul's lack of attention to this topic, more recent scholarship presents wealth and poverty in Pauline epistles not as a peripheral or isolated concern but as an integral and corollary part of his *ministry rooted in the *grace of the *Lord Jesus *Christ.

1. Socioeconomic Level of Pauline Communities
2. Generous Use of Wealth and Warning Against Love of Money
3. "Remember the Poor"
4. The Collection

1. Socioeconomic Level of Pauline Communities.

For the last century or so, Pauline scholars have argued that Paul's communities reflected a relative cross-section of society, meaning that Pauline communities mostly consisted of members from the lower strata with a few members having greater resources, minus the wealthiest and the poorest sectors. Steven Friesen and Bruce Longenecker's respective heuristic Poverty Scale (PS) and Economic Scale (ES) in the urban context of the Roman Empire (see table 1) have advanced this discussion by providing a more detailed and concrete socioeconomic mapping of Roman urban society and Pauline communities within it.

The first three categories identify the formal ranks of imperial, regional, and municipal elites (*honestiores*). While the rest of the categories fall under the generic umbrella of the nonelites (*humiliores*), scale 4 identifies a middling group of some merchants, traders, artisans, and military veterans who enjoyed moderate surplus of wealth (Friesen, 7 percent). The relatively poor (*penētes*; PS 5-6, 22 percent, 40 percent respectively; ES 5-6) are the ones who could afford to provide at least an adequate subsistence for themselves and their families, that is, a suitable dwelling, food, and clothing. Scale 7 consists of the destitute (*ptōchoi*), such as beggars, unskilled day laborers, and unattached widows and orphans who lived at or below the level of minimum existence, lacking necessary subsistence for food, shelter, and clothing (Friesen, 28 percent). Longenecker's more optimistic economic scale significantly expands the middling group (ES 4) to 15 percent of urban population and the "stable near subsistence" level (ES 5) to 27 percent of urban population, while reducing the last two groups of living at and below subsistence level (ES 6 and ES 7) to 30 percent and 25 percent of urban population, respectively.

Judging from the evidence from the Pauline letters (both undisputed and disputed), in the Pauline communities of the Greco-Roman urban setting, their members were drawn predominantly from merchants, free laborers and artisans, *slaves, and recent immigrants, groups that constituted the urban plebs (PS 5/6; ES 5/6)—compared to Acts's portrayal of some in the upper strata such as leading men and women of Berea (PS/ES 2-3; e.g., Acts 13:50; 17:12, 34; 18:7-8), which points to Acts' apologetic concern for upward vertical spread of the *gospel in concert with geographical spread of the gospel.

As a group, the Pauline Christians would have shared the typical anxieties and insecurities of urban plebs over their severe socioeconomic realities. Paul, whose Roman *citizenship is apologetically highlighted in Acts (Acts 16:37-39; 22:25-29), mentions not his Roman citizenship but his own poverty and afflictions to defend his apostolic ministry and to highlight the spiritual riches it offers (1 Cor 4:9-13; 2 Cor 4:8-10; 6:10; 11:21-33). Paul's (possible) voluntary downward mobility (Friesen, PS 6 or 7) might have been based on Christ's own example of "poverty," which primarily meant the *kenōsis* of Christ but also evokes the image of Jesus' earthly poverty (2 Cor 8:9; cf. 2 Cor 6:10).

At the same time, despite such harsh realities, a degree of moderate wealth was to be expected in the house churches founded by Paul: that is, the middling group of the relatively prosperous and stable (PS 4/5; ES 4/5), those who could offer their places for assemblies and hospitality for Paul and his associates and therefore act as patrons for the communities (e.g., Phoebe in Rom 16:1-2; Gaius and Crispus in 1 Cor 1:14-16; Erastus in Rom 16:23; Philemon in Philem 1-2).

The Pauline communities were not exempt from the tension between the rich and the poor, particularly surrounding the *Lord's Supper, including social pretensions and prejudices (1 Cor 1:11-12; 6:12-20; 11:17-34). Some wealthier members (thus with greater leisure time) of the Corinthian community were apparently arriving at the meal earlier, consuming much of the food and drink without sharing them, and thus humiliating the have-nots by their selfish and greedy behavior (1 Cor 11:21-22, 33). This practice resembled the customary practices and values of the Greco-Roman banquets in the *patronage system, where wealthy patrons would have assigned the best and the largest part of food to their privileged guests and patrons, while the patron's (poor) clients would be treated with shame.

Table 1. Comparison of Population Percentage in Poverty Scale (PS) of Friesen and Economic Scale (ES) of Longenecker in the Urban Context of the Roman Empire

Scale: Friesen/ Longenecker	Categories	Includes	Friesen %	Longenecker %
PS 1/ES 1	**Imperial elites**	imperial dynasty, Roman senatorial families, a few retainers, local royalty, a few freedpersons	0.04%	**ES 1-3: 3%** (the same percentage for the total elite groups; no further breakdown given)
PS 2/ES 2	**Regional or provincial elites**	equestrian families, provincial officials, some retainers, some decurial families, some freedpersons, some retired military officers	1%	See above
PS 3/ES 3	**Municipal elites**	most decurial families, wealthy men and women who did not hold office, some freedpersons, some retainers, some veterans, some merchants	1.76%	See above
PS 4/ES 4	**Moderate surplus resources**	some merchants, some traders, some freedpersons, some artisans (especially those who employed others), and military veterans Longenecker adds two particular groups: *apparitores*, those "working for civic magistrates as scribes, messengers, lectors, and heralds"; and *Augustales*, mostly freedmen who comprised the priesthood of the cult of Augustus	7% (estimated)	15%

Scale: Friesen/ Longenecker	Categories	Includes	Friesen %	Longenecker %
PS 5/ES 5	**Stable near subsistence level** (with reasonable hope of remaining above the minimum level to sustain life)	many merchants and traders, regular wage earners, artisans, large shop owners, freedpersons, some farm families	**22%** (estimated)	**27%**
PS 6/ES 6	**At subsistence level** (and often below minimum level to sustain life)	small farm families, laborers (skilled and unskilled), artisans (especially those employed by others), wage earners, most merchants and traders, small shop/tavern owners	**40%**	**30%**
PS 7/ES 7	**Below subsistence level**	some farm families, unattached widows, orphans, beggars, disabled, unskilled day laborers, prisoners	**28%**	**25%**

Paul refuses to commend the Corinthians in this behavior and division (1 Cor 11:22) and reminds them of the true theology and practice of the Lord's Supper, rooted in Christ's self-giving on behalf of the people so that they might proclaim Christ's *death until he comes (1 Cor 11:23-26). Paul then warns the Corinthians to partake in the Lord's Supper with self-examination that their eating and drinking without "discerning the *body" of believers will incur God's *judgment (1 Cor 11:27-32). Therefore, when they gather for the meal, they should wait for one another (1 Cor 11:33). In order for the Corinthians to truly proclaim Christ's death through the Lord's Supper, the community must have unity and show genuine concern for others, especially the poor, to share in the table of the Lord.

2. Generous Use of Wealth and Warning Against Love of Money.

The standard Pauline teachings concerning use of wealth are sharing/charity (good works) and *hospitality for fellow believers, which are shared by the rest of the NT (Heb 13:2, 16; 1 Pet 4:9; 3 Jn 5-8). These teachings follow traditional Jewish piety based on the concern and activity of God and Christ: caring for the poor (Gal 2:10), working with one's own hands as to avoid idleness and dependence (1 Thess 4:11-12; 2 Thess 3:6-12; Eph 4:28), warnings against greed (*pleonexia*; 1 Cor 5:11; 1 Tim 3:8; Titus 1:7), and generosity and hospitality toward others, particularly fellow believers (Rom 12:8, 13; 1 Cor 16:2; 2 Cor 8:2; Eph 4:28), rooted in Christ's own generosity (2 Cor 8:9). Paul lists giving economic assistance (1 Cor 12:28) and also economic generosity and acts of *mercy in cheerfulness among spiritual gifts (Rom 12:8) given for the benefit of the whole body of Christ.

In the (later) Pastoral Epistles, Christians are exhorted to "do good works/deeds" (i.e., *almsgiving/charity for those in need; Titus 2:14; 3:8, *kalōn ergōn*; cf. Gal 6:9-10, "to work the good," *ergazōmetha to agathon*). The rich believers are especially commanded to be humble, put their *hope in God rather than in uncertainty of riches, and practice generosity (1 Tim 6:17-8), which will result in spiritual blessing in the age to come (1 Tim 6:19; for spiritual blessings in this life, see 2 Cor 9:10-15; Phil 4:14-20). The *church should also assist "real" widows, who are proven upright and needy with accountability (1 Tim 5:3-16). Warnings against "*love of money" (*philargyria*) and "pursuing dishonest gain" are prominent for qualifications for church *leadership (1 Tim 3:3, 8; cf. 1 Tim 6:10; Heb 13:5; 1 Pet 5:2) in direct contrast to descriptions of false *teachers and the people in the last days as "lovers of money" and those seeking "dishonest gain" (2 Tim 3:2, 4; Titus 1:11; cf. 2 Pet 2:3, 14). In a Pauline corpus, there are further adaptations from Greco-Roman moral teachings of the time: importance of "cheerful giving" (2 Cor 9:7), contentment (1 Tim 6:6-8; cf.

Heb 13:5a), and self-sufficiency (*autarkēs*) in all circumstances (Phil 4:11; cf. 1 Tim 6:7-8).

3. "Remember the Poor."
According to Longenecker, Paul was uncompromising in advancing care for the poor as integral to the theology and practice of Jesus-followers. In Galatians 2:9-10, Paul recounts his meeting with James, Peter, and John in *Jerusalem, where they recognized God's grace given to him as the *apostle to the *Gentiles and gave him and Barnabas the "right hand of *fellowship." The one thing they asked was for Paul and Barnabas to "remember the poor," which Paul was actually eager to do. This shows the Jerusalem apostles' concern that Jewish piety of caring for the poor might be abandoned in Gentile *mission, and Paul's assurance that it would continue to characterize his mission to Gentiles as a common *identity (with the Jerusalem Jesus-followers) in conformity to the *truth of the gospel. Thus Paul was committed to caring for the poor wherever he established his mission in the Gentile world; the poor in this context, then, are best understood as the indigenous poor in any location, as indicated in his teachings above (see section 2 above).

4. The Collection.
If remembering the poor was the general identity marker of Christian communities for Paul, his *collection to "the poor among the saints at Jerusalem" (Rom 15:26 NRSV) was a particular application of that principle. Based on Romans 15:26-27; 1 Corinthians 16:1-4; and 2 Corinthians 8:1–9:15, it appears that Paul has spent a significant amount of time and effort in organizing this collection. In 1 Corinthians 16:1-2, Paul advises the Corinthians to set aside a weekly amount of whatever they can offer on Sundays. In 2 Corinthians 8:1–9:15, Paul provides much theological rationale and several motivations for the collection: first, Paul highlights the example of the Macedonians, who, despite their extreme poverty, had contributed to the fund with a gift (*charis*) with abundant *joy and overflowing generosity (2 Cor 8:1-6); second, this generosity is in fact rooted and enabled by the grace (*charis*) of the Lord Jesus Christ, "that though he was rich, yet for your sakes he became poor, so that by his poverty you might become rich" (2 Cor 8:9 NRSV); third, Paul appeals to the principle of equality or "fair balance" (*isotēs*) between the abundance of the Corinthians and the deficiency of the Jerusalemites (2 Cor 8:13-14); fourth, he likens giving to this relief fund to sowing seed, which will bring about God's generous abundance in and on the act of the Corinthians' generosity (2 Cor 9:6-10); finally, this generosity is in fact a necessary effect and obligation of the gospel: "you glorify God by your obedience to the confession of the gospel of Christ and by the generosity of your sharing with them" (2 Cor 9:13 NRSV).

This generosity has indeed born fruit, since Paul in Romans 15:26-27 secured the collection from Achaia (along with Macedonia) and says they were pleased to do this. In fact, Gentile believers owed it to the Jerusalem believers, "for if the Gentiles have come to share in their spiritual blessings, they ought also to be of service to them in material things" (Rom 15:27 NRSV). Therefore, his appeal to equality or fair balance in 2 Corinthians 8 is fulfilled in Romans 15:27. Hence, the collection not only had a goal of assisting the poor Jerusalem followers of Jesus but also served as a demonstration of unity and equality between Jewish and Gentile congregations and therefore of legitimacy of his apostolic ministry (to the Gentiles). Furthermore, as David Downs argues, the collection for the Gentile congregations was depicted in cultic terms (e.g., "the offering of the Gentiles"; "service") and served as an act of *worship on the part of the Gentile followers of Jesus (1 Cor 16:1-2; 2 Cor 8:6, 11-12; 9:12; Rom 15:16, 27-28).

See also Almsgiving and Rewards; Collection for the Saints; Financial Support; Lord's Supper; Social-Scientific Approaches to Paul; Urban Setting of Paul's Churches.

BIBLIOGRAPHY. **E. Bammel,** "πτωχός, κτλ.," *TDNT* 6:885-916; **T. R. Blanton IV and R. Pickett,** eds., *Paul and Economics* (Minneapolis: Fortress, 2017); **C. L. Blomberg,** *Neither Poverty nor Riches* (Downers Grove, IL: InterVarsity Press, 1999); **D. Downs,** *The Offering of the Gentiles* (Tübingen: Mohr Siebeck, 2008); **S. J. Friesen,** "Poverty in Pauline Studies: Beyond the So-Called New Consensus," *JSNT* 26 (2004): 323-61; **D. Georgi,** *Remembering the Poor* (Nashville: Abingdon, 1992); **F. Hauck and W. Kasch,** "πολοῦτος, κτλ.," *TDNT* 6:318-32; **T. C. Hoklotubbe,** *Civilized Piety: The Rhetoric of* Pietas *in the Pastoral Epistles and the Roman Empire* (Waco, TX: Baylor University Press, 2017); **B. W. Longenecker,** *Remember the Poor* (Grand Rapids, MI: Eerdmans, 2010); **W. Meeks,** *The First Urban Christians* (New Haven, CT: Yale University Press, 1983); **J. Meggitt,** *Paul, Poverty and Survival* (Edinburgh: T&T Clark, 1998); **J. Punt,** "Remember the Poor: Pauline Perspectives on Poverty," *Dutch Reformed Theological Journal,* Supplement 1 (2004): 256-65; **T. E. Schmidt,** "Riches and Poverty," in *DPL,* 826-27; **T. D. Still and**

D. G. Horrell, eds., *After the First Urban Christians* (New York: T&T Clark, 2009); **G. Theissen,** *The Social Setting of Pauline Christianity* (Philadelphia: Fortress, 1982); **V. D. Verbrugge and K. R. Krell,** *Paul and Money* (Grand Rapids, MI: Zondervan, 2015); **S. Walton and H. Swithinbank,** *Poverty in the Early Church and Today: A Conversation* (London: T&T Clark, 2019); **L. L. Wellborn,** "'That There May Be Equality': The Contexts and Consequences of a Pauline Ideal," *NTS* 59 (2013): 73-90.

H. Rhee

WISDOM

The Hebrew words found in Proverbs 1:2-7 and their LXX Greek equivalents provide a basic lexicon of wisdom terminology, beginning with *ḥokmâ* and *sophia.* Wisdom terms describe patterns of behavior (e.g., *dikaiosynē,* "*righteousness"), speech (including *paideia,* "instruction"), and thought (related to the *nous,* "mind") (Schnabel, "Wisdom"; Wahlen). The latter includes the faculty for mental action (e.g., *synesis,* "understanding"), engagement in mental activity (e.g., *phroneō,* "think"), and the results of mental processing (e.g., *gnōsis,* "*knowledge") (see Fox).

Peter speaks of Paul's wisdom (2 Pet 3:15-16). His words support three conclusions: Paul received wisdom, Paul communicated wisdom in his *letters, and Paul's wisdom was for the *church.

1. The Background of Paul's Wisdom
2. The Form of Paul's Wisdom
3. The Ecclesiology of Paul's Wisdom
4. Conclusion

1. The Background of Paul's Wisdom.

If Paul's wisdom was "given to him," as Peter claims, it is reasonable to assume it was God-given (Ex 36:1-2; 1 Kings 4:29), an assumption affirmed by Jewish sages (Prov 2:6; Sir 43:33; Bar 3:36; Wis 9:17; Jas 1:5). Yet, this givenness cannot be separated from the influence of Hellenistic Jewish wisdom.

While quotations of Proverbs reveal his knowledge of OT wisdom traditions, Paul's use of Proverbs LXX (e.g., Rom 2:6 [Prov 24:12]; Rom 12:16-17 [Prov 3:4, 7]; Rom 12:20 [Prov 25:21-22]), a product of Hellenistic Judaism (Cook), demonstrates the influence of Hellenistic Jewish wisdom. In fact, Paul is the only NT author to use the wisdom term *aisthēsis* ("perception," Phil 1:9), which is found in the LXX predominantly in Proverbs. Paul was aware of the works of Hellenistic Jewish sages, quoting Ben Sira (see Rom 12:15 [Sir 7:34]; 1 Cor 6:12 [Sir 37:28]; 1 Thess 4:6 [Sir 5:3]) and borrowing language and concepts from Wisdom of Solomon (e.g., Rom 5:12 [Wis 2:24]; 1 Cor 15:32 [Wis 2:5-6]; 2 Cor 5:1 [Wis 9:15]). Scholars find that Hellenistic Jewish wisdom informs Paul's argument in Romans (Dodson; Linebaugh), his thinking about *sophia* in 1 Corinthians (Lamp), and his *Christology (Witherington), though there are good reasons to reject Wisdom Christology (Fee). Cornelis Bennema identifies intertwining "strands" of Jewish wisdom emerging from the OT, which form the background of Paul's wisdom: Torah, Spirit, apocalyptic.

1.1. Torah and Wisdom. Paul rejects the *law as law-*covenant but reappropriates the law as wisdom-instruction (Rosner). The OT hints at the connection of law and wisdom (e.g., Deut 4:6; Ps 119:98; Ezra 7:14, 25), but the relationship became explicit in Hellenistic Judaism.

The sages held that the Scriptures of *Israel were a source of wisdom (Sir 38:24, 34; 39:1-3; Philo, *Post.* 18; Josephus, *Ant.* 20.261-265), and Torah observance was emphasized in the acquisition of wisdom (Prov 4:5 LXX; Sir 1:26; 19:20). More specifically, they associated law with wisdom, a move Paul interacts with (Schnabel 1985; Pate). Ben Sira and Baruch affirm that wisdom is the special possession of Israel because Israel has the law. Wisdom is not with *Gentile nations (Bar 3:22-23; cf. Tob 4:18-19), but *God appointed Wisdom (personified) a dwelling place in Israel (Sir 24:8; Bar 3:36), concentrated in the Jerusalem *temple (Sir 24:3-12; cf. Sir 51:13-14). Wisdom is identified with the law (Sir 24:23; Bar 4:1), which overflows with wisdom (*sophia*), understanding (*synesis*), and instruction (*paideia*; Sir 24:25-34). The association of the law with wisdom is found in a variety of texts (e.g., Prov 9:10 LXX; 4Q525 [Beatitudes] 2-3 ii, 1-6; 2 Bar. 48.22-24; T. Levi 13.1-9) and in the practice of the sages (e.g., Pseudo-Phocylides's subtle use of the law as wisdom instruction and Josephus's retelling of Josiah's reign in *Ant.* 10.4.1).

The association may have been occasioned by the rise of the Mosaic law in Jewish life (Sanders), or the needs of Jews in a Hellenistic context. Regarding the latter, in Sirach 17 the connection of *creation and the law demonstrates a compatibility between universal wisdom and the wisdom of Israel found in the law (Collins). Whatever the reason, the purpose was ethical, offering a guide for behavior in "norms of moral conduct" (Schnabel 1985, 163). Right thinking and right living are bound together, and the law is the source of wisdom leading to ethical behavior (e.g., 4 Macc 1:15-18; 2:7-14). Yet, the ethical thrust of the association of law and wisdom served various ends (Pate). Nationalistic interpretations anchored hope for restoration in a return to Torah observance (e.g., Sirach; Baruch). Apologetic interpretations supported Jewish particularism through the association of law with universalistic wisdom (e.g., 4 Maccabees). Sectarian interpretations made the *teaching of the community an extension of the law (e.g., Dead Sea Scrolls).

1.2. Spirit and Wisdom. Jewish sages developed the OT connection between wisdom and the Spirit (e.g., Is 11:2).

1.2.1. Spirit-Empowered Skill. In the OT, wisdom (*ḥokmâ*) is the skill to do something well, and occasionally the Spirit is involved in acquiring that skill, for example, craftsmanship (Ex 31:2-4), leadership (Deut 34:9), discernment (Job 32:8-9), or divination (Dan 5:11-14). The sages attempted to focus the OT association of the Spirit and wisdom. According to John Levison, in his retelling of Daniel, Josephus guards against any notion that Daniel's interpretations were given through the Spirit unconsciously. To do this Josephus makes two key alterations to his Greek source (Theod. Dan 5:14) in *Jewish Antiquities* 10.239. First, adding a definite article, he sharpens "a spirit" to "the Spirit." Second, he replaces language of a spirit in Daniel with the presence of the Spirit "that attended him" (from *sympareimi*), which indicates in *Antiquities* divine accompaniment, not overpowering. In contrast with his depiction of Balaam, who loses mental control in *prophecy (*Ant.* 4.118-121), Josephus describes Daniel's experience of the Spirit as a prompting to wisdom. This may have a bearing on Paul's thinking about *gifts of the Spirit, especially gifts of wisdom and knowledge (1 Cor 12:8).

1.2.2. Spirit-Led Ethics. Wisdom is also the skill to live well in God's world, and the Spirit is needed to access that wisdom. As a craftswoman (Wis 7:22; 8:6), personified Wisdom was present with God at creation and understands what is right and pleasing to God (Wis 9:9). Therefore, Pseudo-Solomon asks God to send Wisdom to work with him (*sympareimi*, Wis 9:10; cf. Prov 8:27 LXX) as a guide to wise living. Wisdom is apparently equated with the Spirit when Solomon acknowledges that it is not possible to know God's mind or what pleases him unless "you have given wisdom and sent your *Holy Spirit" (Wis 9:17-18; cf. 1QH VI, 8-9, 12-13). Indeed, the answer to Solomon's prayer is that he received understanding and a spirit of wisdom (*pneuma sophias*, Wis 7:7).

1.2.3. Spirit-Inspired Exegesis. A significant innovation in the association of the Spirit and wisdom is Spirit-inspired exegesis of the Scriptures. According to Ben Sira, the pursuit of wisdom requires complete devotion (lit. "giving his life") to the study of the law and other Scriptures (Sir 38:34–39:1-3). Since the locus of wisdom is the law, "the Spirit of understanding [*synesis*]" is needed to access the wisdom of the law in the process of interpretation (Sir 39:6). Spirit-inspired exegesis is seen in Philo, who explains how the Spirit guides him to deeper meanings of Scripture (*Somn.* 2.252), and at *Qumran in the Teacher of Righteousness, who has wisdom through the Holy Spirit (1QH XX, 10-13) to interpret the mysteries of the prophets (1QpHab VII, 1-5).

1.3. Apocalyptic and Wisdom. Wisdom and apocalyptic traditions appear to overlap in Paul's thinking (E. E. Johnson). While these categories seem incompatible, arising from alternate worldviews, a fusion of the two can be found in texts of both genres.

1.3.1. Revelatory Wisdom. According to Proverbs, the ability to seek wisdom is God-given (Prov 20:12), and the book is optimistic about the endeavor, as long as one begins with "the fear of the Lord" (Prov 1:7; 9:10). Ben Sira seems to agree but expresses ambivalence. Although Wisdom resides with Israel as the law, Wisdom has her secrets (Sir 4:18; 14:21), which only God knows and reveals through wisdom (cf. Sir 42:17-21; 43:32-33). Some sages, confronted with the reality of human limitation, despaired of having wisdom without supernatural revelation. The apparent hiddenness of wisdom (Job 28:12-22; Bar 3:29-31) and the transcendence of God (Wis 9:13-16; 1QS XI, 18-19; 1 En. 93.12) required revelatory wisdom. Through revelation come cosmological wisdom (Sir 1:1-10; 1QH IX, 7-21) and knowledge of God and his will (Wis 9:17-18).

1.3.2. Eschatology. The eschatological divine plan of *salvation and *judgment is also revealed. Enoch received revelatory wisdom in what he calls "the vision of wisdom" (1 En. 37.1-5), which includes the judgment and destruction of the wicked and the eternal dwelling of the righteous in the presence of the Lord (1 En. 38–39). Wisdom leads to immortality (Wis 8:17; 9:18) and eschatological salvation at the time of judgment (1QH VI, 3-5; 4Q185 II, 1-13; cf. Prov 28:26 LXX). Apocalyptic *eschatology becomes the context for sapiential *ethics, as seen in 4QInstruction, which is wisdom offered in an apocalyptic framework (4Q416 I, 10-13). The wisdom of the text is wrapped up in the enigmatic phrase "the mystery that is to be" (*raz nihyeh*), which "seems to encompass the entire divine plan, from creation to eschatological judgment" (Collins, 122). Wisdom is acquired through contemplation of the revealed mystery. The particular blend of wisdom and apocalyptic in 4QInstruction is reflected in 1 Corinthians (Goff).

2. The Form of Paul's Wisdom.

Although Paul uses wisdom literary forms (e.g., *maxim*, Gal 6:7), the basic form of his wisdom is the paraenetic letter. Abraham Malherbe argues that Paul's use of the paraenetic letter form serves his pastoral purpose in 1 Thessalonians (1987) and Titus (2005). On Malherbe's reading, Paul appropriates the form from Hellenistic moral *philosophy. The letter, even the friendly letter, in the hands of the philosopher is a form of philosophical pedagogy aimed at the formation of character. Andrew Pitts, alternatively, argues that Paul's letters are not philosophical paraenesis but the epistolary paraenesis of the private letter.

As a form of paraenesis, Jeff de Waal Dryden suggests Paul's letters are wisdom discourses, and he identifies several wisdom strategies evident in Paul's letters: commands, vice and virtue lists, conversion and antithesis (e.g., "old self/new self"), and moral exemplars. These strategies are employed for "promoting virtuous habits," "critiquing and reforming core devotions," and "fostering a mature moral discernment" (171-77). By employing these strategies Paul intentionally attempts to shape the character of his churches. Pauline paraenesis resembles patterns of ethical teaching in Hellenistic Judaism (Wilson), especially the concern for maintaining *identity among Diaspora Jews (Thompson), for example, 4 Maccabees (Westerholm).

Furthermore, in paraenetic letters didactic teaching and ethical exhortation work together. According to Dryden, wisdom deals with actions, reasons, and motivations. In paraenetic letters, the indicative sections provide motivations and reasons for the practical wisdom of the imperative sections. Accordingly, the "purpose of theological reflection in paraenetic letters is to project a moral vision that renders certain ethical actions intelligible and praiseworthy" (Dryden, 187). As wisdom discourses, Paul's letters are not theological treatises; rather, theology serves paraenetic concerns. In this light, even letters that seem disinterested in the themes of wisdom may be considered wisdom discourses (e.g., Galatians).

3. The Ecclesiology of Paul's Wisdom.

For Ben Sira the pursuit of wisdom required leisure (Sir 38:24). Paul, however, offers wisdom through letters composed in less-than-ideal circumstances (e.g., imprisonment) and with great concern for the welfare of his churches (2 Cor 11:28). The lexicon of wisdom terminology in his letters witnesses a pastoral concern for wisdom to be embodied in the life of the church.

3.1. Romans. Paul's argument, directed at the divisions among the Jewish and Gentile believers in Rome, moves from lack of wisdom to renewed wisdom.

3.1.1. Lack of Wisdom. It is generally agreed that Romans 1:18-32 reflects a Jewish perspective on Gentile *sin: lack of wisdom leads to sexual immorality and *idolatry (see 3.2.2). Yet, in agreement with the characterization of Gentile sin in Wisdom of Solomon 13–15, Paul subtly alludes to Israel's idolatry in Romans 1:23 (echoing Ps 105:20 LXX) and therefore also has Israel's sin in view (Linebaugh). Gentiles and Jews are guilty of false claims to wisdom (Rom 1:22).

In Romans 1:18-32 Paul characterizes sin as a lack of wisdom. Those described here are "senseless" (*asynetos*, Rom 1:21, 31), the antithesis of "understanding" (*synesis*), a term synonymous with wisdom (Prov 1:7; 2:2-3, 6 LXX). Furthermore, sin is failure of discernment (*ouk edokimasan*, Rom 1:28). Discernment (*dokimazō*) is the mental process of testing (see Job 34:3 LXX) resulting in rejection or approval (see 1 Tim 3:10) and is needed for knowing the difference between good and evil (see 1 Thess 5:21-22; cf. Rom 16:19b). Failure to discern the knowledge of God results in a worthless mind (*adokimon noun*, Rom 1:28), having knowledge without action (Rom 1:32).

In Romans 2:17-24 Jewish foolishness is exposed with the only direct reference to the association of law and wisdom in Paul, likely reflecting the thinking of Jewish Christians among the Roman believers. Unlike Gentiles, Jews know God's will and have discernment (*dokimazeis*), and the source of this wisdom is the law (Rom 2:18). Thus, Jewish Christians in Rome may have seen themselves as instructors of foolish Gentile Christians (cf. Sir 39:1-10). Inasmuch as Gentiles are in view in Romans 1:18-32, their senselessness probably results from not having the law, since in the LXX *synesis* results from keeping the law (Deut 4:6; Josh 1:8; 1 Kings 2:3; Neh 8:2-3). However, those would-be teachers have not taught themselves (Rom 2:21). Knowing God's will from the law, they dishonor God by breaking the law (Rom 2:23), displaying their own failure of discernment.

In Romans 3:9-18 Jews and Gentiles, together under sin, lack wisdom: "there is no one understanding [*syniōn*]" (Rom 3:11). Significantly, Paul claims that they do not fear God (Rom 3:18). Fear of the Lord is perhaps the central concept of Jewish wisdom, as references throughout Proverbs and Sirach demonstrate. Its meaning is rooted in a covenant relationship with God, in which fear (and love) envision fulfillment of covenant obligations (Deut 10:12-13). Fear of God grounds wisdom in a relationship with God. Lack of wisdom reveals a relational breach with God and among the Roman believers. Thus, false claims of wisdom reveal patterns of thought resulting in division (Rom 12:16). Paul depicts community strife as a violation of the murder prohibition (Rom 13:9; cf. Ex 20:13): having described sin as murderous (Rom 1:29; 3:13-16), he warns that the believers are in danger of harming one another (Rom 14:15, 20-21). Lacking wisdom, they lack *peace.

3.1.2. Renewed Wisdom. Commentators note the reversal of Romans 1:18-32 in Paul's exhortation in Romans 12:1-2, which is a programmatic statement introducing a wisdom discourse (Rom 12:3-21; Wilson). The antithesis of transformation and nonconformity to the world is not a contrast between inner and outer dimensions of life, as if transformation affects the mind without affecting behavior. The renewal of the mind is a communally embodied transformation (Rom 12:4-5), which leads to right thinking, emphasized with the repetition of *phron-* terms (Rom 12:3, 16). Right thinking and right living are bound together, and an external agent is needed to maintain the bond. The agent is left unspecified, yet it is likely the Holy Spirit (Rom 8:5-8; cf. Eph 4:17, 23; Titus 3:5). Whereas in 4 Maccabees the law activates intrinsic reason, for Paul the Spirit enacts transformation (Dunson).

Renewed wisdom's purpose is discernment of God's will. By describing God's will as "good" and "acceptable," Paul takes aim at the divisions among the congregations in Rome. The good they need to discern is how to please and build up fellow believers (Rom 15:2), and discerning what is acceptable looks forward to the end of passing judgment on fellow believers who think differently (Rom 14:13-17), resulting in divine acceptance and human approval (Rom 14:18). Thus, the Spirit who knows God's will (Rom 8:27) empowers moral discernment to mend the relational breach.

In Romans 14:1–15:13 Paul applies his argument directly to the division of weak (Jewish) and *strong (Gentile) believers. Reinforcing his argument here, Paul states his desire for wisdom in Rome in a hortatory section of the letter's closing (Rom 16:17-20). Some commentators see no connection to the preceding argument, yet a reference to divisions (Rom 16:17) echoes Paul's concern for mutual welcome (Rom 14:1; 15:7). Moreover, key terms are repeated from Romans 14:1–15:13: "offenses" (Rom 16:17; 14:13), "serve" (Rom 16:18; 14:18), "good" (Rom 16:19; 14:16; 15:2), "peace" (Rom 16:20; 14:17, 19; 15:13). Thus, wisdom is needed to address the division of the Roman believers, which centers on differing opinions about the law, especially identity markers, most notably *food regulations (Rom 14:2-4). Paul allows for differences of opinion (Rom 14:5), indicating that both groups are able to discern (*dokimazō*) the Lord's will, even if that means they do not think the same with regard to food (Rom 14:22). More importantly, however, wisdom is needed to discern behaviors of mutual welcome and peace.

The example of Christ and the law of *love guide moral discernment. Paul disassociates law and wisdom, relocating wisdom to Christ (Rom 10:6-8; see Pate). So, if the association of law and wisdom provided ethical norms, then Christ has become the norm. Following the example of Christ is pivotal in connecting the transformation through the Spirit and moral discernment (L. T. Johnson). Accordingly, the believers will "think the same" (*to auto phronein*, Rom 15:5; cf. Rom 13:14) as Christ, who did not please himself (Rom 15:3), and they will welcome one another as Christ welcomed them (Rom 15:7). The wisdom of Christ's example is the very antithesis of false claims of wisdom and prideful patterns of thought (Rom 12:16). Moreover, although Christ is the end of the law (Rom 10:4), Paul reappropriates the law as wisdom instruction (Rom 15:4). The love command is wisdom for discerning behavior toward one another as fellow believers (Rom 13:8-10; cf. Lev 19:18). Without love they live as if they lack wisdom, but through love they will discern the way of peace.

3.2. 1 Corinthians. Paul uses *sophia* and cognates predominantly in 1 Corinthians 1–3, especially in 1 Corinthians 1:18–2:16, a theological discourse on wisdom. These polemical chapters are Paul's most sustained treatment of wisdom, and they lend coherence to the entire letter.

3.2.1. Corinthian Wisdom and the Wisdom of the Cross. Paul's discourse on wisdom is rhetorically connected to the issue of factionalism (1 Cor 1:10-17; 3:3-4; Lampe). His concern is not simply with status-seeking behavior in *Corinth, but the wisdom behind it (see Kwon), the reasons and motivations resulting in a secular way of life (1 Cor 3:3). Paul critiques this wisdom theologically, providing reasons and motivations for a different ethic, the apocalyptic wisdom of the *cross (see Brown).

Paul's argument centers on the eschatological revelation of God's wisdom and the destruction of human wisdom. The cross reveals God's wisdom (1 Cor 1:22-23), which those being destroyed regard as foolish (1 Cor 1:18). Yet, the wisdom by which they evaluate the cross is under God's judgment (1 Cor 1:19). The eschatological destruction of human wisdom (see Is 29:14) has already occurred through the cross (1 Cor 1:25); it has been rendered foolish (1 Cor 1:20) and is part of the order that is perishing (1 Cor 2:6). This destruction is demonstrated by human inability to know God and his wisdom (1 Cor 1:21; 2:8). God's wisdom is communicated "in a *mystery" (1 Cor 2:7), which relates to the limits of human comprehension, rather than the intention of the speaker (Lang). The incomprehensibility of God (1 Cor 2:9) requires divine revelation: God's wisdom is revealed (*apekalypsen*) through God's Spirit (1 Cor 2:10-13).

The theological discourse aims to change the way the Corinthians think, so that they become fools in order to become wise (1 Cor 3:18), which means giving up worldly wisdom and living according to cruciform wisdom. In 1 Corinthians 1:30 Paul says, "Christ [crucified] became wisdom for us from God." Commentators generally agree that this cruciform wisdom is soteriological: Christ crucified is God's saving wisdom, further described in salvific terms—*righteousness, sanctification, redemption.* Yet, it is also possible that cruciform wisdom is ethical: Christ crucified is the wisdom of God given to the church for moral discernment. Since the sages held wisdom and ethical righteousness together (e.g., Prov 1:2-3; 2:6-9; 3:13, 16 LXX; Sir 45:26; 4 Macc 1:18), a closer look at *dikaiosynē* in the Corinthian correspondence illuminates the embodied ethics of cruciform wisdom.

By understanding *dikaiosynē* as merely salvific, the forensic concept of the *dikaio-* word group is separated from its moral counterpart. Michael Gorman argues that the two should remain together, so that righteous status creates a just community. In 1 Corinthians 6:1-11, "justified" (*edikaiōthēte*, 1 Cor 6:11) may be a saving verb. However, in context Paul is addressing unjust (*adikeō*) treatment of fellow believers (1 Cor 6:7-8) and the pursuit of justice before unjust (*adikos*) judges (1 Cor 6:1), demonstrating a lack of wisdom in the church (1 Cor 6:5). Those who are justified (*edikaiōthēte*) should instead become a community of *dikaiosynē*, which includes following the wisdom of the cross by absorbing injustice (1 Cor 6:7). In 2 Corinthians 5:21 the church is transformed into the *dikaiosynē* of God, participating in *dikaiosynē* by embodying the reconciliation achieved through the cross (2 Cor 5:18-19). Finally, *dikaiosynē* surfaces with Paul's appeal for generosity in 2 Corinthians 8–9. God's generous *dikaiosynē* directed toward the poor (2 Cor 9:9) is the grounds for the *dikaiosynē* of the church embodied in generosity (2 Cor 9:10), after the example of Christ (2 Cor 8:9). In these texts *dikaiosynē* is cruciform behavior.

Thus, by identifying cruciform wisdom with *dikaiosynē* in 1 Corinthians 1:30, Paul may have in mind wisdom given to the church for moral discernment. Indeed, in the immediate context, the formation of the community is an example of God's cruciform wisdom and justice, displayed in God's choice of those without status (1 Cor 1:26-28). Therefore, the church's "social composition" embodies cruciform wisdom (Hays), which will be demonstrated in justice for the weak and poor. The other terms identified with cruciform wisdom are affected by this interpretation: wisdom is relational *holiness and *freedom from the pursuit of status, which leads to boasting and strife. The concluding indicative reinforces that cruciform wisdom is the wisdom God gives to the church: "we have the mind of Christ" (1 Cor 2:16). The mind of Christ receives the wisdom of the cross imparted by the Spirit for a cruciform way of thinking that will guide moral discernment. That thinking is exemplified in the cruciform example of the apostles (1 Cor 4:9-13), especially Paul, whom they are to imitate (1 Cor 4:16; 8:1–11:1).

3.2.2. Wisdom and the Coherence of Paul's Argument. As the first of the issues Paul addresses, wisdom has a bearing on the coherence of the letter. The wisdom discourse is tied to the rest of the letter in two ways. First, Roy Ciampa and Brian Rosner have shown that Paul views Gentile sin in Corinth from a perspective resembling that found in Jewish wisdom (Wis 13–15; Let. Aris. 134-139, 152; T. Jud. 18-19; Sib. Or. 5). Paul has structured the letter with this in mind (cf. Rom 1:18-31; Eph 5:3, 5, 15): lack of true wisdom (1 Cor 1:10–4:17) leads to sexual immorality (1 Cor 4:18–7:20) and idolatry (1 Cor 8:1–11:1).

Second, Susan Eastman argues that the theme of love unites themes of speech and knowledge in 1 Corinthians 1–4 with the ethical instructions beginning in 1 Corinthians 5. Although the Corinthians possess all knowledge and all speech (1 Cor 1:5), they are disconnected from the "larger relational matrix" in which these must operate: rather than finding their identity as a church belonging to God (1 Cor 1:2), they find it in smaller, competitive factions centered on belonging to certain leaders

(1 Cor 1:12). Knowledge severed from relational bonds produces pride, but knowledge determined by love builds up (1 Cor 8:1-3). Paul undermines spiritual gifts of speech and knowledge performed without love (1 Cor 13:1-2), but such gifts exercised in relationship edify (1 Cor 14:3-5, 12). Thus, love becomes the basis for "interpersonal discernment" in the church, so that love, rather than wisdom, sums up Paul's argument (1 Cor 16:14).

*3.3. **Ephesians.*** The prominence of wisdom in *Ephesus, displayed in the statue of Sophia at the Library of Celsus, is matched by its importance in Paul's letter. God's wisdom frames the opening chapters (Eph 1:8; 3:10), which center on the revelation of the mystery, namely, God's eschatological plan to unite Jews and Gentiles in one *body through the *gospel (Eph 1:8-10; 2:11-22; 3:3-6). Although this mystery was hidden, it has been revealed through the Spirit (Eph 3:5). The church plays a vital role in displaying God's wisdom (Eph 3:10) and therefore needs the Spirit of wisdom (*pneuma sophias*) and revelation (*apokalypseōs*) to grasp their place in God's unfolding plan (Eph 1:17).

The revelation of the mystery provides reasons and motivations for the exhortations to practical wisdom in the latter half of the letter, embodied in a "walk" that is worthy (Eph 4:1; cf. Eph 4:17; 5:2, 8, 15). Practical wisdom focuses on the body growing toward maturity in Christ (Eph 4:12-16), which is reinforced by reminders of conversion and antitheses of old and new patterns of life (Eph 4:17-24; 5:6-14), lists of vices and virtues (Eph 4:25-32; 5:3-5), and a call to imitate God's love (Eph 5:1-2).

The Spirit is not only the agent of revelation but also the guide to ethical wisdom. In Ephesians 5:18 Paul's contrast of drunkenness with Spirit filling is the third of three contrastive exhortations (*mē . . . alla*). The contrastive exhortations parallel one another synonymously, so that the negative and positive ideas are repeated three times in different terms: "not as unwise, but as wise" (Eph 5:15); "do not be foolish but understand what the will of the Lord is" (Eph 5:17); "do not get drunk . . . but be filled with the Spirit" (Eph 5:18). Thus, drunkenness is synonymous with foolishness and unwise living, while being filled with the Spirit is synonymous with wise living and knowing the Lord's will (cf. Prov 23:29-35 LXX). The Spirit of wisdom fills the church, renewing the mind and guiding the body of Christ in moral discernment on the path to maturity (cf. Eph 4:18, 23; 5:10). Four participles explain the results of the filling, culminating with "submitting" (Eph 5:19-21). Submission introduces the *household instructions (Eph 5:22–6:9), marking them as Spirit-led ethical wisdom for mutual relationships in the church.

*3.4. **Philippians.*** In the context of opposition and *suffering Paul calls the church to gospel *citizenship, embodied in unity and perseverance (Phil 1:27-30), both of which begin with Christ-shaped patterns of thought.

Unity is achieved through humility (Phil 2:3-4), which is shaped by a relational way of thinking (*phroneō*, Phil 2:2), moral discernment rooted in love (Phil 1:9-11). Indeed, love motivates the thinking that leads to unity (Phil 2:1); it is the antithesis of selfish ambition (Phil 1:16-17). The way of thinking Paul wants to motivate was embodied by Jesus, whom Paul offers as an example of humility: the believers must think the same (*touto phroneite*) as Christ (Phil 2:5). Paul wants the church to cultivate the Christ-shaped humility described in the Christ *hymn (Phil 2:6-8). The example of Jesus is paradigmatic, and it would have been understood that only the virtuous aspects of his *death are offered for emulation. By imitating Jesus, the Philippians will grow in discernment of how to regard others above themselves, thereby developing habits of humility.

In Philippians 3:4-14 Paul offers his personal story as a paradigm for the Philippians to follow. Paul's story conforms to the pattern of Christ's: giving up advantage, suffering, and *glory. Yet, the glory Christ presently enjoys remains in the future for Paul. The same is true for the church, and Paul wants them to share his way of thinking (*touto phronōmen*, Phil 3:15, echoing Phil 2:5) about present reality and future *hope. Paul exhorts them to imitate his example (Phil 3:17), because he embodies "the normativity of the Christ-story" (Bird and Gupta, 155). By imitating Paul, the Philippians will think about their own story in light of his (and therefore Christ's) and persevere through humiliation to glory (Phil 3:20-21). Imitating Paul is enhanced as they think about (*logizesthe*) and practice virtues exemplified by Paul (Phil 4:8-9).

*3.5. **Colossians.*** Ethical wisdom frames Paul's letter of encouragement (see Heil). Paul's desire for wisdom in the church finds expression in his *prayer for knowledge (*epignōsis*) of God's will through the Spirit's "wisdom" (*sophia*) and "understanding" (*synesis*, Col 1:9). This knowledge will be embodied in a "walk" that is worthy of and pleasing to the Lord (Col 1:10), as Paul emphasizes, saying, "walk in wisdom [*sophia*]" (Col 4:5).

Wisdom is centered in Paul's response to false teaching in the church. Although the exact nature of the Colossian philosophy is debated, it centered on the pursuit of wisdom (DeMaris). Indeed, Paul acknowledges that it has the appearance of wisdom (*sophia*) in the way it promotes ethical behavior aimed at curbing fleshly indulgence (Col 2:23). However, philosophy is ultimately worthless apart from Christ (Col 2:8, 23) and is an insufficient ethical guide for those "*in Christ" (Col 1:2).

Paul seeks to establish the Colossians on the true foundation of wisdom, namely, Christ, struggling for them to know Christ (Col 2:2), so that they will not be deceived (Col 2:4). The high Christology of the letter (Col 1:15-20), probably owing more to regal imagery than Wisdom Christology (Dunne), is part of Paul's response to the philosophy, giving reasons and motivations for ethical behavior. Indeed, "walk in Christ" (Col 2:6) is an exhortation to ethical wisdom, for Christ is the true source of wisdom (*sophia*, Col 2:3), and thinking (*phroneite*) focused on the exalted Christ (Col 3:1-4) is the basis for the ethical wisdom of conversion, ethical antitheses (Col 3:5-17), and the household instructions (Col 3:18–4:1).

Pauline paraenesis includes instructions to *slaves (Col 3:22-25; Eph 6:5-8; 1 Tim 6:1-2; Titus 2:9). In Greco-Roman and Jewish thought, slaves were not considered wise because they lacked moral agency. However, by addressing slaves directly, Paul grants moral agency and capacity for wisdom. This is particularly relevant in Colossians because Tychicus and Onesimus, both slaves (Col 4:7-9), delivered and performed the letter (Shiell). By hearing these slaves included in the "we" of Colossians 1:28, the church is motivated to see slaves included in the "one another" of Colossians 3:16 and recognize their capacity for wisdom. In fact, slaves who fear the Lord (Col 3:22) are exemplars, motivating the Christian household toward wisdom (Lincoln).

3.6. Philemon. Paul wants Philemon's *faith to generate a capacity for understanding (*epignōsis*) every good thing (Philem 6). This may refer to knowledge of benefits enjoyed in Christ or of actions performed for Christ. The latter is probable since in the scope of Paul's personal appeal, "every good thing" points toward a specific good, namely, that Philemon will welcome and reconcile with Onesimus, which is the referent of "good" in Philemon 14. Thus, understanding is needed to discern the course of action Paul could have otherwise commanded (Philem 8).

3.7. 2 Timothy. Timothy's knowledge and learning directly contrast (*Sy de*, 2 Tim 3:10, 14) the *opponents (2 Tim 3:7-8) and their lack of wisdom (*anoia*, 2 Tim 3:9). Timothy "followed" (*parēkolouthēsas*) Paul's example in *ministry (2 Tim 3:10-12) in the sense that he understood it (see 2 Tim 1:15) in such a way that it could determine his course of action (see 1 Tim 4:6; 2 Macc 9:27). In particular, Paul's example gives Timothy wisdom for enduring suffering (2 Tim 1:8; 2:3; 4:5).

Furthermore, Scripture is an effective source of wisdom, making Timothy wise for salvation (2 Tim 3:15; Paul's example may have a similar result, 1 Tim 1:16) and ready for every good work (2 Tim 3:17). The latter results from Scripture's usefulness (2 Tim 3:16), which Paul describes as actions associated with wisdom (Rosner): "teaching" (*didaskalia*, Prov 4:11; 30:3 LXX; Wis 7:21-22; Sir 39:8; Col 1:28; 3:16), "reproof" (*elegmos*, Sir 21:6), "training" (*paideia*, Prov 1:2, 7; 6:23 LXX; Sir 24:25-27; 4 Macc 1:16-17), "righteousness" (*dikaiosynē*, see 3.2.1). The wisdom imparted possibly results from Timothy's early education (2 Tim 3:15), in which Scripture's teaching, reproof, and so on were applied to him as a guide for moral behavior (cf. 2 Tim 2:21). More probable, Scripture finds purpose as a resource for ministry. Indeed, the terms of Scripture's usefulness are the actions of Timothy's ministry in the face of opposition (2 Tim 2:24-25; 4:2). Thus, readiness for every good work entails discernment of ministry practices. The Holy Spirit, at least implied in Scripture's inspiration (*theopneustos*, cf. 2 Pet 1:20-21), empowers Timothy for ministry (2 Tim 1:7, 14) and likely guides his understanding of the Scriptures (cf. 1 Cor 2:13), following Paul's example of inspired exegesis (2 Tim 2:19; 3:8).

4. Conclusion.

Thoroughly shaped by developments in Hellenistic Jewish wisdom, Paul appropriated the paraenetic letter form for the formation of embodied wisdom in his churches. Paul would have likely felt at home among Jewish sages who sought to instill their own wisdom in their adherents. For example, although the law was the source of wisdom for Ben Sira, he never cited it, offering instead his own wisdom to those who were receptive (Sir 6:23, 33-35; 51:23-27). Similarly, Paul offers his own advice (*gnōmē*, 1 Cor 7:25, 40; 2 Cor 8:10; cf. Wis 7:15; Sir 6:23) and his example as worthy of emulation. Yet he differs from the sages on a key point. Paul's chief concern is the formation of wisdom in the church through "christoformity," the embodiment of Christ's wisdom through the Spirit, making Paul a pastor-sage (see McKnight 2019).

See also Apocalypticism; Colossians, Letter to the; Corinthians, First Letter to the; Ephesians, Letter to the; Holy Spirit; Knowledge and Mind; Old Testament in Paul; Philippians, Letter to the; Righteousness; Romans, Letter to the; Teaching, Teachers; Tradition.

BIBLIOGRAPHY. **C. Bennema,** "The Strands of Wisdom Tradition in Intertestamental Judaism: Origins, Developments and Characteristics," *TynBul* 52 (2001): 61-82; **M. F. Bird and N. K. Gupta,** *Philippians,* NCBC (Cambridge: Cambridge University Press, 2020); **A. R. Brown,** *The Cross and Human Transformation: Paul's Apocalyptic Word in 1 Corinthians* (Minneapolis: Fortress, 1995); **R. E. Ciampa and B. S. Rosner,** *The First Letter to the Corinthians,* PNTC (Grand Rapids, MI: Eerdmans, 2010); **J. J. Collins,** *Jewish Wisdom in the Hellenistic Age* (Louisville, KY: Westminster John Knox, 1997); **J. Cook,** *The Septuagint of Proverbs—Jewish and/or Hellenistic Proverbs? Concerning the Hellenistic Colouring of LXX Proverbs* (Leiden: Brill, 1997); **R. E. DeMaris,** *Colossian Controversy: Wisdom in Dispute at Colossae* (Sheffield: Sheffield Academic, 1994); **J. R. Dodson,** *The "Powers" of Personification: Rhetorical Purpose in the "Book of Wisdom" and the Letter to the Romans* (Berlin: de Gruyter, 2008); **J. de W. Dryden,** *A Hermeneutic of Wisdom: Recovering the Formative Agency of Scripture* (Grand Rapids, MI: Baker, 2018); **J. A. Dunne,** "The Regal Status of Christ in the Colossian 'Christ-Hymn': A Re-evaluation of the Influence of Wisdom Traditions," *TrinJ* 32 (2011): 3-18; **B. C. Dunson,** "4 Maccabees and Romans 12:1-21: Reason and the Righteous Life," in *Reading Romans in Context: Paul and Second Temple Judaism,* ed. B. C. Blackwell (Grand Rapids, MI: Zondervan, 2015), 136-42; **S. G. Eastman,** "Love's Folly: Love and Knowledge in 1 Corinthians," *Int* 72 (2018): 7-16; **G. D. Fee,** "Wisdom Christology in Paul: A Dissenting View," in *The Way of Wisdom: Essays in Honor of Bruce K. Waltke* (Grand Rapids, MI: Zondervan, 2000), 251-79; **M. V. Fox,** "Words for Wisdom," *Zeitschrift für Althebräistik* 6 (1993): 149-69; **M. Goff,** "The Mystery of God's Wisdom, the Parousia of the Messiah, and Visions of Heavenly Paradise: 1 and 2 Corinthians in the Context of Jewish Apocalypticism," in *The Jewish Apocalyptic Tradition and the Shaping of New Testament Thought,* ed. B. Reynolds and L. Stuckenbruck (Minneapolis: Fortress, 2017), 175-92; **M. J. Gorman,** "Justification and Justice in Paul, with Special Reference to the Corinthians," *JSPHL* 1 (2011): 23-40; **R. B. Hays,** "Wisdom According to Paul," in *Where Shall Wisdom Be Found? Wisdom in the Bible, the Church and the Contemporary World,* ed. S. C. Barton (Edinburgh: T&T Clark, 1999), 111-23; **J. P. Heil,** *Colossians: Encouragement to Walk in All Wisdom as Holy Ones in Christ* (Atlanta: Society of Biblical Literature, 2010); **E. E. Johnson,** "Wisdom and Apocalyptic in Paul," in *In Search of Wisdom: Essays in Memory of John G. Gammie,* ed. L. G. Perdue (Louisville, KY: Westminster John Knox, 1993), 263-84; **L. T. Johnson,** "Transformation of the Mind and Moral Discernment in Paul," in *Contested Issues in Christian Origins and the New Testament* (Leiden: Brill, 2013), 255-75; **O.-Y. Kwon,** "A Critical Review of Recent Scholarship on the Pauline Opposition and the Nature of Its Wisdom (Σοφία) in 1 Corinthians 1–4," *CurBR* 8 (2010): 386-427; **J. S. Lamp,** *First Corinthians 1–4 in Light of Jewish Wisdom Traditions: Christ, Wisdom, and Spirituality* (Lewiston, NY: Edwin Mellen, 2000); **P. Lampe,** "Theological Wisdom and the 'Word About the Cross': The Rhetorical Scheme in 1 Corinthians 1–4," *Int* 44 (1990): 117-31; **T. J. Lang,** "We Speak in a Mystery: Neglected Greek Evidence for the Syntax and Sense of 1 Corinthians 2:7," *CBQ* 78 (2016): 68-89; **J. R. Levison,** *The Spirit in First Century Judaism* (Leiden: Brill, 1997); **A. T. Lincoln,** "The Household Code and Wisdom Mode of Colossians," *JSNT* 74 (1999): 93-112; **J. A. Linebaugh,** *God, Grace, and Righteousness in Wisdom of Solomon and Paul's Letter to the Romans: Texts in Conversation* (Boston: Brill, 2013); **A. J. Malherbe,** *Paul and the Thessalonians: The Philosophic Tradition of Pastoral Care* (Philadelphia: Fortress, 1987); idem, "Paraenesis in the Epistle to Titus," in *Early Christian Paraenesis in Context,* ed. J. Starr and T. Engberg-Pedersen (Berlin: de Gruyter, 2005), 297-317; **S. McKnight,** *Pastor Paul: Nurturing a Culture of Christoformity in the Church* (Grand Rapids, MI: Brazos, 2019); **C. M. Pate,** *The Reverse of the Curse: Paul, Wisdom, and the Law* (Tübingen: Mohr Siebeck, 2000); **A. W. Pitts,** "Philosophical and Epistolary Contexts for Pauline Paraenesis," in *Paul and the Ancient Letter Form,* ed. S. E. Porter and S. A. Adams, Pauline Studies 6 (Leiden: Brill, 2010), 269-306; **B. S. Rosner,** *Paul and the Law: Keeping the Commandments of God,* NSBT (Downers Grove, IL: InterVarsity Press, 2013); **J. T. Sanders,** "When Sacred Canopies Collide: The Reception of the Torah of Moses in the Wisdom Literature of the Second-Temple Period," *JSJ* 32 (2001): 121-36; **E. J. Schnabel,** *Law and Wisdom from Ben Sira to Paul: A Tradition Historical Enquiry into the Relation of Law, Wisdom, and Ethics* (Tübingen: Mohr Siebeck, 1985); idem, "Wisdom," in *DPL,* 967-73; **W. D. Shiell,** "Wisdom in the

Workplace," in *Wise Church*, ed. S. McKnight and D. J. Hanlon (Eugene, OR: Wipf & Stock, 2021), 47-67; **J. W. Thompson,** *Moral Formation According to Paul: The Context and Coherence of Pauline Ethics* (Grand Rapids, MI: Baker, 2011); **C. L. Wahlen,** "Greek Wisdom," in *DOTWPW*, 842-47; **S. Westerholm,** "Four Maccabees: A Paraenetic Address?," in *Early Christian Paraenesis in Context*, ed. J. Starr and T. Engberg-Pedersen (Berlin: de Gruyter, 2005), 191-216; **W. T. Wilson,** *Love Without Pretense: Romans 12.9-21 and Hellenistic-Jewish Wisdom Literature* (Tübingen: Mohr Siebeck, 1991); **B. Witherington III,** *Jesus the Sage: The Pilgrimage of Wisdom* (Minneapolis: Augsburg Fortress, 1994).

D. J. Hanlon

WISDOM CHRISTOLOGY. *See* Christology; Lord; Wisdom.

WITCHCRAFT. *See* Ephesians, Letter to the; Magic.

WITNESS

"Witness"/"testimony" language connotes a person or message deemed trustworthy. It can therefore describe any kind of *truth telling, including Paul's *preaching of the *gospel ("the testimony of *Christ," 1 Cor 1:6). By extension, the terminology often refers to the *mission of Christians generally, as they *bear witness* to Christ in a nonbelieving world. Paul's letters provide rich evidence of Christian witness in this broad sense.

1. Etymology and Usage
2. Witness as Gospel Preaching
3. Witness as Gospel Partnership

1. Etymology and Usage.

The root *martyr-* is thought to derive from an Indo-European root meaning "to remember" (hence the Sanskrit term for certain Hindu Scriptures: *smriti*, "remembered writings"). By extension, the Greek *martyria* (testimony), *martyreō*, (bear witness), *martys* (one who bears witness), and so on all convey the sense that the testimony offered derives from genuine remembrance or experience (Silva). The terminology is thus particularly frequent in ancient legal contexts: "I, [NAME], testify [*martyreō*]" is a common formula in papyri contracts (e.g., P.Dura 29.23, 24; see further Spicq).

Perhaps equally important for understanding Paul's usage is the presence of witness terminology (complete with legal connotations) in LXX Isaiah: the Servant and/or *Israel is a "witness" to God's faithfulness in the world (Is 43:10, 12; 44:8 LXX); the descendant of David is "given as a witness among the *Gentiles" (*martyrion en ethnesin dedōka*, Is 55:4 LXX).

Paul frequently uses "witness" terminology in what might be described as oath taking: he testifies on behalf of unbelieving Jews that they have zeal for *God (Rom 10:2), his own conscience testifies to his integrity (2 Cor 1:12), he testifies to Macedonian generosity in the matter of the *collection (2 Cor 8:3), he testifies that circumcision obliges a person to keep the whole law (Gal 5:3), and he testifies about the hard work of Epaphras (Col 4:13). The most trustworthy witness is, of course, God himself, and Paul calls "God as [his] witness" to the genuineness of his motives in a change of *travel plans (2 Cor 1:23), to the constancy of his prayers on behalf of the Romans (Rom 1:9), to the depth of his affection for the Philippians (Phil 1:8), and to the moral and financial integrity of his ministry in Thessalonica (1 Thess 1:8). Of special importance is Paul's use of "witness" language to refer to the gospel itself (1 Cor 1:6; 2 Thess 1:10; possibly 1 Tim 2:6; and 2 Tim 1:8) and to his activity of bearing witness to Christ (1 Cor 15:15, twice; Gal 5:3; 1 Thess 2:12). These perhaps reflect the Isaianic background. Similar "missionary" usage, frequently in connection with Paul, is found throughout Acts (Acts 1:8, 22; 14:3; 22:15, 18; 23:11; 26:16, 22).

Paul does not explicitly describe his converts, or even his *coworkers (2 Tim 1:8?), as bearing witness to the gospel. Yet, his letters are replete with mentions of his converts commending Christ to the world in less formal ways, witnessing in the broader sense.

2. Witness as Gospel Preaching.

Unsurprisingly, most references to evangelistic preaching in Paul's letters describe his own *ministry (1 Thess 2:4; Gal 1:15-16; 1 Cor 1:17; 9:14; 15:9:11; 2 Cor 4:1-5; Rom 1:1, 9, 14-15; 15:17-20; Col 1:23-27; Eph 3:1-6; 1 Tim 1:11; 2 Tim 1:11). His coworkers share in that ministry: Timothy and Silvanus (1 Thess 1:5, 9; 3:2; see 2 Tim 4:5), *Peter and Barnabas (Gal 2:7, 9), Epaphras (Col 1:3-8), and the unnamed "brother" who is "famous among all the churches for his preaching of the gospel" (2 Cor 8:18 ESV). By contrast, Paul's converts are never said to preach the gospel. Rather, the gospel is preached to them (1 Thess 2:9) and handed on to them (1 Cor 15:3); they receive it (Gal 1:9), believe it (1 Cor 15:11), and are saved by it (1 Cor 15:2). This seemingly *passive* role in evangelism led Kenneth Scott Latourette in his classic *History of the Expansion of Christianity* to conclude that nowhere in the NT "does any hint occur that the rank and file of Christians regarded it as even a minor part of their duty to communicate their faith to others" (Latourette, 117). Similar claims have been made by scholars focusing specifically on Paul's letters (Ollrog; Bowers; Donaldson).

More recent scholarship (Ware; Plummer; Keown) has sought to reinstate the missionary witness of Paul's converts, interpreting certain key texts as evidence that believers in general are called to bear witness to the gospel, just like Paul and his coworkers. While exegetically rich, such treatments are not conclusive. For example, it might be argued that 1 Thessalonians 1:8 indicates missionary proclamation on the part of the Thessalonian *church (Ware 1992): "The Lord's message rang out [*exēchētai*] from you not only in Macedonia and Achaia—your *faith in God has become known everywhere" (NIV). Yet, the key verb *exēchētai* signals an *echo* or *reverberation* and may simply refer to *Paul's own preaching* in Thessalonica, which reverberated (via reports) throughout Macedonia and Achaia. Again, the reference in Philippians 1:14 to "most of the brothers" being encouraged to "speak the word of God more courageously" might refer to Christians in general, since the anarthrous *adelphos* (brother, sister) frequently means believers generally. Yet the articular *ho adelphos*/*hoi adelphoi* in Paul's letters more commonly refers specifically to the apostle's coworkers (Rom 16:14, 23; 1 Cor 1:1; 16:11-12, 20; 2 Cor 1:1; 2:13; 8:18, 22-23; 9:3, 5; 11:9; 12:18; Gal 1:2; Phil 1:14; 2:25; 4:21; 1 Thess 3:2; Philem 1, 7, 20). Finally, some have interpreted Ephesians 6:15 as referring to evangelistic preaching on the part of Paul's converts: "As shoes for your feet put on whatever will make you ready to proclaim the gospel of *peace." Yet, this NRSV translation hides the ambiguity of the original: literally "fitting the feet in readiness/security of the gospel of peace," or as the NIV renders it, "with your feet fitted with the readiness that comes from the gospel of peace."

3. Witness as Gospel Partnership.

Whether or not Paul hoped his converts would preach the gospel as he did, his letters provide clear evidence that he expected them to bear witness to the world in numerous other verbal and nonverbal ways. One passage opens a window on Paul's thought about Christian witness. In Philippians 1:5, the *apostle gives thanks for the Philippians' "partnership in the gospel from the first day until now" (Phil 1:5 NRSV), widely acknowledged as a reference to the church's decade-long **financial support* of Paul's mission. The letter's conclusion reiterates the theme of partnership/sharing (*koinōn-*) with an explicit mention of the Philippians' recent "gift" (Phil 4:14-18). This notion of "partnership in/for the gospel" (*koinōnia eis to euangelion*) underscores Paul's key idea of Christian witness. Believers are called on to *promote* the gospel mission through a variety of activities.

Financial partnership in the evangelistic cause is a recurring theme, beyond Philippians. Paul urges his churches to assist him and other missionaries in their journeys for the gospel. The key term is *propempō*, "to send with assistance" (Rom 15:24; 1 Cor 16:6; Titus 3:13; see 3 Jn 1:5-8). The theme derives from the Jesus *tradition (Mt 10:10//Lk 10:7), which Paul explicitly cites in connection with gospel preachers in 1 Corinthians 9:14.

Paul also expects his converts to *pray* for the work of the gospel, as part of their evangelistic witness. Not only is it his own practice to pray for the *salvation of nonbelievers (Rom 10:1), but he enjoins others to pray for the preachers of the gospel (Col 4:2-4; Eph 6:19-20) and for the rapid advance (*trechō*) of the gospel itself (2 Thess 3:1).

Christians bear witness to the world through their *good deeds*. They must labor to present a "good appearance" (*euschēmonōs*) to nonbelievers (1 Thess 4:11-12). They should "walk in *wisdom toward outsiders [*pros tous exō*]," making "the most of every opportunity" (Col 4:5 NIV). Even *slaves are to "make the teaching about God our *Savior attractive [*kosmeō*]" through their diligent and trustworthy dealings (Titus 2:9-10 NIV). Here the relationship between good deeds and the preaching of the good news is clarified: the virtues of humility, integrity, and truthfulness displayed in a Christian slave can serve to highlight the beautiful character of the gospel teaching about the Savior.

In one passage, Paul urges believers to bear witness to nonbelievers by *answering questions* (Col 4:3-6). There is a deliberate parallelism in this paragraph between Paul's obligation ("must," *dei*) to speak the Word (*logos*) of the "*mystery of Christ" (Col 4:3-4) and the Colossians' obligation ("must," *dei*) to "answer everyone" with a gracious "word" (*logos en chariti*; Col 4:6). The parallelism reveals an analogy between the apostolic witness and the witness of ordinary Christians; it also highlights the difference. Both Paul and his recipients have a *logos* to offer the world, but whereas Paul has a duty to declare the mystery of Christ, Christians in general have a duty simply to be ready to give an answer (see 1 Pet 3:15).

A collective form of Christian witness to the world is *public *worship*. Paul urges the Corinthians to modify church services so that nonbelievers might understand what is being said and thus "fall down and worship God" (1 Cor 14:24-25 NIV). Finally, Paul expects his converts to modify even their *dining habits* for the sake of Christian witness: in order to bring "*glory to God" among "Jews and Greeks," in the hope of "saving" some (1 Cor 10:31–11:1).

In these various elements of Christian witness Paul is likely indebted to his Jewish heritage (Dickson). While evidence of direct Jewish proselytizing is limited (e.g., Josephus, *Ant.* 20.17-96), many Jewish texts indicate that Israel was to bear witness to the Gentiles: through *good deeds* (T. Levi 14.1-4; Philo, *Ios.* 86-87), **prayer* for the enlightenment of Gentiles (Philo, *Spec.* 1.84-97; *Mos.* 1.149), *public worship* to which Gentiles were invited (Philo, *Mos.* 2.41-44; Josephus, *J.W.* 7.45), and *giving an answer* to Gentile inquirers (Let. Aris. 187-193; m. Abot 2:14).

See also FINANCIAL SUPPORT; GOSPEL; MISSION; PREACHING, FIRST-CENTURY; TRUTH.

BIBLIOGRAPHY. **P. Bowers,** "Church and Mission in Paul," *JSNT* 44 (1991): 89-111; **J. P. Dickson,** *Mission-Commitment in Ancient Judaism and in the Pauline Communities: The Shape, Extent, and Background of Early Christian Mission*, WUNT 2/159 (Tübingen: Mohr Siebeck, 2003); **T. Donaldson,** "The Absence in Paul's Letters of Any Injunction to Evangelize" (paper presented at the Annual Meeting of the Society of Biblical Literature, Nashville, 2000); **M. J. Gorman,** *Becoming the Gospel: Paul, Participation, and Mission* (Grand Rapids, MI: Eerdmans, 2015); **M. Keown,** *Congregational Evangelism in Philippians: The Centrality of an Appeal for Gospel Proclamation to the Fabric of Philippians* (Milton Keynes, UK: Paternoster, 2008); **K. S. Latourette,** *A History of the Expansion of Christianity: The First Five Centuries*, vol. 1 (New York: Harper & Brothers, 1937); **W. Ollrog,** *Paulus und seine Mitarbeiter: Untersuchungen zu Theorie und Praxis der paulinischen Mission*, ed. F. Hahn and O. Steck, WMANT 50 (Neukirchen-Vluyn: Neukirchener Verlag, 1979); **R. L. Plummer,** *Paul's Understanding of the Church's Mission: Did the Apostle Paul Expect the Early Christian Communities to Evangelize?* (Milton Keynes, UK: Paternoster, 2006); **E. J. Schnabel,** *Early Christian Mission*, vol. 2, *Paul and the Early Church* (Downers Grove, IL: InterVarsity Press, 2005); **M. Silva,** "μαρτυρια, etc.," *NIDNTT*, 2nd ed. (Grand Rapids, MI: Zondervan, 2014), 3:234-46; **C. Spicq,** "μαρτυς, etc.," *TLNT* 2:447-52; **H. Strathmann,** "μαρτυς, etc.," *TDNT* 4:474-514; **J. Ware,** "The Thessalonians as a Missionary Congregation: 1 Thessalonians 1:5-8," *ZNW* 83 (1992): 126-31; idem, *The Mission of the Church in Paul's Letter to the Philippians in the Context of Ancient Judaism* (Leiden: Brill, 2005); **K. L. Yinger,** "Paul and Evangelism: A Missiological Challenge from New Testament Specialists," *Missiology* 37 (2009): 385-96.

J. P. Dickson

WOMEN

Although all topics in relation to Pauline study are marked by disagreement in some form or another, there may not be a topic characterized by such widely divergent views as Paul's *teaching on the role and place of women—in the *church, in *marriage, and in society. Paul's letters are well known to contain contentious texts for and about women, even among those who have never read them. In the course of the history of the church, it would probably be true to say that his letters have been solely responsible for some of the most uncompromisingly repressive attitudes toward women in various denominations and expressions of church. For this reason, these texts have also been the cause of some making the decision either to leave the church or to avoid church altogether. In short, the significance of Paul's letters for women, how women are perceived, how they perceive themselves in relation to *God, and what roles and ministries they might or might not exercise is immense. Not only this, but their significance for the corresponding role of men in relation to women and in relation to God, how men are perceived, how they perceive themselves, and their roles and ministries is also vast. It should not be imagined, therefore, that the topic of women in Paul's letters is a discrete topic with relevance only to the female sex. It is a topic that touches on fundamental issues of what it means to be human as part of the living body of the church.

Throughout most of church history, the passages on women in Paul's letters have been understood as expressing a fundamental belief that a woman's place in church governance, marriage, and possibly even society should be one of submission to men, who have been placed in authority over them. Although this has undoubtedly been the majority view, it is now recognized that there have always been groups of women (and men) who have resisted this idea, on the basis that certain women have been clearly gifted by God in a way that has been obvious to all. In other words, a charismatic approach to church life and practice has many times taken precedence over the strict adherence to what it appeared the Pauline letters were mandating in certain instances. If the Spirit was authenticating and validating women's *ministry by the fruit of those same ministries, who were the men and women around them to doubt this? Throughout the ages, therefore, there have been men who have recognized and welcomed the ministry of *leadership, teaching, and preaching by women, even coming under their authority, and there have been women who have responded to what they believe is God's *call to take up those tasks. That there has been consistent and in some senses persistent resistance to the aforementioned hierarchical view of male authority and female submission/subordination tells something of the enduring disquiet among Christians regarding this teaching.

One of the reasons that there is now more awareness of the times and places in the history of the church where women's ministry and leadership has been acknowledged is that there is a worldwide movement within the academy as a whole to turn its attention to the previously ignored and undocumented role of women in history: in literature, politics, science, medicine, philosophy, education, and so on. This is also having an impact in biblical studies and theology, so stones, as it were, are being unturned. Although this move might largely be associated with feminism in a broad sense, it is misleading to assume, first, that feminism exists in only one identifiable form, and second, that the impact of feminism has given rise to a unified response to Paul. It is, in fact, the opposite. Feminist readings of Paul, along with *all* readings of Paul, are hugely diverse, and thus, although the topic of this article is Paul and women, it will not focus on feminist approaches to Paul as such but on the broader response to Paul through the ages and the current situation at this time.

1. Current Positions
2. Methodology
3. In Support of a Mutualist View
4. The Texts
5. Household Codes
6. Applying Paul's Apostolic Teaching

1. Current Positions.

The world is now in an unusual position where scholars and churchmen and -women have adopted diametrically opposed views of Paul. There are those who see Paul's letters as mandating an order of male authority and female submission and/or subordination (whether in the church, the home, society, or all three) (e.g., Grudem; Hodge; Piper), and those who see in Paul's letters a revolutionary message that frees women to serve in all ministries in the church and to have an equal place with men in marriage and society (e.g., McKnight; Peppiatt). Although among evangelicals these two perspectives have been labeled as complementarian and egalitarian, respectively, there is a move to rename these perspectives as hierarchicalist and mutualist on the grounds that these terms are more descriptive of the foundational ideologies of both perspectives (McKnight; Peppiatt). In addition, *hierarchicalist* and *mutualist* can be more easily applied to nonevangelical traditions within the church, such as the Roman Catholic and Orthodox churches, in which all the authoritative positions within the church hierarchy are held by men.

As mentioned above, much of Western culture in the last century has been shaped by feminism. This development is not always viewed favorably in Christian circles, and feminism is often "blamed" for what is viewed by hierarchicalists as a progressive reading of Paul. It is sometimes implied that Paul's letters are only now interpreted differently because of social and cultural pressure to give women an equal place with men. In reality, the impact of feminism is a much more nuanced force in the world and has, in general, improved the lot of women in the home, in education, in the workplace, and in the world. Long-standing inequalities and injustices are being addressed, and Christians should welcome these moves. However, whether one sees feminism as a friend or foe, it would be wrong to assume a direct causal link between rereadings of Paul and feminism *per se*. It should be noted that many feminists, both Christian and secular, would dismiss Paul and his writings altogether.

Further, whereas feminism has undoubtedly had an impact in all areas of life, it is not true to say that feminism or cultural change is the sole driving force behind the mutualist perspective. Factors that have had a significant impact on a mutualist reading of Paul include the rise in number of female scholars (in all disciplines, not just biblical scholarship and theology) and all scholars (male and female) looking more closely at the place of women in the Bible. The result of this is that scholars are now highlighting the role of women in the Bible and in history, where previously they were ignored. In theology, scholars are uncovering erstwhile disregarded data, changing the way the role that women have had in the church, society, and *mission is understood. Where the events of history have often been distorted in the past, they are now being revisited, giving rise to a reexamination of Scripture and how it should be interpreted, understood, and applied in relation to women and men.

Thus, as female and male scholars turn their attention to the depiction of women in the Bible and church history, it is now argued that the call for women to have a role in leading, preaching, and teaching is certainly not rooted solely in a cultural shift. Culture has played its part, to be sure, affording women education and opportunity, but the really radical shift for the church is that this is a call that is seen to arise both from the Scriptures themselves and from the testimony of church history. It is now recognized that the foundations for women to participate in all aspects of ministry in the church, to take up an equal role in marriage and the home, and to occupy positions of leadership come from within the Christian tradition. Hence, today one finds readings of the same Scriptures yielding the opposite result: the texts that were formerly read as endorsing the subordination or submission of women are now read in ways that communicate the opposite. This essay will explore this development.

A number of factors have contributed to this radical shift, and in order to understand how it is possible to have two such diametrically opposed readings of Paul, it is necessary to turn to the question of method.

2. Methodology.

The developments in scholarship cited above mean that someone trying to make sense of "what Paul *really* said about women" might well be overwhelmed by the dizzying array of conflicting views around the texts where women are mentioned. Having said that, it is possible to identify four distinct assumptions that operate behind these various and conflicting readings of Paul, and thus one can identify how and where these four main assumptions give rise to divergent views. This article classifies these four assumptions as three distinct versions of a hierarchicalist view, plus a mutualist view. These different views are determined by where one chooses to begin and which data one chooses to prioritize in making decisions regarding what women should or should not be permitted to do. There is also the matter of coherence. Scholars are divided on whether Paul can be read as having a coherent theology/position on women. As will become clear, if coherence is a goal, this will drive readers toward a mutualist reading of Paul. This article will begin with the hierarchicalist perspective, which will then be broken down into three different versions.

2.1. The Hierarchicalist Perspective. As noted, the most dominant reading of Paul throughout history is that Paul himself held to a hierarchicalist view of the place and role of women: men have been placed in a preeminent and authoritative position in *creation, society, marriage, and the church, and women should be in submission to men due to their subordinate role. The more extreme versions of this view claim that Paul believed in the submission of women to men because they are by nature, that is, God's design, subordinate. Inherent in this position is an assumption, which was dominant in the ancient world, that women were created with some form of deficiency or natural inferiority to men, and this should be reflected in marriage, church, and society. This view has also dominated for much of church history, with women frequently depicted as more prone to deception and *sin, emotionally unstable, less intelligent, less able to understand spiritual truths, and generally weaker in all areas of life than men. As the rationale for these views was often attributed to Paul and the views expressed in his letters, it is for this reason that Paul has been labeled a misogynist by recent generations.

The key text underpinning the view that women are by nature inferior to men is found in 1 Corinthians 11:2-16. Here Paul refers to *man as the "*head" of woman (1 Cor 11:3), where woman herself is the head of no one. Also here one finds the statement that "[man] is the *image and *glory of God," and woman is "the glory of man" (1 Cor 11:7 NIV). These function as two central claims in the hierarchicalist view. In recent years, for obvious and good reasons, the idea that women are by *nature* inferior to men has been exposed as a gross fallacy and is rarely found as the warrant for the submission of women to men. Instead, hierarchicalist views have been transmuted to the idea that men and women, though equal before God, are assigned different "roles" in creation, marriage, the church, and society. These claims are rooted in a tapestry of cross-referencing the following biblical texts: Genesis 2:18-24; 3:6, 16; 1 Corinthians 11:2-16; 14:34-35; Ephesians 5:22-33; Colossians 3:18; 1 Timothy 2:8-15; 3:1-13.

As an example of how this works, 1 Corinthians 11:3, 7-9 in particular are then cross-referenced back to Genesis 2, where it is believed that God himself established a hierarchical relation between all men and all women at creation by creating man first and then woman second as "a suitable helper." Even though there is no reference to man or the husband as the "head," in Genesis it is assumed that man's preeminence signifies an authoritative and leadership role for all men over all women. These assumptions are then also read forward to the *household codes, especially Ephesians 5, where one does read Paul referring to the husband as the "head" of his wife and where Paul instructs wives that they should "submit" to their husbands. The reference to the submission of wives is also found in Colossians 3:18.

Two further texts that are seen to endorse male authority and female submission, especially within the *ekklēsia* (and so applied to church governance), are 1 Corinthians 14:33-35, where it appears Paul tells married women they should remain silent in church and ask their husbands at home if they desire to know anything, and 1 Timothy 2:11-12, where it is believed there is incontrovertible evidence that Paul was prohibiting women in general to teach men. Instead women are to stay silent and learn in quietness and submission. Finally, in 1 Timothy 3 it is assumed that Paul was referring to men only for the office of bishop and deacon, and thus it is argued that each text endorses the submission of women to men.

A fundamental assumption is that Paul's understanding of the husband/man as the "head" of his wife/all women, and as the sole bearer of the "glory and image of God," led him to the rule that men alone should assume positions of authority in the church and the home and that the women should submit to their male leaders and husbands. In this view, it seems clear that Paul sees a divine order whereby men are given authority to rule, to teach the Scriptures, and to make decisions. Women, in contrast, are given a subordinate role in creation, the church, and society, and married women are to submit to their husbands. In short, all women in some form or another are to be under male authority.

2.2. The Three Versions of Hierarchicalist Views. The hierarchicalist perspective on Paul can be subdivided into three categories: affirming, disavowing, and ambivalent hierarchicalists. (1) Affirming hierarchicalists are those who see an unqualified hierarchy of men in authority over women in the Bible and who are sympathetic to this view. They also believe that this should be the norm for the present-day church (Piper and Grudem). (2) Disavowing hierarchicalists are those who believe that Paul held to a straightforwardly hierarchicalist view but believe that this contradicts the overall will of God for men and women, and so they reject what they see as Paul's view as either outdated, culturally irrelevant, and/or pernicious (Lakey). (3) Ambivalent hierarchicalists are those who see an ambivalence in Paul's writings on this issue (Gundry-Volf).

The ambivalence in question might be thought to be either in Paul himself (thus explaining some contradictory data in relation to women in his letters) or between Paul and his later followers/disciples (i.e., Paul was more of a libertarian than later elders, overseers, or bishops in the church). In the first category, then, there are some who argue that Paul is genuinely ambivalent on the issue of women's participation in church and that this explains a kind of flip-flopping or double-mindedness evident, at times, in his letters. There are others who argue that the ambivalence comes from an evolution in Paul's own thought and is reflected in a shift from his earlier letters to his later ones. As the church grew and took root in society, it is argued, Paul became more concerned that Christians were seen to be respecting cultural hierarchical norms to guard against persecution and opposition. Others see a shift from Paul's own thought in his earlier letters to that of his followers, signaling a shift in later epistles that they attribute to his disciples, that is, Colossians, Ephesians, and the Pastorals. The difference between these perspectives is clearly dependent on a prior decision regarding authorship. In addition, one can identify an ambivalence in the reception of Paul among scholars and churchmen and -women over this issue. It is really far from clear how a hierarchical perspective in Paul should be applied to the contemporary church. The confusion over what Paul might have intended in concrete terms for the universal and thus the contemporary church is reflected in the bewildering muddle over what women may or may not be permitted to do in the church, the home, and the workplace by their own denominations.

2.3. The Mutualist View. A stark contrast to a hierarchicalist view is a mutualist perspective, and this has come to the fore in recent years. According to this view, Paul championed women in all forms of ministry, which can be seen in the number of women around him, the responsibilities that they held, and their role in the church. Mutualist readings of Paul see this reflected in both church governance and marriage. As mentioned above, many affirming hierarchicalists worry that this recent shift in perspective has arisen from a desire to conform to "worldly" standards in relation to men and women and therefore believe it should be resisted in favor of what they see as a more "biblical" view. Mutualists, however, argue that it is their view that has the strongest support from Scripture, given the weight of evidence that women were created equal to men for all forms of ministry and *service, and for equality within marriage if they are married.

There is no doubt that this disagreement represents an impasse between two parties within the church. This also reflects widely divergent views across denominational lines having a bearing, as it does, on all aspects of male and female *identity and relations, marriage, and church governance. The significance of this debate for women and men cannot be overstated.

3. In Support of a Mutualist View.

There are four main reasons for questioning whether the hierarchicalist perspective is either really Paul's view and/or whether this reflects a truly Christian teaching on men and women. These include the teachings and actions of Jesus and the evidence of female leadership in the OT (both of which would have informed Paul's thinking), along with the existence of Paul's female *coworkers and his own baptismal and *temple theology of the *body of *Christ.

3.1. Jesus. It is generally acknowledged that the hierarchicalist view stated above cannot be found in the teachings and actions of Jesus. In fact, in the Gospels, one finds the opposite is true in Jesus' relations to women. Although there are twelve male apostles appointed by Jesus, women play an equally prominent role in the reception of the *faith, the *witness to the faith, and the transmission of the faith. God chooses to incarnate God the *Son in and through a woman. Jesus chooses to reveal his identity as the Messiah to women (Jn 4:26; 11:25-27). Jesus appears in his resurrected form to women, appointing them as the first "witnesses" (Mt 28:1-10; Mk 16:1-11; Lk 24:1-10; Jn 20:11-18). Jesus' teaching on marriage is blatantly both defensive and protective of women's rights within marriage (Mt 19:4-9; Lk 16:18). Women are not treated as secondary in their status, as unclean, as objects of shame, or as marginal to the transmission of the *truth. Instead, here in the Gospels one finds that women are consistently elevated by Jesus and are recognized as both witnesses and disciples. The question here, then, revolves around the relationship of Jesus to Paul. Can one claim that there is a continuity and synthesis of Jesus and Paul's views in relation to women, or is there a significant departure?

3.2. The Old Testament Stories of Women. In recent years, much more attention has been paid to the role of women in the OT, focusing on the crucial role that women play in the grand *narrative of *salvation. In the OT one finds women leaders, judges, prophets, warriors, and defenders of the faith, all of which entail that they have authoritative roles over men. Their key role in the history of *Israel, both Jesus' and Paul's own history, adds weight to the view that Paul would have given more credence to the idea that God might appoint women for the task of *preaching the *gospel, making disciples, and leading the people of God.

3.3. Paul's Female Coworkers. The third reason is the evidence in Paul's letters that he clearly appointed women to leadership, teaching, and preaching roles. This blatantly contradicts any injunctions that indicate he taught the opposite as a universal rule for the church and thus has caused many to revisit the texts that imply that women should remain silent. The very obvious role of women in Paul's churches, clearly appointed by Paul himself, directly challenges claims that Paul placed all women in submission to men and prohibited them from teaching and leading and so on. An indication of how scholarship has shifted quite radically on this in a short period of time is that in the first edition of this dictionary, published in 1993, the only female coworker cited in the essay "Co-Workers, Paul and His," is Priscilla. Junia is ruled out as an *apostle, and although there is an acknowledgment that Paul had women coworkers, none of them are mentioned by name (Ellis).

Now, however, it is widely recognized that Paul uses different terms to refer to the people who labor or toil with him: coworker (*synergos*), apostle (*apostolos*), brother or sister (*adelphos* or *adelphē*), minister (*diakonos*), fellow servant (*syndoulos*), fellow-soldier (*systratiōtēs*), and "fellow-prisoner" (*synaichmalōtos*). Hence there are many women who are fall into these categories. There are also numerous women who are named in the NT who were influential in the spread of the gospel and church leadership. These include Tabitha (Acts 9:36-42), Lydia (Acts 16:14-15, 40), Phoebe, Priscilla, Mary, Junia, Tryphaena and Tryphosa, Persis, Rufus's mother, Julia, the sister of Nereus (Rom 16), Chloe (1 Cor 1:11), Euodia and Syntyche (Phil 4:2-3), Nympha (Col 4:15), Lois and Eunice (2 Tim 1:5), Claudia (2 Tim 4:21), Apphia (Philem 1:2), the mother of John Mark (Acts 12:12), the "elect lady" (2 Jn 1:1), Philip's four prophet daughters (Acts 21:9), and the women who are encouraged to prophesy in *Corinth (1 Cor 11:2-16).

Priscilla is prominent among these women. She is mentioned not just in Romans 16:3 but in Acts 18:2, 18, 26; 1 Corinthians 16:19; and 2 Timothy 4:19, where she is listed with her husband, Aquila. Four of the six times she is named first, giving a clear indication that she is deemed to be the most prominent of the pair. In addition to this, she had a crucial role in instructing Apollos in the faith (Acts 18:26). Note, also, that the list in Romans 16 includes more women than men. Prisca, Mary, Tryphaena, Tryphosa, and Persis all "worked" with Paul. Beverly Gaventa writes, "That bland verb does not convey a great deal in English, but this is the language he uses elsewhere when he is speaking about apostolic labor (as in 1 Cor 3:9; 4:12; 15:10; Gal 4:11; 1 Thess 5:12)" (Gaventa, 7-8). The term *coworker* is also the term used of Euodia and Syntyche in Philippians 4:2-3. It is also often noted that they are named with no reference to the men to whom they are related, which is unusual for an ancient text. Instead, they are named as women in their own right, which serves as an indication of their standing with Paul and in the community. Of all these women, two in particular deserve a special mention: Phoebe and Junia.

3.3.1. Phoebe. Paul commends his sister Phoebe to the Roman churches, a deacon of the church at Cenchrae and a benefactor or patron of many, including himself (Rom 16:1-2). The words he uses to describe her are *diakonos* and *prostatis*, which in the past were often translated as "servant" and "helper," respectively. It turns out that not only are these inadequate translations of these two words, but they have served to mislead as to the significance of Phoebe's position and role in the church and in relation to Paul. One can find instances when the word *servant* is used to translate *diakonos* in relation to men, although when referring to a man, it is more commonly found as *minister.* As Elizabeth McCabe points out, *diakonos* is the word "Paul uses to describe his own ministry (1 Cor 3:5; 2 Cor 3:6; 6:4, 11:23; Eph 3:7; Col 1:23, 25)," and so it might be expected that Phoebe is understood as an equal to Paul and other men in terms of her ministry, "but it is unlikely that this parallel could ever be gleaned from English translations alone" (McCabe, 99). Phoebe is still often referred to as a "servant" even now, but this choice of word here does not convey to the reader the import of Paul's description. McCabe makes the point that Paul describes Phoebe as "being" (the participle *ousan*) "of the church in Cenchreae" (the genitive *ekklēsias*), implying a recognized position or ministry in a specific congregation (McCabe, 100). She was a deacon *of* the church, not just a servant *from* the church.

In addition to this, it has now been established that Phoebe was the courier of the letter to the Roman churches. This tells of her central role within the church, her leadership capacities, and her relationship to Paul. Acting as a courier of a *letter in the ancient world entailed not simply delivering the letter but taking responsibility for reading (even "performing") the letter to the recipients, acting as the representative of the author, delivering it as he or she would have wished. In other words, Phoebe's comprehension of the content and import of the letter was so thorough that Paul entrusted the task to her. For him to have chosen a woman to deliver, convey, and take questions on the most theologically dense of his letters tells us as much about him as it does about her.

On the question of Phoebe delivering and reading/interpreting the letter, Gaventa writes, "If Phoebe is the carrier of the letter, and most scholars agree on that point, then she was almost certainly engaged in discussing its content in advance" (Gaventa, 12). She understood the letter thoroughly and knew what Paul wanted to achieve by it. Gaventa adds, "Almost inevitably, Phoebe shaped the hearing of the letter by the way she read it" (Gaventa, 13). She also speculates, "Phoebe may even have had a hand in shaping the content of the letter" (Gaventa, 12-13).

In addition, Paul uses the word *prostatis*, which has been translated in the past as "helper." However, as *prostatis* is a *hapax legomenon* (it occurs only once in the Bible), one can only glean its meaning from cognate (related) terms. Its derivation from the verb *proistēmi* leads to a range of options associated with functions such as presiding, ruling over, directing, or maintaining. Phoebe was one who ruled and led (McCabe). The word *prostatis* also indicates that she was a patron or benefactor, and as a woman of means, she funded Paul's and others' ministries. The overall picture of Phoebe is that she was a great and trusted friend of Paul's and one who was given the task (presumably among other tasks) of delivering his teaching to a strategic church in a key city.

3.3.2. Junia the Apostle. Another highly contested figure among Paul's female friends and coworkers is Junia (Rom 16:7). It is now largely accepted that Junia, with Andronicus, was notable or outstanding among the apostles. This has not always been the case, as in the past translators of the Bible adapted Junia (a woman's name) to Junias (a man's name), on the grounds that a woman could not have been an apostle. Two things are disturbing about the history of the translation of Junia's name and how—once it was established that she was a woman—the idea that she was also an apostle was rejected. First is the refusal to let the text speak for itself, and second is that this is a modern perspective, not an ancient one. John Chrysostom, who was not *that* favorable to women in general, although better than some, writes this in his commentary on Romans:

> To be an apostle is something great. But to be outstanding among the apostles—just think what a wonderful song of praise that is! They

> were outstanding on the basis of their works and virtuous actions. Indeed, how great the wisdom of this woman must have been that she was even deemed worthy of the title of apostle! But even here he does not stop, but adds another song of praise besides, and says "*Who were also in Christ before me.*" (John Chrysostom, *Hom. Rom.* 31 [PG])

So despite the fact that Junia was considered to be a woman within the early church, she was still glossed out of the Bible in later centuries. Now, however, she is recognized as both a woman and an apostle who was *in Christ before Paul. (For more detail on the history of translation, see Scot McKnight, *Junia Is Not Alone*, as well as other recent material on this subject [Epp; Pederson.])

3.4. Paul's Christic Baptismal and Temple Theology. Much hinges on what is understood by the concrete and social implications of Paul's "in Christ" baptismal theology, and his teaching on the body of Christ as one new humanity (Eph 2:14-18). It is quite clear that Paul advocates for full inclusion of the *Gentiles into the initially Jewish church, the body of Christ, on the basis of faith in Jesus Christ. This inclusion entails full equality as co-heirs and "sons" in the Son, which applies also to women. The dividing wall of hostility between Jew and Gentile is destroyed through the *cross of Christ, and two hitherto unreconciled people groups are able to find *peace and unity in Christ. Paul raises this issue with the Galatian church, emphasizing again the equality of all the children of God through faith, "for all of you who were baptized into Christ have clothed yourselves with Christ." He goes on to make the following lapidary statement, "There is neither Jew nor Gentile, neither *slave nor free, nor is there male and female, for you are all one in Christ Jesus" (Gal 3:27-28 NIV). What this means is a matter of much debate.

Most commentators are agreed that Paul is not suggesting that there is now no longer any differentiation whatsoever between Jew and Gentile, slave and free, male and female. The question that it raises, which is much debated, is whether Paul entirely subverts established hierarchies within both the Jewish and Greco-Roman worlds or not. A growing number of scholars hold to the view that Paul was "revolutionary" in his challenge to established hierarchies and social distinctions based on perceptions of who was superior (and thus honored) and who was inferior (and thus shamed). In other words, it is argued that his "in Christ" theology dominated his perspective on how Christians should behave toward one another, leading some to posit that all those baptized into Christ and filled with the *Holy Spirit might participate fully in all aspects of church life and service. Again, scholars and churchmen and -women are divided on whether this idea of unity within the body functions as an overarching theme with implications for concrete relations between Jew and Gentile, slave and free, and male and female, or whether Paul had some sort of eschatological vision of unity but held to more traditional patterns and hierarchies within his churches for the sake of decorum.

The data cited above all serves to dismantle Paul's reputation as one who prohibited women from full participation in leadership and ministries of all kinds and serves to build a picture of Paul as an apostle who recognized the gifts of the women around him and appointed them to all forms of leadership and ministries, including as apostles, church leaders, and teachers. However, there are still the knotty texts themselves, to which this article will now turn in order to demonstrate how differently these texts are received within contemporary scholarship.

4. The Texts.

4.1. 1 Corinthians 11:2-16. These fifteen verses are known to contain some of the most difficult interpretive challenges for scholars of the Bible. Questions abound as the interpreter attempts to make sense of the passage as a whole, within the Pauline corpus, and within the canon. There are, however, identifiable patterns in the history of interpretation of these verses by which one can categorize different readings. These can be classified in five categories.

1. Straightforwardly hierarchical: readings in which the passage is seen to endorse the authority of men over women due to the dependent and subordinate status of women in creation, with head coverings as a sign of that authority and submission. This has been a majority reading throughout most of history. There are a number of contemporary scholars who endorse this reading and argue that as every male is God's image and glory and women are not, and that a woman should be subordinated to a man. They may or may not agree with applying this in a straightforward manner for the universal church. (Grudem; Hodge; Piper)
2. Tensive: readings in which scholars see two different approaches to men and women and their relations spelled out in the text, with a

break at 1 Corinthians 11:11. First Corinthians 11:11-16, in which Paul emphasizes the interdependence of men and women, is deemed to soften the blow of 1 Corinthians 11:3-10, where he appears to assert the preeminence of men and the need for women to be covered in order not to shame men, Christ, God, even the angels. Many scholars see the second half as qualifying the first half in some way but will also admit that the two views expressed in one passage do not present a unified whole. (Gundry-Volf; Johnson)

3. Mutualist: readings in which it is asserted that Paul is not even hinting at the subordination of woman in this passage and that the woman's authority is her own authority to dress as she wills. This is an extremely difficult reading to defend given that the warrant for the enforcement of head coverings is plainly given in 1 Corinthians 11:7-10 and is rooted in the idea that man is the image and glory of God and woman is the glory of man, and man was not made for woman but woman for man. It is a stretch to claim that there is no hint of hierarchy and the subordination of women in this passage. (Payne; Westfall)
4. Rhetorical: readings in which it is suggested that the first half of the passage, 1 Corinthians 11:4-10, contains ideas and theology from the Corinthian male leaders whom Paul was opposing and that he gives his response in 1 Corinthians 11:11-16. These readings see the break in 1 Corinthians 11:11 and following verses not simply as a qualification of the preceding verses but as a contradiction. In these readings, Paul is opposed to the practice of head coverings for women and informs the churches at Corinth that a woman's hair is her glory and thus has been given to her instead of a covering. He ends by informing them that they have no such custom (of head coverings) in any of the churches. (Peppiatt; Schirrmacher; Shoemaker)
5. Hairstyles, not head coverings: readings in which it is thought Paul is referring to hairstyles that would shame persons themselves and the people around them in the ancient world, that is, men who had long hair and thus appeared effeminate, and women who had short hair and thus appeared manly or lesbian. Although often argued in great detail, this is not a majority view. (Murphy-O'Connor; Payne)

One of the main, most contentious verses regarding men and women is this passage is 1 Corinthians 11:3, which reads, "the head of every man is Christ, and the head of the woman is man, and the head of Christ is God" (NIV). Paul uses the word *kephalē* for "head" in this instance, which is normally translated as the physical head but has multiple meanings in ancient texts. It has a wide semantic range, including "source," "origin," "first principle," "leader," "ruler," "one in authority," "crown," "completion," "the coping of a wall," or "the capital of a column." Hierarchicalists and mutualists are unable to agree on the meaning of *kephalē*, as hierarchicalists insist that it means "to have authority over" and mutualists insist that it has connotations of "source" or "origin" with no hint of hierarchy. Views on *kephalē* and its meaning are bound up with a doctrine of God and what it is supposed of the relation of God to Christ. Hierarchicalists root their views in the eternal functional subordination of the Son. Mutualists reject this understanding of the Father/Son relation on the grounds that it is associated with a subordinationist heresy. Clues as to what Paul may have meant may be found in Colossians and Ephesians, where Paul refers to Christ as the "head" of the church. Some scholars argue that Paul is reframing the concept of headship as Christlike in terms of both servant leadership and one in whom everything is nourished and grows to maturity.

There is a strong tendency among modern scholars to persuade readers that the practice of head coverings or maintaining certain hairstyles was simply Paul's concern for adhering to cultural norms. It is then argued that these cultural codes do not function in our modern societies in the West and so may be ignored. As the warrant for the practice of head coverings is clearly given and equally clearly rooted in creation theology and *cosmology, this is a tenuous reading. In sum, 1 Corinthians 11:2-16 continues to perplex and challenge scholars who wish to find a "plain meaning." In the light of the intractable interpretive complexities, it should be acknowledged that this passage should not bear the weight of entire theologies of men and women before God and in relation to one another on its own. Nor should it be allowed to be a controlling passage for church life and practice if and when it is in plain contradiction to other foundational creation accounts.

4.2. 1 Corinthians 14:33b-35. These verses similarly pose difficulties in terms of how one understands them first in their own context and then for the contemporary church. The most obvious difficulty that strikes the reader of 1 Corinthians 14:34-35 is that the instruction here for women to remain silent cuts across the reference to women prophesying in the public assembly in 1 Corinthians 11:5. Women clearly were not entirely silent in the assembly, nor were they expected to be. Readings of this passage similarly fall into the different categories, including hierarchicalist, cultural/contextual, and rhetorical readings. In addition to this, it has been proposed that 1 Corinthians 14:34-35 are an interpolation, as the passage would make more sense if these verses had not been inserted (Fee; Payne).

A hierarchicalist reading of 1 Corinthians 14:34-35 claims that Paul wished women to remain silent in church and to be under the authority of their husbands. A cultural/contextual reading posits that the women/wives were being unruly and disrespectful, chattering during the service and disrupting the *worship. In this context, Paul rebukes them and tells them that they should remain silent and ask their husbands what they want to know at home. In other words, he is not prohibiting godly and prayerful contributions to the services but addressing disruptive behavior. A rhetorical reading sees 1 Corinthians 14:33b-35 in quotation marks as expressing the Corinthian perspective and Paul's response to it in 1 Corinthians 14:36-38. It is difficult to read this passage from a mutualist perspective without seeing it as having a rhetorical structure.

4.3. 1 Timothy 2:11-15. First Timothy 2:11-15 is often deemed by hierarchicalists to be an incontrovertible indication that Paul prohibited women from teaching, speaking, or having any authoritative office over men. Naturally, as the case is built drawing from the other hierarchicalist readings of the passages cited above (1 Cor 11:2-16; 14:33-36; Gen 2:18-24; 3:6, 16, and household codes where wives are instructed to submit to their husbands), 1 Timothy 2:11-15 is seen as irrefutable evidence of Paul's prohibitions. Mutualists will argue that it is possible to put a positive spin on these verses as Paul is clearly allowing women to *learn* albeit in quietness and submission. They claim, therefore, that Paul is supportive of educating women. In addition to this, they cite poor translations that do not convey the gentler and less dictatorial tone that occurs in some translations. Examples of this would be that the text is better translated, "I am not permitting a woman to teach" rather than "I do not permit," that *authentein* as another *hapax legomenon* should be translated "to domineer" rather than "to have authority over," and that women are enjoined to learn in "quietness" rather than "silence." There is no doubt that nuances of translation give a different picture.

Recent scholarship on this passage also draws on a number of newly found ancient sources in relation to the Artemis cult and first-century *Ephesus that shed some light on some of the more obscure references in this passage that are not easily explained away (Glahn; Hoag). This scholarship highlights specific links Paul is making between the cult and the women he is referring to in the letter, including (1) the reference to a particular style of dress that Paul describes as linked to the Artemis cult and the "braided hair," (2) the reference to Adam not being deceived and only the woman being portrayed as the transgressor as linked to a blend of the Isis myth and the Artemis myth, and (3) the reference to women being "saved" through childbearing as derived from Artemis of the Ephesians being a virgin goddess of midwifery. Thus, pregnant Ephesian women would have been accustomed to looking to Artemis for protection during childbirth when Christian women were to put their trust in God and continue in faith, *love, *holiness, and propriety.

4.4. 1 Timothy 3:1-13 and Titus 1:5-9. These texts are often cited to support male-only leadership in the church, as it is argued that Paul is addressing only men in describing the moral qualifications of the offices of bishop or elder and deacon. This hinges on the one reference to a bishop being a "one-woman man" in 1 Timothy 3:2, but as many point out, after this reference there are no male pronouns used. It is possible that Paul is addressing both men and women in these texts. First, he simply refers to "anyone." Second, as Ben Witherington points out, the logic of the passage in 1 Timothy 3 hangs on the verb *must* in 1 Timothy 3:2, which is then followed through to deacons, who "likewise" must follow this pattern of behavior (1 Tim 3:8), and then further extended to women, who also must "likewise" conform to certain moral codes (1 Tim 3:11). Witherington sees this logic as evidence that Paul is referring to women deacons (Witherington, 241). This is further supported by the fact that Paul calls Phoebe a deacon in Romans 16:2 and evidence from church history supporting the idea that there were female deacons in the early church.

5. Household Codes.

The other relevant passages for husband-wife relations occur in Paul's household codes found in Ephesians 5:22-33 and Colossians 3:18-19. As there is a separate article on marriage in this volume, this article will not deal with these passages in detail here. As many note, however, although Paul does exhort wives in particular to submit to their husbands, he never commands the wholesale submission of women to men, and nowhere does he claim that men should have authority over women. The only passage where one does find the word for authority (*exousia*) in relation to husbands and wives is in 1 Corinthians 7, where Paul makes a radically countercultural claim that a Christian wife has "authority" over her husband's *body in precisely the same manner that he has authority over his wife's. Husbands and wives are called into a relationship marked entirely by radical equality and mutuality.

What is becoming apparent through recent scholarship is that a selective reading of Paul's texts on wives through the lens of submission has become the basis for the claim that all women, in all churches everywhere, should be in submission to all men. What is further becoming increasingly apparent is that whereas Paul did not reject certain forms of hierarchy and social mores acceptable in the ancient world, he did redraw boundaries in a way that challenged traditional categories of shame and *honor, which redefined what was expected of those who were in positions of power and had others in their care.

6. Applying Paul's Apostolic Teaching.
A brief survey of Paul and women makes it abundantly clear that there is not a "plain reading" of Paul that justifies a hierarchicalist perspective on men and women. In addition to this, where hierarchical readings of Paul are used to justify the exclusion of women from various ministries in the church or leadership roles, this has resulted simply in considerable confusion and illogicality as to how and when this should be applied. What one sees in the contemporary era is that Paul's writings on men/husbands and women/wives, his acknowledgment of numerous women as coworkers, and his radical view of marriage are now, with ease, understood to demonstrate that Paul was a champion of women. Thus, where the church has often been in considerable confusion as to why Paul would encourage women to share in the task of preaching the gospel, teaching, and leading, on the one hand, and appear to (sometimes totally) prohibit their involvement, on the other, there are now the scholarly resources available to resolve this tension and to make sense of conflictual texts. With the work being done on translation, context, and theological interpretation of Paul's writings, one is now able to build a coherent picture of Paul as an apostle who acknowledged the gifting of women and promoted them to all ministries of the church.

See also CHURCH STRUCTURE; CORINTHIANS, FIRST LETTER TO THE; COWORKERS, PAUL AND HIS; HERMENEUTICS/INTERPRETING PAUL; HOUSEHOLDS AND HOUSEHOLD CODES; LEADERSHIP; MAN AND WOMAN; MARRIAGE AND DIVORCE, ADULTERY AND INCEST; PASTORAL EPISTLES.

BIBLIOGRAPHY. **L. Cohick,** *Women in the World of the Earliest Christians: Illuminating Ancient Ways of Life* (Grand Rapids, MI: Baker Academic, 2009); **L. H. Cohick and A. B. Hughes,** *Christian Women in the Patristic World: Their Influence, Authority, and Legacy in the Second Through Fifth Centuries* (Grand Rapids, MI: Baker Academic, 2017); **E. E. Ellis,** "Co-worker, Paul and His," *DPL*, 183-89; **E. J. Epp,** *Junia: The First Woman Apostle* (Minneapolis: Augsburg Fortress, 2005); **G. E. Fee,** *The First Epistle to the Corinthians*, NICNT (Grand Rapids, MI: Eerdmans, 1991); **B. R. Gaventa,** *When in Romans: An Introduction to Linger with the Gospel According to Paul* (Grand Rapids, MI: Baker Academic, 2016); **S. L. Glahn,** "The Identity of Artemis in First-Century Ephesus," *BSac* 172 (July–September 2015): 316-34; idem, "The First-Century Ephesian Artemis: Ramifications of Her Identity," *BSac* 172 (October–December 2015): 450-69; **J. M. Gundry-Volf,** "Gender and Creation in 1 Cor 11:2-16: A Study in Paul's Theological Method," in *Evangelium, Schriftauslegung, Kirche: Festschrift für P. Stuhlmacher*, ed. J. Adna, S. J. Hafeman, and O. Hofius (Göttingen: Vandenhoeck & Ruprecht, 1997), 151-71; **G. G. Hoag,** *Wealth in Ancient Ephesus and the First Letter to Timothy: Fresh Insights from Ephesiaca by Xenophon of Ephesus* (Winona Lake, IN: Eisenbrauns, 2015); **C. Hodge,** *An Exposition of the First Epistle to the Corinthians* (London: Banner of Truth Trust, 1959); **A. F. Johnson,** *1 Corinthians*, IVPNTC (Downers Grove, IL: IVP Academic, 2004); **M. J. Lakey,** *Image and Glory of God: 1 Corinthians 11:2-16 as a Case Study in Bible, Gender, and Hermeneutics* (London: T&T Clark, 2010); **E. A. McCabe,** "A Reevaluation of Phoebe in Romans 16:1-2 as a *Diakonos* and *Prostatis*: Exposing the Inaccuracies of English Translations," in *Women in the Biblical World: A Survey of Old and New Testament Perspectives*, ed. E. A. McCabe (New York: University Press of America, 2009), 99-116; **S. McKnight,** *The Blue Parakeet: Rethinking How You Read the Bible* (Grand Rapids, MI: Zondervan, 2010); idem, *Junia Is Not Alone: Breaking Our Silence About Women in the Bible and the Church Today* (Englewood, CO: Patheos, 2011); **J. Murphy-O'Connor,** *Keys to First Corinthians: Revisiting the Major Issues* (Oxford: Oxford University

Press, 2009); **P. B. Payne,** *Man and Woman, One in Christ: An Exegetical and Theological Study of Paul's Letters* (Grand Rapids, MI: Zondervan, 2009); **R. Pederson,** *The Lost Apostle: Searching for the Truth About Junia* (Chichester, UK: Jossey-Bass, 2006); **L. Peppiatt,** *Women and Worship at Corinth: Paul's Rhetorical Arguments in 1 Corinthians 11–14* (Eugene, OR: Cascade, 2015); idem, *Unveiling Paul's Women: Making Sense of 1 Corinthians 11:2-16* (Eugene, OR: Cascade, 2018); idem, *Rediscovering Scripture's Vision for Women: Fresh Perspectives on Disputed Texts* (Downers Grove, IL: IVP Academic, 2019); **J. Piper and W. Grudem,** *Recovering Biblical Manhood and Womanhood: A Response to Evangelical Feminism* (Wheaton, IL: Crossway, 1991); **E. Schüssler Fiorenza,** "Missionaries, Apostles, Coworkers: Romans 16 and the Reconstruction of Women's Early Christian History," *WW* 6 (1986): 420-33; **T. Schirrmacher,** *Paul in Conflict with the Veil: An Alternative Interpretation of 1 Corinthians 11:2-16* (Germany: VTR, 2007); **T. P. Shoemaker,** "Unveiling of Equality: 1 Corinthians 11:2–16," *BTB* 17 (1987): 60-63; **C. L. Westfall,** *Paul and Gender: Reclaiming the Apostle's Vision for Men and Women in Christ* (Grand Rapids, MI: Baker Academic, 2016); **B. Witherington III,** *Letters and Homilies for Hellenized Christians: A Socio-historical Commentary on Titus, 1–2 Timothy and 1–3 John* (Downers Grove, IL: IVP Academic, 2006).

L. Peppiatt

WOMEN NAMED IN PAUL

When assessing Paul's views regarding the participation of *women in the *worship and *leadership of the local *church, it is essential not to divorce his teaching from his praxis. In his letters Paul names sixteen women as co-laborers in the *ministry of the *gospel, using the same language to describe their contributions to the ministry as he applies to the contributions and work of their male counterparts. Identifying these women and their contributions to the early church is an essential step toward reading Paul consistently and with integrity. Because each text should be read within its proper context, these women will be addressed alphabetically within the Pauline corpus in which they are named: first Romans and the Corinthian correspondence, then Paul's general epistles, followed finally by his personal epistles.

1. Romans.

It is striking that over half of the women named by Paul in his letters are found in the final chapter of his letter to the Romans. In more Greek-influenced areas of the Mediterranean world, women who achieved public honor and status were frequently praised in terms of their incarnation of the idealized roles of wife, house manager, and mother—even if their actual public role was very different (e.g., financier, benefactor, or ambassador). In Rome, however, women tended to be praised using the same terms as for men (Forbis, 493-98, 504-5), and Paul's sensitivity to this difference is apparent in his greetings to and praise of women in Romans 16. Of the nine women he mentions in Romans 16, only Rufus's mother (Rom 16:13) remains unnamed. It is possible that many of the twenty-six individuals he mentions were Jewish Christians, expelled (like Priscilla and Aquila) from Rome due to Claudius's edict and newly returned upon that emperor's death.

1.1. Julia (Romans 16:15). Paul greets Julia and Philologus together, which may indicate that they were a married couple involved in ministry together (e.g., 1 Cor 9:5). She and her husband may have been leaders of a specific house church or core leaders within the Roman church body. *Julia* was a common Latin name in the first century; she could have been a member of the *Julii* gens, in which case she would have been of very high status indeed (coming from the same family line as Julius Caesar, for example). Alternatively, she could have been a freedwoman previously belonging to that family. However, naming conventions for women had also relaxed in the first century; many women were known by their first names (*praenomen*) instead of their *nomen* or family name. Since Julius Caesar's rise to power, *Julia* as a *praenomen* had become very popular across all levels of society, regardless of the woman's biological relationship to the *Julii* gens.

1.2. Junia (Romans 16:7). Like Julia, Junia is linked with a male counterpart, Andronicus, which suggests another couple ministering together. Paul's description of them as *syngeneis* or "kin" indicates that Junia and Andronicus were Jewish Christians (it could indicate a closer family relationship, but at the very least Paul is including them as extended kin). Like *Julia*, the name *Junia* could indicate that she was born into or freed out of the *Junii* gens: given that *Andronicus* was a name commonly given *slaves or freedmen, it is likely that both Junia and her husband were manumitted Jewish Christians, named by or in honor of the family who had owned and freed them. Richard Bauckham argues that

Junia is the Latinized form of Joanna, who traveled with Jesus and supported his ministry (Bauckham, 109-202; see Lk 8:3; 24:10).

There has been some debate surrounding Junia due to Paul's praise of her ministry and her link to the *apostles: Is she prominent "among" the apostles or well known "to" them? In short, where there is some hesitancy to accept women in roles of leadership in the church, either Junia's gender or her role (or both) have been questioned.

1.2.1. Junia Versus Junias. The debate over the gender of Junia(s) centers on the question of Greek accents: if the accent is acute and positioned over the *iota*, the name is the feminine *Junia*. But if the accent is a circumflex and positioned over the *alpha*, then it refers to the masculine *Junias*. The debate is clouded significantly by the fact that the earliest Greeks manuscripts were unaccented; the accents were added by scribes in the seventh century.

The historical *tradition is by far in favor of the feminine *Junia*. The early fathers unanimously read Romans 16:7 to refer to a female Junia, and in fact John Chrysostom (349–407) praised her, saying "Indeed, how great the wisdom of this woman must have been that she was even deemed worthy of the title apostle" (*Hom. Rom.* 31.2 [on Rom 16:7], trans. PG 60:669-670). The earliest translations of the NT into Latin, Coptic, and Syriac all translate Junia's name in feminine terms. In addition, when accents were added to the Greek manuscripts in the seventh century, the *iota* was consistently accented, reflecting the scribes' understanding that Paul was naming a woman.

Yet it is clear that not all interpreters read *Junias* as feminine: Giles of Rome (1243–1316) apparently described Junia and Andronicus as "those honorable men" (Epp, 35), and Martin Luther used the masculine article before Junia's name in his German translation (1534). However, from the sixteenth century through the early twentieth century, Greek editions of the NT consistently affirmed Junia as a woman (including Erasmus [1516], Melanchthon [1545], Stephanus [1551], Oxford Sheldonian [1675], Van Maaastricht [1711], Cyprian [1715], Griesbach [1777, 1796–1806, 1809], Alexander/Isa. Thomas [1800], Schott [1805, 1811], Tischendorf [1824, 1869–1872], Tregelles [1857–1879, 1870, Emphatic Diaglott [1864, 1942], Westcott-Hort [1881], Gebhardt [1881, 1886], Oxford Greek [1881], Baljon [1898]; see Epp, 62, for an exhaustive listing), and most translations translated the name as feminine (including Wycliffe [1382, 1392], Göttingen Gutenberg Bible [1454], Erasmus Greek-Latin NT [1519], Tyndale [1525], Coverdale [1535], Matthew [1537], Great Bible [1539–1541], Taverner [1539], Geneva NT [1557], Bishops [1568], Spanish "Bear" Bible [1569], Rheims [1582], Geneva Bible [1583–1599], Hutter Polyglot [1599], Reina-Valera [1602, 1858, 1909], KJV [1611], Giovanni Diodati [1649], Wycliffe NT [1731], Webster [1833], Murdock NT [1852], and Julia Smith [1876]). Erwin Nestle's 1927 edition was the first Greek NT to accent the name as masculine, and other Greek editions following this influential publication mirrored this change. It was a shift that echoed the cultural shift of the nineteenth and twentieth centuries away from women serving in leadership capacities in the local church, and the masculine *Junias* is particularly mirrored in English-language NT translations published from 1940 to 1980 (including RSV, ASV, NASB 1995, Young's Literal Translation, and the Message Bible; for an exhaustive listing of the translations, see Epp, 63). Most of the commonly used English-language translations reverted to the feminine *Junia* shortly before the turn of the century (including NIV; many changed the text to Junia and added notes indicating *Junias* as an alternative translation, including ESV, RSV, NLT, HCSB, NET). The twenty-eighth edition of the Nestle-Aland Greek NT reflects the feminine *Junia* as well.

In addition to an overwhelming historical tradition that favors the feminine *Junia*, the first-century secular historical evidence also favors the feminine as well. The name *Junias* simply is not attested as a masculine name; on the other hand, *Junia* is well-attested, in over 250 inscriptions. It was a common name for women of all levels of society, especially given the relaxed naming conventions of the first century and the tendency of freed slaves to take as *praenomen* the *gens* of the manumitter. Arguments that *Junias* is simply irregular or that it is a contraction of *Junianus* are unconvincing, especially since Latin nicknaming conventions tend to lengthen, not contract, a given name (e.g., *Prisca* to *Priscilla*).

1.2.2. "Prominent Among" Versus "Known To." Paul's description of Junia and Andronicus has given rise to debate as well: Are they "prominent among" the apostles or "well known to/by" the apostles? Here the history of interpretation falls in favor of Junia being counted among the apostles, making her the only woman described in the NT as an apostle. Early church fathers unanimously read Roman 16:7 as "among" (e.g., John Chrysostom, *Hom. Rom.* 31 [on Rom 16:7], Origen, *Comm. Rom.* 10, Jerome, *Nom. hebr.* 72.15; *Expositio epistula ad Romanos* 16:7; Theodoret of Cyrus, *Interpretatio epistolum ad Romanos*; John Damascene, *In epistolum ad Romanos*; Peter Abelard, *Commentarius in epistolum ad Romanos* 16.7).

Significant proponents of Junia being "well known to" the apostles include Michael Burer and Daniel Wallace, who argued in 2001 that the grammar of the phrase contraindicates Junia being counted as an apostle. Eldon Jay Epp published a definitive rebuttal of this view in his *Junia, the First Woman Apostle*. Burer claims to have unearthed new evidence to support his reading, but closer examination reveals that the linguistic markers are an inexact match and cannot be legitimately applied to Paul's phrasing in Romans 16:7. Instead, linguistic evidence both biblical and secular supports "among" as the standard reading for this construction of dative *en* + *episemos* (adjective). Further, it is unlikely that Paul would use the favor of "the apostles" as a seal of approval, let alone use it as a means of aligning himself with another's ministry. Paul nowhere else appeals to the opinion of "the apostles." In fact, the sense of disdain and frustration communicated in Galatians 2:6-9 in relation to the supposed influence and approval of precisely these individuals over Paul's own ministry and gospel makes it even less likely that Paul would use an appeal to the good favor of "the apostles" as a rhetorical tool to bolster the ethos of Christians already known to the Roman church for their sacrificial ministry. In short, both historical and linguistic evidence overwhelmingly support the identification of Junia as a woman Paul counted as prominent among the apostles.

1.3. Mary (Romans 16:6). Paul's greetings to Mary suggest that, like the others he names, he knew her personally. Her name could indicate that she was a Jewish Christian, but since Paul calls her *Marian* instead of *Miriam*, she may be connected to the *gens* Marius instead. Paul uses the word *kopiaō* ("to work hard") to describe her service to the church; this is the same verb he applies to himself and other leaders elsewhere (1 Cor 15:10; 16:16; Phil 2:16; 1 Thess 5:12). Curiously, he applies this verb only to women in Romans 16. Whatever his reasons, Paul's usage clearly indicates that he saw their labor for the church in the same regard as his own, a view Chrysostom echoes: "The women of those days were more spirited than lions, sharing with the Apostles their labors for the Gospel's sake. In this way they went traveling with them and also performed all other ministries" (*Hom. Rom.* 31 [on Rom 16:6], trans. PG 60:669; see *NPNF*[1] 11). Much later, Theodoret of Cyrus (ca. 393–458) described both Andronicus and Junia as "not among the pupils but among the teachers, and not among the ordinary teachers but among the apostles" (*Interpretatio epistolum ad Romanos*, trans. PG 82:219-29; see Bray, *Romans*, 392).

1.4. Persis (Romans 16:12). Persis receives this same commendation from Paul for her hard work in ministry. Paul's words place her in the same category as other leaders, both male and female, whom he praised using similar terms in his letters to Corinth, Philippi, and Thessalonika (see 1 Cor 15:10; 16:16; Phil 2:16; 1 Thess 5:12). *Persis* was a name commonly given to slaves imported from Persia, suggesting that she may also have been a slave or freedwoman. Unlike in his greetings in Romans 16:5, 8-9, he describes Persis as "the beloved," possibly because Persis was well-loved and well-known throughout the Roman church as a whole.

1.5. Phoebe (Romans 16:1-2). Unlike most believers in Rome whom Paul greets in Romans 16, Phoebe's name suggests that she is a *Gentile. Phoebe also receives the most extended description of any in Paul's final greetings. He names her "sister," which could simply refer to her belonging to the family of believers, but it may also be argued that *kinship language is frequently used by Paul to describe those who hold leadership roles within the local church (e.g., see Apphia, Philem 2). Further, Paul names her "our" sister, subtly reminding the Roman church that geography and *ethnicity no longer determine kinship and in-group status: *faith is now the sole qualification, and as a sister, Phoebe should be welcomed and cared for by the Roman believers as if she were one of their own. Finally, Paul describes Phoebe as both *prostatis* and *diakonos*, two titles that refer to positions of authority and leadership within society and, later, the church.

1.5.1. Ambassador. Paul's request to the Roman believers to "receive" (*prosdechomai*) their sister Phoebe is also weighted with cultural overtones. The verb *prosdechomai* was used in diplomatic letters to indicate proper reception of official messengers and ambassadors (see also 1 Macc 12:43; 2 Macc 9:25). Paul's usage in his epistles corresponds to this diplomatic context (e.g., 2 Cor 3:1; Phil 2:25-30; Col 4:7-9). The purpose of this official phrasing was to commend the letter bearer as an official representative of the sender, especially if he or she was unknown to its recipients.

While the "help" Paul refers to could indicate her own reason for traveling to Rome, it could also be her commission to carry and read the letter to the Roman believers. Either way, Paul is extending an official request that Phoebe be treated as his representative, his ambassador, both in the matter of his letter and regarding any arrangements needed to prepare for Paul's hoped-for arrival. As Paul's ambassador, she would be privy to Paul's intentions regarding the letter, and she would be the church's source for interpreting Paul's words as he had intended them to be understood (for examples of the roles of and expectations regarding letter-carriers, see, e.g., Xenophon, *Cyr.* 4.5.34; Cicero, *Fam.* 1.6.1; 3.1.1; 9.2.1; 12.30.3).

She may also have been called on to read the letter in the various gatherings of the local church. Although rare, women were known to have been well-educated, and in elite families even rhetorically educated (Plutarch, *Pomp.* 55); it would not be surprising that a woman of Phoebe's resources would also be literate. Given the rhetorical nature of the letter, it is possible that Phoebe would be expected to perform a dramatic reading of Romans, in keeping with rhetorical conventions for speeches in the first century. However, the manuscript evidence available suggests that dramatic reading was not the norm for letter carriers, but rather that they served as the sender's official representative, responsible primarily to ensure that the letter was understood as intended and that any actions required of the recipient by the sender were in fact carried out. Phoebe thus served first as Paul's ambassador and guarantor of the letter's interpretation.

1.5.2. Prostatis. Paul also named Phoebe *prostatis*, a title he gives no one else in his letters. Throughout the Hellenistic world, *prostatis* referred to one's patron or the officer of an organization; when paired with the genitive construction indicating "of," the term consistently indicates *patronage (see also 1 Thess 5:12; 1 Tim 3:4-5; 5:17; Philo, *Virt.* 155; Josephus, *Ant.* 14.157, 144; CIJ 100, 365).

That Paul names Phoebe as his patron would not seem at all unusual to the church in Rome. Within Hellenistic culture (and particularly Roman culture), inscriptional evidence bears witness that influence, ability, and *wealth were more important in the patronage system than was gender (*NewDocs* 4:74-82, 242-44), and this attitude was accepted within certain Jewish circles as well. There is evidence as early as the middle of the first century BCE of women patrons. However, Greek and Roman (Italian, specifically) accolades of women patrons differed in that Greek inscriptions followed the tradition of praising women patrons in terms of their realization of cultural ideals for women (even if the action motivating the praise was entirely commercial or civic) (VanBremen, 223-42), while Roman inscriptions praised men and women alike using the same terms and honorifics (see Forbis, 493-98, 504-5).

Paul's description of Phoebe not only affirms her roles as ambassador and patron but also suggests that Phoebe had been actively and consistently using her resources to serve others in a way that did not prioritize her profit—or her clients' reciprocity—but rather sacrificed her status and wealth to benefit and build the church in Cenchreae.

1.5.3. Diakonos. When Paul identifies Phoebe's home church as Cenchreae, he does so by describing Phoebe as a *diakonos* of that church; Ernst Käsemann argues that the genitive construction suggests a recognized ministry (Käsemann, 411).

In the first and early second centuries CE, deacons such as Phoebe were frequently commissioned to serve as ambassadors from their local church to other churches as well as to assist missionary endeavors (2 Cor 8; 1 Cor 16:1-5; Acts 20:4; Phil 2:25; see also Ign. *Phld.* 10.1; Ign. *Eph.* 2.1). Both men and women were recognized as deacons, with no distinction made in the expression of their leadership. Pliny the Younger (early second century) mentions to Trajan the torture of two female slaves who were called *ministrae* by local believers; *ministrae* likely is the Latin translation of *diakonos* and may be translated as "minister" or "deacon" (Pliny, *Ep.* 10.96.8). An inscription from the late fourth century (or perhaps later) in Jerusalem refers to Sophia the *diakonos*, "the second Phoebe" (*hē deutera Phoibē*) (see *NewDocs* 4 and *CIIP* 1004). Around the same time, John Chrysostom understood *diakonos* to indicate a leadership role in the local church (*Hom. Rom.* 31 [on Rom 16:1]).

It is naive to assume that the office of a deacon as recognized by a local church today is a direct reflection of the role of a *diakonos* in the first century. For this reason, the qualifications and activities of a *diakonos* in the first century must be found within the NT texts and their historical context. While the term *diakonos* is frequently translated as "servant" in the NT, in Paul's use (in comparison to what one finds in the Gospels) the semantic range shades away from a generic servant to a specific role of service such as a representative or intermediary. NT references provide ample insight into the activities of early deacons. First, both Acts and Paul's letters consistently describe deacons in the context of the general ministry of the gospel and service to the church. The first example of *diakonos* in the NT canon is found in Acts 6, where faithful men who were gifted in *teaching and *preaching were commissioned to serve the church. In addition to Stephen and his companions, others described as *diakonos* include *Christ (Rom 15:8), Apollos (1 Cor 3:5), Tychicus (Eph 6:21; Col 4:7), Epaphras (Col 1:7), Paul (1 Cor 3:5; 2 Cor 3:6; 6:4; 11:23;

Eph 3:7; Col 1:23, 25), and of course Phoebe. Paul specifically mentions teaching and preaching the gospel among the activities of a deacon (Col 1:7; regarding himself, Eph 3:7; Col 1:23, 25; 2 Cor 3:6; 11:23), and in fact a full third of instances of *diakon-* in the NT and early church literature are linked to preaching the gospel. Arguing that Phoebe's activities as a deacon differed in any way from those of Epaphras or any other individual described by Paul as a *diakonos* is unsupported by NT texts.

The spiritual qualifications of a leader within the NT church are best rooted in Paul's teaching on gifts in Romans 12, and Paul provides a secondary list of external qualifications for a deacon in 1 Timothy 3:8-13. Spiritually mature competence, in which Paul prioritizes gifting by the *Holy Spirit, is thus the primary qualification for ministry roles within the church (Rom 12; 1 Tim 3:8-11). Paul's identification of Phoebe as a *diakonos* suggests that in his assessment, she was gifted by the Holy Spirit as a leader in the church—a leadership position that likely involved teaching the gospel. It is significant here that Paul commends Phoebe for her role as *diakonos*; there is no condemnation of Phoebe's leadership or gender.

1.6. Priscilla (Romans 16:3-5; 1 Corinthians 16:19; 2 Timothy 4:19; cf. Acts 18:1-3, 18-19, 26). Priscilla and Aquila were Jewish Christians who met Paul in *Corinth after Claudius's edict expelled Jews from Rome (Acts 18:1-3). As they were tentmakers by trade, Paul worked with them in both trade and ministry in Corinth and later Ephesus. Priscilla and Aquila stayed in Ephesus to lead a house church, but Paul's greeting to them in Romans 16 indicates that they returned to Rome upon Claudius's death in AD 54. That they led a house church in their home in multiple cities suggests that their business was profitable enough to afford a property that could accommodate a small gathering, though the leatherworking trade was not one associated with wealth in the first century.

When they first appear in Acts, Aquila is mentioned first. All other occurrences except for one (1 Cor 16:19) list Priscilla first, including when the couple takes aside Apollos to explain the Way more completely to him (see Acts 28:23). The order of names was frequently significant in the classical era, and multiple explanations have been offered for the order and shift in order of Aquila and Priscilla's names. Some have argued that Priscilla's primacy reflected her higher social status or education (e.g., Schreiner, 279; Keener, 2713), while others argue that the shift reflected her growing ministry role, indicating that she was the more prominent evangelist and teacher (e.g., Bassler, 136). Linda Belleville observes that Aquila is listed first in the context of household and business (which echoes first-century conventions to name the head of the household first), but Priscilla is named first in the context of ministry, which would support the argument that Priscilla was the more prominent of the two in their ministry together (Belleville 2004, 121-22).

1.7. Tryphena and Tryphosa (Romans 16:12). The similarity and pairing of these names suggest they may either be sisters (possibly twins?) or slaves in the same *household. Paul does not provide any details regarding their work, but identifying their ministry as "in the *Lord" does indicate that the two worked together in some capacity for the growth and benefit of the church in Rome.

2. Other Letters to the Churches.

2.1. Chloe (1 Corinthians 1:11). Corinth was a colony heavily influenced by Roman culture, yet its position as a major seaport brought many other cultures, ideas, and religions into the city. Several of these, including the cult of Isis, brought with them an expanded concept of women's role in society and religion, making Corinth a city that was accustomed to women playing larger roles in these arenas than might be true of more Greek and Macedonian cities.

Paul here addresses Chloe as the head of her household, which may indicate that she was a widow. There is no mention of her role within the church, but the loyalty of her household to Paul is evident in the report he mentions. Since he names Chloe, it is likely that the message did come from her via members of her house.

The phrase Paul uses suggests "people belonging to Chloe," quite likely indicating that the message bearers were slaves. Family members were often referred to by their familial relationship, and "those of Chloe" carries a strong sense of ownership. Slavery was common in the first century, and a slave's experience was wholly dependent on his or her owner. Paul nowhere explicitly condemns slavery, but makes clear the equality of all people in God's eyes by reminding slaveowners that they do not own themselves either but are slaves of God, bound to obey him and treat others as he does (Eph 6:9).

2.2. Euodia and Syntyche (Philippians 4:2-3). In the middle of a letter devoted to encouraging unity within the church, Paul directly addresses two individuals, challenging them to overcome their differences and reunite in the *mission of the church. This is an unusual rhetorical move in two ways: first, it is out of character for Paul to so publicly name fellow believers he corrects, even if the individual or situation he obliquely refers to is well-known within the church (e.g., 1 Cor 5). Second, women were rarely publicly named unless due to fame or infamy. These factors strongly suggest that Euodia and Syntyche were far more than just women whose quarreling was disrupting church gatherings.

Inscriptional evidence makes clear that these names do refer to women; there are no equivalent male names extant. In addition, these are Greek names, suggesting that these are Macedonian women. Although traditionally Macedonian cultural mores favored a more private role for women, Philippi's status as a distinctly Roman colony combined with historical evidence of women in civic and commercial roles in Philippi argue that, as in other Romanized cultural centers, influence and wealth weighed more heavily than gender in determining one's role in society (IG 329). In fact, Chrysostom read Paul's description in Philippians 4:3—"who have fought at my side for [the sake of] the gospel"—in the context of his introduction of Phoebe in Romans 16:1-2, concluding that Euodia and Syntyche were the leaders or heads (*to kephalaion*) of the Philippian church (Chrysostom, *Hom. Phil.* 13).

Further, Paul includes Euodia and Syntyche in his list of *synergoi*, a term that is found only thirteen times in the NT (twelve uses are by Paul) and which uses to refer exclusively to those who have been *coworkers in his ministry of evangelism and church planting (1 Cor 3:9; 1 Thess 3:2; Rom 16:3; 9:21; Phil 2:25; Philem 24; 2 Cor 1:24; 8:23). That Paul assumes such individuals are leading within the early church is evident in 1 Corinthians 16:16-18. In fact, he further describes Euodia and Syntyche particularly as those who have labored (*synathleō*) together in the ministry. Here he explicitly evokes the imagery of gladiators who fought as a team within the arena (compare Phil 2:25).

It is apparent from Paul's letter that he considers the conflict between the women to threaten the unity and stability of the church, yet he corrects them gently through an appeal instead of challenge or condemnation. Unlike the situation in Corinth, the significance of the problem in Philippi is not that *sin threatens the church, but rather the conflict itself, which further supports the prominence of Euodia and Syntyche within the Philippian church: the whole church will follow the example they set, either of conflict or of reconciliation. David Garland structures Paul's rhetorical argument around this as the central conflict of the letter and the crux of the issue Paul seeks to address. Whether or not Paul is putting a rhetorical spotlight on these leaders, what is truly significant is that Paul describes Euodia and Syntyche as leaders within the church, and does so with only praise. He neither criticizes them for their roles nor in any way suggests that their gender excludes them from a role of leadership within the Philippian church.

2.3. Nympha (Colossians 4:15). There is some textual debate regarding Paul's greeting to Nympha and the church gathering in her house. The manuscripts disagree on whether this name is masculine or feminine, since *Nymphan* is the accusative form of both. However, appealing first to historical evidence demonstrates that while the feminine *Nympha* is attested over sixty times in inscriptions and texts, the masculine version never appears. Also, the well-recognized textual-critical rule of favoring the more difficult reading clearly supports the feminine *Nympha* (see Aland and Aland, 280-81).

The question arises because of Paul's addition of "the church in [his/her] house." If *Nymphan* is masculine, there are no voices arguing that he is not the leader of the church gathering on his property, but if *Nymphan* is feminine, the discussion changes to consider whether she was simply a wealthy widow who hosted the church or was indeed its leader (see, e.g., Moo, 349; Dunn, 285; see Witherington 2007, 206, for a discussion of the textual issues as well). Given the average lifespan of men in the first century, many women became widows who managed their husbands' property, affairs, and households for their children. Paul greets this woman without mentioning a male counterpart or relative, which indicates that she was the functional head of the house in which the church met and its patron. The absence of a separate greeting to the church's leader further suggests that Nympha was its spiritual leader.

3. Personal Epistles.

Although the authorship of some of the personal epistles is disputed, they are grouped here together due to their contextual and cultural similarities.

3.1. Apphia (Philemon 2). Paul's greeting does not make clear whether Apphia was related to either Philemon or Archippus, though many assume she was Philemon's wife or daughter. However, her inclusion by name in the greeting indicates that Paul expected her to have a voice in Philemon's response to his request. Paul greets her as a sister, which indicates that she was a believer (Gal 6:10; 1 Thess 4:10). In addition, since Paul frequently uses kinship language to indicate leadership roles (e.g., Rom 16; 1 Thess 3:2; 2 Cor 1:1; Col 1:1), she was possibly a leader in the church. Further, the church met in Philemon's house (Philem 2), which suggests that many believers in that church were probably members of Philemon's household. If this were the case, any influence Apphia held in the household may have also extended to the church as well. Pheme Perkins suggests that Apphia and Archippus were indeed both leaders in the church, and by naming them in this letter Paul was subtly putting pressure on Philemon by bringing the issue of Onesimus's *freedom into the domain of the church instead of leaving the issue a personal one for Philemon to deal with discreetly (Perkins, 453).

3.2. ***Claudia (2 Timothy 4:21).*** *Claudia* was a very popular Latin name, especially since the Emperor Claudius's rise to power. Given the general relaxation of naming conventions for women in the first century, Claudia could have belonged to any level of society. However, her name traditionally would have associated her with the prestigious *gens* Claudii, suggesting that she was born into or freed out of that tribe.

Paul's wording gives no indication of her role in the ministry of the church, aside from the fact that she and the other believers knew Timothy. She may have been married to one of the men Paul mentions (some speculations name Pudens), and tradition identifies her as Linus's mother.

3.3. ***Eunice and Lois (2 Timothy 1:5).*** Eunice and Lois were Timothy's mother and grandmother, respectively. Their names are Greek, though tradition holds that they were Jewish. Timothy's father is never mentioned, which may indicate that he was not a believer or that he had died.

Paul praises their piety and Christian faith (2 Tim 1:5), perhaps referring to them later (2 Tim 3:15) when he describes Timothy's education in the faith from a young age. If so, the direct reference to "holy writings" suggests that these women were educated and able to read Scripture. Paul's praise casts these women in the company of devout mothers, much like Mary, who were responsible for the education of their young children. If, however, 2 Timothy was written later, it could reflect tradition or norms of Christian education from the second century.

5. Conclusion.

The historical evidence demonstrates that throughout the first-century Mediterranean world, wealth, status, and ability were prioritized over gender when it came to recognizing leadership and influence: while political and civic offices were limited to men, women who were wealthy, high status, and capably held a variety of prominent and public leadership roles, both civic and religious. The NT texts, however, confront the biases of wealth and status head-on, excluding them from the list of qualifications required of church leaders. Instead, Paul redefines ability in terms of spiritual gifting and spiritually mature competency (Rom 12; 1 Tim 3:8-13).

Further, while Paul's teaching indicates that a certain amount of gender-based tension existed in his churches (e.g., 1 Tim 2), his own praxis clearly included women within the leadership structures of the early church, without any indication of differing gender-based expressions of the role. In short, Paul's public recognition of Junia, Phoebe, Priscilla, and many more women who served as leaders in the ministry of the gospel challenges readers to examine Paul's teaching in light of his praxis and his context.

See also Apostle; Church Structure; Coworkers, Paul and His; Patronage; Romans, Letter to the; Servant, Service; Slave, Slavery; Women.

BIBLIOGRAPHY. **K. Aland and B. Aland,** *The Text of the New Testament* (Grand Rapids, MI: Eerdmans, 1995); **J. M. Bassler,** "Prisca/Priscilla," in *Women in Scripture: A Dictionary of Named and Unnamed Women in the Hebrew Bible, the Apocrypha/Deuterocanonical Books, and the New Testament*, ed. Carol Meyers (Grand Rapids, MI: Eerdmans, 2000), 136-37; **R. Bauckham,** *Gospel Women: Studies of the Names Women in the Gospels* (Grand Rapids, MI: Eerdmans, 2002); **L. L. Belleville,** "Women Leaders in the Bible," in *Discovering Biblical Equality*, ed. R. W. Pierce and R. M. Groothius (Downers Grove, IL: InterVarsity Press, 2004), 110-25; idem, "Ιουνιαν . . . Ἐπισημοι Ἐν Τοις Ἀποστολοις: A Re-examination of Romans 16.7 in Light of Primary Source Materials," *NTS* 51 (2017): 231-49; **M. Bird,** *Romans*, SGBC (Grand Rapids, MI: Zondervan, 2016); **G. Bray,** ed., *Romans*, Ancient Christian Commentary on Scripture 6 (Downers Grove, IL: IVP Academic, 1998); **B. Brooten,** "Junia . . . Outstanding Among the Apostles," in *Women Priests*, ed. A. Swidler and L. Swidler (New York: Paulist, 1977), 141-44; **C. Bryan,** *A Preface to Romans: Notes on the Epistle in Its Literary and Cultural Setting* (New York: Oxford University Press, 2000); **M. Burer,** "ΕΠΙΣΗΜΟΙ ἘΝ ΤΟΙΣ ἈΠΟΣΤΟΛΟΙΣ in Rom 16:7 as 'Well Known to the Apostles': Further Defense and New Evidence," *JETS* 58 (2015): 731-55; **M. H. Burer and D. B. Wallace,** "Was Junia Really an Apostle? A Re-examination of Rom 16.7," *NTS* 47 (2001): 76-91; **L. H. Cohick,** *Women in the World of the Earliest Christians: Illuminating Ancient Ways of Life* (Grand Rapids, MI:

Baker Academic, 2009); **J. N. Collins,** *Diakonia: Reinterpreting the Ancient Sources* (Oxford: Oxford University Press, 1990); **J. D. G. Dunn,** *The Epistles to the Colossians and to Philemon: A Commentary on the Greek Text,* NIGTC (Grand Rapids, MI: Eerdmans, 1996). **E. J. Epp,** *Junia, the First Woman Apostle* (Minneapolis: Fortress, 2005); **E. P. Forbis,** "Women's Public Image in Italian Inscriptions," *AJP* 111 (1990): 493-512; **D. Garland,** "The Composition and Unity of Philippians: Some Neglected Literary Features," *NovT* 27 (1985): 141-73; **B. R. Gaventa,** *When in Romans: An Introduction to Linger with the Gospel According to Paul* (Grand Rapids, MI: Baker Academic, 2016); **P. M. Head,** "Named Letter Carriers Among the Oxyrhynchus Papyri," *JSNT* 31, no. 3 (2009): 279-300; **E. Käsemann,** *Commentary on Romans,* trans. and ed. G. W. Bromiley (Grand Rapids, MI: Eerdmans, 1980); **R. A. Kearsley,** "Women in Public Life in the Roman East: Iunia Theodora, Claudia Metrodora, and Phoebe Benefactress of Paul," *TynBul* 50 (1999): 189-211; **C. S. Keener,** *Acts: An Exegetical Commentary,* vol. 3 (Grand Rapids, MI: Baker Academic, 2014); **C. W. Keyes,** "The Greek Letter of Introduction," *AJP* 56 (1935): 28-48; **P. Lampe,** "The Roman Christians of Romans 16," in *The Romans Debate,* ed. K. P. Donfried (Peabody, MA: Hendrickson, 1991); **B. W. Longenecker,** *In Stone and Story: Early Christianity in the Roman World* (Grand Rapids, MI: Baker Academic, 2020); **D. J. Moo,** *The Letters to the Colossians and to Philemon,* PNTC (Grand Rapids, MI: Eerdmans, 2008); **A. Peeler,** "Junia/Joanna: Herald of the Good News," in *Vindicating the Vixens: Revisiting Sexualized, Vilified, and Marginalized Women of the Bible,* ed. S. Glahn (Grand Rapids, MI: Kregel, 2017); **L. Peppiat,** *Rediscovering Scripture's Vision for Women* (Downers Grove, IL: IVP Academic, 2019); **P. Perkins,** "Philemon," in *Women's Bible Commentary,* ed. C. Newsom and S. Ringe (Louisville: Westminster John Knox, 1998); **E. R. Richards,** *The Secretary in the Letters of Paul* (Tübingen: Mohr Siebeck, 1991); **R. Ruether,** "Women Priests and Church Tradition," in *Women Priests,* ed. A. Swidler and L. Swidler (New York: Paulist, 1977), 234-37; **T. Schreiner,** "Women in Ministry: Another Complementarian Perspective," in *Two Views of Women in Ministry,* ed. S. Gundry and J. Beck (Grand Rapids, MI: Zondervan, 2005): 263-322; **W. D. Shiell,** *Reading Acts: The Lector and the Early Christian Audience* (Boston: Brill Academic, 2004); **R. VanBremen,** "Women and Wealth," in *Images of Women in Antiquity,* ed. A. Cameron and A. Kuhrt (Routledge: London, 1983), 223-42; **J. Walters,** "Phoebe and Junia(s), Rom. 16:12, 7," in *Essays on Women in Earliest Christianity* (Eugene, OR: Wipf & Stock, 2007), 1:167-90; **J. L. White,** "Light from Ancient Letters," in *Foundation and Facets: New Testament,* ed. R. W. Funk (Philadelphia: Fortress, 1986), 186-220; **W. Willis,** "Priscilla and Aquila: Co-workers in Christ," in *Essays on Women in Earliest Christianity,* ed. C. D. Osburn (Eugene, OR: Wipf & Stock, 2007), 2:261-76; **J. Wiseman,** "A Distinguished Macedonian Family in the Roman Imperial Period," *American Journal of Archaeology* 88 (1984): 567-82; **B. Witherington III,** *Conflict and Community in Corinth: A Socio-Rhetorical Commentary on 1 and 2 Corinthians* (Grand Rapids, MI: Eerdmans, 1995); idem, *The Letters to Philemon, the Colossians, and the Ephesians: A Socio-Rhetorical Commentary on the Captivity Epistles* (Grand Rapids: Eerdmans, 2007); idem, *Paul's Letter to the Philippians: A Socio-Rhetorical Commentary* (Grand Rapids, MI: Eerdmans, 2011); **B. Witherington III and D. Hyatt,** *Paul's Letter to the Romans: A Socio-Rhetorical Commentary* (Grand Rapids, MI: Eerdmans, 2004).

J. A. Odor

WORKS. *See* James and Paul; Judgment; Law; Works of the Law.

WORKS OF THE LAW

Within Pauline interpretation, the term "works of the *law" (*erga nomou*) has given rise to levels of controversy that few others can rival. Mentioned in six verses in Romans and Galatians within the context of Jew-*Gentile disputes over *faith and *justification, this term is hotly contested in modern debates between the "old" and "new" perspectives on Paul, with varying interpretations leading to strikingly divergent accounts of the *gospel that Paul proclaimed.

This article will proceed in four sections. First, it will give an overview of the Pauline passages themselves, showing the contexts in which "works of the law" are discussed by the *apostle. Second, it will provide an overview of contemporary interpretation of the phrase by the old and new perspectives on Paul, examining the meaning, significance, and reasons for opposing the practice of these works by major interpreters. Third, it will provide an overview of early Christian reception history in this area, which holds potential to provide common ground for reconciling these competing perspectives and to shed light on the apostle's own meaning. Finally, it will return to the Pauline passages and evaluate Paul's conception of works of the law in conjunction with the early historical evidence.

1. Overview
2. Old and New Perspectives

3. Early Perspectives
4. Works of the Law in Paul's Thought

1. Overview.

The phrase "works of the law" is found in two Pauline letters, Romans and Galatians, with eight usages total in six verses: Galatians 2:16 (3×); 3:2, 5, 10; and Romans 3:20, 28 (along with a B-rated textual variant at Rom 9:32). Paul does not define the term in either epistle, and the impression given is that it is commonly understood by his audiences: in Galatians, Paul appeals to shared ground with Peter by stating "we know" that one is not justified by works of the law (Gal 2:16), and in Romans, Paul assumes the term will be understood not only without defining it but even without having ever visited the *church personally.

In Galatians, Paul recounts his confrontation with *Peter and the Jewish believers at Antioch over their separation from the Gentile brethren:

> But when I saw that they were not acting consistently with the truth of the gospel, I said to Cephas before them all, "If you, though a Jew, live like a Gentile and not like a Jew, how can you compel the Gentiles to live like Jews?" We ourselves are Jews by birth and not Gentile sinners; yet we know that a person is justified not by the works of the law but through faith in Jesus Christ. And we have come to believe in Christ Jesus, so that we might be justified by faith in Christ, and not by doing the works of the law, because no one will be justified by the works of the law. (Gal 2:14-16 NRSV)

At the beginning of Galatians 3, Paul directly confronts the Galatians regarding their misguided turn to works of the law. Appealing to *Abraham, who was considered righteous by God through faith, Paul recounts the promised blessing to the Gentile nations through him (see Gen 12:3), and contrasts this with the curse that accompanies the works of the law: "For all who rely on the works of the law are under a *curse; for it is written, 'Cursed is everyone who does not observe and obey all the things written in the book of the law'" (Gal 3:10 NRSV; cf. Deut 27:26).

In Romans, Paul again mentions works of the law (Rom 3:20 NRSV: "deeds prescribed by the law") in the context of a discussion regarding the relative status of Jews and Gentiles before *God. Following his lengthy catena of OT passages that demonstrate that Jews are no different from Gentiles in being held under the power of *sin, Paul writes: "Now we know that whatever the law says, it speaks to those who are under the law, so that every mouth may be silenced, and the whole world may be held accountable to God. For 'no human being will be justified in his sight' by deeds prescribed by the law, for through the law comes the knowledge of sin" (Rom 3:19-20 NRSV; cf. Ps 143:2). After announcing that God's justifying gift is now given through faith in *Christ, Paul continues that this shows that the works of the law (NRSV: "works prescribed by the law") are thus unnecessary:

> Then what becomes of boasting? It is excluded. By what law? By that of works? No, but by the law of faith. For we hold that a person is justified by faith apart from works prescribed by the law. Or is God the God of Jews only? Is he not the God of Gentiles also? Yes, of Gentiles also, since God is one; and he will justify the circumcised on the ground of faith and the uncircumcised through that same faith. (Rom 3:27-30 NRSV)

2. Old and New Perspectives.

What works of what law is Paul referring to? What is the significance of practicing them? And finally, why does Paul regard them as unnecessary for those justified by faith in Christ? These questions are given widely varying answers by the modern old and new perspectives on Paul, and the reasoning behind their rejection is disputed even within these respective camps.

The old perspective traces its heritage back to Martin Luther and John Calvin, and continues to be represented in modern biblical studies by those within Lutheran and Reformed traditions. For both Luther and Calvin, the works of the law represent anything that one might do to seek to earn justification before God. While both figures regard the practices of the Jewish Torah as the inciting referents in Paul's conflicts, Luther and Calvin both see the target of Paul's antithesis as neither the Mosaic law nor the particular practices it prescribes, but rather *works* in a general sense. Nor are works of the law limited to works done apart from God, as even those empowered by his *grace are similarly understood to belong to this category. Luther and Calvin similarly agree on the significance of these works, which are performed on an *individual* basis to gain merit with God and thus earn *salvation. In modern usage, this is often conveyed in terms of moral effort or legalism.

Luther and Calvin diverge on Paul's reasoning for rejecting these works. While Luther recognizes that the human condition is such that no one can perfectly practice the law's works so as to be justified by God, he also regards the attempt itself as futile, since faith in Christ (rather than works) is what justifies. Further, it is precisely the attempt to be justified by works of the law that is actually the epitome of sin: since only Christ can save, those who attempt to save themselves by the works of the law become self-idolaters, making themselves into false messiahs. Calvin affirms the Lutheran reasoning that humanity's sinful condition is such that no one can observe them perfectly and be justified by God, so that one must have Christ's obedience imputed to the believer instead. However, Calvin does not follow Luther in similarly problematizing either the nature of works or the attempt to be justified by them; the issue is not that these works are inherently misdirected, but rather that humanity can never produce them to the required degree to attain salvation.

Modern representatives of the old perspective remain largely within the vein of either Luther or Calvin on this issue. For example, Rudolf Bultmann, while defining "works of the law" in the distinct terminology of twentieth-century existentialism ("man's self-powered striving to undergird his own existence in forgetfulness of his creaturely existence"), nevertheless still follows Luther in summarizing the attempt to be justified by them as "legalism," a self-reliant form of *idolatry that is actually humanity's fundamental sin (Bultmann, 1:264). Others, such as Douglas Moo, have engaged constructively with the new perspective by conceding that Luther and Calvin too quickly jumped from Paul's concerns over the Mosaic law to their own about works in general, while still affirming the traditional old view that the Pauline dichotomy ultimately relates to "doing" versus "believing" (Moo 1983, 88-89, 98-99; 2011, 167).

The new perspective, inaugurated by E. P. Sanders's *Paul and Palestinian Judaism* in 1977 and popularized by figures such as James Dunn and N. T. Wright in the following years, offers a substantially dissimilar account of works of the law in Paul's conflicts. According to Sanders, the views rejected by Luther and Calvin were simply not held by Jews in Paul's time, and the Reformers' account of works of the law represented a projection of their critiques of the late medieval church onto the *opponents of Paul. For the new perspective as represented by these figures, the law in question is the Mosaic law, with the particular practices under dispute being *circumcision, *food laws, and the observance of Sabbath and other days of the Jewish calendar. Rather than practiced on an individual basis to accord merit with God, these works have a *communal* significance: to adopt them is to become part of the Jewish nation, God's *covenant people. While the new perspective figures are not uniform on how Paul's objections relate to the broader injunctions of the Mosaic law, they are agreed that Paul's target is not its moral commandments or good works, which he commends quite strenuously elsewhere.

Like the old perspective, new perspective figures diverge on Paul's reasoning for rejecting these works. Sanders sees Paul's arguments as primarily *experiential*: having witnessed Gentiles receive the Spirit apart from becoming Jews, and himself having been dramatically called as the apostle to the Gentiles, Paul rejects those works that constituted boundary markers that separated the Jews from the surrounding nations (Sanders 1977, 496; 1991, 55). Dunn regards Paul's primary line of reasoning as *social*: these works served to exclude Gentile Christians from Jewish ones, and boundary markers that give rise to an attitude of exclusivity should be relativized in the new covenant (Dunn 1998, 656; 2005, 25, 131, 417-18). Wright's understanding of Paul's reasoning can be summarized as *covenantal* and has three aspects: the covenant promises to Abraham were universal in scope, rather than simply directed toward Jews; the Torah, which constitutes Israel as a nation, did not heal the underlying anthropological issue of human sinfulness that the Abrahamic blessing was promised to resolve; and Christ's advent fulfills these universal promises and inaugurates a new age of salvation history, in which the sin of Adam is healed and boundaries that separated ethnic Israel from the Gentiles can now be left behind (Wright 1978, 66, 71; 2009, 97-98, 105, 186; 2013, 363-67).

Each side of this debate voices concern that the other—at least in unnuanced forms—fails to take account of the entirety of Paul's thought. For example, if the problem with works of the law is entirely social and not also anthropological (as the new perspective logic appears to some old adherents), why would Paul bother writing a passage such as Romans 7? Conversely, if these passages are simply about rejecting salvation by moral effort (as the old view is understood by some new adherents), why does Paul only employ this language in the context of Jew-Gentile debates, and why is the primary work mentioned—that of circumcision—curiously unrelated to moral effort? Despite the constructive engagement of interpreters on each side (such as Moo and Wright), objections such as these have kept the two parties separated in modern Pauline studies to the present day.

3. Early Perspectives.

How might early reception history help adjudicate between these competing interpretations of works of the law? As a prefatory note, it is worth mentioning the one instance of the term found prior to Paul in ancient Jewish writings, which is in the *Qumran scroll known as 4QMMT (ca. 150 BC). In it, the Qumran community prescribes "some works of the law" for priests in *Jerusalem, which consist of twenty-four regulations concerning various aspects of the Torah. This evidence is sometimes taken as supporting a new perspective interpretation of works of the law, in that the practices relate to the Torah and focus on matters of *purity and separation (such as the purity of vessels and liquids) rather than debates regarding good works or moral effort.

Two cautionary notes should be made, however. First, the language of the text is sufficiently flexible ("some works of the law") that a strict definition of the term is difficult to arrive at: as Martin Abegg comments, the phrase "is quite agile and allows for any number of strictures, the only condition being that they find their source in Torah and are concerned with practice which defines relationship to God in a particular sort of Judaism" (141). Second, there is a lack of evidence that either the usage at Qumran was a direct parallel to the views of the parties in Paul's debates two hundred years later or that the Qumran usage bears witness to a more widely held definition of the term. Without such evidence, caution should be exercised in assuming that Peter, Paul, and the *Judaizers were using "works of the law" in a manner that related to the way the phrase was employed at Qumran two centuries prior.

As noted in the introduction, Paul's own usage of "works of the law" appears to have been readily understood in his historical context, so much so that even in writing to an unfamiliar church (that of Rome) he saw no need to expressly define his terms. As such, Christian reception in nearest proximity to this context represents a promising avenue for identifying Paul's meaning by the phrase. An evaluation of reception in the century and a half after the apostle's *death finds that this testimony is remarkably cohesive on the meaning and significance of these works and, surprisingly, that it aligns closely with the so-called new perspective in modern debates. However, the reasons for rejecting these works in early reception do not map precisely onto either modern perspective and show correspondence with both old and new concerns.

The earliest extant sources that employ specific Pauline verses discussing "works of the law" are Justin Martyr's *Dialogue with Trypho* and Irenaeus's *Against Heresies* and *Demonstration of the Apostolic Preaching.* Justin (ca. AD 100–165), writing near the outset of the *Dialogue*, recounts the Jew Trypho's explanation of Jewish conflicts with Christians regarding the law and its practices: "But this is what we are most puzzled about, that you who claim to be pious and believe yourselves to be different from the others do not segregate yourselves from them, nor do you observe a manner of life different from that of the Gentiles, in that you do not keep the feasts or Sabbaths, nor do you practice the rite of circumcision" (*Dial.* 10.3).

Throughout the *Dialogue*, the practice of such works of the Mosaic law—circumcision, Sabbath ordinances, feasts and new moons and festivals—represents the substance of Trypho's contention with Justin, which Justin frequently refutes using Pauline arguments drawn from Romans 2–4 and Galatians 2–3, including a clear reference to Galatians 3:10-13 at *Dialogue* 95-96. Justin makes clear that Christian objections are not to God's everlasting righteous requirements (*Dial.* 28.4; cf. Rom 2:26) or to the works contained in the Torah that "in themselves are good, and holy, and just," which the righteous patriarchs also kept (*Dial.* 44.1-45.4). Justin and Trypho concur on the role of the Mosaic practices as signifying membership in the Jewish nation and covenant: as Justin states, Jewish proselytes are "circumcised in order to be incorporated into the body of your [Trypho's] people like a native-born" (*Dial.* 123.1), and reliance on such practices means supposing that the "descendants of Abraham according to the flesh" will inherit God's promises (*Dial.* 44.1-2; cf. Rom 4:1, 16; Gal 3:3-9).

In response to Trypho's puzzlement as to why Christians worship the Jews' God without adherence to Moses and the law, Justin states:

> Now indeed, for I have read, Trypho, that there should be a definitive law and a covenant more binding than all others, which now must be respected by all those who aspire to the heritage of God. The law promulgated at Horeb is already obsolete, and was intended for you Jews only, whereas the law of which I speak is simply for all men. Now a later law in opposition to an older law abrogates the older; so, too, does a later covenant void an earlier one. An everlasting and final law, Christ himself, and a trustworthy covenant has been given to us, after which there shall be no law, or commandment, or precept. (*Dial.* 11.2)

Throughout the *Dialogue*, Justin presents an array of arguments against Christian observance of the Mosaic law. These include the testimony of the Hebrew prophets; the arrival of the new law and covenant with Christ, which abrogates the old; the nature of this new covenant as intended for all nations; the lives and experiences of Christians in confirming the new covenant's arrival; and the examples of Abraham and the righteous patriarchs, who were similarly justified by faith without circumcision and the Mosaic law (*Dial.* 23.4, 92.3; cf. Rom 4:3-11; Gal 3:5-9). Interestingly, because Trypho agrees that the Messiah's law will take precedence over that of Moses in the new covenant (*Dial.* 67.4-11), the second half of the *Dialogue* shifts away from debating observance of the Torah to whether Jesus is actually the Christ, which proves to be the real crux of the conflict.

Irenaeus (ca. AD 130/140–200), whose apostolic ties reach back via Polycarp to the apostle John, is often regarded as the first great Pauline interpreter. In *Against Heresies* and the *Demonstration*, Irenaeus regards the "works of the law" as referring to the body of legislation delivered by Moses in the desert, which he identifies as the "yoke of bondage" (*Haer.* 4.15.1; Gal 5:1), including such practices as circumcision, Sabbath, the construction of the *temple, and the elaborate practices of *worship and *sacrifice. Like Justin, Irenaeus makes clear that Christian rejections of "works of the law" are not directed against the commandments of the Decalogue, which are "the entrance into life" and "which, if any one does not observe, he has no salvation" (*Haer.* 4.12.5, 4.15.1). Nor are Christian objections directed against the natural precepts of the law that the righteous patriarchs observed, which Irenaeus sees as closely linked with justification by faith and which Christ fulfills and extends (*Haer.* 4.13.1; cf. 4.12.3).

Interestingly, in the *Demonstration* Irenaeus portrays even the Decalogue's commandments as superfluous, though this is because these have now been intensified and surpassed by the precepts of Christ, such as the commandment against adultery being surpassed by Christ's command against adulterous thoughts (Irenaeus, *Epid.* 96). Like Justin, Irenaeus describes how these works serve to identify with the Jewish nation and their covenant, with circumcision and Sabbath given to distinguish the Jews from other nations (*Haer.* 3.12.11; 4.16.1-2). From a salvation-historical perspective, the practice of this former legislation also represents identification with humanity's juvenile state before its renewal by Christ (*Haer.* 4.15.1; *Epid.* 96; cf. Gal 3:23-26).

For Irenaeus, the primary reasons for rejecting works of the law relate to the arrival of the new covenant and law with Christ's advent, which so transform humanity that they render the Mosaic "yoke of bondage" unnecessary and allow the "laws of liberty" to be extended for those now set free (*Haer.* 4.13.2). This "law that gives life" has gone forth from Zion by the apostles' preaching and transformed the Gentile nations, fulfilling Scripture's prophecies and thus confirming the new covenant's arrival (*Haer.* 4.34.4; cf. Mic 4:1-5; Is 2:2-4). In addition, Irenaeus argues that the works of this law were not given for humanity's justification, as illustrated by the examples of Abraham and the righteous patriarchs, but rather to constrain rebellious *Israel; that the new covenant is for all nations (and not simply the Jews); and that the Hebrew prophets foretell the annulment of these works and the acceptance of the Gentiles *qua* Gentiles.

The lines of interpretation found in Justin and Irenaeus cohere with other second-century sources that draw on Paul and contain similar Jew-Gentile conflicts to Paul's own in Romans and Galatians, such as Ignatius of Antioch's writings against Judaizers in his epistles (*Philadelphians* and *Magnesians*), the Epistle to Diognetus, and Melito of Sardis's *Peri Pascha.* For example, the Epistle to Diognetus (which is saturated with Pauline allusions) rejects a number of Jewish practices contained in the Torah, including animal sacrifices, food regulations, the observance of Sabbaths, circumcision, and the new moons, feasts, and fasts of the Jewish calendar (4.1-6). In contrast with the ethnically delimited Jews, Christians "are not distinguished from the rest of humanity by country, language, or custom" (5.1), and are instead marked out by their fidelity and beneficent deeds toward all people. Among early Christian sources for which Pauline influence is less clear (such as the Didache, the Epistle of Barnabas, and Aristides's *Apology*), these same practices are found to be the points in dispute between Jewish and Gentile-Christian parties, such as *Barnabas*'s rejection of the Torah's sacrifices, Sabbaths, and festivals (see Is 1:11-13) in favor of the offering of "the new law of our Lord Jesus Christ" (*Barn.* 2.6).

Another fascinating witness to early interpretation in this area is the heretical Ebionites, whom Tertullian identifies as holding to the position of Paul's opponents in Galatians (*Praescr.* 33.5). The Ebionites are attested to insist on adherence to the Mosaic law, including such practices as circumcision, the observance of Sabbath and Jewish feasts, food regulations, and a focus on Jerusalem. For the

Ebionites, performing such works signifies both identification with Israel and the path to *righteousness, since (in contrast to mainstream Christianity) they understand Jesus himself to have been justified by such works. Contra Paul, then, works of the law *are* necessary for Christians, because faith in Christ and a life in accordance with his teachings do not suffice for salvation (Eusebius, *Hist. eccl.* 3.27.2). Rather, Christ was sent only to Israel according to the *flesh, and so Christians must join this people by adopting the Mosaic law. Following the logic of Paul's Galatian opponents, the Ebionites retain the works of the law and instead reject Paul as an apostate.

As seen by these early figures, the law and works in question align quite closely with those identified by the new perspective, with the focus being on the *law* (that of Moses) rather than works in general. Within this law, certain practices such as circumcision, food regulations, and the observance of Sabbath and the days of the Jewish calendar recur as the points in conflict between Jewish and early Christian parties (though the sacrificial system, seldom discussed by the new perspective, is noted by some early interpreters as well). Like the new perspective, these early interpreters regard the significance of practicing these works as *communal* rather than individualistic, as they represent the symbols of covenant membership within the Jewish nation. However, the picture is varied on the reasons for rejecting them, as both anthropological and social concerns are represented: while the Mosaic law did not heal humanity's broken condition and limited Abraham's universal promises to a single nation, Christ's new covenant heals humankind and breaks down the walls meant to preserve Israel's distinct identity until the time when these promises would be fulfilled. On the other hand, certain emphases particular to portions of each perspective are not found in early reception: these figures do not understand Paul's rejection of works of the law to be a general rejection of working or of a broader attitude of exclusivity.

Moving forward in Christian history, these lines of interpretation remain ubiquitous among early Pauline interpreters such as Tertullian, who writes that the apostle's conflict over works of the law in Galatians was based on the Jews "insisting on circumcision, and observing the seasons and days and months and years of those Jewish ceremonies which they ought to have known were now revoked" (*Marc.* 1.20.4-6; see similarly *An Answer to the Jews*). Likewise Origen, the author of the earliest extant commentary on Romans, writes as follows:

> One should know that the works that Paul repudiates and frequently criticizes are not the works of righteousness that are commanded in the law, but those in which those who keep the law according to the flesh boast; i.e., the circumcision of the flesh, the sacrificial rituals, the observance of Sabbaths or new moon festivals. These, then, and works of this nature are the ones on the basis of which he says no one can be saved. (Origen, *Comm. Rom.* 8.7.6)

In the fourth century this early perspective continues on with the Greek and Latin churches' most prominent exegetes, John Chrysostom and Jerome (as observed by Calvin in his Romans commentary at Rom 3:20). The earliest variation of this early position is found in the writings of Augustine: while the traditional interpretation is found in his early works, within the context of the Pelagian controversy Augustine interprets "works of the law" as any works done apart from God's grace, which he contrast with meritorious works that are empowered by this grace (see *Spir. et litt.* 50). While distinct from the preceding tradition, Augustine's interpretative move was necessitated by the conditions of the Pelagian controversy, in which the traditional Jew-Gentile conflict had been transposed into an intra-Christian soteriological debate. Nevertheless, the two positions are broadly compatible in that neither regards works done apart from God's grace as soteriologically availing, and later Augustine himself continues articulating the traditional early position in his *Answer to the Jews*. Both the early and Augustinian interpretations are preserved in the medieval period, which, due to their compatibility, did not become an occasion of controversy.

4. Works of the Law in Paul's Thought.
What light does this early reception-historical evidence shed on Paul's own meaning in Galatians and Romans? The uniformity of early Christian testimony regarding the points in conflict with Jews, including those sources that clearly show Pauline influence, suggests that the new perspective is correct in identifying the Mosaic law as Paul's specific target. Indeed, this testimony appears to be confirmed in Galatians 3:17, when Paul contrasts the covenant promises given to Abraham with "the law, which came four hundred thirty years later" (NRSV), a temporal indicator that corresponds with Moses' delivery of the law in the desert.

The specific works identified in early reception are likewise the same found in the Pauline epistles.

In Galatians, the Torah's dietary regulations incite the conflict between Peter and Paul at Antioch (Gal 2:12); Paul later reprimands the Galatians for adopting the Jewish calendar observances ("You are observing special days, and months, and seasons, and years," Gal 4:10 NRSV), and the preaching of circumcision prompts Paul's bitter counteroffer of emasculation in Galatians 5:11-12 (cf. Gal 2:3; 5:3; 6:12). In Romans, circumcision is the primary practice under discussion (cf. Rom 2:25–3:1, 4:9-12). These practices are similarly noted in Pauline conflicts elsewhere: in Colossians, for example, Paul describes true circumcision as *baptism into Christ (Col 2:11-12) and continues: "Therefore do not let anyone condemn you in matters of food and drink or of observing festivals, new moons, or sabbaths" (Col 2:16 NRSV). In 1 Corinthians, circumcision is relativized in terms reminiscent of Galatians: "Circumcision is nothing, and uncircumcision is nothing; but obeying the commandments of God is everything" (1 Cor 7:19 NRSV).

The significance of practicing these works is most clearly seen in Romans 3:28-29. Having stated that justification comes apart from works of the law, Paul's counterfactual question puts their communal function in clear relief: "Or is God the God of the Jews only? Is he not also the God of the Gentiles?" Here, as in early patristic reception, the practice of works of the law represents incorporation into the Jewish people, and to insist on their universal adoption would be to deny that the one God is sovereign over all the nations. Likewise in Galatians 2:14, these practices signify "living like a Jew" (*ioudaizein*), and circumcision's connection with membership in the Jewish people is so strong that *circumcision* can simply mean "Jews" or "Jewish" in Paul's writings (Gal 2:7-9, 12; Rom 15:8; cf. Eph 2:11).

Paul's reasoning against works of the law is clearly multifaceted, and here this article will highlight major themes with reference to current debates. First, *pace* certain reductionistic new perspective readings, Paul's conflicts over works of the law do indeed carry an anthropological aspect. The issue is not simply social (in that these practices divide Jewish from Gentile believers) but that being a Jew itself never healed humanity's underlying sinful condition, as Paul's lengthy catena of OT passages in Romans 3:10-18 demonstrates. Indeed, the reality of Israel's continued bondage to sin is what left it subject to the Torah's curses for disobedience (Gal 3:10; cf. Deut 27:26). Conversely, Christ himself does give this new life by the Spirit in the new covenant (Gal 2:20; 3:21), providing the remedy for the underlying condition that Torah could only diagnose (Rom 3:20).

While Paul does distinguish these practices of the law from righteous deeds in general (see Rom 2:25-29; 1 Cor 7:19), to deny that good works or moral effort are Paul's target with "works of the law" is not to thus conclude that one receives God's justifying grace by good works. Paul makes clear elsewhere that the source of justification is God himself and that no prior deeds serve as prerequisites to receive it: as Paul states in Romans 5, it was precisely when we were weak and still sinners that Christ died for us (cf. Eph 2:8). Here the language of John Barclay is helpful: while God's gift in Christ is not unconditional in the sense of holding no future obligations, it is *unconditioned* in that no prior deeds (whether of the Mosaic law or otherwise) are required to receive it. Having received this free gift, what Paul identifies as essential for the believer is neither circumcision nor uncircumcision; rather, it is "faith working through *love" (Gal 5:6 NRSV), the "obedience of faith" (Rom 1:5; 16:26 NRSV), through which the law's righteous requirement is fulfilled by those led by the Spirit (Rom 8:4).

Together with this anthropological reasoning is the clear universal argument found in Romans 3:29. The one God promises to bless every nation through Abraham's seed, and the Mosaic law serves to constitute Israel as a single nation separated from the others. If the Mosaic law were to be imposed on Gentiles once this promised Abrahamic blessing arrived, this would only invalidate the terms of the promises to Abraham, which were made for every people and not simply the Jews (see Gal 3:8).

Along with these arguments, the prominence in early Pauline reception of Christ's law as a reason for no longer adhering to the Mosaic legislation suggests that Paul's own appeals to a Christian law are not mere rhetorical ploys (as is sometimes thought) but rather real expressions of how Paul understands authority to function within the new covenant. In Romans 3:27-28, Paul appeals to the "law of faith" just before stating that works of the law are unnecessary for justification, and to "the law of the Spirit of life in Christ Jesus" in Romans 8:2 (NRSV), which frees humanity to fulfill the law's righteous requirement. Following his arguments against circumcision in Galatians 5, Paul exhorts the Galatians to fulfill "the law of Christ" in Galatians 6:2, and in 1 Corinthians 9:21 he describes himself as not under the law with respect to the Jews, "though I am not free from God's law but am under Christ's law"

(NRSV) As Moo (2013) comments on Galatians 6:2, this "law of Christ" serves as the new covenant counterpart to Moses' law in the old, and thus naturally refers to "all those teachings and commandments set forth by Christ and by his inspired apostles—including Paul" (378). Within the context of Galatians, this law can be witnessed as based in Christ's teachings (Gal 6:2), administered by his apostles (Gal 1:6-9), and enacted in ordinances such as baptism, the spiritual circumcision through which one is raised to new life in Christ (Gal 3:27; cf. Rom 6:4; Col 2:11-12; Titus 3:5).

The reality of such a law explains why certain practices of the Torah always recur in Paul's conflicts with the Jews and early Pauline reception, even while the Torah as a whole is understood as now subordinate. This is because Christ's law in the new covenant, which the prophets foresaw would come forth from Zion to transform the Gentile nations (Mic 4:1-5; Is 2:2-4; 42:4; 51:4), itself reaffirms many Mosaic precepts (such as on the priority of loving God and neighbor) and intensifies others (such as prohibitions of murder and adultery extending to anger and lust). As a result, it is only those points of discontinuity between the two covenants that recur as flashpoints in early conflicts between Jewish parties and Christians: while the old covenant is fully subordinated to the new, the new nevertheless retains and indeed amplifies much of the old.

Finally, as Justin and Trypho's *Dialogue* makes clear, the dispute over works of the law is ultimately subordinate to the question of whether Jesus is indeed the Messiah. If he is, then he inaugurates the promised new covenant, the terms of which take precedence over the prior covenant; if he is not, then the Mosaic covenant and its terms still remain binding. Seen from this standpoint, it is clear why Paul's sharpest vitriol (Gal 5:14) is saved for those who continue to require adherence to the Mosaic law after Christ's advent. Such a move is, in effect, a denial that Christ has come and established the new covenant, and Paul does not overstate the matter by insisting that this means being cut off from Christ (Gal 5:4). For Paul, it is because Jesus is indeed the Messiah and has established this new covenant that he implores the Galatians to become like him, as he similarly describes himself in 1 Corinthians 9:21—not bound by the Mosaic legislation and its works, but yet under the law of God, that is, the *law of Christ.

See also Covenant; Faith; Galatians, Letter to the; Gentiles; Interpretation: Calvin; Interpretation: Luther; Interpretation: New Perspective; Interpretation: Patristic; Justification; Law; Law of Christ; Old Testament in Paul; Paul and Judaism; Romans, Letter to the.

BIBLIOGRAPHY. **M. Abegg,** "'4QMMT C 27, 31 and 'Works Righteousness,'" *DSD* 6, no. 2 (1999): 139-47; **J. M. G. Barclay,** *Paul and the Gift* (Grand Rapids, MI: Eerdmans, 2015); idem, "Did Paul Believe in the One-Way Gift?," *Proceedings of the Irish Biblical Association* 39 (2016): 30-42; **R. Bultmann,** *Theology of the New Testament*, trans. K. Grobel, 2 vols. (London: SCM Press, 1952); **J. D. G. Dunn,** "4QMMT and Galatians," *NTS* 43 (1997): 147-53; idem, *Theology of Paul the Apostle* (Grand Rapids, MI: Eerdmans, 1998); idem, *The New Perspective on Paul* (Grand Rapids, MI: Eerdmans, 2005); **R. B. Eno,** "Some Patristic Views on the Relationship of Faith and Works in Justification," *Recherches Augustiniennes et Patristiques* 19, no. 1 (1984): 3-27; **Justin Martyr,** *Dialogue with Trypho*, trans. T. B. Falls, rev. T. P. Halton (Washington, DC: Catholic University of America Press, 2003); **A. E. McGrath,** *Iustitia Dei* (Cambridge: Cambridge University Press, 2020); **D. J. Moo,** "'Law,' 'Works of the Law,' and Legalism in Paul," *WTJ* 45 (1983): 73-100; idem, "Justification in Galatians," in *Understanding the Times: New Testament Studies in the 21st Century; Essays in Honor of D. A. Carson on the Occasion of His 65th Birthday*, ed. A. J. Köstenberger and R. W. Yarbrough (Wheaton, IL: Crossway, 2011), 160-95; idem, *Galatians* (Grand Rapids, MI: Baker Academic, 2013); **E. P. Sanders,** *Paul and Palestinian Judaism* (Philadelphia: Fortress, 1977); idem, *Paul, the Law, and the Jewish People* (Philadelphia: Fortress, 1983); idem, *Paul* (New York: Oxford University Press, 1991); **T. R. Schreiner,** "'Works of Law' in Paul," *NovT* 33 (1991): 217-44; **M. J. Thomas,** *Paul's "Works of the Law" in the Perspective of Second-Century Reception* (Downers Grove, IL: IVP Academic, 2020); **N. T. Wright,** "The Paul of History and the Apostle of Faith," *TynBul* 29 (1978): 61-88; idem, *Justification: God's Plan and Paul's Vision* (London: SPCK, 2009); idem, *Paul and the Faithfulness of God* (London: SPCK, 2013); **K. L. Yinger,** "The Continuing Quest for Jewish Legalism," *BBR* 19, no. 3 (2009): 375-91.

M. J. Thomas

WORLD. *See* Cosmology; Creation and New Creation; Ecological Paul.

WORSHIP

A discussion of worship in Paul's letters should begin with the recognition that the word *worship* has a plethora of meanings. Andrew McGowan points out that, within the contemporary North American context, *worship* can refer to anything from "ritual" to "personal belief or orientation" to "musical experience" (McGowan, 2). By contrast, as David Peterson argues, worship for a first-century Jew like Paul would have pertained to the whole of life lived in service to the God of Israel (Peterson, 167). McGowan, too, agrees that in the NT and its Hellenistic context, *worship* denotes *service, devotion, and homage to *God, rather than specific rituals, actions, and practices. At the same time, however, worship is implicated in a "wider reality" that rituals and practices both "create" and "represent" (McGowan, 2-3, 7).

Considering worship according to Paul's teaching in his letters, this article will follow a similar definition to those outlined above: worship refers to the service and devotion rendered to God by the whole of life. For Paul, this approach to life is oriented by service to the God of Israel and the confession that "Jesus *Christ is *Lord" (Rom 10:9; 1 Cor 12:3; 2 Cor 4:5). At the same time, that orientation of life manifests in certain ways of living; it is embodied by particular practices that come to make sense within this way of approaching the world—beginning with gathering together and including *baptism, participation in the *Lord's Supper, *prayer, corporate song, *preaching and *prophecy, and the collection of financial resources to share with the poor, particularly in *Jerusalem. Some of these practices bear similarities to the cultural context in which Paul and the communities to which he writes find themselves, while others come into conflict with that context. The following will consider Paul's teaching about practices belonging to the worship of God, beginning first with the cultural context in which they developed.

1. Hellenistic Context
2. Pauline Worship Practices

1. Hellenistic Context.

Paul planted and counseled church communities in major cities throughout modern-day Turkey and Greece (Meeks, 9). These cities, however, already had patterns of worship in service of Greek and Roman gods and goddesses as well as in service to the God of *Israel. In this Hellenistic context, the worship practices in Paul's churches arose within a Jewish matrix and were influenced by the surrounding Greco-Roman culture (Porter).

1.1. Practices for the Worship of Gods and Goddesses. When walking through the ruins of these cities today, one cannot help but notice the prominence of *temples to Zeus, Artemis, Apollo, and other gods and goddesses. In the first century, from these temples would have come the sounds of sacrifice and strains of *hymns sung by choirs, often of virgins and boys. Sometimes choirs would sing *paeans* and sometimes dithyrambs, depending on the occasion and the god or goddess to be honored (see Plutarch, *E Delph.* 9 [383-389c]). The city streets would have echoed with the sounds of processionals to honor the gods. The participants in these processions would sing hymns and perform intricate dancing as well as instrumental music of the flute and *kithara* (Quasten, 1-4). Choirs singing hymns to flute accompaniment would stand near the altar during the *sacrifices. For the city's citizens, such song and musical accompaniment had a purpose: they kept the city well-ordered (Plato, *Resp.* 424b-d; *Leg.* 700a-701b; also West, 14).

Mystery cults, such as that of Isis, were also prevalent in these cities. Those who wanted to join would take part in certain initiatory rites. While these main rites remain unknown, there are vivid descriptions of processionals (for example, Apuleius, *Metam.* 11.1-17) with bands of instruments, choirs, dancers, and priests (Bremmer, 110-25). The processions concluded in the temple of the deity, where various prayers, songs, and rites would take place.

Temples for the cult of the emperor also dotted these urban landscapes, particularly in modern-day Asia Minor. Additionally, images of the emperor appeared on coins and buildings throughout the city, as well as in the form of statues (Price, 170-206). While the practices of the imperial cult varied throughout the *empire, they concerned devotion of the emperor of the day. Whole cities would celebrate raucous festivals and make lively processions to honor the emperor (Price, 102-10). At these public gatherings (as well as at private ones), sacrifices were offered to the accompaniment of hymns sung by choirs. Priests would offer sacrifices in the sanctuaries, but also in civic centers such as the theater and marketplace (Price, 208-9). For instance, a procession would come from the temples of Asclepius and Hygeia, the deities responsible for good health, to the emperor's temple, where a sacrifice would be offered "on behalf of the emperor" for health and safety. Another sacrifice would then be offered in the marketplace, before still another would be offered in the theater in front of images of emperors past and present. Less frequently, sacrifices would be made directly "to" the living emperor (Price, 210-11, 216, 221).

1.2. Practices for the Worship of the God of Israel. Jewish people also inhabited cities throughout the Roman Empire. Away from Jerusalem, where the temple was the center of worship, they continued to honor and serve the God of Israel. Their orientation to the God of Abraham, Isaac, and Jacob involved a different way of life from that of their pagan neighbors—not least in their exclusive service to this God (Ex 20:2-6; Deut 6:4-6). That different way of life included celebrating feasts such as Passover in their homes and taking part in domestic worship practices such as singing Scripture (4 Macc 18:14-15). They also built synagogues as houses of prayer and learning. Scholars debate whether the synagogues were sites for worship; some have argued that no singing took place here (J. A. Smith 1984). This is a difficult judgment to make, given that the Scriptures may have been read in a musically heightened, singsong manner (J. A. Smith 2011, xvii). Unlike pagan worship, which used flutes, *sistra*, *kitharas*, and other instruments liberally, Jewish synagogues notably lacked instruments, expect for the shofar, used at New Year and Purim (J. A. Smith 2011, 132-33, citing m. Rosh Hash. 4:5; m. Meg. 2:5).

This Hellenistic setting constituted the cultural backdrop for Paul's letters to church communities across the Roman Empire.

2. Pauline Worship Practices.

Paul's letters do not supply a full description of worship practices for the fledgling *church communities to which he wrote. However, his letters do remind the members of the churches about the good news of the life, death, and resurrection of Jesus Christ, and they also reveal the expectation that that the members of the churches take part in certain practices.

2.1. Gathering Together of the Church Community. When Paul composed his *letters, he expected them to be read in a communal gathering of those who confessed Jesus Christ as Lord (1 Thess 5:27; see also 1 Cor 5:1-5; Col 4:16). The worship practices Paul discusses in these letters—baptism, the Lord's Supper, and so on—all presuppose such a corporate gathering.

As Wayne Meeks points out, these gatherings bear similarities to other types of gatherings in the Hellenistic context—households, voluntary pagan associations, synagogues, and philosophical schools—but the church gathering also differs from them in meaningful ways. First, while Paul refers to these church communities as the "*household of God," and the members of these communities referred to each other as "brother" and "sister" (Meeks, 87-88), the household model cannot account for the rituals, the emerging types of *leadership roles, or the unity both within local congregations and between church communities across cities, regions, and provinces. Second, like with voluntary associations, such as burial societies, membership in the church gathering involved a free decision, included common meals, and relied on *patronage. However, unlike these pagan associations, the church gatherings demanded exclusive loyalty, making claims that oriented the members' lives around Jesus Christ in ways that caused tension with other communities. Moreover, the ultimate goal was *salvation, not conviviality. The church gatherings also included a broader cross-section of society: *women and men, enslaved persons and free. Third, like the synagogues, the church gatherings met in private houses, and the members took part in similar activities (Scripture reading, interpretation, prayer, meals, prophecy, admonition, and settling of disputes) and did not perform sacrifices. However, Paul did not seem to imitate the synagogue intentionally; his letters make no comparison between the church gathering and synagogue. He does not refer to the gathering as *synagōgē*, preferring rather the term *ekklēsia*. Finally, the church gatherings resembled philosophic schools in their didactic purposes—but the church community differed meaningfully in the practices and beliefs taught to followers. Meeks concludes that these four models make good, albeit insufficient, analogies to the church gatherings (Meeks, 74-84).

The confession of Jesus Christ as Lord created a new community and was the departure point of difference. As Meeks points out, Paul's baptismal language dramatizes "the break with the past and integration into a new community" (Meeks, 88). The baptized put on the "new human" and come into "one body" (1 Cor 12:13; Gal 3:26-29; also Col 3:10-11). The metaphor of the *body (1 Cor 12:12-31) was a common enough metaphor in the ancient world (especially among the Stoics), but Paul employs it specifically to stand for "Christ's body" (Meeks, 89). Working from this metaphor, Paul stresses the interdependence of the members of the congregation as well as the community's orientation to God through Jesus Christ and in the Spirit (1 Cor 12:12-31; see also Eph 4:5-6).

Other aspects of the letters reinforce the importance of the new community. Paul concludes four of his letters by instructing the church members to greet each other with a "holy kiss" (Rom 16:16; 1 Cor 16:20; 2 Cor 13:12; 1 Thess 5:26). Culturally, the kiss was a common familial and social act, and only sometimes a sexual one. That Paul exhorts the congregations to greet each other this way witnesses to the familial, interdependent dimension of the church community (McGowan, 55; see also Phillips).

Participation in the community is key for learning how to live *"in Christ," a consistent point of Pauline emphasis. Douglas Campbell points out that humans learn by imitation, and the early Christians learned in "dense" community. Campbell talks about Pauline churches as "intense communities"—communities of learning and virtue formation" (Campbell, 368-73).

These early church communities became places of learning a new way of life, in which worship practices played a vital role. Gathering together enabled this way of life and so undergirded the worship practices that Paul teaches the congregations to follow.

2.2. Baptizing into the Church Community. The practices of baptism and the Lord's Supper had special significance for the early church. McGowan sums up this significance well: "Paul suggests that baptism effects the incorporation of its members into the body . . . , which is itself made by sharing in the one broken bread" (McGowan, 7). Paul appeals to baptism as initiation into the church community as well as the beginning of Christian life (Rom 13:14; 1 Cor 12:13; Gal 3:27-28; also Eph 4:24; Col 3:10-11). In baptism, members receive the seal of the *Holy Spirit, signifying that they belong to God (2 Cor 1:22; see also Eph 1:13; 4:30).

Some scholars have argued that Paul's concept of baptism borrows from Greek mystery religions in that performance of the ritual led to "rebirth." However, others, such as McGowan, reject this origin, instead connecting baptism to Jewish practices of daily washing in ritual baths (Gen 1; Ex 14; 30; Lev 13–15; Josh 3). McGowan also finds resonance with John the Baptist's *ministry, which emphasized reorientation and transformation (McGowan, 136-42).

Significantly, according to Paul, in addition to receiving cleansing in baptism (1 Cor 6:11; also Eph 5:26; Titus 3:5), members are baptized "into Christ," into his *death and *resurrection (Rom 6:3-14; Gal 3:27; also Col 2:12; 3:1). As C. F. D. Moule comments, "Baptism is not merely turning over a new leaf" (Moule, 57). Instead, baptism entails nothing less than one's death to an old way of life and entry into a new life, oriented to God in Christ, in a new community (Rom 6:1-4; 8:14; also Col 2:11-12; Eph 4:1-6, 17-32). Paul illustrates baptism's transformative significance with the image of removing old clothes and putting on new ones (Gal 3:27; Col 2:12; 3:1, 9-11; see Martin 1974, 105-8). This image underscores the belief that the members of the church community have become a "new *creation" in Christ (2 Cor 5:17; Gal 6:15; also Col 3:10-11).

Furthermore, for Paul, baptism has an ethical dimension. As Romans 6:3-4 and Colossians 2:12 make clear, because of and based on their baptism, the church members should live in certain ways. Receiving baptism as new life *entails* a new way of life.

2.3. Partaking in Lord's Supper as a Church Community. While the practice of baptism marks entry into the church, the Lord's Supper provides sustenance for the new life in Christ. One finds Paul's main teaching on the Lord's Supper in his letter to the Corinthians, where the practice of the Lord's Supper—as well as *food more generally—had divided the church community. In 1 Corinthians 8; 10, Paul addresses the general issue of eating meat sacrificed to idols. Not eating any meat sacrificed to idols would have shut believers out of society; sacrifice to the pagan gods was ubiquitous in the Greco-Roman world (McGowan, 31-32). Even a meal would involve a series of libations to the gods (Plutarch, *Sept. sap. conv.* 5 [150]; *Quaest. conv.* 7.8.4 [712-713]; see also Quasten, 14). Paul tells the Corinthian Christians they have the *freedom to eat any meat (1 Cor 10:25), but they also have responsibility to care for their brothers' and sisters' consciences (1 Cor 10:23-24). In 1 Corinthians 10:16-21, he teaches the Corinthians how to think about food in relation to pagan sacrifice; in doing so, he also teaches them about participation in the Lord's table. As McGowan notes, "Paul's notion of the body eaten is focused communally rather than individually, finding the Savior's presence in the corporate consumption rather than in the elements taken in isolation" (McGowan, 32).

In 1 Corinthians 11:17, Paul shifts to discussing the meal within the community, the practice of the Lord's Supper. He reproves the Corinthian church sternly; some were bringing enough food for a private—and hearty—meal, while others went hungry (1 Cor 11:21-22). Paul instructs them to wait for one another instead and also to share with one another. He exhorts them to follow Christ's example of humility at the table and to practice the Lord's Supper according to the *tradition he taught them (1 Cor 11:23-30). Here Paul emphasizes the "vertical" and "horizontal" dimensions of *fellowship at the table—unity with the Lord and with the Lord's people. On this basis, Paul rebukes the Corinthian church for its divisions (1 Cor 11:17-22).

According to Martin, "It is true to say that the doctrine of the Lord's Supper in the New Testament is distinctively Pauline doctrine" (Martin 1974, 120). Yet, Martin also notes that Paul does not offer innovations on this doctrine. He is consistent with dominical and apostolic teaching in several ways: first, the Lord's Supper involves a common meal with bread and wine and yet is a sharing in Christ's body and blood, and thus with one another as the body of Christ (1 Cor 10:16-17; Rom 12:4-5; also Col 3:15; Eph 4:4-6). Second, it invokes the Lord's presence "in remembrance of me" (1 Cor 11:24-25). Third, it points to a future *hope (1 Cor 11:26; see Martin 1974, 122-29).

2.4. Prayer in the Church Community. When the members of the church community came together, prayer played a vital role. McGowan claims that understanding early Christian prayer is challenging for North Americans, who tend to conceptualize prayer as primarily inner and individual (McGowan, 183-84). For the early church, while private prayer was significant, corporate prayer was foundational. Paul exhorts the congregations to pray together; his instructions to pray are grammatically plural—to the corporate gathering (Rom 12:12; 1 Cor 7:5; Phil 4:6; 1 Thess 5:17; also Col 4:2; Eph 6:18). Furthermore, he stresses that they are united with other geographically disparate churches in calling on Jesus Christ (1 Cor 1:2).

While Paul's letters do not contain reference to the corporate confession of *sin (Delling, 125), they do contain much about intercession. Paul frequently appeals for the congregation's prayers on his and his coworkers' behalf (for example, Rom 15:30; 2 Cor 1:11; 1 Thess 5:25; also Eph 6:19; Col 4:3; 2 Thess 3:1-2). As Delling notes, "Paul frequently expresses his desire that the congregation, at its meetings, should entreat for the 'open door' for the apostle's message, and that it should plead before God for the proclamation of the mystery of Christ with power" (see Eph 6:19; Col 4:3; 2 Thess 3:1). Such prayer aids and supports Paul's work (2 Cor 1:11; also Delling, 126). Paul not only asks for their prayers; he intercedes in prayer for the congregations (Rom 1:9-10; Phil 1:9; 1 Thess 1:2, 3:10; Philem 4-6; also Col 1:3, 9; Eph 1:16; 2 Thess 1:11), and his *coworkers follow his example (see Col 4:12-13).

Martin notes three unique features of prayer in the early church, particularly in Paul's letters to churches (Martin 1974, 34-38): First, Paul uses the Aramaic word *Abba* for God. Jesus uses this word of God (Mk 14:32-39) and teaches his disciples to call God "father" (*patēr*; Mt 6:9). For Paul, the members of the church can approach God as *Abba* through the Holy Spirit (Rom 8:15; Gal 4:6; see also Delling, 71). Second, the affirmation "amen"—a word found in the synagogue as the response of the people—appears at the conclusion of Paul's letters (1 Cor 16:24; see also 1 Cor 14:16; 2 Cor 1:20), and also at the end of doxologies to God and Christ in his letters (Rom 1:25; 9:5; 11:36; 16:27; Gal 1:5; Phil 4:20; also Eph 3:21 [Martin 1974, 37; Delling, 71]). Third, Paul's letters are full of "thanksgiving." The particle "the" in 1 Corinthians 14:16 (also 2 Cor 4:15) implies a fixed prayer of thanksgiving. Perhaps he is referring to a specific prayer at the Lord's Table, but Paul does not record the contents of the prayer (Martin 1974, 37-38). Other passages (for example, 2 Cor 1:11; 9:12; 1 Thess 5:18) convey a general sense of thanksgiving. Paul also frequently offers thanks to God (Rom 1:21; 14:6; also Col 1:3 and "to the Father" in Col 1:12), and his letters often reference thanking God (1 Cor 1:14; 10:30; 14:16-18; 2 Cor 1:11; 4:15; 9:11-12; also Eph 5:4). He exhorts the congregations to give thanks (1 Thess 5:18) and to "be thankful" (Col 3:15), instructing them to pray with thanksgiving (Phil 4:6; Col 4:2), even to overflow with thanksgiving (Col 2:7). Paul also gives thanks for openness to the word in particular congregations (1 Thess 2:13), and he thanks God for congregations (Rom 1:8; 1 Cor 1:4; Phil 1:3; 1 Thess 3:9; Philem 4; also 2 Thess 1:2-3; 2:13). In short, his letters indicate that thanksgiving should characterize Christian prayer (Delling, 124).

As Delling notes, Jesus is never the object of "giving thanks" (Delling, 117). However, one does find Paul referring to calling "upon" the name of Jesus (1 Cor 1:2). Delling points out, "The epiclesis [. . .] does not denote a prayer but, rather, a calling upon in the sense of confessing, but generally simply confessing (it can, of course, be used as form of address)" (Delling, 118). Significantly, though, Paul gives thanks to God *through* Jesus Christ (Rom 1:8; also Eph 5:20).

According to Paul, prayer takes place in the Spirit (Rom 8:26; 1 Cor 14:13-15; also Eph 6:18). The Spirit in turn takes an active role in prayer. Additionally, Paul's letter to the Corinthian church shows that glossolalia (speaking in *tongues) is a prominent activity in the communal gathering. As he instructs the congregation regarding this gift, Paul clarifies that glossolalia is meant for the upbuilding (*oikodomē*) of the whole church community (1 Cor 14:1-40; see also Delling, 21).

2.5. *Singing Together as the Church Community.* The practice of corporate singing is of vital importance to Paul's churches. In the words of Martin, "The Christian Church was born in song" (Martin 1974, 39). While Paul does not provide a detailed description of song in the church gatherings, his letters imply that the members should sing both to God and to humans (W. S. Smith, 174-75). Regarding singing to God, Delling comments, "In services in the Pauline area, at least, it is plain that alongside kerygma and doctrine and 'spiritual' utterances in the narrower sense, a not insignificant place is given to praising, glorifying and giving thanks to God, in exalted language and fixed forms, in the presence of the congregation" (Delling, 86). In 1 Corinthians 14:15, Paul regards the practice of singing as connected to the indwelling of the Spirit (see Eph 5:19; Col 3:16; also W. S. Smith, 76, 167). The practice of singing connects the human to God. Paul's letters further imply that, in addition to its divine orientation, singing has a human, social orientation. Singing serves the purpose of edification (*oikodomē*; 1 Cor 14:26), bringing about unity in the church (1 Cor 12–14; see also Rom 12:4-8) and contributing to the members' instruction. Per 1 Corinthians 14:15, 26 (see also Col 3:16), song engages the mind, thus involving a didactic component (see also W. S. Smith, 175).

2.5.1. Hymns. Some have argued that there are early christological hymns (or fragments of hymns) in Philippians 2:6-11; Colossians 1:15-20; and 1 Timothy 3:16 in light of these passages' unique vocabulary, praise-like attributions, and other stylistic features. If they are indeed early hymns, as Delling stresses, "The content of the primitive Christian hymns which have been handed down to us is not . . . subjective effusions of the emotions." Rather, these hymns "express in clear-cut sentences praise for the saving activity of God in Christ; hence they *often have the character of a confession of faith*" (Delling, 87-88, emphasis original). In fact, they may have a didactic function (see Gordley 2007, 257-69; 2011, 300-302).

2.5.2. Creeds. While Paul's letters contain these hymn-like passages that bear similarity to confessions of *faith, there are not explicit longer creedal formulations in his correspondence with the churches (Delling, 82; Martin 1974, 53). However, Romans 10:9 and 1 Corinthians 12:3 indicate that the brief confession "Jesus Christ is Lord" was used in the worship gatherings (see also 2 Cor 4:5). Delling notes, "It is agreed that primitive Christianity, at any rate in some areas, did possess something in the nature of a *creed.* The wording is also well established: 'Jesus is Lord.' Where it is uttered it is wrought by the Holy Spirit. In it the whole content of Christian preaching can be summarised" (Delling, 77; see also Martin 1974, 53-60). This confession makes sense of the practices and way of life Paul teaches, and it orients their service and devotion to the God of Israel.

2.6. *Preaching and Prophecy in the Church Community.* Across his letters, Paul references his and his coworkers' preaching (*kēryssō*, Rom 10:8; 1 Cor 1:23; 9:27; 15:11; 2 Cor 1:19; 4:5; 11:4; Gal 2:2; 5:11; 1 Thess 2:9; *euangelizō*, Rom 1:15; 15:20; 1 Cor 1:17; 9:16-18; 15:1-2; 2 Cor 10:16; 11:7; Gal 1:8, 11, 16, 23; 4:13; see also Eph 3:8). In 1 Corinthians, Paul reminds the Corinthian church that he preaches Jesus Christ, who was crucified (1 Cor 1:23, 17-25) and raised from the dead (1 Cor 15:12). Much scholarly attention has focused on finding the form of the NT *kerygma*, the public proclamation of the *gospel (see Dodd). Yet, as Delling points out, "The distinguishing mark of the Christian message is that God in Christ has authentically bound Himself to man, by an action valid for today and tomorrow and to eternity" (Delling, 102). Thus, the message is one of *joy, and one that necessitates conversion—a conversion in Christ and through the Spirit. "*The Spirit of God is the inner motivating force of primitive Christian preaching*" (Delling, 102, emphasis original).

For Paul, preaching belongs to congregational worship (Delling, 103). In his letters, though, one does not find one person dominating the gathering but rather corporate participation. The gathering implied in 1 Corinthians 14:26 bears more similarities to a banquet than a lecture (McGowan, 74). Prophecy plays a key role in these gatherings (see Aune, 247-62), and, significantly, Paul's discussion of the gathering in 1 Corinthians 12–14 leads one to envision a "procession of prophets" rather than a single teacher (McGowan, 74-75). In 1 Corinthians 12–14, Paul writes to the Corinthians about spiritual *gifts, which include practices such as prophecy and glossolalia. He makes it clear that these spiritual gifts are in fact *gifts* in the Holy Spirit and should be used to edify the church community (1 Cor 12:7). For instance, Paul instructs them to have an interpreter for the whole church when speaking in tongues (1 Cor 14:5, 13, 28), as the practice of speaking in tongues merely confuses and obstructs without interpretation (1 Cor 14:6, 9, 23). As noted earlier, he employs the familiar Greco-Roman image of the "body" in order to illustrate how the church community should function together (1 Cor 12:12-27, esp. 1 Cor 12:27). He further emphasizes this point by extolling *love (1 Cor 13). The exercise of spiritual gifts should be done in love for the edification of the whole community (see also Martin 1974, 131-33).

2.6.1. Women. A discussion of spiritual gifts raises the question: *Who* could exercise these gifts, and who participated in the gathering? Some have interpreted Paul's teaching on the role of women in the church based on the statement "Women should keep silence in the church" in 1 Corinthians 14:34. However, comments elsewhere his letters attest to women's active participation—even leadership—in the early churches. For instance, in Romans 16:1-2, Paul commends Phoebe, a "deacon" (*diakonos*) in the church in Cenchreae and a benefactor (*prostatis*) to him. He names Priscilla as a coworker (Rom 16:3-5), Mary as one who "labored" for the Roman church (Rom 16:6), and Tryphaena, Tryphosa, and Persis as those who "labored" in the Lord (Rom 16:12). He also mentions Junia as an *apostle—one who even suffered imprisonment (Rom 16:7; see also Epp).

In her recent book, Lucy Peppiatt argues that within 1 Corinthians 11:2-16; 14:20-25, 33b-36, Paul employs the rhetorical device of "speech in character" (already acknowledged by scholars to be at work in 1 Cor 6:12-13; 7:1; 8:1, 4; 10:23; 15:12). In Peppiatt's reading, Paul quotes Corinthian ideas, theology, and slogans about enforcing women's head coverings, preventing women from speaking in tongues, and stopping married women from speaking in the gatherings in order to argue *against* these notions. She argues this reading coheres better with the aforementioned closing greetings in Romans and Paul's discussion of prophecy as a gift to the whole church in 1 Corinthians 14:23.

2.6.2. Scripture. Preaching and prophecy played an important part in these early church gatherings, but did the reading of Scripture? Some scholars doubt that the Scriptures now known at the OT were read in early Christian gatherings. Delling argues that Paul does not "emphasise the *authority* of the OT, but that of the *Christian tradition*" (Delling, 95, emphasis original). Paul himself bases his authority on revelation and emphasizes that he follows a tradition he received directly from the Lord (Gal 1:11-24, esp. Gal 1:12). He often reminds the congregations of the teaching and gospel that was "handed over" to them (Rom 6:17; 1 Cor 11:2; see Delling, 92-95). Given Paul's emphasis on a tradition given by direct revelation, some scholars, Delling included, conclude that the OT was not read in early church gatherings.

Others, such as Ralph Martin, disagree. Martin points out that the allusions and echoes in Paul's letters to his *Gentile congregations assume a familiarity with the stories from the OT (for example, see Rom 4:1-23; 9:7-9; 1 Cor 6:16; 10:1-5; 2 Cor 3:7-18; Gal 3:6-9; 4:21; see Martin 1974, 70). Paul also assumes the OT as preparation for the gospel (2 Cor 3:14; Gal 3:22; Martin 1974, 69; see also McGowan, 80). As such, Martin concludes that the congregations must have read the OT when they came together.

Additionally, while his letters were not canonized for several more centuries, Paul clearly did expect that the congregations to which he wrote would read his letters aloud in their gatherings (see specifically 1 Thess 5:27; Philem 2; also Martin 1974, 71). Moreover, as implied by Colossians 4:16, the early congregations exchanged their letters.

2.7. Giving Money as a Church Community. Finally, in several letters, Paul mentions the practice of putting aside money as a church community to give to the poor among the Jerusalem church (Rom 15:26; 1 Cor 16:1-4; 2 Cor 8:1-24; 9:1-15). As Douglas Campbell comments,

> This collection was an important gesture of unity between the pagan converts in Paul's churches and the Jewish communities who were loyal to Jesus and lived in Judea (Rom 15:25-28). It was also a token of appreciation for the great gift that the Judean people had given to the rest of humanity in the figure of the Jew Jesus, although many other Jewish gifts could be acknowledged as well, like the Jewish Scriptures. (Campbell, 284)

The practice of setting aside and sharing financial resources reinforces the responsibility of the whole church to care for the poor (Gal 2:10; see also Martin 1974, 77) and also reorients money dealings for the upbuilding of the body of Christ.

In conclusion, as the members of the church direct their prayers, thanksgiving, songs, and life together to God through Jesus Christ, these acts of worship serve to edify the whole community in love (1 Cor 14:1-40). These worship practices have a horizontal dimension in addition to their vertical one. By taking part in them, the members of the church learn what it means to live in Christ. These practices bear similarities in some ways to practices in their Hellenistic context, and yet they have unique characteristics that take their peculiar shape from, and come to make sense within, the confession "Jesus Christ is Lord."

See also BAPTISM; BODY OF CHRIST; CHURCH; EMPIRE; GIFTS OF THE SPIRIT; HOLY SPIRIT; HOUSEHOLDS AND HOUSEHOLD CODES; HYMNS, HYMN FRAGMENTS, CONFESSIONS; IN CHRIST; KINSHIP LANGUAGE IN PAUL; LORD; LORD'S SUPPER; LOVE; PRAYER; PREACHING, FIRST-CENTURY; PROPHECY,

Prophesying; Religions, Greco-Roman; Sacrifice, Offering; Temple; Tongues.

BIBLIOGRAPHY. **D. E. Aune,** *Prophecy in Early Christianity and the Ancient Mediterranean World* (Grand Rapids, MI: Eerdmans, 1983); **P. E. Bradshaw,** *The Search for the Origins of Early Christian Worship: Sources and Methods for the Study of Early Liturgy*, 2nd ed. (New York: Oxford University Press, 2002); **J. N. Bremmer,** *Initiation into the Mysteries of the Ancient World*, Münchner Vorlesungen zu Antiken Welten 1 (Berlin: de Gruyter, 2014); **D. Campbell,** *Pauline Dogmatics: The Triumph of God's Love* (Grand Rapids, MI: Eerdmans, 2020); **R. Deichgräber,** *Gotteshymnus und Christushymnus in der frühen Christentum* (Göttingen: Vandenhoeck & Ruprecht, 1984); **G. Delling,** *Worship in the New Testament* (London: Darton, Longman & Todd, 1962); **C. H. Dodd,** *The Apostolic Preaching and Its Developments: Three Lectures, with an Appendix on Eschatology and History*, 2nd ed. (New York: Harper, 1954); **E. J. Epp,** *Junia: The First Woman Apostle* (Minneapolis: Fortress, 2005); **S. E. Fowl,** *The Story of Christ in the Ethics of Paul: An Analysis of the Function of the Hymnic Material in the Pauline Corpus*, JSNTSup 36 (Sheffield: Sheffield Academic Press, 2005); **M. E. Gordley,** *The Colossian Hymn in Context: An Exegesis in Light of Jewish and Greco-Roman Hymnic and Epistolary Conventions*, WUNT 2/228 (Tübingen: Mohr Siebeck, 2007); idem, *Teaching Through Song in Antiquity: Didactic Hymnody Among Greeks, Romans, Jews, and Christians*, WUNT 2/302 (Tübingen: Mohr Siebeck, 2011); idem, *New Testament Christological Hymns: Exploring Texts, Contexts, and Significance* (Downers Grove, IL: IVP Academic, 2018); **N. Gupta,** *Worship That Makes Sense to Paul: A New Approach to the Theology and Ethics of Paul's Cultic Metaphors* (Berlin: de Gruyter, 2010); **M. Hengel,** "Hymns and Christology," in *Between Jesus and Paul* (Philadelphia: Fortress, 1983), 78-96; **L. W. Hurtado,** *One God, One Lord: Early Christian Devotion and Ancient Jewish Monotheism* (Philadelphia: Fortress, 1988); **R. P. Martin,** *Worship in the Early Church*, rev. ed. (Grand Rapids, MI: Eerdmans, 1974); idem, *Carmen Christi: Philippians 2:5–11*, rev. ed. (Grand Rapids, MI: Eerdmans, 1983); **A. B. McGowan,** *Ancient Christian Worship: Early Church Practices in Social, Historical, and Theological Perspective* (Grand Rapids, MI: Baker Academic, 2014); **W. A. Meeks,** *The First Urban Christians: The Social World of the Apostle Paul*, 2nd ed. (New Haven, CT: Yale University Press, 2003); **C. F. D. Moule,** *Worship in the New Testament*, Ecumenical Studies in Worship 9 (Richmond, VA: John Knox, 1961); **L. Peppiatt,** *Women and Worship at Corinth: Paul's Rhetorical Arguments in 1 Corinthians* (Eugene, OR: Cascade Books, 2015); **D. Peterson,** *Engaging with God: A Biblical Theology of Worship* (Downers Grove, IL: IVP Academic, 1992); **L. E. Phillips,** *The Ritual Kiss in Early Christian Worship*, Alcuin/GROW Liturgical Study 36 (Cambridge: Grove Books, 1996); **W. J. Porter,** "Misguided Missals: Is Early Christian Music Jewish or Is It Graeco-Roman?," in *Christian-Jewish Relations Through the Centuries*, ed. S. E. Porter and B. W. R. Pearson, JSNTSup 192 (Sheffield: Sheffield Academic Press, 2000), 202-27; **S. R. R. Price,** *Rituals and Power: The Roman Imperial Cult in Asia Minor* (Cambridge: Cambridge University Press, 1984); **J. Quasten,** *Music and Worship in Pagan & Christian Antiquity*, trans. B. Ramsey, NPM Studies in Church Music and Liturgy (Washington, DC: National Association of Pastoral Musicians, 1983); **J. A. Smith,** "The Ancient Synagogue, the Early Church and Singing," *Music & Letters* 65 (1984): 1-16; idem, *Music in Ancient Judaism and Early Christianity* (Farnham, UK: Ashgate, 2011); **W. S. Smith,** *Musical Aspects of the New Testament* (Amsterdam: Uitgeverij W. ten Have N. V., 1962); **M. L. West,** *Ancient Greek Music* (Oxford: Clarendon, 1992).

A. Whisenand Krall

WRATH, DESTRUCTION

While the highest density of *orgē* vocabulary occurs in Romans, there is a wide range of uses of terms of wrath and destruction interspersed throughout the Pauline literature. Paul consistently sees God's wrath as personal and righteous, and almost always as future. He fairly often recalls the dichotomy of those who are saved and those who perish, but without a notion of glee at the fate of the wicked. While God's wrath is seen as righteous, human anger is more often than not problematized.

1. The Divine Wrath/Destruction as God's Eschatological Judgment
2. The Divine Wrath in Romans
3. Human Wrath

1. The Divine Wrath/Destruction as God's Eschatological Judgment.

In his earliest letter Paul sums up the new believers' *faith: They have "turned to *God from idols, to serve a living and true God, and to wait for his *Son from heaven, whom he raised from the dead—Jesus, who rescues us from the wrath that is coming" (1 Thess 1:9-10 NRSV). Here and elsewhere in the NT (Mt 3:7 and pars.), "the coming wrath" (*orgē* *erchoumenē*) is used almost synonymously for God's eschatological *judgment. With many other Jewish groups of his time Paul shares in the intense expectation of such a final divine intervention, which will destroy an evil world, punish the persecutors of God's people, and rescue God's elect (see T. Mos. 10.3; 1 En. 62.12; Sir 36:8-9).

All of humanity is headed toward this final chapter, which will have a dual outcome (see Mt 25). Toward the end of 1 Thessalonians Paul reassures the believers that they have not been "destined for wrath [*orgē*] but for obtaining *salvation [*sōteria*] through our *Lord Jesus *Christ" (1 Thess 5:9 NRSV). Believers once were "by nature children of wrath, like everyone else" (Eph 2:3 NRSV) but now are saved by God's grace.

God's wrath is depicted as intense, passionate, and personal but never arbitrary (Travis, 55). The righteous wrath of the heavenly judge will bring irreversible destruction to those who persist in opposing God's will. People can become so intimately intertwined with a rebellious and sinful attitude that they might rightly be called "sons of disobedience" (Eph 5:6; Col 3:6) or even "sons of perdition" (*apōleia*, 2 Thess 2:3; cf. Jn 17:12; 18:9 as well as the Qumran literature). Paul admonishes the believers in Philippi to stand firm in the face of opposition by such people. For their opponents this is "evidence of their destruction [*apōleia*], but of your salvation [*sōteria*]" (Phil 1:28 NRSV). God's wrathful intervention brings relief to the persecuted elect, as outlined in 2 Thessalonians 1:7. In this letter the fate of the wicked is narrated at some length; they "will suffer the punishment of eternal destruction, separated from the presence of the Lord and from the *glory of his might" (2 Thess 1:9 NRSV). Apart from these verses Paul is remarkably restrained in picturing the fate of the "sons of wrath" or taking delight in the punishment of the wicked.

At present the *church has to contend with "enemies of the cross of Christ" not just outside but inside the church (Phil 3:18 NRSV). Paul reassures his readers that "their end is destruction" (*apōleia*, Phil 3:19 NRSV), whereas the Philippian believers are eagerly awaiting their heavenly *Savior (*sōtēr*, Phil 3:20). In a very similar fashion Paul contrasts how the word of the *cross is "foolishness to those who are perishing [*apollymi*], but to us who are being saved [*sōzō*] it is the power of God" (1 Cor 1:18 NRSV). This is echoed in 2 Corinthians 2:15-16, where Paul describes himself and his fellow missionaries as God's aroma—to those who are being saved (*sōzō*), a fragrance from life to life, and for those who are perishing (*apollymi*), a fragrance from *death to death (see also 2 Cor 4:3).

In varying vocabulary the wicked are told about their future destruction: 1 Timothy 6:9 warns against riches, which trap people in senseless desires, plunging them into ruin (*apōleia*) and destruction (*olethron*). While this example could have a present aspect of moral ruin that precedes the spiritual one, 2 Thessalonians 1:9 speaks unambiguously about the eternal destruction (*olethron aiōnion*), while 1 Thessalonians 5:3 emphasizes its suddenness, coming on people who feel secure like labor pain on a pregnant woman with no escape. Paul warns his readers in Romans with the same eschatological seriousness not to "destroy [*katalyō*, the opposite of building up; see 2 Cor 5:1] the work of God for the sake of *food" (Rom 14:20 NIV; see 1 Cor 3:17; 8:11). In some cases Paul uses the more neutral or multifaceted *katargeō*, which can mean "disable," "abolish," "terminate," and can be positive in many cases, depending on what is being destroyed, such as the veil that lies over the minds of those under the old *covenant (2 Cor 3:14). Christ will further annihilate the lawless one with the breath of his mouth (2 Thess 2:8); he will destroy all powers and *principalities (1 Cor 15:24) and finally the last enemy, death (1 Cor 15:26). This future perspective can be attributed to Christ's work in the past; in a sense he has already "destroyed death" (2 Tim 1:10).

Compared to the clear future perspective of the divine wrath read as judgment resulting in destruction, passages dealing with God's wrath in the past or present are in the minority: in his warnings against *idolatry and generally rebellious attitudes, Paul references the people of Israel's desert wanderings and how "they were destroyed [*apollymi*] by the destroyer [*olouthreutēs*]," clearly meaning God by the latter (1 Cor 10:10 NRSV). In 1 Thessalonians 2:16 Paul states that God's wrath has finally overtaken the Jews who are resisting the Christian *mission. In a somewhat enigmatic statement Paul counsels the Corinthian believers to hand a notorious sinner over to *Satan "for the destruction of the *flesh, so that his spirit may be saved in the day of the Lord" (1 Cor 5:5 NRSV), thus for once not contrasting destruction and salvation but making the first the condition for the second.

2. The Divine Wrath in Romans.

Romans presents a more systematized account of how God's wrath fits into the picture of salvation. Out of thirty-six occurrences of *orgē*, twelve are found in Romans. The letter famously opens by proclaiming the *gospel as the revelation of God's *righteousness

(Rom 1:17), which is immediately followed by the revelation of God's wrath from heaven (Rom 1:18). This wrath has a present aspect, handing over people who indulge in idolatry and immorality to all kinds of sinful attitudes and deeds (Rom 1:28). By abusing God's kindness, which is meant to lead to repentance (Rom 2:4), people are storing up "wrath for the day of wrath" (Rom 2:5). Paul paints God as wholly impartial (Rom 2:11): Jews and *Gentiles have exactly the same chance to fulfill the law and to receive either "glory and *honor and immortality" (Rom 2:7 NRSV) or "wrath and fury" (Rom 2:8 the only occurrence where *thymos* is used for God in Paul).

Orgē is closely related to the eschatological judgment here, but as just one of two possible outcomes. The further development of Paul's argument shows, however, that this possibility of two outcomes is very much a theoretical one. At present even circumcised Jews are found guilty as long as their *circumcision is only an outward sign (Rom 2:28). Paul briefly digresses in Romans 3:1-4 to deal with the difficult problem of whether God's faithfulness as the covenant God can ever be broken by the human partner, a problem he will more fully unfold in Romans 9–11. For now it is important that God has the right to "inflict wrath" on the sinner; otherwise God cannot judge the world (Rom 3:5-6).

Paul's first argument accumulates in the great indictment of Romans 3:20: "For no human being will be justified in his sight" (NRSV). Paul's dense statement of God's *justification for all who believe in Romans 3:21-31 does not mention wrath anymore. God's attitude toward sins in the past is described as "divine forbearance" (Rom 3:25 NRSV). In the present God has put Christ forward as an atoning *sacrifice (Rom 3:25). The language is cultic rather than judicial, though metaphors can of course be mixed. Readers are not told whether Christ's sacrifice absorbs, satisfies, or averts the divine wrath. Paul is simply adamant that the same divine impartiality that gives Jews and Gentiles the same chance and finds them equally guilty has also extended the offer of justification by faith to all, making no distinction (Rom 3:30). More and more Paul brings in the category of *law now, and he is under pressure to explain why the (Jewish) law does nothing for its adherents. In a short statement to be more fully unfolded in Romans 5 and Romans 7 Paul claims that "the law brings wrath; but where there is no law, neither is there violation" (Rom 4:15 NRSV).

Romans 5 describes the effect of justification as *peace with God, which is anchored in God's *love shown to sinners and enemies (Rom 5:6-8). In an argument from the lesser to the greater Paul expresses his confidence that if Christ's death has wrought reconciliation in the past, God's salvation from the (future) wrath is completely assured (Rom 5:9). As in his earlier statement of 1 Thessalonians 1:9-10, "the wrath" is not specified as God's, though most translations supply the genitive. In Romans 5:12–8:17 Paul drops the notion of wrath altogether as he describes the reality of salvation as *grace, justification, and life in contrast to the twin powers of *sin and death, who manage to conscript even the law for their evil schemes. The emphasis shifts from notions of accountability and judgment to highlighting the plight of people outside Christ as those who are "sold into *slavery under sin" (Rom 7:14 NRSV). Those who died in baptism with Christ "to sin" have a new master (Rom 6), or are rather God's sons and daughters, empowered by the Spirit (Rom 8). Though there is an element of an ongoing battle with the flesh trying to drag believers back into the reality of sin, this happens under the signature of the love of God in Christ, from which nothing can separate (Rom 8:38-39). The open-ended horizon of a dual outcome and the universal horizon of divine wrath has given way to a singular picture of love and life because "there is now no condemnation for those who are in Christ Jesus" (Rom 8:1 NRSV).

In Romans 9–11 Paul picks up the theme of wrath again in order to explain the present, worrying, upside-down situation of how Gentiles who did not strive for righteousness have attained it, while zealous *Israel missed the mark (Rom 9:30-31). This is rooted and foreknown in God's unsearchable judgments (Rom 11:33) and *freedom to make for himself vessels of *mercy destined for glory and vessels for destruction (*apōleia*) destined for wrath (*orgē*; Rom 9:22-23). There is, however, an intriguing dynamic in this seemingly static dualism, when there is "a shift from symmetry to teleology" (Watson, 315). God shows his wrath and power paradoxically by enduring with much patience the objects of wrath, and God does the latter in order to "make known the riches of his glory for the objects of mercy" (Rom 9:23 NRSV). The weight is on the startling fact that mercy was given to those who were "not my people" (Rom 9:25, quoting Hos 2:23), the Gentiles.

As Paul develops his argument, he reinforces the central claim that Jews and Gentiles have been brought to leveling ground through God's work in Christ, and salvation is available through faith for all (Rom 10:4). In Romans 11 Paul's thinking takes yet another turn to emphasize God's abiding faithfulness toward those he called. The hardening brought over Israel is neither complete (there is a remnant), nor without purpose (it is oriented toward the salvation of Gentiles), nor permanent. Instead God has imprisoned all in disobedience so that he may be merciful to all (Rom 11:32). "The mystery is that hardened Israel will follow Gentiles through the door of salvation: wrath leads to mercy" (Dixon, 578). (The two last occurrences in Romans will be discussed in the next section.)

Paul unapologetically speaks of God's coming wrath on the day of judgment, which will destroy all those who sin. Despite a level playing field, Paul finds that both Gentiles and Jews stand condemned before God. However, the universal wrath is closely interwoven with and read in the light of the universal and victorious grace offered to all without distinction. As Paul speaks about the implications of this grace, his language shifts from sin as trespass and accountability toward the language of domination and slavery. The righteous wrath of God is slanted toward mercy, which is the defining context for all believers if they are content to continue their lives in such goodness (Rom 11:22).

3. Human Wrath.

Unlike the divine wrath, human anger (often but not exclusively rendered as *thymos*) is problematic. Together with strife, jealousy, and quarrels, (certain types of) anger is a manifestation of the works of the flesh (Gal 5:19-21), which believers have crucified together with its passions and desires (Gal 5:24). In a very similar list Paul fears to find contention, jealousy, (types of) anger, and rivalry among the Corinthian believers (2 Cor 12:20). Colossians 3:6 announces the wrath (*orgē*) of God on all those who indulge in sinful passions and warns the believers not to indulge in them anymore, and in particular to remove anger (*thymos*) and wrath (*orgē*) from their mouth, together with malice, blasphemy, and filthy or abusive language (Col 3:8). This is equaled to stripping oneself of the old human being to be clothed with Christ (Col 3:9-10). Ephesians 4:31 gives a crescendo of bitterness (*pikria*), anger (*thymos*), and wrath (*orgē*), very similar to Aristotle's comment in *Rhetoric* 2.2.1.

Earlier in the letter believers are admonished to "be angry" but not to sin (Eph 4:26) and not to let the sun go down over their anger. Passions must be reined in and managed so as not to give "room to the devil" (Eph 4:27). "Anger becomes sinful . . . if it undermines the eschatological identity and oneness of the Church" (Barton, 23).

Interestingly, Paul omits vocabulary of wrathful passions in his great indictment of Romans 1:18–3:20, though bitterness (*pikria*) is mentioned in Romans 3:14, echoing Psalm 10:7 LXX. In Romans 12:19 Paul urges the believers not to take revenge by themselves but rather to "make room for the wrath." Paul invokes the important *tradition of God's partisan wrath on behalf of his elect in this passage (Bertschmann, 290-91). God's wrath will vindicate his own people suffering oppression and persecution. In the present the (non-Christian) state authorities offer glimpses of this future judgment as they are God's *servants and "avengers into wrath" (Rom 13:4).

Believers, on the other hand, are called to love their enemies as they overcome evil with good (Rom 12:20-21). Far from merely submitting to the authorities out of *fear ("on account of the wrath"), they obey on account of their conscience (Rom 13:5). Ultimately Christians are motivated by love, which fulfills the law and reassures them of the authorities' benevolence (Rom 13:3, 8). It is this love, which is long-suffering, not irritable or self-seeking, that endures and wins the day over anger, transcending any discourse of sin and wrath, read as punishment.

See also CURSE, ACCURSED, ANATHEMA; ESCHATOLOGY; JUDGMENT; LAW; MAN OF LAWLESSNESS AND RESTRAINING POWER; RIGHTEOUSNESS; ROMANS, LETTER TO THE; SACRIFICE, OFFERING; SALVATION; SIN, GUILT.

BIBLIOGRAPHY. **S. Barton,** "'Be Angry but Do Not Sin' (Ephesians 4:26a): Sin and the Emotions in the New Testament with Special Reference to Anger," in *Studies in Christian Ethics* 28 (2015): 21-34; **D. H. Bertschmann,** "'Revenge Is Mine, I Will Pay Back'—Has Mercy Not the Last Word After All? Reading Romans 12:19 as Part of an Implicit Discourse of Justice and Mercy," in *Biblical Ethics: Tensions Between Justice and Mercy, Law and Love*, ed. Z. Markus and P. Wick (Piscataway, NJ: Gorgias, 2019), 273-300; **T. P. Dixon,** "Judgment for Israel: The Marriage of Wrath and Mercy in Romans 9–11," *NTS* 66 (2020): 565-81; **K. Kinghorn and S. Travis,** *But What About God's Wrath? The Compelling Love Story of Divine Anger* (Downers Grove, IL: IVP Academic, 2019); **A. Kretzer,** "ἀπόλλυμι, ἀπώλεια," *EDNT* 1:135-36; **W. Pesch,** "ὀργή," *EDNT* 2:529-30; **S. H. Travis,** "The Wrath of God," in *Christ and the Judgment of God: The Limits of Divine Retribution in New Testament Thought*, 2nd ed. (Peabody, MA: Hendrickson, 2008), 53-73; **F. Watson,** *Paul, Judaism, and the Gentiles: Beyond the New Perspective*, rev. and exp. ed. (Grand Rapids, MI: Eerdmans, 2007).

D. H. Bertschmann

ZION. *See* JERUSALEM, CITY OF.

Subject Index

Scripture Index

Jeremiah

Luke

1 Corinthians

Galatians

Ephesians